WEBSTER'S

New Thesaurus of the English Language

Created in Cooperation with the Editors of
Merriam-Webster

POPULAR PUBLISHING
New York

This 2001 edition published by arrangement with Federal Street Press,
a division of Merriam-Webster, Incorporated.

Popular Publishing Company, LLC
3 Park Avenue
New York, New York 10016

ISBN 1-59027-001-0

Printed in the United States of America
01 02 03 04 05   5 4 3 2 1

Preface

This book is based on the idea that people use a thesaurus to find a more appropriate word for the meaning they want to express. It is designed to make it as easy as possible for users to find just the right word.

The main entries for synonyms are arranged in alphabetical order. In addition to a list of synonyms, main entries include a brief, straightforward statement of the meaning shared by the group of synonyms, along with lists of antonyms, related and contrasted words, and idiomatic expressions (common words or phrases that have a meaning similar to that of the entry word). These lists are presented to help users recognize slight differences in meaning or tone that may affect word choice and are organized to make the search for an appropriate term as easy as possible. The Explanatory Notes that follow the Introduction should be read carefully. They contain an explanation of how the book is organized and discuss the kinds of information that may be found at each entry.

This thesaurus was created in cooperation with the editors of Merriam-Webster Inc., a company that has been publishing dictionaries for over 150 years.

Introduction

The word *thesaurus* derives from the Greek *thesauros* meaning "a storehouse or treasury." As you become familiar with this book, you will find it to be a storehouse of useful words waiting to give precision and sparkle to your speech and writing. This Introduction and the following Explanatory Notes describe the features of your new thesaurus and will guide you in understanding and using this valuable reference.

The Synonym

English is a very complex language. With its intricate interweaving of strands of Celtic, earlier Roman and later churchly Latin, northern and western Germanic tongues, and, through Norman-French, the whole body of Romance languages, it is not surprising that it is a language peculiarly rich in synonyms.

Synonyms lend character and flexibility to writing and speech. They relieve monotony and enhance expressiveness. But just what are synonyms? To the earlier writers the meaning was clear; they viewed synonyms as words meaning the same thing. Unfortunately, during the last century or so this simple, clearcut meaning has become blurred. To many, the term *synonym* has come to mean little more than words that are somewhat similar in meaning. We feel this loose definition to be unsuitable for the selection of terms in a thesaurus since it deprives you of the guidance you have a right to expect.

As a result, we looked for a new approach and were soon convinced that to identify synonyms we had to isolate a segment of meaning that two or more words had in common. In order to analyze each word carefully, then, we had to think of synonymy not just as a relationship between words, nor even between dictionary senses of words. We had to look for separate objective denotations not marked by such peripheral aspects of meaning as connotations, implications, or quirks of idiomatic usage. Only by taking apart senses could we reach the word's ultimate meaning, which for the sake of simplicity we call an *elementary meaning*. Perhaps if we explain this approach by using an example, it will be clearer to you. In Webster's Third New International Dictionary, a sense of the noun *input* reads:

> : power or energy put into a machine or system for storage (as into a storage battery) or for conversion in kind (as into a mechanically driven electric generator or a radio receiver) or conversion of characteristics (as into a transformer or electric amplifier) usu. with the intent of sizable recovery in the form of output

Much of this definition contains peripheral matter, and from the dictionary point of view it is necessary to include it because it helps guide and orient you in knowing how and when to use the word. However, the fundamental meaning of this sense, its denotation, may be restated as:

> power or energy put into a machine or system for storage or for conversion in kind or conversion of characteristics

When we express this graphically

power	machine	storage
put into a		for	conversion in kind
energy	system	conversion of characteristics

you can see that there are twelve simple statements of denotation or individual elementary meanings associated in this single sense of *input*. Of these twelve only one, "energy put into a system for storage," can reasonably be considered a synonym of *charge* as applied to a storage battery. If we were compiling a list of synonyms for *charge* as applied to a storage battery, we would consider *input* a synonym because of this shared elementary meaning. For the purposes of this thesaurus then, we consider a word to be a synonym only if it or one of its senses shares with another word or a sense of another word one or more such elementary meanings.

When we look at the synonymous relationship of words in terms of elementary meanings, the process of choosing synonyms is simpler and more exact. For example, it is easy to see that no term more restricted in definition than the pertinent meaning of the headword can be its synonym, i.e., *station wagon* cannot be a synonym of *automobile,* and *biceps* cannot be a synonym of *muscle.* Even though a very definite relationship exists between the members of each pair, *station wagon* is a type of automobile and *biceps* is a type of muscle, and so are narrower in their range of application. On the other hand, a word more broadly defined than another word in the dictionary may be considered a synonym of the other word so long as the two words share one or more elementary meanings. In order to pin down the area of shared meaning for you, each main entry in this thesaurus contains before its synonym list a *meaning core* (see p. 9a) which states the elementary meaning or meanings that are shared by all the words in that particular synonym group.

The Antonym

Like *synonym, antonym* has been used by some writers with a great deal of vagueness and often applied loosely to words which show no real oppositeness when compared one to another. We feel that a reappraisal of the antonym concept is long overdue. As in the case of synonyms, the relation needs to be seen as one between segments of meaning which can be isolated, rather than between words or dictionary senses of words. For the purpose of this book, we consider a word to be an antonym when one or more of its elementary meanings precisely opposes or negates the same area of meaning of another word. This definition excludes from consideration as antonyms several classes of words that are sometimes treated as antonyms but that actually contain words which neither directly oppose nor directly negate the words with which they are said to be antonymous. Three such groups seem worth a little attention.

1. *Relative terms* have such a relationship to each other that one can scarcely be used without suggesting the other (as *husband* and *wife, father* and *son, buyer* and *seller*), yet there is no real opposition or real negation between such pairs. Their relation is reciprocal or correlative rather than antonymous.

2. *Complementary terms* in a similar way are usually paired and have a reciprocal relationship to the point that one seems incomplete without the other (as in such pairs as *question* and *answer, seek* and *find*). This relation which involves no negation is better seen as sequential than antonymous.

3. *Contrastive terms* differ sharply from their "opposites" only in some parts of their meaning. They neither oppose nor negate fully, since they are significantly different in range of meaning and applicability, in emphasis, and in the suggestions they convey. For example, *destitute* (a strong word carrying suggestions of misery and distress) is contrastive rather than antonymous with respect to *rich* (a rather neutral and matter-of-fact term), while *poor* (another neutral and matter-of-fact term) is the appropriate antonym of *rich.* Basically, contrastive words are only opposed incidentally; they do not meet head on.

In this thesaurus such words, where appropriate, appear as contrasted words.

What then do we consider antonyms? In this thesaurus three classes of words have been accepted as truly antonymous and as sources from which antonyms may reasonably be drawn. These are:

1. *Opposites without intermediates.* These are words that are so opposed that they are mutually exclusive and leave no middle ground between them. Each denies, point by point and item by item, whatever its opposite affirms. Thus, what is *perfect* can be in no way *imperfect* and what is *imperfect,* to however slight a degree, cannot be viewed as *perfect;* you cannot at the same time *accept* and *reject* or *agree* and *disagree.*

2. *Opposites with intermediates.* Such words make up the extremes in a range of difference and are so completely opposed that the language allows no wider difference. Thus, a scale of excellence might include *superiority, adequacy, mediocrity,* and *inferiority,* but only *superiority* and *inferiority* are so totally opposed that each exactly negates what its opposite affirms.

3. *Reverse opposites.* These are words that are opposed in such a way that each means the

undoing or nullification of what the other affirms. Such reverse opposites exactly oppose and fully negate the special features of their opposites. Thus, *disprove* and its synonym *refute* so perfectly oppose and so clearly negate the implications of *prove* that they fit the concept of antonyms as well as does *unkind* with respect to *kind,* or *come* with respect to *go.*

Related and Contrasted Words

What if you are not looking for an exact synonym or antonym, but are looking for a word somewhat similar or somewhat opposed to a known word? To meet such needs, this thesaurus includes lists of related and contrasted words wherever these seem appropriate and likely to be helpful. We can thus offer a wider range of material for use in word finding and vocabulary building without doing violence to our rather strict interpretation of the synonym and antonym. Related words (near-synonyms) and contrasted words (near-antonyms) are so closely related to, or so clearly contrastable with, the members of a synonym group that you have a right to expect them under the appropriate headings.

Phrases and Idiomatic Equivalents

In the search for longer synonym lists, synonymists increasingly have included phrases among their synonyms. These phrases fall into three classes:

1. *Word equivalents.* These are phrases that act as if they were single words. More often than not they are combinations of noun and attributive noun (as *county agent*) or noun and adjective (as *hard sell*) or of verb and adverb (as *make up*). However, such phrases may be made up of any kinds of word elements and may act as any part-of-speech (as in *passing,* adverb; *except for,* preposition; ‖*half-seas over,* adjective; *as long as,* conjunction). These fixed combinations that act as if they were single words cannot be entirely excluded from word lists. This thesaurus includes such combinations when they are so firmly fixed in usage that they are entered in major modern dictionaries with part-of-speech labels.

2. *Glosses.* These are phrases that say the meaning of a word in another way. Essentially, they are brief definitions. There is no definition of synonym that reasonably can be used to justify including these restatements or definitions in synonym lists. Thus "do heavy menial service" is a gloss rather than a synonym of *drudge,* "have an opinion" is a gloss of *opine,* and "in a state of inferiority to" is a gloss of *under.* Such glosses are excluded from this thesaurus since they add nothing useful to the vocabulary of the user of a thesaurus.

3. *Idioms.* These are phrases that have a meaning different from the overall meaning of the words that make them up. For example, there are no literal meanings of *compare* and *note* that allow the phrase "compare notes" to mean "to exchange observations and views"; yet, this is what it does mean. There are no literal meanings of the words that allow the phrase "come a long way" to mean "make progress, succeed"; yet, it does mean this. When idiomatic phrases mean the same thing as particular words it is difficult not to include them in relevant synonym lists. Such phrases, however, do not have the qualities that allow word equivalents to be included in synonym lists — they do not function as words but, rather, as different ways of conveying the same meaning as particular words do. As in the case of glosses there is no definition of synonym that justifies including idioms in a synonym list. Still, we think that such idiomatic equivalents can be helpful to you since they can add force and variety to your expression. This thesaurus has arrived at a compromise and included selected idiomatic equivalents of synonym groups or of particular words in synonym lists in separate lists that follow the relevant lists of synonyms or related words.

Explanatory Notes

How to use this thesaurus

If you expect to make effective use of this thesaurus, you should read and study these Explanatory Notes. In the paragraphs that follow you will find brief explanations of the order of entries, the kinds of entries, and how each entry is put together. The explanations are illustrated with the actual examples taken from the book. In addition you will find a keyline at the foot of every other page of the main vocabulary to serve as a reminder of the information contained in these Explanatory Notes.

A thesaurus consists mostly of lists of words. It is often difficult for the user to be sure what meaning of a word the editor intended when including it in a list. This thesaurus has been edited with features — such as the meaning cores and verbal illustrations — which will help keep you aware of the meaning intended. But because the English language has so many different ways of combining words and so many subtle shades of meaning, you should always use this thesaurus along with an adequate dictionary. Most of the time you will find that a good desk-size dictionary will be extremely helpful.

Scope of this thesaurus

This thesaurus is concerned with the general vocabulary of English. Most obsolete and archaic words and highly technical terms have been left out. Since the vocabulary of this thesaurus is based on Webster's Third New International Dictionary, its editors feel that enough unusual words have been retained to satisfy the student in search of a sprinkling of out-of-the-ordinary terms to use. Some of these words will not be found in a desk-size dictionary and it then may be necessary for you to use an unabridged dictionary to check the suitability of a particular term. If you do not have ready access to an unabridged dictionary, you may not be able to be sure about some of the rarer words. You should use rare or unusual terms, therefore, with caution. Most of you will find that the words entered in a good desk-size dictionary will provide adequate stimulus for the growth of your vocabulary.

Entry Order

The body of the book consists of main entries and secondary entries. These entries are arranged in alphabetical order. Each main and secondary entry is introduced by a boldface headword, as seen in the following examples:

hang *n* the special method of doing, using, or dealing with something <can't get the *hang* of this gadget>
syn knack, swing, trick
rel art, craft, skill

hang around *vb syn* see FREQUENT
hanger-on *n syn* see PARASITE
rel bystander, follower, spectator, syncophant

In the above examples, *hang, hang around, hanger-on* are the headwords introducing either a main entry, as **hang** *n* does, or a secondary entry, as **hang around** *vb* or **hanger-on** *n* do.

Homograph headwords, that is words which are spelled alike, are entered in historical order. The one first used in English is entered first, as:

till *prep*
till *conj*
till *vb*

Verbs used frequently with one or two prepositions or adverbs may be headwords introducing main entries or secondary entries. If they are used as headwords, they are entered with the verb part in boldface type followed by the preposition or adverb in parentheses in lightface type. Such combinations immediately follow the base verb in alphabetical order. In the following example, you can see that the base verb **put** comes first and is followed in alphabetical order by the entries with preposition or adverb in parentheses, **put** (back), **put** (on), and **put** (on or upon):

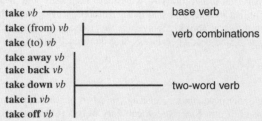

All of these verb entries are then followed by the noun **put**. Two-word verbs (verbs regularly followed by an adverb) that are commonly entered in dictionaries have been entered in boldface at their own alphabetical places in this book. However, they follow in alphabetical order all of those entries showing a verb with a preposition or adverb in parentheses. You can see this in the following example:

Headwords are entered according to normal dictionary practices. This means that nouns appear in the singular and verbs in the infinitive form. Special situations such as those showing plural usage or variant spellings are signaled by showing them in boldface subheads, as at the following entries:

> **crossroad** n, usu **crossroads** pl but sing or pl in constr **syn** see JUNCTURE 2
>
> **woe** n 3 usu **woes** pl **syn** see DISASTER
>
> **catercorner** or **catty-corner** or **kitty-corner** adv **syn** see DIAGONALLY

In the above, **crossroads** and **woes** are subheads indicating plural usage of the headwords. **Catty-corner** and **kitty-corner** are subheads showing variant spellings of the headword.

The Main Entry and Its Elements

Each main entry is made up of a boldface headword followed by a part-of-speech label, a sense number when needed, a meaning core with a short verbal illustration, and a list of synonyms. Nearly all the time, the main entry also has lists of related words, idiomatic equivalents, contrasted words, and antonyms. A typical main entry is:

> **calm** adj 1 free from storm or rough activity <the wind died and the sea became calm>
> *syn* halcyon, hushed, placid, quiet, still, stilly, untroubled
> *rel* inactive, quiescent, reposing, resting; pacific, smooth, tranquil, unruffled
> *idiom* calm as a millpond, still as death
> *con* agitated, disturbed, perturbed, restless, turbulent, uneasy
> *ant* stormy

The headword **calm** is followed by the italic part-of-speech label *adj* which indicates that this word is an adjective. Other part-of-speech labels used in the book are *adv* (adverb), *conj* (conjunction), *interj* (interjection), *n* (noun), *prep* (preposition), *pron* (pronoun), and *vb* (verb).

Individual senses of entries such as **calm** *adj* with more than one sense are introduced by a boldface sense number.

The meaning core indicates the area of meaning in which a group of words are synonymous. At **calm 1**, for example, this reads "free from storm or rough activity". This is the meaning in which the words *calm, halcyon, hushed, placid, quiet, still, stilly,* and *untroubled* can be viewed as synonyms. In other words, the meaning core pinpoints the exact relationship between the main-entry headword and its synonyms.

Material showing a typical or occasionally a single object of reference is enclosed in parentheses, as in the meaning core of **express** *vb* **2**

> to give expression to (as a thought, an opinion, or an emotion)

The parenthesized material is included to alert you to the fact that when this sense of **express** is used, it is usually in connection with "a thought, an opinion, or an emotion".

A meaning core also may have a usage note introduced by a lightface dash. This is used when more information or comments on usage are needed, as in the following example:

> **yet** *adv* **1** beyond this — used as an intensive to stress the comparative degree

Some interjections express feelings but cannot be translated into a simple meaning; in such cases, the meaning core itself may be replaced by a usage note which describes the function of the interjection:

> **good-bye** *interj* — used as a conventional expression of good wishes at parting

Each meaning core is followed by a verbal illustration enclosed by angle brackets, as

> <the wind died and the sea became *calm*>

Here, the verbal illustration shows a typical use of the headword calm in the sense expressed by the meaning core.

The verbal illustration has another use. You can use it as a frame in which to test the suitability of a synonym or a related term in this particular context. At **calm 1** , for instance, you might want to see if the synonym *hushed* can be used exactly the same way *calm* can be. If you substitute *hushed* for *calm* in the verbal illustration, you will get:

> <the wind died and the sea became *hushed*>

You will probably notice at once that this sounds a bit odd. Apparently *hushed* cannot always be used where *calm* can be used. English is full of similar slight differences in meaning and it is for this reason that you are urged to consult the more specific definitions in a good dictionary for any case that seems doubtful to you.

The boldface italic abbreviation *syn* introduces a synonym list that appears at each main entry on a line below the meaning core and the verbal illustration. In the Introduction on page 4a, you read about the aspects which governed the choosing of synonyms. The *syn* list may have only one synonym, as at the entry **hitherto** *adv* **2**, where *here* is the only synonym, or the list may have many synonyms, as *halcyon, hushed, placid, quiet, still, stilly*, and *untroubled* which are shown at **calm** *adj* **1**. Each synonym in a main-entry list is entered in boldface at its own alphabetical place.

A compare cross-reference may appear at the end of a main-entry *syn* list. This cross-reference is introduced by the italic word *compare*. You will find it when two or more groups of synonyms are very closely related and the editors felt that the user looking at one list should know of the existence of the other list. Examples of compare cross-references are found at the entries **assassin** and **murderer:**

> **assassin** *n* a person hired or hirable to commit murder <found out who paid the *assas-sin*> *syn* bravo, cutthroat, gun, gunman, ‖gunsel, gunslinger, hatchet man, hit man, torpedo, triggerman; *compare* MURDERER

> **murderer** *n* one who kills a human being <a *murderer* who wouldn't hesitate to kill in cold blood> *syn* homicide, killer, manslayer, slayer; *compare* ASSASSIN

You will notice that although the headwords are related, there are differences between **assassin** and **murderer** and their respective synonyms. It will help you, then, to find exactly the word you are looking for if you check out these compare cross-references when you see them.

The compare cross-reference is also used when closely related entries such as **ration** and

share 1 both include some of the same words as synonyms. This results from the way language tends to change, sometimes narrowing, sometimes broadening or even subdividing meanings. When this has happened the compare cross-reference warns you of words that, though appropriate to more than one synonym list, may in some contexts blur fine distinctions that you would like to make. A comparison of the main entries of **ration** *n* and **share** *n* **1** will point this up:

> **ration** *n* an amount allotted or made available especially from a limited supply <saved up their gasoline *ration* for a vacation trip>
> *syn* allotment, allowance, apportionment, measure, need, part, portion, quantum, quota, share; *compare* SHARE 1
>
> **share** *n* **1** something belonging to, assumed by, or falling to one (as in division or apportionment) <wanted his *share* of the prize money>
> *syn* allotment, allowance, bite, cut, lot, part, partage, portion, quota, slice; *compare* RATION

You will see that the synonyms *allotment, allowance, part, portion, quota,* and *share* are found in both lists. By taking these synonyms and substituting them in the verbal illustrations, you will find that they sound right, and can be interchanged. If, on the other hand, you take a synonym found in one list, but not in the other, for instance *cut* from the list at **share,** and substitute it in the verbal illustration at **ratio** *n,* you will find that the differences between the meaning cores become more obvious. If you say <wanted his *cut* of the prize money>, you are choosing a word which fits the context. If you try using *cut* in the verbal illustration at *ration*, <saved up their gasoline *cut* for a vacation trip> you will find that *cut* doesn't sound right. So, even though some of the same synonyms appear in both lists, you must be careful to distinguish among all the synonyms in every list. Don't forget to keep a good dictionary on hand to help you do this.

Many main entries include lists of related words, idiomatic equivalents, contrasted words, and antonyms. If an entry has all of these lists, they are shown in the order mentioned above. The boldface italic abbreviation *rel* introduces a list of related words. The related words are ones that are almost but not quite synonymous with the headword. These come immediately after the *syn* list. For example, at the main entry:

> **splendid** *adj* . . . **2** extraordinary or transcendently impressive <a *splendid* new city>
> *syn* glorious, gorgeous, magnificent, proud, resplendent, splendiferous, splendorous, sublime, superb
> *rel* eminent, illustrious; grand, impressive, lavish, luxurious, royal, sumptuous; divine, exquisite, lovely; incomparable, matchless, peerless, superlative, supreme, unparalleled, unsurpassed; surpassing, transcendent

the *rel* list is made up of twenty words separated by semicolons into five subgroups. Each of these subgroups shares a common relation to the headword and its synonyms. Related words are not entered in boldface at their own alphabetical places unless they are synonyms in other lists or head their own main entries.

The boldface italic abbreviation *idiom* introduces a list of idiomatic phrases that are essentially the same in meaning as the words of a synonym group. For a more detailed discussion of these phrases, you might look again at pages 5a & 6a in the Introduction. An *idiom* list at a main entry includes phrases that are generally pertinent to the entire *syn* list and the headword, as the ones at:

> **speak** *vb* **1** to articulate words in order to express thoughts <always *speak* clearly>
> *syn* talk, utter, verbalize, vocalize, voice
> *rel* . . .
> *idiom* break silence, give voice (*or* tongue *or* utterance) to, let fall, make public (*or* known), open one's mouth (*or* lips), put in (*or* into) words, say one's say, speak one's piece

Some idiomatic expressions may be used in more than one form. Such variation is shown in this thesaurus by including the variant word in parentheses. At **slavery** *n* **2**

> *idiom* the yoke (*or* chains) of slavery

gives you the choice of using either *yoke* or *chains* in the phrase.

Idiomatic phrases, including those fixed verb plus preposition combinations that act as idioms rather than as literal meanings of the verb are not entered in boldface at their own alphabetical places in this book.

The boldface italic abbreviation **con** introduces a list of contrasted words. This category contains terms that may be strongly contrasted with the headword, but are not quite antonyms of the headword. An example of a **con** list is:

> **watchful** *adj* paying close attention usually with a view to anticipating approaching
> danger or opportunity <adopted a policy of *watchful* waiting>
> *syn* alert, open-eyed, unsleeping, vigilant, wakeful, wide-awake
> *rel* . . .
> *idiom* . . .
> *con* careless, heedless, thoughless; inadvertent; absentminded, abstracted, faraway
> *ant* . . .

At this main entry, the **con** list is made up of seven words separated by semicolons into three subgroups. Each of these words may be contrasted with the headword *watchful* and with the words in its *syn* list. Contrasted words are not entered in boldface at their own alphabetical places unless they are synonyms in other lists or head their own main entries.

The boldface italic abbreviation **ant** introduces the last possible part of an entry. This is an antonym, as at the entry:

> **perfect** *adj* . . . 2 . . .
> *ant* imperfect

where *imperfect* is the antonym of **perfect 2**, or a list of antonyms as at the entry

> **quiet** *adj.* . . **4** not showy or obtrusive
> *ant* gaudy, loud

In the Introducton to this book on page 5a, you learned about the different classes of opposites to which antonyms belong. When antonyms come from different classes of opposites, they are separated by a semicolon, as at:

> **assistance** *n*
> *syn* see HELP 1
> *rel* backing, supporting, upholding; advantage, avail, profit, use; appropriation, grant,
> subsidy, subvention
> *con* checking, hampering, hindering, hindrance; balking, foiling, frustrating,
> thwarting
> *ant* impediment, impeding; obstructing, obstruction

In the above, *impediment* and *impeding* belong to the class of antonyms that are opposites with intermediates. If you study the *rel* and *con* lists at **assistance** you will see that the first sets of each group form a continuous series:

> backing, supporting, upholding *and* checking, hampering, hindering, hindrance

of which *assistance* forms one extreme and *impeding* (or *impediment*) forms the other. The second pair of antonyms are separated from the first by a semicolon because they belong to a different class — that of antonyms that are reverse opposites. The difference should be plain; *obstruction* (or *obstructing*) amounts to the undoing of whatever is implied by *assistance*.

You may find material in parentheses following antonyms, as at **abrogate** *vb* **2**:

> *ant* establish, fix (*as a right, a quality, or a custom*)

In such cases an antonym or group of antonyms is associated with a particular object or objects of reference. This information will help orient you in choosing the best word possible. Like related and contrasted words, antonyms are not entered in boldface at their own alphabetical places unless they are synonyms in other lists or head their own main entries.

The Secondary Entry

A secondary entry consists of a boldface headword followed by a part-of-speech label, a boldface sense number when needed, and most importantly, a *syn* see cross-reference in small capital letters directing you to the appropriate main entry in whose *syn* list the secondary entry appears. If this main entry has more than one sense, a lightface number follows the see cross-reference to tell you the sense to look for at the main entry.

Like the main entry, the secondary entry may also have lists of related words, idiomatic phrases, contrasted words, and antonyms. If it does, as at:

short *adj* . . . 7
　syn see CONCISE
　rel compact; pointed
　idiom to the point
　con extended, protracted, spun-out
　ant lengthy, long-drawn-out

the terms in the lists apply only to the boldface headword and not necessarily to all of the synonyms at the main entry to which there is a cross-reference. Normally, only a few related words, idiomatic phrases, contrasted words, and antonyms found at the main entry are repeated at the secondary entry. For this reason you should check the main entry for the most complete collection of terms.

Main and Secondary Entries: the One Arbitrary Rule

There is one rule in particular which the editors have followed in working with both main and secondary entries: *no word may appear in more than one list at any single sense of a main or a secondary entry*. For example, *nice* is a synonym at **pleasant** *adj* **1,** which has the meaning core "highly acceptable to the mind or senses". You might reasonably consider other senses of *nice* to qualify it as a related word at **pleasant** *adj* **1,** in addition to its entry as a synonym. This could be the sense meaning "mild", in <the *nice* weather of late spring> or that meaning "suitable", as in <the *nice* clothes she wears>. Further, there is even a sense of *nice* which means "unpleasant", as in <got into a *nice* fix> which could qualify it as a contrasted word or even as an antonym. You can see how confusing the entry would have looked with *nice* shown at three or four places. In order to be as clear as possible, then, each entry shows a word in only one list at any one sense.

Labels

As we mentioned earlier, the part-of-speech label found at each entry is one of the following: *adj* (adjective), *adv* (adverb), *conj* (conjunction), *interj* (interjection), *n* (noun), *prep* (preposition), *pron* (pronoun), and *vb* (verb).

Words that are labeled *cap* or *usu[ally] cap* in Webster's Third New International Dictionary are capitalized in this book:

Gehenna *n*
　syn see HELL

If only one entered sense of a word is capitalized, an italic cap label followed by the boldface capitalized form is shown at the appropriate sense:

pandemonium *n* **1** *cap* **Pandemonium** *syn* see HELL
　2 *syn* see SINK 1
　3 *syn* see DIN 1

Pandemonium should be capitalized when it is used as a synonym of *hell*. When *pandemonium* is used as a synonym of *sink* (sense 1) or *din* (sense 1), it is not capitalized. In addition to the part-of-speech label, an italic label *pl* may be present to indicate that a word or a sense of a word is used in the plural.

Some words are always used in the plural. A typical example is:

years *n pl syn* see OLD AGE

The *pl* label shows that the headword **years** is plural in form and takes a plural verb when used to mean *old age*.

Some words are often used in the plural and are so labeled:

> **road** *n* **1** *often* **roads** *pl syn* see HARBOR 3
> **2** *syn* see WAY 1
> **3** *syn* see WAY 2

This label means that about half the time the word is used in the plural and about half the time it is used in the singular. In the above example, only sense 1 of the headword is often used in the plural.

Some words are usually used in the plural and are so labeled. This means that more often than not, the word will be found in the plural:

> **minutia** *n, usu* **minutiae** *pl* **1** *syn* see INS AND OUTS
> **2** *syn* see TRIVIA

The placing of the label before both senses indicates that the headword **minutia** is usually but not always used in the plural in both senses.

There are words which are plural in form, but which may sometimes take a singular verb in construction. An example is:

> **trivia** *n pl but sometimes sing in constr* . . .

Other words are plural in form but are as likely to take a plural verb as a singular one. The first entered sense of **common** is such a case:

> **common** *n* **1** **commons** *pl but sing or pl in constr*
> *syn* see COMMONALTY

The label shows that in this use *common* occurs only in plural form but may take either a plural or a singular verb.

Finally, there are nouns which are plural in form and always take a singular verb:

> **outdoors** *n pl but sing in constr* the space where air is unconfined <every night he let
> the dog run in the *outdoors*>

One other label which you will see used a few times in this thesaurus is an italic subject guide phrase. The subject guide phrase precedes the meaning core and indicates that the meaning core is limited in application. At **set** *vb*

> **set** *vb* **11** *of a fowl* to incubate eggs by crouching upon them . . .

the phrase *of a fowl* indicates that in this sense **set** is used of a fowl (and not, for instance, of people or crocodiles).

Symbol

One warning symbol is used in this book: double bars ‖. This is placed before a word to alert you that its usage is in some way restricted. Whenever this symbol appears you should check the word in a good dictionary if you are unfamiliar with it. A double-barred word might be slang, as ‖*fat cat* at the entry **notable** *n*. A word may be used by only one segment of the English-speaking population, as ‖*nipper* at **kid** *n* which is chiefly British, or ‖*swarf* at **faint** *vb* which is Scottish. The word might also be an American regional term, such as the Western word ‖*Rocky Mountain Canary* which is a synonym of **donkey** *n*, or the Southern word ‖*glade* which is a related word at **swamp** *n*. These words have been included in this thesaurus to introduce you to the extensive range of the English language and to help you stretch your vocabulary. In order to know exactly which restriction the double bars for each term carries, you are urged to consult a good dictionary.

All double-barred words in this thesaurus follow the labels shown in Webster's Third New International Dictionary.

A

aback *adv syn* see UNAWARES

abaft *adv* toward or at the stern (of a vessel) <headed *abaft* for a smoke>
syn aft, astern
rel after, back, behind
ant forward

abaft *prep* to the rear of <huddled in a nook *abaft* the chimney>
syn back of, behind

abalienate *vb syn* see TRANSFER 4

abandon *vb* **1** to give up without intent to return or reclaim <*abandoned* his family>
syn chuck, desert, forsake, quit, renounce, throw over
rel cast (off), discard, disuse, drop, junk, scrap; reject, repudiate
idiom have done with, leave flat, quit cold, run out on, turn one's back on (*or* upon), walk out on
con hold, keep, possess, retain; redeem, rescue, save; acquire, gain, get, procure, win; cherish, foster
ant reclaim
2 *syn* see RELINQUISH
ant retain

abandon *n* **1** *syn* see UNCONSTRAINT
2 carefree disregard for consequences <behave with *abandon*>
syn impulsiveness, uninhibitedness, unrestraint; *compare* UNCONSTRAINT
rel freedom, liberty, license; exuberance, heedlessness, laxity, laxness, looseness, unruliness, wildness; incontinence, licentiousness, wantonness; fun, games, play, sport
con constraint, inhibitedness, inhibition, restraint; repression, suppression
ant self-restraint

abandoned *adj* **1** *syn* see DERELICT 1
2 free from moral restraint <led a thoroughly *abandoned* life>
syn dissolute, licentious, profligate, reprobate, self-abandoned, unprincipled
rel debased, debauched, depraved, perverted, riotous; incorrigible; lascivious, lecherous, lewd, wanton; corrupt, degenerate
idiom dead to honor, gone to the bad, lost to shame, rotten (to *or* at) the core
con ethical, high-principled, moral, reputable, virtuous; correct, decent, decorous, proper, seemly
ant scrupulous, upright

abase *vb syn* see HUMBLE
rel demote, diminish, downgrade, reduce; fawn, grovel, toady; cower, cringe, truckle
con elevate, lift, raise
ant exalt; extol

abash *vb syn* see EMBARRASS 1

rel abase, demean, humble, humiliate
idiom make one eat humble pie
ant embolden, reassure

abashment *n syn* see EMBARRASSMENT

abate *vb* **1** *syn* see ABOLISH 1
2 *syn* see ANNIHILATE 2
3 *syn* see DECREASE
4 to lessen in force or intensity <the storm *abated* slowly>
syn ‖bate, die (down *or* away), ease off, ebb, fall, let up, lull, moderate, relent, slacken, subside, wane
rel decrease, diminish, dwindle, lessen, weaken
idiom run its course
con augment, expand, extend, increase; mount, rage, soar, surge
ant revive; rise

abatement *n syn* see DEDUCTION 1
con enlargement, increase
ant addition

abbreviate *vb syn* see SHORTEN
rel attenuate, extenuate
con enlarge, increase; amplify, dilate, expand
ant lengthen; extend

ABC *n* **1** *usu* **ABC's** *pl syn* see ALPHABET 1
2 *often* **ABC's** *pl syn* see ALPHABET 2

abdicate *vb* **1** to part formally or definitely with a position of honor or power <the king *abdicated* the throne in order to marry a commoner>
syn demit, renounce, resign; *compare* RELINQUISH
rel abandon, leave, relinquish, surrender; drop; withdraw
con appropriate, arrogate, confiscate; grab, seize, take over, wrest
ant assume, usurp
2 *syn* see DISCARD
con keep, retain, treasure

abdomen *n* the part of the body between the chest and the pelvis <intense pain in the lower *abdomen*>
syn belly, ‖gut, paunch, stomach, tummy, venter
rel bay window, ‖breadbasket, corporation, pod, pot, potbelly; middle, midriff, midsection

abduct *vb syn* see KIDNAP
rel grab, seize

abecedarian *n syn* see AMATEUR 2

aberrant *adj* **1** *syn* see ABNORMAL 1
rel different, disparate, divergent; eccentric, odd, peculiar, strange; exceptional, unusual
con natural, normal, regular, typical; customary, usual, wonted

---

syn synonym(s)   *rel* related word(s)
ant antonym(s)   *con* contrasted word(s)
idiom idiomatic equivalent(s)
‖ use limited; if in doubt, see a dictionary

ant true (*to a type*)
2 *syn* see ERRANT 2

aberration *n* **1** *syn* see DEVIATION 1
rel abnormality; mistake, slip; curiosity, oddity, prodigy, rarity
con average, mean, norm; normality
ant conformity; regularity
2 *syn* see INSANITY 1
ant soundness (*of mind*)

abet *vb* **1** *syn* see INCITE
rel egg, exhort, goad, prod, spur, urge; advocate, countenance, encourage, endorse
con forbid, prevent, prohibit; debar, deter, discourage
2 *syn* see HELP 1

abettor *n* *syn* see CONFEDERATE

abeyance *n* a state of temporary inactivity <the warm dry weather kept his asthma in *abeyance*>
syn abeyancy, cold storage, doldrums, dormancy, intermission, interruption, latency, quiescence, quiescency, suspension
rel break, interval, pause, respite
con activeness, activity, stir
ant continuance

abeyancy *n* *syn* see ABEYANCE
ant continuancy

abeyant *adj* *syn* see LATENT
rel deferred, intermitted, postponed, stayed, suppressed; repressed
con refreshed, renewed, restored
ant active, operative; revived

abhor *vb* **1** *syn* see HATE
2 *syn* see DESPISE
con dote (on *or* upon), like, love
ant admire

abhorrence *n* *syn* see ABOMINATION 2
rel distaste, repellency; dismay, horror
con affection, attachment, love
ant admiration; enjoyment

abhorrent *adj* **1** *syn* see HATEFUL 2
ant admirable
2 *syn* see REPUGNANT 1
rel antipathetic; uncongenial, unsympathetic
con alluring, attractive, captivating; enticing, seductive, tempting
ant congenial

abide *vb* **1** *syn* see STAY 2
rel adhere, cleave, cling, stick; dwell, live, reside
con go, leave, quit; move, remove, shift
ant depart
2 *syn* see CONTINUE 1
rel linger; exist, subsist
con avoid, elude, escape, evade
ant pass
3 *syn* see BEAR 10
rel accept, receive; accede, consent
idiom put up with
4 *syn* see RESIDE 1

abiding *adj* *syn* see SURE 2
rel durable, lasting, perdurable, persistent
con ephemeral, impermanent, short-lived, transient, transitory

ability *n* **1** physical, mental, or legal power to perform <he has the *ability* to accomplish whatever he sets his mind to>
syn adequacy, capability, capacity, competence, might, qualification, qualifiedness
rel address, adroitness, cleverness, dexterity; aptitude, aptness, facility, knack
idiom what it takes
con impotence, inadequacy, incapability, incompetence
ant inability
2 natural or acquired proficiency especially in a particular activity <he has unusual *ability* in planning and designing>
syn command, expertise, expertism, expertness, knack, know-how, mastership, mastery, skill
rel adroitness, deftness, efficiency, handiness, proficiency; ingenuity, resourcefulness; talent
con inadequacy, incompetence, ineffectualness, unfitness; fatuity, futility, inanity

abject *adj* *syn* see DOWNTRODDEN

abjure *vb* to give up (something formerly adhered to) irrevocably and usually solemnly or formally <an immigrant solemnly *abjuring* allegiance to his former country>
syn forswear, palinode, recall, recant, retract, take back, unsay, withdraw
rel disavow, disown, renounce, repudiate; abandon, desert, forsake; cede, relinquish, surrender
idiom eat one's words

ablaze *adj* **1** *syn* see BURNING 1
2 *syn* see ALIGHT 2

able *adj* possessed of or marked by a high level of efficiency and ability <an *able* student always near the head of his class>
syn au fait, capable, competent, good, proper, qualified, wicked
rel effective, effectual, efficient; expert, proficient, skilled, skillful; alert, clever, keen, sharp; brainy, brilliant, intelligent, smart; enterprising, go-ahead, up-and-coming
con ineffective, ineffectual, inefficient; incapable, incompetent, unqualified; fair, indifferent, mediocre; lackluster, maladroit
ant inept; unable

abnegation *n* *syn* see RENUNCIATION

abnormal *adj* **1** departing significantly from the normal or a norm <the *abnormal* rains caused flooding>
syn aberrant, anomalous, atypical, deviant, deviative, heteroclite, preternatural, unrepresentative, untypical
rel divergent, offtype; irregular, unnatural; uncustomary, unusual, unwonted; heteromorphic; paratypic
con common, familiar, natural, ordinary, regular, typical; customary, usual, wonted
ant normal
2 *syn* see IRREGULAR 1

abode *n* *syn* see HABITATION 2

abolish *vb* **1** to bring to an end often by formal or concerted action <*abolish* a tax>
syn abate, abrogate, annihilate, annul, circumduct, invalidate, negate, nullify, quash, undo, vitiate

rel cancel, disallow, disannul, repeal, rescind, revoke, vacate
idiom bring to naught, make void, set aside
con conserve, preserve, save; keep, retain
2 *syn* see ANNIHILATE 2
con found, institute
ant establish
abominable *adj syn* see HATEFUL 2
rel accursed, cursed; loathsome, offensive, repugnant, revolting
con applaudable, commendable
ant laudable (*as practices, customs*); delightful, enjoyable
abominate *vb syn* see HATE
rel curse, damn, objurgate
idiom hold in abomination, take an aversion to
con admire, regard
ant enjoy; esteem
abomination *n* **1** one that is a source of utter disgust or intense dislike <found the new tax form an *abomination* of confused complexity>
syn anathema, bête noire, black beast, bugbear, detestation, hate
rel annoyance, pest, plague, trial; bogey, bugaboo, incubus
con delectation, delight, joy, pleasure; treasure
2 a feeling of extreme disgust and dislike <they hold every indulgence in *abomination*>
syn abhorrence, aversion, detestation, hate, hatred, horror, loathing, repugnance, repugnancy, repulsion, revulsion
rel contempt, despite, disdain, scorn; disfavor, dislike, disrelish, distaste
con admiration, regard, respect; fondness, liking, relish, taste; approbation, approval, countenance, favor; acceptance, tolerance
ant esteem; enjoyment
aboriginal *adj syn* see NATIVE 2
rel primeval, primitive, primordial, pristine; barbarian, barbaric, barbarous, savage
con advanced, progressive; civilized, cultured; sequent, successive
abort *vb syn* CANCEL 2
rel end, terminate; scrap, scratch
abortion *n syn* see FREAK 2
abortive *adj syn* see FUTILE
rel unformed; immature, unmatured, unripe
con accomplished, completed, concluded, finished
ant consummated
abound *vb syn* see TEEM
abounding *adj syn* see ALIVE 5
rel full, jammed, packed, stuffed
about *adv* **1** in every direction <looked carefully *about*>
syn around, round, round about
2 in a circuitous way or course <took the long way *about*>
syn circuitously, round about
3 *syn* see NEARLY
4 here or there without plan or order <left his tools lying *about*>
syn anyhow, any which way, anywise, around, at random, haphazard, haphazardly, helter-skelter, random, randomly

rel back and forth, hither and thither, to and fro; aimlessly, carelessly, casually
5 in the vicinity <talked to the people standing *about*>
syn near, near-at-hand, nearby
idiom close by
6 in the opposite direction <he turned *about* and saw her>
syn again, around, back, backward, in reverse, round, round about
idiom in one's course
about *prep* **1** in the vicinity of <*about* five miles to go>
syn around, circa, close on, near, nearby, nigh
idiom hard by, not far from
2 *syn* see APROPOS
idiom in point of, with regard to
3 *syn* see OVER 3
4 here and there upon or within <traveled *about* the country>
syn round, through, throughout
idiom all over
about-face *n syn* see REVERSAL 1
above *adv* **1** *syn* see OVER 4
ant below
2 higher on the same page or on a preceding page <earlier examples appear *above*>
syn supra
ant below, infra
above *prep* **1** *syn* see OVER 1
ant below
2 *syn* see BEYOND 2
aboveboard *adj syn* see STRAIGHTFORWARD 2
rel open, scrupulous; artless, ingenuous, unsophisticated
con clandestine, covert, furtive, secret, surreptitious; deceitful; crooked, devious, oblique
ant underhand, underhanded
abracadabra *n syn* see GIBBERISH 3
rel mystification; argot, cant, jargon
abrade *vb* **1** to injure or flaw by frictional action <wind-driven sand *abraded* the glass>
syn chafe, corrade, erode, gall, graze, rub, ruffle, wear
rel corrode, eat away, fret; grate, rasp, scrape
2 *syn* see CHAFE 3
rel burn
3 *syn* see ANNOY 1
rel disorganize, disturb, flurry, rattle; confuse, distract, perturb
con calm, relieve, soothe
Abraham's bosom *n syn* see HEAVEN 2
abreast *adj* **1** *syn* see UP-TO-DATE
2 *syn* see FAMILIAR 3
abridge *vb* **1** to make less by in some manner restricting <laws that *abridge* freedom of speech>
syn curtail, diminish, lessen, minify
rel limit, narrow, reduce, restrict; minimize
con augment, broaden, enlarge, extend

---

syn synonym(s)   *rel* related word(s)
ant antonym(s)   *con* contrasted word(s)
idiom idiomatic equivalent(s)
‖ use limited; if in doubt, see a dictionary

ant amplify
2 *syn* see SHORTEN
con amplify, augment, enlarge, increase
ant expand, extend

abridgment *n* a shortened version of a larger work or treatment produced by condensing and omitting without basic alteration of intent and language <an *abridgment* of a dictionary>
syn abstract, boildown, breviary, breviate, brief, condensation, conspectus, epitome, synopsis
rel aperçu, compendium, digest, outline, précis, sketch, syllabus; capsule, summary; sum, summation, summing-up
con elaboration; paraphrase
ant expansion

abroad *adv syn* see OVERSEAS

abrogate *vb* **1** *syn* see ANNUL 4
rel abate, extinguish
con establish, found; confirm, ratify
ant institute (*as by enacting or decreeing*)
2 *syn* see ABOLISH 1
rel extinguish; blot out, cancel, obliterate; ruin, wreck
con support, uphold
ant establish, fix (*as a right, a quality, or a custom*)

abrupt *adj* **1** *syn* see PRECIPITATE 1
rel hastened; casual, informal, unceremonious; quick, speedy
con dilatory, laggard; easy, relaxed
ant deliberate, leisurely
2 *syn* see BLUFF
rel brisk, crisp, sharp; impetuous, quick, ready
con calm, easy, relaxed
3 *syn* see STEEP 1
rel perpendicular, plumb, vertical
con inclined, slanting; flat, level, plane, smooth
ant sloping

abruptly *adv syn* see SHORT 1

abscess *n* a localized swollen area of infection containing pus <had an *abscess* on his leg>
syn boil, carbuncle, furuncle, pimple, pustule
rel lesion, sore, trauma; botch, ulcer

abscond *vb syn* see ESCAPE 1
rel go, leave, quit, withdraw
idiom do the disappearing act, skip out, take French leave
con render, surrender, yield
ant give (oneself) up

absence *n* the state of being absent or missing <the *absence* of news was disturbing>
syn dearth, default, defect, lack, ‖miss, privation, want; *compare* FAILURE 3
rel deficiency, drought, inadequacy, insufficiency; exigency, necessity, need; vacuum, void; nonappearance, nonattendance
con abundance, copiousness, plenty
ant presence

absent *adj* **1** not now present <all missed their *absent* friend>
syn away, gone, lacking, missing, omitted, wanting
ant present
2 *syn* see ABSTRACTED

rel absorbed; forgetful, heedless
con attending, hearkening, listening; considerate, thoughtful
ant attentive

absentminded *adj syn* see ABSTRACTED
rel unnoticing, unobserving, unperceiving, unseeing; heedless, inattentive
idiom lost in thought
con alert; aware
ant wide-awake

absolute *adj* **1** *syn* see PERFECT 2
rel pure, sheer, simple
con circumscribed, limited, partial, restricted
2 *syn* see PURE 2
rel abstract, ideal; real, true
con imperfect, incomplete
ant mixed, qualified
3 *syn* see UTTER
4 exercising power or authority without external restraint <an *absolute* monarch>
syn arbitrary, autarchic, autocratic, despotic, monocratic, tyrannical, tyrannous; *compare* TOTALITARIAN 1
rel dictatorial, magisterial; authoritarian, totalitarian; domineering, imperious, masterful; plenipotential, plenipotentiary, unlimited
con circumscribed, limited, restrained, restricted; constitutional, lawful
5 *syn* see ACTUAL 2
6 *syn* see ULTIMATE 3
rel ideal, transcendent, transcendental; autonomous, free, independent, sovereign; boundless, eternal, infinite
con circumscribed, limited, restricted; conditional, contingent, dependent

absolutely *adv syn* see EASILY 2

absolution *n syn* see PARDON
rel condonation
con censure, reprehension, reprobation
ant condemnation

absolve *vb* **1** *syn* see EXEMPT
2 *syn* see EXCULPATE
rel discharge, free, release
con condemn, doom, sentence; chasten, discipline, punish
ant charge (with), hold (to)

absorb *vb* **1** to take in and make a part of one's being <*absorb* knowledge from reading>
syn assimilate, imbibe, incorporate, inhaust, insorb
rel embody, imbue, impregnate, infuse, permeate
con disgorge, eject, expel, vomit; discharge, eliminate, emit, give off, pass
ant exude, give out
2 *syn* see MONOPOLIZE
rel concern, engage, immerse, involve, preoccupy
con diffuse, disperse, scatter
ant dissipate (*as time, attention*)

absorbed *adj syn* see INTENT
rel involved
idiom caught up in, up to the elbows (*or* ears) in
con apathetic, disinterested, indifferent, unconcerned; uninterested; absent, abstracted

ant distracted

absorbing *adj syn* see ENGROSSING
ant irksome

abstain *vb* **1** *syn* see DENY 3
rel abnegate, eschew, forgo; decline, refuse, reject, spurn
idiom dispense with, do without, let alone
con pamper; gratify, regale; sate, satiate, surfeit
ant indulge
2 *syn* see REFRAIN 1

abstemious *adj* marked by restraint in satisfying desires (as for food, drink, or pleasure) <an *abstemious* man, little given to self-indulgence>
syn abstentious, abstinent, continent, self-restraining, sober, temperate; *compare* SOBER 3
rel self-abnegating, self-denying; ascetic, austere; sparing
con greedy, rapacious, voracious; epicurean, sybaritic, voluptuous
ant gluttonous

abstentious *adj syn* see ABSTEMIOUS
ant gluttonous

abstinence *n syn* see TEMPERANCE 2
rel renunciation
con gorging, sating, surfeiting; immoderateness, overdoing, unrestraint; crapulence, excess, extravagance
ant self-indulgence

abstinent *adj syn* see ABSTEMIOUS
ant gluttonous

abstract *adj* **1** having conceptual rather than concrete existence <the *abstract* perfect society>
syn hypothetical, ideal, theoretical, transcendent, transcendental
rel academic, impractical, utopian, visionary; speculative, undemonstrable; conceptual, notional; inconcrete
con corporeal, material, objective, phenomenal, physical; actual, factual, real
ant concrete
2 *syn* see NEUTRAL

abstract *n syn* see ABRIDGMENT
con enlargement, expansion
ant amplification

abstract *vb* **1** *syn* see DETACH
rel divide, part, separate
con insinuate, interpolate, interpose
ant insert, introduce
2 *syn* see STEAL 1

abstracted *adj* withdrawn in mind and inattentive to external matters <seemed *abstracted* and remote>
syn absent, absentminded, bemused, distrait, faraway, inconscient, lost, preoccupied
rel engrossed, intent, rapt; oblivious, unmindful, unminding; heedless, inattentive
idiom in a brown study, lost in thought, lost to the world
con attentive, vigilant, watchful, wide-awake; noticing, noting, observant, seeing
ant alert

abstruse *adj syn* see RECONDITE
rel complex, complicated, intricate, knotty; abstract, hypothetical, ideal

con clear, evident, manifest, palpable; clear, lucid, perspicuous; easy, facile, simple
ant obvious, plain

absurd *adj syn* see FOOLISH 2
rel comic, droll, funny; asinine, fatuous, simple; irrational, unreasonable
con logical, ratiocinative, subtle
ant rational, sensible

absurdity *n syn* see FOOLISHNESS

abundance *n syn* see PROSPERITY 2
rel adequacy, competence, enough, plenty, sufficiency; lavishness, prodigality
idiom enough and to spare
con deficiency, inadequacy, insufficiency, lack, paucity

abundant *adj syn* see PLENTIFUL
rel lavish, lush, luxuriant, profuse; crammed, crowded, thick; common
idiom in good supply
con infrequent, rare, uncommon; inadequate, scanty
ant scarce

abuse *vb* **1** *syn* see DECRY 2
ant praise
2 to put to a bad or improper use <*abuse* the prerogatives of office>
syn misapply, misemploy, mishandle, misimprove, misuse, pervert, prostitute
rel mar, spoil; corrupt, debase, desecrate, profane
idiom make ill use of
con esteem, honor, respect
3 *syn* see EXPLOIT 2
4 to treat without compassion and usually in a hurtful manner <parents who *abuse* children>
syn ill-treat, ill-use, maltreat, mistreat, misuse, outrage
rel damage, harm, hurt, impair, injure; oppress, persecute, wrong; manhandle, mess (up)
idiom do one dirt, do violence to
con cherish, prize, treasure; esteem, revere, reverence, venerate
ant honor, respect

abuse *n* vehemently and usually coarsely expressed condemnation or disapproval <had an unequaled vocabulary of *abuse*>
syn billingsgate, contumely, invective, obloquy, scurrility, vituperation
rel calumny, defamation, malignment, mud, vilification; cursing, profanity, swearing; berating, railing, rating, reviling
con acclaim, laudation, praise; applause, commendation, compliment
ant adulation

abusive *adj* coarse, insulting, and contemptuous in character or utterance <an *abusive* denunciation>

---

syn synonym(s)   *rel* related word(s)
ant antonym(s)   *con* contrasted word(s)
idiom idiomatic equivalent(s)
|| use limited; if in doubt, see a dictionary

syn contumelious, invective, opprobrious, scurrile, scurrilous, truculent, vituperative, vituperatory, vituperous

rel affronting, insulting, offending, outraging; dirty, odious, offensive; aspersing, maligning, vilifying

con acclaiming, extolling, lauding, praising; eulogistic, panegyrical; flattering

ant complimentary; respectful

abut *vb syn* see ADJOIN

abutting *adj syn* see ADJACENT 3

rel connecting, joining; impinging

con detached, disengaged; disassociated, disconnected, disjoined, parted, separated

abysm *n syn* see GULF 2

abysmal *adj* **1** *syn* see BOTTOMLESS 2

2 *syn* see DEEP 1

rel illimitable, infinite

abyss *n* **1** *syn* see HELL

2 *syn* see GULF 2

3 *syn* see DEPTH 2

academic *adj* **1** *syn* see PEDANTIC

con ignorant, illiterate, unlettered; down-to-earth, everyday, practical, realistic, straightforward

2 *syn* see THEORETICAL 1

rel impractical, utopian, visionary; chimerical, imaginary

accede *vb syn* see ASSENT

rel concur, cooperate; allow, let, permit

con decline; balk, shy, stick; expostulate, kick, object, protest; fight, oppose, resist, withstand

ant demur

accelerate *vb syn* see SPEED 3

rel drive, impel

idiom get going, make up for lost time

con clog, hamper; delay, detain, slow

ant decelerate; retard

accent *n* **1** *syn* see INFLECTION

2 *syn* see EMPHASIS

rel cadence, meter, rhythm; beat, pulsation, pulse, throb

accentuation *n syn* see EMPHASIS

con evenness, sameness, steadiness, uniformity

ant inaccentuation

accept *vb* **1** *syn* see APPROVE 1

rel fancy, like, relish; admire, esteem

con discountenance, disesteem, dislike, disrelish

ant reject

2 to take or sustain without protest or repining <a losing candidate must *accept* the decision of the electorate>

syn bear (with), endure, pocket, swallow, tolerate, tough (out); *compare* BEAR 10

rel acquiesce (in), agree (to *or* with), assent (to), subscribe (to); respect; bow, capitulate, yield

idiom abide by, put up with

con disavow, disown; brush (aside), deny, reject, repudiate

3 *syn* see BELIEVE 1

4 *syn* see APPREHEND 1

acceptable *adj syn* see DECENT 4

rel average, commonplace, ordinary; bearable, endurable, supportable

con insupportable, intolerable, unbearable, unendurable

ant unacceptable

acceptably *adv syn* see WELL 4

acceptant *adj syn* see RECEPTIVE 1

acceptation *n syn* see MEANING 1

accepted *adj* **1** *syn* see USUAL 1

rel conventional, established, recognized; correct, orthodox, proper, right

idiom according to custom (*or* use)

con irregular, questionable, unacceptable, unconventional; incongruent, unconformable, unorthodox

2 *syn* see ORTHODOX 1

acceptive *adj syn* see RECEPTIVE 1

access *n* **1** *syn* see ATTACK 3

rel onset; taking; pang, stitch, twinge

2 *syn* see OUTBURST 1

3 *syn* see DOOR 2

rel passage, route

con departure, retreat, withdrawal

ant egress; outlet

accessible *adj* **1** *syn* see OPEN 4

rel approachable

con limited, restricted; remote

2 *syn* see OPEN 5

ant inaccessible

accession *n syn* see ADDITION

ant discard

accessory *n* **1** *syn* see APPENDAGE

rel accompaniment, concomitant; accretion, addition, increment

2 *syn* see CONFEDERATE

ant principal

accessory *adj syn* see AUXILIARY

rel secondary, subordinate, tributary; coincident, concomitant, concurrent; adventitious, incidental

con constitutional, ingrained, inherent, intrinsic; cardinal, fundamental, vital; essential, indispensable, necessary

ant constituent, integral

accident *n* **1** absence of positive plan or intent <we stopped there by *accident*>

syn chance, fortuity, hap, luck

rel fluke, fortune, hazard

con design, premeditation

ant intent

2 a chance event bringing injury, loss, or distress <the school was closed by an *accident* to the heating system>

syn casualty, misadventure, mischance, mishap

rel calamity, catastrophe, disaster, tragedy; misfortune; chance, destiny, fate, kismet

con foreordination, predestination

accidental *adj* resulting from chance <an *accidental* meeting>

syn casual, chance, contingent, fluky, fortuitous, incidental, odd; *compare* RANDOM, UNINTENTIONAL

rel conditional, dependent; coincident, coincidental; inadvertent, undesigned, unintended, unintentional, unmeant, unplanned, unpurposed, unwitting

con designed, intended, purposed; constitutional, inherent, intrinsic; innate
ant planned; essential

accidentally *adv syn* see INCIDENTALLY 1

acclaim *vb syn* see COMMEND 2
rel cheer, root (for); exalt, magnify; glorify, honor
con berate, rate, revile; damn, execrate, objurgate; censure, denounce
ant vituperate

acclaim *n syn* see APPLAUSE
rel homage, honor, reverence; éclat, glory
con abuse, invective, obloquy; censure, condemnation, denunciation, reprobation
ant vituperation

acclamation *n syn* see APPLAUSE

acclimate *vb syn* see HARDEN 2

acclimatize *vb syn* see HARDEN 2

accolade *n syn* see HONOR 2

accommodate *vb* 1 *syn* see ADAPT
rel bow, defer, submit, yield; alter, change, modify, vary
con alienate, estrange
ant constrain
2 *syn* see HARMONIZE 3
3 *syn* see OBLIGE 2
rel cater (to), humor, indulge
con annoy, harass, harry; irk, vex, worry
ant incommode
4 *syn* see CONTAIN 2
rel encase, enclose
5 *syn* see HARBOR 2

accommodations *n pl* shelter, food, and services (as at a hotel) <searched for *accommodations* as night drew near>
syn lodging, lodgment, room and board
rel bed, room; keep; housing, shelter
idiom bed and breakfast

accompaniment *n* 1 something added to a principal thing usually to increase its impact or effectiveness <her song had a soft orchestral *accompaniment*>
syn augmentation, complement, enhancement, enrichment
rel accessory, addition, supplement; aid, assistance, help
2 an accompanying individual, situation, or occurrence <smog is an inevitable *accompaniment* of excessive numbers of automobiles>
syn associate, companion, concomitant, consort, fellow, mate
rel attendant, colleague, comrade, partner; corollary, equivalent

accompany *vb* to go or be together with <*accompanied* his wife to the theater>
syn attend, bear, ‖bring, ‖carry, chaperon, companion, company, conduct, consort (with), convoy, escort
rel associate, combine, join, link; defend, guard, protect, safeguard, shield; guide, lead, pilot, steer
idiom bear one company, go along with, go hand in hand with
con leave, quit, withdraw; abandon, forsake

accompanying *adj syn* see CONCOMITANT

accomplice *n syn* see CONFEDERATE
rel aider, assistant, helper; flunky, stooge

accomplish *vb syn* see GAIN 1

accomplished *adj syn* see CONSUMMATE 1
rel adept, expert, masterly, proficient; all-around, many-sided, versatile

accomplishment *n* 1 *syn* see ACQUIREMENT
rel art, craft, skill; adeptness, expertise, expertness, proficiency
2 *syn* see ACTION 1

accord *vb* 1 *syn* see AGREE 4
rel coincide, concur; blend, coalesce, fuse, merge
con differ, disagree; compare, contrast
ant conflict
2 *syn* see GRANT 1
rel allot
con deny, gainsay; refuse; detain, hold, reserve
ant withhold
3 *syn* see GIVE 2

accord *n* 1 *syn* see HARMONY 2
rel affinity, attraction, empathy, sympathy; solidarity, union
idiom community of interest(s)
con conflict, contention, difference; animosity, antipathy, hostility
ant dissension, strife; antagonism
2 *syn* see AGREEMENT 2
3 *syn* see HARMONY 1

accordant *adj syn* see HARMONIOUS 2

accordingly *adv syn* see THEREFORE
idiom by reason of that (*or* this), for that (*or* this) reason

according to *prep syn* see BY 5

accost *vb* 1 *syn* see ADDRESS 7
rel buttonhole
con ignore, overlook, slight; avoid, elude, evade, shun
2 to approach boldly or in a challenging or sometimes a defensive manner <*accosted* by a beggar who demanded money>
syn confront, face, front
rel affront, insult, offend, outrage; annoy, bother; challenge, dare, outface
idiom come face to face with, meet face to face
3 *syn* see ADDRESS 4
rel call (to), hail, halloo; buttonhole; dog, hound, pester, worry

accouchement *n syn* see CONFINEMENT 2

account *n* 1 *syn* see BILL 1
2 *syn* see USE 3
con immateriality, inconsequence, insignificance, unimportance; bootlessness, fruitlessness, futility
3 *syn* see WORTH 1
4 *syn* see REGARD 4
rel consequence, dignity, distinction, note; reputation, repute

---

syn synonym(s)   *rel* related word(s)
ant antonym(s)   *con* contrasted word(s)
idiom idiomatic equivalent(s)
‖ use limited; if in doubt, see a dictionary

5 syn see EXPLANATION 2

6 syn see SCORE 4

7 a statement of real or purported events, occurrences, or conditions <wrote an *account* of his travels>

syn chronicle, history, narrative, report, story, version; *compare* STORY 2

account *vb* **1 syn** see CONSIDER 3

rel appraise, assess, estimate, evaluate, rate; esteem

con underestimate, underrate, undervalue

2 syn see EXPLAIN 3

rel answer, elucidate, expound, interpret

accountable *adj* **syn** see RESPONSIBLE

con absolute, arbitrary, autocratic; imperious, magisterial, masterful

ant unaccountable

accouter *vb* **syn** see FURNISH 1

rel attire, dress; adorn, deck, decorate, embellish; fix (up), prepare, ready

accouterment *n, usu* **accouterments** *pl* **syn** see EQUIPMENT

rel appointment(s); furnishing(s); bravery, regalia, trappings

accredit *vb* **1 syn** see APPROVE 2

rel commend, recommend; attest, certify, vouch (for)

con belittle, deprecate, depreciate, disapprove; reject, repudiate

2 syn see ASCRIBE

3 syn see AUTHORIZE 1

rel introduce, present

accretion *n* **syn** see ADDITION

rel enlargement; attachment, joining, uniting; adjunct, appendage

accroach *vb* **1 syn** see ARROGATE 1

2 syn see APPROPRIATE 1

accumulate *vb* to bring together and form a store of <*accumulate* knowledge>

syn amass, cumulate, garner, hive, lay up, roll up, stockpile, store (up), uplay; *compare* HOARD

rel assemble, collect, gather, lay by, lay down, lay in; heap, mass, pile, stock; fund, hoard, treasure

idiom squirrel away

con decrease, diminish, lessen; deal, dispense, distribute, dole (out); dispel, disperse, scatter; consume, expend, spend, use, use up

ant dissipate

accumulation *n* a mass, quantity, or number that has accumulated <an *accumulation* of rubbish>

syn agglomeration, aggregation, amassment, collection, conglomeration, cumulation, hoard, trove

rel bank, heap, mass, pile; cumulus, reserve, stock, store

con dispersal, dispersion, scattering

accumulative *adj* **syn** see CUMULATIVE

rel aggregative, conglomerative; augmentative, multiplicative

con contractile, contractive, reducing, reductive; dispelling, dispersing, dispersive, dissipative, scattering

accuracy *n* **syn** see PRECISION

accurate *adj* **1 syn** see CORRECT 2

con slipshod, slovenly; careless, heedless, lax

ant inaccurate

2 syn see CERTAIN 3

accurately *adv* **syn** see JUST 1

accursed *adj* **syn** see EXECRABLE 1

rel abhorrent, abominable, detestable, hateful, odious; offensive, repugnant, revolting

con admirable, estimable; honorable; divine, holy, sacred

ant blessed

accuse *vb* to declare one guilty of a fault or offense <*accused* her daughter of neglecting her children>

syn arraign, charge, criminate, impeach, incriminate, inculpate, indict, tax

rel blame, censure, criticize, denounce, reprobate; complain

idiom bring charges (against), point the finger at, prefer charges (against)

con absolve, acquit, exonerate, vindicate; accept, approve, endorse, sanction

ant exculpate

accustom *vb* to make something familiar or acceptable through use or experience <*accustom* oneself to city life>

syn familiarize, habituate, inure, use, wont

rel accommodate, adapt, adjust; acclimatize, harden, season

con alienate, estrange, wean; abjure, reject, repudiate; rebuff, repel, repulse, scorn

ant disaccustom

accustomed *adj* **1 syn** see HABITUAL 2

2 syn see USUAL 1

rel commonplace, everyday; conventional, regulation, standard

con infrequent, occasional, uncommon; erratic, odd, peculiar, queer, singular

ant unaccustomed

ace *n* **1 syn** see HAIR

2 syn see PARTICLE

acedia *n* **syn** see SLOTH 2

acerb *adj* **1 syn** see SOUR 1

2 syn see SARCASTIC

acerbate *vb* **syn** see EXACERBATE

acerbic *adj* **1 syn** see SOUR 1

2 syn see SARCASTIC

acerbity *n* **1 syn** see ACRIMONY

rel acidity, sourness, tartness; crabbedness, dourness, saturninity, surliness; acridity, bitterness; harshness, roughness

con blandness, gentleness, mildness, smoothness; amiability, complaisance, good nature

ant mellowness

2 syn see SARCASM

acetose *adj* **syn** see SOUR 1

ache *vb* **1 syn** see HURT 4

2 syn see COMPASSIONATE

rel deplore; sorrow (over); comfort, console, solace

3 syn see LONG

ache *n* **syn** see PAIN 1

rel injury; rack

con alleviation, assuagement, mitigation, relief; comfort, ease

acheronian *adj syn* see GLOOMY 3

acherontic *adj syn* see GLOOMY 3

achieve *vb* **1** *syn* see PERFORM 2
rel complete, conclude, finish; conquer, overcome, surmount
idiom bring to a happy issue, bring to pass
con begin, commence, start
ant fail (in *or* to do)
2 *syn* see GAIN 1
rel acquire, get, obtain, secure; actualize; arrive, come
idiom gain one's end
con depart, deviate, swerve; avoid, elude, escape, shun
ant miss

achievement *n* **1** *syn* see FEAT 2
con omission, slighting
ant failure
2 *syn* see ACQUIREMENT

Achilles' heel *n syn* see SOFT SPOT 2

aching *adj syn* see PAINFUL 1
rel achy

acicular *adj syn* see POINTED 1

aciculate *adj syn* see POINTED 1

acid *adj syn* see SOUR 1
con bland, mild, neutral
ant sweet; alkaline, basic

acidulous *adj syn* see SOUR 1
rel biting, cutting, sharp; piquant, pungent
con bland, mild, neutral; mellow, smooth, suave
ant saccharine

acknowledge *vb* **1** to show often grudgingly by word or deed that one knows of and agrees to or with something <*acknowledge* the justice of a complaint>
syn admit, allow, avow, concede, confess, fess (up), grant, let on, own, own up
rel disclose, divulge, reveal, tell; announce, declare, proclaim, publish
con disallow, disavow, disown, ‖nix, reject; contradict, gainsay, impugn, negate, negative
ant deny
2 to take notice of and accept as being as stated <he is generally *acknowledged* to be the leader in his profession>
syn admit, agree, recognize
rel accept, receive; concede, consider, deem, hold, view
con disregard, neglect, slight; reject, repudiate, spurn
ant ignore

acknowledgment *n syn* see CREDIT 4

acme *n syn* see APEX 2

acoustic *adj syn* see AUDITORY

acquaint *vb* **1** *syn* see INTRODUCE 4
idiom make acquainted
2 *syn* see INFORM 2
rel disclose, divulge, reveal; accustom, habituate
con hold, hold back, reserve, withhold; conceal, hide

acquaintance *n* **1** knowledge of something based on personal exposure <had a considerable *acquaintance* with modern poetry>

syn experience, familiarity, intimacy, inwardness
rel apprehension, grasp, ken; appreciation, awareness, consciousness
con inexperience, unfamiliarity; greenness, verdancy
2 *syn* see FRIEND
rel associate, companion, comrade, crony
con outsider, stranger

acquainted *adj syn* see FAMILIAR 3

acquiesce *vb syn* see ASSENT
rel accommodate, adapt, adjust, reconcile; bow, coincide, concur
con balk, demur, shy (away); kick, protest, remonstrate; differ, dissent
ant object

acquiescence *n* weak or passive agreement to what is asked or demanded <his childish *acquiescence* to all claims on his time>
syn compliance, conformity, resignation
rel complaisance; submissiveness; deference
con contumaciousness, insubordination; independence, self-assurance
ant rebellion, rebelliousness

acquiescent *adj syn* see PASSIVE 2

acquire *vb* **1** *syn* see GET 1
rel achieve, reach; add
con alienate, convey, transfer; abandon, relinquish, surrender, yield
ant forfeit
2 *syn* see EARN 1
rel accumulate, amass, collect, cumulate, garner
3 *syn* see DEVELOP 4

acquirement *n* a power or skill that results from persistent endeavor and cultivation <proud of his scholastic *acquirements*>
syn accomplishment, achievement, acquisition, attainment, finish
rel accretion, addition; advance, advancement; education, erudition, knowledge
con dearth, defect, lack, privation, want

acquisition *n syn* see ACQUIREMENT
rel accession, increment; assets, belongings, means, possessions

acquisitive *adj syn* see COVETOUS
rel demanding, exacting, exigent
con eschewing, forbearing, forgoing; sacrificing
ant abnegating, self-denying

acquit *vb* **1** *syn* see EXCULPATE
rel discharge, free, liberate, release; justify
con condemn, damn, doom, proscribe, sentence
ant convict
2 *syn* see BEHAVE 1

acres *n pl syn* see ESTATE 3

acrid *adj* having or being a noticeable, persistent, and usually unpleasant flavor or sometimes odor <the tonic had an *acrid* aftertaste>
syn amaroidal, astringent, austere, bitter, harsh, sharp

---

syn synonym(s)   *rel* related word(s)
ant antonym(s)   *con* contrasted word(s)
idiom idiomatic equivalent(s)
‖ use limited; if in doubt, see a dictionary

rel biting, caustic, cutting; piquant, pungent; cloying, oversweet, saccharine
con palatable, sapid, tasty, toothsome; delectable, delicious, luscious
ant savory

acrimonious *adj syn* see ANGRY
rel cranky, cross, irascible, splenetic, testy; belligerent, contentious, quarrelsome
con benign, benignant, kind, kindly
ant irenic, peaceable

acrimony *n* sharpness or rancor manifested in words, manner, or disposition <the dispute was renewed with increasing *acrimony*>
syn acerbity, asperity, mordancy
rel bitterness, ill will, malevolence, malice, malignity, spite, spleen; animosity, animus, antipathy, rancor
con civility, courtesy, graciousness, politeness; diplomacy, urbanity
ant suavity

acroamatic *adj syn* see RECONDITE

across *adv* **1** so as to intersect the length of something <cut the board *across*>
syn athwart, crossways, crosswise
2 *syn* see OVER 1

across *prep* from one side to the other <drew the curtain *across* the window>
syn athwart, cross, over

act *vb* **1** to present a role or performance on or as if on the stage <*acted* the part of Hamlet's father>
syn discourse, do, enact, impersonate, perform, personate, play, playact
rel characterize, portray, represent; masquerade; counterfeit, feign, sham, simulate
2 *syn* see ASSUME 4
idiom act a part, put on an act (of)
3 *syn* see BEHAVE 1
rel perform
4 to perform the duties or function of <he *acted* as president for over a year>
syn function, officiate, serve
idiom do duty (as), discharge the office (of), serve in the office (*or* capacity) of
5 to perform especially in an indicated way <the laxative *acted* quickly>
syn behave, function, operate, perform, react, take, work
idiom take effect
6 *syn* see FUNCTION 3

act *n syn* see ACTION 1
rel exploit, feat

actify *vb syn* see VITALIZE

acting *adj syn* see TEMPORARY

action *n* **1** something done or effected <a kindly *action*>
syn accomplishment, act, deed, doing, thing
rel discharge, effectuation, execution, fulfillment, performance; activity, behavior, operation, reaction, work; procedure, proceeding, process
2 *syn* see BATTLE
rel affray, combat, conflict, fray
3 *syn* see SERVICE 1
4 *syn* see SUIT 1

activate *vb syn* see VITALIZE
rel arouse, awaken, rally, rouse, stir, wake, waken
ant arrest

active *adj* **1** being at work or in effective operation <marginal mines that are *active* only when prices are high>
syn alive, dynamic, functioning, live, operative, running, working
rel assiduous, busy, diligent, industrious; energetic, strenuous, vigorous; alert, wide-awake; rushing
con dormant, latent, quiescent; idle, inert, passive, supine; dead, dull, slow
ant inactive; abeyant
2 *syn* see AGILE
rel animated, spirited, vivacious; flexible, graceful, supple
con inert, lumpish, torpid
ant inactive
3 *syn* see ENERGETIC 2
rel expeditious, prompt, ready
con disinterested, indifferent, unconcerned

actively *adv syn* see SERIOUSLY 1

activity *n syn* see EXERCISE 2

activize *vb syn* see VITALIZE

actor *n* **1** one who takes part in an exhibition simulating happenings in real life <had been an *actor* on the stage and in television>
syn impersonator, mime, mimic, mummer, performer, playactor, player, thespian, trouper
2 *syn* see PARTICIPANT
rel mainstay, supporter, sustainer, upholder
con abettor, backer, patron, promoter

actual *adj* **1** existing in act <our *actual* intentions>
syn existent, extant
ant possible, potential
2 existing in or based on fact <problems of *actual* life>
syn absolute, factual, genuine, hard, positive, sure-enough
rel commonplace, everyday, ordinary, routine, usual; concrete, real, tangible
con conjectural, hypothetical, theoretical; putative, reputed, supposititious
ant apparent, nominal
3 *syn* see REAL 3
rel material, objective, phenomenal, physical; authentic, bona fide, legitimate
con abstract, transcendent, transcendental; academic, speculative, theoretical; fabulous, fictitious, mythical
ant ideal; imaginary

actuality *n* **1** *syn* see EXISTENCE 1
rel actualization, externalization, incarnation, materialization; achievement, attainment
con abstraction, ideality, transcendence
ant possibility, potentiality
2 something that has existence <a predicted downturn in the stock market was received as if it were an *actuality*>
syn materiality, reality
rel basis, essence, substance; embodiment, incarnation

3 *syn* see FACT 1

actually *adv syn* see VERY 2

actuate *vb* **1** *syn* see MOVE 5
   2 *syn* see MOBILIZE 1
   rel excite, galvanize, provoke; arouse, rouse, stir; vitalize

act up *vb syn* see CUT UP 2

acumen *n syn* see WIT 3
   rel acuteness, sharpness
   con denseness, density, slowness
   ant obtuseness, obtusity

acuminate *adj syn* see POINTED 1

acuminous *adj syn* see POINTED 1

acute *adj* **1** *syn* see POINTED 1
   rel barbed, prickly, spiky, spined, spiny
   ant blunt
   2 *syn* see SHARP 4
   rel cutting, incisive, trenchant; piercing
   con crass, dense, dull, slow, stupid
   ant obtuse
   3 perceiving clearly and sensitively <an *acute* ear>
   syn keen, perceptive, sensitive, sharp
   rel observant, penetrating, probing; accurate, meticulous, precise
   con imperceptive, insensitive; imprecise, inaccurate; inexact, uncritical
   ant dull
   4 elevated in pitch <an *acute* note>
   syn argute, high, piercing, piping, sharp, shrill, thin, treble
   rel penetrating; reedy, screechy, shrieky, shrilly, squeaky; tinny
   con bass, deep, low
   ant grave
   5 *syn* see SHARP 8
   6 serious to the point of approaching a crisis <an *acute* housing shortage>
   syn climacteric, critical, crucial, desperate, dire
   rel afflictive, grave, serious; aggravated, intensified; dangerous, hazardous, menacing, perilous, precarious, threatening; exigent, urgent

adage *n syn* see SAYING

adamant *adj syn* see INFLEXIBLE 2
   rel immobile, immovable; unsubmitting
   con placable, relenting, submitting; complaisant, obliging; subdued, submissive
   ant yielding

adamantine *adj syn* see INFLEXIBLE 2
   rel immobile, immovable; unsubmitting
   con placable, relenting, submitting; complaisant, obliging; subdued, submissive
   ant yielding

adapt *vb* to bring into correspondence or make suitable <*adapted* himself easily to the company he found himself with>
   syn accommodate, adjust, conform, fit, quadrate, reconcile, square, suit, tailor, tailor-make
   rel qualify, temper; acclimate, acclimatize
   ant unfit

adaptable *adj* **1** *syn* see VERSATILE
   2 *syn* see PLASTIC
   con intractable, irreconcilable, nonconforming, refractory, unaccommodating

ant inadaptable, unadaptable

adapted *adj syn* see ASSORTED 2

add *vb* **1** to bring in or join on something more so as to form a larger or more inclusive whole <*added* music to his accomplishments>
   syn annex, append, subjoin, superadd, take on
   rel affix, attach, fasten, superimpose, tack (on); augment, enlarge, increase; burden, clutter, cumber, encumber, saddle
   con abstract, detach; curtail, decrease, diminish, lessen, reduce
   ant deduct, subtract
   2 to combine numbers or quantities into one sum <*add* up a column of figures>
   syn cast, figure, foot, sum, summate, tot, total, totalize, tote
   rel calculate, compute, estimate, reckon; score, tally

added *adj syn* see ADDITIONAL

addendum *n, sometimes* **addenda** *pl but sing or pl in constr syn* see APPENDIX 1

addict *vb syn* see HABITUATE 2
   rel bias, dispose, incline, predispose; address, apply, direct
   con alienate, estrange; detach, disengage, disincline, indispose
   ant wean

addict *n* a person who by habit or strong inclination indulges in something <a science fiction *addict*>
   syn aficionado, buff, devotee, fan, habitué, hound, lover, votary
   rel enthusiast, fanatic, zealot; hobbyist, putterer, tinkerer

addition *n* something that tends to increase something else (as in size, number, or content) <there are several new *additions* to our staff>
   syn accession, accretion, augmentation, increase, increment, raise, rise
   rel accessory, adjunct, appanage, appurtenance, supplement; continuation, extension, rider; accrual, accruement, accumulation
   con deduction, lessening, reduction

additional *adj* being or coming by way of addition <gave *additional* reasons to justify his position>
   syn added, another, else, farther, fresh, further, more, new, other
   rel accessory, adscititious, collateral, extra, supplemental, supplementary

additionally *adv* **1** *syn* see ALSO 2
   2 *syn* see AGAIN 4

additive *adj syn* see CUMULATIVE
   rel component, constituent, elemental

additory *adj syn* see CUMULATIVE

addle *vb syn* see CONFUSE 2
   rel confound, dumbfound, nonplus; amaze, astound, flabbergast
   idiom addle one's wits
   con animate, enliven, quicken, vivify

---

syn synonym(s)   *rel* related word(s)
ant antonym(s)   *con* contrasted word(s)
idiom idiomatic equivalent(s)
‖ use limited; if in doubt, see a dictionary

ant refresh (*mentally*)

address *vb* **1** *syn* see DIRECT 2
  2 *syn* see SEND 1
  3 to occupy (oneself or one's attention or efforts) with something <*addressed* himself to the job and soon finished it>
  syn apply, bend, buckle (down), devote, direct, give, throw, turn
  rel associate, connect, couple, link, relate; aim, level, point
  idiom bring (oneself) into relation with something, tax (one's energies) with something
  con disregard, ignore, overlook
  4 to communicate directly to or with <*addressed* the governor with his petition>
  syn accost, apply (to), approach, bespeak, memorialize
  rel speak (to), talk (with); appeal (to); apostrophize; petition
  con ignore, overlook, pass up, slight; avoid, cut, disregard
  5 *syn* see TALK 7
  6 to affix directions for delivery <*address* a letter>
  syn direct, superscribe
  7 to seek the attention of usually orally and in order to gain recognition <*address* a stranger to ask directions>
  syn accost, call (to), greet, hail, salute
  rel converse, speak, talk
  idiom attract one's attention
  8 to direct one's attention to in the role of a suitor <ready to marry the first man that *addressed* her>
  syn court, make up (to), pursue, spark, sue, sweetheart, woo
  rel attend, escort, squire; neck, pet, romance, rush, smooch, spoon
  idiom make a play for, pay (one's) addresses to, run after

address *n* **1** the quality or state of being ready or skillful <to bring off such a coup requires *address*>
  syn adroitness, deftness, dexterity, dexterousness, prowess, readiness, skill, sleight; *compare* TACT
  rel competence, efficiency, expertise, know-how, proficiency; craft, finesse; ingeniousness, ingenuity, resourcefulness
  con inadequacy, ineptitude, ineptness, unskillfulness; awkwardness, clumsiness, gawkiness, lubberliness, stupidity
  2 *syn* see TACT
  rel dexterity, ease, facility; cleverness, readiness; affability, graciousness
  con awkwardness, clumsiness, gaucheness; boorishness, churlishness
  ant maladroitness
  3 *syn* see BEARING 1
  4 *syn* see SPEECH 2

adduce *vb* to bring forward for consideration <*adduce* evidence in support of a hypothesis>
  syn advance, allege, cite, lay, offer, present

  rel animadvert, comment, commentate, remark; document, exemplify, illustrate; prefer, proffer, propose, submit, suggest, tender

add up *vb* *syn* see AMOUNT 1

add up (to) *vb* *syn* see MEAN 2

adept *n* *syn* see EXPERT
  ant bungler, incompetent

adept *adj* *syn* see PROFICIENT
  rel clever; adroit, deft, dexterous
  con amateurish, dabbling, dilettantish; awkward, clumsy, maladroit
  ant bungling, inapt, inept

adequacy *n* **1** *syn* see ABILITY 1
  rel equality, satisfactoriness, sufficiency
  idiom enough on the ball
  ant inadequacy, inadequateness
  2 *syn* see ENOUGH

adequate *adj* **1** *syn* see SUFFICIENT 1
  con meager, scanty, sparse
  ant inadequate, unadequate
  2 *syn* see DECENT 4

adequately *adv* **1** *syn* see ENOUGH 1
  2 *syn* see WELL 4

adequation *n* *syn* see EQUIVALENCE

adhere *vb* *syn* see STICK 2
  rel combine, join, link, unite
  con disjoin, disunite

adherence *n* **1** a physical adhering <the close *adherence* of scales to a plant bud>
  syn adhesion, bond, cling, clinging, coherence, cohesion, stickage, sticking
  rel agglutination, cementation, concretion, conglutination; congelation, set, setting, solidification
  con detachment, disjunction, parting, separation
  2 *syn* see ATTACHMENT 1
  con fickleness, inconstancy

adherent *n* *syn* see FOLLOWER
  rel backer, champion, upholder
  con apostate, recreant; deserter, forsaker; adversary, antagonist, opponent
  ant renegade

adhesion *n* **1** *syn* see ADHERENCE 1
  ant nonadhesion
  2 *syn* see ATTACHMENT 1
  con fickleness, inconstancy

adhesive *adj* *syn* see STICKY 1

adieu *interj* *syn* see GOOD-BYE

adieu *n* *syn* see PARTING

ad interim *adj* *syn* see TEMPORARY
  ant permanent

adipose *adj* *syn* see FATTY 1

adiposity *n* *syn* see OBESITY

adit *n* *syn* see DOOR 2

adjacent *adj* **1** *syn* see NEIGHBORING
  ant remote
  2 *syn* see CONVENIENT 2
  3 having a common border <the brothers built on *adjacent* lots>
  syn abutting, adjoining, approximal, bordering, conterminous, contiguous, juxtaposed, touching
  rel closest, nearest, next; consecutive, successive; attached, connected, joined, linked

con distant, far, remote, removed; parted, separated
ant nonadjacent
adjoin *vb* to be contiguous or adjacent to <the new suburb *adjoins* farmland>
syn abut, border, butt (on *or* against), communicate, join, line, march, neighbor, touch, verge
rel meet, run (into); end
adjoining *adj syn* see ADJACENT 3
ant detached
adjourn *vb* **1** *syn* see DEFER
rel curb, hold back, restrain
con advance, expedite, further, promote
2 to bring to a formal close <*adjourn* the legislature>
syn dissolve, prorogate, prorogue, recess, rise, terminate
rel break up, close, disband, discontinue, disperse; stay, suspend
con open; mobilize, muster, rally
ant convene, convoke
adjudge *vb syn* see JUDGE 1
rel accord, allot, assign, award, grant
adjudicate *vb syn* see JUDGE 1
adjunct *n syn* see APPENDAGE
rel accretion, addition; appanage; affix, attachment, fixture
adjust *vb* **1** *syn* see ADAPT
rel accord, correspond; attune, harmonize
2 to alter so as to make efficient or more efficient <*adjust* a carburetor>
syn fix, regulate, tune (up)
rel correct, rectify, right; balance, stabilize, steady, trim, true; arrange, order, rig
idiom make right, put (*or* set) in order, put right (*or* to rights), set right (*or* to rights)
con disarrange, disorder, disturb, upset
ant derange
3 *syn* see HABITUATE 2
adjuvant *adj syn* see AUXILIARY
rel synergistic
con antagonistic, negating, negativing, neutralizing; hindering, impeding, obstructing
ant counteractive
ad–lib *vb syn* see IMPROVISE
admeasure *vb syn* see ALLOT
admeasurement *n syn* see SIZE 1
adminicular *adj syn* see CORROBORATIVE
administer *vb* **1** to supervise the affairs or the provision, use, or conduct of especially in the capacity of an agent or steward <*administer* justice>
syn administrate, carry out, execute, govern, render
rel conduct, direct, manage, run, supervise
2 to provide in appropriate amount <*administer* a laxative>
syn apportion, deal (out), dispense, dole (out), mete (out), portion (out), share out
rel distribute, give, give out, issue; allot, assign, consign; allocate, ration
3 *syn* see GIVE 10
administrate *vb syn* see ADMINISTER 1
administrator *n syn* see EXECUTIVE
admirable *adj syn* see WORTHY 1

admiration *n* **1** *syn* see WONDER 2
rel surprise; ecstasy, rapture, transport
con aloofness, indifference, unconcern
2 *syn* see REGARD 4
rel appreciation; adoration, reverence, veneration, worship
con detestation, hate, hatred, loathing; dislike, disrelish, distaste
ant abhorrence
admire *vb* **1** to view with an elevated feeling of pleasure <*admired* the scene that spread out before them>
syn appreciate, cherish, delight (in), relish; *compare* APPRECIATE 1
rel adore, revere, reverence, venerate, worship
idiom go into raptures over, take delight in
con disesteem, disfavor, dislike, disrelish, mislike
ant disdain
2 to hold in high esteem <*admired* his ability to get things done>
syn consider, esteem, regard, respect
rel appreciate, cherish, prize, treasure, value
idiom have (*or* hold) a high opinion of, rate highly, set (great) store by, think much (*or* highly) of
con abominate, detest, hate, loathe; contemn, despise, disdain, scorn
ant abhor
admirer *n syn* see AMATEUR 1
admissible *adj syn* see PERMISSIBLE
admission *n syn* see DOOR 2
admit *vb* **1** *syn* see TAKE 10
rel allow, permit, suffer; entertain, harbor, house, lodge, shelter
con debar, exclude, shut out; bar, block, hinder, obstruct
ant eject, expel
2 *syn* see ACKNOWLEDGE 1
rel acquiesce, agree, assent, subscribe
ant gainsay
3 *syn* see ENTER 2
rel induct, initiate, install; insert, interject, interpose
con debar, shut out; eject, expel, oust
ant exclude
4 *syn* see ACKNOWLEDGE 2
admittance *n syn* see DOOR 2
admix *vb syn* see MIX 1
admixture *n* **1** an added ingredient that alters the character of something <her love had a marring *admixture* of selfishness>
syn adulterant, alloy, denaturant
rel doctor, fortification, taint; accretion, addition; bit, dash, shade, smack, spice, tinge
2 *syn* see MIXTURE
admonish *vb syn* see REPROVE
rel caution, forewarn, warn
idiom have a word with

---

syn synonym(s)   *rel* related word(s)
ant antonym(s)   *con* contrasted word(s)
idiom idiomatic equivalent(s)
‖ use limited; if in doubt, see a dictionary

con applaud, approve, compliment
ant commend

admonishing *adj syn* see MONITORY

admonishment *n syn* see REBUKE

admonition *n* **1** *syn* see REBUKE
2 *syn* see WARNING

admonitory *adj syn* see MONITORY

ado *n syn* see STIR 1
rel effort, exertion, pains, trouble; confusion, hurly-burly, turmoil, uproar
con calm, peace, serenity, tranquillity; quiet, silence, stillness

adolescence *n syn* see YOUTH 1
ant senescence

adopt *vb* to make one's own what in some fashion one owes to another <*adopt* a new style>
syn embrace, espouse, take on, take up
rel affect, assume; appropriate, arrogate, take, usurp; domesticate, naturalize
idiom adapt to one's own ends, go in for
con reject, spurn; abjure, forswear, renounce
ant discard; repudiate

adoption *n syn* see ESPOUSAL 4

adorable *adj* **1** *syn* see LOVABLE
2 *syn* see DELIGHTFUL

adoration *n* deep, ardent, and often excessive attachment or love <the *adoration* given popular heroes>
syn idolatry, idolization, worship
rel affection, attachment, devotion, love; crush, infatuation, passion, weakness
con antipathy, aversion; disfavor, dislike, distaste
ant detestation

adore *vb* **1** *syn* see REVERE
rel extol, laud, praise
con curse, execrate
2 *syn* see LOVE 2
3 to love, admire, or enjoy excessively <she *adores* and spoils her grandchildren>
syn dote (on *or* upon), idolize, worship
rel admire, esteem, love; coddle, indulge, pamper, spoil
idiom be silly over
con abhor, abominate, hate, loathe; contemn, despise, disdain, scorn
ant detest
4 *syn* see LOVE 1

adorn *vb* to add something nonessential to enhance the appearance or beauty of <a hat *adorned* with feathers>
syn beautify, bedeck, deck, decorate, dress (up), embellish, garnish, ornament, prank, trim
rel enrich, furbish, smarten, spruce (up); bedizen, dandify, fancy up; enhance, heighten, intensify
con clear, divest, expose, strip, uncover; deface, mar, scar, spoil
ant disfigure

ad rem *adj syn* see RELEVANT

adroit *adj* **1** *syn* see DEXTEROUS 1
ant maladroit
2 *syn* see SKILLFUL 2
3 *syn* see CLEVER 4

rel astute, perspicacious, shrewd; intelligent, quick-witted, smart; artful, subtle
con dense, dull, stupid; apathetic, heavy, impassive, phlegmatic, stodgy
ant stolid

adroitness *n* **1** *syn* see ADDRESS 1
2 *syn* see ART 1

adscititious *adj syn* see ADVENTITIOUS

adulation *n syn* see FLATTERY
rel acclaim, applause
ant abuse

adult *adj syn* see MATURE 1
rel aged
con adolescent, pubescent
ant juvenile, puerile

adulterant *n syn* see ADMIXTURE 1

adulterate *vb* to alter fraudulently usually for profit <sausage *adulterated* with cereal products>
syn debase, doctor, dope (up), load, sophisticate, weight
rel cut, dilute; denaturalize, denature, manipulate, tamper (with); defile, impurify, pollute, taint; deacon
con better, improve; augment, fortify, supplement
ant refine

adumbrate *vb* **1** to give a hint or indication of something to come <social unrest that *adumbrated* the revolt>
syn foreshadow, hint, prefigurate, prefigure, shadow (forth); *compare* SUGGEST 5
rel augur, bode, forebode, foretell, portend, presage; lower, menace, threaten; symbolize, typify
idiom cast its shadow before
2 *syn* see FORETELL
rel argue, bespeak, betoken, indicate
3 *syn* see SKETCH
4 *syn* see SUGGEST 5
rel denote, mean, signify
5 *syn* see OBSCURE

adumbration *n syn* see SHADE 1
rel hint, intimation, suggestion; sign, symptom, token; emblem, symbol, type
con disclosure, discovery, divulgence
ant revelation

advance *vb* **1** to cause to proceed or progress toward a goal <warm rains *advanced* the crops>
syn encourage, forward, foster, further, promote, serve
rel aid, assist, help; accelerate, quicken, speed
con hinder, impede; delay, slow; curb, restrain
ant retard; check
2 to raise in rank or position <was *advanced* to the presidency>
syn elevate, prefer, promote, upgrade
rel aggrandize, exalt, raise, uplift; glorify, immortalize, magnify
ant hold back; reduce (*in rank*)
3 *syn* see LEND
4 *syn* see ADDUCE
rel air, broach, expose
5 to go forward in space or time or toward an objective <prices *advanced* sharply>

syn get along, get on, march, move, proceed, progress

rel heighten, increase, intensify; develop, mature

idiom forge ahead, gain ground, get ahead, make headway (*or* progress), make one's way, make rapid strides

con retire, retreat, retrograde, withdraw

ant recede

advance *n* **1** *syn* see PROGRESS 2

2 forward movement especially on a course of action or development <the recent *advance* of technology>

syn advancement, anabasis, headway, march, ongoing, proficiency, progress

rel betterment, furtherance, improvement; development, evolution; breakthrough

con retreat, retrogression; ebbing, retiring, withdrawal

ant recession

3 *syn* see OVERTURE 1

rel offer, proffer

advanced *adj* **1** *syn* see PRECOCIOUS

con retrograde, retrogressive

ant backward

2 *syn* see LIBERAL 3

rel adventurous, daring, venturesome

ant conservative

advancement *n* **1** the act of raising or the status of being raised in grade, rank, or dignity <his *advancement* in his profession was rapid>

syn elevation, preference, preferment, prelation, promotion, upgrading

rel aggrandizement, dignification, magnification, raising, uplifting

con demotion, downgrading, reduction

ant degradation

2 *syn* see ADVANCE 2

advantage *n* **1** *syn* see BETTER 2

2 *syn* see WELFARE

3 something giving one person or side a position of superiority (as in a contest) <he had the *advantage* of greater height>

syn allowance, bulge, ‖deadwood, draw, edge, handicap, head start, odds, ‖overhand, start, vantage; *compare* BETTER 2

rel drop, jump, lead, running start; ascendancy, domination, leadership; mastery, superiority, upper hand, whip hand

idiom ace in the hole, inside track

con embarrassment, hamper, hindrance, impediment, inconvenience

ant disadvantage

4 *syn* see USE 3

rel betterment, improvement; enhancement; heightening

con damage, harm, hurt, injury

ant detriment

5 *syn* see GOOD 1

advantage *vb* *syn* see BENEFIT

advantageous *adj* **1** yielding a profit <sold on very *advantageous* terms>

syn gainful, good, lucrative, moneymaking, paying, profitable, remunerative, well-paying, worthwhile

rel acceptable, agreeable, desirable, pleasing, satisfactory, satisfying

idiom in the black, paying its (own) way

con disadvantageous, unfavorable, unprofitable; damaging, hurtful

2 *syn* see GOOD 1

rel remedial, salutary; conducive, contributory, implemental, instrumental; advisable, expedient

con unfavorable; inconvenient; deleterious, detrimental

ant disadvantageous

advenient *adj* *syn* see ADVENTITIOUS

advent *n* *syn* see ARRIVAL 1

rel approach, nearing

ant exit

advential *adj* *syn* see ADVENTITIOUS

adventitious *adj* coming from without and not participating in the fundamental nature of something <*adventitious* notions that have corrupted the primitive doctrine>

syn adscititious, advenient, advential, supervenient

rel accidental, casual, contingent, fortuitous, incidental

con constitutional, essential, intrinsic; inborn, inbred, innate

ant inherent

adventure *n* an undertaking or experience that involves hazard and requires boldness <recounted the *adventures* of his solitary voyage>

syn emprise, enterprise, exploit, feat, gest, venture

rel hazard, peril, risk; quest; achievement

adventure *vb* *syn* see VENTURE 1

adventuresome *adj* *syn* see ADVENTUROUS

ant unadventurous; cautious

adventurous *adj* courting danger or exposing oneself to danger beyond the call of duty or courage <*adventurous* boys scrambled over the cliff face>

syn adventuresome, audacious, daredevil, daring, foolhardy, rash, reckless, temerarious, venturesome, venturous

rel bold, doughty, intrepid; brash, harebrained, hotheaded, impetuous, imprudent, madcap, overconfident

con shrinking, timid, timorous; afraid, alarmed, fearful, scared; apprehensive, uneasy

ant unadventurous; cautious

adversary *n* *syn* see OPPONENT

rel assaulter, attacker

con backer, supporter, upholder

ant ally

adverse *adj* **1** acting against or in a contrary direction <hindered by *adverse* forces>

syn antagonistic, anti, antipathetic, opposed, opposing, oppugnant

rel contrary, counter, counteractive; hindering, impeding, obstructive; hostile, unfriendly

---

syn synonym(s)   *rel* related word(s)
ant antonym(s)   *con* contrasted word(s)
idiom idiomatic equivalent(s)
‖ use limited; if in doubt, see a dictionary

con coactive, collaborative, cooperative; adjuvant, synergistic; favorable, propitious
2 being opposed to one's interests <an *adverse* balance of trade>
syn detrimental, negative, unfavorable
rel deleterious, harmful, hurtful, injurious; disadvantageous, prejudicial, unpropitious, unsatisfactory
con advantageous, favorable, positive, propitious, satisfactory
adversity *n syn* see MISFORTUNE
rel distress, misery, suffering; deprivation, destitution, indigence, poverty
con bliss, felicity, happiness; comfort, ease
ant prosperity
advert *vb syn* see REFER 3
rel animadvert, note, notice, observe, remark
con disregard, ignore, neglect, overlook
advertent *adj syn* see ATTENTIVE 1
advertise *vb* **1** *syn* see DECLARE 1
rel recount, relate, report; communicate, impart; ballyhoo, promote, propagandize, publicize
con conceal, repress, suppress; bury, hide, obscure
2 *syn* see PUBLICIZE
3 *syn* see PROMOTE 3
advertisement *n syn* see DECLARATION
rel ballyhoo, promotion, propaganda, publicity
advertising *n syn* see PUBLICITY
advice *n* **1** recommendation regarding a decision or course of conduct <benefited from his *advice* on study habits>
syn advisement, counsel
rel direction, guidance, instruction, teaching; input; admonition; caution, cautioning, forewarning, warning
2 *syn* see NEWS
advisable *adj syn* see EXPEDIENT
rel commendable, desirable; becoming, seemly, suitable; sensible
ant inadvisable
advise *vb* **1** *syn* see COUNSEL
rel caution, forewarn, warn; coax, induce, persuade, win (over)
con bedazzle, misadvise, mislead
2 *syn* see CONFER 2
rel deliberate
3 *syn* see INFORM 2
rel disclose, let out, reveal; communicate, impart
advised *adj syn* see DELIBERATE 1
rel intended, intentional, meant; knowing, purposeful, willful
advisement *n syn* see ADVICE 1
advocate *n syn* see EXPONENT
advocate *vb* **1** *syn* see ENCOURAGE 2
2 *syn* see SUPPORT 2
rel justify, vindicate; advance, forward, promote
idiom hold a brief for
con assail, attack; combat, fight, oppose
ant impugn
aegis *n* **1** *syn* see DEFENSE 1

2 *syn* see BACKING
aeneous *adj syn* see BRAZEN 4
aeon *n syn* see AGE 2
aerial *adj* **1** *syn* see AIRY 1
2 *syn* see LOFTY 6
3 *syn* see AIRY 3
rel immaterial, incorporeal; impalpable, imperceptible, imponderable
aesthete *n syn* see CONNOISSEUR
rel perfectionist, stickler; fussbudget, old maid
con barbarian; clod, lout, oaf
affable *adj* **1** *syn* see GRACIOUS 1
rel courteous, polite; suave, urbane; loquacious, talkative
con crabbed, glum, surly; reticent, withdrawn; silent, taciturn, uncommunicative
ant reserved
2 *syn* see GENTLE 2
affair *n* **1** something done or dealt with <trying to get at the truth of the *affair*>
syn business, concern, matter, shooting match, thing
rel care, lookout, responsibility; pie, proceeding
idiom cup of tea
2 *syn* see BUSINESS 8
3 *syn* see LOVE AFFAIR
4 *syn* see AMOUR 2
affect *vb* **1** *syn* see ASSUME 4
2 *syn* see FREQUENT
affect *vb* to produce a usually mental or emotional effect on one capable of reaction <much *affected* by the touching scene>
syn carry, get, impress, influence, inspire, move, strike, sway, touch
rel actuate, draw, drive, impel; penetrate, pierce
idiom work on
affectation *n syn* see POSE 2
rel ostentation, pretentiousness
con ingenuousness, naiveté, naturalness, simplicity, unsophistication
ant artlessness
affected *adj* **1** *syn* see INTERESTED
2 *syn* see SELF-CONSCIOUS
3 *syn* see GENTEEL 3
4 *syn* see PRECIOUS 4
5 *syn* see ARTIFICIAL 3
affecting *adj syn* see MOVING 2
rel piteous, pitiable, pitiful; distressful, distressing, disturbing, troubling
affection *n* **1** *syn* see FEELING 3
rel leaning, penchant, propensity; bias, predilection; bent, faculty, turn
con aversion, hate, hatred; dislike, distaste
ant antipathy
2 *syn* see LOVE 1
rel sympathy, tenderness, warmth; attention, concern, interest; doting, enjoying
con coolness, frigidity
ant coldness
affection *vb syn* see LOVE 2
affection *n* **1** *syn* see DISEASE 1
rel access, attack, paroxysm, spell; derangement, disordering, disturbance
2 *syn* see QUALITY 1

affectionate *adj syn* see LOVING
　rel sympathetic, tender, warm
　con apathetic, impassive, stolid; remote, uninterested, withdrawn
　ant cold; undemonstrative
affective *adj syn* see EMOTIONAL 2
affectivity *n syn* see FEELING 3
affianced *adj syn* see ENGAGED 2
affianced *n syn* see BETROTHED
affiche *n syn* see POSTER
affiliated *adj syn* see RELATED
　con autonomous, free, independent
　ant unaffiliated
affiliation *n syn* see ASSOCIATION 1
affinity *n* **1** *syn* see ATTRACTION 2
　con antipathy, aversion; dislike, distaste; repugnance, repellency, repulsion
　2 *syn* see LIKENESS
　rel accord
affirm *vb syn* see ASSERT 1
　rel attest, certify, guarantee, vouch, witness; say, state
　con debate
affirmative *adj syn* see POSITIVE 6
affix *vb syn* see FASTEN 1
　rel add, annex, append, subjoin
　con disengage, disjoin
　ant detach
afflation *n syn* see INSPIRATION
afflatus *n syn* see INSPIRATION
afflict *vb* to inflict upon one something hard to endure <he was *afflicted* with boils>
　syn agonize, crucify, excruciate, harrow, martyr, martyrize, rack, smite, strike, torment, torture, try, wring
　rel annoy, harass, harry, pester, plague, press, worry; bother, irk, vex; lacerate, wound
　con console, delight, gladden, please, rejoice; ease, relieve, solace
　ant comfort
afflicted *adj syn* see WOEFUL 1
affliction *n* **1** *syn* see TRIAL 1
　rel mischance, mishap
　con alleviation, assuagement, easement, relief
　ant consolation, solace
　2 *syn* see SORROW
　3 *syn* see SICKNESS 1
afflictive *adj* **1** *syn* see PAINFUL 1
　2 *syn* see DEPLORABLE
　3 *syn* see BITTER 2
affluent *adj syn* see RICH 1
　rel acquisitive, grasping
　con poor; bankrupt, impoverished
　ant impecunious; straitened
affranchise *vb syn* see ENFRANCHISE
affray *n* **1** *syn* see BRAWL 2
　2 *syn* see CLASH 2
affright *vb syn* see FRIGHTEN
　rel bewilder, confound
　con animate, fire, inspire
　ant embolden, nerve
affront *vb* **1** *syn* see OFFEND 3
　rel criticize, dispraise
　con compliment; laud, praise; dignify, honor

　2 *syn* see CONFRONT 1
affront *n* a speech or an action designed to impugn the honor or worth of someone or something <her costume was an *affront* to the solemnity of the occasion>
　syn contumely, despite, indignity, insult, slap
　rel dishonor, flouting, offense, outrage, slight; aspersion, barb, defamation, dig
　idiom slap in the face
　con deference, homage, honor; adulation, compliment, flattery
aficionado *n syn* see ADDICT
afield *adj syn* see AMISS 2
afire *adj* **1** *syn* see BURNING 1
　2 *syn* see ALIGHT 2
aflame *adj* **1** *syn* see BURNING 1
　2 *syn* see ALIGHT 2
aflicker *adj syn* ALIGHT 2, ablaze, afire, aflame, aglow
à fond *adv syn* see WELL 3
aforementioned *adj syn* see SUCH 1
aforesaid *adj syn* see SUCH 1
aforethought *adj syn* see DELIBERATE 1
afraid *adj* **1** suffering the effects of apprehension, fear, or terror <too *afraid* to even cry for help>
　syn aghast, anxious, ‖ascared, fearful, frightened, scared, scary, terrified; *compare* FEARFUL 2
　rel shrinking, shy, timid, timorous; cautious, chary, wary; jumpy, skittish
　idiom frightened out of one's wits, in a (blue) funk, scared to death, terror stricken
　con confident, dauntless, fearless; assured, collected, poised, self-possessed
　ant unafraid
　2 *syn* see FEARFUL 2
　idiom all of a twitter (*or* flutter)
　ant unafraid; sanguine
　3 *syn* see DISINCLINED
afresh *adv* **1** *syn* see OVER 7
　2 *syn* see NEW
‖**African dominoes** *n pl syn* see DICE
aft *adv syn* see ABAFT
　rel hind, posterior
　con ahead, before, forward
　ant fore
after *adv* so as to follow in time or space <*after*, we turned toward home>
　syn afterward, afterwhile, behind, by and by, infra, later, latterly, next, subsequently
　rel abaft, aft, astern
　idiom after a time (*or* while), in the wake of
　con ahead, forward
　ant before
after *prep* **1** so as to resemble or follow in some respect <named *after* his father>
　syn for, from
　2 later in time or lower in place or rank <*after* our discussion>

---

syn synonym(s)　　*rel* related word(s)
ant antonym(s)　　*con* contrasted word(s)
idiom idiomatic equivalent(s)
‖ use limited; if in doubt, see a dictionary

syn behind, below, following, next, since, subsequent to
con ante, ere, in advance of, preceding, prior to
ant before
3 *syn* see BEYOND 1
after *adj* **1** *syn* see SUBSEQUENT 1
2 *syn* see POSTERIOR 2
con antecedent, preceding, prior
after all *adv syn* see HOWEVER
aftereffect *n syn* see EFFECT 1
rel remainder, residual, residuum
afterlife *n* **1** *syn* see ETERNITY 2
2 *syn* see HEREAFTER 2
afterlight *n syn* see REVIEW 5
aftermath *n syn* see EFFECT 1
rel remainder, residual, residuum
aftertime *n syn* see FUTURE
afterward *adv syn* see AFTER
afterward *n syn* see FUTURE
afterwhile *adv syn* see AFTER
afterword *n syn* see EPILOGUE 1
afterworld *n syn* see HEREAFTER 2
again *adv* **1** *syn* see ABOUT 6
2 *syn* see OVER 7
3 *syn* see THEN 1
4 as another point, fact, or instance <*again*, consider taxes>
syn additionally, also, besides, further, in addition, then; *compare* ALSO 2
idiom by the same token, into the bargain, on top of that
5 as an alternative and especially a converse <he may win and *again* he may not>
syn contra, contrariwise, contrary, contrawise, conversely, oppositely, vice versa; *compare* HOWEVER
idiom at the same time, be that as it may, just the same, on the other hand
again and again *adv syn* see OFTEN
against *prep* **1** directly opposite <stood *against* the crowd and shouted for order>
syn contra, facing, fronting, over against, toward, vis-à-vis
idiom counter to, face to face with
2 so as to touch <vines trained *against* the wall>
syn to, touching
idiom in contact with, next to
3 *syn* see VERSUS 1
4 without being prevented or obstructed by <succeeded *against* grave handicaps>
syn despite, in spite of, notwithstanding, regardless of
idiom in the face of
5 *syn* see FROM 2
6 *syn* see APROPOS
agape *adj syn* see AGHAST 2
age *n* **1** *syn* see OLD AGE
ant youth
2 *often* **ages** *pl* a long or seemingly long period of time <haven't seen her for *ages*>
syn aeon, blue moon, coon's age, dog's age, donkey's years, eternity, long
idiom month of Sundays, ‖right smart spell
con flash, instant, minute, moment, second, split second, trice

3 *syn* see PERIOD 2
age *vb syn* see MATURE
aged *adj* **1** being in the declining phase of life <*aged* pensioners>
syn ancient, elderly, old, olden
rel pensioned (off), retired, superannuated; senior; hoary, patriarchal, venerable; doddering, senescent, senile, tottery
idiom along in years, getting on, getting on (or along) in years, gray with age, on one's last legs, stricken with years
con juvenile, puerile
ant youthful
2 *syn* see ANCIENT 1
3 *syn* see RIPE 3
ageless *adj syn* see ETERNAL 4
agency *n syn* see MEAN 2
rel antecedent, cause, determinant; gear
agenda *n syn* see PROGRAM 1
agent *n* **1** *syn* see MEAN 2
rel doer, executive, executor, performer; actor, worker; activator, energizer
2 one who acts for another <diplomatic *agents* serving abroad>
syn assignee, attorney, deputy, factor, proxy; *compare* DELEGATE
rel go-between, middleman; instrument, minister, tool; commissioner, proctor, procurator, representative, steward; buyer, commissionaire
ant principal
3 *syn* see SPY
age–old *adj syn* see ANCIENT 1
agglomerate *n syn* see AGGREGATE 1
rel heap, mass, pile
agglomeration *n* **1** *syn* see ACCUMULATION
rel association, combination
2 *syn* see AGGREGATE 1
aggrandize *vb* **1** *syn* see INCREASE 1
rel amplify, build up
2 *syn* see EXALT 1
ant belittle
aggrandizement *n syn* see APOTHEOSIS 2
aggravate *vb* **1** *syn* see INTENSIFY
rel augment, enlarge, increase, multiply; aggrandize
con extenuate, palliate
ant alleviate
2 *syn* see IRRITATE
rel disturb, perturb, upset; annoy, bedevil
con calm, tranquilize
ant appease
aggravation *n syn* see ANNOYANCE 2
aggregate *vb syn* see AMOUNT 1
aggregate *n* **1** a mass or body formed of particles or parts that retain their individuality <an *aggregate* of ill-planned arguments>
syn agglomerate, agglomeration, aggregation, conglomerate, conglomeration; *compare* ACCUMULATION
ant constituent, element
2 *syn* see BODY 5
ant individual, unit; particular
3 *syn* see WHOLE 1
aggregation *n* **1** *syn* see AGGREGATE 1

ant constituent, element
2 *syn* see ACCUMULATION
rel backlog, reserve, stockpile
3 *syn* see GATHERING 2
aggress *vb syn* see ATTACK 1
aggression *n* **1** *syn* see ATTACK 1
2 *syn* see ATTACK 2
rel incursion, inroad, invasion, raid; irruption
ant resistance
aggressive *adj* marked by bold determination and readiness for conflict <an *aggressive* fighter>
syn assertive, assertory, militant, pushful, pushing, pushy, self-assertive
rel belligerent, combative, contentious, scrappy; domineering, imperious, masterful, tough; energetic, hard-hitting, strenuous, vigorous
con passive, unassertive; meek, submissive, yielding
aggressiveness *n syn* see ATTACK 2
aggrieve *vb* **1** *syn* see DISTRESS 2
rel abuse, misuse, outrage; pain
con delight, gladden, please
2 *syn* see WRONG
rel afflict, torment, try; annoy, harass, harry, plague, worry
con benefit, profit
aghast *adj* **1** *syn* see AFRAID 1
rel appalled, horrified, horror-struck; undone, unmanned
idiom scared stiff (*or* white)
2 struck by an intense emotional reaction (as surprise, disgust, or bewilderment) <*aghast* at the lack of discipline>
syn agape, confounded, dismayed, dumbfounded, overwhelmed, shocked, thunderstruck
rel agog, amazed, startled; awed, awestricken; astonished, flabbergasted, surprised
idiom struck all of a heap, taken aback, unable to believe one's eyes (*or* senses)
con acceptant, acquiescent, tolerant
agile *adj* acting or moving with easy alacrity <an *agile* athlete with superior flexibility>
syn active, brisk, brisky, catty, lively, nimble, sprightly, spry, volant, yare, zippy
rel adroit, deft, dexterous; fleet, quick, speedy; limber, lissome, lithe, supple; light-footed, tripping
con inactive, inert, passive; heavy, lethargic, logy; dull, slow, sluggish
ant torpid
agitable *adj syn* see EXCITABLE
agitate *vb* **1** *syn* see SHAKE 4
rel bounce, joggle, jounce; actuate, drive, impel, move
con lull, quiet, still
2 *syn* see DISCOMPOSE 1
rel exasperate, irritate, peeve, provoke, rile, ruffle
ant calm, tranquilize
3 *syn* see DISCUSS 1
rel air, broach, ventilate; consider; assail, attack
agitation *n syn* see COMMOTION 2
rel ado, bustle, disturbance, stir

ant tranquillity
agitator *n syn* see INSTIGATOR
aglow *adj syn* see ALIGHT 2
rel gleaming, glowing, shining; lucent, luminous, radiant
agnate *adj* **1** *syn* see RELATED
2 *syn* see LIKE
agog *adj syn* see EAGER
rel aroused, roused, stirred; excited, galvanized, stimulated; restive; zestful
ant aloof
agonize *vb* **1** *syn* see AFFLICT
rel distress, trouble; chafe, fret, gall
2 *syn* see WRITHE 1
rel bear, endure, suffer
agonizing *adj syn* see EXCRUCIATING
rel exquisite, fierce, intense, vehement, violent
agony *n syn* see DISTRESS
con repose, rest
agrarian *adj syn* see WILD 1
agree *vb* **1** *syn* see ACKNOWLEDGE 2
rel allow, concede, grant, own
con except, exclude
ant deny
2 *syn* see ASSENT
rel allow, concede, grant; receive; acknowledge, admit
con expostulate, kick, object, remonstrate; balk, demur, jib; oppose, resist, withstand
ant protest (against); differ (with)
3 to achieve harmony (as of opinion, feeling, or purpose) <they *agreed* finally on all major issues>
syn coincide, concert, concord, concur, harmonize
rel coact, cooperate, unite
idiom fall in with, hit it off with
con bicker, quarrel, squabble, wrangle; argue, debate, dispute, hassle
ant differ; disagree
4 to exist or go together without conflict or incongruity <his conclusion *agrees* with the evidence>
syn accord, check, check out, cohere, comport, conform, consist, consort, correspond, dovetail, fit (in), ‖gee, go, harmonize, jibe, march, quadrate, rhyme, square, suit, tally
rel approach, equal, match, rival, touch; complete, fulfill, round out, supplement
idiom go hand in hand
con negate, negative, nullify; clash, conflict, jar
ant differ (from)
agree (with) *vb syn* see SUIT 4
agreeability *n syn* see AMENITY 1
agreeable *adj* **1** *syn* see PLEASANT 1
rel delectable, delightful
ant disagreeable
2 *syn* see CONSONANT 1

---

syn synonym(s)   *rel* related word(s)
ant antonym(s)   *con* contrasted word(s)
idiom idiomatic equivalent(s)
‖ use limited; if in doubt, see a dictionary

con conflicting, inharmonious, jarring, uncongenial

agreeableness *n syn* see AMENITY 1

agreed *adv syn* see YES 1

agreement *n* **1** *syn* see HARMONY 2
ant disagreement
2 a settlement reached by parties to a dispute or negotiation <the company has reached an *agreement* with the striking workers>
syn accord, deal, understanding; *compare* CONTRACT
rel cartel, concordat, convention, entente, pact; compact, contract, covenant, treaty; engagement; consensus
3 *syn* see TREATY
4 *syn* see CONTRACT

agrestal *adj syn* see WILD 1

agrestic *adj syn* see RURAL

agriculture *n* the science or business of raising useful plants and animals <opening the country for *agriculture*>
syn farming, husbandry

aground *adj* being or becoming forced onto the ground or shore <the boat is *aground* and breaking up>
syn beached, grounded, stranded
idiom high and dry, on the rocks
ant afloat

ahead *adv* **1** *syn* see BEFORE 1
con after
ant behind
2 further on in the direction in question <the road stretched *ahead* toward the west>
syn alee, forth, forward, onward

ahead of *prep syn* see BEFORE 1

aid *vb syn* see HELP 1
rel alleviate, lighten, mitigate, relieve
ant impede

aid *n* **1** *syn* see HELP 1
2 *syn* see HELP 2
rel alleviation, assuagement, mitigation; backing, support
idiom a leg up
con check, curb, restraint; bar, obstacle, obstruction
ant impediment
3 *syn* see HELPER
4 *syn* see ASSISTANT 2
rel aider, befriender, benefactor, ministrant, succorer; striker

aidant *adj syn* see HELPFUL 1

aide *n syn* see ASSISTANT 2

aide–de–camp *n syn* see ASSISTANT 2

aiding *adj syn* see HELPFUL 1

ail *vb syn* see TROUBLE 1
rel afflict, try
idiom be the matter (with), give one trouble
con alleviate, ease, relieve; comfort, console, solace

ailing *adj syn* see UNWELL
rel debilitated, enfeebled, gone, strengthless, weak; droopy, limp, sapless, spiritless
con hale, lusty, robust, rugged, vigorous

ailment *n* **1** *syn* see DISEASE

2 *syn* see UNREST

aim *vb* **1** *syn* see DIRECT 2
rel concentrate, fix, focus
idiom draw a bead on, take aim
2 to have as a controlling desire something that transcends one's present capacity for attainment <from a boy he had *aimed* at high office>
syn aspire, pant
rel attempt, endeavor, essay, strive, try; design, intend, propose, purpose; covet, crave, yearn (for)
idiom have an eye to, reach for the stars, set one's eyes upon
3 *syn* see INTEND 2
rel choose, desire, want, wish; expect
idiom have (*or* keep) in view, promise oneself (to)
4 *syn* see SLANT 2

aim *n syn* see AMBITION 2
rel desideratum, desire, idol, urge
idiom end in view

aimless *adj syn* see RANDOM

air *n* **1** *syn* see BEARING 1
rel manner, style
2 *usu* **airs** *pl syn* see POSE 2
rel loftiness, ostentation, pretentiousness, show; complacency, self-importance, vainglory, vanity
3 a pervading influence that colors outward appearance or apparent character <the village had an *air* of decay>
syn atmosphere, aura, feel, feeling, mood, semblance
rel character, property, quality
con basis, essence, reality
4 *syn* see MELODY

air *vb syn* see EXPRESS 2
rel discover, divulge, reveal; broadcast, declare, proclaim, publish
idiom make public, noise (*or* sound) abroad, spread far and wide

airless *adj syn* see STUFFY 1

airman *n syn* see PILOT 2

airy *adj* **1** of or relating to air <clouds drifting on *airy* currents>
syn aerial, atmospheric, pneumatic
rel gaseous, vaporous
2 *syn* see LOFTY 6
rel exposed, windswept; supernal
3 resembling or suggesting air especially in lightness or lack of substance <*airy* persiflage>
syn aerial, ethereal, vaporous, vapory
rel frivolous, light, volatile; rare, rarefied, tenuous, thin; dainty, delicate, diaphanous, exquisite, spirituel
con corporeal, material, physical; bulky, massive, massy
ant substantial
4 *syn* see ELASTIC 2
rel animated, high-spirited, spirited
5 *syn* see WINDY 1

akin *adj* **1** *syn* see RELATED
2 *syn* see LIKE
rel kindred; according, agreeing, conforming, harmonizing

con extraneous, foreign
ant alien
alacrity *n* promptness in responding or acting <accepted the invitation with *alacrity*>
syn dispatch, expedition, goodwill, promptitude, readiness
rel briskness, eagerness; enthusiasm, fervor, heartiness, zeal; promptness, quickness
con hesitation, procrastination, temporization, vacillation; apathy, indifference, lethargy, phlegm, sluggishness
ant dilatoriness
a la mode *adj syn* see STYLISH
alarm *n* **1** a signal that warns or calls to action <the *alarm* consisted of two quick flashes of light>
syn alert, SOS, tocsin
rel caution, forewarning, prenotice, warning
2 *syn* see FEAR 1
rel upset; strain, stress, tension
con calm, calmness, serenity, tranquillity; equanimity, sangfroid
ant assurance; composure
alarm *vb syn* see FRIGHTEN
rel amaze, astonish, surprise
idiom give one a turn
con comfort, console, solace
ant assure, relieve
alarmable *adj syn* see EXCITABLE
albeit *conj syn* see THOUGH
album *n syn* see ANTHOLOGY
alcohol *n syn* see LIQUOR 2
alcoholic *adj syn* see SPIRITUOUS
alcoholized *adj syn* see INTOXICATED 1
alcove *n syn* see SUMMERHOUSE
alee *adv syn* see AHEAD 2
alehouse *n* an establishment serving primarily beer and ale <an *alehouse* specializing in beers actually brewed on the premises>
syn beer garden, beer hall, ‖beerhouse, bierstube, mughouse, stube; *compare* BAR 5
rel barrelhouse, bistro, bottle club, brasserie, cabaret, café, honky-tonk, nightclub, rathskeller, roadhouse, wineshop
alembicated *adj syn* see PRECIOUS 4
alert *adj* **1** *syn* see WATCHFUL
rel attentive, heedful, mindful; careful
idiom all eyes and ears, on (one's) guard, on the alert
con inattentive, unmindful; aloof, detached, indifferent, unconcerned
2 *syn* see INTELLIGENT 2
rel apt, prompt, quick, ready
con lackadaisical, languid, listless
3 *syn* see LIVELY 1
rel frisky; mercurial
idiom full of life
con inactive, indolent
ant inert
alert *n syn* see ALARM 1
alfresco *adj syn* see OUTDOOR
algetic *adj syn* see PAINFUL 1
alias *n syn* see PSEUDONYM
alibi *n syn* see EXCUSE 1

alien *adj syn* see EXTRINSIC
rel exotic, outlandish, strange; incompatible, incongrous, inconsonant
con cognate, kindred, related; compatible, congenial, congruous, consonant; germane, material, pertinent, relevant
ant akin; assimilable
alien *n syn* see STRANGER
con national, subject
ant citizen
alien *vb* **1** *syn* see ESTRANGE
rel alter, change, convert
con accommodate, adjust, conform, reconcile
ant unite; reunite
2 *syn* see TRANSFER 4
rel give up, hand over, relinquish
alienate *vb* **1** *syn* see TRANSFER 4
rel give up, hand over, relinquish
2 *syn* see ESTRANGE
rel alter, change, convert
con accommodate, adjust, conform, reconcile
ant unite; reunite
alienation *n* **1** *syn* see ESTRANGEMENT
2 *syn* see INSANITY 1
alight *vb* to come to rest after or as if after a flight, a descent, or a fall <snowflakes *alighting* on the bare trees>
syn land, light, perch, roost, set down, settle, sit down, touch down
rel drop, fall, tumble
con arise, ascend, rise, soar
alight *adj* **1** *syn* see BURNING 1
2 made bright by or as if by fire <her face *alight* with joy>
syn ablaze, afire, aflame, aflicker, aglow
rel bright, effulgent, fulgent, refulgent; blazing, flaming, flaring, glowing
con dark, dusky, gloomy, heavy, lowery, shadowed, shadowy
align *vb syn* see LINE 1
rel adjust, fix, regulate
con unsettle
alike *adj syn* see LIKE
con separate
ant unlike; different
alikeness *n syn* see LIKENESS
aliment *n syn* see FOOD 2
alimentary *adj syn* see NUTRITIVE 1
alimentation *n syn* see LIVING
alimentative *adj syn* see NUTRITIVE 1
alimony *n syn* see LIVING
alive *adj* **1** *syn* see LIVING 1
con inactive, inert
ant dead, defunct
2 *syn* see EXTANT 1
3 *syn* see ACTIVE 1
rel fresh, green, verdant
con dormant, inactive, quiescent
ant dead, extinct

---

syn synonym(s)   *rel* related word(s)
ant antonym(s)   *con* contrasted word(s)
idiom idiomatic equivalent(s)
‖ use limited; if in doubt, see a dictionary

4 syn see AWARE
rel vigilant, watchful, wide-awake; intelligent, quick, quick-witted
con heedless, inattentive, oblivious, unmindful; careless, neglectful, negligent
ant blind (to)
5 full of vigorous life, animation, or activity <the streets were *alive* with shoppers>
syn abounding, overflowing, replete, rife, swarming, teeming, thronged
rel crowded, populous, thick; filled, flush, full
con barren, empty, vacant, void; unoccupied, unpopulated, untenanted
all *adj* **1 syn** see WHOLE 4
rel full, plenary
2 each member or individual of <*all* my friends came with me>
syn each, every
ant no
all *adv* **1** without exception <the money was *all* spent>
syn all in all, altogether, exactly, in toto, just, purely, quite, stick, totally, utterly, wholly
idiom in its entirety
2 syn see APIECE
all *pron* **1 syn** see EVERYTHING
2 syn see EVERYBODY
all *n* **syn** see WHOLE 1
all–around *adj* **1 syn** see VERSATILE
rel complete, consummate
2 not narrowly particularized <taking an *all-around* view of the problem>
syn comprehensive, general, global, inclusive, overall, sweeping
rel broad, extensive, panoramic, wide; all-inclusive, unexcluding, unexclusive, wide-ranging; synoptic
con express, particular, specific; narrow, precise, restricted; individual, singular
allay *vb* **1 syn** see RELIEVE 1
con arouse, rouse, stir; excite, provoke, stimulate; aggravate, enhance
ant intensify
2 syn see CALM
rel ease, soften, subdue; deaden, dull, temper; disburden, disembarrass, disencumber; deliver, free, release
con aggravate, enhance, heighten, magnify, worsen
ant intensify
all but *adv* **1 syn** see NEARLY
2 syn see ALMOST 2
allege *vb* **syn** see ADDUCE
rel affirm, assert, avouch, avow, declare, profess; recite, recount, rehearse, state
con contradict, deny, gainsay, impugn, negate, negative; controvert, disprove, rebut, refute
ant contravene
alleged *adj* of questionable truth or genuineness <had doubts of the *alleged* miracle>
syn ostensible, pretended, professed, purported, so-called, supposed; *compare* SUPPOSED 1
rel credible, plausible, specious; doubtful, dubious, questionable; self-styled, soi-disant, would-be

idiom in name only
con authentic, bona fide, genuine, veritable; actual, real, true; delusory, erroneous, fallacious, false, illusory, imaginary, unreal
allegiance *n* **syn** see FIDELITY 1
rel firmness; consecration, dedication; deference, homage, honor
con alienation, disaffection; disloyalty, treason
allegiant *adj* **syn** see FAITHFUL 1
allegory *n* **1** a method of indirect representation (as in literature or art) of ideas or truths <by *allegory* such abstractions as love and fear can be depicted>
syn figuration, symbolism, symbolization, typification
2 a literary form that tells a story to present a truth or enforce a moral <Orwell's *Animal Farm* is a well-known English *allegory*>
syn apologue, fable, myth, parable; *compare* MYTH 1
allergy *n* **syn** see ANTIPATHY 2
rel rejection, repulsion, revulsion
con affinity, attraction, sympathy
alleviate *vb* **syn** see RELIEVE 1
rel cure, remedy
idiom temper the wind to the shorn lamb
con augment, heighten, intensify
ant aggravate
alleviation *n* **syn** see EASE 3
all–fired *adj* **syn** see UTTER
alliance *n* **1 syn** see ASSOCIATION 1
2 an association (as of nations) for a common object <a world *alliance* in support of peace>
syn anschluss, coalition, confederacy, confederation, federation, league, union; *compare* UNIFICATION
rel association, club, order, society
allied *adj* **syn** see RELATED
rel linked, united; parallel, similar
con alien, extraneous, foreign; discrete, separate, several
ant unallied
all in *adj* **syn** see EFFETE 2
idiom at last gasp
all in all *adv* **1 syn** see ALL 1
2 syn see ALTOGETHER 3
allineate *vb* **syn** see LINE 1
allness *n* **syn** see ENTIRETY 1
allocate *vb* **1 syn** see ALLOT
con reserve, sequester, stockpile
2 syn see DESIGNATE 3
allocution *n* **syn** see SPEECH 2
allot *vb* to give as one's share, portion, role, or place <*allotted* himself a daily hour for exercise>
syn admeasure, allocate, allow, apportion, assign, give, lot, mete (out)
rel deal (out), dispense, distribute, dole (out); equip, fit out, furnish; accord, grant, vouchsafe; appoint, ordain, prescribe
con detain, hold, hold back, keep, retain, withhold; appropriate, arrogate, confiscate
allotment *n* **1 syn** see SHARE 1
2 syn see RATION
all–out *adj* **syn** see TOTAL 5

all over *adv syn* see EVERYWHERE 1
allover *adj syn* see OMNIPRESENT
||**all–overs** *n pl syn* see JITTERS
allow *vb* **1** *syn* see ALLOT
  rel bestow, confer
  con refuse
  2 *syn* see ACKNOWLEDGE 1
  rel accede, acquiesce, assent
  con confute, refute, reject
  ant disallow
  3 *syn* see LET 2
  rel brook, endure, stand, tolerate; defer, submit, yield
  con avert, prevent, ward (off)
  ant inhibit
allowable *adj syn* see PERMISSIBLE
allowance *n* **1** *syn* see RATION
  rel assignment; appropriation, grant, subsidy
  2 *syn* see SHARE 1
  3 *syn* see ADVANTAGE 3
  rel aid, assistance, help; bounty, grant, subsidy
  4 *syn* see PERMISSION
  rel countenance, favor; indulgence, toleration
  con refusal, rejection; contradiction, contravention, negation
  5 a taking into account of extenuating circumstances or of contingencies <we must make *allowance* for the inexperience of youth>
  syn concession
  rel accommodation, adaptation, adjustment; extenuation, mitigation, palliation
alloy *n* **1** *syn* see ADMIXTURE 1
  2 *syn* see MIXTURE
all–powerful *adj syn* see OMNIPOTENT
all right *adv syn* see YES 1
all right *adj syn* see DECENT 4
all round (*or* **all around**) *adv syn* see EVERYWHERE 1
all there *adj syn* see SANE 2
all told *adv syn* see ALTOGETHER 3
allude *vb syn* see REFER 3
  rel hint, imply, intimate, suggest
allure *vb* **1** *syn* see ATTRACT 1
  rel delude; woo
  con avoid, elude, eschew, shun; alienate, disaffect, estrange, wean
  2 *syn* see LURE
allure *n syn* see CHARM 3
allurement *n* **1** *syn* see ATTRACTION 1
  2 *syn* see LURE 2
alluring *adj syn* see ATTRACTIVE 1
  rel appetizing; beguiling, delusive
  con repellent; disagreeable, displeasing, uninviting, unlikable, unpleasant
  ant repulsive
almighty *adj syn* see OMNIPOTENT
almost *adv* **1** *syn* see NEARLY
  2 not actually but in effect <he paid *almost* nothing for it>
  syn all but, as good as, as much as, essentially, practically, well-nigh; *compare* VIRTUALLY
  idiom for all practical purposes, in effect, just about, to all intents and purposes
alms *n pl syn* see DONATION
aloft *adv syn* see OVER 4

  rel high; skyward, upward
  idiom in the clouds
alone *adj* **1** separated from others <the house was *alone* on a windy ridge>
  syn apart, detached, isolate, isolated, removed, unaccompanied
  rel out-of-the-way, private, remote, retired, secluded, withdrawn
  idiom off the beaten track
  con adjacent, close-by, near-at-hand, nearly, neighboring, nigh
  2 *syn* see LONE 1
  3 having no equal or rival and being single in kind or excellence <a drug *alone* in its curative powers>
  syn matchless, only, peerless, unequaled, unique, unmatched, unparalleled, unrivaled; *compare* SUPREME
  rel inimitable; incomparable, unexcelled, unsurpassed; excellent, good, superior
  idiom second to none
  con common, commonplace, everyday, ordinary, usual; accustomed, conventional, customary, regular
  4 *syn* see ONLY 2
alone *adv syn* see ONLY 1
aloneness *n syn* see SOLITUDE
along *adv* **1** so as to make forward progress <hurrying *along* toward town>
  syn forth, forward, on, onward; *compare* AHEAD 2
  2 *syn* see ALSO 2
alongside *prep syn* see BESIDE 1
aloof *adj* **1** *syn* see INDIFFERENT 2
  rel arrogant, disdainful, haughty, proud; chilly, cold, cool, frigid; constrained, reserved, restrained, reticent, standoffish
  con affable, companionable, gregarious, sociable, social; friendly, neighborly
  ant familiar; outgoing
  2 *syn* see UNSOCIABLE
alp *n syn* see MOUNTAIN 1
alpha *n syn* see BEGINNING
  ant omega
alphabet *n* **1** a set of characters in which a language can be written <the Greek *alphabet*>
  syn ABC(s), christcross-row, letters
  2 the simplest fundamental part or level <learning the *alphabet* of computer science>
  syn ABC's, elements, fundamentals, grammar, principles, rudiments
  rel beginning, commencement, start; outset
  idiom first steps
  con entirety, total, whole; details, minutiae, trivia
already *adv* **1** *syn* see BEFORE 2
  2 *syn* see EVEN 2
also *adv* **1** in the same manner <they *also* serve who nurse the wounded soldiers>

syn synonym(s)   *rel* related word(s)
ant antonym(s)   *con* contrasted word(s)
idiom idiomatic equivalent(s)
|| use limited; if in doubt, see a dictionary

syn correspondingly, likewise, similarly, so
idiom in like manner
2 in addition to that <he was stern but *also* just>
syn additionally, along, as well, besides, furthermore, item, likewise, more, moreover, still,
too, withal, yea, yet
idiom into the bargain, on top of that, to boot
3 *syn* see AGAIN 4
alter *vb* **1** *syn* see CHANGE 1
rel accommodate, adapt, adjust, moderate,
modulate, temper; doctor
idiom work a change (in)
con conserve, keep, preserve, retain
ant fix
2 *syn* see STERILIZE
alteration *n* **1** *syn* see CHANGE 1
rel accommodation, adaptation, adjustment;
conversion, metamorphosis, transformation;
fluctuation, shilly-shally, vacillation, wavering
con perdurability, permanence, stability; continuance, endurance, persistence
ant fixation, fixity
2 *syn* see TRANSITION
3 *syn* see CONVERSION 2
altercate *vb* *syn* see QUARREL
rel agitate, argue, debate, dispute
con accord, get along; accommodate, adapt, adjust, conform
ant concur
altercation *n* *syn* see QUARREL
rel argument; combat, contest
con agreement, concord, consonance, harmony;
empathy, like-mindedness, sympathy, understanding
ant accord; concurrence
alterity *n* *syn* see DISSIMILARITY
alternate *adj* **1** *syn* see INTERMITTENT
rel alternant, alternating, rotating; complementary, corresponding, reciprocal
con sequent, successive
ant consecutive
2 *syn* see SUBSTITUTE 1
rel equivalent, proxy, replacing; exchangeable,
interchangeable; makeshift, provisional, tentative
alternate *vb* *syn* see ROTATE 2
rel fluctuate, oscillate, sway, waver; recur, return, revert
con follow, succeed
alternate *n* *syn* see SUBSTITUTE
alternately *adv* *syn* see INSTEAD
alternation *n* *syn* see SUCCESSION 2
rel recurrence, return, reversion; reappearance,
repetition
alternative *adj* *syn* see SUBSTITUTE 1
rel equivalent, proxy, replacing; exchangeable,
interchangeable; makeshift, provisional, tentative
alternative *n* *syn* see CHOICE 1
rel attainable, contingency, possibility
alternatively *adv* *syn* see INSTEAD
although *conj* *syn* see THOUGH
altitude *n* *syn* see HEIGHT
rel apex, eminence, peak, summit

con depth
altitudinous *adj* *syn* see HIGH 1
altogether *adv* **1** *syn* see WELL 3
2 *syn* see ALL 1
3 as a total <*altogether* it cost over a thousand
dollars>
syn all told, in all, quite
idiom taken together
4 with minor exceptions or flaws <*altogether* the
party was a success>
syn all in all, by and large, en masse, generally,
on the whole
idiom all things considered, as a whole, for the
most part, generally speaking, in the main
altruistic *adj* *syn* see CHARITABLE 1
rel considerate, kind, unselfish; bounteous,
bountiful, generous, liberal, openhanded; bighearted, magnanimous, noble-minded
con egotistic, self-centered, selfish, self-seeking;
illiberal, mean, niggardly, stingy, ungenerous
ant egoistic
always *adv* **1** on every relevant occasion <*always*
made the same mistake>
syn constantly, continuously, ever, invariably,
perpetually
rel frequently, often, regularly, usually
idiom in every case (*or* instance), without exception
con rarely, seldom
ant never
2 *syn* see EVER 2
‖**amah** *n* *syn* see NURSEMAID
amalgam *n* *syn* see MIXTURE
amalgamate *vb* *syn* see MIX 1
rel compact, consolidate, unify
con crumble, decompose, disintegrate; disperse,
dissipate, scatter
amalgamation *n* **1** *syn* see MIXTURE
2 *syn* see CONSOLIDATION 2
amaranthine *adj* *syn* see EVERLASTING 1
amaroidal *adj* *syn* see ACRID
amass *vb* *syn* see ACCUMULATE
ant distribute
amassment *n* *syn* see ACCUMULATION
amateur *n* **1** one having a marked and usually informed taste or liking for something <an *amateur* of fine fabrics>
syn admirer, devotee, fan, fancier, votary
rel crank, enthusiast, faddist, infatuate, ‖nut,
zealot; aesthete, cognoscente, connoisseur, dilettante; illuminato, illuminist
con abecedarian, dabbler, tyro; adept, expert
2 one who follows a pursuit without attaining
mastery or professional status <a nation handicapped by *amateurs* in high office>
syn abecedarian, dabbler, dilettante, nonprofessional, smatterer, tyro, uninitiate
rel beginner, greenhorn, neophyte; apprentice,
novice, probationer; potterer, putterer, tinker
con adept, virtuoso, wizard
ant expert, master; professional
amateurish *adj* lacking or marked by lack of expert skill or finish <an *amateurish* actor>

syn dabbling, dilettante, dilettantish, dilettantist, jackleg, unaccomplished, unfinished, ungifted, unskilled
rel clumsy, crude, green, raw, untutored; defective, deficient, faulty, flawed
con accomplished, expert, gifted, skilled
ant professional

amative *adj syn* see EROTIC

amatory *adj syn* see EROTIC
rel admiring, attracted, yearning

amaze *vb syn* see SURPRISE 2
rel affect, impress, move, strike, touch

amaze *n syn* see WONDER 2
rel confoundment; surprise

amazement *n syn* see WONDER 2
rel confoundment; surprise

amazing *adj syn* see MARVELOUS 1

amazon *n syn* see VIRAGO

ambidextrous *adj* **1** *syn* see TWO-HANDED 2
2 *syn* see VERSATILE
3 *syn* see INSINCERE

ambience *n syn* see ENVIRONMENT

ambient *n syn* see ENVIRONMENT

ambiguity *n* expression or an expression obscure because subject to more than one interpretation <a speech full of *ambiguities*>
syn amphibology, double entendre, double meaning, equivocality, equivocation, equivoque, tergiversation
rel dodge, evasion, hedge, quibble, shift, subterfuge; cavil, haggling, hairsplitting, quibbling; obscurity, uncertainty, vagueness
con definiteness, expressness, specificity; clearness, exactness, precision
ant explicitness; lucidity

ambiguous *adj* **1** *syn* see OBSCURE 3
rel doubtful, dubious, questionable
con clear, lucid, perspicuous; categorical, express, specific
ant explicit
2 *syn* see DOUBTFUL 1

ambit *n* **1** *syn* see CIRCUMFERENCE
2 *syn* see RANGE 2

ambition *n* **1** strong desire for advancement <a life ruled by *ambition*>
syn ambitiousness, aspiration, pretension
rel drive, go-ahead, push; anxiety, avidity, eagerness, keenness; energy, enterprise, spirit; goad, incentive, motive, spur
con contentment, satisfaction; faineance, indolence, lethargy, sloth
2 an object of desire or intent <his *ambition* was to have enough to live on without working>
syn aim, goal, mark, objective, quaesitum, target; *compare* INTENTION
rel design, intent, purpose; desire, fancy, hope, wish; dream, ideal, nirvana
3 *syn* see ENTERPRISE 4

ambitious *adj* **1** marked by intense desire for advancement (as in power, fame, or wealth) <a ruthlessly *ambitious* politician>
syn aspiring, emulous, vaulting
rel aggressive, enterprising, go-ahead, pushing, up-and-doing; energetic, hardworking, indefatigable; anxious, avid, eager, keen

con apathetic, phlegmatic, stolid; faineant, indolent, lazy, slothful
2 of a kind to try or exceed one's powers of performance <an *ambitious* scheme to corner the gold market>
syn grandiose, lofty, pretentious, utopian, visionary
rel audacious, bold, daring; chimerical, extravagant, high-flown, impractical, quixotic, unrealistic
con easy, plain, straightforward; feasible, practicable, realistic; unpretentious
ant modest

ambitiousness *n syn* see AMBITION 1

ambivalent *adj syn* see EQUIVOCAL 2

amble *vb syn* see SAUNTER
rel dally, dawdle, dillydally, loiter

ambrosial *adj* **1** *syn* see DELIGHTFUL
2 *syn* see SWEET 2

ambulant *adj syn* see ITINERANT
ant bedfast, bedridden

ambulate *vb syn* see WALK 1

ambulatory *adj syn* see ITINERANT

ambuscade *n syn* see AMBUSH

ambush *vb syn* see SURPRISE 1
rel assail, assault, attack; ensnare, entrap, snare, trap

ambush *n* a device to entrap an enemy by lying in hiding until a surprise attack is feasible <planned an *ambush* on the cliff above the trail>
syn ambuscade, ambushment
rel lure, snare, trap; blind, cover, hideout, retreat

ambushment *n syn* see AMBUSH

ameliorate *vb* **1** *syn* see IMPROVE 1
rel alleviate, lighten, mitigate, relieve
con damage, harm, hurt, impair, injure, mar, spoil; aggravate, intensify
ant worsen; deteriorate
2 *syn* see IMPROVE 3

amenable *adj* **1** *syn* see RESPONSIBLE
rel open, subject; dependent, subordinate
con autarchic, free
ant independent (of); autonomous
2 *syn* see OBEDIENT
rel subdued, tame; receptive, responsive, willing; adaptable, impressionable, malleable, plastic, pliable, pliant
con fierce, mulish, obstinate, stubborn, truculent
ant recalcitrant, refractory

amend *vb* **1** *syn* see CORRECT 1
rel repair; elevate, lift, raise
con corrupt, debauch, deprave, pervert, vitiate
ant debase
2 *syn* see IMPROVE 1
rel advance, forward, promote
ant worsen; impair

amends *n pl syn* see REPARATION

---

syn synonym(s)   **rel** related word(s)
ant antonym(s)   **con** contrasted word(s)
idiom idiomatic equivalent(s)
‖ use limited; if in doubt, see a dictionary

amenity *n* **1** the quality of being pleasant or agreeable <a discussion conducted in perfect *amenity*><the *amenity* of the climate>
syn agreeability, agreeableness, amiability, cordiality, enjoyableness, geniality, gratefulness, pleasance, pleasantness, sweetness and light
rel attractiveness, charm, delightfulness; fascination, pleasingness
con disagreeableness, distastefulness, unattractiveness, unpleasantness
2 a feature that makes for pleasantness or ease <among the *amenities* of the house is central air-conditioning>
syn comfort, convenience, facility
rel betterment, enhancement, enrichment, improvement; excellence, merit, quality, virtue
con difficulty, hardship, trial, vicissitude
3 *pl* **amenities** *syn* see MANNER 5
4 *syn* see LUXURY
5 *syn* see COURTESY 1
rel civility, courteousness, politeness; affability, cordiality, geniality, graciousness, sociability
con discourtesy, impoliteness, incivility; affront, indignity, insult; acrimony
ant rudeness
ament *n* *syn* see FOOL 4
amerce *vb* *syn* see PENALIZE
amercement *n* *syn* see FINE
amiability *n* *syn* see AMENITY 1
amiable *adj* **1** of a generally agreeable nature especially in social interaction <the meeting ended on an *amiable* note>
syn complaisant, easy, good-humored, good-natured, good-tempered, lenient, mild, obliging
rel affable, cordial, genial, gracious; courteous, mannerly; benign, benignant, kind, kindly; responsive, warm, warmhearted
idiom easy to get along with
con discourteous, ill-mannered, ill-natured, impolite, rude; crabbed, dour, unsociable
ant unamiable; surly
2 *syn* see GENTLE 2
amicable *adj* **1** characterized by peaceableness and goodwill <the negotiators joined in *amicable* discussion>
syn friendly, neighborly
rel empathic, like-minded, sympathetic, understanding; accordant, agreeing, concordant, frictionless, harmonious; pacific, peaceable, peaceful
con bellicose, belligerent, combative, contentious, pugnacious, quarrelsome; antipathetic, hostile, suspicious, uncooperative
2 *syn* see HARMONIOUS 3
amical *adj* *syn* see HARMONIOUS 3
amid *prep* **1** in or into the central part of <the bomb burst *amid* the crowd>
syn among, mid, midst
idiom in (*or* into) the middle of, in (*or* into) the midst of, in (*or* into) the thick of
2 *syn* see AMONG 1
3 *syn* see DURING
amigo *n* *syn* see FRIEND
amiss *adv* **1** in a mistaken, inappropriate, or reprehensible way <I feel you judge him *amiss*>

syn faultily, incorrectly, wrongly
rel inaccurately; indiscreetly, unwisely
con accurately, correctly, properly, rightly; cleverly, wisely
ant right
2 out of the proper course <our planning had gone *amiss*>
syn afield, astray, awry, badly, unfavorably, wrong; *compare* HARD 5
idiom beside (*or* off) the mark
con auspiciously, famously, favorably, promisingly, propitiously, well
ant aright
amiss *adj* **1** *syn* see BAD 1
2 *syn* see FAULTY
3 *syn* see BLAMEWORTHY
amity *n* *syn* see GOODWILL 1
rel accord, agreement, concord, harmony; amicableness, neighborliness
con animosity, antagonism, antipathy, hostility; conflict, contention, discord, dissension, strife
ant enmity
amnesty *n* *syn* see PARDON
among *prep* **1** surrounded by <the valley nestled *among* high mountains>
syn amid, mid, midst
2 *syn* see AMID 1
3 *syn* see BETWEEN
amorist *n* *syn* see GALLANT 2
amorous *adj* *syn* see EROTIC
rel enamored, infatuated; lustful
con aloof, detached, indifferent; cold, cool; apathetic, impassive, unconcerned
ant frigid
amorousness *n* *syn* see LOVE 2
amorphous *adj* *syn* see FORMLESS
amount *vb* **1** to make up as a total <their expenses *amounted* to just a hundred dollars>
syn add up, aggregate, come, number, run (to *or* into), sum (to *or* into), total
rel comprehend, comprise, embody, include, incorporate, reach, subsume
2 to be essentially equivalent <that utter terror that *amounts* to madness>
syn approach, correspond (to), equal, match, partake (of), rival, touch
rel hint, imply, intimate, smack (of), suggest
idiom be near to, come to the same thing as, have all the earmarks (*or* features) of
amount *n* **1** *syn* see BODY 5
2 *syn* see SUBSTANCE 2
amour *n* **1** *syn* see LOVE AFFAIR
2 an illicit or informal sexual relation <memoirs devoted to accounts of his *amours*>
syn affair, intrigue, liaison
rel entanglement, intimacy, relationship; love affair, romance
3 *syn* see LOVE 2
amour propre *n* **1** *syn* see PRIDE 2
2 *syn* see CONCEIT 2
rel complacency, self-complacency, self-satisfaction, smugness; pride
amphibological *adj* *syn* see OBSCURE 3
amphibology *n* *syn* see AMBIGUITY

ample *adj* **1** *syn* see SPACIOUS
rel distended, expanded, inflated, swollen
con scant, skimpy, spare; cramped, exiguous, narrow, strait
ant meager; circumscribed
2 *syn* see PLENTIFUL
rel lavish, prodigal, profuse; handsome
idiom enough and to spare
con scrimpy, spare, sparse; beggarly, miserable, niggardly
ant meager, scant

amplify *vb* **1** *syn* see EXPAND 4
rel augment, extend, increase; unfold
con abbreviate, shorten
ant abridge, condense
2 *syn* see EXPAND 3

amplitude *n* **1** *syn* see SIZE 2
2 *syn* see BREADTH 2
con closeness, limitation, restriction, straitness
ant narrowness
3 *syn* see EXPANSE
rel bigness, greatness, largeness; capaciousness, commodiousness, roominess, spaciousness
con circumscription, restriction
ant straitness; limitation

amply *adv* *syn* see WELL 4

amulet *n* *syn* see CHARM 2
rel lucky piece, rabbit-foot

amuse *vb* to pass or cause to pass time in pleasant or agreeable activity <simple toys to *amuse* children on long trips>
syn divert, entertain, recreate
rel absorb, distract, engross; animate, enliven, fleet, quicken; beguile, charm, delight, enchant, fascinate, wile; while
con fatigue, irk, jade, pall (on), tire, wear (on), weary; bore, ennui

amusement *n* *syn* see ENTERTAINMENT

ana *n* *syn* see ANTHOLOGY

anabasis *n* *syn* see ADVANCE 2

anachronism *n* **1** a chronological error <*anachronisms* of several centuries mar some earlier chronicles>
syn misdate, misdating, mistiming, parachronism
rel antedate, anticipation, prochronism, prolepsis; postdate
2 one that is inappropriately situated especially in time <born centuries too late, he was an *anachronism* in modern urban society>
syn solecism
rel faux pas, gaffe; defect, flaw, mistake, slip

anagogic *adj* *syn* see MYSTICAL 1
rel esoteric, occult, recondite; allegorical, symbolical

analects *n pl* *syn* see ANTHOLOGY

analgesic *n* *syn* see ANODYNE 1
ant irritant

analogous *adj* *syn* see LIKE
rel convertible, corresponding, interchangeable; kindred

analogue *n* *syn* see PARALLEL
rel cognate, congener

analogy *n* **1** *syn* see LIKENESS

2 expression or an expression involving explicit or implied comparison of things basically unlike but with some striking similarities <God can be described only by *analogy*>
syn metaphor, simile, similitude
rel ambiguity, equivocation, equivoque, tergiversation
con demonstration, description, formulation

analphabet *n* *syn* see ILLITERATE

analysis *n* **1** separation of a whole into its fundamental elements or constituent parts <*analysis* of a problem>
syn breakdown, breakup, dissection, resolution
rel division, separation; decomposition, disintegration
con combination, union; concatenation, integration, unification
ant synthesis
2 *syn* see EXAMINATION

analytic *adj* *syn* see LOGICAL 2
rel deep, profound; acute, keen, sharp; penetrating, piercing
con constructive, creative, inventive

analytical *adj* *syn* see LOGICAL 2

analyze *vb* to divide a complex whole into its constituent parts or elements <*analyze* the plot of a novel>
syn anatomize, break down, decompose, decompound, dissect, resolve
rel divide, part, separate; assort, classify, pigeonhole; examine, inspect, investigate, scrutinize
con articulate, concatenate, integrate
ant compose, compound; construct

anamnesis *n* *syn* see MEMORY 2

Ananias *n* *syn* see LIAR

anarch *n* *syn* see REBEL

anarchism *n* **1** a political theory opposed to all forms of government and advocating voluntary cooperation and interaction of individuals and groups in satisfying their common needs <the doubtful premises of *anarchism* about human nature>
syn anarchy
rel utopianism; communism, Marxism, syndicalism
con absolutism, authoritarianism, dictatorship; elitism
2 *syn* see DISORDER 2

anarchist *n* *syn* see REBEL

anarchy *n* **1** absence of effective government or the resulting social disorder <complete *anarchy* followed the breakdown of communications>
syn chaos, lawlessness, mobocracy, ochlocracy
rel confusion, disorder, disorganization
idiom mob rule (*or* law), reign of terror
2 *syn* see ANARCHISM
3 *syn* see DISORDER 2

anastomose *vb* *syn* see INTERJOIN

---

syn synonym(s)   *rel* related word(s)
ant antonym(s)   *con* contrasted word(s)
idiom idiomatic equivalent(s)
‖ use limited; if in doubt, see a dictionary

anathema *n* **1** *syn* see CURSE 1
  rel censure, condemnation, denunciation, reprehension, reprobation, reproof
  con eulogy, laudation, praise
  2 *syn* see ABOMINATION 1
  rel leper, pariah, outcast, untouchable
anathematize *vb* *syn* see EXECRATE 1
  rel impugn, reproach
  con approbate, approve, countenance, endorse, favor
anatomize *vb* *syn* see ANALYZE
ancestor *n* **1** a person from whom one is descended <proud of his pioneer *ancestors*>
  syn antecedent (s), ascendant, forebear, forefather, primogenitor, progenitor
  ant descendant
  2 *syn* see FORERUNNER 2
ancestry *n* one's progenitors or their character or quality as a whole <a man of noble *ancestry*>
  syn blood, descent, extraction, lineage, origin, pedigree
  rel family, kindred, line, race, stock; derivation, source; breed, breeding
  ant descendants; posterity
anchor *vb* *syn* see FASTEN 2
  rel imbed, plant
  idiom make fast (*or* secure)
anchorage *n* *syn* see HARBOR 3
ancient *adj* **1** persisting from the distant past <an *ancient* monument>
  syn aged, age-old, antediluvian, antique, hoary, Noachian, old, timeworn, venerable; *compare* OBSOLETE
  rel primal, primeval, primordial, pristine; forgotten, immemorial, remote, traditional; ageless, dateless
  idiom old as time, older than God (*or* the hills), out of the dim past
  con current, fresh, new, novel, prevailing, up-to-date
  ant modern
  2 *syn* see AGED 1
  rel doddering, doting, fading, sinking, waning, wasting
  idiom old as Methuselah (*or* the hills)
ancient *n* *syn* see OLDSTER
ancilla *n* *syn* see HELPER
ancillary *adj* **1** *syn* see AUXILIARY
  2 *syn* see CONCOMITANT
androgynous *adj* *syn* see BISEXUAL
android *n* *syn* see ROBOT 1
anecdote *n* *syn* see STORY 2
  rel recital, relation; episode, event, incident
anemic *adj* *syn* see PALE 2
anent *prep* *syn* see APROPOS
anesthetic *adj* *syn* see INSENSIBLE 5
  rel impenetrable, impermeable, impervious; obtuse
  con responsive, sensitive
anesthetic *n* *syn* see ANODYNE 1
  ant stimulant
anesthetized *adj* *syn* see NUMB 1
anew *adv* **1** *syn* see OVER 7
  2 *syn* see NEW

anfractuous *adj* *syn* see WINDING
angel *n* *syn* see SPONSOR
  rel ‖butter-and-egg man
angelic *adj* *syn* see SAINTLY
anger *n* emotional excitement induced by intense displeasure <a man easily aroused to *anger*>
  syn fury, indignation, ire, mad, rage, wrath
  rel ‖dander, dudgeon, ‖Dutch, huff, ‖monkey, pet, pique, temper; annoyance, exasperation, infuriation, irritation
  ant forbearance
anger *vb* **1** to make angry <their constant heedless interruptions *angered* her>
  syn enrage, incense, infuriate, ire, mad, madden, steam up, umbrage
  rel annoy, irk, vex; aggravate, exasperate, irritate, nettle, provoke, rile; affront, offend, outrage
  idiom burn one up, make one hot under the collar, put (*or* get) one's dander up, set one by the ears
  con appease, conciliate, mollify, placate, propitiate, soothe
  ant gratify; pacify
  2 to be or become angry <he *angers* easily>
  syn blow up, boil, boil over, bristle, burn, flare (up), fume, rage, seethe
  rel chafe, fret, stew; rant, rave, storm
  idiom breathe fire, fly into a rage, get hot under the collar, get one's blood (*or* dander) up, hit the ceiling, lose one's temper, see red
  ant calm (down)
angle *vb* *syn* see HINT 4
angle *n* **1** *syn* see VIEWPOINT 2
  2 *syn* see PHASE
  rel detail, item, particular
  3 *syn* see TURN 4
angle *vb* **1** *syn* see SLANT 2
  2 *syn* see SLANT 3
angry *adj* feeling or showing strong displeasure or bad temper <*angry* at the children's lack of consideration>
  syn acrimonious, choleric, heated, indignant, irate, ireful, mad, shirty, waxy, wrathful, wrathy, wroth, wrothful, wrothy
  rel aggravated, exasperated, perturbed, put out, riley, upset, uptight, worked up, wrought (up); angered, enraged, incensed, infuriate, infuriated, maddened, sore, vexed; orey-eyed, red-faced, wild-eyed
  idiom foaming at the mouth, hot under the collar, in a taking, in a temper (*or* rage), mad as a hornet (*or* wet hen)
  con calm, placid, tolerant; content, pleased, satisfied
anguish *n* *syn* see SORROW
  rel anxiety, worry; ache, pain, pang, throe; torment, torture
  con comfort, consolation, solace; alleviation, assuagement, mitigation
  ant relief
angular *adj* **1** *syn* see RUDE 1
  2 *syn* see LEAN
  rel lathy, ribby, weedy

con chubby, chuffy
ant rotund
anima *n syn* see SOUL 1
animadversion *n* a remark or statement that constitutes an adverse and usually uncharitable criticism <her spiteful *animadversions* on her neighbors' children>
syn aspersion, obloquy, reflection, slam, slur, stricture
rel censure, criticism, reprehension; accusation, imputation, insinuation; captiousness, carping, caviling, faultfinding
con acclaim, extolling, laudation, praise; approbation, approval
ant commendation
animadvert *vb syn* see REMARK 2
rel declare, say, state, tell, utter; descant, dilate, expatiate, perorate; adduce, offer, present
con disregard, ignore, overlook
animal *n syn* see BEAST
animal *adj* **1** *syn* see BRUTISH
2 *syn* see CARNAL 2
rel bestial, brutal, brutish
con intellectual, mental, psychic; reasoning, thinking; nonphysical, spiritual
ant rational
animalism *n syn* see ANIMALITY
rel lasciviousness, lecherousness, lechery, licentiousness, lustfulness, unchastity; sensualism, sensuality, voluptuousness
animality *n* the animal aspect or quality of human beings or human nature <his violent reaction was sheer *animality*>
syn animalism, carnality, fleshliness
rel maleness, masculinity, virility; sensuality; brutishness, coarseness, grossness
ant spirituality
animalize *vb syn* see DEBASE 1
animate *adj* **1** *syn* see LIVING 1
rel breathing, viable
ant inanimate
2 *syn* see LIVELY 1
rel active, dynamic, live; activated, energized, vitalized
con dead, inanimate, lifeless; passive
ant inert
animate *vb* **1** *syn* see ENCOURAGE 1
rel invigorate, refresh, renew; fortify, reinforce, strengthen
idiom give a lift (to), put on (*or* upon) one's mettle, raise the spirits of
2 *syn* see QUICKEN 1
3 *syn* see FIRE 2
rel activate, actuate, motivate; drive, impel, move
con check, curb, restrain; frustrate, thwart
ant inhibit
animated *adj* **1** *syn* see LIVING 1
rel activated, energized, vitalized
con passive
ant inert
2 *syn* see LIVELY 1
rel exuberant, high-spirited, zestful
con enervated, spiritless; comatose

ant dejected, depressed
animating *adj syn* see INVIGORATING
animation *n syn* see SPIRIT 5
animosity *n syn* see ENMITY
con amity; esteem
ant goodwill
animus *n* **1** *syn* see INTENTION
2 *syn* see SOUL 1
3 *syn* see ENMITY
rel grudge; bias, discrimination, prejudice
con partiality, predilection; sympathy
ant favor
annals *n pl syn* see HISTORY 2
annex *vb* **1** *syn* see ADD 1
rel associate, connect, join, link, unite
con disengage; divorce, part, separate
2 *syn* see GET 1
3 *syn* see APPROPRIATE 1
4 *syn* see STEAL 1
annex *n* a subsidiary structure associated with a main building <built an *annex* to the museum to hold a new collection>
syn arm, block, ell, extension, wing
rel addition, continuation
annihilate *vb* **1** *syn* see ABOLISH 1
2 to destroy utterly <matter cannot be *annihilated*>
syn abate, abolish, blot out, eradicate, exterminate, extinguish, extirpate, murder, root out, uncreate, uproot, wipe (out)
rel cancel, efface, erase, expunge, obliterate
con renew, restore; create, discover, invent; fashion, forge, form, make, shape
3 *syn* see DESTROY 1
4 *syn* see SLAUGHTER 3
rel rout
5 *syn* see CRUSH 5
annihilative *adj syn* see DESTRUCTIVE
annotate *vb* to add or append comment <*annotate* a volume of poems>
syn gloss
rel construe, elucidate, explain, expound; comment, commentate, remark
announce *vb* **1** *syn* see DECLARE 1
rel communicate, impart
con hush (up), smother, stifle, suppress
2 to point to as a future occurrence or development <the shortening days *announce* the coming of winter>
syn forerun, foreshow, harbinger, herald, preindicate, presage
rel augur, forebode, forecast, foretell, predict
3 *syn* see INDICATE 2
rel present, set forth, show (forth)
announcement *n syn* see DECLARATION
rel affirmation, assertion, averment, statement
annoy *vb* **1** to disturb and upset nervously <her persistent prying soon *annoyed* her hostess>

syn synonym(s)   *rel* related word(s)
ant antonym(s)   *con* contrasted word(s)
idiom idiomatic equivalent(s)
‖ use limited; if in doubt, see a dictionary

syn abrade, bother, ||bug, chafe, exercise, fret, gall, irk, provoke, ruffle, vex; *compare* IRRITATE
rel agitate, disturb, perturb, upset
idiom get in one's hair
con comfort, console, solace; content, gratify, please, satisfy
ant soothe
2 *syn* see WORRY 1
rel badger, bait, chivy, heckle, hector; chafe, distress, gall, rub
idiom get (*or* grate) on one's nerves, rub one the wrong way
con disregard, ignore, overlook; appease, calm, dulcify, mollify; cool, lull, subdue
annoyance *n* **1** the act of annoying <devoted himself to the *annoyance* of his patient wife>
syn bothering, harassment, irking, provocation, provoking, vexation, vexing
rel pestering, teasing
2 the state or feeling of being annoyed <her *annoyance* increased as he continued to pester her>
syn aggravation, bother, botheration, exasperation, pother
rel anger, indignation, ire, wrath; aversion, repugnance, repulsion, revulsion; disgust, dislike, distaste
con appreciation, enjoyment, liking, pleasure
3 something that causes an annoyed state or feeling <his constant baiting was an *annoyance* to her>
syn besetment, bother, botheration, botherment, exasperation, irritant, nuisance, pest, pester, ||pesterment, plague
rel affliction, aggravation, distress, provocation, trial; riding
annual *n* *syn* see YEARBOOK
annuary *n* *syn* see YEARBOOK
annul *vb* **1** *syn* see ERASE
rel abstract, dispose (of), eliminate, remove
2 *syn* see NEUTRALIZE
rel outweigh, overbalance
3 *syn* see ABOLISH 1
rel counteract, negative, neutralize; blot out, cancel, efface, obliterate; extinguish
idiom make void, set aside
con enact, ordain, pass
4 to deprive of legal validity, force, or authority <*annul* a marriage>
syn abrogate, discharge, dissolve, quash, vacate, void
rel abolish, cancel, countermand, invalidate, nullify, undo
idiom make void
annunciate *vb* *syn* see DECLARE 1
rel affirm, assert, asseverate, aver; profess, protest; pronounce, state
anodyne *n* **1** something used to relieve or prevent pain <opium and its derivatives are still our most potent *anodynes*>
syn analgesic, anesthetic, pain-killer
rel calmative, depressant, sedative, tranquilizer; hypnotic, somnifacient, soporific, stupefacient
2 something that soothes or, often, dulls or deadens the senses or sensibilities <the kind of religion that is no more than an *anodyne*>

syn narcotic, nepenthe, opiate
ant energizer, stimulant; irritant
anomalous *adj* **1** *syn* see IRREGULAR 1
rel monstrous, prodigious
2 *syn* see ABNORMAL 1
rel foreign, peculiar, singular, strange; monstrous, prodigious
con accustomed, customary, usual, wonted
anon *adv* **1** *syn* see PRESENTLY 1
2 *syn* see THEN 1
anonym *n* *syn* see PSEUDONYM
anonymous *adj* not identified by name <saved by an *anonymous* hero>
syn innominate, nameless, undesignated, unnamed
rel incognito, unidentified, unknown, unrecognized, unspecified
ant named, onymous
another *adj* **1** *syn* see THAT 1
2 *syn* see ADDITIONAL
rel second
anschauung *n* *syn* see INTUITION
anschluss *n* *syn* see ALLIANCE 2
answer *n* **1** something spoken or written by way of return to a question or demand <a sullen *answer*>
syn antiphon, rejoinder, reply, respond, response, retort, return
rel comment, observation, remark; defense, justification; rebuttal, refutation; replication
con inquiry, interrogation, query, question, quiz
2 something attained by mental effort and especially by computation <got the *answer* by trial-and-error methods>
syn result, solution
answer *vb* **1** to say, write, or do something in response (as to a question) <*answered* his critics with documented facts>
syn come in, rejoin, reply, respond, retort, return
rel acknowledge, recognize; disprove, rebut, refute; countercharge, recriminate
idiom come back (at), make reply (to)
con ask, inquire, interrogate, query, question, quiz
2 *syn* see SATISFY 5
answerable *adj* *syn* see RESPONSIBLE
rel bound, compelled, constrained, duty-bound, obligated, obliged
Antaean *adj* *syn* see HUGE
antagonism *n* **1** *syn* see ENMITY
rel opposition, oppugnancy, resistance, withstanding; clashing, conflict, difference, disagreement, discord, friction
con concord, consonance, harmony; agreement, understanding
ant accord; comity
2 an opposing state, action, or position <the natural *antagonism* of predators and prey>
syn antithesis, con, contradistinction, contraposition, contrariety, opposition, opposure
rel disagreement, discrepancy, disparity, incongruity; annulling, negation, nullification; counteraction

con agreement, congruity; alliance, association, rapport; empathy, sympathy

antagonist *n syn* see OPPONENT
con adherent, henchman, partisan
ant supporter

antagonistic *adj* **1** *syn* see BITTER 3
2 *syn* see ADVERSE 1
rel discordant, incompatible, inconsonant; averse, disinclined, indisposed, unwilling; conflicting, hostile
con advantageous, beneficial; auspicious, benign, propitious
ant favorable
3 *syn* see ANTIPATHETIC 1
rel adverse, counter, counteractive, reactive; discordant; antonymous, opposing, oppugnant

ante *adv syn* see BEFORE 1

ante *prep syn* see BEFORE 1

ante *n syn* see BET

antecede *vb syn* see PRECEDE 2

antecedence *n syn* see PRIORITY

antecedent *n* **1** *syn* see CAUSE 1
rel forebear, forerunner, precursor; agency, instrumentality, means
con sequel; upshot
ant consequence
2 *syn* see FORERUNNER 2
3 antecedents *pl syn* see ANCESTOR 1

antecedent *adj syn* see PRECEDING
ant consequent; subsequent

antecedently *adv syn* see BEFORE 1

antecessor *n syn* see FORERUNNER 2

antedate *vb syn* see PRECEDE 2

antediluvian *adj syn* see ANCIENT 1

antediluvian *n syn* see FOGY

anterior *adj syn* see PRECEDING
con after, back, hind, hinder, rear
ant posterior

anthology *n* a collection of selected artistic and especially literary pieces or passages <an *anthology* of sacred music>
syn album, ana, analects, florilegium, garland, miscellany, omnibus, posy
rel collection, compilation; delectus, treasurehouse, treasury

anthropoid *adj* resembling man <*anthropoid* extraterrestrials>
syn anthropomorphic, anthropomorphous, humanoid, manlike

anthropomorphic *adj syn* see ANTHROPOID

anthropomorphous *adj syn* see ANTHROPOID

anti *n syn* see OPPONENT

anti *adj syn* see ADVERSE 1
ant pro

antic *n syn* see PRANK
rel artifice, wile; romp

antic *adj* **1** *syn* see FANTASTIC 2
rel foolish; comic, comical, farcical, laughable, ludicrous
con prudent, sensible, wise; conventional, formal; grave, sedate, serious, solemn, somber
2 characterized by a light gay quality <a briskly *antic* and delightful tale>
syn frolicsome, playful, rollicking, sprightly

rel gay, lively, spirited; light, whimsical; casual, easy, suave
con constrained, controlled, curbed, guarded, inhibited, restrained
3 *syn* see PLAYFUL 1

anticipant *adj syn* see EXPECTANT 1

anticipate *vb* **1** *syn* see PREVENT 1
rel forecast, foretell, presage
idiom be one step ahead of
con disregard, ignore, neglect, overlook, slight
2 *syn* see FORESEE
rel await, contemplate, expect; foretaste
idiom be on the lookout (*or* watch) for, look forward to, look (*or* watch) out for

anticipation *n syn* see EXPECTANCY 1

anticipative *adj syn* see EXPECTANT 1

anticipatory *adj syn* see EXPECTANT 1

antidote *n syn* see REMEDY 2
rel negator, neutralizer, nullifier, offset; backfire

antipasto *n syn* see APPETIZER

antipathetic *adj* **1** having a natural or inherent opposition <national needs *antipathetic* to peace>
syn antagonistic, clashing, conflicting, contrariant, contrary, discordant
rel antipodal, antithetical, antonymous, contradictory, opposite
idiom at cross purposes, at daggers drawn, at war with one another
con agreeing, consonant, correspondent, harmonious; coactive, collaborative, cooperative
ant concordant
2 arousing marked aversion or dislike <found his sister's husband in every way *antipathetic*>
syn aversive, kindless, repellent, repugnant, uncongenial, ungenial, unsympathetic
rel abhorrent, obnoxious; disgustful, disgusting, distasteful, loathsome, repulsive
con compatible, consonant, sympathetic; alluring, attractive, charming; agreeable, pleasant, pleasing, satisfying, soothing
ant congenial
3 *syn* see ADVERSE 1

antipathy *n* **1** *syn* see ENMITY
rel disrelish, distaste, repellency, repugnance; avoidance, escape, eschewal, evasion
con liking, partiality, predilection, prepossession; attachment, love; attraction, taste (for)
ant affection (for)
2 the state of mind induced by what is antipathetic <a strong *antipathy* to modern art>
syn allergy, aversion, dyspathy
rel abhorrence, dislike, disrelish, distaste, repellency, repugnance; avoidance, escape, eschewal, evasion
con liking, partiality, predilection, prepossession; affection, attachment, love; attraction
ant taste (for)

antiphon *n syn* see ANSWER 1

antipodal *adj syn* see OPPOSITE

---

syn synonym(s)   *rel* related word(s)
ant antonym(s)   *con* contrasted word(s)
idiom idiomatic equivalent(s)
‖ use limited; if in doubt, see a dictionary

antipode *n syn* see OPPOSITE

antipodean *adj syn* see OPPOSITE

antipole *n syn* see OPPOSITE

antiquate *vb syn* see OUTDATE

antiquated *adj syn* see OLD-FASHIONED
  con modern, new, novel
  ant modernistic

antique *adj* **1** *syn* see ANCIENT 1
  rel ancestral, dateless, immemorial, legendary, time-honored, traditional
  con advanced, current, recent
  2 *syn* see OLD-FASHIONED

antisocial *adj* averse to the society of others <a pure scholar, remote and *antisocial*>
  syn eremitic, misanthropic, reclusive, reserved, solitary, standoffish
  rel ascetic, austere, cold, remote; cynical, introverted, withdrawn
  con affable, friendly, gregarious; communicative, outgoing, sociable
  ant social

antithesis *n* **1** *syn* see ANTAGONISM 2
  2 *syn* see OPPOSITE

antithetical *adj syn* see OPPOSITE

anxiety *n syn* see CARE 2
  rel doubt, mistrust, uncertainty; distress, misery, suffering; dread; panic
  con composure, equanimity, sangfroid; aplomb, confidence, self-possession; certainty, certitude, faith, trust
  ant security

anxious *adj* **1** *syn* see AFRAID 1
  rel agitated, apprehensive, jittery, perturbed, upset, worried; alarmed, bothered, disquieted, troubled, uneasy
  idiom ill at ease
  con calm, collected, cool, easy, imperturbable, unruffled; assured, confident, sanguine, sure
  2 *syn* see EAGER
  rel importunate, pressing, urgent
  idiom all agog, bursting to
  con averse, disinclined, hesitant, indisposed, reluctant
  ant loath

anyhow *adv syn* see ABOUT 4

anytime *adv syn* see EVER 4

anyway *adv syn* see EVER 5

any which way *adv syn* see ABOUT 4

anywise *adv* **1** *syn* see ABOUT 4
  2 *syn* see EVER 5

A1 *adj syn* see EXCELLENT

apace *adv syn* see FAST 2

apart *adv* **1** as a discrete item <taken *apart*, his view seemed sound enough>
  syn independently, individually, one by one, separately, severally, singly
  idiom one at a time
  2 excluded from consideration <these slips *apart*, he had done very well>
  syn aside
  idiom to one side
  3 in or into parts <tore the sheets *apart*>
  syn asunder, sky-high
  idiom all to pieces, to bits (*or* flinders)

apart *adj syn* see ALONE 1

apart from *prep syn* see EXCEPT

apartheid *n syn* see SEGREGATION

apartment *n* **1** a set of rooms (as in a private house or a block) rented or leased for use as a dwelling place <had a tiny top-floor *apartment*>
  syn ‖chambers, flat, lodging(s), rental, rooms, suite, tenement
  2 *syn* see ROOM 1

apathetic *adj syn* see IMPASSIVE 1
  rel dull, inert, languid, sluggish, torpid; anesthetic, impassible, insensible, insensitive; callous, unmoved, untouched; limp, spiritless
  con aroused, awake, aware, conscious, impressionable, perceptive, receptive; vigilant, watchful, wide-awake
  ant alert

apathy *n* **1** lack of emotional responsiveness <hid her sorrow behind a dull brooding *apathy*>
  syn impassivity, insensibility, phlegm, stoicism, stolidity, unresponsiveness
  rel inertness, passivity, supineness; aloofness, detachment, indifference, unconcern; lethargy, torpidity, torpor; listlessness, numbness, stupefaction, stupor
  con ardor, fervor, passion, responsiveness, warmth; alertness, awareness, concern, solicitude
  ant zeal; enthusiasm
  2 lack of interest or concern <public *apathy* toward the school crisis>
  syn disinterest, disregard, heedlessness, indifference, insouciance, lassitude, lethargy, listlessness, unconcern, unmindfulness
  rel callousness, hardness, insensitivity, obduracy, unawareness; coldness, halfheartedness, lukewarmness; calmness, dispassion, dispassionateness
  con attentiveness, concern, heedfulness, interest; awareness, mindfulness, sensitivity, solicitude; ardency, fervency, passion, warmth, zeal

ape *vb syn* see MIMIC
  rel caricature; emulate, rival
  idiom make like

aperçu *n syn* see COMPENDIUM 1

aperitive *adj syn* see PALATABLE

aperture *n* a discontinuity allowing passage <the mouse squeezed through a narrow *aperture* in the wall>
  syn hole, opening, orifice, outlet, vent
  rel discontinuity, gap, hiatus, interstice; bore, perforation, pinhole, prick, puncture; chasm, cleft, cut, gash, slash, slit; breach, break, rupture

apery *n syn* see MIMICRY

apex *n* **1** *syn* see TOP 1
  rel extremity, limit, spire
  ant nadir
  2 the culminating point <the *apex* of his career>
  syn acme, apogee, capsheaf, capstone, climax, comble, crescendo, crest, crown, culmen, culmination, meridian, ne plus ultra, noon, noontide, peak, pinnacle, sublimity, summit, zenith
  rel last word, prime, quintescence, ultimate; achievement, attainment, consummation, realization

ant nadir
3 *syn* see POINT 9
rel cap, crest, peak, prominence, spire
aphorism *n syn* see MAXIM
aphrodisia *n syn* see LUST 2
aphrodisiac *adj syn* see EROTIC
ant anaphrodisiac
apiarist *n syn* see BEEKEEPER
apical *adj syn* see TOP 1
apiculturist *n syn* see BEEKEEPER
apiece *adv* by, for, or to each one <gave the boys a
dollar *apiece*>
syn all, aside, each, ‖per, per capita, per caput
rel individually, one by one, respectively, severally, singly, successively
apish *adj syn* see SLAVISH 3
aplomb *n syn* see CONFIDENCE 2
rel poise, savoir faire; coolness, imperturbability, levelheadedness, nonchalance; composure,
ease, easiness, equanimity, sangfroid
idiom presence of mind
con bewilderment, distraction, perplexity; befuddlement, confusion, fluster, fuddlement; discomfiture, embarrassment, perturbation
ant shyness
apocalypse *n syn* see REVELATION
rel envisioning, foresight, precognition, prevision
apocalyptic *adj* **1** *syn* see PROPHETIC
2 *syn* see OMINOUS
apocryphal *adj syn* see SPURIOUS 3
rel false, erroneous, inaccurate, incorrect, untrue, wrong; doubtful, dubious, questionable
idiom open to question
con accurate, correct, established, factual, true,
truthful, veracious; authentic
apogee *n syn* see APEX 2
Apollyon *n syn* see DEVIL 1
apologetic *adj syn* see REMORSEFUL
apologetic *n syn* see APOLOGY 1
apologia *n syn* see APOLOGY 1
rel clarification, elucidation, explanation, interpretation
apologue *n syn* see ALLEGORY 2
apology *n* **1** a presentation intended to justify or
defend something <the white paper is essentially
an *apology* for recent foreign policy>
syn apologetic, apologia, defense, justification;
compare EXCUSE 1
rel excuse, extenuation, mitigation, palliation;
advocating, advocation, championing, espousal,
espousing, support
idiom pleading one's cause, putting in a good
word for, speaking up for
con blame, censure, condemnation, decrial, reprehension, reprobation
2 an acknowledgment expressing regret for a
wrong, improper, or discommoding act <mur-
mured a brief *apology* for her lateness>
syn excuse, regrets; *compare* EXCUSE 1
rel amends, atonement; acknowledgment, admission, concession, confession, mea culpa; reparation, redress, satisfaction
3 *syn* see EXCUSE 3

aporetic *adj syn* see INCREDULOUS
apostasy *n syn* see DEFECTION
rel perfidy, treacherousness
apostate *n syn* see RENEGADE
rel bolter; dissenter, nonconformist, recusant
con adherent, follower, partisan; convert, proselyte
apostatize *vb syn* see DEFECT
a posteriori *adj syn* see INDUCTIVE
apostle *n syn* see MISSIONARY
apothecary *n syn* see DRUGGIST
apothegm *n syn* see MAXIM
apotheosis *n* **1** the consummate form, example, or
instance (as of a quality) <the *apotheosis* of vul-
garity>
syn epitome, last word, quintessence, ultimate;
compare EMBODIMENT
rel acme, culmination, height, peak, summit
idiom ‖the living end
2 a raising to a state of eminent triumph or glory
<the *apotheosis* of a folk hero>
syn aggrandizement, deification, dignification,
exaltation, glorification
rel elevation, ennoblement, enshrinement, idolization, immortalization, lionization
con debasement, defamation, degradation, deni-
gration, sullying
appall *vb syn* see DISMAY 1
rel awe, faze, overawe
con brace (up), buck up, cheer (up); assure,
hearten, inspire, inspirit
ant embolden, nerve
appalling *adj syn* see FEARFUL 3
rel daunting, dismaying, horrifying; bewildering, confounding, dumbfounding
con assuring, heartening, inspiriting
ant reassuring
appanage *n syn* see RIGHT 2
apparatus *n syn* see EQUIPMENT
rel implement, instrument, tool, utensil; furnishings, provisions, supplies
apparel *vb syn* see CLOTHE
rel appoint
con bare, denude
ant divest
apparel *n syn* see CLOTHES
apparent *adj* **1** *syn* see CLEAR 5
rel ponderable; noticeable, prominent; discernible, observable, perceivable
idiom plain as day, plain to be seen
con ambiguous, hidden, obscure
ant inapparent
2 being other than seems to be the case <her *apparent* goodwill masked an inner loathing>
syn Barmecidal, illusive, illusory, ostensible,
seeming, semblant
rel deceptive, delusive, delusory, misleading;
credible, plausible, specious; factitious, fake,
false, pseudo, sham, supposititious, supposititious

---

syn synonym(s)   *rel* related word(s)
ant antonym(s)   *con* contrasted word(s)
idiom idiomatic equivalent(s)
‖ use limited; if in doubt, see a dictionary

con genuine, true, valid; basic, essential, fundamental, inherent, intrinsic
ant actual, real

apparently *adv syn* see OSTENSIBLY

apparition *n* a visible appearance of something not present and especially of a dead person <illusions that the superstitious see as *apparitions*>
syn bogey, eidolon, ghost, ‖haunt, phantasm, phantom, revenant, shade, shadow, specter, spectrum, spirit, ‖spook, umbra, wraith
rel delusion, hallucination, illusion; corposant, fox fire, ignis fatuus, jack-o'-lantern, marshfire, Saint Elmo's fire, will-o'- the-wisp

appeal *n* **1** *syn* see PRAYER
rel asking, requesting, solicitation
con claim, demand, exaction; kick, objection, protest
2 *syn* see ATTRACTION 1
3 *syn* see CHARM 3
rel draw; pleasantness
con disagreeableness, unpleasantness

appeal *vb* **1** *syn* see BEG
2 *syn* see PETITION
3 *syn* see INTEREST

appealing *adj syn* see ATTRACTIVE 1

appear *vb* **1** to become visible <the sun *appeared* from behind a cloud>
syn emerge, loom, show
rel arrive, come; arise, emanate, issue, materialize, outcrop, rise, spring
idiom come in sight, come into view, meet (*or* strike) the eye, show one's face
con go, leave; depart, retire, withdraw
ant disappear, vanish
2 *syn* see SEEM
idiom give an appearance of, strike one as

appearance *n* **1** the state or form in which one appears <his disheveled *appearance* surprised his guests>
syn aspect, look, mien, seeming
rel air, bearing, countenance, demeanor, manner
2 *usu* **appearances** *pl* outward and often deceptive indication or look <to all *appearances* he was guilty>
syn face, guise, seeming, semblance, show, showing, simulacrum; *compare* MASK
rel fiction, make-believe, pretense, pretension; disguise, facade, front, masquerade, outside, pose
idiom outward show
con fact, reality, truth

appease *vb* **1** *syn* see PACIFY
rel calm (down), ease, soothe; extenuate, gloss (over), palliate, whitewash
con annoy, bother, irk, vex; anger, enrage, incense, infuriate; discompose, disturb, perturb, upset
ant exasperate
2 *syn* see SATISFY 3
rel ease, relieve; cater (to), coddle, pamper, spoil
ant aggravate

appellation *n syn* see NAME 1

appellative *n syn* see NAME 1

append *vb syn* see ADD 1

appendage *n* something accompanying or attached to another thing to which it is usually subordinate or nonessential <people to whom culture is a mere *appendage* to life>
syn accessory, adjunct, appendix, appurtenance
rel auxiliary, incidental, subsidiary, supplement; collateral, extra, nonessential

appendix *n* **1** additional material subjoined to a writing and especially a book <a dictionary with an *appendix* of new words>
syn addendum, codicil, rider, supplement
2 *syn* see APPENDAGE

apperception *n syn* see RECOGNITION 1
rel apprehension, grasp, perception; comprehension, understanding

appertain *vb* **1** *syn* see BELONG 2
2 *syn* see BEAR (on *or* upon)

appetence *n syn* see APPETITE 1

appetent *adj syn* see EAGER
rel craving, desirous, lusting, yearning
idiom consumed with desire

appetite *n* **1** a natural enjoyment of food <all fell to with a hearty *appetite*>
syn appetence, stomach, taste
rel gluttony, greed, hunger, voracity; epicurism, gourmandise
2 *syn* see DESIRE 1
rel cupidity, greed, urgency
con abnegation, asceticism, renunciation, self≠denial; distaste, revulsion
3 an attraction toward something <had a great *appetite* for gossip>
syn fondness, inclination, liking, soft spot, taste, weakness
rel bent, bias, flair, leaning, penchant, proclivity, propensity
con disinclination, dislike, distaste; disinterest, unconcern

appetition *n syn* see DESIRE 1

appetizer *n* food or drink served before a meal to stimulate appetite <*appetizers* such as cocktails and canap>
syn antipasto, hors d'oeuvre, whet, zakuska
rel dainty, delicacy, goody, tidbit; savory

appetizing *adj syn* see PALATABLE
ant disgusting, nauseating

applaud *vb* **1** *syn* see COMMEND 2
rel boost, plug
ant admonish; censure
2 to express enthusiastic approval <*applauded* wildly when his team won a point>
syn cheer, rise (to), root
rel acclaim, extol, laud, praise; eulogize, glorify, magnify, panegyrize
con deride, mock, ridicule, taunt; contemn, disdain, scorn, scout
ant boo, hiss

applause *n* public expression of approbation <her appearance was greeted with *applause*>
syn acclaim, acclamation, plaudit(s)
rel cheers, hand, ovation, round; cheering, clapping, rooting
con derision, mockery, ridicule, taunting; Bronx cheer, raspberry

ant booing, hissing

‖**apple knocker** *n syn* see RUSTIC

apple–polish *vb syn* see FAWN

apple–polisher *n syn* see SYCOPHANT

‖**applesauce** *n syn* see NONSENSE 2

appliance *n syn* see USE 1

applicability *n syn* see USE 3
con irrelevance, unsuitability
ant inapplicability

applicable *adj* **1** *syn* see RELEVANT
rel alliable, associable, compatible, congenial, connective
con incompatible, uncongenial; inappropriate, unfit, unsuitable
ant inapplicable
2 *syn* see FIT 1
rel correct, good, seemly
idiom as it ought to be, as it should be
con improper, incorrect

applicant *n syn* see CANDIDATE

application *n* **1** *syn* see ATTENTION 1
rel busyness, zeal; energy, indefatigability
con bemusement, wool-gathering; faineance, laziness, sloth
ant indolence
2 *syn* see USE 1
3 *syn* see EXERCISE 1
4 *syn* see PRAYER

applicative *adj syn* see RELEVANT

applicatory *adj syn* see RELEVANT

apply *vb* **1** *syn* see ADDRESS 3
rel set about, take on, undertake; drudge, grind, toil
idiom burn the midnight oil, keep one's nose to the grindstone, work like a horse (*or* dog); concern (oneself) with something, set (one's hand) to something
con let slide, neglect, pass over, slight
2 *syn* see BEAR (on *or* upon)
idiom come into relation with
3 *syn* see RESORT 2
rel appeal, petition; beg, beseech, entreat, implore, supplicate; importune, press, urge
idiom make application to
4 *syn* see USE 2

apply (to) *vb syn* see ADDRESS 4

appoint *vb* **1** *syn* see DESIGNATE 2
rel accredit, authorize, commission
con cashier, discharge, dismiss; debar, exclude, reject
2 *syn* see FURNISH 1
rel embellish, enrich, furbish, garnish; dress up, set off, spruce (up)
con denude, dismantle, divest, strip

appointment *n* **1** *syn* see JOB 2
2 *syn* see ENGAGEMENT 3

apportion *vb* **1** *syn* see ALLOT
rel divide, partition, share
con assemble, collect, gather
2 to separate something into shares with care and accuracy and distribute it among a number <Christ *apportioned* the loaves and fishes>
syn divide, ‖divvy, parcel, portion, prorate, quota, ration, share, ‖shift

rel accord, award, bestow, distribute; give, grant, present; part, separate, split
3 *syn* see ADMINISTER 2
rel dish out, serve

apportionment *n syn* see RATION

apposite *adj syn* see RELEVANT
rel felicitous, happy; opportune, pat, seasonable, timely
idiom to the point (*or* purpose)
con awkward, inept; casual, haphazard, hit-or-miss, random
ant inapposite, inapt

appositeness *n syn* see ORDER 11

appraisal *n* **1** *syn* see ESTIMATE 1
2 *syn* see ESTIMATION 1

appraise *vb syn* see ESTIMATE 1
rel adjudge, deem, esteem, judge; audit, examine, inspect, scrutinize
idiom set (*or* place) a value on, take the measure of

appraisement *n* **1** *syn* see ESTIMATE 1
2 *syn* see ESTIMATION 1

appreciable *adj syn* see PERCEPTIBLE
rel noticeable; apparent, clear, evident, manifest, obvious, plain; concrete, material, real, substantial
con impalpable, imperceptible, imponderable, insensible, intangible
ant inappreciable

appreciate *vb* **1** to hold in high estimation <*appreciate* the kindness of a friend>
syn apprize, cherish, esteem, prize, treasure, value; *compare* ADMIRE 1
rel admire, regard, respect; adore, ‖eat up, enjoy, like, love, relish
idiom rate highly, set great store by, think much (*or* well) of
con contemn, disapprove, disdain, scorn; decry, depreciate, disparage
ant despise
2 *syn* see ADMIRE 1
rel enjoy, like, savor
con contemn, disdain, scorn
3 *syn* see KNOW 1
rel catch, seize, take in

appreciation *n syn* see TESTIMONIAL 2

apprehend *vb* **1** to recognize the existence or meaning of <as a child learns to *apprehend* the relation between naughtiness and punishment>
syn accept, catch, compass, comprehend, conceive, cotton (to *or* on to), ‖dig, follow, grasp, make out, see, take, take in, tumble (to), twig, understand
rel realize, recognize, sense; absorb, digest, seize; catch on, wise (up); penetrate
idiom catch (*or* get) the drift of, get the idea, get through one's head, make head or tail of
ant misapprehend
2 *syn* see ARREST 2

---

syn synonym(s) | *rel* related word(s)
ant antonym(s) | *con* contrasted word(s)
idiom idiomatic equivalent(s)
‖ use limited; if in doubt, see a dictionary

3 *syn* see FORESEE

rel dread, fear

idiom be on pins and needles, have one's heart in one's mouth, wait with bated breath

4 *syn* see KNOW 1

idiom be acquainted with, be cognizant of

apprehensible *adj syn* see UNDERSTANDABLE

apprehension *n* **1** *syn* see IDEA

2 *syn* see ARREST

3 fear that something is going or will go wrong <had the strongest *apprehension* about her sister's health>

syn apprehensiveness, foreboding, misgiving, premonition, prenotion, presage, presentiment

rel agitation, angst, anxiety, care, concern, disquiet, disquietude, solicitude, unease, uneasiness, worry; alarm, dread, fear, panic

idiom the anxious seat

con assurance, composure, equanimity, sangfroid, self-possession; faith, reliance, trust

ant confidence

apprehensive *adj* **1** *syn* see AWARE

2 *syn* see FEARFUL 2

ant confident

apprehensiveness *n syn* see APPREHENSION 3

apprentice *n syn* see NOVICE

rel starter; amateur

con adept, expert, specialist

apprenticed *adj syn* see BOUND 2

apprise *vb syn* see INFORM 2

rel announce, communicate, declare, proclaim, publish; disclose, discover, divulge, reveal, tell

idiom make known to, serve (one) notice

apprize *vb syn* see APPRECIATE 1

approach *vb* **1** to come or go near or nearer <as a boy *approaches* manhood>

syn approximate, near, nigh

rel achieve, arrive (at), attain, gain, hit, make, reach; draw on

idiom come to close quarters with

con recede, retire, retreat, withdraw; depart, go, leave

2 *syn* see ADDRESS 4

rel advise, confer, consult, counsel, negotiate, parley; beg, beseech, entreat, implore, plead, supplicate

3 *syn* see REACH 3

4 *syn* see AMOUNT 2

con depart, deviate, digress; differ, disaccord, disharmonize, vary

5 *syn* see BORDER 3

approach *n syn* see OVERTURE 1

rel attempt, endeavor, essay, try; call, invitation

ant withdrawal

approaching *adj syn* see FORTHCOMING

approbate *vb syn* see APPROVE 1

approbation *n* warmly commending acceptance or agreement <expressed *approbation* of their progress>

syn approval, benediction, blessing, favor, OK (*or* okay)

rel commendation, countenance, goodwill, sanction; admiration, esteem, liking, regard, respect; pleasure, satisfaction

con censure, condemnation, criticism, disapproval, disfavor, reprehension; annoyance, disgust, irritation; distress, regret, sorrow

ant disapprobation

approbative *adj syn* see FAVORABLE 1

approbatory *adj syn* see FAVORABLE 1

appropinquity *n syn* see PROXIMITY

appropriate *vb* **1** to take over as if by preeminent right <limitations on the right of the state to *appropriate* private property>

syn accroach, annex, arrogate, commandeer, confiscate, expropriate, preempt, seize, sequester, take; *compare* ARROGATE 1

rel grab, grasp, snatch; claim, exact, extort, wrench; conscript, draft, press

idiom help oneself to, lay hold of, make free with, take possession of

2 *syn* see STEAL 1

rel despoil, spoil; forage, raid

3 *syn* see ARROGATE 1

appropriate *adj* **1** *syn* see FIT 1

rel apposite, germane, pertinent, relevant; opportune, pat, seasonable, timely

con incompatible, incongruous, inconsonant

ant inappropriate

2 *syn* see GOOD 2

rel agreeable, desirable, enjoyable, pleasant; acceptable, admissible, eligible, entitled, right, worthy

con disagreeable undesirable, unpleasant; inadmissible, ineligible, unworthy, wrong

ant inappropriate

3 *syn* see JUST 3

con unfair, unjustified, unmerited, unreasonable; unsuitable

ant inappropriate

4 *syn* see TRUE 7

ant inappropriate

appropriately *adv syn* see WELL 4

appropriateness *n* **1** *syn* see USE 3

2 *syn* see ORDER 11

appropriation *n* property (as money) set apart or given by official or formal action for a predetermined use by others <an increased *appropriation* for public housing>

syn grant, subsidy, subvention

rel allotment, allowance, stipend; aid, assistance, grant-in-aid, help

approval *n syn* see APPROBATION

rel applause, commendation, compliment; acceptance, endorsement, sanction, suffrage

con depreciation, derogation, disparagement

ant disapproval

approve *vb* **1** to find acceptable <they don't *approve* of their daughter's life-style>

syn accept, approbate, countenance, favor, go (for), hold (with)

rel back (up), stand by, support, sustain, uphold; bear, endure, put up (with), tolerate

idiom be in favor of, pat on the back, take kindly to, think well (*or* highly) of, view with approval (*or* favor)

con deprecate, disfavor, dislike, frown (on *or* upon); object (to), oppose *ant* disapprove

2 to give an often formal expression of approval and support <the committee *approved* the plans for the new clubhouse>
syn accredit, certify, endorse, OK (*or* okay), sanction
rel applaud, commend, compliment; confirm, initial, ratify; clear
con refuse, reject, repudiate, spurn; censure, condemn, criticize, reprehend, reprobate
ant disapprove

approving *adj syn* see FAVORABLE 1
approximal *adj syn* see ADJACENT 3
approximate *adj* **1** *syn* see COMPARATIVE
2 *syn* see RUDE 3
approximate *vb* **1** *syn* see APPROACH 1
idiom be in the neighborhood of
2 *syn* see ESTIMATE 3
approximately *adv syn* see NEARLY
idiom in round numbers, right about
ant exactly, precisely
appulse *n syn* see IMPACT 1
appurtenance *n syn* see APPENDAGE
rel appointment (*usu* appointments *pl*), equipment, furnishings, furniture
appurtenant *adj syn* see AUXILIARY
a priori *adj syn* see DEDUCTIVE
apriorism *n syn* see ASSUMPTION 2
apropos *adj syn* see RELEVANT
rel meet, proper
con clumsy, gauche, inappropriate, inept
ant malapropos
apropos *prep* in reference to <it is impossible to reach a decision *apropos* this matter at present>
syn about, against, anent, as for, as regards, as respects, as to, concerning, in re, in respect to, re, regarding, respecting, touching, toward, with respect to
apt *adj* **1** having a tendency or inclination <it is *apt* to be cool late in the evening>
syn given, inclined, liable, likely, prone
rel disposed, minded, predisposed
con averse, disinclined, indisposed, loath; doubtful, improbable, unlikely
2 *syn* see FIT 1
rel apposite, apropos, pertinent, relevant; compelling, convincing, telling; exact, nice, precise
con awkward, clumsy, maladroit
ant inapt, inept
3 *syn* see QUICK 2
rel alert, brainy, bright; gifted, talented
con laggard
aptness *n* **1** *syn* see ORDER 11
rel helpfulness, propitiousness
2 *syn* see GIFT 2
‖**apurpose** *adv syn* see INTENTIONALLY
apyrous *adj syn* see NONCOMBUSTIBLE
aquake *adj syn* see TREMULOUS
aqua vitae *n syn* see LIQUOR 2
aqueduct *n syn* see CHANNEL 1
aquiculture *n syn* see HYDROPONICS
aquiver *adj syn* see TREMULOUS
arab *n* **1** *syn* see VAGABOND
‖**2** *syn* see PEDDLER

arable *adj* suitable for tilling and for growing crops <used their *arable* land intensively>
syn cultivable, cultivatable, tillable
rel fat, fertile, fruitful, productive
con barren, sterile, unfertile, unfruitful, unproductive
arbiter *n syn* see JUDGE 1
rel moderator
arbitrary *adj* **1** characterized by or given to willful and often unwise or irrational choices and demands <a proud fitful *arbitrary* nature>
syn capricious, erratic, freakish, vagarious, wayward, whimsical, whimsied
rel undisciplined, unruly, wild, willful; arrogant, unconstrained, unreasonable; careless, heedless, impetuous, indiscreet, precipitate, rash; kooky, screwball, zany
con circumspect, discreet, heedful, judicious, politic, reflective; calculating, discriminative, judicial, prudent, well-advised
2 *syn* see ABSOLUTE 4
rel authoritarian, dictatorial, magisterial, oracular
con lawful, legal, licit, rightful
ant legitimate
arbitrate *vb syn* see JUDGE 1
rel intermediate, intervene, mediate; appease, placate, soothe
arbitrator *n* **1** *syn* see MODERATOR
2 *syn* see JUDGE 1
arbor *n* a shelter (as in a garden) formed of vines or branches or of latticework covered with climbing shrubs or vines <the children picnicked under the *arbor*>
syn bower, pergola
rel belvedere, casino, gazebo, summerhouse
arc *n syn* see CURVE
arcadia *n syn* see UTOPIA
arcane *adj syn* see MYSTERIOUS
rel eerie, uncanny, weird; anagogic, mystical
arced *adj syn* see CURVED
arch *n syn* see CURVE
arch *adj* **1** *syn* see FIRST 3
rel conspicuous, notable, noteworthy; extraordinary, extreme
2 *syn* see SAUCY 1
rel impish, mischievous, playful, roguish, waggish; bold, cheeky, cocky, flippant, fresh; derisive, mocking, twitting
con modest, quiet, respectful, submissive
3 *syn* see COY 2
archaic *adj* **1** *syn* see OLD-FASHIONED
idiom behind the times, of the old school
con fresh, modern, new, novel; fashionable
ant up-to-date
2 *syn* see PRIMITIVE 3
arched *adj syn* see CURVED
archetypal *adj syn* see TYPICAL 1
archetype *n* **1** *syn* see ORIGINAL 1

---

syn synonym(s)   *rel* related word(s)
ant antonym(s)   *con* contrasted word(s)
idiom idiomatic equivalent(s)
‖ use limited; if in doubt, see a dictionary

2 *syn* see MODEL 2

archfiend *n syn* see DEVIL 2

archilochian *adj syn* see SARCASTIC

archimage *n syn* see MAGICIAN 1

architect *n syn* see FATHER 2

architecture *n syn* see MAKEUP 1

archive *n, usu* **archives** *pl* **1** *syn* see LIBRARY
  2 *syn* see DOCUMENT 1
  rel papers, parchments, scrolls, writings; clippings, cuttings, excerpts, extracts, fragments, gleanings, remains

arciform *adj syn* see CURVED

arctic *adj syn* see COLD 1
  rel bitter, boreal, hyperborean; numbing, rigorous; hibernal, hiemal
  idiom cold as charity, cold enough to freeze a brass monkey
  ant torrid

ardent *adj* **1** *syn* see IMPASSIONED
  rel enthusiastic, urgent; avid, desirous, eager, keen
  con calm, composed, imperturbable, nonchalant; apathetic, impassive, phlegmatic; disinterested, dispassionate, impartial, uninterested
  ant cool
  2 very deep or moving <had an *ardent* longing for knowledge>
  syn extreme, intense
  rel crying, importunate, insistent, urgent; great, mighty, powerful, strong
  con feeble, minimal, slight, trivial
  3 *syn* see EAGER
  rel hasty, impetuous, impulsive, precipitate; fervid, fiery, hectic, hot; uncontrolled, ungoverned; earnest, intent, urgent, vehement
  con dull, heavy, inert, leaden, lumpish; languid, lethargic, listless; apathetic, impassive, phlegmatic
  ant easygoing
  4 *syn* see FAITHFUL 1
  5 *syn* see HOT 1
  6 *syn* see SPIRITUOUS

ardor *n* **1** *syn* see PASSION 6
  rel avidity; gusto, spirit, verve, zest; excitement, galvanization, quickening, stimulation
  con aloofness, detachment, disinterest, unconcern; apathy, lackadaisy, languor, listlessness
  ant coolness; indifference
  2 *syn* see EAGERNESS
  rel ardency, fervor, warmth
  3 *syn* see FIDELITY 1
  rel adoration, love, worship

arduous *adj* **1** *syn* see HARD 6
  2 *syn* see STEEP 1
  3 *syn* see TIGHT 4

arduously *adv syn* see HARD 8
  con easily, facilely
  ant effortlessly

area *n* **1** a distinguishable extent of surface and especially of the earth's surface <a large wooded *area*>
  syn belt, region, territory, tract, zone
  rel expanse, stretch; district, locality, place; lot, plot, section; terrain; circuit

2 *syn* see LOCALITY 1

arena *n syn* see SCENE 4

arete *n syn* see EXCELLENCE

argent *adj syn* see SILVERY

argentate *adj syn* see SILVERY

argenteous *adj syn* see SILVERY

argentine *adj syn* see SILVERY

argot *n syn* see DIALECT 2

arguable *adj syn* see MOOT

argue *vb* **1** *syn* see DISCUSS 1
  rel analyze, investigate, review, sift, study, ventilate; expostulate, object, protest, remonstrate
  2 to contend in words <*arguing* about who should answer the phone>
  syn argufy, bicker, dispute, hassle, quibble, squabble, wrangle; *compare* QUARREL
  rel differ, disaccord, disagree, dissent; balk, demur, jib; clash, conflict
  idiom bandy words, have it out, join (*or* take) issue
  con accord, agree, concur
  3 *syn* see INDICATE 2
  4 *syn* see MAINTAIN 2

argue (into) *vb syn* see INDUCE 1

argufy *vb syn* see ARGUE 2

argument *n* **1** *syn* see REASON 3
  rel basis, foundation; position, posture, stance, standpoint
  2 a vigorous often heated discussion of a moot question <their continuing *argument* over household expenses>
  syn contention, controversy, dispute, hurrah, rumpus
  rel argumentation, debate, disputation, polemic; disagreement, dissension, squabbling; embroilment, fuss, hassle, wrangle
  3 *syn* see SUBJECT 2
  rel position, proposition, statement, thesis

argumentation *n* the act or art or an exercise of one's powers of argument <noted for his skill in *argumentation*>
  syn debate, dialectic, disputation, forensic, mooting
  rel argument, controversy, dispute; declamation, elocution, eloquence, oratory, rhetoric

argumentative *adj syn* see CONTENTIOUS 2

argute *adj* **1** *syn* see SHREWD
  2 *syn* see ACUTE 4

aria *n syn* see SONG 2

arid *adj* **1** *syn* see DRY 1
  rel barren, infertile, sterile, unfruitful
  con fecund, fertile, fruitful
  2 lacking in interest or liveliness <some of the most *arid* prose ever written>
  syn bromidic, dry, dryasdust, dull, dusty, insipid, tedious, uninteresting, weariful, wearisome; *compare* TEPID 2, UNORIGINAL
  rel drab, dreary, flat, heavy, lackluster, leaden, unanimated, unlively; academic, bookish, pedantic; boring, humdrum, monotonous, unimaginative, uninspired
  con appealing, bright, lively, sparkling, stimulating, vigorous, vivid

aright *adv syn* see WELL 1

arise *vb* **1** *syn* see RISE 4
ant recline; slump
2 *syn* see ROLL OUT
3 *syn* see SPRING 1
rel ensue, follow, succeed
4 *syn* see BEGIN 2
aristarch *n* *syn* see CRITIC
‖**aristo** *n* *syn* see GENTLEMAN 1
aristocracy *n* the highest stratum of a society <the self-centered attitude of some *aristocracies*>
syn aristoi, blue blood, carriage trade, crème de la crème, elite, flower, gentility, gentry, haut monde, optimacy, patriciate, quality, society, upper class, upper crust, who's who
rel nobility, noblesse, patricians; county; beau monde, bon ton, jet set, smart set
con canaille, mob, rabble, riffraff; commoners, commons, masses, people, plebeians
aristocrat *n* *syn* see GENTLEMAN 1
ant commoner
aristoi *n* *syn* see ARISTOCRACY
arithmetic *n* *syn* see COMPUTATION
arm *n* **1** *syn* see INLET
2 *syn* see ANNEX
3 *syn* see POWER 4
arm *vb* *syn* see FURNISH 1
rel prepare, ready
idiom put in (*or* into) shape
ant disarm
armament *n* *syn* see DEFENSE 1
armamentarium *n* *syn* see SUPPLY
armed forces *n pl* *syn* see TROOP 2
armistice *n* *syn* see TRUCE
armor *n* *syn* see DEFENSE 1
rel cloak, mantle, shroud, veil; buckler, cover, screen, shelter
armory *n* a place where military arms and supplies are stored <the problem of weapon theft from *armories*>
syn arsenal, depot, dump, magazine
army *n* *syn* see MULTITUDE 1
rel crush, horde, mob, press, throng
aroma *n* **1** *syn* see FRAGRANCE
2 *syn* see SMELL 1
rel fetor, mephitis, reek, stench, stink
aromal *adj* *syn* see SWEET 2
rel penetrating, piquant, pungent
ant acrid
aromatic *adj* *syn* see SWEET 2
ant acrid
aromatize *vb* *syn* see SCENT 2
around *adv* **1** *syn* see ABOUT 1
2 *syn* see THROUGH 1
3 *syn* see ABOUT 4
4 *syn* see ABOUT 6
around *prep* *syn* see ABOUT 1
around *adj* *syn* see EXTANT 1
around-the-clock *adj* *syn* see CONTINUAL
arouse *vb* *syn* see STIR 1
rel alert, excite, work up; electrify, thrill; fire, inflame
idiom fan the fire (*or* flame), raise to fever heat, set on fire, stir one's blood (*or* feelings)
con allay, alleviate, assuage, ease, mitigate, relieve; mollify, pacify, placate

ant calm, quiet
arraign *vb* *syn* see ACCUSE
rel cite, summon; test, try
idiom bring to book, call to account
con absolve, acquit, exculpate, exonerate, vindicate; defend, justify
arrange *vb* **1** *syn* see ORDER 1
rel assort, categorize, pigeonhole, sort
con disorder, disorganize, disturb, unsettle; confuse, jumble, muddle, tumble; disperse, scatter
ant derange, disarrange
2 *syn* see DESIGN 3
3 *syn* see PLAN 2
4 *syn* see NEGOTIATE 1
rel design, plan, project, scheme
5 *syn* see HARMONIZE 4
arrangement *n* *syn* see ORDER 3
rel layout, lineup, setup; method, system
ant disarrangement
arrant *adj* **1** *syn* see UTTER
rel plain, pure, regular, sheer
2 *syn* see SHAMELESS
array *vb* **1** *syn* see ORDER 1
ant disarray
2 *syn* see CLOTHE
array *n* **1** *syn* see GROUP 3
2 *syn* see DISPLAY 2
rel exhibition, exposing, showing; arranging, marshaling, ordering
arrear *n, usu* **arrears** *pl* *syn* see DEBT 3
arrearage *n* **1** *syn* see DEBT 3
2 *syn* see INDEBTEDNESS 1
arrect *adj* **1** *syn* see ERECT
2 *syn* see ATTENTIVE 1
arrest *vb* **1** to bring to a halt <science cannot yet *arrest* the process of aging>
syn check, halt, interrupt, stall, stay; *compare* STOP 3
rel balk, frustrate, thwart; choke, obstruct, stop (up); delay, detain, hamper, hinder, restrain, retard; interfere, interpose, intervene; contain, stem, withstand
idiom bring to a halt (*or* stand *or* standstill), bring up short, check in full career, cut short
con advance, forward, further, promote; expedite, hasten, quicken, speed
2 to take and hold in custody under authority of the law <*arrested* for murder>
syn apprehend, ‖bust, detain, nab, pick up, pinch, pull in, run in; *compare* CATCH 1
rel immure, imprison, incarcerate, jail, lock (up), ‖slough; attach
idiom lay by the heels, lay hands on
con discharge, free, liberate, release
arrest *n* the taking and holding of a person in custody under authority of the law <unwilling to submit to *arrest*>

---

syn synonym(s)   *rel* related word(s)
ant antonym(s)   *con* contrasted word(s)
idiom idiomatic equivalent(s)
‖ use limited; if in doubt, see a dictionary

syn apprehension, arrestation, arrestment, ‖bust, detention, ‖nab, pickup, pinch
rel capture, catch, collar, seizure, taking
con discharge, freeing, liberation, release

arrestation *n syn* see ARREST

arresting *adj syn* see NOTICEABLE
rel attractive, enchanting, fascinating; affective, appealing, impressive, moving, touching
idiom enough to make one stop and take notice
con common, familiar, ordinary, run-of-the=mill; hackneyed, stereotyped, trite

arrestive *adj syn* see NOTICEABLE

arrestment *n syn* see ARREST

arride *vb syn* see PLEASE 2
rel beguile, divert, entertain, recreate
idiom tickle one's fancy
con bore, ennui, jade, weary

arrival *n* **1** the reaching of a destination <the train was late in its *arrival*>
syn advent, coming
rel appearance, emergence, entrance, issuance, manifestation
con disappearance, going, leaving, withdrawal; recession, retirement, retreat
ant departure
2 *syn* see SUCCESS

arrive *vb* **1** *syn* see COME 1
con get away, go, retire
ant depart
2 *syn* see SUCCEED 3

arriviste *n syn* see UPSTART

arrogance *n syn* see PRIDE 3
ant humility

arrogant *adj* **1** *syn* see PROUD 1
rel domineering, imperative, peremptory; affected, artificial, highfalutin, mannered, showy
idiom too big for one's britches
con humble; deferential, submissive; abject, obsequious, subservient, truckling
ant meek
2 *syn* see POMPOUS 1

arrogate *vb* **1** to claim or take over in a high=handed manner <*arrogated* to himself the right to make all decisions>
syn accroach, appropriate, assume, commandeer, preempt, usurp; *compare* APPROPRIATE 1
rel annex, preempt, preoccupy, sequester; grab, seize, take, take over
idiom help oneself to, make free with, take into one's own hands
con cede, relinquish, resign, surrender, yield
ant renounce
2 *syn* see APPROPRIATE 1

arrondi *adj syn* see CURVED

arroyo *n syn* see RAVINE

arsenal *n* **1** *syn* see ARMORY
2 *syn* see DEPOT 2

arsonist *n syn* see INCENDIARY

arsy–varsy *adj syn* see UPSIDE-DOWN 2

art *n* **1** a usually acquired proficiency in doing or performing <there's an *art* to competent public speaking>
syn adroitness, craft, cunning, dexterity, expertise, know-how, skill

rel capability, competence, handiness, proficiency; address, finesse, ‖savvy
con clumsiness, maladroitness
2 *syn* see CUNNING 2
rel acuteness, astuteness
con candor, frankness, sincerity; directness, straightforwardness, bluffness, bluntness
3 *syn* see TRADE 1

artery *n syn* see WAY 1

artful *adj syn* see SLY 2
rel diplomatic, oily, politic, smooth, suave; facile, specious, superficial; adroit, dexterous
ant artless

artfulness *n syn* see CUNNING 2

article *n* **1** *syn* see POINT 1
rel division, section, segment
2 *syn* see ESSAY 2
rel critique, manifesto, report, statement, study, survey
3 *syn* see THING 3
rel detail, particular

articled *adj syn* see BOUND 2

articulate *adj* **1** *syn* see VOCAL 1
rel clear, distinct, intelligible
ant inarticulate; dumb
2 *syn* see VOCAL 3
rel meaningful, significant; garrulous, prolix, talkative; uttering, venting
ant inarticulate

articulate *vb* **1** *syn* see INTEGRATE 3
rel connect, join, relate; methodize, order, organize, systematize; adjust, coordinate, harmonize, regulate; assemble, collect, gather; unify
con dissect, resolve; divide, part, separate
2 to form speech sounds <regional differences in *articulating* the letter *r*>
syn enunciate, phonate, pronounce, say
rel sound, utter

articulation *n syn* see VOCALIZATION

artifice *n* **1** *syn* see CUNNING 2
rel ingenuity, inventiveness, originality; adroitness, cleverness, keenness, quickness, shrewdness; adeptness, proficiency
2 *syn* see TRICK 1
rel chicane, chicanery, trickery; knavery, rascality, skulduggery; deceit, dissimulation, duplicity, guile

artificial *adj* **1** *syn* see SYNTHETIC
rel fabricated, fashioned, made
con native
ant natural
2 taking the place of something else and especially of something finer or more costly <*artificial* diamonds>
syn dummy, ersatz, false, imitation, mock, sham, simulated, spurious, substitute; *compare* FICTITIOUS 2, SPURIOUS 3
rel fake, papier-mâché, ‖pretend, unreal; hollow, painted
con authentic, bona fide, genuine, real, sure=enough, true, veritable
3 lacking in spontaneity and genuineness <exchanged *artificial* smiles>
syn affected, assumed, feigned, put-on, spurious

rel histrionic, insincere, overdone, quaint, stagy, theatrical, unnatural; cute, cutesy, goody=goody, mincing, overrefined, simpering; contrived, forced, labored

con genuine, sincere, spontaneous, unaffected

artist *n syn* see EXPERT

rel ace, crackerjack, first-rater, shark, top-notcher; genius, prodigy, wonder

artiste *n syn* see EXPERT

artless *adj syn* see NATURAL 5

rel free, relaxed; aboveboard, forthright, straightforward; childlike, trusting, unsuspicious; untouched, virginal

con cunning, insidious, sly, wily; calculating, designing, intriguing, scheming; artificial, insincere

ant artful; affected

arty *adj syn* see PRETENTIOUS 3

arty–crafty *adj syn* see PRETENTIOUS 3

as *conj syn* see BECAUSE

as a rule *adv syn* see USUALLY 2

‖**ascared** *adj syn* see AFRAID 1

ascend *vb* **1** to move upward to or toward a summit <*ascend* a mountain>

syn climb, escalade, escalate, mount, scale, upclimb, upgo

rel clamber, get up, scramble, shin; crest, surmount, top

idiom scale the heights, work one's way up

ant descend

2 *syn* see RISE 4

ascendancy *n syn* see SUPREMACY

ascendant *n* **1** *syn* see SUPREMACY

2 *syn* see ANCESTOR 1

rel forerunner, precursor, predecessor

ant descendant

ascendant *adj syn* see DOMINANT 1

ascension *n syn* see ASCENT

ascent *n* a moving upward or an upward movement <the slow *ascent* of the creaky old elevator>

syn ascension, rise, rising

rel elevation, raising, uplifting

ant descent

ascertain *vb syn* see DISCOVER 3

rel ask, inquire, interrogate, query, question; appraise, inspect, observe, survey, view; consider, contemplate, study, weigh

con assume, presume; conjecture, guess, surmise

ascetic *adj syn* see SEVERE 1

rel abstemious, abstinent, forbearing; self-abasing, self-abnegating, self-denying, self-forgetful, selfless; disciplined, restrained, schooled, trained

con epicurean, sensual, sensuous, sybaritic; abandoned, dissolute, licentious, self-indulgent

ant luxurious, voluptuous

ascribe *vb* to refer especially to a supposed cause, source, or author <a manuscript commonly *ascribed* to Saint Augustine>

syn accredit, assign, attribute, charge, credit, impute, lay, refer

rel attach (to), connect (with), fix (on *or* upon), pin (on), saddle (on *or* upon *or* with); affix, fas-

ten; conjecture, guess, surmise; adduce, advance, allege, cite

aseptic *adj syn* see UNDEMONSTRATIVE

as for *prep syn* see APROPOS

as good as *adv* **1** *syn* see NEARLY

2 *syn* see ALMOST 2

ash *n* the residue left when material is consumed by fire <cold whitened *ash* on the hearth>

syn ashes, cinders, clinkers

rel dross, scoria, slag; charcoal, coal(s), coke, ember(s); fumes, smoke, soot

ashake *adj syn* see TREMULOUS

ashamed *adj* humiliated or disconcerted usually by feelings of guilt, disgrace, or impropriety <*ashamed* of her brother's noisy boasting>

syn chagrined, mortified, shamed

rel abashed, discomfited, embarrassed; abased, humbled, humiliated; abject, hangdog, mean; contrite, penitent, repentant

idiom unable to show one's face

con arrogant, assured, overbearing, self-assured; vain, vainglorious

ant proud

ashen *adj syn* see PALE 1

rel corpselike, ghostly, macabre; blanched, bleached, decolorized, faded

ashes *n pl syn* see ASH

ashiver *adj syn* see TREMULOUS

ashy *adj syn* see PALE 1

aside *adv* **1** in a slanting or sloping direction <his head hung *aside* as if he lacked the strength to hold it up>

syn aslant, aslope, obliquely, sideways, sidewise, slant, slantingly, slantingways, slantly, slantways, slantwise, ‖slaunchways, slopeways; *compare* SIDEWAYS 1

rel askance, askant, askew, awry; downgrade, downhill

con erectly, uprightly, vertically

2 *syn* see APART 2

3 *syn* see APIECE

‖**aside** *prep syn* see NEAR 2

aside *n syn* see DIGRESSION

aside from *prep syn* see EXCEPT

asinine *adj syn* see SIMPLE 3

rel puerile; absurd, irrational, unreasonable

con prudent, sage, sane, sapient, wise; clever, intelligent, knowing, smart; rational, reasonable

ant judicious, sensible

ask *vb* **1** to call upon for an answer or information <*asked* him to explain his behavior>

syn catechize, examine, inquire, interrogate, query, question, quiz

rel argue, canvass, debate, deliberate, discuss, review, talk (over)

con answer, rejoin, reply, respond, retort

2 to seek to obtain by making one's needs or desires known <*asked* for time to consider the problem>

---

syn synonym(s) *rel* related word(s)
ant antonym(s) *con* contrasted word(s)
idiom idiomatic equivalent(s)
‖ use limited; if in doubt, see a dictionary

syn bespeak, desire, request, solicit
rel claim, demand, exact, require; beg, beseech, entreat, implore, importune
idiom put in for
3 *syn* see DEMAND 2
4 *syn* see INVITE
rel canvass, request, seek
askance *adv* **1** *syn* see AWRY 1
ant directly
2 with absence of approval or trust <a proceeding one must view more than a little *askance*>
syn distrustfully, doubtfully, mistrustfully, skeptically, suspiciously
rel captiously, critically, cynically, doubtingly; deprecatingly, depreciatively, disparagingly
con approvingly, favorably
askant *adv syn* see AWRY 1
ant directly
asker *n syn* see SUPPLIANT
askew *adv syn* see AWRY 1
ant straight
aslant *adv syn* see ASIDE 1
asleep *adj* **1** *syn* see DEAD 1
2 *syn* see NUMB 1
3 *syn* see INACTIVE
as long as *conj syn* see BECAUSE
aslope *adv syn* see ASIDE 1
as much as *adv syn* see ALMOST 2
asomatous *adj syn* see IMMATERIAL 1
aspect *n* **1** *syn* see APPEARANCE 1
rel countenance, face, visage; air, bearing, port, presence
2 *syn* see PHASE
rel point of view, slant, standpoint
asperity *n* **1** *syn* see DIFFICULTY 1
rel austerity, bitterness, grimness, harshness, inclemency, severity, stringency
con blandness, gentleness, mildness, softness
2 *syn* see INEQUALITY 1
3 *syn* see ACRIMONY
rel harshness, keenness, roughness, sharpness; irritability, snappishness, tartness, waspishness
con blandness, smoothness, suavity, urbanity; courtesy, gallantry
ant amenity
asperous *adj syn* see ROUGH 1
asperse *vb* **1** *syn* see MALIGN
rel deride, mock, taunt; affront, insult, offend
con applaud, commend, compliment
2 *syn* see BAPTIZE
aspersion *n syn* see ANIMADVERSION
rel abuse, invective, muck, vituperation; backbiting, calumny, detraction, scandal, slander; lampoon, libel, pasquinade, skit, squib
con eulogy, extolling, laudation, praise; acclaim, acclamation, applause, plaudits; commendation, compliment
asphyxiate *vb syn* see SUFFOCATE
aspirant *n syn* see CANDIDATE
aspiration *n syn* see AMBITION 1
rel aim, direction, goal, objective; desire, lust, passion, urge
aspire *vb* **1** *syn* see AIM 2
rel hunger, long, pine, thirst; bid (for), strain (for *or* after), struggle (for), try (for)

idiom cry for the moon, have at heart, have one's heart set on, reach for (*or* keep one's eyes on) the stars
con condescend, deign, look down (on); grovel, stoop, wallow
2 *syn* see RISE 4
aspiring *adj syn* see AMBITIOUS 1
rel desirous, impassioned, urgent; wanting, wishful, yearning
as regards *prep syn* see APROPOS
as respects *prep syn* see APROPOS
ass *n* **1** *syn* see DONKEY 1
2 *syn* see FOOL 1
assail *vb syn* see ATTACK 1
rel beat, belabor, buffet, pound, pummel
idiom round on
assailment *n syn* see ATTACK 1
assassin *n* a person hired or hirable to commit murder <found out who paid the *assassin*>
syn bravo, cutthroat, gun, gunman, ‖gunsel, gunslinger, hatchet man, hit man, torpedo, triggerman; *compare* MURDERER
rel apache, desperado, goon, ‖gorilla, highbinder, strong arm, thug
assassinate *vb syn* see MURDER 1
assault *n syn* see ATTACK 1
rel brush, clash, invasion, melee, skirmish; brawl, contest, fracas, set-to
assault *vb syn* see ATTACK 1
rel battle, fight, war; clash, collide, encounter, engage; skirmish
assay *vb* **1** *syn* see TRY 5
rel venture
idiom make an effort to
2 *syn* see ESTIMATE 1
rel demonstrate, prove, test, try; analyze, resolve; calculate, compute, reckon
assemblage *n syn* see GATHERING 1
assemble *vb* **1** *syn* see CONVOKE
2 *syn* see GATHER 6
rel associate, combine, unite; convene, convoke
con dispel, dissipate, scatter; leave, part, quit, separate
ant disperse
3 *syn* see GROUP 1
rel accumulate, aggregate, amass, garner; bunch, clump; bank, heap, mound, pile, stack
con dispel, dissipate, scatter; leave, part, quit, separate; break up, disband
ant disperse
4 *syn* see MAKE 3
assembly *n* **1** *syn* see GATHERING 2
rel association, band, conclave, party, troupe
2 *syn* see GROUP 1
rel crowd, push; faction, interest, sect, wing; brotherhood, fellowship, fraternity
con masses, multitude; canaille, rabble, riffraff, ruck, trash
assent *vb* to give or express one's consent or concurrence <*assented* grudgingly to her plans for the evening>
syn accede, acquiesce, agree, consent, subscribe, yes
rel adopt, embrace, espouse; accept; abide, bear (with), endure, stand, suffer, tolerate; down,

stomach, swallow, take; defer, relent, submit, yield
idiom be at one with, cast one's vote for, give the nod of approval, go along with, see eye to eye with
con rebuff, refuse, reject, scorn, scout, spurn; deny, gainsay
ant dissent

assert *vb* **1** to state firmly, positively, or assuredly <he continued to *assert* his innocence>
syn affirm, aver, avouch, avow, constate, declare, depose, predicate, profess, protest
rel adduce, advance, allege, cite, claim, pretend; announce, broadcast, disseminate, proclaim, promulgate, publish, spread
idiom have it
con contradict, contravene, dispute, gainsay, negate, negative, traverse; confute, disprove, rebut, refute
ant deny; controvert
2 *syn* see MAINTAIN 2
rel declare, express, utter, voice; advance, state, stipulate, submit

assertive *adj* **1** *syn* see EMPHATIC
2 *syn* see AGGRESSIVE
rel affirmative; arbitrary, dogmatic, peremptory, positive; assured, certain, cocksure, opinionated, opinionative, self-assured, sure; confident, presumptuous, sanguine, self-confident
con bashful, diffident, modest, shy; amenable, biddable, docile, submissive
ant retiring; acquiescent

assertory *adj syn* see AGGRESSIVE

assess *vb* **1** *syn* see LEVY
2 *syn* see ESTIMATE 1
rel calculate, compute; account, consider, deem, reckon, weigh

assessment *n* **1** *syn* see ESTIMATION 1
2 *syn* see ESTIMATE 1
3 *syn* see TAX 1

asset *n* **1** **assets** *pl syn* see MEAN 3
rel bankroll, money; equity; principal
ant liabilities
2 *syn* see CREDIT 3
rel distinction, glory, honor, ornament
con detriment, disadvantage, discredit, liability
ant handicap

asshead *n syn* see FOOL 1

assiduous *adj* marked by careful attention or persistent application <learned to speak French fluently by *assiduous* practice>
syn diligent, industrious, operose, sedulous; *compare* BUSY 1
rel hardworking, laborious, moiling; indefatigable, tireless, untiring, unwearied, zealous
idiom hard at it
con casual, haphazard, happy-go-lucky, hit-or-miss, intermittent, random; careless, lax, remiss, slack, sloppy, slovenly; indolent, lazy, slothful
ant desultory

assiduously *adv syn* see HARD 3

assign *vb* **1** *syn* see TRANSFER 4
2 *syn* see ALLOT
rel establish, fix, set, settle

3 *syn* see ASCRIBE
rel associate, link, relate; classify, pigeonhole
4 *syn* see PRESCRIBE 2
rel decide, determine; commit, consign, entrust, relegate

assignation *n syn* see ENGAGEMENT 3
rel agreement, arrangement, understanding; get-together

assignee *n syn* see AGENT 2

assignment *n syn* see TASK 1
rel incumbency, liability, obligation, responsibility

assimilate *vb* **1** *syn* see ABSORB 1
rel imbue, infuse, ingrain, inoculate, leaven, suffuse; adopt, embrace, espouse; corner, engross, monopolize
2 *syn* see EQUATE 2

assimilation *n syn* see RECOGNITION 1
rel awareness, consciousness, mindfulness

assist *vb syn* see HELP 1
rel accompany, attend, escort; concur, cooperate
con clog, fetter, trammel; forestall, prevent; burden, encumber, handicap, tax, weigh down
ant hamper; impede

assist *n syn* see HELP 1

assistance *n syn* see HELP 1
rel backing, supporting, upholding; advantage, avail, profit, use; appropriation, grant, subsidy, subvention
con checking, hampering, hindering, hindrance; balking, foiling, frustration, thwarting
ant impediment, impeding; obstructing, obstruction

assistant *n* **1** *syn* see HELPER
2 a person who takes over part of the duties of a superior <started as *assistant* to the secretary>
syn aid, aide, aide-de-camp, coadjutant, coadjutor, lieutenant
rel acolyte, attendant, second; flunky, henchman, minion, stooge; girl Friday, right-hand man; agent, attorney, deputy, factor, proxy; fall guy, patsy; co-worker, workfellow, yokemate

assistive *adj syn* see HELPFUL 1

assize *n* **1** *syn* see LAW 1
2 *syn* see STANDARD 4

associate *vb syn* see JOIN 1
rel amalgamate, blend, coalesce, merge, mingle, mix; ally, confederate, federate, league
con alienate, estrange; divide, divorce, part

associate *n* **1** *syn* see PARTNER
rel affiliate, ally, confederate, leaguer; abettor, accomplice, collaborator
2 *syn* see COLLEAGUE
3 a person regularly frequenting the company of another <a man is judged by the *associates* he keeps>

---

syn synonym(s)   *rel* related word(s)
ant antonym(s)   *con* contrasted word(s)
idiom idiomatic equivalent(s)
|| use limited; if in doubt, see a dictionary

syn buddy, chum, comate, companion, comrade, crony, ‖cully, pal, running mate; *compare* FRIEND

rel acquaintance, friend, sympathizer; confidant, familiar, intimate; brother-in-arms, comrade-in-arms

4 *syn* see ACCOMPANIMENT 2

rel complement, correlate, correlative, counterpart, match; correspondent

con competitor, rival; adversary, antagonist, opponent

association *n* **1** the quality or state of being associated <worked in close *association* with the courts>

syn affiliation, alliance, cahoots, combination, conjointment, conjunction, connection, hookup, partnership, tie-up, togetherness

rel coaction, collaboration, concert, cooperation, teamwork; conviviality, gaiety, joviality, sociability

con aloofness, apartness, disjunction, disunion, isolation, separation

ant disassociation, dissociation

2 an organization of persons sharing a common interest or purpose <a buyers' *association*>

syn brotherhood, club, congress, fellowship, fraternity, guild, league, order, society, sodality, union

rel alliance, axis, bloc, coalition, federation, organization; faction, interest, sect, wing; combine, gang, machine, ring

3 *syn* see LEAGUE 4

4 something (as a feeling or recollection) associated in the mind with a particular person or thing <the thought of her childhood home always carried an *association* of loving warmth>

syn connotation, hint, implication, overtone, suggestion, undertone

rel image, picture, vision; appearance, fantasy, illusion, mirage

assort *vb* to arrange systematically <*assort* yarn by color>

syn categorize, class, classify, group, pigeonhole

rel arrange, methodize, order, systematize; distribute, divide, separate; screen, sift; stratify

con derange, disarrange, disorder, disorganize; commingle, jumble, mingle, mix, scramble

assorted *adj* **1** *syn* see MISCELLANEOUS

con chosen, picked, preferred, selected

2 corresponding in such manner or degree as to be appropriately associated <they made a well≠ *assorted* pair>

syn adapted, conformable, fitted, matched, suited

rel chosen, picked, preferred, selected; associated, bracketed, coupled, linked

con confused, disordered, fouled-up, haywire, jumbled, muddled, scrambled

assortment *n* **1** *syn* see VARIETY 2

2 *syn* see MISCELLANY 1

assuage *vb* **1** *syn* see RELIEVE 1

rel placate

con augment, increase, recruit, reinforce; enhance, exaggerate, heighten, intensify, magnify, strengthen

ant exacerbate

2 *syn* see PACIFY

rel calm, ease, relax, slack, slacken, soothe

con annoy, inflame, nettle, provoke, ruffle, vex

as such *adv syn* see PER SE

assumably *adv syn* see PRESUMABLY

assume *vb* **1** *syn* see DON 2

2 *syn* see DON 1

3 *syn* see ARROGATE 1

rel grab, seize, snatch, take

idiom take over the helm, take possession (*or* command)

4 to take on or present a false or deceptive appearance <their gaiety was *assumed*>

syn act, affect, bluff, counterfeit, fake, feign, pretend, put on, sham, simulate

rel camouflage, cloak, conceal, disguise, dissemble, hide, mask

idiom make believe

5 *syn* see PRESUPPOSE

rel affirm, assert, aver, predicate, profess; allow, concede, grant

6 *syn* see UNDERSTAND 3

assumed *adj syn* see ARTIFICIAL 3

rel factitious, synthetic; deceptive, delusory, illusory, insubstantial, unreal

con authentic, bona fide, genuine, veritable; real, true

assumption *n* **1** *syn* see PRESUPPOSITION

2 something that is taken for granted or advanced as fact <decisions based on *assumptions* about the nature of society>

syn apriorism, posit, postulate, postulation, premise, presumption, presupposition, supposition, thesis

rel conjecture, guess, surmise; hypothesis, theory; axiom, fundamental, law, principle, theorem

assurance *n* **1** *syn* see WORD 8

rel parole, promise, troth; plight; agreement, compact, covenant, pact, understanding

2 *syn* see CERTAINTY

rel credit; dependence, reliance, trust

con suspicion, uncertainty; disbelief, incredulity, unbelief

ant mistrust; dubiousness

3 *syn* see SAFETY

4 *syn* see CONFIDENCE 2

rel composure, equanimity, sangfroid

con agitation, disquiet, jumpiness, nervousness, shakiness, skittishness; anxiety, doubt, foreboding, funk, perturbation, trepidation

ant alarm

5 *syn* see TEMERITY

rel brazenness, cockiness, presumption; conceit, self-conceit, self-importance, vanity

con diffidence, modesty, shyness, timidity; self≠ depreciation, self-effacement, unassumingness, unpretentiousness

assure *vb* **1** *syn* see ENSURE

con abash, discomfit, embarrass; buffalo, bulldoze, cow, daunt, intimidate, shake; demoralize, disquiet, unman, unnerve

ant alarm

2 to make one sure or certain of something <pinched his arm to *assure* himself he was awake>
syn convince, persuade, satisfy
idiom bring (*or* drive) home to, lead one to believe, sell one on something
assured *adj* **1** *syn* see CONFIDENT 1
rel collected, composed, cool, imperturbable, unflappable, unruffled; game, plucky, resolute, spunky
con abashed, discomfited, disconcerted, embarrassed, rattled; hesitant, insecure, reluctant, uncertain; apprehensive, timorous
2 *syn* see DECIDED 1
rel certain, fixed, set
con ambiguous, uncertain; enigmatic, mysterious, obscure
assuredness *n* *syn* see CERTAINTY
astern *adv* *syn* see ABAFT
rel rear
con ahead, before, forward
as to *prep* **1** *syn* see APROPOS
2 *syn* see BY 5
astonish *vb* *syn* see SURPRISE 2
rel overwhelm; affright, alarm, terrify
astonishing *adj* *syn* see MARVELOUS 1
astound *vb* *syn* see SURPRISE 2
astounding *adj* *syn* see MARVELOUS 1
astral *adj* **1** *syn* see STELLAR 1
2 *syn* see DREAMY 1
3 *syn* see EXALTED 1
astray *adv* *syn* see AMISS 2
astricted *adj* *syn* see CONSTIPATED
astringent *adj* **1** *syn* see ACRID
rel puckery
con bland, mellow, mild
2 *syn* see SEVERE 1
rel biting, cutting, incisive, penetrating, piercing, stabbing; brisk, caustic, keen, sharp
con lax, loose, relaxed, slack, weak; unexacting
3 *syn* see TONIC 1
astucious *adj* *syn* see SHREWD
astucity *n* *syn* see WIT 3
astute *adj* **1** *syn* see SHREWD
rel discreet, foresighted, prudent; cunning, sly, wily
con ingenuous, naive, simple, unsophisticated; dull, heavy, obtuse, slow; arid, barren, staid, stuffy, uninspired
ant gullible
2 *syn* see SLY 2
rel subtle, subtle; keen, knowing, sharp
idiom slippery as an eel, too clever by half
con aboveboard, forthright, straightforward; ingenuous, naive, simple, unsophisticated
astuteness *n* *syn* see WIT 3
asudden *adv* *syn* see SHORT 1
asunder *adv* *syn* see APART 3
idiom all to pieces, one part from the other, to shreds
as usual *adv* *syn* see USUALLY 1
asweat *adj* *syn* see SWEATY
as well *adv* **1** *syn* see ALSO 2
idiom over and above

2 *syn* see EVEN 1
as well as *prep* *syn* see BESIDES 1
as yet *adv* *syn* see HITHERTO 1
asylum *n* **1** *syn* see SHELTER 1
2 *syn* see REFUGE 1
rel inviolability; security
3 an institution for the care of the insane <demand for improved *asylums*>
syn booby hatch, ‖bughouse, crazy house, ‖funny farm, loony bin, madhouse, ‖nuthouse
rel farm, home, institution, sanatorium
idiom insane (*or* lunatic) asylum, mental hospital (*or* institution), state hospital
asymmetric *adj* *syn* see LOPSIDED
at all *adv* **1** *syn* see EVER 5
2 *syn* see EVER 4
ataraxy *n* *syn* see EQUANIMITY
atavism *n* *syn* see REVERSION 1
ataxia *n* *syn* see CONFUSION 3
at close hand *adv* *syn* see CLOSE
atelier *n* *syn* see STUDIO
athenaeum *n* *syn* see LIBRARY
athirst *adj* **1** *syn* see THIRSTY 1
rel dehydrated, desiccated, dried up
2 *syn* see EAGER
con lackadaisical, languid, listless; autistic, withdrawn
athletic *adj* *syn* see MUSCULAR 2
rel active, energetic, strenuous, vigorous
con delicate; decadent, effete, flabby, soft
athletics *n pl* physical activities engaged in for exercise or pleasure <went in heavily for *athletics*>
syn games, sports
rel calisthenics, exercise, gymnastics; drill, practice, workout; amusement, diversion, entertainment, pastime, recreation
athwart *adv* **1** *syn* see ACROSS 1
2 *syn* see OVER 1
athwart *prep* *syn* see ACROSS
atiptoe *adj* *syn* see EXPECTANT 1
atmosphere *n* **1** *syn* see AIR 3
rel character, flavor, property, quality; characteristic, individuality, peculiarity; impression, suggestion
2 *syn* see ENVIRONMENT
atmospheric *adj* *syn* see AIRY 1
atom *n* *syn* see PARTICLE
rel dash, touch, trace; shade, smack, spice, soupçon, suggestion, suspicion, tincture, tinge
atomize *vb* *syn* see DESTROY 1
at once *adv* **1** *syn* see TOGETHER 1
2 *syn* see AWAY 3
atone *vb* *syn* see EXPIATE
rel compensate, pay, recompense, satisfy; appease, conciliate, propitiate
idiom set one's house in order
atone (for) *vb* *syn* see COMPENSATE 1
atramentous *adj* *syn* see BLACK 1
at random *adv* *syn* see ABOUT 4

---

syn synonym(s)   *rel* related word(s)
ant antonym(s)   *con* contrasted word(s)
idiom idiomatic equivalent(s)
‖ use limited; if in doubt, see a dictionary

atrocious *adj* **1** *syn* see OUTRAGEOUS 2
  rel flagitious, infamous, iniquitous, vicious; barbarous, savage; glaring, rank; abominable, contemptible, despicable, execrable, odious, vile
  con fine, righteous, upright, virtuous; benign, gentle, kindly
  ant humane
  2 *syn* see OFFENSIVE
  rel displeasing, distasteful
  con alluring, magnetic

atrociousness *n syn* see ENORMITY 1

atrocity *n syn* see ENORMITY 1

atrophy *n syn* see DETERIORATION 1

attach *vb syn* see FASTEN 1
  rel associate; add, annex, append; bind, tie
  con disassociate, dissociate; disembarrass, disencumber, disengage, disentangle
  ant detach

attachment *n* **1** the state of being firmly attached to someone or something (as by affection, sympathy, or self-interest) <his *attachment* to an outworn code>
  syn adherence, adhesion, constancy, faithfulness, fidelity, loyalty
  rel firmness, staunchness, steadfastness; allegiance, devotion, fealty
  con disloyalty, faithlessness, infidelity, unfaithfulness; aloofness, distance, remoteness; disinterest, disregard, unconcern, unmindfulness
  ant detachment
  2 *syn* see LOVE 1
  rel piety; devotedness
  con antipathy, disinclination, dislike; alienation, disaffection, estrangement
  ant aversion

attack *vb* **1** to act in violent opposition <cavalry *attacked* the Indian camp>
  syn aggress, assail, assault, beset, fall (on or upon), storm, strike
  rel invade, irrupt; charge, raid, rush; besiege, blockade, encompass, invest; beleaguer, beset, harass, harry, press; turn (on)
  idiom gang up on, light into, sail into, set upon, take the offensive
  con defend, guard, protect, shield; combat, oppose, resist, withstand
  2 to begin to work vigorously (as at a task) <*attack* a problem>
  syn bang away (at), tackle
  rel buckle (to or down or down to), fall to, pitch in, wade (in or into)
  idiom address (or apply or devote) oneself to, give oneself up to
  con dawdle, lag, poke, putter

attack *n* **1** an act of attacking especially in the form of an attempt to injure, destroy, or defame <insecticides that are essential for successful *attack* on insect pests>
  syn aggression, assailment, assault, offense, offensive, onfall, onset, onslaught
  rel charge, descent, drive, foray, push, raid, sally, sortie; blitz, incursion, inroad, surprise; action, battle

  con championing, justification, protection, support, vindication; opposition, resistance; defending, guarding, protecting, sheltering
  ant defense
  2 action or an attitude in a struggle that calls for or is opposed by defense <his policy had always been one of *attack*>
  syn aggression, aggressiveness, belligerence, combativeness, fight, pugnacity
  rel bellicosity, chauvinism, jingoism, warmongering; activation, militarization, mobilization, muster
  con submissiveness, yielding
  3 an episode of bodily or mental disorder <a sudden *attack* of dizziness>
  syn access, fit, seizure, spell, throe, turn; *compare* SIEGE
  rel outbreak, paroxysm, spasm; affection, ailment, complaint, disease, disorder

attain *vb syn* see GAIN 1
  idiom gain one's end, make good

attainable *adj syn* see AVAILABLE 1

attainment *n syn* see ACQUIREMENT

attempt *vb syn* see TRY 5
  rel begin, commence, inaugurate, initiate, start; venture
  idiom give (something) a try, take a crack (or whack) at
  con accomplish, achieve, effect, execute, fulfill, perform; attain, compass, gain, reach
  ant succeed

attempt *n* an effort made to do or accomplish something <made a determined *attempt* to improve her writing>
  syn endeavor, essay, hassle, striving, struggle, trial, try, undertaking
  rel care, effort, pains, trouble; beginning, commencement, initiation, offer, shy, start
  con accomplishment, achievement, attainment, finish, fulfillment

attend *vb* **1** *syn* see LISTEN
  idiom be attentive (to), give heed (to)
  2 *syn* see TEND 2
  rel govern, oversee, supervise; direct, handle, manage, regulate, run; aid, assist, help
  3 *syn* see ACCOMPANY
  rel associate, fraternize, join, mingle, mix

attendant *adj syn* see CONCOMITANT

attendant *n syn* see HELPER

attending *adj syn* see CONCOMITANT

attention *n* **1** a focusing of the mind on something <gave the problem careful *attention*>
  syn application, concentration, consideration, debate, deliberation, heed, study
  rel assiduity, diligence, industry, sedulity, sedulousness; notice, observation, regard, remark; absorption, engrossment, immersion, intentness
  con absence, absentmindedness, abstraction, detachment, remoteness, withdrawal; disinterest, indifference, unconcern, unmindfulness
  ant inattention
  2 *syn* see NOTICE 1
  rel awareness, consciousness, mindfulness, sensibility

con disregard, heedlessness, insensibility, un-awareness, unconsciousness
3 syn see COURTESY 1
rel deference, homage, honor, reverence; benignity; considerateness, consideration, kindliness, solicitude
con neglect, negligence; aloofness, indifference, unconcern; discourtesy

attentive *adj* **1** concentrating one's attention on something <listeners *attentive* to the speaker's appeal>
syn advertent, arrect, heedful, intentive, observant, regardful
rel alert, aware, mindful; agog, eager, interested, keen; concentrating, earnest, intent; open-eared, open-eyed
idiom all ears (*or* eyes), on the ball, paying attention
con absorbed, abstracted, bemused, preoccupied; absentminded, daydreaming, faraway, oblivious, wandering, woolgathering
ant absent; inattentive
2 syn see THOUGHTFUL 3
con aloof, indifferent
ant inattentive; neglectful

attenuate *vb* **1 syn** see THIN 1
rel lessen; sap; dissipate; constrict, contract, deflate, shrink
con amplify, dilate, distend, expand, inflate, swell; augment, enlarge, increase; enrich
2 syn see WEAKEN 1
3 syn see THIN 2

attenuate *adj* **1 syn** see THIN 1
2 syn see THIN 2

attenuated *adj* **syn** see THIN 2

attest *vb* **1 syn** see CERTIFY 1
rel confirm, corroborate, substantiate, verify; support, sustain, uphold, warrant; affirm, asseverate, depone, swear, testify
con confute, controvert, disprove, refute; contradict, deny, gainsay
2 syn see INDICATE 2
rel authenticate, confirm, substantiate
con falsify, misrepresent; distort, garble, pervert, twist, warp
ant belie
3 syn see TESTIFY 1

attestation *n* **syn** see TESTIMONY
at times *adv* **syn** see SOMETIMES
attire *vb* **syn** see CLOTHE
rel accouter, appoint, arm, equip, outfit
con bare, denude, dismantle, strip
ant divest

attire *n* **syn** see CLOTHES
attirement *n* **syn** see CLOTHES
attitude *n* **1 syn** see POSTURE 1
rel air, demeanor, port, presence
2 syn see POSITION 1
rel point of view; bias, predilection, prejudice, prepossession

attitudinize *vb* **syn** see POSE 4
attorney *n* **1 syn** see AGENT 2
rel alternate, locum tenens, stand-in, substitute, supply

2 syn see LAWYER
attorney-at-law *n* **syn** see LAWYER
attract *vb* **1** to exert an irresistible or compelling influence on <her beauty *attracted* all eyes>
syn allure, bewitch, captivate, charm, draw, enchant, fascinate, magnetize, take, wile
rel entice, lure, seduce, tempt; beguile, draw (in), intrigue, inveigle, suck (in); enrapture, entrance; court, invite, solicit
con fend (off), hold (off *or* away), rebuff, repulse; disgust, offend, revolt
ant repel
2 syn see INTEREST

attracting *adj* **syn** see ATTRACTIVE 1
attraction *n* **1** a quality that elicits admiration or pleased responsiveness <yielding to the *attraction* of the balmy afternoon>
syn allurement, appeal, attractiveness, call, draw, drawing power, lure, pull, seduction
rel charm, glamour, interest; delight, pleasure; bait, hook, snare
con offensiveness, repulsiveness, ugliness
2 a relationship characteristic of individuals that are drawn together naturally or involuntarily and exert a degree of influence on one another <the *attraction* between iron and the magnet>
syn affinity, sympathy
rel accord, concord, harmony
idiom drawing together
con conflict, discord, friction, tension

attractive *adj* **1** having the power to attract <an area *attractive* to wildlife>
syn alluring, appealing, attracting, bewitching, captivating, charming, drawing, enchanting, engaging, fascinating, glamorous, magnetic, mesmeric, prepossessing, seductive, siren
rel beautiful, bonny, comely, fair, lovely, pretty; Circean, enticing, fetching, luring, tempting; interesting, taking, winning; beckoning, come-hither, inviting, provocative, tantalizing, teasing; likable, simpatico
con abhorrent, distasteful, obnoxious, repugnant; loathsome, offensive, repulsive, revolting; antipathetic, unsympathetic
ant repellent, repelling; forbidding
2 syn see BEAUTIFUL
rel agreeable, goodly, ||likely, pleasing, sightly
con homely, ill-favored, plain, uncomely, unprepossessing
ant unattractive

attractiveness *n* **syn** see ATTRACTION 1
attribute *n* **1 syn** see QUALITY 1
rel particularity, singularity, specialty; brand, earmark, impress, stamp
2 syn see SYMBOL 1
attribute *vb* **syn** see ASCRIBE
rel calendar, chronologize, date, place
attrition *n* **syn** see PENITENCE
attritional *adj* **syn** see REMORSEFUL

---

syn synonym(s)   **rel** related word(s)
ant antonym(s)   **con** contrasted word(s)
idiom idiomatic equivalent(s)
|| use limited; if in doubt, see a dictionary

attune *vb syn* see HARMONIZE 3
rel balance, compensate, counterbalance; accord, agree; fix, rectify, regulate
idiom put in tune, set to rights (*or* in order)
con divide, separate, wean
‖**atween** *prep syn* see BETWEEN 2
‖**atwixt** *prep syn* see BETWEEN 2
atypical *adj syn* see ABNORMAL 1
rel irregular, unnatural; different, divergent; exceptional, odd, peculiar, queer, strange
con customary, usual
ant typical; representative
auberge *n syn* see HOTEL
au courant *adj* 1 *syn* see AWARE
2 *syn* see UP-TO-DATE
3 *syn* see FAMILIAR 3
audacious *adj* 1 *syn* see BRAVE 1
rel adventurous, daredevil, daring, foolhardy, rash, reckless, venturesome; brash, brazen, shameless
con calculating, cautious, chary, wary; judicious, prudent, sane, wise; careful, circumspect, discreet
2 *syn* see ADVENTUROUS
rel fearless, valiant, valorous
con careful, circumspect, discreet; calculating, cautious, chary, wary
3 *syn* see INSOLENT 2
4 free from constraint and formality <found life an *audacious* ever-changing adventure>
syn uncurbed, ungoverned, unhampered, uninhibited, unrestrained, untrammeled
rel emancipated, free, independent; easy, relaxed; careless, heedless, thoughtless; self-absorbed, self-centered, selfish
con checked, curbed, governed, hampered, inhibited, restrained, trammeled; careful, cautious, heedful, mindful, thoughtful; considerate, generous, self-abnegating, self-effacing; drab, dull, pedestrian
audacity *n syn* see TEMERITY
rel cheek, effrontery, face, gall; brass, brazenness, cockiness; forwardness, impudence, resolution; courage, mettle, spirit
con calculation, caution, wariness; shyness, timidity, timorousness; agitation, disquiet, nervousness, perturbation, trepidation
ant circumspection
audible *adj syn* see AURAL 1
ant inaudible
audience *n* 1 *syn* see HEARING 2
rel attention, consideration, ear
2 *syn* see FOLLOWING 2
rel admirers, devotees, fanciers, fans, votaries
audile *adj syn* see AUDITORY
audit *n syn* see EXAMINATION
rel investigation, probe; check, control, corrective
audition *n syn* see HEARING 2
auditory *adj* of, relating to, or experienced through the sense of hearing <*auditory* disorders>
syn acoustic, audile, aural; *compare* AURAL 1
au fait *adj* 1 *syn* see ABLE

2 *syn* see FAMILIAR 3
3 *syn* see DECOROUS 1
au fond *adv syn* see ESSENTIALLY 1
Augean stable *n syn* see SINK 1
aught (*or* **ought**) *n syn* see ZERO 1
augment *vb* 1 *syn* see INCREASE 1
2 *syn* see INCREASE 2
augment *n syn* see INCREASE 1
rel exalt, hike, raise
con attenuate, decrease, dwindle; abridge; alleviate, assuage, relieve
ant abate
augmentation *n* 1 *syn* see ACCOMPANIMENT 1
rel adjunct, annex, attachment, fixture, reinforcement; bonus, boot, extra, plus
2 *syn* see ADDITION
con subtraction
augur *n syn* see PROPHET
augur *vb* 1 *syn* see FORETELL
rel argue, bespeak, indicate
2 to indicate or suggest a future probability <their enthusiasm *augurs* well for the success of the enterprise>
syn betoken, bode, forebode, foreshadow, foreshow, foretoken, omen, portend, presage, promise
rel hint, imply, intimate, suggest; prefigure, shadow (forth)
idiom bid fair to, give promise (*or* fair promise) of, hold out hope of, lead one to believe (*or* expect)
augury *n syn* see FORETOKEN
rel anticipation, premonition, presentiment
con accomplishment, effecting, effectuation, fulfillment; actualization, materialization, realization; appearance, emergence, forthcoming, issuance
august *adj syn* see GRAND 1
rel splendid, sublime, superb; impressive, moving, striking; awe-inspiring, awful, fearful, overwhelming
au naturel *adj syn* see NUDE 2
aura *n syn* see AIR 3
rel appearance, aspect, suggestion; aureole, radiance
aural *adj* 1 heard or perceived with the ear <responded to *aural* stimuli>
syn audible, auricular; *compare* AUDITORY
2 *syn* see AUDITORY
aureate *adj syn* see RHETORICAL
rel baroque, rococo
con moderate, quiet, restrained, sober, temperate
ant austere
auricular *n syn* see AURAL 1
aurora *n syn* see DAWN 1
auslander *n syn* see STRANGER
auspex *n syn* see PROPHET
auspices *n pl syn* see BACKING
auspicious *adj* 1 *syn* see FAVORABLE 5
rel hopeful; golden, halcyon, roseate, rosy
con ominous, portentous, unpropitious; adverse, antagonistic
ant inauspicious; ill-omened

2 syn see TIMELY 1

austere *adj* **1 syn** see SEVERE 1
rel bald, bare, simple, unadorned, undecorated, unembellished, unornamented; earnest, grave, serious, sober, somber
con complicated, elaborate, fancy, flamboyant, fussy, ornate; frivolous, light, light-minded, shallow, superficial
2 syn see ACRID
rel biting, keen, rough
con bland, mellow, smooth, soft
3 syn see GRIM 2

autarchic *adj* **1 syn** see ABSOLUTE 4
rel commanding, dogmatic, imperious; nonconstitutional, undemocratic
2 syn see FREE 1
rel self-dependent, self-reliant, self-sufficient

autarkic *adj* **syn** see FREE 1
rel self-dependent, self-reliant, self-sufficient

authentic *adj* **1** worthy of acceptance because of accuracy <an *authentic* portrayal of ancient customs>
syn convincing, credible, faithful, trustworthy, trusty
rel accurate, dependable, factual, reliable, sure; solid, sound, straight, valid; authoritative, cathedral, official, standard
idiom all wool and a yard wide; to be depended (*or* relied) on
con incredible, unconvincing, untrustworthy; equivocal, obscure, uncertain, vague; hypothetical, purported, putative, supposed, supposititious; debatable, doubtful, questionable; nonstandard
ant inauthentic
2 being exactly as appears or is claimed <an *authentic* masterpiece>
syn blown-in-the-bottle, bona fide, genuine, indubitable, pukka, questionless, real, right, simon-pure, sure-enough, true, undoubted, undubitable, unquestionable, veritable, very
rel cognizable, identifiable, knowable, recognizable; honest, pure, unadulterated, unalloyed
con deceptive, delusive, delusory, false, misleading, wrong; unidentifiable, unrecognizable
ant spurious
3 syn see CERTAIN 3

authenticate *vb* **1 syn** see CONFIRM 2
rel accredit, approve, endorse; demonstrate, prove, test, try; avouch, vouch (for)
con reject, repudiate, spurn; contradict, deny, negate
ant impugn

author *n* **syn** see FATHER 2
rel origin, source; ancestor, parent, procreator

authoritarian *adj* **1 syn** see DICTATORIAL
rel heavy-handed, high-handed, oppressive, strict, stringent
ant libertarian; anarchistic
2 syn see TOTALITARIAN 1
rel fascistic, nazi; patriarchal
ant democratic

authoritative *adj* **1 syn** see OFFICIAL
2 syn see TRUE 9

rel attested, authenticated, circumstantiated, confirmed, proven, validated, verified; convincing, indisputable, irrefutable, sure, unrefutable; cathedral, cathedratic
con contestable, controversial, debatable, disputable, refutable; dubious, questionable, suspect, unreliable
3 syn see DICTATORIAL
4 syn see ORTHODOX 1

authority *n* **1 syn** see EXPERT
2 syn see POWER 1
rel governance, government, rule
3 syn see INFLUENCE 1
rel example, exemplar, ideal, model, pattern, standard; force, power, pressure

authorization *n* **syn** see PERMISSION

authorize *vb* **1** to invest with power or the right to act <I did not *authorize* him to speak for me>
syn accredit, commission, empower, enable, license
rel approve, countenance, endorse; aid, assist, help, support, subserve; advance, facilitate, forward, further, promote
con bar, disallow, enjoin, forbid, interdict, prohibit
2 syn see ENTITLE 2
rel allow, let, permit; approve, countenance, endorse
idiom give one the right to
3 syn see INVEST 2

auto *n* **syn** see CAR

auto *vb* **1 syn** see DRIVE 5
2 syn see RIDE 1

autobiographer *n* **syn** see BIOGRAPHER
autobiographist *n* **syn** see BIOGRAPHER
autobiography *n* **syn** see BIOGRAPHY
rel diary, journal, letters

autocar *n* **syn** see CAR

autochthonous *adj* **syn** see NATIVE 2
con alien, extraneous, extrinsic, foreign; imported, introduced
ant naturalized

autocracy *n* **syn** see TYRANNY

autocratic *adj* **syn** see ABSOLUTE 4
rel arrogant, haughty, overbearing, overweening
con deferential, submissive, yielding; forbearing, indulgent, lenient, tolerant

autodidactic *adj* **syn** see SELF-TAUGHT
autograph *vb* **syn** see SIGN 1
autognosis *n* **syn** see SELF-KNOWLEDGE
autoist *n* **syn** see MOTORIST
automatic *adj* **1 syn** see SPONTANEOUS
rel prompt, quick, ready; accustomed, confirmed, habitual, habituated
2 syn see PERFUNCTORY

automaton *n* **1 syn** see ROBOT 1
2 syn see ROBOT 2

automobile *n* **syn** see CAR

---

syn synonym(s)   *rel* related word(s)
ant antonym(s)   *con* contrasted word(s)
idiom idiomatic equivalent(s)
‖ use limited; if in doubt, see a dictionary

automobilist *n syn* see MOTORIST

autonomous *adj syn* see FREE 1
rel self-governed; unconstrained, uncontrolled, unsubordinated
con controlled, subordinated; governed, ruled; affiliated, allied

autopsy *n* examination of the body after death usually to determine the cause of death <the *autopsy* of a murder victim>
syn necropsy, ‖post, postmortem, postmortem examination

autoschediasm *n syn* see IMPROVISATION

autoschediastic *adj syn* see EXTEMPORANEOUS

auxiliary *adj* capable of supplying or intended to supply aid or support <an *auxiliary* police unit>
syn accessory, adjuvant, ancillary, appurtenant, collateral, contributory, subservient, subsidiary
rel complementary, supplementary; peripheral, secondary, subordinate, tributary; backing, supporting, upholding; aiding, assisting, helping
con chief, leading, main, principal; sole, solitary, unique

avail *vb syn* see BENEFIT
rel answer, fill, fulfill, meet, satisfy
con damage, harm, hurt, injure

avail *n syn* see USE 3
rel interest; appositeness, suitability
con inappropriateness, unsuitableness

available *adj* **1** that is accessible or may be obtained <the best pen *available* at the present time>
syn attainable, disponible, gettable, obtainable, procurable, securable
rel accessible, convenient, handy
idiom to be had
con unattainable, unobtainable; absent, deficient, lacking, missing
ant unavailable
2 *syn* see PURCHASABLE 1

avarice *n syn* see CUPIDITY
rel frugality, parsimony, thrift; miserliness, niggardliness, parsimoniousness, stinginess; acquisitiveness, covetousness, graspingness, piggishness
con extravagance; bountifulness, bounty, generosity, liberality, munificence, openhandedness
ant prodigality

avariciousness *n syn* see CUPIDITY

avenge *vb* to inflict punishment by way of repayment for <*avenge* an insult>
syn redress, revenge, venge, vindicate
rel compensate, pay (back), pay out, recompense, repay, requite, retaliate, retribute; chasten, chastise, punish; correct, right
idiom get an eye for an eye, get even with, settle accounts, wreak one's vengeance
con condone, disregard, ignore, overlook; absolve, amnesty, forgive, pardon, remit; bear, endure, stand, suffer, tolerate

avengement *n syn* see RETALIATION

avenging *n syn* see RETALIATION

avenue *n* **1** *syn* see WAY 1
‖**2** *syn* see DRIVEWAY

aver *vb syn* see ASSERT 1

rel defend, hold, justify, maintain
con deny

average *n* something (as a number, quantity, or condition) that represents a middle point between extremes <somewhat sweeter than *average*>
syn mean, median, norm, par
ant maximum; minimum

average *adj syn* see MEDIUM
rel common, familiar, ordinary; customary, usual
idiom common or garden variety
con choice, excellent, exceptional, prime, superior; conspicuous, noticeable, outstanding, prominent; bad, inferior, low-grade, poor, punk

averagely *adv syn* see ENOUGH 2

avernal *adj syn* see INFERNAL 2

averse *adj syn* see DISINCLINED
rel balky, contrary, perverse; flinching, quailing, recoiling, resistant, shrinking; uncongenial, unsympathetic
ant avid (of *or* for)

aversion *n* **1** *syn* see DISLIKE
rel antagonism, antipathy, hostility; dread, fear, horror
con bias, partiality; leaning, propensity, taste
ant predilection
2 *syn* see ANTIPATHY 2
rel abhorrence, distaste, repellency, repugnance, repulsion, revulsion; disgust, dread, loathing
con bias, partiality, penchant; flair, inclination, leaning, taste
ant attachment; predilection
3 *syn* see ABOMINATION 2
ant delight

aversive *adj syn* see ANTIPATHETIC 2

avert *vb* **1** *syn* see TURN 6
rel remove, transfer
2 *syn* see PREVENT 2
rel anticipate; balk, foil, frustrate, thwart; check, halt, stay, stop
con advance, further, promote

aviary *n* a house, enclosure, or large cage for confining live birds <the zoo's *aviary*>
syn birdhouse
rel dovecote, dovehouse; columbary, pigeon house

aviator *n syn* see PILOT 2

avid *adj syn* see EAGER
rel covetous, craving, desirous, wanting, wishful; importunate, insistent, pressing, urgent; gluttonous, omnivorous
con aloof, disinterested, uninterested; disinclined, indisposed, loath
ant indifferent; averse

avidity *n syn* see CUPIDITY

avoid *vb syn* see ESCAPE 2
rel avert, deflect, divert, obviate, prevent, ward (off); debar, exclude, preclude; forbid, prohibit
idiom give a miss (*or* a wide berth), have no truck with, set one's face against, steer clear of, turn one's back on
con court, invite, solicit

ant face; meet

avoidance *n syn* see ESCAPE 2

avouch *vb syn* see ASSERT 1
rel confirm, corroborate; acknowledge, admit, confess, own
con deny, impugn

avow *vb* **1** *syn* see ASSERT 1
rel defend, maintain, vindicate; asseverate, swear, testify
2 *syn* see ACKNOWLEDGE 1
con repudiate, withdraw

avowry *n syn* see PATRON SAINT

await *vb syn* see EXPECT 1
rel abide, stay, wait
idiom bide one's time, sweat (*or* tough) it out

awake *vb syn* see WAKE 1

awake *adj syn* see AWARE
rel vigilant, watchful; aroused, awakened, roused, stirred up; excited
con drowsy, sleepy, slumberous, somnolent; inactive, inert, supine

awaken *vb* **1** *syn* see WAKE 1
2 *syn* see STIR 1
rel fire, inflame; alert
idiom stir the feelings (*or* blood) of
con arrest, check, retard, subdue; calm, compose, restrain

awanting *prep syn* see WITHOUT 2

award *vb* **1** *syn* see GRANT 1
rel allocate, allot, apportion, assign; dower, endow, endue
2 *syn* see GIVE 2

award *n syn* see HONOR 2

aware *adj* marked by realization, perception, or knowledge often of something not generally realized, perceived, or known <*aware* of her own inner weakness>
syn alive, apprehensive, au courant, awake, cognizant, conscious, conversant, knowing, mindful, sensible, sentient, ware, witting
rel acquainted, apprised, informed; alert, heedful; impressionable, perceptive, receptive
con anesthetic, impassible, insensible, insensitive; ignorant, unknowing
ant unaware

awash *adj syn* see FULL 1

away *adv* **1** from this or that place <come *away* at once>
syn hence, thence
rel forth, out, therefrom
2 at some distance from a place expressed or implied <he lived several blocks *away*>
syn off, over
rel afar, far; apart, aside

3 without hesitation or delay <fire *away* when you see the target>
syn at once, directly, first off, forthwith, immediately, instanter, instantly, now, PDQ, right, right away, right off, straight, straight away, straight off, straightway
rel momentarily, promptly, ‖pronto, punctually; expeditiously, quickly, speedily, swiftly

away *adj syn* see ABSENT 1

awe *n syn* see REVERENCE 2
rel esteem, regard, respect, veneration, worship; admiration, amazement, wonder, wonderment
con despite, scorn; arrogance, insolence, superciliousness

awe *vb syn* see FRIGHTEN

aweless *adj syn* see BRAVE 1

awful *adj syn* see FEARFUL 3
rel impressive, moving; august, imposing, majestic; splendid, superb; grave, serious, solemn; ominous, portentous

‖**awful** *adv syn* see VERY 1

awfully *adv syn* see VERY 1

awkward *adj* **1** *syn* see CLUMSY 1
rel blundering, bumbling, bungling; clownish, lubberly, oafish; cumbrous, hulking, ponderous
idiom all thumbs
2 marked by a lack of grace, ease, skill, or fitness (as in action or speech) <his *awkward* approach to the problem>
syn bumbling, clumsy, gauche, halting, ham=handed, heavy-handed, inept, lumbering, maladroit, unhandy, unhappy, wooden; *compare* CLUMSY 1
rel rigid, stiff; discomfited, disconcerted, embarrassed; bunglesome, bungling, inefficient, inexpert, unskillful
con adept, adroit, dexterous, expert, finished, polished, proficient, skilled, skillful, smooth; easy, effortless, facile, simple
ant deft; graceful
3 *syn* see INCONVENIENT
4 *syn* see INFELICITOUS

awry *adv* (*or adj*) **1** deviating from a straight line or direction <the coverlet was pulled *awry*>
syn askance, askant, askew, ‖cam, cock-a-hoop, cockeyed, crookedly
rel aside, aslant, obliquely, slantways
con even, straight, true; directly, undeviatingly
2 *syn* see AMISS 2
rel erroneously, faultily, untruly; aside

ax *vb syn* see DISMISS 3

axiom *n* **1** *syn* see PRINCIPLE 1
2 *syn* see MAXIM

‖**ayah** *n syn* see NURSEMAID

aye *adv syn* see YES 1

---

syn synonym(s)   *rel* related word(s)
ant antonym(s)   *con* contrasted word(s)
idiom idiomatic equivalent(s)
‖ use limited; if in doubt, see a dictionary

B

Babbitt *n syn* see PHILISTINE

babblative *adj syn* see TALKATIVE

babble *vb* **1** *syn* see GIBBER

2 to talk nonsensically <silly people *babbling* on about trivia>
syn blabber, blather, drivel, drool, gabble, prate, prattle, twaddle, ‖waffle
rel clack, jaw, rattle, run on, yak, yammer, yap
idiom run off at the mouth

3 *syn* see CHAT 1

babble *n* **1** *syn* see CHATTER

2 *syn* see GIBBERISH 1

babe *n syn* see BABY 1

babel *n syn* see DIN
con hush, noiselessness; peace, quiet, silence

babushka *n syn* see KERCHIEF 1

baby *n* **1** a very young child especially in the first year of life <the love of a mother for her *baby*>
syn babe, bantling, infant, neonate, newborn
rel bambino, little one, toddler, tot; nursling, suckling, weanling; bratling
idiom babe in arms

2 *syn* see WEAKLING

‖**3** *syn* see GIRL FRIEND 2

baby *vb* to treat with special, excessive, or fond care <*baby* a sick husband>
syn cater (to), cocker, coddle, cosset, cotton, humor, indulge, mollycoddle, pamper, spoil
rel dry-nurse, wet-nurse; dote (on *or* upon), favor; gratify, please, satisfy
con control, discipline, restrain; abuse, ill-treat, ill-use, mistreat, oppress; neglect, overlook, slight

baby buggy *n syn* see BABY CARRIAGE

baby carriage *n* a four-wheeled push carriage with a folding top for a baby <a park popular with young mothers pushing *baby carriages*>
syn baby buggy, bassinet, ‖perambulator, ‖pram

babyhood *n syn* see INFANCY 1

babyish *adj syn* see CHILDISH

bacchanal *n syn* see ORGY 2

bacchanalia *n syn* see ORGY 2

back *n* **1** the surface or part most remote from the front <the *back* of his neck>
syn posterior, rear, rearward
rel extremity, tail; reverse
con anterior
ant front

2 *syn* see SPINE

back *adv syn* see ABOUT 6

back *adj* **1** distant from settled areas <*back* regions in the hill country>
syn frontier, outlandish, remote, unsettled
rel uncultivated, uninhabited, unoccupied, unpopulated, wild
con built-up, settled, urban

2 *syn* see POSTERIOR 2

ant front

back *vb* **1** *syn* see SUPPORT 2
rel aid, assist, help; abet

2 *syn* see CAPITALIZE

3 *syn* see MOUNT 5

4 *syn* see RECEDE 1
con advance, progress

back answer *n syn* see RETORT 2

backbiting *n syn* see DETRACTION
rel animadversion, reflection, stricture; abuse, invective, obloquy, vituperation
con accolade, commendation, encomium, eulogy, laudation, paean, panegyric, praise, tribute; adulation, blarney, compliment, flattery, soft soap

backbiting *adj syn* see LIBELOUS

backbone *n* **1** *syn* see SPINE

2 *syn* see FORTITUDE
rel hardihood; heart
con irresoluteness, irresolution
ant backbonelessness, spinelessness

3 *syn* see MAINSTAY

backchat *n syn* see BANTER

backcountry *n syn* see FRONTIER 2

‖**backdoor trots** *n pl but sing or pl in constr syn* see DIARRHEA

back down *vb* to withdraw from a previous agreement or stand <a politician *backing down* on an earlier promise>
syn back off, back out, backpedal, backwater, cop out, crawfish (out), cry off, declare off, renege, resile, welsh
rel disavow, recall, recant, retract, take back, withdraw; backtrack; beg off, weasel (out); balk, demur, hold back, stickle
idiom get out of, go back on

backer *n syn* see SPONSOR
rel ally, protagonist; bankroller, ‖grubstaker, ‖meal ticket, promoter

backer–up *n syn* see SPONSOR

backfire *vb* to have the reverse of the desired effect <the new policy *backfired* disastrously>
syn backlash, boomerang, bounce (back), kick back
rel fall (through), fizzle, miscarry, miss, ricochet
idiom come to grief, go on the rocks, ‖lay an egg
con come off, succeed, work out

backhouse *n syn* see PRIVY 1

backing *n* aid or support given to an undertaking <the project had the *backing* of the city fathers>
syn aegis, auspices, patronage, sponsorship
rel championship, cooperation, fosterage; guidance, tutelage; encouragement; assistance, help, support

backland *n syn* see FRONTIER 2

backlash *vb syn* see BACKFIRE

backlog *n syn* see RESERVE

back of *prep syn* see ABAFT

back off *vb syn* see BACK DOWN

back out *vb syn* see BACK DOWN

backpack *n* a carrying case (as of canvas or nylon) held on the back by shoulder straps <carried his supplies in a *backpack*>
syn haversack, knapsack, pack, packsack, rucksack

backpedal *vb syn* see BACK DOWN
rel dodge, duck, elude, evade, get around, shirk, sidestep

backset *n syn* see SETBACK

backside *n syn* see BUTTOCKS

backslide *vb syn* see LAPSE
rel regress, retrovert, return, revert; defect, desert, tergiversate, turn
idiom fall away, fall (*or* sink *or* slide *or* slip) back into, give in to

backsliding *n syn* see LAPSE 2

backstabbing *n syn* see DETRACTION

backstage *adj or adv* off or away from the part of the stage visible to the audience <*backstage* sounds that gave the impression of a storm>
syn offstage
idiom behind the scenes
ant onstage

backstop *vb syn* see SUPPORT 2

back talk *n* impudent and insolent talk <do as you're told and no *back talk*>
syn guff, ‖jaw, ‖lip, mouth, sass, sauce
rel cheek, impudence, insolence

backup *n syn* see SUBSTITUTE 1

backup *adj syn* see SUBSTITUTE 1

‖**backveld** *n syn* see FRONTIER 2

backward *adv syn* see ABOUT 6

backward *adj* **1** directed, turned, or executed backward <the *backward* swimming of the crayfish>
syn retral, retrograde
rel inverted, reversed
ant advance, forward
2 *syn* see DISINCLINED
rel bashful, diffident
3 *syn* see SHY 1
4 *syn* see RETARDED
5 holding to outworn or traditional views, ideas, or principles <had a *backward* attitude toward social inferiors>
syn benighted, ignorant, unenlightened, unprogressive
rel conservative, reactionary; obtuse, stupid, thickheaded; bigoted, hidebound, narrow; blind; unenlightened, uninformed
con advanced, aware, enlightened, forward-looking, progressive, unbenighted
6 not developing or progressing especially in economic and social areas <*backward* nations using primitive farming methods>
syn behindhand, underdeveloped, undeveloped, unprogressive
rel poor, struggling; medieval; benighted, retarded, uncultivated, uncultured
idiom behind the times
con forward-looking, progressive; civilized, cultivated, cultured; modern

ant advanced

backwash *n syn* see FRONTIER 2

backwater *n syn* see FRONTIER 2

backwater *vb syn* see BACK DOWN
rel dodge, duck, elude, evade, get around, shirk, sidestep

backwoods *n pl but sing or pl in constr syn* see FRONTIER 2

‖**backwoodser** *n syn* see RUSTIC

backwoodsman *n syn* see RUSTIC

bad *adj* **1** falling short of a standard of what is satisfactory <a *bad* repair job>
syn amiss, ‖bum, ‖crappy, dissatisfactory, poor, ‖punk, rotten, unsatisfactory, up, wrong
rel deficient, inadequate, inferior; careless, slipshod; defective, disordered, off, unsound; execrable, ‖lousy, miserable, wretched; inadmissible, objectionable, unacceptable; insufferable, intolerable
idiom below par, not up to snuff (*or* scratch)
con excellent, fine, meritorious; acceptable, adequate, sound
2 *syn* see WRONG 1
rel arrant, peccant; graceless, improper, indecorous, untoward; disorderly, misbehaving, naughty, rowdy, ruffianly, unruly; froward, perverse
ant good
3 *syn* see EVIL 5
4 *syn* see EVIL 6
5 having undergone decay <one *bad* apple can spoil the barrel>
syn decayed, putrid, rotten, spoiled
rel fusty, stale; mildewed, moldered, moldy, moth-eaten, musty, rancid, worm-eaten, decomposed, putrefied, putrifacted; tainted, turned
con crisp, dewy, fresh, sweet, unspoiled; choice, picked, prime
ant good
6 *syn* see NAUGHTY 1
7 *syn* see TOUGH 8
8 arousing discomfort or distaste <a *bad* smell>
syn ‖chiselly, disagreeable, displeasing, rotten, sour, unhappy, unpleasant
rel disgusting, foul, nauseating, noisome, noxious, offensive, repulsive, sickening; abhorrent, hateful, loathsome, obnoxious; uneasy; thankless, ungrateful; distasteful, distressing, sticky; ungracious, unhandsome
con agreeable, pleasant, pleasing, refreshing, soothing; unoffensive
9 *syn* see HARMFUL
10 *syn* see DOWNCAST
11 *syn* see NULL

bad actor *n syn* see TROUBLEMAKER

bad books *n pl syn* see DISLIKE

badge *n* **1** *syn* see INSIGNIA
2 *syn* see HONOR 2

badger *vb syn* see BAIT 2

---

syn synonym(s)   *rel* related word(s)
ant antonym(s)   *con* contrasted word(s)
idiom idiomatic equivalent(s)
‖ use limited; if in doubt, see a dictionary

rel plague, tease, worry

badinage *n syn* see BANTER
rel chaffing, guying, japery, joshing, kidding, sport

badland *n syn* see WASTE 1

‖**bad lot** *n syn* see WASTREL 1

badly *adv* **1** *syn* see HARD 5
2 *syn* see AMISS 2
ant well

badman *n syn* see OUTLAW
rel criminal, villain; hood, hoodlum, hooligan, thug; blackguard, devil, knave, rapscallion, rascal, rascallion, rogue, scoundrel

bad–mouth *vb syn* see DECRY 2

bad–tempered *adj syn* see ILL-TEMPERED
rel cantankerous, cranky, crusty, temperamental, touchy
con forbearing, long-suffering, patient
ant good-tempered

Baedeker *n syn* see HANDBOOK

baffle *vb syn* see FRUSTRATE 1
rel confound, dumbfound, flummox, mystify, nonplus, puzzle; addle, ball up, befuddle, confuse, fog, mix up, muddle; discomfit, disconcert, embarrass, faze, rattle
con enlighten, illuminate

bag *n* **1** a container made of a flexible material and open or opening at the top <a grocery *bag*>
syn ‖poke, pouch, sack
‖**2** *syn* see HAG 2

bag *vb syn* see CATCH 1
rel clench, ‖cop, ‖glom, hook, land, nab, net, sack, scoop
idiom lay by the heels

baggage *n syn* see WANTON

‖**bagged** *adj syn* see INTOXICATED 1

bagnio *n syn* see BROTHEL

bail *n syn* see GUARANTEE 1

bail *vb syn* see DIP 2

bailiwick *n syn* see FIELD
rel district, jurisdiction, neighborhood, place, quarter, realm; beat, circuit, round, walk

bait *vb* **1** *syn* see MOLEST
2 to persist in tormenting or harassing another <*baiting* him with gibes about his humble origin>
syn badger, bullyrag, chivy, heckle, hector, hound, ride
rel annoy, bother, bedevil, devil, rag, worry; harass, harry, haze, vex; ‖bug, nag, pester, push around
3 *syn* see LURE

bait *n* **1** *syn* see LURE 2
‖**2** *syn* see SNACK

bake *vb* **1** *syn* see BURN 3
2 *syn* see FIRE 6

baking *adj syn* see HOT 1

balance *n* **1** the stability resulting from the equalization of opposing forces <keeping his emotional *balance* when under stress>
syn counterpoise, equilibrium, equipoise, poise, stasis
rel collectedness, composure, cool, coolness, coolth, equanimity, repose, sangfroid; aplomb, assurance, self-assurance, self-possession; control, self-control, stability, steadiness; stagnancy, stagnation
con imbalance, unbalance; instability, nervousness, shakiness, uncontrol, unsteadiness
2 *syn* see SYMMETRY
rel congruity, consistency, correspondence, sameness
con disbalance, disharmony, disproportion, incongruity, inconsistency, irregularity, overbalance, unbalance
ant imbalance
3 *syn* see REMAINDER

balance *vb syn* see COMPENSATE 1
rel adjust, attune, harmonize, tune; accord, agree, correspond; even, level, square
idiom strike a balance

bald *adj* **1** *syn* see HAIRLESS
rel bobbed, clipped, cropped, polled, shaven, sheared
con bushy, hairy, hirsute, shaggy; unshaven, unshorn; fleecy, furry, woolly; downy, fuzzy, pilose, pubescent
2 *syn* see BARE 1
rel austere, severe; plain, unadorned, undecorated, unembellished, ungarnished, unornamented; colorless, lackluster, lifeless, lusterless, uncolored

balderdash *n syn* see NONSENSE 2

baldhead *n* one who has a bald head
syn baldpate, ‖baldy, ‖skinhead

baldpate *n syn* see BALDHEAD

‖**baldy** *n syn* see BALDHEAD

balefire *n syn* see BEACON 1

baleful *adj syn* see SINISTER
rel deadly, evil, harmful, pernicious; bodeful, foreboding; unfavorable, unpromising
con auspicious, benign, favorable, promising, propitious; advantageous, beneficial
ant beneficent
2 *syn* see OMINOUS

balk *n syn* see TIMBER 2

balk *vb* **1** *syn* see FRUSTRATE 1
idiom stand in the way of
con back, support, uphold; aid, assist, help
ant forward
2 *syn* see DEMUR
rel decline, refuse, turn down; flinch, hang back, quail, recoil, shrink
con capitulate, give in

balky *adj syn* see CONTRARY 3
rel immovable, inflexible, unbending, unmanageable; averse, disinclined, hesitant, indisposed, loath, reluctant
con subdued, submissive, tame

ball *n* a more or less spherical body or mass <a *ball* of string>
syn globe, orb, rondure, round, sphere
rel egg, oval, ovoid

ball *vb* to form into a more or less spherical body or mass <*balled* the cookie dough with her hands>
syn conglobate, conglobe, ensphere, round, sphere
rel bead, pill; clot, wad

balladmonger *n syn* see POETASTER

ball and chain *n* **1** *syn* see RESTRICTION 1

‖**2** *syn* see WIFE

ballast *vb syn* see STABILIZE

ballerina *n syn* see DANCER

ballet girl *n syn* see DANCER

ballot *n* **1** a piece of paper used to cast a vote in an election <deliberately spoiled his *ballot*>
syn ticket, vote
rel Australian ballot, Indiana ballot, Massachusetts ballot, office-block ballot, office-group ballot, party-column ballot, secret ballot
2 *syn* see SUFFRAGE

ballot *vb syn* see ELECT 2

‖**ballup** *n syn* see CONFUSION 3

ball up *vb syn* see CONFUSE 2

ballyhoo *vb syn* see TOUT

balm *n* **1** *syn* see OINTMENT
2 *syn* see FRAGRANCE

balm *vb syn* see CALM

balmy *adj* **1** *syn* see SWEET 2
rel musky; refreshing, rejuvenating, restorative; pleasant, pleasing
2 *syn* see GENTLE 1
rel agreeable, delightful, gratifying, pleasant, pleasing; allaying, assuaging, balsamic, easing, lightening, relieving, soothing
con annoying, bothering, bothersome, irking, irksome, vexing
‖**3** *syn* see FOOLISH 2

‖**baloney** *n syn* see NONSENSE 2

balustrade *n syn* see RAILING

bamboozle *vb syn* see DUPE
rel bilk, diddle, swindle

ban *vb syn* see FORBID
rel illegalize, outlaw
con approve, authorize; suffer, tolerate

ban *n syn* see TABOO

banal *adj syn* see INSIPID 3
rel hackneyed, pedestrian, trite, warmed-over; bromidic, commonplace, corny, platitudinous, stock; bewhiskered, hoary, old; asinine, fatuous, silly, simple
con fresh, new, novel; different, uncommon, unusual; stimulating, zesty; choice, rare, recherché
ant original

banality *n syn* see COMMONPLACE

bananas *adj syn* see INSANE 1

banausic *adj* **1** *syn* see DULL 9
2 *syn* see MATERIALISTIC

band *n syn* see STRIP 1
rel belt, border, edge, line; tape; fascia, taenia; streak, vein

band *vb* **1** *syn* see BELT 1
2 *syn* see UNITE 2
rel amalgamate, unionize; consociate; club, team (up)
con disintegrate, disperse, dissolve, separate
ant break up, disband

band *n* **1** *syn* see COMPANY 4
rel assembly, bevy, body, bunch, covey, group; detachment, detail
2 *syn* see GROUP 1
3 *syn* see ORCHESTRA

bandage *vb* to cover with a bandage <*bandage* wounds>
syn bind, dress

bandanna *n syn* see KERCHIEF 1

bandar–log *n syn* see CHATTERBOX

bandbox *adj syn* see DAPPER

bandeau *n syn* see STRIP 1

banderole *n syn* see FLAG

‖**bandido** *n syn* see OUTLAW
rel brigand, footpad, highwayman, holdup man; bravo, cutthroat, gunman, villain; gangster, mobster, racketeer

banding *n syn* see STRIP 1

bandit *n* **1** *syn* see OUTLAW
rel brigand, footpad, highwayman, holdup man; bravo, cutthroat, villain; gangster, mobster, racketeer; jayhawker
2 *syn* see MARAUDER

bandwagon *n syn* see FASHION 3

bandy *vb syn* see EXCHANGE 3
rel chuck, flip, pitch, throw, toss; banter; answer, repay, retort
idiom bat (*or* beat) back and forth

bandy *adj syn* see BOWLEGGED

bandy–legged *adj syn* see BOWLEGGED

bane *n* **1** *syn* see POISON
2 *syn* see DOWNFALL 2

baneful *adj* **1** *syn* see PERNICIOUS
rel injurious; insalubrious, noisome, unhealthy, unwholesome
con benign, favorable, propitious; advantageous, helpful, profitable; healthful, salubrious, salutary, wholesome
ant beneficial
2 *syn* see OMINOUS

‖**bang** *vb syn* see SURPASS 1

bang *n* **1** *syn* see BLOW 1
2 a loud percussive or explosive noise <slammed the book shut with a *bang*>
syn blast, boom, burst, clap, crack, crash, slam, smash, wham
rel noise, report, sound; discharge, explosion, pop, shot; howl, roar, roll, rumble, thunder
3 *syn* see THRILL
4 *syn* see SMASH 6
5 *syn* see VIGOR 2

bang *adv syn* see JUST 1

bang away (at) *vb syn* see ATTACK 2

bang–up *adj syn* see EXCELLENT

banish *vb* to eject by force or authority from a country, state, or sovereignty <*banish* an enemy of the king>
syn cast out, deport, displace, exile, expatriate, expel, expulse, ‖lag, ostracize, oust, relegate, run out, transport; *compare* EJECT 1
rel disfellowship, excommunicate, rusticate; debar, exclude, shut out; drive out, eject, evict, turn out; bump, can, cashier, discharge, dismiss, fire, put out, sack; blackball, blacklist, boycott

---

syn synonym(s)   *rel* related word(s)
ant antonym(s)   *con* contrasted word(s)
idiom idiomatic equivalent(s)
‖ use limited; if in doubt, see a dictionary

banishment *n syn* see EXILE 1

banister *n syn* see RAILING

bank *n* **1** *syn* see PILE 1
rel snowbank, snowdrift; cloudage, fogbank
2 *syn* see SHORE
rel bankside, levee, riverfront, streamside; lake-front, lakeshore, lakeside, margin; oceanfront, seabank, seabeach, seaboard, seafront, sea front-age, sea line, sea sands, shingle
idiom water's edge

bank *vb syn* see HEAP 1
rel compact, concentrate

bank *vb* to place money in a bank <*banks* half his paycheck every week>
syn deposit
rel invest, lay aside, lay away, salt away, salt down, save, set aside, sock away; cache, coffer, hoard, squirrel (away), stash
con draw out, take out, withdraw; disburse, ex-pend, fork (over *or* out), lay out, pay (out), spend

bank (on *or* upon) *vb syn* see RELY (on *or* upon)
rel intend, plan; bet (on), gamble (on), stake, venture, wager
idiom bank the rent on, bet one's bottom dollar on, go bail on, lay money on

bankroll *vb syn* see CAPITALIZE

bankrupt *vb* **1** *syn* see DEPLETE
rel break, impair, incapacitate
con rebuild, repair, restore, revive; augment, bolster, fortify, strengthen
2 *syn* see STRIP 2
3 *syn* see RUIN 3
4 *syn* see RUIN 2

banned *adj* **1** *syn* see FORBIDDEN
2 *syn* see CONTRABAND

banner *n syn* see FLAG
rel banneret

banner *adj syn* see EXCELLENT

bannerol *n syn* see FLAG

banquet *n syn* see DINNER
rel bridale, feed, ‖gaudy, harvest home, repast, ‖tuck, ‖tuck-in, ‖tuck-out

bantam *adj* **1** *syn* see SMALL 1
2 *syn* see SAUCY 1

banter *vb* **1** to make fun of good-naturedly <the students resented their teacher's *bantering* them about mistakes>
syn chaff, fool, fun, jest, ‖jive, joke, jolly, josh, kid, rag, razz, rib
rel deride, guy, mock, quiz, rally, ridicule, sati-rize, taunt, tease, twit
idiom make fun of, make merry with, poke fun at
‖**2** *syn* see FACE 3
‖**3** *syn* see COAX

banter *n* animated back-and-forth exchange of remarks <entertained the group with their jolly *banter*>
syn backchat, badinage, ‖cross talk, persiflage, repartee, snip-snap
rel chitchat, gossip, gossipry, small talk; rally-ing, teasing; exchange, give-and-take
con debate, deliberation, discussion

bantling *n syn* see BABY 1

baptismal name *n syn* see GIVEN NAME

baptize *vb* **1** to administer the rite of baptism <a child *baptized* in the Catholic Church>
syn asperse, christen, immerse, sprinkle
rel cleanse, purify, regenerate
2 *syn* see NAME 1

bar *n* **1** a solid piece of material usually rectangu-lar and considerably longer than it is wide <a *bar* of gold>
syn billet, ingot, rod, slab, stick, strip
2 something that stands in the way of some ob-jective <his religion was a *bar* to membership in that exclusive club>
syn barricade, barrier, blank wall, block, block-ade, fence, roadblock, stop, wall
rel clog, encumbrance, hamper, hindrance, im-pediment; hurdle, obstacle, obstruction, stum-bling block; check, checkrein, control, curb; bamboo curtain, iron curtain; difficulty, hard-ship, vicissitude
3 *syn* see OBSTACLE
rel check, checkrein, control, curb
con accommodation, convenience, facility, ser-vice
ant advantage
4 *syn* see COURT 2
5 a room or public establishment where alco-holic beverages are served <nightly discussions in the *bar*>
syn barroom, ‖boozer, ‖bucket shop, buvette, cantina, cocktail lounge, drinkery, drunkery, ‖gin mill, ‖groggery, ‖grogshop, lounge, pot-house, pub, ‖public house, ‖rum-hole, rummery, ‖rum-mill, rumshop, saloon, tap, taproom, tav-ern, watering hole, watering place; *compare* ALE-HOUSE
rel barrelhouse, bistro, bottle club, cabaret, café, dive, honky-tonk, nightclub, rathskeller, roadhouse, wineshop

bar *vb* **1** *syn* see LIMIT 2
2 *syn* see EXCLUDE
rel block, hinder; leave out, omit, pass over; banish, deport, exile, ostracize
con accept, receive, welcome; allow, let, permit
ant admit, include
3 *syn* see HINDER
rel halt, stop
con back, support, uphold

bar *prep syn* see EXCEPT

barathrum *n syn* see HELL

barb *n syn* see SHAFT 2

barbarian *adj* **1** of, relating to, or characteristic of people that are not fully civilized <the *barbarian* tribes that sacked Rome>
syn barbaric, barbarous, Gothic, Hunnic, Hun-nish, rude, savage, uncivil, uncivilized, uncul-tivated, wild
rel heathenish, vandal, vandalic; backward, coarse, crude, ill-mannered, primitive, rough; untamed; uncouth, uncultured; beastish, blood-thirsty, brutal, cruel, ferocious, inhuman
con gentle, peaceful, subdued, submissive, tame; cultured, enlightened, humane, sophisticated; genteel, refined, well-bred, well-mannered

ant civilized

2 syn see BARBARIC 1

barbaric *adj* **1** marked by a lack of restraint, cultivated taste, and refinement <the *barbaric* use of color and ornament>

syn barbarian, barbarous, graceless, outlandish, tasteless, vulgar, wild

rel coarse, crude, rough, rude, uncouth; flamboyant, florid, ornate, ostentatious, showy; blatant, flashy, garish, gaudy, loud, tawdry; cacophonous, harsh, raucous; aggressive

con quiet, restrained, soft, subdued; concinnous, cultivated, elegant, polished, refined; smooth, sophisticated, urbane

2 syn see BARBARIAN 1

barbarism *n* a word or expression which in form or use offends against contemporary standards of correctness or purity in a language <many writers consider *irregardless* a *barbarism*>

syn corruption, impropriety, slangism, solecism, vernacularism, vernacularity, vulgarism

rel neologism; colloquialism, foreignism; shibboleth; Goldwyn- ism, Irish bull, malaprop, malapropism, spoonerism; caconym; error, lapse, misuse, slip

barbarous *adj* **1 syn** see BARBARIAN 1

2 syn see OUTRAGEOUS 1

3 syn see BARBARIC 1

rel backward, benighted, cretinous, ignorant, illiterate, lowbrow, philistine, uneducated, unlettered, unread, unschooled, untaught, untutored

con aware, informed, sophisticated, with-it; finished, polished, rounded; well-bred, well-mannered; educated, intelligent, learned, schooled; erudite, well-read

4 syn see FIERCE 1

rel heartless, uncompassionate, unmerciful; atrocious, monstrous, outrageous; bloody, butcherly, sanguinary; fiendish, sadistic

con forbearing, lenient, merciful, tolerant; compassionate, sympathetic, tender; benevolent, humane, humanitarian

ant clement

barbate *adj syn* see BEARDED

barber *n* one whose occupation is primarily cutting hair

syn haircutter

rel coiffeur, coiffeuse, friseur, hairdresser, hair stylist; beautician, cosmetologist; clipper, cropper, shaver

bard *n* **1** a poet-singer who sang or recited verse to the accompaniment of a stringed instrument (as a harp) <*bards* were the theater of olden times>

syn jongleur, minstrel, troubadour

rel meistersinger, minnesinger, rhapsodist; gleeman; skald; conteur

2 syn see POET

bardlet *n syn* see POETASTER

bardling *n syn* see POETASTER

bare *adj* **1** lacking a natural or usual cover or finish <the room looked *bare* without curtains and pictures>

syn bald, naked, nude

rel denuded, dismantled, divested, peeled, stripped, uncovered; baldish, depilated, hairless; unattired, unclad, unclothed, undressed, unrobed; arid, bleak, desert, desolate

con attired, clad, clothed, dressed, garbed; furry, hairy; green, leafy, luxuriant, verdant; complete, consummate, finished, perfect

ant covered

2 syn see OPEN 2

3 syn see EMPTY 1

rel barren, depleted, destitute, dried-up, emptied, exhausted; unfilled, unstocked, unsupplied

con bountiful, bursting, chock-full, complete, crammed, laden, overflowing, overfull, replete, stuffed; full, stocked, supplied

4 syn see VERY 4

bare *vb syn* see STRIP 2

rel disclose, exhibit, expose, reveal, show, unveil

con camouflage, cloak, disguise, dissemble, mask; apparel, attire, dress, garb, invest, robe

ant cover

barefaced *adj syn* see SHAMELESS

rel blunt, candid, frank, open, plain, temerarious; indecent, indecorous, unseemly

con covert, secret, secretive, stealthy; cautious, circumspect, discreet, tactful

ant furtive

barefisted *adj or adv syn* see BARE-HANDED

barefoot *adj* **1** wearing no shoes or stockings <always went *barefoot* in the summer>

syn shoeless, unsandaled, unshod

con socked, stockinged; sockless; booted, sandaled, shod

2 syn see DISCALCED

bare–handed *adj or adv* without covering on the hands <box *bare-handed*>

syn barefisted, bareknuckle

ant gloved

bareknuckle *adj or adv syn* see BARE-HANDED

barely *adv syn* see JUST 2

con amply; adequately, enough, sufficiently

barf *vb syn* see VOMIT

bargain *n* **1** an advantageous purchase <at that price the car is a *bargain*>

syn buy, closeout, pennyworth, steal

rel deal; giveaway

con cheat, flimflam, gouge, sticking, sting

2 syn see CONTRACT

bargain *vb* **1 syn** see HAGGLE 2

rel arrange, confer, negotiate; compromise

2 syn see TRADE 1

barge *vb syn* see LUMBER

bark *vb syn* see SNAP 1

barkeeper *n* **1 syn** see SALOONKEEPER

2 syn see BARTENDER

barmaid *n syn* see BARTENDER

barman *n syn* see BARTENDER

Barmecidal *adj syn* see APPARENT 2

barnacle *n syn* see PARASITE

---

syn synonym(s)   *rel* related word(s)
ant antonym(s)   *con* contrasted word(s)
idiom idiomatic equivalent(s)
‖ use limited; if in doubt, see a dictionary

‖**barney** *n syn* see QUARREL

barnyard *adj syn* see OBSCENE 2

baron *n syn* see MAGNATE

baronial *adj syn* see GRAND 1

baroque *adj syn* see ORNATE
  rel embellished, gilt, ornamented, scrolled
  con austere, gray

barrage *n* a vigorous expulsion or projection of many things at once <the announcement was met with a *barrage* of protests>
  syn bombardment, broadside, burst, cannonade, drumfire, fusillade, hail, salvo, shower, storm, volley
  rel burst, eruption, flare, outburst, stream, surge, tornado

barrel *n* **1** *syn* see CASK
  2 *syn* see MUCH

barrel *vb syn* see HURRY 2

barrelhouse *n syn* see DIVE

barrelhouse *vb syn* see HURRY 2

barren *adj* **1** *syn* see STERILE 1
  rel childless, fallow, heirless, issueless
  con pregnant; fertile
  ant fecund
  2 deficient in production of vegetation and especially crops <*barren* deserts and wastelands>
  syn hardscrabble, infertile, unbearing, unfertile, unproductive
  rel fallow; irreclaimable, uncultivable, unhusbanded, untillable, wild; bleak, depleted, impoverished, poor, worn-out; vegetationless, verdureless; arid, desert, dry, parched
  con arable, fruitful, productive; fat, rich; lush, luxuriant; green, verdant, verdurous
  ant fertile

barren *n syn* see WASTE 1

barricade *n syn* see BAR 2

barrier *n syn* see BAR 2

barring *prep syn* see EXCEPT

barroom *n syn* see BAR 5

bar sinister *n syn* see STIGMA

bartender *n* one who serves alcoholic beverages at a bar <worked for some years as a *bartender*>
  syn barkeeper, barmaid, barman, mixologist, tapster; *compare* SALOONKEEPER

barter *vb syn* see TRADE 1

basal *adj* **1** *syn* see FUNDAMENTAL 1
  rel pedimental; bottommost, lowermost, lowest, nethermost, undermost
  con highest, uppermost
  2 *syn* see ELEMENTARY 1

base *n* **1** something on which another thing is reared or built or by which it is supported or fixed in place <the *base* of a lamp>
  syn basement, basis, bed, bedrock, bottom, footing, foundation, ground, groundwork, hardpan, infrastructure, rest, seat, seating, substratum, substruction, substructure, underpinning, understructure; *compare* BASIS 1
  rel bolster, buttress, framework, prop, stand, stay, support; foot
  2 *syn* see BASIS 1
  3 *syn* see BOTTOM 3

base *vb* to supply or to serve as a basis <*based* his accusation on sound evidence>
  syn bottom, establish, found, ground, predicate, rest, stay
  rel build, construct, fix, plant, seat, set up

base *adj* **1** *syn* see IGNOBLE 1
  2 *syn* see CHEAP 2
  3 contemptible because beneath minimal standards of human decency <a *base* lying cheat>
  syn despicable, ignoble, low, low-down, servile, sordid, squalid, ugly, vile, wretched; *compare* CONTEMPTIBLE
  rel beggarly, lousy, sorry; abominable, disgraceful, loathsome; bad, evil, wicked; base-minded, low-minded, meanspirited; caitiff, cowardly, dastardly, recreant; unworthy; dirty, filthy; degrading, humiliating, ignominious
  con honest, honorable, upright; virtuous; ethical, moral, righteous; fair, forbearing, open-minded, patient, reasonable, tolerant, understanding
  ant noble

baseborn *adj* **1** *syn* see IGNOBLE 1
  2 *syn* see ILLEGITIMATE 1

baseless *adj* being without cause or occasion <anxious old ladies with their *baseless* fears>
  syn bottomless, foundationless, gratuitous, groundless, un-called-for, unfounded, ungrounded, unwarranted
  rel false, wrong; indefensible, reasonless, unjustifiable, unsolid, unsupported, unsustained, untenable; empty, idle, vain; needless, pointless, senseless, unnecessary, unneeded
  con actual, real, reasonable, true; authentic, bona fide, genuine, valid

basement *n syn* see BASE 1

bash *n* **1** *syn* see BLOW 1
  2 *syn* see SHINDIG 1

bashful *adj syn* see SHY 1
  rel timorous; recoiling, shrinking; mousy; abashed, embarrassed; blushful
  con assured, bold, intrepid; arrogant, barefaced, brazen, impudent, shameless; loquacious, talkative
  ant brash, forward

basic *adj* **1** *syn* see FUNDAMENTAL 1
  rel capital, chief, main, principal
  2 *syn* see ELEMENTAL 1

basic *n syn* see ESSENTIAL 1

basically *adv syn* see ESSENTIALLY 1

basin *n syn* see DEPRESSION 2

basis *n* **1** something that supports or sustains anything immaterial <his argument rested on a *basis* of conjecture>
  syn base, bedrock, footing, foundation, ground, groundwork, infrastructure, root, substratum, underpinning; *compare* BASE 1
  rel axiom, fundamental, law, principle, theorem; assumption, postulate, premise, presumption, presupposition; essence, heart
  2 *syn* see BASE 1
  3 something serving as a reason or justification for an action or opinion <resented such a challenge without *basis* or reason>
  syn foundation, warrant
  rel call, justification, right; ground(s), reason

bask *vb* **1** *syn* see SUN
  2 *syn* see WALLOW 3
bassinet *n* *syn* see BABY CARRIAGE
bastard *n* **1** one born out of wedlock <bore a *bastard* before she was fifteen>
  syn by-blow, catch colt, chance child, come-by=chance, filius nullius, filius populi, illegitimate, love child, mamzer (*or* momzer *or* momser), natural child, whoreson, woods colt
  2 *syn* see HYBRID
bastard *adj* **1** *syn* see ILLEGITIMATE 1
  2 *syn* see SPURIOUS 3
bastardize *vb* *syn* see DEBASE 1
bastardy *n* *syn* see ILLEGITIMACY 1
baste *vb* **1** *syn* see BEAT 1
  rel clobber, ‖larrup, mill, whip
  2 *syn* see SCOLD 1
bastille *n* *syn* see JAIL
bastille *vb* *syn* see IMPRISON
bastinado *n* *syn* see BLOW 1
bastion *n* *syn* see BULWARK
bat *n* **1** *syn* see BLOW 1
  2 *syn* see CUDGEL
  ‖**3** *syn* see SPEED 2
  4 *syn* see BINGE 1
‖**bat** *n* *syn* see HAG 2
bat *vb* *syn* see WANDER 1
bat *vb* *syn* see WINK
batch *n* *syn* see GROUP 3
bate *vb* ‖**1** *syn* see ABATE 4
  ‖**2** *syn* see DECREASE
  3 *syn* see EXCLUDE
bath *n, usu* **baths** *pl syn* see SPA 1
‖**bath** *vb* *syn* see BATHE 1
bathe *vb* **1** to clean oneself with a bath <*bathed* only on Saturday nights>
  syn ‖bath, shower, tub, wash
  rel soap; douse, soak
  2 to flow or splash against <waves *bathed* the rocky shore>
  syn lap, lave, lip, wash
  rel drench, soak, sop, souse; flush
bathetic *adj* **1** *syn* see TRITE
  2 *syn* see SENTIMENTAL
bathtub gin *n* *syn* see MOONSHINE 2
bating *prep* *syn* see EXCEPT
baton *n* *syn* see CUDGEL
batter *vb* **1** to affect (as by repeated blows) so severely as to disfigure or damage <so *battered* in the fight he couldn't even crawl away> <a boat *battered* to pieces by stormy seas>
  syn ‖bung up, mangle, maul
  rel disable, disfigure; maim, mutilate; cripple, lame; bruise, contuse, lacerate; baste, clobber, pummel; shatter, wreck
  idiom beat black and blue, beat to pieces (*or* shreds), beat within an inch of one's life
  2 *syn* see BEAT 1
battery *n* *syn* see GROUP 3
battle *n* a hostile meeting between opposing military forces <the *battle* continued until nightfall>
  syn action, engagement
  rel brush, clash, encounter, pitched battle, scrimmage, skirmish; assault, attack, onset, onslaught, sortie; combat, conflict, contest, fight; hostilities
battle *vb* *syn* see CONTEND 1
  rel clash, scrimmage; assail, assault, attack, bombard
battle cry *n* a word or phrase used as a slogan by a faction <"death to the invader" was the *battle cry*>
  syn cry, motto, rallying cry, war cry; *compare* CATCHWORD
battlesome *adj* *syn* see QUARRELSOME 2
‖**batty** *adj* *syn* see INSANE 1
bauble *n* *syn* see KNICKKNACK
bavardage *n* *syn* see SMALL TALK
bawd *n* *syn* see PROSTITUTE
bawdy house *n* *syn* see BROTHEL
bawl *vb* **1** *syn* see ROAR
  rel holler, scream, screech, shout, shrick, squall, yammer, yell
  2 to cry and weep loudly or lustily especially from distress <the baby *bawled* and kicked when its bottle was taken away>
  syn howl, squall, wail, yowl; *compare* CRY 2, ROAR
  rel blubber, boohoo, cry, sob, weep
bawl out *vb* *syn* see SCOLD 1
  rel condemn, denounce
  idiom read a lecture (*or* lesson)
bay *n, usu* **bays** *pl syn* see HONOR 2
bay *vb* *syn* see HOWL 1
bay *n* *syn* see INLET
baygall *n* *syn* see SWAMP
bayou *n* *syn* see INLET
bay window *n* *syn* see POTBELLY
bazoo *n* ‖**1** *syn* see MOUTH 1
  2 *syn* see RASPBERRY
be *vb* to have actuality or reality <I think, therefore I *am*>
  syn breathe, exist, live, move, subsist
  rel hold, obtain, stand; abide, continue, endure, go on, persist, prevail, remain; come
beach *n* *syn* see SHORE
  rel oceanfront; lakeshore, lakeside
beach *vb* *syn* see SHIPWRECK 1
beached *adj* *syn* see AGROUND
beacon *n* **1** a signal fire usually on an elevated place <a *beacon* on the hill to warn of danger>
  syn balefire, watchfire
  rel flare; bonfire
  2 *syn* see LIGHTHOUSE
beak *n* **1** *syn* see BILL 1
  2 *syn* see NOSE 1
  3 *syn* see PROMONTORY
  ‖**4** *syn* see JUDGE 2
beak *vb* *syn* see PECK 1
be–all and end–all *n* **1** *syn* see ESSENCE 2
  2 *syn* see WHOLE 1
beam *n* **1** *syn* see TIMBER 2
  2 *syn* see RAY 1

---

syn synonym(s)   *rel* related word(s)
ant antonym(s)   *con* contrasted word(s)
idiom idiomatic equivalent(s)
‖ use limited; if in doubt, see a dictionary

3 *syn* see BUTTOCKS

beam *vb* **1** *syn* see SHINE 1

2 *syn* see SMILE

beaming *adj syn* see BRIGHT 1

‖**bean** *n syn* see HEAD 1

beanery *n syn* see EATING HOUSE

beany *adj syn* see SPIRITED 2

bear *vb* **1** *syn* see CARRY 1
   rel shoulder
   2 *syn* see BEHAVE 1
   3 to have attached to one <the bottle *bears* the label "poisonous">
   syn carry, have, possess
   rel display, exhibit, show
   con lack, need, want
   4 *syn* see ACCOMPANY
   5 to give birth to offspring <she has *borne* several children>
   syn ‖birth, ‖born, bring forth, deliver
   idiom bring abed, bring to bed, bring to birth, give birth to, have a baby
   con abort, miscarry
   6 *syn* see PRESS 8
   7 *syn* see PRESS 1
   8 *syn* see PROCREATE 1
   9 to bring forth a product <the apple trees *bear* every year>
   syn produce, turn out, yield
   rel breed, engender, generate, propagate, reproduce; fructify, fruit; fabricate, fashion, form, make, shape; create, invent
   10 to put up with something trying or difficult <can't *bear* the tension of the work>
   syn abide, brook, digest, endure, go, lump, stand, ‖stick, stick out, stomach, suffer, support, sustain, swallow, sweat out, take, tolerate; *compare* ACCEPT 2
   rel afflict, torment, torture, try; allow, condone, countenance, permit; acquiesce, bow, defer, submit, yield
   idiom make do, put up with, take lying down
   con decline, refuse, reject, spurn; avoid, bypass, elude, evade, shun
   11 *syn* see HEAD 3

bear (on *or* upon) *vb* to have a connection especially logically <this situation *bears* directly upon the question under discussion>
   syn appertain, apply, pertain, relate
   rel refer; affect, concern, involve, touch; correspond, parallel
   idiom have to do with, tie in with

bear (with) *vb syn* see ACCEPT 2

bearable *adj* capable of being borne <his outrageous behavior is hardly *bearable*>
   syn endurable, livable, sufferable, supportable, sustainable, tolerable
   rel acceptable, admissible, allowable, satisfactory
   con insufferable, insupportable, intolerable, unendurable, unsupportable
   ant unbearable

beard *n* the natural growth of hair on a man's face <some men look better with *beards*>
   syn beaver, whiskers; *compare* SIDE-WHISKERS
   rel charley, galways, goatee, imperial, spade beard, Vandyke; fuzz

beard *vb syn* see FACE 3
   idiom beard the lion in his den

bearded *adj* having a beard <an old *bearded* philosopher>
   syn barbate, bewhiskered, whiskered
   rel beardy; goateed; hairy; stubbed, stubbly, unshaven
   con barefaced, clean-faced, clean-shaven, shaven, smooth-faced, whiskerless
   ant beardless

bear down *vb syn* see CONQUER 1

bearer *n* **1** *syn* see MESSENGER
   2 a man who carries baggage and supplies for travelers <native *bearers* serving the safari>
   syn carrier, drogher, porter
   rel boy, cargador, coolie; redcap, skycap

bearing *n* **1** the way in which or the quality by which a person outwardly manifests his personality <a dowager with a regal *bearing*>
   syn address, air, comportment, demeanor, deportment, mien, port, presence, set
   rel aspect, brow, look; attitude, carriage, pose, posture, stand; poise; display, front; behavior, conduct
   2 *syn* see BIRTH 1

bearish *adj syn* see CANTANKEROUS

bear out *vb syn* see CONFIRM 2

bear up *vb syn* see SUPPORT 4

beast *n* a lower animal as distinguished from man <*beasts* of the field>
   syn animal, brute, creature, ‖critter
   rel beastie, varmint; quadruped

beastly *adj syn* see BRUTISH

beat *vb* **1** to strike repeatedly <robbed and *beaten* by thugs>
   syn baste, batter, belabor, buffet, drub, ‖dump, hammer, lam, lambaste, paste, pelt, pound, pummel, thrash, tromp, wallop, whop
   rel bastinado, baton, bludgeon, cudgel, fustigate, pistol-whip; flog, lace, lash, tan, whip; lay on, maul, muss up, rough (up)
   idiom give one beans, rain blows on
   2 *syn* see WHIP 2
   3 *syn* see SCOUR 2
   4 *syn* see WHIP 3
   5 *syn* see WAG
   6 *syn* see HAMMER 1
   7 *syn* see SURPASS 1
   idiom beat (all) hollow
   8 *syn* see NONPLUS 1
   9 *syn* see CHEAT
   10 *syn* see FRUSTRATE 1
   11 *syn* see SCOOP 3
   12 *syn* see PULSATE
   13 *syn* see WIN 1

beat *n* **1** *syn* see RHYTHM
   2 *syn* see SCOOP

beat down *vb syn* see CONQUER 1

beating *n syn* see DEFEAT 1
   rel lump(s)

beatitude *n syn* scc HAPPINESS
   rel ecstasy, rapture, transport

con affliction, trial, tribulation; anguish, grief, sorrow, woe; agony, suffering
ant despair, dolor
beau *n* 1 *syn* see BOYFRIEND 1
2 *syn* see BOYFRIEND 2
Beau Brummel *n syn* see FOP
beau ideal *n syn* see MODEL 2
idiom shining example
‖**beaut** *n syn* see BEAUTY
beauteous *adj syn* see BEAUTIFUL
beautiful *adj* very pleasing or delightful to look at <the most *beautiful* woman in the world>
syn attractive, beauteous, ‖bonny, comely, dishy, fair, foxy, good-looking, handsome, lovely, pretty, pulchritudinous, stunning, well=favored
rel choice, elegant, exquisite; glorious, resplendent, splendid, sublime, superb; eye-appealing, eye-filling, ‖proper; personable, pleasing
con offensive, repugnant, repulsive, revolting; homely, ordinary, plain, unattractive, unbeauteous, uncomely, unhandsome, unlovely, unpretty
ant ugly, unbeautiful
beautiful people *n pl syn* see SMART SET
beautify *vb syn* see ADORN
rel glamorize, prettify
con deface, disfigure; damage, mar, spoil
ant uglify
beauty *n* a physically attractive woman <a charming woman and a *beauty* to boot>
syn ‖beaut, bunny, eyeful, knockout, looker, lovely, stunner
rel charmer, dazzler, dream, eye-opener, good=looker, peach; belle, toast
idiom raving beauty
con dog, gorgon, hag, slattern, witch
beaver *n syn* see BEARD
becalm *vb syn* see CALM
because *conj* for the reason that <I left *because* I was bored>
syn as, as long as, ‖being, 'cause, considering, for, inasmuch as, now, seeing, since, whereas
idiom in view of the fact
because of *prep syn* see OVER 6
becloud *vb* 1 *syn* see OBSCURE
rel befuddle, confuse, perplex, puzzle
con illuminate
2 *syn* see CONFUSE 4
become *vb* 1 to commence to be <*became* sick yesterday>
syn come, ‖come over, get, go, grow, run, turn, wax
rel arise, mount, rise, soar
idiom get to be, turn out to be
2 *syn* see SUIT 4
3 *syn* see FLATTER
becoming *adj syn* see DECOROUS 1
rel attractive, flattering; tasteful
con unattractive, unflattering; distasteful; inappropriate, unfitting, unrespectable, unsuitable
ant unbecoming
becomingly *adv syn* see WELL 4
becrush *vb syn* see CRUSH 2
bed *n syn* see BASE 1

bed *vb* 1 to put to bed <getting the children *bedded*>
syn tuck (in)
rel cradle
2 *syn* see RETIRE 4
bedamn *vb syn* see SWEAR 3
bedaub *vb syn* see SMEAR 1
bedaze *vb syn* see DAZE 2
bedazzle *vb syn* see DAZE 1
bedcover *n syn* see BEDSPREAD
bedeck *vb syn* see ADORN
rel bedaub, bedizen
bedevil *vb syn* see WORRY 1
bedfast *adj syn* see BEDRIDDEN
bedim *vb syn* see OBSCURE
con highlight, illuminate
bedlamite *n syn* see LUNATIC 1
bedlamite *adj syn* see INSANE 1
bedog *vb syn* see TAIL
bedraggled *adj syn* see SHABBY 1
bedridden *adj* confined to one's bed by illness or injury <a *bedridden* invalid>
syn bedfast
rel confined, incapacitated, laid up; feeble, infirm, sickly, weak
idiom flat on one's back
con healed, well; hale, healthy, whole
ant ambulant, ambulatory
bedrock *n* 1 *syn* see BASE 1
2 *syn* see BASIS 1
bedspread *n* an often ornamental outer covering for a bed <an appliquéd *bedspread*>
syn bedcover, counterpane, coverlet, ‖coverlid, spread
bee *n syn* see CAPRICE
rel idea; impulse
beef *n* 1 *syn* see MUSCLE 1
2 *syn* see POWER 4
3 *syn* see QUARREL
‖**beef** *vb syn* see GRIPE
beef (up) *vb syn* see INCREASE 1
beefheaded *adj syn* see STUPID 1
beef–witted *adj syn* see STUPID 1
beefy *adj syn* see HUSKY 1
beekeeper *n* one who engages in the production of and caring for bees and honey <special masks and gloves for *beekeepers*>
syn apiarist, apiculturist, beeman, beemaster
beeline *n syn* see HURRY 2
Beelzebub *n syn* see DEVIL 1
beeman *n syn* see BEEKEEPER
beemaster *n syn* see BEEKEEPER
beer garden *n syn* see ALEHOUSE
beer hall *n syn* see ALEHOUSE
‖**beerhouse** *n syn* see ALEHOUSE
beetle *vb* 1 *syn* see HANG 4
2 *syn* see BULGE
beetlehead *n syn* see DUNCE
beetleheaded *adj syn* see STUPID 1

‖**beezer** *n syn* see NOSE 1
befall *vb syn* see HAPPEN 1
befit *vb syn* see SUIT 4
befitting *adj* **1** *syn* see FIT 1
 ant unbefitting
 2 *syn* see DECOROUS 1
befittingly *adv syn* see WELL 1
befog *vb* **1** *syn* see OBSCURE
 2 *syn* see CONFUSE 4
 3 *syn* see PUZZLE
befool *vb syn* see DUPE
before *adv* **1** so as to precede something in order
 or time <racing on *before* to give warning>
 syn ahead, ante, antecedently, beforehand, fore,
 forward, in advance, precedently, previous
 con behind; abaft, aft, astern
 ant after
 2 in time past <had heard that joke *before*>
 syn already, earlier, erstwhile, formerly, heretofore, once, previously; *compare* THEN 1
 ant after
 3 until now or then <you'll get it tomorrow and
 not *before*>
 syn beforehand, earlier, sooner
before *prep* **1** coming before in space or time <be
 home *before* dark>
 syn ahead of, ante, ere, in advance of, preceding,
 prior to, to; *compare* UNTIL
 con since, subsequent to
 ant after
 2 in the presence of <stood *before* the court>
 syn confronting, facing
 idiom face to face with
 3 *syn* see UNTIL
beforehand *adv* **1** *syn* see BEFORE 1
 2 *syn* see BEFORE 3
befoul *vb* **1** *syn* see CONTAMINATE 2
 2 *syn* see MALIGN
befuddle *vb syn* see CONFUSE 2
 rel daze
befuddlement *n syn* see HAZE 2
 rel confusion, mix-up
 con clearheadedness, lucidness
beg *vb* to ask for or ask one for something urgently
 <*beg* one's life from an attacker><*beg* a stranger
 for help>
 syn appeal, beseech, brace, conjure, crave, entreat, implore, importune, invoke, plead, pray,
 supplicate
 rel ask, call (on), request, solicit; petition, sue;
 besiege, demand, press; nag, worry
 idiom throw oneself at the feet of (*or* on the
 mercy of)
 con hint, intimate, suggest
‖**begats** *n pl* **1** *syn* see GENEALOGY
 2 *syn* see OFFSPRING
begem *vb syn* see BEJEWEL
beget *vb* **1** *syn* see FATHER
 2 *syn* see PROCREATE 1
beggar *n* **1** one who begs especially habitually or
 as a livelihood <*beggars* crying out to tourists>
 syn bummer, cadger, moocher, panhandler,
 ‖schnorrer
 rel deadbeat, freeloader, sponge, sponger; ‖bin-
 dle stiff, hobo, tramp

 2 *syn* see SUPPLIANT
 3 *syn* see PAUPER
beggared *adj syn* see POOR 1
beggarly *adj syn* see CONTEMPTIBLE
 rel wretched; ‖cheesy, trashy; measly, paltry
beggary *n* **1** *syn* see POVERTY 1
 2 *syn* see MENDICANCY
begin *vb* **1** to carry out the first act or step of an
 action or operation <*began* his lecture with a
 joke>
 syn commence, embark (on *or* upon), enter, get
 off, inaugurate, initiate, jump (off), kick off,
 launch, lead off, open, set to, start, take up, tee
 off
 rel establish, found, institute; introduce, usher
 in; broach; attack, tackle; prepare; break in; dig
 in
 idiom get the show on the road, get to work, get
 underway
 con cease, desist, discontinue, quit, stop; close,
 complete, conclude, finish, terminate; abandon,
 forsake, leave, quit; back out, renege, withdraw
 ant end
 2 to come into existence <not since civilization
 began has there been such distress>
 syn arise, commence, originate, start; *compare*
 SPRING 1
 rel spring; open
 idiom raise its head
 con end, finish, terminate
beginner *n syn* see NOVICE
beginning *n* the first part or stage of a process or
 development <the first few chapters at the *beginning* of the novel>
 syn alpha, birth, commencement, dawn, dawning, day spring, genesis, onset, opening, opening
 gun, outset, outstart, setout, start
 rel creation, inception, origin, origination, root,
 source, spring; anlage, rudiment, sprout; prologue; appearance, emergence, rise; incipiency,
 infancy
 idiom the word go
 con consummation, termination; closing, completion, conclusion; omega
 ant end, ending
beginning *adj* **1** *syn* see INITIAL 1
 2 *syn* see ELEMENTARY 1
begird *vb* **1** *syn* see BELT 1
 2 *syn* see SURROUND 1
begirdle *vb syn* see BELT 1
begone *vb syn* see GET OUT 1
begrime *vb syn* see SOIL 2
begrudge *vb syn* see ENVY
beguile *vb* **1** *syn* see MANIPULATE 2
 2 *syn* see DECEIVE
 rel entice, lure, seduce
 3 *syn* see WHILE
beguiling *adj syn* see MISLEADING
béguin *n syn* see INFATUATION
behave *vb* **1** to act in a specified way <*behave* as
 people of good breeding should>
 syn acquit, act, bear, carry, comport, conduct,
 demean, deport, disport, do, go on, move, quit
 rel control, direct, manage

idiom make as if (*or* as though); be on one's best behavior, mind one's p's and q's
ant misbehave, misconduct
2 *syn* see ACT 5

behavior *n* one's actions in general or on a particular occasion <his flustered *behavior* before women>
syn comportment, conduct, deportment, tenue
rel bearing, demeanor, mien; action, manner, way
con misbehavior, misconduct

behead *vb* to sever the head <nobles *beheaded* for treason>
syn decapitate, decollate, guillotine, head, neck
idiom bring to the block

behemoth *n* *syn* see GIANT

behemothic *adj* *syn* see HUGE

behest *n* *syn* see COMMAND 1
rel demand; prompting, request, solicitation

behind *adv* *syn* see AFTER

behind *prep* **1** *syn* see ABAFT
2 *syn* see AFTER 2

behind *n* *syn* see BUTTOCKS

behindhand *adj* **1** *syn* see NEGLIGENT
2 *syn* see BACKWARD 6
3 *syn* see TARDY
ant beforehand

behold *vb* *syn* see SEE 1

beholden *adj* *syn* see INDEBTED

beholder *n* *syn* see SPECTATOR

being *n* **1** *syn* see EXISTENCE 1
rel character, individuality, personality
ant nonbeing
2 *syn* see THING 5
3 *syn* see ENTITY 1
4 *syn* see ESSENCE 1
5 *syn* see HUMAN

‖**being** *conj* *syn* see BECAUSE

bejewel *vb* to ornament with or as if with jewels <a *bejeweled* headdress> <cobwebs all *bejeweled* with glittering morning dew>
syn begem, beset, enjewel, gem, jewel
rel bespangle, spangle; diamond; encrust

belabor *vb* *syn* see BEAT 1

belated *adj* **1** *syn* see TARDY
2 *syn* see OLD-FASHIONED

belch *vb* **1** to expel gas suddenly from the stomach through the mouth <ate and ate until he *belched*>
syn burp, eruct, eructate
2 *syn* see ERUPT 1

beldam *n* **1** a woman of advanced years <a crotchety *beldam* hunched over the fire>
syn dame, gammer, grandam; *compare* GAFFER, OLDSTER
rel grandmother, granny; grand dame; matron; matriarch
idiom old girl
con damsel, lass, maid, miss
2 *syn* see HAG 2

beleaguer *vb* **1** *syn* see BESIEGE
rel siege, storm
idiom set upon from all sides
2 *syn* see WORRY 1

belfry *n* **1** *syn* see BELL TOWER
‖**2** *syn* see HEAD 1

belie *vb* *syn* see MISREPRESENT
rel contradict, contravene, negative; controvert, disprove; conceal, disguise, hide
con bespeak, betoken, indicate; disclose, discover, reveal
ant attest

belief *n* **1** the act of assenting intellectually to something proposed as true or the state of mind of one who so assents <offered ready *belief* to anyone he trusted>
syn credence, credit, faith
rel assurance, certainty, certitude, conviction, sureness; acquiescence, assent; trust; credibility, trustworthiness
con distrust, doubt, mistrust, uncertainty; incredulity; question
ant disbelief, unbelief
2 *syn* see OPINION
rel doctrine, dogma, fundamental, law, precept, principle; concept, idea

believable *adj* worthy of belief <the author's bizarre characterizations are hardly *believable*>
syn colorable, credible, creditable, plausible
rel likely, possible, probable, tenable; conceivable, rational, reasonable; presumable, supposable; unquestionable; convincing, impressive, persuasive, satisfying; meaningful, solid, substantial
con improbable, unlikely; doubtable, doubtful, dubious, fishy, questionable, specious; implausible, incredible; inconceivable, untenable; fabulous, mythological
ant unbelievable

believe *vb* **1** to have a firm conviction in the reality of something <*believes* in ghosts>
syn accept, ‖buy, swallow
rel accredit, credit, trust; admit
idiom have no doubts about, hold the belief that, take (*or* accept) as gospel, take at one's word, take one's word for
con discredit, distrust, doubt, mistrust, question, suspect; challenge, dispute; reject, turn down
ant disbelieve, misbelieve
2 *syn* see FEEL 3
3 *syn* see UNDERSTAND 3

belittle *vb* *syn* see DECRY 2
rel criticize, discredit; underestimate, underrate, undervalue
con intensify; boast, crow
ant aggrandize; magnify

belittlement *n* *syn* see DETRACTION

bell *vb* *syn* see RING

‖**bell cow** *n* *syn* see LEADER 1

bellicose *adj* *syn* see BELLIGERENT
rel aggressive, assertive; factious, fighting, rebellious

---

syn synonym(s)   *rel* related word(s)
ant antonym(s)   *con* contrasted word(s)
idiom idiomatic equivalent(s)
‖ use limited; if in doubt, see a dictionary

idiom full of fight
con gentle, moderate, temperate
ant amicable; pacific
belligerence *n syn* see ATTACK 2
belligerent *adj* having or taking an aggressive or fighting attitude <a *belligerent* reply to a diplomatic note>
syn bellicose, combative, contentious, gladiatorial, militant, pugnacious, quarrelsome, ‖ructious, scrappy, truculent, warlike; *compare* QUARRELSOME 2
rel battling, fighting, warring; attacking, invading; aggressive, antagonistic, fierce, hostile; ardent, hot, hot-tempered
con neutral; pacific, pacifist, peaceable, peaceful; conciliatory; amicable
ant friendly
‖**belling** *n syn* see SHIVAREE
bellow *vb syn* see ROAR
rel bark, bay, yelp; cry, wail; low, moo
bell ringer *n syn* see SMASH 6
bell tower *n* a tower that supports or shelters a bell or group of bells <a *bell tower* stood free from the church>
syn belfry, campanile, carillon
bellwether *n syn* see LEADER 1
belly *n syn* see ABDOMEN
bellyache *n syn* see STOMACHACHE
‖**bellyache** *vb syn* see GRIPE
‖**bellyacher** *n syn* see GROUCH
belong *vb* **1** to be suitable, appropriate, or advantageous or to be in a proper or fitting place or situation <the boxes *belong* in the attic>
syn fit, go, set
rel become, befit, suit; accord, agree, chime, harmonize; correspond, match, tally
idiom have one's place
2 to be the property of (a person or thing) <the books *belong* to the library>
syn appertain, pertain, vest
3 to be an attribute, part, adjunct, or function (of a person or thing) <good humor and wit *belong* to his personality>
syn indwell, inhere
idiom run in one's blood (*or* family)
belongings *n pl syn* see POSSESSION 2
beloved *adj syn* see FAVORITE 1
beloved *n* **1** *syn* see SWEETHEART 1
2 *syn* see GIRL FRIEND 2
3 *syn* see BOYFRIEND 2
below *adv* **1** in or at a lower position than something expressed or implied <several business establishments were situated *below*>
syn beneath, under, underneath
ant above
2 lower on the same page or on a following page <for additional examples see *below*>
syn infra
ant above, supra
below *prep* **1** in a lower position relative to some other object or place <lives just *below* me>
syn beneath, under, underneath
con over
ant above

2 *syn* see AFTER 2
belt *n* **1** a strip of flexible material worn around the waist <a leather *belt*>
syn ceinture, cincture, girdle, sash, waistband
rel baldric, cummerbund; band
2 *syn* see AREA 1
rel stretch, strip
belt *vb* **1** to bind about or around with or as if with a belt <gold lamé *belting* the gown>
syn band, begird, begirdle, cincture, encincture, engird, engirdle, gird, girdle
rel tie (up); loop; sash; circle, encircle, ring
2 *syn* see SLAM 1
belt *n syn* see BLOW 1
belvedere *n syn* see SUMMERHOUSE
bemean *vb syn* see HUMBLE
bemedaled *adj* having or wearing decorations especially as awarded by the military <the general's *bemedaled* uniform>
syn beribboned, decorated
bemired *adj syn* see MUDDY 1
bemoan *vb syn* see DEPLORE 1
rel regret; complain
con applaud, cheer, huzzah; delight, jubilate, rejoice
ant exult
bemuse *vb syn* see DAZE 2
rel addle; perplex, puzzle
con enlighten, illuminate
bemused *adj syn* see ABSTRACTED
benchmark *n syn* see STANDARD 3
bend *vb* **1** *syn* see CURVE
rel arch, curl, double, hook
ant straighten
2 *syn* see GIVE 12
3 *syn* see INCLINE 3
4 *syn* see ADDRESS 3
bend (over) *vb syn* see HANG 4
bend *n* **1** *syn* see TURN 2
2 *syn* see TURN 4
3 *syn* see CURVE
bender *n syn* see BINGE 1
bending *adj syn* see CROOKED 1
beneath *adv syn* see BELOW 1
beneath *prep syn* see BELOW 1
ant above, over
benediction *n* **1** *syn* see BLESSING 1
2 *syn* see GRACE 1
3 *syn* see APPROBATION
4 *syn* see GOOD 1
benefact *vb syn* see HELP 1
benefaction *n syn* see DONATION
benefic *adj syn* see GOOD 1
rel desirable, pleasing, satisfying
con damaging, harmful, injurious
ant malefic
beneficence *n syn* see DONATION
beneficial *adj syn* see GOOD 1
rel salutary, wholesome
con baneful, deleterious, noxious, pernicious
ant detrimental, harmful
benefit *n* **1** *syn* see GOOD 1
2 *syn* see WELFARE
rel account, behalf, sake; gain, profit

con catastrophe, disaster, misfortune; detriment
ant harm, ill

benefit *vb* to be useful or profitable to <medicines that *benefit* mankind>
syn advantage, avail, profit, serve, work (for)
rel advance, ameliorate, better, contribute (to), favor, improve; relieve, succor; build, further, promote; aid, assist, help
idiom do a world of good
con hinder, impede; damage, impair, injure; distress, upset; afflict, anguish; oppose
ant harm, hurt

benet *vb syn* see CATCH 3

benevolence *n* **1** *syn* see GOODWILL 1
con animosity, bitterness, ill will; antagonism, hostility; inimicality, unkindliness; stinginess
2 *syn* see GIFT 1

benevolent *adj* **1** *syn* see GENEROUS 1
rel beneficent; charitable; humane; compassionate, tenderhearted
con cruel, inhuman, malicious, spiteful
ant malevolent
2 *syn* see CHARITABLE 1
rel bighearted, freehearted, generous, greathearted, largehearted, liberal, openhanded; public-spirited; do-good
con niggardly, stingy; callous, indifferent, insensitive, unconcerned, unfeeling

benighted *adj* **1** *syn* see IGNORANT 1
rel backward, unenlightened; uninformed
idiom in the dark
con informed, intelligent
2 *syn* see BACKWARD 5

benightedness *n syn* see IGNORANCE 1

benign *adj* **1** *syn* see KIND
rel gracious
con malevolent, malicious, malignant, spiteful; acrid, caustic, mordant
ant malign
2 *syn* see FAVORABLE 5
rel gentle, mild; benevolent, charitable, humane; clement, forbearing, merciful
con menacing, threatening
ant malign

benignant *adj syn* see KIND
rel mild; gracious
con malevolent, malicious, spiteful; relentless
ant malignant

benison *n syn* see BLESSING 1

bent *n* **1** *syn* see LEANING 2
2 *syn* see GIFT 2
con antipathy, aversion; inability, incapacity

bent *adj* **1** *syn* see CURVED
2 *syn* see DECIDED 2

benumb *vb* **1** *syn* see DEADEN 1
2 *syn* see DAZE 2

benumbed *adj syn* see NUMB 1

bequeath *vb* **1** *syn* see WILL
con disinherit, exheridate
2 *syn* see HAND DOWN

bequest *n syn* see LEGACY 1

berate *vb syn* see SCOLD 1
con acclaim, praise; applaud; commend, compliment

berceuse *n syn* see LULLABY

bereave *vb syn* see DEPRIVE 2

bereaved *adj* suffering the death of a loved one <the *bereaved* family>
syn bereft
rel distressed, sorrowing

bereft *adj syn* see BEREAVED

beribboned *adj syn* see BEMEDALED

berth *n* **1** *syn* see WHARF
2 *syn* see JOB 2

beseech *vb syn* see BEG

beset *vb* **1** *syn* see BEJEWEL
2 *syn* see ATTACK 1
3 *syn* see BESIEGE
4 *syn* see INFEST 1
5 *syn* see SURROUND 1
idiom come at from all directions (*or* sides)

besetment *n syn* see ANNOYANCE 3

beside *prep* **1** at or by the side of <left the car *beside* the road>
syn alongside, by, ‖fornent, next to
rel near, opposite
2 *syn* see NEAR 2
3 *syn* see BESIDES 1
4 *syn* see EXCEPT

besides *adv* **1** *syn* see ALSO 2
idiom at that
2 *syn* see AGAIN 4

besides *prep* **1** in addition to <*besides* being tall, he's thin>
syn as well as, beside, beyond, over and above
idiom along with, together with
2 *syn* see EXCEPT

besides *adj syn* see ADDITIONAL

besiege *vb* to surround an enemy in a fortified or strong position so as to prevent ingress and egress <Troy was *besieged* by Greeks for ten years>
syn beleaguer, beset, blockade, invest
rel encircle, encompass, hem (in), surround; trap; assail, assault, attack

besmear *vb* **1** *syn* see SMEAR 1
2 *syn* see TAINT 1

besmirch *vb syn* see TAINT 1

besoil *vb syn* see SOIL 2

besotted *adj syn* see INFATUATED

bespangle *vb syn* see SPANGLE 1

bespatter *vb* **1** *syn* see SPOT 1
2 *syn* see MALIGN

bespeak *vb* **1** *syn* see RESERVE 2
2 *syn* see ADDRESS 4
3 *syn* see ASK 2
idiom put in for
4 *syn* see INDICATE 2

bespeckle *vb syn* see SPECKLE 1

bespectacled *adj* having or wearing glasses <*bespectacled* thesaurists>
syn spectacled

bespot *vb syn* see SPOT 1

---

syn synonym(s) **rel** related word(s)
ant antonym(s) **con** contrasted word(s)
idiom idiomatic equivalent(s)
‖ use limited; if in doubt, see a dictionary

besprinkle *vb syn* see SPRINKLE 1

best *adj* much more than half <passed the *best* part of a month at the shore>
syn better, ‖bettermost, greater, largest, most

best *vb* 1 *syn* see CONQUER 2
2 *syn* see SURPASS 1
3 *syn* see DEFEAT 2

best *n* the choicest one or part <always gave the *best* that she had>
syn choice, cream, elite, fat, flower, pick, pride, prime, primrose, prize, top
rel gem; nonesuch, nonpareil; exemplar, model, paragon, pattern
idiom cock of the walk, flower of the flock, one in a thousand (*or* million)
ant worst

bestain *vb syn* see STAIN 1

‖**best bib and tucker** *n syn* see FINERY

best girl *n syn* see GIRL FRIEND 1

bestial *adj syn* see BRUTISH

bestialize *vb syn* see DEBASE 1

bestir *vb syn* see STIR 1

bestow *vb* 1 *syn* see USE 2
2 *syn* see STOW
3 *syn* see HARBOR 2
4 *syn* see GIVE 1

bestower *n syn* see DONOR

bestrew *vb syn* see STREW 1

bestride *vb* 1 *syn* see MOUNT 5
2 to sit with one leg on each side <boys *bestriding* a fallen log>
syn straddle, ‖striddle, stride

bet *n* something of value (as money) staked on a winner-take-all basis on the outcome of an uncertainty <laid a *bet* at three to one on the champion>
syn ante, pot, stake, wager

bet *vb syn* see GAMBLE 1

bête noire *n syn* see ABOMINATION 1

bethink *vb syn* see REMEMBER

betide *vb syn* see HAPPEN 1

betimes *adv* 1 *syn* see EARLY 1
2 *syn* see EARLY 2
‖3 *syn* see SOMETIMES

betoken *vb* 1 *syn* see INDICATE 2
2 *syn* see AUGUR 2

betray *vb* 1 *syn* see DECEIVE
rel ensnare, entrap, snare, trap
2 to prove faithless or treacherous <*betrayed* his own people by going over to the enemy>
syn cross, double-cross, sell, sell out, ‖split
rel desert, renegade; give away, inform, turn in; collaborate; apostatize
idiom act (*or* play) the traitor, break faith, round on, sell down the river
3 *syn* see REVEAL 1
rel demonstrate, evidence, evince, manifest, show; betoken, indicate
con defend, guard, protect, safeguard, shield

betrayer *n syn* see INFORMER

betrothal *n syn* see ENGAGEMENT 2

betrothed *n* either member of a couple engaged to be married
syn affianced, intended

rel fiancé, husband-to-be; bride-to-be, fiancée, wife-to-be

betrothed *adj syn* see ENGAGED 2

betrothing *n syn* see ENGAGEMENT 2

betrothment *n syn* see ENGAGEMENT 2

better *adj* 1 *syn* see BEST
2 more worthy or pleasing than an alternative <it is *better* to lose gracefully than to win arrogantly>
syn ‖bettermost, preferable, superior; *compare* GOOD
rel exceeding, exceptional, surpassing; choice, desirable, excellent
idiom more than a match for
ant worse

better *adv syn* see MORE 2
ant worse

better *n* 1 *syn* see SUPERIOR
2 a superior or winning position <had the *better* of the argument>
syn advantage, superiority, upper hand, victory, whip hand; *compare* ADVANTAGE 3
rel success, triumph, win
con collapse, defeat, disadvantage, loss; beating, drubbing, licking
ant worse

better *vb* 1 *syn* see IMPROVE 1
ant worsen
2 *syn* see SURPASS 1

‖**bettermost** *adj* 1 *syn* see BETTER 2
2 *syn* see BEST

between *prep* 1 in common to (as in position, in a distribution, or in participation) <a treaty *between* three powers>
syn among
2 in the time, space, or interval that separates <*between* the ages 12 and 20>
syn ‖atween, ‖atwixt, ‖betwixt, in between, tween, twixt

‖**betwixt** *prep syn* see BETWEEN 2

bevel *adj syn* see DIAGONAL

beveled *adj syn* see DIAGONAL

‖**bever** *n syn* see SNACK

beverage *n syn* see DRINK 1

bevy *n syn* see GROUP 1

bewail *vb syn* see DEPLORE 1
ant rejoice

beware *vb* to be cautious <*beware* of the dog>
syn look out, mind, watch out
rel attend, heed, notice, watch
idiom be on one's guard, be on the lookout (*or* watch), keep at a safe distance, take care (*or* heed)
con disregard, ignore, neglect

bewhiskered *adj syn* see BEARDED

bewilder *vb* 1 *syn* see PUZZLE
rel baffle, fuddle, muddle
2 *syn* see CONFUSE 2

bewitch *vb* 1 to practice witchcraft on <medicine men who *bewitch* ignorant tribesmen>
syn charm, enchant, ensorcell, hex, spell, voodoo, witch
rel bedevil, demonize, overlook, possess, sorcerize; beglamour, dazzle, trick

idiom cast a spell on (*or* over), give (*or* cast) the evil eye, put a curse on
2 *syn* see ATTRACT 1
rel beglamour, ‖snow
bewitched *adj syn* see ENAMORED 3
bewitching *adj syn* see ATTRACTIVE 1
con forbidding, grim
bewitchment *n syn* see MAGIC 1
beyond *adv* **1** on or to the farther side <a house with mountains *beyond*>
syn farther, further, ‖yon, yonder
2 *syn* see OVER 1
beyond *prep* **1** on or to the farther side of <the store is just *beyond* the next house>
syn after, outside, past, without
2 out of the reach, sphere, or comprehension of <it's *beyond* me how he did it>
syn above, past
idiom beyond one's depth (*or* power), over (*or* above) one's head, too deep (*or* much) for
3 *syn* see BESIDES 1
beyond *adj syn* see ADDITIONAL
beyond *n syn* see HEREAFTER 2
‖**b'hoy** *n syn* see TOUGH
bias *n* **1** *syn* see LEANING 2
2 *syn* see PREJUDICE
rel inclination, predisposition; slant, standpoint, viewpoint
con dispassionateness; fairness, justness
bias *adj syn* see DIAGONAL
bias *vb* **1** *syn* see SLANT 3
2 *syn* see INCLINE 3
3 *syn* see PREJUDICE 2
biased *adj* **1** *syn* see DIAGONAL
2 exhibiting or characterized by a highly personal and unreasoned distortion of judgment <a *biased* estimate of the book's worth>
syn colored, jaundiced, one-sided, partial, partisan, prejudiced, prepossessed, tendentious, unindifferent, unneutral, warped
rel bent, disposed, inclined, predisposed; influenced, interested, swayed; opinionated
con detached, dispassionate, impartial, neutral, open-minded; fair, honest, just
ant unbiased
bibber *n syn* see DRUNKARD
bibble–babble *n syn* see CHATTER
bibelot *n syn* see KNICKKNACK
Bible *n* the sacred volume of Christians <students of the *Bible*>
syn Book, Holy Writ, Sacred Writ, Scripture
idiom Book of Books, Good Book, Word of God
bibliopole *n syn* see BOOKDEALER
bicker *vb* **1** *syn* see ARGUE 2
rel battle, contend, fight, war
2 *syn* see QUARREL
3 *syn* see RATTLE 1
bickering *n syn* see QUARREL
bicycle *n* a pedal-propelled vehicle with two wheels tandem, a steering handle, and a saddle seat <ten-speed *bicycles*>
syn bike, cycle, two-wheeler, velocipede
bid *vb* **1** *syn* see COMMAND

rel summon
con interdict, prohibit
ant forbid
2 *syn* see INVITE
rel request
biddable *adj syn* see OBEDIENT
rel amiable, good-natured, obliging
con mulish, obstinate, stiff-necked, stubborn
ant recalcitrant
bidding *n syn* see COMMAND 1
rel call, summoning
biddy *n* **1** *syn* see MAID 2
2 *syn* see HAG 2
bide *vb* **1** *syn* see STAY 2
rel continue
2 *syn* see RESIDE 1
bierstube *n syn* see ALEHOUSE
biff *n syn* see BLOW 1
‖**biff** *vb syn* see STRIKE 2
‖**biffy** *n syn* see PRIVY 1
bifold *adj syn* see TWOFOLD 1
big *adj* **1** of significant size or scope <a *big* expanse of mud> <*big* plans>
syn considerable, extensive, hefty, large, large-scale, major, sizable
rel bumper, hulking, whacking, whopping; clumsy, unwieldy; ample, biggish, capacious, commodious, comprehensive, copious, roomy, spacious, voluminous; distended, inflated, swollen
con paltry, piddling, trivial; slight, small; insignificant; minute, tiny, wee
ant little
2 *syn* see LARGE 1
3 *syn* see PREGNANT 1
4 *syn* see FULL 1
rel flushed, overflowing; cloyed, glutted, sated, satiated, satisfied
idiom full to bursting (*or* overflowing), full to the ears, stuffed to the gills
con empty
5 *syn* see IMPORTANT 1
6 *syn* see PRETENTIOUS 3
7 *syn* see GENEROUS 1
‖**big** *adv syn* see VERY 1
big *n syn* see NOTABLE 1
big boy *n syn* see NOTABLE 1
‖**big bug** *n syn* see NOTABLE 1
‖**big cheese** *n syn* see NOTABLE 1
‖**big chief** *n syn* see NOTABLE 1
‖**biggety** *adj syn* see WISE 5
‖**biggie** *n syn* see NOTABLE 1
big gun *n syn* see NOTABLE 1
‖**big house** *n syn* see JAIL
bight *n syn* see INLET
big name *n syn* see CELEBRITY 2
bigness *n syn* see SIZE 2
‖**big noise** *n syn* see NOTABLE 1
bigot *n syn* see ENTHUSIAST

---

syn synonym(s)   *rel* related word(s)
ant antonym(s)   *con* contrasted word(s)
idiom idiomatic equivalent(s)
‖ use limited; if in doubt, see a dictionary

rel approver, liker, relisher; mumpsimus, racist, segregationist
con depreciator, disparager, knocker; disliker, disrelisher, hater, loather, misliker

bigoted *adj syn* see ILLIBERAL
rel lily-white; conservative

big shot *n syn* see NOTABLE 1

big-timer *n syn* see NOTABLE 1

‖**big wheel** *n syn* see NOTABLE 1

bigwig *n syn* see NOTABLE 1

bike *n syn* see BICYCLE

bilge *n syn* see NONSENSE 2

bilk *vb* **1** *syn* see FRUSTRATE 1
con fulfill
2 *syn* see CHEAT
3 *syn* see ESCAPE 2
rel dodge, shake

bill *n* **1** the jaws of a bird with their projecting horny covering <the huge *bill* of the toucan>
syn beak, neb, nib, pecker
2 *syn* see PROMONTORY
3 *syn* see VISOR 1

bill *n* **1** a statement of the amount due a creditor <*bills* from the grocer and doctor>
syn account, invoice, reckoning, score, statement, tab
rel charges, damage
idiom statement of account
2 *syn* see CHECK 2
3 *syn* see POSTER
4 *syn* see DOLLAR

billet *n syn* see JOB 2

billet *vb* **1** to assign quarters to soldiers <the troops were *billeted* in private homes>
syn canton, quarter
rel bed, house, lodge, put up; bestow
2 *syn* see HARBOR 2

billet *n syn* see BAR 1

billet–doux *n syn* see LOVE LETTER

billingsgate *n syn* see ABUSE

billy *n syn* see CUDGEL

billy club *n syn* see CUDGEL

‖**bim** *n syn* see WANTON

bimanal *adj syn* see TWO-HANDED 2

bimanual *adj syn* see TWO-HANDED 1

‖**bimbo** *n syn* see WANTON

binary *adj syn* see TWOFOLD 1

bind *vb* **1** *syn* see TIE 1
con release
ant unloose
2 *syn* see BANDAGE

‖**bindle stiff** *n syn* see VAGABOND

‖**bing** *n syn* see PILE 1

binge *n* **1** a drunken revel <hung over after a weekend *binge*>
syn bat, bender, blowoff, booze, brannigan, bum, bust, carousal, carouse, compotation, drunk, jag, orgy, ran-tan, rowdydow, soak, souse, spree, tear, ‖time, toot, wassail
rel bacchanal, bacchanalia, debauch; blast, ‖blowout; ‖bun
2 *syn* see SPREE 1

bio *n syn* see BIOGRAPHY

biocide *n syn* see PESTICIDE

biographer *n* one who writes a biography <irresponsible *biographers* whose work is more fiction than fact>
syn autobiographer, autobiographist, Boswell, memoirist

biography *n* a more or less detailed account of the events and circumstances of a person's life <wrote a *biography* of his grandfather>
syn autobiography, bio, confessions, life, memoir
rel diary, journal, letters; adventures, history, story; profile; obit, obituary

biologic *n syn* see DRUG 1

bird *n* **1** *syn* see RASPBERRY
‖**2** *syn* see GIRL 1

birdbrain *n syn* see SCATTERBRAIN

birdhouse *n syn* see AVIARY

birdman *n syn* see PILOT 2

bird–witted *adj syn* see GIDDY 1

birr *n syn* see ENERGY 2

birth *n* **1** the act or process of bringing forth young from the womb <had a very hard *birth* after a prolonged labor>
syn bearing, ‖birthing, childbearing, childbirth, delivery, parturition
rel abortion, miscarriage, slip
2 *syn* see BEGINNING

birth *vb* ‖**1** *syn* see BEAR 5
2 *syn* see SPRING 1

birth control *n* control of the number of children born especially by preventing or lessening the frequency of conception <cultural and religious aspects of *birth control*>
syn contraception
rel rhythm method; planned parenthood; vasectomy; (the) pill

‖**birthing** *n syn* see BIRTH 1

birthmark *n* **1** a congenital pigmented area on the skin <*birthmarks* often appear on the neck>
syn mole, nevus
2 *syn* see CHARACTERISTIC 1

birth pang *n, usu* **birth pangs** *pl syn* see LABOR 2

birthright *n* **1** *syn* see RIGHT 2
2 *syn* see HERITAGE 1

bisexual *adj* being structurally and functionally both male and female <many lower animals are *bisexual*>
syn androgynous, hermaphrodite, hermaphroditic

bistered *adj syn* see DARK 3

bistro *n syn* see NIGHTCLUB

bit *n* **1** *syn* see MORSEL 1
2 *syn* see PARTICLE
3 *syn* see END 4
4 *syn* see WHILE 1

bit *vb syn* see RESTRAIN 1

bit by bit *adv syn* see GRADUALLY

bite *vb* **1** to seize with the teeth so that they enter <*bite* into a pear>
syn champ, chomp
rel gnaw, nibble, tooth; ‖chaw, chew, crunch, masticate, munch, scrunch; eat
idiom sink one's teeth into
2 *syn* see EAT 3

3 *syn* see SMART
bite *n* **1** *syn* see MORSEL 1
  2 *syn* see SNACK
  3 *syn* see SHARE 1
biting *adj syn* see INCISIVE
||**bitsy** *adj syn* see TINY
bitter *adj* **1** *syn* see ACRID
  rel acerb, acid, bitterish
  con delicious; bland, flat, insipid
  2 difficult to accept mentally <the *bitter* truth>
  syn afflictive, distasteful, galling, grievous, painful, unpalatable
  rel annoying, distressing, disturbing, woeful; bad, disagreeable, displeasing, offensive, unpleasant; galling, provoking, vexatious
  con agreeable, gratifying, satisfying
  3 marked by intense animosity <*bitter* contempt>
  syn antagonistic, hostile, rancorous, virulent, vitriolic
  rel alienated, divided, estranged; irreconcilable
  4 *syn* see SEVERE 3
  con mild, springlike, summery
bitter–ender *n syn* see DIEHARD 1
bitterly *adv syn* see HARD 6
bivouac *vb syn* see CAMP
||**bivvy** *vb syn* see CAMP
bizarre *adj* **1** *syn* see STRANGE 4
  2 *syn* see FANTASTIC 2
  con normal, ordinary, regular
blab *n syn* see CHATTER
blab *vb syn* see GOSSIP
blab (out) *vb syn* see REVEAL 1
blabber *vb syn* see BABBLE 2
blabber *n syn* see CHATTER
blabber *n syn* see CHATTERBOX
blabbermouth *n syn* see CHATTERBOX
blabmouth *n syn* see CHATTERBOX
black *adj* **1** having the color of soot or coal <a *black* hearse>
  syn atramentous, ebon, ebony, inky, jet, jetty, onyx, pitch-black, pitch-dark, pitchy, raven, sable
  rel blackish; charcoal, slate; piceous; dusky, swart, swarthy; brunet
  idiom black as a crow (or a shoe or the ace of spades), black as hell (or night)
  ant white
  2 *syn* see DIRTY 1
  3 *syn* see GLOOMY 3
  4 *syn* see UTTER
black *vb syn* see BRUISE 1
black (out) *vb syn* see ERASE
black and white *n syn* see PRINT 2
black–a–vised *adj syn* see DARK 3
black beast *n syn* see ABOMINATION 1
||**blackcoat** *n syn* see CLERGYMAN
black dog *n syn* see SADNESS
blacken *vb syn* see MALIGN
  idiom blacken one's good name, give one a black eye, throw mud at
black eye *n* **1** a bruise about the eye <got a *black eye* in a fight>
  syn mouse, shiner

rel contusion
  2 *syn* see STIGMA
blackguard *n syn* see VILLAIN 1
black out *vb syn* see FAINT
blackout *n syn* see FAINT
blague *n syn* see NONSENSE 2
blah *n syn* see NONSENSE 2
blah *adj syn* see DULL 9
blamable *adj syn* see BLAMEWORTHY
blame *vb syn* see CRITICIZE
  rel accuse, charge; impute
  idiom lay at one's door (or doorstep), lay (or put) the blame on
  con exculpate, vindicate; praise
blame *n* responsibility for misdeed or delinquency <accepted the *blame* for his foolish act>
  syn culpability, fault, onus
  rel accountability, answerability, liability; accusation, charge, imputation; censure, condemnation, denunciation, reprehension
  idiom burden of guilt
  con commendation, compliment; acclaim, applause, praise
blamed *adj* **1** *syn* see DAMNED 2
  2 *syn* see UTTER
blameful *adj syn* see BLAMEWORTHY
blameless *adj* **1** *syn* see INNOCENT 2
  2 *syn* see GOOD 11
  rel unimpeachable
  ant blameworthy
blameworthy *adj* deserving reproach and punishment <though not criminal, his behavior was certainly *blameworthy*>
  syn amiss, blamable, blameful, censurable, culpable, demeritorious, guilty, reprehensible, sinful, unholy
  rel illaudable, uncommendable, unpraiseworthy, unpretty; delinquent, faultful; punishable; foolish, irresponsible, reckless
  idiom at fault, to blame
  con faultless, flawless, impeccable, irreproachable, unimpeachable; guiltless, innocent, sinless; creditable, high-principled, upright
  ant blameless; unblamable
blanch *vb syn* see WHITEN 1
blanch (over) *vb syn* see PALLIATE
blanch *vb syn* see RECOIL
blanched *adj syn* see PALE 1
bland *adj* **1** *syn* see SUAVE
  rel good-natured, ingratiating
  con bluff, crusty, gruff
  ant brusque
  2 *syn* see GENTLE 1
  3 *syn* see INSIPID 3
  con pungent, savory, spicy, zestful
blandish *vb syn* see COAX
  rel flatter; beguile, charm
  con threaten
blandishment *n syn* see FLATTERY

---

blank *adj* **1** *syn* see EXPRESSIONLESS
2 *syn* see UTTER
blank *n syn* see OMISSION
blank check *n syn* see CARTE BLANCHE
blanket *vb syn* see COVER 3
blankety–blank *adj* **1** *syn* see DAMNED 2
2 *syn* see UTTER
blankness *n syn* see VACUITY 2
blank wall *n syn* see BAR 2
blare *vb* **1** *syn* see BLAZE
2 *syn* see SCREAM 4
blaring *adj syn* see LOUD 1
blarney *vb syn* see COAX
blarney *n syn* see FLATTERY
blasé *adj syn* see SOPHISTICATED 2
 con awed, wide-eyed; artless, naive, natural, unsophisticated
blasphemous *adj syn* see SACRILEGIOUS
blasphemy *n* **1** impious or irreverent language
 <cursing God is *blasphemy*>
 syn cursing, cussing, execration, imprecation,
 profanity, swearing
 rel affront, indignity, insult; abuse, billingsgate,
 scurrility, vituperation
 con reverence, veneration, worship
 ant adoration
2 *syn* see PROFANATION
 rel abuse, befouling, shaming
blast *n syn* see BANG 2
blast *vb* **1** to ruin or to injure severely, suddenly,
 or surprisingly <we'll have no peaches; frost
 blasted the blossoms this year>
 syn blight, dash, nip
 rel destroy, ruin, wreck; damage, injure, spoil;
 shrivel, stunt, wither
2 *syn* see SLAM 1
3 *syn* see WHIP 2
blasted *adj* **1** *syn* see DAMNED 2
2 *syn* see UTTER
blat *vb syn* see EXCLAIM
blatant *adj* **1** *syn* see VOCIFEROUS
 rel screaming; obtrusive
 con modest, soft-spoken
2 *syn* see GAUDY
3 *syn* see SHAMELESS
blather *vb syn* see BABBLE 2
blather *n syn* see NONSENSE 2
blatherskite *n syn* see NONSENSE 2
‖**blatter** *n syn* see CHATTER
blaze *vb* to burn or appear to burn brightly <the
 hot sun *blazed* down>
 syn blare, flame, flare, glare, glow
 rel illuminate, illumine, light; radiate, shine;
 coruscate, fulgurate, scintillate, sparkle; incandesce
blaze (abroad) *vb syn* see DECLARE 1
blazes *n pl syn* see HELL
blazing *adj* **1** *syn* see BURNING 1
2 *syn* see IMPASSIONED
blazon *vb syn* see DECLARE 1
bleach *vb syn* see WHITEN 1
bleak *adj* **1** *syn* see GRIM 2
2 *syn* see GLOOMY 3
blear *vb syn* see DULL 4

blear *adj syn* see FAINT 2
blear–eyed *adj syn* see STUPID 1
blear–witted *adj syn* see STUPID 1
bleary *adj* **1** *syn* see FAINT 2
2 *syn* see EFFETE 2
bleat *vb syn* see GRIPE
bleed *vb* **1** *syn* see EXUDE
2 *syn* see FLEECE 1
bleeding *adj* **1** *syn* see DAMNED 2
2 *syn* see UTTER
blemish *vb syn* see INJURE 1
blemish *n* an imperfection (as a spot or crack) <a
 blemish on the face>
 syn defect, flaw, vice
 rel fault, scar; blister, blotch, disfigurement,
 pockmark, wart; catch, snag, tear
blench *vb syn* see RECOIL
blench *vb syn* see WHITEN 1
blend *vb* **1** *syn* see MIX 1
 rel combine, integrate
 con resolve, separate
2 *syn* see HARMONIZE 4
blend *n syn* see MIXTURE
blending *adj syn* see HARMONIOUS 1
bless *vb* **1** to make holy by religious rite or word
 <the priest *blessed* the water and wine>
 syn consecrate, hallow, sanctify
 rel dedicate
 con defile, desecrate, profane
2 *syn* see PRAISE 2
blessed *adj* **1** *syn* see HOLY 1
2 *syn* see DAMNED 2
3 *syn* see UTTER
blessedness *n syn* see HAPPINESS
 con agony, suffering
 ant misery
blessing *n* **1** an expression or utterance of good
 wishes <on departing, he received his father's
 blessing>
 syn benediction, benison
 rel Godspeed, valediction
2 *syn* see APPROBATION
3 *syn* see GOOD 1
4 *syn* see GRACE 1
‖**bless out** *vb syn* see SCOLD 1
blight *vb syn* see BLAST 1
blighted *adj* **1** *syn* see DAMNED 2
2 *syn* see UTTER
‖**blighter** *n syn* see WRETCH 1
blimp *n* **1** *syn* see FATTY
2 *cap syn* see REACTIONARY
3 *cap syn* see STUFFED SHIRT
blind *adj* **1** lacking the power to see <kittens are
 blind at birth>
 syn ‖dark, eyeless, sightless, stone-blind, visionless
 rel dim-sighted, purblind, short-sighted; blind-
 ish; blindfolded; unseeing
 idiom blind as a bat
 con seeing, sighted; keen, sharp
2 *syn* see INTOXICATED 1
3 *syn* see DULL 7
blind *vb syn* see DAZE 1
blind *n* **1** *syn* see FRONT 3

2 syn see DECOY 2
blind alley *n syn* see DEAD END
blinding *adj* **1 syn** see DAMNED 2
  2 syn see UTTER
blink *vb* **1 syn** see WINK
  2 to shine intermittently <we'll signal by *blinking* the headlights>
  syn flash, flicker, twinkle
  rel glimmer, scintillate, shimmer
blink (at) *vb syn* see CONNIVE 1
blink (at *or* away) *vb syn* see NEGLECT
‖**blinking** *adj* **1 syn** see DAMNED 2
  2 syn see UTTER
blip *vb* **1 syn** see SLAP 1
  2 syn see CENSOR
bliss *n* **1 syn** see HAPPINESS
  con dolor, misery, woe
  ant anguish
  2 syn see HEAVEN 2
blissfulness *n syn* see HAPPINESS
  rel ecstasy, euphoria, exaltation; heaven, paradise
blister *vb syn* see LAMBASTE 3
blistering *adj* **1 syn** see HOT 1
  ‖**2 syn** see DAMNED 2
blithe *adj* **1 syn** see CHEERFUL 1
  2 syn see MERRY
  ant atrabilious, morose
blithering *adj syn* see UTTER
blithesome *adj syn* see MERRY
blitz *vb syn* see BOMBARD
‖**bloat** *n syn* see DRUNKARD
bloated *adj syn* see POMPOUS 1
bloc *n syn* see COMBINATION 2
block *n* **1 syn** see BAR 2
  2 syn see ANNEX
block *vb* **1 syn** see HINDER
  2 syn see INTERCEPT
  3 syn see FILL 1
block (out) *vb syn* see SKETCH
blockade *n* **1 syn** see BAR 2
  ‖**2 syn** see MOONSHINE 2
blockade *vb syn* see BESIEGE
block and block *adj syn* see FULL 1
blockhead *n syn* see DUNCE
blockheaded *adj syn* see STUPID 1
blockish *adj syn* see STUPID 1
block out *vb syn* see SCREEN 3
‖**bloke** *n syn* see MAN 3
blond *adj* **1** of a pale soft yellow color <*blond* hair>
  syn flaxen, golden, straw
  rel blondish; platinum; champagne, towheaded
  con dark; brunet
  2 syn see FAIR 3
blood *n* **1** the fluid that circulates in the heart, arteries, capillaries, and veins of a vertebrate animal <*blood* covered the battlefield>
  syn ‖claret, gore
  rel ichor; humor
  2 syn see ANCESTRY
  3 syn see MURDER
  4 syn see FOP
blood–and–guts *adj syn* see INTENSIVE

bloodbath *n syn* see MASSACRE
bloodless *adj* **1 syn** see PALE 2
  rel colorless; lifeless
  con alive; vigorous; florid
  ant plethoric; sanguine
  2 syn see INSENSIBLE 5
bloodshed *n syn* see MASSACRE
bloodstained *adj syn* see BLOODY 1
bloodsucker *n syn* see PARASITE
bloodthirsty *adj syn* see MURDEROUS
bloody *adj* **1** affected by or involving the shedding of blood <a *bloody* knife> <when will this long and *bloody* conflict cease?>
  syn bloodstained, ensanguined, gory, imbrued, sanguinary, sanguine, sanguineous
  rel bloodthirsty, grim, murderous, slaughterous; cutthroat, red-handed
  2 syn see MURDEROUS
bloom *n* **1 syn** see FLOWER 1
  2 a state or time of beauty, freshness, and vigor <the *bloom* of youth>
  syn blossom, flush
  rel glow
  3 a rosy appearance of the cheeks <recovered all her health and *bloom*>
  syn blossom, blush, flush, glow
bloom *vb syn* see BLOSSOM
‖**blooming** *adj* **1 syn** see DAMNED 2
  2 syn see UTTER
blooper *n* **1 syn** see ERROR 2
  2 syn see FAUX PAS
blossom *n* **1 syn** see FLOWER 1
  rel capitulum, corymb, cyme, inflorescence, panicle, raceme, spike, umbel
  2 syn see BLOOM 2
  3 syn see BLOOM 3
blossom *vb* to produce flowers or be in flower <lilacs *blossom* in the spring>
  syn bloom, blow, burgeon, effloresce, flower, outbloom
  rel bud; leaf; shoot; open, unfold
  idiom burst into bloom, come into flower, put forth blossoms (*or* flowers *or* bloom)
  con fade, fall, wither
blot *n syn* see STIGMA
  rel blemish, flaw, defect
blot *vb syn* see STAIN 1
blotch *vb syn* see SPLOTCH
blot out *vb* **1 syn** see ERASE
  2 syn see ANNIHILATE 2
‖**blotter** *n syn* see DRUNKARD
‖**blotto** *adj syn* see INTOXICATED 1
bloviate *vb syn* see ORATE
blow *vb* **1** to produce a current of air on <let the wind *blow* your hair dry>
  syn fan, ruffle, wind, winnow
  2 syn see BOAST
  3 syn see PANT 1
  4 syn see WASTE 2

---

syn synonym(s)   *rel* related word(s)
ant antonym(s)   *con* contrasted word(s)
idiom idiomatic equivalent(s)
‖ use limited; if in doubt, see a dictionary

5 *syn* see TREAT 3
‖**6** *syn* see BOTCH
‖**7** *syn* see GO 2
blow *n syn* see BREAK 4
blow *vb syn* see BLOSSOM
blow *n* **1** a forceful sharp stroke (as with the fist or an instrument) <struck him a sudden *blow*>
   syn bang, bash, bastinado, bat, belt, biff, bop, crack, ‖ding, ‖douse, pound, slam, slosh, smack, smash, sock, ‖swap, thwack, wallop, ‖welt, whack, whop; *compare* CUFF, HIT 1
   rel recumbentibus, slug, ‖souse; clip, pelt, plug, punch, swat
   2 *syn* see IMPACT 1
blow–by–blow *adj syn* see CIRCUMSTANTIAL
blowen *n syn* see HARLOT 1
blower *n syn* see BRAGGART
blowhard *n syn* see BRAGGART
‖**blow in** *vb syn* see COME 1
blown–in–the–bottle *adj syn* see AUTHENTIC 2
‖**blow off** *vb syn* see GRIPE
blowoff *n syn* see BINGE 1
‖**blowout** *n syn* see SHINDIG 1
blowsy *adj syn* see SLATTERNLY
   ant spruce
blow up *vb* **1** *syn* see EXPLODE 1
   2 *syn* see DISCREDIT 2
   3 *syn* see ANGER 2
blowy *adj syn* see WINDY 1
blub *vb syn* see CRY 2
blubber *vb syn* see CRY 2
bludgeon *n syn* see CUDGEL
bludgeon *vb syn* see INTIMIDATE
blue *adj* **1** *syn* see DOWNCAST
   2 *syn* see RISQUÉ
   3 *syn* see UTTER
blue *n syn* see OCEAN
blue blood *n* **1** *syn* see GENTLEMAN 1
   2 *syn* see ARISTOCRACY
‖**bluebottle** *n syn* see POLICEMAN
bluecoat *n syn* see POLICEMAN
blue–eyed *adj syn* see FAVORITE 1
blue moon *n syn* see AGE 2
bluenose *n syn* see PRUDE
bluenosed *adj syn* see PRIM 1
blueprint *n syn* see PLAN 1
   rel outline, sketch
blueprint *vb syn* see PLAN 2
blue–ribbon *adj syn* see EXCELLENT
blues *n pl but sometimes sing in constr syn* see SADNESS
bluff *adj* direct and unceremonious in speech or manner <*bluff* aggressive questions>
   syn abrupt, blunt, breviloquent, brief, brusque, crusty, curt, gruff, rough, short, short-spoken, snippety, snippy
   rel hearty, honest, sincere; barefaced, candid, direct, forthright, frank, no-nonsense, outspoken, plainspoken, straightforward; bearish, rude, tactless; sharp, tart; laconic, terse
   idiom to the point
   con civil, courteous, courtly, gallant, polite; diplomatic, urbane
   ant smooth, suave

bluff *vb* **1** *syn* see DECEIVE
   rel fool, joke, trick
   2 *syn* see ASSUME 4
blunder *vb* **1** *syn* see STUMBLE 3
   2 *syn* see WALLOW 2
   3 *syn* see BOTCH
blunder (away) *vb syn* see WASTE 2
blunder *n syn* see ERROR 2
blunderbuss *n syn* see STUMBLEBUM
blunderer *n syn* see STUMBLEBUM
blunt *adj* **1** *syn* see DULL 6
   rel unpointed, unsharp; insensitive
   con acuminate, acute
   ant keen, sharp
   2 *syn* see BLUFF
   con politic, smooth, suave
   ant subtle; tactful
blunt *vb* **1** *syn* see DULL 3
   2 *syn* see DEADEN 1
   3 *syn* see DULL 5
   4 *syn* see WEAKEN 1
‖**blunt** *n syn* see MONEY
blur *n syn* see STIGMA
blur *vb* **1** *syn* see TAINT 1
   2 *syn* see CONFUSE 4
   3 *syn* see DULL 4
blurb *n syn* see PUFF 3
blurt (out) *vb syn* see EXCLAIM
blush *vb* to turn or glow red in the face <*blushed* from embarrassment>
   syn color, crimson, flush, glow, mantle, pink, pinken, redden, rose, rouge
blush *n syn* see BLOOM 3
bluster *vb* **1** *syn* see ROAR
   rel blast, storm, rage
   2 *syn* see INTIMIDATE
blustering *adj syn* see WILD 6
blustery *adj syn* see WILD 6
board *vb* **1** to get aboard of <*boarded* the wrong bus>
   syn embark
   rel embus, emplane, entrain
   idiom get on
   con debus, deplane, detrain; land
   ant debark, disembark, get off
   2 *syn* see HARBOR 2
   rel care (for), cherish, nurture, tend
board *n* **1** **boards** *pl syn* see DRAMA
   2 *syn* see TABLE 1
boast *vb* to express pride in oneself or one's accomplishments <*boasting* about all the girl friends he had>
   syn blow, brag, cock-a-doodle-doo, crow, gasconade, mouth, prate, puff, rodomontade, vaunt
   rel pique, plume, preen, pride, quack; gush, vapor; aggrandize, exalt, glory, triumph; bluster, ‖bounce, bully, ruffle, swash, swashbuckle, swagger; flaunt, parade, show off
   idiom blow one's horn, congratulate oneself, hug oneself, pat oneself on the back
   con belittle, decry, degrade, disparage, knock, minimize, run down
   ant depreciate
boaster *n syn* see BRAGGART

boastful *adj* given to or characterized by boasting
<a *boastful* old windbag>
syn braggadocian, braggart, braggy, rodomontade, self-glorifying, vaunting
rel arrogant, pretentious; cock-a-hoop, exultant; big-headed, conceited, swelled-headed; self-aggrandizing, self-applauding, self-flattering, vainglorious
idiom having a high opinion of oneself, seeing oneself larger than life
con self-depreciating, self-effacing, unassuming; bashful, demure, sheepish, shy, timid; quiet, reserved, restrained, retiring
ant modest

bob *vb syn* see TAP 1

bobbery *n syn* see BRAWL 2

bobble *vb syn* see BOTCH

‖**bobby** *n syn* see POLICEMAN

‖**bodacious** *adj syn* see NOTEWORTHY

bode *vb syn* see AUGUR 2

bodement *n syn* see FORETOKEN

bodiless *adj syn* see IMMATERIAL 1

bodily *adj* of or relating to the human body
<*bodily* pain>
syn carnal, corporal, corporeal, fleshly, physical, somatic
rel animal, sensual
con intellectual, mental, psychic, psychological; spiritual, unworldly

boding *n syn* see FORETOKEN

body *n* 1 *syn* see HUMAN
2 *syn* see CORPSE
3 the main, central, or essential part <the *body* of the discussion dealt with ways to ensure equal opportunities for all>
syn bulk, core, corpus, mass, staple, substance; *compare* ESSENCE 2, SUBSTANCE 2, TENOR 1
rel majority; sum, total, whole; basis, crux, fundamental, gravamen; gist, pith
con angle, aspect, facet, feature, side; accessory, extension, offshoot, side issue
4 a discrete portion of matter <unknown *bodies* in space>
syn bulk, mass, object, volume
5 a determinable or measurable whole <collected a large *body* of evidence>
syn aggregate, amount, budget, bulk, quantity, quantum, total
rel input; extent, range; number, stock, sum, whole
6 *syn* see GROUP 3
7 *syn* see SUBSTANCE 2

body (forth) *vb syn* see REPRESENT 2

boeotian *n syn* see PHILISTINE

bog *n syn* see SWAMP

bog (down) *vb syn* see DELAY 1

bogey *n syn* see APPARITION

boggle *vb* 1 *syn* see DEMUR
2 *syn* see BOTCH
3 *syn* see STAGGER 5

bogus *adj syn* see COUNTERFEIT
rel forged; imitation
con bona fide, good
ant authentic, genuine, real

Bohemian *n* a person (as an artist) who has an unconventional life-style that often reflects protest against or indifference to convention <a gathering place for radicals and *Bohemians*>
syn maverick, nonconformist
rel beat, beatnik, dropout, hippie; iconoclast; eccentric, original; recusant
con conformer, conventionalist, formalist, pedant

bohunk *n syn* see OAF 2

boil *n syn* see ABSCESS

boil *vb* 1 *syn* see SEETHE 4
2 to prepare (as food) in a liquid heated to the point that it begins to give off steam <*boil* eggs>
syn parboil, seethe, simmer, stew
rel coddle, poach; decoct; steam
3 *syn* see ANGER 2
4 *syn* see RUSH 1

boil down *vb syn* see SIMPLIFY

boildown *n syn* see ABRIDGMENT

‖**boiled** *adj syn* see INTOXICATED 1

boiling *adj syn* see HOT 1

boil over *vb syn* see ANGER 2

boisterous *adj* 1 *syn* see TURBULENT 1
2 *syn* see VOCIFEROUS
rel brawling, noisy, riotous, rollicking, rowdy
con sedate, sober, staid; noiseless

‖**boko** *n syn* see NOSE 1

bold *adj* 1 *syn* see BRAVE 1
con pusillanimous, shrinking, timid, timorous
ant cowardly
2 *syn* see WISE 5
rel audacious; bluff
con mousy, quiet, shy
3 *syn* see INSOLENT 2

‖**boldacious** *adj syn* see INSOLENT 2

bold–faced *adj syn* see WISE 5

boldhearted *adj syn* see BRAVE 1

boldness *n syn* see INSOLENCE

bollix *vb syn* see BOTCH

Bolshevik *n syn* see COMMUNIST

‖**Bolshie** *n syn* see COMMUNIST

bolster *vb* 1 *syn* see SUPPORT 4
rel reinforce, strengthen
2 *syn* see SUPPORT 5

bolt *n syn* see THUNDERBOLT

bolt *vb* 1 *syn* see START 1
2 *syn* see RUSH 1
3 *syn* see RUN 2
4 *syn* see EXCLAIM
5 *syn* see GULP

bomb *n* 1 *syn* see FAILURE 5
‖2 *syn* see FORTUNE 4

bomb *vb* 1 *syn* see BOMBARD
2 *syn* see FAIL 4

bombard *vb* to assault with bombs or shells <cities *bombarded* by planes and artillery>
syn blitz, bomb, cannonade, shell
rel barrage, strafe, strike

---

syn synonym(s) *rel* related word(s)
ant antonym(s) *con* contrasted word(s)
idiom idiomatic equivalent(s)
‖ use limited; if in doubt, see a dictionary

idiom open up on, pour a broadside into

bombardment *n syn* see BARRAGE

bombast *n* pretentious inflated speech or writing <adolescent *bombast* about Youth and Destiny>
syn fustian, highfalutin, rant, rhapsody, rhetoric, rodomontade
rel grandiloquence, magniloquence; flatulence, orotundity, tumidity, turgidity; heroics, pyrotechnics, sesquipedality; Johnsonese; spread= eagleism; nonsense
idiom purple prose

bombastic *adj syn* see RHETORICAL
rel flatulent
con unimpassioned; unaffected

‖**bombed** *adj syn* see INTOXICATED 1

bombinate *vb syn* see HUM

bona fide *adj syn* see AUTHENTIC 2

bona fides *n syn* see GOOD FAITH

bonanza *n* a place of great abundance or a source of great wealth or opportunity <the town proved to be a *bonanza* for entrepreneurs>
syn eldorado, Golconda, gold mine, mine, treasure-house, treasure trove, treasury

bond *n* **1** *usu* **bonds** *pl syn* see SHACKLE
2 *syn* see CONTRACT
3 a uniting or binding element or force <the *bonds* of friendship>
syn knot, ligament, ligature, link, nexus, tie, vinculum, yoke
rel bridge, connection, connective, liaison; interrelationship, relationship
4 *syn* see ADHERENCE 1
5 *syn* see GUARANTEE 1

bondage *n* the state of subjection to an owner or master <prisoners sold into *bondage*>
syn enslavement, helotry, peonage, serfage, serfdom, servility, servitude, slavery, thrall, thralldom, villenage, yoke
rel subjection, subjugation
con freedom, independence, liberty

bondman *n syn* see SLAVE 1

bondslave *n syn* see SLAVE 1

bondsman *n syn* see SLAVE 1

bone *n* **1** **bones** *pl syn* see DICE
‖**2** *syn* see DOLLAR

bone (up) *vb syn* see CRAM 4

bone–dry *adj* **1** *syn* see DRY 1
2 *syn* see DRY 3

bonehead *n syn* see DUNCE

boneless *adj syn* see WEAK 4

boner *n* **1** *syn* see ERROR 2
2 *syn* see FAUX PAS

‖**boneyard** *n syn* see CEMETERY

bong *vb syn* see RING

boniface *n syn* see SALOONKEEPER

‖**bonkers** *adj syn* see INSANE 1

bonne bouche *n syn* see DELICACY

‖**bonnet** *n syn* see DECOY 2

‖**bonny** *adj syn* see BEAUTIFUL

bon vivant *n syn* see EPICURE
rel bon viveur, boulevardier, high liver, high roller, man-about-town, sport

bony *adj syn* see LEAN

boo *n syn* see RASPBERRY

boo *n syn* see MARIJUANA

boob *n* **1** *syn* see DUNCE
2 *syn* see PHILISTINE

‖**boo–boo** *n syn* see FAUX PAS

boob tube *n syn* see TELEVISION

booby *n syn* see DUNCE

booby hatch *n syn* see ASYLUM 3

booby trap *n syn* see PITFALL

boodle *n* **1** *syn* see FORTUNE 4
2 *syn* see SPOIL

boodle *vb syn* see CHEAT

boohoo *vb syn* see CRY 2

book *n* **1** a collection of folded, cut, bound, and usually printed sheets <a *book* of poems>
syn tome, volume
rel publication, work, writing; scroll; booklet, brochure, folder, leaflet, magazine, pamphlet; compendium, handbook, manual, monograph, textbook, tract, treatise; codex; novel
2 *cap* **Book** *syn* see BIBLE

book *vb* **1** *syn* see LIST 3
2 *syn* see TIME 1
3 *syn* see RESERVE 2

bookdealer *n* one who deals in books <sold his library to a *bookdealer*>
syn bibliopole, bookman, bookseller
rel bouquiniste

bookie *n syn* see BOOKMAKER

bookish *adj syn* see PEDANTIC
rel booksy, highbrow

book–learned *adj syn* see PEDANTIC

bookmaker *n* one who determines odds and receives and pays off bets <*bookmakers* who welsh on paying off winners>
syn bookie, layer
rel pricemaker; runner

bookman *n syn* see BOOKDEALER

bookseller *n syn* see BOOKDEALER

booky *adj syn* see PEDANTIC

boom *n* **1** *syn* see BANG 2
2 *syn* see PROSPERITY 4

boomerang *vb syn* see BACKFIRE

booming *adj syn* see FLOURISHING

boon *n* **1** *syn* see GIFT 1
2 *syn* see GOOD 1

boon *adj syn* see MERRY

‖**boondocks** *n pl syn* see FRONTIER 2

‖**boonies** *n pl syn* see FRONTIER 2

boor *n* an uncouth ungainly fellow <an ill-mannered *boor*>
syn ‖bosthoon, chuff, churl, clodhopper, clown, grobian, mucker
rel barbarian, vulgarian; looby, lubber; farmer, loon, rustic, swain; ‖carl; bohunk; boob, buffoon, oaf
con slicker, smoothy; gentleman; cosmopolitan, cosmopolite, sophisticate

boorish *adj* uncouth in manner or appearance <a *boorish* fellow lacking all grace>
syn churlish, cloddish, clodhopping, clownish, ill-bred, loutish, lowbred, lubberly, lumpish, robustious, rugged, swainish, uncivilized, uncultured, unpolished, unrefined; *compare* COARSE 3

rel barbarian, barbaric, outlandish, tasteless, vulgar; bucolic, countrified, inurbane, provincial, rustic, yokelish; ill-mannered, impolite, rude, uncivil, ungracious; graceless, unpoised
con cultivated, cultured, refined; suave, urbane; courteous, courtly, genteel, polite, well-bred; graceful, gracious, poised

boost *vb* **1** *syn* see RAISE 9
 2 *syn* see INCREASE 1
 3 *syn* see PROMOTE 3
 ‖**4** *syn* see SHOPLIFT

boost *n* *syn* see RISE 3

‖**booster** *n* *syn* see DECOY 2

boot *n* **1** *syn* see THRILL
 2 *syn* see NOVICE

boot (out) *vb* **1** *syn* see EJECT 1
 2 *syn* see DISMISS 3

‖**boot hill** *n* *syn* see CEMETERY

bootleg *n* *syn* see MOONSHINE 2

bootleg *vb* *syn* see SMUGGLE

bootless *adj* *syn* see FUTILE
 rel frustrating; profitless, worthless

bootlick *vb* *syn* see FAWN

bootlick *n* *syn* see SYCOPHANT

bootlicker *n* *syn* see SYCOPHANT

bootlicking *adj* *syn* see FAWNING

booty *n* *syn* see SPOIL

booze *vb* *syn* see DRINK 3

booze *n* **1** *syn* see LIQUOR 2
 2 *syn* see BINGE 1

‖**boozed** *adj* *syn* see INTOXICATED 1

boozehound *n* *syn* see DRUNKARD

boozer *n* **1** *syn* see DRUNKARD
 ‖**2** *syn* see BAR 5

‖**boozy** *adj* *syn* see INTOXICATED 1

bop *n* *syn* see BLOW 1

borasca *n* *syn* see POVERTY 1

bordello *n* *syn* see BROTHEL

border *n* **1** a line or relatively narrow space that marks the outermost bound of something <the *border* of the rug>
 syn brim, brink, edge, fringe, hem, margin, perimeter, periphery, rim, selvage, skirt, verge; *compare* CIRCUMFERENCE
 rel butts and bounds, lines, metes and bounds; bound, circumference, confine, end, extremity, limit, termination; boundary, frontier, march, pale; beginning, door, entrance, threshold; sideline; lip
 con inside, interior; recesses; center; body, bulk, mass, whole
 2 *syn* see FRONTIER 1

border *vb* **1** to form a border to <hedges *border* the park>
 syn bound, define, edge, fringe, hem, margin, outline, rim, skirt, surround, verge
 rel circumscribe, encircle, enclose, frame; contour, delineate, mark (off), outline, set off; flank, line, side; trim
 2 *syn* see ADJOIN
 3 to come to be closely similiar to a specified thing <ideas that *border* on the absurd>
 syn approach, trench, verge
 rel approximate, compare, near

idiom come close (*or* near) to

bordering *adj* *syn* see ADJACENT 3

borderland *n* *syn* see FRONTIER 1

borderline *adj* *syn* see DOUBTFUL 1

bore *vb* **1** *syn* see PERFORATE
 2 *syn* see GAZE 1

bore *vb* to induce a state of boredom in <*bored* to death by his endless sermon>
 syn ennui, pall, tire, weary
 rel jade; fatigue, wear; annoy, irk, irritate; afflict, bother, discomfort
 idiom put one to sleep
 con amuse, entertain; excite, fascinate, intrigue; absorb, beguile, engross, enthrall, grip; enliven, freshen, invigorate, quicken, stimulate
 ant interest

bore *n* someone or something that is boring <cocktail parties frequented mainly by *bores*>
 syn drag, ‖dullsville, ‖pill
 rel bad news; downer; soporific
 idiom crashing bore

boreal *adj* *syn* see COLD 1

boredom *n* *syn* see TEDIUM
 rel fatigue, weariness; disgust, distaste
 con amusement, diversion, entertainment; excitement, fascination; engrossment, enthrallment

boresome *adj* *syn* see IRKSOME
 rel deadly, dreary, dull, humdrum, monotonous
 con amusing, entertaining; exciting, fascinating, intriguing; absorbing, engrossing, enthralling, gripping, stimulating
 ant interesting

boring *adj* *syn* see IRKSOME

born *adj* *syn* see INHERENT

‖**born** *vb* *syn* see BEAR 5

borné *adj* *syn* see LITTLE 2

bosh *n* *syn* see NONSENSE 2

bosom *n* *syn* see HEART 1

bosomy *adj* *syn* see BUXOM

boss *n* *syn* see LEADER 2

‖**boss** *adj* *syn* see EXCELLENT

boss *vb* *syn* see SUPERVISE

bossy *adj* *syn* see MASTERFUL 1

‖**bosthoon** *n* *syn* see BOOR

Boswell *n* *syn* see BIOGRAPHER

botch *vb* to do or proceed ineffectively or badly through clumsiness, stupidity, or lack of ability <a complete incompetent —*botches* everything he puts his hand to>
 syn ‖blow, blunder, bobble, boggle, bollix, bugger up, bumble, bungle, cobble, dub, flub, fluff, foozle, fumble, goof (up), gum (up), louse up, mess, ‖muck, mucker, muff, ‖screw (up)
 rel butcher, mangle, murder, mutilate; mar, ruin, spoil; destroy, wreck; hash; tinker; misconduct, mishandle, mismanage; confuse, disorder
 idiom ‖drop a clanger, play (*or* wreak) havoc with, play hell with, pull a boner (*or* rock)

---

syn synonym(s)   *rel* related word(s)
ant antonym(s)   *con* contrasted word(s)
idiom idiomatic equivalent(s)
‖ use limited; if in doubt, see a dictionary

botch *n syn* see MESS 3
botchery *n syn* see MESS 3
botchy *adj syn* see SLIPSHOD 3
bother *vb* **1** *syn* see DISCOMPOSE 1
  2 *syn* see ANNOY 1
bother *n* **1** *syn* see ANNOYANCE 2
  2 *syn* see ANNOYANCE 3
  3 *syn* see INCONVENIENCE
botheration *n* **1** *syn* see ANNOYANCE 2
  2 *syn* see ANNOYANCE 3
bothering *n syn* see ANNOYANCE 1
botherment *n syn* see ANNOYANCE 3
bothersomeness *n syn* see INCONVENIENCE
bottega *n syn* see STUDIO
bottle (up) *vb* **1** *syn* see RESTRAIN
  2 *syn* see CORNER
bottom *n* **1** the under surface as opposed to the top surface <gum was stuck to the *bottom* of her shoe>
  syn sole, underneath, underside, undersurface
  rel belly, underbelly, underbody; base, floor, foot, ground
  con acme, apex, cap, crest, crown, tip, upper
  ant top
  2 *syn* see BUTTOCKS
  3 the lower or lowest point <the *bottom* of the page>
  syn base, foot, nadir
  rel basement, floor, ground; end; low
  con acme, apex, pinnacle, zenith
  ant top
  4 *syn* see BASE 1
  5 *syn* see ESSENCE 2
bottom *vb syn* see BASE
bottom *adj* **1** *syn* see BOTTOMMOST
  2 *syn* see FUNDAMENTAL 1
bottom dog *n syn* see VICTIM 2
bottomless *adj* **1** *syn* see BASELESS
  rel reasonless, unjustifiable, unsupportable
  2 extremely deep <the *bottomless* sea>
  syn abysmal, fathomless, plumbless, plummetless, soundless, unfathomable; *compare* DEEP 1
  rel endless, infinite
bottommost *adj* that is at the very bottom <the ladder's *bottommost* rung>
  syn bottom, lowermost, lowest, nethermost, rock-bottom, undermost
  con top, upper, uppermost
  ant topmost
bough *n syn* see LIMB
bought *adj syn* see READY-MADE
‖boughten *adj syn* see READY-MADE
boulevard *n syn* see WAY 1
bounce *vb* **1** *syn* see JUMP 1
  2 *syn* see DISMISS 3
  ‖3 *syn* see INTIMIDATE
bounce (back) *vb* **1** *syn* see RECOVER 3
  2 *syn* see BACKFIRE
bouncer *n* **‖1** *syn* see LIE
  rel exaggeration, hyperbole, overstatement
  idiom tall tale
  2 a person employed to restrain or eject disorderly persons (as at a bar) <tossed out by the *bouncer*>

syn chucker, ‖chucker-out, houseman
  rel goon, muscleman, strong arm
bouncy *adj syn* see ELASTIC 2
bound *n* **1** *usu* **bounds** *pl syn* see ENVIRONS 1
  2 *syn* see LIMIT 1
bound *vb* **1** *syn* see DEMARCATE 1
  2 *syn* see BORDER 1
bound *adj* **1** *syn* see FINITE
  2 obliged to serve a master or in a clearly defined capacity for a certain length of time by the terms of a contract or mutual agreement <brought to the American colonies as a *bound* servant>
  syn apprenticed, articled, indentured
  rel contracted; enslaved
  con free, freed
  3 *syn* see CONSTIPATED
bound *vb syn* see JUMP 1
boundary *n syn* see ENVIRONS 1
bounded *adj syn* see FINITE
  ant unbounded
bounder *n syn* see CAD
boundless *adj syn* see LIMITLESS
bounteous *adj* **1** *syn* see LIBERAL 1
  con cheap, illiberal, scant
  ant niggardly
  2 *syn* see PLENTIFUL
  con insufficient, scant, sparse
bountiful *adj* **1** *syn* see LIBERAL 1
  2 *syn* see PLENTIFUL
bouquet *n* **1** cut flowers arranged for wear or display <a *bouquet* of spring flowers>
  syn nosegay, posy
  rel arrangement; boutonniere, corsage; spray; wreath; garland, festoon; lei
  2 *syn* see COMPLIMENT 1
  3 *syn* see FRAGRANCE
Bourbon *n syn* see REACTIONARY
bout *n* **1** *syn* see SPELL 1
  2 *syn* see SIEGE
boutade *n syn* see CAPRICE
bow *vb syn* see YIELD 2
bow *n* **1** *syn* see CURVE
  2 *syn* see TURN 4
bow *vb syn* see CURVE
bowdlerize *vb syn* see CENSOR
bowed *adj* **1** *syn* see CURVED
  2 *syn* see BOWLEGGED
bowel *vb syn* see EVISCERATE
bower *n syn* see ARBOR
bowery *n syn* see SKID ROW
bowl *n syn* see STADIUM
‖bowl (down *or* out) *vb syn* see WHIP 2
bowl (down *or* over) *vb syn* see FELL 1
bowlegged *adj* having legs bent outward <a *bowlegged* cowboy>
  syn bandy, bandy-legged, bowed
  rel bent, crooked, curved, misshapen
bowwow *n syn* see DOG 1
box *n* **‖1** *syn* see HUT
  ‖2 *syn* see PREDICAMENT
  3 *syn* see TELEVISION
box *n syn* see CUFF
box *vb syn* see SLAP 1

boxing *n* the art of attack and defense with the fists practiced as a sport <he liked *boxing* —at least as a spectator sport>
syn fisticuffs, prizefighting, pugilism, ring

boy *n* **1** a male person not fully matured <a *boy* of nine>
syn lad, laddie, shaveling, son, stripling, tad
rel gamin, ragamuffin, street arab, urchin; hobbledehoy, whippersnapper; schoolboy
idiom little shaver, small fry
2 *syn* see MAN 3

boyfriend *n* **1** a man who is a woman's usual or preferred escort or companion <went to the movies with her *boyfriend*>
syn beau, gentleman friend, swain, young man
rel admirer
2 a man who shares with a woman a strong and usually sexually oriented mutual attraction <this was the *boyfriend* she hoped to marry>
syn beau, beloved, flame, inamorato, lover, steady, sweetheart, truelove
rel crush, heartthrob; fiancé
3 *syn* see LOVER 1

brabble *vb syn* see QUARREL

brabble *n* **1** *syn* see QUARREL
2 *syn* see CHATTER

brace *n* **1** *syn* see COUPLE
2 *syn* see SUPPORT 3
3 braces *pl syn* see SUSPENDERS

brace *vb* **1** *syn* see GIRD 3
2 *syn* see SUPPORT 4
3 *syn* see BEG

bracing *adj syn* see INVIGORATING

bracket *vb* **1** *syn* see JOIN 1
2 *syn* see COMPARE 2

brag *vb syn* see BOAST
con apologize, deprecate

braggadocian *adj syn* see BOASTFUL

braggadocio *n syn* see BRAGGART

braggart *n* one who boasts <too much of a *braggart* about his strength>
syn blower, blowhard, boaster, braggadocio, bragger, ‖gasbag, puckfist, rodomont, rodomontade, vaunter
rel bluffer, blusterer, loudmouth, miles gloriosus, ranter, raver, windbag
con Milquetoast

braggart *adj syn* see BOASTFUL

bragger *n syn* see BRAGGART

braggy *adj syn* see BOASTFUL

Brahmin *n syn* see INTELLECTUAL 2

brain *n* **1** *syn* see MIND 1
2 *syn* see INTELLECT 2
3 *often* **brains** *pl syn* see INTELLIGENCE 1

brainchild *n syn* see INVENTION

brainless *adj syn* see SIMPLE 3

brainpower *n syn* see INTELLIGENCE 1

brainsick *adj syn* see INSANE 1

brainwork *n syn* see THOUGHT 1

brainy *adj syn* see INTELLIGENT 2

brake *vb syn* see HINDER
rel slow, stop

branch *n* **1** *syn* see LIMB
rel branchlet

2 *syn* see CREEK 2

brand *n* **1** *syn* see MARK 7
2 *syn* see STIGMA

brandish *vb syn* see SHOW 4

brand name *n syn* see MARK 7

brand–new *adj* conspicuously new and unused <a *brand-new* car right out of the showroom>
syn fire-new, mint, spang-new, spanking-new, span-new, spick-and-span
rel untouched, unused; clean, fresh, pristine
con hand-me-down, secondhand, used; outworn, shabby, worn, worn-out
ant old

brannigan *n* **1** *syn* see BINGE 1
2 *syn* see QUARREL

brash *adj* **1** *syn* see RASH 1
2 *syn* see EXUBERANT 1
3 *syn* see TACTLESS
4 *syn* see PRESUMPTUOUS
rel bold, brazen; rash, reckless; headlong, impetuous; cocksure

brashness *n* **1** *syn* see TEMERITY
2 *syn* see EFFRONTERY

brass *n* ‖**1** *syn* see MONEY
2 *syn* see EFFRONTERY

brassbound *adj* **1** *syn* see ILLIBERAL
2 *syn* see INFLEXIBLE 2
3 *syn* see PRESUMPTUOUS

brass hat *n syn* see SUPERIOR

brassy *adj* **1** *syn* see SHAMELESS
2 *syn* see BRAZEN 4

brave *adj* **1** having or showing no fear when faced with something dangerous, difficult, or unknown <made a *brave* attempt to save the burning house>
syn audacious, aweless, bold, boldhearted, bravehearted, chin-up, courageous, dauntless, doughty, fearless, gallant, game, greathearted, ‖gutsy, heroic, intrepid, lionhearted, manful, manly, ‖plucked, plucky, soldierly, spunky, stalwart, stout, stouthearted, unafraid, unblenched, unblenching, undauntable, undaunted, unfearful, unfearing, valiant, valorous
rel daring, defiant, gritty, hardy, mettlesome, resolute, spirited, steadfast, unapprehensive, undismayed, unflinching, unfrightened, unquailing, unshrinking, unswerving, unwincing, unyielding, venturesome; chivalrous, noble, preux; confident
con cringing, flinching, frightened, pusillanimous, scared, shrinking, timid; chickenhearted, fainthearted, lily-livered, nerveless, soft, spineless, unmanly, weakhearted, weak-kneed, yellow
ant cowardly, craven
2 *syn* see COLORFUL
3 *syn* see GOOD 1

brave *vb syn* see FACE 3
con avoid

bravehearted *adj syn* see BRAVE 1

---

syn synonym(s)   *rel* related word(s)
ant antonym(s)   *con* contrasted word(s)
idiom idiomatic equivalent(s)
‖ use limited; if in doubt, see a dictionary

bravery *n syn* see FINERY

bravo *n syn* see ASSASSIN

brawl *vb syn* see QUARREL

brawl *n* **1** *syn* see QUARREL

2 a rough, noisy, and often prolonged hand-to-hand fight usually involving several people <windows and furniture were broken in the barroom *brawl*>
syn affray, bobbery, broil, dogfight, donnybrook, fight, fracas, fray, free-for-all, knockdown-and-drag-out, maul, melee, mellay, ‖muss, rough-and-tumble, row, rowdydow, ruction, scrap, scrimmage, scuffle, set-to; *compare* QUARREL
rel fistfight, fisticuffs, slugfest; struggle, tussle; conflict, contention, contest, riot; altercation, embroilment, imbroglio, quarrel, wrangle; commotion, disturbance, eruption, hubbub, pandemonium, ruckus, rumpus, turn-to, ‖turnup, upheaval, uproar; incident, ‖rumble
idiom a coming to blows, exchange of blows

brawling *adj syn* see QUARRELSOME 2

brawlsome *adj syn* see QUARRELSOME 2

brawly *adj syn* see QUARRELSOME 2

brawn *n syn* see MUSCLE 1

brawny *adj syn* see MUSCULAR 2
rel lusty, red-blooded, vigorous, vital; tough
con lanky, lean, rawboned, skinny, thin
ant scrawny

bray *vb syn* see PULVERIZE 1

brazen *adj* **1** *syn* see INSOLENT 2

2 *syn* see SHAMELESS

3 *syn* see GAUDY

4 of the color of polished brass <a *brazen* sky at sunset>
syn aeneous, brassy
rel bronze

brazenfaced *adj syn* see SHAMELESS

breach *n* **1** the act or offense of failing to keep the law or to do what law, duty, or obligation requires <sued for *breach* of contract> <his behavior was a gross *breach* of good manners>
syn contravention, infraction, infringement, transgression, trespass, violation
rel disregard, nonobservance; delinquency, dereliction, neglect
con conformance, conformity, observance
ant observance

2 *syn* see GAP 1

3 an interruption of accustomed friendly relations <a trivial misunderstanding caused a *breach* between the brothers>
syn break, fissure, fracture, rent, rift, rupture, schism, split; *compare* SCHISM 3
rel division, separation, severance; alienation, estrangement; difference, discord, disharmony, dissension, disunity, strife, variance; secession, withdrawal; falling-out, quarrel
idiom parting of ways
con integrity, solidarity, union, unity; communion, community; accord, concord, harmony

4 *syn* see GAP 2

breach *vb* **1** *syn* see OPEN 3
rel bore, penetrate

2 *syn* see VIOLATE 1

bread *n* **1** *syn* see FOOD 1

2 *syn* see LIVING

‖**3** *syn* see MONEY

bread and butter *n syn* see LIVING

breadth *n* **1** *syn* see EXPANSE

2 spaciousness of extent <the *breadth* of his knowledge on the subject is awesome>
syn amplitude, comprehensiveness, fullness, scope, wideness
rel compass, gamut, orbit, range, reach, sweep; expanse, spread, stretch
con limitation, restriction
ant narrowness

breadthen *vb syn* see BROADEN

break *vb* **1** *syn* see GIVE 12

2 *syn* see PLOW

3 *syn* see VIOLATE 1
ant observe

4 *syn* see ESCAPE 1

5 *syn* see FAIL 5
idiom go broke

6 *syn* see RUIN 3

7 *syn* see DEGRADE 1

8 *syn* see DISPROVE 1

9 *syn* see COMMUNICATE 1

10 *syn* see SOLVE 2

11 *syn* see DECODE

12 *syn* see HAPPEN 1

13 *syn* see GET OUT 2

‖**14** *syn* see CLEAR 9

break *n* **1** *syn* see GAP 1

2 *syn* see GAP 3

3 *syn* see INTERLUDE

4 a usually short rest period <took a *break* for coffee>
syn blow, breath, breather, breathing space (or spell), respite, ten; *compare* PAUSE

5 *syn* see BREACH 3

6 *syn* see FAUX PAS

7 *syn* see OPPORTUNITY

breakable *adj syn* see FRAGILE 1

break down *vb* **1** *syn* see ANALYZE

2 *syn* see DECAY

3 *syn* see COLLAPSE 2

breakdown *n* **1** *syn* see NERVOUS BREAKDOWN

2 *syn* see COLLAPSE 2

3 *syn* see ANALYSIS 1

break in *vb* **1** *syn* see HOUSEBREAK
idiom break and enter

2 *syn* see INTERRUPT 2

breakneck *adj syn* see FAST 3

break out *vb syn* see ERUPT 2

breakout *n syn* see ESCAPE 1

breakthrough *n syn* see RISE 3

break up *vb* **1** *syn* see SEPARATE 1

2 *syn* see DISBAND

breakup *n syn* see ANALYSIS 1

breast *n syn* see HEART 1

breast–feed *vb syn* see NURSE 1

breastwork *n syn* see BULWARK

breath *n* **1** *syn* see HINT 2

2 *syn* see BREAK 4

breathe *vb* **1** *syn* see BE

2 *syn* see REST 3

3 to draw (as air) into and expel from the lungs <*breathe* clean air>

syn respire

rel exhale, inhale

4 *syn* see CONFIDE 1

breathe (in) *vb* *syn* see INHALE

breathe (out) *vb* *syn* see EXHALE

breather *n* *syn* see BREAK 4

breathing *n* *syn* see INSTANT 1

breathing space (*or* spell) *n* *syn* see BREAK 4

breathless *adj* **1** *syn* see EAGER

2 *syn* see STUFFY 1

bred–in–the–bone *adj* *syn* see INVETERATE 1

breech *n* *syn* see BUTTOCKS

breed *vb* **1** *syn* see PROCREATE 1

2 *syn* see FATHER 1

3 *syn* see GENERATE 3

4 *syn* see GROW 1

breed *n* *syn* see TYPE

breeding *n* *syn* see CULTURE

rel civility, courtesy, gentility, grace

con barbarism, boorishness; coarseness, grossness; discourtesy, rudeness

ant vulgarity

breeding ground *n* a place or environment which favors growth <the slum was a *breeding ground* for crime>

syn forcing bed, forcing house, hotbed, hothouse

breeze *n* *syn* see SNAP 1

breeze *vb* to proceed quickly and easily <*breezed* through customs>

syn waltz, zip

rel skim, slide, slip

con drag, falter, flag, lag, trail

breezy *adj* **1** *syn* see WINDY 1

2 *syn* see EASYGOING 3

breviary *n* *syn* see ABRIDGMENT

breviate *n* *syn* see ABRIDGMENT

breviloquent *adj* **1** *syn* see CONCISE

2 *syn* see BLUFF

brew *vb* *syn* see LOOM 2

brew *n* *syn* see MISCELLANY 1

bribable *adj* *syn* see VENAL 1

bribe *vb* to give or promise money or favor to a person in a position of trust to influence his judgment or conduct <*bribed* a building inspector>

syn buy, buy off, fix, have, ‖lubricate, sop, square, tamper (with)

rel approach; corrupt, instigate, suborn; soften (up), sweeten

idiom grease the palm (*or* hand), oil the palm (*or* hand), tickle the palm

bridal *n* *syn* see WEDDING

bridewell *n* *syn* see JAIL

bridle *vb* *syn* see RESTRAIN 1

rel repress, suppress; control, manage; govern, rule

con air, express, utter, ventilate, voice

ant vent

brief *adj* **1** *syn* see SHORT 1

rel fleeting, momentary, passing, transient

ant long

2 *syn* see CONCISE

3 *syn* see BLUFF

brief *n* *syn* see ABRIDGMENT

briefly *adv* in a few words <he answered *briefly* and to the point>

syn concisely, in brief, in short, laconically, shortly, succinctly, tersely

rel accurately, crisply, exactly, precisely

idiom in a capsule, in a nutshell, in a word, to make a long story short

con diffusely, long-windedly, profusely, prolixly, protractedly, verbosely, wordily; at length, comprehensively, fully

‖**brig** *n* *syn* see JAIL

brigand *n* *syn* see MARAUDER

bright *adj* **1** shining or glowing with light <the *bright* sun>

syn beaming, brilliant, effulgent, fulgent, incandescent, lambent, lucent, lucid, luminous, lustrous, radiant, refulgent

rel clear, light, undimmed; illuminated, lighted; coruscating, flashing, gleaming, glistening, glittering, scintillating, shimmering, sparkling; blazing, flaming, glowing; burnished, polished, shiny; sunshiny

con dark, dusky, gloomy, murky, tenebrous; colorless, drab, dreary, lackluster, leaden; somber; cloudy, gray, overcast, shadowy; moonless, starless, sunless; faint, pale, weak

ant dim; dull

2 *syn* see COLORFUL

3 *syn* see GLAD 2

4 *syn* see FAVORABLE 5

5 *syn* see INTELLIGENT 2

rel advanced, precocious

con retarded

ant dense, dull

6 *syn* see LIVELY 1

brilliant *adj* **1** *syn* see BRIGHT 1

ant subdued

2 *syn* see INTELLIGENT 2

rel erudite, learned; sage, wise

brim *n* *syn* see BORDER 1

brimful *adj* **1** *syn* see FULL 1

2 *syn* see BIG 3

brimming *adj* **1** *syn* see FULL 1

2 *syn* see BIG 3

brine *n* *syn* see OCEAN

bring *vb* **1** *syn* see CONVERT 1

‖**2** *syn* see ACCOMPANY

3 *syn* see SELL 4

bring about *vb* *syn* see EFFECT 1

bring around *vb* *syn* see INDUCE 1

bring down *vb* *syn* see FELL 1

bring forth *vb* *syn* see BEAR 5

bring in *vb* **1** *syn* see YIELD 5

2 *syn* see SELL 4

3 *syn* see EARN 1

---

syn synonym(s)   *rel* related word(s)

ant antonym(s)   *con* contrasted word(s)

idiom idiomatic equivalent(s)

‖ use limited; if in doubt, see a dictionary

bring off *vb syn* see EFFECT 2

bring out *vb syn* see SAY 1

bring up *vb* **1** to give a child a parent's fostering care <the orphan was *brought up* by his aunt>
syn ‖fetch up, raise, rear
rel breed, cultivate, foster, nurture; feed, nourish, provide (for); discipline, educate, train
con abuse, ill-use, maltreat; neglect
2 *syn* see STOP 4
3 *syn* see REFER 3
4 *syn* see BROACH
5 *syn* see VOMIT

brink *n* **1** *syn* see BORDER 1
2 *syn* see VERGE 2

‖**briny** *n syn* see OCEAN

brio *n syn* see SPIRIT 5

brisk *adj syn* see AGILE
rel adroit; quick
con inactive, torpid
ant sluggish

brisky *adj syn* see AGILE

bristle *vb syn* see ANGER 2

brittle *adj syn* see SHORT 6

broach *n syn* see BROOCH

broach *vb* to open up (a subject) for discussion <would be awkward to *broach* the matter now>
syn bring up, introduce, moot, ventilate
rel interject, interpose; mention, speak (about); propose, suggest
con hush (up), quash, stifle, suppress; black out, censor

broad *adj* **1** *syn* see LIBERAL 3
2 *syn* see EXTENSIVE 1
3 *syn* see RISQUÉ

broadcast *n syn* see DECLARATION

broadcast *vb* **1** *syn* see STREW 1
2 *syn* see DECLARE 1
rel communicate, radio, televise, transmit
idiom spread a report, spread far and wide

broaden *vb* to grow or become broad or broader <the street *broadens* into an avenue>
syn breadthen, widen
rel expand; spread (out); open
con contract, shrink; slim, thin
ant narrow

broad–minded *adj syn* see LIBERAL 3

broadside *n syn* see BARRAGE

Brobdingnagian *adj syn* see HUGE

brocard *n syn* see MAXIM

‖**brogue** *vb syn* see IDLE

broil *vb syn* see BURN 3

broil *n syn* see BRAWL 2

broiling *adj syn* see HOT 1

broke *adj syn* see POOR 1

broken–down *adj syn* see SHABBY 1

broker *n syn* see GO-BETWEEN 2

bromide *n syn* see COMMONPLACE

bromidic *adj syn* see ARID 2

‖**Bronx cheer** *n syn* see RASPBERRY

brooch *n* an ornament with a pin or clasp now worn usually by women <a diamond *brooch*>
syn broach, clip, pin

brood *n syn* see OFFSPRING

brood *vb* **1** *syn* see SET 11

2 *syn* see MOPE 1

brook *vb syn* see BEAR 10

brook *n syn* see CREEK 2

brothel *n* an establishment where prostitutes ply their trade <madam of the local *brothel*>
syn bagnio, bawdy house, bordello, call house, cathouse, crib, disorderly house, fancy house, ‖hookshop, ‖joyhouse, lupanar, parlor house, seraglio, sporting house, stew, whorehouse
idiom house of ill fame (*or* repute), house of prostitution

brotherhood *n syn* see ASSOCIATION 2

brouhaha *n* **1** *syn* see DIN
2 *syn* see COMMOTION 3

brow *n syn* see FOREHEAD

browbeat *vb syn* see INTIMIDATE

browbeater *n syn* see BULLY 1

brownie *n syn* see FAIRY

‖**brownnose** *vb syn* see FAWN

‖**brownnose** *n syn* see SYCOPHANT

‖**brownnoser** *n syn* see SYCOPHANT

brown study *n syn* see REVERIE

browse *vb* to read through, study, or examine cursorily <*browsed* through the book looking for illustrations>
syn dip (into), flip (through), glance (at *or* over), leaf (through), riff (through), riffle (through), run (through *or* over), scan, skim (through), thumb (through)
rel go (through *or* over), look (over), peruse, skip (through)
idiom give the once over, run the eye over
con examine, study; delve (into), dig (into)
ant pore (over)

bruise *n* an injury involving rupture of small blood vessels and discoloration without break in the overlying skin <got an ugly *bruise* when he fell>
syn contusion; *compare* BLACK EYE
rel ‖boo-boo; abrasion, scrape, scratch
idiom black-and-blue spot (*or* mark)

bruise *vb* **1** to inflict a bruise on <fell down and *bruised* his hip>
syn black, contuse
rel batter, ‖bung up
2 *syn* see CRUSH 2

bruit (about) *vb syn* see DECLARE 1
rel hint, intimate, rumor, suggest

bruja *n syn* see WITCH 1

brume *n syn* see HAZE 1

brummagem *adj syn* see COUNTERFEIT

brunet *adj syn* see DARK 3

brush *vb* to touch or strike lightly (as in passing) <they *brushed* fenders but no real damage was done>
syn glance, graze, kiss, shave, skim
rel bump, clash, collide, sideswipe; clip, contact, scrape, touch

brush *n* **1** *syn* see ENCOUNTER
rel clash, engagement
2 *syn* see CLASH 2

brush up *vb syn* see TOUCH UP

brusque *adj syn* see BLUFF

brutal *adj* **1** *syn* see BRUTISH

2 syn see SEVERE 3

brutalize *vb syn* see DEBASE 1

brute *adj syn* see BRUTISH

brute *n syn* see BEAST

brutish *adj* marked by animal traits and by a lack of man's dignity or refinement <a graceless *brutish* hulk of a man>
syn animal, beastly, bestial, brutal, brute, feral, ferine, swinish
rel animalistic; coarse, crude; base, low, mean, scurvy, vile

bubble *vb* **1 syn** see SLOSH 1
  2 syn see SEETHE 4

bubble *n syn* see PIPE DREAM

buccaneer *n syn* see PIRATE

buck *n* **1 syn** see MAN 3
  2 syn see FOP
  ‖**3 syn** see DOLLAR
  4 syn see SAWHORSE

buck *vb* **1 syn** see RESIST
  2 syn see CARRY 1
  3 syn see PASS 9

buck (off) *vb syn* see THROW 2

buck *vb syn* see PULVERIZE 1

‖**bucket** *n syn* see JAIL

bucket *vb syn* see HURRY 2

‖**bucket shop** *n syn* see BAR 5

buckle (down) *vb* **1 syn** see ADDRESS 3
  2 syn see PITCH IN 1

buckle (under) *vb syn* see YIELD 2

buckram *adj syn* see STIFF 4

buck up *vb syn* see COMFORT

bucolic *adj syn* see RURAL
  ant urbane

bucolic *n syn* see RUSTIC

bud *n* **1 syn** see CHILD 1
  2 syn see SEED 2

buddy *n syn* see ASSOCIATE 3

‖**buddy–buddy** *adj syn* see INTIMATE 4

‖**budge** *n syn* see LIQUOR 2

budget *n syn* see BODY 5

budtime *n syn* see SPRING 5

buff *n syn* see ADDICT

buff *vb syn* see POLISH 1

buffalo *vb* **1 syn** see FRUSTRATE 1
  2 syn see NONPLUS 1

buff–bare *adj syn* see NUDE 2

buffet *n syn* see CUFF

buffet *vb* **1 syn** see SLAP 1
  2 syn see BEAT 1

‖**buffet** *n syn* see EATING HOUSE

‖**bufflehead** *n syn* see DUNCE

‖**buffle–headed** *adj syn* see SIMPLE 3

buffoon *n syn* see CLOWN 3

‖**buffy** *adj syn* see INTOXICATED 1

bug *n syn* see ENTHUSIAST

‖**bug** *vb syn* see ANNOY 1

bugbear *n syn* see ABOMINATION 1

‖**bugger** *n syn* see SNOT 1

‖**bugger** *vb syn* see EXHAUST 4

bugger up *vb syn* see BOTCH

‖**buggy** *adj* **1 syn** see ENTHUSIASTIC
  2 syn see INSANE 1

‖**buggy** *n syn* see CAR

‖**bughouse** *n syn* see ASYLUM 3

‖**bughouse** *adj syn* see INSANE 1

bug off *vb syn* see GET OUT 1

‖**bugs** *adj* **1 syn** see INSANE 1
  2 syn see ENTHUSIASTIC

build *vb* **1** to form or fashion a structure <will *build* either a garage or carport>
syn construct, erect, put up, raise, rear, uprear; *compare* ERECT 3, MAKE 3
rel fabricate, fashion, frame, manufacture; run up, throw up; prefabricate
con demolish, destroy, dismantle, level, pull down, raze, take down, tear down, wreck
  2 syn see MAKE 3
  3 syn see INCREASE 1
  4 syn see INCREASE 2

build (on) *vb syn* see RELY (on *or* upon)

build *n syn* see PHYSIQUE
rel conformation

building *n* a usually roofed and walled structure built for permanent use <a *building* with four apartments>
syn fabric, structure; *compare* EDIFICE, HUT

build up *vb* **1 syn** see ERECT 5
  2 syn see PUBLICIZE

buildup *n syn* see PUBLICITY

‖**built** *adj* **1 syn** see CURVACEOUS
  2 syn see BUXOM

built–in *adj syn* see INHERENT

bulge *vb* to extend outward beyond the usual or normal line <the box was so full that the sides *bulged*>
syn beetle, jut, overhang, poke, pouch, pout, project, protrude, protuberate, stand out, stick out
rel bag, belly, dilate, distend, expand, swell

bulge *n* **1 syn** see PROJECTION 1
rel bump, lump, swelling
con depression, hollow, pit
  2 syn see ADVANTAGE 3

bulk *n* **1** a body of usually material substance that constitutes a thing or unit <his industry was proven by the *bulk* of his accomplishment> <a great dark *bulk* blocked the alley>
syn mass, volume
rel bigness, greatness, largeness, magnitude, quantity, totality
  2 syn see BODY 4
  3 syn see BODY 5
  4 syn see BODY 3

bulk *vb syn* see LOOM 3

bull *n* **1 syn** see ERROR 2
  ‖**2 syn** see NONSENSE 2
  ‖**3 syn** see POLICEMAN

bull *adj syn* see LARGE 1

‖**bull band** *n syn* see SHIVAREE

bulldoze *vb* **1 syn** see INTIMIDATE
rel menace, threaten; harass, harry
  2 syn see PUSH 2

---

syn synonym(s)   *rel* related word(s)
ant antonym(s)   *con* contrasted word(s)
idiom idiomatic equivalent(s)
‖ use limited; if in doubt, see a dictionary

bulldozer *n syn* see BULLY 1

bullet *vb syn* see HURRY 2

bullfighter *n* one who fights bulls <moved with the grace of an experienced *bullfighter*>
syn matador, toreador, torero
rel banderillero; cuadrillero, picador; cuadrilla

bullheaded *adj syn* see OBSTINATE

bullwork *n syn* see WORK 2

bully *n* 1 an insolent, overbearing person who persists in tormenting another <a big *bully* who picked on little kids>
syn browbeater, bulldozer, harasser, harrier, hector, intimidator; *compare* TOUGH
rel annoyer, antagonizer, heckler, persecutor, pest, tease, tormenter
2 *syn* see PIMP 1

bully *adj syn* see EXCELLENT

bully *vb syn* see INTIMIDATE
rel torment, torture; menace, threaten
ant coax

bullyboy *n syn* see TOUGH

bullyrag *vb* 1 *syn* see INTIMIDATE
2 *syn* see BAIT 2

bulwark *n* an aboveground defensive structure that forms part of a fortification <the *bulwarks* were woefully undermanned>
syn bastion, breastwork, parapet, rampart
rel citadel, fort, fortress, stronghold
con bunker, dugout

bulwark *vb syn* see DEFEND 1

‖**bum** *vb syn* see HUM

bum *vb syn* see IDLE

bum *n* 1 *syn* see VAGABOND
2 *syn* see SLUGGARD

‖**bum** *adj syn* see BAD 1

bum *n syn* see BINGE 1

bumble *vb syn* see HUM

bumble *vb* 1 *syn* see BOTCH
2 *syn* see STUMBLE 3

bumbling *adj syn* see AWKWARD 2

‖**bumfuzzle** *vb syn* see CONFUSE 2

bummel *vb syn* see SAUNTER

bummer *n* 1 *syn* see BEGGAR 1
2 *syn* see MARAUDER
3 *syn* see FAILURE 5

bumming *n syn* see MENDICANCY

bump *vb* 1 to meet with or come up against forcibly <the two cars *bumped* with a great crumpling of fenders>
syn clash, collide, ‖prang
rel bang, carom, crash, hit, knock, slam, strike; impinge; jar, jolt
idiom whang together
2 *syn* see HAPPEN 2
3 *syn* see DEGRADE 1

bump *n* 1 *syn* see IMPACT 1
2 a swelling of tissue usually resulting from a blow <fell and got a *bump* on his head>
syn bunch, knot, lump, ‖pumpknot
rel protuberance, swelling
3 a marked unevenness in a road surface likely to jolt a passing vehicle
syn ‖cahot, thank-you-ma'am
rel chuckhole, mudhole, pothole, rut

4 *syn* see GIFT 2

bumpkin *n syn* see RUSTIC

bump off *vb syn* see MURDER 1

‖**bump-off** *n syn* see MURDER

bunch *n* 1 *syn* see BUMP 2
2 *syn* see GROUP 3
3 *syn* see SET 5
4 *syn* see GROUP 1

bunco steerer *n syn* see SWINDLER

bundle *n* 1 *syn* see GROUP 3
2 *syn* see FORTUNE 4

bundle up *vb* to dress warmly <*bundle up*, it's cold outside>
syn ‖hap, muffle, wrap (up)
rel envelop, mummify, swaddle, swathe

‖**bung** *vb syn* see THROW 1

bung-full *adj syn* see FULL 1

bungle *vb syn* see BOTCH

bungle *n syn* see ERROR 2

bungler *n syn* see STUMBLEBUM

‖**bung up** *vb syn* see BATTER 1

bunk *vb syn* see HARBOR 2

‖**bunk** *vb syn* see ESCAPE 1

‖**bunk** *n syn* see NONSENSE 2

‖**bunk** *vb syn* see DECEIVE

bunkum *n syn* see NONSENSE 2

‖**bunkum** *adj* 1 *syn* see EXCELLENT
2 *syn* see HEALTHY 1

bunny *n syn* see BEAUTY
rel bimbo

buns *n pl syn* see BUTTOCKS

Bunyanesque *adj syn* see HUGE

buoy (up) *vb syn* see SUPPORT 5

buoyancy *n syn* see EBULLIENCE

buoyant *adj syn* see ELASTIC 2

burble *vb* 1 *syn* see SLOSH 1
2 *syn* see CHAT 1

burden *n* 1 *syn* see LOAD 1
2 *syn* see LOAD 3

burden *vb* to lay a heavy load on or to lie like a heavy load on a person or thing <*burdened* his men with needless heavy work><I won't *burden* you with this lengthy story>
syn charge, clog, cumber, encumber, lade, load, lumber, saddle, task, tax, weigh, weight
rel overburden, overload, overweigh; handicap; afflict, oppress
idiom bear down on (*or* upon)
con alleviate, ease, lighten, relieve, unload; disburden, disencumber
ant unburden

burden *n syn* see SUBSTANCE 2

burdensome *adj syn* see ONEROUS

burdensomely *adv syn* see HARD 8

bureaucrat *n* a member of a bureaucracy <*bureaucrats* were blamed for the error>
syn mandarin
rel civil servant, functionary, official

burg *n* a small, insignificant, remote town <the *burg* had only two stores and one gas station>
syn hick town, jerkwater town, mudhole, one-horse town, Podunk, tank town, whistle-stop
rel cowtown; crossroads; jumping-off place; hamlet, village

con city, metropolis
burgee *n syn* see FLAG
burgeon *vb* **1** *syn* see INCREASE 2
   2 *syn* see BLOSSOM
burghal *adj syn* see URBAN
burgher *n syn* see TOWNSMAN
burglarize *vb* to commit an act of breaking open and entering with a felonious purpose the dwelling house of another by night <that night several homes were *burglarized*>
   syn burgle; *compare* HOUSEBREAK, ROB 1
   rel knock over, rob; ransack, rifle; screw
burgle *vb syn* see BURGLARIZE
burial *n* **1** *syn* see GRAVE
   2 the act or ceremony of burying <his *burial* took place yesterday>
   syn entombment, inhumation, interment, sepulture
   rel burying, exequies, funeral, obsequies; deposition; deep six
   con disinterment, exhumation
burial ground *n syn* see CEMETERY
buried *adj syn* see ULTERIOR
burke *vb* **1** *syn* see SUPPRESS 3
   2 *syn* see SKIRT 3
burlesque *n* **1** *syn* see MOCKERY 2
   2 *syn* see CARICATURE 2
burlesque *vb syn* see MIMIC
burly *adj syn* see HUSKY 1
‖**burn** *n syn* see CREEK 2
burn *vb* **1** *syn* see SHINE 1
   2 to undergo combustion <the wood is too green to *burn*>
   syn combust
   rel fire, flame, ignite, incinerate, kindle, light; consume, use; smolder, sputter
   3 to be hot as if on fire <sand *burning* in the blazing sun>
   syn bake, broil, cook, melt, roast, scorch, swelter
   rel parch, toast, warm; char
   con chill, cool, freeze
   4 *syn* see ANGER 2
   5 *syn* see SMART
   6 *syn* see FIRE 6
   ‖**7** *syn* see CHEAT
burn (up) *vb syn* see IRRITATE
burnable *adj syn* see COMBUSTIBLE 1
burning *adj* **1** on fire <the *burning* house>
   syn ablaze, afire, aflame, alight, blazing, conflagrant, fiery, flaming, flaring, ignited, lighted
   rel aglow, glowing, incandescent
   idiom in flames
   con burned-out, cold
   2 *syn* see HOT 1
   ant icy
   3 *syn* see FEVERISH 2
   4 *syn* see IMPASSIONED
   5 *syn* see PRESSING
burnish *vb syn* see POLISH 1
burnished *adj syn* see LUSTROUS 1
burn off *vb syn* see CLEAR 9
burnsides *n pl syn* see SIDE-WHISKERS
burp *vb syn* see BELCH 1

burro *n syn* see DONKEY 1
burrow *n* **1** *syn* see LAIR 1
   2 *syn* see HOVEL
burrow *vb syn* see SNUGGLE
burst *vb* **1** *syn* see EXPLODE 1
   2 *syn* see SHATTER 1
   3 *syn* see PLUNGE 2
burst (forth) *vb syn* see ERUPT 2
burst *n* **1** *syn* see OUTBREAK 1
   2 *syn* see OUTBURST 1
   3 *syn* see BANG 2
   4 *syn* see BARRAGE
bury *vb* **1** to deposit (a corpse) in or as if in the earth <the pharaohs were *buried* in pyramids> <*buried* at sea>
   syn entomb, inhume, inter, lay away, plant, put away, sepulcher, sepulture, tomb; *compare* ENTOMB 1
   rel inurn; coffin
   idiom consign to the grave, lay to rest, put six feet under
   con dig (up), disentomb, disinter, exhume, untomb; burn, cremate
   2 *syn* see HIDE
burying ground *n syn* see CEMETERY
‖**bus** *n syn* see CAR
bush *n syn* see FRONTIER 2
bush *adj syn* see MINOR 2
bush–league *adj syn* see MINOR 2
‖**bush up** *vb syn* see HIDE
bushwa *n syn* see NONSENSE 2
business *n* **1** *syn* see FUNCTION 1
   2 *syn* see PATRONAGE 2
   3 *syn* see WORK 1
   4 activity concerned with the supplying and distribution of commodities <the lumber *business* depends heavily on the housing *business*>
   syn commerce, industry, trade, traffic
   5 *syn* see ENTERPRISE 3
   6 *syn* see AFFAIR 1
   7 *syn* see DOODAD
   8 something personal to oneself <that is none of your *business*>
   syn affair, concern, lookout, occasions, palaver
businessman *n syn* see MERCHANT
buss *vb syn* see KISS 1
bust *vb* **1** *syn* see RUIN 3
   2 *syn* see DEGRADE 1
   ant promote
   3 *syn* see FAIL 5
   ‖**4** *syn* see ARREST 2
bust *n* ‖**1** *syn* see CUFF
   2 *syn* see FAILURE 5
   3 *syn* see BINGE 1
   4 *syn* see RAID 2
   ‖**5** *syn* see ARREST
‖**busthead** *n syn* see MOONSHINE 2
bustle *vb syn* see HURRY 2
bustle *n* **1** *syn* see STIR 1

---

syn synonym(s)   *rel* related word(s)
ant antonym(s)   *con* contrasted word(s)
idiom idiomatic equivalent(s)
‖ use limited; if in doubt, see a dictionary

2 *syn* see COMMOTION 4

bustling *adj* full of activity <a *bustling* frontier town>
  syn busy, fussy, hopping, humming, hustling, lively, popping
  rel active, brisk, energetic
  idiom on its way, on the go (*or* move), up and doing

busty *adj syn* see BUXOM

busy *adj* **1** engaged in activity <I can't stop to talk. I'm *busy*>
  syn employed, engaged, occupied, working; *compare* ASSIDUOUS
  idiom at work, on the fly
  con idle, inactive
  ant free
  2 *syn* see BUSTLING
  3 *syn* see IMPERTINENT 2

busy *vb syn* see ENGAGE 4

busybody *n* one who concerns himself with affairs not his own <a meddlesome *busybody* who saw all and tattled all she saw>
  syn butt-in, ‖buttinsky, intermeddler, kibitzer, meddler, Meddlesome Mattie, nose, nosey Parker, Paul Pry, polypragmatist, pragmatic, pragmatist, prier (*or* pryer), quidnunc, rubber, rubberneck, snoop, ‖stickybeak; *compare* GOSSIP 1, INFORMER
  rel gossip, gossipmonger, newsmonger, rumormonger, scandalmonger, tabby, talebearer, telltale
  idiom curiosity shop, question box

busybody *vb* **1** *syn* see SNOOP
  2 *syn* see MEDDLE

but *conj* **1** *syn* see ONLY
  2 *syn* see EXCEPT 1

but *prep syn* see EXCEPT

but *adv* **1** *syn* see ONLY 1
  2 *syn* see JUST 3

butcher *vb* **1** *syn* see SLAUGHTER 1
  2 *syn* see SLAUGHTER 2

butchery *n syn* see MASSACRE

butt *n* **1** *syn* see TARGET 1
  2 *syn* see LAUGHINGSTOCK
  3 *syn* see FOOL 3

butt (on *or* against) *vb syn* see ADJOIN

‖**butt** *n* **1** *syn* see BUTTOCKS
  2 *syn* see CIGARETTE

butt *n syn* see CASK

butterball *n syn* see FATTY

butt in *vb* **1** *syn* see INTRUDE 1
  con abstain, forbear, restrain
  2 *syn* see MEDDLE

butt–in *n syn* see BUSYBODY

‖**buttinsky** *n syn* see BUSYBODY

buttocks *n pl* the part of the back on which a person sits <gave the boy a whack across the *buttocks*>
  syn backside, beam, behind, bottom, breech, buns, ‖butt, ‖can, cheeks, derriere, ‖duff, fanny, fundament, hams, haunches, heinie (*or* hiney), hind end, ‖hinder, hunkers, ‖keister, nates, podex, posterior, rear, rear end, rump, seat, ‖stern, tail, tail end, ‖tokus

idiom seat of one's pants

button–down *adj syn* see CONVENTIONAL 1

buttress *n syn* see SUPPORT 3

buttress *vb syn* see SUPPORT 4

buvette *n syn* see BAR 4

buxom *adj* having an amply developed bosom <a *buxom* young woman>
  syn bosomy, ‖built, busty, chesty, full-bosomed, ‖stacked; *compare* CURVACEOUS
  rel full-figured, Junoesque, shapely, well-developed, well-proportioned

buy *vb* **1** to acquire something for money or the equivalent <*bought* a new car>
  syn purchase, take
  rel acquire, get, obtain, procure
  ant sell
  2 *syn* see RANSOM
  3 *syn* see BRIBE
  ‖**4** *syn* see BELIEVE 1

buy *n syn* see BARGAIN 1

buyable *adj syn* see VENAL 1

buyer *n syn* see PURCHASER

buy off *vb syn* see BRIBE

buzz *vb* **1** *syn* see HUM
  2 *syn* see HISS
  ‖**3** *syn* see TELEPHONE

buzz *n syn* see REPORT 1

‖**buzzed** *adj syn* see INTOXICATED 1

buzz off *vb syn* see GET OUT 1

by *prep* **1** *syn* see BESIDE 1
  2 *syn* see NEAR 2
  3 *syn* see VIA 1
  4 *syn* see VIA 2
  5 with reference to <sorted *by* color>
  syn according to, as to

by *adv syn* see OVER 5

by *interj syn* see GOOD-BYE

by all odds *adv syn* see FAR AND AWAY

by a long shot *adv syn* see FAR AND AWAY

by and by *adv* **1** *syn* see AFTER
  2 *syn* see PRESENTLY 1

by–and–by *n syn* see FUTURE

by and large *adv syn* see ALTOGETHER 3

by–blow *n syn* see BASTARD 1

by dint of *prep syn* see VIA 2

bye–bye *interj syn* see GOOD-BYE

by far *adv syn* see FAR AND AWAY

bygone *adj* **1** *syn* see FORMER 2
  2 *syn* see OLD-FASHIONED
  3 *syn* see EXTINCT 2

by long odds *adv syn* see FAR AND AWAY

by means of *prep syn* see VIA 2

byname *n syn* see NICKNAME

by odds *adv syn* see FAR AND AWAY

by ordinary *adv syn* see USUALLY 2

bypass *vb* **1** *syn* see SKIRT 2
  2 *syn* see SKIRT 3

byplace *n syn* see NOOK

by–product *n syn* see OUTGROWTH 2

by–sitter *n syn* see SPECTATOR

bystander *n syn* see SPECTATOR

by stealth *adv syn* see SECRETLY

by–talk *n syn* see SMALL TALK

by the bye *adv syn* see INCIDENTALLY 2

by the way *adv syn* see INCIDENTALLY 2
by–the–way *adj syn* see INDIFFERENT 2
by virtue of *prep syn* see VIA 2
by way of *prep* 1 *syn* see VIA 1
  2 *syn* see VIA 2

byword *n* 1 *syn* see SAYING
  2 *syn* see CATCHWORD
  3 *syn* see NICKNAME
Byzantine *adj syn* see COMPLEX 2

---

syn synonym(s)   *rel* related word(s)
ant antonym(s)   *con* contrasted word(s)
idiom idiomatic equivalent(s)
‖ use limited; if in doubt, see a dictionary

C

cab *n syn* see TAXICAB

‖**cab** *n syn* see CRUD

cabal *n* **1** *syn* see CLIQUE

  2 *syn* see PLOT 2

cabalistic *adj syn* see MYSTERIOUS

cabaret *n syn* see NIGHTCLUB

‖**cabbage** *n syn* see MONEY

cabbage *vb syn* see STEAL 1

cabbagehead *n syn* see DUNCE

cabin *n syn* see HUT

‖**caboose** *n syn* see HUT

‖**caboose** *n syn* see JAIL

‖**ca' canny** *n syn* see SLOWDOWN 2

cache *vb syn* see HIDE

  con discover, unearth

cachet *n syn* see STATUS 2

‖**cack** *vb syn* see VOMIT

cackle *vb syn* see CHAT 1

cackle *n syn* see CHATTER

cacophonic *adj syn* see DISSONANT 1

cacophonous *adj syn* see DISSONANT 1

cad *n* a person without gentlemanly instincts
  <gloated over his rival's distress like the *cad* that
  he was>
  syn bounder, cur, rotter, yellow dog
  rel boor, churl, clown, lout; guttersnipe,
  mucker, vulgarian; ‖creep; bastard, heel, louse,
  rat, stinker
  idiom Jack Nasty
  ant gentleman

cadaver *n syn* see CORPSE

cadaverous *adj* **1** *syn* see GHASTLY 2

  2 *syn* see EMACIATED

  rel careworn, haggard, pinched, worn

cadence *n syn* see RHYTHM

  rel accent, accentuation, emphasis, stress; pulsation, pulse, throb

cadency *n syn* see RHYTHM

‖**cadet** *n syn* see PIMP 1

cadger *n syn* see BEGGAR 1

cadging *n syn* see MENDICANCY

caducity *n syn* see OLD AGE

  rel dotage, dotingness, second childhood

café *n* **1** *syn* see EATING HOUSE

  2 *syn* see NIGHTCLUB

‖**caff** *n syn* see EATING HOUSE

cage *vb syn* see ENCLOSE 1

  rel imprison, incarcerate, jail

cagey *adj syn* see SHREWD

cageyness *n syn* see CUNNING 2

cahoots *n pl syn* see ASSOCIATION 1

‖**cahot** *n syn* see BUMP 3

cajole *vb syn* see COAX

  rel beguile, deceive, delude; tantalize; crowd,
  push

cake *vb* **1** to cover with a surface layer <the floor
  was *caked* with filth>
  syn crust, encrust (*or* incrust), incrustate, rime

  rel besmear, coat, smear, spread; cover, daub

  2 *syn* see HARDEN 1

  rel compress, condense, contract, shrink

cakewalk *n syn* see RUNAWAY

‖**calaboose** *n syn* see JAIL

calamitous *adj* **1** *syn* see FATAL 2

  2 *syn* see DEPLORABLE

calamity *n syn* see DISASTER

  rel collapse, ruin, wreck; affliction, cross, trial,
  tribulation, visitation
  con fortune, luck; benefaction; favor, gift
  ant boon

calamity howler *n syn* see PESSIMIST

calculate *vb* to determine or approximate a mathematical value (as speed, cost, or quantity) <*calculate* the cost of a new car>
  syn cipher, compute, estimate, figure, reckon
  rel consider, study, weigh; ascertain, determine,
  discover; appraise, evaluate, price, value; assess,
  prize, rate
  con conjecture, guess, surmise

calculate (on *or* upon) *vb syn* see RELY (on *or*
  upon)

calculating *adj syn* see CAUTIOUS

  rel artful, crafty, cunning, guileful, sly, wily
  con improvident, imprudent, indiscreet
  ant rash, reckless

calculation *n syn* see COMPUTATION

calembour *n syn* see PUN

calendar *n syn* see PROGRAM 1

calenture *n syn* see PASSION 6

caliber *n* **1** *syn* see QUALITY 2

  rel ability, capability, capacity; force, power

  2 *syn* see QUALITY 3

caliginous *adj syn* see DARK 1

call *vb* **1** to speak or utter in a loud distinct carrying voice <*call* for help>
  syn cry, hallo, holler, hollo, shout, vociferate,
  yell; *compare* SHOUT 1
  rel bawl, bellow, hoot, howl, roar, scream,
  screech, shriek, shrill, whoop, yowl
  con murmur, whisper

  2 *syn* see DEMAND 1

  3 *syn* see SUMMON 2

  rel assemble, collect, gather, round up; bid, invite

  4 *syn* see CONVOKE

  5 *syn* see TELEPHONE

  6 *syn* see NAME 1

  7 *syn* see PREDICT 2

  8 *syn* see ESTIMATE 3

  9 *syn* see FORETELL

  10 *syn* see VISIT 2

call (for) *vb syn* see DEMAND 2

call (to) *vb syn* see ADDRESS 7

call *n* **1** the natural vocal sound of an animal and
  especially a bird <the clear *call* of a bellbird>
  syn cry, note, song

rel cheep, chirp, peep, twitter, warble
2 *syn* see ATTRACTION 1
3 *syn* see OCCASION 3
4 *syn* see VISIT 1
call down *vb syn* see REPROVE
caller *n syn* see VISITOR 1
‖**callet** *n syn* see PROSTITUTE
call girl *n syn* see PROSTITUTE
call house *n syn* see BROTHEL
calligraphy *n syn* see HANDWRITING
call in *vb syn* see SUMMON 2
calling *n* **1** *syn* see MISSION
2 *syn* see TRADE 1
3 *syn* see WORK 1
‖**callithump** *n syn* see SHIVAREE
call off *vb syn* see CANCEL 2
callous *adj syn* see UNFEELING 2
rel indurated, set
callow *adj* **1** *syn* see YOUNG 1
2 *syn* see INEXPERIENCED
callowness *n syn* see INEXPERIENCE
call up *vb* to summon for active military duty
<*called up* the army reserves>
syn order up; *compare* DRAFT 1
rel mobilize
idiom call to the colors
ant discharge, muster out
calm *n syn* see QUIET 1
calm *adj* **1** free from storm or rough activity <the
wind died and the sea became *calm*>
syn halcyon, hushed, placid, quiet, still, stilly,
untroubled
rel inactive, quiescent, reposing, resting; pacific,
smooth, tranquil, unruffled
idiom calm as a millpond, still as death
con agitated, disturbed, perturbed, restless, turbulent, uneasy
ant stormy
2 free from mental or emotional distress or agitation <a man who remained *calm* under stress>
syn collected, composed, easy, easygoing,
placid, poised, possessed, self-composed, self≈
possessed, serene, tranquil
rel cool, imperturbable, laid-back, nonchalant,
unflappable, unruffled; even-tempered, impassive, phlegmatic, steady; firm, stable, staunch
con discomposed, disturbed, perturbed, upset;
anxious, bothered, confused, nervous; fidgety,
jittery, jumpy, shaky, tense
ant agitated
calm *vb* to relieve from or bring to an end whatever distresses, agitates, or disturbs <that inner
faith that *calms* the troubled spirit>
syn allay, balm, becalm, compose, lull, quiet,
‖quieten, settle, soothe, ‖soother, still, tranquilize
rel alleviate, assuage, mitigate, relieve; appease,
mollify, pacify, placate; relax, steady
con bother, discompose, disquiet, disturb,
flurry, perturb, stir up, upset
ant agitate; arouse
calmant *n syn* see SEDATIVE
calmative *n syn* see SEDATIVE
calmness *n syn* see EQUANIMITY

calumniate *vb syn* see MALIGN
ant eulogize; vindicate
calumnious *adj syn* see LIBELOUS
calumny *n syn* see DETRACTION
rel animadversion, reflection, stricture
con encomium, panegyric, tribute; adulation,
compliment, flattery
ant eulogy; vindication
calvary *n syn* see TRIAL 1
‖**cam** *adv syn* see AWRY 1
camaraderie *n* a spirit of friendly goodwill typical
of comrades <the easy *camaraderie* of a cozy
neighborhood bar>
syn comradery, good-fellowship
rel affability, friendliness, gregariousness, sociability; cheer, conviviality, jollity
con aloofness, coldness, frigidity, inaccessibil-
ity, reclusiveness, remoteness, self-containment;
exclusiveness, self-sufficiency, unsociability
camarilla *n syn* see CLIQUE
cameraman *n syn* see PHOTOGRAPHER
camerist *n syn* see PHOTOGRAPHER
camouflage *vb syn* see DISGUISE
rel becloud, befog, dim
camp *n* **1** a place where a number of people (as vacationers or soldiers) live temporarily together in
usually more or less casual housing <planned to
summer at a fishing *camp* in Maine>
syn campground, encampment
2 *syn* see CLIQUE
3 *syn* see HUT
camp *vb* to live temporarily in a camp or the outdoors <*camped* under the trees for the night>
syn bivouac, ‖bivvy, encamp, ‖laager, ‖maroon,
tent
idiom rough it
con decamp
campanile *n syn* see BELL TOWER
camper *n syn* see TRAILER
campestral *adj syn* see RURAL
camp follower *n syn* see PROSTITUTE
campground *n syn* see CAMP 1
‖**cample** *vb syn* see SCOLD 1
‖**can** *n* **1** *syn* see JAIL
2 *syn* see TOILET
3 *syn* see BUTTOCKS
‖**can** *vb syn* see DISMISS 3
Canaan *n syn* see HEAVEN 2
canaille *n syn* see RABBLE 2
canal *n syn* see CHANNEL 1
canard *n syn* see LIE
rel hoax, humbug, mare's nest, sell, spoof; artifice, dodge, trick
‖**canary** *n syn* see INFORMER
cancel *vb* **1** *syn* see ERASE
2 to give up something previously arranged or
agreed on <decided to *cancel* his appointment
with the dentist>
syn abort, call off, drop, scrub

---

syn synonym(s)   *rel* related word(s)
ant antonym(s)   *con* contrasted word(s)
idiom idiomatic equivalent(s)
‖ use limited; if in doubt, see a dictionary

rel end, terminate; annul, invalidate, rescind, revoke; give up, relinquish, surrender

cancel (out) *vb syn* see NEUTRALIZE

candid *adj* **1** *syn* see FAIR 4
rel aboveboard, forthright, straightforward; honest, scrupulous, upright
2 *syn* see FRANK
ant evasive

candidate *n* one who seeks an office, honor, position, or award <examining *candidates* for editorial positions>
syn applicant, aspirant, hopeful, seeker
rel nominee; dark horse; also-ran, has-been; campaigner, electioneerer, stumper, whistle-stopper

candy *vb syn* see SUGARCOAT 1

canine *n syn* see DOG 1

canker *vb syn* see DEBASE 1

cankered *adj syn* see CANTANKEROUS

cannabis *n syn* see MARIJUANA

canned *adj* **1** *syn* see CONDENSED
‖**2** *syn* see INTOXICATED 1

cannibalic *adj syn* see FIERCE 1

canniness *n* **1** *syn* see PRUDENCE 1
2 *syn* see CUNNING 2

‖**cannon** *n syn* see PICKPOCKET

cannonade *n syn* see BARRAGE

cannonade *vb syn* see BOMBARD

canny *adj* **1** *syn* see CLEVER 4
2 *syn* see SPARING
3 *syn* see WISE 4

canon *n* **1** *syn* see LAW 1
2 *syn* see DOCTRINE

canonical *adj syn* see ORTHODOX 1

‖**cant** *adj syn* see LIVELY 1

cant *vb syn* see SLANT 1

cant *n* **1** *syn* see DIALECT 2
rel diction, language, phraseology, vocabulary; idiom, speech
2 *syn* see TERMINOLOGY
3 *syn* see HYPOCRISY

cantankerous *adj* habitually ill-humored, irritable, and disagreeable <one of our more *cantankerous* fellow workers>
syn bearish, cankered, cranky, cross-grained, crotchety, ornery, rantankerous, vinegarish, vinegary, waspish, waspy; *compare* IRASCIBLE, IRRITABLE
rel dour, morose, sour; crabbed, cross, crusty, huffy, petulant, prickly, snappish; dyspeptic, ill-conditioned, ill-natured; liverish
idiom like a bear with a sore paw
con benign, kindly, mellow, mild; amiable, congenial, friendly, pleasant, well-disposed; benevolent, gracious, kind

canter *n syn* see VAGABOND

cantina *n syn* see BAR 5

canting *adj syn* see HYPOCRITICAL

canton *vb syn* see BILLET 1

‖**canty** *adj syn* see LIVELY 1

canvass *vb* **1** *syn* see SCRUTINIZE 1
2 *syn* see DISCUSS 1
3 *syn* see SOLICIT 1

cap *vb* **1** *syn* see SURMOUNT 3

‖**2** *syn* see PUZZLE
3 *syn* see COVER 3
4 *syn* see SURPASS 1
5 *syn* see CLIMAX

capability *n* **1** *syn* see ABILITY 1
rel art, craft, cunning, skill
con inability, disability
ant incapability, incompetence
2 *syn* see EFFICACY 1

capable *adj syn* see ABLE
ant incapable

capacious *adj syn* see SPACIOUS
rel dilatable, distensible, expandable, expansive, extensile; abundant, copious, plentiful
ant exiguous

capacity *n* **1** *syn* see ABILITY 1
rel bent, faculty, gift, knack, talent, twin; caliber, stature
con impotence, ineffectiveness, powerlessness
ant incapacity
2 *syn* see STATUS 1

cape *n syn* see PROMONTORY

caper *vb syn* see GAMBOL
idiom cut capers

caper *n* **1** *syn* see ESCAPADE
2 *syn* see PRANK
rel devilment, impishness, mischief, roguery, waggishness

‖**capernoited** *adj syn* see INTOXICATED 1

capital *adj* **1** *syn* see EGREGIOUS
2 *syn* see CHIEF 2
rel cardinal, essential, vital; basic, fundamental, underlying
3 *syn* see EXCELLENT

capital *n syn* see MEAN 3

capitalize *vb* to supply capital for or to <agreed to *capitalize* the venture>
syn back, bankroll, finance, grubstake, stake
rel aid, assist, help, subsidize, support; fund; promote, sponsor

capitulate *vb syn* see YIELD 2

capitulation *n syn* see SURRENDER

capper *n syn* see DECOY 2

caprice *n* an arbitrary, impulsive, and often illogical notion or change of mind <given to sudden *caprices* and random fancies>
syn bee, boutade, conceit, crank, crotchet, fancy, freak, humor, maggot, megrim, notion, vagary, whigmaleerie, whim, whimsy
rel mood, temper, vein; contrariety, inconsistency, perversity; characteristic, foible, habit, mannerism, peculiarity, trait, trick

capricious *adj* **1** *syn* see ARBITRARY 1
2 *syn* see INCONSTANT 1
rel humorsome, moody; effervescent
con constant, steady
ant steadfast
3 *syn* see UNCERTAIN 1

capsheaf *n syn* see APEX 2

capstone *n syn* see APEX 2

capsule *adj syn* see CONDENSED

caption *n* an explanatory or identifying comment accompanying a pictorial illustration <the *captions* were under the wrong figures>

syn legend, underline

captious *adj syn* see CRITICAL 1
rel demanding, exacting, finicky; contrary, perverse; irritable, peevish, petulant, snappish, snappy, testy
con judicious, sensible, wise; rational, reasonable; knowing, knowledgeable
ant appreciative

captivate *vb syn* see ATTRACT 1
rel delight, gratify, please; enthrall, grip, hold, mesmerize, spellbind
ant repulse

captivated *adj syn* see ENAMORED 3

captivating *adj syn* see ATTRACTIVE 1

capture *vb syn* see CATCH 1

Capuan *adj syn* see LUXURIOUS 3

car *n* a usually private passenger-carrying automotive vehicle <drove a shabby old *car*>
syn auto, autocar, automobile, buggy, ‖bus, machine, motor, motorcar
rel beach wagon, coach, compact, convertible, coupe, fastback, hardtop, hatchback, limousine, notchback, phaeton, roadster, runabout, sedan, station wagon, subcompact, touring car; ‖clunker, ‖crate, ‖heap, ‖jalopy, junker, ‖wreck

‖**caravan** *n syn* see TRAILER

caravansary *n syn* see HOTEL

carbon *n syn* see REPRODUCTION

carbon copy *n syn* see REPRODUCTION

carbuncle *n syn* see ABSCESS

carcass *n syn* see CORPSE

‖**carcel** *n syn* see JAIL

card *n* **1** *syn* see WAG 1
2 *syn* see PROGRAM 1
3 *syn* see MENU

card *vb syn* see SCHEDULE 1

cardboard *adj syn* see STIFF 4
rel unlifelike, unreal, unrealistic

cardinal *adj* **1** *syn* see ESSENTIAL 2
2 *syn* see CENTRAL 1

care *n* **1** *syn* see SORROW
rel strain, stress, tension
2 a burdened or disquieted state of mind <a mind full of *care* and sadness>
syn anxiety, concern, concernment, disquiet, disquietude, solicitude, unease, uneasiness, worry
rel apprehension, foreboding, misgiving, suspense; agitation, disturbance, perturbation; alarm, consternation, dismay, fear
con calm, ease, peace, quietude; assurance, comfort, easiness
3 *syn* see TRIAL 2
4 serious and heedful attentiveness <attended his words with *care*>
syn carefulness, concern, consciousness, heed, heedfulness, regard; *compare* ATTENTION 1
rel curiosity; enthusiasm, interest; consideration, solicitude, thoughtfulness; effort, exertion, pains, trouble; alertness, vigilance, watchfulness
con carelessness, disregard, heedlessness, unconcern; boredom, disinterest, ennui
5 *syn* see OVERSIGHT 1

6 *syn* see CUSTODY

care (for) *vb* **1** *syn* see TEND 2
2 *syn* see MINISTER (to)
idiom take care of

careen *vb syn* see LURCH 2

career *vb syn* see COURSE

carefree *adj* **1** *syn* see HAPPY-GO-LUCKY
2 *syn* see IRRESPONSIBLE

careful *adj* **1** *syn* see CAUTIOUS
rel attentive, heedful, observant
2 closely attentive to details or showing such attention <*careful* workmanship>
syn conscientious, conscionable, exact, fussy, heedful, meticulous, painstaking, punctilious, punctual, scrupulous
rel accurate, nice, precise; deliberate, studied; foresighted, provident, prudent; critical, discriminating, finical, finicky; observant, particular, religious; duteous, dutiful, intent
con disorderly, lax, negligent, slack, slipshod, slovenly; heedless, neglectful, remiss
ant careless

carefulness *n syn* see CARE 4

careless *adj* **1** lacking in or showing lack of care and attention <*careless* of the harm his neglect might do to others> <unwilling to accept such *careless* shoddy work>
syn feckless, heedless, inadvertent, irreflective, thoughtless, uncaring, unheeding, unrecking, unreflective, unthinking; *compare* INCAUTIOUS, RASH 1
rel forgetful, inattentive, oblivious, unmindful; lax, neglectful, negligent, slack, unconcerned, uninterested; inadequate, incapable, unfit, unqualified
con careful, heedful, thoughtful; concerned, considerate, punctilious, scrupulous
ant careful
2 *syn* see IRRESPONSIBLE
3 *syn* see NEGLIGENT
4 *syn* see SLIPSHOD 3
5 *syn* see SLOVENLY 1

caress *vb* to express interest, affection, or love by touching or handling <*caress* a frightened child>
syn cosset, cuddle, dandle, fondle, love, pet
rel cocker, coddle, indulge, pamper; coquet, dally, flirt, toy, trifle; nuzzle, pat, stroke

careworn *adj syn* see HAGGARD
rel distressed, troubled; exhausted, fagged, jaded, tuckered
ant carefree

cargo *n syn* see LOAD 1

caricature *n* **1** *syn* see MOCKERY 2
2 a grotesque or bizarre imitation <a doting attentiveness that was a sickly *caricature* of motherhood>
syn burlesque, parody, takeoff, travesty

---

syn synonym(s)   *rel* related word(s)
ant antonym(s)   *con* contrasted word(s)
idiom idiomatic equivalent(s)
‖ use limited; if in doubt, see a dictionary

rel lampoon, libel, pasquinade; laughingstock, mockery; cheat, fake, imitation, phony, sham; bosh, bunk, gammon, hokum, moonshine; clinquant, pinchbeck, shoddy, tinsel

carillon *n syn* see BELL TOWER

caritas *n syn* see MERCY

cark *vb* **1** *syn* see TROUBLE 1
2 *syn* see WORRY 3

carnage *n syn* see MASSACRE

carnal *adj* **1** *syn* see BODILY
rel material, substantial; earthly, earthy
2 characterized by physical rather than intellectual or spiritual day-to-day <giving too much heed to the *carnal* aspects of day-to-day life>
syn animal, fleshly, sensual; *compare* SENSUOUS
rel bodily, corporal, corporeal, physical; coarse, gross, obscene, vulgar; earthly, earthy, mundane, temporal, worldly; lascivious, lewd, lustful, wanton; Pandemic, sensuous
con ethical, moral, noble, righteous, virtuous; aerial, ethereal, otherworldly, supernal; chaste, decent, modest, pure
ant spiritual; intellectual

carnality *n syn* see ANIMALITY

carom *vb syn* see GLANCE 1

carousal *n syn* see BINGE 1

carouse *n syn* see BINGE 1

carouse *vb syn* see REVEL 1

carp (at) *vb syn* see NAG

carper *n syn* see CRITIC

‖**carpet** *vb syn* see SCOLD 1
idiom call on the carpet, take to task

carpet knight *n syn* see HEDONIST

carping *adj syn* see CRITICAL 1
rel blaming, criticizing, reprehending, reprobating; jawing, railing, upbraiding; blameful, condemnatory, damnatory, objurgatory, reproachful, reprobatory
con applauding, commendatory, complimentary; approving, endorsing; extolling, laudatory, praiseful
ant fulsome

carriage *n* **1** *syn* see TRANSPORTATION 1
2 *syn* see POSTURE 1

carriageable *adj syn* see PORTABLE

carriage trade *n syn* see ARISTOCRACY

carrier *n* **1** *syn* see BEARER 2
2 *syn* see MESSENGER
3 *syn* see VECTOR

carrot *n syn* see REWARD

carry *vb* **1** to be the agent or means by which someone or something is shifted from one place to another <*carried* the child on his shoulder>
syn bear, buck, convey, ferry, ‖hump, ‖jag, lug, pack, tote, transport
rel bring, fetch, take; move, remove, shift, transfer; send, transmit
‖**2** *syn* see ACCOMPANY
3 *syn* see AFFECT
4 *syn* see BEAR 3
5 *syn* see CONDUCT 4
6 *syn* see BEHAVE 1
7 *syn* see SUPPORT 4
8 *syn* see STOCK

carrying *n syn* see TRANSPORTATION 1

carry off *vb syn* see KILL 1

carry on *vb* **1** *syn* see CONDUCT 3
2 *syn* see CUT UP 2
3 *syn* see PERSEVERE

carry out *vb* **1** *syn* see ADMINISTER 1
rel complete, finalize; discharge, effect, effectuate, fulfill; prosecute, transact
idiom put in force (*or* into effect); sign, seal, and deliver
2 *syn* see EFFECT 2

carrytale *n syn* see GOSSIP 1

carry through *vb* **1** *syn* see EFFECT 2
2 *syn* see CONTINUE 1

carte blanche *n* full discretionary power <was given *carte blanche* to build, landscape, and furnish the house>
syn blank check, free hand
rel license, prerogative, right; authority, power; say, say-so
idiom power of attorney

carte d'entrée *n syn* see TICKET 2

carte du jour *n syn* see MENU

cartel *n* **1** *syn* see DEFIANCE 1
rel gage, gauntlet, glove; blow, slap
2 *syn* see SYNDICATE
rel corporation; multinational; consortium, merger

carve *vb* **1** *syn* see CUT 5
2 *syn* see SCULPTURE

Casanova *n* **1** *syn* see GALLANT 2
2 *syn* see WOLF

cascade *n syn* see WATERFALL

‖**cascade** *vb syn* see VOMIT

case *n* **1** *syn* see EVENT 4
2 *syn* see ORDER 9
3 *syn* see SUIT 1
4 *syn* see INSTANCE
rel circumstance, episode, event, incident, occurrence; condition, situation, state
5 *syn* see ECCENTRIC

case *n syn* see HULL

‖**case** *vb syn* see SCRUTINIZE 1

case history *n syn* see INSTANCE

cash *n syn* see MONEY

cashier *vb* **1** *syn* see DISMISS 3
rel eject, expel, oust; bar, eliminate, exclude; pass over, shelve
con appoint, designate, elect, name; employ, engage, hire
2 *syn* see DISCARD

cash in *vb syn* see DIE 1

cask *n* a vessel made of staves, headings, and hoops <a *cask* of cider>
syn barrel, butt, hogshead, keg, pipe, tun

Cassandra *n syn* see PESSIMIST

cassock *n syn* see CLERGYMAN

cast *vb* **1** *syn* see THROW 1
rel broadcast, disperse, distribute, scatter
2 *syn* see DIRECT 2
3 *syn* see DISCARD
rel abandon, leave, relinquish, surrender, yield; dismiss, drop
‖**4** *syn* see VOMIT

5 *syn* see ADD 2
6 *syn* see PLAN 2
cast *n* **1** *syn* see LOOK 2
  2 *syn* see PREDICTION
  3 *syn* see COLOR 1
  4 *syn* see HINT 2
  5 *syn* see TYPE
  6 *syn* see FORM 1
cast about *vb* *syn* see SEEK 1
cast away *vb* **1** *syn* see WASTE 2
  2 *syn* see SHIPWRECK 1
castaway *n* *syn* see OUTCAST
cast down *vb* *syn* see HUMBLE
cast down *adj* *syn* see DOWNCAST
castigate *vb* **1** *syn* see PUNISH 1
  rel baste, beat, belabor, drub, pummel, thrash; berate, rail, rate, tongue-lash, upbraid, wig; penalize
  2 *syn* see LAMBASTE 3
castigation *n* *syn* see PUNISHMENT
castigatory *adj* *syn* see PUNITIVE
castle *n* *syn* see MANSION
castle-builder *n* *syn* see DREAMER
cast out *vb* **1** *syn* see BANISH
  ‖**2** *syn* see QUARREL
castrate *vb* **1** *syn* see STERILIZE
  2 *syn* see UNNERVE
  rel bleed, drain, empty, exhaust
casual *adj* **1** *syn* see ACCIDENTAL
  rel unplanned, unpremeditated; extemporaneous, extempore, impromptu, improvised, offhand; impulsive, spontaneous
  con advised, considered, deliberate, intentional, planned, premeditated, studied
  ant deliberate
  2 *syn* see INDIFFERENT 2
  3 *syn* see EASYGOING 3
  con ceremonial, conventional, formal
  4 *syn* see LITTLE 3
casually *adv* *syn* see INCIDENTALLY 1
casualty *n* **1** *syn* see ACCIDENT 2
  2 *syn* see FATALITY 2
  3 *syn* see VICTIM 2
casuistry *n* *syn* see FALLACY 2
‖**cat** *n* *syn* see MAN 3
‖**cat** *vb* *syn* see VOMIT
cataclysm *n* **1** *syn* see FLOOD 2
  2 *syn* see DISASTER
cataclysmic *adj* *syn* see FATAL 2
catacomb *n* *syn* see CRYPT
catalog *n* *syn* see LIST
  rel program, prospectus, syllabus
catalog *vb* **1** *syn* see INVENTORY
  2 *syn* see LIST 3
  rel admit, enter, introduce; count, enumerate, number
catalyst *n* *syn* see STIMULUS
cataplasm *n* *syn* see POULTICE
cataract *n* **1** *syn* see WATERFALL
  2 *syn* see FLOOD 2
catastrophe *n* *syn* see DISASTER
catastrophic *adj* *syn* see FATAL 2
catcall *n* *syn* see RASPBERRY
catch *vb* **1** to obtain physical mastery and possession of <the cat *caught* a mouse>

syn bag, capture, collar, ‖cotch, get, nail, prehend, secure, take; *compare* ARREST 2, SEIZE 2
rel clutch, grab, snatch; clasp, grasp, grip; ensnare, entangle, entrap, snare, tangle, trap
con free, release
ant miss
  2 *syn* see SEIZE 2
  3 to put at a disadvantage or bring under control by or as if by enmeshing in a net <*caught* in the fallacy of his own argument>
syn benet, catch up, ensnare, entangle, entrap, snare, tangle, trap; *compare* ENTANGLE 3
rel baffle, confound, nonplus, perplex, stick, stump; abash, disturb, embarrass, put out; confuse, flurry, fluster, rattle
  4 *syn* see DUPE
  5 *syn* see FIND 1
  6 *syn* see MARRY 1
  7 to come up with often unexpectedly <the storm *caught* them unawares>
syn ‖cotch, overhaul, overtake, take
rel reach
idiom come upon
  8 *syn* see SEIZE 3
  9 *syn* see INTERCEPT
  10 *syn* see CONTRACT 1
idiom fall ill (of *or* with), fall victim to
  11 *syn* see FASTEN 2
  12 *syn* see STRIKE 2
  13 *syn* see APPREHEND 1
catch colt *n* *syn* see BASTARD
catching *adj* **1** *syn* see INFECTIOUS 2
  2 *syn* see INFECTIOUS 3
catch on *vb* *syn* see DISCOVER 3
catchphrase *n* *syn* see CATCHWORD
catchpole *n* *syn* see DELEGATE
catch up *vb* **1** *syn* see CATCH 3
  2 *syn* see ENTHRALL 2
catchword *n* a word or phrase that catches the eye or ear and is repeated so often that it becomes representative of a political party, school of thought, or point of view <"new deal" became the *catchword* of supporters and critics of Franklin Roosevelt>
syn byword, catchphrase, phrase, shibboleth, slogan, watchword; *compare* BATTLE CRY
rel household word; maxim, motto
catchy *adj* *syn* see FITFUL
catechize *vb* *syn* see ASK 1
categorical *adj* **1** *syn* see ULTIMATE 3
  con conjectural, hypothetical, supposititious; conditional, contingent, dependent, relative
  2 *syn* see EXPLICIT
  rel certain, positive, sure; direct, downright, forthright
  con ambiguous; doubtful, dubious, problematic, questionable
  3 *syn* see POSITIVE 1
categorically *adv* *syn* see EXPRESSLY 1

---

syn synonym(s)　　　*rel* related word(s)
ant antonym(s)　　　*con* contrasted word(s)
idiom idiomatic equivalent(s)
‖ use limited; if in doubt, see a dictionary

categorize *vb syn* see ASSORT
  rel identify, nail down, peg, put down
category *n syn* see CLASS 1
cater (to) *vb* **1** *syn* see BABY
  idiom make much of
  2 *syn* see INDULGE 1
cateran *n syn* see MARAUDER
catercorner (*or* **catty-corner** *or* **kitty-corner**) *adv*
  syn see DIAGONALLY
cater–cousin *n syn* see FRIEND
caterwaul *vb syn* see QUARREL
catharsis *n syn* see PURIFICATION
catholic *adj* **1** *syn* see UNIVERSAL 2
  rel comprehensive, inclusive; general, generic,
  indeterminate; extensive, large-scale
  ant parochial; provincial
  2 *syn* see ECLECTIC 2
catholicon *n syn* see PANACEA
cathouse *n syn* see BROTHEL
catlike *adj syn* see STEALTHY 2
catnap *n syn* see NAP
catnap *vb syn* see NAP
‖**catouse** *n syn* see COMMOTION 3
cat's–paw *n syn* see TOOL 2
catty *adj* **1** *syn* see STEALTHY 2
  2 *syn* see AGILE
  3 *syn* see MALICIOUS
‖**caulk** (off) *vb syn* see NAP
‖**caulker** *n syn* see DRAM
causatum *n syn* see EFFECT 1
cause *n* **1** that (as a person, fact, or condition)
  which is responsible for an effect <the storm was
  the *cause* of all our difficulties>
  syn antecedent, determinant, occasion, reason
  rel goad, impulse, incentive, inducement, motive, spring; origin, prime mover, root, source;
  author, creator, generator, originator
  con consequence, effect, issue, outcome, result
  2 *syn* see MOTIVE 1
  3 *syn* see OCCASION 3
  4 *syn* see SUIT 1
cause *vb* **1** *syn* see GENERATE 3
  2 *syn* see EFFECT 1
  rel elicit, evoke, provoke
  idiom be at the root of, give origin to, set on foot
'cause *conj syn* see BECAUSE
causerie *n syn* see CHAT 2
caustic *adj* **1** marked by sharp and often witty incisiveness <a *caustic* critic>
  syn mordacious, mordant, salty, scathing, trenchant; *compare* SARCASTIC
  rel biting, cutting, incisive; acrid, bitter, pungent, tart; acute, keen, sharp; ironic, sarcastic,
  satiric, stinging; harsh, rough, severe, stringent;
  crisp, pithy, succinct, terse
  con gentle, mild; cordial, gracious; bland, diplomatic, suave, urbane
  ant genial
  2 *syn* see SARCASTIC
causticity *n syn* see SARCASM
caution *n* **1** *syn* see WARNING
  2 *syn* see PRUDENCE 1
caution *vb syn* see WARN 1
cautionary *adj syn* see MONITORY

cautioning *adj syn* see MONITORY
cautious *adj* marked by careful prudence especially in reducing or avoiding risk or danger <a
  cautious approach to marriage>
  syn calculating, careful, chary, circumspect,
  considerate, discreet, gingerly, guarded, safe,
  wary
  rel alert, vigilant, watchful; cagey, canny, cozy,
  foresighted, precautious, shrewd; forethoughtful, prethoughtful, provident, prudent; calculating, scheming, shrewd; expedient, judicious, politic
  idiom on one's guard, on the safe side, playing it
  safe
  con daring, rash, reckless, venturesome; headlong, impetuous, precipitate
  ant adventurous, temerarious
cavalier *adj syn* see PROUD 1
cave *n* a usually natural underground chamber
  <the limestone *caves* of Kentucky>
  syn cavern, grotto, subterrane, subterranean
cave *vb* **1** *syn* see GIVE 12
  2 *syn* see YIELD 2
cave (in) *vb syn* see COLLAPSE 2
caveat *n syn* see WARNING
cavern *n syn* see CAVE
cavernous *adj* **1** suggestive of a cave <a *cavernous*
  fireplace that gulped in wood>
  syn chasmal, gaping, yawning
  rel commodious, vast
  2 *syn* see HOLLOW 1
cavil *vb syn* see QUIBBLE 1
caviler *n syn* see CRITIC
caviling *adj syn* see CRITICAL 1
  rel contrary, perverse; demanding, exacting;
  finicky, fussy, picky; mean, petty, small; hairsplitting, niggling, nitpicking
  con amiable, complaisant, good-natured, tolerant; accommodating, easy, obliging
cavillous *adj syn* see CRITICAL 1
cavity *n syn* see HOLE 3
cavort *vb syn* see GAMBOL
  rel carry on, cut up, horse (around), horseplay,
  roughhouse
caw *vb syn* see SQUALL 1
cease *vb syn* see STOP 3
  rel close, conclude, end, finish, terminate; intermit
  con continue, persist; extend, prolong, protract;
  arise, originate, rise, spring
cease *n syn* see END 2
cease-fire *n syn* see TRUCE
ceaseless *adj* **1** *syn* see CONTINUAL
  2 *syn* see EVERLASTING 1
cede *vb* **1** *syn* see RELINQUISH
  rel accord, concede, grant, vouchsafe
  con hold, hold back, keep back, retain, withhold
  2 *syn* see TRANSFER 4
ceinture *n syn* see BELT 1
‖**celeb** *n syn* see CELEBRITY 2
celebrate *vb* **1** *syn* see KEEP 2
  2 *syn* see PRAISE 2
celebrated *adj syn* see FAMOUS 2
celebrious *adj syn* see FAMOUS 2

celebrity *n* **1** *syn* see FAME 2
 ant obscurity
 2 a widely known and popularly esteemed person <youngsters making a great to-do over sports *celebrities*>
 syn big name, ||celeb, luminary, name, notability, notable, somebody
 rel hero, immortal, mahatma, star, superstar; lion; personage, worthy; cynosure
 idiom center of attraction, person of note (*or* mark)
 con back number; nobody

celerity *n* **1** *syn* see HASTE 1
 rel alacrity, briskness, legerity
 2 *syn* see SPEED 2

celestial *adj* of, relating to, or befitting heaven or the heavens <*celestial* music from an angelic choir>
 syn empyreal, empyrean, heavenly
 rel ethereal, supernal, transcendental; otherworldly, unearthly, transmundane; beatific, blessed, elysian, Olympian
 con earthly, earthy, mundane, sublunary, worldly; chthonian, hellish, infernal
 ant terrestrial, uncelestial

cemetery *n* a piece of land used for burying the dead <the quiet peace of a country *cemetery*>
 syn ||boneyard, ||boot hill, burial ground, burying ground, God's acre, graveyard, memorial park, necropolis, polyandrium, potter's field
 rel churchyard; catacomb
 idiom city of the dead

censor *vb* to remove matter considered objectionable by expurgation or alteration <*censor* a movie>
 syn blip, bowdlerize, expurgate, screen
 rel cut out, excise, exscind; blue-pencil, delete, edit, red-pencil; bleach, clean (up), purge, purify; narrow, restrain, restrict

censorious *adj* *syn* see CRITICAL 1
 rel chiding, reproachful, reproaching; condemnatory, condemning, denouncing, denunciatory, reprehending; accusatory, culpatory
 con acclaiming, acclamatory, extolling, laudatory, lauding, praising; adulatory, complimentary, flattering
 ant eulogistic

censurable *adj* *syn* see BLAMEWORTHY
 rel improper, incorrect, objectionable, wrong, wrongful; discreditable, doubtful, questionable; inadmissible, unacceptable
 con correct, proper, right; acceptable, admissible; creditable
 ant uncensurable

censure *vb* *syn* see CRITICIZE
 rel rebuke, reprimand, reproach, reprove; contemn, disdain, scorn, scout, strafe; disallow, disapprove, oppose, reject, stigmatize
 con applaud, compliment, recommend; allow, approve, support
 ant commend

center *n* **1** a point or part in a surface or solid more or less equidistant from the periphery <the *center* of the earth>
 syn core, middle, midpoint, midst
 rel inside, interior
 con circumference, compass, perimeter, periphery; bounds, confines, limits
 2 one eminent in or central to a particular activity, condition, or interest <a *center* of international trade>
 syn focal point, focus, heart, hub, nerve center, polestar, seat; *compare* ESSENCE 2
 3 a source or point of origin (as of an influence, pressure, or effect) <the group proved a *center* of discontent>
 syn core, heart, pith, quick, root
 rel activator, dynamo, energizer, stimulant

center *adj* **1** *syn* see MIDDLE 1
 2 *syn* see MIDDLE 2

centermost *adj* *syn* see MIDDLE 1

central *adj* **1** occupying a dominant or supremely important position <the *central* theme of American foreign policy>
 syn cardinal, overriding, overruling, pivotal, ruling
 rel dominant, paramount, predominant, preponderant; important, significant; outstanding, salient, signal; chief, essential, foremost, leading, main; all-absorbing, controlling, master; focal, key; basic, fundamental, primary, radical
 con insignificant, minor, trivial, unimportant; borderline, marginal
 ant peripheral
 2 *syn* see MIDDLE 2

centralizing *adj* *syn* see INTEGRATIVE

centripetal *adj* *syn* see INTEGRATIVE

||**cep** *prep* *syn* see EXCEPT

cerate *n* *syn* see OINTMENT

cerberus *n* *syn* see CUSTODIAN

cerebral *adj* **1** *syn* see MENTAL 1
 2 *syn* see INTELLECTUAL 2

cerebrate *vb* *syn* see THINK 5

cerebration *n* *syn* see THOUGHT 1

ceremonial *adj* stressing or concerned with careful attention to form and detail <his *ceremonial* approach to everyday life>
 syn ceremonious, conventional, formal, solemn, stately
 rel mannered, studied, stylized; liturgical, ritual, ritualistic; august, courtly, imposing, lofty; fixed, rigid, set, starchy, stiff
 con casual, easy, informal, relaxed; artless, ingenuous, open, sincere

ceremonial *n* **1** *syn* see FORM 2
 2 *syn* see RITE 2

ceremonious *adj* *syn* see CEREMONIAL
 rel decorous, proper, seemly; impressive, moving, striking; grandiose, imposing, majestic
 ant unceremonious

ceremony *n* **1** *syn* see FORM 2
 2 *syn* see RITE 2

certain *adj* **1** *syn* see FIRM 4

---

syn synonym(s)   *rel* related word(s)
ant antonym(s)   *con* contrasted word(s)
idiom idiomatic equivalent(s)
|| use limited; if in doubt, see a dictionary

rel assured, certified, guaranteed, warranted; ensured, insured, sure

2 constituting an indeterminate and otherwise unidentified part of a group or whole <*certain* students dispute this finding>

syn some, various

rel a, an, one; many, numerous; divers, several, sundry

con no; all

3 being such beyond a doubt <no *certain* likeness of this saint survives>

syn accurate, authentic, dependable, reliable

rel credible, plausible, well-grounded

con counterfeit, false, spurious; controversial, doubtful, dubious, questionable

ant uncertain

4 syn see INFALLIBLE 2

5 syn see POSITIVE 3

rel confirmable, demonstrable, establishable, provable, verifiable; doubtless, trustworthy, unerring

con controversial, iffy

ant uncertain

6 syn see INEVITABLE

rel indefeasible, irrevocable, unalterable, written; fated, predestinated, predetermined

ant uncertain

7 syn see SURE 5

rel assured, confident, sanguine

con hesitant, indecisive, vague, wavering; doubtful, dubious, questionable

ant uncertain

certainty *n* a state of mind in which one is free from doubt <answered with complete *certainty*>

syn assurance, assuredness, certitude, confidence, conviction, sureness, surety

rel belief, credence, faith; absoluteness, definiteness, dogmatism, positiveness, positivism; firmness, staunchness, steadiness

con doubt, mistrust, skepticism, unsureness; fluctuation, irresolution, shifting, trimming, vacillation, wavering; obscurity, vagueness

ant uncertainty

certification *n syn* see CREDENTIALS

certify *vb* **1** to testify usually formally and in writing to the truth or genuineness of something <*certify* a student's college transcript>

syn attest, vouch, witness

rel assert, aver, avouch, avow, profess

2 syn see WARRANT 2

3 syn see APPROVE 2

rel authorize, commission, license

con antagonize, counter, oppose

certitude *n syn* see CERTAINTY

rel cocksureness

con uncertainty

ant doubt

‖**cess** *n syn* see TAX 1

cessation *n syn* see END 2

cesspit *n syn* see SINK 1

cesspool *n syn* see SINK 1

‖**chack** *n syn* see SNACK

chafe *vb* **1 syn** see ANNOY 1

2 syn see ABRADE 1

3 to make sore or raw through friction <the high stiff collar *chafed* his neck>

syn abrade, excoriate, fret, gall, rub

rel damage, hurt, impair, injure; flay, peel, skin; inflame, irritate; graze, scrape, scratch

con ease, relieve, soothe

chaff *vb syn* see BANTER 1

idiom make merry over

chaffer *vb syn* see HAGGLE 2

rel beg, coax, plead

chafing *adj syn* see IMPATIENT 1

chagrined *adj syn* see ASHAMED

rel crushed, disconcerted; discomposed, perturbed, upset

idiom put out of countenance

chain *n* **1 chains** *pl syn* see SHACKLE

2 syn see SUCCESSION 2

3 syn see SYNDICATE

chain *adj* **1 syn** see CUMULATIVE

2 syn see TRITE

chair *vb syn* see PRESIDE

chair car *n syn* see PARLOR CAR

chalk (out) *vb syn* see SKETCH

chalk up *vb syn* see GET 1

challenge *vb* **1 syn** see DEMAND 1

2 syn see QUESTION 2

3 syn see FACE 3

rel question; dispute; strive, struggle, try

idiom throw down the (*or* one's) gage

con bypass, evade

4 syn see STIR 1

challenge *n* **1 syn** see DEMUR 2

2 syn see DEFIANCE 1

rel calling, claiming, demanding, exacting; importuning, insistence

chamber *n* **1 syn** see ROOM 1

‖**2 chambers** *pl syn* see APARTMENT 1

chamber *vb syn* see HARBOR 1

champ *vb* **1 syn** see CHEW 1

rel crush, macerate, mash, smash

2 syn see BITE 1

rel nibble, nip; gum, mouth, mumble; peck, pick

champaign *n syn* see FIELD

champion *n syn* see EXPONENT

champion *vb syn* see SUPPORT 2

rel battle, contend, fight (for)

idiom put in a good word for, stand behind (*or* back of), stand up for

con condemn, denounce

ant combat

champion *adj* **1 syn** see EXCELLENT

rel distinguished, illustrious, outstanding, splendid

2 syn see FIRST 3

chance *n* **1 syn** see ACCIDENT 1

con certainty, inevitability, necessity; destiny, fate, foreordination, predestination

ant law

2 an unpurposed, unpredictable, and uncontrollable master force <the folly of depending on *chance* for success in life>

syn fortune, hazard, luck

rel advantage, break, fluke; fate, lot; contingency

3 *syn* see OPPORTUNITY
rel likelihood, possibility, probability; outlook, prospect
chance *vb* **1** *syn* see HAPPEN 1
2 *syn* see HAPPEN 2
3 *syn* see GAMBLE 2
4 *syn* see VENTURE 1
idiom put at (*or* in) hazard
con cherish, protect, safeguard, secure
chance *adj syn* see ACCIDENTAL
rel careless, heedless, offhand
chance child *n syn* see BASTARD 1
chancy *adj* **1** *syn* see UNCERTAIN 1
rel hazardous, risky, speculative, unsound; precarious, ticklish, touchy, tricky
idiom hanging by a thread, on thin ice (*or* slippery ground)
con safe, secure, sound, stable
2 *syn* see DANGEROUS 1
change *vb* **1** to make or become different <*changed* her will again and again> <our needs *change* as we grow older>
syn alter, modify, mutate, refashion, turn, vary; *compare* TRANSFORM
rel convert, metamorphose, transform, transmute; diversify, variegate; exchange, interchange
idiom go (*or* pass through) a change
con establish, fix, set
2 *syn* see TRANSFORM
3 *syn* see REVERSE 1
4 *syn* see STERILIZE
5 to make substitution for or among <it's time to *change* the subject>
syn replace, shift
rel exchange, swap, trade; substitute
6 *syn* see EXCHANGE 2
change *n* **1** a making different <saw a gradual *change* of attitude in the community>
syn alteration, modification, mutation, turn, variation
rel aberration, deviation, divergence; diversification; shift, innovation
ant uniformity
2 a result of such change <amazed at the *changes* in the town>
syn innovation, mutation, novelty, permutation, sport, vicissitude
rel conversion, metamorphosis, transformation, transmutation; shift, substitute, surrogate; avatar
changeable *adj* **1** alterable or changing under slight provocation <*changeable* April weather>
syn changeful, fluid, mobile, mutable, protean, unsettled, unstable, unsteady, variable, weathery; *compare* INCONSTANT 1, MUTABLE 2
rel adaptable, impressionable, plastic, pliant; ever-changing, kaleidoscopic; restless, unfixed; inconstant, uncertain, vicissitudinous
con constant, invariable, permanent; certain, fixed, immutable, unalterable, unmodifiable; abiding, enduring, persistent
ant unchangeable; unchanging
2 *syn* see MUTABLE 2

3 *syn* see INCONSTANT 1
changeabout *n syn* see REVERSAL 1
changeful *adj syn* see CHANGEABLE 1
rel active, dynamic, live; lively, vigorous
con durable, lasting, perdurable, stable; steady, uniform
ant changeless, unchanging
changeover *n syn* see CONVERSION 2
channel *n* **1** passage through which a fluid (as water) flows or is led <the river cut a new *channel* to the sea>
syn aqueduct, canal, conduit, course, duct, watercourse
rel pass, passage, way
2 *syn* see MEAN 2
3 *syn* see PIPELINE
channel *vb syn* see CONDUCT 4
chant *vb syn* see SING 1
chaos *n* **1** *syn* see CONFUSION 3
2 *syn* see ANARCHY 1
rel misrule, unruliness
chap *n syn* see MAN 3
chaperon *vb* **1** *syn* see ACCOMPANY
rel guide, overlook, oversee, supervise
2 *syn* see SUPERVISE
chapfallen *adj syn* see DOWNCAST
chaplet *n syn* see WREATH
character *n* **1** an arbitrary or conventional device used in writing or printing <an inscription in runic *characters*>
syn mark, sign, symbol
rel cipher, device, monogram; letter
2 *syn* see CHARACTERISTIC 1
3 *syn* see QUALITY 1
rel distinction, uniqueness, uniquity
4 *syn* see TYPE
5 *syn* see DISPOSITION 3
rel soul, spirit; courage, mettle, resolution; intellect, intelligence, mind
6 *syn* see ROLE 1
7 *syn* see STATUS 1
8 *syn* see NOTABLE 1
9 *syn* see ECCENTRIC
‖**10** *syn* see HUMAN
11 *syn* see REPUTATION 2
character assassination *n syn* see DETRACTION
characteristic *adj* being or revealing a quality specific or identifying to an individual or group <her *characteristic* down-to-earth approach to a problem>
syn diacritic, diagnostic, distinctive, idiosyncratic, individual, peculiar, proper
rel especial, particular, special, specific; natural, normal, regular, typical
con general, generic, universal
ant uncharacteristic
characteristic *n* **1** something that marks or sets apart <*characteristics* that distinguish man from lower primates>

---

syn synonym(s)   *rel* related word(s)
ant antonym(s)   *con* contrasted word(s)
idiom idiomatic equivalent(s)
‖ use limited; if in doubt, see a dictionary

syn birthmark, character, feature, point, trait; *compare* QUALITY 1
rel badge, mark, sign, token; flavor, odor, savor, smack, tang; differentia; singularity
2 *syn* see QUALITY 1

characterize *vb* **1** *syn* see SKETCH
2 to be a peculiar or significant quality or feature of something <a man *characterized* by quiet dignity>
syn distinguish, individualize, individuate, mark, qualify, signalize, singularize
rel define, describe, differentiate, identify; peculiarize, personalize
idiom be a feature of

characterless *adj* lacking in character or solid qualities <a drab *characterless* little man that no one ever seemed to notice>
syn namby-pamby, pantywaist, wishy-washy
rel childish, infantile; sissified, sissy, unmanly; futile, weak; impotent, powerless
con manly, strong, vigorous, virile

charade *n* *syn* see PRETENSE 2

chare *n* *syn* see TASK 1

charge *vb* **1** *syn* see BURDEN
2 *syn* see LOAD 3
3 *syn* see PERMEATE
4 *syn* see ENTRUST 1
5 *syn* see COMMAND
rel ask, request, solicit; adjure
6 *syn* see ACCUSE
rel impugn, reprehend, reproach
idiom bring (*or* prefer) charges
con excuse, forgive, pardon, remit; acquit
ant absolve
7 *syn* see ASCRIBE
8 *syn* see RUSH 1

charge *n* **1** *syn* see LOAD 3
rel business, devoir, place
2 *syn* see OBLIGATION 2
3 *syn* see OVERSIGHT 1
4 *syn* see COMMAND 1
5 *syn* see PRICE 1

chargeless *adj* *syn* see FREE 5

charger *n* *syn* see COURSER

charioteer *vb* *syn* see DRIVE 5

charisma *n* *syn* see CHARM 3

charitable *adj* **1** having or showing interest in or concern for the welfare of others <spent generously for *charitable* aid to the needy>
syn altruistic, benevolent, eleemosynary, good, humane, humanitarian, philanthropic
rel accommodating, helpful, obliging; benign, kindhearted, kindly, sympathetic
2 *syn* see FORBEARING
rel benevolent, considerate, kindly, thoughtful
con cold, harsh, heartless, unfeeling
ant uncharitable

charity *n* **1** *syn* see MERCY
rel affection, attachment, love; altruism, benevolence, humaneness; kindliness; amity, friendliness, goodwill
con malevolence, malignancy, malignity, spite, spleen
ant ill will, malice

2 *syn* see DONATION

charivari *n* *syn* see SHIVAREE

charlatan *n* one who pretends unscrupulously to knowledge or skill <the medical establishment called him a *charlatan*>
syn mountebank, quack, quacksalver, quackster, saltimbanque; *compare* IMPOSTOR
rel bluff, four-flusher, sham

Charlie McCarthy *n* *syn* see STOOGE 1

charm *n* **1** *syn* see SPELL
2 an object worn or cherished to ward off evil or attract good fortune <the American Indian medicine bag is essentially a *charm*>
syn amulet, fetish, juju, luck, mascot, periapt, phylactery, talisman, zemi
3 a quality or combination of qualities that is wholly attractive and irresistible <the *charm* of her smile>
syn allure, appeal, charisma, fascination, glamour, magnetism, witchcraft, witchery
rel allurement, attraction, attractiveness, lure; agreeableness, delightfulness, gratefulness
con hatefulness, obnoxiousness, odiousness, repulsiveness; distastefulness, unpleasantness

charm *vb* **1** *syn* see ATTRACT 1
2 *syn* see BEWITCH 1

charmed *adj* *syn* see ENAMORED 3

charmer *n* *syn* see MAGICIAN 1

charming *adj* *syn* see ATTRACTIVE 1
ant charmless

chart *n* **1** a stylized or symbolic depiction of something incapable of direct verbal or pictorial representation (as because of complexity or abstractness) <a *chart* of anticipated economic progress>
syn graph, map
rel plan, plat, plot, scheme
2 *syn* see TABLE 2

chart *vb* *syn* see PLAN 2

charter *n* *syn* see DEED 3

charter *vb* *syn* see HIRE 1

chary *adj* **1** *syn* see CAUTIOUS
rel disinclined, hesitant, loath, reluctant; economical, frugal, sparing, thrifty; constrained, inhibited, restrained
2 *syn* see SPARING

chase *vb* **1** *syn* see FOLLOW 2
con flee, fly
2 *syn* see HUNT 1
3 *syn* see EJECT 1
4 *syn* see RUSH 1
5 *syn* see COURSE

chase *n* *syn* see HUNTING
2 *syn* see GAME 3

chaser *n* *syn* see WOLF

chasm *n* **1** *syn* see GULF 2
2 *syn* see RAVINE
3 *syn* see OMISSION
4 *syn* see SCHISM 3

chasmal *adj* *syn* see CAVERNOUS 1

chaste *adj* free from every trace of the lewd or salacious <was as *chaste* in language as in conduct>

syn clean, decent, immaculate, modest, pure, spotless, stainless, unblemished, undefiled, unsullied

rel ethical, moral, righteous, virtuous; maidenly, virgin, virginal; becoming, decorous, proper, seemly; abstinent, continent

con coarse, gross, obscene, ribald, vulgar; lascivious, lecherous, licentious, lustful; gluttonous, incontinent, self-indulgent

ant unchaste

chasten *vb syn* see PUNISH 1

rel abase, humble, humiliate; afflict, try

con baby, humor, indulge, spoil

ant pamper

chastise *vb syn* see PUNISH 1

rel baste, beat, belabor, pummel, thrash

chastisement *n syn* see PUNISHMENT

chat *vb* **1** to emit a ready flow of inconsequential talk <*chats* on the phone for hours>

syn babble, burble, cackle, chatter, chin-chin, clack, clatter, ‖dish, dither, gab, gabble, ‖gas, jaw, ‖natter, patter, prate, prattle, rattle, run on, smatter, talk, tinkle, twaddle, twiddle, twitter, yak, yakety-yak, yammer, yatter; *compare* CONVERSE

rel yap; blab, gossip; gush, lallygag; confabulate

idiom beat one's gums, ‖chew the fat (*or* rag), ‖shoot (*or* bat) the breeze, ‖shoot (*or* sling) the bull

con discourse, expound; declaim, harangue, hold forth, orate, preach

2 *syn* see CONVERSE

chat *n* **1** *syn* see CHATTER

2 an informal conversation <had a satisfactory little *chat* with the new assistant>

syn causerie, chin, prose, rap, talk, yarn; *compare* CONVERSATION 2

rel gossip, tête-à-tête

idiom bull session, rap session

con debate, deliberation, discussion

3 *syn* see CONVERSATION 1

chateau *n syn* see MANSION

chattel *n* **1** chattels *pl syn* see POSSESSION 2

2 *syn* see SLAVE 1

chatter *vb* **1** *syn* see GIBBER

2 *syn* see CHAT 1

chatter *n* idle and often loud and incessant talk <schoolgirl *chatter*>

syn babble, bibble-babble, blab, blabber, ‖blatter, brabble, cackle, chat, chin-chin, ‖chin music, chitchat, chitter-chatter, clack, gab, gabble, gibble-gabble, jabber, palaver, prate, prattle, stultiloquence, talkee-talkee, tittle-tattle, yak, yakety-yak, yak-yak, yatter

rel ‖bull, gossip, small talk

idiom tongue wagging

chatterbox *n* one who engages in chatter <that old *chatterbox* will talk your arm off>

syn bandar-log, blabber, blabbermouth, blabmouth, chatterer, chewet, gabber, jabberer, magpie, prater, prattler

rel busybody, gossip, newsmonger, quidnunc, scandalmonger, tabby, tattletale

chatterer *n syn* see CHATTERBOX

chatty *adj syn* see TALKATIVE

‖**chaw** *vb* **1** *syn* see CHEW 1

2 *syn* see PONDER 2

chawbacon *n syn* see RUSTIC

cheap *adj* **1** costing little <produce is usually *cheaper* in summer>

syn inexpensive, low, low-cost, low-priced, popular, reasonable, uncostly, undear

rel bargain-basement, bargain-counter, cut-rate, reduced; dirt-cheap

con dear, high, high-priced

ant costly, expensive

2 of inferior quality <*cheap* furniture is never a bargain>

syn base, cheesy, common, mean, ‖ornery, paltry, poor, rubbishing, rubbishly, rubbishy, shoddy, sleazy, tatty, trashy, trumpery; *compare* INFERIOR 2

rel cheap-jack, valueless, worthless; flashy, garish, meretricious, tawdry; brummagem, fake, phony, sham; bad, rotten, terrible

con capital, excellent, fine, good; first-class, first-rate, high-class, high-grade, superior, tip-top, top-notch

ant precious

3 *syn* see CONTEMPTIBLE

rel wrong; base, low, vile; measly, paltry, petty, trifling

ant noble

4 *syn* see STINGY

cheapen *vb syn* see DEPRECIATE 1

cheap–jack (*or* cheap–john) *n syn* see PEDDLER

cheapskate *n syn* see MISER

cheat *n* **1** *syn* see DECEPTION 1

2 *syn* see IMPOSTURE

rel bamboozlement, cozening, hoaxing; chicane, chicanery, trickery

3 *syn* see SWINDLER

cheat *vb* to obtain something (as money) from or an advantage over by dishonesty and trickery <*cheated* out of his inheritance by a grasping lawyer>

syn beat, bilk, boodle, ‖burn, chisel, chouse, cozen, ‖crook, defraud, diddle, do, ‖doodle, ‖dry-shave, ‖duff, flimflam, gyp, ‖mace, ‖mump, overreach, ream, ‖screw, sucker, swindle, take; *compare* EXTORT 1, FLEECE 1

rel befool, dupe, fool, gull, slick; bunco, con, fudge, short; beguile, deceive, delude, double-cross, mislead

cheater *n syn* see SWINDLER

check *vb* **1** *syn* see ARREST 1

rel cease, desist, discontinue, stop; repress, suppress; circumvent, foil, frustrate, thwart

ant expedite

2 *syn* see RESTRAIN 1

rel baffle, balk; obviate, preclude, prevent

ant accelerate (*of speed*); advance (*as of hopes, plans*); release (*of feelings, energies*)

---

syn synonym(s)   *rel* related word(s)
ant antonym(s)   *con* contrasted word(s)
idiom idiomatic equivalent(s)
‖ use limited; if in doubt, see a dictionary

3 *syn* see TRY 1

4 *syn* see AGREE 4

check *n* **1** *syn* see SETBACK

2 a statement of charges for food and drink consumed (as at a restaurant) <shocked at the size of the *check*>
syn bill, tab
rel damage, score

check out *vb* ‖**1** *syn* see DIE 1

2 *syn* see AGREE 4

check over *vb* *syn* see SCRUTINIZE 1

check–over *n* *syn* see EXAMINATION

check up *vb* *syn* see SCRUTINIZE 1

checkup *n* *syn* see EXAMINATION

cheek *n* **1** **cheeks** *pl* *syn* see BUTTOCKS

2 *syn* see EFFRONTERY

cheeky *adj* *syn* see WISE 5

cheep *vb* *syn* see CHIRP

cheer *vb* **1** *syn* see COMFORT

2 *syn* see ENCOURAGE 1

3 *syn* see APPLAUD 2

cheerful *adj* **1** marked by or suggestive of lighthearted ease of mind and spirit <a *cheerful* smile>
syn blithe, cheery, ‖chirk, chirpy, chirrupy, lightsome, sunbeamy, sunny; *compare* LIVELY 1
rel airy, carefree, debonair, jaunty; animated, gay, lighthearted, lively, vivacious; buoyant, corky
idiom in good (*or* high) spirits, of good cheer
con blue, dejected, depressed, melancholy; dispirited, heavyhearted; joyless, mournful, sorrowful, woeful; dour, morose, saturnine, sullen; doleful, lugubrious; austere, forbidding, grim, stern
ant gloomy, glum

2 *syn* see GLAD 2
ant cheerless

‖**cheerio** *interj* *syn* see GOOD-BYE

cheerless *adj* *syn* see GLOOMY 3
rel dejecting
ant cheerful

cheery *adj* **1** *syn* see GLAD 2

2 *syn* see CHEERFUL 1

cheeseparer *n* *syn* see MISER

cheeseparing *adj* *syn* see STINGY
rel cheap, grudging, mean, shabby; illiberal

cheesy *adj* *syn* see CHEAP 2

chef d'oeuvre *n* **1** *syn* see MASTERPIECE 1

2 *syn* see SHOWPIECE

‖**chemist** *n* *syn* see DRUGGIST

cherish *vb* **1** *syn* see NURSE 2
rel conserve, preserve, save; entertain, harbor, keep, shelter; defend, guard, safeguard, shield
con reject, repudiate, scorn
ant abandon

2 *syn* see APPRECIATE 1
rel revere, reverence, venerate
idiom hold in high esteem
con disregard, forget, ignore, overlook, slight
ant neglect

3 *syn* see ADMIRE 1

chest *n* *syn* see TREASURY 2

chesty *adj* *syn* see BUXOM

chew *vb* **1** to crush or grind with the teeth <*chew* your food well>
syn champ, ‖chaw, chomp, ‖chonk, chumble, chump, crunch, masticate, munch, ruminate, scrunch
rel bite; gnaw, nibble; consume, devour, eat; gum, mumble
‖**2** *syn* see SCOLD 1

chewet *n* *syn* see CHATTERBOX

‖**chew out** *vb* *syn* see SCOLD 1

chiaus *n* *syn* see SWINDLER

chic *n* *syn* see FASHION 3

chic *adj* *syn* see STYLISH

chicane *vb* **1** *syn* see QUIBBLE 1

2 *syn* see DUPE

chicane *n* *syn* see DECEPTION 1
rel artifice, feint, gambit, maneuver, ploy, ruse, stratagem, trick, wile; furtiveness, surreptitiousness, underhandedness
con forthrightness, straightforwardness

chicanery *n* *syn* see DECEPTION 1
rel intrigue, machination, plot; furtiveness, surreptitiousness, underhandedness
con forthrightness, straightforwardness; honesty, honor, integrity, probity

chichi *adj* **1** *syn* see SHOWY

2 *syn* see PRECIOUS 4

chick *n* **1** *syn* see CHILD 1

‖**2** *syn* see GIRL FRIEND 1

chickabiddy *n* *syn* see CHILD 1

chicken *n* *syn* see COWARD

‖**chicken** *adj* *syn* see COWARDLY

chide *vb* *syn* see REPROVE
rel berate, rate, scold, upbraid
con applaud, compliment; approve, endorse, sanction
ant commend

chiding *n* *syn* see REBUKE

chief *n* **1** *syn* see LEADER 2
rel dictator, duce, führer

2 *syn* see NOTABLE 1

chief *adj* **1** *syn* see FIRST 3

2 standing apart by reason of superior importance, significance, or influence <his *chief* claim to consideration is his unquestionable uprightness>
syn capital, ‖cock, dominant, main, major, number one, outstanding, predominant, preeminent, principal, star, stellar
rel primal, primary, prime; important, prominent, significant; consequential, momentous, weighty; effective, potent, telling; controlling, master, ruling
con inconsequential, minor, trivial, unimportant; collateral, contingent, secondary

chiefly *adv* *syn* see GENERALLY 1

chieftain *n* *syn* see LEADER 2

chiffer *n* *syn* see NUMBER

child *n* **1** a young person <a movie for both *children* and adults>
syn bud, chick, chickabiddy, chit, juvenile, kid, moppet, ‖nipper, puss, youngling, young one, youngster, youth

rel minor; adolescent, teenager, teener, teeny-bopper; brat, bratling, dickens, runabout; cherub, innocent, lamb, sweetling
idiom a slip of a boy (*or* girl), small fry, young hopeful
ant adult, grown-up
2 children *pl syn* see OFFSPRING
childbearing *n* **1** *syn* see BIRTH 1
2 *syn* see LABOR 2
childbed *n* *syn* see CONFINEMENT 2
childbirth *n* **1** *syn* see BIRTH 1
2 *syn* see LABOR 2
childing *adj* **1** *syn* see PREGNANT 1
2 *syn* see FERTILE
childish *adj* significantly deficient in maturity <a *childish* and spiteful attitude>
syn babyish, immature, infantile, infantine, pre-kindergarten, puerile
rel asinine, fatuous, foolish, silly, simple; naive, unsophisticated; arrested, backward, moronic, retarded, slow, ‖wanting
ant adult
child's play *n* *syn* see SNAP 1
chill *vb* *syn* see DISCOURAGE 1
chill *adj* **1** *syn* see COLD 1
2 *syn* see COLD 2
rel distant, formal, reserved, solitary, standoffish, uncompanionable, withdrawn; abstracted, disinterested, uninterested
con easy, gregarious, informal; sociable
chiller *n* *syn* see THRILLER
chillsome *adj* *syn* see COLD 1
chilly *adj* *syn* see COLD 1
chime *n* *syn* see HARMONY 2
chime *vb* *syn* see RING
chime in *vb* **1** *syn* see INTERRUPT 2
2 *syn* see SAY 1
chimera *n* *syn* see PIPE DREAM
chimerical *adj* *syn* see FICTITIOUS 1
rel ambitious, pretentious, utopian; deceptive, delusive, delusory; fabulous, mythical; absurd, preposterous
con believable, plausible, rational, reasonable; possible, practicable
ant feasible
chiming *adj* *syn* see HARMONIOUS 1
chin *n* *syn* see CHAT 2
chin *vb* *syn* see CONVERSE
chin–chin *vb* *syn* see CHAT 1
chin–chin *n* *syn* see CHATTER
‖**chinchy** *adj* *syn* see STINGY
chine *n* *syn* see RIDGE 1
Chinese puzzle *n* *syn* see MYSTERY
Chinese wall *n* *syn* see OBSTACLE
chink *n* *syn* see CRACK 3
rel interruption
chink *vb* *syn* see JINGLE
‖**chink** *n* *syn* see MONEY
chinkle *vb* *syn* see JINGLE
‖**chin music** *n* *syn* see CHATTER
chintzy *adj* **1** *syn* see GAUDY
2 *syn* see STINGY
chin–up *adj* *syn* see BRAVE 1
chip *vb* *syn* see CHIRP

chip in *vb* **1** *syn* see CONTRIBUTE 1
2 *syn* see INTERRUPT 2
chipper *vb* *syn* see CHIRP
chipper *adj* **1** *syn* see LIVELY 1
2 *syn* see NEAT 2
‖**chippy** *n* *syn* see DOXY 1
‖**chips** *n* *pl* *syn* see MONEY
‖**chirk** *adj* **1** *syn* see LIVELY 1
2 *syn* see CHEERFUL 1
chirk (up) *vb* *syn* see ENCOURAGE 1
‖**chirm** *n* *syn* see DIN
‖**chirm** *vb* *syn* see CHIRP
chirography *n* *syn* see HANDWRITING
chirp *vb* to make a short, sharp, and usually repetitive sound <sparrows *chirping* on the lawn>
syn cheep, chip, chipper, ‖chirm, chirrup, clutter, peep, tweedle, tweet, twitter
chirpy *adj* *syn* see CHEERFUL
chirrup *vb* *syn* see CHIRP
chirrupy *adj* *syn* see CHEERFUL 1
chisel *vb* **1** *syn* see SCULPTURE
2 *syn* see CHEAT
chisel (in) *vb* *syn* see INTRUDE 1
‖**chiselly** *adj* *syn* see BAD 8
chit *n* *syn* see CHILD 1
chit *n* *syn* see NOTE 2
chitchat *n* **1** *syn* see CHATTER
2 *syn* see SMALL TALK
chitter *vb* *syn* see CHIRP
chitter–chatter *n* **1** *syn* see CHATTER
2 *syn* see SMALL TALK
chivalrous *adj* *syn* see GENEROUS 1
rel knightly, manly, noble
con churlish common, low
chivy *vb* **1** *syn* see FOLLOW 2
2 *syn* see BAIT 2
rel afflict, torment, try; chase, pursue, trail
choate *adj* *syn* see WHOLE 3
chockablock *adj* *syn* see FULL 1
chock–full *adj* *syn* see FULL 1
choice *n* **1** the act, right, opportunity, or faculty of choosing or deciding <the *choice* lies with the electorate>
syn alternative, ‖druthers, election, option, preference, selection
rel decision, determination, finding, judgment, verdict; appraisal, evaluation, rating
2 *syn* see BEST
choice *adj* having qualities that appeal to a fine or highly refined taste <a few *choice* spirits gathered nightly to discuss the day's events>
syn dainty, delicate, elegant, exquisite, rare, recherché, select, superior
rel incomparable, peerless, preeminent, prime, superlative, supreme, surpassing, transcendent, unsurpassed; chosen, culled, picked, selected
con common, ordinary; average, fair, mediocre, medium, middling, run-of-the-mill, second-rate; drab, dull, lackluster, lusterless

---

syn synonym(s)   *rel* related word(s)
ant antonym(s)   *con* contrasted word(s)
idiom idiomatic equivalent(s)
‖ use limited; if in doubt, see a dictionary

ant indifferent

||**choicy** *adj syn* see NICE 1

choke *vb* **1** to check normal breathing especially by compressing or obstructing the windpipe <*choked* by a bone in the throat>
syn strangle, throttle; *compare* SUFFOCATE
2 *syn* see SUFFOCATE
3 *syn* see FILL 1
4 *syn* see LOAD 3

choke (off) *vb syn* see SILENCE

||**chokey** *n syn* see JAIL

choking *n syn* see REPRESSION 1

choleric *adj* **1** *syn* see IRASCIBLE
rel acrimonious, angry, fiery, indignant, irate, mad, spunky, wrathful, wroth; captious, carping, faultfinding
con calm, serene, tranquil; composed, cool, nonchalant
ant placid
2 *syn* see ANGRY

chomp *vb* **1** *syn* see CHEW 1
2 *syn* see BITE 1

||**chonk** *vb syn* see CHEW 1

choose *vb* **1** to fix upon one among alternatives as the one to be taken, accepted, or adopted <*chose* the largest apple but found it sour>
syn cull, elect, mark, opt (for), optate, pick, pick out, prefer, select, single (out), take
rel adopt, embrace, espouse; crave, desire, love, want, wish
con decline, refuse, repudiate, spurn; abnegate, forbear, forgo
ant reject; eschew
2 *syn* see WILL
rel favor, prefer
||**3** *syn* see DESIRE 1

choosy *adj syn* see NICE 1

chop *vb* **1** *syn* see FELL 2
2 to cut into fragments by repeated strokes <*chop* meat and onions for hash>
syn hash, mince
rel cut up, dice, fragment
idiom cut to bits, make mincemeat of

chop *n syn* see CUFF

chop–chop *adv syn* see FAST 2

chore *n* **1** *syn* see TASK 1
2 *syn* see TASK 2
rel trial, tribulation

chortle *vb syn* see LAUGH

chorus *n syn* see HARMONY 1

chosen *adj syn* see SELECT 1

chouse *n syn* see TRICK 1

chouse *vb syn* see CHEAT

||**chow** *n* **1** *syn* see FOOD 1
2 *syn* see MEAL

chowchow *adj syn* see MISCELLANEOUS

chowchow *n syn* see MISCELLANY 1

chowderhead *n syn* see DUNCE

chrism *n syn* see OINTMENT

christcross–row *n syn* see ALPHABET 1

christen *vb* **1** *syn* see BAPTIZE
2 *syn* see NAME 1

Christian *adj syn* see DECOROUS 1

Christian name *n syn* see GIVEN NAME

Christmas *n* a festival or holiday commemorating the birth of Christ <gave presents on *Christmas*>
syn Nativity, noel, Xmas, yule, yuletide

chronic *adj* **1** *syn* see HABITUAL 2
2 *syn* see USUAL 1

chronicle *n* **1** *syn* see HISTORY 2
2 *syn* see ACCOUNT 7
rel narration, recital, recountal

chthonian *adj syn* see INFERNAL 1

chthonic *adj syn* see INFERNAL 1

chubby *adj syn* see ROTUND 2
ant slim

chuck *vb* **1** *syn* see DISCARD
2 *syn* see EJECT 1
3 *syn* see ABANDON 1
4 *syn* see THROW 1

||**chuck** *n syn* see HARBOR 3

chucker *n syn* see BOUNCER 2

||**chucker–out** *n syn* see BOUNCER 2

chuckhole *n syn* see POTHOLE

chuckle *vb syn* see LAUGH

chucklehead *n syn* see DUNCE

chuckleheaded *adj syn* see STUPID 1

chuff *n* **1** *syn* see BOOR
2 *syn* see MISER

||**chuff** *adj syn* see SULLEN

||**chuffy** *adj syn* see STOCKY

||**chuffy** *adj syn* see SULLEN

chum *n syn* see ASSOCIATE 3

chumble *vb syn* see CHEW 1

chummy *adj* **1** *syn* see FAMILIAR 1
2 *syn* see INTIMATE 4

chump *n* ||**1** *syn* see HEAD 1
2 *syn* see DUNCE
3 *syn* see FOOL 3

chump *vb syn* see CHEW 1

||**chumpy** *adj syn* see STOCKY

chunk *n syn* see LUMP 1

chunky *adj syn* see STOCKY
rel chubby, rotund

||**chunter** *vb syn* see MUMBLE

church *n* **1** *syn* see HOUSE OF WORSHIP
2 *syn* see RELIGION 2

church *adj syn* see ECCLESIASTICAL

churchly *adj syn* see ECCLESIASTICAL

churchman *n syn* see CLERGYMAN

churchmanly *adj syn* see ECCLESIASTICAL

churl *n syn* see BOOR
ant aristocrat, gentleman

churlish *adj syn* see BOORISH
rel crude, discourteous; blunt, brusque, crusty, curt, gruff; dour, surly; naive, unschooled
con bland, politic, smooth; polished, sophisticated
ant courtly

churn *vb syn* see SEETHE 4

chute *n syn* see WATERFALL

chutzpah *n syn* see EFFRONTERY

cicatrix *n syn* see SCAR

cicatrize *vb syn* see SCAR

||**cig** *n syn* see CIGARETTE

cigarette *n* a paper-wrapped tube of finely cut smoking tobacco <dependence on *cigarettes*>

syn ‖butt, ‖cig, ‖coffin nail, fag, ‖gasper, ‖pill, ‖skag, smoke

cimmerian *adj syn* see INFERNAL 2

cinch *n syn* see SNAP 1

cinch *vb syn* see ENSURE

cincture *n syn* see BELT 1

cincture *vb syn* see BELT 1

cinders *n pl syn* see ASH

cine *n syn* see MOVIE

‖**cinema** *n syn* see MOVIE

cipher *n* **1** *syn* see ZERO 1
2 *syn* see NUMBER
3 *syn* see MONOGRAM
4 *syn* see NONENTITY

cipher *vb* **1** *syn* see CALCULATE
‖**2** *syn* see SOLVE 2

ciphering *n syn* see COMPUTATION

circa *prep syn* see ABOUT 1

Circean *adj syn* see ENTICING

circle *n* **1** *syn* see RANGE 2
2 *syn* see CYCLE 1
3 *syn* see SET 5
rel acquaintance; cronies, friends, intimates; associates, companions, comrades
4 *syn* see CLIQUE

circle *vb* **1** *syn* see SURROUND 1
2 *syn* see TURN 1

circuit *n* **1** *syn* see CIRCUMFERENCE
rel course, route, way; journey, tour, travels, trip
2 *syn* see REVOLUTION 1
3 *syn* see TOUR 2
4 *syn* see LEAGUE 4

circuitous *adj syn* see INDIRECT 1
ant straight

circuitously *adv syn* see ABOUT 2

circular *adj* **1** *syn* see ROUND 1
2 *syn* see INDIRECT 1

circulate *vb* **1** *syn* see SPREAD 1
rel exchange, interchange; flow; revolve, rotate
2 *syn* see MOBILIZE 1

circulation *n syn* see REVOLUTION 1

circulator *n syn* see GOSSIP 1

circumambages *n pl syn* see VERBIAGE 1

circumambulate *vb syn* see WANDER 1

circumbendibus *n syn* see VERBIAGE 1

circumduct *vb* **1** *syn* see TURN 1
2 *syn* see ABOLISH 1

circumference *n* a continuous line or course about an area <strolled along the *circumference* of the reservoir>
syn ambit, circuit, compass, perimeter, periphery; *compare* BORDER 1
rel boundary, bounds, confines, limits; border, margin, rim

circumlocution *n syn* see VERBIAGE 1
con conciseness, concision, pithiness, succinctness, terseness; compactness

circumnavigate *vb syn* see SKIRT 2

circumscribe *vb syn* see LIMIT 2
rel fetter, hamper, trammel
con amplify, distend, inflate, swell; enlarge
ant dilate, expand

circumscribed *adj syn* see DEFINITE 1

rel bound, bounded, finite; confined, cramped, strait

circumscription *n* **1** *syn* see RESTRICTION 1
2 *syn* see RESTRICTION 2

circumspect *adj syn* see CAUTIOUS
rel meticulous, punctilious, scrupulous
con adventurous, daredevil, foolhardy; careless, heedless; bold
ant audacious

circumstance *n* **1** *syn* see OCCURRENCE
rel detail, item, particular; component, constituent, element, factor
2 *syn* see FATE

circumstantial *adj* marked by careful attention to relevant details <gave a *circumstantial* account of his adventure>
syn blow-by-blow, clocklike, detailed, full, itemized, minute, particular, particularized, thorough
rel accurate, exact, nice, precise; complete, replete; close, strict
con compendious, concise, laconic, pithy, short, succinct, terse; abbreviated, curtailed, cut, pruned, shortened, trimmed
ant abridged; summary

circumvent *vb* **1** *syn* see FRUSTRATE 1
rel befool, dupe, hoodwink, trick; avoid, elude, escape, evade
ant conform (*to laws, orders*); cooperate (*with persons*)
2 *syn* see SKIRT 2
3 *syn* see SKIRT 3

circumvolution *n syn* see REVOLUTION 1

cit *n syn* see TOWNSMAN

citadel *n syn* see FORT

citation *n syn* see ENCOMIUM
rel award, guerdon, reward

cite *vb* **1** *syn* see REMEMBER
2 *syn* see MENTION
3 *syn* see ADDUCE
rel count, enumerate, number, tell

citizen *n* **1** *syn* see TOWNSMAN
2 a person regarded as a member of a sovereign state, entitled to its protection, and subject to its laws <the subtle bond between the *citizen* and the nation>
syn national, subject
con foreigner, stranger
ant alien

city *adj syn* see URBAN

civic *adj syn* see PUBLIC 1

civil *adj* **1** *syn* see PUBLIC 1
2 adequate in courtesy <made a *civil* inquiry about their health>
syn courteous, genteel, mannerly, polite, well-mannered; *compare* COURTLY
rel cultivated, refined, well-bred; accommodating, affable, cordial, obliging; bland, diplomatic, gracious, politic, suave, urbane

---

con boorish, churlish, loutish, uncouth; discourteous, ill-mannered, impolite, ungracious
ant uncivil; rude

civilities *n pl syn* see MANNER 5

civilized *adj* **1** *syn* see DECOROUS 1
2 *syn* see SUAVE

Civitas Dei *n syn* see HEAVEN 2

‖**clabber** *vb syn* see CURDLE

clack *vb* **1** *syn* see CHAT 1
2 *syn* see RATTLE 1

clack *n* **1** *syn* see CHATTER
2 *syn* see GOSSIP 1

clad *vb* **1** *syn* see CLOTHE
2 *syn* see SHEATHE

‖**claggy** *adj* **1** *syn* see STICKY 1
2 *syn* see MUDDY 1

claim *vb* **1** *syn* see DEMAND 1
rel adduce, advance, allege; assert, defend, justify, maintain, vindicate
con abnegate, forgo; refuse, reject, repudiate; disavow, disown
ant disclaim; renounce
2 *syn* see MAINTAIN 2

claim *n* **1** a real or assumed right to demand something as one's own or one's due <his genial wit was his greatest *claim* to fame>
syn ‖dibs, pretense, pretension, title
rel birthright, prerogative, privilege, right; affirmation, assertion, declaration, protestation
2 *syn* see INTEREST 1

clamant *adj syn* see PRESSING

clamber *vb syn* see SCRAMBLE 1

clamor *n* **1** *syn* see COMMOTION 4
2 *syn* see DIN
3 *syn* see COMMOTION 1

clamor *vb syn* see ROAR
rel claim, demand; agitate, debate, dispute
idiom make the welkin ring, raise the roof

clamorous *adj* **1** *syn* see VOCIFEROUS
rel articulate, eloquent, vocal, voluble; adjuring, begging, imploring, importunate
ant taciturn
2 *syn* see PRESSING

clamp *n syn* see HOLD

clampdown *n syn* see REPRESSION 2

clan *n* **1** *syn* see FAMILY 1
2 *syn* see CLIQUE

clandestine *adj syn* see SECRET 1
rel illegitimate, illicit; artful, foxy, sly
con aboveboard, forthright, straightforward
ant open

clandestinely *adv syn* see SECRETLY

‖**clanger** *n syn* see ERROR 2

clangorous *adj syn* see NOISY

clap *n syn* see BANG 2

‖**clapped–out** *adj* **1** *syn* see EFFETE 2
2 *syn* see TIRED 1

claptrap *n syn* see NONSENSE 2

‖**claret** *n syn* see BLOOD 1

clarify *vb* **1** *syn* see PURIFY 1
2 to make clear and understandable <felt a need to *clarify* his position on the question>
syn clear, clear up, elucidate, explain, illuminate, illustrate; *compare* EXPLAIN 1

rel settle, straighten out; define, delineate, formulate; analyze, break down, simplify
idiom make plain
con befog, cloud, obfuscate, obscure; confuse, foul up, muddle, ‖snafu

clarion *adj syn* see FAIR 2

clarity *n* notable precision of thought or expression <*clarity* of expression depends on use of exactly the right words in precisely the right way>
syn clearness, limpidity, lucidity, perspicuity, plainness
rel articulateness, articulation; care, exactitude, fussiness, meticulousness, nicety, precision; accuracy, correctitude, propriety
con haziness, imprecision, indefiniteness, unclearness, vagueness; inexactness, laxity, looseness, sloppiness, slovenliness
ant obscurity

‖**clarty** *adj* **1** *syn* see MUDDY 1
2 *syn* see STICKY 1

clash *vb* **1** *syn* see BUMP 1
2 to be markedly out of harmony <garish colors that *clashed* almost painfully>
syn conflict, disaccord, discord, disharmonize, jangle, jar, mismatch
rel fret, gall, grate, try
idiom swear at one another
con accord, blend, conform, correspond; fit, meet, suit
ant harmonize

clash *n* **1** *syn* see IMPACT 1
2 a sharp and usually brief conflict especially between military units <recurrent border *clashes*>
syn affray, brush, fray, melee, mellay, scrimmage, skirmish
rel brawl, broil, fracas, riot, row, rumpus, scrap, set-to; action, battle, conflict, engagement; embroilment, encounter
idiom clash of arms, passage at (*or* of) arms

clashing *adj syn* see ANTIPATHETIC 1

clasp *n syn* see HOLD

clasp *vb* **1** *syn* see EMBRACE 1
2 *syn* see TAKE 4

class *n* **1** a unit or a subunit of a larger whole made up of members sharing one or more characteristics <miniaturization of circuitry made possible a whole new *class* of small computers and calculators>
syn category, grade, group, grouping, league, pigeonhole, tier
rel brand, color, description, feather, genre, grain, ilk, kidney, kind, nature, order, sort, stamp, style, type; bracket, branch, denomination, division, head, section; genus, species
2 *syn* see QUALITY 3
3 *syn* see TYPE

class *vb* **1** *syn* see ASSORT
2 to put into an appropriate class <he is generally *classed* among our leading theoretical physicists>
syn classify, evaluate, grade, rank, rate
rel appraise, gauge, judge; divide, part, separate; allot, assign; account, assess, consider, hold, reckon, regard; mark, score

classic *adj* **1** *syn* see EXCELLENT
  2 *syn* see VINTAGE 1
  3 *syn* see TYPICAL 1
classic *n syn* see MASTERPIECE 1
classical *adj* **1** *syn* see EXCELLENT
  2 *syn* see VINTAGE 1
  3 *syn* see TYPICAL 1
classify *vb* **1** *syn* see ASSORT
  2 *syn* see CLASS 2
‖**classy** *adj syn* see STYLISH
clatter *vb* **1** *syn* see RATTLE 1
  2 *syn* see CHAT 1
clatter *n syn* see COMMOTION 4
clattery *adj syn* see NOISY
claviger *n syn* see CUSTODIAN
‖**clawback** *n syn* see SYCOPHANT
clean *adj* **1** free from dirt <kept a *clean* house in a dirty neighborhood>
  syn cleanly, immaculate, spotless, taintless, unsoiled, unsullied
  rel bright, shining, sparkling; fresh, pure, untainted, wholesome
  idiom clean as a whistle (*or* new penny)
  con dingy, grimy, grubby, messy, mussy, slovenly; filthy, foul, noisome
  ant dirty, unclean
  2 *syn* see INNOCENT 2
  3 *syn* see CHASTE
  ant unclean
  4 *syn* see FAIR 5
clean *vb* **1** *syn* see PURIFY 1
  2 to make clean <*cleaned* his car every week>
  syn cleanse, clean up
  rel do, neaten, order, police, spruce, straighten (up), tidy, trim; brighten, freshen, furbish, recondition; renew, renovate
  idiom make spick-and-span
  con begrime, daub, dirty, sully; besmirch, defile, foul, pollute
  ant soil
  3 *syn* see DRESS 3
clean–cut *adj syn* see EXPLICIT
clean–limbed *adj syn* see SHAPELY
cleanly *adj syn* see CLEAN 1
  rel neat, orderly, spick-and-span, tidy, trim; dainty, fastidious, fussy, nice
  con disheveled, disorderly, slipshod, sloppy, slovenly, unkempt
  ant uncleanly
cleanse *vb* **1** *syn* see CLEAN 2
  rel disinfect, sanitize, sterilize
  2 *syn* see PURIFY 1
  3 *syn* see PURIFY 2
cleansing *n syn* see PURIFICATION
clean up *vb* **1** *syn* see CLEAR 6
  2 *syn* see CLEAN 2
  3 *syn* see SETTLE 7
‖**clean up** (on) *vb syn* see WHIP 2
clear *adj* **1** *syn* see FAIR 2
  2 *syn* see TRANSPARENT 1
  3 *syn* see TRANSLUCENT 3
  rel milky, opalescent
  4 free from obscurity or ambiguity <his account of the accident was perfectly *clear*>

  syn clear-cut, crystal, lucent, lucid, luculent, luminous, pellucid, perspicuous, translucent, transparent, transpicuous, unambiguous, unblurred; *compare* UNDERSTANDABLE
  rel apprehensible, comprehensible, graspable, knowable, understandable; plain, simple, straightforward, uncomplicated, unperplexed; defined, definite
  idiom clear as day (*or* crystal), plain as the nose on one's face
  con clouded, dark, mysterious, unclear; hazy, ill-defined, vague
  ant obscure
  5 readily perceived or apprehended <a *clear* case of embezzlement>
  syn apparent, conspicuous, distinct, evident, manifest, obvious, open-and-shut, openhanded, palpable, patent, plain, straightforward, unambiguous, unequivocal, univocal, unmistakable; *compare* SELF-EXPLANATORY, UNDERSTANDABLE
  rel appreciable, perceptible, recognizable, sensible, tangible; overt, public, published, unhidden, unobscured; exact, precise
  con dim, dusky, gloomy, murky; cryptic, dark, enigmatic, equivocal, indistinct, vague; arcane, esoteric, mysterious, occult
  ant obscure
  6 *syn* see EMPTY 1
clear *adv syn* see WELL 3
clear *vb* **1** *syn* see EXCULPATE
  2 *syn* see CLARIFY 2
  3 *syn* see VACATE 2
  4 *syn* see RID
  rel eliminate, rule out; clean, cleanse
  5 to make right by presenting what is due <*clear* one's accounts>
  syn clear off, discharge, liquidate, pay, pay up, quit, satisfy, settle, square
  rel close, pay off, repay, sink, solve
  6 to obtain as a profit or return <he *cleared* several thousand on the deal>
  syn clean up, gain, make, net
  rel acquire, get, obtain, secure; earn, win; accumulate, gather, glean, pick up
  7 *syn* see EXTRICATE 2
  8 to pass over or by <*cleared* the hurdle with perfect form>
  syn hurdle, leap, negotiate, over, overleap, surmount, vault
  9 to become fair <the weather *cleared* later in the day>
  syn ‖break, burn off
  rel ameliorate, better, improve, meliorate; settle, stabilize
  10 *syn* see VANISH
clear away *vb* **1** *syn* see REMOVE 4
  2 *syn* see EXTRICATE 2
clear–cut *adj* **1** *syn* see CLEAR 4
  2 *syn* see EXPLICIT

---

syn synonym(s)   *rel* related word(s)
ant antonym(s)   *con* contrasted word(s)
idiom idiomatic equivalent(s)
‖ use limited; if in doubt, see a dictionary

3 *syn* see INCISIVE

rel clear, distinct, manifest, plain; definite, explicit, express; exact, nice, precise

con fogged, hazy, misty; confused, muddled; obscured, overcast

4 *syn* see DECIDED 1

rel indubitable, undisputed, undoubted, unquestioned

idiom beyond a shade (*or* shadow) of doubt, past dispute

clearness *n syn* see CLARITY

clear off *vb syn* see CLEAR 5

clear out *vb syn* see GET OUT 1

clear–sightedness *n syn* see WIT 3

clear up *vb* **1** *syn* see CLARIFY 2

  2 *syn* see SOLVE 2

cleavage *n syn* see SCHISM 3

cleave *vb syn* see STICK 2

rel associate, combine, conjoin, join, link, unite

con alienate, disaffect, disunite, estrange, separate

cleave *vb* **1** *syn* see CUT 5

  2 *syn* see TEAR 1

rel divide, divorce, separate; chop, hew

con join, link, unite; attach, fasten

cleft *n* **1** *syn* see CRACK 3

  2 *syn* see RAVINE

  3 *syn* see SCHISM 3

clemency *n* **1** *syn* see MERCY

rel gentleness, mildness; equitableness, fairness, justness

con austerity, severity, sternness; rigidity, rigorousness, strictness; inexorableness, inflexibility, obduracy

ant harshness

  2 *syn* see FORBEARANCE 2

rel endurance, sufferance

con firmness, hardness, inflexibility, obdurateness, relentlessness, rigidity

ant harshness

clement *adj syn* see FORBEARING

rel compassionate, sympathetic, tender; benign, benignant, kind, kindly; benevolent, charitable, humane

con austere, severe, stern; rigid, rigorous, strict, stringent

ant harsh; barbarous

clench *n syn* see HOLD

clergyman *n* one duly ordained to the service of God in the Christian church <the responsibility of the *clergyman* to the whole community>

syn ‖blackcoat, cassock, churchman, cleric, clerical, clerk, ‖devil-dodger, divine, ‖dominie, ecclesiast, ecclesiastic, ‖Holy Joe, minister, parson, preacher, pulpitarian, pulpiteer, pulpiter, reverend, sermonizer, sky pilot

rel evangelist, missionary; chaplain, curate, pastor, vicar; father, priest, shepherd; predicant

idiom man of God, man of the cloth

cleric *n syn* see CLERGYMAN

clerical *n syn* see CLERGYMAN

clerisy *n syn* see INTELLIGENTSIA

clerk *n syn* see CLERGYMAN

clerkish *adj syn* see NICE 1

clever *adj* **1** *syn* see SKILLFUL 2

  2 *syn* see DEXTEROUS 1

  3 *syn* see INTELLIGENT 2

rel apt, prompt, quick, ready; able, capable, competent; all-around, many-sided, versatile

idiom quick as a flash, sharp (*or* smart) as a whip

con asinine, fatuous, foolish, simple

ant dull

4 highly skilled in devising or contriving <very *clever* about getting her own way>

syn adroit, canny, ‖coony, cunning, dexterous, ingenious, ‖sleighty, slim, sly; *compare* SKILLFUL 2

rel able, adept, expert, handy, masterly, proficient, skilled, skillful; capable, competent, qualified; crafty, deceitful, slick, tricky

con awkward, clumsy, gauche, inept, maladroit; dilatory, ‖laggard, slow, sluggish; incapable, incompetent, inept, unqualified

5 pleasing because of aptness, sparkle, and usually wit <delighted her audience with a series of *clever* comparisons>

syn good, scintillating, smart, sprightly

rel bright, brilliant, coruscating, dazzling, sparkling; piquant, racy, salty; fanciful, whimsical; amusing, entertaining, pleasing; facetious, funny, humorous, witty; laughable, risible

con drab, dull, humdrum, monotonous, stodgy; barren, empty, inane; fatuous, pointless; absurd, foolish, nonsensical, ridiculous

ant stupid

‖cleverly *adv syn* see WELL 3

cliché *n syn* see COMMONPLACE

cliché *adj syn* see TRITE

clichéd *adj syn* see TRITE

click *vb syn* see SUCCEED 2

client *n syn* see CUSTOMER

clientage *n syn* see FOLLOWING 2

clientele *n syn* see FOLLOWING 2

climacteric *adj syn* see ACUTE 6

climate *n syn* see ENVIRONMENT

climatize *vb syn* see HARDEN 2

climax *n syn* see APEX 2

climax *vb* to bring to or come to a satisfying termination <the feast was *climaxed* by a glorious plum pudding>

syn cap, crown, culminate, finish off, round off, top off

rel content, please, satisfy; conclude, end, finish, terminate

climb *vb syn* see ASCEND 1

‖clinch *vb syn* see EMBRACE 1

clinch *n syn* see HOLD

clincher *n syn* see TRUMP CARD

cling *vb syn* see STICK 2

cling *n syn* see ADHERENCE 1

clinging *n syn* see ADHERENCE 1

clink *vb syn* see JINGLE

‖clink *n syn* see JAIL

clinkers *n pl syn* see ASH

‖clip *vb syn* see EMBRACE 1

clip *n syn* see BROOCH

clip *vb* **1** *syn* see CUT 6

2 syn see MOW
3 syn see REDUCE 2
4 syn see OVERCHARGE 1
clique *n* a narrowly exclusive group of people usually held together by a common often selfish interest or purpose <there was a politically minded *clique* on the campus>
syn cabal, camarilla, camp, circle, clan, coterie, in-group, mob, ring; *compare* SET 5
clitter *vb syn* see RATTLE 1
cloak *n syn* see MASK 2
cloak *vb syn* see DISGUISE
rel blanket, curtain, screen, shroud, veil
ant uncloak
clobber *vb* ‖**1 syn** see WHIP 2
2 syn see SLAM 1
clochard *n syn* see VAGABOND
clock *vb syn* see TIME 2
‖**clock** *vb syn* see SET 11
clocklike *adj syn* see CIRCUMSTANTIAL
clockwise *adj syn* see RIGHT-HANDED
clod *n* **1 syn** see LUMP 1
2 syn see DUNCE
cloddish *adj syn* see BOORISH
clodhopper *n* **1 syn** see RUSTIC
2 syn see BOOR
clodhopping *adj syn* see BOORISH
clodpate *n syn* see DUNCE
clodpoll *n syn* see DUNCE
clog *n syn* see ENCUMBRANCE
clog *vb* **1 syn** see BURDEN
2 syn see HAMPER
3 syn see FILL 1
cloggy *adj syn* see STICKY 1
cloister *vb syn* see SECLUDE
cloistered *adj syn* see SECLUDED
clonk *vb syn* see THUD
‖**Cloot** *n, usu* **Cloots** *pl syn* see DEVIL 1
‖**Clootie** *n syn* see DEVIL 1
close *vb* **1** to fill an opening with an appropriate closure <be sure to *close* the gate>
syn ‖put to, shut
rel bang, clap, slam; block, choke, clog, obstruct, occlude, stop; debar, exclude
ant open
2 syn see SCREEN 3
3 to bring or come to a limit or to a natural or appropriate stopping point <*closed* the meeting as soon as the discussion was over>
syn complete, conclude, consummate, determine, do, end, finish, halt, terminate, ultimate, wind up, wrap up
rel cease, desist, quit, stop; finalize, write off
idiom call it a day, set a period to
con begin, commence, enter (on *or* upon), inaugurate, initiate, start
4 syn see FILL 1
5 syn see DECREASE
6 syn see MEET 6
close *n* **1 syn** see END 2
2 syn see FINALE
ant opening
‖**close** *n syn* see COURT 1
close *adj* **1 syn** see SILENT 3

idiom close as a clam
con candid, frank, plain
ant open
2 syn see STUFFY 1
rel humid, muggy, sticky
3 syn see STINGY
ant liberal
4 having the constituent parts massed closely together <a paper of fine *close* texture>
syn compact, crowded, dense, thick, tight
rel compacted, compressed, condensed, consolidated, constricted, contracted; firm, solid, substantial; impenetrable, impermeable; close-grained
con lax, loose, slack; unconsolidated
5 syn see TIGHT 3
6 not far removed (as in space, time, or relationship) from something stipulated or understood <true and veritable are *close* synonyms> <the park is very *close* to the river> <it is *close* to closing time>
syn immediate, near, near-at-hand, nearly, nigh, proximate; *compare* NEIGHBORING
rel abutting, adjacent, adjoining, contiguous; convenient, handy; nearest, nearmost, next
idiom at hand, at one's fingers' ends (*or* fingertips), under one's nose
con distant, far, faraway, far-off, removed
ant remote
7 syn see FAMILIAR 1
con cool, remote, withdrawn
ant aloof
close *adv* into proximity with respect to space, time, or approach <hoping to come *closer* to the truth of the matter>
syn at close hand, hard, near, nearby, nigh
rel almost, nearabout, nearly
idiom as near as no matter (*or* never mind), in hailing (*or* spitting) distance, within an inch (*or* an ace) of, within a stone's throw
con afar, distantly, far
ant remotely
close–at–hand *adj* **1 syn** see NEIGHBORING
2 syn see CONVENIENT 2
close–by *adj* **1 syn** see NEIGHBORING
2 syn see CONVENIENT 2
closed *adj syn* see SELF-SUFFICIENT
closed book *n syn* see MYSTERY
closed–minded *adj syn* see OBSTINATE
closefisted *adj syn* see STINGY
rel clinging, clutching, grasping, keeping, tenacious
close in *vb syn* see ENCLOSE 1
close–lipped *adj syn* see SILENT 3
closely *adv syn* see HARD 4
rel carefully, heedfully, mindfully, thoughtfully; meticulously, minutely, punctiliously, scrupulously
con carelessly, heedlessly, thoughtlessly

---

syn synonym(s)   *rel* related word(s)
ant antonym(s)   *con* contrasted word(s)
idiom idiomatic equivalent(s)
‖ use limited; if in doubt, see a dictionary

closemouthed *adj syn* see SILENT 3

close off *vb syn* see ISOLATE

close on *prep syn* see ABOUT 1

close out *vb syn* see SELL OUT 1

closeout *n syn* see BARGAIN 1

‖**closet** *n syn* see PRIVY 1

closet *adj* **1** *syn* see PRIVATE 2
  2 *syn* see THEORETICAL 1

close–tongued *adj syn* see SILENT 3

closing *n syn* see END 2

closing *adj syn* see LAST

closure *n syn* see END 2

clot *n syn* see GROUP 3

clot *vb syn* see COAGULATE

clothe *vb* to cover with or as if with garments <forests *clothe* the rocky slopes>
  syn apparel, array, attire, clad, dress, enclothe, garb, garment, raiment
  rel costume, do up, dress up, tog (up *or* out); cloak, mantle, robe; accouter, equip, outfit, rig (out); bedrape, drape, swathe; endue, invest
  con dismantle, divest, strip
  ant unclothe

clothes *n pl* a person's garments as a whole <dressed in new *clothes* from the skin out>
  syn apparel, attire, attirement, clothing, dress, duds, habiliment(s), rags, raiment, rigging, things, togs
  rel array, garb, toggery, vestments, vesture; costume, getup, outfit, rig

clothing *n* **1** *syn* see CLOTHES
  2 *syn* see ROLE 1

cloud *n syn* see MULTITUDE 1

cloud *vb* **1** *syn* see OBSCURE
  rel addle, befuddle, confuse, muddle; distract, perplex, puzzle
  2 *syn* see CONFUSE 4
  3 *syn* see TAINT 1

clouded *adj syn* see DOUBTFUL 1

cloudless *adj syn* see FAIR 2

cloudy *adj* **1** *syn* see OVERCAST
  2 *syn* see HAZY
  3 *syn* see MURKY 3

clough *n syn* see RAVINE

clout *n* **1** *syn* see CUFF
  2 *syn* see PULL 2

clout *vb* **1** *syn* see STRIKE 2
  ‖**2** *syn* see STEAL 1

clove *n syn* see RAVINE

clown *n* **1** *syn* see RUSTIC
  2 *syn* see BOOR
  3 a performer (as in a circus) who entertains by grotesque appearance and actions <children delighted by the antics of the *clowns*>
  syn buffoon, harlequin, merry-andrew, zany
  rel comedian; fool, jester, mountebank; mime, mummer
  4 *syn* see ZANY 2

clownish *adj syn* see BOORISH
  rel awkward, clumsy, gauche; green, raw, rough, rude, uncouth
  ant urbane

cloy *vb syn* see SATIATE
  con excite, pique, provoke, stimulate

  ant whet

club *n* **1** *syn* see CUDGEL
  2 *syn* see ASSOCIATION 2

club car *n syn* see PARLOR CAR

‖**cluck** *n syn* see DUNCE

clue *n syn* see HINT 1

clue (*or* clew) *vb syn* see INFORM 2

clump *n* **1** *syn* see GROUP 3
  rel clutter, hodgepodge, jumble, omnium≠gatherum
  2 *syn* see LUMP 1

clump *vb syn* see LUMBER

clumsy *adj* **1** lacking in physical ease and grace usually because of coarse cumbersome build or poor coordination <a *clumsy* boy constantly stumbling over his own feet> <the *clumsy* gait of a young puppy>
  syn awkward, gawky, lumbering, lumpish, splathering, splay, ungainly; *compare* AWKWARD 2
  rel butterfingered, heavy-handed, left-handed, unhandy; graceless, inelegant, uncouth; bulky, hulking, unwieldy
  idiom all thumbs, fingers all thumbs
  con comely, shapely, well-formed, well-proportioned; apt, deft, handy, quick, ready
  2 *syn* see AWKWARD 2

clunk *vb syn* see THUD

clunker *n syn* see JALOPY

cluster *n* **1** *syn* see GROUP 3
  2 *syn* see GROUP 1

cluster *vb syn* see GROUP 1
  rel accumulate, aggregate, associate, cumulate; bundle, package, parcel

clutch *vb syn* see SEIZE 2
  rel clench, clinch, gripe; cherish, harbor, hold, keep

clutch *n syn* see HOLD

clutch *n syn* see GROUP 3

clutter *n* **1** *syn* see CONFUSION 3
  2 a disordered nondescript mass or group <a *clutter* of ornaments on the mantel>
  syn hash, hugger-mugger, jumble, jungle, litter, mash, mishmash, muddle, rummage, scramble, shuffle, tumble
  rel hodgepodge, macédoine, medley, mélange; disarray, mess, muss, ruck
  con arrangement, array, order; grouping, ordering, pigeonholing, ranking, sorting

‖**cly** *vb syn* see STEAL 1

coact *vb syn* see INTERACT

coacting *adj syn* see COOPERATIVE

coactive *adj syn* see COOPERATIVE

coadjutant *n syn* see ASSISTANT 2

coadjute *vb syn* see UNITE 2

coadjutor *n syn* see ASSISTANT 2

coadunate *vb syn* see JOIN 1

coadunation *n syn* see UNIFICATION

coagment *vb syn* see JOIN 1

coagulate *vb* to alter by chemical reaction from a liquid to a more or less firm jelly <the blood *coagulated* and closed the wound>
  syn clot, congeal, gel, gelate, gelatinize, jell, jellify, jelly, set

rel concrete, harden, solidify; curdle, inspissate; compact, concentrate, consolidate; coalesce; freeze; dehydrate, dry; condense, thicken
con deliquesce, fluidify, liquefy, liquesce; flux, fuse, melt, run

coalesce *vb syn* see JOIN 1
rel adhere, cleave, cling, stick; blend, fuse, merge, mingle, mix

coalition *n* **1** *syn* see UNIFICATION
2 *syn* see COMBINATION 2
3 *syn* see ALLIANCE 2

coarct *vb syn* see RESTRAIN 1

coarse *adj* **1** made up of relatively large particles <*coarse* sand>
syn grainy, granular
rel caked, cakey, lumpy, particulate
2 *syn* see CRUDE 5
3 deficient in refinement of manner and delicacy of feeling <a *coarse* practical man lacking all social graces>
syn crass, crude, gross, incult, inelegant, low, raw, rough, rude, uncouth, uncultivated, uncultured, unrefined, vulgar; *compare* BOORISH
rel raffish, roughneck, rowdy, vulgarian; common, tacky
con considerate, courtly, gracious; cultivated, polished, refined
4 *syn* see OBSCENE 2
||**5** *syn* see WILD 6

coast *n syn* see SHORE

coast *vb syn* see SLIDE 6

coax *vb* to influence or persuade by artful ingratiation <*coaxed* her friend to help her with her work>
syn ||barter, blandish, blarney, cajole, con, soft=soap, sweet-talk, wheedle
rel pester, plague, tease; importune, press, urge; get, induce, persuade, prevail; entice, inveigle, lure, tempt; butter (up)
con coerce, compel, constrain, force, oblige; browbeat, bulldoze, cow, intimidate
ant bully

cob *vb syn* see SURPASS 1

cobble *vb syn* see BOTCH
rel confuse, foul up, snafu, snarl (up)

||**cobblers** *n syn* see NONSENSE 2

cobweb *n syn* see WEB 2

cock *n* **1** *syn* see FAUCET
2 *syn* see LEADER 2
||**3** *syn* see NONSENSE 2

||**cock** *adj syn* see CHIEF 2

cock *vb syn* see LORD

cock *n syn* see PILE 1

cock *vb syn* see HEAP 1

cock-a-doodle-doo *vb syn* see BOAST

cock-a-hoop *adj* **1** *syn* see EXULTANT
2 *syn* see AWRY 1

Cockaigne *n syn* see UTOPIA

cockamamie *adj syn* see FOOLISH 2

cock-and-bull story *n syn* see LIE

cock-a-whoop *adj syn* see EXULTANT

cockcrow *n syn* see DAWN 1

cockcrowing *n syn* see DAWN 1

cocker *vb syn* see BABY

||**cocket** *adj syn* see SAUCY 1

cockeyed *adj* **1** *syn* see AWRY 1
2 *syn* see INTOXICATED 1

cockle *vb syn* see RIPPLE

cocksure *adj syn* see SURE 5

cocktail lounge *n syn* see BAR 5

||**coco** *n syn* see HEAD 1

coconspirator *n syn* see CONFEDERATE

||**coconut** *n syn* see HEAD 1

cocotte *n syn* see PROSTITUTE

coddle *vb syn* see BABY

codicil *n syn* see APPENDIX 1

||**codswallop** *n syn* see NONSENSE 2

coefficient *adj syn* see COOPERATIVE

coerce *vb syn* see FORCE 2
rel beset, push, urge; browbeat, bulldoze, bully, cow, intimidate; menace, terrorize, threaten

coercion *n syn* see FORCE 4
rel menace, menacing, threat, threatening

coetaneous *adj syn* see CONTEMPORARY 1

coeval *adj syn* see CONTEMPORARY 1

coexistent *adj syn* see CONTEMPORARY 1

coexisting *adj syn* see CONTEMPORARY 1

coffee shop *n syn* see EATING HOUSE

coffer *n syn* see TREASURY 2

||**coffin nail** *n syn* see CIGARETTE

cogency *n syn* see POINT 3
rel pertinence, relevance; bearing, concern, connection

cogent *adj* **1** *syn* see VALID
rel compelling, constraining, forceful, forcible, potent, powerful, puissant; inducing, persuasive; justified, well-founded, well-grounded
con ineffective, ineffectual, inefficacious; feeble, forceless, impotent, powerless, weak
2 *syn* see WELL-FOUNDED
rel consequential, influential, momentous, weighty; meaningful, significant

cogitable *adj syn* see THINKABLE 1

cogitate *vb* **1** *syn* see THINK 5
rel conceive, envisage, envision, imagine
2 *syn* see PLOT

cogitation *n syn* see THOUGHT 1

cogitative *adj syn* see THOUGHTFUL 1

cognate *adj syn* see RELATED
rel common, general, generic, universal
con different, disparate, divergent, diverse, various

cognizance *n syn* see NOTICE 1

cognizant *adj syn* see AWARE
con forgetful, oblivious, unmindful; heedless, ignoring, neglectful, slighting, unmindful
ant ignorant

cognize *vb syn* see KNOW 1

cognomen *n syn* see NAME 1

cognoscente *n syn* see CONNOISSEUR
rel ||dab, proficient, specialist; authority, critic, judge

cohere *vb* **1** *syn* see STICK 2

---

syn synonym(s)   *rel* related word(s)
ant antonym(s)   *con* contrasted word(s)
idiom idiomatic equivalent(s)
|| use limited; if in doubt, see a dictionary

rel blend, coalesce, fuse, merge; associate, combine, connect, join, unite
con disembarrass, disentangle, untangle
2 *syn* see AGREE 4

coherence *n* **1 *syn*** see ADHERENCE 1
rel integrity, solidarity, union, unity
ant incoherence
2 *syn* see CONSISTENCY

cohesion *n* **1 *syn*** see ADHERENCE 1
ant incohesion
2 *syn* see SOLIDARITY

cohort *n* **1 *syn*** see PARTNER
2 *syn* see FOLLOWER

coil *n syn* see COMMOTION 3

coil *vb syn* see WIND 2
rel revolve, rotate, turn

‖**coin** *n syn* see MONEY
idiom coin of the realm

coinage *n syn* see INVENTION

coincide *vb syn* see AGREE 3
rel accord, correspond, jibe, tally; equal, match
con deviate, divagate, divaricate, diverge; bias, skew, twist, warp
ant differ

coincident *adj syn* see CONCOMITANT

coincidentally *adv syn* see TOGETHER 1

coincidently *adv syn* see TOGETHER 1

coinstantaneously *adv syn* see TOGETHER 1

cold *adj* **1** marked by a deficiency of warmth <a *cold* day>
syn arctic, chill, chillsome, chilly, cool, freezing, frigid, frore, frosty, gelid, glacial, icy, nippy, shivery
rel biting, bleak, chilling, cutting, nipping, polar, raw, sharp; frozen, iced, wintry; bracing, brisk, crisp, snappy
con genial, mild
ant warm
2 lacking cordiality or emotional warmth <a *cold* greeting>
syn chill, emotionless, frigid, glacial, icy, indifferent, unemotional
rel unenthusiastic, unresponsive, unsympathetic
con cordial, friendly, genial, hearty, warm; empathic, sympathetic
3 *syn* see MATTER-OF-FACT 3
4 *syn* see FRIGID 3
ant hot
5 *syn* see GLOOMY 3
6 *syn* see DEAD 1
7 *syn* see INSENSIBLE 2

cold–blooded *adj* **1 *syn*** see UNFEELING 2
2 *syn* see MATTER-OF-FACT 3

cold feet *n syn* see FEAR 1

coldhearted *adj syn* see UNFEELING 2
ant warmhearted

‖**cold meat** *n syn* see CORPSE

cold–shoulder *vb syn* see CUT 7

cold storage *n syn* see ABEYANCE

colic *n syn* see STOMACHACHE

coliseum *n syn* see STADIUM

‖**coll** *vb syn* see EMBRACE 1

collapse *vb* **1 *syn*** see GIVE 12

rel break up, disintegrate, shatter
idiom fall to pieces
2 to lose energy, stamina, or control under stress <exhausted to the point of *collapsing* helplessly on the bed>
syn break down, cave (in), drop, ‖flake out, give out, peg out, succumb, wilt
rel droop, fail, languish, weaken; exhaust, fag, flag, play out, tire, weary
con enliven, invigorate, stimulate

collapse *n* **1 *syn*** see NERVOUS BREAKDOWN
2 a sudden and grave failure <the *collapse* of an overextended market>
syn breakdown, crack-up, crash, debacle, smash, smashup, wreck
rel breakup, disorganization, disruption, undoing; cataclysm, catastrophe; destruction, ruination, ruining; failure

collar *vb* **1 *syn*** see CORNER
2 *syn* see CATCH 1
3 *syn* see STEAL 1

collate *vb syn* see COMPARE 2

collateral *adj* **1 *syn*** see CONCOMITANT
2 *syn* see INDIRECT 1
3 *syn* see CORROBORATIVE
4 *syn* see SUBORDINATE
rel allied, cognate, kindred, related; complementary, corresponding, reciprocal
con major, prominent
5 *syn* see AUXILIARY

‖**collateral** *n syn* see REFUSE

colleague *n* one affiliated with another usually through a common office or profession <he claims to speak for his *colleagues* in the Senate>
syn associate, compatriot, compeer, confrere
rel consociate, copartner, fellow, partner; coworker, workfellow; buddy, chum, companion, crony, pal; aide, assistant, helper

collect *vb* **1 *syn*** see GATHER 6
con assort, sort; sever, sunder; deal, dispense, divide, dole
ant disperse; distribute
2 *syn* see INFER
3 *syn* see COMPOSE 4
4 *syn* see GROUP 1
rel align, array, dispose, marshal, order, rank
con broadcast, disperse, distribute, scatter

collected *adj* **1 *syn*** see CALM 2
rel peaceful, quiet, still
ant distraught
2 *syn* see COOL 2
rel assured, confident, sanguine, sure; complacent, self-satisfied, smug
con disordered, troubled

collection *n* **1 *syn*** see GATHERING 2
rel band, crew, outfit, party
2 *syn* see ACCUMULATION
rel assortment, medley, miscellany, variety; bunch, clump, cluster, group; armamentarium; caboodle, kit, lot

‖**college** *n syn* see JAIL

collide *vb syn* scc BUMP 1
rel atomize, fragment, pulverize, shatter, smash, splinter; break up, crunch, scrap

collimate *vb syn* see PARALLEL 2
collision *n syn* see IMPACT 1
  rel dilapidation, ruin, wreck; demolishment, destruction
collocate *vb syn* see PARALLEL 2
collogue *vb* ‖1 *syn* see PLOT
  2 *syn* see CONFER 2
colloque *vb syn* see CONVERSE
colloquial *adj syn* see VERNACULAR
colloquial *n syn* see VERNACULAR 3
colloquium *n syn* see CONFERENCE 2
colloquy *n* 1 *syn* see CONVERSATION 1
  2 *syn* see CONVERSATION 2
  3 *syn* see CONFERENCE 2
collude *vb syn* see PLOT
collusion *n syn* see COMPLICITY
colluvies *n syn* see MISCELLANY 1
collywobbles *n pl but sing or pl in constr syn* see STOMACHACHE
Colonel Blimp *n* 1 *syn* see STUFFED SHIRT
  2 *syn* see REACTIONARY
color *n* 1 a property of a visible thing recognizable only when rays of light fall upon it and serving to distinguish things otherwise visually identical (as in size, shape, or texture) <the green *color* of foliage turns red and gold in autumn>
  syn cast, hue, shade, tinge, tint, tone
  2 *syn* see MASK 2
  3 *syn* see VERISIMILITUDE
  4 *syn* see POSITION 1
  5 *syn* see FLAG
  6 something used to impart visible color to something <dyed her curtains with one of the new easy-to-use *colors*>
  syn colorant, dye, dyestuff, pigment, stain, tincture
color *vb* 1 *syn* see EMBROIDER
  rel disguise, distort, fake, misrepresent
  con constrain, minimize, reduce, soften, temper; blue-pencil, censor, edit
  2 *syn* see MISREPRESENT
  3 *syn* see BLUSH
colorable *adj syn* see BELIEVABLE
  rel cogent, compelling, convincing, sound, telling, valid
colorant *n syn* see COLOR 6
colored *adj syn* see BIASED 2
colorful *adj* making a fine display of usually showy color <a *colorful* bed of asters>
  syn brave, bright, colory, gay, vivid
  rel blatant, florid, garish, gaudy, loud; flashy, showy, splashy
  con blanched, bleached, pallid, wan; dim, dull, faint, pale, weak
  ant colorless
coloring *n* 1 *syn* see MASK 2
  2 *syn* see EXAGGERATION
colorless *adj* 1 *syn* see PALE 1
  2 lacking in sparkle and vitality <an accurate but *colorless* recital of facts>
  syn drab, dull, flat, lackluster, lifeless, lusterless, prosaic, prosy
  rel blurry, hazy, obscure, vague; feeble, insipid, milk-and-water, namby-pamby, weak, wishy-washy; unimaginative, uninspired

  con clear, concise, exact, precise; exciting, provocative, rousing, stimulating, stirring
  ant colorful
  3 *syn* see NEUTRAL
  rel aloof, remote, withdrawn
colory *adj syn* see COLORFUL
colossal *adj syn* see HUGE
colporteur *n syn* see MISSIONARY
colt *n syn* see NOVICE
coltish *adj syn* see PLAYFUL 1
columbary *n syn* see DOVECOTE
column *n* 1 *syn* see PILLAR 1
  2 *syn* see SUPPORT 3
coma *n* 1 *syn* see FAINT
  2 *syn* see LETHARGY 1
comate *n syn* see ASSOCIATE 3
comatose *adj* 1 *syn* see INSENSIBLE 2
  2 *syn* see LETHARGIC
  rel anesthetic, impassible, insensitive
  ant awake
comb *vb* 1 *syn* see SORT 2
  2 *syn* see SCOUR 2
  rel examine, inspect, scrutinize; investigate, probe, sift
combat *vb syn* see RESIST
  rel battle, contend, war
combat *n syn* see SERVICE 1
combative *adj syn* see BELLIGERENT
  rel energetic, strenuous, vigorous; manful, manly, virile
  ant pacifistic
combativeness *n syn* see ATTACK 2
‖**combe** *n syn* see VALLEY
combination *n* 1 *syn* see UNIFICATION
  2 individuals or organized interests banded together to further a common end <a *combination* of citizens devoted to holding down taxes>
  syn bloc, coalition, combine, faction, party, ring
  rel cartel, pool, syndicate, trust; cabal, circle, clique, coterie, set
  3 *syn* see ASSOCIATION 1
combine *vb* 1 *syn* see JOIN 1
  rel amalgamate, blend, commingle, fuse, mingle, mix; consolidate, unify
  con divide, divorce, part
  ant separate
  2 *syn* see EMBODY 2
  3 *syn* see UNITE 2
  rel agree, coincide; merge, pool
combine *n* 1 *syn* see COMBINATION 2
  2 *syn* see SYNDICATE
comble *n syn* see APEX 2
combust *vb syn* see BURN 2
combustible *adj* 1 capable of catching or being set on fire <*combustible* materials should be stored away from open fire>
  syn burnable, flammable, ignitable, inflammable

---

syn synonym(s)   *rel* related word(s)
ant antonym(s)   *con* contrasted word(s)
idiom idiomatic equivalent(s)
‖ use limited; if in doubt, see a dictionary

rel comburent, combustive; burning, firing, igniting, kindling
con fireproof; flameproof, nonflammable; fire‑resistant, fire-resistive, fire-retardant
ant incombustible, noncombustible
2 *syn* see EXCITABLE
come *vb* **1** to attain to a destination <when will they *come*>
syn arrive, ‖blow in, get, get in, reach, show, show up, turn up
rel approach, near, nigh
con depart, leave, quit, retreat, withdraw
ant go
2 *syn* see AMOUNT 1
3 *syn* see HAPPEN 1
4 *syn* see BECOME 1
come (from) *vb* **1** *syn* see SPRING
2 *syn* see ORIGINATE 5
come (in) *vb* *syn* see ENTER 1
comeback *n* *syn* see RETORT 2
come by *vb* *syn* see VISIT 2
come–by–chance *n* *syn* see BASTARD 1
comedian *n* **1** *syn* see HUMORIST 2
2 *syn* see WAG 1
come down (with) *vb* *syn* see CONTRACT 1
comedown *n* a loss of status <bitter over their *comedown* in the world>
syn descent, discomfiture, down; *compare* SET-BACK
rel collapse, crash, downfall, fall, ruin, smash, undoing, wreck
con advance, headway, progress
ant rise
comedy *n* *syn* see HUMOR 4
come in *vb* *syn* see ANSWER 1
comely *adj* **1** *syn* see BEAUTIFUL
ant homely
2 *syn* see DECOROUS 1
come off *vb* **1** *syn* see SUCCEED 2
2 *syn* see HAPPEN 1
come–off *n* *syn* see ESCAPE 2
come–on *n* **1** *syn* see LURE 2
‖**2** *syn* see FOOL 3
3 *syn* see SWINDLER
come out *vb* **1** *syn* see GET OUT 2
2 *syn* see DEBUT
come out (with) *vb* *syn* see SAY 1
come over *vb* **1** *syn* see VISIT 2
2 *syn* see BECOME 1
come round *vb* *syn* see RECOVER 2
comestible *adj* *syn* see EDIBLE
comestibles *n pl* *syn* see FOOD 1
come through *vb* **1** *syn* see SURVIVE 2
2 *syn* see CONTRIBUTE 1
comeuppance *n* *syn* see DUE 1
comfort *n* **1** *syn* see HELP 1
2 *syn* see AMENITY 2
comfort *vb* to cheer or try to cheer a person overcome by grief or misery <*comforting* her widowed sister with words of hope>
syn buck up, cheer, console, solace, upraise
rel brighten, gladden, lighten; allay, alleviate, assuage, mitigate, relieve; refresh, renew, restore; reassure; commiserate, condole, sympathize

idiom give a lift to
con torment, torture, try; distress, trouble, worry; annoy, irk, vex
ant afflict; bother
comfortable *adj* **1** *syn* see SUFFICIENT 1
2 enjoying or providing conditions that make for comfort and security <lived in a *comfortable* home on a quiet street>
syn comfy, cozy, cushy, easeful, easy, snug, soft
rel agreeable, grateful, gratifying, welcome; pleasant, pleasing; restful; comforting, consoling, solacing; content, pleased, satisfied
con distressing, perturbing, troubling; annoying, bothering, irking, vexing; inferior, miserable, poor, substandard, wretched
ant uncomfortable
3 *syn* see PROSPEROUS 3
idiom in comfortable circumstances
‖**comfortable** *n* *syn* see QUILT
comforter *n* *syn* see QUILT
comfortless *adj* *syn* see UNCOMFORTABLE
comfy *adj* *syn* see COMFORTABLE 2
comic *adj* *syn* see LAUGHABLE
rel antic, fantastic, grotesque; mocking, ridiculing
ant tragic
comic *n* *syn* see HUMORIST 2
comical *adj* *syn* see LAUGHABLE
rel absurd, foolish, silly; impish, roguish, sportive, waggish
con doleful, dolorous, lugubrious, melancholy
ant pathetic
comicality *n* *syn* see HUMOR 4
comicalness *n* *syn* see HUMOR 4
coming *n* *syn* see ARRIVAL 1
coming *adj* **1** *syn* see FORTHCOMING
2 *syn* see NEXT
coming in *n, usu* **comings in** *pl syn* see REVENUE
comingle *vb* *syn* see MIX 1
comity *n* *syn* see GOODWILL 1
rel accord, concord, harmony; camaraderie, companionship, comradeship, good-fellowship
comma *n* *syn* see PAUSE
command *vb* to issue orders or an order to <the general *commanded* the troops to advance>
syn bid, charge, direct, enjoin, instruct, order, tell, warn
rel demand, exact, require; coerce, compel, constrain, force, oblige; conduct, control, manage; ask, call (on), request, say
ant comply, obey
command *n* **1** a direction that must or should be obeyed <failure to obey a direct *command* subjects the soldier to grave penalties>
syn behest, bidding, charge, dictate, injunction, mandate, order, word
rel direction, directive, instruction; canon, law, ordinance, precept, rule, statute; devoir, duty, obligation, responsibility
2 *syn* see POWER 1
rel rule
3 *syn* see ABILITY 2
rel aplomb, assurance, confidence, poise
con incertitude, insecurity, uncertainty, unsureness; indecisiveness, vagueness

commandeer *vb* **1** *syn* see APPROPRIATE 1
 2 *syn* see ARROGATE 1
comme il faut *adj* *syn* see DECOROUS 1
commemorate *vb* **1** *syn* see KEEP 2
 2 *syn* see MEMORIALIZE 2
commemorative *adj* *syn* see MEMORIAL
commemoratory *adj* *syn* see MEMORIAL
commence *vb* **1** *syn* see BEGIN 1
 2 *syn* see BEGIN 2
 idiom come into being (*or* existence)
commencement *n* *syn* see BEGINNING
commend *vb* **1** *syn* see COMMIT 1
 rel resign, yield; proffer, tender
 2 to indicate one's warm approval <the teacher
 commended her pupils' studious attitude>
 syn acclaim, applaud, compliment, hail, kudize,
 praise, recommend, ‖roose
 rel eulogize, extol; approve, countenance, endorse, support
 con blame, criticize, reprehend, reprobate;
 chide, rebuke, reprimand, reproach, reprove
 ant censure; admonish
commendable *adj* *syn* see WORTHY 1
commensurable *adj* *syn* see PROPORTIONAL
commensurate *adj* *syn* see PROPORTIONAL
comment *n* **1** *syn* see REMARK 2
 2 *syn* see CRITICISM 1
comment *vb* *syn* see REMARK 2
 rel construe, elucidate, explain, explicate, expound; annotate, gloss
commentary *n* *syn* see REMARK 2
commentate *vb* *syn* see REMARK 2
commerce *n* **1** *syn* see CONTACT 2
 2 a situation characterized by mutual exchange
 (as of ideas) <those who feel that art should have
 no *commerce* with morality>
 syn communion, dealings, intercourse, traffic,
 truck
 rel communication, congress, contact, exchange, interchange, intercommunication; basis,
 common ground, takeoff
 3 *syn* see BUSINESS 4
commie *n* *syn* see COMMUNIST
commination *n* *syn* see CURSE 1
commingle *vb* *syn* see MIX 1
 rel integrate, unify
comminute *vb* *syn* see PULVERIZE 1
commiserable *adj* *syn* see PITIFUL 1
commiserate *vb* *syn* see COMPASSIONATE
commiseration *n* *syn* see PITY
commission *vb* **1** *syn* see AUTHORIZE 1
 rel appoint, designate, name, nominate; bid,
 charge, command, enjoin, instruct, order
 2 *syn* see DELEGATE
commit *vb* **1** to assign (as to a person) especially
 for use or safekeeping <it is unwise to *commit* all
 power and authority to one man> <sainted beings who *commit* their spirits to God>
 syn commend, confide, consign, entrust, hand
 over, relegate, turn over
 rel allocate, allot, assign, destine, ordain; move,
 remove, shift, transfer; deliver, give, offer, submit; delegate, deputize
 idiom give into the charge (*or* hands) of

 2 to be responsible for or guilty of (an offense or
 wrongdoing) <*commit* a crime>
 syn perpetuate, pull
 rel accomplish, achieve, do, effectuate, execute,
 perform, pull off; contravene, transgress, trespass, violate; offend, scandalize, sin
commitment *n* *syn* see OBLIGATION 2
committal *n* *syn* see OBLIGATION 2
commix *vb* *syn* see MIX 1
commixture *n* *syn* see MIXTURE
commodious *adj* *syn* see SPACIOUS
 con cramped, narrow, strait
 ant incommodious
commodities *n* *pl* *syn* see MERCHANDISE
 rel articles, items, things
common *adj* **1** generally shared in or participated
 in by members of a community <our *common*
 civic responsibilities>
 syn communal, conjoint, conjunct, intermutual,
 joint, mutual, public, shared
 rel general, generic, universal; like, reciprocal,
 similar; corporate
 con personal, private, restricted
 ant individual
 2 *syn* see GENERAL 2
 rel popular, public
 3 *syn* see IMPURE 3
 4 taking place often <a *common* occurrence>
 syn customary, everyday, familiar, frequent
 rel repetitious, routine, usual
 con infrequent, occasional, unfrequent; casual,
 chance, incidental
 ant rare, uncommon
 5 *syn* see GENERAL
 6 conforming to a type without noteworthy ex-
 cellences or faults <just a *common* everyday sort
 trying to get by in life>
 syn commonplace, ordinary, prosaic, uneventful, unexceptional, unnoteworthy
 rel down-to-earth, matter-of-fact, prosy, unex-
 citing; dull, flat, trite, stale, uninteresting
 con exceptional, noteworthy, remarkable; excellent, marvelous, prodigious, wonderful; aberrant, divergent, eccentric
 ant extraordinary
 7 *syn* see DECENT 4
 8 *syn* see CHEAP 2
 9 *syn* see INFERIOR 2
 ‖10 *syn* see EASYGOING 3
common *n* **1** commons *pl but sing or pl in constr*
 syn see COMMONALTY
 2 an often improved and ornamentally planted
 open space for public use in a built-up area <in
 summer a band played on the village *common*>
 syn green, plaza, square
 rel garden, park, pleasance, pleasure ground
commonage *n* *syn* see COMMONALTY
commonalty *n* persons without rank or authority
 or the political estate made up of these <laws

---

syn synonym(s)   *rel* related word(s)
ant antonym(s)   *con* contrasted word(s)
idiom idiomatic equivalent(s)
‖ use limited; if in doubt, see a dictionary

that both the gentles and the *commonalty* recognized as just>
syn commonage, commoners, common men, commune, people, plebeians, plebes, plebs, populace, rank and file, third estate
rel masses, mob, multitude, proletariat, public
con aristocracy, elite, gentility, nobility; classes, gentry, nobs
commoners *n pl syn* see COMMONALTY
commonition *n syn* see WARNING
commonly *adv syn* see USUALLY 2
idiom more often than not
common men *n pl syn* see COMMONALTY
commonplace *n* an idea or expression deficient in originality or freshness <lazily exchanging *commonplaces* over their beer>
syn banality, bromide, cliché, platitude, prosaicism, prosaism, rubber stamp, shibboleth, tag, truism
rel chestnut, corn, prose, stereotype; inanity, shallowness, wishy-washiness; threadbareness, triteness
ant profundity
commonplace *adj* **1** *syn* see COMMON 6
2 *syn* see GENERAL 1
3 *syn* see PROSAIC 3
4 *syn* see TRITE
idiom a dime a dozen, as everyday as breakfast
common sense *n syn* see SENSE 6
commorancy *n syn* see HABITATION 2
commotion *n* **1** a state of often disorderly civic unrest <the whole city was in *commotion* over the new restrictions>
syn clamor, convulsion, ferment, outcry, tumult, upheaval, upturn
rel insurgence, insurrection, mutiny, rebellion, revolt, riot, uprising
2 a state of usually mental or emotional excitement <this challenge threw him into great *commotion* of mind>
syn agitation, confusion, dither, flap, lather, pother, stew, tumult, turbulence, turmoil
rel discomposure, disquiet, flurry, fluster, perturbation, upset; annoyance, bother, irritation, vexation; strain, tension
con calm, placidity, quietude, relaxation, serenity
3 a noisy and often unruly disturbance <the children created a *commotion* over missing the circus>
syn brouhaha, ‖catouse, coil, foofaraw, furore, fuss, hurrah, ruckus, rumpus, shindig, shindy, to-do, uproar
rel din, hubbub, hullabaloo, pandemonium, racket; fracas, ruction, row
4 a state of noisy confusion <never saw such *commotion* as the time the old sow got out and knocked the preacher into the midden>
syn bustle, clamor, clatter, hassle, hubbub, hurly-burly, lather, moil, pother, rowdydow, ruction, storm, to-do, tow-row, tumult, turmoil, uproar, whirl, whoopla; *compare* DIN, STIR 1
con calmness, order, peace, quiet
commove *vb syn* see ELATE

communal *adj syn* see COMMON 1
commune *n syn* see COMMONALTY
communicable *adj* **1** *syn* see INFECTIOUS 2
2 *syn* see COMMUNICATIVE
communicate *vb* **1** to make known <*communicated* the whole story under a pledge of secrecy>
syn break, convey, impart, pass on, transmit
rel betray, disclose, discover, divulge, ‖let out, reveal, tell; hint, imply, let on, suggest; broadcast, disseminate, publicize
con conceal, hide, obscure, screen, veil; dissemble; distort, garble, twist, warp; camouflage, disguise
2 *syn* see ADJOIN
communication *n* **1** *syn* see MESSAGE 1
2 *syn* see CONTACT 2
3 interchange of thoughts or opinions through shared symbols <the difficulties of *communication* between people of different cultural backgrounds>
syn communion, converse, intercommunication, intercourse
rel exchange, interchange; conversing, discussing, talking; conversation, discussion, talk; advice, intelligence, news, tidings
communicative *adj* inclined to talk freely and sometimes indiscreetly <too *communicative* to be trusted with a secret>
syn communicable, expansive; *compare* FRANK
rel garrulous, loquacious, talkative, voluble; conversational; demonstrative, effusive, gushing
con constrained, guarded, inhibited, restrained; bridled, controlled, curbed
communion *n* **1** *syn* see COMMERCE 2
2 *syn* see COMMUNICATION 3
3 *syn* see CONTACT 2
4 *syn* see RELIGION 2
Communist *n* a member of the Russian Communist party <restructuring of Russia by the *Communists*>
syn Bolshevik, ‖Bolshie, commie, comrade, Red
rel fellow traveler, pink, pinko; Leninist, Marxist, Stalinist, Trotskyist; apparatchik
community *n syn* see SOCIETY 3
commutable *adj syn* see INTERCHANGEABLE
commute *vb syn* see TRANSFORM
compact *adj* **1** *syn* see PITHY
2 *syn* see CLOSE 4
rel hard; appressed, bunched, packed
con loose, slack, unconstrained; rare, tenuous, thin
compact *vb syn* see UNIFY 1
rel compress, condense, contract; combine, unite; set, solidify
con disperse, dissipate; fluff, loosen
compact *n syn* see CONTRACT
compacting *adj syn* see INTEGRATIVE
companion *n* **1** *syn* see ASSOCIATE 3
rel colleague, fellow, partner; chaperon, escort
2 *syn* see MATE 5
3 *syn* see ACCOMPANIMENT 2
companion *vb syn* see ACCOMPANY
companionable *adj syn* see SOCIAL 1
rel amiable, complacent, good-natured

con uncongenial, unsympathetic; reserved, taciturn, uncommunicative

companionship *n syn* see COMPANY 1

company *n* **1** association between individuals especially on pleasant or intimate terms <we always enjoyed his *company*>
syn companionship, fellowship, society
rel camaraderie, comradeship, consociation
2 persons visiting especially in one's house <invited *company* for dinner>
syn guests, visitors; *compare* VISITOR 1
3 *syn* see GATHERING 2
4 a group of persons associated in a joint effort or for a common purpose <a *company* of thieves lay in wait by the highway>
syn band, corps, outfit, party, troop, troupe; *compare* GROUP 1
rel crew, gang, pack, team; circle, clique, coterie, set; association, club, order, society; crowd, horde, mob, throng; group
5 *syn* see ENTERPRISE 3

company *vb syn* see ACCOMPANY

comparable *adj syn* see LIKE
ant disparate

comparative *adj* being such in comparison with an expressed or implied standard or absolute <living in *comparative* poverty>
syn approximate, near, relative
rel equivalent, like, similar
con genuine, real, true
ant absolute

compare *vb* **1** *syn* see EQUATE 2
2 to examine side by side or point by point in order to establish likenesses and differences <*compare* the effects of two diets on weight loss>
syn bracket, collate, contrast
rel approach, equal, match, rival, touch; examine, inspect, observe, scan, scrutinize, size (up); consider, contemplate, ponder, study, weigh

comparison *n syn* see LIKENESS

compass *vb* **1** *syn* see SURROUND 1
2 *syn* see GET 1
3 *syn* see APPREHEND 1

compass *n* **1** *syn* see CIRCUMFERENCE
rel domain, field, sphere; enclosure
2 *syn* see ENVIRONS 1
3 *syn* see RANGE 2
rel bounds, limits; circumscription, limitation, restriction

compassion *n* **1** *syn* see SYMPATHY 2
rel charity, clemency, grace, lenity, mercy; benevolence, humaneness, humanity
con aloofness, indifference, unconcern; cruelty, harshness, mercilessness; implacability, relentlessness
2 *syn* see PITY

compassionate *adj syn* see TENDER
rel clement, forbearing; piteous, pitiful
con grim, implacable, merciless, relentless, unrelenting; adamant, inexorable, inflexible, obdurate

compassionate *vb* to feel or express compassion for <a kindly man who *compassionated* all human misery>

syn ache, commiserate, feel (for), pity, sympathize (with)
rel grieve (over), regret, repine; lament, mourn, sorrow (for *or* over); deplore
con accept, endure, tolerate; disregard, ignore, overlook, pass over

compassionless *adj syn* see UNFEELING 2

compatible *adj syn* see CONSONANT 1
rel appropriate, fit, fitting, meet, proper, suitable
ant incompatible

compatriot *n syn* see COLLEAGUE

compeer *n syn* see COLLEAGUE

compel *vb syn* see FORCE 2

compellation *n syn* see NAME 1

compendiary *adj syn* see CONCISE

compendious *adj syn* see CONCISE
rel close, compact
con amplified, elaborated, expanded, inflated; complete, full

compendium *n* **1** a condensed treatment of a subject <prepared a *compendium* of the state laws dealing with education>
syn aperçu, digest, pandect, précis, sketch, survey, syllabus, sylloge
rel abridgment, abstract, brief, conspectus, epitome; overview
con elaboration, expansion
2 *syn* see HANDBOOK

compenetrate *vb syn* see PERMEATE

compensate *vb* **1** to make good the defects of <her kind heart *compensated* for her nosy ways>
syn atone (for), balance, counterbalance, counterpoise, countervail, make up, offset, outweigh, redeem, set off
rel abrogate, annul, invalidate, negate, nullify; counteract, negative, neutralize; better, fix (up), improve, repair; redress
idiom make amends (*or* reparations), make matters right
2 *syn* see PAY 1
3 to make proper payment to (as for injury, loss, or damage) <*compensated* a worker injured on the job>
syn indemnify, pay, recompense, reimburse, remunerate, repay, requite
rel recoup, refund
idiom make restitution (*or* reparation)

compensation *n syn* see REPARATION

compete *vb* **1** to strive to gain mastery or obtain a prize <students *competing* for a scholarship>
syn contend, contest, rival, vie
rel dispute; battle, fight, strive, struggle; attempt, essay, try
2 *syn* see RIVAL 2
rel approach, equal, match, touch

competence *n* **1** *syn* see ENOUGH
2 *syn* see ABILITY 1
rel appropriateness, fitness, suitability

---

syn synonym(s)   *rel* related word(s)
ant antonym(s)   *con* contrasted word(s)
idiom idiomatic equivalent(s)
|| use limited; if in doubt, see a dictionary

ant incompetence

competent *adj* **1** *syn* see ABLE
  rel adept, finished, masterly, polished
  ant incompetent
  2 *syn* see SUFFICIENT 1

competition *n* **1** *syn* see CONTEST 1
  2 *syn* see CONTEST 2
  3 *syn* see RIVAL

competitor *n* *syn* see RIVAL

complacence *n* *syn* see CONCEIT 2

complacency *n* *syn* see CONCEIT 2

complacent *adj* feeling or showing an often excessive or unjustified satisfaction and pleasure in one's status, possessions, or attainments <had the *complacent* air of superiority that often mars an ignorant self-made man>
  syn priggish, self-complacent, self-contented, self-pleased, self-satisfied, smug
  rel assured, confident, self-assured, self-confident, self-possessed; conceited, egoistic, egotistic
  con humble, modest; diffident, shy

complain *vb* to express discontent, resentment, or regret usually peaceably and as if seeking sympathy <a nice girl but given to *complaining* over trifles>
  syn fuss, kick, murmur, repine, wail, whine; *compare* GRIPE 2, GRUMBLE 1
  rel fret, worry; nag, pester
  idiom air a grievance, find fault, register a complaint, sing (*or* cry) the blues
  con accept, condone, countenance, tolerate

complainer *n* *syn* see GROUCH

complaint *n* *syn* see DISEASE 1

complaisant *adj* *syn* see AMIABLE 1
  rel accommodating, agreeable, generous, indulgent; submissive
  con harsh, rigorous, stern; determined, firm, masterful

complement *n* **1** something that makes up a deficiency in another thing <bought the farm with its *complement* of equipment and livestock>
  syn supplement
  rel correlate, counterpart; makeweight
  2 *syn* see ACCOMPANIMENT 1
  3 *syn* see COUNTERPART 1

complete *adj* **1** *syn* see WHOLE 3
  2 *syn* see UNABRIDGED
  3 *syn* see WHOLE 4
  4 brought to completion <each *complete* revolution of the earth>
  syn completed, concluded, done, down, ended, finished, terminated, through
  rel accomplished, achieved, effected, executed, realized; attained, compassed
  idiom all over, done with, set at rest
  ant incomplete
  5 *syn* see EXHAUSTIVE
  ant incomplete
  6 *syn* see UTTER

complete *vb* **1** *syn* see CLOSE 3
  rel accomplish, achieve, discharge, effect, execute, fulfill, perform
  idiom carry through, go through with
  2 *syn* see FULFILL 1

completed *adj* *syn* see COMPLETE 4

completely *adv* **1** *syn* see DOWN 2
  idiom down to the ground
  2 *syn* see THOROUGHLY 2
  3 *syn* see WELL 3

completeness *n* **1** *syn* see ENTIRETY 1
  2 *syn* see INTEGRITY 2

complex *adj* **1** made up of two or more separable or identifiable elements <the *complex* vascular system of higher plants>
  syn composite, compound
  rel blended, compounded, mingled, mixed; heterogeneous, varied; elaborate, intricate, involved; complicated, confused, mixed-up
  con homogeneous, uniform
  ant simple
  2 difficult to comprehend because of a multiplicity of interrelated elements <a *complex* plot to undermine the government by discrediting its leaders>
  syn Byzantine, complicated, daedal, elaborate, gordian, intricate, involved, knotty, labyrinthine, sophisticated
  rel bewildering, confusing, distracting, disturbing; baffling, confounding, mysterious, mystifying, perplexing, puzzling; equivocal, obscure, vague; involute, involuted, reticular
  con clear, defined, definite, distinct, plain, recognizable, uncomplicated, uninvolved; comprehensible, explicable, intelligible, knowable
  ant simple

complex *n* *syn* see SYSTEM 1
  con constituent, element, factor; member, part, piece, portion; detail, item, particular
  ant component

complexion *n* *syn* see DISPOSITION 3
  rel kind, sort, style, type

complexion *vb* *syn* see TINT

complexionless *adj* *syn* see PALE 1

compliance *n* *syn* see ACQUIESCENCE
  rel amenability, docility, obedience, tractability; deference, submission, submissiveness
  con contumacy, obstinacy, stubbornness
  ant frowardness

complicate *vb* to make complex, involved, or difficult <a disagreement *complicated* by intense personal animosities>
  syn entangle, ‖muck, muddle, perplex, ravel, snarl, tangle
  rel jumble, ‖snafu; derange, disarrange, disorder, mix up, upset
  con arrange, order; disentangle, straighten (out), untangle
  ant simplify

complicated *adj* **1** *syn* see ELABORATE 2
  2 *syn* see COMPLEX 2
  rel arduous, difficult, hard; abstruse, recondite
  con easy, facile, light; clear-cut, precise, straightforward
  ant simple

complicity *n* association with an improper or unlawful activity <failed to prove his *complicity* in the cover-up>
  syn collusion, connivance

rel implication, involvement; engineering, machination, manipulation, wire-pulling

compliment *n* **1** an expression of regard or praise <a man meriting the *compliments* and homage of his fellows>
syn bouquet, kudo, orchid(s)
rel trade-last; laud, laudation, praise; accolade, commendation, honor; blessing(s), congratulation(s), felicitation(s); encomium, eulogy, tribute
con dig, gibe, jeer, slam
ant taunt
‖ **2** *syn* see GIFT 1

compliment *vb syn* see COMMEND 2
idiom take off one's hat to
con belittle, decry, denigrate, depreciate, disparage, run down

complimentary *adj syn* see FREE 5

comply *vb syn* see OBEY

component *n syn* see ELEMENT 2
con admixture, amalgam, blend, compound, mixture
ant composite; complex

comport *vb* **1** *syn* see AGREE 4
2 *syn* see BEHAVE 1

comportment *n* **1** *syn* see BEARING 1
2 *syn* see BEHAVIOR

compose *vb* **1** *syn* see CONSTITUTE 1
rel consist (of)
2 to bring into being by mental and especially artistic effort <*compose* a ballad or a history of England>
syn create
rel devise, invent, make up, originate; dream up
3 *syn* see CALM
rel ease, lessen, soften; comfort, console, solace
con agitate, embroil, trouble, unsettle
ant discompose
4 to bring oneself or one's emotions under control <*composed* himself and turned to face the new attack>
syn collect, contain, control, cool, re-collect, rein, repress, restrain, simmer down, smother, suppress
rel down, mitigate, moderate, modulate, pocket, temper, tune down; bottle (up), check, hold in; ease (off *or* up), let up, relax, slacken
idiom calm down, control one's feelings (*or* emotions), get hold of oneself, master one's feelings, pull oneself together

composed *adj* **1** *syn* see CALM 2
2 *syn* see COOL 2
rel quiet, still; sedate, serious, staid; repressed, suppressed
con concerned, worried
ant discomposed, ruffled

composite *adj syn* see COMPLEX 1

composite *n syn* see MIXTURE
rel combination, union

composition *n* **1** *syn* see MAKEUP 1
2 *syn* see COMPROMISE
3 *syn* see ESSAY 2

compos mentis *adj syn* see SANE 2

compost *n syn* see MIXTURE

composure *n syn* see EQUANIMITY

ant discomposure, perturbation

compotation *n syn* see BINGE 1

compound *vb* **1** *syn* see JOIN 1
2 *syn* see MIX 1
3 *syn* see INCREASE 1

compound *adj syn* see COMPLEX 1

compound *n syn* see MIXTURE

comprehend *vb* **1** *syn* see APPREHEND 1
2 *syn* see KNOW 1
rel envisage, envision, see
3 *syn* see INCLUDE

comprehendible *adj syn* see UNDERSTANDABLE
ant incomprehensible

comprehensible *adj syn* see UNDERSTANDABLE
ant incomprehensible

comprehensive *adj* **1** *syn* see ENCYCLOPEDIC
2 *syn* see ALL-AROUND 2
idiom in depth

comprehensiveness *n syn* see BREADTH 2

compress *vb* **1** *syn* see CONTRACT 3
rel compact, consolidate; cram, crowd, press, squeeze
con disperse, dissipate, scatter
ant stretch; spread
2 *syn* see PRESS 1

comprise *vb syn* see CONSTITUTE 1

compromise *n* a settlement reached by mutual concession <the company and the union agreed to a *compromise* on fringe benefits>
syn composition
rel golden mean, mean, middle ground, middle way; agreement, compact, contract, pact; arrangement, bargain, understanding
idiom happy medium

compromise *vb syn* see ENDANGER
rel blast, blight, mar, queer, ruin, spoil
idiom cook one's goose; play havoc (*or* hob) with, settle one's hash

compulsatory *adj syn* see MANDATORY

compulsion *n syn* see FORCE 4
rel driving, impelling, pressing; exigency, necessity, need; pressure, stress
con coaxing, inducing, persuasion; choice, election, option, preference

compulsory *adj syn* see MANDATORY

compunction *n* **1** *syn* see PENITENCE
rel conscience, conscientiousness, punctiliousness, scrupulosity, scrupulousness
con brazenness, callousness, hardness, insensitivity; disinterest, indifference, unconcern; obduracy, recalcitrance
2 *syn* see QUALM
rel disinclination; hesitancy, hesitation

compunctious *adj syn* see REMORSEFUL

computation *n* the act or action of calculating mathematically <by his *computation* they could not possibly afford a new car>
syn arithmetic, calculation, ciphering, estimation, figuring, reckoning

---

syn synonym(s)   *rel* related word(s)
ant antonym(s)   *con* contrasted word(s)
idiom idiomatic equivalent(s)
‖ use limited; if in doubt, see a dictionary

compute *vb syn* see CALCULATE
comrade *n* **1** *syn* see ASSOCIATE 3
  rel consort, fellow, mate; adjunct, ally, auxiliary
  2 *syn* see COMMUNIST
comradery *n syn* see CAMARADERIE
comstock *n syn* see PRUDE
con *vb* **1** *syn* see SCRUTINIZE 1
  2 *syn* see MEMORIZE
con *n* **1** *syn* see OPPONENT
  ant pro
  2 *syn* see ANTAGONISM 2
con *vb* **1** *syn* see DUPE
  2 *syn* see COAX
‖**con** *n syn* see CONVICT
concatenate *vb syn* see INTEGRATE 3
concavity *n syn* see DEPRESSION 2
conceal *vb syn* see HIDE
  rel camouflage, disguise, dissemble
  idiom keep (something) dark
  con betray, divulge; evidence, evince, manifest
  ant reveal
concealed *adj syn* see ULTERIOR
concede *vb* **1** *syn* see ACKNOWLEDGE 1
  rel cede, relinquish, waive
  con agitate, argue, debate, discuss; answer, confute, refute; controvert
  ant dispute
  2 *syn* see GRANT 1
  con refuse, reject
  ant deny
conceit *n* **1** *syn* see IDEA
  2 an attitude of regarding oneself with favor <his constant boasting was an indication of *conceit*>
  syn amour propre, complacence, complacency, conceitedness, consequence, egoism, egotism, narcissism, outrecuidance, pride, self-admiration, self-complacency, self-conceit, self-consequence, self-esteem, self-exaltation, self-glory, self-importance, self-love, self-opinion, self-pride, swelled head, swellheadedness, vainglory, vainness, vanity
  rel assurance, pomposity, self-partiality, smugness, stuffiness
  con humbleness, humility, self-depreciation, unpretentiousness
  ant modesty
  3 *syn* see CAPRICE
‖**conceit** *vb syn* see UNDERSTAND 3
conceited *adj syn* see VAIN 3
conceitedness *n syn* see CONCEIT 2
‖**conceity** *adj syn* see VAIN 3
conceivable *adj* **1** *syn* see THINKABLE 2
  2 *syn* see PROBABLE
conceive *vb* **1** *syn* see THINK 1
  rel excogitate; cogitate, speculate; meditate, ponder, ruminate
  2 *syn* see APPREHEND 1
  rel heed, mark, note, notice, observe, remark
  3 *syn* see UNDERSTAND 3
  rel judge; deem, feel
concenter *vb* **1** *syn* see FASTEN 3
  2 *syn* see CONVERGE
concentrate *vb* **1** *syn* see FASTEN 3
  rel establish, set, settle

  2 *syn* see UNIFY 1
  rel assemble, collect, gather; heap, mass, pile
  con dispel, disperse; attenuate, dilute, extenuate, rarefy, thin; dispense, distribute
  ant dissipate
  3 *syn* see CONTRACT 3
  4 *syn* see CONVERGE
concentrated *adj* **1** *syn* see STRONG 3
  2 *syn* see WHOLE 5
  rel complete, entire, total
  3 *syn* see INTENSE 1
concentrating *adj syn* see INTEGRATIVE
concentration *n syn* see ATTENTION 1
  rel enthrallment, raptness
  ant distraction
concept *n syn* see IDEA
  con percept, sensation, sense-datum, sensum
conception *n syn* see IDEA
conceptual *adj* existing or dealing with what exists only in the mind <*conceptual* analysis of a problem>
  syn ideal, ideational, notional
  rel abstract, transcendent, transcendental; absolute, categorical, ultimate; obscure, remote; fanciful, imaginary, visionary
  con practical, pragmatic, realistic; concrete, material, substantial, tangible
concern *n* **1** *syn* see INTEREST 3
  2 *syn* see AFFAIR 1
  3 *syn* see BUSINESS 8
  4 *syn* see CARE 4
  5 *syn* see CONSIDERATION 3
  6 *syn* see UNCERTAINTY
  rel faltering, irresolution; apprehension, misgiving; inquietude, suspense
  7 *syn* see CARE 2
  rel attention, consideration, thoughtfulness
  con aloofness, incuriousness, indifference
  ant unconcern
  8 *syn* see ENTERPRISE 3
  9 *syn* see GADGET 1
concerned *adj syn* see INTERESTED
concerning *prep syn* see APROPOS
concernment *n syn* see CARE 2
concert *vb* **1** *syn* see NEGOTIATE 1
  rel argue, debate, discuss; concur, cooperate, unite
  2 *syn* see AGREE 3
concert *n syn* see HARMONY 1
concession *n syn* see ALLOWANCE 5
conciliate *vb syn* see PACIFY
  rel intervene, mediate; persuade, prevail; calm, quiet, soothe, tranquilize
  con alienate, disaffect, estrange; foment, incite; excite, pique, provoke, stimulate
  ant antagonize
concise *adj* presented with or given to brevity of expression <a *concise* statement of the problem> <a very *concise* thinker>
  syn breviloquent, brief, compendiary, compendious, curt, laconic, short, short and sweet, succinct, summary, terse; *compare* PITHY
  rel abridged, compressed, condensed; marrowy, meaty, pithy; lean

con diffuse, long-winded, prolix, rambling, voluble, wordy
ant redundant; verbose

concisely *adv syn* see BRIEFLY

conclude *vb* **1** *syn* see DECIDE
2 *syn* see CLOSE 3
idiom ring down the curtain
ant open
3 *syn* see INFER

concluded *adj syn* see COMPLETE 4

concluding *adj syn* see LAST
ant opening

conclusion *n* **1** *syn* see INFERENCE 2
2 *syn* see FINALE
3 *syn* see END 2
4 *syn* see DECISION 1

conclusive *adj* putting an end to debate or question usually by reason of irrefutability <the evidence was *conclusive* and no defense was possible>
syn definitive
rel cogent, compelling, convincing, telling; incontrovertible, irrefragable, irrefrangible, irrefutable, unanswerable; deciding, decisive, determinant, determinate, determinative; clear, precise, unambiguous
con doubtful, dubious, problematic, questionable; credible, plausible, specious; ambiguous, cryptic, enigmatic, obscure
ant inconclusive

concoct *vb syn* see CONTRIVE 2
rel conceive, envisage, envision; create, discover, originate

concomitant *adj* occurring in company with <good manners are likely to be *concomitant* with good behavior>
syn accompanying, ancillary, attendant, attending, coincident, collateral, incident, satellite
rel accessory, adjuvant, supplementary; correlative, corresponding

concomitant *n syn* see ACCOMPANIMENT 2

concord *n* **1** *syn* see HARMONY 2
rel amity, comity, friendship, goodwill; calmness, peace, placidity, serenity, tranquillity
con conflict, contention, difference, dissension, strife, variance
ant discord
2 *syn* see HARMONY 3
3 *syn* see HARMONY 1
4 *syn* see TREATY

concord *vb syn* see AGREE 3

concordance *n syn* see HARMONY 2

concordant *adj syn* see HARMONIOUS 2

concours *n syn* see CONTEST 2

concourse *n* a coming, flocking, or flowing together <they doubt the universe originated in a chance *concourse* of atoms>
syn concursion, confluence, gathering, junction, meeting
rel association, joining, linkage
con disassociation, parting, separation

concrete *vb* **1** *syn* see HARDEN 1
2 *syn* see JOIN 1

concupiscence *n syn* see LUST 2

concupiscent *adj syn* see LUSTFUL 2

concur *vb* **1** *syn* see UNITE 2
rel accord, agree, harmonize, jibe
2 *syn* see AGREE 3
rel accede, acquiesce, assent, consent
ant contend; altercate

concurrent *adj syn* see CONTEMPORARY 1

concurrently *adv syn* see TOGETHER 1

concursion *n syn* see CONCOURSE

concuss *vb* **1** *syn* see SHAKE 4
2 *syn* see FORCE 2

concussion *n syn* see IMPACT 1
rel beating, buffeting, jarring, jolting, pounding, shaking; blow, clip, clout

condemn *vb* **1** *syn* see CRITICIZE
rel belittle, decry, depreciate, disparage; deprecate, disapprove
idiom damn with faint praise, find fault with
con applaud, commend, compliment; acclaim, eulogize, extol, laud, praise; condone, excuse, forgive, pardon
2 *syn* see SENTENCE
con deliver, redeem, rescue, save

condemned *adj syn* see DAMNED 1
rel fallen, fated

condensation *n syn* see ABRIDGMENT

condense *vb* **1** *syn* see CONTRACT 3
rel compact, consolidate; curtail, minimize
con amplify
2 *syn* see EPITOMIZE 1
con broaden, expand, extend, widen
ant amplify

condensed *adj* made shorter and typically simpler <a *condensed* biography>
syn canned, capsule, epitomized, pocket, potted
rel abbreviated, abridged, bobbed, bobtail, bobtailed, curtailed, shortened
con elaborated, polished, refined; amplified, enlarged, expanded

condescend *vb syn* see STOOP 1

condign *adj syn* see JUST 3
rel grim, rigorous, stern, strict, stringent; atrocious, awful, dreadful, horrible

condition *n* **1** something that limits or qualifies an agreement or offer <included the *condition* that any heir contesting the will would be automatically disinherited>
syn provision, proviso, reservation, stipulation, strings, terms
rel prerequisite, requirement, requisite; exception, exemption, limitation, modification, qualification, restriction, saving clause
2 *syn* see ESSENTIAL 2
3 *syn* see STATE 1
4 *syn* see ORDER 9
5 *syn* see ORDER 10
6 *syn* see DISEASE 1

---

syn synonym(s)   *rel* related word(s)
ant antonym(s)   *con* contrasted word(s)
idiom idiomatic equivalent(s)
‖ use limited; if in doubt, see a dictionary

conditional *adj* **1** containing or dependent on a condition <our agreement is *conditional* on your raising the needed funds>
syn provisional, provisionary, provisory, tentative
rel iffy, obscure, uncertain; limited, modified, qualified, restricted
con fixed, set, sure
ant unconditional
2 *syn* see DEPENDENT 1
rel provisional, tentative; problematic, questionable; fortuitous, incidental
ant unconditional
condonable *adj syn* see JUSTIFIABLE
rel acceptable, tolerable
condone *vb syn* see EXCUSE 1
rel disregard, forget, ignore, overlook
con deplore, deprecate, disapprove; impugn, reproach
conduce *vb syn* see CONTRIBUTE 2
conduct *n* **1** *syn* see OVERSIGHT 1
2 *syn* see BEHAVIOR
rel bearing, demeanor, mien, posture, stance
conduct *vb* **1** *syn* see GUIDE
2 *syn* see ACCOMPANY
rel convey, transmit
3 to have the direction of and responsibility for <he had *conducted* a small market for many years>
syn carry on, direct, keep, manage, operate, ordain, run
rel administer, handle, head, oversee, supervise; arrange, control, keep up, order, regulate, rule; engineer, lead, pilot, steer
4 to act as a conduit for <shady transactions that *conducted* profits away from the stockholders>
syn carry, channel, convey, funnel, pipe, siphon, traject, transmit
rel remove, separate, take away, withdraw
5 *syn* see BEHAVE 1
conduit *n* **1** *syn* see CHANNEL 1
2 *syn* see PIPELINE
confab *vb syn* see CONFER 2
confabulate *vb syn* see CONFER 2
confabulation *n* **1** *syn* see CONVERSATION 1
2 *syn* see CONVERSATION 2
3 *syn* see CONFERENCE 1
confederacy *n syn* see ALLIANCE 2
confederate *n* one associated with another or others in a wrong or unlawful act <conspiring with his *confederates* to overthrow the government>
syn abettor, accessory, accomplice, coconspirator, conspirator
rel collaborator, fellow traveler; associate, colleague, fellow, partner
confederation *n syn* see ALLIANCE 2
confer *vb* **1** *syn* see GIVE 2
rel allot, provide; vouchsafe
2 to carry on a conversation or discussion usually directed toward reaching a decision or settlement <the President *conferred* with his cabinet about the scandal>
syn advise, collogue, confab, confabulate, consult, huddle, parley, powwow, treat

rel bargain, chaffer, deal, negotiate; argue, debate, discuss; converse, speak, talk
idiom put one's head together with
conference *n* **1** an interchanging of views <took several hours of *conference* to find a solution to the problem>
syn confabulation, deliberation, discussion, rap, ventilation
2 a meeting for the purpose of serious discussion and interchange of views <the association held a *conference* on the problems of aging>
syn colloquium, colloquy, palaver, rap session, seminar
rel round robin, round table
3 *syn* see TALK 4
4 *syn* see LEAGUE 4
conferrer *n syn* see DONOR
confess *vb syn* see ACKNOWLEDGE 1
idiom make a clean breast, open one's heart
confessions *n pl syn* see BIOGRAPHY
confidant *n syn* see FRIEND
confide *vb* **1** to tell confidentially <shyly *confided* her secret>
syn breathe, whisper
rel hint, insinuate, intimate, suggest
con advertise, broadcast, proclaim, publish
2 *syn* see COMMIT 1
rel bestow, present
confidence *n* **1** *syn* see TRUST 1
con distrust, mistrust; despair, hopelessness
ant doubt; apprehension
2 a feeling or showing of adequacy and reliance on oneself and one's powers <had serene *confidence* in his own ability to win>
syn aplomb, assurance, self-assurance, self-assuredness, self-confidence, self-trust; *compare* EQUANIMITY
rel courage, mettle, resolution, spirit, tenacity; brashness, impudence, presumption
con apprehension, incertitude, misgiving, self-depreciation, self-doubt, uncertitude
ant diffidence
3 *syn* see CERTAINTY
4 *syn* see EFFRONTERY
confidence man *n syn* see SWINDLER
confident *adj* **1** marked by a strong, fearless, and bold belief in oneself and one's capacities <faced his accusers with a *confident* air>
syn assured, sanguine, secure, self-assured, self-confident, undoubtful
rel certain, cocksure, cocky, perky, positive, sure; self-possessed, self-reliant; bold, brave, courageous, dauntless, fearless, intrepid, unafraid, undaunted, valiant
con jittery, nervous, uneasy; afraid, daunted, fearful; doubtful, dubious
ant apprehensive
2 *syn* see SURE 5
3 *syn* see PRESUMPTUOUS
confidential *adj* **1** *syn* see PRIVATE 2
2 *syn* see FAMILIAR 1
rel secret; tried, trustworthy, trusty
configuration *n syn* see FORM 1
confine *vb* **1** *syn* see LIMIT 2

2 syn see IMPRISON
confine *n, usu* **confines** *pl* **1 syn** see ENVIRONS 1
  2 syn see LIMIT 1
  rel circumference, compass, periphery
  3 syn see RANGE 2
confined *adj syn* see CRAMPED
confinement *n* **1 syn** see RESTRICTION 2
  2 the state attending and consequent to childbirth <had a long difficult *confinement*>
  syn accouchement, childbed, lying-in
  rel parturition; labor, travail
confirm *vb* **1 syn** see RATIFY
  rel accede, acquiesce, assent, consent, subscribe; validate
  idiom make good
  con decline, refuse, reject
  2 to attest to the truth, genuineness, accuracy, or validity of something <a surprise witness *confirmed* his account of the incident>
  syn authenticate, bear out, corroborate, justify, substantiate, validate, verify
  rel attest, certify, vouch, witness; back, support, underpin, uphold, warrant; check, check out
  con confute, controvert, disprove, refute; contravene, gainsay, impugn, negative, traverse
  ant deny; contradict
confirm (in) *vb syn* see HABITUATE 2
confirmation *n syn* see TESTIMONY
confirmative *adj syn* see CORROBORATIVE
confirmatory *adj syn* see CORROBORATIVE
confirmed *adj* **1 syn** see HABITUAL 2
  2 syn see INVETERATE 1
confiscate *vb syn* see APPROPRIATE 1
confiture *n syn* see JAM
conflagrant *adj syn* see BURNING 1
conflagration *n syn* see FIRE 1
conflict *n* **1 syn** see CONTEST 1
  rel argument, controversy, dispute
  2 syn see CONTEST 2
  3 syn see DISCORD
conflict *vb syn* see CLASH 2
  rel differ, disagree, vary; disturb, interfere
  idiom run against the tide
conflicting *adj* **1 syn** see ANTIPATHETIC 1
  2 syn see INCONSONANT 1
confluence *n syn* see CONCOURSE
conform *vb* **1 syn** see ADAPT
  rel attune, harmonize, tune
  2 syn see AGREE 4
  con conflict, differ, disagree
  ant diverge
  3 syn see HARMONIZE 3
  4 syn see OBEY
  idiom toe the line
conformable *adj syn* see ASSORTED 2
  rel appropriate, fitting, suitable; applicable, usable
conformation *n syn* see FORM 1
conforming *adj syn* see DECOROUS 1
conformity *n* **1 syn** see CONSISTENCY
  2 syn see ACQUIESCENCE
confound *vb* **1 syn** see PUZZLE
  idiom take aback
  2 syn see MISTAKE 1

ant discriminate, distinguish
  3 syn see EMBARRASS
  4 syn see DISPROVE 1
confounded *adj* **1 syn** see AGHAST 2
  2 syn see DAMNED 2
  3 syn see UTTER
confoundedly *adv syn* see EVER 6
confrere *n* **1 syn** see COLLEAGUE
  2 syn see PARTNER
confront *vb* **1** to stand over against in the role of an adversary or enemy <he *confronted* his accusers with perfect aplomb>
  syn affront, encounter, face, meet; *compare* MEET 6
  rel beard, brave, challenge, defy; flout, scorn, scout; oppose, resist, withstand
  idiom come to close quarters with, come up against
  con avoid, elude, evade
  2 syn see ACCOST 2
confronting *prep syn* see BEFORE 2
confuse *vb* **1 syn** see EMBARRASS
  2 to make unclear in mind or purpose <found the city hustle and noise very *confusing*>
  syn addle, ball up, befuddle, bewilder, ‖bumfuzzle, discombobulate, distract, dizzy, fluster, fuddle, mix up, ‖mizzle, ‖momble, muddle, mull, throw off, throw out
  rel misguide, mislead; agitate, bother, discompose, disquiet, flurry, perturb, upset
  3 syn see PUZZLE
  4 to make indistinct the elements or true character of (as a discussion) <*confuse* an issue in a debate>
  syn becloud, befog, blur, cloud, fog, muddy
  rel complicate, confound, involve, mix up
  idiom lose in a fog
  con clarify, elucidate; simplify
  5 to throw into disorder <surging waves *confused* the waters> <her accounts were totally *confused*>
  syn foul up, jumble, mix up, muddle, ‖snafu, snarl up, tumble; *compare* DISORDER 1
  rel derange, disarrange, disorder, disorganize, disturb, mess (up), unsettle
  idiom put in a flutter, throw into confusion
  6 syn see MISREPRESENT
  7 syn see MISTAKE 1
  ant differentiate
confusion *n* **1 syn** see RUIN 3
  2 syn see EMBARRASSMENT
  3 a condition in which things are out of their normal or proper places or relationships <the room was in complete *confusion*>
  syn ataxia, ‖ballup, chaos, clutter, disarray, disorder, huddle, misorder, muddle, ‖mullock, pell-mell, snarl, topsy-turviness

---

syn synonym(s)   *rel* related word(s)
ant antonym(s)   *con* contrasted word(s)
idiom idiomatic equivalent(s)
‖ use limited; if in doubt, see a dictionary

rel derangement, disarrangement, disturbance; foul-up, mess, mix-up, muck, ‖mux, ‖snafu; babel, din, hullabaloo, pandemonium

con methodization, ordering, organization, systematization; method, order, system

4 *syn* see COMMOTION 2

rel disorder, disorganization, disturbance; discomfiture, embarrassment

confute *vb syn* see DISPROVE 1

congé *n syn* see PARTING

congeal *vb* **1** *syn* see HARDEN 1

rel chill, cool, freeze

2 *syn* see COAGULATE

congenial *adj* **1** *syn* see HARMONIOUS 3

ant uncongenial

2 *syn* see CONSONANT 1

rel companionable, cooperative, social; affable, cordial, genial, gracious, sociable; pleasant, pleasing

ant uncongenial; antipathetic (*of persons*); abhorrent (*of tasks, responsibilities*)

3 *syn* see PLEASANT 1

4 *syn* see GRACIOUS 1

congenital *adj* **1** *syn* see INNATE 1

2 *syn* see INHERENT

congeries *n syn* see GATHERING 2

congest *vb syn* see FILL 1

conglobate *vb syn* see BALL

conglobe *vb syn* see BALL

conglomerate *adj syn* see MISCELLANEOUS

conglomerate *n* **1** *syn* see AGGREGATE 1

2 *syn* see SYNDICATE

conglomeration *n* **1** *syn* see ACCUMULATION

2 *syn* see AGGREGATE 1

congratulate *vb* to express to another one's pleasure in his good fortune or success <*congratulate* a friend when she wins a race>

syn felicitate

rel applaud, laud, praise; bless, compliment

idiom pat one on the back, tender (*or* offer) congratulation, wish one joy, wish one well

con belittle, depreciate, disparage, knock, run down, slur

congregate *vb syn* see GATHER 6

rel swarm, teem

ant disperse

congregation *n syn* see GATHERING 2

rel audience, disciples, following, public

congress *n syn* see ASSOCIATION 2

congress *vb syn* see GATHER 6

congruity *n syn* see CONSISTENCY

congruous *adj* **1** *syn* see CONSONANT 1

rel appropriate, fit, fitting, meet; proper, seemly

ant incongruous

2 *syn* see HARMONIOUS 2

conjectural *adj syn* see SUPPOSED 1

con demonstrated; unquestionable

conjecture *n syn* see THEORY 2

ant fact

conjecture *vb* to draw an inference from slight or inadequate evidence <when he failed to arrive on time she *conjectured* that he was drinking again>

syn guess, presume, pretend, suppose, surmise, think; *compare* INFER, UNDERSTAND 3

rel assume, expect, suspect; believe, deem, feel; conceive, fancy, imagine; conclude, estimate, gather, glean, infer, judge

idiom hazard a guess, take for granted

con demonstrate, prove, test, try; ascertain, determine, discover, learn

conjoin *vb* **1** *syn* see JOIN 1

2 *syn* see UNITE 2

conjoint *adj* **1** *syn* see COMMON 1

2 *syn* see COOPERATIVE

conjointly *adv syn* see TOGETHER 3

conjointment *n syn* see ASSOCIATION 1

conjugal *adj syn* see MATRIMONIAL

conjugality *n syn* see MARRIAGE 1

conjugate *vb syn* see JOIN 1

conjunct *adj syn* see COMMON 1

conjunction *n syn* see ASSOCIATION 1

conjuration *n syn* see SPELL

conjure *vb syn* see BEG

conjurer *n* **1** *syn* see MAGICIAN 1

2 *syn* see MAGICIAN 2

conjuring *n* **1** *syn* see MAGIC 1

2 *syn* see MAGIC 2

conjury *n syn* see MAGIC 1

‖conk *n* **1** *syn* see NOSE 1

2 *syn* see HEAD 1

‖conk *n syn* see HIT 1

conk *vb syn* see DIE 1

con man *n syn* see SWINDLER

rel shill

con mark, sucker, victim; greenhorn

connate *adj* **1** *syn* see INNATE 1

2 *syn* see INHERENT

3 *syn* see RELATED

connatural *adj* **1** *syn* see INNATE 1

2 *syn* see RELATED

connect *vb syn* see JOIN 1

ant disconnect

connection *n* **1** *syn* see ASSOCIATION 1

2 *syn* see JOINT 1

3 *syn* see JOB 2

4 *syn* see RELIGION 2

connivance *n syn* see COMPLICITY

connive *vb* **1** to secretly favor or sympathize with something improper or illicit <*connive* at treason>

syn blink (at), wink (at)

rel condone, disregard, ignore, overlook, tolerate

idiom close (*or* shut) one's eyes to, let go by (*or* get by) one's eye, regard with indulgence

con disapprove, disfavor, frown (at *or* upon); disallow, reject, repudiate; disdain, scorn, scout, spurn

2 *syn* see PLOT

connoisseur *n* a person who enjoys with discrimination and appreciation of subtleties and details especially in matters of culture or art <a *connoisseur* of fine wines>

syn aesthete, cognoscente, dilettante

rel bon vivant, epicure, gourmet; adept, authority, critic, expert

con abecedarian, amateur, dabbler, tyro

connotation *n syn* see ASSOCIATION 4

connote *vb* **1** *syn* see MEAN 2
  2 *syn* see SUGGEST 1
connubial *adj* *syn* see MATRIMONIAL
connubiality *n* *syn* see MARRIAGE 1
conquer *vb* **1** to overcome or gain dominion over by force of arms <leaders who have tried and failed to *conquer* the world>
  syn bear down, beat down, crush, defeat, overpower, reduce, subdue, subjugate, vanquish; *compare* DEFEAT 2, OVERTHROW 2, WHIP 1, WIN 1
  rel baffle, balk, circumvent, foil, frustrate, outwit, override, thwart; bend, control, master, overmaster, subject, worst
  idiom bring one to one's knees, trample in the dust, trample underfoot
  con bow, cave, give up, succumb, yield; capitulate, submit, surrender
  2 to gain mastery over something by getting the better of obstacles and difficulties <trials faced by the men who *conquered* Mount Everest>
  syn best, master, overcome, prevail, triumph; *compare* OVERCOME 1
  3 *syn* see OVERCOME 1
conqueror *n* *syn* see VICTOR 1
conquest *n* *syn* see VICTORY 1
  rel defeating, overthrow, rout, routing, subdual
consanguine *adj* *syn* see RELATED
‖**consarned** *adj* **1** *syn* see DAMNED 2
  2 *syn* see UTTER
conscience *n* *syn* see QUALM
conscienceless *adj* *syn* see UNSCRUPULOUS
  rel devious, shifty, tricky, unfair
  ant conscientious
conscientious *adj* **1** *syn* see UPRIGHT 2
  ant conscienceless
  2 *syn* see CAREFUL 2
conscionable *adj* *syn* see CAREFUL 2
conscious *adj* **1** *syn* see AWARE
  rel noticing, noting, observing, perceiving, remarking; vigilant, watchful
  con forgetful, oblivious, unmindful; disregarding, ignoring, overlooking
  ant unconscious
  2 *syn* see SELF-CONSCIOUS
consciousness *n* *syn* see CARE 4
conscribe *vb* *syn* see DRAFT 1
conscript *vb* *syn* see DRAFT 1
consecrate *vb* **1** *syn* see DEVOTE 1
  con desecrate, profane; defile, pollute
  2 *syn* see BLESS 1
consecrated *adj* *syn* see HOLY 1
consecution *n* **1** *syn* see ORDER 5
  2 *syn* see SUCCESSION 2
consecutive *adj* following one after another in orderly fashion <it rained for five *consecutive* days>
  syn sequent, sequential, serial, subsequent, subsequential, succedent, succeeding, successional, successive; *compare* NEXT
  rel after, ensuing, following, later; enlarging, increasing, progressive
  con antecedent, preceding, prior
consecutively *adv* *syn* see TOGETHER 2
consent *vb* *syn* see ASSENT

  rel allow, let, permit; approve, sanction; concur
  con decline; balk, demur, stick, stickle
consent *n* **1** *syn* see PERMISSION
  2 *syn* see AGREEMENT 2
consentaneous *adj* *syn* see UNANIMOUS
consentient *adj* *syn* see UNANIMOUS
consequence *n* **1** *syn* see EFFECT 1
  con origin, root, source
  ant antecedent
  2 *syn* see IMPORTANCE
  rel exigency, need; fame, honor, renown, reputation, repute
  3 *syn* see STATUS 2
  4 *syn* see CONCEIT 2
consequent *adj* *syn* see RATIONAL
consequential *adj* *syn* see IMPORTANT 1
consequently *adv* *syn* see THEREFORE
conservancy *n* *syn* see CONSERVATION 1
conservation *n* **1** a deliberate planned guarding and protecting of something felt as precious <*conservation* of our natural resources>
  syn conservancy, husbanding, preserval, preservation, salvation, saving
  rel attention, care, cherishing, protection; control, directing, governing, management, managing, supervising, supervision
  con neglect, squandering, waste
  2 *syn* see PRESERVATION 1
conservative *adj* **1** tending to resist or oppose change <took a very *conservative* stance politically>
  syn die-hard, fogyish, old-line, orthodox, reactionary, right, tory, traditionalistic
  con modern, progressive, radical
  ant advanced
  2 kept or keeping within bounds <equally *conservative* in speech and action>
  syn controlled, discreet, moderate, reasonable, restrained, temperate, unexcessive, unextreme
  rel cautious, chary, wary; circumspect, politic, proper, prudent
  con expansive, unconstrained; excessive, freewheeling, uncontrolled, unrestrained
conservative *n* *syn* see DIEHARD 1
conservatory *n* *syn* see GREENHOUSE
conserve *vb* *syn* see SAVE 3
  rel keep up, maintain, support, sustain
  con dissipate, fritter, squander, waste
conserve *n* *syn* see JAM
consider *vb* **1** to give serious thought to <*consider* the risk you would be taking>
  syn contemplate, excogitate, mind, perpend, ponder, study, think (out *or* over), weigh
  rel meditate, muse, ruminate; cogitate, reason, reflect, speculate, think; examine, inspect, look (at), scan, scrutinize, see
  idiom bestow thought to, chew the cud over, revolve (*or* turn over) in one's mind
  con disregard, ignore, neglect, overlook, slight

---

syn synonym(s)   *rel* related word(s)
ant antonym(s)   *con* contrasted word(s)
idiom idiomatic equivalent(s)
‖ use limited; if in doubt, see a dictionary

2 *syn* see EYE 1
rel envisage, envision
3 to come to view, judge, or classify <he *considered* thrift essential to success>
syn account, deem, reckon, regard, view; *compare* FEEL 3
rel conceive, fancy, imagine, think; conclude, gather, infer, judge, rule
4 *syn* see ADMIRE 2
5 *syn* see FEEL 3

considerable *adj* 1 *syn* see IMPORTANT 1
2 tending more to the large than the small <buckled down with his ax and made a *considerable* impression on the woodpile>
syn good, respectable, ‖right smart, sensible, sizable, ‖smart
rel able, capable, competent; active, effective, efficacious; important, notable, significant; goodly, pretty, substantial, tidy
con insignificant, meager, slight, trivial; big, grand, great, huge
3 *syn* see BIG 1

considerably *adv* *syn* see WELL 8

considerate *adj* 1 *syn* see CAUTIOUS
2 *syn* see THOUGHTFUL 3
rel kind, kindly; compassionate, sympathetic, tender, warmhearted; amiable, complaisant, obliging
ant inconsiderate
3 *syn* see GENEROUS 1

considerately *adv* *syn* see WELL 2
rel solicitously, tenderly; altruistically, benevolently, charitably
con austerely, harshly, severely, strictly

considerateness *n* *syn* see CONSIDERATION 3

consideration *n* 1 *syn* see ATTENTION 1
2 *syn* see MOTIVE 1
3 thoughtful and sympathetic attention <showed great *consideration* to the needs of others>
syn concern, considerateness, regard, solicitude
rel awareness, heed, heedfulness, mindfulness; forbearance, mercy, quarter
con disregard, heedlessness, unconcern, unmindfulness; inconsiderateness; contempt, despite, disdain, disinterest, scorn
4 *syn* see REGARD 4

considered *adj* *syn* see DELIBERATE 1
rel intentional, voluntary, willful
con impulsive, instinctive, spontaneous; headlong, impetuous, precipitate
ant unconsidered

considering *conj* *syn* see BECAUSE

consign *vb* 1 *syn* see COMMIT 1
rel resign, surrender, yield
2 *syn* see SEND 1

consist *vb* 1 to have existence or a place <our national strength *consists* not solely in military readiness>
syn dwell, exist, inhere, lie, reside
rel be, subsist; abide, repose, rest
idiom have one's (*or* a) place
2 *syn* see AGREE 4

consistency *n* agreement or harmony of parts, traits, or features <his adversary had to admit the *consistency* of his position>
syn coherence, conformity, congruity, correspondence; *compare* HARMONY 2
rel agreement, concord, consonance; likeness, similarity; apposition, aptness, felicity, fitness, suitability
con incoherence, incongruity; impropriety, inappropriateness, unsuitability
ant inconsistency

consistent *adj* 1 *syn* see SAME 3
2 *syn* see CONSONANT 1

consistently *adv* *syn* see USUALLY 1

consociate *n* *syn* see PARTNER

console *vb* *syn* see COMFORT
rel calm, relieve, tranquilize; animate, hearten, inspirit
idiom lift the spirits of
con agitate, discompose, disquiet, disturb, perturb, upset

consolidate *vb* *syn* see UNIFY 1
rel amalgamate, blend, fuse, merge; set, solidify
con part, sever, sunder; liquefy, melt

consolidating *adj* *syn* see INTEGRATIVE

consolidation *n* 1 *syn* see UNIFICATION
2 a union of two or more businesses <*consolidation* is often accompanied by a new corporate name>
syn amalgamation, merger
ant dissolution

consonance *n* 1 *syn* see HARMONY 2
con discrepancy, incompatibility, incongruousness
ant discord
2 *syn* see HARMONY 1
ant dissonance

consonant *adj* 1 conforming (as to a pattern, a standard, or a relationship) without discord or difficulty <his performance was seldom *consonant* with his very real abilities>
syn agreeable, compatible, congenial, congruous, consistent, sympathetic; *compare* HARMONIOUS 2
rel accordant, conformable, harmonious; coincident, concurrent; en rapport
con discordant, discrepant; incompatible, incongruous, inconsistent
ant inconsonant
2 *syn* see HARMONIOUS 1
ant dissonant
3 *syn* see LIKE
4 *syn* see RESONANT

consort *n* 1 *syn* see ACCOMPANIMENT 2
2 *syn* see SPOUSE

consort *vb* *syn* see AGREE 4

consort (with) *vb* *syn* see ACCOMPANY

consortium *n* *syn* see ASSOCIATION 2

conspectus *n* *syn* see ABRIDGMENT

conspicuous *adj* 1 *syn* see CLEAR 5
2 *syn* see NOTICEABLE
rel celebrated, eminent, illustrious; showy
con common, everyday, ordinary; covert, secret; concealed, hidden

ant inconspicuous

conspiracy *n syn* see PLOT 2
 rel sedition, treason; disloyalty, faithlessness, falsity, perfidiousness, perfidy, treacherousness, treachery
 con faith, faithfulness, fealty, loyalty

conspirator *n syn* see CONFEDERATE

conspire *vb syn* see PLOT

‖**constable** *n syn* see POLICEMAN

constancy *n syn* see ATTACHMENT 1

constant *adj* **1** *syn* see FAITHFUL 1
 rel abiding, clinging, enduring, lasting, persistent, persisting
 con capricious, mercurial
 ant fickle, inconstant
 2 *syn* see INFLEXIBLE 3
 con fluctuant, fluctuating, fluctuational, unstable
 ant inconstant, variable
 3 *syn* see SAME 3
 4 *syn* see STEADY 2
 5 *syn* see CONTINUAL
 rel chronic, confirmed, inveterate; dogged, obstinate, pertinacious; persevering
 con alternate, intermittent, recurrent; infrequent, occasional, sporadic
 ant fitful

constantly *adv syn* see ALWAYS 1
 idiom day after day, day in, day out
 ant occasionally

constate *vb syn* see ASSERT 1

consternate *vb syn* see DISMAY 1

consternation *n syn* see FEAR 1
 rel confusion, muddle, muddlement; bewilderment, distraction, perplexity
 con composure, equanimity, phlegm, sangfroid; aplomb, poise, self-command, self-possession

constipate *vb syn* see STULTIFY

constipated *adj* being unable to defecate regularly and without difficulty <complained that she was constantly *constipated*>
 syn astricted, bound, costive, obstipated

constituent *n syn* see ELEMENT 2
 rel division, fraction, part, portion
 con complex, economy, organism, system; amalgam, blend, composite, compound
 ant aggregate, whole

constitute *vb* **1** to be all or a fundamental part of the substance of <water *constitutes* the greater part of the human body>
 syn compose, comprise, form, make, make up
 rel embody, incorporate, integrate; complement, complete, fill out, flesh (out)
 2 *syn* see ENACT 1
 3 *syn* see FOUND 2

constitution *n* **1** *syn* see PHYSIQUE
 2 *syn* see MAKEUP 1

constitutional *adj syn* see INHERENT
 con anomalous, irregular, unnatural
 ant advenient

constitutional *n syn* see WALK 1
 rel ambulation, footwork, legwork, perambulation

constitutive *adj syn* see ESSENTIAL 2

constrain *vb* **1** *syn* see FORCE 2
 2 *syn* see RESTRAIN 1
 3 *syn* see DENY 3
 rel abridge, curtail, deprive; ban, bar, disallow, enjoin
 4 *syn* see IMPRISON
 5 *syn* see PRESS 1
 6 *syn* see DISTRESS 2

constrained *adj syn* see RESERVED 1

constrainment *n syn* see RESTRICTION 2

constraint *n* **1** *syn* see FORCE 4
 rel repression, suppression; driving, impelling, impulsion; goad, motive, spring, spur
 2 *syn* see RESTRICTION 2

constrict *vb* **1** *syn* see CONTRACT 3
 rel curb, restrain; circumscribe, confine, limit, restrict
 con enlarge, expand, increase, maximize
 2 to make narrow or narrower <the muscles that *constrict* the sphincter>
 syn constringe, narrow
 rel gather, plait, pucker; compress, constrain, squeeze; astringe
 con broaden, dilate, distend, widen
 ant expand

constringe *vb syn* see CONSTRICT 2

construal *n syn* see EXPLANATION 1

construct *vb* **1** *syn* see MAKE 3
 2 *syn* see BUILD 1
 3 *syn* see ERECT 5

construction *n* **1** *syn* see MAKEUP 1
 2 *syn* see EXPLANATION 1

constructive *adj syn* see IMPLICIT 2
 rel inferential, ratiocinative; construable, interpretable, renderable
 con clear, evident, obvious, patent
 ant manifest

construe *vb syn* see EXPLAIN 1

consuetude *n syn* see HABIT 1

consult *vb syn* see CONFER 2
 rel cogitate, counsel, deliberate; consider, examine, review

consume *vb* **1** to bring to an end by or as if by the action of a destroying force <the village was *consumed* by fire>
 syn devour, eat, eat up, exhaust, use up
 rel destroy, raze, ruin, wreck; annihilate, extinguish; crush, overwhelm, suppress
 con bolster, brace, buttress, hold up, prop, stay, support, sustain; build, construct, create, make, produce; renew, restore
 2 *syn* see WASTE 2
 3 *syn* see GO 4
 4 *syn* see EAT 1
 5 to eat or drink usually gluttonously or without measure <*consumed* dozens of burgers and a case of beer>
 syn polish off, punish, put away, put down, shift, swill; *compare* EAT 1

---

syn synonym(s)　　　*rel* related word(s)
ant antonym(s)　　　*con* contrasted word(s)
idiom idiomatic equivalent(s)
‖ use limited; if in doubt, see a dictionary

rel absorb, ingest; devour, gobble (up), gorge, wolf; down, gulp, guzzle, inhale, swallow
idiom dispose of
6 syn see MONOPOLIZE
consumedly *adv syn* see EVER 6
consuming *adj syn* see ENGROSSING
consummate *adj* **1** brought to the highest possible point of perfection <the difficult allegro passages displayed her *consummate* skill>
syn accomplished, finished, perfected, ripe, virtuosic; *compare* PERFECT 2
rel faultless, flawless, impeccable, perfect; practiced, skilled, trained; able, gifted, talented; inimitable, peerless, superb, superlative, supreme, transcendent, unsurpassable
con callow, crude, green, raw, rough, uncouth; defective, deficient, inadequate
2 syn see UTTER
consummate *vb syn* see CLOSE 3
consumption *n syn* see TUBERCULOSIS
contact *n* **1** the state of being in or coming into close association or connection <shuddered at the *contact* of his icy hand>
syn contingence, touch
rel closeness, contiguity, nearness, propinquity, proximity; impingement, taction, touching; association, connection, relation; oneness, union, unity
con breach, break, rift, rupture, split; insularity, isolation, seclusion, segregation, separation; distance, farness, remoteness
2 a situation permitting exchange of ideas and opinions <tried for several days to get in *contact* with her brother>
syn commerce, communication, communion, intercommunication, intercourse
rel association, companionship, fellowship; oneness, union, unity; accord, concord, harmony, rapport; empathy, sympathy, understanding
contact *vb syn* see REACH 4
contagion *n syn* see POISON
rel contamination, corruption, pollution, taint; miasma
contagious *adj* **1** *syn* see INFECTIOUS 2
2 syn see INFECTIOUS 3
contain *vb* **1** *syn* see COMPOSE 4
2 to have or be capable of having within <the box *contained* family papers> <a mug that will *contain* a quart of ale>
syn accommodate, hold
rel harbor, house, lodge, shelter; admit, receive, take, take in
3 syn see INCLUDE
contaminate *vb* **1** to debase by making impure or unclean <feared her child's morals would be *contaminated* by others>
syn defile, pollute, soil, taint; *compare* TAINT 1
rel corrupt, debase, debauch, deprave, pervert, vitiate; harm, injure, spoil
con better, elevate, improve
ant purify
2 to render unfit for use by the introduction of unwholesome or undesirable elements <water *contaminated* by sewage>

syn befoul, foul, pollute
rel infect; poison; dirty, soil
ant purify
contemn *vb syn* see DESPISE
contemplate *vb* **1** *syn* see EYE 1
rel ponder, reflect, study; examine, inspect, scan, scrutinize
2 syn see CONSIDER 1
rel drift, roam
3 syn see INTEND 2
idiom have in view
contemplative *adj syn* see THOUGHTFUL 1
rel musing, weighing; reasoning
idiom in a brown study
contemporaneous *adj syn* see CONTEMPORARY 1
contemporary *adj* **1** existing or occurring at the same time <the story has come down from several *contemporary* sources>
syn coetaneous, coeval, coexistent, coexisting, concurrent, contemporaneous, simultaneous, synchronal, synchronic, synchronous
rel accompanying, attendant, attending, coincident, concomitant; current, existing, present; associated, connected, linked, related
con antecedent, foregoing, preceding, previous, prior; ensuing, following, succeeding
2 syn see PRESENT
3 syn see UP-TO-DATE
contempt *n* **1** *syn* see DESPITE 1
rel antipathy, aversion; distaste, repugnance
con awe, fear, reverence
ant regard
2 syn see DISGRACE
3 syn see DEFIANCE 2
contemptible *adj* arousing or meriting scorn or disdain <a *contemptible* attempt to blame his wife for his failure>
syn beggarly, cheap, despicable, despisable, mean, pitiable, pitiful, scummy, scurvy, shabby, sorry; *compare* BASE 3
rel abhorrent, abominable, detestable, hateful, odious; abject, ignoble, sordid; bad, inferior, poor, sad; disgusting, scrimy, shameful; outcast
con creditable, estimable, honorable, noble; high-minded, high-principled, principled, true, upright; honest, square, straight
ant admirable
contend *vb* **1** to strive in opposition to someone or something <*contending* against the temptation to look behind him>
syn battle, fight, oppugn, tug, war
rel combat, oppose, resist, withstand; contest, cope (with), vie
2 syn see MAINTAIN 2
rel report, say, tell; charge, enjoin, urge; dictate, prescribe
3 syn see COMPETE 1
rel combat, oppose, resist, withstand; confront, encounter, face, meet, stand
content *vb syn* see SATISFY 3
rel delight, thrill, tickle; bewitch, captivate, charm, enrapture
con disappoint, dishearten, displease
ant discontent

contention *n* **1** *syn* see DISCORD
rel altercation, quarrel, squabble, wrangle; argument, controversy, dispute
con agreement, coincidence, concurrence
2 *syn* see ARGUMENT 2
3 *syn* see THESIS 1

contentious *adj* **1** *syn* see BELLIGERENT
rel contrary, froward, perverse; captious, carping, caviling, faultfinding
con calm, serene, tranquil; amiable, complaisant, good-natured, obliging
ant peaceable
2 prone to wordy contention <a *contentious* old chap, always ready for an argument>
syn argumentative, controversial, disputatious, litigious, polemical
rel fiery, hasty, hotheaded, impetuous, peppery; bellicose, belligerent, scrappy
con amiable, complaisant, good-natured, obliging; agreeable, cooperative, understanding

conterminous *adj* *syn* see ADJACENT 3

contest *vb* **1** *syn* see COMPETE 1
rel endeavor
2 *syn* see RESIST

contest *n* **1** an earnest struggle for superiority or victory <the rival factions continued in *contest* for several years>
syn competition, conflict, emulation, rivalry, strife, striving, tug-of-war, warfare
rel brush, encounter, skirmish; action, battle, engagement
2 a competitive encounter between groups or individuals <there were *contests* of skill and endurance>
syn competition, concours, conflict, meet, meeting, rencontre
rel proving, testing, trial, trying

contestation *n* *syn* see THESIS 1

contiguity *n* *syn* see PROXIMITY

contiguous *adj* **1** *syn* see ADJACENT 3
rel close, near, nearby, nigh
con apart, separate; distant, remote
2 *syn* see NEIGHBORING

contiguously *adv* *syn* see IMMEDIATELY 1

contiguousness *n* *syn* see PROXIMITY

continence *n* *syn* see TEMPERANCE 2
rel self-restraint; moderation, temperateness; chasteness, chastity, purity
con self-indulgence; excessiveness, inordinateness; lasciviousness, lecherousness, lewdness, licentiousness, wantonness
ant incontinence

continent *adj* *syn* see ABSTEMIOUS
rel bridled, curbed, inhibited, restrained; chaste, pure
con self-indulgent, spoiled
ant incontinent

contingence *n* *syn* see CONTACT 1

contingency *n* *syn* see JUNCTURE 2
rel break, chance, occasion, opportunity

contingent *adj* **1** *syn* see ACCIDENTAL
rel unanticipated, unforeseeable, unforeseen; likely, possible, probable
con certain, inevitable, necessary

2 *syn* see DEPENDENT 1

continual *adj* continuing without intermission and seemingly without end <they were tired of her *continual* nagging>
syn around-the-clock, ceaseless, constant, continuous, endless, everlasting, incessant, interminable, minutely, perpetual, timeless, unceasing, unending, unintermitted, unintermittent, uninterrupted, unremitting
rel abiding, enduring, persistent, persisting, staying; unvarying; unchanging, unfailing, unflagging, unwaning; relentless, running, steady
con ephemeral, evanescent, impermanent, short-lived, temporary, transient, transitory

continually *adv* *syn* see TOGETHER 2

continuance *n* *syn* see RUN 2
rel constancy, longevity, permanence; survival

continuation *n* **1** uninterrupted existence or succession <the *continuation* of political disorder in Northern Ireland>
syn continuity, duration, endurance, persistence
rel extension, prolongation, protraction
ant termination
2 *syn* see RUN 2
ant cessation

continue *vb* **1** to remain indefinitely in existence or in a particular state or course <many traditional beliefs still *continue*> <do you expect to *continue* in school for the rest of your life?>
syn abide, carry through, endure, last, perdure, persist
rel carry on, carry over, ride, run on; outlast, outlive, survive; remain, stay
con cease, desist, discontinue, quit; arrest, check, interrupt; defer, intermit, postpone, stay, suspend
ant discontinue
2 *syn* see RESUME 2

continuing *adj* *syn* see OLD 2

continuity *n* *syn* see CONTINUATION 1

continuous *adj* *syn* see CONTINUAL
ant discontinuous

continuously *adv* **1** *syn* see TOGETHER 2
2 *syn* see ALWAYS 1

contort *vb* *syn* see DEFORM
rel bend, curve, twist

contour *n* *syn* see OUTLINE

contra *prep* *syn* see AGAINST 1

contra *adv* *syn* see AGAIN 5

contra *n* *syn* see OPPOSITE

contraband *adj* prohibited or excluded by law or treaty <fur or feathers from endangered species are *contraband* in advanced nations>
syn banned, hot
rel disapproved, proscribed, taboo; forbidden, prohibited; excluded, shut out

contraband *vb* *syn* see SMUGGLE

contraception *n* *syn* see BIRTH CONTROL

---

syn synonym(s)   *rel* related word(s)
ant antonym(s)   *con* contrasted word(s)
idiom idiomatic equivalent(s)
‖ use limited; if in doubt, see a dictionary

contract *n* a usually legally enforceable arrangement between two or more parties <a *contract* for a new roof>
  syn agreement, bargain, bond, compact, convention, covenant, pact, transaction; *compare* AGREEMENT 2, TREATY

contract *vb* **1** to become affected by a disease or disorder <*contracted* a severe cold that later turned into pneumonia>
  syn catch, come down (with), get, sicken (with *or* of), take
  rel acquire, obtain; decline, fail, sink, weaken; afflict, derange, disorder, indispose, upset; bring on, cause, induce; succumb (to)
  idiom be laid by the heels by, fall (a) victim to
  2 *syn* see INCUR
  3 to make or become smaller in bulk or volume <*contract* a muscle>
  syn compress, concentrate, condense, constrict, shrink
  rel decrease, diminish, dwindle, lessen, reduce
  con dilate, distend, inflate, swell
  ant expand

contracted *adj syn* see ENGAGED 2

contradict *vb syn* see DENY 4
  rel dispute; belie, falsify, garble
  con authenticate, substantiate, verify
  ant corroborate; confirm

contradiction *n syn* see DENIAL 2

contradictory *n syn* see OPPOSITE

contradictory *adj syn* see OPPOSITE
  rel negating, nullifying; adverse, antagonistic, counteractive
  con agreeing, jibing, squaring, tallying
  ant corroboratory; confirmatory

contradistinction *n syn* see ANTAGONISM 2

contraposition *n syn* see ANTAGONISM 2

contraption *n syn* see DEVICE 2

contrariant *n syn* see ANTIPATHETIC 1

contrariety *n syn* see ANTAGONISM 2

contrariwise *adv syn* see AGAIN 5
  idiom on (*or* to) the contrary

contrary *n syn* see OPPOSITE

contrary *adj* **1** *syn* see OPPOSITE
  2 *syn* see ANTIPATHETIC 1
  3 obstinately self-willed in refusing to concur, conform, or submit <why be *contrary* about something that you cannot change>
  syn balky, cross-grained, froward, ornery, perverse, restive, wayward, wrongheaded
  rel headstrong, intractable, recalcitrant, refractory, unruly; contumacious, insubordinate, rebellious; dissentient, dissident, nonconforming, nonconformist, recusant; obstinate, stubborn
  con amenable, biddable, docile, obedient, tractable; amiable, obliging; acquiescent, compliant; forbearing, long-suffering, tolerant
  ant complaisant

contrary *adv syn* see AGAIN 5

contrast *vb syn* see COMPARE 2

contravene *vb* **1** *syn* see VIOLATE 1
  rel encroach, intrude, overstep, trespass
  2 *syn* see DENY 4
  rel combat, fight, oppose, resist; abjure, disclaim, disown, exclude, reject, repudiate, spurn

con accept, agree, subscribe (to); admit, allow, own
  ant uphold (*as a principle*); allege (*as a right or claim*)

contravention *n syn* see BREACH 1
  rel crime, offense, sin, vice

contrawise *adv syn* see AGAIN 5

contretemps *n syn* see MISFORTUNE

contribute *vb* **1** to give in common with others <*contribute* to a fund for handicapped children>
  syn chip in, come through, kick in, pitch in, subscribe; *compare* GIVE 1
  idiom put something in the pot, sweeten the kitty
  2 to have a share in something (as an act or effect) <careful planning *contributed* greatly to the success of the project>
  syn conduce, redound, tend
  rel aid, help, assist; add (to), augment, supplement; fortify, recruit, reinforce, strengthen
  idiom do one's bit, have a hand in
  con detract, minus, subtract, take away

contribution *n syn* see DONATION

contributory *adj syn* see AUXILIARY

contrite *adj syn* see REMORSEFUL

contriteness *n syn* see PENITENCE

contrition *n syn* see PENITENCE

contriturate *vb syn* see PULVERIZE 1

contrivance *n* **1** *syn* see DEVICE 2
  2 *syn* see INVENTION

contrive *vb* **1** *syn* see PLOT
  rel develop, elaborate, work out
  2 to use ingenuity in making or doing or achieving an end <*contrived* a useful camp stove from a few bricks and a piece of screen>
  syn concoct, cook (up), devise, dream up, formulate, frame, hatch (up), invent, make up, vamp (up)
  rel plan, plot, project, scheme; fabricate, fashion, make, manufacture; handle, manipulate, move; rig

control *vb* **1** *syn* see COMPOSE 4
  rel adjust, regulate; curb, master, quell, subdue
  2 *syn* see GOVERN 3
  rel regulate, supervise; discipline
  idiom put through the mill (*or* a course of sprouts), take in hand

control *n syn* see POWER 1

controlled *adj syn* see CONSERVATIVE 2

controversial *adj syn* see CONTENTIOUS 2

controversy *n* **1** *syn* see ARGUMENT 2
  2 *syn* see QUARREL

controvert *vb syn* see DISPROVE 1
  rel challenge, oppugn, question

contumacious *adj syn* see INSUBORDINATE
  rel contrary, froward, perverse; alienated, disaffected, estranged, irreconcilable
  con acquiescent, compliant, resigned
  ant obedient

contumacy *n syn* see DEFIANCE 2

contumelious *adj* **1** *syn* see ABUSIVE
  2 *syn* see INSOLENT 2
  ant obsequious

contumely *n* **1** *syn* see ABUSE

rel animadversion, aspersion, reflection, stricture

idiom hard (*or* bitter) words

2 *syn* see AFFRONT

contuse *vb syn* see BRUISE 1

contusion *n syn* see BRUISE

conundrum *n syn* see MYSTERY

convalesce *vb syn* see IMPROVE 3

convenance *n syn* see FORM 3

convene *vb* **1** to begin a session (as of a legislature or conference) <the council *convened* at 10 o'-clock>

syn meet, open, sit

idiom hold a meeting (*or* session)

2 *syn* see SUMMON 2

rel convoke, muster

3 *syn* see CONVOKE

convenience *n* **1** *syn* see AMENITY 2

2 *syn* see TOILET

convenience *vb syn* see OBLIGE 2

convenient *adj* **1** *syn* see GOOD 2

2 situated within easy reach <left his glasses *convenient* to his book>

syn adjacent, close-at-hand, close-by, handy, near-at-hand, nearby

rel close, near, nigh; immediate, next

idiom at one's beck and call, at one's fingertips, in one's immediate neighborhood, under one's nose

ant inconvenient

convention *n* **1** *syn* see TREATY

2 *syn* see CONTRACT

rel accord, understanding

3 *syn* see FORM 3

rel canon, law, precept, rule; custom, practice

conventional *adj* **1** according with or based on generally accepted and well-established usage <took a very *conventional* view of his duty>

syn button-down, orthodox, square, straight; *compare* TRADITIONAL 1

rel moderate, sober, temperate; constrained, restrained; dependable, reliable, responsible; conscientious, fastidious, nice, punctilious, scrupulous; conservative, traditionalistic

ant unconventional

2 *syn* see TRADITIONAL 1

3 *syn* see CEREMONIAL

rel decent, decorous, proper, seemly; correct, precise, right

con lax, negligent, remiss, slack; artless, ingenuous, naive, natural, simple, unsophisticated

ant unconventional

converge *vb* to come to or trend toward a common point <the main streets *converge* on a central square>

syn concenter, concentrate, focus, meet

idiom come to a center, come (*or* run) together

conversant *adj* **1** *syn* see AWARE

ant ignorant

2 *syn* see FAMILIAR 3

rel sensible; up-to-date; apprehending, comprehending, perceptive, percipient

con unfamiliar; nescient

ant unconversant

conversation *n* **1** oral exchange of information or ideas <leaned against the fence in casual *conversation*>

syn chat, colloquy, confabulation, converse, dialogue, parley

rel discussion; discourse, speech, talk

2 an instance of conversational exchange <had a long *conversation* about family problems>

syn colloquy, confabulation, dialogue, talk; *compare* CHAT 2

rel debate, deliberation, discussion, ventilation; comment, observation, remark; cross talk, repartee

conversation piece *n syn* see CURIOSITY 2

converse *vb* to engage in conversation <they *conversed* quietly while waiting for their friend>

syn chat, chin, colloque, talk, visit, yarn; *compare* CHAT 1

converse (in) *vb syn* see SPEAK 3

converse *n* **1** *syn* see CONVERSATION 1

2 *syn* see COMMUNICATION 3

converse *adj syn* see OPPOSITE

converse *n syn* see OPPOSITE

conversely *adv syn* see AGAIN 5

conversion *n* **1** fundamental alteration in one's system of beliefs <Judaism does not encourage *conversion* of gentiles>

syn metanoia, rebirth

rel about-face, reversal, turning; reclamation, regeneration

idiom change of heart

2 change of one thing to another usually by substitution <*conversion* of locomotives from steam to diesel power>

syn alteration, changeover, shift, transformation

rel change, modification, qualification; metamorphosis, mutation, permutation, transmutation; innovation, novelty

convert *vb* **1** to induce (another or others) to accept the validity of something (as a belief, course of action, or point of view) <Chinese missionaries *converted* many Japanese to Buddhism>

syn bring, lead, move, persuade

rel redeem, reform, save; bend, bias, incline, sway; actuate, budge, impel; proselyte, proselytize

2 *syn* see TRANSFORM

rel fabricate, forge, make, manufacture; apply, employ, use, utilize

convey *vb* **1** *syn* see CARRY 1

2 *syn* see COMMUNICATE 1

rel project, put across

3 *syn* see TRANSFER 4

rel commit, consign, relegate

4 *syn* see CONDUCT 4

conveyance *n* **1** *syn* see TRANSPORTATION 1

2 *syn* see DEED 3

3 *syn* see VEHICLE 3

---

syn synonym(s)   *rel* related word(s)

ant antonym(s)   *con* contrasted word(s)

idiom idiomatic equivalent(s)

‖ use limited; if in doubt, see a dictionary

convict *n* a person serving time in prison after conviction as a criminal <mixing hardened *convicts* with juvenile offenders>
  syn ‖con, jailbird, ‖lag, loser, prison bird
  rel long-termer, longtimer; ‖stir bug; recidivist, repeater

conviction *n* **1** *syn* see CERTAINTY
  con dubiety, dubiosity, uncertainty; disbelief, incredulity, unbelief
  2 *syn* see OPINION
  rel doctrine, dogma, tenet

convince *vb* **1** *syn* see ASSURE 2
  2 *syn* see INDUCE 1

convincing *adj* **1** *syn* see AUTHENTIC 1
  2 *syn* see VALID

convivial *adj* *syn* see SOCIAL 1
  rel lively, vivacious; jocund, jolly, merry
  con grave, sedate, serious, sober, solemn, somber; reserved, reticent, silent
  ant taciturn; stolid

convoke *vb* to bring together by or as if by summons <the ruler *convoked* his council>
  syn assemble, call, convene, summon; *compare* SUMMON 2
  rel collect, congregate, gather; ask, bid, invite, request; meet, sit
  con adjourn, close, dissolve, prorogue, recess, suspend; disperse, scatter

convoluted *adj* *syn* see WINDING

convoy *vb* *syn* see ACCOMPANY
  rel defend, guard, protect, safeguard, shield

convulse *vb* *syn* see SHAKE 4

convulsion *n* *syn* see COMMOTION 1
  rel cataclysm, disaster; quaking, rocking, shaking, tottering, trembling

cook *vb* **1** to make ready or fit for eating by the use of heat <liked everything well-*cooked*>
  syn do
  2 *syn* see BURN 3

cook (up) *vb* *syn* see CONTRIVE 2

cookshop *n* *syn* see EATING HOUSE

cool *adj* **1** *syn* see COLD 1
  ant warm
  2 freed or giving the impression of freedom from all agitation or excitement <they looked *cool* and very formidable>
  syn collected, composed, disimpassioned, imperturbable, nonchalant, unflappable, unruffled; *compare* HAPPY-GO-LUCKY
  rel calm, placid, serene, tranquil; aloof, detached, indifferent; impassive, phlegmatic, stolid; assured, confident, self-possessed
  con fervent, fervid, impassioned, passionate, perfervid; discomposed, disturbed, flurried, flustered, perturbed, upset
  ant ardent; agitated
  3 *syn* see UNSOCIABLE
  ‖**4** *syn* see MARVELOUS 2

cool *vb* **1** *syn* see COMPOSE 4
  2 *syn* see MURDER 1

cooler *n* *syn* see JAIL

coolness *n* *syn* see EQUANIMITY

‖**coon** *vb* *syn* see STEAL 1

coon's age *n* *syn* see AGE 2

‖**coony** *adj* *syn* see CLEVER 4

coop *n* *syn* see JAIL

coop *vb* *syn* see ENCLOSE 1
  rel bar, block, hinder, impede, obstruct

cooperate *vb* *syn* see UNITE 2
  rel agree, coincide
  con annul, negate, nullify; negative, neutralize
  ant counteract

cooperative *adj* involving joint action in producing a result <the need of *cooperative* efforts to effect lasting social change>
  syn coacting, coactive, coefficient, conjoint, synergetic, synergic
  rel collaborative, concerted; noncompetitive, uncompetitive
  con competitive, emulous, rivaling, vying; antagonistic, conflicting, oppugnant
  ant counteractive

coordinate *vb* *syn* see HARMONIZE 3

coordinate *n* **1** *syn* see OPPOSITE NUMBER
  2 *syn* see MATE 5

‖**cop** *vb* *syn* see STEAL 1

cop *n* *syn* see POLICEMAN

copartner *n* *syn* see PARTNER

copious *adj* *syn* see PLENTIFUL
  rel exuberant, lush, luxuriant
  con exiguous, scant, scanty, scrimpy, spare, sparse; slender, slight, slim, tenuous, thin
  ant meager

cop out *vb* ‖**1** *syn* see DIE 1
  2 *syn* see BACK DOWN

‖**copper** *n* *syn* see POLICEMAN

copy *n* **1** *syn* see IMITATION
  2 *syn* see REPRODUCTION
  rel counterpart, parallel; impress, impression, imprint, print; effigy, image, likeness
  ant original

copy *vb* to make a copy of <*copied* the speech word for word>
  syn duplicate, imitate, reduplicate, replicate, reproduce
  rel ditto, repeat; counterfeit, fake, sham, simulate; ape, burlesque, mock, parody, take off, travesty
  ant originate

coquet *vb* *syn* see TRIFLE 1

coquette *n* *syn* see FLIRT

coquettish *adj* *syn* see COY 2

cordial *adj* *syn* see GRACIOUS 1
  rel responsive, sympathetic, tender, warm, warmhearted; heartfelt, hearty, sincere, wholehearted
  con cold, cool, frigid, frosty; aloof, detached, disinterested, indifferent; reserved, silent, taciturn

cordiality *n* *syn* see AMENITY 1
  rel responsiveness, sympathy, understanding, warmth; mutuality, reciprocity; approbation, approval, favor
  con cross-purposes, difference, disagreement, misunderstanding, odds, variance; disapprobation, disapproval, disfavor

core *n* **1** *syn* see CENTER 1
  2 *syn* see BODY 3

3 *syn* see SUBSTANCE 2
rel consequence, import, importance, significance
4 *syn* see CENTER 3
rel base, basis, foundation; beginning, commencement, origin, start
‖**corker** *n syn* ‖DILLY, crackerjack, ‖daisy, dandy, humdinger, jim-dandy, knockout, ‖lalapalooza, ‖lulu, nifty
corkscrew *vb syn* see WIND 2
corner *n* **1** *syn* see PREDICAMENT
2 *syn* see MONOPOLY
corner *vb* to get into one's control or a position from which escape is difficult <*cornered* him at a party and tried to borrow a hundred dollars>
syn bottle (up), collar, tree
rel bother, disturb, put out, trouble; capture, catch, nab, seize, trap
idiom chase up a tree, drive (*or* run) into a corner, get (*or* have) on the ropes
cornerwise *adv syn* see DIAGONALLY
corny *adj syn* see TRITE
corollary *n syn* see EFFECT 1
coronal *n syn* see WREATH
coronet *n syn* see WREATH
corporal *adj syn* see BODILY
corporation *n syn* see POTBELLY
corporeal *adj* **1** *syn* see BODILY
2 *syn* see MATERIAL 1
corps *n syn* see COMPANY 4
corpse *n* a dead body especially of a human being <concealed the *corpse* under some rubbish>
syn body, cadaver, carcass, ‖cold meat, ‖deader, mort, remains, stiff
rel carrion; bones
corpselike *adj* **1** *syn* see DEATHLY 1
2 *syn* see GHASTLY 2
corpsy *adj syn* see DEATHLY 1
corpulence *n syn* see OBESITY
corpulent *adj syn* see FAT 2
corpus *n* **1** *syn* see BODY 3
2 *syn* see OEUVRE
corrade *vb syn* see ABRADE 1
corral *vb syn* see ENCLOSE 1
correct *vb* **1** to set right something that is wrong <*correct* a misstatement>
syn amend, emend, mend, rectify, right
rel ameliorate, better, improve; redress, remedy, revise; make over, reform; adjust, fix, regulate
con damage, harm, hurt, impair, injure, mar, spoil
2 *syn* see PUNISH 1
con baby, coddle, cosset, humor, indulge, pamper, spoil
correct *adj* **1** *syn* see DECOROUS 1
rel careful, meticulous, punctilious, scrupulous
2 conforming to or agreeing with fact <the *correct* solution to the problem>
syn accurate, exact, nice, precise, proper, right, rigorous
rel faithful, true, undistorted, veracious, veridical; faultless, flawless, impeccable, perfect
con fallacious, false, wrong; defective, faulty, flawed, imperfect

ant incorrect
correction *n syn* see PUNISHMENT
correctitude *n syn* see ORDER 7
corrective *n syn* see REMEDY 2
correctly *adv syn* see WELL 1
correctness *n* **1** *syn* see ORDER 7
2 *syn* see PRECISION
correlate *n* **1** *syn* see COUNTERPART 1
2 *syn* see PARALLEL
correspond *vb syn* see AGREE 4
correspond (to) *vb syn* see AMOUNT 2
correspondence *n syn* see CONSISTENCY
ant divergence
correspondent *n syn* see PARALLEL
corresponding *adj syn* see LIKE
correspondingly *adv syn* see ALSO 1
corridor *n syn* see PASSAGE 4
corrival *n syn* see RIVAL
corroborate *vb syn* see CONFIRM 2
con invalidate, negate, nullify
ant contradict
corroborative *adj* serving or tending to corroborate <*corroborative* evidence>
syn adminicular, collateral, confirmative, confirmatory, corroboratory, verificatory
rel ancillary, auxiliary, supplementary, supportive; assisting, helping
con confutative, refutative, refutatory; contradictory, negatory
corroboratory *adj syn* see CORROBORATIVE
corrode *vb syn* see EAT 3
corrosive *adj syn* see SARCASTIC
corrosiveness *n syn* see SARCASM
corrugation *n syn* see WRINKLE
corrupt *vb* **1** *syn* see DEBASE 1
rel abase, degrade; ruin, wreck
con amend, correct, reform
2 *syn* see DECAY
rel befoul, defile, foul; smirch, tarnish
corrupt *adj* **1** *syn* see VICIOUS 2
rel crooked, devious, oblique; baneful, deleterious, detrimental, noxious, pernicious; abased, degraded, low
2 seeking sordid advantage with little regard to moral or legal bars <a *corrupt* politician>
syn mercenary, praetorian, unethical, unprincipled, unscrupulous, venal; *compare* CROOKED 2, VENAL 1
rel undependable, unreliable, untrustworthy; faithless, inconstant, unfaithful; double-dealing, perfidious, treacherous, two-faced; bribable, corruptible; blackguardly, knavish, reprobate
con ethical, principled, scrupulous, upright; dependable, reliable, trustworthy, trusty
3 *syn* see CROOKED 2
corrupted *adj syn* see DEBASED
corruptible *adj syn* see VENAL 1
corruption *n* **1** *syn* see VICE 1
2 *syn* see BARBARISM

---

syn synonym(s)   *rel* related word(s)
ant antonym(s)   *con* contrasted word(s)
idiom idiomatic equivalent(s)
‖ use limited; if in doubt, see a dictionary

corsair *n syn* see PIRATE
coruscate *vb syn* see FLASH 1
coruscation *n syn* see FLASH 1
corybantic *adj syn* see FURIOUS 2
coryphée *n syn* see DANCER
cosmic *adj syn* see UNIVERSAL 2
cosmopolitan *adj* **1** exhibiting or characterized by a sophistication and savoir faire arising from cultured urban life and wide travel <had a thoroughly *cosmopolitan* outlook on life>
syn metropolitan, urbane; *compare* SOPHISTICATED 2
rel civilized, polished, smooth; sophisticated, worldly-wise; cultivated, cultured
con boorish, cloddish, rude, rustic; insular, parochial, provincial
2 *syn* see UNIVERSAL 2
cosmos (*or* **kosmos**) *n syn* see UNIVERSE
cosset *vb* **1** *syn* see CARESS
2 *syn* see BABY
cost *n* **1** *syn* see PRICE 1
2 *syn* see EXPENSE 1
3 *syn* see EXPENSE 2
costive *adj* **1** *syn* see CONSTIPATED
2 *syn* see STINGY
costless *adj syn* see FREE 5
costly *adj* **1** commanding or being a large price <the scarcer an item becomes the more *costly* it is>
syn dear, expensive, high; *compare* PRECIOUS 1
rel excessive, exorbitant, extravagant, inordinate, steep, stiff; fancy, premium, top
con inexpensive, low, low-priced, reasonable
ant cheap
2 *syn* see PRECIOUS 1
costume *n* style of clothing and adornment <her *costume* was always suitable to the occasion>
syn dress, getup, guise, outfit, rig, setout, turnout
rel fashion, mode, style
cot *n syn* see HUT
‖**cotch** *vb* **1** *syn* see SEIZE 2
2 *syn* see CATCH 1
3 *syn* see CATCH 7
coterie *n syn* see CLIQUE
cottage *n syn* see HUT
cotton *vb* **1** *syn* see BABY
2 *syn* see FAWN
cotton (*to or* on *to*) *vb syn* see APPREHEND 1
cottony *adj syn* see SOFT 3
couch *vb* **1** *syn* see WORD
2 *syn* see LOWER 3
couch *n syn* see LAIR 1
couleur de rose *adj syn* see HOPEFUL 2
couloir *n syn* see PASSAGE 4
counsel *n syn* see ADVICE 1
counsel *vb* to give advice to or about <*counseled* him to wait for a more propitious occasion>
syn advise, recommend
rel admonish, reprehend, warn; direct, order, prescribe; charge, enjoin, prompt, urge; advocate, suggest
count *vb* **1** to ascertain the total of units in a collection by noting one after another <*counted* the sheep in the pasture>

syn enumerate, number, numerate, tale, tally, tell
rel add, cast, figure, foot, sum, tot, total; calculate, compute, estimate, reckon; tell off
2 *syn* see MATTER
3 *syn* see WEIGH 3
count (on) *vb syn* see RELY (on *or* upon)
count (on *or* upon) *vb syn* see EXPECT 1
countenance *n* **1** *syn* see LOOK 2
idiom (the) cut of one's jib
2 *syn* see FACE 1
countenance *vb* **1** *syn* see ENCOURAGE 2
rel applaud, commend; back, champion, support, uphold
con deride, ridicule; criticize, reprehend, reprobate; reproach, reprove
ant discountenance
2 *syn* see APPROVE 1
counter *vb syn* see OPPOSE 1
rel baffle, balk, beat, bilk, circumvent, dash, disappoint, foil, frustrate, ruin
counter *n syn* see OPPOSITE
counter *adj syn* see OPPOSITE
rel hostile, inimical; adverse, antagonistic, anti, oppugnant; hindering, impeding, obstructive
counteract *vb syn* see NEUTRALIZE
rel correct, fix, rectify, right
con cooperate, coordinate, synergize; back, reinforce, support
counteractant *n syn* see REMEDY 2
counteractive *n syn* see REMEDY 2
counteragent *n syn* see REMEDY 2
counterbalance *vb syn* see COMPENSATE 1
rel amend, correct, rectify
con overbalance, unbalance
counterblow *n syn* see RETALIATION
countercheck *vb syn* see NEUTRALIZE
counterfactual *adj syn* see FALSE 1
counterfeit *vb syn* see ASSUME 4
rel ape, copy, imitate, mimic
counterfeit *adj* being an imitation intended to mislead or deceive <*counterfeit* money> <*counterfeit* sympathy>
syn bogus, brummagem, fake, false, phony, pinchbeck, pseudo, sham, snide, spurious; *compare* SPURIOUS 3
rel feigned, pretended, simulated; deceptive, delusive, delusory, misleading; fraudulent
con authentic, veritable; actual, real, true; unquestionable, valid
ant bona fide, genuine
counterfeit *n syn* see IMPOSTURE
rel copy, facsimile, reproduction; dummy, simulacrum
countermeasure *n syn* see REMEDY 2
counterpane *n syn* see BEDSPREAD
counterpart *n* **1** something that completes or complements <export controls as a *counterpart* of domestic distribution controls>
syn complement, correlate, pendant; *compare* PARALLEL
rel analogue, correlate, correspondent; equal, equivalent, like, match
con counterpoint, opposite

2 *syn* see PARALLEL

3 *syn* see EQUAL

4 *syn* see OPPOSITE NUMBER

counterpoise *n syn* see BALANCE 1

counterpoise *vb syn* see COMPENSATE 1

rel ballast, poise, stabilize, steady, trim

con capsize, overturn, upset

counterpole *n syn* see OPPOSITE

countersign *n syn* see PASSWORD 1

counterstep *n syn* see REMEDY 2

countertype *n syn* see PARALLEL

countervail *vb syn* see COMPENSATE 1

rel amend, correct, rectify; foil, frustrate, thwart; overcome, surmount

countless *adj syn* see INNUMERABLE

count out *vb syn* see EXCLUDE

countrified *adj syn* see RURAL

country *n* the nation-state to which one belongs or from which one originated <returned to his own *country* after years of exile>

syn fatherland, home, homeland, land, mother country, motherland, soil

country *adj syn* see RURAL

country jake *n syn* see RUSTIC

countryman *n syn* see RUSTIC

couple *vb* **1** *syn* see JOIN 1

2 *syn* see HITCH 2

rel hook up, ‖inspan

couple *n* two individuals of the same or a similar kind that occur, function, or are considered together <a *couple* of ideas for improving the book> <the happiest *couple* I know>

syn brace, doublet, duo, dyad, pair, twosome

rel span, team, yoke

coupling *n syn* see JOINT 1

courage *n* a quality of mind or temperament that enables one to stand fast in the face of opposition, hardship, or danger <had the kind of *courage* that could appreciate a danger yet steadfastly face it>

syn dauntlessness, guts, heart, mettle, ‖moxie, pluck, resolution, spirit, spunk; *compare* FORTITUDE

rel audacity, boldness, bravery, doughtiness, fearlessness, intrepidity; gallantry, heroism, valor; backbone, fortitude, grit, sand; assurance, determination, firmness, persistence, tenacity

con chickenheartedness, faintheartedness, unmanliness, yellowness; baseness, cravenness, poltroonery, pusillanimity; timidity, timorousness

ant cowardice

courageous *adj syn* see BRAVE 1

rel fiery, high-spirited; strong, tenacious

con afraid, apprehensive, fearful

ant pusillanimous

courier *n syn* see MESSENGER

course *n* **1** *syn* see WAY 2

rel circuit, orbit, range, scope

2 *syn* see CHANNEL 1

3 way of acting or proceeding <hard to decide on the best *course* to follow>

syn line, policy, polity, procedure, program

rel design, pattern, plan, platform, scheme; manner, system, way

idiom course of action

4 *syn* see PROGRESS 2

5 *syn* see SUCCESSION 2

course *vb* to proceed with great celerity (as in pursuing or competing) <the fox *coursed* after the hare>

syn career, chase, race, rush, speed, tear; *compare* RUSH 1

rel hasten, hurry, hustle; dart, dash, scamper, scoot, scurry; run, sprint

idiom step on the gas, stir one's stumps

courser *n* a strong vigorous horse formerly used in mounted combat <heroes mounted on great fiery *coursers*>

syn charger, war-horse

court *n* **1** an open space wholly or partly enclosed (as by buildings or walls) <the apartment overlooks the *court*>

syn ‖close, courtyard, curtilage, enclosure, quad, quadrangle, yard

2 a place or the persons assembled for the administration of justice <the *court* was called to order>

syn bar, lawcourt, tribunal

3 *syn* see JUDGE 2

court *vb syn* see ADDRESS 8

rel allure, attract, captivate, charm

courteous *adj syn* see CIVIL 2

rel attentive, considerate, thoughtful

con blunt, brusque, curt, gruff; insolent, overbearing, supercilious

ant discourteous

courtesan *n syn* see HARLOT 1

courtesy *n* **1** courteous behavior or a courteous act <noted for her *courtesy* and graciousness> <such little *courtesies* take little time but often brighten lonely lives>

syn amenity, attention, gallantry

rel affability, cordiality, geniality, graciousness; comity, complaisance; chivalry, civility, courteousness, courtliness; attentiveness, considerateness, consideration, thoughtfulness

con boorishness, churlishness; impoliteness, incivility, rudeness, ungraciousness

ant discourtesy

2 *syn* see FAVOR 4

courtly *adj* marked by elaborate and often ceremonious courtesy <a *courtly* gentleman of the old school>

syn gallant, gracious, preux, stately; *compare* CIVIL 2

rel august, dignified, imposing, lofty; prim, starchy, stiff, stilted, studied; ceremonious, conventional, formal; civilized

con discourteous, ill-mannered, impolite, rude, uncivil, ungracious; boorish, coarse, gross, loutish, uncouth, vulgar

ant churlish

courtyard *n syn* see COURT 1

---

syn synonym(s)   *rel* related word(s)

ant antonym(s)   *con* contrasted word(s)

idiom idiomatic equivalent(s)

‖ use limited; if in doubt, see a dictionary

cousinage *n syn* see KIN 2

cousinhood *n syn* see KIN 2

cove *n syn* see INLET

covenant *n syn* see CONTRACT

covenant *vb syn* see VOW
  rel agree, concur

cover *vb* **1** *syn* see DEFEND 1
  2 *syn* see HIDE
  3 to spread over or put something over <fog *covered* the ground> <*covered* the bed with a quilt>
  syn blanket, cap, crown, overcast, overlay, overspread
  rel conceal, hide, screen; defend, protect, shield; enclose, enfold, envelop, shroud, wrap; superimpose, superpose
  con display, exhibit, expose
  ant bare, uncover
  4 *syn* see TRAVEL 2
  5 *syn* see SET 11

cover *n* **1** *syn* see SHELTER 1
  rel concealment, hiding, screen; safety, security
  ant exposure
  2 *syn* see MASK 2

coverlet *n syn* see BEDSPREAD

‖**coverlid** *n syn* see BEDSPREAD

covert *adj* **1** *syn* see SECRET 1
  rel camouflaged, cloaked, disguised, dissembled, masked
  con candid, frank, open
  ant overt
  2 *syn* see ULTERIOR
  con direct, forthright; honest, square, straight

covert *n syn* see SHELTER 1

covertly *adv syn* see SECRETLY

covet *vb syn* see DESIRE 1
  con abjure, forswear
  ant renounce

covetous *adj* having or marked by an urgent and often unscrupulous desire for possessions <the *covetous* eye of an avid collector>
  syn acquisitive, desirous, grabby, grasping, greedy, itchy, prehensile
  rel esurient, gluttonous, rapacious, ravenous, voracious; hoggish, lickerish, piggish, swinish; avid, eager, keen; envious, jealous; grudging, selfish
  con generous, liberal, munificent; ungrudging, unselfish; abstemious, abstinent, ascetic, austere; moderate, restrained, temperate

covey *n syn* see GROUP 1

covin *n syn* see PLOT 2

cow *vb syn* see INTIMIDATE
  rel appall, daunt, dismay; abash, discomfit, disconcert, embarrass, faze, rattle
  con cower, cringe, fawn, toady, truckle

coward *n* one who shows or yields to ignoble fear <a treacherous *coward* who betrayed his friends to save his own skin>
  syn chicken, craven, dastard, funk, funker, poltroon, quitter, yellowbelly
  rel baby, fraidycat, invertebrate, jellyfish, milksop, scaredy-cat; caitiff, recreant
  con gallant, hero, palladin, stalwart; ideal, model, pattern, standard

coward *adj syn* see COWARDLY

cowardly *adj* marked by or arising from a base lack of courage <a *cowardly* desertion>
  syn ‖chicken, coward, cowhearted, craven, gutless, lily-livered, milk-livered, poltroon, poltroonish, poor-spirited, pusillanimous, spunkless, unmanly, white-livered, yellow
  rel afraid, chickenhearted, fainthearted, fearful, timid, timorous; funky, panicky; caitiff, dastardly, recreant, vile, worthless
  con courageous, fearless, intrepid, valiant; daring, reckless, temerarious
  ant brave

cower *vb syn* see FAWN
  rel blench, flinch, quail, recoil, shrink, wince
  con browbeat, bulldoze, bully, cow, intimidate; bristle, strut, swagger

cowering *adj syn* see FAWNING

cowhearted *adj syn* see COWARDLY

coxcomb *n syn* see FOP

coy *adj* **1** *syn* see SHY 1
  rel decent, decorous, nice, proper, seemly
  con brash, brazen, impudent
  2 marked by a light playful artlessness <glanced up with a *coy* twinkle in her eye>
  syn arch, coquettish, roguish
  rel capricious, kittenish, lively, mischievous, playful, skittish
  con serious, sober, thoughtful

cozen *vb* **1** *syn* see CHEAT
  2 *syn* see DECEIVE

cozy *adj* **1** *syn* see COMFORTABLE 2
  rel safe, secure
  2 *syn* see INTIMATE 4

crab *vb syn* see GRIPE
  idiom fret and fume

crab *n syn* see GROUCH

crabbed *adj syn* see SULLEN
  rel blunt, brusque, crusty, gruff; choleric, cranky, splenetic, testy; huffy, irascible, irritable, snappish
  con amiable, complaisant, good-natured, obliging; benign, benignant, kind, kindly; agreeable, pleasing; affable, genial, gracious

crabber *n syn* see GROUCH

crabby *adj syn* see SULLEN

crabwise *adv syn* see SIDEWAYS 1

crack *vb syn* see DECODE
  rel puzzle out

crack *n* **1** *syn* see BANG 2
  rel splintering, splitting; percussion
  2 *syn* see JOKE 1
  rel dig, fling, potshot
  idiom flash of wit
  3 a usually narrow opening, break, or discontinuity made by splitting and rupture <a *crack* in the ice>
  syn chink, cleft, fissure, rift, rima, rimation, rime, split
  rel rent; discontinuity, interstice, interval; cranny, niche; crevasse, crevice
  4 *syn* see INSTANT 1
  idiom flash of lightning
  5 *syn* see BLOW 1

6 *syn* see FLING 1
crack *adj syn* see PROFICIENT
  rel excellent, superior
crackbrain *n syn* see CRACKPOT
  idiom cracked wit
crackbrained *adj syn* see INSANE 1
crackdown *n syn* see REPRESSION 2
  rel quashing
  idiom lowering the boom
cracked *adj syn* see INSANE 1
  idiom ||off in the upper story
crackerjack *n syn* see ||DILLY
crackerjack *adj syn* see PROFICIENT
||**crackers** *adj syn* see INSANE 1
cracking *adj syn* see MONSTROUS 1
crackpot *n* one given to extremely eccentric or lunatic ideas or actions <a *crackpot* who wrote
  threatening letters to public figures>
  syn crackbrain, crank, cuckoo, ding-a-ling,
  harebrain, kook, lunatic, nut, screwball
  rel case, character, ||dingbat, eccentric, oddball,
  oddity, ||wack; loon, loony, madman, maniac
crack–up *n* **1** *syn* see NERVOUS BREAKDOWN
  2 *syn* see CRASH 3
  3 *syn* see COLLAPSE 2
  rel decline, deterioration
||**cracky** *adj syn* see INSANE 1
cradlesong *n syn* see LULLABY
craft *n* **1** *syn* see ART 1
  2 *syn* see TRADE 1
  rel job
  3 *syn* see CUNNING 2
craftiness *n syn* see CUNNING 2
crafty *adj syn* see SLY 2
  rel adroit, clever, tidy; acute, keen, sharp; de-
  ceitful, fawning, ||sleekit, ||sleeky
cragged *adj syn* see ROUGH 1
craggy *adj syn* see ROUGH 1
cram *vb* **1** to fill (a limited space) forcibly with
  more than is practicable or fitting <*crammed* the
  suitcase chock-full and had to sit on it to close
  it>
  syn jam, jam-pack, ||pang, ram, stuff, tamp;
  compare LOAD 3, PRESS 7
  rel pack, stive; fill, heap; chock, choke; press,
  shove, thrust; drive, force; squeeze, wedge
  2 *syn* see PRESS 7
  3 *syn* see GULP
  rel overeat
  idiom pack it in
  4 to study intensively or under pressure <had to
  cram all night before the exam>
  syn bone (up), ||mug (up)
  rel study; review
  idiom burn the midnight oil
cram–full *adj syn* see FULL 1
crammed *adj syn* see FULL 1
  idiom crammed full, crammed to the bursting
  point, fit (*or* ready) to burst
  ant emptied
cramp *n* **1** *syn* see RESTRICTION 1
  rel shackle
  2 *syn* see RESTRICTION 2
  rel constipation, stultification

cramp *adj syn* see CRAMPED
cramped *adj* having insufficient size or capacity
  <a *cramped* cubbyhole of an office>
  syn confined, cramp, incommodious, squeezy,
  ||tucked up
  rel close, narrow, tight, two-by-four; little, minute, small, tiny
  con commodious, unconfined
  ant spacious
crank *n* **1** *syn* see CAPRICE
  2 *syn* see CRACKPOT
  rel freak
  3 *syn* see GROUCH
cranky *adj* **1** *syn* see INSANE 1
  2 *syn* see CANTANKEROUS
  rel contrary, difficult, froward, perverse
  3 *syn* see IRASCIBLE
  rel bad-humored, ill-humored; disagreeable;
  ugly
  idiom out of sorts
cranny *n syn* see NOOK
||**crap** *n syn* see NONSENSE 2
||**crap out** *vb syn* see FAINT
||**crappy** *adj syn* see BAD 1
crash *vb syn* see FAIL 5
  ant skyrocket
crash *n* **1** *syn* see BANG 2
  2 *syn* see IMPACT 1
  3 a wrecking or smashing especially of a vehicle
  <an air *crash*>
  syn crack-up, pileup, ||prang, smash, smashup,
  ||stramash, wreck
  rel accident; collision
  4 *syn* see COLLAPSE 2
crashing *adj syn* see UTTER
crass *adj syn* see COARSE 3
  rel churlish, loutish
  ant refined
crate *n syn* see JALOPY
crave *vb* **1** *syn* see BEG
  2 *syn* see DESIRE 1
  con contemn, despise, disdain, scorn
  ant spurn
  3 *syn* see LONG
  idiom have a craving for
  4 *syn* see DEMAND 2
craven *adj syn* see COWARDLY
craven *n syn* see COWARD
craving *n syn* see DESIRE 1
crawfish (out) *vb syn* see BACK DOWN
crawl *vb* **1** *syn* see CREEP 1
  rel grovel; worm
  2 *syn* see TEEM
  ||**3** *syn* see LAMBASTE 3
craze *vb syn* see MADDEN 1
craze *n syn* see FASHION 3
  rel enthusiasm, fever
crazed *adj syn* see INSANE 1
craziness *n syn* see FOOLISHNESS

---

syn synonym(s)   *rel* related word(s)
ant antonym(s)   *con* contrasted word(s)
idiom idiomatic equivalent(s)
|| use limited; if in doubt, see a dictionary

crazy *adj* **1 syn** see INSANE 1
rel doting, gaga, moonstruck; beeheaded, silly; erratic, possessed
idiom as crazy as a loon, having a screw loose, having bats in one's belfry, not having all one's marbles (*or* buttons)
ant sane
2 syn see FOOLISH 2
rel goofy, senseless
idiom beyond the realm of reason, out of all reason
con practical, reasonable, reasoned, sensible
ant sane
‖**crazy** *adv syn* see VERY 1
crazy house *n syn* see ASYLUM 3
cream *n* **1 syn** see OINTMENT
2 syn see BEST
idiom (the) top cream
‖**cream** *vb syn* see WHIP 2
crease *n syn* see WRINKLE
create *vb* **1 syn** see GENERATE 1
idiom call into being
2 syn see FOUND 2
3 syn see COMPOSE 2
rel conceive, formulate; imagine
creation *n syn* see UNIVERSE
creative *adj syn* see INVENTIVE
rel causal, institutive, occasional; Promethean
ant uncreative
creator *n syn* see FATHER 2
rel brain(s), brainpower, mastermind
creature *n* **1 syn** see BEAST
2 syn see HUMAN
3 syn see SYCOPHANT
credence *n syn* see BELIEF 1
rel acceptance, accepting, admission, admitting; confidence, reliance, trust
con skepticism; distrust, mistrust; disbelief, incredulity, unbelief
credentials *n pl* something presented or held by one as proof that he is what or who he claims to be <her academic *credentials* were excellent>
syn certification, document(s), documentation, paper(s)
rel voucher; accreditation, endorsement, sanction; character, recommendation, reference, testimonial
credible *adj* **1 syn** see BELIEVABLE
rel satisfactory, satisfying; solid, sound, straight, valid
idiom to be believed
con unsatisfactory; preposterous, ridiculous
ant incredible
2 syn see AUTHENTIC 1
rel likely, probable; rational, reasonable; conclusive, determinative
ant incredible
credit *n* **1 syn** see BELIEF 1
rel confidence, reliance, trust
2 syn see INFLUENCE 1
rel fame, renown, reputation, repute
con disrepute, ignominy, obloquy, opprobrium
ant discredit
3 one that enhances another <he is a *credit* to his family>

syn asset
rel honor
4 favorable notice or attention resulting from an action or achievement <took all the *credit* for the idea>
syn acknowledgment, recognition
rel attention, notice; distinction, fame, honor; glory, kudos
credit *vb* **1 syn** see FEEL 3
con disbelieve, pooh-pooh
ant discredit
2 syn see ASCRIBE
creditable *adj* **1 syn** see BELIEVABLE
ant discreditable
2 syn see RESPECTABLE 1
rel satisfactory; suitable
ant discreditable
credo *n syn* see IDEOLOGY
credulous *adj* ready or inclined to believe especially on slight or insufficient evidence <deceiving the *credulous* young girls>
syn unsuspecting, unsuspicious, unwary
rel believing; accepting, unquestioning; trustful, trusting; green, inexperienced; naive, simple, unsophisticated; dupable, gullible
con mistrustful, suspecting, suspicious; careful, wary; doubtful, doubting, questioning
ant incredulous, skeptical
creed *n* **1 syn** see RELIGION 1
2 syn see RELIGION 2
3 syn see IDEOLOGY
creek *n* ‖**1 syn** see INLET
rel ria
2 a natural stream of water normally smaller than and often tributary to a river <went wading in the *creek*>
syn ‖branch, brook, ‖burn, ‖crick, gill, race, ‖rindle, ‖rithe, rivulet, ‖run, runnel, stream
rel ‖beck, brooklet, ‖rigolet, rill, rillet, runlet, streamlet; freshet; ditch, watercourse; wadi
creep *vb* **1** to move along a surface in a prone or crouching position <a cat *creeping* through the grass>
syn crawl, slide, snake
rel glide, slither; sneak, steal, tiptoe; edge, inch; sniggle, wriggle
2 syn see STEAL 3
3 syn see SNEAK
crème de la crème *n syn* see ARISTOCRACY
crepehanger *n syn* see PESSIMIST
crescendo *n syn* see APEX 2
crest *n* **1 syn** see TOP 1
rel cap
2 syn see RIDGE 1
3 syn see APEX 2
crest *vb syn* see SURMOUNT 3
crestfallen *adj syn* see DOWNCAST
idiom ‖in a funk
ant elated
cretin *n syn* see FOOL 4
rel zombie
crew *n syn* see GROUP 1
rel aggregation, collection, congregation; gang, retinue, set

crib *n* **1** *syn* see BROTHEL
  2 *syn* see PONY
  rel plagiarism
‖**crib** *vb* *syn* see GRIPE
‖**crick** *n* *syn* see CREEK 2
crime *n* **1** a serious breach of the public law
  <armed robbery is a *crime*>
  syn misdeed, offense
  rel criminality, illegality, lawlessness; delict,
  delictum; breach, break, infringement, transgression, violation; wrong, wrongdoing; felony
  2 *syn* see EVIL 3
crimeless *adj* *syn* see INNOCENT 2
criminal *adj* *syn* see UNLAWFUL
criminal *n* one who has committed a usually serious offense <car thieves and other *criminals*>
  syn felon, lawbreaker, malefactor, offender
  rel scofflaw; transgressor, trespasser, wrongdoer; crook, ‖twicer; gangster, hood, mobster,
  racketeer, thug; fugitive, outlaw; convict, jailbird
criminate *vb* *syn* see ACCUSE
  ant exonerate
crimp *vb* **1** *syn* see CRUMPLE 1
  2 *syn* see RESTRAIN 1
crimp *n* *syn* see OBSTACLE
crimple *vb* *syn* see CRUMPLE 1
crimson *vb* *syn* see BLUSH
  ant blanch
cringe *vb* *syn* see FAWN
  rel blench, flinch, quail, recoil, wince; ‖croodle,
  crouch, shrink
  idiom bow and scrape, eat dirt
cringing *adj* *syn* see FAWNING
  rel obeisant, prostrate
  idiom bowing and scraping, eating dirt, eating
  humble pie, on one's hands and knees
crinkle *vb* *syn* see CRUMPLE 1
crinkle *n* *syn* see WRINKLE
  rel crimp
cripple *vb* **1** *syn* see MAIM
  rel lame
  2 *syn* see PARALYZE 1
  3 *syn* see WEAKEN 1
crisis *n* *syn* see JUNCTURE 2
crisp *adj* **1** *syn* see SHORT 6
  con flabby, flaccid, limp
  2 *syn* see INCISIVE
  rel piquing, provoking, stimulating
crisscross *vb* *syn* see INTERSECT
criterion *n* *syn* see STANDARD 3
  rel adjudgment, judgment
critic *n* one given to harsh or captious judgment
  <chronic *critics* of the administration>
  syn aristarch, carper, caviler, criticizer, faultfinder, knocker, momus, smellfungus, Zoilus
  rel Monday morning quarterback; nitpicker,
  quibbler; belittler, disparager; complainer; cen-
  surer; muckraker, mudslinger
  con backer, supporter; partisan; advocate,
  champion, protagonist
critic *adj* *syn* see CRITICAL 1
critical *adj* **1** exhibiting the spirit of one who looks
  for and points out faults and defects <constant
  critical comments about her attire>

  syn captious, carping, caviling, cavillous, censorious, critic, faultfinding, hypercritical, overcritical
  rel discerning, discriminating, penetrating; finicky, fussy, particular; belittling, demeaning,
  disparaging, humbling, lowering
  con cursory, shallow, superficial; encouraging,
  flattering, praising
  ant uncritical
  2 *syn* see ACUTE 6
  rel conclusive, decisive, determinative; consequential, important, momentous, significant,
  weighty
criticism *n* **1** a discourse that evaluates or analyzes
  something (as a work of art or literature) <read
  every *criticism* of the new play>
  syn comment, critique, notice, review, reviewal
  rel analysis, examination, study; commentary,
  observation; opinion; appraisal, assessment, estimate, rating
  2 an unfavorable observation or commentary
  <her recent theatrical offerings have met only
  with *criticism*>
  syn flak, knock, ‖pan, rap, swipe
  rel cavil, nit-picking, quibble; aspersion, censure, denunciation; blast; roast
  idiom bad press
  con blurb, puff; hype, plug, promo
  ant commendation
criticize *vb* to make adverse comments about
  (someone or something) openly, often publicly,
  and with varying severity <*criticized* his opponent's liberal views>
  syn blame, censure, condemn, cut up, denounce,
  denunciate, knock, pan, rap, reprehend, reprobate, skin; *compare* LAMBASTE 3, REPROVE, SCOLD 1
  rel blast, castigate, fulminate (against), fustigate, roast, scathe
  idiom find fault with, pull (*or* pick *or* tear) to
  pieces, take to task
  con approve, countenance, endorse, OK (*or*
  okay)
  ant praise
criticizer *n* *syn* CRITIC, aristarch, carper, caviler,
  faultfinder, knocker, momus, smellfungus,
  Zoilus
critique *n* *syn* see CRITICISM 1
‖**critter** *n* *syn* see BEAST
croak *vb* **1** *syn* see GRUMBLE 1
  rel complain, quarrel
  ‖**2** *syn* see DIE 1
‖**croaker** *n* *syn* see PHYSICIAN
croaking *adj* *syn* see HOARSE 1
croaky *adj* *syn* see HOARSE 1
crock *n* *syn* see NONSENSE 2
‖**crocked** *adj* *syn* see INTOXICATED 1
crone *n* *syn* see HAG 2
  rel frump, slattern, sloven
crony *n* *syn* see ASSOCIATE 3

---

syn synonym(s)   *rel* related word(s)
ant antonym(s)   *con* contrasted word(s)
idiom idiomatic equivalent(s)
‖ use limited; if in doubt, see a dictionary

idiom bosom buddy

‖**crooch** *vb syn* see CROUCH

‖**croodle** *vb syn* see SNUGGLE

crook *vb* **1** *syn* see CURVE
  ‖**2** *syn* see STEAL 1
  ‖**3** *syn* see CHEAT

crooked *adj* **1** departing from a straight line or course <a *crooked* road>
  syn bending, curving, devious, twisting; *compare* CURVED, WINDING
  rel oblique; circuitous, indirect, roundabout; errant, meandering, rambling, serpentine, snaky, tortuous, winding; zigzag
  con direct, undeviating
  ant straight
  2 deviating from rectitude <*crooked* police officers on the take>
  syn corrupt, dishonest, snide; *compare* CORRUPT 2, VENAL 1
  rel devious, indirect, shifty, underhand; double-dealing, fraudulent; deceitful, lying, untruthful; ruthless, unscrupulous
  con aboveboard, forthright, straightforward; conscientious, honorable, just, proper, righteous, scrupulous, upright
  ant honest, straight

crookedly *adv syn* see AWRY 1
  ant straight

crop *n syn* see HARVEST 2

crop *vb* **1** *syn* see TOP 1
  rel chop, hew, slash; detach, disengage
  2 *syn* see MOW
  3 *syn* see CUT 6
  rel snip

cropping *n syn* see HARVEST 1

cross *n* **1** *syn* see TRIAL 1
  idiom a cross to bear
  2 *syn* see HYBRID

cross *vb* **1** *syn* see DENY 4
  2 *syn* see BETRAY 2
  idiom bite the hand that feeds one, stab in the back
  3 *syn* see TRAVERSE 4
  4 to cause (an animal or plant) to breed with one of a different kind <*crossing* a horse with an ass results in a mule>
  syn crossbreed, cross-mate, hybridize, interbreed, intercross
  rel mongrelize
  5 *syn* see INTERSECT
  idiom lie (*or* be) athwart

cross *adj syn* see IRASCIBLE
  rel captious, carping, caviling, faultfinding
  idiom cross as a bear

cross *prep syn* see ACROSS

crossbred *n syn* see HYBRID

crossbreed *vb syn* see CROSS 4

crossbreed *n syn* see HYBRID

crosscut *vb syn* see INTERSECT

cross–examination *n* a thorough, typically formal questioning for full information <*cross-examination* of a hostile witness>
  syn grill, grilling, interrogation, third degree
  rel debriefing; questioning

cross–grained *adj* **1** *syn* see CANTANKEROUS
  2 *syn* see CONTRARY 3
  rel difficult

crossing *adj syn* see TRANSVERSE

cross–mate *vb syn* see CROSS 4

crosspatch *n syn* see GROUCH

crossroad *n, usu* **crossroads** *pl but sing or pl in constr syn* see JUNCTURE 2

‖**cross talk** *n syn* see BANTER

crossways *adv syn* see ACROSS 1
  rel transversely; askew, awry, crisscross
  con lengthwise
  ant longways

crosswise *adv syn* see ACROSS 1
  con longways
  ant lengthwise

crosswise *adj syn* see TRANSVERSE
  ant lengthwise

crotchet *n syn* see CAPRICE
  rel eccentricity, kink, kinkiness, quirk, twist
  idiom bee in one's bonnet (*or* brain), flea in one's nose, kink in one's horn, maggot in one's brain

crotchety *adj syn* see CANTANKEROUS

crouch *vb* to stoop low with the limbs close to the body <*crouched* behind a rock and watched>
  syn ‖crooch, huddle, hunch, scrooch (down); *compare* SQUAT
  rel bend, bow, dip, duck; hunker (down), ‖quat, squat, stoop, ‖swat; cower, cringe, flinch, quail, wince; grovel

crow *vb syn* see BOAST
  rel cry, exult, jubilate

crowd *vb* **1** *syn* see PRESS 1
  rel ram, shove
  2 *syn* see PRESS 7
  rel bunch, cluster

crowd *n* **1** a usually large group of people <a *crowd* gathered before the palace>
  syn crush, drove, horde, multitude, press, push, squash, throng; *compare* MULTITUDE 1
  rel army, host, legion; flock, gaggle, herd, swarm; mob, rabble, rout
  2 *syn* see GATHERING 2
  rel huddle, parley; troop; herd; rally
  3 *syn* see MULTITUDE 1
  4 *syn* see SET 5

crowded *adj* **1** *syn* see FULL 1
  rel overcharged, overloaded
  ant uncrowded
  2 *syn* see CLOSE 4
  ant uncrowded

crown *n* **1** *syn* see TOP 1
  2 *syn* see WREATH
  rel diadem, tiara
  3 *syn* see APEX 2

crown *vb* **1** *syn* see SURMOUNT 3
  2 *syn* see COVER 3
  3 *syn* see CLIMAX

crown (with) *vb syn* see ENDOW 1

crucial *adj syn* see ACUTE 6
  rel deciding, decisive, important; necessary, vital; clamorous, compelling, crying, imperative, insistent, pressing

crucible *n syn* see TRIAL 1

crucify *vb syn* see AFFLICT
rel bedevil, bother, browbeat
idiom kill by inches, nail to the cross, put on the rack

crud *n* a deposit or incrustation of something filthy, greasy, or sticky <machinery all covered with *crud*>
syn ‖cab, goo, gook, gunk; *compare* GOO 1
rel filth, muck, slime, sludge; debris, junk, rubbish, trash

‖**cruddle** *vb syn* see CURDLE

crude *adj* **1** *syn* see UNREFINED 3
2 *syn* see COARSE 3
rel backward, ignorant, unenlightened; boorish, cloddish, clodhopping, ill-bred, loutish, low-bred; savage; insensible
3 *syn* see RUDE 1
rel immature, unmatured; coarse, graceless
con cultivated, cultured, refined; developed, matured, ripened
ant consummate, finished
4 *syn* see OBSCENE 2
rel blue, risqué
idiom rated X
5 rough in plan or execution <*crude* imitations, completely lacking in the original artistry>
syn coarse, inexpert, prentice; *compare* RUDE 1
rel amateurish, unproficient, unskilled, untaught, untrained; raw, rough, rude, unfinished, unpolished; inadequate, ineffective, inferior, poor
con finished, perfected, polished
ant expert

cruel *adj syn* see FIERCE 1
rel atrocious, heinous, monstrous, outrageous; bestial, bloodthirsty, brutish; heartless, implacable, relentless; impiteous, unpitying
con compassionate, sympathetic, tender; clement, forbearing, lenient, merciful; humane, kindly

‖**cruise** *vb syn* see GO 1

cruise *n syn* see VOYAGE
rel sail

‖**cruiser** *n syn* see PROSTITUTE

crumb *n syn* see PARTICLE

crumble *vb syn* see DECAY
rel mush, squash

crumbly *adj syn* see SHORT 6
rel rubbery

‖**crump** *adj syn* see SHORT 6

crumple *vb* **1** to press or twist into folds or wrinkles <*crumple* a piece of paper>
syn crimp, crimple, crinkle, ‖crunkle, rimple, ruck (up), ‖ruckle, rumple, screw, scrunch, wrinkle
rel crease, fold; buckle, cockle; wad
ant smooth
2 *syn* see GIVE 12

crunch *vb syn* see CHEW 1

crunchy *adj syn* see SHORT 6

‖**crunkle** *vb syn* see CRUMPLE 1

crusading *adj syn* see EVANGELICAL

crush *vb* **1** *syn* see PRESS 3
rel ‖scruze, squeeze

2 to reduce or be reduced to a pulpy or broken mass <*crushed* rose petals>
syn becrush, bruise, mash, ‖mush (up), pulp, squash
rel press, squeeze; contuse; batter, maim; beat, pound; dash, quash, ‖quat, smash; comminute, powder, pulverize, triturate
3 *syn* see PULVERIZE 1
4 *syn* see PRESS 1
5 to bring to an end by destroying or defeating <the police *crushed* the rebellion>
syn annihilate, extinguish, put down, quash, quell, quench, squash, suppress; *compare* SUPPRESS 2
rel ‖quelch, repress, squelch, strangle; beat down, conquer, defeat, subdue, subjugate; ruin, wreck; abolish, demolish, destroy; blot out, obliterate
idiom crush (*or* grind) under one's heel, ride down into the dust, roll (*or* trample) in the dust
6 *syn* see CONQUER 1
idiom bring one to his knees
7 *syn* see PRESS 7

crush *n* **1** *syn* see CROWD 1
2 *syn* see INFATUATION
rel calf love, puppy love

‖**crust** *n syn* see EFFRONTERY

crust *vb syn* see CAKE 1

crusty *adj* **1** *syn* see BLUFF
rel irritable, snappish, waspish; choleric, cranky, irascible, splenetic, testy; crabbed, dour, saturnine, surly
2 *syn* see OBSCENE 2

crux *n syn* see SUBSTANCE 2

cry *vb* **1** *syn* see CALL 1
rel bleat
2 to show distress, grief, or pain by tears and usually incoherent utterances <the little girl *cried* when she fell down>
syn blub, blubber, boohoo, ‖pipe, sob, wail, weep; *compare* BAWL 2, WHIMPER
rel sniff, snivel, whimper, whine; break down, choke up; groan, moan, sigh; bemoan, bewail, keen, lament, mourn, sorrow; bawl, howl, squall, yowl
idiom cry one's eyes (*or* heart) out, ‖pipe one's eye, shed tears
3 *syn* see SHOUT 1
4 *syn* see PUBLICIZE

cry *n* **1** *syn* see BATTLE CRY
rel slogan
2 *syn* see REPORT 1
3 *syn* see FASHION 3
4 *syn* see CALL 1
rel screech, squawk; squeak; caw

cry down *vb syn* see DECRY 2
ant cry up

crying *adj* **1** *syn* see PRESSING
rel necessary, needed

---

syn synonym(s)　　*rel* related word(s)
ant antonym(s)　　*con* contrasted word(s)
idiom idiomatic equivalent(s)
‖ use limited; if in doubt, see a dictionary

2 *syn* see OUTRAGEOUS 2

cry off *vb syn* see BACK DOWN

cry out *vb syn* see EXCLAIM

crypt *n* a subterranean chamber <a burial *crypt*>
syn catacomb, undercroft, vault
rel cell; chamber, compartment, room; cave, cavern, grotto

cryptanalyze *vb syn* see DECODE

cryptic *adj* being intentionally obscure and mysterious <the senator made some *cryptic* statements about intelligence operations>
syn dark, Delphian, enigmatic, mystifying; *compare* OBSCURE 3
rel equivocal, murky, obscure, opaque, tenebrous, unclear, uninformative, vague; incomprehensible, inexplicable, strange, unfathomable; abstruse, mysterious; evasive, secretive

crystal *adj syn* see CLEAR 4
idiom clear as crystal, crystal clear

cry up *vb syn* see PRAISE 2
idiom beat the drum for, praise to the skies
ant cry down

cubby *n syn* see CUBBYHOLE

cubbyhole *n* an excessively small room or place <a cramped *cubbyhole* of an office>
syn cubby, mousehole, pigeonhole
rel recess; niche; cubicle
idiom hole in the wall

‖**cubes** *n pl syn* see DICE

cuckoo *n syn* see CRACKPOT

cuckoo *adj syn* see INSANE 1

cuddle *vb* **1** *syn* see CARESS
rel embrace, enfold, hold
2 *syn* see SNUGGLE

cudgel *n* a short solid stick used as a weapon or an instrument of punishment <beat the prisoner with a *cudgel*>
syn bat, baton, billy, billy club, bludgeon, club, knobkerrie, mace, nightstick, ‖shillelagh, spontoon, truncheon, war club
rel birch, cane, ferule, hickory, paddle, rattan, rod, switch; blackjack; quarterstaff; bastinado

cue *n syn* see HINT 1

cuff *vb syn* see SLAP 1

cuff *n* a sharp blow typically delivered with the hand <gave him a good *cuff* in the face>
syn box, buffet, ‖bust, chop, clout, haymaker, ‖paste, poke, punch, slap, smack, sock, spank, ‖spat, ‖swack; *compare* BLOW 1, HIT 1
rel bat, blow, clip, wallop

cul–de–sac *n syn* see DEAD END
rel stalemate

cull *vb* **1** *syn* see GLEAN
rel accumulate, amass, collect, round up
2 *syn* see CHOOSE 1
rel discriminate
idiom separate the sheep from the goats, separate the wheat from the chaff

‖**cull** *n syn* see FOOL 3

‖**cully** *n syn* see ASSOCIATE 3

culmen *n syn* see APEX 2

culminate *vb syn* see CLIMAX

culmination *n syn* see APEX 2
rel extremity, limit, maximum

culpability *n syn* see BLAME
con blamelessness, innocence
ant inculpability

culpable *adj syn* see BLAMEWORTHY
rel impeachable, indictable
ant inculpable

cult *n* **1** *syn* see RELIGION 1
2 *syn* see RELIGION 2

cultivable *adj syn* see ARABLE
ant uncultivable

cultivatable *adj syn* see ARABLE
ant uncultivatable

cultivate *vb* **1** *syn* see TILL
rel crop, farm, manage
2 *syn* see NURSE 2
rel raise, rear; educate, instruct, teach, train; ameliorate, better, improve
con disregard, ignore, neglect, slight
3 *syn* see GROW 1
rel develop, mature, ripen

cultivated *adj syn* see GENTEEL 1
rel courteous, polite
ant uncultivated

cultivation *n syn* see CULTURE

culture *n* enlightenment and excellence of taste acquired by intellectual and aesthetic training <a man of *culture* is known by his reading>
syn breeding, cultivation, polish, refinement
rel education, enlightenment, erudition, learning; gentility, manners; discrimination, taste; savoir-faire, sophistication, urbanity; class, elegance
con greenness, ignorance, inexperience, verdancy; crudeness, vulgarity

cultured *adj syn* see GENTEEL 1
rel educated, enlightened, erudite, learned, literate; civilized
ant uncultured

culverhouse *n syn* see DOVECOTE

cumber *vb syn* see BURDEN

cumbersome *adj syn* see UNWIELDY
rel irksome, tiresome, wearisome

cumbrance *n syn* see ENCUMBRANCE
rel burden, charge, pressure

cumbrous *adj syn* see UNWIELDY
rel clogging, hampering, hindering, impeding

cumshaw *n syn* see GRATUITY

cumulate *vb syn* see ACCUMULATE
rel obtain, secure
ant dissipate

cumulation *n syn* see ACCUMULATION
rel stockpile; snowball

cumulative *adj* increasing or produced by addition of like or similar things <the *cumulative* effect of several drugs>
syn accumulative, additive, additory, chain, summative
rel accumulated, amassed; augmenting, increasing, multiplying; advancing, heightening, intensifying, magnifying, snowballing
con dispersed, dissipated, scattered

cunning *adj* **1** *syn* see CLEVER 4
rel well-devised, well-laid, well-planned; crackerjack, masterful

idiom too clever by half
2 *syn* see SLY 2
rel acute, keen, sharp; knowing, smart; wary
idiom not to be caught with chaff
con artless, naive, unsophisticated

cunning *n* **1 *syn*** see ART 1
rel deftness, dexterousness; adeptness, expertness; cleverness, ingeniousness, ingenuity
2 skill in devising or using indirect or subtle methods <a woman able to maneuver people with great *cunning*>
syn art, artfulness, artifice, cageyness, canniness, craft, craftiness, foxiness, slyness, wiliness
rel savvy, sharpness, shrewdness; cleverness, ingeniousness, ingenuity; agility, facility, finesse, slickness; subtlety; insidiousness, shiftiness, trickiness
3 *syn* see DECEIT 1
idiom satanic cunning, the cunning of the serpent

cupidity *n* intense desire for possessions and wealth <the sight of so much money aroused his *cupidity*>
syn avarice, avariciousness, avidity, greed, rapacity
rel acquisitiveness, greediness, possessiveness, rapaciousness; eagerness, voracity; craving, desire; lust; infatuation, passion

cur *n* **1 *syn*** see SNOT 1
rel riffraff
2 *syn* see CAD

curative *adj* restoring or tending to restore to a state of normalcy or health <a *curative* drug>
syn curing, healing, remedial, remedying, restorative, sanative, sanatory, vulnerary, wholesome
rel medicable, medicative, medicinal; corrective, therapeutic; invigorating, tonic; beneficial, helpful, salutary, wholesome

curb *vb* **1 *syn*** see HAMPER
2 *syn* see DENY 3
rel repress, suppress
ant goad
3 *syn* see RESTRAIN 1
rel fetter, hamper, hog-tie, manacle, shackle
idiom hold in leash, keep a tight rein on
con unbridle, unleash
ant spur

curd *vb* *syn* see CURDLE

curdle *vb* to cause to become coagulated or thickened and often sour <hot weather will *curdle* milk>
syn ‖clabber, ‖cruddle, curd, ‖lopper, turn
rel clot, coagulate, condense, thicken; ferment; go off, sour, spoil

cure *n* **1 *syn*** see REMEDY 1
2 *syn* see REMEDY 2

cure *vb* to rectify an unhealthy or undesirable condition <aspirin *cured* his headache>
syn heal, remedy
rel doctor, medicate; restore; ameliorate, better, improve

cure–all *n* *syn* see PANACEA

cureless *adj* *syn* see HOPELESS 2

curing *adj* *syn* see CURATIVE

curio *n* *syn* see KNICKKNACK

curiosity *n* **1 *syn*** see INTEREST 3
rel inquisitiveness, questioning
ant disinterest
2 something that arouses interest especially because of uncommon or exotic characteristics <an architectural *curiosity*>
syn conversation piece, oddity
rel exception, nonesuch, rarity; marvel, prodigy, wonder; anomaly; freak, monstrosity
idiom something to write home about

curious *adj* **1 *syn*** see INQUISITIVE 1
rel searching; analytical; prurient
ant incurious
2 interested in what is not one's personal or proper concern <a *curious* old woman prying into her neighbors' affairs>
syn inquisitive, inquisitorial, inquisitory, ‖nibby, nosy, peery, prying, snoopy
rel interfering, intermeddling, meddling, tampering; examining, inspecting, scrutinizing; impertinent, intrusive, meddlesome
idiom consumed (*or* burning *or* eaten up) with curiosity, curious as a cat (*or* monkey)
con aloof, detached, disinterested, indifferent, unconcerned, uninterested; apathetic, impassive, phlegmatic, stolid
ant incurious
3 *syn* see STRANGE 4

curl *vb* *syn* see WIND 2
rel crook; roll; ringlet; kink
con straighten, unkink, unwind
ant uncurl

currency *n* *syn* see MONEY

current *adj* **1 *syn*** see PRESENT
rel topical, up-to-date
con antiquated, antique, obsolete
2 *syn* see PREVAILING
rel accustomed, customary; a la mode, fashionable, modern, popular
ant antique

current *n* **1 *syn*** see FLOW
2 *syn* see TENDENCY 1

curry *vb* *syn* see WHIP 2

curse *n* **1** a denunciation that conveys a wish or threat of evil <the dying man's *curse* against his family>
syn anathema, commination, imprecation, malediction, malison
rel execration, objurgation; damning, denunciation; blasphemy, profanation, profanity, sacrilege
ant blessing
2 *syn* see SWEARWORD
3 *syn* see PLAGUE 1

curse *vb* **1 *syn*** see EXECRATE 1
rel blaspheme; blight; doom

---

syn synonym(s)   *rel* related word(s)
ant antonym(s)   *con* contrasted word(s)
idiom idiomatic equivalent(s)
‖ use limited; if in doubt, see a dictionary

idiom call down curses on the head of, call down evil on
ant bless
2 syn see SWEAR 3
idiom ‖curse up a storm
cursed *adj* **1 syn** see DAMNED 2
rel hateful
2 syn see EXECRABLE 1
rel disgusting; odious
ant blessed
cursing *n syn* see BLASPHEMY 1
cursive *adj syn* see EASY 9
cursory *adj syn* see SUPERFICIAL 2
rel fast, hasty, hurried, quick, rapid, speedy, swift; brief, short; casual, desultory, haphazard, random
con careful, meticulous, scrupulous
ant painstaking
curt *adj* **1 syn** see CONCISE
2 syn see BLUFF
rel imperious, peremptory
ant voluble
curtail *vb* **1 syn** see SHORTEN
ant prolong, protract
2 syn see ABRIDGE 1
ant extend
curtains *n pl but sing in constr syn* see DEATH 1
curtilage *n syn* see COURT 1
curvaceous *adj* having a shapely figure marked by pronounced curves <*curvaceous* bikini-clad girls swarmed over the beach>
syn ‖built, curvesome, curvilinear, curvy, Junoesque, rounded, ‖stacked, well-developed; *compare* BUXOM, SHAPELY
rel shapeful, shapely, statuesque, well-proportioned; attractive, charming, pleasing
curvation *n syn* see CURVE
curvature *n syn* see CURVE
curve *vb* to swerve or cause to swerve from a straight line or course <the road *curves* to the right>
syn bend, bow, crook, round; *compare* WIND 2
rel deflect, divert, turn; deviate, swerve, veer; coil, curl, spiral, twist, wind; incurve
ant straighten
curve *n* something (as a line or surface) that curves or is curved <a slight *curve* to her eyebrows>
syn arc, arch, bend, bow, curvation, curvature, round
rel incurvation, incurvature; inflection; rondure; circuit, circumference, compass
curved *adj* having or characterized by a curve or curves <a *curved* vault>
syn arced, arched, arciform, arrondi, bent, bowed, curvilinear, round, rounded; *compare* CROOKED 1
rel declinate; embowed, incurvate, incurved; excurved; bending, twisted, twisting
ant straight
curvesome *adj syn* see CURVACEOUS
curvilinear *adj* **1 syn** see CURVED
2 syn see CURVACEOUS
curving *adj syn* see CROOKED 1
curvy *adj syn* see CURVACEOUS

cushy *adj syn* see COMFORTABLE 2
cusp *n syn* see POINT 9
cuspidate *adj syn* see POINTED 1
cuss *n* **1 syn** see SWEARWORD
2 syn see MAN 3
cuss *vb syn* see SWEAR 3
idiom ‖cuss up a blue streak
cussed *adj syn* see DAMNED 2
cussing *n syn* see BLASPHEMY 1
cussword *n syn* see SWEARWORD
custodian *n* one that guards, protects, or maintains (as property or records) <was the *custodian* of the manor for many years>
syn cerberus, claviger, ‖custodier, custos, guardian, keeper, warden, watchdog
rel curator, steward; castellan, governor; overseer, supervisor
‖custodier *n syn* see CUSTODIAN
custody *n* the act or duty of guarding and preserving <the government has *custody* of all state gifts>
syn care, guardianship, keeping, safekeeping, trust, ward
rel caretaking; charge, management, supervision; protection
custom *n* **1 syn** see HABIT 1
rel precedent; ritual; mold; fixture, institution; prescription, rubric; canon, law, precept, rule
idiom matter of course
con departure, deviation, shift; exception; irregularity
2 syn see PATRONAGE 2
custom *adj syn* see CUSTOM-MADE
customarily *adv syn* see USUALLY 1
rel conventionally, traditionally; normally, ordinarily; routinely
idiom as a matter of course
con rarely; never
ant occasionally
customary *adj* **1 syn** see USUAL 1
rel acknowledged, recognized, understood; standard; conventional, orthodox, traditional; prescriptive, regulation, stipulated
idiom being the customary (*or* usual) thing
con occasional; infrequent, inhabitual, sporadic, uncommon; irregular
ant uncustomary
2 syn see COMMON 4
rel household, popular; general, universal
ant uncustomary
custom–built *adj syn* see CUSTOM-MADE
customer *n* one that patronizes or uses the services of something (as a store or restaurant) <many *customers* in the shop>
syn client, patron
rel buyer, consumer, purchaser, shopper
customized *adj syn* see CUSTOM-MADE
custom–made *adj* made according to personal order and individual specifications <he always wore a *custom-made* suit>
syn custom, custom-built, customized, custom-tailored, made-to-order, tailor-made
ant mass-produced
custom–tailored *adj syn* see CUSTOM-MADE

custos *n syn* see CUSTODIAN

cut *vb* **1** to penetrate with or as if with a sharp edge <*cut* his hand on a broken bottle>
syn gash, incise, pierce, slash, slice, slit
rel cleave, dissever, sever, sunder; rend, rip, rive, tear; lacerate, wound
2 *syn* see SHORTEN
3 *syn* see REDUCE 2
4 *syn* see MOW
5 to penetrate and divide with an edged tool or instrument <*cut* the melon into slices>
syn carve, cleave, dissect, dissever, sever, slice, split, sunder
rel divide, part, separate; chop, dice, hash, mince, mow
idiom lay open
6 to reduce by severing parts <the barber *cut* his hair too short>
syn clip, crop, pare, prune, shave, shear, skive, trim
rel cut back, dock, lop, poll, pollard, shrub; amputate; curtail
7 to refuse social recognition especially by way of rebuke <his friends *cut* him after the scandal broke>
syn cold-shoulder, ostracize, snob, snub
rel disdain, ignore, rebuff, reject, slight, turn away; affront, insult, offend
idiom give the cold shoulder (to), show one his place, slam the door in one's face, slam the door on, slap one in the face, turn aside (*or* away) from, turn one's back (on *or* upon)
8 *syn* see DILUTE
9 *syn* see FELL 2
10 *syn* see OPERATE 2
cut *n* **1** *syn* see PART 1
2 *syn* see SHARE 1
3 *syn* see TRENCH
4 *syn* see TYPE

cut *adj syn* see INTOXICATED 1
cut back *vb* **1** *syn* see SHORTEN
2 *syn* see REDUCE 2
cut down *vb syn* see REDUCE 2
cut in *vb syn* see INTRUDE 1
cut off *vb* **1** *syn* see KILL 1
2 *syn* see INTERCEPT
3 *syn* see ISOLATE
4 *syn* see DISINHERIT 1
cutoff *n syn* see SHORTCUT
cut out *vb* **1** *syn* see EXCISE
2 *syn* see SUPPLANT 1
cutpurse *n syn* see PICKPOCKET
cutthroat *n syn* see ASSASSIN
cutting *adj syn* see INCISIVE
rel piercing, probing
cut up *vb* **1** *syn* see CRITICIZE
2 to behave in a boisterously comic or unruly manner <children *cutting* up in front of company>
syn act up, carry on, horse, horseplay
rel caper, cavort, romp; clown; show off; roughhouse; misbehave
idiom cut a dido (*or* shine), cut up rough, ‖kick up a shindy, raise Cain (*or* Ned), whoop it up
cutup *n syn* see ZANY 2
cycle *n* **1** a complete course of recurrent operations or events <a 24-hour *cycle* of medication>
syn circle, round, wheel; *compare* SUCCESSION 2
rel chain, sequel, sequence, series; course, run; circuit, loop, ring
2 *syn* see BICYCLE
cyclone *n syn* see TORNADO
cyclopean *adj syn* see HUGE
ant lilliputian
cynical *adj syn* see SARDONIC
cyprian *n syn* see WANTON
czar *n syn* see MAGNATE

---

syn synonym(s)   *rel* related word(s)
ant antonym(s)   *con* contrasted word(s)
idiom idiomatic equivalent(s)
‖ use limited; if in doubt, see a dictionary

D

dab *vb syn* see SMEAR 1

‖**dab** *n syn* see EXPERT

dabbler *n syn* see AMATEUR 2
 con adept, artist, connoisseur; expert, master, professional

dabbling *adj syn* see AMATEURISH
 rel sciolistic, shallow, sophomoric, superficial
 con adept, capable, competent

‖**dabster** *n syn* see EXPERT

dad *n syn* see FATHER 1

dada *n syn* see FATHER 1

dad–blamed *adj* **1** *syn* see DAMNED 2
 2 *syn* see UTTER

dad–blasted *adj* **1** *syn* see DAMNED 2
 2 *syn* see UTTER

dad–burned *adj* **1** *syn* see DAMNED 2
 2 *syn* see UTTER

daddy *n syn* see FATHER 1

daedal *adj syn* see COMPLEX 2

daffy *adj* **1** *syn* see INSANE 1
 2 *syn* see FOOLISH 2

daft *adj syn* see INSANE 1

daily *adj* of each or every day <*daily* prayers for the dead>
 syn diurnal, quotidian
 con nocturnal; alternate, intermittent, periodic, recurrent, spasmodic; erratic, fitful, fluctuating, infrequent, irregular; occasional, sporadic
 ant nightly

dainty *n syn* see DELICACY

dainty *adj* **1** *syn* see CHOICE
 rel beautiful, bonny, fair, lovely, pretty; delectable, delicious, delightful; airy, diaphanous, ethereal, light
 con coarse, vulgar
 ant gross
 2 *syn* see NICE 1
 rel acute, penetrative, perceptive
 con careless, neglectful, negligent, thoughtless

‖**daisy** *n syn* ‖DILLY, ‖corker, crackerjack, dandy, humdinger, jim-dandy, knockout, ‖lalapalooza, ‖lulu, nifty

dale *n syn* see VALLEY

dally *vb* **1** *syn* see TRIFLE 1
 rel frolic, gambol, play, rollick, romp, sport; caress, cosset, cuddle, dandle, fondle, pet
 2 *syn* see DELAY 2
 con fleet, rush, scurry, skedaddle
 ant hasten

dam *vb syn* see HINDER
 rel repress, suppress
 con air, express, utter, vent

damage *n syn* see INJURY 1
 rel impairment, marring; deterioration, dilapidation, disrepair, ruining, wrecking; deleteriousness, disadvantage, drawback
 con amelioration, betterment, improvement; benefit, profit; advantage, service, use

 ant repair

damage *vb syn* see INJURE 1
 rel demolish, destroy, raze, ruin, wreck; deteriorate, dilapidate; abuse, ill-treat, maltreat, mistreat, misuse, outrage
 con ameliorate, amend, better, improve; mend
 ant repair

damaged *adj* having been injured <*damaged* merchandise>
 syn flawed, impaired, marred, spoiled
 rel blemished, broken, imperfect, injured, unsound
 con flawless, good, intact, unbroken, unhurt, unimpaired, uninjured, unmarred, whole; corrected, improved, rectified, repaired
 ant undamaged

damaging *adj syn* see HARMFUL

dame *n* **1** *syn* see MATRIARCH
 2 *syn* see BELDAM 1
 ‖**3** *syn* see WOMAN 1

damn *vb* **1** *syn* see SENTENCE
 rel castigate, discipline, penalize, punish; banish, cast out, expel
 con deliver, ransom, redeem, rescue; reward
 ant save
 2 *syn* see EXECRATE 1
 rel abominate; vituperate
 3 *syn* see SWEAR 3

damn *n syn* see PARTICLE

damnable *adj* **1** *syn* see EXECRABLE 1
 rel abhorrent, abominable, detestable, hateful, odious; damned
 con admirable, commendable, estimable; laudable, praiseworthy
 2 *syn* see DAMNED 2
 3 *syn* see UTTER

damned *adj* **1** being doomed to eternal punishment <a *damned* soul>
 syn condemned, doomed, lost
 rel anathematized, cursed, reprobate; done for
 idiom gone to blazes, hell bound
 con delivered, ransomed, redeemed
 ant saved
 2 deserving censure or strong disapproval — often used as a generalized expression of annoyance <this *damned* door won't open>
 syn blamed, blankety-blank, blasted, bleeding, blessed, blighted, blinding, ‖blinking, ‖blistering, ‖blooming, confounded, ‖consarned, cursed, cussed, dad-blamed, dad-blasted, dad-burned, damnable, dang, darn (*or* durn), dashed, doggone, dratted, execrable, goldarn, infernal, perishing, so-and-so
 3 *syn* see UTTER

damned *adv syn* see VERY 1

damp *adj* slightly or relatively wet <her dress was still *damp*>
 syn dampish, dank, moist, moisty, wettish

rel drenched, saturated, soaked, soaking; soggy, water-logged
con arid, dry
dampen *vb syn* see MUFFLE 2
dampish *adj syn* see DAMP
damsel *n syn* see GIRL 1
dance *vb* **1** to perform a rhythmic and patterned succession of steps usually to music <the band was good enough to *dance* to>
syn foot (it), hoof (it), prance, step, tread
rel shuffle, trip, truck
idiom ‖cut a rug, trip the light fantastic
2 *syn* see FLIT 2
rel quaver, quiver, shake, tremble, wobble
dancer *n* a professional performer of dances <*dancers* performing a ballet>
syn ballerina, ballet girl, coryphée, dancing girl, danseur, danseuse, figurant, figurante, hoofer
rel chorine, chorus boy, chorus girl, chorus man; danseur noble, premier danseur, premiere danseuse, prima ballerina
dancing girl *n syn* see DANCER
dandle *vb syn* see CARESS
rel disport, play, sport
dandy *n* **1** *syn* see FOP
con clod, lout, lump, oaf, slob, slouch
ant sloven
2 *syn* ‖DILLY, ‖corker, crackerjack, ‖daisy, humdinger, jim-dandy, ‖lalapalooza, ‖lulu, nifty, peach
‖**dandy** *adj* **1** *syn* see MARVELOUS 2
2 *syn* see EXCELLENT
rel grand, hunky-dory, keen, nifty, swell
idiom fine and dandy
con ‖bum, ‖crummy, grim, ‖lousy, ‖putrid, rotten
ant blah
dang *adj* **1** *syn* see DAMNED 2
2 *syn* see UTTER
danger *n* the state of being exposed to injury, pain, or loss <they are seeking a place where children can play without *danger*>
syn hazard, jeopardy, peril, risk
rel menace, precariousness, threat; emergency, exigency, pass; precipice
idiom dangerous ground, thin ice
con safety; exemption, immunity; defense, guard, protection, safeguard, shield
ant security
dangerous *adj* **1** attended by or involving the possibility of injury, pain, or loss <a *dangerous* crossing>
syn chancy, ‖dangersome, hairy, hazardous, jeopardous, parlous, perilous, risky, treacherous, unhealthy, unsound, wicked; *compare* GRAVE 3
rel insecure, precarious, uncertain, unsafe; chance, haphazard, hit-or-miss, random; critical, menacing, serious, threatening
idiom beset (*or* fraught) with danger, on a collision course
con certain, reliable; harmless, innocent
ant safe, secure
2 *syn* see GRAVE 3

‖**dangersome** *adj syn* see DANGEROUS 1
dangle *vb syn* see HANG 1
dank *adj syn* see DAMP
danseur *n syn* see DANCER
danseuse *n syn* see DANCER
dap *vb syn* see GLANCE 1
dapper *adj* trimly neat and tidy <a *dapper* dresser, always neat as a pin>
syn bandbox, doggish, doggy, natty, sassy, sparkish, spiffy, spruce, sprucy, well-groomed; *compare* NEAT 2, STYLISH
rel chichi; jaunty, rakish; showy
con dowdy, drab, unstylish; disheveled, disordered, slipshod, sloppy, slovenly, unkempt, untidy; blowsy, dowdy, frowsy, shabby, slatternly
dappled *adj syn* see VARIEGATED
con pure, smooth, spotless, unbroken, uniform
dare *vb syn* see FACE 3
rel change, hazard, risk
idiom take the bull by the horns
con avoid, evade; flee, run
dare *n syn* see DEFIANCE 1
daredevil *adj syn* see ADVENTUROUS
con timid, timorous; cautious, chary, circumspect, wary; discreet, judicious, prudent, sane, sensible
daring *adj syn* see ADVENTUROUS
dark *adj* **1** deficient in light <a *dark* room>
syn caliginous, dim, dun, dusk, dusky, gloomy, lightless, murky, obscure, somber, tenebrous, unilluminated
rel cloudy, dull, shadowy, shady; pitch-black, pitch-dark
con bright, brilliant, luminous, radiant; enlightened, illuminated, illumined, lighted
ant light
2 *syn* see CRYPTIC
rel abstruse, esoteric, hidden, occult, recondite; anagogic, cabalistic, darkling, mystic, mystical; complicated, intricate, knotty
con clear, perspicuous; easy, facile, light, simple
ant lucid
3 of dark complexion <her *dark* good looks>
syn bistered, black-a-vised, brunet, dark-skinned, dusky, swart, swarth, swarthy
con blond, fair, light; ruddy, tawny
‖**4** *syn* see BLIND 1
darken *vb syn* see OBSCURE
ant illuminate
dark-skinned *adj syn* see DARK 3
darling *n syn* see SWEETHEART 1
darling *adj* **1** *syn* see FAVORITE 1
2 *syn* see DELIGHTFUL
darn (*or* **durn**) *adj* **1** *syn* see DAMNED 2
2 *syn* see UTTER
dart *n syn* see SHAFT 2
dart *vb syn* see FLY 1
rel hasten, hurry, precipitate, speed; run, scamper, scoot, scurry, sprint, spurt

---

syn synonym(s)　　*rel* related word(s)
ant antonym(s)　　*con* contrasted word(s)
idiom idiomatic equivalent(s)
‖ use limited; if in doubt, see a dictionary

con dally, dawdle, delay, linger, tarry; lumber, plod, slog, trudge

dash *vb* **1** *syn* see RUSH 1
rel run, scamper, scoot, scurry, sprint
con dally, dawdle, delay, linger, tarry; lumber, plod, slog, trudge
2 *syn* see RUN 1
3 *syn* see BLAST 1
4 *syn* see FRUSTRATE 1

dash *n* **1** *syn* see SPIRIT 5
rel energy, force, might, power, strength; intensity, vehemence; impressiveness
con apathy, dullness, languor, lethargy, listlessness, sluggishness, stagnation, torpor
2 *syn* see HINT 2
rel impress, impression, stamp

dashed *adj* **1** *syn* see DAMNED 2
2 *syn* see UTTER

dashing *adj* **1** *syn* see LIVELY 1
2 *syn* see STYLISH
rel flashy, flaunting; dapper, jaunty, spiffy, spruce
idiom cutting a fine figure
con unfashionable, unstylish; modest, unostentatious, unpretentious
ant drab

dastard *n* *syn* see COWARD

date *vb* to go or take on a date <he *dated* her several times that winter>
syn see, take out
rel accompany, escort; court, woo
idiom go out with

date *n* **1** *syn* see ENGAGEMENT 3
2 *syn* see ESCORT 1

dated *adj* *syn* see OLD-FASHIONED
ant up-to-the-minute

dateless *adj* *syn* see ETERNAL 4
ant ephemeral

daub *vb* *syn* see SMEAR 1
rel spatter, speckle, spot; dapple, fleck, variegate

daunt *vb* *syn* see DISMAY 1
rel browbeat, bully, cow, intimidate; baffle, foil, frustrate, thwart
con arouse, awaken, rally, rouse, stir, waken; actuate, drive, impel, move; activate, energize, vitalize
ant enhearten

dauntless *adj* *syn* see BRAVE 1
rel indomitable, invincible, unconquerable
con hesitant, reluctant
ant poltroon

dauntlessness *n* *syn* see COURAGE
ant poltroonery

dawdle *vb* **1** *syn* see IDLE 1
2 *syn* see DELAY 2
rel amble, saunter, stroll; stay, wait; toy, trifle; fritter, waste
idiom fritter away time
con arouse, rally, rouse, stir; hasten, hurry, speed

dawdler *n* *syn* see LAGGARD

dawn *n* **1** the first appearance of light in the morning <birds which sing at *dawn*>

syn aurora, cockcrow, cockcrowing, dawning, daybreak, daylight, light, morn, morning, sunrise, sunup
rel prime
idiom break of day, crack of dawn, first blush (*or* flush) of day, first light, peep of day, the wee small hours
2 *syn* see BEGINNING
ant sunset

dawning *n* **1** *syn* see DAWN 1
2 *syn* see BEGINNING
ant sunset

day *n* **1** the time of light between one night and the next <waiting for *day* to dawn>
syn daylight, daytime
rel light, sunlight, sunshine
con dark, nighttime
ant night
2 *usu* **days** *pl* *syn* see PERIOD 2

daybreak *n* *syn* see DAWN 1

daydream *n* *syn* see FANCY 4
rel conceiving, fancying, imagination, imagining
con substantiality, tangibility; authenticity, truth, verity

daydreaming *adj* *syn* see DREAMY 1

daydreamy *adj* *syn* see DREAMY 1

daylight *n* **1** *syn* see DAWN 1
syn see DAY 1

dayspring *n* *syn* see BEGINNING

daystar *n* *syn* see SUN 1

daytime *n* *syn* see DAY 1

daze *vb* **1** to confuse with light <the bright sunlight *dazed* him>
syn bedazzle, blind, dazzle
rel overcome, overpower, overwhelm; dizzy
2 to dull or deaden the powers of the mind through some disturbing experience or influence <*dazed* by the news of the accident>
syn bedaze, bemuse, benumb, paralyze, petrify, stun, stupefy
rel bewilder, confound, disorder, distract, dumbfound, mystify; befuddle, confuse, fuddle, muddle; dazzle, dizzy; rock
con enhance, expand, heighten, sharpen; alert, arouse, waken

daze *n* *syn* see HAZE 2

dazzle *vb* *syn* see DAZE 1

dead *adj* **1** devoid of life <a *dead* person>
syn asleep, cold, deceased, defunct, departed, exanimate, extinct, inanimate, late, lifeless, spiritless, unanimated
rel bloodless, breathless; gone, reposing; inactive, inert; belowground, buried
idiom dead as a doornail, gone the way of all flesh, out of one's misery, pushing up daisies
con animate, animated, living, vital; being, existing; active, live
ant alive
2 *syn* see DEATHLY 1
rel insensible, insentient, numb, unfeeling, unresponsive; inanimate, unconscious
con feeling, responsive, sensitive, sentient; animate, animated, living, spirited, vivacious

ant alive
3 *syn* see NUMB 1
4 *syn* see OBSOLETE
ant living; viable
5 *syn* see EXTINCT 2
6 *syn* see DULL 7
rel bleak, dismal
con glorious, resplendent
7 *syn* see UTTER
dead *adv syn* see DIRECTLY 1
deaden *vb* **1** to impair in vigor, force, activity, or
sensation <the news *deadened* his distress>
syn benumb, blunt, desensitize, dull, mull,
numb
rel anesthetize, paralyze, unnerve; stun, stupefy
con animate, vivify; energize, invigorate; activate, vitalize
ant enliven
2 *syn* see MUFFLE 2
dead end *n* a course which leads to nothing further
<had reached a *dead end* in negotiations>
syn blind alley, cul-de-sac, impasse, pocket
rel corner, hole; deadlock, halt, standstill; bot-
tleneck
deadened *adj* **1** *syn* see DEATHLY 1
2 *syn* see NUMB 1
‖**deader** *n syn* see CORPSE
deadfall *n syn* see PITFALL
deadliness *n syn* see FATALITY 1
deadlock *n syn* see DRAW 4
rel condition, posture, situation, state; dilemma,
plight, predicament, quandary
con decision, determination, resolution, solution
deadly *adj* **1** causing or causative of death <a
deadly disease>
syn deathly, fatal, lethal, mortal, mortiferous,
pestilent, pestilential; *compare* PERNICIOUS
rel destroying, destructive; killing, slaying; internecine; baneful, noxious, pernicious; poisonous, toxic, virulent
con healthful, healthy, wholesome; advantageous, beneficial, restorative, sanative
2 *syn* see PERNICIOUS
con harmless, innocuous, inoffensive, unoffending
3 *syn* see DEATHLY 1
deadpan *adj syn* see EXPRESSIONLESS
dead to rights *adv syn* see RED-HANDED
deadweight *n syn* see LOAD 3
‖**deadwood** *n syn* see ADVANTAGE 3
deaf *adj syn* see OBSTINATE
deal *vb* **1** *syn* see DISTRIBUTE 1
rel partake, participate, share
con receive, take; detain, hold, hold back, keep,
retain, withhold; appropriate, arrogate, confiscate
2 *syn* see GIVE 10
rel impart, mete, render
con annul, cancel, remove, rescind, revoke
deal (out) *vb syn* see ADMINISTER 2
rel dish, dish out, help, serve; offer, present,
proffer, tender
con hold, hold back, keep, retain, withhold

deal (with) *vb syn* see TREAT 2
rel control, direct; clear, rid, unburden
con misconduct, misdirect, mishandle, mismanage; disregard, ignore, neglect; burden, cumber,
encumber
deal *n* **1** *syn* see AGREEMENT 2
2 treatment received in a transaction from another <a fair *deal*>
syn shake
dealer *n syn* see MERCHANT
dealings *n pl syn* see COMMERCE 1
rel affairs, business, concerns, doings, matters,
things; proceedings
deambulatory *adj syn* see ITINERANT
dean *n syn* see LEADER 1
dear *adj* **1** *syn* see FAVORITE 1
2 *syn* see LOVING
3 *syn* see COSTLY 1
con inexpensive, low, moderate, modest, nominal
ant cheap
dear *n syn* see SWEETHEART 1
dearth *n syn* see ABSENCE
rel infrequency, rareness, scarcity, uncommonness; exiguousness, meagerness, scantiness,
scantness; insufficiency, paucity
con superfluity, surplus; lavishness, prodigality,
profusion
ant excess
death *n* **1** the end or the ending of life <*death* of a
man><*death* of an enterprise>
syn curtains, decease, defunction, demise, dissolution, grim reaper, (the) Pale Horse, passing,
quietus, silence, sleep
rel annihilation, ending, expiration, extinction,
grave, termination
idiom crossing the bar
ant life
2 *syn* see FATALITY 2
deathful *adj syn* see DEATHLY 1
deathless *adj syn* see IMMORTAL 1
rel eternal; abiding, lasting, persisting
deathlike *adj* **1** *syn* see DEATHLY 1
2 *syn* see GHASTLY 2
deathly *adj* **1** suggesting death (as in inertness or
appearance) <fell in a *deathly* faint>
syn corpselike, corpsy, dead, deadened, deadly,
deathful, deathlike
rel cadaverous, haggard, wasted; ghastly, grisly,
gruesome, macabre; appalling, dreadful, horrible
con healthy, hearty, robust; stout, sturdy; energetic, strenuous, vigorous
2 *syn* see DEADLY 1
debacle *n* **1** *syn* see DEFEAT 1
2 *syn* see COLLAPSE 2
debar *vb syn* see EXCLUDE
rel forbid, interdict; block, hinder, impede, obstruct

---

syn synonym(s)   *rel* related word(s)
ant antonym(s)   *con* contrasted word(s)
idiom idiomatic equivalent(s)
‖ use limited; if in doubt, see a dictionary

con accept, receive; allow, let, permit
ant admit
debark *vb syn* see DISEMBARK
debase *vb* 1 to cause to become impaired in quality
or character <vulgarly outrageous movies that
debase the taste of the people>
syn animalize, bastardize, bestialize, brutalize,
canker, corrupt, debauch, demoralize, deprave,
pervert, poison, rot, stain, vitiate, warp; *compare*
ADULTERATE
rel damage, harm, impair, injure, mar, spoil;
contaminate, defile, dishonor, pollute, taint;
commercialize
con enhance, heighten; lift, raise; ameliorate,
better, improve
ant elevate; amend
2 *syn* see HUMBLE
rel cripple, debilitate, disable, enfeeble, sap, undermine, weaken
con acclaim, laud, praise; refresh, rejuvenate,
renew, restore
3 *syn* see ADULTERATE
rel damage, impair, worsen; corrupt, defile,
spoil
idiom play the devil (*or* the mischief) with
con amend, upgrade
debased *adj* being lowered in quality or character
<became *debased* in his greed for money>
syn corrupted, debauched, depraved, perverted,
vitiate, vitiated
rel decadent, degenerate, degenerated, deteriorated; abandoned, dissolute, profligate, reprobate
con ameliorated, bettered, improved; elevated,
lifted, raised
ant elevated
debatable *adj syn* see MOOT
ant undebatable
debate *n* 1 *syn* see ARGUMENTATION
rel controverting, rebutting, refuting
2 *syn* see ATTENTION 1
debate *vb syn* see DISCUSS 1
rel altercate, quarrel, wrangle; confute, controvert, disprove, rebut, refute; demonstrate, prove;
contend, contest
con agree, coincide, concur; affirm, aver, maintain, profess
debauch *vb* 1 *syn* see DEBASE 1
rel decoy, inveigle, lure, seduce, tempt
con amend, remedy; clean, cleanse, purge, purify; preserve, reclaim, save
2 *syn* see SEDUCE 2
debauch *n syn* see ORGY 2
debauched *adj syn* see DEBASED
rel lascivious, lecherous, lewd, libertine, libidinous, licentious, wanton
con delivered, reclaimed, redeemed, rescued,
saved; chaste, decent, pure; moral, virtuous; continent, temperate
debilitate *vb syn* see WEAKEN 1
rel devitalize; attenuate, extenuate; harm, hurt,
mar, spoil
con energize, vitalize; fortify, reinforce,
strengthen; refresh, rejuvenate, renew, restore;
rally, rouse, stir

ant invigorate
debility *n syn* see INFIRMITY 1
debris *n syn* see REFUSE
rel dregs, dross, rubble
debt *n* 1 *syn* see EVIL 2
2 *syn* see INDEBTEDNESS 1
3 something (as money) that is owed <struggling
to keep ahead of his *debts*>
syn arrear(s), arrearage, due, indebtedness, liability; *compare* INDEBTEDNESS 1
rel default, deficit, delinquency, nonpayment,
outstandings; debit, demurrage
con asset, credit; compensation, refund, reim-
bursement, remuneration
debunk *vb syn* see EXPOSE 4
debut *vb* to make one's formal entrance into society <she *debuted* on her 20th birthday>
syn come out
idiom make one's bow
decadence *n syn* see DETERIORATION 1
rel regress, regression, regressiveness, retrogradation, retrograding, retrogression, retrogressiveness; debasement, degradation
con advance, progress, progression; amelioration, bettering, betterment, improvement
ant rise; flourishing
decadent *adj syn* see EFFETE 3
decamp *vb* 1 *syn* see GET OUT 1
2 *syn* see ESCAPE 1
rel exit, go, leave, quit, retire, withdraw; avoid,
elude, evade, shun
con arrive, come
decapitate *vb* 1 *syn* see BEHEAD
2 *syn* see DESTROY 1
decay *vb* to undergo or to cause to undergo destructive changes <apples *decaying* in the bas-
ket>
syn break down, corrupt, crumble, decompose,
disintegrate, molder, ‖perish, putrefy, putresce,
rot, spoil, taint, turn
rel deteriorate; debilitate, enfeeble, sap, undermine, weaken; contaminate, defile, pollute; dilapidate, ruin, wreck; curdle, ferment, sour,
work; dry-rot
idiom go bad, go to pot, go to seed, go to wrack
and ruin
con mature, ripen; refresh, renew, restore; activate, energize, vitalize; cleanse, purify; galvanize,
quicken, stimulate, strengthen
decayed *adj* 1 *syn* see EFFETE 3
2 *syn* see BAD 5
decease *n syn* see DEATH 1
decease *vb syn* see DIE 1
deceased *adj syn* see DEAD 1
deceit *n* 1 the act or practice of imposing upon the
credulity of others by dishonesty, fraud, or trickery <he was full of *deceit* in his business deal-
ings>
syn cunning, dissemblance, dissimulation, duplicity, guile
rel chicane, chicanery, deception, double-dealing, fraud, trickery; artifice, craft; cheating, cozening, defrauding, entrapping, overreaching,
trapping

con honesty, scrupulosity, scrupulousness, uprightness; candidness, candor, frankness, openness; forthrightness, straightforwardness
2 syn see IMPOSTURE

deceitful *adj syn* see DISHONEST 1
rel artful, crafty, cunning, foxy, guileful, insidious, sly, tricky, wily; clandestine, furtive, stealthy, underhand, underhanded; deceptive, delusive, delusory, misleading
con assuring, convincing, reassuring
ant trustworthy

deceive *vb* to lead astray or frustrate by underhandedness <advertising that *deceives* the public>
syn beguile, betray, bluff, ||bunk, cozen, delude, double-cross, four-flush, humbug, illude, juggle, mislead, mock, sell out, suck in, take in, two=time
rel cheat, defraud, do, overreach; circumvent, outwit; bamboozle, befool, dupe, gull, hoax, hoodwink, spoof, trick, victimize; throw off
idiom pull one's leg, pull the wool over one's eyes, put something over (*or* across), take for a ride, take into camp, throw off the scent (*or* track)
con correct, disabuse, rectify, unblind; acquaint, advise, apprise, inform
ant undeceive; enlighten

deceiving *adj syn* see MISLEADING
ant undeceiving; enlightening

decelerate *vb syn* see DELAY 1
ant accelerate

decency *n syn* see DECORUM 1
rel appropriateness, fitness, fittingness, suitability; ceremoniousness, conventionality, formality
con impropriety, indecorousness, unseemliness; inappropriateness, unfitness, unsuitability; discourteousness, impoliteness, rudeness
ant indecency

decent *adj* 1 *syn* see DECOROUS 1
con awkward, clumsy, gauche, inept, maladroit; discomfiting, disconcerting, embarrassing; crude, rough, rude, uncouth
2 syn see CHASTE
rel noble; good, right; rigid, strict; ascetic, austere, severe
con lewd; libertine, wanton; abandoned, dissolute, profligate, reprobate
ant indecent; obscene
3 syn see RESPECTABLE 5
4 better than mediocre but less than excellent <the accommodations were *decent*>
syn acceptable, adequate, all right, common, good, respectable, right, satisfactory, sufficient, tolerable, unexceptionable, unexceptional, unimpeachable, unobjectionable; *compare* RESPECTABLE 5, SUFFICIENT 1
rel average, fair, mediocre, middling
con imperfect, inadequate, unacceptable, unsatisfactory; excellent, fine, superior
5 syn see SUFFICIENT 1

decently *adv syn* see WELL 1

deception *n* **1** the act of deliberately deceiving <resort to falsehood and *deception* in avoiding the tax>

syn cheat, chicane, chicanery, dipsy-doodle, dirt, dishonesty, double-dealing, dupery, fourberie, fraud, hanky-panky, highbinding, indirection, sharp practice, subterfuge, ||suck-in, trickery
rel cunning, deceit, dissimulation, duplicity, guile; cheating, cozening, defrauding, overreaching; bamboozling, befooling, duping, gulling, hoaxing, hoodwinking; manipulation; ride, ||snow job
con candidness, frankness, openness; honesty, integrity, probity; artlessness, ingenuousness, naiveté
2 syn see IMPOSTURE
rel delusion, hallucination, illusion, mirage
3 syn see FALLACY 2

deceptive *adj syn* see MISLEADING
rel colorable, plausible, specious; apparent, illusory, ostensible, seeming
con authentic, bona fide, genuine, veritable; actual, real, true; dependable, reliable, trustworthy

deceptiveness *n syn* see FALLACY 2

decide *vb* to come or to cause to come to a conclusion <he *decided* how to solve the problem>
syn conclude, determine, figure, resolve, rule, settle
rel gather; adjudge, adjudicate, judge; conjecture, guess, surmise; establish, fix, set
idiom cast the die, make up one's mind, settle in one's mind
con falter, hesitate, vacillate, waver; fluctuate, oscillate; balk, demur, scruple, shy

decided *adj* **1** beyond any doubt or ambiguity <a *decided* advantage over her opponent>
syn assured, clear-cut, definite, pronounced
rel determined, resolved; certain, positive, sure; categorical, explicit, express, unequivocal; clear, obvious, runaway, unmistakable
con doubtful, dubious, problematic, uncertain; equivocal, obscure, vague
ant questionable
2 free from doubt or wavering <he had a *decided* manner>
syn bent, decisive, determined, intent, resolute, resolved, set, settled
rel certain, cocksure, positive, sure; iron-jawed; established, fixed; earnest, purposeful, serious; unfaltering, unhesitating, unwavering
con doubtful, dubious, irresolute, uncertain; faltering, hesitant, vacillating, wavering; undetermined, unresolved, unsettled, unsure
ant undecided
3 syn see POSITIVE 1

decidedness *n syn* see DECISION 2

decimate *vb* **1** *syn* see DESTROY 1
2 syn see SLAUGHTER 3

decipher *vb* **1** *syn* see DECODE
ant cipher, encipher
2 syn see SOLVE 2

---

syn synonym(s)   **rel** related word(s)
ant antonym(s)   **con** contrasted word(s)
idiom idiomatic equivalent(s)
|| use limited; if in doubt, see a dictionary

rel paraphrase, translate; analyze, break down
idiom find the key of
con misconstrue, misinterpret, misunderstand; confuse, muddle; bewilder, confound, mystify, puzzle; jumble, mix, scramble

decision *n* **1** a position arrived at after consideration <the *decision* of the committee remains firm>
syn conclusion, determination, resolution, settlement
rel accord, agreement, understanding; accommodation, adjustment, arrangement; compromise, reconciliation; choice, preference, selection
con deadlock, draw, stalemate, standoff, tie
2 freedom from doubt or wavering <a man of unusual *decision*>
syn decidedness, determination, firmness, purposefulness, purposiveness, resoluteness, resolution, resolve
rel doggedness, obstinacy, obstinance, perseverance, persistence, stubbornness; earnestness, seriousness; backbone, fortitude, grit, pluck
con changeableness, indetermination, irresolution; uncertainty, unsureness; faltering, fluctuation, hesitation, vacillation, wavering
ant indecision

decisive *adj syn* see DECIDED 2
rel imperative, imperious, masterful, peremptory; assured, self-assured, self-confident; steadfast, unswerving, unwavering
con fluctuating, oscillating; hesitant, reluctant; doubtful, dubious, irresolute, uncertain, undecided
ant indecisive

deck *vb syn* see ADORN
rel apparel, array, attire, clothe, dress; accouter, appoint, furnish
con deface, disfigure; impair, mar, spoil; contort, deform, distort; dismantle, divest, strip

deck (out) *vb syn* see DRESS UP 1

declaim *vb syn* see ORATE

declamatory *adj syn* see RHETORICAL

declaration *n* the act of declaring, proclaiming, or publicly announcing <a *declaration* of war>
syn advertisement, announcement, broadcast, proclamation, promulgation, pronouncement, pronunciamento, publication
rel information, notice, notification; communication; disclosure, revelation; report, statement; acknowledgment, avowal
con concealment, hiding; denial, disaffirmation; recall, recantation, retraction, revocation

declare *vb* **1** to make known openly or publicly <*declared* his intention to run for the senate>
syn advertise, announce, annunciate, blaze (abroad), blazon, broadcast, bruit (about), disseminate, proclaim, promulgate, publish, sound, toot, vend
rel acquaint, advise, apprise, inform, notify; communicate, impart; pronounce; disclose, discover, divulge, reveal; report
idiom declare oneself, make public (*or* known)
con hold, hold back, keep back, reserve, withhold; recall, recant, retract, revoke

2 *syn* see ASSERT 1
rel air, broach, express, utter, vent, ventilate, voice; acknowledge, admit, own
idiom have one's say
con controvert; deny; repress, suppress; conceal, hide
3 *syn* see SAY 1
rel broach, express, voice
idiom speak one's piece

declare off *vb syn* see BACK DOWN

declass *vb syn* see DEGRADE 1
rel disbar, exclude, rule out; abash, discomfit, disconcert
con aggrandize, exalt, magnify

déclassé *adj syn* see INFERIOR 2

declension *n syn* see DETERIORATION 1
rel regression, regressiveness, retrogression, retrogressiveness; dilapidation, ruination
con ascension, ascent; rise, rising; advance, progress, progression; development, maturation

declination *n* **1** *syn* see DETERIORATION 1
2 *syn* see FAILURE 4

decline *vb* **1** *syn* see SET 12
ant ascend
2 *syn* see FAIL 1
rel backslide, lapse, relapse; slide; return, revert; recede, retrograde; abate, ebb, subside, wane
idiom go downhill, take a turn for the worse
con advance, progress; develop, mature; gain, recover
3 *syn* see DETERIORATE 1
4 to turn away by not accepting, receiving, or considering <he *declined* the invitation>
syn disapprove, dismiss, refuse, reject, reprobate, repudiate, spurn, turn down
rel balk, boggle, demur, jib, scruple, shy, stick, stickle; abstain, forbear, refrain; deny, gainsay; abjure, renounce; bypass
idiom send regrets
con receive, take; accede, acquiesce, assent, consent; choose, select; adopt, embrace, espouse
ant accept

decline *n* **1** *syn* see FAILURE 4
rel devitalization, weakening
con advancement, progress; recovery; development, maturation
2 *syn* see DETERIORATION 1
rel comedown, descent, drop, fall, falling off, slump; ebb, wane; backsliding, lapse, relapse
con development, evolution
3 a downward movement (as in price or value) <stocks suffered a *decline* in the market>
syn dip, downslide, downswing, downtrend, downturn, drop, falloff, sag, slide, slip, slump
rel lapse, loss, lowering; depression; decrease, drop-off, sell-off
con upswing, uptrend, upturn
4 *syn* see DESCENT 4

declivate *adj syn* see INCLINED 3

declivitous *adj syn* see INCLINED 3

declivity *n syn* see DESCENT 4
ant acclivity

decode *vb* to convert code into ordinary language <*decode* a message>

syn break, crack, cryptanalyze, decipher, decrypt
rel anagram; render, translate; ‖dope out, figure out, make out; resolve, solve, unfold, unravel, unriddle, work, work out; elucidate, explain, interpret
con cipher, codify, encipher; anagrammatize
ant code, encode, encrypt

decollate *vb syn* see BEHEAD

decolor *vb syn* see WHITEN 1
rel wash out; achromatize, fume, peroxide
con blacken; dye, imbue, stain, tinge, tint; paint, shade
ant color

decolorize *vb syn* see WHITEN 1
ant color

decompose *vb* **1** *syn* see ANALYZE
con combine, join, link, write; synthesize, unify; amalgamate, merge, mix
ant compound
2 *syn* see DECAY
rel deliquesce, liquefy, melt; break up, dissolve

decompound *vb syn* see ANALYZE
ant compound

decorate *vb syn* see ADORN
rel accouter, appoint, equip, furnish, outfit
con impair, injure, mar, spoil; blot, blotch, foul, mutilate, scar, uglify; dismantle, divest, strip

decorated *adj syn* see BEMEDALED

decoration *n syn* see HONOR 2

decorous *adj* **1** conforming to an accepted standard of propriety or good form <*decorous* behavior seems regrettably out of fashion>
syn au fait, becoming, befitting, Christian, civilized, comely, conforming, correct, decent, de rigueur, done, nice, proper, respectable, right, seemly
rel ceremonial, ceremonious, conventional, formal; dignified, elegant; appropriate, fit, fitting, meet, seasonable, suitable; prim, punctilious, rigid, stiff, stuffy
con blatant, clamorous, obstreperous, strident; aggressive, assertive, pushing, pushy; coarse, gross, vulgar; easy, fast, loose; improper, incorrect, unbecoming
ant indecorous
2 *syn* see GOOD 13

decorously *adv syn* see WELL 1

decorousness *n syn* see ORDER 7
rel ceremoniousness, conventionality, formality, solemnity; convenance, convention, form, usage
con inappropriateness, incorrectness; unfitness, unsuitability, unsuitableness; disorder, misbehavior, misconduct, misdeed, misdemeanor
ant indecorousness

decorticate *vb syn* see SKIN 2
rel bark; scalp; denude, divest

decorum *n* **1** socially acceptable behavior or accepted standards of this <they found his conduct quite lacking in *decorum*>
syn decency, dignity, etiquette, propriety, seemliness
rel convenance, convention, form, usage

con laxity, laxness, license, slackness; carelessness, heedlessness, inconsiderateness, mannerlessness; inappropriateness, incorrectness
ant indecorum
2 *syn* see ORDER 7
rel ceremoniousness, conventionality, formality, solemnity; convenance, convention, form, usage
con inappropriateness, incorrectness; unfitness, unsuitability, unsuitableness; disorder, misbehavior, misconduct, misdeed, misdemeanor
ant indecorum; license
3 *usu* **decorums** *syn* see MANNER 3

decoy *n* **1** *syn* see LURE 2
rel chicane, chicanery, deception, trickery; drawing card
con rebuff, repellence, repellency, repellent, repugnance, repulse, repulsion
2 a person used as a lure <used the detective as a *decoy* to catch the pushers>
syn blind, ‖bonnet, ‖booster, capper, shill, shillaber, stick
rel lugger, roper, steerer; come-on, front, plant, stall

decoy *vb syn* see LURE
rel deceive, delude, mislead; ensorcell, wile
con disgust, repel, sicken; offend, repulse, revolt

decrease *vb* to grow less especially gradually <his influence *decreased* as a new generation grew up>
syn abate, bate, close, diminish, drain (away), dwindle, lessen, peak (out), peter (out), rebate, recede, reduce, taper, taper off
rel abbreviate, abridge, clip, curtail, retrench, shorten, trim; contract, shrink; allay, alleviate, ease, lighten, mitigate; ebb, subside; cut, cut back, cut down, lower; deduct, subtract
con augment, enlarge, multiply; elongate, extend, lengthen, prolong, protract; amplify, dilate, distend, expand, swell; accumulate, amass
ant increase

decree *n* **1** *syn* see EDICT 1
2 *syn* see LAW 1
rel behest, bidding, injunction, order; charge, charging, direction, instruction; announcement, declaration, proclamation, promulgation, pronouncement

decree *vb syn* see DICTATE
rel compel, constrain, force, oblige; demand, require

decrepit *adj* **1** *syn* see WEAK 1
rel haggard, wasted, worn; aged, old, superannuated; creaky, quavering, shaking, tottering
con strong; lusty; hale, healthy, hearty, robust, sound, well
ant sturdy
2 *syn* see SHABBY 1

---

syn synonym(s)   *rel* related word(s)
ant antonym(s)   *con* contrasted word(s)
idiom idiomatic equivalent(s)
‖ use limited; if in doubt, see a dictionary

rel damaged, impaired, injured, marred, spoiled; cast-off, ragged, used; slipshod, sloppy, unkempt

decrepitude *n syn* see INFIRMITY 1
ant vigor

decretum *n syn* see LAW 1

decry *vb* **1** *syn* see DEPRECIATE 1
2 to indicate one's low opinion of something <*decrying* his opponent's character>
syn abuse, bad-mouth, belittle, cry down, depreciate, derogate, detract (from), diminish, discount, disparage, dispraise, downcry, ‖low-rate, minimize, opprobriate, put down, run down, take (from), take away, write off
rel deprecate, disapprove; censure, condemn, criticize, denounce, reprehend, reprobate; asperse, calumniate, defame, malign, traduce, vilify; discredit, disgrace
idiom bring into discredit, cast a slur upon, cast blame upon, dump on, throw stones at
con acclaim, eulogize, laud, praise; aggrandize, exalt, magnify; applaud, commend, compliment, recommend; endorse, sanction; approve, countenance, favor
ant extol, puff

decrypt *vb syn* see DECODE

decumbent *adj syn* see PRONE 4

decussate *vb syn* see INTERSECT

dedicate *vb syn* see DEVOTE 1
rel address, apply, direct, give, surrender; commit, confide, consign, entrust; allot, appropriate, assign, set (aside)
idiom give over to

dedition *n syn* see SURRENDER

deduce *vb syn* see INFER
rel cogitate; consider, deem, regard; conceive, fancy, imagine; assume, presume, presuppose; read (into)
idiom take to mean

deducible *adj syn* see DEDUCTIVE

deduct *vb* **1** to take away one quantity from another <*deduct* the cost from his bill>
syn discount, draw back, knock off, substract, subtract, take, take away, take off, take out
rel decrease, diminish, lessen, reduce; roll back
con cast, figure, sum, tot, total
ant add
2 *syn* see INFER

deduction *n* **1** an amount subtracted from a sum <*deductions* from gross income>
syn abatement, discount, rebate, reduction, subtraction
rel allowance, credit, cut; decrease, decrement, depreciation, diminution; charge-off, offtake, takeoff, write-off; dockage
con accession, accretion, augmentation, increase, increment, raise, rise; appreciation
ant addition
2 *syn* see INFERENCE 1
3 *syn* see INFERENCE 2
rel cogitation, deliberation, reasoning, reflection, speculation, thinking; consideration, contemplation; meditation, mulling, musing, pondering, rumination

deductive *adj* that can be deduced or developed from premises <*deductive* laws>
syn a priori, deducible, derivable, dogmatic, reasoned
rel illative, inferential, ratiocinative; conjectural, hypothetical, purported, putative, supposed, suppositious; academic, speculative, theoretical
con categorical, definite, explicit, express; instinctive, intuitive

deed *n* **1** *syn* see ACTION 1
2 *syn* see FEAT 2
rel gaining, securing, winning; adventure, enterprise, quest; cause, crusade
idiom bold stroke
3 a written, signed, and usually sealed instrument that spells out some bargain, transfer, or contract <the *deed* to the property>
syn charter, conveyance
rel bargain, compact, contract, covenant, pact

deed *vb syn* see TRANSFER 4

deem *vb* **1** *syn* see CONSIDER 3
rel conjecture, guess, surmise, suspect, ‖suspicion, understand; ‖allow, assume, believe, ‖calculate, daresay, divine, expect, presume, suppose
idiom hold to be true
2 *syn* see FEEL 3
idiom take for granted

de–emphasize *vb syn* see SOFT-PEDAL

deep *adj* **1** having great extension downward or inward <a *deep* well><a *deep* closet>
syn abysmal, profound; *compare* BOTTOMLESS 2
con depthless, shallow, superficial, unprofound; flat, level, plain, plane
ant shallow
2 *syn* see INTENSIVE
3 *syn* see RECONDITE
rel complex, complicated, intricate; arcane, mysterious; concealed, hidden
con easy, facile, simple; apparent, clear, distinct, evident, manifest, obvious; lucid, perspicuous; depthless, shallow, superficial, unprofound
4 *syn* see SLY 2
rel shrewd; acute, keen, knowing, sharp; contriving, intriguing, plotting
con ingenuous, naive, simple, unsophisticated; aboveboard, forthright, straightforward
5 *syn* see INTENT
rel abstracted, concentrated; centered, fixed, focused, set
con distracted, diverted; detached, disinterested, indifferent, unconcerned, uninterested

deep *n syn* see OCEAN

deep–dyed *adj syn* see INVETERATE 1

deepen *vb syn* see INTENSIFY

deepness *n* **1** *syn* see DEPTH 1
ant shallowness
2 *syn* see DEPTH 2

deep–rooted *adj syn* see INVETERATE 1

deep–seated *adj* **1** *syn* see INHERENT
2 *syn* see INVETERATE 1
rel constitutional, immanent, indwelling, ingrained, inherent, intrinsic; deep, profound; inner, internal, inward; implanted; infixed

con peripheral, shallow, superficial, surface; adventitious, casual, chance, incidental
ant skin-deep

‖**deep–six** *vb syn* see DISCARD

deep water *n syn* see PREDICAMENT

deface *vb* to mar the appearance of <*deface* the wall with graffiti>
syn disfashion, disfeature, disfigure
rel blemish, damage, harm, impair, injure, mar, spoil; contort, deform, distort, misshape; batter, mangle, mutilate; demolish, destroy; dilapidate, ruin, wreck
con mend, patch, repair; freshen, improve, refurbish, renew, restore; adorn, beautify, deck, decorate, embellish, ornament

defacer *n syn* see VANDAL

de facto *adv syn* see VERY 2

defalcation *n syn* see FAILURE 3
rel laxness, negligence, remissness, slackness; failing, fault
con discharge, effectuation, execution, fulfillment; completion, conclusion

defamation *n syn* see DETRACTION
ant puffery

defamatory *adj syn* see LIBELOUS

defame *vb syn* see MALIGN
rel belie, misrepresent
idiom cast a slur on, throw mud at
con applaud, commend, compliment; exalt, magnify; back, champion, support, uphold
ant laud; puff

default *n* **1** *syn* see FAILURE 1
rel deficiency, fault, imperfection, shortcoming; lapse, weakness; disregard, omission, overlooking, slight
2 *syn* see ABSENCE

defeasance *n syn* see DEFEAT 1

defeat *vb* **1** *syn* see CONQUER 1
rel bar, block, hinder, impede, obstruct; repress, suppress
idiom beat all hollow, get the better of, grind into the dust
con capitulate, defer, give in, submit; back down, withdraw
2 to win a victory over <*defeated* his opponent in the race>
syn best, down, outdo, ‖pip, worst; *compare* CONQUER 1, WHIP 2
rel outfight, outgame; nose out
idiom get the better of

defeat *n* **1** an overthrow especially of an army in battle <the brigade suffered a *defeat*>
syn beating, debacle, defeasance, discomfiture, downcast, downthrow, drubbing, ‖dusting, licking, overthrow, rout, shellacking, thrashing, trouncing, vanquishment, warming
rel bafflement, check, foil, frustration; rebuff, repulse, reversal, reverse, setback; ‖cleaning, ‖cleanup, clobbering, lambasting
con conquest, triumph; gaining, securing, winning; ascendancy, supremacy
ant victory
2 *syn* see FAILURE 2

defeater *n syn* see VICTOR 1

ant defeated

defect *n* **1** *syn* see BLEMISH
rel failing, fault, foible, frailty; infirmity, weakness; deficiency, imperfection, shortcoming
con excellence, faultlessness, impeccability; merit, perfection, virtue
2 *syn* see ABSENCE
rel scantiness, scarceness, scarcity, shortage
con overage, overplus, superfluity, surplus, surplusage
ant excess

defect *vb* to desert a cause or party often in order to espouse another <he *defected* from the Communist party>
syn apostatize, desert, rat, renounce, repudiate, tergiversate, tergiverse, turn
rel abandon, forsake; back out, renege, withdraw; depart, go, leave, quit; reject, spurn
idiom change sides, go back on, go over, turn one's coat, walk (*or* run) out on
con adhere (to), cling (to), hang on, stick (to *or* with); cherish, cultivate, foster

defection *n* conscious abandonment of allegiance or duty <*defection* from family responsibilities in times of trouble>
syn apostasy, desertion, falseness, recreancy, tergiversation
rel alienation, disaffection, estrangement; disloyalty, faithlessness; abandonment, forsaking; divorce, parting, runout, separation, sundering; disownment, rejection, repudiation
idiom running out on, ‖taking a runout powder
con constancy, faithfulness, loyalty, resoluteness, staunchness, steadfastness; allegiance, fealty, fidelity; dependability, reliability, trustworthiness

defective *adj* **1** *syn* see FAULTY
rel broken, damaged, impaired, injured
con faultless, flawless, impeccable, unblemished, undamaged
ant defectless
2 *syn* see DEFICIENT 1
rel corrupted, debased, vitiated; deranged, disordered, disturbed, unsettled; unhealthy, unsound
con entire, perfect, whole; complete, full, plenary; healthy, sound
ant intact; defectless

defector *n syn* see RENEGADE

defend *vb* **1** to keep safe (as from danger or against attack) <*defend* the country from aggression>
syn bulwark, cover, fend, guard, protect, safeguard, screen, secure, shield
rel avert, prevent, ward; oppose, resist, withstand; battle, contend, fight, war; conserve, preserve, save
idiom stand on the defensive, stave off from

---

syn synonym(s)   *rel* related word(s)
ant antonym(s)   *con* contrasted word(s)
idiom idiomatic equivalent(s)
‖ use limited; if in doubt, see a dictionary

con aggress, assail, assault, fall (on *or* upon); bombard, storm; beset, besiege, overrun; capitulate, cave, submit, yield
ant attack
2 *syn* see MAINTAIN 2
rel air, express, utter, vent, voice; account, explain, justify, rationalize; back, champion, support, uphold
idiom speak (*or* stand *or* stick) up for
con contradict, deny, gainsay, traverse; confute, controvert, disprove, rebut, refute
defendable *adj syn* see TENABLE 1
ant undefendable
defense *n* **1** means or method of defending <the skunk's powerful *defense* against attackers>
syn aegis, armament, armor, guard, protection, safeguard, security, shield, ward
rel arms, munitions, weaponry, weapons; fastness, fort, fortress, stronghold
con aggression, offense, offensive
ant attack
2 *syn* see APOLOGY 1
rel answer, rejoinder, reply, response, retort, return; exculpation, excuse, explanation, rationalization
con censure, condemnation, criticism, decrial, reprehension, reprobation, reproof; assault, attack, onset, onslaught
defenseless *adj syn* see HELPLESS 1
defensible *adj* **1** *syn* see TENABLE 1
ant indefensible
2 *syn* see JUSTIFIABLE
ant indefensible
defer *vb* to delay an action or proceeding <decided to *defer* voting until the next meeting>
syn adjourn, delay, hold off, hold over, hold up, intermit, lay over, postpone, prorogue, put off, put over, remit, shelve, stand over, stay, suspend, waive
rel detain, retard, slow; block, hinder, impede, obstruct; stall; extend, lengthen, prolong, protract
idiom hold up on, lay to one side, put on ice, set aside
con accelerate, hasten, hurry, speed; expedite, further, promote
ant advance
defer *vb syn* see YIELD 2
rel accede, acquiesce, agree, assent; accommodate, adapt, adjust, conform; cringe, fawn, truckle
con combat, fight, oppose, resist; object, remonstrate; balk, demur, stickle, strain
ant withstand
deference *n syn* see HONOR 1
rel acquiescence, compliance; submission, submissiveness
con insolence, irreverence; disesteem, disfavor; discourtesy, incivility, rudeness
ant disrespect
deferential *adj* **1** *syn* see RESPECTFUL
2 *syn* see INGRATIATING
defi *n syn* see DEFIANCE 1
defiance *n* **1** the act or an instance of defying <presented a *defiance* to his rival>

syn cartel, challenge, dare, defi, defy, stump
rel call, muster, summons; command, enjoinder, order
con capitulation, submission, surrender
2 disposition to resist or unwillingness to brook opposition <exhibited *defiance* toward his teacher>
syn contempt, contumacy, despite, recalcitrance, stubbornness
rel factiousness, insubordination, insurgency, rebelliousness; headstrongness, intractableness, unruliness; boldness, bravado, brazenness, impudence, insolence; audacity, effrontery, hardihood, temerity; contrariness, perversity
con acquiescence, compliance; amenableness, docility, obedience, tractableness; submissiveness
deficiency *n* **1** *syn* see FAILURE 3
rel absence, default, defect, want
con copiousness, plenty; great deal, heap, lot, much
2 *syn* see IMPERFECTION
rel dearth, defect, lack, privation, want; default, dereliction, miscarriage, neglect
ant excess
deficient *adj* **1** showing lack of something necessary <*deficient* in judgment>
syn defective, inadequate, incomplete, insufficient, lacking, uncomplete, wanting
rel faulty, flawed, imperfect, unsound; damaged, impaired, injured, marred; amiss, bad, unsatisfactory
idiom in want of
con complete, entire, intact, whole; acceptable, adequate, sufficient
2 *syn* see SHORT 3
rel infrequent, rare, uncommon
idiom found wanting
con excessive, extravagant, immoderate, inordinate; enough, satisfactory, sufficing
ant adequate, sufficient
deficit *n syn* see FAILURE 3
con copiousness, plenty; excess, surplus, surplusage
defile *vb* **1** *syn* see CONTAMINATE 1
rel desecrate, profane; befoul, dirty, foul, sully, tarnish
con consecrate, hallow
ant cleanse; purify
2 *syn* see RAPE
rel dishonor, shame, soil, sully
3 *syn* see TAINT 1
defiled *adj syn* see IMPURE
define *vb* **1** *syn* see PRESCRIBE 2
rel circumscribe, limit, mark (off), mark (out); designate; delineate, describe
con confound, confuse, mistake
2 *syn* see BORDER 1
3 *syn* see ETCH 2
rel explain, expound, interpret
definite *adj* **1** having distinct or certain limits <*definite* dimensions>
syn circumscribed, determinate, fixed, limited, narrow, precise, restricted

rel assigned, defined, prescribed; established, set; decided, determined, settled
con ambiguous, obscure, vague; unconditional, unlimited, unqualified, unrestricted; indeterminate, uncircumscribed; imprecise, loose, undefined
ant indefinite
2 *syn* see EXPLICIT
rel complete, full; downright, forthright; incisive
con doubtful, dubious, questionable; ambiguous
ant indefinite; equivocal
3 *syn* see POSITIVE 1
4 *syn* see DECIDED 1
ant uncertain
definitely *adv* **1** *syn* see EXPRESSLY 1
2 *syn* see EASILY 2
definiteness *n syn* see PRECISION
ant indefiniteness
definitive *adj* **1** *syn* see CONCLUSIVE
rel determining, settling; concluding, final, last, terminal, ultimate; closing, completing, ending, finishing, terminating; absolute, categorical
con inconclusive, indecisive; temporary, transitory
ant provisional, tentative
2 *syn* see EXPLICIT
rel actual, real
con doubtful, dubious, questionable; ambiguous
ant indefinitive
definitiveness *n syn* see PRECISION
ant indefinitiveness, indefinitude
definitude *n syn* see PRECISION
ant indefinitiveness, indefinitude
deflect *vb* **1** *syn* see TURN 6
rel disperse, swerve; hook, skew
2 *syn* see WARD 1
rel hold off, keep off
deflection *n* **1** *syn* see DEVIATION 1
rel bending, curving, twisting; departing, swerve, swerving, veer, veering
2 *syn* see TURN 2
deflorate *vb syn* see RAPE
deflower *vb* **1** *syn* see RAPE
2 *syn* see RAVAGE
deform *vb* to mar or spoil by or as if by twisting <a face *deformed* by bitterness>
syn contort, distort, misshape, torture, warp, wind
rel batter, cripple, maim, mangle, mutilate; deface, disfigure; damage, impair, injure, mar, spoil; blemish, flaw; screw (up), squinch
deformity *n* a physical blemish or disfigurement <the dwarf's humpback *deformity*>
syn distortion, malconformation, malformation, misshape
rel defacement, deformation, disfigurement; damage, impairment, injury; aberration, abnormality; irregularity, unnaturalness
defraud *vb syn* see CHEAT
rel bamboozle, hoax, trick; circumvent, foil, outwit; fleece, milk, stick; take in

idiom do out of, put over a fast one, take to the cleaner's
defrauder *n syn* see SWINDLER
deft *adj syn* see DEXTEROUS 1
rel agile, brisk, fleet; apt, prompt, quick, ready; adept, crack, crackerjack; ingenious, neat
con heavy-handed, unskillful; blundering, bungling, butterfingered; rigid, stiff, wooden
ant awkward, unhandy
deftness *n syn* see ADDRESS 1
rel agility, fleetness, nimbleness; assuredness, confidence
con incompetence, inefficiency; clumsiness, heavy-handedness, maladroitness
ant awkwardness
defunct *adj* **1** *syn* see DEAD 1
rel inactive, inert
ant alive; live
2 *syn* see EXTINCT 2
ant surviving
defunction *n syn* see DEATH 1
defy *vb syn* see FACE 3
rel deride, mock, ridicule; gibe, flout; scorn, scout, spurn; disregard, ignore
idiom fling (*or* throw) down the gauntlet, hurl defiance at
con blench, flinch, quail, shrink
ant recoil
defy *n syn* see DEFIANCE 1
dégagé *adj syn* see EASYGOING 3
ant mannered
degeneracy *n syn* see DETERIORATION 1
degenerate *adj* **1** *syn* see EFFETE 3
rel deteriorating, retrograde, retrogressive, worsening; failing, sinking
2 *syn* see VICIOUS 2
rel degraded, demeaned
con ethical, moral, virtuous; honorable, just, upright
ant regenerate
degenerate *vb syn* see DETERIORATE 1
rel corrupt, deprave, vitiate; backslide, lapse; return, revert
con improve, upgrade; lift, uplift
degeneration *n syn* see DETERIORATION 1
rel regression, regressiveness, retrogression, retrogressiveness; depreciation; corruption, depravation, depravedness, depravity, perversion
con regeneracy, regenerateness; progress, progression
ant regeneration
degradation *n syn* see DEMOTION
ant advancement; elevation
degrade *vb* **1** to lower in station, rank, or grade <*degraded* in rank for misconduct>
syn break, bump, bust, declass, demerit, demote, disgrade, disrate, downgrade, put down, reduce

---

syn synonym(s) *rel* related word(s)
ant antonym(s) *con* contrasted word(s)
idiom idiomatic equivalent(s)
|| use limited; if in doubt, see a dictionary

rel abase, debase, humble, humiliate, lower; disbar, rule out

con advance, further; boost, lift, raise; enhance, heighten

ant elevate

2 syn see HUMBLE

rel belittle, decry, derogate, detract, disparage; diminish, lessen, reduce

con elevate, raise; acclaim, extol, laud, praise

ant uplift

degree *n* **1** a unitary component of a process, course, or order of classification <advanced by *degrees*>

syn grade, notch, rung, stage, step

2 relative size or character of the parts or components in a complex whole compared with other like things <the *degree* of difference between the two jobs> <his work demands a high *degree* of intelligence>

syn proportion, rate, ratio, scale

rel dimension; extent, magnitude, measure, size

dégringolade *n syn* see DETERIORATION 1

dehydrate *vb syn* see DRY 1

ant hydrate; rehydrate

deific *adj* **1 syn** see DIVINE 1

2 syn see DIVINE 2

deification *n syn* see APOTHEOSIS 2

deign *vb syn* see STOOP 1

deject *vb syn* see DISCOURAGE 1

ant exhilarate; cheer

dejected *adj syn* see DOWNCAST

idiom down in the dumps (*or* mouth), in the dumps

ant animated

dejection *n syn* see SADNESS

rel despair, desperation

ant exhilaration

‖**dekko** *vb syn* see SEE 2

delay *vb* **1** to cause to be late or behind in movement or progress <was *delayed* by traffic>

syn bog (down), decelerate, detain, embog, hang up, mire, retard, set back, slacken, slow (up *or* down)

rel block, hinder, impede, obstruct; defer, hold over, hold up, intermit, postpone, put off, stay, suspend; arrest, check, interrupt

idiom hang fire

con accelerate, hasten, hurry, precipitate, quicken, speed; advance, forward, further, promote

ant expedite

2 to move or act slowly so that progress or work is retarded <their landlord kept *delaying* in making repairs>

syn dally, dawdle, dilly, dillydally, drag, lag, linger, loiter, mull, poke, procrastinate, put off, tarry, trail

rel hang back, idle, wait; drone; falter, hesitate, vacillate, waver

idiom take one's own sweet (*or* good) time

ant hasten, hurry

3 syn see DEFER

delectable *adj syn* see DELIGHTFUL

rel choice, dainty, delicate, exquisite, rare; palatable, sapid, savory, tasty, toothsome

con loathsome, offensive, repulsive, revolting

ant distasteful

delectate *vb syn* see PLEASE 2

delectation *n* **1 syn** see PLEASURE 2

rel gratification, gratifying, regalement, regaling; enjoyment, relish

ant distaste

2 syn see ENJOYMENT 1

‖**deleerit** *adj syn* see INTOXICATED 1

delegate *n* a person standing in the place of another or others <was a *delegate* to the convention>

syn catchpole, deputy, representant, representative; *compare* AGENT 2

rel agent, factor, proxy; alternate, replacement, stand-in, substitute, surrogate; mouthpiece, spokesman; emissary, envoy

delegate *vb* to appoint as one's representative <*delegated* her to watch the children>

syn commission, depute, deputize

rel ascribe, assign, charge; appoint, designate, name; choose, pick, select

delete *vb syn* see ERASE

rel eliminate, exclude, rule out; omit

deleterious *adj syn* see HARMFUL

rel destroying, destructive; ruining, ruinous

con advantageous, profitable; healthful, healthy, salubrious, wholesome

ant salutary

deliberate *adj* **1** arrived at after due thought <a *deliberate* judgment>

syn advised, aforethought, considered, designed, premeditated, prepense, studied, studious, thought-out

rel planned, projected, schemed; calculated; careful, meticulous, scrupulous; foresighted, forethoughtful, provident, prudent

con chance, chancy, desultory, haphazard, happy-go-lucky, hit-or-miss, random; aimless, designless, purposeless; hasty, hurried; abrupt, impetuous, sudden; automatic, instinctive, spontaneous

ant casual

2 syn see VOLUNTARY

rel intended, meant, meditated, purposed; determined, purposeful; aware, cognizant, conscious

con careless, heedless, inadvertent, thoughtless; unintended, unpurposed

ant impulsive

3 syn see SLOW 2

rel calculating, cautious, chary, circumspect, wary; careful, heedful; collected, composed, cool, imperturbable

con hasty, headlong, impetuous, sudden

ant abrupt, precipitate

deliberate *vb* **1 syn** see PONDER 2

2 syn see THINK 5

rel excogitate, study, weigh; argue, debate, discuss, talk over

deliberately *adv syn* see INTENTIONALLY

deliberation *n* **1 syn** see ATTENTION 1

2 syn see THOUGHT 1

3 syn see CONFERENCE 1

delicacy *n* something special and delicious to eat <fresh fruit in the winter was once an uncommon *delicacy*>
syn bonne bouche, dainty, goody, kickshaw, morsel, tidbit (*or* titbit), treat
rel banquet, feast, regale; cosseting, indulgence, luxury
idiom choice bit, dish fit for a king

delicate *adj* **1** *syn* see CHOICE
rel delectable, delicious, delightful; balmy, gentle, lenient, mild, soft; aerial, airy, ethereal
con coarse, crude, vulgar
ant gross
2 *syn* see FINE 1
3 *syn* see NICE 1
rel perceptive, sensitive
con insensitive, undiscriminating, unperceptive
4 *syn* see FRAGILE 1
5 lacking in strength or substance <a *delicate* constitution>
syn flimsy, slight
rel feeble, fragile, frail, weak; sickly, unhealthy; decrepit, infirm
con stalwart, stout, strong, sturdy, tenacious, tough; hale, healthy, robust, sound, well, wholesome
6 *syn* see TACTFUL
rel adept, expert, masterly, proficient; discreet, foresighted, prudent; careful, heedful; cautious, wary
con impolitic; imprudent, indiscreet; awkward, clumsy, gauche, inept, maladroit; unskillful
7 marked by or requiring tact <a *delicate* situation>
syn precarious, sensitive, ticklish, touchy, tricky
rel uncertain, unpredictable; hair-trigger, volatile; sticky

delicatesse *n syn* see TACT
ant indelicacy

delicious *adj syn* see DELIGHTFUL
rel appetizing, palatable, sapid, savory, toothsome; choice, dainty, delicate, exquisite, rare
con banal, flat, inane, insipid, jejune, wishy≠washy

delight *vb* **1** *syn* see EXULT
2 *syn* see PLEASE 2
rel amuse, divert, entertain; allure, attract, charm, enchant, fascinate; enrapture, entrance, transport
con aggrieve, distress, pain, trouble; afflict, try; grieve; bother, irk; bore

delight (in) *vb* **1** *syn* see ADMIRE 1
rel enjoy, like, savor; eat up, luxuriate (in)
con abhor, abominate, hate, loathe
2 *syn* see LOVE 1

delight *n syn* see PLEASURE 2
rel glee, hilarity, jollity, mirth; ecstasy, rapture, transport; contentment, satisfaction; relish
con abhorrence, detestation, hate, hatred; dislike, distaste; discontent, dissatisfaction
ant aversion; disappointment

delightful *adj* highly pleasing to the senses or to aesthetic taste <a *delightful* view>
syn adorable, ambrosial, darling, delectable, delicious, heavenly, luscious, lush, scrumptious, yummy
rel charming, enchanting, fascinating; alluring, attractive; beautiful, fair, lovely; ineffable; agreeable, gratifying, pleasant, pleasing; satisfying
con miserable, wretched; distasteful, obnoxious, repellent, repugnant; abhorrent, detestable, hateful, odious; boring, irksome, tedious; distressing, troubling
ant abominable, horrid

delimit *vb* **1** *syn* see DEMARCATE 1
rel decide
2 *syn* see LIMIT 2

delimitate *vb* **1** *syn* see DEMARCATE 1
2 *syn* see LIMIT 2

delineate *vb* **1** *syn* see REPRESENT 1
rel design, plan; evoke, paint
2 *syn* see ETCH 2

delineation *n* **1** *syn* see REPRESENTATION
rel design, plan; evocation, painting; account, story, version
2 *syn* see OUTLINE

delinquency *n syn* see FAILURE 1
rel nonobservance; nonfulfillment; lapse, weakness

delinquent *adj syn* see NEGLIGENT

deliquesce *vb syn* see LIQUEFY
rel decay, decompose, disintegrate
con cake, harden, indurate, set, solidify

delirious *adj* **1** disordered in mind especially temporarily <*delirious* from the fever>
syn raving, wandering
rel deranged, disarranged, disordered, disturbed, unsettled; bewildered, confused, distracted; rambling; irrational, unreasonable; crazed, crazy, demented, insane, lunatic, mad, maniac
idiom out of one's head (*or* mind)
con rational, reasonable; sane, sensible; comatose, unconscious
2 *syn* see FURIOUS 2
rel overexcited, overwrought; ecstatic, rapturous, transported; delighted, enthused, thrilled
idiom all agog, beside oneself
con collected, composed, easy, relaxed; unexcited, unmoved, unstimulated

delirium *n* frenzied excitement or wild enthusiasm <in a *delirium* of patriotic feeling>
syn frenzy, furor
rel ardor, enthusiasm, fervor, passion, zeal; ecstasy, rapture, transport
con nonchalance, sangfroid; indifference, unconcern
ant apathy

deliver *vb* **1** *syn* see RESCUE
con immure, imprison, incarcerate, intern, jail; capture, catch, ensnare, entrap, snare, trap; condemn, damn, doom

---

syn synonym(s)   *rel* related word(s)
ant antonym(s)   *con* contrasted word(s)
idiom idiomatic equivalent(s)
‖ use limited; if in doubt, see a dictionary

2 *syn* see GIVE 3
rel relinquish, resign, surrender, yield
con keep, retain
3 *syn* see BEAR 5
4 *syn* see SAY 1
rel broach, express, vent, voice; communicate, impart
5 *syn* see GIVE 10
rel dispatch, send, transmit; fling, hurl, pitch, throw
delivery *n syn* see BIRTH 1
Delphian *adj* 1 *syn* see PROPHETIC
2 *syn* see CRYPTIC
delude *vb syn* see DECEIVE
idiom play tricks (*or* a trick) on
con enlighten, illume, illuminate, illustrate, light, lighten; elucidate, explain
deluding *adj syn* see MISLEADING
deluge *n syn* see FLOOD 2
rel flux; overrunning
deluge *vb* 1 to flow over so as to submerge or enclose <the lowlands were completely *deluged*>
syn drown, engulf, flood, inundate, overflow, overwhelm, submerge, swamp, whelm
rel overrun; flush, gush, pour, sluice, stream
2 *syn* see WET
con dehydrate, desiccate, dry, parch
3 to affect overwhelmingly as if by a deluge of water <he was *deluged* by telephone calls>
syn flood, overwhelm, swamp, whelm
rel overcome; oversupply; abound, teem
delusion *n* 1 something accepted as true that is actually false or unreal <people who suffer from *delusions* of persecution>
syn hallucination, ignis fatuus, illusion, mirage, phantasm
rel chicane, chicanery, deception, trickery; cheat, counterfeit, deceit, fake, fraud, humbug, imposture, sham; daydream, dream, fancy, fantasy, figment, vision; apparition, eidolon, ghost, phantom, shade
ant reality
2 *syn* see FALLACY 2
ant verity
delusive *adj syn* see MISLEADING
rel chimerical, fanciful, fantastic, imaginary, quixotic, visionary; apparent, illusory, ostensible, seeming
con authentic, bona fide, genuine, veritable; actual, real, true
delusory *adj syn* see MISLEADING
deluxe *adj syn* see LUXURIOUS 3
rel choice, dainty, delicate, elegant, exquisite, rare, recherché
con coarse, common, ordinary; inelegant
delve *vb* ‖1 *syn* see DIG 1
rel gouge (out), hollow (out), quarry (out), scoop (out); burrow, tunnel; comb, ferret out, search, seek
2 *syn* see MINE
delve (into) *vb syn* see EXPLORE
delve *n syn* see HOLE 1
delving *n syn* see INQUIRY 1
demagogue *n* a leader who makes use of popular prejudices and false claims especially for politi-

cal advantage <*demagogues* who endanger the orderly processes of democratic government>
syn rabble-rouser
rel fomenter, inciter, instigator; agitator, firebrand, hothead, incendiary, inflamer; troublemaker
demand *n* 1 *syn* see REQUIREMENT 1
2 *syn* see NEED 3
demand *vb* 1 to ask for something as or as if one's right or due <the physician *demanded* payment of his bill>
syn call, challenge, claim, exact, postulate, require, requisition, solicit
rel ask, request; bid, charge, command, direct, enjoin, order; cite, summon, summons; coerce, compel, constrain, force, oblige; necessitate
con cede, relinquish, resign, waive; allow, concede, grant; give, offer, tender
2 to have as a need or requirement <it *demands* considerable practice to master the piano>
syn ask, call (for), crave, necessitate, require, take
rel fail, lack, need, want
idiom need (*or* want), doing, stand in need of
demanding *adj syn* see ONEROUS
rel rigid, rigorous, severe, stern, strict, stringent; crying, imperative, importunate, instant, pressing, urgent
ant undemanding
demarcate *vb* 1 to mark the limits of <*demarcate* the boundary between two countries>
syn bound, delimit, delimitate, determine, limit, mark (out), measure
rel establish, fix, set; assign, define, prescribe; circumscribe, confine, restrict
2 *syn* see DISTINGUISH
rel insulate, isolate, seclude, segregate, sequester
demean *vb syn* see BEHAVE 1
demean *vb syn* see HUMBLE
rel belittle, decry, derogate, detract, disparage; contemn, despise, scorn
con elevate, enhance, heighten
demeanor *n syn* see BEARING 1
rel behavior, conduct
dement *n syn* see LUNATIC 1
demented *adj syn* see INSANE 1
rel delirious, frenzied, hysterical
demerit *n syn* see IMPERFECTION
demerit *vb syn* see DEGRADE 1
demeritorious *adj syn* see BLAMEWORTHY
ant meritorious
demesne *n syn* see FIELD
demigod *n syn* see SUPERMAN
demimondaine *n syn* see HARLOT 1
demimonde *n syn* see HARLOT 1
demirep *n syn* see HARLOT 1
demise *vb syn* see DIE 1
demise *n syn* see DEATH 1
rel annihilation, ending, expiration, extinction
demit *vb syn* see ABDICATE 1
demit *vb syn* see LOWER 3
demiurgic *adj syn* see INVENTIVE
‖**demob** *vb syn* see DISCHARGE 7

ant mobilize

demobilize *vb syn* see DISCHARGE 7
rel break up, disband, dispel, disperse, scatter; retire, withdraw
ant mobilize

democratic *adj* of or relating to a political system in which the supreme power is held and exercised by the people <a *democratic* government>
syn popular, self-governing, self-ruling
rel representative; libertarian
con totalitarian; absolute, arbitrary, autocratic, despotic; tyrannical, tyrannous; fascistic, nazi, patriarchal
ant authoritarian; undemocratic

démodé *adj syn* see OLD-FASHIONED
ant a la mode

demoded *adj syn* see OLD-FASHIONED
ant a la mode

demolish *vb syn* see DESTROY 1
rel dilapidate; crush, smash; break, burst, crack
con build, erect, frame, raise, rear
ant construct; rebuild
2 *syn* see TOTAL 3

demon *n syn* see DEVIL 2

demoniac *adj syn* see FIENDISH
rel crazed, crazy, insane, maniac; fired, inspired
con celestial, heavenly
ant angelic

demonian *adj syn* see FIENDISH
rel crazed, crazy, insane, maniac; fired, inspired
con celestial, heavenly
ant angelic

demonic *adj syn* see FIENDISH
rel crazed, crazy, insane, maniac; fired, inspired
con celestial, heavenly
ant angelic

demonstrate *vb* **1** *syn* see SHOW 2
rel display, exhibit, expose, flaunt, parade; explain, set forth
idiom go to show
con conceal, hide, secrete; camouflage, cloak, disguise, dissemble, mask
2 *syn* see PROVE 1
rel authenticate, validate
3 *syn* see ESTABLISH 6

demonstration *n syn* see EXHIBITION 1

demonstrative *adj* marked by display of feeling <was *demonstrative* in his welcome>
syn expansive, outgoing, unconstrained, unreserved, unrestrained
rel affectionate, loving; effusive, outpouring, profuse; candid, frank, open, outspoken, plain
con constrained, reserved, restrained, reticent, taciturn; bashful, shy; retiring, shrinking; introverted; aloof, detached, indifferent, unconcerned; chilly, cold, frigid, glacial, icy
ant undemonstrative

demoralize *vb* **1** *syn* see DEBASE 1
rel debilitate, undermine, weaken; damp, dampen
2 *syn* see DISCOURAGE 1
rel agitate, disturb, upset; disarrange, disorder, disorganize, unsettle; confuse, jumble, muddle, snarl; debilitate, undermine, weaken; unman, unnerve

con arrange, order, organize; energize, fortify, invigorate, strengthen

demote *vb syn* see DEGRADE 1
rel demean, lower
ant promote

demotion *n* the action or an instance of demoting <received a *demotion* from sergeant to corporal>
syn degradation, downgrading, reduction
rel debasement, humbling, humiliation; blackballing, disbarment, exclusion, suspension
con advancement, preferment, upgrading; aggrandizement; boost, elevation, lift, raise
ant promotion

demur *vb* to object or have scruples <he *demurred* at any horseplay>
syn balk, boggle, gag, jib, scruple, shy, stick, stickle, strain, stumble
rel falter, hesitate, vacillate, waver; combat, fight, oppose, resist; expostulate, object, protest, remonstrate; deprecate, disapprove
con accept, admit, receive, take; acquiesce, agree, assent, consent, subscribe, yes; concur; defer, relent, submit, succumb, yield
ant accede

demur *n* **1** *syn* see QUALM
rel faltering, hesitancy, hesitation; aversion, disinclination, loathness; expostulation, protest
con promptness, quickness, readiness
2 the act of objecting or taking exception <accepted without *demur*>
syn challenge, demurral, demurrer, difficulty, objection, protest, question, remonstrance, remonstration
rel reluctance, unwillingness; faltering, hesitancy, hesitation; deprecation, disapproval; protestation; difference, disagreement, dissent, variance
con acquiescence, agreement, assent, consent; concurrence; submission

demure *adj syn* see SHY 1
rel decent, decorous, nice, proper, seemly; prim; earnest, serious, solemn; close, reserved, reticent, silent
con impertinent, intrusive, meddlesome, obtrusive, officious; brash, forward, unbashful, unretiring

demurral *n syn* see DEMUR 2

demurrer *n syn* see DEMUR 2

den *n* **1** *syn* see LAIR 1
2 *syn* see HIDEOUT
3 *syn* see SINK 1

denaturant *n syn* see ADMIXTURE 1

denial *n* **1** refusal to satisfy a request or desire <*denial* of his visiting privileges>
syn disallowance, refusal, rejection
rel declination, nonacceptance
con allowing, conceding, grant, letting; leave, permission, sufferance

---

syn synonym(s)   *rel* related word(s)
ant antonym(s)   *con* contrasted word(s)
idiom idiomatic equivalent(s)
‖ use limited; if in doubt, see a dictionary

2 refusal to admit the truth <his *denial* that he took the money>
syn contradiction, gainsaying, negation
rel controversion, disproof, rebuttal, refutal, refutation; refusal, rejection, repudiation
con acknowledgment, avowal, confession; affirmation, assertion, confirmation
ant admission
3 *syn* see RENUNCIATION
rel abstaining, refraining
con indulgence, self-indulgence; overdoing, overindulgence

denigrate *vb syn* see MALIGN

denizen *n* **1** *syn* see INHABITANT
rel citizen, national, subject
2 *syn* see HABITUÉ 1

denominate *vb syn* see NAME 1

denomination *n* **1** *syn* see NAME 1
2 *syn* see RELIGION 2

denotative *adj syn* see INDICATIVE

denote *vb syn* see MEAN 2
rel insinuate; announce, argue, bespeak, prove

denotive *adj syn* see INDICATIVE

denounce *vb syn* see CRITICIZE
rel accuse, arraign, charge, impeach, incriminate, indict, tax; revile, vituperate; delate, inform
idiom cry harrow (*or* haro)
con panegyrize, praise
ant eulogize

de novo *adv syn* see OVER 7

dense *adj* **1** *syn* see CLOSE 4
rel heaped, massed, piled; crammed, crowded, jam-packed
con dispersed, dissipated, scattered; rare, thin; exiguous, meager, scant, scanty, spare
ant sparse; tenuous
2 *syn* see STUPID 1
rel obtuse; impassive, phlegmatic, stolid; lethargic, sluggish, torpid
ant subtle; bright

denticulate *adj syn* see SERRATE

denudate *vb syn* see STRIP 2

denude *vb* **1** *syn* see STRIP 1
2 *syn* see STRIP 2

denuded *adj syn* see OPEN 2

denunciate *vb syn* see CRITICIZE
rel delate, inform; menace, threaten
ant eulogize

deny *vb* **1** *syn* see DISCLAIM
rel abandon, desert, forsake
con adopt, embrace, espouse; recognize
ant acknowledge; admit
2 to refuse to grant <he was unwilling to *deny* the child's request>
syn disallow, keep back, refuse, withhold
idiom say no to, turn thumbs down on
con allow, concede, let, permit; afford, give
ant grant
3 to restrain (as oneself) from or forgo what is pleasant or satisfying <decided to *deny* himself a second piece of pie>
syn abstain, constrain, curb, hold back, refrain
rel eschew, forbear, forgo, sacrifice; inhibit, restrain; avoid, shun

con overdo, overindulge
ant indulge
4 to refuse to accept as true, valid, or worthy of consideration <*denying* the existence of witches>
syn contradict, contravene, cross, disaffirm, gainsay, impugn, negate, negative, traverse
rel decline, refuse, reject, repudiate; confute, controvert, disprove, rebut, refute; downface
con affirm, assert, aver; allow, grant; authenticate, corroborate, substantiate, validate, verify; avow, confess; claim, submit
ant concede; confirm

depart *vb* **1** *syn* see GO 2
rel set out, start, strike out, toddle
con linger, stay, tarry, wait; come; approach, near
ant arrive; abide, remain
2 *syn* see DIE 1
con exist, live, survive
3 *syn* see SWERVE 2
rel abandon, desert, forsake; reject, repudiate; cast, discard; differ, disagree, dissent, vary
4 *syn* see DIGRESS 2

departed *adj* **1** *syn* see DEAD 1
idiom called home, gone to a better land
2 *syn* see EXTINCT 2

departing *adj syn* see PARTING

departure *n* **1** the act of going, coming out, or leaving a place <the hasty *departure* of the refugees>
syn egress, egression, exit, exiting, exodus, offgoing, setting-out, withdrawal
rel going, leaving, quitting, retreat; decampment, flight; farewell, leave-taking
con coming, entering, ingress
ant arrival
2 *syn* see DEVIATION 1
rel rambling, straying, wandering

depend *vb syn* see HANG 1

depend (on *or* upon) *vb* **1** to rest or to be contingent upon something uncertain, variable, or indeterminable <our trip *depends* upon the weather>
syn hang (on *or* upon), hinge (on *or* upon), ‖pend, stand (on *or* upon), turn (on *or* upon)
rel base, bottom, found, ground, rest, stay
idiom hang in the balance
2 *syn* see RELY (on *or* upon)
rel incline, lean

dependable *adj* **1** *syn* see RELIABLE 1
rel assured, confident, sure; responsible; constant, faithful, loyal, staunch, steadfast, steady
idiom as good as one's word, to be counted on
con capricious, fickle, inconstant, mercurial, unstable; dishonest, lying, mendacious, untruthful
ant independable, undependable
2 *syn* see TRUE 9
3 *syn* see CERTAIN 3

dependence *n syn* see TRUST 1

dependent *adj* **1** determined or conditioned by another <a conclusion that is *dependent* on a premise>

syn conditional, contingent, relative, reliant

rel exposed, liable, open, subject, susceptible; iffy, provisional, provisory; uncertain; circumscribed, limited, restricted

con categorical, ultimate; boundless, eternal, illimitable, uncircumscribed; basal, basic, fundamental, primary, underived

ant absolute; infinite; original

2 *syn* see SUBORDINATE

rel counting, depending, reckoning, relying, trusting; accessory, ancillary, appurtenant; abased, debased, humbled

con principal; paramount, predominant, preponderant, preponderating, sovereign

ant independent

depict *vb syn* see REPRESENT 1

rel narrate, recite, recount, rehearse, relate, report, state; outline, sketch

depiction *n syn* see REPRESENTATION

deplete *vb* to bring to a low estate by depriving of something essential <an epidemic which *depletes* an army of manpower>

syn bankrupt, drain, draw, draw down, exhaust, impoverish, use up

rel cripple, debilitate, disable, enfeeble, sap, undermine, weaken; decrease, diminish, lessen, reduce; bleed, draw off, dry up, empty, milk; consume, expend, finish, spend, wash up

idiom dig into

con augment, enlarge, increase; bolster, fortify, strengthen; rebuild, repair, restore, revive

ant renew, replace

depleted *adj syn* see EFFETE 2

rel sapped, weakened

con augmented, enlarged, increased

deplorable *adj* of a kind to cause great distress <a *deplorable* loss of life>

syn afflictive, calamitous, dire, distressing, dolorous, grievous, heartbreaking, heartrending, lamentable, mournful, regrettable, unfortunate, woeful

rel awful, dreadful, terrible; horrifying, intolerable, overwhelming, sickening, unbearable; miserable, wretched; disastrous

idiom as bad as bad can be, as bad as can be

con beneficial, helpful, salutary; advantageous, favorable, propitious

deplore *vb* **1** to manifest grief or sorrow for something <*deplore* the death of a close friend>

syn bemoan, bewail, grieve, lament, moan, weep

rel deprecate, disapprove; mourn, sorrow; cry, keen, wail

con boast, brag, crow, vaunt; rejoice

2 *syn* see REGRET

depone *vb syn* see TESTIFY 2

deport *vb* **1** *syn* see BEHAVE 1

2 *syn* see BANISH

deportation *n syn* see EXILE 1

deportment *n* **1** *syn* see BEHAVIOR

2 *syn* see BEARING 1

depose *vb* **1** to remove from a throne or other high position <trying to *depose* the king in favor of his brother> <*deposed* industrial leaders>

syn dethrone, discrown, disenthrone, displace, disthrone, uncrown, unmake

rel overthrow, subvert, upset; chuck, dismiss, eject, oust, throw out

con inaugurate, induct, install, instate, invest; crown, enthrone, throne

2 *syn* see ASSERT 1

3 *syn* see TESTIFY 2

deposit *vb syn* see BANK

rel put by, store, stow

deposit *n syn* see SEDIMENT

depository *n syn* see DEPOT 2

depot *n* **1** *syn* see ARMORY

2 a place where something is deposited or stored <a gasoline *depot*>

syn arsenal, depository, magazine, repository, store, storehouse

rel storeroom, warehouse

3 *syn* see RAILROAD STATION

rel terminal, terminus

deprave *vb syn* see DEBASE 1

con elevate, ennoble, exalt, raise, uplift

depraved *adj* **1** *syn* see DEBASED

rel degenerate, infamous, vicious, villainous; degraded; twisted, warped

con scrupulous, upright

2 *syn* see VICIOUS 2

depravity *n syn* see VICE 1

deprecate *vb syn* see DISAPPROVE 1

rel bemoan, bewail, deplore, lament; derogate, detract

ant endorse

depreciate *vb* **1** to reduce the value of <*depreciate* the dollar>

syn cheapen, decry, devalorize, devaluate, devalue, downgrade, lower, mark down, soften, underprize, underrate, undervalue, write down, write off

rel depress; abate, decrease, diminish, dwindle, lessen, reduce; erode

con augment, increase; bloat, blow up, expand, inflate; amplify, magnify

ant appreciate

2 *syn* see DECRY 2

rel underestimate, underrate, undervalue; discountenance, disesteem, disfavor

con cherish, prize, treasure, value; comprehend, understand

ant appreciate

depreciation *n syn* see DETRACTION

depreciative *adj syn* see DEROGATORY

rel underestimating, underrating, undervaluing

ant appreciative

depreciatory *adj syn* see DEROGATORY

rel underestimating, underrating, undervaluing

ant appreciative

depredate *vb syn* see RAVAGE

depredator *n syn* see MARAUDER

depress *vb* **1** *syn* see LOWER 3

2 to lower in spirit or mood <the thought of all his debts *depressed* him>

---

syn synonym(s)   *rel* related word(s)
ant antonym(s)   *con* contrasted word(s)
idiom idiomatic equivalent(s)
‖ use limited; if in doubt, see a dictionary

syn oppress, press, sadden, weigh down
rel ail, distress, trouble; afflict, torment, try; contrist, deject, discourage, dishearten, dispirit; bother, disturb, perturb, upset
con delight, gladden, gratify, please, rejoice; excite, inspire, stimulate; brighten, cheer up, encourage; buoy, elevate
ant elate, exhilarate; cheer

depressant *adj syn* see GLOOMY 3

depressed *adj* **1** *syn* see DOWNCAST
rel lugubrious, melancholy
ant exhilarated; animated
2 *syn* see UNDERPRIVILEGED

depressing *adj* **1** *syn* see GLOOMY 3
con cheering, elevating, uplifting; exciting, inspiring
ant exhilarating
2 *syn* see SAD 2

depression *n* **1** *syn* see SADNESS
rel boredom, doldrums, ennui, tedium
con glee, hilarity, mirth
ant buoyancy; elation
2 a low spot <a *depression* in the land>
syn basin, concavity, dip, hollow, sag, sink, sinkage, sinkhole; *compare* NOTCH 1
rel cavity, hole, pocket, vacuity, vacuum, void; crater, pit; scoop
3 a period of lowered economic activity and extensive unemployment <indicators that warn of a coming *depression*>
syn recession, slump, stagnation
rel crash, decline, dislocation, drop; sag; paralysis; ‖stagflation
con expansion; booming, development, growth; advancement, progress
ant boom

depressive *adj syn* see GLOOMY 3

deprivation *n syn* see PRIVATION 2

deprive *vb* **1** *syn* see STRIP 2
2 to prevent one from possessing <to *deprive* a person of his civil rights>
syn bereave, disinherit, dispossess, divest, lose, oust, rob; *compare* STRIP 2
rel dock; bare, denude, dismantle, strip
con furnish, give, supply; clothe, endow, equip, fit (out), invest, outfit
ant provide

deprived *adj syn* see UNDERPRIVILEGED

deprivement *n syn* see PRIVATION 2

depth *n* **1** the perpendicular extent or measurement downward from a surface <measured the *depth* of the river>
syn deepness, drop
rel profoundness, profundity; lowness; sounding; draft
con shallowness; altitude, elevation
2 the quality of being profound (as in insight) or full (as of knowledge) <her answer showed she had great *depth* in that subject>
syn abyss, deepness, profoundness, profundity
rel sense, wisdom, wiseness; brain, intellect, intelligence; keenness, sharpness
con shallowness, superficiality, unprofoundness; sciolism, smatter, smattering

depthless *adj syn* see SUPERFICIAL 2

depurate *vb syn* see PURIFY 1

depute *vb syn* see DELEGATE

deputize *vb syn* see DELEGATE

deputy *n* **1** *syn* see AGENT 2
rel substitute, surrogate; replacement
2 *syn* see DELEGATE

derange *vb* **1** *syn* see DISORDER 1
rel perturb; discommode, incommode, inconvenience
con compose, settle
ant arrange; adjust
2 *syn* see UPSET 5
3 *syn* see MADDEN 1

deranged *adj syn* see INSANE 1
rel disarranged, disordered, disturbed

derangement *n syn* see INSANITY 1
rel disarrangement, disorder; confusion; disturbance; unsoundness

derelict *adj* **1** given up especially by the owner or occupant <a *derelict* old home>
syn abandoned, deserted, desolate, forsaken, lorn, solitary, uncouth
rel dilapidated, dingy, faded, run-down, seedy, shabby, threadbare
con cherished, prized, treasured; attended, kept up, maintained
2 *syn* see NEGLIGENT
rel irresponsible, undependable, unreliable, untrustworthy
con dependable, reliable, responsible, trustworthy; careful, heedful, thoughtful
ant faithful

derelict *n* **1** *syn* see OUTCAST
2 *syn* see VAGABOND

dereliction *n syn* see FAILURE 1
rel abuse, misuse, outrage
ant faithfulness

deride *vb syn* see RIDICULE
rel banter, chaff, jolly, kid, rag, rib

de rigueur *adj syn* see DECOROUS 1

derision *n syn* see LAUGHINGSTOCK

derivable *adj syn* see DEDUCTIVE

derivate *adj syn* see SECONDARY 2

derivation *n syn* see SOURCE

derivational *adj syn* see SECONDARY 2

derivative *adj syn* see SECONDARY 2
ant underivative

derivative *n syn* see OUTGROWTH 2

derive *vb* **1** to reach (as a conclusion) as an end point of reasoning and observation <evidence from which he *derived* a startling new set of axioms>
syn educe, evolve, excogitate
rel conclude, deduce, gather, infer, judge; arrive (at), elicit, extract, reach; develop, elaborate, formulate, put (together), work out
2 *syn* see INFER
3 *syn* see TAKE 14

derive (from) *vb syn* see SPRING 1

derived *adj syn* see SECONDARY 2

dernier cri *n syn* see FASHION 3

dernier ressort *n syn* see RESOURCE 3

derogate *vb syn* see DECRY 2

rel decrease, lessen, reduce; discredit, disgrace
con enhance, heighten, intensify

derogatory *adj* designed or tending to belittle <*derogatory* comments about the actor's performance>
syn depreciative, depreciatory, detracting, disadvantageous, disparaging, dyslogistic, pejorative, slighting, uncomplimentary
rel belittling, decrying, minimizing; aspersing, calumnious, defamatory, maligning, vilifying; degrading, demeaning, humiliating; despiteful, malevolent, malicious, spiteful; contumelious, disdainful, scornful
con admiring, esteeming; acclaiming, laudatory, praising; appreciative
ant complimentary

derout *vb syn* see ROUT 1

derriere *n syn* see BUTTOCKS

descant *n* **1** *syn* see MELODY
2 *syn* see SONG 2

descant *vb syn* see DISCOURSE 1

descend *vb* **1** *syn* see FALL 1
ant rise
2 *syn* see STOOP 2
3 *syn* see DETERIORATE 1

descendant *n* **1** **descendants** *pl syn* see OFFSPRING
ant ancestors, ascendants
2 *syn* see OUTGROWTH 2

descent *n* **1** the act or process of passing from a higher to a lower level or state <a parachute *descent*><his slow *descent* to the gutter>
syn drop, fall
rel plummeting, plunging, sinking
con rise, upswing, upturn; advance, headway, progress, progression; betterment, improvement
ant ascent
2 *syn* see COMEDOWN
3 *syn* see ANCESTRY
4 an inclination downward <the steep *descent* of the mountain>
syn decline, declivity, dip, drop, fall
rel downgrade, grade, gradient, incline, slope; drop, drop-off
con acclivity, upgrade, uphill
ant ascent, rise

describe *vb* **1** *syn* see RELATE 1
rel communicate, impart; transmit; construe, elucidate, explain, explicate, expound; exemplify, illustrate; characterize, distinguish
2 *syn* see REPRESENT 1

description *n* **1** *syn* see REPRESENTATION
2 a descriptive statement <a fascinating *description* of his adventures>
syn narration, recital, recountal, recounting
rel anecdote, narrative, story, tale, yarn; account, chronicle, version; report, statement
3 *syn* see TYPE

descry *vb* **1** *syn* see SEE 1
2 *syn* see FIND 1
rel appreciate, comprehend, understand; realize

desecrate *vb syn* see RAVAGE

desecrated *adj syn* see IMPURE 3

desecration *n syn* see PROFANATION
ant consecration

desensitize *vb syn* see DEADEN 1
ant sensitize

desert *n syn* see WASTE 1

desert *n usu* **deserts** *pl syn* see DUE 1
rel chastening, chastisement, discipline, disciplining, punishment
idiom just deserts

desert *vb* **1** *syn* see ABANDON 1
rel depart, go, leave
con adhere, cohere
ant cleave (to), stick (to)
2 *syn* see DEFECT
rel abscond, decamp, escape, flee, fly
idiom go over the hill
con abide, remain, stay

deserted *adj syn* see DERELICT 1
rel empty, vacant; uninhabited, unoccupied; bare, barren

desertion *n syn* see DEFECTION
rel perfidiousness, perfidy, treacherousness, treachery

deserve *vb syn* see EARN 2
rel gain, get, win; demand
idiom have it coming

deserved *adj syn* see JUST 3
ant undeserved

deserving *n syn* see DUE 1

deserving *adj syn* see WORTHY 1
ant undeserving

desexualize *vb syn* see STERILIZE

desiccate *vb* **1** *syn* see DRY 1
2 to drain or be drained of emotional or intellectual vitality <this book is *desiccated* by undue concentration on statistics>
syn devitalize, dry up
rel deplete, drain, exhaust; divest; decay, fade, shrivel, wither, wizen
con brighten, enliven

desiderate *vb syn* see DESIRE 1

desight *n syn* see EYESORE

design *vb* **1** *syn* see INTEND 2
2 *syn* see PLAN 2
rel delineate, diagram; create, invent; construct, fashion, form, frame, produce; contrive
con accomplish, achieve, effect, execute, fulfill, perform
3 to work out the arrangement of the parts of <*design* an urban center>
syn arrange, lay out, map (out), plan, set out; *compare* PLAN 2
rel delineate, diagram, draft, outline, sketch

design *n* **1** *syn* see PLAN 1
rel delineation, diagram, draft, outline, sketch, tracing; creation, invention
con accomplishment, achievement, execution, fulfillment, performance
2 *syn* see INTENTION

---

syn synonym(s)   *rel* related word(s)
ant antonym(s)   *con* contrasted word(s)
idiom idiomatic equivalent(s)
‖ use limited; if in doubt, see a dictionary

rel conation, volition, will; deliberation, reflection, thinking, thought; intrigue, machination, plot

con accident, chance, fortuity, hap; impulse

3 *syn* see FIGURE 3

4 *syn* see MAKEUP 1

designate *vb* **1** *syn* see NAME 1

2 to declare a person one's choice <*designated* him to fill the position>

syn appoint, finger, make, name, nominate, tap

rel choose, elect, opt, pick, select, single; assign, delegate, depute; dictate

con disapprove, disfavor, object (to), oppose; disallow, reject, turn down

3 to set aside (as funds) for a specific use <*designated* the income to be used for charity>

syn allocate, earmark

rel specify; appropriate, reserve; stipulate; allot, apportion, mete (out)

designation *n* *syn* see NAME 1

rel identification, recognition; classification, pigeonhole, pigeonholing

designative *adj* *syn* see INDICATIVE

designed *adj* *syn* see DELIBERATE 1

rel decided, determined, resolved

con casual, chance, contingent, fluky, fortuitous, incidental; impulsive, spontaneous; natural, normal, regular, typical

ant accidental

designedly *adv* *syn* see INTENTIONALLY

designless *adj* *syn* see RANDOM

desire *n* **1** a longing for something that promises enjoyment or satisfaction <he had a strong *desire* for fame and fortune>

syn appetite, appetition, craving, itch, lust, passion, urge

rel hankering, hunger, hungering, longing, pining, thirst, thirsting, yearning; desideratum, desiderium; avarice, cupidity, greed, rapacity; concupiscence, eros

con abhorrence, repellency, repugnance, repulsion; aversion, disfavor, dislike

ant distaste

2 *syn* see LUST 2

desire *vb* **1** to have a longing for something <women who *desire* success>

syn ‖choose, covet, crave, desiderate, want, wish

rel hanker, hunger, long, pine, thirst, yearn; enjoy, fancy, like; aim, aspire, pant

idiom set one's eyes (*or* heart) upon

con abhor, abominate, detest, hate, loath; decline, refuse, reject, repudiate, spurn

2 *syn* see ASK 2

desired *adj* *syn* see TRUE 7

desirous *adj* *syn* see COVETOUS

desist *vb* *syn* see STOP 3

rel abstain, forbear; abandon, relinquish, resign, yield

idiom have done with

con continue; persevere

ant persist

desistance *n* *syn* see END 2

desk *n* a table, frame, or case with a sloping or horizontal surface especially for writing <sat meditating at her *desk*>

syn escritoire, secretaire, secretary, writing desk

rel lectern, reading desk

desolate *adj* **1** *syn* see DERELICT 1

rel empty, vacant; uninhabited, unoccupied

2 *syn* see INCONSOLABLE

3 *syn* see GLOOMY 3

rel bare, barren; destitute, poor, poverty‑stricken; dark, murky

desolate *vb* *syn* see RAVAGE

despair *vb* to lose all hope or confidence <*despaired* of winning>

syn despond, give up

rel abandon, drop, relinquish, renounce, resign, surrender, yield

idiom lose heart (*or* courage *or* faith *or* hope)

con await, count (on), depend (on), hope, look (for); trust (in *or* to)

ant expect

despairing *adj* *syn* see DESPONDENT

rel atrabilious, melancholic, melancholy; cynical, misanthropic, pessimistic; depressed, oppressed, weighed down

con optimistic, roseate, rose-colored; assured, confident, sanguine, sure

ant hopeful

desperado *n* *syn* see OUTLAW

rel convict, criminal, lawbreaker

desperate *adj* **1** *syn* see DESPONDENT

rel foolhardy, rash, reckless, venturesome; headlong, precipitate; baffled, balked, circumvented, foiled, frustrated, outwitted, thwarted

con collected, composed, cool, nonchalant; assured, confident, sanguine, sure

2 *syn* see ACUTE 6

3 *syn* see INTENSE 1

4 *syn* see OUTRAGEOUS 2

despicable *adj* **1** *syn* see CONTEMPTIBLE

rel disgraceful, disreputable, ignominious, infamous, loathsome

con applaudable, commendable

ant laudable, praiseworthy

2 *syn* see BASE 3

despisable *adj* *syn* see CONTEMPTIBLE

despisal *n* *syn* see DESPITE 1

despise *vb* to regard as beneath one's notice and unworthy of consideration or interest <he had always *despised* the weak>

syn abhor, contemn, disdain, look down, scorn, scout

rel abominate, detest, execrate, hate, loathe; reject, repudiate, spurn; avoid, eschew, renounce, shun; disregard, ignore, overlook, slight, snub

idiom have no use for, look down one's nose at

con apprize, cherish, prize, treasure, value; admire, regard, respect

ant appreciate, esteem

despisement *n* *syn* see DESPITE 1

despite *n* **1** the feeling or attitude of despising <felt *despite* toward the lowly>

syn contempt, despisal, despisement, disdain, disparagement, scorn

rel disdainfulness, insolence, superciliousness; abhorrence, abomination, detestation, hate, hatred, loathing; rejection, repudiation, spurning;

aversion, disfavor, dislike, distaste; cold shoulder, rebuff, slight, snub; disgust, loathing
con admiration, esteem, honor, regard, respect; attraction, liking
2 syn see MALICE
rel contempt, disdain, scorn; abhorrence, abomination, detestation, hate, hatred, loathing
con admiration, esteem, respect; awe, fear, reverence
ant appreciation
3 syn see DEFIANCE 2
rel harm, hurt, injury
4 syn see AFFRONT
rel cut, discourtesy, incivility; rebuff, slight, snub
despite *prep syn* see AGAINST 4
despiteful *adj syn* see MALICIOUS
despitefulness *n syn* see MALICE
despoil *vb syn* see RAVAGE
despoiler *n* **1 syn** see MARAUDER
2 syn see VANDAL
despond *vb* **1 syn** see DESPAIR
rel droop, sag; languish
idiom reach the depths
con expect, hope, look
2 syn see MOPE 1
despondent *adj* having lost all or nearly all hope <*despondent* about his health>
syn despairing, desperate, desponding, forlorn, hopeless
rel grieving, mourning, sorrowful; dejected, depressed, melancholy, sad; disconsolate, dispirited, downcast, woebegone; discouraged, disheartened
con cheerful, glad, happy, joyful, joyous; buoyant, elastic, resilient, volatile; hopeful, optimistic
ant lighthearted
desponding *adj syn* see DESPONDENT
despot *n syn* see TYRANT
despotic *adj syn* see ABSOLUTE 4
despotism *n syn* see TYRANNY
despotize *vb syn* see TYRANNIZE
desquamate *vb syn* see SCALE 2
destine *vb syn* see PREDESTINE 1
destiny *n syn* see FATE
rel design, goal, intent, intention, objective
destitute *adj* **1 syn** see DEVOID
rel deficient; bankrupt, bankrupted, depleted, drained, exhausted; divested, stripped
con complete, full, replete
2 syn see POOR 1
rel depleted, drained, exhausted
idiom on one's uppers, on the rocks
con comfortable, prosperous, well-fixed, well-off, well-to-do
ant opulent
destituteness *n syn* see POVERTY 1
rel absence, dearth, lack; adversity, misfortune
con competence, sufficiency
ant opulence
destitution *n syn* see POVERTY 1
rel absence, dearth, lack, privation, want; adversity, misfortune
con competence, sufficiency

ant opulence
destroy *vb* **1** to bring to ruin <the army *destroyed* the enemy village><his health was finally *destroyed* by drink>
syn annihilate, atomize, decapitate, decimate, demolish, destruct, discreate, dismantle, dissolve, dynamite, pull down, pulverize, quench, raze, rub out, ruin, ‖ruinate, shatter, shoot, smash, tear down, unbuild, undo, unframe, unmake, wrack, wreck; *compare* TOTAL 3
rel abolish, extinguish; devastate, pillage, ravage, sack, waste; eradicate, exterminate, extirpate, wipe; mangle, mutilate; rubble; doom
idiom blow to bits, bring to an end, dispose of, tear to shreds
con establish, found, institute, organize; fabricate, fashion, forge, form, make, manufacture, shape; conserve, preserve, protect, save
2 syn see KILL 1
destroyer *n* **1 syn** see VANDAL
2 syn see DOWNFALL 2
destruct *vb syn* see DESTROY 1
destruction *n* **1 syn** see DOWNFALL 2
2 syn see RUIN 3
destructive *adj* having the capability, property, or effect of destroying <a *destructive* windstorm> <his brother was a *destructive* influence in his life>
syn annihilative, ruinous, shattering, wrackful, wreckful
rel calamitous, deadly, disastrous, fatal, lethal, mortal; consumptive; internecine; baneful, deleterious, detrimental
con creative, formative; harmless, innocuous, inoffensive; helpful, improving
ant constructive
desuetude *n* **1 syn** see END 2
2 syn see DISUSE
desultory *adj* **1 syn** see FITFUL
rel erratic; shifting, vagrant, wavering
con constant, invariable, unchanging, unfailing
ant steady
2 syn see RANDOM
rel fitful, spasmodic; disorderly, unmethodical, unsystematic; capricious, fickle, inconstant, mercurial
con orderly, systematic
ant assiduous; methodical
detach *vb* to remove one thing from another with which it is in union or association <*detach* sheets from a loose-leaf book>
syn abstract, disassociate, disconnect, disengage, dissociate, uncouple, unfix
rel cut off, divorce, part, separate, sever, sunder; disjoin, disunite; disassemble, dismantle, dismember, dismount; disaffiliate
idiom take apart
con fasten, fix; bind, tie; combine, conjoin, unite
ant affix, attach

---

syn synonym(s)   *rel* related word(s)
ant antonym(s)   *con* contrasted word(s)
idiom idiomatic equivalent(s)
‖ use limited; if in doubt, see a dictionary

detached *adj* **1** *syn* see ALONE 1
  rel separate, unconnected
  con abutting, adjacent; connected, joined, linked
  ant adjoining; attached
  2 *syn* see INDIFFERENT 2
  con anxious, concerned, solicitous; self-centered, selfish
  ant interested
  3 *syn* see NEUTRAL
  rel distant, remote, removed
detachment *n* *syn* see SEPARATION 1
detail *n* *syn* see POINT 1
  con anatomy, framework, skeleton, structure; bulk, mass; design, plan
detail *vb* *syn* see SPECIFY 3
detailed *adj* *syn* see CIRCUMSTANTIAL
  rel abundant, copious; exhausting, exhaustive, thoroughgoing
detailedly *adv* *syn* see THOROUGHLY 2
detain *vb* **1** *syn* see ARREST 2
  rel buttonhole, hold, restrain
  2 *syn* see KEEP 5
  3 *syn* see DELAY 1
  rel check, curb, inhibit, restrain
detect *vb* *syn* see FIND 1
detectable *adj* *syn* see PERCEPTIBLE
detection *n* *syn* see DISCOVERY
detective *n* one employed or engaged in detecting lawbreakers or in getting information that is not readily or publicly accessible <used *detectives* to locate the missing witness>
  syn dick, ‖eye, gumshoe, hawkshaw, investigator, plainclothesman, Sherlock, Sherlock Holmes, sleuth, ‖tec; *compare* INFORMER, PRIVATE DETECTIVE
  rel G-man; roper; shoofly; ‖nare
detention *n* *syn* see ARREST
  rel imprisonment, incarceration, internment
deter *vb* **1** *syn* see DISSUADE
  rel prevent; block, hinder, impede, obstruct; debar, shut out; frighten, scare; inhibit, restrain
  con abet, incite, instigate; excite, provoke, stimulate; actuate, motivate
  2 *syn* see PREVENT 2
deteriorate *vb* **1** to pass from a higher to a lower type or condition <the road quickly *deteriorated* into a bumpy path>
  syn decline, degenerate, descend, disimprove, disintegrate, retrograde, rot, sink, worsen
  rel crumble, decay, decompose; impair, mar, spoil; debilitate, undermine, weaken; depreciate, lessen
  idiom be the worse for wear, go downhill, go to pot (*or* the dogs)
  con better, improve; advance, progress; enhance, heighten
  ant ameliorate
  2 *syn* see FAIL 1
deterioration *n* **1** a falling from a higher to a lower level (as of quality or character) <the *deterioration* of business during the depression>
  syn atrophy, decadence, declension, declination, decline, degeneracy, degeneration, dégrin-

golade, devaluation, devolution, downfall, downgrade, ruin
  rel impairment, spoiling; crumbling, decay, decaying, decomposition, disintegration, dissolution, dry rot, rotting; debasement, degradation; depreciation, lessening; dislocation, disruption
  con betterment, help; enhancement, heightening, improvement
  ant amelioration
  2 *syn* see FAILURE 4
  con convalescence, recovering, recuperation
  ant improvement
determinable *adj* *syn* see TERMINABLE
determinant *n* *syn* see CAUSE 1
  rel factor; authority, influence, weight
determinate *adj* **1** *syn* see INFLEXIBLE 3
  2 *syn* see DEFINITE 1
  ant indeterminate
determinate *vb* *syn* see IDENTIFY
determination *n* **1** *syn* see DECISION 1
  2 *syn* see DECISION 2
  ant indetermination
determine *vb* **1** *syn* see ESTABLISH 6
  rel fix, set; settle
  2 *syn* see PREDESTINE 1
  3 *syn* see DEMARCATE 1
  4 *syn* see DECIDE
  rel bias, dispose, incline, predispose; actuate, drive, impel, move; induce, persuade
  5 *syn* see CLOSE 3
  6 *syn* see DISCOVER 3
determined *adj* *syn* see DECIDED 2
  rel earnest, purposeful, serious; unfaltering, unhesitating, unwavering
  con unresolved, unsettled; hesitant, hesitating, wavering
  ant undetermined
detest *vb* *syn* see HATE
  rel reject, repudiate, spurn
  con love; appreciate, treasure, value
  ant adore
detestable *adj* *syn* see HATEFUL 2
  rel sorry; atrocious, heinous, monstrous, outrageous
  ant adorable
detestation *n* **1** *syn* see ABOMINATION 2
  rel antipathy, disgust
  con affection, attachment, love; forbearance, indulgence, tolerance
  ant adoration
  2 *syn* see ABOMINATION 1
  ant adoration
dethrone *vb* *syn* see DEPOSE 1
  ant enthrone, throne
detonate *vb* *syn* see EXPLODE 1
detour *n* an indirect course often temporarily replacing part of a usual route <a *detour* around road construction> <took a *detour* to show him the lake>
  syn roundabout, runaround
  rel bypass
detour *vb* *syn* see SKIRT 2
detract (from) *vb* *syn* see DECRY 2

rel libel, slander; decrease, lessen, reduce
con enhance, heighten, intensify

detracting *adj* **1** *syn* see DEROGATORY
2 *syn* see LIBELOUS

detraction *n* the expression of damaging or malicious opinions <his persistent *detraction* of his rival's motives was wholly unfair>
syn backbiting, backstabbing, belittlement, calumny, character assassination, defamation, depreciation, disparagement, scandal, slander, sycophancy, tale
rel damage, harm, hurt, injury; injustice, wrong; aspersion, calumniation, libel, libeling, maligning, slandering, traducing, vilification
con enhancement, heightening, laudation, praise; approbation, approval
ant commendation

detractive *adj* *syn* see LIBELOUS

detractory *adj* *syn* see LIBELOUS

detriment *n* *syn* see DISADVANTAGE
rel damage, harm, hurt, injury, mischief; impairment, marring, spoiling
ant advantage, benefit

detrimental *adj* *syn* see HARMFUL
con aiding, helpful, helping; harmless
ant beneficial
2 *syn* see ADVERSE 2

de trop *adj* *syn* see SUPERFLUOUS

detruncate *vb* *syn* see TOP 1

deuced *adj* *syn* see UTTER

‖**deval** *vb* *syn* see STOP 3

devalorize *vb* *syn* see DEPRECIATE 1

devaluate *vb* *syn* see DEPRECIATE 1

devaluation *n* *syn* see DETERIORATION 1

devalue *vb* *syn* see DEPRECIATE 1

devast *vb* *syn* see RAVAGE

devastate *vb* *syn* see RAVAGE

devastation *n* *syn* see RUIN 3

‖**devel** *vb* *syn* see STRIKE 2

develop *vb* **1** *syn* see EXPAND 4
2 *syn* see UNFOLD 3
rel actualize, materialize, realize
3 *syn* see MATURE
rel dilate, expand; enroot, establish; flourish, prosper, thrive
con shrivel, wither, wizen
4 to come to have usually gradually <*develop* a taste for dry wine>
syn acquire, form
rel gain, get, obtain; achieve, attain, reach
5 *syn* see HAPPEN 1

development *n* progressive advance from a lower or simpler to a higher or more complex form <*development* of a seed into a plant><*development* of an industry>
syn evolution, evolvement, flowering, growth, progress, progression, unfolding, upgrowth
rel advance, advancement, ongoing
con decadence, declension, degeneration, deterioration, devolution
ant decline

deviant *adj* **1** *syn* see ABNORMAL 1
con normal; natural
2 *syn* see IRREGULAR 1

deviate *vb* **1** *syn* see SWERVE 2
2 *syn* see ERR
idiom deviate from the path of virtue

deviation *n* **1** departure from a course or procedure or from a norm or standard <no *deviation* from traditional methods was permitted>
syn aberration, deflection, departure, divergence, diversion, turning
rel alteration, change, modification, variation; breach, transgression, violation; anomaly, failing, fault; blunder, error, lapse
con accordance, agreement, conformance, conformity, correspondence
2 *syn* see TURN 2

deviative *adj* *syn* see ABNORMAL 1

device *n* **1** *syn* see TRICK 1
2 something (as a mechanical device) that performs a function or effects a desired end <invented many handy household *devices*>
syn contraption, contrivance; *compare* GADGET 1
rel appliance, implement, instrument, tool, utensil; apparatus, machine, mechanism; expedient, makeshift, resort, resource, shift; creation, invention; dingus, doohickey, hickey, thingumbob
3 *syn* see FIGURE 3
rel attribute, emblem, symbol, type; insignia, motto

deviceful *adj* *syn* see INVENTIVE

devil *n* **1** *often cap* the personal supreme spirit of evil and unrighteousness in Jewish and Christian theology
syn Apollyon, Beelzebub, ‖Cloot(s), ‖Clootie, diablo, fiend, Lord Harry, Lucifer, Old Gooseberry, Old Nick, Old Scratch, Satan, serpent
rel cacodemon; dybbuk
idiom Prince of Darkness
2 an extremely and malignantly wicked person <he was a *devil* who would stop at nothing to get what he wanted>
syn Archfiend, demon, fiend, Satan, succubus; *compare* SCAMP, VILLAIN 1
rel blackguard, caitiff, knave; scoundrel, villain; beast, brute
3 *syn* see SCAMP

‖**devil–devil** *n* *syn* see SPELL

‖**devil–dodger** *n* *syn* see CLERGYMAN

deviling *n* *syn* see IMP 1

devilish *adj* **1** *syn* see FIENDISH
rel iniquitous, nefarious, villainous; accursed, cursed, damnable, execrable; bad, evil, wicked
ant angelic
2 *syn* see SATANIC 1

devilkin *n* *syn* see IMP 1

devil–may–care *adj* *syn* see WILD 7
rel rash, reckless
con careful, heedful, responsible, thoughtful

devilment *n* *syn* see MISCHIEVOUSNESS

devilry *n* *syn* see MISCHIEVOUSNESS

---

syn synonym(s)   *rel* related word(s)
ant antonym(s)   *con* contrasted word(s)
idiom idiomatic equivalent(s)
‖ use limited; if in doubt, see a dictionary

‖**devil's–bones** *n pl syn* see DICE
deviltry *n syn* see MISCHIEVOUSNESS
devious *adj* **1** *syn* see OBSCURE 2
  2 *syn* see CROOKED 1
  rel deviating, digressing, diverting
  ant straightforward
  3 *syn* see ERRATIC 1
  4 *syn* see ERRANT 2
  rel artful, crafty, cunning, foxy, insidious, sly, tricky
  5 *syn* see UNDERHAND
  ant straightforward
devise *n syn* see LEGACY 1
devise *vb* **1** *syn* see PLAN 2
  2 *syn* see CONTRIVE 2
  rel create, discover; forge, form, shape; design
  3 *syn* see PLOT
  4 *syn* see WILL
devitalize *vb syn* see DESICCATE 2
  rel deprive; eviscerate, weaken
  ant vitalize
devoid *adj* showing a want or lack <a poem *devoid* of worth>
  syn destitute, empty, innocent, void
  rel bare, barren; lacking, wanting; deficient
  con filled, full; furnished, provided, supplied
  ant replete
devoir *n* **1** *syn* see OBLIGATION 2
  2 *syn* see TASK 1
devolution *n syn* see DETERIORATION 1
  rel regression, regressiveness, retrogression, retrogressiveness; receding, recession, retrogradation, retrograding
  con development; progress, progression
  ant evolution
devote *vb* **1** to set apart for a particular and often a better or higher use or end <a woman who *devotes* her life to helping others>
  syn consecrate, dedicate, hallow
  rel sanctify, vow; commit, confide, consign, entrust
  idiom set apart
  2 *syn* see GIVE 1
  3 *syn* see ADDRESS 3
  rel attempt, endeavor, strive, struggle, try; employ, use, utilize
devote (to) *vb syn* see HABITUATE 2
  rel attach, wrap (up)
devoted *adj syn* see LOVING
  rel constant, faithful, loyal, true; thoughtful; fervid, zealous
devotee *n* **1** *syn* see ADDICT
  2 *syn* see AMATEUR 1
devotion *n* **1** *syn* see FIDELITY 1
  rel enthusiasm, fervor, passion, zeal; affection, attachment, love; consecration, dedication, devotement
  2 *syn* see LOVE 1
devour *vb* **1** *syn* see EAT 1
  2 *syn* see EAT UP 1
  idiom eat like a horse, eat one's head off
  3 *syn* see CONSUME 1
  4 *syn* see RAVAGE
  rel demolish, destroy; ruin, wreck; dissipate, squander

5 to exhibit avid interest in or enjoyment of <the crowd *devoured* the lurid scene>
  syn ‖eat up
  rel delight (in), enjoy, rejoice (in), relish, revel (in); feast (on), gloat (over *or* on)
  con avoid, eschew, shun
devout *adj* showing fervor in the practice of religion <a *devout* churchgoer>
  syn godly, holy, pietistic, pious, prayerful, religious
  rel ardent, fervent, fervid, zealous; adoring, revering, venerating, worshiping
  con impious, irreligious, ungodly, unholy; irreverent; apostate, backsliding
  ant undevout
dexter *adj syn* see FAVORABLE 5
  ant sinister
dexterity *n* **1** *syn* see ADDRESS 1
  rel adeptness, skillfulness; effortlessness, smoothness
  con awkwardness, maladroitness
  ant clumsiness
  2 *syn* see ART 1
dexterous *adj* **1** ready and skilled in physical movements <a *dexterous* worker>
  syn adroit, clever, deft, handy, neat-handed, nimble
  rel agile; adept, expert, masterly, proficient, skilled, skillful; easy, effortless, facile, smooth
  con awkward, gauche, inept, maladroit
  ant clumsy
  2 *syn* see CLEVER 4
dexterousness *n syn* see ADDRESS 1
  ant clumsiness
dextrorotatory *adj syn* see RIGHT-HANDED
  ant levorotatory
diablerie *n* **1** *syn* see MISCHIEVOUSNESS
  2 *syn* see EVIL 3
diablo *n syn* see DEVIL 1
diabolic *adj* **1** *syn* see SATANIC 1
  2 *syn* see FIENDISH
  rel evil, ill, wicked
  ant angelic
diabolism *n syn* see SATANISM
diabolonian *adj syn* see FIENDISH
diacritic *adj syn* see CHARACTERISTIC
diagnose *vb syn* see IDENTIFY
diagnostic *adj syn* see CHARACTERISTIC
diagnosticate *vb syn* see IDENTIFY
diagonal *adj* between horizontal and vertical in direction <cloth with a *diagonal* stripe>
  syn bevel, beveled, bias, biased, slanted, slanting; *compare* INCLINED 3
diagonally *adv* in a line running across from corner to corner <decided to place the couch *diagonally* at the end of the room>
  syn catercorner (*or* catty-corner *or* kitty-corner), cornerwise, slantingways, slantways, slantwise, ‖slaunchways
  idiom on the bias
  con parallelly, square, straight
‖**dial** *n syn* see FACE 1
dial *vb syn* see TUNE 3
dialect *n* **1** *syn* see LANGUAGE 1

2 a form of language that is not recognized as standard <the Doric *dialect* of ancient Greece>
syn argot, cant, jargon, lingo, patois, patter, slang, vernacular; *compare* TERMINOLOGY, VERNACULAR 3
rel localism, provincialism, regionalism

dialectic *n syn* see ARGUMENTATION

dialogue *n* **1** *syn* see CONVERSATION 1
2 *syn* see CONVERSATION 2

diametric *adj syn* see OPPOSITE

diapason *n* **1** *syn* see MELODY
2 *syn* see RANGE 5

diaphanous *adj syn* see FILMY

diarrhea *n* abnormally frequent intestinal evacuations with more or less fluid stools <they were taken with severe *diarrhea*>
syn ‖backdoor trots, dysentery, flux, Montezuma's revenge, ‖runs, scour(s), ‖squirts, summer complaint, ‖trots
idiom Montezuma's revenge, summer complaint

diatribe *n syn* see TIRADE

‖**dibs** *n pl* **1** *syn* see MONEY
2 *syn* see CLAIM 1

dice *n pl, sing* **die** a pair or set of small cubes marked on each face with from one to six spots and used in various games and in gambling by being shaken and thrown to come to rest at random <staked everything on a cast of the *dice*>
syn ‖African dominoes, bones, ‖cubes, ‖devil's bones, ‖ivory, ‖tats

dice *vb syn* see DISCARD

dicey *adj syn* see UNCERTAIN 1

dichotomize *vb syn* see SEPARATE 1

dick *n* **1** *syn* see DETECTIVE

dicker *vb syn* see HAGGLE 2

dickey *adj syn* see WEAK 2

dictate *vb* to promulgate expressly something to be followed, observed, obeyed, or accepted <the commission *dictated* the policies to be followed>
syn decree, impose, lay down, ordain, prescribe, set
rel control, direct, manage; guide, lead; govern, rule; say, tell, utter; bid, charge, command, enjoin, instruct, order

dictate *n syn* see COMMAND 1

dictative *adj syn* see DICTATORIAL

dictator *n syn* see TYRANT

dictatorial *adj* imposing one's will or opinions on others <the chief was inclined to be *dictatorial* with his subordinates>
syn authoritarian, authoritative, dictative, doctrinaire, dogmatic, magisterial; *compare* TOTALITARIAN 1
rel bossy, domineering, imperative, imperious, masterful, peremptory; absolute, arbitrary, autocratic, despotic, tyrannical; arrogant, haughty, overbearing, proud; firm, stern
con amenable, biddable, docile, obedient, tractable; menial, obsequious, servile, slavish, subservient

dictatorship *n syn* see TYRANNY

diction *n syn* see WORDING

dictionary *n syn* see TERMINOLOGY

dictum *n syn* see MAXIM

‖**dicty** *adj syn* see SNOBBISH

didactic *adj* overburdened with instruction and the proprieties <his speech to the new freshmen was painfully *didactic*>
syn moral, moralizing, preachy, schoolmasterish, sermonic, sermonizing, teachy
rel advisory, exhortative, hortative; preceptive
ant undidactic

‖**didder** *vb syn* see SHAKE 1

diddle *vb* **1** *syn* see IDLE
2 *syn* see CHEAT

diddle–daddle *vb syn* see IDLE

diddler *n syn* see SWINDLER

dido *n* **1** *usu* **didoes** *pl syn* see PRANK
2 *syn* see KNICKKNACK

die *vb* **1** to pass from physical life <he *died* at an advanced age>
syn cash in, ‖check out, conk, ‖cop out, ‖croak, decease, demise, depart, drop, expire, go, ‖kick in, ‖kick off, pass, pass away, pass out, peg out, perish, pip, pop off, ‖snuff (out), succumb, ‖swelt
idiom be gathered to one's fathers, bite the dust (*or* ground), breathe one's last, cash in one's checks (*or* chips), give up the ghost, ‖kick the bucket, ‖kick up one's heels, meet one's end, shuffle off this mortal coil, ‖snuff it, turn up one's toes (to the daisies)
con be, exist, subsist; flourish, thrive
ant live
2 *syn* see PERISH 2

die (down *or* away) *vb syn* see ABATE 4
rel recede; disappear
con ascend, mount, rise
ant come up

die *n* **1** *see* DICE
‖**2** *syn* see TOY 2

die–away *adj syn* see LANGUID

diehard *n* **1** an irreconcilable opponent of change <party *diehards* who would make no concessions>
syn bitter-ender, conservative, fundamentalist, old liner, praetorian, pullback, right, rightist, right wing, right-winger, standpat, standpatter, tory; *compare* REACTIONARY
rel mossback, old fogy, stick-in-the-mud; intransigent; true blue; right-center
con liberal, progressive, radical
2 *syn* see REACTIONARY

die–hard *adj syn* see CONSERVATIVE 1

differ *vb* **1** to be unlike or distinct in nature, form, or characteristics <the houses *differ* only in a few minor details>
syn disagree, vary
rel depart, deviate, diverge
con accord, conform, correspond
ant agree
2 to be of unlike or opposite opinion <men who *differ* on religious matters>

---

syn synonym(s)   *rel* related word(s)
ant antonym(s)   *con* contrasted word(s)
idiom idiomatic equivalent(s)
‖ use limited; if in doubt, see a dictionary

syn disaccord, disagree, discord, dissent, divide, vary

rel clash, conflict, jar; bicker, quarrel, squabble; argue, debate, dispute; oppose, protest (against)

idiom differ in opinion, hold opposite views

con coincide, concert, concur, harmonize; accord, conform, correspond

ant agree

difference *n* **1** *syn* see DISSIMILARITY

rel modification, variation

con equivalence, equivalency, sameness

ant resemblance

2 *syn* see DISCORD

rel clash, conflict

3 *syn* see VARIANCE 1

difference *vb* *syn* see KNOW 4

different *adj* **1** unlike in kind or character <could hardly be more *different*>

syn disparate, dissimilar, distant, divergent, diverse, other, otherwise, unalike, unequal, unlike, unsimilar, various

rel particular, single; distinctive, individual, peculiar; divers, sundry

con akin, analogous, comparable, like, parallel, similar, uniform; equal, equivalent, self-same

ant alike, identical, same

2 *syn* see DISTINCT 1

differential *adj* *syn* see DISCRIMINATORY

differentiate *vb* *syn* see KNOW 4

rel comprehend, understand

con confound, mistake

ant confuse

differently *adv* *syn* see OTHERWISE 1

difficile *adj* *syn* see HARD 6

difficult *adj* *syn* see HARD 6

rel problem, problematic

idiom easier said than done, no picnic, tough sledding

ant simple

difficultly *adv* *syn* see HARD 8

difficulty *n* **1** something obstructing one's course and demanding effort and endurance if one's end is to be attained <she encountered great *difficulties* on her way to success>

syn asperity, hardness, hardship, rigor, vicissitude

rel impediment, obstacle, obstruction, snag; dilemma, fix, jam, pickle, plight, predicament, quandary, scrape; emergency, exigency, pass, pinch, strait; bother, inconvenience, problem, trouble

idiom hard nut to crack, hard row to hoe, heavy sledding

2 *syn* see DEMUR 2

3 *syn* see QUARREL

diffident *adj* *syn* see SHY 1

rel blenching, flinching, shrinking; hesitant, reluctant

con assured, presumptuous, sanguine, sure; self-assured, self-confident, self-possessed, self-reliant; brazen, impudent, shameless

ant confident

difform *adj* *syn* see LOPSIDED

diffuse *adj* *syn* see WORDY

rel exuberant, lavish, profuse; casual, desultory, random; lax, loose, slack; lengthy, long

con concentrated; condensed

ant succinct

diffuse *vb* **1** *syn* see SPREAD 1

rel extend; expand

con compact, consolidate; center, centralize, focus

ant concentrate

2 *syn* see INTERFUSE 2

dig *vb* **1** to loosen and turn over or remove (as soil) with or as if with a spade <*dig* for potatoes> <*dug* through her drawer looking for the scarf>

syn ‖delve, excavate, grub, shovel, spade

rel quarry; enter, penetrate, pierce, probe; dig up, root, rootle, root out

2 to form by digging <*dig* a trench>

syn dig out, excavate, scoop, shovel, spade

3 *syn* see THRUST 2

‖**4** *syn* see RESIDE 1

5 *syn* see POKE 1

‖**6** *syn* see APPREHEND 1

7 *syn* see ENJOY 1

dig (into) *vb* *syn* see EXPLORE

dig *n* **1** *syn* see POKE 1

2 *syn* see SITE 3

digest *n* *syn* see COMPENDIUM 1

rel abridgment, synopsis

digest *vb* **1** *syn* see BEAR 10

2 *syn* see EPITOMIZE 1

digit *n* *syn* see NUMBER

dignification *n* *syn* see APOTHEOSIS 2

dignify *vb* *syn* see EXALT 1

con abase, debase

ant demean

dignitary *n* *syn* see NOTABLE 1

dignity *n* **1** *syn* see STATUS 2

2 *syn* see DECORUM 1

rel excellence, merit, perfection, virtue; ethicalness, ethics, morality, nobility, nobleness

con impropriety, indecency, indecorum, unseemliness

3 *syn* see ELEGANCE

rel augustness, grandeur, grandness, magnificence, majesty, nobility, nobleness; address, poise

dig out *vb* **1** *syn* see DIG 2

2 *syn* see RUMMAGE 3

digress *vb* **1** *syn* see SWERVE 2

2 to turn aside from the main subject of attention or course of argument <he *digressed* into too many side issues>

syn depart, divagate, diverge, excurse, ramble, stray, wander

rel drift, roam

idiom get off the subject, go off on a tangent

con advance, proceed, progress

digression *n* a departure from a subject or theme <a *digression* from the main point of the speech>

syn aside, discursion, divagation, excursion, excursus, parenthesis

rel episode, excurse, incident, underaction; deflection, deviation, divergence; departure; drifting, rambling, straying, wandering

||**dike** (out *or* up) *vb syn* see DRESS UP 1

dilapidate *vb syn* see RUIN 2
  rel crumble, decay, decompose, disintegrate; disregard, forget, ignore, neglect, overlook, slight
  con mend, rebuild, repair; rejuvenate, renew, renovate, restore

dilapidated *adj syn* see SHABBY 1
  rel damaged, impaired, injured, marred; crumbled, decayed

dilate *vb syn* see EXPAND 3
  rel augment, enlarge, increase; extend, lengthen, prolong, protract; broaden, widen
  con compress, condense, contract, shrink; attenuate
  ant circumscribe; constrict

dilate (on *or* upon) *vb syn* see DISCOURSE 1
  rel describe, narrate, recite, recount, rehearse, relate
  con abbreviate, abridge, curtail, shorten

dilatory *adj syn* see SLOW 2
  rel lax, neglectful, negligent, remiss, slack
  con assiduous, busy, industrious, sedulous; prompt, quick, ready; hasty, impetuous, precipitate
  ant diligent

dilemma *n syn* see PREDICAMENT
  rel bewilderment, mystification, perplexity
  idiom horns of a dilemma

dilettante *n* **1** *syn* see CONNOISSEUR
  2 *syn* see AMATEUR 2

dilettante *adj syn* see AMATEURISH

dilettantish *adj syn* see AMATEURISH

dilettantist *adj syn* see AMATEURISH

diligent *adj syn* see ASSIDUOUS
  rel persevering, persistent, persisting; unflagging
  con deliberate, laggard, leisurely, slow; desultory
  ant dilatory

||**dilly** *adj syn* see FOOLISH 2

||**dilly** *n* one that is remarkable or extraordinary of its kind <came up with a *dilly* of an idea to sell the product>
  syn ||corker, crackerjack, ||daisy, dandy, ||dinger, ||doozer, humdinger, jim-dandy, knockout, ||lalapalooza, ||lulu, nifty, peach, ||pip, pippin, ripper, ripsnorter, rouser

dilly *vb syn* see DELAY 2

dillydally *vb syn* see DELAY 2

dilute *vb* to make less strong or concentrated <*dilute* acid>
  syn cut, thin, weaken
  rel moderate, qualify, temper; deliquesce, liquefy; alter, modify
  con enrich, fortify, richen, upgrade; condense, densify, evaporate, thicken
  ant concentrate

dilute *adj* of relatively low strength or concentration <*dilute* acid>
  syn diluted, thin, washy, watered-down, waterish, watery, weak
  rel reduced; adulterated, sophisticated; impaired, impoverished, weakened

  con condensed, densified, thickened
  ant concentrated

diluted *adj syn* see DILUTE
  ant concentrated

dim *adj* **1** *syn* see DARK 1
  ant bright
  2 *syn* see DULL 7
  ||**3** *syn* see DULL 9
  4 *syn* see FAINT 2
  con manifest, plain
  ant distinct

dim *vb* **1** *syn* see OBSCURE
  2 *syn* see DULL 1
  3 *syn* see DULL 4

dime novel *n* a usually paperback melodramatic novel <read mostly *dime novels*>
  syn dreadful, penny dreadful, shilling shocker, shocker, yellowback
  rel bloodcurdler, chiller, ||killer-diller; thriller; pulp

dimension *n* **1** *usu* dimensions *pl syn* see SIZE 1
  2 *usu* dimensions *pl syn* see RANGE 2

dimensionality *n syn* see SIZE 1

diminish *vb* **1** *syn* see ABRIDGE 1
  2 *syn* see DECREASE
  rel ebb, subside, wane; moderate, temper; attenuate, extenuate
  con aggravate, enhance, heighten, intensify
  3 *syn* see DECRY 2

diminutive *adj syn* see TINY

||**dimmet** *n syn* see EVENING 1

dimple *vb syn* see RIPPLE

||**dimps** *n syn* see EVENING 1

||**dimpsy** *n syn* see EVENING 1

dim–sighted *adj syn* see PURBLIND

dimwit *n syn* see DUNCE

dim–witted *adj syn* see RETARDED
  con alert, keen

din *n* a welter of discordant sounds <the *din* of a machine shop>
  syn babel, brouhaha, ||chirm, clamor, hubbub, hullabaloo, jangle, music, pandemonium, racket, racketry, tintamarre, tumult, uproar; *compare* COMMOTION 4
  rel blatancy, boisterousness, clamorousness, stridency; bedlam; clangor, clatter, rattle; clash, percussion; ||row; noise, sound
  con calm, lull, quietude, stillness; concord, consonance, harmony; melody, musicality, tunefulness

diner *n syn* see EATING HOUSE

||**dinero** *n syn* see MONEY

ding *vb* **1** *syn* see STRIKE 2
  2 *syn* see SURPASS 1

||**ding** *n syn* see BLOW 1

ding–a–ling *n syn* see CRACKPOT

dingdong *adv syn* see HARD 3

dinge *n syn* see SADNESS

---

syn synonym(s)   *rel* related word(s)
ant antonym(s)   *con* contrasted word(s)
idiom idiomatic equivalent(s)
|| use limited; if in doubt, see a dictionary

‖**dinger** *n syn* ‖DILLY, ‖corker, crackerjack, ‖daisy, dandy, humdinger, jim-dandy, knockout, ‖lalapalooza, ‖lulu

dingus *n syn* see DOODAD

dingy *adj syn* see SHABBY 1
  rel grimed, smirched, soiled, sullied, tarnished; dull; dusky, gloomy, murky
  con bright, brilliant, luminous, shining; clean, cleanly

dining table *n syn* see TABLE 1

dinky *adj syn* see MINOR 2

‖**dinky–di** *adj syn* see FAITHFUL 1

dinner *n* a usually elaborate meal served to guests or a group often to mark an occasion or honor an individual <the annual club *dinner*>
  syn banquet, feast, regale, spread
  rel ‖blowout, festival, fete, junket; breakfast, collation, luncheon

dinner table *n syn* see TABLE 1

dinosauric *adj syn* see HUGE

‖**dinsome** *adj syn* see VOCIFEROUS

dint *n syn* see POWER 4

dip *vb* **1** to plunge or thrust momentarily or partially under the surface of a liquid <*dip* a dress in cleansing fluid>
  syn douse, duck, dunk, immerse, souse, submerge, submerse
  rel pitch, plunge
  2 to lift a portion of by reaching below the surface with something shaped to hold liquid <*dip* drinking water from a spring>
  syn bail, lade, ladle, scoop
  rel dish, spoon; bucket (up *or* out), draw
  ‖**3** *syn* see PAWN
  4 *syn* see DUCK 2
  5 *syn* see PLUMMET
  6 *syn* see SET 12
  7 *syn* see SWERVE 1

dip (into) *vb syn* see BROWSE

dip *n* **1** *syn* see DESCENT 4
  2 *syn* see DECLINE 3
  3 *syn* see DEPRESSION 2
  ‖**4** *syn* see PICKPOCKET

diplomacy *n syn* see TACT

diplomatic *adj syn* see TACTFUL
  rel bland, smooth; courteous, polite; astute, shrewd; artful, crafty, guileful, wily
  ant undiplomatic

‖**dippy** *adj syn* see FOOLISH 2

‖**dipsy–doodle** *n syn* see DECEPTION 1

dire *adj* **1** *syn* see FEARFUL 3
  2 *syn* see DEPLORABLE
  rel depressing, oppressing
  3 *syn* see OMINOUS
  4 *syn* see PRESSING
  5 *syn* see ACUTE 6

direct *vb* **1** *syn* see ADDRESS 6
  2 to turn something toward its appointed or intended mark or goal <*directed* her eyes to the door>
  syn address, aim, cast, head, incline, lay, level, point, present, set, train, turn, zero (in)
  rel beam; divert; fasten, focus
  3 *syn* see ADDRESS 3

  rel fix, set, settle
  con deflect, divert; deviate, digress, diverge, swerve
  4 *syn* see GUIDE
  ant misdirect
  5 *syn* see GOVERN 3
  6 *syn* see CONDUCT 3
  7 *syn* see COMMAND
  rel assign, define, prescribe

direct *adj* **1** being or passing in a straight line of descent from parent to offspring <*direct* ancestors>
  syn lineal
  2 admitting free or continuous passage <a *direct* route to the beach>
  syn straight, straightforward, through, uninterrupted
  rel linear; continuous, unbroken, undeviating, unswerving
  con circuitous, roundabout
  ant indirect
  3 *syn* see FRANK
  ant devious
  4 marked by absence of an intervening agency, instrumentality, or influence <he had no *direct* knowledge of the crime>
  syn firsthand, immediate, primary
  rel contiguous, next, proximate
  ant indirect

direct *adv* **1** *syn* see DIRECTLY 1
  2 *syn* see VERBATIM

direction *n* **1** *syn* see VIEWPOINT 2

directive *n* **1** *syn* see EDICT 1
  2 *syn* see MEMORANDUM 2
  3 *syn* see MESSAGE 1

directly *adv* **1** without deviation of course <the turnpike runs *directly* east and west>
  syn dead, direct, due, right, straight, straightly, undeviatingly
  idiom as the crow flies, in a beeline
  con circuitously, deviously, round about; discursively, ramblingly
  ant indirectly
  2 *syn* see VERBATIM
  3 *syn* see IMMEDIATELY 1
  4 *syn* see AWAY 3
  5 *syn* see PRESENTLY 1

direful *adj* **1** *syn* see FEARFUL 3
  2 *syn* see OMINOUS

dirt *n* **1** *syn* see EARTH 2
  2 *syn* see DECEPTION 1

dirt poor *adj syn* see POOR 1

dirty *adj* **1** soiled or begrimed with dirt <wash those *dirty* hands>
  syn black, dungy, filthy, foul, grimy, grubby, grungy, impure, mucky, murky, nasty, soily, sordid, squalid, unclean, uncleanly
  rel contaminated, defiled, polluted, tainted; dreggy; draggled, draggletailed, draggly
  idiom dirty as a pig
  con immaculate, spotless; unsoiled, unspotted, unsullied
  ant clean
  2 *syn* see IMPURE 1

ant clean
3 *syn* see OBSCENE 2
4 *syn* see WILD 6
dirty *vb* **1** *syn* see SOIL 2
ant clean
2 *syn* see TAINT 1
idiom dirty one's hands
disability *n syn* see DISADVANTAGE
disable *vb* **1** *syn* see DISQUALIFY
2 *syn* see PARALYZE 1
3 *syn* see WEAKEN 1
rel harm, hurt, mar, spoil; batter, maim, mangle, mutilate; ruin, wreck
con restore, resuscitate, revive, revivify
ant rehabilitate
disabuse *vb* to set free from mistakes (as in reasoning or judgment) <he was *disabused* of the notion that he was indispensable to the company>
syn purge, undeceive, undelude
rel amend, correct, emend, rectify, redress; disillude, disillusion, unblind; enlighten, illuminate; free, liberate, release
idiom open one's eyes, prick the (*or* one's) bubble, puncture one's balloon, set (*or* put) right (*or* straight)
con deceive, delude, mislead; dupe, gull
disaccord *vb* **1** *syn* see CLASH 2
2 *syn* see DIFFER 2
ant accord
disaccord *n syn* see DISCORD
ant accord
disacknowledge *vb syn* see DISCLAIM
disadvantage *n* an unfavorable or prejudicial quality or circumstance <the machine has two serious *disadvantages*>
syn detriment, disability, drawback, handicap
rel bar, impediment, obstacle, obstruction; blocking, hamper, hindrance, imposition
con aid, assistance, help; service, usefulness, utility, value, worth
ant advantage
disadvantaged *adj syn* see UNDERPRIVILEGED
ant advantaged
disadvantageous *adj syn* see DEROGATORY
disadvise *vb syn* see DISSUADE
disaffect *vb syn* see ESTRANGE
rel agitate, discompose, disquiet, disturb, upset
ant win (over)
disaffection *n syn* see ESTRANGEMENT
disaffirm *vb syn* see DENY 4
disagree *vb* **1** *syn* see DIFFER 1
ant agree
2 *syn* see DIFFER 2
ant agree
disagreeable *adj* **1** *syn* see BAD 8
rel annoying, distressing, disturbing, woeful
ant agreeable
2 *syn* see IRRITABLE
ant agreeable
disallow *vb* **1** *syn* see DENY 2
con accede, acquiesce, assent
ant allow
2 *syn* see DISCLAIM
rel debar, exclude, shut out

ant allow
disallowance *n syn* see DENIAL 1
disappear *vb syn* see VANISH
rel go, leave
ant appear
disappoint *vb syn* see FRUSTRATE 1
disapprove *vb* **1** to feel or express an objection <*disapprove* of his actions>
syn deprecate, discommend, discountenance, disesteem, disfavor, frown, object
rel blame, censure, condemn, criticize, denounce, reprehend, reprobate; decry, depreciate, detract, disparage, dispraise; expostulate, remonstrate
idiom look askance at, make a wry face at, not go for, take a dim view of, take exception to
con applaud, commend, compliment, recommend; accredit, certify, endorse, sanction; approbate, countenance, favor
ant approve
2 *syn* see DECLINE 4
disarm *vb* **1** *syn* see PARALYZE 1
2 to influence favorably by persuasive words or acts <*disarmed* by her smile>
syn unarm, unsteel, win (over)
rel allure, attract, bewitch, captivate, charm, enchant, fascinate
con alert, caution, tip (off), warn
ant arm
disarming *adj syn* ingratiating, deferential, ingratiatory, insinuating, insinuative, saccharine, silken, silky
disarrange *vb syn* see DISORDER 1
rel mislay, misplace; displace, replace; overturn
ant arrange
disarray *n syn* see CONFUSION 3
con arrangement, marshaling
disarray *vb syn* see DISORDER 1
ant array
disassemble *vb syn* see DISMOUNT
disassociate *vb syn* see DETACH
disaster *n* a sudden calamitous event bringing great damage, loss, or destruction <a flood *disaster* struck the valley>
syn calamity, cataclysm, catastrophe, misadventure, tragedy, woe(s)
rel accident, casualty, fatality, mishap; adversity, distress, misadventure, mischance, misfortune; rock(s)
disastrous *adj syn* see FATAL 2
rel hapless, luckless, unfortunate; destructive
con fortunate, happy, lucky, providential
disavow *vb syn* see DISCLAIM
rel impugn, negate, negative
con allow, concede, grant; assert, justify, maintain
ant avow
disband *vb* to cease to exist as a unit <the dance group *disbanded* after a farewell concert>

---

syn synonym(s)   *rel* related word(s)
ant antonym(s)   *con* contrasted word(s)
idiom idiomatic equivalent(s)
‖ use limited; if in doubt, see a dictionary

syn break up, disperse, dissolve

rel dispel, dissipate, scatter; dichotomize, disjoin, disjoint, dissect, dissever, disunite, divide, divorce, part, separate, sever, sunder

idiom go their several ways, part company

con combine, concur, conjoin, cooperate, unite; assemble, collect, congregate, gather; call up, summon

ant band

disbelief *n syn* see UNBELIEF

rel atheism, deism; rejection, repudiation, spurning

con credence, credit, faith

ant belief

disbelieve *vb* to hold not to be true or real <*disbelieved* his professions of sincerity>

syn discredit, unbelieve

rel distrust, doubt, mistrust, question, suspect; eschew, reject, scorn, scout

con accept, ‖buy, swallow

ant believe

disbelieving *adj syn* see INCREDULOUS

disbodied *adj syn* see IMMATERIAL 1

disburden *vb syn* see UNLOAD

disburse *vb* **1** *syn* see SPEND 1

2 *syn* see DISTRIBUTE 1

disbursement *n syn* see EXPENSE 1

discalceate *adj syn* see DISCALCED

discalced *adj* wearing only sandals on the feet <*discalced* monks>

syn barefoot, discalceate

con calced, shod

discard *vb* to get rid of <*discard* old clothes> <people who *discard* traditional values>

syn abdicate, cashier, cast, chuck, ‖deep-six, ‖dice, ditch, dump, jettison, junk, lay aside, reject, scrap, shed, ‖shoot, shuck (off), slough, throw away, throw out, wash out

rel abandon, desert, forsake; repudiate, spurn; dismiss, eject, oust

idiom do away with, let go by the board

con adopt, embrace, espouse, take on, take up; employ, use, utilize; hold, hold back, keep, retain; cherish, esteem, nurture

discarding *n syn* see DISPOSAL 2

discarnate *adj syn* see IMMATERIAL 1

ant carnate, incarnate

discept *vb syn* see DISCUSS 1

discern *vb* **1** *syn* see SEE 1

rel ascertain, discover; anticipate, apprehend, divine, foresee

2 *syn* see KNOW 4

discernible *adj syn* see PERCEPTIBLE

ant indiscernible

discerning *adj syn* see WISE 1

ant undiscerning

discernment *n syn* see WIT 3

rel intuition, reason; sagaciousness, sagacity

con crassness, density, slowness; blindness

discharge *vb* **1** *syn* see UNLOAD

2 *syn* see EXEMPT

3 *syn* see SHOOT 1

4 *syn* see FREE

rel dismiss, eject, expel, oust; eliminate, exclude

5 to give outlet to <the river *discharges* its waters into the bay>

syn disembogue, emit, flow, give off, pour, void

rel eject, exude, release

6 *syn* see DISMISS 3

rel displace, replace, supersede, supplant

con hire; contract

ant engage

7 to release from service with the armed forces <*discharged* from the army with the rank of sergeant>

syn ‖demob, demobilize, muster out, separate

rel disenroll; deactivate, inactivate; bounce, cashier, dismiss, drop, fire, sack

8 *syn* see CLEAR 5

9 *syn* see ANNUL 4

discinct *adj syn* see NEGLIGENT

disciple *n syn* see FOLLOWER

rel enthusiast, fanatic, zealot

disciplinary *adj syn* see PUNITIVE

discipline *n* **1** *syn* see PUNISHMENT

2 *syn* see WILL 3

discipline *vb* **1** *syn* see PUNISH 1

rel overcome, reduce, subdue, subjugate; bridle, check, curb, inhibit, restrain

2 *syn* see TEACH

rel guide, lead; conduct, control, direct, manage

disclaim *vb* to refuse to admit, accept, or approve <the senator *disclaimed* the comment attributed to him> <*disclaim* responsibility for a subordinate's mistake>

syn deny, disacknowledge, disallow, disavow, disown, repudiate

rel contradict, contravene, gainsay, traverse; refuse, reject, spurn; deprecate; belittle, disparage, minimize; abjure, forswear, recant, renounce, retract; challenge, criticize

idiom turn one's back on, wash one's hands of

con acknowledge, avow, own; accept, admit, receive, take

ant claim

disclose *vb* **1** *syn* see OPEN 2

2 *syn* see REVEAL 1

rel acknowledge, admit, avow, confess, own

idiom make public

con conceal, hide; camouflage, cloak, disguise, dissemble, mask

discolor *vb* **1** *syn* see TAINT 1

2 *syn* see STAIN 1

discolor *adj syn* see VARIEGATED

discombobulate *vb* **1** *syn* see DISCOMPOSE 1

2 *syn* see CONFUSE 2

discomfit *vb syn* see EMBARRASS

rel annoy, bother, irk, vex; disturb, perturb, upset

discomfiture *n* **1** *syn* see DEFEAT 1

2 *syn* see COMEDOWN

3 *syn* see EMBARRASSMENT

rel agitation, disquiet, perturbation, upset; commotion; prickles

discomforting *adj syn* see UNCOMFORTABLE

ant comforting

discommend *vb syn* see DISAPPROVE 1

rel admonish; criticize, reprehend; censure

con approve, endorse, sanction
ant commend; recommend
discommode *vb syn* see INCONVENIENCE
rel flurry, fluster, perturb, upset; bother, irk, vex
discommoding *adj syn* see INCONVENIENT
discommodious *adj syn* see INCONVENIENT
discompose *vb* **1** to destroy or impair one's capacity for collected thought or decisive action <*discomposed* by the rudeness of his friend>
syn agitate, bother, discombobulate, dismay, disquiet, disturb, flurry, fluster, perturb, unhinge, unsettle, untune, upset; *compare* EMBARRASS
rel disagree; annoy, irk, vex; harass, harry, pester, plague, worry
con calm, quiet, settle, soothe, tranquilize; allay, alleviate, assuage; appease, conciliate, mollify, pacify, placate, propitiate
ant compose
2 *syn* see DISORDER 1
ant compose
discomposure *n syn* see EMBARRASSMENT
ant composure
disconcert *vb syn* see EMBARRASS
rel bewilder, nonplus, perplex, puzzle
disconcertion *n syn* see EMBARRASSMENT
disconcertment *n syn* see EMBARRASSMENT
disconfirm *vb syn* see DISPROVE 1
disconnect *vb syn* see DETACH
ant connect
disconnected *adj syn* see INCOHERENT 2
ant connected
disconsolate *adj* **1** *syn* see DOWNCAST
rel comfortless, inconsolable; sorrowful, woeful; doleful, melancholy; unhappy
ant cheerful
2 *syn* see INCONSOLABLE
3 *syn* see GLOOMY 3
ant cheerful, cheery
disconsonant *adj syn* see INCONSONANT 1
discontent *adj syn* see DISCONTENTED
ant content
discontented *adj* showing or expressing a sense of grievance or thwarted aspirations or desires <*discontented* with his position>
syn discontent, disgruntled, dissatisfied, malcontent, malcontented, uncontent, uncontented, ungratified
rel disquieted, disturbed, perturbed, restless, upset; displeased; unhappy
con satisfied; gratified, pleased; happy; elated, exultant, jubilant, triumphant
ant contented
discontinuance *n syn* see END 2
ant continuance, continuation
discontinuation *n syn* see END 2
ant continuance, continuation
discontinue *vb syn* see STOP 3
ant continue
discontinuity *n syn* see GAP 1
ant continuity
discontinuous *adj syn* see INCOHERENT 2
ant continuous

‖**disconvenience** *n syn* see INCONVENIENCE
ant convenience
‖**disconvenience** *vb syn* see INCONVENIENCE
ant convenience
discord *n* the state of those who disagree and lack harmony <a household full of turmoil and *discord*>
syn conflict, contention, difference, disaccord, disharmony, dispeace, dissension, dissent, dissidence, dissonance, disunion, disunity, division, inharmony, mischief, strife, unpeace, variance
rel discrepancy, incompatibility, incongruity, inconsistency, inconsonance, uncongeniality; animosity, antagonism, antipathy, enmity, hostility, rancor; polarization; collision
con accord, consonance; agreement, concordance, concurrence
ant concord, harmony
discord *vb* **1** *syn* see CLASH 2
ant concord, harmonize
2 *syn* see DIFFER 2
ant accord
discordant *adj* **1** *syn* see INHARMONIOUS 2
2 *syn* see INCONSONANT 1
con according, agreeing, congenial, harmonious, harmonizing
ant concordant
3 *syn* see ANTIPATHETIC 1
ant concordant
4 *syn* see DISSONANT 1
discotheque *n syn* see NIGHTCLUB
discount *n syn* see DEDUCTION 1
discount *vb* **1** *syn* see DEDUCT 1
con boost, hike, increase, mark up, raise
2 *syn* see NEGLECT
3 *syn* see DECRY 2
discountenance *vb* **1** *syn* see EMBARRASS
idiom put out of countenance
2 *syn* see DISAPPROVE 1
rel reproach, reprove
con encourage, favor
ant countenance
discourage *vb* **1** to weaken the stamina, interest, or zeal of <the long winter and lack of fuel *discouraged* the settlers>
syn chill, deject, demoralize, dishearten, disparage, dispirit
rel depress, weigh; afflict, try; damp, dampen, droop; distress, trouble; bother, irk, vex
idiom take the heart out of
con cheer, embolden, hearten, inspirit, nerve, steel
ant encourage
2 *syn* see DISSUADE
rel check, inhibit, restrain; prevent; frighten, scare
idiom lay a wet blanket on, throw cold water on
con advocate, countenance, favor; approve, back, endorse

---

syn synonym(s)   *rel* related word(s)
ant antonym(s)   *con* contrasted word(s)
idiom idiomatic equivalent(s)
‖ use limited; if in doubt, see a dictionary

ant encourage

discouraging *adj syn* see GLOOMY 3
rel deterring; hindering
ant encouraging

discourse *n* **1** *syn* see SPEECH 1
2 a systematic, serious, and often learned exposition of a subject or topic <his *discourses* during the seminar were long remembered>
syn disquisition, dissertation, memoir, monograph, monography, thesis, tractate, treatise
rel article, essay, paper; lecture, sermon; rhetoric, speech, talk

discourse *vb* **1** to express oneself especially formally and at length <*discourses* knowledgeably about the laws of nature>
syn descant, dilate (on *or* upon), discuss, dissert, dissertate, expatiate, sermonize
rel converse, speak, talk, voice; argue, dispute; harangue, lecture, orate, perorate; amplify, develop, elaborate, enlarge, expand; explain, expound; comment, commentate, remark
2 *syn* see ACT 1

discourteous *adj syn* see RUDE 6
con chivalrous, civil, courtly, gallant
ant courteous

discover *vb* **1** *syn* see EXPOSE 4
2 *syn* see REVEAL 1
rel advertise, proclaim, publish
con repress, suppress
3 to become or be made aware of something not previously known <*discover* a secret>
syn ascertain, catch on, determine, find out, hear, learn, see, tumble, unearth
rel descry, detect, encounter, espy, hit (on *or* upon), meet (with), spot; discern, note, observe, perceive
idiom get wise to
con miss, overlook; disregard, ignore

discovery *n* the gaining knowledge of or ascertaining the existence of something previously unknown or unrecognized <the *discovery* of a new chemical element>
syn detection, espial, find, strike, unearthing
rel disclosure, exposition, exposure, revelation, uncovering

discreate *vb syn* see DESTROY 1

discredit *vb* **1** *syn* see DISBELIEVE
ant credit
2 to deprive of credibility <he *discredited* the rumor immediately>
syn blow up, disprove, explode, puncture, shoot
rel expose, show up; destroy, ruin
idiom bring to naught, knock the bottom out of, not leave a leg to stand on
con accept, believe, credit

discredit *n syn* see DISGRACE
ant credit

discreditable *adj syn* see DISREPUTABLE 1

discreet *adj* **1** *syn* see CAUTIOUS
con foolhardy
ant indiscreet
2 *syn* see PLAIN 1
3 *syn* see CONSERVATIVE 2

discreetness *n syn* see PRUDENCE 1

ant indiscreetness

discrepancy *n syn* see DISSIMILARITY

discrepant *adj syn* see INCONSONANT 1
rel different, disparate, divergent, diverse; disagreeing, varying
con agreeing, conforming, corresponding, jibing, squaring, tallying; alike, identical, like, parallel, similar, uniform

discrepate *vb syn* see KNOW 4

discrete *adj syn* see DISTINCT 1
con blended, fused, merged, mingled
ant indiscrete

discretion *n syn* see PRUDENCE 1
rel moderation, restraint; gumption, judgment, sense, wisdom
con asininity, fatuousness, foolishness, simplicity; foolhardiness, rashness, recklessness
ant indiscretion

discretionary *adj syn* see OPTIONAL

discriminate *vb syn* see KNOW 4
rel note, perceive, remark; collate, compare, contrast
ant confound

discriminating *adj syn* see ECLECTIC 1
rel careful; judicious, prudent, wise
ant undiscriminating

discrimination *n syn* see WIT 3
rel judgment, sense
con crassness, density, slowness

discriminative *adj syn* see DISCRIMINATORY
ant undiscriminative

discriminatory *adj* applying or favoring discrimination in treatment <*discriminatory* employment practices against women>
syn discriminative
rel biased, inequitable, partial, partisan, prejudiced, prepossessed, unfair, unjust
con dispassionate, equal, equitable, fair, impartial, just, objective, unbiased, uncolored, unprejudiced
ant nondiscriminatory

discrown *vb syn* see DEPOSE 1

disculpate *vb syn* see EXCULPATE
ant inculpate

discumber *vb syn* see EXTRICATE 2

discursion *n syn* see DIGRESSION

discuss *vb* **1** to exchange views about something in order to arrive at the truth or to convince others <met to *discuss* community needs>
syn agitate, argue, canvass, debate, discept, dispute, ‖kick around, moot, pro-and-con, thrash out, toss (around)
rel deliberate, hash over, reason (out), talk over; consider, weigh
idiom consider pro and con, go into, reason the point
2 *syn* see DISCOURSE 1
rel elucidate, explicate, interpret

discussion *n syn* see CONFERENCE 1

disdain *n* **1** *syn* see DESPITE 1
rel antipathy, aversion; arrogance, haughtiness, insolence, superciliousness
con awe, fear, reverence
2 *syn* see PRIDE 3

disdain *vb syn* see DESPISE
con accept, receive, take; acknowledge, admit, own; esteem, respect
ant admire
disdainful *adj syn* see PROUD 1
rel rejecting, repudiating, spurning; contemning, despising, scorning, scouting; antipathetic, averse, unsympathetic
ant admiring; respectful
disdainfulness *n syn* see PRIDE 3
disease *n* **1** a kind or instance of impairment of a living being that interferes with normal bodily function <tuberculosis has become a controllable *disease*>
syn affection, ailment, complaint, condition, disorder, ill, infirmity, malady, sickness, syndrome; *compare* INFIRMITY 1, SICKNESS 1
rel bug, ‖epizootic, ‖misery, virus
2 *syn* see INFIRMITY 1
ant health
diseasedness *n syn* see SICKNESS 1
disedge *vb syn* see DULL 3
disembark *vb* to go ashore out of a ship <*disembark* at the next port>
syn debark, land
rel put in
con board, get on
ant embark
disembarrass *vb syn* see EXTRICATE 2
rel clear, rid, unburden
ant embarrass
disembodied *adj syn* see IMMATERIAL 1
disembogue *vb syn* see DISCHARGE 5
disembowel *vb syn* see EVISCERATE
disembroil *vb syn* see EXTRICATE 2
ant embroil
disemploy *vb syn* see DISMISS 3
disenable *vb syn* see DISQUALIFY
disenchanted *adj syn* see SOPHISTICATED 2
disencumber *vb syn* see EXTRICATE 2
rel alleviate, lighten, relieve
con depress, oppress, weigh
ant encumber
disenfranchise *vb syn* see DISFRANCHISE
disengage *vb* **1** *syn* see DETACH
rel free, liberate, release
con associate, connect, join, link, unite
ant engage
2 *syn* see LOOSE 3
disentangle *vb syn* see EXTRICATE 2
rel detach, disengage; part, separate, sever, sunder
con enmesh, involve
ant entangle, tangle
disenthrall *vb syn* see FREE
disenthrone *vb syn* see DEPOSE 1
disentranced *adj syn* see SOPHISTICATED 2
disentwine *vb syn* see EXTRICATE 2
disesteem *vb syn* see DISAPPROVE 1
disesteem *n syn* see DISGRACE
ant esteem
disfashion *vb syn* see DEFACE
disfavor *n* **1** *syn* see DISLIKE
rel distrust, mistrust

con approbation, approval; admiration, esteem, liking, regard, respect
ant favor
2 *syn* see DISGRACE
disfavor *vb syn* see DISAPPROVE 1
con accept, approbate, approve, countenance, go (for), hold (with)
ant favor
disfeature *vb syn* see DEFACE
disfigure *vb syn* see DEFACE
ant adorn
disfranchise *vb* to deprive of a legal right and especially of the right to vote <people subtly *disfranchised* by community apathy>
syn disenfranchise
rel deprive, take away
ant affranchise, enfranchise, franchise
disgorge *vb* **1** *syn* see VOMIT
2 *syn* see ERUPT 1
disgrace *n* the state of one who has lost esteem and good repute <retired in *disgrace* after the scandal became public>
syn contempt, discredit, disesteem, disfavor, dishonor, disrepute, ignominy, infamy, obloquy, odium, opprobrium, shame
rel abasement, debasement, debasing, degradation, humbling, humiliation; black eye, blot, brand, spot, stain, stigma
con admiration, regard; awe, fear, reverence; fame, glory, honor, renown, repute
ant esteem, respect
disgraceful *adj syn* see DISREPUTABLE 1
ant respectable; respectworthy
disgracious *adj syn* see RUDE 6
ant gracious
disgrade *vb syn* see DEGRADE 1
disgruntled *adj syn* see DISCONTENTED
disguise *vb* to alter so as to hide the true appearance or character of <*disguised* herself with a wig> <*disguised* his anger behind a false geniality>
syn camouflage, cloak, dissemble, dissimulate, dress up, mask
rel conceal, hide; obfuscate, obscure; belie, falsify, garble, misrepresent; affect, assume, counterfeit, feign, pretend, sham, simulate
con display, exhibit, expose, flaunt, parade, show; betray, disclose, discover, reveal
disguise *n* **1** *syn* see MASK 2
rel deception, delusion; speciousness
2 *syn* see PRETENSE 2
disguised *adj syn* see INTOXICATED 1
disguisement *n syn* see MASK 2
disgust *vb* to be offensive to the taste or sensibilities of <the sight of filth *disgusted* him>
syn nauseate, reluct, repel, repulse, revolt, sicken
rel offend, outrage

---

syn synonym(s)   *rel* related word(s)
ant antonym(s)   *con* contrasted word(s)
idiom idiomatic equivalent(s)
‖ use limited; if in doubt, see a dictionary

idiom make one sick, stick in one's craw (*or* crop *or* gizzard), turn one's stomach
con charm, entice, tempt; delight, gratify, please, rejoice, tickle

disgusted *adj syn* see FED UP

disgusting *adj syn* see OFFENSIVE

‖**dish** *vb syn* see CHAT 1

disharmonic *adj syn* see DISSONANT 1
ant harmonic, harmonious

disharmonious *adj syn* see DISSONANT 1
ant harmonic, harmonious

disharmonize *vb syn* see CLASH 2
ant harmonize

disharmony *n syn* see DISCORD
ant harmony

dishearten *vb syn* see DISCOURAGE 1
ant hearten

disheartening *adj syn* see GLOOMY 3
rel despondent, pessimistic
con encouraging, optimistic
ant heartening

disheveled *adj syn* see SLOVENLY 1

dishonest *adj* **1** unworthy of trust or belief <made a *dishonest* report on their progress>
syn deceitful, knavish, lying, mendacious, roguish, shifty, unhonest, untruthful
rel crooked, devious, furtive, oblique; faithless, false, perfidious, untrustworthy; cheating, cozening, ‖cronk, defrauding, double-dealing, fraudulent, swindling, two-faced; insidious, tricky
con conscientious, honorable, just, scrupulous, upright; aboveboard, forthright, straightforward; candid, fair, frank, open, plain; dependable, reliable, sure, trustworthy, trusty
ant honest
2 *syn* see CROOKED 2

dishonesty *n syn* see DECEPTION 1

dishonor *n syn* see DISGRACE
con reverence, veneration; authority, credit, influence, prestige, weight
ant honor

dishonorable *adj syn* see DISREPUTABLE 1
ant honorable

dish out *vb syn* see GIVE 3

dishy *adj syn* see BEAUTIFUL

disillusioned *adj syn* see SOPHISTICATED 2
con beguiled, deceived, deluded, misled

disimpassioned *adj syn* see COOL 2
ant heated, impassioned

disimprison *vb syn* see FREE
ant imprison

disimprove *vb syn* see DETERIORATE 1
ant improve

disinclination *n syn* see DISLIKE
ant inclination

disinclined *adj* lacking the will or desire to do something <*disinclined* to accept her story>
syn afraid, averse, backward, hesitant, indisposed, loath, reluctant, shy, uneager, unwilling, unwishful
rel antipathetic, unsympathetic; doubtful, dubious; opposing, resisting; balking, boggling, shying, sticking, stickling; objecting, protesting

con anxious, avid, eager, keen; disposed, predisposed, ready, willing
ant inclined

disingenuous *adj* lacking in candor and often giving a false appearance of simple frankness <had a *disingenuous* way of asking for advice when he really wanted help>
syn uncandid, unfrank
rel false, feigned, insincere, left-handed; artful, crafty, cunning, foxy, guileful, insidious, sly, tricky, wily; devious, indirect, oblique
con artless, naive, natural, simple, unsophisticated; candid, frank, open, plain; sincere, unfeigned; aboveboard, direct, straightforward
ant ingenuous

disinherit *vb* **1** to deprive (an heir apparent) of the right to inherit <the father *disinherited* his wayward son in his will>
syn cut off
rel disown, repudiate; dispossess
idiom cut off without a cent
2 *syn* see DEPRIVE 2

disinhume *vb syn* see EXHUME
ant inhume

disintegrate *vb* **1** *syn* see DECAY
rel deliquesce; disperse, dissipate, scatter
con articulate, concatenate; blend, coalesce, fuse, merge; associate, combine, conjoin, connect, join, link, unite
2 *syn* see DETERIORATE 1

disinter *vb syn* see EXHUME
ant inter

disinterest *n syn* see APATHY 2
ant interest

disinterested *adj* **1** *syn* see INDIFFERENT 2
rel negative, neutral
con concerned, curious; fervent, impassioned, passionate
ant interested
2 *syn* see NEUTRAL
rel fair, just, impartial, unbiased
con biased, prejudiced; involved
ant concerned

disject *vb syn* see STREW 1

disjoin *vb syn* see SEPARATE 1

disjoint *vb* **1** *syn* see SEPARATE 1
2 *syn* see DISORDER 1

disjointed *adj syn* see INCOHERENT 2

dislike *n* a state of mind or feeling marked by an inner avoidance of something usually felt as unpleasant or repugnant <a pronounced *dislike* for mathematics>
syn aversion, bad books, disfavor, disinclination, disliking, displeasure, disrelish, dissatisfaction, distaste, indisposition
rel detestation, hate, hatred; deprecation, disapproval; prejudice, scunner
idiom ‖a derry on
con affection, attachment, love; partiality, predilection, preference
ant liking

disliking *n syn* see DISLIKE
ant liking

dislimb *vb syn* see MAIM

dislimn *vb syn* see OBSCURE

dislocate *vb* **1** *syn* see DISORDER 1
  2 *syn* see MOVE 4

disloyal *adj syn* see FAITHLESS
  rel alienated, disaffected, estranged
  ant loyal

disloyalty *n* **1** *syn* see INFIDELITY
  ant loyalty
  2 *syn* see TREACHERY
  ant loyalty

dismal *adj syn* see GLOOMY 3
  con animated, gay, lively; cheerful

dismals *n pl, used with the syn* see SADNESS

dismantle *vb* **1** *syn* see STRIP 2
  con appoint, equip, outfit
  2 *syn* see DESTROY 1
  3 *syn* see REVOKE 2
  4 *syn* see DISMOUNT

dismay *n syn* see FEAR 1
  con aplomb, assurance, confidence, self-possession; mettle, resolution, spirit

dismay *vb* **1** to unnerve and check by arousing
  fear, apprehension, or aversion <*dismayed* by
  the task that lay ahead>
  syn appall, consternate, daunt, horrify, shake
  rel bewilder, confound, dumbfound, mystify,
  nonplus, perplex, puzzle; abash, discomfit, disconcert, embarrass, faze, rattle; discourage, dishearten; affright, alarm, frighten, scare, terrify
  idiom set one back on one's heels, take aback
  con assure, ensure, secure; excite, galvanize,
  pique, provoke, quicken, stimulate
  2 *syn* see DISCOMPOSE 1

dismayed *adj syn* see AGHAST 2
  rel discomfited, disconcerted, fazed, rattled
  ant undismayed

dismember *vb* **1** *syn* see MAIM
  rel part, separate, sever, sunder
  2 *syn* see DISMOUNT

dismiss *vb* **1** *syn* see DIVORCE 2
  2 *syn* see DECLINE 4
  3 to let go from one's employ or service <during
  the recession thousands of employees were *dis-
  missed*>
  syn ax, boot (out), bounce, ‖can, cashier, discharge, disemploy, drop, fire, kick out, let out,
  sack, terminate, turn off
  rel depose, deselect, displace, furlough, lay off,
  remove, retire, suspend, unseat; reject, turn
  away; riff
  idiom give one the gate (*or* one's walking papers), let go; give the ax (*or* the can) to
  con hire; contract, engage; get, obtain, procure,
  secure
  ant employ
  4 *syn* see EJECT 1
  rel cast, discard, shed, slough
  idiom send one to Coventry
  5 to refuse to consider seriously <*dismisses* the
  other performers as mere amateurs>
  syn kiss off, pooh-pooh
  rel deride, mock, rally, ridicule, taunt, twit;
  flout, gibe, gird, jeer, scoff; contemn, despise,
  disdain, scorn, scout; reject

dismissive *adj syn* see PROUD 1

dismount *vb* to take down or apart from an assembled position <*dismount* a revolver for
  cleaning>
  syn disassemble, dismantle, dismember, take
  down
  rel detach, disengage; disconnect, disjoin, disunite, separate
  idiom take apart, take to pieces
  con assemble, construct, put together; combine,
  unite

disobedient *adj* refusing or neglecting to obey
  <the *disobedient* child refused to come in>
  syn naughty, obstreperous, unruly; *compare*
  CONTRARY 3, NAUGHTY 1
  rel headstrong, recalcitrant, willful; contumacious, insubordinate, rebellious
  con amenable, biddable, docile, tractable; decorous, good, well-behaved
  ant obedient

disoblige *vb syn* see INCONVENIENCE
  con accommodate, convenience, favor
  ant oblige

disorder *n* **1** *syn* see CONFUSION 3
  con orderliness; pattern, plan
  ant order
  2 breach of public order <the overthrow of the
  government caused *disorder* in the country>
  syn anarchism, anarchy, distemper, misrule,
  riot
  rel anomie; agitation, commotion, convulsion,
  tumult, turbulence, turmoil, upheaval
  ant order
  3 *syn* see DISEASE 1
  4 *syn* see SICKNESS 1

disorder *vb* **1** to undo the fixed or proper order of
  something <*disorder* the carefully arranged
  contents of a drawer>
  syn derange, disarrange, disarray, discompose,
  disjoint, dislocate, disorganize, disrupt, distemper, disturb, jumble, ‖mammock, mess (up), mix
  up, muddle, muss (up), ‖mux, rummage, shuffle,
  tumble, unsettle, upset; *compare* CONFUSE 5
  rel ball up, embroil; dishevel, rumple
  idiom make hay of
  con arrange, marshal, methodize, organize, systematize; align, array, line, line up, range; adjust,
  fix, regulate
  ant order
  2 *syn* see UPSET 5

disordered *adj* **1** *syn* see INCOHERENT 2
  2 *syn* see INSANE 1

disorderly *adj syn* see TURBULENT 1

disorderly house *n syn* see BROTHEL

disorganize *vb syn* see DISORDER 1
  ant organize

disown *vb syn* see DISCLAIM
  ant own

disparage *vb* **1** *syn* see DECRY 2

---

syn synonym(s)   *rel* related word(s)
ant antonym(s)   *con* contrasted word(s)
idiom idiomatic equivalent(s)
‖ use limited; if in doubt, see a dictionary

ant applaud
2 syn see DISCOURAGE 1

disparagement *n* **1 syn** see DETRACTION
rel animadversion, aspersion, reflection, stricture
2 syn see DESPITE 1

disparaging *adj syn* see DEROGATORY
rel underestimating, underrating, undervaluing
con acclaiming, extolling, praising; exalting, magnifying

disparate *adj syn* see DIFFERENT 1
rel discordant, discrepant, incompatible, inconsistent, inconsonant; distinct, separate
ant analogous, comparable

disparity *n* the state of being different (as in degree, rank, excellence, or number) <the *disparity* between the rich and the poor> <their stories showed significant *disparity*>
syn disproportion, imparity, inequality, unevenness
rel alterity, difference, dissemblance, dissimilarity, dissimilitude, distinction, divergence, divergency, otherness, unlikeness
con adequation, equality, equatability, equivalence, equivalency, sameness; correlation, correspondence, likeness; evenness
ant parity

dispassionate *adj* **1 syn** see NEUTRAL
rel imperturbable, unflappable, unruffled
con fervent, vehement; intemperate
2 syn see FAIR 4
rel aloof, indifferent; frank, open; aboveboard, straightforward

dispatch *vb* **1 syn** see SEND 1
rel hasten, quicken, speed
2 syn see KILL 1
3 syn see EAT UP 1

dispatch *n* **1 syn** see HASTE 1
con dawdling, loitering, procrastination
ant delay
2 syn see ALACRITY
rel diligence, industriousness

dispeace *n syn* see DISCORD

dispel *vb syn* see SCATTER 1
rel dismiss, eject, expel, oust; crumble, disintegrate

dispensable *adj* capable of being dispensed with <many household gadgets are readily *dispensable*>
syn nonessential, unessential, unrequired
rel needless, unnecessary, unneeded; minor, trivial, unimportant
con essential, imperative, necessary, necessitous, required; vital
ant indispensable

dispensation *n syn* see FAVOR 4

dispense *vb* **1 syn** see DISTRIBUTE 1
2 syn see GIVE 3
rel portion, prorate
3 syn see ADMINISTER 2
4 syn see HANDLE 2
5 syn see EXEMPT

disperse *vb* **1 syn** see SCATTER 1
rel discharge, dismiss

con call, cite, convene, convoke, summon
ant assemble, congregate; collect
2 syn see DISTRIBUTE 1
3 syn see SPREAD 1
4 syn see DISBAND

dispirit *vb syn* see DISCOURAGE 1
idiom dampen (*or* lower) one's spirits
ant inspirit

dispirited *adj syn* see DOWNCAST
rel melancholy, sad
ant high-spirited, inspirited

dispiriting *adj syn* see GLOOMY 3
rel dejecting, distressing; oppressing
ant inspiriting

displace *vb* **1 syn** see BANISH
2 syn see DEPOSE 1
3 syn see SUPPLANT 1

displaced person *n syn* see REFUGEE

displacement *n syn* see EXILE 1

display *vb* **1 syn** see OPEN 2
rel demonstrate, evidence, evince, lay out, manifest, show
con camouflage, cloak, disguise, dissemble, mask; conceal, hide, secrete
2 syn see SHOW 4
3 syn see SHOW 1

display *n* **1 syn** see EXHIBITION 1
2 a striking or spectacular exhibition <a parvenu's *display* of wealth>
syn array, fanfare, panoply, parade, pomp, shine, show
rel ostentation, ostentatiousness, pretension, pretentiousness, showiness; setout

displeasing *adj syn* see BAD 8
rel annoying, bothersome, irksome, vexing
con agreeable, gratifying, pleasant
ant pleasing

displeasure *n syn* see DISLIKE
rel anger; vexation
con delight, enjoyment
ant pleasure

disponible *adj syn* see AVAILABLE 1

disport *n syn* see PLAY 1
rel jollity, merriment

disport *vb* **1 syn** see SHOW 4
2 syn see BEHAVE 1
3 syn see PLAY 1

disposal *n* **1 syn** see ORDER 3
2 the act of ridding oneself of something <incinerators used for the *disposal* of trash>
syn discarding, disposition, dumping, jettison, junking, relegation, riddance, scrapping, throwing away
rel chucking, clearance; demolishing, demolition, destroying, destruction
con acquirement, acquisition; accumulation, collection, cumulation, deposit, hoard, trove

dispose *vb* **1 syn** see INCLINE 3
ant indispose
2 syn see ORDER 1

disposed *adj syn* see WILLING 1
ant indisposed

disposition *n* **1 syn** see DISPOSAL 2
rel control, controlling, direction, management

2 *syn* see ORDER 3

3 the complex of especially mental and emotional qualities that distinguish an individual <a man of irritable *disposition*>
syn character, complexion, humor, individualism, individuality, makeup, nature, personality, temper, temperament
rel mood, tone, vein; cast, stamp, tenor, type; being; identity
idiom frame of mind

4 *syn* see LEANING 2

dispossess *vb syn* see DEPRIVE 2
con provide, supply

dispossession *n syn* see PRIVATION 2

dispraise *vb syn* see DECRY 2
ant praise

disproportion *n syn* see DISPARITY

disproportional *adj syn* see LOPSIDED

disproportionate *adj syn* see LOPSIDED
ant proportionate

disprove *vb* **1** to show by presenting evidence that something is not true <the defendant's claims were *disproved* by the testimony>
syn break, confound, confute, controvert, disconfirm, evert, rebut, refute
rel contravene, impugn, negative, traverse; overthrow, overturn
con evidence, show; demonstrate, display, illustrate, manifest; argue, bespeak, tell
ant prove

2 *syn* see DISCREDIT 2

disputable *adj syn* see MOOT

disputation *n syn* see ARGUMENTATION

disputatious *adj syn* see CONTENTIOUS 2

dispute *vb* **1** *syn* see ARGUE 2
con give in, surrender

2 *syn* see DISCUSS 1
rel confute, controvert, disprove, rebut, refute
con allow, grant
ant concede

3 *syn* see QUESTION 2

4 *syn* see RESIST

dispute *n* **1** *syn* see ARGUMENT 2
rel conflict, discord, dissension, strife

2 *syn* see QUARREL

disqualified *adj syn* see UNFIT 2
ant qualified

disqualify *vb* to deprive of a power, right, or privilege <a conviction of perjury *disqualified* him from being a witness>
syn disable, disenable, incapacitate
rel bar, bate, debar, eliminate, except, exclude, rule out, suspend
con empower, enable
ant qualify

disquiet *vb syn* see DISCOMPOSE 1
rel distress, trouble
con calm, compose, lull, still
ant quiet, soothe, tranquilize

disquiet *n* **1** *syn* see CARE 2
ant quiet

2 *syn* see UNREST
ant quiet

disquietude *n* **1** *syn* see CARE 2

2 *syn* see UNREST
ant quietness, quietude

disquisition *n syn* see DISCOURSE 2
rel inquiry, investigation; argumentation, debate, disputation

disquisitive *adj syn* see INQUISITIVE 1

disrate *vb syn* see DEGRADE 1

disregard *vb syn* see NEGLECT
con attend, mind, tend, watch; note, notice, observe, remark
ant regard

disregard *n syn* see APATHY 2
rel forgetting, ignoring, neglecting, omission, omitting, overlooking, slighting
con consideration, thoughtfulness

disregardful *adj syn* see NEGLIGENT
ant regardful

disrelish *n syn* see DISLIKE
ant relish

disremember *vb syn* see FORGET 1

disreputable *adj* **1** not reputable or decent <was punished for his *disreputable* conduct>
syn discreditable, disgraceful, dishonorable, ignominious, inglorious, shabby, shady, shameful, shoddy, unrespectable
rel abject, mean, sordid; beggarly, cheap, contemptible, despicable, pitiable, scurvy, sorry
con admirable, creditable, estimable, honorable, respectable
ant reputable

2 *syn* see SHABBY 1

disrepute *n syn* see DISGRACE
ant repute

disrespect *n syn* see INSOLENCE
ant respect

disrespectful *adj syn* see RUDE 6
ant respectful

disrobe *vb* **1** *syn* see STRIP 1

2 *syn* see STRIP 2

disrupt *vb* **1** *syn* see OPEN 3

2 *syn* see DISORDER 1

dissatisfaction *n syn* see DISLIKE
ant satisfaction

dissatisfactory *adj syn* see BAD 1
ant satisfactory

dissatisfied *adj syn* see DISCONTENTED
rel annoyed, bothered, irked, vexed
con content, contented, gratified
ant satisfied

dissect *vb* **1** *syn* see SEPARATE 1

2 *syn* see CUT 5
rel penetrate, pierce, probe

3 *syn* see ANALYZE

dissection *n syn* see ANALYSIS 1
rel examination, inspection, review, scrutiny; criticism, critique

dissemblance *n syn* see DISSIMILARITY
ant resemblance, semblance

dissemblance *n syn* see DECEIT 1

---

syn synonym(s) *rel* related word(s)
ant antonym(s) *con* contrasted word(s)
idiom idiomatic equivalent(s)
|| use limited; if in doubt, see a dictionary

dissemble *vb syn* see DISGUISE
  con demonstrate, evidence, evince, manifest, show
dissembler *n syn* see HYPOCRITE
disseminate *vb* **1** *syn* see SPREAD 1
  2 *syn* see DECLARE 1
  3 *syn* see STREW 1
dissension *n syn* see DISCORD
  rel altercation, bickering, quarrel, wrangle; argument, controversy, dispute
  con amity, friendship, goodwill
  ant accord; comity
dissent *vb syn* see DIFFER 2
  rel balk, boggle, demur, shy, stickle
  con accede, acquiesce, agree, subscribe
  ant assent; concur
dissent *n* **1** *syn* see DISCORD
  2 *syn* see HERESY
  rel disagreement, nonagreement, nonconcurrence
dissenter *n syn* see HERETIC
dissert *vb syn* see DISCOURSE 1
dissertate *vb syn* see DISCOURSE 1
dissertation *n syn* see DISCOURSE 2
  rel exposition; argumentation, disputation
dissever *vb* **1** *syn* see SEPARATE 1
  2 *syn* see CUT 5
dissidence *n* **1** *syn* see DISCORD
  2 *syn* see HERESY
dissident *adj syn* see HERETICAL
dissident *n syn* see HERETIC
dissimilar *adj syn* see DIFFERENT 1
  rel antithetical, antonymous, contradictory, contrary, opposite
  ant similar
dissimilarity *n* lack of agreement or correspondence or an instance of this <the *dissimilarities* in the cultures of the two countries>
  syn alterity, difference, discrepancy, dissemblance, dissimilitude, distance, distinction, divarication, divergence, divergency, otherness, unlikeness
  rel disparity, diversity; discordance, incongruity, inconsistency, inconsonance; discord, variance; severance; offset; margin
  con affinity, analogy, likeness, resemblance, similitude; accordance, congruity, consistency, consonance; agreement, conformity, correspondence
  ant similarity
dissimilitude *n syn* see DISSIMILARITY
  ant similitude
dissimulate *vb syn* see DISGUISE
dissimulation *n syn* see DECEIT 1
  rel camouflaging, cloaking, disguising, dissembling, masking; concealing, hiding, secreting; feigning, pretending, pretense, shamming; hypocrisy, pharisaism, sanctimony
dissimulator *n syn* see HYPOCRITE
dissipate *vb* **1** *syn* see SCATTER 1
  rel crumble, disintegrate
  ant accumulate; concentrate (*as efforts, thoughts*)
  2 *syn* see WASTE 2

  rel disappear, evanesce, evaporate, vanish
  ant absorb (*as time, attention*)
dissipation *n syn* see ENTERTAINMENT
dissociate *vb syn* see DETACH
  rel alienate, estrange
  ant associate
dissolute *adj syn* see ABANDONED 2
  rel lax, light, loose, slack, wanton, wayward; fast, raffish, rakish, wild
dissolution *n* **1** *syn* see SEPARATION 1
  2 *syn* see DEATH 1
dissolve *vb* **1** *syn* see DESTROY 1
  2 *syn* see ADJOURN 2
  3 *syn* see ANNUL 4
  4 *syn* see LIQUEFY
  5 *syn* see SOLVE 2
  6 *syn* see DISBAND
dissonance *n syn* see DISCORD
dissonant *adj* **1** marked by a mingling of discordant sounds <the two bands playing different pieces at the same time sounded *dissonant*>
  syn cacophonic, cacophonous, discordant, disharmonic, disharmonious, immusical, inharmonic, inharmonious, rude, unharmonious, unmusical
  rel grating, harsh, hoarse, jarring, raucous, rugged, strident
  con blending, chiming, concerted, harmonic, symphonious; euphonious, harmonious, mellifluous, mellow, melodious, musical; agreeable, pleasing
  ant consonant
  2 *syn* see INCONSONANT 1
dissuade *vb* to turn one aside from a purpose, a project, or a plan <they tried to *dissuade* a friend from making a mistake>
  syn deter, disadvise, discourage, divert
  rel derail, throw off; advise, counsel; exhort, prick, urge
  idiom talk out of
  con get, induce, prevail; affect, influence, touch
  ant persuade
distance *n* **1** an extent of areal or linear measure <he did not know the *distance* he had walked>
  syn length, stretch
  rel area, extent; ambit, compass, extension, orbit, purview, radius, range, reach, scope, sweep
  2 the length of a literal or figurative course traversed or to be traversed <she had come a long *distance* from her pitiful beginnings>
  syn way, ways
  rel extent, size; piece, spell
  3 *syn* see EXPANSE
  4 *syn* see DISSIMILARITY
distance *vb syn* see OUTSTRIP 1
distant *adj* **1** not close in space, time, or relationship <traveling to a more *distant* place> <the *distant* days of the Pilgrim fathers> <a *distant* cousin>
  syn far, faraway, far-flung, far-off, off-lying, outlying, remote, removed
  rel apart, isolated, obscure, out-of-the-way, retired, secret; secluded, sequestered
  idiom at a distance

con close, near, nearby, next, nigh; adjacent, adjoining, contiguous
2 syn see DIFFERENT 1
3 syn see UNSOCIABLE
rel arrogant, haughty, proud; modest, retiring, shy
con forward, presuming, ||pushy, self-assertive
distaste *n syn* see DISLIKE
rel abhorrence, repugnance, repulsion, revulsion; antipathy, hostility
con relish, zest; appetite, desire; enjoyment
ant taste
distasteful *adj* **1 syn** see UNPALATABLE 1
ant tasteful, tasty
2 syn see BITTER 2
rel obnoxious, repellent, repugnant, repulsive; abominable, detestable, hateful, odious
con agreeable, grateful, gratifying, pleasant, pleasing, welcome
distemper *vb syn* see DISORDER 1
distemper *n syn* see DISORDER 2
distend *vb syn* see EXPAND 3
rel augment, enlarge, increase; extend, lengthen
ant constrict
disthrone *vb syn* see DEPOSE 1
distill *vb syn* see DRIP
distinct *adj* **1** capable of being distinguished as differing <the novel has two related, but nevertheless *distinct*, plots>
syn different, discrete, diverse, separate, several, various
rel distinctive, individual, peculiar; particular, single, sole; especial, individual, special, specific; disparate, dissimilar, divergent
con identical, same, selfsame; corresponding, equivalent, like, similar
ant indistinguishable
2 syn see CLEAR 5
rel defined, prescribed; categorical, definite, explicit, express, specific; lucid, perspicuous; clear-cut, incisive, trenchant
con faint, obscure
ant indistinct; nebulous
distinction *n* **1 syn** see DISSIMILARITY
con affinity, analogy, likeness, similarity, similitude
ant indistinction, resemblance
2 syn see EMINENCE 1
3 syn see HONOR 2
distinctive *adj syn* see CHARACTERISTIC
rel separate, single, unique; discrete, distinct, several
con common, familiar, ordinary, popular, vulgar; alike, analogous, comparable, identical, like, parallel; equal, equivalent, same
distinctively *adv syn* see ESPECIALLY 1
distinctiveness *n syn* see INDIVIDUALITY 3
distingué *adj syn* see GENTEEL 1
distinguish *vb* **1 syn** see KNOW 4
rel divide, part; detach, disengage; demarcate, set off
con confuse, mistake
ant confound
2 syn see EXALT 1

3 syn see CHARACTERIZE 2
idiom set apart
4 syn see SEE 1
5 syn see IDENTIFY
distinguished *adj syn* see FAMOUS 2
rel courtly, dignified, grand, imposing, stately
ant undistinguished
distort *vb* **1 syn** see MISREPRESENT
rel misconstrue, misinterpret; alter, change
2 syn see DEFORM
rel bend, curve, twist
distortion *n syn* see DEFORMITY
distract *vb* **1 syn** see CONFUSE 2
2 syn see MADDEN 1
distracted *adj syn* see DISTRAUGHT
distraction *n* **1 syn** see INSANITY 1
2 syn see ENTERTAINMENT
distrait *adj* **1 syn** see ABSTRACTED
2 syn see DISTRAUGHT
distraught *adj* **1** agitated with doubt or mental conflict <*distraught* over the health of her child>
syn distracted, distrait, distressed, harassed, tormented, troubled, worried
rel agitated, concerned, discomposed, flustered, perturbed, upset; addled, confused, muddled; bewildered, nonplussed
idiom beside oneself
con composed, cool, imperturbable, nonchalant, unflappable, unruffled; calm, tranquil; unconcerned, undisturbed, unworried
ant collected
2 syn see INSANE 1
distress *n* the state of being in serious trouble or in mental or physical anguish <in great *distress* over the decision she had to make>
syn agony, dolor, misery, passion, suffering
rel affliction, cross, trial, tribulation, visitation; anguish, grief, heartbreak, sorrow, woe; exigency, pass, pinch, strait; difficulty, hardship, rigor, vicissitude; ache, pain, pang, throe, twinge
con comfort, comforting, consolation, solace, solacing; allaying, alleviation, assuagement, ease, relief, relieving; peace, security, tranquility
distress *vb* **1 syn** see TRY 2
rel afflict, rack, torment, torture
con allay, alleviate, assuage, lighten, mitigate, relieve
2 to cause pain or suffering to <the death of his longtime friend *distressed* him deeply>
syn aggrieve, constrain, grieve, hurt, injure, pain
rel harass, strain, stress, try, trouble; depress, oppress, weigh
con comfort, console, solace; aid, assist, help
3 syn see TROUBLE 1
rel annoy, harry, pester, plague
distressed *adj syn* see DISTRAUGHT
distressing *adj syn* see DEPLORABLE

---

syn synonym(s)   **rel** related word(s)
ant antonym(s)   **con** contrasted word(s)
idiom idiomatic equivalent(s)
|| use limited; if in doubt, see a dictionary

distribute *vb* **1** to give out, usually in shares, to each member of a group <*distributed* his possessions among his heirs>
syn deal, disburse, dispense, disperse, divide, ||divvy, dole (out), lot (out), measure (out), partition
rel allocate, allot, apportion, assign, mete (out); parcel, portion, prorate, ration; administer; dribble; bestow, donate, give, present
con assemble, gather; accumulate, hoard
ant amass; collect
2 *syn* see SPREAD 1
distribution *n syn* see ORDER 3
district *n* **1** *syn* see QUARTER 2
2 *syn* see LOCALITY 1
rel division, parcel
distrust *vb* to have no trust or confidence in <he *distrusted* most politicians>
syn doubt, misdoubt, mistrust, suspect, ||suspicion
rel disbelieve, discredit, unbelieve
con bank, count, depend, reckon, rely; commit, confide, consign, entrust
ant trust
distrustful *adj syn* see SUSPICIOUS 2
distrustfully *adv syn* see ASKANCE 2
disturb *vb* **1** *syn* see MOVE 4
2 *syn* see DISCOMPOSE 1
rel alarm, frighten, scare, terrify; bewilder, distract, perplex, puzzle; discommode, incommode, inconvenience, trouble
3 *syn* see DISORDER 1
rel displace, replace; move, remove, shift; interfere, intermeddle, meddle, tamper
con establish, fix, set, settle; adjust, regulate
disunify *vb syn* see ESTRANGE
disunion *n* **1** *syn* see SEPARATION 1
2 *syn* see DISCORD
disunite *vb* **1** *syn* see SEPARATE 1
2 *syn* see ESTRANGE
disunity *n syn* see DISCORD
disusage *n syn* see DISUSE
disuse *n* cessation of use, practice, or exercise <to keep the mind from falling into *disuse,* one must exercise one's reading abilities> <his muscles became atrophied from *disuse*>
syn desuetude, disusage
con appliance, application, employment, operation, play, usance; exercise
ant use
disused *adj syn* see OBSOLETE
ditch *n syn* see TRENCH
ditch *vb* **1** *syn* see DISCARD
||**2** *syn* see HIDE
||**dite** *n syn* see PARTICLE
dither *vb* **1** *syn* see SHAKE 1
2 *syn* see HESITATE
3 *syn* see CHAT 1
dither *n* **1** *syn* see JITTERS
2 *syn* see COMMOTION 2
dithyrambic *adj syn* see IMPASSIONED
ditto *n syn* see REPRODUCTION
ditty *n syn* see SONG 2
diurnal *adj syn* see DAILY

ant nocturnal
diuturnal *adj syn* see LASTING
divagate *vb syn* see DIGRESS 2
divagation *n syn* see DIGRESSION
divarication *n syn* see DISSIMILARITY
dive *vb syn* see PLUNGE 2
rel bound, jump, leap, spring; impel, move
dive *n* a shabby or disreputable place for drinking or entertainment <got a schooner of beer at the *dive* down the street>
syn barrelhouse, hangout, honky-tonk, joint
rel dump, hole; bar, barroom, lounge, pothouse, pub, saloon, taproom, tavern
||**diver** *n syn* see PICKPOCKET
diverge *vb* **1** *syn* see SWERVE 2
rel differ, disagree, vary; divide, part, separate
ant converge; conform
2 *syn* see DIGRESS 2
divergence *n* **1** *syn* see DISSIMILARITY
rel diversity, variety
con accord, concord, consonance, harmony
ant conformity, correspondence
2 *syn* see DEVIATION 1
rel division, parting, separation; differing, disagreeing, varying
con agreement, coincidence, concurrence
ant convergence
divergency *n syn* see DISSIMILARITY
divergent *adj* **1** *syn* see DIFFERENT 1
rel antithetical, contradictory, contrary, opposite; aberrant, abnormal, atypical
con alike, identical, parallel, same
ant convergent
2 *syn* see IRREGULAR 1
divers *adj syn* see SEVERAL 3
divers *pron, pl in constr syn* see SUNDRY
diverse *adj* **1** *syn* see DIFFERENT 1
rel contrasted, contrasting, contrastive; contradictory, contrary, opposite
con equal, equivalent, same
ant identical, selfsame
2 *syn* see DISTINCT 1
idiom of every description
3 *syn* see MANIFOLD
diversely *adv syn* see OTHERWISE 1
diverseness *n syn* see VARIETY 1
diversiform *adj syn* see MANIFOLD
diversion *n* **1** *syn* see DEVIATION 1
2 *syn* see PLAY 1
3 *syn* see ENTERTAINMENT
rel frivolity, levity
4 *syn* see ENJOYMENT 1
diversity *n syn* see VARIETY 1
rel difference, dissimilarity, distinction, divergence, divergency, unlikeness
ant uniformity; identity
divert *vb* **1** *syn* see TURN 6
rel swerve; alter, change, modify
con fix, set, settle
2 *syn* see DISSUADE
rel abstract, detach, disengage
3 *syn* see AMUSE
rel delight, gladden, please, regale, tickle
divertissement *n syn* see ENTERTAINMENT

divest *vb* **1** *syn* see STRIP 2
  ant invest, vest; apparel, attire, clothe
  2 *syn* see DEPRIVE 2
  rel despoil, plunder, spoil
  ant invest, vest
divestiture *n syn* see PRIVATION 2
divide *vb* **1** *syn* see SEPARATE 1
  rel carve, chop, cut
  ant unite
  2 *syn* see DISTRIBUTE 1
  3 *syn* see APPORTION 2
  rel allocate, allot, assign
  4 *syn* see DIFFER 2
  rel part, separate
  con combine, concur, conjoin, cooperate
  ant unite
dividend *n syn* see REWARD
divine *n syn* see CLERGYMAN
divine *vb syn* see FORESEE
divine *adj* **1** of or relating to God or a god <the *divine* will>
  syn deific, godly
  rel chthonian
  2 like or like that of God or a god <men who aspire to *divine* honors>
  syn deific, godlike
  rel extramundane, superhuman, superphysical, transmundane
  3 *syn* see MARVELOUS 2
division *n* **1** *syn* see PART 1
  2 *syn* see SEPARATION 1
  3 *syn* see DISCORD
divorce *n syn* see SEPARATION 1
divorce *vb* **1** *syn* see SEPARATE 1
  rel disaffect, wean
  2 to end a marriage by legal action <unable to agree, they decided to *divorce*><*divorced* his wife>
  syn dismiss, put away, unmarry
  rel break up, separate, split; annul, cancel
divorcement *n syn* see SEPARATION 1
divulge *vb syn* see REVEAL 1
  rel proclaim; gossip, tattle
‖**divvy** *vb* **1** *syn* see DISTRIBUTE 1
  2 *syn* see APPORTION 2
‖**dizzard** *n syn* see DUNCE
dizzy *adj* **1** *syn* see GIDDY 1
  rel asinine, fatuous, foolish; inane
  2 affected by a sensation of being whirled about or around <the speed with which she dispatched her tasks made the onlookers *dizzy*>
  syn giddy, light, light-headed, swimming, swimmy, vertiginous
  rel reeling, whirling; bewildered, confounded, distracted, puzzled; addled, befuddled, confused, dazed, dazzled, fuddled, muddled
  idiom with spots before one's eyes
  3 *syn* see EXCESSIVE 1
dizzy *vb syn* see CONFUSE 2
do *vb* **1** *syn* see PERFORM 2
  2 *syn* see CLOSE 3
  3 *syn* see ACT 1
  4 *syn* see CHEAT
  idiom do out of, sell one a bill of goods

  5 *syn* see COOK 1
  6 *syn* see BEHAVE 1
  7 *syn* see SHIFT 5
  8 *syn* see HAPPEN 1
  9 *syn* see TRAVEL 2
  10 *syn* see SERVE 3
  11 *syn* see SERVE 5
‖**do** *n syn* see SUCCESS
doable *adj syn* see POSSIBLE 1
doc *n syn* see PHYSICIAN
docile *adj syn* see OBEDIENT
  rel adaptable, pliable, pliant
  con obstinate, self-willed, stubborn, willful
  ant indocile; ungovernable, unruly
‖**docious** *adj syn* see OBEDIENT
dock *n syn* see WHARF
docket *n syn* see PROGRAM 1
doctor *n syn* see PHYSICIAN
doctor *vb* **1** *syn* see TREAT 4
  2 *syn* see MEND 2
  3 *syn* see ADULTERATE
doctrinaire *adj syn* see DICTATORIAL
  rel bullheaded, dogged, mulish, obstinate, pertinacious, pigheaded, stiff-necked, stubborn
  ant undoctrinaire
doctrine *n* a principle accepted as valid and authoritative <the *doctrine* of evolution>
  syn canon, dogma, tenet
  rel instruction, teaching; axiom, basic, fundamental, principle
  idiom article of belief (*or* faith)
document *n* **1** something preserved and serving as evidence (as of an event, a situation, or the culture of a period) <ceramic and flint artifacts provide our only *document* of this ancient people>
  syn archive(s), monument, record
  rel evidence, testimony
  2 *usu* **documents** *pl syn* see CREDENTIALS
documentation *n syn* see CREDENTIALS
doddering *adj syn* see SENILE
doddery *adj syn* see SENILE
dodge *vb* **1** to avoid or evade by some maneuver or shift <*dodging* in and out among the crowd> <*dodged* his pursuer with ease>
  syn duck, fence, parry, shirk, sidestep
  rel malinger; avoid, elude, escape, evade, skirt; slide, slip; short-circuit
  idiom fight shy of
  con ‖banter, beard, brave, challenge, dare, defy, front, venture; confront, encounter, meet
  ant face
  2 *syn* see EQUIVOCATE 2
dodo *n syn* see DUNCE
‖**dods** *n pl syn* see SULK
‖**dodunk** *n syn* see DUNCE
doff *vb syn* see REMOVE 3
do for *vb syn* see HELP 1
dofunny *n syn* see DOODAD

---

syn synonym(s)   *rel* related word(s)
ant antonym(s)   *con* contrasted word(s)
idiom idiomatic equivalent(s)
‖ use limited; if in doubt, see a dictionary

dog *n* **1** a highly variable carnivorous domesticated mammal <many households have *dogs* as pets>
syn bowwow, canine, hound, ‖pooch, tyke
rel pup, puppy; cur, ‖feist, mongrel, mutt
2 *syn* see SNOT 1
3 *syn* see FRANKFURTER
4 *syn* see JALOPY
dog *vb syn* see TAIL
Dogberry *n syn* see POLICEMAN
dogfall *n syn* see DRAW 4
dogfight *n syn* see BRAWL 2
dogged *adj* **1** *syn* see INFLEXIBLE 2
2 *syn* see PERSISTENT 1
doggery *n syn* see RABBLE 2
doggish *adj syn* see DAPPER
doggone *adj* **1** *syn* see DAMNED 2
2 *syn* see UTTER
doggy *adj syn* see DAPPER
dogma *n syn* see DOCTRINE
rel belief, conviction, persuasion, view
dogmatic *adj* **1** *syn* see DICTATORIAL
2 *syn* see DEDUCTIVE
dog nap *n syn* see NAP
dog's age *n syn* see AGE 2
‖**dogsbody** *n syn* see SLAVE 2
do in *vb* **1** *syn* see RUIN 2
2 *syn* see MURDER 1
3 *syn* see EXHAUST 4
doing *n syn* see ACTION 1
doit *n syn* see PARTICLE
doldrums *n pl* **1** *syn* see TEDIUM
rel blues, dejection, depression, dumps, gloom; apathy, disinterest, indifference, listlessness
con high spirits, spirits
2 *syn* see ABEYANCE
rel depression, retardation, slump, stagnation; inactivity
dole (out) *vb* **1** *syn* see ADMINISTER 2
2 *syn* see DISTRIBUTE 1
‖**dole** *n* **1** *syn* see SORROW
2 *syn* see MISFORTUNE
doleful *adj* **1** *syn* see DOWNCAST
2 *syn* see WOEFUL 1
3 *syn* see MELANCHOLY 2
rel grieving, mourning, sorrowing; piteous, pitiful
con blithe, blithesome, radiant, sparkling, sunny
ant cheerful, cheery
dolefuls *n pl, used with* the *syn* see SADNESS
dolent *adj syn* see WOEFUL 1
dolesome *adj syn* see MELANCHOLY 2
dolittle *n syn* see SLUGGARD
‖**doll** *n syn* see WOMAN 1
dollar *n* a currency bill representing one hundred cents <had a single *dollar* left>
syn bill, ‖bone, ‖buck, ‖fish, ‖frogskin, ‖iron man, oner, rock, ‖skin, ‖smacker, ‖smackeroo
dollop *n syn* see DRAM 1
doll out *vb syn* see DRESS UP 1
doll up *vb syn* see DRESS UP 1
dolor *n syn* see DISTRESS
con blessedness, bliss, felicity, happiness

ant beatitude
dolorous *adj* **1** *syn* see DEPLORABLE
2 *syn* see WOEFUL 1
3 *syn* see MELANCHOLY 2
dolt *n syn* see DUNCE
dolthead *n syn* see DUNCE
doltish *adj syn* see STUPID 1
domain *n syn* see FIELD
‖**dome** *n syn* see HEAD 1
domestic *adj* **1** of or relating to the household or family <*domestic* chores required to maintain a home>
syn family, home, household
con civic, public; personal, private; business, occupational, professional
2 of, relating to, or carried on within an indicated or implied country <charts of *domestic* as well as foreign waters>
syn home, ‖inland, internal, intestine, municipal, national, native
ant foreign
3 *syn* see TAME
domesticate *vb* to adapt (an animal or plant) to life in intimate association with and to the advantage of man <the man who *domesticated* the first dog>
syn domesticize, domiciliate, master, tame
rel gentle, subdue; housebreak; break, bust, train
domesticated *adj syn* see TAME
domesticize *vb syn* see DOMESTICATE
domicile *n syn* see HABITATION 2
domicile *vb syn* see HARBOR 2
domiciliate *vb* **1** *syn* see HARBOR 2
2 *syn* see DOMESTICATE
dominance *n syn* see SUPREMACY
dominant *adj* **1** superior to all others in power, influence, or importance <the Sumerians were a *dominant* race of ancient times>
syn ascendant, master, outweighing, overbalancing, overbearing, overweighing, paramount, predominant, predominate, preponderant, prevalent, regnant, sovereign
rel prevailing; preeminent, supreme, surpassing, transcendent; chief, first, foremost, leading, main, principal; governing, ruling
con collateral, dependent, secondary, subject, tributary; unimportant
ant subordinate
2 *syn* see CHIEF 2
dominate *vb* **1** *syn* see GOVERN 3
2 *syn* see RULE 2
3 *syn* see OVERLOOK 2
domination *n* **1** *syn* see SUPREMACY
2 *syn* see POWER 1
dominator *n syn* see LEADER 2
domineer *vb syn* see RULE 2
domineering *adj syn* see MASTERFUL 1
rel arrogant, insolent, lordly
con obsequious, servile, slavish; bootlicking, groveling, sycophantic, toadying
ant subservient; fawning
‖**dominie** *n syn* see CLERGYMAN
dominion *n* **1** *syn* see SUPREMACY

2 *syn* see FIELD

3 *syn* see OWNERSHIP

domino *n syn* see MASK 1

domitae naturae *adj syn* see TAME

don *vb* **1** to place on one's person (an article of clothing) <*donned* a raincoat for his trip>
syn assume, draw on, get on, huddle (on), put on, slip (on), throw
rel apparel, array, attire, clad, clothe, dress, enclothe, garb, garment, raiment
con cast, pull (off), remove, take off, throw off; unclothe, undress; disrobe
ant doff
2 to clothe or envelop oneself in <able to *don* a new personality at will>
syn assume, pull, put on, strike, take on
rel camouflage, color, disguise; belie, falsify, garble, misrepresent

donate *vb syn* see GIVE 1

donation *n* a gift of money or its equivalent to a charity, humanitarian cause, or public institution <sought *donations* for victims of the flood>
syn alms, benefaction, beneficence, charity, contribution, offering
rel aid, assistance, help, relief; philanthropy; bequest, endowment; appropriation, grant, subsidy, subvention; allowance, dole, pittance, ration

donator *n syn* see DONOR

done *adj* **1** *syn* see DECOROUS 1

2 *syn* see COMPLETE 4

3 *syn* see EFFETE 2

4 *syn* see THROUGH 4

done for *adj syn* see THROUGH 3

done in *adj syn* see EFFETE 2

‖**doney** *n syn* see GIRL FRIEND 1

‖**donicker** *n syn* see TOILET

Don Juan *n* **1** *syn* see GALLANT 2

2 *syn* see WOLF

donk *n syn* see DONKEY 1

donkey *n* **1** the domestic ass <the *donkey,* a typical pack animal>
syn ass, burro, donk, jackass, ‖moke, ‖neddy, ‖Rocky Mountain canary
rel ‖dickey, jack; hinny, mule; jennet, jenny, jenny ass
2 *syn* see FOOL 1

donkeyish *adj syn* see FOOLISH 2

donkey's years *n pl syn* see AGE 2

donkeywork *n syn* see WORK 2

donnybrook *n syn* see BRAWL 2

donor *n* one that gives something to another <a *donor* of funds to research foundations>
syn bestower, conferrer, donator, giver, presenter
rel contributor, subscriber

do–nothing *n syn* see SLUGGARD

‖**donsie** *adj syn* see UNWELL

doodad *n* something trivial which is hard to classify or whose name is unknown <wondered what the little round *doodad* was for>
syn business, dingus, dofunny, doohickey, gadget, gizmo, ‖hootenanny, jigger, rigamajig, thingum, thingumajig, thingumbob, thingummy; *compare* GADGET 1, WHAT-DO-YOU-CALL-IT

doodle *n syn* see FOOL 1

‖**doodle** *vb syn* see CHEAT

doodle *vb syn* see FIDDLE 2

doohickey *n syn* see DOODAD

doom *n syn* see FATE
rel calamity, cataclysm, catastrophe, disaster, tragedy

doom *vb syn* see SENTENCE

doom (to) *vb syn* see PREDESTINE 1

doomed *adj syn* see DAMNED 1

doomful *adj syn* see OMINOUS

door *n* **1** an opening by which one can enter or leave a structure and especially a building <looked through the front *door*>
syn doorway, entrance, entranceway, entry, entryway, portal
2 a means or right of entering, approaching, or participating <viewed education as the *door* to success>
syn access, adit, admission, admittance, entrance, entrée, entry, ingress, way

doormat *n syn* see WEAKLING

doorway *n syn* see DOOR 1

‖**doozer** *n syn* ‖DILLY, ‖corker, ‖daisy, dandy, ‖dinger, humdinger, jim-dandy, ‖lalapalooza, ‖lulu, peach

dope *n* **1** *syn* see DRUG 2

2 *syn* see DUNCE

dope (up) *vb syn* see ADULTERATE

doped *adj syn* see DRUGGED

‖**dope out** *vb* **1** *syn* see SOLVE 2

2 *syn* see INFER

3 *syn* see PLAN 2

dopey *adj syn* see LETHARGIC

‖**do–re–mi** *n syn* see MONEY

‖**dorm** *vb syn* see DOZE

dormancy *n syn* see ABEYANCE

dormant *adj syn* see LATENT
ant active

‖**dort** *vb syn* see SULK

‖**dorts** *n pl syn* see SULK

‖**dorty** *adj syn* see SULLEN

‖**doss** *n syn* see SLEEP 1

‖**doss** *vb syn* see SLEEP

dot *n syn* see POINT 11

dot *vb* **1** *syn.* see SPECKLE 1

2 *syn* see SPOT 2

dot *n syn* see DOWRY

dotage *n* advanced age accompanied by a decline of mental poise and alertness <a doddering eighty-year-old entering his *dotage*>
syn second childhood, senility; *compare* OLD AGE
rel decrepitude, feebleness, infirmity; age, elderliness, senectitude
con adolescence, youth; maturity

dote (on *or* upon) *vb syn* see ADORE 3
rel enjoy, fancy, like
idiom be sweet on
ant loathe

---

syn synonym(s)   *rel* related word(s)
ant antonym(s)   *con* contrasted word(s)
idiom idiomatic equivalent(s)
‖ use limited; if in doubt, see a dictionary

‖**doted** *adj syn* see SENILE
doting *adj* **1** *syn* see SENILE
  2 *syn* see LOVING
  rel asinine, fatuous, foolish, silly, simple
dottiness *n syn* see FOOLISHNESS
dotty *adj* **1** *syn* see INFATUATED
  2 *syn* see FOOLISH 2
double *adj* **1** *syn* see TWOFOLD 1
  2 *syn* see TWIN
  3 *syn* see TWOFOLD 2
  4 *syn* see INSINCERE
double *n* **1** *syn* see MATE 5
  2 *syn* see IMAGE 1
  3 *syn* see TURN 2
  rel departure, digression, divergence, swerving, veering
double *vb* **1** to make twice as great or as many <*doubled* the amount of his salary>
  syn dualize, dupe, duplicate
  rel replicate; amplify, augment, enlarge, increase, magnify; supplement
  con decrease, lessen, minimize
  ant halve
  2 to make of two thicknesses by turning or bending usually in the middle <he *doubled* the towel for better absorbency>
  syn fold
  rel pleat, plicate, turn over
  3 *syn* see ESCAPE 2
  4 *syn* see DUB
double–barreled *adj* **1** *syn* see TWOFOLD 2
  2 *syn* see TWOFOLD 1
double–cross *vb* **1** *syn* see DECEIVE
  2 *syn* see BETRAY 2
double–dealer *n syn* see SWINDLER
double–dealing *n syn* see DECEPTION 1
double–dealing *adj syn* see INSINCERE
double–distilled *adj syn* see UTTER
‖**double–dog dare** *vb syn* see FACE 3
double–dome *n syn* see INTELLECTUAL 2
double–dyed *adj syn* see UTTER
double–edged *adj syn* see OBSCURE 3
double entendre *n syn* see AMBIGUITY
double–faced *adj* **1** *syn* see OBSCURE 3
  2 *syn* see INSINCERE
doublehearted *adj syn* see INSINCERE
double meaning *n syn* see AMBIGUITY
double–minded *adj* **1** *syn* see VACILLATING 2
  idiom of two minds
  2 *syn* see INSINCERE
doublet *n syn* see COUPLE
double–talk *n* **1** *syn* see NONSENSE 2
  2 *syn* see GOBBLEDYGOOK
double–tongued *adj syn* see INSINCERE
doubt *vb* **1** *syn* see QUESTION 2
  2 *syn* see DISTRUST
  con accredit, credit, trust; accept, believe, ‖buy, swallow
doubt *n syn* see UNCERTAINTY
  rel dubiousness, questionableness; disbelief, incredulity, unbelief
  con dependence, faith, reliance, trust
  ant certitude; confidence
doubtable *adj syn* see DOUBTFUL 1

  ant undoubtable
doubter *n syn* see SKEPTIC
doubtful *adj* **1** not having or affording assurance of the certainty or soundness of something or someone <their chance of success is *doubtful*>
  syn ambiguous, borderline, clouded, doubtable, dubious, dubitable, equivocal, fishy, impugnable, indecisive, open, precarious, problematic, queasy, shady, shaky, suspect, suspicious, uncertain, unclear, undecided, uneasy, unsettled, unstable, unsure; *compare* MOOT
  rel question-begging; touch-and-go; chancy, insecure, questionable, speculative; hazy, obscure; unlikely; contingent, iffy
  idiom at issue, in dispute, in doubt, in question
  con decisive, open-and-shut, positive, sure; inarguable, incontestable, unarguable, undeniable, undoubted, unquestionable
  ant indubitable
  2 *syn* see MOOT
  3 *syn* see IMPROBABLE 1
doubtfully *adv syn* see ASKANCE 2
doubtfulness *n syn* see UNCERTAINTY
doubting Thomas *n syn* see SKEPTIC
doubtless *adv* **1** *syn* see EASILY 2
  2 *syn* see PRESUMABLY
doubtlessly *adv* **1** *syn* see WELL 7
  ant doubtfully
  2 *syn* see EASILY 2
dough *n syn* see MONEY
doughface *n syn* see MASK 1
‖**doughhead** *n syn* see DUNCE
doughty *adj syn* see BRAVE 1
doughy *adj syn* see PALE 1
do up *vb syn* see MEND 2
dour *adj* **1** *syn* see GRIM 2
  rel rigid, rigorous, strict; implacable
  2 *syn* see SULLEN
‖**douse** *n syn* see BLOW 1
douse *vb syn* see REMOVE 3
douse *vb* **1** *syn* see DIP 1
  2 *syn* see WET
  con bake, dehydrate, desiccate, dry, parch
  3 *syn* see SPLASH
  4 *syn* see EXTINGUISH 1
‖**dout** *vb syn* see EXTINGUISH 1
dove *n syn* see PACIFIST
  ant hawk
dovecote *n* a small compartmented raised house or box for domestic pigeons <old countryseats with elaborate stone *dovecotes*>
  syn columbary, culverhouse, dovehouse, pigeon house, pigeonry
  rel aviary, birdhouse; perch, roost
dovehouse *n syn* see DOVECOTE
‖**dover** *n syn* see NAP
dovetail *vb syn* see AGREE 4
dowager *n syn* see MATRIARCH
dowd *n syn* see SLATTERN 1
dowdy *n syn* see SLATTERN 1
dowdy *adj* **1** *syn* see SLATTERNLY
  con chic, fashionable, modish, stylish; flashy, garish, gaudy
  ant smart

2 syn see TACKY 2
ant smart
3 syn see OLD-FASHIONED
dower *n syn* see DOWRY
dower *vb syn* see ENDOW 1
  rel accouter, appoint, equip, furnish, outfit
||**dowly** *adj syn* see OVERCAST
down *adv* **1** from a higher to a lower level <the land sloped *down* toward the sea>
  syn downward, downwardly, downwards, netherwards
  rel below, earthward, groundward; downgrade, downhill, downslope
  con aloft, upward, upwardly, upwards
  ant up
  2 to completion <wash *down* the car>
  syn completely, fully, through-and-through
  idiom from top to bottom
  3 syn see SERIOUSLY 1
down *adj* **1 syn** see SLOW 3
  2 syn see DOWNCAST
  ant up
  3 syn see SICK 1
  4 syn see LOWER
  ant up
  5 syn see COMPLETE 4
down *n syn* see COMEDOWN
down *vb* **1 syn** see SWALLOW 1
  2 syn see DEFEAT 2
  3 syn see FELL 1
  4 syn see KILL 1
  5 syn see OVERCOME 1
down *n* a soft fluffy material or covering <the *down* on a peach>
  syn floss, flue, fluff, fur, fuzz, lint, pile
down–and–out *n syn* see PAUPER
down–at–heel *adj syn* see SHABBY 1
downcast *n syn* see DEFEAT 1
downcast *adj* low in spirits <felt *downcast* by the rejection>
  syn bad, blue, cast down, chapfallen, crestfallen, dejected, depressed, disconsolate, dispirited, doleful, down, downhearted, down-in-the-mouth, downthrown, droopy, dull, heartsick, heartsore, hipped, low, low-spirited, mopey, soul-sick, spiritless, sunk, woebegone; *compare* SAD 1
  rel discouraged, disheartened; oppressed, weighed down; distressed, troubled; despondent, forlorn; listless; broody, moody; gloomy, glum, morose
  idiom in the depths
  con cheerful, happy, joyous, lighthearted; excited, exhilarated, intoxicated; buoyed up, gladdened; encouraged, heartened; animated, gay, lively, sprightly, vivacious; delighted, pleased
  ant elated
downcry *vb syn* see DECRY 2
downfall *n* **1 syn** see DETERIORATION 1
  rel comedown, descent, discomfiture, down
  2 something that causes a downfall <drink was his *downfall*>
  syn bane, destroyer, destruction, ruin, ruination, undoing

  rel headache, problem, trouble
  idiom road to ruin
  con aid, help, support
downgrade *n syn* see DETERIORATION 1
  ant upgrade
downgrade *vb* **1 syn** see DEPRECIATE 1
  ant upgrade
  2 syn see DEGRADE 1
  ant upgrade
downgrading *n syn* see DEMOTION
  ant upgrading
downhearted *adj syn* see DOWNCAST
down–in–the–mouth *adj syn* see DOWNCAST
downright *adj* **1 syn** see UTTER
  2 being what is stated beyond any possibility of doubt <a *downright* lie>
  syn flat, indubitable, unquestionable, up-and-down; *compare* POSITIVE 3
  rel out-and-out, sure-enough; absolute, positive; certain, clear
downside–up *adj syn* see UPSIDE-DOWN 2
downslide *n syn* see DECLINE 3
downswing *n syn* see DECLINE 3
downthrow *n syn* see DEFEAT 1
downthrown *adj syn* see DOWNCAST
down–to–date *adj syn* see UP-TO-DATE
down–to–earth *adj syn* see REALISTIC
downtrend *n syn* see DECLINE 3
downtrodden *adj* oppressed by superior power <the *downtrodden* peasants>
  syn abject, underfoot
  rel oppressed, persecuted; abused, maltreated, mistreated
downturn *n syn* see DECLINE 3
downward *adv syn* see DOWN 1
  ant upward
downwardly *adv syn* see DOWN 1
  ant upwardly
downwards *adv syn* see DOWN 1
  ant upwards
||**downy** *adj syn* see SLY 2
dowry *n* the money, goods, or estate that a woman brings to her husband in marriage <from a poor family, she came to her marriage with no *dowry*>
  syn dot, dower, marriage portion
  con bride-price, bridewealth; settlement
doxy *n* **1** a usually young woman who is sexually promiscuous <a *doxy* who frequented singles bars>
  syn ||chippy, floozy, grisette, light-o'-love, nymph, nymphet, party girl, tart, ||tootsie
  rel groupie
  idiom woman of easy virtue
  ||**2 syn** see MISTRESS
doyen *n* **1 syn** see LEADER 1
  2 syn see EXPERT
doze *vb* to sleep lightly <he was inclined to *doze* at his desk>

---

syn synonym(s)   *rel* related word(s)
ant antonym(s)   *con* contrasted word(s)
idiom idiomatic equivalent(s)
|| use limited; if in doubt, see a dictionary

syn ||dorm, drowse, ||sloom, slumber, ||snoozle, ||sog; *compare* NAP, SLEEP

doze (off) *vb* to fall into a light sleep <*dozed* off while sitting before the fire>
syn drop off, drowse (off)
idiom drift off

doze *n* a light sleep <was caught in a *doze* at her desk>
syn drowse, ||sloom, slumber; *compare* NAP, SLEEP 1

dozy *adj syn* see SLEEPY 1

DP *n syn* see REFUGEE

drab *n* 1 *syn* see HAG 2
    2 *syn* see SLATTERN 1
    3 *syn* see PROSTITUTE

drab *adj* 1 *syn* see DULL 8
    2 *syn* see COLORLESS 2
    rel bleak, desolate, dismal, dispiriting, dreary; dingy, faded
    con bright, brilliant, luminous

draconian *adj syn* see RIGID 3

draffy *adj syn* see WORTHLESS 1

draft *n* DRINK 3, drag, drain, drench, ||peg, swig, swill

draft *vb* 1 to enroll in the armed forces by compulsion <*drafted* when he was barely eighteen>
syn conscribe, conscript; *compare* CALL UP
rel induct; enlist, enroll, muster (in *or* out); impress, press
    2 *syn* see SKETCH
    3 to formulate and produce <*drafting* plans to meet an emergency>
    syn draw up, formulate, frame, make, prepare
    rel concoct, contrive, devise, invent; fabricate, fashion, forge, form, manufacture, shape; plan, project; outline, sketch
    4 *syn* see DRAIN 1

drag *n* 1 *syn* see DRAW 1
    2 *syn* see DRINK 3
    ||3 *syn* see PULL 2
    ||4 *syn* see WAY 1
    5 *syn* see BORE

drag *vb* 1 *syn* see PULL 2
    con propel, push, shove, thrust; drive, impel, move
    2 *syn* see DELAY 2
    idiom drag one's feet (*or* heels)
    con hasten, hurry
    3 to hang down and be drawn behind <her dress *dragged* in the dust>
    syn draggle, trail, traipse
    rel droop, hang, sag

||drag down *vb syn* see EARN 1

dragging *adj syn* see LONG 2

draggle *vb syn* see DRAG 3

draggle–tail *n syn* see SLATTERN 1

draggletailed *adj syn* see SLATTERNLY

dragoon *vb syn* see INTIMIDATE

drain *vb* 1 to draw off (liquid) by degrees <*drain* the water from the swimming pool>
syn draft, draw, draw off, pump, siphon, tap
rel milk; bleed; suck; empty, exhaust
    2 *syn* see TIRE 1
    3 *syn* see DEPLETE

idiom bleed white

drain (away) *vb syn* see DECREASE

drain *n syn* see DRINK 3

drained *adj syn* see EFFETE 2

dram *n* 1 a small quantity of something (as alcoholic liquor) to drink <a *dram* of brandy helped to break his chill>
syn ||caulker, dollop, drop, jolt, nip, shot, slug, snifter, snort, snorter, spot, toothful, tot, ||wet
rel draft, drink, ||peg, potation, pull, swig, swill; finger; jigger; dash; ||splash; snack; quick one
    2 *syn* see PARTICLE

drama *n* dramatic art, literature, or affairs <was interested in *drama* during her college years>
syn boards, footlights, (the) stage, theater
rel show business

dramatic *adj* 1 of or relating to drama <made no objections to his son's *dramatic* ambitions>
syn dramaturgic, histrionic, theatral, theatric, theatrical, thespian
    2 *syn* see THEATRICAL 2
ant undramatic

dramatist *n syn* see PLAYWRIGHT

dramatizer *n syn* see PLAYWRIGHT

dramaturge *n syn* see PLAYWRIGHT

dramaturgic *adj syn* see DRAMATIC 1

drape *vb* 1 *syn* see SWATHE
    2 *syn* see SPRAWL 1

dratted *adj syn* see DAMNED 2

draw *vb* 1 *syn* see PULL 2
    rel bring, fetch; educe, elicit, evoke, extract
    con propel, push, shove, thrust; drive, impel, move
    2 *syn* see DRAIN 1
    3 *syn* see ATTRACT 1
    4 *syn* see INDUCE 1
    5 *syn* see TAKE 14
    6 *syn* see INFER
    7 *syn* see EXTEND 3
    8 *syn* see DEPLETE
    9 *syn* see EVISCERATE

draw *n* 1 a sucking pull on something (as a sipping straw or cigarette) <took a long *draw* on his pipe before answering>
syn drag, puff, pull
rel smoke; inhale
    2 *syn* see ADVANTAGE 3
    3 *syn* see ATTRACTION 1
    4 an indecisive ending to a contest or competition <the prizefight ended in a *draw*>
    syn deadlock, dogfall, stalemate, standoff, tie
    rel dead heat, photo finish; standstill
    con loss; win

draw back *vb syn* see DEDUCT 1

drawback *n syn* see DISADVANTAGE
    rel evil, ill; inconvenience, trouble
    con advantage, edge

draw down *vb* 1 *syn* see EARN 1
    2 *syn* see DEPLETE

draw in *vb syn* see INDUCE 1

drawing *adj syn* see ATTRACTIVE 1

drawing power *n syn* see ATTRACTION 1

drawing room *n syn* see SALON 1

drawn *adj syn* see HAGGARD

con hale, robust

drawn–out *adj syn* see LONG 2

draw off *vb syn* see DRAIN 1
　rel abstract; withdraw; move, remove, shift, transfer

draw on *vb* **1** *syn* see EFFECT 1
　2 *syn* see INDUCE 1
　3 *syn* see DON 1

draw out *vb syn* see EXTEND 3

draw up *vb* **1** *syn* see DRAFT 3
　2 *syn* see STOP 4

dray horse *n syn* see SLAVE 2

dread *n syn* see FEAR 1

dreadful *adj syn* see FEARFUL 3

‖**dreadful** *adv syn* see VERY 1

dreadful *n syn* see DIME NOVEL

dreadfully *adv syn* see VERY 1

dream *n* **1** *syn* see FANCY 4
　2 *syn* see PIPE DREAM

dream *vb syn* see LONG

dreamer *n* one whose conduct is guided more by ideals than practicalities <a *dreamer* proposing glorious plans impossible to make work>
　syn castle-builder, idealist, ideologue, utopian, visionary
　rel daydreamer, illusionist, lotus-eater, wishful thinker; Don Quixote; theorist
　con pragmatist, realist; Babbitt, Philistine; pedant

dream up *vb syn* see CONTRIVE 2

dreamy *adj* **1** given to dreaming, reverie, or fancy <a *dreamy* and most impractical person>
　syn astral, daydreaming, daydreamy, otherworldly, unworldly, visionary
　rel fanciful, idealistic, romantic, whimsical
　con down-to-earth, practical, pragmatic, realistic; actual, factual
　2 *syn* see MARVELOUS 2

drear *adj syn* see GLOOMY 3

dreary *adj* **1** *syn* see GLOOMY 3
　2 *syn* see DULL 9

dreck *n syn* see REFUSE

dreg *n, usu* **dregs** *pl* **1** *syn* see SEDIMENT
　2 *syn* see RABBLE 2

‖**dreich** *adj syn* see LONG 2

drench *n syn* see DRINK 3

drench *vb* **1** *syn* see WET
　rel dip, duck, dunk, immerse, submerge
　2 *syn* see SOAK 1
　3 *syn* see POUR 3

drenched *adj syn* see WET 1

dress *vb* **1** *syn* see CLOTHE
　ant undress
　2 *syn* see BANDAGE
　3 to remove the entrails from <*dress* fish, fowl, or game>
　syn clean, gut
　rel butcher, slaughter
　4 *syn* see TILL
　rel fertilize, topdress

dress (up) *vb syn* see ADORN

dress *n* **1** *syn* see CLOTHES
　2 *syn* see COSTUME

dress down *vb syn* see SCOLD 1

dress up *vb* **1** to attire in best or formal clothes <*dressed up* to go to the theater>
　syn deck (out), ‖dike (out *or* up), doll out, doll up, ‖dude up, fix up, gussy up, prank, ‖prick (up), primp, prink (up), slick, smarten (up), smug, spiff, spruce (up), tog (out *or* up), ‖toggle, trick (off, out, *or* up)
　rel prettify, pretty (up); apparel, array, attire, clad, clothe, dress, enclothe, garb, garment, raiment; overdress; preen; prim (up)
　idiom dress fit to kill, dress to the nines, put on the dog
　2 *syn* see DISGUISE

drib *vb syn* see DRIP

drib *n syn* see DROP 1

dribble *vb* **1** *syn* see DRIP
　2 *syn* see DROOL 2

dribble (away) *vb syn* see WASTE 2

dribble *n syn* see PITTANCE

driblet *n* **1** *syn* see PITTANCE
　2 *syn* see DROP 1

drift *n* **1** *syn* see FLOW
　2 *syn* see PILE 1
　rel array, batch, bunch, bundle, clump, cluster, clutch, group, lot, parcel, set
　‖**3** *syn* see DROVE 2
　4 *syn* see TENDENCY 1
　rel motion, movement, progress, progression; aim, intent, intention, purpose
　5 *syn* see LEANING 2
　6 *syn* see TENOR 1
　rel direction, line, set

drift *vb* **1** to become carried or floated along <cakes of ice *drifting* along the stream>
　syn float, ride, wash
　rel dart, fly, sail, scud, shoot, skim; dance, flicker, flit, flitter, flutter, hover
　2 *syn* see SAUNTER
　3 *syn* see WANDER 1
　4 *syn* see SLIDE 6
　5 *syn* see HEAP 1

drifter *n* **1** *syn* see ROVER
　2 *syn* see VAGABOND

driftwood *n* vagrant impoverished people <the *driftwood* of skid row>
　syn flotsam, jetsam, wreckage

drill *vb* **1** *syn* see PERFORATE
　2 *syn* see EXERCISE 3
　rel accustom, habituate

drill *n syn* see EXERCISE 3

drilling *n syn* see EXERCISE 3

drink *vb* **1** to take in (potable liquid) <the boys *drank* all the soda>
　syn imbibe, quaff, sip, sup (off *or* up), swallow, toss
　rel drain, gulp, guzzle, slosh, slurp, swig, swill; wash down
　idiom wet one's whistle

---

syn synonym(s)　　　*rel* related word(s)
ant antonym(s)　　　*con* contrasted word(s)
idiom idiomatic equivalent(s)
‖ use limited; if in doubt, see a dictionary

2 to salute and wish honor and health to (a person) by raising and then drinking from a vessel <*drink* to the bride and groom>
syn pledge, toast
rel honor, salute; wet
3 to partake of alcoholic liquors especially habitually or to excess <he *drinks* but does not smoke>
syn booze, guzzle, imbibe, liquor (up), ‖lush (up), nip, soak, swig, swill, swizzle, tank up, tipple, tope
idiom bend the elbow, cheer the inner man, drink like a fish, go on a binge, hit the bottle, take a nip
drink *n* **1** liquid suitable for swallowing <able to make palatable *drink* from seawater>
syn beverage, drinkable, liquor, potable
rel liquid; brew; potion
2 *syn* see LIQUOR 2
3 a portion of potable liquid <took a *drink* from the cup>
syn draft, drag, drain, drench, ‖peg, swig, swill
rel draw, pull; finger, jigger; libation
4 *syn* see OCEAN
drinkable *adj syn* see POTABLE
drinkable *n syn* see DRINK 1
drinkery *n syn* see BAR 5
drip *vb* to let fall drops of moisture or liquid <trees *dripping* after the rain>
syn distill, drib, dribble, drop, trickle, trill, weep
rel spatter, sprinkle, spurtle; gush, pour, sluice, stream
‖**drip** *n* **1** *syn* see NONSENSE 2
2 *syn* see DUNCE
dripping *adj syn* see WET 1
drippy *adj syn* see SENTIMENTAL
drive *vb* **1** *syn* see MOVE 5
rel coerce, compel, force; incite, instigate
con check, curb, inhibit, restrain; guide, lead, pilot, steer
2 *syn* see PUSH 1
3 to urge along (as cattle) <cowboys *driving* the great herds north>
syn ‖drove, herd, run
rel shepherd; wrangle; egg, exhort, goad, prick, prod, punch, sic, spur, urge
4 *syn* see THRUST 2
5 to operate and steer (a motor vehicle) <*drive* a car>
syn auto, charioteer, motor, pilot, tool, wheel
rel operate, run, work; guide, steer; roll; chauffeur
6 *syn* see IMPRESS 3
7 *syn* see PLUNGE 2
8 *syn* see LABOR 1
drive *n* **1** a short trip in a vehicle <took a *drive* around town>
syn ride, spin, turn; *compare* TRIP 1
rel whirl; joyride; excursion, outing
2 *syn* see DRIVEWAY
3 *syn* see ENTERPRISE 4
4 *syn* see VIGOR 2
rel impetus, momentum, speed, velocity
drivel *vb* **1** *syn* see DROOL 2

2 *syn* see BABBLE 2
3 *syn* see WASTE 2
drivel *n* **1** *syn* see NONSENSE 2
2 *syn* see GIBBERISH 1
driveling *adj syn* see INSIPID 3
driver *n syn* see MOTORIST
driveway *n* a private road giving access from a public way <the *driveway* to a house>
syn ‖avenue, drive
rel court, place, row, street
driving *adj syn* see ENERGETIC 2
drizzle *vb syn* see SPRINKLE 5
drogher *n syn* see BEARER 2
drôlerie *n syn* see JOKE 1
droll *adj syn* see LAUGHABLE
rel absurd, preposterous
droll *n syn* see HUMORIST 2
drollery *n* **1** *syn* see JOKE 1
2 *syn* see HUMOR 4
drollness *n syn* see HUMOR 4
drone *vb* **1** *syn* see HUM
2 *syn* see IDLE
drony *adj syn* see LAZY
drool *vb* **1** to secrete or become filled with saliva usually in anticipation of food <mouths *drooled* as we waited for dinner>
syn water
idiom water at the mouth
2 to let saliva or some other substance flow from the mouth <babies often *drool* uncontrollably>
syn dribble, drivel, salivate, slabber, slaver, slobber
3 *syn* see ENTHUSE 2
4 *syn* see BABBLE 2
drool *n syn* see NONSENSE 2
droop *vb* **1** *syn* see SLOUCH
2 *syn* see LOWER 3
3 to become literally or figuratively limp through loss of vigor or freshness <he walked along, his shoulders *drooping* from exhaustion>
syn flag, sag, swag, wilt
rel drop, fall, sink, slump, subside; dangle, hang, loll, lop, sling, suspend; decline, deteriorate, ‖dwine, fade, fail, languish, weaken
droopy *adj syn* see DOWNCAST
drop *n* **1** the quantity of fluid that falls in one spherical mass <a *drop* of rain>
syn drib, driblet, droplet, globule, gobbet
rel dribble, drip, trickle
2 *syn* see PARTICLE
3 *syn* see DRAM
4 *syn* see DESCENT 4
5 *syn* see DESCENT 1
6 *syn* see DECLINE 3
7 *syn* see DEPTH 1
drop *vb* **1** *syn* see FALL 2
2 *syn* see FALL 1
ant mount
3 *syn* see PLUMMET
rel slide, slip
con rally, rebound; ascend, climb; soar
ant mount
4 *syn* see COLLAPSE 2
rel backslide, lapse, relapse

5 *syn* see DIE 1
6 *syn* see DRIP
7 *syn* see FELL 1
8 *syn* see QUIT 6
9 *syn* see CANCEL 2
10 *syn* see DISMISS 3
11 *syn* see LOSE 2
12 *syn* see LOSE 1
drop (in *or* by) *vb syn* see VISIT 2
drop (off) *vb syn* see SLIP 6
droplet *n syn* see DROP 1
drop off *vb syn* see DOZE (off)
dropsical *adj syn* see INFLATED
dropsied *adj syn* see INFLATED
drossy *adj syn* see WORTHLESS 1
droughty *adj syn* see DRY 1
‖drouk *vb syn* see SOAK 1
drove *n* **1** *syn* see CROWD 1
　2 a group of domestic animals reared or handled
　as a unit <a *drove* of cattle>
　syn ‖drift, flock, herd
　rel drive; pack; school
‖drove *vb syn* see DRIVE 3
drown *vb* **1** *syn* see OVERWHELM 4
　2 *syn* see DELUGE 1
　3 *syn* see WET
drowse *vb syn* see DOZE
drowse (off) *vb syn* see DOZE (off)
drowse *n syn* see DOZE
drowsy *adj syn* see SLEEPY 1
　rel lackadaisical, languid, languorous
　con alert, vigilant, watchful; active, dynamic,
　live; animated, lively, vivacious
drub *vb* **1** *syn* see BEAT 1
　2 *syn* see LAMBASTE 3
　3 *syn* see WHIP 2
drubbing *n syn* see DEFEAT 1
drudge *vb* to perform hard, menial, or monoto-
　nous work <*drudged* all day washing floors>
　syn grind, grub, ‖muck, plod, slave, slog, toil
　rel hammer, peg (away *or* at *or* on), plow, plug,
　pound (away); perform, work
　idiom keep one's nose to the grindstone
　con idle, laze, loaf, lounge; dally, dawdle, pot-
　ter, putter; cheat, chisel
drudge *n* **1** *syn* see SLAVE 2
　2 *syn* see WORK 2
　3 *syn* see HACK 2
drudgery *n syn* see WORK 2
drudging *adj syn* see IRKSOME
drug *n* **1** a substance used by itself or in a mixture
　in the treatment or diagnosis of disease <a life-
　sustaining *drug*>
　syn biologic, medicinal, pharmaceutic, pharma-
　ceutical
　rel cure, medicament, medication, medicine,
　physic, remedy, specific; simple
　2 a narcotic substance or preparation <de-
　pended on *drugs* to make life bearable>
　syn dope, ‖hop, narcotic, opiate
drugged *adj* being under the influence of a drug
　taken for nonmedical purposes <was *drugged* on
　LSD>

　syn doped, high, hopped-up, spaced-out,
　stoned, tripped out, turned on, ‖wiped out,
　zonked
　idiom on a trip
　ant straight
druggist *n* one who deals in medicinal drugs
　syn apothecary, ‖chemist, pharmacist
　rel pharmacologist
drum *vb syn* see SOLICIT 1
drumfire *n syn* see BARRAGE
drumhead *adj syn* see SUMMARY 2
drum up *vb syn* see SOLICIT 1
drunk *adj syn* see INTOXICATED 1
　rel drinking, drinky
　idiom roaring drunk
　con bone-dry, dry
　ant sober
drunk *n* **1** *syn* see BINGE 1
　2 *syn* see DRUNKARD
drunkard *n* one who drinks alcoholic liquors to
　excess <*drunkards* lurching homeward when the
　bar finally closes>
　syn bibber, ‖bloat, ‖blotter, boozehound,
　boozer, drunk, fuddler, guzzler, inebriate, lush,
　‖lusher, rumdum, rummy, ‖rumpot, ‖shicker,
　soak, soaker, sot, sponge, stiff, swillbowl,
　swiller, tippler, toper, tosspot
　rel alcoholic, dipsomaniac; wino; drammer
　idiom elbow bender (*or* crooker)
　ant teetotaler
drunken *adj syn* see INTOXICATED 1
drunkery *n syn* see BAR 5
‖druthers *n syn* see CHOICE 1
dry *adj* **1** devoid of or deficient in moisture <pre-
　ferred a *dry* climate>
　syn arid, bone-dry, droughty, moistureless,
　sere, thirsty, unwatered, waterless
　rel baked, dehydrated, desiccated, parched;
　bald, bare, barren; depleted, drained, exhausted,
　impoverished; juiceless, sapless, sapped
　con drenched, dripping, saturated, soaked,
　soaking, sodden, sopping, soppy, soused, wring-
　ing-wet; damp, dank, humid, moist; exuberant,
　lush, luxuriant, prodigal, profuse
　ant wet
　2 *syn* see THIRSTY 1
　3 marked by the absence of or abstention from
　alcoholic beverages <a *dry* party>
　syn bone-dry, teetotal
　ant wet
　4 *syn* see IMPASSIVE 1
　5 *syn* see ARID 2
　6 *syn* see PLAIN 1
　7 *syn* see SOUR 1
　ant sweet
　8 *syn* see HARSH 3
dry *vb* **1** to treat or affect so as to deprive of mois-
　ture <clothes *dried* in the wind>
　syn dehydrate, desiccate, exsiccate, parch, sear

---

syn synonym(s)　　　*rel* related word(s)
ant antonym(s)　　　*con* contrasted word(s)
idiom idiomatic equivalent(s)
‖ use limited; if in doubt, see a dictionary

rel evaporate; anhydrate; deplete, drain, exhaust; shrivel, wither, wizen
con deluge, douse, drench, soak, sop, souse; damp, dampen, moisten
ant wet
2 *syn* see HARDEN 1
dryasdust *adj syn* see ARID 2
dry land *n syn* see EARTH 2
‖**dry–shave** *vb syn* see CHEAT
dry up *vb* **1 *syn*** see DESICCATE 2
2 *syn* see WITHER
3 *syn* see SHUT UP 2
dual *adj* **1 *syn*** see TWOFOLD 1
2 *syn* see TWIN
dualistic *adj syn* see TWOFOLD 1
dualize *vb syn* see DOUBLE 1
dub *vb* **1 *syn*** see NAME 1
2 *syn* see BOTCH
dub *vb* to provide (a motion-picture film) with a new sound track (as by substituting dialogue in a foreign language) <*dubbed* the Italian movie into English>
syn double
dubiety *n syn* see UNCERTAINTY
rel hesitancy; faltering, vacillation, wavering
con decidedness, decisiveness
ant decision
dubiosity *n syn* see UNCERTAINTY
rel addlement, confusion, muddlement; faltering, vacillation, wavering
con cocksureness, positiveness
ant decidedness
dubious *adj* **1 *syn*** see MOOT
2 *syn* see DOUBTFUL 1
rel skeptical; mistrustful; disinclined, hesitant, reluctant
con dependable, tried, trustworthy, trusty; certain, positive, sure
ant cocksure; reliable
3 *syn* see IMPROBABLE 1
4 *syn* see UNRELIABLE 1
ant trustworthy
dubitable *adj syn* see DOUBTFUL 1
ant indubitable
dubitancy *n syn* see UNCERTAINTY
duce *n syn* see TYRANT
‖**duck** *n syn* see ECCENTRIC
duck *vb* **1 *syn*** see DIP 1
2 to lower (as the head or body) quickly <had to *duck* his head to get through the door>
syn dip, stoop
rel bend; bow
3 *syn* see DODGE 1
rel avert, prevent, ward
4 *syn* see ESCAPE 2
duck soup *n syn* see SNAP 1
duct *n syn* see CHANNEL 1
ductile *adj syn* see PLASTIC
rel responsive; submitting; fluid, liquid
con intractable, refractory; adamant, obdurate
ductus *n syn* see HANDWRITING
dud *n syn* see FAILURE 5
dude *n syn* see FOP
‖**dude up** *vb syn* see DRESS UP 1

dudgeon *n syn* see OFFENSE 2
rel fury, ire, rage, wrath; humor, mood, temper
duds *n pl* **1 *syn*** see CLOTHES
‖**2 *syn*** see RAGS 1
due *adj* **1 *syn*** see JUST 3
rel good, right; equitable, fair, just; coming, earned
con excessive, exorbitant, extravagant, immoderate, inordinate; deficient
ant undue
2 having reached the date at which payment is required <a note that would become *due* after eighteen months>
syn mature, payable
3 *syn* see UNPAID 2
due *n* **1** what one fairly has coming <the artist has finally been accorded her *due*>
syn comeuppance, desert(s), deserving, lumps, merit, right(s)
rel deservedness, dueness, entitlement; compensation, payment, recompense, recompensing, repayment, satisfaction; reprisal, retaliation, retribution, revenge, vengeance; guerdon, need, reward
idiom what is coming to one
2 *syn* see DEBT 3
due *adv syn* see DIRECTLY 1
duel *vb syn* see RESIST
due to *prep syn* see OVER 6
‖**duff** *vb syn* see CHEAT
‖**duff** *n syn* see BUTTOCKS
duffer *n* ‖**1 *syn*** see PEDDLER
2 *syn* see DUNCE
dulcet *adj* **1 *syn*** see MELODIOUS 1
con grinding, rasping, scraping, scratching
ant grating
2 *syn* see SWEET 1
dull *adj* **1 *syn*** see STUPID 1
ant sharp
2 *syn* see RETARDED
con advanced, precocious
3 *syn* see INSENSIBLE 5
4 *syn* see DOWNCAST
5 *syn* see COLORLESS 2
ant bright
6 lacking sharpness of edge or point <a knife with a *dull* blade>
syn blunt, obtuse
rel blunted, dulled, unsharpened
con honed, keen, razor-sharp, unblunted, whetted
ant sharp
7 lacking warmth, luster, or brilliance <a smooth *dull* finish>
syn blind, dead, dim, flat, lackluster, lusterless, mat, muted
rel cold, dingy, drab, dun, leaden, somber; deadened, lifeless
con beaming, bright, brilliant, effulgent, fulgent, incandescent, lambent, lucent, lucid, luminous, lustrous, radiant, refulgent; burnished, polished, shiny
8 cloudy in color <a *dull* brown>
syn drab, muddy, murky, subfusc

rel blurry, cloudy, hazy; flat, lackluster, lifeless, lusterless; mousy
ant clear; rich
9 being so unvaried or uninteresting as to provoke boredom or tedium <any routine constantly repeated can become *dull*>
syn banausic, blah, ‖dim, dreary, humdrum, monotone, monotonous, pedestrian, plodding, poky, stodgy
rel boring, irksome, tedious, tiring, wearisome; brainless; exhausting, fagging, fatiguing
con animating, exciting, stimulating; gay, spritely
ant lively
10 *syn* see OVERCAST
11 *syn* see ARID 2
rel matter-of-fact, prosaic, prosy; bloodless
idiom dull as ditchwater
con exciting, stimulating
ant lively
dull *vb* **1** to make less clear, distinct, or bright <colors *dulled* by the sun>
syn dim, fade, muddy, pale, tarnish
rel discolor, wash out; blur
con brighten, freshen, intensify
2 *syn* see DEADEN 1
ant sharpen
3 to deprive of sharpness (as of edge or point) <*dull* a spade>
syn blunt, disedge, obtund, turn
idiom take the edge off
con edge, hone
ant sharpen
4 to impair one or more of the senses <age had *dulled* his hearing>
syn blear, blur, dim
rel debilitate, enfeeble, weaken; darken; retard, slow
ant sharpen
5 to make slow or obtuse <his mind had been *dulled* by drink>
syn blunt, hebetate, stupefy
rel becloud, befog, cloud, darken, dim; benumb, deaden, numb; retard, slow
con quicken, stimulate, whet
ant sharpen
dullard *n syn* see DUNCE
dullhead *n syn* see DUNCE
dullness *n syn* see LETHARGY 1
rel denseness, stupidity
con edge, incisiveness, keenness
ant sharpness
‖**dullsville** *n* **1** *syn* see BORE
rel burg, hick town, jerkwater town, mudhole, one-horse town, Podunk, tank town, whistle-stop
2 *syn* see TEDIUM
dumb *adj* **1** lacking the power to speak <deaf and *dumb* from birth>
syn inarticulate, mute, silent, speechless, unarticulate, voiceless; *compare* SILENT 2
ant articulate
2 *syn* see SILENT 2
rel incoherent, indistinct, maundering, tongue-tied

3 *syn* see SILENT 3
con speaking, talking; talkative, verbose
4 *syn* see STUPID 1
idiom dumb as an ox
dumb (up) *vb syn* see SHUT UP 2
dumbbell *n syn* see DUNCE
‖**dumb bunny** *n syn* see DUNCE
‖**dumb cluck** *n syn* see DUNCE
dumbfound *vb* **1** *syn* see SURPRISE 2
2 *syn* see STAGGER 5
dumbfounded *adj syn* see AGHAST 2
‖**dumbhead** *n syn* see DUNCE
‖**dummkopf** *n syn* see DUNCE
dummy *n* **1** *syn* see DUNCE
2 *syn* see STOOGE 1
dummy *adj syn* see ARTIFICIAL 2
‖**dummy** (up) *vb syn* see SHUT UP 2
dump *vb* **1** *syn* see DISCARD
‖**2** *syn* see BEAT 1
dump *n* **1** *syn* see ARMORY
2 *syn* see STY 1
dumping *n syn* see DISPOSAL 2
dumpling *n syn* see FATTY
dumps *n pl syn* see SADNESS
idiom low spirits
dumpy *adj syn* see STOCKY
rel formless, shapeless, unformed
dun *adj syn* see DARK 1
dun *vb syn* see WORRY 1
dunce *n* a dull-witted person <the traditional *dunce* in pointed cap>
syn beetlehead, blockhead, bonehead, boob, booby, ‖bufflehead, cabbagehead, chowderhead, chucklehead, chump, clod, clodpate, clodpoll, ‖cluck, dimwit, ‖dizzard, dodo, ‖dodunk, dolt, dolthead, dope, ‖doughhead, ‖drip, duffer, dullard, dullhead, dumbbell, ‖dumb bunny, ‖dumb cluck, ‖dumbhead, ‖dummkopf, dummy, dunderhead, dunderpate, fathead, featherweight, goof, ‖goon, hammerhead, idiot, ignoramus, ironhead, knothead, knucklehead, lackwit, lame-brain, lunk, lunkhead, ‖moonraker, moron, muddlehead, mug, muggins, mutt, muttonhead, nitwit, noddy, noodle, numskull, oaf, pinhead, poke, prune, pumpkin head, put, ‖schnook, simp, simpleton, ‖spoon, squarehead, ‖stunpoll, ‖stupe, stupid, thickhead, thickskull, turnip, wantwit, woodenhead, zombie
rel lightweight; ass, donkey, fool, imbecile, jackass, jerk, nincompoop, ninny, ‖schmo, ‖schmuck; birdbrain, featherbrain, scatterbrain
idiom dumb ox, Simple Simon
con brain, highbrow, intellectual, thinker, wit; pundit, sage, savant, scholar, wise man; prodigy, wizard; genius, mastermind
duncical *adj syn* see STUPID 1
dunderhead *n syn* see DUNCE
dunderpate *n syn* see DUNCE
dundrearies *n pl syn* see SIDE-WHISKERS

---

syn synonym(s)   *rel* related word(s)
ant antonym(s)   *con* contrasted word(s)
idiom idiomatic equivalent(s)
‖ use limited; if in doubt, see a dictionary

dungeon *n* a close dark prison or vault commonly underground <the prisoners were kept in lightless *dungeons*>
  syn oubliette
  rel vault; black hole; cell; jail, prison
dungy *adj syn* see DIRTY 1
dunk *vb syn* see DIP 1
  rel saturate, soak, sop
duo *n syn* see COUPLE
dupe *n syn* see FOOL 3
dupe *vb* to delude by underhand methods <the public is easily *duped* by extravagant claims in advertising>
  syn bamboozle, befool, catch, chicane, con, dust, flimflam, fool, gull, hoax, hoodwink, hornswoggle, job, kid, pigeon, ||rig, spoof, trick, victimize
  rel beguile, betray, deceive, delude, double≠cross, mislead; cheat, cozen, defraud, overreach; baffle, circumvent, outwit
  idiom pull one's leg, put something over (*or* across)
  con enlighten, inform, wise (up)
dupe *vb syn* see DOUBLE 1
dupery *n syn* see DECEPTION 1
duple *adj syn* see TWOFOLD 1
duplex *adj syn* see TWOFOLD 1
duplicate *adj syn* see SAME 2
duplicate *n* 1 *syn* see REPRODUCTION
  rel analogue, counterpart, parallel
  2 *syn* see MATE 5
duplicate *vb* 1 *syn* see DOUBLE 1
  2 *syn* see COPY
duplicitous *adj syn* see UNDERHAND
duplicity *n syn* see DECEIT 1
  rel faithlessness, perfidiousness, perfidy, treacherousness, treachery
durable *adj syn* see LASTING
  rel stout, strong, tenacious
  con feeble, fragile, frail, weak
duration *n* 1 *syn* see CONTINUATION 1
  2 *syn* see RUN 2
  3 *syn* see TERM 2
duress *n syn* see FORCE 4
during *prep* in the course of <*during* the disorder some men kept their heads>
  syn amid, mid, midst, over, throughout
dusk *adj syn* see DARK 1
dusk *n syn* see EVENING 1
||**dusk dark** *n syn* see EVENING 1
dusky *adj* 1 *syn* see DARK 3
  2 *syn* see DARK 1
  3 *syn* see GLOOMY 3
  4 *syn* see OBSCURE 3
dust *n* 1 *syn* see DUSTING
  2 *syn* see QUARREL
  ||3 *syn* see REFUSE
dust *vb* 1 *syn* see SPRINKLE 1
  2 *syn* see WHIP 2
  3 *syn* see DUPE

  idiom throw dust in one's eyes
  ||4 *syn* see HURRY 2
dusting *n* 1 a small quantity lightly applied to or sprinkled on <a *dusting* of sugar on the cake>
  syn dust, powdering, sprinkling
  ||2 *syn* see DEFEAT 1
||**dust off** *vb syn* see MURDER 1
dustup *n syn* see QUARREL
dusty *adj syn* see ARID 2
Dutch *n syn* see TROUBLE 3
duteous *adj syn* see RESPECTFUL
dutiful *adj syn* see RESPECTFUL
duty *n* 1 *syn* see OBLIGATION 2
  rel accountability, amenability, answerability, liability
  2 *syn* see FUNCTION 1
  3 *syn* see LOAD 3
  4 *syn* see TAX 1
  5 *syn* see TASK 1
  6 *syn* see USE 4
dwarf *n* a very small person <she was a tiny little thing, almost a *dwarf*>
  syn homunculus, hop-o'-my-thumb, Lilliputian, manikin, midge, midget, peewee, pygmy, runt, Tom Thumb
  rel half-pint, ||ribe, ||shrimp, wart; dwarfling; minimus
  ant giant
dwarf *vb syn* see STUNT
dwarf *adj syn* see TINY
dwarfish *adj syn* see TINY
dwell *vb* 1 *syn* see RESIDE 1
  2 *syn* see CONSIST 1
dweller *n syn* see INHABITANT
dwelling *n syn* see HABITATION 2
dwindle *vb* 1 *syn* see DECREASE
  rel ebb, subside, wane; attenuate, extenuate, thin; moderate; disappear
  2 *syn* see FAIL 3
||**dwine** *vb syn* see FAIL 1
dyad *n syn* see COUPLE
dye *n syn* see COLOR 6
dyed–in–the–wool *adj syn* see INVETERATE 1
dyestuff *n syn* see COLOR 6
dying *adj syn* see MORIBUND
dynamic *adj* 1 *syn* see ACTIVE 1
  rel activating, energizing, vitalizing
  ant static
  2 *syn* see VIGOROUS
  rel forceful, forcible; intense, vehement, violent
  con idle, inactive, passive
  ant inert
dynamite *vb syn* see DESTROY 1
dynamo *n syn* see HUSTLER 1
dysentery *n syn* see DIARRHEA
dyslogistic *adj syn* see DEROGATORY
  ant eulogistic
dyspathy *n syn* see ANTIPATHY 2
dyspeptic *adj syn* see ILL-TEMPERED
dysphoria *n syn* see SADNESS

E

each *adj syn* see ALL 2
  rel any, several, various; particular, respective, specific
each *adv syn* see APIECE
  idiom a shot, a throw, a whack
eager *adj* moved by a strong and urgent desire or interest <young executives *eager* to succeed>
  syn agog, anxious, appetent, ardent, athirst, avid, breathless, impatient, keen, raring, solicitous, thirsty
  rel enthusiastic, gung ho, heated, hot; ambitious, intent; acquisitive, covetous, craving, desirous, hankering, ‖honing, hungry, longing, pining, wishful, yearning; impatient, restive, restless
  idiom champing at the bit, ready and willing
  con aloof, disinterested, incurious, indifferent, unconcerned, uninterested; apathetic, detached, impassive, stolid
  ant listless
eagerness *n* a strong and urgent desire or interest <an *eagerness* to learn>
  syn ardor, enthusiasm, zing
  rel alacrity, avidity, keenness, quickness; ambition; gusto, ‖mustard, zest
  con lackadaisicality, languor, lethargy; aloofness, disinterest; apathy, deliberation, detachment, impassivity, stolidity
  ant listlessness
eagle eye *n syn* see EYE 3
eagle–eyed *adj syn* see SHARP-EYED
ear *n syn* see NOTICE 1
earlier *adv* **1** *syn* see BEFORE 2
  2 *syn* see HITHERTO 1
  3 *syn* see BEFORE 3
earliest *adj syn* see FIRST 2
  con final, terminal, ultimate
  ant latest
early *adv* **1** at or nearly at the beginning of a period, course, process, or series <it is much too *early* to guess the outcome>
  syn betimes, seasonably, soon, timely
  rel first
  2 in advance of the expected or usual time <these apples bear *early* and heavy>
  syn betimes, oversoon, prematurely
  rel beforehand
  idiom ahead of time, bright and early
early *adj* **1** of, relating to, or occurring near the beginning of a period of time, a development, or a series <*early* Renaissance><*early* art forms>
  syn primitive, primordial
  rel original, pristine; ancient, antediluvian, antiquated, primal, primeval; antecedent, preceding, prevenient, prior
  con conclusive, final, last, terminal, ultimate; eventual; intermediate, middle, midmost
  ant late

  2 occurring before the expected or usual time <an *early* death><an *early* peach>
  syn overearly, oversoon, premature, previous, ‖soon, untimely; *compare* PRECOCIOUS
  rel anticipative, anticipatory, precipitant, precocious; unanticipated, unexpected
  con slow, tardy; anticipated, expected
  ant late
earmark *vb syn* see DESIGNATE 3
earn *vb* **1** to receive as return for effort <*earn* a living wage>
  syn acquire, bring in, ‖drag down, draw down, gain, get, knock down, make, win
  rel attain, effect, obtain, procure, realize, receive, secure
  2 to be or make worthy of <his devotion to duty *earned* him a promotion>
  syn deserve, merit, rate
  rel bag, come by, harvest, net, reap, score
earnest *n syn* see EARNESTNESS
  rel attention, interest; enthusiasm, warmth, zeal
  ant jest, play
earnest *adj syn* see SERIOUS 1
  rel ardent, enthusiastic, passionate, pressing, warm, zealous; assiduous, busy, diligent, industrious, perseverant, sedulous; sincere, wholehearted, whole-souled
  con buoyant, effervescent, elastic, flippant, light
  ant frivolous
earnest *n syn* see PLEDGE 1
earnestly *adv* **1** *syn* see HARD 3
  rel seriously, soberly, solemnly, thoughtfully; zealously
  2 *syn* see SERIOUSLY 1
earnestness *n* a state of freedom from all jesting or trifling <he studied with great *earnestness*>
  syn earnest, intentness, serious-mindedness, seriousness
  rel doggedness, perseverance, persistence; decision, determination, firmness, purposefulness, resolve; absorption, attentiveness, concentration, engrossment; deliberation; gravity, sobriety
  con levity, lightness; shallowness, superficiality; carelessness, slackness
  ant frivolity
earnings *n pl syn* see PROFIT
earshot *n* the range within which something (as a voice) may be heard <the gossips were still within *earshot* of her>
  syn hearing, sound
  idiom carrying (*or* hearing) distance

---

syn synonym(s)   *rel* related word(s)
ant antonym(s)   *con* contrasted word(s)
idiom idiomatic equivalent(s)
‖ use limited; if in doubt, see a dictionary

earsplitting *adj syn* see LOUD 1
rel penetrating, shrill

earth *n* **1** the entire area in which man lives and acts <expect the destruction of the *earth*>
syn globe, (the) planet, world
rel orb, sphere; cosmos, creation, macrocosm, universe, vale
2 areas of land as distinguished from sea and air <clayey *earth*, difficult to drain>
syn dirt, dry land, ground, land, soil, terra firma
rel clay, gravel, humus, loam, mud, sand; fill, subsoil; terrain, turf; clod

earthlike *adj syn* see EARTHY 1

earthly *adj* **1** of, relating to, or characteristic of this earth or man's life on earth <*earthly* pursuits>
syn earthy, mundane, sublunary, tellurian, telluric, terrene, terrestrial, uncelestial, worldly
rel carnal, corporeal, earthbound, physical; material, temporal; unspiritual
con celestial, empyreal, empyrean, heavenly; ideal, utopian; divine, spiritual
2 *syn* see PROBABLE
rel imaginable, potential

earthquake *n* a shaking or trembling of the earth that is volcanic or tectonic in origin <homes destroyed by *earthquakes*>
syn quake, ‖quaker, shake, shock, temblor (*or* tremblor), tremor

earthy *adj* **1** consisting of, resembling, or suggesting earth <a stale *earthy* smell>
syn earthlike, terrene, terrestrial
rel clayey, dusty, muddy, sandy
2 *syn* see EARTHLY 1
3 *syn* see MATERIALISTIC
4 *syn* see REALISTIC
ant impractical

ease *n* **1** *syn* see REST 1
rel idleness, inactivity, inertia, inertness, passivity, supinity; calmness, security
con labor, toil, travail; adversity, difficulty; burden, care, worry
2 *syn* see UNCONSTRAINT
3 freedom from or mitigation of pain <medication brought him instant *ease*>
syn alleviation, easement, mitigation, relief
rel decrease, diminishment, moderation, reduction; calming, soothing
con discomfort, unrest; agony, pain
4 *syn* see READINESS 3
rel adroitness, artfulness, cleverness, deftness, effortlessness, expertise, expertness, fluency, knack, poise, skillfulness, smoothness; dispatch, efficiency
con awkwardness, clumsiness, maladroitness, stiffness, woodenness; constraint; inconvenience, pains; exertion
ant effort
5 *syn* see PROSPERITY 2

ease *vb* **1** *syn* see RELIEVE 1
rel deaden, dull; ameliorate, help
con afflict, torment
2 *syn* see LOOSE 5
rel disengage, free, release

con bind, restrain, tighten
3 to make less difficult <new laws that will *ease* voting requirements>
syn facilitate
rel aid, assist, better, help, improve; forward, further, promote, speed
idiom clear (*or* prepare) the way (for), grease the wheels, open the door (to *or* for)
con hinder, impede, retard

easeful *adj syn* see COMFORTABLE 2

easement *n syn* see EASE 3
rel allayment, appeasement, assuagement, mollification

ease off *vb* **1** *syn* see LOOSE 5
2 *syn* see ABATE 4
3 *syn* see RELAX 2

easily *adv* **1** without discomfort, difficulty, or reluctance <*easily* translated the document>
syn effortlessly, facilely, freely, lightly, readily, smoothly, well
rel competently, dexterously, efficiently, fluently, handily, simply
idiom hands down, slick as a whistle
con awkwardly, clumsily, ineptly, stiffly; arduously, wearily
ant laboriously
2 without question <this is *easily* the best course of action>
syn absolutely, definitely, doubtless, doubtlessly, positively, unequivocally, unquestionably
rel actually, assuredly, certainly, clearly, decidedly, indeed, really, truly, undoubtedly
idiom no doubt
con apparently, perhaps, probably, seemingly; doubtfully, equivocally, questionably
3 *syn* see WELL 7

easy *adj* **1** causing or involving little or no difficulty <an *easy* solution>
syn effortless, facile, light, royal, simple, smooth, untroublesome
rel apparent, clear, distinct, evident, manifest, obvious, plain; clear-cut, straightforward, uncomplicated, uncompounded, uninvolved
idiom easy as falling off a log, easy as pie, nothing to it
con arduous, difficult, troublesome; abstruse, complex, complicated, intricate, knotty
ant hard
2 *syn* see FORBEARING
rel compassionate, condoning, excusing, forgiving, pardoning, sympathetic; benign, kindly; lax, moderate, soft; humoring, mollycoddling, pampering, spoiling
con austere, exacting, rigid, severe, stern, strict, stringent
3 easily taken advantage of or imposed upon <he was *easy* prey to her wiles>
syn fleeceable, gullible, naive, susceptible
rel credulous, trusting, unmistrusting, unsuspicious; deceivable, deludable, dupable, exploitable; artless, dewy-eyed, green, simple, unsophisticated
con critical, cynical, disbelieving, mistrustful, scoffing, skeptical, suspicious, unbelieving

4 syn see FAST 7

5 syn see COMFORTABLE 2
rel secure
con discontented, dissatisfied; miserable
ant uncomfortable

6 syn see AMIABLE 1
rel familiar, gregarious, informal; courtly, diplomatic, pleasant, polite, sociable; smooth, suave, urbane
con brusque, curt, unfriendly, unpleasant; constrained, embarrassed, formal, restrained; discourteous, impolite, undiplomatic, ungracious; stiff, unsocial, withdrawn, wooden
ant ill at ease

7 syn see CALM 2
rel relaxed; lethargic, unambitious
con agitated, tense, troubled, uptight

8 syn see PROSPEROUS 3
rel successful, thriving
idiom in easy circumstances, on easy street
con straitened

9 marked by ready facility (as of expression) <an *easy* style of writing>
syn cursive, effortless, flowing, fluent, running, smooth
rel facile; graceful
con effortful, labored
ant difficult

easygoing *adj* **1 syn** see CALM 2
con agitated, flurried, flustered, harassed; anxious, concerned, upset, worried
ant uptight

2 syn see LAZY
rel apathetic, careless, indifferent, unconcerned; unambitious
con active, ambitious, diligent, dynamic, energetic, industrious, live, vigorous

3 not constrained or bound by rigid standards <enjoyed the *easygoing* morality of a commune>
syn breezy, casual, ‖common, dégagé, hang=loose, informal, low-pressure, relaxed, ‖sonsy, unconstrained, unfussy, unreserved
rel affable, folksy; flexible, lax, moderate, offhand, off-handed, unaffected; carefree, devil=may-care, happy-go-lucky; outgiving; uninhibited
idiom free and easy
con ceremonious, decorous, formal, proper, stuffy; constrained, inflexible, inhibited, restrained, rigid, starchy, stiff

easy mark *n* **1 syn** see FOOL 3

2 syn see SOFT TOUCH 1

‖easy rider *n* **1 syn** see SYCOPHANT

2 syn see PIMP 1

easy street *n* **syn** see PROSPERITY 2

eat *vb* **1** to take in as food <they quickly *ate* a light breakfast>
syn consume, devour, feed (on), ingest, meal, partake (of), take; *compare* CONSUME 5
rel banquet, feast, gormandize; eat up, gobble (up *or* down), gorge (on), ‖mop (up), polish off, scoff; breakfast, dine, lunch, nosh, snack, sup; mouth, ‖muckamuck; nibble, pick
idiom break bread, get away with, have (*or* take) a bite, take nourishment, ‖put on the feed bag

2 syn see CONSUME 1

3 to consume gradually <the acid *ate* the surface of the copper>
syn bite, corrode, eat away, erode, gnaw, scour, wear (away)
rel nibble (away); consume, decompose, disintegrate, dissolve

eatable *adj* **syn** see EDIBLE

eat away *vb* **syn** see EAT 3

eating house *n* a cheap often small restaurant <grabbed a quick sandwich at a local *eating house*>
syn beanery, ‖buffet, café, ‖caff, coffee shop, cookshop, diner, ‖greasy spoon, ‖hashery, ‖hash house, lunch counter (*or* bar), luncheonette, lunchroom, lunch wagon (*or* cart), quick-lunch, sandwich shop, snack bar (*or* counter)
rel cafeteria, eatery, tearoom; trattoria

‖eats *n pl* **syn** see FOOD 1

eat up *vb* **1** to eat completely and without delay <*eat up* your dinner before it gets cold>
syn devour, dispatch, polish off
rel down, eat; bolt, gobble (up *or* down), gorge (on), ‖mop (up), wolf

2 syn see CONSUME 1

‖3 syn see DEVOUR 5
rel luxuriate (in), riot (in), wallow (in)
idiom be beside oneself over, be thrilled to death by, smack one's lips over, take delight in

‖4 syn see LOVE 1

ebb *vb* **syn** see ABATE 4
rel decline, peter (out); recede, retreat, retrograde
con ascend, increase, mount, rise; advance, progress
ant flow

ebbing *n* **syn** see FAILURE 4
rel declining, sinking

ebon *adj* **syn** see BLACK 1

ebony *adj* **syn** see BLACK 1

ebullience *n* lively or enthusiastic expression of thoughts or feelings <her bubbling *ebullience* was infectious>
syn buoyancy, effervescence, exuberance, exuberancy
rel animation, enthusiasm, gaiety, high-spiritedness, liveliness, vitality, vivaciousness, vivacity; agitation, excitement, exhilaration, ferment
con apathy, impassivity, languor, lethargy, listlessness, passivity, sluggishness, stolidity, torpidity, torpor; enervation, inactivity, inertia, lifelessness; disinterest, unconcern, uninterest

ebullient *adj* **syn** see EXUBERANT 1

eccentric *adj* **1** not having the same center <not concentric but *eccentric* circles>
syn off-center
rel uncentered; off-balance, unbalanced
con centered; balanced
ant concentric

---

syn synonym(s)   *rel* related word(s)
ant antonym(s)   *con* contrasted word(s)
idiom idiomatic equivalent(s)
‖ use limited; if in doubt, see a dictionary

2 syn see STRANGE 4
rel anomalous, irregular, unnatural; exceptionable, exceptional, quirky, quizzical; beeheaded, ‖dippy, wacky; fantastic, grotesque
con customary, habitual; natural, normal, regular, typical

eccentric *n* one who deviates from established patterns especially in odd or whimsical ways <an *eccentric* who filled his house with statues of himself>
syn case, character, ‖duck, oddball, oddity, original, quiz, ‖spook, ‖wack, zombie
rel bohemian, maverick, nonconformist, unconformist; dissenter, heretic; caution, coot, ‖geezer; crackpot, crank, freak, kook, screwball
idiom queer duck (*or* potato)
con conformer, conformist, conventionalist, traditionalist; bore, bromide, dullard

ecclesiast *n syn* see CLERGYMAN

ecclesiastic *n syn* see CLERGYMAN

ecclesiastical *adj* of, relating to, or belonging to a church especially as an established institution <*ecclesiastical* law>
syn church, churchly, churchmanly, spiritual
rel apostolic, canonical, episcopal, episcopalian, evangelistic, theological; clerical, ministerial, papal, pastoral, patriarchal, pontifical, prelatial, priestly, rabbinical, sacerdotal; cathedralesque, churchlike, pantheonic, synagogal, synagogical, tabernacular, templelike
con lay, secular

ecdysiast *n syn* see STRIPTEASER

echelon *n syn* see LINE 5

echoic *adj syn* see ONOMATOPOEIC

éclat *n syn* see FAME 2
rel bang, brilliance, brilliancy, display, luster, noticeableness, prominence, remarkableness; distinction, standing; kudos
con oblivion, obscurity; contempt, derision, scorn

eclectic *adj* **1** selecting what appears to be the best from various doctrines, methods, or styles <an *eclectic* taste in music>
syn discriminating, select, selective
rel elective, selecting; choosing, choosy, discerning, fastidious, finicky, fussy, particular, picky
2 composed of elements drawn from various sources <an *eclectic* art incorporating romanticism and impressionism>
syn catholic
rel broad, comprehensive, inclusive; assorted, mingled, mixed; diverse, diversified, heterogeneous, multifarious, multiform, varied; derived, unoriginal
con distinctive, narrow; new, original

eclipse *vb syn* see OBSCURE

economical *adj syn* see SPARING
rel careful, forehanded, prudent; economizing, penny-wise; cheeseparing, close, mean, miserly, niggardly, penny-pinching, penurious, scrimping, skimping, spare, stingy
con generous, lavish, wasteful
ant extravagant

economic poison *n syn* see PESTICIDE

economize *vb* to avoid unnecessary waste or expense <*economize* on food by using leftovers>
syn save
rel conserve; scrimp, skimp
con dissipate, scatter, waste
ant squander, throw away

economy *n* careful management of material resources <retired people often must learn to practice *economy*>
syn forehandedness, frugality, husbandry, providence, prudence, thrift, thriftiness
rel meanness, miserliness, niggardliness, parcity, parsimony, scrimping, skimping, stinginess; carefulness, discretion
con improvidence, lavishness, prodigality, squandering, thriftlessness, wastefulness
ant extravagance

ecstasy *n* intense exaltation of mind and feelings <was in *ecstasy* over flying>
syn heaven, rapture, rhapsody, seventh heaven, transport; *compare* EXHILARATION
rel beatitude, blessedness, bliss, blissfulness, felicity, gladness, happiness; delectation, delight, elation, joy, joyfulness, overjoyfulness, pleasure; enchantment, euphoria, intoxication, madness; exaltation, inspiration; paradise; afflatus, frenzy, fury
idiom cloud nine
con dejection, downheartedness, lowness, low-spiritedness, oppression; blues, dumps, melancholy
ant depression

ecumenical *adj syn* see UNIVERSAL 2
rel heaven-wide; all-comprehending, all-comprehensive, all-covering, all-including, all-pervading; comprehensive, general, inclusive
con diocesan, local, parochial, provincial; circumscribed, insular, limited, narrow, restricted

edacious *adj syn* see VORACIOUS

eddy *n* a swirling mass especially of water <dark *eddies* in the flooded stream>
syn maelstrom, vortex, whirl, whirlpool
rel gurge, surge, swirl, twirl, whirl; back current, back stream, countercurrent, counterflow, counterflux; backwash, backwater

eddy *vb syn* see SWIRL

edge *n* **1 syn** see BORDER 1
rel end, extremity; ledge, side
con area, surface
2 a cutting quality <there was an *edge* to his voice as he answered>
syn incisiveness, keenness, sharpness
rel bite, cut, sting; knife-edge, razor-edge; acerbity, acidity, acridity, causticity; astringency, stringency; acuteness, penetration, shrillness, thinness
3 syn see VERGE 2
4 syn see ADVANTAGE 3
con bar, encumbrance, obstacle; disadvantage

edge *vb* **1 syn** see SHARPEN
2 syn see BORDER 1
3 syn see SIDLE

edge in *vb syn* see INSINUATE 3

edgy *adj* **1 syn** see TENSE 2
  rel skittish; excitable, excited, high-strung, overstrung; irritable, touchy; impatient, restless
  idiom on edge
  con detached; peaceful, placid; patient
  2 syn see EXCITABLE

edible *adj* suitable for use as food <*edible* plant products>
  syn comestible, eatable, esculent
  rel digestible; nourishing, nutritious, nutritive; palatable, savory, succulent, tasty, toothsome
  ant inedible

edibles *n pl* **syn** see FOOD 1

edict *n* **1** a publicly proclaimed order or rule of conduct by a competent authority <a government *edict* regarding curfew enforcement>
  syn decree, directive, ruling, ukase
  rel instrument; order; manifesto, proclamation, pronouncement, pronunciamento; bull
  2 syn see LAW 1

edifice *n* a large, magnificent, or massive building <a marble *edifice* now used as a museum>
  syn erection, pile, structure; *compare* BUILDING, HUT

edify *vb* **syn** see ILLUMINATE 2
  rel better, enhance; elucidate; educate, instruct, teach
  con debase, deprave

edition *n* the total number of copies of the same work printed during a stretch of time <the initial *edition* of 50,000 copies was exhausted in a month>
  syn impression, printing, reissue, reprinting

educate *vb* **syn** see TEACH
  rel cultivate, nurture; brief, explain, inform

education *n* **1** the act or process of educating <devoted herself to the *education* of illiterate adults>
  syn instruction, schooling, teaching, training, tuition, tutelage
  rel coaching, pedagogy, tutorage, tutoring, tutorship; direction, guidance
  2 the product or result of being educated <obtained his *education* in local schools and in college>
  syn erudition, knowledge, learning, scholarship, science
  rel culture, edification, enlightenment, learnedness, literacy
  con ignorance, illiteracy

educational *adj* **syn** see INFORMATIVE

educative *adj* **syn** see INFORMATIVE

educe *vb* **1** to draw out something hidden, latent, or reserved <*educed* important information from the witness>
  syn elicit, evince, evoke, extort, extract, milk
  rel drag, draw, draw out, pull, wrest, wring; gain, get, obtain, procure, secure; distill
  con miss, overlook, pass over
  2 syn see DERIVE 1
  rel reason (out), think (out)

eerie *adj* **syn** see WEIRD 1
  rel bizarre, fantastic, grotesque; arcane; crawly

efface *vb* **syn** see ERASE

  rel eradicate, extirpate; eliminate, exclude, rule out

effect *n* **1** a condition or occurrence traceable to a cause <the *effect* of the medicine was dizziness>
  syn aftereffect, aftermath, causatum, consequence, corollary, end product, event, eventuality, issue, outcome, precipitate, result, sequel, sequence, upshot
  rel pursuance; development, fruit, outgrowth, ramification; denouement, repercussion; conclusion, end; side effect
  con antecedent, determinant, occasion, reason; base, basis, foundation, ground, groundwork
  ant cause
  2 effects *pl* **syn** see POSSESSION 2
  3 the force of impression of one thing on another <had a profound *effect* on our lives>
  syn impact, imprint, influence, mark, repercussion
  rel backlash, backwash; recoil, reflex, response; aftereffect, aftermath

effect *vb* **1** to induce to come into being <specific genes *effect* specific bodily characters>
  syn bring about, cause, draw on, make, produce, secure
  rel conceive, create, generate; bring on, induce; enact, render, turn out, yield
  con impede, limit, restrict; repress, suppress
  2 to carry to a successful conclusion <found a pass that allowed them to *effect* passage through the mountains>
  syn bring off, carry out, carry through, effectuate; *compare* FULFILL 1, PERFORM 2
  rel actualize, realize; achieve, procure
  con fail, fall down
  3 syn see ENFORCE

effective *adj* producing or capable of producing a result <an *effective* rebuke>
  syn effectual, efficacious, efficient, virtuous
  rel adequate, capable, competent; cogent, compelling, convincing, sound, telling, valid; able, active, dynamic; operative, useful; direct
  con abortive, bootless, fruitless, futile, vain; empty, hollow, idle, nugatory, otiose, pointless; inoperative, useless, worthless
  ant ineffective

effectiveness *n* **1 syn** see POINT 3
  rel forcefulness, potency, power, strength, verve, vigor
  con impotence, weakness
  ant ineffectiveness
  2 syn see EFFICIENCY 1
  3 syn see EFFICACY 1

effectual *adj* **syn** see EFFECTIVE
  rel accomplishing, achieving, effecting, fulfilling; practicable, sound, useful, valid, workable; conclusive, decisive, determinative, influential; authoritative, potent, powerful, strong, toothy
  con impotent, weak

---

syn synonym(s)   **rel** related word(s)
ant antonym(s)   **con** contrasted word(s)
idiom idiomatic equivalent(s)
‖ use limited; if in doubt, see a dictionary

ant ineffectual

effectuate *vb syn* see EFFECT 2

effeminate *adj* lacking manly strength and purpose <a young man with extravagant and *effeminate* mannerisms>
syn epicene, Miss-Nancyish, pansified, prissy, sissified, sissy, unmanly
rel chichi, old-maidish, overnice, precious; foppish, sappy, silken
ant manly, masculine

effervescence *n syn* see EBULLIENCE
rel bubbling, ebullition, fizzing, foaming
con deadness, flatness, staleness

effervescent *adj* **1** *syn* see EXUBERANT 1
2 *syn* see ELASTIC 2
rel animated, boiling, bubbly, excited, gay, lively, sparkling, sprightly, vivacious; gleeful, hilarious, jolly, mirthful
con lifeless, listless, subdued; earnest, sedate, serious, solemn

effete *adj* **1** *syn* see STERILE 1
2 having lost energy or drive <*effete*, weary, burned-out revolutionaries>
syn all in, bleary, ‖clapped-out, depleted, done, done in, drained, exhausted, far-gone, spent, used up, washed-out, worn-out
rel consumed; debilitated, enfeebled, fatigued
idiom on one's last legs, out on one's feet
con alive, lively, vigorous, vital
3 having lost character <a soft, *effete* society>
syn decadent, decayed, degenerate, overripe
rel decaying, declining; soft, weak; dissolute, immoral

efficacious *adj syn* see EFFECTIVE
rel active, operative, productive; influential, potent, powerful, puissant, strong
con abortive; impotent, powerless, useless, vain, weak
ant inefficacious

efficacy *n* **1** the power to produce an effect <*efficacy* of the drug>
syn capability, effectiveness, efficiency, potency
rel capableness, productiveness, use; adequacy, capacity, sufficiency
con ineffectiveness, inefficiency; uselessness, worthlessness
ant inefficacy
2 *syn* see EFFICIENCY 1

efficiency *n* **1** the capacity to produce desired results with a minimum expenditure of energy, time, or resources <demands a high degree of *efficiency* on the job>
syn effectiveness, efficacy, performance
rel ability, address, adeptness, competence, expertise, know-how, proficiency, prowess, skill; capability, resourcefulness; productivity
con inadequacy, incompetence, ineffectiveness; unproductiveness
ant inefficiency
2 *syn* see EFFICACY 1

efficient *adj syn* see EFFECTIVE
rel able, capable, competent, fitted, qualified; adept, expert, masterly, proficient, skilled, skillful

con incapable, incompetent, inexpert, unadept, unproficient, unqualified, unsuitable; unproductive; ineffectual
ant inefficient

effloresce *vb syn* see BLOSSOM

effort *n* **1** the active use of energy in producing a result <thought the job wasn't worth the *effort*>
syn elbow grease, exertion, pains, trouble, while
rel labor, toil, travail, work; energy, force, might, power, puissance; attempt, endeavor, essay
idiom sweat of one's brow
con adroitness, facility, smoothness; do-nothingness, inaction, indolence, inertia, lackadaisicalness, languor, laziness
ant ease
2 *syn* see TASK 2

effortful *adj syn* see HARD 6

effortless *adj* **1** *syn* see EASY 1
rel adept, expert, masterly, proficient, ready, skilled, skillful
con laborious, toilsome, trying
ant painstaking
2 *syn* see EASY 9

effortlessly *adv syn* see EASILY 1
rel adeptly, adroitly, efficiently, expertly, proficiently, skillfully
con painstakingly
ant arduously, laboriously

effrontery *n* flagrant disregard of courtesy or propriety and an arrogant assumption of privilege <had the *effrontery* to insult her father>
syn brashness, brass, cheek, chutzpah, confidence, ‖crust, face, gall, nerve, presumption; *compare* INSOLENCE
rel audacity, hardihood, temerity; assurance, self-assurance, self-confidence; brazenness, impudence; impertinence, insolence
con courtesy, grace, propriety

effulgent *adj syn* see BRIGHT 1
rel vivid; glorious, resplendent, splendid
con dark, dusky, gloomy, murky

effusive *adj* unduly demonstrative <*effusive* assurances of undying love>
syn gushing, gushy, slobbering, slobbery, sloppy
rel expansive, fulsome, outpouring, profuse; demonstrative, unconstrained, unreserved, unrestrained; cloying, slushy; smarmy
con close, restrained, reticent, taciturn; bashful, modest, shy
ant reserved

egg (on) *vb syn* see URGE
rel agitate, excite, pique, stimulate; instigate; arouse, drive, rally, stir up, whip (on *or* up)
con arrest, bridle

egghead *n syn* see INTELLECTUAL 2

egocentric *adj* **1** concerned with the individual person rather than society <an *egocentric* approach to world problems>
syn individualist, individualistic
rel self-centered, selfish
2 concerned only with one's own activities or needs and usually tending to self-assertion or

self-satisfaction <an *egocentric* man, lacking feeling for others>
syn egoistic, egomaniacal, egotistic, self-absorbed, self-centered, self-concerned, self-interested, self-involved, selfish, self-seeking, self-serving; *compare* POMPOUS 1
rel conceited, narcissistic, self-affected, self-applauding, self-conceited, self-concentered, self-indulgent, self-loving, stuck-up, vainglorious; megalomaniac
idiom wrapped up in oneself

egoism *n* **1** **syn** see EGOTISM 1
rel self-assurance, self-confidence, self-possession
ant altruism
2 syn see CONCEIT 2
rel self-satisfaction
con meekness, modesty
ant humility

egoistic *adj* **syn** see EGOCENTRIC 2
rel individualistic; self-satisfied, swellheaded
con humble, modest
ant altruistic

egomaniacal *adj* **syn** see EGOCENTRIC 2
rel self-exalting, self-glorifying, vainglorious

egotism *n* **1** an exaggerated sense of one's own importance <in believing that he was indispensable, he exhibited consummate *egotism*>
syn egoism, self-importance
rel conceit, conceitedness, narcissism, self-esteem, self-love, vainness; boastfulness, boasting, bragging, gasconade, gasconism, megalomania, vaunting
con humility, lowliness; bashfulness, diffidence, shyness; modesty
ant altruism
2 syn see CONCEIT 2
rel arrogance, superiority; contempt
con humbleness, self-effacement
ant humility

egotistic *adj* **syn** see EGOCENTRIC 2
rel boastful, cocky, inflated, pretentious, proud, puffed up, self-satisfied; conceited, stuck-up
idiom in love with oneself, stuck on oneself
con humble, modest; self-effacing, shy

egregious *adj* conspicuously bad or objectionable <an *egregious* mistake>
syn capital, flagrant, glaring, gross, rank
rel arrant, outright, stark; infamous, nefarious, notorious; atrocious, deplorable, heinous, monstrous, outrageous, preposterous
con measly, minor, petty, piddling, slender, slight, trifling, trivial

egress *n* **1** **syn** see DEPARTURE 1
rel emergence, emerging
con coming, entering; arrival
ant ingress
2 a place or means of going out <a gate providing *egress* from the pasture>
syn exit, outlet
rel opening, passage; escape
idiom way out
con entrance, entry, entryway
ant access, ingress

egression *n* **syn** see DEPARTURE 1
con entrance, entering
ant ingression

eidolon *n* **syn** see APPARITION

ejaculate *vb* **syn** see EXCLAIM
rel call (out), shout, vociferate, yell

eject *vb* **1** to drive or force (somebody) out <*eject* an intruder from one's home>
syn boot (out), chase, chuck, dismiss, evict, extrude, kick out, out, throw out; *compare* BANISH
rel displace, dispossess; drive off, rout, run off; debar, disbar, eliminate, exclude, rule out, shut out; bump, cashier, discharge, fire, sack; discard, shed; reject, repudiate, spurn
idiom give one his walking papers, send packing, show one the door
con accept, admit, install, receive; entertain, harbor, house, lodge, shelter
2 syn see ERUPT 1

elaborate *adj* **1** **syn** see COMPLEX 2
2 marked by complexity of detail or ornament <an *elaborate* coiffure>
syn complicated, fancy, intricate
rel detailed, highly-wrought; decorated, dressy, embellished, ornate; elegant; busy, overdone, overworked, overwrought
con common, ordinary, plain, unpolished; inartificial, inornate, natural
ant simple

elaborate *vb* **1** **syn** see EXPAND 4
rel comment, discuss, dwell (upon); clarify, explain, expound, interpret
2 syn see UNFOLD 3

élan *n* **syn** see SPIRIT 5
rel impetus

élan vital *n* **syn** see SOUL 1

elapse *vb* **syn** see PASS 3
rel flow, glide, pass (by), slide, slip (by); lapse, run out

elastic *adj* **1** able to withstand strain without being permanently affected or injured <a rubber band is *elastic*>
syn flexible, resilient, springy, stretch, stretchy, supple, whippy
rel ductile, malleable, pliable, pliant, plastic, rubberlike, rubbery; adaptable, moldable, stretchable, yielding; bouncy, limber, lithe
con brittle; inflexible, stiff, tense
ant rigid
2 able to recover quickly from depression and maintain high spirits <had an *elastic* optimistic nature>
syn airy, bouncy, buoyant, effervescent, expansive, resilient, volatile
rel animated, gay, lively, sprightly, vivacious; ebullient, high-spirited, mettlesome, soaring, spirited; adaptable, recuperative
con blue, dejected, depressed, gloomy, melancholy, sad; flaccid, limp

---

syn synonym(s)   **rel** related word(s)
ant antonym(s)   **con** contrasted word(s)
idiom idiomatic equivalent(s)
|| use limited; if in doubt, see a dictionary

elate *vb* to elevate the spirits of <the phenomenal sales record *elated* him>
syn commove, excite, exhilarate, inspire, set up, spirit (up), stimulate
rel brighten, cheer, cheer up, encourage; delight, gladden, gratify, overjoy; buoy, elevate, exalt, uplift
con distress; oppress, weigh; weary
ant depress

elated *adj syn* see INTOXICATED 2
rel enchanted, enraptured, exalted, transported; delighted, ecstatic, euphoric, exultant, jubilant, overjoyed
idiom in heaven, in seventh heaven, on cloud nine
con blue, deflated, unhappy

elation *n* **1** the quality or state of being elated <felt great *elation* when he won the presidential nomination>
syn euphoria, exaltation, exhilaration
rel buoyancy; happiness, joy; excitement; rapture, transport
idiom stars in one's eyes
con blues, depression; distress, misery, sadness, unhappiness
ant deflation
2 *syn* see EUPHORIA 2
ant depression

elbow *vb syn* see PUSH 2

elbowroom *n syn* see ROOM 3
rel space

elder *n* **1** *syn* see SENIOR 2
2 *syn* see OLDSTER
3 *syn* see SUPERIOR

elderliness *n syn* see OLD AGE

elderly *adj syn* see AGED 1
rel aging, declining
con juvenile, young
ant youthful

eldorado *n syn* see BONANZA

elect *adj syn* see SELECT 1
rel choice, rare; hand-picked, singled out; designated, destined, ordained; delivered, redeemed, saved
con refused, rejected, repudiated, spurned; disdained, scorned; damned, doomed, reprobate

elect *vb* **1** *syn* see CHOOSE 1
rel decide, determine, resolve, settle; conclude, judge; accept, admit, receive
con reject; dismiss, eject, expel, oust
ant abjure
2 to select by or as if by ballot <the board of directors *elected* a new chairman>
syn ballot, vote (in)
rel choose, designate, name, opt, pick, select, single; nominate; appoint
3 *syn* see WILL

election *n syn* see CHOICE 1

elective *adj syn* see OPTIONAL

electrify *vb syn* see THRILL
rel provoke; jar, stagger, stun

eleemosynary *adj syn* see CHARITABLE 1
rel beneficent, generous, liberal, munificent, openhanded

con close, parsimonious, tight

elegance *n* impressive beauty of form, appearance, or behavior <the sumptuous *elegance* of the furnishings>
syn dignity, grace
rel beauty, charm; cultivation, culture, polish, refinement, sophistication, style, taste, tastefulness; lushness, magnificence, ornateness, poshness, richness, splendor, sumptuousness
con grotesqueness, ugliness; clumsiness, crudeness, roughness, rudeness; austerity, bareness, inornateness, severity

elegant *adj syn* see CHOICE
rel august, grand, majestic, noble, stately; beautiful, graceful, handsome, lovely; cultivated, cultured, finished, polished, refined, tasteful; luxurious, opulent, sumptuous
con crude, rough, rude, uncouth; grotesque

element *n* **1** *syn* see ESSENTIAL 1
2 one of the parts, substances, or principles that make up a compound or complex whole <analyzed the various *elements* of the problem>
syn component, constituent, factor, ingredient; *compare* POINT 1
rel fundamental, principle; item, member, part, particle, piece, portion; detail, particular; aspect, facet, feature, view
con bulk, mass, volume; entirety, whole; sum, total, totality
ant composite, compound
3 elements *pl syn* see ALPHABET 2
rel basics, basis, foundations, groundwork; outlines
4 *syn* see POINT 1
rel division, member, section, sector, segment

elemental *adj* **1** of, relating to, or being an ultimate and irreducible element <such *elemental* aspects of life as sex and nutrition>
syn basic, elementary, essential, fundamental, primitive, substratal, underlying
rel primary, prime, primordial; inherent, intrinsic, radical
con secondary, subordinate; casual, incidental, trivial, unimportant
2 *syn* see ELEMENTARY 1
3 *syn* see INHERENT

elementary *adj* **1** of, relating to, or dealing with the simplest principles of something <can't handle the most *elementary* decision-making>
syn basal, beginning, elemental, rudimental, rudimentary, simplest
rel introductory, prefatory, preliminary; easy, simple; rude, unsubtle
con complex, complicated, elaborate, intricate, labyrinthine; sophisticated
ant advanced
2 *syn* see ELEMENTAL 1

elephantine *adj* **1** *syn* see HUGE
con slender, slight, slim, thin; dainty
2 *syn* see PONDEROUS 2
rel awkward, clumsy, graceless, maladroit, ungraceful
con graceful, nimble, quick

elevate *vb* **1** *syn* see LIFT 1

rel ensky, erect
con cut (down), deflate, depress, scale (down)
ant lower
2 *syn* see ADVANCE 2
rel boost; enhance, glorify, heighten
con demote, downgrade, lower, reduce; abase, debase, degrade
elevated *adj* **1** being positioned above a surface <an *elevated* monorail>
syn lifted, raised, upheaved, uplifted, upraised, uprisen
rel high; aerial
con ground-level, low, lowered, low-lying, un-elevated
ant sunken
2 being on a high moral or intellectual plane <*elevated* ideas>
syn high-minded, moral, noble
rel ethical, honorable, righteous, upright, upstanding, virtuous
con base, ignoble, mean; immoral, low, unethical; intolerable, unacceptable
3 *syn* see GRAND 3
4 being exceedingly dignified in form, tone, or style <an *elevated* prose style>
syn eloquent, high, lofty
rel dignified, formal; grand, grandiloquent, grandiose, high-flown, majestic, stately, towering
con informal; lowly, unassuming
elevation *n* **1 *syn*** see HEIGHT
rel acclivity, ascent, rise
con depression, descent; flatness, levelness
2 *syn* see ADVANCEMENT 1
rel advance, boost, raise; ennoblement, exaltation, glorification, lionization; apotheosis, deification, immortalization, magnification
con downgrading; depreciation, detraction, disparagement
ant degradation
elf *n syn* see FAIRY
elicit *vb syn* see EDUCE 1
rel bring, fetch
con eschew, forego; abandon
elide *vb syn* see NEGLECT
eligible *adj* qualified to be or worthy of being chosen <an *eligible* bachelor>
syn fit, suitable
rel acceptable, desirable, likely, preferable, seemly; capable, fitted, qualified, suited, worthy; marriageable, nubile; visitable
con undesirable; disqualified, unfit, unqualified, unsuitable, unworthy
ant ineligible
eliminate *vb* **1 *syn*** see EXCLUDE
rel freeze out, shut out; dismiss, ‖dump, eject, evict, expel, oust; delete, erase, expunge
con accept, receive
2 *syn* see REMOVE 4
3 *syn* see PURGE 3
elite *n* **1 *syn*** see BEST
rel elect, pink, select; ‖hoi polloi
idiom cream of the crop, crème de la crème, pick of the bunch

2 *syn* see ARISTOCRACY
rel drawing rooms; Four Hundred; beautiful people, jet set, smart set
idiom high society, horsey set
con hoi polloi, (the) masses, mob, peasantry, people, proletariat, rabble
elixir *n syn* see PANACEA
rel balm, cure, therapy, therapeutic
ell *n syn* see ANNEX
elocution *n syn* see ORATORY
elongate *vb syn* see EXTEND 3
rel drag (out); string
con contract, draw in; compress; curtail, retrench; shrink
ant abbreviate, shorten
elongate *adj syn* see LONG 1
rel lengthened
ant abbreviated, shortened
elongated *adj syn* see LONG 1
rel drawn (out), lengthened, prolonged, prolonged, protracted, stretched
con contracted, drawn (in), shrunken
ant shortened
elongation *n syn* see EXTENSION 1
elope *vb* to go away secretly usually with the intention of marrying <decided to *elope* rather than endure a big wedding>
syn run away
idiom go to Gretna Green
eloquence *n* discourse marked by force and persuasiveness suggesting strong feeling <read the poem with *eloquence*>
syn expression, expressiveness, expressivity, facundity
rel meaningfulness, persuasiveness; fervor, force, forcefulness, passion, power, spirit, vigor
eloquent *adj* **1 *syn*** see VOCAL 3
rel forceful, potent, powerful; ardent, fervent, fervid, impassioned, passionate; glib, silver-tongued, voluble
con inarticulate, ineffective, weak
2 *syn* see EXPRESSIVE
rel graphic, indicative, revealing, suggestive, telling; affecting, impressive, moving, poignant, touching
3 *syn* see ELEVATED 4
else *adv syn* see OTHERWISE 2
else *adj syn* see ADDITIONAL
‖elseways *adv syn* see OTHERWISE 2
elsewise *adv syn* see OTHERWISE 2
elucidate *vb syn* see CLARIFY 2
rel exemplify; demonstrate, prove; annotate, spell out; enlighten
con confuse; darken
elude *vb syn* see ESCAPE 2
rel baffle, circumvent, foil, frustrate, outwit, thwart; flee, fly
idiom give the slip

---

syn synonym(s)   *rel* related word(s)
ant antonym(s)   *con* contrasted word(s)
idiom idiomatic equivalent(s)
‖ use limited; if in doubt, see a dictionary

con accost, face; chase, follow, pursue, tag, tail, trail

elusion *n syn* see ESCAPE 2

elusive *adj* not easily perceived, grasped, comprehended, pinned down, or isolated <inspiration need not be forever *elusive* > <they finally isolated the *elusive* virus that caused the disease>
syn elusory, evasive, intangible
rel evanescent, fleeting, fugitive; baffling, imponderable, incomprehensible, mysterious; insubstantial, phantom

elusory *adj syn* see ELUSIVE
rel nebulous, vague

elvish *adj syn* see PLAYFUL 1

elysium *n syn* see HEAVEN 2

emaciated *adj* being very lean through loss of flesh (as from hunger or disease) <*emaciated* bony hands clutched at him>
syn cadaverous, gaunt, skeletal, wasted
rel bony, lean, scrawny, skinny, wizened; starved, underfed, undernourished
idiom all skin and bones, thin as a rail
con fit, husky, solid, well-fed, well-nourished; chubby, plump, portly, rotund, stocky, stout; corpulent, obese
ant fleshy

emanate *vb syn* see SPRING 1
rel initiate; emit, exude, radiate

emancipate *vb syn* see FREE
ant enslave

emasculate *vb syn* see UNNERVE
rel debilitate, devitalize
con energize, vitalize

emasculate *adj syn* see WEAK 4

embark *vb syn* see BOARD 1

embark (on *or* upon) *vb syn* see BEGIN 1

embarrass *vb* to throw into a state of self-conscious distress <bawdy stories *embarrassed* her>
syn abash, confound, confuse, discomfit, disconcert, discountenance, faze, rattle; *compare* DISCOMPOSE 1
rel agitate, bother, discompose, flurry, fluster, perturb; nonplus; chagrin, distress, vex; queer
idiom put on the spot, put to the blush
con calm, relieve, soothe

embarrassing *adj syn* see INCONVENIENT

embarrassment *n* the quality, state, or condition of being embarrassed <felt great *embarrassment* when she fell down>
syn abashment, confusion, discomfiture, discomposure, disconcertion, disconcertment, unease, uneasiness
rel constraint, strain; agitation, discombobulation, perturbation; chagrin, distress, vexation; humiliation, mortification; difficulty, Queer Street
con assurance, calm, imperturbability, savoir faire

embed *vb syn* see ENTRENCH 1

embellish *vb* **1** *syn* see ADORN
rel apparel, array, ‖doll up, dress up, emblaze, embroider, enrich, furbish
con bare, denude, divest, strip
2 *syn* see EMBROIDER

embellishment *n syn* see EXAGGERATION
rel floridity, ostentation

embezzle *vb* to appropriate dishonestly and fraudulently to one's own use <*embezzled* a trust fund>
syn misappropriate, peculate
rel loot, pilfer, steal, thieve

embitter *vb syn* see EXACERBATE
rel bitter, sour

emblem *n* **1** *syn* see SYMBOL 1
2 *syn* see INSIGNIA

emblematize *vb syn* see REPRESENT 2

embodiment *n* a concrete or actual entity in which something (as an idea, principle, or type) is embodied <he is the *embodiment* of all our hopes>
syn incarnation, personification; *compare* APOTHEOSIS 1
rel manifestation; prosopopoeia; archetype; apotheosis, epitome, quintessence

embody *vb* **1** to make an abstraction concrete or perceptible often by representation in human or animal form <Dickens *embodied* hypocrisy in his Uriah Heep>
syn exteriorize, externalize, incarnate, manifest, materialize, objectify, personalize, personify, personize, substantiate; *compare* REPRESENT 2
rel actualize, hypostatize, realize, reify, symbolize, typify; demonstrate, evince, exemplify, exhibit, illustrate, show (forth)
ant disembody
2 to cause to become a body or part of another body <*embodied* a revenue provision in the new law>
syn combine, incorporate, integrate
rel absorb, amalgamate, assimilate, blend, consolidate, fuse, merge, unify
3 *syn* see INCLUDE
rel compose, consist (of), constitute
4 *syn* see REPRESENT 2

embog *vb syn* see DELAY 1

embolden *vb syn* see ENCOURAGE 1
rel impel; inspire; chance, hazard, venture
con deter, discourage
ant abash

embouchement *n syn* see MOUTH 5

embouchure *n syn* see MOUTH 5

embowel *vb syn* see EVISCERATE

embrace *vb* **1** to gather into one's arms usually as a gesture of affection <*embraced* his wife>
syn clasp, ‖clinch, ‖clip, ‖coll, enfold, hug, press, squeeze
rel cling, grip, hold; encircle, entwine, envelop, enwind, fold, lock, twine, wrap; cuddle, fondle, nuzzle, snuggle; cradle, hold
idiom ‖go into a clinch
2 *syn* see ADOPT
rel accept, accommodate, admit, incorporate, receive, take (over), take in; seize (upon), welcome
con reject; abjure, deny, forswear, renounce
ant spurn
3 *syn* see INCLUDE
rel compose, cover, enclose, hold

embracement *n syn* see ESPOUSAL 4

embracing *n syn* see ESPOUSAL 4

embrangle *vb syn* see ENTANGLE 3

embroider *vb* to give an elaborate account of, often with florid language and fictitious details <*embroidered* the story of his adventures in the army>
syn color, embellish, exaggerate, fudge, magnify, overcharge, overdraw, overpaint, overstate, pad, stretch
rel aggrandize, amplify, build up, distend, elaborate, enhance, enlarge (upon), expand; dramatize, hyperbolize, overdo, overelaborate, overembellish, overemphasize, overestimate
idiom lay it on thick, stretch (*or* strain) the truth
con deemphasize, minimize, play (down), underestimate, understate

embroidering *n syn* see EXAGGERATION

embroil *vb syn* see INVOLVE 1

embroilment *n* 1 *syn* see QUARREL
2 *syn* see ENTANGLEMENT 1

embryo *n syn* see SEED 2

emend *vb syn* see CORRECT 1
rel alter, edit, emendate; polish, retouch

emerge *vb syn* see APPEAR 1
rel derive, originate, spring, stem; arise, materialize, rise; come (forth), come out, emanate, flow, issue (forth); proceed
idiom appear on the horizon, come on the scene, come out in the open, come to light, make its appearance
con disappear, fade, fade (out); evaporate; dissolve

emergency *n syn* see JUNCTURE 2
rel difficulty, extremity; clutch, fix, hole, pinch, push, squeeze, vicissitude; climax
idiom turn of events

emigrant *n* one that leaves one place to settle in another <a city teeming with *emigrants* from many lands>
syn immigrant, migrant
rel alien, displaced person, DP, émigré, evacuee, exile, expatriate, fugitive, refugee; migrator, migratory
con aborigine, native

emigrate *vb syn* see MIGRATE

émigré *n* 1 a person forced to immigrate usually for political reasons <a city filled with White Russian *émigrés*>
syn exile, expatriate, expellee
rel emigrant, immigrant; alien, displaced person, DP, evacuee, fugitive, refugee
2 *syn* see REFUGEE

eminence *n* 1 a condition, position, or state of great importance or superiority <the *eminence* of the presidency>
syn distinction, illustriousness, kudos, preeminence, prestige, prominence, prominency, renown
rel greatness, loftiness, prepotency, significance, superiority; authority, credit, dignity, importance, influence, power, weight; fame, famousness, glory, honor, reputation, repute
con insignificance, unimportance; obscurity
2 *syn* see NOTABLE 1

3 a natural elevation <the house stood on an *eminence* overlooking the river>
syn projection, prominence
rel peak, raise, rise, uprise; altitude, elevation, height; highness, loftiness
con cavity, depression, dip

eminency *n syn* see FORTE

eminent *adj syn* see FAMOUS 2
rel well-known; august, dominant, exalted, important, lofty, noble, preeminent; big league, big-name, big-time
con uncelebrated, unremarkable, unrenowned; common, lowly

eminently *adv syn* see VERY 1

emissary *n syn* see MESSENGER

emit *vb* 1 *syn* see DISCHARGE 5
2 to discharge something such as moisture, vapor, or fumes <a smokestack *emitting* effluents>
syn give off, give out, issue, release, throw off, vent
rel discharge, evacuate, expel; let out, loose, pass (off); pour (out), reek; drip, emanate, excrete, extrude, exude, ooze, secrete; exhale, expire

emolument *n syn* see WAGE
rel guerdon

emote *vb* to give expression to emotion especially on or as if on the stage <she *emotes*, postures, and harangues at the slightest provocation>
syn emotionalize
rel gush, sentimentalize; carry on, rage, rant, storm, take on

emotion *n syn* see FEELING 3
rel excitability, responsiveness, sensibility, sensitiveness, sensitivity, susceptibilities; sensation
con coldness, detachment, reserve, unfeelingness

emotionable *adj syn* see EMOTIONAL 1

emotional *adj* 1 dominated by, prone to, or moved by emotion <an irritable *emotional* woman who was easily upset by trivialities>
syn emotionable, feeling, sensitive, sentient
rel responsive, susceptible, susceptive; softhearted, sympathetic; ardent, fervent, passionate; rhapsodic, rhapsodical
con cold, detached, insensitive, reserved, taciturn, unfeeling
ant emotionless, unemotional
2 appealing to or arousing emotion <an *emotional* sermon>
syn affective, emotive, moving; *compare* MOVING 2
rel affecting, stirring, touching

emotionalize *vb syn* see EMOTE

emotionless *adj* 1 *syn* see COLD 2
rel nonemotional, undemonstrative; cool, dispassionate, distant, immovable, impassive, remote, reserved; heartless, unfeeling

---

syn synonym(s)   *rel* related word(s)
ant antonym(s)   *con* contrasted word(s)
idiom idiomatic equivalent(s)
‖ use limited; if in doubt, see a dictionary

con responsive, softhearted, sympathetic; ardent, fervent, passionate
ant emotional
2 syn see MATTER-OF-FACT 3
emotive *adj syn* see EMOTIONAL 2
empathy *n syn* see SYMPATHY 2
rel accord, affinity, communion, compatibility, concord, congeniality, fellow feeling, rapport, responsiveness, warmth; appreciation, comprehension, understanding
idiom community of interests
con animosity, animus, antagonism, antipathy, enmity
emphasis *n* force brought to bear on something to bring out what is important <the school's *emphasis* on discipline>
syn accent, accentuation, stress
rel attention; force, insistence; weight
emphasize *vb* to give emphasis to especially by displaying more or less prominently <the papers *emphasized* crime stories>
syn feature, italicize, play (up), stress, underline, underscore
rel accent, accentuate, charge, highlight, mark, pinpoint, point (up), punctuate, spotlight; assert, press
idiom bear down on (*or* upon)
con depreciate, minimize, play (down), shrug off, underrate, understate
ant de-emphasize
emphatic *adj* marked by, uttered with, or made prominent by stress or emphasis <made his point in an *emphatic* argument>
syn assertive, forceful, insistent, resounding
rel aggressive, energetic, insistive, vigorous; accented, accentuated, assertative, decided, emphasized, marked, pointed, stressed, underlined
con insipid, milk-and-water, unaggressive, unassertive, weak, wishy-washy; de-emphasized, played (down), understated
ant unemphatic
empirical *adj* originating in, relying on, or based on factual information, observation, or direct sense experience <an *empirical* basis for an ethical theory>
syn experient, experiential, experimental
rel observational; factual
con conjectural, speculative, unproved, unsubstantiated; ideal, imagined
ant theoretical
employ *vb* **1 syn** see USE 2
rel avail, exert, practice, work; devote, engross, monopolize
2 to provide with a job that pays wages <*employed* a new draftsman>
syn engage, hire, put on, take on
rel add, contract (for), obtain, procure, retain, secure, sign (on *or* up)
employable *adj syn* see OPEN 5
employed *adj syn* see BUSY 1
employment *n* **1 syn** see USE 1
rel purpose; disposition, exercise, exploitation, handling, utilization
2 syn see EXERCISE 1

3 syn see WORK 1
rel assignment, mission; office, position, post, situation; function
4 the act of employing for wages <handled the *employment* of new workers>
syn engagement, engaging, hiring
rel enlistment, enrollment, recruitment, signing on
empower *vb* **1 syn** see INVEST 2
2 syn see AUTHORIZE 1
3 syn see ENABLE 2
rel endow, invest; authorize, charge, commission, entitle, entrust, license, privilege, sanction
con debar, disallow, disbar, exclude, rule out, shut out
emprise *n syn* see ADVENTURE
emptiness *n syn* see VACUITY 2
emptor *n syn* see PURCHASER
empty *adj* **1** lacking contents that could or should be present <an *empty* apartment> <the whole book is *empty* of meaning>
syn bare, clear, stark, vacant, vacuous, void
rel barren, blank; abandoned, deserted, emptied, forsaken, godforsaken, unfilled, unfurnished, uninhabited, untenanted, vacated; destitute, devoid; depleted, drained, exhausted
con complete, replete; filled, occupied, packed, teeming
ant full
2 syn see VAIN 1
rel paltry, petty, trifling, trivial; banal, flat, inane, ineffectual, insipid, jejune, vapid; dumb, fatuous, foolish, ignorant, silly, simple
con meaningful, pregnant, significant; authentic, bona fide, genuine, veritable
3 syn see EXPRESSIONLESS
4 syn see DEVOID
empty *vb syn* see VACATE 2
empty–headed *adj* **1 syn** see GIDDY 1
rel brainless, rattleheaded; ignorant, simple
2 syn see VACUOUS 2
3 syn see IGNORANT 1
empyreal *adj syn* see CELESTIAL
rel aerial, airy; extraterrestrial; divine, holy, spiritual, sublime
ant terrestrial
empyrean *adj syn* see CELESTIAL
empyrean *n* **1 syn** see HEAVEN 2
2 syn see SKY
emulate *vb syn* see RIVAL 2
rel challenge, outvie
emulation *n syn* see CONTEST 1
emulative *adj syn* see SLAVISH 3
emulous *adj syn* see AMBITIOUS 1
rel aiming, striving; agog, athirst; competitive, vying
con unambitious, unaspiring; detached, disinterested, uninterested
enable *vb* **1 syn** see AUTHORIZE 1
rel allow, let, permit, sanction
2 to render able often by giving power, strength, or competence to <her education *enabled* her to find an excellent job>
syn empower

rel allow, let, permit; condition, fit, prepare, qualify, ready
con inhibit, preclude, prevent; disallow, enjoin, forbid, prohibit
enact *vb* **1** to cause to be by legal and authoritative act <*enact* a law>
syn constitute, establish, make
rel bring about, institute; authorize, decree, proclaim; accomplish, carry (through), effect, effectuate, execute, legislate, pass, put (through), ratify
con abolish, abrogate, annul, cancel, invalidate, nullify, rescind, revoke; overturn
ant repeal
2 *syn* see ACT 1
rel depict, portray, represent
enamored *adj* **1** moved by intense sexual attraction <became more desperately *enamored* of the man every day>
syn mashed, smitten, soft (on), spoony (over *or* on)
rel infatuated; crazy (over *or* about), mad (about), nuts (about), silly (over *or* about), wild (about); amorous, devoted, loving
idiom head over heels in love, stuck on, sweet on
2 *syn* see INFATUATED
3 taking great pleasure in something <found herself *enamored* of those huge English teas>
syn bewitched, captivated, charmed, enchanted, entranced, fascinated
rel fond
encamp *vb* *syn* see CAMP
encampment *n* *syn* see CAMP 1
enceinte *adj* *syn* see PREGNANT 1
enchant *vb* **1** *syn* see BEWITCH 1
2 *syn* see ATTRACT 1
rel delight, enthrall, please, send, thrill; mesmerize
idiom carry away, knock dead
con disillusion, dissatisfy, let down
ant disenchant
enchanted *adj* *syn* see ENAMORED 3
rel delighted, pleased; pixilated
ant disenchanted
enchanter *n* *syn* see MAGICIAN 1
enchanting *adj* *syn* see ATTRACTIVE 1
rel attractive, pleasing; delectable, delightful; beguiling, enthralling, entrancing, intriguing, witching; exciting, sirenic
con repellent
enchantment *n* *syn* see MAGIC 1
enchantress *n* *syn* see WITCH 1
enchiridion *n* *syn* see HANDBOOK
rel book, text
encincture *vb* *syn* see BELT 1
encircle *vb* *syn* see SURROUND 1
rel band, cincture, circuit, enring; halo, wreathe
enclose *vb* **1** to shut up or confine by or as if by barriers <a valley *enclosed* by mountains>
syn cage, close in, coop, corral, envelop, fence, hedge, hem, immure, mew, mure, pen, shut in, wall
rel bound, circumscribe, confine, contain, limit, restrict; circle, compass, encircle, encompass, surround; environ; enlock

2 *syn* see ENFOLD 1
enclosure *n* *syn* see COURT 1
enclothe *vb* *syn* see CLOTHE
encomiastic *adj* *syn* see EULOGISTIC
encomium *n* a formal expression of praise <an unstinted *encomium* of a national hero>
syn citation, eulogy, panegyric, salutation, tribute
rel approval, kudos, laud, laudation, magnification, praise; acclaim, acclamation, applause, plaudits; accolade, commendation, compliment
con abuse, invective, obloquy, vituperation; criticism, critique, faultfinding
encompass *vb* **1** *syn* see SURROUND 1
rel bound, delimit
2 *syn* see INCLUDE
encounter *vb* **1** *syn* see CONFRONT 1
rel clash, collide, conflict
2 *syn* see ENGAGE 5
3 *syn* see MEET 6
rel ‖bump (into), come (across), run (across), run (into)
idiom cross the path of, fall in with, meet up with
con miss, pass (by)
4 *syn* see FIND 1
encounter *n* a sudden, hostile, and usually brief confrontation or dispute between factions or persons <a sharp courtroom *encounter* between opposing lawyers>
syn brush, run-in, set-to, skirmish, velitation
rel conflict, contest; scrap; fight, fray; battle; argument, contention, quarrel
encourage *vb* **1** to fill with courage or strength of purpose especially in preparation for a hard task <the teacher's praise *encouraged* the student to try harder>
syn animate, cheer, chirk (up), embolden, enhearten, hearten, inspirit, nerve, ‖pearten (up), steel, strengthen; *compare* SUPPORT 5
rel assure, reassure; boost, excite, galvanize, pique, provoke, quicken, stimulate; buck up, buoy (up), energize, fortify, invigorate; rally, stir
idiom give a shot in the arm
con deject, depress, discourage, dishearten, dispirit; affright, caution, frighten
ant discourage
2 to give the support of one's approval to <the government openly *encouraged* East-West détente>
syn advocate, countenance, favor
rel approve, back, endorse, go (for), sanction, subscribe (to); abet, assist, reinforce, support, sustain; incite, instigate; induce, prevail
idiom lend one's countenance to, lend one's favor (or support) to, smile upon
con deter, dissuade, divert, hinder; inhibit, restrain; disapprove
ant discourage

syn synonym(s)   *rel* related word(s)
ant antonym(s)   *con* contrasted word(s)
idiom idiomatic equivalent(s)
‖ use limited; if in doubt, see a dictionary

3 syn see ADVANCE 1
rel patronize, push, support; develop, improve, subsidize
con weaken; check, retard, slow
ant discourage
encouraging *adj syn* see HOPEFUL 2
encroach *vb syn* see TRESPASS 2
rel barge (in), ‖bust (in), butt (in), chisel (in), horn (in), muscle (in), worm (in); interfere, interpose, intervene, meddle; overstep
idiom foist oneself upon, stick one's nose in (*or* into)
con ignore, let (alone), pass over; avoid
encrust (*or* **incrust**) *vb syn* see CAKE 1
encumber *vb syn* see BURDEN
rel freight; discommode, incommode, inconvenience; fetter, hamper, handicap; block, impede, obstruct; oppress, overburden
encumbrance *n* something that impedes and makes action difficult <told his story simply without the *encumbrance* of unnecessary details>
syn clog, cumbrance, hindrance, impedance, impediment
rel disadvantage, handicap, load; difficulty, hardship, inconvenience
con aid; catalyst, impetus, stimulus
ant assist, assistance
encyclopedic *adj* embracing, comprehensively treating, or informed in a wide range of subjects <an *encyclopedic* article on world history>
syn comprehensive, inclusive
rel all-comprehensive, all-embracing, all-inclusive, complete; extensive, general; discursive
end *n* **1 syn** see LIMIT 1
rel borderline, tip; extreme, extremity
con center, hub, middle
2 ceasing of a course (as of action or activity) or the point at which something ceases <the *end* of the war>
syn cease, cessation, close, closing, closure, conclusion, desistance, desuetude, discontinuance, discontinuation, ending, finish, period, stop, termination, terminus; *compare* FINALE
rel consummation, culmination; expiration; coda, curtains, finale, finality, finis, terminal, windup
idiom cutoff point, end of the line, stopping point
con genesis, inception
ant beginning
3 syn see FINALE
4 something residual <melted down candle *ends*>
syn bit, fragment, scrap
rel butt end, fag end, leaving, remainder, remnant, residue; part, particle, piece
end *vb syn* see CLOSE 3
ant begin
endable *adj syn* see TERMINABLE
endanger *vb* to bring into peril (as of harm or disaster) <conspirators who were *endangering* the cause of freedom>
syn compromise, hazard, imperil, jeopard, jeopardize, jeopardy, menace, peril, risk

rel expose, lay (open); chance, venture
con guard, protect, shelter, shield; preserve, save
endeavor *vb syn* see TRY 5
rel determine, intend, purpose; address, apply, bid (for), drive (at), go (for); strain
endeavor *n syn* see ATTEMPT
rel exertion, push; labor, toil, travail, work
ended *adj syn* see COMPLETE 4
endemic *adj syn* see NATIVE 2
rel home-bred, native-born
con pandemic; extraneous, extrinsic
ant exotic
ending *n* **1 syn** see END 2
ant beginning
2 syn see FINALE
endless *adj* **1 syn** see LIMITLESS
2 syn see EVERLASTING 1
rel constant, continuous; deathless, immortal, undying; boundless, limitless, unbounded, unlimited; self-perpetuating
3 syn see CONTINUAL
rel overlong
endorse *vb syn* see APPROVE 2
rel attest, authenticate, pass (on *or* upon), vouch, witness; command, recommend; advocate, back (up), champion, stand by, support, uphold
con deprecate, disapprove; anathematize, denounce
endorsement *n syn* see SANCTION
endow *vb* **1** to furnish or provide with a gift, talent, or good quality <poets *endowed* with genius>
syn crown (with), dower, endue
rel bestow, confer; accord, award, grant; empower, enable; enhance, enrich, heighten
con bare, denude, divest, strip; despoil, ravage, spoliate; deplete, drain, exhaust
2 to furnish, (as an institution) with a store of capital <*endowed* a hospital>
syn finance, fund, subsidize
rel found, organize; bequeath, contribute, donate, subscribe, support; award, grant; back, promote, sponsor; provide, supply
con beggar, impoverish, pauperize; drain, draw (on)
end product *n syn* see EFFECT 1
endue *vb syn* see ENDOW 1
rel clothe, invest, vest; accouter, equip, furnish, outfit
endurable *adj syn* see BEARABLE
endurance *n* **1 syn** see CONTINUATION 1
2 syn see TOLERANCE 1
endure *vb* **1 syn** see CONTINUE 1
rel bide, linger
con crumble, decay, disintegrate; collapse, fall
ant perish
2 syn see ACCEPT 2
rel stand, submit (to), suffer, sustain; undergo
con break, collapse, give in, resign
3 syn see BEAR 10
enduring *adj* **1 syn** see LASTING
ant fleeting
2 syn see OLD 2

3 syn see SURE 2
rel durable, resolute, solid, sound, stable, staunch, sturdy, substantial
con capricious, changeable, fickle, inconstant, mercurial, unstable, variable

endways *adv syn* see LENGTHWISE

endwise *adv syn* see LENGTHWISE

enemy *n* an individual or group that is hostile toward another <the senator was blackmailed by a political *enemy*>
syn foe
rel adversary, antagonist, opponent; assailant, attacker, combatant, invader; competitor, contender, emulator, rival
con benefactor, friend, supporter; ally, collaborator, colleague, confederate, friendly; adherent, follower, partisan, upholder

energetic *adj* **1 syn** see VIGOROUS
rel aggressive, emphatic, vibrant; indefatigable
con easygoing; faineant, idle, languorous, lethargic
2 disposed to or having a capacity for action <an *energetic* campaign worker>
syn active, driving, enterprising, lively
rel animated, breezy, brisk, fresh, kinetic, peppy, spirited, sprightly, spry, vivacious, zippy
idiom full of go (*or* life *or* pep *or* zip)
con apathetic, inert; lethargic, limp, listless, passive, phlegmatic, spiritless, spunkless
ant inactive

energetically *adv syn* see HARD 1
rel firmly, strenuously; busily, industriously, zealously
idiom at full tilt
con idly, lazily, lethargically, listlessly; slowly
ant unenergetically

energize *vb* **1 syn** see VITALIZE
idiom put pep (*or* zip) into
con emasculate, enervate; debilitate, enfeeble
2 syn see STRENGTHEN 2
rel arm, empower, enable; build (up), sustain
con daunt

energy *n* **1 syn** see POWER 4
rel activity, operativeness; forcefulness, mightiness, powerfulness
con impotence; decrepitude, feebleness, weakness; powerlessness
ant inertia
2 vigorous and effectual application and operation of power <work with *energy*>
syn birr, go, hardihood, ‖moxie, pep, potency, tuck, vigor; *compare* VIGOR 2
rel application, effectiveness, efficacy; effort, operativeness; toughness
con kef, languor, lethargy, listlessness, sluggishness; ergophobia

enervate *vb syn* see UNNERVE
rel debilitate, devitalize, disable; exhaust, fatigue, jade, tire, weary
con activate, energize, vitalize; galvanize, quicken, stimulate

enervated *adj syn* see LANGUID
rel debilitated, devitalized, enfeebled, undermined, weakened; exhausted, fatigued, run=

down, tired, weary; decadent, degenerate, degenerated, deteriorated
con active, animated, energetic, lusty, strenuous, vigorous, vital; strong, sturdy, tenacious, tough

enfant terrible *n syn* see SCAMP

enfeeble *vb syn* see WEAKEN 1
rel devitalize, exhaust
con galvanize; harden, strengthen
ant fortify

enfold *vb* **1** to surround or cover closely <a heavy fog *enfolded* the ships>
syn enclose, enshroud, envelop, enwrap, invest, shroud, veil, wrap; *compare* SWATHE
rel cover, drape; encase, ensheathe; encircle, encompass, environ, gird, girdle, surround
2 syn see EMBRACE 1

enforce *vb* to put something into effect or operation <*enforce* a law>
syn effect, implement, invoke
rel accomplish, administer, carry (out *or* through), discharge, execute, fulfill, perform; compel, force, oblige
con disregard, forget, ignore, neglect; relax

enfranchise *vb* to admit to full political rights as a freeman or citizen <slaves were emancipated in 1863 but were not *enfranchised* until the Fifteenth Amendment went into effect in 1870>
syn affranchise, franchise
rel emancipate, free, liberate, release; deliver, extricate, rescue
con enslave, oppress, subject
ant disenfranchise, disfranchise

engage *vb* **1** to come into contact and interlock with <the teeth of one gear wheel *engaging* those of another>
syn intermesh, mesh
rel interact, interlace, interlock, interplay
con free, release
ant disengage
2 syn see PROMISE 1
rel commit; bind, tie; affiance, betroth, troth
3 syn see EMPLOY 2
con dismiss, eject, fire
ant discharge
4 to hold the attention of <the puzzle *engaged* him all evening>
syn busy, engross, immerse, occupy, soak
rel absorb, imbue, involve; arrest, captivate, enthrall, fascinate, grip; monopolize, preengage, preoccupy
5 to enter into contest or conflict with <ordered to seek out and *engage* the enemy fleet>
syn encounter, face, meet, take on
rel assault, attack, strike; battle, fight
idiom do battle with, join battle with
con elude, escape, evade

engaged *adj* **1 syn** see BUSY 1
ant unengaged

---

syn synonym(s)   **rel** related word(s)
ant antonym(s)   **con** contrasted word(s)
idiom idiomatic equivalent(s)
‖ use limited; if in doubt, see a dictionary

2 pledged in marriage <the *engaged* couple made a charming pair>
syn affianced, betrothed, contracted, intended, plighted, ‖promised
rel committed, pledged
con free, uncommitted, unpledged
ant unengaged
3 *syn* see INTENT

engagement *n* **1** *syn* see PROMISE
2 the act or state of being engaged to be married <the couple recently announced their *engagement*>
syn betrothal, betrothing, betrothment, espousal, troth
rel pledge, plight, promise
ant disengagement
3 a promise to be in an agreed place at a specified time, usually for a particular purpose <had an *engagement* with him for nine that evening>
syn appointment, assignation, date, rendezvous, tryst
rel arrangement, invitation; interview; get-together, meeting, visit
4 *syn* see EMPLOYMENT 4
5 *syn* see BATTLE

engaging *adj* **1** *syn* see ATTRACTIVE 1
2 *syn* see SWEET 1
rel alluring, appealing, attractive, captivating, charming, enchanting, entrancing, fetching; fascinating, interesting, intriguing
con repellent, repelling, repulsive; unappealing, unattractive, uninteresting
ant loathsome

engaging *n* *syn* see EMPLOYMENT 4

engender *vb* *syn* see GENERATE 3
rel develop; excite, stimulate; arouse, quicken, rouse, stir

engineer *vb* to contrive or plan out usually with subtle skill or craft <*engineered* an agreement between the two rival governments>
syn finagle, machinate, maneuver, wangle; *compare* MANIPULATE 2
rel arrange, contrive, devise, mastermind, plan (out), set up; intrigue, plot, scheme; manage, manipulate, negotiate; put (over), put (through), swing
idiom pull strings (*or* wires)

engird *vb* *syn* see BELT 1

engirdle *vb* *syn* see BELT 1

englut *vb* *syn* see GULP

engrave *vb* **1** to cut into a surface usually with a graving tool in order to form an inscription or a pictorial illustration <*engraved* a banknote design on the copper plate>
syn etch, grave, incise
rel chase, enchase; carve; inscribe
2 to impress deeply <the incident was *engraved* in his memory>
syn etch, impress, imprint, inscribe
rel carve; fix; instill; print; embed, entrench, infix, ingrain, root

engross *vb* **1** *syn* see WRITE
rel enscroll, scroll; superscribe
2 *syn* see MONOPOLIZE

rel apply, fill, occupy, preoccupy; assimilate, take up; arrest, engage, grip, ‖hog, hold, immerse, involve; attract, captivate, enthrall
con bewilder, distract; disperse, dissipate, scatter
3 *syn* see ENGAGE 4

engrossed *adj* *syn* see INTENT
rel consumed, monopolized, occupied; submerged; assiduous, busy, diligent, industrious, sedulous
idiom caught up in, lost in, taken up with
con detached, disinterested, indifferent, unconcerned, uninterested

engrossing *adj* gripping the attention completely so as to exclude everything else <the *engrossing* nature of his task made the time pass quickly>
syn absorbing, consuming, monopolizing
rel all-consuming, controlling, gripping; interesting, intriguing; exciting, provoking, stimulating; obsessing, preoccupying
con boring, drab, dull, monotonous; unentertaining, unexciting, uninteresting

engulf *vb* *syn* see DELUGE 1

enhance *vb* **1** *syn* see INTENSIFY
rel elevate, lift, raise; enlarge (upon), exaggerate, strengthen; augment, build (up), increase; adorn, beautify, embellish, embroider
con belittle, deprecate, detract, minimize
2 *syn* see FLATTER

enhancement *n* *syn* see ACCOMPANIMENT 1
rel improvement, intensification

enhearten *vb* *syn* see ENCOURAGE 1

enigma *n* *syn* see MYSTERY
rel crux, knot, puzzler, sticker; bewilderment, perplexity, question, question mark
idiom hard nut to crack

enigmatic *adj* *syn* see CRYPTIC

enisle *vb* *syn* see ISOLATE

enjewel *vb* *syn* see BEJEWEL

enjoin *vb* **1** *syn* see COMMAND
rel decree, dictate, impose, prescribe, rule; adjure, advise, counsel; admonish, caution, forewarn
con acquiesce, agree, comply, conform, obey, submit, yield
2 *syn* see FORBID
rel deny, disallow

enjoy *vb* **1** to take pleasure in or receive satisfaction from <*enjoyed* the meal>
syn ‖dig, go, like, ‖mind, relish
rel cotton (to); take (to); appreciate, dote (on *or* upon), fancy, love; delight (in), drink (in), eat up, luxuriate (in), savor
con abhor, abominate, detest, hate, loathe; condemn, despise, scorn
2 *syn* see HAVE 1
rel fill, occupy, maintain; boast, command

enjoyableness *n* *syn* see AMENITY 1
rel attractiveness, pleasingness, pleasurableness; niceness

enjoyment *n* **1** an attitude, circumstance, or favorable response to a stimulus that tends to make one gratified or happy <gave himself up to vigorous *enjoyment* of his pipe>

syn delectation, diversion, pleasure, relish; *compare* PLEASURE 2
rel delight, joy; amusement, entertainment; indulgence, savor; recreation, relaxation; gratification, satisfaction
con abhorrence, antipathy, aversion; repugnance, repulsion
2 syn see PLEASURE 2

enkindle *vb syn* see LIGHT 1

enlarge *vb* **1** *syn* see INCREASE 1
rel add (to), embroider, exaggerate; grow, stretch, widen
con attenuate; abridge; compress
2 syn see EXPAND 4
3 syn see INCREASE 2

enlargement *n syn* see EXPANSION 2

enlighten *vb syn* see ILLUMINATE 2
rel direct, educate, guide, inform, instruct, school, teach, train; acquaint, advise, apprise, inform
con bewilder, confuse, mystify, perplex, puzzle; addle, fuddle, muddle

enlightening *adj* tending to dissipate ignorance or increase knowledge and awareness <an *enlightening* glimpse of government in action>
syn illuminant, illuminating, illuminative, illumining
rel broadening, edifying, educational, instructive; clarifying, elucidative, explanatory
con unedifying, uninstructive; confusing, obfuscatory, obscuring

enlist *vb syn* see ENTER 3

enliven *vb syn* see QUICKEN 1
rel refresh, rejuvenate, renew, restore; excite, galvanize, invigorate, jazz (up), pep (up), provoke, stimulate; amuse, cheer, divert, entertain, recreate; exhilarate, fire, inspire
idiom give (new) life to
con depress, oppress, weigh
ant subdue

en masse *adv syn* see ALTOGETHER 3

enmesh *vb syn* see ENTANGLE 3
rel drag (into), draw (in), hook, tangle; embarrass, implicate
idiom make party to
con disembarrass, disentangle
ant extricate

enmeshment *n syn* see ENTANGLEMENT 1

enmity *n* deep-seated dislike or ill will or a manifestation of such feeling <the country had experienced generations of racial *enmity*>
syn animosity, animus, antagonism, antipathy, hostility, rancor
rel uncordiality, unfriendliness; alienation, dead set, disaffection, estrangement; abhorrence, detestation, dislike, hate, hatred, loathing; aversion; bad blood, bitterness, daggers, gall, ill will, malevolence, malice, malignancy, malignity, spite, spleen
con amicability, cordiality, friendliness, neighborliness; comity, empathy, friendship, goodwill, sympathy, understanding
ant amity

ennoble *vb syn* see EXALT 1

ennui *n syn* see TEDIUM
rel blues, dejection, depression, dumps, melancholy, sadness; fatigue, languidness, languor, listlessness, spiritlessness, tiredness, weariness; satiety, surfeit

ennui *vb syn* see BORE
con enliven, stimulate, vitalize

enormity *n* **1** the quality or state of being abnormally, monstrously, or outrageously evil <the utter *enormity* of the crime>
syn atrociousness, atrocity, heinousness, monstrousness
rel grossness, outrage, outrageousness, rankness; depravity; flagrancy
con excusableness, remissibility, veniality; bearableness, tolerability
2 the quality or state of being huge <the *enormity* of the task confounded him>
syn enormousness, hugeness, immensity, magnitude, tremendousness, vastness
rel bigness, greatness, massiveness; graveness, seriousness, weightiness
con diminutiveness, minuteness, smallness, tininess; triviality, unimportance

enormous *adj syn* see HUGE
rel stupendous
ant tiny

enormousness *n syn* see ENORMITY 2
rel monstrousness, prodigiousness, stupendousness

enough *adj syn* see SUFFICIENT 1

enough *adv* **1** in or to a degree or quantity that satisfies some condition <unstable *enough* to react with water>
syn adequately, sufficiently
rel abundantly, amply; acceptably, admissibly, satisfactorily; commensurately, proportionately
2 in a tolerable degree <she sang well *enough*>
syn averagely, fairly, moderately, passably, rather, so-so, tolerably
rel acceptably, decently, satisfactorily

enough *n* as much as is needed or wanted <we have *enough* for all of our needs>
syn adequacy, competence, sufficiency, sufficient
rel abundance, ampleness, plenty
con inadequateness; deficiency, deficit, lack, shortage, want; outage, ullage, wantage
ant inadequacy, insufficiency

enounce *vb syn* see ENUNCIATE 1

enrage *vb syn* see ANGER 1
idiom make one's blood boil, work up into a passion
ant placate

enrapture *vb syn* see TRANSPORT 2
rel elate, gladden, gratify, please, rejoice; allure, attract, captivate, charm, enchant, enthrall, fascinate

enravish *vb syn* see TRANSPORT 2

---

syn synonym(s)   *rel* related word(s)
ant antonym(s)   *con* contrasted word(s)
idiom idiomatic equivalent(s)
‖ use limited; if in doubt, see a dictionary

enrich *vb* to make financially rich or richer <*enriched* himself through speculation>
syn richen
enrichment *n syn* see ACCOMPANIMENT 1
enroll *vb* **1** to take in (as a person) by entering identification in a list, catalog, or roll <the school *enrolls* about 800 students>
syn list, register
rel enter, insert; catalog, inscribe, record; enlist, line (up), recruit, sign (up); join, matriculate
con discard, omit, reject
2 *syn* see LIST 3
3 *syn* see ENTER 3
ensample *n* **1** *syn* see MODEL 2
2 *syn* see EXAMPLE 3
ensanguined *adj syn* see BLOODY 1
ensconce *vb* **1** *syn* see HIDE
2 to establish or place firmly, comfortably, or snugly <was happily *ensconced* on the sofa before the fire>
syn install, settle
rel establish, fix, locate, place, plant, seat, set, situate, station
ensepulcher *vb syn* see ENTOMB 1
enshroud *vb syn* see ENFOLD 1
rel cloak, conceal, curtain, hide
con disclose, display, illustrate, open (up), reveal, show, uncover, unveil
ensign *n syn* see FLAG
enslave *vb* to reduce to and hold in a state of servitude <free peasants reduced to serfdom or *enslaved*>
syn enthrall, subjugate
rel disenfranchise, disfranchise; subject; oppress, shackle, yoke
con affranchise, enfranchise; free, liberate
ant emancipate
enslavement *n syn* see BONDAGE
ensnare *vb syn* see CATCH 3
rel decoy, entice, inveigle, lure; hook, net, snag; bag, capture
ensnarl *vb* **1** *syn* see ENTANGLE 1
2 *syn* see ENTANGLE 3
ensorcell *vb syn* see BEWITCH 1
ensorcellment *n syn* see MAGIC 1
ensphere *vb syn* see BALL
ensue *vb syn* see FOLLOW 1
rel derive, emanate, issue, proceed, stem; attend, result
idiom be subsequent (to), come next
con antecede, forerun, preface
ensuing *adj* **1** *syn* see SUBSEQUENT 1
2 *syn* see NEXT
ensure *vb* to make something certain or sure <provisions *ensuring* that the rank and file have a voice in union policy-making>
syn assure, cinch, insure, secure
rel certify, guarantee, warrant; arrange, establish, provide, set out
enswathe *vb syn* see SWATHE
entangle *vb* **1** to twist or interweave so as to make separation difficult <*entangled* the yarn>
syn ensnarl, intertangle, perplex, snarl, tangle
rel intertwine, interweave, ‖snirl, twist; ball up

2 *syn* see COMPLICATE
3 to catch or hold as if in a net from which escape is difficult <a firm hopelessly *entangled* in financial difficulties>
syn embrangle, enmesh, ensnarl, trammel; *compare* CATCH 3, INVOLVE 1
rel burden, clog, fetter, hamper, impede; bag, capture, catch, ensnare, entrap, snare, trap; discomfit, embarrass, embroil
con extricate, untangle; detach, disengage; clear, free; disburden, unfetter
ant disentangle
4 *syn* see CATCH 3
entanglement *n* **1** the condition of being deeply involved or closely linked often in an embarrassing or compromising way <*entanglements* with underworld figures tarnished his reputation>
syn embroilment, enmeshment, involvement; *compare* WEB 2
rel ensnarement; affair, intrigue, liaison; association, contact
2 *syn* see WEB 2
enter *vb* **1** to come or go into some place or thing <he *entered* the room>
syn come (in), go in, ingress, penetrate
rel pierce, probe
idiom set foot in
con egress, exit, go out, leave; come out, emerge, sally; escape, flee
ant issue
2 to cause or permit to go in or into <*enter* synonyms in a thesaurus>
syn admit, introduce
rel inject, insert, intercalate, interpolate, put (in), set down; docket, inscribe, list, post, record, register; enroll
3 to make or become a member of <decided to *enter* the army>
syn enlist, enroll, join (up), muster, sign on, sign up
rel come (into), go (into)
idiom get oneself into, take up (*or* out) membership (in)
4 *syn* see BEGIN 1
enterprise *n* **1** *syn* see ADVENTURE
rel attempt, effort, endeavor, striving, struggle; campaign, cause, project, pursuit, task, undertaking; deed
2 *syn* see PROJECT 2
rel speculation
3 a unit of economic or business organization or activity <an economy encouraging the expansion of small, privately owned *enterprises*>
syn business, company, concern, establishment, firm, house, outfit
rel interest; organization; corporation; industry
4 readiness to attempt or engage in what requires energy or daring <complained about his brother's lack of *enterprise*>
syn ambition, drive, get-up-and-go, initiative, push; *compare* VIGOR 2
rel ambitiousness, eagerness, energy, enthusiasm, ‖hustle, vigor; boldness, courage, daring, venturesomeness; inventiveness, self-reliance

con languor, lethargy; indolence, laziness, sloth; apathy, inertia

enterprising *adj* **1 syn** see ENERGETIC 2
rel aggressive, ambitious, busy, eager, hustling, pushing, up-and-coming; adventurous, venturesome
2 showing initiative, resolution, and determined effort (as in pursuing a course or a career) <an *enterprising* young woman likely to go far>
syn go-ahead, gumptious, up-and-coming
rel aggressive, pushing; diligent, hardworking, industrious, zealous; ambitious, aspiring, craving, hungry, itching, lusting, yearning; audacious, daring, dashing, venturesome
idiom on one's toes
ant unenterprising

entertain *vb* **1 syn** see HARBOR 2
rel invite; admit, receive; cherish, cultivate, foster; feed, nourish
con banish, eject, throw out; ignore, neglect
2 syn see AMUSE
rel delight, enliven, gladden, gratify, please, regale, rejoice

entertainment *n* something diverting, amusing, or entertaining <staged a floor show as *entertainment* for her guests>
syn amusement, dissipation, distraction, diversion, divertissement, recreation
rel disport, play, sport; enjoyment, gaiety, pleasure; relaxation, relief

enthrall *vb* **1 syn** see ENSLAVE
rel master, subdue
con emancipate
2 to hold spellbound <told mystery stories that *enthralled* his playmates>
syn catch up, fascinate, grip, hold, mesmerize, spellbind
rel absorb, engage, preoccupy; charm, enchant, engross, intrigue
con bore, ennui, weary

enthuse *vb* **1 syn** see THRILL
2 to show great enthusiasm <tourists *enthusing* over the medieval towns>
syn drool, rave, rhapsodize, rhapsody
con censure, criticize; belittle, depreciate, disparage, dispraise, knock, undervalue

enthusiasm *n* **1 syn** see PASSION 6
rel craze, fascination, infatuation, mania
con impassivity, phlegm, stolidity; aloofness, detachment, indifference, unconcern
ant apathy
2 syn see EAGERNESS
rel earnest, interest; ebullience, élan

enthusiast *n* a person who manifests extreme and often uncritical ardor, fervor, or devotion in an attachment <an increasing number of ecology *enthusiasts*>
syn bigot, bug, fanatic, fiend, freak, maniac, nut, zealot
rel addict, aficionado, buff, bum, devotee, fan, habitué, lover, votary; partisan, supporter; bear, extremist
con depreciator, detractor, disparager, knocker

enthusiastic *adj* filled with or marked by enthusiasm <was *enthusiastic* about golf>
syn ‖buggy, ‖bugs, gung ho, keen, nutty, warm, zealous
rel ardent, devoted, eager, fervent, hearty, spirited; gaga, ‖gone (on), hopped-up; hipped, obsessed; passionate, vascular; rabid
con apathetic, detached, indifferent, reluctant, uninterested
ant unenthusiastic

entice *vb* **syn** see LURE
con alarm, fright, frighten (off), terrify
ant scare (off)

enticement *n* **syn** see LURE 2

enticing *adj* being extremely and often dangerously attractive <she looked at him with an *enticing* smile>
syn Circean, fetching, luring, tempting
rel attractive, beguiling, bewitching, enchanting, fascinating, intriguing, inviting, siren, witching; captivating; likable, pleasant, pleasing

entify *vb* **syn** see MATERIALIZE 2

entire *adj* **1 syn** see WHOLE 3
rel all, gross; plenary
con incomplete, unfinished; limited, qualified
ant partial
2 syn see WHOLE 1
rel concatenated, integrated; compacted, consolidated, unified
con broken (up); faulty
ant impaired
3 syn see WHOLE 4

entirely *adv* **1 syn** see WELL 3
2 syn see ONLY 1

entireness *n* **1 syn** see ENTIRETY 1
con incompleteness
2 syn see INTEGRITY 2

entirety *n* **1** the state of being complete <the striking *entirety* and self-sufficiency of the feudal community>
syn allness, completeness, entireness, oneness, totality, wholeness
rel collectiveness, unity; integrity, plenitude; comprehensiveness, omneity, universality
con disunity, division, separateness; fragmentation, incompleteness
2 syn see WHOLE 1
rel collectivity, complex, everything
con component, detail, element, item, part
ant particular

entitle *vb* **1 syn** see NAME 1
2 to furnish with proper authority or grounds for seeking or claiming something <this ticket *entitles* the bearer to free admission>
syn authorize, qualify
rel empower, license; allow, enable, let, permit

entity *n* **1** one that has real and independent existence <each *entity* of the series requires separate study>
syn being, existence, existent, individual, something, thing

---

syn synonym(s)   *rel* related word(s)
ant antonym(s)   *con* contrasted word(s)
idiom idiomatic equivalent(s)
‖ use limited; if in doubt, see a dictionary

rel body, object

2 *syn* see THING 5

3 *syn* see WHOLE 2

entomb *vb* **1** to deposit in or as if in a tomb <relics *entombed* in pyramids>

syn ensepulcher, sepulcher, sepulture, tomb; *compare* BURY 1

rel bury, inhume, inter, ‖plant; inurn; enshrine, shrine

con dig (up), disinhume, disinter, exhume, unbury

ant disentomb

2 *syn* see BURY 1

entombment *n syn* see BURIAL 2

entourage *n* one's attendants or subordinates <the queen's *entourage*>

syn following, retinue, suite, train

rel associates, attendants, courtiers, followers, retainers; hangers-on, sycophants, toadies

entrails *n pl* the internal organs of the body <some of the *entrails* are valued as food>

syn gut(s), innards, insides, internals, inwards, ‖pudding(s), stuffing, tripes, viscera

rel bowels, intestines; vitals; giblets, pluck, purtenance

entrammel *vb syn* see HAMPER

con assist, expedite, facilitate; extricate

entrance *n* **1** the act or fact of going in or coming in <awaited the *entrance* of the army into the city>

syn entry, ingress, ingression

rel arrival, coming, incoming, ingoing; penetration

con departure, egress, emergence, emerging, emigration, exit

ant egression, exiting

2 *syn* see DOOR 1

rel access, aperture, opening, threshold

ant exit

3 *syn* see DOOR 2

rel open door

entrance *vb syn* see TRANSPORT 2

rel gladden, please, rejoice; attract, bewitch, captivate, charm, enchant, fascinate; enthrall, hypnotize, spellbind

con disappoint, disgust, repel, repulse; bore

entranced *adj syn* see ENAMORED 3

entranceway *n syn* see DOOR 1

entrap *vb* **1 *syn*** see CATCH 3

2 *syn* see LURE

entreat *vb syn* see BEG

rel blandish, coax, wheedle; pester, plague, press, urge

entreaty *n syn* see PRAYER

entrée *n syn* see DOOR 2

rel introduction; open door

entrench *vb* **1** to establish so solidly or strongly as to make dislodgment or change extremely difficult <prejudices *entrenched* for generations>

syn embed, fix, infix, ingrain, lodge, root

rel found, ground; implant; confirm, define, establish, settle, strengthen

con eliminate, eradicate, root out, uproot; banish, cast out, eject, expel; remove

ant dislodge

2 *syn* see TRESPASS 2

rel interfere, intervene

idiom break in upon, stick one's nose into

entrenched *adj syn* see INVETERATE 1

entrepreneur *n* **1** one who owns, launches, manages, and assumes the risks of an economic venture <theatrical *entrepreneurs* making fortunes from successful shows>

syn undertaker

rel organizer; backer, impresario; contractor; administrator, manager; producer; promoter

2 *syn* see GO-BETWEEN 2

entrust *vb* **1** to confer a trust upon <*entrusted* him with responsibility for completing the work>

syn charge, trust

rel confer, impose; delegate, relegate; allocate, allot, assign

2 *syn* see COMMIT 1

rel deliver, deposit, leave, trust; bank, count, depend, reckon, rely

idiom give in trust

entry *n* **1 *syn*** see ENTRANCE 1

2 *syn* see DOOR 1

rel access, opening, threshold

con egress

ant exit

3 *syn* see DOOR 2

entryway *n syn* see DOOR 1

rel threshold

con egress

ant exit

entwine *vb syn* see WIND 2

rel entangle, entwist, interlace, interplait, intertwine, interweave; enmesh

con uncoil, undo, unravel, untwine, untwist, unwind, unwrap; straighten (out)

enumerate *vb* **1 *syn*** see COUNT 1

2 to specify one after the other <*enumerated* the advantages of his position>

syn list, numerate, tick off

rel run (over), tell off; identify, mention, recite, recount, relate, specify

3 *syn* see ITEMIZE 1

enunciate *vb* **1** to make a definite or systematic statement of <was the first to *enunciate* the modern principle of inertia>

syn enounce, state

rel develop, formulate, outline, postulate; advance, lay down, submit; announce, declare, proclaim; affirm; show

idiom set forth

2 *syn* see ARTICULATE 2

rel express, intone, modulate, vocalize, voice

envelop *vb* **1 *syn*** see ENFOLD 1

rel cloak, hide, mask

2 *syn* see SWATHE

3 *syn* see ENCLOSE 1

rel guard, protect, shield

envenom *vb syn* see EXACERBATE

envious *adj* maliciously grudging another's advantages <*envious* of her rival's charm>

syn envying, green-eyed, invidious, jealous

rel coveting, covetous, grasping, greedy; begrudging, grudging; appetent, desirous, longing, yearning; resentful, umbrageous
idiom green with envy
con benign, benignant; generous, kind; tolerant; unconcerned, uninterested

enviousness *n syn* see ENVY

environ *vb syn* see SURROUND 1
rel enclose, fence, go (around)

environment *n* surrounding or associated matters that influence or modify a course of development <the socioeconomic *environment* in Germany that produced Hitler>
syn ambience, ambient, atmosphere, climate, medium, milieu, mise-en-scène, surroundings
rel habitat; backdrop, background, context, setting; situation, status

environs *n pl* **1** an enclosing line or margin <several thousand businesses located within the *environs* of the city>
syn bound(s), boundary, compass, confine(s), limits, precinct(s), purlieus; *compare* LIMIT 1
rel fringes
2 the suburban areas or districts around a city or heavily populated area <a new system of parks for the national capital and its *environs*>
syn outskirt(s), purlieus, suburbs
rel locality, neighborhood, vicinity; surroundings

envisage *vb syn* see THINK 1
rel behold, grasp, look (upon), picture, regard, survey, view; externalize, materialize, objectify; foresee
idiom form a mental picture of, have a picture of, picture to oneself, view in the mind's eye

envision *vb syn* see THINK 1
rel call up, conjure up, summon up; picture, view; foresee
idiom have a mental picture of, picture to oneself, view in the mind's eye

envoy *n* **1** a representative with a rank between an ambassador and a minister resident who is accredited to a foreign government <the President received the *envoy* from Spain>
syn envoy extraordinary, minister plenipotentiary
rel ambassador, attaché, chargé d'affaires, consul, councillor, internuncio, legate, minister, nuncio; diplomat
2 *syn* see MESSENGER

envoy extraordinary *n syn* see ENVOY 1

envy *n* spiteful malice and resentment over another's advantage <his lavish life-style provoked *envy* among his colleagues>
syn enviousness, invidiousness, jealousy
rel covetousness; grudging; resentment

envy *vb* to experience envy <while she outwardly criticized her sister's looks, she secretly *envied* them>
syn begrudge, grudge
rel covet, crave, desire, hanker, long, want, yearn
idiom be green with envy

envying *adj syn* see ENVIOUS

enwrap *vb* **1** *syn* see SWATHE
2 *syn* see ENFOLD 1
rel enswathe, swaddle, swathe; sheathe

ephemeral *adj syn* see TRANSIENT
rel brief, short, temporary, unenduring; episodic
idiom here today and gone tomorrow
con endless, enduring, eternal, everlasting, lasting
ant perpetual

epicene *adj syn* see EFFEMINATE

epicure *n* one who takes great and fastidious pleasure in eating and drinking <was a real *epicure*, and his dinners were excellent>
syn bon vivant, gastronome, gastronomer, gastronomist, gourmand, gourmet
rel amateur, connoisseur, epicurean; glutton, ravener; high liver

epicurean *adj syn* see SENSUOUS

epidemic *n* the sudden widespread occurrence of something felt to resemble an epidemic disease <an *epidemic* of art forgeries>
syn outbreak, plague, rash; *compare* OUTBREAK 1

epigrammatic *adj syn* see PITHY

epilogue *n* **1** the final part that rounds out or completes the design of a nondramatic literary work <the author wrote an *epilogue* to his book explaining that some of his earlier impressions were wrong>
syn afterword
rel postlude; conclusion, ending
con prelude; foreword, introduction, preface
ant prologue
2 something that resembles an epilogue in rounding out or giving point to something else <an incident that can be regarded as an *epilogue* to the history of Roman Britain>
syn sequel
rel follow-up, postscript
ant prologue

episode *n syn* see OCCURRENCE

epistle *n syn* see LETTER 2
rel communication

epitaph *n* an inscription on a tombstone in memory of the one buried there
syn hic jacet

epitome *n* **1** *syn* see ABRIDGMENT
2 *syn* see SUMMARY
3 *syn* see APOTHEOSIS 1

epitomize *vb* **1** to make or give an epitome of <a report which *epitomizes* one of the most complex theories of all time>
syn condense, digest, inventory, nutshell, sum, summarize, summate, sum up, synopsize
rel boil down, capsulize; outline, tabulate
con elaborate, enlarge (on), expand
2 to serve as the typical representation or ideal expression of <he *epitomized* safe, dull conservatism>

---

syn synonym(s)	*rel* related word(s)
ant antonym(s)	*con* contrasted word(s)
idiom idiomatic equivalent(s)	
‖ use limited; if in doubt, see a dictionary	

syn exemplify, typify
rel embody, incarnate, incorporate, personify, represent, symbolize
3 *syn* see REPRESENT 2
epitomized *adj syn* see CONDENSED
epoch *n syn* see PERIOD 2
rel interval, term
epochal *adj* uniquely or highly significant <had to make an *epochal* decision: whether or not to declare war>
syn momentous
rel consequential, far-reaching, important; unmatched, unparalleled
con inconsequential, minor, petty, small-time, trivial, unimportant
equable *adj syn* see STEADY 2
rel methodical, orderly, regular, systematic; immutable, invariable, unchangeable; equal, equivalent, same
con variable; fitful, spasmodic
ant inequable, unequable
equal *adj* **1** *syn* see SAME 2
rel equable, even, uniform; alike, like; commensurate, corresponding, proportionate
idiom one and the same
con different, disparate, divergent, diverse, varied; unalike, unequable, uneven; irregular
ant unequal
2 *syn* see FAIR 4
idiom without distinction
con discriminating, discriminative, unfair
ant inequitable
3 *syn* see EVEN 3
4 *syn* see EVEN 4
5 *syn* see PROPORTIONAL
equal *n* one that is equal to another in status, achievement, value, meaning, or effect <he has no *equal* in common sense and honesty>
syn counterpart, equivalent, like, match; *compare* OPPOSITE NUMBER, PARALLEL
rel companion, fellow, mate, peer; alter ego, double, twin; competitor, rival; similar
equal *vb* **1** *syn* see AMOUNT 2
rel compare, parallel; accord, agree, square, tally; reach
idiom amount to the same thing
2 *syn* see EVEN 2
3 to make or produce something equal to (as in quality or value) <*equal* that if you can>
syn match, measure up, meet, rival, tie, touch
rel beat, top
equality *n syn* see EQUIVALENCE
equalize *vb* **1** to make equal in amount, degree, or status <*equalize* educational opportunities>
syn equate, even
rel balance, level, square
2 *syn* see EVEN 2
equally *adv* **1** *syn* see EVENLY 1
2 *syn* see EVENLY 2
equanimity *n* the characteristic quality of one who is self-possessed and not easily disturbed or perturbed <faced disaster with bland *equanimity*>
syn ataraxy, calmness, composure, coolness, imperturbability, phlegm, sangfroid, self-possession; *compare* CONFIDENCE 2

rel balance, equilibrium, equipoise, poise; aplomb, assurance, confidence, self-assurance; detachment; placidity, serenity, tranquillity
con alarm, anxiety, apprehension; excitability, nervousness; agitation, discomposure, disquiet, disturbance, perturbation
equatability *n syn* see EQUIVALENCE
equate *vb* **1** *syn* see EQUALIZE 1
2 to treat, represent, or regard as equal, equivalent, or comparable <*equated* retreat with cowardice>
syn assimilate, compare, liken, match, paragon, parallel
rel associate, relate, similize; consider, hold, regard, represent, treat
equidistant *adj syn* see MIDDLE 1
equilibrium *n syn* see BALANCE 1
rel stabilization, steadiness, steadying; counterbalance, counterpoise
con top-heaviness
equip *vb syn* see FURNISH 1
rel provide, supply; fit (out), rig (up *or* out), turn (out); gear, prepare, qualify
equipment *n* items needed for the performance of a task or useful in effecting an end <the *equipment* for the polar expedition included ships, instruments, sleds, dogs, and supplies>
syn accouterment(s), apparatus, gear, habiliments, machinery, material(s), matériel, outfit, paraphernalia, tackle, tackling
rel accessories, appurtenances, attachments, fittings, trappings; baggage, belonging(s), impedimenta, rig, things, traps; equipage, provisioning, provisions
equipoise *n syn* see BALANCE 1
rel counterbalance, counterpoise, counterweight
equitable *adj* **1** *syn* see FAIR 4
rel level, stable; equivalent, identical, same
idiom fair and square
con discriminatory
ant inequitable, unfair
2 *syn* see EVEN 3
equity *n syn* see JUSTICE 1
rel equitableness, justness
con bias, discrimination, partiality, unfairness
ant inequity
equivalence *n* the state or property of being equivalent or the result of making equivalent <the *equivalence* of paper money and coins>
syn adequation, equality, equatability, equivalency, par, parity, sameness
rel likeness; compatibility, correlation, correspondence; exchangeability, interchangeability
con discrepancy, disparity, divergence, incompatibility, inequality, unlikeness
ant difference
equivalency *n syn* see EQUIVALENCE
equivalent *adj* **1** *syn* see SAME 2
rel commensurate, proportionate; convertible, correlative, corresponding, parallel, reciprocal, substitute
con disparate, divergent, diverse, various; discordant, discrepant, incompatible, inconsonant

ant different
2 syn see LIKE
equivalent *n syn* see EQUAL
  rel obverse, reciprocal, substitute; parallel
equivocal *adj* **1 syn** see OBSCURE 3
  rel hazy, indistinct; doubtful, dubious, questionable; indeterminate, multivocal
  idiom clear as mud
  con clear, distinct, understandable; categorical, explicit, unambiguous, univocal; certain, conclusive
  ant unequivocal
  2 characterized by a mixture of opposing feelings <an *equivocal* attitude toward the expensive proposal>
  syn ambivalent
  rel uncertain, undecided
  idiom having mixed (*or* divided) feelings
  con assured, certain, decided, sure
  3 syn see DOUBTFUL 1
  rel disreputable
  idiom open to question
  con credible
equivocality *n syn* see AMBIGUITY
equivocate *vb* **1 syn** see LIE
  rel elude, escape, evade
  2 to avoid committing oneself by speaking evasively <he'd rather be brutally frank with them than *equivocate* on that issue>
  syn dodge, evade, hedge, pussyfoot, shuffle, sidestep, tergiversate, tergiverse, weasel; *compare* SKIRT 3
  rel cavil, prevaricate, quibble; fence, parry; avoid, elude, eschew
  idiom beat around (*or* about) the bush, beg the question, mince words
equivocating *adj syn* see EVASIVE 1
  rel deceptive, delusive, misleading
equivocation *n* **1 syn** see AMBIGUITY
  rel hedging; coloring, distortion, misrepresentation; deceit, dissimulation, duplicity
  ant explicitness
  2 syn see FALLACY 2
  rel haggling, quibbling; fib, fibbing, lie, lying
equivoque *n syn* see AMBIGUITY
era *n syn* see PERIOD 2
  rel term; stage
eradicate *vb syn* see ANNIHILATE 2
  rel demolish, destroy, raze; liquidate, purge
  con establish, fix, set; implant, inculcate, instill; breed, engender, generate, propagate
erase *vb* to eliminate or neutralize with or as if with a stroke of the pen <time has *erased* their sad memories> <*erase* an error>
  syn annul, black (out), blot out, cancel, delete, efface, expunge, obliterate, wipe (out), x (out)
  rel disannul, negate, nullify; abolish, blank (out), cross (off *or* out), cut out, dele, eliminate, excise, extirpate, rub out, scrape, sponge (out), strike (out); neutralize; remove, take out, withdraw
  con impress, imprint, print, stamp; insert; reinstate, renew, restore
ere *prep syn* see BEFORE 1

erect *adj* standing up straight <the dog's *erect* ears pricked forward>
  syn arrect, raised, stand-up, straight-up, upright, upstanding
  rel erectile; elevated, lifted, upraised; perpendicular, standing, vertical
  con decumbent, flat, prostrate, recumbent; drooping, hanging, pendent
erect *vb* **1 syn** see BUILD 1
  2 syn see MAKE 3
  rel compose, create; make up, run up
  con demolish, destroy, tear up, unbuild, wreck
  3 to fix in an upright position <*erected* a flagpole>
  syn put up, raise, rear, set up; *compare* BUILD 1
  rel elevate, heighten, hoist, lift, upraise, uprear; upend
  4 syn see EXALT 1
  idiom put on a pedestal
  ant abase
  5 to bring into existence as if by raising a building <*erect* social barriers along religious lines>
  syn build up, construct, establish, hammer (out), set up
  rel fabricate, fashion, forge, form, shape; bring about, effect
  con break down, tear down; liquidate, purge; dispose (of), eliminate, remove
erection *n syn* see EDIFICE
eremitic *adj syn* see ANTISOCIAL
ergo *adv syn* see THEREFORE
erode *vb* **1 syn** see EAT 3
  rel crumble, decay, deteriorate, disintegrate; consume
  2 syn see ABRADE 1
  rel grate, rub (off *or* away), scrape (off *or* away)
erotic *adj* of, devoted to, affected by, or tending to arouse sexual love or desire <*erotic* art>
  syn amative, amatory, amorous, aphrodisiac
  rel ardent, fervent, fervid, impassioned, lovesome, passionate; earthy; carnal, epicurean, fleshly, voluptuous; bawdy, sexy, spicy; concupiscent, lecherous; lascivious, lewd, lickerish, prurient, salacious, sensual
eroticism *n syn* see LUST 2
err *vb* to depart from a standard (as of wisdom or morality) <the human tendency to *err*>
  syn deviate, stray, wander
  rel miscalculate; lapse, slip (up), stumble, trip; transgress, trespass; offend; sin
  idiom go astray (*or* amiss *or* wrong), leave the straight and narrow
errable *adj syn* see FALLIBLE
errant *adj* **1 syn** see ERRATIC 1
  rel drifting, itinerant, meandering, rambling, ranging, roaming, roving, shifting, straying
  con static, unmoving
  2 deviating from an accepted pattern or standard <a parent scolding her *errant* child>

---

syn aberrant, devious, erring
rel deviating, straying, wandering; misbehaving, mischievous, naughty
idiom off the straight and narrow
3 *syn* see FALLIBLE
rel aberrant, erring; unreliable
con perfect, trustworthy
ant inerrant

erratic *adj* **1** moving about aimlessly or irregularly without a fixed course <an *erratic* breeze barely stirred the leaves of the tree>
syn devious, errant, stray, wandering
rel curving, meandering, roundabout, winding; shifting, undirected
con fixed, stable, unmoving; active, animated, brisk, lively, sprightly
ant static
2 *syn* see UNCERTAIN 1
rel doubtful, dubious
ant stable
3 *syn* see ARBITRARY 1
rel changeable, inconsistent, inconstant, unpredictable, variable; mercurial, unstable, volatile
con consistent, conventional, predictable, stable
4 *syn* see STRANGE 4
rel anomalous, irregular, unnatural
con natural, normal, regular, typical; customary, usual

erring *adj syn* see ERRANT 2

erroneous *adj* **1** *syn* see FALSE 1
rel amiss, askew, awry, off; defective; mistaken
idiom all off, all wrong, way off the mark
con right, true
ant accurate, correct
2 *syn* see MISTAKEN

erroneousness *n syn* see FALLACY 1
rel inaccurateness, mistakenness
con accuracy, accurateness, rightness
ant correctness

error *n* **1** an often unintentional deviation from truth or accuracy <made an *error* in adding the figures>
syn mistake, x
rel inaccuracy; miscalculation, miscomputation; oversight, slip
2 something (as an act, statement, or belief) that departs from what is or is generally held to be acceptable <spying on the opposing party proved to be a grave *error*>
syn blooper, blunder, boner, bull, bungle, ‖clanger, fluff, goof, lapse, miscue, misstep, mistake, rock, slip, slipup, trip; *compare* FAUX PAS
rel fault, misdoing, misjudgment, stumble; ‖boo-boo, botch, fumble, muff, howler, screamer; impropriety, indecorum
3 *syn* see FALLACY 1
rel misreading, misunderstanding; delusion, illusion

errorless *adj syn* see IMPECCABLE 1
con imprecise, inaccurate, incorrect, unexact, wrong

ersatz *adj syn* see ARTIFICIAL 2
rel factitious, synthetic; fake

ersatz *n syn* see IMITATION

erstwhile *adv syn* see BEFORE 2
erstwhile *adj syn* see FORMER 2
eruct *vb* **1** *syn* see BELCH 1
idiom bring up gas
2 *syn* see ERUPT 1
eructate *vb syn* see BELCH 1
erudite *adj syn* see LEARNED
rel lettered, well-read; studious
ant illiterate
eruditeness *n syn* see ERUDITION 2
erudition *n* **1** *syn* see EDUCATION 2
2 the quality or state of being erudite <a scholar of great cultivation and *erudition*>
syn eruditeness, learnedness, scholarliness, scholarship
rel cultivation, culture, education, intellectuality, literacy; bookishness, pedantry, studiousness
ant illiteracy

erupt *vb* **1** to give off or release (as something pent up) forcefully <the volcano *erupted* gouts of lava>
syn belch, disgorge, eject, eruct, expel, irrupt, spew
rel cast (out *or* up), hurl, throw off; boil, discharge, emit; jet, spout, spurt; extravasate
2 to break away or burst from limits or restraint <riots *erupted* in the ghetto>
syn break out, burst (forth), explode
rel detonate, touch off; go off

eruption *n* **1** *syn* see OUTBURST 1
2 *syn* see OUTBREAK 1

escalade *vb syn* see ASCEND 1
con clamber (down), climb (down); go (down)

escalate *vb* **1** *syn* see ASCEND 1
2 to increase in extent, volume, amount, number, intensity, or scope <a little war threatens to *escalate* into a huge, ugly one>
syn expand, grow
rel broaden, enlarge, heighten, increase, intensify, spread, widen
con decrease, limit, minimize; constrict, contract, narrow; collapse, shrink, shrivel
ant de-escalate

escapade *n* a usually adventurous action that runs counter to approved or conventional conduct <childish *escapades* on Halloween>
syn caper, lark, rollick; *compare* PRANK
rel antic, frolic, vagary; prank; fling, spree; mischief, roguery

escape *vb* **1** to run away especially from something that limits one's freedom and threatens one's well-being <trying to *escape* from prison>
syn abscond, break, ‖bunk, decamp, flee, fly, scape
rel get away, make off, mosey, run away; bail out, ‖ditch, double, duck out, flit, jump, skip; depart; disappear, vanish
idiom cut and run, cut loose, fly the coop, take it on the lam
con come back, return; abide, remain, stay; chase, follow, pursue, tag, trail
2 to get away or keep away from what one does not wish to incur, endure, or encounter <made every effort to *escape* suspicion>

syn avoid, bilk, double, duck, elude, eschew, evade, shun, shy; *compare* SHAKE 5, SKIRT 3
rel burke, bypass, circumvent; dodge, shake, shun, skit; miss
idiom fight shy of, give the slip
con catch, contract, incur; abide, bear, brook, endure, stand, suffer, tolerate; dare, face, meet

escape *n* **1** the act or fact of escaping or having escaped physically <succeeded in making his *escape* from the prison>
syn breakout, escapement, escaping, flight, getaway, lam, ‖scape, slip
rel departure; deliverance, liberation, release
con return; grasp, grip, hold, retention; imprisonment, incarceration
2 the act or fact of escaping or having escaped what one does not wish to incur, encounter, or endure <sought *escape* from responsibility>
syn avoidance, come-off, elusion, escaping, eschewal, evasion, runaround, shunning
rel bypassing, circumvention, dodging, ducking, sidestepping; elusiveness, evasiveness
con abidance, abiding, bearing, endurance, enduring, submission, submitting, toleration; facing

escapement *n syn* see ESCAPE 1

escaping *n* **1** *syn* see ESCAPE 1
2 *syn* see ESCAPE 2

eschew *vb* **1** *syn* see ESCAPE 2
idiom shy away from, steer clear of
con adopt, embrace, espouse
ant choose
2 *syn* see FORGO
rel abstain, refrain
idiom let well enough alone

eschewal *n syn* see ESCAPE 2
rel shirking; shying

escort *n* **1** a boy or man who goes on a date with a girl or woman <had her pick of *escorts* to the dance>
syn date
rel beau, boyfriend, fellow; cavalier, gallant, squire, vis-à-vis
2 a person who leads or directs another or others in a way or course (as through difficult terrain) <served as our *escort* when we drove through the desert>
syn guide
rel attendant, companion, guard

escort *vb* **1** *syn* see ACCOMPANY
2 *syn* see GUIDE
rel bring; squire

escritoire *n syn* see DESK

esculent *adj syn* see EDIBLE

esoteric *adj syn* see RECONDITE

especial *adj* **1** *syn* see SPECIAL 1
rel preeminent, supreme, surpassing; dominant, paramount, predominant, preponderant; exceptional, notable, singular, unusual
con unexceptional, usual
ant general
2 *syn* see EXPRESS 2

especially *adv* **1** in a special way <was *especially* good at math>

syn distinctively, particularly, special, specially, specifically
rel remarkably, unusually; exceptionally, markedly, peculiarly, singularly, uniquely; eminently, notably, preeminently, supremely
idiom before all else
2 *syn* see EXPRESSLY 2

espial *n syn* see DISCOVERY

espionage *n* systematic secret observation in order to accumulate information <agents engaged in industrial *espionage*>
syn spying
rel observation, reconnaissance, sleuthing, surveillance, watching

espousal *n* **1** *syn* see ENGAGEMENT 2
2 *often* **espousals** *pl syn* see WEDDING
3 *syn* see MARRIAGE
rel mating; union
idiom getting hitched, taking on the ball and chain, tying the knot
con estrangement, separation
4 ready acceptance of or the taking up of a cause or belief <his wholehearted *espousal* of left-wing philosophies worried his family>
syn adoption, embracement, embracing
rel acceptance, approval; advocacy; aid, promotion, support
con denial, rejection; disapproval, dislike, distaste; antipathy, aversion, intolerance
ant repudiation

espouse *vb* **1** *syn* see MARRY 1
2 *syn* see ADOPT
rel accept, approve; advocate, back, champion, support, uphold
con abandon, desert, forsake; deny, reject; disapprove, dislike
ant repudiate

esprit *n* **1** *syn* see SPIRIT 5
rel acumen, acuteness, brains, brightness, cleverness, intelligence, mind, quick-wittedness, sharpness, wit; courage, mettle, tenacity; fervor, passion
2 *syn* see MORALE
rel camaraderie, fellowship; devotion, loyalty; enthusiasm, fervor, passion
3 *syn* see WIT 5

esprit de corps *n syn* see MORALE
rel camaraderie, comradeship, fellowship; partisanism, partisanship; devotion, loyalty; enthusiasm, spirit

espy *vb* **1** *syn* see SEE 1
rel recognize, take in; sight, spot, spy; witness
idiom catch sight of, get a load of
2 *syn* see FIND 1
rel spy; make out; notice

essay *vb syn* see TRY 5
rel venture; labor, toil, travail, work
idiom give it a try (*or* fling *or* go), have at it, make a stab at, take a crack (*or* whack) at

---

syn synonym(s) *rel* related word(s)
ant antonym(s) *con* contrasted word(s)
idiom idiomatic equivalent(s)
‖ use limited; if in doubt, see a dictionary

essay *n* **1** *syn* see ATTEMPT
rel exertion; labor, toil, travail, work; go, venture
2 a relatively brief discourse written for others' reading or consideration <an *essay* on free will>
syn article, composition, paper, theme
rel discourse, discussion, explication, exposition, study; piece; tract, treatise; dissertation, thesis

essence *n* **1** a basic underlying or constituting entity, substance, or form <succeeds in conveying completely the cruel *essence* of loneliness>
syn being, essentia, essentiality, nature, texture
rel entity, form, substance
2 the most basic, significant, and indispensable element, attribute, quality, property, or aspect of a thing <the very *essence* of Machiavellianism is the belief that in politics there is neither good nor evil>
syn be-all and end-all, bottom, essentiality, marrow, pith, quintessence, quintessential, rock bottom, root, soul, stuff, substance, virtuality; *compare* BODY 3, CENTER 2, SUBSTANCE 2
rel timber; element, fiber, property; aspect, attribute, quality, spirit; inwardness, significance; crux, gist, kernel, nub, nubbin; distillate, distillation

essentia *n syn* see ESSENCE 1

essential *adj* **1** *syn* see INHERENT
con conditional, contingent, dependent
ant accidental
2 so important to the nature and essence of a thing as to be indispensable <the *essential* ingredient in this medicine is a new drug>
syn cardinal, constitutive, fundamental, vital
rel basal, basic, underlying; capital, chief, foremost, leading, main, principal; primal, primary, prime
con dependent, secondary, subordinate; accessory, auxiliary, contributory, subsidiary
3 *syn* see ELEMENTAL 1
4 urgently required <raw materials *essential* to industry>
syn imperative, indispensable, necessary, necessitous, prerequisite
rel needed, needful; required, requisite, wanted; right-hand; vital
con dispensable, unnecessary, unneeded, unrequired, unwanted
ant nonessential

essential *n* **1** something that forms part of the minimal body, character, or structure of a thing <prosperity is an *essential* of the good life>
syn basic, element, fundamental, part and parcel, rudiment
rel essence, stuff, substance; must, necessary, prerequisite, sine qua non
2 something necessary, required, or unavoidable <work was an *essential* to survival>
syn condition, must, necessity, precondition, prerequisite, requirement, requisite, sine qua non
idiom name of the game

essentiality *n* **1** *syn* see ESSENCE 1

2 *syn* see ESSENCE 2

essentially *adv* **1** in regard to the essential points <*essentially* the problem is this: he is unreliable>
syn au fond, basically, fundamentally, in essence
rel actually, really
idiom at bottom
2 *syn* see ALMOST 2
rel substantially, virtually
idiom in the main

establish *vb* **1** *syn* see SET 1
rel enroot, entrench, implant, inculcate, infix, instill, root; set down, set up; moor, rivet, secure; found, ground
con eradicate, exterminate, extirpate, uproot, wipe (out)
ant abrogate
2 *syn* see BASE
idiom lay the foundation for (*or* of)
3 *syn* see ENACT 1
rel formulate; authorize, decree, legislate, prescribe
ant repeal
4 *syn* see FOUND 2
rel endow, provide; originate; build
con disestablish; demolish, tear down
ant abolish
5 *syn* see ERECT 5
6 to make clear beyond a reasonable doubt <*established* an alibi for the time of the crime>
syn demonstrate, determine, make out, prove, show
rel authenticate, confirm, corroborate, document, substantiate, verify; attest; clarify
idiom afford (*or* offer) proof of
con discredit, expose, show up; confute, invalidate, parry, rebut, refute
ant disprove

established *adj syn* see FIRM 3

establishment *n* **1** *syn* see ENTERPRISE 3
rel workplace; institute, institution; foundation
2 *often cap* a group of influential leaders who represent an established order of society <the literary *establishment*>
syn Old Guard
rel conservative(s), diehard(s)
con liberal(s)

estate *n* **1** *syn* see ORDER 9
rel form, state
2 a class of people in a community distinguishable by social or political duties or privileges <a party platform appealing to people of every *estate*>
syn grade, rank
rel bracket, category; footing, level, order, standing; place, position, station; caste, class
3 an extensive landed property <spent the weekend at his country *estate*>
syn acres, land, manor, quinta
rel farm, ranch; plantation; villa

esteem *n syn* see REGARD 4
rel approval, liking; appreciation, valuation
ant abomination

esteem *vb* **1** *syn* see APPRECIATE 1
rel idolize, revere, worship
idiom hold dear, think the world of
ant despise
2 *syn* see ADMIRE 2
rel revere, venerate
idiom hold in esteem (*or* high regard)
con abhor
ant abominate

estimable *adj* **1** *syn* see WORTHY 1
2 *syn* see RESPECTABLE 1
rel admired, esteemed, respected
con disreputable, unworthy; bad
3 *syn* see HONORABLE 1

estimate *vb* **1** to judge something with respect to its worth <*estimated* the value of the jewels>
syn appraise, assay, assess, evaluate, rate, set (at), survey, valuate, value
rel adjudge, adjudicate, judge; ascertain, determine, discover; price, prize; decide, settle
2 *syn* see CALCULATE
rel cast, sum; count, enumerate
3 to fix some value (as size, distance, or composition) more or less accurately <*estimated* the rainfall at over six inches>
syn approximate, call, judge, place, put, reckon
rel round, round off; conjecture, guess, suppose, surmise; fancy, imagine; deduce, infer
con calculate, compute; measure

estimate *n* **1** the act of appraising or valuing the nature, character, quality, status, or worth of something <his influence as President is beyond *estimate*>
syn appraisal, appraisement, assessment, estimation, evaluation, valuation
rel calculation, measurement, reckoning; sizing up; projection
2 *syn* see ESTIMATION 1
idiom point of view

estimation *n* **1** the result of evaluating something <his *estimation* of the man's ability proved incorrect>
syn appraisal, appraisement, assessment, estimate, evaluation, judgment, stock
rel impression; opinion
2 *syn* see COMPUTATION
3 *syn* see ESTIMATE 1
4 *syn* see REGARD 4

estrange *vb* to cause one to break a bond or tie of affection or loyalty <her arrogance *estranged* her children and friends>
syn alien, alienate, disaffect, disunify, disunite, wean
rel break up, divide, divorce, part, separate, sever, split, sunder
idiom set at odds
con appease, conciliate, pacify, propitiate; associate, espouse, join, link, unite
ant reconcile

estrangement *n* the act of estranging or the condition of being estranged <a petty dispute resulted in total *estrangement*>
syn alienation, disaffection
rel division, divorce, schism; withdrawal

con appeasement, conciliation, propitiation
ant reconciliation

etceteras *n pl* *syn* see SUNDRIES

etch *vb* **1** *syn* see ENGRAVE 1
2 to set forth in a sharp, clear-cut manner with minute attention to detail <the most sharply *etched* character in the novel>
syn define, delineate
rel outline, set forth; depict, describe, picture, portray, represent
3 *syn* see ENGRAVE 2

eternal *adj* **1** *syn* see INFINITE 1
rel endless, interminable, unceasing, unending; lasting, permanent, perpetual; deathless, immortal, undying
con ephemeral, evanescent, momentary, passing, short-lived, temporary, transient
ant mortal
2 *syn* see EVERLASTING 1
rel deathless, undying
3 *syn* see CONTINUAL
con interrupted, sporadic
4 valid or existing unaltered at all times <right and wrong are *eternal* verities that cannot be changed>
syn ageless, dateless, intemporal, timeless
rel immemorial, lasting, perdurable, permanent, perpetual; immutable, inalterable, unalterable, unchangeable, unchanging
con alterable, changeable, changing, fluctuating, varying; debatable, questionable, suspect

eternalize *vb* *syn* see PERPETUATE

eternally *adv* *syn* see EVER 2

eternity *n* **1** a totality of infinite time <in *eternity* there is no change or passing away>
syn infinity, sempiternity
rel endlessness, infiniteness, infinitude, perpetuity, timelessness
con ephemerality, impermanence, transience; limitedness, restrictedness
ant finiteness
2 unending existence after death <belief in the *eternity* of our spiritual nature>
syn afterlife, everlastingness, eviternity, immortality, world-without-end
3 *syn* see AGE 2
idiom forever and a day, forever and ever

eternize *vb* *syn* see PERPETUATE

ethereal *adj* *syn* see AIRY 3
rel celestial, empyreal, empyrean, heavenly; vaporish, vaporlike, unsubstantial; filmy, gossamer; delicate, fragile, light
con heavy, thick
ant substantial

ethic *n* **1** ethics *pl but usu sing in constr* the discipline dealing with what is good and bad and with moral duty and obligation <*ethics* has been called the science of the ideal of human character>

---

syn synonym(s)   *rel* related word(s)
ant antonym(s)   *con* contrasted word(s)
idiom idiomatic equivalent(s)
‖ use limited; if in doubt, see a dictionary

syn morals

2 a group of moral principles or set of values <the Christian *ethic*>

syn morality, morals, mores

3 ethics *pl* the code of conduct or behavior governing an individual or a group (as the members of a profession) <medical *ethics*>

syn principles

rel moralities, morals, mores; criteria, standards

4 the complex of ideals, beliefs, or standards that characterizes or pervades a group, community, or people <the American work *ethic*>

syn ethos

rel belief, ideal, standard, value

ethical *adj syn* see MORAL 1

rel high-principled; elevated; upright, upstanding

con flagitious, iniquitous, nefarious; improper, indecent, indecorous, unbecoming, unseemly; immoral, low

ethnic *adj* **1** *syn* see HEATHEN

rel non-Christian, unchristian

2 of, relating to, or originating from the traits shared by members of a group as a product of their common heredity and cultural tradition <only a person thoroughly familiar with Yiddish can recognize the *ethnic* quality of the pun> <*ethnic* cookery>

syn racial

rel national; tribal

ethos *n syn* see ETHIC 4

etiquette *n* **1** *syn* see MANNER 5

2 *syn* see DECORUM 1

rel behavior, conduct, deportment, manners; amenities, civilities, formalities; convention, form, protocol

idiom social graces

eulogistic *adj* of, relating to, characterized by, or bestowing praise <the speaker made *eulogistic* remarks on the group's accomplishment>

syn encomiastic, laudative, laudatory, panegyrical, praiseful

rel approbatory, approving, commendatory, complimentary

con uncomplimentary; critical, disapproving, disparaging; abusive

ant dyslogistic

eulogize *vb syn* see PRAISE 2

rel applaud; belaud, bepraise

idiom praise to the skies, sing the praises of

ant vilify

eulogy *n syn* see ENCOMIUM

rel adulation, glorification

con calumny, slander

ant vilification

euphemism *n* an agreeable or inoffensive expression that is substituted for one that might offend or suggest unpleasantness <vandalism that goes under the *euphemism* of souvenir hunting>

syn nice Nelly, nice-nellyism

ant dysphemism

euphonic *adj syn* see MELODIOUS 1

euphonious *adj syn* see MELODIOUS 1

euphoria *n* **1** *syn* see ELATION 1

ant deflation, dysphoria

2 an often groundless or excessive feeling of well-being and happiness <drug-induced *euphoria*>

syn elation, exaltation, intoxication

rel ecstasy, frenzy; madness; glee

con anxiety, unease, uneasiness

ant depression

euphuistic *adj syn* see RHETORICAL

rel elaborate; colorful; verbose; elevated

con concise, simple, straightforward; lean

evacuee *n syn* see REFUGEE

evade *vb* **1** *syn* see ESCAPE 2

rel flee, fly, slip (away); foil, outwit, thwart

idiom keep (*or* know) one's distance

con accost, confront, dare, face

2 *syn* see EQUIVOCATE 2

rel bypass, circumvent, duck; parry, turn (aside)

idiom give (someone) the runaround

con confront, face; elucidate, explain

evaluate *vb* **1** *syn* see ESTIMATE 1

rel appreciate; class, gauge, rank; criticize

2 *syn* see CLASS 2

evaluation *n* **1** *syn* see ESTIMATE 1

rel interpreting; judging, rating

2 *syn* see ESTIMATION 1

rel appreciation; interpretation; decision

evanesce *vb syn* see VANISH

rel disintegrate, dispel, disperse, dissipate, dissolve, scatter

idiom go up in smoke, vanish into thin air

con appear; coalesce

ant materialize

evanescent *adj syn* see TRANSIENT

rel temporary; flying; dissolving, fading, melting; disappearing, vanishing

evangelical *adj* characterized by or reflecting a missionary, reforming, or redeeming impulse or purpose <a mood of *evangelical* nationalism>

syn crusading, evangelistic

rel ardent, fervid, impassioned, militant, zealous; missionary, propagandizing, proselytizing

evangelist *n syn* see MISSIONARY

evangelistic *adj syn* see EVANGELICAL

rel missionary, reforming

evangelize *vb syn* see PREACH 1

evanish *vb syn* see VANISH

idiom pass out of the picture

evaporate *vb syn* see VANISH

rel escape, pass (away *or* off); weaken; vaporize

idiom go pouf

evasion *n syn* see ESCAPE 2

rel dodging, equivocating, equivocation, evading, excuse, subterfuge; haggling, quibbling; escapism

con confrontation, confronting; daring

ant facing

evasive *adj* **1** tending to evade or avoid confrontation <his answers were ambiguous and *evasive*>

syn equivocating, prevaricative, prevaricatory, shifty, shuffling

rel ambiguous, equivocal, unclear, vague; sliding, slippery, sly

con categorical, definite, explicit, unambiguous, univocal; candid, forthright

ant direct
2 *syn* see ELUSIVE
even *adj* **1 *syn*** see LEVEL
con bent, crooked, curved, twisted
ant uneven
2 *syn* see STEADY 2
rel equal, identical, same; consistent, continual, continuous, undeviating, unvaried
3 giving no advantage to either side < an *even* exchange>
syn equal, equitable, fair
rel balanced, fair and square, square; honest, straightforward, unprejudiced
con inequitable, unequal, unfair
ant uneven
4 being nicely in balance <his chances for success or failure are *even*>
syn equal, even-up, fifty-fifty
rel balanced, comparable, proportionate
con disproportionate, unbalanced
ant uneven
5 being neither more nor less than the named or understood amount, extent, or number <an *even* mile>
syn exact, square
con approximate, imprecise, inaccurate
even *adv* **1** in a like manner <they can learn *even* as others do>
syn as well, exactly, expressly, just, precisely
2 at the very time <perhaps *even* now the moment has come to consider a retreat>
syn already
3 not this merely but also — used as an intensive to emphasize the identity or character of something <a huge, *even* monstrous animal>
syn indeed, nay, truly, verily, yea
rel absolutely, positively; quite, really
4 — used as an intensive to indicate an extreme, hypothetical, or unlikely case or instance <refused *even* to look at her> <*even* if this were so, it should not change our plans>
syn so much as
idiom even so much as
5 *syn* see YET 1
even *vb* **1** to make (as a surface) smooth, even, level, or flat <*even* the soil with a spade>
syn flatten, flush, lay, level, plane, smooth, smoothen
rel grade, roll; align; symmetrize; uniform; pancake
con rough, roughen
2 to make even or balanced in advantage <hoped to *even* the odds by training>
syn equal, equalize
rel balance, square
con unbalance, unequalize, upset; derange, disarrange
3 *syn* see EQUALIZE 1
evening *n* **1** the closing part of day and the early part of night <the last light of *evening*>
syn ‖dimmet, ‖dimps, ‖dimpsy, dusk, ‖dusk dark, eventide, gloaming, nightfall, owl-light, twilight
rel afternoon; sundown, sunset; duskiness, duskness

con sunrise; dawn
ant morning
2 a latter portion or a period of decline <in the *evening* of life>
syn sunset, twilight
3 a party taking place in the evening <their *evenings* were notable affairs>
syn soiree
rel reception; salon; party
evenly *adv* **1** in equal parts <a career divided *evenly* between stage and screen>
syn equally, fifty-fifty, squarely
rel commensurably, proportionately
con disproportionately, unequally
ant unevenly
2 in a just or fair manner <she was *evenly* polite to everyone>
syn equally, impartially
rel fairly, justly
con unfairly, unjustly
3 without variation or fluctuation <spread the paint *evenly*>
syn flatly, smooth, smoothly, uniformly
con irregularly, roughly
ant unevenly
event *n* **1 *syn*** see OCCURRENCE
rel act, action, deed; achievement, exploit, feat; accident, chance, fortune
2 a matter worthy of remark <the trip was an *event* in their dull routine>
syn milepost, milestone, occasion
rel affair, landmark; delight, treat
idiom historic event
con insignificancy, trifle, triviality
3 *syn* see EFFECT 1
rel offshoot, outgrowth; product, resultant, sequent
idiom end result
4 a postulated outcome, condition, or contingency <in the *event* of rain, we will not meet>
syn case, eventuality
rel chance, fortuity, hap, happenstance
5 any of the contests in a sports program <track-and-field *events*>
syn match, meet
rel competition, contest
6 *syn* see FACT 2
eventide *n* *syn* see EVENING 1
eventual *adj* *syn* see LAST
rel consequent, ensuing, inevitable, succeeding; ending, endmost
con antecedent, beginning, inceptive, initial, original
eventuality *n* **1 *syn*** see EVENT 4
rel contingency, possibility
2 *syn* see EFFECT 1
con antecedent, beginning, root
eventually *adv* *syn* see YET 2
idiom in the long run

---

syn synonym(s)   *rel* related word(s)
ant antonym(s)   *con* contrasted word(s)
idiom idiomatic equivalent(s)
‖ use limited; if in doubt, see a dictionary

even–up *adj syn* see EVEN 4

ever *adv* **1** *syn* see ALWAYS 1
2 through all or an indefinite time <a name that will *ever* be respected>
syn always, eternally, evermore, forever, forevermore, in perpetuum
3 in each and every case <war and suffering have *ever* gone hand in hand>
syn invariably
rel consistently, regularly, usually
4 at any time or on any occasion <he is seldom if *ever* absent>
syn anytime, at all
5 in any way <nor was it *ever* important>
syn anyway, anywise, at all, once
6 — used as an intensive after an inverted verb-subject construction <is he *ever* proud of himself>
syn confoundedly, consumedly, excessively, extremely, immensely, inordinately, over, overfull, overly, overmuch, super, too, unduly
rel annoyingly, plaguey; grievously, mortally; consummately

ever and again *adv syn* see SOMETIMES

ever and anon *adv syn* see SOMETIMES

everlasting *adj* **1** lasting or enduring through all time <*everlasting* laws governing the physical universe>
syn amaranthine, ceaseless, endless, eternal, immortal, never-ending, unending, world-without-end; *compare* IMMORTAL 1
rel lasting, perdurable, permanent, perpetual; boundless, infinite, limitless, termless
con ephemeral, evanescent, momentary, short-lived, transitory
2 *syn* see CONTINUAL
con interrupted, off-and-on, periodic, sporadic

everlastingness *n syn* see ETERNITY 2

evermore *adv syn* see EVER 2

evert *vb syn* see DISPROVE 1

every *adj syn* see ALL 2

everybody *pron* every person <*everybody* must do what his conscience dictates>
syn all, everyman, everyone
idiom all and sundry
ant nobody

everyday *adj* **1** *syn* see COMMON 4
con distinctive, singular, unique; uncommon, unusual
ant exceptional
2 *syn* see PROSAIC 3
3 *syn* see ORDINARY 1

everyman *pron syn* see EVERYBODY
idiom the man in the street

everyone *pron syn* see EVERYBODY
ant no one

everyplace *adv syn* see EVERYWHERE 1
idiom all over the place

everything *pron* the whole amount <lost *everything* in the fire>
syn all
idiom all in all, the lot, the whole ball of wax, the whole bit (*or* shebang), the whole kit and kaboodle, the works

everywhere *adv* **1** in every place or in all places <poverty anywhere is a danger to peace and prosperity *everywhere*>
syn all over, all round (*or* all around), everyplace, far and near, far and wide, high and low, overall, throughout
idiom in all quarters, in every quarter
2 *syn* see WHEREVER

evict *vb syn* see EJECT 1
rel dislodge, dispossess, force (out), put out, shut out, turn out
idiom turn (*or* put) out bag and baggage, turn out of doors, turn out of house and home
con harbor, house, lodge, shelter

evidence *n* **1** *syn* see INDICATION 3
2 *syn* see TESTIMONY

evidence *vb syn* see SHOW 2
rel display, expose; attest, bespeak, betoken, confirm, indicate, prove, testify

evident *adj syn* see CLEAR 5
rel noticeable, prominent, pronounced
idiom as plain as the nose on one's face, plain as day
con inconspicuous; ambiguous, unapparent, unrecognizable; concealed, hidden
ant inevident

evidently *adv syn* see OSTENSIBLY

evil *n* **1** whatever is harmful, distressing, or disastrous <attempts to grasp the nature of *evil*>
syn ill
rel bad, badness, devilry, diablerie, diabolism, evilness, satanism, satanity, wickedness, wrong
con goodness, virtue
ant good
2 whatever is morally unacceptable <return good for *evil*>
syn debt, sin, wickedness, wrong
rel evildoing, misconduct, sinfulness, wrongdoing
con rectitude, righteousness, virtue
ant good
3 a particular thing (as an act) that is evil <choose the lesser of two *evils*>
syn crime, diablerie, iniquity, sin, tort, wrong, wrongdoing
rel badness, evilness, maleficence, vice, wickedness; misdeed, offense

evil *adj* **1** *syn* see WRONG 1
rel base, low, vile; flagitious, nefarious; baneful, pernicious; black, damnable, execrable
con high, noble; exemplary, salutary
ant good
2 *syn* see OFFENSIVE
rel distasteful, repellent; fetid, putrid, stinking
3 *syn* see MALICIOUS
rel angry, disagreeable, ugly, unpleasant, wrathful; harmful, hurtful, injurious, mischievous; destructive
4 *syn* see HARMFUL
rel calamitous, destructive, disastrous
con harmless, noninjurious
ant innocuous
5 reporting or predicting harm or misfortune <messengers bearing *evil* tidings>

syn bad, ill, unfavorable; *compare* OMINOUS
rel baleful, baneful, inauspicious; ill-boding, ill=
omened, ominous
con auspicious, favorable
ant good
6 marked by misfortune or calamity <the family
fell upon *evil* times>
syn bad, inauspicious
rel unfavorable, unfortunate, unlucky; difficult,
hard, trying; calamitous, disastrous
con favorable; lucky; easy, prosperous; auspicious, halcyon, happy
ant good

evince *vb* **1** *syn* see SHOW 2
rel argue, attest, bespeak, betoken, confirm, indicate, prove; display, exhibit, expose, illustrate,
signify
con repress, suppress; conceal, hide
2 *syn* see EDUCE 1
rel bring (about), cause; provoke, stimulate

eviscerate *vb* to take out the entrails of <*eviscerate*
a turkey>
syn bowel, disembowel, draw, embowel, exenterate, gut, paunch

eviternity *n syn* see ETERNITY 2

evocative *adj* serving or tending to call something
(as a mood) forth <conduct *evocative* of the utmost contempt>
syn evocatory, suggestive
rel meaningful, pregnant, weighty; arousing,
moving, stimulating, stirring; causing, effecting,
inducing, producing

evocatory *adj syn* see EVOCATIVE

evoke *vb syn* see EDUCE 1
rel excite, provoke, stimulate; arouse, awaken,
rally, rouse, stir, waken; call forth, call up, conjure (up), raise, summon (forth *or* up)

evolution *n syn* see DEVELOPMENT
rel change, transformation

evolve *vb* **1** *syn* see DERIVE 1
rel get (at), obtain; advance
2 *syn* see UNFOLD 3
rel advance, progress; mature, open (up), ripen

evolvement *n syn* see DEVELOPMENT
rel metamorphosis, transformation

evulse *vb syn* see EXTRACT 1

exacerbate *vb* to cause to become increasingly bitter or severe <foolish words that only *exacer-
bated* the quarrel>
syn acerbate, embitter, envenom
rel annoy, exasperate, irritate, provoke; aggravate, heighten, intensify; inflame
idiom add fuel to the flame, fan the flames, feed
the fire, pour oil on the fire
con appease, mollify, pacify, placate, quell;
lessen, moderate
ant assuage

exact *vb* **1** *syn* see EXTORT 1
2 *syn* see LEVY
3 *syn* see DEMAND 1
rel coerce, compel, constrain, force, oblige; extort, extract, squeeze, wrest, wring

exact *adj* **1** *syn* see CORRECT 2
idiom on the money

2 *syn* see EVEN 5
ant imprecise, inexact
3 *syn* see SAME 1
4 *syn* see CAREFUL 2
5 *syn* see PRECISE 4

exacting *adj syn* see ONEROUS
rel rigid, rigorous, severe, stern, strict, stringent; finicky, fussy, particular; critical, hypercritical
con laissez-faire, lenient
ant unexacting

exactitude *n syn* see PRECISION

exactly *adv* **1** *syn* see JUST 1
rel ‖plumb, plunk; specifically
idiom on the dot (*or* nose), right on the nail
con about, around, more or less, roughly
ant approximately
2 *syn* see ALL 1
rel absolutely, expressly, positively; completely
3 as you say or state — used to express agreement or concurrence <"You are accusing me of
lying?" he asked. "*Exactly*," she replied.>
syn precisely, yes
idiom quite so, (that's) for sure (*or* certain)
4 *syn* see EVEN 1

exactness *n syn* see PRECISION

exaggerate *vb syn* see EMBROIDER
rel hyperbolize, overcolor, romance, romanti-
cize
idiom blow up out of (all) proportion, draw the
long bow, make the eagle scream
ant understate

exaggeration *n* an overstepping of the bounds of
truth <the passage shows the author's penchant
for grotesque *exaggeration*>
syn coloring, embellishment, embroidering, hyperbole, overstatement
rel aggrandizement, amplification, enlargement; overcoloring, overdrawing, romance,
stretching
idiom flight of fancy, tall talk
con minimizing, underestimation
ant understatement

exalt *vb* **1** to enhance the status of <propaganda
that *exalts* nationalism to the level of religion>
syn aggrandize, dignify, distinguish, ennoble,
erect, glorify, honor, magnify, pedestal, stellify,
sublime, uprear
rel boost, build up, elevate, lift, promote, raise,
upgrade, uplift; enhance, heighten, intensify; acclaim, enhalo, extol, laud, praise; apotheosize
con debase, degrade, demean, humble, humiliate; belittle, decry, depreciate, derogate, detract,
disparage, downgrade, minimize
ant abase
2 *syn* see FIRE 2
rel pique, quicken, stimulate; deepen, enhance,
sharpen; encourage, inspirit, spirit (up), uplift

exaltation *n* **1** *syn* see APOTHEOSIS 2

---

syn synonym(s) **rel** related word(s)
ant antonym(s) **con** contrasted word(s)
idiom idiomatic equivalent(s)
‖ use limited; if in doubt, see a dictionary

rel upgrading, uplifting; extolment, laudation, praise

con debasement, degradation, demeanment, humiliation; belittlement, depreciation, derogation, disparagement, downgrading

ant abasement

2 syn see ELATION 1

rel delectation, delight; bliss, joy, rapture

ant deflation

3 syn see EUPHORIA 2

ant depression

exalted *adj* **1** raised to or having high rank <moved in *exalted* circles> <Alexander was *exalted* to the papal throne in 1492>

syn astral, highest, highest-ranking, top=drawer, top-ranking

rel august, noble; eminent, illustrious, prominent; high, high-ranking; foremost, number one; first, leading, outstanding

con low, lowly, low-ranking, unimportant; minor; humble, plebeian

ant abject

2 syn see GRAND 3

ant abject

examination *n* a careful, detailed, and often formal study designed to uncover pertinent information <the doctor gave him a physical *examination*>

syn analysis, audit, check-over, checkup, inspection, perlustration, review, scan, scrutiny, survey, view

rel assay, breakdown, diagnosis, dissection; sifting, winnowing; canvass, catechization, inquiry, questioning, quizzing, testing

examine *vb* **1 syn** see SCRUTINIZE 1

rel check (out), go (over), investigate, look (into); contemplate, look (at *or* over), observe

idiom give a going over, give the once-over, go over with a fine-toothed comb

2 syn see TRY 1

3 syn see ASK 1

rel cross-examine; grill; pump

idiom give the third degree to, put to the question

example *n* **1 syn** see INSTANCE

2 syn see MODEL 2

idiom shining example

3 an instance that illustrates a rule or provides practice in its application <worked out his arithmetic *examples*>

syn ensample, illustration, problem

idiom case in point

exanimate *adj* **syn** see DEAD 1

exasperate *vb* **syn** see IRRITATE

rel agitate, work up

idiom try one's temper (*or* patience)

ant appease; mollify

exasperation *n* **1 syn** see ANNOYANCE 2

rel irritation, vexation; displeasure; resentment

2 syn see ANNOYANCE 3

ex cathedra *adj* **syn** see OFFICIAL

excavate *vb* **1 syn** see DIG 1

rel gouge (out), hollow (out), scoop (out), scrape (out), quarry (out)

2 syn see DIG 2

exceed *vb* **1** to go or be beyond a natural or set limit <the policeman *exceeded* his authority> <this task *exceeds* my powers>

syn outstep, overrun, overstep, surpass

rel outreach, overreach; dare, presume, venture

2 syn see SURPASS 1

exceedingly *adv* **syn** see VERY 1

excel *vb* **syn** see SURPASS 1

excellence *n* something that gives especial worth or value <the particular *excellence* of this cake is its lightness>

syn arete, excellency, merit, perfection, quality, virtue

rel value, worth; distinction, fineness, superiority; goodness, niceness, superbness; class

con blemish, defect, flaw; failing, foible, frailty, vice

ant fault

excellency *n* **syn** see EXCELLENCE

excellent *adj* meritoriously near the standard or model and eminently good of its kind <an *excellent* restaurant specializing in French cuisine>

syn A1, bang-up, banner, blue-ribbon, ‖boss, bully, ‖bunkum, capital, champion, classic, classical, ‖dandy, famous, fine, first-class, first-rate, first-string, five-star, front-rank, Grade A, number one, par excellence, prime, quality, royal, skookum, ‖slap-up, sovereign, stunning, superior, ‖swingeing, top, top-notch, whiz-bang; *compare* MARVELOUS 2, SUPREME

rel high-class, high-grade, proper; ‖rum; distinguished, exceptional, premium; brag, incomparable, magnificent, nobby, sensational, smart, superb, superlative, terrific, tip-top, unsurpassed

idiom all wool and a yard wide, beyond compare, out of this world

con mediocre; bad, inadequate, inferior, low, low-grade, low-quality, substandard; fourth=rate, second-class, second-rate; poor, shoddy, sorry, unsatisfactory, wretched; commonplace, mediocre, ordinary

ant execrable

except *vb* **1 syn** see EXCLUDE

rel omit, pass over; exempt; reject

con incorporate, receive, work in

ant admit

2 syn see OBJECT 1

except *prep* with the exclusion or exception of <*except* Christmas, we had no long holiday>

syn apart from, aside from, bar, barring, bating, beside, besides, but, ‖cep, except for, excluding, exclusive of, outside, outside of, save, saving

except *conj* **1** on any other condition than that <wouldn't go near that woman *except* I had to>

syn but, save, saving, unless, ‖without

2 syn see ONLY

except for *prep* **syn** see EXCEPT

exceptionable *adj* **syn** see OBJECTIONABLE

con unimpeachable; exemplary

ant unexceptionable

exceptional *adj* **1** being out of the ordinary <an *exceptional* opportunity>

syn extraordinary, phenomenal, rare, remarkable, singular, uncommon, uncustomary, un-

imaginable, unique, unordinary, unthinkable, unusual, unwonted; *compare* STRANGE 4
rel infrequent, scarce; distinct, notable, noteworthy
con frequent; common, commonplace, familiar, ordinary, usual
ant unexceptional
2 syn see SUPERIOR 4
rel good; excellent, marvelous, outstanding, phenomenal, wonderful; extraordinary, singular, special
con common, ordinary, run-of-the-mill
ant average
exceptionally *adv syn* see VERY 1
rel especially, particularly; extraordinarily, unusually; marvelously, phenomenally, stupendously, wonderfully
excerpt *vb* to select (passages or details) as typical of a larger store <quotations *excerpted* from many authors>
syn extract
rel cull, glean; choose, pick, pick out, select, single; cite, quote
excess *n* **1** whatever exceeds a limit, measure, bound, or accustomed degree <the proper balance between sufficiency and *excess*>
syn fat, overabundance, overflow, overkill, overmuch, overplus, plethora, superfluity, surfeit, surplus, surplusage
rel overbalance, overspill; oversupply; profusion; superabundance
idiom enough and then some, enough and to spare, too much of a good thing
con insufficiency, lack, scarcity
ant deficiency; dearth
2 the amount or degree by which a thing or number exceeds another <an *excess* of 10 bushels over what was needed>
syn overage, overstock, oversupply, plus, surplus, surplusage
rel overproduction; overmeasure
ant deficit, shortfall
3 *often* **excesses** *pl* undue or immoderate personal indulgence especially in eating and drinking <*excess* at table is seldom healthful> <his *excesses* led to his failure in business>
syn immoderation, inordinateness, intemperance, overindulgence
rel extravagance, overdoing; indulgence, self-indulgence; immoderacy, immoderateness; dissipation, prodigality, saturnalia
con moderation; sobriety, temperateness; restraint, self-discipline, self-restraint
ant temperance
excess *adj syn* see SUPERFLUOUS
rel redundant; unessential
excessive *adj* **1** going beyond a normal or acceptable limit <spend an *excessive* amount on clothes>
syn dizzy, exorbitant, extravagant, extreme, immoderate, inordinate, sky-high, steep, stiff, stratospheric, supernatural, towering, unconscionable, undue, unmeasurable
rel boundless, limitless, unbounded; over, overboard, overmuch, overweening; super

idiom out of bounds
con exiguous, meager, narrow, scant, scanty, skimpy, sparse, tight
ant deficient
2 given to personal excesses <an *excessive* drinker, often drunk and never quite sober>
syn immoderate, inordinate, intemperate, overindulgent, unrestrained, untempered
rel extravagant; indulgent, self-indulgent; dissipated, prodigal
con conservative, moderate, sober, temperate
ant restrained
excessively *adv syn* see EVER 6
exchange *vb* **1 syn** see TRADE 1
2 to give up, taking in return something else <*exchanged* his uniform for civilian clothes>
syn change, substitute, swap, switch, trade; *compare* TRADE 1
rel displace, replace
3 to give and receive reciprocally <*exchanged* a few words with her neighbor>
syn bandy, interchange
rel pay back, reciprocate
idiom give as much as one takes, give tit for tat, return the compliment
exchangeable *adj syn* see INTERCHANGEABLE
exchequer *n syn* see TREASURY 2
excise *vb* to remove by or as if by dissecting <*excise* a tumor> <*excised* some wordy passages>
syn cut out, exsect, extirpate, resect
rel amputate, cut off; elide, remove, strike out; eradicate, root out; delete, expurgate, exscind, slash
excitable *adj* easily excited <an *excitable* child who needs a firm hand>
syn agitable, alarmable, combustible, edgy, skittery, skittish, startlish, volatile
rel high-strung, mercurial, temperamental, unstable; touchy
idiom like a bundle of nerves, likely to go off at half cock, on edge, on the ragged edge
con calm, collected, cool, easy, easygoing, phlegmatic, placid, quiet
ant unexcitable
excite *vb* **1 syn** see PROVOKE 4
rel agitate, discompose, disquiet, disturb, perturb, stir up; impassion; charge (up), energize, touch off, turn on
idiom set astir, set on fire, stir the blood
con allay, placate, soothe
ant quiet
2 syn see ELATE
rel move; fire
con depress, dishearten
3 syn see INTEREST
excited *adj syn* see INTOXICATED 2
rel animated, atwitter; agitated, charged (up), inflamed, pink; delighted, enthusiastic
idiom all fired up, all of a twitter, beside oneself

---

syn synonym(s)   *rel* related word(s)
ant antonym(s)   *con* contrasted word(s)
idiom idiomatic equivalent(s)
‖ use limited; if in doubt, see a dictionary

con apathetic, unmoved; deflated
ant unexcited

exciting *adj* absorbingly interesting <the most *exciting* day of her life><an *exciting* personality>
syn exhilarant, exhilarating, exhilarative, eye-popping, inspiring, intoxicating, rousing, stimulating, stirring
rel arresting, interesting, intriguing; moving, provocative; heady, thrilling
con blah, dull, uninteresting, unintriguing; humdrum, monotonous, tedious
ant unexciting

exclaim *vb* to speak or utter suddenly and usually sharply, vehemently, or passionately <*exclaimed* in delight at the sight of the toy>
syn blat, blurt (out), bolt, cry out, ejaculate
rel burst (out); roar, snort

exclude *vb* to prevent the participation, consideration, or inclusion of <*excluded* that subject from discussion>
syn bar, bate, count out, debar, eliminate, except, rule out, suspend
rel ban; close out, estop, obviate, preclude, prevent, prohibit, ward (off); blackball, blacklist, ostracize; block; disbar; lock out, put out, shut out
idiom close (*or* shut) the door on
con comprehend, involve; embrace, take in
ant admit; include

excluding *prep syn* see EXCEPT

exclusionary *adj syn* see EXCLUSIVE 1

exclusive *adj* **1** having or exercising the power to limit or exclude <a tangle of *exclusive* laws>
syn exclusionary, exclusory
rel barring, debarring, excluding; limitative, limiting, restrictive; preclusive, prohibitive
con free, unlimited, unrestricted, unrestrictive
ant admissive
2 *syn* see SELECT 1
rel aristocratic, elite, preferred, privileged, tony; aloof, clannish, cliquey, cliquish; high-hat, snobbish, standoffish
con catholic, cosmopolitan, universal; common, familiar, ordinary, popular, vulgar
ant inclusive
3 *syn* see STYLISH
con tasteless; frumpy, unfashionable
4 *syn* see SOLE 4
rel individual, lone, only
con common, general, public
5 *syn* see WHOLE 5
con divided, partial

exclusive *n syn* see SCOOP

exclusively *adv syn* see ONLY 1
rel completely, wholly; particularly

exclusive of *prep syn* see EXCEPT

exclusory *adj syn* see EXCLUSIVE 1

excogitate *vb* **1** *syn* see CONSIDER 1
2 *syn* see DERIVE 1
rel contrive, invent, think (up); develop, think (out)

excoriate *vb* **1** *syn* see CHAFE 3
2 *syn* see LAMBASTE 3

idiom tear into

excorticate *vb syn* see SKIN 2

excrescence *n syn* see OUTGROWTH 1

excrescency *n syn* see OUTGROWTH 1

excruciate *vb syn* see AFFLICT
rel inflame, irritate; hurt, pain, wound; convulse
idiom prolong the agony

excruciating *adj* intensely or unbearably painful <his suffering was *excruciating*>
syn agonizing, harrowing, racking, tearing, tormenting, torturing, torturous
rel acute, extreme; piercing, sharp, shooting, stabbing; consuming, rending

exculpate *vb* to free from alleged fault or guilt <the court *exculpated* him after a thorough investigation>
syn absolve, acquit, clear, disculpate, exonerate, vindicate
rel explain, justify, rationalize; condone, excuse, forgive, pardon, remit; amnesty, free, let off
idiom clear the (*or* one's) record, wipe the slate clean
con blame, censure, denounce, reprehend, reprobate; incriminate; accuse, charge; arraign, indict; impeach; convict
ant inculpate

excurse *vb syn* see DIGRESS 2

excursion *n* **1** a trip not involving a prolonged or definite separation from one's usual abode or way of life <an afternoon *excursion* to the city>
syn jaunt, junket, outing, roundabout, sally
rel expedition, journey, trek, trip, safari; circuit, tour; one-way trip, pleasure trip, round trip; ‖pasear, paseo, walk, ‖walkabout
2 *syn* see DIGRESSION

excursus *n syn* see DIGRESSION

excusable *adj* **1** *syn* see VENIAL
2 *syn* see JUSTIFIABLE

excuse *vb* **1** to exact neither punishment nor redress for or from <she was much too ready to *excuse* her children's faults>
syn condone, forgive, pardon, remit
rel alibi, apologize (for), explain, justify, pretext, rationalize; absolve, acquit, clear, exculpate, exonerate, vindicate; extenuate, gloss (over), gloze, overlook, palliate, pass over, shrug off, whitewash, wink (at)
con blame, censure, criticize, reprehend, reprobate; castigate, chasten, chastise, correct, discipline; admonish, chide, rebuke, reprimand
ant punish
2 *syn* see EXEMPT

excuse *n* **1** a justifying explanation of a fault or defect <what's your *excuse* for being late>
syn alibi, plea, pretext, ‖right; *compare* APOLOGY 1, 2
rel defense; explanation, justification, rationalization; reason
2 *syn* see APOLOGY 2
3 an inferior example of a specified kind <this heap is a sorry *excuse* for a car>
syn apology
rel makeshift, shift, stopgap, substitute
idiom a sorry specimen

con nonpareil, paragon; gem, jewel, treasure

exec *n syn* see EXECUTIVE

execrable *adj* **1** so odious as to be utterly detestable <an *execrable* crime>
syn accursed, cursed, damnable
rel atrocious, heinous, horrific, horrifying, monstrous; base, despicable, foul, low, vile; detestable, loathsome, nauseating, repulsive, revolting
idiom beneath (*or* below) contempt, not to be put up with (*or* endured)
2 *syn* see DAMNED 2

execrate *vb* **1** to denounce violently <*execrated* those responsible for the concentration camps>
syn anathematize, curse, damn, objurgate
rel censure, condemn, denounce, reprehend, reprobate, reprove; ban; revile; accurse, imprecate
con applaud, commend, compliment; acclaim, extol, laud, praise; admire
ant eulogize
2 *syn* see HATE
3 *syn* see SWEAR 3

execration *n syn* see BLASPHEMY 1

execute *vb* **1** *syn* see PERFORM 2
rel act; bring about, cause; carry out, complete, discharge, transact
2 *syn* see ADMINISTER 1
rel discharge, dispatch, transact; conduct, handle
3 *syn* see FULFILL 1
rel put through
4 *syn* see MURDER 1
rel eliminate, purge
idiom put to death

executive *n* one who holds an administrative or managerial position <a senior sales *executive*>
syn administrator, exec, manager, officer, official
rel businessman, businesswoman; entrepreneur; higher-up; director, leader, supervisor

exegesis *n syn* see EXPLANATION 1

exegetic *adj syn* see EXPLANATORY

exemplar *n syn* see MODEL 2
rel soul; exponent, illustration; prototype

exemplary *adj* **1** *syn* see GOOD 11
rel ideal, model; admirable, commendable, praiseworthy, worthy
con evil, corrupt; unworthy
2 *syn* see TYPICAL 1

exemplify *vb* **1** to use examples in order to clarify <a good teacher *exemplifies* each complex point>
syn illustrate, instance
rel clarify, clear up, spell out; cite, quote; enlighten, illuminate
2 *syn* see EPITOMIZE 2
rel demonstrate; illustrate
3 *syn* see REPRESENT 2

exempt *vb* to free from a liability or requirement <*exempt* a man from military service>
syn absolve, discharge, dispense, excuse, let off, privilege (from), relieve, spare
rel except; free
idiom give (one) exemption

exemption *n* freeing or the state of being free or freed from a charge or obligation to which others are subject <received a tax *exemption*>
syn immunity, impunity
rel exception; discharge, freedom, release

exenterate *vb syn* see EVISCERATE

exercise *n* **1** the act of bringing into play or realizing in action <one can usually avoid accidents by the *exercise* of foresight>
syn application, employment, exercising, exertion, operation, use; *compare* USE 1
con dereliction, disregard, neglect; carelessness, heedlessness, inattention, laxity
2 regular or repeated appropriate use of a faculty, power, or bodily organ <muscular atrophy from lack of *exercise*>
syn activity, exercising, exertion
rel action, movement; practice, use, workout
con inactiveness, inactivity; idleness, unemployment
3 something practiced or performed in order to develop, improve, or display a specific power or skill <spelling *exercises*>
syn drill, drilling, practice
4 a performance having a strongly marked secondary or ulterior aspect <his writing is an *exercise* in confusion>
syn lesson, study

exercise *vb* **1** *syn* see USE 2
idiom put into practice
2 *syn* see EXERT
3 to use repeatedly in order to master or strengthen <beginning swimmers *exercising* their new skill> <games that *exercise* the muscles>
syn drill, practice, rehearse
rel break in, condition, groom, prepare, train; cultivate, develop, foster, improve; fix, set
4 *syn* see ANNOY 1

exercising *n* **1** *syn* see EXERCISE 1
2 *syn* see EXERCISE 2

exert *vb* to bring to bear especially with sustained effort or lasting effect <*exerted* tremendous influence over his son's development>
syn exercise, ply, put out, throw, wield
rel apply, employ, use
idiom put forth

exertion *n* **1** *syn* see EXERCISE 1
2 *syn* see EFFORT 1
rel strain, striving, struggle
idiom hard (*or* long) pull
con ease, leisure, relaxation, repose, rest; inactivity, idleness
ant inertia
3 *syn* see EXERCISE 2

exfoliate *vb syn* see SCALE 2

exhale *vb* to let or force out of the lungs <*exhaled* a cloud of cigarette smoke>
syn breathe (out), expire, outbreathe

---

syn synonym(s)   *rel* related word(s)
ant antonym(s)   *con* contrasted word(s)
idiom idiomatic equivalent(s)
‖ use limited; if in doubt, see a dictionary

rel emit, let (out); blow
ant inhale, inspire
exhaust *vb* **1** *syn* see DEPLETE
rel dispel, disperse, dissipate, scatter; run out
idiom suck dry
con conserve, preserve, save; renew, restore
2 *syn* see CONSUME 1
3 *syn* see GO 4
4 to tire utterly
syn ‖bugger, do in, fag, frazzle, knock out, out-tire, outwear, ‖poop, prostrate, sew up, tucker, wear out; *compare* TIRE 1
rel overdo, overdrive, overexert, overextend, overply, overwork; debilitate, enfeeble, weaken
idiom run one ragged, tire to death
con relax, rest, unlax
exhausted *adj syn* see EFFETE 2
rel run-down, weak, weakened; ‖beat, dog-tired, tired, ‖tucked up; limp; dead
idiom all done in (*or* for)
exhaustion *n syn* see FATIGUE
rel collapse, prostration
exhaustive *adj* testing all possibilities or considering all the elements of <an *exhaustive* search>
syn complete, full-dress, thorough, thoroughgoing, whole-hog
rel all-encompassing, all-out, comprehensive, full-blown, full-scale, out-and-out, profound, total; intensive, radical, sweeping
con cursory, shallow; incomplete, partial; slipshod, unthorough
ant superficial
exhaustively *adv* **1** *syn* see HARD 3
con cursorily, superficially; incompletely, partially
2 *syn* see THOROUGHLY 2
exhibit *vb* **1** *syn* see SHOW 2
2 *syn* see LOOK 4
3 *syn* see SHOW 4
idiom parade one's wares, strut one's stuff
exhibit *n syn* see EXHIBITION 2
exhibition *n* **1** an act or instance of showing, evincing, or showing off <she gave an incredible *exhibition* of bad manners>
syn demonstration, display, show, spectacle
rel manifestation, sight
2 a public display of objects of interest <a trade *exhibition*>
syn exhibit, exposition, fair, show
rel demonstration, display, offering, presentation, showing
exhibitive *adj syn* see INDICATIVE
exhilarant *adj syn* see EXCITING
exhilarate *vb syn* see ELATE
rel animate, enliven, invigorate, vitalize; boost, buoy, exalt, inspirit, lift, pep (up), uplift; cheer, delight, gladden, ‖send, thrill
idiom send into ecstasies
con deject, dishearten, dispirit, weigh down
ant depress
exhilarated *adj syn* see INTOXICATED 2
rel buoyed up, exalted, gladdened, pepped up, uplifted
idiom in ecstasies, on cloud nine

con blue, dispirited, down, low, unhappy, weighed down
ant depressed
exhilarating *adj* **1** *syn* see EXCITING
rel animating, animative, enlivening, inspiriting, invigorating, quickening; cheering, elevating, uplifting; breathtaking, electric
con deflating, disheartening, dispiriting
ant depressing
2 *syn* see INVIGORATING
exhilaration *n syn* see ELATION 1 *compare* ECSTASY
rel animation, enlivenment, firing, invigoration, quickening, stimulation, vitalization, vivification; electrification, excitation, excitement, galvanization; elevation, inspiration, uplift
ant dejection
exhilarative *adj* **1** *syn* see EXCITING
2 *syn* see INVIGORATING
exhort *vb syn* see URGE
rel admonish, plead; call upon, insist; stimulate
con block, deter, discourage, impede
exhumate *vb syn* see EXHUME
exhume *vb* to take out of a place of burial <the body was *exhumed* and burned>
syn disinhume, disinter, exhumate, unbury, uncharnel
rel dig up, disentomb, unearth; disembalm
con bury, entomb, inter, ‖plant
ant inhume
exigency *n* **1** *syn* see JUNCTURE 2
rel difficulty, hardship, rigor, vicissitude; dilemma, fix, jam, pickle, scrape; pressure, urgency
2 *syn* see NEED 4
rel demand, imperativeness, insistence, requirement; coercion, compulsion, constraint; duress, pressure, urgency
idiom matter of life and death
exigent *adj* **1** *syn* see PRESSING
rel acute; necessary; menacing, threatening
2 *syn* see ONEROUS
exiguous *adj syn* see MEAGER 2
rel diminutive, little, small, tiny; slender, slight, tenuous, thin; confined, limited, narrow, restricted, straitened
ant ample
exile *n* **1** forced removal from one's native country <a deposed king living in *exile* in Rome>
syn banishment, deportation, displacement, expulsion, ostracism, relegation
rel exclusion; extradition; expatriation; diaspora, dispersion, migration, scattering
con recall, restoration
2 *syn* see ÉMIGRÉ
rel nonperson, outcast, unperson
idiom man without a country
exile *vb syn* see BANISH
rel dispossess; evacuate; extradite; drive out
idiom turn out of house and home
con recall, restore
exist *vb* **1** *syn* see BE
2 *syn* see CONSIST 1
existence *n* **1** the state or fact of having independent reality <customs that have recently come into *existence*>

syn actuality, being
rel life; presence; reality; perseity
ant nonexistence
2 syn see ENTITY 1
rel essence; individuality
existent *adj* **1 syn** see ACTUAL 1
rel existing; present
2 syn see EXTANT 1
3 syn see PRESENT
existent *n* **syn** see ENTITY 1
existing *adj* **syn** see EXTANT 1
exit *n* **1 syn** see DEPARTURE 1
ant entry
2 syn see EGRESS 2
ant entrance, entry
exit *vb* **syn** see GO 2
idiom make an (*or* one's) exit
con arrive, come
ant enter
exiting *n* **syn** see DEPARTURE 1
ant entering
exodus *n* **syn** see DEPARTURE 1
rel emigration, migration; flight
con immigration; ingress
ant influx
ex officio *adj* **syn** see OFFICIAL
exonerate *vb* **syn** see EXCULPATE
rel disburden, free
ant incriminate
exorbitant *adj* **syn** see EXCESSIVE 1
rel overboard, overmuch; unwarranted; outrageous, preposterous; exacting, extortionate
idiom out of sight
con equitable, fair, just; rational, reasonable
exordium *n* **syn** see INTRODUCTION
rel preliminary
con afterword, conclusion, epilogue, postscript
exotic *adj* **1** not native to the place where found <*exotic* fish>
syn foreign
rel imported, introduced, naturalized; alien, extrinsic, strange
con aboriginal, autochthonous, endemic, native; domestic, local
ant indigenous
2 excitingly or enticingly different or unusual <he was moved by her *exotic* beauty>
syn romanesque, romantic, strange
rel different, unusual; alluring, enticing, fascinating, glamorous, mysterious
expand *vb* **1 syn** see OPEN 4
2 syn see INCREASE 1
3 to increase or become increased in bulk, volume, or size <water *expands* when heated>
syn amplify, dilate, distend, inflate, swell
rel grow; bulk (up), enlarge, fill (out); bolster; mushroom, ‖plim, puff (up)
con condense, decrease, deflate, shrink, shrivel; dwindle, lessen
ant contract
4 to express more fully and in greater detail <*expanded* his notes into an essay>
syn amplify, develop, elaborate, enlarge
rel detail, explicate; augment; discourse, expatiate

con compress, condense, contract
ant abridge
5 syn see INCREASE 2
6 syn see ESCALATE 2
rel prolong, protract
con de-escalate; circumscribe
ant limit, restrict
expanse *n* a significantly large area or range <a trackless *expanse* of moor>
syn amplitude, breadth, distance, expansion, space, spread, stretch
rel compass, extent, orbit, range, reach, scope, sweep; area, domain, field, sphere, territory; immensity, magnitude
expansion *n* **1 syn** see EXPANSE
2 the act or process of increasing in some way <the recent *expansion* of science>
syn enlargement, extension, spread
con contraction, decrease, shrinking
expansive *adj* **1 syn** see ELASTIC 2
rel communicative, demonstrative, extroverted, gregarious, unconstrained, unreserved, unrestrained; effusive, gushy, lavish; generous, liberal, openhanded
con austere, severe, stern; reserved, reticent, silent, taciturn
2 syn see DEMONSTRATIVE
ant withdrawn
3 syn see COMMUNICATIVE
4 syn see EXTENSIVE 1
rel ample, large; big, great
ant limited
expatiate *vb* **syn** see DISCOURSE 1
rel narrate, recite, recount, rehearse, relate; ramble
expatriate *vb* **syn** see BANISH
ant repatriate
expatriate *n* **syn** see ÉMIGRÉ
ant repatriate
expect *vb* **1** to anticipate in the mind <did not *expect* him for dinner>
syn await, count (on *or* upon), hope, look
rel anticipate, apprehend, divine, foreknow, foresee
idiom bargain on (*or* for), look for
ant despair (of)
2 syn see UNDERSTAND 3
rel feel, sense; presume, presuppose
expectancy *n* **1** the state of one who looks forward to something <had an air of wistful *expectancy*>
syn anticipation, expectation
rel presensation, presentiment
2 syn see EXPECTATION 2
expectant *adj* **1** characterized by expectation <an *expectant* crowd>
syn anticipant, anticipative, anticipatory, atiptoe, expecting
rel open-eyed, openmouthed; hopeful; eager; alert, watchful

---

syn synonym(s)   **rel** related word(s)
ant antonym(s)   **con** contrasted word(s)
idiom idiomatic equivalent(s)
‖ use limited; if in doubt, see a dictionary

con apathetic, indifferent, uninterested; unconcerned, unimpressed, unmoved
2 *syn* see PREGNANT 1
idiom anticipating a blessed event, waiting for the stork

expectation *n* **1** *syn* see EXPECTANCY 1
2 something that is expected <each had his own dreams and *expectations*>
syn expectancy
rel design, hope, intention, motive, notion; prospect

expecting *adj* **1** *syn* see EXPECTANT 1
2 *syn* see PREGNANT 1

expediency *n* **1** *syn* see ORDER 11
rel propitiousness; convenience
2 *syn* see RESOURCE 3
rel design, strategy, tactic; measure, step
idiom card up one's sleeve, means to an end

expedient *adj* dictated by practical or prudential motives <decided it was not *expedient* to interfere yet>
syn advisable, politic, prudent, tactical, wise
rel advantageous, beneficial, convenient, practical, profitable, useful, utilitarian; opportune, seasonable, timely, well-timed; feasible, possible, practicable; appropriate, fit, fitting, suitable; judicious
con deleterious, detrimental; harmful, hurtful, injurious; fruitless, futile, vain; inappropriate, uncalled-for, unfitting, unsuitable; impolite, imprudent, inadvisable, injudicious, unwise
ant inexpedient

expedient *n* *syn* see RESOURCE 3
rel agency, instrument, instrumentality, means, medium

expedition *n* **1** *syn* see JOURNEY
rel campaign; entrada, exploration
2 *syn* see HASTE 1
rel alacrity, promptitude
con delay, retardation, slackening, slowing
ant procrastination
3 *syn* see ALACRITY
rel expeditiousness, speediness, swiftness; punctuality
con dawdling, delaying, faltering, hesitation

expeditious *adj* *syn* see FAST 3
rel effective, effectual, efficacious, efficient; prompt, ready
con ineffective, ineffectual, inefficacious, inefficient; dilatory, laggard, leisurely, slow
ant sluggish

expeditiously *adv* *syn* see FAST 2
rel effectively, efficaciously; punctually
con ineffectively; deliberately, dilatorily, leisurely, slowly
ant sluggishly

expeditiousness *n* *syn* see HASTE 1

expeditive *adj* *syn* see FAST 3

expel *vb* **1** *syn* see ERUPT 1
rel blow off, blow out, ejaculate, exhaust
2 *syn* see BANISH
rel drum out, read out; eliminate, turn out; ‖bounce

idiom give (one) the boot, give the bum's rush, give the old heave-ho, send to Coventry, throw out on one's ear
ant admit

expellee *n* *syn* see ÉMIGRÉ

expend *vb* **1** *syn* see SPEND 1
rel dispense, distribute; blow, exhaust, use up
idiom loose (*or* untie) the purse strings, open one's purse
con hoard, lay up, save
2 *syn* see GO 4

expenditure *n* *syn* see EXPENSE 1

expense *n* **1** something expended to secure a benefit or bring about a result <spared no *expense* in furnishing their home>
syn cost, disbursement, expenditure, outlay
2 a loss incurred in the course of gaining something <won the war at the *expense* of many lives>
syn cost, price, toll
rel decrement, forfeit, forfeiture, sacrifice; deprivation, loss

expensive *adj* *syn* see COSTLY 1
rel immoderate, uneconomical; big-ticket, high-priced
con economical, moderate; bargain, low-cost, low-priced, thrifty; cheap
ant inexpensive

experience *n* *syn* see ACQUAINTANCE 1
rel background; observation; know-how, practice, skill; savoir faire, sophistication; wisdom
ant inexperience

experience *vb* **1** to meet with directly (as through participation or observation) <*experience* pain> <trying to *experience* the problems of a different culture>
syn have, know, see, suffer, sustain, undergo
rel encounter, meet; accept, receive
2 *syn* see FEEL 2
rel behold, see, survey, view

experienced *adj* made skillful or wise through practice <an *experienced* sales executive>
syn old, old-time, practical, practiced, seasoned, skilled, versed, vet, veteran; *compare* PROFICIENT
rel broken in; accomplished, skillful; expert, qualified; old-line, wise
idiom having been around, knowing the score (*or* the ropes)
con apprentice, beginning, freshman, green, new, novice, raw, untested, untried
ant experienceless, inexperienced

experient *adj* *syn* see EMPIRICAL

experiential *adj* *syn* see EMPIRICAL

experiment *n* an operation or process carried out to resolve an uncertainty <*experiments* that added much to our understanding of nutritional needs>
syn experimentation, test, trial, trial and error, trial run
rel probe, research, search; examination, investigation; analysis, study

experiment *vb* to engage in experimentation <*experimenting* with regional solutions to urban problems>

syn experimentalize, experimentize, test (out), try (out), try on
rel investigate, probe, research, search; analyze, scrutinize, study, weigh
idiom play around with

experimental *adj* **1** *syn* see EMPIRICAL
2 of, relating to, or having the characteristics of experiment <*experimental* missile flights>
syn experimentative, test, trial
rel preliminary, preparatory; developmental; provisional, temporary, tentative
con tested, tried; permanent, proved; accepted, established, standard

experimentalize *vb* *syn* see EXPERIMENT

experimentation *n* *syn* see EXPERIMENT

experimentative *adj* *syn* see EXPERIMENTAL 2

experimentize *vb* *syn* see EXPERIMENT

expert *adj* *syn* see PROFICIENT
rel schooled, trained; adroit, deft, dexterous; pro, professional
con unpracticed; unschooled
ant amateur, inexpert

expert *n* one who has acquired special skill in or knowledge and mastery of something <a fingerprint *expert*>
syn adept, artist, artiste, authority, ‖dab, ‖dabster, doyen, master, master-hand, maven, passed master, past master, pro, professional, proficient, swell, virtuoso, whiz, wiz, wizard
rel ‖darb; specialist
con dabbler, dilettante, tyro; apprentice, novice, probationer
ant amateur

expertise *n* **1** *syn* see ABILITY 2
rel readiness; competence; skillfulness
2 *syn* see ART 1
rel quickness; cleverness, ingeniousness; finesse; savvy

expertism *n* *syn* see ABILITY 2

expertness *n* *syn* see ABILITY 2
rel prowess; facility

expiate *vb* to make amends or give satisfaction for wrong done <*expiated* his crime with his life>
syn atone
rel amend, compensate (for), correct, rectify, redress, remedy
idiom make up for, put right

expiative *adj* *syn* see PURGATIVE

expiatory *adj* *syn* see PURGATIVE

expire *vb* **1** *syn* see DIE 1
idiom draw one's last breath; give up the breath of life
con live, thrive
2 *syn* see PASS 3
3 *syn* see EXHALE
ant inspire

explain *vb* **1** to make something comprehensible or more comprehensible <a commentary that *explains* the allegory>
syn construe, explicate, expound, interpret, spell out; *compare* CLARIFY 2
rel decipher, disentangle, undo, unravel, unriddle, unscramble, untangle; analyze, break down; clear up, resolve, solve

idiom put into plain English
con confound, confuse, puzzle
ant obfuscate
2 *syn* see CLARIFY 2
3 to give the reason for or cause of <unable to *explain* his strange conduct>
syn account, explain away, justify, rationalize
rel condone, excuse; absolve, acquit, exculpate, exonerate, vindicate

explain away *vb* *syn* see EXPLAIN 3

explanation *n* **1** something that makes clear what is obscure <sought some *explanation* of the difficult passage>
syn construal, construction, exegesis, explication, exposé, exposition, interpretation
rel disentanglement, unscrambling; enlightenment, illumination; definition, meaning; resolution, solution; demonstration, example, exemplification, illustration
2 a statement of causes, grounds, or motives <refused an *explanation* for her act>
syn account, justification, rationale, rationalization, reason
rel grounds; motive

explanative *adj* *syn* see EXPLANATORY

explanatory *adj* serving to explain <*explanatory* notes in a book>
syn exegetic, explanative, explicative, explicatory, expositional, expositive, expository, interpretive
rel enlightening, illuminating; discursive; demonstrative, illustrative
con baffling, bewildering, confusing, misleading, mystifying, puzzling
ant obfuscatory

expletive *n* *syn* see SWEARWORD

explicate *vb* *syn* see EXPLAIN 1
rel amplify, develop, dilate, enlarge (upon), expand, expatiate; demonstrate
idiom dot the *i*'s (and cross the *t*'s)

explication *n* *syn* see EXPLANATION 1
rel amplification, development, enlargement, expansion, expatiation

explicative *adj* *syn* see EXPLANATORY
rel annotative, exemplificative, scholiastic

explicatory *adj* *syn* see EXPLANATORY

explicit *adj* characterized by full precise expression <gave the guard *explicit* orders about whom to admit>
syn categorical, clean-cut, clear-cut, definite, definitive, express, specific, unambiguous
rel certain, clear, distinct, lucid, perspicuous, plain, sure, understandable, unequivocal; accurate, correct, exact, precise
con cryptic, dark, enigmatic, equivocal, obscure, unclear, vague; implicit, implied, inferred; imprecise, inaccurate, incorrect, inexact
ant ambiguous

explicitly *adv* *syn* see EXPRESSLY 1

---

syn synonym(s)   *rel* related word(s)
ant antonym(s)   *con* contrasted word(s)
idiom idiomatic equivalent(s)
‖ use limited; if in doubt, see a dictionary

explode *vb* **1** to burst violently and noisily usually due to pressure within <the bomb *exploded*>
syn blow up, burst, detonate, go off, mushroom
rel blast, discharge
idiom blow sky-high, blow to kingdom come
con fail, fizzle, peter (out)
2 *syn* see ERUPT 2
rel flame (up), flare (up)
idiom blow a fuse (*or* gasket)
3 *syn* see DISCREDIT 2
rel invalidate; deflate
idiom shoot full of holes

exploit *n* **1** *syn* see ADVENTURE
rel effort, job; maneuver
2 *syn* see FEAT 2
rel do, performance, stunt; blow, coup, stroke
idiom bold stroke

exploit *vb* **1** *syn* see USE 2
rel cultivate, work
2 to take unfair advantage of <*exploits* his friend's good nature>
syn abuse, impose (on *or* upon), use
rel manipulate; bleed, fleece, skin, soak, stick
3 *syn* see MANIPULATE 2

explore *vb* to search through or into <*explored* the possibilities of reaching an agreement>
syn delve (into), dig (into), go (into), inquire (into), investigate, look (into), probe, prospect, sift
rel burrow, mouse (out); quarry, search; examine, test, try; inquisite, question
idiom nose around

explosion *n* *syn* see OUTBURST 1

exponent *n* one who actively promotes or backs something <an *exponent* of arbitration in labor disputes>
syn advocate, champion, expounder, proponent, supporter
rel backer, booster, partisan, promoter, protagonist; defender, upholder
con antagonist, enemy; opposition
ant opponent

expose *vb* **1** to make accessible to something detrimental or dangerous <he needlessly *exposed* his troops to enemy fire>
syn lay (open), subject, uncover
rel endanger, hazard, imperil, jeopard, jeopardize, jeopardy, peril, risk
idiom put (*or* leave) in harm's way
con cover, shelter; guard, protect
ant shield
2 *syn* see OPEN 2
rel unfold, unshroud
3 *syn* see SHOW 4
rel advertise, air, broadcast, publish
4 to reveal the faults, frailties, unsoundness, or pretensions of <the monograph *exposed* the theory as being pure myth>
syn debunk, discover, show up, uncloak, undress, unmask, unshroud
rel disclose, reveal, uncover
idiom lay bare

exposé *n* *syn* see EXPLANATION 1

exposed *adj* **1** *syn* see OPEN 2

rel apparent, evident, manifest; unconcealed, unhidden; revealed; visible
idiom laid bare
con covered, enveloped, sheathed
2 *syn* see LIABLE 2
rel likely; menaced, threatened
con defended, guarded, protected, safeguarded, shielded

exposition *n* **1** *syn* see EXPLANATION 1
rel presentation; discourse, discussion, disquisition, expounding; statement; delineation, enunciation
2 *syn* see EXHIBITION 2
rel display, production

expositional *adj* *syn* see EXPLANATORY

expositive *adj* *syn* see EXPLANATORY
rel depictive, descriptive, graphic; illuminative; delineative

expository *adj* *syn* see EXPLANATORY
rel disquisitional; critical

expostulate *vb* *syn* see OBJECT 1
rel combat, fight, oppose, resist; argue, debate, discuss, dispute
idiom raise one's voice against

exposure *n* the condition of being exposed to something detrimental <*exposure* to attack>
syn liability, openness, vulnerability, vulnerableness
rel susceptibility, susceptiveness, susceptivity; defenselessness, helplessness, unprotection; danger, jeopardy, peril, risk
con bulwark, cover, protection, safeguard, shelter, shield, shielding

expound *vb* *syn* see EXPLAIN 1
rel express, present, state; comment, discourse; clarify, delineate, describe, exemplify, illustrate

expounder *n* *syn* see EXPONENT
rel explainer, expositor

express *adj* **1** *syn* see EXPLICIT
rel expressed, uttered, voiced; out-and-out, unmistakable; unconditional, unqualified
con unexpressed, unsaid, unstated; ambiguous, equivocal; conditional, qualified
2 of a particular or exact sort <came for the *express* purpose of buying a car>
syn especial, set, special, specific
rel individual; definite, particular; explicit; intended, intentional, premeditated
ant vague

express *vb* **1** *syn* see WORD
2 to give expression to (as a thought, an opinion, or an emotion) <*expressed* his views freely>
syn air, give, put, state, vent, ventilate; *compare* SAY 1, WORD
rel broach, circulate, put about; disclose, tell; frame; enunciate, phrase; announce, declare, proclaim, pronounce; discharge, drain
con hint, insinuate, intimate, suggest
ant imply
3 *syn* see MEAN 2
rel communicate, convey, impart
4 *syn* see PRESS 3

expression *n* **1** an act, process, or instance of expressing in words <his anger found *expression* in a string of oaths>

syn statement, utterance, vent, voice
rel issue; manifestation, representation; observation, reflection
con hint, insinuation, intimation, suggestion
2 *syn* see PHRASE 2
rel word; verbalism; idiom; clause
3 one thing that calls to mind another often symbolically <sent flowers as an *expression* of sympathy>
syn gesture, indication, reminder, sign, token
rel embodiment, manifestation, representation, symbol; demonstration, show
4 *syn* see ELOQUENCE
rel graphicness, vividness
5 *syn* see LOOK 2

expressionless *adj* lacking expression <cold *expressionless* eyes>
syn blank, deadpan, empty, inexpressive, unexpressive, vacant
rel dull, lackluster, lusterless, vacuous; impassive, inscrutable, stolid, wooden; dead
con lustrous; responsive; alive, vital
ant expressive

expressive *adj* clearly conveying or manifesting something <a forceful and *expressive* word>
syn eloquent, facund, meaningful, pregnant, rich, sententious, significant
rel revealing, revelatory, suggestive; graphic, pictorial, vivid; alive, demonstrative, lively, responsive, senseful, spirited
con banal, commonplace, drab, dull, flat, jejune, inane, insipid, vacuous, vapid; impassive, indifferent; austere, severe, stern, stiff, wooden; blank, deadpan, empty, expressionless, vacant; dead
ant inexpressive, unexpressive

expressiveness *n* *syn* see ELOQUENCE
ant inexpressiveness

expressivity *n* *syn* see ELOQUENCE

expressly *adv* **1** in direct and unmistakable terms <his beliefs *expressly* repudiate the church's teachings>
syn categorically, definitely, explicitly, specifically
rel directly; unmistakably
con ambiguously, equivocally; conditionally; likely, possibly, probably
2 for the express purpose <programs designed *expressly* to serve immediate political objectives>
syn especially, in specie, specially, specifically
3 *syn* see EVEN 1

expropriate *vb* *syn* see APPROPRIATE 1
rel dispossess; take (away)

expulse *vb* *syn* see BANISH
rel ‖bounce; eject
con admit, receive

expulsion *n* *syn* see EXILE 1
rel driving out, forcing out; ejection, ousting; removal
idiom the boot, the old heave-ho

expunge *vb* *syn* see ERASE
rel discard, drop, exclude, omit; annihilate, eradicate

expurgate *vb* **1** *syn* see PURIFY 2
2 *syn* see CENSOR

expurgation *n* *syn* see PURIFICATION

expurgatorial *adj* *syn* see PURGATIVE

expurgatory *adj* *syn* see PURGATIVE

exquisite *adj* **1** *syn* see CHOICE
rel consummate, finished; faultless, flawless, impeccable
2 *syn* see IMPECCABLE 1
rel superb, superlative
con faulty, flawed, imperfect
3 *syn* see INTENSE 1
rel acute, extreme; consummate, transcending

exquisite *n* *syn* see FOP

exsect *vb* *syn* see EXCISE

exsiccate *vb* *syn* see DRY 1

extant *adj* **1** that is in existence <the most talented writer *extant*>
syn alive, around, existent, existing, living
con dead, defunct, destroyed, exterminated, extinct; departed, gone, lost
ant nonextant
2 *syn* see ACTUAL 1
rel current, immediate, present
con possible, potential
3 *syn* see PRESENT

extemporaneous *adj* composed, devised, or done at the moment rather than beforehand <made an *extemporaneous* speech after the dinner>
syn autoschediastic, extemporary, extempore, impromptu, improvised, offhand, spur-of-the‒moment, unrehearsed, unstudied; *compare* UNINTENTIONAL
rel casual, informal; unprepared, unthought‒out; impulsive, snap, spontaneous
idiom off the cuff, on the spur of the moment
con designed, planned, prepared, projected, schemed, thought-out; considered, deliberated, premeditated, studied

extemporary *adj* *syn* see EXTEMPORANEOUS

extempore *adj* *syn* see EXTEMPORANEOUS

extemporization *n* *syn* see IMPROVISATION

extemporize *vb* *syn* see IMPROVISE
rel dash off, knock off, toss off
idiom do offhand, play (it) by ear
con cook up, plan, prepare, think out

extend *vb* **1** *syn* see OPEN 4
con close, fold
2 *syn* see OFFER 1
rel allocate, allot; accord, advance, award, bestow, confer, grant; donate
idiom place at one's disposal
3 to make or become longer <*extended* her visit by a week>
syn draw, draw out, elongate, lengthen, prolong, prolongate, protract, spin (out), stretch
rel amplify, enlarge, expand, increase
con abridge; curtail
ant shorten

---

syn synonym(s)	*rel* related word(s)
ant antonym(s)	*con* contrasted word(s)
idiom idiomatic equivalent(s)	

‖ use limited; if in doubt, see a dictionary

4 syn see INCREASE 1
5 syn see RUN 8
rel advance, proceed; continue
6 syn see RANGE 3
7 to reach a certain point <his education doesn't *extend* beyond elementary school>
syn go
rel reach, run; advance; attain
extended *adj* **1 syn** see LONG 1
rel prolonged, protracted, spread out, stretched out (*or* forth)
ant contracted
2 syn see EXTENSIVE 1
rel far-flung, widespread
con narrow; inextensive
ant unextended
extension *n* **1** the act or state of extending or being extended <a one-month *extension* of the price freeze seems likely>
syn elongation, lengthening, production, prolongation, prolongment, protraction
rel continuation, continuing; drawing out, stretch, stretch-out
con abridgment, shortening; contraction, curtailment, shrinking
2 syn see EXPANSION 2
rel augmentation, increase; spreading out
con abridgment, curtailment; reduction
ant contraction
3 syn see RANGE 2
rel magnitude, size, spread; comprehensiveness
4 syn see ANNEX
extensity *n* *syn* see RANGE 2
extensive *adj* **1** widely ranging in scope or application <*extensive* privileges>
syn broad, expansive, extended, scopic, scopious, wide
rel comprehensive, general, inclusive; far-reaching, far-spreading, spacious, wide-ranging; all-encompassing, all-inclusive, blanket, boundless, indiscriminate, unrestricted, wholesale
con circumscribed, constricted, limited, narrow, restricted; unextended
2 syn see BIG 1
con little, small
extent *n* **1 syn** see RANGE 2
rel domain, field, province, sphere
2 syn see SIZE 1
rel compass, extension, orbit, radius, reach, scope, sweep
3 syn see ORDER 4
extenuate *vb* **1 syn** see THIN 1
rel mitigate; moderate, qualify, temper
con aggravate, enhance, heighten
2 syn see PALLIATE
rel explain, justify, rationalize; apologize
idiom put a gloss on (*or* upon *or* over), put a good face upon
exterior *adj* *syn* see OUTER
rel outermost, outmost
con inner, ingrained, inherent, intrinsic
ant interior
exteriorize *vb* *syn* see EMBODY 1
ant interiorize

exterminate *vb* **1 syn** see ANNIHILATE 2
rel finish off; execute; kill (off)
idiom do away with, put an end to, put out of the way
2 syn see SLAUGHTER 3
idiom wipe off the face of the earth, wipe off the map
external *adj* *syn* see OUTER
rel out, outermost, outmost, peripheral
con ingrained, inherent, intrinsic
ant internal
externalize *vb* *syn* see EMBODY 1
ant internalize
extinct *adj* **1 syn** see DEAD 1
2 that has died out altogether <an *extinct* civilization>
syn bygone, dead, defunct, departed, gone, lost, vanished
rel nonexistent; collapsed, fallen, overthrown; disappeared
idiom gone from the face of the earth
con existent, existing, living; active; contemporary, current
ant extant
3 syn see OBSOLETE
rel antiquated, archaic, old-fashioned
con modern; contemporary
ant current
extinguish *vb* **1** to cause to cease burning <firemen *extinguishing* the blaze>
syn douse, ‖dout, out, put out, quench, ‖squench
rel blow out, snuff out; smother
con fire, kindle, start; torch
ant ignite
2 syn see ANNIHILATE 2
rel erase, expunge, obliterate
3 syn see CRUSH 5
rel check; smother, stifle; snuff (out); choke (out), trample (down)
idiom put the lid (*or* the kibosh) on
con encourage, fire (up)
ant inflame
extinguishment *n* *syn* see REPRESSION 1
extirpate *vb* **1 syn** see ANNIHILATE 2
rel efface, erase, expunge, demolish, destroy, raze; kill off
con breed, engender, generate, propagate
2 syn see EXCISE
extol *vb* *syn* see PRAISE 2
idiom beat the drum for, make much of
ant decry
extort *vb* **1** to obtain something by pressure or intimidation <racketeers *extorting* protection money>
syn exact, gouge, pinch, screw, shake down, squeeze, wrench, wrest, wring; *compare* CHEAT, FLEECE 1
rel demand; coerce, force; extract, get, obtain, secure; bleed, fleece, skin
idiom bleed one white, make one pay through the nose, put the screws to
2 syn see EDUCE 1
extra *adj* *syn* see SUPERFLUOUS

rel added, additional, supplemental, supplementary

extra *adv* to a degree or extent beyond the usual <she was *extra* smart>
syn extremely, rarely, ‖uncommon, uncommonly, unusually
rel especially; particularly; considerably, markedly, noticeably
con barely, scarcely

extract *vb* **1** to draw out forcibly or with effort <*extract* a confession> <*extract* a tooth>
syn evulse, pull, tear, yank
rel pry; avulse
2 *syn* see EKE OUT 3
3 *syn* see GLEAN
4 *syn* see EDUCE 1
5 *syn* see EXCERPT
rel abridge, condense, shorten

extraction *n syn* see ANCESTRY

extraneous *adj* **1** *syn* see EXTRINSIC
rel accidental, adventitious, incidental
con constitutional, ingrained, inherent; germane, material, pertinent
2 *syn* see IRRELEVANT
rel incidental; unessential; unrelated; pointless; inappropriate
idiom beside the point
ant relevant

extraordinary *adj syn* see EXCEPTIONAL 1
rel amazing; stupendous, terrific, wonderful
idiom out of the ordinary
con customary, normal, regular, usual
ant ordinary

extravagance *n* **1** *syn* see LUXURY
2 the quality, state, fact, or an instance of being extravagant <by living simply and avoiding *extravagance* they saved enough for the trip>
syn extravagancy, lavishness, overdoing, prodigality, squander, unthrift, waste, wastefulness
rel improvidence, spendthriftness; excess, indulgence, overindulgence
con moderation, temperateness; care, forehandedness, frugality; austerity
ant economy

extravagancy *n syn* see EXTRAVAGANCE 2

extravagant *adj* **1** grossly exaggerated <*extravagant* accusations>
syn fantastic, preposterous, wild
rel unbalanced, unrestrained; absurd, foolish, ludicrous, nonsensical, ridiculous, silly; bizarre, crazy; exaggerated, implausible
con plausible, sensible; restrained
ant reasonable
2 *syn* see EXCESSIVE 1
rel exuberant, lavish, profuse; prodigal, profligate, wasteful
con economical, frugal, sparing
ant restrained

extreme *adj* **1** very great <the project demanded *extreme* secrecy>
syn utmost, uttermost
2 *syn* see ARDENT 2
rel deep, moving
3 departing sharply from the traditional or usual <*extreme* political views>

syn extremist, fanatic, rabid, radical, revolutional, revolutionary, revolutionist, ultra, ultraist; *compare* OUTLANDISH 3
rel excessive, immoderate; desperate, drastic; extravagant, unreasonable; violent, wild
con conservative, moderate, restrained; reasonable, sensible
4 *syn* see EXCESSIVE 1
rel intolerable, unwarranted
5 most distant from a center <the *extreme* edge of the city>
syn farthest, furthermost, furthest, outermost, outmost, remotest, utmost, uttermost

extreme *n* **1** an extreme state or condition <an *extreme* of poverty>
syn extremity
rel excess, inordinancy
2 something situated at or marking one end or the other of a range <*extremes* of heat and cold>
syn extremity, limit
rel climax, consummation, culmination; ceiling, crest, crown, height; peak, pinnacle, summit, top; maximum, utmost, uttermost

extremely *adv* **1** *syn* see EVER 6
2 *syn* see VERY 1
3 *syn* see EXTRA

extremist *n syn* see RADICAL

extremist *adj syn* see EXTREME 3

extremity *n* **1** *syn* see EXTREME 2
rel acme, apex, apogee, vertex, zenith
2 *syn* see EXTREME 1

extricate *vb* **1** *syn* see KNOW 4
2 to free from an undesirable situation or condition <*extricate* himself from financial difficulties>
syn clear, clear away, discumber, disembarrass, disembroil, disencumber, disentangle, disentwine, unentangle, unscramble, untangle, untie, untwine
rel unravel; abstract, detach, disengage; disburden, disemburden; deliver, disinvolve, free, liberate, release, rescue; resolve
con embroil, entangle, tangle; clog, fetter, hogtie, manacle, shackle, trammel; block, hamper, hinder, impede, obstruct

extrinsic *adj* not properly part of a thing <a point *extrinsic* to his basic thesis>
syn alien, extraneous, foreign
rel acquired, gained; exterior, external, outer, outside, outward
con native; inner, inside, interior, internal, inward; individual, personal
ant intrinsic

extrude *vb syn* see EJECT 1

exuberance *n syn* see EBULLIENCE
rel gayness; friskiness, life, liveliness, sprightliness, zest, zestfulness; abandon, ardor

exuberancy *n syn* see EBULLIENCE

---

syn synonym(s)   *rel* related word(s)
ant antonym(s)   *con* contrasted word(s)
idiom idiomatic equivalent(s)
‖ use limited; if in doubt, see a dictionary

exuberant *adj* **1** joyously unrestrained and enthusiastic <his warm *exuberant* personality>
syn brash, ebullient, effervescent, high-spirited, vivacious
rel gay, lively, spirited, sprightly, zestful; frolicsome; ardent, passionate
con constrained, inhibited, repressed, restrained, subdued; calm, impassive, quiet
ant austere
2 *syn* see PROFUSE
rel fecund, fertile, fruitful, prolific; rampant, rank; diffuse
con scant, scanty, spare

exude *vb* to flow slowly out <a sticky resin *exuded* from the bark>
syn bleed, ooze, percolate, ‖screeve, seep, ‖sew, ‖sicker, strain, sweat, transude, weep
rel emanate; discharge, emit; trickle

exult *vb* to rejoice especially with feelings or display of triumph or self-satisfaction <the players were *exulting* in their victory>
syn delight, glory, jubilate, triumph
rel rejoice; celebrate; boast, brag, crow, show off
con lament, mourn
ant bemoan

exultance *n syn* see EXULTATION

exultant *adj* manifesting proud elation <*exultant* over her successes>
syn cock-a-hoop, cock-a-whoop, exulting, jubilant, triumphal, triumphant
rel happy, joyous, overjoyed; delighting, rejoicing; elated, flushed
idiom in high feather
con depressed, mournful, unhappy

exultation *n* the act of exulting or the state of being exultant <the *exultation* of victory and the thrill of power>
syn exultance, jubilance, jubilation, triumph
rel delight, elation, satisfaction; celebration, rejoicing; gloating

exulting *adj syn* see EXULTANT

exuviate *vb syn* see SHED 2

eye *n* **1** an organ of sight <turned his *eyes* to the view>
syn lamp, ocular, oculus, ‖ogle, orb, peeper, winker
2 the faculty of seeing with or as if with the eyes <had a keen *eye* for details>
syn eyesight, seeing, sight, vision
3 very close watching or observation <kept an *eye* on him>
syn eagle eye, scrutiny, surveillance, tab, watch
4 *often* **eyes** *pl* a way of looking at something <in the *eyes* of the law, a man is innocent until proven guilty>
syn view, viewpoint; *compare* VIEWPOINT 2
rel attitude, position, thinking; conception, grasp; conclusion, judgment
5 *syn* see OPINION
6 *syn* see LOOP 1
7 *syn* see LOOP 2
‖**8** *syn* see DETECTIVE

eye *vb* **1** to fix the eyes on <the child *eyed* the presents with delight>
syn consider, contemplate, gaze (upon), look (at *or* upon), view; *compare* LOOK 7
rel regard; stare (at)
2 to keep a close watch on <the detective *eyed* the suspect>
syn eyeball, scrutinize, watch; *compare* TAIL
rel stare (at); size up
idiom keep a close (*or* an eagle) eye on
3 *syn* see LOOK 7

eyeball *vb syn* see EYE 2

eye–catching *adj syn* see NOTICEABLE

eyeful *n syn* see BEAUTY

eyeless *adj syn* see BLIND 1

eye–popping *adj syn* see EXCITING

eyesight *n syn* see EYE 2

eyesore *n* something offensive to the sight <the old abandoned house was a neighborhood *eyesore*>
syn desight, fright, mess, monstrosity, sight

eyewash *n syn* see NONSENSE 2

eyewitness *n syn* see SPECTATOR

F

fable *n* **1 syn** see FICTION
  2 syn see ALLEGORY 2
fabric *n* **1 syn** see BUILDING
  2 syn see TEXTURE 2
fabricate *vb* **syn** see MAKE 3
  rel turn out; create, formulate, invent; concoct, contrive, devise
fabrication *n* **syn** see FICTION
  rel creation; deceit, fib; artifact, opus, product, production, work
fabulous *adj* **syn** see MYTHICAL
  rel amazing, astonishing, astounding, incredible, marvelous, unbelievable, wonderful; exorbitant, extravagant, inordinate, outrageous, preposterous; monstrous, prodigious, stupendous
  con believable, colorable, credible
facade *n* **syn** see MASK 2
face *n* **1** the front part of the head including the eyes, nose, mouth, cheeks, chin, and forehead <hid his *face* from the camera>
  syn countenance, ‖dial, features, ‖kisser, ‖map, mug, ‖mush, muzzle, ‖pan, phiz, ‖puss, visage
  rel lineaments, physiognomy
  2 syn see LOOK 2
  3 syn see APPEARANCE 2
  4 syn see MASK 2
  5 syn see EFFRONTERY
  6 a distortion of the face usually as an expression of contempt or distaste <the old man made a *face* at the flat beer>
  syn grimace, moue, mouth, mouthing, mow, mug
  rel frown, glower, lower, pout, scowl
  idiom wry face, wry mouth
  con grin, simper, smile, smirk
  7 syn see MAKEUP 3
  8 syn see TOP 2
face *vb* **1** to have the face or front in a specified direction <the house *faces* toward the river>
  syn front, look
  rel border, meet
  ant back
  2 syn see MEET 6
  rel watch; gaze, glare, stare; await, expect, look (for)
  3 to confront with courage or boldness <ready to *face* her accusers>
  syn ‖banter, beard, brave, challenge, dare, defy, ‖double-dog dare, front, outdare, outface, venture
  rel confront, encounter, meet; oppose, resist, withstand; contend, fight
  idiom brazen it out, face the music, face up to, take the bull by the horns
  con elude, escape, eschew, evade, shun
  ant avoid
  4 syn see CONFRONT 1
  5 syn see ACCOST 2

  rel beard, brave, challenge, dare, defy
  idiom stand up to
  6 syn see ENGAGE 5
  7 syn see SHEATHE
facet *n* **syn** see PHASE
  rel face, front
facetious *adj* **syn** see WITTY
  rel jesting, joking, quipping, wisecracking; blithe, jocund, jolly, jovial, merry; comic, comical, droll, funny, laughable, ludicrous
  con grave, serious, sober, solemn, somber
  ant lugubrious
facile *adj* **syn** see EASY 1
  rel adroit, deft, dexterous; fluent, glib, voluble; cursory, shallow, superficial, uncritical
  con awkward, clumsy, constrained, cumbersome, labored, maladroit; tongue-tied; deep, profound, thorough
  ant arduous
facilely *adv* **syn** see EASILY 1
  ant arduously
facilitate *vb* **syn** see EASE 3
facility *n* **1 syn** see READINESS 3
  rel skill, wit; aptitude, bent, leaning, propensity, turn; abandon, spontaneity, unconstraint; address, poise, tact; effortlessness, lightness, smoothness
  con awkwardness, clumsiness, ineptness, maladroitness; rigidity, stiffness, woodenness; effort, exertion, pains
  2 syn see AMENITY 2
  rel accommodation, advantage, aid, fitting
  con difficulty, hardship, inconvenience
facing *prep* **1 syn** see AGAINST 1
  con side by side
  2 syn see BEFORE 2
facsimile *n* **syn** see REPRODUCTION
  con archetype, model, original, pattern, prototype, standard
fact *n* **1** the quality of being actual <the realm of *fact* is distinct from fancy>
  syn actuality, reality
  rel authenticity, genuineness, truth
  con fancy, fantasy, fiction
  2 something that has actual existence <stubborn *facts* that cannot be confuted>
  syn event, phenomenon
  rel circumstance, detail, episode, particular; happening, incident, occurrence; observable
  con contingency, eventuality, hope, possibility, potentiality, probability
  ant illusion

---

syn synonym(s)   **rel** related word(s)
ant antonym(s)   **con** contrasted word(s)
idiom idiomatic equivalent(s)
‖ use limited; if in doubt, see a dictionary

faction *n syn* see COMBINATION 2
rel camp, offshoot, wing
idiom splinter group

factious *adj syn* see INSUBORDINATE
rel contending, fighting, warring; belligerent, contentious, quarrelsome; alienated, disaffected, estranged
con companionable, gregarious, social; acquiescent, compliant; faithful, loyal, true
ant cooperative

factitious *adj syn* see SYNTHETIC
rel affected, assumed, counterfeited, false, feigned, forced, pretended, sham, shammed, simulated
con authentic, bona fide, genuine, veritable; artless, naive, simple, spontaneous
ant natural

factor *n* **1** *syn* see ELEMENT 2
rel antecedent, cause, determinant; agency, agent, instrument, instrumentality, means
2 *syn* see AGENT 2
rel bailiff, majordomo, seneschal, steward; adjutant, aid, assistant, coadjutor, helper

factory *n* an establishment for the manufacturing of goods <a shoe *factory*>
syn manufactory, mill, plant, works

factual *adj syn* see ACTUAL 2
rel certain, undoubted, veritable; authentic, legitimate, unquestionable, valid
con erroneous, false, questionable, wrong
ant illusory

facultative *adj syn* see OPTIONAL

faculty *n* **1** *syn* see GIFT 2
rel instinct; property, quality; leaning, penchant, proclivity, propensity; predilection
con inability, incapability, incapacity, ineptness
2 *syn* see POWER 3

facund *adj syn* see EXPRESSIVE

facundity *n syn* see ELOQUENCE

fad *n syn* see FASHION 3
rel caprice, conceit, fancy, vagary, whim, whimsy
con custom, habit, practice, usage

fade *vb* **1** *syn* see FAIL 1
2 *syn* see DULL 1
3 *syn* see VANISH
rel deliquesce, dissolve, melt; abate, diminish, dwindle, ebb, lessen, moderate, wane; attenuate, rarefy, thin
idiom fade like a shadow
con intensify; eternalize, immortalize, perpetuate

faded *adj syn* see SHABBY 1
rel haggard, washed-out, wasted, worn; dim, murky; achromatic, colorless; ashen, pale, pallid, wan
con energetic, lusty, vigorous; colorful; vivid

fag *n syn* see CIGARETTE

fag *vb syn* see EXHAUST 4
con refresh, relax, rest, restore

‖**fag** *n syn* see HOMOSEXUAL

‖**faggot** *n syn* see HOMOSEXUAL

fail *vb* **1** to lose strength, power, vitality, or intensity <his health *failed* and he retired early>

syn decline, deteriorate, ‖dwine, fade, flag, languish, weaken
rel jade, sink, slip, waste (away), worsen
idiom go downhill, hit the skids
con better, improve, strengthen
2 to become used up <food *failed* before they got back to civilization>
syn give out, run out
rel dwindle, shrink, wane
3 to be or become inadequate or deficient <the spring gradually *failed* as the drought persisted>
syn dwindle, shrink, wane, waste (away), weaken
rel decrease, diminish, lessen; give out, run out; short
idiom be found wanting
con appreciate, gain, grow, increase, wax
4 to be less than adequate or successful <the attack *failed*>
syn bomb, ‖flop, flummox, wash out
rel bankrupt, deplete, drain, exhaust, impoverish; bust out, flunk, ‖spin
idiom come to grief, fall flat (*or* short), go on the rocks, ‖lay an egg, ‖take the count
ant succeed
5 to be unable to meet financial engagements <the bank *failed*>
syn break, bust, crash, fold
rel gazette; close, end, finish, terminate
idiom be ruined, go bankrupt, go broke, go on the rocks, go to the wall, go under
con boom, prosper
6 *syn* see NEGLECT
idiom be found wanting, come (*or* fall) short of

failing *n syn* see FAULT 2
rel imperfection, shortcoming
idiom weak point

failing *adj syn* see SHORT 3

failure *n* **1** omission of performance of an action or task <the mechanic's *failure* to adjust the brakes>
syn default, delinquency, dereliction, neglect, oversight
rel laxity, negligence, remissness, slackness; indifference, unconcern
con accomplishment, achievement, discharge, effectuation, fulfillment
2 lack of satisfactory performance or effect <the *failure* of the candidate in the election>
syn defeat, insuccess, nonsuccess, unsuccess, unsuccessfulness
rel failing, fault, imperfection, shortcoming
idiom no go
ant success
3 the fact or state of being inadequate <the crop *failure* brought on a near famine>
syn defalcation, deficiency, deficit, inadequacy, insufficience, insufficiency, lack, scantiness, shortage, underage; *compare* ABSENCE, SCARCITY
rel inferiority, meagerness, poorness, skimpiness; dearth, paucity
con abundance, adequacy, sufficiency
4 a marked weakening <felt a gradual *failure* of physical strength>

syn declination, decline, deterioration, ebbing, waning

rel debilitation, enfeeblement, exhaustion, flagging, weakness

con improvement; invigoration, revitalization, strengthening

5 one that has failed <he is a *failure* in school because of inattention>

syn bomb, bummer, bust, dud, flop, lemon, loser

rel botch, fiasco, fizzle, hash, muddle, washout; has-been, might-have-been

ant success

fain *adj syn* see WILLING 1

faineant *n syn* see SLUGGARD

faineant *adj syn* see LAZY

rel apathetic, impassive, phlegmatic

con active, energetic, vigorous; busy, industrious

faint *adj* **1** *syn* see GENTLE 1

2 scarcely or imperfectly perceptible <he had only a *faint* idea of how he could help>

syn blear, bleary, dim, fuzzy, ill-defined, indistinct, obscure, shadowy, unclear, undefined, undetermined, undistinct, vague; *compare* OBSCURE 3

rel blurred, dusty, pale, wan, weak; hushed, inaudible, low, muffled, small, soft, stifled, thin

con bright, distinct, evident, obvious, patent, unmistakable; certain, sure

ant clear

faint *n* the act or condition of losing consciousness <was so frightened she fell into a *faint*>

syn blackout, coma, swoon, syncope

rel grayout, swim; dizziness, vertigo; knockout

idiom a dead faint

faint *vb* to lose consciousness <*fainted* at the sight of blood>

syn black out, ‖crap out, pass out, ‖swarf, ‖swelt, swoon

rel gray out

idiom faint dead away, fall in a faint, go out like a light, pass out cold

faintly *adv syn* see SOTTO VOCE

fair *adj* **1** *syn* see BEAUTIFUL

rel dainty, delicate, exquisite; charming, enchanting; chaste, pure

con ill-favored, ugly

ant foul

2 not stormy <a *fair* day>

syn clarion, clear, cloudless, fine, pleasant, rainless, sunny, sunshine, sunshining, sunshiny, unclouded, undarkened

rel calm, placid, tranquil, unthreatening; balmy, clement, mild, pretty

con overcast, stormy, threatening

3 of light complexion <*fair* people often sunburn badly>

syn blond, light

rel ruddy, tawny

con brunet, dark, swarthy

4 characterized by honesty, justice, and freedom from improper influence <a *fair* decision by the judge>

syn candid, dispassionate, equal, equitable, impartial, impersonal, indifferent, just, nondiscriminatory, nonpartisan, objective, square, unbiased, uncolored, undistinctive, unprejudiced, unprepossessed

rel detached, disinterested; balanced, rational, reasonable, sane; open-minded, straight

con biased, inequitable, partial, partisan, prejudiced, prepossessed, unjust

ant unfair

5 observing the rules <a *fair* fight>

syn clean, sportsmanlike, sportsmanly

rel decent, honest, lawful

con dirty, dishonest, fixed

ant unfair

6 *syn* see EVEN 3

7 *syn* see MEDIUM

rel common, ordinary

con choice, good, prime, right; bad, poor, wrong

fair *n syn* see EXHIBITION 2

rel carnival, festival

fair–haired *adj syn* see FAVORITE 1

fairish *adj syn* see MEDIUM

fairly *adv* **1** *syn* see ENOUGH 2

2 *syn* see SOMEWHAT 2

fairy *n* a benevolent mythical being <children who believe in *fairies*>

syn brownie, elf, fay, nisse, pixie, sprite

rel gremlin, imp, leprechaun, puck; dwarf, gnome, goblin, kobold

con ogre, troll

fairyland *n syn* see UTOPIA

faith *n* **1** *syn* see BELIEF 1

con dubiety, dubiosity, skepticism, uncertainty

2 *syn* see TRUST 1

con disbelief, incredulity, unbelief; apprehension, misgiving

3 *syn* see RELIGION 1

4 *syn* see RELIGION 2

rel doctrines, dogmas, tenets

faithful *adj* **1** firm in adherence to whatever one is bound to by duty or promise <a *faithful* public official, conscientious and above reproach>

syn allegiant, ardent, constant, ‖dinky-di, fast, liege, loyal, resolute, staunch, steadfast, steady, true

rel dependable, reliable, tried, trustworthy; affectionate, devoted, loving; dyed-in-the-wool

con disloyal, false, perfidious, traitorous, treacherous; fickle, inconstant, unstable

ant faithless

2 *syn* see TRUE 3

idiom at one with, on all fours with

3 *syn* see AUTHENTIC 1

faithfulness *n* **1** *syn* see ATTACHMENT 1

2 *syn* see FIDELITY 1

faithless *adj* not true to allegiance or duty <a *faithless* husband>

---

syn synonym(s)   *rel* related word(s)

ant antonym(s)   *con* contrasted word(s)

idiom idiomatic equivalent(s)

‖ use limited; if in doubt, see a dictionary

syn disloyal, false, perfidious, recreant, traitorous, treacherous, unfaithful, unloyal, untrue

rel capricious, fickle, inconstant, unstable; fluctuating, wavering; changeable, changeful

con constant, loyal, resolute, staunch, steadfast, true

ant faithful

faithlessness *n* **1** *syn* see TREACHERY

2 *syn* see INFIDELITY

fake *vb* *syn* see ASSUME 4

fake *n* **1** *syn* see IMPOSTURE

2 *syn* see IMPOSTOR

fake *adj* **1** *syn* see COUNTERFEIT

rel fabricated, forged; concocted, framed, invented

con bona fide, genuine

2 *syn* see FICTITIOUS 2

faker *n* *syn* see IMPOSTOR

rel cheat, cheater, cozener, defrauder, swindler

fall *vb* **1** to pass downward <fruit *falling* off a tree> <the temperature *fell* sharply>

syn descend, drop, lower

rel decline, dip, plummet, sink; decrease, diminish, lessen; dangle, drag, droop, trail

ant rise

2 to come down suddenly and involuntarily <*fell* on the ice>

syn drop, go down, keel (over), pitch, plunge, slump, topple, tumble

rel slip, sprawl, stumble, trip

idiom come a cropper, take a header, take a spill

con ascend, climb

3 to suffer ruin, defeat, or failure <the city *fell* after a long siege>

syn go down, go under, submit, succumb, surrender

rel give up, yield

con endure, prevail, resist; conquer, triumph, vanquish, win

4 *syn* see ABATE 4

ant rise

5 *syn* see PLUMMET

fall (off *or* away) *vb* *syn* see SLIP 6

fall (on *or* upon) *vb* *syn* see ATTACK 1

fall *n* **1** *syn* see DESCENT 1

2 *syn* see DESCENT 4

3 *usu* falls *pl but sing or pl in constr* *syn* see WATERFALL

fallacious *adj* **1** *syn* see ILLOGICAL

ant sound, valid

2 *syn* see MISLEADING

ant veritable

fallaciousness *n* *syn* see FALLACY 1

rel ambiguity, equivocation; deception, deluding, misleading; faultiness, illogicality, unreasonableness

ant soundness, validity

fallacy *n* **1** a false or erroneous idea <his argument is based on a *fallacy*>

syn erroneousness, error, fallaciousness, falsehood, falseness, falsity, untruth

rel misconception, misconstrual, misinterpretation, misunderstanding

con comprehension, grasp, understanding; correctitude, correctness, truth

ant verity

2 unsound and misleading reasoning <the *fallacy* of her theory is clearly evident>

syn casuistry, deception, deceptiveness, delusion, equivocation, sophism, sophistry, speciousness, spuriousness

rel elusion, evasion, inconsistency, quibble, quibbling

fall back *vb* **1** *syn* see RETREAT 2

2 *syn* see RECEDE 1

fall flat *vb* *syn* see FAIL 4

fall guy *n* **1** *syn* see SCAPEGOAT

2 *syn* see FOOL 3

fallible *adj* liable or inclined to error <a *fallible* rule>

syn errable, errant

rel careless, faulty, heedless

con careful, heedful; inerrable, inerrant, unerring; exact, perfect, precise

ant infallible

falling–out *n* *syn* see QUARREL

falloff *n* *syn* see DECLINE 3

fall out *vb* **1** *syn* see HAPPEN 1

2 *syn* see QUARREL

fall to *vb* *syn* see PITCH IN 1

false *adj* **1** not in conformity with what is true <the information turned out to be *false*>

syn counterfactual, erroneous, inaccurate, incorrect, specious, unsound, untrue, wrong; *compare* ILLOGICAL

rel deceptive, delusive, delusory, distorted, fallacious, misleading; deceitful, dishonest, fraudulent, lying, mendacious, untruthful

idiom contrary to fact, off the mark

con accurate, correct, established, factual, truthful, veracious, veridical

ant true

2 *syn* see MISLEADING

3 *syn* see FAITHLESS

rel apostate, backsliding, renegade; crooked, devious; hollow

ant true

4 *syn* see COUNTERFEIT

rel apparent, ostensible, seeming

con bona fide, genuine

ant real

5 *syn* see ARTIFICIAL 2

false face *n* *syn* see MASK 1

false front *n* *syn* see MASK 2

falsehood *n* **1** *syn* see FALLACY 1

2 *syn* see LIE

rel fakery, feigning, pretense, sham; deceit, dissimulation, fraud

ant truth

3 *syn* see MENDACITY

falseness *n* **1** *syn* see FALLACY 1

2 *syn* see INFIDELITY

3 *syn* see DEFECTION

falsifier *n* *syn* see LIAR

falsify *vb* **1** *syn* see LIE

2 *syn* see MISREPRESENT

rel alter, change; cook, doctor; contort; contradict, contravene, deny, traverse

falsity *n* **1** *syn* see LIE

2 syn see FALLACY 1
rel bluff, fabrication, fake, sham; disingenuousness, hypocrisy, insincerity, uncandidness
ant verity
3 syn see INFIDELITY

falter *vb* **1 syn** see TEETER
2 syn see HESITATE
rel blench, flinch, quail, recoil, shrink; quake, quaver, shake, shudder, tremble; tick over
con persevere, persist; decide, determine, resolve

faltering *adj syn* see VACILLATING 2

fame *n* **1 syn** see REPUTATION 2
2 the state of being widely known for one's deeds <his *fame* was short-lived>
syn celebrity, éclat, notoriety, renown, ‖rep, reputation, repute
rel acclaim, acclamation, applause; acknowledgment, recognition; conspicuousness, prominence; distinction, eminence, glory, greatness, honor, illustriousness, note, preeminence
con disgrace, dishonor, disrepute, ignominy, obloquy, odium, opprobrium, shame
ant obscurity; infamy

famed *adj syn* see FAMOUS 2
ant obscure; ill-famed

familiar *n syn* see FRIEND

familiar *adj* **1** closely associated <time and interests have made them *familiar*>
syn chummy, close, confidential, intimate, thick
rel amicable, friendly, neighborly; affable, boon, cordial, genial, gracious, sociable; comfortable, cozy, easy, snug; forward, fresh, impertinent, intrusive, obtrusive, officious
con detached, disinterested, incurious, indifferent, remote, unconcerned; ceremonial, ceremonious, conventional, formal
ant aloof
2 syn see COMMON 4
rel accustomed, habitual, wonted; commonplace, prosaic
con new, newfangled, new-fashioned, novel; rare, strange, uncommon; chimerical, fantastic
ant unfamiliar
3 well-informed especially through study or experience <*familiar* with what is being taught in the schools>
syn abreast, acquainted, au courant, au fait, conversant, informed, up, versant, versed
rel aware, cognizant, conscious, mindful
con unacquainted, unconversant, uninformed, unversed; insensible, unaware, unconscious, unmindful; ignorant, unenlightened, unknowing
ant unfamiliar

familiarity *n syn* see ACQUAINTANCE 1
rel awareness, cognition, comprehension, knowledge, understanding
ant unfamiliarity

familiarize *vb syn* see ACCUSTOM
rel acquaint, adapt, adjust, condition, naturalize, season

family *n* **1** a group of persons of or regarded as of common ancestry <traditionally all people belong to the *family* of Noah>
syn clan, folk, house, kin, kindred, lineage, race, stock, tribe
rel brood, dynasty, line, stirp, strain; issue, offspring, progeny
idiom kith and kin, one's own flesh and blood
2 a group of usually related persons living in one house and under one head <was the only child in her *family*>
syn folks, house, household, ménage

family *adj syn* see DOMESTIC 1

family tree *n syn* see GENEALOGY

famished *adj syn* see HUNGRY

famous *adj* **1 syn** see WELL-KNOWN
2 widely known and honored for achievement <a *famous* physician>
syn celebrated, celebrious, distinguished, eminent, famed, great, illustrious, notable, prestigious, prominent, redoubtable, renowned; *compare* WELL-KNOWN
rel estimable, honorable, reputable, respectable, well-thought-of
idiom held in esteem
con humble, inconspicuous, undistinguished, unimportant, unknown
ant obscure; infamous
3 syn see EXCELLENT
ant wretched

fan *n* **1 syn** see ADDICT
2 syn see AMATEUR 1

fan *vb* **1 syn** see BLOW 1
‖**2 syn** see SEARCH 2

fan (out) *vb syn* see OPEN 4

fanatic *adj syn* see EXTREME 3

fanatic *n syn* see ENTHUSIAST

fancied *adj syn* see IMAGINARY 1

fancier *n syn* see AMATEUR 1

fanciful *adj* **1 syn** see IMAGINARY 1
rel apocryphal, fabulous, fictitious, legendary, mythical; bizarre, fantastic, grotesque; absurd, preposterous; false, wrong
con matter-of-fact, prosaic; truthful, veracious
ant realistic
2 syn see FICTITIOUS 1
ant veridical

fancy *n* **1 syn** see WILL 1
2 syn see CAPRICE
rel idea; irrationality, unreasonableness; contrariness, perverseness
3 syn see IMAGINATION
rel envisagement, envisioning, objectification
idiom flight of fancy
con awareness, experience, perception
4 an idea or image present in the mind but having no concrete or objective reality <unable to tell fact from *fancy*>
syn daydream, dream, fantasy (*or* phantasy), nightmare, phantasm, vision
rel fable, fabrication, fiction, figment, invention; concept, conception, idea, notion; chimera, delu-

---

syn synonym(s)   **rel** related word(s)
ant antonym(s)   **con** contrasted word(s)
idiom idiomatic equivalent(s)
‖ use limited; if in doubt, see a dictionary

sion, illusion; fata morgana, hallucination, mirage
idiom figment of the imagination
con actuality, fact, reality
fancy *vb* **1** *syn* see LIKE
rel approve, endorse, sanction
idiom have a fancy (*or* hankering) for; have one's heart set on
con deprecate, disapprove; abhor, abominate, detest, dislike, hate, loathe
2 *syn* see THINK 1
con demonstrate, prove, test, try
fancy *adj* *syn* see ELABORATE 2
fancy–free *adj* *syn* see FREE 6
fancy house *n* *syn* see BROTHEL
fancy man *n* **1** *syn* see LOVER 1
2 *syn* see PIMP 1
fancy woman *n* *syn* see HARLOT 1
fanfare *n* *syn* see DISPLAY 2
fanny *n* *syn* see BUTTOCKS
fantastic *adj* **1** *syn* see FICTITIOUS 1
rel implausible, incredible, unbelievable; absurd, preposterous; irrational, unreasonable; deceptive, delusive, delusory, misleading
con common, commonplace, everyday, familiar, ordinary; customary, prevailing, universal, usual
2 conceived or made without reference to reality <their explanation was *fantastic*>
syn antic, bizarre, grotesque
rel adroit, clever, ingenious; eccentric, erratic, odd, queer, singular, strange; absurd, nonsensical, preposterous, ridiculous
con factual, solid, sound, valid, well-grounded; plausible, reasonable
3 *syn* see FOOLISH 2
4 *syn* see MONSTROUS 1
5 *syn* see EXTRAVAGANT 1
fantasy (*or* **phantasy**) *n* **1** *syn* see IMAGINATION
rel conceiving, envisioning, fancying, imagining; externalizing, objectifying
2 *syn* see FANCY 4
rel caprice, freak, vagary, whim, whimsy; bizarrerie, grotesquerie
con actuality, fact, reality
3 *syn* see PIPE DREAM
far *adv* *syn* see WELL 8
far *adj* *syn* see DISTANT 1
idiom a long day's journey
ant near
far and away *adv* by a considerable margin <he was *far and away* the best man for the job>
syn by all odds, by a long shot, by far, by long odds, by odds, out and away
rel decidedly, definitely; doubtless, unconditionally, undoubtedly, unequivocally, unquestionably; absolutely, positively; just, quite, very
con barely; slightly; possibly
far and near *adv* *syn* see EVERYWHERE 1
far and wide *adv* *syn* see EVERYWHERE 1
faraway *adj* **1** *syn* see DISTANT 1
ant near-at-hand
2 *syn* see ABSTRACTED
rel disregardful, heedless, oblivious, stargazing, unheeding, unmindful

idiom off one's guard
farce *n* *syn* see MOCKERY 2
farceur *n* *syn* see ZANY 2
farcical *adj* *syn* see LAUGHABLE
rel absurd, extravagant, nonsensical, outrageous, preposterous
fare *vb* **1** *syn* see GO 1
rel advance, progress
idiom make headway
con stay, stop
2 *syn* see SHIFT 5
farewell *interj* *syn* see GOOD-BYE
farewell *n* *syn* see PARTING
farewell *adj* *syn* see PARTING
farfetched *adj* *syn* see FORCED
rel bizarre, fantastic, grotesque; eccentric, erratic, queer, strange
con accustomed, usual, wonted
far–flung *adj* *syn* see DISTANT 1
far–gone *adj* *syn* see EFFETE 2
farming *n* *syn* see AGRICULTURE
rel cultivation, tillage; agronomy, geoponics, hydroponics
far–off *adj* *syn* see DISTANT 1
idiom behind the farthest range
ant nearby
far–out *adj* *syn* see OUTLANDISH 3
farther *adv* *syn* see BEYOND 1
farther *adj* *syn* see ADDITIONAL
farthest *adj* *syn* see EXTREME 5
ant nearest
fascinate *vb* **1** *syn* see ENTHRALL 2
2 *syn* see ATTRACT 1
rel affect, impress, influence, strike, sway, touch; delight, gladden, please, rejoice; absorb, engage, engross, occupy, preoccupy
con disgust, horrify, repel; affront, insult, offend, outrage, shame
3 *syn* see INTEREST
fascinated *adj* *syn* see ENAMORED 3
fascinating *adj* *syn* see ATTRACTIVE 1
rel delectable, delightful; seducing
fascination *n* *syn* see CHARM 3
fashion *n* **1** *syn* see METHOD 1
rel custom, habit, practice, usage, wont
2 *syn* see VEIN 1
3 the prevailing or accepted custom <follow the *fashion*>
syn bandwagon, chic, craze, cry, dernier cri, fad, furore, mode, rage, style, thing, ton, trend, ‖twig, vogue
rel drift, tendency; convention, form, usage
idiom the in thing, the last word, the latest thing
fashion *vb* *syn* see MAKE 3
rel contrive, devise; design, plan, plot; turn out
fashionable *adj* *syn* see STYLISH
rel current, popular, prevalent, up-to-the-minute
idiom all the rage
ant unfashionable
fast *adj* **1** *syn* see SURE 1
rel fixed, held, inextricable, stuck, wedged
con insecure, loose, shaky, unstable
2 *syn* see FAITHFUL 1

3 moving, proceeding, or acting with great celerity <a *fast* horse>
syn breakneck, expeditious, expeditive, fleet, harefooted, hasty, posthaste, quick, raking, rapid, snappy, speedy, swift
rel active, alert, brisk, keen, lively
idiom quick as lightning, quick as thought, swift as an arrow
con lethargic, logy, poky, sluggish, tardy, torpid; languid, languorous; deliberate, gradual
ant slow
4 persistent in adhering to something <a *fast* grip>
syn firm, fixed, secure, set, tenacious, tight; *compare* STABLE 4, SURE 1
idiom stuck fast
con insecure, loose, relaxed, unfirm, weak; free, unattached, unfixed
5 *syn* see WILD 7
6 *syn* see LICENTIOUS 2
7 sexually promiscuous—usually used of a woman <she's said to be *fast*>
syn easy, light, loose, ‖riggish, unchaste, wanton, whorish
rel careless, heedless, lax, slack; bawdy, indecent; lascivious, lecherous, lewd, libertine, licentious, lickerish, riotous
idiom no better than one should be, of easy virtue
con chaste, decent, decorous, modest, moral, pure, virtuous
fast *adv* **1** *syn* see HARD 7
2 in a rapid manner <run up the hill as *fast* as you know how>
syn apace, chop-chop, expeditiously, flat-out, fleetly, full tilt, hastily, lickety-split, posthaste, presto, promptly, pronto, quick, quickly, rapidly, soon, speedily, swift, swiftly
idiom by leaps and bounds, in a flash, in a twinkling, in nothing flat, in short order, like a bat out of hell, like a blue streak, like a flash, like a house afire, like a shot, like a streak, like greased lightning, like wildfire
con deliberately, leisurely; apathetically, lethargically, sluggishly
ant slow, slowly
fasten *vb* **1** to cause one thing to hold to another <*fasten* a feather to a hat>
syn affix, attach, fix, rivet
rel connect, join, link, unite; adhere, cleave, cling, cohere, stick
con divide, divorce, part, separate, sever, sunder; loose, loosen
ant unfasten
2 to fix in place or in a desired position <*fasten* the door>
syn anchor, catch, fix, moor, secure
rel bed, implant, infix, lodge, set, settle; embed, join, wedge; establish; bar, hitch, hook
idiom make fast (*or* secure *or* sure)
con loose, undo, unloose, unloosen
ant unfasten
3 to direct (as attention or hope) directly and steadily <*fastened* his whole mind on the problem>

syn concenter, concentrate, fix, fixate, focus, put, rivet
rel address, apply, devote, direct, train, turn
con falter, vacillate, waver
fastidious *adj syn* see NICE 1
rel demanding, exacting; captious, critical, hypercritical
con cursory, uncritical
fastigium *n syn* see TOP 1
fastness *n syn* see FORT
rel retreat, shelter; defense, guard, protection; adytum, sanctum
fat *adj* **1** *syn* see FATTY 1
2 having excess adipose tissue <a *fat* woman overflowing her chair>
syn corpulent, fleshy, gross, heavy, obese, overblown, overweight, porcine, portly, pursy, stout, upholstered, weighty; *compare* ROTUND 2
rel beefy, bulky, chunky, dumpy, full-bodied, heavyset, squat, stocky, stubby, thick, thickset; paunchy, potbellied; brawny, burly, husky
idiom broad in the beam, fat as a pig
con angular, gaunt, lank, lanky, rawboned, scrawny, skinny, spare; slender, slight, slim, thin
ant lean
3 *syn* see LARGE 1
rel broad, deep, wide
con narrow, skinny
4 *syn* see RESONANT
‖**5** *syn* see REMOTE 4
fat *n* **1** *syn* see BEST
2 *syn* see EXCESS 1
fatal *adj* **1** *syn* see DEADLY 1
2 bringing on an adverse fate <to accept his word was a *fatal* mistake>
syn calamitous, cataclysmic, catastrophic, disastrous, fateful, ruinous
rel baneful, pernicious; baleful, malefic, maleficent, malign, sinister; ill-fated, ill-starred, unlucky
con advantageous, beneficial, profitable; auspicious, benign, favorable, propitious
fatal *n syn* see FATALITY 2
fatality *n* **1** the condition of causing death <the tuberculosis *fatality* remains high>
syn deadliness, lethality, mortality
rel malignancy, noxiousness, perniciousness, poisonousness, virulence
2 an instance of dying especially as the result of accident or disaster <two *fatalities* over the weekend>
syn casualty, death, fatal
‖**fat cat** *n syn* see NOTABLE 1
fate *n* whatever is destined or inevitably decreed for one <the *fate* of the bill has not been decided>
syn circumstance, destiny, doom, kismet, lot, moira, portion, weird

---

syn synonym(s)   *rel* related word(s)
ant antonym(s)   *con* contrasted word(s)
idiom idiomatic equivalent(s)
‖ use limited; if in doubt, see a dictionary

rel consequence, effect, issue, outcome, result, upshot; end, ending, termination; ineluctability, inescapableness, inevitability, inevitableness, unavoidability

con accident, chance, fortune, hazard, luck

fate *vb syn* see PREDESTINE 1

fateful *adj* **1** *syn* see OMINOUS

rel important, momentous, significant; conclusive, decisive, determinative; acute, critical, crucial

con inconclusive, insignificant, trivial, unimportant

2 *syn* see FATAL 2

fathead *n syn* see DUNCE

fatheaded *adj syn* see STUPID 1

father *n* **1** a male human parent <scarcely knew his *father*>

syn dad, dada, daddy, ‖governor, ‖old man, pa, ‖pap, papa, ‖pappy, ‖pater, pop, poppa; *compare* MOTHER 1

2 one that originates or institutes <the *father* of radiotelegraphy>

syn architect, author, creator, founder, generator, inventor, maker, originator, patriarch, sire

rel builder, encourager, motor, mover, organizer, prime mover, producer, promoter, promulgator, supporter; inaugurator, initiator, introducer

con disciple, follower

father *vb* **1** to be the male parent in reproduction <didn't know who *fathered* the child>

syn beget, breed, get, procreate, progenerate, sire

rel engender, generate, ingenerate; spawn

2 *syn* see GENERATE 1

fatherland *n syn* see COUNTRY

fatherless *adj syn* see ILLEGITIMATE 1

fathom *vb* **1** *syn* see SOUND

2 *syn* see KNOW 1

rel penetrate, pierce, probe; perceive, recognize; ‖dig, savvy

fathomable *adj syn* see UNDERSTANDABLE

fathomless *adj syn* see BOTTOMLESS 2

fatidic *adj syn* see PROPHETIC

fatigue *n* complete depletion of strength <suffering from *fatigue*>

syn exhaustion, lassitude, tiredness, weariness

rel enervation, ennui, languor, listlessness; debilitation, faintness, feebleness, weakness

con briskness, energy, liveliness, vigor, vitality; endurance, strength

fatigue *vb syn* see TIRE 1

rel deplete; exhaust, fag, tucker, wear out; debilitate, disable, weaken; annoy, bother, irk, vex

con refresh, rejuvenate, renew, restore; assuage, relieve

fatigued *adj syn* see TIRED 1

fatness *n syn* see OBESITY

‖**fatso** *n syn* see FATTY

fatty *adj* **1** containing fat especially in unusual amounts <a rather *fatty* steak>

syn adipose, fat

rel blubbery, lardy, suety

ant lean

2 having the qualities of fat <the constant frying left a *fatty* deposit on the kitchen woodwork>

syn greasy, oily, oleaginous, unctuous

fatty *n* a fat person <*fatties* trying to diet>

syn blimp, butterball, dumpling, ‖fatso, ‖tub

rel overweight; pudge, roly-poly, strapper; potbelly

idiom tons of fun

ant skinny

fatuous *adj syn* see SIMPLE 3

rel idiotic, imbecile, moronic; besotted, fond, infatuated, insensate; absurd, dumb, silly, stupid

con judicious, prudent, sage, sane, sapient, wise

ant sensible

faucet *n* a fixture for controlling the passage of fluid <turn off the *faucet*>

syn cock, gate, hydrant, petcock, spigot, stopcock, tap, valve

rel bung, spile

fault *n* **1** *syn* see IMPERFECTION

rel infirmity, weakness

con faultlessness, impeccability; meticulousness, preciseness, precision

2 an imperfection in character or an ingrained moral weakness <he has few *faults*>

syn failing, foible, frailty, vice

rel infirmity, weakness; blemish, defect, flaw

con excellence, perfection, virtue; desirability, goodness, rightness

ant merit

3 *syn* see BLAME

rel accountability, answerability, liability, responsibility; crime, error, offense, sin, transgression

faultfinder *n* **1** *syn* see CRITIC

2 *syn* see GROUCH

faultfinding *adj syn* see CRITICAL 1

rel particular, persnickety; ultracritical

con appreciative, cherishing, prizing, valuing

faultily *adv syn* see AMISS 1

rel erroneously, fallaciously, inaccurately, mistakenly, unfairly

con correctly, right

faultless *adj* **1** *syn* see IMPECCABLE 1

rel entire, intact, perfect, whole; blameless

con defective, deficient, imprecise, inaccurate, inexact, uncorrect

ant faulty

2 *syn* see INNOCENT 2

faulty *adj* marked by a fault or defect <a *faulty* mechanism>

syn amiss, defective, flawed, imperfect, sick

rel imprecise, inaccurate, inexact, uncorrect; deficient, inadequate, incomplete; erroneous, fallacious, fallible, specious, wrong; blemished, damaged, defaced, disfigured, marred

con accurate, correct, exact, nice, precise, right; complete, entire, intact, perfect, whole; excellent, good; unflawed, unimpaired

ant faultless

faux pas *n* a breach of etiquette or of social convention <hustled him out of the room before he could commit another *faux pas*>

syn blooper, boner, ‖boo-boo, break, gaffe, impropriety, indecorum, solecism; *compare* ERROR 2 *rel* bungle, misstep, stumble; howler, screamer; indiscretion, misjudgment, oversight, pratfall

favor *n* **1** *syn* see REGARD 4
ant disfavor
2 *syn* see APPROBATION 1
con depreciation, derogation, disparagement
ant disfavor
3 *syn* see GIFT 1
rel aid, assistance, backing, encouragement, help, support
4 a special privilege <willing to grant a *favor* to a good friend>
syn courtesy, dispensation, indulgence, kindness, service
rel aid, assistance, cooperation, help

favor *vb* **1** *syn* see APPROVE 1
rel endorse, OK (*or* okay), sanction; appreciate, prize, value
idiom set great store by
con decry, depreciate, disparage
ant disfavor
2 *syn* see OBLIGE 2
rel humor, indulge, pamper
idiom do one a favor (*or* service), do right by
con baffle, circumvent, foil, frustrate, thwart
3 *syn* see ENCOURAGE 2
4 *syn* see RESEMBLE
con contradict, differ

favorable *adj* **1** expressing approval <a *favorable* recommendation>
syn approbative, approbatory, approving
rel benignant, kind, kindly; recommendatory, well-disposed; commendatory, complimentary, laudatory, praiseful
idiom in one's favor
con depreciative, disapprobatory, disapproving, disparaging, uncomplimentary; censorious, condemnatory, critical, faultfinding
ant unfavorable
2 *syn* see PLEASANT 1
3 *syn* see GOOD 1
rel healthful, salutary, wholesome
con disadvantageous, unpropitious; damaging, hampering
ant unfavorable
4 *syn* see TIMELY 1
5 indicative of a successful outcome <*favorable* conditions for opening a new business>
syn auspicious, benign, bright, dexter, fortunate, propitious, white
rel advantageous, beneficial, profitable; happy, lucky, promising, providential; cheering, encouraging, reassuring
idiom full of promise
con calamitous, cataclysmic, catastrophic, disastrous, fatal, fateful, ruinous; baleful, malefic, maleficent, malign, sinister; ill-fated, ill-starred, unlucky; inauspicious, unpromising, unpropitious
ant unfavorable

favorably *adv* *syn* see WELL 5
favored *adj* *syn* see FAVORITE 2
favoring *adj* *syn* see GOOD 1
favorite *adj* **1** accorded special treatment or attention <a *favorite* daughter>

syn beloved, blue-eyed, darling, dear, fair-haired, loved, pet, precious, white-haired, white-headed
rel admired, adored, esteemed, revered; cherished, prized, treasured
idiom dear as the apple of one's eye, dear to one's heart, held dear
con contemned, despised, disdained; abhorrent, detested, hated
2 constituting a favorite <*favorite* melodies>
syn favored, popular, preferred, well-liked
rel laudable, pleasant, praiseworthy; cherished, prized, treasured
con despised, detested, disliked, hated, unpopular; eschewed, rejected

fawn *vb* to act or behave with abjectness in the presence of a superior <*fawn* on the master>
syn apple-polish, bootlick, ‖brownnose, cotton, cower, cringe, grovel, honey (up), kowtow, slaver, toady, truckle
rel blandish, cajole, coax, wheedle; butter (up), flatter, make up (to); cater (to), pander (to); crawl; abase, debase, demean; bow, cave, defer, submit, yield; court, invite, woo
idiom be at one's beck and call, curry favor, dance attendance, kiss one's feet, lick one's shoes (*or* boots), make a doormat of oneself
con contemn, despise, disdain, scorn, scout; reject, repudiate, spurn; flout, gibe, jeer, scoff; deride, mock, ridicule, taunt
ant domineer

fawning *adj* characteristic of one that fawns <sent *fawning* greetings>
syn bootlicking, cowering, cringing, groveling, kowtowing, parasitic, sycophant, sycophantic, sycophantical, sycophantish, toadying, toadyish, truckling
rel flunkyish, obsequious, servile, slavish, subservient; compliant, deferential, humble, submissive, yielding; ingratiating; adulatory, flattering, mealy-mouthed; crawling, spineless; abject, ignoble, mean
con arrogant, disdainful, haughty, insolent, lordly, overbearing, proud, supercilious; contemptuous, insulting, scathing, scornful; authoritative, imperious, magisterial, masterful
ant domineering

fay *n* *syn* see FAIRY

faze *vb* *syn* see EMBARRASS
rel confound, dumbfound, mystify, nonplus, perplex, puzzle; confuse, muddle; appall, daunt, dismay, horrify; annoy, bother, irritate, vex
con calm, compose, quiet, relax, soothe; ease, relieve

fealty *n* *syn* see FIDELITY 1
rel faith, trueness, truth; dependability, reliability, trustworthiness; devotedness, support
con disloyalty, traitorousness, treacherousness
ant perfidy

---

fear *n* **1** agitation or dismay in the anticipation of or in the presence of danger <living in *fear* of what the future might hold>
syn alarm, cold feet, consternation, dismay, dread, fright, horror, panic, terror, trepidation, trepidity
rel apprehension, foreboding, misgiving, presentiment; angst, anxiety, concern, worry; agitation, discomposure, disquietude, perturbation; chickenheartedness, cowardice, cowardliness, faintheartedness, timidity, timorousness; funk, scare
idiom cold sweat
con boldness, bravery, courage, courageousness, dauntlessness, fortitude, gallantry, intrepidity, prowess, valiancy, valor
ant fearlessness
2 *syn* see REVERENCE 2
rel esteem, respect
con contempt, scorn
fearful *adj* **1** *syn* see AFRAID 1
rel agitated, alarmed, discomposed, disquieted, disturbed, perturbed
con audacious, bold, brave, courageous, dauntless, unafraid, valiant
ant fearless
2 inspired or moved by fear <*fearful* of loud noises>
syn afraid, apprehensive; *compare* AFRAID 1
rel alarmed, disquieted, disturbed; aflutter, agitated, jittery, nervous, perturbed, uneasy; anxious, concerned, solicitous, worried
con assured, confident, sanguine, sure; collected, composed, cool, imperturbable, nonchalant, unflappable, unperturbed
ant unafraid
3 causing fear <a *fearful* sight>
syn appalling, awful, dire, direful, dreadful, formidable, frightful, horrible, horrific, redoubtable, shocking, terrible, terrific, tremendous
rel alarming, frightening, terrifying; ghastly, grim, grisly, gruesome, lurid, macabre; baleful, malign, sinister; overwhelming, sublime
con attractive, charming, delightful, enchanting, pleasant, pleasing
ant reassuring
fearless *adj syn* see BRAVE 1
rel assured, confident, sanguine, sure
con afraid, frightened, scared, terrified
ant fearful
feasible *adj syn* see POSSIBLE 1
rel practical; advantageous, beneficial, profitable; appropriate, fit, fitting, suitable
con impossible, impracticable, unachievable, unattainable, unworkable; ambitious, pretentious, utopian
ant infeasible, unfeasible
feast *n syn* see DINNER
rel entertainment, festivity; refreshment, repast; meal
feat *n* **1** *syn* see ADVENTURE
idiom bold stroke, deed of derring-do
2 a remarkable act or performance <Washington's *feat* of tossing a dollar across the river>

syn achievement, deed, exploit, tour de force
rel act, action; accomplishment, consummation, execution, performance; conquest, triumph, victory
3 *syn* see TRICK 3
feather *n syn* see TYPE
featherbrain *n syn* see SCATTERBRAIN
featherbrained *adj syn* see GIDDY 1
rel capricious, fickle, impulsive, whimsical; shallow, superficial, unprofound
featherhead *n syn* see SCATTERBRAIN
featherlight *adj syn* see LIGHT 1
featherweight *n syn* see DUNCE
featherweight *adj syn* see LIGHT 1
feature *n* **1** *syn* see QUALITY 1
2 *syn* see CHARACTERISTIC 1
rel article, detail, item, particular; component, constituent, element, factor, ingredient; individuality, particularity, peculiarity, speciality, specialty; attribute, property, quality
3 **features** *pl syn* see FACE 1
feature *vb* ‖**1** *syn* see RESEMBLE
2 *syn* see THINK 1
3 *syn* see EMPHASIZE
febrile *adj syn* see FEVERISH 1
feckless *adj* **1** having no real worth or purpose <after years of *feckless* negotiations>
syn fustian, good-for-nothing, meaningless, purposeless, unpurposed, useless, worthless
rel bootless, fruitless, futile, unavailing, vain; ineffective, ineffectual, inefficacious
con meaningful, purposeful, worthwhile; fruitful; effective, effectual, efficacious; consequential, important, momentous, significant, weighty
ant efficient, ‖feckful
2 *syn* see CARELESS 1
rel carefree, easygoing, happy-go-lucky, lackadaisical, nonchalant; remiss; irresponsible, undependable, unreliable, untrustworthy
con attentive, considerate, thoughtful; meticulous, punctilious, punctual, scrupulous; dependable, reliable, responsible, trustworthy
3 *syn* see IRRESPONSIBLE
ant ‖feckful
fecund *adj syn* see FERTILE
rel breeding, generating, propagating, reproducing
con infertile, sterile
ant barren
fecundity *n* **1** *syn* see FERTILITY
rel productiveness, productivity; exuberance, lavishness, lushness, luxuriance, prodigality, profuseness, profusion
con infertility, sterility, unproductiveness
ant barrenness, infecundity
2 *syn* see ELOQUENCE
federation *n syn* see ALLIANCE 2
fed up *adj* disgusted and completely out of patience <*fed up* with her bad behavior>
syn disgusted, sick, tired, weary
rel bored; glutted, sated, satiated, surfeited
idiom fed to the gills (*or* teeth), full up to here with, sick and tired of, sick (*or* tired) to death
con enchanted, enraptured, enthralled; delighted, excited, exhilarated, pleased, thrilled

fee *n syn* see WAGE
 rel consideration; charge, cost, expense, price
‖**feeb** *n syn* see FOOL 4
feeble *adj* **1** *syn* see WEAK 1
 rel emasculated, enervated, unmanned, unnerved; helpless; aged, doddering, senile; ailing, sapless
 con hale, healthy, sound; lusty, strenuous; strong
 ant robust
 2 *syn* see TENUOUS 3
feebleminded *adj syn* see RETARDED
 ant strong-minded
feebleness *n syn* see INFIRMITY 1
feed *vb syn* see GIVE 3
feed (on) *vb syn* see EAT 1
 idiom have (*or* take) a bite, ‖put on the feed bag (*or* nose bag)
feed *n* **1** *syn* see MEAL
 2 *syn* see FOOD 1
 rel banquet, feast, meal, repast
feel *vb* **1** *syn* see TOUCH 1
 rel manipulate, ply, wield; explore, sound; fumble, grope
 2 to have as an emotional response <*felt* pleasure in her company>
 syn experience, know, savor, taste
 rel apprehend; notice, observe, perceive; encounter, meet; endure, suffer, undergo
 idiom be aware (*or* conscious) of, be sensible of
 con disregard, ignore
 3 to view as right or true <we *feel* that he should retire soon>
 syn believe, consider, credit, deem, hold, sense, think; *compare* CONSIDER 3
 rel assume, presume, suppose, suspect; conclude, deduce, gather, infer, judge; conjecture, guess, surmise; esteem; repute
 idiom take (it) into one's head
 con challenge, distrust, doubt, misdoubt, mistrust, question
 4 *syn* see GROPE
feel (for) *vb syn* see COMPASSIONATE
feel *n* **1** *syn* see TOUCH 3
 2 *syn* see TOUCH 4
 3 *syn* see AIR 3
 con basis, essence, reality
feeler *n* an attempt to ascertain opinion <the letter was a *feeler* to see how they would react>
 syn trial balloon
 rel query, question; inquiry, probe, test; leader, leading question; sounding board; intimation, representation; prospectus; kiteflying
feeling *n* **1** *syn* see SENSATION 1
 rel action, behavior, reaction; responsiveness; palpability, palpableness, perceptibility, perceptibleness, tangibility, tangibleness
 con apathy, indifference, insensibility, numbness
 2 *syn* see TOUCH 4
 3 subjective response or reaction (as to a person or situation) <a *feeling* of sadness>
 syn affection, affectivity, emotion, passion, sentiment

rel humor, mood, temper, vein; attitude, outlook; belief, opinion, view; concept, idea, impression, notion, thought
 4 *syn* see OPINION
 5 *syn* see AIR 3
 rel impress, impression, imprint
feeling *adj syn* see EMOTIONAL 1
 con numb, unmoved, unresponsive
 ant unfeeling
feel out *vb syn* see PROBE 2
feign *vb syn* see ASSUME 4
feigned *adj syn* see ARTIFICIAL 3
 rel counterfeit, false, sham
 con heartfelt, hearty, sincere, wholehearted, whole-souled
feint *n syn* see TRICK 1
 rel make-believe, pretense, pretension; befooling, hoax, hoodwinking; cheat, counterfeit, deceit, fake, humbug, imposture, sham; expedient, resort, shift
felicitate *vb syn* see CONGRATULATE
 rel commend, compliment, recommend; salute
 con comfort, console, solace; commiserate, condole (with), pity; gibe, jeer, scoff; deride, mock, ridicule, taunt; contemn
felicitous *adj syn* see FIT 1
 rel convincing, telling; opportune, pat, seasonable, timely, well-timed; apposite, apropos, germane, pertinent, relevant
 con awkward, clumsy, gauche, inept, maladroit; unfortunate, unhappy, unlucky
 ant infelicitous
feline *adj syn* see STEALTHY 2
fell *vb* **1** to force an opponent off his feet <*felled* the heckler with a single blow>
 syn bowl (down *or* over), bring down, down, drop, flatten, floor, ground, knock down, knock over, lay low, level, mow (down), prostrate, throw down, tumble
 rel shoot, shoot down
 idiom lay level with the ground
 con pick up, raise
 2 to bring down by cutting <*felled* the great oak by the driveway>
 syn chop, cut, hew
 rel flatten, level, raze; cleave, rive, split; sever, sunder; gash, hack, mangle, slash
fell *adj* **1** *syn* see FIERCE 1
 rel baleful, malefic, maleficent, malign, sinister; implacable, relentless, unrelenting; fearful, horrible, horrific, terrific
 con compassionate, sympathetic, tender; clement, forbearing, lenient, merciful; humane
 2 *syn* see GRAVE 3
fell *n syn* see HIDE
fellow *n* **1** *syn* see PARTNER
 2 *syn* see ACCOMPANIMENT 2
 3 *syn* see MATE 5
 4 *syn* see MAN 3

---

syn synonym(s)   *rel* related word(s)
ant antonym(s)   *con* contrasted word(s)
idiom idiomatic equivalent(s)
‖ use limited; if in doubt, see a dictionary

fellow feeling *n syn* see SYMPATHY 2
fellowship *n* **1** *syn* see COMPANY 1
  2 *syn* see ASSOCIATION 2
felo–de–se *n syn* see SUICIDE
felon *n syn* see CRIMINAL
female *n syn* see WOMAN 1
female *adj syn* see FEMININE
feminine *adj* of, relating to, or characterized by qualities considered typical of a woman <clothing for the career woman that manages to be both *feminine* and businesslike>
  syn female, muliebral, womanish, womanlike, womanly
  rel effeminate; ladylike
  con male, manlike, manly, masculine, virile; manful, mannish
femme fatale *n syn* see SIREN
fen *n syn* see SWAMP
fence *n syn* see BAR 2
fence *vb* **1** *syn* see ENCLOSE 1
  2 *syn* see DODGE 1
  rel feint, maneuver; baffle, foil, outwit
fend *vb* **1** *syn* see DEFEND 1
  2 *syn* see WARD 1
fend (off) *vb* to give a sharp check to <tried to *fend* off his attentions>
  syn hold off, keep off, rebuff, rebut, repel, repulse, stave off, ward (off)
  rel refuse, reject; snub, spurn; avert, avoid
  idiom hold (*or* keep) at bay, keep at a distance, keep at arm's length
  con allure, attract, captivate, charm, enchant, fascinate; embolden, hearten
feral *adj* **1** *syn* see BRUTISH
  rel barbaric, barbarous, ferocious, fierce, inhuman, savage, vicious
  con gentle, mild, tame
  2 *syn* see SAVAGE 1
ferine *adj syn* see BRUTISH
ferment *vb syn* see SEETHE 4
ferment *n* **1** *syn* see UNREST
  2 *syn* see COMMOTION 1
ferocious *adj* **1** *syn* see FIERCE 1
  rel rapacious, ravening, ravenous, voracious; implacable, relentless
  ant tender
  2 *syn* see SAVAGE
ferret out *vb syn* see SEEK 1
  rel elicit, extract; nose out, pry (out); penetrate, pierce, probe; chase, follow, pursue, trail; ascertain, determine, discover, learn
  con conceal, hide, screen, secrete; camouflage, disguise; cover (up), hush (up), suppress
  ant squirrel (away)
ferry *vb syn* see CARRY 1
fertile *adj* marked by abundant productivity <*fertile* soil><a *fertile* mind>
  syn childing, fecund, fruitful, productive, proliferant, prolific, rich, spawning
  rel bearing, producing, yielding; abundant, bountiful, copious, exuberant, generous, lush, luxuriant, plenteous, plentiful, teeming; creative, ingenious, inventive, pregnant, resourceful; exciting, galvanizing, provoking, quickening, stimulating

  con barren, impotent, unfruitful; dull, imitative, stupid, unproductive
  ant infertile, sterile
fertility *n* the quality or state of being fertile <insure the *fertility* of the soil>
  syn fecundity, fruitfulness, prolificacy
  rel abundance, copiousness, plentifulness; creativity, ingenuity, inventiveness, resourcefulness
  con barrenness, impotence, unfruitfulness
  ant infertility, sterility
fervent *adj syn* see IMPASSIONED
  rel devout, pious, religious; responsive, tender, warm, warmhearted; heartfelt, hearty, sincere, unfeigned, wholehearted, whole-souled; earnest, serious; eager, enthusiastic
  con apathetic, impassive, phlegmatic; aloof, detached, indifferent, unconcerned
fervid *adj* **1** *syn* see IMPASSIONED
  con collected, composed, cool, imperturbable, nonchalant
  ant gelid
  2 *syn* see FEVERISH 2
fervor *n syn* see PASSION 6
  rel devoutness, piety, piousness; earnestness, seriousness, solemnity; heartiness, sincerity, wholeheartedness; empressement, warmth
  con apathy, impassiveness, impassivity; aloofness, detachment, indifference, unconcern; languor, lethargy, torpor
fescennine *adj syn* see OBSCENE 2
fess (up) *vb syn* see ACKNOWLEDGE 1
fester *vb syn* see RANKLE
festive *adj syn* see MERRY
festivity *n syn* see MERRYMAKING
fetch *vb syn* see SELL 4
fetching *adj syn* see ENTICING
fetch up *vb* ‖**1** *syn* see BRING UP 1
  2 *syn* see STOP 4
fetid *adj syn* see MALODOROUS 1
  rel loathsome, repugnant, repulsive, revolting
  con aromatic, balmy, odorous, redolent
  ant fragrant
fetish *n* **1** *syn* see CHARM 2
  2 irrational reverence or attachment <had a *fetish* for red hair>
  syn fixation, mania, obsession, thing
  rel preoccupation, prepossession; bias, partiality, predilection, prejudice; leaning, penchant, proclivity, propensity
  con antipathy, aversion, repugnance, repulsion; dislike, disrelish, distaste
fetter *n, usu* **fetters** *pl syn* see SHACKLE
fetter *vb syn* see HAMPER
  con disembarrass, disencumber, disentangle, extricate, untangle; detach, disengage
fettle *n syn* see ORDER 10
feud *n* **1** *syn* see VENDETTA
  2 *syn* see QUARREL
  rel argument; combat, contest
fevered *adj* **1** *syn* see FEVERISH 1
  ant afebrile
  2 *syn* see FEVERISH 2
feverish *adj* **1** abnormally heated by fever <the child's forehead felt *feverish*>

syn febrile, fevered, fiery

rel burning, flushed, hectic, hot, inflamed, pyretic

ant afebrile

2 marked by intense emotion or activity <a *feverish* imagination>

syn burning, fervid, fevered, heated, hectic

rel excited, high-strung, nervous, overwrought; frenzied, furious, passionate

idiom keyed up

con calm, composed, cool, serene, tranquil; apathetic, languid, lethargic, listless, phlegmatic

few *adj syn* see INFREQUENT

few *n* a small quantity or number <sold a *few* of the books>

syn handful, scattering, smatch, smatter, smattering, spatter, spattering, sprinkling

con abundance, many, multitude, numbers

fiat *n syn* see SANCTION

fib *n syn* see LIE

rel equivocation, evasiveness; mendacity, untruthfulness

idiom tall tale

fib *vb syn* see LIE

rel concoct, fabricate, make up, trump up

idiom draw the long bow, stretch the truth

fibber *n syn* see LIAR

fibbery *n syn* see MENDACITY

fiber *n syn* see TEXTURE 2

fibrous *adj syn* see MUSCULAR 1

fibster *n syn* see LIAR

fickle *adj syn* see INCONSTANT 1

rel unfaithful; undependable, unreliable

con stable, unchanging

ant constant, true

fiction *n* a story, account, explanation, or conception which is an invention of the human mind <his belief was based on a *fiction*>

syn fable, fabrication, figment

rel concoction, fantasy, invention; falsehood, lie, misrepresentation, untruth; anecdote, narrative, story, tale, yarn; fish story

con actuality, reality

ant fact

fictional *adj syn* see FICTITIOUS 1

fictitious *adj* **1** suggestive of fiction especially in lacking a sound factual basis <*fictitious* values in logic>

syn chimerical, fanciful, fantastic, fictional, fictive, illusory, imaginary, suppositious, supposititious, unreal

rel concocted, created, invented, made; fabricated, fashioned; cooked-up, false, made-up, trumped-up, untrue; romantic

con actual, real, true; authentic, genuine; factual, veritable; truthful, veracious, verisimilar

2 not genuine <the gigolo wooed the heiress with *fictitious* ardor>

syn fake, mock, sham, simulated; *compare* ARTIFICIAL 2

rel deceptive, delusive, delusory, misleading; dishonest, unreal, untrue; artificial, ersatz, factitious, synthetic

con authentic, bona fide, veritable; actual, honest, real, true

ant genuine

fictive *adj syn* see FICTITIOUS 1

fiddle *vb* **1** to handle something nervously or absently <always *fiddling* with his tie>

syn fidget, play, trifle, twiddle

rel feel, handle, touch

2 to work aimlessly, fruitlessly, or pointlessly <*fiddled* around with the engine for hours>

syn doodle, mess, mess around, potter, puddle, putter, tinker

rel dabble, fool, monkey

fiddle *n syn* see IMPOSTURE

fiddle–faddle *n syn* see NONSENSE 2

fiddlesticks *n pl syn* see NONSENSE 2

fidelity *n* **1** constancy to something to which one is bound by a pledge or duty <we must practice *fidelity* to our word>

syn allegiance, ardor, devotion, faithfulness, fealty, loyalty, piety

rel constancy, staunchness, steadfastness; dependability, reliability, trustworthiness

con disloyalty, falseness, falsity, perfidiousness, traitorousness, treacherousness, treachery; undependableness, unreliability, untrustworthiness

ant perfidy; faithlessness

2 *syn* see ATTACHMENT 1

ant infidelity

fidget *vb syn* see FIDDLE 1

fidgety *adj syn* see NERVOUS

field *n* a limited area of knowledge or endeavor to which pursuits, activities, and interests are confined <a lawyer eminent in her *field*>

syn bailiwick, champaign, demesne, domain, dominion, precinct, province, region, sphere, terrain, territory, walk

rel bounds, confines, limits; area, department; compass, orbit, purview, range, reach, scope, sweep

con terra incognita

fiend *n syn* see DEVIL 1

2 *syn* see DEVIL 2

3 *syn* see ENTHUSIAST

fiendish *adj* having or manifesting qualities associated with devils, demons, and fiends <inflicted *fiendish* tortures on his captive>

syn demoniac, demonian, demonic, devilish, diabolic, diabolonian, satanic, serpentine, unhallowed

rel hellish, infernal; baleful, malefic, maleficent, malign, sinister; malevolent, malicious, malignant; atrocious, heinous, monstrous, outrageous; barbarous, cruel, ferocious, inhuman, savage, vicious

con benign, benignant, kind, kindly; gentle, mild; compassionate, sympathetic, tender

fierce *adj* **1** displaying fury or malignity in looks or actions <*fierce* native tribes>

---

syn synonym(s)   *rel* related word(s)
ant antonym(s)   *con* contrasted word(s)
idiom idiomatic equivalent(s)
‖ use limited; if in doubt, see a dictionary

syn barbarous, cannibalic, cruel, fell, ferocious, grim, inhuman, inhumane, savage, truculent, wolfish
rel menacing, threatening; enraged, infuriated, maddened; aggressive, bellicose, belligerent, pugnacious; brutal, merciless, pitiless, ruthless, vicious, wild
con benign, benignant, gentle, kind, kindly; peaceful; subdued, submissive, tame
ant mild
2 *syn* see INTENSE 1
rel excessive, extreme, inordinate; penetrating, piercing; superlative, supreme, transcendent
con gentle, mild, subdued
fiercely *adv syn* see HARD 2
fiery *adj* **1** *syn* see BURNING 1
2 *syn* see HOT 1
ant frigid, icy
3 *syn* see FEVERISH 1
4 *syn* see SPIRITED 2
rel headlong, hotheaded, impetuous, madcap, precipitate; fervid, impassioned, perfervid; fierce, intense, vehement, violent; enthusiastic, excitable, impulsive, unrestrained; irascible, irritable
con deliberate, leisurely, slow; apathetic, dull, impassive, lethargic, phlegmatic, sluggish; enervated, listless, spiritless
5 *syn* see IMPASSIONED
ant icy
fifty–fifty *adv syn* see EVENLY 1
fifty–fifty *adj syn* see EVEN 4
fight *vb* **1** *syn* see CONTEND 1
rel strive, struggle; rowdy, scuffle, tussle; debate, dispute; altercate, bicker, quarrel, scrap, spat, squabble, tiff, wrangle
idiom ‖mix it, mix it up, put up a fight
con bow, capitulate, submit, succumb, yield
2 *syn* see RESIST
con abide, bear, endure, suffer; advocate, back, champion, support, uphold; defend, guard, protect, shield
fight *n* **1** *syn* see BRAWL 2
2 *syn* see QUARREL
3 *syn* see ATTACK 2
fighter *n syn* see SOLDIER
fighting man *n syn* see SOLDIER
figment *n syn* see FICTION
rel daydream, dream, fancy, nightmare; bubble, chimera, illusion; creation
figurant *n syn* see DANCER
figurante *n syn* see DANCER
figuration *n* **1** *syn* see OUTLINE
2 *syn* see ALLEGORY 1
figure *n* **1** *syn* see NUMBER
rel character, symbol
2 *syn* see FORM 1
rel delineation; appearance, build, frame, physique
3 a unit in a decorative composition (as in a fabric) <a rug with geometrical *figures* in blue and red>
syn design, device, motif, motive, pattern
rel decoration, embellishment, ornamentation

figure *vb* **1** *syn* see CALCULATE
2 *syn* see ADD 2
rel count, enumerate, number
3 *syn* see DECIDE
figure out *vb syn* see SOLVE 2
rel disentangle, unscramble, untangle; crack, decode
con obfuscate, obscure; conceal, hide, screen
figuring *n syn* see COMPUTATION
filch *vb syn* see STEAL 1
filcher *n syn* see THIEF
file *n syn* see LINE 5
filius nullius *n syn* see BASTARD 1
filius populi *n syn* see BASTARD 1
fill *vb* **1** to make full in a way or to a degree that prevents further entry or passage <*fill* a cavity in a tooth>
syn block, choke, clog, close, congest, obstruct, occlude, plug, stop, stopper
rel bar, dam, jam; ‖bung, pug
con clear, free
2 *syn* see LOAD 3
3 *syn* see SATISFY 5
4 *syn* see SATIATE
rel overfeed, overfill, overstuff
fille de joie *n syn* see PROSTITUTE
fillet *n syn* see STRIP 1
fill in *vb* **1** *syn* see INTRODUCE 6
2 *syn* see INFORM 2
fill–in *n syn* see SUBSTITUTE 1
film *n* **1** *syn* see HAZE 1
2 *syn* see MOVIE
filmy *adj* characterized by fineness and delicacy of texture <*filmy* curtains>
syn diaphanous, flimsy, gauzy, gossamer, sheer, tiffany, transparent
rel dainty, delicate, fine
con coarse, heavy, opaque, rough
filthy *adj* **1** *syn* see DIRTY 1
rel disheveled, slipshod, sloppy, slovenly, unkempt; loathsome, offensive, repulsive, revolting, verminous; coarse, gross, obscene, ribald, vulgar
con cleaned, cleansed; clean, cleanly; neat, shipshape, tidy, trig, trim
ant immaculate, spick-and-span
2 *syn* see OBSCENE 2
filthy lucre *n syn* see MONEY
finagle *vb syn* see ENGINEER
final *adj syn* see LAST
rel crowning, ending, finishing; conclusive, decisive, definitive, determinative; irrefutable, unanswerable, unappealable
con earliest, maiden, original, primary; beginning, incipient, introductory; inaugural
ant initial
finale *n* a final part or element (as of a sequence, series, or action) <the solution of the mystery forms the *finale* of the play>
syn close, conclusion, end, ending, finish, windup; *compare* END 2
rel climax, consummation, culmination; denouement, payoff; cessation, termination
con beginning, genesis, initiation, rise, start; inception, origin, root, source

ant prologue

finally *adv syn* see YET 2
  idiom at last, at length, at long last, in the long run, when all is said and done

finance *vb* **1** *syn* see CAPITALIZE
  idiom put up the money, raise the dough
  2 *syn* see ENDOW 2
  rel back, bank, bankroll, grubstake, stake, underwrite; patronize, promote, sponsor, support

financial *adj* of or relating to finance <the *financial* interests of the country>
  syn fiscal, monetary, pecuniary, pocket
  rel business, commercial, economic

find *vb* **1** to come upon <they soon *found* what they needed>
  syn catch, descry, detect, encounter, espy, hit (on *or* upon), meet (with), spot, turn up
  rel discern, discover, note, sight; distinguish, identify, recognize; dig up, scare up
  idiom bring to light, come up with, fall in with, lay one's finger (on *or* upon), lay one's hand (on *or* upon)
  con miss, overlook, pass (over)
  ant lose
  2 *syn* see GIVE 3

find *n* **1** one of unexpected worth or merit obtained or encountered more or less by chance <the young understudy proved to be a remarkable *find*>
  syn treasure, treasure trove
  rel boast, gem, jewel, pride
  idiom one in a thousand (*or* million)
  2 *syn* see DISCOVERY

find out *vb syn* see DISCOVER 3

fine *n* a pecuniary penalty exacted by an authority <paid a *fine* of ten dollars>
  syn amercement, forfeit, mulct, penalty
  rel damages, reparation; punishment; assessment

fine *vb syn* see PENALIZE
  rel distrain, exact, levy, tax; confiscate, sequestrate

fine *adj* **1** marked by subtlety of perception or discrimination <I cannot follow these *fine* distinctions>
  syn delicate, finespun, hairline, hairsplitting, nice, refined, subtle
  rel abstruse, esoteric, recondite; cryptic, enigmatic, obscure; minute, petty, trifling
  con definite, explicit, express, specific; clear, lucid, perspicuous; broad, extensive, general, generic, indefinite, wide
  2 consisting of small particles <*fine* sand>
  syn impalpable, powdery, pulverized
  rel light, loose, porous
  ant coarse
  3 *syn* see EXCELLENT
  rel beautiful, splendid; enjoyable, pleasant
  idiom fine and dandy
  con miserable, wretched; atrocious, awful, objectionable, unpleasant
  4 *syn* see FAIR 2

finecomb *vb syn* see SCOUR 2

finery *n* dressy clothing <decked out in all her *finery*>

syn ‖best bib and tucker, bravery, frippery, full dress, ‖glad rags, regalia, Sunday best, war paint
  rel apparel, clothes; foofaraw, frill, gewgaw, ornament, trimming
  con rags, tatters

finespun *adj syn* see FINE 1

finesse *vb syn* see MANIPULATE 2

fine–tooth–comb *vb syn* see SCOUR 2

finger *vb* **1** *syn* see TOUCH 1
  2 *syn* see DESIGNATE 2
  3 *syn* see IDENTIFY

finical *adj syn* see NICE 1
  con slipshod, sloppy, slovenly; blowsy, dowdy, frowzy, slatternly

finicking *adj syn* see NICE 1

finicky *adj syn* see NICE 1

finish *vb* **1** *syn* see CLOSE 3
  rel accomplish, achieve, effect, fulfill
  idiom have done with
  2 *syn* see GO 4
  3 *syn* see KILL 1
  4 *syn* see MURDER 1

finish *n* **1** *syn* see END 2
  2 *syn* see FINALE
  3 *syn* see ACQUIREMENT
  rel correctness, discrimination, propriety, refinement; elegance, grace, polish; cultivation, taste

finished *adj* **1** *syn* see COMPLETE 4
  2 *syn* see THROUGH 3
  3 *syn* see CONSUMMATE 1
  rel cultivated, cultured, refined; smooth, suave, urbane; elegant, exquisite; all-around, many‡sided, versatile
  con imperfect, incomplete
  ant crude; unfinished

finish off *vb syn* see CLIMAX

finite *adj* having definite or definable limits or boundaries <a *finite* thickness>
  syn bound, bounded, limited
  rel confined, restricted; definable, defined, definite, determinate, fixed, terminable; exact, precise, specific
  con boundless, unbounded, unlimited; absolute, complete, total
  ant infinite

‖**fink** *n syn* see INFORMER

fire *n* **1** a destructive burning <the house was destroyed by *fire*>
  syn conflagration, holocaust, inferno
  rel blaze, flame, flare, glare; burning, charring, scorching, searing
  idiom sea of flames, sheet of fire
  2 *syn* see PASSION 6
  rel animation, exhilaration, liveliness; dash, drive, energy, ginger, gusto, heartiness, pep, punch, snap, spirit, starch, verve, vigor, vim, zest, zing, zip

---

syn synonym(s)   *rel* related word(s)
ant antonym(s)   *con* contrasted word(s)
idiom idiomatic equivalent(s)
‖ use limited; if in doubt, see a dictionary

fire *vb* **1** *syn* see LIGHT 1
idiom set fire to, set on fire
con extinguish, quench, smother
2 to stimulate (as mental powers) to higher or more intense activity <a painting that *fired* the viewer's imagination>
syn animate, exalt, inform, inspire; *compare* PROVOKE 4
rel arouse, enliven, rouse, stir; electrify, excite; heighten, intensify; enthuse, thrill
con appall, dismay; alarm, frighten, terrify
ant daunt
3 *syn* see DISMISS 3
rel eject, expel, oust
idiom give the pink slip, give the sack, strike off the rolls
con engage; appoint, designate, elect, name
ant hire
4 *syn* see SHOOT 1
5 *syn* see THROW 1
6 to dry or harden by subjecting to heat <*fire* bricks>
syn bake, burn, kiln
firebug *n* *syn* see INCENDIARY
fire–new *adj* *syn* see BRAND-NEW
firewater *n* *syn* see LIQUOR 2
firm *adj* **1** *syn* see FAST 4
2 *syn* see STABLE 4
3 having a texture or consistency that resists deformation by external force <*firm* flesh>
syn hard, solid
rel close, compact, dense, thick; inelastic, inflexible, rigid, stiff, unyielding; sturdy, substantial, tough
con flaccid, flimsy, floppy, limp, loose, slack, sleazy, soft, squishy
ant flabby
4 that has been established and is not usually subject to change <a *firm* price>
syn certain, fixed, set, settled, stated, stipulated
rel established, going, prevailing; consistent, stable, steady, unwavering; definite, exact, explicit, specific, undeviating; flat
con changeable, fluctuating, shaky, shifting, unsteady, variable
5 *syn* see SURE 1
6 *syn* see SURE 2
firm *adv* *syn* see HARD 7
firm *n* *syn* see ENTERPRISE 3
firmament *n* *syn* see SKY
firmly *adv* **1** *syn* see HARD 7
2 *syn* see HARD 9
firmness *n* **1** *syn* see STABILITY
2 *syn* see DECISION 2
first *adj* **1** being number one in a series <the *first* day of the week>
syn foremost, headmost, inaugural, initial, leading
con final, terminal, ultimate; interjacent, intermediary, intermediate, intervenient, intervening
ant last

2 preceding all others <succeeded at her *first* try>
syn earliest, initial, maiden, original, pioneer, primary, prime
rel early, pristine; primal, primogenial, primordial
con derivative, imitative, secondary
ant final
3 exceeding all others <he was the *first* statesman of his era>
syn arch, champion, chief, foremost, head, leading, premier, principal
rel eminent, highest, preeminent, primary, prime, supreme; dominant, paramount, predominant, sovereign; main, outstanding
con ancillary, auxiliary, secondary, subsidiary
ant subordinate
4 most rudimentary <had not the *first* chance of success>
syn least, slightest, smallest
rel measly, slight, slim, trifling, trivial
con considerable, goodly, significant, substantial, tolerable, worthwhile
first *adv* *syn* see FIRSTLY
first–class *adj* *syn* see EXCELLENT
idiom in a class by itself
con fair, indifferent, middling; unexceptional, unnoteworthy, unremarkable
firsthand *adj* *syn* see DIRECT 4
firstly *adv* as the first thing to be mentioned <*firstly*, we wish to consider the economic problem>
syn first, initially
rel incipiently, originally, primarily
idiom before all (*or* anything) else, first of all, first off, to begin with
con ultimately
ant finally, lastly
first off *adv* *syn* see AWAY 3
first–rate *adj* *syn* see EXCELLENT
con fair, indifferent, middling, poor; unexceptional, unnoteworthy, unremarkable
first–string *adj* *syn* see EXCELLENT
firth *n* *syn* see INLET
fiscal *adj* *syn* see FINANCIAL
fish *n* **1** *syn* see FOOL 3
‖**2** *syn* see DOLLAR
fish *vb* *syn* see HINT 4
fishwife *n* *syn* see VIRAGO
fishy *adj* *syn* see DOUBTFUL 1
fissure *n* **1** *syn* see CRACK 3
rel abyss, chasm, gorge, ravine; breach, rent, rupture; gash, hole, opening
2 *syn* see BREACH 3
fist *n* *syn* see HANDWRITING
fisticuffs *n pl* *syn* see BOXING
fit *n* *syn* see ATTACK 3
fit *adj* **1** adapted to an end or use by nature or art <food *fit* for a king>
syn applicable, appropriate, apt, befitting, felicitous, fitting, happy, just, meet, proper, right, rightful, suitable; *compare* JUST 3
rel adapted, adjusted; congruous, consonant; decent, decorous; acceptable, adequate, tolerable

con improper, inadequate, inappropriate, unsuitable; false, wrong
ant unfit
2 syn see ELIGIBLE
rel able, competent
3 syn see GOOD 2
4 syn see HEALTHY 1
idiom fit as a fiddle
ant unfit
fit *vb* **1 syn** see SUIT 4
2 syn see BELONG 1
3 syn see PREPARE 1
4 syn see ADAPT
fit (in) *vb* **syn** see AGREE 4
fitful *adj* lacking steadiness or regularity in course, movement, or succession <a *fitful* breeze>
syn catchy, desultory, on-again-off-again, spasmodic, sporadic, spotty
rel intermittent, interrupted, irregular, periodic, recurrent; haphazard, hit-or-miss, random; changeable, variable; capricious, inconstant, unstable
con equable, even, steady, uniform; methodical, orderly, regular, systematic
ant constant
fitly *adv* **syn** see WELL 1
fitness *n* **1 syn** see ORDER 10
2 syn see ORDER 11
rel decency, decorum, harmony
ant unfitness
3 syn see USE 3
fit out *vb* **syn** see FURNISH 1
fitted *adj* **syn** see ASSORTED 2
fitting *adj* **1 syn** see FIT 1
rel apposite, apropos, germane, pertinent, relevant, seemly; accordant, concordant, harmonious
2 syn see TRUE 7
fittingly *adv* **1 syn** see WELL 1
2 syn see WELL 4
fivefold *adj* **syn** see QUINTUPLE
five-star *adj* **syn** see EXCELLENT
fix *vb* **1 syn** see SET 1
rel stabilize, steady; decide, determine, rule; specify
con change, modify, vary
ant alter; abrogate
2 syn see ENTRENCH 1
rel inculcate, instill
con overthrow, overturn, subvert, upset
3 syn see FASTEN 1
4 syn see FASTEN 2
con dislodge, displace
5 syn see FASTEN 3
6 syn see PREPARE 1
7 syn see MEND 2
8 syn see ADJUST 2
rel mend, patch, rebuild, repair; amend, emend, revise
con disorganize, unsettle
9 syn see SOLVE 1
10 syn see STERILIZE
11 syn see BRIBE

fix *n* **syn** see PREDICAMENT
fixate *vb* **syn** see FASTEN 3
fixation *n* **syn** see FETISH 2
rel craze, fascination, infatuation
idiom bee in one's bonnet
fixed *adj* **1 syn** see FAST 4
2 syn see IMMOVABLE 1
3 syn see DEFINITE 1
4 syn see INFLEXIBLE 3
5 syn see FIRM 4
con changing, variable, varying
6 syn see SURE 2
7 syn see WHOLE 5
con distracted, erratic, wandering
fixedly *adv* **syn** see HARD 7
rel stubbornly, tenaciously
fixture *n* **syn** see INSTITUTION
fix up *vb* **syn** see DRESS UP 1
fizz *vb* **syn** see HISS
fizzle *vb* **syn** see HISS
flabbergast *vb* **syn** see SURPRISE 2
rel overwhelm, shock
flabby *adj* **syn** see LIMP 1
rel soft, yielding; impotent, powerless; enervated, languid, listless, spiritless
con taut, tense, tight; strong, sturdy, tenacious, tough; gritty, plucky
ant firm
flaccid *adj* **syn** see LIMP 1
rel emasculated, enervated, unnerved; debilitated, enfeebled, sapped, weakened
con elastic, flexible, springy, supple; limber, lithe; energetic, lusty, nervous, vigorous
ant resilient
flag *n* a piece of fabric that is used as a symbol (as of a nation) or as a signaling device <we respect the *flag* of our fathers>
syn banderole, banner, bannerol, burgee, color, ensign, gonfalon, gonfanon, jack, oriflamme, pendant, pennant, pennon, standard, streamer
flag *vb* **syn** see SIGNAL
flag *vb* **1 syn** see FAIL 1
2 syn see DROOP 3
rel abate, ebb, wane
flagellate *vb* **syn** see WHIP 1
flagitious *adj* **syn** see VICIOUS 2
rel criminal, scandalous, sinful, wicked; disgraceful, shameful; flagrant, glaring, gross
con good, upstanding, virtuous
flagrant *adj* **syn** see EGREGIOUS
rel bold, conspicuous, obvious, striking; heinous; flagitious, wicked; disgraceful, scandalous, shameful, shocking
con hidden, inconspicuous, obscure; excusable, unimportant
flagrante delicto *adv* **syn** see RED-HANDED
flag-waver *n* **syn** see PATRIOTEER
flair *n* **syn** see GIFT 2
flak *n* **syn** see CRITICISM 2

---

syn synonym(s)   **rel** related word(s)
ant antonym(s)   **con** contrasted word(s)
idiom idiomatic equivalent(s)
‖ use limited; if in doubt, see a dictionary

flake (off) *vb syn* see SCALE 2

‖**flake out** *vb syn* see COLLAPSE 2

flam *n syn* see IMPOSTURE

flamboyant *adj* **1** *syn* see ORNATE
 2 *syn* see SHOWY

flame *n* **1** *syn* see SWEETHEART 1
 2 *syn* see GIRL FRIEND 2
 3 *syn* see BOYFRIEND 2

flame *vb syn* see BLAZE
 rel coruscate, glint; fire, ignite, kindle, light

flaming *adj* **1** *syn* see BURNING 1
 2 *syn* see IMPASSIONED

flammable *adj syn* see COMBUSTIBLE 1
 ant incombustible, nonflammable

flap *n syn* see COMMOTION 2

flapdoodle *n syn* see NONSENSE 2

flare *vb syn* see BLAZE
 rel dart, shoot; flicker, flutter
 idiom burst into flame
 ant gutter out

flare (up) *vb syn* see ANGER 2
 idiom ‖blow one's stack (*or* top *or* lid), fly into a passion, fly off the handle
 con calm (down), cool (off *or* down), simmer down

flare *n syn* see OUTBREAK 1

flare–up *n syn* see OUTBURST 1

flaring *adj syn* see BURNING 1

flash *vb* **1** to shoot forth light (as in rays or sparks) <lightning *flashed* in the sky>
 syn coruscate, glance, gleam, glimmer, glint, glisten, glitter, scintillate, shimmer, spangle, sparkle, twinkle
 rel dart, shoot; blare, blaze, burn, flame, flare, glare, glow, incandesce; blink, flicker, spark; dazzle; beam, radiate, shine
 2 *syn* see BLINK 2
 3 *syn* see SHOW 4

flash *n* **1** a sudden brief light <saw a *flash* sweep across the sky>
 syn coruscation, glance, gleam, glimmer, glint, glisten, glitter, quiver, scintillation, shimmer, sparkle, twinkle
 rel blare, blaze, flame, flare, glare, glow; flicker; beam, ray
 2 *syn* see INSTANT 1
 idiom half a second (*or* shake), twinkling of an eye

flashy *adj syn* see GAUDY
 rel flamboyant, florid, ornate; flashing, glittering, sparkling
 con dowdy, slatternly; natural, simple, unaffected; chic, modish, smart

flat *adj* **1** *syn* see LEVEL
 idiom flat as a billiard table (*or* pancake)
 con rugged, scabrous, uneven; hilly, mountainous
 2 *syn* see PRONE 4
 3 *syn* see DOWNRIGHT 2
 4 *syn* see COLORLESS 2
 5 *syn* see INSIPID 3
 rel dull, lifeless; flavorless, stale, tasteless
 6 *syn* see UNPALATABLE 1
 7 *syn* see POOR 1

 8 *syn* see DULL 7

flat *n syn* see APARTMENT 1

‖**flatfoot** *n syn* see POLICEMAN

flatly *adv syn* see EVENLY 3

flat–out *adj syn* see UTTER

flat–out *adv syn* see FAST 2

flatten *vb* **1** *syn* see EVEN 1
 2 *syn* see FELL 1

flatter *vb* to be becoming to <a neckline designed to *flatter* the stylishly stout>
 syn become, enhance, suit
 rel adorn, beautify, decorate, embellish, ornament; finish, perfect
 idiom put in the best light
 con deface, disfigure; distort; mar, spoil

flattery *n* flattering speech or attentions <*flattery* will get you nowhere>
 syn adulation, blandishment, blarney, incense, oil, soft soap
 rel compliments; laud, laudation, praise; cajolery, coaxing, wheedling; fulsomeness, unctuousness; bootlicking, fawning, ingratiation, obsequiousness, sycophancy, toadying, truckling
 idiom honeyed words
 con censure, condemnation, criticism, reprehension, reprobation; castigation, excoriation; aspersion, insult; contempt, disdain, scorn; belittling, depreciation, derogation, detraction, disparagement

flatulent *adj syn* see INFLATED
 rel empty, hollow, vain; shallow, superficial
 con weighty, cogent, compelling, convincing, telling; forceful, forcible, potent

flaunt *vb syn* see SHOW 4
 rel boast, brag, gasconade, vaunt; disclose, discover, divulge, reveal; advertise, broadcast, declare, proclaim, publish; flourish, wave
 idiom dangle before the (*or* one's) eyes
 con camouflage, cloak, disguise, dissemble, mask; bury, conceal, hide, screen, secrete

flavor *n syn* see TASTE 3

flavorless *adj syn* see UNPALATABLE 1
 ant flavorsome

flavorsome *adj syn* see PALATABLE
 con flat, insipid, vapid, wishy-washy; bland, mild; displeasing, tasteless, unflavored, unpalatable, unpleasant, unsavory
 ant flavorless

flaw *n syn* see BLEMISH
 rel cleavage, rent, rip, riving, split, tear

flawed *adj* **1** *syn* see DAMAGED
 ant flawless
 2 *syn* see FAULTY
 ant flawless

flawless *adj* **1** *syn* see WHOLE 1
 ant flawed
 2 *syn* see PERFECT 2
 3 *syn* see IMPECCABLE 1
 con defective, faulty, flawed, imperfect, unsound
 4 *syn* see IDEAL 3

flaxen *adj syn* see BLOND 1

flay *vb syn* see LAMBASTE 3
 rel assail, attack, berate, tongue-lash

fleckless *adj syn* see PERFECT 2

flection *n syn* see TURN 4

fledgling *n syn* see NOVICE

flee *vb* **1** *syn* see ESCAPE 1
rel avoid, elude, evade, shun
idiom take a (runout) powder
2 *syn* see RUN 2
con stand, stay

fleece *vb* **1** to obtain something valuable from by improper means <a corrupt mayor who *fleeced* the town treasury>
syn bleed, milk, mulct, rook, stick, sweat; *compare* CHEAT, EXTORT 1
rel cheat, cozen, defraud, do, hustle, ‖rope (in), swindle, take; pluck
idiom sell one a bill of goods, take for a sucker, take to the cleaner's
2 *syn* see OVERCHARGE 1

fleeceable *adj syn* see EASY 3

fleecy *adj syn* see HAIRY 1

fleer *vb* **1** *syn* see SNEER 1
2 *syn* see SCOFF
rel grin, smile, smirk
idiom cast in one's teeth, curl one's lip at, laugh one out of court

fleet *vb* **1** *syn* see WHILE
rel dally, fritter, idle, potter, squander, waste
2 *syn* see FLY 4
idiom go like the wind (or lightning), make (good) time
3 *syn* see HURRY 2

fleet *adj syn* see FAST 3
rel agile, brisk, nimble, spry; alert, animated, lively, spirited, sprightly, vivacious

fleeting *adj syn* see TRANSIENT
con abiding, enduring, persistent
ant lasting

fleetly *adv syn* see FAST 2

flesh *n syn* see MANKIND

fleshiness *n syn* see OBESITY

fleshliness *n syn* see ANIMALITY

fleshly *adj* **1** *syn* see BODILY
2 *syn* see CARNAL 2
rel epicurean, luxurious, sensuous, sybaritic, voluptuous; lay, profane, secular, temporal
con divine, religious, spiritual; intellectual, mental, psychic

fleshy *adj syn* see FAT 2
ant emaciated

flexible *adj syn* see ELASTIC 1
rel amenable, docile, manageable, tractable; acquiescent, compliant
con brittle, crisp, fragile, frangible; firm, hard, rigid, stiff, unyielding, wooden; intractable, recalcitrant, refractory, ungovernable; callous, hardened, indurated
ant inflexible

flexuous *adj syn* see WINDING

flexure *n syn* see TURN 4

flibbertigibbet *n syn* see SCATTERBRAIN

flick *n syn* see MOVIE

flicker *vb* **1** *syn* see FLIT 2
2 *syn* see BLINK 2
rel fluctuate, oscillate, swing, vibrate, waver; blaze, flame, flare, glare; coruscate, glance, gleam, glint, glitter, sparkle; quaver, quiver, tremble

flier *n syn* see PILOT 2

flight *n syn* see ESCAPE 1

flightiness *n syn* see LIGHTNESS
rel capriciousness, fickleness, inconstancy, instability, mercurialness
con constancy, equableness, steadfastness
ant steadiness

flighty *adj syn* see GIDDY 1
rel changeable, inconstant, mercurial, unstable; buoyant, effervescent, volatile; gay, lively, sprightly; irresponsible
con constant, dependable, reliable, responsible, trustworthy; stable; sedate
ant steady

flimflam *n* **1** *syn* see IMPOSTURE
2 *syn* see NONSENSE 2

flimflam *vb* **1** *syn* see DUPE
2 *syn* see CHEAT

flimflammer *n syn* see SWINDLER

flimsy *adj* **1** *syn* see FILMY
2 *syn* see IMPLAUSIBLE
ant substantial
3 *syn* see DELICATE 5
4 *syn* see WEAK 1
ant sturdy
5 *syn* see LIMP 1

flinch *vb syn* see RECOIL
rel avoid, elude, escape, eschew, evade, shun; retire, withdraw; recede, retreat

fling *vb* **1** *syn* see RUSH 1
2 *syn* see THROW 1
con catch, grab, receive

fling *n* **1** a casual attempt <I'm willing to take a *fling* at almost any job>
syn crack, go, pop, shot, slap, stab, ‖stagger, try, whack, whirl
rel attempt, effort, essay, trial
con best, limit, maximum
ant utmost
2 *syn* see SPREE 1

flip (through) *vb syn* see BROWSE

flippancy *n syn* see LIGHTNESS
rel archness, pertness, sauciness; impishness, mischievousness, playfulness, roguishness, waggishness; cheekiness, cockiness, freshness
con earnestness, gravity, soberness, solemnity
ant seriousness

flirt *vb syn* see TRIFLE 1
rel disport, play, sport; caress, fondle, pet

flirt *n* a woman who trifles amorously <a charming girl but an outrageous *flirt*>
syn coquette, vamp

flit *vb* **1** *syn* see HURRY 2
2 to move briskly, irregularly, and usually intermittently <the hummingbird *flitted* from flower to flower>
syn dance, flicker, flitter, flutter, hover

---

syn synonym(s)   *rel* related word(s)
ant antonym(s)   *con* contrasted word(s)
idiom idiomatic equivalent(s)
‖ use limited; if in doubt, see a dictionary

rel dart, float, fly, scud, skim
3 *syn* see FLY 4
flitter *vb syn* see FLIT 2
rel quaver, quiver, teeter
float *vb* **1** *syn* see DRIFT 1
2 *syn* see HANG 3
3 *syn* see FLY 1
rel drift, waft
floater *n syn* see VAGABOND
flock *n* **1** *syn* see MULTITUDE 1
2 *syn* see DROVE 2
flog *vb syn* see WHIP 1
flood *n* **1** *syn* see FLOW
2 a great or overwhelming flow of or as if of water <a *flood* of messages>
syn cataclysm, cataract, deluge, flooding, inundation, niagara, overflow, pour, spate, torrent
rel current, flow, stream, tide; excess, superfluity, surplus; outgushing, outpouring
con dribble, drip, dropping
ant trickle
flood *vb* **1** *syn* see DELUGE 1
2 *syn* see DELUGE 3
flooding *n syn* see FLOOD 2
floor *vb syn* see FELL 1
floozy *n syn* see DOXY 1
‖**flop** *vb* **1** *syn* see RETIRE 4
2 *syn* see FAIL 4
con come off, go over, succeed
flop *n syn* see FAILURE 5
floppy *adj syn* see LIMP 1
florid *adj* **1** *syn* see RHETORICAL
2 *syn* see ORNATE
rel ostentatious, pretentious, showy
con bald, bare, barren; austere, unadorned
3 *syn* see RUDDY
ant pallid
florilegium *n syn* see ANTHOLOGY
floss *n syn* see DOWN
flotsam *n syn* see DRIFTWOOD
flounce *vb syn* see SASHAY
flounder *vb syn* see WALLOW 2
rel strive, struggle; labor, toil, travail
flourish *vb syn* see SUCCEED 3
rel bloom, blossom, flower; augment, increase, multiply; amplify, expand; develop, grow, wax
con shrivel, wither; contract, shrink; abate, ebb, subside, wane
ant languish
flourishing *adj* enjoying a vigorous growth <a *flourishing* economy>
syn booming, prospering, prosperous, roaring, robust, thrifty, thriving; *compare* SUCCESSFUL
rel vigorous; rampant, rank; exuberant, lush, luxuriant, profuse
idiom going strong, in full swing
con decadent, declining, deteriorating; failing; decreasing, dwindling
ant languishing
flout *vb syn* see SCOFF
rel disregard, slight; repudiate, spurn; insult; defy
idiom thumb one's nose at
con admire, esteem, regard, respect

ant revere
flow *vb* **1** *syn* see POUR 2
rel cascade, jet, spout, spurt; well; course, ripple, run
2 *syn* see SPRING 1
3 *syn* see TEEM
4 *syn* see DISCHARGE 5
flow *n* something suggestive of running water <she expressed herself in a *flow* of words>
syn current, drift, flood, flux, rush, spate, stream, tide
rel progression, sequence, series, succession; continuance, continuation, continuity
flower *n* **1** the often showy part of a seed plant that bears reproductive organs <children picking *flowers* in the meadow>
syn bloom, blossom, posy
rel bud, floret; shoot, spray
2 *syn* see BEST
3 *syn* see ARISTOCRACY
flower *vb syn* see BLOSSOM
flowering *n syn* see DEVELOPMENT
ant fading
flowery *adj syn* see RHETORICAL
rel diffuse, prolix, redundant, verbose, wordy
con compendious, concise, laconic, pithy, succinct, summary, terse
flowing *adj syn* see EASY 9
flub *vb syn* see BOTCH
fluctuant *adj* **1** *syn* see WEAK 2
2 *syn* see UNCERTAIN 1
flue *n syn* see DOWN
fluent *adj* **1** *syn* see VOCAL 3
rel loquacious, talkative; easy, effortless, facile, smooth; apt, prompt, quick, ready
con stammering, stuttering; tongue-tied; dumb; fettered, hampered, trammeled
2 *syn* see EASY 9
fluff *n* **1** *syn* see DOWN
2 *syn* see ERROR 2
fluff *vb syn* see BOTCH
fluid *adj syn* see CHANGEABLE 1
fluky *adj syn* see ACCIDENTAL
flummadiddle *n syn* see NONSENSE 2
flummox *vb syn* see FAIL 4
flurry *n syn* see STIR 1
rel confusion, excitement, turbulence, turmoil; haste, hurry
flurry *vb syn* see DISCOMPOSE 1
rel bewilder, distract, perplex; excite, galvanize, provoke, quicken, stimulate
flush *n* **1** *syn* see BLOOM 3
2 *syn* see BLOOM 2
flush *vb* **1** *syn* see BLUSH
2 *syn* see EVEN 1
flush *adj* **1** *syn* see RICH 1
2 *syn* see RUDDY
3 *syn* see LEVEL
flushed *adj syn* see RUDDY
fluster *vb* **1** *syn* see DISCOMPOSE 1
rel bewilder, confound, distract, mystify, nonplus, perplex, puzzle; addle, confuse, fuddle, muddle
ant steady

2 syn see CONFUSE 2

flutter *vb syn* see FLIT 2
  rel quaver, quiver, shake, tremble, wobble; beat, palpitate, pulsate, throb; fluctuate, oscillate, swing, vibrate; flap

flux *n* **1 syn** see DIARRHEA
  2 syn see FLOW

flux *vb syn* see LIQUEFY

fly *vb* **1** to pass lightly or quickly over or above a surface <clouds *flying* across the sky>
  syn dart, float, sail, scud, shoot, skim, skirr
  rel dance, flicker, flit, flitter, flutter, hover; arise, ascend, mount, rise, soar; glide, slide, slip
  2 syn see RUN 2
  rel hide; retreat, withdraw
  3 syn see ESCAPE 1
  4 to pass swiftly as if on wings <how time *flies* when we are happy>
  syn fleet, flit, sail, sweep, wing
  rel soar; hasten, hurry, speed; barrel, skim, whisk, whiz, zip; breeze, dart, dash, rush, tear
  idiom go like the wind (*or* lightning), outstrip the wind
  con dally, dawdle, dillydally, drift; lag, linger, loiter, trail; crawl, creep, poke
  ant drag
  5 syn see HURRY 2

fly–boy *n syn* see PILOT 2

fly–by–night *adj syn* see UNRELIABLE 1

flying colors *n pl syn* see SUCCESS

flyspeck *n syn* see POINT 11

foam *n* a mass of bubbles gathering in or on the surface of a liquid or something as insubstantial as such a mass <a *foam* of delicate lace at her throat>
  syn froth, lather, spume, suds, yeast

fob off *vb syn* see FOIST 3

focal point *n syn* see CENTER 2

focus *n syn* see CENTER 2
  idiom center of attraction (*or* interest), focus of attention

focus *vb* **1 syn** see FASTEN 3
  2 syn see CONVERGE
  idiom come to a focus

foe *n syn* see ENEMY
  con associate, companion, comrade
  ant friend

fog *n syn* see HAZE 2

fog *vb* **1 syn** see OBSCURE
  rel bewilder, distract, mystify, perplex, puzzle
  2 syn see CONFUSE 4
  rel addle, muddle

foggy *adj syn* see HAZY
  idiom in a fog

fogram *n syn* see FOGY

fogy *n* a person who is behind the times or over-conservative <his father is an old *fogy*>
  syn antediluvian, fogram, fossil, fuddy-duddy, mid-Victorian, moldy fig, mossback, square, stick-in-the-mud
  rel conservative, diehard; back number
  idiom regular old fogy
  ant modern

fogyish *adj syn* see CONSERVATIVE 1

  ant up-to-the-minute

foible *n syn* see FAULT 2
  rel imperfection, shortcoming

foil *vb syn* see FRUSTRATE 1
  rel discomfit, disconcert, embarrass, faze, rattle; curb, restrain

foist *vb* **1 syn** see INSINUATE 3
  2 syn see IMPOSE 4
  3 to pass or offer (something spurious) as genuine or worthy <his theory was far more reasonable than many *foisted* on the public>
  syn fob off, palm (on *or* upon), palm off, pass off, work off; *compare* IMPOSE 4
  rel beguile, deceive, delude, mislead; bamboozle, dupe, gull, hoax, hoodwink, trick; cheat, defraud, overreach, swindle; impose, inflict, wish

fold *n syn* see WRINKLE

fold *vb* **1 syn** see DOUBLE 2
  2 syn see FAIL 5

fold up *vb* **1 syn** see GIVE 12
  2 syn see RUIN 3

foliage *n* the leaves of plants <a tree with handsome *foliage*>
  syn leafage, umbrage, verdure
  rel greenness, herbage; growth, vegetation

folk *n* **1 syn** see FAMILY 1
  2 folks *pl syn* see FAMILY 2

folklore *n syn* see LORE 2

follow *vb* **1** to come after in time <a juggling act *followed* the singer>
  syn ensue, succeed, supervene
  rel displace, replace, supersede, supplant; postdate
  con herald, lead, preface, usher (in); antedate, predate
  ant precede
  2 to go after or on the track of <*followed* the boys to their hiding place>
  syn chase, chivy, pursue, trail; *compare* TAIL
  rel trace, track; hunt, search, seek; dog, hound, tag; accompany, attend, convoy; ape, copy, imitate; exercise, practice
  con guide, lead, pilot, steer; elude, escape, evade; abandon, desert
  ant precede; forsake
  3 syn see OBEY
  4 syn see APPREHEND 1

follower *n* one who attaches himself to another <he is a born *follower*>
  syn adherent, cohort, disciple, henchman, partisan, satellite, sectary, sectator, supporter
  rel addict, devotee, freak, habitué, votary; admirer, fan, fancier; advocate; bootlicker, hanger-on, lickspittle, parasite, sycophant, toady
  ant leader

following *adj syn* see NEXT

following *n* **1 syn** see ENTOURAGE
  2 the body of persons who attach themselves to another especially as disciples, patrons, or ad-

---

syn synonym(s)   **rel** related word(s)
ant antonym(s)   **con** contrasted word(s)
idiom idiomatic equivalent(s)
‖ use limited; if in doubt, see a dictionary

mirers <he has a strong *following* in this country>
syn audience, clientage, clientele, public
following *prep syn* see AFTER 2
folly *n syn* see FOOLISHNESS
  rel fatuity, stupidity
  ant wisdom
foment *vb syn* see INCITE
  rel goad, spur; cultivate, foster, nurse, nurture
  con repress, suppress
  ant quell
fomenter *n syn* see INSTIGATOR
fond *adj* **1** *syn* see OPTIMISTIC
  2 *syn* see LOVING
  rel responsive, romantic, sentimental, sympathetic, tender, warm; indulgent
  idiom silly over
fondle *vb syn* see CARESS
  rel clasp, embrace, hug; nestle, snuggle
fondness *n* **1** *syn* see LOVE 1
  2 *syn* see APPETITE 3
  rel partiality, predilection; relish
  con disgust; hate
font name *n syn* see GIVEN NAME
food *n* **1** things that are edible <conserve a nation's supply of *food*>
  syn bread, ‖chow, comestibles, ‖eats, edibles, feed, foodstuff, grub, meat, ‖muckamuck, nurture, provender, provisions, scoff, ‖tuck, viands, victuals, vivres
  2 material which feeds and supports the mind or spirit <*food* for thought>
  syn aliment, nourishment, nutriment, pabulum, pap, sustenance
foodstuff *n syn* see FOOD 1
foofaraw *n syn* see COMMOTION 3
fool *n* **1** a person lacking in judgment or prudence <stop acting like a *fool*>
  syn ass, asshead, donkey, doodle, idiot, imbecile, jackass, jerk, madman, mooncalf, nincom, nincompoop, ninny, ninnyhammer, poop, ‖schmo, ‖schmuck, tomfool
  rel blockhead, dimwit, dope, dumbbell, dummy, nitwit, numskull, pinhead; birdbrain, featherbrain, featherhead, rattlebrain, scatterbrain; goose, silly
  2 a retainer formerly kept to provide casual entertainment <a king's *fool*>
  syn idiot, jester, motley
  rel buffoon, clown, comedian, comic, merry=andrew
  3 one who is victimized or made to appear foolish <she's nobody's *fool*>
  syn butt, chump, ‖come-on, ‖cull, dupe, easy mark, fall guy, fish, gudgeon, gull, mark, monkey, ‖mug, patsy, pigeon, sap, saphead, ‖schlemiel, simple, sucker, victim
  rel pushover; laughingstock; loser; instrument, tool
  4 one who is mentally deficient <a badly retarded child, little more than a *fool*>
  syn ament, cretin, ‖feeb, half-wit, idiot, imbecile, moron, natural, simpleton, softhead, underwit, zany

fool *vb* **1** *syn* see TRIFLE 1
  2 *syn* see MEDDLE
  3 *syn* see BANTER
  4 *syn* see DUPE
fool (around) *vb syn* see PHILANDER
fool (away) *vb syn* see WASTE 2
foolhardy *adj syn* see ADVENTUROUS
  rel headlong, impetuous, precipitate
  con calculating, cautious, circumspect; careful, prudent
  ant wary
fooling *n syn* see HORSEPLAY
foolish *adj* **1** *syn* see SIMPLE 3
  rel idiotic, imbecilic, moronic; daft, feebleminded, half-witted; half-cocked; irrational
  con bright, clever, intelligent, quick-witted
  ant smart
  2 felt to be ridiculous because not exhibiting good or conventional sense <a *foolish* investment>
  syn absurd, ‖balmy, cockamamie, crazy, daffy, ‖dilly, ‖dippy, donkeyish, dotty, fantastic, harebrained, idleheaded, insane, kooky, loony, loopy, lunatic, mad, nutty, ‖potty, preposterous, sappy, silly, tomfool, unearthly, wacky, zany
  rel laughable, ludicrous, ridiculous; half-baked, headless, jerky, nonsensical; offbeat, unacceptable, unconventional, unorthodox
  con judicious, sage, sapient; discreet, foresighted, prudent; canny, shrewd, slick
  ant sensible; wise
foolishness *n* the quality or state of being foolish <the *foolishness* of so many of her schemes>
  syn absurdity, craziness, dottiness, folly, inanity, insanity, lunacy, preposterousness, senselessness, silliness, witlessness
  rel imprudence, indiscretion, injudiciousness, insensibility, unwiseness; irrationality, unreasonableness; impracticality; absurdness, ludicrousness, ridiculousness; bull, bunk, nonsense
  con discretion, judiciousness, prudence, sensibility, wiseness; rationality, reasonableness; practicality; soundness; canniness, shrewdness
  ant sense, wisdom
foot *n syn* see BOTTOM 3
foot *vb syn* see ADD 2
foot (it) *vb* **1** *syn* see DANCE 1
  2 *syn* see WALK 1
footing *n* **1** *syn* see BASIS 1
  2 *syn* see STATUS 1
  3 *syn* see BASE 1
  4 *syn* see TERM 5
footlicker *n syn* see SYCOPHANT
footlights *n pl syn* see DRAMA
footprint *n* the mark or impression made by a foot <*footprints* in the sand>
  syn footstep, spoor, step, track, tract, vestige
  rel sign, trace; pug, pugmark
footslog *vb syn* see PLOD 1
footstep *n syn* see FOOTPRINT
footstone *n syn* see TOMBSTONE
foozle *vb syn* see BOTCH
fop *n* a man who is conspicuously fashionable or elegant in dress or appearance <felt contempt for the mincing overdressed *fop*>

syn Beau Brummel, blood, buck, coxcomb, dandy, dude, exquisite, gallant, lounge lizard, macaroni, petit-maître, popinjay
rel fashion plate, silk stocking; blade, cavalier, man-about-town, spark, sport, swell; ladies' man, lady-killer, masher
idiom man of the world

for *prep* **1** *syn* see TO 5
2 on the side of <I'm *for* Smith all the way>
syn in favor of, pro, with
con anti, contra
ant against
3 *syn* see AFTER 1

for *conj* *syn* see BECAUSE

forage *vb* *syn* see SCOUR 2

forager *n* *syn* see MARAUDER

foray *vb* **1** *syn* see INVADE 1
2 *syn* see RAID 1

foray *n* *syn* see INVASION

forbear *vb* **1** *syn* see FORGO
rel bridle, curb, inhibit, restrain; avoid, escape, evade, shun; cease, desist
2 *syn* see REFRAIN 1
rel bear, endure, suffer, tolerate

forbearance *n* **1** *syn* see PATIENCE
rel restraint, temperance; endurance
2 the quality of being forbearing <she is known for her *forbearance* with children>
syn clemency, indulgence, lenience, leniency, mercifulness, tolerance, toleration; *compare* MERCY
rel longanimity, long-suffering, patience; charity, grace, lenity, mercy
con firmness, inflexibility, rigidity, sternness, strictness; austerity, harshness, inexorability
ant vindictiveness

forbearing *adj* disinclined to be severe or rigorous <*forbearing* toward her husband's weaknesses>
syn charitable, clement, easy, indulgent, lenient, merciful, tolerant
rel gentle, mild; longanimous, long-suffering, patient; considerate, thoughtful
con grim, implacable, merciless, relentless; impatient, nervous, restive; firm, inflexible, rigid, stern, strict; austere, harsh
ant unrelenting

forbid *vb* to debar one from using, doing, or entering or something from being used, done, or entered <smoking is *forbidden* here> <security regulations *forbid* the entry of unauthorized persons>
syn ban, enjoin, inhibit, interdict, outlaw, prohibit, taboo
rel debar, exclude, rule out, shut out; estop, obviate, preclude, prevent; forestall; proscribe, veto; check, curb, halt, restrain, stop; bar, block, hinder, impede, obstruct
con allow, let, suffer; authorize, license; approve, endorse, sanction; command, order; abide, bear, endure, tolerate
ant permit; bid

forbiddance *n* *syn* see TABOO

forbidden *adj* not permitted or allowed <accepting bribes is *forbidden*>

syn banned, prohibited, verboten
ant permitted

force *n* **1** *syn* see POWER 4
rel pressure, strain, stress, tension; headway, impetus, momentum, speed, velocity; vigor
2 *syn* see POINT 3
3 forces *pl* *syn* see TROOP 2
4 the exercise of power in order to impose one's will on a person or to have one's will with a thing <move a huge boulder by main *force*>
syn coercion, compulsion, constraint, duress, violence
rel fierceness, intensity, vehemence; effort, exertions, pains, trouble
con compliance, submission, yielding; impotence, powerlessness, weakness
ant forcelessness

force *vb* **1** *syn* see RAPE
2 to cause a person or thing to yield to pressure <hunger *forced* him to steal the food>
syn coerce, compel, concuss, constrain, make, oblige, shotgun
rel drive, impel, move; command, enjoin, order; demand, exact, require; press, pressure, sandbag; cause, occasion
con blandish, cajole, coax, wheedle; get, induce, persuade, prevail; entice, inveigle, lure, seduce, tempt

force (on *or* upon) *vb* *syn* see INFLICT 2

||**force** *n* *syn* see WATERFALL

forced *adj* produced or kept up through effort <a *forced* laugh>
syn farfetched, labored, strained
rel coerced, compelled, constrained; artificial, factitious; unnatural; inflexible, rigid, stiff, wooden; exhausting, fatiguing
con easy, effortless, smooth; impulsive, instinctive, spontaneous; artless, natural, normal, unaffected, unsophisticated
ant unforced

forceful *adj* **1** *syn* see POWERFUL 2
rel compelling, constraining; manful, virile; cogent, telling
con decrepit, frail, infirm
ant feeble
2 *syn* see EMPHATIC

forcefully *adv* *syn* see HARD 1

forceless *adj* *syn* see WEAK 4

forcible *adj* *syn* see POWERFUL 2
rel intense, vehement, violent; aggressive, assertive, militant, self-assertive; coercive

forcibly *adv* *syn* see HARD 1

forcing bed *n* *syn* see BREEDING GROUND

forcing house *n* *syn* see BREEDING GROUND

fore *adv* *syn* see BEFORE 1

forebear *n* *syn* see ANCESTOR 1

forebode *vb* *syn* see AUGUR 2

foreboding *n* *syn* see APPREHENSION 3

---

syn synonym(s)   *rel* related word(s)
ant antonym(s)   *con* contrasted word(s)
idiom idiomatic equivalent(s)
|| use limited; if in doubt, see a dictionary

rel augury, foretoken, omen, portent, prognostic; forewarning, warning

forecast *vb syn* see FORETELL
rel conjecture, guess, surmise; conclude, gather, infer

forecast *n syn* see PREDICTION

forecaster *n syn* see PROPHET

foredestine *vb syn* see PREDESTINE 2

forefather *n syn* see ANCESTOR 1

forefeel *vb syn* see FORESEE

foregoer *n syn* see FORERUNNER 2

foregoing *adj syn* see PRECEDING
ant following

forehandedness *n syn* see ECONOMY

forehead *n* the part of the face above the eyes <his broad noble *forehead*>
syn brow, frons, front

foreign *adj* 1 *syn* see EXOTIC 1
ant native
2 *syn* see EXTRINSIC
rel incompatible, incongruous, inconsistent, inconsonant; distasteful, obnoxious, repellent, repugnant; accidental, adventitious
con applicable, apposite, apropos, material, pertinent, relevant; akin, alike, uniform
ant germane
3 *syn* see IRRELEVANT

foreigner *n syn* see STRANGER

foreknow *vb syn* see FORESEE
rel conclude, gather, infer

foreland *n syn* see PROMONTORY

foremost *adj* 1 *syn* see FIRST 1
2 *syn* see FIRST 3

forename *n syn* see GIVEN NAME

forenoon *n syn* see MORNING 2

forensic *n syn* see ARGUMENTATION

foreordain *vb* 1 *syn* see PREDESTINE 1
2 *syn* see PREDESTINE 2

forerun *vb* 1 *syn* see PRECEDE 2
2 *syn* see ANNOUNCE 2

forerunner *n* 1 one that goes before and in some way announces the coming of another <a coma is often a *forerunner* of death>
syn harbinger, herald, outrider, precursor
rel anticipator; advertiser, announcer; advertisement, announcement, augury, foretoken, omen, portent, presage, prognostic; forewarning, warning; mark, sign, symptom, token; foreshadow
2 one belonging to an early developmental period of something contemporary or fully developed <the water-driven dynamo that was a *forerunner* of present-day giant atomic power plants>
syn ancestor, antecedent, antecessor, foregoer, precursor, predecessor, prototype
rel example, exemplar, model, pattern; pioneer; author, initiator, originator
con consequence, result; effect, event, issue, outgrowth; conclusion, consummation, culmination
ant end product

foresee *vb* to know or expect in advance that something will happen or come into existence or

be made manifest <he had not *foreseen* his present problems>
syn anticipate, apprehend, divine, forefeel, foreknow, preknow, previse, prevision, see, visualize
rel forebode, forecast, foretell, predict, presage, prognosticate, prophesy; descry, discern, espy, perceive
idiom look for, look forward to

foreseer *n syn* see PROPHET

foreshadow *vb* 1 *syn* see ADUMBRATE 1
2 *syn* see AUGUR 2

foreshow *vb* 1 *syn* see AUGUR 2
2 *syn* see ANNOUNCE 2

foresight *n syn* see PRUDENCE
rel clairvoyance, discernment, perception
ant hindsight

forest *n* a heavily wooded area
syn timber, timberland, weald, wood(s), woodland
rel coppice, copse, grove, thicket; wildwood, woodlot
con field, meadow, plain, prairie

forestall *vb* 1 *syn* see PREVENT 2
con court, invite, woo; advance, forward, further, promote
2 *syn* see PREVENT 1

foretell *vb* to tell something before it happens through or as if through special knowledge or occult power <the prophet *foretold* the fall of the city>
syn adumbrate, augur, call, forecast, portend, predict, presage, prognosticate, prophesy, soothsay, vaticinate
rel anticipate, apprehend, divine, foreknow, foresee; announce, declare, proclaim; disclose, divulge, reveal; forewarn, warn; bode, forebode, foreshadow, foreshow, foretoken, promise; prefigure

foreteller *n syn* see PROPHET

foretelling *n syn* see PREDICTION

forethink *vb syn* see PREMEDITATE

forethought *n syn* see PRUDENCE 1
rel deliberation, premeditation; gumption, judgment, sense
ant rashness; impetuosity

foretime *n syn* see PAST

foretoken *n* something that serves as a sign of future happenings <they felt that her new job was a *foretoken* of good fortune>
syn augury, bodement, boding, omen, portent, presage, prognostic
rel badge, indication, mark, note, sign, symptom, token; forerunner, harbinger, herald, precursor; forewarning, shadow, warning; intimation, promise; ostent; hint, inkling, suggestion

foretoken *vb syn* see AUGUR 2

forever *adv syn* see EVER 2

forevermore *adv syn* see EVER 2

forewarn *vb syn* see WARN 1

forewarning *n syn* see WARNING

foreword *n syn* see INTRODUCTION

forfeit *n syn* see FINE

forfeit *vb syn* see LOSE 1

forfend *vb syn* see PREVENT 2

forgather *vb syn* see GATHER 6

forge *vb syn* see MAKE 3
rel beat, pound, turn out; copy, imitate

forget *vb* **1** to lose the remembrance of <I soon *forgot* his name>
syn disremember, ‖misremember, unknow
rel misrecollect; blow up, fluff; unlearn
idiom clean forget, draw a blank
con recall, recollect
ant remember
2 *syn* see NEGLECT
con bethink, mind, recall, recollect
ant remember

forgetful *adj* tending to lose or let go from one's mind something once known or learned <she is growing *forgetful*>
syn oblivious, unmindful, unwitting
rel lax, neglectful, negligent, remiss, slack; careless, heedless, thoughtless; absent, absent-minded, abstracted, bemused
con alert, alive, awake, aware, cognizant, conscious, sensible; attentive, considerate, thoughtful

forgetfulness *n syn* see OBLIVION

forgivable *adj syn* see VENIAL

forgive *vb syn* see EXCUSE 1
idiom forgive and forget

forgo *vb* to deny oneself something for the sake of an end <he vowed to *forgo* all luxuries until the debt was paid>
syn eschew, forbear, sacrifice
rel abandon, relinquish, surrender, waive; abdicate, renounce, resign; forsake, give up

fork (out) *vb syn* see SPEND 1

forlorn *adj* **1** dejected and saddened especially by reason of being alone <a *forlorn* lost child>
syn lonely, lonesome, lorn
rel abandoned, deserted, desolate, forgotten, forsaken; miserable, wretched; friendless, homeless; defenseless, helpless; depressed, oppressed, weighed down; alone, solitary
2 *syn* see DESPONDENT
rel cynical, pessimistic; fruitless, futile, vain
con hopeful, optimistic, roseate, rose-colored

form *n* **1** outward appearance of something as distinguished from the substance of which it is made <the carefully graded *form* of the curves>
syn cast, configuration, conformation, figure, shape
rel contour, outline, profile, silhouette; anatomy, framework, skeleton, structure; economy, organism, scheme, system
2 conduct regulated by an external control (as custom or a formal protocol of procedure) <observing the *forms* of polite society>
syn ceremonial, ceremony, formality, liturgy, rite, ritual
rel procedure, proceeding, process; custom, habit, practice, usage; canon, law, precept, regulation, rule; method, mode; decorum, etiquette, propriety
3 a fixed or accepted way of doing or sometimes of expressing something <good *form* in swimming>

syn convenance, convention, usage
rel fashion, manner, mode, style, way

form *vb* **1** *syn* see MAKE 3
rel devise; create, invent; turn out; design, plan, plot, project, scheme; establish, found, organize
con demolish, destroy, ruin, wreck
2 *syn* see DEVELOP 4
3 *syn* see CONSTITUTE 1

formal *adj* **1** *syn* see CEREMONIAL
rel methodical, orderly, regular, systematic; decorous, proper, seemly; prim, unbending; distant, reserved
ant informal
2 *syn* see NOMINAL

formality *n* **1** *syn* see FORM 2
rel convenance, convention
ant informality
2 *syn* see RITE 2

formation *n syn* see MAKEUP 1

former *adj* **1** *syn* see PRECEDING
con following, succeeding, supervening
ant latter
2 having been such at some previous time <*former* friends>
syn bygone, erstwhile, late, old, once, onetime, past, quondam, sometime, whilom
con current, present; future, prospective

formerly *adv syn* see BEFORE 2

formidable *adj* **1** *syn* see FEARFUL 3
ant comforting
2 *syn* see HARD 6
ant simple

formless *adj* having no definite or recognizable form <a *formless* fear>
syn amorphous, inchoate, shapeless, unformed, unshaped
rel chaotic, orderless, unordered, unorganized; indistinct, obscure, unclear, vague; indefinite, indeterminate, undefined; crude, raw, rough, rude
con distinct, formed; definite, explicit, express, specific; ordered, organized

formulate *vb* **1** *syn* see WORD
2 *syn* see CONTRIVE 2
3 *syn* see DRAFT 3

‖**fornent** *prep syn* see BESIDE 1

for real *adv syn* see SERIOUSLY 1

forsake *vb syn* see ABANDON 1
rel spurn; leave; abdicate, resign
ant return (to), revert (to)

forsaken *adj syn* see DERELICT 1

forswear *vb* **1** *syn* see ABJURE
2 *syn* see PERJURE

fort *n* a structure or place offering resistance to a hostile force <settlers fled to the *fort*>
syn citadel, fastness, fortress, redoubt, stronghold

forte *n* that in which one excels <writing is her strongest *forte*>

---

syn synonym(s)   *rel* related word(s)
ant antonym(s)   *con* contrasted word(s)
idiom idiomatic equivalent(s)
‖ use limited; if in doubt, see a dictionary

syn eminency, long suit, medium, métier, oyster, strong suit

rel ableness, effectiveness, efficiency; ability, competence; bag, thing

idiom cup of tea, dish of tea, strong point

con inadequacy, incapability, incompetence, inefficiency; greenness, rawness

forth *adv* **1** *syn* see AHEAD 2

2 *syn* see ALONG 1

forthcome *vb* *syn* see LOOM 2

forthcoming *adj* being soon to appear or take place <the *forthcoming* holidays>

syn approaching, coming, nearing, oncoming, upcoming

rel future; imminent, impending, pending; anticipated, awaited, expected

con distant, far-off, remote; bygone, former, gone, gone-by, past

forthright *adj* **1** *syn* see STRAIGHTFORWARD 2

con covert, secret, stealthy, surreptitious, underhand; deceitful, mendacious, untruthful

ant furtive

2 *syn* see FRANK

forthwith *adv* **1** *syn* see AWAY 3

2 *syn* see SHORT 1

fortify *vb* **1** *syn* see STRENGTHEN 2

rel arouse, rally, rouse, stir; refresh, renew, restore

con dilute, thin

ant enfeeble

2 *syn* see GIRD 3

fortitude *n* a quality of character combining courage and staying power <she bore up under all her problems with admirable *fortitude*>

syn backbone, grit, guts, intestinal fortitude, ‖moxie, nerve, sand, spunk; *compare* COURAGE

rel courage, mettle, pith, resoluteness, resolution, spirit, stick-to-itiveness, tenacity; boldness, bravery, courageousness, dauntlessness, fearlessness, intrepidity, valiancy, valor, valorousness; endurance, stamina, strength; constancy, determination, perseverance; bottom

con cowardliness, fearfulness, timidity, timorousness; faintheartedness, milksoppiness, weakness; cowardice, yellowness

ant pusillanimity

fortress *n* *syn* see FORT

fortuitous *adj* *syn* see ACCIDENTAL

con activated, actuated, motivated; projected, schemed

ant deliberate

fortuitously *adv* *syn* see INCIDENTALLY 1

ant deliberately

fortuity *n* *syn* see ACCIDENT 1

ant deliberation

fortunate *adj* **1** *syn* see FAVORABLE 5

ant disastrous

2 *syn* see LUCKY

ant unfortunate

fortunately *adv* *syn* see WELL 5

fortunateness *n* *syn* see LUCK 3

ant unfortunateness

fortune *n* **1** *syn* see CHANCE 2

rel destiny, doom, portion

con design, intent, intention

2 *syn* see LUCK 3

ant misfortune

3 *syn* see WEALTH 2

4 a very large amount of money <those furs must have cost a *fortune*>

syn ‖bomb, boodle, bundle, mint, packet, pile, pot, ‖roll, wad

idiom king's ransom, pretty penny, tidy sum

fortuneless *adj* *syn* see POOR 1

forty winks *n pl but sing or pl in constr* *syn* see NAP

forward *adj* **1** *syn* see PRESUMPTUOUS

2 *syn* see WISE 5

ant bashful

3 *syn* see PRECOCIOUS

con regressive, retrograde, retrogressive

ant backward

forward *adv* **1** *syn* see BEFORE 1

2 *syn* see AHEAD 2

ant backward

3 *syn* see ALONG 1

forward *vb* **1** *syn* see ADVANCE 1

rel back, champion, support, uphold

con baffle, circumvent, foil, frustrate, outwit, thwart

ant balk

2 *syn* see SEND 1

fossil *n* *syn* see FOGY

foster *vb* **1** *syn* see NURSE 2

rel back, champion, support, uphold; entertain, harbor, house, lodge, shelter; accommodate, assist, favor, help, oblige

con combat, fight, oppose, resist, withstand; curb, inhibit, restrain; ban, forbid, interdict, prohibit; abuse, disregard, neglect

2 *syn* see ADVANCE 1

foul *adj* **1** *syn* see OFFENSIVE

2 *syn* see DIRTY 1

rel fetid, malodorous, noisome, putrid, stinking; loathsome, offensive, repulsive, revolting

ant fair; undefiled

3 *syn* see OBSCENE 2

foul *vb* **1** *syn* see SOIL 2

rel contaminate, defile, pollute; desecrate, profane

2 *syn* see CONTAMINATE 2

foul play *n* *syn* see MURDER

foul up *vb* *syn* see CONFUSE 5

found *vb* **1** *syn* see BASE

rel support, sustain; erect, raise, rear

2 to set going or to bring into existence <*founded* a new school for graduate studies>

syn constitute, create, establish, institute, organize, set up, start

rel begin, commence, inaugurate, initiate; fashion, form

con close, conclude, end, finish, terminate; arrest, check, halt, stay, stop

foundation *n* **1** *syn* see BASIS 1

2 *syn* see BASIS 3

3 *syn* see BASE 1

foundational *adj* *syn* see FUNDAMENTAL 1

foundationless *adj* *syn* see BASELESS

founder *n* *syn* see FATHER 2

founder *vb syn* see SINK 1

fount *n syn* see SOURCE

fountain *n syn* see SOURCE

fountainhead *n syn* see SOURCE

four *n syn* see QUARTET

fourberie *n syn* see DECEPTION 1

four–flush *vb syn* see DECEIVE

foursome *n syn* see QUARTET

foursquare *adj syn* see SQUARE 1

fourth *n syn* see QUARTER 1

foxiness *n syn* see CUNNING 2

foxy *adj* **1** *syn* see SLY 2
  rel deceitful, dishonest
  con aboveboard, forthright, straightforward
  2 *syn* see BEAUTIFUL

foyer *n syn* see VESTIBULE

fracas *n* **1** *syn* see QUARREL
  2 *syn* see BRAWL 2

fractional *adj syn* see INCOMPLETE 1

fractious *adj* **1** *syn* see UNRULY 1
  ant orderly
  2 *syn* see IRRITABLE
  ant peaceable

fracturable *adj syn* see FRAGILE 1

fracture *n syn* see BREACH 3

fragile *adj* **1** easily broken <a *fragile* dish of the finest porcelain>
  syn breakable, delicate, fracturable, frail, frangible, shatterable, shattery
  rel brittle, crisp, crumbly, crunchy, friable, short
  con infrangible, unbreakable; elastic, flexible, resilient; stout, strong, sturdy, tenacious
  ant tough
  2 *syn* see WEAK 1
  ant durable

fragment *n* **1** *syn* see PARTICLE
  2 *syn* see END 4

fragment *vb syn* see SHATTER 1

fragmentary *adj syn* see INCOMPLETE 1

fragrance *n* a sweet or pleasant odor <the *fragrance* of flowers>
  syn aroma, balm, bouquet, incense, perfume, redolence, scent, spice
  rel odor, smell
  con fetidness, fetor, malodor, noisomeness, rancidness, rankness
  ant stench, stink

fragrant *adj syn* see SWEET 2
  rel delectable, delicious, delightful
  ant fetid

frail *adj* **1** *syn* see WEAK 1
  rel slender, slight, slim, tenuous, thin; petty, puny
  con hale, healthy, sound
  ant robust
  2 *syn* see FRAGILE 1
  con solid, substantial

frailty *n syn* see FAULT 2

frame *vb* **1** *syn* see CONTRIVE 2
  2 *syn* see DRAFT 3
  3 *syn* see MAKE 3

framework *n syn* see STRUCTURE 3

franchise *n syn* see SUFFRAGE

franchise *vb syn* see ENFRANCHISE

frangible *adj syn* see FRAGILE 1

frank *adj* marked by free, forthright, and sincere expression <a *frank* answer>
  syn candid, direct, forthright, man-to-man, open, openhearted, plain, plainspoken, single, single-eyed, single-hearted, single-minded, straightforward, unconcealed, undisguised, undissembled, undissembling, unmannered, unreserved, unvarnished; *compare* COMMUNICATIVE, STRAIGHTFORWARD 2
  rel ingenuous, naive, natural, simple, unsophisticated; bluff, blunt; heart-to-heart, sincere; honest, scrupulous, upright; dispassionate, fair, impartial, just, unbiased; barefaced, brazen, outspoken, uninhibited
  con reserved, reticent, secretive, silent, taciturn, uncommunicative; covert, furtive, secret, sneaking, underhand; deceitful, deceptive, dishonest, evasive, false, lying, mendacious, tricky, untruthful; insincere
  ant reticent

frank *n syn* see FRANKFURTER

frankfurter *n* a seasoned beef or beef and pork sausage <baked beans served with the obligatory *frankfurters*>
  syn dog, frank, hot dog, wiener, wienerwurst, ‖wienie

frantic *adj syn* see FURIOUS 2

frantically *adv syn* see HARD 2

fraternity *n syn* see ASSOCIATION 2

fraud *n* **1** *syn* see DECEPTION 1
  2 *syn* see IMPOSTURE
  rel bamboozlement, bamboozling, dupery, duping, hoodwinking
  3 *syn* see IMPOSTOR

fray *n* **1** *syn* see BRAWL 2
  rel contention, discord, dissension, strife
  2 *syn* see CLASH 2

frayed *adj syn* see RAGGED

frazzle *vb syn* see EXHAUST 4

frazzled *adj syn* see RAGGED

freak *n* **1** *syn* see CAPRICE
  2 one that is physically abnormal <pitiful *freaks* displayed in sideshows>
  syn abortion, lusus, miscreation, monster, monstrosity
  rel aberration, chimera, malconformation, malformation, misshape, mosaic, mutation, sport; abnormality, anomaly, curiosity, oddity; rara avis, rarity; androgyne, hermaphrodite
  idiom freak of nature
  3 *syn* see ENTHUSIAST

freakish *adj syn* see ARBITRARY 1

freckle *vb syn* see SPECKLE 1

free *adj* **1** not subject to the rule or control of another <a *free* country>
  syn autarchic, autarkic, autonomous, independent, separate, sovereign

---

syn synonym(s)	*rel* related word(s)
ant antonym(s)	*con* contrasted word(s)
idiom idiomatic equivalent(s)	
‖ use limited; if in doubt, see a dictionary	

rel free-born, unenslaved; delivered, emancipated, enfranchised, freed, liberated, released; democratic, self-directing, self-governing, self-ruling; sui juris; individualistic, unregimented
con coerced, compelled, constrained, forced, obliged; dependent, restricted, subject; inferior, subordinate, subservient; captive, enslaved, enthralled, subjugated
ant bond
2 not bound, confined, or detained by force <the prisoner was now *free*>
syn loose, unconfined, unrestrained
rel unbound, unchained, unfettered, unshackled, untied; clear, loose, scot-free; emancipated, freed, liberated; independent
idiom at liberty, free as a bird, free as air, free to come and go
con confined, restrained; impounded, imprisoned, incarcerated, interned, jailed; bound, chained, fettered, shackled, tied
3 *syn* see LIBERAL 1
ant close
4 *syn* see OUTSPOKEN
5 not costing or charging anything <a *free* public school>
syn chargeless, complimentary, costless, gratis, gratuitous
rel unpaid, unrecompensed, unremunerated
idiom for free, for love, for nothing, on the cuff, on the house
con charged, paid; costly, dear, expensive, high, high priced
6 not having the affections fixed on a particular object <she was happy to be *free* and in no hurry to fall in love again>
syn fancy-free, heart-whole
free *vb* to relieve from constraint or restraint <*free* an oppressed people>
syn discharge, disenthrall, disimprison, emancipate, liberate, loose, loosen, manumit, redeem, release, ‖spring, unbind, unchain, unshackle
rel clear, detach, disencumber, disengage, disentangle, extricate; deliver, ransom, redeem, rescue; affranchise, enfranchise
idiom cut loose
con fetter, hamper, hog-tie, manacle, shackle, trammel; immure, imprison, incarcerate, intern, jail; circumscribe, confine, limit, restrict; curb, inhibit, restrain; enslave, enthrall, subjugate
freebooter *n* **1** *syn* see MARAUDER
2 *syn* see PIRATE
freedom *n* the power or condition of acting without compulsion <*freedom* of the press>
syn liberty, license
rel exemption, immunity; prerogative, privilege, right; compass, latitude, scope, sweep
con coercion, compulsion, constraint; restraint
ant necessity
free-for-all *n* *syn* see BRAWL 2
free hand *n* *syn* see CARTE BLANCHE
freehanded *adj* *syn* see LIBERAL 1
freeloader *n* *syn* see PARASITE
freely *adv* EASILY 1, effortlessly, facilely, lightly, readily, smoothly, well

free–minded *adj* *syn* see HAPPY-GO-LUCKY
free–spoken *adj* *syn* see OUTSPOKEN
freezer *n* *syn* see JAIL
freezing *adj* *syn* see COLD 1
ant scorching
freight *n* *syn* see LOAD 1
frenetic *adj* *syn* see FURIOUS 2
frenzied *adj* *syn* see FURIOUS 2
frenziedly *adv* *syn* see HARD 2
frenzy *n* *syn* see DELIRIUM
frenzy *vb* *syn* see MADDEN 1
frequent *adj* *syn* see COMMON 4
ant infrequent, rare
frequent *vb* to go to or be in often <he *frequents* the bar down the street>
syn affect, hang around, hang out, haunt, resort
rel attend, go (to), visit; infest, overrun
con avoid, miss, sidestep
ant shun
frequenter *n* *syn* see HABITUÉ 1
frequently *adv* **1** *syn* see OFTEN
ant infrequently
2 *syn* see USUALLY 2
fresh *adj* **1** *syn* see NEW 1
rel gleaming, glistening, sparkling; striking, vital, vivid; virginal, youthful; crude, green, raw, uncouth; artless, naive, natural, unsophisticated
con hackneyed, shopworn, stereotyped, threadbare, trite
ant stale
2 *syn* see ADDITIONAL
3 *syn* see INEXPERIENCED
4 *syn* see WISE 5
freshman *n* *syn* see NOVICE
freshness *n* *syn* see INEXPERIENCE
fret *vb* **1** *syn* see WORRY 3
rel chafe, fume; brood, mope
idiom eat one's heart out
2 *syn* see ANNOY 1
3 *syn* see CHAFE 3
4 *syn* see RIPPLE
fretful *adj* **1** *syn* see IRRITABLE
rel captious, carping, caviling, critical, fault-finding; contrary, perverse
con forbearing, long-suffering, patient, resigned; subdued, submissive, tame
2 *syn* see IMPATIENT 1
friable *adj* *syn* see SHORT 6
fribble *adj* *syn* see GIDDY 1
fribbling *adj* *syn* see GIDDY 1
fried *adj* *syn* see INTOXICATED 1
friend *n* a person with whom one is on good and, usually, familiar terms <he is one of my closest *friends*>
syn acquaintance, amigo, cater-cousin, confidant, familiar, intimate, mate; *compare* ASSOCIATE 3
rel alter ego, best friend, bosom friend; ally, colleague, partner; nodding acquaintance
con enemy; adversary, antagonist, opponent; competitor, rival
ant foe
friendliness *n* *syn* see GOODWILL 1
rel affability, amiability, congeniality, cordiality, neighborliness, sociability

ant unfriendliness

friendly *adj* **1** *syn* see AMICABLE 1
rel close, familiar, intimate; affectionate, devoted, loving
ant unfriendly; belligerent
2 *syn* see HARMONIOUS 3
3 *syn* see SYMPATHETIC 2
ant unfriendly

friendship *n* *syn* see GOODWILL 1
rel affinity, attraction; empathy; accord, concord, consonance, harmony; alliance, coalition, federation, fusion, league
con antagonism, antipathy, hostility, rancor; hate
ant animosity

fright *n* **1** *syn* see FEAR 1
2 *syn* see EYESORE

fright *vb* *syn* see FRIGHTEN

frighten *vb* to strike or to fill with fear or dread <the puppy was *frightened* by the unfamiliar noises>
syn affright, alarm, awe, fright, scare, ‖spook, startle, terrify, terrorize
rel appall, astound, daunt, disconcert, dismay, faze, horrify, shock; demoralize, unman, unnerve; browbeat, bulldoze, cow, intimidate; agitate, discompose, disquiet, perturb, upset
idiom curdle the blood, curl the hair, freeze the blood, frighten one out of one's wits, give one a scare, give one a turn, make one's blood run cold, make one's flesh creep, make one's hair stand on end, make one's teeth chatter, make one tremble, put one's heart in one's mouth, scare hell out of, scare one spitless, scare one stiff, scare the life out of, scare the pants off of, scare to death, strike terror into, take one's breath away
con embolden, encourage, hearten, reassure

frightened *adj* *syn* see AFRAID 1
idiom in a fright
ant unfrightened

frightful *adj* *syn* see FEARFUL 3

frigid *adj* **1** *syn* see COLD 1
2 *syn* see COLD 2
3 free from or deficient in passion <claimed his wife was a *frigid* woman>
syn cold, inhibited, passionless, undersexed, unresponsive
idiom as cold as an iceberg
con affectionate, demanding, loving
ant ardent; amorous

frill *n* *syn* see LUXURY
fringe *n* *syn* see BORDER 1
fringe *vb* *syn* see BORDER 1
frippery *n* *syn* see FINERY
frisk *vb* **1** *syn* see GAMBOL
2 *syn* see SEARCH 2
frisky *adj* *syn* see PLAYFUL 1
fritter *vb* *syn* see WASTE 2
frivol away *vb* *syn* see WASTE 2
frivolity *n* *syn* see LIGHTNESS
rel coquetting, dallying, flirting, toying, trifling; fun, game, jest, play, sport
ant seriousness; staidness

frivolous *adj* *syn* see GIDDY 1
rel shallow, superficial, unprofound; gay, light, playful
ant serious

‖frogskin *n* *syn* see DOLLAR

frolic *vb* **1** *syn* see REVEL 1
2 *syn* see GAMBOL

frolic *n* *syn* see PRANK

frolicsome *adj* **1** *syn* see ANTIC 2
2 *syn* see PLAYFUL 1

from *prep* **1** *syn* see AFTER 1
2 in the face of <protect them *from* exploitation>
syn against

frondeur *n* *syn* see REBEL

frons *n* *syn* see FOREHEAD

front *n* **1** *syn* see FOREHEAD
2 *syn* see MASK 2
3 a person, group, or thing used to mask the identity or true character of a controlling agent <the export company was a *front* for illegal activities>
syn blind
rel disguise, facade, mask

front *vb* **1** *syn* see FACE 1
2 *syn* see FACE 3
3 *syn* see MEET 6
4 *syn* see ACCOST 2

frontier *n* **1** a region between two countries <lived on the *frontier* between Mexico and the U.S.>
syn border, borderland, march, marchland
2 a rural region that forms the margin of settled or developed territory <settlers found living on the *frontier* was a hard life>
syn backcountry, backland, ‖backveld, backwash, backwater, backwoods, ‖boondocks, ‖boonies, bush, hinterland, ‖outback, sticks, up≠country
idiom the back of beyond

frontier *adj* *syn* see BACK 1
fronting *prep* *syn* see AGAINST 1
front–rank *adj* *syn* see EXCELLENT
frore *adj* *syn* see COLD 1
frosty *adj* *syn* see COLD 1
froth *n* *syn* see FOAM
rel flippancy, frivolity, levity, lightness
froward *adj* *syn* see CONTRARY 3
frown *vb* **1** to put on a dark or malignant countenance or aspect <he *frowned* at the naughty child>
syn gloom, glower, lower, scowl
rel glare; grimace; pout, sulk
idiom look black, look daggers
con grin, laugh
ant smile
2 *syn* see DISAPPROVE 1

frowsy *adj* **1** *syn* see SLATTERNLY
rel lax, neglectful, negligent, remiss, slack
ant trim; smart

---

syn synonym(s)   *rel* related word(s)
ant antonym(s)   *con* contrasted word(s)
idiom idiomatic equivalent(s)
‖ use limited; if in doubt, see a dictionary

2 syn see MALODOROUS 1

frugal *adj syn* see SPARING
rel careful, meticulous; discreet, prudent; conserving, preserving; cheeseparing, penny-pinching, scrimping, stinting
ant wasteful

frugality *n syn* see ECONOMY

‖**fruit** *n syn* see HOMOSEXUAL

fruitage *n syn* see HARVEST 2

fruitful *adj syn* see FERTILE
rel breeding, propagating, reproducing; abounding
con abortive, bootless, futile, vain
ant unfruitful; fruitless

fruitfulness *n syn* see FERTILITY

fruition *n syn* see PLEASURE 2
rel actualization, materialization, realization; accomplishment, fulfillment; achievement, attainment

fruitless *adj syn* see FUTILE
rel barren, infertile, sterile, unfruitful; foiled, frustrated, thwarted; infructuous, unprofitable
con fecund, fertile, prolific
ant fruitful

‖**fruity** *adj syn* see INSANE 1

frumpish *adj syn* see TACKY 2

frumpy *adj syn* see TACKY 2

frustrate *vb* **1** to come between a person and his aim or desire or to defeat another's plan <my efforts are *frustrated* at every turn>
syn baffle, balk, beat, bilk, buffalo, circumvent, dash, disappoint, foil, ruin, thwart; *compare* OUTWIT
rel annul, cancel, counteract, negative, neutralize, nullify; anticipate, forestall; conquer, defeat, lick, overcome; forbid, inhibit, prohibit; obviate, preclude, prevent; bar, block, hinder, impede, obstruct; arrest, check, halt, interrupt
idiom cut the ground from under one, dash one's hope, defeat expectation, throw a monkey wrench into the works, upset one's applecart
con accomplish, achieve, bring about, effect, perform; advance, forward, further, promote; abet, foment, incite, instigate
ant fulfill

2 syn see NEUTRALIZE

frying pan *n* a pan with a handle used for frying food <some still prefer the sturdy cast-iron *frying pan*>
syn skillet, spider

fuddle *vb syn* see CONFUSE 2
ant clarify, clear

fuddler *n syn* see DRUNKARD

fuddy–duddy *n* **1 syn** see FOGY

2 syn see STUFFED SHIRT

3 syn see FUSSBUDGET

fudge *vb syn* see EMBROIDER

fudge *n syn* see NONSENSE 2

fugacious *adj syn* see TRANSIENT

fugitive *adj syn* see TRANSIENT

fugitive *n syn* see REFUGEE

fulfill *vb* **1** to do what is required by the terms of so as to make effective <found themselves unable to *fulfill* their contract>

syn complete, execute, implement, perform; *compare* EFFECT 2
rel effect, effectuate; discharge

2 syn see SATISFY 5

fulgent *adj syn* see BRIGHT 1

full *adj* **1** containing as much as is possible <the hamper is *full*>
syn awash, big, block and block, brimful, brimming, bung-full, chockablock, chock-full, cram≠full, crammed, crowded, jam-full, jammed, jam≠packed, loaded, packed, ‖packed out, replete, stuffed, ‖trig
rel abounding, teeming
idiom full to bursting (*or* overflowing), ready to burst
con blank, vacant, void; bare, barren
ant empty

2 syn see CIRCUMSTANTIAL
ant incomplete

3 syn see WHOLE 2
con denuded, dismantled, divested, stripped

4 syn see SATIATED

full–blooded *adj* **1 syn** see PUREBRED

2 syn see RUDDY

full–blown *adj* **1 syn** see MATURE 1

2 syn see TOTAL 5

full–bodied *adj syn* see STRONG 3

full–bosomed *adj syn* see BUXOM

full dress *n syn* see FINERY

full–dress *adj syn* see EXHAUSTIVE

full–fledged *adj syn* see MATURE 1

full–grown *adj syn* see MATURE 1

full–mouthed *adj syn* see LOUD 1

fullness *n syn* see BREADTH 2

full–out *adj syn* see TOTAL 5

full–scale *adj syn* see TOTAL 5

full tilt *adv syn* see FAST 2

fully *adv* **1 syn** see DOWN 2

2 syn see WELL 3

fulsome *adj* too obviously extravagant or ingratiating to be accepted as genuine or sincere <offering sickeningly *fulsome* praise>
syn oily, oleaginous, slick, smarmy, soapy, unctious, unctuous
rel canting, holier-than-thou, hypocritical, pecksniffian, pharisaical, sanctimonious; bland, glib, honey-mouthed, honey-tongued, ingratiating, mealy-mouthed, oily-tongued, smooth, smooth-tongued, suave; buttery, flattering, wheedling; excessive, extravagant, exuberant, lavish, profuse; cloying, satiating, sating; bombastic, grandiloquent, magniloquent
con earnest, genuine, heartfelt, hearty, sincere, true, truthful, unfeigned, wholehearted, whole≠souled

fumble *vb* **1 syn** see GROPE

2 syn see BOTCH
rel flounder, stumble

3 syn see MUMBLE

fume *n syn* see SNIT

fume *vb syn* see ANGER 2

fun *vb syn* see BANTER

fun *n* **1** action or speech intended to amuse or arouse laughter <you know he only said it in *fun*>

syn game, jest, joke, play, sport
rel amusement, diversion, entertainment, recreation; blitheness; jocundity, joviality, merriment; glee, hilarity, jollity, mirth; mischief, teasing
con soberness, thoughtfulness
ant earnestness, seriousness
2 *syn* see PLAY 1
function *n* 1 the acts or operations expected of a person or thing <fulfill one's *function* as a mother>
syn business, duty, office, province, role
rel affair, concern; job, task, work
2 *syn* see USE 4
3 *syn* see POWER 3
rel action, behavior, operation
function *vb* 1 *syn* see ACT 4
2 *syn* see ACT 5
3 to operate in the proper or expected manner <finally succeeded in getting the motor to *function*>
syn act, go, run, work
rel do, operate, perform
functional *adj syn* see PRACTICAL 2
functioning *adj syn* see ACTIVE 1
fund *n syn* see SUPPLY
fund *vb syn* see ENDOW 2
fundament *n syn* see BUTTOCKS
fundamental *adj* 1 forming or affecting the groundwork, roots, or lowest part of something <the *fundamental* rules of poetry>
syn basal, basic, bottom, foundational, meat-and-potatoes, primary, radical, underlying
rel primal, prime, primordial; elemental, elementary
con incidental
2 *syn* see ELEMENTAL 1
3 *syn* see ESSENTIAL 2
rel indispensable, necessary, needful, requisite; dominant, paramount
fundamental *n* 1 *syn* see PRINCIPLE 1
rel component, constituent, element, factor
2 *syn* see ESSENTIAL 1
3 *usu* **fundamentals** *pl syn* see ALPHABET 2
fundamentalist *n syn* see DIEHARD 1
fundamentally *adv syn* see ESSENTIALLY 1
ant superficially
funeral director *n syn* see MORTICIAN
funereal *adj syn* see GLOOMY 3
rel grave, solemn
con animated, gay, lively, sprightly, vivacious; blithe, jocund, jolly, jovial, merry
ant festive
fungible *adj syn* see INTERCHANGEABLE
funk *vb syn* see SMELL 3
funk *n syn* see COWARD
funker *n syn* see COWARD
funky *adj syn* see MALODOROUS 1
funnel *vb syn* see CONDUCT 4
funniness *n syn* see HUMOR 4
funny *adj syn* see LAUGHABLE
rel antic, bizarre, fantastic, grotesque
idiom too funny for words
con doleful, dolorous, lugubrious, melancholy, plaintive

ant unfunny
‖**funny farm** *n syn* see ASYLUM 3
funnyman *n syn* see HUMORIST 2
fur *n* 1 *syn* see HIDE
2 *syn* see DOWN
furbish *vb syn* see POLISH 1
furious *adj* 1 *syn* see WILD 6
2 marked by uncontrollable excitement often under the stress of a powerful emotion <in a state of *furious* activity>
syn corybantic, delirious, frantic, frenetic, frenzied, mad, rabid, wild
rel excited, provoked, stimulated; enthusiastic, fanatic; desperate, feverish, hasty, impetuous; fierce, intense, vehement, violent; excessive, extravagant, extreme, inordinate; enraged, incensed, infuriated, maddened; hysterical, irrational, unreasonable; bewildered, distracted, upset; crazed, demented, insane, mad, maniac
con calm, composed, peaceful, placid, quiet, serene, subdued, tranquil; apathetic, impassive, imperturbable, inexcitable
3 *syn* see INTENSE 1
furiously *adv syn* see HARD 2
furl *vb syn* see ROLL 3
furnish *vb* 1 to supply one with what is needed (as for daily living or a particular activity) <*furnished* him the papers for his application>
syn accouter, appoint, arm, equip, fit out, gear, outfit, rig, turn out
rel dower, endow, endue; apparel, array, clothe; mount; give, provide, supply
con denude, dismantle, divest, strip; despoil, spoliate; relieve (of), take away
2 *syn* see GIVE 3
furor *n syn* see DELIRIUM
furore *n* 1 *syn* see STIR 1
2 *syn* see FASHION 3
3 *syn* see COMMOTION 3
furrow *n syn* see WRINKLE
rel channel, groove, rut
further *adv* 1 *syn* see BEYOND 1
2 *syn* see AGAIN 4
further *adj syn* see ADDITIONAL
further *vb syn* see ADVANCE 1
rel engender, generate, propagate
con bar, block, impede, obstruct; forestall, prevent
ant hinder; retard
furthermore *adv syn* see ALSO 2
furthermost *adj syn* see EXTREME 5
furthest *adj syn* see EXTREME 5
furtive *adj* 1 *syn* see SECRET 1
rel artful, crafty, cunning, foxy, guileful, insidious, scheming, shifty, sly, sneaky, tricky, wily; calculating, cautious, circumspect, wary; cloaked, disguised, masked
con brash, impudent, presumptuous
ant forthright; barefaced, brazen

---

syn synonym(s)   *rel* related word(s)
ant antonym(s)   *con* contrasted word(s)
idiom idiomatic equivalent(s)
‖ use limited; if in doubt, see a dictionary

2 *syn* see STEALTHY 2
ant open
furtively *adv* *syn* see SECRETLY
ant openly
furuncle *n* *syn* see ABSCESS
fury *n* *syn* see ANGER
rel passion; furor; acerbity, acrimony, asperity
fuse *vb* **1** *syn* see LIQUEFY
2 *syn* see MIX 1
rel compact, consolidate, unify
fusillade *n* *syn* see BARRAGE
fusion *n* *syn* see MIXTURE
fuss *n* **1** *syn* see STIR 1
rel fluster, perturbation; bother, flap, stew; racket, rumpus; haste, hurry, speed
2 *syn* see COMMOTION 3
3 *syn* see QUARREL
fuss *vb* **1** *syn* see WORRY 3
idiom fret and fume
2 *syn* see COMPLAIN
3 *syn* see GRIPE
4 *syn* see NAG
fussbudget *n* one who becomes upset over trifles <he is the biggest *fussbudget* I know, always going into a tizzy over nothing>
syn fuddy-duddy, fusser, fusspot, granny, old lady, old maid
rel perfectionist, precisionist, stickler
fusser *n* *syn* see FUSSBUDGET
fusspot *n* *syn* see FUSSBUDGET
fussy *adj* **1** *syn* see BUSTLING

2 *syn* see CAREFUL 2
3 *syn* see NICE 1
rel fretful, irritable, querulous
fustian *n* *syn* see BOMBAST
fustian *adj* *syn* see FECKLESS 1
fusty *adj* **1** *syn* see MALODOROUS 1
rel close, moldy; dirty, filthy, squalid; disheveled, slipshod, sloppy, slovenly, unkempt
2 *syn* see OLD-FASHIONED

futile *adj* barren of results <efforts to convince him were *futile*>
syn abortive, bootless, fruitless, ineffective, ineffectual, unavailable, unavailing, unprevailing, unproductive, useless, vain
rel empty, hollow, idle, nugatory, otiose; inadequate, inefficacious, inefficient, insufficient; unsatisfactory, unsuccessful
idiom in vain, no dice, of no avail, to no effect
con effectual, efficacious, fruitful; advantageous, beneficial, profitable
ant effective

future *n* time that is to come <you must try to do better in the *future*>
syn aftertime, afterward, by-and-by, hereafter, offing, to-be; *compare* PRESENT
idiom time to come
ant past
fuzz *n* **1** *syn* see DOWN
‖**2** *syn* see POLICEMAN
fuzzy *adj* *syn* see FAINT 2

G

gab *vb syn* see CHAT 1

gab *n syn* see CHATTER

gabber *n syn* see CHATTERBOX

gabble *vb* **1** *syn* see GIBBER

  2 *syn* see BABBLE 2

  3 *syn* see CHAT 1

gabble *n syn* see CHATTER

gabby *adj syn* see TALKATIVE

gad *vb syn* see WANDER 1

gadget *n* **1** a usually small and often novel mechanical or electronic device or contrivance <a new kitchen *gadget* for separating egg whites>
  syn concern, gimmick, gizmo, jigger, widget; *compare* DEVICE 2, DOODAD, WHAT-DO-YOU-CALL-IT
  rel apparatus, appliance, contraption, tool, utensil
  2 *syn* see DOODAD

gaffe *n syn* see FAUX PAS

gaffer *n* a man of advanced years <doddering *gaffers* on the park benches>
  syn graybeard, patriarch; *compare* BELDAM 1, OLDSTER
  rel duffer, geezer, grandfather, old boy, veteran

gag *vb* **1** *syn* see RETCH
  2 *syn* see DEMUR

gag *n syn* see JOKE 1
  rel ruse, trick, wile

gaiety *n* **1** *syn* see MERRYMAKING
  2 *syn* see MIRTH
  rel cheerfulness, gladness, happiness; geniality, pleasantness, winsomeness; animation, conviviality, entertainment, exhilaration, liveliness, merrymaking, radiance, spiritedness, vivacity
  con blues, cheerlessness, dismalness, dreariness, gloom, grief, infelicity, joylessness, misery, moodiness, moroseness, pensiveness, solemnity, somberness, sorrow, sullenness, uncheerfulness, wistfulness, woe

gain *n syn* see PROFIT
  rel cut, rake-off, share, take, winnings; ice
  ant loss

gain *vb* **1** to arrive at a goal, point, or end <*gained* success in the theater>
  syn accomplish, achieve, attain, rack up, reach, realize, score, win
  rel complete, consummate, fulfill, perfect, produce; succeed
  con falter, flop, flounder, flunk, lose
  2 *syn* see IMPROVE 3
  rel invigorate, renew, strengthen; cure, heal, remedy
  3 *syn* see EARN 1
  4 *syn* see GET 1
  ant lose
  5 *syn* see CLEAR 6
  ant lose

gainful *adj syn* see ADVANTAGEOUS 1

rel fat, fruitful, generous, lush, productive, rich; satisfying, substantial

gainsay *vb syn* see DENY 4
  rel combat, fight, oppose, resist, withstand
  ant admit

gainsaying *n syn* see DENIAL 2
  ant admission; admitting

gait *n syn* see SPEED 2

gal *n* **1** *syn* see GIRL 1
  2 *syn* see GIRL FRIEND 1
  3 *syn* see WOMAN 1

gall *n syn* see EFFRONTERY
  rel arrogance, conceit, haughtiness, loftiness, lordliness, overbearance, pomposity, pride, priggishness, self-importance, smugness
  con bashfulness, humbleness, humility, lowliness, modesty, shyness
  ant meekness

gall *vb* **1** *syn* see ABRADE 1
  rel bark, burn, file, fray, frazzle, grate, graze, scrape, scratch, scuff, skin
  2 *syn* see CHAFE 3
  rel distress, pain; cut, score, wound
  3 *syn* see ANNOY 1
  4 *syn* see IRRITATE
  rel chide, disturb, harass, harry, torment, worry; bedevil, needle, trouble

gallant *n* **1** *syn* see FOP
  2 an individual who is amorously attracted to the opposite sex <his fiancee accused him of being a trifling *gallant*>
  syn amorist, Casanova, Don Juan, lothario, paramour, Romeo
  rel dirty old man, lecher, libertine, rake, satyr; admirer, adorer, beau, date, escort, lover, sparker, suitor, swain, wooer
  idiom gay blade

gallant *adj* **1** *syn* see COURTLY
  rel suave, urbane; attentive, considerate, thoughtful
  con heedless, inattentive, indifferent, thoughtless, unconcerned
  ant ungallant
  2 *syn* see BRAVE 1
  ant dastardly

gallantry *n* **1** *syn* see COURTESY 1
  rel deference, duty, homage, honor; reverence, suavity, urbanity; address, poise, savoir faire, tact
  con boorishness, churlishness, clownishness, loutishness; discourteousness
  ant discourtesy

---

syn synonym(s)   *rel* related word(s)

ant antonym(s)   *con* contrasted word(s)

idiom idiomatic equivalent(s)

‖ use limited; if in doubt, see a dictionary

2 *syn* see HEROISM
rel bravery, dauntlessness; mettle, resolution, spirit
ant dastardliness

gallery *n syn* see MUSEUM

galley slave *n syn* see SLAVE 2

gallimaufry *n syn* see MISCELLANY 1

galling *adj syn* see BITTER 2

gallivant *vb syn* see WANDER 1

‖**gallows** *n pl syn* see SUSPENDERS

‖**galluptious** *adj syn* see MARVELOUS 2

‖**galluses** *n pl syn* see SUSPENDERS

galoot *n syn* see MAN 3

galumph *vb syn* see LUMBER

galvanize *vb syn* see PROVOKE 4
rel activate, energize, vitalize

gambit *n syn* see TRICK 1
rel design, plan, plot

gamble *vb* **1** to engage in a game of chance for something of value <swore he would never *gamble* for high stakes again>
syn bet, game, lay, play, put (on), set, stake, wager
rel chance, hazard, lot, risk, speculate, venture
idiom buck the odds, take a flyer (on), try one's luck
2 to take a chance on something <*gambled* on the train being late>
syn chance, hazard, risk, venture; *compare* VENTURE 1
rel brave, challenge, dare, defy, face; endanger, imperil, jeopardize
idiom go it blind, take a chance (*or* one's chances), tempt fortune, trust to luck

gambol *vb* to leap or tumble about playfully <young lambs *gamboling* in the meadow>
syn caper, cavort, frisk, frolic, rollick, romp
rel lark, revel, roister; bound, leap, spring
idiom kick up one's heels, let off steam

game *n* **1** *syn* see FUN 1
con business, duty, labor, study, toil
2 games *pl syn* see ATHLETICS
3 animals under pursuit <hunting big *game* is a risky and expensive sport>
syn chase, prey, quarry
rel kill, ravin, victim

game *vb syn* see GAMBLE 1

game *adj syn* see BRAVE 1

game plan *n syn* see PLAN 1

gamesome *adj syn* see PLAYFUL 1

gamin *n syn* see URCHIN

gamine *n syn* see TOMBOY

gammer *n syn* see BELDAM 1

gamut *n syn* see RANGE 5

gamy *adj syn* see MALODOROUS 1

‖**gander** *n syn* see PEEP

gangling *adj* being tall, thin, and usually loose-jointed <a *gangling* high-school boy>
syn gangly, lanky, rangy, spindling, spindly
rel bony, gaunt, lank, lean, scrawny, skinny, spare, tall, thin
con low, low-set, low-statured, short, squat, stocky, sturdy, thickset

gangly *adj syn* see GANGLING

‖**gangrel** *n syn* see VAGABOND

gap *n* **1** an open space in a barrier <the sheep got through a *gap* in the fence>
syn breach, break, discontinuity, hole, opening
rel fracture, rupture; chink, cleavage, cleft, crack, crevice, fissure, slit, slot; division, interspace, interval, separation; aperture, cranny, orifice
2 *syn* see RAVINE
3 a period of discontinuity <a *gap* of an hour between speakers>
syn breach, break, hiatus, interim, interruption, interval, lacuna; *compare* PAUSE
rel caesura, intermission, lull, pause, respite, rest

gape *vb* **1** *syn* see GAZE 1
2 *syn* see LOOK 7
3 *syn* see YAWN

gaping *adj syn* see CAVERNOUS 1

garb *vb syn* see CLOTHE

garbage *n syn* see REFUSE
rel dregs, rubble; filth, sewage, slop

garble *vb syn* see MISREPRESENT
rel becloud, conceal, hide, obfuscate, obscure

garden house *n syn* see SUMMERHOUSE

gargantuan *adj syn* see HUGE
ant lilliputian

garish *adj syn* see GAUDY
rel overdone, overwrought
con dark, dim, dreary, dull, dusky, murky; quiet, unpretentious
ant somber

garland *n* **1** *syn* see WREATH
2 *syn* see ANTHOLOGY

garment *vb syn* see CLOTHE

garner *vb* **1** *syn* see REAP
2 *syn* see GLEAN
3 *syn* see ACCUMULATE
rel gather, glean, harvest, reap; hoard, store
con disseminate, spread

garnish *vb syn* see ADORN

garrulous *adj syn* see TALKATIVE
rel blabbing, prattling, prolix, verbose, windy, wordy
con concise; terse; blunt, brusque, curt
ant taciturn

‖**gas** *n syn* see NONSENSE 2

‖**gas** *vb syn* see CHAT 1

‖**gasbag** *n syn* see BRAGGART

gasconade *vb syn* see BOAST

gash *vb syn* see CUT 1
rel carve, split; injure, wound; furrow, mark, notch; lance, nip

gasp *vb syn* see PANT 1

‖**gasper** *n syn* see CIGARETTE

gastronome *n syn* see EPICURE
rel aesthete, connoisseur, dilettante

gastronomer *n syn* see EPICURE

gastronomist *n syn* see EPICURE

gate *n syn* see FAUCET

gather *vb* **1** *syn* see GROUP 1
rel choose, cull, pick, select; accumulate, amass
idiom separate the wheat from the chaff (*or* the sheep from the goats)

con dispel, disperse, dissipate
ant scatter
2 syn see REAP
rel cull, pick, pluck; heap, mass, pile, stack
3 syn see GLEAN
4 syn see INFER
rel catch, fathom, follow, grasp, take in
idiom put two and two together
5 syn see UNDERSTAND 3
6 to bring or come together <a crowd *gathered* to watch the fight>
syn assemble, collect, congregate, congress, forgather, muster, raise, rendezvous; *compare* GROUP 1
rel aggregate, troop; affiliate, ally, associate, league; encounter, meet
con break up, disband, disperse, part, separate; disintegrate, disorganize, dissolve
ant scatter
7 syn see LOOM 2
gathering *n* **1 syn** see CONCOURSE
2 a number of individuals come or brought together <a *gathering* in the town park>
syn aggregation, assemblage, assembly, collection, company, congeries, congregation, crowd, group, muster, ruck; *compare* GROUP 1
rel bunch, crew, crush, flock, gang, horde, mass, press, rout, swarm, turnout
3 syn see HARVEST 1
gauche *adj* **syn** see AWKWARD 2
rel crude, green, unpolished
con bland, smooth, suave, urbane
ant adroit
gaudy *adj* cheaply or vulgarly showy <*gaudy* sideshow posters>
syn blatant, brazen, chintzy, flashy, garish, glaring, loud, meretricious, tawdry, tinsel
rel obtrusive, ostentatious, pretentious, showy, tasteless; coarse, crude, gross, vulgar; brummagem, fake, phony, sham
con restrained, tasteful, unobtrusive; factual, illuminating, informative
ant quiet
gauge *n* **syn** see STANDARD 3
rel check, mark, model, norm, pattern, rule, type
gauge *vb* **syn** see MEASURE 2
‖**gaum** *n* **syn** see OAF 2
gaunt *adj* **1 syn** see LEAN
2 syn see EMACIATED
ant bloated
‖**gaup** (*or* **gawp**) *vb* **1 syn** see LOOK 7
2 syn see GAZE 1
gauzy *adj* **syn** see FILMY
gawk *vb* **syn** see GAZE 1
gawk *n* **syn** see OAF 2
gawky *adj* **syn** see CLUMSY 1
gay *adj* **1 syn** see MERRY
2 syn see LIVELY 1
rel frolicsome, playful, sportive
con earnest, sedate, serious, solemn, somber, staid; quiet, silent, still
ant grave, sober
3 syn see COLORFUL

4 syn see WILD 7
5 syn see HOMOSEXUAL
6 syn see PRESUMPTUOUS
gaze *vb* **1** to look long and usually attentively <*gazed* out the window>
syn bore, gape, ‖gaup (*or* gawp), gawk, glare, gloat, goggle, peer, stare; *compare* LOOK 7
rel look, see, watch; peek, peep; contemplate, inspect, observe, scrutinize, survey; admire, ogle, regard
con glance, skim, skip
2 syn see LOOK 7
gaze (upon) *vb* **syn** see EYE 1
gazebo *n* **syn** see SUMMERHOUSE
gear *n* **syn** see EQUIPMENT
rel accessories, adjuncts, appendages, appurtenances; belongings, effects, means, possessions
gear *vb* **syn** see FURNISH 1
‖**gee** *n* **syn** see MAN 3
‖**gee** *vb* **syn** see AGREE 4
Gehenna *n* **syn** see HELL
gel *vb* **syn** see COAGULATE
gelastic *adj* **syn** see LAUGHABLE
gelate *vb* **syn** see COAGULATE
gelatinize *vb* **syn** see COAGULATE
geld *vb* **syn** see STERILIZE
gelid *adj* **syn** see COLD 1
con ardent, burning, fervent, scorching, sweltering, torrid
ant fervid
‖**gelt** *n* **syn** see MONEY
gem *vb* **syn** see BEJEWEL
‖**gendarme** *n* **syn** see POLICEMAN
genealogy *n* an account often in chart form recording a line of ancestors <decided to prepare a *genealogy* of his family>
syn ‖begats, family tree, pedigree, stemma
general *adj* **1** conforming to what is expected in the ordinary course of events <the *general* problems of everyday life>
syn common, commonplace, matter-of-course, natural, normal, prevalent, regular, run-of-the-mill, typic, typical, usual
rel everyday, popular; familiar, universal; habitual, humdrum, routine, uneventful
con abnormal, extraordinary, irregular, novel, strange, unexpected, unforeseeable, unusual
2 belonging or relating to the whole <a *general* change in the weather>
syn common, generic, universal
rel natural, normal, regular, typical; broad, inclusive, wide
con individual, particular, special; characteristic, distinctive, peculiar
3 syn see ALL-AROUND 2
4 syn see PUBLIC 4
generally *adv* **1** in a reasonably inclusive manner <the forest was *generally* coniferous>

---

syn synonym(s)   *rel* related word(s)
ant antonym(s)   *con* contrasted word(s)
idiom idiomatic equivalent(s)
‖ use limited; if in doubt, see a dictionary

syn chiefly, largely, mainly, mostly, overall, predominantly, primarily, principally
rel about, approximately, practically, roughly, roundly
con altogether, totally, wholly
2 *syn* see ALTOGETHER 3
3 *syn* see USUALLY 2

generate *vb* **1** to bring into existence <*generate* new business>
syn create, father, hatch, make, originate, parent, procreate, produce, sire, spawn
rel bring about, effect, impose, occasion; introduce; cause; found, inaugurate, institute, set up; develop, induce, whip (up)
idiom bring to pass, give birth to, give rise to
con demolish, destroy, extinguish, ruin; degenerate, deteriorate, impair, worsen
2 *syn* see PROCREATE 1
3 to be the cause or source of something immaterial <actions that *generated* a good deal of suspicion>
syn breed, cause, engender, get up, hatch, induce, muster (up), occasion, produce, provoke, work up
rel accomplish, achieve, perform
idiom give birth to, give rise to

generator *n* *syn* see FATHER 2

generic *adj* *syn* see GENERAL 2
ant specific

generous *adj* **1** marked by a noble or forbearing spirit <*generous* toward the weakness of others>
syn benevolent, big, chivalrous, considerate, greathearted, lofty, magnanimous
rel altruistic, charitable, kindhearted, kindly, thoughtful, ungrudging, unselfish; fair, honest; long-suffering, tolerant; helpful, willing
con base, ignoble, mean, self-centered, selfish; grim, hard, harsh, intolerant
ant ungenerous
2 *syn* see LIBERAL 1
ant stingy
3 *syn* see PLENTIFUL
rel lavish; luxuriant; affluent, wealthy
con scant, scanty, sparse

generously *adv* *syn* see WELL 2

genesis *n* *syn* see BEGINNING
rel provenance, provenience
con cessation, conclusion, culmination, end, finish, termination

genial *adj* **1** *syn* see GRACIOUS 1
rel amicable, friendly, neighborly; blithe, cheerful, jocund, jolly, jovial, merry
con discourteous, rude, uncivil, ungracious; crabbed, morose, sullen; ironic, sarcastic, sardonic, satiric
ant caustic (*remarks, comments*); saturnine (*manner, disposition, aspect*)
2 *syn* see GENTLE 2

geniality *n* *syn* see AMENITY 1

genitalia *n pl* the external components of the reproductive system <nude bathers were reminded of the local ordinance prohibiting public exposure of the *genitalia*>

syn genitals, parts, private parts, privates, privities, privy parts, pudendum (*usu* pudenda *pl*), secrets

genitals *n pl* *syn* see GENITALIA

genius *n* *syn* see GIFT 2
rel creativity, ingenuity, inventiveness, originality; astuteness, brains, grasp, intellect, intelligence, understanding

gent *n* *syn* see MAN 3

genteel *adj* **1** having characteristics or qualities befitting the upper classes <in those days croquet was a very *genteel* sport> <his manner was perfectly *genteel*>
syn cultivated, cultured, distingué, polished, refined, urbane, well-bred
rel elegant, fashionable, graceful, stylish; chivalrous, gentlemanly, knightly, ladylike, noble; mannerly, well-mannered
con coarse, common, crude, ill-bred, rough, rude, uncouth, uncultured, unpolished, vulgar
ant ungenteel
2 *syn* see CIVIL 2
rel well-behaved; aristocratic, cultured
con crude, discourteous, inconsiderate, rough, rude
3 involving or excessively preoccupied with the airs and forms of middle-class or upper-class proprieties <a shy *genteel* girl terrified of blundering socially>
syn affected, la-di-da, ‖lardy-dardy, mincing, pretentious, stilted, too-too; *compare* PRECIOUS 4, PRIM 1
rel artificial, formal, highfalutin
con cultured, genuine, honest, refined; gracious, polished; gentlemanly, ladylike
4 *syn* see PRIM 1
rel narrow; intolerant, uncharitable; confined, insular, parochial, provincial
idiom nasty nice
con charitable, tolerant, understanding; broad-minded, easy, relaxed

gentile *adj* *syn* see HEATHEN

gentility *n* *syn* see ARISTOCRACY

gentle *adj* **1** free from all harshness, roughness, or intensity <a *gentle* summer breeze>
syn balmy, bland, faint, lenient, mild, smooth, soft
rel delicate, mellow, tender; hushed, low, soothing; calm, halcyon, peaceful, placid, quiet, serene, tranquil
con coarse, harsh, rough; exquisite, fierce, intense, savage, vehement, violent; forceful, forcible, powerful
2 having a pleasant easygoing nature <a *gentle* person in everything she does>
syn affable, amiable, genial
rel kind, pleasant, pleasing, tender; agreeable, benign, mild; compassionate, kindly, softhearted, sympathetic, warmhearted
con belligerent, cantankerous, contentious, ill-natured, petty, quarrelsome; aggressive, demanding, overbearing
ant harsh, stern

gentleman *n* **1** a person of good or noble birth <the contributions of the country *gentleman* to social stability>
syn ‖aristo, aristocrat, blue blood, patrician
rel Brahmin; chevalier; nob, swell
con churl, clown, lout
ant boor
2 *syn* see MAN 3
gentleman friend *n syn* see BOYFRIEND 1
gentlewoman *n syn* see WOMAN 1
gentry *n syn* see ARISTOCRACY
genuine *adj* **1** *syn* see AUTHENTIC 2
con artificial, ersatz, factitious; counterfeited, sham, simulated; sophisticated
ant fraudulent
2 *syn* see ACTUAL 2
con uncommon, unordinary, unusual; alleged, apocryphal, apparent, fabulous, fictitious, mythical
3 free from hypocrisy or pretense <a *genuine* love for his fellowman>
syn heart-whole, honest, real, sincere, true, undesigning, undissembled, unfeigned; *compare* NATURAL 5, SINCERE 1
rel reliable, trustworthy, unaffected, unimpeachable, veritable
con affected, hyprocritical
ant insincere
genuinely *adv syn* see VERY 2
germ *n syn* see SEED 2
germane *adj syn* see RELEVANT
con incompatible, incongruous, inconsonant
ant foreign
gest *n syn* see ADVENTURE
gestapo *adj syn* see TERRORISTIC
gestation *n syn* see PREGNANCY
gesture *n syn* see EXPRESSION 3
gesture *vb syn* see SIGNAL
get *vb* **1** to come into possession of <hoped to *get* a fortune from his invention>
syn acquire, annex, chalk up, compass, gain, have, land, obtain, pick up, procure, pull, secure, win
rel educe, elicit, evoke, extort, extract, ‖promote; accept, receive; clutch, grab, grasp, take; accomplish, achieve, effect; capture, carry; draw
idiom come by
con abnegate, eschew, forbear, forgo, give up, sacrifice; abandon, forsake, renounce
2 *syn* see EARN 1
3 *syn* see BECOME 1
rel achieve, attain, effect, realize
idiom get to be, turn out to be
4 *syn* see CONTRACT 1
5 *syn* see FATHER 1
6 *syn* see PREPARE 1
rel arrange, order, right; adjust, coordinate, organize
7 *syn* see CATCH 1
8 *syn* see AFFECT
rel bend, bias, dispose, predispose, prompt
con benumb, deaden, numb; blunt, dull, harden
9 *syn* see NONPLUS 1
rel bother, distress, disturb, perturb, upset; discomfit, disconcert, embarrass

10 *syn* see IRRITATE
idiom try one's temper
con calm, compose, cool, lull, soothe, subdue
11 *syn* see LEARN 1
idiom get into one's head
12 *syn* see MEMORIZE
13 *syn* see INDUCE 1
rel provoke; beg, coax, press, pressure, urge
14 *syn* see REACH 4
15 *syn* see COME 1
get along *vb* **1** *syn* see ADVANCE 5
rel depart, go
con recede, regress, retreat, retrogress, reverse, revert
2 *syn* see SHIFT 5
rel flourish, prosper, succeed, thrive
get away *vb syn* see GO 2
getaway *n syn* see ESCAPE 1
get back *vb syn* see RECOVER 1
get by *vb syn* see SHIFT 5
get in *vb syn* see COME 1
get off *vb* **1** *syn* see GO 2
rel advance, progress
2 *syn* see BEGIN 1
get on *vb* **1** *syn* see DON 1
2 *syn* see ADVANCE 5
3 *syn* see SHIFT 5
get out *vb* **1** to go away quickly, immediately, and often secretly <had to *get out* before the police arrived>
syn begone, bug off, buzz off, clear out, decamp, hightail, kite, scram, skedaddle, skiddoo, take off, ‖vamoose
rel depart, duck (out), egress, exit, go, leave, split
idiom beat it, be off, make tracks, take a powder, take a runout powder
con abide, remain, reside, stay
2 to become known <we can't let this story *get out*>
syn break, come out, leak, out, transpire
3 *syn* see PUBLISH 2
gettable *adj syn* see AVAILABLE 1
get up *vb* **1** *syn* see ROLL OUT
2 *syn* see RISE 1
3 *syn* see GENERATE 3
getup *n* **1** *syn* see COSTUME
2 *syn* see VIGOR 2
get–up–and–go *n* **1** *syn* see VIGOR 2
2 *syn* see ENTERPRISE 4
gewgaw *n syn* see KNICKKNACK
ghastly *adj* **1** disturbingly frightening or repellent in appearance or aspect <the *ghastly* sight of burned and rotting bodies>
syn grim, grisly, gruesome, hideous, horrible, horrid, horrifying, lurid, macabre, terrible, terrifying

---

syn synonym(s)   *rel* related word(s)
ant antonym(s)   *con* contrasted word(s)
idiom idiomatic equivalent(s)
‖ use limited; if in doubt, see a dictionary

rel appalling, awful, dreadful, frightening, frightful, shocking; disgustful, disgusting, nauseant, nauseating, sickening
con appealing, attractive, charming, pleasant, touching; acceptable, bearable; trivial, unimportant
2 resembling or suggestive of a ghost <a *ghastly* form slightly visible through the fog>
syn cadaverous, corpselike, deathlike, ghostlike, ghostly, shadowy, spectral
rel ashen, livid, lurid, pale; uncanny, weird; gruesome, haggard, macabre; dim, faint, weak; charnel, mortuary, sepulchral
ghost *n syn* see APPARITION
rel demon, devil
ghost *vb syn* see GHOSTWRITE
ghostlike *adj syn* see GHASTLY 2
ghostly *adj syn* see GHASTLY 2
ghostwrite *vb* to write for and in the name of another <a *ghostwritten* autobiography>
syn ghost, ‖spook
GI *n syn* see SOLDIER
giant *n* something of monstrous size, appearance, or power <a *giant* of a tractor>
syn behemoth, leviathan, mammoth, monster, whale
rel cyclops, polypheme
giant *adj syn* see HUGE
rel gross, hulking
con paltry, petty, puny, trifling, trivial
ant dwarf
gibber *vb* to utter or speak rapidly, inarticulately, and usually unintelligibly <a *gibbering* idiot>
syn babble, chatter, gabble, jabber
rel blather, drivel, prate, prattle, yammer; stammer, stutter; mumble, mutter; mow
idiom run off at the mouth
con articulate, enunciate, pronounce
gibberish *n* **1** unintelligible or meaningless talk <the *gibberish* of an imbecile>
syn babble, drivel, Greek, jabber, jabberwocky, nonsense, skimble-skamble; *compare* GIBBERISH 3
rel blather, bunkum, claptrap, twaddle; blabber, gabble, palaver, prattle
2 *syn* see GOBBLEDYGOOK
3 speech or actions that are esoteric in nature and suggest the magical, strange, or unknown <the shaman's strange *gibberish*>
syn abracadabra, hocus-pocus, mumbo jumbo, mummery
rel magic, sorcery, thaumaturgy
gibbet *vb syn* see HANG 2
gibble–gabble *n syn* see CHATTER
gibe *vb syn* see SCOFF
rel rail, rally, revile, scold, twit
giddy *adj* **1** having a lightheartedly silly nature <tried to teach a bunch of *giddy* Girl Scouts how to make a fire>
syn bird-witted, dizzy, empty-headed, featherbrained, flighty, fribble, fribbling, frivolous, harebrained, hoity-toity, light, light-headed, rattlebrained, scatterbrained, silly, skittish, volage, yeasty
rel capricious, fickle, impulsive, whimsical; brainless, exuberant, thoughtless, witless

idiom giddy as a goose
con earnest, pensive, sedate, serious, sober, solemn, staid, thoughtful
2 *syn* see DIZZY 2
rel bemused, flustered
idiom going around in circles, like a chicken with its head cut off, seeing double
gift *n* **1** something freely given by one person to another for his benefit or pleasure <the watch was a graduation *gift*>
syn benevolence, boon, ‖compliment, favor, largess, present
rel alms, benefaction, contribution, donation; award, bestowal, grant, presentation; legacy; offering, reward, tip; remembrance, souvenir, token
2 a natural or special facility or capableness <has a *gift* for electronics>
syn aptness, bent, bump, faculty, flair, genius, head, knack, nose, set, talent, turn; *compare* LEANING 2
rel ability, aptitude, capability; accomplishment, acquirement, attainment; instinct, numen, power; forte, leaning, propensity, specialty
con awkwardness, clumsiness, maladroitness
gigantean *adj syn* see HUGE
gigantesque *adj syn* see HUGE
gigantic *adj syn* see HUGE
rel hulking, stupendous
con paltry, petty, puny, trifling, trivial
giggle *vb syn* see LAUGH
gill *n syn* see CREEK 2
gimcrack *n syn* see KNICKKNACK
gimmick *n* **1** *syn* see GADGET 1
2 *syn* see TRICK 1
rel cheat, counterfeit, deceit, dodge, fake, humbug, imposture; fun, game, jest, method, sport
gimp *n syn* see SPIRIT 5
gingerly *adj syn* see CAUTIOUS
gingery *adj syn* see SPIRITED 2
con lethargic, listless, poky, slow; dead, dull, flat, insipid, stuffy; dreary; blasé, lackadaisical, nonchalant
‖gin mill *n syn* see BAR 5
gird *vb* **1** *syn* see BELT 1
ant ungird
2 *syn* see SURROUND 1
rel wrap, wreathe
3 to prepare oneself for action <*girded* himself for the coming trial>
syn brace, fortify, prepare, ready, steel, strengthen
rel bolster, buttress, support, sustain; harden, reinforce, shore (up); invigorate; dispose, forearm, prepare
idiom gird one's loins, whet the knife
gird *vb syn* see SCOFF
girdle *n syn* see BELT 1
girdle *vb* **1** *syn* see BELT
2 *syn* see SURROUND 1
girl *n* **1** a young unmarried female person <hired a *girl* to babysit>
syn ‖bird, damsel, gal, lass, lassie, maid, maiden, miss, missy, ‖quail, ‖quiff, wench

rel hoyden, tomboy; deb, debutante, subdeb, subdebutante; bobby-soxer; schoolgirl; gamine
‖**2 syn** see WOMAN 1
3 syn see MAID 2
4 syn see GIRL FRIEND 1

girl Friday *n syn* see RIGHT-HAND MAN

girl friend *n* **1** a woman who is a man's usual or preferred companion <took his *girl friend* out every weekend>
syn best girl, ‖chick, ‖doney, gal, girl, lady friend, lass, mouse, popsy
2 a woman who shares with a man a strong and usually sexually oriented mutual attraction <his wife caught him with his *girl friend*>
syn ‖baby, beloved, flame, honey, inamorata, ladylove, steady, sweetheart, sweetie, truelove
3 syn see MISTRESS

gist *n syn* see SUBSTANCE 2
rel sap, soul, spirit; subject, theme, topic; bearing, drift, tenor

give *vb* **1** to provide gratuitously <*gave* their labor to rebuild the burned church>
syn bestow, devote, donate, give away, hand out, present; *compare* CONTRIBUTE 1
rel accord, award, confer, grant, hand; afford, contribute, furnish, provide; aid, assist, benefact, help
con keep, retain, withhold; lease, sell
2 to provide by or as if by formal action <he was *given* a diploma>
syn accord, award, confer, grant; *compare* GRANT 1
rel bestow, hand over, present; allocate, appropriate, assign
con decline, refuse; hold back, withhold
3 to put into the possession of another usually for use or consumption <*gave* the dog a drink of water>
syn deliver, dish out, dispense, feed, find, furnish, hand, hand over, provide, supply, transfer, turn over
rel administer, commit, offer; deal, disburse, disperse, distribute, divide, dole (out), lot (out); afford, lend
con have, hold, hold back, keep, keep back, reserve, retain, withhold
4 syn see OFFER 1
rel bestow, confer, render; administer, dispense, issue
5 syn see EXPRESS 2
6 syn see ALLOT
7 to furnish as a result or product <6 +6 *gives* 12>
syn produce, yield
rel be, equal, make; afford, furnish, offer, supply
8 syn see SPEND 1
9 syn see SELL 2
10 to bestow or dispense by some action <*gave* him a punch in the nose>
syn administer, deal, deliver, inflict, strike
rel bestow, dispense; fetch
11 syn see ADDRESS 3
12 to fail in response to physical stress <the bridge *gave* under the heavy load>

syn bend, break, cave, collapse, crumple, fold up, go, yield
rel fail, relax, relent, slacken, weaken
idiom cave in, give way
13 syn see HAPPEN 1

give away *vb* **1 syn** see GIVE 1
2 syn see REVEAL 1

give back *vb* **1 syn** see RETREAT 2
rel back out, backtrack, backwater; crumble, fail, falter, weaken
2 syn see RESTORE 5

given *adj syn* see APT 1

given name *n* the name that precedes one's surname <arguing over the baby's *given name*>
syn baptismal name, Christian name, font name, forename, personal name, prename
rel first name, middle name; appellation, appellative, compellation, denomination, style; praenomen; epithet, label, tag

give off *vb* **1 syn** see EMIT 2
2 syn see DISCHARGE 5

give out *vb* **1 syn** see EMIT 2
2 syn see COLLAPSE 2
3 syn see FAIL 2

give over *vb syn* see STOP 3

giver *n syn* see DONOR

give up *vb* **1 syn** see RELINQUISH
2 syn see DESPAIR

gizmo *n* **1 syn** see DOODAD
2 syn see GADGET

glabrous *adj syn* see HAIRLESS
rel beardless, shaven, smooth-shaven
con bristled, bristly, hairy, hirsute, stubbled, stubbly

glacial *adj* **1 syn** see COLD 1
2 syn see COLD 2
rel aloof, distant, remote, reserved, standoffish, withdrawn; exclusive, inaccessible, seclusive, unapproachable
con affable, gregarious, sociable

glad *adj* **1** characterized by or expressing the mood of one who is pleased or delighted <she was *glad* to be on vacation>
syn happy, joyful, joyous, lighthearted
rel delighted, gratified, pleased, rejoiced, tickled; blithe, exhilarated, jocund, jolly, jovial, merry; gleeful, hilarious, mirthful
idiom filled with (*or* full of) delight
con blue, dejected, depressed, downcast, melancholy; despondent, dispirited, heavyhearted, sadhearted, unhappy; forlorn, joyless, sorrowful, woeful
ant sad
2 full of brightness and cheerfulness <a *glad* spring morning>
syn bright, cheerful, cheery, radiant
rel beaming, sparkling; beautiful; genial, pleasant
con dark, dim, dull, gloomy, somber

---

syn synonym(s)   *rel* related word(s)
ant antonym(s)   *con* contrasted word(s)
idiom idiomatic equivalent(s)
‖ use limited; if in doubt, see a dictionary

gladden *vb syn* see PLEASE 2
  rel comfort, console, solace; animate, enliven, exhilarate, invigorate, liven, quicken, vivify
  con depress, oppress, weigh; discourage, dishearten, dispirit; damp, dampen; bother, irk
  ant sadden
gladiatorial *adj syn* see BELLIGERENT
‖**glad rags** *n pl syn* see FINERY
glamorous *adj syn* see ATTRACTIVE 1
glamour *n syn* see CHARM 3
glance *vb* **1** to strike a surface obliquely so as to go off at an angle <the bullet *glanced* off the stone wall>
  syn carom, dap, graze, ricochet, skim, skip
  rel brush, kiss, scrape, shave, slant; contact, hit, strike, touch; bounce, careen, rebound
  con center, focus
  2 *syn* see BRUSH
  3 *syn* see FLASH 1
glance (at *or* over) *vb syn* see BROWSE
glance *n* **1** *syn* see FLASH 1
  2 *syn* see PEEP
glance *vb syn* see POLISH 1
glare *vb* **1** *syn* see BLAZE
  rel dazzle, flash, gleam, glisten, glitter
  2 *syn* see GAZE 1
  rel frown, glower, lower, scowl
glaring *adj* **1** *syn* see EGREGIOUS
  rel conspicuous, noticeable, outstanding; excessive, extreme, inordinate; obtrusive
  ant unnoticeable
  2 *syn* see GAUDY
  rel cheap, coarse, crude, gross
  con elegant, tasteful
glass *n syn* see MIRROR 1
glass *vb syn* see REFLECT 1
‖**glasshouse** *n syn* see GREENHOUSE
glassy *adj syn* see SLEEK
glaze *vb syn* see POLISH 1
glaze *n syn* see LUSTER
gleam *n syn* see FLASH 1
gleam *vb* **1** *syn* see SHINE 1
  2 *syn* see FLASH 1
  rel burn
gleaming *adj syn* see LUSTROUS 1
glean *vb* to gather by effort and usually bit by bit <evidence *gleaned* from various testimonies>
  syn cull, extract, garner, gather, pick up
  rel sift, winnow; ascertain, conclude, deduce, learn
  con amass, heap, pile
glee *n syn* see MIRTH
  rel delectation, delight, enjoyment, joy, pleasure; blitheness; joyousness
  ant gloom
gleeful *adj syn* see MERRY
glen *n syn* see VALLEY
glib *adj* characterized by very fluent often superficial address toward others <*glib* chatter>
  syn silver-tongued, vocative, voluble, well=hung; *compare* TALKATIVE
  rel articulate, eloquent, facile, fluent, vocal
  con inarticulate, unfluent
glide *vb* **1** *syn* see SLIDE 1

  rel float, fly, sail, scud, shoot, skim
  2 *syn* see STEAL 3
  3 *syn* see SNEAK
glimmer *vb syn* see FLASH 1
glimmer *n syn* see FLASH 1
glimpse *n syn* see PEEP
glint *vb syn* see FLASH 1
glint *n* **1** *syn* see FLASH 1
  2 *syn* see LUSTER
glissade *vb syn* see SLIDE 1
  rel float, fly, sail, scud, shoot, skim
glisten *vb syn* see FLASH 1
glisten *n syn* see FLASH 1
glistening *adj syn* see LUSTROUS 1
glitter *vb* **1** *syn* see FLASH 1
  2 *syn* see SPANGLE 1
glitter *n syn* see FLASH 1
gloaming *n syn* see EVENING 1
gloat *vb syn* see GAZE 1
  con begrudge, covet, envy, grudge
global *adj* **1** *syn* see UNIVERSAL 2
  ant parochial
  2 *syn* see ALL-ROUND 2
  rel all-inclusive, blanket, catholic, grand, universal
globe *n* **1** *syn* see BALL
  2 *syn* see EARTH 1
globule *n syn* see DROP 1
gloom *vb* **1** *syn* see FROWN 1
  rel brood, mope
  con smile; bubble, effervesce, enthuse, sparkle
  2 *syn* see OBSCURE
gloom *n syn* see SADNESS
  con hilarity, jollity, mirth; gaiety, gladness
  ant glee
gloomy *adj* **1** *syn* see DARK 1
  rel bleak, dismal, dreary
  ant brilliant
  2 *syn* see SULLEN
  rel cheerless, dejected, depressed, downcast, joyless, melancholy, oppressed, solemn, unhappy, weary
  con glad, happy, joyful, joyous, lighthearted; blithe, jocund, jovial, merry
  ant cheerful
  3 causing or marked by gloom <the *gloomy* atmosphere of the dungeon>
  syn acheronian, acherontic, black, bleak, cheerless, cold, depressant, depressing, depressive, desolate, disconsolate, discouraging, disheartening, dismal, dispiriting, drear, dreary, dusky, funereal, joyless, lugubrious, morne, oppressive, somber, tenebrific, unhappy, woebegone
  rel despondent, mirthless, pessimistic; melancholy, mournful, sad; drab, dull, muzzy
  con bright, cheerful, happy; cheering, emboldening, encouraging, heartening, optimistic
  ant gloomless
glorification *n syn* see APOTHEOSIS 2
glorify *vb* **1** *syn* see PRAISE 2
  2 *syn* see EXALT 1
glorious *adj* **1** *syn* see SPLENDID 2
  rel brilliant, effulgent, lustrous, radiant; imposing, impressive; majestic, noble; ravishing, stunning; beautiful

ant inglorious
  2 *syn* see MARVELOUS 2
glory *vb syn* see EXULT
gloss *n syn* see LUSTER
  rel glossiness, silkiness, sleekness, slickness;
  burnish
gloss *vb syn* see POLISH 1
gloss (over) *vb syn* see PALLIATE
  rel account, explain, justify, rationalize; belie,
  falsify, miscolor, misrepresent
gloss *vb syn* see ANNOTATE
glossy *adj* **1** *syn* see LUSTROUS 1
  2 *syn* see SLEEK
glow *vb* **1** *syn* see BLAZE
  rel burn; ignite, kindle, light
  2 *syn* see BLUSH
glow *n syn* see BLOOM 3
glower *vb syn* see FROWN 1
  rel stare; look, watch
glowing *adj* **1** *syn* see RUDDY
  2 *syn* see IMPASSIONED
  rel enthusiastic; avid, desirous, eager, fierce,
  keen; burning, heated
gloze (over) *vb syn* see PALLIATE
  rel account, explain, justify, rationalize; belie,
  falsify, miscolor, misrepresent
gluey *adj syn* see STICKY 1
glum *adj syn* see SULLEN
  rel close-lipped, silent, taciturn, tight-lipped;
  depressed, oppressed, weighed down
  con glad, happy, joyful, joyous, lighthearted
  ant cheerful
glut *vb syn* see SATIATE
  rel cram, feast, stuff
  idiom make a pig of (oneself)
  con scant, skimp
  ant stint
glutted *adj syn* see SATIATED
gluttonous *adj syn* see VORACIOUS
  rel hoggish, piggish; indulgent, intemperate
  con sober, temperate; ascetic, austere; sparing
  ant abstemious
gnaw *vb* **1** *syn* see WORRY 1
  rel haunt, irritate, rankle
  2 *syn* see EAT 3
  rel abrade, fret; consume, crumble
gnome *n syn* see MAXIM
gnostic *adj syn* see WISE 1
go *vb* **1** to move on a course <they were glad to be
  going toward home>
  syn ‖cruise, fare, hie, journey, pass, proceed,
  ‖process, push on, repair, travel, wend
  rel advance; approach, near
  idiom gain ground, get over the ground, make
  one's way
  ant stay; stop
  2 to move out of and away from where one is
  <it's time to *go* now>
  syn ‖blow, depart, exit, get away, get off, leave,
  ‖mog, move, pop off, pull out, push off, quit, retire, run along, shove off, take off, withdraw
  rel abscond, decamp, escape, flee, fly, hightail
  idiom take a powder
  con abide, remain, stay; arrive

ant come
  3 *syn* see RUN 8
  4 to be brought to or toward an end <his money
  will soon be *gone*>
  syn consume, exhaust, expend, finish, run
  through, spend, use up, wash up
  rel deplete, devour, dissipate, fritter (away),
  overspend, squander, waste
  con conserve, preserve, save
  5 *syn* see DIE 1
  6 *syn* see PASS 3
  7 *syn* see GIVE 12
  8 *syn* see HAPPEN 1
  9 *syn* see BECOME 1
  10 *syn* see RANGE 3
  11 *syn* see SUCCEED 3
  12 *syn* see SUCCEED 2
  13 *syn* see RESORT 2
  14 *syn* see FUNCTION 3
  15 *syn* see EXTEND 7
  16 *syn* see AGREE 4
  17 *syn* see BELONG 1
  18 *syn* see BEAR 10
  19 *syn* see ENJOY 1
go (for) *vb syn* see APPROVE 1
go (into) *vb syn* see EXPLORE
go (together *or* with) *vb syn* see SUIT 4
go *n* **1** *syn* see OCCURRENCE
  2 *syn* see VIGOR 2
  3 *syn* see ENERGY 2
  4 *syn* see FLING 1
  5 *syn* see SPELL 1
  6 *syn* see SIEGE
  7 *syn* see SUCCESS
goad *n syn* see STIMULUS
  rel compulsion, drive, impulsion; desire, lust,
  passion, urge, zeal
  ant curb
goad *vb syn* see URGE
  rel impel, move; coerce, compel, force; instigate
go–ahead *adj syn* see ENTERPRISING 2
goal *n* **1** *syn* see AMBITION 2
  2 *syn* see USE 4
goat *n syn* see SCAPEGOAT
goatish *adj syn* see LUSTFUL 2
gob *n* **1** *syn* see LUMP 1
  2 *usu* **gobs** *pl syn* see SCAD
gob *n syn* see MOUTH 1
gobbet *n syn* see DROP 1
gobble *vb syn* see GULP
gobbledygook *n* wordy unintelligible language
  <the *gobbledygook* of bureaucrats>
  syn double-talk, gibberish
  rel double Dutch, Greek, jabberwocky; ‖bull,
  bunkum, claptrap, drivel, garbage, malarkey,
  nonsense, poppycock, twaddle
go–between *n* **1** *syn* see MARRIAGE BROKER

---

syn synonym(s)   *rel* related word(s)
ant antonym(s)   *con* contrasted word(s)
idiom idiomatic equivalent(s)
‖ use limited; if in doubt, see a dictionary

2 an intermediate agent between individuals or groups <served as a *go-between* in the labor dispute>
syn broker, entrepreneur, interagent, interceder, intercessor, intermediary, intermediate, intermediator, mediator, middleman
rel agent, attorney, deputy, factor, proxy; emissary, envoy, messenger; delegate, representative; arbitrator, negotiator

godless *adj syn* see IRRELIGIOUS
rel agnostic, atheistic, infidel
ant godly

godlike *adj syn* see DIVINE 2

godly *adj* **1** *syn* see DIVINE 1
2 *syn* see SAINTLY
3 *syn* see DEVOUT
ant godless

go down *vb* **1** *syn* see FALL 2
rel droop, sag, sink; cave (in), collapse, crumple, fold
2 *syn* see SET 12
3 *syn* see SINK 1
4 *syn* see FALL 3
5 *syn* see HAPPEN 1

God's acre *n syn* see CEMETERY

godsend *n syn* see GOOD 1

go–getter *n syn* see HUSTLER 1

goggle *vb* **1** *syn* see LOOK 7
2 *syn* see GAZE 1

go in *vb syn* see ENTER 1

Golconda *n syn* see BONANZA

goldarn *adj* **1** *syn* see DAMNED 2
2 *syn* see UTTER

goldbrick *n syn* see SLACKER

goldbrick *vb syn* see IDLE

golden *adj* **1** *syn* see BLOND 1
2 *syn* see MELLIFLUOUS

golden–ager *n syn* see OLDSTER

gold mine *n syn* see BONANZA

golem *n syn* see ROBOT 2

gone *adj* **1** *syn* see EXTINCT 2
2 *syn* see ABSENT 1
3 *syn* see LOST 2
4 *syn* see PREGNANT 1

gonfalon *n syn* see FLAG

gonfanon *n syn* see FLAG

goo *n* **1** a sticky substance <slipped on a patch of greasy *goo* on the walk>
syn gook, goop, gumbo, gunk, muck; *compare* CRUD
rel dope
2 *syn* see CRUD

good *adj* **1** having a helpful or auspicious character <a *good* wind>
syn advantageous, benefic, beneficial, brave, favorable, favoring, helpful, propitious, toward, useful
rel convenient, suitable; desirable, needed; appropriate, proper, right
con disadvantageous, unfavorable; damaging, hampering, harmful; unwanted
ant ill
2 adapted to the end in view <they doubted that the fruit was *good* to eat>

syn appropriate, convenient, fit, meet, proper, suitable, useful
rel all right, apt, becoming, conformable, congruous, fitting, seemly
con inadequate, inappropriate, undesirable, unfit, unsuitable, useless
3 *syn* see WHOLE 1
con blemished, damaged, defective, flawed, impaired, imperfect, unsound
ant bad
4 *syn* see ADVANTAGEOUS 1
5 *syn* see PLEASANT 1
6 *syn* see HEALTHFUL
7 *syn* see CLEVER 5
8 *syn* see CONSIDERABLE 2
9 *syn* see WELL-FOUNDED
10 *syn* see DECENT 4
11 conforming to a high standard of morality or virtue <if you can't be *good*, be careful>
syn blameless, exemplary, guiltless, inculpable, innocent, irreprehensible, irreproachable, lily=white, pure, righteous, unblamable, virtuous
rel incorrupt, sound, uncorrupted, untainted
con blameworthy, impure, unrighteous; evil, iniquitous, reprobate, sinful
ant bad
12 *syn* see CHARITABLE 1
13 behaving in an acceptable or desirable manner <a *good* child>
syn decorous, well-behaved
rel polite, proper; considerate, kindly, thoughtful
con ill-behaved, indecorous, naughty; careless, heedless, inconsiderate, mischievous, thoughtless
ant bad
14 *syn* see SKILLFUL 2
ant bad
15 *syn* see ABLE

good *n* **1** something that is desirable or beneficial <it's an ill wind that blows no *good*>
syn advantage, benediction, benefit, blessing, boon, godsend
con bane, harm, misfortune; detriment, jinx
ant evil, ill
2 *syn* see RIGHT 1
3 *syn* see WELFARE
4 goods *pl syn* see POSSESSION 2
5 goods *pl syn* see MERCHANDISE

good–bye *interj* — used as a conventional expression of good wishes at parting <the party was over; the time had come to say *good-bye*>
syn adieu, by, bye-bye, ‖cheerio, farewell, so long, ‖toodle-oo
rel good day, good evening, good morning, good night
idiom be good, be seeing you, fare you well, keep in touch, see you (later)
con hello, how do, howdy, hullo

good–bye *n syn* see PARTING

good–bye *adj syn* see PARTING

good faith *n* a state of mind characterizing one free from fraud, deceit, or misconduct <determined to act in *good faith*>

syn bona fides, sincereness, sincerity, uberrima
fides

rel decency, decorum, propriety, seemliness;
ethicality, morality, virtuousness

good–fellowship *n syn* see CAMARADERIE

good–for–nothing *n syn* see WASTREL 1

good–for–nothing *adj* **1** *syn* see FECKLESS 1

2 *syn* see WORTHLESS 1

ant precious

good–hearted *adj syn* see KIND

good–humored *adj syn* see AMIABLE 1

rel buoyant, cheerful, cheery, genial, smiling

ant ill-humored

good–looking *adj syn* see BEAUTIFUL

ant ill-looking

good–natured *adj syn* see AMIABLE 1

rel altruistic, benevolent, charitable; acquiescent, compliant

con choleric, cranky, cross, irascible, splenetic,
touchy; crabbed, gloomy, glum, morose, splenetic

ant contrary; ill-natured

goodness *n* the quality or state of being morally
excellent <that eternal *goodness* that burns away
evil>

syn morality, probity, rectitude, righteousness,
rightness, uprightness, virtue

rel honesty, honor, integrity; grace, merit, quality, superiority

ant badness, evil

good sense *n syn* see SENSE 6

good–tasting *adj syn* see PALATABLE

good–tempered *adj syn* see AMIABLE 1

con crabbed, surly; snappish, touchy; irascible

ant bad-tempered, ill-tempered

goodwill *n* **1** benevolent interest or concern <try-
ing to promote interracial *goodwill*>

syn amity, benevolence, comity, friendliness,
friendship, kindliness

rel altruism, charity, favor, generosity, helpfulness, kindness, rapport, sympathy, tolerance

con animus, disfavor, enmity, hatred, intolerance, malevolence

ant animosity, ill will

2 *syn* see ALACRITY

goody *n syn* see DELICACY

goody–goody *n syn* see PRUDE

gooey *adj* **1** *syn* see STICKY 1

2 *syn* see SENTIMENTAL

goof *n* **1** *syn* see DUNCE

2 *syn* see ERROR 2

‖**goof** (off) *vb syn* see IDLE

goof (up) *vb syn* see BOTCH

go off *vb syn* see EXPLODE 1

gook *n* **1** *syn* see GOO

2 *syn* see CRUD

3 *syn* see NONSENSE 2

go on *vb* **1** *syn* see PERSEVERE

2 *syn* see BEHAVE 1

‖**goon** *n syn* see DUNCE

goop *n syn* see GOO 1

goose egg *n syn* see ZERO 1

goosey *adj* **1** *syn* see STUPID 1

2 *syn* see NERVOUS

go over *vb syn* see SUCCEED 2

gordian *adj syn* see COMPLEX 2

gore *n syn* see BLOOD 1

gorge *n syn* see RAVINE

gorge *vb syn* see SATIATE

rel bolt, devour, gobble, guzzle, raven, wolf;
overeat, overindulge, stuff

idiom eat like a horse, eat one out of house and
home

gorged *adj syn* see SATIATED

gorgeous *adj* **1** *syn* see SPLENDID 2

rel elegant, luxurious, opulent, plush, sumptuous; flamboyant, garish, gaudy, ostentatious,
pretentious, showy; beautiful, colorful

2 *syn* see GRAND 2

‖**gorilla** *n syn* see THUG 1

gory *adj syn* see BLOODY 1

gospel *n syn* see VERACITY 2

gossamer *adj syn* see FILMY

gossip *n* **1** a person who habitually retails private,
scandalous, or sensational and often inaccurate
information <her life ruined by a vicious old *gossip*>

syn carrytale, circulator, clack, gossiper, gossipmonger, ‖long tongue, mumblenews, newsmonger, quidnunc, rumorer, rumormonger, scandalizer, scandalmonger, sieve, tabby, talebearer,
telltale; *compare* BUSYBODY, INFORMER

2 *syn* see REPORT 1

rel account, chronicle, conversation, story, tale;
babble, banter, chatter, prate

gossip *vb* to disclose something, often of questionable veracity, that is better kept to oneself <*gos-
siped* about his neighbor's business>

syn blab, noise (about *or* abroad), rumor, talk,
tattle

rel babble, chat, chatter, prate, prattle; hint, imply, insinuate, intimate, suggest

idiom dish the dirt, spill the beans, tell idle tales,
tell tales out of school

gossiper *n syn* see GOSSIP 1

gossipmonger *n syn* see GOSSIP 1

Gothic *adj syn* see BARBARIAN 1

rel brutal, coarse, crude

gouge *vb syn* see EXTORT 1

rel cheat, con, swindle; overcharge

go under *vb* **1** *syn* see FALL 3

2 *syn* see SINK 1

gourmand *n syn* see EPICURE

gourmet *n syn* see EPICURE

govern *vb* **1** to exercise sovereign authority <a dictator may *govern* in a thoroughly enlightened
manner>

syn overrule, reign, rule, sway

rel captain, command, head; administer, conduct, control, direct, manage, master; regulate,
supervise

2 *syn* see ADMINISTER 1

---

syn synonym(s)   *rel* related word(s)

ant antonym(s)   *con* contrasted word(s)

idiom idiomatic equivalent(s)

‖ use limited; if in doubt, see a dictionary

3 to exercise a decisive role in influencing the actions and conduct of <parents who *govern* their children wisely>
syn control, direct, dominate, handle, manage
rel directionalize, guide, lead, shepherd, steer; boss, oversee, supervise
idiom be at the helm (*or* wheel), be in the driver's seat, hold the reins

‖**governor** *n syn* see FATHER 1

grab *vb syn* see SEIZE 2

grabble *vb syn* see GROPE

grabby *adj syn* see COVETOUS

grace *n* **1** a short prayer either asking a blessing before or giving thanks after a meal <taught each child a *grace* of his own>
syn benediction, blessing, thanks, thanksgiving
rel invocation, petition
2 *syn* see MERCY
rel compassionateness, responsiveness, tenderness; forbearance, indulgence, leniency; goodness
3 *syn* see ELEGANCE

graceless *adj* **1** *syn* see BARBARIC 1
2 *syn* see INFELICITOUS
ant graceful

gracious *adj* **1** marked by kindly courtesy <her *gracious* attitude toward those around her>
syn affable, congenial, cordial, genial, sociable, ‖sonsy
rel amiable, complaisant, easy, obliging; benign, benignant, kind, kindly; chivalrous, courteous, courtly; approachable, bonhomous, clubby, forthcoming, forthgoing, outgoing
con boorish, churlish; blunt, brusque, crabbed, crusty, curt, gruff, short, sullen, surly
ant ungracious
2 *syn* see COURTLY
rel mannered, starchy

gradation *n* the difference or variation between two things that are nearly alike <the *gradations* were too small to be seen with the unaided eye>
syn nuance, shade
rel difference, distinction, divergence; change, modification, variation

grade *n* **1** *syn* see DEGREE 1
2 *syn* see ESTATE 2
3 *syn* see CLASS 1
4 *syn* see QUALITY 3
5 *syn* see SLOPE

grade *vb syn* see CLASS 2
rel arrange, order; assort, sort

Grade A *adj syn* see EXCELLENT

gradient *n syn* see SLOPE

gradual *adj* proceeding slowly usually by minute or imperceptible steps or degrees <his health showed *gradual* improvement>
syn piecemeal, step-by-step
rel deliberate, dilatory, lagging, poky, sluggish
con acute, sharp, sudden
ant abrupt

gradually *adv* by small degrees or amounts <*gradually* he learned the new job>
syn bit by bit, little by little, piecemeal
idiom a little at a time, by degrees

con quickly, rapidly, speedily; at once, immediately, suddenly

grain *n syn* see PARTICLE

grainy *adj syn* see COARSE 1

grammar *n syn* see ALPHABET 2

grand *adj* **1** large and impressive in size, scope, extent, or conception <the platform provided a *grand* view of the canyon>
syn august, baronial, grandiose, imposing, lordly, magnific, magnificent, majestic, noble, princely, royal, stately; *compare* HUGE
rel monumental, prodigious, stupendous, tremendous; towering; gorgeous, splendid, sublime, superb
con measly, paltry, petty, puny, trifling, trivial
2 marked by great magnificence, display, and usually ceremony or formality <delighted to attend the *grand* presidential fete>
syn gorgeous, impressive, lavish, luxurious, splendid, sumptuous
rel magnificent, majestic; flashy, garish, gaudy, ornate, ostentatious, showy
con crude, meretricious, obtrusive, vulgar; flimsy, tawdry
3 noble in character or spirit <a *grand* outlook on life>
syn elevated, exalted, lofty, sublime, superb
rel magnificent, splendid
con average, common, commonplace, ordinary; base, lowly, mean, poor

grandam *n syn* see BELDAM 1

grande dame *n syn* see MATRIARCH

grandiloquent *adj syn* see RHETORICAL

grandiose *adj* **1** *syn* see GRAND 1
rel ostentatious, pretentious, showy; cosmic, overwhelming, unfathomable, vast
2 *syn* see AMBITIOUS 2

granny *n syn* see FUSSBUDGET

grant *vb* **1** to give as a favor or right <*granted* him an extension of payments>
syn accord, award, concede, vouchsafe
rel bestow, confer, donate, give, present; allow, permit; cede, relinquish, yield
con decline, refuse, turn down
2 *syn* see ACKNOWLEDGE 1
con differ, disagree, dissent; challenge, dispute, object, protest
3 *syn* see GIVE 2

grant *n syn* see APPROPRIATION
rel gift; assistance, benefaction, contribution, donation; alms, charity, dole, handout

granular *adj syn* see COARSE 1

grapevine *n syn* see REPORT 1

graph *n syn* see CHART 1
rel diagram, outline, sketch

graphic *adj* **1** giving a clear visual impression especially in words <gave a *graphic* description of the whole incident>
syn photographic, pictorial, picturesque, vivid
rel clear, lucid, perspicuous; clear-cut, incisive; cogent, compelling, convincing, telling; definite, explicit, precise, realistic, striking, visual
con confused, hazy, indistinct, obscure
2 *syn* see PICTORIAL 1

grapple *n syn* see HOLD
grapple *vb* **1** *syn* see SEIZE 2
   2 *syn* see WRESTLE
grasp *vb* **1** *syn* see TAKE 4
   2 *syn* see APPREHEND 1
   rel envisage, fathom, perceive
   3 *syn* see KNOW 1
grasp *n syn* see HOLD
graspable *adj syn* see UNDERSTANDABLE
   ant ungraspable
grasping *adj syn* see COVETOUS
   rel extorting, extortionate
grass *n syn* see MARIJUANA
grate *vb* **1** *syn* see SCRAPE 1
   rel abrade, bark, chafe, fray, gall, scuff, skin
   2 *syn* see IRRITATE
grateful *adj* **1** feeling or expressing gratitude <was *grateful* for the gift>
   syn obliged, thankful
   rel appreciative, beholden; gratified, pleased
   idiom filled with gratitude
   ant ungrateful
   2 *syn* see PLEASANT 1
   rel comforting, consoling, solacing; refreshing, rejuvenating, renewing, restorative, restoring; delectable, delicious, delightful
   ant obnoxious
gratefulness *n syn* see AMENITY 1
gratify *vb* **1** *syn* see PLEASE 2
   rel appease, baby, cater (to), coddle, favor, humor, indulge, oblige, pamper
   con bother, irk; aggravate, exasperate, irritate, nettle, rile; agitate, disturb, perturb, upset
   2 *syn* see SATISFY 3
   3 *syn* see INDULGE 1
   idiom do one proud
gratifying *adj syn* see PLEASANT 1
   rel contenting, satisfying; delighting, gladdening, regaling, rejoicing
   con invidious, obnoxious; offensive, revolting
grating *adj syn* see HARSH 3
gratis *adj syn* see FREE 5
gratuitous *adj* **1** *syn* see FREE 5
   rel voluntary, willing
   2 *syn* see SUPEREROGATORY
   3 *syn* see BASELESS
   rel indefensible, reasonless, unsupportable
gratuity *n* something given over and above what is due, generally in return for or expectation of good service <he found that an occasional *gratuity* smoothed his path>
   syn cumshaw, lagniappe, largess, ‖palm grease, ‖palm oil, ‖perk(s), perquisite, pourboire, tip
   rel alms, benefaction, contribution, donation; offering, reward
grave *vb* **1** *syn* see ENGRAVE 1
   2 *syn* see IMPRESS 3
grave *n* a place of interment <his *grave* is in the church burial ground>
   syn burial, ‖pit, sepulcher, sepulture, tomb
   rel catacomb, crypt, vault; mausoleum; ossuary; cinerarium
   idiom final resting place
grave *adj* **1** *syn* see SERIOUS 2

2 *syn* see SERIOUS 1
   rel heavy, ponderous; grim, sad, saturnine; awful, dreadful, horrible, terrible
   con flippant, light, light-minded
   ant gay
   3 involving marked risk of impairment or destruction <a *grave* illness>
   syn dangerous, fell, grievous, major, serious, ugly; *compare* DANGEROUS 1
   rel deadly, destructive, dire, fatal, killing, murderous; frightening, ghastly, terrible; afflictive, severe
   con paltry, petty, trivial; harmless, innocuous; temporary, transitory
gravely *adv syn* see SERIOUSLY 2
grave marker *n syn* see TOMBSTONE
gravestone *n syn* see TOMBSTONE
graveyard *n syn* see CEMETERY
gravid *adj syn* see PREGNANT 1
gravidity *n syn* see PREGNANCY
graybeard *n syn* see GAFFER
gray matter *n syn* see MIND 1
graze *vb* **1** *syn* see BRUSH
   2 *syn* see GLANCE 1
   3 *syn* see ABRADE 1
   rel harm, hurt, injure; bruise, contuse, wound
greasy *adj* **1** *syn* see FATTY 2
   2 *syn* see SLICK 1
‖**greasy spoon** *n syn* see EATING HOUSE
great *adj* **1** *syn* see LARGE 1
   con measly, paltry, petty, puny, trifling, trivial
   ant little
   2 *syn* see FAMOUS 2
   rel superlative, supreme, surpassing, transcendent
great deal *n syn* see MUCH
greater *adj* **1** *syn* see BEST
   2 *syn* see SUPERIOR 1
great gun *n syn* see NOTABLE 1
greathearted *adj* **1** *syn* see BRAVE 1
   2 *syn* see GENEROUS 1
greatly *adv syn* see VERY 1
greatness *n syn* see SIZE 2
greed *n syn* see CUPIDITY
   rel gluttonousness, gluttony, rapaciousness, ravenousness, voraciousness
greedy *adj syn* see COVETOUS
   con bounteous, bountiful, generous, liberal, munificent, openhanded; exuberant, lavish, prodigal, profuse
Greek *n syn* see GIBBERISH 1
green *adj* **1** *syn* see YOUNG 1
   2 *syn* see INEXPERIENCED
   con grown-up, ripe, mature, matured; educated, instructed, trained; proficient, skilled, skillful
   ant experienced
green *n syn* see COMMON 2
‖**greenbacks** *n pl syn* see MONEY
green-eyed *adj syn* see ENVIOUS

---

syn synonym(s)   *rel* related word(s)
ant antonym(s)   *con* contrasted word(s)
idiom idiomatic equivalent(s)
‖ use limited; if in doubt, see a dictionary

greenhorn *n syn* see RUSTIC

greenhouse *n* a glass-enclosed structure for the cultivation and protection of tender plants <a small window *greenhouse* full of bloom>
syn conservatory, ‖glasshouse
rel coolhouse, hotbed, hothouse

greenness *n* **1** *syn* see YOUTH 1
2 *syn* see INEXPERIENCE

greet *vb syn* see ADDRESS 7

greeting *n* the ceremonial words or acts of one who meets, welcomes, or formally addresses another <after the *greeting* the chairman called the roll>
syn salutation, salute
rel address, hail, hello, welcome
con farewell, good-bye
ant valediction

gregarious *adj syn* see SOCIAL 2

grief *n syn* see SORROW
rel bemoaning, bewailing, deploring, lamenting
con comfort, comforting, consolation, solace, solacing
ant joy

grievance *n syn* see INJUSTICE 2
rel hardship, rigor; affliction, cross, trial, tribulation

grieve *vb* **1** *syn* see DISTRESS 2
2 to feel or express deep distress <*grieved* at the loss of so many lives>
syn mourn, sorrow
rel bear, endure, suffer; bemoan, bewail, deplore, lament; cry, keen, wail, weep
ant rejoice
3 *syn* see DEPLORE 1

grievous *adj* **1** *syn* see ONEROUS
2 *syn* see BITTER 2
3 *syn* see GRAVE 3
4 *syn* see DEPLORABLE

‖**grifter** *n syn* see SWINDLER

grill *n syn* see CROSS-EXAMINATION

grilling *n syn* see CROSS-EXAMINATION

grim *adj* **1** *syn* see FIERCE 1
rel foreboding, ominous
2 forbidding in action or appearance <had a *grim* and determined expression on his face>
syn austere, bleak, dour, hard, harsh, severe, stringent
rel cold, forbidding, ‖off-putting; fixed, rigid, set; determined, firm, stern
con calm, mellow, mild, soft, warm; attractive, beautiful, pleasing
ant pleasant
3 being extremely obdurate or firm in action or purpose <fought with *grim* determination>
syn implacable, ironfisted, merciless, mortal, relentless, ruthless, unappeasable, unflinching, unrelenting, unyielding
rel adamant, inexorable, inflexible, obdurate, resolute, stubborn, unforgiving, vindictive; certain, inevitable; determined, dogged
con considerate, gentle, mild; clement, forbearing, indulgent
ant lenient
4 *syn* see GHASTLY 1

rel loathsome, offensive, repugnant, repulsive, revolting

grimace *n syn* see FACE 6

grimace *vb* to distort one's face by way of expressing a feeling <*grimaced* with pain>
syn mop, mouth, mow, mug, ‖mump
rel contort, deform, distort, misshape
idiom make a face (*or* mouth), make a wry face (*or* mouth), pull a face, screw up one's face

grime *vb syn* see SOIL 2

grim reaper *n syn* see DEATH 1

grimy *adj syn* see DIRTY 1

grin *vb syn* see SMILE
con frown, gloom
ant grimace

grind *vb syn* see DRUDGE

grind *n* **1** *syn* see WORK 2
2 *syn* see ROUTINE

grip *vb* **1** *syn* see TAKE 4
2 *syn* see ENTHRALL 2

grip *n syn* see HOLD
rel coercion, constraint, duress, restraint

gripe *vb* to complain emphatically and often petulantly <students *griping* about the cafeteria food>
syn ‖beef, ‖bellyache, bleat, ‖blow off, crab, ‖crib, fuss, kvetch, squawk, yammer, yawp (*or* yaup); *compare* COMPLAIN
rel brawl, kick, take on; croak, grouch, grouse, grumble, murmur, mutter
con applaud, approve, cheer; rejoice; accept, bear, endure, tolerate

gripe *n* **1** *syn* see HOLD
2 *usu* **gripes** *pl syn* see STOMACHACHE

griper *n syn* see GROUCH

grisette *n syn* see DOXY 1

grisly *adj syn* see GHASTLY 1
rel eerie, uncanny, weird

grit *n syn* see FORTITUDE
con faltering, hesitation, vacillation, wavering
ant faintheartedness

grobian *n syn* see BOOR 2

grog *n syn* see LIQUOR 2

‖**groggery** *n syn* see BAR 5

‖**grogshop** *n syn* see BAR 5

groove *n syn* see ROUTINE

groovy *adj syn* see MARVELOUS 2

grope *vb* to reach out or about blindly (as in testing or searching) <*groped* along the wall in search of a door>
syn feel, fumble, grabble
rel poke, pry, root; examine, explore, search

gross *adj* **1** *syn* see EGREGIOUS
rel excessive, exorbitant, extreme, immoderate, inordinate
con paltry, trifling, trivial
ant petty
2 *syn* see UTTER
3 *syn* see FAT 2
4 *syn* see WHOLE 4
ant net
5 *syn* see MATERIAL 1
6 *syn* see COARSE 3
7 *syn* see OBSCENE 2

rel animal, carnal, fleshy, sensual; loathsome, offensive, repulsive, revolting; improper, unrefined

con decent, decorous, proper, refined

gross *n syn* see WHOLE 1

grotesque *adj syn* see FANTASTIC 2

rel baroque, flamboyant, rococo; eerie, uncanny, weird; extravagant, extreme; comic, comical, droll, ludicrous

grotto *n syn* see CAVE

grouch *n* an habitually irritable or complaining person <it's hard to live with a *grouch*>

syn ‖bellyacher, complainer, crab, crabber, crank, crosspatch, faultfinder, griper, grouser, growler, grumbler, grump, kicker, malcontent, sorehead, sourpuss

con optimist, Pollyanna

grouch *vb syn* see GRUMBLE 1

ground *n* **1** *syn* see BASIS 1

2 *syn* see BASE 1

3 *syn* see REASON 3

rel evidence, testimony; antecedent, cause, determinant; demonstration, test, trial

4 grounds *pl syn* see SEDIMENT

5 *syn* see EARTH 2

ground *vb* **1** *syn* see FELL 1

2 *syn* see BASE

rel buttress, support, sustain

grounded *adj syn* see AGROUND

groundless *adj syn* see BASELESS

ant well-founded, well-grounded

groundwork *n* **1** *syn* see BASIS 1

2 *syn* see BASE 1

group *n* **1** a usually comparatively small assemblage of individuals <people gathered in *groups* about the hall>

syn assembly, band, bevy, bunch, cluster, covey, crew, party; *compare* COMPANY 4, GATHERING

rel circle, clique, coterie, set

con crowd, crush, horde, mob, press, rout, throng

2 *syn* see GATHERING 2

3 an assemblage of things constituting a unit <a *group* of houses behind the church>

syn array, batch, battery, body, bunch, bundle, clot, clump, cluster, clutch, lot, parcel, passel, platoon, set, sort, suite

rel assemblage, collection, mess, shooting match

4 *syn* see SET 5

5 *syn* see SYNDICATE

6 *syn* see CLASS 1

group *vb* **1** to make into or bring together in a group <*grouped* the children according to age>

syn assemble, cluster, collect, gather, round up; *compare* GATHER 6

rel adjust, arrange, harmonize, organize, systematize; allocate, dispose, distribute, place; bunch, crowd, huddle

idiom bring together, get together

con disband, disperse, scatter, separate

2 *syn* see ASSORT

‖**group grope** *n syn* see ORGY 2

grouping *n syn* see CLASS 1

grouse *vb syn* see GRUMBLE 1

grouser *n syn* see GROUCH

grovel *vb syn* see FAWN

idiom lick the dust (*or* one's boots)

groveler *n syn* see SYCOPHANT

groveling *adj syn* see FAWNING

grow *vb* **1** to cause (something living) to exist or flourish <*grew* a crop of wheat>

syn breed, cultivate, produce, propagate, raise

rel care (for), foster, nurse, nurture, rear, tend

2 *syn* see MATURE

3 *syn* see ESCALATE 2

4 *syn* see BECOME 1

growl *vb syn* see RUMBLE

growler *n syn* see GROUCH

grown *adj* **1** *syn* see MATURE 1

2 *syn* see OVERGROWN

grown–up *adj syn* see MATURE 1

ant childish; callow

growth *n syn* see DEVELOPMENT

grow up *vb syn* see MATURE

grub *vb* **1** *syn* see DIG 1

rel burrow, poke, root

2 *syn* see SCOUR 2

3 *syn* see DRUDGE

grub *n* **1** *syn* see HACK 2

2 *syn* see FOOD 1

grubber *n syn* see HACK 2

grubby *adj syn* see DIRTY 1

ant immaculate

grubstake *vb syn* see CAPITALIZE

grudge *vb syn* see ENVY

rel deny; refuse

grudge *n syn* see MALICE

rel grievance, injury, injustice

gruesome *adj syn* see GHASTLY 1

rel appalling, daunting; horrendous, horrific; baleful, sinister

gruff *adj* **1** *syn* see BLUFF

rel crabbed, dour, morose, saturnine, sullen, surly; boorish, churlish; fierce, truculent

con bland, smooth, suave, urbane; fulsome, oily, slick, soapy, unctuous

2 *syn* see HOARSE 1

grumble *vb* **1** to complain in a low harsh voice and often in a surly manner <workers *grumbling* about the low wages>

syn croak, grouch, grouse, ‖grunt, murmur, mutter, scold; *compare* COMPLAIN

rel ‖beef, ‖bellyache, brawl, crab, fuss, gripe, holler, squawk, whine; groan, moan; complain, kick

con applaud, cheer; rejoice

2 *syn* see RUMBLE

grumbler *n syn* see GROUCH

grump *n* **1** **grumps** *pl syn* see SULK

2 *syn* see GROUCH

grump *vb syn* see SULK

---

syn synonym(s)   *rel* related word(s)

ant antonym(s)   *con* contrasted word(s)

idiom idiomatic equivalent(s)

‖ use limited; if in doubt, see a dictionary

Grundy *n syn* see PRUDE

grungy *adj syn* see DIRTY 1

‖**grunt** *vb syn* see GRUMBLE 1

guarantee *n* **1** an assurance for the fulfillment of a condition <gave him a *guarantee* that the work would be done according to specifications>
syn bail, bond, guaranty, security, surety, warranty; *compare* PLEDGE 1
rel earnest, pledge, promise, token, undertaking, word; oath, vow
2 *syn* see WORD 8

guarantee *vb syn* see WARRANT 2

guarantor *n syn* see SPONSOR

guaranty *n syn* see GUARANTEE 1
rel bargain, contract

guaranty *vb syn* see WARRANT 2

guard *n* **1** *syn* see DEFENSE 1
2 a person or group on sentinel duty <posted six *guards* around the diamond necklace><turned out the *guard*>
syn lookout, picket, sentinel, sentry, ward, watch, watchman
rel guardian, jailer, keeper, turnkey, warden, warder; patrolman; outguard, patrol

guard *vb syn* see DEFEND 1
rel attend, mind, tend, watch; accompany, chaperon, conduct, convoy, escort

guarded *adj* **1** *syn* see ULTERIOR
2 *syn* see CAUTIOUS
ant unguarded

guardian *n syn* see CUSTODIAN

guardianship *n syn* see CUSTODY

guardroom *n syn* see JAIL

gudgeon *n syn* see FOOL 3

guerdon *n syn* see REWARD

guerdon *vb syn* see PAY 1

guerrilla *n syn* see PARTISAN 2

guess *vb* **1** *syn* see CONJECTURE
rel reason, speculate; deduce; estimate, reckon
idiom venture a guess
2 *syn* see PREDICT 2

guest *n* **1** *syn* see VISITOR 1
2 guests *pl syn* see COMPANY 2

guff *n* **1** *syn* see NONSENSE 2
2 *syn* see BACK TALK

guffaw *vb syn* see LAUGH

guide *vb* to put or lead on a course or into the way to be followed <*guided* them safely through the minefields>
syn conduct, direct, escort, lead, pilot, route, see, shepherd, show, steer
rel accompany, chaperon, convoy; control, manage; contrive, engineer, maneuver
idiom set one on one's way
con bewilder, distract, mystify, perplex, puzzle; beguile, deceive, delude, mislead
ant misguide

guide *n* **1** *syn* see LEADER 1
2 *syn* see ESCORT 2
rel conductor, director, leader, pilot
3 *syn* see HANDBOOK

guidebook *n syn* see HANDBOOK

guild *n syn* see ASSOCIATION 2

guile *n syn* see DECEIT 1

ant ingenuousness; candor

guileful *adj* **1** *syn* see SLY 2
ant guileless
2 *syn* see UNDERHAND

guileless *adj syn* see NATURAL 5
ant guileful

guillotine *vb syn* see BEHEAD

guilt *n syn* see BLAME
rel crime, offense, sin; responsibility
ant innocence; guiltlessness

guiltless *adj* **1** *syn* see GOOD 11
2 *syn* see INNOCENT 2
ant guilty

guilty *adj syn* see BLAMEWORTHY
rel accountable, answerable, responsible; impeached, incriminated, indicted
ant innocent; guiltless

guise *n* **1** *syn* see COSTUME
2 *syn* see APPEARANCE 2
3 *syn* see MASK 2

gulch *n syn* see RAVINE

gulf *n* **1** *syn* see INLET
2 a hollow place of vast width and depth <a *gulf* extending deep into the earth>
syn abysm, abyss, chasm
rel cave, cavity, hollow; crevasse, gulch, ravine; pit, shaft, well

gull *vb syn* see DUPE

gull *n syn* see FOOL 3

gullible *adj syn* see EASY 3
ant astute

gulp *vb* to swallow hurriedly or greedily or in one swallow <*gulped* his lunch and ran off>
syn bolt, cram, englut, gobble, guzzle, ingurgitate, slop, slosh, wolf
rel devour, glut, stuff
con nibble, pick

gum (up) *vb syn* see BOTCH

gumbo *n syn* see GOO 1

gummy *adj syn* see STICKY 1

gumption *n syn* see SENSE 6
rel astuteness, perspicaciousness, perspicacity, sagaciousness, sagacity, shrewdness

gumptious *adj syn* see ENTERPRISING 2

gumshoe *n* **1** *syn* see DETECTIVE
2 *syn* see POLICEMAN

gumshoe *vb syn* see SNEAK

gun *n syn* see ASSASSIN

gung ho *adj syn* see ENTHUSIASTIC

gunk *n* **1** *syn* see GOO 1
2 *syn* see CRUD

gunman *n syn* see ASSASSIN

‖**gunsel** *n syn* see ASSASSIN

gunslinger *n syn* see ASSASSIN

gurge *vb syn* see SWIRL

gurgle *vb syn* see SLOSH 1

gush *vb syn* see POUR 2
rel flood, flush; emanate, issue, spring

gushing *adj syn* see EFFUSIVE

gushy *adj syn* see EFFUSIVE

gussy up *vb syn* see DRESS UP 1

gust *n syn* see OUTBURST 1

gusto *n syn* see TASTE 4
rel delectation, delight, enjoyment, pleasure; ardor, enthusiasm, fervor, passion, zeal

gusty *adj syn* see WINDY 1

‖**gusty** *adj syn* see PALATABLE

gut *n* **1** *usu* **guts** *pl syn* see ENTRAILS

 ‖**2** *syn* see ABDOMEN

  3 guts *pl syn* see COURAGE

  4 guts *pl syn* see FORTITUDE

gut *vb* **1** *syn* see EVISCERATE

  2 *syn* see DRESS 3

gut *adj syn* see INNER 2

gutless *adj syn* see COWARDLY

 ant ‖gutsy

‖**gutsy** *adj syn* see BRAVE 1

guy *n syn* see MAN 3

guzzle *vb* **1** *syn* see DRINK 3

  2 *syn* see GULP

guzzler *n syn* see DRUNKARD

gyp *n* **1** *syn* see SWINDLER

  2 *syn* see IMPOSTURE

gyp *vb syn* see CHEAT

gypper *n syn* see SWINDLER

gyrate *vb* **1** *syn* see TURN 1

  2 *syn* see SPIN 1

gyration *n syn* see REVOLUTION 1

gyre *vb* **1** *syn* see TURN 1

  2 *syn* see SPIN 1

gyre *n syn* see REVOLUTION 1

gyve *n, usu* **gyves** *pl syn* see SHACKLE

---

syn synonym(s)   *rel* related word(s)
ant antonym(s)   *con* contrasted word(s)
idiom idiomatic equivalent(s)
‖ use limited; if in doubt, see a dictionary

H

habiliment *n* **1** habiliments *pl syn* see EQUIPMENT
2 *usu* habiliments *pl syn* see CLOTHES

habit *n* **1** a mode of behaving or doing fixed by constant repetition <it was his *habit* to rise early>
syn consuetude, custom, habitude, manner, practice, praxis, trick, usage, use, way, wont
rel bent, disposition, inclination, proclivity, tendency, turn; convention, fashion, form, mode, pattern, style; addiction; groove, rote, routine, rut, set
2 *syn* see PHYSIQUE
rel carcass; framework; contour, outline

habitable *adj syn* see LIVABLE 1
ant unhabitable, uninhabitable

habitant *n syn* see INHABITANT

habitat *n* the physical environment natural to a kind of being <the watery *habitat* of the eel>
syn haunt, home, locality, range, site, stamping ground
rel environment, locale, surroundings, territory

habitation *n* **1** the act of inhabiting or the state of being inhabited <places suitable for *habitation*>
syn inhabitancy, inhabitation, occupancy, occupation, residence, settlement
rel colonization, domiciliation, peopling; sojourning
2 the place where one lives <*habitations* unfit for human occupancy>
syn abode, commorancy, domicile, dwelling, home, house, residence, residency
rel apartment, flat, tenement; housing, lodging, lodgment, quarters; haunt, haven, homeplace, homestead, place, seat; ‖digs, nest, nook, ‖pad, ‖roost; astre, fireside, hearth, hearthside, hearthstone, roof, rooftree
idiom roof over one's head, where one hangs one's hat

habitual *adj* **1** *syn* see USUAL 1
rel constant, established, ingrained, inveterate, persistent, steady
con infrequent, irregular, sporadic, uncommon
ant occasional
2 acting by force of habit <*habitual* smokers who blue the air>
syn accustomed, chronic, confirmed, habituated
rel continual, inveterate, persistent, regular, steady; automatic, instinctive, involuntary; addicted; customary, wonted
con conscious, deliberate, premeditative, purposive, witting

habitually *adv syn* see USUALLY 1
ant occasionally

habituate *vb* **1** *syn* see ACCUSTOM
2 to make acceptable or desirable (as to oneself) through use <*habituate* oneself to poverty>
syn addict, adjust, confirm (in), devote (to), take (to)

rel bear, endure, inure, support, tolerate; condition, familiarize, season
con balk (at), object (to), resist

habituated *adj syn* see HABITUAL 2

habitude *n syn* see HABIT 1
rel attitude, position, stand; condition, situation, state
con humor, mood, temper; caprice, freak, vagary, whim

habitué *n* **1** one who frequents a place <an *habitué* of libraries>
syn denizen, frequenter, haunter
rel customer, devotee, patron, sojourner; employer, user
2 *syn* see ADDICT

habitus *n syn* see PHYSIQUE

hack *vb* to cut with repeated crude or ruthless blows <*hack* a path through the jungle>
syn hackle, haggle, slash
rel gash, mangle; chop, cut, fell, hew

hack *n* **1** *syn* see TAXICAB
2 one who surrenders intellectual or personal integrity for an assured reward (as a regular income) <party *hacks* and hangers-on>
syn drudge, grub, grubber, hireling, mercenary, slavey
rel grind, lackey, servant, slave; machine, plodder; potboiler

hack *adj* **1** *syn* see INFERIOR 2
rel commonplace, dull, ordinary, trite, usual; inconsequential, petty, trivial
con individual, original, uncommon, unusual
2 *syn* see TRITE
rel antiquated, old, outmoded, outworn
con lively; unfamiliar

hackle *vb syn* see HACK

hackneyed *adj syn* see TRITE
rel antediluvian, antiquated, archaic, obsolete, outmoded, out-of-date; conventional, everyday, quotidian, stock; moth-eaten
ant unhackneyed

Hadean *adj syn* see INFERNAL 1
rel gloomy, murky, stygian

hades *n syn* see HELL

hag *n* **1** *syn* see WITCH 1
2 an ugly or evil-looking old woman <a pitiful homeless *hag*>
syn ‖bag, ‖bat, beldam, biddy, crone, drab, trot, witch
rel gammer, grandam; ‖battle-ax, fishwife, gorgon, harpy, harridan, shrew, slattern, virago, vixen

haggard *adj* thin and contracted by or as if by fatigue or inner distress <*haggard* from their long vigil>
syn careworn, drawn, pinched, worn
rel angular, gaunt, lank, lean, scraggy, scrawny, skinny, spare; ashen, faded, pale, pallid, wan;

exhausted, fagged, fatigued, tired, wearied, worn-down
con energetic, lusty, strenuous, vigorous; easy, relaxed
haggle *vb* **1** *syn* see HACK
  2 to argue as to terms <*haggle* over prices>
  syn bargain, chaffer, dicker, higgle, huckster, palter
  rel barter, deal, horse-trade, trade; bicker, cavil, dispute, quibble, squabble, stickle, wrangle
hagridden *adj syn* see OBSESSED
hagride *vb syn* see WORRY 1
hail *n syn* see BARRAGE
hail *vb* **1** *syn* see ADDRESS 7
  rel hallo, hallow, holler, shout
  2 *syn* see COMMEND 2
  con belittle, depreciate, disparage, downgrade; berate, censure, condemn, libel, rap; dismiss, reject
hail (from) *vb syn* see ORIGINATE 5
hair *n* a minute distance, degree, or margin <won the election by a *hair*>
  syn ace, hairbreadth, whisker; *compare* HINT 2
  rel bit, fraction, jot, mite, particle, trace, trifle
hairbreadth *n syn* see HAIR
haircutter *n syn* see BARBER
hairless *adj* lacking hair <he had a shining *hairless* head>
  syn bald, glabrous, smooth
  rel baldish; shaved, shaven, shorn, tonsured
  ant hairy
hairline *adj syn* see FINE 1
hairsplitting *adj syn* see FINE 1
hair–trigger *adj syn* see INSTANTANEOUS
hairy *adj* **1** covered with or as if with hair <wore a *hairy* overcoat>
  syn fleecy, hirsute, pileous, pilose, whiskered, woolly
  rel bristly, bushy, downy, fluffy, fuzzy, lanate, nappy, pubescent, rough, shaggy, tomentose, tufted, unshorn, villous
  con bald, barefaced, beardless, glabrous, shaved, shaven, shorn, smooth
  ant hairless
  2 *syn* see DANGEROUS 1
  3 *syn* see ROUGH 1
halcyon *adj syn* see CALM 1
  con blustery, fevered, foul, raging, rough, stormy, tempestuous, troubled, tumultuous, wild
hale *adj syn* see HEALTHY 1
  rel husky, stout, strapping
  idiom hale and hearty
  ant infirm
haleness *n syn* see HEALTH
half–blind *adj syn* see PURBLIND
half blood *n syn* see HYBRID
  ant full blood
half–breed *n syn* see HYBRID
  ant full blood
halfhearted *adj syn* see TEPID 2
‖half–seas over *adj syn* see INTOXICATED 1
halfway *adj syn* see MIDDLE 1
half–wit *n syn* see FOOL 4

half–witted *adj syn* see RETARDED
hall *n syn* see PASSAGE 4
hallo *vb syn* see CALL 1
hallow *vb* **1** *syn* see BLESS 1
  2 *syn* see DEVOTE 1
  con defile, desecrate, pollute, profane
hallowed *adj syn* see HOLY 1
hallucination *n syn* see DELUSION 1
  rel apparition, fata morgana, phantom, wraith
hallway *n syn* see PASSAGE 4
halt *vb syn* see LIMP 1
halt *vb* **1** *syn* see STOP 4
  ant proceed
  2 *syn* see STOP 3
  3 *syn* see ARREST 1
  4 *syn* see HESITATE
  5 *syn* see CLOSE 2
halting *adj* **1** *syn* see AWKWARD 2
  2 *syn* see VACILLATING 2
ham–handed *adj syn* see AWKWARD 2
hammer *vb* **1** to strike or shape with or as if with a hammer <brass *hammered* into bowls and trays>
  syn beat, malleate, pound
  rel elaborate, fashion, form, shape
  2 *syn* see BEAT 1
  3 *syn* see IMPRESS 3
  ‖4 *syn* see STAMMER 1
hammer (out) *vb syn* see ERECT 5
hammerhead *n syn* see DUNCE
hammerheaded *adj syn* see STUPID 1
hamper *vb* to impede in moving, progressing, or acting freely <the long dress *hampered* her escape>
  syn clog, curb, entrammel, fetter, hobble, hog⹀tie, leash, shackle, tie, tie up, trammel; *compare* HINDER, RESTRAIN 1
  rel cumber, encumber, handicap, hinder, impede, lumber, obstruct; baffle, balk, bar, block, foil, frustrate, thwart; restrain, restrict, retard; discomfit, embarrass; check, inconvenience, inhibit
  idiom tie one's hands
  con free, liberate, loose, release, unfetter, unleash, unshackle
  ant aid, facilitate
hamper *n syn* see OBSTACLE 1
hams *n pl syn* see BUTTOCKS
hand *n* **1** *syn* see SIDE 1
  2 *syn* see PHASE
  3 *syn* see HANDWRITING
  4 *syn* see HELP 1
  5 *syn* see WORKER
  6 *syn* see TOUCH 6
hand *vb* **1** *syn* see GIVE 3
  2 *syn* see PASS 9
handbill *n syn* see POSTER
handbook *n* a concise reference book <a *handbook* of wild flowers>

---

syn synonym(s) **rel** related word(s)
ant antonym(s) **con** contrasted word(s)
idiom idiomatic equivalent(s)
‖ use limited; if in doubt, see a dictionary

syn Baedeker, compendium, enchiridion, guide, guidebook, manual, vade mecum
con cyclopedia, encyclopedia

hand down *vb* to convey in succession <a skill *handed down* from father to son>
syn bequeath, hand on, pass (on), transmit
con get, obtain, receive

handful *n syn* see FEW

handicap *n* **1** *syn* see DISADVANTAGE
rel burden, encumbrance, load; embarrassment
ant asset
2 *syn* see ADVANTAGE 3

handicraft *n syn* see TRADE 1

hand in *vb syn* see SUBMIT 2

handkerchief *n* a small usually square piece of cloth used especially for blowing the nose <carry a pocket *handkerchief*>
syn hankie, kerchief, ‖wipe, ‖wiper

‖handle *n* **1** *syn* see NAME 1
2 *syn* see NICKNAME

handle *vb* **1** *syn* see TOUCH 1
rel test, try; manipulate
2 to deal with or manage usually with dexterity or efficiency <*handles* his tools with great skill>
syn dispense, maneuver, manipulate, ply, swing, wield
rel direct, guide, manage, operate, run, work; brandish, flourish, shake, wave; aim, lay, level, point
3 *syn* see OPERATE 3
4 *syn* see TREAT 2
rel conduct, control, direct, manage
5 *syn* see GOVERN 3
6 *syn* see USE 2

handling *n syn* see OVERSIGHT 1

handmaid *n syn* see MAID 2

hand on *vb syn* see HAND DOWN

hand out *vb syn* see GIVE 1

hand over *vb* **1** *syn* see RELINQUISH
2 *syn* see GIVE 3
3 *syn* see COMMIT 1

hand running *adv syn* see TOGETHER 2

handsome *adj* **1** *syn* see LIBERAL 1
con economical, frugal, sparing; scrimpy, skimpy
2 *syn* see BEAUTIFUL
rel august, majestic, noble, stately; chic, dashing, fashionable, modish, smart, stylish
con inelegant, unsightly
ant unhandsome

handwriting *n* writing in which the letters are formed by a hand-guided implement (as a pen) <legible *handwriting*>
syn calligraphy, chirography, ductus, fist, hand, penmanship, script
rel longhand

handy *adj* **1** *syn* see CONVENIENT 2
idiom at one's hand (*or* elbow), ready to hand
ant unhandy
2 *syn* see PRACTICAL 2
rel adaptable, advantageous, beneficial, wieldy
con clumsy, cumbersome, cumbrous, unwieldy
ant unhandy
3 *syn* see DEXTEROUS 1

hang *vb* **1** to place or be placed so as to be supported at one point or side usually at the top <*hang* the washing on the line>
syn dangle, depend, sling, suspend
rel attach, hook; fix, pin, tack (up); adhere, cling, stick
2 to put to death by suspending by the neck <was *hanged* for stealing a sheep>
syn gibbet, noose, scrag, string (up), turn off
rel execute, lynch
idiom bring to the gallows, hang by the neck, make dance on air (*or* nothing)
3 to remain poised or stationary as if suspended in midair <clouds *hanging* in the west>
syn float, hover, poise
4 to project outward or incline downward <children *hanging* out the windows to watch a parade>
syn beetle, bend (over), jut, lean (over), overhang
rel drape, droop, loll, lop, sag, trail

hang (on *or* upon) *vb syn* see DEPEND (on *or* upon) 1

hang *n* the special method of doing, using, or dealing with something <can't get the *hang* of this gadget>
syn knack, swing, trick
rel art, craft, skill

hang around *vb syn* see FREQUENT

hanger–on *n syn* see PARASITE
rel bystander, follower, spectator, sycophant

hanging *adj syn* see SUSPENDED

hand–loose *adj syn* see EASYGOING 3

hang on *vb syn* see PERSEVERE

hang out *vb* **1** *syn* see RESIDE 1
2 *syn* see FREQUENT

hangout *n* **1** *syn* see RESORT 2
2 *syn* see DIVE

hang up *vb syn* see DELAY 1

hanker *vb syn* see LONG
rel covet, desire, wish

hankie *n syn* see HANDKERCHIEF

hanky–panky *n syn* see DECEPTION 1

hap *n syn* see ACCIDENT 1
rel destiny, fate, lot, portion

hap *vb syn* see HAPPEN 1

‖hap *vb syn* see BUNDLE UP

haphazard *adj syn* see RANDOM
rel accidental; careless, helter-skelter, slipshod; unorganized, unsystematic
con deliberate, designed, intentional, voluntary, willful
ant planned

haphazard *adv syn* see ABOUT 4
rel accidentally, aimlessly, carelessly, casually, promiscuously

haphazardly *adv syn* see ABOUT 4
rel accidentally, aimlessly, carelessly, casually, promiscuously

hapless *adj syn* see UNLUCKY
rel infelicitous; miserable, woeful, wretched

happen *vb* **1** to take place or come about <the incident *happened* at midnight>

syn befall, betide, break, chance, come, come off, develop, do, fall out, give, go, go down, hap, occur, pass, rise, transpire
rel go off, turn out
idiom come to pass
2 to come by chance <he unexpectedly *happened* on a new method>
syn bump, chance, hit, light, luck, meet, stumble, tumble
rel befall

happening *n syn* see OCCURRENCE

happify *vb syn* see PLEASE 2

happily *adv syn* see WELL 5

happiness *n* a state of well-being or pleasurable satisfaction <felt *happiness* at her husband's success>
syn beatitude, blessedness, bliss, blissfulness
rel content, contentedness, satisfaction; cheer, cheerfulness, felicity, gladness; gaiety, jollity, joy; delectation, delight, enjoyment, pleasure
con discontent, dissatisfaction, vexation; cheerlessness, despair, desperation, despondency, hopelessness; distress, misery, wretchedness
ant unhappiness

happy *adj* **1** *syn* see LUCKY
rel accidental, casual, fortuitous, incidental; opportune, seasonable, timely
ant unhappy
2 *syn* see FIT 1
rel effective, effectual, efficacious, efficient; cogent, convincing, telling; pat, seasonable, well-timed; correct, nice, right
ant unhappy
3 *syn* see GLAD 1
rel content, contented, satisfied
ant unhappy; disconsolate

happy–go–lucky *adj* disposed to accept cheerfully whatever happens <enjoyed a *happy-go-lucky* existence without needlessly worrying>
syn carefree, free-minded, insouciant, lighthearted, lightsome; *compare* COOL 2
rel casual, easy, easygoing; blithe, careless, cheerful, feckless, heedless, lackadaisical; debonair, nonchalant, unconcerned; devil-may-care, reckless
con careful, cautious, circumspect, discreet, guarded, prudent

happy hunting ground *n syn* see HEAVEN 2

hara–kiri *n syn* see SUICIDE

harangue *n syn* see TIRADE

harangue *vb syn* see ORATE

harass *vb* **1** *syn* see RAID 1
2 *syn* see WORRY 1
rel badger, bait, bullyrag, chivy, devil, heckle, hector, hound, ride
idiom give a bad (*or* hard) time
3 *syn* see TRY 2

harassed *adj syn* see DISTRAUGHT

harasser *n syn* see BULLY 1

harassment *n syn* see ANNOYANCE 1
rel aggravation, disturbance, exasperation, irritation, perturbation

harbinger *n syn* see FORERUNNER 1

harbinger *vb syn* see ANNOUNCE 2

harbor *n* **1** *syn* see SHELTER 1
2 *syn* see INLET
3 a place where seacraft may ride secure <a small craft retreated to the safety of the *harbor*>
syn anchorage, ‖chuck, harborage, haven, port, riding, road(s), roadstead

harbor *vb* **1** to provide with shelter or a refuge <*harbored* the refugees in our homes>
syn chamber, haven, house, roof, shelter, shield
rel cherish, foster, nurse, nurture; conceal, hide, secrete; guard, protect, safeguard, screen
idiom give shelter (*or* asylum) to
con eject, evict, expel, oust; banish, deport, exile; eliminate, exclude, shut out
2 to provide with a usually temporary place to live <the miners were *harbored* in camps>
syn accommodate, bestow, billet, board, bunk, domicile, domiciliate, entertain, house, hut, lodge, put up, quarter, room, roost
rel cabin, camp, encamp

harborage *n syn* see SHELTER 1
2 *syn* see REFUGE 1
3 *syn* see HARBOR 3

hard *adj* **1** *syn* see FIRM 2
rel compacted, compressed, concentrated, consolidated, packed; callous, hardened, indurate, indurated, set; adamantine, flinty, granitic, iron, ironhard
con fluid, liquid; flabby, limp; ductile, malleable, plastic, pliable, pliant; elastic, flexible, limber, resilient, supple
ant soft
2 *syn* see SPIRITUOUS
ant soft
3 *syn* see REALISTIC
4 *syn* see INSENSIBLE 5
5 *syn* see INTENSIVE
6 demanding great toil and effort <a *hard* but rewarding task>
syn arduous, difficile, difficult, effortful, formidable, heavy, knotty, labored, laborious, operose, rough, rugged, serious, severe, slavish, sticky, strenuous, terrible, toilful, toilsome, tough, uphill
rel burdensome, exacting, onerous; complex, complicated, intricate, involved, scabrous; backbreaking, distressing, exhausting, fatiguing, grinding, tiring, wearing, wearisome, wearying; bothersome, demanding, irksome, rocky, straining, troublesome, trying; merciless, unsparing
con effortless, facile, light, simple, smooth
ant easy
7 *syn* see ACTUAL 2
8 *syn* see GRIM 2
9 *syn* see SEVERE 3

hard *adv* **1** with great or utmost force <hit the nail *hard*>

---

syn synonym(s)   *rel* related word(s)
ant antonym(s)   *con* contrasted word(s)
idiom idiomatic equivalent(s)
‖ use limited; if in doubt, see a dictionary

syn energetically, forcefully, forcibly, hardly, might and main, mightily, powerfully, strongly, vigorously

rel actively, animatedly, briskly, snappily, spiritedly, sprightly, vivaciously; earnestly, intensely, keenly, seriously, urgently, wholeheartedly

idiom with all one's might

con faintly, feebly, nervelessly, softly, strengthlessly, unenergetically, weakly

ant easily, easy

2 in a violent manner <the wind blew *hard* all the next day>

syn fiercely, frantically, frenziedly, furiously, hardly, madly, stormily, tumultuously, turbulently, violently, wildly

rel boisterously, exuberantly, rowdily, uproariously; angrily, brutally, ferociously, savagely, viciously

idiom like a house afire, like fury, like mad

con gently, mildly, softly

3 with intentness and determination <made up her mind to study *hard*>

syn assiduously, dingdong, earnestly, exhaustively, intensely, intensively, painstakingly, thoroughly, unremittingly

rel conscientiously, meticulously, punctiliously

con carelessly, casually, desultorily, fitfully, haphazardly

4 in a fixed and intensive manner <stared *hard* at the offender>

syn closely, intently, searchingly, sharply

con casually, cursorily, idly, offhand

5 in such manner as to cause hardship, difficulty, or defeat <things will go *hard* with him if he doesn't reform>

syn badly, hardly, harshly, painfully, rigorously, roughly, severely; *compare* AMISS 2

rel cruelly; relentlessly; meanly, shabbily, unfairly

con comfortably, pleasantly, smoothly; acceptably, satisfactorily, satisfyingly

ant easily, easy

6 with great or excessive resentment or grief <don't take your setback so *hard*>

syn bitterly, hardly, keenly, rancorously, resentfully, sorely

con casually, lightly, nonchalantly, offhandedly

7 in a firm manner <hold on *hard*>

syn fast, firm, firmly, fixedly, solidly, steadfastly, tight, tightly

con easily, easy, loose, loosely, slackly

8 with difficulty <breathing *hard* after the climb>

syn arduously, burdensomely, difficultly, hardly, laboriously, onerously, toilsomely

rel exhaustingly, gruelingly, painfully, tiredly; awkwardly, cumbersomely, cumbrously, inconveniently, ponderously, unhandily, unwieldily

con effortlessly, evenly, handily, readily, smoothly

ant easily, easy

9 to the point of hardness <the pond is frozen *hard*>

syn firmly, hardly, solid, solidly

10 *syn* see CLOSE

hard–boiled *adj* **1** *syn* see UNFEELING 2

rel coarse, crude, rough; seasoned, sophisticated, worldly-wise

idiom not born yesterday

con artless, guileless, naive, simple-hearted, unsophisticated; kindly, mild, soft

2 *syn* see REALISTIC

harden *vb* **1** to make or become physically hard or solid <this substance *hardens* immediately on exposure to air>

syn cake, concrete, congeal, dry, indurate, set, solidify

rel compact, consolidate, densify, firm, stiffen; anneal, caseharden, temper; calcify, fossilize, lithify, ossify, petrify

con deliquesce, dissolve, fuse, liquefy, melt

ant soften

2 to make proof against hardship, strain, or exposure <frontier life *hardened* most men quickly to rough conditions>

syn acclimate, acclimatize, climatize, season, toughen

rel accustom, habituate, indurate, inure; accommodate, adapt, adjust, conform

con emasculate, enervate; debilitate, devitalize, enfeeble, sap, undermine, weaken

ant soften

hardened *adj* *syn* see UNFEELING 2

hardfisted *adj* *syn* see STINGY

ant openhanded

hardhanded *adj* *syn* see STINGY

ant openhanded

hardheaded *adj* **1** *syn* see OBSTINATE

2 *syn* see REALISTIC

hardhearted *adj* *syn* see UNFEELING 2

hardihood *n* **1** *syn* see TEMERITY

rel boldness, intrepidity; brazenness, cockiness; fortitude, grit, guts, pluck, sand

ant cowardice; timidity

2 *syn* see INSOLENCE

3 *syn* see ENERGY 2

hardiness *n* *syn* see TEMERITY

ant cowardice; timidity

hard–line *adj* *syn* see TOUGH 3

hardly *adv* **1** *syn* see HARD 1

2 *syn* see HARD 2

3 *syn* see HARD 5

4 *syn* see HARD 6

5 *syn* see HARD 8

6 *syn* see JUST 2

7 *syn* see HARD 9

hardly ever *adv* *syn* see SELDOM

hardness *n* *syn* see DIFFICULTY 1

ant easiness

hardpan *n* *syn* see BASE 1

hardscrabble *adj* *syn* see BARREN 2

hard–shell *adj* *syn* see INVETERATE 1

hardship *n* *syn* see DIFFICULTY 1

rel adversity, mischance, misfortune; danger, hazard, peril; affliction, trial, tribulation; drudgery, toil, travail; discomfort, distress

con comfort, ease

hardy *adj syn* see TOUGH 4
  ant tender

harebrain *n* **1** *syn* see SCATTERBRAIN
  2 *syn* see CRACKPOT

harebrained *adj* **1** *syn* see GIDDY 1
  2 *syn* see FOOLISH 2

harefooted *adj syn* see FAST 3

hark *vb syn* see LISTEN
  rel mark, mind, note, notice, remark
  idiom be all ears, not miss a trick

harlequin *n syn* see CLOWN 3

harlot *n* **1** a woman who engages in unlawful or socially unacceptable sexual intercourse often for material gain <ply the trade of a *harlot*>
  syn blowen, courtesan, demimondaine, demimonde, demirep, fancy woman, hetaera, kept woman, paphian, whore
  2 *syn* see PROSTITUTE

harlotry *n syn* see PROSTITUTION

harm *n syn* see INJURY 1
  rel deleteriousness; banefulness, noxiousness, perniciousness; mischance, misfortune, misuse; impairment, marring
  con aid, help; accommodation, benefaction; charity, favor, service
  ant benefit

harm *vb syn* see INJURE 1
  rel abuse, ill-use, maltreat, mistreat, misuse, molest; dilapidate, ruin; discommode, incommode, inconvenience; sabotage, sap, undermine
  idiom do violence to
  con ameliorate, better, improve; avail, profit
  ant benefit

harmful *adj* inflicting or capable of inflicting injury <a *harmful* drug>
  syn bad, damaging, deleterious, detrimental, evil, hurtful, ill, injurious, mischievous, nocent, nocuous, prejudicial, prejudicious
  rel baleful, baneful, malefic, malign, malignant, noisome, noxious, pernicious, toxic; insalubrious, unhealthful, unhealthy, unwholesome; dangerous, hazardous, risky, unsafe
  con innocuous, inoffensive, nontoxic; beneficent, beneficial, benign, benignant, favorable, helpful, salutary, useful; safe, unhazardous
  ant harmless

harmless *adj* not having hurtful or injurious qualities <*harmless* pastimes>
  syn innocent, innocuous, innoxious, inobnoxious, inoffensive, unoffending, unoffensive; compare SAFE 3
  rel guiltless; nontoxic, painless, safe
  con baneful, dangerous, malignant, noxious, pernicious, toxic, virulent; damaging, destructive, detrimental, hurtful, injurious; deadly, fell, ruinous; improper, unsuitable, wrong
  ant harmful

harmonic *adj syn* see HARMONIOUS 1

harmonious *adj* **1** musically concordant <a *harmonious* morning chorus of birds>
  syn blending, chiming, consonant, harmonic, musical, symphonic, symphonious
  rel canorous, dulcet, euphonious, mellifluous, mellisonant, melodious, musical, silvery, sonorous, sweet, tuneful; chordal, contrapuntal, counterpointed, polyphonic
  idiom in concert, in tune
  con clashing, discordant, dissonant, grating, harsh, jangling, jarring, raucous, shrill, strident, tuneless, unmusical, untuneful; atonal
  ant disharmonious, inharmonious, unharmonious

  2 having the parts agreeably related <a building with *harmonious* proportions>
  syn accordant, concordant, congruous; compare CONSONANT 1
  rel agreeable, pleasing, satisfying; concinnate, symmetrical
  con clashing, incongruous, unsymmetrical; askew, distorted, skewed
  ant inharmonious, unharmonious

  3 marked by accord in sentiment or action <a *harmonious* effort to reach a practicable agreement>
  syn amicable, amical, congenial, friendly
  rel coactive, collaborative, cooperative; empathetic, empathic, simpatico, sympathetic; calm, irenic, pacific, peaceful
  idiom of one accord
  con incompatible, uncongenial, uncooperative, unfriendly, unsympathetic; belligerent, contentious, pugnacious
  ant inharmonious, unharmonious

harmonize *vb* **1** *syn* see AGREE 3
  rel cooperate, match, unite
  con differ, disagree
  ant clash; conflict
  2 *syn* see AGREE 4
  ant differ (from)
  3 to bring into consonance or accord <*harmonize* the factions of a political party>
  syn accommodate, attune, conform, coordinate, integrate, proportion, reconcile, reconciliate, tune
  rel adapt, adjust, correlate; coapt, relate
  con alienate, disrupt, estrange
  ant disharmonize
  4 to combine or adapt so as to achieve a desired effect <*harmonize* the elements of a story>
  syn arrange, blend, integrate, orchestrate, symphonize, synthesize, unify
  rel coordinate, correlate

harmonizing *n syn* see RECONCILIATION

harmony *n* **1** musical agreement of sounds <singing in *harmony*>
  syn accord, chorus, concert, concord, consonance, tune
  rel mellifluousness, melodiousness, melody, musicality, sonority, tunefulness; diapason, polyphony
  con cacophony, discord, discordance, discordancy, dissonance, harshness, inharmoniousness, jangle, stridency, tunelessness, unharmoni-

---

syn synonym(s)   *rel* related word(s)
ant antonym(s)   *con* contrasted word(s)
idiom idiomatic equivalent(s)
‖ use limited; if in doubt, see a dictionary

ousness, unmusicalness, untunefulness; atonality

ant disharmony, inharmony

2 the effect produced when different things come together without clashing or disagreement <goals that are in *harmony* with our capabilities>

syn accord, agreement, chime, concord, concordance, consonance, tune; *compare* CONSISTENCY

rel conformance, conformity, correspondence; articulation, coaptation, compatibility, congruity; concatenation, concurrence, integration, oneness, togetherness, unity

con disagreement, discord, disparity, dissidence, disunity, variance

ant conflict

3 the state of persons who are in full and perfect agreement <friends who live in *harmony*>

syn concord, rapport, unity

rel affinity, empathy, fellow-feeling, kinship; peace, tranquillity

idiom meeting of minds

con contention, dissension, strife

ant discord

4 *syn* see SYMMETRY

rel concinnity, consonance; dignity, elegance, grace; integrity, unity

con asymmetry, discordance, discordancy, imbalance

ant inharmony

harness *vb syn* see HITCH 2

‖**harness bull** (*or* **cop**) *n syn* see POLICEMAN

harpy *n syn* see VIRAGO

harrier *n syn* see BULLY 1

harrow *vb syn* see AFFLICT

rel fret, irritate, pester; badger, bait, bedevil, devil, heckle, hector, needle, tantalize, tease

harrowing *adj syn* see EXCRUCIATING

harry *vb* **1** *syn* see RAVAGE

2 *syn* see RAID 1

3 *syn* see WORRY 1

rel disturb, irk, perturb, upset; badger, irritate

harsh *adj* **1** *syn* see ROUGH 1

rel coarse, granular, loose; bristly, scraggly, scratchy, shaggy, stubbly

con glossy, satiny, silken, silky, sleek, slick, velvety

2 *syn* see ACRID

rel acerb, acerbic, biting, burning, mordant; pungent, tangy; dry, sour, tart

con mild, smooth, sweet, velvety

3 disagreeable to the ear <many birds have *harsh* cries>

syn dry, grating, hoarse, jarring, rasping, raucous, rough, rugged, rusty, squawky, strident, stridulent, stridulous

rel discordant, dissonant, immelodious, ineuphonious, inharmonious, unmelodious, unmusical; grinding, jangling, scraping; blaring, brassy; ear-piercing, piercing, shrill, squeaky

con euphonious, harmonious, mellow, melodic, melodious, musical, sonorous, sweet; low, soft; agreeable, pleasing

4 *syn* see UNCOMFORTABLE

5 *syn* see GRIM 2

6 *syn* see SEVERE 3

ant mild

harshly *adv syn* see HARD 5

con considerately; gently, lightly, well; famously

ant smoothly

haruspex *n syn* see PROPHET

harvest *n* **1** the act, process, or occasion of gathering a crop <the time of *harvest*>

syn cropping, gathering, harvesting, ingathering, reaping

rel garnering, storing

con planting, seedtime, sowing

2 the gathered produce of land <a bountiful *harvest* saved the settlers>

syn crop, fruitage

rel yield; bearing, vintage

harvest *vb syn* see REAP

rel assemble, collect; accumulate, amass, bin, store (up), stow (away); cache, hide, hoard, squirrel, stash

harvesting *n syn* see HARVEST 1

hash *vb syn* see CHOP 2

hash *n* **1** *syn* see MISCELLANY 1

2 *syn* see CLUTTER 2

3 *syn* see MESS 3

‖**hashery** *n syn* see EATING HOUSE

‖**hash house** *n syn* see EATING HOUSE

hassle *n* **1** *syn* see QUARREL

2 *syn* see COMMOTION 4

3 *syn* see ATTEMPT

hassle *vb* **1** *syn* see ARGUE 2

rel cavil; brawl, fight, spar, struggle

2 *syn* see WORRY 1

haste *n* **1** rapidity of motion or action <we finished our job with great *haste*>

syn celerity, dispatch, expedition, expeditiousness, hurry, hustle, rustle, speed, speediness, swiftness

rel fastness, fleetness, quickness, rapidity; pace, velocity; dash, drive

con languidness, languor, leisureliness, reluctance, slowness; lethargy, sluggishness, torpor

ant deliberateness, deliberation

2 rash or headlong action <oversights due to *haste*>

syn hastiness, hurriedness, precipitance, precipitancy, precipitateness, precipitation, rush

rel impetuosity, impetuousness, impulsiveness

con care, carefulness, circumspection, hastelessness, unhurriedness

ant deliberateness, deliberation

haste *vb syn* see HURRY 2

hasten *vb syn* see SPEED 3

2 *syn* see HURRY 2

hastily *adv syn* see FAST 2

rel agilely, nimbly; impetuously, impulsively, unpremeditatedly; carelessly, recklessly, thoughtlessly; precipitately, prematurely, suddenly

con carefully, designedly, studiedly, thoughtfully; gradually, leisurely, slowly, sluggishly

ant deliberately

hastiness *n syn* see WASTE 2

hasty *adj* **1 *syn*** see FAST 3
rel agile, brisk, nimble; hurried, quickened
con dilatory, laggard, leisured, leisurely
2 *syn* see PRECIPITATE 1
ant deliberate
3 *syn* see RASH 1
rel devil-may-care, slambang, slapdash

hatch *vb* **1 *syn*** see GENERATE 3
2 *syn* see GENERATE 1

hatch (up) *vb syn* see CONTRIVE 2

hatchet man *n syn* see ASSASSIN

hate *n* **1 *syn*** see ABOMINATION 2
rel animosity, animus, antipathy, hostility, ill will, rancor; disgust, scorn, spite
con affection; toleration; adoration, veneration
ant love
2 *syn* see ABOMINATION 1
rel bother, grievance, gripe, irritant, nuisance, ‖pain, trouble
ant delight

hate *vb* to feel extreme enmity or dislike <Cain *hated* his brother> <*hate* to meet strangers>
syn abhor, abominate, detest, execrate, loathe
rel contemn, despise, disdain, dislike, scorn; deprecate, disapprove; resent
con cherish, enjoy, fancy, like, relish; favor, prefer, prize; esteem, respect, revere; dote; idolize, worship
ant love

hateable *adj syn* see HATEFUL 2
ant lovable

hateful *adj* **1 *syn*** see MALICIOUS
rel acrimonious, ill-natured; bitter, resentful; mean
con benevolent, charitable, cordial, genial, good-humored, good-natured, kind, kindly, pleasant
2 deserving of or arousing hate <found herself in a *hateful* situation>
syn abhorrent, abominable, detestable, hateable, horrid, odious
rel distasteful, distressing, obnoxious, repellent, repulsive; contemptible, despicable, execrable, opprobrious, reprehensible, scurvy; foul, infamous, vile; accursed, blasphemous, damnable, unspeakable
con compatible, congenial, consonant; alluring, appealing, attractive, charming, enchanting; agreeable, delectable, delightful, likable, pleasant, pleasing
ant lovable; sympathetic

hatred *n syn* see ABOMINATION 2
rel antipathy, dislike; animosity, enmity, hostility, rancor
con affability, benevolence, benignity, charitableness, cordiality
ant love; admiration

haughtiness *n syn* see PRIDE 3
ant lowliness

haughty *adj syn* see PROUD 1
rel aloof, detached, distant, indifferent, reserved; egotistic; contemptuous, scornful
con humble; obsequious, servile, subservient
ant lowly

haul *vb syn* see PULL 2
rel move, remove, shift; boost, elevate, hoist, lift, raise

haul *n syn* see LOAD 1

haul up *vb syn* see STOP 4

haunches *n pl syn* see BUTTOCKS

haunt *vb syn* see FREQUENT

haunt *n* **1 *syn*** see RESORT 2
2 *syn* see HABITAT
3 *syn* see APPARITION

haunter *n syn* see HABITUÉ 1

hauteur *n syn* see PRIDE 3
ant lowliness

haut monde *n syn* see ARISTOCRACY

have *vb* **1** to keep, control, or experience as one's own <can't *have* your cake and eat it too>
syn enjoy, hold, own, possess, retain
idiom to be possessed of, have in hand
con lack, need, want
2 *syn* see INCLUDE
rel admit, compose, comprise
3 *syn* see BEAR 3
4 *syn* see GET 1
5 *syn* see EXPERIENCE 1
6 *syn* see LET 2
7 *syn* see KNOW 1
8 *syn* see OUTWIT
9 *syn* see BRIBE
10 *syn* see MUST 2

haven *n* **1 *syn*** see HARBOR 3
2 *syn* see SHELTER 1

haven *vb syn* see HARBOR 1

haversack *n syn* see BACKPACK

havoc *n syn* see RUIN 3
rel calamity, cataclysm, catastrophe; despoiling, pillaging, ravaging; vandalism

havoc *vb syn* see RAVAGE

hawk *vb syn* see PEDDLE 2

hawker *n syn* see PEDDLER

hawk–eyed *adj syn* see SHARP-EYED

hawkshaw *n syn* see DETECTIVE

haymaker *n syn* see CUFF

hayseed *n syn* see RUSTIC
ant city slicker, slicker

hazard *n* **1 *syn*** see CHANCE 2
2 *syn* see DANGER

hazard *vb* **1 *syn*** see VENTURE 1
2 *syn* see GAMBLE 2
3 *syn* see ENDANGER

hazardous *adj syn* see DANGEROUS 1
ant safe; unhazardous

haze *vb syn* see OBSCURE

haze *n* **1** an atmospheric condition that is characterized by the presence of fine particulate material in the air and that deprives the air of its transparency <*haze* obscured the distant hills>
syn brume, film, mist, smaze

---

syn synonym(s)   *rel* related word(s)
ant antonym(s)   *con* contrasted word(s)
idiom idiomatic equivalent(s)
‖ use limited; if in doubt, see a dictionary

rel cloud, ‖drisk, fog, murk, ‖smeech, smog, smoke, vapor; cloudiness, mistiness, murkiness, smokiness

2 a state of mental vagueness or obtuseness <lived in a *haze* of pleasant memories>
syn befuddlement, daze, fog, ‖maze, muddledness, muddleheadedness, muddlement
rel dream, reverie, stupor, trance; absentmindedness, abstraction, bemusement, preoccupation, woolgathering
con alertness, attentiveness, awareness

hazy *adj* obscured or made dim by or as if by haze <had only a *hazy* idea of where they were>
syn cloudy, foggy, misty, mushy, vague, vaporous, vapory
rel blurred, clouded, dim, indefinite, indistinct, murky, nebulous, obscure; bemused, dreamy, tranced, stuporous; dazed, ‖mazed, muzzy

he *n syn* see MAN 3

head *n* **1** the upper division of the body that contains the brain, the chief sense organs, and the mouth <put your hat on your *head*>
syn ‖bean, ‖belfry, ‖chump, ‖coco, ‖coconut, ‖conk, ‖dome, headpiece, noddle, noggin, noodle, ‖nut, ‖pallet, pate, poll, sconce
rel brainpan, cranium, crown, scalp
2 *syn* see MIND 1
3 *syn* see GIFT 2
4 *syn* see LEADER 2
con subordinate; aide, assistant, helper
5 *syn* see PROMONTORY
6 *syn* see TOILET
7 *syn* see HEADLINE
8 *syn* see SUBJECT 2

head *adj syn* see FIRST 3

head *vb* **1** *syn* see BEHEAD
2 *syn* see DIRECT 2
3 to commence to go in an indicated direction <the cowboys *headed* for town>
syn bear, light out, make, set out, strike out, take off
rel go, proceed, start
idiom make a beeline for
4 *syn* see SPRING 1

heading *n syn* see HEADLINE

headland *n syn* see PROMONTORY

headline *n* a word or group of words usually in large type introducing and summarizing a newspaper story <*headlines* that screamed the news of the president's death>
syn head, heading
rel banner, banner head, bannerline, scarehead, screamer, spreadhead

headlong *adj syn* see PRECIPITATE 1
rel daredevil, daring, foolhardy, rash, reckless

headman *n syn* see LEADER 2

headmost *adj syn* see FIRST 1

headpiece *n syn* see HEAD 1

headshaker *n syn* see SKEPTIC

head start *n syn* see ADVANTAGE 3

headstone *n syn* see TOMBSTONE

headstrong *adj syn* see OBSTINATE
con subdued, tame; amenable, biddable, docile, meek, obedient, tractable

headway *n* **1** *syn* see ADVANCE 2

heady *adj syn* see SHREWD

heal *vb syn* see CURE

healing *adj syn* see CURATIVE

health *n* the state of being sound in body or mind <the patient was nursed back to *health*>
syn haleness, healthiness, soundness, wholeness
rel stamina, vitality, well-being; euphoria
con debility, decrepitude, feebleness; ill health, illness, sickliness
ant disease, infirmity

healthful *adj* conducive or beneficial to the health or soundness of body or mind <regular exercise is a *healthful* practice>
syn good, healthy, hygienic, salubrious, salutary, salutiferous, wholesome
rel advantageous, beneficial, profitable, useful; corrective, curative, remedial; aiding, alleviative, helpful, mitigative, restorative, sanative
con insalubrious, unhealthy, unhygienic, unwholesome; damaging, deleterious, detrimental, harmful, injurious, mischievous, pernicious
ant unhealthful

healthiness *n syn* see HEALTH
ant unhealthiness

healthy *adj* **1** enjoying or manifesting health <a *healthy* baby>
syn ‖bunkum, fit, hale, right, sane, sound, well, well-conditioned, well-liking, whole, wholesome
rel hearty, iron, lusty, robust, thriving, vigorous; rugged, stalwart, strong, sturdy, tough; agile, chipper, spry; blooming, rosy, thriving
idiom fit as a fiddle, in (top) condition, in fine fettle, in shape, in trim, sound as a dollar, up to snuff
con decrepit, delicate, feeble, fragile, frail, weak; infirm, ‖poorly, sickly
ant unhealthy
2 *syn* see HEALTHFUL
ant unhealthful
3 *syn* see SAFE 3

heap *n* **1** *syn* see PILE 1
rel congeries, gathering
2 *syn* see MUCH
3 *syn* see SCAD
4 *syn* see JALOPY

heap *vb* **1** to throw or collect in a pile <*heap* up leaves for a bonfire>
syn bank, cock, drift, hill, mound, pile, stack
rel cord, ‖dess, rick, shock; bunch, clump, lumber, lump, mass; deposit, dump; accumulate, amass, assemble, collect, gather, group
con broadcast, disperse, distribute, scatter, separate, spread, strew
2 *syn* see LOAD 3

hear *vb* **1** *syn* see LISTEN
idiom get wind of
2 *syn* see DISCOVER 3

hearing *n* **1** *syn* see EARSHOT
2 an opportunity to be heard <they finally obtained a *hearing* on their complaints>
syn audience, audition
rel conference, interview, meeting, parley; test, tryout; discussion, negotiation

hearken *vb syn* see LISTEN
hearsay *n syn* see REPORT 1
heart *n* **1** the seat or center of secret thoughts and emotions <in his *heart* he knew he was seriously in the wrong>
syn bosom, breast, soul
idiom bottom of the heart, cockles of the heart
2 *syn* see COURAGE
3 *syn* see TASTE 4
4 *syn* see CENTER 2
5 *syn* see CENTER 3
heartache *n syn* see SORROW
idiom aching heart, heavy heart
heartbreak *n* **1** *syn* see SORROW
rel agony, bale, torment
idiom bleeding heart
heartbreaking *adj syn* see DEPLORABLE
hearten *vb syn* see ENCOURAGE 1
rel energize, enliven; arouse, rally, rouse, stir
con damp, dampen; weigh
ant dishearten
heartfelt *adj syn* see SINCERE 1
rel bona fide, genuine, honest, true, unfeigned; deep, profound
con hypocritical, insincere; false, pretended
heartless *adj syn* see UNFEELING 2
heartrending *adj syn* see DEPLORABLE
heart–searching *n syn* see INTROSPECTION
heartsick *adj syn* see DOWNCAST
heartsore *adj syn* see DOWNCAST
heartthrob *n syn* see SWEETHEART 1
heart–whole *adj* **1** *syn* see FREE 6
2 *syn* see GENUINE 3
hearty *adj syn* see SINCERE 1
rel responsive, warm, warmhearted; deep, profound; exuberant, profuse
con cold, dispassionate, emotionless
ant hollow
‖**heat** *n syn* see POLICEMAN
heated *adj* **1** *syn* see HOT 1
ant chilled
2 *syn* see FEVERISH 2
3 *syn* see ANGRY
heathen *adj* of or relating to people who do not acknowledge the God of the Bible <ancient *heathen* sacrificial rites>
syn ethnic, gentile, infidel, infidelic, pagan, profane
rel heathenish, paganish
heave *vb* **1** *syn* see THROW 1
2 *syn* see TOSS 2
3 *syn* see PANT 1
4 *syn* see RETCH
‖**5** *syn* see VOMIT
heaven *n* **1** *usu* **heavens** *pl syn* see SKY
2 an abode of blissful spiritual life after death <the religious conceptions of *heaven* and hell>
syn Abraham's bosom, bliss, Canaan, Civitas Dei, elysium, empyrean, happy hunting ground, kingdom come, New Jerusalem, nirvana, paradise, Zion
rel afterworld, eternity, glory, hereafter, promised land; everlastingness, immortality
idiom Beulah Land (*or* Land of Beulah), City of God, Kingdom of God, Kingdom of Heaven

con earth, world; Gehenna, hades, inferno, netherworld, perdition, pit, Sheol, Tartarus, Tophet, underworld
ant hell
3 *syn* see UTOPIA
4 *syn* see ECSTASY
heavenly *adj* **1** *syn* see CELESTIAL
con hadean, Tartarean
ant hellish
2 *syn* see DELIGHTFUL
heavy *adj* **1** having great or relatively great weight <a *heavy* load>
syn hefty, massive, ponderous, weighty; *compare* UNWIELDY
rel awkward, bulky, clumsy, lumbering, lumbersome; unhandy, unmanageable, unwieldy; cumbersome, cumbrous
con airy, buoyant, weightless; handy, manageable, wieldy
ant light
2 *syn* see FAT 2
3 *syn* see SERIOUS 2
4 *syn* see RECONDITE
5 *syn* see PREGNANT 1
6 *syn* see LETHARGIC
7 *syn* see OVERCAST
8 *syn* see HARD 6
9 *syn* see RICH 3
heavy *n syn* see NOTABLE 1
heavy–footed *adj syn* see PONDEROUS 2
heavy–handed *adj* **1** *syn* see AWKWARD 2
2 *syn* see PONDEROUS 2
heavyhearted *adj syn* see SAD 1
ant lighthearted
heavyheartedness *n syn* see SADNESS
ant lightheartedness
heavyset *adj syn* see STOCKY
heavyweight *n syn* see NOTABLE 1
con lightweight
hebetate *vb syn* see DULL 5
hebetude *n syn* see LETHARGY 1
hebetudinous *adj syn* see LETHARGIC
heckle *vb* **1** *syn* see BAIT 2
rel plague, worry; discomfit, disconcert, embarrass, faze, rattle; tease, torment
2 *syn* see MOLEST
hectic *adj syn* see FEVERISH 2
hector *n syn* see BULLY 1
hector *vb* **1** *syn* see INTIMIDATE
2 *syn* see BAIT 2
hedge *vb* **1** *syn* see EQUIVOCATE 2
2 *syn* see ENCLOSE 1
hedonist *n* one given to the zealous pursuit of pleasure <lead the life of a *hedonist*>
syn carpet knight, pleasuremonger, sybarite
rel bon vivant, man-about-town; epicure, epicurean, gourmand, gourmet; debauchee, libertine, rake; sensualist, voluptuary; pleasure-seeker
ant ascetic

---

syn synonym(s)   *rel* related word(s)
ant antonym(s)   *con* contrasted word(s)
idiom idiomatic equivalent(s)
‖ use limited; if in doubt, see a dictionary

hedonistic *adj syn* see SYBARITIC
  con austere, self-denying, self-disciplined, self-restricted
  ant ascetic
heebie–jeebies *n pl syn* see JITTERS
heed *vb syn* see LISTEN
  rel mark, mind, note; observe, see, watch
  idiom give (*or* pay) heed to
heed *n* **1** *syn* see NOTICE 1
  rel awareness, interest, mindfulness; audience, hearing
  2 *syn* see ATTENTION 1
  rel concern, interest
  con inattention, unconcern
  3 *syn* see CARE 4
heedful *adj* **1** *syn* see ATTENTIVE 1
  ant heedless, unheeding
  2 *syn* see MINDFUL 2
  ant heedless, unheeding
  3 *syn* see CAREFUL 2
heedfully *adv syn* see WELL 2
  ant heedlessly, unheeding
heedfulness *n syn* see CARE 4
  ant heedlessness
heedless *adj syn* see CARELESS 1
  ant heedful, heeding
heedlessness *n syn* see APATHY 2
  ant heedfulness
hee–haw *vb syn* see LAUGH
heel *n* **1** *syn* see REMAINDER
  2 *syn* see VILLAIN 1
heel *vb syn* see SLANT 1
hefty *adj* **1** *syn* see HEAVY 1
  2 *syn* see HUSKY 1
  3 *syn* see BIG 1
height *n* the distance a thing rises above the level on which it stands <the *height* of a building>
  syn altitude, elevation
  rel highness, loftiness, rise, tallness, stature
  con lowness, profundity
  ant depth
heighten *vb* **1** *syn* see INCREASE 1
  2 *syn* see INCREASE 2
  rel elevate, lift, raise; better, improve; enlarge, increase
  con diminish, lessen, shrink
  3 *syn* see INTENSIFY
heinie (*or* **hiney**) *n syn* see BUTTOCKS
heinous *adj syn* see OUTRAGEOUS 2
  con paltry, petty, trifling, trivial
  ant venial
heinousness *n syn* see ENORMITY 1
heir *n* one who inherits <died without *heirs*>
  syn heritor, inheritor
‖**heist** *vb syn* see STEAL 1
hell *n* a place or state of the dead or of the damned <went to *hell* for his sins>
  syn abyss, barathrum, blazes, Gehenna, hades, inferno, netherworld, Pandemonium, perdition, pit, Sheol, Tophet
  rel limbo, Styx, Tartarus
  idiom the hot place, infernal regions, place of torment
  ant heaven

hell *vb syn* see REVEL 1
hell–fired *adj syn* see UTTER
hellish *adj syn* see INFERNAL 2
helotry *n syn* see BONDAGE
help *n* **1** an act or instance of giving what will benefit or assist <the stranded travelers received *help* from passersby>
  syn aid, assist, assistance, comfort, hand, lift, relief, secours, succor, support
  rel benefit, cooperation, service
  ant hindrance
  2 something that is beneficial <the rain was a real *help* to late crops>
  syn aid, support
  rel benefit, use
  3 *syn* see HELPER
help *vb* **1** to give assistance or support <*help* the children with their lessons>
  syn abet, aid, assist, benefact, do for, help out, stead
  rel back, bolster, boost, champion, second, support, uphold; avail, benefit, profit; advance, facilitate, forward, further, promote, serve; befriend, succor
  idiom give a lift, lend a hand (*or* a helping hand), stand back of (*or* behind)
  con bar, block, impede, obstruct, oppose; baffle, balk, foil, frustrate, thwart; discomfit, embarrass; damage, harm, hurt, injure
  ant hinder
  2 *syn* see IMPROVE 1
  rel alleviate, mitigate, palliate, relieve
  con harm, impair, worsen
helper *n* one that helps <was made boss and assigned a dozen *helpers*>
  syn aid, ancilla, assistant, attendant, help, striker
  rel helpmate, helpmeet; auxiliary, deputy, subordinate; associate, follower; employee, laborer, servant, worker
  idiom helping hand, right-hand man
helpful *adj* **1** of service or assistance <*helpful* suggestions>
  syn aidant, aiding, assistive, serviceable
  rel beneficial, effective, profitable, salutary, usable; constructive, practical, useful
  con timeserving, uncooperative, unreliable; impractical, ineffectual
  ant unhelpful
  2 *syn* see GOOD 1
helpless *adj* **1** lacking protection or support <*helpless* nestlings>
  syn defenseless, unprotected
  rel abandoned, desolate, forlorn, forsaken, friendless; feeble, weak
  2 *syn* see POWERLESS
helplessly *adv syn* see WILLY-NILLY
help out *vb syn* see HELP 1
helter–skelter *adv* **1** *syn* see PELL-MELL
  2 *syn* see ABOUT 4
hem *n syn* see BORDER 1
hem *vb* **1** *syn* see BORDER
  2 *syn* see ENCLOSE 1
  3 *syn* see SURROUND 1

hence *adv* **1** *syn* see AWAY 1
   2 *syn* see THEREFORE
henceforth *adv* from this time forward <made up his mind to keep out of trouble *henceforth*>
   syn henceforward, hereafter; *compare* THENCE-FORTH
   idiom from now on
henceforward *adv syn* see HENCEFORTH
henchman *n syn* see FOLLOWER
   rel attendant; lackey, minion, stooge
henpeck *vb syn* see NAG
hep *adj syn* see WISE 4
herald *n syn* see FORERUNNER 1
   rel courier, crier, messenger
herald *vb* **1** *syn* see ANNOUNCE 2
   2 *syn* see TOUT
Herculean *adj syn* see HUGE
herd *n syn* see DROVE 2
herd *vb syn* see DRIVE 3
here *adv syn* see HITHERTO 2
hereafter *adv syn* see HENCEFORTH
hereafter *n* **1** *syn* see FUTURE
   2 an existence or place of existence after this life <buried pots and tools with the dead for use in the *hereafter*>
   syn afterlife, afterworld, beyond, otherworld
   idiom great beyond (*or* hereafter), life after death, next world (*or* life), world beyond the grave, world to come
   con here and now
here and there *adv syn* see SOMETIMES
heresy *n* defection from a dominant belief or ideology <the *heresy* of the flat-earth theory>
   syn dissent, dissidence, heterodoxy, misbelief, nonconformism, nonconformity, schism, unorthodoxy
   rel impiety, infidelity; apostasy, defection, revisionism; error, fallacy
heretic *n* one who is not orthodox in his beliefs <a *heretic* in religion>
   syn dissenter, dissident, misbeliever, nonconformist, schismatic, schismatist, sectary, separatist
   rel apostate, defector, iconoclast, recreant, recusant, renegade; infidel, unbeliever; deviationist, revisionist
   ant orthodox
heretical *adj* of, relating to, or characterized by heresy <*heretical* beliefs>
   syn dissident, heterodox, nonconformist, schismatic, sectarian, unorthodox
   rel apostate, infidel, miscreant, revisionist; differing, disagreeing, dissentient, dissenting, dissentive, misbelieving, unbelieving
   con conventional, established; agreeing, conforming, conformist
   ant orthodox
heretofore *adv syn* see BEFORE 2
heritage *n* **1** something that one receives or is entitled to receive by succession (as from a parent) <the *heritage* of freedom>
   syn birthright, heritance, inheritance, legacy, patrimony
   2 *syn* see TRADITION 1

heritance *n syn* see HERITAGE 1
heritor *n syn* see HEIR
hermaphrodite *adj syn* see BISEXUAL
hermaphroditic *adj syn* see BISEXUAL
hermetic *adj* **1** *syn* see RECONDITE
   2 *syn* see SECLUDED
hermit *n syn* see RECLUSE
heroic *adj* **1** *syn* see BRAVE 1
   ant pusillanimous
   2 *syn* see HUGE
heroism *n* conspicuous courage or bravery <received an award for *heroism*>
   syn gallantry, prowess, valiance, valiancy, valor, valorousness
   rel boldness, bravery, courage, doughtiness, fearlessness, intrepidity, spirit; chivalry, nobility
   con cowardice, spiritlessness, timidity, timorousness, weakness
   ant pusillanimity
hesitancy *n syn* see HESITATION
hesitant *adj* **1** *syn* see DISINCLINED
   con resolute, staunch, steadfast
   2 *syn* see VACILLATING 2
hesitate *vb* to show irresolution or uncertainty <*hesitate* to buy a new car just now>
   syn dither, falter, halt, shilly-shally, stagger, vacillate, waver, whiffle, wiggle-waggle
   rel balk, boggle, demur, scruple, stick, stickle; fluctuate, oscillate, swing; dawdle, delay, dilly-dally, hang back, procrastinate, stall, temporize; pause
hesitating *adj syn* see VACILLATING 2
hesitation *n* the act or action of hesitating <several persons volunteered without *hesitation*>
   syn hesitancy, indecision, indecisiveness, irresolution, shilly-shally, to-and-fro, vacillation, wavering
   rel doubt, dubiety, dubiosity, mistrust, uncertainty; dawdling, delay, procrastination; averseness, indisposition, reluctance
   con alacrity, eagerness; courage, mettle, resolution, spirit, tenacity; aplomb, assurance, confidence
hetaera *n syn* see HARLOT 1
heteroclite *adj syn* see ABNORMAL 1
heterodox *adj syn* see HERETICAL
   ant orthodox
heterodoxy *n syn* see HERESY
   ant orthodoxy
heterogeneous *adj syn* see MISCELLANEOUS
   ant homogeneous
hew *vb syn* see FELL 2
hex *vb syn* see BEWITCH 1
hex *n* **1** *syn* see JINX
   2 *syn* see WITCH 1
hiatus *n syn* see GAP 3
hic jacet *n syn* see EPITAPH
hick *n syn* see RUSTIC
hick town *n syn* see BURG

---

syn synonym(s)   *rel* related word(s)
ant antonym(s)   *con* contrasted word(s)
idiom idiomatic equivalent(s)
‖ use limited; if in doubt, see a dictionary

hidden *adj syn* see ULTERIOR
  ant open
hide *vb* to withdraw or withhold from sight or observation <they *hid* their loot in a cave>
  syn bury, ‖bush up, cache, conceal, cover, ‖ditch, ensconce, occult, plant, screen, secrete, stash
  rel mantle, mask, obscure, shade, shield; entomb, inter; cloak, curtain, shroud, veil; harbor, lodge, seclude, shelter
  con bare, disclose, discover, display, exhibit, expose, reveal, show; uncover, unmask, unveil, unwrap; flaunt, parade, show off
hide *n* an animal skin <tanned *hides* for shoe leather>
  syn fell, fur, jacket, pelt, skin
hide *vb syn* see WHIP 1
hideaway *n syn* see HIDEOUT
hidebound *adj syn* see ILLIBERAL
hideous *adj* **1** *syn* see UGLY 2
  ant lovely
  2 *syn* see OFFENSIVE
  3 *syn* see GHASTLY 1
hideout *n* a place of retreat or concealment <a gangsters' *hideout*>
  syn den, hideaway, lair
  rel covert, haven, hermitage, refuge, retreat, sanctuary, shelter; robbers' roost
hie *vb syn* see GO 1
hierarch *n syn* see LEADER 2
hieratic *adj syn* see SACERDOTAL
higgle *vb syn* see HAGGLE 2
higgler *n syn* see PEDDLER
high *adj* **1** having a relatively great upward extension <a *high* building>
  syn altitudinous, tall; *compare* LOFTY 6
  rel aerial, eminent, lofty, soaring, towering; big, gigantic, grand, large, prominent
  idiom tall (*or* high) as a steeple
  con little, short, squat
  ant low
  2 *syn* see COSTLY 1
  ant low
  3 *syn* see MALODOROUS 1
  4 *syn* see ELEVATED 4
  5 *syn* see ACUTE 4
  6 *syn* see DRUGGED
high and low *adv syn* see EVERYWHERE 1
high–and–mighty *adj syn* see PROUD 1
highball *vb syn* see HURRY 2
highbinding *n syn* see DECEPTION 1
highbrow *n syn* see INTELLECTUAL 2
highbrow *adj syn* see INTELLECTUAL 2
highbrowed *adj syn* see INTELLECTUAL 2
  ant lowbrow, low-browed
higher *adj syn* see SUPERIOR 1
higher–up *n syn* see SUPERIOR
highest *adj* **1** *syn* see TOP 1
  ant lowest
  2 *syn* see EXALTED 1
highest–ranking *adj syn* see EXALTED 1
highfalutin *adj syn* see RHETORICAL
  con down-to-earth, matter-of-fact
highfalutin *n syn* see BOMBAST

high–flown *adj syn* see RHETORICAL
high–handed *adj syn* see MASTERFUL 1
high hat *n syn* see SNOB
high–hat *adj syn* see SNOBBISH
high–hearted *adj syn* see SPIRITED 2
high jinks *n pl* **1** *syn* see HORSEPLAY
  2 *syn* see REVELRY 2
highly *adv syn* see VERY 1
high–minded *adj syn* see ELEVATED 2
  ant low-minded
high–muck–a–muck *n syn* see NOTABLE 1
high–principled *adj syn* see HONORABLE 1
high roller *n syn* see SPENDTHRIFT
high sign *n* **1** *syn* see SIGN 1
  2 a private usually covert signal, warning, or cue <I gave him the *high sign* when I saw the police approaching>
  syn ‖office
  rel tip, tip-off, wink; nod; alarm, SOS, warning
high–sounding *adj syn* see PRETENTIOUS 3
high–spirited *adj* **1** *syn* see SPIRITED 2
  rel jolly, lighthearted, merry, mirthful
  ant low-spirited
  2 *syn* see EXUBERANT 1
high–strung *adj* **1** *syn* see TENSE 3
  2 *syn* see NERVOUS
hightail *vb syn* see GET OUT 1
highway *n syn* see WAY 1
high yellow *n syn* see MULATTO
hike *vb* **1** *syn* see RAISE 9
  2 to travel about or through on foot <*hiked* through the woods>
  syn tramp, tromp
  rel footslog; stroll, walk; ramble, rove, wander; explore
hike *n* **1** *syn* see TRAMP 3
  2 *syn* see RISE 3
hilarity *n syn* see MIRTH
hill *n syn* see PILE 1
hill *vb syn* see HEAP 1
hillbilly *n syn* see RUSTIC
hillman *n syn* see RUSTIC
hind *adj syn* see POSTERIOR 2
hind end *n syn* see BUTTOCKS
hinder *vb* to put obstacles in the way of <their cause was *hindered* by the excesses of overzealous supporters>
  syn bar, block, brake, dam, impede, obstruct, overslaugh; *compare* HAMPER
  rel arrest, check, interrupt, retard; clog, entrammel, fetter, hamper, hog-tie, manacle, shackle, trammel; curb, deter, hamstring, inhibit, restrain, tie (down); embog, mire; burden, handicap, lumber; baffle, balk, frustrate, thwart
  idiom bog down
  con abet, advance, aid, assist, ease, encourage, facilitate, forward, promote; accelerate, hasten, quicken, speed
  ant further, help
hinder *adj syn* see POSTERIOR 2
  ant fore, front
‖**hinder** *n syn* see BUTTOCKS
hindmost *adj* **1** *syn* see POSTERIOR 2
  con foremost, headmost

2 syn see LAST

hindrance *n syn* see ENCUMBRANCE
  ant help

hinge (on *or* upon) *vb syn* see DEPEND (on *or* upon) 1

hint *n* **1** a slight or indirect pointing out of something and especially of the way to an end <give me a *hint* on how you would deal with the matter>
  syn clue, cue, indication, inkling, intimation, notion, suggestion, telltale, wind
  rel innuendo, insinuation; inspiration, prompting; aiming, direction, pointing; key, pointer, tip; advice, assistance
  con command, directive, instruction, order
  2 a very small amount or admixture <add a *hint* of garlic to the salad>
  syn breath, cast, dash, intimation, lick, shade, shadow, smack, smatch, smell, soupçon, spice, sprinkling, strain, streak, suggestion, suspicion, taste, tincture, tinge, touch, trace, trifle, twang, vein, whiff, whisper, wink; *compare* HAIR
  rel adumbration, taint, vestige; particle, scintilla
  con abundance, heap, lot
  ant oodles
  3 syn see ASSOCIATION 4

hint *vb* **1 syn** see SUGGEST 1
  2 syn see POINT 2
  3 syn see ADUMBRATE 1
  4 to seek to obtain by sly or indirect means <kept *hinting* for an invitation to the party>
  syn angle, fish
  rel beg, coax, plead; importune, press; seek, solicit
  con ask (for), demand, insist (on *or* upon)

hinterland *n syn* see FRONTIER 2

hipped *adj* **1 syn** see DOWNCAST
  2 syn see OBSESSED

hire *n syn* see WAGE

hire *vb* **1** to take or engage something or grant the use of something for a stipulated price or rate <*hire* a conveyance>
  syn charter, lease, let, rent
  rel contract (for), engage; sublease, sublet, subrent
  2 syn see EMPLOY 2
  ant fire

hired girl *n syn* see MAID 2

hireling *n syn* see HACK 2

hiring *n syn* see EMPLOYMENT 4

hirsute *adj syn* see HAIRY 1
  ant hairless

hiss *vb* to make a sibilant sound <he thought he heard a snake *hiss*>
  syn buzz, fizz, fizzle, sibilate, sizz, sizzle, swish, wheeze, whish, whisper, whiz, whoosh

hiss *n syn* see RASPBERRY

history *n* **1 syn** see ACCOUNT 7
  2 a chronological record of events <a *history* of the American Revolution>
  syn annals, chronicle
  rel account, recital, relation, report; diary, journal, memoir; epic, saga, tale

histrionic *adj syn* see DRAMATIC 1

hit *vb* **1 syn** see STRIKE 2
  rel buffet, pound, stroke
  idiom give one a clip
  2 syn see OCCUR 2
  3 syn see HAPPEN 2

hit (on *or* upon) *vb syn* see FIND 1

hit *n* **1** a stroke delivered with a part of the body or an instrument <gave the disobedient boy a *hit* on the head with her ruler>
  syn ‖conk, knock, lick, rap, swat, swipe, wipe; *compare* BLOW 1, CUFF
  2 syn see SMASH 6
  3 syn see MURDER

hitch *vb* **1 syn** see LIMP 1
  2 to attach as a means of motive power <*hitched* the team to a wagon>
  syn couple, harness, yoke
  idiom make fast
  con free, release, unfasten; uncouple, unharness, unyoke
  ant unhitch
  ‖**3 syn** see MARRY 2
  4 syn see HITCHHIKE

hitchhike *vb* to travel by securing free rides <*hitchhiked* to California>
  syn hitch, thumb
  idiom bum (*or* hook) a ride

hitherto *adv* **1** up to this particular point or time <imposed order upon what was *hitherto* haphazard>
  syn as yet, earlier, so far, thus far, yet
  rel before, formerly, heretofore, once, previously
  idiom up to now (*or* then)
  2 to this place <the appointed delegate shall come *hitherto*>
  syn here

hit man *n syn* see ASSASSIN

hit—or—miss *adj syn* see RANDOM

hive *vb syn* see ACCUMULATE

hoard *n* **1 syn** see ACCUMULATION
  2 syn see RESERVE

hoard *vb* to store up beyond one's present or reasonable need <*hoarding* sugar during war>
  syn squirrel, stash; *compare* ACCUMULATE, SAVE 4
  rel ‖sock away; garner, lay by, lay up
  idiom take all one can lay one's hands on
  con consume, use up; blow, dissipate, tool (away), fritter, frivol away, prodigalize, throw away, trifle (away), waste

hoarse *adj* **1** rough or dry in sound <developed a *hoarse* cough>
  syn croaking, croaky, gruff, husky
  rel coarse, dry, guttural, thick
  2 syn see HARSH 3
  con honeyed, mellifluent, mellifluous, smooth

hoary *adj syn* see ANCIENT 1

hoax *vb syn* see DUPE

---

syn synonym(s)   *rel* related word(s)
ant antonym(s)   *con* contrasted word(s)
idiom idiomatic equivalent(s)
‖ use limited; if in doubt, see a dictionary

hoax *n syn* see IMPOSTURE
hobble *vb* **1** *syn* see LIMP 1
  2 *syn* see HAMPER
hobo *n syn* see VAGABOND
hoboism *n syn* see VAGRANCY
hock *vb syn* see PAWN
hocus–pocus *n syn* see GIBBERISH 3
‖**hodge** *n syn* see RUSTIC
hodgepodge *n syn* see MISCELLANY 1
hogback *n syn* see RIDGE 1
hogshead *n syn* see CASK
hog–tie *vb syn* see HAMPER
hogwash *n syn* see NONSENSE 2
hoi polloi *n syn* see RABBLE 2
hoist *vb syn* see LIFT 1
hoity–toity *adj syn* see GIDDY 1
hokum *n syn* see NONSENSE 2
hold *vb* **1** *syn* see KEEP 5
  2 *syn* see ENTHRALL 2
  3 *syn* see HAVE 1
  4 *syn* see CONTAIN 2
  5 *syn* see FEEL 3
hold (with) *vb syn* see APPROVE 1
hold *n* the act or manner of grasping or holding
  <lost his *hold* on the side of the boat>
  syn clamp, clasp, clench, clinch, clutch, grapple,
  grasp, grip, gripe, tenure
  rel handclasp, handhold; purchase
hold back *vb* **1** *syn* see RESTRAIN 1
  2 *syn* see KEEP 5
  3 *syn* see DENY 3
hold down *vb syn* see RESTRAIN 1
holder *n syn* see OWNER
hold in *vb syn* see RESTRAIN 1
hold off *vb* **1** *syn* see FEND (off)
  2 *syn* see DEFER
hold out *vb syn* see OFFER 1
hold over *vb syn* see DEFER
hold up *vb syn* see DEFER
hole *n* **1** *syn* see APERTURE
  2 *syn* see GAP 1
  3 a space within the substance of a body or mass
  <buried their trash in a *hole* in the ground>
  syn cavity, hollow, vacuity, void
  rel gap, hiatus, lacuna; cranny, interstice, niche;
  fissure, rent, rift; vacancy, vacuum
  4 *syn* see HOVEL
  5 *syn* see PREDICAMENT
hole *vb syn* see OPEN 3
hole–and–corner *adj syn* see SECRET 1
holiday *n syn* see VACATION
holiness *n* a state of spiritual soundness and unimpaired virtue <the *holiness* of the saints>
  syn saintliness, sanctity
  rel blessedness, divineness, divinity, sacredness;
  consecration, devotion, devoutness, piety, piousness, spirituality
holler *vb syn* see CALL 1
hollo *vb syn* see CALL 1
hollow *adj* **1** having a muffled or reverberating
  quality <had a deep *hollow* gloomy voice>
  syn cavernous, reverberant, sepulchral
  rel echoing, resonant, resounding, reverberating, sounding

  con dead, dull, flat, toneless
  2 *syn* see VAIN 1
hollow *n* **1** *syn* see DEPRESSION 2
  2 *syn* see HOLE 3
holocaust *n syn* see FIRE 1
holy *adj* **1** dedicated to the service of or set apart
  by religion <pilgrimages to *holy* places>
  syn blessed, consecrated, hallowed, sacred,
  sanctified, unprofane; *compare* SACRED 2
  rel adored, glorified, revered, reverenced, venerated, worshiped; divine, religious, spiritual
  2 *syn* see SAINTLY
  ant unholy
  3 *syn* see DEVOUT
‖**Holy Joe** *n syn* see CLERGYMAN
holy place *n syn* see SHRINE
Holy Writ *n syn* see BIBLE
homage *n syn* see HONOR 1
home *n* **1** *syn* see HABITATION 2
  2 *syn* see HABITAT
  3 *syn* see COUNTRY
home *adj* **1** *syn* see DOMESTIC 1
  2 *syn* see DOMESTIC 2
homeland *n syn* see COUNTRY
homely *adj* **1** *syn* see PLAIN 1
  rel commonplace, familiar, intimate
  2 *syn* see PLAIN 5
  idiom homely as a mud (*or* hedge) fence, homely
  enough to sour milk
  ant comely
homicidal *adj syn* see MURDEROUS
homicide *n* **1** *syn* see MURDERER
  2 *syn* see MURDER
homilize *vb syn* see PREACH 1
hominine *adj syn* see HUMAN
hominoid *n syn* see ANTHROPOID
‖**homo** *n syn* see HOMOSEXUAL
homoerotic *adj syn* see HOMOSEXUAL
homophile *adj syn* see HOMOSEXUAL
Homo sapiens *n syn* see MANKIND
homosexual *adj* relating to or exhibiting sexual
  desire toward a member of one's own sex <*homosexual* acts between consenting adults>
  syn gay, homoerotic, homophile, inverted,
  ‖queer, uranian
  rel androgynous, bisexual, epicene; transvestite;
  lesbian, sapphic; camp, effeminate, ‖swishy
homosexual *n* one who is inclined to or practices
  homosexuality <a bar frequented by *homosexu-
  als*>
  syn ‖fag, ‖faggot, ‖fruit, ‖homo, invert, ‖queer,
  uranian, uranist
  rel transvestite; ‖fairy, ‖nance, ‖nancy, ‖pansy,
  ‖queen, ‖swish; lesbian, sapphist
homunculus *n syn* see DWARF
honcho *n syn* see LEADER 2
hone *vb syn* see SHARPEN
honed *adj syn* see SHARP 1
honest *adj* **1** *syn* see GENUINE 3
  rel reliable, unaffected, unimpeachable
  2 *syn* see UPRIGHT 2
  rel candid, forthright, frank, open, plain; dispassionate, objective; truthful, veracious
  ant dishonest

honestness *n syn* see HONESTY
  ant dishonesty
honesty *n* uprightness as evidenced in character and actions <he was generally known as a person of scrupulous *honesty*>
  syn honestness, honor, honorableness, incorruption, integrity
  rel conscientiousness, justness, probity, scrupulousness, uprightness; dependability, reliability, trustworthiness; goodness, morality, rectitude, virtue
  con deceitfulness, mendaciousness, mendacity, untruthfulness; deceit, duplicity, guile
  ant dishonesty
honey *n* **1** *syn* see SWEETHEART 1
  2 *syn* see GIRL FRIEND 2
honey *vb syn* see SUGARCOAT 1
honey (up) *vb syn* see FAWN
honeybunch *n syn* see SWEETHEART 1
honeyed *adj syn* see MELLIFLUOUS
honky–tonk *n syn* see DIVE
honor *n* **1** respect or esteem shown one as his due or claimed by one as a right <received the *honor* due his rank>
  syn deference, homage, obeisance, reverence
  rel admiration, esteem; adoration, adulation, devotion, veneration, worship; acknowledgment, compliment, recognition, regard, respect
  con contempt, despite, disdain, scorn; disregard, neglect, slighting
  ant dishonor
  2 an evidence or symbol of distinction <received many *honors* for her devoted public service>
  syn accolade, award, badge, bays, decoration, distinction, kudos, laurels
  rel deference, esteem, respect; admiration, approval
  3 *syn* see HONESTY
  con disgrace, ignominy, shame
  ant dishonor, dishonorableness
honor *vb syn* see EXALT 1
  ant dishonor
honorable *adj* **1** deserving of or entitled to honor (as because of rank, achievements, or service) <medicine is an *honorable* profession>
  syn estimable, high-principled, noble, sterling, worthy; *compare* VENERABLE 1
  rel august, illustrious, reverend, venerable, worshipful
  ant dishonorable
  2 *syn* see UPRIGHT 2
  ant dishonorable
honorableness *n syn* see HONESTY
  ant dishonor, dishonorableness
‖**hooch** *n* **1** *syn* see LIQUOR 2
  2 *syn* see MOONSHINE 2
‖**hood** *n syn* see THUG 1
hoodlum *n syn* see THUG 1
hoodoo *n syn* see JINX
hoodwink *vb syn* see DUPE
hooey *n syn* see NONSENSE 2
hoof *vb syn* see WALK 1
hoof (it) *vb syn* see DANCE 1
hoofer *n syn* see DANCER

hook *vb syn* see STEAL 1
‖**hooker** *n syn* see PROSTITUTE
‖**hookshop** *n syn* see BROTHEL
hookup *n syn* see ASSOCIATION 1
hooligan *n syn* see THUG 1
‖**hoosegow** *n syn* see JAIL
hoosier *n syn* see RUSTIC
hoot *n* **1** *syn* see RASPBERRY
  2 *syn* see PARTICLE
‖**hootenanny** *n syn* see DOODAD
hop *vb* **1** *syn* see SKIP 1
  2 *syn* see JUMP 1
‖**hop** *n syn* see DRUG 2
hope *vb syn* see EXPECT 1
hope *n syn* see TRUST 1
hopeful *adj* **1** full of hope or inclined to hope <the candidate was *hopeful* of winning>
  syn hoping; *compare* CONFIDENT 1, EXPECTANT 1, OPTIMISTIC
  rel anticipative, assured, satisfied, secure; cheerful, content, easy, undisturbed; fond, optimistic, Pollyannaish, rose-colored, sanguine, upbeat
  con doubtful, insecure, pessimistic, uncertain; discouraged, disheartened, gloomy, glum
  ant hopeless
  2 exhibiting qualities that inspire hope <a *hopeful* prospect for improvement>
  syn couleur de rose, encouraging, likely, promiseful, promising, roseate, rose-colored, rosy
  rel advantageous, auspicious, propitious; bright, cheering, cheery, golden, halcyon, happy, sunny; budding, up-and-coming
  con discouraging, disheartening, dismal, dreary, gloomy, pessimistic
  ant hopeless
hopeful *n syn* see CANDIDATE
hopeless *adj* **1** *syn* see DESPONDENT
  rel gloomy, glum, morose
  con cheerful; assured, confident, optimistic, sanguine, sure
  ant hopeful
  2 offering no prospect of change for the better <his case was *hopeless* and beyond all human aid>
  syn cureless, immedicable, impossible, incurable, insanable, irremediable, irreparable, uncorrectable, uncurable, unrecoverable
  rel insoluble; incorrigible, irredeemable
  idiom beyond hope (*or* remedy *or* repair), beyond human aid
  con correctable, curable, medicable, remediable, reparable
  ant hopeful
hoper *n syn* see OPTIMIST
hoping *adj syn* see HOPEFUL 1
hop-o'-my-thumb *n syn* see DWARF
hopped–up *adj syn* see DRUGGED
hopping *adj syn* see BUSTLING

---

syn synonym(s)   *rel* related word(s)
ant antonym(s)   *con* contrasted word(s)
idiom idiomatic equivalent(s)
‖ use limited; if in doubt, see a dictionary

horde *n syn* see CROWD 1

horizon *n syn* see KEN

horn in *vb* **1** *syn* see MEDDLE
  2 *syn* see INTRUDE 1

‖**horning** *n syn* see SHIVAREE

hornswoggle *vb syn* see DUPE

horrible *adj* **1** *syn* see GHASTLY 1
  rel abhorrent, abominable, detestable, hateful;
  loathsome, obnoxious, offensive, repulsive, revolting
  con gratifying, pleasing, soothing
  2 *syn* see FEARFUL 3
  3 *syn* see OFFENSIVE

horrid *adj* **1** *syn* see GHASTLY 1
  2 *syn* see HATEFUL 2
  3 *syn* see OFFENSIVE

horrific *adj syn* see FEARFUL 3

horrify *vb syn* see DISMAY 1

horrifying *adj syn* see GHASTLY 1

horror *n* **1** *syn* see FEAR 1
  rel distress, pain, shock, throe, wrench
  2 *syn* see ABOMINATION 2

hors d'oeuvre *n syn* see APPETIZER

horse *n syn* see SAWHORSE

horse *vb syn* see CUT UP 2

‖**horsefeathers** *n pl syn* see NONSENSE 2

horse opera *n syn* see WESTERN

horseplay *n* rough or boisterous play <their
  friendly *horseplay* almost ended in tragedy>
  syn fooling, high jinks, roughhouse, roughhousing, rowdiness, skylarking
  rel buffoonery, clowning

horseplay *vb syn* see CUT UP 2

horse sense *n syn* see SENSE 6

hospice *n syn* see HOTEL

hospitable *adj syn* see SOCIAL
  ant inhospitable

host *n syn* see MULTITUDE 1

hostage *n syn* see PLEDGE
  rel guaranty, security, surety

hostel *n syn* see HOTEL

hostelry *n syn* see HOTEL

hostile *adj* **1** marked by lack of friendliness or by
  opposition <takes a *hostile* view of a tax in-
  crease><*hostile* tribes>
  syn ill, inimicable, inimical, unfriendly
  rel argumentative, competitive, contrary, dim,
  disaffected, disapproving, opposed, opposite,
  unfavorable; dour, sour; bellicose, belligerent,
  contentious, pugnacious; militant, warlike
  con amicable, benign, friendly
  ant unhostile
  2 *syn* see BITTER 3

hostility *n syn* see ENMITY

hot *adj* **1** marked by a notable amount of heat <a
  hot day>
  syn ardent, baking, blistering, boiling, broiling,
  burning, fiery, heated, red-hot, scalding, scorching, sizzling, sultry, sweltering, sweltry, torrid,
  white-hot
  rel febrile, fevered, feverish, feverous, hectic;
  summery, tropic, tropical; mild, warm
  idiom hot as a firecracker (*or* furnace), hot as an
  oven, hot as hell

  con chilly, cool, frigid, icy
  ant cold
  2 *syn* see LUSTFUL 2
  3 *syn* see MARVELOUS 2
  4 *syn* see CONTRABAND

hot air *n syn* see NONSENSE 2

hotbed *n syn* see BREEDING GROUND

hot–blooded *adj syn* see IMPASSIONED
  con callous, hard, unfeeling
  ant cold-blooded

hotchpotch *n syn* see MISCELLANY 1

hot dog *n syn* see FRANKFURTER

hotel *n* an establishment for the lodging and entertainment especially of transients <spent their
  vacation at a resort *hotel*>
  syn auberge, caravansary, hospice, hostel, hostelry, inn, lodge, public house, roadhouse, tavern
  rel boardinghouse, lodging house, pension,
  rooming house, spa; boatel, motel, motor inn;
  ‖fleabag, ‖flophouse

hotfoot *adv syn* see PELL-MELL

hotfoot *vb syn* see HURRY 2

hotheaded *adj syn* see RASH 1
  ant cool

hothouse *n syn* see BREEDING GROUND

hot spot *n syn* see NIGHTCLUB

hot–tempered *adj* **1** *syn* see ILL-TEMPERED
  2 *syn* see IRASCIBLE

hot water *n* **1** *syn* see PREDICAMENT
  2 *syn* see TROUBLE 3

hound *n* **1** *syn* see DOG 1
  2 *syn* see ADDICT

hound *vb syn* see BAIT 2

house *n* **1** *syn* see HABITATION 2
  2 *syn* see FAMILY 2
  3 *syn* see FAMILY 1
  4 *syn* see ENTERPRISE 3

house *vb* **1** *syn* see HARBOR 1
  2 *syn* see HARBOR 2

housebreak *vb* to commit an act of breaking open
  and entering with a felonious purpose the dwelling of another by day or night <was arrested
  again in September for *housebreaking*>
  syn break in; *compare* BURGLARIZE, ROB 1
  rel knock over, rob; ransack, rifle
  idiom break and enter

household *n syn* see FAMILY 2

household *adj syn* see DOMESTIC 1

housemaid *n syn* see MAID 2

houseman *n syn* see BOUNCER 2

house of God *syn* see HOUSE OF WORSHIP

house of prayer *syn* see HOUSE OF WORSHIP

house of worship a building for religious exercises
  <there are many *houses of worship* in this city>
  syn church, house of God, house of prayer, tabernacle, temple
  rel abbey, basilica, bethel, cathedral, chantry,
  chapel, conventicle, ‖fane, ‖kirk, masjid, meet-
  inghouse, minster, mosque, oratory, pagoda,
  sanctuary, shrine, stupa, synagogue
  idiom the Lord's house

house trailer *n syn* see TRAILER

housing *n syn* see SHELTER 2

hovel *n* a small wretched dwelling place <mi-
  grants forced to live in *hovels*>

syn burrow, hole; *compare* HUT
rel hut, hutch, shack, shanty; pigpen, pigsty, sty

hover *vb* **1** *syn* see FLIT 2
  2 *syn* see HANG 3

howbeit *adv syn* see HOWEVER

howbeit *conj syn* see THOUGH

however *conj syn* see ONLY

however *adv* in spite of that <I accept your decision; I cannot, *however*, approve of it>
  syn after all, howbeit, nevertheless, nonetheless, notwithstanding, per contra, still, still and all, though, withal, yet
  idiom all the same, be that as it may, for all that, on the other hand

howl *vb* **1** to utter or emit a loud sustained doleful sound or outcry <the dogs *howled* through the night>
  syn bay, quest, ululate, wail
  rel bark, growl, yelp; blubber, cry, keen, weep, whimper; bawl, squall, yowl
  2 *syn* see YELL 2
  3 *syn* see BAWL 2

howl *n syn* see RIOT 2

hoyden *n syn* see TOMBOY

hub *n syn* see CENTER 2

hubbub *n* **1** *syn* see DIN
  2 *syn* see COMMOTION 4

‖**hubby** *n syn* see HUSBAND

hubristic *adj syn* see PROUD 1

huckster *n syn* see PEDDLER

huckster *vb* **1** *syn* see HAGGLE 2
  2 *syn* see PEDDLE 2

huddle *vb* **1** *syn* see CROUCH
  2 *syn* see CONFER 2

huddle (on) *vb syn* see DON 1

huddle *n syn* see CONFUSION 3

hue *n syn* see COLOR 1

huff *vb* **1** *syn* see PANT 1
  2 *syn* see IRRITATE

huff *n syn* see OFFENSE 2

huffy *adj* **1** *syn* see PROUD 1
  2 *syn* see IRRITABLE

hug *vb syn* see EMBRACE 1

huge *adj* exceedingly or excessively large <*huge* corporations> <ate a *huge* dinner>
  syn Antaean, behemothic, Brobdingnagian, Bunyanesque, colossal, cyclopean, dinosauric, elephantine, enormous, gargantuan, giant, gigantean, gigantesque, gigantic, Herculean, heroic, immense, jumbo, leviathan, lusty, mammoth, massive, massy, mastodonic, mighty, monster, monstrous, monumental, mountainous, planetary, prodigious, pythonic, ‖swapping, Titan, titanic, tremendous, unfathomed, untold, vast, walloping, whacking, whaling, whopping; *compare* GRAND 1
  rel bulky, extensive, great, immeasurable, magnificent, towering; outsize, oversize
  con diminutive, little, miniature, minute, petite, small, teeny, tiny, wee, weeny

hugely *adv syn* see VERY 1

hugeness *n syn* see ENORMITY 2

hugger–mugger *n* **1** *syn* see SECRECY
  2 *syn* see CLUTTER 2

hugger–mugger *adv syn* see SECRETLY

hugger–mugger *adj syn* see SECRET 1

hugger–muggery *n syn* see SECRECY

hull *n* an outer covering of a fruit or seed <peanut *hulls*>
  syn case, husk, pod, shell, shuck, skin, ‖slough
  rel chaff; bark, peel, rind

hull *vb syn* see SHUCK

hullabaloo *n syn* see DIN

hum *vb* to make a low prolonged sound <the wind *hummed* in the chimney>
  syn bombinate, ‖bum, bumble, buzz, drone, ‖sowf, strum, thrum
  rel moan, murmur, purr, vibrate, whisper
  con howl, roar, shriek

human *adj* of, relating to, or characteristic of mankind <problems of *human* relationships>
  syn hominine, mortal
  rel anthropological, ethnologic, ethological; anthropoid, hominid, hominoid
  con angelic, divine, superhuman; animal, brute, subhuman

human *n* a member of the human race <every *human* has a right to live>
  syn being, body, ‖character, creature, individual, life, man, mortal, party, person, personage, soul, wight; *compare* MAN 3, MANKIND

humane *adj syn* see CHARITABLE 1
  rel chickenhearted, compassionate, kindhearted, soft-hearted; benevolent, gentle, kind, kindly, mild
  ant inhuman, inhumane

humanitarian *adj syn* see CHARITABLE 1

humanity *n syn* see MANKIND

humankind *n syn* see MANKIND

humanoid *adj syn* see ANTHROPOID

humble *adj* **1** lacking all signs of pride, aggressiveness, or self-assertiveness <accepted her success with *humble* appreciation>
  syn lowly, meek, modest, unassuming
  rel simple, unobtrusive, unostentatious, unpretentious; acquiescent, compliant, resigned; quiet, subdued, submissive
  con ostentatious, pretentious, showy; vain, vainglorious; arrogant, disdainful, haughty, lordly, overbearing, proud, toplofty
  ant conceited
  2 *syn* see IGNOBLE 1

humble *vb* to make lower in status, prestige, or esteem <his devotion to duty *humbled* his critics>
  syn abase, bemean, cast down, debase, degrade, demean, humiliate, lower, sink
  rel chagrin, mortify; abash, discomfit, embarrass
  idiom bring low, take down a peg or two
  con aggrandize, exalt, magnify

humbug *n* **1** *syn* see IMPOSTURE
  2 *syn* see IMPOSTOR
  3 *syn* see NONSENSE 2

---

syn synonym(s)   *rel* related word(s)
ant antonym(s)   *con* contrasted word(s)
idiom idiomatic equivalent(s)
‖ use limited; if in doubt, see a dictionary

humbug *vb syn* see DECEIVE
humdinger *n syn* ‖DILLY, ‖corker, crackerjack, ‖daisy, dandy, jim-dandy, ‖lulu, nifty, peach, ‖pip
humdrum *adj syn* see DULL 9
humdrum *n syn* see MONOTONY
humid *adj* containing or characterized by an uncomfortable amount of atmospheric warmth and moisture <a *humid* climate>
syn mucky, muggy, soggy, sticky, sultry; *compare* STIFLING 1, STUFFY 1
rel clammy, dank, sodden; close, oppressive, stuffy; sweltering
con arid, dry; cool, crisp, fresh
humiliate *vb syn* see HUMBLE
humming *adj syn* see BUSTLING
humor *n* **1** *syn* see DISPOSITION 3
2 *syn* see MOOD 1
3 *syn* see CAPRICE
4 that quality or element which appeals to a sense of the ludicrous or incongruous <see the *humor* in a situation>
syn comedy, comicality, comicalness, drollery, drollness, funniness, humorousness, wittiness
rel jocosity, jocularity, jocundity, jocundness; flippancy, levity, lightness; banter, chaffing, jesting, joking, kidding
con earnestness, seriousness, solemnity; depth, profundity
5 something that is or is designed to be humorous <his heavy *humor* fell flat>
syn wit
rel banter, chitchat, pleasantry, repartee
6 *syn* see WIT 5
ant humorlessness
humor *vb* **1** *syn* see INDULGE 1
2 *syn* see BABY
humorist *n* **1** *syn* see WAG 1
2 a person noted for or specializing in humor <a writer best known as a *humorist*>
syn comedian, comic, droll, funnyman, jester, joker, jokester, quipster, wag, wit
rel buffoon, card, clown, cutup, gagman, gagster, jokesmith, merry-andrew, prankster, punster, zany; banterer, kidder
humorous *adj syn* see WITTY
humorousness *n syn* see HUMOR 4
humorsome *adj syn* see MOODY
‖**hump** *vb syn* see CARRY 1
hunch *vb syn* see CROUCH
hunch *n syn* see LUMP 1
hunger *vb syn* see LONG
hungry *adj* feeling distressed from lack of food <a group of *hungry* children>
syn famished, ‖peckish, ravenous, starved, starving
rel rapacious, voracious
con full, glutted, gorged, sated, satiated
ant surfeited
hunk *n syn* see LUMP 1
hunker (down) *vb syn* see SQUAT
hunkers *n pl syn* see BUTTOCKS
hunks *n pl but sing or pl in constr syn* see MISER
hunky-dory *adj syn* see MARVELOUS 2

Hunnic *adj syn* see BARBARIAN 1
Hunnish *adj syn* see BARBARIAN 1
hunt *vb* **1** to search for or pursue (game or prey) for the purpose of capturing or killing <*hunted* deer in bow-and-arrow season only>
syn chase, run
rel dog, ferret, hawk, hound; course, drive, stalk, start, still-hunt, track; capture, kill, snare; gun, shoot
idiom go hunting
2 *syn* see SEEK 1
hunt (down *or* out *or* up) *vb syn* see RUMMAGE 3
hunting *n* the act or practice of seeking and taking wild and especially game animals <lived by *hunting* and fishing>
syn chase, venery
rel angling, coursing, falconry, fishing, gunning, hawking, shooting
hurdle *n syn* see OBSTACLE
hurdle *vb* **1** *syn* see CLEAR 8
2 *syn* see JUMP 1
3 *syn* see OVERCOME 1
hurl *vb syn* see THROW 1
hurly-burly *n syn* see COMMOTION 4
hurrah *n* **1** *syn* see PASSION 6
2 *syn* see COMMOTION 3
3 *syn* see ARGUMENT 2
hurricane *n* a violent rotating storm or system of winds originating in the tropics and often moving into temperate latitudes <the *hurricane* struck the coast early today>
syn tropical cyclone, tropical storm, typhoon, ‖willy-willy; *compare* TORNADO, WHIRLWIND 1
rel williwaw
hurried *adj syn* see PRECIPITATE 1
ant unhurried
hurriedness *n syn* see HASTE 2
hurry *vb* **1** *syn* see SPEED 3
2 to proceed or move with dispatch <*hurry* home after school>
syn barrel, barrelhouse, beeline, bucket, bullet, bustle, ‖dust, fleet, flit, fly, haste, hasten, highball, hotfoot, hustle, ‖nip, pelt, rock, rocket, run, rush, scoot, scour, ‖skeet, skin, smoke, speed, stave, ‖tatter, whirl, whish, whisk, whiz, zip; *compare* RUSH 1
rel jog, peg, skelp, trot; bowl (along), breeze; dig in; post
idiom get a move on, go (*or* move) like lightning, make tracks, step on it, step on the gas
con creep, dally, dawdle, drag, lag, linger, loiter, poke, saunter, stroll
hurry *n syn* see HASTE 1
hurry-scurry *adv syn* see PELL-MELL
hurt *vb* **1** *syn* see INJURE 1
rel abuse, afflict, mistreat, misuse
ant benefit
2 *syn* see INJURE 3
3 *syn* see DISTRESS 2
4 to experience or be the seat of sharp physical distress <my arm still *hurts*>
syn ache, pain, ‖suffer; *compare* SMART
hurt *n syn* see INJURY 1
hurtful *adj* **1** *syn* see HARMFUL

con harmless, innocuous
2 syn see PAINFUL 1
hurting *adj syn* see PAINFUL 1
husband *n* the male partner in a marriage <ne-
glected his responsibilities as a *husband*>
  syn ‖hubby, lord, man, ‖master, mister, Mr.,
‖old man
  rel consort, helpmate, helpmeet, mate, other
half, spouse; benedict, bridegroom
husbanding *n syn* see CONSERVATION 1
  ant squandering
husbandry *n* **1 syn** see ECONOMY
  2 syn see AGRICULTURE
hush *vb syn* see SILENCE
hush (up) *vb syn* see SUPPRESS 3
hush *adj syn* see STILL 3
hush *n* **1 syn** see QUIET 1
  2 syn see SECRECY
hushed *adj* **1 syn** see CALM 1
  2 syn see PRIVATE 2
hushful *adj syn* see STILL 3
hush–hush *adj syn* see SECRET 1
hush–hush *n syn* see SECRECY
husk *n syn* see HULL
husk *vb syn* see SHUCK
husky *adj syn* see HOARSE 1
husky *adj* **1** big and muscular <a *husky* man carried in the trunks>
  syn beefy, burly, hefty
  rel brawny, muscular, well-built; stalwart,
stout, strapping, strong, sturdy; Herculean,
mighty, powerful; Bunyanesque, gigantic
  con delicate, fragile, frail; puny, scrawny, slight;
elfin; mousey
  2 syn see LARGE 1
hussy *n* **1 syn** see WANTON
  2 syn see MINX
hustle *vb* **1 syn** see PUSH 2
  2 syn see HURRY 2
hustle *n syn* see HASTE 1
hustler *n* **1** an alert enterprising individual <he's a
hustler, eager to get ahead in the world>
  syn dynamo, go-getter, live wire, peeler, rustler,
self-starter
  rel humdinger, hummer; new broom; doer,
powerhouse
  idiom busy bee
  con dawdler, idler; slow coach, slowpoke, stick=
in-the-mud
  2 syn see PROSTITUTE
hustling *adj syn* see BUSTLING
hut *n* a small, simply constructed dwelling often
for temporary or intermittent occupancy <the
shepherds lived in *huts* in the summer>
  syn ‖box, cabin ‖caboose, camp, cot, cottage,
lodge, shack, shanty; *compare* BUILDING, EDIFICE,
HOVEL
  rel bungalow, cabana, chalet, crib, dacha,
hooch (*or* hootch), hovel, hutch, lean-to, shed,
summer house
hut *vb syn* see HARBOR 2
Hyblaean *adj syn* see MELLIFLUOUS
hybrid *n* an offspring produced by parents of different strains, breeds, varieties, species, or gen-

era <the mule is a *hybrid* of the ass and the
horse>
  syn bastard, cross, crossbred, crossbreed, half
blood, half-breed, mongrel, mule
  rel incross, incrossbred, outcross; combination,
composite, mixture
  con pureblood, purebred, thoroughbred
hybridize *vb syn* see CROSS 4
hydrant *n syn* see FAUCET
‖**hydro** *n syn* see SPA 1
hydroponics *n* the growing of plants in nutrient
solution and without soil <tomatoes grown by
hydroponics>
  syn aquiculture, nutriculture
  idiom soilless agriculture
hygienic *adj syn* see HEALTHFUL
  ant unhygienic
hymeneal *adj syn* see MATRIMONIAL
hymn *n syn* see SONG 2
hymn *vb* **1 syn** see PRAISE 2
  2 syn see SING
hypaethral *adj syn* see OUTDOOR
hype *n syn* see PUBLICITY
hype *vb syn* see PUBLICIZE
hyperbole *n syn* see EXAGGERATION
  con depreciation, minimization, understatement
  ant litotes
hypercritical *adj syn* see CRITICAL 1
hypercriticize *vb syn* see QUIBBLE 1
hypnotic *adj syn* see SOPORIFIC 1
hypocorism *n syn* see NICKNAME
hypocrisy *n* the pretense or affectation of having
virtues, principles, or beliefs that one does not
actually have <political *hypocrisy*>
  syn cant, hypocriticalness, pecksniffery, pharisaicalness, pharisaism, sanctimoniousness, sanctimony, sham, Tartuffery, Tartuffism
  rel pietism, religiosity; casuistry, glibness, insincerity, self-righteousness, unctiousness; charla-
tanry, humbug, quackery
  con candidness, fairness, openness; honesty,
probity, truthfulness
  ant sincerity
hypocrite *n* one who affects virtues, qualities, or
attitudes he does not have <don't be a *hypocrite*
— if you don't approve, say so>
  syn dissembler, dissimulator, lip server, pharisee, Tartuffe, whited sepulcher
  rel pietist; actor, attitudinizer, bluffer, charlatan, faker, four-flusher, fraud, humbug, impostor, masquerader, phony, poser, poseur, pretender, quack, sham
hypocritical *adj* **1** characterized by hypocrisy
<*hypocritical* compliments>
  syn canting, pecksniffian, pharisaic, pharisaical,
sanctimonious, self-righteous
  rel goody-goody, holier-than-thou, moralistic,
pietistic, religiose; casuistic; affected, insincere;

---

syn synonym(s)   *rel* related word(s)
ant antonym(s)   *con* contrasted word(s)
idiom idiomatic equivalent(s)
‖ use limited; if in doubt, see a dictionary

bland, glib, mealymouthed, oily, smooth,
smooth-spoken, smooth-tongued, unctuous
con honest, open, straightforward
ant sincere
2 *syn* see INSINCERE
hypocriticalness *n syn* see HYPOCRISY

ant sincerity
hypostatize *vb syn* see MATERIALIZE 2
hypothesis *n syn* see THEORY 1
hypothetical *adj* **1** *syn* see SUPPOSED 1
rel doubtful, problematic
2 *syn* see ABSTRACT 1

I

icky *adj syn* see OFFENSIVE

iconographic *adj syn* see PICTORIAL 1

icy *adj* **1** *syn* see COLD 1
ant fiery
2 *syn* see COLD 2
ant fiery

idea *n* what exists in the mind as a representation (as of something comprehended) or as a formulation (as of a plan) <that's not my *idea* of a good time>
syn apprehension, conceit, concept, conception, image, impression, intellection, notion, perception, thought
rel assumption, belief, conclusion, conviction, estimation, feeling, inclination, judgment, opinion, persuasion, presumption, reaction, reflection, sentiment, view; conjecture, guess, hypothesis, speculation, supposition, surmise, suspicion, theory; caprice, fancy, fantasy, vagary, whim, whimsy; brainstorm, inspiration

ideal *adj* **1** *syn* see ABSTRACT 1
ant actual
2 *syn* see CONCEPTUAL
3 constituting a standard (as of perfection or excellence) <the *ideal* man of letters>
syn flawless, indefectible, model
rel archetypal, archetypical, prototypal, prototypical
con average, normal, representative, typical
4 *syn* see PERFECT 3
5 *syn* see TYPICAL 1

ideal *n* **1** *syn* see MODEL 2
2 *syn* see PARAGON

idealist *n syn* see DREAMER

idealist *adj syn* see IDEALISTIC

idealistic *adj* characterized by idealism <made an *idealistic* speech on human rights>
syn idealist, utopian, visionary
rel impractical, poetical, quixotic, romantic, starry, starry-eyed, unrealistic
con empirical, matter-of-fact, practical, pragmatic, rational, realistic
ant unidealistic

ideational *adj syn* see CONCEPTUAL

identic *adj syn* see SAME 2
ant nonidentical

identical *adj* **1** *syn* see SAME 1
2 *syn* see SAME 2
ant nonidentical

identicalness *n syn* see IDENTITY 1

identification *n syn* see RECOGNITION 1

identify *vb* to establish the identity of <the culprit was *identified* by his fingerprints>
syn determinate, diagnose, diagnosticate, distinguish, finger, pinpoint, place, recognize, spot
rel find; determine, establish, make out, pick out, select, separate (out)

identity *n* **1** the quality of being the same in all that constitutes the objective reality of separate things <the *identity* of the two texts is exact>
syn identicalness, oneness, sameness, selfsameness
rel agreement, likeness, resemblance, semblance, similarity, similitude; correspondence, equality, equivalence; uniformity
con dissimilarity, dissimilitude, unlikeness, unsimilarity
ant nonidentity
2 *syn* see INDIVIDUALITY 4

ideologue *n syn* see DREAMER

ideology *n* an overall view of or attitude toward life <an *ideology* based on tolerance>
syn credo, creed, weltanschauung
rel outlook, philosophy, view

idiom *n syn* see LANGUAGE 1

idiosyncratic *adj* **1** *syn* see CHARACTERISTIC
2 *syn* see STRANGE 4

idiot *n* **1** *syn* see FOOL 1
2 *syn* see FOOL 2
3 *syn* see FOOL 4
4 *syn* see DUNCE

‖**idiot box** *n syn* see TELEVISION

idle *adj* **1** *syn* see VAIN 1
2 *syn* see VACANT 4
3 *syn* see INACTIVE
ant busy

idle *vb* to spend time in idleness <people *idling* in the park>
syn ‖brogue, bum, dawdle, diddle, diddle-daddle, drone, goldbrick, ‖goof (off), ‖lallygag, laze, lazy, loaf, loiter, loll, lounge
rel relax, repose, rest; amble, linger, mooch, mosey, saunter, stroll, tarry; hang around, sit around, sit back, sit by
idiom dog it, kill time, lie around, mark time

idleheaded *adj syn* see FOOLISH 2

idleness *n syn* see SLOTH 1

idler *n syn* see SLUGGARD

idolatry *n syn* see ADORATION

idolization *n syn* see ADORATION

idolize *vb syn* see ADORE 3
idiom worship the ground one walks on

iffy *adj syn* see UNCERTAIN 1

ignis fatuus *n syn* see DELUSION 1

ignitable *adj syn* see COMBUSTIBLE 1

ignite *vb syn* see LIGHT 1

ignited *adj syn* see BURNING 1

ignoble *adj* **1** belonging to or characteristic of socially or economically inferior classes <a person of *ignoble* antecedents>

---

syn base, baseborn, humble, low, lowborn, lowly, mean, plebeian, unennobled, unwashed
rel coarse, common, homely, inferior, inglorious, modest, ordinary, peasant, plain, poor, popular, simple, vulgar
con highborn, highbred, wellborn, well-bred; eminent, high, lofty, proud, superior
ant noble
2 *syn* see BASE 3
ant noble
ignominious *adj syn* see DISREPUTABLE 1
ignominy *n syn* see DISGRACE
rel contempt, despite, disdain, scorn; chagrin, mortification
con glory, honor; esteem, respect
ignoramus *n syn* see DUNCE
ignorance *n* **1** the state of being unlearned <the blight of *ignorance*>
syn benightedness, illiteracy
rel callowness, greenness, inexperience, naiveté, rawness, simpleness, simplicity, uncouthness, uncultivation, unsophistication; empty-headedness, unintelligence, witlessness; know-nothingism, philistinism
con education, enlightenment, erudition, learning, literacy
2 the state of being unaware or uninformed <*ignorance* of the law>
syn innocence, inscience, nescience, unacquaintance, unacquaintedness, unawareness, unfamiliarity, unknowingness
con acquaintance, acquaintanceship, experience; awareness, familiarity, knowledgeableness
ignorant *adj* **1** lacking knowledge or education <an *ignorant* boy with no taste for school>
syn benighted, empty-headed, illiterate, know-nothing, rude, uneducated, uninstructed, unlettered, unschooled, untaught, untutored
rel lowbrow, uncultured, unintellectual; callow, green, inexperienced; crude, gross, raw, uncouth; ingenuous, naive, simple, unsophisticated
con educated, erudite, learned, literate
2 lacking information on or awareness of something <was *ignorant* of the circumstances surrounding the affair>
syn incognizant, inconversant, oblivious, unacquainted, unaware, unfamiliar, uninformed, uninstructed, unknowing, unwitting
idiom in the dark
con aware, conscious, conversant, informed, knowing, knowledgeable
3 *syn* see BACKWARD 5
ignore *vb syn* see NEGLECT
rel avoid, evade
ilk *n syn* see TYPE
ill *adj* **1** *syn* see EVIL 5
ant good
2 *syn* see HARMFUL
3 *syn* see SICK 1
4 *syn* see RUDE 6
5 *syn* see HOSTILE 1
ill *n* **1** *syn* see EVIL 1
ant benefit
2 *syn* see DISEASE 1

ill–adapted *adj syn* see UNFIT 1
ill–advised *adj* **1** *syn* see RASH 1
2 *syn* see INADVISABLE
ant well-advised
3 *syn* see UNWISE
ant well-advised
illation *n* **1** *syn* see INFERENCE 1
2 *syn* see INFERENCE 2
ill–behaved *adj syn* see NAUGHTY 1
ill–boding *adj syn* see OMINOUS
ill–bred *adj* **1** *syn* see BOORISH
ant well-bred
2 *syn* see RUDE 6
ant well-bred, well-mannered
ill–chosen *adj syn* see INFELICITOUS
ill–defined *adj syn* see FAINT 2
ant well-defined
illegal *adj syn* see UNLAWFUL
rel banned, forbidden, interdicted, prohibited, proscribed, outlawed, unauthorized, unlicensed, unwarranted; felonious; contraband, hot; actionable, irregular
con authorized, lawful, licensed, licit, permitted, regular, right
ant legal
illegality *n* the quality or state of being illegal <the *illegality* of an act>
syn illegitimacy, illicitness, unlawfulness
rel badness, impropriety, wrongness
con lawfulness, legitimacy, licitness; propriety
ant legality
illegible *adj* incapable of being read or deciphered <an *illegible* signature>
syn indecipherable, undecipherable, unreadable
rel faint, indistinct, obscure, unclear
ant legible, readable
illegitimacy *n* **1** the state or condition of being born out of wedlock <he accepted the fact of his *illegitimacy*>
syn bastardy, illegitimateness, supposititiousness
rel bar sinister
ant legitimacy, legitimateness
2 *syn* see ILLEGALITY
ant legitimacy, legitimateness
illegitimate *adj* **1** not recognized by law as lawful offspring <an *illegitimate* child>
syn baseborn, bastard, fatherless, misbegotten, natural, spurious, supposititious, unfathered
rel birthless; adulterine
ant legitimate
2 *syn* see UNLAWFUL
ant legitimate
illegitimate *n syn* see BASTARD 1
ant legitimate
illegitimateness *n syn* see ILLEGITIMACY 1
ant legitimacy, legitimateness
ill–famed *adj syn* see INFAMOUS 1
ill–fated *adj syn* see UNLUCKY
ill–favored *adj* **1** *syn* see UGLY 2
ant well-favored
2 *syn* see OBJECTIONABLE
ill–flavored *adj syn* see UNPALATABLE 1
ill–humored *adj syn* see ILL-TEMPERED

ant good-humored, good-natured

illiberal *adj* unwilling or unable to grasp the point of view of others <had the *illiberal* outlook of an old-time schoolmaster>
syn bigoted, brassbound, hidebound, intolerant, narrow, narrow-minded, small-minded, unenlarged
rel biased, jaundiced, one-sided, opinionated, partial, partisan, prejudiced; grudging, little, mean, paltry, petty, small, uncharitable, ungenerous; insular, parochial, provincial; rigid, rigorous, stringent
con broad-minded, open-minded, tolerant, unbigoted; advanced, progressive, radical
ant liberal

illicit *adj syn* see UNLAWFUL
ant licit

illicitness *n syn* see ILLEGALITY

illimitable *adj syn* see INFINITE 1
rel endless, interminable
ant limitable; limited

illiteracy *n syn* see IGNORANCE 1

illiterate *adj syn* see IGNORANT 1
ant literate; erudite

illiterate *n* one who cannot read or write <the training of adult *illiterates*>
syn analphabet
rel functional illiterate, semiliterate, subliterate
ant literate

ill–judged *adj syn* see UNWISE

ill–kempt *adj syn* see SLOVENLY 1

ill–looking *adj syn* see UGLY 2
ant good-looking, ||well-looked

ill–mannered *adj syn* see RUDE 6
ant well-bred, well-mannered

ill–natured *adj syn* see ILL-TEMPERED
ant good-humored, good-natured

illness *n syn* see SICKNESS 1
ant health

illogical *adj* contrary to or devoid of logic <came to an *illogical* conclusion from the facts presented>
syn fallacious, invalid, irrational, mad, nonrational, reasonless, sophistic, unreasonable, unreasoned; *compare* FALSE 1
rel inconsistent; specious; unscientific, unsound; absurd, meaningless, senseless
idiom without rhyme or reason
con rational, reasonable, sensible; plausible, sane, sound, valid
ant logical

ill–omened *adj syn* see OMINOUS
ant auspicious

ill–seasoned *adj syn* see UNSEASONABLE 1
ant seasonable

ill–starred *adj syn* see UNLUCKY
rel bodeful, fateful, foreboding, ominous, portentous; baleful, malefic, malign, sinister; unfavorable, unpromising, unpropitious

ill–suited *adj syn* see UNFIT 1

ill–tempered *adj* having a bad temper <an *ill-tempered* old man>
syn bad-tempered, dyspeptic, hot-tempered, ill≈humored, ill-natured, ||rusty, tempersome

rel crabbed, surly; fractious, huffy, irritable, peevish, petulant, querulous, snappish, sour, waspish; shrewish, vixenish
con calm, easy, placid, serene, tranquil; amiable, complaisant, considerate, good-natured, kindly, obliging, tolerant
ant good-tempered, sweet-tempered, well-tempered

ill–timed *adj* **1** *syn* see UNSEASONABLE 1
ant seasonable
2 *syn* see IMPROPER 1

ill–treat *vb syn* see ABUSE 4
rel aggrieve, harass, harry, molest
con befriend, relieve, succor; countenance, encourage, favor, patronize

illude *vb syn* see DECEIVE

illume *vb* **1** *syn* see ILLUMINATE 1
2 *syn* see ILLUMINATE 2

illuminant *adj syn* see ENLIGHTENING

illuminate *vb* **1** to supply with physical light <a room dimly *illuminated* by firelight>
syn illume, illumine, light, lighten
rel brighten; irradiate; floodlight, highlight, spotlight; fire, ignite, kindle
con blur, cloud, darken, dim, dull, obscure, pale
2 to supply with spiritual or intellectual light <the worth of a truly *illuminating* book>
syn edify, enlighten, illume, illumine, improve, irradiate, uplift
rel better, improve; ennoble, exalt, refine; finish, mature, perfect, polish
con becloud, cloud, darken, obfuscate, obscure, overshadow, shadow
3 *syn* see CLARIFY 2
rel construe, define, dramatize, expound, express, gloss, interpret
idiom shed light on (*or* upon)
con baffle, confound, confuse, mystify, pose, puzzle, stump

illuminati *n pl syn* see INTELLIGENTSIA

illuminating *adj syn* see ENLIGHTENING

illuminative *adj syn* see ENLIGHTENING

illumine *vb* **1** *syn* see ILLUMINATE 1
2 *syn* see ILLUMINATE 2

illumining *adj syn* see ENLIGHTENING

ill–use *vb syn* see ABUSE 4
con befriend, relieve, succor; countenance, encourage, favor, patronize

illusion *n* **1** *syn* see DELUSION 1
rel invention; bubble, chimera, dream, will-o'≈the-wisp; appearance, seeming, semblance
2 *syn* see PIPE DREAM

illusionist *n syn* see MAGICIAN 2

illusive *adj syn* see APPARENT 2

illusory *adj* **1** *syn* see FICTITIOUS 1
ant factual
2 *syn* see APPARENT 2

---

syn synonym(s)   *rel* related word(s)
ant antonym(s)   *con* contrasted word(s)
idiom idiomatic equivalent(s)
|| use limited; if in doubt, see a dictionary

rel chimerical, fanciful, fantastic, imaginary, unreal, visionary; deceptive, delusive, delusory, misleading
con actual, real, veritable; authentic, true, valid
ant factual

illustrate *vb* **1** *syn* see CLARIFY 2
rel display, exhibit, expose, show; disclose, discover, reveal
con cloak, conceal, enshroud, mask, screen, shroud, veil
2 *syn* see EXEMPLIFY 1
rel elucidate, explain, expound, interpret; demonstrate, manifest, show; enliven, vivify
3 *syn* see REPRESENT 2
4 *syn* see SHOW 2

illustration *n* **1** *syn* see EXAMPLE 3
2 *syn* see INSTANCE

illustrational *adj syn* see PICTORIAL 1

illustrative *adj syn* see PICTORIAL 1

illustratory *adj syn* see PICTORIAL 1

illustrious *adj syn* see FAMOUS 2
rel glorious, resplendent, splendid, sublime; conspicuous, lofty, outstanding, signal, striking
con abject, inglorious, mean; disgraceful, dishonorable, ignoble, ignominious, shameful
ant infamous

illustriousness *n syn* see EMINENCE 1
ant infamy

ill will *n syn* see MALICE
rel hostility, rancor, venom
ant goodwill

image *n* **1** one strikingly like another especially in appearance or manner <she was the *image* of her mother>
syn double, picture, portrait, ringer, simulacrum, spit, spitting image
rel counterpart, equal, equivalent, match
idiom chip off the old block, dead ringer, speaking likeness, spit and image
2 *syn* see IDEA

image *vb* **1** *syn* see REPRESENT 1
2 *syn* see THINK 1
3 *syn* see REFLECT 1

imaginable *adj syn* see THINKABLE 2
ant unimaginable

imaginary *adj* **1** having no real existence but existing in imagination <elves are *imaginary* beings>
syn fancied, fanciful, imagined, notional, shadowy
rel imaginative; abstract, hypothetical, ideal, visionary; apparitional, chimerical, fantastic, figmental, hallucinatory, illusory, phantasmal, phantasmic, quixotic, spectral; unreal, unsubstantial
con genuine, true, valid
ant actual, real
2 *syn* see FICTITIOUS 1
ant actual, real

imagination *n* the power or function of the mind by which mental images are formed or the exercise of that power <children have great *imagination*>
syn fancy, fantasy (*or* phantasy), imaginativeness

rel creativity, inspiration, invention, inventiveness, visualization
con literalness, matter-of-factness, prosaism, unimaginativeness

imaginativeness *n syn* see IMAGINATION
ant unimaginativeness

imagine *vb* **1** *syn* see THINK 1
2 *syn* see UNDERSTAND 3

imagined *adj syn* see IMAGINARY 1
con known, recognized, seen

imbecile *adj syn* see RETARDED

imbecile *n* **1** *syn* see FOOL 4
2 *syn* see FOOL 1

imbibe *vb* **1** *syn* see ABSORB 1
2 *syn* see DRINK 1
3 *syn* see DRINK 3

imbricate *vb syn* see OVERLAP

imbroglio *n syn* see QUARREL

imbrued *adj syn* see BLOODY 1

imbue *vb syn* see INFUSE 1

imitate *vb* **1** *syn* see COPY
2 *syn* see MIMIC

imitation *adj syn* see ARTIFICIAL 2
ant real

imitation *n* something made or produced as an often inferior likeness of something else <usually wore *imitations* of her costly jewels>
syn copy, ersatz, simulacrum
rel counterfeit, fake, forgery, phony, sham, simulation; counterpart, duplicate, replica, reproduction; likeness, semblance
ant original

imitative *adj* **1** *syn* see ONOMATOPOEIC
2 *syn* see SLAVISH 3

immaculate *adj* **1** *syn* see CHASTE
ant maculate
2 *syn* see IMPECCABLE 1
3 *syn* see CLEAN 1

immalleable *adj syn* see STIFF 1
ant malleable

immaterial *adj* **1** not composed of matter <*immaterial* forces>
syn asomatous, bodiless, disbodied, discarnate, disembodied, incorporeal, insubstantial, metaphysical, nonmaterial, nonphysical, spiritual, unbodied, ‖uncorporal, unembodied, unfleshly, unmaterial, unphysical, unsubstantial
rel impalpable, imponderable; psychic, subjective; aerial, airy, ethereal; insensible, unearthly, unworldly; supernatural; celestial, heavenly; apparitional, ghostly, shadowy
con bodily, corporeal, fleshly, incarnate; material, objective, palpable, physical, substantial; mundane, terrestrial, worldly
ant material
2 *syn* see IRRELEVANT
ant material

immature *adj* **1** *syn* see YOUNG 1
rel precocious, premature
ant mature
2 *syn* see CHILDISH
ant mature

immeasurable *adj* **1** *syn* see INCALCULABLE 1
2 *syn* see LIMITLESS

immediacy *n syn* see PROXIMITY
immediate *adj* **1** *syn* see DIRECT 4
  ant distant (*of relatives*)
  2 *syn* see INSTANTANEOUS
  3 *syn* see CLOSE 6
immediately *adv* **1** in direct connection without intermediary <*immediately* in front of the viewers>
  syn contiguously, directly
  2 *syn* see AWAY 3
  rel anon, shortly, soon
  idiom right now
immedicable *adj syn* see HOPELESS 2
  ant medicable
immense *adj syn* see HUGE
immensely *adv syn* see EVER 6
immensity *n syn* see ENORMITY 2
immerse *vb* **1** *syn* see DIP 1
  rel saturate, soak
  2 *syn* see BAPTIZE
  3 *syn* see ENGAGE 4
immersed *adj syn* see INTENT
immigrant *n syn* see EMIGRANT
imminent *adj* **1** about to take place <their departure is *imminent*>
  syn impending, proximate
  rel approaching, coming, nearing, upcoming; brewing, gathering; pending; likely, possible, probable; ineluctable, inescapable, inevasible, inevitable, unavoidable, unescapable
  idiom in prospect, in store, in the cards, in the offing, in the wind, in view
  con distant, far-off, remote
  2 menacingly near <a thunderstorm was *imminent*>
  syn lowering (*or* louring), lowery (*or* loury), menacing, overhanging, threatening
  rel alarming, ominous, sinister; brewing, gathering; minatory
immingle *vb syn* see MIX 1
immix *vb syn* see MIX 1
immixture *n syn* see MIXTURE
immobile *adj* **1** *syn* see IMMOVABLE 1
  ant mobile, movable
  2 *syn* see STATIC
immobilize *vb syn* see PARALYZE 1
immoderate *adj* **1** *syn* see EXCESSIVE 1
  ant moderate
  2 *syn* see EXCESSIVE 2
  ant moderate
immoderation *n syn* see EXCESS 3
  ant moderation
immolate *vb syn* see SACRIFICE 1
immoral *adj* **1** *syn* see IMPURE 1
  ant moral
  2 *syn* see WRONG 1
  ant moral
immorality *n syn* see VICE 1
  ant morality
immortal *adj* **1** not subject to death <the *immortal* gods>
  syn deathless, undying; *compare* EVERLASTING 1
  rel endless, enduring, imperishable, indestructible, perpetual, sempiternal, timeless

con ephemeral, evanescent, fleeting, fugitive, passing, short-lived, transient, transitory
  ant mortal
  2 *syn* see EVERLASTING 1
immortality *n syn* see ETERNITY 2
  ant mortality
immortalize *vb syn* see PERPETUATE
immotile *adj syn* see IMMOVABLE 1
  ant motile
immotive *adj syn* see IMMOVABLE 1
immovable *adj* **1** incapable of moving or being moved <an *immovable* rock>
  syn fixed, immobile, immotile, immotive, irremovable, ‖sitfast, steadfast, unmovable
  rel adamant, fast, rooted, stable, stationary, stuck, unmoving, unyielding
  con portable, removable, transferable, transportable
  ant movable
  2 *syn* see INFLEXIBLE 3
immunity *n syn* see EXEMPTION
  ant susceptibility
immure *vb* **1** *syn* see ENCLOSE 1
  2 *syn* see IMPRISON
immusical *adj syn* see DISSONANT 1
  ant musical
immutable *adj syn* see INFLEXIBLE 3
  ant mutable
imp *n* **1** a small demon, devil, or wicked spirit <the *imps* of hell>
  syn deviling, devilkin
  rel elf, gnome, goblin, gremlin, ‖hob, hobgoblin, kobold, ouph, pixie, puck, sprite, troll
  2 *syn* see URCHIN
impact *n* **1** a forcible or enforced contact between two or more things <a crater formed by the *impact* of a meteorite>
  syn appulse, blow, bump, clash, collision, concussion, crash, impingement, jar, jolt, jounce, percussion, shock, smash, wallop
  rel brunt; buffet, hit, pound, punch, rap, slap, smiting, strike, stroke; bounce, quake, quiver, rock, shake, tremble, tremor; encounter, meeting
  2 *syn* see EFFECT 3
impair *vb syn* see INJURE 1
  rel sap, undermine, weaken
  con ameliorate, better
  ant improve; repair
impaired *adj syn* see DAMAGED
impale *vb* to pierce or fix with or as if with something pointed <an insect *impaled* on a pin>
  syn lance, skewer, skiver, spear, spike, spit, transfix, transpierce
  rel perforate, pierce, prick, punch, puncture, stab
impalpable *adj* **1** *syn* see IMPERCEPTIBLE
  ant palpable
  2 *syn* see FINE 2
imparity *n syn* see DISPARITY

---

syn synonym(s)   *rel* related word(s)
ant antonym(s)   *con* contrasted word(s)
idiom idiomatic equivalent(s)
‖ use limited; if in doubt, see a dictionary

ant parity

impart *vb syn* see COMMUNICATE 1

impartial *adj syn* see FAIR 4
ant partial

impartially *adv syn* see EVENLY 2

impassable *adj* **1** not allowing passage <an *impassable* barrier>
syn impenetrable, impermeable, imperviable, impervious, unpierceable
con penetrable, permeable, pervious
ant passable
2 *syn* see INSUPERABLE

impasse *n* **1** *syn* see DEAD END
2 *syn* see PREDICAMENT

impassible *adj syn* see INSENSIBLE 5
rel cold, emotionless, passionless, unemotional, unfeeling; inert, unresponsive
ant passible

impassioned *adj* actuated by or showing intense feeling <*impassioned* oratory>
syn ardent, blazing, burning, dithyrambic, fervent, fervid, fiery, flaming, glowing, hot-blooded, overheated, passionate, perfervid, red-hot, torrid, white-hot
rel feverish, fierce, furious, intense, vehement, violent; deep, profound, warm, zealous; gushing, gushy, maudlin, melodramatic, mushy, overemotional, romantic, sentimental
con cold, cool, dispassionate, frigid, icy, unemotional; objective
ant unimpassioned

impassive *adj* **1** unresponsive to what might normally excite interest or emotion <*impassive* endurance of pain>
syn apathetic, dry, matter-of-fact, phlegmatic, stoic, stolid
rel calm, cold, cool; collected, composed, dispassionate, emotionless, imperturbable, inexcitable, unexcitable, unflappable; inexpressive, reserved, reticent, taciturn, unemotional, unexpressive; bovine, passionless, placid, spiritless, unconcerned, wooden; callous, hardened, indurated, insensible; cold-blooded, coldhearted, heartless
con compassionate, sympathetic, tender, warm, warmhearted
ant responsive
2 *syn* see INSUSCEPTIBLE

impassivity *n syn* see APATHY 1

impatient *adj* **1** lacking power to endure hardship, distress, or opposition <married to an *impatient* self-centered man>
syn chafing, fretful, unpatient
rel abrupt, hasty, headlong, impetuous; anxious, edgy, itchy, nervous; irascible, irritable
idiom all of a stew
con enduring, forbearing, tolerant; self-controlled, Spartan, stoic
ant patient
2 *syn* see INTOLERANT 1
rel demanding, harsh
3 *syn* see EAGER
ant patient

impeach *vb syn* see ACCUSE

impeccable *adj* **1** absolutely correct and beyond criticism <*impeccable* manners>
syn errorless, exquisite, faultless, flawless, immaculate, irreproachable
rel accurate, clean, correct, exact, nice, perfect, precise, right; infallible, unerring
con defective, deficient, faulty; blameworthy, censurable, criticizable, culpable; cursory, shallow, superficial, uncritical
ant peccant
2 *syn* see PERFECT 2

impecunious *adj syn* see POOR 1
ant affluent; flush

impecuniousness *n syn* see POVERTY 1
ant affluence; flushness

impedance *n syn* see ENCUMBRANCE

impede *vb syn* see HINDER
rel discomfit, disconcert, embarrass, faze, rattle
ant aid, assist

impediment *n* **1** *syn* see ENCUMBRANCE
ant aid, assistance
2 *syn* see OBSTACLE

impel *vb syn* see MOVE 5
rel compel, constrain, force; foment, incite, instigate; goad, spur; inspire, motivate
con check, curb, inhibit
ant restrain

impend *vb syn* see LOOM 2

impending *adj syn* see IMMINENT 1

impenetrable *adj* **1** *syn* see IMPASSABLE 1
rel firm, solid, substantial
ant penetrable
2 *syn* see INCOMPREHENSIBLE 1
ant penetrable
3 *syn* see MYSTERIOUS

impenetrate *vb syn* see PERMEATE

impenitent *adj syn* see REMORSELESS
ant penitent

imperative *adj* **1** *syn* see MASTERFUL 1
rel bidding, commanding, ordering; harsh, stern
con begging, entreating, imploring; lenient, mild, soft
2 *syn* see PRESSING
rel acute, critical, crucial
3 *syn* see ESSENTIAL 4
rel basic, fundamental; claimed, demanded, exacted
4 *syn* see MANDATORY

imperceptible *adj* incapable of being apprehended by the senses or intellect <*imperceptible* changes in temperature>
syn impalpable, imponderable, inappreciable, indiscernible, insensible, intangible, invisible, unapparent, unappreciable, undiscernible, unobservable, unperceivable
rel faint, inconspicuous, indistinct, indistinguishable, insignificant, obscure, undistinguishable, unnoticeable, vague; ephemeral, evanescent, fugitive, momentary; slight, trivial
con apparent, appreciable, discernible, observable, palpable, ponderable, sensible, visible
ant perceivable, perceptible

imperceptive *adj* lacking perception or insight <*imperceptive* criticism that misses the point of the play>
syn impercipient, unperceiving, unperceptive
rel unappreciative, undiscerning, unobservant; cursory, shallow, slapdash, superficial
con astute, discerning, discriminating, judicious, perspicacious; delicate, nice, refined, sensitive, subtle
ant perceiving, perceptive, percipient
impercipient *adj syn* see IMPERCEPTIVE
ant perceiving, perceptive, percipient
imperfect *adj syn* see FAULTY
ant perfect
imperfection *n* an instance of failure to reach a standard of excellence or perfection <watch for *imperfections* in the cloth>
syn deficiency, demerit, fault, shortcoming, sin
rel blemish, defect, flaw; failing, foible, frailty
ant perfection
imperial *adj syn* see MASTERFUL 1
imperil *vb syn* see ENDANGER
imperious *adj* **1** *syn* see MASTERFUL 1
rel heavy-handed, oppressive, strict, stringent; absolute, arbitrary
con considerate, easy, gentle, kindly
2 *syn* see MANDATORY
imperishable *adj syn* see INDESTRUCTIBLE
impermanent *adj syn* see TRANSIENT
ant permanent
impermeable *adj syn* see IMPASSABLE 1
ant permeable
impersonal *adj* **1** *syn* see NEUTRAL
2 *syn* see FAIR 4
3 *syn* see MATTER-OF-FACT 3
impersonate *vb syn* see ACT 1
impersonator *n syn* see ACTOR 1
impertinence *n syn* see INSOLENCE
impertinent *adj* **1** *syn* see IRRELEVANT
ant pertinent
2 going beyond what is proper or acceptable in thrusting oneself into the affairs of others <*impertinent* interference with her sister's family>
syn busy, intrusive, meddlesome, ‖nebby, obtrusive, officious, polypragmatic
rel arrogant, bold, brash, brazen, fresh, impudent, pert, presumptuous, saucy; inquisitive, interfering, meddling, nosy, prying; offensive, rude
con decent, decorous, proper, seemly; reserved, reticent, silent; apposite, germane, pertinent, relevant
3 *syn* see RUDE 6
4 *syn* see INSOLENT 2
imperturbability *n syn* see EQUANIMITY
imperturbable *adj syn* see COOL 2
rel complacent, self-satisfied, smug; unaffected, unmoved, untouched
con discomfited, disconcerted, fazed, rattled; irascible, splenetic, testy
ant choleric; touchy
imperviable *adj syn* see IMPASSABLE 1
impervious *adj syn* see IMPASSABLE 1
ant pervious
impetuous *adj syn* see PRECIPITATE 1

rel spontaneous; restive; ardent, fervid, impassioned, passionate
con equable, even, steady; advised, considered, deliberate, planned, premeditated
impetuously *adv syn* see PELL-MELL
impetus *n syn* see STIMULUS
impignorate *vb syn* see PAWN
impingement *n syn* see IMPACT 1
impious *adj* **1** lacking reverence for holy or sacred matters <made *impious* remarks about the church>
syn irreverent, irreverential, profane, ungodly, unhallowed, unholy
rel godless, iconoclastic, irreligious, sacrilegious, scandalous, undevout
con devout, godly, religious, spiritual
ant pious
2 lacking due respect (as toward one's parents) <an *impious* son>
syn unduteous, undutiful
rel disobedient, froward, unfaithful, wayward; contrary, perverse, wrongheaded
con duteous, dutiful
impish *adj syn* see PLAYFUL 1
rel arch, pert, saucy; flippant, fresh, giddy; casual, devil-may-care, free and easy, offhand
impishness *n syn* see MISCHIEVOUSNESS
implacable *adj syn* see GRIM 3
con peaceable, tractable; kindly, tolerant
ant placable
implant *vb* to introduce into the mind <*implanted* worthy ideals in their children>
syn inculcate, infix, inseminate, instill
rel imbue, infuse, ingrain, inoculate, leaven, root; impenetrate, impregnate, penetrate, permeate, pervade, saturate; inspire
implausible *adj* not plausible or readily believable <an *implausible* explanation>
syn flimsy, improbable, inconceivable, incredible, thick, thin, unbelievable, unconceivable, unconvincing, unsubstantial, weak; *compare* TENUOUS 3
rel doubtful, dubious, fishy; problematic, puzzling, suspect
idiom a bit thick
con meaty, pithy; solid, sound, substantial; believable, conceivable, credible; likely, probable
ant plausible
implement *n* a usually relatively simple device for performing a mechanical or manual operation <spades, hoes, and other gardener's *implements*>
syn instrument, tool, utensil
rel apparatus, appliance; contrivance, device; contraption, gadget
implement *vb* **1** *syn* see FULFILL 1
2 *syn* see ENFORCE
rel actualize, materialize, realize
implemental *adj syn* see INSTRUMENTAL

---

syn synonym(s)   *rel* related word(s)
ant antonym(s)   *con* contrasted word(s)
idiom idiomatic equivalent(s)
‖ use limited; if in doubt, see a dictionary

impliable *adj syn* see STIFF 1
  ant pliable
implicate *vb syn* see INVOLVE 1
  rel affect, concern; incriminate
  con absolve, acquit, exculpate, exonerate
implicated *adj syn* see INTERESTED
implication *n syn* see ASSOCIATION 4
implicit *adj* **1** *syn* see TACIT 1
  idiom taken for granted
  ant explicit
  2 being such in essential character <our *implicit* freedom is better than your nominal liberty>
  syn constructive, practical, virtual
  rel absolute, complete, unqualified, wholehearted; genuine, real
  ant spelled out
implied *adj syn* see TACIT 1
imploration *n syn* see PRAYER
implore *vb syn* see BEG
imply *vb* **1** *syn* see POINT 2
  2 *syn* see SUGGEST 1
  con state; express; affirm, assert, declare
impolite *adj syn* see RUDE 6
  ant polite
impolitic *adj* **1** *syn* see UNWISE
  ant politic
  2 *syn* see INADVISABLE
  ant politic
  3 *syn* see TACTLESS
imponderable *adj syn* see IMPERCEPTIBLE
  ant appreciable, ponderable
imponderous *adj syn* see LIGHT 1
  ant ponderous
import *vb* **1** *syn* see MEAN 2
  2 *syn* see MATTER
import *n* **1** *syn* see MEANING 1
  rel construction, interpretation
  2 *syn* see IMPORTANCE
  rel value, worth; design, intent, object, objective, purpose; emphasis, stress
importance *n* the quality or state of being of notable worth or influence <persons of national and worldwide *importance*>
  syn consequence, import, magnitude, moment, momentousness, pith, significance, ‖signification, weight, weightiness
  rel conspicuousness; distinction, eminence, mark, prominence, salience; notability, note, noteworthiness, reputation, standing; substance, value, worth, worthiness; gravity, seriousness
  con inconsequence, insignificance, paltriness, pettiness, triviality
  ant unimportance
important *adj* **1** marked by or indicative of notable worth or consequence <an *important* discovery> <his manner was grave and *important*>
  syn big, consequential, considerable, material, meaningful, momentous, significant, substantial, weighty
  rel conspicuous, distinctive, exceptional, impressive, marked, memorable, notable, noteworthy, noticeable, outstanding, prominent, remarkable, salient, unusual; essential; valuable, worthwhile; worthy; effective, potent, powerful, telling; big-time, first-class, first-rate, front-

page, top-notch; distinguished, eminent, famous, noted
  con inconsiderable, little, minor, paltry, petty, slight, trivial
  ant unimportant
  2 *syn* see POMPOUS 1
importunate *adj syn* see PRESSING
  rel persevering, persistent; dogged, pertinacious
importune *vb syn* see BEG
impose *vb* **1** *syn* see DICTATE
  rel charge, command, enjoin, order; demand, exact, require; compel, constrain, oblige
  2 *syn* see LEVY
  3 *syn* see INFLICT 2
  4 to force another to accept <*imposed* all the dirty jobs on her sister>
  syn foist, wish; *compare* FOIST 3, INFLICT 2
  rel burden, lade, saddle; fob, fob off, palm off
  idiom take advantage of
  5 to take usually unwarranted advantage <did not wish to *impose* by turning up unannounced>
  syn infringe, intrude, obtrude, presume
  rel encroach, trespass
  idiom make free, take liberties
impose (on *or* upon) *vb syn* see EXPLOIT 2
imposing *adj* **1** *syn* see GRAND 1
  rel impressive, moving; imperial, regal
  ant unimposing
  2 *syn* see PRETENTIOUS 3
impossible *adj* **1** not capable of being realized or attained <*impossible* goals>
  syn impracticable, impractical, infeasible, irrealizable, unattainable, unfeasible, unrealizable, unworkable
  rel absurd, inexecutable, unobtainable, unreasonable, unthinkable
  idiom out of the question
  con attainable, feasible, realizable; practicable, practical, rational, reasonable
  ant possible
  2 *syn* see HOPELESS 2
impost *n syn* see TAX 1
impostor *n* one who passes himself off as something or someone he is not <the presumed heir was discovered to be an *impostor*>
  syn fake, faker, fraud, humbug, phony, pretender; *compare* CHARLATAN
  rel imitator, mimic; beguiler, deceiver, misleader; cheat, pettifogger, shyster, trickster; hypocrite; charlatan, mountebank, quack; bluffer, dissembler, four-flusher, shammer
  idiom wolf in sheep's clothing
imposture *n* the act, practice, or an instance of imposing on another by use of an assumed character or name <his claims were based on *imposture*>
  syn cheat, counterfeit, deceit, deception, fake, flam, flimflam, fraud, gyp, hoax, humbug, mare's nest, phony, put-on, ‖rig, sell, sham, spoof, swindle
  rel copy, imitation; fabrication, forgery; artifice, feint, gambit, maneuver, ploy, ruse, sleight, stratagem, trick, wile; make- believe, pretense, pretension

impotent *adj* **1** *syn* see POWERLESS
rel crippled, disabled, enfeebled
con able, capable, competent
ant potent
2 *syn* see WEAK 4
con forceful, powerful, puissant, strenuous, vigorous
ant potent
3 *syn* see STERILE 1

impoverish *vb* **1** *syn* see DEPLETE
ant enrich
2 *syn* see RUIN 3

impoverished *adj* *syn* see POOR 1

impoverishment *n* *syn* see POVERTY 1

impracticable *adj* **1** *syn* see IMPOSSIBLE 1
ant feasible, practicable
2 incapable of being successfully used or turned to account <a route through the mountains that is *impracticable* in winter>
syn impractical, nonfunctional, unfunctional, unserviceable, unusable, unworkable, useless
rel disadvantageous, unacceptable, undesirable, unsatisfactory; awkward, inconvenient, troublesome
con functional, practical, serviceable, usable, useful, workable
ant practicable

impractical *adj* **1** incapable of dealing prudently with practical matters <a very *impractical* person whose checkbook never balanced>
syn ivory-tower, ivory-towered, ivory-towerish, nonrealistic, unpractical, unrealistic, viewy
rel idealistic, otherworldly, quixotic, romantic, starry-eyed, visionary
con commonsensible, commonsensical, realistic, sensible, worldly-wise
ant practical
2 *syn* see IMPRACTICABLE 2
ant practical
3 *syn* see IMPOSSIBLE 1

imprecate *vb* *syn* see SWEAR 3

imprecation *n* **1** *syn* see BLASPHEMY 1
2 *syn* see PRAYER
3 *syn* see CURSE 1
con blessing

impregnable *adj* *syn* see INVINCIBLE 1
rel safe, secure; defended, guarded, protected, safeguarded, shielded
con exposed, open, susceptible

impregnate *vb* **1** *syn* see PERMEATE
rel inoculate, leaven
2 *syn* see SOAK 1

impress *vb* **1** *syn* see ENGRAVE 2
2 *syn* see AFFECT
rel enthuse, electrify, thrill; excite, galvanize, pique, provoke, stimulate
idiom make (*or* leave) one's mark
3 to fix in the mind or memory by emphasis or repetition <the speaker *impressed* his principal thesis upon his audience>
syn drive, grave, hammer, pound, stamp
rel establish, fix, set
idiom drive home to one, fix in one's mind, get into one's head

impress *n* *syn* see IMPRESSION 1

impressible *adj* *syn* see SENTIENT 3

impression *n* **1** the perceptible trace or traces left by pressure <the *impression* made by a die>
syn impress, imprint, indentation, print, stamp
rel dent, dint, hollow; trace, track, vestige; mark, sign
2 *syn* see IDEA
3 *syn* see EDITION

impressionable *adj* *syn* see SENTIENT 3
rel affectable, influenceable

impressive *adj* **1** *syn* see MOVING 2
rel august, grand, imposing, majestic, noble; splendid, superb; arresting, notable, striking
ant unimpressive
2 *syn* see GRAND 2

imprint *vb* *syn* see ENGRAVE 2

imprint *n* **1** *syn* see IMPRESSION 1
2 *syn* see EFFECT 3

imprison *vb* to shut up closely so that escape is impossible or unlikely <the offender was quickly sentenced and *imprisoned*>
syn bastille, confine, constrain, immure, incarcerate, intern, jail, jug, ‖prison, ‖quod
rel circumscribe, limit, restrict; check, curb, restrain
idiom put under lock and key
con free, liberate, release

improbable *adj* **1** not likely to be true or to occur <the immediate success of their plan is *improbable*>
syn doubtful, dubious, questionable, unlikely
ant probable
2 *syn* see IMPLAUSIBLE

impromptu *n* *syn* see IMPROVISATION

impromptu *adj* *syn* see EXTEMPORANEOUS
rel prompt, quick

improper *adj* **1** unsuited to the circumstances or the occasion <wore quite *improper* dress for such a formal reception>
syn ill-timed, inadmissible, inappropriate, inapt, inept, intempestive, malapropos, unapt, unbecoming, unbefitting, uncomely, undue, unfitting, unseasonable, unseemly, unsuitable, untimely
rel infelicitous, unhappy; inapplicable, inapposite; fresh, impertinent, sassy; crude, gauche, tactless
idiom out of place, out of season
con apposite, appropriate, apropos, apt, becoming, befitting, felicitous, fitting, germane, happy, opportune, pat, pertinent, seasonable, suitable, timely, well-timed
ant proper
2 *syn* see INDECOROUS
rel informal, unceremonious, unconventional
con correct, right
ant proper

---

syn synonym(s)   *rel* related word(s)
ant antonym(s)   *con* contrasted word(s)
idiom idiomatic equivalent(s)
‖ use limited; if in doubt, see a dictionary

impropriety *n* **1** the quality or state of being improper (as in social behavior) <was shocked by the *impropriety* of their actions>
syn incorrectness, indecorousness, indecorum, inelegance, unbecomingness, unmeetness, unseemliness, untowardness
rel inadmissibility, objectionableness, unacceptableness
con becomingness, decency, decorousness, decorum, meetness
ant propriety, seemliness
2 *syn* see FAUX PAS; *compare* ERROR 2
3 *syn* see BARBARISM

improve *vb* **1** to make more acceptable or bring nearer to some standard <studied hard to *improve* her chances of success>
syn ameliorate, amend, better, help, meliorate
rel cultivate, develop, perfect; correct, emend, rectify, reform, remedy; edit, revise; enhance, enrich, refine, rub up, upgrade
con diminish, downgrade, lessen, lower
2 *syn* see ILLUMINATE 2
3 to grow or become better (as in health or well≠being) <the invalid is steadily *improving*>
syn ameliorate, convalesce, gain, look up, mend, perk (up), recuperate
rel advance, better, progress; recover; rally, revive, strengthen
idiom gain ground, make progress
con decline, deteriorate, fail, flag, languish, run down, sink, weaken

improvident *adj* not foreseeing or providing for the future <an *improvident* way of life>
syn thriftless, unthrift, unthrifty
rel careless, heedless, imprudent; extravagant, prodigal, profligate, spendthrift; lavish, profuse, reckless; uneconomical, wasteful
con careful, economical, frugal, parsimonious, prudent, saving, sparing
ant provident, thrifty

improvisate *vb syn* see IMPROVISE

improvisation *n* something that is improvised <the pianist played several clever *improvisations*>
syn autoschediasm, extemporization, impromptu

improvise *vb* to perform or provide on the spur of the moment <*improvise* an excuse for being late>
syn ad-lib, extemporize, improvisate
rel concoct, contrive, devise, invent

improvised *adj syn* see EXTEMPORANEOUS

imprudent *adj* **1** *syn* see UNWISE
ant prudent
2 *syn* see INADVISABLE
ant prudent

impudence *n syn* see INSOLENCE

impudent *adj* **1** *syn* see WISE 5
2 *syn* see INSOLENT 2
3 *syn* see SHAMELESS

impugn *vb syn* see DENY 4
rel assail, attack
idiom call in (*or* into) question (*or* doubt), throw doubt on

con back, support, uphold
ant advocate; authenticate

impugnable *adj syn* see DOUBTFUL 1

impulse *n syn* see STIMULUS
rel excitant; lust, passion, urge; actuation, drive, impulsion

impulsive *adj syn* see SPONTANEOUS
rel abrupt, hasty, headlong, impetuous, precipitate, sudden
con considered, designed, premeditated; calculating, cautious, circumspect
ant deliberate

impulsiveness *n syn* see ABANDON 2

impunity *n syn* see EXEMPTION

impure *adj* **1** morally or mentally unclean <*impure* thoughts>
syn dirty, immoral, unchaste, unclean, uncleanly
rel belowstairs, carnal, immodest, indecent, indecorous, lascivious, lewd, lustful, prurient, scarlet, sensual; filthy, vile
con chaste, clean, cleanly, decent, decorous, immaculate, modest, virtuous; moral
ant pure
2 *syn* see DIRTY 1
3 made unfit for ceremonial purposes <altars overturned and sacred vessels made *impure* by the touch of profane hands>
syn common, defiled, desecrated, polluted, profaned, unclean
rel unhallowed, unholy
con clean, consecrated, undefiled
ant pure
4 *syn* see UNREFINED 3

impute *vb syn* see ASCRIBE
rel accuse, indict; adduce; hint, insinuate, intimate

in *adj syn* see STYLISH

in *n syn* see PULL 2

inability *n* lack of sufficient power, resources, or capacity to perform <suffered from an *inability* to make quick decisions>
syn inadequacy, incapability, incapacity, incompetence, ineffectiveness, ineffectualness, inefficacy
rel inadeptness, inaptitude, inaptness, inefficiency, ineptitude, ineptness
con adequacy, capability, capacity; competence, efficiency
ant ability

inaccessible *adj* not capable of being achieved <an *inaccessible* goal>
syn inapproachable, unapproachable, unattainable, un-come-at-able, ungetatable, unobtainable, unreachable
rel distant, far, faraway, far-off, out-of-the-way, remote
ant accessible

inaccurate *adj syn* see FALSE 1
con right, true
ant accurate

inaction *n* lack of action or activity <the delay was due to the committee's *inaction*>
syn inactiveness, inactivity

rel drift, idleness, indolence, inertness, lethargy, quiescence, slackness, slothfulness, torpidity
con activeness, activity

inactive *adj* not characterized by or engaged in usual or normal activity <forced by illness to lead an *inactive* life>
syn asleep, idle, inert, passive, quiet, sleepy
rel abeyant, dormant, inoperative, latent, quiescent; do-nothing, indolent, lethargic, lymphatic, slack, slothful, sluggish, torpid; motionless, sedentary, static; disengaged, jobless, unemployed, unoccupied, unworking; ossified
con busy, employed, engaged, occupied; energetic, strenuous, vigorous; animated, brisk, lively
ant active

inactiveness *n syn* see INACTION
inactivity *n syn* see INACTION
ant activity
in addition *adv syn* see AGAIN 4
inadept *adj syn* see UNSKILLFUL 1
ant adept
inadequacy *n* **1** *syn* see INABILITY
2 *syn* see FAILURE 3
ant adequacy
inadequate *adj* **1** *syn* see DEFICIENT 1
ant adequate
2 *syn* see SHORT 3
ant adequate
3 *syn* see MEAGER
ant adequate
4 *syn* see WEAK 4
ant adequate
inadmissible *adj* **1** *syn* see IMPROPER 1
2 *syn* see OBJECTIONABLE
ant admissible
in advance *adv syn* see BEFORE 1
in advance of *prep* **1** *syn* see BEFORE 1
2 *syn* see UNTIL
inadvertent *adj* **1** *syn* see CARELESS 1
ant advertent
2 *syn* see UNINTENTIONAL
inadvisable *adj* not likely to have a satisfactory outcome <it seemed *inadvisable* to go any farther because of threatening weather>
syn ill-advised, impolitic, imprudent, inexpedient, unadvisable, unexpedient
rel careless, inappropriate, incautious, rash, undesirable, unsensible; foolish, indiscreet, pointless, unwise; foolhardy, harebrained
con expedient, judicious, politic, prudent, sensible, wise
ant advisable
in all *adv syn* see ALTOGETHER 2
in all probability *adv syn* see PRESUMABLY
inalterable *adj syn* see INFLEXIBLE 3
ant alterable
inamorata *n* **1** *syn* see GIRL FRIEND 2
2 *syn* see MISTRESS
inamorato *n syn* see BOYFRIEND 2
in and out *adv syn* see THOROUGHLY 2
inane *adj syn* see INSIPID 3
rel asinine, fatuous, foolish, silly; idle, vain; blank, empty, hollow

con expressive, meaningful, pregnant, significant, weighty
ant deep, profound
inanimate *adj* **1** *syn* see INSENSATE 1
ant animate
2 *syn* see DEAD 1
ant animate; living
inanity *n syn* see FOOLISHNESS
inapplicable *adj syn* see IRRELEVANT
ant applicable
inapposite *adj syn* see IRRELEVANT
ant apposite
inappreciable *adj* **1** *syn* see IMPERCEPTIBLE
ant appreciable
2 *syn* see MEAGER
inapproachable *adj syn* see INACCESSIBLE
ant approachable
inappropriate *adj* **1** *syn* see UNFIT 1
rel indecorous, unseemly; inconsonant
con felicitous, fitting, happy, meet, proper; fit, suitable
ant appropriate
2 *syn* see IMPROPER 1
inapt *adj* **1** *syn* see UNFIT 1
rel awkward, clumsy, gauche, maladroit; banal, flat, insipid, jejune
con apposite, germane, pertinent, relevant
ant apt
2 *syn* see IMPROPER 1
ant apt
3 *syn* see UNSKILLFUL 1
ant adept
inarguable *adj syn* see POSITIVE 3
ant arguable
inarticulate *adj* **1** *syn* see DUMB 1
ant articulate
2 *syn* see TACIT 1
3 failing to give or incapable of giving clear or effective verbal expression to one's ideas or feelings <made some *inarticulate* explanation for being late> <was completely *inarticulate* when it came to expressing affection>
syn incoherent, maundering, tongue-tied, unvocal
rel faltering, halting, hesitating, mumbling, stammered, stammering; blurred, indistinct
con facile, glib, smooth
ant articulate
inartificial *adj syn* see NATURAL 5
ant artificial
inasmuch as *conj syn* see BECAUSE
inattentive *adj* not paying proper attention <an *inattentive* pupil dozing at his desk>
syn inobservant, unheeding, unnoticing, unobservant, unobserving, unperceiving, unwatchful
rel distracted, distrait, distraught; careless, heedless, thoughtless, undiscerning, unmindful, unthinking; bored, ennuyé
ant attentive; observant

---

syn synonym(s)   *rel* related word(s)
ant antonym(s)   *con* contrasted word(s)
idiom idiomatic equivalent(s)
‖ use limited; if in doubt, see a dictionary

inaugural *adj syn* see FIRST 1
inaugural *n syn* see INITIATION
inaugurate *vb* **1** *syn* see INITIATE 3
  2 *syn* see BEGIN 1
  3 *syn* see INTRODUCE 3
inauguration *n syn* see INITIATION
inauspicious *adj* **1** *syn* see OMINOUS
  ant auspicious
  2 *syn* see EVIL 6
in between *prep syn* see BETWEEN 2
inborn *adj* **1** *syn* see INNATE 1
  ant acquired
  2 *syn* see INHERENT
inbred *adj syn* see INHERENT
in brief *adv syn* see BRIEFLY
incalculable *adj* **1** being great beyond calculation
  <*incalculable* damage>
  syn immeasurable, inestimable, measureless, uncountable, unmeasurable, unmeasured, unreckonable
  rel countless, innumerable, unnumbered, untold; boundless, enormous, infinite, limitless, vast
  con minimal, slight, trivial
  ant infinitesimal
  2 *syn* see UNCERTAIN 1
  ant calculable
in camera *adv syn* see SECRETLY
incandescent *adj syn* see BRIGHT 1
incantation *n* **1** *syn* see SPELL
  2 *syn* see MAGIC 1
incapability *n syn* see INABILITY
  ant capability
incapable *adj* **1** *syn* see UNFIT 2
  ant capable
  2 *syn* see INEFFICIENT 2
  ant capable
incapacitate *vb* **1** *syn* see PARALYZE 1
  2 *syn* see DISQUALIFY
  ant capacitate
incapacity *n syn* see INABILITY
  ant capacity
incarcerate *vb syn* see IMPRISON
incarnadine *vb syn* see REDDEN 1
incarnate *vb syn* see EMBODY 1
incarnation *n syn* see EMBODIMENT
incautious *adj* **1** lacking in caution <made an *incautious* prediction>
  syn unalert, unguarded, unvigilant, unwary, unwatchful; *compare* CARELESS 1
  rel imprudent, indiscreet, injudicious; bold, brash, impetuous, rash, reckless; neglectful, negligent, regardless, thoughtless, unmindful; hasty
  idiom caught napping, off one's guard
  con careful, circumspect, judicious, wary, watchful; discreet, judicious, prudent; sensible, thoughtful, wise
  ant cautious
  2 *syn* see RASH 1
  ant cautious
  3 *syn* see IRRESPONSIBLE
incendiary *n* a person who deliberately and unlawfully sets fire to a building or other property <a fire set by an *incendiary*>

  syn arsonist, firebug, torch
  rel pyromaniac
incendiary *adj syn* see INFLAMMATORY
incense *n* **1** *syn* see FRAGRANCE
  2 *syn* see FLATTERY
incense *vb syn* see ANGER 1
  ant placate
incentive *n syn* see STIMULUS
inception *n syn* see SOURCE
  con closing, completion, conclusion
  ant termination
inceptive *adj syn* see INITIAL 1
  ant terminal
incertitude *n syn* see UNCERTAINTY
  ant certitude
incessant *adj syn* see CONTINUAL
  ant intermittent
inchoate *adj* **1** *syn* see FORMLESS
  2 *syn* see INCOHERENT 2
incident *n syn* see OCCURRENCE
incident *adj* **1** *syn* see CONCOMITANT
  ant essential, fundamental
  2 *syn* see RELATED
incidental *adj syn* see ACCIDENTAL
  ant essential
incidentally *adv* **1** by chance <in this discussion grave questions were brought up *incidentally*>
  syn accidentally, casually, fortuitously
  ant deliberately
  2 by way of interjection or digression <another leading industry, *incidentally*, has quadrupled its business in four years>
  syn by the bye, by the way, in passing, obiter, parenthetically
  idiom in the bygoing
incipient *adj syn* see INITIAL 1
incise *vb* **1** *syn* see CUT 1
  2 *syn* see ENGRAVE 1
incisive *adj* having, manifesting, or suggesting a keen alertness of mind <a man well known for his *incisive* wit>
  syn biting, clear-cut, crisp, cutting, ingoing, penetrating, trenchant
  rel acute, drilling, keen, sharp; acerb, acerbic, caustic, mordant, scathing, slashing, tart; concise, laconic, succinct, terse
  con diffuse, prolix, verbose, wordy; feeble, limp, pithless, sapless
  ant unincisive
incisiveness *n syn* see EDGE 2
incitation *n syn* see STIMULUS
incite *vb* to aid or promote the activity or development of <*incite* a riot>
  syn abet, foment, instigate, provoke, raise, set, set on, stir (up), whip (up)
  rel forward, further, promote, stimulate; set off, trigger; agitate, solicit; encourage, motivate, motive; excite, inflame, rouse
  con check, curb, discourage, inhibit, restrain; calm, quiet, subdue
incitement *n syn* see STIMULUS
  ant restraint; inhibition
inciter *n syn* see INSTIGATOR
incivil *adj syn* see RUDE 6

ant civil

inclement *adj syn* see SEVERE 3
ant clement

inclination *n* **1** *syn* see LEANING 2
ant disinclination
2 *syn* see WILL 1
ant disinclination
3 *syn* see APPETITE 3
ant disinclination
4 *syn* see SLOPE

incline *vb* **1** *syn* see TEND 1
2 *syn* see SLANT 1
rel deflect, turn
3 to have an attitude toward or to influence one to take an attitude <*inclined* to believe the story> <his argument *inclined* me to share his view>
syn bend, bias, dispose, predispose; *compare* PREJUDICE 2, TEND 1
rel affect, influence, prompt, sway; drive, impel, induce, move, persuade
ant disincline, indispose
4 *syn* see DIRECT 2

incline *n* *syn* see SLOPE

inclined *adj* **1** *syn* see WILLING 1
ant disinclined
2 *syn* see APT 1
ant disinclined
3 sloping from the horizontal or perpendicular <cars running on an *inclined* track>
syn declivate, declivitous, inclining, leaning, oblique, pitched, pitching, sloped, sloping, tilted, tilting, tipped; *compare* DIAGONAL
rel dipping, graded, raked

inclining *n* *syn* see LEANING 2

inclining *adj* *syn* see INCLINED 3

include *vb* to possess as an integral part of a whole <the park *includes* a zoo and a botanical garden>
syn comprehend, contain, embody, embrace, encompass, have, involve, subsume, take in
rel comprise, cover, encircle, enclose, hold; number; admit, receive
con leave out, omit; preclude, reject; debar; eliminate, rule out
ant exclude

inclusive *adj* **1** *syn* see ALL-AROUND 2
2 *syn* see ENCYCLOPEDIC

incogitable *adj* *syn* see INCREDIBLE 1
ant cogitable

incogitant *adj* *syn* see RASH 1

incognizable *adj* *syn* see INCOMPREHENSIBLE 1
ant cognizable

incognizant *adj* *syn* see IGNORANT 2
ant cognizant

incoherent *adj* **1** *syn* see LOOSE 3
2 lacking cohesion or continuity <an *incoherent* presentation>
syn disconnected, discontinuous, disjointed, disordered, inchoate, incohesive, muddled, unconnected, uncontinuous, unorganized
rel discordant, incompatible, incongruous, inconsistent, inconsonant, inharmonious
con ordered, orderly; connected; organized; planned, plotted

ant coherent
3 *syn* see INARTICULATE 3

incohesive *adj* *syn* see INCOHERENT 2
ant cohesive

incombustible *adj* *syn* see NONCOMBUSTIBLE
ant combustible

income *n* *syn* see REVENUE

incommode *vb* *syn* see INCONVENIENCE
rel block, hinder, impede, obstruct; annoy, bother, irk, vex
con favor, oblige; humor, indulge; gratify, please
ant accommodate

incommodious *adj* **1** *syn* see INCONVENIENT
ant commodious
2 *syn* see CRAMPED
ant commodious

incommunicable *adj* **1** *syn* see UNUTTERABLE
ant communicable
2 *syn* see RESERVED 1
ant communicable, communicative

incomparable *adj* *syn* see SUPREME
rel matchless
con common, commonplace, ordinary; indifferent, mediocre, medium, middling
ant average

incompatible *adj* *syn* see INCONSONANT 1
rel adverse, antagonistic, counter; antipathetic; antipodal, antipodean, antithetical, contradictory, contrary, opposite; irreconcilable, unadaptable, unconformable
ant compatible
2 *syn* see IRRECONCILABLE
ant compatible

incompetence *n* *syn* see INABILITY

incompetent *adj* **1** *syn* see UNFIT 2
ant competent
2 *syn* see INEFFICIENT 2
ant competent

incomplete *adj* **1** lacking a part or parts <an *incomplete* text of a speech>
syn fractional, fragmentary, part, partial
rel broken, deficient, incoherent, lacking, short, wanting; bitty, composite, scrappy
con intact, undamaged, whole
ant complete
2 *syn* see DEFICIENT 1
ant complete

incompliant *adj* **1** *syn* see OBSTINATE
ant compliant
2 *syn* see STIFF 1

incomprehensible *adj* **1** lying above or beyond the reach of the human mind <the *incomprehensible* universe>
syn impenetrable, incognizable, uncomprehensible, unfathomable, ungraspable, unintelligible, unknowable

---

syn synonym(s)	*rel* related word(s)
ant antonym(s)	*con* contrasted word(s)
idiom idiomatic equivalent(s)	
‖ use limited; if in doubt, see a dictionary	

rel inscrutable, mysterious, mystifying, unsearchable; cryptic, enigmatic, obscure, unclear; imperceptible, indistinguishable
con cognizable, fathomable, graspable, intelligible, knowable; clear, lucid, plain, simple, straightforward; rational, reasonable
ant comprehensible, understandable
2 *syn* see INCONCEIVABLE 1
ant comprehensible, graspable
inconceivable *adj* **1** impossible to comprehend in the absence of actual experience or knowledge <color is *inconceivable* to those born blind>
syn incomprehensible, unimaginable, unknowable, ununderstandable
idiom beyond one's grasp
con comprehensible, imaginable, knowable, understandable
ant conceivable
2 *syn* see INCREDIBLE 1
ant conceivable
3 *syn* see IMPLAUSIBLE
con believable, convincing, credible, plausible
ant conceivable
inconclusive *adj* leading to no conclusion or definite result <the report was *inconclusive*>
syn indecisive
rel open, uncertain, undecided, unsettled; incomplete, unfinished
con clarifying, illuminating; decisive
ant conclusive
incondite *adj* *syn* see RUDE 6
inconformable *adj* *syn* see IRRECONCILABLE
ant conformable
incongruent *adj* *syn* see INCONSONANT 1
ant congruent, congruous
incongruous *adj* *syn* see INCONSONANT 1
rel alien, extraneous, foreign; bizarre, fantastic, grotesque
idiom out of place
con appropriate, fit, fitting, meet, seemly, suitable
ant congruent, congruous
inconnu *n* *syn* see STRANGER
inconquerable *adj* **1** *syn* see INVINCIBLE 1
2 *syn* see INSUPERABLE
inconscient *adj* *syn* see ABSTRACTED
ant conscient, conscious
inconscious *adj* *syn* see INSENSIBLE 2
ant conscious
inconsequent *adj* *syn* see PETTY 2
inconsequential *adj* *syn* see PETTY 2
ant consequential
inconsiderable *adj* **1** *syn* see LITTLE 3
ant considerable
2 *syn* see MEAGER
ant considerable
3 *syn* see PETTY 2
ant considerable
inconsiderate *adj* **1** *syn* see RASH 1
ant considerate
2 *syn* see SHORT 5
ant considerate
inconsistent *adj* **1** *syn* see INCONSTANT 1
ant consistent

2 *syn* see INCONSONANT 1
ant consistent
3 *syn* see IRRECONCILABLE
ant consistent
inconsolable *adj* incapable of being consoled <she was *inconsolable* over the loss of her child>
syn desolate, disconsolate, unconsolable
rel comfortless, dejected, forlorn, heartsick
ant consolable
inconsonant *adj* **1** not in agreement with one another or not agreeable one to the other <his actions are *inconsonant* with his words>
syn conflicting, disconsonant, discordant, discrepant, dissonant, incompatible, incongruent, incongruous, inconsistent, unmixable
rel ill-matched, ill-suited, mismated, uncongenial; inappropriate, unsuitable
con accordant, compatible, congenial, congruous, consistent
ant consonant
2 *syn* see INHARMONIOUS 2
ant consonant
inconspicuous *adj* not readily noticeable <occupied an *inconspicuous* position>
syn obscure, unconspicuous, unemphatic, unnoticeable
rel indistinct, insignificant, unnoticeable, unobtrusive, vague
con eye-catching, showy, striking; distinct, noticeable
ant conspicuous, prominent
inconstant *adj* **1** lacking firmness or steadiness (as in purpose or devotion) <depended too much on an *inconstant* friend>
syn capricious, changeable, fickle, inconsistent, lubricious, mercurial, temperamental, ticklish, uncertain, unstable, variable, volatile; *compare* CHANGEABLE 1, MUTABLE 2, UNCERTAIN 1
rel changeful, mutable, protean, unsettled, unsteady; elusive, erratic, vacillating, vagrant, wavering, wayward; irresolute, shifty, shilly-shally; undependable, unreliable; disloyal, faithless, false, perfidious, traitorous, treacherous, untrue; frivolous, light, light-minded
con dependable, reliable, trustworthy, trusty; faithful, loyal, resolute, staunch, steadfast, true
ant constant
2 *syn* see MUTABLE 2
ant constant
incontestable *adj* *syn* see POSITIVE 3
ant contestable
incontinent *adj* *syn* see LICENTIOUS 2
ant continent
incontinently *adv* *syn* see PELL-MELL
incontrovertible *adj* *syn* see POSITIVE 3
ant controvertible
inconvenience *n* the quality or state of being inconvenient <hated the *inconvenience* of not having a telephone>
syn bother, bothersomeness, ‖disconvenience, troublesomeness
rel aggravation, annoyance, exasperation, trial; fuss, pother, stew
ant convenience

inconvenience *vb* to subject to disturbance or discomfort <was not seriously *inconvenienced* by the bad weather>
  syn discommode, ‖disconvenience, disoblige, incommode, put about, put out, trouble
  rel discompose, disturb; interfere, intermeddle, meddle; aggravate, exasperate, try
  idiom put to trouble
  ant convenience
inconvenient *adj* not conducive to physical, mental, or social ease and comfort <he came at an *inconvenient* time>
  syn awkward, discommoding, discommodious, embarrassing, incommodious
  rel bothersome, pestiferous, troublesome; inexpedient; detrimental, disadvantageous, prejudicial
  con appropriate, becoming, fitting, suitable; acceptable, bearable, tolerable; advantageous, desirable, helpful
  ant convenient
inconversable *adj syn* see SILENT 3
  ant conversable
inconversant *adj syn* see IGNORANT 2
  ant conversant
incorporate *vb* **1** *syn* see ABSORB 1
  2 *syn* see EMBODY 2
incorporeal *adj syn* see IMMATERIAL 1
  ant corporeal
incorrect *adj syn* see FALSE 1
  ant correct
incorrectly *adv syn* see AMISS 1
  ant correctly
incorrectness *n syn* see IMPROPRIETY 1
  ant correctitude, correctness
incorruptible *adj syn* see INDESTRUCTIBLE
  ant corruptible
incorruption *n syn* see HONESTY
  ant corruption
increase *vb* **1** to make greater or more numerous <*increase* crops by good cultural practices>
  syn aggrandize, augment, beef (up), boost, build, compound, enlarge, expand, extend, heighten, magnify, manifold, multiply, plus, push
  rel aggravate, enhance, intensify; amplify, dilate, distend, inflate, swell; elongate, lengthen, prolong, protract; reinforce, strengthen
  con abate, abbreviate, condense, contract; depreciate, diminish, lessen, lower, reduce; curtail, shorten, shrink; minimize
  ant decrease
  2 to become greater or more numerous <his wealth *increased* over the years>
  syn augment, build, burgeon, enlarge, expand, heighten, mount, multiply, rise, run up, snowball, upsurge, wax
  rel dilate, distend, inflate, intensify, lengthen, strengthen, swell; pullulate, swarm, teem
  con abate, condense, contract, diminish, lessen, lower, reduce, shorten, shrink; die off, die (out), end, terminate
  ant decrease
  3 *syn* see RAISE 9

increase *n* **1** *syn* see ADDITION
  ant decrease
  2 *syn* see RISE 3
increate *adj syn* see SELF-EXISTENT
  ant created
incredible *adj* **1** too extraordinary or improbable to admit of belief <an *incredible* story of privations overcome>
  syn incogitable, inconceivable, insupposable, unbelievable, unimaginable, unthinkable
  rel absurd, outlandish, preposterous, ridiculous; impossible, untenable
  idiom beyond belief, out of the question
  con acceptable, believable, conceivable, likely, plausible, reasonable
  ant credible
  2 *syn* see IMPLAUSIBLE
  ant credible
incredulity *n syn* see UNBELIEF
  con gullibility, naiveté
  ant credulity, credulousness
incredulous *adj* unwilling to admit or accept what is offered as true <his explanation met an *incredulous* response from his listeners>
  syn aporetic, disbelieving, questioning, quizzical, show-me, skeptical, unbelieving
  rel hesitant, suspicious, uncertain, wary; distrustful, distrusting, mistrustful; doubting, dubious, unconvinced, unsatisfied
  con trustful, trusting; unsuspecting, unsuspicious, unwary; gullible, naive
  ant credulous
increment *n syn* see ADDITION
incriminate *vb syn* see ACCUSE
  rel implicate, involve
  ant exonerate
incrustate *vb syn* see CAKE 1
inculcate *vb syn* see IMPLANT
  rel educate, instruct, teach; communicate, impart
inculpable *adj* **1** *syn* see GOOD
  ant culpable
  2 *syn* see INNOCENT 2
  ant culpable
inculpate *vb syn* see ACCUSE
  ant exculpate
incult *adj syn* see COARSE 3
incur *vb* to bring (something usually unpleasant) upon oneself <he foolishly *incurred* debts beyond his ability to pay>
  syn contract
  rel acquire, get; bring on, induce
  idiom bring down on (*or* upon)
  con avoid, elude, escape, eschew, evade, shun; discharge, pay, settle
incurable *adj syn* see HOPELESS 2
  ant curable
incurious *adj syn* see INDIFFERENT 2

---

syn synonym(s)   *rel* related word(s)
ant antonym(s)   *con* contrasted word(s)
idiom idiomatic equivalent(s)
‖ use limited; if in doubt, see a dictionary

rel absent, absentminded, abstracted, distraught, preoccupied

con nosy, prying, snoopy; impertinent, intrusive, meddlesome; observant, observing

ant curious, inquisitive

incursion *n syn* see INVASION

indebted *adj* owing gratitude or recognition (as for a favor or service rendered) <was *indebted* to the book for most of her information>

syn beholden, obligated, obliged

rel duty-bound, honor-bound

indebtedness *n* **1** a state of owing something <unable to escape from *indebtedness*>

syn arrearage, debt, liability, obligation; *compare* DEBT 3

rel delinquency, nonpayment; bankruptcy, failure, insolvency

con discharge, liquidation, satisfaction; exoneration, freeing, release

2 *syn* see DEBT 3

indecent *adj* **1** *syn* see INDECOROUS

ant decent

2 *syn* see OBSCENE 2

ant decent

indecipherable *adj syn* see ILLEGIBLE

ant decipherable

indecision *n syn* see HESITATION

ant decision, decisiveness

indecisive *adj* **1** *syn* see INCONCLUSIVE

ant decisive

2 *syn* see DOUBTFUL 1

con certain, incontrovertible, undebatable, unequivocal

ant decisive

3 *syn* see VACILLATING 2

rel undecided, unsettled

idiom of two minds

con decided, determined, firm, positive, resolved, settled, unfaltering, unhesitant, unhesitating, unwavering

ant decisive

indecisiveness *n syn* see HESITATION

ant indecision, indecisiveness

indecorous *adj* not conforming with accepted standards of propriety or good taste <they regarded argument in public as *indecorous*>

syn improper, indecent, indelicate, malodorous, ridiculous, rough, unbecoming, undecorous, ungodly, unseemly, untoward

rel inappropriate, incorrect, unbefitting, unfit, unfitting; immodest, inelegant, undignified; coarse, gross, loose, offensive, shameful, tasteless, vulgar; discourteous, ill-mannered, impolite, rude, uncivil; irregular, unlawful

idiom in bad form

con becoming, courteous, decent, nice, proper, seemly; conventional, formal

ant decorous

indecorousness *n syn* see IMPROPRIETY 1

ant decorousness

indecorum *n* **1** *syn* see FAUX PAS

2 *syn* see IMPROPRIETY 1

ant decorum

indeed *adv* **1** *syn* see WELL 7

2 *syn* see EVEN 3

indefatigable *adj* capable of prolonged and arduous effort <a teacher who has *indefatigable* patience with slow learners>

syn inexhaustible, tireless, unflagging, untiring, unweariable, unwearying, weariless

rel assiduous, diligent, painstaking, sedulous; determined, dogged, patient, persevering, persistent, pertinacious, relentless, steadfast, stubborn, tenacious, unfaltering, unflinching, unrelenting, unwavering; energetic, strenuous, vigorous

con dawdling, dilatory, laggard, lagging, procrastinating; fainéant, indolent, lackadaisical, lazy, slothful, sluggish

ant fatigable

indefectible *adj* **1** *syn* see PERFECT 2

2 *syn* see IDEAL 3

indefensible *adj syn* see INEXCUSABLE

ant defensible

indefinable *adj syn* see UNUTTERABLE

ant definable

indefinite *adj* **1** having no exact limits <a region with *indefinite* boundaries>

syn indeterminate, indistinct, inexact, undeterminable

rel unclear, undefined, unfixed, unspecific; broad, loose, wide; general, obscure, vague

con exact, measured; known

ant definite

2 *syn* see LIMITLESS

ant definite

indelible *adj* that cannot be removed or erased <made an *indelible* impression on his hearers>

syn ineffaceable, ineradicable, inerasable, inexpungible, inextirpable, uneradicable, unerasable

rel indestructible, undestroyable; enduring, permanent

con effaceable, eradicable, erasable, removable; ephemeral, evanescent, passing, temporary, transitory

ant delible

indelicate *adj syn* see INDECOROUS

rel callow, crude, rude, uncouth; lewd, wanton

con chaste, modest, pure

ant delicate

indemnification *n syn* see REPARATION

indemnify *vb syn* see COMPENSATE 3

indemnity *n syn* see REPARATION

indentation *n* **1** *syn* see NOTCH 1

2 *syn* see IMPRESSION 1

indenture *n syn* see NOTCH 1

indentured *adj syn* see BOUND 2

independent *adj* **1** *syn* see FREE 1

2 *syn* see SELF-SUFFICIENT

ant dependent

independently *adv syn* see APART 1

idiom on one's own

indescribable *adj syn* see UNUTTERABLE

ant describable

indestructible *adj* incapable of being destroyed <*indestructible* idealism>

syn imperishable, incorruptible, inexterminable, inextinguishable, inextirpable, irrefragable, irrefrangible, quenchless, undestroyable, unperishable

rel changeless, immutable, unalterable, unchangeable; deathless, immortal, perpetual, undying; durable, enduring, lasting, permanent; indelible, ineradicable; unextinguishable, unquenchable

con alterable, changeable, corruptible, impermanent, temporary, transient, unlasting; mortal, temporal; evanescent

ant destroyable, destructible, perishable

indeterminate *adj syn* see INDEFINITE 1
ant determinate

index *n syn* see INDICATION 3

Indian sign *n syn* see JINX

indicate *vb* **1** *syn* see POINT 2
2 to give evidence of or serve as ground for a valid or reasonable inference <several polls *indicate* a landslide for the incumbent>
syn announce, argue, attest, bespeak, betoken, testify, witness
rel denote, import, mean, signify; demonstrate, prove; evidence, evince, manifest, show; display, exhibit, express, illustrate; connote, hint, imply, suggest
3 *syn* see SHOW 5

indication *n* **1** *syn* see HINT 1
2 *syn* see EXPRESSION 3
3 something that is an outward manifestation of something else <such *indications* of prosperity as second cars and color TVs>
syn evidence, index, indicia, mark, sign, significant, symptom, token; *compare* SYMBOL 1, TESTIMONY
rel expression, manifestation; hint, suggestion; proof; prefiguration, type

indicative *adj* serving to indicate <the roar of the crowd was *indicative* of its approval>
syn denotative, denotive, designative, exhibitive, indicatory, indicial, significative
rel characteristic, demonstrative, evidential, evincive, expressive, suggestive, symbolic, symptomatic, testatory

indicatory *adj syn* see INDICATIVE

indicia *n pl syn* see INDICATION 3

indicial *adj syn* see INDICATIVE

indict *vb syn* see ACCUSE

indifference *n syn* see APATHY 2

indifferent *adj* **1** *syn* see FAIR 4
2 marked by a lack of interest or concern <was *indifferent* to suffering and poverty>
syn aloof, by-the-way, casual, detached, disinterested, incurious, numb, pococurante, remote, unconcerned, uncurious, uninterested, withdrawn; *compare* UNSOCIABLE
rel apathetic, impassive, insensible; dispassionate; careless, heedless, negligent, regardless, uncaring, unmindful; inattentive, unobserving
con attentive, considerate, heedful, interested, mindful, regardful, sympathetic
ant concerned
3 *syn* see COLD 2
4 *syn* see MEDIUM

indigence *n syn* see POVERTY 1

ant affluence, opulence

indigency *n syn* see POVERTY 1
ant affluence, opulence

indigenous *adj* **1** *syn* see NATIVE 2
con alien, extraneous, foreign
ant exotic; naturalized
2 *syn* see INNATE 1

indigent *adj syn* see POOR 1
ant affluent, opulent

indignant *adj syn* see ANGRY
ant gratified

indignation *n syn* see ANGER
ant gratification

indignity *n syn* see AFFRONT
rel grievance, injury, injustice, wrong

indirect *adj* **1** deviating from a direct line or straightforward course <made *indirect* inquiries about the new neighbor>
syn circuitous, circular, collateral, oblique, roundabout
rel circumlocutory, crooked, devious; meandering, serpentine, sinuous, tortuous, twisting, winding; errant, vagrant, wandering
ant direct; forthright, straightforward
2 *syn* see UNDERHAND
ant straight

indirection *n syn* see DECEPTION 1

indiscernible *adj syn* see IMPERCEPTIBLE
ant discernible, distinguishable

indiscreet *adj syn* see UNWISE
ant discreet

indiscriminate *adj* **1** including all or nearly all within the range of choice, operation, or effectiveness <her charity was *indiscriminate* but generous>
syn indiscriminating, indiscriminative, sweeping, undiscriminated, undiscriminating, undistinguishing, wholesale
rel assorted, heterogeneous, miscellaneous, promiscuous; shallow, superficial, uncritical; broad, extensive, wide
con discretionary, discriminative; choosy, picky; critical, perfectionist
ant selective; discriminate, discriminated
2 *syn* see RANDOM
3 *syn* see MISCELLANEOUS

indiscriminating *adj syn* see INDISCRIMINATE 1
ant discriminating

indiscriminative *adj syn* see INDISCRIMINATE 1
ant discriminative

indispensable *adj syn* see ESSENTIAL 4
rel cardinal, fundamental
ant dispensable

indisposed *adj* **1** *syn* see UNWELL
2 *syn* see DISINCLINED
rel antagonistic, antipathetic, hostile, inimical
con amicable, neighborly; responsive, sympathetic
ant disposed

---

syn synonym(s)   *rel* related word(s)
ant antonym(s)   *con* contrasted word(s)
idiom idiomatic equivalent(s)
‖ use limited; if in doubt, see a dictionary

indisposition n 1 syn see DISLIKE
2 syn see SICKNESS 1
indisputable adj 1 syn see POSITIVE 3
ant disputable
2 syn see REAL 3
indistinct adj 1 syn see INDEFINITE 1
ant distinct
2 syn see FAINT 2
ant distinct
indistinguishable adj syn see SAME 2
ant distinguishable
indite vb syn see WRITE
individual adj 1 syn see PERSONAL 1
ant common, popular
2 syn see SPECIAL 1
rel separate, single, sole
con generic, universal
ant general
3 syn see CHARACTERISTIC
ant common
4 syn see SEVERAL 1
individual n 1 syn see ENTITY 1
2 syn see THING 5
3 syn see HUMAN
individualism n 1 syn see DISPOSITION 3
2 syn see INDIVIDUALITY 3
individualist adj syn see EGOCENTRIC 1
individualistic adj syn see EGOCENTRIC 1
individuality n 1 syn see DISPOSITION 3
2 syn see UNITY 1
3 distinctive character <a person of marked *individuality*>
syn distinctiveness, individualism, particularity, singularity
rel character, personality
4 individual identity <a teacher who respects children's *individualities*>
syn identity, ipseity, personality, seity, selfdom, selfhood, selfness, singularity
rel independence, separateness, uniqueness; difference, dissimilarity, unlikeness
con likeness, resemblance, similarity
individualize vb syn see CHARACTERIZE 2
individually adv syn see APART 1
individuate vb syn see CHARACTERIZE 2
indocile adj syn see UNRULY 1
ant docile
indolence n syn see SLOTH 1
ant industry
indolent adj syn see LAZY
con active, diligent, energetic, vigorous
ant industrious
indomitable adj 1 syn see INVINCIBLE 1
ant domitable
2 syn see INSUPERABLE
rel dogged, pertinacious, stubborn; resolute, staunch, steadfast
ant domitable
3 syn see UNRULY 1
indoors adv in or into a building <stayed *indoors* during the storm>
syn inside, within, withindoors, withinside
con outdoors, outside, without, withoutdoors
ant outdoors

indubitable adj 1 syn see POSITIVE 3
ant dubitable, questionable
2 syn see AUTHENTIC 2
ant doubtful, dubious
3 syn see DOWNRIGHT 2
induce vb 1 to move another to do or agree to something <*induced* him to give up smoking for the sake of his health>
syn argue (into), bring around, convince, draw, draw in, draw on, get, oversway, persuade, prevail (on or upon), procure, prompt, talk (into), win (over)
rel influence, sway; abet, incite, lead; actuate, impel, move; activate, motivate
con check, curb, hold back, restrain
2 syn see GENERATE 3
inducible adj syn see INDUCTIVE
induct vb syn see INITIATE 3
induction n syn see INITIATION
inductive adj 1 derived or derivable by reasoning from a part to a whole, from particulars to generals, or from the individual to the universal <used an *inductive* approach to the problem>
syn a posteriori, inducible
rel Baconian, epagogic
2 syn see PRELIMINARY
indulge vb 1 to give free rein to (as curiosity or a desire) <*indulged* their taste for gourmet foods>
syn cater (to), gratify, humor
rel favor, oblige, satisfy; delight, please, regale
idiom give rein to
con bridle, check, constrain, curb, restrain
2 syn see BABY
3 syn see WALLOW 3
indulgence n 1 syn see FORBEARANCE 2
rel benignancy, benignity, benignness, kindliness, kindness; gentleness, mildness
con rigor, severity, sternness; rigidity, rigorousness; harshness
ant strictness
2 syn see FAVOR 4
indulgent adj syn see FORBEARING
rel cosseting, pampering, permissive; condoning, excusing, forgiving, pardoning; benign, benignant, kind, kindly
con severe, stern; harsh, rigorous, stringent
ant strict
indurate vb syn see HARDEN 1
industrious adj syn see ASSIDUOUS
rel active, busy, live, dynamic; persevering, persistent
con idle, inactive; lethargic, sluggish
ant indolent, slothful; unindustrious
industry n syn see BUSINESS 4
indwell vb syn see BELONG 3
indweller n syn see INHABITANT
indwelling adj syn see INHERENT
inebriant n syn see LIQUOR 2
inebriate n syn see DRUNKARD
inebriated adj syn see INTOXICATED 1
inebrious adj syn see INTOXICATED 1
inedible adj not fit for food <an *inedible* plant>
syn inesculent, uneatable
rel indigestible, unwholesome; insipid, unappetizing; baneful, noxious, poisonous

con eatable, esculent; digestible, wholesome; appetizing, savory, tasty; harmless, innocuous, innoxious, nonpoisonous
ant edible

ineffable *adj syn* see UNUTTERABLE
rel celestial, empyreal, empyrean, heavenly; ethereal; divine, holy, sacred, spiritual; abstract, ideal, transcendent, transcendental
con expressible; utterable

ineffaceable *adj syn* see INDELIBLE

ineffective *adj* **1** *syn* see FUTILE
ant effective
2 *syn* see WEAK 4
3 not producing or not capable of producing a required result <*ineffective* remedies>
syn ineffectual, inefficacious, inefficient
rel inadequate, incompetent, inferior; useless, worthless
con active, effectual, efficacious; esteemed, valuable
ant effective

ineffectiveness *n syn* see INABILITY
ant effectiveness

ineffectual *adj* **1** *syn* see FUTILE
ant effectual
2 *syn* see INEFFECTIVE 3
ant effectual
3 *syn* see WEAK 4
4 *syn* see LITTLE 2

ineffectualness *n syn* see INABILITY
ant effectualness

inefficacious *adj syn* see INEFFECTIVE 3
ant efficacious

inefficacy *n syn* see INABILITY
ant efficacy

inefficient *adj* **1** *syn* see INEFFECTIVE 3
ant efficient
2 incapable of the proper performance of duties <*inefficient* workmen>
syn incapable, incompetent, inept, inexpert, unexpert, unskilled, unskillful, unworkmanlike
rel careless, slipshod, slovenly; unfitted, unprepared, unqualified, untrained; unskilled, unskillful
con able, adept, capable, competent, expert, proficient, qualified, skilled, skillful, workmanlike
ant efficient

inelaborate *adj syn* see PLAIN 1
ant elaborate

inelastic *adj syn* see STIFF 1
ant elastic

inelegance *n syn* see IMPROPRIETY 1
ant elegance

inelegant *adj syn* see COARSE 3

ineligible *adj syn* see UNFIT 2
ant eligible

ineluctable *adj syn* see INEVITABLE
con doubtful, dubious, questionable; likely, possible, probable

ineludible *adj syn* see INEVITABLE

inenarrable *adj syn* see UNUTTERABLE

inept *adj* **1** *syn* see IMPROPER 1
ant apt

2 *syn* see INFELICITOUS
ant apropos, apt
3 *syn* see AWKWARD 2
ant apt; adept
4 *syn* see UNSKILLFUL 1
ant able
5 *syn* see INEFFICIENT 2
ant competent, efficient

inequable *adj syn* see INEQUITABLE
ant equable

inequality *n* **1** the quality of being uneven <hampered by the *inequality* of the ground>
syn asperity, irregularity, roughness, unevenness
rel cragginess, jaggedness, ruggedness, rugosity
con equality, evenness, levelness, smoothness
2 *syn* see DISPARITY
ant equality

inequitable *adj* not fair or just <an *inequitable* tax burden>
syn inequable, unequitable, unfair, unjust, unrighteous
rel undeserved, undue, unmerited; bad, wrong, wrongful; arbitrary, high-handed, oppressive
con fair, just
ant equitable

inequitableness *n syn* see INJUSTICE 1
ant equitableness

inequity *n syn* see INJUSTICE 1
ant equity

ineradicable *adj syn* see INDELIBLE
ant eradicable

inerasable *adj syn* see INDELIBLE
ant erasable

inerrable *adj syn* see INFALLIBLE 1
ant errable

inerrant *adj syn* see INFALLIBLE 1
rel accurate, correct, exact, precise; dependable, reliable, trustworthy
ant errant

inert *adj syn* see INACTIVE
rel impotent, powerless; apathetic, impassive, phlegmatic, stolid; dead, inanimate, lifeless
con animated, awake; alert, vigilant, watchful; live, operative
ant animated; dynamic

inerudite *adj syn* see UNSCHOLARLY
ant erudite, learned

inescapable *adj syn* see INEVITABLE
ant escapable

inescapably *adv syn* see WILLY-NILLY

inesculent *adj syn* see INEDIBLE
ant esculent

in essence *adv* **1** *syn* see ESSENTIALLY 1
2 *syn* see VIRTUALLY

inessential *adj syn* see UNNECESSARY
ant crucial, essential

inestimable *adj* **1** *syn* see INCALCULABLE 1
2 *syn* see PRECIOUS 1

---

syn synonym(s)　　**rel** related word(s)
ant antonym(s)　　**con** contrasted word(s)
idiom idiomatic equivalent(s)
‖ use limited; if in doubt, see a dictionary

inevasible *adj syn* see INEVITABLE

inevitable *adj* incapable of being avoided or escaped <the effect of the scandal on the election was *inevitable*>
syn certain, ineluctable, ineludible, inescapable, inevasible, necessary, returnless, unavoidable, unescapable, unevadable
rel ineliminable, sure, unpreventable; decided, settled; destined, foreordained; inexorable, inflexible
idiom as sure to follow as night follows day, in the cards
con eludible, escapable, evadable
ant avoidable, evitable

inevitably *adv syn* see WILLY-NILLY

inexact *adj syn* see INDEFINITE 1
ant exact

inexcusable *adj* being without excuse or justification <an *inexcusable* blunder>
syn indefensible, inexpiable, unforgivable, unjustifiable, unpardonable, untenable
rel blamable, blameworthy, censurable, criticizable; impermissible, unallowable, unpermissible; intolerable, reprehensible
con allowable, blameless, defensible, forgivable, justifiable, pardonable, venial
ant excusable

inexhaustible *adj syn* see INDEFATIGABLE

inexorable *adj syn* see INFLEXIBLE 2
rel resolute; immobile, immovable
con compassionate, responsive, sympathetic, tender; clement, forbearing, indulgent, lenient

inexpedient *adj syn* see INADVISABLE
ant expedient

inexpensive *adj syn* see CHEAP 1
ant expensive

inexperience *n* lack or serious deficiency of practical wisdom <his failure was due to his *inexperience*>
syn callowness, freshness, greenness, rawness
rel ignorance, naiveté; amateurishness; unfamiliarity; unsophistication, verdancy
con grasp, understanding; polish, sophistication; skill, training
ant experience

inexperienced *adj* lacking knowledge, skill, or practice based on direct observation and participation <hired *inexperienced* help>
syn callow, fresh, green, inexpert, raw, rude, unconversant, unexperienced, unfleshed, unpracticed, unseasoned, untried, unversed, young
rel ignorant, immature, inept, naive; prentice, unacquainted, unfamiliar, unskilled, untrained
con expert, old, practiced, seasoned, skilled, versed, veteran
ant experienced

inexpert *adj* 1 *syn* see INEXPERIENCED
ant expert
2 *syn* see UNSKILLFUL 1
ant expert
3 *syn* see INEFFICIENT 2
ant expert
4 *syn* see CRUDE 5

inexpiable *adj syn* see INEXCUSABLE

ant expiable

inexplainable *adj syn* see INEXPLICABLE
ant explainable, explicable

inexplicable *adj* not capable of being explained or accounted for <an *inexplicable* discrepancy in the accounts>
syn inexplainable, unaccountable, unexplainable; *compare* MYSTERIOUS
rel indecipherable, indescribable, inscrutable, undefinable, unfathomable, unsolvable; mysterious, odd, peculiar, strange
con clear, obvious, plain; comprehensible, graspable, intelligible
ant explainable, explicable

inexpressible *adj syn* see UNUTTERABLE
ant expressible

inexpressive *adj syn* see EXPRESSIONLESS
ant expressive

inexpugnable *adj syn* see INVINCIBLE 1
rel irresistible, unopposable
con assailable, attackable
ant expugnable

inexpungible *adj syn* see INDELIBLE

inexterminable *adj syn* see INDESTRUCTIBLE

inextinguishable *adj syn* see INDESTRUCTIBLE
ant extinguishable

inextirpable *adj* 1 *syn* see INDESTRUCTIBLE
2 *syn* see INDELIBLE

inextricable *adj syn* see INSOLUBLE
ant extricable

infallible *adj* 1 incapable of being in error <an *infallible* ear for pitch in music>
syn inerrable, inerrant, sure, unerring
rel faultless, flawless, impeccable, undeceivable; correct, exact, perfect
con deceivable, faulty, unsure; doubtful, dubious, questionable
ant fallible
2 not liable to mislead, deceive, or disappoint <an *infallible* remedy>
syn certain, sure, surefire, unfailing
rel effective, efficacious, efficient; handy, helpful, useful; acceptable, agreeable, satisfying; satisfactory
con doubtful, questionable, uncertain, unsure; useless, worthless; unacceptable, unsatisfying; unsatisfactory
ant fallible

infamous *adj* 1 having an extremely and deservedly bad reputation <one of the most *infamous* of the dictator's henchmen>
syn ill-famed, notorious, opprobrious
rel abominable, atrocious, evil, hateful, heinous, iniquitous, odious, scandalous, vile, villainous; contemptible, despicable, scurvy, sorry
con distinguished, eminent, esteemed, honored, illustrious, notable, prestigious, reputable
2 *syn* see VICIOUS 2
rel disgraceful, disreputable, ignominious, shameful
con glorious, splendid, sublime
ant illustrious

infamy *n syn* see DISGRACE
rel notoriety, notoriousness

infancy *n* **1** early childhood <the helplessness of *infancy*>
  syn babyhood, infanthood
  rel childhood, immaturity, juvenility, nonage
  con adulthood, maturity, old age, senescence
2 the state or period of being under the age established by law for the attainment of full civil rights <his heirs were still in *infancy*>
  syn minority, nonage
  rel immaturity, juniority, juvenility
  con adulthood, adultness, maturity, seniority
  ant majority

infant *n syn* see BABY 1

infant *adj syn* see YOUNG 1

infanthood *n syn* see INFANCY 1

infantile *adj syn* see CHILDISH
  ant adult

infantine *adj syn* see CHILDISH
  ant adult

infatuate *adj syn* see INFATUATED

infatuated *adj* possessed with or marked by a strong attachment or foolish or unreasoning love or desire <*infatuated* with a woman he can't have>
  syn besotted, dotty, enamored, infatuate
  rel bewitched, captivated, enraptured, obsessed; foolish, silly
  con detached, dispassionate, objective, undazzled, unprepossessed

infatuation *n* a strong and unreasoning but transitory attachment <went through a series of *infatuations* before she settled down>
  syn béguin, crush, ‖pash, passion
  rel ardor, craze, devotion, fascination, obsession, rage

in favor of *prep syn* see FOR 1

infeasible *adj syn* see IMPOSSIBLE 1
  ant feasible

infectious *adj* **1** capable of causing infection <viruses and other *infectious* agents>
  syn infective
  rel mephitic, miasmic, noxious, pestilent, pestilential, poisonous, toxic, virulent
  con healthful, hygienic, salutary, wholesome
2 transmissible by infection <*infectious* diseases>
  syn catching, communicable, contagious
3 easily communicated or diffused <her enthusiasm was *infectious*>
  syn catching, contagious, taking
  rel irresistible, sympathetic

infective *adj syn* see INFECTIOUS 1

infecund *adj syn* see STERILE 1
  ant fecund

infelicitous *adj* marked by a lack of appropriateness and grace of expression <made a very *infelicitous* remark>
  syn awkward, graceless, ill-chosen, inept, unfortunate, unhappy
  rel inappropriate, inapropos, inapt, malapropos, unapt; deplorable, gauche, regrettable
  con fortunate, graceful, happy
  ant felicitous

infer *vb* to arrive at by reasoning from evidence or from premises <we *inferred* from his questions that he was a stranger in the vicinity>
  syn collect, conclude, deduce, deduct, derive, ‖dope out, draw, gather, judge, make, make out; *compare* CONJECTURE
  rel induce; conjecture, glean, guess, reckon, speculate, surmise, think; ascertain, construe, interpret, reason, understand
  idiom come to (*or* draw *or* reach) a conclusion; read between the lines

inference *n* **1** the deriving of a conclusion by reasoning <the answer was obtainable by *inference*>
  syn deduction, illation, judgment, ratiocination
  rel conjecture, guessing, reckoning, supposition, surmise
2 a determination arrived at by reasoning <a wrong *inference* based on incomplete evidence>
  syn conclusion, deduction, illation, judgment, ratiocination, sequitur
  rel assumption, conjecture, guess, presumption, reckoning, supposition, surmise

inferior *adj* **1** being or regarded as being below the level of another thing <the *inferior* latitudes of the northern hemisphere>
  syn lesser, low, lower, nether, subjacent, under
  rel junior, minor, secondary, subaltern, subordinate
  con greater, higher, over, overlying
  ant superior
2 of little or less importance, value, or merit <sold *inferior* goods at high prices>
  syn common, déclassé, hack, low-grade, mean, poor, second-class, second-drawer, second-rate; *compare* CHEAP 2
  rel average, fair, indifferent, mediocre, middling, ordinary; bad, base, paltry, punk, shoddy, sleazy, sorry, tawdry, tin-pot, wretched; good-for-nothing, lousy, ‖no-account, no-good, unworthy, valueless, worthless
  con choice, excellent, first-class, first-rate, high-grade, prime
  ant superior

inferior *n* one lower than another (as in station or worth) <a man inclined to be disdainful of his social *inferiors*>
  syn poor relation, scrub, secondary, subaltern, subordinate, underling, understrapper
  rel attendant, auxiliary, deputy; retainer, satrap, subject, vassal; hanger-on, heeler, henchman, hireling, minion, satellite, sycophant; adherent, disciple, follower
  con chief, head, leader, master, principal
  ant superior

infernal *adj* **1** of or relating to a nether world of the dead <the *infernal* regions>
  syn chthonian, chthonic, Hadean, plutonian, plutonic, sulphurous, Tartarean

---

syn synonym(s)   *rel* related word(s)
ant antonym(s)   *con* contrasted word(s)
idiom idiomatic equivalent(s)
‖ use limited; if in doubt, see a dictionary

con celestial, elysian, Hesperidean, paradisaic, paradisal, paradisiacal
ant supernal
2 resembling or appropriate to hell or its inhabitants <an *infernal* glow in the sky>
syn avernal, cimmerian, hellish, pandemoniac, plutonian, plutonic, stygian
rel demoniac, devilish, diabolic, fiendish; sulphurous
ant celestial, heavenly
3 *syn* see DAMNED 2
4 *syn* see UTTER
inferno *n* **1** *syn* see HELL
2 *syn* see FIRE 1
inferred *adj* *syn* see TACIT 1
infertile *adj* **1** *syn* see STERILE 1
rel depleted, drained, exhausted, impoverished
con breeding, generating, propagating, reproducing
ant fertile
2 *syn* see BARREN 2
ant fertile
infest *vb* **1** to spread or swarm over in a troublesome manner <lawns *infested* with weeds>
syn beset, overrun, overspread, overswarm
rel abound, crawl, swarm, teem; annoy, harass, harry, pester, plague, worry
2 to live in or on as a parasite <a dog *infested* by fleas>
syn parasite, parasitize
infidel *adj* *syn* see HEATHEN
infidelic *adj* *syn* see HEATHEN
infidelity *n* betrayal of a moral obligation <a leader guilty of *infidelity* to the responsibilities he had accepted>
syn disloyalty, faithlessness, falseness, falsity, perfidiousness, perfidy, unfaithfulness; *compare* TREACHERY
rel fickleness, inconstancy; treacherousness, treachery, treason
idiom bad faith
con devotion, faithfulness, fealty; constancy, loyalty, steadfastness
ant fidelity
infiltrate *vb* *syn* see INSINUATE 3
infinite *adj* **1** being without known limits <the idea of an *infinite* universe>
syn eternal, illimitable, perdurable, sempiternal, supertemporal
rel everlasting, perpetual
con bounded, circumscribed, limited, restricted
ant finite
2 *syn* see LIMITLESS
ant finite
infinity *n* *syn* see ETERNITY 1
infirm *adj* *syn* see WEAK 1
ant hale
infirmity *n* **1** the quality or state of being enfeebled and weakened in health <suffering from old age and attendant physical *infirmity*>
syn debility, decrepitude, disease, feebleness, infirmness, malaise, sickliness, unhealthiness; *compare* DISEASE 1, SICKNESS 1
rel debilitation, decay, enfeeblement, failing, frailty, weakening, weakness; diseasedness, un-

wellness; illness, indisposition, sickness, unhealth
ant haleness
2 *syn* see DISEASE 1
3 *syn* see SICKNESS 1
infirmness *n* *syn* see INFIRMITY 1
infix *vb* **1** *syn* see ENTRENCH 1
2 *syn* see IMPLANT
inflame *vb* **1** *syn* see LIGHT 1
ant extinguish
2 *syn* see IRRITATE
inflammable *adj* *syn* see COMBUSTIBLE 1
ant nonflammable, noninflammable
inflammatory *adj* exciting or tending to excite anger, animosity, or disorder <*inflammatory* speeches designed to spark rebellion>
syn incendiary
rel exciting, incitive, instigative, provocative; revolutionary, seditionary, seditious
con calming, moderating, soothing, temperate
inflate *vb* *syn* see EXPAND 3
ant deflate
inflated *adj* swollen with or as if with something insubstantial <had an *inflated* idea of his own importance>
syn dropsical, dropsied, flatulent, overblown, tumescent, tumid, turgid, windy
rel aureate, bombastic, flowery, grandiloquent, magniloquent, rhetorical; ostentatious, pretentious, showy; fustian, ranting, rhapsodical; diffuse, prolix, verbose, wordy
con compendious, concise, laconic, pithy, succinct, summary, terse
inflatus *n* *syn* see INSPIRATION
inflection *n* a particular manner of employing the sounds of the voice in speech <questions end on a rising *inflection*>
syn accent, intonation, tone
rel articulation, enunciation, pronunciation; timbre, tonality
idiom tone of voice
inflexible *adj* **1** *syn* see STIFF 1
rel immobile, immovable
con elastic, resilient, springy, supple; ductile, malleable, plastic, pliable, pliant; fluid, liquid
ant flexible
2 rigidly firm in will or purpose <a person of *inflexible* resolution>
syn adamant, adamantine, brassbound, dogged, inexorable, iron, obdurate, relentless, rigid, rockbound, rock-ribbed, single-minded, steadfast, stubborn, unbendable, unbending, uncompliant, uncompromising, unswayable, unyielding; *compare* STIFF 1
rel intractable, obstinate; indomitable, invincible, unconquerable; grim, hard, implacable, unrelenting; dyed-in-the-wool, fixed, set, ‖sot
con agreeable, amenable, compliant, docile, pliant, responsive, swayable, yielding; mild, open
ant flexible
3 incapable of changing or being changed <*inflexible* rules>
syn constant, determinate, fixed, immovable, immutable, inalterable, invariable, ironclad, un-

alterable, unchangeable, unmodifiable, unmovable

rel strict; rigorous; established, set, settled; changeless, unchanging

con adaptable, adjustable, alterable, changeable, mutable, variable

ant flexible

4 *syn* see TOUGH 3

inflict *vb* **1** *syn* see GIVE 10

2 to cause one to endure (something damaging or painful) <*inflict* retribution>

syn force (on *or* upon), impose, visit, wreak, wreck; *compare* IMPOSE 4

rel expose, subject

idiom lay open to, put on the spot

con guard, protect, shelter, shield

inflow *n* *syn* see INFLUX

ant outflow, outflux

influence *n* **1** power exerted over the minds or behavior of others <a person of great *influence* in national politics>

syn authority, credit, prestige, weight; *compare* PULL 2

rel command, domination, dominion, mastery; ascendancy, dominance, eminence, predominance; consequence, importance, moment; ||drag, in, pull

2 *syn* see PULL 2

3 *syn* see EFFECT 3

influence *vb* **1** *syn* see AFFECT

2 *syn* see PREJUDICE 2

influenceable *adj* *syn* see RECEPTIVE 1

influx *n* a flowing in <anticipated an *influx* of immigrants>

syn inflow, influxion, inpour, inpouring, inrush

rel accession, augmentation, increase; illapse

con outpour, outpouring, outrush; efflux, effluxion, exodus

ant outflow, outflux

influxion *n* *syn* see INFLUX

ant effluxion

inform *vb* **1** *syn* see FIRE 2

rel imbue, infuse, leaven, permeate; enlighten, illuminate; endow, endue

2 to make aware or cognizant of something <was kept *informed* of developments>

syn acquaint, advise, apprise, clue (*or* clew), fill in, notify, post, tell, warn, wise (up)

rel educate, enlighten, instruct, teach; familiarize; caution, forewarn

idiom keep posted

3 to give information about someone especially as an informer <his suspicions aroused, he *informed* on his neighbor to the police>

syn ||nark, peach, ||pimp, rat, ||sing, snitch, squeak, squeal, ||stool; *compare* TALK 6

rel blab, tattle, tell; betray, give away, turn in

informal *adj* **1** conducted or carried out without rigidly prescribed procedure <carried on an *informal* investigation>

syn irregular, unceremonious, unofficial

rel casual, spontaneous; unauthorized; unconventional; private, special

con authorized, ceremonious, conventional, official, regular

ant formal

2 *syn* see EASYGOING 3

rel familiar, natural, simple

con affected, mannered, prim, rigid, stiff, stilted

ant formal

information *n* **1** *syn* see KNOWLEDGE 2

2 *syn* see NEWS

informational *adj* *syn* see INFORMATIVE

informative *adj* imparting information <gave an *informative* talk>

syn educational, educative, informational, informatory, instructional, instructive

rel edifying, elucidative, enlightening, explanatory, illuminating

ant uninformative

informatory *adj* *syn* see INFORMATIVE

informed *adj* *syn* see FAMILIAR 3

ant uninformed

informer *n* one who informs against another <his arrest was brought about by an *informer*>

syn betrayer, ||canary, ||fink, ||nark, ||pimp, snitch, squawker, ||squeaker, squealer, stool, stoolie, stool pigeon, talebearer, tattler, tattletale, tipster; *compare* BUSYBODY, DETECTIVE, GOSSIP 1, SPY

infra *adv* **1** *syn* see BELOW 2

ant above, supra

2 *syn* see AFTER

infract *vb* *syn* see VIOLATE 1

infraction *n* *syn* see BREACH 1

rel crime, offense, sin; error, faux pas, lapse, slip

infrastructure *n* **1** *syn* see BASE 1

ant superstructure

2 *syn* see BASIS 1

infrequent *adj* appearing, happening, or met with so seldom as to attract attention <held only *infrequent* press conferences>

syn few, occasional, rare, scarce, seldom, semioccasional, sporadic, uncommon, unfrequent

rel isolated, scattered; meager, scant, scanty, sparse; exceptional, limited, unusual; odd, spasmodic, stray

idiom few and far between

con abundant, common, numerous, regular; ordinary, routine

ant frequent

infrequently *adv* **1** *syn* see SELDOM

ant frequently

2 *syn* see OCCASIONALLY

ant frequently

infringe *vb* **1** *syn* see TRESPASS 2

2 *syn* see VIOLATE 1

3 *syn* see IMPOSE 5

infringement *n* *syn* see BREACH 1

infuriate *vb* *syn* see ANGER 1

infuse *vb* **1** to introduce one thing into another so as to change or affect it <a teacher who *infused* her pupils with the desire to learn>

---

syn synonym(s)   *rel* related word(s)
ant antonym(s)   *con* contrasted word(s)
idiom idiomatic equivalent(s)
|| use limited; if in doubt, see a dictionary

syn imbue, ingrain, inoculate, invest, leaven, steep, suffuse

rel animate, fire, inform, inspire; implant, inculcate, instill; impregnate, permeate, pervade, saturate; indoctrinate

2 *syn* see INTERFUSE 2

ingather *vb syn* see REAP

ingathering *n syn* see HARVEST 1

ingeminate *vb syn* see REPEAT

ingenerate *adj syn* see INHERENT

ingenious *adj* **1** *syn* see INVENTIVE

2 *syn* see CLEVER 4

ingenuous *adj syn* see NATURAL 5

con covert, furtive, stealthy, surreptitious, underhand; artful, crafty, foxy, guileful, insidious, sly, tricky, wily

ant disingenuous

ingest *vb syn* see EAT 1

inglorious *adj syn* see DISREPUTABLE 1

ant glorious

ingoing *adj syn* see INCISIVE

ingot *n syn* see BAR 1

ingrain *vb* **1** *syn* see ENTRENCH 1

rel engrave, etch, grave, incise

2 *syn* see INFUSE 1

ingrained *adj syn* see INHERENT

rel chronic, confirmed, deep-rooted, inveterate

con exterior, external, outer, outside, outward

ingratiating *adj* intended or designed to gain favor <an *ingratiating* smile>

syn deferential, disarming, ingratiatory, insinuating, insinuative, saccharine, silken, silky

rel adulatory; fawning, sycophantic

ingratiatory *adj syn* see INGRATIATING

ingredient *n syn* see ELEMENT 2

ingress *n* **1** *syn* see ENTRANCE 1

ant egress

2 *syn* see DOOR 2

ant egress

ingress *vb syn* see ENTER 1

ant egress

ingression *n syn* see ENTRANCE 1

ant egression

in-group *n syn* see CLIQUE

ant outgroup

ingurgitate *vb syn* see GULP

inhabit *vb* to dwell in as a place of settled residence <islands *inhabited* by Polynesians>

syn occupy, people, populate, tenant

rel settle; abide, dwell, live

inhabitable *adj syn* see LIVABLE 1

ant uninhabitable

inhabitancy *n syn* see HABITATION 1

inhabitant *n* one that occupies a particular place regularly <*inhabitants* of large cities>

syn denizen, dweller, habitant, indweller, liver, occupant, resident, ‖residenter, resider

rel aborigine, autochthon, indigene, native

inhabitation *n syn* see HABITATION 1

inhale *vb* to draw (as air) into the lungs <*inhaling* smoke>

syn breathe (in), inspire

ant exhale, expire

inharmonic *adj syn* see DISSONANT 1

ant harmonic

inharmonious *adj* **1** *syn* see DISSONANT 1

ant harmonious

2 lacking harmony especially in sentiment <the committee meeting was singularly *inharmonious*>

syn discordant, inconsonant, uncongenial, unharmonious

rel antagonistic, cat-and-dog, conflicting, conflictive, differing, disagreeing, incompatible, incongruous, quarrelsome

con concordant, congenial, consonant; amiable, compatible; collaborative

ant harmonious

inharmony *n syn* see DISCORD

ant harmony

inhaust *vb syn* see ABSORB 1

inhere *vb* **1** *syn* see CONSIST 1

2 *syn* see BELONG 3

inherent *adj* being a part, element, or quality of a thing's inmost being <*inherent* rights of every citizen>

syn born, built-in, congenital, connate, constitutional, deep-seated, elemental, essential, inborn, inbred, indwelling, ingenerate, ingrained, innate, intimate, intrinsic

rel inner, internal, inward, resident; basic, elementary, fundamental, immanent, integral; characteristic, distinctive, individual, peculiar; natural, normal, regular, typical; bred-in-the-bone

con shallow, superficial; accidental, fortuitous, incidental; alien, extraneous, extrinsic, foreign

ant adventitious

inheritance *n* **1** *syn* see HERITAGE 1

2 *syn* see LEGACY 1

inherited *adj syn* see INNATE 1

inheritor *n syn* see HEIR

inhibit *vb* **1** *syn* see FORBID

rel avert, ward

ant allow

2 *syn* see RESTRAIN 1

ant activate; animate

inhibited *adj syn* see FRIGID 3

ant uninhibited

inhuman *adj syn* see FIERCE 1

rel malicious, malign, malignant; implacable, relentless, unrelenting; devilish, diabolical, fiendish

con altruistic, benevolent, charitable, eleemosynary, humanitarian, philanthropic; compassionate, tender

ant humane

inhumane *adj syn* see FIERCE 1

ant humane

inhumation *n syn* see BURIAL 2

ant exhumation

inhume *vb syn* see BURY 1

ant disinhume, exhume

inimicable *adj syn* see HOSTILE 1

inimical *adj syn* see HOSTILE 1

iniquitous *adj syn* see WRONG 1

iniquity *n syn* see EVIL 3

initial *adj* **1** marking a commencement or constituting a start <*initial* symptoms of the disease>

syn beginning, inceptive, incipient, initiative, initiatory, introductory, nascent

rel basic, elementary, first, fundamental; embryonic, germinal; early, infant; antecedent; earliest, introductory, primary

con closing; concluding, conclusive; terminal, terminative; last, ultimate

ant final

2 syn see FIRST 2

3 syn see FIRST 1

ant final

initially *adv* **1** in the beginning <*initially* we were confused but soon enough we fully understood>

syn originally, primarily, primitively

rel first, firstly, incipiently

idiom at first, at the first go-off, from the word go

con lastly, ultimately

ant finally

2 syn see FIRSTLY

initiate *vb* **1 syn** see BEGIN 1

ant terminate

2 syn see INTRODUCE 3

3 to put through the formalities for becoming a member or official <the club *initiated* four new members>

syn inaugurate, induct, install, instate, invest

rel institute; admit, enter, introduce, take in

initiation *n* the process or an instance of being formally introduced into an office or made a member of an organization <a fraternity *initiation*>

syn inaugural, inauguration, induction, installation, investiture

rel baptism; institution, introduction

initiative *adj* **syn** see INITIAL 1

initiative *n* **syn** see ENTERPRISE 4

initiatory *adj* **syn** see INITIAL 1

injudicious *adj* **syn** see UNWISE

ant judicious

injunction *n* **syn** see COMMAND 1

injure *vb* **1** to deplete the soundness, strength, effectiveness, or perfection of something <*injured* her prestige by making rash statements>

syn blemish, damage, harm, hurt, impair, mar, prejudice, spoil, tarnish, vitiate

rel disserve; disadvantage; endamage, weaken; blight, queer; foul up, louse up; contort, deface, deform, disfigure, distort; bespatter, foul, smirch; disable, incapacitate

con assist, help, succor; better, enhance, improve; benefit; strengthen

ant aid

2 syn see DISTRESS 2

idiom do dirt to

3 to inflict bodily hurt on <was *injured* in an auto accident>

syn hurt, wound

rel damage, harm; afflict, torment, torture; batter, cripple, maim, mangle, mutilate

idiom draw blood

injurious *adj* **syn** see HARMFUL

injury *n* **1** an act or the result of inflicting something that causes loss or pain <we cannot forgive his *injury* of the painting> <his falsehood caused grave *injury* to his brother's reputation>

syn damage, harm, hurt, mischief, outrage, ruin

rel agony, discomfiture, distress, misery, suffering; pain, pang; detriment, disservice, loss; bad, evil, ill

2 syn see INJUSTICE 2

injustice *n* **1** absence of justice <preached against *injustice*>

syn inequitableness, inequity, unfairness, unjustness, wrong

rel crime, malfeasance, malpractice, villainy, wrongdoing; favoritism, inequality, partiality, partisanship

con equity, fairness, right

ant justice, justness

2 an act or instance of unjustness <pointed out various *injustices* in the law> <you do him an *injustice* when you call him lazy>

syn grievance, injury, wrong

rel damage, harm, hurt, mischief, outrage, ruin; breach, infraction, infringement, tort, transgression, trespass, violation

ink *vb* **syn** see SIGN 1

inkling *n* **syn** see HINT 1

inky *adj* **syn** see BLACK 1

‖**inland** *adj* **syn** see DOMESTIC 2

ant foreign

inlet *n* a recess in the shores of a body of water <*inlets* of lakes and rivers>

syn arm, bay, bayou, bight, cove, ‖creek, firth, gulf, harbor, ‖loch, ‖lough, slough

inn *n* **syn** see HOTEL

innards *n pl* **syn** see ENTRAILS

innate *adj* **1** existing in or belonging to an individual inherently <*innate* vigor>

syn congenital, connate, connatural, inborn, indigenous, inherited, native, natural, unacquired

rel constitutional, deep-seated, essential, ingrained, inherent, intrinsic; hereditary; normal, regular, standard, typical

con accidental, adventitious, fortuitous, incidental; affected, assumed, feigned, simulated; cultivated, fostered, nurtured

ant acquired

2 syn see INHERENT

inner *adj* **1** situated further in <the *inner* layers were less worn>

syn ‖innermore, inside, interior, internal, intestine, inward

rel central, focal, middle, nuclear; close, familiar, intimate; constitutional, essential, inherent, intrinsic

con exterior, external, outside, outward

ant outer

2 arising from one's inmost self <*inner* thoughts and feelings>

syn gut, interior, internal, intimate, visceral, viscerous

---

syn synonym(s)   *rel* related word(s)
ant antonym(s)   *con* contrasted word(s)
idiom idiomatic equivalent(s)
‖ use limited; if in doubt, see a dictionary

rel individual, personal, private; concealed, hidden, secret
con exterior, outer; open, public
‖**innermore** *adj syn* see INNER 1
innervate *vb syn* see PROVOKE 4
innerve *vb syn* see PROVOKE 4
innholder *n syn* see SALOONKEEPER
innkeeper *n syn* see SALOONKEEPER
innocence *n syn* see IGNORANCE 2
innocent *adj* 1 *syn* see GOOD 11
rel unstained, unsullied, white, white-handed
2 free from legal guilt or fault <the defendant was found *innocent*>
syn blameless, clean, crimeless, faultless, guiltless, inculpable, unguilty
idiom in the clear
ant guilty
3 *syn* see LAWFUL
4 *syn* see DEVOID
5 *syn* see NATURAL 5
6 *syn* see HARMLESS
con harmful, injurious, mischievous
innocuous *adj* 1 *syn* see HARMLESS
con harmful, injurious; evil; troublesome
ant pernicious
2 *syn* see INSIPID 3
innominate *adj syn* see ANONYMOUS
innovation *n syn* see CHANGE 2
rel deviation, introduction, wrinkle
innovational *adj syn* see INVENTIVE
innovative *adj syn* see INVENTIVE
innovator *n* one who introduces something new <an *innovator* of bold ideas in the field of computers>
syn introducer, inventor, original, originator
rel author, creator, maker, producer; architect, builder, developer
innovatory *adj syn* see INVENTIVE
innoxious *adj syn* see HARMLESS
ant noxious
innuendo *n syn* see INSINUATION
innumerable *adj* too many to be counted <received *innumerable* requests for help>
syn countless, innumerous, numberless, uncountable, uncounted, unnumberable, unnumbered, untold
ant numberable, numerable
innumerous *adj syn* see INNUMERABLE
inobnoxious *adj syn* see HARMLESS
ant obnoxious
inobservant *adj syn* see INATTENTIVE
ant observant
inobtrusive *adj syn* see QUIET 4
ant obtrusive
inoculate *vb syn* see INFUSE 1
rel admit, enter, introduce
inodorous *adj syn* see ODORLESS
ant odorous; smelly
inoffensive *adj syn* see HARMLESS
con loathsome, repulsive, revolting; distasteful, obnoxious, repellent, repugnant
ant offensive
inopportune *adj syn* see UNSEASONABLE 1
ant opportune

inordinate *adj* 1 *syn* see EXCESSIVE 1
rel irrational, unreasonable; gratuitous, supererogatory, uncalled-for, wanton; extra, superfluous, surplus
con moderate, temperate; checked, curbed, inhibited, restrained
2 *syn* see EXCESSIVE 2
inordinately *adv syn* see EVER 6
inordinateness *n syn* see EXCESS 3
in passing *adv syn* see INCIDENTALLY 2
in perpetuum *adv syn* see EVER 2
inpour *n syn* see INFLUX
ant outpour, outpouring
inpouring *n syn* see INFLUX
ant outpour, outpouring
inquest *n syn* see INQUIRY 1
inquietude *n syn* see UNREST
rel anxiety, uneasiness
ant quiet, quietness, quietude
inquire *vb syn* see ASK 1
rel investigate, probe, search; scrutinize, study
inquire (into) *vb syn* see EXPLORE
inquiring *adj syn* see INQUISITIVE 1
inquiry *n* 1 the act or an instance of seeking truth, information, or knowledge about something <an exhaustive *inquiry* revealed no evidence of a conspiracy>
syn delving, inquest, inquisition, investigation, probe, probing, quest, research
rel catechizing, interrogation, questioning; audit, check, examination, inspection, scrutiny; hearing; inquirendo
2 a request for information <addressed his *inquiry* to the personnel director>
syn interrogation, interrogatory, query, question, questioning
inquisition *n syn* see INQUIRY 1
inquisitive *adj* 1 given to examination or investigation <an *inquisitive* child who was interested in everything around her>
syn curious, disquisitive, inquiring, investigative, questioning
rel nosy, prying, snoopy
con indifferent, unconcerned, uninquisitive, uninterested
ant incurious
2 *syn* see CURIOUS 2
ant incurious, uninquiring
inquisitorial *adj syn* see CURIOUS 2
inquisitory *adj syn* see CURIOUS 2
in re *prep syn* see APROPOS
in respect to *prep syn* see APROPOS
in reverse *adv syn* see ABOUT 6
inroad *n syn* see INVASION
inroad *vb syn* see INVADE 1
inrush *n syn* see INFLUX
ant outrush
insalubrious *adj syn* see UNWHOLESOME 1
ant salubrious, salutary
insalutary *adj syn* see UNWHOLESOME 1
ant salubrious, salutary
insanable *adj syn* see HOPELESS 2
ins and outs *n pl* characteristic peculiarities or technicalities <soon learned the *ins and outs* of his job>

syn minutiae, ropes
rel details, incidentals, particulars; ramifications; oddities, peculiarities, quirks
insane *adj* **1** being afflicted by or manifesting unsoundness of mind or an inability to control one's rational processes <adjudged *insane* after a period of observation>
syn bananas, ‖batty, bedlamite, ‖bonkers, brainsick, ‖buggy, ‖bughouse, ‖bugs, crackbrained, cracked, ‖crackers, ‖cracky, ‖cranky, crazed, crazy, cuckoo, daffy, daft, demented, deranged, disordered, distraught, ‖fruity, ‖loco, loony, lunatic, mad, maniac, ‖mental, mindless, non compos mentis, nuts, nutsy, nutty, reasonless, screwy, teched, unbalanced, unsane, unsound, wacky, witless, wrong
rel irrational, unreasonable; bewildered, distracted; dotty, eccentric, off, rocky, strange, touched; ‖dippy
idiom around the bend, crazy as a coot, not all there, not right in one's head, ‖off one's dot, off one's nut (*or* rocker), ‖off one's onion, out of (*or* off) one's head, out of one's mind, touched in the head
con judicious, sapient, sensible, wise; rational, reasonable; balanced; logical, subtle; healthy, sound; clear, lucid
ant sane
2 syn see FOOLISH 2
rel fanciful, fantastic, imaginary, visionary; impractical, unrealistic
con feasible, possible, practicable, usable; rational, reasonable, sane, sensible; practical, realistic
insaneness *n syn* see INSANITY 1
ant saneness, sanity
insanity *n* **1** grave disorder of mind that impairs one's capacity to function safely or normally in society <his *insanity* required confinement in a mental institution>
syn aberration, alienation, derangement, distraction, insaneness, lunacy, madness, psychopathy, unbalance
rel acromania; delirium, frenzy, hysteria; delusion, hallucination, illusion; irrationality, unreasonableness; dotage
con judiciousness, sageness, sensibility, wiseness; rationality, reasonableness; healthiness, soundness, wholesomeness
ant saneness, sanity
2 syn see FOOLISHNESS
rel asininity, fatuousness, stupidity; impracticality
insatiable *adj* incapable of being satisfied or appeased <an *insatiable* lust for glory>
syn insatiate, quenchless, unappeasable, unquenchable, unsatiate, unsatisfiable
rel unsatiated, unsatisfied; demanding, exigent, importunate, insistent, urgent; clamorous, crying, pressing, yearning
con appeasable, quenchable, satisfiable; satiate, satiated, satisfied; controlled, curbed, restrained
ant satiable
insatiably *adv syn* see VERY 1
insatiate *adj syn* see INSATIABLE

ant satiate, satiated
inscience *n syn* see IGNORANCE 2
inscribe *vb* **1 syn** see WRITE
rel engrave, enscroll
2 syn see LIST 3
3 syn see ENGRAVE 2
inscrutable *adj syn* see MYSTERIOUS
insecure *adj* **1** not confident or sure <feels very *insecure* about his future>
syn unassured, unconfident, unsure
rel hesitant, questioning, uncertain
idiom in suspense, up in the air
con assured, confident, self-assured, self-confident, sure
ant secure
2 syn see WEAK 2
ant secure
inseminate *vb syn* see IMPLANT
insensate *adj* **1** lacking animate awareness or sensation <would often talk to stones and other *insensate* objects>
syn inanimate, insensible, insentient, senseless, unfeeling
rel exanimate, unanimated; anesthetic, insensitive
con aware, cognizant, conscious; feeling, sensible, sensient
ant sensate
2 syn see SIMPLE 3
3 syn see INSENSIBLE 5
insensibility *n syn* see APATHY 1
ant sensibility
insensible *adj* **1 syn** see INSENSATE 1
ant sensible
2 deprived of consciousness <knocked *insensible* by a sudden punch>
syn cold, comatose, inconscious, senseless, unconscious
idiom out cold
3 syn see NUMB 1
4 syn see IMPERCEPTIBLE
ant sensible
5 devoid or insusceptible of emotion or passion <*insensible* to love or compassion>
syn anesthetic, bloodless, dull, hard, impassible, insensate, insensitive, rocky
rel blunt, obtuse; apathetic, impassive, phlegmatic, stoic, stolid; callous, hardened, indurated, pachydermatous, thick-skinned; absorbed, engrossed, intent, rapt
con alert, alive, awake, aware, cognizant, conscious; affected, impressed, influenced, touched
ant sensible
insensitive *adj* **1 syn** see INSENSIBLE 5
rel aloof, incurious, indifferent, unconcerned
con compassionate, responsive, tender
ant sensitive
2 syn see NUMB 1
ant sensitive

---

syn synonym(s)   **rel** related word(s)
ant antonym(s)   **con** contrasted word(s)
idiom idiomatic equivalent(s)
‖ use limited; if in doubt, see a dictionary

3 *syn* see INSUSCEPTIBLE
ant sensitive
insentient *adj* **1** *syn* see INSENSATE 1
ant sentient
2 *syn* see INSUSCEPTIBLE
insert *vb* *syn* see INTRODUCE 6
rel interlope, intrude, obtrude; implant, inculcate, instill; admit, enter
con detach, disengage
ant abstract, extract
in short *adv* *syn* see BRIEFLY
inside *n* **1** *syn* see INTERIOR
ant outside
2 insides *pl* *syn* see ENTRAILS
inside *adj* **1** *syn* see INNER 1
ant outside
2 *syn* see PRIVATE 2
inside *adv* *syn* see INDOORS
ant outside
inside out *adv* *syn* see THOROUGHLY 2
insidious *adj* *syn* see SLY 2
rel perfidious, treacherous; dangerous, perilous; gradual, subtle
insight *n* **1** *syn* see SAGACITY
2 *syn* see INTUITION
insighted *adj* *syn* see WISE 1
insightful *adj* *syn* see WISE 1
rel discriminating, penetrating; inseeing
insignia *n* a distinguishing mark of authority, office, or honor <wore a coronet with the strawberry leaf *insignia* of his ducal rank > <displayed her military *insignia* with pride>
syn badge, emblem
rel decoration; regalia
insignificancy *n* *syn* see NONENTITY
insignificant *adj* **1** *syn* see SENSELESS 5
ant significant
2 *syn* see MINOR 2
3 *syn* see LITTLE 3
ant significant
insincere *adj* not being or expressing what one appears to be or express <an *insincere* person who could not be trusted>
syn ambidextrous, double, double-dealing, double-faced, doublehearted, double-minded, double-tongued, hypocritical, left-handed, mala fide
rel deceitful, dishonest, lying, mendacious, untruthful; shifty, slippery, tricky
con candid, frank, open, plain; direct, forthright, straight, straightforward
ant sincere
insinuate *vb* **1** *syn* see INTRODUCE 6
2 *syn* see SUGGEST 1
rel ascribe, impute
con affirm, assert, aver, avouch, avow, declare, profess; air, broach, express, state, voice
3 to introduce (as oneself) by stealthy, smooth, or artful means <*insinuated* himself into the confidence of others>
syn edge in, foist, infiltrate, work in, worm
rel insert, intercalate, interject, interpolate, interpose, introduce
insinuating *adj* *syn* see INGRATIATING

insinuation *n* a stealthy or indirect hinting or suggestion <*insinuations* about her opponent's probity>
syn innuendo, insinuendo
rel hint, hinting, implication, implying, intimation, suggestion; animadversion, aspersion, reflection; ascription, imputation
insinuative *adj* *syn* see INGRATIATING
insinuendo *n* *syn* see INSINUATION
insipid *adj* **1** *syn* see UNPALATABLE 1
rel bland, mild
con appetizing, flavorable, tasty
ant sapid, savory
2 *syn* see ARID 2
rel commonplace, ordinary, plain; mundane, prosaic, unimaginative
3 devoid of qualities that make for spirit and character <an *insipid* little story of teenage puppy love>
syn banal, bland, driveling, flat, inane, innocuous, jejune, milk-and-water, namby-pamby, sapless, swashy, vapid, waterish, watery, wishy-washy
rel slight, tenuous, thin; feeble, weak; subdued, tame; mild, soft; pointless
con piquant, poignant, pungent, racy, spicy; fiery, gingery, high-spirited, mettlesome, peppery, spirited, spunky; exciting, piquing, provocative, provoking
ant sapid
insistent *adj* **1** *syn* see PERSISTENT 1
2 *syn* see EMPHATIC
rel persevering, persistent, pressing; obtrusive
3 *syn* see PRESSING
insociable *adj* *syn* see UNSOCIABLE
ant sociable
insolate *vb* *syn* see SUN
insolence *n* the quality, state, or an instance of being insulting or grossly lacking in respect <court-martialed because of *insolence* to an officer>
syn boldness, disrespect, hardihood, impertinence, impudence, insolency, insolentness; *compare* EFFRONTERY
rel brazenness; presumption; arrogance; rudeness; contempt
con deference; correctness, decency, decorum, decorousness, properness, seemliness
ant respect, respectfulness
insolency *n* *syn* see INSOLENCE
ant respect, respectfulness
insolent *adj* **1** *syn* see PROUD 1
rel imperative, peremptory; dictatorial, magisterial
ant deferential
2 exhibiting boldness or effrontery <an *insolent* child with no respect or regard for anyone>
syn audacious, bold, ‖boldacious, brazen, contumelious, impertinent, procacious, saucy
rel arrogant, disdainful, overbearing; discourteous, impolite, rude, uncivil, ungracious
con humble, lowly, meek, modest, unassertive; civil, courteous, polite

ant deferential

insolentness *n syn* see INSOLENCE

ant respect, respectfulness

insoluble *adj* admitting of no solution <seemingly *insoluble* problems faced the city council>

syn inextricable, insolvable, irresoluble, irresolvable, unsoluble, unsolvable

rel inexplicable, unexplainable; inconceivable, unaccountable; mysterious

con answerable, explicable, understandable; resolvable; clear, plain, straightforward

ant soluble, solvable

insolvable *adj syn* see INSOLUBLE

ant soluble, solvable

insomnia *n* prolonged inability to obtain adequate sleep <sleeping pills failed to relieve his *insomnia*>

syn insomnolence, sleeplessness

rel restlessness, wakefulness; stress, tension

insomnolence *n syn* see INSOMNIA

insorb *vb syn* see ABSORB 1

insouciance *n syn* see APATHY 2

insouciant *adj syn* see HAPPY-GO-LUCKY

inspect *vb syn* see SCRUTINIZE 1

rel notice, observe; catechize, inquire, interrogate, question; review

inspection *n syn* see EXAMINATION

rel inquest, inquiry, inquisition, investigation, probe, research; oversight, supervision, surveillance

inspiration *n* a divine or seemingly divine imparting of knowledge or power <*inspiration* is the only plausible explanation for his exquisite work>

syn afflation, afflatus, inflatus

rel animus, genius, muse, vision; enlightenment, illumination; brainstorm, brain wave

inspire *vb* 1 *syn* see INHALE

ant expire

2 *syn* see FIRE 2

rel quicken, stimulate; infect, infuse; endow, endue

3 *syn* see ELATE

4 *syn* see AFFECT

inspiring *adj syn* see EXCITING

ant uninspiring

inspirit *vb syn* see ENCOURAGE 1

rel exalt, fire, inform, inspire

ant dispirit

in spite of *prep syn* see AGAINST 4

instability *n* the state or quality of not being firm or fixed <the *instability* of the economy>

syn precariousness, shakiness, unfixedness, unsettledness, unstability, unstableness, unsteadfastness, unsteadiness

rel undependability, unreliability; inconstancy, insecurity

con firmness, soundness, stoutness, sturdiness; fixity, solidity

ant stability, stableness

install *vb* 1 *syn* see INITIATE 3

2 *syn* see ENSCONCE 2

installation *n syn* see INITIATION

instance *n* an individual that clearly belongs to an indicated class <their rescue was an *instance* of great courage>

syn case, case history, example, illustration, representative, sample, sampling, specimen

rel ground, proof, reason; detail, item, particular; exponent

instance *vb* 1 *syn* see EXEMPLIFY 1

2 *syn* see MENTION

rel exemplify, illustrate

instant *n* 1 an infinitesimal space of time <came not an *instant* too soon>

syn breathing, crack, flash, ‖jiff, jiffy, minute, moment, second, shake, split second, ‖tick, trice, twinkle, twinkling, wink

2 *syn* see POINT 7

3 *syn* see OCCASION 5

instant *adj* 1 *syn* see PRESSING

2 *syn* see PRESENT

3 *syn* see INSTANTANEOUS

instantaneous *adj* done, occurring, or acting without any perceptible duration of time <*instantaneous* answers to tough questions>

syn hair-trigger, immediate, instant; *compare* QUICK 2

rel spontaneous; fast, quick, rapid; momentary, transitory

con late, tardy; slow, sluggish

instanter *adv syn* see AWAY 3

instantly *adv syn* see AWAY 3

idiom in a flash, on a dime, on the spot

instate *vb syn* see INITIATE 3

instead *adv* as an alternative to something expressed or implied <longed *instead* for a quiet country life>

syn alternately, alternatively, in lieu, rather

insteep *vb syn* see SOAK 1

instigate *vb syn* see INCITE

rel activate, actuate; hint, insinuate, suggest; plan, plot, scheme; goad, urge; fire, inflame

instigation *n syn* see STIMULUS

instigator *n* one that goads or urges forward <the *instigator* of the riot>

syn agitator, fomenter, inciter, mover

rel firebrand, incendiary, inflamer, rabble-rouser

instill *vb syn* see IMPLANT

instinctive *adj* 1 prompted by natural instinct or propensity <was quite unable to control her *instinctive* fear of snakes>

syn instinctual, intuitive, visceral

rel congenital, inborn, innate; ingrained, inherent, intrinsic; natural

ant reasoned

2 *syn* see SPONTANEOUS

rel natural, normal, regular, typical

ant intentional

instinctual *adj syn* see INSTINCTIVE 1

institute *vb* 1 *syn* see FOUND 2

---

syn synonym(s)   *rel* related word(s)
ant antonym(s)   *con* contrasted word(s)
idiom idiomatic equivalent(s)
‖ use limited; if in doubt, see a dictionary

ant abrogate
2 *syn* see INTRODUCE 3
institute *n syn* see LAW 1
institution *n* something or someone well established in a customary relationship <he's been in the office so long that he has become an *institution*>
syn fixture
rel custom, habit; establishment, rite
instruct *vb* **1** *syn* see TEACH
rel acquaint, apprise, inform; engineer, guide, lead, pilot, steer
2 *syn* see COMMAND
rel assign, define, prescribe
instruction *n syn* see EDUCATION 1
instructional *adj syn* see INFORMATIVE
instructive *adj syn* see INFORMATIVE
rel didactic, moralistic, moralizing
instrument *n* **1** *syn* see MEAN 2
2 *syn* see IMPLEMENT
rel equipment, gear, machinery, paraphernalia, tackle
instrumental *adj* serving as a means, agent, or tool <was *instrumental* in organizing the strike>
syn implemental, ministerial
rel conducive, helpful; serviceable, useful
instrumentality *n syn* see MEAN 2
rel energy, force, might, power
instrumentation *n syn* see MEAN 2
insubordinate *adj* unwilling to submit to authority <*insubordinate* soldiers are court-martialed>
syn contumacious, factious, insurgent, mutinous, rebellious, seditious
rel intractable, recalcitrant, refractory, ungovernable, unruly; indocile, uncompliant, uncomplying; disaffected, dissentious
con amenable, biddable, docile, obedient, tractable; subdued, submissive, tame
ant subordinate
insubstantial *adj* **1** *syn* see IMMATERIAL 1
ant substantial
2 *syn* see WEAK 1
ant substantial
3 *syn* see TENUOUS 3
ant substantial
insuccess *n syn* see FAILURE 2
ant success, successfulness
insufferable *adj* incapable of being endured <that man is an *insufferable* bore>
syn insupportable, intolerable, unbearable, unbrookable, unendurable, unsufferable, unsupportable
rel distressing, painful; unacceptable
ant sufferable
insufficience *n* **1** *syn* see FAILURE 3
ant sufficiency
2 *syn* see SCARCITY
ant sufficiency
insufficiency *n* **1** *syn* see FAILURE 3
ant sufficiency
2 *syn* see SCARCITY
ant sufficiency
insufficient *adj* **1** *syn* see DEFICIENT 1
ant sufficient

2 *syn* see SHORT 3
ant sufficient
insular *adj* having the narrow and limited outlook characteristic of geographic isolation <the *insular* thinking of peasant communities>
syn local, ‖parish-pump, parochial, provincial, sectarian, small-town
rel regional, sectional; insulated, isolated, secluded; circumscribed, confined, limited, restricted; illiberal, narrow, narrow-minded
con broad-minded, liberal; cosmopolitan, metropolitan, urban
insulate *vb syn* see ISOLATE
insult *vb syn* see OFFEND 3
rel abase, debase, degrade, humble, humiliate; fleer, flout, gibe, gird, jeer, scoff, sneer; deride, mock, ridicule, taunt; rump
con admire, esteem, respect
ant honor
insult *n syn* see AFFRONT
rel abuse, invective, obloquy, vituperation; disgrace, ignominy, opprobrium, shame; disdainfulness, insolence, superciliousness; contempt, disdain, scorn; unpleasantry
con deference, homage, honor, obeisance, reverence
insuperable *adj* incapable of being surmounted, overcome, or passed over <they met with *insuperable* difficulties>
syn impassable, inconquerable, indomitable, insurmountable, invincible, unconquerable, unsurmountable
rel unachievable, unattainable; unsurpassable; impenetrable, impregnable, invulnerable
con surmountable; achievable, negotiable
ant superable
insupportable *adj syn* see INSUFFERABLE
ant bearable, supportable
insupposable *adj syn* see INCREDIBLE 1
ant supposable
insuppressible *adj syn* see IRREPRESSIBLE
ant suppressible
insuppressive *adj syn* see IRREPRESSIBLE
insure *vb syn* see ENSURE
rel guard, protect, safeguard, shield
insurgent *n syn* see REBEL
insurgent *adj syn* see INSUBORDINATE
insurmountable *adj syn* see INSUPERABLE
ant surmountable
insurrect *vb syn* see REVOLT 1
insurrectionist *n syn* see REBEL
insusceptible *adj* incapable of being moved, affected, or impressed <*insusceptible* to flattery>
syn impassive, insensitive, insentient, unimpressible, unimpressionable, unresponsive, unsusceptible
con impressible, impressionable, responsive, sensitive, sentient
ant susceptible
intact *adj* **1** *syn* see WHOLE 1
ant defective
2 *syn* see VIRGIN 1
ant deflowered
intangible *adj* **1** *syn* see IMPERCEPTIBLE

rel rare, tenuous, thin; slender, slight; aerial, aeriform, airy, ethereal; eluding, elusive, evading, evasive; touchless
ant tangible
2 *syn* see ELUSIVE
integer *n syn* see NUMBER
integral *adj syn* see WHOLE 3
integral *n syn* see WHOLE 2
integrate *n syn* see WHOLE 2
integrate *vb* **1** *syn* see HARMONIZE 4
2 *syn* see HARMONIZE 3
3 to join together systematically <an economic system that successfully *integrates* private gain with public responsibility>
syn articulate, concatenate
rel combine, conjoin, link, unite; compact, concentrate, consolidate, unify; blend, coalesce, fuse, merge; organize, systematize
con disperse, dissipate, scatter; analyze, break down, resolve
ant disintegrate
4 *syn* see UNIFY 1
5 *syn* see EMBODY 2
integrative *adj* tending to integrate <*integrative* forces in a fragmented society>
syn centralizing, centripetal, compacting, concentrating, consolidating, unifying
ant disintegrative
integrity *n* **1** *syn* see HONESTY
rel forthrightness, straightforwardness
2 the quality or state of being complete or undivided <trying to maintain the *integrity* of the empire>
syn completeness, entireness, perfection, wholeness
rel soundness, stability; absoluteness, purity, simplicity
intellect *n* **1** *syn* see REASON 5
rel comprehension; intuition
2 a person with great intellectual powers <one of the great *intellects* of his time>
syn brain, intellectual, intelligence
rel genius; egghead, pundit; thinker
intellection *n syn* see IDEA
intellective *adj syn* see MENTAL 1
intellectual *adj* **1** *syn* see MENTAL 1
con animal, fleshly, sensual
ant carnal
2 devoted to or engaged in the creative use of the intellect <the play appealed to the *intellectual* members of the audience>
syn cerebral, highbrow, highbrowed, intellectualistic
intellectual *n* **1** *syn* see INTELLECT 2
2 a person who possesses or has pretensions of strong intellectual interest or superiority <accused of being an *intellectual* and a snob>
syn Brahmin, double-dome, egghead, highbrow
3 intellectuals *pl syn* see INTELLIGENTSIA
intellectualistic *adj syn* see INTELLECTUAL 2
intelligence *n* **1** the ability to learn and to cope <what he lacked in education, he made up in *intelligence*>
syn brain(s), brainpower, mentality, mother wit, sense, wit

rel acumen, discernment, insight, judgment; perspicacity, sagacity, wisdom
2 *syn* see INTELLECT 2
3 *syn* see NEWS
intelligent *adj* **1** *syn* see RATIONAL
con irrational, unreasonable
ant unintelligent
2 mentally keen or quick <quite *intelligent* for his age>
syn alert, brainy, bright, brilliant, clever, knowing, knowledgeable, quick-witted, ready-witted, sharp, smart; *compare* WISE 4
rel astute, perspicacious, sagacious, shrewd; acute, keen; adroit, cunning, ingenious
con foolish, idiotic, imbecilic, moronic; crass, dense, dull, dumb, slow, stupid
ant unintelligent
intelligentsia *n* a class of articulate persons devoted to intellectual, cultural, and social matters <the *intelligentsia* posed a threat to the new regime>
syn clerisy, illuminati, intellectuals, literati
rel avant-garde, vanguard
intelligible *adj syn* see UNDERSTANDABLE
ant unintelligible
intemperance *n syn* see EXCESS 3
rel drunkenness, insobriety; debauchery
ant temperance
intemperate *adj* **1** *syn* see EXCESSIVE 2
rel bibacious, bibulous, crapulous, drunken; gluttonous
ant temperate, tempered
2 *syn* see SEVERE 3
ant temperate
intempestive *adj syn* see IMPROPER 1
intemporal *adj syn* see ETERNAL 4
ant temporal
intend *vb* **1** *syn* see MEAN 2
2 to have in mind as a purpose <*intended* to read the book>
syn aim, contemplate, design, mean, ‖mind, plan, propose, purpose
rel attempt, endeavor, essay, strive, try; plot, scheme; assign, designate, destine
idiom figure on, have in mind to, look forward to
intendance *n syn* see OVERSIGHT 1
intended *adj syn* see ENGAGED 2
intended *n syn* see BETROTHED
intendment *n* **1** *syn* see INTENTION
2 *syn* see MEANING 1
intensate *vb syn* see INTENSIFY
intense *adj* **1** extreme in degree, power, or effect <*intense* hatred>
syn concentrated, desperate, exquisite, fierce, furious, terrible, vehement, vicious, violent
rel aggravated, enhanced, heightened, intensified; accentuated, emphasized, stressed
ant subdued

---

syn synonym(s)   *rel* related word(s)
ant antonym(s)   *con* contrasted word(s)
idiom idiomatic equivalent(s)
‖ use limited; if in doubt, see a dictionary

2 *syn* see INTENSIVE
3 *syn* see ARDENT 2
ant slight
intensely *adv* **1** *syn* see HARD 3
rel fiercely, furiously, vehemently, viciously, violently
2 *syn* see SERIOUSLY 2
intensify *vb* to increase markedly in measure or degree <both companies *intensified* their efforts to win the contract> <the pain *intensified* sharply>
syn aggravate, deepen, enhance, heighten, intensate, magnify, mount, redouble, rise, rouse
rel accent, accentuate, emphasize, stress; aggrandize, exalt; sharpen
con moderate, qualify; alleviate, ease, lighten, relieve; decrease, diminish, lessen, reduce
ant abate; allay, mitigate; temper
intensive *adj* highly concentrated <an *intensive* study of the causes of the war>
syn blood-and-guts, deep, hard, intense, profound
con casual, shallow, superficial
intensively *adv* *syn* see HARD 3
intent *n* **1** *syn* see INTENTION
rel conation, volition, will
con chance, fortune, hap, hazard, luck
ant accident
2 *syn* see MEANING 1
intent *adj* **1** having one's mind or attention deeply fixed <the student was too *intent* on his work to hear the phone>
syn absorbed, deep, engaged, engrossed, immersed, preoccupied, rapt, wrapped, wrapped up
rel attending, attentive, minding, watching; concentrated, riveted
con absent, absent-minded, abstracted, bemused, faraway, preoccupied; daydreaming, napping, oblivious
ant distracted
2 *syn* see DECIDED 2
intention *n* what one purposes to accomplish or do <her *intention* was to finish by noon>
syn animus, design, intendment, intent, meaning, plan, purpose; *compare* AMBITION 2
rel project, scheme; desire, hope, wish
intentional *adj* *syn* see VOLUNTARY
rel intended, meant, proposed, purposed; advised, considered, designed, designful, premeditated, studied
con accidental, casual, fortuitous; careless, heedless, inadvertent, thoughtless
ant unintentional
intentionally *adv* with intention <hurt her *intentionally*>
syn ‖apurpose, deliberately, designedly, on purpose, prepensely, purposedly, purposely, purposively
ant unintentionally
intentive *adj* *syn* see ATTENTIVE 1
intently *adv* *syn* see HARD 4
intentness *n* *syn* see EARNESTNESS
inter *vb* *syn* see BURY 1

ant disinter
interact *vb* to act upon one another <humor and pathos *interacted* to make a moving drama>
syn coact, interplay, interreact
rel collaborate, cooperate; combine, join, merge, unite
interagent *n* *syn* see GO-BETWEEN 2
interblend *vb* *syn* see MIX 1
interbreed *vb* *syn* see CROSS 4
intercalate *vb* *syn* see INTRODUCE 6
intercede *vb* *syn* see INTERPOSE 2
interceder *n* *syn* see GO-BETWEEN 2
intercept *vb* to stop, seize, or interrupt in progress or course <*intercept* a forward pass>
syn block, catch, cut off
rel grab, seize, take; check, curb
con fumble, miss; loose, release
intercessor *n* *syn* see GO-BETWEEN 2
interchange *vb* *syn* see EXCHANGE 3
rel reverse, transpose
interchangeable *adj* permitting mutual substitution <*interchangeable* parts>
syn commutable, exchangeable, fungible, interconvertible, substitutable
rel changeable, convertible; reciprocal, reciprocative
interchurch *adj* *syn* see NONSECTARIAN
intercommunication *n* **1** *syn* see COMMUNICATION 3
2 *syn* see CONTACT 2
intercomparable *adj* *syn* see LIKE
interconnect *vb* *syn* see INTERJOIN
interconvertible *adj* *syn* see INTERCHANGEABLE
intercourse *n* **1** *syn* see COMMERCE 2
2 *syn* see COMMUNICATION 3
3 *syn* see CONTACT 2
intercreedal *adj* *syn* see NONSECTARIAN
intercross *vb* **1** *syn* see INTERSECT
2 *syn* see CROSS 4
interdenominational *adj* *syn* see NONSECTARIAN
interdict *vb* *syn* see FORBID
ant sanction
interdiction *n* *syn* see TABOO
ant sanction
interest *n* **1** participation in advantage, profit, and responsibility <he owned a half *interest* in a furniture store>
syn claim, share, stake
2 *syn* see WELFARE
3 readiness to be concerned with or moved by something <had an *interest* in art>
syn concern, curiosity, interestedness, regard
rel enthusiasm, excitement, passion; attention, care, concernment; absorption, engrossment
con apathy, indifference, unconcern
ant disinterest
interest *vb* to engage the attention and interest of <his appeal failed to *interest* his listeners>
syn appeal, attract, excite, fascinate, intrigue
rel arouse, tantalize, titillate; lure, pull, snare, tempt; pique
ant bore
interested *adj* having a share or concern in some affair <all *interested* parties met for the reading of the will>

syn affected, concerned, implicated, involved
rel biased, partial, partisan, prejudiced
con aloof, incurious, indifferent, unconcerned; apathetic, bored, ennuyé
ant detached, disinterested
interestedness *n syn* see INTEREST 3
interfere *vb* **1** *syn* see INTERPOSE 2
rel bar, block, hinder, impede, obstruct
2 *syn* see MEDDLE
rel discommode, incommode, inconvenience, trouble; baffle, balk, foil, frustrate, thwart
interflow *vb syn* see MIX 1
interfuse *vb* **1** *syn* see MIX 1
2 to cause to pass into or through <*interfused* illuminating anecdotes with the informative text>
syn diffuse, infuse, interlard, intersow, intersperse, intersprinkle
rel impenetrate, impregnate, interpenetrate, penetrate, pervade, saturate
3 *syn* see PERMEATE
interfusion *n syn* see MIXTURE
interim *n syn* see GAP 3
interim *adj syn* see TEMPORARY
interior *adj* **1** *syn* see INNER 1
con extraneous, extrinsic, foreign
ant exterior
2 *syn* see INNER 2
interior *n* the internal or inner part <the *interior* of the house>
syn inside, inward(s), within
rel center, heart; belly, bosom; innards, internals
ant exterior, outside
interject *vb syn* see INTRODUCE 6
interjoin *vb* to join mutually <*interjoined* several stations into a new system>
syn anastomose, interconnect, interlink, intertie
rel interdigitate, interlace, interlock, interrelate
con disunite, part, separate, sunder
ant disjoin
interknit *vb syn* see INTERWEAVE
interlace *vb syn* see INTERWEAVE
interlard *vb syn* see INTERFUSE 2
interlink *vb syn* see INTERJOIN
interlope *vb* **1** *syn* see INTRUDE
2 *syn* see MEDDLE
interlude *n* an intervening or interruptive period or space <an *interlude* of happiness in a tragic story> <woodland broken by *interludes* of meadow>
syn break, intermission, interregnum, interval, parenthesis
rel breather, lull, pause, respite, rest; episode, idyll; meantime, meanwhile, spell; entr'acte
intermeddle *vb syn* see MEDDLE
rel encroach, entrench, invade, trespass
intermeddler *n syn* see BUSYBODY
intermediary *adj syn* see MIDDLE 2
intermediary *n* **1** *syn* see GO-BETWEEN 2
2 *syn* see MEAN 2
intermediate *vb syn* see INTERPOSE 2
intermediate *adj* **1** *syn* see MIDDLE 2
2 *syn* see MEDIUM

intermediate *n syn* see GO-BETWEEN 2
intermediator *n syn* see GO-BETWEEN 2
interment *n syn* see BURIAL 2
ant disinterment
intermesh *vb syn* see ENGAGE 1
interminable *adj syn* see CONTINUAL
rel eternal, infinite; lasting, permanent
con intermittent, periodic; discontinued, stopped; closed, completed, ended, finished, terminated
intermingle *vb syn* see MIX 1
intermission *n* **1** *syn* see ABEYANCE
2 *syn* see INTERLUDE
intermit *vb syn* see DEFER
rel arrest, check, interrupt
con continue, persist; iterate, reiterate, repeat
intermittent *adj* occurring or appearing in interrupted sequence <they predict *intermittent* rain throughout the day>
syn alternate, isochronal, isochronous, periodic, periodical, recurrent, recurring
rel cyclic, cyclical, iterant, iterative, metrical, rhythmic, rhythmical, seasonal, serial; arrested, checked, interrupted; fitful, spasmodic; infrequent, occasional, sporadic; discontinuing, discontinuous
con constant, perpetual; everlasting, interminable
ant continual, continuous; incessant, unceasing
intermix *vb syn* see MIX 1
intermixture *n syn* see MIXTURE
intermutual *adj syn* see COMMON 1
intern *vb syn* see IMPRISON
internal *adj* **1** *syn* see INNER 1
ant external
2 *syn* see INNER 2
3 *syn* see DOMESTIC 2
ant external
internals *n pl syn* see ENTRAILS
internuncio *n syn* see MESSENGER
interpenetrate *vb syn* see PERMEATE
interplay *vb syn* see INTERACT
interpolate *vb syn* see INTRODUCE 6
rel admit, enter; interlope, intrude; add, annex, append, superadd
con cancel, delete, erase, expunge
interpose *vb* **1** *syn* see INTRODUCE 6
rel cast, throw, toss; push, shove, thrust
2 to come between disagreeing elements <forced to *interpose* when the argument grew heated>
syn intercede, interfere, intermediate, intervene, mediate, step in
rel butt in, interlope, intrude, obtrude; intermeddle, meddle; arbitrate, moderate, negotiate
interpret *vb* **1** *syn* see EXPLAIN 1
rel exemplify, illustrate; annotate, gloss; comment, commentate
con contort, deform, distort; garble, misrepresent; misconstrue, misunderstand

---

syn synonym(s)   *rel* related word(s)
ant antonym(s)   *con* contrasted word(s)
idiom idiomatic equivalent(s)
‖ use limited; if in doubt, see a dictionary

2 *syn* see REPRESENT 1

interpretation *n* **1** *syn* see EXPLANATION 1
2 manner of artistic presentation in performance or adaptation or an instance of this <*interpretation* involves a re-creative effort by the performer>
syn reading, rendering, rendition, version

interpretive *adj syn* see EXPLANATORY

interreact *vb syn* see INTERACT

interregnum *n syn* see INTERLUDE

interrogate *vb syn* see ASK 1

interrogation *n* **1** *syn* see CROSS-EXAMINATION
2 *syn* see INQUIRY 2

interrogatory *n syn* see INQUIRY 2

interrupt *vb* **1** *syn* see ARREST 1
rel defer, intermit, postpone, suspend
2 to ask questions or make remarks while another is speaking <a chatterbox who habitually *interrupts* everyone>
syn break in, chime in, chip in
rel cut in, put in
idiom break in on (*or* upon)

interruption *n* **1** *syn* see GAP 3
rel rent, rift, rupture, split
2 *syn* see ABEYANCE

intersect *vb* to divide by passing through or across <parallel lines can never *intersect*>
syn crisscross, cross, crosscut, decussate, intercross
rel traverse; bisect

intersow *vb syn* see INTERFUSE 2

intersperse *vb syn* see INTERFUSE 2

intersprinkle *vb syn* see INTERFUSE 2

intertangle *vb syn* see ENTANGLE 1

intertie *vb syn* see INTERJOIN

intertrude *vb syn* see INTRUDE 1

intertwine *vb syn* see INTERWEAVE

intertwist *vb syn* see INTERWEAVE

interval *n* **1** *syn* see PAUSE
2 *syn* see INTERLUDE
3 *syn* see GAP 3

intervene *vb syn* see INTERPOSE 2
rel divide, part, separate, sever

intervolve *vb syn* see INTERWEAVE

interweave *vb* to blend or unite intimately <joy and melancholy are often closely *interwoven*>
syn interknit, interlace, intertwine, intertwist, intervolve, interwind, interwork, interwreathe, inweave
rel associate, join, link; blend, fuse, mix

interwind *vb syn* see INTERWEAVE

interwork *vb syn* see INTERWEAVE

interwreathe *vb syn* see INTERWEAVE

intestinal fortitude *n syn* see FORTITUDE

intestine *adj* **1** *syn* see DOMESTIC 2
2 *syn* see INNER 1

intimacy *n syn* see ACQUAINTANCE 1

intimate *vb syn* see SUGGEST 1
rel attest, bespeak, betoken, indicate
con air, express, utter, vent, voice; affirm, assert, aver, avouch, declare, profess

intimate *adj* **1** *syn* see INHERENT
2 *syn* see INNER 2
3 *syn* see FAMILIAR 1

rel nearest, next; affectionate, devoted, fond, loving; privy, secret
con distant, remote
4 having or marked by a warm personal relation <*intimate* friends for many years><an *intimate* friendship>
syn ‖buddy-buddy, chummy, cozy, pally, ‖palsy-walsy
idiom thick as thieves

intimate *n syn* see FRIEND
rel associate, companion, comrade, crony
con outsider, stranger

intimation *n* **1** *syn* see HINT 1
2 *syn* see HINT 2

intimidate *vb* to frighten or coerce into submission or obedience <refused to be *intimidated* by the manager>
syn bludgeon, bluster, ‖bounce, browbeat, bulldoze, bully, bullyrag, cow, dragoon, hector, ‖ruffle, strong-arm, terrorize
rel alarm, disquiet, frighten, scare, terrify; badger, bait, chivy, hound, ride; coerce, compel, constrain, force, oblige; ‖ruffianize
con blandish, cajole, coax, wheedle; induce, persuade, prevail

intimidator *n syn* see BULLY 1

into *prep syn* see TO 1

intolerable *adj syn* see INSUFFERABLE
ant tolerable

intolerant *adj* **1** unwilling or unable to endure with composure <he was inclined to be very *intolerant* of interruption>
syn impatient, unforbearing, unindulgent
rel contemptuous, disdainful; fractious, irritable, snappish, waspish; indignant, irate, outraged, stuffy, upset, worked up
con forbearing, indulgent, long-suffering, patient; resigned, uncomplaining
ant tolerant
2 *syn* see ILLIBERAL
rel inflexible, obdurate; antipathetic, averse, unsympathetic
con forbearing, indulgent, lenient
ant tolerant

intonation *n syn* see INFLECTION

in toto *adv syn* see ALL 1

intoxicant *n syn* see LIQUOR 2

intoxicated *adj* **1** significantly under the influence of alcoholic liquor <some people become *intoxicated* more easily than others>
syn alcoholized, ‖bagged, blind, ‖blotto, ‖boiled, ‖bombed, ‖boozed, ‖boozy, ‖buffy, ‖buzzed, ‖canned, ‖capernoited, cockeyed, ‖crocked, cut, ‖deleerit, disguised, drunk, drunken, fried, ‖half-seas over, inebriated, inebrious, ‖jagged, ‖juiced, ‖lit, ‖lit up, ‖loaded, looped, ‖lushed, muddled, ‖oiled, ‖organized, ‖pickled, ‖pie-eyed, ‖piped, pixilated, ‖plastered, polluted, ‖potted, rum-dum, ‖screwy, ‖shick, ‖shicker, ‖shot, slewed, slopped, sloppy, ‖smashed, soshed, sozzled, ‖spiflicated, squiffed, ‖stewed, stiff, ‖stinking, ‖stinko, stoned, ‖swacked, tanked, ‖tiddly, tight, unsober, wet, zonked

rel befuddled, bemused, besotted, dazed, dopey, fuddled, loopy, maudlin, sodden, soppy, sotted, tipsy

idiom disguised with drink, full as a tick, in drink (*or* liquor), in one's cups, in the bag, stewed to the gills, the worse for drink, three sheets in (*or* to) the wind, under the table, under the weather, with drink taken

con abstemious, abstinent, moderate, temperate

ant sober

2 profoundly and usually pleasantly moved <*intoxicated* with the beauty of the scene>

syn elated, excited, exhilarated, turned-on

rel affected, concerned, interested, moved; galvanized, piqued, quickened, stimulated

con disinterested, unconcerned; depressed, disheartened, distressed, saddened

intoxicating *adj syn* see EXCITING

intoxication *n syn* see EUPHORIA 2

intractable *adj* **1** *syn* see UNRULY 1

ant tractable

2 *syn* see OBSTINATE

ant tractable

intransigent *adj syn* see OBSTINATE

intrepid *adj syn* see BRAVE 1

ant craven

intricate *adj* **1** *syn* see COMPLEX 2

rel arduous, difficult, hard

2 *syn* see ELABORATE 2

intrigue *vb* **1** *syn* see INTEREST

2 *syn* see PLOT

intrigue *n* **1** *syn* see PLOT 2

2 *syn* see AMOUR 2

intrinsic *adj syn* see INHERENT

con added, annexed, appended, superadded

ant extrinsic

intrinsically *adv syn* see PER SE

introduce *vb* **1** *syn* see ENTER 2

rel inaugurate, induct, install; bring forward

2 *syn* see BROACH

3 to bring into practice or use <*introduce* reforms in the welfare system>

syn inaugurate, initiate, institute, launch, originate, set up, usher in

rel establish, found, organize; innovate, invent; unveil; pioneer

4 to cause to know each other personally <planned to *introduce* her to his mother>

syn acquaint, present, ‖quaint

5 *syn* see PRECEDE 3

6 to put among or between others <*introduced* several new lines of dialogue>

syn fill in, insert, insinuate, intercalate, interject, interpolate, interpose, throw in

rel inlay, inlet, inset; inject, instill; work in

con eject, evict, oust; eliminate, exclude

ant abstract; withdraw

introducer *n syn* see INNOVATOR

introduction *n* something that serves as a preliminary or antecedent <the crisis could be the *introduction* to a general war>

syn exordium, foreword, overture, preamble, preface, prelude, prelusion, proem, prolegomenon, prologue

introductory *adj* **1** *syn* see PRELIMINARY

ant closing, concluding

2 *syn* see INITIAL 1

introspection *n* the examination of one's own thought and feeling <a man much given to *introspection*>

syn heart-searching, self-contemplation, self-examination, self-observation, self-questioning, self-reflection, self-scrutiny, self-searching, soul-searching

rel contemplation, meditation, reflection; self-analysis

ant extrospection

intrude *vb* **1** to thrust or force in without permission, welcome, or fitness <constantly *intruded* himself into his sister's affairs>

syn butt in, chisel (in), cut in, horn in, intertrude, obtrude

rel encroach, entrench, infringe, invade, muscle, trespass; insinuate, intercalate, interject, interpolate, interpose, introduce; interfere, intervene; intermeddle, meddle; bother, disturb, pester

con retire, stand off, withdraw

2 *syn* see IMPOSE 5

intrusive *adj syn* see IMPERTINENT 2

rel butting in, intruding, obtruding

con bashful, coy, diffident, modest, retiring, shy

ant unintrusive

intuition *n* immediate apprehension or cognition <skeptical of the traditional woman's *intuition*>

syn anschauung, insight, intuitiveness

rel second sight, sixth sense

ant ratiocination

intuitive *adj syn* see INSTINCTIVE 1

rel direct, immediate, presentative

ant ratiocinative

intuitiveness *n syn* see INTUITION

inumbrate *vb syn* see SHADE

inundate *vb syn* see DELUGE 1

inundation *n syn* see FLOOD 2

inurbane *adj syn* see RUDE 6

ant urbane

inure *vb syn* see ACCUSTOM

rel discipline, train

inutile *adj syn* see WORTHLESS 1

ant utile

invade *vb* **1** to enter for conquest or plunder <the Danes *invaded* England>

syn foray, inroad, overrun, overswarm, raid

rel loot, pillage, plunder, ravage

2 *syn* see TRESPASS 2

rel impenetrate, interpenetrate, permeate, pervade

invalid *adj* **1** *syn* see ILLOGICAL

ant valid

2 *syn* see NULL

invalidate *vb syn* see ABOLISH 1

rel counteract, counterbalance, negative, neutralize, offset; discredit

---

syn synonym(s)   *rel* related word(s)
ant antonym(s)   *con* contrasted word(s)
idiom idiomatic equivalent(s)
‖ use limited; if in doubt, see a dictionary

ant validate
invaluable *adj syn* see PRECIOUS 1
ant worthless
invariable *adj* **1** *syn* see INFLEXIBLE 3
ant variable
2 *syn* see SAME 3
ant variable, varying
invariably *adv* **1** *syn* see ALWAYS 1
2 *syn* see EVER 3
invasion *n* a hostile entrance into the territory of
another <Hitler's *invasion* of Poland>
syn foray, incursion, inroad, irruption, raid
rel aggression, attack, offense, offensive; breach,
infraction, infringement, transgression, trespass,
violation; encroachment, entrenchment
invective *adj syn* see ABUSIVE
rel censorious, condemnatory, damnatory, denunciatory, reproachful
invective *n syn* see ABUSE
rel diatribe, jeremiad, philippic, tirade
inveigh (against) *vb syn* see OBJECT 1
inveigle *vb syn* see LURE
inveiglement *n syn* see LURE 2
invent *vb syn* see CONTRIVE 2
rel conceive, envision, imagine; create, mint,
produce, turn out; inaugurate, initiate
invention *n* a product of creative imagination <his
most famous *invention* is the electric light bulb>
syn brainchild, coinage, contrivance
rel concoction, contraption, innovation, novelty; creation, opus, original
inventive *adj* adept or prolific at producing new
things and ideas <had a very *inventive* turn of
mind> <she was an *inventive* genius>
syn creative, demiurgic, deviceful, ingenious,
innovational, innovative, innovatory, original,
originative
rel fertile, fruitful, productive, teeming; causative, constructive, formative
con sterile, uncreative, unproductive
ant uninventive
inventor *n* **1** *syn* see INNOVATOR
2 *syn* see FATHER 2
inventory *n* **1** *syn* see SUPPLY
2 *syn* see RESERVE
inventory *vb* **1** to make an itemized report or record of <will *inventory* all office supplies>
syn catalog, itemize, tally
rel list, record, register; enumerate, tabulate
idiom take account (*or* stock) of
2 *syn* see ITEMIZE 1
3 *syn* see EPITOMIZE 1
inveracity *n syn* see LIE
ant veracity
inverse *vb syn* see REVERSE 1
inversion *n syn* see REVERSAL 1
invert *vb syn* see REVERSE 1
rel flip, turn down, turn over
invert *n syn* see HOMOSEXUAL
invertebrate *n syn* see WEAKLING
invertebrate *adj syn* see WEAK 4
rel disorganized, structureless
inverted *adj* **1** *syn* see UPSIDE-DOWN 1
2 *syn* see HOMOSEXUAL

invest *vb* **1** *syn* see INITIATE 3
rel endow, endue; consecrate, honor
ant divest, strip
2 to make a formal grant of power or authority
<the Constitution *invests* the Congress with tax-
ation powers>
syn authorize, empower, vest
rel bequeath, endow
con hold back, keep back, reserve, withhold
ant divest
3 *syn* see ENFOLD 1
4 *syn* see BESIEGE
5 *syn* see INFUSE 1
investigate *vb syn* see EXPLORE
rel muckrake, poke, pry
investigation *n syn* see INQUIRY 1
rel observation, observing; sounding, survey,
surveying
investigative *adj syn* see INQUISITIVE 1
investigator *n syn* see DETECTIVE
investiture *n syn* see INITIATION
inveterate *adj* **1** firmly established or having
something firmly established <the *inveterate*
tendency to overlook the obvious>
syn bred-in-the-bone, confirmed, deep-dyed,
deep-rooted, deep-seated, dyed-in-the-wool, entrenched, hard-shell, irradicable, settled, sworn
rel accustomed, addicted, chronic, habituated;
customary, habitual, usual; hardened, indurated; established, fixed, set; inbred, innate;
abiding, enduring, persistent, persisting
2 *syn* see OLD 2
invidious *adj* **1** *syn* see LIBELOUS
2 *syn* see ENVIOUS
rel bitter; hateful
3 *syn* see REPUGNANT 1
rel abominable, detestable, hateful, odious
con agreeable, grateful, gratifying, pleasant,
pleasing
invidiousness *n syn* see ENVY
invigorate *vb syn* see STRENGTHEN 2
rel refresh, rejuvenate, renew, restore; rally,
rouse, stir; activate, animate, stimulate, vitalize,
vitaminize
ant debilitate
invigorating *adj* having an enlivening effect <an
invigorating discussion>
syn animating, bracing, exhilarating, exhilarative, quickening, stimulating, stimulative, tonic,
vitalizing
rel brisk, lively; fascinating, interesting
con anesthetic, numbing, somniferous
ant deadening
invincible *adj* **1** incapable of being conquered
<the team proved to be *invincible*>
syn impregnable, inconquerable, indomitable,
inexpugnable, invulnerable, unassailable, unbeatable, unconquerable, undefeatable
rel inviolable, untouchable; unattackable
con conquerable, subduable, surmountable,
vanquishable
ant vincible
2 *syn* see INSUPERABLE
ant vincible

inviolable *adj syn* see SACRED 3
 rel consecrated, hallowed; blessed, divine, holy; chaste, pure
 ant violable
inviolate *adj syn* see SACRED 3
 rel intact, perfect; faultless, flawless
 con desecrated, profaned; defiled, polluted
invisible *adj syn* see IMPERCEPTIBLE
 rel hidden, unseeable
 ant visible
invitation *n syn* see PROPOSAL
invite *vb* to request the presence or participation of <*invited* guests to dinner> <*invited* the major nations to confer>
 syn ask, bid
 rel call, call in, summon; court, solicit, woo; entice, inveigle, lure, tempt
invoice *n syn* see BILL 1
invoke *vb* 1 *syn* see BEG
 2 *syn* see ENFORCE
involuntary *adj syn* see SPONTANEOUS
 rel unintended, unintentional, unwitting
 ant voluntary
involve *vb* 1 to bring a person or thing into circumstances or a situation from which extrication is difficult <nations *involved* in war>
 syn embroil, implicate, mire, tangle; *compare* ENTANGLE 3
 rel catch up; draw (into)
 2 *syn* see INCLUDE
involved *adj* 1 *syn* see COMPLEX 2
 rel confused, muddled
 con easy, facile, simple
 2 *syn* see INTERESTED
 rel enmeshed, entangled
 ant uninvolved
involvement *n syn* see ENTANGLEMENT 1
invulnerable *adj syn* see INVINCIBLE 1
 ant vulnerable
inward *adj syn* see INNER 1
 con alien, extraneous, extrinsic, foreign
 ant outward
inward *n* 1 often **inwards** *pl syn* see INTERIOR
 2 **inwards** *pl syn* see ENTRAILS
inwardness *n syn* see ACQUAINTANCE 1
inweave *vb syn* see INTERWEAVE
iota *n syn* see PARTICLE
ipseity *n syn* see INDIVIDUALITY 4
irascible *adj* easily aroused to anger <an *irascible* fellow and hard to get along with>
 syn choleric, cranky, cross, hot-tempered, ireful, passionate, peppery, quick-tempered, ratty, ‖stomachy, temperish, testy, tetchy, touchy; *compare* CANTANKEROUS, IRRITABLE
 rel fractious, huffy, irritable, peevish, petulant, querulous, snappish, waspish; impatient, jittery, jumpy, nervous, restive; bristly, crabbed, surly
 con amiable, complaisant, good-natured, obliging; calm, quiet, relaxed; long-suffering, patient, tolerant
irate *adj syn* see ANGRY
ire *n syn* see ANGER
ire *vb syn* see ANGER 1
ireful *adj* 1 *syn* see ANGRY

 2 *syn* see IRASCIBLE
irenic *adj syn* see PACIFIC
 ant acrimonious
irk *vb* 1 *syn* see ANNOY 1
 rel discommode, incommode, inconvenience, trouble
 2 *syn* see TRY 2
irking *n syn* see ANNOYANCE 1
irksome *adj* tending to cause boredom or tedium <an *irksome* task>
 syn boresome, boring, drudging, tedious, tiresome, tiring
 rel dull, stupid; exhausting, fagging, fatiguing, wearisome
 con exciting, inspiring, provocative, stimulative, stirring
 ant absorbing, engrossing
iron *n, usu* **irons** *pl syn* see SHACKLE
iron *adj syn* see INFLEXIBLE 2
ironbound *adj syn* see ROUGH 1
ironclad *adj syn* see INFLEXIBLE 3
ironfisted *adj* 1 *syn* see STINGY
 2 *syn* see GRIM 3
ironhanded *adj syn* see RIGID 3
ironhead *n syn* see DUNCE
ironhearted *adj syn* see UNFEELING 2
 ant softhearted
ironic *adj syn* see SARDONIC
 rel biting, cutting, incisive, trenchant; caustic, mordant, scathing
‖**iron man** *n syn* see DOLLAR
irradiate *vb syn* see ILLUMINATE 2
irradicable *adj syn* see INVETERATE 1
irrational *adj syn* see ILLOGICAL
 rel crazy, demented, insane
 con logical, reasonable, sensible
 ant rational
irrealizable *adj syn* see IMPOSSIBLE 1
 ant realizable
irrebuttable *adj syn* see POSITIVE 3
 ant rebuttable
irreclaimable *adj syn* see IRRECOVERABLE
 ant reclaimable
irreconcilable *adj* incapable of being made consistent <the two versions of the story are completely *irreconcilable*>
 syn incompatible, inconformable, inconsistent
 rel discordant, discrepant, dissonant, inaccordant, incongruent, incongruous, inharmonious
 ant reconcilable
irrecoverable *adj* not capable of being recovered, regained, remedied, or rectified <suffered an *irrecoverable* loss in the fire>
 syn irreclaimable, irredeemable, irremediable, irreparable, irretrievable
 ant recoverable
irredeemable *adj syn* see IRRECOVERABLE
 ant redeemable
irreflective *adj syn* see CARELESS 1

---

syn synonym(s)   *rel* related word(s)
ant antonym(s)   *con* contrasted word(s)
idiom idiomatic equivalent(s)
‖ use limited; if in doubt, see a dictionary

ant reflective

irrefragable *adj syn* see INDESTRUCTIBLE

irrefrangible *adj syn* see INDESTRUCTIBLE

irrefutable *adj syn* see POSITIVE 3
ant refutable

irregular *adj* **1** not according with or explainable by law, rule, or custom <unusual problems require *irregular* solutions>
syn abnormal, anomalous, deviant, divergent, off-key, unnatural, unregular
rel aberrant, atypical; exceptional, odd, peculiar, queer, singular, strange, unique
con natural, normal, typical; accustomed, customary, habitual, usual, wonted
ant regular
2 *syn* see INFORMAL 1
3 *syn* see LOPSIDED
ant regular
4 *syn* see RANDOM
rel occasional, sporadic; erratic, fitful, spasmodic; inconstant, uneven, unsteady
5 *syn* see SPOTTY 1

irregular *n syn* see PARTISAN 2

irregularity *n syn* see INEQUALITY 1
ant regularity

irregularly *adv syn* see OCCASIONALLY
ant regularly

irrelative *adj syn* see IRRELEVANT
ant relative

irrelevant *adj* not applicable or pertinent <age should be *irrelevant* to employability>
syn extraneous, foreign, immaterial, impertinent, inapplicable, inappote, irrelative
rel inconsequential, insignificant, unimportant
idiom beside the point, neither here nor there, out of the question
con applicable, appurtenant, germane, material, pertinent, significant
ant relevant

irreligious *adj* lacking religious emotions, doctrines, or practices <an *irreligious* person but not openly hostile to organized religion>
syn godless, nonreligious, unreligious
rel indevout, undevout; ungodly, unholy, unsanctimonious; blasphemous, impious, profane, sacrilegious; amoral, unmoral
con devout, pious
ant religious

irremediable *adj* **1** *syn* see IRRECOVERABLE
ant remediable
2 *syn* see HOPELESS 2

irremovable *adj syn* see IMMOVABLE 1
ant removable

irreparable *adj* **1** *syn* see IRRECOVERABLE
ant reparable
2 *syn* see HOPELESS 2

irreprehensible *adj syn* see GOOD 11
ant reprehensible

irrepressible *adj* impossible to repress, restrain, or control <an *irrepressible* joy over his brother's good fortune>
syn insuppressible, insuppressive, irrestrainable, uncontainable, uncontrollable, unrestrainable

rel bubbling over, effervescent, enthusiastic, rhapsodical
ant repressible

irreproachable *adj* **1** *syn* see GOOD 11
2 *syn* see IMPECCABLE 1

irresoluble *adj syn* see INSOLUBLE
ant resoluble

irresolute *adj syn* see VACILLATING 2
ant resolute

irresolution *n syn* see HESITATION
ant resolution

irresolvable *adj syn* see INSOLUBLE
ant resolvable

irresponsible *adj* lacking in responsibility <*irresponsible* behavior>
syn carefree, careless, feckless, incautious, reckless, uncareful, wild
rel undependable, unreliable, untrustworthy; unaccountable, unanswerable
con careful, cautious, discreet, heedful; dependable, reliable, trustworthy
ant responsible

irrestrainable *adj syn* see IRREPRESSIBLE
ant restrainable

irretrievable *adj syn* see IRRECOVERABLE
ant retrievable

irreverent *adj syn* see IMPIOUS 1
ant reverent

irreverential *adj syn* see IMPIOUS 1
ant reverential

irreversible *adj syn* see IRREVOCABLE
ant reversible

irrevocable *adj* incapable of being recalled or revoked <an *irrevocable* decision of the Supreme Court>
syn irreversible, nonreversible, unrepealable
rel constant, established, fixed; immutable, unchangeable, unmodifiable
con repealable, reversible; alterable, changeable, modifiable
ant revocable

irritable *adj* easily exasperated <the miserable weather made us all *irritable*>
syn disagreeable, fractious, fretful, huffy, peevish, pettish, petulant, ‖pindling, prickish, prickly, querulent, querulential, querulous, raspish, raspy, snappish, snappy, twitty, waspish, waspy, whiny; *compare* CANTANKEROUS, IRASCIBLE
rel cranky, cross, testy, touchy; choleric, irascible, splenetic
con amiable, complaisant, good-natured, obliging; affable, cordial, genial, gracious, sociable
ant easygoing

irritant *n syn* see ANNOYANCE 3

irritate *vb* to excite to angry annoyance <his rude interruptions really *irritated* her>
syn aggravate, burn (up), exasperate, gall, get, grate, huff, inflame, nettle, peeve, pique, provoke, put out, rile, roil; *compare* ANNOY 1
rel abrade, bother, ‖bug, chafe, exercise, fret, irk, ruffle, try, vex; anger, enrage, incense, infuriate, madden; affront, offend
con appease, conciliate, mollify, pacify, placate, propitiate; delight, gladden, gratify, please

irrupt *vb syn* see ERUPT 1
irruption *n syn* see INVASION
Ishmael *n syn* see OUTCAST
Ishmaelite *n syn* see OUTCAST
island *vb syn* see ISOLATE
isochronal *adj syn* see INTERMITTENT
isochronous *adj syn* see INTERMITTENT
isolate *vb* to set apart from others <the jury was *isolated* for several days>
  syn close off, cut off, enisle, insulate, island, segregate, separate, sequester
  rel quarantine; block (off); abstract, detach, disengage, remove; divide, part, sever, sunder
  con associate, connect, join, link, unite
isolate *adj syn* see ALONE 1
isolated *adj syn* see ALONE 1
  rel retired, secluded, withdrawn; abandoned, deserted, forsaken, stranded
isolation *n syn* see SOLITUDE
issue *n* **1** *syn* see OFFSPRING
  2 *syn* see EFFECT 1
  3 *syn* see PROBLEM 2
  rel matter; subject, topic
issue *vb* **1** *syn* see SPRING 1
  2 *syn* see EMIT 2
  3 *syn* see PUBLISH 2
italicize *vb syn* see EMPHASIZE
itch *n* **1** *syn* see DESIRE 1
  2 *syn* see LUST 2
itch *vb syn* see LONG
itchy *adj syn* see COVETOUS

item *adv syn* see ALSO 2
item *n syn* see POINT 1
  rel component, piece; incidental, minutia
itemize *vb* **1** to set down in detail or by particulars <*itemize* deductions on a tax form>
  syn enumerate, inventory, list, particularize, specialize, specify; *compare* SPECIFY 3
  rel circumstantiate, document; count, number; cite, instance, mention; spell out
  ant summarize
  2 *syn* see INVENTORY
itemized *adj syn* see CIRCUMSTANTIAL
  ant summarized
iterate *vb syn* see REPEAT

itinerant *adj* traveling from place to place <*itinerant* preachers>
  syn ambulant, ambulatory, deambulatory, itinerate, nomadic, perambulant, perambulatory, peripatetic, roving, vagabond, vagrant, wandering, wayfaring
  rel rambling, ranging, roaming; moving, shifting
itinerate *adj syn* see ITINERANT
itsy–bitsy *adj syn* see TINY
itty–bitty *adj syn* see TINY
||**ivory** *n often* **ivories** *pl syn* see DICE
ivory–tower *adj syn* see IMPRACTICAL 1
  ant down-to-earth
ivory–towered *adj syn* see IMPRACTICAL 1
ivory–towerish *adj syn* see IMPRACTICAL 1

J

jab *vb syn* see POKE 1
jab *n* **1** *syn* see POKE 1
  2 *syn* see PRICK
jabber *vb syn* see GIBBER
jabber *n* **1** *syn* see GIBBERISH 1
  2 *syn* see CHATTER
jabberer *n syn* see CHATTERBOX
jabberwocky *n syn* see GIBBERISH 1
jack *n* **1** *syn* see MARINER
  2 *syn* see FLAG
  ‖**3** *syn* see MONEY
jack (up) *vb syn* see RAISE 9
jackass *n* **1** *syn* see DONKEY 1
  2 *syn* see FOOL 1
jacket *n syn* see HIDE
jackleg *adj syn* see AMATEURISH
jackleg lawyer *n syn* see PETTIFOGGER
jackpot *n syn* see POT 3
jack-tar *n syn* see MARINER
jade *n* **1** *syn* see WANTON
  2 *syn* see MINX
jade *vb* **1** *syn* see TIRE 1
  rel cloy, pall, sate, satiate, surfeit; emasculate,
  enervate, unman, unnerve; depress, oppress,
  weigh
  con rejuvenate, renew, restore
  ant refresh
  2 *syn* see SATIATE
jaded *adj* **1** *syn* see TIRED 1
  ant refreshed
  2 *syn* see SATIATED
‖jag *n syn* see PRICK
jag *n syn* see BINGE 1
‖jag *vb syn* see CARRY 1
jagged *adj syn* see ROUGH 1
‖jagged *adj syn* see INTOXICATED 1
jail *n* a building or institution for the confinement
  of persons held in lawful custody <sent to *jail* for
  perjury>
  syn bastille, ‖big house, bridewell, ‖brig,
  ‖bucket, ‖caboose, ‖calaboose, ‖can, ‖carcel,
  ‖chokey, ‖clink, ‖college, cooler, coop, freezer,
  guardroom, ‖hoosegow, jug, keep, lockup, pen,
  penitentiary, ‖pokey, prison, reformatory, rock
  pile, skookum-house, slammer, ‖stir, stockade
  idiom house of correction
jail *vb syn* see IMPRISON
  ant release
jailbird *n syn* see CONVICT
jake *n syn* see RUSTIC
jakes *n pl but sing or pl in constr syn* see PRIVY 1
jalopy *n* a dilapidated old automobile <bought a
  jalopy for $50>
  syn clunker, crate, dog, heap, junker, wreck
jam *vb* **1** *syn* see PRESS 1
  rel tamp, wad
  2 *syn* see CRAM 1
  3 *syn* see PRESS 7

jam *n syn* see PREDICAMENT
jam *n* a rich spread prepared by boiling fruit and
  sugar until the mixture thickens <enjoyed his
  mother's tasty berry *jams*>
  syn confiture, conserve, preserve
  rel jelly, marmalade
jam-full *adj syn* see FULL 1
jammed *adj syn* see FULL 1
jam-pack *vb syn* see CRAM 1
jam-packed *adj syn* see FULL 1
jangle *vb syn* see CLASH 2
jangle *n syn* see DIN
jape *n syn* see JOKE 1
jar *vb* **1** *syn* see CLASH 2
  2 *syn* see SHAKE 2
jar *n syn* see IMPACT 1
  rel fluctuation, sway, vibration; agitation, disturbance, upset
jargon *n* **1** *syn* see TERMINOLOGY
  2 *syn* see DIALECT 2
  rel idiom, speech; abracadabra, gibberish
jarring *adj syn* see HARSH 3
  ant soothing
jaundiced *adj syn* see BIASED 2
jaunt *n syn* see EXCURSION 1
‖jaw *n syn* see BACK TALK
jaw *vb* **1** *syn* see SCOLD 1
  2 *syn* see CHAT 1
jay *n syn* see RUSTIC
jazz *n syn* see NONSENSE 2
jealous *adj* **1** intolerant of rivalry or unfaithfulness
  <her husband was *jealous* of her flirting with
  other men>
  syn possessive, possessory
  rel covetous, demanding; grasping, grudging;
  envious, green-eyed, invidious; mistrustful, suspicious; doubting, questioning
  con tolerant, trusting, understanding
  2 *syn* see ENVIOUS
  3 *syn* see SUSPICIOUS 2
jealousy *n syn* see ENVY
jeer *vb syn* see SCOFF
  con fawn, toady, truckle; approve, endorse, OK,
  sanction
jejune *adj syn* see INSIPID 3
  rel slight, slim, tenuous, thin; arid, dry
jell *vb syn* see COAGULATE
  rel stiffen, thicken; cohere, stick
jellify *vb syn* see COAGULATE
jelly *vb syn* see COAGULATE
jellyfish *n syn* see WEAKLING
jeopard *vb syn* see ENDANGER
jeopardize *vb syn* see ENDANGER
jeopardous *adj syn* see DANGEROUS 1
jeopardy *n syn* see DANGER
  rel exposure; liability, openness, sensitiveness,
  susceptibility; accident, chance, hap
  ant safety

jeopardy *vb syn* see ENDANGER

jeremiad *n syn* see TIRADE

jerk *vb* to act on with or make a sudden sharp quick movement <*jerked* to one side> <*jerk* a root from the ground>
syn lug, lurch, snap, twitch, vellicate, yank
rel drag, pull; fling, sling, throw, toss; wrench, wrest, wring

jerk *n syn* see FOOL 1

jerkwater town *n syn* see BURG

jerry–build *vb syn* see THROW UP 1

jest *n* 1 *syn* see JOKE 1
rel banter, chaff, jolly; derision, ridicule, twit
2 *syn* see FUN 1
con gravity, seriousness, soberness
ant earnest
3 *syn* see LAUGHINGSTOCK

jest *vb* 1 *syn* see SCOFF
2 *syn* see BANTER

jestee *n syn* see LAUGHINGSTOCK

jester *n* 1 *syn* see FOOL 2
2 *syn* see HUMORIST 2

jet *adj syn* see BLACK 1

jet *vb syn* see SQUIRT

jetsam *n syn* see DRIFTWOOD

jet set *n syn* see SMART SET

jettison *n syn* see DISPOSAL 2

jettison *vb syn* see DISCARD
ant salvage

jetty *n syn* see WHARF

jetty *adj syn* see BLACK 1

jewel *n syn* see PARAGON

jewel *vb syn* see BEJEWEL

jezebel *n syn* see WANTON

jib *vb syn* see DEMUR

jibe *vb syn* see AGREE 4

‖**jiff** *n syn* see INSTANT 1

jiffy *n syn* see INSTANT 1

jig *n syn* see TRICK 1

jigger *n* 1 *syn* see DOODAD
2 *syn* see GADGET 1

‖**jiggery–pokery** *n syn* see NONSENSE 2

jiggle *vb syn* see SHAKE 3

jillion *n syn* see SCAD

jim–dandy *n syn* see ‖DILLY

‖**jimjams** *n syn* see JITTERS

‖**jimmies** *n syn* see JITTERS

jimmy *vb syn* see PRY

jingle *vb* to make a repeated sharp light ringing sound <the coins *jingled* in his pocket>
syn chink, chinkle, clink, tingle, tinkle
rel clack, clatter, rattle

jinx *n* something that is felt or meant to bring bad luck <her continual bad luck seemed due to a *jinx*>
syn hex, hoodoo, Indian sign, voodoo, whammy
rel charm, enchantment, spell; curse, evil eye

jitters *n pl* a sense of panic or extreme nervousness <got the *jitters* whenever he thought of the money he had lost>
syn ‖all-overs, dither, heebie-jeebies, ‖jimjams, ‖jimmies, jumps, shakes, shivers, whim-whams, willies

jittery *adj syn* see NERVOUS

‖**jive** *vb syn* see BANTER

job *n* 1 *syn* see TASK 1
rel affair, concern, matter, thing
2 a regular remunerative employment <held two *jobs* to make ends meet>
syn appointment, berth, billet, connection, office, place, position, post, situation, spot; *compare* WORK 1
rel assignment, engagement, posting; calling, employment, occupation, pursuit; profession, trade, vocation; niche, opening, slot
3 *syn* see WORK 1
4 *syn* see TASK 2

job *vb syn* see DUPE

jobless *adj syn* see UNEMPLOYED

jockey *vb syn* see MANIPULATE 2

jocose *adj syn* see WITTY
rel playful, roguish, sportive, waggish, whimsical; comic, comical, droll, laughable, ludicrous; blithe, jocund, jolly, jovial
con demure, earnest, grave, sedate, serious, sober, solemn, staid
ant lugubrious

jocular *adj syn* see WITTY
rel jolly, jovial, merry; playful, sportive; comic, comical, droll, laughable, ludicrous
con earnest, grave, serious, sober, solemn

jocularity *n syn* see MIRTH

jocund *adj syn* see MERRY
rel mischievous, playful, sportive
con dour, gloomy, glum, morose, saturnine, sullen; grave, sedate, serious, solemn, somber, staid

jocundity *n syn* see MIRTH

jog *vb syn* see POKE 1
rel agitate, shake

joggle *vb syn* see SHAKE 3

john *n syn* see TOILET

John Law *n syn* see POLICEMAN

johnny *n syn* see TOILET

join *vb* 1 to bring or come together into some manner of union <the couple were *joined* in marriage soon thereafter>
syn associate, bracket, coadunate, coagment, coalesce, combine, compound, concrete, conjoin, conjugate, connect, couple, link, marry, one, relate, unite, wed, yoke
rel agree, concur, cooperate; articulate, concatenate, integrate; affix, attach, fasten; knit, weave; bind, tie, tie up
con separate, sever, sunder; detach, disengage; disembarrass, disentangle, untangle
ant disjoin, part
2 *syn* see ADJOIN

join (up) *vb syn* see ENTER 3

joining *n syn* see JOINT 1

joint *n* 1 a place where two or more things are united <the leak was found at a *joint* in the pipeline>

---

syn synonym(s)   *rel* related word(s)
ant antonym(s)   *con* contrasted word(s)
idiom idiomatic equivalent(s)
‖ use limited; if in doubt, see a dictionary

syn connection, coupling, joining, junction, juncture, seam, union
rel crux, link, tie; interconnection; abutment, articulation, suture; concourse, confluence, meeting
2 *syn* see DIVE

joint *adj syn* see COMMON 1

jointly *adv syn* see TOGETHER 3

joke *n* **1** a remark, story, or action intended to evoke laughter <had a good memory for *jokes*>
syn crack, drôlerie, drollery, gag, jape, jest, quip, sally, waggery, wisecrack, witticism, ‖yak
rel antic, caper, dido, monkeyshine, prank; bijouterie, bon mot; burlesque, caricature, parody, quiz, rib; badinage, persiflage, raillery; facetiousness, humorousness, jocoseness, jocularity, wittiness; humor, repartee, sarcasm, wit
2 *syn* see FUN 1
3 *syn* see LAUGHINGSTOCK

joke *vb syn* see BANTER

joker *n* **1** *syn* see WAG 1
2 *syn* see HUMORIST 2
3 *syn* see ZANY 2

jokester *n* **1** *syn* see HUMORIST 2
2 *syn* see ZANY 2

jollity *n* **1** *syn* see MIRTH
rel blitheness; disport, frolic, gambol, play, rollick, romp, sport
con earnestness, gravity, sedateness, seriousness, solemnity, staidness
ant somberness
2 *syn* see MERRYMAKING

jolly *adj syn* see MERRY
rel frolicsome, mischievous, playful, roguish, sportive, waggish
con earnest, grave, sedate, serious, solemn, staid; doleful, dolorous, lugubrious, rueful
ant somber

jolly *vb syn* see BANTER
rel blandish, cajole

jolt *vb syn* see SHOCK 2

jolt *n* **1** *syn* see IMPACT 1
2 *syn* see DRAM

jongleur *n syn* see BARD 1

josh *vb syn* see BANTER

joskin *n syn* see RUSTIC

jostle *vb syn* see PUSH 2

jot *n syn* see PARTICLE

jounce *n syn* see IMPACT 1

journal *n* a publication that appears at regular intervals <a monthly scientific *journal*>
syn magazine, newspaper, organ, periodical, review

journey *n* passing or a passage from one place to another <at that time it was a four day *journey* from Boston to New York> <she was tired though their *journey* was barely begun>
syn expedition, peregrination(s), travel(s), trek, trip; *compare* TRIP 1
rel excursion, jaunt, junket, sally, tour; cruise, voyage; pilgrimage, progress, safari

journey *vb syn* see GO 1

jovial *adj syn* see MERRY

rel facetious, humorous, jocose, jocular; affable, genial, sociable; amiable, good-natured; bantering, chaffing, jollying, joshing
con dour, gloomy, glum, morose, saturnine, sullen; grave, sedate, serious, solemn, staid

joviality *n syn* see MIRTH

joy *n syn* see PLEASURE 2
rel ecstasy, rapture, transport
ant sorrow; misery

joyance *n syn* see PLEASURE 2

joyful *adj syn* see GLAD 1
rel buoyant, effervescent, expansive
con despairing, desperate, despondent, forlorn, hopeless; depressed, oppressed, weighed down
ant joyless

‖**joy girl** *n syn* see PROSTITUTE

‖**joyhouse** *n syn* see BROTHEL

‖**joy-juice** *n syn* see LIQUOR 2

joyless *adj* **1** *syn* see SAD 2
2 *syn* see GLOOMY 3

joyous *adj syn* see GLAD 1
rel ecstatic, rapturous, transported
con doleful, dolorous, melancholy; miserable, wretched
ant lugubrious

jubilance *n syn* see EXULTATION

jubilant *adj syn* see EXULTANT

jubilate *vb syn* see EXULT

jubilation *n syn* see EXULTATION

judge *n* **1** a person who impartially decides unsettled questions or controversial issues <the *judge* declared the ruling invalid>
syn arbiter, arbitrator, referee, umpire
rel intermediary, mediator, negotiator; conciliator, peacemaker, reconciler
2 an official entrusted with administration of laws <the *judge* gave the defendant a suspended sentence>
syn ‖beak, court, justice, magistrate

judge *vb* **1** to decide something in dispute or controversy upon its merits and upon evidence <the committee will *judge* the truth of the testimony>
syn adjudge, adjudicate, arbitrate, referee, umpire
rel decide, determine, rule, settle
2 *syn* see INFER
rel demonstrate, prove, show; check, test, try
3 *syn* see ESTIMATE 3

judgmatic *adj syn* see WISE 2

judgment *n* **1** *syn* see INFERENCE 1
rel decision, determination, ruling; belief, conviction, opinion, persuasion, view
2 *syn* see INFERENCE 2
3 *syn* see ESTIMATION 1
4 *syn* see SENSE 6
rel astuteness, perspicacity, sagacity, shrewdness; acumen, discernment, insight, penetration

judicious *adj syn* see WISE 2
rel rational, reasonable; dispassionate, equitable, fair, objective
con irrational, thoughtless, unreasonable; ill-considered
ant injudicious; asinine

jug *n syn* see JAIL

jug *vb syn* see IMPRISON
juggle *vb syn* see DECEIVE
‖**juice** *n syn* see LIQUOR 2
‖**juiced** *adj syn* see INTOXICATED 1
juicy *adj syn* see SUCCULENT
juju *n syn* see CHARM 2
jumble *vb* **1** *syn* see CONFUSE 5
  2 *syn* see DISORDER 1
jumble *n* **1** *syn* see CLUTTER 2
  2 *syn* see MISCELLANY 1
jumbo *adj syn* see HUGE
jump *vb* **1** to move suddenly through space by or
  as if by muscular action <*jumped* across the
  open trench>
  syn bounce, bound, hop, hurdle, leap, lop, saltate, spring, vault
  2 *syn* see START 1
  3 *syn* see RAISE 9
jump (in *or* into) *vb syn* see PITCH IN 1
jump (off) *vb syn* see BEGIN 1
jumps *n pl syn* see JITTERS
jumpy *adj syn* see NERVOUS
  idiom on pins and needles
junction *n* **1** *syn* see CONCOURSE
  2 *syn* see JOINT 1
juncture *n* **1** *syn* see JOINT 1
  2 a critical or crucial time or state of affairs <was
  at a *juncture* where he had to make a decision>
  syn contingency, crisis, crossroad(s), emergency, exigency, pass, pinch, strait, turning
  point, zero hour
  rel condition, posture, situation, state, status;
  plight, predicament, quandary
  3 *syn* see POINT 7
jungle *n* **1** *syn* see CLUTTER 2
  2 *syn* see MAZE 1
junk *n syn* see REFUSE
junk *vb syn* see DISCARD
junker *n syn* see JALOPY
junket *n syn* see EXCURSION 1
junking *n syn* see DISPOSAL 2
Junoesque *adj syn* see CURVACEOUS
jurisdiction *n syn* see POWER 1
  rel bounds, confines, limits; compass, range,
  reach, scope; bailiwick, domain, field, province,
  sphere, territory
just *adj* **1** *syn* see WELL-FOUNDED
  2 *syn* see TRUE 3
  3 being what is called for by circumstances or
  accepted standards <punishments once considered fair and *just* are now held to be cruel, excessive, and unreasonable>
  syn appropriate, condign, deserved, due, merited, requisite, rhadamanthine, right, rightful,
  suitable; *compare* FIT 1
  rel fit, fitting, meet, proper
  con farfetched, irrelevant, remote, unconnected;
  improper, inapplicable, inapposite, inappropriate; abusive, cruel, harsh
  ant unjust
  4 *syn* see UPRIGHT 2
  rel rigid, strict; dependable, reliable, tried,
  trustworthy
  5 *syn* see FAIR 4

  rel aloof; condign, due, rightful
  ant unjust
  6 *syn* see FIT 1
just *adv* **1** as stated or indicated without deviation
  <*just* six inches long>
  syn accurately, bang, exactly, precisely, right,
  sharp, ‖smack-dab, spang, square, squarely
  rel definitely, directly, expressly, unmistakably
  con almost, nearly; approximately, imprecisely,
  inaccurately, inexactly, loosely
  2 by a very small margin <*just* enough food for
  one meal>
  syn barely, hardly, scarce, scarcely
  rel almost, approximately, nearly
  con copiously, fully, generously, lavishly, un-
  stintedly, unstintingly
  3 no more than <*just* a note to remind you>
  syn but, merely, only, simply
  idiom nothing but
  4 *syn* see ALL 1
  5 *syn* see EVEN 1
just about *adv syn* see NEARLY
justice *n* **1** the action, practice, or obligation of
  awarding each his just due <his *justice* was stern
  but absolutely fair>
  syn equity
  rel evenness, fairness, impartiality
  con foul play, inequity, unjustness; bias, leaning, one-sidedness, partiality
  ant injustice
  2 *syn* see JUDGE 2
justifiable *adj* capable of being justified <thought
  her absence was not *justifiable*>
  syn condonable, defensible, excusable, tenable,
  vindicable, warrantable
  rel admissible, allowable, legitimate, reasonable; forgivable, pardonable, remissible
  ant unjustifiable
justification *n* **1** *syn* see EXPLANATION 2
  2 *syn* see APOLOGY 1
justified *adj syn* see WELL-FOUNDED
  ant unjustified
justify *vb* **1** *syn* see MAINTAIN 2
  rel demonstrate, prove; back, support, uphold
  con confute, disprove, refute
  2 *syn* see CONFIRM 2
  3 *syn* see EXPLAIN 3
  rel extenuate, gloss, gloze, palliate, whitewash
  con accuse, arraign, incriminate, indict; blame,
  condemn, denounce
  4 to constitute sufficient grounds <thought the
  storm warning *justified* his leaving early>
  syn warrant
  rel allow, permit; approve, authorize, sanction
justly *adv syn* see WELL 1
jut *vb* **1** *syn* see BULGE
  rel elongate, extend, lengthen
  2 *syn* see HANG 4
jut *n syn* see PROJECTION 1

---

syn synonym(s)   *rel* related word(s)
ant antonym(s)   *con* contrasted word(s)
idiom idiomatic equivalent(s)
‖ use limited; if in doubt, see a dictionary

juvenile *adj syn* see YOUNG 1
 ant adult
juvenile *n syn* see CHILD 1

juvenility *n syn* see YOUTH 1
juxtaposed *adj syn* see ADJACENT 3

K

‖**kale** *n* *syn* see MONEY

keck *vb* *syn* see RETCH

keel (over) *vb* *syn* see FALL 2

keen *adj* **1** *syn* see SHARP 1
  2 *syn* see ENTHUSIASTIC
  3 *syn* see EAGER
  rel fervent, fervid, perfervid; fierce, intense, vehement; fired
  con apathetic, impassive, phlegmatic, stolid; languid, listless
  4 *syn* see SHARP 4
  5 *syn* see ACUTE 3
  con dull, obtuse
  6 *syn* see LIVELY 1
  ‖**7** *syn* see MARVELOUS 2

keenly *adv* *syn* see HARD 6

keenness *n* **1** *syn* see EDGE 2
  2 *syn* see WIT 3

keep *vb* **1** *syn* see OBEY
  ant neglect
  2 to notice or honor a day, occasion, or deed <*keep* the Sabbath by refraining from work>
  syn celebrate, commemorate, observe, solemnize
  rel regard, respect; bless, consecrate, sanctify; honor, laud, praise
  idiom keep the faith
  con disregard, forget, ignore, neglect, omit, overlook, slight; contravene, infringe, transgress, violate
  ant break
  3 *syn* see STOCK
  4 *syn* see RESTRAIN 1
  ant release
  5 to hold in one's possession or under one's control <*kept* all the money for himself>
  syn detain, hold, hold back, keep back, keep out, reserve, retain, withhold
  rel conserve, preserve, save; enjoy, have, own, possess; conduct, control, direct, manage
  con cast, discard, junk; refuse, reject, repudiate, spurn; abandon, resign, surrender, yield
  ant relinquish
  6 *syn* see REFRAIN 1
  7 *syn* see CONDUCT 3

keep *n* **1** *syn* see LIVING
  2 *syn* see JAIL

keep back *vb* **1** *syn* see KEEP 5
  2 *syn* see DENY 2

keeper *n* *syn* see CUSTODIAN

keeping *n* **1** *syn* see CUSTODY
  2 *syn* see PRESERVATION 1

keep off *vb* *syn* see FEND (off)

keep out *vb* *syn* see KEEP 5

keepsake *n* *syn* see REMEMBRANCE 3

keep up *vb* *syn* see MAINTAIN 1

keg *n* *syn* see CASK

‖**keister** *n* *syn* see BUTTOCKS

kelter *n* *syn* see REFUSE

ken *n* the extent of one's recognition, comprehension, perception, understanding, or knowledge <abstractions that are beyond the *ken* of small children>
  syn horizon, purview, range, reach
  rel comprehension, grasp, perception, understanding

kept woman *n* *syn* see HARLOT 1

kerchief *n* **1** a square of cloth used as a head covering or scarf <wore a *kerchief* around his neck>
  syn babushka, bandanna
  2 *syn* see HANDKERCHIEF

kernel *n* *syn* see SUBSTANCE 2

key *n* *syn* see PASSPORT

kibitzer *n* *syn* see BUSYBODY

kick *vb* **1** *syn* see OBJECT 1
  rel combat, fight, oppose, resist, withstand; anathematize, condemn, curse, damn, execrate
  idiom put up a fight (against)
  2 *syn* see COMPLAIN

kick *n* *syn* see THRILL

‖**kick around** *vb* *syn* see DISCUSS 1

kick back *vb* *syn* see BACKFIRE

kicker *n* *syn* see GROUCH

‖**kick in** *vb* **1** *syn* see CONTRIBUTE 1
  2 *syn* see DIE 1

kick off *vb* **1** *syn* see BEGIN 1
  ‖**2** *syn* see DIE 1

kick out *vb* **1** *syn* see DISMISS 3
  2 *syn* see EJECT 1

kickshaw *n* *syn* see DELICACY

kid *n* *syn* see CHILD 1

kid *vb* **1** *syn* see DUPE
  2 *syn* see BANTER

kidnap *vb* to carry off a person surreptitiously for an illegal purpose <an ex-convict *kidnapped* the child for ransom>
  syn abduct, ‖snatch, spirit (away)
  rel shanghai, waylay; coax, decoy, entice, inveigh, lure, seduce
  idiom make off with
  con deliver, ransom, redeem, rescue; bring (back), give back, restore, return

kidney *n* *syn* see TYPE

kid stuff *n* *syn* see SNAP 1

kill *vb* **1** to deprive of life <found it hard to *kill* animals>
  syn carry off, cut off, destroy, dispatch, down, finish, lay low, put away, scrag, slay, take off; *compare* MURDER 1

---

syn synonym(s)   *rel* related word(s)
ant antonym(s)   *con* contrasted word(s)
idiom idiomatic equivalent(s)
‖ use limited; if in doubt, see a dictionary

rel butcher, choke, drown, massacre, poison, shoot, slaughter, suffocate; knife, sacrifice, stifle; annihilate, exterminate, ruin
idiom do (*or* make) away with, do for, put out of the way, put (*or* do) to death, put to sleep, take one's life
2 syn see VETO
killer *n syn* see MURDERER
killing *n syn* see MURDER
kiln *vb syn* see FIRE 6
kilter *n syn* see ORDER 10
kin *n* **1 syn** see FAMILY 1
2 the members of one's immediate or extended family <all our *kin* gathered to celebrate great grandma's birthday>
syn cousinage, cousinhood, kinfolk, kinsmen
3 syn see RELATIVE
kind *n syn* see TYPE
kind *adj* showing or having a gentle considerate nature <mother was a *kind* person, always willing to help others>
syn benign, benignant, good-hearted, kindly
rel altruistic, benevolent, charitable, eleemosynary, humane, humanitarian, openhearted, philanthropic, propitious; compassionate, kindhearted, responsive, sympathetic, tender, warm, warmhearted; clement, forbearing, indulgent, lenient, merciful, tolerant; affable, amiable, cordial, genial, good-humored, good-natured, good-tempered, sweet-tempered; complaisant, obliging, gentle, good
con cruel, fell, fierce, inhuman, savage; hard, harsh, rough; grim, implacable, merciless, unrelenting
ant unkind
kindhearted *adj syn* see TENDER
kindle *vb* **1 syn** see LIGHT 1
rel blaze, flame, flare, glow; excite, provoke, stimulate; arouse, foment, incite, instigate, rouse, stir
ant smother
2 syn see STIR 1
ant stifle
kindless *adj syn* see ANTIPATHETIC 2
kindliness *n syn* see GOODWILL 1
ant unkindliness
kindly *adj syn* see KIND
rel gracious, sociable; friendly, neighborly; attentive, considerate, thoughtful
con malevolent, malicious, malign, spiteful
ant unkindly; acrid (*of temper, attitudes, comments*)
kindly *adv syn* see WELL 2
kindness *n syn* see FAVOR 4
kind of *adv syn* see SOMEWHAT 2
kindred *n syn* see FAMILY 1
kindred *adj syn* see RELATED
ant alien
kinfolk *n pl syn* see KIN 2
king *n syn* see MAGNATE
kingdom come *n syn* see HEAVEN 2
kinglike *adj syn* see KINGLY
kingly *adj* of, relating to, or befitting a king <a *kingly* entourage>

syn kinglike, majestic, monarchal, monarchial, monarchical, regal, royal, sovereign
rel imperious, lordly, masterful, powerful, puissant; imperial, princely, queenly
kinky *adj syn* see OUTLANDISH 3
kinsman *n* **1 syn** see RELATIVE
2 kinsmen *pl syn* see KIN 2
kinswoman *n syn* see RELATIVE
kismet *n syn* see FATE
kiss *vb* **1** to touch with the lips especially as a sign of affection <*kissed* his mother good night>
syn buss, lip, osculate, peck, smack, smooch, ‖smoodge, ‖smouch
2 syn see BRUSH
‖**kisser** *n syn* see FACE 1
kiss off *vb syn* see DISMISS 5
kite *vb syn* see GET OUT 1
kittenish *adj syn* see PLAYFUL 1
kitty *n syn* see POT 3
klutz *n syn* see OAF 2
knack *n* **1 syn** see GIFT 2
rel quickness, readiness
ant ineptitude
2 syn see ABILITY 2
3 syn see HANG
knapsack *n syn* see BACKPACK
knave *n syn* see VILLIAN 1
knavish *adj syn* see DISHONEST
knell *vb syn* see RING
knickknack *n* a small or trivial ornamental article <a collection of pretty *knickknacks* was displayed on the mantel>
syn bauble, bibelot, curio, dido, gewgaw, gimcrack, novelty, objet d'art, pretty-pretty, rattletrap(s), toy, trifle, trinket, whatnot, whigmaleerie
rel souvenir; bric-a-brac, virtu; miniature; kickshaw, notion; trumpery
knifelike *adj syn* see SHARP 8
ant dull
knobkerrie *n syn* see CUDGEL
knock *vb* **1 syn** see TAP 1
2 syn see CRITICIZE
ant boost
knock *n* **1 syn** see HIT 1
2 syn see CRITICISM 2
knock about *vb syn* see MANHANDLE
knock down *vb* **1 syn** see FELL 1
2 syn see EARN 1
knock–down–and–drag–out *n* **1 syn** see BRAWL
2 syn see QUARREL
knocker *n syn* see CRITIC
knock off *vb* **1 syn** see STOP 3
2 syn see DEDUCT 1
3 syn see MURDER 1
‖**4 syn** see ROB 1
knock out *vb syn* see EXHAUST 4
knockout *n* **1 syn** see ‖DILLY
2 syn see BEAUTY
knock over *vb* **1 syn** see FELL 1
2 syn see OVERTURN 1
3 syn see OVERWHELM 4
4 syn see ROB 1
knot *n* **1 syn** see BOND 3

2 *syn* see BUMP 2
3 *syn* see MAZE 1
knothead *n* *syn* see DUNCE
knotty *adj* **1** *syn* see COMPLEX 2
  2 *syn* see HARD 6

know *vb* **1** to possess an intellectual hold of
<*knows* several languages>
  syn appreciate, apprehend, cognize, comprehend, fathom, grasp, have, understand
  rel apperceive; differentiate, discern, discriminate, distinguish, realize
  idiom have at one's fingertips, see through
2 *syn* see EXPERIENCE 1
3 *syn* see FEEL 2
4 to recognize the differences between <*know*
right from wrong>
  syn difference, differentiate, discern, discrepate,
discriminate, distinguish, extricate, separate,
sever, severalize
  con confound, mingle, mix
  ant confuse, mix up
5 *syn* see RECOGNIZE 1

knowable *adj* *syn* see UNDERSTANDABLE
  ant unknowable
know-how *n* **1** *syn* see ABILITY 2
  2 *syn* see ART 1
knowing *adj* **1** *syn* see INTELLIGENT 2
  rel vigilant, watchful; discerning, observant,
perceptive

  con blunt, obtuse
  2 *syn* see WISE 1
  3 *syn* see WISE 4
  4 *syn* see AWARE
  5 *syn* see SOPHISTICATED 2
know-it-all *n* *syn* see SMART ALECK
knowledge *n* **1** *syn* see EDUCATION 2
  ant ignorance
  2 the body of things known about or in science
<made major contributions to scientific *knowl-
edge*>
  syn information, lore, science, wisdom
  rel advice, intelligence, news; data, evidence,
facts, input
knowledgeable *adj* **1** *syn* see INTELLIGENT 2
  2 *syn* see WISE 1
know-nothing *adj* *syn* see IGNORANT 1
know-nothing *n* *syn* see DUNCE
knuckle *vb* *syn* see YIELD 2
knucklehead *n* *syn* see DUNCE
knuckle under *vb* *syn* see YIELD 2
kook *n* *syn* see CRACKPOT
kooky *adj* *syn* see FOOLISH 2
kowtow *vb* *syn* see FAWN
kowtowing *adj* *syn* see FAWNING
kudize *vb* *syn* see COMMEND 2
kudo *n* *syn* see COMPLIMENT 1
kudos *n* **1** *syn* see EMINENCE 1
  2 *syn* see HONOR 2
kvetch *vb* *syn* see GRIPE

---

syn synonym(s)   *rel* related word(s)
ant antonym(s)   *con* contrasted word(s)
idiom idiomatic equivalent(s)
‖ use limited; if in doubt, see a dictionary

L

laager *vb syn* see CAMP

label *n syn* see TICKET 1
  rel mark, marker

labor *n* **1** *syn* see WORK 2
  rel endeavor, struggle
  con ease, leisure, relaxation, repose, rest; amusement, diversion, entertainment, recreation; idleness, inactivity, inertia, inertness, passiveness
  2 the physical activities involved in parturition <first *labors* are sometimes difficult>
  syn birth pang(s), childbearing, childbirth, travail

labor *vb* **1** to exert one's powers of mind or body especially with painful or strenuous effort <*labored* all day to make a living>
  syn drive, moil, strain, strive, toil, tug, work
  idiom break one's neck
  con idle, laze, loaf, lounge; goof (off), shirk; dawdle, poke, putter
  ‖**2** *syn* see TILL

labored *adj* **1** *syn* see HARD 6
  2 *syn* see FORCED
  rel heavy, ponderous, weighty; awkward, clumsy, inept, maladroit

laborer *n syn* see WORKER

laborious *adj syn* see HARD 6
  ant easy, effortless

laboriously *adv syn* see HARD 8
  ant easily, effortlessly

labyrinth *n syn* see MAZE 1

labyrinthine *adj syn* see COMPLEX 2

lacerated *adj* having jagged cuts or breaks <the *lacerated* area was badly swollen>
  syn mangled, rent, torn
  rel gashed, mutilated, ripped, slashed; jagged, ragged, saw-toothed, scalloped, scored; serrated

lachrymose *adj syn* see TEARFUL

lack *vb* to be without something and especially something essential or greatly needed <the building *lacks* a fire escape>
  syn need, require, want
  con enjoy, have, hold, own, possess

lack *n* **1** *syn* see ABSENCE
  2 *syn* see FAILURE 3

lackadaisical *adj syn* see LANGUID
  rel incurious, indifferent, unconcerned; faineant, indolent, lazy, slothful; idle, passive; emasculated; romantic, sentimental
  con energetic, lusty, strenuous, vigorous; active, dynamic, live

lacking *adj* **1** *syn* see ABSENT 1
  2 *syn* see DEFICIENT 1

lacking *prep syn* see WITHOUT 2

lackluster *adj* **1** *syn* see DULL 7
  2 *syn* see COLORLESS 2
  rel dead, leaden, rusty, tarnished
  con lustrous

lackwit *n syn* see DUNCE

laconic *adj syn* see CONCISE
  rel brusque
  con garrulous, glib, loquacious, talkative
  ant verbose, wordy

laconically *adv syn* see BRIEFLY

lacuna *n syn* see GAP 3

lad *n syn* see BOY 1

laddie *n syn* see BOY 1

lade *vb* **1** *syn* see BURDEN
  2 *syn* see DIP 2

la–di–da *adj* **1** *syn* see PRECIOUS 4
  2 *syn* see GENTEEL 3

ladies' man *n syn* see WOLF

lading *n syn* see LOAD 1

ladle *vb syn* see DIP 2

lady *n* **1** *syn* see WOMAN 1
  2 *syn* see WIFE

lady friend *n syn* see GIRL FRIEND 1

lady–killer *n syn* see WOLF

ladylove *n syn* see GIRL FRIEND 2

lag *vb syn* see DELAY 2
  rel retard, slacken, slow; stay

lag *adj syn* see LAST

‖**lag** *vb syn* see BANISH

‖**lag** *n syn* see CONVICT

laggard *adj syn* see SLOW 2
  rel dawdling, delaying, loitering, procrastinating; comatose, lethargic, sluggish; apathetic, impassive, phlegmatic
  con alert, vigilant, watchful, wide-awake; expeditious, fast, fleet, speedy
  ant prompt, quick

laggard *n* one that delays unnecessarily or falls behind <no room for *laggards* on the expedition>
  syn dawdler, lingerer, loiterer, slow coach, slowpoke, straggler
  rel lazybones, loafer
  con dynamo, go-ahead, go-getter, hustler, live wire, rustler; eager beaver

lagniappe *n syn* see GRATUITY

lair *n* **1** a resting or living place of a wild animal <photographed the wolf at the entrance to his *lair*>
  syn burrow, couch, den, lodge
  2 *syn* see HIDEOUT

‖**lalapalooza** *n syn* ‖DILLY, ‖corker, crackerjack, ‖daisy, dandy, humdinger, jim-dandy, ‖lulu, peach, ‖pip

‖**lallygag** *vb syn* see IDLE

lam *vb syn* see BEAT 1

lam *n syn* see ESCAPE 1

lambaste *vb* **1** *syn* see BEAT 1
  2 *syn* see WHIP 2
  3 to assail with withering oral or written denunciation <the senator has been publicly *lambasted* for taking bribes>

syn blister, castigate, ‖crawl, drub, excoriate, flay, lash (into), roast, scarify, scathe, scorch, score, scourge, slam, slap, slash, ‖slate; *compare* CRITICIZE, REPROVE, SCOLD 1
rel censure, criticize, denounce, pan; berate, scold, tongue-lash; assail, attack, squabash
idiom burn one's ears, ‖crawl all over, give (one) a roasting, pin one's ears back, rake (one) over the coals, read the riot act, rip into
con applaud, extol, praise; approve, countenance, endorse

lambent *adj syn* see BRIGHT 1

lame–brain *n syn* see DUNCE

lament *vb syn* see DEPLORE 1
ant exult; rejoice

lamentable *adj* **1** *syn* see DEPLORABLE
2 *syn* see MELANCHOLY 2

lamia *n syn* see WITCH 1

lamp *n syn* see EYE 1

lampoonery *n syn* see SATIRE

lampooning *adj syn* see SATIRIC

lance *vb syn* see IMPALE

land *n* **1** *syn* see EARTH 2
2 *syn* see COUNTRY
3 *syn* see ESTATE 3

land *vb* **1** *syn* see DISEMBARK
2 *syn* see ALIGHT
3 *syn* see GET 1

‖**lang syne** *n syn* see PAST

language *n* **1** a body or system of words and phrases used by a large community or by a people, a nation, or a group of nations <the English and French *languages*>
syn dialect, idiom, speech, tongue, vernacular
rel argot, cant, jargon, lingo, patois, slang
2 *syn* see TERMINOLOGY

languid *adj* lacking in vim or energy <doing the job in a slow and *languid* manner>
syn die-away, enervated, lackadaisical, languishing, languorous, limp, listless, spiritless
rel comatose, lethargic, sluggish, torpid; apathetic, impassive, phlegmatic; inactive, inert, supine
con alert, awake, ‖fly, keen, lively, wide-awake
ant vivacious; chipper

languish *vb syn* see FAIL 1
ant flourish

languishing *adj syn* see LANGUID
rel debilitated, enfeebled, weakened; faineant, indolent; longing, pining, yearning
con hale, healthy, robust, sound; energetic, lusty, vigorous
ant flourishing, thriving; unaffected

languor *n syn* see LETHARGY 1
rel exhaustion, fatigue, weariness; blues, depression, dumps; doldrums, ennui, tedium
con celerity, legerity; gusto, zest
ant alacrity

languorous *adj syn* see LANGUID
rel dilatory, laggard, leisurely, slow; faineant, indolent, slothful; passive; lax, loose, relaxed, slack; indulged, pampered
ant vigorous; strenuous (*of times, seasons*)

lank *adj syn* see LEAN

rel attenuated, extenuated
con chubby
ant burly

lanky *adj* **1** *syn* see GANGLING
2 *syn* see LEAN

lap *vb syn* see OVERLAP

lap *vb* **1** *syn* see SLOSH 1
2 *syn* see BATHE 2

lapse *n* **1** *syn* see ERROR 2
rel crime, offense, sin, vice; failing, foible, frailty; breach, transgression, trespass, violation
2 a temporary deviation or fall especially from a higher to a lower state <a *lapse* into nonproductiveness> <ashamed of his *lapse* from grace>
syn backsliding, relapse
rel decadence, declension, decline, degeneration, deterioration, devolution; recession, retrogradation; regression, retrogression
con advance, progress; development, maturation; amendment; betterment, improvement

lapse *vb* to fall from a better or higher state into a lower or poorer one <*lapsed* into his old vulgar ways>
syn backslide, recidivate, relapse
rel return, revert; slide, slip; decline, degenerate, deteriorate; subside; descend; recede, retrograde; apostatize
con advance, progress; develop, mature; amend, mend; better, improve

larcener *n syn* see THIEF

larcenist *n syn* see THIEF

larcenous *adj* prone to committing larceny <*larcenous* employees were robbing the company blind>
syn sticky-fingered, thieving, thievish
rel burglarious; light-fingered

larceny *n syn* see THEFT

‖**lardy–dardy** *adj syn* see GENTEEL 3

lares and penates *n pl syn* see POSSESSION 2

large *adj* **1** above the average of its kind in magnitude <a *large* increase in the tax rate>
syn big, bull, fat, great, husky, oversize
rel colossal, enormous, gigantic, huge, immense, mammoth, vast, voluminous; monstrous, monumental, prodigious, stupendous, tremendous; excessive, exorbitant, extravagant, extreme, immoderate, inordinate
con diminutive, little, minute, tiny, wee; slender, slight, slim, thin
ant small
2 *syn* see BIG 1

largely *adv syn* see GENERALLY 1

largeness *n syn* see SIZE 2

large–scale *adj syn* see BIG 1

largess *n* **1** *syn* see GIFT 1
2 *syn* see GRATUITY

largest *adj syn* see BEST

lark *n* **1** *syn* see ESCAPADE
2 *syn* see PRANK

---

syn synonym(s)   **rel** related word(s)
ant antonym(s)   **con** contrasted word(s)
idiom idiomatic equivalent(s)
‖ use limited; if in doubt, see a dictionary

larkish *adj syn* see PLAYFUL 1

‖**larrup** *vb* **1** *syn* see WHIP 1
   2 *syn* see WHIP 2

‖**larruping** *adv syn* see VERY 1

lascivious *adj* **1** *syn* see LICENTIOUS 2
   rel coarse, gross, obscene
   2 *syn* see LUSTFUL 2

lash *vb* **1** *syn* see RUSH 1
   2 *syn* see POUR 3
   3 *syn* see WHIP 1
   4 *syn* see WAG
   5 *syn* see SCOLD 1

lash (into) *vb syn* see LAMBASTE 3

lashings *n pl syn* see MUCH

lass *n* **1** *syn* see GIRL 1
   2 *syn* see GIRL FRIEND 1

lassie *n syn* see GIRL 1

lassitude *n* **1** *syn* see FATIGUE
   2 *syn* see APATHY 2
   3 *syn* see LETHARGY 1
   rel doldrums, ennui, tedium; blues, depression, dumps; impotence, powerlessness
   con energy, force, might, power, strength
   ant vigor

last *vb syn* see CONTINUE 1

last *adj* following all relevant others (as in time, order, or importance) <he was the *last* one in line>
   syn closing, concluding, eventual, final, hindmost, lag, latest, latter, rearmost, terminal, terminating, ultimate
   rel bottommost, end, extreme, furthest, outermost, remotest, utmost, uttermost
   con beginning, inaugural, initial, introductory, original, primary, prime
   ant first

lasting *adj* existing or continuing for so long a time as to seem fixed or established <his reading made a *lasting* impression on him>
   syn diuturnal, durable, enduring, perdurable, perduring, permanent, stable; *compare* OLD 2
   rel abiding, continuing, persisting; endless, everlasting, unceasing; continual, continuous, incessant, perennial, unremitting; eternal, sempiternal; indelible, indissoluble, inexhaustible, inexpugnable, inexpungible
   con ephemeral, evanescent, fugitive, momentary, passing, short-lived, transient, transitory
   ant fleeting

last word *n syn* see APOTHEOSIS 1

late *adj* **1** *syn* see TARDY
   con opportune, seasonable, well-timed
   ant early; prompt, punctual
   2 *syn* see DEAD 1
   3 *syn* see FORMER 2
   4 *syn* see MODERN 1

lated *adj syn* see TARDY

lately *adv syn* see NEW

latency *n syn* see ABEYANCE

latent *adj* not now manifest or showing signs of existence or activity <a *latent* infection>
   syn abeyant, dormant, lurking, potential, prepatent, quiescent
   rel concealed, hidden; idle, inactive, inert; immature, unmatured, unripe

   con active, dynamic, live, operative; activated, energized, vitalized
   ant patent

later *adj syn* see SUBSEQUENT 1

later *adv syn* see AFTER
   ant earlier

laterally *adv syn* see SIDEWAYS 1

latest *adj syn* see LAST
   ant earliest

lather *n* **1** *syn* see FOAM
   2 *syn* see COMMOTION 4
   3 *syn* see COMMOTION 2

lather *vb syn* see WHIP 1

latitude *n syn* see ROOM 3

latrine *n syn* see TOILET

latter *adj syn* see LAST
   ant former

latterly *adv syn* see AFTER

laud *vb syn* see PRAISE 2
   rel adore, revere, reverence, venerate, worship; admire; flatter
   con blame, condemn; anathematize, curse, damn, execrate, objurgate
   ant revile

laudable *adj syn* see WORTHY 1
   ant illaudable

laudative *adj syn* see EULOGISTIC

laudatory *adj syn* see EULOGISTIC

laugh *vb* to show mirth, joy, or scorn with a smile and a usually explosive sound <*laughed* at all the funny things that happened>
   syn chortle, chuckle, giggle, guffaw, hee-haw, snicker, ‖sniggle, tehee, titter
   rel cachinnate, cackle, crow, roar, whoop; beam, grin, simper, smile, smirk

laughable *adj* provoking laughter or mirth <the *laughable* antics of the clowns>
   syn comic, comical, droll, farcical, funny, gelastic, ludicrous, ridiculous, risible
   rel amusing, diverting, entertaining, rich; facetious, humorous, jocose, jocular, witty; derisive, derisory, mocking
   con grave, serious, solemn; boring, irksome, tedious, tiresome, wearisome; affecting, impressive, moving, pathetic, poignant, touching

laughingstock *n* an object of ridicule <totally unaware that he was the *laughingstock* of the entire office>
   syn butt, derision, jest, jestee, joke, mock, mockery, pilgarlic, sport
   rel gazingstock; mark, target

launch *vb* **1** *syn* see THROW 1
   2 *syn* see BEGIN 1
   3 *syn* see INTRODUCE 3

laurels *n pl syn* see HONOR 2

lavatory *n syn* see TOILET

lave *vb syn* see BATHE 2

lavish *adj* **1** *syn* see PROFUSE
   con scant, scanty; economical, frugal, thrifty; discreet, provident, prudent; miserly, niggardly, parsimonious, penurious, stingy
   ant sparing
   2 *syn* see GRAND 2

lavishness *n syn* see EXTRAVAGANCE 2

ant sparingness

law *n* **1** a principle governing conduct, action, or procedure <found it hard to live by outdated *laws*>
syn assize, canon, decree, decretum, edict, institute, ordinance, precept, prescript, prescription, regulation, rule, statute
rel command, dictate, mandate
2 *syn* see PRINCIPLE 1
rel exigency, necessity
ant chance

lawbreaker *n* *syn* see CRIMINAL

lawcourt *n* *syn* see COURT 2

lawful *adj* being in accordance with law <obtained *lawful* custody of the child>
syn innocent, legal, legitimate, licit
rel condign, due, rightful; allowable, permissible; justifiable, warrantable; bona fide
idiom of right
con flagitious, iniquitous, nefarious; improper, unjustifiable, wrong; criminal, guilty, peccant; illegitimate, illicit
ant lawless, unlawful

lawless *adj* *syn* see UNLAWFUL
ant lawful

lawlessness *n* *syn* see ANARCHY 1
rel conflict, contention, difference, discord, dissension, strife, variance

lawsuit *n* *syn* see SUIT 1

lawyer *n* a person authorized to practice law in the courts or to serve clients in the capacity of legal agent or adviser <took the problem to his family *lawyer*>
syn attorney, attorney-at-law; *compare* PETTIFOGGER
rel advocate, ‖barrister, counsel, counselor, ‖mouthpiece, pleader, ‖solicitor; jurisconsult, jurisprudent, jurist; legist

lax *vb* *syn* see LOOSE 5

lax *adj* **1** *syn* see LOOSE 1
con firm, hard, solid; elastic, resilient, springy
ant rigid
2 *syn* see NEGLIGENT
rel forgetful, oblivious, unmindful
con austere, severe, stern; rigid, rigorous; conscientious, honest, scrupulous, upright
ant strict, stringent

lay *vb* **1** *syn* see SET 1
2 *syn* see GAMBLE 1
3 *syn* see EVEN 1
4 *syn* see ASCRIBE
5 *syn* see DIRECT 2
6 *syn* see SET 5
7 *syn* see ADDUCE

lay (for) *vb* *syn* see SURPRISE 1

lay (open) *vb* *syn* see EXPOSE 1

lay *n* **1** *syn* see MELODY
2 *syn* see SONG 2

lay *adj* *syn* see PROFANE 1
con professional

lay aside *vb* **1** *syn* see DISCARD
2 *syn* see SAVE 4

lay away *vb* **1** *syn* see SAVE 4
2 *syn* see BURY 1

lay by *vb* *syn* see SAVE 4

lay down *vb* **1** *syn* see RELINQUISH
2 *syn* see PRESCRIBE 2
3 *syn* see DICTATE

layer *n* *syn* see BOOKMAKER

lay in *vb* *syn* see SAVE 4

lay low *vb* **1** *syn* see FELL 1
2 *syn* see KILL 1

lay off *vb* *syn* see REST 3

lay out *vb* **1** *syn* see DESIGN 3
2 *syn* see SPEND 1

lay over *vb* *syn* see DEFER

lay up *vb* **1** *syn* see ACCUMULATE
2 *syn* see SAVE 4

laze *vb* *syn* see IDLE
con drudge, grind, labor, toil, travail, work

laze *n* *syn* see SLOTH 1

laziness *n* *syn* see SLOTH 1
ant industriousness

lazy *adj* not easily aroused to action or activity <the hot humid weather made them *lazy*>
syn drony, easygoing, faineant, indolent, slothful, slowgoing, work-shy
rel idle, inactive, inert, passive, supine, trifling; comatose, lethargic, sluggish, torpid; lackadaisical, languid, languorous, listless, unenergetic, unindustrious; lax, neglectful, negligent, remiss, shiftless, slack
con diligent, hardworking; brisk, chipper, energetic, vigorous; active, animated, lively, spry, vivacious; prompt, quick, ready
ant industrious

lazy *vb* *syn* see IDLE

lazybones *n* *syn* see SLUGGARD

lead *vb* **1** *syn* see GUIDE
rel get, induce, persuade, prevail
con drive, impel; coerce, compel, constrain, force, oblige
ant follow
2 *syn* see PRECEDE 3
3 *syn* see CONVERT 1

lead *n* *syn* see LEADER 1

leader *n* **1** one that takes the lead or initiative <each group selected its own *leader* for the tour>
syn ‖bell cow, bellwether, dean, doyen, guide, lead, pilot
rel pacemaker, pacesetter; forerunner, harbinger, herald, precursor; conductor, director, rector
con adherent, dependent, hanger-on, henchman, satellite
ant follower
2 a person in whom resides authority or ruling power <the company had only one *leader*>
syn boss, chief, chieftain, cock, dominator, head, headman, hierarch, honcho, master

---

syn synonym(s)   *rel* related word(s)
ant antonym(s)   *con* contrasted word(s)
idiom idiomatic equivalent(s)
‖ use limited; if in doubt, see a dictionary

rel captain, commander, general; director, principal, superintendent, superior; foreman, manager, straw boss
con inferior, subaltern, subordinate, underling, understrapper
3 *syn* see NOTABLE 1
leading *adj* **1** *syn* see FIRST 1
2 *syn* see FIRST 3
ant subordinate
3 *syn* see WELL-KNOWN
lead off *vb* *syn* see BEGIN 1
lead on *vb* **1** *syn* see LURE
2 *syn* see TRIFLE 1
leaf (through) *vb* *syn* see BROWSE
leafage *n* *syn* see FOLIAGE
league *n* **1** *syn* see ALLIANCE 2
2 *syn* see ASSOCIATION 2
3 *syn* see CLASS 1
4 a group of sports clubs or teams that play one another competitively <the new baseball *league*>
syn association, circuit, conference, loop, wheel
rel division
league *vb* *syn* see UNITE 2
leak *vb* *syn* see GET OUT 2
lean *vb* **1** *syn* see SLANT 1
rel bend, curve; deflect, divert, sheer, turn
2 *syn* see TEND 1
lean (over) *vb* *syn* see HANG 4
lean *n* *syn* see SLOPE
lean *adj* thin because of absence of superfluous flesh <a *lean* strong horse>
syn angular, bony, gaunt, lank, lanky, meager, rawboned, scraggy, scrawny, skinny, spare; *compare* THIN 1
rel slender, slight, slim, spare-set, stringy, thin; cadaverous, haggard, pinched, wasted, worn; wizened
con brawny, burly, husky, muscular, sinewy; stalwart, stout, strong, sturdy; corpulent, fat, fatty, flabby, obese, plump, portly, rotund
ant fleshy
leaning *n* **1** *syn* see SLOPE
2 an attraction to a particular activity, thing, or end <a strong *leaning* toward liberal views>
syn bent, bias, disposition, drift, inclination, inclining, lurch, partiality, penchant, predilection, predisposition, proclivity, propensity, sentiment, tendency; *compare* GIFT 2, PREJUDICE
rel favor, favoritism, odds
con avoidance, evasion, shunning; disdaining, scorning, scouting, spurning; disinterest, dislike, distaste
leaning *adj* *syn* see INCLINED 3
leap *vb* **1** *syn* see JUMP 1
rel arise, ascend, mount, rise, soar
con drop, fall, sink, slump
2 *syn* see CLEAR 8
learn *vb* **1** to acquire knowledge of or skill in by study and experience <*learn* a trade>
syn get, master, pick up
rel con, peruse, study
idiom make oneself master of
2 *syn* see MEMORIZE

3 *syn* see DISCOVER 3
learned *adj* possessing or manifesting unusually wide and deep knowledge <a most *learned* scholar in his field>
syn erudite, scholarly, scholastic
rel cultivated, cultured; academic, bookish, pedantic, professorial; abstruse, esoteric, polymath, recondite
con ignorant, illiterate, uneducated, unlearned, unlettered, untutored
learnedness *n* *syn* see ERUDITION 2
learning *n* *syn* see EDUCATION 2
lease *vb* *syn* see HIRE 1
leash *vb* *syn* see HAMPER
least *adj* *syn* see FIRST 4
leave *vb* **1** *syn* see WILL
rel commit, confide, consign, entrust; allot, apportion, assign
2 *syn* see LET 2
3 *syn* see GO 2
4 *syn* see QUIT 6
5 *syn* see RELINQUISH
leave *n* **1** *syn* see PERMISSION
rel assent
con refusal, rejection; forbiddance, interdiction, prohibition
2 *syn* see VACATION
leaven *vb* *syn* see INFUSE 1
rel moderate, qualify, temper; enliven, quicken, vivify
leave off *vb* *syn* see STOP 3
leave-taking *n* *syn* see PARTING
leaving *n*, *usu* **leavings** *pl* *syn* see REMAINDER
rel fragments, pieces, portions; discards, junk, scrap
lecherous *adj* *syn* see LICENTIOUS 2
lecture *n* *syn* see SPEECH 2
lecture *vb* *syn* see TALK 7
ledger *n* *syn* see TOMBSTONE
leech *n* *syn* see PARASITE
leer *vb* *syn* see SNEER 1
lees *n* *pl* *syn* see SEDIMENT
leeway *n* *syn* see ROOM 3
left-handed *adj* *syn* see INSINCERE
legacy *n* **1** a gift by will especially of money or personal property <received a *legacy* of $5,000 from her late uncle>
syn bequest, devise, inheritance
2 *syn* see HERITAGE 1
legal *adj* *syn* see LAWFUL
ant illegal
legal tender *n* *syn* see MONEY
legate *vb* *syn* see WILL
legend *n* **1** *syn* see MYTH 1
2 *syn* see CAPTION
3 *syn* see LORE 2
legendary *adj* *syn* see MYTHICAL
legerdemain *n* *syn* see MAGIC 2
legion *n* *syn* see MULTITUDE 1
legion *adj* *syn* see MANY
legitimate *adj* **1** *syn* see LAWFUL
rel cogent, sound, valid; acknowledged, recognized; customary, usual; natural, normal, regular, typical

ant illegitimate
2 syn see TRUE 8
ant arbitrary

leisure *n syn* see REST 1
con drudgery, grind, labor
ant toil

leisurely *adj syn* see SLOW 2
rel lax, relaxed, slack; delayed, retarded, slackened; comfortable, easy, restful
con fast, hasty, quick, rapid, speedy; headlong, impetuous, precipitate
ant hurried; abrupt

leitmotiv *n* a dominant recurring thematic element or feature (as in a work of art) <the *leitmotiv* of man against nature often appears in his paintings>
syn motif
rel motive, theme

lemon *n syn* see FAILURE 5

lend *vb* to give into another's keeping for temporary use on condition that the borrower return the same or its equivalent <I do not have another copy of the book to give, but I can *lend* you mine>
syn advance, loan
rel lease-lend, lend-lease; allow, furnish, give; accommodate, oblige

length *n* **1 syn** see DISTANCE 1
2 syn see RANGE 2

lengthen *vb syn* see EXTEND 3
ant shorten; abbreviate

lengthening *n syn* see EXTENSION 1
ant shortening

lengthways *adv syn* see LENGTHWISE
ant widthways, widthwise

lengthwise *adv* in the direction of the length <the students folded their papers *lengthwise*>
syn endways, endwise, lengthways, longitudinally, longways, longwise
con latitudinally, widthways; broadside, broadway, broadwise
ant widthways, widthwise

lengthy *adj* **1 syn** see LONG 2
ant short
2 syn see LONG 1

lenience *n syn* see FORBEARANCE 2

leniency *n syn* see FORBEARANCE 2

lenient *adj* **1 syn** see GENTLE 1
ant caustic
2 syn see FORBEARING
rel condoning, excusing, forgiving, pardoning; benign, benignant, kindly; compassionate, tender; humoring, indulging, pampering, mollycoddling, spoiling
con rigid, rigorous, stringent; austere, severe
ant stern; exacting
3 syn see AMIABLE 1

lenity *n syn* see MERCY
rel tenderness; benevolence, charitableness, humaneness
con rigidity, rigorousness, strictness, stringency; austerity, sternness
ant severity

leper *n syn* see OUTCAST

lessen *vb* **1 syn** see ABRIDGE 1
rel amputate, clip, crop, truncate
2 syn see DECREASE
rel attenuate, dilute, thin, weaken

lesser *adj* **1 syn** see INFERIOR 1
2 syn see MINOR 2

lesson *n syn* see EXERCISE 4

lesson *vb syn* see REPROVE

let *vb* **1 syn** see HIRE 1
2 to neither forbid nor prevent <*let* the boy go to the movies>
syn allow, have, leave, permit, suffer
rel accredit, approve, certify, endorse, sanction; authorize, commission, license; concede, grant
con ban, enjoin, forbid, inhibit, interdict, prohibit; bar, block, hinder, impede, obstruct; circumvent, foil, frustrate, thwart

let down *vb syn* see LOWER 3

lethal *adj syn* see DEADLY 1
con renewing, restorative, restoring

lethality *n syn* see FATALITY 1

lethargic *adj* deficient in alertness or activity <became *lethargic* after taking the drug>
syn comatose, dopey, heavy, hebetudinous, sluggish, slumberous, stupid, torpid
rel dormant, idle, inactive, inert, passive, supine; apathetic, impassive, phlegmatic, spiritless, stolid; lackadaisical, languid, languorous, listless; dilatory, laggard, slow
con alert, aware, responsive; apt, prompt, quick, ready; brisk, gingery, peppery, spirited
ant energetic

lethargy *n* **1** physical and mental inertness <disgusted, he sank into a state of *lethargy*>
syn coma, dullness, hebetude, languor, lassitude, sleep, slumber, stupor, torpidity, torpidness, torpor
rel comatoseness, sluggishness; indolence, laziness, sloth, slothfulness; idleness, inactivity, inertia, inertness, passiveness, supineness; apathy, impassivity, inanition, phlegm
con aptness, promptness, quickness, readiness; alertness, quick-wittedness
ant vigor
2 syn see APATHY 2

lethe *n syn* see OBLIVION

let off *vb syn* see EXEMPT

let on *vb* **1 syn** see ACKNOWLEDGE 1
2 syn see REVEAL 1

let out *vb* ‖**1 syn** see REVEAL 1
2 syn see DISMISS 3

letter *n* **1 letters** *pl syn* see ALPHABET 1
2 a direct or personal written or printed message addressed to a person or organization <wrote several *letters* to her friends>
syn epistle, missive, note
rel dispatch, memorandum, message, report

‖**lettuce** *n syn* see MONEY

let up *vb syn* see ABATE 4

---

syn synonym(s) *rel* related word(s)
ant antonym(s) *con* contrasted word(s)
idiom idiomatic equivalent(s)
‖ use limited; if in doubt, see a dictionary

levee *n* **1** *syn* see WHARF
  2 *syn* see RED-LIGHT DISTRICT
level *vb* **1** *syn* see EVEN 1
  2 *syn* see DIRECT 2
  3 *syn* see FELL 1
level *adj* having a surface without bends, curves, or irregularities <looked for a *level* spot to land the plane>
  syn even, flat, flush, planate, plane, smooth
  rel akin, alike, identical, like, parallel, similar, uniform; aligned; regular; equal, equivalent, same
  con bumpy, irregular, lumpy, uneven; unaligned, unparallel; changing, varying; fluctuating, rolling, swaying, undulating; coarse, rough
lever *vb* *syn* see PRY
leviathan *n* *syn* see GIANT
leviathan *adj* *syn* see HUGE
levity *n* *syn* see LIGHTNESS
  rel absurdity, folly, foolishness, silliness
  con collection, quietude, sobriety
  ant gravity
levy *n* *syn* see TAX 1
levy *vb* to determine and require satisfaction of (as a tax or obligation) <several broad-based taxes were *levied*>
  syn assess, exact, impose, put (on *or* upon)
  rel extort, wrest, wring; charge, lay (on *or* upon), place, set
  con remit; abate, diminish, lessen
lewd *adj* *syn* see LICENTIOUS 2
  rel coarse, gross, obscene; improper, indecent, indelicate
  con modest, proper, self-restrained; temperate
  ant chaste
lexicon *n* **1** *syn* see VOCABULARY 1
  2 *syn* see TERMINOLOGY
liability *n* **1** *syn* see DEBT 3
  ant asset
  2 *syn* see INDEBTEDNESS 1
  3 *syn* see EXPOSURE
liable *adj* **1** *syn* see RESPONSIBLE
  rel bound, tied
  con exempt, immune; free, independent
  2 being likely to be affected by some usually adverse contingency or action <without the heat shield he was *liable* to be burned>
  syn exposed, obnoxious, open, prone, sensitive, subject, susceptible
  rel assailable, penetrable, vulnerable; attackable, beatable, conquerable, vincible
  ant unliable
  3 *syn* see APT 1
  ant unliable
liaison *n* *syn* see AMOUR 2
liar *n* one that tells lies <he is a compulsive *liar*>
  syn Ananias, falsifier, fibber, fibster, perjurer, prevaricator, storyteller
libel *vb* *syn* see MALIGN
  rel burlesque, caricature, travesty
libelous *adj* injurious to reputation <the campaign degenerated into an exchange of *libelous* statements>
  syn backbiting, calumnious, defamatory, detracting, detractive, detractory, invidious, ma-

ligning, scandalous, slanderous, traducing, vilifying
  rel depreciative, depreciatory, derogative, disparaging, pejorative; contumelious, debasing, malevolent, vituperative
  con adulating, adulatory, applauding, commendatory, eulogistic, eulogizing, laudatory, praising
liberal *adj* **1** marked by generosity and openhandedness <a *liberal* allowance for his son>
  syn bounteous, bountiful, free, freehanded, generous, handsome, munificent, openhanded, unsparing
  rel exuberant, lavish, prodigal, profuse; benevolent, charitable, eleemosynary, philanthropic
  con closefisted, miserly, niggardly, parsimonious, penurious, stingy, tight, tightfisted; meager, scanty
  ant close
  2 *syn* see PLENTIFUL
  3 not bound by authoritarianism, orthodoxy, or traditional forms <modern young people usually have a *liberal* attitude toward sex>
  syn advanced, broad, broad-minded, progressive, radical, tolerant, wide
  rel forbearing, indulgent, lenient
  con rigid, rigorous, strict, stringent; dictatorial, doctrinaire, dogmatic, oracular; conservative, reactionary
  ant authoritarian
liberate *vb* *syn* see FREE
  rel detach, unhook; untangle; disembarrass
  con bind, tie; ensnare, entrap, snare, trap; constrain, restrain, restrict
libertine *adj* *syn* see LICENTIOUS 2
  con ethical; continent, sober, temperate
  ant straitlaced
liberty *n* *syn* see FREEDOM
  rel autonomy, independence; delivery, emancipation, enfranchisement, liberation
  con circumscription, confinement, limitation, restriction
  ant restraint
libidinous *adj* **1** *syn* see LICENTIOUS 2
  rel coarse, gross, obscene
  2 *syn* see LUSTFUL 2
library *n* a place in which literary, musical, artistic, or reference materials (as books or films) are kept for use but not for sale <planned to study all evening in the *library*>
  syn archive(s), athenaeum
  rel reading room
license *n* *syn* see FREEDOM
  rel laxity, looseness, relaxation, slackness
  con duty, obligation; decency, propriety; continence, sobriety, temperance
  ant decorum
license *vb* *syn* see AUTHORIZE 1
  rel allow, let, permit, suffer; certify, sanction
  con check, curb, restrain
  ant ban
licentious *adj* **1** *syn* see ABANDONED 2
  2 disregarding sexual restraints <a coarse *licentious* man>

syn fast, incontinent, lascivious, lecherous, lewd, libertine, libidinous, lustful, randy, salacious, satyric
rel animal, carnal, fleshly, oversexed, sensual; abandoned, dissolute, profligate, reprobate; corrupt, debauched, depraved, scabrous; amoral, immoral, unmoral; lax, loose, relaxed
con chaste, decent, pure; moral, virtuous; rigid, strict; ascetic, austere, severe
ant continent

licit *adj syn* see LAWFUL
rel approved, sanctioned; authorized, licensed
con banned, forbidden, inhibited, interdicted, prohibited
ant illicit

lick *vb* **1** *syn* see WHIP 2
2 *syn* see OVERCOME 1

lick *n* **1** *syn* see HINT 2
2 *syn* see HIT 1

lickerish *adj syn* see LUSTFUL 2
lickerishness *n syn* see LUST 2
lickety–split *adv syn* see FAST 2
licking *n syn* see DEFEAT 1
lickspit *n syn* see SYCOPHANT
lickspittle *n syn* see SYCOPHANT
lie *vb* **1** *syn* see REST 1
2 *syn* see CONSIST 1

lie *vb* to be untruthful directly or indirectly <*lying* under oath is a crime>
syn equivocate, falsify, fib, palter, prevaricate
rel beguile, deceive, delude, misguide, misinform, misinstruct, mislead; distort, exaggerate, misstate

lie *n* a statement or declaration that is not true <was sued for printing *lies* about the candidate>
syn ‖bouncer, canard, cock-and-bull story, falsehood, falsity, fib, inveracity, misrepresentation, misstatement, prevarication, ‖rapper, story, tale, taradiddle, untruism, untruth
rel deceitfulness, dishonesty, distortion, fraudulence, inaccuracy, mendacity; fable, flam, myth; falsification, forgery, libel, perjury; fish story, song and dance
con veracity, verisimilitude, verity
ant truth

lie by *vb syn* see REST 3
lied *n syn* see SONG 2
lie down *vb syn* see REST 1
liege *adj syn* see FAITHFUL 1
lieutenant *n syn* see ASSISTANT 2
life *n* **1** *syn* see BIOGRAPHY
2 *syn* see HUMAN
3 *syn* see SPIRIT 5
lifeless *adj* **1** *syn* see DEAD 1
ant living
2 *syn* see COLORLESS 2
ant lifeful
lifelong *adj syn* see OLD 2
lifework *n syn* see MISSION
lift *vb* **1** to remove from a lower to a higher place or position <*lifted* the sack to his shoulder>
syn elevate, hoist, pick up, raise, rear, take up, uphold, uplift, upraise, uprear
rel arise, ascend, levitate, mount, rise, rocket, soar, surge, tower; aggrandize, exalt, magnify

con decrease, diminish, lessen, reduce; abase, debase, degrade, demean, humble, humiliate; depress, oppress, weigh
ant lower
2 *syn* see REVOKE 2
ant invoke
3 *syn* see STEAL 1
4 *syn* see RISE 4
lift *n* **1** *syn* see THEFT
2 *syn* see HELP 1
lifted *adj syn* see ELEVATED 1
ligament *n syn* see BOND 3
ligature *n syn* see BOND 3
light *n syn* see DAWN 1
light *adj syn* see FAIR 3
light *vb* **1** to cause something to start burning <*lighted* the fuse on the dynamite>
syn enkindle, fire, ignite, inflame, kindle
con douse, ‖dout, put out, quench, snuff; damp (down), smother, stamp (out)
ant extinguish
2 *syn* see ILLUMINATE 1
light *adj* **1** having little weight <the package was *light*>
syn featherlight, featherweight, imponderous, lightweight, unheavy, weightless
rel inconsequential, trifling, trivial; little, petty, small; flimsy, meager, slender, slight
idiom light as a feather
con bulky, burdensome, cumbersome, huge, massive, overweight, ponderous, portly, unwieldy, weighty
ant heavy
2 *syn* see EASY 1
ant arduous
3 *syn* see FAST 7
4 *syn* see GIDDY 1
5 *syn* see LITTLE 3
6 *syn* see DIZZY 2
light *vb* **1** *syn* see ALIGHT
2 *syn* see HAPPEN 2
lighted *adj syn* see BURNING 1
ant unlighted, unlit
lighten *vb syn* see ILLUMINATE 1
ant darken
lighten *vb syn* see RELIEVE 1
rel attenuate, dilute, extenuate, thin
con depress, oppress, weigh
light–headed *adj* **1** *syn* see GIDDY 1
2 *syn* see DIZZY 2
lighthearted *adj* **1** *syn* see HAPPY-GO-LUCKY
ant heavyhearted
2 *syn* see GLAD 1
rel buoyant, effervescent, expansive, resilient, volatile; high-spirited, spirited; gay, lively, sprightly, vivacious
con gloomy, glum, morose, sullen
ant despondent
3 *syn* see MERRY

---

syn synonym(s)   **rel** related word(s)
ant antonym(s)   **con** contrasted word(s)
idiom idiomatic equivalent(s)
‖ use limited; if in doubt, see a dictionary

ant heavyhearted

lighthouse *n* a building equipped to guide sea navigators by means of a powerful light <rowed out to the *lighthouse*>
  syn beacon, pharos
  rel direction, guidance

lightless *adj syn* see DARK 1
  ant bright, ‖lightful

lightly *adv syn* see EASILY 1

light–mindedness *n syn* see LIGHTNESS

lightness *n* gaiety or indifference where seriousness and attention are called for <a crisis that allowed no room for *lightness*>
  syn flightiness, flippancy, frivolity, levity, light=mindedness, volatility
  rel buoyancy, effervescence, elasticity, expansiveness, resiliency; gaiety, liveliness, vivacity; cheerfulness, lightheartedness
  con earnestness, gravity, sedateness, soberness, somberness, staidness
  ant seriousness

light–o'–love *n syn* see DOXY 1

light out *vb syn* see HEAD 3

lightsome *adj* 1 *syn* see CHEERFUL 1
  2 *syn* see HAPPY-GO-LUCKY

lightweight *adj syn* see LIGHT 1

like *vb* 1 *syn* see ENJOY 1
  rel choose, elect, prefer, select; admire, esteem, regard, respect; approve, endorse; appreciate, comprehend, understand
  ant dislike
  2 *syn* see WILL

like *adj* being so similar as to appear to be the same or nearly the same (as in appearance, character, or quantity) <shirts of *like* design>
  syn agnate, akin, alike, analogous, comparable, consonant, corresponding, equivalent, intercomparable, parallel, similar, such, suchlike, undifferenced, undifferentiated, uniform; *compare* SAME 2
  rel equal, equivalent, identical, same, selfsame; allied, cognate, close, related, resembling; coextensive, commensurate
  idiom of that ilk, on the order of
  con different, disparate, divergent, diverse, various; dissimilar, distinct; discordant, discrepant, inconsistent, inconsonant
  ant unlike

like *n syn* see EQUAL

likely *adj* 1 *syn* see PROBABLE
  con problematic; certain, inevitable, necessary
  ant unlikely
  2 *syn* see APT 1
  ant unlikely
  3 *syn* see HOPEFUL 2

likely *adv syn* see PRESUMABLY

liken *vb syn* see EQUATE 2

likeness *n* agreement or correspondence in details (as of appearance, structure, or quality) <the remarkable *likeness* of the two cousins>
  syn affinity, alikeness, analogy, comparison, resemblance, semblance, similarity, simile, similitude
  rel equality, equivalence, identicalness, identity, sameness; agreement, conformity, correspondence; analogousness, comparableness, parallelism, uniformity
  con difference, dissimilarity, distinction, divergence, divergency; disaffinity, opposition
  ant unlikeness

likewise *adv* 1 *syn* see ALSO 1
  2 *syn* see ALSO 2

liking *n* 1 *syn* see APPETITE 3
  ant disliking
  2 *syn* see WILL 1

lilliputian *adj syn* TINY, diminutive, minute, teensy, teensy-weensy, teenty, teeny, teeny=weeny, wee, weeny
  ant Brobdingnagian

lilliputian *n syn* see DWARF

lily–livered *adj syn* see COWARDLY

lily–white *adj syn* see GOOD 11

limb *n* 1 a member of a woody plant that is an outgrowth from a main stem or from one of its divisions <hung the swing from a tree's *limb*>
  syn bough, branch
  rel shoot, spray, sprig, switch, twig; arm
  2 *syn* see SCAMP

limber *adj syn* see SUPPLE 3
  rel plastic, pliable, pliant; elastic, flexible, resilient, springy
  con inflexible, rigid, stark, stiff, tense, wooden

limit *n* 1 a material or immaterial point beyond which something does not or cannot extend <there seemed no *limit* to the problems they faced>
  syn bound, confine(s), end, limitation, term; *compare* ENVIRONS 1
  rel circumscription, confinement, restriction, termination; border, brim, brink, edge, margin, rim, verge
  2 **limits** *pl syn* see ENVIRONS 1
  3 *syn* see EXTREME 2

limit *vb* 1 *syn* see DEMARCATE 1
  2 to prescribe or serve as a restricting boundary <*limited* the naughty child to the house for three days> <ignorance that *limits* spiritual growth>
  syn bar, circumscribe, confine, delimit, delimitate, prelimit, restrict
  rel constrict, contract, lessen, narrow, pinch; check, curb, hinder, inhibit, restrain; appoint, assign, define, prescribe, set
  con enlarge, expand, extend, increase, widen; develop, grow
  ant broaden

limitation *n* 1 *syn* see LIMIT 1
  2 *syn* see RESTRICTION 1

limited *adj* 1 *syn* see DEFINITE 1
  rel inexhaustive, inextensive
  con boundless, infinite
  ant unlimited
  2 *syn* see FINITE
  3 *syn* see QUALIFIED 2
  4 *syn* see LITTLE 2

limitless *adj* having no limits <the *limitless* black of deep space>
  syn boundless, endless, immeasurable, indefinite, infinite, measureless, unbounded, unlimited, unmeasured

rel bottomless, countless, incalculable, incomprehensible, inexhaustible, innumerable, undrainable, unfathomable, vast, wasteless
con bound, bounded, finite, fixed, limited, measurable; comprehensible, fathomable; confined, restricted
ant limited
limn *vb syn* see REPRESENT 1
limp *vb* **1** to walk lamely <*limped* across the floor after his fall>
syn halt, hitch, hobble
rel toddle, totter, waddle; falter, stagger, stumble, wobble
2 syn see STUMBLE 6
limp *adj* **1** deficient in firmness of texture, substance, or structure <plants going *limp* from lack of water>
syn flabby, flaccid, flimsy, floppy, sleazy
rel lax, loose, relaxed, slack; limber, supple
con inflexible, rigid, stark, stiff, tense, wooden; firm, hard, solid; brittle, crisp
2 syn see LANGUID
limpid *adj syn* see TRANSPARENT 1
limpidity *n syn* see CLARITY
line *n* **1 syn** see WAY 2
2 syn see COURSE 3
3 syn see WORK 1
‖**4 syn** see SPIEL
5 a series of things arranged in continuous or uniform order <a *line* of cars waiting at the light>
syn echelon, file, queue, rank, row, string, tier
rel column, progression, succession, train; sequence, series
6 syn see OUTLINE
7 syn see MERCHANDISE
line *vb* **1** to arrange in a line or lines <*lined* the bottles along the shelf>
syn align, allineate, line up, range
rel arrange, array, marshal, order, ordinate
con derange, disarrange, disorder, disturb; disperse, dissipate, scatter
2 syn see ADJOIN
lineage *n* **1 syn** see ANCESTRY
2 syn see FAMILY 1
lineal *adj syn* see DIRECT 1
lineament *n syn* see OUTLINE
lineation *n syn* see OUTLINE
line up *vb syn* see LINE 1
linger *vb* **1 syn** see STAY 2
2 syn see DELAY 2
3 syn see SAUNTER
lingerer *n syn* see LAGGARD
lingo *n syn* see DIALECT 2
link *n syn* see BOND 3
link *vb syn* see JOIN 1
lint *n syn* see DOWN
lion *n syn* see NOTABLE 1
lionhearted *adj syn* see BRAVE 1
‖**lip** *n syn* see BACK TALK
lip *vb* **1 syn** see KISS 1
2 syn see BATHE 2
lip server *n syn* see HYPOCRITE
liquefy *vb* to convert or to become converted to a liquid state <*liquefy* a block of ice by heating>

syn deliquesce, dissolve, flux, fuse, liquesce, melt, run, thaw
rel soften; thin
con clot, coagulate, congeal; harden, set; gel, jellify, jelly; condense, inspissate, thicken
ant solidify
liquesce *vb syn* see LIQUEFY
liquid *adj syn* see MELLIFLUOUS
liquidate *vb* **1 syn** see CLEAR 5
2 syn see PURGE 3
3 syn see MURDER 1
liquor *n* **1 syn** see DRINK 1
2 an intoxicating beverage usually distilled after being fermented <belted down a slug of *liquor*>
syn alcohol, aqua vitae, booze, ‖budge, drink, firewater, grog, ‖hooch, inebriant, intoxicant, ‖joy-juice, ‖juice, ‖lush, ‖sauce, spirit(s), ‖strunt, tipple
idiom Demon Rum, the bottle
liquor (up) *vb syn* see DRINK 3
lissome *adj syn* see SUPPLE 3
list *n* a series of items (as names) written down or printed especially as a memorandum or record <all the people on the *list* were present>
syn catalog, register, roll, roll call, roster, schedule
rel checklist, handlist; index; inventory
list *vb* **1 syn** see ENUMERATE 2
2 syn see ITEMIZE 1
3 to enter in a list <his name was not *listed* in the telephone book>
syn book, catalog, enroll, inscribe
rel file, index, note, post, schedule, tabulate; record, register, roster
4 syn see ENROLL 1
list *vb syn* see SLANT 1
listen *vb* to perceive by ear usually with careful or responsive attention <now hear me; *listen* to my words>
syn attend, hark, hear, hearken, heed
idiom give a hearing to, give ear to, hang upon the lips (*or* words) of, keep one's ears open, lend one's (*or* an) ear, prick up one's ears, strain one's ears
listless *adj syn* see LANGUID
rel careless, heedless, thoughtless
con agog, anxious, avid, keen; alert, vigilant, watchful; energetic, lusty, vigorous; prompt, quick, ready
ant eager
listlessness *n syn* see APATHY 2
‖**lit** *adj syn* see INTOXICATED 1
literal *adj syn* see VERBATIM
literally *adv syn* see VERBATIM
literati *n pl syn* see INTELLIGENTSIA
literatim *adv syn* see VERBATIM
lithe *adj syn* see SUPPLE 3
rel slender, slight, slim, thin; lean, spare

---

syn synonym(s)   **rel** related word(s)
ant antonym(s)   **con** contrasted word(s)
idiom idiomatic equivalent(s)
‖ use limited; if in doubt, see a dictionary

con awkward, clumsy, gauche, inept, maladroit; inflexible, stiff, tense, wooden

lithesome *adj syn* see SUPPLE 3

litigious *adj syn* see CONTENTIOUS 2

litter *n* **1** *syn* see REFUSE

2 *syn* see CLUTTER 2

little *adj* **1** *syn* see SMALL 1

ant big

2 contemptibly limited <men with *little* minds picking at flaws in a great leader>

syn borné, ineffectual, limited, mean, narrow, paltry, set, small

rel bigoted, hidebound, illiberal, narrow=minded, provincial; contemptible; niggard, niggardly, self-centered, selfish

ant great

3 lacking importance <the nagging *little* details of a job>

syn casual, inconsiderable, insignificant, light, minor, minute, petty, ‖potty, shoestring, small, small-beer, trivial, unimportant; *compare* PETTY 2

rel fortuitous; incidental; collateral, secondary, subordinate, subsidiary

con consequential, meaningful, significant, substantial, weighty; basal, basic, essential, foundational, fundamental

ant important

little *adv syn* see SELDOM

ant much

little by little *adv syn* see GRADUALLY

‖**little woman** *n syn* see WIFE

‖**lit up** *adj syn* see INTOXICATED 1

liturgy *n* **1** *syn* see FORM 2

2 *syn* see RITE 2

livable *adj* **1** suitable for living <a very *livable* apartment>

syn habitable, inhabitable, lodgeable, occupiable, tenantable

rel cozy, homelike, homey, snug; acceptable, bearable, tolerable

ant unlivable

2 *syn* see BEARABLE

live *vb* **1** *syn* see BE

2 *syn* see RESIDE 1

live *adj syn* see ACTIVE 1

rel effective, effectual, efficacious, efficient

ant inactive, inert; dormant (*as a volcano*); defunct (*as an institution, journal*)

livelihood *n syn* see LIVING

rel art, craft, handicraft, profession, trade; emolument, fee, pay, salary, stipend, wage

lively *adj* **1** keenly alive and brisk <always thought of as a *lively* teacher>

syn alert, animate, animated, bright, ‖cant, ‖canty, chipper, ‖chirk, dashing, gay, keen, ‖peart, peppy, pert, rousing, spirited, ‖spirity, sprightful, sprightly, unpedantic, vivacious; *compare* CHEERFUL 1

rel agile, brisk, nimble, spry; buoyant, effervescent, elastic, expansive, resilient, volatile; blithe, cock-a-hoop, jocund, jolly, merry; gleeful, hilarious, mirthful; chirping, chirpy, chirrupy

con lethargic, sluggish, torpid; lackadaisical, languid, languorous, listless; apathetic, impassive, phlegmatic, stolid; boring, irksome, tedious

ant dull, unlively

2 *syn* see AGILE

idiom full of pep

3 *syn* see ENERGETIC 2

4 *syn* see BUSTLING

ant unanimated

liven *vb syn* see QUICKEN 1

liver *n syn* see INHABITANT

live wire *n syn* see HUSTLER 1

livid *adj* **1** *syn* see PALE 1

rel grisly; dusky, gloomy, murky

con bright, brilliant, effulgent, lucent, luminous, lustrous, radiant

2 *syn* see SENSATIONAL 2

living *adj* **1** having or showing life <the *living* things of a locality>

syn alive, animate, animated, vital, zoetic

rel being, existing, subsisting; active, dynamic, live, operative

con dead, deceased, defunct, demised, departed, gone, inanimate

ant lifeless

2 *syn* see EXTANT 1

living *n* supplies or resources needed to live <kept trying to earn a *living* the honest way>

syn alimentation, alimony, bread, bread and butter, keep, livelihood, maintenance, salt, subsistence, support, sustenance

rel sustainment, sustentation

load *n* **1** something which is carried, conveyed, or transported from one place to another <a *load* of grain just arrived>

syn burden, cargo, freight, haul, lading, payload

rel bale, pack, parcel, shipment

2 something heavy <could not lift the *load*>

syn weight

3 a burdensome or laborious responsibility <considered taking care of the children a heavy *load*>

syn burden, charge, deadweight, duty, millstone, onus, task, tax, weight

rel care, liability, obligation, responsibility; drag, drain, pressure

idiom millstone around one's neck

con breeze, child's play, cinch, duck soup, picnic, ‖pipe, pushover, snap

ant sinecure

4 *usu* **loads** *pl syn* see SCAD

load *vb* **1** *syn* see BURDEN

rel bear, carry, convey, transport

ant unload

2 *syn* see ADULTERATE

3 to make full or overfull <a basket *loaded* with fresh fruit>

syn charge, choke, fill, heap, pack, pile; *compare* CRAM 1

rel glut, gorge, surfeit; flood, oversupply, swamp

loaded *adj* **1** *syn* see FULL 1

‖**2** *syn* see INTOXICATED 1

loaf *vb syn* see IDLE

con labor, toil, travail, work

loafer *n syn* see SLUGGARD

loan *vb syn* see LEND

loan shark *n* one who lends money to individuals at exorbitant rates of interest <got involved with *loan sharks*>
  syn Shylock, usurer
  rel lender, loaner, moneylender; shark
loath *adj syn* see DISINCLINED
  ant anxious
loathe *vb syn* see HATE
  rel decline, refuse, reject, repudiate, spurn
  con covet, crave, desire, want, wish
  ant tolerate
loathing *n syn* see ABOMINATION 2
  ant tolerance
loathsome *adj syn* see OFFENSIVE
  rel hateful, invidious, obnoxious
  con bearable, endurable, sufferable, supportable; engaging, inviting; alluring, bewitching, charming, enchanting, fascinating
  ant tolerable
lobby *n syn* see VESTIBULE
lobster *n syn* see OAF 2
local *adj syn* see INSULAR
  ant cosmopolitan
locale *n syn* see SCENE 3
  rel area, district, neighborhood, vicinage, vicinity
locality *n* 1 a more or less definitely circumscribed place or region <searched for the child in the *locality* of the waterfront>
  syn area, district, neighborhood, vicinage, vicinity
  rel belt, region, tract, zone; section, sector; bailiwick, domain, field, province, sphere, territory
  idiom neck of the woods
  2 *syn* see HABITAT
located *adj syn* see SITUATED
location *n syn* see PLACE 1
‖**loch** *n syn* see INLET
lockup *n syn* see JAIL
‖**loco** *adj syn* see INSANE 1
locum tenens *n syn* see SUBSTITUTE 1
locus *n syn* see PLACE 1
locution *n syn* see PHRASE 2
lodge *vb* 1 *syn* see HARBOR 2
  rel accept, admit, receive, take; accommodate, contain, hold
  2 *syn* see ENTRENCH 1
lodge *n* 1 *syn* see HUT
  2 *syn* see HOTEL
  3 *syn* see LAIR 1
lodgeable *adj syn* see LIVABLE 1
lodging *n* 1 *syn* see ACCOMMODATIONS
  2 usu **lodgings** *pl syn* see APARTMENT 1
lodgment *n syn* see ACCOMMODATIONS
loftiest *adj syn* see TOP 1
loftiness *n syn* see PRIDE 3
lofty *adj* 1 *syn* see PROUD 1
  2 *syn* see AMBITIOUS 2
  3 *syn* see GRAND 3
  4 *syn* see GENEROUS 1
  5 *syn* see ELEVATED 4
  6 extending or rising high in the air so as to have great or imposing height <a *lofty* monument to human aspiration>

  syn aerial, airy, skyscraping, soaring, spiring, topless, towering, towery; *compare* HIGH 1
  rel elevated, lifted, raised; aggrandized, exalted, magnified; august, imposing, majestic, stately
  con humble, low, modest
logical *adj* 1 *syn* see RATIONAL
  ant illogical
  2 having or showing skill in thinking or reasoning <a *logical* argument>
  syn analytic, analytical, ratiocinative, subtle
  rel cogent, compelling, convincing, sound, telling, valid; clear, lucid, perspicuous; rational, reasonable; discriminating
  con instinctive, intuitive; irrational, unreasonable; casuistical, sophistical
  ant illogical
logo *n syn* see MARK 7
logotype *n syn* see MARK 7
loiter *vb* 1 *syn* see DELAY 2
  2 *syn* see IDLE
loiterer *n syn* see LAGGARD
loll *vb* 1 *syn* see SLOUCH
  2 *syn* see IDLE
‖**lollop** *vb syn* see SLOUCH
lone *adj* 1 having no company <a *lone* figure walking through the snow>
  syn alone, lonely, lonesome, solitary
  rel single, sole, unique; abandoned, deserted, forsaken; isolated, secluded
  con attended, chaperoned, companioned, convoyed, escorted
  ant accompanied
  2 *syn* see ONLY 2
  3 *syn* see SINGLE 2
lonely *adj* 1 *syn* see LONE 1
  2 *syn* see FORLORN 1
loneness *n syn* see SOLITUDE
lonesome *adj* 1 *syn* see LONE 1
  2 *syn* see FORLORN 1
  3 *syn* see OBSCURE 2
long *adj* 1 having considerable extension in space or time <a *long* road> <it has been a *long* time since we have seen you>
  syn elongate, elongated, extended, lengthy
  rel extensive, longish, outstretched
  con brief, curtailed
  ant short
  2 unduly extended <went through many *long* days of misery>
  syn dragging, drawn-out, ‖dreich, lengthy, long-drawn-out, longsome, overlong, prolonged, protracted
  rel diffuse, diffusive, long-winded, prolix; flatulent, verbose, wordy
  con ephemeral, evanescent, fleeting, fugacious, fugitive, impermanent, passing, short-lived, transient, transitory; abbreviated, abridged, curtailed, shortened
  ant brief

---

syn synonym(s)   *rel* related word(s)
ant antonym(s)   *con* contrasted word(s)
idiom idiomatic equivalent(s)
‖ use limited; if in doubt, see a dictionary

long *n syn* see AGE 2

long *vb* to desire urgently <*long* for peace>
　syn ache, crave, dream, hanker, hunger, itch, lust, pine, sigh, suspire, thirst, yearn, yen
　rel aim, aspire, want; miss
　idiom have an appetite (*or* a longing) for
　con abhor, detest, dread, fear, loathe

longanimity *n syn* see PATIENCE

long-drawn-out *adj syn* see LONG 2
　ant short; curtailed

‖long green *n syn* see MONEY

longitudinally *adv syn* see LENGTHWISE
　ant horizontally

long-lasting *adj syn* see OLD 2
　ant ephemeral

long-lived *adj syn* see OLD 2
　ant short-lived

longsome *adj syn* see LONG 2

long-suffering *n syn* see PATIENCE
　rel subduedness; humility, lowliness, meekness
　con impatience, uneasiness; irksomeness, tediousness, wearisomeness; boredom, ennui, tedium

long suit *n syn* see FORTE
　rel specialism, specialization, specialty

longtimer *n syn* see VETERAN
　con apprentice, neophyte, novice; newcomer, rookie, tenderfoot

‖long tongue *n syn* see GOSSIP 1

longways *adv syn* see LENGTHWISE

long-winded *adj syn* see WORDY
　rel extended, lasting, lengthy, long, long-drawn-out, prolonged, protracted
　con brief, close, compact

longwise *adv syn* see LENGTHWISE

‖loo *n syn* see TOILET

looby *n syn* see OAF 2

look *vb* **1** to make sure or take care (that something is or is not done) <*look* that you accuse no one unjustly>
　syn mind, see, watch
　rel attend, heed, tend; note, notice, observe; beware
　2 *syn* see SEE 2
　rel note, notice, observe, spot
　idiom get a load of, take a gander at
　3 *syn* see EXPECT 1
　rel divine, forecast, foretell
　ant despair (of)
　4 to make apparent by the expression of the eyes or countenance <*looked* her annoyance at this interruption>
　syn exhibit, show; *compare* SHOW 2
　rel display, express, indicate, manifest
　5 *syn* see SEEM
　idiom strike one as
　6 *syn* see FACE 1
　7 to gaze in wonder or surprise <you should have seen them *look*>
　syn eye, gape, ‖gaup (*or* gawp), gaze, goggle, ogle, rubberneck, stare; *compare* GAZE 1
　rel gawk; glare, gloat, glower; peer
　8 *syn* see TEND 1

look (at *or* upon) *vb syn* see EYE 1

look (into) *vb syn* see EXPLORE

look *n* **1** the directing of one's eyes in order to see <he wanted one last *look* before departing>
　syn sight, view
　rel glance, glimpse, peek, peep, squint; cast, slant; eye, ‖gander, ‖look-see, regard; eyeful, gaze, stare, survey
　2 facial aspect especially as indicative of mood or feeling <you should have seen the *look* on her face>
　syn cast, countenance, expression, face, visage
　rel mug, physiognomy, ‖puss
　3 *syn* see APPEARANCE 1

look down *vb* **1** *syn* see OVERLOOK 2
　2 *syn* see DESPISE
　3 *syn* see STARE DOWN

looker *n syn* see BEAUTY

looker-on *n syn* see SPECTATOR

look in *vb syn* see VISIT 2

look-in *n syn* see OPPORTUNITY

looking glass *n syn* see MIRROR 1

look out *vb syn* see BEWARE

lookout *n* **1** *syn* see GUARD 2
　2 an elevated place affording a wide view for observation <guards posted at a *lookout* to watch for enemy troops entering the valley>
　syn observatory, outlook, overlook
　rel watchtower; crow's nest; cupola, widow's walk; fire tower
　3 a careful looking or watching <kept a constant *lookout* for new developments>
　syn surveillance, tout, vigil, vigilance, watch, watch and ward
　rel observance, observation
　4 *syn* see VISTA
　5 *syn* see BUSINESS 8

look up *vb* **1** *syn* see IMPROVE 3
　2 *syn* see VISIT 2

loom *vb* **1** *syn* see APPEAR 1
　2 to take shape as an impending occurrence <an international economic crisis *looms* ahead>
　syn brew, forthcome, gather, impend
　rel approach, come on, make up, near
　con disappear, fade, pass, vanish; die (down *or* away), diminish, dwindle, wane; recede, retreat, withdraw
　3 to appear in an impressively great or exaggerated form <the power of the enemy *loomed* in the soldiers' imagination>
　syn bulk, stand out
　rel lower, rear, threaten, tower
　con die (down *or* away), diminish, dwindle, wane

loon *n syn* see LUNATIC 1

loony *adj* **1** *syn* see FOOLISH 2
　2 *syn* see INSANE 1

loony *n syn* see LUNATIC 1

loony bin *n syn* see ASYLUM 3

loop *n* **1** a curving or doubling of a line so as to form a closed or partly open curve <the transit makes a *loop* around town>
　syn eye, ring
　rel circlet, circuit, circumference, hoop, wreath; curve

2 a circular or curved piece used often to form a fastening or a handle <one of his belt *loops* is broken>
syn eye, ring, staple
rel hook
3 *syn* see LEAGUE 4
loop *vb syn* see SURROUND 1
rel arc, arch, bend, coil, curve
looped *adj syn* see INTOXICATED 1
loopy *adj syn* see FOOLISH 2
loose *adj* **1** not tightly bound, held, restrained, or stretched <*loose* rope>
syn lax, relaxed, slack
rel detached, free; flabby, flaccid, limp; desultory, negligent, remiss
con rigid, rigorous, stringent, taut, tense; exact, precise; bound, checked, curbed, inhibited, restrained, tied
ant strict; tight
2 *syn* see FREE 2
rel clear; disconnected, unattached, unconnected, undone, unfastened
con fast
3 not dense, close, or compact in structure <*loose* soil>
syn incoherent, nonadhesive
rel disconnected, disjointed, separate, unconnected
con compressed, condensed, contracted; concentrated, crammed, crowded, localized; close, compact, dense, thick
4 *syn* see FAST 7
rel capricious, extravagant, free, inconstant, reckless, unrestrained
loose *vb* **1** *syn* see FREE
2 *syn* see TAKE OUT (on)
3 to set free from a fastened or fixed condition <*loose* a knot>
syn disengage, unbind, undo, unfasten, unfix, unloose, unloosen
rel unbandage, unbar, unbolt, unbuckle, unbutton, unchain, unclasp, unglue, unhitch, unhook, unlace, unlash, unlatch, unlock, unpin, unscrew, unsnap, unstick, unstrap, untie
con bind, engage, fasten, fix, secure
4 *syn* see SHOOT 1
5 to make less rigid or tight <exercise *loosed* his muscles>
syn ease, ease off, lax, loosen, relax, slack, slacken, untighten
rel abate, alleviate, bate, lessen, let up, mitigate
con anchor, cement, clamp, clinch, fasten, knit, secure, set, tauten
ant tighten
loose–lipped *adj syn* see TALKATIVE
ant closemouthed
loosen *vb* **1** *syn* see LOOSE 5
ant tighten
2 *syn* see FREE
loosen up *vb syn* see RELAX 2
ant tighten (up)
loose–tongued *adj syn* see TALKATIVE
ant closemouthed
loot *n* **1** *syn* see SPOIL

rel lift, pillage, seizure
2 *syn* see MONEY
loot *vb syn* see ROB 1
looter *n syn* see MARAUDER
lop *vb* **1** *syn* see SLOUCH
2 *syn* see JUMP 1
lope *vb syn* see SKIP 1
rel run, sprint; romp, trip
‖lopper *vb syn* see CURDLE
lopsided *adj* lacking in balance, symmetry, or proportion <the arrangement of the furniture was *lopsided*>
syn asymmetric, difform, disproportional, disproportionate, irregular, nonsymmetrical, off-balance, overbalanced, proportionless, unbalanced, unequal, uneven, unproportionate, unsymmetrical
rel cockeyed, crooked, top-heavy, unsteady
con balanced, even, regular, symmetrical
loquacious *adj syn* see TALKATIVE
rel jabbering, overtalkative; prolix, verbose, wordy
con breviloquent, concise, succinct, taciturn, terse; abrupt, brusque, curt
lord *n syn* see HUSBAND
lord *vb* to affect an air of superiority and authority <nouveau riche love to *lord* it>
syn cock, peacock, pontificate, swagger, swank, swell
rel affect, pretend, put on; boss, order (about *or* around), overawe, overbear; tyrannize
idiom put on airs
Lord Harry *n syn* see DEVIL 1
lordly *adj* **1** *syn* see GRAND 1
2 *syn* see PROUD 1
rel egotistic, puffed; affected, snobbish, swollen; authoritarian, dictatorial, magisterial
con humble; abject, mean; subdued, submissive
lore *n* **1** *syn* see KNOWLEDGE 2
2 a body of traditions relating to a person, institution, or place <the Scottish Highlands are rich in local *lore*>
syn folklore, legend, myth, mythology, mythos, tradition
rel custom, folkway, traditionalism; fable, old wives' tale, saga, superstition, tale
Lorelei *n syn* see SIREN
lorn *adj* **1** *syn* see DERELICT 1
2 *syn* see FORLORN 1
lose *vb* **1** to suffer deprivation of <*lost* all his savings in a poor investment>
syn drop, forfeit, sacrifice
rel mislay, misplace, miss; give up, relinquish, surrender, yield
con cash in, profit; clear, make, realize, take in; obtain, win
ant gain
2 to fail to win, gain, or obtain <*lost* every contest she entered>

---

syn synonym(s)   *rel* related word(s)
ant antonym(s)   *con* contrasted word(s)
idiom idiomatic equivalent(s)
‖ use limited; if in doubt, see a dictionary

syn drop, lose out
rel decline, fall, succumb, yield
ant win
3 syn see DEPRIVE 2
4 syn see SHAKE 5
5 syn see RID
lose out *vb syn* see LOSE 2
loser *n* **1 syn** see FAILURE 5
rel also-ran, underdog
ant winner
2 syn see CONVICT
losing *n syn* see LOSS 1
loss *n* **1** the action of having something go out of one's control or possession <took precautions against *loss* or theft of his property>
syn losing, mislaying, misplacement, misplacing; *compare* PRIVATION 2
rel forfeit, forfeiture, sacrifice; bereavement, deprivation, deprivement, dispossession, divestiture, divestment, privation
2 syn see PRIVATION 2
3 syn see RUIN 3
lost *adj* **1 syn** see DAMNED 1
rel incorrigible, irreclaimable, irredeemable, irreformable, unconverted, unregenerate; graceless
2 no longer possessed <earned his *lost* reputation by his outrageous behavior>
syn gone, missing
rel absent, lacking; past; irrecoverable, irretrievable, irrevocable
con cherished, protected, treasured
3 syn see EXTINCT 2
4 syn see ABSTRACTED
rel absorbed; daydreamy, musing, unconscious
lot *n* **1 syn** see SHARE 1
2 syn see FATE
rel decree, fortune; foreordination, predestination, predetermination
3 a measured portion of land having fixed boundaries <building *lots*>
syn parcel, plat, plot, tract
rel clearing, field, patch; part, plottage; block, frontage, real estate
4 syn see GROUP 3
rel aggregate, aggregation, conglomerate, conglomeration
5 syn see SET 5
6 syn see TYPE
7 syn see MUCH
lot *vb syn* see ALLOT
‖**lot** (on *or* upon) *vb syn* see RELY (on*or* upon)
lot (out) *vb syn* see DISTRIBUTE 1
lothario *n syn* see GALLANT 2
loud *adj* **1** marked by intensity or volume of sound <a *loud* blast on a trumpet>
syn blaring, earsplitting, full-mouthed, piercing, roaring, stentorian, stentorious, stentorophonic
rel booming, deafening, ear-piercing, fulminating, pealing, ringing, thunderous; resonant, resounding, sonorous; harsh, hoarse, raucous, stertorous, strident
con dulcet, gentle, mellifluous, mellow, quiet, smooth

ant low, soft
2 syn see GAUDY
rel brassy, vulgar; obnoxious, offensive; obtrusive
loudmouthed *adj syn* see VOCIFEROUS
‖**lough** *n syn* see INLET
lounge *vb syn* see IDLE
rel drift, vegetate; dally, slack; lie, lie down, recline
lounge *n syn* see BAR 5
lounge car *n syn* see PARLOR CAR
lounge lizard *n* **1 syn** see FOP
2 syn see PARASITE
louse *n syn* see SNOT 1
louse up *vb syn* see BOTCH
lout *n syn* see OAF 2
rel boor, bumpkin, churl, clodhopper, hayseed, hick, peasant, rube, rustic, yokel; dolt
lout *vb syn* see RIDICULE
loutish *adj syn* see BOORISH
rel awkward, bungling, clumsy, inept, maladroit, rusty; callow, crude, gauche, raw, rough, uncouth
lovable *adj* gifted with traits and qualities that attract affection <a *lovable* child>
syn adorable, lovesome
rel admirable, agreeable, attractive, desirable, genial, likable, pleasing, winning, winsome; alluring, appealing, bewitching, captivating, charming, enchanting, engaging, enthralling, entrancing, fetching, ravishing, seductive
con dislikable, displeasing, distasteful, unattractive, unlikable, unpleasing; odious, offensive; abhorrent, abominable, obnoxious, repellent; contemptible, despicable, detestable
ant hateful; unlovable
love *n* **1** the feeling which animates a person who is genuinely fond of someone or something <a mother's *love* for her child>
syn affection, attachment, devotion, fondness
rel like(s), liking, regard; adoration, idolatry, piety, worship; allegiance, fealty, fidelity, loyalty; emotion, sentiment; crush, infatuation, passion, yearning; ardency, ardor, enthusiasm, fervor, zeal
con antipathy, aversion; animosity, animus, enmity, hostility, rancor; abhorrence, detestation, hatred
ant hate
2 the affection and tenderness felt by lovers <the ability to distinguish between *love* and lust was the mark of her maturity>
syn amorousness, amour, passion
rel crush, infatuation; desire, lust, yearning; ardency, ardor, fervor
idiom (the) tender passion
3 syn see LOVE AFFAIR
4 syn see SWEETHEART 1
love *vb* **1** to like or desire actively <she *loves* her material possessions all too dearly>
syn adore, delight (in), ‖eat up
rel appreciate, cherish, prize, treasure, value; dote (on *or* upon), fancy
idiom hold dear

con abjure, give up, reject, relinquish
2 to feel a lover's passion, devotion, or tenderness for <in spite of all their misfortunes, they continued to *love* each other devotedly>
syn adore, affection, worship
rel deify, exalt, idolize, revere, venerate; cherish, dote (on *or* upon); admire, fancy, like
con avoid, disregard, ignore, neglect, overlook, shun, slight
3 *syn* see CARESS

love affair *n* a romantic attachment or episode between lovers <saddened by the end of a summer *love affair*>
syn affair, amour, love, romance
rel flirtation, intrigue; triangle, ménage à trois

love child *n syn* see BASTARD 1

loved *adj syn* see FAVORITE 1

love letter *n* a letter expressing a lover's affection <she had never received a *love letter*>
syn billet-doux, mash note
rel valentine

loveling *n syn* see SWEETHEART 1

lovely *adj syn* see BEAUTIFUL
rel alluring, bewitching, captivating, charming, enchanting, engaging, entrancing, lovesome; delectable, delightful; dainty, delicate, exquisite, rare; graceful
ant hideous; unlovely

lovely *n syn* see BEAUTY

lover *n* **1** a man who is a woman's regular partner in nonmarital sexual activity
syn boyfriend, fancy man, man, master, paramour
rel cavalier servente, sugar daddy
2 *syn* see BOYFRIEND 2
3 *syn* see ADDICT
4 *syn* see MISTRESS

lovesome *adj* **1** *syn* see LOVABLE
2 *syn* see LOVING

lovey–dovey *adj syn* see SENTIMENTAL

loving *adj* feeling or expressing love <his *loving* son unfailingly waited upon him during his last years>
syn affectionate, dear, devoted, doting, fond, lovesome
rel adoring, attached, benevolent, cordial, kind, tender, warmhearted; attentive, caring, considerate, solicitous; amatory, amorous, erotic; enamored, infatuated; ardent, fervent, impassioned, passionate; faithful; bound up
con aloof, detached, indifferent, unconcerned; chilly, cold, frigid
ant unloving

low *adj* ‖**1** *syn* see SHORT 2
rel squatty; unelevated
2 *syn* see INFERIOR 1
3 *syn* see POOR 1
4 *syn* see IGNOBLE 1
rel lowbred, rude
5 *syn* see BASE 3
rel scrubby, scruffy; miserable, woebegone, woeful
con decent, decorous, proper, seemly; ethical, moral, noble; high, lofty

6 *syn* see COARSE 3
7 *syn* see UNWELL
rel declining, weak; dizzy, faint, feverish
8 *syn* see DOWNCAST
9 of lesser degree, size, or amount than average or ordinary <the energy crisis resulted in *lower* speed limits for all vehicles>
syn subaverage, subnormal
rel fallen, reduced; brief, short; mediocre, moderate; atypical
10 *syn* see CHEAP 1
rel economical; moderate, nominal; cut, cut-rate, marked down, slashed
con elevated, enhanced, increased, raised

lowborn *adj syn* see IGNOBLE 1
ant highborn

lowbred *adj syn* see BOORISH
ant highbred

low-cost *adj syn* see CHEAP 1

low-down *adj syn* see BASE 3

lower *vb syn* see FROWN 1
rel peer, stare; intimidate, menace, threaten

lower *adj syn* see INFERIOR 1
ant higher

lower *vb* **1** *syn* see FALL 1
ant rise
2 *syn* see DEPRECIATE 1
rel demote; de-escalate, deflate
con raise
3 to cause or allow to descend <*lowered* the landing gear of the aircraft>
syn couch, demit, depress, droop, let down, sink
rel detrude, submerge; debase, reduce
con elevate, hoist, lift, pull up, raise
4 *syn* see REDUCE 2
ant raise
5 *syn* see HUMBLE
ant elevate

lowering (*or* **louring**) *adj* **1** *syn* see IMMINENT 2
rel frowning, gloomy, sullen; black, dark; foreboding, impending, portentous
2 *syn* see OVERCAST

lowermost *adj syn* see BOTTOMMOST
ant uppermost

lowery (*or* **loury**) *adj syn* see IMMINENT 2

lowest *adj syn* see BOTTOMMOST
ant highest

low-grade *adj syn* see INFERIOR 2

low-key *adj syn* see SUBDUED 2

low-keyed *adj syn* see SUBDUED 2

lowlife *n* **1** *syn* see WRETCH 1
2 *syn* see VILLAIN 1

lowly *adj* **1** *syn* see HUMBLE 1
rel retiring, withdrawing; deferential, obeisant, reverential; obsequious, servile
ant haughty
2 *syn* see IGNOBLE 1
3 *syn* see PROSAIC 3

low-pressure *adj syn* see EASYGOING 3

---

syn synonym(s)   *rel* related word(s)
ant antonym(s)   *con* contrasted word(s)
idiom idiomatic equivalent(s)
‖ use limited; if in doubt, see a dictionary

ant high-pressure
low-priced *adj syn* see CHEAP 1
‖**low-rate** *vb syn* see DECRY 2
low-set *adj syn* see SHORT 2
low-spirited *adj syn* see DOWNCAST
  ant high-spirited
low-statured *adj syn* see SHORT 2
loyal *adj syn* see FAITHFUL 1
  con faithless; alienated, disaffected, estranged;
  contumacious, factious, insubordinate, mutinous, rebellious, seditious
  ant disloyal
loyalist *n syn* see PATRIOT 1
loyalty *n* **1** *syn* see FIDELITY 1
  rel trueness, truth
  ant disloyalty
  2 *syn* see ATTACHMENT 1
lubber *n syn* see OAF 2
lubberland *n syn* see UTOPIA
lubberly *adj syn* see BOORISH
‖**lubricate** *vb syn* see BRIBE
lubricious *adj* **1** *syn* see INCONSTANT 1
  2 *syn* see SLICK 1
lucent *adj* **1** *syn* see BRIGHT 1
  2 *syn* see CLEAR 4
lucid *adj* **1** *syn* see BRIGHT 1
  2 *syn* see SANE 2
  3 *syn* see UNDERSTANDABLE
  4 *syn* see CLEAR 4
  con dusky, gloomy, murky; muddy, turbid
lucidity *n* **1** *syn* see CLARITY
  rel comprehensibility, intelligibility, under-
  standability; distinctness, explicitness
  ant ambiguity
  2 *syn* see WIT 2
Lucifer *n syn* see DEVIL 1
luck *n* **1** *syn* see CHANCE 2
  rel break, occasion, opportunity
  2 *syn* see ACCIDENT 1
  3 success dependent on chance <he had all the
  luck in the world and was greatly envied by every one of his associates>
  syn fortunateness, fortune, luckiness
  rel advantage, break, fluke, godsend, opportunity, windfall; weal; hap, kismet
  ant ill-fortune
  4 *syn* see CHARM 2
luck *vb syn* see HAPPEN 2
luckiness *n syn* see LUCK 3
luckless *adj syn* see UNLUCKY
  rel miserable, wretched
  ant lucky
lucky *adj* having a favorable outcome or an unforeseen or unpredictable success <he can only
  be described as *lucky,* as his success and fame are
  unearned>
  syn fortunate, happy, providential, ‖sonsy, well
  rel auspicious, benign, favorable, propitious;
  advantageous, beneficial, profitable; felicitous
  idiom in luck
  con baleful, malefic, maleficent, malign, sinister
  ant luckless, unlucky
lucrative *adj syn* see ADVANTAGEOUS 1
lucre *n* **1** *syn* see PROFIT

  2 *syn* see MONEY
luculent *adj syn* see CLEAR 4
ludicrous *adj syn* see LAUGHABLE
  rel absurd, foolish, preposterous, silly; antic,
  bizarre, fantastic, grotesque
  con doleful, dolorous, lugubrious, melancholy
lug *vb* **1** *syn* see PULL 2
  2 *syn* see CARRY 1
  3 *syn* see JERK
‖**lug** *n syn* see OAF 2
‖**lugs** *n pl syn* see POSE 2
lugubrious *adj* **1** *syn* see MELANCHOLY 2
  rel depressing, oppressing, oppressive; dour,
  glum, morose, saturnine, sullen
  con blithe, jocund, jolly, jovial, merry; cheerful,
  glad, joyful
  ant facetious
  2 *syn* see GLOOMY 3
lukewarm *adj* **1** *syn* see TEPID 1
  2 *syn* see TEPID 2
  rel irresolute, irresolved, uncommitted, unresolved; hesitant, indecisive, uncertain, undecided; cool; wishy-washy
  ant icy; boiling
lull *vb* **1** *syn* see CALM
  rel moderate, qualify, temper
  ant agitate
  2 *syn* see ABATE 4
lull *n* **1** *syn* see QUIET 1
  2 *syn* see PAUSE
  rel abeyance, quiescence
lullaby *n* a song to quiet children or lull them to
  sleep <sang a *lullaby* to the baby every night>
  syn berceuse, cradlesong
‖**lulu** *n syn* see ‖DILLY
lumber *vb* to tread heavily or clumsily <the tired
  old man slowly *lumbered* home>
  syn barge, clump, galumph, stumble, stump
  rel plod, trudge; shamble, slog
lumber *vb syn* see BURDEN
lumbering *adj* **1** *syn* see CLUMSY 1
  rel cumbersome, cumbrous, ponderous; hulking, hulky
  2 *syn* see AWKWARD 2
luminary *n* **1** *syn* see CELEBRITY 2
  rel leading light
  2 *syn* see NOTABLE 1
luminous *adj* **1** *syn* see BRIGHT 1
  2 *syn* see CLEAR 4
  3 *syn* see UNDERSTANDABLE
lummox *n syn* see OAF 2
lump *n* **1** a compact mass of indefinite size and
  shape <dropped a large *lump* of butter into the
  steaming chowder>
  syn chunk, clod, clump, gob, hunch, hunk, nugget, wad
  rel particle, piece, portion; batch, bunch, ‖swad;
  bit, chip, crumb, morsel, scrap; wedge; block,
  bulk
  2 *syn* see MUCH
  3 *syn* see BUMP 2
  rel bulge, protuberance, swelling
  4 *syn* see OAF 2
  5 lumps *pl syn* see DUE 1

lump *vb syn* see BEAR 10
lumpish *adj* **1** *syn* see BOORISH
  2 *syn* see CLUMSY 1
lumpkin *n syn* see OAF 2
lumpy *adj syn* see RUDE 1
lunacy *n* **1** *syn* see INSANITY 1
  rel absurdity, folly, foolery, foolishness; asininity, fatuity, inanity, ineptitude, stupidity
  2 *syn* see FOOLISHNESS
lunatic *adj* **1** *syn* see INSANE 1
  2 *syn* see FOOLISH 2
lunatic *n* **1** a person who is insane or of unsound mind <Bedlam was a famous old English asylum for *lunatics*>
  syn bedlamite, dement, loon, loony, madling, madman, maniac, non compos, nut, Tom o' Bedlam
  rel demoniac, energumen; raver; neuropath, neurotic, paranoid, psycho, psychoneurotic
  2 *syn* see CRACKPOT
lunch counter (*or* **bar**) *n syn* see EATING HOUSE
luncheonette *n syn* see EATING HOUSE
lunchroom *n syn* see EATING HOUSE
lunch wagon (*or* **cart**) *n syn* see EATING HOUSE
lunge *vb syn* see PLUNGE 2
lunk *n syn* see DUNCE
lunkhead *n syn* see DUNCE
lupanar *n syn* see BROTHEL
lurch *n syn* see LEANING 2
lurch *vb* **1** *syn* see SEESAW
  2 to move forward unsteadily while swaying from side to side <the sodden drunk *lurched* uncertainly toward the door>
  syn careen, stagger, ‖stoit, ‖stoiter, ‖stot, sway, swing, weave, wobble; *compare* TEETER
  rel reel, rock, roll, swag, toss, totter, whirl; bob; wave, waver
  con march, stride
  3 *syn* see TEETER
  rel pitch, plunge
  4 *syn* see JERK
  5 *syn* see WALLOW 2
  6 *syn* see STUMBLE 3
lure *n* **1** *syn* see ATTRACTION 1
  2 something that leads an individual into a place or situation from which escape is difficult <used her charm as a *lure* to trap the unsuspecting youth>
  syn allurement, bait, come-on, decoy, enticement, inveiglement, seducement, siren song, snare, ‖stale, temptation, trap
  rel appeal, attraction, incentive, inducement; con game, gimmick, suck-in, trick; ambush, blind, camouflage, delusion, fake, illusion
  con caution, caveat, warning
lure *vb* to draw from a usual, desirable, or proper course or situation into one felt as unusual, undesirable, or wrong <the promise of money *lured* him away from his steady job>
  syn allure, bait, decoy, entice, entrap, inveigle, lead on, seduce, tempt, toll, train
  rel bag, capture, catch, draw in, ensnare, rope, snare, suck in; attract, beguile, bewitch, captivate, charm, enchant, fascinate, invite; draw, draw on; blandish, cajole, wheedle

  idiom bait the hook, give the come-on
  con drive (away *or* off), rebuff, repulse
  ant repel
lurid *adj* **1** *syn* see PALE 1
  2 *syn* see GHASTLY 1
  rel ashen, ashy, livid, pale, pallid, wan; baleful, malefic, maleficent, malign, sinister
  3 *syn* see SENSATIONAL 2
luring *adj syn* see ENTICING
  ant repellent, repelling
lurk *vb syn* see SNEAK
lurking *adj syn* see LATENT
luscious *adj* **1** *syn* see DELIGHTFUL
  rel appetizing, flavorsome, nectarious, palatable, piquant; choice, distinctive, exquisite, rare, rich
  ant austere
  2 *syn* see LUXURIOUS 3
  3 *syn* see SENSUOUS
  4 *syn* see ORNATE
lush *adj* **1** *syn* see PROFUSE
  rel luxurious, sumptuous
  2 *syn* see DELIGHTFUL
  3 *syn* see SENSUOUS
  4 *syn* see LUXURIOUS 3
lush *n* ‖**1** *syn* see LIQUOR 2
  2 *syn* see DRUNKARD
lush (up) *vb syn* see DRINK 3
‖**lushed** *adj syn* see INTOXICATED 1
‖**lusher** *n syn* see DRUNKARD
lust *n* **1** *syn* see DESIRE 1
  rel coveting, yearning, yen
  2 sexual appetency <they mistakenly thought that *lust* was lasting love>
  syn aphrodisia, concupiscence, desire, eroticism, itch, lickerishness, lustfulness, passion, prurience, pruriency
  rel nymphomania, priapism, satyriasis, satyrism; excitement, heat, hunger, libido, rut; fervor; carnality, lasciviousness, lecherousness, lechery, lubricity, salacity
lust *vb syn* see LONG
  rel desire, wish
luster *n* the quality or condition of shining by reflected light <the satiny *luster* of fine pearls>
  syn glaze, glint, gloss, polish, sheen, shine
  rel iridescence, opalescence; brilliance, brilliancy, effulgence, luminosity, radiance, refulgence; afterglow, gleam, glow; candescence, incandescence
lusterless *adj* **1** *syn* see DULL 7
  ant lustrous
  2 *syn* see COLORLESS 2
lustful *adj* **1** *syn* see LICENTIOUS 2
  2 sexually excited <*lustful* old man>
  syn concupiscent, goatish, hot, lascivious, libidinous, lickerish, passionate, prurient, ruttish, rutty, satyric

---

syn synonym(s)   *rel* related word(s)
ant antonym(s)   *con* contrasted word(s)
idiom idiomatic equivalent(s)
‖ use limited; if in doubt, see a dictionary

rel burning, hot-blooded, itching; lecherous, salacious

lustfulness *n syn* see LUST 2

lustral *adj syn* see PURGATIVE

lustrate *vb syn* see PURIFY 2

lustration *n syn* see PURIFICATION

lustratory *adj syn* see PURGATIVE

lustrous *adj* **1** having a high gloss or shine <a *lustrous* star sapphire>
syn burnished, gleaming, glistening, glossy, polished, sheeny, shining, shiny
rel gleamy, glimmering, glinting, sparkling; radiant
con dull, flat, lackluster, mat
ant lusterless
2 *syn* see BRIGHT 1
rel glorious, resplendent, splendid

lusty *adj* **1** *syn* see VIGOROUS
rel hale, healthy
ant effete
2 *syn* see STRONG 3
3 *syn* see HUGE

lusus *n syn* see FREAK 2

luxuriant *adj* **1** *syn* see PROFUSE
rel fecund, fertile, fruitful, prolific; rampant, rank
con barren, infertile, sterile, unfruitful
2 *syn* see LUXURIOUS 3

luxuriate *vb syn* see WALLOW 3
rel overindulge, overdo; eat up, enjoy, feast, love, riot

luxurious *adj* **1** *syn* see SENSUOUS
rel self-indulging, self-pampering; languishing, languorous

con self-abnegating, self-denying; austere, severe, stern
ant ascetic
2 *syn* see GRAND 2
rel imposing, majestic, stately
3 ostentatiously rich or magnificent <the robber barons built *luxurious* homes which rivaled the palaces of Europe>
syn Capuan, deluxe, luscious, lush, luxuriant, opulent, palace, palatial, plush, plushy, sumptuous, upholstered
rel extravagant, grandiose, ostentatious, posh, pretentious, showy; awful, grand, imposing, magnificent, majestic, stately; Lucullan; elaborate, fancy; costly, expensive, precious
con economical, frugal, sparing, thrifty; exiguous, meager, scant, scanty, scrimpy, skimpy, spare

luxury *n* something adding to pleasure but not absolutely necessary <the poor cannot even afford the essentials, let alone occasional *luxuries*>
syn amenity, extravagance, frill, luxus, superfluity
rel comfort; embellishment, redundancy, self-indulgence; dainty, delicacy
con basics, essential(s), fundamental(s)

luxus *n syn* see LUXURY

lying *adj syn* see DISHONEST
rel false, wrong; deceptive, delusive, delusory, misleading

lying–in *n syn* see CONFINEMENT 2

lyncean *adj syn* see SHARP-EYED

lynx–eyed *adj syn* see SHARP-EYED

M

ma *n syn* see MOTHER 1

macabre *adj syn* see GHASTLY 1
 rel deadly, deathlike, deathly; ghostlike, ghostly

macaroni *n syn* see FOP

mace *n syn* see CUDGEL

‖**mace** *n syn* see SWINDLER

‖**mace** *vb syn* see CHEAT

machinate *vb* **1** *syn* see ENGINEER
 2 *syn* see PLOT

machination *n syn* see PLOT 2

machine *n* **1** *syn* see CAR
 2 *syn* see ROBOT 2

machinery *n syn* see EQUIPMENT
 rel agency, agent, channel, instrument, instrumentality, means, medium, organ, vehicle; contraption, contrivance, device, gadget; appliance, implement, instrument, tool, utensil

‖**mack** *n syn* see PIMP 1

macquereau *n syn* see PIMP 1

macrocosm *n syn* see UNIVERSE
 ant microcosm

macrocosmos *n syn* see UNIVERSE
 ant microcosm

mad *adj* **1** *syn* see INSANE 1
 rel delirious, frantic, frenetic, furious, rabid, wild
 2 *syn* see FOOLISH 2
 3 *syn* see ILLOGICAL
 4 *syn* see ANGRY
 rel sore, worked up; affronted, offended, outraged
 5 *syn* see FURIOUS 2

mad *vb syn* see ANGER 1

mad *n syn* see ANGER

mad–brained *adj syn* see RASH 1

madcap *adj syn* see RASH 1

madden *vb* **1** to make insane <prolonged solitary confinement had *maddened* the prisoners>
 syn craze, derange, distract, frenzy, unbalance, unhinge
 rel shatter; possess
 idiom drive insane (*or* mad *or* crazy)
 2 *syn* see ANGER 1
 con allay, assuage, mitigate, relieve

made–to–order *adj syn* see CUSTOM-MADE

madhouse *n syn* see ASYLUM 3

madid *adj syn* see WET 1

madling *n syn* see LUNATIC 1

madly *adv syn* see HARD 2
 rel foolishly, insanely, irrationally; hastily, rashly

madman *n* **1** *syn* see LUNATIC 1
 2 *syn* see FOOL 1

madness *n syn* see INSANITY 1

maelstrom *n syn* see EDDY
 rel commotion, confusion, fury, storm, turmoil

mafia *n syn* see CLIQUE

magazine *n* **1** *syn* see DEPOT 2

 rel cache, lumber room
 2 *syn* see ARMORY
 3 *syn* see JOURNAL
 rel publication; digest, gazette; annual, bimonthly, biweekly, daily, monthly, quarterly, semiweekly, weekly

mage *n syn* see MAGICIAN 1

maggot *n syn* see CAPRICE

magian *n syn* see MAGICIAN 1

magian *adj syn* see MAGIC

magic *n* **1** the use of means (as charms or spells) believed to have supernatural power over natural forces <the practice of *magic*>
 syn bewitchment, conjuring, conjury, enchantment, ensorcellment, incantation, magicking, necromancy, sorcery, thaumaturgy, witchcraft, witchery, witching, wizardry
 rel abracadabra, alchemy, augury, charm, divining, exorcism, fortune-telling, mumbo jumbo, occultism, soothsaying, sortilege, voodooism; devilry, deviltry, diablerie, diabolism, satanism; wicca
 2 the art of producing mysterious effects by illusion and sleight of hand <the club presented a program of clever *magic* to raise funds>
 syn conjuring, legerdemain
 idiom sleight of hand

magic *adj* having seemingly supernatural qualities or powers <modern medicine has developed a host of *magic* drugs>
 syn magian, magical, mystic, necromantic, sorcerous, thaumaturgic, witchy, wizardly
 rel extraordinary, marvelous, prodigious, remarkable, stupendous, unbelievable, unprecedented

magical *adj syn* see MAGIC

magician *n* **1** one who practices magical arts <a *magician* cast a spell over the child>
 syn archimage, charmer, conjurer, enchanter, mage, magian, magus, necromancer, sorcerer, voodoo, voodooist, warlock, wizard; *compare* WITCH 1
 rel augurer, brujo, diviner, exorciser, exorcist, invocator, thaumaturge, thaumaturgist; medicine man, shaman; prophet, seer, soothsayer; fortune-teller, medium; diabolist, satanist
 2 one who practices tricks of illusion and sleight of hand <a *magician* performed tricks for the children at the party>
 syn conjurer, illusionist, trickster

magicking *n syn* see MAGIC 1

magisterial *adj* **1** *syn* see DICTATORIAL

---

syn synonym(s) *rel* related word(s)
ant antonym(s) *con* contrasted word(s)
idiom idiomatic equivalent(s)
‖ use limited; if in doubt, see a dictionary

rel disdainful, insolent, lordly, supercilious
2 *syn* see MASTERFUL 1
3 *syn* see POMPOUS 1
magistrate *n syn* see JUDGE 2
magnanimous *adj syn* see GENEROUS 1
rel altruistic, liberal, unselfish; great, high=
minded, knightly, noble, nobleminded, princely
con measly, paltry, petty, picayune, picayunish
magnate *n* a businessman of exceptional wealth,
influence, or power <the oil and steel *magnates*
who controlled whole nations>
syn baron, czar, king, merchant prince, mogul,
prince, tycoon
rel figure, name, personage; ‖biggie, big gun,
big-timer, ‖big wheel, fat cat, lion, nabob; plutocrat
idiom captain of industry
magnetic *adj syn* see ATTRACTIVE 1
rel arresting, irresistible; charismatic
con repellent, repugnant, repulsive
magnetism *n syn* see CHARM 3
magnetize *vb syn* see ATTRACT 1
magnific *adj syn* see GRAND 1
magnificent *adj* **1** *syn* see GRAND 1
rel glorious, resplendent, splendid, sublime, superb; luxurious, opulent, sumptuous
con abject, ignoble, mean, sordid; humble,
lowly, meek; paltry
ant modest
2 *syn* see SPLENDID 2
3 *syn* see SUPERB 3
magnify *vb* **1** *syn* see PRAISE 2
2 *syn* see EXALT 1
rel augment, enlarge, increase; amplify, dilate,
distend, expand, inflate, swell
ant belittle, minimize
3 *syn* see INCREASE 1
ant minify
4 *syn* see INTENSIFY
5 *syn* see OVERPLAY 2
6 *syn* see EMBROIDER
magniloquent *adj syn* see RHETORICAL
magnitude *n* **1** *syn* see ENORMITY 2
2 *syn* see SIZE 1
3 *syn* see SIZE 2
4 *syn* see ORDER 4
5 *syn* see IMPORTANCE
magnum opus *n syn* see MASTERPIECE 1
magpie *n syn* see CHATTERBOX
magus *n syn* see MAGICIAN 1
mahogany *n syn* see TABLE 1
maid *n* **1** *syn* see GIRL 1
2 a woman hired to do housework <in addition
to her other duties the *maid* was expected to care
for the baby>
syn biddy, girl, handmaid, hired girl, housemaid, maidservant
rel au pair girl; chambermaid, nursemaid, par-
lormaid; handmaiden; domestic, factotum, ‖mu-
chacha, servant
idiom maid of all work
maiden *n syn* see GIRL 1
maiden *adj* **1** *syn* see VIRGIN 1
rel husbandless; old-maidish, spinsterish, spin-
sterly

2 *syn* see FIRST 2
maidenhead *n syn* see VIRGINITY
maidenhood *n syn* see VIRGINITY
maiden lady *n syn* see SPINSTER
maidservant *n syn* see MAID 2
maim *vb* to wound so severely as to deprive of the
use of or to cause loss of a limb or member <an
arm hanging useless, *maimed* in an auto acci-
dent>
syn cripple, dislimb, dismember, mayhem, mutilate; *compare* PARALYZE 1
rel disable, disfigure, hamstring; batter, break,
‖bung up, mangle, massacre, maul
con rehabilitate, restore, salvage; cure, fix, heal,
mend, remedy, repair
main *n syn* see OCEAN
main *adj syn* see CHIEF 2
rel foremost, head, leading, paramount; cardinal, controlling, essential, fundamental, vital;
prevailing
‖**main** *adv syn* see VERY 1
‖**mainline** *vb syn* see SHOOT UP 2
mainly *adv syn* see GENERALLY 1
mainstay *n* a chief reliance <the *mainstay* of the
organization held things together>
syn backbone, pillar, sinew(s)
rel brace, buttress, crutch, maintainer, prop,
staff, standby, stay, support, supporter, sustainer, upholder
maintain *vb* **1** to keep in a state of repair, efficiency, or validity <he followed a careful regi-
men to *maintain* his good health>
syn keep up, preserve, save, sustain; *compare*
SAVE 3
rel husband, manage; care (for), cultivate;
guard, protect
con disregard, ignore, neglect, omit, overlook,
slight
2 to uphold as true, right, proper, or acceptable
often in the face of challenge or indifference <I
maintain that his actions were justified by the
circumstances>
syn argue, assert, claim, contend, defend, justify, vindicate, warrant
rel affirm, aver, avouch, avow, declare, profess,
protest; emphasize, insist, persist, stress; correct,
rectify, right
con contradict, deny, gainsay, traverse; challenge, query, question
3 *syn* see SUPPORT 3
maintenance *n syn* see LIVING
majestic *adj* **1** *syn* see GRAND 1
rel courtly, dignified; ceremonious; imperial
2 *syn* see KINGLY
major *adj* **1** *syn* see CHIEF 2
rel better, greater, higher, superior
2 *syn* see BIG 1
3 *syn* see GRAVE 3
make *vb* **1** *syn* see EFFECT 1
rel initiate, originate, start
2 *syn* see GENERATE 1
rel brew
3 to bring something into being by forming,
shaping, combining, or altering materials
<*made* a dress from odd bits of material>

syn assemble, build, construct, erect, fabricate, fashion, forge, form, frame, manufacture, mold, produce, put together, shape; *compare* BUILD 1
4 *syn* see DRAFT 3
5 *syn* see CONSTITUTE 1
6 *syn* see PREPARE 1
7 *syn* see DESIGNATE 2
8 *syn* see ENACT 1
9 *syn* see INFER
10 *syn* see EARN 1
rel harvest, reap
11 *syn* see CLEAR 6
12 *syn* see FORCE 2
13 *syn* see HEAD 3
rel break (for)
‖**14** *syn* see MEDDLE
15 *syn* see RUN 8
make–believe *n syn* see PRETENSE 2
make off *vb syn* see RUN 2
rel depart, go, leave, quit, retire, withdraw; abscond, decamp, escape
make out *vb* **1** *syn* see APPREHEND 1
2 *syn* see ESTABLISH 6
3 *syn* see INFER
‖**4** *syn* see SHIFT 5
5 *syn* see SUCCEED 3
make over *vb syn* see TRANSFER 4
make–peace *n syn* see PEACEMAKER
maker *n syn* see FATHER 2
rel executor, operator; manufacturer
makeshift *n syn* see RESOURCE 3
makeshift *adj* serving as a temporary expedient <forced to make *makeshift* plans>
syn provisional, rough-and-ready, rough-and=tumble, stopgap
make up *vb* **1** *syn* see CONTRIVE 2
2 *syn* see MIX 1
3 *syn* see PREPARE 1
4 *syn* see CONSTITUTE 1
5 *syn* see COMPENSATE 1
make up (to) *vb syn* see ADDRESS 8
makeup *n* **1** the way in which parts or constituents are related in an organized whole <the complex *makeup* of the eye>
syn architecture, composition, constitution, construction, design, formation
rel arrangement, ordering, organization, plan, setup; form, shape, style
2 *syn* see DISPOSITION 3
rel cast, fiber, grain, mold, stamp, stripe, vein; constitution, frame
3 cosmetics used to color and beautify the face or body <with *makeup* on, she didn't look bad>
syn face, maquillage, paint, war paint
rel powder; blackface, grease paint
maladroit *adj* **1** *syn* see AWKWARD 2
rel blundering, floundering, stumbling, ungraceful; left-handed, unskilled
con deft, dexterous, handy; clever, cunning, ingenious
ant adroit
2 *syn* see TACTLESS
malady *n syn* see DISEASE 1
mala fide *adj syn* see INSINCERE

ant bona fide
malaise *n syn* see INFIRMITY 1
malapert *adj syn* see SAUCY 1
malapert *n syn* see MINX
malapropos *adj* **1** *syn* see IMPROPER 1
ant apropos
2 *syn* see UNSEASONABLE 1
malarkey *n syn* see NONSENSE 2
malconformation *n syn* see DEFORMITY
malcontent *n* **1** *syn* see GROUCH
2 *syn* see REBEL
malcontent *adj syn* see DISCONTENTED
rel alienated, disaffected, estranged; disobedient, ungovernable, unruly; restless; contumacious, factious, insubordinate, mutinous, rebellious, seditious
malcontented *adj syn* see DISCONTENTED
male *adj syn* see VIRILE
rel macho
male *n syn* see MAN 3
malediction *n syn* see CURSE 1
ant benediction
malefactor *n syn* see CRIMINAL
rel blackguard, knave, miscreant, rascal, rogue, scoundrel; evildoer, sinner, wrongdoer
malefic *adj syn* see SINISTER
ant benefic
maleficent *adj syn* see SINISTER
ant beneficent
maleness *n syn* see VIRILITY
rel machismo, macho
malevolence *n syn* see MALICE
rel antagonism, hostility; abhorrence, abomination, detestation
ant benevolence
malevolent *adj syn* see MALICIOUS
rel baleful, malefic, maleficent, sinister
con benign, benignant, kind, kindly
ant benevolent
malformation *n syn* see DEFORMITY
malice *n* a desiring or wishing pain, injury, or distress to another <they sought to ruin his reputation out of pure *malice*>
syn despite, despitefulness, grudge, ill will, malevolence, maliciousness, malignancy, malignity, spite, spitefulness, spleen
rel bane, poison, venom; bile; animosity, animus, antipathy, down, enmity; hate, hatefulness, hatred, invidiousness, meanness; bitterness, resentment, umbrage
con benevolence, benignancy, benignity, charity, kindliness, kindness
malicious *adj* having, showing, or indicative of intense often vicious ill will <the helpless victim of *malicious* rumors>
syn catty, despiteful, evil, hateful, malevolent, malign, malignant, nasty, rancorous, spiteful, spitish, vicious, wicked

---

syn synonym(s)   *rel* related word(s)
ant antonym(s)   *con* contrasted word(s)
idiom idiomatic equivalent(s)
‖ use limited; if in doubt, see a dictionary

rel poisonous, poison-pen, venomous, virulent; baneful, deleterious, detrimental, noxious, pernicious; envious, green, green-eyed, jealous; mean, petty

con benevolent, charitable, friendly, kind, kindly; considerate, thoughtful

maliciousness *n syn* see MALICE

malign *adj* **1** *syn* see SINISTER

rel baneful, deleterious, detrimental, injurious, noxious, pernicious

con auspicious, favorable, propitious; fortunate, happy, lucky, providential

ant benign

2 *syn* see MALICIOUS

rel antagonistic, antipathetic, hostile, inimical

con benignant, kind, kindly

ant benign

malign *vb* to speak evil of for the purpose of injuring and without regard for the truth <the candidates increasingly *maligned* each other as the campaign degenerated>

syn asperse, befoul, bespatter, blacken, calumniate, defame, denigrate, libel, ‖scandal, scandalize, slander, slur, smear, spatter, tear down, traduce, vilify, villainize

rel decry, depreciate, derogate, detract, disparage; opprobriate, revile, vituperate; backbite, besmirch, defile, pollute, smirch, soil, stain, sully, taint, tarnish

idiom blow upon, cast aspersion(s) on (*or* upon)

con acclaim, applaud, eulogize, extol, laud, praise; defend, justify, maintain, vindicate

malignancy *n syn* see MALICE

malignant *adj syn* see MALICIOUS

rel devilish, diabolical, fiendish

con altruistic, benevolent, charitable, humane

ant benignant

maligning *adj syn* see LIBELOUS

malignity *n syn* see MALICE

rel revengefulness, vengefulness, vindictiveness

ant benignity

malison *n syn* see CURSE 1

ant benison

‖**malkin** *n syn* see SLATTERN 1

malleable *adj syn* see PLASTIC

rel governable, manageable; transformable

con intractable, recalcitrant, ungovernable, unmanageable, unruly

ant refractory

malleate *vb syn* see HAMMER 1

malodorous *adj* **1** having an unpleasant smell <*malodorous* cheeses>

syn fetid, frowsy, funky, fusty, gamy, high, mephitic, musty, nidorous, noisome, olid, putrid, rancid, rank, reeking, reeky, ‖smellful, smelly, stale, stenchful, stenchy, stinking, stinky, strong, whiffy; *compare* ODOROUS

rel bad, foul, nauseating, offensive, vile; decayed, decomposed, fuggy, off, rotten, spoiled, tainted; nasty, noxious, pestilential, poisonous, polluted

con clean, deodorized, fresh

ant fragrant, sweet

2 *syn* see INDECOROUS

maltreat *vb syn* see ABUSE 4

‖**mam** *n syn* see MOTHER 1

mama (*or* **mamma**) *n syn* see MOTHER 1

‖**mammock** *vb syn* see DISORDER 1

mammoth *n syn* see GIANT

mammoth *adj syn* see HUGE

mammy *n syn* see MOTHER 1

mamzer (*or* **momzer** *or* **momser**) *n syn* see BASTARD 1

man *n* **1** *syn* see HUMAN

2 *syn* see MANKIND

3 a male human being <just an average *man* trying to get by>

syn ‖bloke, boy, buck, ‖cat, chap, cuss, fellow, galoot, ‖gee, gent, gentleman, guy, he, male, ‖mun, skate, snap, ‖stirra; *compare* HUMAN

4 *syn* see HUSBAND

5 *syn* see LOVER 1

6 *syn* see POLICEMAN

manage *vb* **1** *syn* see CONDUCT 3

rel superintend; guide

2 *syn* see GOVERN 3

3 *syn* see SHIFT 5

rel bring about, carry out, contrive, effect, execute; accomplish, achieve, succeed

idiom sink or swim on one's own

con collapse, fail, fall down; give up, poop (out)

management *n syn* see OVERSIGHT 1

manager *n syn* see EXECUTIVE

rel handler, impresario, producer

man–at–arms *n syn* see SOLDIER

mancipium *n syn* see SLAVE 1

mandarin *n syn* see BUREAUCRAT

mandate *n syn* see COMMAND 1

rel decree, fiat, imperative; authority, authorization

mandatory *adj* containing or constituting a command <*mandatory* entrance examinations>

syn compulsatory, compulsory, imperative, imperious, obligatory, required

rel essential, indispensable, irremissible, necessary, needful, requisite; binding, commanding, compelling, de rigueur; forced, involuntary

con discretionary, elective, voluntary

ant optional

maneuver *n* **1** *syn* see MEASURE 7

2 *syn* see TRICK 1

rel contrivance, device; intrigue, machination, manipulation, plot; demarche, movement, plan; finesse, subterfuge

maneuver *vb* **1** *syn* see ENGINEER

rel navigate; finesse; design

2 *syn* see HANDLE 2

rel navigate

3 *syn* see MANIPULATE 2

man Friday *n syn* see RIGHT-HAND MAN

manful *adj syn* see BRAVE 1

manfulness *n syn* see VIRILITY

rel machismo, macho

mangle *vb syn* see BATTER 1

rel damage, impair, injure, mar; deface, disfigure; contort, deform, distort; butcher, hack

mangled *adj syn* see LACERATED

mangy *adj syn* see SHABBY 1

manhandle *vb* to treat roughly <riot police *manhandled* innocent bystanders>
syn knock about, mishandle, rough (up), roughhouse, slap around
rel abuse, maltreat, mistreat; batter, ‖bung up, mangle, maul

mania *n syn* see FETISH 2
rel craze, enthusiasm, fancy, fascination, infatuation, passion; compulsion, fixed idea, hang-up, idée fixe

maniac *adj syn* see INSANE 1
rel berserk, delirious, frantic, frenetic, frenzied, furious, rabid, raging, ranting, violent, wild

maniac *n* **1** *syn* see LUNATIC 1
2 *syn* see ENTHUSIAST

manifest *adj syn* see CLEAR 5
rel disclosed, divulged, revealed, told; evidenced, evinced, shown; noticeable, prominent
con implicit; obscure

manifest *vb* **1** *syn* see EMBODY 1
2 *syn* see SHOW 2
rel display, expose; express, utter, vent, voice
con adumbrate, shadow
ant suggest

manifold *adj* comprehending or uniting various features <a *manifold* operation>
syn diverse, diversiform, multifarious, multifold, multiform, multiplex, multivarious
rel multiphase, polymorphic, polymorphous
con homogeneous, pure, uniform; plain, simple, straightforward, uncomplex, uncomplicated

manifold *vb syn* see INCREASE 1

manikin *n syn* see DWARF

manipulate *vb* **1** *syn* see HANDLE 2
2 to control or play upon by artful, unfair, or insidious means <the sycophant cleverly *manipulated* his master>
syn beguile, exploit, finesse, jockey, maneuver, play; *compare* ENGINEER
rel machinate, use; conduct, control, direct, engineer, manage

mankind *n* the human race <all *mankind* will benefit from this new discovery>
syn flesh, Homo sapiens, humanity, humankind, man, mortality; *compare* HUMAN

manlike *adj* **1** *syn* see ANTHROPOID
2 *syn* see VIRILE
rel macho

manliness *n syn* see VIRILITY
rel machismo, macho

manly *adj* **1** *syn* see VIRILE
rel macho
2 *syn* see BRAVE 1

man–made *adj syn* see SYNTHETIC

manner *n* **1** *syn* see HABIT 1
2 *syn* see METHOD 1
rel custom, habit, habitude, practice, usage, use, wont; form, style
3 *syn* see STYLE 4
4 *syn* see VEIN 1
rel form, turn; affectation, affectedness, mannerism; idiosyncrasy, peculiarity
5 manners *pl* habitual conduct or deportment in social intercourse evaluated according to some conventional standard of politeness or civility <a person with impeccable *manners*>
syn amenities, civilities, decorum(s), etiquette, mores, proprieties
rel formalities, protocol; elegancies; bearing, behavior, demeanor, deportment, mien, p's and q's; mannerliness
idiom conduct becoming a gentleman
con mannerlessness, unmannerliness

mannered *adj syn* see SELF-CONSCIOUS

mannerism *n syn* see POSE 2
rel eccentricity, idiosyncrasy; oddness, peculiarity, queerness, singularity

mannerless *adj syn* see RUDE 6
ant mannerly

mannerly *adj syn* see CIVIL 2
ant mannerless, unmannerly

manor *n* **1** *syn* see MANSION
2 *syn* see ESTATE 3

mansion *n* a large imposing residence <the governor's *mansion*>
syn castle, chateau, manor, villa
rel estate, hall, house

manslaughter *n syn* see MURDER

manslayer *n syn* see MURDERER

mantic *adj syn* see PROPHETIC

mantle *vb syn* see BLUSH

man–to–man *adj syn* see FRANK

manual *n syn* see HANDBOOK
rel abecedarium, hornbook, primer; text, textbook

manufactory *n syn* see FACTORY

manufacture *vb syn* see MAKE 3

manumit *vb syn* see FREE
ant enslave

many *adj* consisting of a goodly but indefinite number <*many* lives were lost in the flood>
syn legion, multifarious, multitudinal, multitudinous, numerous, populous, ‖several, sundry, various, voluminous
rel divers, manifold, multiple, multiplicate, multiplied, myriad; abounding, abundant, bounteous, bountiful, copious, plentiful
con meager, scant, scanty, sparse; only, sole
ant few

many *pron syn* see SUNDRY

many–sided *adj* **1** *syn* see MULTILATERAL
2 *syn* see VERSATILE

map *n* **1** *syn* see CHART 1
rel picture, portrayal; delineation, design, diagram, draft, outline, sketch, tracing
‖**2** *syn* see FACE 1

map (out) *vb syn* see DESIGN 3

maquillage *n syn* see MAKEUP 3

mar *vb syn* see INJURE 1
rel bruise, scar, scratch, warp; ruin, wreck
con adorn, beautify, decorate, embellish; mend, patch, repair; amend, correct, emend, rectify, reform, revise

---

syn synonym(s)   *rel* related word(s)
ant antonym(s)   *con* contrasted word(s)
idiom idiomatic equivalent(s)
‖ use limited; if in doubt, see a dictionary

maraud *vb syn* see RAID 1

marauder *n* one who raids in search of plunder
<*marauders* sacked village after village>
syn bandit, brigand, bummer, cateran, depredator, despoiler, forager, freebooter, looter, pillager, plunderer, raider, ravager, ravisher,
sacker, spoiler, spoliator
rel buccaneer, desperado, pirate; wrecker

marblehearted *adj syn* see UNFEELING 2
ant softhearted

marbles *n pl syn* see WIT 2

march *n syn* see FRONTIER 1
rel boundary, periphery; territory; outlands,
provinces

march *vb syn* see ADJOIN
rel fringe, hem, rim, skirt; extend; parallel

march *vb* **1** *syn* see AGREE 4
2 *syn* see STRIDE 1
3 *syn* see ADVANCE 5

march *n syn* see ADVANCE 2

marchland *n syn* see FRONTIER 1

mare's nest *n syn* see IMPOSTURE
rel babel, clamor, din, hubbub, hullabaloo,
racket, uproar

margin *n* **1** *syn* see BORDER 1
rel frame, trimming; shore; side
2 *syn* see ROOM 3
3 *syn* see MINIMUM

margin *vb syn* see BORDER 1
rel abut, connect, join, line, neighbor, touch

marijuana *n* the dried leaves and flowering tops of
the pistillate hemp plant sometimes smoked for
their intoxicating effect <*marijuana* was smoked
by several students at the party>
syn boo, cannabis, grass, ‖Mary Jane, moocah,
pot, ‖tea, weed
rel joint, reefer; hash, hashish

marine *adj* **1** of or relating to the sea <*marine* biol-
ogy>
syn maritime, oceanic, thalassic
rel hydrographic, oceanographic; abyssal,
bathyal, bathybic, bathysmal, benthic, dipsey,
neritic, pelagic; aquatic, fluvial, fluviatile, lacus-
trine
2 of or relating to the navigation of the sea <*marine* charts and maps>
syn maritime, nautical, navigational
rel naval; seamanlike, seamanly; deep-sea,
oceangoing, seafaring, seagoing

mariner *n* one engaged in sailing or handling a
ship <the tanker crew was made up mostly of
experienced *mariners*>
syn jack, jack-tar, sailor, sailorman, salt, seaman, tar, tarpaulin
rel bluejacket, gob, rating, ‖swab, ‖swabbie;
‖lascar, ‖limey; old salt, sea dog, shellback

marital *adj syn* see MATRIMONIAL

maritime *adj* **1** *syn* see MARINE 2
2 *syn* see MARINE 1

mark *n* **1** *syn* see AMBITION 2
2 *syn* see TARGET 1
3 *syn* see USE 4
4 *syn* see FOOL 3
5 *syn* see INDICATION 3

rel attribute, emblem, symbol, type; character,
property, quality
6 *syn* see QUALITY 1
7 a device (as a word) pointing distinctly to the
origin or ownership of merchandise to which it is
applied and legally reserved to the exclusive use
of the owner <the company was brought to
court for illegally using the *mark* of its rival>
syn brand, brand name, logo, logotype, trademark
rel label, stamp
8 *syn* see CHARACTER 1
9 *syn* see NOTICE 1
10 *syn* see EFFECT 3

mark *vb* **1** *syn* see CHOOSE 1
2 *syn* see SHOW 5
3 *syn* see SHOW 2
4 *syn* see CHARACTERIZE 2
rel bespeak, betoken, denote, signify
idiom set apart
5 *syn* see SEE 1
rel record, register; attend, heed, regard

mark (out) *vb syn* see DEMARCATE 1
rel lay off, mark off; chart, lay out, map

mark down *vb* **1** *syn* see REDUCE 2
ant mark up
2 *syn* see DEPRECIATE 1

marked *adj syn* see NOTICEABLE
rel distinguished, noted; considerable

market *n syn* see STORE 4

market *vb* **1** *syn* see SELL 3
rel wholesale
2 *syn* see SELL 2

marketable *adj* capable of being sold <*marketable* commodities>
syn merchandisable, merchantable, salable, sellable, trafficable, vendible
rel commercial; profitable, selling; fit, good,
sound, wholesome
con unmerchantable, unsalable
ant unmarketable

‖**maroon** *vb syn* see CAMP

marred *adj syn* see DAMAGED
rel banged-up, battered, bruised, mutilated; ruined, wrecked
ant unmarred

marriage *n* **1** the state of being united to a person
of the opposite sex as husband or wife <*marriage*
was not in the plans of this couple>
syn conjugality, connubiality, matrimony, wedlock
rel match, union
2 *syn* see WEDDING

marriage broker *n* one who arranges marriages
<the old widow served as the town's *marriage
broker*>
syn go-between, matchmaker
rel shadchan

marriage portion *n syn* see DOWRY

married *adj syn* see MATRIMONIAL

marrow *n syn* see ESSENCE 2
rel core, heart, kernel, meat

marrowy *adj syn* see PITHY

marry *vb* **1** to take as spouse <he *married* her for
her money>

syn catch, espouse, wed
rel wive
idiom get hitched, get married, tie the knot
con annul, divorce, separate
2 to join in wedlock <the minister *married* all three daughters in one ceremony>
syn ‖hitch, mate, splice, tie, wed
idiom tie the knot, unite in marriage
3 syn see JOIN 1

marsh *n syn* see SWAMP

marshal *vb* **1 syn** see ORDER 1
rel distribute, space; escort, guide, shepherd, usher
2 syn see MOBILIZE 3

marshland *n syn* see SWAMP

martial *adj* belonging to, engaged in, or appropriate to the affairs of war <the reviewing officer saw the company standing in *martial* array>
syn military, warlike
rel bellicose, belligerent, combative, pugnacious; aggressive, militant; high-spirited, mettlesome, spirited
con civil, civilian; irenic, pacific, peaceable, peaceful
ant unmartial

martyr *vb syn* see AFFLICT

martyrize *vb syn* see AFFLICT

marvel *n syn* see WONDER 1

marveling *n syn* see WONDER 2
rel surprise

marvelous *adj* **1** causing or exciting wonder <the way in which he could bring together opposing forces was truly *marvelous*>
syn amazing, astonishing, astounding, miraculous, prodigious, spectacular, staggering, strange, stupendous, surprising, wonderful, wondrous
rel awe-inspiring, awesome, awful, awing; incomprehensible, inconceivable, incredible, unimaginable; fabulous, phenomenal, supernatural; exceptional, extraordinary; bewildering, confounding, striking, stunning
con commonplace, ordinary, routine; blah, unexciting, uninteresting
2 superior or outstanding of its kind <had a *marvelous* weekend>
syn ‖cool, ‖dandy, divine, dreamy, ‖galluptious, glorious, groovy, hot, hunky-dory, ‖keen, ‖neat, nifty, peachy, ripping, sensational, super, swell, terrific, wonderful; *compare* EXCELLENT, SUPERIOR 4, SUPREME
rel agreeable, enjoyable, pleasant, pleasurable; rewarding, satisfying
con dreary, dull, humdrum, monotonous, tedious; inferior, low-grade, mean, poor, punk

‖Mary Jane *n syn* see MARIJUANA

mascot *n syn* see CHARM 2

masculine *adj syn* see VIRILE
ant effeminate, unmasculine
rel macho

masculinity *n syn* see VIRILITY
rel machismo, macho

mash *n syn* see CLUTTER 2

mash *vb* **1 syn** see CRUSH 2

‖2 syn see PRESS 1

mashed *adj syn* see ENAMORED 1

masher *n syn* see WOLF

mash note *n syn* see LOVE LETTER

mask *n* **1** a cover or partial cover for the face that has openings for the eyes and is used especially for disguise <on Halloween he wore a pirate's *mask*>
syn domino, doughface, false face, visor, vizard
rel disguise, masquerade; veil
2 an outward appearance that seeks to obscure an underlying true character <he was able to maintain a *mask* of dignity and tranquillity in his time of anxiety>
syn cloak, color, coloring, cover, disguise, disguisement, facade, face, false front, front, guise, masquerade, muffler, pretense, pretext, put-on, semblance, show, veil, veneer, window dressing; *compare* APPEARANCE 2
rel affectation, air, pose, posture; fakery, sham; dissembling, dissimulation, seeming, simulation; appearance, aspect

mask *vb syn* see DISGUISE
rel screen, secrete, veil; blur; defend, guard, protect, safeguard, shield

masquerade *n syn* see MASK 2

masquerade *vb syn* see POSE 4

mass *n* **1 syn** see BODY 4
2 syn see PILE 1
3 syn see BULK 1
rel aggregate, aggregation, conglomerate, conglomeration; sum, whole
4 syn see BODY 3
5 syn see MUCH
6 *usu* **masses** *pl syn* see RABBLE 2

massacre *vb syn* see SLAUGHTER 3

massacre *n* the act or an instance of killing a considerable number of human beings under circumstances of atrocity or cruelty <the *massacre* of the Indians by the soldiers and settlers>
syn bloodbath, bloodshed, butchery, carnage, slaughter
rel blood purge, decimation, genocide, pogrom; internecion; assassination, killing, murder, slaying

massive *adj* **1 syn** see HEAVY 1
rel hulking, hulky, massy
2 syn see HUGE
3 syn see MONSTROUS 1

massy *adj syn* see HUGE

master *n* **1 syn** see EXPERT
rel maestro, savant; genius, mastermind; guru, swami
2 syn see LEADER 2
rel overlord, overman, overseer
3 syn see VICTOR 1
‖4 syn see HUSBAND
5 syn see LOVER 1

master *vb* **1 syn** see OVERCOME 1

---

syn synonym(s)   **rel** related word(s)
ant antonym(s)   **con** contrasted word(s)
idiom idiomatic equivalent(s)
‖ use limited; if in doubt, see a dictionary

2 *syn* see DOMESTICATE
rel dominate, govern, predominate, rule
3 *syn* see CONQUER 2
4 *syn* see LEARN 1

master *adj* **1** *syn* see DOMINANT 1
2 *syn* see PROFICIENT

masterdom *n* *syn* see SUPREMACY

masterful *adj* **1** disposed to exercise or flaunt dictatorial authority in a way to override any protestation <the royal favorite was pompous and *masterful* when dealing with subordinates>
syn bossy, domineering, high-handed, imperative, imperial, imperious, magisterial, overbearing, peremptory
rel absolute, arbitrary, authoritarian, authoritative, dictative, dictatorial, doctrinaire, dogmatic; autocratic, despotic, tyrannical; high-and≠mighty, self-willed
con humble, modest, unpretentious; indecisive, irresolute; submissive, yielding; feeble, weak
2 *syn* see PROFICIENT
rel adroit, deft, dexterous; preeminent, superlative, supreme, transcendent

master–hand *n* *syn* see EXPERT

masterly *adj* *syn* see PROFICIENT
rel preeminent, superlative, supreme, transcendent

masterpiece *n* **1** something done or made with extraordinary skill or brilliance <his latest work is unquestionably a *masterpiece*>
syn chef d'oeuvre, classic, magnum opus, masterwork, tour de force
rel objet d'art, masterstroke
con botch, disaster, fiasco
2 *syn* see SHOWPIECE

mastership *n* *syn* see ABILITY 2

masterwork *n* *syn* see MASTERPIECE 1

mastery *n* **1** *syn* see POWER 1
2 *syn* see ABILITY 2

masticate *vb* *syn* see CHEW 1
rel bruise, crush, macerate, mash, pulp, pulpify, smash, squash

mastodonic *adj* *syn* see HUGE

mat *adj* *syn* see DULL 7

matador *n* *syn* see BULLFIGHTER

match *n* **1** *syn* see OPPONENT
2 *syn* see EQUAL
rel analogue, parallel
3 *syn* see MATE 5
4 *syn* see PARALLEL
5 *syn* see EVENT 5
rel bout, engagement, game

match *vb* **1** *syn* see OPPOSE 1
2 *syn* see EQUATE 2
3 *syn* see AMOUNT 2
rel complement, supplement
4 *syn* see EQUAL 3
rel compare, stack up
idiom hold a candle to

matched *adj* *syn* see ASSORTED 2
rel balanced, equated, evened, similar; coordinated, harmonized; coupled, joined, mated, paired, yoked
ant unmatched

matchless *adj* *syn* see ALONE 3
ant matchable

matchmaker *n* *syn* see MARRIAGE BROKER

mate *n* **1** *syn* see PARTNER
2 *syn* see ACCOMPANIMENT 2
3 *syn* see FRIEND
rel bedmate, classmate, co-mate, helpmate, playmate, roommate, schoolmate, teammate
4 *syn* see SPOUSE
rel match, parti
5 one of a pair matched in one or more qualities <the *mate* of a shoe>
syn companion, coordinate, double, duplicate, fellow, match, reciprocal, twin
rel alter ego, complement, sosie; compeer, equal, equivalent, peer

mate *vb* *syn* see MARRY 2
rel breed, crossbreed, pair; generate, procreate

‖**mater** *n* *syn* see MOTHER 1

material *adj* **1** of or belonging to actuality <for him the *material* world is the only world>
syn corporeal, gross, objective, phenomenal, physical, sensible, substantial, tangible
rel actual, real, true; appreciable, palpable, perceptible; earthly, worldly; animal, carnal, fleshly, sensual
con impalpable, imperceptible, intangible, unsubstantial; spiritual
ant immaterial, nonmaterial
2 *syn* see IMPORTANT 1
ant immaterial
3 *syn* see RELEVANT
rel consequential, important, momentous, significant; cardinal, essential, fundamental, vital
ant immaterial

material *n* **1** *syn* see THING 5
rel component, constituent, element, ingredient; apparatus, equipment, machinery
2 *usu* **materials** *pl* *syn* see EQUIPMENT

materialistic *adj* of or relating to a preoccupation with or stress upon material rather than intellectual or spiritual things <*materialistic* values characterize the modern age>
syn banausic, earthy, mundane, sensual, temporal, worldly
rel carnal, profane; earthly, terrestrial; secular, unspiritual
con intellectual, mental; spiritual, unfleshly, unworldly; heavenly

materiality *n* *syn* see ACTUALITY 2

materialize *vb* **1** *syn* see EMBODY 1
rel appear, emerge, loom, show; issue, rise, spring
2 to convert mentally into something concrete <with the help of graphs and figures abstract ideas can be *materialized*>
syn entify, hypostatize, reify
rel actualize, pragmatize, realize; corporealize; symbolize, typify

matériel *n* *syn* see EQUIPMENT

matriarch *n* a dignified, usually elderly woman of some rank or authority <the local *matriarchs* controlled the town's social functions>
syn dame, dowager, grande dame, matron

rel materfamilias, mother

matrimonial *adj* of, relating to, or characteristic of marriage <the *matrimonial* bond between husband and wife>
syn conjugal, connubial, hymeneal, marital, married, nuptial, spousal, wedded
rel bridal, epithalamic

matrimony *n syn* see MARRIAGE 1

matron *n syn* see MATRIARCH

matter *n* **1** *syn* see SUBJECT 2
2 *syn* see AFFAIR 1
rel complication, grievance, to-do, worry; circumstance, predicament
3 *syn* see SUBSTANCE 2
4 *syn* see THING 5
5 *syn* see ORDER 4

matter *vb* to be of importance <being your own self is what really *matters*>
syn count, import, mean, signify, weigh
idiom carry weight

matter-of-course *adj syn* see GENERAL 1

matter-of-fact *adj* **1** *syn* see REALISTIC
rel objective, sound
2 *syn* see PROSAIC 1
3 involving no display of emotion <the *matter-of-fact* reading of the judge masked his inner anguish>
syn cold, cold-blooded, emotionless, impersonal, unimpassioned
rel unaffected, unsentimental; prosaic
con emotional, impassioned, personal
4 *syn* see IMPASSIVE 1

maturate *vb syn* see MATURE

mature *adj* **1** having attained the normal peak of natural growth and development <*mature* plants ready to bear fruit>
syn adult, full-blown, full-fledged, full-grown, grown, grown-up, matured, ripe, ripened
rel developed, ready
idiom of age
con childish, childlike; boyish, green, juvenile, maiden, puerile, youthful
ant immature
2 *syn* see DUE 2
3 *syn* see UNPAID 2

mature *vb* to become fully developed or ripe <she *matured* as an actress after several years of summer stock>
syn age, develop, grow, grow up, maturate, mellow, ‖ripe, ripen
rel blossom, flower; advance, progress, round; season; decline, deteriorate, olden, wane
idiom come of age

matured *adj* **1** *syn* see MATURE 1
rel completed, finished; advised, considered, deliberate, designed, premeditated, studied
con callow, crude, green, raw, rough, rude, uncouth
ant premature, unmatured
2 *syn* see RIPE 3

maudlin *adj syn* see SENTIMENTAL
rel addled, befuddled, confused, fuddled, muddled; silly

maul *n syn* see BRAWL 2

maul *vb syn* see BATTER 1
rel flagellate, flail, lash, whip; bang, bash, buffet, pound; abuse, maltreat, manhandle, molest, rough (up)

maunder *vb syn* see WANDER 1

maundering *adj syn* see INARTICULATE 3

maven *n syn* see EXPERT

maverick *n syn* see BOHEMIAN

mawkish *adj syn* see SENTIMENTAL
rel banal, flat; cloying, nauseating, sickening

maxim *n* a general truth or fundamental principle usually expressed sententiously <Francis Bacon is noted for his fondness for *maxims*>
syn aphorism, apothegm, axiom, brocard, dictum, gnome, moral, rule, truism
rel commonplace, motto, platitude; law, precept, prescript; theorem; proverb
idiom rule of thumb

maximal *adj syn* see MAXIMUM
ant minimal

maximize *vb syn* see OVERPLAY 2
ant minimize

maximum *adj* greatest in quantity or highest in degree attainable or attained <apply *maximum* pressure above the point of injury>
syn maximal, outside, top, topmost, utmost; *compare* SUPREME
rel greatest, highest, largest
con least, lowest, slightest, smallest
ant minimum

maybe *adv syn* see PERHAPS

mayhem *vb syn* see MAIM

maze *n* **1** something intricately or confusingly elaborate or complicated <the landscape soon became a *maze* of superhighways>
syn jungle, knot, labyrinth, mesh, mizmaze, morass, skein, snarl, tangle, web
rel fog, haze; gordian knot; conglomeration, hodgepodge, miscellany, mishmash
‖**2** *syn* see HAZE 2

‖**mazuma** *n syn* see MONEY

MD *n syn* see PHYSICIAN

meager *adj* **1** *syn* see LEAN
2 being smaller than what is normal, necessary, or desirable <the remains of dinner provided only a *meager* meal that evening>
syn exiguous, poor, scant, scanty, scrimp, scrimpy, skimp, skimpy, spare, sparse; *compare* SHORT 3
rel deficient, inadequate, insufficient; inappreciable, inconsiderable, slight; bare, mere, minimum; miserable, shabby
con adequate, enough, sufficient; appreciable, considerable; copious, plentiful
ant ample

meal *n* the portion of food taken at one time to satisfy appetite <the noonday dinner was the big *meal* of the day in those times>
syn ‖chow, feed, ‖nosh, refection, repast

---

syn synonym(s)   *rel* related word(s)
ant antonym(s)   *con* contrasted word(s)
idiom idiomatic equivalent(s)
‖ use limited; if in doubt, see a dictionary

rel feast, ‖nosh-up, spread; refreshment, regalement; collation, snack; fare, grub, meat, mess, victuals; board, table

meal *vb syn* see EAT 1

mean *adj* **1** *syn* see IGNOBLE 1
ant wellborn
2 *syn* see INFERIOR 2
3 *syn* see LITTLE 2
4 *syn* see CONTEMPTIBLE
5 *syn* see CHEAP 2
6 *syn* see STINGY
7 *syn* see TROUBLESOME
rel difficult, formidable, rough, rugged, tough
8 *syn* see UNWELL

mean *vb* **1** *syn* see INTEND 2
rel desire, want, wish
2 to convey (as an idea) to the mind <your answer *means* nothing to me>
syn add up (to), connote, denote, express, import, intend, signify, spell
rel designate, name; attest, betoken, indicate; hint, imply, intimate, suggest
3 *syn* see MATTER

mean *n* **1** *syn* see AVERAGE
2 *usu* **means** *sing or pl in constr* one by which work is accomplished or an end effected <careful planning is a major *means* of improving output> <use any *means* to secure peace>
syn agency, agent, channel, instrument, instrumentality, instrumentation, intermediary, medium, ministry, organ, vehicle
rel fashion, manner, method, mode, system, way; apparatus, equipment, machinery, paraphernalia
3 **means** *pl* one's total property including real property and intangibles <people of moderate *means* are feeling the effects of inflation worse>
syn assets, capital, resources, wealth
rel finances, fortune, funds, moneybags, pocket, purse; ‖bundle, nest egg, pile, reserves, savings; estate, holdings, possessions; intangibles

mean *adj* **1** *syn* see MIDDLE 2
2 *syn* see MEDIUM

meander *vb syn* see WANDER 1
rel snake, turn, twist, wind

meanderer *n syn* see ROVER

meandering *adj syn* see WINDING

meandrous *adj syn* see WINDING

meaning *n* **1** the idea that something conveys to the mind <critics have endlessly debated the *meaning* of the poem>
syn acceptation, import, intendment, intent, message, purport, sense, significance, significancy, signification, sum and substance, understanding; *compare* SUBSTANCE 2, TENOR 1
rel drift, effect, essence, tenor; force, point, value; hint, implication, intimation, suggestion; connotation, definition, denotation
2 *syn* see INTENTION

meaningful *adj* **1** *syn* see EXPRESSIVE
ant meaningless
2 *syn* see IMPORTANT 1

meaningless *adj* **1** *syn* see SENSELESS 5
rel blank, empty, vacant

ant meaningful
2 *syn* see FECKLESS 1

measly *adj syn* see PETTY 2

measure *n* **1** *syn* see RATION
2 *syn* see TEMPERANCE 1
3 *syn* see SIZE 1
4 *syn* see MELODY
5 *syn* see RHYTHM
6 *syn* see STANDARD 3
7 an action planned or taken toward the accomplishment of a purpose <developed a new set of safety *measures*>
syn maneuver, move, procedure, proceeding, step
rel effort, project, proposal, proposition; expedient, makeshift, resort, resource, shift, stopgap

measure *vb* **1** *syn* see DEMARCATE 1
2 to ascertain the quantity, mass, extent, or degree of in terms of a standard unit or fixed amount <*measure* the depth of the water>
syn gauge, scale
rel size, size up; calculate, compute, estimate, figure, reckon

measure (out) *vb syn* see DISTRIBUTE 1

measureless *adj* **1** *syn* see INCALCULABLE 1
ant measurable
2 *syn* see LIMITLESS
ant measurable

measure up *vb syn* see EQUAL 3

meat *n* **1** *syn* see FOOD 1
2 *syn* see SUBSTANCE 2

meat–and–potatoes *adj syn* see FUNDAMENTAL 1

meathead *n syn* see OAF 2

meaty *adj syn* see PITHY

mechanical *adj syn* see PERFUNCTORY

meddle *vb* to concern oneself with officiously, impertinently, or indiscreetly <continually *meddling* in other people's affairs>
syn busybody, butt in, fool, horn in, interfere, interlope, intermeddle, ‖make, mess around, monkey (with), tamper (with)
rel intervene, intrude, invade, obtrude; pry, snoop, trespass
idiom put (*or* shove *or* stick) one's oar in, stick one's nose into
con disregard, ignore, neglect, omit, overlook, slight; avoid, eschew, shun

meddler *n syn* see BUSYBODY

meddlesome *adj syn* see IMPERTINENT 2

Meddlesome Mattie *n syn* see BUSYBODY

medial *adj* **1** *syn* see MIDDLE 1
2 *syn* see MIDDLE 2
3 *syn* see MEDIUM

median *n syn* see AVERAGE
rel center, middle

median *adj* **1** *syn* see MIDDLE 1
2 *syn* see MIDDLE 2

mediate *vb syn* see INTERPOSE 2

mediator *n* **1** *syn* see GO-BETWEEN 2
rel arbitrator, judge; conciliator, peacemaker; negotiator, troubleshooter
2 *syn* see MODERATOR

medical *n syn* see PHYSICIAN

medicament *n syn* see REMEDY 1

medicant *n syn* see REMEDY 1
medication *n syn* see REMEDY 1
medicinal *n syn* see DRUG 1
medicine *n syn* see REMEDY 1
mediciner *n syn* see PHYSICIAN
medico *n syn* see PHYSICIAN
mediocre *adj syn* see MEDIUM
  rel bad, inferior, poor; common, commonplace, ordinary, unexceptional
  idiom no great shakes, nothing to write home about
meditate *vb syn* see PONDER 2
meditative *adj* **1** *syn* see THOUGHTFUL 1
  rel musing, ruminant; wistful
  2 *syn* see PENSIVE 2
medium *adj* midway between the extremes of a scale, measurement, or evaluation <bought a suit of *medium* quality>
  syn average, fair, fairish, indifferent, intermediate, mean, medial, mediocre, middle-rate, middling, moderate, run-of-mine, run-of-the-mill, so-so
  rel median, par; passable, tolerable; neutral; popular, vulgar; normal, standard
  idiom fair to middling
  con inferior, low-grade, poor; excellent, first-class, high-grade, prime, superior
medium *n* **1** *syn* see MEAN 2
  rel intermediate, intermedium
  2 *syn* see ENVIRONMENT
  3 *syn* see FORTE
medley *n syn* see MISCELLANY 1
‖**meech** *vb syn* see SNEAK
meed *n* **1** *syn* see REWARD
  rel recompensing, satisfaction
  2 *syn* see RATION
  rel desert, due, merit
meek *adj syn* see HUMBLE 1
  rel gentle, mild; tame; forbearing, lenient, tolerant; long-suffering, patient
  con high-spirited, mettlesome, spirited, spunky; contumacious, insubordinate, rebellious
  ant arrogant
meet *vb* **1** *syn* see HAPPEN 2
  2 *syn* see CONFRONT 1
  3 *syn* see ENGAGE 5
  rel brave, oppose
  4 *syn* see EQUAL 3
  5 *syn* see SATISFY 5
  rel approach, equal, match, rival, tie, touch
  6 to come together face-to-face or as if face-to-face <the two leaders agreed to *meet* in a series of summit talks>
  syn close, encounter, face, front; *compare* CONFRONT 1
  rel accost, greet, salute; bump, clash, collide, cross; grapple, tussle, wrestle; experience, suffer, sustain, undergo
  con elude, escape, evade, shun
  ant avoid
  7 *syn* see CONVERGE
  8 *syn* see CONVENE 1
meet (with) *vb syn* see FIND 1
meet *n* **1** *syn* see EVENT 5

  2 *syn* see CONTEST 2
meet *adj* **1** *syn* see FIT 1
  rel accommodated, conformed, reconciled; good, right; equitable, fair, just
  ant unmeet
  2 *syn* see GOOD 2
  ant unmeet
meeting *n* **1** *syn* see CONTEST 2
  2 *syn* see CONCOURSE
  3 *syn* see TALK 4
  rel congress, moot
meetness *n syn* see ORDER 11
  ant unmeetness
megacosm *n syn* see UNIVERSE
  ant microcosm
megrim *n syn* see CAPRICE
  rel impulse, urge
melancholic *adj syn* see SAD 2
melancholy *n syn* see SADNESS
  rel miserableness, misery, wretchedness; despair, desperation; boredom, ennui, tedium
  con hopefulness, optimism
  ant exhilaration
melancholy *adj* **1** *syn* see SAD 1
  2 expressing or suggesting sorrow or mourning <the gloomy day led him to a *melancholy* train of thought>
  syn doleful, dolesome, dolorous, lamentable, lugubrious, moanful, mournful, plaintive, rueful, sighful, sorrowful, wailful, woeful; *compare* SAD 1, SAD 2
  rel pensive, reflective, thoughtful; discomposing, disquieting, disturbing, perturbing; dismal, dreary, funereal, gloomy, lachrymose, somber, sombrous
  con cheerful, glad, happy, joyful, joyous, lighthearted; gay, lively, vivacious
  3 *syn* see SAD 2
mélange *n syn* see MISCELLANY 1
meld *vb syn* see MIX 1
melding *n syn* see UNIFICATION
melee *n* **1** *syn* see CLASH 2
  rel dogfight, scuffle
  2 *syn* see BRAWL 2
  3 *syn* see MISCELLANY 1
meliorate *vb syn* see IMPROVE 1
melisma *n syn* see MELODY
mellay *n* **1** *syn* see BRAWL 2
  2 *syn* see CLASH 2
mellifluent *adj syn* see MELLIFLUOUS
mellifluous *adj* having a smooth rich flow <his *mellifluous* voice held his audience in a trance>
  syn golden, honeyed, Hyblaean, liquid, mellifluent, mellow; *compare* MELODIOUS 1
  rel accordant, canorous, euphonic, euphonious, harmonious, mellisonant, silvery; golden-tongued, silver-tongued; dulcet, sweet; resonant, sonorous

---

syn synonym(s)   *rel* related word(s)
ant antonym(s)   *con* contrasted word(s)
idiom idiomatic equivalent(s)
‖ use limited; if in doubt, see a dictionary

con blatant, boisterous, clamorous, obstreperous, strident, vociferous; discordant, grating, harsh

mellisonant *adj syn* see MELODIOUS 1

mellow *adj* **1** *syn* see RIPE 3
2 *syn* see MELLIFLUOUS

mellow *vb syn* see MATURE

melodia *n syn* see MELODY

melodic *adj* **1** *syn* see MELODIOUS 2
2 *syn* see MELODIOUS 1

melodious *adj* **1** pleasing to the ear <*melodious* sounds of the forest>
syn dulcet, euphonic, euphonious, mellisonant, melodic, sweet, tuneful; *compare* MELLIFLUOUS
rel canorous, harmonious
con discordant, grating, harsh
ant unmelodious
2 containing, constituting, or characterized by melody <her voice shows marked improvement and a new richly *melodious* quality>
syn melodic, musical, songful, tuned, tuneful
rel cantabile, lyric, melic

melody *n* a rhythmic succession of single tones organized as an aesthetic whole <took out his flute and played a simple *melody*>
syn air, descant, diapason, lay, measure, melisma, melodia, strain, tune, warble; *compare* SONG 2
rel song; bel canto, canto, vocalise; lyrics

melt *vb* **1** *syn* see LIQUEFY
rel heat, warm
con coagulate, harden, set
ant freeze; solidify
2 *syn* see BURN 3
rel perspire, sweat

member *n syn* see PART 1

memento *n* **1** *syn* see REMEMBRANCE 3
2 *syn* see VESTIGE 1

memo *n* **1** *syn* see NOTE 2
2 *syn* see MEMORANDUM 2

memoir *n* **1** *syn* see BIOGRAPHY
rel anecdote; memory, recollection, remembrance, reminiscence
2 *syn* see DISCOURSE 2

memoirist *n syn* see BIOGRAPHER

memorable *adj syn* see NOTEWORTHY
rel momentous, rememberable; deathless, unfadable, unforgettable
ant unmemorable

memorandum *n* **1** *syn* see NOTE 2
2 a communication that contains directive, advisory, or informative matter <the *memorandum* announced the holiday schedule>
syn directive, memo, notice
rel announcement, dispatch, minute; epistle, letter, missive, note; reminder, tickler; message; diary

memorial *adj* serving to preserve remembrance <a *memorial* plaque>
syn commemorative, commemoratory
rel celebrative, consecrative, dedicatory, enshrining

memorial *n* **1** *syn* see REMEMBRANCE 3
2 *syn* see MONUMENT 2

memorialize *vb* **1** *syn* see ADDRESS 4
2 to record or honor the memory of by or as if by a monument <the new library *memorializes* the late President>
syn commemorate, monument, monumentalize
rel etch, grave, impress, imprint; jog, nudge, remind
idiom bring to mind, fix in the (*or* one's) mind (*or* memory), impress on one's mind, treasure in one's heart
con forget, neglect, overlook

memorial park *n syn* see CEMETERY

memorize *vb* to commit to memory <the actors hadn't even *memorized* their lines>
syn con, get, learn
rel study
idiom get (*or* learn) by heart, get (*or* learn) word for word
con forget

memory *n* **1** the power or process of reproducing or recalling what has been learned <blessed with a good *memory*>
syn recollection, remembrance, reminiscence
rel reflection, retrospection; retention, retentiveness; mind, recall; mind's eye; awareness, cognizance, consciousness
con forgetfulness, obliviousness, unmindfulness; lethe, oblivion
2 a particular act of recalling <her *memory* of her wedding day remains vivid>
syn anamnesis, recall, recollection, remembrance, reminiscence
rel memento, souvenir

menace *vb* **1** *syn* see THREATEN
rel alarm, frighten, scare; endanger, torment; loom, lower
2 *syn* see ENDANGER

menacing *adj syn* see IMMINENT 2

ménage *n syn* see FAMILY 2
rel ménage à trois

mend *vb* **1** *syn* see CORRECT 1
2 to put into good shape or working order again <*mends* garments in her spare time>
syn doctor, do up, fix, overhaul, patch, rebuild, recondition, reconstruct, repair, revamp, ‖right, ‖rightle, vamp
rel condition, ready, service; refurbish, rejuvenate, renew, renovate, restore; correct, emend, rectify, redress, reform; heal
3 *syn* see IMPROVE 3

mendacious *adj syn* see DISHONEST
rel false, wrong; erroneous, fallacious, spurious; equivocating, fibbing, paltering, prevaricating
ant veracious

mendaciousness *n syn* see MENDACITY
ant veraciousness, veracity

mendacity *n* the practice or an instance of lying <he was ultimately caught by his own outrageous *mendacity*>
syn falsehood, fibbery, mendaciousness, truthlessness, untruthfulness, unveracity
rel boggling, caviling, dodging, equivocation, hedging, quibbling, shifting, sidestepping
ant veraciousness, veracity

mendicancy *n* the practice or act of begging <the city passed an ordinance against *mendicancy*>
syn beggary, bumming, cadging, mendicity, mooching, panhandling
rel sponging
mendicity *n syn* see MENDICANCY
menial *adj syn* see SUBSERVIENT 2
mental *adj* 1 of or relating to the mind <the *mental* aspects of the problem>
syn cerebral, intellective, intellectual, psychic, psychical, psychological
rel immaterial, inner, spiritual; telepathic; intelligent, rational, reasoning, thinking; ideological
con bodily, corporal, corporeal, physical, somatic; perceptive; sensual, sensuous
‖ **2** *syn* see INSANE 1
mentality *n syn* see INTELLIGENCE 1
mention *vb* to refer to someone or something in a clear unmistakable manner <several donors were *mentioned* in the article>
syn cite, instance, name, specify
rel denominate, designate; detail; advert, allude, refer; quote
idiom make mention of
con disregard, ignore, neglect, overlook, pass by, pass over, slight
menu *n* a list of the dishes that may be ordered (as at a restaurant) or that are to be served (as at a banquet) <hoped to find something tasty on the *menu*><he saved the elaborate *menu* as a souvenir of the awards banquet>
syn card, carte du jour
idiom bill of fare
Mephistophelian *adj syn* see SATANIC 1
mephitic *adj* 1 *syn* see MALODOROUS 1
2 *syn* see POISONOUS
mercenary *n syn* see HACK 2
mercenary *adj syn* see CORRUPT 2
ant unmercenary
merchandisable *adj syn* see MARKETABLE
ant unmerchantable, unsalable
merchandise *n* the products that are bought and sold in business <*merchandise* of inferior quality>
syn commodities, goods, line, vendible(s), wares
rel effects; job lot, stock; staples
merchandise *vb syn* see SELL 3
rel advertise, publicize
merchandiser *n syn* see MERCHANT
merchant *n* a buyer and seller of commodities for profit <a *merchant* of dry goods>
syn businessman, dealer, merchandiser, trader, tradesman, trafficker
rel jobber, retailer, wholesaler
merchantable *adj syn* see MARKETABLE
ant unmerchantable, unsalable
merchant prince *n syn* see MAGNATE
merciful *adj syn* see FORBEARING
rel compassionate, pitiful, softhearted; benign, kind, kindly; condoning, forgiving, pardoning
ant merciless, unmerciful
mercifulness *n syn* see FORBEARANCE 2
rel commiseration, pity, ruth
con severeness, severity, sternness

ant mercilessness, unmercifulness
merciless *adj* 1 *syn* see PITILESS
ant merciful
2 *syn* see GRIM 3
rel compassionless, cutthroat, pitiless; gratuitous, uncalled-for, wanton
con charitable, lenient, tolerant; easy, easygoing
ant merciful
mercurial *adj syn* see INCONSTANT 1
rel buoyant, effervescent, elastic, expansive, resilient; mobile, movable; adroit, clever, cunning, ingenious
ant saturnine
mercy *n* a show of or a disposition to show kindness or compassion <the *mercy* of the Lord knows all seasons>
syn caritas, charity, clemency, grace, lenity; *compare* FORBEARANCE 2
rel commiseration, compassion, pity, ruth; benevolence, benignancy, benignity, kindliness, kindness; generosity, goodwill
con reprisal, retaliation, retribution, revenge, vengeance; castigation, chastening, chastisement, punishment
mere *adj syn* see VERY 4
merely *adv syn* see JUST 3
meretricious *adj syn* see GAUDY
rel deceptive, delusive, delusory, misleading, spurious; insincere
meretrix *n syn* see PROSTITUTE
merge *vb syn* see MIX 1
mergence *n syn* see UNIFICATION
merger *n* 1 *syn* see CONSOLIDATION 2
2 *syn* see UNIFICATION
merging *n syn* see UNIFICATION
meridian *n syn* see APEX 2
merit *n* 1 *syn* see EXCELLENCE
ant fault
2 *syn* see QUALITY 2
3 *syn* see DUE 1
rel gaining(s), winning(s)
merit *vb syn* see EARN 2
rel award, reward; recompense, repay, requite; entitle, justify, warrant
meritable *adj syn* see WORTHY 1
ant meritless
merited *adj syn* see JUST 3
rel entitled, justified, warranted
ant unmerited
meritorious *adj syn* see WORTHY 1
merriment *n* 1 *syn* see MIRTH
2 *syn* see MERRYMAKING
merry *adj* indicative of or marked by high spirits or lightheartedness <the *merry* life of the town folk was a joy to see>
syn blithe, blithesome, boon, festive, gay, gleeful, jocund, jolly, jovial, lighthearted, mirthful, riant

---

syn synonym(s)   *rel* related word(s)
ant antonym(s)   *con* contrasted word(s)
idiom idiomatic equivalent(s)
‖ use limited; if in doubt, see a dictionary

rel animated, lively, sprightly, vivacious; cheerful, glad, happy, joyful, joyous; hilarious, mad, unconstrained, wild
con gloomy, glum, melancholy; grave, sober, somber; earnest, sedate, serious, staid
merry–andrew *n syn* see CLOWN 3
merrymaking *n* gay or festive activity <a night of *merrymaking*>
syn festivity, gaiety, jollity, merriment, revel, reveling, revelment, revelry, whoopee
rel enjoyment, indulgence, pleasure, self-indulgence
mesh *n* **1** *usu* **meshes** *pl syn* see WEB 2
   2 *syn* see MAZE 1
   rel net, network
mesh *vb syn* see ENGAGE 1
meshuggaas *n syn* see NONSENSE 2
mesmeric *adj syn* see ATTRACTIVE 1
mesmerize *vb syn* see ENTHRALL 2
   rel entrance, hypnotize
mess *n* ‖**1** *syn* see MUCH
   2 *syn* see EYESORE
   3 a confused or disordered state, condition, or situation <upon becoming president, he proceeded to make a *mess* of the government>
   syn botch, botchery, hash, mess-up, mix-up, muddle, mull, muss, shambles; *compare* MISCELLANY 1
   rel confusion, disorder; wreck, wreckage
   idiom kettle of fish
mess *vb* **1** *syn* see BOTCH
   rel confuse, disorder, jumble
   idiom make a mess of
   2 *syn* see FIDDLE 2
mess (up) *vb syn* see DISORDER 1
   rel damage, mar, ruin, spoil; ‖muck, mucker, muff
message *n* **1** something (as information) conveyed by writing, speech, or signals <left a *message* before he went out>
   syn communication, directive, word
   rel communiqué, dispatch, report; memo, memorandum; epistle, letter, missive, note
   2 *syn* see MEANING 1
mess around *vb* **1** *syn* see FIDDLE 2
   2 *syn* see MEDDLE
   3 *syn* see PHILANDER
messenger *n* one who bears a message or does an errand <blamed the *messenger* for the bad news he brought>
   syn bearer, carrier, courier, emissary, envoy, internuncio
   rel herald; go-between, intermediary, mediator; dispatcher, post
mess–up *n syn* see MESS 3
messy *adj* **1** *syn* see SLOVENLY 1
   rel dirty, grimy, grubby
   con clean
   ant neat
   2 *syn* see SLIPSHOD 3
metagrobolize *vb syn* see PUZZLE
metamorphize *vb syn* see TRANSFORM
metamorphose *vb syn* see TRANSFORM
   rel age, develop, mature, ripen

metanoia *n syn* see CONVERSION 1
metaphor *n syn* see ANALOGY 2
   rel comparison, trope; allegory, personification
   idiom figure of speech
metaphysical *adj* **1** *syn* see IMMATERIAL 1
   rel supernatural, transcendent, transcendental
   2 *syn* see SUPERNATURAL 1
mete (out) *vb* **1** *syn* see ADMINISTER 2
   rel measure
   2 *syn* see ALLOT
meter *n syn* see RHYTHM
method *n* **1** the means or procedures used in attaining an end <he claimed that his ends justified his *methods*>
   syn fashion, manner, mode, modus, system, technique, way, wise
   rel design, plan, schema, scheme; form, style; course, line; modus operandi, practice, procedure, process, routine; wrinkle
   2 *syn* see ORDER 8
methodic *adj syn* see ORDERLY 1
   ant desultory, unmethodical
methodical *adj syn* see ORDERLY 1
   rel methodized, organized, systematized; analytical, logical; careful, meticulous, scrupulous
   con casual, hit-or-miss, random; confused, jumbled
   ant desultory, unmethodical
methodize *vb syn* see ORDER 1
   rel establish, fix, set, settle
meticulous *adj syn* see CAREFUL 2
   rel fastidious, pernickety, picky; cautious, strict, thorough; microscopic
métier *n* **1** *syn* see TRADE 1
   2 *syn* see FORTE
metropolitan *adj syn* see COSMOPOLITAN 1
mettle *n syn* see COURAGE
mettlesome *adj syn* see SPIRITED 2
   rel edgy, excitable, high-strung, skittish, startlish
mew *vb syn* see ENCLOSE 1
Mickey Mouse *adj syn* see PETTY 2
mid *adj* **1** *syn* see MIDDLE 2
   2 *syn* see MIDDLE 1
mid *prep* **1** *syn* see AMID 1
   2 *syn* see AMONG 1
   3 *syn* see DURING
middle *adj* **1** equally distant from the extremes <the *middle* finger>
   syn center, centermost, equidistant, halfway, medial, median, mid, middlemost, midmost
   2 being at neither extreme <paid a *middle* price for it>
   syn center, central, intermediary, intermediate, mean, medial, median, mid
middle *n syn* see CENTER 1
middlebrow *n syn* see PHILISTINE
middleman *n syn* see GO-BETWEEN 2
middlemost *adj syn* see MIDDLE 1
middle–of–the–road *adj syn* see MODERATE 4
middle–rate *adj syn* see MEDIUM
middle–road *adj syn* see MODERATE 4
middling *adj syn* see MEDIUM
   rel inferior, poor, second-rate

midge *n syn* see DWARF

midget *n syn* see DWARF

midget *adj syn* see TINY

midmost *adj syn* see MIDDLE 1

midpoint *n syn* see CENTER 1

midst *n syn* see CENTER 1

midst *prep* **1** *syn* see AMID 1

   2 *syn* see AMONG 1

   3 *syn* see DURING

mid–Victorian *n syn* see FOGY

   rel bluenose, goody-goody, Mrs. Grundy, prig, prude, puritan; Victorian

mien *n* **1** *syn* see BEARING 1

   rel expression, manner, mannerism

   2 *syn* see APPEARANCE 1

miff *n* **1** *syn* see OFFENSE 2

   rel conniption, fit

   2 *syn* see QUARREL

might *n* **1** *syn* see POWER 1

   2 *syn* see POWER 4

   rel energeticness, lustiness, strenuousness, vigor, vigorousness; forcefulness, forcibleness, powerfulness

   3 *syn* see ABILITY 1

   4 *syn* see MUSCLE 1

might and main *adv syn* see HARD 1

mightily *adv* **1** *syn* see HARD 1

   rel arduously, laboriously, strenuously, toilsomely

   2 *syn* see VERY 1

mighty *adj* **1** *syn* see POWERFUL 2

   2 *syn* see STRONG 1

   3 *syn* see HUGE

   rel eminent, illustrious, renowned; august, grand, imposing, impressive, moving

mighty *adv syn* see VERY 1

migrant *adj syn* see MIGRATORY

migrant *n syn* see EMIGRANT

   rel in-migrant, out-migrant; drifter, mover, nomad, traveler, wanderer

migrate *vb* to move from one country, place, or locality to another <his father had *migrated* to the Far West years before>

   syn emigrate, transmigrate

   rel immigrate, in-migrate, out-migrate, remigrate; drift, trek; nomadize, range, roam, rove, wander

migrative *adj syn* see MIGRATORY

   ant nonmigratory

migratorial *adj syn* see MIGRATORY

   ant nonmigratory

migratory *adj* moving habitually or occasionally from one region or climate to another <the study of *migratory* birds>

   syn migrant, migrative, migratorial, mobile, transmigratory

   rel errant, nomad, nomadic, ranging, roving, wandering

   ant nonmigratory

mild *adj* **1** *syn* see GENTLE 1

   rel choice, dainty, delicate, exquisite; moderate, temperate; benign, benignant

   con intense, severe, sharp, vehement

   ant fierce, harsh

   2 *syn* see AMIABLE 1

   rel docile, meek; subdued, submissive; deferential, obeisant, subservient

milepost *n syn* see EVENT 2

milestone *n syn* see EVENT 2

milieu *n syn* see ENVIRONMENT

militant *adj* **1** *syn* see BELLIGERENT

   rel martial, military

   2 *syn* see AGGRESSIVE

military *adj syn* see MARTIAL

   rel chauvinistic, jingoistic, militaristic, warmongering; soldierlike, soldierly

   ant unmilitary

military *n syn* see TROOP 2

militate *vb syn* see WEIGH 3

milk *vb* **1** *syn* see FLEECE 1

   rel exact, exploit, extort; drain, empty, exhaust, pump, suck, wring

   2 *syn* see EDUCE 1

milk–and–water *adj syn* see INSIPID 3

milk–livered *adj syn* see COWARDLY

milksop *n syn* see WEAKLING

   rel effeminate; coward

milk–warm *adj syn* see TEPID 1

mill *n syn* see FACTORY

million *n syn* see SCAD

millstone *n syn* see LOAD 3

Milquetoast *n syn* see WEAKLING

mime *n syn* see ACTOR 1

mimic *n syn* see ACTOR 1

mimic *vb* to copy or exaggerate (as manner or gestures) often by way of mockery <*mimicked* her halting speech>

   syn ape, burlesque, imitate, mock, parody, take off, travesty

   rel hit off, mime, mum; act, do, enact, impersonate, perform, personate, play; copycat; pantomime

mimicry *n* the art or practice of closely imitating another in speech, gestures, or manners <engaged in *mimicry* of café society>

   syn apery

   rel imitation, mimesis, mimetism; mock, mockery; caricature, parody

miminy–piminy *adj syn* see NICE 1

mince *vb* **1** *syn* see CHOP 2

   2 *syn* see SASHAY

mincing *adj syn* see GENTEEL 3

   rel dainty, delicate, fastidious, finical, finicking, finicky, fussy, nice, particular, pernickety, persnickety, squeamish

‖**mincy** *adj syn* see NICE 1

mind *n* **1** the element or complex of elements in an individual that feels, perceives, thinks, wills, and especially reasons <sad to see such a *mind* dulled by drink and drugs>

   syn brain, gray matter, head, ‖upper story, ‖upperworks, wit

---

syn synonym(s)   *rel* related word(s)

ant antonym(s)   *con* contrasted word(s)

idiom idiomatic equivalent(s)

‖ use limited; if in doubt, see a dictionary

rel brainpower, intellect, intelligence; consciousness, mentality; faculty, function, power
2 syn see WILL 1
rel disposition, temper, temperament
con aversion, disinclination, indisposition
3 syn see WIT 2
4 syn see OPINION
5 syn see MOOD 1
‖**6 syn** see NOTICE 1
mind *vb* ‖**1 syn** see REMEMBER
‖**2 syn** see ENJOY 1
3 syn see SEE 1
‖**4 syn** see INTEND 2
5 syn see OBEY
6 syn see LOOK 1
7 syn see BEWARE
8 syn see TEND 2
rel oversee, superintend, supervise; discipline, govern
con forget, slight
9 syn see CONSIDER 1
minded *adj syn* see WILLING 1
rel contemplating, intending, planning, purposing
mindful *adj* **1 syn** see AWARE
ant unmindful
2 inclined to be aware <*mindful* of the ever‍changing social scene>
syn heedful, observant, observative, observing, regardful, thoughtful
rel attentive, conscientious; aware, cognizant, conscious, conversant, sensible; alert, vigilant, watchful
con heedless, inattentive
ant mindless, unmindful
mindless *adj* **1 syn** see SIMPLE 3
2 syn see INSANE 1
mine *n syn* see BONANZA
rel lode, quarry, vein; spring, well, wellspring
mine *vb* to dig into for the purpose of obtaining items of use or value <*mined* manuscripts looking for undiscovered masterpieces>
syn delve, quarry
rel burrow, drill, excavate, sap, scoop; work
mingle *vb* **1 syn** see MIX 1
2 syn see SOCIALIZE
mingle–mangle *n syn* see MISCELLANY 1
mingy *adj syn* see STINGY
miniature *n syn* see MODEL 1
miniature *adj syn* see TINY
rel small-scale, subminiature
con large-scale
minify *vb syn* see ABRIDGE 1
rel dwarf, miniaturize, shrink
minikin *adj syn* see TINY
minim *n syn* see PARTICLE
minimal *adj* constituting the least possible <*minimal* differences of opinion>
syn minimum
rel littlest, lowest, slightest, smallest; basal, basic, essential, fundamental
con maximum, topmost, utmost; greatest, highest, largest, most
ant maximal

minimize *vb syn* see DECRY 2
rel dwarf, reduce
ant magnify, maximize
minimum *n* the least quantity assignable, admissible, or possible <testing the use of a *minimum* of security at the prison>
syn margin
rel dab, hair, iota, jot, modicum, particle, pittance, smidgen, speck, whit
con abundance, bushel(s), gob(s), ‖lashings, load(s), lot(s), mass(es), much, oodles, profusion, scads, slather(s), ton(s), world(s)
ant maximum
minimum *adj syn* see MINIMAL
ant maximum
minion *n syn* see SYCOPHANT
minister *n syn* see CLERGYMAN
minister (to) *vb* to attend to the wants and comforts of someone <*minister* to the sick and dying>
syn care (for), mother, nurse, serve, wait (on)
rel cure, heal, remedy; doctor, treat; pander
ministerial *adj syn* see INSTRUMENTAL
minister plenipotentiary *n syn* see ENVOY 1
ministry *n syn* see MEAN 2
minor *adj* **1 syn** see LITTLE 3
rel dependent; inferior, piddling, trifling; junior, lower
con meaningful, significant
ant major
2 lower in standing or reputation than others of the same class <a *minor* poet of the late eighteenth century>
syn bush, bush-league, dinky, insignificant, lesser, minor-league, secondary, small, small‍fry, small-time
rel average, fair, indifferent, mediocre, medium, middling, second-rate, undistinguished, unnoticeable; trivial, unimportant
con chief, foremost, leading, principal
ant major
minor *n syn* see INFANT 2
minority *n syn* see INFANCY 2
ant majority
minor–league *adj syn* see MINOR 2
minstrel *n syn* see BARD 1
rel balladist, singer, wait
mint *n syn* see FORTUNE 4
mint *adj syn* see BRAND-NEW
rel intact, original, perfect, unmarred
minus *prep syn* see WITHOUT 2
ant plus
minute *n syn* see INSTANT 1
minute *adj* **1 syn** see TINY
2 syn see LITTLE 3
3 syn see CIRCUMSTANTIAL
rel careful, meticulous, punctilious, scrupulous
con abstract; general, universal; comprehending, comprehensive, embracing, embracive, including, inclusive
minutely *adj syn* see CONTINUAL
minutia *n, usu* **minutiae** *pl* **1 syn** see INS AND OUTS
2 syn see TRIVIA
minx *n* a pert girl <her rivals called her a brazen *minx*>

syn hussy, jade, malapert, saucebox, slut, snip
rel broad, brat, upstart; baggage, chippy, drab, floozy, strumpet, tart, trollop, trull

miracle *n syn* see WONDER 1

miraculous *adj* **1** *syn* see SUPERNATURAL 1
2 *syn* see MARVELOUS 1
con natural, normal

mirage *n syn* see DELUSION 1

mire *n syn* see SWAMP
rel muck

mire *vb* **1** *syn* see DELAY 1
rel bemire, sink; adhere, cleave, cling, cohere, stick; enmesh, ensnare, entangle, entrap, involve, snare, trap
2 *syn* see INVOLVE 1

mirror *n* **1** a polished or smooth surface (as of glass) that forms images by reflection <spent hours looking at herself in the *mirror*>
syn glass, looking glass, ‖seeing glass
rel cheval glass, pier glass, reflector, speculum
2 *syn* see MODEL 2

mirror *vb* **1** *syn* see REFLECT 1
2 *syn* see REPRESENT 2

mirth *n* a mood or temper characterized by joy and high spirits and usually manifested in laughter and merrymaking <a man of contentment, but seldom of *mirth*>
syn glee, hilarity, jocularity, jocundity, jollity, joviality, merriment
rel cheer, cheerfulness, joyfulness, lightheartedness; gladness, happiness; frivolity, levity
con blues, dejection, depression, dumps, gloom, sadness; boredom, ennui, tedium; anguish, misery, woe; infelicity, wretchedness
ant melancholy

mirthful *adj syn* see MERRY
ant mirthless

miry *adj syn* see MUDDY 1

misadventure *n* **1** *syn* see DISASTER
2 *syn* see ACCIDENT 2
rel blunder, boner, bull, error, faux pas, howler, lapse, slip

misanthropic *adj syn* see ANTISOCIAL
rel misogynic
con altruistic, benevolent, charitable, humane, humanitarian
ant philanthropic

misapply *vb syn* see ABUSE 2
rel misappropriate, misdirect, mismanage

misapprehend *vb* **1** *syn* see MISUNDERSTAND 1
ant apprehend
2 *syn* see MISUNDERSTAND 2
ant apprehend

misappropriate *vb syn* see EMBEZZLE

misbegotten *adj syn* see ILLEGITIMATE 1

misbehaving *adj syn* see NAUGHTY 1
ant well-behaved

misbehavior *n syn* see MISCONDUCT

misbelief *n syn* see HERESY

misbeliever *n syn* see HERETIC

miscalculate *vb* to calculate wrongly <*miscalculate* the distance> <he seriously *miscalculated* the effect of his remark>
syn misestimate, misjudge, misreckon

rel discount, disregard, overlook; misconstrue, misinterpret, misunderstand; overestimate, overprize, overrate, overvalue; understimate, underprize, underrate, undervalue

miscarry *vb* to go wrong or amiss <her plans *miscarried* almost from the start>
syn misfire, miss
rel abort; fail, flop
idiom fall through, miss fire, miss the mark
con come off, prevail, succeed

miscellaneous *adj* consisting of diverse things or members <gathered together a *miscellaneous* lot of books for sale>
syn assorted, chowchow, conglomerate, heterogeneous, indiscriminate, mixed, motley, multifarious, promiscuous, unassorted, unsorted, varied
rel different, disparate, divergent, diverse, various; divers, many, sundry; odd; commingled, jumbled, mingled, scrambled
con akin, alike, identical, like, parallel, similar, uniform

miscellany *n* **1** an unorganized mixture of various dissimilar items or elements <sold a *miscellany* of old household effects>
syn assortment, brew, chowchow, colluvies, gallimaufry, hash, hodgepodge, hotchpotch, jumble, medley, mélange, melee, mingle-mangle, mishmash, mixed bag, motley, odds and ends, olio, olla podrida, omnium-gatherum, pasticcio, pastiche, patchwork, porridge, potpourri, rumble-bumble, salad, salmagundi, smorgasbord, stew
rel mess, muddle; accumulation, aggregation, congeries, conglomeration, cumulation; combination, mix, mixture
2 *syn* see ANTHOLOGY

mischance *n* **1** *syn* see MISFORTUNE
2 *syn* see ACCIDENT 2

mischief *n* **1** *syn* see INJURY 1
rel difficulty, hardship, trouble
2 *syn* see SCAMP
3 *syn* see MISCHIEVOUSNESS
4 *syn* see DISCORD

‖**mischiefful** *adj syn* see PLAYFUL 1

mischief-maker *n syn* see TROUBLEMAKER

mischievous *adj* **1** *syn* see HARMFUL
rel dangerous, hazardous, perilous, precarious, risky
2 *syn* see NAUGHTY 1
rel annoying, bothering, bothersome, irking, irksome, vexatious, vexing
3 *syn* see PLAYFUL 1
rel artful, foxy, insidious, sly, tricky

mischievousness *n* action or conduct that annoys or irritates without causing or meaning serious harm <a wag who was forever engaging in *mischievousness*>

---

syn synonym(s)   *rel* related word(s)
ant antonym(s)   *con* contrasted word(s)
idiom idiomatic equivalent(s)
‖ use limited; if in doubt, see a dictionary

syn devilment, devilry, deviltry, diablerie, impishness, mischief, roguery, roguishness, sportiveness, waggery, waggishness

rel doggery, odiousness, offensiveness; evil, harm, hurt, injury; annoying, pestering, teasing

miscolor *vb syn* see MISREPRESENT

miscomprehend *vb syn* see MISUNDERSTAND 1

misconceive *vb syn* see MISUNDERSTAND 2

misconduct *n* improper behavior <was charged with *misconduct*>

syn misbehavior, misdoing, wrongdoing

rel impropriety; malfeasance, malversation, misfeasance

misconstrue *vb syn* see MISUNDERSTAND 2

miscreant *adj syn* see VICIOUS 2

miscreant *n syn* see VILLAIN 1

miscreation *n syn* see FREAK 2

rel deformation, deformity

miscue *n syn* see ERROR 2

misdate *n syn* see ANACHRONISM 1

misdating *n syn* see ANACHRONISM 1

misdeed *n syn* see CRIME 1

misdeem *vb* **1** *syn* see MISJUDGE 2

  2 *syn* see MISTAKE 1

misdoing *n syn* see MISCONDUCT

misdoubt *vb syn* see DISTRUST

rel apprehend, dread, fear

mise–en–scène *n* **1** *syn* see SCENE 1

  2 *syn* see SCENE 3

  3 *syn* see ENVIRONMENT

misemploy *vb syn* see ABUSE 2

miser *n* a mean grasping person <an old *miser* who loved only his bank account>

syn cheapskate, cheeseparer, chuff, hunks, moneygrubber, muckworm, nabal, niggard, ‖nipcheese, penny pincher, piker, scrooge, skin, skinflint, stiff, tightwad

rel glutton, hog, pig

miserable *adj syn* see WOEFUL 1

rel despairing, despondent, forlorn, hopeless; piteous, pitiable, pitiful; melancholy

con cheerful, glad, happy, joyful, joyous, lighthearted

miserly *adj syn* see STINGY

rel avaricious, covetous, grasping, greedy; abject, ignoble, sordid

con bountious, generous; altruistic, benevolent, charitable

misery *n* **1** a state of suffering and want that is the result of poverty or conditions beyond one's control <the poor learn to live with *misery*> <*the utter misery* in which the flood victims survived>

syn unhappiness, woe, wretchedness

rel agony, anguish; despondency, grief, sorrow; desolation, squalor

con beatitude, blessedness, bliss, felicity, happiness; content, ease, satisfaction

  2 *syn* see DISTRESS

rel adversity, misfortune; dejection, depression, melancholy, sadness

ant blessedness

‖**3** *syn* see PAIN 1

misesteem *vb syn* see MISJUDGE 2

misestimate *vb syn* see MISCALCULATE

misfire *vb syn* see MISCARRY

misfortunate *adj syn* see UNLUCKY

ant fortunate

misfortune *n* adverse fortune or an instance of this <her hopes and dreams soon ended in *misfortune*> <unable to grasp why he had been struck by such a *misfortune*>

syn adversity, contretemps, ‖dole, mischance, mishap, tragedy, ‖unluck

rel calamity, cataclysm, catastrophe, disaster; accident, casualty; affliction, cross, trial, tribulation, visitation

con break, chance, luck, opportunity

ant fortune

misgiving *n syn* see APPREHENSION 3

rel doubt, fear, qualm, suspicion; distrust, mistrust

misguided *adj syn* see MISTAKEN

mishandle *vb* **1** *syn* see MANHANDLE

  2 *syn* see ABUSE 2

mishap *n* **1** *syn* see MISFORTUNE

  2 *syn* see ACCIDENT 2

mishmash *n* **1** *syn* see MISCELLANY 1

  2 *syn* see CLUTTER 2

misidentify *vb syn* see MISTAKE 1

misimprove *vb syn* see ABUSE 2

misinterpret *vb syn* see MISUNDERSTAND 2

misjudge *vb* **1** *syn* see MISCALCULATE

  2 to have a mistaken opinion of <her first impression led her to *misjudge* the girl>

syn misdeem, misesteem, mistake

rel misapprehend, miscomprehend, misconceive, misconstrue, misinterpret, misunderstand

con catch on (to), penetrate, tumble (to), wise (up)

misknow *vb syn* see MISUNDERSTAND 1

mislaying *n syn* see LOSS 1

mislead *vb syn* see DECEIVE

rel lie, misguide, misinform; entice, inveigle, lure, seduce, tempt

misleading *adj* having an appearance or character that leads one astray or into error <the president made several *misleading* statements to the people>

syn beguiling, deceiving, deceptive, deluding, delusive, delusory, fallacious, false

rel casuistical, sophistical, specious; wrong; bewildering, confounding, distracting, perplexing, puzzling; deceitful, inaccurate

con clarifying, elucidative, explanatory, illuminating

‖**mismannered** *adj syn* see RUDE 6

mismatch *vb syn* see CLASH 2

misorder *n syn* see CONFUSION 3

misplacement *n syn* see LOSS 1

misplacing *n syn* see LOSS 1

misread *vb syn* see MISUNDERSTAND 2

misreckon *vb syn* see MISCALCULATE

‖**misremember** *vb syn* see FORGET 1

misrepresent *vb* to give a false, imperfect, or misleading representation of <the summary totally *misrepresents* the facts of the case>

syn belie, color, confuse, distort, falsify, garble, miscolor, misstate, pervert, twist, warp, wrench, wrest

rel dress, embellish, embroider, gild, gloss, varnish; camouflage, cloak, disguise, dissemble, mask; counterfeit, feign, simulate; equivocate, lie, palter, prevaricate, weasel

idiom give a false coloring, put a false construction (*or* appearance) on

misrepresentation *n syn* see LIE

misrule *n syn* see DISORDER 2

miss *vb* **1** *syn* see NEGLECT

2 *syn* see MISUNDERSTAND 1

3 *syn* see MISCARRY

‖**miss** *n syn* see ABSENCE

miss *n syn* see GIRL 1

misshape *vb syn* see DEFORM

misshape *n syn* see DEFORMITY

missing *adj* **1** *syn* see ABSENT 1

2 *syn* see LOST 2

mission *n* a continuing task or responsibility that one is destined or fitted to do or specially called upon to undertake <his *mission* in life was to serve humanity>

syn calling, lifework, vocation

rel goal, purpose; business, profession, trade

missionary *n* one who attempts to convert others to a specific way of life, set of ideas, or course of action <served as a *missionary* for the feminist cause>

syn apostle, colporteur, evangelist, missioner, propagandist

rel revivalist; promoter

missioner *n syn* see MISSIONARY

missish *adj syn* see PRIM 1

missive *n syn* see LETTER 2

Miss–Nancyish *adj syn* see EFFEMINATE

misstate *vb syn* see MISREPRESENT

misstatement *n syn* see LIE

misstep *n syn* see ERROR 2

‖**missus** *n syn* see WIFE

missy *n syn* see GIRL 1

mist *n syn* see HAZE 1

mist *vb syn* see OBSCURE

mistake *vb* **1** to take one thing to be another <he *mistakes* sarcasm for wit>

syn confound, confuse, misdeem, misidentify, mix, mix up

rel misconceive, misknow; addle, jumble, muddle, tumble

con discern, distinguish, grasp, perceive; differentiate, separate

ant recognize

2 *syn* see MISUNDERSTAND 2

3 *syn* see MISJUDGE 2

mistake *n* **1** *syn* see ERROR 2

rel confounding, confusion, mistaking; inadvertence; disregarding, neglect, neglecting, omission, omitting, slight, slighting

2 *syn* see ERROR 1

mistaken *adj* acting, thinking, or judging in a manner at variance with truth or the facts <he is *mistaken* in his evaluation of the crisis>

syn erroneous, misguided, wrong

rel confounded, confused; deceived, deluded, misinformed

idiom all wet, off base, off the track

con accurate, correct, right, unerring; exact, precise

mister *n syn* see HUSBAND

mistimed *adj syn* see UNSEASONABLE 1

ant well-timed

mistiming *n syn* see ANACHRONISM 1

mistreat *vb syn* see ABUSE 4

mistress *n* a woman who is a man's regular partner in nonmarital sexual activity <gave up his *mistress* when he married>

syn ‖doxy, girl friend, inamorata, lover, paramour, woman

rel bedmate; concubine; kept woman; dulcinea

mistrust *n syn* see UNCERTAINTY

rel apprehension, foreboding, misgiving, presentiment

con dependence, faith, reliance

ant assurance, trust

mistrust *vb* **1** *syn* see DISTRUST

rel anticipate, apprehend, foresee; alarm, frighten, scare; appall, dismay

ant trust

2 *syn* see QUESTION 2

mistrustful *adj syn* see SUSPICIOUS 2

ant trustful, trusting

mistrustfully *adv syn* see ASKANCE 2

ant trustfully, trustingly

misty *adj syn* see HAZY

misunderstand *vb* **1** to fail to understand <he *misunderstood* the full meaning of the novel>

syn misapprehend, miscomprehend, misknow, miss

rel misconceive, misconstrue, misinterpret, misread, mistake

con apprehend, conceive, know, realize; fathom, follow, grasp, seize, take in

ant comprehend, understand

2 to interpret incorrectly <*misunderstood* the instructions>

syn misapprehend, misconceive, misconstrue, misinterpret, misread, mistake

rel misexplain, mistranslate; miscomprehend, misknow

con fathom, follow, take in

ant understand

misuse *vb* **1** *syn* see ABUSE 2

2 *syn* see ABUSE 4

mite *n syn* see PARTICLE

mitigate *vb syn* see RELIEVE 1

rel extenuate, palliate

con aggravate, enhance, heighten; augment, increase

ant intensify

mitigation *n syn* see EASE 3

---

syn synonym(s)   **rel** related word(s)
ant antonym(s)   **con** contrasted word(s)
idiom idiomatic equivalent(s)
‖ use limited; if in doubt, see a dictionary

mix *vb* **1** to combine or be combined into a more or less uniform whole <*mixed* the ingredients to make a thick sauce>
syn admix, amalgamate, blend, comingle, commingle, commix, compound, fuse, immingle, immix, interblend, interflow, interfuse, intermingle, intermix, make up, meld, merge, mingle
rel associate, combine, conjoin, inosculate, join, link, unite; braid, lump, work in; coalesce; blunge
con divide, part, separate, sever, sunder
2 *syn* see MISTAKE 1

mix *n syn* see MIXTURE

mixed *adj syn* see MISCELLANEOUS
rel amalgamated, blended, fused, merged, mingled

mixed bag *n syn* see MISCELLANY 1

mixologist *n syn* see BARTENDER

mixture *n* a product formed by the combination of two or more things <the tea is actually a *mixture* of several varieties>
syn admixture, alloy, amalgam, amalgamation, blend, commixture, composite, compost, compound, fusion, immixture, interfusion, intermixture, mix, mix-up
rel brew, concoction, confection, mélange

mix up *vb* **1** *syn* see CONFUSE 2
ant straighten (out)
2 *syn* see CONFUSE 5
3 *syn* see MISTAKE 1
4 *syn* see DISORDER 1
ant straighten (out *or* up)

mix–up *n* **1** *syn* see MESS 3
2 *syn* see MIXTURE

mizmaze *n syn* see MAZE 1

‖**mizzle** *vb syn* see SPRINKLE 5

‖**mizzle** *vb syn* see CONFUSE 2

moan *vb syn* see DEPLORE 1

moanful *adj syn* see MELANCHOLY 2

mob *n* **1** *syn* see RABBLE
2 a large disorderly crowd of people usually bent on riotous or destructive action <the *mob* screamed for a lynching>
syn rabble, rout
rel posse; crowd, crush, horde, press, push, throng; herd, swarm
3 *syn* see CLIQUE

‖**mob** *vb syn* see SCOLD 1

mobile *adj* **1** *syn* see MOVABLE
rel fluid, liquid; protean; capricious, fickle, inconstant, mercurial
con immutable, invariable, unchangeable
ant immobile
2 *syn* see CHANGEABLE 1
ant immobile, stable
3 *syn* see VERSATILE
4 *syn* see MIGRATORY

mobile home *n syn* see TRAILER

mobilize *vb* **1** to put into movement or circulation <an increase in prices *mobilizes* the whole cycle of inflation>
syn actuate, circulate, set off
rel activate; impel, propel
idiom set in motion

con inactivate, slow (down *or* up)
ant immobilize
2 *syn* see MOVE 5
3 to assemble (as resources) and make ready for use or action <the president tried to *mobilize* support for the new proposal>
syn marshal, muster, organize, rally

mobocracy *n syn* see ANARCHY 1

mock *vb* **1** *syn* see RIDICULE
rel buffoon, burlesque, caricature, parody, travesty
2 *syn* see DECEIVE
3 *syn* see MIMIC
rel affect, assume, counterfeit, feign, simulate

mock *n* **1** *syn* see LAUGHINGSTOCK
2 *syn* see MOCKERY 2

mock *adj* **1** *syn* see ARTIFICIAL 2
rel pseudo, quasi, so-called
2 *syn* see FICTITIOUS 2
rel bogus, phony

mockery *n* **1** *syn* see LAUGHINGSTOCK
2 an insincere, contemptible, or impertinent imitation of something worthwhile <arbitrary methods that make a *mockery* of justice>
syn burlesque, caricature, farce, mock, sham, travesty
rel derision, ridicule, sport; parody, satire, take=off; joke, laughingstock

mode *n* **1** *syn* see VEIN 1
2 *syn* see METHOD 1
3 *syn* see STATE 1

mode *n syn* see FASHION 3

model *n* **1** a miniature representation of something <a *model* of the dam that was accurate down to the last detail>
syn miniature, pocket edition
rel copy, mock-up, replica, reproduction; dummy, effigy
2 something set or held before one for guidance or imitation <Samuel Johnson's literary style is often used as a *model* for writers seeking precision and clarity>
syn archetype, beau ideal, ensample, example, exemplar, ideal, mirror, paradigm, pattern, standard; *compare* PARAGON
rel apotheosis, nonesuch, nonpareil, paragon; emblem, symbol, type; embodiment, epitome, quintessence; criterion, gauge, touchstone

model *adj* **1** *syn* see IDEAL 3
rel commendable, exemplary
2 *syn* see PERFECT 3
3 *syn* see TYPICAL 1

moderate *adj* **1** *syn* see SOBER 3
2 not excessive in degree, amount, or intensity <the new proposals were met with only *moderate* enthusiasm> <the snowfall is expected to be no more than *moderate*>
syn modest, reasonable, temperate
rel bland, gentle, mild, soft; inconsequential, inconsiderable, slight, small; paltry, piddling, trifling, trivial
con excessive, extreme, inordinate, intemperate, radical, unreasonable
ant immoderate

3 *syn* see MEDIUM
rel constant, equable, even, steady
4 avoiding extreme political or social measures <party policy became increasingly *moderate*>
syn middle-of-the-road, middle-road, soft-shell
con conservative, right, tory; left, radical, red; extremist, fanatical, ultra
5 *syn* see CONSERVATIVE 2
moderate *vb* **1** to modify as to avoid an extreme or keep within bounds <actors *moderate* their voices and gestures to fit the size of the theater>
syn modulate, restrain, temper
rel abate, decrease, diminish, lessen, reduce; alleviate, cushion, lighten, mitigate, mollify, relieve, slacken, slow; constrain, control, qualify; chasten, cool, subdue, tone (down)
con aggravate, enhance, heighten, intensify; augment, increase
2 *syn* see ABATE 4
moderately *adv* **1** *syn* see ENOUGH 2
2 *syn* see SOMEWHAT 2
ant extremely, immoderately
moderateness *n* *syn* see TEMPERANCE 1
ant immoderateness, immoderation
moderation *n* *syn* see TEMPERANCE 1
ant immoderateness, immoderation
moderator *n* one who arbitrates <the labor dispute was finally referred to a *moderator*>
syn arbitrator, mediator
rel arbiter, judge; conciliator, negotiator, peacemaker
modern *adj* **1** having taken place, existed, or developed in times close to the present <*modern* concepts of engineering made the bridge possible>
syn late, recent
rel contemporary, present-day; latter
con antiquated, old-fashioned, old hat, outdated, outmoded, outworn
ant old-time
2 *syn* see NEW 1
rel coincident, concomitant, concurrent, contemporaneous, contemporary; current, prevailing, prevalent
ant ancient, antique
modernistic *adj* *syn* see NEW 1
rel futuristic
ant antiquated
modernize *vb* *syn* see RENEW 1
modest *adj* **1** *syn* see HUMBLE 1
rel moderate, temperate; retiring, withdrawing; unboastful; unpresuming, unpresumptuous, unpretending
con barefaced, brazen, impudent, shameless
ant ambitious
2 *syn* see SHY 1
rel reticent, silent; nice, proper, seemly
3 *syn* see CHASTE
rel priggish, prim, prissy, prudish, puritanical, straitlaced, stuffy
con improper, indecent, indecorous, indelicate, unseemly
ant immodest
4 *syn* see MODERATE 2
5 *syn* see PLAIN 1

modicum *n* *syn* see PARTICLE
modification *n* *syn* see CHANGE 1
rel conversion, metamorphosis, transformation, transmogrification; qualification, tempering
modified *adj* *syn* see QUALIFIED 2
modify *vb* *syn* see CHANGE 1
rel modulate, restrain, temper; qualify
modish *adj* *syn* see STYLISH
rel voguish
modulate *vb* *syn* see MODERATE 1
modus *n* *syn* see METHOD 1
‖**mog** *vb* *syn* see GO 2
mogul *n* *syn* see MAGNATE
moiety *n* *syn* see PART 1
moil *vb* **1** *syn* see LABOR 1
‖**2** *syn* see SEETHE 4
moil *n* **1** *syn* see WORK 2
2 *syn* see COMMOTION 4
moira *n* *syn* see FATE
moist *adj* **1** *syn* see DAMP
2 *syn* see SENTIMENTAL
moistureless *adj* *syn* see DRY 1
ant moist
moisty *adj* *syn* see DAMP
‖**moke** *n* *syn* see DONKEY 1
mold *n* *syn* see TYPE
mold *vb* *syn* see MAKE 3
moldable *adj* *syn* see PLASTIC
molder *vb* *syn* see DECAY
moldy *adj* *syn* see OLD-FASHIONED
moldy fig *n* *syn* see FOGY
mole *n* *syn* see BIRTHMARK 1
molecule *n* *syn* see PARTICLE
molest *vb* to annoy or disturb with hostile intent or injurious effect <he was specifically warned by the court not to *molest* his former wife>
syn bait, heckle, persecute, torment
rel annoy, badger, bother, irk, pester; pother, tease; bedevil, beset, devil, trouble; harass, harry, vex
moll *n* *syn* see PROSTITUTE
mollify *vb* **1** *syn* see PACIFY
rel lighten; temper; abate, decrease, lessen, reduce
ant exasperate
2 *syn* see RELIEVE 1
‖**molly** *n* *syn* see WEAKLING
mollycoddle *n* *syn* see WEAKLING
rel ‖mollycot
mollycoddle *vb* *syn* see BABY
ant neglect; abuse
molt *vb* *syn* see SHED 2
mom *n* *syn* see MOTHER 1
‖**momble** *vb* *syn* see CONFUSE 2
moment *n* **1** *syn* see INSTANT 1
ant eternity
2 *syn* see POINT 7
3 *syn* see OCCASION 5
4 *syn* see IMPORTANCE

---

syn synonym(s)   *rel* related word(s)
ant antonym(s)   *con* contrasted word(s)
idiom idiomatic equivalent(s)
‖ use limited; if in doubt, see a dictionary

rel advantage, avail, profit, use

momentaneous *adj syn* see TRANSIENT

momentary *adj syn* see TRANSIENT
rel brief, quick, short; impulsive
ant agelong

momentous *adj* **1** *syn* see IMPORTANT 1
ant trivial
2 *syn* see EPOCHAL

momentousness *n syn* see IMPORTANCE
ant triviality

mommy *n syn* see MOTHER 1

momus *n syn* see CRITIC

monarchal *adj syn* see KINGLY

monarchial *adj syn* see KINGLY

monarchical *adj syn* see KINGLY

mondaine *adj syn* see SOPHISTICATED 2

monetary *adj syn* see FINANCIAL
rel numismatic

money *n* something (as pieces of stamped metal or paper certificates) customarily and legally used as a medium of exchange <the only thing that he liked about his job was the *money*>
syn ‖blunt, ‖brass, ‖bread, ‖cabbage, cash, ‖chink, ‖chips, ‖coin, currency, ‖dibs, ‖dinero, ‖do-re-mi, dough, filthy lucre, ‖gelt, ‖greenbacks, ‖jack, ‖kale, legal tender, ‖lettuce, ‖long green, loot, lucre, ‖mazuma, ‖moolah, ‖mopus, needful, ‖ooftish, pelf, rhino, rocks, ‖scratch, ‖shekels, ‖smash, stuff, ‖stumpy, ‖sugar, swag, ‖wampum
rel bankroll, capital, coinage, finances, funds, mammon, resources, riches, treasure, wealth, wherewithal; boodle, hay; ‖stiff

moneyed *adj syn* see RICH 1
ant penniless, unmoneyed

moneygrubber *n syn* see MISER

moneymaking *adj syn* see ADVANTAGEOUS 1

monger *n syn* see PEDDLER

monger *vb syn* see PEDDLE 2

mongerer *n syn* see PEDDLER

mongrel *n syn* see HYBRID

‖moniker *n* **1** *syn* see NAME 1
2 *syn* see NICKNAME

monish *vb syn* see REPROVE

monition *n syn* see WARNING

monitorial *adj syn* see MONITORY

monitory *adj* giving a warning <the parents wrote their son a *monitory* letter>
syn admonishing, admonitory, cautionary, cautioning, monitorial, warning
rel advisory, counseling; critical, expostulatory, remonstratory; exhortatory, hortatory; moralistic, moralizing, preachy

monkey *n* **1** *syn* see FOOL 3
2 *syn* see URCHIN

monkey *adj syn* see SMALL 1

monkey (with) *vb syn* see MEDDLE

monkeyshine *n usu* **monkeyshines** *pl*
syn see PRANK

monocratic *adj syn* see ABSOLUTE 4
con democratic

monogram *n* a sign of identity usually formed of the combined initials of a name <everything he owned had his *monogram* on it>
syn cipher
rel device, initials; John Hancock, signature

monograph *n syn* see DISCOURSE 2

monography *n syn* see DISCOURSE 2

monopolize *vb* to take up completely <he would attempt to *monopolize* every conversation>
syn absorb, consume, engross, sew up
rel corner, hog; devour; have, hold, own, possess; employ, use, utilize; control, manage
con contribute, participate, share

monopolizing *adj syn* see ENGROSSING

monopoly *n* exclusive possession <neither party has a *monopoly* on morality>
syn corner
rel cartel, consortium, pool, syndicate, trust; copyright; ownership, possessorship, proprietorship

monotone *n syn* see MONOTONY

monotone *adj syn* see DULL 9

monotonous *adj syn* see DULL 9
rel samely, uniform, unvaried; repetitious; jogtrot, singsong
con changing, varying; fresh, new, novel; absorbing, engrossing, interesting

monotonousness *n syn* see MONOTONY

monotony *n* a tedious sameness or reiteration <the *monotony* of his job finally got to him>
syn humdrum, monotone, monotonousness
rel boredom, ennui, tedium; dryness, flatness, uniformity
con variability, variation; diversification, diversity, multifariousness, variety

monster *n* **1** *syn* see FREAK 2
rel demon, devil, fiend, hellhound; bandersnatch
2 *syn* see GIANT

monster *adj syn* see HUGE

monstrosity *n* **1** *syn* see FREAK 2
2 *syn* see EYESORE

monstrous *adj* **1** extremely impressive <the traditional burial ceremonies turned into a *monstrous* spectacle>
syn cracking, fantastic, massive, monumental, mortal, prodigious, stupendous, towering, tremendous
rel grandiose, impressive, magnificent, showy, splendid, superb; colossal, enormous, huge, immense, mammoth, vast
con mean, petty, picayune, poky, small-time
2 *syn* see HUGE
3 *syn* see OUTRAGEOUS 2
rel glaring, rank; fateful, ominous, portentous; flagitious, infamous

‖monstrous *adv syn* see VERY 1

monstrousness *n syn* see ENORMITY 1

Montezuma's revenge *n syn* see DIARRHEA

monument *n* **1** *syn* see DOCUMENT 1
2 a lasting evidence or reminder of someone or something notable <the whole body of students who learned from him form his *monument*>
syn memorial, testimonial
rel memento, tribute
3 *syn* see TOMBSTONE

monument *vb syn* see MEMORIALIZE 2

monumental *adj* **1** *syn* see HUGE
2 *syn* see MONSTROUS 1
3 *syn* see TOWERING 4
monumentalize *vb syn* see MEMORIALIZE 2
moocah *n syn* see MARIJUANA
mooch *vb syn* see WANDER 1
moocher *n syn* see BEGGAR 1
mooching *n syn* see MENDICANCY
mood *n* **1** a state of mind in which an emotion or set of emotions gains ascendancy <a melancholy *mood* induced by the sight of ancient ruins>
syn humor, mind, strain, temper, tone, vein
rel character, disposition, individuality, personality, temperament; soul, spirit; affection, emotion, feeling, response
2 *syn* see TEMPER 1
3 *syn* see AIR 3
moody *adj* subject to moods <a *moody* person whose behavior was erratic and whose actions were unpredictable>
syn humorsome, temperamental
rel capricious, fickle, inconstant, mercurial, unstable, whimsical; broody
con calm, dispassionate, stable, steady, unexcitable; bovine, impassive, stolid
‖**moolah** *n syn* see MONEY
mooncalf *n syn* see FOOL 1
‖**moonraker** *n syn* see DUNCE
moonshine *n* **1** *syn* see NONSENSE 2
2 illegally distilled liquor <his death was caused by bad *moonshine*>
syn bathtub gin, ‖blockade, bootleg, ‖busthead, ‖hooch, mountain dew, white lightning
rel homebrew; ‖bug juice, grappa, ‖jake, smoke, squareface
moor *vb syn* see FASTEN 2
moot *vb* **1** *syn* see BROACH
2 *syn* see DISCUSS 1
moot *adj* open to question <it is a *moot* point whether he would have been tried and convicted>
syn arguable, debatable, disputable, doubtful, dubious, mootable, problematic, questionable, uncertain; *compare* DOUBTFUL 1
rel controversial, suspect; unsettled
con confirmed, established, settled; inarguable, indisputable, undebatable, unproblematic, unquestionable; certain, sure
mooting *n syn* see ARGUMENTATION
mootable *adj syn* see MOOT
mop *vb syn* see GRIMACE
mop (up) *vb syn* see WHIP 2
mope *vb* **1** to become listless or dejected <*moped* for several days after the divorce>
syn brood, despond
rel ache, grieve, grump, pout, sulk
2 *syn* see SAUNTER
mopes *n pl syn* see SADNESS
mopey *adj syn* see DOWNCAST
moppet *n syn* see CHILD 1
‖**mopus** *n syn* see MONEY
moral *adj* **1** conforming to a standard of what is right and good <*moral* goodness may be distinguished from intellectual goodness>

syn ethical, moralistic, noble, principled, righteous, right-minded, virtuous
rel good, right; conscientious, honest, honorable, just, scrupulous, upright; chaste, decent, modest, pure
con amoral, nonmoral, unmoral
ant immoral
2 *syn* see DIDACTIC
3 *syn* see ELEVATED 2
moral *n syn* see MAXIM
morale *n* a sense of common purpose or a degree of dedication to a common task regarded as characteristic of or dominant in a group <*morale* was high among the troops>
syn esprit, esprit de corps
rel drive, spirit, vigor; assurance, confidence, self-confidence, self-possession
con enervation; aimlessness, purposelessness; egoism, egotism, self-centeredness
moralistic *adj syn* see MORAL 1
rel didactic
morality *n* **1** *syn* see GOODNESS
rel godliness, saintliness
2 *syn* see ETHIC 2
moralize *vb* to make moral reflections usually in an officious or tiresome manner <people avoided him as he was always *moralizing*>
syn preach, preachify, sermonize
rel lecture, pontificate
moralizing *adj syn* see DIDACTIC
morally *adv syn* see VIRTUALLY
morals *n pl* **1** *syn* see ETHIC 1
2 *syn* see ETHIC 2
rel conduct, habits, standards
morass *n* **1** *syn* see SWAMP
2 *syn* see MAZE 1
rel dunghill
moratorium *n syn* see SUSPENSION 2
morbid *adj* abnormally susceptible to or characterized by gloomy or unwholesome feelings <his *morbid* poetry is the product of his lifelong frustrations>
syn morose, sick, sickly
rel gloomy, melancholic; psychotic; dark, moody, saturnine, sullen
con healthy, sound, well, wholesome; solid, stable, stolid, sturdy
mordacious *adj syn* see CAUSTIC 1
mordancy *n syn* see ACRIMONY
rel incisiveness, pungency, trenchancy; acidity, acridity, causticity, mordacity
mordant *adj syn* see CAUSTIC 1
more *adj syn* see ADDITIONAL
more *adv syn* see ALSO 2
2 to a greater or higher degree <were *more* evenly matched>
syn better
more or less *adv* **1** *syn* see SOMEWHAT 2
2 *syn* see NEARLY

---

syn synonym(s)   *rel* related word(s)
ant antonym(s)   *con* contrasted word(s)
idiom idiomatic equivalent(s)
‖ use limited; if in doubt, see a dictionary

moreover *adv syn* see ALSO 2
mores *n pl* **1** *syn* see ETHIC 2
  2 *syn* see MANNER 5
morgue *n syn* see PRIDE 3
moribund *adj* approaching death or a final end
  <found lying *moribund* in her bed> <with its
  mills shut down the city's economy was *moribund*>
  syn dying
  rel expiring, fading, going; decadent, deteriorating, regressing
  idiom at death's door, on one's last legs, with
  one foot in the grave
  con booming, flourishing, prospering, thriving;
  lively, viable
morn *n* **1** *syn* see DAWN 1
  2 *syn* see MORNING 2
morne *adj syn* see GLOOMY 3
morning *n* **1** *syn* see DAWN 1
  con sundown, sunset
  2 the time before noon <it rained most of the
  morning>
  syn forenoon, morn
  con afternoon, evening; day, night
moron *n* **1** *syn* see FOOL 4
  2 *syn* see DUNCE
moronic *adj syn* see RETARDED
morose *adj* **1** *syn* see SULLEN
  rel choleric, cranky, irascible, splenetic, testy;
  irritable, waspish; brusque, gruff
  con jocund, jolly, jovial, merry
  ant blithe
  2 *syn* see MORBID
morsel *n* **1** a small piece or quantity of food
  <tossed a *morsel* of meat to the dog>
  syn bit, bite, mouthful
  rel taste; tidbit; crumb, ort, scrap
  2 *syn* see SNACK
  3 *syn* see DELICACY
mort *n syn* see CORPSE
‖**mortacious** *adv syn* see VERY 1
mortal *adj* **1** *syn* see DEADLY 1
  rel implacable, relentless, unrelenting
  2 *syn* see GRIM 3
  3 *syn* see MONSTROUS 1
  4 *syn* see HUMAN
  rel finite, temporal; frail, weak
  5 *syn* see PROBABLE
mortal *n syn* see HUMAN
mortality *n* **1** *syn* see FATALITY 1
  2 *syn* see MANKIND
mortally *adv syn* see VERY 1
mortgage *vb syn* see PAWN
mortician *n* one whose business is to prepare the
  dead for burial and to arrange and manage fu-
  nerals <*morticians* must be certified>
  syn funeral director, undertaker
  rel embalmer
mortiferous *adj syn* see DEADLY 1
mortified *adj* **1** *syn* see SEVERE 1
  2 *syn* see ASHAMED
  rel annoyed, harassed, harried, worried
mortuary *adj syn* see SEPULCHRAL 1
mosey *vb syn* see SAUNTER

‖**moss** *n syn* see SWAMP
mossback *n* **1** *syn* see RUSTIC
  2 *syn* see FOGY
most *adj syn* see BEST
  rel greatest, highest, maximum, utmost, uttermost
most *adv syn* see VERY 1
most *adv syn* see NEARLY
mostly *adv syn* see GENERALLY 1
  idiom for the most part
mote *n syn* see POINT 11
moth–eaten *adj* **1** *syn* see SHABBY 1
  2 *syn* see OLD-FASHIONED
mother *n* **1** a female human parent <the *mother* of
  seven children>
  syn ma, ‖mam, mama (*or* mamma), mammy,
  ‖mater, mom, mommy, ‖mum, mummy, ‖old
  lady, ‖old woman; *compare* FATHER 1
  2 *syn* see SOURCE
mother *vb syn* see MINISTER (to)
mother country *n syn* see COUNTRY
motherland *n syn* see COUNTRY
mother–naked *adj syn* see NUDE 2
mother wit *n syn* see INTELLIGENCE 1
motif *n* **1** *syn* see LEITMOTIV
  2 *syn* see SUBJECT 2
  3 *syn* see FIGURE 3
motion *n* **1** the act or an instance of moving <the
  motion of the planets>
  syn move, movement, stir, stirring
  rel agitation, fluctuation, oscillation, sway,
  swing, wavering; locomotion
  con inertia, inertness, passivity
  2 an impulse or inclination of the mind or will <a
  motion of the will toward what appears good>
  syn movement
  rel goad, impulse, incentive, inducement, motive, spring, spur
  con inertia, stagnation, vegetation
motion *vb syn* see SIGNAL
motionless *adj* being without motion <stood *motionless* so that he would remain undiscovered>
  syn still, stock-still, stone-still
  rel stagnant, static, stationary, unmoving; fixed,
  immobile, immotile, immotive, immovable, irremovable, ‖sitfast, steadfast, unmovable
  con active, changing, mobile, moving
motion picture *n syn* see MOVIE
motivate *vb syn* see PROVOKE 4
motivation *n syn* see STIMULUS
motive *n* **1** the object influencing a choice or
  prompting an action <trying to discover what
  was his *motive* in killing the girl>
  syn cause, consideration, reason, spring; *compare* STIMULUS
  rel antecedent, determinant; emotion, feeling,
  passion; aim, end, intent, intention, purpose
  2 *syn* see FIGURE 3
  3 *syn* see SUBJECT 2
motley *adj* **1** *syn* see VARIEGATED
  2 *syn* see MISCELLANEOUS
  rel discrepant, incompatible, incongruous, uncongenial
motley *n* **1** *syn* see FOOL 2

2 *syn* see MISCELLANY 1

motor *n syn* see CAR

motor *vb* **1** *syn* see RIDE 1
2 *syn* see DRIVE 5

motorcar *n syn* see CAR

motor home *n syn* see TRAILER

motorist *n* a person who travels by automobile
<the roads were crowded with *motorists* going to
work>
syn autoist, automobilist, driver, operator

mottle *vb syn* see SPLOTCH

motto *n syn* see BATTLE CRY
rel byword, catchphrase, catchword, shibboleth, slogan, watchword, word

moue *n syn* see FACE 6

mound *vb syn* see HEAP 1

mound *n syn* see PILE 1

mount *n syn* see MOUNTAIN 1

mount *vb* **1** *syn* see INCREASE 2
2 *syn* see ASCEND 1
con descend, fall, lower
ant drop
3 *syn* see RISE 4
ant drop
4 *syn* see INTENSIFY
5 to get on (something) as a means of conveyance <*mount* a horse>
syn back, bestride
rel seat, settle
ant dismount
‖6 *syn* see TESTIFY 2
7 *syn* see STAGE

mountain *n* **1** a relatively steep and high elevation
of land <why are *mountains* in New England
considered no more than hills in Colorado>
syn alp, mount, peak
rel butte, mesa; bald, dome; hill; bluff; volcano;
sierra
con bottom, bottomland, dale, dell, vale, valley
2 *syn* see PILE 1
3 *syn* see MUCH
4 *syn* see OBSTACLE

mountain dew *n syn* see MOONSHINE 2

mountaineer *n syn* see RUSTIC

mountainous *adj syn* see HUGE

mountebank *n* **1** *syn* see CHARLATAN
2 *syn* see SWINDLER

mourn *vb syn* see GRIEVE 2
con delight, gladden, please, rejoice

mournful *adj* **1** *syn* see SAD 1
2 *syn* see SAD 2
3 *syn* see MELANCHOLY 2
4 *syn* see DEPLORABLE

mournfulness *n syn* see SADNESS

mouse *n* **1** *syn* see GIRL FRIEND 1
2 *syn* see BLACK EYE 1

mouse *vb* **1** *syn* see SNOOP
2 *syn* see STEAL 3

mousehole *n syn* see CUBBYHOLE

mousetrap *n syn* see PITFALL

mouth *n* **1** the opening through which food passes
into the body of an animal <the *mouth* in verte-
brates is one of the features of the face>
syn ‖bazoo, gob, ‖mush, ‖row, ‖trap, ‖yap

rel mug, muzzle
2 *syn* see FACE 6
3 *syn* see SPOKESMAN
4 *syn* see BACK TALK
5 the place where a tributary enters a larger
stream or body of water <the *mouth* of the Mis-
sissippi river is in the Gulf of Mexico>
syn embouchement, embouchure
rel estuary; delta

mouth *vb* **1** *syn* see ORATE
2 *syn* see BOAST
3 *syn* see REVEAL 1
4 *syn* see GRIMACE

mouthful *n syn* see MORSEL 1

mouthing *n syn* see FACE 6

mouthpiece *n syn* see SPOKESMAN

mouth–watering *adj syn* see PALATABLE

‖**mouthy** *adj* **1** *syn* see TALKATIVE
2 *syn* see RHETORICAL

movable *adj* capable of moving or of being moved
<a device with a *movable* attachment>
syn mobile, moving, unstable, unsteadfast, unsteady
rel remotive, removable; motile; changeable,
changeful, mutable, variable; roving
con immobile, immotile, immotive, irremovable, steadfast; established, fixed, set, settled;
stagnant, static, unmoving

movables *n pl syn* see POSSESSION 2

move *vb* **1** *syn* see GO 2
2 *syn* see ADVANCE 5
3 *syn* see BE
4 to change or cause to change from one place to
another <he *moved* quickly down the stair-
case> <*move* the chair across the room>
syn dislocate, disturb, remove, shift, ship, transfer
rel displace, replace, supersede, supplant; bear,
carry, convey, transmit, transport
5 to set or keep in motion or action <the mechanism that *moves* the locomotive>
syn actuate, drive, impel, mobilize, propel
rel activate, motivate
con bring up, draw up, fetch up, halt, haul up,
pull up, stop
6 *syn* see PROVOKE 4
7 *syn* see AFFECT
rel induce, persuade, prevail
8 *syn* see CONVERT 1
9 *syn* see BEHAVE 1

move *n* **1** *syn* see MEASURE 7
2 *syn* see MOTION 1
rel alteration, change, modification, variation

movement *n* **1** *syn* see MOTION 1
rel act, action, deed; activity, dynamism, live-
ness, operation, operativeness
2 *syn* see MOTION 2

mover *n syn* see INSTIGATOR

---

syn synonym(s)	*rel* related word(s)
ant antonym(s)	*con* contrasted word(s)
idiom idiomatic equivalent(s)	
‖ use limited; if in doubt, see a dictionary	

movie *n* a representation (as of a story) by means of motion pictures <tired old *movies* that appear on TV>
syn cine, ‖cinema, film, flick, motion picture, moving picture, photoplay, picture, picture show, show
rel cinematics, cinematography
moving *adj* **1** *syn* see MOVABLE
2 having the power to excite deep and usually somber emotion <made a *moving* appeal for help for the orphaned children>
syn affecting, impressive, poignant, touching; *compare* EMOTIONAL 2
rel eloquent, expressive, facund, meaningful, pregnant, sententious, significant; arousing, awakening, rallying, rousing, stirring; exciting, provoking, quickening, stimulating; breathless, gripping
con unaffecting, unimpressive, untouching; casual, cold, formal
ant unmoving
3 *syn* see EMOTIONAL 2
moving picture *n* *syn* see MOVIE
mow *n* *syn* see PILE 1
mow *vb* to cut down standing grass or grain with a tool or a machine <*mowed* the lawn every week>
syn clip, crop, cut
rel reap; pare, trim
mow (down) *vb* *syn* see FELL 1
mow *n* *syn* see FACE 6
mow *vb* *syn* see GRIMACE
moxie *n* **1** *syn* see ENERGY 2
2 *syn* see COURAGE
3 *syn* see FORTITUDE
‖**mozo** *n* *syn* see WORKER
Mr. *n* *syn* see HUSBAND
Mrs. *n* *syn* see WIFE
Mrs. Grundy *n* *syn* see PRUDE
much *adv* **1** *syn* see VERY 1
2 *syn* see OFTEN
3 *syn* see NEARLY
much *n* a great quantity, amount, extent, or degree <learned *much* worth remembering from his experiences in the army>
syn barrel, great deal, heap, lashings, lot, lump, mass, ‖mess, mountain, multiplicity, pack, peck, pile, plenty, ‖power, ‖sight; *compare* MULTITUDE 1, SCAD
rel excess, overage, oversupply, plethora, superfluity
idiom all kinds of
con bit, crumb, modicum, trifle; deficiency, inadequacy, insufficiency, undersupply
ant little
‖**much** *vb* *syn* see BABY
much as *conj* *syn* see THOUGH
muck *n* **1** *syn* see SLIME
2 *syn* see REFUSE
3 *syn* see GOO 1
muck *vb* **1** *syn* see SOIL 2
‖**2** *syn* see BOTCH
‖**3** *syn* see COMPLICATE
4 *syn* see DRUDGE
‖**5** *syn* see SAUNTER

‖**muckamuck** *n* *syn* see FOOD 1
muckamuck *n* *syn* see NOTABLE 1
mucker *vb* *syn* see BOTCH
mucker *n* **1** *syn* see BOOR
2 *syn* see WRETCH 1
3 *syn* see TOUGH
mucking *adj* *syn* see DAMNED 2
muckworm *n* *syn* see MISER
mucky *adj* **1** *syn* see DIRTY 1
2 *syn* see MURKY 3
3 *syn* see HUMID
‖**mucky** *vb* *syn* see SOIL 2
mucronate *adj* *syn* see POINTED 1
mud *vb* *syn* see ROIL 1
muddle *vb* **1** *syn* see ROIL 1
2 *syn* see MUMBLE
3 *syn* see CONFUSE 2
4 *syn* see DISORDER 1
5 *syn* see CONFUSE 5
6 *syn* see COMPLICATE
7 *syn* see STUMBLE 6
muddle (away) *vb* *syn* see WASTE 2
muddle *n* **1** *syn* see CONFUSION 3
2 *syn* see MESS 3
3 *syn* see CLUTTER 2
muddled *adj* **1** *syn* see INCOHERENT 2
2 *syn* see INTOXICATED 1
muddledness *n* *syn* see HAZE 2
muddlehead *n* *syn* see DUNCE
muddleheadedness *n* *syn* see HAZE 2
muddlement *n* *syn* see HAZE 2
muddle through *vb* *syn* see SHIFT 5
muddy *adj* **1** having a great deal of mud <playing in the wet field, he got his shoes all *muddy*>
syn bemired, ‖claggy, ‖clarty, miry, oozy
rel black, dirty, dungy, filthy, foul, grubby, impure, nasty, soily, sordid, squalid, unclean, uncleanly; bedraggled, draggled
con clean, cleanly, immaculate, spotless, taintless, unsoiled, unsullied
ant mudless
2 *syn* see TURBID
rel gloomy, murky; addled, confused, muddled
3 *syn* see DULL 8
muddy *vb* **1** *syn* see SOIL 2
2 *syn* see ROIL 1
3 *syn* see DULL 1
4 *syn* see CONFUSE 4
rel conceal, hide, screen
con illuminate, illumine, light, lighten
mudhole *n* **1** *syn* see POTHOLE
2 *syn* see BURG
muff *vb* *syn* see BOTCH
muffle *vb* **1** *syn* see BUNDLE UP
rel cover, envelop, overspread, shroud, veil
2 to dull the sound of <closed the door to *muffle* the outside noises>
syn dampen, deaden, mute, stifle
rel mellow, soften, soft-pedal, subdue, tone (down); smother
con amplify, enhance, heighten, magnify, reinforce, strengthen
3 *syn* see SUPPRESS 2
muffler *n* *syn* see MASK 2

mug *n* **1** *syn* see FACE 1
  2 *syn* see FACE 6
  3 *syn* see DUNCE
  ‖**4** *syn* see FOOL 3
  5 *syn* see TOUGH

mug *vb syn* see GRIMACE

‖mug (up) *vb syn* see CRAM 4

muggins *n syn* see DUNCE

muggy *adj syn* see HUMID
  rel damp, dampish, moist, moisty, wettish
  con dry

mughouse *n syn* see ALEHOUSE

mug–up *n syn* see SNACK

mugwump *n syn* see NOTABLE 1

mulatto *n* a person of mixed Caucasian and Negro
ancestry <the special conflicts faced by *mulat-
toes* with both whites and blacks>
  syn high yellow
  rel mulatta, mulattress; octoroon, quadroon;
sambo, zambo; mustee; half-breed

mulct *n syn* see FINE

mulct *vb* **1** *syn* see PENALIZE
  rel claim, demand, exact, require
  2 *syn* see FLEECE 1

mule *n syn* see HYBRID

muleheaded *adj syn* see OBSTINATE

muley *adj syn* see OBSTINATE

muliebral *adj syn* see FEMININE

mulish *adj syn* see OBSTINATE
  rel ungovernable, unruly; fixed, set

mull *n syn* see MESS 3

mull *vb* **1** *syn* see DEADEN 1
  2 *syn* see CONFUSE 2
  3 *syn* see DELAY 2

mull (over) *vb syn* see PONDER 2

mulligrubs *n pl syn* see SULK
  rel blues, dejection, depression, (the) dismals,
dumps, gloom, heavyheartedness, melancholy,
mournfulness, sadness, unhappiness

‖mullock *n* **1** *syn* see REFUSE
  2 *syn* see CONFUSION 3

multeity *n syn* see VARIETY 1

multicolor *adj syn* see VARIEGATED
  ant monotone

multicolored *adj syn* see VARIEGATED
  ant monotone

multifarious *adj* **1** *syn* see MANY
  2 *syn* see MANIFOLD
  3 *syn* see MISCELLANEOUS

multifariousness *n syn* see VARIETY 1

multifold *adj syn* see MANIFOLD

multiform *adj syn* see MANIFOLD
  ant uniform

multiformity *n syn* see VARIETY 1
  ant uniformity

multihued *adj syn* see VARIEGATED
  ant monotone

multilateral *adj* having many sides <*multilateral*
figures>
  syn many-sided
  ant one-sided, unilateral

multiloquent *adj syn* see TALKATIVE

multiloquious *adj syn* see TALKATIVE

multiplex *adj syn* see MANIFOLD

multiplicity *n* **1** *syn* see VARIETY 1
  ant unity
  2 *syn* see MUCH

multiply *vb* **1** *syn* see INCREASE 1
  2 *syn* see INCREASE 2
  3 *syn* see PROCREATE 1

multitude *n* **1** a very large number of individuals
or things <that child always asks a *multitude* of
questions>
  syn army, cloud, crowd, flock, host, legion,
rout, scores; *compare* CROWD 1, MUCH, SCAD
  rel numbers, oodles, quantities
  con few, handful, scattering, smatter, smattering, sprinkling
  ant none
  2 *syn* see CROWD 1

multitudinal *adj syn* see MANY
  rel countless, innumerable, innumerous, numberless, uncountable, uncounted, unnumberable, unnumbered, untold

multitudinous *adj syn* see MANY
  rel countless, innumerable, innumerous, numberless, uncountable, uncounted, unnumberable, unnumbered, untold

multivarious *adj syn* see MANIFOLD

multivocal *adj syn* see VOCIFEROUS

mum *adj syn* see SILENT 2

‖mum *n syn* see MOTHER 1

mumble *vb* to utter with a low inarticulate voice
<embarrassed, he *mumbled* an apology>
  syn ‖chunter, fumble, muddle, ‖mump, murmur, mutter, swallow
  rel maunder; limp, shuffle, stumble; ‖hammer,
stammer, ‖stut, stutter; speak, talk, utter, verbalize, vocalize, voice
  idiom speak with mush in one's mouth
  con speak out, speak up; clamor, cry out, shout,
vociferate

mumble *n syn* see MURMUR 1

mumblenews *n pl but sing or pl in constr syn* see
GOSSIP 1

mumbo jumbo *n syn* see GIBBERISH 3

‖mumchance *adj syn* see SILENT 2

mummer *n syn* see ACTOR 1

mummery *n syn* see GIBBERISH 3

mummify *vb syn* see WITHER

mummy *n syn* see MOTHER 1

mummy *vb syn* see WITHER

‖mump *vb* **1** *syn* see MUMBLE
  2 *syn* see GRIMACE
  3 *syn* see SULK

‖mump *vb syn* see CHEAT

mumpish *adj syn* see SULLEN

mumps *n pl syn* see SULK

‖mun *vb syn* see MUST 2

‖mun *n syn* see MAN 3

munch *vb syn* see CHEW 1

mundane *adj* **1** *syn* see EARTHLY 1
  rel profane, secular, temporal

---

syn synonym(s)   *rel* related word(s)
ant antonym(s)   *con* contrasted word(s)
idiom idiomatic equivalent(s)
‖ use limited; if in doubt, see a dictionary

ant eternal

2 *syn* see MATERIALISTIC

rel animal, carnal, fleshly

3 *syn* see PROSAIC 3

municipal *adj* **1 *syn*** see DOMESTIC 2

2 *syn* see URBAN

munificent *adj* *syn* see LIBERAL 1

con close, mean, niggard, ungiving

murder *n* the crime of killing a person <a *murder* occurred during a gang shoot-out>

syn blood, ‖bump-off, foul play, hit, homicide, killing, manslaughter

murder *vb* **1** to kill (a human being) unlawfully and with premeditated malice <planned a safe way to *murder* his rival>

syn assassinate, ‖bump off, cool, do in, ‖dust off, execute, finish, knock off, liquidate, put away, rub out, scrag, slay; *compare* KILL 1

rel asphyxiate, behead, decapitate, electrocute, garrote, guillotine, hang, lynch, smother, strangle

idiom take for a ride

2 *syn* see ANNIHILATE 2

murderer *n* one who kills a human being <a *murderer* who wouldn't hesitate to kill in cold blood>

syn homicide, killer, manslayer, slayer; *compare* ASSASSIN

rel butcher, slaughterer

murdering *adj* *syn* see MURDEROUS

murderous *adj* characterized by or of a kind to cause murder or bloodshed <made a *murderous* assault on his former friend>

syn bloodthirsty, bloody, homicidal, murdering, sanguinary, sanguine, sanguineous

rel deadly; destructive, devastating, ruinous

con harmless, innocuous, trivial

mure *vb* *syn* see ENCLOSE 1

murk *vb* **1 *syn*** see OBSCURE

2 *syn* see SOIL 2

murky *adj* **1 *syn*** see DARK 1

rel glooming, glowering, lowering

con bright, brilliant, effulgent, radiant

2 *syn* see OBSCURE 3

3 having visible material in suspension <a *murky* liquid>

syn cloudy, mucky

rel muddy, roily, turbid

con clear, limpid, lucent, translucent, transparent; clean, fresh, pure, unpolluted

4 *syn* see DULL 8

5 *syn* see DIRTY 1

murmur *n* **1** a low indistinct but often continuous sound (as of voices) <could hear the *murmur* of the audience throughout the entire performance>

syn mumble, mutter, rumor, susurration, undertone, whisper

rel murmuration; buzz, drone, hum, purr; brool

2 *syn* see REPORT 1

murmur *vb* **1 *syn*** see GRUMBLE 1

2 *syn* see COMPLAIN

3 *syn* see MUMBLE

muscle *n* **1** muscular strength <loading cargo calls for real *muscle*>

syn beef, brawn, might, sinew, thew

rel power, strength

con impotence

2 *syn* see POWER 4

muscle–bound *adj* *syn* see STIFF 4

muscular *adj* **1** marked by good well-developed musculature <his arms were lean but *muscular*>

syn fibrous, ropy, sinewy, stringy, wiry

rel flexible, elastic, resilient, springy, supple

con flabby, flaccid, flimsy, floppy, limp, sleazy; feeble, weak

2 strong and powerful in build or action <a *muscular* lad who could wield an ax like a man>

syn athletic, brawny, sinewy; *compare* STRONG 1

rel stalwart, stout, strong, sturdy; well-built, well-knit, well-set; beefy, burly, husky; Herculean, mighty, powerful

con faint, fragile, frail; delicate, feeble, weak; ‖pindling, puny, slight

muse *vb* *syn* see PONDER 2

rel excogitate, study

muse *n* *syn* see REVERIE

muse *n* *syn* see POET

museum *n* a room, building, or locale where a collection of objects is put on exhibition <an art *museum* with a famous collection of jade>

syn gallery

rel salon; picture gallery, pinacotheka

‖mush *n* **1 *syn*** see MOUTH 1

2 *syn* see FACE 1

‖mush (up) *vb* *syn* see CRUSH 2

mushroom *vb* *syn* see EXPLODE 1

mushy *adj* **1 *syn*** see SOFT 6

2 *syn* see HAZY

3 *syn* see SENTIMENTAL

music *n* *syn* see DIN

musical *adj* **1 *syn*** see HARMONIOUS 1

ant unmusical; musicless

2 *syn* see MELODIOUS 2

ant unmusical; musicless

musician *n* one skilled in music <the one playing the sax is a real *musician*>

syn musicianer, ‖musicker, musico, virtuoso

rel performer, player

musicianer *n* *syn* see MUSICIAN

‖musicker *n* *syn* see MUSICIAN

musico *n* *syn* see MUSICIAN

muskeg *n* *syn* see SWAMP

muss *n* ‖**1 *syn*** see BRAWL 2

2 *syn* see MESS 3

muss (up) *vb* *syn* see DISORDER 1

rel dishevel, rumple, wrinkle

mussy *adj* *syn* see SLOVENLY 1

must *verbal auxiliary* **1 *syn*** see WANT 3

2 — used to indicate requirement by immediate or future need or purpose <we *must* hurry if we want to catch the bus>

syn have, ‖mun, need

rel ought, should want

idiom have got to, must needs

must *n* **1 *syn*** see OBLIGATION 2

2 *syn* see ESSENTIAL 2

muster *vb* **1 *syn*** see ENTER 3

2 *syn* see MOBILIZE 3

3 *syn* see GATHER 6
muster (up) *vb syn* see GENERATE 3
muster *n* **1** *syn* see GATHERING 2
2 *syn* see ROSTER 1
muster out *vb syn* see DISCHARGE 7
ant call up, draft
muster roll *n syn* see ROSTER 1
musty *adj* **1** *syn* see MALODOROUS 1
rel dirty, filthy, squalid
2 *syn* see TRITE
mutable *adj* **1** *syn* see CHANGEABLE 1
rel fluctuating, swaying, swinging, wavering; fickle, inconstant, unstable
con equable, even, steady, uniform; durable, lasting, permanent, stable
ant immutable
2 liable to change or to be changed <a flexible and perhaps too *mutable* policy>
syn changeable, inconstant, shifty, slippery, uncertain, unstable, unsteady, variable; *compare* CHANGEABLE 1, INCONSTANT 1
rel changeful, protean, unsettled; capricious, fickle, inconsistent, lubricious, mercurial, temperamental, ticklish, volatile; fluctuating, shilly≈shally, vacillating, wavering
con constant, established, fixed, immovable, inalterable, invariable, set, unalterable, unchangeable, unmodifiable, unmovable
ant immutable
mutate *vb* **1** *syn* see TRANSFORM
2 *syn* see CHANGE 1
mutation *n* **1** *syn* see CHANGE 1
2 *syn* see CHANGE 2
mute *adj* **1** *syn* see DUMB 1
2 *syn* see SILENT 2
con articulate, eloquent, fluent, glib, vocal, voluble
mute *vb syn* see MUFFLE 2
muted *adj syn* see DULL 7
mutedly *adv syn* see SOTTO VOCE
mutilate *vb* **1** *syn* see MAIM
rel damage, hurt, injure, mar, spoil; deface
2 *syn* see STERILIZE
mutineer *n syn* see REBEL
mutinous *adj syn* see INSUBORDINATE
rel alienated, disaffected
mutiny *vb syn* see REVOLT 1
mutt *n syn* see DUNCE
mutter *vb* **1** *syn* see MUMBLE
2 *syn* see GRUMBLE 1
rel repine, wail
mutter *n syn* see MURMUR 1
muttonchops *n pl syn* see SIDE-WHISKERS
muttonhead *n syn* see DUNCE
mutual *adj syn* see COMMON 1
rel partaken, participated; associated, connected, related, united
mutually *adv syn* see TOGETHER 3
‖**mux** *vb syn* see DISORDER 1
muzzle *n syn* see FACE 1
myopic *adj* affected by a condition in which the visual images come to a focus in front of the retina of the eye resulting especially in defective vision of distant objects <so *myopic* that he used glasses even to read>

syn nearsighted, shortsighted
rel presbyopic; astigmatic
ant farsighted, hyperopic, longsighted
myriad-minded *adj syn* see VERSATILE
mysterial *adj syn* see MYSTERIOUS
mysterious *adj* being beyond one's powers to discover, understand, or explain <he had a *mysterious* sense of humor, laughing when other people did not>
syn arcane, cabalistic, impenetrable, inscrutable, mysterial, mystic, numinous, unaccountable, unexaminable, unguessed, unknowable; *compare* INEXPLICABLE, STRANGE 4
rel impenetrable, incognizable, incomprehensible, uncomprehensible, ungraspable, unintelligible, unknowable; abstruse, esoteric, occult, recondite; ambiguous, cryptic, enigmatic, equivocal, obscure
con explainable, explicable; apprehensible, comprehendible, comprehensible, fathomable, graspable, intelligible, knowable, lucid, scrutable; candid, frank, honest, straightforward
ant unmysterious
mystery *n* something which baffles or perplexes <the *mystery* of her disappearance has never been solved>
syn Chinese puzzle, closed book, conundrum, enigma, mystification, puzzle, puzzlement, riddle, why
rel poser, problem, stumper; perplexity; brainteaser, brain twister
con open book
mystic *adj* **1** *syn* see MYSTICAL 1
rel imaginary, visionary; quixotic
2 *syn* see MYSTERIOUS
3 *syn* see MAGIC
mystical *adj* **1** having a spiritual meaning or reality that is neither apparent to the senses nor obvious to the intelligence <the Church is the *mystical* body of Christ>
syn anagogic, mystic, telestic
rel abysmal, deep, profound; absolute, categorical, ultimate; divine, holy, sacred, spiritual; miraculous, supernatural, supranatural
2 *syn* see SECRET 1
mystification *n syn* see MYSTERY
mystifying *adj syn* see CRYPTIC
myth *n* **1** a traditional story of ostensibly historical content whose origin has been lost <the various Greek *myths* that have come down to us>
syn legend, mythos, mythus; *compare* ALLEGORY 2
rel saga; fable, fabrication, fiction, figment; creation, invention
2 *syn* see ALLEGORY 2
3 *syn* see LORE 2
mythical *adj* lacking factual basis or historical validity <a *mythical* account attributes the founding of the city to Noah>

---

syn synonym(s)   *rel* related word(s)
ant antonym(s)   *con* contrasted word(s)
idiom idiomatic equivalent(s)
‖ use limited; if in doubt, see a dictionary

syn fabulous, legendary, mythological
rel fictional, fictitious, fictive, imaginary, suppositious, unreal; fanciful, fantastic, visionary; created, invented
con actual, real, true; authentic, genuine, veritable; truthful, veracious, verisimilar

   ant historical
mythological *adj syn* see MYTHICAL
mythology *n syn* see LORE 2
mythos *n* **1** *syn* see MYTH 1
  2 *syn* see LORE 2
mythus *n syn* see MYTH 1

N

nab *vb* **1 syn** see ARREST 2
  2 syn see SEIZE 2
  3 syn see STEAL 1
‖**nab** *n* **1 syn** see POLICEMAN
  2 syn see ARREST
nabal *n* **syn** see MISER
nabob *n* **syn** see NOTABLE 1
nada *n* **syn** see NOTHINGNESS
nadir *n* **syn** see BOTTOM 3
  con acme, climax, culmination; peak, summit
  ant apex, zenith
nag *vb* to find fault incessantly <stop *nagging* her over nothing>
  syn carp (at), fuss, henpeck, peck (at)
  rel annoy, harass, harry, pester, plague, tease, worry; bother, irk, vex; badger, bait, chivy, heckle, hector, hound, ride; egg, goad, needle, prod, urge
  idiom give a bad (*or* hard) time, pick at (*or* on), take it out on
  con commend, compliment, praise; acclaim, applaud, hail
nail *vb* **1 syn** see CATCH 1
  ‖**2 syn** see SEIZE 2
  ‖**3 syn** see STEAL 1
  ‖**4 syn** see STRIKE 2
naive *adj* **1 syn** see NATURAL 5
  rel fresh, original
  ant sophisticated
  2 syn see EASY 3
naked *adj* **1 syn** see BARE 1
  2 syn see NUDE 2
  3 syn see OPEN 2
  rel disclosed, discovered, revealed; evident, manifest, obvious, palpable; colorless, uncolored; pure, sheer, simple
namby–pamby *adj* **1 syn** see INSIPID 3
  2 syn see CHARACTERLESS
namby–pamby *n* **syn** see WEAKLING
name *n* **1** the word or combination of words by which something is called and by means of which it can be distinguished or identified <the *name* always given to the eldest son> <what is the *name* of that bird?>
  syn appellation, appellative, cognomen, compellation, denomination, designation, ‖handle, ‖moniker, nomen, rubric, style, title
  rel baptismal name, Christian name, font name, forename, personal name, prename; byname, byword, hypocorism, nickname, pet name, sobriquet; epithet, label, tag; alias, incognito, nom de guerre, nom de plume, pen name, pseudonym
  2 syn see REPUTATION 2
  3 syn see CELEBRITY 2
name *vb* **1** to give a name to <*named* the child for his grandfather>
  syn baptize, call, christen, denominate, designate, dub, entitle, style, term, title
  rel label, tag, ticket; nickname
  idiom give a handle, pin a moniker on
  2 syn see DESIGNATE 2
  rel advertise, announce, declare, publish
  3 syn see MENTION
  rel identify, recognize
nameable *adj* **syn** see NOTEWORTHY
nameless *adj* **1 syn** see OBSCURE 5
  2 syn see ANONYMOUS
  ant named
namely *adv* that is to say <understandably his wife disapproves of his bad habits, *namely* gambling and drinking>
  syn scilicet, to wit, videlicet
  rel especially, expressly, particularly, specially, specifically
nana *n* **syn** see NURSEMAID
‖**nanny** *n* **syn** see NURSEMAID
nap *n* a short sleep <generally took an hour's *nap* after lunch>
  syn catnap, dog nap, ‖dover, forty winks, siesta, snooze; *compare* DOZE, SLEEP 1
  rel dogsleep; break, interlude, intermission, let up, pause, respite, rest
nap *vb* to sleep briefly <*napped* for an hour after lunch>
  syn catnap, ‖caulk (off), siesta, snooze; *compare* DOZE, SLEEP
  rel drowse; relax, rest, unlax
  idiom catch a wink of sleep, catch forty winks, take a nap (*or* siesta *or* snooze)
narcissism *n* **syn** see CONCEIT 2
narcissistic *adj* **syn** see VAIN 3
narcotic *n* **1 syn** see DRUG 2
  2 syn see ANODYNE 2
narcotic *adj* **syn** see SOPORIFIC 1
‖**nark** *n* **syn** see INFORMER
‖**nark** *vb* **syn** see INFORM 3
narrate *vb* **syn** see RELATE 1
  rel descant, dilate, discourse, expatiate
narration *n* **1 syn** see DESCRIPTION 2
  2 syn see STORY 2
narrative *n* **1 syn** see STORY 2
  2 syn see ACCOUNT 7
narrow *adj* **1 syn** see DEFINITE 1
  2 syn see LITTLE 2
  3 syn see ILLIBERAL
  rel inexorable, inflexible, obdurate
  con forbearing, indulgent, lenient, tolerant
  ant broad
  ‖**4 syn** see STINGY
narrow *vb* **syn** see CONSTRICT 2

---

syn synonym(s)   **rel** related word(s)
ant antonym(s)   **con** contrasted w
idiom idiomatic equivalent(s)
‖ use limited; if in doubt, see a dictio

narrow–fisted *adj syn* see STINGY
   ant openhanded
narrowhearted *adj syn* see STINGY
   ant openhearted
narrow–minded *adj syn* see ILLIBERAL
   ant broad-minded
nascent *adj syn* see INITIAL 1
nasty *adj* 1 *syn* see DIRTY 1
   rel coarse, gross, obscene, ribald, vulgar; improper, indecent, indecorous, indelicate, unseemly
   2 *syn* see OFFENSIVE
   3 *syn* see OBSCENE 2
   4 *syn* see MALICIOUS
nates *n pl syn* see BUTTOCKS
national *adj* 1 *syn* see PUBLIC 1
   2 *syn* see DOMESTIC 2
national *n syn* see CITIZEN 2
native *adj* 1 *syn* see INNATE 1
   2 belonging to a locality by birth or origin <a *native* tradition> <delighted with the tasty *native* fruits>
   syn aboriginal, autochthonous, endemic, indigenous
   rel domestic, local
   con adopted, introduced, naturalized
   ant alien, foreign, nonnative
   3 *syn* see DOMESTIC 2
   4 *syn* see WILD 1
   5 *syn* see UNREFINED 3
Nativity *n syn* see CHRISTMAS
‖**natter** *vb syn* see CHAT 1
natty *adj syn* see DAPPER
natural *adj* 1 *syn* see ILLEGITIMATE 1
   2 *syn* see INNATE 1
   ant abnormal, unnatural
   3 *syn* see GENERAL 1
   4 *syn* see WILD 1
   5 free from pretension or calculation <he spoke in a perfectly *natural* manner>
   syn artless, guileless, inartificial, ingenuous, innocent, naive, simple, simplehearted, unaffected, unartful, unartificial, unschooled, unsophisticated, unstudied, untutored, unworldly; *compare* GENUINE 3
   rel impulsive, instinctive, spontaneous; easy, unlabored; constitutional, ingrained, inherent; folksy, homespun, unpretentious; ignorant, primitive, undesigning; unconstrained, unembarrassed; candid, frank, open, plain; sincere, unfeigned; provincial, rustic
   con ceremonial, ceremonious, conventional, formal; ostentatious, pretentious, showy; assumed, contrived, counterfeited, feigned, pretended; artful, sophisticated, studied
   ant affected; artificial, unnatural
natural *n syn* see FOOL 4
natural child *n syn* see BASTARD 1
naturalness *n syn* see UNCONSTRAINT
   ant unnaturalness
nature *n* 1 *syn* see TYPE
   rel anatomy, framework, structure; conformation, figure, shape
   2 *syn* see ESSENCE 1

   3 *syn* see DISPOSITION 3
   4 *syn* see UNIVERSE
naught (*or* **nought**) *n* 1 *syn* see NOTHING 1
   2 *syn* see ZERO
naughty *adj* 1 guilty of misbehavior <a *naughty* boy who teased the cat and upset the milk>
   syn bad, ill-behaved, misbehaving, mischievous, paw; *compare* DISOBEDIENT
   rel contrary, froward, perverse, wayward; headstrong, intractable, recalcitrant, refractory, ungovernable, unruly, willful; disorderly, rowdy, ruffianly; evil, indecorous, wicked
   con decorous, good, well-behaved; amenable, docile, obedient, tractable; amiable, complaisant, good-natured, obliging; polite, proper; considerate, kindly, thoughtful
   2 *syn* see DISOBEDIENT
nausea *n* a stomach distress with an urge to vomit <overcome with *nausea* as the boat continued to pitch and wallow>
   syn qualmishness, queasiness, squeamishness
nauseate *vb syn* see DISGUST
nauseated *adj* affected with nausea <was *nauseated* after taking the drug>
   syn nauseous, squeamish; *compare* SQUEAMISH 1
   rel choking, gagging; heaving; barfing, upchucking, vomiting
   idiom ready (*or* about) to lose one's cookies
nauseating *adj syn* see OFFENSIVE
   ant appetizing
nauseous *adj syn* see NAUSEATED
nautical *adj syn* see MARINE 2
navigable *adj syn* see PASSABLE
   ant unnavigable
navigational *adj syn* see MARINE 2
nawob *n syn* see NOTABLE 1
nay *adv* 1 *syn* see NO
   2 *syn* see EVEN 3
naze *n syn* see PROMONTORY
neanderthal *adj syn* see OLD-FASHIONED
near *adv* 1 *syn* see CLOSE
   ant far
   2 *syn* see ABOUT 5
near *prep* 1 *syn* see ABOUT 1
   2 not far distant from <kept the boy *near* him>
   syn ‖aside, beside, by, nearby, nigh, round
   idiom close to, hard by, within earshot, within reach, within sight
near *adj* 1 *syn* see CLOSE 6
   ant far
   2 *syn* see COMPARATIVE
near *vb syn* see APPROACH 1
   rel equal, match, rival, touch
   con alter, change, modify, vary; differ
‖**nearabout** *adv syn* see NEARLY
near–at–hand *adj* 1 *syn* see NEIGHBORING
   2 *syn* see CLOSE 6
   3 *syn* see CONVENIENT 2
near–at–hand *adv syn* see ABOUT 5
nearby *adv* 1 *syn* see CLOSE
   2 *syn* see ABOUT 5
nearby *prep* 1 *syn* see NEAR 2
   2 *syn* see ABOUT 1
nearby *adj* 1 *syn* see CLOSE 6

2 *syn* see NEIGHBORING

3 *syn* see CONVENIENT 2

nearing *adj syn* see FORTHCOMING

nearly *adv* very close to <our work is *nearly* done for today>
syn about, all but, almost, approximately, as good as, just about, more or less, most, much, ‖nearabout, nigh, practically, roughly, round, roundly, rudely, say, some, somewhere, well≈nigh
rel virtually
idiom as near as never mind(s), in effect, in essence, in substance, in the main, nigh on (*or* onto *or* upon), to all (practical) intents and purposes

nearsighted *adj syn* see MYOPIC

neat *adj* **1** *syn* see STRAIGHT 3
2 manifesting care and orderliness <always kept a *neat* house>
syn chipper, orderly, prim, shipshape, snug, spick-and-span, tidy, trig, trim, uncluttered, well-groomed; *compare* DAPPER
rel clean, immaculate, spotless; dainty, fastidious, finicky, nice; methodical, regular, systematic; accurate, correct, exact, precise
idiom in good order, neat as a pin (*or* bandbox), neat as can be, neat as wax
con disheveled, disordered, slipshod, sloppy, slovenly, unkempt, untidy; dirty, filthy, foul, nasty; lax, negligent, remiss, slack
ant disorderly, messy
‖**3** *syn* see MARVELOUS 2

neat–handed *adj syn* see DEXTEROUS 1

neb *n syn* see BILL 1

nebbish *n syn* see WEAKLING

‖**nebby** *adj syn* see IMPERTINENT 2

‖**necessary** *n syn* see PRIVY 1

necessary *adj* **1** *syn* see ESSENTIAL 4
rel compelling, compulsory, constraining, mandatory, obligatory; important, momentous, significant; cardinal, fundamental
con insignificant, unessential, unimportant
ant unnecessary
2 *syn* see INEVITABLE
rel inerrable, inerrant, infallible, unerring

necessitate *vb syn* see DEMAND 2

necessitous *adj* **1** *syn* see POOR 1
rel depleted, drained, exhausted
2 *syn* see ESSENTIAL 4

necessity *n* **1** *syn* see NEED 4
rel coercion, compulsion, constraint, duress, obligation; indispensableness, needfulness, requisiteness
2 *syn* see OCCASION 3
3 *syn* see ESSENTIAL 2

neck *vb syn* see BEHEAD

necrology *n syn* see OBITUARY

necromancer *n syn* see MAGICIAN 1

necromancy *n syn* see MAGIC 1

necromantic *adj syn* see MAGIC

necropolis *n syn* see CEMETERY

necropsy *n syn* see AUTOPSY

‖**neddy** *n syn* see DONKEY 1

need *n* **1** *syn* see OBLIGATION 2
2 *syn* see REQUIREMENT 1

3 opportunity or requirement to employ <found little *need* for his rifle>
syn demand, occasion, use
rel call, claim, exaction
4 a pressing lack of something essential <he is in *need* of food>
syn exigency, necessity
rel deficiency, deficit, lack, shortage, want
con adequacy, enough, sufficiency
5 *syn* see POVERTY 1

need *vb* **1** *syn* see LACK
rel claim, demand, exact; hanker, hunger, long, pine, thirst, yearn; covet, crave, desire, wish
2 *syn* see MUST 2

needed *adj syn* see NEEDFUL
ant unneeded

needful *adj* necessary for supply or relief <provided them with everything *needful*>
syn needed, required, requisite
rel essential, imperative, indispensable, necessary; lacked, wanted; cardinal, fundamental, vital
con excess, redundant, superfluous; nonessential, unessential; uncalled-for, unnecessary, unneeded
ant needless

needful *n syn* see MONEY

neediness *n syn* see POVERTY 1

needle *vb syn* see WORRY 1

needless *adj syn* see UNNECESSARY
ant needful

needy *adj syn* see POOR 1

ne'er *adv syn* see NEVER

ne'er–do–well *n syn* see WASTREL 1

nefarious *adj syn* see VICIOUS 2
rel atrocious, heinous, monstrous, outrageous; flagrant, glaring, gross, rank
ant exemplary

negate *vb* **1** *syn* see DENY 4
ant affirm
2 *syn* see ABOLISH 1
3 *syn* see NEUTRALIZE

negation *n syn* see DENIAL 2
ant affirmation

negative *adj syn* see ADVERSE 2

negative *vb* **1** *syn* see VETO
2 *syn* see DENY 4
ant affirm
3 *syn* see NEUTRALIZE
rel abrogate, invalidate, nullify

neglect *vb* to pass over without giving due attention <*neglected* his family for the sake of his mistress>
syn blink (at *or* away), discount, disregard, elide, fail, forget, ignore, miss, omit, overleap, overlook, overpass, pass, pass by, pass over, pretermit, slight, slough over, slur (over)
rel brush (off *or* aside), disdain, dismiss, reject, scant, scorn, shrug away, shrug off

---

syn synonym(s)   *rel* related word(s)
ant antonym(s)   *con* contrasted word(s)
idiom idiomatic equivalent(s)
‖ use limited; if in doubt, see a dictionary

idiom pay no attention to, pay no heed (*or* mind), think little of

con appreciate, prize, treasure, value; cultivate, foster, nurse, nurture

ant cherish

neglect *n syn* see FAILURE 1

neglected *adj* not properly or sufficiently attended to or cared for <the whole property had a *neglected* appearance>

syn run-down, uncared-for, untended

rel disregarded, ignored, overlooked, slighted, unheeded

con prized, treasured; fostered, tended; guarded, supervised, watched

ant cherished

neglectful *adj syn* see NEGLIGENT

ant attentive

negligent *adj* failing to give proper attention or care <*negligent* in taking care of the children> <a *negligent* man, prone to forgetfulness>

syn behindhand, careless, delinquent, derelict, discinct, disregardful, lax, neglectful, regardless, remiss, slack

rel heedless, inadvertent, inattentive, inconsiderate, thoughtless, unheedful, unthinking; incurious, indifferent, unconcerned; slipshod, slovenly

con rigid, rigorous, strict; attentive, considerate, heedful, thoughtful; careful, exact, fussy, meticulous, punctilious, punctual, scrupulous

ant attentive

negligible *adj syn* see REMOTE 4

ant significant

negotiable *adj syn* see PASSABLE

ant nonnegotiable

negotiate *vb* **1** to bring about by mutual agreement <*negotiate* a treaty>

syn arrange, concert, settle

rel adjust, compose, transact; agree, bargain, contract, covenant

con break off, intermit, interrupt, suspend; differ, disagree, dissent

2 *syn* see CLEAR 8

neigh *vb* to make the cry typical of a horse <the frightened horse *neighed* and stamped>

syn nicker, whicker, ‖whinner, whinny

neighbor *vb syn* see ADJOIN

neighborhood *n* **1** *syn* see LOCALITY 1

2 *syn* see ORDER 4

neighboring *adj* not distant <the need for understanding between *neighboring* countries>

syn adjacent, close-at-hand, close-by, contiguous, near-at-hand, nearby; *compare* CLOSE 6

rel abutting, adjoining, bordering, conterminous, touching; close, near

con distant, far, faraway, far-off, remote, removed; parted, separated

neighborly *adj syn* see AMICABLE

rel cooperative, gregarious, hospitable, social; cordial, gracious, sociable

ant unneighborly; ill-disposed

neonate *n syn* see BABY 1

neophyte *n syn* see NOVICE

neoteric *adj syn* see NEW 1

nepenthe *n syn* see ANODYNE 2

ne plus ultra *n syn* see APEX 2

nerve *n* **1** *syn* see FORTITUDE

2 *syn* see TEMERITY

3 *syn* see EFFRONTERY

nerve *vb syn* see ENCOURAGE 1

nerve center *n syn* see CENTER 2

nervous *adj* easily upset or irritated <a *nervous* fretful woman>

syn fidgety, goosey, high-strung, jittery, jumpy, nervy, spooky, twittery, unrestful

rel agitated, edgy, excitable, skittish, volatile; fretful, irritable, querulous, snappish, waspish

con calm, placid, serene, steady, tranquil; collected, composed, cool, imperturbable, inexcitable, poised, unflappable, unruffled

ant nerveless

nervous breakdown *n* an emotional disorder often characterized by depression, tenseness, irritability, headache, and susceptibility to fatigue <worked and worried himself into a *nervous breakdown*>

syn breakdown, collapse, crack-up, nervous prostration

rel neurasthenia; prostration

nervous prostration *n syn* see NERVOUS BREAKDOWN

nervy *adj* **1** *syn* see WISE 5

2 *syn* see NERVOUS

rel excitable, fidgety, jerky, tense, twitchy

idiom tied up in knots

con composed, easy, relaxed

ant phlegmatic

3 *syn* see TENSE 2

nescience *n syn* see IGNORANCE 2

nest egg *n syn* see RESERVE

nestle *vb syn* see SNUGGLE

net *vb syn* see CLEAR 6

nether *adj syn* see INFERIOR 1

nethermost *adj syn* see BOTTOMMOST

ant uppermost

netherwards *adv syn* see DOWN 1

ant upwards

netherworld *n syn* see HELL

nettle *vb syn* see IRRITATE

rel agitate, discompose, disturb, perturb, upset

nettlesome *adj syn* see THORNY

neuter *vb syn* see STERILIZE

neutral *adj* not experiencing or generating a strong emotional commitment or response <made a *neutral* response to his challenge>

syn abstract, colorless, detached, disinterested, dispassionate, impersonal, poker-faced, unpassioned

rel clinical, collected, composed, cool, nonchalant; calm, easy, relaxed; aloof, indifferent

con intemperate, loaded; fervent, impassioned, passionate, vehement

neutralize *vb* to make inoperative or ineffective usually by means of an opposite force, influence, or effect <attacked by the kind of propaganda that is difficult to *neutralize*>

syn annul, cancel (out), counteract, countercheck, frustrate, negate, negative, redress

rel balance, compensate, counterbalance, counterpoise, countervail, offset; abrogate, invali-

date, nullify; conquer, defeat, overcome, subdue; override, overrule
con activate, animate, dynamize, vitalize

never *adv* not at any time <they had *never* seen him before>
syn ne'er
idiom never in all one's born days, never in one's life, never in the world, never on earth
con constantly, continuously, ever, invariably, perpetually
ant always

never–ending *adj syn* see EVERLASTING 1
ant ended; transitory

never–failing *adj syn* see SURE 2

nevertheless *adv syn* see HOWEVER

nevus *n syn* see BIRTHMARK 1

new *adj* **1** recently come into existence or use or a particular state or relation <*new* styles that flatter stout figures>
syn fresh, modern, modernistic, neoteric, newfangled, new-fashioned, new-sprung, novel, recent
rel first-hand, independent, primary
con dated, outdated, outmoded, out-of-date; shabby, worn; hackneyed, old hat, trite
ant old
2 *syn* see UNFAMILIAR 1
3 *syn* see ADDITIONAL
4 *syn* see REFRESHED

new *adv* within recent time <the scent of new-mown grass>
syn afresh, anew, lately, newly, of late, recently
con aforetime, before, earlier, formerly; heretofore, hitherto
ant once

newborn *n syn* see BABY 1

newcomer *n syn* see NOVICE

newfangled *adj syn* see NEW 1
ant oldfangled

new–fashioned *adj syn* see NEW 1
ant old-fashioned

New Jerusalem *n syn* see HEAVEN 2

newly *adv syn* see NEW

news *n pl but sing in constr* a report of events or conditions not previously known <her friend gave her the bad *news*>
syn advice, information, intelligence, speerings, tidings, word
rel announcement, report; dope, lowdown, ‖poop; gossip, rumor, tattle

newsmonger *n syn* see GOSSIP 1

newspaper *n syn* see JOURNAL

new–sprung *adj syn* see NEW 1

next *adj* being the one that comes immediately after another <the *next* day>
syn coming, ensuing, following; *compare* CONSECUTIVE
rel proximate

next *adv syn* see AFTER

next *prep syn* see AFTER 2

next to *prep syn* see BESIDE 1

nexus *n syn* see BOND 3

niagara *n syn* see FLOOD 2

nib *n syn* see BILL 1

‖**nibby** *adj syn* see CURIOUS 2

nice *adj* **1** having or displaying exacting standards <too *nice* about his food to like camp cooking>
syn ‖choicy, choosy, clerkish, dainty, delicate, fastidious, finical, finicking, finicky, fussy, miminy-piminy, ‖mincy, niminy-piminy, old-maidish, old-womanish, particular, pernickety, persnickety, picksome, picky, precious, squeamish, squeamy
rel discerning, discriminating, penetrating; overparticular; queasy; careful, meticulous, punctilious, scrupulous; judicious, sage, sapient, wise
con coarse, gross, vulgar; callow, crude, green, raw, uncouth; lax, neglectful, negligent, remiss, slack; careless, sloppy, slovenly
2 *syn* see FINE 1
3 *syn* see PLEASANT 1
4 *syn* see CORRECT 2
rel rigid, strict, stringent; exquisite, rare
con haphazard, happy-go-lucky, hit-or-miss, random; careless, heedless, inadvertent
5 *syn* see DECOROUS 1

nicely *adv syn* see WELL 1

nice Nelly *n* **1** *syn* see PRUDE
2 *syn* see EUPHEMISM

nice–nellyism *n syn* see EUPHEMISM

niche *n syn* see NOOK

nick *n syn* see NOTCH 1

‖**nick** *vb syn* see STEAL 1

nicker *vb syn* see NEIGH

nickname *n* a descriptive or familiar name that is used instead of or in addition to one's proper name <because he was a redhead his friends gave him the *nickname* "Red">
syn byname, byword, ‖handle, hypocorism, ‖moniker, sobriquet
rel first name, middle name; appellation, appellative, compellation, denomination, style; epithet, label, tag

nictate *vb syn* see WINK

nictitate *vb syn* see WINK

nidorous *adj syn* see MALODOROUS 1

nifty *adj syn* see MARVELOUS 2

nifty *n syn* see ‖DILLY

niggard *n syn* see MISER

niggard *adj syn* see STINGY

niggardly *adj syn* see STINGY
ant bounteous, bountiful

niggling *adj syn* see PETTY 2

nigh *adv* **1** *syn* see CLOSE
2 *syn* see NEARLY

nigh *adj syn* see CLOSE 6

nigh *prep* **1** *syn* see NEAR 2
2 *syn* see ABOUT 1

nigh *vb syn* see APPROACH 1

night *n* the time from dusk to dawn <stayed up all *night*>
syn nighttide, nighttime

---

syn synonym(s)		*rel* related word(s)
ant antonym(s)		*con* contrasted word(s)
idiom idiomatic equivalent(s)		
‖ use limited; if in doubt, see a dictionary		

con day, daytime

night *adj syn* see NIGHTLY

night and day *adv syn* see TOGETHER 2

nightclub *n* a restaurant serving liquor and providing entertainment <Las Vegas *nightclubs*>
syn bistro, cabaret, café, discotheque, hot spot, nightery, night spot, nitery, supper club, watering hole, watering place

nightery *n syn* see NIGHTCLUB

nightfall *n syn* see EVENING 1

nightly *adj* of, relating to, or associated with the night <*nightly* noises>
syn night, nocturnal
con daily, diurnal; matutinal, morning; evening, twilight, vespertine

nightmare *n syn* see FANCY 4

night spot *n syn* see NIGHTCLUB

nightstick *n syn* see CUDGEL

nighttide *n syn* see NIGHT

nighttime *n syn* see NIGHT

nightwalker *n syn* see PROSTITUTE

nihility *n syn* see NOTHINGNESS

nil *n syn* see NOTHING 1

nim *vb syn* see STEAL 1

nimble *adj* **1** *syn* see AGILE
rel light, lightsome; alert, vigilant, watchful, wide-awake
2 *syn* see DEXTEROUS 1

nimble-witted *adj syn* see WISE 4
ant slow-witted

niminy–piminy *adj syn* see NICE 1

nimmer *n syn* see THIEF

nincom *n syn* see FOOL 1

nincompoop *n syn* see FOOL 1

ninny *n syn* see FOOL 1

ninnyhammer *n syn* see FOOL 1

nip *vb* **1** *syn* see BLAST 1
rel arrest, check; press, squeeze; balk, frustrate, thwart
2 *syn* see STEAL 1
‖**3** *syn* see HURRY 2

nip *n syn* see DRAM

nip *vb syn* see DRINK 3

‖**nipcheese** *n syn* see MISER

‖**nipper** *n syn* see CHILD 1

nipping *adj syn* see COLD 1

nippy *adj syn* see COLD 1

nirvana *n syn* see HEAVEN 2

nisse *n syn* see FAIRY

‖**nit** *adv syn* see NO

nitery *n syn* see NIGHTCLUB

nitwit *n syn* see DUNCE

nitwitted *adj syn* see SIMPLE 3

‖**nix** *n syn* see NOTHING 1

‖**nix** *adv syn* see NO

‖**nix** *vb syn* see VETO

no *adv* — used as a function word to express negation, dissent, denial, or refusal <*no*, you can't come with me>
syn nay, ‖nit, ‖nix, ‖nope
idiom by no manner of means, by no means, in no case, no dice, not at any price, not for love or money, not for the life of me, not for the world, nothing doing, not on your life, no way, on no

account, on no condition, under no circumstances
ant yes

‖**no-account** *adj syn* see WORTHLESS 1

Noachian *adj syn* see ANCIENT 1

noble *adj* **1** *syn* see GRAND 1
rel eminent, illustrious
con beggarly, contemptible, despicable, scurvy, sorry
ant cheap, ignoble, unnoble
2 *syn* see ELEVATED 2
ant base
3 *syn* see HONORABLE 1
ant ignoble
4 *syn* see MORAL 1

nobody *pron syn* see NO ONE
ant everybody; somebody

nobody *n syn* see NONENTITY
ant somebody

nocent *adj syn* see HARMFUL
ant innocent

nocturnal *adj syn* see NIGHTLY
con daily, diurnal

nocuous *adj syn* see HARMFUL
ant innocuous

nodding *adj syn* see SLEEPY 1

noddle *n syn* see HEAD 1

noddy *n syn* see DUNCE

noel *n syn* see CHRISTMAS

noggin *n syn* see HEAD 1

no–good *adj syn* see WORTHLESS 1

no–good *n* **1** *syn* see WASTREL 1
2 *syn* see WRETCH 1

noise *n syn* see SOUND 1
rel babel, clamor, din, hubbub, pandemonium, racket, uproar
con quiet, silence, stillness

noise (about *or* abroad) *vb syn* see GOSSIP

noiseful *adj syn* see NOISY
ant noiseless, silent

noiseless *adj syn* see STILL 3
con boisterous, clamorous, strident, vociferous
ant noiseful, noisy

noiselessness *n syn* see SILENCE 1
ant noisiness

noisome *adj* **1** *syn* see UNWHOLESOME 1
ant wholesome
2 *syn* see MALODOROUS 1
rel dirty, filthy, squalid; loathsome, revolting
ant balmy
3 *syn* see OFFENSIVE

noisy *adj* making noise <the *noisiest* car you ever heard>
syn clangorous, clattery, noiseful, rackety, sonorous, uproarious
rel blatant, boisterous, clamorous, obstreperous, strepitous, strident, vociferous; tumultuous, turbulent
con quiet, silent, still, stilly
ant noiseless

nomadic *adj syn* see ITINERANT

no man *pron syn* see NO ONE
ant everybody, everyman

nom de guerre *n syn* see PSEUDONYM

nomen *n syn* see NAME 1

nominal *adj* being something in name or form only <the *nominal* head of his party>
syn formal, so-called, titular
rel apparent, ostensible, seeming; alleged, pretended, professed
idiom in name only
con genuine, real, true
ant actual

nominate *vb syn* see DESIGNATE 2
rel intend, mean, propose, purpose; offer, present, proffer, tender

nonadhesive *adj syn* see LOOSE 3

nonage *n syn* see INFANCY 2
ant age

nonchalant *adj syn* see COOL 2
rel cheerful, glad, lighthearted; easy, effortless, light, smooth
con anxious, careful, concerned, solicitous, worried

noncombustible *adj* incapable of being burned <*noncombustible* material was used whenever possible>
syn apyrous, incombustible, nonflammable, noninflammable, uninflammable
rel fireproof, fire-resistant, fire-resistive, fire-retardant, flameproof
con flammable, inflammable
ant combustible

noncommittal *adj syn* see RESERVED 1

noncompos *n syn* see LUNATIC 1

non compos mentis *adj syn* see INSANE 1

nonconformism *n syn* see HERESY
ant conformism

nonconformist *n* 1 *syn* see HERETIC
ant conformist
2 *syn* see BOHEMIAN
ant conformist

nonconformist *adj syn* see HERETICAL

nonconformity *n syn* see HERESY
ant conformity

noncreative *adj syn* see UNORIGINAL
ant creative

nondiscriminatory *adj syn* see FAIR 4
ant discriminatory

none *pron syn* see NO ONE

nonentity *n* an utterly insignificant person <tired of dealing with subordinates and *nonentities*>
syn cipher, insignificancy, nobody, nothing, nullity, rushlight, whiffet, whippersnapper, whipster, zero, zilch
rel lightweight, obscurity, sad sack, small beer, small fry
idiom blank space in the rear rank, man in the street, no great shakes

nonesuch *n syn* see PARAGON
idiom one in a million

nonessential *adj syn* see DISPENSABLE
ant essential

nonetheless *adv syn* see HOWEVER

nonexistence *n syn* see NOTHINGNESS
ant existence; reality

nonflammable *adj syn* see NONCOMBUSTIBLE
ant flammable, inflammable

nonfunctional *adj syn* see IMPRACTICABLE 2
ant functional

noninflammable *adj syn* see NONCOMBUSTIBLE
ant flammable, inflammable

nonliterate *adj syn* see PRIMITIVE 6

nonmaterial *adj syn* see IMMATERIAL 1
ant material

nonobligatory *adj syn* see OPTIONAL
ant obligatory

no–nonsense *adj syn* see SERIOUS 1

nonpareil *n syn* see PARAGON

nonpartisan *adj syn* see FAIR 4
ant partisan

nonphysical *adj syn* see IMMATERIAL 1
ant physical

non–placet *vb syn* see VETO

nonplus *vb* 1 to cause to be at a total loss as to how to act or decide <was totally *nonplussed* by the economic problems>
syn beat, buffalo, get, stick, stump; *compare* PUZZLE
rel baffle, frustrate, stymie, thwart; confound, perplex; mystify; dumbfound; overcome, throw; paralyze; confuse, flurry, fluster, muddle, rattle
idiom put (*or* drive) to one's wit's end, put up a tree (*or* stump), throw on one's beam end
2 *syn* see STAGGER 5
rel faze, rattle; baffle, balk, frustrate

nonprofessional *n syn* see AMATEUR 2
ant professional

nonrational *adj syn* see ILLOGICAL
ant rational

nonrealistic *adj syn* see IMPRACTICAL 1
ant realistic

nonreligious *adj syn* see IRRELIGIOUS
rel lay, profane, secular, temporal
ant religious

nonresistant *adj syn* see PASSIVE 2
ant resistant, resisting

nonresisting *adj syn* see PASSIVE 2
ant resistant, resisting

nonreversible *adj syn* see IRREVOCABLE
ant reversible

nonsectarian *adj* not affiliated with or restricted to a particular religious group <the problems facing *nonsectarian* colleges>
syn interchurch, intercreedal, interdenominational, undenominational, unsectarian
con denominational
ant sectarian

nonsense *n* 1 *syn* see GIBBERISH 1
2 something uttered or proposed that seems senseless or absurd <his theories are mere *nonsense*>
syn ‖applesauce, balderdash, ‖baloney, bilge, blague, blah, blather, blatherskite, bosh, ‖bull, ‖bunk, bunkum, bushwa, claptrap, ‖cobblers, ‖cock, ‖codswallop, ‖crap, crock, double-talk, ‖drip, drivel, drool, eyewash, fiddle-faddle, fid-

---

syn synonym(s)   *rel* related word(s)
ant antonym(s)   *con* contrasted word(s)
idiom idiomatic equivalent(s)
‖ use limited; if in doubt, see a dictionary

dlesticks, flapdoodle, flimflam, flummadiddle, fudge, ‖gas, gook, guff, hogwash, hokum, hooey, ‖horsefeathers, hot air, humbug, jazz, ‖jiggery≠ pokery, malarkey, meshuggaas, moonshine, piffle, pishposh, poppycock, punk, rot, rubbish, slipslop, tomfoolery, tommyrot, tosh, trash, trumpery, twaddle, whangdoodle, windbaggery
idiom stuff and nonsense

nonsuccess *n syn* see FAILURE 2
ant success, successfulness

nonsymmetrical *adj syn* see LOPSIDED
ant symmetrical

nonviolent *adj syn* see PACIFIC
ant violent

noodle *n* **1** *syn* see DUNCE
2 *syn* see HEAD 1

nook *n* a secluded or sheltered place <resting in a shady *nook*>
syn byplace, cranny, niche
rel alcove, recess; cubbyhole, hole

noon *n syn* see APEX 2

no one *pron* no person <*no one* will be allowed to leave early>
syn nobody, no man, none
idiom never a one, nobody on earth, nobody under the sun, not a blessed soul, not a soul
con all, everyman; many, some
ant everybody, everyone

noontide *n syn* see APEX 2

noose *vb syn* see HANG 2

‖nope *adv syn* see NO
ant ‖yep, ‖yup

norm *n syn* see AVERAGE

normal *adj* **1** *syn* see SANE 2
2 *syn* see GENERAL 1

nose *n* **1** the prominent part of the human face that bears the nostrils and covers the nasal passage <had a large *nose*>
syn beak, ‖beezer, ‖boko, ‖conk, pecker, proboscis, ‖schnozzle, smeller, ‖sneezer, ‖snitch, snoot, snout
2 *syn* see BUSYBODY
3 *syn* see GIFT 2

nose *vb* **1** *syn* see SMELL 1
2 *syn* see SNOOP

nose-dive *vb syn* see PLUMMET

nosegay *n syn* see BOUQUET 1

nosey Parker *n syn* see BUSYBODY

nosh *n* ‖**1** *syn* see MEAL
2 *syn* see SNACK

Nostradamus *n syn* see PROPHET

nostrum *n syn* see PANACEA

nosy *adj syn* see CURIOUS 2

notability *n* **1** *syn* see NOTABLE 1
2 *syn* see CELEBRITY 2

notable *adj* **1** *syn* see NOTEWORTHY
2 *syn* see FAMOUS 2

notable *n* **1** a person of consequence or prominence <*notables* of Congress and the diplomatic corps>
syn big, big boy, ‖big bug, ‖big cheese, ‖big chief, ‖biggie, big gun, ‖big noise, big shot, big≠ timer, ‖big wheel, bigwig, character, chief, dignitary, eminence, ‖fat cat, great gun, heavy, heavyweight, high-muck-a-muck, leader, lion, lumi-

nary, muckamuck, mugwump, nabob, nawob, notability, personage, personality, pooh-bah, pot, somebody, VIP
rel figure; baron, czar, king, magnate, mogul, prince; light, star; power
idiom big-time operator, his nibs, Mr. Big
con cipher, nobody, nonentity; functionary, underling
2 *syn* see CELEBRITY 2

notably *adv syn* see VERY 1

notandum *n syn* see NOTE 2

notation *n syn* see NOTE 2

notch *n* **1** a usually V-shaped depression in an edge or surface <a *notch* in the table>
syn indentation, indenture, nick; *compare* DEPRESSION 2
rel cut, gash, incision, score, scratch; cleft, gap, nock
2 *syn* see DEGREE 1

note *vb syn* see SEE 1

note *n* **1** *syn* see CALL 1
2 a written reminder <made a *note* to return the call>
syn chit, memo, memorandum, notandum, notation
3 *syn* see REMARK 2
rel reminder
4 *syn* see LETTER 2
5 *syn* see NOTICE 1

noted *adj syn* see WELL-KNOWN
ant unnoted

note-perfect *adj syn* see PERFECT 2

noteworthy *adj* having a quality that attracts one's attention <a *noteworthy* event>
syn ‖bodacious, memorable, nameable, notable, observable, red-letter, rubric
rel conspicuous, noticeable, outstanding, prominent, remarkable; evident, manifest, patent; exceptional, extraordinary
con blah, common, commonplace, inconsequential, insignificant, ordinary, quotidian, unimportant, unremarkable
ant unnoteworthy

nothing *n* **1** something that does not exist <his hopes were based on *nothing*>
syn naught (*or* nought), nil, ‖nix, wind
idiom nothing at all, nothing whatever
con something
2 *syn* see ZERO 1
3 *syn* see NONENTITY
idiom (the) little end of nothing whittled down to a point

nothing *adj syn* see WORTHLESS 1

nothingness *n* the quality or state of being nothing <the house was blown into *nothingness* by the force of the explosion>
syn nada, nihility, nonexistence, nullity, vacuity
rel emptiness; vacuum, void
con concreteness, solidity, substantiality; materiality, reality
ant somethingness

notice *n* **1** a noting of or concerning oneself with something <take *notice* of the gathering clouds>

syn attention, cognizance, ear, heed, mark, ‖mind, note, observance, observation, regard, remark
rel care, concern, consideration, thought; apprehension, grasp, understanding
con disinterest, disregard, indifference, unconcern; carelessness, heedlessness, unmindfulness; insouciance, negligence, recklessness
2 syn see MEMORANDUM 2
3 syn see CRITICISM 1
notice *vb* **syn** see SEE 1
rel acknowledge, recognize; advert, allude, refer
con disregard, ignore, neglect, overlook, slight
noticeable *adj* attracting or compelling notice or attention <they both showed a *noticeable* aversion to his company>
syn arresting, arrestive, conspicuous, eye-catching, marked, outstanding, pointed, prominent, remarkable, salient, sensational, signal, striking
rel notable, noteworthy; evident, manifest, obvious, palpable, patent; spectacular
con obscure, vague; concealed, hidden, shrouded; insignificant, undistinguished
ant unnoticeable
notify *vb* **syn** see INFORM 2
rel announce, broadcast, declare, proclaim, promulgate, publish; disclose, discover, divulge, reveal
notion *n* **1 syn** see IDEA
2 syn see CAPRICE
3 syn see HINT 1
notional *adj* **1 syn** see CONCEPTUAL
2 syn see IMAGINARY 1
ant real
notoriety *n* **syn** see FAME 2
rel ballyhoo, promotion, propaganda, publicity
notorious *adj* **1 syn** see WELL-KNOWN
2 syn see INFAMOUS 1
notwithstanding *prep* **syn** see AGAINST 4
notwithstanding *adv* **syn** see HOWEVER
nourish *vb* **1 syn** see NURSE 1
2 syn see NURSE 2
nourishing *adj* **syn** see NUTRITIOUS
ant unnourishing
nourishment *n* **syn** see FOOD 2
rel keep, living, maintenance, support
nouveau riche *n* **syn** see UPSTART
novel *adj* **syn** see NEW 1
rel different, odd, peculiar, singular, special, strange, uncommon, unfamiliar, unique, unusual
con customary, habitual, usual; common, familiar, ordinary
novelty *n* **1 syn** see CHANGE 2
con old story
2 syn see KNICKKNACK
novice *n* one who is just entering a field in which he has no previous experience <a *novice* in the theater —had never even had a walk-on role>
syn apprentice, beginner, boot, colt, fledgling, freshman, neophyte, newcomer, novitiate, prentice, punk, recruit, rookie, tenderfoot, tyro
rel amateur; cub; postulant, probationer; greenhorn, greeny; learner, student, trainee, undergraduate

con expert, pro, professional
ant doyen, old hand, old-timer, veteran
novitiate *n* **syn** see NOVICE
now *adv* **1 syn** see TODAY
ant then
2 syn see AWAY 3
now *conj* **syn** see BECAUSE
now *n* **syn** see PRESENT
nowadays *adv* **syn** see TODAY
now and again *adv* **syn** see SOMETIMES
now and then *adv* **syn** see SOMETIMES
noxious *adj* **1 syn** see UNWHOLESOME 1
ant wholesome; sanitary
2 syn see PERNICIOUS
rel fetid, noisome, putrid, stinking
ant innocuous, innoxious
nuance *n* **syn** see GRADATION
rel dash, soupçon, suggestion, suspicion, tinge, touch; nicety, refinement, subtlety
nub *n* **syn** see SUBSTANCE 2
nubbin *n* **syn** see SUBSTANCE 2
nubilous *adj* **1 syn** see OVERCAST
2 syn see OBSCURE 3
nucleus *n* **syn** see SEED 2
nude *adj* **1 syn** see BARE 1
con covered
2 not wearing any clothes <all the boys liked to swim *nude*>
syn au naturel, buff-bare, mother-naked, naked, raw, stark, ‖starkers, stark-naked, stripped, unclad, unclothed, undressed
rel peeled, uncovered; dishabille, garmentless, unattired, unrobed
idiom ‖buck naked, in a state of nature, in one's birthday suit, in one's skin, in the altogether, in the buff, in the raw, stripped to the buff, without a stitch on, without a stitch to one's name
con attired, robed; decent; covered
ant clad, clothed, dressed
nudge *vb* **syn** see POKE 1
nudnick *n* **syn** see PEST 2
nugatory *adj* **syn** see VAIN 1
nugget *n* **syn** see LUMP 1
nuisance *n* **1 syn** see PEST 2
2 syn see ANNOYANCE 3
null *adj* having no legal or binding force or validity <a *null* ballot>
syn bad, invalid, null and void, void
rel ineffective, ineffectual, inefficacious, useless, worthless
con acceptable, good, valid
null and void *adj* **syn** see NULL
nullify *vb* **syn** see ABOLISH 1
rel counteract, neutralize; compensate, counterbalance, countervail, offset; confine, limit, restrict
nullity *n* **1 syn** see NOTHINGNESS
2 syn see NONENTITY

---

syn synonym(s)   **rel** related word(s)
ant antonym(s)   **con** contrasted word(s)
idiom idiomatic equivalent(s)
‖ use limited; if in doubt, see a dictionary

numb *adj* **1** devoid of sensation or feeling <my arm is *numb*>
syn anesthetized, asleep, benumbed, dead, deadened, insensible, insensitive, numbed, senseless, unfeeling
rel insensate, insentient, stupefied; comatose, unconscious
con alert; aware, conscious; sensitive
2 *syn* see INDIFFERENT 2

numb *vb syn* see DEADEN 1
rel chill, freeze, frost

numbed *adj syn* see NUMB 1

number *n* a character by which an arithmetical value is designated <you must add the *numbers* of the first column>
syn chiffer, cipher, digit, figure, integer, numeral, whole number

number *vb* **1** *syn* see COUNT 1
2 *syn* see AMOUNT 1

numberless *adj syn* see INNUMERABLE
ant numberable

number one *adj* **1** *syn* see CHIEF 2
2 *syn* see EXCELLENT

numeral *n syn* see NUMBER

numerate *vb* **1** *syn* see ENUMERATE 2
2 *syn* see COUNT 1

numerous *adj syn* see MANY
rel big, great, large

numinous *adj* **1** *syn* see SUPERNATURAL 1
2 *syn* see SACRED 2
3 *syn* see SPIRITUAL 4
4 *syn* see MYSTERIOUS

numskull *n syn* see DUNCE

numskulled *adj syn* see STUPID 1

nuptial *adj syn* see MATRIMONIAL

nuptial *n, usu* **nuptials** *pl syn* see WEDDING

nurse *n syn* see NURSEMAID

nurse *vb* **1** to feed from the breast <decided to *nurse* her baby>
syn breast-feed, nourish, suckle
rel bottle-feed
2 to promote the growth, development, or progress of <*nursed* the flame into a blaze>
syn cherish, cultivate, foster, nourish, nursle, nurture
rel feed; advance, forward, further, promote; humor, indulge, pamper
con check, hold back, retard, slow
3 *syn* see MINISTER (to)

nursemaid *n* one who is regularly employed to look after children <the *nursemaid* had three children in her charge>
syn ‖amah, ‖ayah, nana, ‖nanny, nurse, nurserymaid
rel babysitter, ‖minder, sitter; chaperon; governess

nurserymaid *n syn* see NURSEMAID

nursle *vb syn* see NURSE 2

nurture *n syn* see FOOD 1

nurture *vb syn* see NURSE 2
rel bring up, raise, rear; discipline, educate, school, train; back, bolster, support, sustain, uphold
con disregard, ignore, neglect, overlook, pass over, slight

nut *n* **1** *syn* see PROBLEM 2
‖**2** *syn* see HEAD 1
3 *syn* see CRACKPOT
4 *syn* see LUNATIC 1
5 *syn* see ENTHUSIAST

‖**nuthouse** *n syn* see ASYLUM 3

nutriculture *n syn* see HYDROPONICS

nutrient *adj syn* see NUTRITIOUS

nutriment *n syn* see FOOD 2
rel bread, bread and butter, keep, livelihood, living, maintenance, subsistence, support

nutrimental *adj syn* see NUTRITIOUS

nutritional *adj syn* see NUTRITIVE 1

nutritious *adj* promoting growth and repairing natural waste <*nutritious* food>
syn nourishing, nutrient, nutrimental, nutritive
rel good, healthful, salubrious, salutary, wholesome; balanced
con indigestible; bad, insalubrious, unhealthful, unwholesome
ant innutritious

nutritive *adj* **1** relating to or concerned with nutrition <*nutritive* organs of the body>
syn alimentary, alimentative, nutritional
rel digestive, metabolic; constructive, creative, formative, productive
2 *syn* see NUTRITIOUS

nuts *adj syn* see INSANE 1

nutshell *vb syn* see EPITOMIZE 1

nutsy *adj syn* see INSANE 1

nutty *adj* **1** *syn* see ENTHUSIASTIC
2 *syn* see INSANE 1
3 *syn* see FOOLISH 2

nuzzle *vb syn* see SNUGGLE

nymph *n syn* see DOXY 1

nymphet *n syn* see DOXY 1

oaf *n* **1** *syn* see DUNCE

2 a big clumsy, usually slow-witted person <an *oaf* who bumped into everything he passed>
syn bohunk, ‖gaum, gawk, klutz, lobster, looby, lout, lubber, ‖lug, lummox, lump, lumpkin, meathead, palooka, schlepp (*or* schlepper), slouch
rel ‖baboon, beast, bruiser, brute, bull, gorilla, hulk, missing link, ox; clod, clown, dub, galoot, slob; blunderbuss, blunderer, blunderhead

oar *vb* *syn* see ROW

oater *n* *syn* see WESTERN

oath *n* *syn* see SWEARWORD

obdurate *adj* **1** *syn* see UNFEELING 2
con tender

2 *syn* see INFLEXIBLE 2
rel mulish, stiff-necked; immovable
con relenting, submitting

obedient *adj* submissive to the will, guidance, or control of another <children should always be *obedient* to their parents>
syn amenable, biddable, docile, ‖docious, tractable
rel acquiescent, compliant, sheeplike, submissive, yielding; duteous, dutiful, loyal; law-abiding; obeisant, subservient
con insubordinate, rebellious; contrary, froward, perverse, wayward, willful; headstrong, intractable, recalcitrant, refractory, uncontrollable, ungovernable, unruly
ant contumacious, disobedient

obeisance *n* *syn* see HONOR 1
rel allegiance, fealty, loyalty

obeisant *adj* *syn* see SUBSERVIENT 2

obese *adj* *syn* see FAT 2
ant skinny

obesity *n* a condition characterized by excessive bodily fat <could barely walk because of his *obesity*>
syn adiposity, corpulence, fatness, fleshiness
rel chubbiness, chunkiness, embonpoint, grossness, plumpness, portliness, pudginess, rotundity, stockiness, stoutness, tubbiness
con lankiness, leanness, scrawniness, slenderness, slimness
ant skinniness

obey *vb* to act or behave in conformity with (as an order) or in duty to (as a parent) <*obey* a superior's order>
syn comply, conform, follow, keep, mind, observe
rel bow, defer, submit, yield; accede, acquiesce, agree, assent; fulfill, satisfy; carry out; heed, regard
idiom abide by
con break, disregard, transgress, violate; command, order
ant disobey

obfuscate *vb* *syn* see OBSCURE
ant clarify

obit *n* *syn* see OBITUARY

obiter *adv* *syn* see INCIDENTALLY 2

obiter dictum *n* *syn* see REMARK 2

obituary *n* a notice of a person's death usually with a short biographical account <always read the *obituaries* in the paper>
syn necrology, obit

object *n* **1** *syn* see THING 3
rel doodad; gadget

2 *syn* see THING 5

3 *syn* see BODY 4

4 *syn* see VIEW 6

5 *syn* see USE 4

object *vb* **1** to oppose by arguing against <*objecting* because the evidence was unclear>
syn except, expostulate, inveigh (against), kick, protest, remonstrate
rel balk, boggle, demur, dissent, jib, stickle; complain; criticize; challenge; spurn; rail, rant, rave, storm
con accede, agree, assent, consent; accredit, approve, sanction
ant acquiesce

2 *syn* see DISAPPROVE 1

objectify *vb* *syn* see EMBODY 1

objection *n* *syn* see DEMUR 2

objectionable *adj* arousing or likely to arouse objection <the language in that movie is *objectionable*>
syn exceptionable, ill-favored, inadmissible, unacceptable, undesirable, unwanted, unwelcome
rel abhorrent, loathsome, offensive, repellent, repugnant, repulsive, revolting; disagreeable, distasteful, invidious, obnoxious, unpleasant; unfit, unsuitable; censurable, reprehensible
con acceptable, agreeable, gratifying, pleasant, pleasing, welcome
ant unobjectionable

objective *adj* **1** *syn* see MATERIAL 1
rel external, outer, outside, outward
ant subjective

2 *syn* see FAIR 4
ant subjective

objective *n* **1** *syn* see AMBITION 2

2 *syn* see USE 4

objectless *adj* *syn* see RANDOM

objet d'art *n* *syn* see KNICKKNACK

objurgate *vb* *syn* see EXECRATE 1
rel castigate, censure

obligated *adj* *syn* see INDEBTED

---

syn synonym(s)   *rel* related word(s)
ant antonym(s)   *con* contrasted word(s)
idiom idiomatic equivalent(s)
‖ use limited; if in doubt, see a dictionary

obligation *n* **1** *syn* see OCCASION 3
2 something one is bound to do or forbear <it is our *obligation* to obey the law>
syn charge, commitment, committal, devoir, duty, must, need, ought, ‖right
rel compulsion, constraint, restraint; burden, requirement, responsibility; business, part, place
con choice, discretion, free will, option; decision, determination, pleasure, will
3 *syn* see INDEBTEDNESS 1
obligatory *adj* *syn* see MANDATORY
ant nonobligatory
oblige *vb* **1** *syn* see FORCE 2
2 to do a service or courtesy <you will *oblige* me greatly if you will get there on time>
syn accommodate, convenience, favor
rel gratify, please; avail, benefit, profit; aid, assist, contribute, help
con bother, discommode, incommode, inconvenience, trouble
ant disoblige
obliged *adj* **1** *syn* see GRATEFUL 1
2 *syn* see INDEBTED
obliging *adj* *syn* see AMIABLE 1
ant disobliging
oblique *adj* **1** *syn* see INCLINED 3
2 *syn* see INDIRECT 1
ant straight
obliquely *adv* *syn* see ASIDE 1
ant straight
obliterate *vb* *syn* see ERASE
oblivion *n* a state of forgetting or the fact of having forgotten <the *oblivion* of sleep>
syn forgetfulness, lethe, obliviousness
rel nirvana; insensibleness
con alertness, awareness, consciousness; memory, recall, recalling, recollection, remembrance
oblivious *adj* **1** *syn* see FORGETFUL
rel absorbed, unaware, unconscious
idiom turned off
2 *syn* see IGNORANT 2
obliviousness *n* *syn* see OBLIVION
obloquy *n* **1** *syn* see ABUSE
2 *syn* see ANIMADVERSION
3 *syn* see DISGRACE
obnoxious *adj* **1** *syn* see LIABLE 2
ant unobnoxious
2 *syn* see REPUGNANT 1
con congenial, likable, simpatico
ant grateful; unobnoxious
obnubilate *vb* *syn* see OBSCURE
obscene *adj* **1** *syn* see OFFENSIVE
2 marked by the use of words regarded as taboo in polite usage <knew all the *obscene* expressions for the genitalia>
syn barnyard, coarse, crude, crusty, dirty, fescennine, filthy, foul, gross, indecent, nasty, paw, profane, rank, raunchy, ‖raw, rocky, scatological, scurrilous, smutty, vulgar; *compare* RISQUÉ
rel bawdy, ribald, smoking-room; impure, lascivious, lewd, warm; lurid, pornographic, salacious, scabrous, sultry; earthy, rich; unprintable; foulmouthed
con acceptable, proper, tolerable; appropriate, fit, suitable; clean, decent, decorous, seemly

obscure *adj* **1** *syn* see DARK 1
rel clouded, cloudy, fuliginous; shadowy, shady, umbrageous
con clear, lucid; bright, brilliant, luminous
2 withdrawn from the main centers of human activity <was exiled to an *obscure* Siberian village>
syn devious, lonesome, out-of-the-way, remote, removed, retired, secret
rel distant, far, far-off; close, hidden, odd, secluded, sequestered, solitary; blind; inaccessible
idiom back of beyond, off the beaten track (*or* path), in the boondocks (*or* sticks)
con central; urban; populous
3 not readily understood or grasped <an *obscure* textual reference>
syn ambiguous, amphibological, double-edged, double-faced, dusky, equivocal, murky, nubilous, opaque, sibylline, tenebrous, uncertain, unclear, unexplicit, unintelligible, vague; *compare* CRYPTIC, FAINT 2
rel difficult, incomprehensible, inexplicable, puzzling, unfathomable; illegible; abstruse, Delphian, enigmatic, esoteric, inscrutable, mysterious, mystic, mystical; inconclusive, indecisive, indefinite
con definite, explicit, obvious; clear, express, unambiguous, unequivocal
ant lucid
4 *syn* see INCONSPICUOUS
rel humble, lowly, minor, unimportant
5 lacking the prominence, showiness, or worth by which attention might be attracted <an *obscure* Roman poet>
syn nameless, uncelebrated, unfamed, unheard-of, unknown, unnoted, unrenowned
rel inconspicuous; minor, undistinguished, unimportant
con celebrated, distinguished, named, notable, noted, noteworthy, renowned, well-known
ant famed, famous
6 *syn* see FAINT 2
ant clear
obscure *vb* to make dark, dim, or indistinct <fog *obscured* our view>
syn adumbrate, becloud, bedim, befog, cloud, darken, dim, dislimn, eclipse, fog, gloom, haze, mist, murk, obfuscate, obnubilate, overcast, overcloud, overshadow, shadow
rel blear, blur, fuzz; blind, conceal, dim out, hide, screen, shade, shroud; bemask, camouflage, cloak, cover, disguise, mask, veil; belie, falsify, misrepresent
con brighten, light (up), lighten; clarify, enlighten; elucidate, exemplify, explain
ant illuminate, illumine
obscured *adj* *syn* see ULTERIOR
obsequious *adj* *syn* see SUBSERVIENT 2
rel deferential; parasitic, sycophantic, toadying
con self-assertive
observable *adj* **1** *syn* see PERCEPTIBLE
ant unobservable
2 *syn* see NOTEWORTHY
observance *n* **1** *syn* see RITE 2

2 syn see NOTICE 1
ant nonobservance, unobservance
observant *adj* **1 syn** see ATTENTIVE 1
rel awake
ant unobservant
2 syn see MINDFUL 2
observation *n* **1 syn** see NOTICE 1
2 syn see REMARK 2
observative *adj* **syn** see MINDFUL 2
observatory *n* **syn** see LOOKOUT 2
observe *vb* **1 syn** see OBEY
2 syn see KEEP 2
rel revere, reverence, venerate
ant break, violate
3 syn see SEE 1
4 syn see REMARK 2
observer *n* **syn** see SPECTATOR
observing *adj* **syn** see MINDFUL 2
ant unobserving
obsessed *adj* preoccupied intensely or abnormally <*obsessed* with cleanliness>
syn hagridden, hipped, queer
rel bewitched, dominated, gripped, held, possessed, prepossessed; bedeviled, beset, dogged, harassed, haunted, plagued, troubled; overcome
idiom have on the brain
con detached, unconcerned, uninterested; indifferent, neutral; cool, easygoing
obsession *n* **syn** see FETISH 2
obsolesce *vb* **syn** see OUTDATE
obsolete *adj* no longer active or in use <*obsolete* social customs>
syn dead, disused, extinct, outmoded, outworn, passé, superseded; *compare* ANCIENT 1
rel old-fashioned, old hat, old-time, old-timey, out-of-date, unfashionable; dusty, fusty, moldy, moth-eaten, musty, stale, timeworn
idiom behind the times
con contemporary, modern, new-fashioned, up=to-date, up-to-the-minute; novel, original, unique
ant current
obsolete *vb* **syn** see OUTDATE
obstacle *n* something that seriously hampers action or progress <lack of education is an *obstacle* to advancement>
syn bar, Chinese wall, crimp, hamper, hurdle, impediment, mountain, obstruction, rub, snag, stumbling block, traverse
rel clog, encumbrance, handicap, hindrance; bump, difficulty, hardship, vicissitude; catch, hitch; disincentive
con aid, assist, assistance, help
ant advantage
obstinate *adj* unwilling to submit (as to reason or control) <he had an *obstinate* determination to live as he pleased>
syn bullheaded, closed-minded, deaf, hard-headed, headstrong, incompliant, intractable, intransigent, muleheaded, muley, mulish, pertinacious, perverse, pervicacious, pigheaded, refractory, self-willed, ‖sot, stiff, stiff-necked, stubborn, tough, unpliable, unpliant, unyielding, willful, wrongheaded; *compare* UNRULY 1

rel resistant, unsubmissive, withstanding; contrary, crabbed, recalcitrant, renitent; inexorable, inflexible, obdurate; opinionated; resolute, staunch, steadfast, unbudging
con acquiescent, complaisant, compliant; submissive, yielding; agreeable, cooperative, willing
ant pliable, pliant
obstipated *adj* **syn** see CONSTIPATED
obstreperous *adj* **1 syn** see VOCIFEROUS
2 syn see DISOBEDIENT
obstruct *vb* **1 syn** see FILL 1
2 syn see HINDER
3 syn see SCREEN 3
obstruction *n* **syn** see OBSTACLE
obtain *vb* **syn** see GET 1
obtainable *adj* **1 syn** see AVAILABLE 1
rel derivable
2 syn see PURCHASABLE 1
obtrude *vb* **1 syn** see IMPOSE 5
2 syn see INTRUDE 1
obtrusive *adj* **syn** see IMPERTINENT 2
ant unobtrusive
obtund *vb* **syn** see DULL 3
obtuse *adj* **syn** see DULL 6
obviate *vb* **syn** see PREVENT 2
rel anticipate; interfere, interpose, intervene
obvious *adj* **syn** see CLEAR 5
ant abstruse, obscure; unobvious
occasion *n* **1 syn** see OPPORTUNITY
2 syn see CAUSE 1
3 something that provides a reason for something else <there is no *occasion* for alarm>
syn call, cause, necessity, obligation
rel basis, foundation, ground, warrant; justification, right; excuse
4 syn see OCCURRENCE
5 a particular point of time at which something takes place <we always spoke, but on that *occasion* we didn't>
syn instant, moment, time, while
idiom point in time
6 syn see NEED 3
7 occasions *pl* **syn** see BUSINESS 8
8 syn see EVENT 2
occasion *vb* **syn** see GENERATE 3
occasional *adj* **syn** see INFREQUENT
rel incidental; casual, random
con accustomed, habitual, usual; constant, continual, continuous
ant customary
occasionally *adv* on a few occasions <*occasionally* she'll walk instead of drive>
syn infrequently, irregularly, on occasion, sporadically, uncommonly; *compare* SOMETIMES
rel off and on, once or twice
idiom every now and then, from time to time, ‖once in a way, once in a while

---

syn synonym(s)   **rel** related word(s)
ant antonym(s)   **con** contrasted word(s)
idiom idiomatic equivalent(s)
‖ use limited; if in doubt, see a dictionary

con continually, continuously, frequently; commonly, customarily, habitually, often; hardly ever, rarely, scarcely, seldom; never
ant constantly

occlude *vb syn* see FILL 1

occult *vb syn* see HIDE

occult *adj syn* see RECONDITE
rel arcane, mysterious; cabalistic, mystical, supernatural; eerie, unearthly, weird

occupancy *n syn* see HABITATION 1

occupant *n syn* see INHABITANT

occupation *n* 1 *syn* see WORK 1
2 *syn* see HABITATION 1

occupiable *adj syn* see LIVABLE 1

occupied *adj syn* see BUSY 1
ant unoccupied

occupy *vb* 1 *syn* see ENGAGE 4
2 *syn* see INHABIT

occur *vb* 1 *syn* see HAPPEN 1
2 to enter one's mind <it just *occurred* to me: she can't drive>
syn hit, strike
idiom come into one's head, come to mind, cross one's mind, flash across one's mind, go through one's head

occurrence *n* something that happens or takes place <the chance encounter turned out to be a fortunate *occurrence*>
syn circumstance, episode, event, go, happening, incident, occasion, thing
rel contingency, emergency, exigency, juncture, pass; condition, situation, state; adventure, experience

ocean *n* the body of water that covers nearly three-fourths of the earth <pulled the downed pilot from the *ocean*>
syn blue, brine, ‖briny, deep, drink, main, sea

oceanic *adj syn* see MARINE 1

ochlocracy *n syn* see ANARCHY 1

ocular *adj* 1 *syn* see VISUAL 2
2 *syn* see VISUAL 1

ocular *n syn* see EYE 1

oculus *n syn* see EYE 1

odd *adj* 1 being without a corresponding mate <had only an *odd* glove; the other was lost>
syn unmatched, unpaired
rel lone, only, single
con matched, paired
2 *syn* see ACCIDENTAL
3 *syn* see STRANGE 4

oddball *n syn* see ECCENTRIC

oddball *adj syn* see STRANGE 4

oddity *n* 1 *syn* see ECCENTRIC
2 *syn* see CURIOSITY 2

oddments *n pl syn* see SUNDRIES

odds *n pl syn* see ADVANTAGE 3

odds and ends *n pl* 1 *syn* see SUNDRIES
2 *syn* see MISCELLANY 1

odiferous *adj syn* see ODOROUS

odious *adj syn* see HATEFUL 2

odium *n* 1 *syn* see DISGRACE
rel hate, hatred
ant honor
2 *syn* see STIGMA

odor *n syn* see SMELL 1

odoriferous *adj syn* see ODOROUS

odorize *vb syn* see SCENT 2

odorless *adj* having no odor <*odorless* castor oil>
syn inodorous, scentless, smell-less
rel deodorant, deodorizing; unscented
con scented, smelly
ant odorous

odorous *adj* having or emitting an odor <*odorous* chemicals are often malodorous>
syn odiferous, odoriferous, scented; *compare* MALODOROUS 1, SWEET 2
rel redolent, reeking, smelling, smelly; heady, pungent, strong; olfactive, olfactory
ant inodorous, odorless, scentless

o'er *prep syn* see OVER 1

oeuvre *n* a substantial body of work constituting the lifework of a writer, composer, or artist <one of the more popular operas in the Mozart *oeuvre*>
syn corpus, opera omnia
rel output

off *adv syn* see AWAY 2

off *adj* 1 *syn* see REMOTE 4
2 *syn* see SLOW 3

offal *n syn* see REFUSE

off–balance *adj syn* see LOPSIDED

off–center *adj syn* see ECCENTRIC 1

off–color *adj* 1 *syn* see UNWELL
2 *syn* see RISQUÉ

offend *vb* 1 *syn* see TRESPASS 1
2 *syn* see VIOLATE 1
3 to cause hurt feelings or deep resentment <*offended* her by his cruel remark>
syn affront, insult, outrage
rel aggrieve, hurt, sting, wound; exasperate, gall, irritate, nettle; excite, provoke; appall, horrify, scandalize, shock; disoblige, displease, distress, disturb, miff, pique, upset
idiom hurt one's feelings, ruffle one's feathers, step (*or* tread) on one's toes
con delight, gratify, please, tickle; captivate, charm, enchant; flatter

offender *n syn* see CRIMINAL

offense *n* 1 *syn* see ATTACK 1
2 an emotional response to a slight or indignity <he is so sensitive that he takes *offense* at the slightest criticism>
syn dudgeon, huff, miff, pique, resentment, ‖snuff, umbrage
rel affront, indignity, insult; anger, indignation; displeasure; catfit, conniption, fit, tantrum; pet, tizzy; explosion, flare-up, outburst, scene
con delight, pleasure
3 *syn* see CRIME 1

offensive *adj* utterly unpleasant or distasteful to the senses or sensibilities <the *offensive* odor of garbage> <her arrogant assurance was more than a little *offensive*>
syn atrocious, disgusting, evil, foul, hideous, horrible, horrid, icky, loathsome, nasty, nauseating, noisome, obscene, repellent, repugnant, repulsive, revolting, sickening, ungrateful, unwholesome, vile

rel abhorrent, bad, disagreeable, objectionable, uncongenial, unpleasant; abominable, detestable, fulsome, odious; rank; appalling, awful, beastly, dreadful, frightful, ghastly, grim, grisly, gruesome, lurid, shocking, terrible; unappetizing, unpalatable, unsavory
con agreeable, appealing, attractive, pleasant, pleasing; favorable, unobjectionable, welcome; appetizing, palatable, savory; divine
ant inoffensive, unoffensive
offensive *n syn* see ATTACK 1
offer *vb* 1 to put something before another for acceptance or consideration <he was soon *offered* another job>
syn extend, give, hold out, pose, present, proffer, tender
rel display, exhibit, show
con accept, receive, take; decline, refuse, reject
2 *syn* see ADDUCE
3 *syn* see TRY 5
4 *syn* see SHOW 1
offering *n* 1 *syn* see VICTIM 1
2 *syn* see DONATION
offgoing *n syn* see DEPARTURE 1
offhand *adj syn* see EXTEMPORANEOUS
office *n* 1 *syn* see JOB 2
2 *syn* see FUNCTION 1
‖3 *syn* see PRIVY 1
‖4 *syn* see HIGH SIGN 2
officer *n* 1 *syn* see POLICEMAN
2 *syn* see EXECUTIVE
official *n syn* see EXECUTIVE
official *adj* derived from the proper office, officer, or authority <the mayor's office issued an *official* statement>
syn authoritative, ex cathedra, ex officio
rel approved, authorized, certified, cleared, endorsed, OK'd, sanctioned; canonical, cathedral
ant officious (*in diplomatic use*), unofficial
officially *adv syn* see OSTENSIBLY
officiate *vb syn* see ACT 4
officious *adj syn* see IMPERTINENT 2
offing *n syn* see FUTURE
offish *adj* 1 *syn* see UNSOCIABLE
2 *syn* see UNWELL
off-key *adj syn* see IRREGULAR 1
off-load *vb syn* see UNLOAD
off-lying *adj syn* see DISTANT 1
offscouring *n syn* see OUTCAST
offset *vb syn* see COMPENSATE 1
rel check, stop
offshoot *n syn* see OUTGROWTH 2
offspring *n pl* those who follow in direct parental line <a mother of numerous *offspring*>
syn ‖begats, brood, children, descendants, issue, posterity, progeniture, progeny, scions, seed
rel hatch, swarm; produce, spawn, young
con antecedents, ascendants, forebears, forefathers, progenitors
ant ancestors
offstage *adj or adv syn* see BACKSTAGE
ant onstage
‖**off-the-peg** *adj syn* see READY-MADE
off-the-rack *adj syn* see READY-MADE

off-the-shelf *adj syn* see READY-MADE
of late *adv syn* see NEW
oft *adv syn* see OFTEN
often *adv* many times <we called *often* but still could not reach you>
syn again and again, frequently, much, oft, oftentimes, ofttimes, over and over, repeatedly, time and again
idiom a number of times, many a time, many times over, time and time again
con infrequently, rarely; now and then, occasionally
ant seldom
oftentimes *adv syn* see OFTEN
ofttimes *adv syn* see OFTEN
ogle *vb syn* see LOOK 7
‖**ogle** *n syn* see EYE 1
ogress *n syn* see VIRAGO
oil *n syn* see FLATTERY
‖**oiled** *adj syn* see INTOXICATED 1
oily *adj* 1 *syn* see FATTY 2
2 *syn* see FULSOME
ointment *n* a semisolid medicinal or cosmetic preparation for application to the skin <put *ointment* on the burned skin>
syn balm, cerate, chrism, cream, salve, unction, unguent
rel embrocation, liniment; demulcent, emollient; lotion; dressing
OK (*or* **okay**) *adv syn* see YES 1
OK (*or* **okay**) *vb syn* see APPROVE 2
OK (*or* **okay**) *n syn* see APPROBATION
‖**okeydoke** *adv syn* see YES 1
old *adj* 1 *syn* see ANCIENT 1
con contemporary, current, recent; advanced
ant new
2 of long standing <the ending of such an *old* friendship was tragic>
syn continuing, enduring, inveterate, lifelong, long-lasting, long-lived, perennial; *compare* LASTING
rel constant, perpetual, staying; established, firm, solid, steady
con newfound, recent; brief, short-lived; casual, temporary, transitory, weak
ant new
3 *syn* see OLD-FASHIONED
rel primitive; traditional
con newish
ant modern, new
4 *syn* see AGED 1
idiom along in years, getting on
con juvenile, young
ant youthful
5 *syn* see EXPERIENCED
con young
ant new
6 *syn* see FORMER 2

---

syn synonym(s)   *rel* related word(s)
ant antonym(s)   *con* contrasted word(s)
idiom idiomatic equivalent(s)
‖ use limited; if in doubt, see a dictionary

old age *n* the final stage of the normal life span <spent his *old age* in a nursing home>
  syn age, caducity, elderliness, senectitude, senescence, years; *compare* DOTAGE
  rel decrepitude, feebleness; infirmity
  idiom advanced years, declining years, winter of life
  ant youth

olden *adj* **1** *syn* see ANCIENT 1
  2 *syn* see AGED 1

oldest profession *n* *syn* see PROSTITUTION

oldfangled *adj* *syn* see OLD-FASHIONED
  ant newfangled

old–fashioned *adj* typical of an earlier time and often replaced by something more modern or fashionable <*old-fashioned* high-buttoned shoes>
  syn antiquated, antique, archaic, belated, bygone, dated, démodé, demoded, dowdy, fusty, moldy, moth-eaten, neanderthal, old, oldfangled, old hat, old-time, old-timey, outdated, outmoded, out-of-date, passé, rococo, unmodern, vintage
  rel aged, ancient; discarded, disused, obsolete; outworn, unfashionable; crusty, fogyish, fuddy-duddy, fusty, moss-backed, moss-grown, mossy, stodgy; Victorian; old-line
  con modernistic, modish, newfangled, stylish, ‖trendy; current, recent, timely; new-fashioned, up-to-date, up-to-the-minute
  ant contemporary; modern

Old Gooseberry *n* *syn* see DEVIL 1

Old Guard *n* *syn* see ESTABLISHMENT 2

old hand *n* *syn* see VETERAN

old hat *adj* **1** *syn* see OLD-FASHIONED
  2 *syn* see TRITE

old lady *n* ‖**1** *syn* see WIFE
  ‖**2** *syn* see MOTHER 1
  3 *syn* see FUSSBUDGET

old–line *adj* *syn* see CONSERVATIVE 1

old liner *n* *syn* see DIEHARD 1

old maid *n* **1** *syn* see SPINSTER
  2 *syn* see FUSSBUDGET

old–maidish *adj* *syn* see NICE 1

‖**old man** *n* **1** *syn* see HUSBAND
  2 *syn* see FATHER 1

Old Nick *n* *syn* see DEVIL 1

Old Scratch *n* *syn* see DEVIL 1

oldster *n* a person of advanced years <an *oldster* long retired from the business world>
  syn ancient, elder, golden-ager, old-timer, senior, senior citizen; *compare* BELDAM 1, GAFFER
  ant youngster, youth

old–time *adj* **1** *syn* see OLD-FASHIONED
  2 *syn* see EXPERIENCED

old–timer *n* **1** *syn* see VETERAN
  2 *syn* see OLDSTER

old–timey *adj* *syn* see OLD-FASHIONED

‖**old woman** *n* **1** *syn* see WIFE
  2 *syn* see MOTHER 1

old–womanish *adj* *syn* see NICE 1

oleaginous *adj* **1** *syn* see FATTY 2
  2 *syn* see FULSOME

olid *adj* *syn* see MALODOROUS 1

olio *n* *syn* see MISCELLANY 1

olla podrida *n* *syn* see MISCELLANY 1

omen *n* *syn* see FORETOKEN

omen *vb* *syn* see AUGUR 2

ominous *adj* indicative of future misfortune or calamity <dark *ominous* clouds preceded the storm>
  syn apocalyptic, baleful, baneful, dire, direful, doomful, fateful, ill-boding, ill-omened, inauspicious, threatening, unlucky, unpropitious; *compare* EVIL 5, SINISTER
  rel portentous; malefic, maleficent, malign, sinister; comminatory, forbidding, grim, lowering, menacing; hostile, inhospitable, unfriendly
  con auspicious, benign, favorable, promising, propitious; beneficial

omission *n* something omitted or missing <several *omissions* in the list>
  syn blank, chasm, overlook, oversight, preterition, pretermission, skip
  rel inadvertence, inadvertency, lapse, slip; break, gap, hiatus, lacuna
  con inclusion; accession, addition, augmentation, increase, reinforcement; superaddition

omit *vb* *syn* see NEGLECT

omitted *adj* *syn* see ABSENT 1
  ant included

omnibus *n* *syn* see ANTHOLOGY

omnipotent *adj* having virtually unlimited authority or influence <an *omnipotent* leader>
  syn all-powerful, almighty
  rel divine, godlike; unlimited, unrestricted
  con impotent, powerless; limited, restricted

omnipresent *adj* present at all places at all times <*omnipresent* God>
  syn allover, ubiquitous, universal
  rel boundless, endless, immeasurable, infinite, limitless, unending
  con bounded, finite, limited, restricted; cramped, straitened; narrow, strait

omnium–gatherum *n* *syn* see MISCELLANY 1

on *prep* **1** *syn* see OVER 4
  2 *syn* see OVER 3

on *adv* *syn* see ALONG 1

on–again–off–again *adj* *syn* see FITFUL

onanism *n* *syn* see SELF-GRATIFICATION

onanistic *adj* *syn* see SYBARITIC

once *adv* **1** *syn* see EVER 5
  2 *syn* see BEFORE 2

once *adj* *syn* see FORMER 2

once and again *adv* *syn* see SOMETIMES

once more *adv* *syn* see OVER 7

oncoming *adj* *syn* see FORTHCOMING

on–dit *n* *syn* see REPORT 1

one *adj* *syn* see SINGLE 2

one *n* *syn* see DOLLAR

one *vb* *syn* see JOIN 1

one by one *adv* *syn* see APART 1

one–horse town *n* *syn* see BURG

oneness *n* **1** *syn* see UNITY 1
  ant multiplicity
  2 *syn* see UNIQUENESS
  3 *syn* see ENTIRETY 1
  4 *syn* see IDENTITY 1

onerous *adj* imposing great hardship or strain <found the care of his old mother an *onerous* task>
  syn burdensome, demanding, exacting, exigent, grievous, oppressive, superincumbent, taxing, tough, trying, weighty
  rel arduous, difficult, hard, laborious; heavy, hefty, ponderous; cumbersome, unruly, unwieldy; driving, heavy-handed
  con easy, effortless; facile, light, simple, smooth, unexacting, untaxing
onerously *adv syn* see HARD 8
one–sided *adj syn* see BIASED 2
  rel lopsided, weighted
  con many-sided
one–sidedness *n syn* see PREJUDICE
  con manysidedness
onetime *adj syn* see FORMER 2
onfall *n syn* see ATTACK 1
ongoing *n syn* see ADVANCE 2
  rel development, growth
onlooker *n syn* see SPECTATOR
only *adj* 1 *syn* see ALONE 3
  2 being one or more of which there exist no others <the *only* survivors of the wreck>
  syn alone, lone, singular, sole, solitary, solo, unexampled, unique, unrepeatable
  rel incomparable, inimitable, matchless, peerless, transcendent, unequaled, unparalleled, unrivaled; companionless, separate, unaccompanied, unattended, uncompanied, uncompanioned
  con divers, many, multifarious, numerous, sundry, various
  3 *syn* see SINGLE 2
only *adv* 1 to the exclusion of any alternative or competitor <he will confess *only* to you>
  syn alone, but, entirely, exclusively, solely
  2 *syn* see JUST 3
only *conj* in spite of which <it looks delicious, *only* I'm not hungry>
  syn but, except, however, save, yet
on occasion *adv syn* see OCCASIONALLY
on offer *adj syn* see PURCHASABLE 1
onomatopoeic *adj* formed in imitation of a natural sound <*buzz* is an *onomatopoeic* word to describe the sound of bees>
  syn echoic, imitative, onomatopoetic
  rel emulative, simulative; mimetic, mimic, mimical
onomatopoetic *adj syn* see ONOMATOPOEIC
on purpose *adv syn* see INTENTIONALLY
onset *n* 1 *syn* see ATTACK 1
  2 *syn* see BEGINNING
onslaught *n syn* see ATTACK 1
on the whole *adv syn* see ALTOGETHER 3
onus *n* 1 *syn* see LOAD 3
  2 *syn* see BLAME
  3 *syn* see STIGMA
onward *adv* 1 *syn* see AHEAD 2
  2 *syn* see ALONG 1
onyx *adj syn* see BLACK 1
oodles *n pl but sometimes sing in constr syn* see SCAD

||**ooftish** *n syn* see MONEY
||**oofy** *adj syn* see RICH 1
ooid *adj syn* see OVAL
oomph *n syn* see SPIRIT 5
ooze *vb syn* see EXUDE
oozy *adj syn* see MUDDY 1
opaque *adj syn* see OBSCURE 3
  ant transparent, transpicuous
ope *vb syn* see OPEN 1
open *adj* 1 not closed or obstructed <escaped through the *open* gate>
  syn patent, unclosed, unobstructed
  rel agape, dehiscent, gaping, patulous, ringent, wide, yawning; ajar; unbarred, unbolted, unfastened, unlocked, unsealed; clear, unimpeded
  con blocked, obstructed; constricted, cramped, narrow, strait
  ant closed, shut
  2 lacking a cover or covering <an *open* wound that continued to ooze blood> <his chest *open* to the sun>
  syn bare, denuded, exposed, naked, peeled, stripped, uncovered
  3 *syn* see LIABLE 2
  ant closed
  4 not restricted to a particular group or situation <favored *open* enrollment in the schools>
  syn accessible, open-door, public, unrestricted
  rel attainable, available, obtainable, reachable, securable
  idiom to be had, within reach
  con limited, restricted; inaccessible, private
  ant closed
  5 available for use or consideration or decision <there are only two courses *open* to us>
  syn accessible, employable, operative, practicable, usable
  rel appropriate, fit, proper, suitable; acceptable, agreeable, pleasing
  idiom within reach
  con inaccessible, inoperative, unusable
  ant closed
  6 *syn* see DOUBTFUL 1
  7 *syn* see FRANK
  ant close; clandestine
open *vb* 1 to change from a closed to an open condition <*open* the window>
  syn ope, unblock, unclose, undo, unshut, unstop
  rel clear, free, release; bare, disclose, expose, reveal
  idiom lay open, swing open, throw open
  con block, occlude, stop
  ant close, shut
  2 to make physically or mentally visible <dawn *opened* a surprising scene to his startled eyes>
  syn disclose, display, expose, reveal, unclothe, uncover, unveil
  rel adumbrate, hint, shadow, suggest

---

syn synonym(s)   *rel* related word(s)
ant antonym(s)   *con* contrasted word(s)
idiom idiomatic equivalent(s)
|| use limited; if in doubt, see a dictionary

idiom bring to light, bring to (*or* into) view, lay bare, make plain, show forth

con cloak, conceal, hide, screen, secrete, shroud

3 to make an opening in <decided to *open* a can of beans>

syn breach, disrupt, hole, rupture

rel break, broach, tap, undo; cut, gash, slash; perforate, pierce

idiom lay open

con occlude, shut; fasten, secure

ant close

4 to spread out <the eagle slowly *opened* its mighty wings>

syn expand, extend, fan (out), outspread, outstretch, spread, unfold

rel billow, dilate, distend, swell; cover, mantle, overspread

con collect, concentrate, contract, gather (in)

ant close

5 *syn* see BEGIN 1

ant close

6 *syn* see CONVENE 1

open *n syn* see OUTDOORS

open air *n syn* see OUTDOORS

open–air *adj syn* see OUTDOOR

con indoor, inside; enclosed

open–and–shut *adj syn* see CLEAR 5

open–door *adj syn* see OPEN 4

open–eyed *adj syn* see WATCHFUL

openhanded *adj* **1** *syn* see LIBERAL 1

ant closefisted, tightfisted

2 *syn* see CLEAR 5

openhearted *adj syn* see FRANK

opening *n* **1** *syn* see BEGINNING

ant closing

2 *syn* see APERTURE

3 *syn* see GAP 1

4 *syn* see OPPORTUNITY

opening gun *n syn* see BEGINNING

openmouthed *adj syn* see VOCIFEROUS

openness *n syn* see EXPOSURE

open sesame *n syn* see PASSPORT

open up *vb syn* see OPERATE 2

opera omnia *n syn* see OEUVRE

operate *vb* **1** *syn* see ACT 5

2 to perform surgery <*operated* on him to remove a brain tumor>

syn cut, open up

3 to cause to function <knew how to *operate* earth-moving equipment>

syn handle, run, use, work

rel play; manage, maneuver; drive, pilot, steer; ply, wield

idiom make go

4 *syn* see CONDUCT 3

operation *n* **1** *syn* see EXERCISE 1

2 *syn* see USE 1

operative *adj* **1** *syn* see ACTIVE 1

ant inoperative

2 *syn* see OPEN 5

operative *n* **1** *syn* see WORKER

2 *syn* see PRIVATE DETECTIVE

operator *n syn* see MOTORIST

operose *adj* **1** *syn* see HARD 6

2 *syn* see ASSIDUOUS

opiate *adj syn* see SOPORIFIC 1

opiate *n* **1** *syn* see DRUG 2

2 *syn* see ANODYNE 2

opine *vb* to form or express an opinion <he *opined* that the story was true>

syn ‖opinion, opinionate

rel accept, believe, consider, hold, judge, regard, think, view; speculate

con deny, disclaim, disown, reject, repudiate; disbelieve, discredit, doubt

opinion *n* an idea or judgment held as true or valid <seek an expert *opinion* on the authenticity of the painting>

syn belief, conviction, eye, feeling, mind, persuasion, sentiment, view

rel attitude, impression, notion, think, thought; conclusion, estimate, estimation, judgment, reaction; assumption, conjecture, speculation, supposition, theory

idiom point of view

con disbelief, discredit, doubt, unbelief; distrust, mistrust, questioning, skepticism

‖**opinion** *vb syn* see OPINE

opinionate *vb syn* see OPINE

opponent *n* one who expresses or manifests opposition <her *opponent* in the debate>

syn adversary, antagonist, anti, con, match, opposer, oppugnant

rel enemy, foe; competitor, rival; assailant, combatant; counteragent

con ally, colleague, comrade, confederate, partner; advocate, champion

ant exponent, pro, proponent

opportune *adj syn* see TIMELY 1

rel appropriate, felicitous, happy

ant inopportune

opportunity *n* a state of affairs or combination of circumstances favorable to some end <all he asked was an *opportunity* to show what he could do>

syn break, chance, look-in, occasion, opening, shot, show, squeak, time

rel room, space; leisure, liberty; relief, spell, turn; juncture, pass; dog's chance, hope, prayer

oppose *vb* **1** to place over against something to provide resistance or counterbalance <*oppose* one military force with another>

syn counter, match, pit, play (off), vie

rel array, confront, face

idiom set over against

2 *syn* see RESIST

opposed *adj syn* see ADVERSE 1

opposer *n syn* see OPPONENT

opposing *adj syn* see ADVERSE 1

opposite *n* something that is exactly opposed or contrary <virtue and vice are *opposites*>

syn antipode, antipole, antithesis, contra, contradictory, contrary, converse, counter, counterpole, reverse

rel contrast, counterpoint, foil; contrapositive, inverse, obverse; antonym

idiom the other extreme, the other side of the coin

con analogon, analogue, counterpart, like, parallel, similar; equal, equivalent; correlate, correlative; carbon copy, duplicate, replica
ant same

opposite *adj* being so far apart as to be or to seem irreconcilable <held *opposite* views on the solution of the problem>
syn antipodal, antipodean, antithetical, contradictory, contrary, converse, counter, diametric, polar, reverse
rel contrasting; contrapositive, inverse, obverse; antonymous; different, dissimilar, divergent, opposed, unalike, unlike, unsimilar; independent, separate, unconnected, unrelated
con alike, analogous, equivalent, like, parallel, similar; equal; correlative
ant same

opposite *prep syn* see TO 6

oppositely *adv syn* see AGAIN 5

opposite number *n* one holding an equivalent or parallel position <the Secretary of State and his *opposite number*, the Foreign Minister>
syn coordinate, counterpart, vis-à-vis; *compare* EQUAL
rel complement, cousin, equal, equivalent, like, match, tally

opposition *n syn* see ANTAGONISM 2

opposure *n syn* see ANTAGONISM 2

oppress *vb* 1 *syn* see WRONG
rel harass, harry; afflict, torment, torture; conquer, overcome, overthrow, subjugate
2 *syn* see DEPRESS 2
rel burden, distress, trouble

oppressive *adj* 1 *syn* see ONEROUS
ant unoppressive
2 *syn* see GLOOMY 3

oppressor *n syn* see TYRANT

opprobriate *vb syn* see DECRY 2

opprobrious *adj* 1 *syn* see ABUSIVE
2 *syn* see INFAMOUS 1

opprobrium *n syn* see DISGRACE
rel abuse, scurrility, vituperation
con credit, prestige

oppugn *vb syn* see CONTEND 1

oppugnant *adj syn* see ADVERSE 1

oppugnant *n syn* see OPPONENT

opt (for) *vb syn* see CHOOSE 1

optate *vb syn* see CHOOSE 1

optic *adj syn* see VISUAL 1

optical *adj syn* see VISUAL 1

optimacy *n syn* see ARISTOCRACY

optimism *n* an inclination to put the most favorable construction on actions and events or to anticipate the best possible outcome <was a practitioner of *optimism* in his everyday life>
syn Pollyannaism, rose-colored spectacles, sanguineness, sanguinity
rel brightness, buoyancy, happiness; idealism; positivism
con hopelessness; despair, gloom, melancholy; malism; defeatism, fatalism; cynicism
ant pessimism

optimist *n* one given to optimism <was a jaunty *optimist*>

syn hoper, Pollyanna
rel dreamer, idealist, positivist
con defeatist, fatalist; cynic, doubter, skeptic
ant pessimist

optimistic *adj* anticipating only the best to happen and minimizing all other possibilities <was *optimistic* about book sales that year>
syn fond, Pollyannaish, sanguine, upbeat; *compare* HOPEFUL 1
rel bright, cheerful, merry, sunny; hopeful, hoping; assured, confident
idiom feeling on top of the world, looking on the bright side, riding (*or* sitting) on cloud nine
con cynical; doubtful, uncertain
ant pessimistic

option *n syn* see CHOICE 1
rel prerogative, privilege, right

optional *adj* not compulsory <attendance at the meeting is *optional*>
syn discretionary, elective, facultative, nonobligatory
rel free, voluntary; alternative
con demanded, imperative; enforced, involuntary; essential, necessary
ant compulsory, mandatory, obligatory, required

opulent *adj* 1 *syn* see RICH 1
rel lavish, prodigal, profuse; extravagant, ostentatious, pretentious, showy; plush, swank
con modest, simple, unpretentious
2 *syn* see LUXURIOUS 3
3 *syn* see PROFUSE

oracle *n syn* see REVELATION

oracular *adj syn* see PROPHETIC

oral *adj* 1 *syn* see VOCAL 1
2 expressed or transmitted vocally <stories of folk heroes kept alive in *oral* tradition>
syn spoken, traditional, unwritten, verbal, word-of-mouth
rel narrated, recounted, related, told
con chronicled, recorded, written, written down

orate *vb* to talk in a declamatory, grandiloquent, or impassioned manner <*orated* to the crowd about the flag and patriotism>
syn bloviate, declaim, harangue, mouth, perorate, rant, rave, soapbox
rel elocute; bombast, rodomontade, sermonize, speechify; blah-blah

oratorical *adj syn* see RHETORICAL

oratory *n* the art of speaking in public eloquently and effectively <a politician who was a master at *oratory*>
syn elocution, rhetoric, speechcraft

orb *n* 1 *syn* see BALL
2 *syn* see EYE 1

orbit *n syn* see RANGE 2

orchestra *n* a usually large group of musicians who perform together <a string *orchestra* played at the reception>

---

syn synonym(s)   *rel* related word(s)
ant antonym(s)   *con* contrasted word(s)
idiom idiomatic equivalent(s)
|| use limited; if in doubt, see a dictionary

syn band, philharmonic, symphony
rel combo, ensemble

orchestrate *vb syn* see HARMONIZE 4

orchidaceous *adj syn* see SHOWY

orchids *n pl syn* see COMPLIMENT 1

ordain *vb* **1** *syn* see CONDUCT 3
  2 *syn* see DICTATE

ordeal *n syn* see TRIAL 1

order *n* **1** *syn* see ASSOCIATION 2
  2 *syn* see TYPE
  rel bracket, branch, pigeonhole, set; estate, grade, rank, status
  3 sequential occurrence in space or time <changed the *order* of the books on the shelf>
  syn arrangement, disposal, disposition, distribution, ordering, sequence
  rel array, arrayal, collocation; allocation, allotment, apportionment, arrayment, proration
  con disarrangement, disordering; chaos, confusion, disorder, mix-up, muddle
  4 general or approximate size or amount <a loss on the *order* of seven million dollars>
  syn extent, magnitude, matter, neighborhood, range, tune, vicinity
  rel approach, approximation, closeness, nearness, proximity
  5 manner of being arranged in space or of occurring in time <tell everything in the *order* in which it happened>
  syn consecution, procession, sequence, succession
  rel consecutiveness, following, successiveness; chain, progression, series, train
  6 *syn* see SUCCESSION 2
  7 orderly conduct <about to call the meeting to *order* when the interruption occurred>
  syn correctitude, correctness, decorousness, decorum, orderliness, properness, propriety, seemliness
  rel goodness, niceness, rightness; fitness, suitability; integrity, probity, rectitude, uprightness
  con impropriety, indecorousness, indecorum, unseemliness
  ant disorder
  8 orderly arrangement or disposition <troubled by the lack of *order* in their daily lives>
  syn method, orderliness, pattern, plan, system
  con anarchy, chaos, confusion, muddle, ‖snafu
  ant disorder
  9 state with respect to quality, functioning, or status <the equipment was in very poor *order*>
  syn case, condition, estate, repair, shape
  rel fettle, fitness, kilter, trim
  10 a state of soundness <had her car put in *order* for spring>
  syn condition, fettle, fitness, kilter, repair, shape, trim
  rel adjustment, amendment, correction, gear, rectification
  idiom working order
  con disrepair
  11 the state of being appropriate to or required by the circumstances <that remark is definitely out of *order*>

syn appositeness, appropriateness, aptness, expediency, fitness, meetness, propriety, rightness, suitability, suitableness
  rel opportuneness, seasonableness, timeliness; auspiciousness, favorableness; felicity, grace
  con inappropriateness, unfitness, unsuitability, unsuitableness
  12 *syn* see COMMAND 1
  rel authorization, permission

order *vb* **1** to bring about an orderly disposition of individuals, units, or elements <*ordered* his affairs in preparation for marriage>
  syn arrange, array, dispose, marshal, methodize, organize, systematize
  rel adjust, fix, regulate, right; align, line, line up, range; classify, codify, hierarchize; regiment, routine, routinize; streamline
  idiom put (*or* set) in order, put in shape, put (*or* set) to rights, reduce to order, whip into shape (*or* order)
  ant disorder
  2 *syn* see COMMAND

ordering *n syn* see ORDER 3

orderliness *n* **1** *syn* see ORDER 7
  ant disorderliness
  2 *syn* see ORDER 8
  ant disorderliness

orderly *adj* **1** following a set arrangement, design, or pattern <work out an *orderly* procedure and stick to it> <an *orderly* row of houses surrounded the village green>
  syn methodic, methodical, regular, systematic
  rel accurate, correct, exact, precise; alike, uniform; businesslike; conventional, formal
  idiom in apple-pie order
  con haphazard, irregular, unmethodical, unsystematic; careless, casual, free and easy
  ant chaotic, disorderly
  2 *syn* see NEAT 2
  rel picked up
  ant disordered; disorderly

order up *vb syn* see CALL UP

ordinance *n syn* see LAW 1

ordinarily *adv syn* see USUALLY 2

ordinary *adj* **1** of the customary or common type encountered in the normal course of events <*ordinary* traffic had been stopped to let the marchers pass>
  syn everyday, plain, plain Jane, quotidian, routine, unremarkable, usual, workaday
  rel commonplace, natural, normal, regular; customary, familiar, frequent
  con infrequent, rare, uncommon; accidental, casual, chance, fortuitous
  ant extraordinary
  2 *syn* see COMMON 6

organ *n* **1** *syn* see MEAN 2
  2 *syn* see JOURNAL

organize *vb* **1** *syn* see FOUND 2
  rel construct, put together
  2 *syn* see ORDER 1
  rel coordinate, integrate
  3 *syn* see MOBILIZE 3

‖**organized** *adj syn* see INTOXICATED 1

orgulous *adj syn* see PROUD 1

orgy *n* **1** *syn* see BINGE 1
2 an act or occasion of excessive indulgence in sex <the infamous *orgies* of ancient Rome>
syn bacchanal, bacchanalia, debauch, ‖group grope, party, saturnalia
3 *syn* see SPREE 1

orifice *n syn* see APERTURE

oriflamme *n syn* see FLAG

origin *n* **1** *syn* see ANCESTRY
rel maternity, parentage, paternity
2 *syn* see SOURCE

original *n* **1** a first form from which copies or reproductions can be produced <students copying the da Vinci *original*>
syn archetype, protoplast, prototype
rel forerunner, mother, precursor; model, pattern; precedent
con dummy, imitation, simulacrum; counterfeit, fake, forgery
ant copy, reproduction
2 *syn* see INNOVATOR
3 *syn* see ECCENTRIC

original *adj* **1** *syn* see FIRST 2
rel archetypal, prototypal
2 *syn* see PRIMARY 5
3 *syn* see INVENTIVE
con banal, trite; derivative, initative
ant unoriginal

originally *adv syn* see INITIALLY 1

originate *vb* **1** *syn* see GENERATE 1
2 *syn* see INTRODUCE 3
3 *syn* see SPRING 1
4 *syn* see BEGIN 2
5 to have one's origin or home base in <he *originates* from Ohio>
syn come (from), hail (from)
rel derive (from), spring (from), stem (from)

originative *adj syn* see INVENTIVE
ant unoriginative

originator *n* **1** *syn* see FATHER 2
2 *syn* see INNOVATOR

orison *n syn* see PRAYER

ornament *vb syn* see ADORN
rel enrich; embroider

ornate *adj* elaborately and often pretentiously decorated or designed <a very *ornate* room—all marble, gilt, and brocade>
syn baroque, flamboyant, florid, luscious, rich, rococo
rel elaborate, high-wrought, resplendent; labored, overdone, overelaborated, overembellished, overworked, overwrought; luxuriant, luxurious, opulent, sumptuous; aureate, gilded
con natural, plain, quiet, simple; severe, unembellished, unornamented, unostentatious, unpretentious; restrained, subdued
ant austere; chaste

ornery *adj* ‖**1** *syn* see CHEAP 2
2 *syn* see CANTANKEROUS
3 *syn* see CONTRARY 3

orotund *adj* **1** *syn* see RESONANT
rel loud, stentorian
2 *syn* see RHETORICAL

orphan *adj* deprived by death of one and usually both parents <seeking homes for the countless *orphan* children from the disaster area>
syn orphaned, parentless, unparented
rel alone, solitary; abandoned, cast-off, forsaken, lost; disregarded, ignored, neglected, slighted

orphaned *adj syn* see ORPHAN

orphic *adj syn* see RECONDITE

orthodox *adj* **1** conforming to doctrines or practices that are held to be right or true by an authority, standard, or tradition <those who still hold an *orthodox* view about evolution>
syn accepted, authoritative, canonical, received, sanctioned, sound
rel acknowledged, admitted, approved; customary, official, recognized, standard, traditional; correct, proper, right
con heretical, heterodox, unauthoritative, uncanonical
ant unorthodox
2 *syn* see CONVENTIONAL 1
3 *syn* see CONSERVATIVE 1
ant unorthodox

oscillate *vb syn* see SWING 2

osculate *vb syn* see KISS 1

ostend *vb syn* see SHOW 2

ostensible *adj* **1** *syn* see APPARENT 2
2 *syn* see ALLEGED

ostensibly *adv* to all outward appearances <*ostensibly* it was a business trip but actually it was all pleasure>
syn apparently, evidently, officially, outwardly, professedly, seemingly
rel externally, superficially; sensibly
idiom on the face of it, on the surface, to the eye
con genuinely, really, truly; au fond, basically

ostentatious *adj syn* see SHOWY
ant unostentatious

ostracism *n syn* see EXILE 1

ostracize *vb* **1** *syn* see BANISH
con accept, entertain, receive, welcome; harbor, haven, refuge, shelter
2 *syn* see CUT 7

other *adj* **1** *syn* see DIFFERENT 1
2 *syn* see ADDITIONAL

‖othergates *adv syn* see OTHERWISE 1

other half *n syn* see RABBLE 2

otherness *n syn* see DISSIMILARITY

‖otherways *adv syn* see OTHERWISE 2

‖otherwhile *adv syn* see SOMETIMES

otherwise *adv* **1** in a different way or manner <he could not act *otherwise*>
syn differently, diversely, ‖othergates, variously
ant likewise
2 under different conditions <might *otherwise* have left>
syn else, ‖elseways, elsewise, ‖otherways

otherwise *adj syn* see DIFFERENT 1

---

syn synonym(s)   *rel* related word(s)
ant antonym(s)   *con* contrasted word(s)
idiom idiomatic equivalent(s)
‖ use limited; if in doubt, see a dictionary

otherworld *n syn* see HEREAFTER 2

otherworldly *adj* **1** of or relating to a world other than the actual world <believed in the existence of *otherworldly* phenomena>
syn transcendental, transmundane
rel exterrestrial, extramundane, extraterrestrial; unearthly, unworldly
2 *syn* see DREAMY 1

otiose *adj syn* see VAIN 1
rel purposeless, useless; inexcusable; superfluous, supernumerary, surplus

oubliette *n syn* see DUNGEON

ought *vb syn* see WANT 3

ought *n syn* see OBLIGATION 2

ounce *n syn* see PARTICLE

oust *vb* **1** *syn* see DEPRIVE 2
2 *syn* see BANISH

out *adv syn* see OUTDOORS

out *vb* **1** *syn* see EJECT 1
2 *syn* see EXTINGUISH 1
3 *syn* see GET OUT 2

out *n syn* see SHOWING 1

out and away *adv syn* see FAR AND AWAY

out–and–out *adj syn* see UTTER

‖**outback** *n syn* see FRONTIER 2

outbalance *vb syn* see OUTWEIGH 1

outbloom *vb syn* see BLOSSOM

outbreak *n* **1** a sudden or violent beginning of activity <an *outbreak* of new housing starts>
syn burst, eruption, flare, outburst; *compare* EPIDEMIC
rel beginning, commencement, dawn, onset, outset
2 *syn* see EPIDEMIC

outbreathe *vb syn* see EXHALE

outburst *n* **1** a violent expression of emotion <an *outburst* of anger>
syn access, burst, eruption, explosion, flare-up, gust, sally
rel scene, storm, tantrum; frenzy, rapture transport(s)
2 *syn* see OUTBREAK 1

outcast *n* one who is cast out by society <a political *outcast*>
syn castaway, derelict, Ishmael, Ishmaelite, leper, offscouring, pariah, untouchable
rel hobo, tramp, vagabond, vagrant; displaced person; exile, expatriate; reprobate
con big name, bigwig, celebrity, lion, luminary, name, notable, personage, somebody

outcome *n syn* see EFFECT 1

outcomer *n syn* see STRANGER

out–country *adj syn* see RURAL

outcrier *n syn* see PEDDLER

outcry *n syn* see COMMOTION 1

outdare *vb syn* see FACE 3

outdate *vb* to make obsolete or out-of-date <the automobile *outdated* the horse and buggy>
syn antiquate, obsolesce, obsolete, outmode, superannuate
rel age, date, fossilize; replace, supersede

outdated *adj syn* see OLD-FASHIONED
ant up-to-the-minute

outdistance *vb syn* see OUTSTRIP 1

outdo *vb* **1** *syn* see SURPASS 1
idiom out-Herod Herod, steal (*or* get) a march on
2 *syn* see DEFEAT 2

outdoor *adj* taking place, done, or existing in the open air <an *outdoor* restaurant>
syn alfresco, hypaethral, open-air, out-of-door, outside
ant indoor, inside

outdoors *adv* in or into the open air <went *outdoors* for some fresh air>
syn out, out of doors, outside, without, withoutdoors
ant indoors, inside, withindoors

outdoors *n pl but sing in constr* the space where air is unconfined <every night he let the dog run in the *outdoors*>
syn open, open air, out-of-doors, outside, without
idiom God's good (*or* green) earth

outer *adj* being or located outside something <the sheep's thick *outer* coat of wool>
syn exterior, external, outside, outward, over
rel extraneous, extrinsic, superficial, surface; outlying, remote
con inside, interior, internal, inward
ant inner

outermost *adj syn* see EXTREME 5
ant inmost, innermost

outface *vb syn* see FACE 3

outfit *n* **1** *syn* see EQUIPMENT
2 *syn* see COSTUME
3 *syn* see COMPANY 4
4 *syn* see ENTERPRISE 3

outfit *vb syn* see FURNISH 1

outfox *vb syn* see OUTWIT

outgeneral *vb syn* see OUTWIT
rel outfight, outflank, outgame
idiom steal a march

outgo *vb syn* see SURPASS 1

outgoing *adj syn* see DEMONSTRATIVE
ant aloof

outgrowth *n* **1** a projecting part of an organism <a warty *outgrowth* on the skin>
syn excrescence, excrescency, process, processus
rel enlargement, prolongation, swelling; offshoot, shoot
2 something that develops or grows directly out of something else <the new TV series was an *outgrowth* of a popular movie>
syn by-product, derivative, descendant, offshoot, spin-off
rel branch, member; child, offspring, product; aftereffect, consequence, effect, issue, outcome, result
con origin, root, source; antecedent, cause, determinant

outhouse *n syn* see PRIVY 1

outing *n syn* see EXCURSION 1

outjockey *vb syn* see OUTWIT

outland *adj syn* see RURAL

outlander *n syn* see STRANGER

outlandish *adj* **1** *syn* see BARBARIC 1

rel foreign, strange
2 *syn* see STRANGE 4
rel monstrous; outré
con commonplace, everyday
3 marked by sharp departure from the traditional or usual <men who wear beads, earrings, and other *outlandish* ornaments>
syn far-out, kinky, outré, ultra; *compare* EXTREME 3
rel bizarre, extravagant, outrageous, wild; unconventional, unorthodox
con conservative, conventional; compliant, conformable; moderate
4 *syn* see BACK 1
outlast *vb syn* see OUTLIVE
outlaw *n* a criminal of the American Western frontier <*outlaws* held up stagecoaches>
syn badman, ‖bandido, bandit, desperado
rel gunman, gunslinger
idiom bad guy
outlaw *vb syn* see FORBID
outlay *vb syn* see SPEND 1
outlay *n syn* see EXPENSE 1
outlet *n* **1 *syn*** see APERTURE
2 *syn* see EGRESS 2
rel escape; release
3 *syn* see STORE 4
outline *n* the line that gives form or shape to a body or a figure <saw only a dark *outline* of the house through the gloom>
syn contour, delineation, figuration, line, lineament, lineation, profile, silhouette
rel configuration, conformation, figure, form, shape; skyline
con bulk, hulk, mass
outline *vb* **1 *syn*** see BORDER 1
2 *syn* see SKETCH
outlive *vb* to remain in existence longer than <the committee has *outlived* its usefulness>
syn outlast, outwear, survive
rel outstand, outstay
outlook *n* **1 *syn*** see LOOKOUT 2
2 *syn* see VISTA
3 *syn* see VIEW 4
4 *syn* see VIEWPOINT 2
outlying *adj syn* see DISTANT 1
outmaneuver *vb syn* see OUTWIT
idiom steal a march (on)
outmatch *vb syn* see SURPASS 1
outmode *vb syn* see OUTDATE
outmoded *adj* **1 *syn*** see OLD-FASHIONED
2 *syn* see OBSOLETE
3 *syn* see TACKY 2
outmost *adj syn* see EXTREME 5
ant inmost, innermost
out–of–date *adj* **1 *syn*** see OLD-FASHIONED
ant up-to-date
2 *syn* see TACKY 2
out–of–door *adj syn* see OUTDOOR
out–of–doors *n pl but sing in constr syn* see OUTDOORS
out of doors *adv syn* see OUTDOORS
out–of–the–way *adj syn* see OBSCURE 2
outpace *vb syn* see OUTSTRIP 1

outplace *vb syn* see REPLACE 3
output *n* the amount of something produced <an annual *output* of 3,000,000 units>
syn outturn, product, production, turnout, yield
rel gain, get, profit, take; crop, harvest
con input; raw material
outrage *n syn* see INJURY 1
outrage *vb* **1 *syn*** see RAPE
2 *syn* see ABUSE 4
3 *syn* see WRONG
4 *syn* see OFFEND 3
outrageous *adj* **1** exceeding the limits of what is normal or tolerable <*outrageous* prices that threaten our way of life>
syn barbarous, unchristian, uncivilized, unconscionable, ungodly, unholy, wicked
rel abominable, awful, beastly, dreadful, ghastly, horrible, horrid, impossible, intolerable, terrible, unreasonable; scandalous, shocking
con normal, reasonable, tolerable; acceptable, bearable, endurable, supportable
2 enormously or flagrantly bad or horrible <*outrageous* treatment of prisoners>
syn atrocious, crying, desperate, heinous, monstrous, scandalous, shocking
rel enormous, flagrant, gross; egregious, nefarious, notorious, villainous
con condonable, excusable, forgivable, pardonable; defensible, justifiable; legitimate, reasonable; comprehensible, plausible, understandable
outrank *vb syn* see PRECEDE 1
outré *adj syn* see OUTLANDISH 3
outreach *vb syn* see OUTWIT
outrecuidance *n syn* see CONCEIT 2
outrider *n syn* see FORERUNNER 1
outright *adj* **1 *syn*** see UTTER
2 *syn* see WHOLE 4
outrun *vb syn* see OUTSTRIP 1
outset *n syn* see BEGINNING
outshine *vb syn* see SURPASS 1
outside *n syn* see OUTDOORS
outside *adj* **1 *syn*** see OUTER
rel alien, foreign
ant inside
2 *syn* see OUTDOOR
3 *syn* see MAXIMUM
4 *syn* see REMOTE 4
outside *adv syn* see OUTDOORS
outside *prep* **1 *syn*** see BEYOND 1
2 *syn* see EXCEPT
outside of *prep syn* see EXCEPT
outsider *n syn* see STRANGER
con insider
outskirt *n usu* outskirts *pl syn* see ENVIRONS 2
outslick *vb syn* see OUTWIT
outsmart *vb syn* see OUTWIT
outspeed *vb syn* see OUTSTRIP 1

---

syn synonym(s)   *rel* related word(s)
ant antonym(s)   *con* contrasted word(s)
idiom idiomatic equivalent(s)
‖ use limited; if in doubt, see a dictionary

outspoken *adj* speaking without fear or reserve <quite *outspoken* in her views on mandatory retirement>
 syn free, free-spoken, round, vocal
 rel candid, direct, forthright, frank, open, plain, plainspoken, straightforward, unreticent; bluff, blunt; explicit, point-blank, unequivocal; strident
 con reserved, restrained, reticent; private, retiring, shrinking; unassertive
outspread *vb syn* see OPEN 4
 ant folded (*of wings or a fan*)
outstanding *adj* **1** *syn* see UNPAID 2
 2 *syn* see NOTICEABLE
 3 *syn* see CHIEF 2
 4 *syn* see SUPERB 3
outstare *vb syn* see STARE DOWN
outstart *n syn* see BEGINNING
outstep *vb syn* see EXCEED 1
outstretch *vb syn* see OPEN 4
outstrip *vb* **1** to go faster than <could *outstrip* even the fastest horse>
 syn distance, outdistance, outpace, outrun, outspeed
 rel outfly, outsoar, outwing; outfoot, outrace, outride; outsail; outtravel; lose, shake off
 con follow, trail; drag, hang back, lag
 2 *syn* see SURPASS 1
outsweepings *n pl syn* see REFUSE
outthink *vb syn* see OUTWIT
outthrust *n syn* see PROJECTION 1
outtire *vb syn* see EXHAUST 4
outturn *n syn* see OUTPUT
outward *adj syn* see OUTER
 ant inward
outwardly *adv syn* see OSTENSIBLY
 ant inwardly
outwear *vb* **1** *syn* see EXHAUST 4
 2 *syn* see OUTLIVE
 rel endure, hold up
outweigh *vb* **1** to exceed in weight, value, or importance <her brother *outweighed* her by nearly fifty pounds> <the facts *outweigh* his argument>
 syn outbalance, overbalance, overweigh, overweight
 rel overbear
 2 *syn* see COMPENSATE 1
outweighing *adj syn* see DOMINANT 1
outwit *vb* to defeat or get the better of by superior cleverness or ingenuity <*outwitted* the enemy by taking a different route>
 syn have, outfox, outgeneral, outjockey, outmaneuver, outreach, outslick, outsmart, outthink, overreach, undo; *compare* FRUSTRATE 1
 rel bamboozle, befool, dupe, gull, hoax, hoodwink, outtrick, outtrump, trick; outdo; outguess
outworn *adj syn* see OBSOLETE
oval *adj* having the shape of a longitudinal section of an egg <an *oval* pond>
 syn ooid, ovate, oviform, ovoid
 rel ovaloid; ellipsoidal, elliptic
ovate *adj syn* see OVAL
over *adv* **1** from one point to another across intervening space <sailed *over* to the island>

 syn across, athwart, beyond, transversely
 2 *syn* see AWAY 2
 3 *syn* see EVER 6
 4 at a higher point <the plane was directly *over*>
 syn above, aloft, overhead
 idiom on high
 ant under
 5 at or to an end <it's all *over* between them>
 syn by, through
 6 *syn* see THROUGH 1
 7 yet another time <do the work *over*>
 syn afresh, again, anew, de novo, once more
 idiom over again
over *prep* **1** at a higher level <clouds hung *over* the town>
 syn above, o'er
 ant under
 2 *syn* see ACROSS
 3 with respect to <children squabbling *over* toys>
 syn about, on, upon, with
 4 so as to make contact with <hit him *over* the head>
 syn on, upon
 5 *syn* see DURING
 6 as the result of <quarreled *over* money matters>
 syn because of, due to, owing to, through
over *adj* **1** *syn* see SUPERIOR 1
 ant under
 2 *syn* see OUTER
over *vb syn* see CLEAR 8
overabounding *adj syn* see SUPERABUNDANT
overabundance *n syn* see EXCESS 1
overabundant *adj syn* see SUPERABUNDANT
overact *vb* to exaggerate in acting especially on the stage or screen <was criticized for *overacting* the part>
 syn overplay
 rel ham, mug; declaim, rant, spout
 idiom chew the scenery
 ant underact, underplay
over against *prep* **1** *syn* see AGAINST 1
 2 *syn* see VERSUS 2
overage *n syn* see EXCESS 2
 ant shortage, underage
overall *adv* **1** *syn* see EVERYWHERE 1
 2 *syn* see GENERALLY 1
overall *adj syn* see ALL-AROUND 2
over and above *prep syn* see BESIDES 1
over and over *adv syn* see OFTEN
overbalance *vb syn* see OUTWEIGH 1
overbalanced *adj syn* see LOPSIDED
overbalancing *adj syn* see DOMINANT 1
overbearing *adj* **1** *syn* see MASTERFUL 1
 2 *syn* see DOMINANT 1
 3 *syn* see PROUD 1
 rel absolute, autocratic, despotic, tyrannical
 con passive, unassertive; acquiescent, compliant, unresisting
 ant subservient
overblown *adj* **1** *syn* see FAT 2
 2 *syn* see INFLATED
 3 *syn* see RHETORICAL

4 *syn* see PRETENTIOUS 3
overbold *adj syn* see SHAMELESS
overbrim *vb syn* see OVERFLOW 2
overburden *vb syn* see OVERLOAD
overcast *vb* **1** *syn* see OBSCURE
2 *syn* see COVER 3
overcast *adj* clouded over <a gray *overcast* March day>
syn cloudy, ‖dowly, dull, heavy, lowering (*or* louring), nubilous, overclouded
rel brooding, dirty, oppressive, sullen
ant clear, cloudless
overcharge *vb* **1** to charge excessively for service or goods <a clip joint well known for *overcharging* customers>
syn clip, fleece, skin, soak, stick
ant undercharge
2 *syn* see OVERLOAD
3 *syn* see EMBROIDER
overcloud *vb syn* see OBSCURE
overclouded *adj syn* see OVERCAST
overcome *vb* **1** to get the better of <*overcome* a bad habit>
syn conquer, down, hurdle, lick, master, surmount, throw; *compare* CONQUER 2
rel beat, defeat; outlive, prevail
con adopt, embrace, take up; indulge
2 *syn* see CONQUER 2
3 *syn* see OVERWHELM 4
4 *syn* see WIN 1
overconfident *adj syn* see PRESUMPTUOUS
overcritical *adj syn* see CRITICAL 1
overdo *vb* to make excessive use or application of <he has *overdone* that joke to the point that it is no longer funny>
syn overplay, overuse, overwork
idiom go overboard, go to extremes, run into the ground
overdoing *n syn* see EXTRAVAGANCE 2
overdraw *vb syn* see EMBROIDER
overdue *adj* **1** *syn* see UNPAID 2
2 *syn* see TARDY
ant early
overearly *adj syn* see EARLY 2
overemphasize *vb syn* see OVERPLAY 2
ant underemphasize
overesteem *vb syn* see OVERVALUE
overestimate *vb syn* see OVERVALUE
ant underestimate
overfill *vb syn* see OVERFLOW 2
overflow *vb* **1** *syn* see DELUGE 1
2 to flow over the brim <the river *overflowed* its banks>
syn overbrim, overfill, overrun, run over, spill, well over
rel brim, cascade, slop, slosh
con drop, recede, withdraw
overflow *n* **1** *syn* see FLOOD 2
2 *syn* see EXCESS 1
overflowing *adj* **1** *syn* see ALIVE 5
2 *syn* see SUPERABUNDANT
overfull *adv syn* see EVER 6
overgrown *adj* covered with growth or herbage <a vacant lot *overgrown* with weeds>

syn grown, rank
rel braky, brambly, brushy, copsy, jungly, thicketed, thickety; dense, overrun, thick; lush
‖**overhand** *n syn* see ADVANTAGE 3
overhang *vb* **1** *syn* see BULGE
2 *syn* see HANG 4
overhanging *adj syn* see IMMINENT 2
overhaul *vb* **1** *syn* see MEND 2
2 *syn* see CATCH 7
overhead *adv syn* see OVER 4
ant underfoot
overheated *adj syn* see IMPASSIONED
overindulgence *n syn* see EXCESS 3
overindulgent *adj syn* see EXCESSIVE 2
overkill *n syn* see EXCESS 1
overlade *vb syn* see OVERLOAD
overlap *vb* to extend over and cover a part of <each course of shingles should *overlap* the preceding course by several inches>
syn imbricate, lap, overlie, override, ride, shingle
overlay *vb syn* see COVER 3
overleap *vb* **1** *syn* see CLEAR 8
2 *syn* see NEGLECT
overlie *vb syn* see OVERLAP
overload *vb* to load to excess <*overload* a ship>
syn overburden, overcharge, overlade, overtax, overweigh, overweight
con lighten
overlong *adj syn* see LONG 2
overlook *vb* **1** *syn* see SURVEY 3
2 to rise above and afford a view of <the tower *overlooks* the city>
syn dominate, look down, overtop, tower (above *or* over)
rel oversee
3 *syn* see NEGLECT
4 *syn* see SUPERVISE
overlook *n* **1** *syn* see OMISSION
2 *syn* see LOOKOUT 2
overly *adv syn* see EVER 6
overlying *adj syn* see SUPERIOR 1
ant underlying
overmuch *n syn* see EXCESS 1
overmuch *adv syn* see EVER 6
overnice *adj syn* see PRECIOUS 4
overpaint *vb syn* see EMBROIDER
overpass *vb syn* see NEGLECT
overpeopled *adj syn* see OVERPOPULATED
ant underpeopled
overplay *vb* **1** *syn* see OVERACT
ant underact, underplay
2 to give undue attention or emphasis to <*overplaying* the trivial at the expense of the significant>
syn magnify, maximize, overemphasize, overstress

---

syn synonym(s)   *rel* related word(s)
ant antonym(s)   *con* contrasted word(s)
idiom idiomatic equivalent(s)
‖ use limited; if in doubt, see a dictionary

rel accent, accentuate, point up; dramatize, exaggerate, hyperbolize, overdraw, overstate, stretch; overvalue
idiom lay it on thick
con downgrade, downplay; minimize
3 *syn* see OVERDO
overplus *n syn* see EXCESS 1
overpopulated *adj* populated too densely <*overpopulated* cities>
syn overpeopled
rel congested, dense, overcrowded
con empty, vacant, void; unpopulated
ant underpopulated
overpower *vb* 1 *syn* see CONQUER 1
2 *syn* see OVERWHELM 4
overpress *vb syn* see PRESSURE
overprize *vb syn* see OVERVALUE
ant underprize, undervalue
overrate *vb syn* see OVERVALUE
ant underrate
overreach *vb* 1 *syn* see CHEAT
2 *syn* see OUTWIT
overreckon *vb syn* see OVERVALUE
overrefined *adj syn* see PRECIOUS 4
override *vb syn* see OVERLAP
overriding *adj syn* see CENTRAL 1
rel primary, principal
overripe *adj syn* see EFFETE 3
overrule *vb syn* see GOVERN 1
overruling *adj syn* see CENTRAL 1
overrun *vb* 1 *syn* see WHIP 2
2 *syn* see INVADE 1
3 *syn* see INFEST 1
4 *syn* see EXCEED 1
5 *syn* see OVERFLOW 2
oversea *adj syn* see OVERSEAS
overseas *adv* beyond or across the sea <served *overseas* for two years>
syn abroad
con stateside
overseas *adj* situated, originating in, or relating to lands overseas <attempting to tap the potential of *overseas* markets>
syn oversea, transmarine, ultramarine
rel alien, exotic, foreign, strange
con domestic, home; stateside
oversee *vb* 1 *syn* see SURVEY 3
2 *syn* see SUPERVISE
overset *vb* 1 *syn* see OVERTURN 1
2 *syn* see OVERTHROW 2
overshadow *vb syn* see OBSCURE
oversight *n* 1 the function or duty of watching or guarding for the sake of proper direction or control <had *oversight* of the children as they played>
syn care, charge, conduct, handling, intendance, management, running, superintendence, superintendency, supervision
rel custody, guard, guardianship; keeping, maintenance; surveillance; aegis, tutelage; ciceronage; chaperonage; check, control
2 *syn* see FAILURE 1
3 *syn* see OMISSION
oversize *adj syn* see LARGE 1

ant undersized
overslaugh *vb syn* see HINDER
oversoon *adj syn* see EARLY 2
oversoon *adv syn* see EARLY 2
overspread *vb* 1 *syn* see COVER 3
2 *syn* see INFEST 1
overstate *vb syn* see EMBROIDER
ant understate
overstatement *n syn* see EXAGGERATION
ant understatement
overstep *vb syn* see EXCEED 1
rel infringe, transgress, trespass
overstock *n syn* see EXCESS 2
ant understock
overstress *vb syn* see OVERPLAY 2
oversupply *n syn* see EXCESS 2
ant undersupply
overswarm *vb* 1 *syn* see INFEST 1
2 *syn* see INVADE 1
oversway *vb syn* see INDUCE 1
overtake *vb syn* see CATCH 7
overtax *vb syn* see OVERLOAD
overthrow *vb* 1 *syn* see OVERTURN 1
2 to cause the downfall of <*overthrow* the government>
syn overset, overturn, topple, tumble, unhorse; *compare* CONQUER 1
rel depose, dethrone, oust, remove, unseat; liquidate, purge; conquer, defeat, destroy, ruin
con create, establish, found, set up
overthrow *n syn* see DEFEAT 1
overtone *n syn* see ASSOCIATION 4
overtop *vb syn* see OVERLOOK 2
overture *n* 1 action intended to attract favorable attention <made friendly *overtures* to the new member of the class>
syn advance, approach
rel bid, proposal, proposition, tender
2 *syn* see INTRODUCTION
overturn *vb* 1 to turn from an upright or level position <the embarrassed boy backed into the table and *overturned* a lamp>
syn knock over, overset, overthrow, tip (over), topple, turn over, upset
rel capsize, keel (over *or* up), upend, upturn; prostrate; down; roll (over)
con erect, right, set up, straighten (up)
2 *syn* see OVERTHROW 2
overturn *n syn* see SHAKE-UP
overuse *vb syn* see OVERDO
ant underuse
overvalue *vb* to set too high a value on <inclined to *overvalue* his own charm>
syn overesteem, overestimate, overprize, overrate, overreckon
rel cherish, prize, treasure; adore, idolize, worship
con belittle, depreciate
ant underprize, undervalue
overweening *adj syn* see PRESUMPTUOUS
overweigh *vb* 1 *syn* see OUTWEIGH 1
2 *syn* see OVERLOAD
overweighing *adj syn* see DOMINANT 1
overweight *vb* 1 *syn* see OUTWEIGH 1

2 *syn* see OVERLOAD

overweight *adj syn* see FAT 2
  ant underweight

overwhelm *vb* **1** *syn* see DELUGE 1
  2 *syn* see DELUGE 3
  3 *syn* see WHIP 2
  4 to subject to the grip of something overpowering and usually distressing or damaging <*overwhelmed* by the death of his only child> <human wants that tend to *overwhelm* environmental realities>
  syn drown, knock over, overcome, overpower, prostrate, whelm
  rel demoralize, devastate, dumbfound, shatter; floor, sink; disturb, upset; destroy, ruin, wreck; downgrade, lower, subordinate

overwhelmed *adj syn* see AGHAST 2

overwhelming *adj syn* see TOWERING 4

overwork *vb syn* see OVERDO

oviform *adj syn* see OVAL

ovoid *adj syn* see OVAL

owing *adj syn* see UNPAID 2

owing to *prep syn* see OVER 6

owl–light *n syn* see EVENING 1

own *vb* **1** *syn* see HAVE 1
  2 *syn* see ACKNOWLEDGE 1
  con deny, disclaim
  ant disown, repudiate

owner *n* one that has the legal or rightful title <*owner* of the shop>
  syn holder, possessor, proprietor
  rel lord, master
  con lessee, renter, tenant; squatter; interloper, intruder, trespasser

ownership *n* lawful claim or title <would soon have *ownership* of the house>
  syn dominion, possession, possessorship, property, proprietary, proprietorship
  rel hand

own up *vb syn* see ACKNOWLEDGE 1

oyster *n syn* see FORTE

---

syn synonym(s)   *rel* related word(s)
ant antonym(s)   *con* contrasted word(s)
idiom idiomatic equivalent(s)
‖ use limited; if in doubt, see a dictionary

P

pa *n syn* see FATHER 1

pablum *n syn* see PAP 2

pabulum *n syn* see FOOD 2

pace *n* **1** *syn* see TEMPO

  2 *syn* see SPEED 2

  3 *syn* see ROUTINE

pace *vb* **1** *syn* see WALK 1

  2 *syn* see PRECEDE 2

pacific *adj* affording or promoting peace <a *pacific* policy>

  syn irenic, nonviolent, pacificatory, pacifist, peaceable, peaceful

  rel appeasing, conciliating, conciliatory, pacifying, propitiating, propitiatory; dovelike, gentle, inoffensive

  con belligerent, combative, contentious, pugnacious, quarrelsome; unpeaceable, unpeaceful; hawkish, violent, warlike

  ant bellicose, unpacific

pacificator *n syn* see PEACEMAKER

pacificatory *adj syn* see PACIFIC

pacificist *n syn* see PACIFIST

  idiom man of peace

pacifist *n* one who opposes war or violence as a means of settling disputes <*pacifists* mounted a campaign against the war>

  syn dove, pacificist

  rel satyagrahi; ‖conchie, conscientious objector; peacemonger

  con belligerent, combatant; chauvinist, hawk, jingo, jingoist, warmonger

  ant bellicist

pacifist *adj syn* see PACIFIC

  ant combative

pacify *vb* to allay anger or agitation <saw his mounting rage and tried to *pacify* him>

  syn appease, assuage, conciliate, mollify, placate, propitiate, sweeten

  rel dulcify, soften; allay, alleviate, mitigate, relieve; moderate, qualify, smooth (over), temper

  idiom pour balm into, pour oil on (the) troubled waters

  con arouse, stir (up)

  ant anger

pack *n* **1** *syn* see BACKPACK

  2 *syn* see MUCH

pack *vb* **1** *syn* see STOW

  2 *syn* see LOAD 3

  3 *syn* see CARRY 1

packed *adj syn* see FULL 1

  idiom packed like sardines (*or* herrings)

‖**packed out** *adj syn* see FULL 1

packet *n syn* see FORTUNE 4

packman *n syn* see PEDDLER

packsack *n syn* see BACKPACK

pact *n* **1** *syn* see CONTRACT

  rel settlement

  2 *syn* see TREATY

‖**pad** *n syn* see PROTECTION 2

pad *vb syn* see EMBROIDER

paddle *vb syn* see ROW

‖**paddy** *n syn* see POLICEMAN

pagan *adj syn* see HEATHEN

pageant *n syn* see PRETENSE 2

pagoda *n syn* see SUMMERHOUSE

pain *n* **1** a bodily sensation that causes acute discomfort or suffering <suffering from chest *pains*>

  syn ache, ‖misery, pang, stitch, throe, twinge

  rel discomfort, distress, hurt, suffering; agony, torment, torture

  2 pains *pl syn* see EFFORT 1

  rel assiduousness, diligence, industry, sedulousness

pain *vb* **1** *syn* see HURT 4

  rel agonize, convulse, crucify, excruciate, harrow, lacerate

  2 *syn* see DISTRESS 2

  rel afflict; distress, upset; wound; anguish

  idiom ‖hit one where one lives

  3 *syn* see TRY 2

painful *adj* **1** causing, marked by, or affected with pain <a *painful* wound>

  syn aching, afflictive, algetic, hurtful, hurting, sore

  rel raw; acute, piercing, sharp, shooting, stabbing, stinging; agonizing, excruciating, harrowing, racking, tormenting, torturous

  ant painless, unpainful

  2 *syn* see BITTER 2

  rel unappetizing, unsavory

  ant painless

painfully *adv syn* see HARD 5

  ant painlessly

pain-killer *n syn* see ANODYNE 1

painstaking *adj syn* see CAREFUL 2

painstakingly *adv syn* see HARD 3

  rel carefully, meticulously; lovingly

paint *n syn* see MAKEUP 3

pair *n syn* see COUPLE

paired *adj syn* see TWIN

pal *n syn* see ASSOCIATE 3

palace *adj syn* see LUXURIOUS 3

palace car *n syn* see PARLOR CAR

palatable *adj* agreeable or pleasant especially to the sense of taste <a *palatable* meal>

  syn aperitive, appetizing, flavorsome, good≠tasting, ‖gusty, mouth-watering, relishing, sapid, saporous, savorous, savorsome, savory, tasteful, tasty, toothsome, toothy

  rel delectable, delicious, delightful, luscious, scrumptious, yummy; tempting; saporific

  con bad-tasting, disagreeable, distasteful, ill≠flavored, unappetizing

  ant unpalatable

palate *n syn* see TASTE 4

palatial *adj syn* see LUXURIOUS 3
 rel noble, regal; monumental; impressive; rich, splendid
palaver *n* **1** *syn* see CONFERENCE 2
 rel dialogue, discussion; parley
 2 *syn* see CHATTER
 rel gas, guff, hot air
 3 *syn* see TERMINOLOGY
 4 *syn* see BUSINESS 8
palaverous *adj syn* see WORDY
pale *adj* **1** deficient in color or in intensity of color
 <a *pale* face>
 syn ashen, ashy, blanched, colorless, complexionless, doughy, livid, lurid, pallid, paly, wan, waxen
 rel sallow, sick, sickly; gray, pasty, pasty-faced, waxlike; white, whitened; deathlike, ghastly
 con flushed, ruddy; bright, colorful, florid
 2 being weak and thin in substance or in vital qualities <a *pale*, inadequate foreign policy>
 syn anemic, bloodless, pallid, waterish, watery
 rel inane, insipid, jejune, wishy-washy; insubstantial, unsubstantial; ineffective, ineffectual; faint, feeble, weak
 con strong, substantial; effective, effectual; bright, colorful
 ant brilliant
pale *vb syn* see DULL 1
Pale Horse *n, used with* the *syn* see DEATH 1
palinode *vb syn* see ABJURE
pall *vb* **1** *syn* see BORE
 2 *syn* see SATIATE
 rel disgust, weary
‖**pallet** *n syn* see HEAD 1
palliate *vb* to give a speciously fine appearance to what is erroneous, base, or evil <did not try to conceal or *palliate* his errors>
 syn blanch (over), extenuate, gloss (over), gloze (over), prettify, sugarcoat, varnish, veneer, white, whiten, whitewash
 rel alleviate, lighten, mitigate; condone, excuse; moderate, qualify, soften, temper; camouflage, cloak, conceal, cover up, disguise, dissemble, mask; hush (up)
 idiom paper over the cracks, put a good face on (*or* upon)
pallid *adj* **1** *syn* see PALE 1
 2 *syn* see PALE 2
pally *adj syn* see INTIMATE 4
palm (on *or* upon) *vb syn* see FOIST 3
‖**palm grease** *n syn* see GRATUITY
palm off *vb syn* see FOIST 3
‖**palm oil** *n syn* see GRATUITY
palooka *n syn* see OAF 2
palpable *adj* **1** *syn* see TANGIBLE 1
 2 *syn* see PERCEPTIBLE
 rel apparent, ostensible, seeming; believable, colorable, credible, plausible
 3 *syn* see CLEAR 5
 rel certain, positive, sure; arresting, noticeable, remarkable, striking
 con doubtful, dubious, problematic, questionable
 ant impalpable

palpate *vb syn* see TOUCH 1
palpation *n syn* see TOUCH 2
palpitate *vb syn* see PULSATE
 rel pitter-patter
‖**palsy–walsy** *adj syn* see INTIMATE 4
palter *vb* **1** *syn* see LIE
 rel evade, fence
 idiom play false, play fast and loose
 2 *syn* see HAGGLE 2
paltry *adj* **1** *syn* see CHEAP 2
 rel beggarly, shabby; pitiful
 2 *syn* see LITTLE 2
 rel base, low, low-down, vile
 3 *syn* see PETTY 2
 rel insignificant, unimportant
paly *adj syn* see PALE 1
pamper *vb syn* see BABY
 rel regale, tickle; caress, dandle, fondle, pet; overindulge
‖**pan** *n* **1** *syn* see FACE 1
 2 *syn* see CRITICISM 2
pan *vb syn* see CRITICIZE
panacea *n* a remedy for all ills or difficulties <bicycles are not a *panacea* for the traffic problem>
 syn catholicon, cure-all, elixir, nostrum
 rel relief; remedy
 idiom universal (*or* sovereign) remedy
pandect *n syn* see COMPENDIUM 1
pandemoniac *adj syn* see INFERNAL 2
pandemonium *n* **1** *cap* **Pandemonium** *syn* see HELL
 2 *syn* see SINK 1
 3 *syn* see DIN
pander *n syn* see PIMP 1
panegyric *n syn* see ENCOMIUM
panegyrical *adj syn* see EULOGISTIC
panegyrize *vb syn* see PRAISE 2
pang *n syn* see PAIN 1
 rel prick, stab, ‖stang
‖**pang** *vb syn* see CRAM 1
panhandler *n syn* see BEGGAR 1
panhandling *n syn* see MENDICANCY
panic *n* **1** *syn* see FEAR 1
 rel frenzy, hysteria; stampede
 con composure, equanimity, sangfroid, self-possession
 ‖**2** *syn* see RIOT 2
‖**pank** *vb syn* see PANT 1
panoply *n syn* see DISPLAY 2
panorama *n syn* see RANGE 2
pan out *vb syn* see SUCCEED 2
pansified *adj syn* see EFFEMINATE
pant *vb* **1** to breathe quickly, spasmodically, or in a labored manner <was *panting* after running up the stairs>
 syn blow, gasp, heave, huff, ‖pank, ‖pegh, puff
 rel gulp; wheeze; wind; chuff
 idiom be out of breath
 2 *syn* see AIM 2
 rel hunger, long, pine, thirst; desire, want, wish

---

syn synonym(s)   *rel* related word(s)
ant antonym(s)   *con* contrasted word(s)
idiom idiomatic equivalent(s)
‖ use limited; if in doubt, see a dictionary

idiom be consumed with desire (for)
pantywaist *n syn* see WEAKLING
pantywaist *adj syn* see CHARACTERLESS
pap *n* **1** *syn* see FOOD 2
  2 something (as reading matter) lacking in solid value or substance <the sentimental *pap* that he offered his readers>
  syn pablum, rubbish, slop
  rel garbage, trash
‖**pap** *n syn* see FATHER 1
papa *n syn* see FATHER 1
paper *n* **1** *syn* see ESSAY 2
  2 *usu* **papers** *pl syn* see CREDENTIALS
paphian *n syn* see HARLOT 1
pappy *adj syn* see SOFT 6
‖**pappy** *n syn* see FATHER 1
par *n* **1** *syn* see EQUIVALENCE
  2 *syn* see AVERAGE
  rel standard
parable *n syn* see ALLEGORY 2
  rel comparison, similitude
parachronism *n syn* see ANACHRONISM 1
parade *n syn* see DISPLAY 2
  rel exhibition
parade *vb syn* see SHOW 4
  rel disclose, divulge, reveal; advertise, declare, proclaim, publish; boast, brag, gasconade
  idiom parade one's wares
  con camouflage, cloak, disguise, dissemble, mask
paradigm *n syn* see MODEL 2
paradigmatic *adj syn* see TYPICAL 1
paradise *n* **1** *syn* see HEAVEN 2
  idiom the next world (*or* life)
  2 *syn* see UTOPIA
paragon *n* an individual of unequaled excellence often serving as a model <she is a *paragon* of a caring physician>
  syn ideal, jewel, nonesuch, nonpareil, phoenix; *compare* MODEL 2
  rel apotheosis, epitome, last word, quintessence, ultimate; archetype, beau ideal, exemplar, pattern; ‖beaut, beauty, crackerjack, gem, love, lovely, peach, trump; champ, champion; cream, pick, tops
paragon *vb syn* see EQUATE 2
parallel *adj syn* see LIKE
  ant nonparallel, unparallel
parallel *n* one that corresponds to or closely resembles another <we seek in vain a *parallel* for this situation>
  syn analogue, correlate, correspondent, counterpart, countertype, match; *compare* COUNTERPART 1, EQUAL
  rel equivalent; double, duplicate, duplication
parallel *vb* **1** *syn* see EQUATE 2
  2 to place (something) so as to be parallel with another <machines that combed and *paralleled* the fibers>
  syn collimate, collocate, parallelize
  rel align, line up
parallelize *vb syn* see PARALLEL 2
paralyze *vb* **1** to render completely powerless, ineffective, or inert <a general strike that *paralyzed* the nation>

syn cripple, disable, disarm, immobilize, incapacitate, prostrate; *compare* MAIM, WEAKEN 1
  rel deaden, enfeeble, weaken; close, shut (down); freeze; demolish, destroy, knock out
  idiom bring to a grinding halt, tie hand and foot
  2 *syn* see DAZE 2
  rel appall, daunt, dismay, horrify; cripple, disable, enfeeble, weaken; astound, flabbergast, nonplus
  con animate, enliven, pep (up), stimulate
  ant galvanize
paramount *adj syn* see DOMINANT 1
  rel capital, headmost; commanding, controlling; cardinal, crowning
paramour *n* **1** *syn* see GALLANT 2
  2 *syn* see LOVER 1
  3 *syn* see MISTRESS
parapet *n syn* see BULWARK
paraphernalia *n pl but sometimes sing in constr syn* see EQUIPMENT 1
paraphrase *n syn* see VERSION 1
paraphrase *vb* to express or interpret something (as a text or passage) in other words <*paraphrased* the complicated document>
  syn rephrase, restate, reword, translate (into)
  rel summarize; transcribe
  con quote, reproduce
parasite *n* a person who is supported or seeks support from another without making an adequate return <lived as a *parasite* in his father's house>
  syn barnacle, bloodsucker, freeloader, hanger-on, leech, lounge lizard, ‖spiv, sponge, sponger, sucker; *compare* SYCOPHANT
  rel dependent; smell-feast; deadbeat, idler, laze
parasite *vb syn* see INFEST 2
parasitic *adj syn* see FAWNING
  rel freeloading, leechlike, sponging
parasitize *vb syn* see INFEST 2
parboil *vb syn* see BOIL 2
parcel *n* **1** *syn* see PART 1
  2 *syn* see LOT 3
  3 *syn* see GROUP 3
parcel *vb syn* see APPORTION 2
  rel allocate, allot, assign; deal, disburse, disperse; dole (out), lot (out)
parch *vb syn* see DRY 1
‖**pard** *n syn* see PARTNER
pardon *n* a remission of penalty or punishment <the governor granted the prisoner a *pardon*>
  syn absolution, amnesty
  rel acquittal, exculpation, exoneration, indemnification, indemnity; forgiveness, remission; justification, vindication
  con conviction; condemnation
  ant punishment
pardon *vb syn* see EXCUSE 1
  rel justify; accept, tolerate; free, liberate, release
  idiom let bygones be bygones, wipe the slate clean
  con amerce, fine, mulct, penalize
  ant punish
pardonable *adj syn* see VENIAL
  ant unpardonable
pare *vb* **1** *syn* see CUT 6

rel flay, scalp, skin, strip
2 *syn* see REDUCE 2
parent *vb syn* see GENERATE 1
parenthesis *n* **1** *syn* see DIGRESSION
  2 *syn* see INTERLUDE
parenthetically *adv syn* see INCIDENTALLY 2
parentless *adj syn* see ORPHAN
  ant parented
par excellence *adj syn* see EXCELLENT
pariah *n syn* see OUTCAST
  rel déclassé
‖**parish–pump** *adj syn* see INSULAR
parity *n syn* see EQUIVALENCE
  rel analogy, parallelism, similitude; approximation, closeness, nearness
  ant disparity, imparity
parlance *n syn* see WORDING
parley *vb* **1** *syn* see SPEAK 3
  2 *syn* see CONFER 2
parley *n* **1** *syn* see TALK 4
  rel rap session
  2 *syn* see CONVERSATION 1
parlor car *n* a railroad passenger car equipped
with individual revolving and reclining chairs
and providing the services of an attendant
  syn chair car, club car, lounge car, palace car,
tavern car
parlor house *n syn* see BROTHEL
parlous *adj syn* see DANGEROUS 1
parlous *adv syn* see VERY 1
Parnassian *n syn* see POET
parochial *adj syn* see INSULAR
  rel prejudiced; bigoted
  con unprejudiced; uncircumscribed, unlimited;
cosmic, universal
  ant catholic
parody *n syn* see CARICATURE 2
  rel spoof, spoofery, rib, ridicule
parody *vb syn* see MIMIC
paronomasia *n syn* see PUN
parous *adj syn* see PREGNANT 1
parry *vb* **1** *syn* see DODGE 1
  rel preclude, prevent; anticipate, forestall
  2 *syn* see WARD 1
parsimonious *adj syn* see STINGY
  idiom penny-wise and pound-foolish
  ant prodigal
parson *n syn* see CLERGYMAN
part *n* **1** something less than the whole to which it
belongs <a *part* of the road was paved>
  syn cut, division, member, moiety, parcel, piece,
portion, section, segment
  rel component, constituent, element, ingredient; detail, fraction, fragment; bit, chip, scrap
  con aggregate, total; combination, complex; entirety, entity, totality, unity
  ant whole
  2 parts *pl syn* see GENITALIA
  3 *syn* see RATION
  4 *syn* see SHARE 1
  rel chunk
  5 *syn* see SIDE 4
part *vb syn* see SEPARATE 1
  ant unite

part *adj syn* see INCOMPLETE 1
partage *n syn* see SHARE 1
partake *vb syn* see SHARE 2
  rel accept, receive, take
  idiom take part in
partake (of) *vb* **1** *syn* see EAT 1
  2 *syn* see AMOUNT 2
  idiom bear resemblance (to)
partaker *n syn* see PARTICIPANT
part and parcel *n syn* see ESSENTIAL 1
partial *adj* **1** *syn* see BIASED 2
  ant impartial
  2 *syn* see INCOMPLETE 1
  rel halfway
  ant whole
partiality *n* **1** *syn* see PREJUDICE
  2 *syn* see LEANING 2
participant *n* one that takes part in something
<were *participants* in the uprising>
  syn actor, partaker, participator, party, sharer
  rel aide, assistant, helper; colleague, confrere,
fellow, partner
  con bystander, looker-on, nonparticipant, observer, onlooker, spectator, watcher
participate *vb syn* see SHARE 2
  rel enter (into), join (in)
  idiom be a party to, be in on, be (*or* get) in the
act, have to do with
  con observe, watch; retire, withdraw
participator *n syn* see PARTICIPANT
particle *n* a tiny or insignificant amount, part, or
piece <not a *particle* of sense>
  syn ace, atom, bit, crumb, damn, ‖dite, doit,
dram, drop, fragment, grain, hoot, iota, jot,
minim, mite, modicum, molecule, ounce, ray,
‖rissom, scrap, scruple, shred, smidgen, smitch,
snap, speck, spot, syllable, tittle, whit, whoop
  rel morsel; snip; dribbet, dribble; dot
parti–color *adj syn* see VARIEGATED
parti–colored *adj syn* see VARIEGATED
  ant unicolor, unicolorous
particular *adj* **1** *syn* see SINGLE 2
  ant general
  2 *syn* see CIRCUMSTANTIAL
  rel careful, meticulous, punctilious, scrupulous
  3 *syn* see SPECIAL 1
  rel appropriate; distinct; singular
  ant universal
  4 *syn* see SEVERAL 1
  5 *syn* see NICE 1
particular *n syn* see POINT 1
  rel speciality, specific
  con entirety
  ant universal
particularity *n syn* see INDIVIDUALITY 3
particularize *vb* **1** *syn* see SPECIFY 3
  idiom draw it fine
  2 *syn* see ITEMIZE 1
particularized *adj syn* see CIRCUMSTANTIAL

---

syn synonym(s)   *rel* related word(s)
ant antonym(s)   *con* contrasted word(s)
idiom idiomatic equivalent(s)
‖ use limited; if in doubt, see a dictionary

ant generalized

particularly *adv syn* see ESPECIALLY 1

parting *n* a mutual separation of two or more persons <saddened by their approaching *parting*>
syn adieu, congé, farewell, good-bye, leave-taking
rel separation; departure
con joining, meeting; return
ant reunion

parting *adj* given, taken, or performed during leave-taking <remembered his father's *parting* advice>
syn departing, farewell, good-bye, valedictory
rel final, last

partisan *n* **1** *syn* see FOLLOWER
rel backer, champion, upholder; die-hard, stalwart
con adversary, antagonist, opponent
2 an irregular soldier who operates behind enemy lines <a train blown up by *partisans*>
syn guerrilla, irregular, patriot

partisan *adj syn* see BIASED 2
rel denominational, factional, sectarian; blind, devoted, die-hard, fanatic, unreasoning
con impartial, indifferent, unbiased, unprejudiced
ant nonpartisan

partition *n syn* see SEPARATION 1

partition *vb syn* see DISTRIBUTE 1

partner *n* one that is associated in any action with another <*partners* in crime>
syn associate, cohort, confrere, consociate, co-partner, fellow, mate, ‖pard
rel assistant, helper, sidekick; bedfellow, buddy, chum, companion, comrade, crony, pal

partnership *n syn* see ASSOCIATION 1
rel consociation, fellowship

parturient *adj syn* see PREGNANT 1

parturition *n syn* see BIRTH 1

party *n* **1** *syn* see COMBINATION 2
rel alliance, union; side
2 *syn* see PARTICIPANT
3 *syn* see HUMAN
4 *syn* see GROUP 1
5 *syn* see COMPANY 4
6 *syn* see ORGY 2

party girl *n* **1** *syn* see DOXY 1
2 *syn* see PROSTITUTE

parvenu *n syn* see UPSTART
idiom codfish aristocrat, pig in clover

‖**pash** *vb syn* see SHATTER 1

‖**pash** *n syn* see INFATUATION

pass *vb* **1** *syn* see GO 1
rel jog, ‖mog
2 *syn* see DIE 1
idiom pass on to the Great Beyond
con linger
3 to move or come to a termination or end <as time *passes*, the pain too will *pass*>
syn elapse, expire, go, pass away
rel slip (by); roll (on); fade (away), peter (out); cease, close, discontinue, end, stop, terminate
con continue; linger
4 *syn* see HAPPEN 1

idiom come to pass
5 *syn* see SURPASS 1
idiom leave way behind, shoot ahead of
6 *syn* see SPEND 3
7 *syn* see NEGLECT
8 *syn* see PROMISE 1
9 to transfer by hand from one person to another <*pass* the salt>
syn buck, hand, reach, ‖shoot
rel give; fork (over)

pass (as *or* for) *vb syn* see POSE 4

pass (on) *vb syn* see HAND DOWN

pass (over) *vb syn* see TRAVEL 2

pass *n syn* see JUNCTURE 2

passable *adj* capable of being passed, crossed, or traveled <*passable* roads>
syn navigable, negotiable, travelable
rel open, unblocked; ‖motorable; accessible, attainable, reachable
con blocked, closed; unnavigable; inaccessible, unattainable, unreachable
ant impassable

passably *adv syn* see ENOUGH 2

passage *n* **1** movement or transference from one place or point to another <air *passage* from New York to London> <the *passage* of current through a wire>
syn transit, travel
rel traject, trajet, traverse, traversing; transfer, transference, transmission, transmittal, transmittance
2 *syn* see TRANSITION
3 *syn* see WAY 2
4 a typically long narrow way connecting parts of a building <the office building contained endless *passages*>
syn corridor, couloir, hall, hallway, passageway
rel areaway

passageway *n syn* see PASSAGE 3

pass away *vb* **1** *syn* see DIE 1
2 *syn* see PASS 3

pass by *vb syn* see NEGLECT

passé *adj* **1** *syn* see OBSOLETE
2 *syn* see OLD-FASHIONED
ant a la mode

passed master *n syn* see EXPERT

passel *n syn* see GROUP 3

passing *n syn* see DEATH 1

passing *adj syn* see TRANSIENT
con lingering

passion *n* **1** *syn* see DISTRESS
2 *syn* see DESIRE 1
rel coveting; aiming, aspiring, panting
3 *syn* see FEELING 3
ant dispassion
4 *syn* see TEMPER 4
rel outbreak, outburst
5 *syn* see LOVE 2
rel heartthrob
6 intense, high-wrought emotion that compels to action <the *passion* of an evangelist>
syn ardor, calenture, enthusiasm, fervor, fire, hurrah, zeal
rel dedication, devotion; eagerness, lust; lyricism; ecstasy, rapture, transport; fury, rage

7 *syn* see LUST 2
rel amorousness; sensuality, sensuousness
8 *syn* see INFATUATION
passionate *adj* **1 *syn*** see IRASCIBLE
2 *syn* see IMPASSIONED
rel excited, quickened, stimulated; high-powered, high-pressure, steamed up; headlong, impetuous, precipitate
ant dispassionate
3 *syn* see LUSTFUL 2
rel steamy, sultry
ant passionless
passionless *adj* *syn* see FRIGID 3
rel detached, impassive, unsusceptible; unaffected, unmoved; apathetic, indifferent, uncaring, unconcerned, unfeeling; cold-blooded, cold-hearted, frozen, heartless
ant passionate, passionful
passive *adj* **1 *syn*** see INACTIVE
rel apathetic, impassive, phlegmatic, stolid
ant active
2 receiving or enduring without resistance <a *passive* acceptance of her fate>
syn acquiescent, nonresistant, nonresisting, resigned, submissive, unresistant, unresisting, yielding
rel bearing, enduring, patient; compliant, docile, tractable; nonviolent
con resistant, resisting, unresigned, unsubmissive, unyielding
pass off *vb* **1 *syn*** see FOIST 3
2 *syn* see POSE 4
pass on *vb* *syn* see COMMUNICATE 1
pass out *vb* **1 *syn*** see FAINT
2 *syn* see DIE 1
pass over *vb* *syn* see NEGLECT
passport *n* a means of entry into a desirable group, society, or condition of life <her skill at sports was a *passport* to fame and fortune>
syn key, open sesame, password, ticket
password *n* **1** a word or phrase that must be spoken by a person before he may pass a guard <give the *password* before entering the fort>
syn countersign, watchword, word
rel tessera
2 *syn* see PASSPORT
3 something (as a short phrase) used as a sign of recognition among members of the same society, class, or group <a fraternity that has secret handshakes and *passwords*>
syn watchword, word
past *adj* **1 *syn*** see PRECEDING
2 *syn* see FORMER 2
rel bypast, gone-by; late, previous
ant present
past *prep* **1 *syn*** see BEYOND 1
rel by
ant before
2 *syn* see BEYOND 2
past *n* former time <reminisced about the *past*>
syn foretime, ‖lang syne, yesterday, yesteryear, yore; *compare* PRESENT
rel antiquity
idiom bygone days (*or* times), days gone by, the good old days

con here and now; tomorrow
ant present; future
paste *vb* *syn* see BEAT 1
idiom give one a pasting
‖**paste** *n* *syn* see CUFF
pasticcio *n* *syn* see MISCELLANY 1
pastiche *n* *syn* see MISCELLANY 1
past master *n* *syn* see EXPERT
pastoral *adj* *syn* see RURAL
rel agrarian
patch *vb* *syn* see MEND 2
patchwork *n* *syn* see MISCELLANY 1
patchy *adj* *syn* see SPOTTY 1
pate *n* *syn* see HEAD 1
patent *adj* **1 *syn*** see OPEN 1
2 *syn* see CLEAR 5
rel prominent; flagrant, glaring, gross, rank
idiom patently obvious
con impalpable, imperceptible, insensible; concealed, hidden, secreted
ant latent
‖**pater** *n* *syn* see FATHER 1
path *n* **1 *syn*** see TRAIL
2 *syn* see WAY 1
3 *syn* see WAY 2
pathetic *adj* *syn* see PITIFUL 1
pathos *n* a quality that moves one to pity and sorrow <the *pathos* of the play was rarely offset by moments of comedy>
syn poignance, poignancy
rel bathos
pathway *n* *syn* see TRAIL
patience *n* the power or capacity to endure without complaint something difficult or disagreeable <it took a lot of *patience* to put up with him>
syn forbearance, longanimity, long-suffering, patientness, resignation, uncomplainingness
rel composure, cool, equanimity, imperturbability, self-control; endurance, sufferance, suffering, tolerance, toleration; nonresistance, passiveness, passivity, submission, submissiveness
con fretfulness; restiveness, restlessness; hastiness; rebellion, resistance
ant impatience
patientness *n* *syn* see PATIENCE
patois *n* **1 *syn*** see VERNACULAR 3
2 *syn* see DIALECT 2
patriarch *n* **1** *syn* see FATHER 2
2 *syn* see GAFFER
patriarchal *adj* *syn* see VENERABLE 1
patrician *n* *syn* see GENTLEMAN 1
ant plebeian
patriciate *n* *syn* see ARISTOCRACY
ant plebs
patrimony *n* *syn* see HERITAGE 1
patriot *n* **1** a person who loves his country and supports its interests <*patriots* who asked what they could do for their country>

---

syn synonym(s) ***rel*** related word(s)
ant antonym(s) ***con*** contrasted word(s)
idiom idiomatic equivalent(s)
‖ use limited; if in doubt, see a dictionary

syn loyalist
rel nationalist
ant traitor
2 *syn* see PATRIOTEER
3 *syn* see PARTISAN 2

patrioteer *n* one who is ostentatiously and chauvinistically patriotic <bloodthirsty *patrioteers* immersed in political witch-hunts>
syn flag-waver, patriot, superpatriot
rel jingo, jingoist

patrolman *n* *syn* see POLICEMAN

patron *n* **1** *syn* see PATRON SAINT
2 *syn* see SPONSOR
ant client; protégé
3 *syn* see CUSTOMER

patronage *n* **1** *syn* see BACKING
rel benefaction, guardianship, protection; subsidy
2 commercial transactions of customers and patrons <developed a large *patronage* by offering fair prices and courteous service>
syn business, custom, trade, traffic
rel clientage, clientele
3 the power to make appointments to government jobs on a basis other than merit alone <ousted his enemies from office and used *patronage* to support his policies>
syn pork-barreling
rel cronyism

patron saint *n* a saint to whose protection and intercession a person, society, church, or place is dedicated <Saint Christopher is the *patron saint* of travelers>
syn avowry, patron
rel titular; guardian angel

patsy *n* **1** *syn* see SCAPEGOAT
2 *syn* see FOOL 3

patter *vb* *syn* see CHAT 1

patter *n* *syn* see DIALECT 2

pattern *n* **1** *syn* see MODEL 2
rel original
2 *syn* see FIGURE 3
rel patterning
3 *syn* see ORDER 8
rel arrangement, constellation

paucity *n* *syn* see SCARCITY
rel fewness

Paul Pry *n* *syn* see BUSYBODY

paunch *n* **1** *syn* see ABDOMEN
2 *syn* see POTBELLY

paunch *vb* *syn* see EVISCERATE

pauper *n* a person having no financial resources except those derived from charity
syn beggar, down-and-out
rel have-not, indigent; ‖casual; almsman, lazarus
con have, millionaire, plutocrat

pauper *vb* *syn* see RUIN 3

pauperism *n* *syn* see POVERTY 1

pauperize *vb* *syn* see RUIN 3

pausation *n* *syn* see PAUSE

pause *n* a temporary cessation of activity or of an activity <a *pause* in the conversation>
syn comma, interval, lull, pausation; *compare* BREAK 4, GAP 3

rel caesura, hush, lapse, letup, suspension; interlude, intermission; recess, respite; wait; break, gap, interruption; cessation, ‖deval
con continuation, progression

paw *vb* *syn* see TOUCH 1

paw *adj* **1** *syn* see NAUGHTY 1
2 *syn* see OBSCENE 2

pawn *n* *syn* see PLEDGE 1

pawn *vb* to give or deposit as security for the payment of a loan or debt or for the fulfillment of an obligation <had to *pawn* all her jewels>
syn ‖dip, hock, impignorate, mortgage, pledge, ‖pop, ‖spout
ant redeem

pawn *n* *syn* see TOOL 2

pay *vb* **1** to discharge an obligation to usually with money <*paid* the doctor for his services>
syn compensate, guerdon, remunerate
rel indemnify, recompense, satisfy; cough (up), plunk down, pony (up), pungle (up), remit, render, tender; pay off
2 *syn* see CLEAR 5
3 *syn* see SPEND 1
4 *syn* see COMPENSATE 3
idiom make up for
5 *syn* see YIELD 5

pay *n* *syn* see WAGE

payable *adj* **1** *syn* see DUE 2
ant unpayable
2 *syn* see UNPAID 2

pay envelope *n* *syn* see WAGE

paying *adj* *syn* see ADVANTAGEOUS 1
rel productive; sound; solvent

payload *n* *syn* see LOAD 1

pay up *vb* *syn* see CLEAR 5

PDQ *adv* *syn* see AWAY 3

peaceable *adj* *syn* see PACIFIC
rel amicable, friendly, neighborly; amiable, complaisant
ant acrimonious; contentious; warlike

peaceful *adj* *syn* see PACIFIC
rel collected, composed, cool, unruffled; constant, equable, steady
con agitated, discomposed, disquieted, disturbed, perturbed, upset

peacemaker *n* one that makes or seeks to make peace <a president who was remembered as a great *peacemaker*>
syn make-peace, pacificator
rel arbitrator, mediator, negotiator; placater; appeaser, peacemonger; peacekeeper
con chauvinist, jingo, jingoist, militarist, war dog, warmonger; peacebreaker

peace officer *n* *syn* see POLICEMAN

peach *n* *syn* ‖DILLY, crackerjack, ‖daisy, dandy, humdinger, jim-dandy, ‖lalapalooza, ‖lulu, nifty, ‖pip
rel pearl

peach *vb* *syn* see INFORM 3

peachy *adj* *syn* see MARVELOUS 2

peacock *vb* *syn* see LORD

peacockish *adj* *syn* see SHOWY

peacocky *adj* *syn* see SHOWY

peak *n* **1** *syn* see VISOR 1

2 *syn* see TOP 1

3 *syn* see MOUNTAIN 1

4 *syn* see APEX 2

peak (out) *vb syn* see DECREASE

peaked *adj syn* see POINTED 1

peaked *adj syn* see SICKLY 2

‖**peaking** *adj syn* see SICKLY 2

peaky *adj syn* see POINTED 1

peaky *adj syn* see SICKLY 2

peal *vb syn* see RING

peanut *adj syn* see PETTY 2

‖**peart** *adj syn* see LIVELY 1

‖**pearten** (up) *vb syn* see ENCOURAGE 1

peasant *n syn* see RUSTIC

peck *n syn* see MUCH

peck *vb* **1** to strike at or pick up with the beak <a hen *pecking* the scattered grain from the ground>

syn beak, pick

2 *syn* see KISS 1

peck (at) *vb syn* see NAG

pecker *n* **1 *syn*** see BILL 1

2 *syn* see NOSE 1

‖**peckish** *adj syn* see HUNGRY

pecksniffery *n syn* see HYPOCRISY

pecksniffian *adj syn* see HYPOCRITICAL

peculate *vb syn* see EMBEZZLE

peculiar *adj* **1 *syn*** see CHARACTERISTIC

rel unique

2 *syn* see STRANGE 4

rel uncustomary

con normal

peculiarity *n syn* see QUALITY 1

pecuniary *adj syn* see FINANCIAL

pedantic *adj* too narrowly concerned with scholarly matters <intellectual life that was *pedantic* rather than broad and humane>

syn academic, bookish, book-learned, booky, quodlibetic, scholastic

rel erudite, learned; didactic, donnish, inkhorn, schoolish, schoolteacherish; arid, dry, dryas-dust, dull

ant unpedantic

peddle *vb* **1 *syn*** see PUSH 6

2 to sell or offer for sale from place to place <*peddled* fish from a pushcart>

syn hawk, huckster, monger, vend

rel sell; push

peddler *n* one who travels about with merchandise to sell <*peddlers* were once common in rural areas>

syn ‖arab, cheap-jack (*or* cheap-john), ‖duffer, hawker, higgler, huckster, monger, mongerer, outcrier, packman, piepoudre, roadman, vendor

rel colporteur, costermonger; pusher

peddling *adj syn* see PETTY 2

pedestal *vb syn* see EXALT 1

pedestrian *adj syn* see DULL 9

rel commonplace, platitudinous, truistic; banal, inane, jejune, wishy-washy; heavy

pedigree *n* **1 *syn*** see GENEALOGY

2 *syn* see ANCESTRY

pedigree *adj syn* see PUREBRED

pedigreed *adj syn* see PUREBRED

peek (in *or* out) *vb syn* see PEEP

peek *n syn* see PEEP

peel *vb* **1 *syn*** see SKIN 2

2 *syn* see SCALE 2

peeled *adj syn* see OPEN 2

peeler *n* **1 *syn*** see STRIPTEASER

2 *syn* see HUSTLER

‖**peeler** *n syn* see POLICEMAN

peep *vb syn* see CHIRP

rel pip

peep *vb* to peer through or as if through a hole or crevice <*peeped* cautiously under the bed>

syn peek (in *or* out)

rel glance; look; peer, stare

idiom take a peep (*or* peek)

peep *n* a brief and sometimes furtive look <take a *peep* at the new neighbors>

syn ‖gander, glance, glimpse, peek

rel look-over, look-see; oeillade, ogle; stare

peeper *n* **1 *syn*** see PEEPING TOM

2 *syn* see EYE 1

peeping tom *n* a pruriently prying person <a *peeping tom* spying on the couple>

syn peeper, voyeur

rel prowler, snoop, snooper

idiom porch climber, window (*or* transom) peeper

‖**peepy** *adj syn* see SLEEPY 1

peer *vb syn* see GAZE 1

rel eye, rubberneck; pry, snoop

peerless *adj syn* see ALONE 3

rel dominant, paramount, predominant, sovereign

peery *adj syn* see CURIOUS 2

peeve *vb syn* see IRRITATE

rel disturb; miff

idiom make one hot under the collar

peevish *adj syn* see IRRITABLE

rel captious, carping, caviling, critical, fault-finding

idiom being in a peeve

peewee *n syn* see DWARF

peewee *adj syn* see TINY

‖**peg** *n syn* see DRINK 3

‖**pegh** *vb syn* see PANT 1

peg out *vb* **1 *syn*** see COLLAPSE 2

2 *syn* see DIE 1

pejorative *adj syn* see DEROGATORY

con acclaiming, extolling, lauding, praising; aggrandizing, exalting, magnifying

pelf *n* **1 *syn*** see MONEY

‖**2 *syn*** see REFUSE

pell–mell *adv* in or as if in confused haste <barged in *pell-mell* without thinking>

syn helter-skelter, hotfoot, hurry-scurry, impetuously, incontinently

rel hurriedly; indiscreetly; carelessly, heedlessly, rashly, thoughtlessly

idiom on the spur of the moment

---

syn synonym(s)   *rel* related word(s)

ant antonym(s)   *con* contrasted word(s)

idiom idiomatic equivalent(s)

‖ use limited; if in doubt, see a dictionary

pell–mell *n syn* see CONFUSION 3
pell–mell *vb syn* see STAMPEDE 2
pellucid *adj* **1** *syn* see TRANSPARENT 1
 rel sheer
 con muddy, roily, turbid
 2 *syn* see CLEAR 4
pelt *n syn* see HIDE
pelt *vb* **1** *syn* see BEAT 1
 2 *syn* see HURRY 2
pen *vb syn* see ENCLOSE 1
 ant unpen
pen *n syn* see JAIL
penalize *vb* to inflict a penalty on <*penalize* a delinquent taxpayer with a stiff fine>
 syn amerce, fine, mulct
 rel castigate, chasten, chastise, correct, discipline, punish; condemn; judge
penalty *n syn* see FINE
penance *n syn* see PENITENCE
penchant *n syn* see LEANING 2
‖**pend** *vb syn* see DEPEND (on *or* upon) 1
pendant *n* **1** *syn* see FLAG
 2 *syn* see COUNTERPART 1
pendent *adj* **1** *syn* see SUSPENDED
 2 *syn* see PENDING
pending *adj* not yet settled or decided <a claim
still *pending*>
 syn pendent, undecided, undetermined, unsettled
 idiom hanging in the balance, in suspense, up in
the air
 con decided, determined, settled
 ant closed
pendulant *adj syn* see SUSPENDED
pendulate *vb syn* see SWING 2
pendulous *adj* **1** *syn* see SUSPENDED
 2 *syn* see VACILLATING 2
penetrable *adj syn* see PERMEABLE
 ant impenetrable
penetrate *vb* **1** *syn* see ENTER 1
 rel encroach, invade, trespass
 2 to enter or go through by or as if by overcoming resistance <the icy wind *penetrated* the
heavy parka>
 syn pierce
 rel bore, perforate, prick, puncture; jab, knife,
stab; drill, drive
 3 *syn* see PERMEATE
 rel insert, insinuate, interpolate, introduce
penetrating *adj* **1** *syn* see INCISIVE
 rel penetrant, penetrative
 2 *syn* see SHARP 4
penetration *n syn* see WIT 3
 rel penetrativeness
penetrative *adj syn* see SHARP 4
penitence *n* regret for sin or wrongdoing <re-
sponded to true *penitence* with forgiveness>
 syn attrition, compunction, contriteness, contrition, penance, penitency, remorse, remorsefulness, repentance, rue, ruth
 rel qualm, scruple; self-accusation, self-castigation, self-punishment, self-reproach, self-reproof; anguish, distress, grief, regret, sadness,
sorrow; debasement, degradation, humbling,
humiliation

 con adamancy, inexorableness, obduracy, obdurateness, stubbornness
penitency *n syn* see PENITENCE
penitent *adj syn* see REMORSEFUL
penitential *adj syn* see REMORSEFUL
penitentiary *n syn* see JAIL
 idiom correctional institution
penmanship *n syn* see HANDWRITING
pennant *n syn* see FLAG
pennilessness *n syn* see POVERTY 1
pennon *n syn* see FLAG
penny dreadful *n syn* see DIME NOVEL
penny pincher *n syn* see MISER
penny–pinching *adj syn* see STINGY
penny–wise *adj syn* see STINGY
pennyworth *n syn* see BARGAIN
pensile *adj syn* see SUSPENDED
pension (off) *vb syn* see RETIRE 2
pensive *adj* **1** *syn* see THOUGHTFUL 1
 rel musing, ruminating
 2 being musingly sad and thoughtful <gazed out
the window with a *pensive* expression on her
face>
 syn meditative, ‖pensy, wistful
 rel absorbed, abstracted, contemplative, musing, preoccupied, thoughtful, withdrawn; blue,
melancholy, sad, saddened
 con alert, aware, interested, outgoing
‖**pensy** *adj* **1** *syn* see PENSIVE 2
 2 *syn* see THOUGHTFUL 1
 3 *syn* see SQUEAMISH 1
penumbra *n syn* see SHADE 1
penurious *adj* **1** *syn* see POOR 1
 2 *syn* see STINGY
penury *n syn* see POVERTY 1
 ant luxury
peon *n syn* see SLAVE 2
peonage *n syn* see BONDAGE
people *n* **1** *syn* see SOCIETY 3
 2 *syn* see COMMONALTY
people *vb syn* see INHABIT
pep *n* **1** *syn* see ENERGY 2
 2 *syn* see VIGOR 2
pepper *vb syn* see SPECKLE 1
peppery *adj* **1** *syn* see PUNGENT
 2 *syn* see IRASCIBLE
 3 *syn* see SPIRITED 2
 rel pepperish; alert, keen, lively, peppy
peppy *adj syn* see LIVELY 1
per *prep syn* see VIA 2
‖**per** *adv syn* see APIECE
perambulant *adj syn* see ITINERANT
perambulate *vb syn* see TRAVERSE 5
‖**perambulator** *n syn* see BABY CARRIAGE
perambulatory *adj syn* see ITINERANT
per capita *adv syn* see APIECE
per caput *adv syn* see APIECE
perceive *vb syn* see SEE 1
 rel divine, identify, realize, recognize; grasp,
seize, take; apprehend
perceptible *adj* apprehensible as real or existent
<a *perceptible* change in attitude>
 syn appreciable, detectable, discernible, observable, palpable, sensible, tangible; *compare* TANGI-
BLE 1

rel distinguishable, recognizable; cognizable, understandable; clear, lucid, perspicuous; conspicuous, noticeable, signal
con impalpable, indiscernible, intangible, invisible, unappreciable, undetectable, undiscernible, unnoticeable, unobservable
ant imperceptible
perception *n syn* see IDEA
perceptive *adj* **1** *syn* see ACUTE 3
rel responsive
ant imperceptive, unperceptive
2 *syn* see WISE 1
rel prehensile, prehensive, prehensorial
ant imperceptive, unperceptive
perch *vb syn* see ALIGHT
perchance *adv syn* see PERHAPS
percipience *n syn* see WIT 3
percolate *vb* **1** *syn* see PERMEATE
2 *syn* see EXUDE
per contra *adv syn* see HOWEVER
percussion *n syn* see IMPACT 1
rel percussiveness
perdition *n syn* see HELL
perdurable *adj* **1** *syn* see LASTING
ant fleeting
2 *syn* see INFINITE 1
perdure *vb syn* see CONTINUE 1
perduring *adj syn* see LASTING
ant fleeting
peregrination *n, usu* **peregrinations** *pl syn* see JOURNEY
peremptory *adj syn* see MASTERFUL 1
rel certain, positive; decided, decisive; absolute, fixed, uncompromising; obstinate
perennial *adj syn* see OLD 2
rel durable, perdurable
perfect *adj* **1** *syn* see WHOLE 1
ant imperfect
2 being entirely without flaw and meeting supreme standards of excellence <a ballerina whose technique was *perfect*>
syn absolute, flawless, fleckless, impeccable, indefectible, note-perfect, unflawed; *compare* CONSUMMATE 1
rel excellent; consummate; expert, finished, masterful, masterly
con defective, faulty, flawed; deficient, inadequate, wanting; unfinished, unpolished; unsound
ant imperfect
3 precisely appropriate or right <found the *perfect* gift for him>
syn ideal, model, very
rel needed, required, requisite; appropriate, fit, proper, right, suitable; exact, express, precise
idiom being just the thing
con foolish, inappropriate, undesirable, unsuitable
4 *syn* see PURE 2
5 *syn* see WHOLE 3
rel consummate
6 *syn* see UTTER
perfect *vb syn* see POLISH 2
perfected *adj syn* see CONSUMMATE 1

ant unperfected
perfectibilian *n syn* see PERFECTIONIST
perfectibilist *n syn* see PERFECTIONIST
perfection *n* **1** *syn* see INTEGRITY 2
2 *syn* see EXCELLENCE
ant imperfection
perfectionist *n* one that demands or works to achieve perfection <a *perfectionist* who rehearsed one scene fifty times>
syn perfectibilian, perfectibilist, perfectist
rel precisian, precisionist, stickler
perfectist *n syn* see PERFECTIONIST
perfectly *adv syn* see WELL 3
perfervid *adj syn* see IMPASSIONED
rel enhanced, heightened, intensified
perfidious *adj syn* see FAITHLESS
rel mercenary, venal; alienated, disaffected, estranged; deceitful, dishonest
perfidiousness *n* **1** *syn* see INFIDELITY
2 *syn* see TREACHERY
perfidy *n* **1** *syn* see TREACHERY
rel foul play
idiom Judas' kiss
ant fealty
2 *syn* see INFIDELITY
rel betrayal, sellout
perforate *vb* to pierce through so as to leave a hole <*perforate* a sheet of postage stamps>
syn bore, drill, prick, ‖pritch, punch, puncture
rel pit; probe; drive, penetrate, pierce
perforce *adv syn* see WILLY-NILLY
perform *vb* **1** *syn* see FULFILL 1
2 to carry something (as a process) to a successful conclusion <*perform* a surgical procedure>
syn achieve, do, execute; *compare* EFFECT 2
rel accomplish, bring off; complete, end, finish, wind up
idiom carry to completion (*or* a successful conclusion), do to a turn, do up brown
3 *syn* see ACT 1
4 *syn* see ACT 5
performance *n syn* see EFFICIENCY 1
performer *n syn* see ACTOR 1
perfume *n syn* see FRAGRANCE
perfume *vb syn* see SCENT 2
perfumed *adj syn* see SWEET 2
perfumy *adj syn* see SWEET 2
perfunctory *adj* characterized by routine and often done merely as a duty <gave her his usual *perfunctory* nod>
syn automatic, mechanical
rel cursory, superficial; involuntary, unaware; routine, usual; standard, stock; cool, impersonal, indifferent; wooden; unconcerned, uninterested
con cordial, friendly, genial, hearty, warm
pergola *n syn* see ARBOR
perhaps *adv* conceivably but not certainly so <*perhaps* this is true, but I think it's debatable>

---

syn synonym(s)	*rel* related word(s)
ant antonym(s)	*con* contrasted word(s)
idiom idiomatic equivalent(s)	
‖ use limited; if in doubt, see a dictionary	

syn maybe, perchance, possibly
rel conceivably, feasibly, imaginably
idiom as it may be, as the case may be, for all one knows
con certainly, definitely, doubtlessly, surely, undoubtedly, unquestionably
perhaps *n syn* see THEORY 2
periapt *n syn* see CHARM 2
peril *n syn* see DANGER
rel exposure, liability, openness, subjection; endangerment
idiom cause for alarm, rocks (*or* breakers) ahead
peril *vb syn* see ENDANGER
perilous *adj syn* see DANGEROUS 1
rel shaky, tottery, unstable, unsteady; delicate, ticklish, touchy
perimeter *n* **1** *syn* see CIRCUMFERENCE
2 *syn* see BORDER 1
period *n* **1** *syn* see END 2
2 an extent of time set off or typified by someone or something <the Victorian *period*><a *period* of expansion>
syn age, day(s), epoch, era, time
periodic *adj syn* see INTERMITTENT
rel on-again-off-again
periodical *adj syn* see INTERMITTENT
periodical *n syn* see JOURNAL
peripatetic *adj syn* see ITINERANT
periphery *n* **1** *syn* see CIRCUMFERENCE
2 *syn* see BORDER 1
periphrase *n syn* see VERBIAGE 1
periphrasis *n syn* see VERBIAGE 1
perish *vb* **1** *syn* see DIE 1
ant survive
2 to suffer spiritual or moral death <nations *perishing* for lack of true leaders>
syn die
rel decline; collapse, go under; expire, succumb; disappear, vanish; cease, end
con flourish, prosper, thrive
ant endure
‖**3** *syn* see DECAY
perishing *adj syn* see DAMNED 2
perjure *vb* to make a false swearer of oneself by violating one's oath to tell the truth <a *perjured* witness>
syn forswear
rel equivocate; deceive, delude, mislead, trick; lie, prevaricate
idiom commit perjury, lie under oath, swear falsely
perjurer *n syn* see LIAR
perk (up) *vb syn* see IMPROVE 3
‖**perk** *n, usu* **perks** *pl syn* see GRATUITY
perlustrate *vb syn* see SCRUTINIZE 1
perlustration *n syn* see EXAMINATION
permanent *adj syn* see LASTING
rel imperishable, invariable
ant temporary
permeable *adj* capable of being permeated especially by fluids <a *permeable* membrane>
syn penetrable, pervious, porose, porous
rel passable
con impassable, impenetrable, impervious

ant impermeable
permeate *vb* to pass or cause to pass through every part of a thing <air *permeated* with cigar smoke>
syn charge, compenetrate, impenetrate, impregnate, interfuse, interpenetrate, penetrate, percolate, pervade, saturate, transfuse
rel invade; imbrue, imbue, infiltrate, infuse, ingrain; diffuse, suffuse; drench, soak, steep; fill
permissible *adj* that may be permitted <a *permissible* error>
syn admissible, allowable
rel unforbidden, unprohibited; allowed, permitted, tolerated; approved, authorized, endorsed, sanctioned; acceptable, bearable, tolerable
con banned, forbidden, disallowed, prohibited, unpermitted, verboten; unacceptable, unbearable
ant impermissible
permission *n* a sanctioning to act or do something that is granted by one in authority <received *permission* to leave work early>
syn allowance, authorization, consent, leave, permit, sanction, sufferance
rel acceptance, acquiescence; approbation, approval; endorsement
ant prohibition
permit *vb syn* see LET 2
rel tolerate
idiom give one his head
ant forbid, prohibit
permit *n syn* see PERMISSION
permutation *n syn* see CHANGE 2
rel alteration, modification
pernicious *adj* exceedingly harmful or destructive <*pernicious* gossip>
syn baneful, deadly, noxious, pestiferous, pestilent, pestilential; *compare* DEADLY 1
rel damaging, deleterious, detrimental, harmful, hurtful; baleful, malefic, maleficent, malign, sinister; miasmatic, miasmic, poisonous, toxic, venomous; malignant, swart, virulent; destructive, devastating, ruinous; fatal, killing, lethal, mortal
con harmless, uninjurious; nonmalignant, nonpoisonous, nontoxic
ant innocuous
pernickety *adj syn* see NICE 1
perorate *vb syn* see ORATE
perpend *vb syn* see CONSIDER 1
perpendicular *adj syn* see VERTICAL
rel stand-up, straight
ant horizontal
perpendicularity *n syn* see VERTICALITY
rel erectness, uprightness
ant horizontality
perpetrate *vb syn* see COMMIT 2
rel effect; inflict, wreak
idiom ‖up and do
perpetual *adj syn* see CONTINUAL
ant ephemeral, transient
perpetually *adv syn* see ALWAYS 1
perpetuate *vb* to make perpetual or cause to last indefinitely <*perpetuate* his memory for future generations>

syn eternalize, eternize, immortalize
rel bolster, conserve, keep, maintain, preserve, secure, support, sustain
con annihilate, blot out, erase, expunge
ant obliterate
perplex *vb* **1** *syn* see PUZZLE
rel discompose, perturb; balk, thwart; astonish, astound, surprise
idiom put (*or* drive) to one's wit's end
2 *syn* see COMPLICATE
3 *syn* see ENTANGLE 1
perquisite *n* **1** *syn* see GRATUITY
2 *syn* see RIGHT 2
per se *adv* by, of, or in itself or oneself or themselves <not opposed to the death penalty *per se*>
syn as such, intrinsically
rel alone, independently, solely
persecute *vb* **1** *syn* see WRONG
rel dragoon, rack, torment, torture
con back, champion, support, uphold
2 *syn* see MOLEST
rel worry; hound, ride
con humor, indulge, pamper; accommodate, favor, oblige
perseverant *adj* *syn* see PERSISTENT 1
perseverative *adj* *syn* see PERSISTENT 1
persevere *vb* to continue in a state, enterprise, or undertaking in spite of counter influences, opposition, or discouragement <*persevered* in her unpopular economic policy>
syn carry on, go on, hang on, persist
rel continue, get on, press (on), proceed
idiom hang in there, hang tough, keep at it, keep driving, never say die, stick (*or* tough) it out
con falter, hesitate, vacillate, waver; renounce, surrender, yield
ant give up
persevering *adj* *syn* see PERSISTENT 1
persiflage *n* *syn* see BANTER
persist *vb* **1** *syn* see PERSEVERE
con cease, discontinue, quit, stop
ant desist
2 *syn* see CONTINUE 1
rel go on; linger; obtain, prevail
ant desist
persistence *n* **1** *syn* see CONTINUATION 1
2 *syn* see RUN 2
rel course
persistent *adj* **1** continuing in a course of action without regard to discouragement, opposition, or previous failure <a *persistent* suitor>
syn dogged, insistent, perseverant, perseverative, persevering, persisting, persistive
rel determined, steadfast, tenacious, unshakable; relentless, unremitting
con malleable, pliant, tractable, yielding; infirm, invertebrate, spineless; vacillating, wavery, wobbling
2 *syn* see PRIMITIVE 3
persisting *adj* *syn* see PERSISTENT 1
persistive *adj* *syn* see PERSISTENT 1
persnickety *adj* *syn* see NICE 1
person *n* *syn* see HUMAN
rel chap, ‖cookie, coot, fellow, galoot, guy, specimen, stick

personage *n* **1** *syn* see NOTABLE 1
2 *syn* see HUMAN
personal *adj* **1** of, relating to, or affecting a particular person <owed his *personal* allegiance to his wife>
syn individual
rel particular, peculiar, special
con general, universal; common, joint, mutual, shared; commonplace, everyday, ordinary
2 *syn* see PRIVATE 1
personal effects *n pl* privately owned items (as clothing and toilet articles) normally worn or carried on the person <packed his *personal effects* in a small bag>
syn ‖plunder, stuff, things, traps, tricks
rel belongings, goods, possessions
idiom personal belongings
personality *n* **1** *syn* see INDIVIDUALITY 4
2 *syn* see DISPOSITION 3
3 *syn* see NOTABLE 1
personalize *vb* **1** *syn* see EMBODY 1
rel anthropomorphize
2 *syn* see REPRESENT 2
personal name *n* *syn* see GIVEN NAME
personate *vb* **1** *syn* see ACT 1
2 *syn* see REPRESENT 2
personification *n* *syn* see EMBODIMENT
personify *vb* **1** *syn* see EMBODY 1
rel reincarnate
2 *syn* see REPRESENT 2
personize *vb* *syn* see EMBODY 1
perspective *n* *syn* see VISTA
perspicacious *adj* *syn* see SHREWD
rel quick-sighted, sharp-sighted, sharp-witted
perspicacity *n* *syn* see WIT 3
perspicuity *n* *syn* see CLARITY
rel intelligibility; explicitness
perspicuous *adj* *syn* see CLEAR 4
perspiring *adj* *syn* see SWEATY
perspiry *adj* *syn* see SWEATY
persuadable *adj* *syn* see RECEPTIVE 1
ant unpersuadable
persuade *vb* **1** *syn* see INDUCE 1
rel affect, impress, touch; reason; convert
con discourage, hinder, prevent
ant dissuade
2 *syn* see CONVERT 1
3 *syn* see ASSURE 2
ant dissuade
persuasible *adj* *syn* see RECEPTIVE 1
ant unpersuasible
persuasion *n* **1** *syn* see OPINION
rel bias, partiality, predilection, prejudice, prepossession
2 *syn* see RELIGION 1
3 *syn* see RELIGION 2
rel affiliation; order
4 *syn* see TYPE
pert *adj* **1** *syn* see SAUCY 1

---

syn synonym(s)   *rel* related word(s)
ant antonym(s)   *con* contrasted word(s)
idiom idiomatic equivalent(s)
‖ use limited; if in doubt, see a dictionary

rel bold, daring; audacious, brazen
con shy
ant coy
2 *syn* see WISE 5
rel disrespectful, rude
3 *syn* see LIVELY 1
pertain *vb* **1** *syn* see BELONG 2
2 *syn* see BEAR (on *or* upon)
rel associate, combine, connect, join
idiom be pertinent (*or* relevant) to
pertinacious *adj syn* see OBSTINATE
rel fixed, unshakable; dogged, tenacious
pertinent *adj syn* see RELEVANT
rel pertaining
ant impertinent
perturb *vb syn* see DISCOMPOSE 1
rel trouble; unsettle
ant compose
pervade *vb syn* see PERMEATE
idiom spread through and through
perverse *adj* **1** *syn* see VICIOUS 2
2 *syn* see OBSTINATE
rel cranky, irritable, unreasonable
3 *syn* see CONTRARY 3
pervert *vb* **1** *syn* see DEBASE 1
rel abuse, maltreat, mistreat, misuse, outrage;
ruin
2 *syn* see ABUSE 2
rel ill-treat
3 *syn* see MISREPRESENT
perverted *adj syn* see DEBASED
rel defiled, polluted, tainted; contorted, distorted, warped; abused, misused, outraged
pervicacious *adj syn* see OBSTINATE
pervious *adj syn* see PERMEABLE
ant impervious
pesky *adj syn* see TROUBLESOME
pesky *adv syn* see VERY 1
pessimist *n* one who emphasizes adverse aspects
or conditions and expects the worst <*pessimists*
predicting another depression>
syn calamity howler, Cassandra, crepehanger,
worrywart
rel fussbudget; Job's comforter; defeatist; killjoy; cynic, misanthrope
con positivist; idealist; Pollyanna
ant optimist
pest *n* **1** *syn* see ANNOYANCE 3
rel bane, trouble, vexation, worry
idiom pain in the neck, pea in the shoe, thorn in
the flesh
2 one who pesters or annoys <a little *pest* who
constantly asked questions>
syn nudnick, nuisance, pesterer
rel badgerer, heckler, tormentor
idiom pain in the neck
pester *vb syn* see WORRY 1
rel ride
idiom drive (one) crazy, drive (one) up the wall,
pester to death
pester *n syn* see ANNOYANCE 3
pesterer *n syn* see PEST 2
‖**pesterment** *n syn* see ANNOYANCE 3

pesticide *n* a chemical agent used to destroy pests
<the need to control indiscriminate use of *pesti-
cides*>
syn biocide, economic poison
rel bactericide, fungicide, germicide, insecticide,
microbicide, rodenticide, vermicide
pestiferous *adj syn* see PERNICIOUS
pestilence *n syn* see PLAGUE 1
pestilent *adj* **1** *syn* see DEADLY 1
2 *syn* see PERNICIOUS
pestilential *adj* **1** *syn* see DEADLY 1
2 *syn* see PERNICIOUS
pet *adj syn* see FAVORITE 1
pet *vb syn* see CARESS
rel embrace, hug
pet *vb syn* see SULK
petcock *n syn* see FAUCET
peter (out) *vb syn* see DECREASE
Peter Funk *n syn* see SWINDLER
petite *adj syn* see SMALL 1
rel diminutive, dwarf, lilliputian, miniature, wee
petition *n syn* see PRAYER
rel request
petition *vb* to make an earnest, formal, and often
written request <*petitioned* for a hearing before
the labor board>
syn appeal, sue (for *or* to)
rel ask, request; beg, beseech, entreat, implore,
plead, pray, supplicate
con claim, demand, exact, press (for)
petitioner *n syn* see SUPPLIANT
petit–maître *n syn* see FOP
petrify *vb syn* see DAZE 2
rel alarm, frighten, startle, terrify; appall, dismay, horrify; numb
idiom turn to stone
pettifogger *n* an unscrupulous lawyer <done out
of his rights by a slick *pettifogger*>
syn jackleg lawyer, shyster; *compare* LAWYER
rel ambulance chaser, Philadelphia lawyer;
‖bush lawyer
pettifogging *adj syn* see PETTY 2
pettish *adj syn* see IRRITABLE
petty *adj* **1** *syn* see LITTLE 3
2 being often contemptibly insignificant or
unimportant <*petty* quarrels and intrigues>
syn inconsequent, inconsequential, inconsiderable, measly, Mickey Mouse, niggling, paltry,
peanut, peddling, pettifogging, picayune, picayunish, piddling, piffling, pimping, puny, small,
trifling, trivial, unconsequential, unconsidered,
ungenerous, unvital; *compare* LITTLE 3
rel negligible, unimportant; hair-drawn, hairsplitting; impertinent, irrelevant
con consequential, considerable; big, gross; significant, vital
ant important, momentous
petulant *adj syn* see IRRITABLE
rel grouchy, sulky
phantasm *n* **1** *syn* see DELUSION 1
rel fabrication, fiction, invention
2 *syn* see APPARITION
3 *syn* see FANCY 4
phantom *n syn* see APPARITION

pharisaic *adj syn* see HYPOCRITICAL

pharisaical *adj syn* see HYPOCRITICAL

pharisaicalness *n syn* see HYPOCRISY

pharisaism *n syn* see HYPOCRISY

pharisee *n syn* see HYPOCRITE

pharmaceutic *n syn* see DRUG 1

pharmaceutical *n syn* see DRUG 1

pharmacist *n syn* see DRUGGIST

pharmacon *n syn* see REMEDY 1

pharos *n syn* see LIGHTHOUSE

phase *n* one of the possible ways of viewing or being presented to view <the moral *phase* of the problem>
  syn angle, aspect, facet, hand, side
  rel condition, situation, state; position, posture, view, viewpoint; appearance, look, semblance; color, complexion

phenomenal *adj* **1** *syn* see MATERIAL 1
  con ontic
  ant noumenal
  2 *syn* see EXCEPTIONAL 1

phenomenon *n* **1** *syn* see FACT 2
  rel experience; actuality, reality
  2 *syn* see WONDER 1
  rel abnormality; anomaly, paradox; peculiarity, singularity, uniqueness, unusualness

philander *n syn* see WOLF
  idiom ‖skirt chaser

philander *vb* to have many love affairs <his reputation for *philandering* with married women>
  syn fool (around), mess around, play (around), wolf, womanize
  rel dally, flirt, trifle; chase, pursue; ‖tomcat (around)
  idiom ‖chase skirts, play Don Juan, play the femmes

philanderer *n syn* see WOLF

philanthropic *adj syn* see CHARITABLE 1
  rel bighearted, freehearted, greathearted, kindhearted, largehearted, openhearted; contributing, donating, freehanded, giving, magnanimous; civic-minded, public-spirited
  ant misanthropic

philharmonic *n syn* see ORCHESTRA

philippic *n syn* see TIRADE

philistine *n* a crass, prosaic, often priggish individual guided by material rather than artistic or intellectual values <*philistines* who opposed everything new and creative in art>
  syn Babbitt, boeotian, boob, middlebrow
  rel bourgeois; capitalist; materialist; boor, clown, lout, vulgarian
  ant aesthete

phiz *n syn* see FACE 1

phlegm *n* **1** *syn* see APATHY 1
  2 *syn* see EQUANIMITY
  rel nonchalance, unconcern

phlegmatic *adj syn* see IMPASSIVE 1
  rel calm, undemonstrative; aloof, incurious, indifferent, unconcerned; lethargic, sluggish

phoebus *n syn* see SUN 1

phoenix *n syn* see PARAGON

phonate *vb syn* see ARTICULATE 2

phone *vb syn* see TELEPHONE

phony *adj syn* see COUNTERFEIT

phony *n* **1** *syn* see IMPOSTURE
  2 *syn* see IMPOSTOR

photo *vb syn* see PHOTOGRAPH
  idiom take a photo (of)

photog *n syn* see PHOTOGRAPHER

photograph *vb* to use a camera to make a picture, image, or likeness of <*photographed* the whole family>
  syn photo, shoot
  rel cinematize, ‖cinematograph, cinemize, film, filmize, picture; snap, snapshoot, snapshot; mug
  idiom capture on film, take a picture (*or* photograph)

photographer *n* one who takes photographs <a newspaper *photographer*>
  syn cameraman, camerist, photog, photographist, photoist
  rel snapshooter, ‖snapshotter; shutterbug; paparazzo; photojournalist

photographic *adj syn* see GRAPHIC 1
  rel accurate, detailed, exact

photographist *n syn* see PHOTOGRAPHER

photoist *n syn* see PHOTOGRAPHER

photoplay *n syn* see MOVIE

phrase *n* **1** *syn* see WORDING
  rel styling
  2 a group of words which, taken together, express a notion and may constitute part of a sentence <an adverbial *phrase*><a trite *phrase*>
  syn expression, locution
  rel phrasing; idiom; catchword, slogan
  3 *syn* see CATCHWORD

phrase *vb syn* see WORD

phraseology *n syn* see WORDING
  idiom choice of words

phrasing *n syn* see WORDING

phthisis *n syn* see TUBERCULOSIS

phylactery *n syn* see CHARM 2

physic *n syn* see REMEDY 1

physical *adj* **1** *syn* see MATERIAL 1
  rel natural; elemental, elementary
  ant spiritual
  2 *syn* see BODILY
  rel visceral; lusty; brute
  ant mental

physician *n* a doctor of medicine <the shortage of *physicians* in rural areas>
  syn ‖croaker, doc, doctor, MD, medical, mediciner, medico, ‖sawbones
  rel medic; general practitioner, practitioner; surgeon; specialist
  idiom medical doctor, medical man

physique *n* bodily makeup or type <a muscular *physique*>
  syn build, constitution, habit, habitus
  rel anatomy, structure; configuration, shape; body, figure, form, frame

picaroon *n syn* see PIRATE

---

syn synonym(s)   *rel* related word(s)
ant antonym(s)   *con* contrasted word(s)
idiom idiomatic equivalent(s)
‖ use limited; if in doubt, see a dictionary

picayune *adj syn* see PETTY 2
picayunish *adj syn* see PETTY 2
pick *vb* **1** *syn* see CHOOSE 1
  idiom pick and choose
  ant reject
  2 *syn* see PECK 1
pick *n syn* see BEST
pick *adj syn* see SELECT 1
picked *adj syn* see SELECT 1
picket *n syn* see GUARD 2
pickle *n syn* see PREDICAMENT
  idiom pretty pickle, ‖sticky wicket, tight spot
‖pickled *adj syn* see INTOXICATED 1
pick out *vb syn* see CHOOSE 1
pickpocket *n* one who steals from pockets <his
  wallet was lifted by a *pickpocket*>
  syn ‖cannon, cutpurse, ‖dip, ‖diver, purse cutter, ‖wire
  rel ‖ganef, thief; ‖mobsman, ‖swell-mobsman
  idiom ‖pocket prowler
picksome *adj syn* see NICE 1
pick up *vb* **1** *syn* see LIFT 1
  2 *syn* see GLEAN
  3 *syn* see GET 1
  4 *syn* see LEARN 1
  5 *syn* see ARREST 2
  rel book
  idiom ‖take (someone) downtown
  6 *syn* see RESUME 2
  idiom pick up the thread again
pickup *n syn* see ARREST
  rel booking
picky *adj syn* see NICE 1
picnic *n syn* see SNAP 1
pictorial *adj* **1** consisting of or relating to pictures
  <a collection of *pictorial* materials>
  syn graphic, iconographic, illustrational, illustrative, illustratory, pictoric
  rel photographic, pictographic
  2 *syn* see GRAPHIC 1
pictoric *adj syn* see PICTORIAL 1
picture *n* **1** *syn* see REPRESENTATION
  2 *syn* see IMAGE 1
  3 *syn* see MOVIE
picture *vb syn* see REPRESENT 1
  rel draw
picture show *n syn* see MOVIE
picturesque *adj syn* see GRAPHIC 1
piddling *adj syn* see PETTY 2
pie *n syn* see SNAP 1
piece *n* **1** *syn* see PART 1
  ‖**2** *syn* see SNACK
pièce de résistance *n syn* see SHOWPIECE
piecemeal *adv syn* see GRADUALLY
piecemeal *adj syn* see GRADUAL
‖pie–eyed *adj syn* see INTOXICATED 1
piepoudre *n syn* see PEDDLER
pier *n* **1** *syn* see WHARF
  rel pierage, wharfage
  2 *syn* see PILLAR 1
pierce *vb* **1** *syn* see CUT 1
  rel penetrate, perforate
  2 *syn* see PENETRATE 2
  rel run through

piercing *adj* **1** *syn* see SHARP 8
  2 *syn* see LOUD 1
  3 *syn* see ACUTE 4
pietistic *adj syn* see DEVOUT
  rel reverencing, reverential
piety *n syn* see FIDELITY 1
  rel docility, obedience; enthusiasm, fervor, passion, zeal; holiness, sanctity
piffle *n syn* see NONSENSE 2
piffling *adj syn* see PETTY 2
‖pig *n* **1** *syn* see WANTON
  2 *syn* see POLICEMAN
pigeon *n syn* see FOOL 3
pigeon *vb syn* see DUPE
pigeonhole *n* **1** *syn* see CUBBYHOLE
  2 *syn* see CLASS 1
  rel niche, slot
pigeonhole *vb syn* see ASSORT
  rel identify, label, name; place, rank, rate; catalog; break down, subdivide
pigeon house *n syn* see DOVECOTE
pigeonry *n syn* see DOVECOTE
pigheaded *adj syn* see OBSTINATE
  idiom not to be moved (*or* budged)
pigment *n syn* see COLOR 6
pigpen *n syn* see STY 1
pigsty *n syn* see STY 1
piked *adj syn* see POINTED 1
piker *n syn* see VAGABOND
piker *n syn* see MISER
pilaster *n syn* see PILLAR 1
pile *n* **1** a quantity of things heaped or stacked together <a *pile* of dirty clothes>
  syn bank, ‖bing, cock, drift, heap, hill, mass,
  mound, mountain, mow, pyramid, rick, ‖rickle,
  ‖ruck, shock, stack, stockpile, windrow
  rel barrow, pyre, tumulus; ‖dess, haycock, hay-
  rick, haystack; accumulation, aggregate, aggregation, amassment, assemblage, collection, conglomeration, glomeration, hoard, jumble
  2 *syn* see MUCH
  3 *syn* see EDIFICE
  4 *syn* see FORTUNE 4
  idiom a pile of money
pile *vb* **1** *syn* see HEAP 1
  2 *syn* see LOAD 3
pile (in) *vb syn* see RETIRE 4
pile (out) *vb syn* see ROLL OUT
  idiom ‖get the lead out, shake a leg, ‖shake it out
pile *n syn* see DOWN
pileous *adj syn* see HAIRY 1
  con bare; pileless
pile up *vb syn* see SHIPWRECK 1
pileup *n syn* see CRASH 3
pilfer *vb syn* see STEAL 1
pilferer *n syn* see THIEF
pilgarlic *n syn* see LAUGHINGSTOCK
‖pill *n* **1** *syn* see CIGARETTE
  2 *syn* see BORE
pillage *vb* **1** *syn* see RAVAGE
  rel encroach, invade, trespass; appropriate, arrogate, confiscate, usurp
  idiom lay waste
  2 *syn* see STEAL 1

pillager *n syn* see MARAUDER
pillar *n* **1** a firm upright support for a superstructure <stone *pillars* supported the ceiling>
　syn column, pier, pilaster
　rel prop; pedestal; post
　2 *syn* see MAINSTAY
pilose *adj syn* see HAIRY 1
pilot *n* **1** *syn* see LEADER 1
　2 one who flies or is qualified to fly an airplane <jet *pilots*>
　syn airman, aviator, birdman, flier, fly-boy
　rel aerialist
pilot *vb* **1** *syn* see GUIDE
　2 *syn* see DRIVE 5
pimp *n* **1** a man who solicits for a prostitute, lives off her earnings, and often lives with her <after dark, the *pimp* appeared on the street seeking clients for his girls>
　syn bully, ‖cadet, ‖easy rider, fancy man, ‖mack, macquereau, pander
　rel procurer; white slaver
　‖**2** *syn* see INFORMER
‖**pimp** *vb syn* see INFORM 3
pimping *adj syn* see PETTY 2
pimple *n syn* see ABSCESS
　rel ‖plouk
pimple *vb syn* see SPOT 2
pin *n syn* see BROOCH
pinch *vb* **1** *syn* see EXTORT 1
　2 *syn* see STEAL 1
　3 *syn* see ARREST 2
　4 *syn* see SCRIMP
pinch *n* **1** *syn* see JUNCTURE 2
　2 *syn* see THEFT
　3 *syn* see ARREST
pinchbeck *adj syn* see COUNTERFEIT
pinched *adj syn* see HAGGARD
　con stalwart, stout, strong, sturdy; healthy, robust
pinch hitter *n syn* see SUBSTITUTE 1
pinching *adj syn* see STINGY
pinchpenny *adj syn* see STINGY
‖**pindling** *adj syn* see IRRITABLE
pine *vb syn* see LONG
　rel brood, fret, mope; grieve, mourn; agonize
pinhead *n syn* see DUNCE
pinhead *adj syn* see STUPID 1
pinheaded *adj syn* see STUPID 1
pink *vb syn* see BLUSH
pinken *vb syn* see BLUSH
Pinkerton *n syn* see PRIVATE DETECTIVE
pin money *n syn* see POCKET MONEY
pinnacle *n syn* see APEX 2
pinpoint *vb syn* see IDENTIFY
pint–size *adj syn* see TINY
pioneer *adj syn* see FIRST 2
　rel pilot
pious *adj syn* see DEVOUT
　rel priestlike, priestly
　ant impious
pip *vb* ‖**1** *syn* see DEFEAT 2
　2 *syn* see DIE 1
‖**pip** *n syn* ‖DILLY, ‖corker, crackerjack, ‖daisy, dandy, humdinger, jim-dandy, ‖lalapalooza, ‖lulu, nifty

pipe *n* **1** *syn* see CASK
　‖**2** *syn* see PIPE DREAM
　‖**3** *syn* see SNAP 1
pipe *vb* ‖**1** *syn* see CRY 2
　2 *syn* see CONDUCT 4
‖**piped** *adj syn* see INTOXICATED 1
pipe down *vb syn* see SHUT UP 2
pipe dream *n* an illusory or fantastic plan or hope <*pipe dreams* of universal peace>
　syn bubble, chimera, dream, fantasy (*or* phantasy), illusion, ‖pipe, rainbow
　rel expectation, hope, prospect
pipeline *n* a person through whom information is transmitted <she was his news *pipeline* from the mayor's office>
　syn channel, conduit
　rel grapevine; origin, source, wellspring; supplier; connection, contact
piping *adj syn* see ACUTE 4
‖**pipped** *adj syn* see INTOXICATED 1
pippin *n syn* ‖DILLY, ‖corker, crackerjack, dandy, ‖dinger, ‖doozer, humdinger, jim-dandy, ‖lalapalooza, ‖pip
piquant *adj syn* see PUNGENT
　rel high-flavored, well-flavored; appetizing, sparkling
　con inane, jejune
　ant banal
pique *n syn* see OFFENSE 2
　rel annoyance, irk, irking, vexation; exasperation, irritation, provocation
pique *vb* **1** *syn* see IRRITATE
　2 *syn* see PROVOKE 4
　rel prick, punch; ignite
　3 *syn* see PRIDE
pirate *n* a robber on the high seas <little boys dreaming of sailing as *pirates*>
　syn buccaneer, corsair, freebooter, picaroon, rover, sea dog, sea robber, sea rover, sea wolf
　rel viking; privateer; looter, marauder, pillager, plunderer, raider
‖**pirl** *vb syn* see SPIN 1
‖**piroot** *vb syn* see SNOOP
pirouette *vb syn* see SPIN 1
pishposh *n syn* see NONSENSE 2
pit *n* ‖**1** *syn* see GRAVE
　2 *syn* see HELL
pit *vb syn* see OPPOSE 1
pitch *vb* **1** *syn* see THROW 1
　rel hoist, raise; move
　2 *syn* see THROW 2
　‖**3** *syn* see PLANT 1
　4 *syn* see FALL 2
　idiom take a pitch
　5 *syn* see PLUNGE 2
　rel drop, fall, sink
　6 *syn* see TOSS 2
　7 *syn* see SEESAW
pitch *n syn* see SPIEL

---

syn synonym(s)　　　*rel* related word(s)
ant antonym(s)　　　*con* contrasted word(s)
idiom idiomatic equivalent(s)
‖ use limited; if in doubt, see a dictionary

rel persuasion

pitch–black *adj syn* see BLACK 1

pitch–dark *adj syn* see BLACK 1

pitched *adj syn* see INCLINED 3

pitch in *vb* **1** to set about doing something energetically <had a lot to do and decided to *pitch in*>
syn buckle (down), fall to, jump (in *or* into), set to, wade (in *or* into)
rel attack, tackle; launch, tee off; begin, commence, start (off *or* out *or* up)
idiom fall to it, fall to work, get busy (*or* cracking), get down to it, get going, get (*or* have) with it, go to it, hop (*or* jump) to it
con dally, dawdle, procrastinate, stall; vacillate
2 *syn* see CONTRIBUTE 1

pitching *adj syn* see INCLINED 3

pitchy *adj syn* see BLACK 1

piteous *adj syn* see PITIFUL 1
rel beseeching, entreating, imploring, supplicating; doleful, dolorous, melancholy, plaintive; ruined

pitfall *n* a hidden or obscure source of danger, error, or harm <*pitfalls* that trap the unwary investigator>
syn booby trap, deadfall, mousetrap, springe, trapfall
rel danger, hazard, peril, risk; cobweb, entanglement, mesh(es), toil(s), web; bait, lure, snare, trap

pith *n* **1** *syn* see ESSENCE 2
rel center, focus, nucleus; meaning, meaningfulness
2 *syn* see SUBSTANCE 2
idiom the long and (the) short
3 *syn* see CENTER 3
rel fulcrum; hub
4 *syn* see IMPORTANCE

pithy *adj* being rich in meaning and tersely cogent in expression <a *pithy* summary>
syn compact, epigrammatic, marrowy, meaty; *compare* CONCISE
rel brief, concise, lean, short, short and sweet, succinct; crisp, curt, terse; effective, forceful; meaningful, significant, substantial
idiom brief and to the point, down to brass tacks, right to the point
con flatulent, inflated, tumid, turgid; prolix, verbose, wordy
ant diffuse

pitiable *adj* **1** *syn* see PITIFUL 1
2 *syn* see CONTEMPTIBLE
rel miserable, wretched; deplorable, lamentable

pitiful *adj* **1** arousing or deserving pity <*pitiful* refugees driven from their homes>
syn commiserable, pathetic, piteous, pitiable, poor, rueful
rel affecting, moving, touching; miserable, woeful, wretched; heartrending
2 *syn* see CONTEMPTIBLE

pitiless *adj* devoid of or unmoved by pity <a *pitiless* concentration camp guard>
syn merciless, unmerciful, unpitying; *compare* UNFEELING 2
rel coldhearted, hardhearted, heartless, ironhearted, marblehearted, stony, stonyhearted,

uncompassionate, unfeeling; barbarous, brutal, cruel, cutthroat, inhumane, savage
idiom lacking bowels of compassion, without an ounce of pity
con compassionate, humane, sympathetic; clement, merciful; tender, warmhearted
ant pitying

pittance *n* a small, often barely sufficient amount or allowance <a *pittance* of an education> <worked for a mere *pittance*>
syn dribble, driblet, ‖scrimption
rel bit, mite, scrap, smidgen, trace; inadequacy, insufficiency
idiom a drop in the bucket, cheeseparings and candle ends
con abundance, opulence, plenty, wealth

pity *n* sympathetic feeling for one suffering, distressed, or unhappy <felt the deepest *pity* for the prisoners>
syn commiseration, compassion, rue, ruth, sympathy
rel dejection, distress, melancholy, sadness, sorrow; charity, clemency, lenity, mercy
con contempt, disdain, disgust, scorn

pity *vb syn* see COMPASSIONATE

pivot *vb syn* see TURN 6

pivotal *adj syn* see CENTRAL 1
rel essential, vital; momentous; capital, principal

pixie *n* **1** *syn* see FAIRY
2 *syn* see SCAMP

pixie *adj syn* see PLAYFUL 1

pixieish *adj syn* see PLAYFUL 1

pixilated *adj* **1** *syn* see PLAYFUL 1
2 *syn* see INTOXICATED 1

placard *n syn* see POSTER

placard *vb syn* see POST

placate *vb syn* see PACIFY
rel comfort; tranquilize
idiom lay the dust
con anger, incense, infuriate, madden; excite, pique, provoke, stimulate
ant enrage

place *n* **1** the portion of space occupied by or chosen for something <the *place* where we'll meet>
syn location, locus, point, position, site, situation, spot, station, where
rel district, locality, vicinity; area, region, tract, zone; field, province, territory
2 *syn* see STATUS 1
3 *syn* see JOB 2

place *vb* **1** *syn* see SET 1
2 *syn* see ESTIMATE 3
3 *syn* see IDENTIFY
rel know, tell; nail, peg
idiom put one's finger on

placed *adj syn* see SITUATED
ant displaced

placid *adj* **1** *syn* see CALM 1
rel irenic, peaceful, serene, unagitated, unstirring
ant roiled
2 *syn* see CALM 2

rel detached, inexcitable, unmoved
con fidgety, jittery, jumpy, skittery; agitated
ant choleric
plague *n* **1** an epidemic disease causing a high mortality rate <smallpox finally ceased to be a *plague* in those nations>
syn curse, pestilence, scourge
rel infestation, invasion; affliction, disease; epidemic; ravage
2 *syn* see ANNOYANCE 3
rel bane, curse
3 *syn* see EPIDEMIC
plague *vb syn* see WORRY 1
rel chafe, gall; badger, bait, hassle, hector, hound, ride; afflict, torment
plain *adj* **1** free from all ostentation or superficial embellishment <just give the *plain* facts>
syn discreet, dry, homely, inelaborate, modest, simple, unadorned, unbeautified, undecorated, unelaborate, unembellished, unembroidered, ungarnished, unornamented, unostentatious, unpretentious
rel muted, restrained; austere, bald, bare, severe, spartan, stark, unluxurious; homespun
con adorned, beautified, elaborate, embellished, embroidered, exaggerated; high-flown, ostentatious, pretentious; flamboyant, rococo
ant rich
2 *syn* see STRAIGHT 3
3 *syn* see CLEAR 5
rel broad, unmistakable; legible
ant abstruse
4 *syn* see FRANK
rel unfeigned; abrupt
idiom plain and open
5 lacking allure without being positively ugly <a *plain* woman, drably dressed>
syn homely, unalluring, unattractive, unbeauteous, unbeautiful, uncomely, unhandsome, unpretty
rel plain-featured; inelegant; ordinary, plain Jane, unremarkable; ill-favored
idiom not much for looks, not much to look at, short on looks
con alluring, attractive, beautiful, comely, handsome; elegant; striking; knockout, sensational
6 *syn* see ORDINARY 1
plainclothesman *n syn* see DETECTIVE
plain dealing *adj syn* see STRAIGHTFORWARD 2
plain Jane *adj syn* see ORDINARY 1
plainness *n syn* see CLARITY
ant abstruseness
plainspoken *adj syn* see FRANK
plaintive *adj syn* see MELANCHOLY 2
rel deploring, lamenting, wailing; piteous, pitiful; sad, saddening
plan *n* **1** a method devised for making or doing something or attaining an end <each company had a *plan* for increasing profits>
syn blueprint, design, game plan, project, scheme, strategy
rel conception, idea, notion; ground plan, projection, projet; intent, intention, platform, purpose; means, method, way

idiom course (*or* plan) of action
2 *syn* see INTENTION
rel policy
3 *syn* see ORDER 8
plan *vb* **1** *syn* see DESIGN 3
2 to formulate a plan for arranging, realizing, or achieving something <*planned* next year's program>
syn arrange, blueprint, cast, chart, design, devise, ‖dope out, project; *compare* DESIGN 3
rel contemplate, meditate; cut out, draft, outline, sketch; figure (out), think (out); formulate, work out; organize
3 *syn* see INTEND 2
idiom be planning (*or* counting) on, have all intentions of, have every intention of
planate *n syn* see LEVEL
plane *vb syn* see EVEN 1
plane *adj syn* see LEVEL
planet *n, used with* the *syn* see EARTH 1
planetary *adj* **1** *syn* see HUGE
2 *syn* see UNIVERSAL 2
plangent *adj syn* see RESONANT
plant *vb* **1** to put or set into the ground for growth <*plant* corn>
syn ‖pitch, put in, seed, sow
rel drill; broadcast, dust, scatter; seed down
con crop, gather, harvest, reap
2 *syn* see HIDE
3 *syn* see BURY 1
plant *n syn* see FACTORY
plash *vb syn* see SPLASH
plaster *vb syn* see SMEAR 1
‖plastered *adj syn* see INTOXICATED 1
plastic *adj* susceptible of being modified in form or nature <the *plastic* quality of modeling clay>
syn adaptable, ductile, malleable, moldable, pliable, pliant, supple
rel elastic, flexible, resilient, supple, workable; impressionable, influenceable, suggestible, susceptible; amenable, bending, giving, tractable, yielding
con inflexible, rigid, stiff; accepted, customary, prevailing, set, standard, wonted
plat *n syn* see LOT 3
plateau *n* a usually extensive level land area raised sharply above adjacent land on at least one side <the *plateaus* of central Bolivia>
syn table, tableland, upland
rel mesa
con dale, glen, vale, valley; bottom, bottomland, lowland
platitude *n syn* see COMMONPLACE
rel inanity, insipidity, vapidity; mawkishness, sentimentality
platoon *n syn* see GROUP 3
plaudit *n, usu* **plaudits** *pl syn* see APPLAUSE
rel kudos
plausibility *n syn* see VERISIMILITUDE

---

syn synonym(s) *rel* related word(s)
ant antonym(s) *con* contrasted word(s)
idiom idiomatic equivalent(s)
‖ use limited; if in doubt, see a dictionary

plausible *adj syn* see BELIEVABLE
  rel likely, possible, probable; presumable
  con impossible, improbable, unlikely
  ant implausible
play *n* **1** activity engaged in for amusement <children need periods of work and *play*>
  syn disport, diversion, fun, recreation, sport
  rel amusement, entertainment; frolic, gambol, romp; delectation, delight, enjoyment, pleasure
  con business, duty, obligation; labor; drudgery
  ant work
  2 *syn* see FUN 1
  rel sportiveness
  ant earnest
  3 *syn* see TRICK 1
  4 *syn* see USE 1
  5 *syn* see ROOM 3
play *vb* **1** to engage in an activity for amusement or recreation <*played* outside for hours>
  syn disport, recreate, sport
  rel amuse, divert, engage, entertain; frolic, gambol, rollick, romp
  con labor, toil, travail; drudge, fag, slave
  ant work
  2 *syn* see FIDDLE 1
  3 *syn* see TREAT 2
  4 *syn* see MANIPULATE 2
  5 *syn* see ACT 1
  6 *syn* see GAMBLE 1
play (around) *vb syn* see PHILANDER
play (down) *vb syn* see SOFT-PEDAL
  rel restrain; mute, soften
  ant play (up)
play (off) *vb syn* see OPPOSE 1
play (up) *vb syn* see EMPHASIZE
  idiom make a (big) production of
  ant play (down)
playact *vb syn* see ACT 1
playactor *n syn* see ACTOR 1
player *n syn* see ACTOR 1
playful *adj* **1** given to or characterized by play, jests, or tricks <in a *playful* mood>
  syn antic, coltish, elvish, frisky, frolicsome, gamesome, impish, kittenish, larkish, ‖mischiefful, mischievous, pixie, pixieish, pixilated, prankful, prankish, pranky, puckish, roguish, sportive, waggish, wicked
  rel gay, lighthearted, whimsical; dashing, larking, lively, sprightly; blithe, jocund, jolly, jovial, merry; gleeful, hilarious, mirthful
  idiom as playful as a kitten (*or* colt), feeling one's oats
  con grim, stern, stolid; grave, serious
  2 *syn* see ANTIC 2
‖**play–pretty** *n syn* see TOY 2
plaything *n syn* see TOY 2
playwright *n* one who writes plays <a famous Broadway *playwright*>
  syn dramatist, dramatizer, dramaturge
  rel librettist; scenarist
plaza *n syn* see COMMON 2
plea *n* **1** *syn* see EXCUSE 1
  rel extenuation, mitigation, palliation; apology; out; vindication

  2 *syn* see PRAYER
  rel overture; call, cry
  idiom solemn entreaty (*or* plea)
plead *vb syn* see BEG
pleasance *n syn* see AMENITY 1
pleasant *adj* **1** highly acceptable to the mind or senses <a *pleasant* personality><a *pleasant* respite>
  syn agreeable, congenial, favorable, good, grateful, gratifying, nice, pleasing, pleasurable, pleasureful, welcome
  rel cheerful, cheering, cheery, glad, joyful, joyous; alluring, attractive, charming, pretty; convivial, engaging
  con displeasing, distasteful; harsh; obnoxious, repellent, repelling, repugnant, repulsive
  ant unpleasant
  2 *syn* see FAIR 2
pleasantness *n syn* see AMENITY 1
  rel goodness, niceness
  ant unpleasantness
please *vb* **1** *syn* see WILL
  2 to give or be a source of pleasure to <her work *pleased* him>
  syn arride, delectate, delight, gladden, gratify, happify, pleasure
  rel content, satisfy, suit; amuse, tickle, titillate; regale, rejoice; overjoy
  con vex; annoy; anger
  ant displease
  3 *syn* see SUIT 6
pleasing *adj syn* see PLEASANT 1
  rel satisfactory, suitable; enchanting, winning; adorable, darling, delightful
  ant displeasing, repellent
pleasurable *adj syn* see PLEASANT 1
  ant unpleasurable
pleasure *n* **1** *syn* see WILL 1
  2 the agreeable emotion accompanying the expectation, acquisition, or possession of something good or desirable <the *pleasures* and pains of growing up>
  syn delectation, delight, enjoyment, fruition, joy, joyance; *compare* ENJOYMENT 1
  rel bliss, felicity, happiness; kick, thrill
  con vexation; annoyance; anger; affliction, distress, sorrow, trouble
  ant displeasure
  3 *syn* see ENJOYMENT 1
  ant displeasure
pleasure *vb syn* see PLEASE 2
pleasure dome *n syn* see RESORT 3
pleasureful *adj syn* see PLEASANT 1
pleasuremonger *n syn* see HEDONIST
pleb *n* **plebs** *pl syn* see COMMONALTY
plebeian *adj syn* see IGNOBLE 1
  ant patrician
plebeians *n pl syn* see COMMONALTY
  ant patricians
plebs *n* **plebes** *pl syn* see COMMONALTY
  rel peasantry, peasants
  ant patricians, patriciate
pledge *n* **1** something given or held as a sign of another's good faith or intentions <the new school

is the *pledge* given by the community to its children>
  syn earnest, pawn, security, token, warrant; *compare* GUARANTEE 1, PROMISE
  rel bail, bond, guarantee, guaranty, surety, warranty; promise, word; oath, vow
  2 *syn* see WORD 8
pledge *vb* **1** *syn* see PAWN
  2 *syn* see DRINK 2
  3 *syn* see PROMISE 1
  rel bind, tie; commit, confide, consign, entrust
  idiom give (*or* make) a solemn pledge, pledge one's honor
  4 *syn* see VOW
plenteous *adj syn* see PLENTIFUL
  rel full, hearty; fruitful, galore, prolific; luxurious, opulent, sumptuous; lavish, prodigal, profuse, profusive, rampant, rife
plentiful *adj* being more than sufficient without being excessive <a *plentiful* harvest>
  syn abundant, ample, bounteous, bountiful, copious, generous, liberal, plenteous, plenty
  rel enough, sufficient; fulsome, rich, unstinted; excessive, extravagant, overabundant, overflowing, superabundant; abounding, bumper, bursting, swarming, swimming, teeming
  con deficient, exiguous, meager, skimpy; inadequate, insufficient
  ant scant, scanty
plenty *n syn* see MUCH
  rel abundance, cornucopia
plenty *adj syn* see PLENTIFUL
pleonasm *n syn* see VERBIAGE 1
plethora *n syn* see EXCESS 1
  rel much, plenty; many; deluge, flood
pliable *adj syn* see PLASTIC
  rel manipulable, manipulatable
  con unadaptable, unflexible, unmalleable, unpliant
  ant unpliable
pliant *adj syn* see PLASTIC
  rel spongy
  ant unpliant
plica *n syn* see WRINKLE
plight *vb syn* see VOW
  idiom plight one's honor
plight *n syn* see PROMISE
plight *n syn* see PREDICAMENT
  rel quandary
plighted *adj syn* see ENGAGED 2
plink *vb syn* see TINKLE 1
plod *vb* **1** to walk laboriously and heavily <slowly *plodded* across the sodden field>
  syn footslog, ‖plodge, plunther, slog, slop, stodge, toil, ‖trash, trudge; *compare* TRAMP 1
  rel tramp, trample, tromp; stamp, stomp, stump; flounder, wallow
  2 *syn* see DRUDGE
  idiom plug away at it
plodding *adj syn* see DULL 9
‖**plodge** *vb syn* see PLOD 1
plot *n* **1** *syn* see LOT 3
  2 a secret plan for accomplishing a usually evil or unlawful end <an assassination *plot*>

  syn cabal, conspiracy, covin, intrigue, machination, practice, scheme
  rel design, plan; connivance, conniving; collusion, complicity; contraption, contrivance, device; artifice, maneuver, ruse, stratagem, trick
plot *vb* to work out a plan especially for something unlawful or wrong <*plotted* the overthrow of the government>
  syn cogitate, ‖collogue, collude, connive, conspire, contrive, devise, intrigue, machinate, scheme (out)
  rel lay; brew, concoct, cook (up), hatch, set up; finagle, maneuver
plow *vb* to cut into and work the surface of (soil) <*plow* a field>
  syn break, plow up, turn, turn over
  rel cultivate, till; fallow; ‖backset; furrow, list, ridge, trench; harrow, rake
plow up *vb syn* see PLOW
  rel plow out
ploy *n syn* see TRICK 1
pluck *n syn* see COURAGE
‖**plucked** *adj syn* see BRAVE 1
plucky *adj syn* see BRAVE 1
  idiom full of pluck (*or* spunk)
  con feeble, weak
  ant pluckless
plug *n syn* see PUFF 3
plug *vb* **1** *syn* see FILL 1
  rel pack; cork
  2 *syn* see PROMOTE 3
plugging *n syn* see WORK 2
plug–ugly *n syn* see TOUGH
plum *n syn* see REWARD
  rel catch, find
‖**plumb** *adv syn* see WELL 3
plumb *vb syn* see SOUND
plumb *adj syn* see VERTICAL
plumbless *adj syn* see BOTTOMLESS 2
  con plumbable
plumb–line *vb syn* see SOUND
plumbness *n syn* see VERTICALITY
plume *vb syn* see PRIDE
plummet *vb* to decrease suddenly and sharply in financial value or price <the stock *plummeted* 60 points when the story broke>
  syn dip, drop, fall, nose-dive, plunge, skid, tumble
  rel decline, decrease, descend, sink; dump; precipitate; collapse, crash
  idiom take a sudden downturn (*or* downtrend)
  con increase; rise; shoot up
  ant skyrocket, soar
plummetless *adj syn* see BOTTOMLESS 2
plump *adj syn* see ROTUND 2
  rel fleshy, portly
  idiom plump as a partridge
  ant skinny
plumpish *adj syn* see ROTUND 2

---

syn synonym(s)   *rel* related word(s)
ant antonym(s)   *con* contrasted word(s)
idiom idiomatic equivalent(s)
‖ use limited; if in doubt, see a dictionary

idiom like a butterball
plumpy *adj syn* see ROTUND 2
plunder *vb syn* see ROB 1
plunder *n* **1** *syn* see SPOIL
‖**2** *syn* see PERSONAL EFFECTS
plunderage *n syn* see SPOIL
plunderer *n syn* see MARAUDER
plunge *vb* **1** *syn* see THRUST 2
2 to thrust or cast oneself or something into or as if into deep water <*plunged* into the crowd>
syn burst, dive, drive, lunge, pitch, ‖splunge; *compare* RUSH 1
rel dip, immerse, submerge; plump, plunk; propel, push, shove, thrust; boil, charge, fling, rush, tear
idiom plunge headlong
con ease, glide, slide, slip
3 *syn* see FALL 2
idiom take a plunge
4 *syn* see PLUMMET
idiom drop like a rock, take a downward plunge
plunther *vb syn* see PLOD 1
plus *n syn* see EXCESS 2
plus *vb syn* see INCREASE 1
plush *adj syn* see LUXURIOUS 3
idiom fit for the gods
plushy *adj syn* see LUXURIOUS 3
plutonian *adj* **1** *syn* see INFERNAL 1
2 *syn* see INFERNAL 2
plutonic *adj* **1** *syn* see INFERNAL 1
2 *syn* see INFERNAL 2
ply *vb* **1** *syn* see HANDLE 2
rel exercise; function
2 *syn* see EXERT
pneuma *n syn* see SOUL 1
pneumatic *adj syn* see AIRY 1
pocket *n syn* see DEAD END
pocket *vb* **1** *syn* see STEAL 1
2 *syn* see ACCEPT 2
pocket *adj* **1** *syn* see TINY
2 *syn* see CONDENSED
3 *syn* see FINANCIAL
pocket edition *n syn* see MODEL 1
pocket money *n* money for small personal expenses or incidentals <he had spent all his *pocket money* on candy and snacks>
syn pin money, spending money
rel petty cash; change, small change
con fortune, resources; income
pocket–size *adj syn* see TINY
pococurante *adj syn* see INDIFFERENT 2
pod *n* **1** *syn* see HULL
2 *syn* see POTBELLY
podex *n syn* see BUTTOCKS
podgy *adj syn* see ROTUND 2
Podunk *n syn* see BURG
poem *n* a particular example of metrical writing <recited a *poem* by Robert Frost>
syn poesy, poetry, rhyme, rune, verse
poesy *n* **1** *syn* see POEM
2 *syn* see POETRY 1
poet *n* a writer of verse <a *poet* to stir men's souls>
syn bard, muse, Parnassian

rel jongleur, rhapsodist, trouvère, trouveur; balladist, elegist, idyllist, lyricist, lyrist, odist, satirist, sonneteer, sonnetist
poetaster *n* a writer of mediocre or inferior verse <*poetasters* who churn out tasteless verse>
syn balladmonger, bardlet, bardling, poeticule, poetling, rhymer, rhymester, verseman, versemonger, verser, versesmith, versificator, versifier
poeticule *n syn* see POETASTER
poetling *n syn* see POETASTER
poetry *n* **1** metrical language or writing <studied the *poetry* of Milton>
syn poesy, rhyme, song, verse
2 *syn* see POEM
poignance *n syn* see PATHOS
poignancy *n syn* see PATHOS
poignant *adj* **1** *syn* see PUNGENT
ant dull
2 *syn* see MOVING 2
rel agitating, disturbing, perturbing
point *n* **1** one unitary part of a whole made up of two or more parts <listened to each *point* of his opponent's argument>
syn article, detail, element, item, particular, thing; *compare* ELEMENT 2
rel characteristic, feature, trait; constituent, material, part; circumstantial, circumstantiality
con aggregate, sum, total, whole
2 *syn* see CHARACTERISTIC 1
3 the quality of an utterance that arouses interest and produces an effect <a book that lacks *point*>
syn cogency, effectiveness, force, punch, validity, validness
rel appositeness, convincement, significance, suggestiveness; appeal, attraction, charm, fascination, interest
4 *syn* see SUBJECT 2
5 *syn* see TIP
6 *syn* see PLACE 1
7 a particular limited and often critical interval of time <at that *point* he was interrupted>
syn instant, juncture, moment
rel brink, threshold, verge
idiom point in time
8 *syn* see VERGE 2
9 a sharp or slender and tapering terminal part <the *point* of a sword>
syn apex, cusp, tip
rel awn, barb, jag, nib, prong, snag, spike, tag, tine
10 *syn* see PROMONTORY
11 a tiny mark or spot <saw a distant *point* of light>
syn dot, flyspeck, mote, speck
rel bit, fleck, iota, minim, mite, particle, scrap, tittle, trace
point *vb* **1** *syn* see PUNCTUATE
2 to tend to show something as probable <all signs *point* to an economic recovery>
syn hint, imply, indicate, suggest; *compare* SUGGEST 1
idiom lead one to expect, make (*or* give) promise of, offer a good prospect of
3 *syn* see DIRECT 2

point (out) *vb syn* see REFER 3

point (to) *vb syn* see TESTIFY 1

pointed *adj* **1** tapering to a thin tip <a *pointed* rock>
syn acicular, aciculate, acuminate, acuminous, acute, cuspidate, mucronate, peaked, peaky, piked, pointy, sharp
con dull, rounded
ant blunt
2 *syn* see NOTICEABLE

pointer *n syn* see TIP

pointful *adj syn* see RELEVANT

pointless *adj syn* see SENSELESS 5

‖**pointsman** *n syn* see POLICEMAN

pointy *adj syn* see POINTED 1

poise *vb* **1** *syn* see STABILIZE
rel back, support, uphold
con agitate, disturb, upset; overthrow, overturn, subvert
2 *syn* see HANG 3

poise *n* **1** *syn* see BALANCE 1
2 *syn* see TACT
rel aplomb, assurance, confidence, self-possession; calmness, serenity, tranquillity; dignity, elegance, grace

poised *adj syn* see CALM 2

poison *n* something that harms, interferes with, or destroys the activity, progress, or welfare of something else <the negative publicity was *poison* for her political ambitions>
syn bane, contagion, venom, virus
rel adulteration, contamination, corruption, sophistication
con catholicon, elixir, panacea
ant antidote

poison *vb syn* see DEBASE 1

poison *adj syn* see POISONOUS

poisonous *adj* having the properties or effect of poison <*poisonous* propaganda>
syn mephitic, poison, toxic, toxicant, venomous, virulent
rel miasmal, miasmatic, miasmic, pestilent, pestilential; deadly, fatal, lethal, mortal; baneful, deleterious, detrimental, nocuous, noxious, pernicious
con corrective, countervailing, emendatory, healing, remedial
ant antidotal

‖**poke** *n syn* see BAG 1

poke *vb* **1** to thrust something into so as to stir up, urge on, or attract attention <he *poked* the man in front of him to get his attention>
syn dig, jab, jog, nudge, prod, punch
rel push, shove, thrust; arouse, awaken, rouse, stir; excite, galvanize, provoke, quicken, stimulate
2 *syn* see SNOOP
3 *syn* see DELAY 2
4 *syn* see BULGE

poke *n* **1** a quick thrust with or as if with the hand <gave him a *poke* in the ribs with my finger>
syn dig, jab, punch, stab
rel bunt, butt; boost, push, shove
2 *syn* see CUFF

3 *syn* see DUNCE

poker–faced *adj* **1** *syn* see SERIOUS 1
2 *syn* see NEUTRAL

‖**pokey** *n syn* see JAIL

poky *adj syn* see DULL 9

polar *adj syn* see OPPOSITE

polemical *adj syn* see CONTENTIOUS 2

polestar *n syn* see CENTER 2

police *n syn* see POLICEMAN

‖**police constable** *n syn* see POLICEMAN

policeman *n* a member of a police force <ask the *policeman* for directions>
syn ‖bluebottle, bluecoat, ‖bobby, ‖bull, ‖constable, cop, ‖copper, Dogberry, ‖flatfoot, ‖fuzz, ‖gendarme, gumshoe, ‖harness bull (*or* cop), ‖heat, John Law, man, ‖nab, officer, ‖paddy, patrolman, peace officer, ‖peeler, ‖pig, ‖pointsman, police, ‖police constable, police officer, ‖rozzer, ‖trap

police officer *n syn* see POLICEMAN

policy *n syn* see COURSE 3

polish *vb* **1** to make smooth or glossy usually by friction <*polished* the silver>
syn buff, burnish, furbish, glance, glaze, gloss, rub, shine
rel brighten, scour, scrub
con roughen
2 to give an elegant finish to <attended classes to *polish* his manners>
syn perfect, refine, round, sleek, slick, smooth
rel better, improve, mend; brush up, furbish, touch up; mature, perfect

polish *n* **1** *syn* see LUSTER
2 *syn* see CULTURE

polished *adj* **1** *syn* see LUSTROUS 1
2 *syn* see SLEEK
3 *syn* see GENTEEL 1

polish off *vb* **1** *syn* see CONSUME 5
2 *syn* see EAT UP 1

polite *adj syn* see CIVIL 2
rel attentive, considerate, thoughtful
ant impolite

politic *adj* **1** *syn* see EXPEDIENT
rel astute, perspicacious, sagacious, shrewd
2 *syn* see TACTFUL
rel judicious, wise

polity *n syn* see COURSE 3

poll *n syn* see HEAD 1

pollard *vb syn* see TOP 1

polloi *n syn* see RABBLE 2

pollute *vb* **1** *syn* see CONTAMINATE 1
2 *syn* see CONTAMINATE 2

polluted *adj* **1** *syn* see IMPURE 3
2 *syn* see INTOXICATED 1

Pollyanna *n syn* see OPTIMIST
rel daydreamer, wishful thinker

Pollyannaish *adj syn* see OPTIMISTIC

Pollyannaism *n syn* see OPTIMISM

‖**polly–fox** *vb syn* see SKIRT 3

---

syn synonym(s)   *rel* related word(s)
ant antonym(s)   *con* contrasted word(s)
idiom idiomatic equivalent(s)
‖ use limited; if in doubt, see a dictionary

poltroon *n syn* see COWARD
poltroon *adj syn* see COWARDLY
poltroonish *adj syn* see COWARDLY
polyandrium *n syn* see CEMETERY
polychromatic *adj syn* see VARIEGATED
polychrome *adj syn* see VARIEGATED
polypragmatic *adj syn* see IMPERTINENT 2
polypragmatist *n syn* see BUSYBODY
pomp *n syn* see DISPLAY 2
　rel ceremonial, ceremony, form, formality, liturgy, ritual
pom–pom girl *n syn* see PROSTITUTE
pompous *adj* 1 characterized by or exhibiting self≠importance <a *pompous* old fool>
　syn arrogant, bloated, important, magisterial, pontifical, puffy, self-important, stuffy, wiggy; *compare* EGOCENTRIC 2, PROUD 1
　rel conceited, narcissistic, self-conceited, stuck≠up, vain, vainglorious; affected, highfalutin, hoity-toity, pretentious; presumptuous, self-centered, selfish; flaunting, flossy, ostentatious
　con natural, unaffected, unpretentious; humble, meek, plain, simple; modest, unassuming
　2 *syn* see RHETORICAL
ponder *vb* 1 *syn* see CONSIDER 1
　rel appraise, evaluate
　2 to consider or examine attentively or deliberately <*ponder* the best way to do it>
　syn ‖chaw, deliberate, meditate, mull (over), muse, revolve, roll, ruminate, turn over
　rel cogitate, reason, reflect, speculate, think; brood, debate, dwell
pondering *adj syn* see THOUGHTFUL 1
ponderous *adj* 1 *syn* see HEAVY 1
　rel substantial; burdensome, onerous, oppressive
　2 lacking all lightness and grace <a *ponderous* prose style>
　syn elephantine, heavy-footed, heavy-handed, uninspired
　rel dreary, dry, dull, humdrum, lifeless, monotonous, pedestrian, plodding, stodgy, stuffy; arid, barren; flat, insipid, savorless, vapid; buckram, cardboard, muscle-bound, stiff, stilted, wooden
　con sparkling, vivid; easy, natural, relaxed, supple, unlabored
　3 *syn* see UNWIELDY
pontifical *adj syn* see POMPOUS 1
pontificate *vb syn* see LORD
pony *n* a literal translation of a foreign language text used especially surreptitiously by students in rendering a lesson <had his *pony* hidden in his lap>
　syn crib, trot
‖**pooch** *n syn* see DOG 1
pooh *n syn* see RASPBERRY
pooh–bah *n syn* see NOTABLE 1
pooh–pooh *n syn* see RASPBERRY
pooh–pooh *vb syn* see DISMISS 5
pool *n* a small body of standing liquid <saw the *pool* of blood on the floor>
　syn puddle
pool *n* 1 *syn* see POT 3
　2 *syn* see SYNDICATE

poop *n syn* see FOOL 1
‖**poop** *vb syn* see EXHAUST 4
poor *adj* 1 lacking money or material possessions <they were so *poor* that the children had no winter coats>
　syn beggared, broke, destitute, dirt poor, flat, fortuneless, impecunious, impoverished, indigent, low, necessitous, needy, penurious, poverty-stricken, stone-broke, stony, strapped, unprosperous
　rel distressed, embarrassed, pinched, reduced, straitened; bankrupt, bankrupted, insolvent; hardscrabble; moneyless, penceless, penniless, unmoneyed; beggarly, down-and-out, pauperized; underprivileged
　idiom down to one's bottom dollar, flat broke, hard up, in need, in penury, in rags, in want, on one's beam-ends, on one's uppers, out at elbows, out of pocket, poor as a church mouse, unable to keep the wolf from the door, unable to make ends meet
　con affluent, comfortable, moneyed, ‖oofy, opulent, pecunious, prosperous, wealthy, well-fixed, well-heeled, well-off, well-to-do
　ant rich
　2 *syn* see MEAGER 2
　3 *syn* see PITIFUL 1
　4 *syn* see CHEAP 2
　5 *syn* see INFERIOR 2
　6 *syn* see BAD 1
poorly *adj syn* see UNWELL
poorness *n syn* see POVERTY 1
poor relation *n syn* see INFERIOR
poor–spirited *adj syn* see COWARDLY
pop *vb* 1 *syn* see STRIKE 2
　‖2 *syn* see PAWN
pop *n syn* see FLING 1
pop *n syn* see FATHER 1
pop (in) *vb syn* see VISIT 2
popinjay *n syn* see FOP
pop off *vb* 1 *syn* see GO 2
　2 *syn* see DIE 1
poppa *n syn* see FATHER 1
popping *adj syn* see BUSTLING
poppycock *n syn* see NONSENSE 2
popsy *n syn* see GIRL FRIEND 1
populace *n syn* see COMMONALTY
popular *adj* 1 *syn* see PUBLIC 4
　2 *syn* see DEMOCRATIC
　3 *syn* see CHEAP 1
　4 *syn* see PREVAILING
　5 *syn* see FAVORITE 2
　ant unpopular
　6 *syn* see WELL-KNOWN
　ant unpopular
populate *vb syn* see INHABIT
populous *adj syn* see MANY
porcine *adj syn* see FAT 2
pork–barreling *n syn* see PATRONAGE 3
porky *adj syn* see FATTY 2
porose *adj syn* see PERMEABLE
porous *adj syn* see PERMEABLE
porridge *n syn* see MISCELLANY 1
port *n* 1 *syn* see HARBOR 3

2 *syn* see SHELTER 1

port *n syn* see BEARING 1

portable *adj* capable of being carried or moved about <a *portable* TV>
syn carriageable, portative, transportable
rel convenient, handy, manageable, wieldy
con fixed, stationary

portal *n syn* see DOOR 1

portative *adj syn* see PORTABLE

portend *vb* **1** *syn* see AUGUR 2
2 *syn* see FORETELL

portent *n* **1** *syn* see FORETOKEN
2 *syn* see WONDER 1

porter *n syn* see BEARER 2

portion *n* **1** *syn* see SHARE 1
2 *syn* see FATE
3 *syn* see PART 1
4 *syn* see RATION

portion *vb syn* see APPORTION 2

portion (out) *vb syn* see ADMINISTER 2

portly *adj syn* see FAT 2

portrait *n syn* see IMAGE 1

portraiture *n syn* see REPRESENTATION

portray *vb syn* see REPRESENT 1
rel photograph; copy, duplicate, reproduce

portrayal *n syn* see REPRESENTATION

pose *vb* **1** *syn* see OFFER 1
2 *syn* see PROPOSE 1
rel ask, query, question; confound, puzzle; baffle
3 to assume a particular physical posture <they *posed* for a family portrait>
syn posture, sit
rel peacock, strut
4 to assume an artificial or pretended attitude or character usually to deceive or impress <*posed* as a salesman>
syn attitudinize, masquerade, pass (as *or* for), pass off, posture; *compare* ACT 1
rel fake, feign, pretend, sham; profess, purport; grandstand, show off

pose *n* **1** *syn* see POSTURE 1
2 an adopted way of speaking or acting <his reticence is just a *pose*>
syn affectation, air(s), lugs, mannerism, prettyism
rel dog, prettiness; fake, pretense, pretension

pose *vb syn* see OFFER 1

pose *vb syn* see PUZZLE

posh *adj syn* see STYLISH

posit *vb syn* see PRESUPPOSE

posit *n syn* see ASSUMPTION 2

position *n* **1** a firmly held point of view or way of regarding something <took a conservative *position* on educational issues>
syn attitude, color, stance, stand; *compare* SIDE 4
rel belief, judgment, opinion, view; angle, slant, standpoint, viewpoint
2 *syn* see PLACE 1
3 *syn* see STATUS 1
4 *syn* see STATUS 2
5 *syn* see JOB 2

positioned *adj syn* see SITUATED

positive *adj* **1** expressed clearly and usually peremptorily <her answer was a *positive* no>
syn categorical, decided, definite, unequivocal
rel clear, unmistakable; decisive, emphatic, energetic, firm, forceful, forcible; explicit, express, specific, unambiguous
con irresolute, uncertain, undecided, unsure
2 *syn* see SURE 5
ant doubtful
3 not subject to being disputed or called in question <gave *positive* proof that he had been there>
syn certain, inarguable, incontestable, incontrovertible, indisputable, indubitable, irrebuttable, irrefutable, sure, uncontestable, uncontrovertible, undeniable, undisputable, undoubtable, unequivocal, unquestionable; *compare* DOWNRIGHT 2
rel assured, clear, decisive
con contestable, controvertible, debatable, disputable, doubtful, dubious, inconclusive, questionable, unconvincing
4 *syn* see UTTER
5 *syn* see ACTUAL 2
6 capable of being constructively applied <*positive* proposals for improving the city>
syn affirmative
rel practical, reasonable, sound
con impractical, unsound, unusable
ant negative
7 *syn* see RIGHT-HANDED

positively *adv syn* see EASILY 2

positure *n syn* see POSTURE 1

possess *vb* **1** *syn* see HAVE 1
2 *syn* see BEAR 3

possessed *adj syn* see CALM 2

possession *n* **1** *syn* see OWNERSHIP
2 **possessions** *pl* things one owns usually excluding real property and intangibles <lost all their *possessions* in the fire>
syn belongings, chattels, effects, goods, lares and penates, movables, things
rel appointments, fixtures, furnishings, furniture; accessories, appurtenances, baggage, ‖duds, duffle, equipment, impedimenta, paraphernalia, trappings, tricks; havings; tangibles

possessive *adj syn* see JEALOUS 1

possessor *n syn* see OWNER

possessorship *n syn* see OWNERSHIP

possessory *adj syn* see JEALOUS 1

possibilities *n pl syn* see POTENTIAL

possible *adj* **1** capable of being realized <a cure is still *possible*>
syn doable, feasible, practicable, viable, workable
rel advisable, expedient; achievable, attainable, available
con futile, hopeless, impracticable
ant impossible
2 *syn* see PROBABLE
rel dormant, latent, potential
3 *syn* see POTENTIAL 1

---

syn synonym(s)   *rel* related word(s)
ant antonym(s)   *con* contrasted word(s)
idiom idiomatic equivalent(s)
‖ use limited; if in doubt, see a dictionary

possibly *adv syn* see PERHAPS
post *vb* to affix to a usual place (as a wall) for public notices <*posted* the notice on the bulletin board>
  syn placard, poster
post *vb syn* see INFORM 2
post *n syn* see JOB 2
post *vb syn* see STATION
‖**post** *n syn* see AUTOPSY
poster *n* a notice or announcement for posting in a public place <nailed the *poster* to the side of the building>
  syn affiche, bill, handbill, placard
  rel advertisement, announcement, banner, broadside, notice, sign; billboard, signboard
poster *vb syn* see POST
posterior *adj* **1** *syn* see SUBSEQUENT 1
  2 situated at or toward the back <the *posterior* part of the animal>
  syn after, back, hind, hinder, hindmost, rear, retral
  con fore, front
  ant anterior
posterior *n* **1** *syn* see BACK 1
  2 *syn* see BUTTOCKS
posterity *n syn* see OFFSPRING
  ant ancestry
posthaste *adv syn* see FAST 2
posthaste *adj syn* see FAST 3
posthumous *adj* occurring after one's death <*posthumous* fame>
  syn postmortal, postmortem, post-obit, post-obituary
  rel delayed, late, retarded
  con opportune, seasonable, timely
  ant antemortem
postliminary *adj syn* see SUBSEQUENT 1
postmortal *adj syn* see POSTHUMOUS
postmortem *adj syn* see POSTHUMOUS
  ant antemortem
postmortem *n syn* see AUTOPSY
postmortem examination *n syn* see AUTOPSY
post–obit *adj syn* see POSTHUMOUS
post–obituary *adj syn* see POSTHUMOUS
postpone *vb syn* see DEFER
postulate *vb* **1** *syn* see DEMAND 1
  2 *syn* see PRESUPPOSE
  rel affirm, assert, aver, predicate
postulate *n syn* see ASSUMPTION 2
postulation *n syn* see ASSUMPTION 2
posture *n* **1** the position or bearing of the body <erect *posture*>
  syn attitude, carriage, pose, positure, stance
  rel bearing, deportment, mien
  2 *syn* see STATE 1
  rel promptness, quickness, readiness
posture *vb* **1** *syn* see POSE 3
  2 *syn* see POSE 4
posy *n* **1** *syn* see FLOWER 1
  2 *syn* see BOUQUET 1
  3 *syn* see ANTHOLOGY
pot *n* **1** *syn* see FORTUNE 4
  2 *syn* see BET
  3 the total of the bets at stake at one time <lost track of how much was in the *pot*>

  syn jackpot, kitty, pool
  4 *syn* see POTSHOT
  ‖**5** *syn* see POTBELLY
  6 *syn* see NOTABLE 1
  7 *syn* see MARIJUANA
  ‖**8** *syn* see TOILET
potable *adj* suitable for drinking <*potable* water>
  syn drinkable
  rel clean, fresh, pure, uncontaminated, unpolluted
  con dirty, foul, impure, polluted, unclean
  ant impotable
potable *n syn* see DRINK 1
potbelly *n* an enlarged, swollen, or protruding abdomen <he had the biggest *potbelly* we had ever seen>
  syn bay window, corporation, paunch, pod, ‖pot
potency *n* **1** *syn* see POWER 4
  ant impotence
  2 *syn* see EFFICACY 1
  3 *syn* see ENERGY 2
  ant impotence
potent *adj* **1** *syn* see POWERFUL 2
  ant impotent
  2 *syn* see STRONG 3
potential *adj* **1** existing in possibility <a *potential* site for the new factory>
  syn possible
  rel conceivable, imaginable, likely, plausible, probable, thinkable
  idiom within the realm (*or* range) of possibility
  con existent, extant; doubtful, impossible, questionable; impracticable, unsuitable
  ant actual
  2 *syn* see LATENT
potential *n* something that can develop or become actual <industrial *potential*>
  syn possibilities, potentiality
  ant actuality, reality
potentiality *n syn* see POTENTIAL
  ant actuality
pother *n* **1** *syn* see COMMOTION 4
  2 *syn* see STIR 1
  3 *syn* see ANNOYANCE 2
  4 *syn* see COMMOTION 2
pother *vb syn* see WORRY 3
pothole *n* a hole, depression, or rut in a road surface <*potholes* all over that stretch of highway>
  syn chuckhole, mudhole
pothouse *n syn* see BAR 5
potpourri *n syn* see MISCELLANY 1
potshot *n* a critical remark made in a random or sporadic manner <took a few *potshots* at his neighbor's argument>
  syn pot, shy, sideswipe
  rel cut, crack, dig; gibe, jeer; aspersion, criticism, insult
potted *adj* **1** *syn* see CONDENSED
  ‖**2** *syn* see INTOXICATED 1
potter *vb syn* see FIDDLE 2
potter (away) *vb syn* see WASTE 2
potter's field *n syn* see CEMETERY
potty *adj* ‖**1** *syn* see LITTLE 3

||**2** *syn* see FOOLISH 2
3 *syn* see SNOBBISH
||**potty** *n syn* see TOILET
pouch *n syn* see BAG 1
pouch *vb syn* see BULGE
pouf *n syn* see QUILT
poule *n syn* see PROSTITUTE
poultice *n* a soft, usually heated, and sometimes medicated mass spread on cloth and applied to sores or other lesions <slapped a mustard *poultice* over the boil>
syn cataplasm
rel plaster; compress; dressing
pound *vb* **1** *syn* see HAMMER 1
2 *syn* see BEAT 1
3 *syn* see IMPRESS 3
pound *n syn* see BLOW 1
pour *vb* **1** *syn* see DISCHARGE 5
2 to send forth or come forth abundantly <medical supplies *poured* into the stricken area>
syn flow, gush, roll, sluice, stream, surge
rel issue, proceed, spring; course, rill, run, rush, swarm; cascade, cataract; deluge, flood, inundate
3 to rain heavily <it *poured* for two solid days>
syn drench, lash, teem
rel beat; deluge, flood, stream
idiom come down in buckets (*or* torrents), rain cats and dogs
pour *n syn* see FLOOD 2
pourboire *n syn* see GRATUITY
pout *vb* **1** *syn* see SULK
2 *syn* see BULGE
pouts *n pl syn* see SULK
poverty *n* **1** the state of one with insufficient resources <repeated crop failures had reduced the farmers to *poverty*>
syn beggary, borasca, destituteness, destitution, impecuniousness, impoverishment, indigence, indigency, need, neediness, pauperism, pennilessness, penury, poorness, privation, unprosperousness, want
rel exigency, necessity; juncture, pass, pinch, strait; difficulty, distress, embarrassment; hardship, suffering; mendicancy
idiom hand-to-mouth existence, straitened circumstances
con affluence, comfort, luxury, opulence, prosperity, richness, wealth
ant riches
2 *syn* see SCARCITY
poverty-stricken *adj syn* see POOR 1
powder *vb* **1** *syn* see SPRINKLE 1
2 *syn* see PULVERIZE 1
powdering *n syn* see DUSTING
powdery *adj syn* see FINE 2
power *n* **1** the right or prerogative of determining, ruling, or governing or the exercise of that right or prerogative <party in *power*>
syn authority, command, control, domination, jurisdiction, mastery, might, strings, sway
rel birthright, prerogative, privilege, right; direction, management; ascendancy, dominance, dominion, masterdom, sovereignty, supremacy;

superiority; influence, prestige, weight; force, strength
con forcelessness, impotence, weakness
ant impuissance, powerlessness
||**2** *syn* see MUCH
3 the ability of a living being to perform in a given way or a capacity for a particular kind of performance <the *power* to think clearly>
syn faculty, function
rel ability, capability, capacity; aptitude, bent, turn; endowment, gift, talent
con inability, incapability, incapacity; inaptness, ineptitude
4 the ability to exert effort for a purpose <raised the productive *power* of the nation>
syn arm, beef, dint, energy, force, might, muscle, potency, puissance, sinew, steam, strength, strong arm, vigor, virtue
rel ability, capability, capacity; effectiveness; dynamism, powder, voltage; dynamis, potentiality; competence, qualification
con inability, incapability, incapacity; ineffectiveness; incompetence
powerful *adj* **1** *syn* see STRONG 1
2 having or manifesting power to effect great or striking results <a *powerful* leader>
syn forceful, forcible, mighty, potent, puissant
rel able, capable, competent; effective, effectual, efficacious, efficient; dynamic, energetic, strenuous, vigorous; convincing, great, invincible; authoritative, dominant, influential, weighty
con faulty, feeble, flawed; impotent, inadequate, incompetent, weak
ant powerless
powerfully *adv syn* see HARD 1
powerless *adj* unable to effect one's purpose, intention, or end <*powerless* to leave>
syn helpless, impotent
rel inactive, inert, passive, supine; decrepit, feeble, infirm, weak; incapable, incompetent, ineffective, unfit
con effective, effectual, efficient; able, capable, competent; potent, puissant
ant powerful
powwow *syn* see TALK 4
powwow *vb syn* see CONFER 2
||**prabble** *n syn* see QUARREL
practic *adj syn* see REALISTIC
practicable *adj* **1** *syn* see POSSIBLE 1
ant impracticable
2 *syn* see PRACTICAL 2
3 *syn* see OPEN 5
ant impracticable
practical *adj* **1** *syn* see IMPLICIT 2
2 capable of being turned to use or account <a *practical* knowledge of auto mechanics>
syn functional, handy, practicable, serviceable, useful, utile
con abstract, academic, theoretical

ant impractical, unpractical
3 *syn* see REALISTIC
ant impractical, unpractical
4 *syn* see EXPERIENCED
practically *adv* **1** *syn* see VIRTUALLY
2 *syn* see ALMOST 2
3 *syn* see NEARLY
practice *vb* *syn* see EXERCISE 3
rel execute, fulfill, perform; follow, pursue; iterate, repeat
practice *n* **1** *syn* see HABIT 1
rel procedure, proceeding, process; method, mode, system
2 *syn* see PLOT 2
3 *syn* see EXERCISE 3
rel use, usefulness, utility; convenance, convention, form, usage
ant theory; precept
practiced *adj* *syn* see EXPERIENCED
ant unpracticed
praetorian *adj* *syn* see CORRUPT 2
praetorian *n* *syn* see DIEHARD 1
pragmatic *n* *syn* see BUSYBODY
pragmatic *adj* *syn* see REALISTIC
pragmatical *adj* *syn* see REALISTIC
pragmatist *n* *syn* see BUSYBODY
praisable *adj* *syn* see WORTHY 1
praise *vb* **1** *syn* see COMMEND 2
ant censure, criticize
2 to glorify and exalt especially in song or writing <*praised* God for all his blessings>
syn bless, celebrate, cry up, eulogize, extol, glorify, hymn, laud, magnify, panegyrize, psalm, psalmody, resound
rel aggrandize, dignify, distinguish, ennoble, erect, exalt, honor, sublime, uprear; enhance, heighten, intensify; apotheosize; proclaim
idiom sing the praises of
con asperse, calumniate, defame, libel, malign, traduce, vilify; belittle, decry, depreciate, derogate, detract (from), discount, disparage, minimize, opprobriate; censure, criticize, denounce, reprehend, reprobate; abuse, reproach, revile
ant dispraise; blame
praiseful *adj* *syn* see EULOGISTIC
praiseworthy *adj* *syn* see WORTHY 1
ant despicable
‖**pram** *n* *syn* see BABY CARRIAGE
prance *vb* **1** *syn* see SASHAY
2 *syn* see DANCE 1
‖**prang** *vb* *syn* see BUMP 1
‖**prang** *n* *syn* see CRASH 3
prank *n* a mischievous or roguish act <he was always playing *pranks* on his sister>
syn antic, caper, dido(es), frolic, lark, monkeyshine(s), ‖rig, shenanigan, shine(s), ‖skite, tomfoolery, trick, wheeze; *compare* ESCAPADE, TRICK 1
rel fooling, high jinks, horseplay, roughhouse, roughhousing, rowdiness, skylarking; gambol, play, rollick, sport; frivolity, levity, lightness; caprice, conceit, fancy, freak, vagary, whim, whimsy
prank *vb* **1** *syn* see ADORN
2 *syn* see DRESS UP 1

prankful *adj* *syn* see PLAYFUL 1
prankish *adj* *syn* see PLAYFUL 1
pranky *adj* *syn* see PLAYFUL 1
‖**prat** *n* *syn* see TRICK 1
prate *vb* **1** *syn* see CHAT 1
2 *syn* see BOAST
3 *syn* see BABBLE 2
prate *n* *syn* see CHATTER
prater *n* *syn* see CHATTERBOX
prattle *vb* **1** *syn* see CHAT 1
2 *syn* see BABBLE 2
prattle *n* *syn* see CHATTER
prattler *n* *syn* see CHATTERBOX
praxis *n* *syn* see HABIT 1
pray *vb* *syn* see BEG
prayer *n* an earnest and usually a formal request for something <the *prayer* in a bill in equity is the part that specifies the kind of relief sought>
syn appeal, application, entreaty, imploration, imprecation, orison, petition, plea, suit, supplication
rel begging, beseeching, imploring, pleading; adoration, worship
con claim, demand, exaction
prayer *n* *syn* see SUPPLIANT
prayerful *adj* *syn* see DEVOUT
preach *vb* **1** to discourse publicly on a religious subject <*preached* at Sunday services>
syn evangelize, homilize, sermonize
rel minister, mission, missionary; prophesy; address, lecture, speak, talk
2 *syn* see MORALIZE
preach *n* *syn* see SERMON
preacher *n* *syn* see CLERGYMAN
preachify *vb* *syn* see MORALIZE
preaching *n* *syn* see SERMON
preachment *n* *syn* see SERMON
preachy *adj* *syn* see DIDACTIC
preamble *n* *syn* see INTRODUCTION
precarious *adj* **1** *syn* see DOUBTFUL 1
2 *syn* see DELICATE 7
precariousness *n* *syn* see INSTABILITY
precaution *n* *syn* see PRUDENCE 1
precede *vb* **1** to go before in rank, dignity, or importance <the small countries at the conference were *preceded* by the large wealthy ones> <those who still feel that age should *precede* beauty>
syn outrank, rank
2 to go before in time <all-out war was *preceded* by many small raids>
syn antecede, antedate, forerun, pace, predate
rel announce, foreshadow, harbinger, herald, presage
con ensue, supervene
ant follow, succeed
3 to cause to be preceded <*preceded* her address with a welcome to the visitors>
syn introduce, lead, preface, usher
ant follow
precedence *n* *syn* see PRIORITY
precedency *n* *syn* see PRIORITY
precedent *adj* *syn* see PRECEDING
precedently *adv* *syn* see BEFORE 1

preceding *adj* being before especially in time or in arrangement <the *preceding* day>
syn antecedent, anterior, foregoing, former, past, precedent, previous, prior
rel other; preexistent; precursive, precursory; erstwhile, heretofore, hitherto
con coming, ensuing, next, sequent, sequential, subsequent, successive
ant following, succeeding

preceding *prep* *syn* see BEFORE 1

precept *n* *syn* see LAW 1
rel axiom, fundamental, principle; doctrine, dogma, tenet; behest, bidding, injunction
ant practice; counsel

précieux *adj* *syn* see PRECIOUS 4

precinct *n* 1 *syn* see QUARTER 2
2 *syn* see FIELD
3 **precincts** *pl* *syn* see ENVIRONS 1

precious *adj* 1 of such great value that a suitable price is hard to estimate <a *precious* twelfth century painting>
syn costly, inestimable, invaluable, priceless, valuable; *compare* COSTLY 1
rel choice, exquisite, rare, recherché; treasurable; rich; prizable
idiom of price
con base, common, mean, paltry, poor, rubbishy, shabby, trashy; contemptible, despicable, miserable; claptrap, gimcrack, trumpery
ant cheap; worthless
2 *syn* see FAVORITE 1
3 *syn* see NICE 1
4 excessively refined <too *precious* to mingle with the common people>
syn affected, alembicated, chichi, la-di-da, overnice, overrefined, précieux; *compare* GENTEEL 3
rel ostentatious, pretentious, showy; artful, sophisticated, studied
con artless, ingenuous, naive, natural, simple, unaffected, unartful, unschooled, unsophisticated, unstudied, untutored; down-to-earth, matter-of-fact, practical, pragmatic, rational

precipitance *n* *syn* see HASTE 2

precipitancy *n* *syn* see HASTE 2

precipitant *adj* *syn* see PRECIPITATE 1

precipitate *n* 1 *syn* see SEDIMENT
2 *syn* see EFFECT 1

precipitate *adj* 1 characterized by impetuous or unexpected haste <beat a *precipitate* retreat>
syn abrupt, hasty, headlong, hurried, impetuous, precipitant, precipitous, rushing, subitaneous, sudden
rel breakneck, headstrong, hotheaded, impatient, impulsive, madcap, refractory, uncontrolled, willful; unanticipated, unexpected, unforeseen, unlooked-for; overhasty
con leisurely, slow, unhurried
ant deliberate
2 *syn* see STEEP 1

precipitateness *n* *syn* see HASTE 2

precipitation *n* 1 *syn* see HASTE 2
2 *syn* see SEDIMENT

precipitous *adj* 1 *syn* see PRECIPITATE 1
2 *syn* see STEEP 1

précis *n* *syn* see COMPENDIUM 1

precise *adj* 1 *syn* see DEFINITE 1
2 *syn* see CORRECT 2
rel rigid, stringent
con careless, heedless; lax, slack
ant imprecise; loose
3 *syn* see PRIM 1
4 distinguished from every other <arrived just at the *precise* moment when he was needed>
syn exact, very
rel specific; individual; particular
con general, inexact, nonspecific
ant imprecise

precisely *adv* 1 *syn* see JUST 1
idiom on the button
ant imprecisely; approximately
2 *syn* see EVEN 1
3 *syn* see EXACTLY 3

preciseness *n* *syn* see PRECISION
ant impreciseness

precisian *n* *syn* see PURIST

precision *n* the quality or character of what is precise <the *precision* involved in close-tolerance machining>
syn accuracy, correctness, definiteness, definitiveness, definitude, exactitude, exactness, preciseness
rel care, carefulness; attention, heed
con inaccuracy, incorrectness, indefiniteness, inexactness; obscurity, unclearness, vagueness; unreliability, untrustworthiness
ant imprecision

precisionist *n* *syn* see PURIST

preclude *vb* *syn* see PREVENT 2
rel cease, discontinue, quit, stop

precocious *adj* exceptionally early in development <a *precocious* child, smart beyond her years>
syn advanced, forward; *compare* EARLY 2
rel ahead, early, overearly, oversoon, premature, previous, ‖soon; developed, mature
con backward, undeveloped; dull, slow, slow-witted, sluggish
ant retarded

precogitate *vb* *syn* see PREMEDITATE

preconception *n* an attitude, belief, or impression formed beforehand <had a lot of *preconceptions* about a man she'd never met>
syn prejudgment, prepossession; *compare* PREJUDICE
rel illusion; delusion
idiom preconceived notion (*or* idea *or* opinion)

precondition *n* *syn* see ESSENTIAL 2

precursor *n* 1 *syn* see FORERUNNER 1
2 *syn* see FORERUNNER 2

predacious *adj* *syn* see RAPACIOUS 1

predate *vb* *syn* see PRECEDE 2

predative *adj* *syn* see RAPACIOUS 1

predatorial *adj* *syn* see RAPACIOUS 1

predatory *adj* *syn* see RAPACIOUS 1

---

syn synonym(s)   *rel* related word(s)
ant antonym(s)   *con* contrasted word(s)
idiom idiomatic equivalent(s)
‖ use limited; if in doubt, see a dictionary

predecessor *n syn* see FORERUNNER 2

predestinate *vb syn* see PREDESTINE 2

predestine *vb* **1** to fix the future of in advance <his treasured scribblings were *predestined* to light a kitchen fire>
syn destine, determine, doom (to), fate, foreordain, predetermine, preform, preordain
rel predecide; prejudge; preestablish
2 to determine by or as if by divine decree or eternal purpose <some believe that God *predestines* individuals to eternal life or to eternal damnation>
syn foredestine, foreordain, predestinate, predetermine, preordain

predetermine *vb* **1** *syn* see PREDESTINE 2
2 *syn* see PREMEDITATE
3 *syn* see PREDESTINE 1

predicament *n* a difficult, perplexing, or trying situation <was in a *predicament*, trying to decide whether or not to take the job>
syn box, corner, deep water, dilemma, fix, hole, hot water, impasse, jam, pickle, plight, quagmire, scrape, soup, spot
rel emergency, exigency, juncture, pass, pinch, strait; asperity, difficulty, hardness, hardship, rigor, vicissitude; Dutch, trouble; condition, posture, situation, state
idiom ‖in a bind

predicate *vb* **1** *syn* see ASSERT 1
2 *syn* see BASE

predict *vb* **1** *syn* see FORETELL
2 to conjecture correctly <*predicted* the turn of the market months in advance>
syn call, guess
rel conjecture, presume, suppose, surmise, think; conclude, gather, infer, judge
idiom hazard a conjecture (*or* guess)

prediction *n* something that is predicted <the *prediction* was for a good outcome>
syn cast, forecast, foretelling, prevision, prognosis, prognostication, prophecy, weird
rel conjecture, guess, surmising

predictor *n syn* see PROPHET

predilection *n syn* see LEANING 2

predispose *vb syn* see INCLINE 3
rel impress, strike, sway
con disaffect, disincline, disinterest, indispose

predisposed *adj syn* see WILLING 1
ant indisposed

predisposition *n syn* see LEANING 2
ant indisposition

predominant *adj* **1** *syn* see DOMINANT 1
ant subordinate
2 *syn* see CHIEF 2

predominantly *adv syn* see GENERALLY 1

predominate *adj syn* see DOMINANT 1

predominate *vb syn* see RULE 2

preeminence *n* **1** *syn* see SUPREMACY
2 *syn* see EMINENCE 1

preeminent *adj* **1** *syn* see SUPREME
2 *syn* see CHIEF 2

preempt *vb* **1** *syn* see APPROPRIATE 1
2 *syn* see ARROGATE 1

preen *vb syn* see PRIDE

preengage *vb* **1** *syn* see RESERVE 2
2 *syn* see PREPOSSESS 1

preface *n syn* see INTRODUCTION

preface *vb syn* see PRECEDE 3

prefatial *adj syn* see PRELIMINARY

prefatorial *adj syn* see PRELIMINARY

prefatory *adj syn* see PRELIMINARY

prefer *vb* **1** *syn* see ADVANCE 2
2 *syn* see CHOOSE 1
3 *syn* see PROPOSE 1

preferable *adj syn* see BETTER 2

preference *n* **1** *syn* see CHOICE 1
rel partiality, predilection, prepossession
2 *syn* see ADVANCEMENT 1

preferment *n syn* see ADVANCEMENT 1

preferred *adj syn* see FAVORITE 2

prefigurate *vb syn* see ADUMBRATE 1

prefigure *vb syn* see ADUMBRATE 1

preform *vb syn* see PREDESTINE 1

pregnance *n syn* see PREGNANCY

pregnancy *n* the condition of containing unborn young within the body <she was in the last trimester of her *pregnancy*>
syn gestation, gravidity, pregnance, situation

pregnant *adj* **1** containing unborn young within the body <she was *pregnant* with her second child>
syn big, childing, enceinte, expectant, expecting, gone, gravid, heavy, parous, parturient
idiom in an interesting condition, in the family way, with child (*or* young)
con barren, infertile; delivered; postpartum
2 *syn* see EXPRESSIVE
rel consequential, important, momentous, significant, weighty

prehend *vb syn* see CATCH 1

prehensile *adj syn* see COVETOUS

preindicate *vb syn* see ANNOUNCE 2

prejudgment *n syn* see PRECONCEPTION

prejudice *n* the inclination to take a stand (as in a conflict) usually without just grounds or sufficient information <could not review his competitor's work without *prejudice*>
syn bias, one-sidedness, partiality; *compare* LEANING 2, PRECONCEPTION
rel partisanship
idiom jaundiced eye
con detachment, dispassion, impartiality, indifference, neutrality
ant objectivity

prejudice *vb* **1** *syn* see INJURE 1
2 to cause to have opinions formed without due knowledge or examination <*prejudice* a man against his neighbor by innuendo>
syn bias, influence, prepossess; *compare* INCLINE 3, SLANT 3
rel bend, dispose, incline, predispose; angle, skew, slant; prejudge

prejudiced *adj syn* see BIASED 2
ant unprejudiced; disinterested

prejudicial *adj* **1** *syn* see HARMFUL
2 *syn* see DISCRIMINATORY

prejudicious *adj syn* see HARMFUL

prekindergarten *adj syn* see CHILDISH

preknow *vb syn* see FORESEE

prelation *n syn* see ADVANCEMENT 1

prelect *vb syn* see TALK 7

‖**prelim** *adj syn* see PRELIMINARY

preliminary *adj* serving to make ready the way for something that follows <held a *preliminary* discussion to set up the agenda of the conference>
  syn inductive, introductory, prefatial, prefatorial, prefatory, ‖prelim, preludial, prelusive, preparative, preparatory, proemial
  rel primal, primary; elemental, elementary; basic, fundamental; fitting, preparing, readying
  ant postliminary

prelimit *vb syn* see LIMIT 2

preliterate *adj syn* see PRIMITIVE 6

prelude *n syn* see INTRODUCTION

preludial *adj syn* see PRELIMINARY

prelusion *n syn* see INTRODUCTION

prelusive *adj syn* see PRELIMINARY

premature *adj syn* see EARLY 2

prematurely *adv syn* see EARLY 2

premeditate *vb* to think on and revolve in the mind beforehand <carefully *premeditating* each step of his plan of campaign>
  syn forethink, precogitate, predetermine
  rel prearrange, preplan, set up; predecide; prepare

premeditated *adj syn* see DELIBERATE 1
  ant unpremeditated; spontaneous

premier *adj syn* see FIRST 3

premise *n syn* see ASSUMPTION 2

premise *vb syn* see PRESUPPOSE

premium *n syn* see REWARD

premium *adj syn* see SUPERIOR 4

premonition *n syn* see APPREHENSION 3

prename *n syn* see GIVEN NAME

prenotion *n syn* see APPREHENSION 3

prentice *n syn* see NOVICE

prentice *adj syn* see CRUDE 5

preoccupied *adj* 1 *syn* see INTENT
  2 *syn* see ABSTRACTED
  rel absorbed; forgetful
  ant unpreoccupied

preoccupy *vb syn* see PREPOSSESS 1

preordain *vb* 1 *syn* see PREDESTINE 1
  2 *syn* see PREDESTINE 2

preparative *adj syn* see PRELIMINARY

preparatory *adj syn* see PRELIMINARY

prepare *vb* 1 to make ready in advance usually for a particular use or disposition <*prepared* rooms for the expected guests>
  syn fit, fix, get, make, make up, ready
  rel furnish, provide, supply; dower, endow, endue; equip, outfit; dispose, incline, predispose; prime
  idiom set the stage (for)
  ant unprepare
  2 *syn* see DRAFT 3
  3 *syn* see GIRD 3

prepared *adj syn* see READY 1
  ant unprepared

prepatent *adj syn* see LATENT

prepense *adj syn* see DELIBERATE 1

prepensely *adv syn* see INTENTIONALLY

preponderance *n syn* see SUPREMACY

preponderancy *n syn* see SUPREMACY

preponderant *adj syn* see DOMINANT 1

preponderate *vb syn* see RULE 2

preponderation *n syn* see SUPREMACY

prepossess *vb* 1 to influence or affect strongly beforehand <was *prepossessed* with the notion of his own superiority>
  syn preengage, preoccupy
  rel busy, engage, engross, immerse, occupy, soak; absorb, imbue, involve
  2 *syn* see PREJUDICE 2

prepossessed *adj syn* see BIASED 2
  ant unprepossessed

prepossessing *adj syn* see ATTRACTIVE 1

prepossession *n syn* see PRECONCEPTION

preposterous *adj* 1 *syn* see FOOLISH 2
  rel irrational, unreasonable
  2 *syn* see EXTRAVAGANT 1

preposterousness *n syn* see FOOLISHNESS

prepotence *n syn* see SUPREMACY

prepotency *n syn* see SUPREMACY

prerequisite *n syn* see ESSENTIAL 2

prerequisite *adj syn* see ESSENTIAL 4

prerogative *n syn* see RIGHT 2
  rel exemption, immunity

presage *n* 1 *syn* see FORETOKEN
  2 *syn* see APPREHENSION 3

presage *vb* 1 *syn* see AUGUR 2
  rel bespeak, indicate
  2 *syn* see ANNOUNCE 2
  3 *syn* see FORETELL

prescribe *vb* 1 *syn* see DICTATE
  2 to fix arbitrarily or authoritatively for the sake of order or of a clear understanding <the Constitution *prescribes* the conditions under which it may be amended>
  syn assign, define, lay down
  rel establish, fix, set, settle; decide, determine; choose, pick out, select

prescript *n syn* see LAW 1

prescription *n syn* see LAW 1

presence *n syn* see BEARING 1
  rel appearance, aspect, look, seeming

present *n syn* see GIFT 1

present *vb* 1 *syn* see INTRODUCE 4
  2 *syn* see GIVE 1
  3 *syn* see OFFER 1
  4 *syn* see ADDUCE
  5 *syn* see DIRECT 2

present *adj* now existing or in progress <the *present* state of the economy seems to be shaky from all reports>
  syn contemporary, current, existent, extant, instant, present-day, todayish
  rel contemporaneous, modern; newfashioned, up-to-date, up-to-the-minute
  con bygone, erstwhile, late, old, once, onetime, quondam, sometime, whilom

---

syn synonym(s)　　　　*rel* related word(s)
ant antonym(s)　　　　*con* contrasted word(s)
idiom idiomatic equivalent(s)
‖ use limited; if in doubt, see a dictionary

ant past

present *n* the present time <the course covers U.S. history from 1900 to the *present*>
syn now, today; *compare* FUTURE, PAST
idiom here and now, this day and age
ant past; future

presentable *adj syn* see RESPECTABLE 5

present–day *adj syn* see PRESENT

presenter *n syn* see DONOR

presentiment *n syn* see APPREHENSION 3
rel discomposing, discomposure, disquietude, disturbance, perturbation

presently *adv* **1** without undue time lapse <the results will be evident *presently*>
syn anon, by and by, directly, shortly, soon
2 *syn* see TODAY

presentment *n syn* see REPRESENTATION

preserval *n syn* see CONSERVATION 1

preservation *n* **1** the act of preserving or the state of being preserved <the *preservation* of peace in the world>
syn conservation, keeping, safekeeping, salvation, saving, sustentation
rel defense, guard, protection, safeguard, shield; care, guardianship, ward
2 *syn* see CONSERVATION 1

preserve *vb* **1** *syn* see SAVE 3
2 *syn* see MAINTAIN 1

preserve *n syn* see JAM

preside *vb* to occupy the place of authority (as in an assembly) <the chief justice *presides* over the supreme court> <the *presiding* elders of the church>
syn chair
rel carry on, conduct, control, direct, keep, manage, operate, ordain, run; administer, handle, head, oversee, supervise

press *n syn* see CROWD 1

press *vb* **1** to act upon through steady pushing or thrusting force exerted in contact <*pressed* her nose against the window>
syn bear, compress, constrain, crowd, crush, jam, ‖mash, push, ‖squab, squash, squeeze, squish, squush
rel propel, shove, thrust; drive, impel, move
2 *syn* see DEPRESS 2
3 to squeeze out the juice or contents of <*press* grapes>
syn crush, express
rel compress, squeeze
4 *syn* see PUSH 2
5 *syn* see PRESSURE
6 *syn* see EMBRACE 1
7 to crowd closely against or around someone or something <hundreds *pressed* around the performer after the show>
syn cram, crowd, crush, jam, squash, squeeze; *compare* CRAM 1
rel pack, ram, stuff, tamp; mass, pile; assemble, collect, congregate, gather
8 to force or push one's way (as through a crowd or against obstruction) <had to *press* through the traffic to get to the other side of town>
syn bear, squeeze

rel force, push, shove

press–agent *vb syn* see PUBLICIZE

press–agentry *n syn* see PUBLICITY

pressing *adj* demanding or claiming especially immediate attention <he was barely able to pay his most *pressing* debts>
syn burning, clamant, clamorous, crying, dire, exigent, imperative, importunate, insistent, instant, urgent
rel direct, immediate; claiming, demanding, exacting, requiring; compelling, constraining, forcing, obliging; acute, critical, crucial

pressure *n syn* see STRESS 1

pressure *vb* to insist upon unduly <*pressured* him into making the wrong move>
syn overpress, press, push
rel drive, impel; rush

prestige *n* **1** *syn* see STATUS 2
2 *syn* see INFLUENCE 1
rel power, sway
3 *syn* see EMINENCE 1

prestigious *adj syn* see FAMOUS 2

presto *adv syn* see FAST 2

presumably *adv* by reasonable assumption <*presumably* the best qualified for the job should get it>
syn assumably, doubtless, likely, presumptively, probably
rel indubitably, surely, undoubtedly, unquestionably

presume *vb* **1** *syn* see CONJECTURE
2 *syn* see PRESUPPOSE
3 *syn* see IMPOSE 5

presuming *adj syn* see PRESUMPTUOUS
ant unassuming, unpresuming

presumption *n* **1** *syn* see EFFRONTERY
2 *syn* see PRESUPPOSITION 1
3 *syn* see ASSUMPTION 2

presumptively *adv syn* see PRESUMABLY

presumptuous *adj* marked by or based on bold and excessive self-confidence <in such company his demand for attention was utterly *presumptuous*>
syn brash, brassbound, confident, forward, gay, overconfident, overweening, presuming, pushful, pushing, ‖pushy, self-asserting, self-assertive, uppish, uppity
rel pretentious, self-assured, self-conceited; lofty, pompous, supercilious; complacent, self-satisfied, smug; inexcusable, outrageous
idiom too big for one's britches
con deferential, dutiful, respectful, submissive; appropriate, proper

presuppose *vb* to take something for granted or as true or existent especially as a basis for action or reasoning <a lecturer who talks above the heads of his listeners *presupposes* too extensive a knowledge on their part>
syn assume, posit, postulate, premise, presume
rel conjecture, guess, surmise; deduce, infer, judge; believe, expect, gather, imagine, reckon, suppose, suspect, take, think, understand; preconceive

presupposition *n* **1** an act of presupposing <going on her *presupposition* that they would succeed>

syn assumption, presumption

rel conjecture, guess, surmise; deduction, inference, judgment; belief, conviction, opinion, view

2 *syn* see ASSUMPTION 2

pretend *vb* **1** *syn* see ASSUME 4

rel beguile, deceive, delude, mislead; profess, purport

idiom make believe

2 *syn* see CONJECTURE

pretended *adj syn* see ALLEGED

pretender *n syn* see IMPOSTOR

pretense *n* **1** *syn* see CLAIM 1

2 the offering of something false as real or true <there is too much *pretense* in his piety>

syn charade, disguise, make-believe, pageant, pretension, pretentiousness

rel deceit, deception, fake, fraud, humbug, imposture, sham; affectation, air, mannerism, pose

con sincereness; reality, soundness, substantiality, validity; fairness, honesty

ant sincerity

3 *syn* see MASK 2

pretension *n* **1** *syn* see CLAIM 1

2 *syn* see AMBITION 1

3 *syn* see PRETENSE 2

pretentious *adj* **1** *syn* see SHOWY

ant unpretentious

2 *syn* see GENTEEL 3

ant unpretentious

3 flamboyant, turgid, or bombastic in manner or content <a *pretentious* literary style>

syn arty, arty-crafty, big, high-sounding, imposing, overblown

rel affected, feigned, put-on; pompier; aureate, bombastic, euphuistic, flowery, grandiloquent, magniloquent, rhetorical; inflated, tumid, turgid

con heartfelt, hearty, sincere, unfeigned, wholehearted, whole-souled; artless, genuine, natural, simple, unaffected

ant unpretentious

4 *syn* see AMBITIOUS 2

pretentiousness *n syn* see PRETENSE 2

ant unpretentiousness

preterition *n syn* see OMISSION

pretermission *n syn* see OMISSION

pretermit *vb syn* see NEGLECT

preternatural *adj* **1** *syn* see SUPERNATURAL 1

rel anomalous, unnatural; nonnatural

2 *syn* see ABNORMAL 1

ant natural

pretext *n* **1** *syn* see EXCUSE 1

2 *syn* see MASK 2

prettify *vb syn* see PALLIATE

pretty *adj* **1** *syn* see SKILLFUL 2

2 *syn* see BEAUTIFUL

rel darling, ducky; cunning, cute

ant unpretty

pretty *adv syn* see SOMEWHAT 2

idiom pretty much

‖**pretty** *n syn* see TOY 2

prettyism *n syn* see POSE 2

pretty–pretty *n syn* see KNICKKNACK

preux *adj syn* see COURTLY

prevail *vb* **1** *syn* see CONQUER 2

2 *syn* see WIN 1

3 *syn* see RULE 2

prevail (on *or* upon) *vb syn* see INDUCE 1

rel affect, impress

prevailing *adj* general (as in circulation, acceptance, or use) in a given place or at a given time <the *prevailing* point of view among farmers>

syn current, popular, prevalent, rampant, regnant, rife, ruling, widespread

rel dominant, predominant, preponderant; common, familiar, ordinary; general, universal

con exceptional, uncommon, unusual

prevalent *adj* **1** *syn* see DOMINANT 1

2 *syn* see PREVAILING

3 *syn* see GENERAL 1

rel accustomed, customary, wonted

prevaricate *vb syn* see LIE

rel belie, garble, misrepresent

prevarication *n syn* see LIE

prevaricative *adj syn* see EVASIVE 1

prevaricator *n syn* see LIAR

prevaricatory *adj syn* see EVASIVE 1

prevent *vb* **1** to be or get ahead of or to deal with beforehand <many problems are *prevented* easily if one plans wisely>

syn anticipate, forestall

rel baffle, balk, foil, frustrate, thwart; arrest, check, interrupt

2 to stop from advancing or occurring <take steps to *prevent* war> <measures designed to *prevent* the spread of disease>

syn avert, deter, forestall, forfend, obviate, preclude, rule out, stave off, ward

rel bar, block, dam, hinder, impede, obstruct; debar, shut out; forbid, inhibit, interdict, prohibit

con allow, leave, let, suffer

ant permit

previous *adj* **1** *syn* see PRECEDING

ant subsequent; consequent

2 *syn* see EARLY 2

previous *adv syn* see BEFORE 1

previously *adv syn* see BEFORE 2

ant subsequently; consequently

previousness *n syn* see PRIORITY

previse *vb syn* see FORESEE

prevision *n syn* see PREDICTION

prevision *vb syn* see FORESEE

prey *n* **1** *syn* see GAME 3

2 *syn* see VICTIM 1

‖**pribble** *n syn* see QUARREL

price *n* **1** the quantity of one thing that is exchanged or demanded in barter or sale for another <what is the *price* of this book>

syn charge, cost, price tag, rate, tab, tariff

2 *syn* see EXPENSE 2

priceless *adj syn* see PRECIOUS 1

rel cherished, prized, treasured, valued

idiom without price

---

price tag *n syn* see PRICE 1

prick *n* a mark or shallow hole made by or as if by a pointed tool <a needle *prick* in his arm>
syn jab, ‖jag, puncture, stab
rel prickle; hole

prick *vb* **1** *syn* see PERFORATE
rel enter; cut, slash, slit
2 *syn* see URGE
rel excite, pique, stimulate

‖**prick** (up) *vb syn* see DRESS UP 1

prickish *adj syn* see IRRITABLE

prickly *adj* **1** *syn* see THORNY
rel annoying, bothersome
2 *syn* see IRRITABLE

pride *n* **1** *syn* see CONCEIT 2
rel bighead, cockiness, overconfidence, self-assurance
idiom overweening pride
ant humility
2 a reasonable or justifiable sense of one's worth or position <inhumane treatment in prison caused him to lose his *pride*>
syn amour propre, self-esteem, self-regard, self≈respect
rel dignity, face, pridefulness, self-confidence, self-trust
con humiliation, mortification; shamefacedness
ant shame
3 proud or disdainful behavior or actions <her snobbishness and overbearing *pride* were offensive>
syn arrogance, disdain, disdainfulness, haughtiness, hauteur, loftiness, morgue, superbity, superciliousness
rel condescension, snobbishness; contempt, scorn; insolence; smugness; pretentiousness
idiom haughty airs
con humbleness, modesty, unpretentiousness
ant humility
4 *syn* see BEST
idiom pride of the herd

pride *vb* to congratulate (oneself) for something one is, has, or has done or achieved <he *prides* himself on his ancestry>
syn pique, plume, preen
rel boast, brag, crow, gasconade, vaunt; congratulate, felicitate
ant efface

‖**pridy** *adj syn* see PROUD 1

prier (*or* **pryer**) *n syn* see BUSYBODY

priestal *adj syn* see SACERDOTAL

priestish *adj syn* see SACERDOTAL

priestlike *adj syn* see SACERDOTAL

priestly *adj syn* see SACERDOTAL

‖**prig** *vb syn* see STEAL 1

prig *n syn* see THIEF

prig *n syn* see PRUDE

prig *adj syn* see PRIM 1

priggish *adj* **1** *syn* see COMPLACENT
rel self-righteous; self-esteeming, self-loving
2 *syn* see PRIM 1

prim *adj* **1** excessively concerned with what one regards as proper or right <a *prim* woman, easily shocked by vulgar language>

syn bluenosed, genteel, missish, precise, prig, priggish, prissy, proper, prudish, puritanical, straitlaced, stuffy, tight-laced, Victorian; *compare* GENTEEL 3
rel correct, nice, precise; decorous; rigid, stiff, wooden; ceremonial, ceremonious, conventional, formal, straight
idiom prim and proper
con lax, loose, slack; easy, easygoing, free
2 *syn* see NEAT 2

prima facie *adj syn* see SELF-EVIDENT

primarily *adv* **1** *syn* see GENERALLY 1
2 *syn* see INITIALLY 1

primary *adj* **1** *syn* see FIRST 2
2 *syn* see PRIMITIVE 4
3 *syn* see FUNDAMENTAL 1
4 *syn* see DIRECT 4
5 not based on or derived from something else <the *primary* studies in nuclear physics>
syn original, prime, primitive, underivative, underived
rel first, firsthand; basic, foundational, fundamental, principal, underlying
con derivate, derivational, derivative, derived; borrowed, secondhand
ant secondary

prime *n* **1** *syn* see MORNING 1
2 *syn* see YOUTH 1
3 *syn* see BEST

prime *adj* **1** *syn* see FIRST 2
2 *syn* see EXCELLENT
3 *syn* see PRIMARY 5

prime *vb syn* see PROVOKE 4

primeval *adj syn* see PRIMITIVE 4

primevous *adj syn* see PRIMITIVE 4

primitial *adj syn* see PRIMITIVE 4

primitive *adj* **1** *syn* see PRIMARY 5
2 *syn* see EARLY 1
3 closely approximating an early ancestral type <the opossums are *primitive* mammals>
syn archaic, persistent, undeveloped, unevolved
ant advanced
4 of or relating to earlier ages of the world or of human history <archaeology is concerned especially with the study of *primitive* man>
syn primary, primeval, primevous, primitial
ant unprimitive
5 *syn* see ELEMENTAL 1
6 characterized by a lack of written language, simple technology, and a relatively simple social organization
syn nonliterate, preliterate
rel barbarian, uncivilized, uncultivated
con advanced, civilized, cultivated

primitively *adv syn* see INITIALLY 1

primogenitor *n syn* see ANCESTOR 1

primordial *adj* **1** *syn* see EARLY 1
2 *syn* see FIRST

primp *vb syn* see DRESS UP 1

primrose *n syn* see BEST

prince *n syn* see MAGNATE

princely *adj syn* see GRAND 1

principal *adj* **1** *syn* see CHIEF 2
2 *syn* see FIRST 3

principally *adv syn* see GENERALLY 1

principium *n syn* see PRINCIPLE 1

principle *n* **1** a comprehensive and fundamental rule, doctrine, or assumption <the *principle* of free speech>
syn axiom, fundamental, law, principium, theorem
rel basis, foundation, ground; canon, precept, rule; convention, form, usage
2 principles *pl syn* see ETHIC 3
3 principles *pl syn* see ALPHABET 2

principled *adj syn* see MORAL 1
ant unprincipled

‖**prink** *vb syn* see SASHAY

prink (up) *vb syn* see DRESS UP 1

print *n* **1** *syn* see IMPRESSION 1
2 printed state or form <to see his name in *print*>
syn black and white, writing

printing *n syn* see EDITION

prior *adj syn* see PRECEDING
rel ahead, before, forward
con after, behind

priority *n* the act, the fact, or the right of preceding another <the right to inherit a title is dependent mainly on *priority* of birth>
syn antecedence, precedence, precedency, previousness
rel arrangement, order, ordering; ascendancy, supremacy; preeminence, transcendence

prior to *prep* **1** *syn* see BEFORE 1
2 *syn* see UNTIL

prison *n syn* see JAIL

‖**prison** *vb syn* see IMPRISON

prison bird *n syn* see CONVICT

prissy *adj* **1** *syn* see PRIM 1
rel fastidious, finicky, squeamish
2 *syn* see EFFEMINATE

‖**pritch** *vb syn* see PERFORATE

private *adj* **1** belonging to or concerning an individual person, company, or interest <*private* property>
syn personal, privy
rel intimate
con common, general, shared
ant public
2 known only to a select few <the group had *private* information about the strike>
syn closet, confidential, hushed, inside
rel secret; discreet; concealed, hidden
con common, general, open
ant public

private detective *n* a person concerned with the maintenance of lawful conduct or the investigation of crime either as a regular employee of a private interest (as a hotel) or as a contractor for fees <retained a *private detective* to report on his wife's associates>
syn operative, Pinkerton, ‖private eye, ‖shamus; *compare* DETECTIVE

‖**private eye** *n syn* see PRIVATE DETECTIVE

privately *adv syn* see SECRETLY

private parts *n pl syn* see GENITALIA

privates *n pl syn* see GENITALIA

privation *n* **1** *syn* see ABSENCE
2 the state of one deprived of something previously or normally possessed <suffered great *privation* during the famine>
syn deprivation, deprivement, dispossession, divestiture, loss; *compare* LOSS 1
rel distress, misery, suffering; losing, mislaying, misplacement, misplacing
3 *syn* see POVERTY 1

privilege *n syn* see RIGHT 2
rel allowance, concession; boon, favor

privilege (from) *vb syn* see EXEMPT

privities *n pl syn* see GENITALIA

privy *adj* **1** *syn* see PRIVATE 1
2 *syn* see ULTERIOR

privy *n* **1** an outdoor toilet <in less settled areas, *privies* often take the place of indoor plumbing>
syn backhouse, ‖biffy, ‖closet, jakes, ‖necessary, ‖office, outhouse
2 *syn* see TOILET

privy parts *n pl syn* see GENITALIA

prize *n* **1** *syn* see REWARD
2 *syn* see BEST

prize *vb syn* see APPRECIATE 1

prize *n syn* see SPOIL

prize *vb syn* see PRY

prizefighting *n syn* see BOXING

pro *prep syn* see FOR 2
ant anti, con

pro *n syn* see EXPERT

pro–and–con *vb syn* see DISCUSS 1

probable *adj* being such as may become true or actual <seems to be a *probable* candidate>
syn conceivable, earthly, likely, mortal, possible
rel believable, colorable, credible, plausible; rational, reasonable; apparent, illusory, ostensible, seeming
con doubtful, dubious, questionable, unlikely
ant improbable, unprobable

probably *adv syn* see PRESUMABLY
ant improbably

probe *n syn* see INQUIRY 1

probe *vb* **1** *syn* see EXPLORE
2 to try to find out (as by discreet questioning) the views or intentions of <*probed* the neighbors on the subject of political reform>
syn feel out, sound (out)
rel ask, catechize, examine, inquire, interrogate, query, quiz
idiom feel the pulse, launch a trial balloon, put out a feeler, see how the land lies, see which way the wind blows, test the water(s)
3 *syn* see SCOUT

probing *n syn* see INQUIRY 1

probity *n syn* see GOODNESS

problem *n* **1** *syn* see EXAMPLE 3
2 something requiring thought and skill to arrive at a proper conclusion or decision <what to do now is a *problem*>

---

syn synonym(s)   *rel* related word(s)
ant antonym(s)   *con* contrasted word(s)
idiom idiomatic equivalent(s)
‖ use limited; if in doubt, see a dictionary

syn issue, nut, question
rel enigma, mystery, puzzle; bugaboo, bugbear; count, point
idiom a hard nut to crack
problematic *adj* **1** *syn* see DOUBTFUL 1
ant unproblematic
2 *syn* see MOOT
ant unproblematic
proboscis *n* *syn* see NOSE 1
procacious *adj* **1** *syn* see INSOLENT 2
2 *syn* see WISE 5
procedure *n* **1** *syn* see COURSE 3
2 *syn* see MEASURE 7
3 *syn* see PROCESS 1
proceed *vb* **1** *syn* see SPRING 1
2 *syn* see GO 1
3 *syn* see ADVANCE 5
ant recede
proceeding *n* **1** *syn* see MEASURE 7
2 *syn* see PROCESS 1
proceeds *n pl* *syn* see PROFIT
process *n* **1** the series of actions, operations, or motions involved in the accomplishment of an end <the *process* of making sugar from sugarcane>
syn procedure, proceeding
rel fashion, manner, method, mode, modus, system, technique, way, wise; routine; operation
2 *syn* see OUTGROWTH 1
‖**process** *vb* *syn* see GO 1
procession *n* *syn* see ORDER 5
processus *n* *syn* see OUTGROWTH 1
proclaim *vb* **1** *syn* see DECLARE 1
rel utter, vent, ventilate, voice
2 *syn* see SHOW 2
proclamation *n* *syn* see DECLARATION
proclivity *n* *syn* see LEANING 2
procrastinate *vb* *syn* see DELAY 2
rel defer, postpone, stay, suspend; prolong, protract
procreate *vb* **1** to produce offspring <*procreate* children>
syn bear, beget, breed, generate, multiply, produce, propagate, reproduce
rel mother; engender; hatch, spawn; proliferate
idiom give birth to, multiply the earth
2 *syn* see GENERATE 1
3 *syn* see FATHER 1
procumbent *adj* *syn* see PRONE 4
procurable *adj* *syn* see AVAILABLE 1
procure *vb* **1** *syn* see GET 1
2 *syn* see INDUCE 1
prod *vb* **1** *syn* see POKE 1
2 *syn* see URGE
rel instigate; excite, pique, provoke, stimulate
prodigal *adj* *syn* see PROFUSE
ant parsimonious; frugal
prodigal *n* *syn* see SPENDTHRIFT
prodigality *n* *syn* see EXTRAVAGANCE 2
ant parsimoniousness
prodigalize *vb* *syn* see WASTE 2
prodigious *adj* **1** *syn* see MARVELOUS 1
2 *syn* see MONSTROUS 1
3 *syn* see HUGE

prodigy *n* *syn* see WONDER 1
produce *vb* **1** *syn* see PROCREATE 1
2 *syn* see STAGE
3 *syn* see EFFECT 1
4 *syn* see GENERATE 1
5 *syn* see GENERATE 3
6 *syn* see MAKE 3
7 *syn* see BEAR 9
8 *syn* see GIVE 7
9 *syn* see GROW 1
produce *n* *syn* see PRODUCT 1
product *n* **1** something produced by physical labor or intellectual effort <the literary *products* of the Age of Reason>
syn produce, production
rel handiwork; consequence, effect, offshoot, outcome, outgrowth, result; fruit, harvest
2 *syn* see OUTPUT
production *n* **1** *syn* see PRODUCT 1
2 *syn* see EXTENSION 1
3 *syn* see OUTPUT
productive *adj* *syn* see FERTILE
ant unproductive
proem *n* *syn* see INTRODUCTION
proemial *adj* *syn* see PRELIMINARY
profanation *n* a violation or misuse of something normally held sacred <the *profanation* of a religious ritual>
syn blasphemy, desecration, sacrilege, violation
rel contamination, defilement, pollution; corruption, debasement, perversion, vitiation; transgression, trespass
con glorification, hallowing, sanctification
ant purification; consecration
profane *adj* **1** not concerned with religion or religious purposes <he was speaking of *profane* history, not the history found in the Bible>
syn lay, secular, temporal, unsacred
rel earthly, mundane, terrestrial, worldly
con consecrated, hallowed, holy, sanctified; divine, religious, spiritual
ant sacred
2 *syn* see HEATHEN
3 *syn* see IMPIOUS 1
4 *syn* see SACRILEGIOUS
5 *syn* see OBSCENE 2
profaned *adj* *syn* see IMPURE 3
ant unprofaned
profanity *n* *syn* see BLASPHEMY 1
profess *vb* *syn* see ASSERT 1
professed *adj* *syn* see ALLEGED
professedly *adv* *syn* see OSTENSIBLY
profession *n* *syn* see TRADE 1
professional *n* *syn* see EXPERT
ant amateur
proffer *vb* *syn* see OFFER 1
proffer *n* *syn* see PROPOSAL
proficiency *n* *syn* see ADVANCE 2
proficient *adj* having or manifesting the knowledge, skill, and experience needed for sucess in a particular field or endeavor <a *proficient* glider pilot>
syn adept, crack, crackerjack, expert, master, masterful, masterly, skilled, skillful; *compare* EXPERIENCED, SKILLFUL 2

rel checked-out, drilled, exercised, practiced; effective, effectual, efficient; able, capable, competent, qualified; accomplished, consummate, finished
con ignorant, untaught, untrained; inexperienced; unskilled
ant incompetent
proficient *n syn* see EXPERT
profile *n syn* see OUTLINE
profit *n* the excess of returns over expenditure in a transaction or a series of transactions <his *profits* from the business venture were rewarding>
syn earnings, gain, lucre, proceeds, return
rel cleaning, cleanup, killing; receipt(s); output, outturn, product, production, turnout, yield
con cost, expenditure, expense, outgo
ant loss
profit *vb syn* see BENEFIT
ant lose
profitable *adj syn* see ADVANTAGEOUS 1
ant profitless, unprofitable
profligate *adj syn* see ABANDONED 2
profligate *n* 1 *syn* see WASTREL 1
2 *syn* see SPENDTHRIFT
profound *adj* 1 *syn* see RECONDITE
2 *syn* see DEEP 1
3 *syn* see INTENSIVE
profoundness *n syn* see DEPTH 2
profundity *n syn* see DEPTH 2
profuse *adj* proffered in or characterized by great abundance <*profuse* apologies> <a *profuse* flow of blood>
syn exuberant, lavish, lush, luxuriant, opulent, prodigal, profusive, riotous
rel abundant, copious; abounding, swarming, teeming; excessive, extravagant, immoderate; bounteous, bountiful, generous, liberal, munificent, openhanded
con exiguous, meager, scrimpy, skimpy, slight, small, sparse
ant scant, scanty
profusive *adj syn* see PROFUSE
progenerate *vb syn* see FATHER 1
progenitor *n syn* see ANCESTOR 1
progeniture *n syn* see OFFSPRING
progeny *n syn* see OFFSPRING
prognosis *n syn* see PREDICTION
prognostic *n syn* see FORETOKEN
prognosticate *vb syn* see FORETELL
prognostication *n syn* see PREDICTION
prognosticator *n syn* see PROPHET
program *n* 1 a formulated plan listing things to be done or to take place especially in chronological order <the *program* of a concert>
syn agenda, calendar, card, docket, programma, schedule, sked, timetable
rel bill; slate; plan
idiom order of the day
2 *syn* see COURSE 3
programma *n syn* see PROGRAM 1
progress *n* 1 *syn* see ADVANCE 2
ant regression, retrogression
2 a movement onward (as in time or space) <the *progress* of a disease> <they made slow *progress* toward their destination>

syn advance, course, progression
rel passage
3 *syn* see DEVELOPMENT
progress *vb syn* see ADVANCE 5
ant retrogress
progression *n* 1 *syn* see PROGRESS 2
2 *syn* see SUCCESSION 2
3 *syn* see DEVELOPMENT
ant regression, retrogression
progressive *adj syn* see LIBERAL 3
ant reactionary
prohibit *vb syn* see FORBID
ant permit
prohibited *adj syn* see FORBIDDEN
prohibition *n syn* see TABOO
ant permission
project *n* 1 *syn* see PLAN 1
2 something (as a business operation) that one engages in or attempts <large-scale *projects* involving large sums of money>
syn enterprise, undertaking
rel affair, business, concern, matter, proposition, thing; adventure, emprise, exploit, feat, gest, venture
project *vb* 1 *syn* see PLAN 2
rel intend, propose, purpose; delineate, diagram
2 *syn* see THINK 1
‖3 *syn* see WANDER 1
4 *syn* see BULGE
rel extend, lengthen, prolong
projection *n* 1 something which extends beyond a level or a normal outer surface <buttresses are *projections* which serve to support a wall>
syn bulge, jut, outthrust, protrusion, protuberance
rel bump, bunch, swelling; extension, prolongation; hook, knob, point, spine, spur
ant depression
2 *syn* see EMINENCE 3
prolegomenon *n syn* see INTRODUCTION
proletariat *n syn* see RABBLE 2
proliferant *adj syn* see FERTILE
prolific *adj syn* see FERTILE
rel abounding, swarming; breeding, generating, propagating, reproducing, reproductive
ant barren, unfruitful
prolificacy *n syn* see FERTILITY
ant barrenness, unfruitfulness
prolix *adj syn* see WORDY
rel irksome, tedious, tiresome, wearisome; prolonged, protracted
prolixity *n syn* see VERBOSITY
prolixness *n syn* see VERBOSITY
prologue *n syn* see INTRODUCTION
ant epilogue
prolong *vb syn* see EXTEND 3
rel continue, endure, last, persist
con abbreviate, retrench, shorten
ant curtail

---

syn synonym(s)   *rel* related word(s)
ant antonym(s)   *con* contrasted word(s)
idiom idiomatic equivalent(s)
‖ use limited; if in doubt, see a dictionary

prolongate *vb syn* see EXTEND 3

prolongation *n syn* see EXTENSION 1

prolonged *adj syn* see LONG 2
 ant curtailed

prolongment *n syn* see EXTENSION 1

prominence *n* **1** *syn* see EMINENCE 1
 2 *syn* see EMINENCE 3

prominency *n syn* see EMINENCE 1

prominent *adj* **1** *syn* see NOTICEABLE
 ant inconspicuous
 2 *syn* see FAMOUS 2
 3 *syn* see WELL-KNOWN

promiscuous *adj* **1** *syn* see MISCELLANEOUS
 2 *syn* see RANDOM

promise *vb* **1** to give one's word to do, bring
 about, or provide <*promised* to render all possible assistance to the flood victims>
 syn engage, pass, pledge, undertake; *compare*
 VOW
 rel accede, agree, assent, consent; bargain, compact, contract; covenant, plight, swear, vow; assure, ensure, insure; guarantee
 idiom give (*or* make) a promise, pass one's word
 2 *syn* see AUGUR 2

promise *n* a declaration that one will do or refrain
 from doing something specified <never gave a
 promise that he did not intend to keep>
 syn engagement, plight, word; *compare* PLEDGE
 1, WORD 8
 rel earnest, guarantee, pawn, pledge, security,
 token; covenant, swear, vow; assurance, warrant
 idiom word of honor

‖**promised** *adj syn* see ENGAGED 2

promised land *n syn* see UTOPIA

promiseful *adj syn* see HOPEFUL 2

promising *adj syn* see HOPEFUL 2
 ant unpromising

promontory *n* a high point of land or rock projecting into a body of water beyond the line of coast
 <stood on the *promontory* watching boats come
 in with the tide>
 syn beak, bill, cape, foreland, head, headland,
 naze, point

promote *vb* **1** *syn* see ADVANCE 2
 con break, bust, declass, degrade, demerit, disgrade, disrate, downgrade, reduce
 ant bump, demote
 2 *syn* see ADVANCE 1
 3 to encourage public acceptance of (as a policy
 or merchandise) through publicity <official attempts to *promote* energy conservation> <televi-
 sion helped *promote* the new smaller cars>
 syn advertise, boost, plug, push; *compare* PUBLI-
 CIZE
 rel ballyhoo, propagandize; build up, cry, hype,
 press-agent, publicize, puff; communicate, impart
 idiom make much of
 con belittle, decry, depreciate, discredit, knock,
 run down
 ant disparage

promotion *n* **1** *syn* see ADVANCEMENT 1
 ant demotion
 2 *syn* see PUBLICITY

rel advertisement

prompt *vb* **1** *syn* see INDUCE 1
 2 *syn* see URGE

prompt *adj* **1** *syn* see QUICK 2
 rel alert, vigilant, watchful, wide-awake; expeditious, speedy, swift
 con lax, remiss, slack; dilatory
 2 *syn* see PUNCTUAL 2

promptitude *n syn* see ALACRITY

promptly *adv syn* see FAST 2

promulgate *vb syn* see DECLARE 1

promulgation *n syn* see DECLARATION

prone *adj* **1** *syn* see WILLING 1
 2 *syn* see LIABLE 2
 3 *syn* see APT 1
 4 lying down <lying *prone* on the floor>
 syn decumbent, flat, procumbent, prostrate,
 reclining, recumbent
 rel resupine, supine; level
 con arrect, raised, stand-up, straight-up, upright, upstanding
 ant erect

pronounce *vb syn* see ARTICULATE 2

pronounced *adj syn* see DECIDED 1

pronouncement *n syn* see DECLARATION

‖**pronto** *adv syn* see FAST 2

pronunciamento *n syn* see DECLARATION

proof *n* **1** *syn* see REASON 3
 2 *syn* see TESTIMONY

prop *n syn* see SUPPORT 3

prop *vb* **1** *syn* see SUPPORT 4
 2 *syn* see SUPPORT 5

propagandist *n syn* see MISSIONARY

propagate *vb* **1** *syn* see PROCREATE 1
 2 *syn* see GROW 1
 3 *syn* see SPREAD 1

propel *vb* **1** *syn* see PUSH 1
 2 *syn* see MOVE 5
 3 *syn* see URGE

propellant *n syn* see STIMULUS

propensity *n syn* see LEANING 2
 ant antipathy

proper *adj* **1** *syn* see FIT 1
 ant improper
 2 *syn* see TRUE 7
 ant improper
 3 *syn* see DECOROUS 1
 ant improper
 4 *syn* see ABLE
 5 *syn* see GOOD 2
 ant improper
 6 *syn* see CHARACTERISTIC
 ‖**7** *syn* see UTTER
 8 *syn* see CORRECT 2
 9 *syn* see PRIM 1

properly *adv* **1** *syn* see WELL 4
 ant improperly
 2 *syn* see WELL 1
 idiom by rights
 ant improperly

properness *n syn* see ORDER 7
 ant improperness

property *n* **1** *syn* see QUALITY 1
 2 *syn* see WEALTH 2

3 syn see OWNERSHIP

prophecy *n* **1 syn** see REVELATION

  2 syn see PREDICTION

prophesier *n syn* see PROPHET

prophesy *vb syn* see FORETELL

prophet *n* one who predicts events or developments <there have been many *prophets* foretelling the end of the world>

  syn augur, auspex, forecaster, foreseer, foreteller, haruspex, Nostradamus, predictor, prognosticator, prophesier, seer, soothsayer

prophetic *adj* of, relating to, or characteristic of a prophet or prophecy <the old woman seemed to have *prophetic* powers>

  syn apocalyptic, Delphian, fatidic, mantic, oracular, prophetical, sibylline, vatic, vaticinal

  rel revelatory; interpretive; mysterious, mystic, strange, unexplainable

  ant unprophetic

prophetical *adj syn* see PROPHETIC

propinquity *n syn* see PROXIMITY

propitiate *vb syn* see PACIFY

  rel adapt, adjust, conform, reconcile; content, satisfy; intercede, mediate

propitiatory *adj syn* see PURGATIVE

propitious *adj* **1 syn** see FAVORABLE 5

  ant unpropitious; adverse

  2 syn see TIMELY 1

  ant unpropitious

  3 syn see GOOD 1

  ant unpropitious; adverse

‖propone *vb syn* see PROPOSE 1

proponent *n syn* see EXPONENT

  ant opponent

proportion *n* **1 syn** see DEGREE 2

  2 syn see SYMMETRY

  ant disproportion

  3 syn see SIZE 1

proportion *vb syn* see HARMONIZE 3

proportional *adj* being in proportion <a starting salary *proportional* to her experience>

  syn commensurable, commensurate, equal, symmetrical

  rel correlative, corresponding, reciprocal; contingent, dependent, relative

  con asymmetrical, disproportionate, irregular, lopsided, nonsymmetrical, off-balance, overbalanced, unbalanced, unequal, uneven, unsymmetrical

  ant disproportional

proportionless *adj syn* see LOPSIDED

proposal *n* something which is proposed to another for consideration <his *proposal* for a new busing plan>

  syn invitation, proffer, proposition, suggestion

  rel motion; recommendation; idea, plan, project; outline, scheme

propose *vb* **1** to set before the mind for consideration <she *proposed* Mr. Smith for secretary of the club>

  syn pose, prefer, ‖propone, proposition, propound, put, suggest

  rel move (for); offer, present, submit, tender; ask, request, solicit

  idiom put forth (*or* forward)

  ant withdraw

  2 syn see INTEND 2

proposition *n syn* see PROPOSAL

proposition *vb syn* see PROPOSE 1

propound *vb syn* see PROPOSE 1

proprietary *n syn* see OWNERSHIP

proprietor *n syn* see OWNER

proprietorship *n syn* see OWNERSHIP

propriety *n* **1 syn** see ORDER 11

  2 syn see DECORUM 1

  ant impropriety

  3 syn see ORDER 7

  ant impropriety

  4 proprieties *pl syn* see MANNER 5

prorate *vb syn* see APPORTION 2

prorogate *vb syn* see ADJOURN 2

prorogue *vb* **1 syn** see DEFER

  2 syn see ADJOURN 2

prosaic *adj* **1** belonging to or characteristic of prose as distinguished from poetry <his poetry is far more fanciful than his *prosaic* writings>

  syn matter-of-fact, prose, prosing, prosy

  rel actual, factual; literal

  con figurative, metaphorical, symbolic; fanciful, florid, flowery, ornate

  ant poetic

  2 syn see COLORLESS 2

  3 belonging to or suitable to the everyday world <the *prosaic* business of day-to-day housekeeping>

  syn commonplace, everyday, lowly, mundane, workaday, workday

  rel practicable, practical; boring, irksome, tedious

  4 syn see COMMON 6

prosaicism *n syn* see COMMONPLACE

prosaism *n syn* see COMMONPLACE

proscribe *vb syn* see SENTENCE

proscription *n syn* see TABOO

prose *n syn* see CHAT 2

prose *adj syn* see PROSAIC 1

prosing *adj syn* see PROSAIC 1

prospect *n syn* see VISTA

prospect *vb syn* see EXPLORE

prosper *vb syn* see SUCCEED 3

  rel augment, increase, multiply; bear, produce, turn out, yield

prospering *adj syn* see FLOURISHING

prosperity *n* **1 syn** see SUCCESS

  2 a state of good fortune and especially of financial success <his wise investments finally brought him a life of *prosperity*>

  syn abundance, ease, easy street, prosperousness, thriving, well-being

  rel affluence, riches, wealth

  idiom bed of roses, comfortable (*or* easy) circumstances, life of ease, the good life

---

syn synonym(s)   **rel** related word(s)
ant antonym(s)   **con** contrasted word(s)
idiom idiomatic equivalent(s)
‖ use limited; if in doubt, see a dictionary

con misery, suffering; distress, embarrassment, indigence, poverty, straits
ant adversity
3 *syn* see WELFARE
4 a state of high general economic activity marked by relatively full employment <a war economy often generates *prosperity*>
syn boom, prosperousness
rel expansion; growth; inflation
con recession, slump, stagnation; bust
ant depression
prosperous *adj* **1** *syn* see TIMELY 1
rel appropriate, convenient, desirable; felicitous, fortunate, happy, lucky
con ill-seasoned, ill-timed, inauspicious, inopportune, unpropitious, unseasonable, untimely
ant unprosperous
2 *syn* see SUCCESSFUL
3 enjoying or marked by economic well-being <in *prosperous* circumstances>
syn comfortable, easy, ‖snug, substantial, well, well-fixed, well-heeled, well-off, well-to-do
rel affluent, opulent, rich, wealthy; halcyon
idiom comfortably off, comfortably situated, in (the) clover, in good case
con impecunious, necessitous, needy, poor; failing, unfortunate, unsuccessful
ant unprosperous
4 *syn* see FLOURISHING
rel lusty, strong
con decrepit, feeble, spindling, weak
prosperously *adv* *syn* see WELL 5
ant unprosperously
prosperousness *n* **1** *syn* see PROSPERITY 2
ant unprosperousness
2 *syn* see PROSPERITY 4
prostitute *vb* *syn* see ABUSE 2
rel corrupt, debase, debauch, deprave, vitiate
prostitute *n* a woman who engages in promiscuous sexual intercourse especially for money <streets haunted by *prostitutes*>
syn bawd, ‖callet, call girl, camp follower, cocotte, ‖cruiser, drab, fille de joie, harlot, ‖hooker, hustler, ‖joy girl, meretrix, moll, nightwalker, party girl, pom-pom girl, poule, quean, sporting girl, street girl, streetwalker, ‖tomato, whore
rel bar girl, B-girl, pickup; V-girl, victory girl; cocodette
idiom lady of pleasure, lady of the evening, woman of the street (*or* streets), woman of the town
prostitution *n* the act or practice of engaging in promiscuous sexual intercourse especially for money <the problem of *prostitution* around military installations>
syn harlotry, oldest profession, (the) social evil, streetwalking, whoredom
prostrate *adj* *syn* see PRONE 4
prostrate *vb* **1** *syn* see FELL 1
2 *syn* see PARALYZE 1
3 *syn* see OVERWHELM 4
4 *syn* see EXHAUST 4
prosy *adj* **1** *syn* see PROSAIC 1
2 *syn* see COLORLESS 2

protean *adj* *syn* see CHANGEABLE 1
protect *vb* *syn* see DEFEND 1
rel conserve, preserve, save; harbor, shelter
protection *n* **1** *syn* see DEFENSE 1
2 money paid under threat of depredation <offered *protection* to keep his store from being vandalized>
syn ‖pad
rel extortion, shakedown, squeeze; graft; bribe, payola
pro tem *adj* *syn* see TEMPORARY
pro tempore *adj* *syn* see TEMPORARY
protest *n* *syn* see DEMUR 2
protest *vb* **1** *syn* see ASSERT 1
2 *syn* see OBJECT 1
rel demonstrate; combat, fight, oppose, resist
ant agree
protoplast *n* *syn* see ORIGINAL 1
prototypal *adj* *syn* see TYPICAL 1
prototype *n* **1** *syn* see ORIGINAL 1
2 *syn* see FORERUNNER 2
prototypical *adj* *syn* see TYPICAL 1
protract *vb* *syn* see EXTEND 3
ant curtail
protracted *adj* *syn* see LONG 2
ant curtailed
protraction *n* *syn* see EXTENSION 1
rel dallying, dawdling, delay, lag; stay, suspension
ant curtailment
protrude *vb* *syn* see BULGE
protrusion *n* *syn* see PROJECTION 1
protuberance *n* *syn* see PROJECTION 1
protuberate *vb* *syn* see BULGE
proud *adj* **1** showing or feeling superiority toward others <a woman who was too *proud* to do her share of menial tasks>
syn arrogant, cavalier, disdainful, dismissive, haughty, high-and-mighty, hubristic, huffy, insolent, lofty, lordly, orgulous, overbearing, ‖pridy, proudhearted, supercilious, superior, toplofical, toplofty; compare POMPOUS 1, VAIN 3
rel contemptuous, scornful; misproud; ostentatious, pretentious; bloated, important, pompous, self-important, stuffy, wiggy; conceited, narcissistic, self-conceited, stuck-up, vain, vainglorious; domineering, high-handed, imperious, masterful
con lowly, meek, modest, unassuming; chagrined, mortified
ant humble
2 *syn* see SPLENDID 2
proudhearted *adj* *syn* see PROUD 1
prove *vb* **1** to establish a point by appropriate objective means <gathered evidence that *proved* the need for better controls>
syn demonstrate, test, try
rel confirm, corroborate, substantiate, verify; argue, attest, bespeak, betoken, indicate
ant disprove; refute
2 *syn* see TRY 1
3 *syn* see ESTABLISH 6
provenance *n* *syn* see SOURCE
provender *n* *syn* see FOOD 1

provenience *n syn* see SOURCE
prove out *vb syn* see SUCCEED 2
proverb *n syn* see SAYING
provide *vb syn* see GIVE 3
provide (for) *vb syn* see SUPPORT 3
providence *n* **1** *syn* see ECONOMY
  ant improvidence
  2 *syn* see PRUDENCE 1
  ant improvidence
provident *adj syn* see SPARING
  ant improvident
providential *adj syn* see LUCKY
  rel benignant, kind, kindly
province *n* **1** *syn* see FUNCTION 1
  rel calling, pursuit, work
  2 *syn* see FIELD
provincial *n syn* see RUSTIC
provincial *adj* **1** *syn* see RURAL
  2 *syn* see INSULAR
  rel bigoted, hidebound
  con cosmic, universal; progressive
  ant catholic
provision *n syn* see CONDITION 1
provisional *adj* **1** *syn* see CONDITIONAL 1
  rel temporary; contingent, dependent
  ant definitive
  2 *syn* see MAKESHIFT
provisionary *adj syn* see CONDITIONAL 1
provisions *n pl syn* see FOOD 1
proviso *n syn* see CONDITION 1
provisory *adj syn* see CONDITIONAL 1
provocation *n syn* see ANNOYANCE 1
provocative *n syn* see STIMULUS
provoke *vb* **1** *syn* see IRRITATE
  rel insult, outrage
  ant gratify
  2 *syn* see ANNOY 1
  rel anger, incense, madden
  3 *syn* see INCITE
  rel perturb, upset
  4 to lead one into doing or feeling or to produce by so leading a person <was *provoked* into finding a solution to the problem> <this foolish answer *provoked* an outburst of rage>
  syn excite, galvanize, innervate, innerve, motivate, move, pique, prime, quicken, rouse, ‖roust, stimulate, suscitate; *compare* FIRE 2, STIR 1
  rel arouse, awaken, bestir, build up, challenge, kindle, rally, stir, wake, waken, whet; animate, exalt, fire, inform, inspire; electrify, enthuse, thrill; titillate, titivate
  idiom bring (one) to one's feet
  con calm, relax, soothe
  5 *syn* see GENERATE 3
provoking *n syn* see ANNOYANCE 1
prowess *n* **1** *syn* see HEROISM
  2 *syn* see ADDRESS 1
proximate *adj* **1** *syn* see CLOSE 6
  2 *syn* see IMMINENT 1
  3 *syn* see RUDE 3
  ant exact
proximity *n* the quality or state of being near <the two houses are in close *proximity*>
  syn appropinquity, contiguity, contiguousness, immediacy, propinquity

rel togetherness; closeness, nearness; adjacency, juxtaposition
  con farness, remoteness
  ant distance
proxy *n syn* see AGENT 2
prude *n* a person who is excessively or priggishly attentive to propriety or decorum <in that narrow atmosphere she hardened into a rigid, inhibited, censorious person—a thorough *prude*>
  syn bluenose, comstock, goody-goody, Grundy, Mrs. Grundy, nice Nelly, prig, puritan, ‖wowser
  rel spoilsport, stick-in-the-mud, wet blanket; fuddy-duddy, old fogy, stuffed shirt; fussbudget, old maid
  con freethinker, latitudinarian, libertarian
prudence *n* **1** a quality in a person that allows him to choose the sensible course <displayed *prudence* in setting up his business>
  syn canniness, caution, discreetness, discretion, foresight, forethought, precaution, providence; *compare* WIT 3
  rel acumen, astucity, astuteness, clear-sightedness, discrimination, keenness, penetration, percipience, perspicacity, shrewdness, wit; insight, sagaciousness, sagacity, sageness, sapience, wisdom; advisableness, expediency; calculation, circumspection
  con indiscretion, unreasonableness, unwiseness
  ant imprudence
  2 *syn* see ECONOMY
prudent *adj* **1** *syn* see WISE 2
  ant imprudent
  2 *syn* see EXPEDIENT
prudish *adj syn* see PRIM 1
  rel strict; austere, severe, stern
prune *n syn* see DUNCE
prune *vb syn* see CUT 6
  rel brash, lop; thin; eliminate, exclude
prurience *n syn* see LUST 2
pruriency *n syn* see LUST 2
prurient *adj syn* see LUSTFUL 2
  rel bawdy, erotic, lewd; sensual
pry *vb syn* see SNOOP
  idiom nose into
pry *vb* to raise, move, or pull apart with or as if with a pry <*pry* up a floorboard>
  syn jimmy, lever, prize
  rel elevate, hoist, lift, pick up, raise, rear, take up, uphold, uplift, upraise, uprear; turn, twist; disengage, disjoin, divide, separate
prying *adj syn* see CURIOUS 2
  rel obtrusive, officious
psalm *vb syn* see PRAISE 2
psalmody *vb syn* see PRAISE 2
pseudo *adj syn* see COUNTERFEIT
  rel wrong
pseudonym *n* a fictitious or assumed name <used a *pseudonym* in many of his adventures>
  syn alias, anonym, nom de guerre

---

syn synonym(s)   *rel* related word(s)
ant antonym(s)   *con* contrasted word(s)
idiom idiomatic equivalent(s)
‖ use limited; if in doubt, see a dictionary

rel ananym; nom de plume, pen name; stage name; incognito

psychal *adj syn* see PSYCHIC 1

psyche *n syn* see SOUL 1

psychic *adj* **1** sensitive to nonphysical forces and influences <because he foretold many things correctly, people regarded him as *psychic*>
syn psychal, psychical, supersensible, supersensory
rel telepathic; spiritual; impressible, impressionable, responsive, sensible, sensile, sensitive, sentient, susceptible, susceptive
2 *syn* see MENTAL 1

psychical *adj* **1** *syn* see PSYCHIC 1
2 *syn* see MENTAL 1

psychological *adj syn* see MENTAL 1

psychopathy *n syn* see INSANITY 1

pub *n syn* see BAR 5

puberty *n syn* see YOUTH 1

pubescence *n syn* see YOUTH 1

public *adj* **1** of, relating to, or affecting the people as an organized community <*public* affairs>
syn civic, civil, national
rel government, governmental; community; state; municipal, urban
2 *syn* see OPEN 4
rel common, general, universal
con private
3 *syn* see COMMON 1
con private
4 held by or applicable to the majority of the people <*public* opinion>
syn general, popular, vulgar
rel prevalent, usual, widespread
ant private

public *n* **1** *syn* see SOCIETY 3
2 *syn* see FOLLOWING 2
rel hangers-on, suite

‖**publican** *n syn* see SALOONKEEPER

publication *n syn* see DECLARATION
rel dissemination

public house *n* **1** *syn* see HOTEL
‖**2** *syn* see BAR 5

publicity *n* information with news value issued to gain public attention or support <$100,000 was allocated for new-product *publicity*>
syn advertising, buildup, hype, press-agentry, promotion, puffery
rel broadcasting, promulgation, skywriting; réclame; announcement, write-up; blurb, commercial, plug, promo, puff; ballyhoo, hoopla; propaganda; hard sell

publicize *vb* to give publicity to <*publicize* a new book>
syn advertise, build up, cry, hype, press-agent, puff; *compare* PROMOTE 3
rel announce, broadcast, headline, promulgate, skywrite; advance, boost, plug, push; extol; bruit, tout, trumpet; propagandize
idiom bring into the limelight, throw the spotlight on

publish *vb* **1** *syn* see DECLARE 1
rel broach, express, utter, vent, ventilate
idiom bring to public notice, lay before the public, publish (*or* noise *or* spread) abroad, put forth

2 to produce for publication and allow to be distributed and sold <*published* a newspaper>
syn get out, issue, put out
rel produce; bring out; market; distribute

puckfist *n syn* see BRAGGART

puckish *adj syn* see PLAYFUL 1

‖**pudding** *n, usu* **puddings** *pl syn* see ENTRAILS

puddle *n syn* see POOL

puddle *vb syn* see FIDDLE 2

puddy *adj syn* see ROTUND 2

pudendum *n, usu* **pudenda** *pl syn* see GENITALIA

pudgy *adj syn* see ROTUND 2
rel ‖chuffy, ‖chumpy, squab, squdgy, ‖stuggy, stumpy, thick-bodied

puerile *adj syn* see CHILDISH

puff *vb* **1** *syn* see PANT 1
idiom huff and puff, pant and blow
2 *syn* see BOAST
3 *syn* see PUBLICIZE

puff *n* **1** *syn* see DRAW 1
rel inhalation, inhaling
2 *syn* see QUILT
3 a commendatory and often extravagant publicity notice or review <this book fails to deliver what the *puff* promises>
syn blurb, plug, puffing, write-up
rel promo; boost, buildup, push; laudation, praise

puffery *n syn* see PUBLICITY

puffing *n syn* see PUFF 3

puffy *adj syn* see POMPOUS 1

‖**puggy** *adj syn* see SWEATY

pugilism *n syn* see BOXING

pugnacious *adj syn* see BELLIGERENT
rel pushing, pushy, self-assertive; defiant, rebellious; brawling
idiom itching for a fight, itching (*or* ready) to fight, ready to fight at the drop of a hat
con bland, easygoing, mild; calm, peaceful; quiet
ant pacific

pugnacity *n syn* see ATTACK 2

puissance *n syn* see POWER 4
rel clout, influence, sway
con powerlessness, weakness
ant impuissance

puissant *adj syn* see POWERFUL 2
rel influential; commanding, ruling
con ineffectual, inefficacious, powerless
ant impuissant

puke *n syn* see SNOT 1

pukka *adj syn* see AUTHENTIC 2

pulchritudinous *adj syn* see BEAUTIFUL

pule *vb syn* see WHIMPER

pull *vb* **1** *syn* see EXTRACT 1
2 to cause to move toward or after an applied force <*pull* a trunk across the floor>
syn drag, draw, haul, lug, tow, tug
rel strain; heave; jerk, wrench, yank; drive, impel, push, shove
3 *syn* see STRAIN 2
4 *syn* see ROW
idiom pull on the oar (*or* oars)
5 *syn* see COMMIT 2

idiom ‖go and do
6 *syn* see DON 2
7 *syn* see GET 1
pull *n* **1** *syn* see DRAW 1
2 the power or ability to secure special favor or partiality <had lots of *pull* with the government>
syn clout, ‖drag, in, influence; *compare* INFLUENCE 1
rel persuasion; wire-pulling
idiom backstairs influence
3 *syn* see ATTRACTION 1
pullback *n* *syn* see DIEHARD 1
pull down *vb* *syn* see DESTROY 1
pull in *vb* **1** *syn* see RESTRAIN 1
2 *syn* see ARREST 2
pull out *vb* *syn* see GO 2
ant pull in
pull through *vb* *syn* see SURVIVE 2
pullulate *vb* *syn* see TEEM
pull up *vb* *syn* see STOP 4
pulp *vb* *syn* see CRUSH 2
pulpitarian *n* *syn* see CLERGYMAN
pulpiteer *n* *syn* see CLERGYMAN
pulpiter *n* *syn* see CLERGYMAN
pulpous *adj* *syn* see SOFT 6
pulpy *adj* *syn* see SOFT 6
pulsate *vb* to course or move with or as if with rhythmic strokes <blood *pulsating* through his veins>
syn beat, palpitate, pulse, throb
rel fluctuate, oscillate, vibrate; pump; drum, pound, roar, thrum
pulse *vb* *syn* see PULSATE
pulverize *vb* **1** to reduce (as by crushing, beating, or grinding) to minute particles <*pulverized* the ore in a stamp mill>
syn bray, buck, comminute, contriturate, crush, powder, triturate; *compare* SHATTER 1
rel break up; abrade, grate, grind; crumble, crunch, mull; levigate; atomize, fragment, fragmentalize, fragmentize, micronize; beat, shatter, smash, smatter, splinter; flour, mill
2 *syn* see DESTROY 1
pulverized *adj* *syn* see FINE 2
rel pulverous, pulverulent; dusty, granular, splintery
ant unpulverized
pummel *vb* *syn* see BEAT 1
pump *vb* *syn* see DRAIN 1
pumpkin head *n* *syn* see DUNCE
‖**pumpknot** *n* *syn* see BUMP 2
pun *n* the humorous use of a word so as to suggest different meanings, or of words having the same or similar sound but different meanings <"mourning shall come with approaching day" is a *pun*>
syn calembour, paronomasia
rel double entendre
idiom play on words
punch *vb* **1** *syn* see POKE 1
rel hit, slap, strike
2 *syn* see PERFORATE
punch *n* **1** *syn* see CUFF

2 *syn* see POKE 1
3 *syn* see POINT 3
4 *syn* see VIGOR 2
punctilious *adj* *syn* see CAREFUL 2
rel conventional, formal, observant; overconscientious, overscrupulous
punctual *adj* **1** *syn* see CAREFUL 2
ant unpunctual
2 marked by exact adherence to an appointed time <a *punctual* arrival>
syn prompt, timely
rel quick, ready
idiom on the dot, on time
con late, tardy
ant unpunctual
punctuate *vb* to mark or divide (written matter) with punctuation marks <*punctuated* the sentence>
syn point
rel divide, separate
puncture *n* *syn* see PRICK
rel perforation
puncture *vb* **1** *syn* see PERFORATE
rel riddle
2 *syn* see DISCREDIT 2
idiom shoot full of holes
pungent *adj* sharp and stimulating to the mind or senses <his *pungent* wit>
syn peppery, piquant, poignant, racy, snappy, spicy, zesty
rel acute, keen, salt, salty, sharp; biting, bitter, cutting, hot, incisive, trenchant; exciting, provocative, stimulating; rich
con banal, corny, dull, flat, hackneyed, insipid, old hat, platitudinous, prosaic, prosy, stale, stodgy, tasteless, unimaginative, uninteresting
ant bland
punish *vb* **1** to inflict a penalty on in requital for a wrongdoing <*punished* the child for misbehaving>
syn castigate, chasten, chastise, correct, discipline
rel criticize, reprove; amerce, fine, mulct, penalize; avenge, fix, revenge; lambaste, scourge
con overlook; absolve, acquit, exculpate, exonerate, vindicate; let off, release
ant excuse, pardon
2 *syn* see CONSUME 5
punishing *adj* *syn* see PUNITIVE
punishment *n* the act or an instance of punishing <a spanking was his *punishment*>
syn castigation, chastisement, correction, discipline, punition, rod
rel criticism, reproof; amercement, fine, mulct, penalty; avengement, revenge
idiom carrot-and-stick treatment, disciplinary action, dose of strap oil, what for
con overlooking; acquittal, exculpation, exoneration, vindication

---

syn synonym(s)   *rel* related word(s)
ant antonym(s)   *con* contrasted word(s)
idiom idiomatic equivalent(s)
‖ use limited; if in doubt, see a dictionary

ant excuse, pardon

punition *n syn* see PUNISHMENT
  idiom punitive measures
punitive *adj* inflicting, involving, or constituting
  punishment <took *punitive* action against him>
  syn castigating, disciplinary, punishing, punitory
  rel correctional, penal
punitory *adj syn* see PUNITIVE
punk *n* 1 *syn* see NONSENSE 2
  2 *syn* see NOVICE
  3 *syn* see TOUGH
‖**punk** *adj syn* see BAD 1
puny *adj* 1 *syn* see PETTY 2
  rel feeble, weak
  2 *syn* see WEAK 1
pup *n syn* see TWERP
puppet *n syn* see TOOL 2
  rel dupe; slave
puppy *n syn* see TWERP
purblind *adj* partly blind <*purblind* with cata-
  racts>
  syn dim-sighted, half-blind
  rel myopic, nearsighted, shortsighted; dim;
  blind, dark, sightless
purchasable *adj* 1 capable of being bought <*purchasable* goods>
  syn available, obtainable, on offer
  rel marketable, salable
  idiom on (or for) sale, on the market, to be had
  con rare; unavailable, unobtainable
  ant unpurchasable
  2 *syn* see VENAL 1
  rel undependable, unreliable; slippery, tricky;
  treacherous
purchase *vb syn* see BUY 1
  idiom make a purchase
  ant sell
purchaser *n* one to whom something is sold <in-
  struction booklets for new-car *purchasers*>
  syn buyer, emptor, vendee
  rel marketer, shopper; client, customer, patron;
  consumer, user
  con seller, vendor
pure *adj* 1 *syn* see STRAIGHT 3
  ant impure
  2 being such and no other <his solution of the
  problem was *pure* genius>
  syn absolute, perfect, pure and simple, sheer,
  simple, unadulterated, unalloyed, undiluted, unmitigated, unmixed, unqualified; *compare* UTTER
  rel complete, plenary, total; authentic, genuine;
  classic; out-and-out, plain, utter
  con mixed, qualified; doubtful, dubious, questionable, uncertain
  3 *syn* see UTTER
  4 *syn* see GOOD 11
  ant impure
  5 *syn* see CHASTE
  rel fresh, inviolate, unblighted, unprofaned
  idiom as pure as the driven snow
  con contaminated, dirty, sullied
  ant immoral, impure
‖**pure** *adv syn* see VERY 1

pure and simple *adj syn* see PURE 2
pureblood *adj syn* see PUREBRED
purebred *adj* being of unmixed ancestry <a *purebred* collie>
  syn full-blooded, pedigree, pedigreed, pureblood, thoroughbred
  rel registered
  con bastard, hybrid, lowbred, mixed
  ant mongrel
‖**puredee** (or **pure–D**) *adj syn* see UTTER
purely *adv syn* see ALL 1
purgation *n syn* see PURIFICATION
purgative *adj* cleansing or purifying especially
  from sin <confession as a *purgative* ritual>
  syn expiative, expiatory, expurgatorial, expurgatory, lustral, lustratory, propitiatory, purgatorial
purgatorial *adj syn* see PURGATIVE
‖**purgatory** *n syn* see SWAMP
purge *vb* 1 *syn* see DISABUSE
  rel absolve, cleanse; clear, rid
  2 *syn* see PURIFY 2
  3 to get rid of often by exile, imprisonment, or
  murder <Stalin *purged* all the Party dissidents>
  syn eliminate, liquidate, remove
  rel debar, exclude, shut out; dismiss, eject, expel, oust; erase, expunge, wipe (out); exterminate
  con rehabilitate; reinstate; repatriate; accept,
  bear (with), tolerate
  ant depurge
purification *n* a freeing from something morally
  harmful, offensive, or sinful <sought *purification*
  through repentance>
  syn catharsis, cleansing, expurgation, lustration, purgation
  rel atonement, expiation; absolution, forgiveness; grace, redemption, salvation; rebirth, regeneration; sanctification
  con contamination, defilement
purify *vb* 1 to free from material impurities or noxious matter <*purify* the water for drinking>
  syn clarify, clean, cleanse, depurate
  rel elutriate; filter; refine
  con dirty, foul, soil
  ant contaminate, pollute
  2 to free from guilt or moral blemish (often cere-
  monially) <*purify* one's heart through confes-
  sion>
  syn cleanse, expurgate, lustrate, purge
  rel atone, expiate; absolve, remit
  con defile, sully, tarnish
purist *n* one who adheres strictly and often excessively to a tradition <*purists* who believe in prescriptive grammar>
  syn precisian, precisionist, traditionalist
  rel Atticist, classicist; bitter-ender, conservative, diehard, Puritan
  con liberal, radical, young Turk
  ant revisionist
puritan *n syn* see PRUDE
puritanical *adj syn* see PRIM 1
  rel rigorous, strict; bigoted, hidebound, illiberal, intolerant, narrow, narrow-minded
  con liberal, tolerant; modern

purl *vb syn* see SWIRL
‖**purl** *vb syn* see SPIN 1
purlieu *n* **1** *syn* see RESORT 2
 2 purlieus *pl syn* see ENVIRONS 1
 3 purlieus *pl syn* see ENVIRONS 2
purloin *vb syn* see STEAL 1
purloiner *n syn* see THIEF
purloining *n syn* see THEFT
purple *adj* **1** *syn* see RISQUÉ
 2 *syn* see RHETORICAL
purport *n* **1** *syn* see MEANING 1
 2 *syn* see TENOR 1
 rel connotation; implication
 3 *syn* see SUBSTANCE 2
purported *adj syn* see ALLEGED
 rel postulated, presupposed; suppositional, suppositive; academic, speculative, theoretical; reputed, rumored; suspected
purportless *adj syn* see SENSELESS 5
purpose *n* **1** *syn* see INTENTION
 rel destination, direction; aim, goal, mission, objective, point; ambition, aspiration; proposal, proposition
 2 *syn* see USE 4
 rel mission
purpose *vb syn* see INTEND 2
 rel meditate, ponder; consider; conclude, decide, determine, resolve
purposedly *adv syn* see INTENTIONALLY
purposefulness *n syn* see DECISION 2
 rel certainty, confidence, sureness
 con indecision, irresoluteness, irresolution, vacillation, waffling, wavering, weakness; aimlessness, indirection
 ant purposelessness
purposeless *adj* **1** *syn* see FECKLESS 1
 rel unhelpful, unprofitable; purportless, senseless; nonsensical
 con helpful, profitable
 ant purposeful
 2 *syn* see RANDOM
 ant purposeful
purposely *adv syn* see INTENTIONALLY
 rel expressly; explicitly
 con unintentionally
 ant accidentally
purposively *adv syn* see INTENTIONALLY
purposiveness *n syn* see DECISION 2
purse cutter *n syn* see PICKPOCKET
pursual *n syn* see PURSUIT 2
pursuance *n syn* see PURSUIT 2
pursue *vb* **1** *syn* see FOLLOW 2
 rel persevere, persist; oppress, persecute; badger, bait, hound, ride
 idiom go in pursuit (of)
 2 *syn* see ADDRESS 8
pursuing *n syn* see PURSUIT 2
pursuit *n* **1** *syn* see WORK 1
 2 a following with a view to reach, accomplish, or obtain <the *pursuit* of happiness>
 syn pursual, pursuance, pursuing, quest, search, seeking
 rel following; reaching; obtaining; accomplishing, accomplishment

 idiom a going all out (after)
pursy *adj syn* see FAT 2
purview *n* **1** *syn* see RANGE 2
 2 *syn* see KEN
push *vb* **1** to use force so as to cause to move ahead or aside <*push* a wheelbarrow across the yard>
 syn drive, propel, shove, thrust
 rel launch; impel, move; force, ram
 con brake, check, stay
 ant pull
 2 to do, effect, or accomplish by forcing aside obstacles or opposition <*pushed* her way through the crowd> <*pushed* the measure through congress>
 syn bulldoze, elbow, hustle, jostle, press, ‖shog, shoulder, shove
 rel dig, nudge; hunch; drive, force, thrust; bump, butt, ram
 con ease, facilitate, slide (by), slip (through); expedite, help (along)
 3 *syn* see INCREASE 1
 4 *syn* see PRESSURE
 5 *syn* see PROMOTE 3
 rel oversell
 6 to engage in the illicit sale of (narcotics) <*pushing* drugs to teenagers>
 syn peddle, shove
 7 *syn* see PRESS 1
push *n* **1** *syn* see ENTERPRISE 4
 2 *syn* see VIGOR 2
 3 *syn* see STIMULUS
 4 *syn* see CROWD 1
 5 *syn* see SET 5
push around *vb syn* see BAIT 2
pushful *adj* **1** *syn* see AGGRESSIVE
 2 *syn* see PRESUMPTUOUS
 rel imposing, intrusive, obtruding, obtrusive, officious; assured, confident, self-confident
pushing *adj* **1** *syn* see AGGRESSIVE
 idiom ‖not backward in going forward
 2 *syn* see PRESUMPTUOUS
push off *vb syn* see GO 2
push on *vb syn* see GO 1
pushover *n syn* see SNAP 1
pushy *adj* **1** *syn* see AGGRESSIVE
 ‖**2** *syn* see PRESUMPTUOUS
pusillanimous *adj syn* see COWARDLY
puss *n syn* see CHILD 1
‖**puss** *n syn* see FACE 1
pussyfoot *vb* **1** *syn* see SNEAK
 2 *syn* see EQUIVOCATE 2
pustule *n syn* see ABSCESS
put *vb* **1** *syn* see SET 1
 2 *syn* see FASTEN 3
 3 *syn* see PROPOSE 1
 4 *syn* see WORD
 5 *syn* see TRANSLATE 1
 6 *syn* see EXPRESS 2
 7 *syn* see ESTIMATE 3

---

syn synonym(s) *rel* related word(s)
ant antonym(s) *con* contrasted word(s)
idiom idiomatic equivalent(s)
‖ use limited; if in doubt, see a dictionary

put (back) *vb syn* see RESTORE 5

put (on) *vb syn* see GAMBLE 1

put (on *or* upon) *vb syn* see LEVY

put *n syn* see DUNCE

put about *vb syn* see INCONVENIENCE

putative *adj syn* see SUPPOSED 1

put away *vb* **1** *syn* see DIVORCE 2
  2 *syn* see CONSUME 5
  3 *syn* see MURDER 1
  4 *syn* see BURY 1
  5 *syn* see KILL 1

put by *vb syn* see SAVE 4

put down *vb* **1** *syn* see CRUSH 5
  2 *syn* see DEGRADE 1
  3 *syn* see CONSUME 5
  4 *syn* see DECRY 2

put in *vb syn* see PLANT 1

put off *vb* **1** *syn* see DELAY 2
  idiom drag one's feet
  2 *syn* see DEFER
  idiom lay on the table, let the matter stand
  3 *syn* see REMOVE 3
  ant put on

put on *vb* **1** *syn* see DON 1
  ant put off
  2 *syn* see DON 2
  rel affect, feign, sham, simulate; masquerade, pose
  idiom make as if (*or* as though)
  3 *syn* see ASSUME 4
  idiom put on a (false) front, put on an act
  4 *syn* see EMPLOY 2
  5 *syn* see STAGE

put–on *adj syn* see ARTIFICIAL 3
  rel mannered, posed; faked, sham

put–on *n* **1** *syn* see IMPOSTURE
  2 *syn* see MASK 2

put out *vb* **1** *syn* see EXERT
  2 *syn* see EXTINGUISH 1
  3 *syn* see PUBLISH 2
  4 *syn* see IRRITATE

  5 *syn* see INCONVENIENCE
  rel displease, dissatisfy; annoy, irritate
  idiom put out of the way, put to it

put over *vb syn* see DEFER

putrefy *vb syn* see DECAY

putresce *vb syn* see DECAY

putrid *adj* **1** *syn* see BAD 5
  2 *syn* see MALODOROUS 1
  3 *syn* see VICIOUS 2

putter *vb syn* see FIDDLE 2
  rel boondoggle; dawdle

‖**put to** *vb syn* see CLOSE 1

put together *vb syn* see MAKE 3

put up *vb* **1** *syn* see HARBOR 2
  2 *syn* see BUILD 1
  rel forge, make, put together, shape
  3 *syn* see ERECT 3
  4 *syn* see RAISE 9
  rel elevate, escalate

‖**puxy** *n syn* see SWAMP

puzzle *vb* to baffle and disturb mentally <a persistent fever that *puzzled* her doctor>
  syn befog, bewilder, ‖cap, confound, confuse, metagrobolize, perplex, pose, stumble; *compare* NONPLUS 1
  rel baffle, foil, frustrate; befuddle, ‖bumfuzzle, fuddle; disconcert, distract, disturb, upset; addle, muddle; mystify; amaze, dumbfound, flabbergast
  con enlighten, inform

puzzle *n syn* see MYSTERY

puzzlement *n syn* see MYSTERY

puzzle out *vb syn* see SOLVE 2
  idiom find the key to, pick the lock

pygmy *n syn* see DWARF
  ant giant

pygmy *adj syn* see TINY

pyramid *n syn* see PILE 1

Pyrrhonian *n syn* see SKEPTIC

Pyrrhonist *n syn* see SKEPTIC

pythonic *adj syn* see HUGE

Q

quack *n syn* see CHARLATAN
  rel counterfeiter, pretender, shammer, simulator

‖**quackle** *vb syn* see SUFFOCATE
quacksalver *n syn* see CHARLATAN
quackster *n syn* see CHARLATAN
quad *n syn* see COURT 1
quadrangle *n syn* see COURT 1
quadrate *adj syn* see SQUARE 1
quadrate *vb* **1** *syn* see AGREE 4
  2 *syn* see ADAPT
quadratic *adj syn* see SQUARE 1
quadratical *adj syn* see SQUARE 1
quaesitum *n syn* see AMBITION 2
quaff *vb syn* see DRINK 1
quag *n syn* see SWAMP
quaggy *adj syn* see SOFT 6
quagmire *n* **1** *syn* see SWAMP
  2 *syn* see PREDICAMENT
quail *n syn* see GIRL 1
quail *vb syn* see RECOIL
  rel cower, cringe
quaint *adj syn* see STRANGE 4
  rel droll, funny, laughable; antiquated, antique, archaic
‖**quaint** *vb syn* see INTRODUCE 4
quake *vb* **1** *syn* see SHAKE 2
  rel fluctuate, waver
  2 *syn* see SHAKE 1
quake *n syn* see EARTHQUAKE
‖**quaker** *n syn* see EARTHQUAKE
quaking *adj syn* see TREMULOUS
quaky *adj syn* see TREMULOUS
qualification *n syn* see ABILITY 1
qualified *adj* **1** *syn* see ABLE
  rel disciplined, instructed, trained; catechized, examined, quizzed; proved, tested, tried
  con incapable, incompetent, unequipped, unfit
  ant disqualified, unqualified
  2 not unlimited and complete <gave only a *qualified* endorsement to the project>
  syn limited, modified, reserved
  rel circumscribed, definite, determined, fixed, restricted; partial
  con complete, entire, full, total, utter, whole; unlimited, unrestricted
  ant absolute, unqualified
qualifiedness *n syn* see ABILITY 1
qualify *vb* **1** *syn* see CHARACTERIZE 2
  rel ascribe, assign, attribute, impute; predicate
  2 *syn* see ENTITLE 2
quality *n* **1** something inherent and distinctive <learned the special *qualities* of the native herbs>
  syn affection, attribute, character, characteristic, feature, mark, peculiarity, property, savor, trait, virtue; *compare* CHARACTERISTIC 1

  rel individuality; affirmation, predication; element, factor, parameter
  2 a usually high level of merit or superiority <merchandise of *quality*>
  syn caliber, merit, stature, value, virtue, worth
  rel arete, excellence, excellency, perfection, superbness, superiority
  con inferiority, meanness, mediocrity, poorness; inadequacy; deficiency
  3 degree of excellence <upgrading the *quality* of incoming students>
  syn caliber, class, grade
  rel capacity, character, footing, place, position, rank, situation, standing, state, station, status
  4 *syn* see STATUS 1
  5 *syn* see ARISTOCRACY
  6 *syn* see EXCELLENCE
quality *adj syn* see EXCELLENT
qualm *n* a misgiving about what one is going to do <had *qualms* about the secret meeting>
  syn compunction, conscience, demur, scruple, squeam
  rel apprehension, foreboding, misgiving, presentiment; doubt, mistrust, suspicion, uncertainty; agitation, insecurity, perturbation; objection, remonstrance; reluctance, unwillingness; impatience, nervousness, unease, uneasiness
  con aplomb, assurance, confidence, self-assurance, self-confidence, self-possession; certainty, certitude, conviction
qualmish *adj syn* see SQUEAMISH 1
qualmishness *n syn* see NAUSEA
qualmy *adj syn* see SQUEAMISH 1
quantity *n* **1** *syn* see BODY 5
  2 quantities *pl syn* see SCAD
quantum *n* **1** *syn* see BODY 5
  2 *syn* see RATION
quarrel *n* a usually verbal dispute marked by anger or discord <a *quarrel* over who would drive the car>
  syn altercation, ‖barney, beef, bickering, brabble, brannigan, brawl, controversy, difficulty, dispute, dust, dustup, embroilment, falling-out, feud, fight, fracas, fuss, hassle, imbroglio, knock-down-and-drag-out, miff, ‖prabble, ‖pribble, rhubarb, row, ruckus, run-in, set-to, spat, squabble, squall, tiff, to-and-fro, word(s), wrangle; *compare* BRAWL 2
  rel battle royal, catfight; affray, bobbery, broil, donnybrook, fray, free-for-all, melee, ruction, rumpus, scrap, scrimmage, scuffle; conflict, contention, difference, discord, dissension, strife, variance; disagreement, misunderstanding

---

syn synonym(s)   **rel** related word(s)
ant antonym(s)   **con** contrasted word(s)
idiom idiomatic equivalent(s)
‖ use limited; if in doubt, see a dictionary

idiom ‖pribbles and prabbles
con accord, concord, harmony; agreement, like=
mindedness, understanding, unity
quarrel *vb* to contend noisily or captiously <with
his belligerent personality he was always *quar-
reling* with someone>
syn altercate, bicker, brabble, brawl, ‖cast out,
caterwaul, fall out, row, scrap, spat, squabble,
tiff, wrangle; *compare* ARGUE 2
rel differ, disaccord, dissent, divide, vary;
bump, clash, collide, conflict, thwart; battle,
contend, fight, war
idiom have words with, pull caps
con agree, coincide, concur
quarrelsome *adj* **1** *syn* see BELLIGERENT
rel adverse, antagonistic, counter; antipathetic,
hostile, inimical, rancorous
idiom having a chip on one's shoulder
2 apt or disposed to quarrel <when he's in a bad
mood he becomes so *quarrelsome*>
syn battlesome, brawling, brawlsome, brawly,
scrappy; *compare* BELLIGERENT
rel argumentative; disputatious; cankered, crabbed, irascible, irritable
con conciliatory, propitiatory
quarry *n syn* see GAME 3
quarry *vb syn* see MINE
quarter *n* **1** one of four equal parts <ate one *quarter* of the pie>
syn fourth, quartern
rel quadrant
2 a division or part of a town or city <the market
quarter in Paris>
syn district, precinct, section, sector
rel division, part; area; locality; barrio
quarter *vb* **1** *syn* see HARBOR 2
2 *syn* see BILLET 1
quarterage *n syn* see SHELTER 2
quarterback *vb syn* see SUPERVISE
quartern *n syn* see QUARTER 1
quarter–witted *adj syn* see RETARDED
quartet *n* a group consisting of four individuals <a
singing *quartet*>
syn four, foursome, quartetto, quaternion, quatuor, tetrad
rel quadruplet
quartetto *n syn* see QUARTET
quash *vb* **1** *syn* see ANNUL 4
2 *syn* see ABOLISH 1
3 *syn* see CRUSH 5
quashing *n syn* see REPRESSION 1
‖**quat** *vb syn* see SQUAT
quaternion *n syn* see QUARTET
quatuor *n syn* see QUARTET
quaver *vb syn* see SHAKE 1
rel falter, hesitate, vacillate, waver
‖**quawk** *vb syn* see SQUALL 1
quay *n syn* see WHARF
‖**queak** *vb syn* see SQUEAK 1
quean *n syn* see PROSTITUTE
queasiness *n syn* see NAUSEA
queasy *adj* **1** *syn* see DOUBTFUL 1
2 *syn* see SQUEAMISH 1
queer *adj* **1** *syn* see STRANGE 4

rel doubtful, dubious, questionable; droll,
funny, laughable
2 *syn* see OBSESSED
‖**3** *syn* see HOMOSEXUAL
4 *syn* see SQUEAMISH 1
‖**queer** *n syn* see HOMOSEXUAL
‖**quelch** *vb syn* see SUPPRESS 2
quell *vb syn* see CRUSH 5
rel conquer, overcome, subjugate, vanquish
con abet, incite, instigate
ant foment
quench *vb* **1** *syn* see EXTINGUISH 1
2 *syn* see CRUSH 5
rel end, terminate
3 *syn* see DESTROY 1
4 to bring (as thirst) to an end with or as if with a
refreshing drink <after being in the hot sun, he
found it difficult to *quench* his thirst>
syn slake, ‖squench
rel appease, content, gratify, satisfy; sate, satiate; allay, alleviate, assuage, lighten, mitigate,
relieve; decrease, diminish, lessen, reduce
quenching *n syn* see REPRESSION 1
quenchless *adj* **1** *syn* see INSATIABLE
2 *syn* see INDESTRUCTIBLE
querulent *adj syn* see IRRITABLE
querulential *adj syn* see IRRITABLE
querulous *adj syn* see IRRITABLE
rel blubbering, crying, wailing, weeping, whimpering; bemoaning, deploring, lamenting
query *n* **1** *syn* see INQUIRY 2
2 *syn* see UNCERTAINTY
query *vb syn* see ASK 1
quest *n* **1** *syn* see INQUIRY 1
2 *syn* see PURSUIT 2
quest *vb* **1** *syn* see HOWL 1
2 *syn* see SEEK 1
question *n* **1** *syn* see INQUIRY 2
2 *syn* see PROBLEM 2
3 *syn* see DEMUR 2
question *vb* **1** *syn* see ASK 1
2 to express doubt about <*questioned* his decision to take a new job>
syn challenge, dispute, doubt, mistrust
rel suspect, ‖suspicion; hesitate (over), puzzle
(over), wonder (about)
questionable *adj* **1** *syn* see IMPROBABLE 1
ant unquestionable
2 *syn* see MOOT
rel refutable; equivocal, obscure, vague
con dependable, true, trustworthy, trusty; genuine, indubitable, real, undoubted, undubitable,
veritable, very
ant authoritative; unquestionable, unquestioned
3 *syn* see UNRELIABLE 1
questioning *n syn* see INQUIRY 2
questioning *adj* **1** *syn* see INCREDULOUS
ant questionless, unquestioning
2 *syn* see INQUISITIVE 1
questionless *adj syn* see AUTHENTIC 2
queue *n syn* see LINE 5
quibble *vb* **1** to find fault with something usually
on minor grounds <was a peevish critic, always
ready to *quibble*>

syn cavil, chicane, hypercriticize
rel carp, criticize
idiom split hairs
con applaud, commend, compliment, recommend; approve, endorse, sanction
2 *syn* see ARGUE 2

quick *adj* **1** *syn* see FAST 3
rel agile, brisk, nimble; abrupt, impetuous
idiom quick on the trigger
con dilatory, laggard, leisurely, slow, unhasty, unhurried; comatose
ant sluggish
2 able to respond without delay or hesitation or indicative of such ability <very *quick* in perception> <his *quick* eye spotted the trouble>
syn apt, prompt, ready; *compare* INSTANTANEOUS
rel clever, intelligent, quick-witted, smart; adroit, deft, dexterous; acute, keen, sharp; able, capable, competent, effective, effectual
con comatose, lethargic, logy, poky, torpid; crass, dense, dull, dumb, stupid
ant slow; sluggish
3 *syn* see WISE 4

quick *adv* *syn* see FAST 2

quick *n* *syn* see CENTER 3

quicken *vb* **1** to make alive or lively <warm spring days that *quicken* the earth>
syn animate, enliven, liven, vivificate, vivify
rel activate, energize, vitalize; arouse, awaken, rouse, stir, wake
con blunt, dull; slow (down)
ant deaden
2 *syn* see PROVOKE 4
rel activate, actuate, motivate; goad, induce, spur
con check, halt, interrupt, stall, stay; curb, inhibit, restrain
ant arrest
3 *syn* see SPEED 3
con bog (down), detain, embog, hang up, mire
ant slacken

quickening *adj* *syn* see INVIGORATING

quick–lunch *n* *syn* see EATING HOUSE

quickly *adv* *syn* see FAST 2

quickness *n* *syn* see SPEED 2
ant slowness

quick–sighted *adj* *syn* see SHARP 4

quick–tempered *adj* *syn* see IRASCIBLE

quick–witted *adj* **1** *syn* see SHARP 4
2 *syn* see INTELLIGENT 2
rel apt, prompt, quick, ready
3 *syn* see WISE 4
rel acute, keen; facetious, humorous, witty
ant slow-witted

quidnunc *n* **1** *syn* see BUSYBODY
2 *syn* see GOSSIP 1

quiescence *n* *syn* see ABEYANCE

quiescency *n* *syn* see ABEYANCE

quiescent *adj* *syn* see LATENT
rel calm, halcyon, hushed, placid, quiet, still, stilly, untroubled

quiet *n* **1** a period of intensified silence <the *quiet* before the storm>
syn calm, hush, lull

rel cessation, stop, termination
con din, hubbub, racket, uproar
2 *syn* see SILENCE 1

quiet *adj* **1** *syn* see CALM 1
con harsh, rough; disquieted, disturbed, perturbed, upset
ant unquiet
2 *syn* see INACTIVE
3 *syn* see STILL 3
con blatant, boisterous, clamorous, strident, vociferous
4 not showy or obtrusive <always dressed in *quiet* good taste>
syn inobtrusive, restrained, subdued, tasteful, tasty, unobtrusive
rel homely, plain, simple, unpretentious
con blatant, brazen, flashy, garish, glaring, meretricious, tawdry, tinsel; elaborate
ant gaudy, loud

quiet *vb* **1** *syn* see SILENCE
rel abate, decrease, lessen
con excite, provoke, quicken, stimulate; awaken, rally, stir
2 *syn* see CALM
con agitate; unhinge, untune
ant disquiet; excite

‖**quieten** *vb* **1** *syn* see SILENCE
2 *syn* see CALM
ant arouse; excite

quietive *adj* *syn* see SEDATIVE

quietness *n* *syn* see SILENCE 1

quietude *n* *syn* see SILENCE 1

quietus *n* *syn* see DEATH 1

‖**quiff** *n* *syn* see GIRL 1

quilt *n* a bed coverlet made of two layers of cloth with a stuffing (as of cotton, wool, or feathers) between <a warm *quilt* is nice on a winter night>
syn ‖comfortable, comforter, pouf, puff
rel bedcover, bedspread, counterpane; eiderdown

quinary *adj* *syn* see QUINTUPLE

quinta *n* *syn* see ESTATE 3

quintessence *n* **1** *syn* see ESSENCE 2
2 *syn* see APOTHEOSIS 1

quintessential *adj* *syn* see TYPICAL 1

quintessential *n* *syn* see ESSENCE 2

quintuple *adj* consisting of five <the problem is viewed as having *quintuple* aspects>
syn fivefold, quinary
rel quintuplicate

quip *n* *syn* see JOKE 1

quip (at) *vb* *syn* see SCOFF

quipster *n* *syn* see HUMORIST 2

quit *vb* **1** *syn* see CLEAR 5
2 *syn* see BEHAVE 1
3 *syn* see GO 2
4 *syn* see ABANDON 1
rel relinquish, resign, surrender
5 *syn* see STOP 3

---

syn synonym(s)   *rel* related word(s)
ant antonym(s)   *con* contrasted word(s)
idiom idiomatic equivalent(s)
‖ use limited; if in doubt, see a dictionary

6 to give up (as a habit, activity, or employment) especially with finality <*quit* a job> <determined to *quit* smoking>
syn drop, leave, resign, terminate
rel retire, secede, withdraw
idiom draw one's time, give notice
con hire on, hire out
quite *adv* **1** *syn* see WELL 3
   2 *syn* see ALTOGETHER 2
   3 *syn* see ALL 1
   4 *syn* see WELL 8
quittance *n* *syn* see REPARATION
quitter *n* *syn* see COWARD
quiver *n* *syn* see FLASH 1
quiver *vb* *syn* see SHAKE 1
   rel beat, palpatate, pulsate, pulse, throb

quivering *adj* *syn* see TREMULOUS
quivery *adj* *syn* see TREMULOUS
quiz *n* *syn* see ECCENTRIC
quiz *vb* **1** *syn* see RIDICULE
   2 *syn* see ASK 1
quizzical *adj* *syn* see INCREDULOUS
   rel curious, inquisitive; probing, searching
‖**quod** *vb* *syn* see IMPRISON
quodlibetic *adj* *syn* see PEDANTIC
quondam *adj* *syn* see FORMER 2
quota *n* **1** *syn* see SHARE 1
   2 *syn* see RATION
quota *vb* *syn* see APPORTION 2
quotidian *adj* **1** *syn* see DAILY
   2 *syn* see ORDINARY 1

R

rabbity *adj syn* see SHY 1
rabble *n* **1** *syn* see MOB 2
2 the lowest class of people <the *rabble* of the city>
syn canaille, doggery, dreg(s), hoi polloi, mass(es), mob, other half, polloi, proletariat, raff, ‖ragabash, ragtag, ragtag and bobtail, riffraff, roughscuff, rout, scum, scurf, tag and rag, tagrag and bobtail, trash, unwashed
rel bourgeoisie, commonalty, many, people, populace, public, rank and file
idiom the great unwashed, the scum of the earth, the submerged tenth
con aristocracy, aristoi, elite, Four Hundred, gentility, nobility, upper class, upper crust, upper ten, upper ten thousand
rabble–rouser *n syn* see DEMAGOGUE
rabid *adj* **1** *syn* see FURIOUS 2
rel crazed, crazy, demented, deranged, insane
2 *syn* see EXTREME 3
rel enthusiastic, keen, obsessed, zealous
race *n syn* see CREEK 2
race *vb* **1** *syn* see RUSH 1
2 *syn* see COURSE
race *n syn* see FAMILY 1
rel culture, nation, nationality, people; breed, type, variety
rachis *n syn* see SPINE
rachitic *adj syn* see RICKETY
racial *adj syn* see ETHNIC 2
racialism *n syn* see RACISM
racism *n* racial prejudice or discrimination <an act of overt *racism*>
syn racialism
rel discrimination, prejudice; illiberality, unfairness; bias, one-sideness, partiality
con broad-mindedness, liberalness, open-mindedness, tolerance; indifference, neutrality
rack *vb syn* see AFFLICT
rel distress, pain; oppress, persecute
‖**rack back** *vb syn* see REPROVE
racket *n* **1** *syn* see DIN
‖**2** *syn* see WORK 1
racketry *n syn* see DIN
rackety *adj* **1** *syn* see NOISY
2 *syn* see RICKETY
racking *adj syn* see EXCRUCIATING
rel barbarous, cruel, ferocious, fierce, inhuman, savage
rack up *vb syn* see GAIN 1
racy *adj* **1** *syn* see PUNGENT
rel fiery, gingery, mettlesome, spirited
con banal, inane, jejune
2 *syn* see RISQUÉ
radiant *adj* **1** *syn* see BRIGHT 1
2 *syn* see GLAD 2
radiate *vb* **1** *syn* see SHINE 1
2 *syn* see SPREAD 1

rel diverge
radical *adj* **1** *syn* see FUNDAMENTAL 1
rel cardinal, essential, vital; constitutional, inherent, intrinsic
ant superficial
2 *syn* see EXTREME 3
3 *syn* see LIBERAL 3
radical *n* one who favors rapid and sweeping changes <the *radicals* advocated overthrow of the government>
syn extremist, revolutionary, revolutionist, ultraist; *compare* REACTIONARY
rel liberal, progressive, reformer; agitator, insurgent, insurrectionist, rebel; anarchist, nihilist, red, subversive; out-and-outer; secessionist, separatist
con bitter-ender, diehard, fogy, intransigent, mossback, reactionary, rightist, standpatter
ant conservative
radius *n syn* see RANGE 2
raff *n syn* see RABBLE 2
raffish *adj syn* see WILD 7
rag *vb* **1** *syn* see SCOLD 1
2 *syn* see BANTER
‖**ragabash** *n syn* see RABBLE 2
ragamuffin *n* a person dressed in ragged clothing <a poor *ragamuffin* found begging>
syn ragshag, scarecrow, tatterdemalion
rel hobo, tramp, vagabond, vagrant; bum, loafer, wastrel; orphan, waif
con buck, coxcomb, dandy, dude, fop
rage *n* **1** *syn* see ANGER
rel acerbity, acrimony, asperity; frenzy, hysteria, mania; agitation, perturbation, upset
2 *syn* see FASHION 3
rel caprice, conceit, crotchet, fancy, freak, vagary, whim
rage *vb syn* see ANGER 2
ragged *adj* torn or worn to tatters <never saw such *ragged* clothes>
syn frayed, frazzled, shreddy, tattered
rel rent, torn; battered, patched; dilapidated, dingy, faded, seedy, shabby, threadbare, worn-out
raging *adj syn* see WILD 6
rags *n pl* **1** poor or ragged clothing <a beggar in *rags*>
syn ‖duds, tatters
rel odds and ends, ribbons, shreds
2 *syn* see CLOTHES
ragshag *n syn* see RAGAMUFFIN
ragtag *n syn* see RABBLE 2

---

syn synonym(s)   *rel* related word(s)
ant antonym(s)   *con* contrasted word(s)
idiom idiomatic equivalent(s)
‖ use limited; if in doubt, see a dictionary

ragtag and bobtail *n syn* see RABBLE 2

raid *n* **1** *syn* see INVASION
rel assault, onset, onslaught
2 a sudden attack by officers of the law <a *raid* on a gambling joint>
syn ‖bust

raid *vb* **1** to make a raid on <Indians *raided* the settlers frequently>
syn foray, harass, harry, maraud
rel despoil, devastate, ravage, sack, spoliate, waste; loot, plunder, rifle, rob
2 *syn* see INVADE 1

raider *n syn* see MARAUDER

rail *n syn* see RAILING

rail *vb syn* see SCOLD 1

railing *n* a usually protective barrier consisting essentially of an elongated raised member <a staircase without a *railing*>
syn balustrade, banister, rail

raillery *n syn* see SATIRE

railroad station *n* a building containing accommodations for railroad passengers or freight <an old *railroad station* fallen into disrepair>
syn depot, station, station house

raiment *n syn* see CLOTHES

raiment *vb syn* see CLOTHE

rainbow *n syn* see PIPE DREAM

rainless *adj syn* see FAIR 2
ant rainy

raise *vb* **1** *syn* see LIFT 1
ant lower
2 *syn* see INCITE
3 *syn* see RESURRECT 1
4 *syn* see ERECT 3
5 *syn* see BUILD 1
6 *syn* see BRING UP 1
7 *syn* see GROW 1
8 *syn* see GATHER 6
9 to make larger in amount <*raised* the rent>
syn boost, hike, increase, jack (up), jump, put up, up
rel inflate
idiom send through the roof
con cut back, decrease, drop, lessen, reduce, roll back; minimize
ant lower

raise *n syn* see ADDITION

raised *adj* **1** *syn* see ELEVATED 1
2 *syn* see ERECT

rake *vb syn* see SCOUR 2

rakehell *adj syn* see WILD 7

raking *adj syn* see FAST 3

rakish *adj syn* see WILD 7

rally *vb* **1** *syn* see MOBILIZE 3
2 *syn* see STIR 1
rel fire; refresh, renew, restore
3 *syn* see RECOVER 2
rel brace (up), enliven, invigorate, perk (up), pick up

rally *vb syn* see RIDICULE
rel harass, harry, tantalize, tease, worry

rallying cry *n syn* see BATTLE CRY

ram *vb* **1** *syn* see THRUST 2
2 *syn* see CRAM 1

ramble *vb* **1** *syn* see WANDER 1
2 *syn* see DIGRESS 2
3 *syn* see SPRAWL 2

ramble *n syn* see WALK 1

rambler *n syn* see ROVER

rambunctious *adj syn* see TURBULENT 1

rampage *n syn* see SPREE 1
rel turmoil, uproar

rampant *adj* **1** *syn* see RANK 1
rel excessive, immoderate, inordinate
con moderate, temperate; checked, curbed, restrained
2 *syn* see PREVAILING

rampart *n syn* see BULWARK

rancid *adj syn* see MALODOROUS 1
rel ‖reasty; loathsome, repulsive
ant sweet

rancor *n syn* see ENMITY
rel bitterness, vindictiveness, virulence

rancorous *adj* **1** *syn* see MALICIOUS
2 *syn* see BITTER 3

rancorously *adv syn* see HARD 6

random *adj* lacking a definite plan, purpose, or pattern <a *random* choice>
syn aimless, designless, desultory, haphazard, hit-or-miss, indiscriminate, irregular, objectless, promiscuous, purposeless, slapdash, spot, unaimed, unconsidered, unplanned; *compare* ACCIDENTAL
rel contingent, fluky, fortuitous, incidental, odd
con arranged, organized, planned; methodical, systematic; deliberate, purposeful
ant purposive

random *adv syn* see ABOUT 4
ant orderly

randomly *adv syn* see ABOUT 4
ant orderly

randy *adj syn* see LICENTIOUS 2

range *vb* **1** *syn* see LINE 1
rel assort, classify, sort; bias, dispose, incline, predispose
2 *syn* see WANDER 1
3 to change or differ within limits <discounts *range* from 10% to 40%>
syn extend, go, run, vary
rel differ, fluctuate

range *n* **1** *syn* see HABITAT
2 sphere of action, expression, or influence <a political movement worldwide in its *range* and power>
syn ambit, circle, compass, confine(s), dimension(s), extension, extensity, extent, length, orbit, panorama, purview, radius, reach, realm, scope, stretch, sweep, width
rel area, space, span; domain, field, province, sphere, territory; amplitude, expanse, gamut, spread
3 *syn* see KEN
rel compass
idiom range of comprehension
4 *syn* see ORDER 4
5 the distance or extent between possible extremes <the *range* of exhibited photographs went from the extremely good to the extremely bad>

syn diapason, gamut, scale, spectrum
rel compass, radius, reach, scope, stretch, sweep
rangy *adj syn* see GANGLING
ant compact
rank *adj* **1** growing or increasing at an immoderate rate <*rank* weeds>
syn rampant
rel exuberant, lavish, lush, luxuriant, profuse
con scanty, sparse, thin
2 *syn* see OVERGROWN
3 *syn* see OBSCENE 2
4 *syn* see EGREGIOUS
rel conspicuous, noticeable, outstanding
5 *syn* see UTTER
6 *syn* see MALODOROUS 1
rel dank, humid; loathsome, repulsive
rank *n* **1** *syn* see LINE 5
2 *syn* see ESTATE 2
3 *syn* see STATUS 1
4 *syn* see STATUS 2
rank *vb* **1** *syn* see CLASS 2
rel arrange, order; assort, sort
2 *syn* see PRECEDE 1
rank and file *n syn* see COMMONALTY
rankle *vb* to produce continual or progressive anger, irritation, or bitterness <this decision has long *rankled* as an act of injustice>
syn fester
rel annoy, bother, irk, vex; aggravate, exasperate, irritate; harass, obsess, plague, torment
ransack *vb* **1** *syn* see SCOUR 2
2 *syn* see ROB 1
ransom *vb* to liberate by paying a price <*ransomed* the king>
syn buy, redeem
rel recover, regain, retrieve; emancipate, free, liberate; extricate, release
rant *vb* **1** *syn* see ORATE
rel bluster, huff; rage, storm
2 *syn* see SCOLD 1
rant *n syn* see BOMBAST
ran–tan *n syn* see BINGE 1
rantankerous *adj syn* see CANTANKEROUS
rap *n* **1** *syn* see HIT 1
2 *syn* see REBUKE
rap *vb* **1** *syn* see TAP 1
2 *syn* see CRITICIZE
rap *n* **1** *syn* see CHAT 2
2 *syn* see CONFERENCE 1
3 *syn* see CRITICISM 2
rapacious *adj* **1** subsisting on prey <the *rapacious* wolf seized the lamb>
syn predacious, predative, predatorial, predatory, raptorial, vulturine, vulturish, vulturous
2 *syn* see VORACIOUS
rel ferocious, fierce
rapacity *n syn* see CUPIDITY
rel claim, demand, exaction
rape *vb* to have sexual intercourse with a woman without her consent and chiefly by force or deception <*rape* a young girl>
syn defile, deflorate, deflower, force, outrage, ravish, spoil, violate

rel debauch, devirginate, dishonor, ruin; betray, deceive, mislead; entice, lure, seduce, tempt; compromise, shame, wrong
rapid *adj syn* see FAST 3
rel agile, brisk, nimble; hurried, quickened
ant deliberate; leisurely
rapidity *n syn* see SPEED 2
rapidly *adv syn* see FAST 2
rapidness *n syn* see SPEED 2
‖**rapper** *n syn* see LIE
rapport *n syn* see HARMONY 3
rapprochement *n syn* see RECONCILIATION
rapscallion *n syn* see SCAMP
rap session *n syn* see CONFERENCE 2
rapt *adj syn* see INTENT
raptorial *adj syn* see RAPACIOUS 1
rapture *n syn* see ECSTASY
rare *adj* **1** *syn* see THIN 2
2 *syn* see CHOICE
rel excellent, fine, unique
3 *syn* see INFREQUENT
con accustomed, customary, habitual, usual, wonted; abounding, profuse
4 *syn* see EXCEPTIONAL 1
rarefied *adj syn* see THIN 2
rarefy *vb syn* see THIN 2
rarely *adv* **1** *syn* see SELDOM
2 *syn* see EXTRA
raring *adj syn* see EAGER
rascal *n* **1** *syn* see VILLAIN 1
2 *syn* see SCAMP
rash *adj* **1** acting, done, or expressed with undue haste or disregard for consequences <don't do anything *rash*> <that was a very *rash* statement>
syn brash, hasty, hotheaded, ill-advised, incautious, incogitant, inconsiderate, mad-brained, madcap, reckless, thoughtless, unadvised, unconsidered, unwary; *compare* CARELESS 1
rel abrupt, headlong, impetuous, precipitate, precipitous, sudden; foolhardy, foolish, impulsive, silly; careless, heedless, imprudent, indiscreet, injudicious, unthinking, unwise
con careful, cautious, chary, circumspect, wary; advised, considered, deliberate, designed, premeditated, studied; calm, cool, level-headed
ant calculating
2 *syn* see ADVENTUROUS
rash *n syn* see EPIDEMIC
rasp *vb syn* see SCRAPE 1
raspberry *n* a sound of disapproval, contempt, or derision <the crowd gave the umpire a *raspberry*>
syn bazoo, bird, boo, ‖Bronx cheer, catcall, hiss, hoot, pooh, pooh-pooh, ‖razz
rasping *adj syn* see HARSH 3
raspish *adj syn* see IRRITABLE
raspy *adj syn* see IRRITABLE
rat *n* **1** *syn* see RENEGADE

---

syn synonym(s)   *rel* related word(s)
ant antonym(s)   *con* contrasted word(s)
idiom idiomatic equivalent(s)
‖ use limited; if in doubt, see a dictionary

2 *syn* see SNOT 1
rat *vb* **1** *syn* see DEFECT
 2 *syn* see INFORM 3
rate *vb* *syn* see SCOLD 1
rate *n* **1** *syn* see PRICE 1
 2 *syn* see DEGREE 2
rate *vb* **1** *syn* see ESTIMATE 1
 2 *syn* see CLASS 2
 3 *syn* see EARN 2
rather *adv* **1** *syn* see ENOUGH 2
 2 *syn* see INSTEAD
 3 *syn* see SOMEWHAT 2
 4 *syn* see WELL 8
ratherish *adv* *syn* see SOMEWHAT 2
ratify *vb* to make something legally valid or operative usually by formal approval or sanctioning <agreed to *ratify* the treaty>
 syn confirm
 rel accredit, authorize, commission, license; approve, endorse, sanction; authenticate, validate
 con disown, reject, repudiate
ratio *n* *syn* see DEGREE 2
ratiocination *n* **1** *syn* see INFERENCE 1
 ant intuition
 2 *syn* see INFERENCE 2
ratiocinative *adj* *syn* see LOGICAL 2
ration *n* an amount allotted or made available especially from a limited supply <saved up their gasoline *ration* for a vacation trip>
 syn allotment, allowance, apportionment, measure, meed, part, portion, quantum, quota, share; *compare* SHARE 1
 rel assignment, consignment, distribution, division
ration *vb* *syn* see APPORTION 2
 rel allocate, allot, assign, mete (out)
rational *adj* agreeable to reason <offered a *rational* explanation>
 syn consequent, intelligent, logical, reasonable, sensible, sound
 rel calm, cool, level-headed, sober, stable; circumspect, judicious, prudent; lucid, normal, sane
 con rash, reckless, wild; groundless, illogical, unreasonable, unreasoning, unsound; crazy, demented, deranged
 ant animal, irrational; absurd
rationale *n* *syn* see EXPLANATION 2
rationalization *n* *syn* see EXPLANATION 2
rationalize *vb* *syn* see EXPLAIN 3
rattle *vb* **1** to make a rapid succession of short sharp noises <the window *rattled* in the wind>
 syn bicker, clack, clatter, clitter, ‖ruttle, shatter
 2 *syn* see CHAT 1
 3 *syn* see EMBARRASS
 rel addle, muddle; disturb, upset; bewilder, distract, perplex
rattlebrain *n* *syn* see SCATTERBRAIN
rattlebrained *adj* *syn* see GIDDY 1
rattlehead *n* *syn* see SCATTERBRAIN
rattletrap *n*, *usu* **rattletraps** *pl* *syn* see KNICK-KNACK
rattletrap *adj* *syn* see RICKETY
rattling *adv* *syn* see VERY 1

ratty *adj* *syn* see IRASCIBLE
raucous *adj* **1** *syn* see HARSH 3
 rel brusque, gruff
 2 *syn* see TURBULENT 1
raunchy *adj* **1** *syn* see SLOVENLY 1
 2 *syn* see OBSCENE 2
ravage *vb* to lay waste (as by plundering or destroying) <the countryside was *ravaged* by the invading soldiers>
 syn deflower, depredate, desecrate, desolate, despoil, devast, devastate, devour, harry, havoc, pillage, sack, scourge, spoil, spoliate, strip, waste
 rel demolish, destroy, raze; loot, plunder, ransack, rob; ruin, wreck; encroach, invade, trespass; crush, overpower, overrun, overthrow, overwhelm
 idiom lay in ruins, lay waste
 con build, improve, rehabilitate
ravager *n* *syn* see MARAUDER
rave *vb* **1** *syn* see ORATE
 2 *syn* see ENTHUSE 2
ravel *vb* *syn* see COMPLICATE
raven *adj* *syn* see BLACK 1
ravening *adj* *syn* see VORACIOUS
ravenous *adj* **1** *syn* see VORACIOUS
 2 *syn* see HUNGRY
ravine *n* a small narrow steep-sided valley <followed the *ravine* high up into the hills>
 syn arroyo, chasm, cleft, clough, clove, gap, gorge, gulch
 rel cut, notch; defile, pass; abyss, gulf; crevasse, crevice, fissure; ‖dry wash, gully, gutter, ‖wash; canyon
raving *adj* *syn* see DELIRIOUS 1
ravish *vb* **1** *syn* see TRANSPORT 2
 2 *syn* see RAPE
ravisher *n* *syn* see MARAUDER
raw *adj* **1** not cooked <a *raw* egg>
 syn uncooked
 2 *syn* see UNREFINED 3
 3 *syn* see RUDE 1
 4 *syn* see NUDE 2
 5 *syn* see INEXPERIENCED
 rel untaught, untutored; unmatured, unripe
 con drilled, exercised; hardened; adult, grown-up, mature, matured, ripe
 6 *syn* see COARSE 3
 ‖**7** *syn* see OBSCENE 2
rawboned *adj* *syn* see LEAN
rawhider *n* *syn* see SLAVE DRIVER
rawness *n* *syn* see INEXPERIENCE
ray *n* **1** one of the lines of light that appear to radiate from a bright or luminous object <the *rays* of the sun>
 syn beam, shaft, shoot
 rel raylet; pencil, streak, stream; moonbeam, sunbeam
 con gleam, glow, incandescence, shine
 2 *syn* see PARTICLE
raze *vb* *syn* see DESTROY 1
razor–sharp *adj* *syn* see SHARP 1
‖**razz** *n* *syn* see RASPBERRY
razz *vb* **1** *syn* see BANTER
 2 *syn* see RIDICULE

re *prep syn* see APROPOS

reach *vb* **1** *syn* see COME 1

2 *syn* see GAIN 1

3 to get into contact with especially intellectually or emotionally <there was no common ground on which she could *reach* him>
syn approach
rel affect, influence, sway; get, move, touch
idiom establish contact with, find a common denominator, get through to, get to, have a meeting of minds, make advances to, make overtures to, make up to, reach (*or* share) common ground

4 to communicate with <you can *reach* me at this number>
syn contact, get
idiom get in touch (*or* contact) with, get through to, get to, keep in touch (*or* contact) with, maintain connections with

5 *syn* see PASS 9

6 *syn* see RUN 8

reach *n* **1** *syn* see RANGE 2

2 *syn* see KEN

react *vb* **1** *syn* see ACT 5

2 *syn* see RETURN 1

reactionarist *n syn* see REACTIONARY

reactionary *adj syn* see CONSERVATIVE 1

reactionary *n* one who strongly resists change and often favors a prior condition <he is a staunch political *reactionary*>
syn Blimp, Bourbon, Colonel Blimp, diehard, reactionarist, reactionist, royalist, ultraconservative, white; *compare* DIEHARD 1, RADICAL
rel bitter-ender, conservative, intransigent, rightist, right-winger, standpatter; fogy, mossback
con extremist, radical, revolutionary, revolutionist, ultraist; liberal, progressive, reformer

reactionist *n syn* see REACTIONARY

reactivate *vb syn* see REVIVE 3

read *vb syn* see SHOW 5

readily *adv syn* see EASILY 1

readiness *n* **1** *syn* see ALACRITY

2 *syn* see ADDRESS 1

3 the power of doing something without evidence of effort <his *readiness* in repartee>
syn ease, facility
rel eloquence, fluency, volubility
con effort, exertions, pains, trouble

reading *n syn* see INTERPRETATION 2

readjust *vb syn* see REORGANIZE

ready *adj* **1** in a state of mental or physical fitness for some experience or action <*ready* to leave at a moment's notice>
syn prepared, set
rel adjusted, fit, qualified; primed
idiom all ready, all set, champing at the bit
con unprepared, unqualified
ant unready

2 *syn* see WILLING 1

3 *syn* see QUICK 2
rel adept, expert, masterly, proficient, skilled, skillful; active, dynamic, live

ready *vb* **1** *syn* see PREPARE 1

2 *syn* see GIRD 3

ready–made *adj* made for general sale or use rather than prepared according to individual specifications <*ready-made* clothing>
syn bought, ‖boughten, ‖off-the-peg, off-the-rack, off-the-shelf, ready-to-wear, store, store-bought, ‖store-boughten
con custom-built, made-to-order, tailor-made; handmade
ant custom-made

ready–to–wear *adj syn* see READY-MADE

ready–witted *adj syn* see INTELLIGENT 2

real *adj* **1** *syn* see AUTHENTIC 2
ant bogus

2 *syn* see GENUINE 3

3 corresponding to known facts <discovered the *real* reason for her hasty departure>
syn actual, indisputable, true, undeniable, unfabled, veridical
rel being, existing, subsisting; certain, inevitable, necessary; sound, valid, well-grounded
idiom deniable, disputable, doubtful, questionable; improbable, uncertain, unlikely
ant unreal; apparent; imaginary

realistic *adj* having no illusions and facing reality squarely <he made a *realistic* appraisal of his chances for advancement>
syn down-to-earth, earthy, hard, hard-boiled, hardheaded, matter-of-fact, practic, practical, pragmatic, pragmatical, sober, unfantastic, unidealistic, unromantic, unsentimental, utilitarian
rel rational, reasonable, sane, sensible, sound; astute, prudent, shrewd; nonacademic
con dreamy, fantastic, imaginative; idealistic, impractical, irrational, romantic, visionary; theoretical
ant unrealistic; fanciful

reality *n* **1** *syn* see FACT 1

2 *syn* see ACTUALITY 2

realize *vb* **1** *syn* see GAIN 1

2 *syn* see THINK 1

really *adv* **1** *syn* see VERY 2

2 *syn* see WELL 7

realm *n syn* see RANGE 2

ream *n, usu* **reams** *pl syn* see SCAD

ream *vb syn* see CHEAT

‖ream out *vb syn* see SCOLD 1

reanimation *n syn* see REVIVAL

reap *vb* to do the work of collecting ripened crops <storms hampered his *reaping*>
syn garner, gather, harvest, ingather
rel glean

reaping *n syn* see HARVEST 1

reappearance *n syn* see RECURRENCE

rear *vb* **1** *syn* see BUILD 1

2 *syn* see ERECT 3

3 *syn* see LIFT 1

4 *syn* see BRING UP 1
rel foster, nurse, nurture; breed, propagate

---

syn synonym(s) *rel* related word(s)
ant antonym(s) *con* contrasted word(s)
idiom idiomatic equivalent(s)
‖ use limited; if in doubt, see a dictionary

rear *n* **1** *syn* see BACK 1
ant front
2 *syn* see BUTTOCKS
rear *adj* *syn* see POSTERIOR 2
ant front
rear end *n* *syn* see BUTTOCKS
rearmost *adj* *syn* see LAST
rearrange *vb* *syn* see REORGANIZE
rearward *n* *syn* see BACK 1
reason *n* **1** *syn* see EXPLANATION 2
2 *syn* see MOTIVE 1
3 a point or points that support something open to question <he soon gave sensible *reasons* for the proposed change>
syn argument, ground, proof, wherefore, why, whyfor
rel explanation, justification, rationalization
4 *syn* see CAUSE 1
5 the power of the mind by which man attains truth or knowledge <we all must use *reason* to solve this problem>
syn intellect, understanding
rel inference, ratiocination
6 *syn* see WIT 2
reason *vb* *syn* see THINK 5
reasonable *adj* **1** *syn* see CONSERVATIVE 2
2 *syn* see MODERATE 2
3 *syn* see CHEAP 1
ant extravagant
4 *syn* see RATIONAL
ant unreasonable
reasoned *adj* *syn* see DEDUCTIVE
reasonless *adj* **1** *syn* see INSANE 1
2 *syn* see ILLOGICAL
reassume *vb* *syn* see RESUME 1
rebate *vb* *syn* see DECREASE
rebate *n* *syn* see DEDUCTION 1
rebel *n* one who breaks with or opposes constituted authority or the established order <he is a *rebel* among educators>
syn anarch, anarchist, frondeur, insurgent, insurrectionist, malcontent, mutineer, revolter
rel adversary, antagonist, opponent; assailant, attacker; extremist, radical, revolutionary, revolutionist, ultraist; debunker, iconoclast
con authoritarian, intransigent, traditionalist; conservative, reactionary, white
rebel *vb* *syn* see REVOLT 1
rebellious *adj* *syn* see INSUBORDINATE
rel alienated, disaffected, estranged
con acquiescent, resigned; submissive
rebirth *n* **1** *syn* see CONVERSION 1
2 *syn* see REVIVAL
rebound *vb* *syn* see RECOVER 3
rebuff *vb* *syn* see FEND (off)
idiom give the cold shoulder
rebuild *vb* *syn* see MEND 2
rebuke *vb* *syn* see REPROVE
rebuke *n* an expression of strong disapproval <his bad behavior earned him a sharp *rebuke*>
syn admonishment, admonition, chiding, rap, reprimand, reproach, reproof, wig, wigging
rel dressing down, earful, lecture, lesson, scolding, talking-to, tongue-lashing

idiom a flea in one's ear, slap on the wrist
con applause, compliment, praise
rebut *vb* **1** *syn* see FEND (off)
2 *syn* see DISPROVE 1
recalcitrance *n* *syn* see DEFIANCE 2
recalcitrant *adj* *syn* see UNRULY 1
rel obstinate, stubborn; opposing, resisting, withstanding
ant amenable
recall *vb* **1** *syn* see REMEMBER
rel educe, elicit, evoke, extract; arouse, awaken, rouse, stir, waken
2 *syn* see ABJURE
3 *syn* see REVOKE 2
4 *syn* see RESTORE 1
recall *n* *syn* see MEMORY 2
recant *vb* *syn* see ABJURE
recapitulation *n* *syn* see SUMMARY
recede *vb* **1** to move backward <they will return after the floodwaters *recede*>
syn back, fall back, retract, retreat, retrocede, retrograde
rel regress, retrogress; depart, retire, withdraw
ant proceed; advance
2 *syn* see DECREASE
receipts *n pl* *syn* see REVENUE
receive *vb* *syn* see TAKE 10
received *adj* *syn* see ORTHODOX 1
recension *n* *syn* see REVISION 1
recent *adj* **1** *syn* see NEW 1
2 *syn* see MODERN 1
recently *adv* *syn* see NEW
receptive *adj* **1** open to ideas, impressions, or suggestions <he has a most *receptive* mind>
syn acceptant, acceptive, influenceable, persuadable, persuasible, responsive, suasible, swayable
rel open, open-minded; accessible, amenable, suggestible
con closed, closed-minded, inhospitable
ant unreceptive
2 *syn* see SYMPATHETIC 2
recess *vb* *syn* see ADJOURN 2
recession *n* *syn* see DEPRESSION 3
recherché *adj* *syn* see CHOICE
rel fresh, new, novel, original; exotic, uncommon, unusual
ant commonplace
recidivate *vb* *syn* see LAPSE
reciprocal *n* *syn* see MATE 5
reciprocate *vb* to give back, usually in kind or quantity <they were glad of the chance to *reciprocate* her kindness>
syn recompense, requite, retaliate, return
rel exchange, interchange; compensate, repay; retort, serve out
con accept, acquire, pocket, take
recital *n* *syn* see DESCRIPTION 2
rel discourse, story; enumeration
recite *vb* *syn* see RELATE 1
rel count, enumerate, number, tell
reckless *adj* **1** *syn* see ADVENTUROUS
rel desperate, hopeless
2 *syn* see RASH 1

ant calculating
3 *syn* see IRRESPONSIBLE
reckon *vb* **1** *syn* see CALCULATE
rel count, enumerate, number; add, cast, foot, sum, total
2 *syn* see CONSIDER 3
rel conjecture, guess, surmise
3 *syn* see ESTIMATE 3
‖**4** *syn* see UNDERSTAND 3
reckon (on) *vb* *syn* see RELY (on *or* upon)
reckoning *n* **1** *syn* see BILL 1
2 *syn* see COMPUTATION
reclaim *vb* *syn* see RESTORE 3
recline *vb* **1** *syn* see SLANT 1
2 *syn* see REST 1
reclining *adj* *syn* see PRONE 4
recluse *adj* *syn* see SECLUDED
recluse *n* a person who leads a secluded or solitary life <a man who led the life of a *recluse* although living in a busy city>
syn hermit, solitary
rel anchorite, cenobite, eremite
reclusion *n* *syn* see SECLUSION
reclusive *adj* *syn* see ANTISOCIAL
recognition *n* **1** a learning process that relates a perception of something new to knowledge already possessed <*recognition* of a genuine diamond>
syn apperception, assimilation, identification
rel cognizance, realization; awareness, consciousness, sensibility
ant irrecognition
2 *syn* see CREDIT 4
ant unrecognition
recognize *vb* **1** to make out as or perceive to be something previously known <said they would *recognize* that face anywhere>
syn know
rel recall, recollect, remember
2 *syn* see IDENTIFY
3 *syn* see ACKNOWLEDGE 2
rel note, notice, observe, remark
recoil *vb* to draw back usually through fear or disgust <*recoiled* from the snake>
syn blanch, blench, flinch, quail, shrink, squinch, start, wince
rel falter, hesitate, waver; balk, shy, stick, stickle; dodge, duck, swerve; quake, shake, shudder, tremble; reel (back)
con advance, approach, near
ant confront; defy
re–collect *vb* *syn* see COMPOSE 4
recollect *vb* *syn* see REMEMBER
rel arouse, awaken, rally, rouse, stir, waken
recollection *n* **1** *syn* see MEMORY 2
2 *syn* see MEMORY 1
recommence *vb* *syn* see RESUME 2
recommend *vb* **1** *syn* see COMMEND 2
ant discommend
2 *syn* see COUNSEL
recompense *vb* **1** *syn* see COMPENSATE 3
rel accord, award, grant, vouchsafe; balance, offset
2 *syn* see RECIPROCATE

recompense *n* *syn* see REPARATION
reconcile *vb* **1** *syn* see HARMONIZE 3
idiom bury the hatchet, make peace
ant estrange
2 *syn* see ADAPT
reconcilement *n* *syn* see RECONCILIATION
reconciliate *vb* *syn* see HARMONIZE 3
reconciliation *n* establishment of harmony <a *reconciliation* between the two countries was effected after ten years>
syn harmonizing, rapprochement, reconcilement
rel appeasement, conciliation, mollification, propitiation, satisfying
ant disagreement
recondite *adj* beyond the reach of the average intelligence <a *recondite* subject>
syn abstruse, acroamatic, deep, esoteric, heavy, hermetic, occult, orphic, profound, secret
rel erudite, learned, scholarly; academic, pedantic; difficult, hard; dark, enigmatic, obscure; anagogic, cabalistic, mystic, mystical; cryptic, runic, sibylline
con easy, facile, simple, straightforward
recondition *vb* **1** *syn* see RESTORE 3
2 *syn* see MEND 2
reconnoiter *vb* *syn* see SCOUT
reconsider *vb* to consider again with a view to changing or reversing <was asked to *reconsider* his decision>
syn reevaluate, reexamine, rethink, re-treat, review, reweigh, think (over)
rel draw off; sleep (on); amend, correct, revise
idiom revise one's thoughts, think better of, view in a new light
reconsideration *n* *syn* see REVIEW 5
reconstitute *vb* *syn* see REORGANIZE
reconstruct *vb* **1** *syn* see MEND 2
2 *syn* see REORGANIZE
3 *syn* see RESTORE 3
record *vb* *syn* see SHOW 5
record *n* *syn* see DOCUMENT 1
recount *vb* *syn* see RELATE 1
recountal *n* *syn* see DESCRIPTION 2
recounting *n* *syn* see DESCRIPTION 2
recoup *vb* *syn* see RECOVER 1
recourse *n* *syn* see RESOURCE 3
recover *vb* **1** to obtain again <*recover* a lost watch>
syn get back, recoup, recruit, regain, repossess, retrieve
rel reclaim, redeem; reacquire, recapture, retake, rewin; reoccupy, resume; rediscover; balance, compensate, offset
con lose, mislay, misplace; forfeit, sacrifice
2 to regain health <*recovering* from a bout of pneumonia>
syn come round, rally

---

syn synonym(s)   *rel* related word(s)
ant antonym(s)   *con* contrasted word(s)
idiom idiomatic equivalent(s)
‖ use limited; if in doubt, see a dictionary

rel convalesce, improve, mend, recuperate; perk (up), revive; heal; refresh, rejuvenate, renew, restore

idiom get back in shape, get better, sit up and take nourishment, take a turn for the better

con decline, fail, weaken, worsen; die, expire, perish

3 to regain a former or normal state <the textile industry was *recovering* quickly from the depression>

syn bounce (back), rebound, snap back

rel rally, revive

con decline, fail

ant worsen

4 *syn* see RESTORE 3

recreancy *n syn* see DEFECTION

recreant *adj syn* see FAITHLESS

recreant *n syn* see RENEGADE

recreate *vb* **1** *syn* see AMUSE

rel refresh, rejuvenate, renew, restore

2 *syn* see PLAY 1

recreation *n* **1** *syn* see ENTERTAINMENT

rel ease, relaxation, repose; frolic, rollick; hilarity, jollity, mirth

2 *syn* see PLAY 1

recreational vehicle *n syn* see TRAILER

recrementitious *adj syn* see SUPERFLUOUS

recrudesce *vb syn* see RETURN 1

rel refurbish, renew, renovate

con repress, suppress; cease, discontinue, stop

recruit *n syn* see NOVICE

recruit *vb syn* see RECOVER 1

rel refresh, renew, renovate, restore; mend, rebuild, repair

rectify *vb syn* see CORRECT 1

rel rebuild, repair

rectitude *n syn* see GOODNESS

rel conscientiousness, justness, scrupulousness

recumbent *adj syn* see PRONE 4

ant erect, upright

recuperate *vb syn* see IMPROVE 3

recur *vb* **1** *syn* see RETURN 1

rel iterate, reiterate, repeat

2 *syn* see RESORT 2

recurrence *n* a periodic or frequent returning <the *recurrence* of the nightmare upset him>

syn reappearance, reoccurrence, return

rel repetition, reproduction; crebrity, frequency

recurrent *adj syn* see INTERMITTENT

recurring *adj syn* see INTERMITTENT

Red *n syn* see COMMUNIST

red–blooded *adj syn* see VIGOROUS

redden *vb* **1** to make red <blood soon *reddened* the bandage>

syn incarnadine, rubify, rubric, ruby, rud, ruddle, ruddy

2 *syn* see BLUSH

redeem *vb* **1** *syn* see RANSOM

2 *syn* see FREE

3 *syn* see COMPENSATE 1

red–handed *adv* in the act of committing a misdeed <caught *red-handed*>

syn dead to rights, flagrante delicto

rel blatantly, openly

red–hot *adj* **1** *syn* see HOT 1

2 *syn* see IMPASSIONED

3 *syn* see UP-TO-DATE

red–letter *adj syn* see NOTEWORTHY

red–light district *n* a district characterized by brothels <sailors frequented the *red-light district*>

syn levee, stew(s), tenderloin

idiom street of fallen women

red–neck *n syn* see RUSTIC

redolence *n syn* see FRAGRANCE

redolent *adj* **1** *syn* see SWEET 2

2 *syn* see REMINISCENT

redouble *vb syn* see INTENSIFY

redoubt *n syn* see FORT

redoubtable *adj* **1** *syn* see FEARFUL 3

2 *syn* see FAMOUS 2

redound *vb syn* see CONTRIBUTE 2

redraft *n syn* see REVISION 1

redraft *vb syn* see REVISE

redraw *vb syn* see REVISE

redress *vb* **1** *syn* see AVENGE

2 *syn* see NEUTRALIZE

redress *n syn* see REPARATION

rel balancing, offsetting; retaliation, vengeance

reduce *vb* **1** *syn* see DECREASE

2 to decrease in amount <they decided to *reduce* prices to stimulate sales>

syn clip, cut, cut back, cut down, lower, mark down, pare, shave, slash

rel curtail, decrease, diminish, lessen; deflate, depreciate; scale (down), step down; roll back

con boost, hike, jack (up), jump, put up, raise, up

ant increase

3 *syn* see CONQUER 1

rel cripple, disable, enfeeble, undermine, weaken; debase, degrade, humble, humiliate

4 *syn* see DEGRADE 1

ant advance

5 to lose body weight especially by dieting <ate no cake while *reducing*>

syn slenderize, slim (down)

rel bant, diet

idiom lose flesh, take off weight

ant fatten

reduction *n* **1** *syn* see DEDUCTION 1

2 *syn* see DEMOTION

redundancy *n syn* see VERBIAGE 1

rel flatulence, inflatedness, inflation, tumidity, turgidity

redundant *adj syn* see WORDY

rel extra, spare, superfluous, supernumerary, surplus; iterating, reiterating, repetitious

ant concise

reduplicate *vb syn* see COPY

reduplication *n syn* see REPRODUCTION

reedy *adj syn* see THIN 1

reek *vb syn* see SMELL 3

reeking *adj syn* see MALODOROUS 1

reeky *adj syn* see MALODOROUS 1

reel *vb* **1** *syn* see SPIN 2

2 to move uncertainly or uncontrollably (as in intoxication) <*reeled* down the street>

syn stagger, titubate, totter, wheel
rel careen, lurch, ‖swaver, sway, swing, weave, wobble; falter, ‖stammer, stumble, teeter, topple; bob, waver

reestablish *vb syn* see RESTORE 1

reevaluate *vb syn* see RECONSIDER

reexamination *n syn* see REVIEW 5

reexamine *vb syn* see RECONSIDER

refashion *vb syn* see CHANGE 1

refection *n syn* see MEAL

refer *vb* **1** *syn* see ASCRIBE
2 *syn* see SUBMIT 2
3 to call or direct attention to something <no one *referred* to his recent divorce>
syn advert, allude, bring up, point (out)
rel insert, interpolate, introduce; cite, quote; instance, mention, name, specify; glance, touch
idiom make an allusion to
4 *syn* see RESORT 2
rel advise, commune, confer, consult

referee *n syn* see JUDGE 1

referee *vb syn* see JUDGE 1

refine *vb syn* see POLISH 2

refined *adj* **1** *syn* see GENTEEL 1
ant earthy
2 *syn* see FINE 1

refinement *n syn* see CULTURE
rel finish, suavity, urbanity; civility, courtesy, politeness; dignity, elegance, grace
ant vulgarity

reflect *vb* **1** to reproduce or show as a mirror does <the trees on the shore were *reflected* in the water>
syn glass, image, mirror
rel repeat, reproduce
2 *syn* see THINK 5
rel study, weigh

reflecting *adj syn* see THOUGHTFUL 1

reflection *n* **1** *syn* see ANIMADVERSION
rel assault, attack, onset, onslaught; depreciation, derogation, disparagement
2 *syn* see THOUGHT 1

reflective *adj syn* see THOUGHTFUL 1

reformatory *n syn* see JAIL

refractory *adj syn* see OBSTINATE
ant malleable

refrain *vb* **1** to hold oneself back from doing or indulging in something <*refrained* from speaking out of turn>
syn abstain, forbear, keep, withhold
rel arrest, check, halt, interrupt, stop; curb, inhibit, restrain
2 *syn* see DENY 3

refresh *vb syn* see RENEW 1
rel animate, enliven, quicken, vivify; recover, recruit, regain; amuse, divert, recreate
con exhaust, tire
ant addle; jade

refreshed *adj* made or become fresh <awoke a *refreshed* man>
syn new, regenerated, reinvigorated, renewed, revived
rel recreated, renovated; animated, exhilarated, invigorated, stimulated

con exhausted, fagged, fatigued, jaded, tired, tuckered, wearied, worn-down, worn-out

refuge *n* **1** the state of being covered or protected <exiles seeking *refuge* in neutral countries>
syn asylum, harborage, sanctuary, shelter; *compare* SHELTER 1
rel protection, shield; immunity
con exposure, liability, openness; vulnerability
2 *syn* see SHELTER 1
3 *syn* see RESOURCE 3

refugee *n* one who flees for safety <the villagers fed and housed the *refugees* from the bombed city>
syn displaced person, DP, émigré, evacuee, fugitive
rel exile; emigrant, expatriate
idiom stateless person

refulgent *adj syn* see BRIGHT 1

refurbish *vb syn* see RENEW 1

refusal *n syn* see DENIAL 1

refuse *vb* **1** *syn* see DECLINE 4
2 *syn* see DENY 2

refuse *n* matter that is regarded as worthless and fit only for throwing away <heaps of *refuse* left by the former tenant>
syn ‖collateral, debris, dreck, ‖dust, garbage, junk, kelter, litter, ‖muck, ‖mullock, offal, outsweepings, ‖pelf, riffraff, rubbish, ‖sculch, spilth, sweepings, swill, trash, waste
rel dump, dustheap; rejectamenta, scraps; lumber; offscouring(s)

refute *vb syn* see DISPROVE 1

regain *vb syn* see RECOVER 1
rel achieve, attain, compass, gain, reach; reclaim, redeem, save; renew, restore

regal *adj syn* see KINGLY
rel august, imposing, magnificent, stately; glorious, resplendent, splendid, sublime

regale *n syn* see DINNER

regalia *n pl syn* see FINERY

regard *n* **1** *syn* see NOTICE 1
2 *syn* see CONSIDERATION 3
ant disregard
3 *syn* see INTEREST 3
4 a feeling of deferential approval and liking <held in high *regard* by his neighbors>
syn account, admiration, consideration, esteem, estimation, favor, respect
rel deference, homage, honor, reverence; appreciation, cherishing, prizing, valuing; approbation, approval, satisfaction
con deprecation, disapproval; disfavor, disgust, dislike, distaste; contempt, disdain, scorn; detestation, hate, hatred
ant despite
5 *syn* see CARE 4

regard *vb* **1** *syn* see ADMIRE 2
con reject, repudiate, scorn
ant despise

---

syn synonym(s)   *rel* related word(s)
ant antonym(s)   *con* contrasted word(s)
idiom idiomatic equivalent(s)
‖ use limited; if in doubt, see a dictionary

2 *syn* see CONSIDER 3

rel assay, assess, estimate, rate, value

regardful *adj* **1** *syn* see ATTENTIVE 1

2 *syn* see MINDFUL 2

3 *syn* see RESPECTFUL

regarding *prep* *syn* see APROPOS

regardless *adj* *syn* see NEGLIGENT

regardless of *prep* *syn* see AGAINST 4

regenerated *adj* *syn* see REFRESHED

region *n* **1** *syn* see AREA 1

rel neighborhood, vicinity; division, part, section, sector

2 *syn* see FIELD

register *n* *syn* see LIST

register *vb* **1** *syn* see ENROLL 1

2 *syn* see SHOW 5

regnant *adj* **1** *syn* see DOMINANT 1

2 *syn* see PREVAILING

regress *vb* *syn* see REVERT 2

regret *vb* to be very sorry for <*regrets* his mistakes> <*regret* the problems facing minorities>

syn deplore, repent, rue

rel bemoan, bewail, lament; grieve, mourn, sorrow; deprecate, disapprove

regret *n* **1** *syn* see SORROW

rel compunction, contrition, penitence, remorse, repentance; demur, qualm, scruple

2 regrets *pl* *syn* see APOLOGY 2

regretful *adj* *syn* see REMORSEFUL

regretless *adj* *syn* see REMORSELESS

regrettable *adj* *syn* see DEPLORABLE

regular *adj* **1** *syn* see GENERAL 1

rel customary, ordinary

ant irregular

2 *syn* see ORDERLY 1

rel fixed, set, settled; constant, equable, even, steady, uniform

ant irregular; sporadic

3 *syn* see UTTER

regulate *vb* *syn* see ADJUST 2

rel arrange, methodize, order, organize, systematize; moderate, temper

regulation *n* *syn* see LAW 1

rehabilitate *vb* *syn* see RESTORE 3

rehearse *vb* **1** *syn* see RELATE 1

rel iterate, reiterate, repeat

2 *syn* see EXERCISE 3

rel run through

reify *vb* *syn* see MATERIALIZE 2

reign *vb* **1** *syn* see GOVERN 1

idiom sit on the throne

2 *syn* see RULE 2

reimburse *vb* *syn* see COMPENSATE 3

rel recover; balance, compensate, offset

con default, dishonor, repudiate, welsh

rein *vb* *syn* see COMPOSE 4

reinforce *vb* *syn* see STRENGTHEN 2

rel augment, enlarge, increase, multiply; bolster, buttress, pillar, prop, sustain

ant undermine

reinstate *vb* **1** *syn* see RESTORE 5

2 *syn* see RESTORE 1

reintroduce *vb* *syn* see RESTORE 1

reinvigorated *adj* *syn* see REFRESHED

reissue *n* *syn* see EDITION

reiterate *vb* *syn* see REPEAT

reject *vb* **1** *syn* see DECLINE 4

rel debar, eliminate, exclude, shut out

ant accept; choose, select

2 *syn* see DISCARD

rejection *n* *syn* see DENIAL 1

rejoin *vb* *syn* see ANSWER 1

rejoinder *n* *syn* see ANSWER 1

rejuvenate *vb* **1** *syn* see RENEW 1

2 *syn* see RESTORE 3

rekindle *vb* *syn* see REVIVE 3

relapse *n* *syn* see LAPSE 2

relapse *vb* *syn* see LAPSE

relate *vb* **1** to tell orally or in writing the details or circumstances of a situation <*related* the story of his life>

syn describe, narrate, recite, recount, rehearse, report, state

rel disclose, divulge, reveal, tell; detail, itemize, particularize; depict, express, render; pronounce

idiom make public

2 *syn* see JOIN 1

rel ascribe, assign, credit, impute, refer

3 *syn* see BEAR (on *or* upon)

related *adj* connected by or as if by family ties <persons *related* in the first degree> <physics and mathematics are closely *related*>

syn affiliated, agnate, akin, allied, cognate, connate, connatural, consanguine, incident, kindred

rel associated, connected; complementary, convertible, correlative, corresponding, reciprocal; alike, analogous, identical; germane, pertinent, relevant

con different, dissimilar, divergent, unconnected, unlike

ant unrelated

relation *n* *syn* see RELATIVE

relative *n* a person connected with another by blood <all of his *relatives* live out of state>

syn kin, kinsman, kinswoman, relation

rel brother, half brother, half sister, sib, sibling, sister; father, mother, parent; child, daughter, son; grandfather, grandmother, grandparent; grandchild, granddaughter, grandson; aunt, half aunt, half uncle, uncle; half nephew, half niece, nephew, niece; cousin, cross-cousin, half cousin, ortho-cousin; agnate, cognate

relative *adj* **1** *syn* see DEPENDENT 1

2 *syn* see COMPARATIVE

relax *vb* **1** *syn* see LOOSE 5

2 to become less tense or reserved <couldn't *relax* in crowds>

syn ease off, loosen up, unbend, unlax, unwind

rel calm (down), collect (oneself), compose (oneself), cool (off), simmer down

idiom be at ease, breathe easily, feel at home, make oneself at home

con rack (oneself), tense (up)

3 *syn* see REST 2

relaxation *n* *syn* see REST 1

rel amusement, diversion, recreation; alleviation, assuagement, mitigation, relief

ant tension

relaxed *adj* 1 *syn* see LOOSE 1
rel flexuous, sinuous; gentle, lenient, mild, soft
ant stiff
2 *syn* see EASYGOING 3
con ascetic, austere, severe, stern
ant tense

release *vb* 1 *syn* see FREE
rel acquit, exculpate, exonerate; relinquish, resign, surrender, yield
idiom cast loose, set at large
ant detain
2 *syn* see EMIT 2
3 *syn* see TAKE OUT (on)
ant check

relegate *vb* 1 *syn* see BANISH
2 *syn* see COMMIT 1
rel accredit, charge, credit, refer

relegation *n* 1 *syn* see EXILE 1
2 *syn* see DISPOSAL 2

relent *vb* *syn* see ABATE 4

relentless *adj* 1 *syn* see GRIM 3
rel rigorous, strict, stringent; cruel, ferocious, fierce, inhuman
con submissive, yielding
2 *syn* see INFLEXIBLE 2

relevance *n* *syn* see USE 3

relevant *adj* relating to or bearing upon the matter in hand <*relevant* testimony>
syn ad rem, applicable, applicative, applicatory, apposite, apropos, germane, material, pertinent, pointful
rel allied, cognate, related; appropriate, apt, fit, fitting, proper, suitable; important, significant, weighty; admissible, allowable
idiom in point, in question, to the point
con impertinent, inadmissible, inapplicable, inapposite, inappropriate; unallied, unassociated, unconnected, unrelated; alien, extrinsic, foreign
ant irrelevant; extraneous

reliable *adj* 1 having qualities that merit confidence or trust <a *reliable* friend>
syn dependable, secure, tried, tried and true, trustworthy, trusty
rel safe; inerrable, inerrant, infallible, unerring; apposite, cogent, compelling, convincing, meaningful, significant, sound, telling, valid; attested, authenticated, circumstantiated, confirmed, proven, validated, verified; unimpeachable, unquestionable
con doubtful, dubious, problematic, questionable, suspect; independable, undependable, untried, untrustworthy; unattested, unauthenticated, unconfirmed, unvalidated
ant unreliable
2 *syn* see CERTAIN 3

reliance *n* *syn* see TRUST 1

reliant *adj* *syn* see DEPENDENT 1

relic *n* 1 *syn* see REMEMBRANCE 3
2 *syn* see VESTIGE 1

relief *n* 1 *syn* see EASE 3
rel lightening, softening; allayment, appeasement, assuagement, mollification
ant anguish
2 *syn* see HELP 1

relieve *vb* 1 to make less grievous or more tolerable <drugs that *relieve* pain>
syn allay, alleviate, assuage, ease, lighten, mitigate, mollify
rel comfort, console, solace; appease, palliate, soften; quiet, soothe, subdue; moderate, qualify, temper; decrease, diminish, lessen, reduce; aid, benefit, help
con aggravate, enhance, heighten, sharpen; reinforce
ant intensify
2 *syn* see ROB 1
3 to take the place of for a time <sent to *relieve* the sentry>
syn spell, take over
rel fill in, sub, substitute; replace, supply
4 *syn* see EXEMPT

religion *n* 1 a system of religious belief <tolerant of all *religions*>
syn creed, cult, faith, persuasion
rel belief, doctrine
2 the body of persons who accept a system of religious belief <Jerusalem is a city sacred to three great *religions*>
syn church, communion, connection, creed, cult, denomination, faith, persuasion, sect

religious *adj* *syn* see DEVOUT
rel faithful, staunch, steadfast, true; ethical, moral, noble, righteous, virtuous; honest, honorable, just, upright
con godless, ungodly
ant irreligious

relinquish *vb* to let out of one's possession or control completely <few leaders willingly *relinquish* power>
syn abandon, cede, give up, hand over, lay down, leave, resign, surrender, ‖turn up, waive, yield; *compare* ABDICATE 1
rel lay aside; quit, throw up; abdicate, renounce; desert, forsake; abnegate, forbear, forgo, sacrifice; cast, discard, shed
ant keep

relish *n* 1 *syn* see TASTE 3
2 *syn* see TASTE 4
rel enjoying, liking, loving; bias, prejudice; flair, leaning, penchant, propensity
3 *syn* see ENJOYMENT 1

relish *vb* 1 *syn* see ENJOY 1
2 to eat or drink with pleasure <so hungry that he will *relish* plain food>
syn savor
3 *syn* see ADMIRE 1

relishing *adj* *syn* see PALATABLE
rel delighting, gratifying, pleasing, regaling, rejoicing, tickling
con banal, flat, inane, insipid, jejune

reluct *vb* *syn* see DISGUST

reluctant *adj* *syn* see DISINCLINED

---

syn synonym(s)   *rel* related word(s)
ant antonym(s)   *con* contrasted word(s)
idiom idiomatic equivalent(s)
‖ use limited; if in doubt, see a dictionary

rel calculating, cautious, chary, circumspect, wary

rely (on *or* upon) *vb* to place full confidence <*relied* on the doctor for an accurate diagnosis>
syn bank (on *or* upon), build (on), calculate (on *or* upon), count (on), depend (on *or* upon), ‖lot (on *or* upon), reckon (on), trust (in *or* to)
rel commit, confide, entrust; await, expect, hope, look
idiom put faith in, swear by
con distrust, mistrust

remain *vb syn* see STAY 2
ant depart

remainder *n* a remaining group, part, or trace <he spent the *remainder* of his life in prison>
syn balance, heel, leavings, remains, remanet, remnant, residual, residue, residuum, rest
rel excess, surplus; hangover, leftover

remains *n pl* **1** *syn* see REMAINDER
2 *syn* see CORPSE

remanet *n syn* see REMAINDER

remark *vb* **1** *syn* see SEE 1
2 to make observations and pass on one's judgment <she *remarked* on the lack of modern paintings at the gallery>
syn animadvert, comment, commentate, observe
rel mention, note

remark *n* **1** *syn* see NOTICE 1
2 an expression of opinion or judgment <a *remark* that led to a vehement argument>
syn comment, commentary, note, obiter dictum, observation
rel assertion, reflection, saying, statement, utterance; clarification, elucidation, explanation, explication, exposition, interpretation; annotation, exegesis, gloss, postil, scholium

remarkable *adj* **1** *syn* see NOTICEABLE
rel exceptional; important, momentous, significant, weighty; peculiar, singular, strange, unique
2 *syn* see EXCEPTIONAL 1

remarkably *adv syn* see VERY 1

remedial *adj syn* see CURATIVE

remedy *n* **1** something used for the treatment of disease <a cold *remedy*>
syn cure, medicament, medicant, medication, medicine, pharmacon, physic
rel biologic, drug, medicinal, pharmaceutical
2 something that corrects or counteracts <no easy *remedy* for discontent>
syn antidote, corrective, counteractant, counteractive, counteragent, countermeasure, counterstep, cure
rel cure-all, elixir, panacea; nostrum

remedy *vb syn* see CURE

remedying *adj syn* see CURATIVE

remember *vb* to bring an image or idea from the past into the mind <*remembers* the old days>
syn bethink, cite, ‖mind, recall, recollect, remind, reminisce, retain, retrospect, revive, revoke
rel look back (on *or* upon), think (of), treasure; relive; educe, elicit, evoke, extract
con disregard, ignore, neglect, overlook; dismember, lose

ant forget

remembrance *n* **1** *syn* see MEMORY 1
2 *syn* see MEMORY 2
3 something that serves to keep a person or thing in mind <wanted to give her a small *remembrance*>
syn keepsake, memento, memorial, relic, remembrancer, reminder, souvenir, token, trophy
rel favor, gift, present

remembrancer *n syn* see REMEMBRANCE 3

remind *vb syn* see REMEMBER
rel hint, imply, intimate, suggest; admonish, advise, warn; jog, prompt
idiom put in mind

reminder *n* **1** *syn* see EXPRESSION 3
2 *syn* see REMEMBRANCE 3
rel memo, memorandum, note, notice; hint, intimation, suggestion; admonition, warning

remindful *adj syn* see REMINISCENT

reminisce *vb syn* see REMEMBER

reminiscence *n* **1** *syn* see MEMORY 1
2 *syn* see MEMORY 2

reminiscent *adj* tending to remind <shoes *reminiscent* of those worn fifty years ago>
syn redolent, remindful
rel evocative, suggestive
idiom bringing to mind

remise *vb syn* see TRANSFER 4

remiss *adj syn* see NEGLIGENT
rel faineant, indolent, lazy, slothful
ant scrupulous

remit *vb* **1** *syn* see EXCUSE 1
2 *syn* see DEFER
3 *syn* see SEND 1

remittable *adj syn* see VENIAL

remnant *n syn* see REMAINDER

remonstrance *n syn* see DEMUR 2

remonstrate *vb syn* see OBJECT 1
rel combat, fight, oppose, resist, withstand

remonstration *n syn* see DEMUR 2

remorse *n syn* see PENITENCE

remorseful *adj* motivated or marked by remorse <a *remorseful* confession>
syn apologetic, attritional, compunctious, contrite, penitent, penitential, regretful, repentant, sorry
rel mournful, rueful, sorrowful
con impenitent, regretless, unregretful; hard, obdurate
ant remorseless

remorsefulness *n syn* see PENITENCE

remorseless *adj* having no remorse <a *remorseless* villain>
syn impenitent, regretless, uncontrite, unregretful, unremorseful, unrepentant, unsorry
rel compassionless, merciless, pitiless, ruthless, uncompassionate, unmerciful
con penitent, regretful, sorry
ant remorseful

remote *adj* **1** *syn* see DISTANT 1
ant close; adjacent
2 *syn* see BACK 1
3 *syn* see OBSCURE 2
4 small in degree <a *remote* possibility>

syn ‖fat, negligible, off, outside, slender, slight, slim, small

con great, large; important, significant, weighty

5 *syn* see INDIFFERENT 2

remotest *adj syn* see EXTREME 5

remove *vb* **1** *syn* see MOVE 4

2 to take something from a place or position <*removed* the book from the shelf>

syn take away, take off, take out, withdraw

rel move, shift, transfer; extract

3 to take (as a hat) from one's person <*removed* her coat when she entered the house>

syn doff, douse, put off, take off

rel cast off, throw off

idiom off with

con don, put on, replace

4 to get rid of <*remove* the causes of poverty>

syn clear away, eliminate, take out

rel dispose (of), eradicate, exterminate, extirpate; blot out, efface, erase, expunge, obliterate

idiom do away with

5 *syn* see PURGE 3

removed *adj* **1** *syn* see DISTANT 1

ant adjoining

2 *syn* see OBSCURE 2

3 *syn* see ALONE 1

remunerate *vb* **1** *syn* see PAY 1

rel accord, award, grant, vouchsafe

2 *syn* see COMPENSATE 3

remunerative *adj syn* see ADVANTAGEOUS 1

renaissance *n syn* see REVIVAL

renascence *n syn* see REVIVAL

rencontre *n syn* see CONTEST 2

rend *vb syn* see TEAR 1

rel divide, separate

render *vb* **1** *syn* see RETURN 3

2 *syn* see REPRESENT 1

3 *syn* see TRANSLATE 1

4 *syn* see ADMINISTER 1

rendering *n* **1** *syn* see INTERPRETATION 2

2 *syn* see VERSION 1

rendezvous *n* **1** *syn* see ENGAGEMENT 3

2 *syn* see RESORT 2

rendezvous *vb syn* see GATHER 6

rendition *n syn* see INTERPRETATION 2

renegade *n* a person who forsakes his faith, party, cause, or allegiance and aligns himself with another <the *renegade* derided his former beliefs>

syn apostate, defector, rat, recreant, runagate, tergiversator, turnabout, turncoat

rel iconoclast, insurgent, rebel; abandoner, deserter, forsaker; heretic, schismatic

con liege man; disciple, follower

ant adherent

renege *vb syn* see BACK DOWN

renew *vb* **1** to make like new <rested to *renew* their strength>

syn modernize, refresh, refurbish, rejuvenate, renovate, restore, update

rel make over, remodel; mend, rebuild, repair; correct, rectify, reform, revise

con bankrupt, deplete, drain, exhaust, impoverish; consume

ant wear out

2 *syn* see RESTORE 1

3 *syn* see REVIVE 3

4 *syn* see REPEAT

5 *syn* see RESUME 2

renewed *adj syn* see REFRESHED

renounce *vb* **1** *syn* see ABDICATE 1

ant arrogate

2 *syn* see ABANDON 1

idiom wash one's hands of

3 *syn* see DEFECT

renouncement *n syn* see RENUNCIATION

renovate *vb* **1** *syn* see REVIVE 3

2 *syn* see RENEW 1

rel clean, cleanse

renown *n* **1** *syn* see FAME 2

2 *syn* see EMINENCE 1

renowned *adj syn* see FAMOUS 2

rel acclaimed, extolled, lauded, praised; outstanding, signal

rent *vb syn* see HIRE 1

rent *adj syn* see LACERATED

rent *n syn* see BREACH 3

rental *n syn* see APARTMENT 1

renunciation *n* voluntary surrender or putting aside of something desired or desirable <led a life of total *renunciation* as a monk>

syn abnegation, denial, renouncement, self-abnegation, self-denial, self-renunciation

rel abjurement, eschewing, forbearing, forgoing, forswearing, sacrifice, self-sacrifice; rejection, repudiation, surrender, yielding

con gripping, holding, keeping

ant retention

reoccupy *vb syn* see RESUME 1

reoccurrence *n syn* see RECURRENCE

reopen *vb syn* see RESUME 2

reorder *vb syn* see REORGANIZE

reorganization *n syn* see SHAKE-UP

reorganize *vb* to arrange in a different way <*reorganize* a bankrupt company>

syn readjust, rearrange, reconstitute, reconstruct, reorder, reorient, reorientate, reshuffle, retool

rel reestablish, refound, resettle; rebuild, regenerate, renovate

con disarrange, disorder, disorganize

reorient *vb syn* see REORGANIZE

reorientate *vb syn* see REORGANIZE

‖**rep** *n* **1** *syn* see FAME 2

2 *syn* see REPUTATION 2

repair *vb* **1** *syn* see GO 1

2 *syn* see RESORT 2

repair *vb syn* see MEND 2

repair *n* **1** *syn* see ORDER 9

2 *syn* see ORDER 10

reparation *n* a return for something lost or suffered, usually through the fault of another <war *reparations*>

---

syn synonym(s)   *rel* related word(s)

ant antonym(s)   *con* contrasted word(s)

idiom idiomatic equivalent(s)

‖ use limited; if in doubt, see a dictionary

syn amends, compensation, indemnification, indemnity, quittance, recompense, redress, reprisal, restitution

rel atonement, expiation; remuneration, requital, retribution, reward; adjustment, settlement

repartee *n* **1** *syn* see RETORT 2

2 *syn* see BANTER

rel humor, irony, sarcasm, satire, wit; rejoinder, response, retort

repast *n* *syn* see MEAL

repay *vb* *syn* see COMPENSATE 3

rel balance, offset; accord, award

repeal *vb* *syn* see REVOKE 2

ant establish; enact

repeat *vb* to say or do again <*repeat* a command>

syn ingeminate, iterate, reiterate, renew, reprise, resay

rel recite, recount, rehearse, relate; hash over, recapitulate, rehash, restate, retell; chime, din, echo, harp, ring; duplicate, reproduce; copy, ditto, imitate; recrudesce, recur, return, revert

repeatedly *adv* *syn* see OFTEN

idiom day after day, day by day, day in and day out

repel *vb* **1** *syn* see FEND (off)

2 *syn* see RESIST

3 *syn* see DISGUST

ant allure; attract

repellent *adj* **1** *syn* see REPUGNANT 1

con alluring, bewitching, captivating, charming; enticing, luring, seductive, tempting

ant attractive; pleasing

2 *syn* see OFFENSIVE

3 *syn* see ANTIPATHETIC 2

repent *vb* *syn* see REGRET

repentance *n* *syn* see PENITENCE

con complacency, self-complacency, self-satisfaction

repentant *adj* *syn* see REMORSEFUL

repercussion *n* *syn* see EFFECT 3

rephrase *vb* *syn* see PARAPHRASE

repine *vb* *syn* see COMPLAIN

replace *vb* **1** *syn* see RETURN 4

2 *syn* see RESTORE 5

3 to put out of a usual or proper place or into the place of another <the old bridge was *replaced* by a new one last year>

syn outplace, supersede, supplant

rel renew, restore; alter, change; recoup, recover, regain, retrieve

4 *syn* see CHANGE 5

replacement *n* *syn* see SUBSTITUTE 1

replete *adj* **1** *syn* see ALIVE 5

2 *syn* see FULL 1

replica *n* *syn* see REPRODUCTION

replicate *vb* *syn* see COPY

replication *n* *syn* see REPRODUCTION

reply *vb* *syn* see ANSWER 1

con accuse, charge, impeach, indict; address, greet, salute

reply *n* *syn* see ANSWER 1

con argument, dispute; greeting, salute

report *n* **1** common talk or an instance of it that spreads rapidly <spread a false *report*>

syn buzz, cry, gossip, grapevine, hearsay, murmur, on-dit, rumble, rumor, scuttlebutt, talk, tattle, tittle-tattle, whispering, word

rel conversation, speech; chat, chatter, chitchat, prating, small talk; canard, dirt, scandal; advice, intelligence, news, tidings

2 *syn* see REPUTATION 2

3 *syn* see ACCOUNT 7

rel declaration, statement; comment, notice, review; brief, bulletin

report *vb* *syn* see RELATE 1

rel communicate, impart

repose *vb* *syn* see REST 1

repose *n* *syn* see REST 1

rel refreshment, renewal, restoration

con strain, stress; agitation, discomposure, perturbation

repository *n* *syn* see DEPOT 2

repossess *vb* **1** *syn* see RECOVER 1

2 *syn* see RESUME 1

3 to resume possession of (an item purchased on installment) in default of payments due <*repossessed* the car>

syn take back

rel get back, reclaim, recover, retrieve

reprehend *vb* *syn* see CRITICIZE

rel admonish, chide, rebuke, reprimand, reproach, reprove; berate, rate, scold, upbraid

reprehensible *adj* *syn* see BLAMEWORTHY

represent *vb* **1** to present an image or lifelike imitation of (as in art) <the painting *represents* a spring scene>

syn delineate, depict, describe, image, interpret, limn, picture, portray, render

rel express, realize, show; display, exhibit; hint, suggest; draft, outline, sketch; narrate, relate

con color, distort, falsify, garble, misinterpret, pervert, twist, warp

2 to serve as the counterpart or image of <a movie hero who *represents* the ideals of the culture>

syn body (forth), emblematize, embody, epitomize, exemplify, illustrate, mirror, personalize, personate, personify, symbolize, typify; *compare* EMBODY 1

rel denote, mean, signify; impersonate, substitute; copy, imitate, reproduce

con belie, distort, garble, twist, warp

ant misrepresent

representant *n* *syn* see DELEGATE

representation *n* the act of delineating <an exponent of *representation* in art>

syn delineation, depiction, description, picture, portraiture, portrayal, presentment

rel demonstration, exemplification, illustration

representative *adj* *syn* see TYPICAL 1

ant atypical

representative *n* **1** *syn* see INSTANCE

2 *syn* see DELEGATE

repress *vb* **1** *syn* see SUPPRESS 2

2 *syn* see COMPOSE 4

repression *n* **1** the action or process of putting down by authority or force <the *repression* of unpopular opinions>

syn choking, extinguishment, quashing, quenching, smothering, squashing, squelching, stifling, strangling, suppression, throttling
rel check, control, curb, restraint; crushing, quelling, subdual
con emboldening, encouragement, support
2 an instance of putting down by authority or force <*repressions* of racial minorities>
syn clampdown, crackdown, suppression
rel crushing, extinction, smothering; limitation, restriction
reprieve *n syn* see RESPITE 1
reprimand *n syn* see REBUKE
reprimand *vb syn* see REPROVE
reprinting *n syn* see EDITION
reprisal *n* 1 *syn* see REPARATION
  2 *syn* see RETALIATION
reprise *vb syn* see REPEAT
reproach *n syn* see REBUKE
  rel blame, censure, discredit
reproach *vb syn* see REPROVE
reprobate *vb* 1 *syn* see CRITICIZE
  2 *syn* see DECLINE 4
reprobate *adj* 1 *syn* see ABANDONED 2
  2 *syn* see WRONG 1
reprobate *n syn* see VILLAIN 1
reproduce *vb* 1 *syn* see PROCREATE 1
  2 *syn* see COPY
reproduction *n* one thing which closely or essentially resembles another that has already been made, produced, or written <printed *reproductions* of the great masters>
syn carbon, carbon copy, copy, ditto, duplicate, facsimile, reduplication, replica, replication
ant original
reproof *n syn* see REBUKE
reprove *vb* to criticize adversely, especially in order to warn of or to correct a fault <*reproved* him for talking in class>
syn admonish, call down, chide, lesson, monish, ||rack back, rebuke, reprimand, reproach, ||sneap, tick off; *compare* CRITICIZE, LAMBASTE 3, SCOLD 1
rel counsel, warn; blame, censure, criticize, reprehend, reprobate; chasten, correct, discipline, punish
idiom haul over the coals, slap one's wrist, take to task
reptile *n syn* see SYCOPHANT
repudiate *vb* 1 *syn* see DECLINE 4
  con acknowledge, admit, avow, confess, own
  ant adopt
  2 *syn* see DEFECT
  3 *syn* see DISCLAIM
  rel abandon, desert, forsake; cast, discard
  con allow, concede, grant
  ant own
repugnance *n syn* see ABOMINATION 2
repugnancy *n syn* see ABOMINATION 2
repugnant *adj* 1 so alien or unlikable as to arouse antagonism and aversion <the idea of moving again became *repugnant* to her>
syn abhorrent, invidious, obnoxious, repellent, revulsive

rel alien, extraneous, extrinsic, foreign; incompatible, incongruous, inconsonant, uncongenial
con acceptable, bearable, tolerable; agreeable, gratifying, pleasant, pleasing, pleasurable
ant congenial
  2 *syn* see OFFENSIVE
  3 *syn* see ANTIPATHETIC 2
repulse *vb* 1 *syn* see FEND (off)
  2 *syn* see DISGUST
  ant captivate
repulsion *n syn* see ABOMINATION 2
repulsive *adj syn* see OFFENSIVE
  ant alluring
reputable *adj syn* see RESPECTABLE 1
reputation *n* 1 *syn* see FAME 2
  rel authority, credit, influence, prestige, weight
  2 the estimation in which one is generally held <a good *reputation*>
syn character, fame, name, ||rep, report, repute
repute *n* 1 *syn* see FAME 2
  ant disrepute
  2 *syn* see REPUTATION 2
reputed *adj* 1 *syn* see RESPECTABLE 1
  2 *syn* see SUPPOSED 1
request *vb syn* see ASK 2
  rel appeal, petition, pray, sue
requiescence *n syn* see REST 1
require *vb* 1 *syn* see DEMAND 1
  2 *syn* see DEMAND 2
  3 *syn* see LACK
required *adj* 1 *syn* see NEEDFUL
  2 *syn* see MANDATORY
  ant optional
requirement *n* 1 something wanted or needed <production was not sufficient to satisfy *requirements* for cars>
syn demand, need, want
  2 *syn* see ESSENTIAL 2
requisite *adj* 1 *syn* see NEEDFUL
  2 *syn* see JUST 3
requisite *n syn* see ESSENTIAL 2
requisition *vb syn* see DEMAND 1
requital *n syn* see RETALIATION
requite *vb* 1 *syn* see RECIPROCATE
  rel content, satisfy; revenge
  2 *syn* see COMPENSATE 3
resay *vb syn* see REPEAT
rescind *vb syn* see REVOKE 2
rescript *n syn* see REVISION 1
rescue *vb* to set free (as from confinement or risk) <*rescue* a drowning child>
syn deliver, save
rel emancipate, free, liberate, manumit, release; conserve, preserve; disembarrass, disentangle, extricate; recover, regain, retrieve; buy, ransom, redeem
research *n syn* see INQUIRY 1
resect *vb syn* see EXCISE
resemblance *n syn* see LIKENESS

---

syn synonym(s)   **rel** related word(s)
ant antonym(s)   **con** contrasted word(s)
idiom idiomatic equivalent(s)
|| use limited; if in doubt, see a dictionary

rel parallel
ant dissemblance

resemble *vb* to be like or similar to <he *resembles* his father>
syn favor, ‖feature, simulate
idiom be a dead ringer for, bear a resemblance to, be the spit and image of, be the very image of, bring to mind, have all the earmarks of, look like, put one in mind of, remind one of, take after
con differ, vary

resentfully *adv syn* see HARD 6

resentment *n syn* see OFFENSE 2
rel animosity, animus, antagonism, antipathy, rancor; ill will, malice, malignancy, malignity, spite

reservation *n syn* see CONDITION 1
rel circumscription

reserve *vb* **1** *syn* see KEEP 5
2 to set or have set aside or apart <*reserve* a hotel room>
syn bespeak, book, preengage
rel contract, engage, retain

reserve *n* something stored or kept available for future use or need <keep a *reserve* of canned foods on hand>
syn backlog, hoard, inventory, nest egg, reservoir, stock, stockpile, store
rel fund, supply
idiom something for a rainy day, something in the sock

reserved *adj* **1** inclined to cautious restraint in the expression of knowledge or opinions <too *reserved* to offer a spontaneous criticism>
syn constrained, incommunicable, noncommittal, restrained
rel bashful, diffident, modest, shy; ceremonious, conventional, formal
con demonstrative, expansive, unconstrained, unrestrained; boisterous, loud, ostentatious; extroverted, open, outgoing
ant unreserved
2 *syn* see SILENT 3
ant effusive
3 *syn* see UNSOCIABLE
ant affable
4 *syn* see ANTISOCIAL
5 *syn* see QUALIFIED 2

reservoir *n syn* see RESERVE

reshuffle *vb syn* see REORGANIZE

reside *vb* **1** to have as one's habitation or domicile <he *resides* in Boston>
syn abide, bide, ‖dig, dwell, hang out, live
rel inhabit, occupy, people, tenant; continue, endure
2 *syn* see CONSIST 1

residence *n* **1** *syn* see HABITATION 1
2 *syn* see HABITATION 2

residency *n syn* see HABITATION 2

resident *n syn* see INHABITANT

‖**residenter** *n syn* see INHABITANT

resider *n syn* see INHABITANT

residual *n syn* see REMAINDER

residue *n syn* see REMAINDER

residuum *n syn* see REMAINDER

resign *vb* **1** *syn* see RELINQUISH
2 *syn* see ABDICATE 1
3 *syn* see QUIT 6

resignation *n* **1** *syn* see ACQUIESCENCE
rel humbleness, lowliness, meekness, modesty
2 *syn* see PATIENCE

resigned *adj syn* see PASSIVE 2
ant rebellious

resile *vb syn* see BACK DOWN

resilient *adj* **1** *syn* see ELASTIC 1
2 *syn* see ELASTIC 2
ant flaccid

resist *vb* to stand firm against a person or influence <the criminal *resisted* the police> <we must learn to *resist* temptation>
syn buck, combat, contest, dispute, duel, fight, oppose, repel, traverse, withstand
rel assail, assault, attack; contradict, contravene, gainsay, impugn; baffle, balk, foil, frustrate, thwart; check, counter, hinder, obstruct, stem
con bow, capitulate, surrender
ant submit, yield

resolute *adj* **1** *syn* see DECIDED 2
rel obstinate, pertinacious, stubborn
2 *syn* see FAITHFUL 1

resoluteness *n syn* see DECISION 2

resolution *n* **1** *syn* see ANALYSIS 1
2 *syn* see DECISION 1
3 *syn* see DECISION 2
4 *syn* see COURAGE

resolve *vb* **1** *syn* see ANALYZE
ant blend
2 *syn* see SOLVE 1
3 *syn* see SOLVE 2
rel dispel, disperse, dissipate; clear, disabuse, purge, rid
4 *syn* see DECIDE

resolve *n syn* see DECISION 2

resolved *adj syn* see DECIDED 2

resonant *adj* marked by conspicuously full and rich sounds or tones (as of speech or music) <a deep *resonant* voice rang out>
syn consonant, fat, orotund, plangent, resounding, ringing, rotund, round, sonorant, sonorous, vibrant
rel full, mellow, rich; deep, profound; enhanced, heightened, intensified; earsplitting, loud, powerful, stentorian, strident; beating, pulsating, pulsing, throbbing; booming, clangorous, noisy, reverberant, reverberating, sounding, thundering, thunderous; electrifying, thrilling
con faint, low, murmurous, muted, smothered, soft, weak; flat, toneless, unmusical; cacophonous, discordant, inharmonious, off-key

resort *n* **1** *syn* see RESOURCE 3
2 a place that is habitually frequented <a favorite *resort* of teenagers>
syn hangout, haunt, purlieu, rendezvous, stamping ground, watering hole
rel harbor, haven, refuge, retreat; den, nest
3 a place providing recreation and entertainment especially to vacationers <returned to the same *resort* every year>

syn pleasure dome, spa, watering place
rel hotel, inn, lodge; bath(s), hot spring(s), mineral spring(s), spring(s), thermal spring(s)
resort *vb* **1 syn** see FREQUENT
ant avoid
2 to betake oneself or to have recourse when in need of help or relief <they were unwilling to *resort* to her parents for aid>
syn apply, go, recur, refer, repair run, turn
rel address, devote, direct, employ, use, utilize
idiom avail oneself of, fall back on (*or* upon)
resound *vb* **syn** see PRAISE 2
resounding *adj* **1 syn** see RESONANT
2 syn see EMPHATIC
resource *n* **1 resources** *pl* **syn** see MEAN 3
2 resources *pl* **syn** see WEALTH 2
3 something to which one turns for assistance in difficulty or need in the absence of a usual means or source of supply <has exhausted every *resource* he can think of>
syn dernier ressort, expediency, expedient, makeshift, recourse, refuge, resort, shift, stopgap, string, substitute, surrogate
rel contraption, contrivance, device, lash-up; creation, invention; fashion, manner, method, mode, system, way; means, measure, step; artifice, dodge, stratagem, subterfuge; hope, opportunity, possibility, relief
respect *n* **syn** see REGARD 4
rel awe, fear, reverence; adoration, veneration, worship
ant scorn
respect *vb* **syn** see ADMIRE 2
rel revere, reverence, venerate
ant abuse; misuse; scorn
respectable *adj* **1** worthy of esteem or deference <a *respectable* scientist>
syn creditable, estimable, reputable, reputed, well-thought-of
rel honorable, worthy
ant disreputable, unrespectable
2 syn see DECOROUS 1
3 syn see DECENT 4
4 syn see CONSIDERABLE 2
5 acceptable in appearance or standing <wore old but *respectable* clothes>
syn decent, presentable, tolerable; *compare* DECENT 4
rel adequate, satisfactory; acceptable, appropriate, proper, suitable
ant disreputable
respectful *adj* marked by or showing respect or deference <a *respectful* glance>
syn deferential, duteous, dutiful, regardful
rel reverent, reverential, venerating; attentive, civil, courteous, gracious, polite
con abusive, insolent, insulting, offensive; contemptuous, impudent, irreverent, rude
ant disrespectful
respecting *prep* **syn** see APROPOS
respective *adj* **syn** see SEVERAL 1
respire *vb* **syn** see BREATHE 3
respite *n* **1** a temporary suspension of the execution of a capital offender <the murderer won a *respite*>

syn reprieve
2 syn see BREAK 4
rel intermission, lull, pause, recess; ease, leisure, rest
resplendent *adj* **syn** see SPLENDID 2
rel blazing, flaming, glowing
respond *n* **syn** see ANSWER 1
respond *vb* **syn** see ANSWER 1
rel act, behave, react
response *n* **syn** see ANSWER 1
responsible *adj* subject to an authority which may exact redress in case of default <she is *responsible* for the safe delivery of the goods>
syn accountable, amenable, answerable, liable
rel exposed, open, subject
con clear, exempt, immune; irresponsible, unaccountable, unanswerable, unliable
ant irresponsible
responsive *adj* **1 syn** see RECEPTIVE 1
ant unresponsive
2 syn see SENTIENT 3
rel answering, replying, responding
3 syn see TENDER
con cold, cool, indifferent
rest *n* **1** freedom from toil or strain <enjoyed his well-deserved *rest*>
syn ease, leisure, relaxation, repose, requiescence
rel deferring, intermission, suspension; quiet, silence, stillness; calm, peace, peacefulness, placidity, restfulness, serenity, tranquillity
con action, work; restlessness, strain
2 syn see BASE 1
rest *vb* **1** to dispose oneself at ease in order to relieve or avoid fatigue <she is *resting* in the bedroom after a hard day's work>
syn lie, lie down, recline, repose, stretch (out)
rel doze, nap, nod, sleep, slumber, snooze
2 to refrain from labor or exertion <planned to do nothing but *rest* during his vacation>
syn relax, rest up, unbend, unlax
rel loaf, loll, lounge; ease off, ease up, let down, let up, slacken, slack off
idiom take it easy, take life easy
con labor, toil, work; drudge, grind, slave
3 to allow an interval of rest from exertion <they *rested* for ten minutes before going back to work>
syn breathe, lay off, lie by, spell
idiom lie (*or* rest) on one's oars, stop for breath, take a break (*or* rest), take five (*or* ten), take time out
4 syn see BASE
rel depend, hang, hinge; count, rely
rest *n* **syn** see REMAINDER
rel excess, overplus, superfluity, surplus, surplusage
restart *vb* **syn** see RESUME 2
restate *vb* **syn** see PARAPHRASE

---

syn synonym(s)   **rel** related word(s)
ant antonym(s)   **con** contrasted word(s)
idiom idiomatic equivalent(s)
‖ use limited; if in doubt, see a dictionary

restatement *n syn* see VERSION 1

restitute *vb* **1** *syn* see RESTORE 3

2 *syn* see RETURN 4

restitution *n syn* see REPARATION

restive *adj* **1** *syn* see CONTRARY 3

2 *syn* see TENSE 2

restiveness *n syn* see UNREST

restless *adj* lacking rest or giving no rest <the patient was *restless* from pain> <*restless* sleep>
syn uneasy, unpeaceful, unquiet, unrestful, unsettled, untranquil
rel agitated, disturbed, perturbed, troubled; fidgety, jittery, jumpy, nervous, restive; fitful, intermittent, spasmodic
con easy, peaceful, quiet, tranquil
ant restful

restlessness *n syn* see UNREST

restorative *adj* **1** *syn* see CURATIVE

2 *syn* see TONIC 1

restore *vb* **1** to put or bring back (as into existence or use) <*restore* peace in the world>
syn recall, reestablish, reinstate, reintroduce, renew, revive
rel get back, recover, regain, retrieve, win (back)
2 *syn* see RENEW 1
3 to put into a previous good state <made plans to *restore* slum areas>
syn reclaim, recondition, reconstruct, recover, rehabilitate, rejuvenate, restitute
rel redeem, rescue, save; amend, reform, revise; recoup, recruit, regain, retrieve; better, improve; correct, rectify, remedy, right; return
ant deteriorate
4 to help or cause to regain signs of life and vigor <*restore* him to health>
syn resuscitate, revive, revivify
rel cure, heal, remedy; arouse, rally, rouse, stir
5 to put again in possession of something <*restore* the king to his throne>
syn give back, put (back), reinstate, replace, return
6 *syn* see RETURN 4

restrain *vb* **1** to prevent from or control in doing something <*restrained* the child from picking all the flowers>
syn bit, bridle, check, coarct, constrain, crimp, curb, hold back, hold down, hold in, inhibit, keep, pull in, withhold; *compare* HAMPER
rel arrest, interrupt, stop; prevent; forbear, refrain; block, hinder, impede, obstruct; gag, muzzle
idiom keep in line, put (*or* lay) under restraint
con countenance, encourage; incline, induce, move, prompt; persuade; allow, permit
ant impel; incite
2 *syn* see COMPOSE 4
ant abandon
3 *syn* see MODERATE 1

restrained *adj* **1** *syn* see QUIET 4
ant unrestrained
2 *syn* see UNDEMONSTRATIVE
3 *syn* see RESERVED 1
4 *syn* see CONSERVATIVE 2
ant extravagant

restraint *n syn* see RESTRICTION 2

restrict *vb syn* see LIMIT 2
rel bind, tie; shrink

restricted *adj syn* see DEFINITE 1

restriction *n* **1** something that restricts or restrains <they both wanted to be free of the *restriction* of the school>
syn ‖ball and chain, circumscription, cramp, limitation, stint, stricture
rel brake, check, control, curb
2 an act of restricting or the condition of being restricted <undue *restriction* of children>
syn circumscription, confinement, constrainment, constraint, cramp, restraint

rest up *vb syn* see REST 2

restyle *vb syn* see REVISE

result *n* **1** *syn* see EFFECT 1
rel close, conclusion, end, finish, termination; product, production
con origin, root, source
2 *syn* see ANSWER 2

resume *vb* **1** to assume or take again <*resumed* her place in society>
syn reassume, reoccupy, repossess, retake
rel reclaim, recoup, recover, regain, retrieve
2 to return to or begin again after interruption <*resumed* her work>
syn continue, pick up, recommence, renew, reopen, restart, take up
rel carry on, go on, keep up
con cease, discontinue, end, halt, postpone, quit, stop; check, intermit, interrupt

résumé *n syn* see SUMMARY

resurgence *n syn* see REVIVAL

resurrect *vb* **1** to restore to life <believed that his body would be literally *resurrected*>
syn raise
idiom raise from the dead
2 *syn* see REVIVE 3

resurrection *n syn* see REVIVAL

resuscitate *vb* **1** *syn* see RESTORE 4
2 *syn* see REVIVE 3

resuscitation *n syn* see REVIVAL

retail *vb syn* see SELL 3

retain *vb* **1** *syn* see HAVE 1
2 *syn* see KEEP 5
con abdicate, resign; abjure, forswear, recant, renounce, retract
3 *syn* see REMEMBER

retake *vb syn* see RESUME 1

retaliate *vb syn* see RECIPROCATE
rel avenge, revenge
idiom even the score, get back at, get even with, give in kind, give one a dose of his own medicine, give one tit for tat, pay one in his own coin, settle (*or* square) accounts, turn the tables on

retaliation *n* the act of inflicting or the intent to inflict injury in return for injury <they had no opportunity for *retaliation*>
syn avengement, avenging, counterblow, reprisal, requital, retribution, revanche, revenge, vengeance
rel correction, discipline, punishment; indemnification, recompense, repayment; amends, indemnity, redress, reparation, restitution

idiom an eye for an eye, blow for blow, measure for measure, tit for tat
con clemency, grace, lenity, mercy; forgiveness, pardon, remission
retard *vb syn* see DELAY 1
  rel decrease, lessen, reduce; clog, fetter, hamper; baffle, balk
  ant accelerate; advance
retarded *adj* limited in intellectual or emotional development <a *retarded* child>
  syn backward, dim-witted, dull, feebleminded, half-witted, imbecile, moronic, quarter-witted, simple, simpleminded, slow, slow-witted; *compare* SIMPLE 3, STUPID 1
  rel dim, ‖dough-baked, ‖dunny, opaque; exceptional, underachieving; touched
  idiom not all there, soft in the head
  con bright, capable, intelligent
retch *vb* to make an effort to vomit <started to *retch* after drinking it>
  syn gag, heave, keck
rethink *vb syn* see RECONSIDER
reticent *adj syn* see SILENT 3
  con candid, open, plain
  ant frank, unreticent
retinue *n syn* see ENTOURAGE
retire *vb 1 syn* see RETREAT 2
  2 syn see GO 2
  rel recede, retreat; abandon, relinquish, surrender, yield
  ant advance
  3 to cause to withdraw from one's position or occupation <all employees are automatically *retired* at age sixty-five>
  syn pension (off), superannuate
  rel discharge, dismiss; drop, leave, quit, resign, terminate, vacate
  4 to go to bed <youngsters should always *retire* before midnight>
  syn bed, ‖flop, pile (in), roll in, turn in
  idiom go beddie-bye, go night-night, hit the hay (*or* sack)
  con arise, get out, get up, pile (out), roll out, turn out, uprise
  ant rise
retired *adj syn* see OBSCURE 2
retirement *n syn* see SECLUSION
retiring *adj 1 syn* see SHY 1
  ant assertive
  2 syn see UNDEMONSTRATIVE
  ant forward
retool *vb syn* see REORGANIZE
retort *vb syn* see ANSWER 1
retort *n 1 syn* see ANSWER 1
  2 a quick, witty, or cutting reply <he made a very clever *retort*>
  syn back answer, comeback, repartee, riposte
  rel reprisal, retaliation, revenge; crack, gag, jape, jest, joke, quip, sally, wisecrack, witticism
retouch *vb syn* see TOUCH UP
retract *vb 1 syn* see RECEDE 1
  ant protract
  2 syn see ABJURE
  rel eliminate, exclude, rule out, suspend

retral *adj 1 syn* see POSTERIOR 2
  2 syn see BACKWARD 1
retreat *n syn* see SHELTER 1
retreat *vb 1 syn* see RECEDE 1
  rel quail, recoil, shrink
  ant advance
  2 to draw back from action or danger <the army *retreated* in disarray>
  syn fall back, give back, retire, withdraw
  rel abandon, depart, evacuate, go, leave, pull out, quit, vacate; decamp, escape, flee, fly; back down, back out, bow out, climb down
  idiom beat a retreat, drop back, give ground, give way, sound a retreat
  con advance, move, proceed, progress
  ant attack
re–treat *vb syn* see RECONSIDER
retrench *vb syn* see SHORTEN
retribution *n syn* see RETALIATION
  rel affliction, trial, tribulation, visitation
retrieve *vb 1 syn* see RECOVER 1
  2 syn see REVIVE 3
retrocede *vb syn* see RECEDE 1
retrograde *adj syn* see BACKWARD 1
retrograde *vb 1 syn* see RECEDE 1
  rel return, revert; invert, reverse; backslide, lapse, relapse
  2 syn see DETERIORATE 1
retrogress *vb syn* see REVERT 2
retrospect *n syn* see REVIEW 5
retrospect *vb syn* see REMEMBER
retrospection *n syn* see REVIEW 5
return *vb 1* to go or come back (as to a person, place, or condition) <the converted sinner soon *returned* to his old ways>
  syn react, recrudesce, recur, revert, turn back
  rel advert; revolve, rotate, turn; renew, restore; recover, regain; rebound, reflect, repercuss, reverberate
  con abandon, depart, leave, quit
  ant forsake
  2 syn see ANSWER 1
  3 to bring back (as a writ or verdict) to an office or tribunal <*return* a verdict of not guilty>
  syn render
  4 to bring, send, or put back to a former or proper place <*return* the gun to its holster>
  syn replace, restitute, restore, take back
  ant remove
  5 syn see RESTORE 5
  6 syn see YIELD 5
  7 syn see RECIPROCATE
  rel bestow, give
return *n 1 syn* see RECURRENCE
  2 syn see ANSWER 1
  3 syn see PROFIT
  ant outlay
returnless *adj syn* see INEVITABLE
revamp *vb 1 syn* see MEND 2

---

syn synonym(s)   **rel** related word(s)
ant antonym(s)   **con** contrasted word(s)
idiom idiomatic equivalent(s)
‖ use limited; if in doubt, see a dictionary

2 *syn* see REVISE

revanche *n syn* see RETALIATION

reveal *vb* **1** to make known what has been or should be concealed <he solemnly promised he would not *reveal* the truth>
syn betray, blab (out), disclose, discover, divulge, give away, let on, ||let out, mouth, spill, tell, unbosom, unclose, uncover, uncurtain, unveil
rel break, communicate, impart; announce, blow (about *or* abroad), broadcast, declare, give out, publish, vent; breathe, whisper; leak; acknowledge, admit, avow, confess, let on; peach, rat, ||split, squeak, squeal (on), ||stool, talk
idiom let slip, let the cat out of the bag, spill the beans
con cover (up), hide, obscure, veil
ant conceal
2 *syn* see OPEN 2

revel *vb* **1** to be festive in a noisy or riotous manner <they *reveled* all night long>
syn carouse, frolic, hell, riot, roister, spree, wassail
idiom blow off steam, cut loose, kick up one's heels, let go, let loose, paint the town red, whoop it up
2 *syn* see WALLOW 3

revel *n* **1** *syn* see MERRYMAKING
2 *syn* see REVELRY 2

revelation *n* disclosure or something disclosed by or as if by divine or preternatural means <a *revelation* closely guarded by members of the sect>
syn apocalypse, oracle, prophecy, vision
ant adumbration

reveling *n syn* see MERRYMAKING

revelment *n* **1** *syn* see MERRYMAKING
2 *syn* see REVELRY 2

revelry *n* **1** *syn* see MERRYMAKING
2 boisterous partying <they were exhausted after the night of *revelry*>
syn high jinks, revel, revelment, skylarking, wassail, whoop-de-do, whoopee, whoopla, whoop-up

revenant *n syn* see APPARITION

revenge *vb syn* see AVENGE
rel defend, justify
idiom get one's own back, have one's revenge, take an eye for an eye

revenge *n syn* see RETALIATION

revengeful *adj syn* see VINDICTIVE
rel adamant, inexorable, inflexible, obdurate

revenue *n* amount received or gained usually measured in money <still holds property that yields a good *revenue*>
syn coming(s) in, income, receipts
rel earnings, gains, salary, wages; proceeds, profit, returns, yield
con expenditure, expense(s), outgoings, outlay

reverberant *adj syn* see HOLLOW 1

revere *vb* to honor and admire profoundly and respectfully <he is *revered* for his wisdom>
syn adore, reverence, venerate, worship
rel admire, esteem, regard, respect; appreciate, cherish, prize, treasure, value; exalt, magnify; enjoy, love

con contemn, despise, disdain, scorn, scout; insult, mock, scoff
ant flout

revered *adj syn* see VENERABLE 1

reverence *n* **1** *syn* see HONOR 1
rel devotion, fealty, loyalty, piety
2 the emotion inspired by what arouses one's deep respect or veneration <a deep *reverence* for honesty>
syn awe, fear
con contempt, despite, disdain, hatred, scorn; insult, mockery

reverence *vb syn* see REVERE
idiom hold in reverence

reverend *adj syn* see VENERABLE 1

reverend *n syn* see CLERGYMAN

reverential *adj syn* see VENERABLE 1

reverie *n* the condition of being lost in thought <spent the day in *reverie* before the fire>
syn brown study, muse, study, trance
rel absorption, abstraction, preoccupation; contemplation, meditation, thought; castle-building, daydreaming, dreaming

reversal *n* **1** a causing to move or face in an opposite direction or to appear in an inverted position <a *reversal* in policy> <the *reversal* of objects seen through a simple lens>
syn about-face, changeabout, inversion, reverse, reversement, reversion, right-about, right-about-face, turn, turnabout, turning, volte-face
rel bouleversement, overturning
2 *syn* see SETBACK

reverse *adj syn* see OPPOSITE

reverse *vb* **1** to change to the contrary or opposite side or position <the chairman *reversed* the order in which they would speak>
syn change, inverse, invert, revert, transplace, transpose, turn
rel capsize, overturn, upset; exchange, interchange; shift, transfer
2 *syn* see REVOKE 2

reverse *n* **1** *syn* see OPPOSITE
2 *syn* see REVERSAL 1
3 *syn* see SETBACK

reversement *n syn* see REVERSAL 1

reversion *n* **1** a return to an ancestral type or condition or an instance of such a return <the law was a shocking *reversion* to earlier times>
syn atavism, throwback
rel backsliding, lapse, relapse
con advance, amendment, bettering, betterment, improvement; reform
2 *syn* see REVERSAL 1

revert *vb* **1** *syn* see RETURN 1
2 to come or go back to a lower or worse condition <*reverted* to savagery>
syn regress, retrogress, throw back
rel backslide, lapse, relapse; decline, degenerate, deteriorate, retrograde
con advance, progress
3 *syn* see REVERSE 1

review *n* **1** *syn* see REVISION 1
2 *syn* see EXAMINATION
3 *syn* see CRITICISM 1

4 syn see JOURNAL

5 a retrospective view of or meditation on past events <an occurrence that in *review* did not surprise him>

syn afterlight, reconsideration, reexamination, retrospect, retrospection, revision

rel reflection, study; second thought

con anticipation, contemplation, foreseeing

review *vb syn* see RECONSIDER

reviewal *n syn* see CRITICISM 1

revile *vb syn* see SCOLD 1

rel asperse, calumniate, defame, libel, malign, slander, traduce, vilify

con acclaim, eulogize, extol, praise

ant laud

revisal *n syn* see REVISION 1

revise *vb* to make a new, amended, improved, or up-to-date version of <the many problems involved in *revising* a dictionary>

syn redraft, redraw, restyle, revamp, rework, rewrite, work over

rel overhaul, reorganize; perfect, polish, upgrade

con discard, disregard

revise *n syn* see REVISION 1

revision *n* **1** an act of revising <the *revision* of a manuscript>

syn recension, redraft, rescript, review, revisal, revise

rel amendment, correction, emendation, rectification

2 syn see REVIEW 5

revitalize *vb syn* see REVIVE 3

revival *n* a renewal of life, activity, or prominence <a *revival* of weaving>

syn reanimation, rebirth, renaissance, renascence, resurgence, resurrection, resuscitation, revivification, reviviscence, risorgimento

rel regeneration, rejuvenation, renewal, restoration

revive *vb* **1 syn** see RESTORE 4

rel gain, improve, recuperate

2 syn see RESTORE 1

3 to restore from a depressed, inactive, or unused state <*revived* his hope of escape>

syn reactivate, rekindle, renew, renovate, resurrect, resuscitate, retrieve, revitalize, revivify

rel reanimate, regenerate, reinvigorate, rejuvenate; arouse, galvanize, quicken, stimulate; activate, energize, vitalize

con extinguish, put down, put out, quell, quench, suppress; inhibit

4 syn see REMEMBER

revived *adj syn* see REFRESHED

revivification *n syn* see REVIVAL

revivify *vb* **1 syn** see REVIVE 3

2 syn see RESTORE 4

reviviscence *n syn* see REVIVAL

revoke *vb* **1 syn** see REMEMBER

2 to annul by recalling or taking back <*revoke* a privilege>

syn dismantle, lift, recall, repeal, rescind, reverse

rel abrogate, annul, void; cancel, erase, expunge; invalidate, nullify; countermand, counterorder; abjure, forswear, recant, retract

ant confirm

revolt *vb* **1** to renounce allegiance or subjection <*revolted* against the king>

syn insurrect, mutiny, rebel, rise (against)

rel defy, oppose, resist; break, renounce, turn (against); boycott, strike; overthrow, overturn, riot

idiom kick over the traces, take up arms against

con obey, submit; aid, assist, help, succor, support; bolster, prop (up), sustain, uphold

2 syn see DISGUST

revolter *n syn* see REBEL

revolting *adj syn* see OFFENSIVE

revolute *vb syn* see REVOLUTIONIZE

revolution *n* **1** the action or an act of moving around an orbit or circular course <the *revolution* of the earth around the sun>

syn circuit, circulation, circumvolution, gyration, gyre, revolve, rotation, round, turn, wheel, whirl

rel cycle, pirouette, reel, roll, spin, twirl

2 syn see SHAKE-UP

revolution *vb syn* see REVOLUTIONIZE

revolutional *adj syn* see EXTREME 3

revolutionary *adj syn* see EXTREME 3

revolutionary *n syn* see RADICAL

revolutionist *n syn* see RADICAL

revolutionist *adj syn* see EXTREME 3

revolutionize *vb* to change fundamentally or completely <he *revolutionized* manufacturing processes>

syn revolute, revolution

rel alter, change, modify; recast, refashion, reform, remodel; redraw, restyle, revamp, revise; metamorphose, transfigure, transform, transmogrify; overthrow, overturn

idiom break with the past, make a clean sweep, make a radical change

revolve *vb* **1 syn** see PONDER 2

2 syn see TURN 1

revolve *n syn* see REVOLUTION 1

revulsion *n syn* see ABOMINATION 2

revulsive *adj syn* see REPUGNANT 1

reward *n* something that is offered or given for some service or attainment <the miner received a *reward* for his hard work>

syn carrot, dividend, guerdon, meed, plum, premium, prize

rel compensation, recompense, remuneration, requital

reweigh *vb syn* see RECONSIDER

reword *vb syn* see PARAPHRASE

rework *vb syn* see REVISE

rewrite *vb syn* see REVISE

rhadamanthine *adj syn* see JUST 3

rhapsodize *vb syn* see ENTHUSE 2

---

syn synonym(s)	**rel** related word(s)
ant antonym(s)	**con** contrasted word(s)
idiom idiomatic equivalent(s)	

‖ use limited; if in doubt, see a dictionary

rel acclaim, extol, praise
con blame, condemn, denounce; decry, derogate, detract, minimize
rhapsody *n* **1** *syn* see BOMBAST
2 *syn* see ECSTASY
rhapsody *vb* *syn* see ENTHUSE 2
rhetoric *n* **1** *syn* see ORATORY
2 *syn* see BOMBAST
rhetorical *adj* emphasizing style often at the expense of thought <the candidate was given to windy *rhetorical* speeches>
syn aureate, bombastic, declamatory, euphuistic, florid, flowery, grandiloquent, highfalutin, high-flown, magniloquent, ‖mouthy, oratorical, orotund, overblown, pompous, purple, sonorous, stilted, swelling, swollen, tumescent, tumid, turgid
rel chichi, orchidaceous, ostentatious, pretentious, showy; gassy, inflated, windy; exaggerated, overdone, overwrought; grand, grandiose, high-sounding, imposing; flamboyant, ornate; embellished; articulate, eloquent, fluent, glib, vocal, voluble
con homely, literal, plain, simple, unpretentious; unadorned, undecorated, unembellished, ungarnished, unornamented
ant unrhetorical
rhino *n* *syn* see MONEY
rhubarb *n* *syn* see QUARREL
rhyme *n* **1** *syn* see POETRY 1
2 *syn* see POEM
3 *syn* see RHYTHM
rhyme *vb* *syn* see AGREE 4
rhymer *n* *syn* see POETASTER
rhymester *n* *syn* see POETASTER
rhythm *n* the regular rise and fall in intensity of sounds that is associated chiefly with poetry and music <the *rhythm* of the music made it easy to dance to>
syn beat, cadence, cadency, measure, meter, rhyme, rhythmus, swing
rel lilt; accent
rhythmus *n* *syn* see RHYTHM
riant *adj* *syn* see MERRY
‖**rib** *n* *syn* see WIFE
rib *vb* *syn* see BANTER 1
ribald *n* *syn* see SCAMP
ribbon *n* *syn* see STRIP 1
rich *adj* **1** having goods, property, and money in abundance <he was a *rich* man, having accumulated his wealth in business>
syn affluent, moneyed, ‖oofy, opulent, wealthy
rel comfortable, easy, independent, prosperous, well-fixed, well-heeled, well-off, well-to-do; fat, flush
idiom flush with money, having money to burn, in the money, rich as Croesus, rolling in money
con destitute, indigent, penurious, poverty-stricken
ant poor
2 *syn* see ORNATE
3 highly seasoned and fatty, oily, or sweet <ate *rich* desserts every day>
syn heavy

rel cloying, oversweet; filling, satiating, sating; fat
con natural, simple, unseasoned
ant plain
4 *syn* see FERTILE
5 *syn* see EXPRESSIVE
richen *vb* *syn* see ENRICH
riches *n pl* *syn* see WEALTH 2
rick *n* *syn* see PILE 1
‖**rick** *vb* *syn* see SPRAIN
rickety *adj* likely to give way or break down <a *rickety* old chair>
syn rachitic, rackety, rattletrap, shaky, wobbly; compare WEAK 2
rel unsound, unsteady
con firm, rugged, solid, sturdy, substantial, well-made
ant stable
‖**rickle** *n* *syn* see PILE 1
ricochet *vb* *syn* see GLANCE 1
rel bound, rebound, recoil
rid *vb* to set a person or thing free of something that encumbers <*rid* himself of his troubles>
syn clear, lose, shake (off), throw off, unburden
rel free, liberate, release; disembosom, unbosom; eradicate, exterminate, extirpate, remove, uproot; abolish, extinguish
con burden, charge, clog, cumber, encumber, lade, load, lumber, saddle, task, tax, weigh, weight
ant weigh down
riddance *n* *syn* see DISPOSAL 2
riddle *n* *syn* see MYSTERY
ride *vb* **1** to travel by automobile <often *rode* out to the countryside>
syn auto, motor
idiom go for a spin
2 *syn* see DRIFT 1
3 *syn* see BAIT 2
rel oppress, persecute; torment, torture
4 *syn* see OVERLAP
ride (out) *vb* *syn* see SURVIVE 2
ride *n* *syn* see DRIVE 1
rel excursion, expedition, journey, tour, trip
rider *n* *syn* see APPENDIX 1
ridge *n* **1** a top or upper part especially when long and narrow <topped the mountain *ridge*>
syn chine, crest, hogback
2 *syn* see WRINKLE
‖**ridge runner** *n* *syn* see RUSTIC
ridicule *vb* to make an object of laughter <*ridiculed* him for his inability to perform the feat>
syn deride, lout, mock, quiz, rally, razz, scout, taunt, twit
rel ‖barrack, flout, gibe, jape, jeer, scoff, sneer; burlesque, caricature, mimic, travesty; haze, ride, roast
idiom laugh out of court, make fun (or game or sport) of, poke fun at
ridiculous *adj* **1** *syn* see LAUGHABLE
rel absurd, foolish, preposterous, silly; antic, bizarre, fantastic, grotesque
2 *syn* see INDECOROUS
riding *n* **1** *syn* see SHIVAREE

2 *syn* see HARBOR 3
rife *adj* **1** *syn* see PREVAILING
  2 *syn* see ALIVE 5
riff (through) *vb* *syn* see BROWSE
riffle *vb* *syn* see RIPPLE
riffle (through) *vb* *syn* see BROWSE
riffraff *n* **1** *syn* see RABBLE 2
  2 *syn* see REFUSE
rifle *vb* *syn* see ROB 1
rift *n* **1** *syn* see CRACK 3
  2 *syn* see BREACH 3
  rel gap, hiatus, interruption, interval
rig *vb* *syn* see FURNISH 1
rig *n* *syn* see COSTUME
‖**rig** *n* **1** *syn* see IMPOSTURE
  2 *syn* see PRANK
‖**rig** *vb* *syn* see DUPE
rigamajig *n* *syn* DOODAD, business, dingus, dofunny, doohickey, gadget, gizmo, thingum, thingumajig, thingumbob
rigging *n* *syn* see CLOTHES
‖**riggish** *adj* *syn* see FAST 7
right *adj* **1** *syn* see UPRIGHT 2
  2 *syn* see DECOROUS 1
  3 *syn* see JUST 3
  4 *syn* see TRUE 3
  con specious, unsound; misguided, mistaken
  ant unright, wrong
  5 *syn* see CORRECT 2
  6 *syn* see FIT 1
  7 *syn* see AUTHENTIC 2
  8 *syn* see SANE 2
  9 *syn* see HEALTHY 1
  10 *syn* see CONSERVATIVE 1
  11 *syn* see DECENT 4
right *n* **1** qualities (as adherence to duty or obedience to lawful authority) that together constitute the ideal of moral propriety or merit moral approval <the *right* is not all on one side>
  syn good, straight
  rel correctitude, correctness, properness, propriety, rightness
  con debt, sin, wickedness; improperness, impropriety, incorrectness, unrightness
  ant unright, wrong
  2 something to which one has a just claim <the *right* to life, liberty, and the pursuit of happiness>
  syn appanage, birthright, perquisite, prerogative, privilege
  rel claim, interest, title; freedom, liberty, license
  3 *usu* **rights** *pl syn* see DUE 1
  4 *syn* see DIEHARD 1
  ‖**5** *syn* see OBLIGATION 2
  ‖**6** *syn* see EXCUSE 1
right *adv* **1** *syn* see JUST 1
  2 *syn* see WELL 4
  ant wrong, wrongly
  3 *syn* see DIRECTLY 1
  4 *syn* see WELL 3
  5 *syn* see AWAY 3
  6 *syn* see VERY 1
right *vb* **1** *syn* see CORRECT 1
  ‖**2** *syn* see MEND 2

right–about *n* *syn* see REVERSAL 1
right–about–face *n* *syn* see REVERSAL 1
right away *adv* *syn* see AWAY 3
righteous *adj* **1** *syn* see MORAL 1
  con corrupt, flagitious, nefarious; bad, evil, immoral, reprobate, sinful, vicious, wicked, wrong
  ant iniquitous, unrighteous
  2 *syn* see GOOD 11
  ant unrighteous
righteousness *n* *syn* see GOODNESS
  ant unrighteousness
rightful *adj* **1** *syn* see JUST 3
  rel equitable, fair, impartial
  ant unrightful
  2 *syn* see TRUE 8
  ant unrightful
  3 *syn* see FIT 1
right hand *n* *syn* see RIGHT-HAND MAN
right–handed *adj* having the same direction or course as the movement of the hands of a watch viewed from in front <a *right-handed* propeller>
  syn clockwise, dextrorotatory, positive
right–hand man *n* a reliable or indispensable person <the boss viewed his efficient assistant as his *right-hand man*>
  syn girl Friday, man Friday, right hand
rightist *n* *syn* see DIEHARD 1
  ant leftist
‖**rightle** *vb* *syn* see MEND 2
rightly *adv* *syn* see WELL 1
right–minded *adj* *syn* see MORAL 1
rightness *n* **1** *syn* see GOODNESS
  2 *syn* see ORDER 11
right off *adv* *syn* see AWAY 3
‖**right smart** *adj* *syn* see CONSIDERABLE 2
‖**right smart** *adv* *syn* see VERY 1
right wing *n* *syn* see DIEHARD 1
right–winger *n* *syn* see DIEHARD 1
  ant left-winger
rigid *adj* **1** *syn* see STIFF 1
  rel firm, hard, solid
  ant elastic
  2 *syn* see INFLEXIBLE 2
  3 extremely severe or stern <was regarded as a *rigid* disciplinarian>
  syn draconian, ironhanded, rigorist, rigorous, strict, stringent, unpermissive
  rel austere, severe, stern; hard-line, inflexible, tough, uncompromising, unyielding; adamant, adamantine, inexorable, obdurate
  con humoring, indulgent, pampering; loose, relaxed; easy, gentle, mild
  ant lax
rigor *n* *syn* see DIFFICULTY 1
  rel austerity, severity, sternness; harshness, roughness; affliction, trial, tribulation, visitation
  ant amenity
rigorist *adj* *syn* see RIGID 3
rigorous *adj* **1** *syn* see RIGID 3

---

syn synonym(s)   *rel* related word(s)
ant antonym(s)   *con* contrasted word(s)
idiom idiomatic equivalent(s)
‖ use limited; if in doubt, see a dictionary

rel inflexible, stiff; ascetic; burdensome, exacting, onerous, oppressive
con easy, effortless, facile, light, smooth
ant mild
2 *syn* see SEVERE 3
rel drastic
con bland, faint, lenient, smooth
3 *syn* see CORRECT 2
rigorously *adv syn* see HARD 5
rile *vb* **1** *syn* see ROIL 1
  2 *syn* see IRRITATE
riley *adj syn* see TURBID
rim *n syn* see BORDER 1
rim *vb syn* see BORDER 1
rima *n syn* see CRACK 3
rimation *n syn* see CRACK 3
rime *n syn* see CRACK 3
rime *vb syn* see CAKE 1
rimple *n syn* see WRINKLE
rimple *vb syn* see CRUMPLE 1
‖**rimption** *n, usu* **rimptions** *pl syn* see SCAD
‖**rindle** *n syn* see CREEK 2
ring *n* **1** *syn* see LOOP 2
  2 *syn* see LOOP 1
  3 *syn* see BOXING
  4 *syn* see CLIQUE
  5 *syn* see COMBINATION 2
ring *vb syn* see SURROUND 1
ring *vb* to sound clearly and resonantly <the church bells were *ringing*>
syn bell, bong, chime, knell, peal, toll
rel resound, reverberate, sound
‖**ring (up)** *vb syn* see TELEPHONE
ringer *n syn* see IMAGE 1
ringing *adj syn* see RESONANT
‖**ring off** *vb syn* see SHUT UP 2
riot *n* **1** *syn* see DISORDER 2
  2 something or someone wildly amusing <the new comedy is a *riot*>
syn howl, ‖panic, scream, sidesplitter
rel sensation, smash, wow
riot *vb syn* see REVEL 1
riot (away) *vb syn* see WASTE 2
riotous *adj syn* see PROFUSE
rip *vb syn* see TEAR 1
rip (out) *vb syn* see SPUTTER 1
ripe *adj* **1** *syn* see MATURE 1
rel seasonable, timely, well-timed; overdue
con callow, crude, raw, rude; immature, unmatured, unmellow
ant unripe; green
  2 *syn* see CONSUMMATE 1
  3 brought by aging to full flavor or the best state <*ripe* cheese>
syn aged, matured, mellow, ripened
rel ready
ant unripe
‖**ripe** *vb syn* see MATURE
ripen *vb syn* see MATURE
rel better, improve; enhance, heighten, intensify, season
ripened *adj* **1** *syn* see MATURE 1
ant unripened
  2 *syn* see RIPE 3

rip–off *n syn* see THEFT
rip off *vb* **1** *syn* see ROB 1
rel abuse, exploit, impose (on *or* upon), use, bleed, fleece, gouge, skin, soak, stick
  2 *syn* see STEAL 1
riposte *n syn* see RETORT 2
ripper *n syn* ‖DILLY, ‖corker, crackerjack, dandy, ‖dinger, humdinger, jim-dandy, ‖lulu, nifty, peach
ripping *adj syn* see MARVELOUS 2
ripple *vb* to become fretted or lightly ruffled on the surface (as water) <the pond was *rippled* by rain>
syn cockle, dimple, fret, riffle
ripsnorter *n syn* ‖DILLY, ‖corker, crackerjack, ‖daisy, dandy, ‖dinger, ‖doozer, humdinger, jim-dandy, ‖lulu
rise *vb* **1** to assume an upright or standing position <he *rose* from his chair>
syn get up, stand up, uprise, upspring
rel sit up; straighten up
idiom come to one's feet
con lie, lounge, recline, sit; loll, sprawl
  2 *syn* see ROLL OUT
ant retire
  3 *syn* see ADJOURN 2
ant sit
  4 to move or come up from a lower to a higher level <smoke *rose* from the chimneys>
syn arise, ascend, aspire, lift, mount, soar, up, uprear
rel surge, tower; climb, scale; elevate, raise, rear
con descend, drop, lower; dip, plummet, sink
ant fall; decline
  5 *syn* see INTENSIFY
  6 *syn* see SURFACE
  7 *syn* see INCREASE 2
ant abate; fall
  8 *syn* see HAPPEN 1
  9 *syn* see SPRING 1
rise (against) *vb syn* see REVOLT 1
rise (to) *vb syn* see APPLAUD 2
rise *n* **1** *syn* see ASCENT
ant fall
  2 *syn* see ADDITION
  3 an increment in amount, number, or volume <crime is on the *rise*>
syn boost, breakthrough, hike, increase, upgrade, wax
con declension, decline, lessening, letup, reduction, slump; decrement, loss
ant drop
rise and shine *vb syn* see ROLL OUT
risible *adj syn* see LAUGHABLE
ant lachrymose, larmoyant
rising *n syn* see ASCENT
ant falling
risk *n syn* see DANGER
rel accident, chance, fortune, luck; exposedness, exposure, liability, liableness, openness
risk *vb* **1** *syn* see ENDANGER
rel beard, brave, dare, defy, face; confront, encounter, meet
idiom go out of one's depth

2 syn see VENTURE 1

3 syn see GAMBLE 2

riskless *adj syn* see SAFE 2

risky *adj* **1 syn** see DANGEROUS 1
rel delicate, precarious, sensitive, ticklish, touchy; speculative
idiom on thin ice
2 syn see RISQUÉ

risorgimento *n syn* see REVIVAL

risqué *adj* verging on impropriety or indecency <blushed at his *risqué* stories>
syn blue, broad, off-color, purple, racy, risky, salty, sexy, shady, spicy, suggestive, wicked; *compare* OBSCENE 2
rel naughty, warm; coarse, crude, earthy, gross, lewd, obscene, raunchy, raw, ribald, vulgar; dirty, foul; indecent, indecorous, indelicate, inelegant, unrefined
con clean, decent, proper; restrained; euphemistic

‖**rissom** *n syn* see PARTICLE

rite *n* **1 syn** see FORM 2
2 forms (as religious rites) appropriate to a particular event <the marriage *rites*>
syn ceremonial, ceremony, formality, liturgy, observance, ritual, service
rel celebration, occasion, solemnity; sacrament, sacramental; form

‖**rithe** *n syn* see CREEK 2

ritual *n* **1 syn** see RITE 2
2 syn see FORM 2

rival *n* one of two or more striving for what only one can possess <political *rivals* for the nomination>
syn competition, competitor, corrival
rel contender, contestant, entrant; adversary, antagonist, opponent

rival *vb* **1 syn** see COMPETE 1
2 to strive to equal or surpass <*rivaling* each other for the most work done>
syn compete, emulate, rivalize
rel attempt, strive, struggle, try; contend, fight
3 syn see EQUAL 3
4 syn see AMOUNT 2

rivalize *vb syn* see RIVAL 2

rivalry *n syn* see CONTEST 1

rive *vb* **1 syn** see TEAR 1
rel divide, separate; chop, hew
2 syn see SHATTER 1

rivel *n syn* see WRINKLE

rivet *vb* **1 syn** see FASTEN 1
2 syn see FASTEN 3

rivulet *n syn* see CREEK 2

road *n* **1** *often* **roads** *pl syn* see HARBOR 3
2 syn see WAY 1
3 syn see WAY 2

roadblock *n syn* see BAR 2

roadhouse *n syn* see HOTEL

roadman *n syn* see PEDDLER

roadstead *n syn* see HARBOR 3

roadster *n syn* see VAGABOND

roam *vb syn* see WANDER 1

roamer *n syn* see ROVER

roar *vb* to make a very loud and often a continuous or protracted noise <the crowd *roared* their disapproval of the speech>
syn bawl, bellow, bluster, clamor, rout; *compare* BAWL 2
rel rebound, repercuss, reverberate; shout, vociferate, yell; din
con breathe, murmur, mutter, whisper

roaring *adj* **1 syn** see LOUD 1
2 syn see FLOURISHING

roast *vb* **1 syn** see BURN 3
2 syn see LAMBASTE 3

rob *vb* **1** to take possessions unlawfully <*rob* a bank><he was mugged and *robbed*>
syn ‖knock off, knock over, loot, plunder, ransack, relieve, rifle, rip off, stick up; *compare* BURGLARIZE, HOUSEBREAK
rel ‖heist, hold up; jackroll, roll; strong-arm; filch, hijack, lift, pilfer, purloin, steal, thieve; cheat, defraud, hustle, swindle; despoil, pillage, ravage, sack
2 syn see DEPRIVE 2

robber *n* one who commits the crime of robbery <only one *robber* was involved in the holdup>
syn yegg; *compare* THIEF
rel hijacker; sandbagger; crook, swindler; cat burglar, cat man, housebreaker, raffles, second-story man; rifler; holdup man, stickup man; ‖bushranger, highwayman, ‖sticker-up

roborant *adj syn* see TONIC 1

robot *n* **1** a machine that looks like a human being and performs various complex acts (as walking or talking) of a human being <a *robot* that performed household chores>
syn android, automaton
rel golem
idiom bionic man
2 an efficient, insensitive, often brutalized person <working on an assembly line can often turn people into *robots*>
syn automaton, golem, machine

robust *adj* **1 syn** see FLOURISHING
2 syn see STRONG 3

robustious *adj syn* see BOORISH

rock *vb* **1 syn** see SHAKE 4
rel oscillate, sway, swing, undulate; quake, totter, tremble
2 syn see TOSS 2
3 syn see HURRY 2

rock *n* **1 syn** see ERROR 2
2 syn see DOLLAR
3 rocks *pl syn* see MONEY

rock bottom *n syn* see ESSENCE 2

rock–bottom *adj syn* see BOTTOMMOST

rockbound *adj* **1 syn** see ROCKY 1
2 syn see INFLEXIBLE 2

rocket *vb* **1 syn** see SKYROCKET
rel arise, ascend, levitate, mount, surge, tower
2 syn see HURRY 2

---

syn synonym(s)   **rel** related word(s)
ant antonym(s)   **con** contrasted word(s)
idiom idiomatic equivalent(s)
‖ use limited; if in doubt, see a dictionary

rock pile *n syn* see JAIL
rock–ribbed *adj* **1** *syn* see ROCKY 1
  2 *syn* see INFLEXIBLE 2
rocky *adj* **1** abounding in or consisting of rocks <a *rocky* shore>
  syn rockbound, rock-ribbed
  rel bebouldered, bouldery; stony
  2 *syn* see INSENSIBLE 5
rocky *adj* **1** *syn* see UNSTABLE 2
  2 *syn* see OBSCENE 2
||**Rocky Mountain canary** *n syn* see DONKEY 1
rococo *adj* **1** *syn* see OLD-FASHIONED
  2 *syn* see ORNATE
rod *n* **1** *syn* see BAR 1
  2 *syn* see PUNISHMENT
  idiom rod in pickle
rodomont *n syn* see BRAGGART
rodomontade *n* **1** *syn* see BOMBAST
  rel boasting, bragging, vaunting; pride, vainglory, vanity
  2 *syn* see BRAGGART
rodomontade *vb syn* see BOAST
rodomontade *adj syn* see BOASTFUL
rogue *n* **1** *syn* see VILLAIN 1
  rel culprit, delinquent
  2 *syn* see SWINDLER
  3 *syn* see SCAMP
roguery *n syn* see MISCHIEVOUSNESS
roguish *adj* **1** *syn* see DISHONEST
  2 *syn* see PLAYFUL 1
  3 *syn* see COY 2
roguishness *n syn* see MISCHIEVOUSNESS
roil *vb* **1** to make turbid <*roiled* the brook with his splashings>
  syn mud, muddle, muddy, rile
  rel befoul, contaminate, dirty, pollute
  con clear, purify, settle
  2 *syn* see IRRITATE
roily *adj syn* see TURBID
roister *vb syn* see REVEL 1
role *n* **1** characteristic exterior properties and aspects, style, and atmosphere in which something intangible is discerned <the moral *role* of the legislature>
  syn character, clothing
  rel appearance, face, guise, seeming, semblance, show; aspect, look
  2 *syn* see FUNCTION 1
roll *n* **1** *syn* see LIST
  2 *syn* see ROSTER 1
  ||**3** *syn* see FORTUNE 4
roll *vb* **1** *syn* see PONDER 2
  2 *syn* see SWATHE
  3 to wrap around on itself or something else <this cloth *rolls* unevenly>
  syn furl
  4 *syn* see WALLOW 3
  5 *syn* see TURN 1
  6 *syn* see WANDER 1
  7 *syn* see POUR 2
  8 *syn* see RUMBLE
  9 *syn* see TOSS 2
roll call *n syn* see LIST
rollick *vb* **1** *syn* see GAMBOL

  2 *syn* see WALLOW 3
rollick *n syn* see ESCAPADE
rollicking *adj syn* see ANTIC 2
  rel cheerful, glad, happy, joyful, joyous, lighthearted
roll in *vb syn* see RETIRE 4
  ant roll out
rolling stone *n syn* see ROVER
roll out *vb* to leave one's bed <*rolled out* at dawn>
  syn arise, get up, pile (out), rise, rise and shine, turn out, uprise
  ant roll in
roll up *vb syn* see ACCUMULATE
roly–poly *adj syn* see ROTUND 2
romance *n syn* see LOVE AFFAIR
romanesque *adj syn* see EXOTIC 2
romantic *adj syn* see EXOTIC 2
  2 *syn* see SENTIMENTAL
  rel fanciful, fantastic, imaginary, quixotic, visionary; created, invented
  ant unromantic; matter-of-fact
Romeo *n syn* see GALLANT 2
romp *n syn* see RUNAWAY
romp *vb syn* see GAMBOL
  idiom cut capers, horse around
rondure *n syn* see BALL
roof *n syn* see TOP 1
roof *vb syn* see HARBOR 1
rook *vb syn* see FLEECE 1
rookie *n syn* see NOVICE
room *n* **1** space in a building enclosed or set apart by a partition <the house had seven *rooms*>
  syn apartment, chamber
  2 rooms *pl syn* see APARTMENT 1
  3 enough space or range for free movement <no *room* for hope>
  syn elbowroom, latitude, leeway, margin, play, scope
  rel clearance; license, range, rein, sway; rope
room *vb syn* see HARBOR 2
room and board *n syn* see ACCOMMODATIONS
roomy *adj syn* see SPACIOUS
  ant cramped
||**roose** *vb syn* see COMMEND 2
roost *vb* **1** *syn* see ALIGHT
  2 *syn* see HARBOR 2
root *n* **1** *syn* see SOURCE
  rel basis, foundation, ground
  2 *syn* see BASIS 1
  3 *syn* see CENTER 3
  4 *syn* see ESSENCE 2
root *vb syn* see ENTRENCH 1
  ant uproot
root *vb syn* see APPLAUD 2
rootage *n syn* see SOURCE
rootless *adj syn* see WEAK 2
root out *vb syn* see ANNIHILATE 2
  rel demolish, destroy, raze
  ant enroot
rootstock *n syn* see SOURCE
roperipe *n syn* see VILLAIN 1
ropes *n pl syn* see INS AND OUTS
ropy *adj syn* see MUSCULAR 1
rose *vb syn* see BLUSH

roseate *adj syn* see HOPEFUL 2
rose–colored *adj syn* see HOPEFUL 2
rose–colored spectacles *n pl syn* see OPTIMISM
roster *n* **1** a list of officers or enlisted men <an army *roster*>
 syn muster, muster roll, roll
 2 *syn* see LIST
rosy *adj syn* see HOPEFUL 2
rot *vb* **1** *syn* see DECAY
 rel corrupt, debase, vitiate
 2 *syn* see DETERIORATE 1
 3 *syn* see DEBASE 1
rot *n syn* see NONSENSE 2
rotate *vb* **1** *syn* see TURN 1
 2 to succeed or cause to succeed each other in turn <the drivers in the car pool *rotated* each week>
 syn alternate
 rel bandy, exchange, interchange; ensue, follow, succeed; relieve, spell
rotation *n syn* see REVOLUTION 1
rote *n syn* see ROUTINE
rotten *adj* **1** *syn* see BAD 5
 rel foul; tainted, touched; sour
 2 *syn* see VICIOUS 2
 3 *syn* see BAD 8
 4 *syn* see BAD 1
rotter *n syn* see CAD
rotund *adj* **1** *syn* see RESONANT
 2 rounded or swollen with fat <a wheezing *rotund* man lumbered by>
 syn chubby, plump, plumpish, plumpy, podgy, puddy, pudgy, roly-poly, round, roundabout, spuddy, tubby; *compare* FAT 2
 rel beefy, chunky, dumpy, heavyset, squat, stocky, stubby, thick, thickset; paunchy, potbellied; buxom, ‖crummy
 idiom on the plump side
 con angular, gaunt, lank, lanky, lean, rawboned, scrawny, skinny, spare; slender, slight, slim, thin
roturier *n syn* see UPSTART
rouge *vb syn* see BLUSH
rough *adj* **1** not smooth or even <a *rough* undressed block of stone>
 syn asperous, cragged, craggy, hairy, harsh, ironbound, jagged, rugged, scabrous, scraggy, uneven, unlevel, unsmooth
 rel bumpy, choppy; burred; firm, hard, solid; coarse, gross
 con flat, flush, level, plain, plane
 ant smooth
 2 *syn* see WILD 6
 con calm, halcyon, peaceful, placid, serene, tranquil
 3 *syn* see TOUGH 8
 4 *syn* see TIGHT 4
 5 *syn* see INDECOROUS
 6 *syn* see RUDE 1
 idiom in the rough
 7 *syn* see RUDE 3
 8 *syn* see HARSH 3
 9 *syn* see COARSE 3
 rel discourteous, impolite, uncivil, ungracious

 10 *syn* see BLUFF
 11 *syn* see HARD 6
rough *n syn* see TOUGH
rough (out) *vb syn* see SKETCH
rough (up) *vb syn* see MANHANDLE
rough–and–ready *adj syn* see MAKESHIFT
rough–and–tumble *n syn* see BRAWL 2
rough–and–tumble *adj syn* see MAKESHIFT
roughhewn *adj syn* see RUDE 1
roughhouse *n syn* see HORSEPLAY
roughhouse *vb syn* see MANHANDLE
roughhousing *n syn* see HORSEPLAY
roughly *adv* **1** *syn* see HARD 5
 ant smoothly
 2 *syn* see NEARLY
roughneck *n syn* see TOUGH
roughness *n syn* see INEQUALITY 1
 ant smoothness
roughscuff *n syn* see RABBLE 2
round *adj* **1** having every part of the circumference equally distant from a center within <flowers crowded in stiff *round* beds>
 syn circular
 rel annular, globular, orbed, orbicular, rounded, spherical, spiral
 2 *syn* see CURVED
 3 *syn* see ROTUND 2
 4 *syn* see OUTSPOKEN
 5 *syn* see RESONANT
round *adv* **1** *syn* see ABOUT 1
 2 *syn* see NEARLY
 3 *syn* see THROUGH 1
 4 *syn* see ABOUT 6
round *prep* **1** *syn* see NEAR 2
 2 *syn* see ABOUT 4
round *n* **1** *syn* see BALL
 2 *syn* see REVOLUTION 1
 3 *syn* see TOUR 2
 4 *syn* see CYCLE 1
 5 *syn* see CURVE
round *vb* **1** *syn* see BALL
 2 *syn* see SURROUND 1
 3 *syn* see POLISH 2
 4 *syn* see CURVE
round about *adv* **1** *syn* see ABOUT 1
 2 *syn* see ABOUT 6
 3 *syn* see ABOUT 2
roundabout *n* **1** *syn* see DETOUR
 2 *syn* see VERBIAGE 1
 3 *syn* see TOUR 2
 4 *syn* see EXCURSION 1
roundabout *adj* **1** *syn* see INDIRECT 1
 2 *syn* see ROTUND 2
rounded *adj* **1** *syn* see CURVED
 2 *syn* see CURVACEOUS
rounder *n syn* see WASTREL 1
roundly *adv* **1** *syn* see WELL 3
 2 *syn* see NEARLY
round off *vb syn* see CLIMAX

---

syn synonym(s)   *rel* related word(s)
ant antonym(s)   *con* contrasted word(s)
idiom idiomatic equivalent(s)
‖ use limited; if in doubt, see a dictionary

round trip *n syn* see TOUR 2
round up *vb syn* see GROUP 1
rouse *vb* **1** *syn* see WAKE 1
  rel animate, enliven, quicken, vivify; excite, provoke, stimulate; foment, incite, instigate
  con calm, compose, lull, quiet, quieten, settle, soothe, still, tranquilize
  2 *syn* see INTENSIFY
  3 *syn* see PROVOKE 4
  4 *syn* see STIR 1
rouser *n syn* see ‖DILLY
rousing *adj* **1** *syn* see EXCITING
  2 *syn* see LIVELY 1
‖roust *vb syn* see PROVOKE 4
roustabout *n syn* see WORKER
rout *n* **1** *syn* see MOB 2
  2 *syn* see RABBLE 2
  3 *syn* see MULTITUDE 1
rout *vb syn* see ROAR
rout *vb syn* see RUMMAGE 3
rout *n* **1** *syn* see DEFEAT 1
  2 *syn* see RUNAWAY
rout *vb* **1** to put to precipitate flight <the army regrouped and *routed* the enemy>
  syn derout, stampede
  rel chase, dispel, drive, expel
  idiom put to flight
  2 *syn* see WHIP 2
route *n syn* see WAY 2
route *vb* **1** *syn* see SEND 1
  2 *syn* see GUIDE
routine *n* habitual or mechanical and sometimes monotonous performance of an established procedure <settled into the *routine* of factory work>
  syn grind, groove, pace, rote, rut, treadmill
  rel squirrel cage; ‖drill
  idiom the beaten path, the drab monotony of habit
routine *adj* **1** *syn* see ORDINARY 1
  2 *syn* see USUAL 1
rove *vb syn* see WANDER 1
rover *n syn* see PIRATE
rover *n* one who roams habitually <he spent most of his life as a *rover* always on the move>
  syn drifter, meanderer, rambler, roamer, rolling stone, wanderer
  rel gad, gadabout, gadder, runabout; itinerant, peripatetic; floater
  idiom bird of passage
  con homebody
  ant stay-at-home
roving *adj syn* see ITINERANT
row *vb* to propel a boat by means of oars <*rowed* across the lake>
  syn oar, paddle, pull
  rel scull; punt; sail, scud
row *n* **1** *syn* see LINE 5
  2 *syn* see SUCCESSION 2
row *n* **1** *syn* see BRAWL 2
  2 *syn* see QUARREL
  3 *syn* see MOUTH 1
row *vb* ‖**1** *syn* see SCOLD 1
  2 *syn* see QUARREL

rowdiness *n syn* see HORSEPLAY
rowdy *adj syn* see TURBULENT 1
rowdy *n syn* see TOUGH
rowdydow *n* **1** *syn* see COMMOTION 4
  2 *syn* see BRAWL 2
  3 *syn* see BINGE 1
rowdydowdy *adj syn* see TURBULENT 1
rowdyish *adj syn* see TURBULENT 1
royal *adj* **1** *syn* see KINGLY
  rel glorious, resplendent, splendid, superb; august, imposing, stately
  2 *syn* see EASY 1
  3 *syn* see GRAND 1
  4 *syn* see EXCELLENT
royalist *n syn* see REACTIONARY
‖rozzer *n syn* see POLICEMAN
rub *vb* **1** *syn* see ABRADE 1
  2 *syn* see CHAFE 3
  rel aggravate, exasperate, nettle, peeve, provoke, rile; annoy, bother, irk, vex
  3 *syn* see POLISH 1
rub *n syn* see OBSTACLE
rubber *n syn* see BUSYBODY
rubberneck *n* **1** *syn* see BUSYBODY
  2 *syn* see TOURIST
rubberneck *vb syn* see LOOK 7
rubber stamp *n syn* see COMMONPLACE
rubbish *n* **1** *syn* see REFUSE
  2 *syn* see NONSENSE 2
  3 *syn* see PAP 2
rubbishing *adj syn* see CHEAP 2
rubbishly *adj syn* see CHEAP 2
rubbishy *adj syn* see CHEAP 2
rube *n syn* see RUSTIC
rubicund *adj syn* see RUDDY
rubify *vb syn* see REDDEN 1
rub out *vb* **1** *syn* see DESTROY 1
  2 *syn* see MURDER 1
rubric *n syn* see NAME 1
rubric *adj syn* see NOTEWORTHY
rubric *vb syn* see REDDEN 1
ruby *vb syn* see REDDEN 1
ruck *n* ‖**1** *syn* see PILE 1
  2 *syn* see GATHERING 2
ruck *n syn* see WRINKLE
ruck (up) *vb syn* see CRUMPLE 1
‖ruckle *vb syn* see CRUMPLE 1
rucksack *n syn* see BACKPACK
ruckus *n* **1** *syn* see COMMOTION 3
  rel brawl, broil, melee, scrap
  2 *syn* see QUARREL
ruction *n* **1** *syn* see BRAWL 2
  2 *syn* see COMMOTION 4
‖ructious *adj syn* see BELLIGERENT
rud *vb syn* see REDDEN 1
ruddle *vb syn* see REDDEN 1
ruddy *adj* having a healthy reddish color <has a *ruddy* complexion after being out in the cold>
  syn florid, flush, flushed, full-blooded, glowing, rubicund, sanguine
  rel bronzed; blooming; blowsy
  con ashen, ashy, livid, pale, pallid, wan, waxy; anemic, bloodless
ruddy *vb syn* see REDDEN 1

rude *adj* **1** lacking in craftsmanship or artistic finish <a *rude* sketch>
syn angular, crude, lumpy, raw, rough, rough-hewn, undressed, unfashioned, unfinished, unformed, unhewn, unpolished, unworked, unwrought
rel unlicked; unprocessed; primitive, rudimental, rudimentary
con dressed, fashioned, finished, formed, hewn, polished, worked, wrought
2 *syn* see DISSONANT 1
3 hastily executed and admittedly imperfect or imprecise <*rude* estimates for the cost of building the house>
syn approximate, proximate, rough
rel crude, imperfect, imprecise, inexact
idiom ‖in the ball park
con accurate, correct; faultless, perfect; exact, precise; meticulous, scrupulous
4 *syn* see COARSE 3
5 *syn* see IGNORANT 1
6 lacking in social refinement <gave a *rude* reply to a polite question>
syn discourteous, disgracious, disrespectful, ill, ill-bred, ill-mannered, impertinent, impolite, incivil, incondite, inurbane, mannerless, ‖mismannered, uncalled-for, uncivil, uncourteous, uncouth, ungracious, unhandsome, unmannered, unmannerly, unpolished
rel brusque, crusty, curt, gruff; harsh; intrusive, meddlesome; crabbed, surly; boorish, churlish, clownish, loutish
con courteous, genteel, mannerly, polite, well≠mannered; bland, diplomatic, politic, smooth, suave; affable, considerate, gracious
ant civil; urbane
7 *syn* see BARBARIAN 1
8 *syn* see INEXPERIENCED
rudely *adv* *syn* see NEARLY
rudiment *n* **1** *syn* see ESSENTIAL 1
2 rudiments *pl* *syn* see ALPHABET 2
rudimental *adj* *syn* see ELEMENTARY 1
rudimentary *adj* *syn* see ELEMENTARY 1
rue *vb* *syn* see REGRET
rue *n* **1** *syn* see SORROW
2 *syn* see PENITENCE
3 *syn* see PITY
rueful *adj* **1** *syn* see PITIFUL 1
2 *syn* see WOEFUL 1
3 *syn* see MELANCHOLY 2
rel depressed, oppressed, weighed down; piteous, pitiful; despairing, despondent, hopeless
ruffian *n* **1** *syn* see TOUGH
2 *syn* see THUG 1
ruffle *vb* **1** *syn* see BLOW 1
2 *syn* see ABRADE 1
3 *syn* see ANNOY 1
‖**4** *syn* see INTIMIDATE
rugged *adj* **1** *syn* see ROUGH 1
2 *syn* see SEVERE 3
rel arduous, difficult
3 *syn* see HARSH 3
4 *syn* see BOORISH
5 *syn* see TOUGH 4

rel brawny, burly, husky, muscular
ant fragile
6 *syn* see HARD 6
ruin *n* **1** *syn* see DETERIORATION 1
2 *syn* see DOWNFALL 2
3 the bringing about of or the results of disaster <met *ruin* at the hands of the enemy>
syn confusion, destruction, devastation, havoc, loss, ruination
rel crumbling, disintegration; break up, dissolution; disrepair; wreck
con rebuilding, reconstruction, re-creation
4 *syn* see INJURY 1
ruin *vb* **1** *syn* see DESTROY 1
rel deface, disfigure; maim, mangle, mutilate; depredate, desecrate, desolate, despoil, devastate, devour, pillage, sack, spoliate, waste
ant restore
2 to subject to forces that are destructive of soundness, worth, or usefulness <in danger of being *ruined* by prosperity>
syn bankrupt, dilapidate, do in, shipwreck, wreck
rel corrupt, debase, degenerate, vitiate
idiom play hob (*or* the devil) with
con rebuild, renew, restore; reclaim, redeem, retrieve, salvage
3 to overthrow the fortunes of <was *ruined* during the Great Depression>
syn bankrupt, break, bust, fold up, impoverish, pauper, pauperize
rel beggar, clean out, deplete, drain, draw, draw down, exhaust, use up; wipe (out); reduce
idiom go under, lose one's shirt (*or* pants), take to the cleaners
4 *syn* see FRUSTRATE 1
‖**ruinate** *vb* *syn* see DESTROY 1
ruination *n* **1** *syn* see RUIN 3
2 *syn* see DOWNFALL 2
ruinator *n* *syn* see VANDAL
ruiner *n* *syn* see VANDAL
ruinous *adj* **1** *syn* see DESTRUCTIVE
2 *syn* see FATAL 2
rule *n* **1** *syn* see LAW 1
rel order; axiom, fundamental, principle; decorum, etiquette, propriety
2 *syn* see MAXIM
rel fundamental, principle
rule *vb* **1** *syn* see GOVERN 1
rel guide, lead
2 to hold preeminence in (as by ability, strength, or position) <an actor who rightfully *rules* the Shakespearian stage>
syn dominate, domineer, predominate, preponderate, prevail, reign
rel guide, lead; preside
idiom be number one, take first place (in *or* on)
3 *syn* see DECIDE
rel deduce, gather, infer, judge

---

syn synonym(s)   *rel* related word(s)
ant antonym(s)   *con* contrasted word(s)
idiom idiomatic equivalent(s)
‖ use limited; if in doubt, see a dictionary

rule out *vb* **1** *syn* see EXCLUDE
  2 *syn* see PREVENT 2
ruling *n* *syn* see EDICT 1
ruling *adj* **1** *syn* see CENTRAL 1
  con peripheral
  2 *syn* see PREVAILING
‖**rum** *adj* *syn* see STRANGE 4
rumble *vb* to make a low heavy rolling sound
  <thunder *rumbling* in the distance>
  syn growl, grumble, roll
  rel boom, roar, thunder; peal, resound; blast,
  burst, clap, crack, crash
rumble *n* *syn* see REPORT 1
rumble–bumble *n* *syn* see MISCELLANY 1
rumbustious *adj* *syn* see TURBULENT 1
rum–dum *adj* *syn* see INTOXICATED 1
rumdum *n* *syn* see DRUNKARD
‖**rum–hole** *n* *syn* see BAR 5
ruminate *vb* **1** *syn* see PONDER 2
  rel consider, excogitate, weigh
  2 *syn* see CHEW 1
ruminative *adj* *syn* see THOUGHTFUL 1
rummage *n* *syn* see CLUTTER 2
  rel conglomeration, hash, hotchpotch, miscellany, patchwork, potpourri
rummage *vb* **1** *syn* see DISORDER 1
  2 *syn* see SCOUR 2
  3 to produce by searching <*rummaged* an old
  dress out of the attic>
  syn dig out, hunt (down *or* out *or* up), rout
  rel ferret (out), find; fish, search (out), spy (out);
  poke
rummery *n* *syn* see BAR 5
‖**rum–mill** *n* *syn* see BAR 5
rummy *adj* *syn* see STRANGE 4
rummy *n* *syn* see DRUNKARD
rumor *n* **1** *syn* see REPORT 1
  2 *syn* see MURMUR 1
rumor *vb* *syn* see GOSSIP
rumorer *n* *syn* see GOSSIP 1
rumormonger *n* *syn* see GOSSIP 1
rump *n* *syn* see BUTTOCKS
rumple *vb* *syn* see CRUMPLE 1
‖**rumpot** *n* *syn* see DRUNKARD
rumpus *n* **1** *syn* see COMMOTION 3
  2 *syn* see ARGUMENT 2
rumshop *n* *syn* see BAR 5
run *vb* **1** to move at a fast springing gait in which
  both feet are momentarily off the ground in the
  course of each pace <the boy *ran* down the
  walk>
  syn dash, scamper, scoot, scurry, shin, sprint;
  compare SCUTTLE
  rel career, course, race; bustle, hurry, hustle,
  rush, speed; scorch
  con crawl, creep, drag, inch, mosey, poke, saunter, stroll, toddle
  2 to hasten away from something that frightens
  or perturbs <afraid to fight but ashamed to
  run>
  syn bolt, flee, fly, make off, scamper, scoot,
  ‖screw, skedaddle, skip, skirr
  idiom ‖dog it, make a break, run for it, show a
  clean pair of heels, take flight, take French leave,
  take to one's heels

  3 *syn* see HURRY 2
  idiom go all out, go like (greased) lightning
  4 *syn* see RESORT 2
  5 *syn* see FUNCTION 3
  6 *syn* see BECOME 1
  7 *syn* see LIQUEFY
  8 to lie in or take a certain course <the path *runs*
  along the crest of the hill>
  syn extend, go, make, reach, stretch
  9 *syn* see RANGE 3
  10 *syn* see HUNT 1
  11 *syn* see DRIVE 3
  12 *syn* see THRUST 2
  13 *syn* see SMUGGLE
  14 *syn* see OPERATE 3
  15 *syn* see CONDUCT 3
run (through *or* over) *vb* *syn* see BROWSE
run (to *or* into) *vb* *syn* see AMOUNT 1
run *n* **1** ‖*syn* see CREEK 2
  2 an uninterrupted course of occurrence or repetition especially of like things or events <the
  play had a long *run*>
  syn continuance, continuation, duration, persistence
  rel continuity, endurance, prolongation
  3 *syn* see TENDENCY 1
  rel course, set; bearing, direction, line, swing
  4 *syn* see TRIP 1
  ‖**5 runs** *pl but sing or pl in constr* *syn* see DIARRHEA
runagate *n* **1** *syn* see RENEGADE
  2 *syn* see VAGABOND
run along *vb* *syn* see GO 2
runaround *n* **1** *syn* see DETOUR
  2 *syn* see ESCAPE 2
run away *vb* *syn* see ELOPE
runaway *n* a one-sided or overwhelming victory
  <the game was a *runaway*, the home team winning by 30 points>
  syn cakewalk, romp, rout, walkaway, walkover
  rel breather, cinch, duck soup, pushover; setup;
  shutout; conquest, triumph, victory, win
  con photo finish, toss-up
run down *vb* *syn* see DECRY 2
run–down *adj* **1** *syn* see SHABBY 1
  2 *syn* see NEGLECTED
  rel abandoned, derelict, deserted, desolate, forsaken, lorn
rune *n* **1** *syn* see SPELL
  2 *syn* see POEM
rung *n* *syn* see DEGREE 1
run in *vb* **1** *syn* see ARREST 2
  2 *syn* see VISIT 2
run–in *n* **1** *syn* see ENCOUNTER
  2 *syn* see QUARREL
runnel *n* *syn* see CREEK 2
running *n* *syn* see OVERSIGHT 1
running *adj* **1** *syn* see ACTIVE 1
  2 *syn* see EASY 9
running *adv* *syn* see TOGETHER 2
running mate *n* *syn* see ASSOCIATE 3
run–of–mine *adj* **1** *syn* see UNREFINED 3
  2 *syn* see MEDIUM
run–of–the–mill *adj* **1** *syn* see MEDIUM
  rel uncommon, unexceptional

2 *syn* see GENERAL 1

run on *vb syn* see CHAT 1

run out *vb* **1** *syn* see FAIL 2

 2 *syn* see BANISH

run over *vb syn* see OVERFLOW 2

runt *n syn* see DWARF

runted *adj syn* see STUNTED

run through *vb syn* see GO 4

runtish *adj syn* see STUNTED

runty *adj syn* see STUNTED

run up *vb* **1** *syn* see INCREASE 2

 2 *syn* see THROW UP 1

rupture *n* **1** *syn* see BREACH 3

 rel division, divorce, parting

 2 *syn* see SEPARATION 1

rupture *vb* **1** *syn* see OPEN 3

 rel divide, divorce, part, separate, sunder; cleave, rend, rive, split

 2 *syn* see SEPARATE 1

rural *adj* relating to or characteristic of the country <a peaceful *rural* scene>

 syn agrestic, bucolic, campestral, countrified, country, out-country, outland, pastoral, provincial, rustic

 rel arcadian, idyllic; natural, simple, unsophisticated

 con metropolitan, municipal, oppidan; crammed, crowded, packed, populous; bustling, busy, hustling; artificial, mundane, sophisticated, worldly

 ant urban; citified

ruse *n syn* see TRICK 1

rush *vb* **1** to move or cause to move quickly, impetuously, and often heedlessly <*rushed* around madly trying to get things done>

 syn boil, bolt, charge, chase, dash, fling, lash, race, shoot, ‖swither, tear; *compare* COURSE, HURRY 2, PLUNGE 2, STAMPEDE 2

 rel hasten, hurry, speed; dart, fly, scud; break

 idiom go off half-cocked, not look before one leaps

 2 *syn* see HURRY 2

 3 *syn* see COURSE

rush *n* **1** *syn* see HASTE 2

 2 *syn* see FLOW

rushing *adj syn* see PRECIPITATE 1

rushlight *n syn* see NONENTITY

rustic *adj syn* see RURAL

rustic *n* an inhabitant of a rural or remote area who is usually characterized by an utter lack of sophistication and cultivation <an unbelieving *rustic* gawking at the skyscrapers>

 syn ‖apple knocker, ‖backwoodser, backwoodsman, bucolic, bumpkin, chawbacon, clodhopper, clown, country jake, countryman, greenhorn, hayseed, hick, hillbilly, hillman, ‖hodge, hoosier, jake, jay, joskin, mossback, mountaineer, peasant, provincial, redneck, ‖ridge runner, rube, ‖wayback, woodsy, yap, ‖yob, yokel

 rel rural; exurbanite, suburbanite; agriculturalist, farmer, granger, husbandman

 con burgher, oppidan, townsman; cityite, urbanite; cosmopolitan, cosmopolite

 ant city slicker

rustle *n syn* see HASTE 1

rustler *n syn* see HUSTLER 1

rusty *adj syn* see HARSH 3

‖**rusty** *adj syn* see ILL-TEMPERED

rut *n syn* see ROUTINE

ruth *n* **1** *syn* see PITY

 2 *syn* see PENITENCE

ruthful *adj syn* see WOEFUL 1

ruthless *adj syn* see GRIM 3

ruttish *adj syn* see LUSTFUL 2

‖**ruttle** *vb syn* see RATTLE 1

rutty *adj syn* see LUSTFUL 2

RV *n syn* see TRAILER

---

syn synonym(s)   *rel* related word(s)
ant antonym(s)   *con* contrasted word(s)
idiom idiomatic equivalent(s)
‖ use limited; if in doubt, see a dictionary

S

sable *adj syn* see BLACK 1
rel dark, dusky, murky; gloomy, somber

sabotage *n* willful effort by indirect means to hinder, prevent, undo, or discredit (as a plan or activity) <*sabotage* of the project by disgruntled officials>
syn subversion, undermining, wreckage, wrecking
rel subversiveness, subversivism; damage, impairment, injury

sabotage *vb* to practice sabotage on <*sabotaged* his opponent's campaign with rumors and smears>
syn subvert, undermine, wreck
rel frustrate, hamper, hinder; block, obstruct; damage; break up, destroy
idiom throw a monkey wrench into
con assist, back, support

saccharine *adj syn* see INGRATIATING
rel candied, cloying, honeyed, oversweet, sugar-candy, sugar-coated, sugared, sugary, sweet, syrupy

sacerdotal *adj* of, relating to, or belonging to priests or priesthood <*sacerdotal* vestments>
syn hieratic, priestal, priestish, priestlike, priestly, sacerdotical
rel churchly, ecclesiastical, religious; clerical, ministerial; apostolic, papal

sacerdotical *adj syn* see SACERDOTAL

sack *n syn* see BAG 1
rel container; pocket

sack *vb syn* see DISMISS 3
rel expel, ship; ‖bump, ‖chuck
idiom give one the sack, send packing

sack *vb syn* see RAVAGE
rel forage, raid; strip

sacker *n syn* see MARAUDER

sacred *adj* **1** *syn* see HOLY 1
rel sacramental; angelic, godly, saintly; cherished
con lay, secular, temporal; earthly; unhallowed
ant profane
2 dedicated to or hallowed by association with a deity <*sacred* songs>
syn numinous, spiritual; *compare* HOLY 1
rel hallowed, sanctified
3 protected (as by law, custom, or human respect) against abuse <a fund *sacred* to charity>
syn inviolable, inviolate, sacrosanct
rel defended, guarded, protected, shielded; immune, untouchable

Sacred Writ *n syn* see BIBLE
idiom Good Book

sacrifice *n syn* see VICTIM 1
rel burnt offering, oblation; sacrification; hecatomb; sin offering

sacrifice *vb* **1** to offer as a victim in sacrifice <Abraham about to *sacrifice* Isaac>

syn immolate, victimize
rel offer (up); consecrate, dedicate, devote; donate, give, yield
2 *syn* see LOSE 1
idiom kiss good-bye
3 *syn* see FORGO
rel cede, yield
idiom part with

sacrilege *n syn* see PROFANATION
rel irreverence; heresy; crime, impiety, offense, sin

sacrilegious *adj* involving or marked by debasement or defilement of what is sacred <*sacrilegious* despoilers of ancient churches>
syn blasphemous, profane
rel impious, irreverent, ungodly; evil, sinful, wicked; irreligious
con godly, pious, reverent; religious

sacrosanct *adj syn* see SACRED 3
rel esteemed, regarded, respected

sad *adj* **1** affected with or expressing sadness <was *sad* to see him go>
syn heavyhearted, melancholy, mournful, saddened, sorry, unhappy; *compare* DOWNCAST, MELANCHOLY 2
rel blue, dejected, dispirited, down, downbeat, downcast, drear, dumpish, dumpy; grieving, unenjoying; depressed, morose; depressing, dismal, joyless, mirthless, saddening, triste; desolate
con happy, joyful, joyous; blithe, gay, lighthearted; exalted, fired, inspired, uplifted
ant glad
2 causing sadness <felt miserable after listening to that *sad* song>
syn depressing, joyless, melancholic, melancholy, mournful, saddening, triste; *compare* MELANCHOLY 2
rel dismal, gloomy; afflicting, doleful, dreary, lamentable, sorrowful; pathetic, tear-jerking
con bright, gay, lively; exhilarating, heartwarming, stimulating, stirring
ant happy

sadden *vb syn* see DEPRESS 2
idiom make blue, ‖put into a funk
ant gladden

saddened *adj syn* see SAD 1

saddening *adj syn* see SAD 2

saddle *vb syn* see BURDEN
rel hamper, impede, restrict; impose, inflict
idiom hang like a millstone around one's neck

sadness *n* the quality, state, or an instance of being sad <her feelings of *sadness* and longing persisted long after he left>
syn blues, dejection, depression, dinge, (the) dismals, (the) dolefuls, dumps, dysphoria, gloom, heavyheartedness, melancholy, mopes, mournfulness, suds, unhappiness

rel dispiritedness, doldrums, downcastness, downheartedness, downs, ‖funk, listlessness, moodiness; anguish, grief, sorrow, sorrowfulness, woe; desolation, disconsolateness, disconsolation, forlornness, misery, mourning; blue devils, despondency, hopelessness, megrims, melancholia
idiom slough of despond
con happiness, joy, joyfulness, joyousness; cheerfulness, cheeriness, gayness, lightheartedness, liveliness; exhilaration, ups
ant gladness

safe *adj* **1** having been freed from risk, danger, harm, or injury <refugees who found themselves *safe* at last in a neutral country>
syn scatheless, unharmed, unscathed
rel unhurt, uninjured; intact
idiom in (*or* with) a whole skin, out of harm's way, safe and sound
con damaged, harmed, hurt, injured
ant unsafe
2 affording security from threat of harm, injury, risk, or loss <found a *safe* place to hide>
syn riskless, secure
rel guarding, protecting, safeguarding, sheltering, shielding; defended, guarded, protected, sheltered, shielded; unthreatened; impregnable, inviolable, invulnerable, unassailable
idiom safe as a bank vault
con insecure, undefended, unguarded, unprotected, vulnerable; threatened; hazardous, risky
ant dangerous, unsafe
3 not threatening danger <it's *safe* to go there only in the daytime>
syn healthy, uninjurious, wholesome; *compare* HARMLESS
rel innocent, innocuous, inoffensive
con hazardous, perilous, precarious, risky; harmful, injurious, unhealthy
ant dangerous, unsafe
4 *syn* see CAUTIOUS

safeguard *n* *syn* see DEFENSE 1
rel palladium; buffer, screen

safeguard *vb* *syn* see DEFEND 1
rel conserve, preserve, save; assure, ensure, insure

safekeeping *n* **1** *syn* see CUSTODY
2 *syn* see PRESERVATION 1

safeness *n* *syn* see SAFETY

safety *n* the quality, state, or condition of being safe <there's *safety* in numbers>
syn assurance, safeness, security
rel cover, protection, shelter; defense; impregnability, inviolability, invulnerability
con hazard, jeopardy, peril, risk, threat; instability, vulnerability
ant danger

sag *vb* **1** *syn* see SLIP 6
2 *syn* see DROOP 3
rel bend, decline; dangle, flap, flop
idiom ‖have a case of the sags
ant tauten

sag *n* **1** *syn* see DEPRESSION 2

rel settling, sinking
2 *syn* see DECLINE 3

sagacious *adj* **1** *syn* see WISE 1
rel clever, intelligent, smart; far-seeing; judicious, prudent, sapient
idiom wise as an owl
con dumb, stupid, unintelligent; ignorant, unlearned, untaught; unperceptive; unwise
2 *syn* see SHREWD
rel critical, discerning, discriminating
idiom wise in the ways of the world

sagaciousness *n* *syn* see SAGACITY
rel judgment, wiseness

sagacity *n* intelligent application of knowledge <*sagacity* acquired from years of learning and experience>
syn insight, sagaciousness, sageness, sapience, wisdom
rel discernment, penetration, perception, perceptiveness, sensitivity; understanding; judiciousness, prudence; comprehension, grasp

sage *adj* **1** *syn* see WISE 1
rel philosophic; learned; profound
2 *syn* see WISE 2
rel acute, penetrating, probing

sage *n* one distinguished for his breadth of knowledge, experience, wisdom, and sound judgment <was one of the renowned *sages* of constitutional law>
syn savant, scholar, wise man
rel expert, master

sageness *n* *syn* see SAGACITY

said *adj* *syn* see SUCH 1

sail *vb* **1** *syn* see FLY 1
2 *syn* see FLY 4

sailor *n* *syn* see MARINER

sailorman *n* *syn* see MARINER

saintliness *n* *syn* see HOLINESS
rel righteousness, worthiness

saintly *adj* being of deeply religious and wholly upright character <a *saintly* old couple>
syn angelic, godly, holy
rel righteous, upright, upstanding, virtuous, worthy; devout, God-fearing, pious; sainted; seraph, seraphic, seraphlike
idiom pure in mind and heart

salable *adj* *syn* see MARKETABLE
ant unsalable

salacious *adj* *syn* see LICENTIOUS 2

salad *n* *syn* see MISCELLANY 1

salad days *n pl* *syn* see YOUTH 1

salary *n* *syn* see WAGE

salient *adj* *syn* see NOTICEABLE
rel important, pertinent, significant, weighty; impressive, moving; obvious, pronounced; intrusive, obtrusive

saliferous *adj* *syn* see SALTY 1

saline *adj* *syn* see SALTY 1

---

syn synonym(s)   *rel* related word(s)
ant antonym(s)   *con* contrasted word(s)
idiom idiomatic equivalent(s)
‖ use limited; if in doubt, see a dictionary

saliva *n* a liquid secreted into the mouth and helpful to digestion <*saliva* drooled down the baby's chin>
syn slaver, spit, spittle, water
rel sputum

salivate *vb syn* see DROOL 2

sally *n* **1** *syn* see OUTBURST 1
2 *syn* see JOKE 1
3 *syn* see EXCURSION 1

salmagundi *n syn* see MISCELLANY 1

salon *n* **1** a spacious elegant apartment or living room (as in a fashionable house) <her *salon* was decorated à la Louis XV>
syn drawing room, saloon
rel parlor; suite
2 a fashionable assemblage of notables held by custom at the home of a prominent person <was famous for her literary *salons*>
syn saloon
rel at home; reception; levee; evening, soiree

saloon *n* **1** *syn* see SALON 1
rel gallery; hall
2 *syn* see SALON 2
rel gathering, party
3 *syn* see BAR 5

saloonist *n syn* see SALOONKEEPER

saloonkeeper *n* one who owns or manages a bar <the traditional image of the fat cigar-smoking *saloonkeeper*>
syn barkeeper, boniface, innholder, innkeeper, ||publican, saloonist, taverner; *compare* BARTENDER
rel victualler

salt *n* **1** *syn* see LIVING
2 *syn* see MARINER

salt *adj syn* see SALTY 1

saltate *vb syn* see JUMP 1

salt away *vb syn* see SAVE 4

saltimbanque *n syn* see CHARLATAN
rel impostor, pretender; cheat, fraud

salty *adj* **1** of, relating to, or containing salt <*salty* deposits>
syn saliferous, saline, salt
rel brackish, briny, saltish; salted
ant saltless
2 *syn* see RISQUÉ
3 *syn* see CAUSTIC 1

salubrious *adj syn* see HEALTHFUL
rel bracing, invigorating, stimulating
ant insalubrious

salutary *adj syn* see HEALTHFUL
rel restorative, sanative, sanatory, tonic
con debilitating, enfeebling, weakening; bad, evil
ant deleterious; unsalutary

salutation *n* **1** *syn* see GREETING
2 *syn* see ENCOMIUM

salute *vb syn* see ADDRESS 7

salute *n syn* see GREETING

salutiferous *adj syn* see HEALTHFUL

salvage *vb* to rescue and save from wreckage, destruction, or loss <*salvaged* the torpedoed vessel>
syn salve

rel deliver, redeem, rescue, save; reclaim, recover, regain, retrieve; ransom
con dump, jettison

salvation *n* **1** *syn* see PRESERVATION 1
2 *syn* see CONSERVATION 1

salve *n syn* see OINTMENT
rel emollient, lubricant; counterirritant; aid, remedy

salve *vb syn* see SALVAGE

salvo *n* **1** *syn* see BARRAGE
rel discharge; spray
2 *syn* see TESTIMONIAL 2

same *adj* **1** being one rather than another or more <went to the *same* hotel each summer>
syn exact, identical, selfsame, very
rel comparable, like, similar
ant different
2 agreeing fundamentally or absolutely <all the family have the *same* dark eyes>
syn duplicate, equal, equivalent, identic, identical, indistinguishable, tantamount; *compare* LIKE
rel comparable, like, similar; coequal
ant different
3 not changing or fluctuating <treated everyone with the *same* courtesy>
syn consistent, constant, invariable, unchanging, unfailing, unvarying
con changeable, fluctuant, inconsistent, inconstant, irregular, variable, varying

sameness *n* **1** *syn* see IDENTITY 1
rel alikeness; uniformity, uniformness, unity
2 *syn* see EQUIVALENCE
rel analogy; resemblance, similarity

sample *n syn* see INSTANCE
rel indication, sign; fragment, part, piece, portion, segment; constituent, element; individual, unit

sampling *n syn* see INSTANCE

sanative *adj syn* see CURATIVE
rel healthful, hygienic, salutary, sanitary

sanatory *adj syn* see CURATIVE

sanctified *adj syn* see HOLY 1
rel canonized, deified, sainted
ant unsanctified

sanctify *vb syn* see BLESS 1

sanctimonious *adj syn* see HYPOCRITICAL
rel deceiving, false; snuffling
ant unsanctimonious

sanctimoniousness *n syn* see HYPOCRISY
idiom odor of sanctity
ant unsanctimoniousness

sanctimony *n syn* see HYPOCRISY

sanction *n* **1** explicit authoritative permission or recognition that gives validity to acts of a subordinate <a colonial governor acting under the *sanction* of the king>
syn endorsement, fiat
rel approval, authorization, consent, permission; approbation, confirmation, encouragement, ratification, recommendation, support
con restraint; debarment; interdict, prohibition; disapprobation, disapproval, objection
ant interdiction
2 *syn* see PERMISSION

sanction *vb syn* see APPROVE 2
  rel authorize, commission, license
  con ban, disallow, forbid, prohibit
  ant interdict
sanctioned *adj syn* see ORTHODOX 1
  ant unsanctioned
sanctity *n syn* see HOLINESS
  rel godliness; righteousness, uprightness
sanctorium *n syn* see SHRINE
sanctuary *n* **1** *syn* see SHRINE
  2 *syn* see SHELTER 1
  rel bamah; oasis
  3 *syn* see REFUGE 1
sanctum *n syn* see SHRINE
sand *n syn* see FORTITUDE
  rel chutzpah, gall
  idiom true (*or* clear) grit
sandwich shop *n syn* see EATING HOUSE
sane *adj* **1** *syn* see HEALTHY 1
  2 free from mental disorder <a thoroughly *sane* and well-balanced man>
  syn all there, compos mentis, lucid, normal, right
  rel balanced, oriented; levelheaded, rational, sensible, sober, sound
  idiom of sound mind
  con abnormal, unbalanced; neurotic, paranoid, psychopathic, psychotic, schizophrenic; balmy, crazy, ‖cuckoo, non compos, non compos mentis, nuts, screwy; deranged, lunatic, mad, wild
  ant insane
  3 *syn* see WISE 2
  rel logical, rational, reasonable; good, right; cogent, compelling, convincing, sound
  con imprudent, injudicious, unwise
saneness *n syn* see WIT 2
  rel clear-mindedness, perception; comprehension, ‖smarts, understanding
sangfroid *n syn* see EQUANIMITY
  rel self-containment, self-control; aloofness, coolheadedness, indifference, unconcern
sanguinary *adj* **1** *syn* see MURDEROUS
  2 *syn* see BLOODY 1
  ant unsanguinary
sanguine *adj* **1** *syn* see BLOODY 1
  2 *syn* see MURDEROUS
  3 *syn* see RUDDY
  4 *syn* see CONFIDENT 1
  rel expectant; hopeful, undespairing
  idiom full of hope
  ant hopeless
  5 *syn* see OPTIMISTIC
  ant unsanguine
sanguineness *n syn* see OPTIMISM
sanguineous *adj* **1** *syn* see BLOODY 1
  2 *syn* see MURDEROUS
sanguinity *n syn* see OPTIMISM
sanity *n syn* see WIT 2
  rel intelligence; comprehension
  idiom sound mind
  ant insanity
sans *prep syn* see WITHOUT 2
sap *n syn* see FOOL 3
sap *vb syn* see WEAKEN 1

  rel deplete, drain, exhaust, knock out; ruin, wreck; destroy
saphead *n syn* see FOOL 3
  rel ‖boob, jerk
sapid *adj syn* see PALATABLE
  idiom fit for a king
  con bland, tasteless; repulsive, unpalatable
  ant insipid
sapidity *n syn* see TASTE 3
  ant insipidity
sapience *n syn* see SAGACITY
sapient *adj syn* see WISE 2
  rel erudite, learned, scholarly; thinking; discriminating, sapiential
sapless *adj syn* see INSIPID 3
sapor *n syn* see TASTE 3
saporous *adj syn* see PALATABLE
sappy *adj syn* ‖**1** *syn* SUCCULENT, juicy
  2 *syn* see SENTIMENTAL
  3 *syn* see FOOLISH 2
sarcasm *n* a savage bitter form of humor usually intended to hurt or wound <a speech full of personal jabs and *sarcasm*>
  syn acerbity, causticity, corrosiveness, sarcasticness
  rel humor, irony, raillery, satire, wit; jest, repartee; gibe, lampooning; mockery, ridicule, scorn, sneering; acrimony, invective; rancor, sharpness
  con playfulness, waggishness, whimsicality
sarcastic *adj* marked by, expressive of, or given to sarcasm <a critic noted for his *sarcastic* comments on actors' performances>
  syn acerb, acerbic, archilochian, caustic, corrosive, ‖sarky; *compare* CAUSTIC 1
  rel dry; cynical, ironic, sardonic, satiric; jeering, mocking, scornful; biting, cutting, incisive; mordant, scathing, sharp, stinging; pungent, tart, trenchant
  con droll, playful, sportive, waggish, whimsical
sarcasticness *n syn* see SARCASM
  rel bitingness, cuttingness, incisiveness, trenchancy; derision, mocking, taunting
sardonic *adj* characterized by or expressing disdainful, skeptical humor <had a *sardonic* smile that mirrored his fixed expectation of the worst from everyone>
  syn cynical, ironic, wry
  rel contemptuous, disdainful, scornful; derisive, jeering, mocking, saturnine, sneering; caustic, corrosive, sarcastic, satiric
‖**sarky** *adj syn* see SARCASTIC
sash *n syn* see BELT 1
sashay *vb* to move about often self-consciously and usually in a conspicuous manner <*sashaying* around, trying to walk like a model>
  syn flounce, mince, prance, ‖prink, strut
  rel swagger
sass *n syn* see BACK TALK
  rel impertinence, insolence, sassiness

---

syn synonym(s)   *rel* related word(s)
ant antonym(s)   *con* contrasted word(s)
idiom idiomatic equivalent(s)
‖ use limited; if in doubt, see a dictionary

sassy *adj* **1** *syn* see WISE 5
  rel brazen, unabashed; audacious
  2 *syn* see DAPPER
Satan *n* **1** *syn* see DEVIL 1
  rel deuce; Mephistopheles; devil-god
  idiom fallen angel, lord of the underworld, prince of darkness
  2 *syn* see DEVIL 2
  rel renegade, villain; beast, viper
satanic *adj* **1** of, relating to, or characteristic of Satan <*Satanic* rites>
  syn devilish, diabolic, Mephistophelian
  rel saturnine
  2 *syn* see FIENDISH
  rel evil, wicked
satanism *n* the worship of Satan usually marked by the travesty of Christian rites <interpreted *satanism* as an offshoot of the belief in two co-equal and coeternal principles of good and evil>
  syn diabolism
  rel Black Mass
sate *vb* *syn* see SATIATE
  rel overfill, overstuff, stuff
  idiom have (*or* give) a bellyful of, have (*or* give) an overdose of
sated *adj* *syn* see SATIATED
  ant unsated
satellite *n* *syn* see FOLLOWER
  rel favorite, minion
satellite *adj* *syn* see CONCOMITANT
satiate *adj* *syn* see SATIATED
  idiom stuffed to the gills
  con insatiable, unsatiable
  ant insatiate, unsatiate
satiate *vb* to satisfy fully or to repletion <tried to titillate rather than *satiate* his readers' interest>
  syn cloy, fill, glut, gorge, jade, pall, sate, ‖stall, stodge, surfeit; *compare* SATISFY 3
  rel content, fulfill, gratify, indulge, satisfy; overdose, stuff
  con coax, court, invite, pique, tantalize, tempt, titillate
satiated *adj* filled to repletion <the mob, *satiated* with violence, finally dispersed>
  syn full, glutted, gorged, jaded, sated, satiate, surfeited
  rel fulfilled, gratified, indulged, satisfied
  con avid, greedy, ravening; craving, hungering, hungry, lusting, thirsting, thirsty
  ant unsatiated
satiny *adj* *syn* see SOFT 3
satire *n* humorous ridicule often used to convey rebuke or criticism or to expose folly or vice <a brilliant writer noted for her *satire*>
  syn lampoonery, raillery, satiricalness
  rel banter, chaffing; causticity, irony; mockery, ridicule; pasquinade, persiflage, squib; parody, spoof, spoofery, takeoff
satiric *adj* of, relating to, characterized by, or based on satire <witty, eloquent, and *satiric* plays>
  syn lampooning, satirizing
  rel bantering, chaffing; caustic, ironic; mocking, ridiculing; parodying, spoofing; farcical; Rabelaisian

satiricalness *n* *syn* see SATIRE
satirizing *adj* *syn* see SATIRIC
satisfactorily *adv* *syn* see WELL 4
  rel competently, sufficiently
  ant unsatisfactorily
satisfactory *adj* **1** *syn* see SUFFICIENT 1
  ant unsatisfactory
  2 *syn* see VALID
  ant unsatisfactory
  3 *syn* see DECENT 4
  rel fair, goodish, passable
  ant unsatisfactory
satisfy *vb* **1** *syn* see CLEAR 5
  2 *syn* see SUIT 6
  3 to satiate desires or longings <strove to *satisfy* his lust for money and power>
  syn appease, content, gratify; *compare* SATIATE
  rel gladden, humor, indulge, please; sate, satiate; pacify, placate
  con tantalize, tease; excite, pique, provoke, stimulate; arouse
  4 *syn* see ASSURE 2
  rel induce, inveigle, win (over)
  5 measure up to a set of criteria or requirements <courses taken to *satisfy* requirements for graduation>
  syn answer, fill, fulfill, meet
  rel comply (with), conform (to), serve; do, suffice
  idiom fill the bill, make good
satisfying *adj* *syn* see VALID
  ant unsatisfying
satisfyingly *adv* *syn* see WELL 5
  rel gratifyingly, pleasingly
  ant unsatisfyingly
saturate *vb* **1** *syn* see SOAK 1
  rel bathe, douche, wash; imbue, infuse, suffuse
  2 *syn* see PERMEATE
  rel pierce, probe; inoculate, instill
saturate *adj* *syn* see WET 1
saturated *adj* *syn* see WET 1
saturnalia *n* *syn* see ORGY 2
saturnine *adj* *syn* see SULLEN
  rel grave, serious, solemn, somber, staid; moping; dark, funereal; reserved, silent, taciturn, uncommunicative
  con cheerful, cheery, happy; cordial, polite
  ant genial
satyric *adj* **1** *syn* see LICENTIOUS 2
  2 *syn* see LUSTFUL 2
sauce *n* **1** *syn* see BACK TALK
  rel pertness, sauciness
  ‖**2** *syn* see LIQUOR 2
saucebox *n* *syn* see MINX
saucy *adj* **1** flippant and bold in manner or attitude <a *saucy* little flirt>
  syn arch, bantam, ‖cocket, malapert, pert
  rel flippant, frivolous, light-minded, volatile; bold, brash, combative; impertinent, impudent, insolent; intrusive, meddlesome, obtrusive; smart, smart-alecky, wise
  con gentle, meek, mild, quiet, subdued
  ant deferential
  2 *syn* see INSOLENT 2

sault *n syn* see WATERFALL

saunter *vb* to walk slowly in an idle or leisurely manner <*sauntered* about the streets, stopping in at various shops>

syn amble, bummel, drift, linger, mope, mosey, ‖muck, stroll; *compare* WANDER 1

rel meander, ramble, roam, rove, spatiate, ‖stravage, wander; loiter, tarry

con bustle, chase, hustle, scurry, tear

saunter *n syn* see WALK 1

savage *adj* 1 being undomesticated and often destructive or ferocious through lack of restraints or human control <*savage* dogs>

syn feral, vicious, wild; *compare* WILD 1

rel uncivilized, undomesticated, unsocialized; unbroken, unsubdued, untamed; bestial, brutal, brute; ferocious, fierce

con civilized, domesticated, socialized; broken, subdued, tamed; domestic, tame

2 *syn* see FIERCE 1

rel coldhearted, heartless, implacable, relentless, unrelenting; rapacious, ravenous, voracious; bloodthirsty, bloody, butcherly, murderous, rabid

3 *syn* see BARBARIAN 1

rel primeval, primitive; uncontrolled, unharnessed; harsh, rough, rugged

savant *n syn* see SAGE

save *vb* 1 *syn* see RESCUE

rel unchain, unshackle

idiom snatch from the jaws of death

con desert, leave; condemn, damn

2 *syn* see MAINTAIN 1

3 to keep secure or maintain intact from injury, decay, or loss <regular painting helps *save* the wood>

syn conserve, preserve; *compare* MAINTAIN 1

rel defend, guard, protect, safeguard, shield

con draw (out), withdraw; consume, spend, use up

4 to accumulate and store up (a supply) for future use <*saved* his money for college>

syn lay aside, lay away, lay by, lay in, lay up, put by, salt away, ‖spare; *compare* HOARD

rel accumulate, cache, collect, stockpile, store (up); hoard, squirrel, stash (away); conserve, husband, manage; keep, reserve, set by; deposit, stow

idiom feather one's nest, keep as a nest egg, save for a rainy day, save to fall back on

con lose, squander, use up, waste

ant consume, spend

5 *syn* see ECONOMIZE

save *prep syn* see EXCEPT

save *conj* 1 *syn* see ONLY

2 *syn* see EXCEPT 1

save–all *adj syn* see STINGY

saving *n* 1 *syn* see PRESERVATION 1

2 *syn* see CONSERVATION 1

saving *prep syn* see EXCEPT

saving *conj syn* see EXCEPT 1

saving *adj syn* see SPARING

savoir faire *n syn* see TACT

rel manners; dignity, elegance, grace; refinement, savoir vivre, taste; aplomb, confidence,

self-assurance, self-possession; blaséness, experience, sophistication

con awkwardness, clumsiness, gaucherie, ineptness, maladroitness

savor *n* 1 *syn* see TASTE 3

rel scent, tinge

2 *syn* see QUALITY 1

savor *vb* 1 *syn* see SMACK

2 *syn* see FEEL 2

3 *syn* see RELISH 2

savorless *adj syn* see UNPALATABLE 1

rel bland; thin, watery, weak; unpleasing

con appetizing, pleasing, tempting; piquant, spicy

ant savory

savorous *adj syn* see PALATABLE

savorsome *adj syn* see PALATABLE

savory *adj* 1 *syn* see PALATABLE

rel pleasing, tempting; gustful

con acrid, sharp, strong

ant unsavory

2 *syn* see SWEET 2

‖**savvy** *adj syn* see SHREWD

saw *n syn* see SAYING

‖**sawbones** *n syn* see PHYSICIAN

sawbuck *n syn* see SAWHORSE

saw–edged *adj syn* see SERRATE

sawhorse *n* a rack on which something (as a board) is laid for sawing <*sawhorses* in the carpentry shop>

syn buck, horse, sawbuck, trestle, workhorse

sawtooth *adj syn* see SERRATE

saw–toothed *adj syn* see SERRATE

say *vb* 1 to express in words <learn to *say* what you mean>

syn bring out, chime in, come out (with), declare, deliver, state, tell, throw out, utter; *compare* EXPRESS 2

rel breathe; articulate, enunciate, pronounce; announce, proclaim; animadvert, comment, give, remark; cite, quote, recite, repeat; affirm, assert, aver, avow, protest

idiom out with, put in (*or* into) words, put it

2 *syn* see ARTICULATE 2

rel speak, talk

3 *syn* see SHOW 5

say *n syn* see VOICE 2

rel authority; decision

say *adv syn* see NEARLY

saying *n* an oft-repeated statement usually involving common experience or observation <the old *saying* that ignorance is bliss>

syn adage, byword, proverb, saw, word

rel dictum, maxim; truism

say–so *n syn* see VOICE 2

scabrous *adj syn* see ROUGH 1

rel scabby, scaly, scurfy; downy; knobby, knotty; bristly, prickly, thorny

con bald, glabrescent

---

syn synonym(s)   *rel* related word(s)

ant antonym(s)   *con* contrasted word(s)

idiom idiomatic equivalent(s)

‖ use limited; if in doubt, see a dictionary

ant glabrous, smooth

scad *n, usu* **scads** *pl* a great number or abundance <*scads* of opportunities>
syn gob(s), heap, jillion, load(s), million, oodles, quantities, ream(s), ‖rimption(s), slather(s), slew, thousand, trillion, wad(s); *compare* MUCH, MULTITUDE 1
rel great deal, lot
con few, handful, scattering, sprinkle, sprinkling

scalawag *n syn* see SCAMP

scalding *adj syn* see HOT 1
ant freezing

scale *vb* **1** *syn* see SKIN 2
2 to shed scales or fragmentary surface matter <*scaling* skin>
syn desquamate, exfoliate, flake (off), peel
rel chip (off), spall (off)

scale *n* **1** *syn* see DEGREE 2
2 *syn* see RANGE 5

scale *vb* **1** *syn* see ASCEND 1
2 *syn* see MEASURE 2

‖**scamble** *vb syn* see SPRAWL 1

scamp *n* a pleasantly mischievous person <what have those little *scamps* done now>
syn devil, enfant terrible, limb, mischief, pixie, rapscallion, rascal, ribald, rogue, scalawag, skeezicks, slyboots, villain
rel bird, chap, dog, ‖duck; ‖bleeder; joker, prankster
con sobersides

scamper *vb* **1** *syn* see RUN 2
rel hasten (off), hurry (away *or* off), light out, speed (away); dash (off), rush (off), shoot, tear (off), whip (off), whiz (off)
2 *syn* see RUN 1
rel scud, scuddle, scuttle

scan *vb syn* see BROWSE
idiom pass one's eye over

scan *n syn* see EXAMINATION
rel perusal; observation, reconnaissance

scandal *n syn* see DETRACTION
rel aspersion; reproach; discredit, disrepute

‖**scandal** *vb syn* see MALIGN

scandalize *vb* **1** *syn* see MALIGN
2 *syn* see SHOCK 1

scandalizer *n syn* see GOSSIP 1
rel blabber, blabbermouth, talker

scandalmonger *n syn* see GOSSIP 1
rel meddler, snoop; backbiter; muckraker

scandalous *adj* **1** *syn* see LIBELOUS
2 *syn* see OUTRAGEOUS 2

‖**scant** *n syn* see SCARCITY

scant *adj* ‖**1** *syn* see STINGY
2 *syn* see SHORT 3
3 *syn* see MEAGER 2
ant ample

scant *vb syn* see SPARE 3

scantiness *n syn* see FAILURE 3
rel scarceness, scarcity; sparseness, sparsity
con excess, overage, surplus

scanty *adj* **1** *syn* see MEAGER 2
rel scarce, wanting
con ample, enough; profuse

ant plentiful
2 *syn* see SHORT 3

scape *vb syn* see ESCAPE 1

‖**scape** *n syn* see ESCAPE 1

scape *n syn* see VISTA

scapegoat *n* one that bears the blame for another or others <was made the *scapegoat* for his boss's errors>
syn fall guy, goat, patsy, whipping boy
rel mark, target; victim

scapegrace *n syn* see WASTREL 1

scar *n* a mark left by the healing of injured tissue <still had *scars* from the operation>
syn cicatrix, scarification
rel blemish, defect, flaw; blister, pockmark, scab; disfigurement

scar *vb* to mark with a scar <burns that had *scarred* her face>
syn cicatrize, scarify
rel cut, score, scratch; blemish, disfigure, flaw, mar; damage, deface

scarce *adj* **1** *syn* see SHORT 3
rel curtailed, shortened, truncated
con adequate, sufficient, unwanting
ant abundant
2 *syn* see INFREQUENT
idiom scarce as ice water in hell, scarcer than hen's teeth, seldom met with

scarce *adv syn* see JUST 2

scarcely *adv syn* see JUST 2
idiom just barely, only just

scarceness *n syn* see SCARCITY

scarcity *n* smallness of supply, quantity, or number in proportion to demand <a serious *scarcity* of grain>
syn insufficience, insufficiency, paucity, poverty, ‖scant, scarceness; *compare* FAILURE 3
rel deficiency, shortage, underage; meagerness; rareness, uncommonness; absence, dearth, lack
con sufficiency; great deal, much; overabundance, overage, oversupply, surplus
ant abundance

scare *vb syn* see FRIGHTEN
rel panic, shake up; freeze, paralyze, petrify
idiom give a scare to, strike terror into the heart of, throw a scare into

scarecrow *n syn* see RAGAMUFFIN

scared *adj syn* see AFRAID 1
rel startled; panicked, panicky, terror-stricken
con emboldened, heartened, reassured; aggressive, bold
ant unafraid, unscared

scarification *n syn* see SCAR

scarify *vb* **1** *syn* see SCAR
rel deform, disfigure, maim, mar
2 *syn* see LAMBASTE 3

scary *adj syn* see AFRAID 1

scathe *vb syn* see LAMBASTE 3
idiom ‖give holy hell, give the business, rip (someone) up one side and down the other

scatheless *n syn* see SAFE 1

scathing *adj syn* see CAUSTIC 1
rel brutal; burning, scorching, searing, sulphurous

scatological *adj syn* see OBSCENE 2

scatter *vb* **1** to cause to separate or break up <the rain *scattered* the crowd>
syn dispel, disperse, dissipate
rel break up, shatter; disband; diverge, divide, part, separate, sever
con assemble, congregate, convene; accumulate, amass, collect, concentrate, crowd
ant gather
2 *syn* see STREW 1
rel dispense, distribute; cast, discard, shed; besprinkle, sprinkle
con accumulate, amass, concentrate
ant collect

scatterbrain *n* a flighty thoughtless person <his wife is a *scatterbrain*>
syn birdbrain, featherbrain, featherhead, flibbertigibbet, harebrain, rattlebrain, rattlehead, shatterbrain
rel fool, goose, silly, simpleton

scatterbrained *adj syn* see GIDDY 1

scattergood *n syn* see SPENDTHRIFT

scattering *n syn* see FEW

scene *n* **1** the total arrangement of the objects that form the scenic environment in which a drama is enacted <spectacle plays that attempt a realistic, three-dimensional *scene*>
syn mise-en-scène, scenery, set, setting, stage set, stage setting
rel hangings, scene cloth; ‖back cloth, backdrop, background; tableau
2 *syn* see VIEW 4
3 the place of an occurrence or action <the *scene* of the crime>
syn locale, mise-en-scène, site
rel locality, location, place, spot
4 a sphere of activity, interest, or controversy <the drug *scene*>
syn arena
rel compass, field, setting, sphere; culture, environment, milieu

scenery *n syn* see SCENE 1
rel decor; furnishings, furniture; properties, props

scent *vb* **1** *syn* see SMELL 1
2 to imbue or fill with an odor <air *scented* with herbs>
syn aromatize, odorize, perfume

scent *n* **1** *syn* see SMELL 1
rel essence, whiff
2 *syn* see FRAGRANCE

scented *adj* **1** *syn* see SWEET 2
2 *syn* see ODOROUS
ant scentless, unscented

scentless *adj syn* see ODORLESS

schedule *n* **1** *syn* see LIST
rel chart, table
2 *syn* see PROGRAM 1

schedule *vb* **1** to place in a schedule <*schedule* a new train>
syn card, sked
rel list, record, slate
2 *syn* see TIME 1

scheme *n* **1** *syn* see PLAN 1

rel presentation, proposal, proposition, suggestion; arrangement, order, ordering; contrivance, device, expedient
2 *syn* see PLOT 2

scheme (out) *vb syn* see PLOT

schism *n* **1** *syn* see BREACH 3
2 *syn* see HERESY
3 a division of a group into two discordant groups <a *schism* within a political party>
syn chasm, cleavage, cleft, split; *compare* BREACH 3
rel divergence, division, separation; breach, break, rupture; estrangement
con unification, unity; reconciliation

schismatic *n syn* see HERETIC
rel protester; skeptic; radical, Young Turk

schismatic *adj syn* see HERETICAL
rel rebellious; unconventional

schismatist *n syn* see HERETIC

‖**schlemiel** *n syn* see FOOL 3

schlepp (*or* **schlepper**) *n syn* see OAF 2

‖**schmo** *n syn* see FOOL 1

‖**schmuck** *n syn* see FOOL 1

‖**schnook** *n syn* see DUNCE

‖**schnorrer** *n syn* see BEGGAR 1

‖**schnozzle** *n syn* see NOSE 1

scholar *n syn* see SAGE
rel pupil, student; bookman; polymath

scholarliness *n syn* see ERUDITION 2
ant unscholarliness

scholarly *adj syn* see LEARNED
rel studious; intellectual, long-hair; educated, taught, trained
con untaught, untrained
ant unscholarly

scholarship *n* **1** *syn* see EDUCATION 2
2 *syn* see ERUDITION 2

scholastic *adj* **1** *syn* see PEDANTIC
rel lettered, literary; scholarly; formal
2 *syn* see LEARNED
rel conversant, versed
con unconversant, unscholarly

school *vb syn* see TEACH
rel inform; guide, lead, show; advance, cultivate; control, direct, manage

schooling *n syn* see EDUCATION 1
rel knowledge; book learning, booklore

schoolmasterish *adj syn* see DIDACTIC

science *n* **1** *syn* see KNOWLEDGE 2
2 *syn* see EDUCATION 2

scilicet *adv syn* see NAMELY

scintillate *vb syn* see FLASH 1

scintillating *adj syn* see CLEVER 5

scintillation *n syn* see FLASH 1

scions *n pl syn* see OFFSPRING

scoff *vb* to show contempt by derision or mockery <heard his tale and *scoffed* at it>
syn fleer, flout, gibe, gird, jeer, jest, quip (at), scout (at), sneer

---

syn synonym(s)	*rel* related word(s)
ant antonym(s)	*con* contrasted word(s)
idiom idiomatic equivalent(s)	
‖ use limited; if in doubt, see a dictionary	

rel pooh-pooh; deride, mock, rally, ridicule, taunt, twit; contemn, despise, disdain, scorn; boo

con accept, approve, commend; compliment; acclaim, laud, praise

scoff *n syn* see FOOD 1

scold *n syn* see VIRAGO

scold *vb* **1** to reproach angrily and abusively <loudly *scolded* him for staying out late>

syn baste, bawl out, berate, ‖bless out, ‖cample, ‖carpet, ‖chew, ‖chew out, dress down, jaw, lash, ‖mob, rag, rail, rant, rate, ‖ream out, revile, ‖row, tell off, tongue, tongue-lash, ‖tongue-walk, upbraid, vituperate, wig; *compare* CRITICIZE, LAMBASTE 3, REPROVE

rel blame, censure, criticize, denounce, reprehend, reprobate; admonish, chide, rebuke, reprimand, reproach, reprove; execrate, objurate; brace, grill, harass, hound; blister, excoriate

idiom jump down one's throat, rake over the coals, read one the riot act, walk into

2 *syn* see GRUMBLE 1

sconce *n syn* see HEAD 1

scoop *n* a news story first obtained and reported by only one source (as a newspaper) <the story was a *scoop* by just a few hours>

syn beat, exclusive

scoop *vb* **1** *syn* see DIP 2

rel gather; lift, pick up

2 *syn* see DIG 2

rel gouge, grub

3 to report a news item in advance of competitors <CBS *scooped* NBC on that story>

syn beat

scoot *vb* **1** *syn* see HURRY 2

2 *syn* see RUN 1

3 *syn* see RUN 2

scope *n* **1** *syn* see ROOM 3

2 *syn* see RANGE 2

3 *syn* see BREADTH 2

scopic *adj syn* see EXTENSIVE 1

scopious *adj syn* see EXTENSIVE 1

scorch *vb* **1** *syn* see LAMBASTE 3

2 *syn* see BURN 3

rel seethe, simmer, stew; ‖plot

scorching *adj syn* see HOT 1

idiom scorching hot, sizzling hot

score *n* **1 scores** *pl syn* see MULTITUDE 1

2 a slight cut or line made with or as if with a sharp instrument <cut *scores* on the ham before baking it>

syn scotch, scratch

rel line, mark; nick, notch, serration; cut, slit; cleft, furrow, groove, indentation; gash

3 *syn* see BILL 1

4 an obligation or injury kept in mind for future reckoning <had a *score* to settle with him>

syn account

rel grudge

5 the number of points gained by contestants in a game or contest <a record *score* of 263 for 72 holes>

syn tally

rel account, record; summary, total

idiom the final count

score *vb* **1** *syn* see LAMBASTE 3

rel ream out

idiom tear to pieces

2 *syn* see GAIN 1

3 *syn* see SUCCEED 3

scorn *n syn* see DESPITE 1

rel flouting, gibing, jeering, scoffing; derision, mockery, ridicule, taunt, taunting

con consideration, respectfulness

ant respect

scorn *vb syn* see DESPISE

rel flout, gibe, jeer, scoff; mock, ridicule, taunt

idiom hold in utter contempt

con accept, acknowledge, welcome

ant respect

scotch *n syn* see SCORE 2

Scotch *adj syn* see SPARING

scoundrel *n syn* see VILLAIN 1

scour *vb* **1** *syn* see HURRY 2

2 to make a thorough search or examination of <*scoured* the neighborhood for the lost child>

syn beat, comb, finecomb, fine-tooth-comb, forage, grub, rake, ransack, rummage, search

rel rout; look (for), seek; fan, range; rifle; ferret (out), find

idiom beat the bushes, leave no stone unturned, look high and low, look up and down, turn inside out, turn upside down

scour *vb* **1** *syn* see SCRUB 1

2 *syn* see EAT 3

scour *n, usu* **scours** *pl syn* see DIARRHEA

scourge *n syn* see PLAGUE 1

scourge *vb* **1** *syn* see WHIP 1

rel hit; knout; flail, whop

idiom whip to ribbons

2 *syn* see RAVAGE

3 *syn* see LAMBASTE 3

scout *vb* to explore in order to obtain information <forward observers *scouted* the terrain before the attack>

syn probe, reconnoiter

rel look (over), survey; observe; check out, examine; ‖case, inspect

idiom run reconnaissance

scout *vb* **1** *syn* see RIDICULE

2 *syn* see DESPISE

rel mock, ridicule

scout (at) *vb syn* see SCOFF

scowl *vb syn* see FROWN 1

idiom look black as thunder, pull a face (*or* scowl)

scrabble *vb* **1** *syn* see SCRIBBLE

2 *syn* see SCRAMBLE 1

scrag *vb* **1** *syn* see HANG 2

2 *syn* see KILL 1

3 *syn* see MURDER 1

scraggy *adj* **1** *syn* see ROUGH 1

2 *syn* see LEAN

rel gangling, spindling, spindly; skeletal; dwarfed, scrubby, stunted, undersize

scram *vb syn* see GET OUT 1

idiom ‖beat it, ‖cheese it, ‖get the hell out

scramble *vb* **1** to move or climb hastily on all fours <*scrambled* across the rocks>

syn clamber, scrabble, ‖spartle, ‖sprauchle
rel scurry, scuttle
2 *syn* see SPRAWL 2

scramble *n syn* see CLUTTER 2
rel conglomeration

scrap *n* **1** *syn* see END 4
rel chip, cutting; scrappage, waste
2 *syn* see PARTICLE

scrap *vb syn* see DISCARD
idiom consign to the scrap heap

scrap *n syn* see BRAWL 2

scrap *vb syn* see QUARREL

scrape *vb* **1** to rub or slide against something that is often harsh, rough, or sharp <chalk *scraping* on the blackboard>
syn grate, rasp, scratch
rel graze, rub, scuff; abrade, chafe, grind
2 *syn* see SCRIMP
3 to make one's way with great difficulty or succeed by a narrow margin <the student barely *scraped* through the exam>
syn shave
rel struggle; get along, get by
idiom cut it (*or* the corner) pretty close, have a close shave

scrape *n syn* see PREDICAMENT
rel trouble; discomfiture, embarrassment

scrapping *n syn* see DISPOSAL 2

scrappy *adj* **1** *syn* see QUARRELSOME 2
2 *syn* see BELLIGERENT

scratch *vb* **1** *syn* see SCRAPE 1
rel squeak, squeal
2 *syn* see SCRIBBLE

scratch *n* **1** *syn* see SCORE 2
‖**2** *syn* see MONEY

scrawl *vb syn* see SCRIBBLE
rel inscribe; doodle

scrawny *adj syn* see LEAN
idiom just (*or* nothing but) skin and bones
ant brawny

screak *vb syn* see SQUEAL 2

scream *vb* **1** to voice a sudden piercing loud cry often in shock, terror, or pain <*screamed* at the sight of the accident and then fainted>
syn screech, shriek, shrill, squeal; *compare* SHOUT 1
rel screak, squeak; cry, yell; bellow, roar; caterwaul, howl, wail, ‖yawl
idiom let out a scream (*or* shriek *or* screech)
2 *syn* see SQUEAL 2
3 *syn* see YELL 2
rel complain, grumble, protest; blare
idiom raise a howl
4 to produce a vivid, blatant, or startling effect <clothes and furnishings that *screamed* nouveau riche>
syn blare, shout, shriek

scream *n syn* see RIOT 2

screech *vb* **1** *syn* see SCREAM 1
rel penetrate, pierce; vent, voice
2 *syn* see SQUEAL 2

screen *vb* **1** *syn* see DEFEND 1
2 *syn* see SHADE

3 to cut off from view by interposing something resembling a screen <*screen* a view with a tall hedge>
syn block out, close, obstruct, shroud, shut off, shut out
rel conceal, hide; separate, wall off; protect, seclude; embosk
idiom throw up a screen
con bare, disclose, expose, open, reveal
4 *syn* see HIDE
rel defend, guard, protect, safeguard, shield; camouflage, cloak, cover up, disguise
5 to examine carefully and methodically in order to separate, select, or eliminate <the personnel department *screened* seventy candidates for ten jobs>
syn sieve, sift; *compare* SORT 2
rel choose, pick out, select; extract, filter (out), riddle, sort (out), winnow (out)
6 *syn* see CENSOR

‖**screeve** *vb syn* see EXUDE

screw *vb* **1** *syn* see CRUMPLE 1
2 *syn* see EXTORT 1
‖**3** *syn* see CHEAT
4 *syn* see SCRIMP
‖**5** *syn* see RUN 2

‖**screw** (up) *vb syn* see BOTCH
rel confuse, muddle, snafu; spoil

screwball *n syn* see CRACKPOT

screwy *adj* ‖**1** *syn* see INTOXICATED 1
2 *syn* see INSANE 1
idiom having a screw loose

scribble *vb* to write or draw hastily or roughly <*scribbled* a quick note to her on his way out>
syn scrabble, scratch, scrawl, squiggle
rel jot (down); scribe, write

scribe *vb syn* see WRITE

scrimmage *n* **1** *syn* see CLASH 2
rel scuffle; fight; free-for-all
2 *syn* see BRAWL 2

scrimp *adj syn* see MEAGER 2

scrimp *vb* to be extremely frugal and parsimonious in an effort to economize <*scrimped* all year to buy that fur coat>
syn pinch, scrape, screw, skimp, ‖skinch, spare, stint; *compare* SPARE 3
rel scamp; scratch; save (up)
idiom pinch pennies

‖**scrimption** *n syn* see PITTANCE

scrimpy *adj* **1** *syn* see MEAGER 2
2 *syn* see SHORT 3
3 *syn* see STINGY

scrimy *adj syn* see STINGY

script *n syn* see HANDWRITING

Scripture *n syn* see BIBLE

scrooch (down) *vb syn* see CROUCH

scrooge *n syn* see MISER

scrub *n syn* see INFERIOR

---

syn synonym(s)   *rel* related word(s)
ant antonym(s)   *con* contrasted word(s)
idiom idiomatic equivalent(s)
‖ use limited; if in doubt, see a dictionary

scrub *vb* **1** to clean by abrasive action <*scrubbed* the pots and pans>
  syn scour
  rel brush; rub; cleanse, wash; buff, polish
  2 *syn* see CANCEL 2
scrubby *adj syn* see SHABBY 1
scruffy *adj syn* see SHABBY 1
scrumptious *adj syn* see DELIGHTFUL
scrunch *vb* **1** *syn* see CHEW 1
  2 *syn* see CRUMPLE 1
||**scrunty** *adj syn* see STUNTED
scruple *n syn* see PARTICLE
scruple *n syn* see QUALM
  rel faltering, hesitancy, hesitation, pause; reconsideration, second thought
scruple *vb syn* see DEMUR
  rel question; fret, worry
scrupulous *adj* **1** *syn* see UPRIGHT 2
  rel fair-minded; strict; upstanding
  con questionable; shifty, slippery; dishonorable, unprincipled; dishonest
  ant unscrupulous
  2 *syn* see CAREFUL 2
  rel critical, fastidious
  con careless; undiscriminating, unparticular
  ant remiss
scrutinize *vb* **1** to look at or over critically and searchingly <the jeweler *scrutinized* the diamonds to see if they were fakes>
  syn canvass, ||case, check over, check up, con, examine, inspect, perlustrate, study, survey, vet, view
  rel look over, overlook, peruse, pore (over), scan; consider, contemplate, weigh; penetrate, pierce, probe; analyze, dig (into), dissect; comb
  idiom turn a careful (*or* heedful) eye to (*or* on)
  2 *syn* see EYE 2
scrutiny *n* **1** *syn* see EXAMINATION
  rel look-in, look-over, look-see
  2 *syn* see EYE 3
scud *vb syn* see FLY 1
scuddle *vb syn* see SCUTTLE
scuff *vb syn* see SHUFFLE 3
scuffle *vb* **1** *syn* see WRESTLE
  rel cuff, scuff
  2 *syn* see SHUFFLE 3
scuffle *n syn* see BRAWL 2
||**sculch** *n syn* see REFUSE
sculp *vb syn* see SCULPTURE
sculpt *vb syn* see SCULPTURE
sculpture *vb* to form an image or representation from solid material (as wood or stone) <*sculptured* a colossal statue of a horse>
  syn carve, chisel, sculp, sculpt
  rel cast, form; model, mold, shape
scum *n* **1** *syn* see RABBLE 2
  idiom scum of the earth
  2 *syn* see SNOT 1
||**scumbag** *n syn* see SNOT 1
scummy *adj syn* see CONTEMPTIBLE
scurf *n syn* see RABBLE 2
scurrile *adj syn* see ABUSIVE
scurrility *n syn* see ABUSE
  rel scurrilousness; maligning, traducing, vilification

scurrilous *adj* **1** *syn* see ABUSIVE
  rel coarse, gross; filthy, foul; insulting, offending, offensive, outrageous, outraging
  2 *syn* see OBSCENE 2
scurry *vb* **1** *syn* see SCUTTLE
  2 *syn* see RUN 1
  rel shoot, tear; dart, fly; scuffle, skelter
scurvy *adj syn* see CONTEMPTIBLE
  rel base, low, vile
scutter *vb syn* see SCUTTLE
  rel hasten, hurry, run, speed
scuttle *vb* to move with or as if with short rapidly alternating steps <armies of fiddler crabs *scuttled* across the road>
  syn scuddle, scurry, scutter; *compare* RUN 1
  rel scoot; scramble; scud
scuttlebutt *n syn* see REPORT 1
sea *n syn* see OCEAN
sea dog *n syn* see PIRATE
seal *n* an adhesive-backed device bearing a symbolic, pictorial, or official design <the *seal* on a diploma>
  syn stamp, sticker
seam *n syn* see JOINT 1
  rel bond
seaman *n syn* see MARINER
sear *vb* **1** *syn* see DRY 1
  2 to burn or scorch with a sudden application of intense heat <*seared* the steaks in the broiler>
  syn sizzle
  rel parch, scorch, shrivel; burn (up)
search *vb* **1** *syn* see SCOUR 2
  rel run down, scout (around), scrimmage, skirmish
  idiom search high and low
  2 to subject (a person) to a thorough check for concealed or contraband articles <police *searching* the suspects for weapons>
  syn ||fan, frisk, shake down
  rel check, examine; inspect, look over, scan, scrutinize, study
search (for *or* out) *vb syn* see SEEK 1
  rel pry (out), scout (out)
search *n syn* see PURSUIT 2
searchingly *adv syn* see HARD 4
sea robber *n syn* see PIRATE
sea rover *n syn* see PIRATE
season *n* a particular period of the year <the Christmas *season*>
  syn time
  rel period, term
season *vb syn* see HARDEN 2
  rel discipline, school, train; fit, prepare; case harden, steel
seasonable *adj syn* see TIMELY 1
  rel apropos, pertinent, relevant; appropriate, apt; convenient
  con irrelevant; inappropriate, inapt; ill-timed, inconvenient, inopportune
  ant unseasonable
seasonably *adv syn* see EARLY 1
  ant unseasonably
seasoned *adj syn* see EXPERIENCED
  rel acclimated, acclimatized, hardened, toughened; case-hardened, steeled

con inexperienced, unpracticed, unskilled, unversed; unacclimated, unacclimatized, unsteeled, untempered, untried
ant unseasoned

seat *n* **1** *syn* see BUTTOCKS
2 *syn* see CENTER 2
rel fulcrum
3 *syn* see BASE 1

seat *vb* to cause to be seated <an usher *seated* her in the third row>
syn sit
rel establish, place, put

seating *n* *syn* see BASE 1

sea wolf *n* *syn* see PIRATE

seclude *vb* to remove or separate (oneself or another) from external influences <in the convent she was *secluded* from secular life>
syn cloister, sequester
rel retire, separate, withdraw; closet, confine, enclose, immure, isolate; screen, shut off

secluded *adj* disposed to, living in, or characterized by seclusion <*secluded* monks> <they enjoyed *secluded* country living>
syn cloistered, hermetic, recluse, secluse, seclusive, sequestered
rel retired, withdrawn; close, hidden, private, screened, shy; alone, isolated, solitary
con communal, public

secluse *adj* *syn* see SECLUDED

seclusion *n* the act or condition of secluding or of being secluded <the queen went into *seclusion* when her husband died>
syn reclusion, retirement, sequestration; *compare* SOLITUDE
rel detachment, separation, withdrawal; reclusiveness, seclusiveness; privacy, privateness; aloneness, isolation, separateness, solitude

seclusive *adj* *syn* see SECLUDED

second *n* *syn* see INSTANT 1
idiom the flash of an eyelid

secondary *adj* **1** *syn* see SUBORDINATE
rel accessory, subservient
con major, prime; first, first-ranking, first-string
ant primary
2 formed from something original, primary, or basic <a *secondary* historical analysis based on original archives>
syn derivate, derivational, derivative, derived
rel borrowed, secondhand; consequent, resultant, subsequent
con basic, principle; first, firsthand, original, uncopied, underived
ant primary
3 *syn* see MINOR 2

secondary *n* *syn* see INFERIOR
rel second fiddle, second-in-command

second childhood *n* *syn* see DOTAGE
second–class *adj* *syn* see INFERIOR 2
second–drawer *adj* *syn* see INFERIOR 2
second–rate *adj* *syn* see INFERIOR 2
ant first-rate

secours *n* *syn* see HELP 1

secrecy *n* the practice or policy of keeping secrets or maintaining concealment <*secrecy* is an inherent feature of intelligence operations>

syn hugger-mugger, hugger-muggery, hush, hush-hush, secretiveness, secretness, silence
rel clandestineness, covertness, furtiveness; concealment, stealth, subterfuge; censorship, suppression
ant openness

secret *adj* **1** existing or done in such a way as to maintain concealment <was involved in *secret* negotiations with the enemy>
syn clandestine, covert, furtive, hole-and-corner, hugger-mugger, hush-hush, mystical, sneak, stealthy, sub-rosa, surreptitious, undercover, ‖underneath, under-the-table; *compare* STEALTHY 2, UNDERHAND
rel underhand, underhanded; unacknowledged, unavowed, undeclared; concealed, hidden, screened; classified, confidential, eyes only, restricted, top secret
con acknowledged, avowed, declared, revealed; aboveboard, straightforward, unconcealed; declassified, unclassified, unrestricted; clear, evident, manifest, obvious, patent, plain
ant open, public
2 *syn* see OBSCURE 2
3 *syn* see RECONDITE

secret *n* **secrets** *pl* *syn* see GENITALIA

secretaire *n* *syn* see DESK

secretary *n* *syn* see DESK

secrete *vb* *syn* see HIDE
rel deposit; withhold

secretiveness *n* *syn* see SECRECY

secretly *adv* in a secret manner <negotiated *secretly* with both sides>
syn by stealth, clandestinely, covertly, furtively, hugger-mugger, in camera, privately, stealthily, sub rosa, surreptitiously
rel confidentially; privatim, privily
idiom behind closed doors, on the qt, on the quiet, under the rose, under the table
con forthrightly, plainly, publicly; manifestly, overtly
ant openly

secretness *n* *syn* see SECRECY

sect *n* *syn* see RELIGION 2

sectarian *adj* **1** *syn* see HERETICAL
rel splinter
con unified, united
ant nonsectarian
2 *syn* see INSULAR

sectary *n* **1** *syn* see HERETIC
rel beatnik, Bohemian, hippie; maverick; liberal, radical, Young Turk; rebel, revolutionary
con advocate, conformist, follower
2 *syn* see FOLLOWER
rel bigot

sectator *n* *syn* see FOLLOWER

section *n* **1** *syn* see PART 1
rel district, locality, subdivision, vicinity; area, belt, zone; region, tract; field, sphere, territory

---

syn synonym(s)   *rel* related word(s)
ant antonym(s)   *con* contrasted word(s)
idiom idiomatic equivalent(s)
‖ use limited; if in doubt, see a dictionary

2 *syn* see QUARTER 2

section *vb* to divide into sections <*sectioned* the class on the basis of ability>
syn sectionalize, sectionize; *compare* SEGMENT
rel break up, divide, separate, slice, split; sector, segment

sectionalize *vb syn* see SECTION

sectionize *vb syn* see SECTION

sector *n syn* see QUARTER 2

secular *adj syn* see PROFANE 1
rel nonclerical, nonreligious
con clerical, ecclesiastical, ministerial, priestly, regular; eternal
ant religious

securable *adj syn* see AVAILABLE 1
rel convenient, handy, reachable, ready
idiom at one's disposal
con unavailable, unreachable

secure *adj* **1** *syn* see CONFIDENT 1
2 *syn* see SAFE 2
rel firm, stable, strong
con open, wide-open; assailable, weak; dangerous, precarious
ant insecure
3 *syn* see RELIABLE 1
4 *syn* see FAST 4
rel strong; iron
5 *syn* see STABLE 4
6 *syn* see SURE 1
rel established, settled; balanced
con precarious; unbalanced; unstable, wobbly
ant insecure

secure *vb* **1** *syn* see DEFEND 1
2 *syn* see ENSURE
rel underwrite
3 *syn* see CATCH 1
4 *syn* see FASTEN 2
rel batten (down), clamp, clinch, pinion, rivet, tie down; cement
con unfasten, untie
5 *syn* see GET 1
6 *syn* see EFFECT 1

security *n* **1** *syn* see SAFETY
ant insecurity
2 *syn* see STABILITY
3 *syn* see PLEDGE 1
4 *syn* see GUARANTEE 1
rel assurance; certification; pledge
5 *syn* see DEFENSE 1

sedate *adj syn* see SERIOUS 1
rel calm, placid, serene, tranquil; collected, composed, dispassionate, imperturbable, unruffled; decorous, dignified, proper, seemly
con indecorous, undignified, unseemly; airy, flippant, light
ant flighty

sedative *n* an agent or drug that relieves irritability, nervousness, or excitement <took a *sedative* to help her sleep>
syn calmant, calmative, quietive
rel balm; pacifier, tranquilizer; sleeping pill, sleeping tablet; depressant, ‖downer
con energizer; stimulant; ‖upper

sediment *n* matter which settles to the bottom of a liquid <rocks hidden by *sediment* spoiled the cove for diving>
syn deposit, dreg(s), grounds, lees, precipitate, precipitation, settlings
rel bottoms, dross, recrement, scoria, slag; draff, heeltap

sedition *n* an offense against official ruling authority (as a government or sovereign) to which one owes allegiance <considered the defense industry strike to be overt *sedition*>
syn seditiousness, treason
rel alienation, disaffection, estrangement; action, protest, strike; coup, coup d'etat, putsch; insurrection, mutiny, rebellion, revolt, revolution, uprising; quislingism
con allegiance, fealty, fidelity, loyalty; duty, respect, responsibility

seditious *adj syn* see INSUBORDINATE
rel alienated, disaffected, dissident; disloyal, faithless, perfidious, traitorous, treacherous; lawless, violent
con faithful, loyal, patriotic

seditiousness *n syn* see SEDITION

seduce *vb* **1** *syn* see LURE
rel coax, tease; betray, deceive, delude, mislead; enslave, entrance; overpower, overwhelm
2 to persuade or entice into sexual partnership <his pathetic attempts to *seduce* his female coworkers>
syn debauch, undo
rel deflower; rape, ravish, violate; corrupt, degrade, pervert, ruin

seducement *n* **1** *syn* see SEDUCTION 1
rel undoing
2 *syn* see LURE 2

seduction *n* **1** the act or an instance of seducing or being seduced into a sexual relationship <his locker-room accounts of innumerable *seductions* were never taken seriously>
syn seducement
rel deflowering; rape, ravishment, violation; corruption, degradation, perversion, ruin
2 *syn* see ATTRACTION 1
rel Lorelei, siren song, temptation

seductive *adj syn* see ATTRACTIVE 1
rel desirable, mouth-watering, provocative

seductress *n syn* see SIREN

sedulous *adj syn* see ASSIDUOUS
rel active; busy; hustling, persevering, persistent, unremitting

see *vb* **1** to take cognizance of by physical or mental vision <*saw* that the boat was being driven ashore> <the only one who *saw* the truth>
syn behold, descry, discern, distinguish, espy, mark, mind, note, notice, observe, perceive, remark, twig, view
rel sight; make out; examine, inspect, scan, scrutinize; penetrate, pierce, probe; consider, study; appraise, ponder, weigh
idiom fix one's eyes (*or* mind *or* thoughts) on, occupy oneself with, pay heed (*or* attention) to, take notice of
2 to perceive something by means of the eyes <she *sees* clearly with her new glasses>

syn ‖dekko, look, watch
rel gape, gaze, glare, peek, peep, peer, stare
idiom give the eye, hold in view, keep one's eye on, lay eyes on, turn one's eyes to
3 *syn* see EXPERIENCE 1
4 *syn* see DISCOVER 3
5 *syn* see THINK 1
6 *syn* see APPREHEND 1
rel discern, discriminate, recognize
7 *syn* see FORESEE
idiom see the day when
8 *syn* see LOOK 1
rel look out, watch out
idiom see to it that
9 *syn* see VISIT 2
10 *syn* see DATE
11 *syn* see GUIDE
rel accompany, go (with); attend
seeable *adj syn* see VISUAL 2
ant unseeable
seed *n* **1** *syn* see OFFSPRING
2 a beginning or source from which something (as a conception) may later develop <the growing *seeds* of suspicion in her mind>
syn bud, embryo, germ, nucleus, spark
rel rudiment; core, kernel; conceit, concept, conception, image, impression, notion
seed *vb syn* see PLANT 1
seedy *adj syn* see SHABBY 1
rel drooping, droopy, flagging, sagging, wilted, wilting; messy, slovenly, unkempt, untidy; neglected, overgrown
idiom gone to seed
con manicured, polished, shined
seeing *n syn* see EYE 2
seeing *conj syn* see BECAUSE
idiom ‖being as how, in that
‖**seeing glass** *n syn* see MIRROR 1
seek *vb* **1** to look for <has gone to *seek* a doctor>
syn cast about, ferret out, hunt, quest, search (for *or* out)
rel bird-dog, delve, dig, fish, mouse, nose, root, smell out, sniff
idiom go in quest (*or* search) of
2 *syn* see TRY 5
seeker *n syn* see CANDIDATE
rel bidder; petitioner; solicitant; claimant
seeking *n syn* see PURSUIT 2
seem *vb* to give the impression of being without necessarily being so in fact <things are not always the way they *seem*>
syn appear, look, sound
rel resemble, suggest; hint, imply, insinuate, intimate
idiom have (*or* show) every sign of, have the earmarks of
seeming *n* **1** *syn* see APPEARANCE 2
rel feigning, pretense, sham; facade; illusion
idiom false face (*or* front), outward show
2 *syn* see APPEARANCE 1
rel bearing, demeanor, posture; image, style; effect, impression
seeming *adj syn* see APPARENT 2
seemingly *adv syn* see OSTENSIBLY

seemliness *n* **1** *syn* see ORDER 7
2 *syn* see DECORUM 1
ant unseemliness
seemly *adj syn* see DECOROUS 1
rel compatible, congenial, congruous, consistent, consonant; pleasing
con inappropriate, unfit, unseasonable, unsuitable, untimely; incompatible, uncongenial; displeasing, unpleasing
ant unseemly
seep *vb syn* see EXUDE
rel drip; leak; flow
seer *n syn* see PROPHET
seesaw *vb* to move backward and forward or up and down from a central axis usually in a swaying often unsteady way <planes landing on the *seesawing* flight deck>
syn lurch, pitch, swag, tilt, tilter, yaw; *compare* TEETER, TOSS 2
rel cant, incline, lean, list; rock, roll, sway
seethe *vb* **1** *syn* see BOIL 2
2 *syn* see SOAK 1
3 *syn* see ANGER 2
idiom ‖do a slow burn
con calm (down), simmer (down)
ant cool (down)
4 to be in a state of internal and especially mental agitation, excitement, or turmoil <his brain *seethed* with unanswered questions>
syn boil, bubble, churn, ferment, ‖moil, simmer, smolder, stir
rel abound, swarm, teem; fret, fume, sizzle, steam; bubble over, erupt, overflow
see–through *adj syn* see TRANSPARENT 1
segment *n syn* see PART 1
segment *vb* to separate into segments <tried to *segment* the poem into understandable units>
syn segmentalize, segmentize; *compare* SECTION
rel categorize, compartmentalize; divide, separate; isolate, seclude, set off
segmentalize *vb syn* see SEGMENT
segmentize *vb syn* see SEGMENT
segregate *vb syn* see ISOLATE
rel disconnect; choose, select, single
con mix
ant desegregate
segregation *n* the quality, state, or condition of being socially or racially excluded or separated <fought against racial *segregation* in the schools>
syn apartheid, separateness, separation, separatism
rel discrimination, jim crowism; ghettoization; isolation, seclusion
ant desegregation
seity *n syn* see INDIVIDUALITY 4
seize *vb* **1** *syn* see APPROPRIATE 1
rel occupy; usurp

---

syn synonym(s)   *rel* related word(s)
ant antonym(s)   *con* contrasted word(s)
idiom idiomatic equivalent(s)
‖ use limited; if in doubt, see a dictionary

2 to take possession or control of usually suddenly and forcibly <the cat *seized* the fish and made off> <*seized* the rope and dragged the boat ashore>
syn catch, clutch, ‖cotch, grab, grapple, nab, ‖nail, snatch, take; *compare* CATCH 1
rel fasten (onto), grasp, latch (onto), snap (at); apprehend, arrest; capture, secure, take over; abduct, carry off, kidnap, spirit (away *or* off)
idiom get into one's clutches, get one's hands (*or* paws) on, lay hold (on *or* of)
con free, loose, release
3 to affect especially as if by laying hold of <was *seized* with a coughing fit>
syn catch, strike, take
rel overtake; afflict

seizure *n syn* see ATTACK 3
rel convulsion; breakdown

seldom *adv* in few instances <she *seldom* writes home anymore>
syn hardly ever, infrequently, little, rarely, unfrequently, unoften
rel occasionally; semioccasionally; irregularly, sporadically; hardly, scarcely
idiom once in a blue moon
con regularly; frequently; usually
ant often

seldom *adj syn* see INFREQUENT

select *adj* **1** singled out from a number or group by fitness or preference <this hotel caters to a *select* clientele>
syn chosen, elect, exclusive, pick, picked, selected
rel culled, screened, weeded (out), winnowed (out); favored, preferred; best, elite
con random; indiscriminate; average, commonplace, mediocre, run-of-the-mill
2 *syn* see CHOICE
rel blue-chip, fine; best; top
3 *syn* see ECLECTIC 1

select *vb syn* see CHOOSE 1
idiom make a choice (*or* selection)
con ignore, pass (over); drop
ant reject

selected *adj syn* see SELECT 1
rel singled (out); appointed, tagged, tapped

selection *n syn* see CHOICE 1
rel choosing, culling, draft, drafting, picking; acumen, discernment, discrimination, insight
ant rejection

selective *adj syn* see ECLECTIC 1
rel particular, scrupulous

self-abandoned *adj syn* see ABANDONED 2

self-abnegating *adj syn* see SELF-SACRIFICING

self-abnegation *n syn* see RENUNCIATION
rel abandonment, relinquishment, resignation

self-absorbed *adj syn* see EGOCENTRIC 2
rel arrogant, cocky, self-important

self-abuse *n syn* see SELF-REPROACH

self-accusation *n syn* see SELF-REPROACH

self-admiration *n syn* see CONCEIT 2

self-asserting *adj syn* see PRESUMPTUOUS
rel aggressive, militant
con meek, modest, unassuming; docile, passive

ant self-effacing

self-assertive *adj* **1** *syn* see AGGRESSIVE
rel impertinent, intrusive, meddlesome, obtrusive, officious, bold; cocksure, sure
2 *syn* see PRESUMPTUOUS

self-assurance *n syn* see CONFIDENCE 2
rel collectedness, coolness, imperturbability; composure, equanimity, sangfroid
con insecurity, uncertainness

self-assured *adj syn* see CONFIDENT 1
rel self-satisfied, smug

self-assuredness *n syn* see CONFIDENCE 2

self-centered *adj* **1** *syn* see SELF-SUFFICIENT
2 *syn* see EGOCENTRIC 2
idiom wrapped up in oneself

self-centeredness *n syn* see SELFISHNESS

self-command *n syn* see WILL 3
rel self-containment, uncommunicativeness

self-complacency *n syn* see CONCEIT 2

self-complacent *adj syn* see COMPLACENT

self-composed *adj syn* see CALM 2

self-conceit *n syn* see CONCEIT 2

self-conceited *adj syn* see VAIN 3

self-concern *n syn* see SELFISHNESS

self-concerned *adj syn* see EGOCENTRIC 2

self-confidence *n syn* see CONFIDENCE 2
rel sanguineness, sureness; cockiness, overconfidence
con diffidence, shyness; self-distrust; doubt, uneasiness
ant self-doubt

self-confident *adj syn* see CONFIDENT 1

self-conscious *adj* aware of the scrutiny of others to the point of not appearing natural or spontaneous <felt *self-conscious* about wearing platform shoes>
syn affected, conscious, mannered
rel self-aware; anxious, ill at ease, uncomfortable, uneasy; formal, stiff, stilted; artificial; ‖mim, prim; exhibitionist, flaunty, ostentatious
con unaware, unconcerned; blithe, easy; natural, spontaneous, unaffected

self-consequence *n syn* see CONCEIT 2

self-contained *adj syn* see SELF-SUFFICIENT

self-contemplation *n syn* see INTROSPECTION

self-contented *adj syn* see COMPLACENT

self-control *n syn* see WILL 3
rel constraint, reserve, self-containedness; balance, stability; dignity
idiom presence of mind
ant self-abandonment

self-criticism *n syn* see SELF-REPROACH

self-deceit *n syn* see SELF-DECEPTION

self-deception *n* the act or an instance of deceiving oneself or of being so deceived <to presume agreement where none exists is a dangerous form of *self-deception*>
syn self-deceit, self-delusion
rel misconception, misinterpretation, misunderstanding; deception, delusion, illusion
idiom kidding oneself

self-defense *n* an act, instance, or means of defending oneself, one's property, or a close relative <sought some measure of *self-defense* against society's lawless elements>

syn self-protection
rel self-preservation
self–delusion *n syn* see SELF-DECEPTION
self–denial *n syn* see RENUNCIATION
rel abstaining, abstemiousness, abstinence; asceticism, selflessness, self-sacrifice, self-sacrificing; self-forgetful, self-forgetting
ant self-indulgence
self–denying *adj syn* see SELF-SACRIFICING
self–dependence *n syn* see SELF-RELIANCE
self–destruction *n syn* see SUICIDE
self–discipline *n syn* see WILL 3
selfdom *n syn* see INDIVIDUALITY 4
self–educated *adj syn* see SELF-TAUGHT
self–effacing *adj syn* see SHY 1
self–esteem *n* **1** *syn* see PRIDE 2
rel self-content, self-contentment; self-satisfaction
con self-distrust, self-doubt; self-contempt
ant self-hate
2 *syn* see CONCEIT 2
rel self-flattery, self-glorification
con self-distrust, self-doubt; self-hate
ant self-contempt
self–evidencing *adj syn* see SELF-EVIDENT
self–evident *adj* evident in itself without need of argument or proof <*self-evident* truths>
syn prima facie, self-evidencing
rel clear, manifest, obvious, plain; unmistakable, unquestionable
con enigmatic, hidden, mysterious, obscure; doubtable, doubtful, questionable, uncertain
self–exaltation *n syn* see CONCEIT 2
self–examination *n syn* see INTROSPECTION
self–existent *adj* existing of or by itself and having no antecedent cause <argues backward to a first great cause, which is itself *self-existent*>
syn increase, self-existing, unbegotten, uncaused, uncreated, unoriginated
rel self-generated, self-originated, self-produced
con consequent, resultant, sequential
ant derivative
self–existing *adj syn* see SELF-EXISTENT
self–explaining *adj syn* see SELF-EXPLANATORY
self–explanatory *adj* capable of being understood without explanation <his actions are *self-explanatory:* he wants to resign>
syn self-explaining; *compare* CLEAR 5
rel clear, evident, obvious, manifest, plain; self-evident; comprehensible, understandable
con equivocal, obscure, uncertain, unclear, vague; complex; incomprehensible, mysterious; inexplicable, unexplainable
self–forgetful *adj syn* see SELFLESS
self–forgetting *adj syn* see SELFLESS
self–giving *adj syn* see SELF-SACRIFICING
self–glorifying *adj syn* see BOASTFUL
self–glory *n syn* see CONCEIT 2
rel self-aggrandizement, self-glorification
self–governing *adj syn* see DEMOCRATIC
self–government *n syn* see WILL 3
self–gratification *n* the act of pleasing oneself or of satisfying one's desires <human beings driven by unconscious forces toward *self-gratification*>

syn onanism, self-indulgence
rel self-abandonment; self-pleasing, self-satisfaction; autotheism, narcissism, self-worship
selfhood *n* **1** *syn* see INDIVIDUALITY 4
2 *syn* see SELFISHNESS
self–importance *n* **1** *syn* see CONCEIT 2
2 *syn* see EGOTISM 1
rel arrogance, pomposity
self–important *adj syn* see POMPOUS 1
self–imposed *adj* imposed by oneself or itself <insists on working under *self-imposed* handicaps>
syn self-inflicted
rel self-generated, self-produced
self–indulgence *n syn* see SELF-GRATIFICATION
rel indulgence; excess, intemperance, overindulgence
ant abstinence
self–indulgent *adj syn* see SYBARITIC
self–inflicted *adj syn* see SELF-IMPOSED
rel self-determined; accepted; voluntary
self–instructed *adj syn* see SELF-TAUGHT
self–interest *n syn* see SELFISHNESS
self–interested *adj syn* see EGOCENTRIC 2
self–involved *adj syn* see EGOCENTRIC 2
selfish *adj syn* see EGOCENTRIC 2
idiom ‖looking out for number one
con self-denying, selfless, self-sacrificing; altruistic, benevolent, charitable, generous, magnanimous
ant unselfish
selfishness *n* a concern for one's own welfare at the expense of or in disregard of others <his *selfishness* was consummate: he cared for no one but himself>
syn self-centeredness, self-concern, self-hood, self-interest, self-regard, self-seeking
rel egoism, egotism, self-absorption; self, self-ism, selfness; autotheism, self-worship
con self-denial, selflessness, self-sacrificing; benevolence, charity, generosity
ant unselfishness
self–knowledge *n* knowledge or understanding of one's own character, motivations, and capabilities <a poet whose verse reflected deep *self-knowledge* and honesty>
syn autognosis, self-understanding
rel self-awareness; introspection, self-examination, self-observation
selfless *adj* having no concern for oneself <*selfless* service to community, state, and nation>
syn self-forgetful, self-forgetting, unselfish
rel self-giving, self-sacrificing; self-renouncing; elevated, generous, high-minded, magnanimous
con self-devoted, self-loving, self-serving
ant self-centered, selfish
self–love *n syn* see CONCEIT 2
idiom the sixth insatiable sense
con self-abuse, self-accusation, self-reproach; self-forgetfulness, selflessness

---

syn synonym(s)   *rel* related word(s)
ant antonym(s)   *con* contrasted word(s)
idiom idiomatic equivalent(s)
‖ use limited; if in doubt, see a dictionary

ant self-hate

self–mastery *n syn* see WILL 3

self–murder *n syn* see SUICIDE

selfness *n syn* see INDIVIDUALITY 4

self–observation *n syn* see INTROSPECTION

self–opinion *n syn* see CONCEIT 2

self–pleased *adj syn* see COMPLACENT

self–possessed *adj syn* see CALM 2
   rel aloof, reserved; self-contained, self-controlled; self-assured

self–possession *n syn* see EQUANIMITY

self–pride *n syn* see CONCEIT 2

self–proclaimed *adj syn* see SELF-STYLED

self–protection *n syn* see SELF-DEFENSE

self–questioning *n syn* see INTROSPECTION

self–recrimination *n syn* see SELF-REPROACH

self–reflection *n syn* see INTROSPECTION

self–regard *n* **1** *syn* see SELFISHNESS
   2 *syn* see PRIDE 2

self–reliance *n* reliance on one's own resources, efforts, and ability <a strong people characterized by bravery and *self-reliance*>
   syn self-dependence
   rel confidence, self-assurance, self-confidence; self-sufficiency, self-support

self–renouncing *adj syn* see SELF-SACRIFICING

self–renunciation *n syn* see RENUNCIATION

self–reproach *n* an act or instance of reproaching oneself <experienced both guilt and *self-reproach* after the quarrel>
   syn self-abuse, self-accusation, self-criticism, self-recrimination, self-reproof
   rel contrition, regret, remorse; self-castigation, self-condemnation, self-flagellation, self-punishment; self-contempt
   con self-contentment, self-satisfaction; self-applause
   ant self-approbation

self–reproof *n syn* see SELF-REPROACH

self–respect *n syn* see PRIDE 2

self–restraining *adj syn* see ABSTEMIOUS

self–restraint *n syn* see WILL 3
   ant abandon

self–righteous *adj syn* see HYPOCRITICAL

self–ruling *adj syn* see DEMOCRATIC

self–sacrificing *adj* sacrificing or denying oneself for others <a *self-sacrificing* love>
   syn self-abnegating, self-denying, self-giving, self-renouncing
   rel selfless, unselfish; charitable, generous, kindly, philanthropic
   con self-centered, selfish, self-seeking

selfsame *adj syn* see SAME 1
   rel alike, like
   idiom (the) very same
   con different, unalike
   ant diverse

selfsameness *n syn* see IDENTITY
   ant diverseness

self–satisfied *adj syn* see COMPLACENT

self–scrutiny *n syn* see INTROSPECTION

self–searching *n syn* see INTROSPECTION

self–seeking *n syn* see SELFISHNESS

self–seeking *adj syn* see EGOCENTRIC 2

self–serving *adj syn* see EGOCENTRIC 2

self–slaughter *n syn* see SUICIDE

self–starter *n syn* see HUSTLER 1

self–styled *adj* given a specified designation or title by oneself often without justification <a department cluttered with *self-styled* experts>
   syn self-proclaimed, soi-disant
   rel self-appointed, self-created, self-given; so-called; quasi; would-be

self–sufficient *adj* maintaining or able to maintain oneself without outside aid <organisms are not *self-sufficient*, closed systems>
   syn closed, independent, self-centered, self-contained, self-sufficing, self-supported, self-supporting, self-sustained, self-sustaining
   rel self-dependent, self-reliant; self-subsistent, self-subsisting; individual, one-man, unit
   idiom one's own man, sufficient unto oneself (*or* itself)
   con dependent

self–sufficing *adj syn* see SELF-SUFFICIENT

self–supported *adj syn* see SELF-SUFFICIENT

self–supporting *adj syn* see SELF-SUFFICIENT

self–sustained *adj syn* see SELF-SUFFICIENT

self–sustaining *adj syn* see SELF-SUFFICIENT

self–taught *adj* having knowledge or skills acquired by one's own efforts without formal instruction <a *self-taught* painter>
   syn autodidactic, self-educated, self-instructed

self–trust *n syn* see CONFIDENCE 2

self–understanding *n syn* see SELF-KNOWLEDGE

self–violence *n syn* see SUICIDE

self–willed *adj syn* see OBSTINATE
   con weak, weak-willed, wishy-washy; spineless

sell *vb* **1** *syn* see BETRAY 2
   2 to give up (property) to another for money or other valuable consideration <can *sell* you the house now>
   syn give, market, vend
   ant buy, purchase
   3 to deal in or offer (articles) for sale on a regular basis <he *sells* small appliances>
   syn market, merchandise, retail
   rel barter, deal (in), exchange, trade, traffic; hawk, peddle; vend
   ant buy
   4 to command a specified price <that coat *sells* for $300>
   syn bring, bring in, fetch
   rel command, draw; realize, return, yield; gross, net

sell *n syn* see IMPOSTURE

sellable *adj syn* see MARKETABLE

sell off *vb syn* see SELL OUT 1

sell out *vb* **1** to dispose of entirely by selling <*sold out* his share of the business>
   syn close out, sell off, ‖sell up
   rel dump, move, unload; sacrifice
   2 *syn* see DECEIVE
   3 *syn* see BETRAY 2

‖**sell up** *vb syn* see SELL OUT 1

selvage *n syn* see BORDER 1

semblance *n* **1** *syn* see AIR 3
   rel aspect, look

2 *syn* see LIKENESS
3 *syn* see APPEARANCE 2
rel air, pose
4 *syn* see MASK 2

semblant *adj syn* see APPARENT 2

seminar *n syn* see CONFERENCE 2

semioccasional *adj syn* see INFREQUENT

sempiternal *adj syn* see INFINITE 1

sempiternity *n syn* see ETERNITY 1

send *vb* **1** to cause to go or be taken from one place, person, or condition to another <*send* a messenger to the bank> <his cold *sent* him to bed>
syn address, consign, dispatch, forward, remit, route, ship, transmit
rel allocate, assign, commit, delegate; advance, launch; expedite, rush
ant receive
2 *syn* see THRILL

senectitude *n syn* see OLD AGE

senescence *n syn* see OLD AGE

senile *adj* exhibiting the weakness and loss of mental faculties often associated with old age <a *senile* professor now unable to lecture coherently>
syn doddering, doddery, ‖doted, doting
rel aging, senescent; aged, ancient, old; enfeebled, feeble, weak; decrepit, doddered, shattered
idiom in one's second childhood

senility *n syn* see DOTAGE
rel decline; senescence

senior *n* **1** *syn* see OLDSTER
2 one older than another <he was her *senior* by eight years>
syn elder
ant junior
3 *syn* see SUPERIOR
con inferior, subordinate, underling

senior citizen *n syn* see OLDSTER

sensation *n* **1** the power to respond or an act of responding to stimuli <the stage of *sensation* precedes that of rational comprehension>
syn feeling, sense, sensibility, sensitivity
rel susceptibility; consciousness; sensitiveness, sensitivity; impression, perception, response
2 *syn* see WONDER 1
rel bomb, bombshell

sensational *adj* **1** *syn* see SENSORY
2 arousing or designed to arouse a quick, intense, and usually superficial emotional response <*sensational* crime reporting>
syn livid, lurid, sensationalistic, sensationist, sultry, tabloid
rel juicy, piquant, pungent; colored, extravagant; coarse, vulgar
con exact, factual; dignified, formal, proper, restrained
3 *syn* see NOTICEABLE
rel impressive, stunning
4 *syn* see MARVELOUS 2
rel boffo, crashing, rousing, slambang, smash, smashing, superfine

sensationalistic *adj syn* see SENSATIONAL 2

sensationist *adj syn* see SENSATIONAL 2

sensatory *adj syn* see SENSORY

sense *n* **1** *syn* see MEANING 1
rel gist, pith, substance; center, core, focus, nucleus
2 *syn* see SUBSTANCE 2
3 *syn* see SENSATION 1
rel awareness, cognizance; discernment, discrimination, penetration; appreciation; recognition
4 *usu* senses *pl syn* see WIT 2
rel consciousness
5 *syn* see INTELLIGENCE 1
6 ability to make intelligent choices and to reach intelligent conclusions or decisions <had enough *sense* to study something practical>
syn common sense, good sense, gumption, horse sense, judgment, wisdom
rel discretion, foresight, prudence; appreciation, comprehension, understanding; brains, intelligence, ‖smarts, wit
ant folly

sense *vb syn* see FEEL 3
rel anticipate; know, realize

senseless *adj* **1** *syn* see NUMB 1
rel oblivious, unaware; inanimate, wooden
2 *syn* see INSENSATE 1
3 *syn* see INSENSIBLE 2
4 *syn* see SIMPLE 3
rel irrational, surd
5 having no meaning <an ancient custom, now outdated and *senseless*>
syn insignificant, meaningless, pointless, purportless, unmeaning
rel purposeless; trivial, unimportant
idiom without rhyme or reason
con purposeful; important, meaning, meaningful, significant

senselessness *n syn* see FOOLISHNESS
rel illogicality, stupidity

sensibility *n syn* see SENSATION 1
rel discernment, discrimination, insight, keenness, penetration, responsiveness; affection, emotion, heart
con apathy, indifference, insensibleness, insentience, unfeelingness, unresponsiveness
ant insensibility

sensibilize *vb syn* see SENSITIZE

sensible *adj* **1** *syn* see MATERIAL 1
rel concrete, solid
con immaterial, insubstantial; unreal
2 *syn* see PERCEPTIBLE
rel imaginal, perceptual, sensational; weighable; evident, manifest, obvious, patent
con imperceptible; cloudy, unclear
ant insensible
3 *syn* see CONSIDERABLE 2
4 *syn* see SENTIENT 3
5 *syn* see AWARE

---

syn synonym(s)   *rel* related word(s)
ant antonym(s)   *con* contrasted word(s)
idiom idiomatic equivalent(s)
‖ use limited; if in doubt, see a dictionary

rel sensitive, susceptible; noting, observing, perceiving, remarking, seeing; appreciating, comprehending, understanding; intelligent, knowing
con anesthetic, insensate, insensitive
ant insensible
6 *syn* see RATIONAL
rel sensemaking
7 *syn* see WISE 2
rel rational, reasonable; down-to-earth, matter=of-fact
con unreasonable, unsound, unwise; asinine, fatuous
ant absurd, foolish

sensile *adj syn* see SENTIENT 3

sensitive *adj* **1** *syn* see SENTIENT 3
rel hypersensitive, supersensitive
con impervious, insensible, unfeeling, unimpressionable, unresponsive; wooden
ant insensitive, unsensitive
2 *syn* see EMOTIONAL 1
rel high-strung, irritable, nervous, tense; insultable, oversensitive, umbrageous; unstable
con impervious, insensate, insensible, unaffected, unemotional
ant insensitive, unsensitive
3 *syn* see ACUTE 3
rel perceiving, seeing; aware, cognizant, conscious; knowing, understanding
4 *syn* see LIABLE 2
rel affected, impressed, influenced; disposed, inclined, predisposed
ant insensitive
5 *syn* see DELICATE 7
6 *syn* see SENSORY

sensitivity *n syn* see SENSATION 1

sensitize *vb* to cause to become sensitive or more sensitive <*sensitizing* corporate officers to social and environmental problems>
syn sensibilize
rel animate, excite, quicken, sharpen, stimulate, whet
ant desensitize

sensorial *adj syn* see SENSORY

sensory *adj* of or relating to sensation or the senses <*sensory* perception>
syn sensational, sensatory, sensitive, sensorial, sensual
rel sensate; receptive

sensual *adj* **1** *syn* see SENSORY
2 *syn* see CARNAL 2
rel irreligious, unspiritual
3 *syn* see SENSUOUS
4 *syn* see MATERIALISTIC

sensualistic *adj syn* see SENSUOUS

sensuous *adj* producing or characterized by gratification of the senses <*sensuous* pleasures>
syn epicurean, luscious, lush, luxurious, sensual, sensualistic, voluptuous; *compare* CARNAL 2, SYBARITIC
rel bacchic, dionysiac, Dionysian, hedonistic, pleasure-loving, pleasure-seeking; self-indulgent, sybaritic; carnal, fleshly, fleshy
con ascetic, disciplined, restrained

sentence *vb* to decree the fate or punishment of one adjudged guilty, unworthy, or unfit <was *sentenced* to exile>
syn condemn, damn, doom, proscribe
rel adjudge, adjudicate, judge; ordain, rule; blame, denounce; penalize, punish; devote
idiom pass sentence on
con absolve, acquit, exculpate, exonerate, vindicate; discharge, free, liberate, release

sententious *adj syn* see EXPRESSIVE
rel aphoristic, concise, crisp, epigrammatic, piquant, pithy, terse

sentient *adj* **1** *syn* see AWARE
2 *syn* see EMOTIONAL 1
3 capable of receiving and of being readily affected by external stimuli <deeply disturbed in the most *sentient* reaches of her mind>
syn impressible, impressionable, responsive, sensible, sensile, sensitive, susceptible, susceptive
rel sensate; open, receptive, susceptive; reactive
con insensate; closed, unreceptive; unreactive

sentiment *n* **1** *syn* see LEANING 2
2 *syn* see OPINION
rel leaning, predilection, propensity; position, posture
idiom way of thinking
3 *syn* see FEELING 3
rel conception; sensation; emotionalism, sentimentality

sentimental *adj* unduly or affectedly emotional <*sentimental* love stories>
syn bathetic, drippy, gooey, lovey-dovey, maudlin, mawkish, moist, mushy, romantic, sappy, slushy, sobby, sobful, soft-boiled, ‖soppy, soupy, sticky, syrupy, tear-jerking
rel dreamy, misty-eyed, moonstruck, nostalgic, oversentimental; inane, insipid, jejune, namby=pamby, schoolgirlish, vapid; rosewater, saccharine, soft, sugar-candy, sugary, sweet; loving, tender; affectionate, demonstrative, effusive; gushing, gushy; passionate
con unaffectionate, undemonstrative; dispassionate, emotionless, unemotional, unresponsive; unfeeling, unloving; dry
ant unsentimental

sentinel *n syn* see GUARD 2

sentry *n syn* see GUARD 2

separate *vb* **1** to become or cause to become disunited or disjoined <forces that *separate* families>
syn break up, dichotomize, disjoin, disjoint, dissect, dissever, disunite, divide, divorce, part, rupture, sever, split (up), sunder, uncombine
rel alienate, discontinue, disunify, estrange; dislink, uncouple, unjoin, unlink; disaggregate, disassemble, disgregate, dispel, disperse, dissolve, scatter; detach, disengage, disrelate, dissociate; halve, quarter
con assemble, associate, blend, mingle, mix; connect, couple, join, link; unify, unite; agglutinate, bind, cement, fuse, weld
ant combine
2 *syn* see KNOW 4

3 syn see SORT 2
rel compartment, compartmentalize
4 syn see DISCHARGE 7
5 syn see ISOLATE
separate *adj* **1 syn** see SINGLE 2
rel distinctive, peculiar; detached, disconnected, disengaged
2 syn see FREE 1
3 syn see DISTINCT 1
rel free, independent
separately *adv* **syn** see APART 1
rel distinctly; solely
con conjointly, jointly
ant together
separateness *n* **syn** see SEGREGATION
ant togetherness
separation *n* **1** the act, process, or an instance of separating or of being separated <*separation* of church and state> <their *separation* was a sad occasion>
syn detachment, dissolution, disunion, division, divorce, divorcement, partition, rupture, split-up
rel disrelation, dissociation, disunity, parting, shedding; disconnection, disjointedness, disjointure; breakup, disjunction, dissection, sequestration; diffluence, dispersal; dichotomy, diremption, trichotomy
con combination; unification
ant union
2 syn see SEGREGATION
separatism *n* **syn** see SEGREGATION
separatist *n* **syn** see HERETIC
sepulcher *n* **syn** see GRAVE
sepulcher *vb* **1 syn** see ENTOMB 1
2 syn see BURY 1
sepulchral *adj* **1** of, relating to, or serving as a sepulcher or a memorial to the dead <*sepulchral* inscriptions>
syn mortuary, tumulary
rel exequial, funebrial, funeral, funerary, funereal
2 syn see HOLLOW 1
sepulture *n* **1 syn** see BURIAL 2
2 syn see GRAVE
sepulture *vb* **1 syn** see ENTOMB 1
2 syn see BURY 1
sequel *n* **1 syn** see SUCCESSION 2
2 syn see EFFECT 1
rel end, ending, termination; close, closing, finish, finishing
3 syn see EPILOGUE 2
rel continuation, development; aftermath, outcome, result
sequence *n* **1 syn** see SUCCESSION 2
rel arrangement, disposition, ordering; procession
2 syn see ORDER 3
rel classification, grouping; placement
3 syn see EFFECT 1
4 syn see ORDER 5
sequent *adj* **syn** see CONSECUTIVE
sequential *adj* **syn** see CONSECUTIVE
sequester *vb* **1 syn** see ISOLATE

2 syn see SECLUDE
rel hide, secrete
3 syn see APPROPRIATE 1
rel attach; impound; dispossess
sequestered *adj* **syn** see SECLUDED
rel sheltered; closeted
sequestration *n* **syn** see SECLUSION
rel retreat
sequitur *n* **syn** see INFERENCE 2
seraglio *n* **syn** see BROTHEL
sere *adj* **syn** see DRY 1
serene *adj* **syn** see CALM 2
rel noiseless, quiet, still; quiescent, resting; undisturbed
con agitated, disquieted, upset
serfage *n* **syn** see BONDAGE
serfdom *n* **syn** see BONDAGE
serial *adj* **syn** see CONSECUTIVE
series *n* **syn** see SUCCESSION 2
rel continuance, continuation, run; category, group, set; column, tier; gradation, scale
serious *adj* **1** not light or frivolous (as in disposition, appearance, or manner) <he was disturbed by her stern, *serious* look>
syn earnest, grave, no-nonsense, poker-faced, sedate, sober, sobersided, solemn, somber, staid, weighty
rel businesslike, ‖dern, determined, steady, steady-going; intent, serious-minded; contemplative, meditative, pensive, reflective, thoughtful; austere, severe, stern; humorless, unhumorous; grim
idiom serious as a judge
con flighty, ‖flip, flippant, frivolous, volatile; casual, easy, relaxed
ant light, unserious
2 expressing, involving, or characterized by seriousness or gravity (as of consequence) <a *serious* economic situation>
syn grave, heavy, severe, weighty
rel important, significant; sobering; unamusing, unfunny, unhumorous; grim
idiom no joke, no laughing matter
con inconsequential, insignificant, unimportant, unserious
ant trifling, trivial
3 syn see HARD 6
4 syn see GRAVE 3
rel menacing, threatening
seriously *adv* **1** in a serious manner <at last settled *seriously* to work>
syn actively, down, earnestly, for real
rel gravely, soberly, solemnly; intently; vigorously, zealously; determinedly, purposefully, resolutely; fervently, passionately
idiom all joking aside, in all seriousness, in earnest
con airily, casually, flippantly, lightly, unconcernedly; carelessly, haphazardly

---

syn synonym(s)   **rel** related word(s)
ant antonym(s)   **con** contrasted word(s)
idiom idiomatic equivalent(s)
‖ use limited; if in doubt, see a dictionary

2 to a serious extent <the cities are *seriously* overcrowded>
syn gravely, intensely, severely
rel decidedly, quite, very; dangerously; critically, deplorably, regrettably

serious–mindedness *n syn* see EARNESTNESS
rel thoughtfulness; sober-mindedness

seriousness *n syn* see EARNESTNESS
rel sedateness, sobriety, solemnity, staidness
con gaiety, jollity; lightness
ant flippancy, frivolity

sermon *n* a religious discourse delivered in public by a clergyman as part of a worship service <preached his first *sermon* on Sunday>
syn preach, preaching, preachment, sermonizing
rel preachification; sermonary, sermonology; sermonette; exhortation, harangue, lecture, tirade

sermonic *adj syn* see DIDACTIC

sermonize *vb* **1** *syn* see PREACH 1
2 *syn* see DISCOURSE 1
3 *syn* see MORALIZE

sermonizer *n syn* see CLERGYMAN

sermonizing *n syn* see SERMON

sermonizing *adj syn* see DIDACTIC

serpent *n syn* see DEVIL 1

serpentine *adj* **1** *syn* see FIENDISH
2 *syn* see WINDING
rel serpentiform, serpentile, serpentlike, snakelike; crooked, devious

serrate *adj* notched or toothed on the edge <jagged peaks and *serrate* ridges>
syn denticulate, saw-edged, sawtooth, saw-toothed, serrated, serried
rel indented, notched, scored, toothed; serrulate

serrated *adj syn* see SERRATE

serried *adj syn* see SERRATE

serve *vb* **1** *syn* see BENEFIT
2 *syn* see ACT 4
3 to prove adequate or sufficient <will not *serve* as a true translation >
syn do, suffice, suit
rel service; function, work; fit; satisfy; make
idiom fill the bill
4 *syn* see MINISTER (to)
5 to put in (a term of imprisonment) <*served* ten years for armed robbery>
syn do
rel put in, spend; undergo
idiom do a hitch (*or* stretch), serve (out) a sentence, serve time, ‖take a vacation
6 *syn* see ADVANCE 1
7 *syn* see TREAT 2

service *n* **1** the performance of military duty in wartime and especially in a combat zone <saw a year's *service* in Vietnam>
syn action, combat
rel active duty, duty; fighting
2 *syn* see FAVOR 4
3 *syn* see RITE 2
4 *syn* see USE 3

serviceability *n syn* see USE 3
rel serviceableness; durability

serviceable *adj* **1** *syn* see HELPFUL 1
ant unserviceable
2 *syn* see PRACTICAL 2
ant unserviceable

serviceman *n* **1** *syn* see SOLDIER
2 servicemen *pl syn* see TROOP 2

servile *adj* **1** *syn* see SUBSERVIENT 2
rel obedient, submissive; passive, unresisting; bootlicking, groveling, toadyish
con aggressive
ant authoritative
2 *syn* see BASE 3

servility *n syn* see BONDAGE

servitude *n syn* see BONDAGE
con freedom, independence

set *vb* **1** to position (something) in a specified place <*set* the lamp on the table>
syn establish, fix, lay, place, put, settle, stick
rel bestow, deposit, park; emplace, ensconce, install; affix, anchor, wedge
con displace, replace, supplant; remove, take (away); uproot
2 *syn* see DIRECT 2
idiom set one's sights on
3 *syn* see STATION
4 *syn* see DICTATE
rel designate, direct, instruct, specify, stipulate; establish; make, name
5 to put in order for a meal <she quickly *set* the table for dinner>
syn lay, spread
rel fix, prepare, ready; arrange
ant clear
6 *syn* see GAMBLE 1
7 *syn* see INCITE
‖**8** *syn* see SIT 1
9 *syn* see BELONG 1
10 *syn* see COAGULATE
11 *of a fowl* to incubate eggs by crouching upon them <a chicken house filled with hens *setting* on eggs>
syn brood, ‖clock, cover, sit
rel hatch, incubate; hover
12 *of a celestial body* to pass below the horizon <the sun *set* at seven o'clock>
syn decline, dip, go down, sink
rel descend, drop
con ascend, climb, come up
ant rise
13 *syn* see HARDEN 1
rel crystallize, granulate; fix

set (at) *vb syn* see ESTIMATE 1

set *adj* **1** *syn* see SITUATED
2 *syn* see DECIDED 2
3 *syn* see FIRM 4
rel confirmed, entrenched, established, inveterate, rooted, well-set, well-settled; prescribed, specified
4 *syn* see LITTLE 2
rel diehard, inflexible, obstinate, pigheaded, rigid, unbending, unyielding
5 *syn* see FAST 4
rel fastened; close; sound
6 *syn* see EXPRESS 2

7 *syn* see READY 1

set *n* **1 *syn*** see GIFT 2
  2 *syn* see BEARING 1
  3 *syn* see SCENE 1
  4 *syn* see GROUP 3
  rel assortment, gaggle; kit, pack
  5 a number of people having something (as habit, interest, occupation, or age) in common <the horsey *set* was gathered at the bar>
  syn bunch, circle, crowd, group, lot, push; *compare* CLIQUE
  rel clan, clique, crew, gang, mob; cénacle; camp, faction; company

set back *vb* *syn* see DELAY 1

setback *n* a checking of progress <loss of his fellowship was a serious *setback* to his education>
  syn backset, check, reversal, reverse; *compare* COMEDOWN
  rel delay, retardation, slowdown; hindrance, impediment, obstacle, stumbling block; disappointment; rebuff; defeat; regress, regression
  idiom reverse of fortune
  con advancement, forwarding, progressing

set down *vb* *syn* see ALIGHT

set off *vb* **1 *syn*** see COMPENSATE 1
  2 *syn* see MOBILIZE 1

set on *vb* *syn* see INCITE

set out *vb* **1 *syn*** see DESIGN 3
  2 *syn* see HEAD 3
  idiom set one's course for

setout *n* **1 *syn*** see COSTUME
  2 *syn* see BEGINNING

setting *n* *syn* see SCENE 1

setting–out *n* *syn* see DEPARTURE 1

settle *vb* **1 *syn*** see ENSCONCE 2
  2 *syn* see CALM
  rel assure, reassure
  ant unsettle
  3 *syn* see SET 1
  rel found, ground, lodge, seat
  con dislodge, unseat, uproot
  ant unsettle
  4 *syn* see DECIDE
  rel fix, seal
  idiom come to a decision (*or* conclusion), form a judgment, make a decision
  5 *syn* see NEGOTIATE 1
  rel mediate, reconcile, straighten (out)
  idiom bring to terms (*or* agreement)
  6 *syn* see CLEAR 5
  idiom settle the score, settle up (*or* square) accounts
  7 to put in order for final disposal <waiting to *settle* an estate>
  syn clean up, wind up
  8 *syn* see ALIGHT
  rel flop (down), plop (down)

settled *adj* **1 *syn*** see FIRM 4
  rel decided, determined
  con uncertain, undecided
  ant unsettled
  2 *syn* see INVETERATE 1
  3 *syn* see DECIDED 2
  rel certain, fixed

  con irresolute, undecided, undetermined, unresolved, vacillating, wavering
  ant unsettled

settlement *n* **1 *syn*** see HABITATION 1
  2 *syn* see DECISION 1
  rel showdown; quietus

settlings *n pl* *syn* see SEDIMENT

set to *vb* **1 *syn*** see BEGIN 1
  2 *syn* see PITCH IN 1

set–to *n* **1 *syn*** see BRAWL 2
  2 *syn* see QUARREL
  3 *syn* see ENCOUNTER

set up *vb* **1 *syn*** see ERECT 5
  ant tear down
  2 *syn* see ELATE
  3 *syn* see ERECT 3
  con disassemble, take down
  4 *syn* see FOUND 2
  rel generate, originate; start up; open
  5 *syn* see INTRODUCE 3
  6 *syn* see TREAT 3

setup *n* *syn* see SNAP 1

seventh heaven *n* *syn* see ECSTASY
  rel exhilaration; bliss, paradise
  con sadness, unhappiness; blues, doldrums, dumps

sever *vb* **1 *syn*** see SEPARATE 1
  2 *syn* see KNOW 4
  3 *syn* see CUT 5

several *adj* **1** possessed by or attributed to a specific individual <the debaters expressed their *several* opinions>
  syn individual, particular, respective, singular
  rel independent; personal, special, specific
  2 *syn* see DISTINCT 1
  3 consisting of an indefinite number more than two and less than many <*several* days passed>
  syn divers, some, sundry, various
  rel particular, separate, single; few; considerable; many, numerous
  idiom not a few
  ‖**4 *syn*** see MANY

‖**several** *pron* *syn* see SUNDRY

severalize *vb* *syn* see KNOW 4

severally *adv* *syn* see APART 1
  rel discretely; exclusively
  idiom one at a time

severe *adj* **1** given to or characterized by strict discipline and firm restraint <treated all the students with *severe* impartiality>
  syn ascetic, astringent, austere, mortified, stern
  rel exacting, heavy-handed, onerous, oppressive; disciplined, iron-willed, self-disciplined; inflexible, restrictive, rigid, rigorous, strict, stringent, uncompromising, unyielding
  con easy, easygoing, gentle, mild, soft; clement, forbearing, indulgent, lax, lenient, merciful
  ant tender, tolerant
  2 *syn* see GRIM 2

---

syn synonym(s)   *rel* related word(s)
ant antonym(s)   *con* contrasted word(s)
idiom idiomatic equivalent(s)
‖ use limited; if in doubt, see a dictionary

rel serious, sober, stern

3 of a kind to cause discomfort or hardship <a *severe* winter storm>
syn bitter, brutal, hard, harsh, inclement, intemperate, rigorous, rugged
rel crimpy, unpleasant; forbidding, hostile, inhospitable; bleak, disagreeable, grim; painful, raw, sharp, smart; blistering, extreme, intense, savage; blustering, blustery, stormy, wintry
con balmy, calm, equable, gentle, moderate, soft, temperate
ant mild

4 *syn* see HARD 6

5 *syn* see SERIOUS 2
rel consequential; dear, sore

severely *adv* **1** *syn* see HARD 5

2 *syn* see SERIOUSLY 2
rel markedly

‖**sew** *vb* *syn* see EXUDE

sew up *vb* ‖**1** *syn* see EXHAUST 4

2 *syn* see MONOPOLIZE

sexy *adj* *syn* see RISQUÉ

shabby *adj* **1** being ill-kept and showing signs of wear and tear <a *shabby* neighborhood full of depressing tenements>
syn bedraggled, broken-down, decrepit, dilapidated, dingy, disreputable, down-at-heel, faded, mangy, moth-eaten, run-down, scrubby, scruffy, seedy, shoddy, sleazy, slipshod, squalid, tacky, tagrag, tattered, threadbare, tired
rel disfigured, dog-eared; decaying, deteriorated, deteriorating; ramshackle, ratty, rickety; bare, miserable, neglected, poor, poverty=stricken; sordid; worm-eaten; outworn, worn=out; abandoned, desolate, ruined, ruinous, wrecked
idiom gone to seed
con neat, spick-and-span, tidy, trig, trim, well=kept; brand-new, fresh, new; unused
ant spruce

2 *syn* see CONTEMPTIBLE

3 *syn* see DISREPUTABLE 1

‖**shack** *n* *syn* see VAGABOND

shack *n* *syn* see HUT

shackle *n*, *usu* **shackles** *pl* something that confines the legs or arms so as to prevent free movement <slaves in *shackles*>
syn bond(s), chains, fetter(s), gyve(s), iron(s)
rel anklet, bilbo, leg-iron, trammel; bracelet, handcuff, manacle; straitjacket; collar, garrote

shackle *vb* *syn* see HAMPER
rel lash, rope, strap; chain, enchain, manacle; handcuff; pinion, secure
con unchain, unfetter, untie
ant unshackle

shade *n* **1** comparative darkness or obscurity due to interception of light rays <trees providing *shade* from the sunlight>
syn adumbration, penumbra, shadow, umbra, umbrage
rel blackness, darkness, dimness, obscuration, obscurity; cover, shelter
con brightness, brilliancy, effulgence, radiance; blaze, glare, glow

2 *syn* see APPARITION

3 *syn* see COLOR 1
rel intensity, saturation

4 *syn* see GRADATION
rel difference, distinction, variation

5 *syn* see HINT 2

shade *vb* to cast into shadow by intercepting light rays <avenues *shaded* by large trees>
syn inumbrate, screen, shadow, umbrage
rel shelter; cover
con roast, scorch, swelter; expose

shaded *adj* *syn* see SHADY 1
ant unshaded

shadow *n* **1** *syn* see SHADE 1

2 *syn* see APPARITION

3 *syn* see VESTIGE 1

4 *syn* see HINT 2

shadow *vb* **1** *syn* see SHADE

2 *syn* see OBSCURE

3 *syn* see TAIL

shadow (forth) *vb* **1** *syn* see SUGGEST 5

2 *syn* see ADUMBRATE 1
rel forecast, foretell, predict

shadow *adj* *syn* see SHADY 1

shadowed *adj* *syn* see SHADY 1
ant unshadowed

shadowy *adj* **1** *syn* see IMAGINARY 1

2 *syn* see GHASTLY 2

3 *syn* see FAINT 2
rel amorphous; foggy

4 *syn* see SHADY 1
ant bright

shady *adj* **1** producing, affording, or abounding in shade <a *shady* day> <cool, *shady* streets>
syn shaded, shadow, shadowed, shadowy, umbrageous, umbrous
rel bosky, screened, sheltered; dusky; dark
con exposed, unshaded, unshadowed; unsheltered; bright, light
ant sunny

2 *syn* see DOUBTFUL 1

3 *syn* see DISREPUTABLE 1
rel subreputable

4 *syn* see RISQUÉ
rel disreputable, shameful

shaft *n* **1** *syn* see RAY 1

2 a scornful, cutting, or pithily critical remark <the target of her latest *shaft* is the president himself>
syn barb, dart
rel cut, jab, thrust; potshot

shake *vb* **1** to move irregularly to and fro or up and down often in a wavering or oscillating manner <was so frightened that her hands *shook*>
syn ‖didder, dither, quake, quaver, quiver, shiver, shudder, tremble, tremor, twitter
rel palpitate, quail, waver; flicker, flit, flitter, flutter; fluctuate, oscillate; chatter, shimmy, vibrate
idiom shake like an aspen leaf

2 to undergo strong vibration especially as the result of a physical blow or shock <the platform *shook* as the train passed>
syn jar, quake, tremble, tremor, vibrate

rel bounce, jounce; chatter, quiver, shimmy; rock, stagger

3 to cause to move in a quick, jerky manner <rattling and *shaking* the latch>
syn jiggle, joggle
rel bounce, ‖chounse, jounce; jostle; rattle; jerk
4 to cause to move to and fro or up and down violently <an earthquake that *shook* the whole coast>
syn agitate, concuss, convulse, rock
rel jog, jostle, rattle, ‖shog; commove, discompose, disorder, jar, jolt, unsettle; disquiet, disturb, perturb, upset; churn, roil, ruffle, stir up, whip
5 to get or keep away from (a pursuer) <tried unsuccessfully to *shake* the man tailing him>
syn lose, slip, throw off; *compare* ESCAPE 2
rel avoid, elude; outwit
idiom get rid of, give (someone) the shake (or slip), slip from under the eye of
6 *syn* see DISMAY 1
rel disturb, jar, rattle, unsettle, upset; bother, worry; unnerve, unstring
shake (off) *vb syn* see RID
shake *n* **1** *syn* see EARTHQUAKE
2 shakes *pl syn* see JITTERS
3 *syn* see INSTANT 1
4 *syn* see DEAL 2
shake down *vb* **1** *syn* see EXTORT 1
2 *syn* see SEARCH 2
shake up *vb syn* see SPEED 3
shake–up *n* an extensive and often drastic rearrangement <a personnel *shake-up* effected by new management>
syn overturn, reorganization, revolution, turn-over
rel liquidation, purge; cleanout, cleanup, clearing out, clear-up; removal, riddance
idiom break with the past, clean sweep
shakiness *n syn* see INSTABILITY
shaking *adj syn* see TREMULOUS
rel unsettled, unstable, unsteady; tottering
con unshakable, unshaken
shaky *adj* **1** *syn* see WEAK 2
rel unsettled; infirm, unsound, unsteady; precarious, tottering, tottery
2 *syn* see DOUBTFUL 1
3 *syn* see TREMULOUS
4 *syn* see RICKETY
shallow *adj* **1** lacking physical depth <buried in a *shallow* grave>
syn shoal, superficial
rel shallowish; surface
idiom as deep as a mud puddle, no deeper than a heavy dew, not deep enough to float a match
con bottomless, unfathomable
ant deep
2 *syn* see SUPERFICIAL 2
rel paltry, petty, trifling, trivial; empty, hollow, idle, vain; bird-witted, featherbrained, flighty
con heavy, profound; discerning, penetrating
ant deep
shallow *n syn* see SHOAL
ant deep

sham *n* **1** *syn* see IMPOSTURE
rel facade, fakery, false front, Potemkin village
2 *syn* see HYPOCRISY
3 *syn* see MOCKERY 2
sham *vb syn* see ASSUME 4
rel ape, copy, imitate, mock; create, invent; lie, mislead
sham *adj* **1** *syn* see FICTITIOUS 2
rel affected, assumed, feigned; pseudo, so-called; make-believe, pretend
2 *syn* see COUNTERFEIT
3 *syn* see ARTIFICIAL 2
rel plaster, synthetic; adulterated; bogus
shamble *vb syn* see SHUFFLE 3
shambles *n pl but usu sing in constr syn* see MESS 3
shame *n syn* see DISGRACE
rel chagrin, embarrassment; guilt, mortification, self-reproach, self-reproof
con pride, self-admiration, self-love, self-respect
ant glory
shamed *adj syn* see ASHAMED
rel crestfallen; shamefaced, shamefast; crushed, disgraced
idiom loaded (or bowed down) with shame
ant proud
shameful *adj syn* see DISREPUTABLE 1
shameless *adj* characterized by or exhibiting boldness and a lack of shame <a *shameless* hussy>
syn arrant, barefaced, blatant, brassy, brazen, brazenfaced, impudent, overbold, unabashed, unblushing
rel audacious, bold, cheeky, presumptuous; baldfaced, high-handed; abandoned, dissolute, profligate; immodest, lewd; disgraceful, outrageous
idiom bold as brass, dead (or lost) to shame
con bashful, diffident, mousy, shy; chaste, decent, modest, pure
‖shamus *n syn* see PRIVATE DETECTIVE
Shangri–la *n syn* see UTOPIA
shanty *n syn* see HUT
shape *vb syn* see MAKE 3
rel devise, plan, work up; tailor
shape *n* **1** *syn* see FORM 1
rel appearance, aspect, look, semblance
2 *syn* see ORDER 9
3 *syn* see ORDER 10
rel state, whack
shapeful *adj syn* see SHAPELY
ant shapeless
shapeless *adj syn* see FORMLESS
rel unshapely; deformed, misshapen
con proportional, proportionate, proportioned, shapeful, symmetrical
ant shapeful, shapely
shapely *adj* having a regular or pleasing shape <a *shapely* girl>

---

syn synonym(s)   *rel* related word(s)
ant antonym(s)   *con* contrasted word(s)
idiom idiomatic equivalent(s)
‖ use limited; if in doubt, see a dictionary

syn clean-limbed, shapeful, statuesque, trim, well-proportioned, well-turned; *compare* CURVA-CEOUS

rel balanced, clean-cut, proportioned, regular, symmetrical; comely, pleasing; ‖built, full-figured, rounded, ‖stacked; buxom

con dumpy, squat, stumpy; angular, lank, lean; ill-favored, ill-looking

ant shapeless, unshapely

share *n* **1** something belonging to, assumed by, or falling to one (as in division or apportionment) <wanted his *share* of the prize money>

syn allotment, allowance, bite, cut, lot, part, partage, portion, quota, slice; *compare* RATION

rel proportion, quotient, quotum; commission, percentage; divide, ‖divvy; rake-off

idiom piece of the action, slice of the melon

2 *syn* see RATION

3 *syn* see INTEREST 1

share *vb* **1** *syn* see APPORTION 2

rel assign, deal (out), dispense, dole (out), give out, mete (out)

idiom ‖go snucks, share and share alike

con retain, withhold; combine, unite

2 to have, get, or use in common with another or others <she *shared* her husband's fate>

syn partake, participate

rel experience

idiom have a share (*or* part) in, have (*or* take) a hand in

shared *adj* *syn* see COMMON 1

ant unshared

share out *vb* *syn* see ADMINISTER 2

sharer *n* *syn* see PARTICIPANT

sharp *adj* **1** having a fine edge <a *sharp* knife makes a clean cut>

syn honed, keen, razor-sharp, unblunted, whetted

rel acute

idiom sharp as a razor blade

con blunted, dulled; unsharpened

ant blunt, dull

2 *syn* see POINTED 1

3 *syn* see INTELLIGENT 2

4 possessing or indicative of alert competence and clear understanding <people of *sharp* judgment and refined sensibilities>

syn acute, keen, penetrating, penetrative, quick-sighted, quick-witted, sharp-sighted, sharp-witted; *compare* SHREWD

rel alert, bright; clever, cute, ingenious, original, resourceful; fast, quick

idiom sharp as a knife (*or* tack)

con dull-witted; unintelligent; foolish, simple, slow, stupid

ant dull

5 *syn* see ACUTE 3

6 *syn* see WISE 4

rel adroit, nimble; clever, cute; sly, unethical

idiom nobody's fool

7 *syn* see SHORT 5

rel acrimonious, biting, double-edged, incisive, penetrating, piercing, stabbing, stinging; caustic, virulent, vitriolic

8 causing intense mental or physical distress <a *sharp* pain>

syn acute, knifelike, piercing, shooting, stabbing

rel intense, severe, smart; biting, drilling, stinging; penetrating; agonizing, excruciating; paralyzing

9 *syn* see ACRID

rel odorous; strong-scented, strong-smelling; suffocating

10 *syn* see ACUTE 4

11 *syn* see STYLISH

‖**sharp** *vb* *syn* see SHARPEN

sharp *adv* *syn* see JUST 1

sharpen *vb* to give a keen edge to <*sharpen* an ax>

syn edge, hone, ‖sharp, whet

rel dress, file, grind, stroke

idiom hone to a razor edge, hone to razor sharpness

ant blunt, dull

sharper *n* *syn* see SWINDLER

sharp–eyed *adj* having keen vision <the *sharp-eyed* child found all the Easter eggs>

syn eagle-eyed, hawk-eyed, lyncean, lynx-eyed, sharp-sighted

rel alert, attentive, aware, keen, lynxlike, observant, sharp, vigilant, watchful

con myopic, nearsighted, shortsighted; dim-sighted, purblind; blind

sharpie *n* *syn* see SWINDLER

sharply *adv* *syn* see HARD 4

rel intensely, penetratingly, piercingly

sharpness *n* *syn* see EDGE 2

ant bluntness, dullness

sharp practice *n* *syn* see DECEPTION 1

sharp–sighted *adj* **1** *syn* see SHARP-EYED

2 *syn* see SHARP 4

sharp–witted *adj* **1** *syn* see SHARP 4

2 *syn* see WISE 4

shatter *vb* **1** to break into small pieces by or as if by a blow <*shatter* a windowpane with a rock>

syn burst, fragment, ‖pash, rive, shiver, smash, ‖smatter, splinter, splinterize, splitter; *compare* PULVERIZE 1

rel break, crack, rend, snap, ‖spalt, split; crunch, crush; crash, dash; fragmentalize, fragmentize, pulverize; demolish, destroy, disintegrate, ruin, ‖total, wreck

idiom smash to smithereens (*or* bits)

2 *syn* see DESTROY 1

3 *syn* see RATTLE 1

shatterable *adj* *syn* see FRAGILE 1

ant shatterproof

shatterbrain *n* *syn* see SCATTERBRAIN

shattering *adj* *syn* see DESTRUCTIVE

shattery *adj* *syn* see FRAGILE 1

idiom as delicate as an eggshell

shave *vb* **1** *syn* see SLIVER

2 *syn* see CUT 6

rel shingle

3 *syn* see REDUCE 2

4 *syn* see BRUSH

idiom cut (*or* shave) it close

5 *syn* see SCRAPE 3

shaveling *n syn* see BOY 1

she *n syn* see WOMAN 1

shear *vb syn* see CUT 6
rel mow; barb, barber; manicure, snip

sheath *n syn* see SKIN 3

sheathe *vb* to cover (a surface) with something that protects <a house *sheathed* with aluminum siding>
syn clad, face, side, skin
rel envelop, surround, wrap; case, cover, encase, jacket; panel
con bare, expose, strip

sheathing *n syn* see SKIN 3

shed *vb* **1** *syn* see DISCARD
rel drop; divest
2 to cast off (a body covering) in a periodic process of growth or renewal <a snake *shedding* its skin>
syn exuviate, molt, slip, slough
rel cast off, discard; doff, take off

sheen *n syn* see LUSTER
rel finish; shininess

sheeny *adj syn* see LUSTROUS 1

sheepheaded *adj syn* see SIMPLE 3

sheer *adj* **1** *syn* see FILMY
rel airy, chiffon, thin; see-through
2 *syn* see UTTER
3 *syn* see PURE 2
rel arrant, bald-faced, complete, outright
4 *syn* see STEEP 1

sheer *vb* **1** *syn* see TURN 6
2 *syn* see SWERVE 1

‖**shekels** *n pl syn* see MONEY

shell *n syn* see HULL

shell *vb* **1** *syn* see SHUCK
2 *syn* see BOMBARD
rel pepper; rake
idiom open fire on

shellac *vb syn* see WHIP 2

shellacking *n syn* see DEFEAT 1
rel ‖clobbering, whipping

shell out *vb syn* see SPEND 1

shelter *n* **1** something (as a structure or place) that covers or affords protection <a bomb *shelter*>
syn asylum, cover, covert, harbor, harborage, haven, port, refuge, retreat, sanctuary; *compare* REFUGE 1
rel buen retiro, den, hermitage, hide, hideaway, hideout, hidey-hole, retirement, tower
2 dwellings provided for numbers of people or for a community <*shelter* for the aged>
syn housing, quarterage
rel dwellings, lodging; roof
3 *syn* see REFUGE 1

shelter *vb syn* see HARBOR 1

shelve *vb syn* see DEFER
rel dish, drop; give up
idiom put on the shelf

shenanigan *n* **1** *syn* see TRICK 1
rel fast one, game, legerdemain
2 *syn* see PRANK
rel frolic; goings-on, mischievousness; stunt

Sheol *n syn* see HELL

shepherd *vb syn* see GUIDE

Sherlock *n syn* see DETECTIVE

Sherlock Holmes *n syn* see DETECTIVE

shibboleth *n* **1** *syn* see CATCHWORD
rel platitude, truism
2 *syn* see COMMONPLACE

‖**shick** *adj syn* see INTOXICATED 1

‖**shicker** *adj syn* see INTOXICATED 1

‖**shicker** *n syn* see DRUNKARD

shield *n syn* see DEFENSE 1
rel buffer, bumper, screen

shield *vb* **1** *syn* see HARBOR 1
idiom give cover (*or* shelter) to; take (*or* shield) under one's wing
ant expose
2 *syn* see DEFEND 1

shift *vb* ‖**1** *syn* see APPORTION 2
2 *syn* see CHANGE 5
3 *syn* see MOVE 4
rel alter, change, vary; budge, stir; shuffle; relocate
idiom shift place
4 *syn* see CONSUME 5
5 to carry on one's affairs independently and self-sufficiently often under difficult circumstances <after the divorce, she was forced to *shift* for herself>
syn do, fare, get along, get by, get on, ‖make out, manage, muddle through, stagger (on *or* along)
rel contrive, survive; freelance; progress, succeed
idiom fend for oneself, make do, make it alone, make shift, paddle one's own canoe, stand on one's own two feet

shift *n* **1** *syn* see CONVERSION 2
2 *syn* see RESOURCE 3
rel gambit, maneuver, ploy, strategy
3 *syn* see SPELL 1
4 *syn* see TRANSITION
5 *syn* see TURN 2

shifty *adj* **1** *syn* see EVASIVE 1
rel dodging, elusive; cagey, collusive, conniving, crafty, cunning; furtive, shifty-eyed, sneaky, tricky; insidious, shady; deceitful, dishonest, fraudulent; treacherous
idiom shifty as the sand
2 *syn* see DISHONEST
3 *syn* see UNDERHAND
4 *syn* see MUTABLE 2

shill *n syn* see DECOY 2

shillaber *n syn* see DECOY 2

‖**shillelagh** *n syn* see CUDGEL

shilling shocker *n syn* see DIME NOVEL

shilly-shally *adj syn* see VACILLATING 2

shilly-shally *n syn* see HESITATION

shilly-shally *vb syn* see HESITATE

shilly-shallying *adj syn* see VACILLATING 2
rel halfhearted, lukewarm

shimmer *vb syn* see FLASH 1

---

syn synonym(s)   *rel* related word(s)
ant antonym(s)   *con* contrasted word(s)
idiom idiomatic equivalent(s)
‖ use limited; if in doubt, see a dictionary

shimmer *n syn* see FLASH 1
  rel blinking; spangle; spark, sparking
shin *vb syn* see RUN 1
shindig *n* **1** a large, festive, and often overly lavish party <threw the *shindig* of the year for the author>
  syn bash, ‖blowout, shindy
  rel fête, gala; ball, dance; blast, party; affair, shebang; ‖shivoo
  2 *syn* see COMMOTION 3
shindy *n* **1** *syn* see SHINDIG 1
  2 *syn* see COMMOTION 3
shine *vb* **1** to emit rays of light <the storm is over and the sun is *shining*>
  syn beam, burn, gleam, radiate
  rel glimmer, glow; incandesce, luminesce; flash, sparkle, twinkle; flare; glare
  2 *syn* see POLISH 1
shine *n* **1** *syn* see DISPLAY 2
  2 *syn* see LUSTER
  rel finish
  3 *usu* **shines** *pl syn* see PRANK
shiner *n syn* see BLACK EYE 1
shingle *vb syn* see OVERLAP
shining *adj syn* see LUSTROUS 1
shiny *adj syn* see LUSTROUS 1
ship *vb* **1** *syn* see SEND 1
  rel direct; freight; export
  ant receive
  2 *syn* see MOVE 4
shipshape *adj syn* see NEAT 2
shipwreck *vb* **1** to destroy, disable, or seriously damage a ship (as by running aground or causing to founder) <the typhoon *shipwrecked* the entire fishing fleet>
  syn beach, cast away, pile up, strand, wreck
  rel break up; scuttle; founder; capsize; go down, sink
  idiom go aground, go to the bottom (*or* Davy Jones's locker), run on the rocks
  2 *syn* see RUIN 2
shirk *vb* **1** *syn* see SNEAK
  2 *syn* see DODGE 1
  rel bilk, burke; bypass, double, eschew, get around; shuffle off, shun
shirker *n syn* see SLACKER
shirty *adj syn* see ANGRY
shivaree *n* a noisy mock serenade to a newly married couple <*shivarees* and other such disappearing rural customs>
  syn ‖belling, ‖bull band, ‖callithump, charivari, ‖horning, ‖riding, ‖skimmelton
  rel entertainment, reception, welcome
shiver *vb syn* see SHATTER 1
shiver *vb syn* see SHAKE 1
‖shivereens *n pl syn* see SMITHEREENS
shivering *adj syn* see TREMULOUS
shivers *n pl syn* see JITTERS
shivery *adj* **1** *syn* see TREMULOUS
  2 *syn* see COLD 1
shoal *adj syn* see SHALLOW 1
shoal *n* a place where a body of water (as a sea or river) is not deep <dangerous *shoals* in uncharted waters>

  syn shallow
  rel barrier, barrier reef, coral reef, fringing reef, reef, sand reef; bank, bar, sandbank, sandbar, tombolo; hook, spit; seamount
  con abyss, deep, depth
shock *n syn* see PILE 1
shock *n* **1** *syn* see IMPACT 1
  2 *syn* see EARTHQUAKE
  3 *syn* see TRAUMA
  rel prostration, stupefaction
shock *vb* **1** to offend the moral sense of <were *shocked* by pornography>
  syn scandalize
  rel astonish, astound, startle, surprise; jar, jolt, shake up; insult, offend, outrage; appall, horrify; floor, knock out; disgust, nauseate, sicken
  idiom stink in one's nostrils, turn one's stomach
  2 to cause to undergo a physical or psychological shock <his slap *shocked* her out of hysterics>
  syn jolt, startle
  rel shake; jar; electrify
shocked *adj syn* see AGHAST 2
  rel jarred, jolted, shaken up, ‖shook up; offended, outraged; appalled, horrified
shocker *n* **1** *syn* see THRILLER
  2 *syn* see DIME NOVEL
shocking *adj* **1** *syn* see FEARFUL 3
  rel heinous, monstrous
  2 *syn* see OUTRAGEOUS 2
  rel burning, glaring; disgraceful, shameful; unspeakable
shoddy *adj* **1** *syn* see CHEAP 2
  rel makeshift, scambling
  2 *syn* see SHABBY 1
  3 *syn* see DISREPUTABLE 1
shoeless *adj syn* see BAREFOOT 1
  ant shod
shoestring *adj syn* see LITTLE 3
‖shog *vb syn* see PUSH 2
shoo–in *n syn* see SURE THING
‖shool *vb syn* see SHUFFLE
shoot *vb* **1** to cause (a weapon) to drive a projectile forward <*shoot* an arrow at a target>
  syn discharge, fire, loose
  rel trigger; launch, project; expel; blast; poop
  idiom let fly
  2 *syn* see DESTROY 1
  3 *syn* see DISCREDIT 2
  ‖4 *syn* see DISCARD
  5 *syn* see VOMIT
  ‖6 *syn* see PASS 9
  7 *syn* see SHOOT UP 2
  8 *syn* see FLY 1
  9 *syn* see RUSH 1
  rel gallop, highball, hotfoot; spurt
  10 *syn* see PHOTOGRAPH
shoot *n syn* see RAY 1
shooting *adj syn* see SHARP 8
  ant stationary
shooting match *n syn* see AFFAIR 1
shoot up *vb* **1** *syn* see SKYROCKET
  2 to take (a drug) by hypodermic needle <had been *shooting up* heroin for weeks>
  syn ‖mainline, shoot

shop *n syn* see STORE 4
rel boutique

shoplift *vb* to steal displayed goods from a store <the manager caught them *shoplifting* records>
syn ‖boost
rel bag, cop, ‖nick, palm, pilfer, pinch, rip off, snitch, swipe

shopworn *adj syn* see TRITE
rel overused, overworked, overworn

shore *n* the land bordering a usually large body of water <watched the ships while walking along the *shore*>
syn bank, beach, coast, strand
rel coastline, shoreline, waterfront, waterside; coastland, seacoast, seashore; foreshore, littoral, shoreface, shoreside; brink, embankment, riverbank, riverside

shore (up) *vb syn* see SUPPORT 4

shore *n syn* see SUPPORT 3

short *adj* **1** having little length in space or time <a *short* visit>
syn brief
rel abbreviate, abbreviated, abridged, curtailed, decreased, diminished, lessened, shortened; curtate, decurtate
con extensive, lengthy; drawn-out, overlong; extended, prolonged, protracted
ant long
2 having small physical stature <he was the *shortest* boy present>
syn ‖low, low-set, low-statured
rel chunky, dumpy, squat, squatty, stubby, thick, thickset
con gangling, gangly, lanky, rangy; elevated, high, lofty, spiring, towering
ant tall
3 not coming up to a measure or need <fuel was very *short* that year>
syn deficient, failing, inadequate, insufficient, scant, scanty, scarce, scrimpy, shy, skimpy, slender, unsufficient, wanting; *compare* MEAGER 2
rel lacking, needing; exiguous, meager, sparse
con abounding, overflowing, teeming; abundant, ample, copious, plenteous, plentiful
ant long
4 *syn* see BLUFF
ant expansive
5 lacking in graciousness or consideration <her manner was *short* and abrupt>
syn inconsiderate, sharp, thoughtless, unceremonious, ungracious
rel bluff, blunt, brusque, crusty, curt; short-spoken; gruff, irascible
con considerate, gracious, kindly; bland, smooth; ceremonious
6 readily breaking or crumbling <a rich *short* pastry>
syn brittle, crisp, crumbly, ‖crump, crunchy, friable
rel delicate, fragile
con soggy, tough
7 *syn* see CONCISE
rel compact; pointed
idiom to the point

con extended, protracted, spun-out
ant lengthy, long-drawn-out

short *adv* **1** without hesitation or delay <stopped *short*>
syn abruptly, asudden, forthwith, sudden, suddenly
con hesitantly; gradually, slowly
2 *syn* see UNAWARES

short *n syn* see SUBSTANCE 2

short *vb syn* see SPARE 3

shortage *n syn* see FAILURE 3
rel curtailment, pinch, tightness; shortfall
ant overage

short and sweet *adj syn* see CONCISE

shortcoming *n syn* see IMPERFECTION
idiom weak point
con forte, long suit

shortcut *n* a route shorter or more direct than the one ordinarily taken <they took a *shortcut* down the back roads>
syn cutoff
rel bypass
ant detour

shorten *vb* to reduce in extent (as of length or duration) <decided to *shorten* their visit> <*shorten* a skirt for summer wear>
syn abbreviate, abridge, curtail, cut, cut back, retrench, slash
rel decrease, diminish, elide, excerpt, lessen, reduce; compress, condense, contract, shrink; bobtail, clip, dock; minimize
idiom cut short
con draw out, protract
ant elongate; lengthen; extend, prolong

shorthanded *adj* short of the necessary number of people <the office was critically *shorthanded*>
syn underhanded, undermanned, understaffed
rel short, wanting
con overmanned, overstaffed

short–lived *adj syn* see TRANSIENT
rel short-haul, short-run, short-term
con long-run, long-term
ant agelong; long-lived

shortly *adv* **1** *syn* see BRIEFLY
2 *syn* see PRESENTLY 1
rel pronto, quickly

short–range *adj syn* see TACTICAL 1
ant long-range

shortsighted *adj syn* see MYOPIC
ant farsighted, longsighted

short–spoken *adj syn* see BLUFF
ant windy

shot *n* **1** *syn* see FLING 1
2 *syn* see OPPORTUNITY
3 *syn* see DRAM

‖**shot** *adj syn* see INTOXICATED 1

shotgun *vb syn* see FORCE 2

should *vb syn* see WANT 3

shoulder *vb syn* see PUSH 2

---

syn synonym(s)   *rel* related word(s)
ant antonym(s)   *con* contrasted word(s)
idiom idiomatic equivalent(s)
‖ use limited; if in doubt, see a dictionary

shout *vb* **1** to utter a sudden loud cry (as to express joy or triumph or to attract attention) <the mob *shouted* for a speech>
syn cry, whoop, yell; *compare* CALL 1, SCREAM 1
rel exclaim; howl, scream, shriek; bawl, bellow, clamor, roar, vociferate
con murmur, whisper
2 *syn* see SCREAM 4
3 *syn* see CALL 1
rel bark; bray
4 *syn* see TREAT 3
shove *vb* **1** *syn* see PUSH 1
rel cram, jam; dig, jab, poke, prod
idiom push and shove
2 *syn* see PUSH 2
3 *syn* see PUSH 6
shove (off) *vb* *syn* see GO 2
ant pull in
shovel *vb* **1** *syn* see DIG 1
2 *syn* see DIG 2
shovel *vb* *syn* see SHUFFLE
show *vb* **1** to set out or place on view for customers <we're *showing* lots of long dresses this fall>
syn display, offer
rel afford, supply; exhibit; present, proffer, submit; deal (in), sell
2 to reveal outwardly or make apparent <asked a question or two to *show* his intelligence>
syn demonstrate, evidence, evince, exhibit, illustrate, manifest, mark, ostend, proclaim; *compare* LOOK 4
rel disclose, discover, divulge, lay out, reveal, unveil; present, project
con camouflage, conceal, dissemble, hide, obscure
ant disguise
3 *syn* see STAGE
4 to present in such a way as to invite notice, attention, and admiration <she loved to *show* her jewels to everyone>
syn brandish, display, disport, exhibit, expose, flash, flaunt, parade, show off, trot out
rel air, lay out, set out, spread; blazon, flourish, sport, vaunt
con belittle, deprecate, depreciate, minimize
5 to give an exact and usually automatic reading or indication of <the speedometer *shows* 70 MPH>
syn indicate, mark, read, record, register, say
rel point (to); ring up
6 *syn* see LOOK 4
rel lay out, reveal, unveil
7 *syn* see GUIDE
8 *syn* see ESTABLISH 6
rel present; plead; allege
9 *syn* see APPEAR 1
rel come, show up; materialize
10 *syn* see COME 1
idiom ‖make the scene, put in an appearance, show one's face
11 *syn* see TURN UP 3
show *n* *syn* see APPEARANCE 2
rel likeness; effect, impression
idiom outward show

2 *syn* see MASK 2
3 *syn* see DISPLAY 2
4 *syn* see OPPORTUNITY
5 *syn* see EXHIBITION 1
6 *syn* see EXHIBITION 2
7 *syn* see MOVIE
8 *syn* see SHOWING 1
shower *n* *syn* see BARRAGE
rel shatter, spatter, spray
shower *vb* *syn* see BATHE 1
showing *n* **1** performance in a test of skill, power, or effectiveness <he made a good *showing* in the race>
syn out, show
rel record
2 *syn* see APPEARANCE 2
show–me *adj* *syn* see INCREDULOUS
show off *vb* *syn* see SHOW 4
rel boast, brag, swagger
showpiece *n* a prime or outstanding example used or suitable for exhibition <a Fabergé Easter egg was the *showpiece* of the collection>
syn chef d'oeuvre, masterpiece, pièce de résistance
rel gem, jewel; prize
con claptrap, rubbish, trash, trivia, truck
showroom *n* *syn* see STORE 4
show up *vb* *syn* see EXPOSE 4
rel discredit; invalidate
2 *syn* see TURN UP 3
3 *syn* see COME 1
showy *adj* given to or marked by excessive outward display <*showy* decorations>
syn chichi, flamboyant, orchidaceous, ostentatious, peacockish, peacocky, pretentious, splashy, swank
rel sporty; flashy, garish, gaudy, jazzy, meretricious, tawdry; gorgeous, resplendent; luxurious, opulent, ornate, sumptuous; overdone, overwrought; sensational
con muted, quiet, restrained, subdued; elegant, graceful, restrained; appropriate, seemly
ant unshowy
shred *n* *syn* see PARTICLE
shred *vb* *syn* see SLIVER
shreddy *adj* *syn* see RAGGED
shrew *n* *syn* see VIRAGO
rel she-devil, spitfire
shrewd *adj* marked by clever discerning awareness and hardheaded acumen <the captain was a *shrewd* judge of character>
syn argute, astucious, astute, cagey, heady, perspicacious, sagacious, ‖savvy; *compare* SHARP 4, WISE 2, 4
rel canny, crafty, foxy, ingenious, ‖pawky, slick, ‖sly, tidy; clever, intelligent, knowing, quick-witted, smart; polite, smooth; judicious, prudent, sensible, wise; penetrating, piercing, probing; acute, keen, sharp; farsighted, foresighted
con green, naive, simple, soft; foolable, gullible, slow
shrewdness *n* *syn* see WIT 3
rel canniness, foxiness
shriek *vb* **1** *syn* see SCREAM 1

rel squawk, ‖yarm
2 *syn* see SQUEAL 2
3 *syn* see SCREAM 4
shrill *vb syn* see SCREAM 1
shrill *adj syn* see ACUTE 4
shrine *n* a structure or place considered sacred by a religious group <pilgrims going to the *shrine* at Lourdes hoping to be healed>
syn holy place, sanctorium, sanctuary, sanctum
rel reliquary; enshrinement
shrink *vb* **1** *syn* see CONTRACT 3
rel shrivel (up), wither
con amplify, expand
ant swell
2 *syn* see FAIL 3
idiom shrink (*or* dwindle) down to nothing
3 *syn* see RECOIL
rel cower, cringe, crouch, huddle, slink; draw (back), recede, retire, retreat, withdraw; boggle, demur, scruple
shrinking *adj syn* see UNDEMONSTRATIVE
shrivel *vb syn* see WITHER
rel parch; fossilize
shroud *vb* **1** *syn* see ENFOLD 1
2 *syn* see SCREEN 3
shrouded *adj syn* see ULTERIOR
shuck *n syn* see HULL
shuck *vb* to strip, break off, or remove the enclosing case or cover of <*shuck* corn>
syn hull, husk, shell; *compare* SKIN 2
rel decorticate, peel, skin, strip
shuck (off) *vb syn* see DISCARD
shudder *vb syn* see SHAKE 1
rel gyrate, shimmy
shuffle *vb* **1** *syn* see DISORDER 1
2 *syn* see EQUIVOCATE 2
3 to walk awkwardly in a sliding, dragging way without lifting the feet <an old drunk *shuffling* along in filthy bedroom slippers>
syn scuff, scuffle, shamble, ‖shool, shovel
rel drag, pad, scrape, slipper, slip-slop, slur; draggle, straggle, trail (along)
4 *syn* see STUMBLE 6
shuffle *n syn* see CLUTTER 2
shuffling *adj syn* see EVASIVE 1
shun *vb syn* see ESCAPE 2
rel decline, refuse, reject; snub; despise, disdain, scorn
idiom have nothing to do with, keep away from, stand aloof from, steer clear of, turn away from, turn one's back upon
con accept, adopt, welcome
shunning *n syn* see ESCAPE 2
shunt *vb* **1** to push or turn off to one side <*shunt* a railroad car onto a siding>
syn sidetrack, switch; *compare* TURN 6
rel change, move, shift, transfer; avert, deflect, divert, head off
idiom push aside (*or* to the side)
2 *syn* see SHUTTLE
shush *vb* **1** *syn* see SILENCE
2 *syn* see SUPPRESS 2
shut *vb syn* see CLOSE 1
rel lock, seal; batten (down)

ant open
‖**shut–eye** *n syn* see SLEEP 1
shut in *vb syn* see ENCLOSE 1
ant shut out
shut–in *adj syn* see UNSOCIABLE
shut–mouthed *adj syn* see SILENT 3
ant openmouthed
shut off *vb syn* see SCREEN 3
shut out *vb syn* see SCREEN 3
shuttle *vb* to travel back and forth frequently <*shuttled* between New York and Washington every week>
syn shunt
rel shuttlecock; alternate
shut up *vb* **1** *syn* see SILENCE
2 to cease speaking <told the boy to sit down and *shut up*>
syn dry up, dumb (up), ‖dummy (up), pipe down, ‖ring off
rel hush, quiet (down), shush, soft-pedal
idiom button (*or* seal) one's lips, keep quiet
shy *adj* **1** disinclined to obtrude oneself <*shy* in the presence of strangers>
syn backward, bashful, coy, demure, diffident, modest, rabbity, retiring, self-effacing, timid, unassertive, unassured
rel backhanded, hesitant, reluctant; conscious, self-conscious, self-distrustful, shamefaced, sheepish; introversive, introvert, introverted, inturned; circumspect, reserved; cautious, chary, suspicious, wary; apprehensive, fearful, nervous, skittish, timorous
con brash, forward; aggressive, audacious, intrusive, obtruding, pushing, pushy; blunt, crass
ant bold, obtrusive
2 *syn* see DISINCLINED
3 *syn* see SHORT 3
con excess, over, surplus
shy *vb* **1** *syn* see DEMUR
rel blench, quail, recoil, shrink
2 *syn* see ESCAPE 2
shy *n syn* see POTSHOT
Shylock *n syn* see LOAN SHARK
shyster *n syn* see PETTIFOGGER
‖**sib** *adj syn* see SYMPATHETIC 2
sibilate *vb syn* see HISS
sibylline *adj* **1** *syn* see PROPHETIC
2 *syn* see OBSCURE 3
sic *vb syn* see URGE
rel agitate, catalyze, inspirit, instigate; abet, aid, countenance, favor
sick *adj* **1** affected with illness or disease <was *sick* with pneumonia>
syn down, ill; *compare* UNWELL
rel diseased, disordered, fevered; ailing, ‖cronk, ‖crook, funny, indisposed, unwell; debilitated, sickly, unhealthy; rocky, tottering, wobbly; confined, laid up; lousy, mean, rotten
idiom ‖on the sick list, sick as a dog

---

syn synonym(s)   *rel* related word(s)
ant antonym(s)   *con* contrasted word(s)
idiom idiomatic equivalent(s)
‖ use limited; if in doubt, see a dictionary

con healthy, strong
ant well
2 *syn* see MORBID
3 *syn* see FED UP
idiom ‖up to here with
4 *syn* see FAULTY
5 *syn* see SICKLY 2
sick (up) *vb syn* see VOMIT
sicken *vb* **1** *syn* see UPSET 5
2 *syn* see DISGUST
sicken (with *or* of) *vb syn* see CONTRACT 1
sickening *adj syn* see OFFENSIVE
‖**sicker** *vb syn* see EXUDE
sickliness *n syn* see INFIRMITY 1
sickly *adj* **1** *syn* see UNWELL
rel ‖cranky, down
con hale, hearty; healthy, well
ant robust
2 accompanying, indicating, or suggesting sickness <a *sickly* complexion>
syn peaked, ‖peaking, peaky, sick
rel ‖pimping, puny, sickish, weak; diseased; unhealthy
con healthy, hearty
3 *syn* see UNWHOLESOME 1
4 *syn* see MORBID
sickness *n* **1** the condition of being ill <finally recovered from her *sickness*>
syn affliction, diseasedness, disorder, illness, indisposition, infirmity, unhealth; *compare* DISEASE 1, INFIRMITY 1
rel indisposedness, unhealthfulness, unhealthiness, unwellness; affection, ailment, ill
idiom ill health
con haleness, healthiness, heartiness
ant health
2 *syn* see DISEASE 1
side *n* **1** a place, space, or direction with respect to a center or a line of division <lived on the north *side* of the street> <turned to one *side*>
syn hand
rel direction, flank, sector
2 *syn* see PHASE
3 *syn* see VIEWPOINT 2
4 the attitude, position, or action of one person or group as opposed to another <could understand her *side* as well as his in the quarrel>
syn part; *compare* POSITION 1
rel attitude, disposition; posture, stance, stand; position, standpoint, viewpoint
side *vb syn* see SHEATHE
side (with) *vb syn* see SUPPORT 2
side action *n syn* see SIDE EFFECT
sideboards *n pl syn* see SIDE-WHISKERS
sideburns *n pl syn* see SIDE-WHISKERS
side effect *n* a secondary and usually adverse effect (as of a drug) <drowsiness is a common *side effect* of antihistamines>
syn side action, side reaction
rel effect; reaction, response
side–glance *n* a look or glance directed to one side <she shot an impatient *side-glance* at him>
syn side-look
rel glance; stare

sideling *adv syn* see SIDEWAYS 1
sideling *adj syn* see STEEP 1
‖**sidelings** *adv syn* see SIDEWAYS 1
sidelong *adv syn* see SIDEWAYS 1
side–look *n syn* see SIDE-GLANCE
side reaction *n syn* see SIDE EFFECT
sidereal *adj syn* see STELLAR 1
sidesplitter *n syn* see RIOT 2
sidestep *vb* **1** *syn* see EQUIVOCATE 2
2 *syn* see SKIRT 3
3 *syn* see DODGE 1
sideswipe *n syn* see POTSHOT
sidetrack *vb syn* see SHUNT 1
sideward *adv syn* see SIDEWAYS 1
sideways *adv* **1** to, toward, or at one side <slipped *sideways* on the ice>
syn crabwise, laterally, sideling, ‖sidelings, sidelong, sideward, sidewise; *compare* ASIDE 1
rel obliquely; indirectly
con straight; directly
2 *syn* see ASIDE 1
side–whiskers *n pl* the usually shaped growth of whiskers on both sides of a man's face <grew *side-whiskers* and a moustache in order to look older>
syn burnsides, dundrearies, muttonchops, sideboards, sideburns
sidewise *adv* **1** *syn* see SIDEWAYS 1
2 *syn* see ASIDE 1
sidle *vb* to move sideways or obliquely especially in an unobtrusive or furtive manner <a suspicious-looking man *sidled* up to her>
syn edge, ‖slive
rel ease, slip
siege *n* a sometimes prolonged period of disorder or stress (as of body or mind) <endured a three-week *siege* of flu>
syn bout, go; *compare* ATTACK 3
rel attack, onslaught, seizure, spell
siesta *n syn* see NAP
siesta *vb syn* see NAP
sieve *n syn* see GOSSIP 1
sieve *vb syn* see SCREEN 5
sift *vb* **1** *syn* see SCREEN 5
2 *syn* see SORT 2
3 *syn* see EXPLORE
sigh *vb* **1** to take in and let out a deep audible breath (as in weariness, grief, or relief) <flopped down in the chair and *sighed* deeply>
syn ‖sock, sough, suspire
rel breathe, respire; exhale; gasp, pant, wheeze; groan, moan; sob
idiom heave a sigh
2 to make a sound like sighing <the wind *sighed* in the branches>
syn sough
rel blow; murmur, whisper; moan; whine; whistle; howl, roar
3 *syn* see LONG
sighful *adj syn* see MELANCHOLY 2
sight *n* **1** *syn* see EYESORE
‖**2** *syn* see MUCH
3 *syn* see EYE 2
4 *syn* see LOOK 1

5 *syn* see VIEW 4

6 *syn* see VIEW 5

sightless *adj syn* see BLIND 1
ant sighted

sightseer *n syn* see TOURIST

sign *n* **1** a motion, action, gesture, or word by which a command, thought, or wish is expressed <put a finger to her lips as a *sign* to keep quiet>
syn high sign, signal
rel gesticulation, gesture, motion; hint, indication, suggestion, warning
2 *syn* see CHARACTER 1
3 *syn* see EXPRESSION 3
rel symbolization; attestation, evidence, proof
4 *syn* see INDICATION 3
rel earmark, exponent, indicator; exhibit, show

sign *vb* **1** to affix a signature to <he refused to *sign* a confession>
syn autograph, ink, signature, subscribe
idiom put one's John Hancock on, put one's John Henry down (*or* on)
2 *syn* see SIGNAL

sign (over) *vb syn* see TRANSFER 4

signal *n syn* see SIGN 1
rel alarm, alert, tocsin; movement

signal *vb* to notify by or as if by a signal <*signaled* his wife to keep quiet>
syn flag, gesture, motion, sign, signalize
idiom give the high sign (to)

signal *adj syn* see NOTICEABLE
rel characteristic, distinctive, individual, peculiar, significative; eminent, famous, illustrious, renowned

signalize *vb* **1** *syn* see CHARACTERIZE 2
2 *syn* see SIGNAL

signature *vb syn* see SIGN 1

significance *n* **1** *syn* see MEANING 1
2 *syn* see IMPORTANCE
rel authority, credit, influence, merit, prestige; excellence, perfection, virtue
con indifference; triviality, unimportance, worthlessness; irrelevance
ant insignificance

significancy *n syn* see MEANING 1

significant *adj* **1** *syn* see EXPRESSIVE
rel cogent, compelling, convincing, sound, telling, valid; forceful, powerful; important, momentous, weighty
con meaningless, unexpressive; unimportant
ant insignificant
2 *syn* see IMPORTANT 1
con inconsequential, meaningless, unimportant
ant insignificant

significant *n syn* see INDICATION 3

significantly *adv syn* see WELL 8
ant insignificantly

signification *n* **1** *syn* see MEANING 1
rel implying, signifying; construction, implication; essence, gist, substance
||**2** *syn* see IMPORTANCE

significative *adj syn* see INDICATIVE

signify *vb* **1** *syn* see MEAN 2
rel bear, carry, convey; bespeak, purport
2 *syn* see MATTER

sign on *vb syn* see ENTER 3

sign up *vb syn* see ENTER 3

silence *n* **1** absence of sound or noise <the heavy *silence* of the night>
syn noiselessness, quiet, quietness, quietude, soundlessness, still, stillness
rel calm, hush, lull
con din, uproar
ant noise
2 *syn* see SECRECY
3 *syn* see DEATH 1

silence *vb* to compel or reduce to silence <*silenced* the courtroom chatter by pounding her gavel>
syn choke (off), hush, quiet, ||quieten, shush, shut up, still
rel dampen, deaden, dumb, lull, muffle, mute; quash, quell, squash, squelch, suppress; gag, muzzle

silent *adj* **1** *syn* see DUMB 1
2 characterized by absence of speech <was *silent* as he faced the altar>
syn dumb, mum, ||mumchance, mute, speechless, wordless; *compare* DUMB 1
rel inarticulate, muted, tongue-tied, voiceless
con speaking, talking
3 showing marked restraint in speaking <a stern, *silent* man>
syn close, close-lipped, closemouthed, close-tongued, dumb, inconversable, reserved, reticent, shut-mouthed, silentious, speechless, taciturn, tight-lipped, tight-mouthed, uncommunicative, wordless
rel checked, curbed, inhibited, restrained; unconversational, unsociable; inarticulate, incoherent; mute, voiceless; mum, secretive
con articulate, fluent, glib, vocal, voluble; babblative, garrulous, loquacious, windy; blabbering, blabbery, chattering
ant talkative
4 *syn* see STILL 3
idiom silent as a post (*or* stone), silent as the grave (*or* tomb)
ant noisy
5 *syn* see UNSPOKEN 1

silentious *adj syn* see SILENT 3

silhouette *n syn* see OUTLINE
rel ||shade, shadow

silken *adj* **1** *syn* see SOFT 3
2 *syn* see INGRATIATING

silky *adj* **1** *syn* see SOFT 3
2 *syn* see INGRATIATING

silliness *n syn* see FOOLISHNESS
rel illogicality
con logic, logicality, logicalness, sanity, sensibleness; wisdom

silly *adj* **1** *syn* see SIMPLE 3
rel empty, empty-headed, vacuous; irrational, unreasonable; ignorant, unintelligent, unwise
ant sensible

---

syn synonym(s)   *rel* related word(s)
ant antonym(s)   *con* contrasted word(s)
idiom idiomatic equivalent(s)
|| use limited; if in doubt, see a dictionary

2 *syn* see GIDDY 1
rel ‖balmy, crazy, ‖dippy, irrational, off, ‖wacked-out
idiom silly as a goose
con level-headed, practical, rational, serious
ant sensible
3 *syn* see FOOLISH 2
rel funny, senseless
silvern *adj syn* see SILVERY
silver–tongued *adj syn* see GLIB
silvery *adj* relating to, containing, or resembling silver <repeated polishings gave the wood a *silvery* sheen>
syn argent, argentate, argenteous, argentine, silvern
rel silver; brilliant, glittering, shimmering, shining
similar *adj syn* see LIKE
rel complementary, correlative; reciprocal
idiom much of a muchness, much the same
con antithetical, antonymous, contradictory, contrary, opposite
ant dissimilar
similarity *n syn* see LIKENESS
rel approximation; collation, correlation; association, interrelation; parallel; closeness; coincidence, synonymity
con unlikeness, variance
ant dissimilarity
similarly *adv syn* see ALSO 1
idiom by the same token
simile *n* **1** *syn* see ANALOGY 2
2 *syn* see LIKENESS
similitude *n* **1** *syn* see LIKENESS
rel copy, image, replica
ant dissimilitude
2 *syn* see ANALOGY 2
simmer *vb* **1** *syn* see BOIL 2
2 *syn* see SEETHE 4
simmer down *vb syn* see COMPOSE 4
rel quiet (down), subside
idiom ‖cool it, take it easy
con boil, seethe; explode, fulminate
ant boil over
Simon Legree *n syn* see SLAVE DRIVER
simon–pure *adj syn* see AUTHENTIC 2
simp *n syn* see DUNCE
simper *vb syn* see SMIRK
simple *adj* **1** *syn* see NATURAL 5
rel childish, childlike; amateur, green, unexperienced; trusting; ‖square
2 *syn* see PLAIN 1
ant elaborate
3 actually or apparently deficient in intelligence <a poor *simple* woman easily duped>
syn asinine, brainless, ‖buffle-headed, fatuous, foolish, insensate, mindless, nitwitted, senseless, sheepheaded, silly, soft, spoony, unintelligent, unwitty, weak-headed, weak-minded, witless; *compare* RETARDED, STUPID 1
rel amateur, green, inexperienced, inexpert; credulous, gullible; childish, childlike; naive; ignorant, illiterate, uneducated, unschooled, untaught; crass, dense, dopey, dull, dumb, slow,

stupid; doting, feebleminded, idiotic, retarded, simpleminded
con able, competent; alert, clever, keen; bright, intelligent, understanding
ant wise
4 *syn* see RETARDED
5 *syn* see PURE 2
rel inelaborate, stark; bald, bare, mere; fundamental, uncompounded
6 *syn* see EASY 1
rel incomplex, incomplicate
idiom simple as ABC
ant complex, complicated
simple *n syn* see FOOL 3
simplehearted *adj syn* see NATURAL 5
simpleminded *adj syn* see RETARDED
simplest *adj syn* see ELEMENTARY 1
simpleton *n* **1** *syn* see FOOL 4
2 *syn* see DUNCE
rel bungler, ‖clot
simplify *vb* to make simple or simpler <*simplify* a manufacturing process>
syn boil down, streamline
rel clarify, clean up, disentangle, disinvolve, straighten (out), unscramble; abridge, cut down, reduce, shorten; oversimplify
ant complicate
simply *adv syn* see JUST 3
simulacrum *n* **1** *syn* see IMAGE 1
2 *syn* see IMITATION
3 *syn* see APPEARANCE 2
simulate *vb* **1** *syn* see ASSUME 4
rel ape, copy, imitate, mimic; play-act, pose
idiom ‖make out like (*or* as if)
2 *syn* see RESEMBLE
simulated *adj* **1** *syn* see FICTITIOUS 2
ant genuine
2 *syn* see ARTIFICIAL 2
ant genuine
simultaneous *adj syn* see CONTEMPORARY 1
rel agreeing, coinciding, concurring
simultaneously *adv syn* see TOGETHER 1
idiom in one breath
sin *n* **1** *syn* see EVIL 3
2 *syn* see EVIL 2
3 *syn* see IMPERFECTION
sin *vb syn* see TRESPASS 1
since *prep syn* see AFTER 2
ant before
since *conj syn* see BECAUSE
sincere *adj* **1** genuine in feeling or expression <had a *sincere* dislike for politics>
syn heartfelt, hearty, unfeigned, wholehearted, whole-souled; *compare* GENUINE 3
rel candid, frank, frankhearted, open, plain; faithful, honest, truthful; aboveboard, forthright, pretensionless, straightforward, unpretentious; dear, devout, heartful; meant, unaffected
con affected, artificial, feigned, put-on, unmeant
ant insincere
2 *syn* see GENUINE 3
rel authentic, bona fide; serious; actual
idiom honest to God
ant insincere

sincereness *n syn* see GOOD FAITH
sincerity *n syn* see GOOD FAITH
  rel heart; goodwill; singleness, straightforwardness
  con cunning, deceit, guile; ill will
  ant insincerity
sine qua non *n syn* see ESSENTIAL 2
sinew *n* **1** *syn* see POWER 4
  2 *usu* **sinews** *pl syn* see MAINSTAY
sinewy *adj syn* see MUSCULAR 1
  rel strong, sturdy, tenacious, tough
  ant flabby
  2 *syn* see MUSCULAR 2
sinful *adj* **1** *syn* see WRONG 1
  rel base, low, vile; disgraceful, shameful; culpable, damnable
  2 *syn* see BLAMEWORTHY
  ant sinless
sing *vb* **1** to utter words in musical tones and with musical inflections and modulations <children often can *sing* before they converse>
  syn chant, tune, vocalize
  rel descant; carol, serenade, troll; croon, hum, lull, lullaby; cantillate, hymn, intone; singsong; roar
  2 *syn* see TALK 6
  ‖**3** *syn* see INFORM 3
single *adj* **1** being without a spouse <enjoying life as a *single* girl>
  syn sole, spouseless, unmarried, unwed
  rel free, unattached, unfettered; celibate; maiden, virgin
  idiom footloose and fancy-free
  con attached; united; wed
  ant married
  2 one as distinguished from two or more or all others <a *single* instance of dishonesty has been cited>
  syn lone, one, only, particular, separate, sole, solitary, unique
  rel individual, singular; especial, special, specific; distinguished, singled-out; distinct
  con several; manifold, many, numerous
  ant multiple
  3 *syn* see FRANK
  4 *syn* see SOLE 4
single (out) *vb syn* see CHOOSE 1
  rel screen, winnow (out); accept, admit, receive
single–eyed *adj syn* see FRANK
single–hearted *adj syn* see FRANK
single–minded *adj* **1** *syn* see FRANK
  2 *syn* see INFLEXIBLE 2
  rel diehard; bigoted
singleness *n* **1** *syn* see UNIQUENESS
  2 *syn* see UNITY 1
  ant multifariousness
singly *adv syn* see APART 1
  ant together
singular *adj* **1** *syn* see SEVERAL 1
  rel discrete; certain, definite; exclusive
  2 *syn* see EXCEPTIONAL 1
  ant usual
  3 *syn* see ONLY 2
  idiom first and last, one and only, one only

4 *syn* see STRANGE 4
  idiom passing strange
singularity *n* **1** *syn* see INDIVIDUALITY 4
  2 *syn* see INDIVIDUALITY 3
  3 *syn* see UNITY 1
  ant multiplicity
singularize *vb syn* see CHARACTERIZE 2
singularness *n syn* see UNITY 1
  ant multifariousness
sinister *adj* seriously threatening disaster <a *sinister* plot>
  syn baleful, malefic, maleficent, malign; *compare* OMINOUS
  rel fateful, ill-omened, inauspicious, ominous, portentous, unpropitious; apocalyptic, dire, doomful, ill-boding, threatening; lowering, menacing; evil, malicious
  con harmless, innocent, innocuous
sink *vb* **1** to become submerged <the overloaded raft *sank* below the surface>
  syn founder, go down, go under, submerge, submerse
  rel capsize, overturn, tip (over); dive, plunge; scuttle; shipwreck, wreck
  idiom go to Davy Jones's locker, go to the bottom, sink like a rock
  con come up, rise
  ant float
  2 *syn* see SET 12
  3 *syn* see DETERIORATE 1
  ant rise
  4 *syn* see STOOP 2
  5 *syn* see LOWER 3
  6 *syn* see THRUST 2
  7 *syn* see HUMBLE
  ant uplift
sink *n* **1** a place marked by a staggering amount of corruption and filth <that area of the city was a *sink* of vice and crime>
  syn Augean stable, cesspit, cesspool, den, pandemonium, Sodom, sty
  rel hellhole; fleshpot
  idiom Alsatian den, den of iniquity, sink of corruption
  2 *syn* see DEPRESSION 2
sinkage *n syn* see DEPRESSION 2
sinkhole *n syn* see DEPRESSION 2
sinuous *adj syn* see WINDING
  rel twisted; snake-shaped
  idiom twisting and turning
sip *vb syn* see DRINK 1
siphon *vb* **1** *syn* see CONDUCT 4
  2 *syn* see DRAIN 1
sire *n syn* see FATHER 2
sire *vb* **1** *syn* see FATHER 1
  2 *syn* see GENERATE 1
siren *n* an enticingly attractive woman who lures men into dangerous or compromising situations <a slinky *siren* of the silent screen era>

---

syn synonym(s)   *rel* related word(s)
ant antonym(s)   *con* contrasted word(s)
idiom idiomatic equivalent(s)
‖ use limited; if in doubt, see a dictionary

syn femme fatale, Lorelei, seductress, temptress
rel charmer, vamp

siren *adj syn* see ATTRACTIVE 1
rel sirenic

siren song *n syn* see LURE 2

sissified *adj syn* see EFFEMINATE

sissy *n syn* see WEAKLING

sissy *adj syn* see EFFEMINATE

sissy–pants (*or* **sissy-britches**) *n pl but sing or pl in constr syn* see WEAKLING

sit *vb* **1** to rest on the buttocks or haunches <she was *sitting* in a chair>
syn ‖set
rel perch, rest; ‖plop (down), seat, sit down; squat
con arise, get up, rise, stand, stand up
2 *syn* see CONVENE 1
3 *syn* see POSE 3
4 *syn* see SET 11
5 *syn* see SEAT
rel ensconce, install, settle

sit down *vb syn* see ALIGHT

site *n* **1** *syn* see PLACE 1
2 *syn* see SCENE 3
3 a place where an archaeological excavation is made <a burial *site*>
syn dig
4 *syn* see HABITAT

sited *adj syn* see SITUATED

‖sitfast *adj syn* see IMMOVABLE 1

sitting duck *n syn* see TARGET 1
rel sitter

situate *adj syn* see SITUATED

situated *adj* having a site, situation, or location <a town *situated* on a hill>
syn located, placed, positioned, set, sited, situate

situation *n* **1** *syn* see PLACE 1
2 *syn* see PREGNANCY
3 *syn* see JOB 2
4 *syn* see STATUS 1
5 *syn* see STATE 1
rel bargain

sizable *adj* **1** *syn* see CONSIDERABLE 2
2 *syn* see BIG 1
rel man-sized; giant-sized

sizableness *n syn* see SIZE 2

size *n* **1** the amount of measurable space or area occupied by or comprising a thing <the *size* of the card is 3″x 5″>
syn admeasurement, dimension(s), dimensionality, extent, magnitude, measure, proportion
rel area; body, bulk, mass, volume; height; extension, length; amplitude, breadth, expanse, spread, stretch, width; measurement
2 considerable amount, proportion, volume, character, or importance <left an estate of some *size*>
syn amplitude, bigness, greatness, largeness, magnitude, sizableness
rel dimension, extent
con littleness, smallness; minuteness, tininess

sizz *vb syn* see HISS

sizzle *vb* **1** *syn* see SEAR 2

2 *syn* see HISS

sizzling *adj syn* see HOT 1

‖skag *n syn* see CIGARETTE

skate *n syn* see MAN 3

sked *n syn* see PROGRAM 1

sked *vb syn* see SCHEDULE 1

skedaddle *vb* **1** *syn* see RUN 2
rel ‖split; cut out
2 *syn* see GET OUT 1
idiom lift them up and set them down, ‖take off like a bat out of hell

‖skeet *vb syn* see HURRY 2

skeezicks *n syn* see SCAMP

skein *n syn* see MAZE 1

skeletal *adj syn* see EMACIATED

skeleton *vb syn* see SKETCH

skeletonize *vb syn* see SKETCH

‖sken *vb syn* see SQUINT

skeptic *n* a doubting or incredulous person <people of long experience are often *skeptics*>
syn doubter, doubting Thomas, headshaker, Pyrrhonian, Pyrrhonist, unbeliever, zetetic
rel questioner; agnostic; pessimist; scoffer; cynic, misanthrope; disbeliever
con accepter; apostle, disciple, follower; devotee, diehard
ant believer

skeptical *adj syn* see INCREDULOUS
rel freethinking; dissenting; suspicious; cynical
idiom ‖from Missouri
ant believing

skeptically *adv syn* see ASKANCE 2
idiom with a grain of salt, with a note of skepticism, with a skeptical eye
con trustingly
ant gullibly

skepticism *n syn* see UNCERTAINTY
rel qualm, qualmishness
idiom question in one's mind, shadow of doubt
con belief, trust
ant gullibility

sketch *n syn* see COMPENDIUM 1

sketch *vb* to present succinctly <let's *sketch* our plan of action>
syn adumbrate, block (out), chalk (out), characterize, draft, outline, rough (out), skeleton, skeletonize
rel depict; diagram, diagrammatize; blueprint, delineate, line; draw, plot, trace; design, develop; detail, lay out, map (out)

sketchy *adj syn* see SUPERFICIAL 2

skew *vb* **1** *syn* see SLANT 3
2 *syn* see SWERVE 1
rel skid, slide, slip

skewer *vb syn* see IMPALE

skid *vb* **1** *syn* see SLIDE 3
rel sheer, skew, slue, veer
idiom go into a skid
2 *syn* see PLUMMET

skiddoo *vb syn* see GET OUT 1
idiom go (*or* take) off like a shot

skid road *n syn* see SKID ROW

skid row *n* a city street or district notorious for cheap bars, flophouses, and homeless derelicts <boozy old men wandering the *skid row*>

syn bowery, skid road
skill *n* **1** *syn* see ABILITY 2
  2 *syn* see ART 1
  3 *syn* see ADDRESS 1
  rel ease, skillfulness
skilled *adj* **1** *syn* see PROFICIENT
  con skill-less, unproficient
  ant unskilled, unskillful
  2 *syn* see EXPERIENCED
  rel prepared, primed, trained
  con unfit, unqualified, untrained
  ant unskilled
skillet *n* *syn* see FRYING PAN
skillful *adj* **1** *syn* see PROFICIENT
  rel learned, versant, well-versed
  ant unskillful
  2 accomplished or done with proficiency or skill
  <his answer was a very *skillful* evasion>
  syn adroit, clever, good, pretty, ‖skilly, wicked, workmanlike, workmanly; *compare* CLEVER 4, PROFICIENT
  rel expert, masterful
  con clumsy; unskilled
  ant inept, unskillful
‖**skilly** *adj syn* see SKILLFUL 2
skim *vb* **1** *syn* see BRUSH
  2 *syn* see GLANCE 1
  3 *syn* see FLY 1
skim (through) *vb syn* see BROWSE
  con examine, inspect, scrutinize
skimble–skamble *n syn* see GIBBERISH 1
‖**skimmelton** *n syn* see SHIVAREE
skimp *adj syn* see MEAGER 2
skimp *vb* **1** *syn* see SCRIMP
  2 *syn* see SPARE 3
skimpy *adj* **1** *syn* see MEAGER 2
  2 *syn* see SHORT 3
skin *n* **1** *syn* see HIDE
  2 *syn* see HULL
  3 a usually thin casing forming the outside surface of a structure or thing <aircraft *skins* made of aluminum alloys>
  syn sheath, sheathing
  rel facing, siding; case, casing, cover, jacket; shell
  4 *syn* see MISER
  5 *syn* see SWINDLER
  ‖**6** *syn* see DOLLAR
skin *vb* **1** *syn* see SHEATHE
  2 to remove the surface, skin, or thin outer covering of <*skin* a Bermuda onion>
  syn decorticate, excorticate, peel, scale, strip; *compare* SHUCK
  rel cut off, pull off; pare, shave (off), trim; hull, husk, shuck; bark, rind; excoriate, flay, gall
  3 *syn* see OVERCHARGE 1
  4 *syn* see CRITICIZE
  5 *syn* see HURRY 2
‖**skinch** *vb* **1** *syn* see SCRIMP
  2 *syn* see SPARE 3
skinflint *n syn* see MISER
‖**skinhead** *n syn* see BALDHEAD
skinny *adj syn* see LEAN
  rel twiggy, weedy; emaciated; skeletal

idiom mere skin and bones, skinny as a rail
ant fleshy
skip *vb* **1** to move or proceed with a light bounding step <children *skipping* home from school>
  syn hop, lope, skitter, spring, trip
  rel caper, cavort, curvet, frisk, gambol; bounce, hippety-hop; jump; leap; bound
  con hobble, shamble, shuffle; hitch, limp, stagger, totter
  2 *syn* see GLANCE 1
  3 *syn* see RUN 2
  idiom ‖split the scene
skip *n syn* see OMISSION
skirmish *n* **1** *syn* see CLASH 2
  rel assault, attack; ambush
  con pitched battle
  2 *syn* see ENCOUNTER
skirr *vb* **1** *syn* see RUN 2
  2 *syn* see FLY 1
skirt *n* **1** *syn* see BORDER 1
  rel skirting
  ‖**2** *syn* see WOMAN 1
skirt *vb* **1** *syn* see BORDER 1
  2 to make a detour or circuit (as around a congested area) <*skirted* the city to avoid traffic>
  syn bypass, circumnavigate, circumvent, detour
  idiom go around
  3 to avoid (as a topic or question) because of difficulty, complexity, controversy, or danger <*skirted* all touchy issues>
  syn burke, bypass, circumvent, ‖polly-fox, sidestep; *compare* EQUIVOCATE 2, ESCAPE 2
  rel avoid, dodge, duck, evade, hedge; elude, escape; ignore, skip
  idiom get around
  con confront, face, meet, take on
‖**skite** *n syn* see PRANK
skitter *vb syn* see SKIP 1
skittery *adj syn* see EXCITABLE
skittish *adj* **1** *syn* see GIDDY 1
  rel irresponsible, undependable, unreliable
  2 *syn* see EXCITABLE
  rel restive; nervous
skive *vb syn* see CUT 6
skiver *vb syn* see IMPALE
skookum *adj syn* see EXCELLENT
skookum–house *n syn* see JAIL
skulk *vb syn* see SNEAK
skunk *n syn* see SNOT 1
skunk *vb syn* see WHIP 2
sky *n* the expanse of space surrounding the earth <blue *sky* crisscrossed with jet trails>
  syn empyrean, firmament, heaven(s), welkin
  rel azure; celestial sphere
  idiom the wild blue yonder
sky–high *adv syn* see APART 3
sky–high *adj syn* see EXCESSIVE 1
skylarking *n* **1** *syn* see HORSEPLAY
  idiom ‖making whoopee

---

syn synonym(s)   *rel* related word(s)
ant antonym(s)   *con* contrasted word(s)
idiom idiomatic equivalent(s)
‖ use limited; if in doubt, see a dictionary

2 *syn* see REVELRY 2

sky pilot *n syn* see CLERGYMAN
 rel chaplain; padre

skyrocket *vb* to rise abruptly and rapidly (as to an unprecedented level or amount) <when the election was over taxes and prices *skyrocketed*>
 syn rocket, shoot up, soar
 rel climb, rise; upsoar, upspring
 con slide; fall; drop
 ant crash, plummet

skyscraping *adj syn* see LOFTY 6

slab *n syn* see BAR 1
 rel chunk, lump

‖**slab** *n syn* see SLIME

slabber *vb syn* see DROOL 2

slack *adj* **1** *syn* see NEGLIGENT
 rel dilatory, lackadaisical, lethargic, sluggish; faineant, indolent, lazy, slothful; inert, stagnant
 con assiduous, busy, diligent, industrious, sedulous
 2 *syn* see LOOSE 1
 rel feeble, infirm, soft, unsteady, weak; inactive, inert, passive, supine; laggard, leisurely, slow
 con tensed, tightened; constant, equable, even, steady, uniform; firm, hard
 ant taut, tight
 3 *syn* see SLOW 3

slack *vb syn* see LOOSE 5
 idiom ‖cut some slack, make slack
 ant tighten

slack *n syn* see SLOWDOWN 1

slacken *vb* **1** *syn* see DELAY 1
 idiom keep back
 ant quicken
 2 *syn* see ABATE 4
 3 *syn* see LOOSE 5
 ant tighten

slackening *n syn* see SLOWDOWN 1

slacker *n* one who shirks work, responsibility, or an obligation <didn't want any *slackers* in her office>
 syn goldbrick, shirker, slinker, ‖spiv
 rel idler, loafer; slugabed, sluggard

slack–spined *adj syn* see WEAK 4

slake *vb syn* see QUENCH 4

slam *n* **1** *syn* see BLOW 1
 2 *syn* see BANG 2
 3 *syn* see ANIMADVERSION
 rel fling, swipe; crack, potshot; rap, slap; dig, jab

slam *vb* **1** to strike with extreme force or violence <*slammed* the ball out of the park><the car *slammed* into the fence>
 syn belt, blast, clobber, slug, smash, wallop; *compare* STRIKE 2
 rel bang, bat, hit, knock, slap, swat, thwack; cudgel, hammer, mace; batter, beat, pound
 2 *syn* see LAMBASTE 3

‖**slam** *adv syn* see WELL 3

slammer *n syn* see JAIL

slander *n syn* see DETRACTION
 rel black wash, muckraking, mud-slinging, roorback, scandal-mongering

slander *vb syn* see MALIGN

 rel assail, attack; damage, hurt, injure; blackwash, muckrake; belie, strumpet
 idiom dish the dirt, run a smear campaign, sling the mud
 ant panegyrize

slanderous *adj syn* see LIBELOUS
 rel blackwashing, muckraking, scandalmongering
 ant panegyrical

slang *n syn* see DIALECT 2
 rel slanginess, slanguage

slangism *n syn* see BARBARISM

slant *adv syn* see ASIDE 1

slant *vb* **1** to set or be set at an angle <*slanted* the ladder against the wall>
 syn cant, heel, incline, lean, list, recline, slope, tilt, tip
 rel bank, decline, descend; bend, deviate, diverge, splay, swerve, veer
 2 to direct (written or spoken material) to the interests of a particular audience or group <a magazine *slanted* to farm families>
 syn aim, angle
 rel direct, orient, point, train; concentrate, focus; spoon-feed; bias, skew, warp
 3 to orient (material) from objective presentation so as to favor a particular bias <accused the media of *slanting* the news against the president>
 syn angle, bias, skew; *compare* PREJUDICE 2
 rel influence, prejudice; color, distort, twist, warp
 ant objectify, objectivize

slant *n* **1** *syn* see SLOPE
 2 *syn* see VIEWPOINT 2
 rel predilection, predisposition, prejudice

slanted *adj syn* see DIAGONAL

slanting *adj syn* see DIAGONAL

slantingly *adv syn* see ASIDE 1

slantingways *adv* **1** *syn* see ASIDE 1
 2 *syn* see DIAGONALLY

slantly *adv syn* see ASIDE 1

slantways *adv* **1** *syn* see ASIDE 1
 2 *syn* see DIAGONALLY

slantwise *adv* **1** *syn* see ASIDE 1
 2 *syn* see DIAGONALLY

slap *n* **1** *syn* see CUFF
 2 *syn* see AFFRONT
 3 *syn* see FLING 1

slap *vb* **1** to strike quickly and sharply with the hand <*slapped* the hysterical girl>
 syn blip, box, buffet, cuff, smack, spank, ‖wherret; *compare* STRIKE 2
 rel ‖biff, ding, hit, sock, swat, whack; ‖wap, wham; bash
 2 *syn* see LAMBASTE 3

‖**slap** *adv syn* see WELL 3

slap around *vb syn* see MANHANDLE

slapdash *adj* **1** *syn* see RANDOM
 2 *syn* see SLIPSHOD 2

‖**slap–up** *adj syn* see EXCELLENT

slash *vb* **1** *syn* see CUT 1
 2 *syn* see HACK
 3 *syn* see LAMBASTE 3

idiom ‖light into
4 *syn* see REDUCE 2
5 *syn* see SHORTEN
slate *n syn* see TICKET 3
‖**slate** *vb syn* see LAMBASTE 3
slather *n, often* **slathers** *pl syn* see SCAD
slattern *n* **1** an untidy slovenly woman <two blowsy *slatterns* gossiping at the bar>
syn dowd, dowdy, drab, draggle-tail, ‖malkin, slut, ‖streel, traipse
rel frump; slob, ‖slommack, sloven; crone, gammer, hag, witch
2 *syn* see WANTON
rel prostitute, whore
slattern *adj syn* see SLATTERNLY
slatternly *adj* being habitually untidy and very dirty especially in dress or appearance <a filthy, *slatternly* old woman>
syn blowsy, dowdy, draggletailed, frowsy, slattern, sordid; *compare* SLOVENLY 1
rel careless, disordered, neglected, poky; bedraggled, disheveled, draggled, draggly, messy, mussy, slipshod, sloppy, slovenly, unkempt, untidy; dirty, filthy, foul, grimy, squalid
con clean, fresh, neat, tidy, trim; smart; immaculate, spotless
ant bandbox
slaughter *n syn* see MASSACRE
rel slaughtery; annihilation, destruction
slaughter *vb* **1** to kill (animals) for food <*slaughtered* a steer for the winter>
syn butcher, slay
rel stick
2 to kill (a person) in an especially bloody or barbarous manner <Jack the Ripper *slaughtered* his victims with a knife>
syn butcher, slay
rel kill, murder, ‖total, ‖waste; maim, mangle, mutilate, torture
3 to kill (people) in large numbers <millions *slaughtered* in death camps>
syn annihilate, decimate, exterminate, massacre, wipe (out)
‖**slaunchways** *adv* **1** *syn* see DIAGONALLY
2 *syn* see ASIDE 1
slave *n* **1** a person held in servitude or bondage <plantations worked by *slaves*>
syn bondman, bondslave, bondsman, chattel, mancipium
rel help, menial, retainer, servant; helot, serf, thrall, vassal
con freedman, freedwoman; ‖deditician
ant freeman
2 one who works at a hard, monotonous, usually menial task <*slaves* working all night for minimum wage>
syn ‖dogsbody, dray horse, drudge, galley slave, peon, slavey, toiler, workhorse
rel ‖coolie
slave *vb syn* see DRUDGE
idiom work like a slave
slave driver *n* a person in authority who exacts extreme effort from his subordinates <the chief proofreader was a real *slave driver*>

syn rawhider, Simon Legree, taskmaster
rel martinet
idiom a hard taskmaster
slaver *vb* **1** *syn* see DROOL 2
2 *syn* see FAWN
slaver *n syn* see SALIVA
slavery *n* **1** *syn* see WORK 2
2 *syn* see BONDAGE
idiom involuntary servitude, the yoke (*or* chains) of slavery
slavey *n* **1** *syn* see SLAVE 2
2 *syn* see HACK 2
slavish *adj* **1** *syn* see HARD 6
2 *syn* see SUBSERVIENT 2
rel spineless, subdued, tame; miserable, wretched
ant independent
3 copying obsequiously something superior <the painting was a *slavish* copy of an old master>
syn apish, emulative, imitative
rel uninspired; unoriginal
con fresh, new, novel, original; fanciful, imaginative, ingenious, inspired; extravagant, high≠flown
slay *vb* **1** *syn* see KILL 1
2 *syn* see MURDER 1
3 *syn* see SLAUGHTER 2
4 *syn* see SLAUGHTER 1
slayer *n syn* see MURDERER
sleazy *adj* **1** *syn* see LIMP 1
rel slight, tenuous, thin; gossamery
2 *syn* see CHEAP 2
3 *syn* see SHABBY 1
sleek *vb syn* see POLISH 2
sleek *adj* having a very smooth or lustrous surface or texture <the car's *sleek* new paint job>
syn glassy, glossy, polished, ‖sleekit, sleeky, smarmy
rel smooth; glistening, lustrous
‖**sleekit** *adj syn* see SLEEK
sleeky *adj syn* see SLEEK
sleep *n* **1** the natural periodic suspension of consciousness during which the powers of the body are restored <needed eight hours of *sleep* to function efficiently>
syn ‖doss, ‖shut-eye, slumber; *compare* DOZE, NAP
rel repose, rest; slumberland
idiom land of Nod, the arms of Morpheus
con wakefulness
2 *syn* see LETHARGY 1
3 *syn* see DEATH 1
sleep *vb* to rest in a state of sleep <*slept* for over eight hours>
syn ‖doss, slumber; *compare* DOZE, NAP
rel relax, repose, rest; oversleep, sleep in
idiom be in the land of Nod, be sunk in sleep, pound one's ear, rest in the arms of Morpheus, sleep like a top (*or* log)

---

syn synonym(s)   *rel* related word(s)
ant antonym(s)   *con* contrasted word(s)
idiom idiomatic equivalent(s)
‖ use limited; if in doubt, see a dictionary

con arouse, awaken, wake (up)

sleeplessness *n syn* see INSOMNIA

sleepy *adj* **1** having an inclination for or affected by sleep <was *sleepy* after the long day>
syn dozy, drowsy, nodding, ‖peepy, ‖sloomy, slumberous, slumbery, snoozy, somnolent, soporific
rel heavy, heavy-eyed, lethargic, sluggish, torpid; dazed, dopey, listless, oscitant, yawning; asleep, sleeping, slumbering; nepenthean, poppied; comatose, ‖out
con awake, conscious; restless, sleepless, unsleeping; alert, wide-awake
ant wakeful
2 *syn* see INACTIVE
3 *syn* see SOPORIFIC 1

‖**sleer** *vb syn* see SNEER 1

sleight *n* **1** *syn* see ADDRESS 1
2 *syn* see TRICK 1

‖**sleighty** *adj syn* see CLEVER 4

slender *adj* **1** *syn* see THIN 1
rel slenderish, slimmish; lithe, svelte, trim
idiom slender as a reed
2 *syn* see SHORT 3
3 *syn* see REMOTE 4

slenderize *vb syn* see REDUCE 5

sleuth *n syn* see DETECTIVE

slew *n syn* see SCAD

slewed *adj syn* see INTOXICATED 1

slice *n syn* see SHARE 1
rel segment
idiom a slice of the pie (*or* melon)

slice *vb* **1** *syn* see CUT 1
2 *syn* see CUT 5

slick *vb* **1** *syn* see POLISH 2
2 *syn* see DRESS UP 1
3 *syn* see SLIDE 1

slick *adj* **1** having a glassy surface that often offers insecure footing <a floor *slick* with wax>
syn greasy, lubricious, ‖sliddery, ‖slipper, slippery, slippy, slithery
rel oily; ‖slape, smooth; soapy
idiom slick as a greased pig
con coarse, gritty, rough, uneven
2 *syn* see FULSOME
rel glossy; slippery
3 *syn* see WISE 4

slicker *n syn* see SWINDLER

‖**slidder** *vb* **1** *syn* see SLIDE 3
2 *syn* see SLITHER 2

‖**sliddery** *adj syn* see SLICK 1

slide *vb* **1** to go or progress with a smooth continuous motion <goldfish *slid* across the pool>
syn glide, glissade, slick, slip, slither
rel flow, stream
2 *syn* see SLIP 6
3 to fall or nearly fall because of loss of balance or footing <stumbled and *slid* on the ice>
syn skid, ‖slidder, slip, ‖slur
idiom take a slide (*or* a skid)
4 to shift or be shifted out of place or away from one's grasp <the packages *slid* from her arms>
syn slip
rel shift; move; fall, spill, tumble

5 *syn* see CREEP 1
6 to take a natural course <preferred to let the matter *slide* for a while>
syn coast, drift
rel glide
idiom run its course
7 *syn* see STEAL 3
8 *syn* see SNEAK

slide *n syn* see DECLINE 3

slight *adj* **1** *syn* see THIN 1
rel slightish, ‖slighty; smallish; pint-sized
2 *syn* see DELICATE 5
rel gossamery, sleazy
3 *syn* see REMOTE 4

slight *vb syn* see NEGLECT
rel skip; contemn, despise; flout, scoff

slightest *adj syn* see FIRST 4
rel ‖fat, negligible

slighting *adj syn* see DEROGATORY

slim *adj* **1** *syn* see THIN 1
rel lissome, lithe, lithesome, svelte
ant chubby
2 *syn* see CLEVER 4
3 *syn* see REMOTE 4

slim (down) *vb syn* see REDUCE 5

slime *n* a viscous and usually dirty or offensive substance <a layer of *slime* formed in the bottom of the pool>
syn muck, ‖slab, slum
rel ooze, ‖sleech, sludge; scum

sling *vb* **1** *syn* see THROW 1
rel catapult; sock
2 *syn* see STRIDE 1

sling *vb syn* see HANG 1

slink *vb syn* see SNEAK

slink *n syn* see SNEAK

slinker *n syn* see SLACKER

slip *vb* **1** *syn* see SLIDE 1
2 *syn* see SNEAK
3 *syn* see STEAL 3
4 *syn* see SLIDE 4
5 *syn* see SLIDE 3
6 to decline gradually from a standard or accustomed level <sales in some lines *slipped*>
syn drop (off), fall (off *or* away), sag, slide, slump
rel erode, soften; decline, go down, sink; dip, drop; nose-dive, plummet, topple; crash
con better, gain, improve, rally, rebound; ascend, climb, rise; skyrocket, soar
7 *syn* see SHAKE 5
8 *syn* see SHED 2

slip (on) *vb syn* see DON 1
ant slip (off)

slip *n* **1** *syn* see WHARF
2 *syn* see ESCAPE 1
3 *syn* see ERROR 2
4 *syn* see DECLINE 3

‖**slipper** *adj syn* see SLICK 1

slippery *adj* **1** *syn* see SLICK 1
2 *syn* see MUTABLE 2

slippy *adj syn* see SLICK 1

slipshod *adj* **1** *syn* see SHABBY 1
2 *syn* see SLOVENLY 1

3 marked by indifference to exactness, precision, and accuracy <a *slipshod* piece of research>
syn botchy, careless, messy, slapdash, sloppy, slovenly, unthorough, untidy
rel neglected, negligent; haphazard, slaphappy, unmeticulous; botched-up, fouled-up, messed-up, ||screwed-up; faulty, imperfect, inaccurate, inexact
con fastidious, meticulous, neat; accurate, exact, precise; methodical, orderly, systematic; thorough

slipslop *n syn* see NONSENSE 2
slipup *n syn* see ERROR 2
slit *vb syn* see CUT 1
slither *vb* **1** *syn* see SLIDE 1
rel ||sluther
2 to walk or move in a sinuous way <the trout *slithered* among the smooth rocks>
syn ||slidder, snake, undulate
rel creep, glide, sidle, steal; lurk, prowl, slink, sneak
slithery *adj syn* see SLICK 1
||**slive** *vb syn* see SIDLE
sliver *vb* to cut into very thin slices <*slivered* cheese>
syn shave, shred
rel carve, haggle, slice
con chop, dice, mince; comminute, powder, pulverize; crush, mash
slobber *vb syn* see DROOL 2
slobbering *adj syn* see EFFUSIVE
slobbery *adj* **1** *syn* see EFFUSIVE
2 *syn* see SLOVENLY 1
slog *vb* **1** *syn* see STRIKE 2
2 *syn* see PLOD 1
3 *syn* see DRUDGE
slogan *n syn* see CATCHWORD
rel expression, idiom, locution
slogging *n syn* see WORK 2
||**slommacky** *adj syn* see SLOVENLY 1
||**sloom** *n syn* see DOZE
||**sloom** *vb syn* see DOZE
||**sloomy** *adj syn* see SLEEPY 1
slop *n syn* see PAP 2
slop *vb* **1** *syn* see SPILL 1
2 *syn* see SPLASH
3 *syn* see GULP
4 *syn* see PLOD 1
slope *vb syn* see SLANT 1
slope *n* a natural or artificial inclined surface <the steep *slope* of the hill>
syn grade, gradient, inclination, incline, lean, leaning, slant, tilt
rel acclivity, ascent, rise; declivity, descent; deflection, deviation, obliqueness, obliquity; pitch, swag, sway, tip; bend, skew
con champaign, flat, flatland, mesa, plain(s), plateau, tableland
ant level
sloped *adj syn* see INCLINED 3
slopeways *adv syn* see ASIDE 1
sloping *adj syn* see INCLINED 3
slopped *adj syn* see INTOXICATED 1
sloppy *adj* **1** *syn* see SLIPSHOD 3

rel amateurish; mediocre; awkward, clumsy; poor
ant exact, precise
2 *syn* see SLOVENLY 1
3 *syn* see EFFUSIVE
rel soft; oversentimental
4 *syn* see INTOXICATED 1
slosh *n syn* see BLOW 1
slosh *vb* **1** *of a liquid* to move with a gentle lapping motion or sound <heard water *sloshing* in the bottom of the boat>
syn bubble, burble, gurgle, lap, swash, wash
rel babble; ripple; dash, plash, splash, tumble; bespatter, spatter; churn, whirl; gush, rush; roar
2 *syn* see SPLASH
3 *syn* see GULP
||**4** *syn* see STRIKE 2
sloth *n* **1** disinclination to action or labor <a hot summer day is likely to induce *sloth* in all of us>
syn idleness, indolence, laze, laziness, slothfulness, slouch, sluggishness
rel ergophobia, faineancy, idling, lazing, loafing; apathy, heaviness, languidness, languor, lassitude, lethargy, listlessness, torpidity; shiftlessness
con assiduity, assiduousness, busyness, diligence, sedulity, sedulousness
ant industriousness, industry
2 sluggishness and apathy in the practice of virtue <the deadly sin of *sloth*>
syn acedia
rel heedlessness, inattention, inattentiveness
con assiduity
slothful *adj syn* see LAZY
con assiduous, busy, diligent, sedulous
ant industrious
slothfulness *n syn* see SLOTH 1
slouch *n* **1** *syn* see OAF 2
2 *syn* see SLUGGARD
3 *syn* see SLOTH 1
slouch *vb* to assume, have, or move with an awkwardly drooping posture, carriage, or gait <three drunks *slouched* across the room>
syn droop, loll, ||lollop, lop, slump, trollop
rel loaf, lounge, saunter, shamble, shuffle; bend, lean, stoop; sag, wilt
con erect, straighten (up); sit up, stand up
slough *n* **1** *syn* see SWAMP
2 *syn* see INLET
||**slough** *n syn* see HULL
slough *vb* **1** *syn* see SHED 2
2 *syn* see DISCARD
idiom ||get shut (*or* shed) of
slough over *vb syn* see NEGLECT
sloven *adj syn* see SLOVENLY 1
slovenly *adj* **1** negligent of or marked by lack of neatness and order especially in appearance or dress <*slovenly* attire>

---

syn synonym(s)	*rel* related word(s)
ant antonym(s)	*con* contrasted word(s)
idiom idiomatic equivalent(s)	
|| use limited; if in doubt, see a dictionary	

syn careless, disheveled, ill-kempt, messy, mussy, raunchy, slipshod, slobbery, ‖slommacky, sloppy, sloven, uncombed, unfastidious, unkempt, unneat, untidy; *compare* SLATTERNLY
rel down-at-heel, shabby, sleazy, sluttish, slutty; blowsy, dowdy, frowsy, frumpish
con fastidious, neat, tidy, trim; combed, groomed, well-groomed; immaculate
ant neat
2 *syn* see SLIPSHOD 3

slow *adj* **1** *syn* see RETARDED
rel limited; ‖dunch
2 moving, flowing, or proceeding at less than the usual, desirable, or required speed <a *slow* advance toward mutual understanding>
syn deliberate, dilatory, laggard, leisurely, unhasty, unhurried
rel measured, slowish, steady; unhasting, unhurrying; slow-footed, slow-going, slow-paced; plodding, poky, rusty; dragging, flagging, halting, lagging, straggling; dawdling, delaying, postponing, procrastinating; leaden, sluggish; crawling, snaillike, snail-paced, ultra-slow
idiom as slow as a swamp turtle, as slow as molasses in January
con blitz, lightning, quick, rapid, swift; fast-going, fast-moving, fast-paced, rapid-paced
ant fast
3 marked by reduced economic activity (as in sales or patronage) <trading was *slow* on the commodity exchange today>
syn down, off, slack, sluggish
rel moderate; reduced; low; inactive, stagnant
con active; up; heavy

slow (up *or* down) *vb* *syn* see DELAY 1
rel moderate, qualify, temper; abate, decrease, lessen, reduce
ant speed

slow coach *n* *syn* see LAGGARD

slowdown *n* **1** a slowing or gradual decrease in activity <a *slowdown* in car sales this quarter>
syn slack, slackening, slow-up
rel decline, downtrend, downturn; drop, drop-off, falloff; inactivity, stagnation; freeze
con increase, rise, upswing, upturn; acceleration, quickening
ant speedup
2 a deliberate slowing down by workers in the rate and quantity of production <air traffic snarled by a controllers' *slowdown*>
syn ‖ca' canny
rel action; protest; slow-up; sit-down; strike, walkout; stoppage
ant speedup

slowgoing *adj* *syn* see LAZY

slowpoke *n* *syn* see LAGGARD

slow–up *n* *syn* see SLOWDOWN 1

slow–witted *adj* *syn* see RETARDED
ant quick-witted

‖**slubberdegullion** *n* *syn* see VILLAIN 1

slue *vb* *syn* see SWERVE 1

slug *n* *syn* see SLUGGARD
rel slacker, sloven

slug *n* *syn* see DRAM

slug *vb* *syn* see SLAM 1

slugabed *n* *syn* see SLUGGARD

sluggard *n* an habitually lazy, shiftless, and inactive person <a *sluggard* who wanted to sleep all day>
syn bum, dolittle, do-nothing, faineant, idler, lazybones, loafer, slouch, slug, slugabed
rel lie-abed, sleepyhead; dawdler, laggard, slow coach, slowpoke; goldbrick, shirker
idiom ‖his idleship, ‖Weary Willie
con go-getter, hustler, live wire
ant dynamo

sluggish *adj* **1** *syn* see LETHARGIC
rel dragging, draggy, leaden, lumpish; costive, stiff; apathetic, stupefied
con go-getting, hustling, vigorous; expeditious
ant brisk
2 *syn* see SLOW 3

sluggishness *n* *syn* see SLOTH 1

sluice *vb* *syn* see POUR 2
rel flush, wash; douse, drench, soak

slum *n* a densely populated usually urban area marked by run-down housing, poverty, and social disorganization <a *slum* full of vagrants, junkies, pimps, and pushers>
syn stew
rel slumdom, slumland; tobacco road; tenderloin; skid row; ghetto; hive, kennel, rookery, warren
idiom desolation row, the wrong side of the tracks

slum *n* *syn* see SLIME

slumber *vb* **1** *syn* see DOZE
2 *syn* see SLEEP

slumber *n* **1** *syn* see SLEEP 1
2 *syn* see DOZE
3 *syn* see LETHARGY 1

slumberous *adj* **1** *syn* see SLEEPY 1
2 *syn* see SOPORIFIC 1
3 *syn* see LETHARGIC

slumbery *adj* *syn* see SLEEPY 1

slump *vb* **1** *syn* see FALL 2
rel droop, flag, sag
idiom come down like a rock (*or* a ton of bricks)
2 *syn* see SLOUCH
rel cave in, collapse
3 *syn* see SLIP 6

slump *n* **1** *syn* see DECLINE 3
2 *syn* see DEPRESSION 3

slup *vb* *syn* see SLURP

‖**slur** *vb* *syn* see SLIDE 3

slur *vb* *syn* see MALIGN

slur (over) *vb* *syn* see NEGLECT

slur *n* **1** *syn* see ANIMADVERSION
2 *syn* see STIGMA

slurp *vb* to eat or drink noisily <*slurping* soup with a large spoon>
syn slup
rel guzzle, lap (up), slosh, swill; suck; wolf (down); smack
con nibble, pick (at); sip

slushy *adj* *syn* see SENTIMENTAL

slut *n* **1** *syn* see SLATTERN 1
2 *syn* see WANTON

3 *syn* see MINX

sly *adj* **1** *syn* see CLEVER 4
  rel smart; cagey; masterful
  2 attaining or seeking to attain one's ends by devious means <a *sly* way of upping sales>
  syn artful, astute, crafty, cunning, deep, ‖downy, foxy, guileful, insidious, subdolous, subtle, tricky, vulpine, wily; *compare* UNDERHAND
  rel disingenuous, unfrank; calculating, designing, Machiavellian, scheming; cagey, devious, shady, shifty, ‖slanter, slick, slippery, smooth; clandestine, covert, furtive, stealthy; underhand, underhanded, unscrupulous; predatory; crooked, dishonest
  idiom crazy like a fox, cunning as a fox (*or* serpent), sly as a fox
  con candid, forthright, frank, honest, open, sincere, straightforward

sly *vb* *syn* see SNEAK

slyboots *n pl but sing in constr* *syn* see SCAMP

slyness *n* *syn* see CUNNING 2

smack *n* **1** *syn* see TASTE 3
  2 *syn* see HINT 2

smack *vb* to have a trace, vestige, or suggestion of something <that plan *smacks* of radicalism>
  syn savor, smell
  rel resemble, suggest; reek, stink

smack *vb* **1** *syn* see KISS 1
  idiom ‖plant a juicy kiss on
  2 *syn* see SLAP 1

smack *n* **1** *syn* see CUFF
  2 *syn* see BLOW 1

‖**smack–dab** *adv* *syn* see JUST 1

‖**smacker** *n* *syn* see DOLLAR

‖**smackeroo** *n* *syn* see DOLLAR

small *adj* **1** being the opposite of large <a *small* white house>
  syn bantam, little, monkey, petite, smallish; *compare* TINY
  rel cramped, limited, narrow, two-by-four; puny, undersized; paltry, petty, piddling, trivial
  con big, great; considerable, sizable; enormous, huge, immense, vast
  ant large
  2 *syn* see MINOR 2
  3 *syn* see LITTLE 2
  4 *syn* see LITTLE 3
  5 *syn* see PETTY 2
  6 *syn* see REMOTE 4

small beer *n* *syn* see TRIVIA

small–beer *adj* *syn* see LITTLE 3

small change *n* *syn* see TRIVIA

smallest *adj* *syn* see FIRST 4

small–fry *adj* *syn* see MINOR 2

smallish *adj* *syn* see SMALL 1
  ant largish

small–minded *adj* *syn* see ILLIBERAL
  ant large-minded

small potato *n, usu* **small potatoes** *pl but sing or pl in constr* *syn* see TRIVIA

small talk *n* light or casual conversation <had to make *small talk* at the cocktail party>
  syn bavardage, by-talk, chitchat, chitter-chatter, trifling

  rel badinage, banter, repartee; babble, babbling, bibble-babble, chatter, prattle, prattling, prittle-prattle

small–time *adj* *syn* see MINOR 2
  ant big-time

small–town *adj* *syn* see INSULAR

‖**smarm** *vb* *syn* see SMEAR 1

smarmy *adj* **1** *syn* see SLEEK
  2 *syn* see FULSOME

smart *vb* *syn* see HURT 4

smart *vb* to cause or produce a sharp stinging and usually localized pain <gave him a slap that was hard enough to *smart*>
  syn bite, burn, ‖stang, sting; *compare* HURT 4
  rel prick; tingle; hurt

smart *adj* **1** *syn* see INTELLIGENT 2
  ant stupid
  2 *syn* see WISE 4
  idiom knowing the score, on the ball
  ant dull, dumb
  3 *syn* see CLEVER 5
  rel pert, saucy
  4 *syn* see WISE 5
  5 *syn* see STYLISH
  rel dapper, ‖dinky, spruce
  ant dowdy
  ‖**6** *syn* see CONSIDERABLE 2

smart aleck *n* an obnoxiously conceited and self-assertive person with pretensions to smartness or cleverness <was heckled by a *smart aleck* in the back row>
  syn know-it-all, smarty, smarty-pants, wiseacre, wisecracker, wise guy, wisehead, wisenheimer
  rel blowhard, boaster, braggadocio, braggart, gasbag, windbag; exhibitionist, grandstander, show-off
  idiom hot-air artist

smart–alecky *adj* *syn* see WISE 5

smarten (up) *vb* *syn* see DRESS UP 1

smart set *n* ultrafashionable often international society <the *smart set* that suns in Cannes and skis in St. Moritz>
  syn beautiful people, jet set, ton
  rel aristocracy, aristoi, blue bloods, bon ton, elite, Four Hundred, society, upper crust, who's who

smarty *n* *syn* see SMART ALECK

smarty–pants *n pl but sing in constr* *syn* see SMART ALECK

smash *vb* **1** *syn* see SHATTER 1
  2 *syn* see SLAM 1
  3 *syn* see DESTROY 1

smash *n* **1** *syn* see BLOW 1
  2 *syn* see BANG 2
  3 *syn* see IMPACT 1
  4 *syn* see CRASH 3
  5 *syn* see COLLAPSE 2
  6 a striking success <the new musical was a box-office *smash*>

---

syn synonym(s)   *rel* related word(s)
ant antonym(s)   *con* contrasted word(s)
idiom idiomatic equivalent(s)
‖ use limited; if in doubt, see a dictionary

syn bang, bell ringer, hit, succès fou, ten-strike, wow

rel sensation; knockout

idiom howling (*or* roaring) success, smash hit

con disaster, dud, failure

ant flop

‖**smash** *n syn* see MONEY

‖**smashed** *adj syn* see INTOXICATED 1

smashup *n* **1** *syn* see COLLAPSE 2

2 *syn* see CRASH 3

smatch *n* **1** *syn* see HINT 2

2 *syn* see FEW

smatter *vb* ‖**1** *syn* see SHATTER 1

2 *syn* see CHAT 1

smatter *n syn* see FEW

smatterer *n syn* see AMATEUR 2

smattering *n syn* see FEW

smaze *n syn* see HAZE 1

smear *vb* **1** to overspread with something unctuous, viscous, or adhesive <*smeared* the crack with wet concrete>

syn bedaub, besmear, dab, daub, plaster, ‖smarm, smudge

rel rub; coat, cover, overlay, overspread, spread; smirch, soil

2 *syn* see TAINT 1

3 *syn* see MALIGN

idiom use smear tactics (on *or* against)

4 *syn* see WHIP 2

rel foil, frustrate; repulse

idiom mop up the floor (*or* earth) with

smell *vb* **1** to perceive by means of the olfactory organs <*smelled* a dead skunk>

syn nose, scent, sniff, ‖snift, snuff

rel detect, perceive, sense; whiff; ‖snaffle, snuffle

idiom get a whiff of

2 *syn* see SMACK

3 to have or emit an offensive odor <the canal *smells* today>

syn funk, reek, stench, stink

idiom offend the nostrils, smell (*or* stink) to high heaven

smell *n* **1** a quality that makes a thing perceptible to the olfactory sense <the *smell* of a ham cooking>

syn aroma, odor, scent

rel bouquet, fragrance, incense, perfume, redolence, spice; flavor, savor, stench, stink

2 *syn* see HINT 2

smeller *n syn* see NOSE 1

‖**smellful** *adj syn* see MALODOROUS 1

ant odorless, smell-less

smellfungus *n syn* see CRITIC

smell–less *adj syn* see ODORLESS

ant ‖smellful, smelly

smelly *adj syn* see MALODOROUS 1

con odorless, scentless, smell-less; fragrant, fresh, sweet

smidgen *n syn* see PARTICLE

smile *vb* to express amusement, satisfaction, or pleasure by brightening one's eyes and curving the corners of one's mouth upward <*smiled* as she greeted him>

syn beam, grin

rel simper, smirk

idiom break into a smile, crack a smile

con grimace; glare, glower, lower, scowl

ant frown

smirch *vb syn* see SOIL 2

rel discolor; smear

smirk *vb* to smile in an affected manner <*smirking* children imitating their teacher>

syn simper, ‖smirkle; *compare* SNEER 1

rel grin, smile; fleer, leer, sneer

‖**smirkle** *vb syn* see SMIRK

smitch *n syn* see PARTICLE

smite *vb* **1** *syn* see STRIKE 2

rel bat, belt, clobber; dash

idiom smite a blow

2 *syn* see AFFLICT

smithereens *n pl* very small particles or fragments <a house blown to *smithereens* by a bomb>

syn ‖shivereens, smithers

rel fragments, particles, pieces

smithers *n pl syn* see SMITHEREENS

smitten *adj syn* see ENAMORED 1

idiom bitten by the love bug

smoke *n syn* see CIGARETTE

smoke *vb syn* see HURRY 2

smolder *vb syn* see SEETHE 4

rel burst, erupt, explode; fulminate

smooch *vb syn* see SOIL 2

smooch *vb syn* see KISS 1

idiom ‖plant a smooch on

‖**smoodge** *vb syn* see KISS 1

smooth *adj* **1** *syn* see LEVEL

rel glossy, sleek, slick; rippleless, unbroken, unwrinkled

con harsh, rugged, scabrous, uneven

ant rough

2 *syn* see HAIRLESS

3 *syn* see EASY 9

4 *syn* see EASY 1

rel smooth-running

idiom smooth and easy

ant labored

5 *syn* see SUAVE

rel courteous, courtly, polite; smooth-faced, smooth-tongued

con bluff, blunt, brusque, crusty, curt, gruff, harsh

6 *syn* see GENTLE 1

rel agreeable, soothing

smooth *vb* **1** *syn* see EVEN 1

con corrugate; roughen; wrinkle

ant unsmooth

2 *syn* see POLISH 2

smooth *adv syn* see EVENLY 3

smoothen *vb syn* see EVEN 1

smoothly *adv* **1** *syn* see EVENLY 3

con unevenly, ununiformly

ant roughly

2 *syn* see EASILY 1

ant unsmoothly

smooth–spoken *adj syn* see VOCAL 3

ant rough-spoken

smorgasbord *n syn* see MISCELLANY 1

smother *vb* **1** *syn* see SUFFOCATE

2 syn see COMPOSE 4

rel hush up, muffle; cork; quash, quell, squelch; quench

3 syn see WHIP 2

smothering *adj syn* see STIFLING 1

smothering *n syn* see REPRESSION 1

smothery *adj syn* see STIFLING 1

‖**smouch** *vb syn* see KISS 1

smouch *vb syn* see STEAL 1

smudge *vb* **1 syn** see SOIL 2

  rel smear; blotch, splotch

  2 syn see SMEAR 1

  3 syn see TAINT 1

‖**smudgy** *adj syn* see STIFLING 1

smug *adj syn* see COMPLACENT

  idiom pleased with oneself

smug *vb syn* see DRESS UP 1

smuggle *vb* to import or export secretly and in violation of the law <*smuggling* weapons into the country>

  syn bootleg, contraband, run

  idiom run contraband

smut *vb* **1 syn** see STAIN 1

  2 syn see TAINT 1

smutch *vb* **1 syn** see SOIL 2

  2 syn see TAINT 1

smutty *adj syn* see OBSCENE 2

snack *n* food served or taken informally and usually in small amounts and typically under other circumstances than a regular meal <a milk-and-cookie *snack* after school>

  syn ‖bait, ‖bever, bite, ‖chack, morsel, mug-up, nosh, ‖piece, tapa

  rel collation, refreshment, tea

  idiom bite to eat

snack bar (*or* **counter**) *n syn* see EATING HOUSE

‖**snaffle** *vb syn* see STEAL 1

‖**snafu** *vb syn* see CONFUSE 5

snag *n syn* see OBSTACLE

  rel brake, clog, curb, drag; hold-up

  idiom ‖snags and sawyers

snake *n syn* see SNOT 1

snake *vb* ‖**1 syn** see STEAL 1

  2 syn see CREEP 1

  3 syn see SLITHER 2

  ‖**4 syn** see SNEAK

snaky *adj syn* see WINDING

snap *vb* **1** to speak in a curt biting tone <*snapped* at his subordinates for inefficiency>

  syn bark, snarl

  rel growl, grumble, grunt, snort; roar, yell

  idiom bite one's head off, snap off one's head (*or* nose)

  2 syn see JERK

  rel clutch, grab, grasp, seize, snaffle, snatch

snap *n* **1** something easily managed or accomplished <that exam was a *snap*>

  syn breeze, child's play, cinch, duck soup, kid stuff, picnic, pie, ‖pipe, pushover, setup, ‖snip, soft touch

  rel sinecure

  idiom a simple twist of the wrist, simplicity itself, soft snap

  con difficulty, headache, problem, trouble; bother, inconvenience, pain

ant chore

  2 syn see PARTICLE

  3 syn see MAN 3

  4 syn see VIGOR 2

snap back *vb syn* see RECOVER 3

‖**snapper** *vb syn* see STUMBLE 3

snapping *adv syn* see VERY 1

snappish *adj syn* see IRRITABLE

  rel curt, short, ungracious; crabbed, morose, surly

snappy *adj* **1 syn** see IRRITABLE

  2 syn see FAST 3

  3 syn see PUNGENT

  rel animated, lively, vivacious; prompt, quick, ready

  4 syn see STYLISH

snare *n syn* see LURE 2

  rel chicane, chicanery, deception; ensnarement, entrapment

snare *vb syn* see CATCH 3

  rel seduce, tempt; involve; embrangle, enmesh, ensnarl, trammel

‖**snark** *vb syn* see SNORE

snarl *n* **1 syn** see CONFUSION 3

  rel entanglement, tangle; complexity, complication, intricacy, intricateness; labyrinth, maze; mishmash, swarm; jam

  idiom tangled skein, wheels within wheels

  2 syn see MAZE 1

snarl *vb* **1 syn** see ENTANGLE 1

  2 syn see COMPLICATE

snarl *vb syn* see SNAP 1

snarl up *vb syn* see CONFUSE 5

snatch *vb* **1 syn** see SEIZE 2

  rel jerk, wrench, yank; nip (up), whip (up)

  ‖**2 syn** see KIDNAP

sneak *vb* to move or go stealthily and furtively <*sneaked* into the garage and stole the car>

  syn creep, glide, gumshoe, lurk, ‖meech, pussyfoot, shirk, skulk, slide, slink, slip, sly, ‖snake, ‖snook, steal; *compare* STEAL 3

  rel crawl, slither, worm, prowl

  idiom go on (little) cat's feet, move under cover

  con barge, strut, swagger; clump, stamp, stump; stride; march, parade

sneak *n* a person who behaves in a stealthy, furtive, or shifty manner <found out that he was a liar, a cheat, and a *sneak*>

  syn slink, sneaker, sneaksby, weasel

  rel blackguard, knave, scoundrel; cur, heel, louse, reptile, skunk, snake; toad

  idiom Jerry Sneak

sneak *adj syn* see SECRET 1

sneaker *n syn* see SNEAK

sneaking *adj syn* see UNDERHAND

  ant forthright

sneaksby *n syn* see SNEAK

sneaky *adj syn* see UNDERHAND

‖**sneap** *vb syn* see REPROVE

---

syn synonym(s)   **rel** related word(s)

ant antonym(s)   **con** contrasted word(s)

idiom idiomatic equivalent(s)

‖ use limited; if in doubt, see a dictionary

sneer *vb* **1** to smile with attendant facial contortions expressing scorn or contempt <*sneered* haughtily at the beggar>
  syn fleer, leer, ‖sleer; *compare* SMIRK
  rel grin, smile
  idiom curl one's lip, make a scornful (*or* mocking) face
  2 *syn* see SCOFF
  rel belittle, detract, disparage, underrate
  idiom cock a snook at, give the Bronx cheer to, give the raspberry, sneeze at, thumb one's nose at
‖**sneezer** *n syn* see NOSE 1
snicker *vb syn* see LAUGH
  idiom have a case of the snickers
snide *adj* **1** *syn* see COUNTERFEIT
  2 *syn* see CROOKED 2
sniff *vb syn* see SMELL 1
‖**snift** *vb syn* see SMELL 1
  rel ‖snifter
snifter *n syn* see DRAM
‖**sniggle** *vb syn* see LAUGH
snip *n* **1** *syn* see MINX
  ‖**2** *syn* see SNAP 1
snippety *adj syn* see BLUFF
  rel impolite, insolent, rude
snippy *adj syn* see BLUFF
snip–snap *n syn* see BANTER
snit *n* a state of agitation or excited irritation especially over a trivial matter <was in a *snit* because the bus was one minute late>
  syn fume, stew, sweat, swivet, tizzy
  rel huff, pique; conniption, fit, frenzy, seizure, taking; dither, flap, panic, ‖swither
snitch *vb* **1** *syn* see INFORM 3
  2 *syn* see STEAL 1
snitch *n* ‖**1** *syn* see NOSE 1
  2 *syn* see INFORMER
snob *n* one inclined to rebuff or ignore people or things that he regards as inferior (as in culture or social status) <appeals to real lovers of music rather than musical *snobs*>
  syn high-hat, snoot, snot
  rel name-dropper, snobling; bootlicker, hanger-on, lickspittle, sycophant, toady
snob *vb syn* see CUT 7
snobbish *adj* of, relating to, or characteristic of a snob <a *snobbish* group of jet-set sophisticates>
  syn ‖dicty, high-hat, potty, snobby, snooty
  rel aloof, remote; high-flown, pretentious, snotty, supercilious; haughty, hoity-toity, pompous, ritzy; condescending, patronizing; insecure, uncertain, unconfident, unself-confident, unsure
  con certain, confident, secure, self-confident
snobby *adj syn* see SNOBBISH
  rel snubbing, snubby
‖**snook** *vb* **1** *syn* see SNOOP
  2 *syn* see SNEAK
snoop *vb* to look, inquire, or search impertinently or intrusively <he knew he had no right to *snoop* into her private life>
  syn busybody, mouse, nose, ‖piroot, poke, pry, ‖snook

  rel peek, peep, peer, stare; interfere, intrude, meddle, mess
  idiom stick (*or* poke) one's nose into
snoop *n syn* see BUSYBODY
snoopy *adj syn* see CURIOUS 2
snoot *n* **1** *syn* see NOSE 1
  2 *syn* see SNOB
snooty *adj syn* see SNOBBISH
snooze *vb syn* see NAP
snooze *n syn* see NAP
‖**snoozle** *vb syn* see DOZE
snoozy *adj syn* see SLEEPY 1
snore *vb* to breathe during sleep with a rough hoarse noise due to vibration of the soft palate <driven to distraction by her sister's *snoring*>
  syn ‖snark
  rel wheeze; snuffle; snort, ‖snotter
  idiom ‖drive pigs to market, ‖saw logs (*or* wood)
snort *n syn* see DRAM
snorter *n syn* see DRAM
snot *n* **1** an utterly contemptible person <a despicable *snot* whom everyone shunned>
  syn ‖bugger, cur, dog, louse, puke, rat, scum, ‖scumbag, skunk, snake, sod, stinkard, stinkaroo, stinker, toad, wretch; *compare* VILLAIN 1
  rel ‖creep, ‖crumb, lowlife; knave, rogue, scoundrel, ‖skite; pig, reptile
  2 *syn* see SNOB
snout *n syn* see NOSE 1
snowball *vb syn* see INCREASE 2
snub *vb syn* see CUT 7
  rel high-hat, ‖ritz, swank; put down
  idiom look coldly upon, turn a cold shoulder (on *or* upon)
‖**snudge** *vb syn* see SNUGGLE
‖**snuff** *n syn* see OFFENSE 2
snuff *vb syn* see SMELL 1
‖**snuff** (out) *vb syn* see DIE 1
snug *adj* **1** *syn* see NEAT 2
  2 *syn* see COMFORTABLE 2
  idiom snug as a bug in a rug
  ‖**3** *syn* see PROSPEROUS 3
snug *vb syn* see SNUGGLE
snuggle *vb* to assume or be in a warm comfortable position usually near another person or thing <a baby *snuggling* close to his mother>
  syn burrow, ‖croodle, cuddle, nestle, nuzzle, ‖snudge, snug, ‖snuzzle
  rel curl up; huddle; spoon
  idiom snuggle up like a bug in a rug
  con flinch, recoil, shrink
‖**snuzzle** *vb syn* see SNUGGLE
‖**sny** *vb syn* see TEEM
so *adv* **1** *syn* see ALSO 1
  2 *syn* see THUS 1
  3 *syn* see VERY 1
  4 *syn* see THEREFORE
so *conj* with the purpose that <repeated it aloud *so* there'd be no mistake>
  syn so as, so that
  idiom in order that, to the end that, with the intent that
soak *vb* **1** to permeate or be permeated with or as if with water <*soak* a sponge with water> <rain *soaked* her to the skin>

syn drench, ‖drouk, impregnate, insteep, saturate, seethe, sodden, ‖sog, sop, souse, steep, waterlog; *compare* WET

rel dip, immerse, submerge; draw, infuse; infiltrate, penetrate, permeate, pervade; water-soak; drown

2 *syn* see WET
3 *syn* see ENGAGE 4
4 *syn* see OVERCHARGE 1
5 *syn* see DRINK 3
idiom ‖soak it up like a sponge

soak *n* **1** *syn* see DRUNKARD
2 *syn* see BINGE 1

soaked *adj syn* see WET 1

soaker *n syn* see DRUNKARD

soaking *adj syn* see WET 1
idiom soaking wet

so–and–so *adj syn* see DAMNED 2

soapbox *vb syn* see ORATE

soapy *adj syn* see FULSOME

soar *vb* **1** *syn* see RISE 4
rel climb; shoot
2 *syn* see SKYROCKET
ant plummet

soaring *adj syn* see LOFTY 6
idiom high as the sky

so as *conj syn* see SO

sob *vb syn* see CRY 2

sobby *adj syn* see SENTIMENTAL

sober *adj* **1** *syn* see ABSTEMIOUS
rel controlled, restrained; self-possessed
con indulgent, overindulgent; uncontrolled, unrestrained; immoderate, intemperate; excessive; profligate
2 *syn* see SERIOUS 1
rel decorous, proper; calm, placid, serene, tranquil
con flippant, light, light-minded; unstable, volatile
ant gay
3 having or exhibiting self-control and avoiding extremes of behavior <his bearing was *sober*, his comments judicious>
syn moderate, temperate, unimpassioned; *compare* ABSTEMIOUS
rel rational, reasonable; calm, collected, composed, cool, imperturbable; constrained, disciplined, inhibited, reserved, restrained, self-controlled, self-disciplined; abstaining, forbearing, refraining; abnegating, eschewing, forgoing
con irrational, unreasonable; emotional, hotheaded, impassioned, overemotional, passionate; intemperate, uncontained, uncontrolled; excited; drunk, intoxicated; abandoned
ant unsober
4 *syn* see SUBDUED 2
5 *syn* see REALISTIC
rel sober-eyed, sober-minded

sobersided *adj syn* see SERIOUS 1

sobful *adj syn* see SENTIMENTAL

sobriety *n syn* see TEMPERANCE 2
rel gravity, sedateness, seriousness, soberness
con excitement; drunkenness, intoxication; abandonment

ant insobriety

sobriquet *n syn* see NICKNAME

so–called *adj* **1** *syn* see NOMINAL
2 *syn* see ALLEGED

sociable *adj* **1** *syn* see SOCIAL 2
ant nonsocial
2 *syn* see GRACIOUS 1
rel companionable, convivial; gregarious; close, familiar, intimate; good-natured
ant unsociable
3 *syn* see SOCIAL 1
ant unsociable, unsocial

social *adj* **1** conducive to, marked by, or passed in pleasant companionship with one's friends or associates <a relaxed, *social* evening>
syn companionable, convivial, sociable
rel amusing, entertaining, pleasant, pleasurable; cordial, friendly, genial, gracious, hospitable
con unfriendly, unhospitable; eremitic, solitary
ant unsociable, unsocial
2 inclined by nature to association or community life with others of the same species <man is a *social* animal>
syn gregarious, sociable
rel social-minded; intersocial
con eremitic, solitary, unsociable; antisocial, asocial, unsocial; remote, withdrawn
ant nonsocial

social evil *n, used with* the *syn* see PROSTITUTION

socialize *vb* to participate actively in a social group <*socializes* with her colleagues>
syn mingle
rel associate, mix

society *n* **1** *syn* see COMPANY 1
2 *syn* see ASSOCIATION 2
3 an organized aggregate of persons who are responsible for a prevailing social order <rules made in the interests of *society* rather than for the chosen few>
syn community, people, public
rel masses, populace
idiom people in general, society at large, the general public
4 *syn* see ARISTOCRACY
idiom high society (*or* life)

sock *vb syn* see STRIKE 2

sock *n* **1** *syn* see BLOW 1
2 *syn* see CUFF

‖**sock** *vb syn* see SIGH 1

sod *n syn* see SNOT 1

sodality *n syn* see ASSOCIATION 2

sodden *adj syn* see WET 1

sodden *vb syn* see SOAK 1

Sodom *n syn* see SINK 1
rel Babylon

so far *adv syn* see HITHERTO 1
idiom up till now

soft *adj* **1** *syn* see GENTLE 1
rel moderate, temperate

---

2 syn see SUBDUED 2
ant loud
3 smooth or delicate in texture, grain, or fiber <the dog's fur was *soft*>
syn cottony, satiny, silken, silky, velvety
rel smooth; sleek
con coarse, rough
ant harsh
4 syn see COMFORTABLE 2
ant rough
5 syn see SIMPLE 3
idiom ‖soft in the head
6 giving way easily to physical touch or pressure <a *soft cheese*>
syn mushy, pappy, pulpous, pulpy, quaggy, spongy, squashy, squelchy, squishy, squushy, yielding
rel softish; compressible, malleable, pliable, pliant, workable; doughy, formless; flabby, fleshy
idiom soft as butter
con firm, solid; resistant, rigid, tough, unyielding; nail-hard, rock-hard
ant hard
soft (on) *adj syn* see ENAMORED 1
soft–boiled *adj syn* see SENTIMENTAL
ant hard-boiled
soften *vb syn* see DEPRECIATE 1
softened *adj syn* see SUBDUED 2
softhead *n syn* see FOOL 4
softhearted *adj syn* see TENDER
ant hardhearted
soft–pedal *vb* to reduce the emphasis, importance, or effect of something (as an issue) <tried to *soft‗pedal* military spending>
syn de-emphasize, play (down)
rel tone (down), tune (down); cushion, dampen, muffle, subdue; hush (up), silence, suppress; conceal, disguise
con emphasize, play (up); focus (on), spotlight
soft–shell *adj syn* see MODERATE 4
soft soap *n syn* see FLATTERY
rel ‖snow job
soft–soap *vb syn* see COAX
soft spot *n* **1 syn** see APPETITE 3
2 a vulnerable point <the major *soft spot* in the West's armor>
syn Achilles' heel
rel vulnerability, vulnerableness, weakness; chink, loophole
idiom heel of Achilles, weak link (or point), weak link in the chain
con impregnability, invulnerability; invincibility
soft touch *n* **1** someone who can be easily talked into giving help (as a loan) <recognized him as a *soft touch* when she was broke>
syn easy mark
rel softy; dupe, fool, pushover; sucker; mark, sitting duck, target
con cynic, doubting Thomas, hard case, skeptic
2 syn see SNAP 1
‖**sog** *vb syn* see SOAK 1
‖**sog** *vb syn* see DOZE
soggy *adj syn* see HUMID

soi–disant *adj syn* see SELF-STYLED
soil *vb* **1 syn** see CONTAMINATE 1
ant purify
2 to make or become unclean <a shirt *soiled* with grease and grime>
syn begrime, besoil, dirty, foul, grime, muck, ‖mucky, muddy, murk, smirch, smooch, smudge, smutch, tarnish; *compare* STAIN 1
rel ‖becoom, ‖benasty, ‖nasty; bedaub, daub, smear; drabble, draggle; mess, spoil
con brighten, cleanse, freshen, renew; purify
ant clean
3 syn see TAINT 1
soil *n* **1 syn** see EARTH 2
2 syn see COUNTRY
soily *adj syn* see DIRTY 1
soiree *n syn* see EVENING 3
sojourn *n* a temporary but sometimes extended stay <a summer *sojourn* in Nice>
syn stopover, tarriance, visit
rel stay, stop; layover
sojourn *vb syn* see VISIT 3
rel linger; abide
Sol *n syn* see SUN 1
solace *vb syn* see COMFORT
idiom offer (or give) solace to, wipe one's tears away
soldier *n* a person engaged in military service <*soldiers* fighting and dying in futile wars>
syn fighter, fighting man, GI, man-at-arms, serviceman, swad, ‖swaddy, ‖sweat, warrior
rel dogface, doughboy, ‖doughfoot, grunt, infantryman; trooper; guerrilla, partisan; condottiere, free companion, free lance, mercenary, soldier of fortune
soldierly *adj syn* see BRAVE 1
rel martial; aggressive, combative, militant, pugnacious, warlike
con unsoldierly
sole *n syn* see BOTTOM 1
sole *adj* **1 syn** see SINGLE 1
2 syn see SINGLE 2
3 syn see ONLY 2
idiom one and only
4 belonging, granted, or attributed to the one person or group <*sole* rights of publication>
syn exclusive, single, unshared
con multiple; shared
solecism *n* **1 syn** see ANACHRONISM 2
2 syn see BARBARISM
3 syn see FAUX PAS
solely *adv syn* see ONLY 1
solemn *adj* **1 syn** see CEREMONIAL
rel full, plenary; august, grand, impressive, magnificent, majestic, overwhelming; ostentatious
2 syn see SERIOUS 1
idiom as solemn as an owl, grave as an undertaker
solemnize *vb syn* see KEEP 2
rel dignify, honor, solemnify, venerate
solicit *vb* **1** to seek (as advertising, orders, or votes) especially on a large scale <*solicited* contributions all over the district>

syn canvass, drum, drum up
rel ask, request; beg, beseech, implore; claim, demand, exact
2 *syn* see ASK 2
rel apply, go, refer, resort, turn
3 *syn* see DEMAND 1
solicitous *adj syn* see EAGER
solicitude *n* **1** *syn* see CARE 2
rel attention, heed, watchfulness; presentiment; compunction, qualm, scruple
con carelessness, heedlessness, indifference, neglect, negligence
ant unmindfulness
2 *syn* see CONSIDERATION 3
solid *adj* **1** *syn* see FIRM 2
rel compacted, concentrated, consolidated
con spongy; disintegrated; fluid, liquid
2 *syn* see STABLE 4
3 *syn* see VALID
rel firm, hard
ant insubstantial
4 *syn* see UNANIMOUS
solid *adv syn* see HARD 9
solidarism *n syn* see SOLIDARITY
solidarity *n* a feeling of unity (as in interests, standards, and responsibilities) that binds members of a group together <*solidarity* among union members is essential in negotiations>
syn cohesion, solidarism, togetherness
rel cohesiveness; oneness, singleness, undividedness; integrity, solidity, union, unity; esprit, esprit de corps; firmness, fixity
con separation; discord, dissension, schism; confusion, disorder, disorganization
ant division
solidify *vb syn* see HARDEN 1
rel compress, contract
idiom make (*or* become) hard as a rock
con soften; disintegrate, dissolve
ant liquefy
solidly *adv* **1** *syn* see HARD 9
2 *syn* see HARD 7
solitariness *n syn* see SOLITUDE
solitary *adj* **1** *syn* see ANTISOCIAL
ant gregarious
2 *syn* see UNSOCIABLE
3 *syn* see DERELICT 1
4 *syn* see LONE 1
rel companionless, unaccompanied, unattended
ant accompanied
5 *syn* see SINGLE 2
6 *syn* see ONLY 2
solitary *n syn* see RECLUSE
solitude *n* the state of one who is alone <a very social person who could not bear *solitude*>
syn aloneness, isolation, loneness, solitariness; *compare* SECLUSION
rel detachment, separateness; retirement, withdrawal; confinement, quarantine; loneliness, lonesomeness
con companionship, company
solo *adj syn* see ONLY 2
so long *interj syn* see GOOD-BYE
solution *n syn* see ANSWER 2

solve *vb* **1** to find an answer or solution for (a problem or difficulty) <mass transit partially *solved* the traffic problem>
syn fix, resolve, work, work out
rel decide, determine, settle
idiom hit upon a solution
2 to find an explanation or solution for something obscure, mysterious, or incomprehensible <the mystery of the missing cookies has been *solved*>
syn break, ‖cipher, clear up, decipher, dissolve, ‖dope out, figure out, puzzle out, resolve, unfold, unravel, unriddle
rel enlighten, illuminate; construe, elucidate, explain, interpret
idiom get to the bottom of, have it, put two and two together
somatic *adj syn* see BODILY
somber *adj* **1** *syn* see DARK 1
2 *syn* see GLOOMY 3
3 *syn* see SERIOUS 1
idiom as somber as an undertaker
some *adj* **1** *syn* see CERTAIN 2
2 *syn* see SEVERAL 3
some *adv* **1** *syn* see NEARLY
2 *syn* see SOMEWHAT 2
somebody *pron* one or some individual of no certain or known identity <*somebody* should be home>
syn someone
rel anybody, one
con none
ant nobody, no one
somebody *n* **1** *syn* see NOTABLE 1
ant nobody
2 *syn* see CELEBRITY 2
someday *adv syn* see YET 2
‖somegate *adv syn* see SOMEHOW
somehow *adv* in some way not yet known or specified <this thing must be done *somehow*>
syn ‖somegate, someway, somewise
rel anyhow, anyway, anywise
idiom by hook or by crook, in one way or another, in some such way, somehow or other (*or* another)
con nohow, noway, nowise
someone *pron syn* see SOMEBODY
someplace *adv syn* see SOMEWHERE 1
ant no place
something *adv syn* see SOMEWHAT 2
something *n syn* see ENTITY 1
sometime *adv syn* see YET 2
idiom one of these days
sometime *adj syn* see FORMER 2
sometimes *adv* at intervals <illustrated by beautiful and *sometimes* outstanding photographs>
syn at times, ‖betimes, ever and again, ever and anon, here and there, now and again, now and

---

syn synonym(s)   *rel* related word(s)
ant antonym(s)   *con* contrasted word(s)
idiom idiomatic equivalent(s)
‖ use limited; if in doubt, see a dictionary

then, once and again, ‖otherwhile; *compare* OCCA-SIONALLY
rel intermittently, periodically, recurrently; frequently; consistently, constantly
idiom every now and then (*or* again), every once in a while, every so often, from time to time
con continually, continuously, unceasingly, uninterruptedly; endlessly, ever, interminably

someway *adv syn* see SOMEHOW

somewhat *adv* 1 *syn* see WELL 8
2 to some extent or in some degree <felt *somewhat* better but not fine>
syn fairly, kind of, moderately, more or less, pretty, rather, ratherish, some, something, sort of
rel adequately, bearably, tolerably; insignificantly, slightly
idiom rather more than less

somewhen *adv syn* see YET 2

somewhere *adv* 1 to, at, or in some unknown or unspecified location <lived on a farm *somewhere* in the Midwest>
syn someplace, ‖somewheres
rel somewhither; elsewhere, otherwhere
idiom someplace or other
con anyplace, anywhere, ‖anywheres; no place, ‖nowheres
ant nowhere
2 *syn* see NEARLY

‖**somewheres** *adv syn* see SOMEWHERE 1
ant ‖nowheres

somewise *adv syn* see SOMEHOW

somnifacient *adj syn* see SOPORIFIC 1

somniferous *adj syn* see SOPORIFIC 1

somnific *adj syn* see SOPORIFIC 1

somnolent *adj* 1 *syn* see SOPORIFIC 1
2 *syn* see SLEEPY 1
rel inactive, passive, supine

somnorific *adj syn* see SOPORIFIC 1

so much as *adv syn* see EVEN 4

son *n syn* see BOY 1
rel sonny; junior

sonance *n syn* see SOUND 1

sonant *adj syn* see VOCAL 1

song *n* 1 *syn* see POETRY 1
2 music or a piece of music intended for vocal expression <played and sang a *song*>
syn aria, descant, ditty, hymn, lay, lied; *compare* MELODY
rel lyric; piece
3 *syn* see CALL 1

song and dance *n syn* see SPIEL

songful *adj syn* see MELODIOUS 2

sonorant *adj syn* see RESONANT

sonorous *adj* 1 *syn* see RESONANT
2 *syn* see RHETORICAL
3 *syn* see NOISY

‖**sonsy** *adj* 1 *syn* see LUCKY
2 *syn* see GRACIOUS 1
3 *syn* see EASYGOING 3

soon *adv* 1 *syn* see PRESENTLY 1
rel forthwith, instantly, pronto, quickly
idiom in the near future
2 *syn* see FAST 2

3 *syn* see EARLY 1

‖**soon** *adj syn* see EARLY 2

sooner *adv syn* see BEFORE 3

sooner or later *adv syn* see YET 2

soothe *vb syn* see CALM
rel comfort, console; hush, subdue
con annoy, irritate, vex
ant excite

‖**soother** *n syn* see CALM

soothsay *vb syn* see FORETELL

soothsayer *n syn* see PROPHET

sop *n* 1 *syn* see WEAKLING
2 a conciliatory or propitiatory gift or advance <provided the $400 raise as a *sop*> <the new office was a *sop* to his wounded feelings>
syn sugarplum
rel douceur, gratuity; ‖baksheesh, ‖boodle, bribe, ‖palm oil
idiom sop in the pan, sop to Cerberus

sop *vb* 1 *syn* see WET
2 *syn* see SOAK 1
3 *syn* see BRIBE

sophic *adj syn* see WISE 1

sophism *n syn* see FALLACY 2
rel illogicality, irrationality; invalidity, unsoundness; claptrap

sophistic *adj syn* see ILLOGICAL

sophisticate *adj syn* see SOPHISTICATED 2

sophisticate *vb syn* see ADULTERATE

sophisticated *adj* 1 *syn* see COMPLEX 2
ant unsophisticated
2 being experienced in the ways of the world <a *sophisticated*, well-traveled man>
syn blasé, disenchanted, disentranced, disillusioned, knowing, mondaine, sophisticate, worldly, worldly-wise, world-wise; *compare* COSMOPOLITAN 1
rel adult, mature; experienced, practiced, schooled, seasoned; salty, uncelestial; couth, well-bred; smooth, suave, svelte, urbane; bored, jaded, world-weary; brittle; cynical, skeptical
con artless, gee-whiz, ingenuous, natural; green, inexperienced, unseasoned, virginal; unworldly
ant naive, unsophisticated

sophistry *n syn* see FALLACY 2
rel ambiguity, tergiversation

soporiferous *adj syn* see SOPORIFIC 1

soporific *adj* 1 tending to induce sleep <a *soporific* drug> <*soporific* prose>
syn hypnotic, narcotic, opiate, sleepy, slumberous, somnifacient, somniferous, somnific, somnolent, somnorific, soporiferous, soporifical
rel calming, quietening, sedative, tranquilizing; anesthetic, deadening, numbing
con arousing, waking; invigorating, stimulating
2 *syn* see SLEEPY 1

soporifical *adj syn* see SOPORIFIC 1

sopping *adj syn* see WET 1

soppy *adj* 1 *syn* see WET 1
‖2 *syn* see SENTIMENTAL

sorcerer *n syn* see MAGICIAN 1

sorceress *n syn* see WITCH 1

sorcerous *adj syn* see MAGIC

sorcery *n syn* see MAGIC 1

sordid *adj* **1** *syn* see DIRTY 1
2 *syn* see SLATTERNLY
3 *syn* see BASE 3
rel foul, nasty, seamy, sodden
sore *adj syn* see PAINFUL 1
sorehead *n syn* see GROUCH
sorely *adv syn* see HARD 6
sorrow *n* distress of mind <felt great *sorrow* at the
loss of her friend>
syn affliction, anguish, care, ‖dole, grief, heartache, heartbreak, regret, rue, woe
rel mournfulness, sadness, sorrowfulness, unhappiness; grieving, lamentation, mourning, sorrowing; dejection, depression, melancholy; agony, distress, dolor, misery, suffering,
wretchedness
con cheerfulness, gaiety, gladness, happiness,
joyfulness; ecstasy
ant joy
sorrow *vb syn* see GRIEVE 2
rel groan, moan, sob
idiom break one's heart over, eat one's heart out
ant rejoice
sorrowful *adj* **1** *syn* see WOEFUL 1
rel sorrow-laden, sorrow-stricken, sorrow≈
struck
idiom full of (*or* filled with) sorrow
con sorrowless
ant joyful
2 *syn* see MELANCHOLY 2
ant gay
sorry *adj* **1** *syn* see SAD 1
rel bad, regretful, remorseful; miserable,
wretched
ant glad
2 *syn* see REMORSEFUL
3 *syn* see CONTEMPTIBLE
rel inadequate, paltry, poor, trifling; cheesy,
scruffy, shoddy; disgraceful
sort *n* **1** *syn* see TYPE
2 *syn* see GROUP 3
sort *vb* **1** *syn* see ASSORT
2 to analyze and assort (as individuals or things)
to obtain those desired or required <he knew he
must *sort* out facts from fancy>
syn comb, separate, sift, winnow; *compare*
SCREEN 5
rel riddle, screen; choose, cull, pick, select
con consolidate, join, lump, merge; aggregate,
amalgamate, blend, fuse, mix; unify
sort of *adv syn* see SOMEWHAT 2
SOS *n syn* see ALARM 1
soshed *adj syn* see INTOXICATED 1
so–so *adv syn* see ENOUGH 2
so–so *adj syn* see MEDIUM
sot *n syn* see DRUNKARD
‖**sot** *adj syn* see OBSTINATE
so that *conj syn* see SO
sotto voce *adv* in an inaudible or barely audible
voice <made a snide remark to her *sotto voce*>
syn faintly, mutedly, weakly
rel low, quietly, softly; muffledly; mutteringly;
aside, privately

idiom below one's breath, between one's teeth,
in an aside, in an undertone, in a whisper, out of
earshot, under one's breath
con aloud, out, out loud
sough *vb* **1** *syn* see SIGH 2
2 *syn* see SIGH 1
soul *n* **1** an animating essence or principle held to
be inseparably associated with life or living beings <philosophers who teach that life is a manifestation of *soul*>
syn anima, animus, élan vital, pneuma, psyche,
spirit, vital force
rel life, vitality
idiom breath of life
2 the immortal part of man believed to have permanent individual existence <into God's hands I
commit my *soul*>
syn spirit
rel life; noumenon
idiom one's immortal soul
con flesh
ant body
3 *syn* see HEART 1
rel character, personality, psyche; conscience;
spirit
idiom heart of hearts, heart's core, one's inmost
soul (*or* mind), one's secret (*or* inner) self, (the)
secret recesses of the heart
4 *syn* see ESSENCE 2
5 *syn* see HUMAN
soul–searching *n syn* see INTROSPECTION
soul–sick *adj syn* see DOWNCAST
sound *adj* **1** *syn* see HEALTHY 1
rel intact, unimpaired; perfect
idiom sound as a bell (*or* whistle), sound of
mind and body
con impaired; unfit
ant unsound
2 *syn* see WHOLE 1
3 *syn* see STABLE 4
ant unsound
4 *syn* see VALID
rel errorless, faultless, flawless, impeccable; accurate, correct, exact, precise; rational, reasonable; well-founded, well-grounded
con questionable, shaky; invalid
ant unsound
5 *syn* see ORTHODOX 1
6 *syn* see RATIONAL
rel right-minded, sober, sober-minded, sound≈
minded
ant unsound
sound *n* **1** a sensation or effect resulting from stimulation of the auditory receptors <the *sound* of
thunder>
syn noise, sonance
rel vibration; resonance; sonancy; reverberation
con quiet, soundlessness
ant silence

---

syn synonym(s)   *rel* related word(s)
ant antonym(s)   *con* contrasted word(s)
idiom idiomatic equivalent(s)
‖ use limited; if in doubt, see a dictionary

2 *syn* see EARSHOT

sound *vb* **1** *syn* see SEEM

2 *syn* see DECLARE 1

sound *vb* to measure the depth of (as a body of water) typically with a weighted line <*sounding* the distance to the bottom>

syn fathom, plumb, plumb-line

idiom ‖cast (*or* sling) the lead, make a sounding, take soundings

sound (out) *vb* *syn* see PROBE 2

soundless *adj* *syn* see BOTTOMLESS 2

ant soundable

soundless *adj* *syn* see STILL 3

soundlessness *n* *syn* see SILENCE 1

soundness *n* **1** *syn* see HEALTH

ant unsoundness

2 *syn* see STABILITY

3 *syn* see WIT 2

rel level-headedness, sensibleness

idiom sound mind, soundness of mind

ant unsoundness

sound off *vb* *syn* see SPEAK UP

soup *n* *syn* see PREDICAMENT

soupçon *n* *syn* see HINT 2

soupy *adj* *syn* see SENTIMENTAL

sour *adj* **1** causing or characterized by the one of the basic taste sensations produced chiefly by acids <*sour* pickles>

syn acerb, acerbic, acetose, acid, acidulous, dry, tart

rel keen, sharp, tangy; ‖blinky, sourish; fermented, soured, turned; acrid, bitter, vinegary

ant sweet

2 *syn* see BAD 8

source *n* the point at which something begins its course or existence <the *source* of her wisdom was long practical experience>

syn derivation, fount, fountain, fountainhead, inception, mother, origin, provenance, provenience, root, rootage, rootstock, spring, well, wellhead, wellspring, whence

rel birthplace; beginning, commencement, dawn, dawning, onset, opening, start, starting; authorship, origination, rise, rising; antecedent, cause, determinant; parent, paternity

con end, ending, terminus

ant termination; outcome

sourpuss *n* *syn* see GROUCH

rel killjoy

souse *vb* **1** *syn* see DIP 1

2 *syn* see WET

3 *syn* see SOAK 1

souse *n* *syn* see BINGE 1

soused *adj* *syn* see WET 1

souvenir *n* *syn* see REMEMBRANCE 3

idiom token of remembrance

sovereign *adj* **1** *syn* see FREE 1

rel self-determined, self-governed

2 *syn* see DOMINANT 1

rel commanding, directing, guiding; highest, loftiest

3 *syn* see EXCELLENT

4 *syn* see KINGLY

sovereignty *n* *syn* see SUPREMACY

sow *vb* **1** *syn* see PLANT 1

2 *syn* see STREW 1

rel fling, toss; drill

‖**sowf** *vb* *syn* see HUM

sozzled *adj* *syn* see INTOXICATED 1

spa *n* **1** a locality featuring mineral springs or water cures <hoped a week at a *spa* would help his arthritis>

syn baths, ‖hydro, springs, watering place, wells

rel waters

idiom health spa

2 *syn* see RESORT 3

space *n* **1** *syn* see WHILE 1

rel lapse; interval, term; duration

2 *syn* see EXPANSE

rel room, roomage; spaciousness

spaced-out *adj* *syn* see DRUGGED

spacious *adj* larger in extent or capacity than the average <a mansion with *spacious* rooms and gardens>

syn ample, capacious, commodious, roomy, wide

rel big, generous, great, large, spacy; enormous, immense, vast; expansive, extended, extensive; boundless, spaceless

con circumscribed, confined, cramped, limited, narrow, restricted; small, tiny

ant strait

spade *vb* **1** *syn* see DIG 2

2 *syn* see DIG 1

span *n* *syn* see TERM 2

rel interval; space

spang *adv* *syn* see JUST 1

spangle *vb* **1** to adorn with small brilliant objects <a tutu *spangled* with sequins>

syn bespangle, glitter

rel adorn, decorate, ornament, trim

2 *syn* see FLASH 1

spang-new *adj* *syn* see BRAND-NEW

spaniel *n* *syn* see SYCOPHANT

spank *vb* *syn* see SLAP 1

spank *n* *syn* see CUFF

idiom a sound spank

spanking *adv* *syn* see VERY 1

spanking-new *adj* *syn* see BRAND-NEW

span-new *adj* *syn* see BRAND-NEW

spare *vb* **1** *syn* see EXEMPT

2 *syn* see SAVE 4

3 to refrain from the free use or consumption of <don't *spare* the syrup on my pancakes>

syn scant, short, skimp, ‖skinch, stint; *compare* SCRIMP

rel pinch

4 *syn* see SCRIMP

spare *adj* **1** *syn* see SUPERFLUOUS

idiom enough and to spare, more than enough

2 *syn* see LEAN

ant corpulent

3 *syn* see MEAGER 2

ant profuse

sparing *adj* careful in the use of money, goods, or resources <was *sparing* in his expenditures>

syn canny, chary, economical, frugal, provident, saving, Scotch, stewardly, thrifty, unwasteful, wary; *compare* STINGY

rel parsimonious, ‖scant, tight, tightfisted, ungiving
con exuberant, liberal, prodigal, profuse
ant lavish, unsparing
spark *n syn* see SEED 2
spark *n syn* see SUITOR 2
spark *vb syn* see ADDRESS 8
sparker *n syn* see SUITOR 2
sparkish *adj syn* see DAPPER
sparkle *vb syn* see FLASH 1
sparkle *n syn* see FLASH 1
sparse *adj syn* see MEAGER 2
rel dispersed, scattered; infrequent, occasional, sporadic; rare, scarce, uncommon
con close, compact, thick
‖spartle *vb syn* see SCRAMBLE 1
spasmodic *adj syn* see FITFUL
rel spurtive
con continual, continuous, uninterrupted
spat *n* **1** *syn* see QUARREL
‖2 *syn* see CUFF
spat *vb syn* see QUARREL
spate *n* **1** *syn* see FLOOD 2
rel progression, series, succession; rain, river, spurt
2 *syn* see FLOW
spatter *vb* **1** *syn* see SPLASH
rel sparge
2 *syn* see SPOT 1
3 *syn* see MALIGN
4 *syn* see SPUTTER 2
spatter *n syn* see FEW
spattering *n syn* see FEW
spawn *vb syn* see GENERATE 1
spawning *adj syn* see FERTILE
speak *vb* **1** to articulate words in order to express thoughts <always *speak* clearly>
syn talk, utter, verbalize, vocalize, voice
rel drawl, gasp, mouth, mumble, murmur, mutter, shout, splutter, spout, whisper; descant, dilate (on *or* upon), expatiate, perorate; converse, discourse; allege, assert, aver, convey, declare, tell
idiom break silence, give voice (*or* tongue *or* utterance) to, let fall, make public (*or* known), open one's mouth (*or* lips), put in (*or* into) words, say one's say, speak one's piece
con gabble, gibber, jabber; maunder, mumble, mutter; mispronounce, misspeak
2 *syn* see TALK 7
3 to have oral command of (a language) <he *speaks* fluent German>
syn converse (in), parley, talk, use
idiom be at ease in
con falter, hesitate, stumble
speaker *n syn* see SPOKESMAN
speaking *n syn* see SPEECH 1
speak out *vb syn* see SPEAK UP
speak up *vb* to speak strongly, boldly, or vigorously <we'll never know how you feel if you don't *speak up*>
syn sound off, speak out
idiom come out with it, have one's say, let one's voice be heard, make oneself heard, speak one's mind, stand up and be counted

spear *vb syn* see IMPALE
rel stick; bore, drill, penetrate, pierce; gouge, ream
special *adj* **1** of or relating to one thing or class <*special* soap for infants>
syn especial, individual, particular, specific
rel characteristic, distinctive, peculiar; exceptional, occasional, rare, uncommon; unique
con common, familiar, ordinary; customary, habitual, usual
2 *syn* see EXPRESS 2
rel defined, determinate; designated, earmarked
special *adv syn* see ESPECIALLY 1
specialize *vb syn* see ITEMIZE 1
specially *adv* **1** *syn* see ESPECIALLY 1
2 *syn* see EXPRESSLY 2
species *n syn* see TYPE
specific *adj* **1** *syn* see SPECIAL 1
rel limited, reserved, restricted, specialized
con general, generic
ant nonspecific, unspecific
2 *syn* see EXPLICIT
con ambiguous, cloudy, indefinite, uncertain, unexplicit, unspecified, vague
ant nonspecific, unspecific
3 *syn* see EXPRESS 2
ant nonspecific, unspecific
specifically *adv* **1** *syn* see EXPRESSLY 2
2 *syn* see ESPECIALLY 1
3 *syn* see EXPRESSLY 1
specificate *vb syn* see SPECIFY 3
specificize *vb syn* see SPECIFY 3
specify *vb* **1** *syn* see MENTION
2 *syn* see ITEMIZE 1
3 to make something (as a condition or requirement) specific <his will *specified* how the money would be divided>
syn detail, particularize, specificate, specificize, stipulate; *compare* ITEMIZE 1
rel determine, establish, fix, settle; condition, limit, set; pin (down); enumerate, list; precise
specimen *n syn* see INSTANCE
rel sort, species, type, variety
specious *adj syn* see FALSE 1
rel apparent, seeming; colorable, plausible; beguiling; illogical, spurious; empty, hollow, idle, nugatory, vain
ant valid
speciousness *n syn* see FALLACY 2
rel speciosity
ant validity
speck *n* **1** *syn* see POINT 11
rel pinpoint; tick
2 *syn* see PARTICLE
speck *vb syn* see SPECKLE 1
speckle *vb* **1** to produce on or mark with small spots, speckles, or blemishes <a *speckled* egg>
syn bespeckle, dot, freckle, pepper, speck, sprinkle, stipple; *compare* SPOT 1

---

syn synonym(s)   *rel* related word(s)
ant antonym(s)   *con* contrasted word(s)
idiom idiomatic equivalent(s)
‖ use limited; if in doubt, see a dictionary

rel dapple, flake, fleck
2 *syn* see SPOT 2

spectacle *n syn* see EXHIBITION 1

spectacled *adj syn* see BESPECTACLED

spectacular *adj syn* see MARVELOUS 1
rel eye-popping, sensational, striking, thrilling; dramatic, histrionic, stagy, theatrical
ant unspectacular

spectator *n* one who sees or looks upon something <sports *spectators*>
syn beholder, by-sitter, bystander, eyewitness, looker-on, observer, onlooker, stander-by, viewer, watcher, witness
rel gazer; perceiver; seer

specter *n syn* see APPARITION

spectral *adj syn* see GHASTLY 2
rel phantom, phantomlike, shadowlike; disembodied, unearthly; spooky

spectrum *n* 1 *syn* see APPARITION
2 *syn* see RANGE 5

speculate *vb syn* see THINK 5
rel excogitate, review, study, weigh
idiom ‖beat one's brains, turn over in one's mind, ‖use the gray matter

speculation *n* 1 *syn* see THOUGHT 1
rel excogitation, review, studying, weighing
2 *syn* see THEORY 2

speculative *adj* 1 *syn* see THEORETICAL 1
2 *syn* see THOUGHTFUL 1
rel musing, ruminating; curious, inquiring, questioning
ant unspeculative

speech *n* 1 communication, expression, or interchange of thoughts in spoken words <considered *speech* as a means of reproducing for one's listeners the images in one's mind>
syn discourse, speaking, talk, utterance, verbalization; *compare* VOCALIZATION
rel articulation, uttering, vocalization, vocalizing, voice, voicing; expressing, expression; language
idiom oral communication, vocal expression
2 a usually formal discourse delivered to an audience <a televised *speech* to the nation>
syn address, allocution, lecture, talk
rel debate, parlance, parley; declamation, harangue, oration, speechification
3 *syn* see LANGUAGE 1

speechcraft *n syn* see ORATORY

speechless *adj* 1 *syn* see DUMB 1
rel aphonic
2 *syn* see SILENT 2
3 *syn* see SILENT 3

speed *n* 1 *syn* see HASTE 1
rel alacrity, legerity; headway
con dilatoriness, tardiness
2 rate of movement, performance, or occurrence <ran through the exercise at a high *speed*>
syn ‖bat, celerity, gait, pace, quickness, rapidity, rapidness, swiftness, velocity; *compare* TEMPO
rel fastness, fleetness; clip, hickory

speed *vb* 1 *syn* see HURRY 2
idiom make haste
ant slow (up *or* down)

2 *syn* see COURSE
3 to cause to move fast or faster <*sped* our craft forward>
syn accelerate, hasten, hurry, quicken, shake up, step up, swiften
rel advance, aid, ease, encourage, expedite, facilitate, forward, further, help (along), smooth; cheer (on), drive (on), goad (on), spur (on); burn (up)
idiom ‖get the lead out
con hamper, restrain, retard; check, stay; delay, postpone, put off
ant slow (up *or* down)

speedily *adv syn* see FAST 2
idiom against the clock, hell-bent for leather, like a bat out of hell, like all forty, ‖like all get‑ out, on the double, to beat the band
con deliberately, languidly, leisurely; lazily, lethargically, sluggishly; crawlingly, creepingly
ant slow, slowly

speediness *n syn* see HASTE 1
ant slowness

speedy *adj syn* see FAST 3
rel agile, brisk, nimble; prompt, ready
idiom fast as greased lightning, speedy as an arrow
ant dilatory; slow

speerings *n pl syn* see NEWS

‖**spelder** *vb syn* see SPRAWL 1

spell *n* a spoken word or set of words believed to have magic power <cause death by muttering *spells* over her>
syn charm, conjuration, ‖devil-devil, incantation, rune
rel bewitching, enchanting, hexing

spell *vb syn* see BEWITCH 1

spell *vb syn* see MEAN 2

spell *vb* 1 *syn* see RELIEVE 3
2 *syn* see REST 3

spell *n* 1 a limited period or amount of activity <each *spell* of work was followed by a brief rest>
syn bout, go, shift, stint, time, tour, trick, turn
rel streak; ‖patch, period; stretch; relay
2 *syn* see WHILE 1
3 *syn* see ATTACK 3

spellbind *vb syn* see ENTHRALL 2

spell out *vb syn* see EXPLAIN 1

spend *vb* 1 to distribute or consume in payment or expenditure <*spent* fifty dollars for that dress>
syn disburse, expend, fork (out), give, lay out, outlay, pay, shell out
rel blow, drop, hand out; contribute; consume, dissipate, lavish, squander, throw away, waste
ant save
2 *syn* see GO 4
3 to cause or permit to elapse <*spent* the summer at the beach>
syn pass, while (away)

spender *n syn* see SPENDTHRIFT
ant saver

spending money *n syn* see POCKET MONEY

spendthrift *n* one who dissipates his resources foolishly and wastefully <a *spendthrift* who lost his estate through gambling>

syn high roller, prodigal, profligate, scatter-good, spender, squanderer, unthrift, waster, wastethrift, wastrel
con hoarder, miser, saver
spent *adj syn* see EFFETE 2
spew *vb* **1** *syn* see VOMIT
2 *syn* see ERUPT 1
rel flood, gush
sphere *n* **1** *syn* see BALL
2 *syn* see FIELD
rel circle, jurisdiction, realm
sphere *vb syn* see BALL
spice *n* **1** *syn* see HINT 2
2 *syn* see FRAGRANCE
spick–and–span *adj* **1** *syn* see BRAND-NEW
2 *syn* see NEAT 2
spicy *adj* **1** *syn* see SWEET 2
2 *syn* see PUNGENT
rel fiery, gingery, high-spirited, spirited, zestful
3 *syn* see RISQUÉ
rel sophisticated; piquant
spider *n syn* see FRYING PAN
spiel *n* voluble, glib, or extravagant talk often intended to impress, persuade, or deceive <gave her a long sales *spiel*>
syn ‖line, pitch, song and dance
rel demagoguery; dramatics, pyrotechnics, sensationalism
‖**spieler** *n syn* see SWINDLER
spiff *vb syn* see DRESS UP 1
spiffy *adj syn* see DAPPER
‖**spiflicated** *adj syn* see INTOXICATED 1
spigot *n syn* see FAUCET
spike *vb syn* see IMPALE
spill *vb* **1** to cause or allow (something) to fall, flow, or run out and be lost or wasted <accidentally dropped the cup and *spilled* his tea>
syn slop, squab
rel dribble, drip, drop; spatter, splash, spray
2 *syn* see OVERFLOW 2
3 *syn* see REVEAL 1
spilth *n syn* see REFUSE
spin *vb* **1** to turn or cause to turn rapidly <pinwheels *spinning* in the wind>
syn gyrate, gyre, ‖pirl, pirouette, ‖purl, twirl, whirl, whirligig; *compare* TURN 1
rel revolve, rotate, wheel; swirl; oscillate, pendulate, vibrate
idiom spin like a top
2 to feel as if revolving <her head was *spinning* with figures>
syn reel, swim, turn, whirl
rel dizzy, giddy; fluster, mix up, muddle
idiom be in a whirl
spin (out) *vb syn* see EXTEND 3
spin *n syn* see DRIVE 1
spinal column *n syn* see SPINE
spindling *adj syn* see GANGLING
spindly *adj syn* see GANGLING
spine *n* the articulated column of bones that is the central and axial feature of a vertebrate skeleton <fractured his *spine*>
syn back, backbone, rachis, spinal column, vertebrae, vertebral column

rel spinal cord
spineless *adj syn* see WEAK 4
rel weak-kneed, weak-willed
idiom as spineless as an amoeba
con self-willed, strong-willed
spin–off *n syn* see OUTGROWTH 2
spinster *n* a woman who is past the common age for marrying or who seems unlikely ever to marry <a gentle *spinster*, happy in her solitary life>
syn maiden lady, old maid, spinstress, ‖tabby
spinstress *n syn* see SPINSTER
spiny *adj syn* see THORNY
spiral *vb syn* see WIND 2
spiring *adj syn* see LOFTY 6
spirit *n* **1** *syn* see SOUL 1
2 *syn* see APPARITION
3 *syn* see SOUL 2
4 *syn* see TEMPER 1
5 a lively or brisk quality in a person or his actions <a man of great *spirit* and courage>
syn animation, brio, dash, élan, esprit, gimp, life, oomph, verve, vim, zing; *compare* VIGOR 2
rel ardor, briskness, enthusiasm, liveliness; drive, get-up-and-go, ginger, go, pep, snap, starch, vigor, vitality, zip; character, force, substance
6 *syn* see COURAGE
rel ardor, fervor, passion, zeal; energy, force, might, power, strength
7 *often* **spirits** *pl syn* see LIQUOR
spirit (away) *vb syn* see KIDNAP
spirit (up) *vb syn* see ELATE
spirited *adj* **1** *syn* see LIVELY 1
rel sharp; fiery, gingery, peppery
idiom full of life (*or* go)
ant spiritless
2 having or manifesting a high degree of vitality, spirit, and daring <the lawyer gave a *spirited* defense of his client>
syn beany, fiery, gingery, high-hearted, high-spirited, mettlesome, peppery, spunky
rel game, gritty, resolute; audacious, bold, brave, courageous, dauntless, fearless, intrepid, nervy, plucky, valiant; avid, eager, hot, keen; ardent, enthusiastic, fervent, hot, passionate, peppy, zealous
con unenthusiastic; flabby, languid, limp; boneless, spineless
ant spiritless
spiritless *adj* **1** *syn* see DEAD 1
2 *syn* see DOWNCAST
idiom down in the dumps
3 *syn* see LANGUID
rel tame; broken, subdued, submissive
ant spirited
spiritual *adj* **1** *syn* see IMMATERIAL 1
rel supernatural, supramundane
ant physical

---

syn synonym(s)   *rel* related word(s)
ant antonym(s)   *con* contrasted word(s)
idiom idiomatic equivalent(s)
‖ use limited; if in doubt, see a dictionary

2 syn see SACRED 2

3 syn see ECCLESIASTICAL

4 appealing to, coming from, or related to the higher emotions or to the aesthetic senses <man's *spiritual* and intellectual life as opposed to his animal instincts>

syn numinous

rel cerebral, intellectual, mental; elevated, high, high-minded, lofty; saintly

con low, lower; base

ant animal

spirituous *adj* containing a considerable amount of alcohol <*spirituous* liquors>

syn alcoholic, ardent, hard, strong

rel spiked; inebriating, intoxicating, intoxicative; heady

con nonalcoholic, nonintoxicating, soft

‖**spirity** *adj syn* see LIVELY 1

spit *vb syn* see IMPALE

spit *n* **1 syn** see SALIVA

2 syn see IMAGE 1

rel counterpart; look-alike; twin

spit *vb* **1 syn** see SPUTTER 1

2 syn see SPUTTER 2

spite *n syn* see MALICE

rel rancor; revenge, revengefulness, vengeance, vengefulness, vindictiveness

con sympathy; affection, love, tenderness

spiteful *adj syn* see MALICIOUS

rel antagonistic, hostile; revengeful, vengeful, vindictive

con charitable; sympathetic; affectionate, loving

ant spiteless

spitefulness *n syn* see MALICE

spitish *adj syn* see MALICIOUS

spitting image *n syn* see IMAGE 1

rel mirror image

spittle *n syn* see SALIVA

spit up *vb syn* see VOMIT

‖**spiv** *n* **1 syn** see PARASITE

2 syn see SLACKER

splash *vb* to dash a liquid or semiliquid substance upon or against <*splashed* water onto her face>

syn douse, plash, slop, slosh, spatter, splatter, splosh, splurge, spurtle, swash

rel dash, throw; spray; sprinkle; ‖sprent, squirt; drench, drown, soak, sop, wet

splashy *adj syn* see SHOWY

splathering *adj syn* see CLUMSY 1

splatter *vb syn* see SPLASH

splay *adj syn* see CLUMSY 1

spleen *n syn* see MALICE

rel revenge, revengefulness, vindictiveness; wrath

splendid *adj* **1 syn** see GRAND 2

rel baroque, flamboyant

2 extraordinarily or transcendently impressive <a *splendid* new city>

syn glorious, gorgeous, magnificent, proud, resplendent, splendiferous, splendorous, sublime, superb

rel eminent, illustrious; grand, impressive, lavish, luxurious, royal, sumptuous; divine, exquisite, lovely; incomparable, matchless, peerless,

superlative, supreme, unparalleled, unsurpassed; surpassing, transcendent

con common, ordinary, run-of-the-mill

ant unimpressive

splendiferous *adj syn* see SPLENDID 2

rel dazzling, marvelous; smashing, walloping; rattling, ripping, screaming, terrific

splendorous *adj syn* see SPLENDID 2

splice *vb syn* see MARRY 2

splinter *vb syn* see SHATTER 1

splinterize *vb syn* see SHATTER 1

split *vb* **1 syn** see CUT 5

rel crack, rive

2 syn see TEAR 1

‖**3 syn** see BETRAY 2

split (up) *vb syn* see SEPARATE 1

split *n* **1 syn** see CRACK 3

2 syn see SCHISM 3

3 syn see BREACH 3

rel alienating, estranging

split second *n syn* see INSTANT 1

splitter *vb syn* see SHATTER 1

split–up *n syn* see SEPARATION 1

‖**splodge** *vb syn* see SPLOTCH

splosh *vb syn* see SPLASH

splotch *vb* to mark or spot with irregular patches especially of contrasting color <a black horse *splotched* with white>

syn blotch, mottle, ‖splodge

rel blot, stain; dapple, fleck, marble, motley, variegate; bespot, spot; harlequin

‖**splunge** *vb syn* see PLUNGE 2

splurge *n syn* see SPREE 1

rel extravagance; splash

splurge *vb syn* see SPLASH

splurt *vb syn* see SQUIRT

splutter *vb* **1 syn** see SPUTTER 2

2 syn see SPUTTER 1

spoil *n* something taken from another by force or craft <gold, jewels, and paintings are often *spoils* of war>

syn boodle, booty, loot, plunder, plunderage, prize, ‖spreaghery, ‖spulzie, swag

rel acquisition, grab, haul, take; pickings, stealings; pillage, spoliation

spoil *vb* **1 syn** see RAVAGE

2 syn see INJURE 1

rel ‖snafu; ruin, wreck; demolish, destroy

3 syn see RAPE

4 syn see BABY

rel accommodate, favor, oblige

idiom spoil (one) rotten, spoil to death

5 syn see DECAY

spoiled *adj* **1 syn** see DAMAGED

ant unspoiled

2 syn see BAD 5

rel off, tainted; putrefying, rotting

ant unspoiled

spoiler *n syn* see MARAUDER

spoken *adj* **1 syn** see ORAL 2

ant written

2 syn see VOCAL 1

ant unspoken

spokesman *n* one who speaks as a representative of another <selected as *spokesman* for the party's views>
  syn mouth, mouthpiece, speaker, spokesperson, spokeswoman
  rel delegate, deputy, representative; champion, protagonist; prophet
spokesperson *n syn* see SPOKESMAN
spokeswoman *n syn* see SPOKESMAN
spoliate *vb syn* see RAVAGE
  rel raid; maraud; gut, ravish, sweep
spoliator *n syn* see MARAUDER
sponge *n* **1** *syn* see DRUNKARD
  2 *syn* see PARASITE
sponger *n syn* see PARASITE
spongy *adj syn* see SOFT 6
  idiom as soft as a sponge
sponsor *n* one that accepts responsibility for another person or thing <the major *sponsor* of this project is the government>
  syn angel, backer, backer-up, guarantor, patron, surety
  rel advocate, champion, mainstay, supporter, upholder; preferrer, promoter; benefactor, Maecenas
sponsorship *n syn* see BACKING
spontaneity *n syn* see UNCONSTRAINT
  rel extemporaneousness, offhandedness, unpremeditatedness
spontaneous *adj* acting or activated without apparent thought or deliberation <a *spontaneous* burst of applause>
  syn automatic, impulsive, instinctive, involuntary, unmeditated, unpremeditated, unprompted, will-less
  rel unconstrained, unforced; unreasoned, unstudied; extemporaneous, extempore, impromptu, improvised, offhand; natural, simple, unsophisticated
  con deliberate, intended, intentional, planned, predetermined, preplanned, studied, thought-out, voluntary, willed, willful; forced, prompted; conventional, formal, stylized
  ant premeditated
spontoon *n syn* see CUDGEL
spoof *vb syn* see DUPE
spoof *n syn* see IMPOSTURE
spook *n* ‖**1** *syn* see APPARITION
  ‖**2** *syn* see ECCENTRIC
  3 *syn* see SPY
‖**spook** *vb* **1** *syn* see FRIGHTEN
  2 *syn* see GHOSTWRITE
spooky *adj* **1** *syn* see WEIRD 1
  rel spookish; ominous
  2 *syn* see NERVOUS
‖**spoon** *n syn* see DUNCE
spoony *adj syn* see SIMPLE 3
spoony (over *or* on) *adj syn* see ENAMORED 1
spoor *n syn* see FOOTPRINT
sporadic *adj* **1** *syn* see FITFUL
  ant regular
  2 *syn* see INFREQUENT
  rel separate, single
  ant frequent

sporadically *adv syn* see OCCASIONALLY
  ant regularly
sport *vb syn* see PLAY 1
sport *n* **1** *syn* see PLAY 1
  2 sports *pl syn* see ATHLETICS
  3 *syn* see FUN 1
  rel jollification; antics, high jinks, horseplay
  4 *syn* see LAUGHINGSTOCK
  5 *syn* see CHANGE 2
sporting girl *n syn* see PROSTITUTE
sporting house *n syn* see BROTHEL
sportive *adj syn* see PLAYFUL 1
sportiveness *n syn* see MISCHIEVOUSNESS
sportsmanlike *adj syn* see FAIR 5
  ant unsporting, unsportsmanlike
sportsmanly *adj syn* see FAIR 5
  ant unsporting, unsportsmanlike
sporty *adj syn* see WILD 7
spot *n* **1** *syn* see STIGMA
  2 *syn* see DRAM
  3 *syn* see PARTICLE
  4 *syn* see PLACE 1
  rel scene; section, sector
  5 *syn* see JOB 2
  idiom job slot
  6 *syn* see PREDICAMENT
spot *vb* **1** to mark or stain (something) with spots <a white dress *spotted* with red mud>
  syn bespatter, bespot, spatter; *compare* SPECKLE 1
  rel blot, blotch, mottle; fleck, marble, streak, stripe; dot, pepper, speck, speckle, sprinkle, stipple; splash; dirty, soil, stain
  2 to form or appear as spots on <a bleak landscape *spotted* with cottages>
  syn dot, pimple, speckle, sprinkle, stud
  rel intersperse
  3 *syn* see IDENTIFY
  rel ascertain; see
  4 *syn* see FIND 1
spot *adj syn* see RANDOM
spotless *adj* **1** *syn* see CLEAN 1
  rel hygienic, sanitary
  2 *syn* see CHASTE
  ant spotted
spotty *adj* **1** lacking uniformity <*spotty* illumination>
  syn irregular, patchy, uneven
  rel unequal; flickering, fluctuating
  con equal, even, regular, uniform
  2 *syn* see FITFUL
spousal *n syn* see WEDDING
spousal *adj syn* see MATRIMONIAL
spouse *n* a marriage partner <consulted with her *spouse* before buying the car>
  syn consort, mate
spouseless *adj syn* see SINGLE 1
  con espoused
‖**spout** *vb syn* see PAWN

---

syn synonym(s)   *rel* related word(s)
ant antonym(s)   *con* contrasted word(s)
idiom idiomatic equivalent(s)
‖ use limited; if in doubt, see a dictionary

spout *n syn* see WATERFALL
spraddle *vb syn* see SPRAWL 1
sprain *vb* to injure (a joint) by a sudden twisting motion that stretches and lacerates the ligaments <*sprained* her ankle>
   syn ‖rick, turn, twist, wrench
   rel pull, strain, stretch; tear; dislocate, throw; break, fracture
sprangle *vb syn* see SPRAWL 2
sprat *n syn* see TWERP
‖sprauchle *vb syn* see SCRAMBLE 1
sprawl *vb* **1** to lie or sit with arms and legs stretched out carelessly and awkwardly <the dog lay *sprawled* out on the sofa>
   syn drape, ‖scamble, ‖spelder, spraddle, spread-eagle
   rel loll, lounge; slouch, slump
   2 to grow, develop, or spread irregularly and without apparent design or plan <the city *sprawls* down the whole coast>
   syn ramble, scramble, sprangle, spread-eagle, straddle, straggle
   rel extend, stretch; spread
spread *vb* **1** to extend or cause to extend over a considerable area or space <they *spread* the news far and wide> <clouds *spread* over the sky>
   syn circulate, diffuse, disperse, disseminate, distribute, propagate, radiate, strew; *compare* STREW 1
   rel deal, dispense; broadcast, communicate, pass (on), transmit; dissipate, scatter, sow; peddle, push, retail
   idiom spread abroad (*or* far and wide)
   con hold (in); contain; compress
   2 *syn* see OPEN 4
   con fold; close
   3 *syn* see SET 5
spread *n* **1** *syn* see EXPANSION 2
   rel diffusion; profusion; stretch, sweep
   2 *syn* see EXPANSE
   3 *syn* see DINNER
   4 *syn* see BEDSPREAD
spread–eagle *vb* **1** *syn* see SPRAWL 1
   2 *syn* see SPRAWL 2
‖spreaghery *n syn* see SPOIL
spree *n* **1** an unrestrained indulgence in or outburst of an activity <a shopping *spree*>
   syn binge, fling, orgy, rampage, splurge
   2 *syn* see BINGE 1
spree *vb syn* see REVEL 1
sprightful *adj syn* see LIVELY 1
sprightly *adj* **1** *syn* see LIVELY 1
   rel perky; breezy
   2 *syn* see ANTIC 2
   rel sportive; coltish, frisky
   3 *syn* see AGILE
   4 *syn* see CLEVER 5
   rel pungent, sharp; keen-witted, quick-witted
spring *vb* **1** to have something as a source <the primitive cultures from which civilization *springs*>
   syn arise, birth, come (from), derive (from), emanate, flow, head, issue, originate, proceed, rise, stem, upspring; *compare* BEGIN 2

   rel appear, emerge, come out, loom; arrive, come; begin, commence, hatch, start
   2 *syn* see SKIP 1
   3 *syn* see JUMP 1
   4 *syn* see START 1
   ‖5 *syn* see FREE
spring *n* **1** *usu* **springs** *pl syn* see SPA 1
   2 *syn* see SOURCE
   3 *syn* see YOUTH 1
   ant autumn
   4 *syn* see MOTIVE 1
   rel excitant, impetus, incitement, stimulant, stimulus
   5 the season between winter and summer <planting flowers in the *spring*>
   syn budtime, springtide, springtime
   rel ‖blackberry winter
   idiom prime of the year
   con autumn, fall
spring *adj syn* see VERNAL
springe *n syn* see PITFALL
springlike *adj syn* see VERNAL
springtide *n* **1** *syn* see SPRING 5
   2 *syn* see YOUTH 1
   ant autumn
springtime *n* **1** *syn* see SPRING 5
   2 *syn* see YOUTH 1
   ant autumn
springy *adj syn* see ELASTIC 1
   rel rebounding, recoiling
   ant rigid; springless
sprinkle *vb* **1** to scatter (something) in small drops or particles <*sprinkle* chocolate shot on whipped cream>
   syn besprinkle, dust, powder, ‖strinkle; *compare* STREW 1
   rel shake; scatter; pepper; sparge
   2 *syn* see SPECKLE 1
   3 *syn* see SPOT 2
   4 *syn* see BAPTIZE
   5 to rain lightly <it's only *sprinkling,* so we can still take our walk>
   syn drizzle, ‖mizzle
   rel mist; shower; spit
   con pour, stream
sprinkling *n* **1** *syn* see HINT 2
   2 *syn* see DUSTING
   3 *syn* see FEW
sprint *vb syn* see RUN 1
sprit *vb syn* see SQUIRT
sprite *n syn* see FAIRY
‖spritz *vb syn* see SQUIRT
spruce *adj syn* see DAPPER
   ant slouchy
spruce (up) *vb syn* see DRESS UP 1
sprucy *adj syn* see DAPPER
spry *adj syn* see AGILE
   rel prompt, quick, ready; energetic, vigorous; healthy, robust, sound
   ant doddering
spuddy *adj syn* see ROTUND 2
‖spulzie *n syn* see SPOIL
spume *n syn* see FOAM
spunk *n* **1** *syn* see FORTITUDE

rel bulldoggedness, doggedness
idiom clear (*or* true) grit
ant funk
2 syn see COURAGE
spunkless *adj syn* see COWARDLY
ant spunky
spunky *adj* **1 syn** see BRAVE 1
idiom full of spunk
ant spunkless; funky
2 syn see SPIRITED 2
ant funky
spur *n syn* see STIMULUS
rel excitant; activation, actuation
ant checkrein, curb
spur *vb syn* see URGE
rel rowel; arouse, awaken, rally, rouse, stir; in-stigate; countenance, favor
ant curb
spurious *adj* **1 syn** see ILLEGITIMATE 1
2 syn see ARTIFICIAL 2
3 of doubtful authenticity <claimed they had bought a *spurious* painting>
syn apocryphal, bastard, unauthentic, ungenu-ine; *compare* ARTIFICIAL 2, COUNTERFEIT
rel bogus, counterfeit, fake, phony, pseudo, sham; false, unreal
idiom not what (*or* all) it's cracked up to be
con actual, real, true; bona fide, genuine, verita-ble
ant authentic
4 syn see ARTIFICIAL 3
rel make-believe, pretend, pretended, pseudo
5 syn see COUNTERFEIT
spuriousness *n syn* see FALLACY 2
spurn *vb syn* see DECLINE 4
rel conspue, contemn, despise, disdain, scorn, scout; flout, scoff, sneer
con crave, desire, want
ant embrace
spur–of–the–moment *adj syn* see EXTEMPORANEOUS
spurt *vb syn* see SQUIRT
spurtle *vb syn* see SPLASH
sputter *vb* **1** to utter (words or ejaculations) hast-ily, explosively, and sometimes indistinctly <pompously *sputtering* his objections>
syn rip (out), spit, splutter
rel ejaculate, eject, throw (out); gibber, jabber; bluster, heckle, hector, rage, rant, rave, storm
2 to make a series of sudden short crackling or popping sounds <bacon *sputtering* in the pan>
syn spatter, spit, splutter
rel crackle, pop; hiss
spy (on *or* upon) *vb* to make furtive, stealthy, or secret observations of <had private detectives *spying* on his wife>
syn ‖stag
rel stake out; watch
spy *n* one who keeps secret watch to obtain infor-mation <was convicted on evidence produced by a *spy*>
syn agent, spook, undercover man; *compare* IN-FORMER
rel detective, investigator, sleuth; ‖narc; scout; beagle

idiom inside man, secret agent
spying *n syn* see ESPIONAGE
squab *adj syn* see STOCKY
‖**squab** *vb syn* see PRESS 1
squab *vb syn* see SPILL 1
squabble *n syn* see QUARREL
squabble *vb* **1 syn** see QUARREL
rel clash, encounter
idiom have a squabble over
2 syn see ARGUE 2
idiom get into (*or* have) a hassle, have a verbal wrestling match
squalid *adj* **1 syn** see DIRTY 1
rel disheveled, slipshod, sloppy, slovenly, un-kempt; frowzy, slatternly; dingy, shoddy, sleazy
2 syn see SHABBY 1
3 syn see BASE 3
squall *vb* **1** to make a raucous noise <angry street urchins fighting and *squalling* at each other>
syn caw, ‖quawk, squark, squawk, yawp (*or* yaup)
rel bellow, howl, roar, shout, yell; bark, yap, yip; croak
2 syn see BAWL 2
rel squeal; screech, shriek; yelp
squall *n syn* see QUARREL
squander *vb syn* see WASTE 2
idiom make ducks and drakes of, play ducks and drakes with
squander *n syn* see EXTRAVAGANCE 2
squanderer *n syn* see SPENDTHRIFT
square *n* **1 syn** see COMMON 2
2 syn see FOGY
square *adj* **1** having four equal sides and four right angles <a large *square* box>
syn foursquare, quadrate, quadratic, quadrati-cal
rel boxlike, boxy, squarish
2 syn see EVEN 5
3 syn see FAIR 4
4 syn see CONVENTIONAL 1
square *vb* **1 syn** see ADAPT
2 syn see CLEAR 5
3 syn see BRIBE
4 syn see AGREE 4
rel balance; coincide
square *adv syn* see JUST 1
squarehead *n syn* see DUNCE
squarely *adv* **1 syn** see EVENLY 1
2 syn see JUST 1
squark *vb syn* see SQUALL 1
squash *vb* **1 syn** see PRESS 1
2 syn see CRUSH 2
3 syn see CRUSH 5
4 syn see PRESS 7
squash *n* **1 syn** see SQUELCH
2 syn see CROWD 1
squashing *n syn* see REPRESSION 1
squashy *adj syn* see SOFT 6

---

syn synonym(s)   *rel* related word(s)
ant antonym(s)   *con* contrasted word(s)
idiom idiomatic equivalent(s)
‖ use limited; if in doubt, see a dictionary

ant firm

squat *vb* to sit on one's haunches <they were *squatting* around the fire>
syn hunker (down), ‖quat, ‖swat; *compare* CROUCH
rel crouch; hunch; stoop

squat *adj syn* see STOCKY
rel squattish, squatty
con long, tall; twiggy
ant lanky

‖**squaw** *n* **1** *syn* see WIFE
2 *syn* see WOMAN 1

squawk *vb* **1** *syn* see SQUALL 1
2 *syn* see GRIPE
rel yap, yip

squawker *n syn* see INFORMER

squawky *adj syn* see HARSH 3
con liquid, mellow, smooth

squdgy *adj syn* see STOCKY

squeak *vb* **1** to utter or make a short shrill cry or noise <mice *squeaking* in the barn>
syn ‖queak; *compare* SQUEAL 2
rel creak, grate, screak, screech, squeal; pipe; scream
2 *syn* see TALK 6
3 *syn* see INFORM 3

squeak *n syn* see OPPORTUNITY

‖**squeaker** *n syn* see INFORMER

squeal *vb* **1** *syn* see SCREAM 1
idiom squeal like a stuck pig
2 to make a harsh piercing sometimes rasping noise <tires *squealing* on wet pavement>
syn screak, scream, screech, shriek; *compare* SQUEAK 1
rel creak, grate, rasp
3 *syn* see INFORM 3
4 *syn* see TALK 6
5 *syn* see YELL 2
rel bitch, bleat, complain, gripe, squawk
idiom raise a howl, scream bloody murder

squealer *n syn* see INFORMER

squeam *n syn* see QUALM

squeamish *adj* **1** inclined to become nauseated <felt *squeamish* after the heavy meal on the ship>
syn ‖pensy, qualmish, qualmy, queasy, queer, ‖wambly; *compare* NAUSEATED
rel unsettled, upset; dizzy, shaky, vertiginous
2 *syn* see NAUSEATED
idiom sick at (*or* to) one's stomach
3 *syn* see NICE 1

squeamishness *n syn* see NAUSEA

squeamy *adj syn* see NICE 1

squeeze *vb* **1** *syn* see PRESS 1
rel contract, ‖scruze
2 *syn* see EMBRACE 1
3 *syn* see EXTORT 1
4 *syn* see EKE OUT 2
5 *syn* see PRESS 8
6 *syn* see PRESS 7

squeezy *adj syn* see CRAMPED

squelch *n* a sound of or as if of semiliquid matter under suction <the *squelch* of his feet in the mud>

syn squash, squidge, squish

squelch *vb syn* see SUPPRESS 2

squelching *n syn* see REPRESSION 1

squelchy *adj syn* see SOFT 6

‖**squench** *vb* **1** *syn* see EXTINGUISH 1
2 *syn* see QUENCH 4

squidge *n syn* see SQUELCH

squiffed *adj syn* see INTOXICATED 1

squiggle *vb* **1** *syn* see WRIGGLE
2 *syn* see SCRIBBLE

squinch *vb* **1** *syn* see RECOIL
2 *syn* see SQUINT

squinny *vb syn* see SQUINT

squinny *adj syn* see THIN 1

squint *vb* to look or peer with the eyes partly closed <*squinted* in the bright sunlight>
syn ‖sken, squinch, squinny
idiom look asquint, screw up one's eyes
ant goggle

squirm *vb* **1** *syn* see WRIGGLE
2 *syn* see WRITHE 1

squirrel *vb syn* see HOARD

squirt *vb* to come forth in a sudden rapid usually narrow stream <water *squirting* from the hose>
syn jet, splurt, sprit, ‖spritz, spurt, ‖squitter
rel pour, stream, surge; spatter; spray
con dribble, drip, trickle

squirt *n* ‖**1** **squirts** *pl syn* see DIARRHEA
2 *syn* see TWERP

squish *n* **1** *syn* see PRESS 1
2 *syn* see SQUELCH

squishy *adj syn* see SOFT 6

‖**squit** *n syn* see TWERP

‖**squitter** *vb syn* see SQUIRT

squush *vb syn* see PRESS 1

squushy *adj syn* see SOFT 6

stab *n* **1** *syn* see PRICK
2 *syn* see POKE 1
3 *syn* see FLING 1

stab *vb syn* see THRUST 2
rel dagger, dirk, poniard, prong

stabbing *adj syn* see SHARP 8

stabile *adj syn* see STEADY 2

stabilify *vb syn* see STABILIZE

stabilitate *vb syn* see STABILIZE

stability *n* the ability to withstand force or stress without alteration of position and without material change <the structural *stability* of the bridge>
syn firmness, security, soundness, stableness, steadiness, strength
rel dependability, durability, reliability; solidity, solidness, sturdiness; cohesion, toughness
con insecurity, undependability, unreliability, unsoundness, unsteadiness; weakness
ant instability, unstability

stabilize *vb* to make or keep stable, steadfast, or firm <a policy that *stabilized* the economy>
syn ballast, poise, stabilify, stabilitate, steady
rel balance, counterbalance, counterpoise, equalize, equipoise; prop, support, sustain; fix, secure, set, settle
ant unstabilize

stable *adj* **1** *syn* see SURE 1

rel balanced, poised; fixed, set, solid, sound, steadfast
con wobbling, wobbly
ant instable, unstable
2 *syn* see STEADY 2
3 *syn* see LASTING
rel constant, steady; safe, secure, sound; resolute, staunch, steadfast
4 marked by solidity, firmness, and stability especially in design or construction <a *stable* foundation for the building>
syn firm, secure, solid, sound; *compare* FAST 4, SURE 1
rel strong, sturdy; unassailable, unshakable
idiom as firm as (the rock of) Gibraltar, solid as a rock
con insecure, shaky, unsound, weak, wobbling, wobbly
ant instable, unstable
stableness *n syn* see STABILITY
ant unstableness
stack *n syn* see PILE 1
stack *vb syn* see HEAP 1
‖**stacked** *adj* **1 *syn*** see CURVACEOUS
2 *syn* see BUXOM
stade *n syn* see STADIUM
stadium *n* a large usually unroofed structure with tiered seats enclosing a field used especially for sports <a football *stadium*>
syn bowl, coliseum, stade
rel arena, garden, gymnasium
‖**stag** *vb syn* see SPY (on *or* upon)
stage *n* **1** *used with* the *syn* see DRAMA
2 *syn* see DEGREE 1
rel level; phase; period
stage *vb* to present on the stage <*staged* a play>
syn mount, produce, put on, show
rel bring out, open; give, present; do, execute, perform, play
stage set *n syn* see SCENE 1
stage setting *n syn* see SCENE 1
stagger *vb* **1 *syn*** see REEL 2
2 *syn* see LURCH 2
idiom pitch and plunge
3 *syn* see TEETER
rel ‖stiver, ‖stoit, ‖stoiter, ‖stot
4 *syn* see HESITATE
5 to affect with great wonder or bewilderment <a plot so bizarre as to *stagger* the imagination>
syn boggle, dumbfound, nonplus
rel perplex, puzzle, stump; amaze, astonish, astound, flabbergast; bowl (over), floor, knock over; devastate, overpower, overwhelm, shatter; paralyze
idiom take (one) aback
stagger (on *or* along) *vb syn* see SHIFT 5
‖**stagger** *n syn* see FLING 1
staggering *adj syn* see MARVELOUS 1
stagnant *adj syn* see STATIC
stagnate *vb* **1 *syn*** see VEGETATE
2 *syn* see STULTIFY
stagnation *n syn* see DEPRESSION 3
staid *adj syn* see SERIOUS 1
rel decorous, formal; collected, composed, cool; priggish, smug; starchy, stuffy

con breezy, devil-may-care, easy, frivolous; debonair, jaunty; playful, sportive; hoydenish, rakish; fresh, irreverent; uncontrolled, unrestrained
ant unstaid
stain *vb* **1** to soil often permanently with foreign matter <a shirt *stained* with grease>
syn bestain, blot, discolor, smut; *compare* SOIL 2
rel tinge; bedaub, daub, smear; besmirch, smirch, smudge, smutch
2 *syn* see TAINT 1
3 *syn* see DEBASE 1
stain *n* **1 *syn*** see STIGMA
rel blemish, defect, flaw
idiom blot on the escutcheon
2 *syn* see COLOR 6
stainless *adj syn* see CHASTE
con tainted, tarnished
ant stained
stake *n* **1 *syn*** see BET
2 *syn* see INTEREST 1
stake *vb* **1 *syn*** see GAMBLE 1
rel stake down
2 *syn* see CAPITALIZE
stale *adj* **1 *syn*** see MALODOROUS 1
2 *syn* see TRITE
rel dusty, fusty; dead
ant fresh
‖**stale** *n syn* see LURE 2
stalemate *n syn* see DRAW 4
stalk *vb* **1** to pursue (game) stealthily or under cover <*stalk* deer>
syn still-hunt
rel follow, track; drive, chase, pursue; walk up; flush (out); ambush
2 *syn* see STRIDE 1
stalky *adj syn* see THIN 1
stall *vb* ‖**1 *syn*** see SATIATE
2 *syn* see ARREST 1
rel brake, slow (down); hold off, put off, stand off; suspend; shut down
idiom pull the checkstring
con spur
stalwart *adj* **1 *syn*** see STRONG 2
rel athletic, brawny, husky, muscular, sinewy
2 *syn* see BRAVE 1
stamina *n syn* see TOLERANCE 1
stammer *vb* **1** to make involuntary stops and repetitions in uttering syllables and words <the frightened child *stammered* and fell silent>
syn ‖hammer, ‖stut, stutter
rel falter, hesitate; stumble; splutter, sputter; gibber, jabber
‖**2 *syn*** see TEETER
stamp *vb* **1 *syn*** see TRAMPLE 2
rel clomp, clump, stump
2 *syn* see IMPRINT 3
rel etch, imprint, infix, inscribe, print
idiom impress on the mind
stamp *n* **1 *syn*** see IMPRESSION 1

---

syn synonym(s)	*rel* related word(s)
ant antonym(s)	*con* contrasted word(s)
idiom idiomatic equivalent(s)	
‖ use limited; if in doubt, see a dictionary	

2 *syn* see TYPE
3 *syn* see SEAL
stampede *vb* **1** *syn* see ROUT 1
2 to take to sudden headlong flight in panic
<cattle *stampeding* across the plain>
syn pell-mell; *compare* RUSH 1
rel bolt, charge, chase, crash, dash, fling, hurry,
rush, shoot, tear
idiom run like a pack of scalded dogs
stamping ground *n* **1** *syn* see HABITAT
2 *syn* see RESORT 2
stance *n* **1** *syn* see POSTURE 1
2 *syn* see POSITION 1
stanch *vb* *syn* see STEM
stand *vb* **1** *syn* see BEAR 10
idiom ‖hack it, take lying down
2 *syn* see TREAT 3
stand (on *or* upon) *vb* *syn* see DEPEND (on *or* upon)
1
idiom be contingent on
stand *n* *syn* see POSITION 1
standard *n* **1** *syn* see FLAG
2 *syn* see MODEL 2
3 a means of determining what a thing should be
<each generation has its own *standards* of mo-
rality>
syn benchmark, criterion, gauge, measure,
touchstone, yardstick
rel average, mean, median, norm, par; axiom,
belief, fundamental, principle; law, rule; exemplar, model, pattern
idiom rule of thumb
4 a fixed, customary, or official measure (as of
quantity, quality, or price) <governmental *standards* of weights and measures>
syn assize
rel ‖dick
stander–by *n* *syn* see SPECTATOR
stand–in *n* *syn* see SUBSTITUTE 1
rel second; assistant
standing *n* **1** *syn* see TERM 5
2 *syn* see STATUS 1
3 *syn* see STATUS 2
standoff *adj* *syn* see UNSOCIABLE
standoff *n* *syn* see DRAW 4
standoffish *adj* **1** *syn* see UNSOCIABLE
2 *syn* see ANTISOCIAL
stand out *vb* **1** *syn* see BULGE
2 *syn* see LOOM 3
standout *adj* *syn* see SUPERB 3
stand over *vb* *syn* see DEFER
standpat *n* *syn* see DIEHARD 1
standpatter *n* *syn* see DIEHARD 1
standpoint *n* *syn* see VIEWPOINT 2
standstill *n* cessation of movement <the car came
to a *standstill* in the mud>
syn stay, stillstand, stop
rel arrest, check; pause; cessation, halt
con start; movement
ant start-up
stand up *vb* *syn* see RISE 1
stand–up *adj* *syn* see ERECT
con lowered; flat, horizontal
‖**stang** *vb* *syn* see SMART

staple *n* *syn* see LOOP 2
staple *n* *syn* see BODY 3
star *adj* *syn* see CHIEF 2
starch *n* *syn* see VIGOR 2
star–crossed *adj* *syn* see UNLUCKY
stare *vb* **1** *syn* see LOOK 7
idiom ‖take a gander at
2 *syn* see GAZE 1
idiom fix (*or* rivet) one's eyes on
stare down *vb* to overcome (someone) by or as if
by staring <the teacher could not *stare* the boy
down>
syn look down, outstare
rel glare; master, quell, subdue, suppress; overcome, overwhelm
stark *adj* **1** *syn* see UTTER
2 *syn* see NUDE 2
3 *syn* see EMPTY 1
‖**starkers** *adj* *syn* see NUDE 2
stark–naked *adj* *syn* see NUDE 2
idiom bare (*or* naked) as a newborn babe, ‖na-
ked as a jaybird, naked as the day one was born
‖**starny** *adj* *syn* see STELLAR 1
starry *adj* *syn* see STELLAR 1
start *vb* **1** to move suddenly and violently from a
state of stillness or rest <*started* from his bed at
the sound of shots>
syn bolt, jump, spring, startle
rel dart; bounce; bound, leap; draw (back),
flinch, recoil
idiom jump out of one's skin, start aside
ant stay
2 *syn* see RECOIL
3 *syn* see BEGIN 2
rel proceed, spring
ant end
4 *syn* see FOUND 2
5 *syn* see BEGIN 1
ant stop
start *n* **1** *syn* see BEGINNING
ant finish
2 *syn* see ADVANTAGE 3
startle *vb* **1** *syn* see START 1
2 *syn* see SHOCK 2
3 *syn* see FRIGHTEN
rel astonish, surprise
idiom make one jump out of one's skin, ‖scare
the pants off
startlish *adj* *syn* see EXCITABLE
starved *adj* *syn* see HUNGRY
rel underfed, undernourished; weakened; half≠
famished, half-starved
con fed, nourished; overfed
ant well-fed
starving *adj* *syn* see HUNGRY
rel craving, famishing, hungering; dying, perishing
idiom crazy for food
stash *vb* **1** *syn* see HOARD
2 *syn* see HIDE
rel hoard, squirrel
stasis *n* *syn* see BALANCE 1
state *n* **1** the way in which one manifests existence
or the circumstances under which one exists or

by which one is given distinctive character <remained in a weakened *state* for weeks>
syn condition, mode, posture, situation, status
rel circumstances; attitude, position, stand
idiom state of being
2 syn see STATUS 1
3 syn see STATUS 2
state *vb* **1 syn** see RELATE 1
rel elucidate, explain, expound, interpret; set forth
2 syn see ENUNCIATE 1
3 syn see SAY 1
4 syn see EXPRESS 2
ant imply
stated *adj syn* see FIRM 4
stately *adj* **1 syn** see CEREMONIAL
rel dignified, grand, noble; imperial, kingly, princely, regal, royal
2 syn see COURTLY
3 syn see GRAND 1
con lowly, poor; shabby; cheap
statement *n* **1 syn** see EXPRESSION 1
rel outgiving; articulation, presentation, presentment, verbalization, vocalization
2 syn see WORD 1
rel description, narrative, recital
3 syn see BILL 1
static *adj* characterized by relatively little or no movement, progression, or change (as in conditions) <a *static* economy>
syn immobile, stagnant, stationary, unmoving; compare STEADY 2
rel constant, stabile, stable, unchanging, unfluctuating; fixed, immovable, rigid, sticky; inactive, inert; stalled, stopped, stuck
idiom at a standstill, standing still
con active, changing, mobile, moving, progressing; erratic, fluctuating, inconstant, unstable
ant dynamic
station *n* **1 syn** see PLACE 1
2 syn see RAILROAD STATION
3 syn see STATUS 1
station *vb* to appoint or assign to an office or duty <*stationed* guards around the camp>
syn post, set
rel appoint, assign; place, position
stationary *adj syn* see STATIC
rel motionless, stock-still
ant moving
station house *n syn* see RAILROAD STATION
statuesque *adj syn* see SHAPELY
stature *n* **1 syn** see QUALITY 2
rel prestige, standing, status; ability, capacity; competence, qualification
2 syn see STATUS 2
status *n* **1** rating or positioning in relation to others (as in a social order, community, class, or profession) <his *status* as a slave>
syn capacity, character, footing, place, position, quality, rank, situation, standing, state, station
rel rating
2 social or professional importance or distinction <a lawyer of international *status*>
syn cachet, consequence, dignity, position, prestige, rank, standing, state, stature

rel caliber, merit, worth; distinction, renown; eminence, prominence
con inconsequence, insignificance, unimportance
3 syn see STATE 1
rel status quo
idiom state of affairs
statute *n syn* see LAW 1
rel act, enactment
staunch *adj* **1 syn** see SURE 1
2 syn see FAITHFUL 1
rel firm, strong
idiom as staunch as an oak, tried and true
con mercurial; shaky, unsteady
stave *vb syn* see HURRY 2
stave off *vb* **1 syn** see FEND (off)
rel beat off, drive (off), fight (off); block, parry
2 syn see PREVENT 2
staving *adv syn* see VERY 1
ant barely
stay *vb* **1 syn** see ARREST 1
rel postpone, prorogue, put off
2 to continue to be in one place for a noticeable time <*stayed* late at the office>
syn abide, bide, linger, remain, stick around, tarry, wait
rel dally, delay, dillydally, lag, procrastinate; hang around, loiter; outstay, stay out
ant go
3 syn see VISIT 3
rel bide, dwell, live
4 syn see DEFER
stay *n syn* see STANDSTILL
stay *n syn* see SUPPORT 3
stay *vb syn* see BASE
stead *vb syn* see HELP 1
steadfast *adj* **1 syn** see IMMOVABLE 1
2 syn see INFLEXIBLE 2
ant unsteadfast, vacillating
3 syn see SURE 2
ant capricious
4 syn see FAITHFUL 1
rel unfaltering, unflinching, unquestioning, unwavering
steadfastly *adv syn* see HARD 7
rel staunchly, strongly
steadiness *n syn* see STABILITY
ant unsteadiness
steady *adj* **1 syn** see SURE 2
rel unswerving; eternal, never-ending
2 being neither markedly varying nor variable in course or extent <a *steady* rain> <*steady* prices>
syn constant, equable, even, stabile, stable, unchanging, unfluctuating, uniform, unvarying; compare STATIC
rel steady-going; certain, changeless, fixed, set, sure, unchangeable; unflickering, unwavering; durable, reliable

---

syn synonym(s)   **rel** related word(s)
ant antonym(s)   **con** contrasted word(s)
idiom idiomatic equivalent(s)
‖ use limited; if in doubt, see a dictionary

con inconstant, uneven, unstable; changeable; changing, fluctuating, uncertain, undependable, undulating, unsure, varying, wavering
ant unsteady
3 *syn* see FAITHFUL 1
steady *vb syn* see STABILIZE
steady *n* **1** *syn* see BOYFRIEND 2
2 *syn* see GIRL FRIEND 2
steal *vb* **1** to take another's possession illegally and without his knowledge <*stole* a car>
syn abstract, annex, appropriate, cabbage, ‖clout, ‖cly, collar, ‖coon, ‖cop, ‖crook, filch, ‖heist, hook, lift, nab, ‖nail, ‖nick, nim, nip, pilfer, pillage, pinch, pocket, ‖prig, purloin, rip off, smouch, ‖snaffle, ‖snake, snitch, swipe, thieve, vulture
rel mooch; fleece, frisk; grab, grasp, seize, snatch, take; plagiarize; hijack, shanghai; poach, rustle; burglarize, rob; loot, plunder, rifle
idiom make off (*or* away) with, run away (*or* off) with
2 *syn* see SNEAK
3 to move or go quietly so as not to disturb <*stole* out of the sickroom on tiptoe>
syn creep, glide, mouse, slide, slip; *compare* SNEAK
rel tiptoe
con clump, stamp, stomp, stump
steal *n* **1** *syn* see THEFT
2 *syn* see BARGAIN 1
stealage *n* *syn* see THEFT
stealer *n* *syn* see THIEF
stealing *n* *syn* see THEFT
stealthily *adv* *syn* see SECRETLY
ant openly
stealthy *adj* **1** *syn* see SECRET 1
rel crafty, cunning, sly, wily; skulking, slinking, sneaking; catlike
con direct, straight, straightforward
ant open
2 being so quiet, slow, and deliberate in movement as to escape observation <the *stealthy* movements of the cat burglar>
syn catlike, catty, feline, furtive; *compare* SECRET 1
rel noiseless, pantherine, pantherish, quiet, silent; shifty, skulking, sly, sneak, sneaking, sneaky
steam *n* *syn* see POWER 4
steamroller *vb* *syn* see WHIP 2
steam up *vb* *syn* see ANGER 1
steel *vb* **1** *syn* see GIRD 3
rel rally; nerve; buck up; reinforce
idiom grit one's teeth, set one's jaw, take the bit in one's teeth
ant unsteel
2 *syn* see ENCOURAGE 1
steep *adj* **1** having an incline approaching the perpendicular <a *steep* trail up the mountain>
syn abrupt, arduous, precipitate, precipitous, sheer, sideling, steepdown, steep-to, steep-up, ‖stickle
rel elevated, lifted, raised; steepish; high, lofty; prerupt; perpendicular, straight-up; breakneck

con easy, gentle, gradual, moderate; shelfy, shelving, shelvy
2 *syn* see EXCESSIVE 1
steep *vb* **1** *syn* see SOAK 1
2 *syn* see INFUSE 1
steepdown *adj* *syn* see STEEP 1
steep–to *adj* *syn* see STEEP 1
steep–up *adj* *syn* see STEEP 1
steer *vb* *syn* see GUIDE
idiom steer one's course
steer *n* *syn* see TIP
stellar *adj* **1** of, relating to, or suggestive of a star or group of stars <*stellar* light>
syn astral, sidereal, ‖starny, starry, stellular
rel gleaming, luminous, lustrous, shining, starlike, twinkling; star-spangled
con starless
2 *syn* see CHIEF 2
stellify *vb* *syn* see EXALT 1
stellular *adj* *syn* STELLAR 1, astral, sidereal, ‖starny, starry
stem *vb* *syn* see SPRING 1
stem *vb* to hinder or prevent by or as if by damming <*stem* the flow of blood>
syn stanch, stop
rel arrest, check, control
stemma *n* *syn* see GENEALOGY
stench *vb* *syn* see SMELL 3
stenchful *adj* *syn* see MALODOROUS 1
stenchy *adj* *syn* see MALODOROUS 1
stentorian *adj* *syn* see LOUD 1
rel orotund; clamorous, vociferous; gravelly, rough; clarion-voiced, loudmouthed, loud⹀voiced, trumpet-tongued
stentorious *adj* *syn* see LOUD 1
stentorophonic *adj* *syn* see LOUD 1
step *n* **1** *syn* see FOOTPRINT
2 *syn* see DEGREE 1
3 *syn* see MEASURE 7
rel act, action; motion
step *vb* **1** *syn* see WALK 1
2 *syn* see DANCE 1
step–by–step *adj* *syn* see GRADUAL
step in *vb* **1** *syn* see VISIT 2
2 *syn* see INTERPOSE 2
step up *vb* *syn* see SPEED 3
ant step down
stereotyped *adj* *syn* see TRITE
idiom worn thin
stereotypical *adj* *syn* see TRITE
ant original
sterile *adj* **1** lacking the power to bear offspring or produce fruit <a hybrid that is completely *sterile*>
syn barren, effete, impotent, infecund, infertile, unfruitful
rel sterilized; fallow, fruitless, unproductive; unprolific; arid, bare, dry; dead, desolate
con potent, productive, rich; bearing, fruiting, fruitive, producing, turning out, yielding; fecund, fruitful, prolific, teeming
ant fertile
2 *syn* see UNORIGINAL
rel flat, insipid, jejune, vapid; stale; effete, worn⹀out; impotent

con fertile, fruitful, potent, producing, productive, prolific
ant fecund

sterilize *vb* to make incapable of producing offspring <*sterilizing* animals in medical experiments>
syn alter, castrate, change, desexualize, fix, geld, mutilate, neuter, unsex
rel emasculate; caponize, poulardize; spay

sterling *adj syn* see HONORABLE 1
rel pure, true

stern *adj syn* see SEVERE 1
rel grim, implacable, unrelenting; inexorable, inflexible
ant lenient, soft

‖**stern** *n syn* see BUTTOCKS

stew *n* **1** *syn* see BROTHEL
2 *usu* **stews** *pl syn* see RED-LIGHT DISTRICT
3 *syn* see SLUM
4 *syn* see MISCELLANY 1
5 *syn* see SNIT
rel boil
6 *syn* see COMMOTION 2

stew *vb* **1** *syn* see BOIL 2
2 *syn* see WORRY 3
idiom be in a stew

stewardly *adj syn* see SPARING
‖**stewed** *adj syn* see INTOXICATED 1
stick *n* **1** *syn* see BAR 1
2 *syn* see DECOY 2
3 **sticks** *pl, used with* the *syn* see FRONTIER 2
idiom the middle of nowhere

stick *adv syn* see ALL 1

stick *vb* **1** *syn* see THRUST 2
2 to become or cause to become closely and firmly attached <papers all *stuck* together>
syn adhere, cleave, cling, cohere
rel affix, attach, fasten, fix; glue; cement; fuse, weld; braze, solder
idiom stick close, stick like a wet shirt, stick like the paper on the wall, stick like wax, stick to like a barnacle (*or* leech)
con loosen; detach, disengage
ant unstick
3 *syn* see SET 1
4 *syn* see NONPLUS 1
5 *syn* see FLEECE 1
6 *syn* see OVERCHARGE 1
‖**7** *syn* see BEAR 10
8 *syn* see DEMUR

stickage *n syn* see ADHERENCE 1
stick around *vb syn* see STAY 2
stick-at-nothing *adj syn* see UNSCRUPULOUS
sticker *n syn* see SEAL
sticking *n syn* see ADHERENCE 1
stick-in-the-mud *n syn* see FOGY
‖**stickle** *adj syn* see STEEP 1
stickle *vb syn* see DEMUR
rel hold out, stall; contend, kick, object, protest

stick out *vb* **1** *syn* see BULGE
rel outstretch, outthrust, protend, push
2 *syn* see STRIKE 1
3 *syn* see BEAR 10

stick up *vb syn* see ROB 1

sticky *adj* **1** having the quality of sticking by or as if by adhesion <*sticky* syrup>
syn adhesive, ‖claggy, ‖clarty, cloggy, gluey, gooey, gummy, stodgy
rel tacky; viscid, viscous
2 *syn* see HUMID
3 *syn* see HARD 6
4 *syn* see SENTIMENTAL

‖**stickybeak** *n syn* see BUSYBODY
sticky-fingered *adj syn* see LARCENOUS
stiff *adj* **1** incapable of or highly resistant to bending or flexing <a *stiff* cardboard packing box>
syn immalleable, impliable, incompliant, inelastic, inflexible, rigid, unbending, unflexible, unyielding; *compare* INFLEXIBLE 2
rel stiffish; hard, resistant; hardened, petrified; stark
idiom stiff as a board (*or* poker)
con soft, softened; yielding; bendable, pliant; limber, supple, willowy
ant flexible, flexile
2 *syn* see INTOXICATED 1
3 *syn* see OBSTINATE
4 characterized by a lack of ease, grace, or spontaneity especially in style <a play whose dialogue and characters were *stiff* and perfunctory>
syn buckram, cardboard, muscle-bound, stilted, wooden
rel rigid, set, studied; machine-made, mechanical, stereotyped, stock; arid, dry, dull
con expressive, graphic, vivid; easy, fluent, graceful, smooth
5 *syn* see EXCESSIVE 1

stiff *n* **1** *syn* see CORPSE
2 *syn* see DRUNKARD
3 *syn* see MISER

stiff-necked *adj syn* see OBSTINATE
stifle *vb* **1** *syn* see SUFFOCATE
2 *syn* see MUFFLE 2
3 *syn* see SUPPRESS 3
4 *syn* see STULTIFY

stifling *adj* **1** producing or seeming to produce suffocation <*stifling* heat>
syn smothering, smothery, ‖smudgy, suffocating, suffocative; *compare* HUMID, STUFFY 1
rel oppressive, overpowering; unbearable, unendurable
2 *syn* see STUFFY 1

stifling *n syn* see REPRESSION 1
stigma *n* a mark of shame or discredit <the *stigma* of personal cowardice>
syn bar sinister, black eye, blot, blur, brand, odium, onus, slur, spot, stain
rel besmirchment, disfigurement, smudge, smutch, taint, tainting; disgrace, dishonor, shame
con credit, distinction, glory, honor; bay(s), crown, laurel(s)

still *adj* **1** *syn* see MOTIONLESS

---

syn synonym(s)   **rel** related word(s)
ant antonym(s)   **con** contrasted word(s)
idiom idiomatic equivalent(s)
‖ use limited; if in doubt, see a dictionary

2 *syn* see CALM 1
rel peaceful, unperturbed
con roiled, roily, turbid
3 devoid of or making no stir, sound, or noise <the streets were *still* at 3:00 A.M.>
syn hush, hushful, noiseless, quiet, silent, soundless, stilly, whist
rel calm, hushed, peaceful, placid, serene, tranquil; deathlike, deathly
idiom deathly still, still as death
ant noisy

still *vb* **1** *syn* see CALM
ant agitate
2 *syn* see SILENCE

still *adv* **1** *syn* see HOWEVER
2 *syn* see YET 1
idiom still (*or* even) more
3 *syn* see ALSO 2

still *n* *syn* see SILENCE 1

still and all *adv* *syn* see HOWEVER

still–hunt *vb* *syn* see STALK 1

stillness *n* *syn* see SILENCE 1

stillstand *n* *syn* see STANDSTILL

stilly *adj* **1** *syn* see STILL 3
con agitated, disturbed, noisy
ant noiseful
2 *syn* see CALM 1

stilted *adj* **1** *syn* see RHETORICAL
2 *syn* see STIFF 4
3 *syn* see GENTEEL 3
rel conventional, formal; decorous; prim

stimulant *n* *syn* see STIMULUS

stimulate *vb* **1** *syn* see PROVOKE 4
rel enliven, vivify; activate, dynamize, energize, vitalize
idiom build a fire under, get one started (*or* moving)
con unnerve; deaden
2 *syn* see ELATE

stimulating *adj* **1** *syn* see EXCITING
rel enlivening, lively; provocative, seminal, suggestive; incitory, stimulative, stimulatory
2 *syn* see INVIGORATING

stimulative *adj* *syn* see INVIGORATING

stimulus *n* something that rouses the mind or spirits or incites to activity <the war proved a *stimulus* to the economy> <sought a *stimulus* to take her mind off her own troubles>
syn catalyst, goad, impetus, impulse, incentive, incitation, incitement, instigation, motivation, propellant, provocative, push, spur, stimulant; *compare* MOTIVE 1
rel boost, encouragement, inducement, invitation, urging; cause, motive; excitement, piquing, provocation, stimulation

sting *vb* *syn* see SMART

stingy *adj* being unwilling or showing unwillingness to share with others <too *stingy* to tip the waiter>
syn cheap, cheeseparing, ‖chinchy, chintzy, close, closefisted, costive, hardfisted, hardhanded, ironfisted, mean, mingy, miserly, ‖narrow, narrow-fisted, narrowhearted, niggard, niggardly, parsimonious, penny-pinching, penny-wise, penurious, pinching, pinchpenny, save‑

all, ‖scant, scrimpy, scrimy, tight, tightfisted, ungenerous, ungiving; *compare* SPARING
rel economical, frugal, Scotch, sparing, thrifty; scaly, screwy
idiom as close as a vise, as close (*or* tight) as paper on a wall, near (*or* close *or* tight) as the bark on a tree
con bountiful, giving, liberal, munificent, openhanded, philanthropic, unsparing, unstinting; prodigal
ant generous

stink *vb* *syn* see SMELL 3

stinkard *n* *syn* see SNOT 1

stinkaroo *n* *syn* see SNOT 1

stinker *n* *syn* see SNOT 1

stinking *adj* **1** *syn* see MALODOROUS 1
idiom stinking to high heaven
‖**2** *syn* see INTOXICATED 1

‖**stinko** *adj* *syn* see INTOXICATED 1

stinky *adj* *syn* see MALODOROUS 1

stint *vb* **1** *syn* see SCRIMP
2 *syn* see SPARE 3

stint *n* **1** *syn* see RESTRICTION 1
2 *syn* see TASK 1
rel amount, quantity; allotment, apportionment; participation, share
3 *syn* see SPELL 1

stipend *n* *syn* see WAGE
rel award, consideration, payment

stipple *vb* *syn* see SPECKLE 1

stipulate *vb* *syn* see SPECIFY 3
rel designate; state; provide

stipulated *adj* *syn* see FIRM 3
rel designated, pinned down
con implied, unstated, unwritten

stipulation *n* *syn* see CONDITION 1
rel specification; circumscription, limit

stir *vb* **1** to cause to shift from quiescence or torpor into activity <a teacher who *stirred* the minds of his most sluggish students>
syn arouse, awaken, bestir, challenge, kindle, rally, rouse, wake, waken, whet; *compare* PROVOKE 4
rel excite, galvanize, inspire, provoke, quicken, stimulate; agitate, foment, incite, instigate; activate, energize, vitalize; actuate, drive, impel, move; ‖roust, rout
idiom make (*or* have) an impact on, set astir, set on fire
2 *syn* see WAKE 1
3 *syn* see SEETHE 4

stir (up) *vb* *syn* see INCITE
idiom add fuel to the flame, apply the torch, feed the fire, pour oil on the fire, stir the embers

stir *n* **1** signs of excited activity, hurry, or commotion <noticed a *stir* within the crowd>
syn ado, bustle, flurry, furore, fuss, pother, whirl, whirlpool, whirlwind; *compare* COMMOTION 4
rel agitation, disquiet, stir-up; commotion, disturbance; din, hubbub, pandemonium, stirabout, tumult
con calm, peace, placidity; inaction, inactivity
ant tranquillity

2 *syn* see MOTION 1
‖**stir** *n syn* see JAIL
‖**stirra** *n syn* see MAN 3
stirring *n syn* see MOTION 1
stirring *adj syn* see EXCITING
  rel heart-stirring, soul-stirring
stitch *n syn* see PAIN 1
stivy *adj syn* see STUFFY 1
stock *n* **1** *syn* see FAMILY 1
  2 *syn* see ESTIMATION 1
  3 *syn* see TRUST 1
  4 *syn* see SUPPLY
  5 *syn* see RESERVE
stock *vb* to equip, furnish, supply, or have material requisites (as for sale) <a bar that *stocks* all the best brands of liquor>
  syn carry, keep
  rel have; furnish, supply
  idiom have (*or* keep) in stock, keep on hand
stockade *n syn* see JAIL
stockpile *n* **1** *syn* see PILE 1
  2 *syn* see RESERVE
stockpile *vb syn* see ACCUMULATE
stock–still *adj syn* see MOTIONLESS
stocky *adj* being compact and broad in build and often short in stature <a *stocky* but quick and hard-hitting catcher>
  syn ‖chuffy, ‖chumpy, chunky, dumpy, heavyset, squab, squat, squdgy, stubby, ‖stuggy, stumpy, thick, thick-bodied, thickset
  rel plump, stout; bunty, low-set, short; lumpish, lumpy, pudgy; corpulent, fat
  con lean, skinny, thin, wiry
stodge *vb* **1** *syn* see SATIATE
  2 *syn* see PLOD 1
stodgy *adj* **1** *syn* see STICKY 1
  2 *syn* see DULL 9
  rel unexciting; pedantic; heavy, ponderous, weighty
  3 *syn* see TACKY 2
stoic *adj syn* see IMPASSIVE 1
  rel aloof, detached, indifferent, unconcerned; self-controlled, Spartan; indomitable, unassailable; long-suffering, patient, resigned
stoicism *n syn* see APATHY 1
  rel backbone, fortitude, grit, guts, pluck, sand
‖**stoit** *vb syn* see LURCH 2
‖**stoiter** *vb syn* see LURCH 2
stolid *adj syn* see IMPASSIVE 1
  rel blunt, dull, obtuse; dense, dull, dumb, slow, stupid; inactive, inert, passive, supine
  ant sensitive
stolidity *n syn* see APATHY 1
  rel dullness, dumbness, slowness, stupidity; inactiveness, inactivity, inertia, passivity
  con aptness, quickness, readiness; animation, enlivening, quickening; ardor, enthusiasm, fervor, passion, zeal; fire
  ant sensitivity
stomach *n* **1** *syn* see ABDOMEN
  2 *syn* see APPETITE 1
stomach *vb syn* see BEAR 10
stomachache *n* abdominal pain <she has a terrible *stomachache*>

syn bellyache, colic, collywobbles, gripe(s)
  rel distress, misery
‖**stomachy** *adj syn* see IRASCIBLE
stomp *vb syn* see TRAMPLE 2
stone–blind *adj syn* see BLIND 1
stone–broke *adj syn* see POOR 1
stoned *adj* **1** *syn* see INTOXICATED 1
  2 *syn* see DRUGGED
stone–still *adj syn* see MOTIONLESS
stony *adj* **1** *syn* see UNFEELING 2
  ant soft
  2 *syn* see POOR 1
stonyhearted *adj syn* see UNFEELING 2
  rel flinty, hard, stonelike
  idiom as cold as marble
  ant softhearted
stooge *n* **1** one who plays a subordinate or compliant role to a principal <an executive who was only a *stooge* with no real power>
  syn Charlie McCarthy, dummy, yes-man
  2 *syn* see TOOL 2
stool *n syn* see INFORMER
‖**stool** *vb syn* see INFORM 3
‖**stoolie** *n syn* see INFORMER
stool pigeon *n syn* see INFORMER
stoop *vb* **1** to descend from one's level (as of rank or dignity) usually to do something <a king who would not *stoop* to consider the common people>
  syn condescend, deign
  rel relax, thaw, unbend; accord, concede; accommodate, favor, oblige
  idiom be so good as to, come (*or* get) down from one's high horse, lower oneself
  2 to drop in status or dignity by indulgence in pettiness or unworthy behavior <a woman who would not *stoop* to tell a lie>
  syn descend, sink
  idiom act beneath oneself, debase (*or* demean) oneself, lower oneself
  3 *syn* see DUCK 2
stop *vb* **1** *syn* see STEM
  2 *syn* see FILL 1
  rel disrupt, hinder, interrupt; cut off, shut off, turn off
  ant unstop
  3 to suspend or cause to suspend activity <the conversation *stopped*>
  syn cease, desist, ‖deval, discontinue, give over, halt, knock off, leave off, quit, surcease; *compare* ARREST 1
  rel ‖can, refrain (from); arrest, check, cut off, interrupt; stay, suspend; ‖cheese, lay off; break off, break up, end, terminate
  con continue, go on, keep (on), keep up, persist
  ant start
  4 to come to a standstill <the car *stopped* at the intersection>

---

syn synonym(s)   *rel* related word(s)
ant antonym(s)   *con* contrasted word(s)
idiom idiomatic equivalent(s)
‖ use limited; if in doubt, see a dictionary

syn bring up, draw up, fetch up, halt, haul up, pull up
con start; move; pull out
ant go

stop (in *or* by) *vb syn* see VISIT 2
stop (over) *vb syn* see VISIT 3
idiom make a stopover
stop *n* **1** *syn* see END 2
ant start
2 *syn* see BAR 2
3 *syn* see STANDSTILL
stopcock *n syn* see FAUCET
stopgap *adj syn* see MAKESHIFT
stopgap *n syn* see RESOURCE 3
stopover *n syn* see SOJOURN
stopper *vb syn* see FILL 1
ant unstopper
store *vb syn* see STOW
store (up) *vb syn* see ACCUMULATE
rel deposit; cache
store *n* **1** *syn* see RESERVE
2 *syn* see SUPPLY
3 *syn* see DEPOT 2
4 a business establishment where goods are shown for sale <a food *store*>
syn market, outlet, shop, showroom
rel discounter, discount house, discount store, emporium
store *adj syn* see READY-MADE
store–bought *adj syn* see READY-MADE
‖**store–boughten** *adj syn* see READY-MADE
storehouse *n syn* see DEPOT 2
storm *n* **1** *syn* see COMMOTION 4
2 *syn* see BARRAGE
storm *vb syn* see ATTACK 1
storm and stress *n syn* see UNREST
stormful *adj syn* see WILD 6
rel threatening; dusty, murky; foul; howling, riproaring, roaring
ant calm
stormily *adv syn* see HARD 2
stormy *adj syn* see WILD 6
rel threatening; dusty, murky; foul; howling, riproaring, roaring
ant calm
story *n* **1** *syn* see ACCOUNT 7
2 a recital of real or imaginary happenings that is less elaborate than a novel <told the *story* of his escape> <a simple *story* of heartwarming devotion>
syn anecdote, narration, narrative, tale, yarn; *compare* ACCOUNT 7
rel conte; description; fable; folktale, legend, märchen; Canterbury tale, cock-and-bull story, fabrication, fairy tale, fiction
3 *syn* see LIE
storyteller *n syn* see LIAR
‖**stot** *vb syn* see LURCH 2
stout *adj* **1** *syn* see BRAVE 1
idiom bold as a lion
con irresolute; fainthearted
2 *syn* see STRONG 2
rel resolute, steadfast; hard; indomitable, invincible

idiom as strong (*or* stalwart) as an English oak
3 *syn* see FAT 2
rel thick-bodied; ‖plenitudinous
ant spare
stouthearted *adj syn* see BRAVE 1
stow *vb* to put (articles) into a storage space <*stowed* his gear belowdecks>
syn bestow, pack, store, warehouse
ant unstow
straddle *vb* **1** *syn* see BESTRIDE 2
2 *syn* see SPRAWL 2
straggle *vb* **1** *syn* see WANDER 1
2 *syn* see SPRAWL 2
straggler *n syn* see LAGGARD
straight *adv* **1** *syn* see AWAY 3
2 *syn* see DIRECTLY 1
straight *adj* **1** *syn* see DIRECT 2
idiom as straight as an arrow
ant circuitous
2 *syn* see STRAIGHTFORWARD 2
3 free from admixture or extraneous matter <a shot of *straight* liquor>
syn neat, plain, pure, unadulterated, undiluted, unmixed
rel unmodified; concentrated; strong
con adulterated, blended, mixed; watered= down; weak
4 *syn* see CONVENTIONAL 1
straight *n syn* see RIGHT 1
straightaway *adv syn* see AWAY 3
straightforward *adj* **1** *syn* see DIRECT 2
2 free from all that is dishonest or secretive <a *straightforward* answer>
syn aboveboard, forthright, plain dealing, straight; *compare* FRANK
rel pretenseless; honest, honorable, just, upright, upstanding; candid, frank, open, plain, unequivocal; direct, outspoken
con equivocal, evasive, shuffling; indirect; prevaricative; dishonest, untruthful
ant devious
3 *syn* see FRANK
rel barefaced, straight-from-the-shoulder
4 *syn* see CLEAR 5
straightly *adv syn* see DIRECTLY 1
straight off *adv syn* see AWAY 3
straight–out *adj syn* see UTTER
straight–up *adj* **1** *syn* see ERECT
2 *syn* see VERTICAL
straightway *adv syn* see AWAY 3
strain *n* **1** *syn* see HINT 2
2 *syn* see MELODY
3 *syn* see MOOD 1
strain *vb* **1** *syn* see TRY 2
rel stretch
idiom put a strain on
2 to injure (as a body part) by overuse or misuse <*strained* a muscle while lifting weights>
syn pull
3 *syn* see LABOR 1
4 *syn* see EXUDE
5 *syn* see DEMUR
strain *n syn* see STRESS 1
strained *adj syn* see FORCED

rel taut, tense, tight
con unforced, unlabored; unconstrained
ant unstrained
strait *n syn* see JUNCTURE 2
rel bind, squeeze; difficulty, hardship, rigor, vicissitude; bewilderment, mystification, perplexity
straitlaced *adj syn* see PRIM 1
rel hidebound, intolerant, narrow, narrow‍minded; rigorous, strict
idiom prim and proper
con easygoing, relaxed; broadminded, liberal, liberal-minded; libertine
strake *vb syn* see STREAK
‖**stramash** *n syn* see CRASH 3
strand *n syn* see SHORE
strand *vb syn* see SHIPWRECK 1
stranded *adj syn* see AGROUND
idiom high and dry, run aground
strange *adj* **1** *syn* see EXOTIC 2
2 *syn* see UNFAMILIAR 1
rel unknown; alien
3 *syn* see MARVELOUS 1
4 deviating from what is ordinary, usual, or to be expected <a *strange*, unpredictable man>
syn bizarre, curious, eccentric, erratic, idiosyncratic, odd, oddball, outlandish, peculiar, quaint, queer, ‖rum, rummy, singular, uncouth, unusual, weird; *compare* EXCEPTIONAL 1, MYSTERIOUS
rel aberrant, abnormal, atypical, off, off-the‍wall; fishy, funny; far-out, freaky, ‖kinky, kooky, offbeat, outré, ‖scatty; crazy, nutty; fantastic, grotesque
idiom as strange as they come
con common, ordinary, unexceptional, usual; expected, predictable
ant familiar
stranger *n* a nonresident or an unknown person in a community <he felt he had become a *stranger* in a foreign land>
syn alien, auslander, foreigner, inconnu, outcomer, outlander, outsider
rel out-of-stater, outstater; transient; visitor; immigrant; wanderer
idiom stranger within the gates
con inhabitant, resident; aboriginal, aborigine, autochthon, indigene, native
strangle *vb* **1** *syn* see CHOKE 1
2 *syn* see SUPPRESS 2
strangling *n syn* see REPRESSION 1
strapped *adj syn* see POOR 1
stratagem *n syn* see TRICK 1
rel conspiracy, intrigue, machination, plot
strategy *n syn* see PLAN 1
stratospheric *adj syn* see EXCESSIVE 1
straw *adj syn* see BLOND 1
rel strawish, strawy
straw *vb syn* see STREW 1
stray *vb* **1** *syn* see WANDER 1
2 *syn* see ERR
idiom stray from the straight and narrow
3 *syn* see DIGRESS 2
idiom get off the track, get sidetracked

stray *adj syn* see ERRATIC 1
rel random, sporadic
streak *n syn* see HINT 2
streak *vb* to make irregular lines or stripes of contrasting colors on or in <hair *streaked* with gray>
syn strake, striate, stripe
rel dapple, fleck, spot; marble, variegate, vein
stream *n* **1** *syn* see CREEK 2
2 *syn* see FLOW
stream *vb syn* see POUR 2
streamer *n syn* see FLAG
streamline *vb syn* see SIMPLIFY
‖**streel** *n syn* see SLATTERN 1
street *n syn* see WAY 1
rel ruelle, streetlet; drive
street arab *n syn* see VAGABOND
street girl *n syn* see PROSTITUTE
streetwalker *n syn* see PROSTITUTE
streetwalking *n syn* see PROSTITUTION
strength *n* **1** *syn* see POWER 4
rel brawn; sturdiness, toughness; healthiness, soundness
con feebleness
ant weakness
2 *syn* see STABILITY
3 *syn* see SUBSTANCE 2
strengthen *vb* **1** *syn* see ENCOURAGE 1
2 to make strong or stronger <exercise is needed to *strengthen* the body>
syn energize, fortify, invigorate, reinforce
rel brace, support, undergird; anneal, ruggedize, sinew, tone (up), toughen; cheer, embolden, encourage, enhearten, ensteel, hearten, inspirit, nerve, steel
con cripple, debilitate, disable, enfeeble, tear down, undermine; deject, discourage, dishearten, dispirit; emasculate, enervate, unman, unnerve
ant weaken
3 *syn* see GIRD 3
idiom gather one's resources, recruit one's strength
‖**strengthy** *adj syn* see STRONG 1
strenuous *adj* **1** *syn* see VIGOROUS
2 *syn* see HARD 6
rel breathless, energy-consuming; mean, wicked; Herculean
idiom a long hard pull, an uphill climb, tough going
con comfortable, cushy, light, unburdensome
ant effortless
stress *n* the action or effect of force exerted within or upon a thing <the bridge trusses slowly yielded to *stress* and buckled under the weight of the deck>
syn pressure, strain, tension
rel pinch; burden, weight
2 *syn* see EMPHASIS

---

syn synonym(s) *rel* related word(s)
ant antonym(s) *con* contrasted word(s)
idiom idiomatic equivalent(s)
‖ use limited; if in doubt, see a dictionary

rel import, importance

stress *vb* **1** *syn* see TRY 2
  2 *syn* see EMPHASIZE

stretch *vb* **1** *syn* see RUN 8
  rel range, roll
  2 *syn* see EXTEND 3
  con abbreviate, shorten; condense, curtail, cut, trim
  3 *syn* see EMBROIDER

stretch (out) *vb* *syn* see REST 1

stretch *n* **1** *syn* see RANGE 2
  2 *syn* see DISTANCE 1
  3 *syn* see EXPANSE
  rel area, region, tract
  4 *syn* see WHILE 1

stretch *adj* *syn* see ELASTIC 1

stretchy *adj* *syn* see ELASTIC 1

strew *vb* **1** to spread (something) loosely or at intervals usually over a substantial area <*strew* seed for birds>
  syn bestrew, broadcast, disject, disseminate, scatter, sow, straw; *compare* SPREAD 1, SPRINKLE 1
  rel dust, pepper; dissipate; cover
  2 *syn* see SPREAD 1

striate *vb* *syn* see STREAK

strict *adj* **1** *syn* see RIGID 3
  rel exacting, oppressive, unsparing; dour, forbidding, grim, hard-boiled, harsh, tough
  idiom not to be trifled (*or* messed) with
  con easy, easygoing; lax, loose; permissive
  ant lenient
  2 *syn* see TRUE 3

stricture *n* **1** *syn* see RESTRICTION 1
  2 *syn* see ANIMADVERSION

‖**striddle** *vb* **1** *syn* see BESTRIDE 2
  2 *syn* see STRIDE 1

stride *vb* **1** to move or walk with long often purposeful steps <*strode* to the door and slammed it>
  syn march, sling, stalk, ‖striddle
  rel clump, stamp, stomp, tramp, tromp
  2 *syn* see BESTRIDE

strident *adj* **1** *syn* see HARSH 3
  rel loud, stentorian, stertorous
  2 *syn* see VOCIFEROUS

stridulent *adj* *syn* see HARSH 3

stridulous *adj* *syn* see HARSH 3

strife *n* **1** *syn* see DISCORD
  rel argument, controversy, dispute; altercation, quarrel, squabble, wrangle; brawl, broil, fracas; affray, combat, fight, fray
  ant accord
  2 *syn* see CONTEST 1

strike *vb* **1** to engage in a temporary work stoppage to effect compliance with demands made on an employer <they *struck* for higher wages>
  syn stick out, walk out
  idiom go (*or* be) on strike
  2 to deliver (a blow) in a strong, vigorous manner <angrily *struck* the boy>
  syn ‖biff, catch, clout, ‖devel, ding, hit, ‖nail, pop, slog, ‖slosh, smite, sock, swat, whack; *compare* SLAM 1, SLAP 1
  rel beat, pummel, ‖slat, ‖swap, ‖wap, whop; cudgel, hammer, mace; ‖plug, poke, ‖puck,

punch; bang, bash, crash, ‖pandy, slam; ‖stoush, thrash
  idiom hang one on, let one fly
  3 *syn* see GIVE 10
  4 *syn* see AFFLICT
  5 *syn* see SEIZE 3
  6 *syn* see ATTACK 1
  7 *syn* see OCCUR 2
  8 *syn* see AFFECT
  9 *syn* see DON 2

strike *n* *syn* see DISCOVERY

strike out *vb* *syn* see HEAD 3

striker *n* *syn* see HELPER

striking *adj* *syn* see NOTICEABLE
  rel showy; forceful, powerful; cogent, compelling, telling

strikingly *adv* *syn* see VERY 1

string *n* **1** *syn* see LINE 5
  2 *syn* see RESOURCE 3
  3 *syn* see SUCCESSION 2
  4 strings *pl* *syn* see POWER 1

string (up) *vb* *syn* see HANG 2

string along *vb* *syn* see TRIFLE 1
  idiom keep (someone) dangling

stringent *adj* **1** *syn* see RIGID 3
  rel binding, confining, drawing
  2 *syn* see GRIM 2

strings *n pl* *syn* see CONDITION 1

stringy *adj* *syn* see MUSCULAR 1

‖**strinkle** *vb* *syn* see SPRINKLE 1

strip *vb* **1** to remove the clothing of <guards *stripped* and searched the prisoners>
  syn denude, disrobe, unclothe, undress
  rel doff, peel, take off; bare, denudate, expose, uncover; disfrock, unfrock
  idiom strip to the buff
  con clothe, dress, robe; cover
  2 to take something (as honors, privileges, functions, or trappings) away from <an exiled king now *stripped* of his power>
  syn bankrupt, bare, denudate, denude, deprive, dismantle, disrobe, divest; *compare* DEPRIVE 2
  rel bereave; deplenish, disfurnish, ‖displenish, dispossess; despoil, rob
  con clothe, endow, furnish, grant, vest; install
  ant invest
  3 *syn* see RAVAGE
  4 *syn* see SKIN 2

strip *n* *syn* see STRIPTEASE

strip *n* **1** a relatively long and narrow piece or section <tear old linen into *strips* for bandages>
  syn band, bandeau, banding, fillet, ribbon, stripe
  rel piece; section; segment; shred
  2 *syn* see BAR 1

stripe *vb* *syn* see WHIP 1

stripe *n* **1** *syn* see STRIP 1
  2 *syn* see TYPE

stripe *vb* *syn* see STREAK

stripling *n* *syn* see BOY 1

stripped *adj* **1** *syn* see NUDE 2
  con attired; covered
  ant clothed, dressed
  2 *syn* see OPEN 2

con covered, unexposed; protected

stripper *n syn* see STRIPTEASER

stripping *n syn* see STRIPTEASE

striptease *n* entertainment in which a female performer removes her clothing piece by piece in view of an audience <a nightclub featuring *striptease*>
syn strip, stripping
idiom exotic dancing

stripteaser *n* one who performs a striptease <worked part-time as a model and *stripteaser*>
syn ecdysiast, peeler, stripper, stripteuse, teaser
idiom exotic dancer, ‖pantie peeler, ‖strip-and-shake artist, strip artist

stripteuse *n syn* see STRIPTEASER

strive *vb* **1** *syn* see LABOR 1
2 *syn* see TRY 5
rel labor, toil, travail, work; drive, strain

striving *n* **1** *syn* see CONTEST 1
rel contending; combat, fight
2 *syn* see ATTEMPT
rel labor, toil, travail, work

stroll *vb syn* see SAUNTER

stroll *n syn* see WALK 1

strong *adj* **1** having great physical strength <had the *strong* hands and arms of a wrestler>
syn mighty, powerful, ‖strengthy, wieldy; *compare* MUSCULAR 2
rel firm, robust, stark, strapping, sturdy, two-handed; able-bodied, tough; brawny, muscular, sinewy; lusty, vigorous
idiom strong as a bull (*or* ox)
con feeble, frail; puny, weak-bodied; forceless, impotent, powerless, strengthless
ant weak
2 having or manifesting great force or power (as in acting or resisting) <a *strong* constitution>
syn stalwart, stout, sturdy, tenacious, tough
rel hardy, robust, rugged, strapping; firm, solid, staunch; durable, enduring; forceful, potent, powerful; lusty, vigorous
con frail; forceless, impotent, powerless, strengthless; depleted, failing
ant weak
3 being rich in a characteristic ingredient <*strong* coffee>
syn concentrated, full-bodied, lusty, potent, robust
rel strong-flavored, strong-tasting; straight, undiluted, unmixed; rich; heroic, large, powerful
con diluted, mixed, watered-down
ant weak
4 *syn* see SPIRITUOUS
5 *syn* see SURE 1
rel solid, substantial, unmoving, unyielding
6 *syn* see MALODOROUS 1

strong arm *n* **1** *syn* see POWER 4
2 *syn* see THUG 1

strong–arm *vb syn* see INTIMIDATE

stronghold *n syn* see FORT

strongly *adv syn* see HARD 1
ant weakly

strong man *n syn* see TYRANT

strong suit *n syn* see FORTE

structure *n* **1** *syn* see BUILDING
rel construction, erection, pile
2 *syn* see EDIFICE
3 something made up of more or less interdependent elements and having a definite organizational pattern <the complex bureaucratic *structure* of modern government>
syn framework
rel anatomy, skeleton; build, construction, frame; arrangement, composition, form, format, makeup, morphology; complex, network, system

struggle *vb syn* see TRY 5
rel compete, vie
idiom make a valiant attempt (*or* try)
ant give up

struggle *n syn* see ATTEMPT

strum *vb syn* see HUM

strumpet *n syn* see WANTON

‖**strunt** *vb syn* see STRUT 2

‖**strunt** *n syn* see LIQUOR 2

strut *vb* **1** *syn* see SASHAY
2 to walk with an air of pomposity or affected dignity <a pompous general *strutting* off the parade ground>
syn ‖strunt, swagger
rel flaunt, parade
con cower, cringe; slink

stubborn *adj* **1** *syn* see OBSTINATE
rel contumacious, insubordinate, rebellious; cantankerous, ornery; ‖stunkard, ‖stunt
idiom set in one's ways, stubborn as a mule
con adaptable, pliable, pliant; amenable, tractable
ant docile
2 *syn* see INFLEXIBLE 2

stubbornness *n syn* see DEFIANCE 2
rel cantankerousness, orneriness

stubby *adj syn* see STOCKY

stube *n syn* see ALEHOUSE

stuck–up *adj syn* see VAIN 3
idiom too big for one's breeches, wise in one's own conceit

stud *vb syn* see SPOT 2

studied *adj syn* see DELIBERATE 1
rel thoughtful; intentional, voluntary, willful, willing
con natural, offhand
ant unstudied

studio *n* the working place of an artist (as a painter) <moved to a larger *studio*>
syn atelier, bottega
rel shop, workroom, workshop

studious *adj syn* see DELIBERATE 1
ant impromptu

study *n* **1** *syn* see REVERIE
2 *syn* see ATTENTION 1
rel contemplation, weighing; abstraction, meditation, musing, pondering, rumination

---

syn synonym(s)   *rel* related word(s)
ant antonym(s)   *con* contrasted word(s)
idiom idiomatic equivalent(s)
‖ use limited; if in doubt, see a dictionary

3 syn see EXERCISE 4

study *vb* **1 syn** see CONSIDER 1
idiom give careful study to
2 syn see SCRUTINIZE 1

stuff *n* **1 syn** see PERSONAL EFFECTS
2 syn see MONEY
3 syn see THING 5
4 syn see ESSENCE 2

stuff *vb* **syn** see CRAM 1
rel overfill, overstuff
idiom fill to overflowing, fill to the brim

stuffed *adj* **syn** see FULL 1

stuffed shirt *n* a smug usually pompous person with an inflexibly conservative or reactionary outlook <a *stuffed shirt* with a starched mind>
syn Blimp, Colonel Blimp, fuddy-duddy
rel diehard; prig, prude, smug
con freethinker, latitudinarian, liberal, libertarian, libertine; avant-garde

stuffing *n* **syn** see ENTRAILS
rel ‖tar

stuffy *adj* **1** marked by a heavy oppressive quality of air <a *stuffy* room that needed airing>
syn airless, breathless, close, stifling, stivy, suffocating, sultry; *compare* HUMID, STIFLING 1
rel heavy, oppressive, thick; stagnant; shut-up, unventilated
con airy, breezy; open, ventilated; bracing, invigorating, refreshing, stimulating
2 syn see PRIM 1
rel dull, humdrum, stodgy; hidebound, illiberal, narrow, narrow-minded
3 syn see POMPOUS 1

‖stuggy *adj* **syn** see STOCKY

stultify *vb* to deprive of vitality and render futile especially by enfeebling or repressive influences <artistic creativity *stultified* by the intrusion of propaganda>
syn constipate, stagnate, stifle, trammel
rel discourage, inhibit, restrain; check, stunt; enfeeble, impair, weaken; deaden, dull; repress, smother, suffocate, suppress; invalidate, nullify
con encourage, foster, nourish; pique, provoke, stimulate

stultiloquence *n* **syn** see CHATTER

stumble *vb* **1 syn** see WALLOW 2
rel falter, waver; trip; fall
2 syn see DEMUR
3 to move so clumsily and awkwardly as to lose one's balance or trip and fall <*stumbled* across the darkened room and fell>
syn blunder, bumble, lurch, ‖snapper; *compare* WALLOW 2
rel reel, stagger, totter; trip; pitch, topple
4 syn see LUMBER
5 syn see TEETER
rel careen, swing
6 to act, proceed, or execute in a hesitant and clumsily faltering manner <*stumbled* through his Latin translation>
syn limp, muddle, shuffle
rel falter, hesitate, wobble; blunder, bumble; botch, bungle, ‖muck
ant breeze

7 syn see HAPPEN 2
idiom come (*or* run) up against, fall upon, stub one's toe upon (*or* on)
8 syn see PUZZLE

stumblebum *n* a clumsy inept or blundering person <a staff consisting of third-raters and *stumblebums*>
syn blunderbuss, blunderer, bungler
rel incompetent
con crackerjack, ‖dab, ‖darb, expert, topnotcher, whiz; natural; professional

stumbling block *n* **syn** see OBSTACLE

stump *vb* **1 syn** see NONPLUS 1
2 syn see LUMBER

stump *n* **syn** see DEFIANCE 1

stumpy *adj* **syn** see STOCKY

‖stumpy *n* **syn** see MONEY

stun *vb* **syn** see DAZE 2
rel nonplus; amaze, astound, flabbergast; knock out
idiom strike dumb (*or* dead)

stunner *n* **1 syn** see WONDER 1
2 syn see BEAUTY

stunning *adj* **1 syn** see EXCELLENT
2 syn see BEAUTIFUL

‖stunpoll *n* **syn** see DUNCE

‖stunt *adj* **syn** see STUNTED

stunt *vb* to hinder the normal growth and development of <the inhospitable climate had *stunted* all vegetation>
syn dwarf, suppress
rel check, curb, hold back; impair

stunt *n* **syn** see TRICK 3

stunted *adj* having had one's growth and development hindered or arrested <the children were *stunted* from malnutrition>
syn runted, runtish, runty, ‖scrunty, ‖stunt
rel undersized; dwarf
con able-bodied, robust well-set, well-set-up; giant, oversize; healthy, strong, sturdy, vigorous

‖stupe *n* **syn** see DUNCE

stupefy *vb* **1 syn** see DULL 5
2 syn see DAZE 2
rel addle, faze, rattle; nonplus

stupendous *adj* **1 syn** see MARVELOUS 1
2 syn see MONSTROUS 1

stupid *adj* **1** lacking in or exhibiting a lack of power to absorb ideas or impressions <a willing boy but too *stupid* to succeed in school>
syn beefheaded, beef-witted, beetleheaded, blear-eyed, blear-witted, blockheaded, blockish, chuckleheaded, dense, doltish, dull, dumb, duncical, fatheaded, goosey, hammerheaded, numskulled, pinhead, pinheaded, thick, thickheaded, thick-witted; *compare* RETARDED, SIMPLE 3
rel asinine, fatuous, foolish, silly, simple; brute, brutish, dummel, lumbering, oafish, slow, slow= witted, sluggish; crass; backward, half-witted, retarded; idiotic, imbecilic
idiom ‖dead above (*or* between) the ears, ‖dead from the neck up, having a block for a head, having cotton between the ears, ‖muscle-bound between the ears

con acute, alert, bright, clever, keen, knowing, quick, quick-witted, sharp, smart; sage, wise; brilliant; able, competent
ant intelligent
2 *syn* see LETHARGIC
stupid *n syn* see DUNCE
stupor *n syn* see LETHARGY 1
rel sopor; anesthesia, insensibility
sturdy *adj syn* see STRONG 2
rel sound, substantial
ant decrepit
Sturm und Drang *n syn* see UNREST
‖**stut** *vb syn* see STAMMER 1
stutter *vb syn* see STAMMER 1
sty *n* **1** an extremely unkempt or filthy place <the basement was a rat-infested *sty*>
syn dump, pigpen, pigsty
2 *syn* see SINK 1
stygian *adj syn* see INFERNAL 2
style *n* **1** *syn* see VEIN 1
2 *syn* see NAME 1
3 *syn* see FASHION 3
4 an individual's characteristic attitudes and taste as expressed or indicated in his way of life <she liked the man's sophisticated *style*>
syn manner, way
rel behavior; bearing, carriage; characteristic, trait; idiosyncrasy, peculiarity
style *vb syn* see NAME 1
stylish *adj* being in accordance with or conforming to current fashion <she was a *stylish* dresser>
syn a la mode, chic, ‖classy, dashing, exclusive, fashionable, in, modish, posh, sharp, smart, snappy, swank, swish, tonish, tony, ‖trendy, trig, ultrafashionable, with-it; *compare* DAPPER
rel new, new-day, newfangled, new-fashioned; modern, modernistic, up-to-date; chichi, doggish, doggy, natty, rakish, sassy, swagger; ostentatious, pretentious, ritzy, showy, swell; sleek, slick
idiom in fashion, in the mode
con styleless; old-fashioned, outmoded, out-of-date; drab, tasteless
ant dowdy, unstylish
suasible *adj syn* see RECEPTIVE 1
suave *adj* being conspicuously and ingratiatingly tactful and well-mannered <a man of *suave*, well-bred equanimity>
syn bland, civilized, smooth, urbane; *compare* TACTFUL
rel affable, cordial, genial, gracious, sociable; courteous, courtly, polite; diplomatic, politic; cultivated, cultured, distingué, polished, refined, well-bred; sophisticated, worldly; ingratiating, soft, soft-spoken; fulsome, slick, unctuous
con clumsy, unpolished, unskilled; tactless, undiplomatic, untactful
ant bluff
sub *adj syn* see SUBORDINATE
sub *n syn* see SUBSTITUTE 1
subaltern *n syn* see INFERIOR
subaquatic *adj syn* see SUBMARINE
subaqueous *adj syn* see SUBMARINE

subaverage *adj syn* see LOW 9
subconscious *n* mental activities that occur just below the threshold of consciousness <a motive probably rooted in his *subconscious*>
syn underconsciousness, undersense
rel subconsciousness; subliminal self
idiom subconscious (*or* submerged) mind
con consciousness; awareness
subdolous *adj syn* see SLY 2
subdue *vb syn* see CONQUER 1
rel extinguish, put down, quash, quell, quench, squelch, suppress
subdued *adj* **1** *syn* see QUIET 4
2 reduced or lacking in force, intensity, or vividness <*subdued* colors> <the child answered his questions in a timid *subdued* voice>
syn low-key, low-keyed, sober, soft, softened, toned down
rel moderated, tempered; controlled, restrained; mellow; neutral; quiet
con enlivened, intensified; bright, intense, strong; brilliant, vivid; saturated; blaring, glaring, harsh, screaming
3 *syn* see TAME
ant unsubdued
subduer *n syn* see VICTOR 1
subfusc *adj syn* see DULL 8
subitaneous *adj syn* see PRECIPITATE 1
subjacent *adj syn* see INFERIOR 1
ant superjacent
subject *n* **1** *syn* see CITIZEN 2
2 the basic idea or the principal object of attention in a discourse or artistic composition <the Puritan ethic was the *subject* of her paper>
syn argument, head, matter, motif, motive, point, subject matter, text, theme, topic
rel material, substance; problem, question; leitmotiv; core, meat
con elaboration, enlargement, enlarging, expatiation; development, explication
subject *adj* **1** *syn* see SUBORDINATE
rel servile, slavish, subservient
ant dominant, sovereign
2 *syn* see LIABLE 2
rel apt, likely
subject *vb syn* see EXPOSE 1
subjective *adj* peculiar to a particular individual as modified by individual bias and limitations <*subjective* judgments>
syn unobjective
rel biased, prejudiced; abstract, nonobjective, nonrepresentational, nonrepresentative
ant objective
subject matter *n syn* see SUBJECT 2
subjoin *vb syn* see ADD 1
rel combine, conjoin, unite
con part, separate, sever
subjugate *vb* **1** *syn* see CONQUER 1
rel compel, coerce, force

---

syn synonym(s)   *rel* related word(s)
ant antonym(s)   *con* contrasted word(s)
idiom idiomatic equivalent(s)
‖ use limited; if in doubt, see a dictionary

2 *syn* see ENSLAVE
ant liberate
subjugator *n syn* see VICTOR 1
sublease *vb syn* see SUBLET
sublet *vb* to turn over to another one's right of occupancy of (rented or leased housing) <*sublet*
her apartment to a friend>
syn sublease, underlease, underlet
sublime *vb syn* see EXALT 1
sublime *adj* **1** *syn* see GRAND 3
2 *syn* see SPLENDID 2
rel abstract, ideal, transcendent, transcendental; divine, holy, sacred, spiritual; august, majestic, noble, stately
sublimity *n syn* see APEX 2
sublunary *adj syn* see EARTHLY 1
submarine *adj* being, acting, growing, or used under water <a *submarine* camera>
syn subaquatic, subaqueous, underwater
submerge *vb* **1** *syn* see DIP 1
rel drench, impregnate, saturate, soak
2 *syn* see DELUGE 1
3 *syn* see SINK 1
submerse *vb* **1** *syn* see DIP 1
2 *syn* see SINK 1
submission *n syn* see SURRENDER
rel bowing, submitting; acquiescence, compliance, resignation; cringing, servility; prostration
ant resistance
submissive *adj* **1** *syn* see TAME
rel complying, conformable, obeying; bowing
down, unerect; menial, servile, slavish, subservient
ant rebellious
2 *syn* see PASSIVE 2
submit *vb* **1** *syn* see YIELD 2
ant resist, withstand
2 to offer or commit (something) for consideration, study, or decision <*submitted* his report
directly to the general>
syn hand in, refer
rel bring, deliver, present; offer, proffer, tender;
send in; provide
3 *syn* see SUGGEST 4
4 *syn* see FALL 3
ant hold out, resist
subnormal *adj syn* see LOW 9
rel subpar
subordinate *adj* placed in or occupying a lower
class, rank, or status <making the executive *subordinate* to the legislative branch>
syn collateral, dependent, secondary, sub, subject, tributary, under
rel adjuvant, auxiliary, contributory, subsidiary; satellite; inferior, subaltern, subalternate;
accessory, parergal, supplementary
con chief, first, leading, main; dominant, master, superior
subordinate *n syn* see INFERIOR
sub rosa *adv syn* see SECRETLY
ant aboveboard
sub–rosa *adj syn* see SECRET 1
ant aboveboard
subscribe *vb* **1** *syn* see SIGN 1

2 *syn* see CONTRIBUTE 1
3 *syn* see ASSENT
rel approve, endorse, favor, sanction
subsequent *adj* **1** being, occurring, or carried out
at a time after something else <*subsequent* events
disproved his predictions>
syn after, ensuing, later, posterior, postliminary, subsequential
rel following, next, succeeding; consequential,
resultant, resulting
con exordial, introductory, prefatory, preliminary, preludial; anterior, precedent, preceding,
prior
ant antecedent
2 *syn* see CONSECUTIVE
ant antecedent
subsequential *adj* **1** *syn* see SUBSEQUENT 1
2 *syn* see CONSECUTIVE
ant antecedent
subsequently *adv syn* see AFTER
ant antecedently, priorly
subsequent to *prep syn* see AFTER 2
subservient *adj* **1** *syn* see AUXILIARY
2 showing extreme compliance or abject obedience <a *subservient* minor bureaucrat>
syn menial, obeisant, obsequious, servile, slavish
rel acquiescent, compliant, resigned, submissive; cowering, cringing, fawning, truckling; abject, ignoble, mean
idiom as obedient as a dog
con aggressive; arrogant, haughty; rebellious;
independent, irrepressible, uncontainable
ant domineering, overbearing
subside *vb syn* see ABATE 4
idiom dwindle down
subsidiary *adj syn* see AUXILIARY
rel backup; minor, tributary
subsidize *vb syn* see ENDOW 2
rel back; promote; help
subsidy *n syn* see APPROPRIATION
rel subsidization; gift, reward
subsist *vb syn* see BE
subsistence *n syn* see LIVING
substance *n* **1** *syn* see TENOR 1
rel import, meaning
idiom the general drift
2 the inner significance or central meaning of
something written or said <just give me the *substance* of his speech>
syn amount, body, burden, core, crux, gist, kernel, matter, meat, nub, nubbin, pith, purport,
sense, short, strength, sum and substance, sum
total, thrust, upshot; *compare* BODY 3, ESSENCE 2,
MEANING 1, TENOR 1
rel center, focus, heart, nucleus; point; import,
meaningfulness
3 *syn* see BODY 3
rel drift, tenor
4 *syn* see ESSENCE 2
5 *syn* see THING 5
6 *syn* see WEALTH 2
substantial *adj* **1** *syn* see MATERIAL 1
con airy, ethereal

ant unsubstantial
2 syn see IMPORTANT 1
rel key, principal; strong; serious
3 syn see PROSPEROUS 3
rel solid, solvent
substantiate *vb* **1 syn** see EMBODY 1
rel substantialize, substantify
2 syn see CONFIRM 2
rel demonstrate, prove, test, try
substitutable *adj syn* see INTERCHANGEABLE
substitute *n* **1** a person who takes the place of or acts instead of another <found a *substitute* for the sick teacher>
syn alternate, backup, fill-in, locum tenens, pinch hitter, replacement, stand-in, sub, succedaneum, surrogate
rel relay, relief; deputy, procurator, proxy; supply; double, understudy
2 syn see RESOURCE 3
substitute *vb syn* see EXCHANGE 2
substitute *adj* **1** serving or fitted for use as a substitute <a *substitute* driver was needed for the long trip>
syn alternate, alternative, backup, surrogate
rel additional, another; other, second; reserve; supplemental, supplementary, suppletory
2 syn see ARTIFICIAL 2
substract *vb syn* see DEDUCT 1
substratal *adj syn* see ELEMENTAL 1
substratum *n* **1 syn** see BASIS 1
rel core, meat, stuff, substance
2 syn see BASE 1
substruction *n syn* see BASE 1
substructure *n syn* see BASE 1
ant superstructure
subsume *vb syn* see INCLUDE
subterfuge *n syn* see DECEPTION 1
subterrane *n syn* see CAVE
subterranean *adj* being, lying, functioning, or operating under the surface of the earth <*subterranean* hot springs that emerge as geysers>
syn subterrestrial, underearth, underfoot, underground
con aboveground, surface, surficial
subterranean *n syn* see CAVE
subterrestrial *adj syn* see SUBTERRANEAN
subtile *adj syn* see THIN 2
subtle *adj* **1 syn** see THIN 2
2 syn see FINE 1
ant unsubtle
3 syn see LOGICAL 2
rel dexterous, skillful
con blunt; dense
4 syn see SLY 2
ant unsubtle
subtract *vb syn* see DEDUCT 1
ant add
subtraction *n syn* see DEDUCTION 1
ant addition
suburbs *n pl syn* see ENVIRONS 2
rel fringes; suburbia
subvention *n syn* see APPROPRIATION
subversion *n syn* see SABOTAGE
rel demolishing, destroying, destruction

subvert *vb syn* see SABOTAGE
rel overthrow, overturn, upset; demolish, destroy, ruin; corrupt, debase, deprave, pervert
con sustain, uphold
succedaneum *n syn* see SUBSTITUTE 1
succedent *adj syn* see CONSECUTIVE
succeed *vb* **1 syn** see FOLLOW 1
ant precede
2 to result favorably according to plans and desires <that advertising campaign really *succeeded*>
syn click, come off, go, go over, pan out, prove out
rel catch on; prevail
idiom go over big, go over with a bang, hit the mark, make a hit, turn out well
ant fail, flop
3 to attain or be attaining a desired end <how to *succeed* in big business>
syn arrive, flourish, go, make out, prosper, score, thrive
rel ‖dow; get ahead; boom; achieve, attain, gain, reach; accomplish, effect, fulfill; conquer, prevail, triumph, win (out)
idiom do all right by oneself, do well, gain one's end, get places, get somewhere, get to the top of the ladder, make a success, make it (big), make one's mark, ‖make the big time, make the grade
con dwindle, languish; fall down, flounder, founder; lose (out); bust
ant fail
succeeding *adj syn* see CONSECUTIVE
succès fou *n syn* see SMASH 6
success *n* a succeeding fully or in accordance with one's desires <attributed his business *success* to hard work and attention to detail>
syn arrival, ‖do, flying colors, go, prosperity, successfulness
rel accomplishment, achievement, attainment; triumph, victory
ant failure; nonsuccess, unsuccessfulness
successful *adj* resulting in or having gained success <a *successful* business venture>
syn prosperous, thriving; *compare* FLOURISHING
rel extraordinary, notable, noteworthy, outstanding, smash, smashing
idiom crowned (*or* blessed *or* flushed) with success, ‖out front
con failing, thriveless, unprosperous; defeated, disappointed, failed, frustrated; bankrupt, broken, destroyed, ruined
ant successless, unsuccessful
successfully *adv syn* see WELL 5
ant unsuccessfully
successfulness *n syn* see SUCCESS
ant nonsuccess, unsuccessfulness
succession *n* **1 syn** see ORDER 5
2 a number of things that follow each other in some order <another *succession* of price hikes>

---

syn synonym(s) *rel* related word(s)
ant antonym(s) *con* contrasted word(s)
idiom idiomatic equivalent(s)
‖ use limited; if in doubt, see a dictionary

syn alternation, chain, consecution, course, order, progression, row, sequel, sequence, series, string, suite, train; *compare* CYCLE 1
rel successiveness; round, round robin
successional *adj syn* see CONSECUTIVE
successive *adj syn* see CONSECUTIVE
rel alternating, rotating
successively *adv syn* see TOGETHER 2
succinct *adj syn* see CONCISE
rel blunt, brusque
idiom right to the point
ant discursive
succinctly *adv syn* see BRIEFLY
ant discursively
succor *n syn* see HELP 1
rel ministration, ministry; maintenance, nourishment, sustenance
succubus *n syn* see DEVIL 2
succulent *adj* full of juice <a *succulent* roast>
syn juicy, ||sappy
succumb *vb* 1 *syn* see YIELD 2
rel abandon, relinquish, resign
2 *syn* see FALL 3
idiom hand over one's sword, meet one's Waterloo, show (*or* wave) the white flag, strike (*or* haul down) one's colors
3 *syn* see COLLAPSE 2
idiom bite the dust, ||take the count
4 *syn* see DIE 1
idiom yield one's breath
such *adj* 1 being previously characterized or specified <authorized to seize illegally parked cars and impound *such* vehicles>
syn aforementioned, aforesaid, said
2 being of so extreme a degree or quality <*such* nonsense as I had never heard before>
syn that
3 *syn* see LIKE
such *pron* 1 *syn* see SUCH A ONE
2 *syn* see SUCHLIKE
idiom the like
such a one *pron* someone or something that has been, is being, or will be stated, implied, or exemplified <the area is full of caverns; *such a one* may be found here>
syn such
suchlike *adj syn* see LIKE
suchlike *pron* a person or thing of the same or similar kind <airplanes, missiles, rockets, and *suchlike*>
syn such
sucker *n* 1 *syn* see PARASITE
2 *syn* see FOOL 3
idiom easy pickings
sucker *vb syn* see CHEAT
suck in *vb syn* see DECEIVE
||**suck–in** *n syn* see DECEPTION 1
suckle *vb syn* see NURSE 1
sudden *adj syn* see PRECIPITATE 1
rel accelerated, quickened, speeded; expeditious, fast, fleet, rapid, swift
sudden *adv* 1 *syn* see UNAWARES
2 *syn* see SHORT 1
suddenly *adv* 1 *syn* see SHORT 1

2 *syn* see UNAWARES
idiom of (*or* on) a sudden, on the sudden
suds *n pl but sing or pl in constr* 1 *syn* see SADNESS
2 *syn* see FOAM
sue *vb syn* see ADDRESS 8
idiom make (*or* pay) suit to, press one's suit
sue (for *or* to) *vb syn* see PETITION
suffer *vb* 1 *syn* see BEAR 10
rel accept, admit, receive
idiom grin and abide
2 *syn* see EXPERIENCE 1
3 *syn* see LET 2
rel countenance; accept, admit, receive; acquiesce, bow, submit, yield
||4 *syn* see HURT 4
sufferable *adj syn* see BEARABLE
ant insufferable
sufferance *n syn* see PERMISSION
suffering *n syn* see DISTRESS
rel adversity, misfortune
suffice *vb syn* see SERVE 3
sufficiency *n syn* see ENOUGH
ant insufficiency
sufficient *adj* 1 being what is requisite or needed especially without superfluity <there is *sufficient* bread left for breakfast>
syn adequate, comfortable, competent, decent, enough, satisfactory, sufficing; *compare* DECENT 4
rel ample, plenteous, plentiful, plenty; commensurable, commensurate, due, proportionate; acceptable, agreeable, pleasing
con inadequate, unsufficing; deficient; failing, lacking, missing, wanting
ant insufficient
2 *syn* see DECENT 4
idiom fair to middling
sufficient *n syn* see ENOUGH
sufficiently *adv syn* see ENOUGH 1
ant insufficiently
sufficing *adj syn* see SUFFICIENT 1
suffocate *vb* to stop the respiration of (as by asphyxiation) <the child was *suffocated* in an old refrigerator>
syn asphyxiate, choke, ||quackle, smother, stifle; *compare* CHOKE 1
rel stive; strangle
suffocating *adj* 1 *syn* see STIFLING 1
2 *syn* see STUFFY 1
suffocative *adj syn* see STIFLING 1
suffrage *n* the right, privilege, or power of expressing one's choice or wish (as in an election or in the determination of policy) <universal *suffrage*>
syn ballot, franchise, vote
rel voice
suffuse *vb syn* see INFUSE 1
rel interject, interpose, introduce
||**sugar** *n syn* see MONEY
sugar (over) *vb syn* see SUGARCOAT 1
sugarcoat *vb* 1 to make (something difficult or unpleasant) superficially easy or attractive <*sugarcoated* the reproach with a smile>
syn candy, honey, sugar (over), sweeten
rel edulcorate

2 *syn* see PALLIATE

sugarplum *n syn* see SOP 2

suggest *vb* **1** to convey an idea indirectly <designing attractive books with jackets that truly *suggest* their contents>
syn connote, hint, imply, insinuate, intimate; *compare* POINT 2
rel advert, allude, refer; denote
idiom bring to mind
con demonstrate, display, exhibit, manifest, set out, show
ant express
2 *syn* see POINT 2
rel promise
idiom be the sign of, point in the direction of
3 *syn* see PROPOSE 1
4 to offer (as an idea or theory) for consideration <this, I *suggest*, is what really happened>
syn submit, theorize
rel conjecture; imagine
5 to represent another thing indirectly, figuratively, and sometimes obscurely by evoking a thought, image, or conception of it <the meaning of a poem is often *suggested* in its title>
syn adumbrate, shadow (forth); *compare* ADUMBRATE 1
rel outline, sketch; betoken, symbolize; typify
con display, flaunt, parade
ant manifest

suggestion *n* **1** *syn* see PROPOSAL
2 *syn* see HINT 1
rel implication, innuendo
3 *syn* see ASSOCIATION 4
rel allusion; reminder
con demonstration, display, exhibition, manifestation, show
ant expression
4 *syn* see HINT 2

suggestive *adj* **1** *syn* see EVOCATIVE
rel significative
2 *syn* see RISQUÉ
rel erotic, sexy

suicide *n* the act or an instance of taking one's own life voluntarily and intentionally <committed *suicide* by shooting herself>
syn felo-de-se, hara-kiri, self-destruction, self=murder, self-slaughter, self-violence

suit *n* **1** a legal proceeding instituted for the sake of demanding justice or enforcing a right <filed a *suit* to recover her property>
syn action, case, cause, lawsuit
2 *syn* see PRAYER
rel asking, request, requesting, solicitation, soliciting

suit *vb* **1** *syn* see AGREE 4
idiom be in accord with, check out to the letter
2 *syn* see SERVE 3
3 *syn* see ADAPT
4 to be suitable for or to <the right word is the one that *suits* the occasion>
syn agree (with), become, befit, fit, go (together or with); *compare* SUIT 6
rel harmonize (with); benefit; please, satisfy
idiom answer a need (*or* the purpose), hit the spot

con clash, conflict, disaccord, disagree
5 *syn* see FLATTER
6 to meet the needs or desires of <this arrangement *suits* me fine>
syn please, satisfy; *compare* SUIT 4
con discontent, displease, dissatisfy; disappoint, fail, let down

suitability *n syn* see ORDER 11
ant unsuitability

suitable *adj* **1** *syn* see GOOD 2
ant unsuitable
2 *syn* see JUST 3
rel reasonable; advisable, expedient, politic
ant unsuitable
3 *syn* see FIT 1
rel nice, presentable, seemly
ant unbecoming, unsuitable
4 *syn* see ELIGIBLE
ant unsuitable

suitableness *n syn* see ORDER 11
ant unsuitableness

suitably *adv syn* see WELL 4
ant unsuitably

suite *n* **1** *syn* see ENTOURAGE
2 *syn* see GROUP 3
3 *syn* see APARTMENT 1
4 *syn* see SUCCESSION 2

suited *adj syn* see ASSORTED 2
ant unsuited

suitor *n* **1** *syn* see SUPPLIANT
2 one who courts a woman or seeks to marry her <a *suitor* for the king's daughter>
syn spark, sparker, swain, wooer
rel beau, boyfriend; cavalier, gallant; lover, man, paramour

sulk *vb* to be sullen or morose in mood usually because of a grievance <*sulked* all day when he didn't call>
syn ‖dort, grump, ‖mump, pet, pout, ‖sull
rel frown, glower, lower, scowl; brood, gloom, mope, take on
idiom be in a sulk, have the sulks, ‖take the dods

sulk *n*, *often* **sulks** *pl* the state, condition, or mood of one sulking <sat in a *sulk* all day after being reprimanded>
syn ‖dods, ‖dorts, grumps, mulligrubs, mumps, pouts, sullens
rel sourness, sulkiness, surliness; glumness, grouchiness
idiom a case of the sulks

sulky *adj syn* see SULLEN
rel cranky, testy, touchy; cantankerous, irritable, querulous
idiom having the sulks

‖**sull** *vb syn* see SULK

sullen *adj* showing a forbidding or disagreeable mood <stalked out in *sullen* silence>

---

syn synonym(s)   *rel* related word(s)
ant antonym(s)   *con* contrasted word(s)
idiom idiomatic equivalent(s)
‖ use limited; if in doubt, see a dictionary

syn ‖chuff, ‖chuffy, crabbed, crabby, ‖dorty, dour, gloomy, glum, morose, mumpish, saturnine, sulky, surly, ugly
rel moody; tenebrific, tenebrose, tenebrous; frowning, glowering, lowering, scowling; cross, fretful, grumpy, ill-humored, peevish, petulant, pouting, pouty, sour; black, hostile, malevolent, malicious, malign, mean, ‖runty; cynical, pessimistic
con easy, gay, high-spirited, insouciant, light-hearted, smiling

sullens *n pl syn* see SULK

sully *vb syn* see TAINT 1
rel disgrace, shame

sulphurous *adj syn* see INFERNAL 1

sultry *adj* 1 *syn* see HUMID
rel smothering, smothery, ‖smudgy, stifling, suffocating
2 *syn* see STUFFY 1
3 *syn* see HOT 1
idiom hot as Hades, ‖hot as old Billy Hell
4 *syn* see SENSATIONAL 2

sum *n* 1 *syn* see WHOLE 1
2 *syn* see WHOLE 2
rel body, bulk, mass; structure
3 *syn* see SUMMARY

sum *vb* 1 *syn* see ADD 2
2 *syn* see EPITOMIZE 1

sum (to *or* into) *vb syn* see AMOUNT 1

sum and substance *n* 1 *syn* see SUBSTANCE 2
2 *syn* see MEANING 1

summarize *vb syn* see EPITOMIZE 1
rel recapitulate, résumé, retrograde

summary *adj* 1 *syn* see CONCISE
rel compact, compacted
ant circumstantial
2 done or executed on the spot and without formality <a *summary* trial and speedy execution>
syn drumhead

summary *n* a short restatement of the main points <a *summary* of the news>
syn epitome, recapitulation, résumé, sum, summation, summing-up, sum-up
rel outline; run-through; roundup; inventory
con amplification, elaboration, enlargement, expansion

summate *vb* 1 *syn* see ADD 2
2 *syn* see EPITOMIZE 1

summation *n syn* see SUMMARY

summative *adj syn* see CUMULATIVE

summer *n* the season between spring and autumn <liked to swim during the *summer*>
syn summertide, summertime
rel midsummer

summer complaint *n syn* see DIARRHEA

summerhouse *n* a covered structure in a garden or park designed to provide a shady resting place <watched the sea from the *summerhouse*>
syn alcove, belvedere, garden house, gazebo, pagoda

summertide *n syn* see SUMMER

summertime *n syn* see SUMMER

summing–up *n syn* see SUMMARY

summit *n* 1 *syn* see TOP 1

2 *syn* see APEX 2

summon *vb* 1 *syn* see CONVOKE
2 to demand or request the presence or service of <were *summoned* to the principal's office>
syn call, call in, convene, summons; *compare* CONVOKE
rel bid, command, enjoin, order; cite, subpoena
idiom bid come

summons *vb syn* see SUMMON 2

‖**sump** *n syn* see SWAMP

sumptuous *adj* 1 *syn* see LUXURIOUS 3
rel gorgeous, resplendent, splendid, superb; lavish, rich
2 *syn* see GRAND 2
rel awe-inspiring, grandiose, imposing

sum total *n* 1 *syn* see WHOLE 1
2 *syn* see SUBSTANCE 2

sum up *vb syn* see EPITOMIZE 1

sum–up *n syn* see SUMMARY

sun *n* 1 the heavenly body about which the earth rotates <up in time to see the *sun* rise>
syn daystar, phoebus, Sol
rel celestial body, luminary, orb, star
idiom old Sol
2 the radiation of the sun <enjoying the warm spring *sun*>
syn sunlight, sunshine
rel daylight; radiance, radiation

sun *vb* to expose to sunshine <*sunned* himself too long and got badly burned>
syn bask, insolate
rel sunbathe; sunburn, sun-cure, sun-dry, tan

sunbeamy *adj syn* see CHEERFUL 1

Sunday best *n syn* see FINERY
idiom Sunday-go-to-meeting clothes

sunder *vb* 1 *syn* see SEPARATE 1
rel cleave, rend, rive
2 *syn* see CUT 5

‖**sundowner** *n syn* see VAGABOND

sundries *n pl* miscellaneous small articles, details, or items <supplied such *sundries* as needles, pins, and thread>
syn etceteras, oddments, odds and ends, this and that(s)
rel notions

sundry *adj* 1 *syn* MANY, legion, multifarious, multitudinal, multitudinous, numerous, populous, ‖several, various, voluminous
idiom all and sundry
2 *syn* see SEVERAL 3
idiom all sorts of

sundry *pron, pl in constr* an indeterminate number of more than one or two <*sundry* were interviewed; a few were selected>
syn divers, many, ‖several, various
idiom all and sundry, quite a few

sunk *adj syn* see DOWNCAST

sunlight *n syn* see SUN 2

sunny *adj* 1 *syn* see FAIR 2
rel bright, brilliant
idiom bright and sunny
2 *syn* see CHEERFUL 1

sunrise *n syn* see DAWN 1

sunset *n syn* see EVENING 2

sunshine *n syn* see SUN 2
sunshine *adj syn* see FAIR 2
sunshining *adj syn* see FAIR 2
sunshiny *adj syn* see FAIR 2
sunup *n syn* see DAWN 1
sup (off *or* up) *vb syn* see DRINK 1
super *adj syn* see MARVELOUS 2
   idiom out of this world
super *adv* 1 *syn* see VERY 1
   2 *syn* see EVER 6
superabundant *adj* abounding to a great, abnormal, or excessive degree <*superabundant* harvests had brought down prices>
   syn overabounding, overabundant, overflowing
   rel abounding, abundant, cornucopian, plenteous, plentiful; excess, excessive, overmuch, surplus; crawling, teeming; overspilling; epidemic, rampant
superadd *vb syn* see ADD 1
superannuate *vb* 1 *syn* see OUTDATE
   2 *syn* see RETIRE 2
superb *adj* 1 *syn* see GRAND 3
   rel noble; majestic
   2 *syn* see SPLENDID 2
   rel imposing, stately; opulent
   3 consummately impressive and supremely excellent of its kind <the writer's style is brilliant and his command of words and imagery, *superb*>
   syn magnificent, outstanding, standout, superexcellent, superlative; *compare* SUPREME
   rel glorious, gorgeous, marvelous, resplendent; crashing, rousing, sensational, slambang, super, superfine, wonderful; best, optimal, optimum, prime; sublime
   idiom very best
   con inferior, mediocre, poor, substandard; atrocious, awful, dreadful, shocking; deplorable, dismal, lamentable, pitiful, woeful; abominable, execrable, outrageous, shameful
   ant wretched
superbity *n syn* see PRIDE 3
supercilious *adj syn* see PROUD 1
   rel sniffish, sniffy, snifty, snippy, snuffy; sneering
superciliousness *n syn* see PRIDE 3
supererogant *adj syn* see SUPEREROGATORY
supererogative *adj syn* see SUPEREROGATORY
supererogatory *adj* given or done without compulsion, need, or warrant <people who offer *supererogatory* advice>
   syn gratuitous, supererogant, supererogative, unasked, uncalled-for, wanton
   rel nonessential, superfluous, supernumerary, unnecessary, unneeded
   con essential, indispensable, vital; compulsory, obligatory; called-for, needful, required, requisite, sought, wanted
superexcellent *adj syn* see SUPERB 3
   rel incomparable, matchless, unparalleled, unsurpassed
superficial *adj* 1 *syn* see SHALLOW 1
   2 lacking in depth, solidity, and comprehensiveness <wrote only a *superficial* report on the situation>

syn cursory, depthless, shallow, sketchy, uncritical
   rel bird's-eye, general; one-dimensional, skin≈deep; smattery
   con comprehensive, full, inclusive; deep, detailed, in-depth, thorough; critical
   ant exhaustive
superficies *n syn* see TOP 2
superfluent *adj syn* see SUPERFLUOUS
superfluity *n* 1 *syn* see EXCESS 1
   rel overflowing, swarming, teeming
   2 *syn* see LUXURY 1
superfluous *adj* exceeding what is needed or indispensable <omitted all *superfluous* information>
   syn de trop, excess, extra, recrementitious, spare, superfluent, supernumerary, surplus
   rel unnecessary, unneeded, unwanted; needless, useless; dispensable, nonessential; gratuitous, supererogatory, unasked, un- called-for
   con critical, crucial, imperative; essential, fundamental, vital; consequential, important, momentous, notable, noteworthy; defective, inadequate
   ant deficient
superhuman *adj* 1 *syn* see SUPERNATURAL 1
   2 *syn* see SUPERNATURAL 2
superhuman *n syn* see SUPERMAN
superincumbent *adj* 1 *syn* see SUPERIOR 1
   2 *syn* see ONEROUS
superintend *vb syn* see SUPERVISE
superintendence *n syn* see OVERSIGHT 1
   rel direction, presidence
superintendency *n syn* see OVERSIGHT 1
   rel direction, presidence
superior *adj* 1 being or regarded as being above the level of another <the new assistant received a *superior* rating for his work>
   syn greater, higher, over, overlying, superincumbent, superjacent
   rel major, primary, senior
   con lesser, lower, nether, under
   ant inferior
   2 *syn* see SUPERNATURAL 1
   3 *syn* see BETTER 2
   ant inferior
   4 being of higher quality, accomplishment, or merit <a class of *superior* students>
   syn exceptional, premium; *compare* MARVELOUS 2
   rel noteworthy, remarkable, unusual
   con commonplace, ordinary, unexceptional, unremarkable
   ant average
   5 *syn* see CHOICE
   6 *syn* see EXCELLENT
   ant inferior
   7 *syn* see PROUD 1
superior *n* one standing above another in a hierarchy of rank <was always respectful to his *superiors* in the department>

---

syn synonym(s)   *rel* related word(s)
ant antonym(s)   *con* contrasted word(s)
idiom idiomatic equivalent(s)
‖ use limited; if in doubt, see a dictionary

syn better, brass hat, elder, higher-up, senior
rel heavyweight
ant inferior

superiority *n syn* see BETTER 2
rel ascendancy, dominance, supremacy
ant inferiority

superjacent *adj syn* see SUPERIOR 1
ant subjacent

superlative *adj syn* see SUPERB 3
rel accomplished, consummate, finished

superman *n* a person of extraordinary power or achievement <a space program run by scientific *supermen*>
syn demigod, superhuman
idiom Triton among the minnows
con also-ran, loser, underdog
ant subhuman

supermundane *adj syn* see SUPERNATURAL 1

supernatural *adj* 1 of, relating to, or proceeding from an order of existence beyond the visible observable universe <many then believed in a *supernatural* force that directs history>
syn metaphysical, miraculous, numinous, preternatural, superhuman, superior, supermundane, suprahuman, supramundane, supranatural, unearthly
rel paranormal, rare, unusual; spiritual; celestial, heavenly; divine
2 being much more than is natural or normal <had a *supernatural* ability to win money>
syn superhuman, supernormal, superordinary, supranormal, uncanny, unnatural
rel extraordinary, outstanding, phenomenal, remarkable; paranormal
3 *syn* see EXCESSIVE 1

supernormal *adj syn* see SUPERNATURAL 2
ant subnormal

supernumerary *adj syn* see SUPERFLUOUS

superordinary *adj syn* see SUPERNATURAL 2
ant ordinary

superpatriot *n syn* see PATRIOTEER

superscribe *vb syn* see ADDRESS 6

supersede *vb syn* see REPLACE 3
rel reject, repudiate; abandon, desert, forsake; discard

superseded *adj syn* see OBSOLETE

supersensible *adj syn* see PSYCHIC 1

supersensory *adj syn* see PSYCHIC 1

supertemporal *adj syn* see INFINITE 1

supervene *vb syn* see FOLLOW 1

supervenient *adj syn* see ADVENTITIOUS

supervise *vb* to have or exercise the charge, direction, and oversight of <*supervised* the construction of the new stadium>
syn boss, chaperon, overlook, oversee, quarterback, superintend, survey
rel guide, steer; administer, conduct, direct; manage, run; control; monitor, proctor

supervision *n syn* see OVERSIGHT 1

supper club *n syn* see NIGHTCLUB

supplant *vb* 1 to supersede (another) by or as if by force, trickery, or treachery <a wife who found herself *supplanted* by another woman>
syn cut out, displace, usurp

rel crowd (out), force (out); bounce, cast (out), eject, expel, oust
idiom give the bum's rush, give the old heave-ho, step into the shoes of
2 *syn* see REPLACE 3

supple *adj* 1 *syn* see ELASTIC 1
ant stiff
2 *syn* see PLASTIC
3 showing freedom and ease of bodily movement (as in bending or twisting) <the light *supple* spring of a cat>
syn limber, lissome, lithe, lithesome
rel agile, graceful, willowy, wiry, withy
con awkward, clumsy, gawky, maladroit, unhandy; ungraceful; arthritic, creaky, decrepit
ant stiff

supplement *n* 1 *syn* see COMPLEMENT 1
2 *syn* see APPENDIX 1

suppliant *n* one who asks (as for a favor or gift) humbly <a room full of *suppliants* waiting to see the king>
syn asker, beggar, petitioner, prayer, suitor, supplicant, supplicator
rel solicitant, solicitor

supplicant *n syn* see SUPPLIANT

supplicate *vb syn* see BEG
idiom ask on bended knee, ‖come down on one's marrowbones

supplication *n syn* see PRAYER

supplicator *n syn* see SUPPLIANT

supply *vb syn* see GIVE 3
rel fulfill, outfit, provision

supply *n* an accumulation of something that is a source from which things may be drawn <an unending *supply* of new talent>
syn armamentarium, fund, inventory, stock, store
rel accumulation; reserve, reservoir, stockpile, surplus; hoard

supply *adj syn* see TEMPORARY

support *vb* 1 *syn* see BEAR 10
2 to favor actively in the face of opposition <*support* an unpopular economic policy>
syn advocate, back, backstop, champion, side (with), uphold
rel applaud, approve, endorse, favor, plunk (for), pull (for), root; adopt, embrace, espouse; defend, maintain, sustain
idiom align oneself with, be on (someone's) side, take (someone's) side
con battle, combat, counter, fight, oppose; withstand
ant buck
3 to supply what is needed for sustenance <*support* his family>
syn maintain, provide (for)
idiom boil the pot, bring home the bacon, make a living for, take care of
4 to hold up in position by serving as a foundation or base for <pillars *supporting* an arch>
syn bear up, bolster, brace, buttress, carry, prop, shore (up), sustain, upbear, uphold
rel stand

5 to keep from yielding, sinking, or losing courage or stability <her friends *supported* her during the crisis>
syn bolster, buoy (up), prop, sustain, underprop, uphold; *compare* ENCOURAGE 1
rel encourage; fortify, stiffen, strengthen

support *n* **1** *syn* see HELP 1
2 *syn* see HELP 2
3 a supporting means, agency, medium, or device <girders as structural *supports*><strong economic *support* for the government>
syn brace, buttress, column, prop, shore, stay, underpinner, underpinning, underpropping
rel base, foundation; sustentation
4 *syn* see LIVING

supportable *adj* *syn* see BEARABLE
ant insupportable, unsupportable

supporter *n* **1** *syn* see FOLLOWER
2 *syn* see EXPONENT
ant antagonist

supposable *adj* *syn* see THINKABLE 2
ant insupposable

supposal *n* *syn* see THEORY 1

suppose *vb* **1** *syn* see UNDERSTAND 3
rel presuppose
2 *syn* see CONJECTURE

suppose *n* *syn* see THEORY 2

supposed *adj* **1** accepted or advanced as true or real on the basis of less than conclusive evidence <the *supposed* efficiency of the new machine>
syn conjectural, hypothetical, putative, reputed, suppositional, suppositious, supposititious, suppositive, suppository; *compare* ALLEGED
rel assumed, postulated, postulatory, presumed, presupposed; provisional, tentative; academic, speculative, theoretical; alleged
con sure; known, proved, proven; ascertained, demonstrated, observed, recognized
ant certain
2 *syn* see ALLEGED
ant proved, proven

supposition *n* **1** *syn* see ASSUMPTION 2
2 *syn* see THEORY 2

suppositional *adj* *syn* see SUPPOSED 1

suppositious *adj* **1** *syn* see FICTITIOUS 1
2 *syn* see SUPPOSED 1
rel doubtful, dubious, questionable; pretended, simulated

supposititious *adj* **1** *syn* see ILLEGITIMATE 1
2 *syn* see FICTITIOUS 1
3 *syn* see SUPPOSED 1

supposititiousness *n* *syn* see ILLEGITIMACY 1

suppositive *adj* *syn* see SUPPOSED 1

suppository *adj* *syn* see SUPPOSED 1

suppress *vb* **1** *syn* see CRUSH 5
idiom ride roughshod over
2 to hold back more or less forcefully someone or something that seeks an outlet <management tried to *suppress* the workers' discontent> <there was no way to *suppress* her short of murder>
syn muffle, ‖quelch, repress, shush, squelch, strangle; *compare* CRUSH 5

rel curb, restrain; arrest, check, interrupt; put down, slap down; quash, quell, squash; cut off, spike; abolish, annihilate, extinguish
idiom bring to naught, crack (*or* clamp) down on, put the kibosh on
3 to keep from public knowledge <*suppress* all news from the front>
syn burke, hush (up), stifle
rel repress; censor; silence
idiom put the lid on
con disclose, divulge, leak, ‖let out, reveal; broadcast, circulate, diffuse, publish, spread
4 *syn* see COMPOSE 4
rel drown; swallow
5 *syn* see STUNT

suppression *n* **1** *syn* see REPRESSION 1
2 *syn* see REPRESSION 2

supra *adv* *syn* see ABOVE 2
ant infra

suprahuman *adj* *syn* see SUPERNATURAL 1

supramundane *adj* *syn* see SUPERNATURAL 1

supranatural *adj* *syn* see SUPERNATURAL 1

supranormal *adj* *syn* see SUPERNATURAL 2

supremacy *n* the position of being first (as in rank, power, or influence) <Britain once enjoyed *supremacy* on the seas>
syn ascendancy, ascendant, dominance, domination, dominion, masterdom, preeminence, preponderance, preponderancy, preponderation, prepotence, prepotency, sovereignty
rel authority, control, driver's seat, power, sway; mastership, mastery, principality, superiority; transcendence

supreme *adj* developed to the utmost and not exceeded by any other in degree, quality, or intensity <dying for one's principles is an example of *supreme* sacrifice>
syn incomparable, preeminent, surpassing, towering, transcendent, ultimate, unequalable, unmatchable, unsurpassable; *compare* ALONE 3, EXCELLENT, MARVELOUS 2, MAXIMUM, SUPERB 3
rel crowning, master, sovereign; unequaled, unmatched, unparalleled, unrivaled, unsurpassed; final, last; absolute, perfect

surcease *vb* *syn* see STOP 3

sure *adj* **1** firmly settled or established <trying to find a *sure* footing on the rugged slope>
syn fast, firm, secure, stable, staunch, strong; *compare* FAST 4, STABLE 4
2 free from doubt, hesitation, or fear <upheld a *sure* faith>
syn abiding, enduring, firm, fixed, never-failing, steadfast, steady, unfaltering, unqualified, unquestioning, unshakable, unshaken, unwavering, wholehearted
rel assured, changeless, constant, unchangeable, unchanging, uncompromising, unfailing, unvarying; certain, fixed, set

---

syn synonym(s)   *rel* related word(s)
ant antonym(s)   *con* contrasted word(s)
idiom idiomatic equivalent(s)
‖ use limited; if in doubt, see a dictionary

con insecure, uncertain, unreliable; feeble, infirm, shaky, unsound; doubtful, dubious, hesitant
ant unsure
3 *syn* see INFALLIBLE 1
4 *syn* see INFALLIBLE 2
5 marked by unwavering assurance especially as to the rightness of one's views or actions <was *sure* he knew the answer>
syn certain, cocksure, confident, positive
rel assured, self-assured, self-possessed, self-satisfied; arrogant, cocky, pert; decided, decisive
con doubtful, hesitant, uncertain
ant unsure
6 *syn* see POSITIVE 3
rel convincing, telling; absolute, definite; genuine, real, valid
sure–enough *adj* **1** *syn* see ACTUAL 2
2 *syn* see AUTHENTIC 2
surefire *adj syn* see INFALLIBLE 2
sureness *n syn* see CERTAINTY
ant unsureness
sure thing *n* one that is bound to be successful <was deemed a *sure thing* in the race>
syn shoo-in
rel certainty; winner
surety *n* **1** *syn* see CERTAINTY
2 *syn* see GUARANTEE 1
3 *syn* see SPONSOR
surface *n syn* see TOP 2
rel exterior, outside; cover, covering
con body, mass; inside, interior; lining
surface *vb* to come to the surface (as of water) <a submarine *surfaced* outside the harbor>
syn rise
rel come up
con go down, go under; submerge; dive
surfeit *n syn* see EXCESS 1
surfeit *vb syn* see SATIATE
rel overfill, overindulge
idiom have all one can take (*or* stand)
ant whet
surfeited *adj syn* see SATIATED
ant unsatisfied
surge *vb syn* see POUR 2
surly *adj syn* see SULLEN
rel discourteous, ill-mannered, rude, ungracious; bearish, boorish, churlish; fractious, irritable, snappish, waspish
idiom as surly as a bear
con affable, cordial, genial, gracious
ant amiable
surmise *vb syn* see CONJECTURE
rel consider, regard; hypothesize, theorize
idiom risk assuming, venture a guess
surmount *vb* **1** *syn* see OVERCOME 1
rel best, better, outdo, outstrip, outtop, outtower, surpass
idiom rise superior to
2 *syn* see CLEAR 8
3 to stand or lie at the top of <a cross *surmounts* the cupola>
syn cap, crest, crown, top
rel finish; terminate

4 *syn* see TOP
surpass *vb* **1** to be or become greater than or superior to <*surpassed* all his fellows in scholarship>
syn ‖bang, beat, best, better, cap, cob, ding, exceed, excel, outdo, outgo, outmatch, outshine, outstrip, pass, top, transcend, trump
rel distance, outdistance, outpace, outperform, outpoint, outrange, outrival, outrun, outvie; eclipse, outrank, outtop, outtower, outweigh, overshadow, overtop, rank
idiom have it all over, put to shame
2 *syn* see EXCEED 1
surpassing *adj syn* see SUPREME
surpassingly *adv syn* see VERY 1
surplus *n* **1** *syn* see EXCESS 1
ant deficiency
2 *syn* see EXCESS 2
ant shortage
surplus *adj syn* see SUPERFLUOUS
surplusage *n* **1** *syn* see EXCESS 2
ant shortage, underage
2 *syn* see EXCESS 1
ant shortage
surprise *vb* **1** to attack unawares <hijackers *surprised* the truck driver and took his cargo>
syn ambush, lay (for), waylay
rel bushwhack, dry-gulch; capture, catch; grab, grasp, seize, take
2 to impress forcibly through unexpectedness, startlingness, or unusualness <was *surprised* by his violent jealousy>
syn amaze, astonish, astound, dumbfound, flabbergast
rel startle; bewilder, confound, discomfit, disconcert, dismay, nonplus, ‖swan; faze, rattle, rock; bowl (over), floor, stagger; stun, stupefy
idiom leave open-mouthed (*or* aghast), take aback (*or* by surprise)
surprising *adj syn* see MARVELOUS 1
rel unexpected, unforeseen, unlooked-for; eye-opening, eye-popping
surrender *vb* **1** *syn* see RELINQUISH
rel commit, consign, entrust
2 *syn* see FALL 3
rel give in, give up
idiom haul down one's colors, strike the (*or* one's) flag
surrender *n* the yielding of one's person, forces, or possessions to another <the victors demanded unconditional *surrender*>
syn capitulation, dedition, submission
rel appeasement, Munich; relenting, succumbing, yielding; white flag
surreptitious *adj syn* see SECRET 1
rel skulking, slinking, slinky, sneaking, sneaky
con obvious, open, overt
ant brazen
surreptitiously *adv syn* see SECRETLY
con openly, overtly, plainly
ant brazenly
surrogate *n* **1** *syn* see SUBSTITUTE
2 *syn* see RESOURCE 3
surrogate *adj syn* see SUBSTITUTE 1

surround *vb* **1** to close in or as if in a ring about something <a crowd *surrounded* the accident victim>
syn begird, beset, circle, compass, encircle, encompass, environ, gird, girdle, hem, loop, ring, round
rel embosom, enclave, enclose, envelop; circumscribe, circumvent, confine, limit
2 *syn* see BORDER 1
surroundings *n pl syn* see ENVIRONMENT
surveillance *n* **1** *syn* see EYE 3
idiom peeled eye
2 *syn* see LOOKOUT 3
rel surveyance
idiom watchful (*or* weather) eye
survey *vb* **1** *syn* see ESTIMATE 1
rel measure, size, size up
2 *syn* see SUPERVISE
3 to view from or as if from a high place or position <*surveyed* the view from her penthouse window>
syn overlook, oversee
4 *syn* see SCRUTINIZE 1
survey *n* **1** *syn* see EXAMINATION
2 *syn* see COMPENDIUM 1
‖**survigrous** *adj syn* see VIGOROUS
survive *vb* **1** *syn* see OUTLIVE
2 to continue to exist or function in spite of a usually adverse condition or development <a company that managed to *survive* the recession>
syn come through, pull through, ride (out)
rel carry on, carry through, continue, endure, last, persist; live down, outlast, outlive; recover, revive
idiom come out of it, live to fight again, make it through, ride out (*or* weather) the storm
con collapse, crash, fold, fold up, go down, go under; founder, sink; close (down), close up; bankrupt, bust
ant perish
susceptible *adj* **1** *syn* see LIABLE 2
rel disposed, inclined, predisposed
ant immune, unsusceptible
2 *syn* see EASY 3
rel nonresistant, soft; movable, persuadable
ant unsusceptible
3 *syn* see SENTIENT 3
rel affected, impressed, influenced, swayed, touched; aroused, roused, stirred
ant unsusceptible
susceptive *adj syn* see SENTIENT 3
suscitate *vb syn* see PROVOKE 4
suspect *adj syn* see DOUBTFUL 1
idiom ‖a bit thin (*or* thick), open to suspicion
suspect *vb* **1** *syn* see DISTRUST
idiom have doubts about
2 *syn* see UNDERSTAND 3
idiom be inclined to think
suspend *vb* **1** *syn* see EXCLUDE
2 *syn* see DEFER
rel arrest, check, interrupt; cease, discontinue, stop
idiom lay on the table, put on the shelf
3 *syn* see HANG 1

suspended *adj* hung or seeming as if hung from a support <bunches of grapes *suspended* from the vines>
syn hanging, pendent, pendulant, pendulous, pensile
rel dangling, swinging
suspenders *n pl* a pair of adjustable bands for holding up the front and rear of a pair of trousers or a skirt <every stockbroker seemed to be wearing *suspenders* and a yellow tie>
syn braces, ‖gallows, ‖galluses
suspense *n syn* see SUSPENSION 2
suspension *n* **1** *syn* see ABEYANCE
2 a temporary withholding of action or cessation of activity <asked for *suspension* of judgment until all the evidence was in>
syn moratorium, suspense
rel cessation, concluding, conclusion, end, ending, finish, period, termination
con resumption; continuance
suspicion *n* **1** *syn* see UNCERTAINTY
rel apprehension, foreboding, misgiving, presentiment; distrust
2 *syn* see HINT 2
‖**suspicion** *vb syn* see DISTRUST
suspicious *adj* **1** *syn* see DOUBTFUL 1
rel questionable; queer
2 given or prone to suspicion <was *suspicious* of everyone's motives>
syn distrustful, jealous, mistrustful
rel careful, cautious; leery, wary, watchful; skeptical, unbelieving
con trustful, trusting, unsuspecting; naive; dupable, easy, exploitable, gullible
ant unsuspicious
suspiciously *adv syn* see ASKANCE 2
rel distrustingly, mistrustingly
ant unsuspiciously
suspire *vb* **1** *syn* see SIGH 1
idiom draw a long breath
2 *syn* see LONG
sustain *vb* **1** *syn* see MAINTAIN 1
rel nourish, support; prolong
2 *syn* see SUPPORT 4
rel lug, pack, tote
3 *syn* see SUPPORT 5
rel befriend, favor
idiom stand by
con abandon, forsake; ignore
4 *syn* see BEAR 10
5 *syn* see EXPERIENCE 1
rel bear, endure
sustainable *adj syn* see BEARABLE
ant unsustainable
sustenance *n* **1** *syn* see FOOD 2
idiom bodily sustenance
2 *syn* see LIVING
sustentation *n syn* see PRESERVATION 1
susurration *n syn* see MURMUR 1

---

syn synonym(s)   *rel* related word(s)
ant antonym(s)   *con* contrasted word(s)
idiom idiomatic equivalent(s)
‖ use limited; if in doubt, see a dictionary

‖swack *n syn* see CUFF
‖swacked *adj syn* see INTOXICATED 1
swad *n syn* see SOLDIER
swaddle *vb syn* see SWATHE
  rel ‖sweel
  ant unswaddle
‖swaddy *n syn* see SOLDIER
swag *vb* 1 *syn* see SEESAW
  2 *syn* see DROOP 3
swag *n* 1 *syn* see SPOIL
  2 *syn* see MONEY
swagger *vb* 1 *syn* see LORD
  rel swash, swashbuckle
  2 *syn* see STRUT 2
  rel bluster, brandish, flourish
  con blench, quail; shrink, wince; truckle
‖swagger *n syn* see VAGABOND
‖swagman *n syn* see VAGABOND
swain *n* 1 *syn* see BOYFRIEND 1
  2 *syn* see SUITOR 2
swainish *adj syn* see BOORISH
swallow *vb* 1 to receive through the esophagus into the stomach <*swallowed* the pills easily with a sip of water>
  syn down, take
  rel drop, gulp, ‖quilt, toss; ingest, ingurgitate
  2 *syn* see DRINK 1
  3 *syn* see BELIEVE 1
  idiom swallow (something) hook, line, and sinker
  4 *syn* see BEAR 10
  5 *syn* see ACCEPT 2
  6 *syn* see MUMBLE
swamp *n* wet spongy land saturated and sometimes partially covered with water <hunted alligators in the Florida *swamps*>
  syn baygall, bog, fen, marsh, marshland, mire, morass, ‖moss, muskeg, ‖purgatory, ‖puxy, quag, quagmire, slough, ‖sump, swampland, ‖swang, ‖vlei
  rel bottoms, ‖holm; ‖glade; ‖jheel; quake ooze; shaking prairie, trembling prairie
swamp *vb* 1 *syn* see DELUGE 1
  2 *syn* see DELUGE 3
swampland *n syn* see SWAMP
‖swang *n syn* see SWAMP
swank *vb syn* see LORD
swank *adj* 1 *syn* see SHOWY
  2 *syn* see STYLISH
swap *vb* 1 *syn* see EXCHANGE 2
  2 *syn* see TRADE 1
  idiom ‖swap horses, swap out of
‖swap *n syn* see BLOW 1
‖swapping *adj syn* see HUGE
‖swarf *vb syn* see FAINT
swarm *vb syn* see TEEM
  idiom gather (*or* swarm) like bees
swarming *adj syn* see ALIVE 5
swart *adj syn* see DARK 3
swarth *adj syn* see DARK 3
swarthy *adj syn* see DARK 3
swash *vb* 1 *syn* see SLOSH 1
  2 *syn* see SPLASH
swashy *adj syn* see INSIPID 3

swat *vb* ‖1 *syn* see SQUAT
  2 *syn* see STRIKE 2
  rel blip, box, buffet, cuff, smack; belt, clobber, slug, smash, wallop
swat *n syn* see HIT 1
swathe *vb* to cover or bind completely with clothing or material <legs *swathed* in bandages> <the baby was *swathed* in a warm shawl>
  syn drape, enswathe, envelop, enwrap, roll, swaddle, wrap (up); *compare* ENFOLD 1
  rel enfold; encase; cover
  con bare, denude, expose, strip, uncover, unswaddle, unwrap
  ant unswathe
sway *vb* 1 *syn* see SWING 2
  2 *syn* see LURCH 2
  3 *syn* see GOVERN 1
  4 *syn* see AFFECT
  rel bias, dispose, incline, predispose; conduct, control, direct, manage; govern, rule
sway *n syn* see POWER 1
  rel range, reach, scope, sweep; amplitude, expanse, spread, stretch
swayable *adj syn* see RECEPTIVE 1
swear *vb* 1 *syn* see VOW
  idiom swear on a stack of Bibles, swear to God, swear up and down
  2 *syn* see TESTIFY 2
  3 to use profane, blasphemous, or obscene language <*swore* when the horse threw him>
  syn bedamn, curse, cuss, damn, execrate, imprecate
  rel blaspheme; rail, rant; abuse, revile, vilify, vituperate
  idiom ‖chew the dirty rag, curse and swear, fall a-cursing, ‖let out religion, make the air blue, rip (*or* rap) out an oath, swear like a sailor (*or* trooper), use language
swear *n syn* see SWEARWORD
swearing *n syn* see BLASPHEMY 1
swearword *n* a profane, blasphemous, or obscene word <let loose with a string of *swearwords*>
  syn curse, cuss, cussword, expletive, oath, swear
  rel four-letter word, obscenity, scurrility
  idiom blue word, one-horse oath, raw one, ripe (*or* juicy) word, sailor's blessing, six-cornered oath, strong word
sweat *vb* 1 *syn* see EXUDE
  2 *syn* see FLEECE 1
sweat *n* 1 *syn* see WORK 2
  2 *syn* see SNIT
  ‖3 *syn* see SOLDIER
sweatful *adj syn* see SWEATY
sweating *adj syn* see SWEATY
sweat out *vb syn* see BEAR 10
sweaty *adj* producing, accompanied by, or characterized by sweat <he still held the racket tight in *sweaty* hands>
  syn asweat, perspiring, perspiry, ‖puggy, sweatful, sweating
  rel clammy; sticky; wet
  idiom bathed in sweat, covered with sweat, drenched with (*or* in) sweat, in a muck of a sweat, wet with sweat (*or* perspiration)

sweep *vb syn* see FLY 4

sweep *n syn* see RANGE 2

sweeping *n* sweepings *pl syn* see REFUSE

sweeping *adj* 1 *syn* see ALL-AROUND 2
 rel all-embracing, all-encompassing
 2 *syn* see INDISCRIMINATE 1
 rel all-out, out-and-out, whole-hog; across-the-board, blanket

sweet *adj* 1 distinctly pleasing or charming <a *sweet* smile>
 syn dulcet, engaging, winning, winsome
 rel agreeable, pleasant, pleasing; beautiful, fair, lovely; delectable, delicious, delightful, luscious; angelic, heavenly
 con disagreeable, unpleasant; displeasing, obnoxious, repulsive
 ant bitter
 2 having a pleasant smell <the *sweet* odor of flowers and incense>
 syn ambrosial, aromal, aromatic, balmy, fragrant, perfumed, perfumy, redolent, savory, scented, spicy; *compare* ODOROUS
 rel clean, fresh; sweetish
 con funky, fusty, musty, noisome, putrid, rancid, rotten, stale, stinking, strong, whiffy; fetid, foul, olid, rank, smelly
 ant malodorous
 3 *syn* see MELODIOUS 1

sweet *n syn* see SWEETHEART 1

sweeten *vb* 1 *syn* see PACIFY
 2 *syn* see SUGARCOAT 1

sweetheart *n* 1 one who is dearly beloved — often used as a term of endearment <was her childhood *sweetheart*> <*sweetheart*, you know I'll wait>
 syn beloved, darling, dear, flame, heartthrob, honey, honeybunch, love, loveling, sweet, sweetling, turtledove
 rel ‖cutie pie, deary, pigsney; pet, puggy
 2 *syn* see GIRL FRIEND 2
 rel doll baby, lovey-dovey, ‖tootsie
 3 *syn* see BOYFRIEND 2
 rel paramour; ‖dreamboat

sweetheart *vb syn* see ADDRESS 8

sweetie *n syn* see GIRL FRIEND 2
 rel sweetie pie

sweetling *n syn* see SWEETHEART 1

sweetness and light *n syn* see AMENITY 1

sweet–talk *vb syn* see COAX

swell *vb* 1 *syn* see EXPAND 3
 rel balloon, belly, bloat, blow up, bosom; pouch, pout; overblow
 con compress, condense, constrict, contract
 ant shrink
 2 *syn* see LORD
 rel puff
 idiom act the grand seigneur, swell it

swell *n syn* see EXPERT

swell *adj syn* see MARVELOUS 2

swelled head *n syn* see CONCEIT 2

swellheadedness *n syn* see CONCEIT 2

swelling *adj syn* see RHETORICAL

‖swelt *vb* 1 *syn* see DIE 1
 2 *syn* see FAINT

swelter *vb syn* see BURN 3

sweltering *adj syn* see HOT 1
 idiom ‖hot as the hinges of hell
 ant frigid

sweltry *adj syn* see HOT 1

swerve *vb* 1 to turn or be turned away abruptly from a straight line or course <*swerved* the car to avoid collision>
 syn dip, sheer, skew, slue, train off, veer
 2 to be deflected from a fixed or right course of action or conduct <never *swerved* from the concept of duty, honor, country>
 syn depart, deviate, digress, diverge
 rel shift; waver; err, stray, wander
 idiom deviate from the straight and narrow, get off the proper course (*or* path)

swift *adj syn* see FAST 3
 rel headlong, precipitate, sudden; double-quick; supersonic
 ant sluggish

swift *adv syn* see FAST 2
 ant sluggishly

swiften *vb syn* see SPEED 3

swiftly *adv syn* see FAST 2
 con slowly
 ant sluggishly

swiftness *n* 1 *syn* see SPEED 2
 ant sluggishness
 2 *syn* see HASTE 1
 ant slowness

swig *n syn* see DRINK 3

swig *vb syn* see DRINK 3

swill *vb* 1 *syn* see DRINK 3
 2 *syn* see CONSUME 5

swill *n* 1 *syn* see REFUSE
 2 *syn* see DRINK 3

swillbowl *n syn* see DRUNKARD

swiller *n syn* see DRUNKARD

swim *vb syn* see SPIN 2
 idiom have one's head swim

swimming *adj syn* see DIZZY 2
 rel fluctuating, swaying, wavering

swimmingly *adv syn* see WELL 5

swimmy *adj syn* see DIZZY 2

swindle *vb syn* see CHEAT
 rel rogue; victimize
 idiom sell one a bill of goods, take for a ride, take for a sucker

swindle *n syn* see IMPOSTURE

swindler *n* one who defrauds usually of money and especially by imposture or by gaining the victim's confidence <lost their savings to *swindlers* in a get-rich-quick scheme>
 syn bunco steerer, cheat, cheater, chiaus, come-on, confidence man, con man, defrauder, diddler, double-dealer, flimflammer, ‖grifter, gyp, gypper, ‖mace, mountebank, Peter Funk, rogue, sharper, sharpie, skin, slicker, ‖spieler, trickster

---

syn synonym(s) *rel* related word(s)
ant antonym(s) *con* contrasted word(s)
idiom idiomatic equivalent(s)
‖ use limited; if in doubt, see a dictionary

rel bilk, bilker, blackleg, charlatan, chiseler, crook, deceiver, dodger, fraud, gouger, harpy, highbinder, hoaxer, operator, rook, shark, sharp, sharpster, tricker; scoundrel

swing *vb* **1** *syn* see HANDLE 2
 2 to move rhythmically to and fro, up and down, or back and forth <the clock's pendulum *swung* slowly>
 syn oscillate, pendulate, sway
 rel undulate, wave; rock, roll; revolve, rotate, switch, wheel; jiggle, wag, waggle, wiggle, wigwag
 3 *syn* see TURN 6
 4 *syn* see LURCH 2

swing *n* **1** *syn* see RHYTHM
 2 *syn* see HANG

‖**swingeing** *adj syn* see EXCELLENT

swinish *adj syn* see BRUTISH

swipe *n* **1** *syn* see HIT 1
 2 *syn* see CRITICISM 2

swipe *vb syn* see STEAL 1

swirl *vb* to move swiftly in circles, eddies, or undulations <water *swirled* into the storm drains>
 syn eddy, gurge, purl, swoosh, whirl, whirlpool, whorl
 rel boil, roil; gush, surge

swish *vb syn* see HISS

swish *adj syn* see STYLISH

switch *vb* **1** *syn* see WAG
 2 *syn* see EXCHANGE 2
 3 *syn* see SHUNT 1

‖**swither** *vb syn* see RUSH 1

swivet *n syn* see SNIT

swizzle *vb syn* see DRINK 3

swollen *adj syn* see RHETORICAL

swoon *vb syn* see FAINT
 rel die away, drown

swoon *n syn* see FAINT

swoosh *vb syn* see SWIRL

sworn *adj syn* see INVETERATE 1

sybarite *n syn* see HEDONIST

sybaritic *adj* marked by or given to luxury or voluptuous living <the *sybaritic* grandeur of a sultan's harem> <a man of *sybaritic* and self-indulgent habits>
 syn hedonistic, onanistic, self-indulgent, sybaritical, sybaritish; *compare* SENSUOUS
 rel apolaustic, pleasure-loving; epicurean, luxurious; carnal, sensual, voluptuous

sybaritical *adj syn* see SYBARITIC

sybaritish *adj syn* see SYBARITIC

sycophancy *n syn* see DETRACTION

sycophant *n* a base or servilely attentive flatterer and self-seeker <*sycophants* who slavishly curried favor with the king>
 syn apple-polisher, bootlick, bootlicker, ‖brownnose, ‖brownnoser, ‖clawback, creature, ‖easy rider, footlicker, groveler, lickspit, lickspittle, minion, reptile, spaniel, toad, toadeater, toadier, toady, truckler, yes-man; *compare* PARASITE
 rel flunky, gopher, lackey, slave, stooge; flatterer, self-seeker; snob, tuft-hunter

sycophant *adj syn* see FAWNING

sycophantic *adj syn* see FAWNING

sycophantical *adj syn* see FAWNING

sycophantish *adj syn* see FAWNING

syllable *n syn* see PARTICLE

syllabus *n syn* see COMPENDIUM 1

sylloge *n syn* see COMPENDIUM 1

symbol *n* **1** something that stands for something else by reason of relationship, association, convention, or accidental resemblance <the lion is often used as a *symbol* of courage>
 syn attribute, emblem; *compare* INDICATION 3
 rel indication, token, type; badge, mark, note, sign, stamp; character, design, device, figure, motif, pattern; representation
 2 *syn* see CHARACTER 1

symbolism *n syn* see ALLEGORY 1

symbolization *n syn* see ALLEGORY 1

symbolize *vb syn* see REPRESENT 2

symmetrical *adj syn* see PROPORTIONAL

symmetry *n* beauty of form or arrangement arising from balanced proportions <the superb *symmetry* of the design>
 syn balance, harmony, proportion
 rel arrangement, order; agreement, conformity; equality, evenness, regularity; rhythm; finish
 con asymmetry, dissymmetry; disproportion, imbalance, irregularity, unbalance

sympathetic *adj* **1** *syn* see CONSONANT 1
 ant unsympathetic
 2 favorably inclined <found his hearers *sympathetic* to his proposal>
 syn friendly, receptive, ‖sib, well-disposed
 rel agreeable, congenial, favorable; amenable, open, open-minded, receptive, responsive
 con ill-disposed, unfriendly, unreceptive; cool, indifferent, lukewarm; neutral
 ant unsympathetic
 3 *syn* see TENDER
 rel benign, benignant, kind, kindly; appreciating, comprehending, understanding
 ant unsympathetic

sympathize (with) *vb syn* see COMPASSIONATE
 rel appreciate, comprehend, understand

sympathy *n* **1** *syn* see ATTRACTION 2
 ant antipathy
 2 a feeling for or a capacity for sharing in the interests of another <he was in *sympathy* with her desire to succeed>
 syn compassion, empathy, fellow feeling
 rel responsiveness, sensitivity; feelings, heart; tenderness, warmheartedness, warmth; benignancy, benignness, kindliness, kindness
 con disinterest, unconcern
 3 *syn* see PITY

symphonic *adj syn* see HARMONIOUS 1

symphonious *adj syn* see HARMONIOUS 1

symphonize *vb syn* see HARMONIZE 4

symphony *n syn* see ORCHESTRA
 rel concert band, symphony band; symphony orchestra

symptom *n syn* see INDICATION 3

synchronal *adj syn* see CONTEMPORARY 1

synchronic *adj syn* see CONTEMPORARY 1

synchronous *adj syn* see CONTEMPORARY 1

syncope *n syn* see FAINT
syndicate *n* a combination of interlocked companies or enterprises <a large newspaper *syndicate*>
  syn cartel, chain, combine, conglomerate, group, pool, trust
  rel association, organization; partnership, union
syndrome *n syn* see DISEASE 1
synergetic *adj syn* see COOPERATIVE
  ant counteractive
synergic *adj syn* see COOPERATIVE
  ant counteractive
synopsis *n syn* see ABRIDGMENT
synopsize *vb syn* see EPITOMIZE 1
  idiom hit the high spots, put it in a nutshell
synthesize *vb syn* see HARMONIZE 4
synthetic *adj* formed or developed by human art, skill, or effort and not by natural processes <*synthetic* plastics>
  syn artificial, factitious, man-made; *compare* ARTIFICIAL 2
  rel manufactured; constructed, fabricated,

made
  con natural
syrupy *adj syn* see SENTIMENTAL
system *n* **1** an organized integrated whole made up of diverse but interrelated and interdependent parts <the capitalist *system*>
  syn complex; *compare* WHOLE 2
  rel aggregation, array; mesh, network; arrangement, disposition, scheme, setup; order, pattern
  con disorganization; chaos
  2 *syn* see WHOLE 2
  3 *syn* see ORDER 8
  rel procedure, proceeding, process
  4 *syn* see METHOD 1
systematic *adj syn* see ORDERLY 1
  rel arranged, ordered, organized, systematized; analytical, logical
  con disorganized; chaotic
  ant unsystematic
systematize *vb syn* see ORDER 1
  rel contrive, frame
  con confuse, disorder, jumble

---

syn synonym(s)   *rel* related word(s)
ant antonym(s)   *con* contrasted word(s)
idiom idiomatic equivalent(s)
‖ use limited; if in doubt, see a dictionary

T

tab *n* **1** *syn* see EYE 3
  2 *syn* see BILL 1
  3 *syn* see CHECK 2
  4 *syn* see PRICE 1

tabby *n* **1** *syn* see GOSSIP 1
  ‖**2** *syn* see SPINSTER

tabernacle *n* *syn* see HOUSE OF WORSHIP

table *n* **1** a piece of furniture on which food is customarily served <a feast on the *table*>
  syn board, dining table, dinner table, mahogany, ‖table-board
  rel bar, buffet, counter, sideboard
  2 a condensed ordered enumeration of items usually arranged in columns <a *table* of weights and measures>
  syn chart, tabulation
  rel list; diagram
  3 *syn* see PLATEAU

‖**table–board** *n* *syn* see TABLE 1

tableland *n* *syn* see PLATEAU

tabloid *adj* *syn* see SENSATIONAL 2

taboo *n* a restraint imposed by social usage or as a protective measure <a society rife with antiquated moral *taboos*>
  syn ban, forbiddance, interdiction, prohibition, proscription
  rel inhibition, limitation, reservation, restraint, restriction; regulation, sanction; don't
  con acceptance, toleration; approval, authorization, permission, permit, permittance

taboo *vb* *syn* see FORBID

tabulation *n* *syn* see TABLE 2

tacit *adj* **1** expressed or conveyed without words, speech, or forthright reference <they made a *tacit* agreement to work together>
  syn implicit, implied, inarticulate, inferred, undeclared, understood, unexpressed, unsaid, unspoken, unuttered, wordless
  rel alluded (to), hinted (at), intimated, suggested; assumed
  con expressed, spoken, verbal; categorical, explicit, express, unequivocal
  2 *syn* see UNSPOKEN 1

taciturn *adj* *syn* see SILENT 3
  rel laconic, unexpressive; brooding, dour
  con chatty, communicative, loquacious, talkative; convivial, uninhibited, unreserved, unrestrained
  ant garrulous

tack *n* *syn* see TURN 2
  rel alteration; digression, tangent; swerve, zigzag

tackle *n* *syn* see EQUIPMENT

tackle *vb* *syn* see ATTACK 2
  rel take on, undertake; plunge into, set about
  idiom get on the job, put one's shoulder to the wheel, start the ball rolling
  con avoid, delay, hesitate, put off

tackling *n* *syn* see EQUIPMENT

tacky *adj* **1** *syn* see SHABBY 1
  rel dowdy, outmoded, unstylish; messy, sloppy, slovenly, unkempt, untidy; blowsy, frowsy, frumpish
  idiom gone to seed
  2 marked by a lack of style or good taste <an old *tacky* scarf spoiled her outfit>
  syn dowdy, frumpish, frumpy, outmoded, out-of-date, stodgy, unstylish
  rel unbecoming; crude, inelegant, tasteless; incorrect, unsuitable; cheap, gaudy
  con ‖mod, modern, modish, smart, stylish, tasteful; elegant

tact *n* skill and grace in dealing with others <handled the embarrassing situation with great *tact*>
  syn address, delicatesse, diplomacy, poise, savoir faire, tactfulness; *compare* ADDRESS 1
  rel control, head, presence, repose; amenity, courtesy, gallantry; policy, politicness, smoothness, suavity, urbanity; adroitness, deftness, skill; acumen, finesse, perception, sensitivity
  con abruptness, bluntness, coarseness, discourtesy, rudeness
  ant tactlessness

tactful *adj* marked by or exhibiting tact <his *tactful* skill in handling negotiations>
  syn delicate, diplomatic, politic, tactical; *compare* SUAVE
  rel polished, suave, urbane; adroit, deft, skilled, skillful; perceptive, sensitive
  con clumsy, unpolished, unskilled; discourteous, impolite, rude; undiplomatic
  ant blunt, tactless, untactful

tactfulness *n* *syn* see TACT
  rel civility, civilness, politeness; polish
  ant tactlessness

tactic *adj* *syn* see TACTILE 2

tactical *adj* **1** made or carried out with only a limited or immediate end in view <had time only for *tactical* decisions and not strategic planning>
  syn short-range
  con long-range
  ant strategic
  2 *syn* see EXPEDIENT
  3 *syn* see TACTFUL

tactile *adj* **1** *syn* see TANGIBLE 1
  2 of or relating to the sense of touch <*tactile* responses>
  syn tactic, tactual

tactility *n* *syn* see TOUCH 3

taction *n* *syn* see TOUCH 2

tactless *adj* marked by a lack of tact <his *tactless* remark hurt her>
  syn brash, impolitic, maladroit, undiplomatic, unpolitic, untactful
  rel impolite, inconsiderate, indelicate, rude; bungling, inept

con diplomatic, polite, tactical
ant tactful
tactual *adj syn* see TACTILE 2
tad *n syn* see BOY 1
tag *n* **1** *syn* see COMMONPLACE
2 *syn* see TICKET 1
tag *vb syn* see TAIL
tag and rag *n syn* see RABBLE 2
tag end *n syn* see TAIL END 2
tagrag *adj syn* see SHABBY 1
tagrag and bobtail *n syn* see RABBLE 2
tail *n syn* see BUTTOCKS
tail *vb* to follow (someone) for purposes of surveillance <detectives *tailing* the suspects>
syn bedog, dog, shadow, tag, trail; *compare* EYE 2, FOLLOW 2
rel hound, pursue
tail end *n* **1** *syn* see BUTTOCKS
2 the hindmost end of something <watched the *tail end* of the parade march off>
syn tag end
tailor *vb syn* see ADAPT
rel style; dovetail; shape up
tailor–made *adj syn* see CUSTOM-MADE
tailor–make *vb syn* see ADAPT
taint *vb* **1** to touch or affect with something bad or undesirable <his good reputation was *tainted* by the scandal>
syn besmear, besmirch, blur, cloud, defile, dirty, discolor, smear, smudge, smut, smutch, soil, stain, sully, tar, tarnish; *compare* CONTAMINATE 1
rel discredit; brand, stigmatize; blacken; damage, harm, hurt
idiom cast a slur upon; give a bad name to, give a black mark to
con brighten, cleanse, clear
2 *syn* see DECAY
rel befoul, contaminate, foul
3 *syn* see CONTAMINATE 1
taintless *adj syn* see CLEAN 1
ant tainted
take *vb* **1** *syn* see CATCH 1
2 *syn* see SEIZE 2
idiom make off with
con drop, dump, give up, relinquish, surrender
3 *syn* see APPROPRIATE 1
con relinquish, yield
4 to lay hold of (as with the hands or an instrument) <*took* the ax by the handle>
syn clasp, grasp, grip
rel hold; handle
idiom take hold of
con drop, release
5 *syn* see SEIZE 3
rel contract, get; harrow, reach, torment
6 *syn* see CATCH 7
7 *syn* see ATTRACT 1
8 *syn* see SWALLOW 1
9 *syn* see EAT 1
10 to bring into and accept in a particular capacity or relationship <*took* his son as a member of the firm>
syn admit, receive, take in
rel bring; accept; have, include

11 *syn* see BUY 1
12 *syn* see CHOOSE 1
13 *syn* see DEMAND 2
14 to obtain from another source by means of derivation <*takes* his name from his father's>
syn derive, draw
rel get, obtain; borrow
15 *syn* see BEAR 10
rel withstand; undergo; ‖hack
idiom take it lying down, take it on the chin
16 *syn* see CONTRACT 1
idiom take sick with
17 *syn* see APPREHEND 1
18 *syn* see UNDERSTAND 3
19 *syn* see DEDUCT 1
20 *syn* see TREAT 2
21 *syn* see CHEAT
rel bamboozle, hoodwink
idiom take for a ride
22 *syn* see ACT 5
take (from) *vb syn* see DECRY 2
take (to) *vb syn* see HABITUATE 2
rel enjoy, fancy, favor, like
idiom get used to
take away *vb* **1** *syn* see REMOVE 2
rel separate
2 *syn* see DEDUCT 1
3 *syn* see DECRY 2
take back *vb* **1** *syn* see RETURN 4
2 *syn* see REPOSSESS 3
3 *syn* see ABJURE
take down *vb syn* see DISMOUNT
take in *vb* **1** *syn* see TAKE 10
2 *syn* see INCLUDE
3 *syn* see APPREHEND 1
rel perceive; ‖savvy; absorb, assimilate, digest
4 *syn* see DECEIVE
rel flimflam, take; trick
take off *vb* **1** *syn* see REMOVE 2
2 *syn* see REMOVE 3
3 *syn* see DEDUCT 1
4 *syn* see KILL 1
5 *syn* see MIMIC
idiom do a takeoff on
6 *syn* see GET OUT 1
7 *syn* see HEAD 3
idiom hit the road (*or* trail)
8 *syn* see GO 2
takeoff *n syn* see CARICATURE 2
take on *vb* **1** *syn* see DON 2
2 *syn* see ADD 1
3 to proceed to deal with <*took on* a new job with more responsibilities>
syn take up, undertake
rel begin, commence, enter (upon); attempt, endeavor, try; launch, venture
idiom set about, take upon oneself
con abandon, drop, forsake
ant give up

---

syn synonym(s)   **rel** related word(s)
ant antonym(s)   **con** contrasted word(s)
idiom idiomatic equivalent(s)
‖ use limited; if in doubt, see a dictionary

4 *syn* see ENGAGE 5
5 *syn* see EMPLOY 2
6 *syn* see ADOPT
ant give up
take out *vb* **1** *syn* see REMOVE 2
2 *syn* see REMOVE 4
3 *syn* see DEDUCT 1
4 *syn* see DATE
take out (on) *vb* to find release for (as emotions)
<*took out* her anger on the dog>
syn loose, release, unleash, vent
idiom give vent to, let loose (*or* fly)
con control, govern, restrain; bottle (up), check,
keep down, quell, smother; repress, suppress
take over *vb syn* see RELIEVE 3
take up *vb* **1** *syn* see LIFT 1
2 *syn* see BEGIN 1
3 *syn* see TAKE ON 3
rel assume; tackle
idiom address oneself to
4 *syn* see ADOPT
rel support; affiliate
5 *syn* see RESUME 2
taking *adj syn* see INFECTIOUS 3
tale *n* **1** *syn* see STORY 2
rel myth, saga
2 *syn* see DETRACTION
3 *syn* see LIE
rel fiction; yarn
4 *syn* see WHOLE 1
tale *vb syn* see COUNT 1
talebearer *n* **1** *syn* see INFORMER
2 *syn* see GOSSIP 1
talent *n syn* see GIFT 2
rel art, craft, skill; endowment; expertise, forte
talisman *n syn* see CHARM 2
idiom good-luck piece, lucky piece (*or* charm)
talk *vb* **1** *syn* see SPEAK 3
2 *syn* see SPEAK 1
3 *syn* see CONVERSE
4 *syn* see CHAT 1
rel palaver, spout off
idiom talk one's arm (*or* ear *or* leg) off, flap (*or*
wag) the (*or* one's) tongue
5 *syn* see GOSSIP
6 to reveal secret or confidential information
usually concerning illegal acts <at last the suspect *talked* to the police>
syn sing, squeak, squeal; *compare* INFORM 3
rel inform (on); divulge, reveal; confess
idiom spill one's guts, spill the beans, tell all
7 to give a talk <he *talks* to community groups
on ecology>
syn address, lecture, prelect, speak
rel declaim, harangue, hold forth, perorate,
speechify, spout
talk (into) *vb syn* see INDUCE 1
talk *n* **1** *syn* see SPEECH 1
2 *syn* see CONVERSATION 2
3 *syn* see CHAT 2
4 a formal or prearranged discussion, exchange,
or negotiation usually of a political nature
<summit *talks* on nuclear arms>
syn conference, meeting, parley, powwow

rel dialogue, discussion, exchange; negotiation;
deliberation
5 *syn* see REPORT 1
6 *syn* see SPEECH 2
rel spiel; conference, discussion
talkative *adj* given to talk or talking <a *talkative*,
sociable man>
syn babblative, chatty, gabby, garrulous, loose=
lipped, loose-tongued, loquacious, mouthy, multiloquent, multiloquious, talky, tonguey; *compare* GLIB
rel articulate, eloquent, fluent; vocal, voluble;
buzzy, gossipy
con closemouthed, laconic, reserved, reticent,
uncommunicative; speechless
ant silent
talkee–talkee *n syn* see CHATTER
talky *adj syn* see TALKATIVE
tall *adj syn* see HIGH 1
rel high-reaching, sky-high, skyscraping
idiom higher than a cat's back
con abbreviated, truncated; low
ant short
tally *n syn* see SCORE 5
tally *vb* **1** *syn* see INVENTORY
2 *syn* see COUNT 1
3 *syn* see AGREE 4
rel equal, match; balance, complement
con conflict (with), differ (from), disagree (with)
tame *adj* docilely tractable <a *tame* lion>
syn domestic, domesticated, domitae naturae,
subdued, submissive
rel broken (in), ‖busted, housebroken, trained;
amenable, biddable, docile, obedient, tractable;
pliable, pliant; meek, mild
idiom gentle as a lamb
con fierce, savage, tameless; undomesticated,
untrained; unbridled, unbroken
ant untamed, wild
tame *vb syn* see DOMESTICATE
tamp *vb syn* see CRAM 1
rel fill up (*or* in), plug up; concentrate
tamper (with) *vb* **1** *syn* see BRIBE
2 *syn* see MEDDLE
rel interpose, intervene; doctor, manipulate
tang *n syn* see TASTE 3
rel bite, nip, piquancy, twang; aroma, pungency; spiciness, tanginess
tangible *adj* **1** capable of being perceived especially by the sense of touch <a stuffed animal
that provides *tangible* as well as visual stimulation for infants>
syn palpable, tactile, touchable; *compare* PERCEP-
TIBLE
rel corporeal, physical; embodied, material,
real, substantial
con ethereal, spiritual, unreal
ant intangible
2 *syn* see MATERIAL 1
3 *syn* see PERCEPTIBLE
rel distinct, evident, manifest, obvious, patent,
plain
con clouded, cloudy, imperceptible, indistinct,
unclear

ant intangible
tangle *vb* **1** *syn* see INVOLVE 1
  idiom make a party to
  ant untangle
  2 *syn* see CATCH 3
  ant untangle
  3 *syn* see ENTANGLE 1
  rel foul up, mix up
  4 *syn* see COMPLICATE
  ant untangle
tangle *n* *syn* see MAZE 1
tanked *adj* *syn* see INTOXICATED 1
tank town *n* *syn* see BURG
tank up *vb* *syn* see DRINK 3
tantalize *vb* *syn* see WORRY 1
  rel badger, bait; frustrate
tantamount *adj* *syn* see SAME 2
  rel alike, like, uniform; selfsame, very
  idiom as much as to say
tap *n* **1** *syn* see FAUCET
  2 *syn* see BAR 5
tap *vb* *syn* see DRAIN 1
tap *vb* **1** to strike or hit audibly and usually lightly
  <*tapped* her pencil on the desk>
  syn bob, knock, rap, tunk
  rel bang, beat, hammer, hit, pound, smite,
  strike, thud, thump
  2 *syn* see DESIGNATE 2
tapa *n* *syn* see SNACK
taper *vb* *syn* see DECREASE
taper off *vb* *syn* see DECREASE
taproom *n* *syn* see BAR 5
tapster *n* *syn* see BARTENDER
tar *n* *syn* see MARINER
tar *vb* *syn* see TAINT 1
taradiddle *n* *syn* see LIE
tardy *adj* not arriving, occurring, or done at the
  set, due, or expected time <be *tardy* for school>
  syn behindhand, belated, late, lated, overdue,
  unpunctual
  rel delayed, detained; dilatory, laggard, slow;
  delinquent
  con beforehand, early; convenient, opportune,
  seasonable, timely; precise, punctilious
  ant prompt, punctual
target *n* **1** an object of ridicule, attack, or abuse
  <made him the chief *target* of political satire>
  syn butt, mark, sitting duck
  rel victim; fall guy, scapegoat, whipping boy
  2 *syn* see AMBITION 2
  3 *syn* see USE 4
tariff *n* **1** *syn* see TAX 1
  2 *syn* see PRICE 1
‖**tarnation** *adj* *syn* see UTTER
tarnish *vb* *syn* see DULL 1
  2 *syn* see SOIL 2
  rel contaminate, defile, pollute, stain, taint
  con clean, cleanse; shine (up)
  ant polish
  3 *syn* see INJURE 1
  4 *syn* see TAINT 1
  rel defame, disgrace, embarrass; slander
tarpaulin *n* *syn* see MARINER
tarriance *n* *syn* see SOJOURN

tarry *vb* **1** *syn* see DELAY 2
  rel falter, flag
  2 *syn* see STAY 2
  rel dawdle; sojourn
  3 *syn* see VISIT 3
tart *adj* *syn* see SOUR 1
  rel piquant, pungent
  ant flat
tart *n* *syn* see DOXY 1
Tartarean *adj* *syn* see INFERNAL 1
Tartuffe *n* *syn* see HYPOCRITE
Tartuffery *n* *syn* see HYPOCRISY
Tartuffism *n* *syn* see HYPOCRISY
task *n* **1** a piece of work assigned or to be done
  <laboratory *tasks* assigned to chemistry stu-
  dents>
  syn assignment, chare, chore, devoir, duty, job,
  stint
  rel enterprise, project, undertaking; errand, labor, toil, work; charge, function, mission, office,
  province; business, calling, employment, occupation, vocation
  2 a necessary undertaking that is usually difficult, dull, disagreeable, or problematic <deci-
  phering his handwriting is a real *task*>
  syn chore, effort, job, taskwork
  rel burden, onus, strain, tax; bother, headache,
  nuisance, pain, trouble
  idiom a hard (*or* long) row to hoe
  con child's play, cinch, duck soup, picnic, ‖pipe,
  sinecure, snap
  3 *syn* see LOAD 3
task *vb* *syn* see BURDEN
taskmaster *n* *syn* see SLAVE DRIVER
taskwork *n* *syn* see TASK 2
taste *vb* *syn* see FEEL 2
  idiom be exposed to, run up against
taste *n* **1** *syn* see HINT 2
  rel bit, sample, sampling
  2 *syn* see APPETITE 1
  3 the property of a substance which makes it perceptible to the gustatory sense <children often
  dislike the *taste* of olives>
  syn flavor, relish, sapidity, sapor, savor, smack,
  tang
  4 a liking for or enjoyment of something because
  of the pleasure it gives <had a *taste* for fast cars>
  syn gusto, heart, palate, relish, zest
  rel appreciation, comprehension, understanding; partiality, predilection, prepossession; disposition, inclination, predisposition
  con dislike, disrelish; allergy, aversion, repugnance, repulsion
  ant antipathy; distaste
  5 *syn* see APPETITE 3
  ant distaste
  6 the power or practice of discerning and enjoying whatever constitutes excellence (as in the fine

---

syn synonym(s)   *rel* related word(s)
ant antonym(s)   *con* contrasted word(s)
idiom idiomatic equivalent(s)
‖ use limited; if in doubt, see a dictionary

arts) <a room whose decoration reflected her exquisite *taste*>
  syn tastefulness
  rel correctness; finesse, polish, refinement; elegance, grace
  con gracelessness, inelegance, unrefinement; incorrectness, vulgarity
  ant tastelessness
tasteful *adj* **1** *syn* see PALATABLE
  rel rich
  ant savorless, tasteless
  2 *syn* see QUIET 4
  ant tasteless
tastefulness *n* *syn* see TASTE 6
  ant tastelessness
tasteless *adj* **1** *syn* see UNPALATABLE 1
  rel bland, dull, stale, vapid; unflavored; uninteresting
  con flavorful, pleasing
  ant tasteful, tasty
  2 *syn* see BARBARIC 1
  rel inelegant, unpolished, unrefined
  idiom in bad taste
  ant tasteful, tasty
tasty *adj* **1** *syn* see PALATABLE
  idiom fit for a king
  con unsavory; bland, flavorless, unpalatable
  ant savorless, tasteless
  2 *syn* see QUIET 4
  ant tasteless
‖**tats** *n pl* *syn* see DICE
‖**tatter** *vb* *syn* see HURRY 2
tatterdemalion *n* *syn* see RAGAMUFFIN
tattered *adj* **1** *syn* see RAGGED
  2 *syn* see SHABBY 1
tatters *n pl* *syn* see RAGS 1
tattle *vb* *syn* see GOSSIP
  idiom tell tales out of school
tattle *n* *syn* see REPORT 1
tattler *n* *syn* see INFORMER
tattletale *n* *syn* see INFORMER
tatty *adj* *syn* see CHEAP 2
taunt *vb* *syn* see RIDICULE
  rel banter, chaff; provoke; upbraid; disdain, scorn; affront, insult, offend, outrage
taut *adj* *syn* see TIGHT 3
  rel firm, trim; stretched
  con flabby; relaxed
  ant slack
tautology *n* *syn* see VERBIAGE 1
  rel reiteration, repetition, repetitiousness; padding
tavern *n* **1** *syn* see BAR 5
  2 *syn* see HOTEL
tavern car *n* *syn* see PARLOR CAR
taverner *n* *syn* see SALOONKEEPER
tawdry *adj* *syn* see GAUDY
  rel common, sleazy; flaring, screaming
tax *vb* **1** *syn* see BURDEN
  rel overtax
  idiom press hard upon, tax the strength of, weigh heavy on (*or* upon)
  2 *syn* see ACCUSE
tax *n* **1** a charge usually of money imposed by authority upon persons or property for public pur-

poses <federal, state, and local *taxes* bear heavily on the thrifty>
  syn assessment, ‖cess, duty, impost, levy, tariff
  rel tithe, tribute; boodle, boondoggle, giveaway, pork barrel
  2 *syn* see LOAD 3
  rel difficulty, strain; demand, imposition
taxi *n* *syn* see TAXICAB
taxicab *n* an automobile that carries passengers for a fare <took a *taxicab* from the airport to his hotel>
  syn cab, hack, taxi
  rel ‖crawler, nighthawk
taxing *adj* *syn* see ONEROUS
  rel wearing; tedious, troublesome
TB *n* *syn* see TUBERCULOSIS
‖**tea** *n* *syn* see MARIJUANA
teach *vb* to cause to acquire knowledge or skill <*teach* a child to read>
  syn discipline, educate, instruct, school, train
  rel communicate, impart; implant, inculcate, instill; edify, enlighten, indoctrinate; fit, ground, prepare, rear; drill, exercise, practice; coach, tutor; lesson
  idiom give instruction
teaching *n* *syn* see EDUCATION 1
teachy *adj* *syn* see DIDACTIC
tear *vb* **1** to separate (one part of a substance or object from another) forcibly <*tore* a chunk from the loaf on the table>
  syn cleave, rend, rip, rive, split
  rel cut, gash, incise, slash, slit; devil, pull (apart), rift, sever, sunder; ribbon, shred; break, crack, rupture; damage, impair, injure
  2 *syn* see EXTRACT 1
  3 *syn* see RUSH 1
  4 *syn* see COURSE
tear *n* *syn* see BINGE 1
tear down *vb* **1** *syn* see DESTROY 1
  ant build up
  2 *syn* see MALIGN
  ant build up
teardrops *n pl* *syn* see TEARS
tearful *adj* flowing with or accompanied by tears <*tearful* entreaties>
  syn lachrymose, teary, weeping, weepy
  rel lamenting, mournful; sniveling; bawling, blubbering, crying, sobbing
  con dry-eyed
  ant tearless
tearing *adj* *syn* see EXCRUCIATING
tear–jerking *adj* *syn* see SENTIMENTAL
tears *n pl* a profuse secretion of saline fluid that overflows the eyelids and dampens the face <a blow that brought *tears* to his eyes>
  syn teardrops, water
teary *adj* *syn* see TEARFUL
  ant tearless
tease *vb* *syn* see WORRY 1
  rel disturb, importune
  idiom give a bad time
teaser *n* *syn* see STRIPTEASER
tease up *vb* *syn* see TOUCH UP
‖**tec** *n* *syn* see DETECTIVE

teched *adj syn* see INSANE 1

technique *n syn* see METHOD 1

tedious *adj* **1** *syn* see IRKSOME

2 *syn* see ARID 2

rel dragging, mortal, slow, tiresome

tedium *n* a state of dissatisfaction and weariness <incessant routine without variety breeds *tedium*>

syn boredom, doldrums, ‖dullsville, ennui, yawn

rel irksomeness, tediousness, tiresomeness, wearisomeness; dullness, monotony

con enlivenment, interest, invigoration, refreshment

teem *vb* to be abundantly stocked or provided <rivers *teeming* with fish>

syn abound, crawl, flow, pullulate, ‖sny, swarm

rel bristle, bustle; cram, crowd, jam, pack; overbrim, overflow, overrun

con lack, want

teem *vb syn* see POUR 3

teeming *adj syn* see ALIVE 5

rel multitudinous, populous, pregnant; bristling

con rare, sparse, uncommon; empty, lacking, void, wanting

teensy *adj syn* see TINY

teensy–weensy *adj syn* see TINY

teenty *adj syn* see TINY

teeny *adj syn* see TINY

teeny–weeny *adj syn* see TINY

tee off *vb syn* see BEGIN 1

teeter *vb* to progress (as by walking) unsteadily <*teetered* along on 4-inch heels>

syn falter, lurch, stagger, ‖stammer, stumble, topple, totter, wobble; *compare* LURCH 2, SEESAW

rel sway, weave

teethy *adj syn* see TOOTHY 1

teetotal *adj syn* see DRY 3

tehee *vb syn* see LAUGH

telephone *vb* to communicate with (a person) by telephone <*telephoned* him yesterday>

syn ‖buzz, call, phone, ‖ring (up)

idiom ‖get (one) on the horn, give (one) a buzz (or ring)

telestic *adj syn* see MYSTICAL 1

television *n* a medium of communication involving the transmission and reproduction of images by radio waves <it's fashionable to put down *television*>

syn boob tube, box, ‖idiot box, ‖telly, tube, TV, video

tell *vb* **1** *syn* see COUNT 1

2 *syn* see SAY 1

rel communicate, convey, impart

3 *syn* see REVEAL 1

rel recite, recount, rehearse, relate; acquaint, apprise, inform

4 *syn* see INFORM 2

5 *syn* see COMMAND

6 *syn* see WEIGH 3

telling *adj syn* see VALID

rel power-packed; influential, weighty; significant, striking

tell off *vb syn* see SCOLD 1

rel call down; denounce

idiom give (one) a piece of one's mind, tell (one) a thing or two, tell (one) where to get off

telltale *n* **1** *syn* see GOSSIP 1

2 *syn* see HINT 1

tellurian *adj syn* see EARTHLY 1

telluric *adj syn* see EARTHLY 1

‖telly *n syn* see TELEVISION

temblor (or **tremblor**) *n syn* see EARTHQUAKE

temerarious *adj syn* see ADVENTUROUS

rel heedless, imprudent, incautious, injudicious

temerity *n* conspicuous or flagrant boldness (as in speech, behavior, or action) <had the *temerity* to order an attack when hopelessly outnumbered>

syn assurance, audacity, brashness, hardihood, hardiness, nerve

rel daring, foolhardiness, heedlessness, rashness, recklessness, venturesomeness; impetuosity, precipitateness; impertinence, intrusiveness

con deliberation, judgment, judiciousness, prudence; heed, heedfulness

ant caution

temper *vb syn* see MODERATE 1

rel dilute, season; ease, pacify, soften; adjust, modify; curb, tone (down)

idiom take the edge off

temper *n* **1** a general or prevailing quality or characteristic (as of moral or social attitudes and behavior) <the wild fashions reflected the *temper* of the times>

syn mood, spirit, timbre, tone

rel atmosphere, aura, climate; orientation, outlook; disposition, drift, leaning, tendency, trend; character, nature, peculiarity

2 *syn* see DISPOSITION 3

rel condition, posture, state; attribute, property, quality; style, type, way

idiom turn of mind

3 *syn* see MOOD 1

idiom frame (or state) of mind

4 an outbreak or display of anger <a childish fit of *temper*>

syn passion

rel anger, fury, ire, rage; conniption, fit, outburst, tantrum

temperament *n syn* see DISPOSITION 3

rel mentality, mind; kind, type, way

idiom inner nature

temperamental *adj* **1** *syn* see MOODY

2 *syn* see INCONSTANT 1

ant steady

temperance *n* **1** an avoidance of extremes (as in action, thought, or feeling) <a man who knew no *temperance* in his opinions>

syn measure, moderateness, moderation

rel reasonableness; constraint, restraint

idiom happy medium

---

syn synonym(s)   *rel* related word(s)

ant antonym(s)   *con* contrasted word(s)

idiom idiomatic equivalent(s)

‖ use limited; if in doubt, see a dictionary

con extremeness, radicalness; excess, excessiveness; immoderateness, immoderation, unconstraint, unreasonableness, unrestraint
ant intemperance, intemperateness
2 strict habitual and usually complete self-denial in the gratification of appetites or passions <an ascetic who practiced complete *temperance*>
syn abstinence, continence, sobriety
rel abnegation, eschewal, forbearance, forgoing, refrainment, sacrifice, self-denial, self-deprivation; control, restraint, self-control, self-discipline; asceticism, austerity, mortification
con intemperance, intemperancy, intemperateness, prodigality
ant excess
temperate *adj* **1** *syn* see MODERATE 2
rel constant, equable, even, steady; checked, curbed, regulated, restrained
ant intemperate
2 *syn* see ABSTEMIOUS
rel indulgent; self-indulgent
con intemperate; dissipated, prodigal, profligate
ant excessive
3 *syn* see CONSERVATIVE 2
4 *syn* see SOBER 3
temperish *adj* *syn* see IRASCIBLE
tempersome *adj* *syn* see ILL-TEMPERED
tempestuous *adj* *syn* see WILD 6
rel tumultuous, unbridled, unrestrained, violent
ant calm, quiet
temple *n* *syn* see HOUSE OF WORSHIP
tempo *n* rate of performance or delivery <increased sales and production *tempo*>
syn pace, time; *compare* SPEED 2
rel speed; momentum
temporal *adj* **1** *syn* see MATERIALISTIC
ant nontemporal
2 *syn* see PROFANE 1
rel material, physical; nonsacred, nonspiritual, unhallowed, unsanctified, unspiritual
con celestial, heavenly
ant spiritual
temporary *adj* lasting, continuing, or serving for a limited time <was *temporary* president of the company for nine months>
syn acting, ad interim, interim, pro tem, pro tempore, supply; *compare* TRANSIENT
rel alternate, substitute; interimistic, provisional, provisory; jackleg, make-do, makeshift, stopgap
ant permanent
tempt *vb* *syn* see LURE
rel provoke, rouse; court, invite, solicit, vamp, woo
idiom whet the appetite
con discourage; dissuade; repel, repulse, revolt
temptation *n* *syn* see LURE 2
tempting *adj* *syn* see ENTICING
rel appetizing, mouth-watering; provoking, rousing, tantalizing
con repellent, repulsive
ant untempting
temptress *n* *syn* see SIREN
ten *n* *syn* see BREAK 4

tenable *adj* **1** capable of being defended against attack <the platoon's position was no longer *tenable*>
syn defendable, defensible
rel impregnable, secure
con insecure, vulnerable; defenseless, helpless, unprotected; dangerous, precarious, risky
ant untenable
2 *syn* see JUSTIFIABLE
rel believable, credible, maintainable, plausible
con indefensible, inexcusable, unbelievable, unjustifiable
ant untenable
tenacious *adj* **1** *syn* see STRONG 2
rel bulldogged, bulldoggish, bulldoggy, dogged, obstinate, pertinacious, stubborn; resolute, steadfast, true; persevering, persisting
2 *syn* see VISCOUS
rel cohesive; tacky; sticky
3 *syn* see FAST 4
con lax, slack
tenant *vb* *syn* see INHABIT
tenantable *adj* *syn* see LIVABLE 1
idiom fit to live in
con uninhabitable
tend *vb* **1** *syn* see TILL
2 to supervise or take charge of <employed a girl to *tend* the children each day>
syn attend, care (for), mind, watch
rel cherish, cultivate, foster, minister, nurse, nurture, serve; defend, guard, protect, safeguard, shield; supervise
idiom look after, see after, see to, take care of, take under one's wing
con disregard, ignore, neglect
tend *vb* **1** to have or exhibit an inclination or tendency <he *tends* to praise people too highly>
syn incline, lean, look; *compare* INCLINE 3
idiom be disposed
2 *syn* see CONTRIBUTE 2
tendency *n* **1** a movement or course having a particular direction and character <a growing *tendency* to underestimate the potential strength of that nation>
syn current, drift, run, tenor, trend
rel curve, inclination, leaning, propensity; turn; shift; custom, habit, usage, way
2 *syn* see LEANING 2
tendentious *adj* *syn* see BIASED 2
tender *adj* showing or expressing affectionate interest in another <his mother was very *tender* with her wayward son>
syn compassionate, kindhearted, responsive, softhearted, sympathetic, warm, warmhearted
rel gentle, lenient, mild, soft, yielding; considerate, solicitous, thoughtful; affectionate, fond, loving; benevolent, charitable, humane, mild; commiserative; forgiving, merciful, tolerant
con callous, hard, harsh; inhumane, uncharitable, unfeeling
ant rough, severe
tender *vb* *syn* see OFFER 1
rel propose, purpose, submit, suggest
tenderfoot *n* *syn* see NOVICE

tenderloin *n syn* see RED-LIGHT DISTRICT

tenebrific *adj syn* see GLOOMY 3

tenebrous *adj* 1 *syn* see DARK 1
2 *syn* see OBSCURE 3

tenement *n syn* see APARTMENT 1

tenet *n syn* see DOCTRINE
rel belief, conviction, persuasion, view

tenor *n* 1 the course of thought that is retained through something spoken or written <the *tenor* of the book is first expressed in the introduction>
syn drift, purport, substance; *compare* BODY 3, MEANING 1, SUBSTANCE 2
rel intent; inclination, trend; mood, tone; core, gist, meat, stuff
2 *syn* see TENDENCY 1

tense *adj* 1 *syn* see TIGHT 3
rel strained, stretched
ant relaxed
2 feeling or showing nervous tension <the soldiers were *tense* as they waited for the order to advance>
syn edgy, nervy, restive, uneasy, uptight
rel queasy; jittery, rusty, unquiet; anxious, concerned, overanxious
con easy; calm, cool, ‖loose, placid, unconcerned; firm, nerveless, unshaken
ant relaxed

tension *n* 1 *syn* see STRESS 1
rel tautness, tenseness, tightness
idiom stress and strain
ant relaxation
2 emotional strain <was suffering from nervous *tension*>
syn unease, uptightness
rel strain, stress; anxiety, nerves, nervousness, uneasiness; agitation, discomfort, disquiet, misease

ten–strike *n syn* see SMASH 6

tent *vb syn* see CAMP

tentative *adj* 1 *syn* see CONDITIONAL 1
rel acting, ad interim, makeshift, temporary; probationary; experimental, test, trial
con conclusive, decisive, definitive
ant final
2 *syn* see VACILLATING 2
rel disinclined, reluctant

tenue *n syn* see BEHAVIOR

tenuous *adj* 1 *syn* see THIN 2
2 *syn* see THIN 1
rel aerial, airy, ethereal, fine
con abundant
ant dense
3 having little substance or strength and usually not firmly based <only a *tenuous* link in the chain of evidence>
syn feeble, insubstantial, unsubstantial; *compare* IMPLAUSIBLE
rel flimsy, weak; insignificant
con significant, sound, strong
ant substantial

tenure *n syn* see HOLD

tepid *adj* 1 moderately warm <a *tepid* bath>
syn lukewarm, milk-warm, warmish

rel mild, temperate, warm
con cold, cool, freezing, frozen; heated, hot, steaming
2 lacking in animation, force, passion, conviction, or commitment <gave only a *tepid* endorsement to the candidate>
syn halfhearted, lukewarm, unenthusiastic; *compare* ARID 2
rel indifferent; colorless, dull, lifeless, unlively; feeble, marrowless, pithless, sapless, spiritless; dim, faint, forceless, weak
con animated, forceful; fiery, impassioned, passionate, spirited

tergiversate *vb* 1 *syn* see DEFECT
idiom fall away from
2 *syn* see EQUIVOCATE 2
idiom beg the question

tergiversation *n* 1 *syn* see DEFECTION
rel about-face, reversal, reverse; denial, disavowal, forswearing, renunciation, repudiation
2 *syn* see AMBIGUITY

tergiversator *n syn* see RENEGADE

tergiverse *vb* 1 *syn* see DEFECT
2 *syn* see EQUIVOCATE 2

term *n* 1 *syn* see LIMIT 1
rel terminus
2 a limited, definite, or measurable extent of time during which something exists, lasts, or is in progress <the office has a *term* of four years>
syn duration, span, time
rel phase; go, period, spell, stretch; hitch, tour, turn; standing
3 *syn* see WORD 2
4 **terms** *pl syn* see CONDITION 1
rel detail, item, particular, point; limit
5 **terms** *pl* mutual social relationship or relative position <fight on equal *terms*> <the two were on *terms* of great intimacy>
syn footing, standing
rel coequality, equipollence, status; equality, equivalence, par, parity; balance

term *vb syn* see NAME 1

termagant *n syn* see VIRAGO

termagant *adj syn* see TURBULENT 1

terminable *adj* liable to be terminated or subject to termination <marriage is a *terminable* institution>
syn determinable, endable
rel finite, limited; limitable

terminal *adj syn* see LAST
con beginning, starting
ant initial

terminate *vb* 1 *syn* see CLOSE 3
rel abolish, extinguish; discontinue, wind down
idiom put the lid on
ant initiate
2 *syn* see ADJOURN 2
3 *syn* see DISMISS 3
4 *syn* see QUIT 6

---

syn synonym(s)   *rel* related word(s)
ant antonym(s)   *con* contrasted word(s)
idiom idiomatic equivalent(s)
‖ use limited; if in doubt, see a dictionary

terminated *adj syn* see COMPLETE 4

terminating *adj syn* see LAST
 ant initial

termination *n syn* see END 2
 rel issue, outcome, ‖pay-off, result
 con source; beginning, start
 ant initiation

terminology *n* the specialized or technical terms and expressions peculiar to a field, subject, or trade <the *terminology* of the plastics industry>
 syn cant, dictionary, jargon, language, lexicon, palaver, vocabulary; *compare* DIALECT 2
 rel shoptalk; gibberish, gobbledygook

terminus *n syn* see END 2

terra firma *n syn* see EARTH 2

terrain *n* **1** the physical configuration and features of a tract of land <made an analysis of the *terrain* via aerial photos>
 syn topography
 rel contour, form, profile, shape
 2 an area devoted to a specified activity <the whole county had become breeding and racing *terrain*>
 syn territory, turf
 3 *syn* see FIELD

terrene *adj* **1** *syn* see EARTHLY 1
 2 *syn* see EARTHY 1

terrestrial *adj* **1** *syn* see EARTHLY 1
 rel earthbound, prosaic; profane, secular, unspiritual
 ant empyreal
 2 *syn* see EARTHY 1

terrible *adj* **1** *syn* see FEARFUL 3
 2 *syn* see HARD 6
 3 *syn* see INTENSE 1
 4 *syn* see GHASTLY 1

terribly *adv syn* see VERY 1

terrific *adj* **1** *syn* see FEARFUL 3
 rel terrorizing; agitating, disquieting, upsetting
 2 *syn* see MARVELOUS 2
 rel magnificent, superb; rattling, screaming

terrified *adj syn* see AFRAID 1
 rel horrified, shocked; terrorized; frozen, paralyzed
 con unfearful, unfearing, unfrightened
 ant unafraid

terrify *vb syn* see FRIGHTEN
 rel freeze, paralyze, petrify, stun, stupefy
 idiom put the fear of God into, strike fear into the heart of

terrifying *adj syn* see GHASTLY 1
 ant unterrifying

territory *n* **1** *syn* see AREA 1
 2 *syn* see FIELD
 3 *syn* see TERRAIN 2

terror *n syn* see FEAR 1
 rel awe, fearfulness

terroristic *adj* characterized by or practicing terror as a means of coercion <used torture and other *terroristic* tactics to extract confessions>
 syn gestapo
 rel coercive, strong-arm; brutal, cruel, merciless; immoral, improper, unsanctioned

terrorize *vb* **1** *syn* see FRIGHTEN

 idiom scare to death
 2 *syn* see INTIMIDATE
 idiom use gestapo tactics on

terse *adj syn* see CONCISE
 rel close, compact; lean, precise; clear-cut, crisp, incisive; taut
 con circuitous; pleonastic, redundant, repetitious

tersely *adv syn* see BRIEFLY
 rel closely, compactly; crisply, incisively, precisely; abruptly, curtly
 idiom in as few words as possible
 ant prolixly

test *n syn* see EXPERIMENT
 rel inspection, scrutiny; confirmation, corroboration, substantiation, verification

test *vb* **1** *syn* see TRY 1
 rel assay, essay; confirm, substantiate, verify
 idiom bring to test
 2 *syn* see PROVE 1

test (out) *vb syn* see EXPERIMENT

test *adj syn* see EXPERIMENTAL 2
 rel proving, testing, trying; probationary, speculative

testament *n syn* see TESTIMONY

testify *vb* **1** to serve as evidence of <present conditions *testify* to the accuracy of his predictions>
 syn attest, point (to)
 rel affirm; demonstrate, show; prove
 con discredit, disprove, invalidate; confute, refute
 2 to make a solemn declaration under oath for the purpose of establishing a fact (as in court) <*testified* against the defendant>
 syn depone, depose, ‖mount, swear
 idiom give testimony
 3 *syn* see INDICATE 2

testimonial *n* **1** *syn* see TESTIMONY
 rel indication, manifestation, show, sign, symbol, token
 2 an expression of great approval and high esteem <a dinner was planned as a *testimonial* in her honor>
 syn appreciation, salvo, tribute
 rel salute; triumph; jubilee; commemoration, memorialization, remembrance
 3 *syn* see MONUMENT 2

testimony *n* something that serves as tangible verification <the results are remarkable *testimony* to the accuracy of his predictions>
 syn attestation, confirmation, evidence, proof, testament, testimonial, witness; *compare* INDICATION 3
 rel demonstration, illustration; affirmation, corroboration, documentation, substantiation, verification

testy *adj syn* see IRASCIBLE
 rel annoyed, exasperated, grouchy, irritable

tetchy *adj syn* see IRASCIBLE
 rel ill-humored; cantankerous

tête-à-tête *n* a private conversation between two people <had a *tête-à-tête* with her in a quiet corner>
 syn vis-à-vis

rel causerie, chat, coze; conversation, talk; argument, discussion

tetrad *n syn* see QUARTET

‖**tew** *vb syn* see WORRY 3

text *n syn* see SUBJECT 2
rel consideration, issue; fundamentals; idea

texture *n* **1** *syn* see ESSENCE 1
2 a basic often highly complex underlying scheme, structure, or pattern <war destroys the very *texture* of a society>
syn fabric, fiber, web
rel framework, structure; composition, constitution, makeup; pattern, scheme

thalassic *adj syn* see MARINE 1

thankful *adj syn* see GRATEFUL 1
con unappreciative, ungrateful
ant thankless, unthankful

thankless *adj* **1** not inclined to give thanks <a *thankless* guest>
syn unappreciative, ungrateful, unthankful
rel self-centered; careless, heedless, thoughtless; unappreciative, ungrateful, unmindful
con appreciative, grateful, mindful; careful, heedful, thoughtful
ant thankful
2 not likely to obtain thanks <a *thankless* job>
syn unappreciated, ungrateful, unthankful
rel disagreeable, distasteful, unpleasant; miserable, wretched
con thankworthy

thanks *n pl syn* see GRACE 1

thanksgiving *n syn* see GRACE 1

thankworthy *adj syn* see WORTHY 1

thank–you–ma'am *n syn* see BUMP 3

that *adj* **1** being the other <we argued it this way and we argued it *that* way>
syn another
ant this
2 *syn* see SUCH 2

thaumaturgic *adj syn* see MAGIC 1

thaumaturgy *n syn* see MAGIC 1

thaw *vb syn* see LIQUEFY

theater *n syn* see DRAMA

theatral *adj syn* see DRAMATIC 1

theatric *adj syn* see DRAMATIC 1

theatrical *adj* **1** *syn* see DRAMATIC 1
2 having qualities resembling a stage play or an actor's performance <he slowly made an exaggerated *theatrical* bow>
syn dramatic
rel histrionic, melodramatic, staged; affected, artificial, exaggerated, mannered, unnatural

theft *n* the unlawful taking and carrying away of property without the consent of its owner <was found guilty of auto *theft*>
syn larceny, lift, pinch, purloining, rip-off, steal, stealage, stealing, thievery, thieving, ‖touch
rel filching, pilferage, pilfering, swiping; robbery, robbing, ‖stouth, ‖stouthrief; ‖score

theme *n* **1** *syn* see SUBJECT 2
2 *syn* see ESSAY 2

then *adv* **1** at another time <science as it was taught *then*>
syn again, anon, when; *compare* BEFORE 2

rel before, formerly
2 *syn* see AGAIN 4
3 *syn* see THEREFORE

thence *adv* **1** *syn* see AWAY 1
2 *syn* see THEREFROM

thenceforth *adv* from that time forward <the island which was *thenceforth* to be their home>
syn thenceforward, thereafter; *compare* HENCEFORTH
idiom from then on

thenceforward *adv syn* see THENCEFORTH

theorem *n syn* see PRINCIPLE 1

theoretical *adj* **1** concerned principally with abstractions and theories <*theoretical* versus applied physics>
syn academic, closet, speculative
rel conjectural, hypothetical, notional, suppositional, unproved; analytical, problematical
con practical; factual; proved
ant applied
2 *syn* see ABSTRACT 1
rel idealized, ivory-tower
ant concrete

theorize *vb syn* see SUGGEST 4

theory *n* **1** a belief, policy, or procedure proposed or followed as the basis of action <an educational system that was based on the *theory* that men learn best by experience>
syn hypothesis, supposal; *compare* ASSUMPTION 2
rel base, basis, grounds, position, premise, understanding
ant practice
2 something taken for granted especially on trivial or inadequate grounds <her *theory* that the house was haunted>
syn conjecture, perhaps, speculation, suppose, supposition
rel guess, guesswork, surmise; feeling, hunch, impression, presentiment, suspicion
con assurance, certainty, knowledge

there *adv* to or into that place <they seldom go *there* anymore>
syn thither, thitherward, yon
rel yonder
ant here

thereafter *adv syn* see THENCEFORTH

thereby *adv* in consequence of that <lied to the jury, *thereby* negating his testimony>
syn therethrough; *compare* THEREFROM

therefore *adv* for this or that reason <I think, *therefore* I am>
syn accordingly, consequently, ergo, hence, so, then, thereupon, thus
rel thence, therefrom

therefrom *adv* from that thing, fact, or circumstance <public opinion and a policy deriving *therefrom*>
syn thence, thereof; *compare* THEREBY

thereof *adv syn* see THEREFROM

---

syn synonym(s)   *rel* related word(s)
ant antonym(s)   *con* contrasted word(s)
idiom idiomatic equivalent(s)
‖ use limited; if in doubt, see a dictionary

thereon *adv* on or upon that <knew both the text and commentary *thereon*>
syn thereupon
rel therein, thereof, thereto
therethrough *adv syn* see THEREBY
theretofore *adv* up to that time <*theretofore* obscure communities>
syn thereuntil
rel ‖afore, before, previously
idiom before then
thereuntil *adv syn* see THERETOFORE
idiom until then
thereupon *adv* **1** *syn* see THEREON
2 *syn* see THEREFORE
thesis *n* **1** a position assumed or a point made especially in controversy <her *thesis* about the assassination was arguable>
syn contention, contestation
rel point, position; argument; belief, opinion, sentiment(s), view(s)
2 *syn* see ASSUMPTION 2
3 *syn* see DISCOURSE 2
rel exposition; argument, argumentation
thespian *adj syn* see DRAMATIC 1
thespian *n syn* see ACTOR 1
thew *n syn* see MUSCLE 1
thick *adj* **1** *syn* see STOCKY
rel broad, wide; bulky, burly, husky; blubber, blubbery, massive, obese
con slender, slight, slim; lanky, spare; skeletal
2 *syn* see CLOSE 4
rel concentrated, crammed; localized
con dispersed, scattered
ant diffuse
3 *syn* see STUPID 1
4 *syn* see FAMILIAR 1
idiom hand in glove, thick as thieves
5 *syn* see IMPLAUSIBLE
idiom a little too thick
thick–bodied *adj syn* see STOCKY
thickhead *n syn* see DUNCE
rel ‖clot
thickheaded *adj syn* see STUPID 1
thickset *adj syn* see STOCKY
rel fleshy, portly
thickskull *n syn* see DUNCE
rel lout
thick–witted *adj syn* see STUPID 1
thief *n* one who steals <a *thief* took her money>
syn filcher, larcener, larcenist, nimmer, pilferer, prig, purloiner, stealer; *compare* ROBBER
rel burglar, cat burglar, cat man, housebreaker; hijacker, robber; ‖booster, ‖dip, lifter, shoplifter; nip, pickpocket
thieve *vb syn* see STEAL 1
thievery *n syn* see THEFT
thieving *adj syn* see LARCENOUS
thieving *n syn* see THEFT
thievish *adj syn* see LARCENOUS
thin *adj* **1** not thick, heavy, or broad (as in configuration or physique) <a *thin* body>
syn attenuate, reedy, slender, slight, slim, squinny, stalky, tenuous, twiggy; *compare* LEAN

rel lank, lanky, lathy, lean, macilent, spare; cadaverous, gaunt, pinched, skeletal, wasted; meager, puny, small, twiglike
con broad, wide; compact, dense, solid; heavy, massive; corpulent, fat, obese
ant thick
2 characterized by wide separation of component particles <*thin* air at high altitudes>
syn attenuate, attenuated, rare, rarefied, subtile, subtle, tenuous
rel diffuse, diluted, dispersed; fine, refined
con heavy, thick
ant dense
3 *syn* see DILUTE
4 *syn* see ACUTE 4
rel high-pitched
con low, low-pitched; guttural; deep
5 *syn* see IMPLAUSIBLE
rel vapid; transparent; questionable; untenable
idiom a bit thin
con believable, convincing, sound, substantial
thin *vb* **1** to make thin or thinner <a once powerful frame *thinned* by privation>
syn attenuate, extenuate, wiredraw
rel diminish, reduce; weaken
con broaden, enlarge; strengthen
ant thicken
2 to make or become less dense <the air *thinned* at high altitudes>
syn attenuate, rarefy
ant densify
3 *syn* see DILUTE
thing *n* **1** *syn* see AFFAIR 1
2 *syn* see OCCURRENCE
3 *syn* see ACTION 1
rel exploit, feat, stunt
4 whatever is apprehended as having actual, distinct, and demonstrable existence <there is a place for each *thing* in the lab>
syn article, object
rel entity, item
5 that which can be known as having existence in space or time <virtue is not a *thing*, but an attribute of a *thing*>
syn being, entity, individual, material, matter, object, stuff, substance
rel item, particular
con attribute, characteristic, property, quality
6 *syn* see ENTITY 1
ant nonentity, nonexistence
7 things *pl syn* see POSSESSION 2
8 things *pl syn* see PERSONAL EFFECTS
9 things *pl syn* see CLOTHES
10 *syn* see POINT 1
11 *syn* see FASHION 3
12 *syn* see FETISH 2
thingum *n syn* see DOODAD
thingumajig *n syn* see DOODAD
thingumbob *n syn* see DOODAD
thingummy *n syn* see DOODAD
think *vb* **1** to form an idea of something in the mind <try to *think* exactly how the accident happened>

syn conceive, envisage, envision, fancy, feature, image, imagine, project, realize, see, vision, visualize

rel consider, contemplate, study, weigh; appreciate, comprehend, understand; cerebrate, ideate; conjecture, guess, surmise

2 *syn* see UNDERSTAND 3

3 *syn* see CONJECTURE

4 *syn* see FEEL 3

rel estimate; regard

5 to use one's powers of conception, judgment, or inference <the power to *think* sets humans apart from other animals>

syn cerebrate, cogitate, deliberate, reason, reflect, speculate

rel consider, contemplate; brood, meditate, mull, muse, ponder, ruminate; intellectualize, logicalize, logicize, rationalize; conclude, deduce, infer, judge

idiom put on one's thinking cap, set one's brain to work, use one's head, use the old bean

think (out *or* over) *vb syn* see CONSIDER 1

think (over) *vb syn* see RECONSIDER

thinkable *adj* **1** capable of being thought about <concepts that are easy enough to be *thinkable*>

syn cogitable

rel imaginable, presumable, supposable; comprehendible, comprehensible

con unimaginable; incomprehensible, uncomprehensible

ant unthinkable

2 capable of being made actual <nationalism at this time would be scarcely *thinkable*>

syn conceivable, imaginable, supposable

rel likely, possible; convincing, plausible; feasible, practicable, practical

con inconceivable, unimaginable; impossible, unlikely; implausible; impractical, unfeasible

ant unthinkable

thinking *adj syn* see THOUGHTFUL 1

ant unthinking

third degree *n syn* see CROSS-EXAMINATION

third estate *n syn* see COMMONALTY

thirst *vb syn* see LONG

rel covet; desire, wish

thirsting *adj syn* see THIRSTY 1

thirsty *adj* **1** experiencing a desire for drink <the long hot walk had made him *thirsty*>

syn athirst, dry, thirsting

rel juiceless, parched, sapless

2 *syn* see DRY 1

3 *syn* see EAGER

idiom hungry for, itching for, wild for

ant sated, satiated

this and that *n, often* **this and thats** *pl syn* see SUNDRIES

thither *adv syn* see THERE

ant hither

thitherward *adv syn* see THERE

ant hitherward

thorny *adj* bristling with perplexities, points of controversy, or other conflicting elements <the *thorny* question of states' rights>

syn nettlesome, prickly, spiny

rel troublesome, vexatious; difficult; tricky

thorough *adj* **1** *syn* see EXHAUSTIVE

rel absolute

2 *syn* see CIRCUMSTANTIAL

thoroughbred *adj syn* see PUREBRED

con mixed, mongrel

thoroughfare *n syn* see WAY 1

thoroughgoing *adj* **1** *syn* see EXHAUSTIVE

2 *syn* see UTTER

thoroughly *adv* **1** *syn* see WELL 3

2 in a detailed and complete manner <*thoroughly* investigated the accusations>

syn completely, detailedly, exhaustively, in and out, inside out, up and down

idiom item by item, to the last detail

con casually, offhandedly, sketchily, superficially

ant cursorily

3 *syn* see VERY 1

4 *syn* see HARD 3

though *adv syn* see HOWEVER

though *conj* in spite of the fact that <*though* they know the war is lost, they continue to fight>

syn albeit, although, howbeit, much as, when, whereas, while

thought *n* **1** the act or process of thinking <sat immersed in deep *thought*>

syn brainwork, cerebration, cogitation, deliberation, reflection, speculation

rel contemplation; meditation, musing, pondering, rumination

2 *syn* see IDEA

thoughtful *adj* **1** characterized by or exhibiting the power to think <the doctor had a shrewd rather than a *thoughtful* face>

syn cogitative, contemplative, meditative, pensive, ‖pensy, pondering, reflecting, reflective, ruminative, speculative, thinking

rel analytical, calculating, logical, rational; earnest, grave, melancholy, serious, sober, studious; brainy, intellectual; deep, inseeing, introspective

con irrational; dull, slow, stupid, unthinking; empty-headed, shallow, vacuous

ant thoughtless

2 *syn* see MINDFUL 2

3 mindful of others <the thank-you note was a *thoughtful* gesture>

syn attentive, considerate

rel anxious, careful, concerned, heedful, mindful, solicitous; chivalrous, civil, courteous, gallant, gracious, polite, well-bred

con careless, heedless, inattentive, negligent, remiss, unconcerned, unmindful, unthinking; inconsiderate; discourteous, impolite

ant thoughtless, unthoughtful

thoughtfully *adv syn* see WELL 2

rel courteously, politely, solicitously

con discourteously, impolitely; inconsiderately, heedlessly, unkindly

---

syn synonym(s)   *rel* related word(s)

ant antonym(s)   *con* contrasted word(s)

idiom idiomatic equivalent(s)

‖ use limited; if in doubt, see a dictionary

ant thoughtlessly, unthoughtfully

thoughtless *adj* **1** *syn* see RASH 1
2 *syn* see CARELESS 1
con mindful
ant thoughtful
3 *syn* see SHORT 5
rel discourteous, impolite, rude; selfish
ant thoughtful

thought–out *adj* *syn* see DELIBERATE 1
rel investigated; analyzed
idiom thought over (*or* through)

thousand *n* *syn* see SCAD

thrall *n* *syn* see BONDAGE

thralldom *n* *syn* see BONDAGE

thrash *vb* **1** *syn* see BEAT 1
2 *syn* see WHIP 2
3 *syn* see WHIP 1
rel strike; paddywhack, ‖pail

thrashing *n* *syn* see DEFEAT 1

thrash out *vb* *syn* see DISCUSS 1

threadbare *adj* **1** *syn* see SHABBY 1
rel damaged, impaired, injured; frayed, ragged;
shopworn, timeworn, worn
idiom the worse for wear, worn to rags (*or*
threads)
2 *syn* see TRITE
rel common, familiar; imitative, uncreative; set,
stock; banal, corny
con fresh, new; different, novel, original, unconventional, unusual; memorable

threaten *vb* to announce or forecast impending
danger or evil <bullies *threatening* the child with
a beating>
syn menace
rel browbeat, bulldoze, cow, intimidate; augur,
forebode, portend, presage; caution, forewarn,
warn
idiom make (*or* utter) threats against

threatening *adj* **1** *syn* see IMMINENT 2
rel impending; forthcoming, upcoming; close,
near
2 *syn* see OMINOUS

threesome *n* *syn* see TRIAD

threshold *n* *syn* see VERGE 2

thrift *n* *syn* see ECONOMY
rel austerity, economizing; saving; parsimony
ant waste

thriftiness *n* *syn* see ECONOMY
ant thriftlessness

thriftless *adj* *syn* see IMPROVIDENT
ant thrifty

thrifty *adj* **1** *syn* see FLOURISHING
rel blooming, burgeoning; growing
2 *syn* see SPARING
rel foresighted, prudent; conserving, preserving
con extravagant, improvident
ant wasteful

thrill *vb* to fill with emotions that stir or excite or
to be so excited <an audience *thrilled* by the brilliant spectacle>
syn electrify, enthuse, send
rel animate, excite, galvanize, move, quicken,
stimulate; arouse, inspire, rally, rouse, stir
idiom thrill to pieces (*or* to bits)

con bore, ennui, weary

thrill *n* sudden emotional stimulation, excitement,
or enjoyment <they both got a *thrill* out of
small-boat racing>
syn bang, boot, kick, wallop
rel excitement, lift, stimulation, titillation

thriller *n* a work of fiction or drama designed to
hold the interest by use of a high degree of intrigue, adventure, or suspense <wrote cheap detective *thrillers*>
syn chiller, shocker, thriller-diller
rel gothic, mystery; dime novel, penny dreadful,
shilling shocker

thriller–diller *n* *syn* see THRILLER

thrive *vb* **1** *syn* see BOOM
rel come on, develop, grow; increase; prosper
con stagnate; fail; bust
2 *syn* see SUCCEED 3
rel advance, progress
idiom make a go, turn out well

thriving *adj* **1** *syn* see FLOURISHING
rel blooming, growing; advancing, progressing
idiom going strong
con shriveling; dying
2 *syn* see SUCCESSFUL

thriving *n* *syn* see PROSPERITY 2

throb *vb* *syn* see PULSATE
rel thump; resonate

throe *n* **1** *syn* see ATTACK 3
rel convulsion
2 *syn* see PAIN 1
rel stab

throne *n* *syn* see TOILET

throng *n* *syn* see CROWD 1
rel assemblage, assembly, collection, congregation, gathering; bunch, flock, group, pack

thronged *adj* *syn* see ALIVE 5
rel crawling

throttle *vb* *syn* see CHOKE 1
rel garrote

throttling *n* *syn* see REPRESSION 1

through *prep* **1** *syn* see VIA 1
2 *syn* see VIA 2
3 *syn* see OVER 6
4 *syn* see ABOUT 4
idiom clear through

through *adv* **1** from beginning to end <the region
has a mild climate the whole year *through*>
syn around, over, round, throughout
2 *syn* see OVER 5

through *adj* **1** *syn* see DIRECT 2
con obstructed; interrupted
2 *syn* see COMPLETE 4
3 having no further value, strength, or resources
<when he lost his voice, his singing career was
through>
syn done for, finished, washed-up
rel ended; over
4 being at the very end of a course, concern, or
relationship <was *through* with his wife>
syn done, washed-up
rel finished

through–and–through *adv* *syn* see DOWN 2

throughout *adv* **1** *syn* see EVERYWHERE 1

2 *syn* see THROUGH 1

throughout *prep* **1** *syn* see ABOUT 4

2 *syn* see DURING

throw *vb* **1** to cause to move swiftly through space by a propulsive movement or a propelling force <*throw* a ball to first base>
syn ‖bung, cast, chuck, fire, fling, heave, hurl, launch, pitch, sling, toss
rel ding, drive, impel, precipitate, shoot; project, propel, push, shove, thrust; flick, flip; shy, tumble; lift, lob
2 to dislodge from one's seat especially in horseback riding <was *thrown* while taking a fence>
syn buck (off), pitch, unhorse, unseat
rel ding (off), fling (off)
3 *syn* see OVERCOME 1
4 *syn* see DON 1
5 *syn* see EXERT
6 *syn* see ADDRESS 3

throw away *vb* **1** *syn* see DISCARD
ant salvage
2 *syn* see WASTE 2
con lay away, lay by, lay up

throw back *vb* *syn* see REVERT 2

throwback *n* *syn* see REVERSION 1

throw down *vb* *syn* see FELL 1
rel cast down

throw in *vb* *syn* see INTRODUCE 6
rel contribute

throwing away *n* *syn* see DISPOSAL 2
ant salvaging

throw off *vb* **1** *syn* see RID
2 *syn* see SHAKE 5
3 *syn* see EMIT 2
rel disgorge, eject, exhaust, expel
4 *syn* see CONFUSE 2

throw out *vb* **1** *syn* see EJECT 1
2 *syn* see DISCARD
3 *syn* see SAY 1
4 *syn* see CONFUSE 2

throw over *vb* *syn* see ABANDON 1

throw up *vb* **1** to construct or erect hastily and often carelessly <makeshift buildings *thrown up* almost overnight>
syn jerry-build, run up
rel roughcast, roughhew
idiom slap together, throw together
2 *syn* see VOMIT

thrum *vb* *syn* see HUM
rel ‖birr, purr

thrust *vb* **1** *syn* see PUSH 1
rel crowd, jam; bump, elbow, jostle, nudge, prod, shoulder
2 to cause (as a pointed instrument) to penetrate forcibly <*thrust* the dagger through her heart>
syn dig, drive, plunge, ram, run, sink, stab, stick
rel jab, shove; impale; pierce; embed; put

thrust *n* *syn* see SUBSTANCE 2

thud *vb* to make a dull sound by or as if by striking a surface with something thick and heavy <heard footsteps *thudding* down the hall>
syn clonk, clunk, thump
rel tunk; hit, smite, strike; beat, pound

thug *n* **1** a person inclined or hired to treat another roughly, brutally, or murderously <was beaten and robbed by *thugs*>
syn ‖gorilla, ‖hood, hoodlum, hooligan, ruffian, strong arm; *compare* TOUGH
rel bully, ‖larrikan, plug-ugly, roughneck, rowdy, tough; punk; cutthroat, gangster, gunman, mobster; goon, hatchet man
2 *syn* see TOUGH

thumb *vb* *syn* see HITCHHIKE
idiom thumb a ride

thumb (through) *vb* *syn* see BROWSE

thump *vb* *syn* see THUD
rel hammer, knock

thunder *n* the sound that follows a flash of lightning and is caused by sudden expansion of the air in the path of the electrical discharge <he was more afraid of *thunder* than of lightning>
syn thunderclap, thundercrack, thundering
rel fulmination

thunderbolt *n* a single discharge of lightning with the accompanying thunder <she was startled by the *thunderbolt*>
syn bolt, thunderstroke

thunderclap *n* *syn* see THUNDER

thundercrack *n* *syn* see THUNDER

thundering *n* *syn* see THUNDER

thunderstroke *n* *syn* see THUNDERBOLT

thunderstruck *adj* *syn* see AGHAST 2
rel bewildered, staggered; breathless, stunned
idiom struck dumb

thus *adv* **1** in this or that manner <summoned his counselors and spoke *thus* to them>
syn so, thus and so, thus and thus, thusly
2 *syn* see THEREFORE

thus and so *adv* *syn* see THUS 1

thus and thus *adv* *syn* see THUS 1

thus far *adv* *syn* see HITHERTO 1

thusly *adv* *syn* see THUS 1

thwack *n* *syn* see BLOW 1

thwart *adj* *syn* see TRANSVERSE

thwart *vb* *syn* see FRUSTRATE 1
rel curb, restrain, scotch; cross; foul up, gum up, queer; stymie; counter, match, oppose, pit, play(off), vie
con aid, assist, help, support; abet, encourage

‖**tick** *n* *syn* see INSTANT 1

ticket *n* **1** a slip giving information (as of ownership, identity, or price) <the price of the iron is on the *ticket*>
syn label, tag
rel card; slip; sticker
2 a card of admission <theater *tickets*>
syn carte d'entrée
rel pass
3 a list of candidates for appointment, nomination, or election <vote the party *ticket*>
syn slate
rel choice; lineup; list

---

syn synonym(s)   *rel* related word(s)
ant antonym(s)   *con* contrasted word(s)
idiom idiomatic equivalent(s)
‖ use limited; if in doubt, see a dictionary

4 syn see BALLOT 1
5 syn see PASSPORT
ticklish *adj* **1 syn** see UNSTABLE 2
  2 syn see DELICATE 7
  rel critical
  3 syn see INCONSTANT 1
tick off *vb* **1 syn** see ENUMERATE 2
  2 syn see REPROVE
tidbit (*or* **titbit**) *n syn* see DELICACY
‖**tiddly** *adj syn* see INTOXICATED 1
tide *n syn* see FLOW
tidings *n pl syn* see NEWS
tidy *adj syn* see NEAT 2
  rel sleek, spruce
  ant untidy
tie *n* **1 syn** see BOND 3
  rel fastener, fastening; attachment
  2 syn see DRAW 4
tie *vb* **1** to make fast and secure <*tie* a bundle with strong cord>
  syn bind, tie up
  rel attach, fasten; connect, join, link; anchor, moor, rivet, secure; lash, truss (up); band, cinch, gird, rope
  con loose, loosen; disconnect
  ant untie
  2 syn see MARRY 2
  3 syn see HAMPER
  idiom tie hand and foot, tie one's hands
  ant untie
  4 syn see EQUAL 3
tier *n* **1 syn** see LINE 5
  rel layer
  2 syn see CLASS 1
tie up *vb* **1 syn** see TIE 1
  2 syn see HAMPER
tie–up *n syn* see ASSOCIATION 1
  rel linkup
tiff *n syn* see QUARREL
tiff *vb syn* see QUARREL
tiffany *adj syn* see FILMY
tight *adj* **1 syn** see FAST 4
  rel clasped; solid, steadfast
  con lax, limp; shaky
  ant loose
  2 syn see CLOSE 4
  ant loose
  3 fitting, drawn, or stretched so that there is no slackness or looseness <a *tight* drumhead>
  syn close, taut, tense
  rel skintight; constricted, contracted, drawn, tightened; inflexible, rigid, stiff
  con loosened, slack, unconstricted
  ant loose
  4 difficult to cope with, get through, or circumvent <a very *tight* diplomatic situation>
  syn arduous, rough, tricksy, trying
  rel difficult; exacting; tense; critical; punishing; distressing, disturbing, upsetting
  5 syn see STINGY
  6 syn see INTOXICATED 1
  idiom tight as a tick
tight *adv syn* see HARD 7
tightfisted *adj syn* see STINGY

  rel grudging, mean, shabby
tight–laced *adj syn* see PRIM 1
tight–lipped *adj syn* see SILENT 3
  idiom with one's lips sealed
tightly *adv syn* see HARD 7
tight–mouthed *adj syn* see SILENT 3
tightwad *n syn* see MISER
till *prep syn* see UNTIL
till *conj* up to the time when <be sure to wait *till* I come>
  syn until
till *vb* to prepare (soil) for the raising of crops <*till* the soil>
  syn cultivate, dress, ‖labor, tend, work
  rel harrow, hoe, mulch, plow, turn; plant, sow
tillable *adj syn* see ARABLE
  ant untillable
tilt *vb* **1 syn** see SLANT 1
  2 syn see SEESAW
tilt *n syn* see SLOPE
tilted *adj syn* see INCLINED 3
tilter *vb syn* see SEESAW
tilting *adj syn* see INCLINED 3
timber *n* **1 syn** see FOREST
  2 a large squared or dressed piece of wood <roof *timbers*>
  syn balk, beam
  rel girder, rafter
timberland *n syn* see FOREST
timbre *n syn* see TEMPER 1
time *n* **1 syn** see WHILE 1
  rel season
  2 syn see OCCASION 5
  3 syn see OPPORTUNITY
  idiom the proper moment
  4 syn see PERIOD 2
  5 syn see TERM 2
  6 syn see SEASON
  7 syn see TEMPO
  8 syn see SPELL 1
  ‖**9 syn** see BINGE 1
time *vb* **1** to arrange or set the time of <*timed* his visits to coincide with her vacations>
  syn book, schedule
  rel plan, program, set up
  2 to ascertain or record the time, duration, or rate of <*timed* the car at 100 mph>
  syn clock
  idiom hold the clock on
time and again *adv syn* see OFTEN
timeless *adj* **1 syn** see CONTINUAL
  2 syn see ETERNAL 4
timely *adv syn* see EARLY 1
timely *adj* **1** done or occurring at a suitable time <await a more *timely* moment>
  syn auspicious, favorable, opportune, propitious, prosperous, seasonable, timeous, well≈timed
  rel appropriate, fit, fitting, meet, proper, suitable; likely, promising
  con improper, inappropriate, unfitting; inauspicious, inopportune, unfavorable, unpropitious, unsuitable; ill-timed
  ant untimely

2 *syn* see PUNCTUAL 2

timeous *adj syn* see TIMELY 1

timetable *n syn* see PROGRAM 1
rel table; plan

timeworn *adj* **1** *syn* see ANCIENT 1
2 *syn* see TRITE

timid *adj* **1** *syn* see SHY 1
rel humble; shrinking
ant bold
2 marked by or exhibiting a lack of boldness, courage, or determination <was too *timid* to ski>
syn timorous, ‖timorsome, undaring
rel gentle, mild, milk-toast, milky; cautious, chary, wary; jumpy, nervous, skittish; afraid, apprehensive, fainthearted, fearful; chicken, chickenhearted, henhearted, mouselike, mousy, pigeonhearted; cowardly, yellow; funky, panicky
con audacious, brave, courageous, daring, doughty, fearless, intrepid, lionhearted, unafraid, valiant, valorous
ant bold
3 *syn* see VACILLATING 2

timorous *adj syn* see TIMID 2
rel quailing, recoiling, shrinking; quivering, shivering, shuddering, trembling
ant assured

‖**timorsome** *adj syn* see TIMID 2

tincture *n* **1** *syn* see COLOR 6
2 *syn* see HINT 2
rel smattering

tincture *vb syn* see TINT
rel pigment; stain

ting *vb syn* see TINKLE 1

tinge *vb syn* see TINT
rel streak

tinge *n* **1** *syn* see COLOR 1
rel coloration, coloring, tincture; stain
2 *syn* see HINT 2

tingle *vb* **1** *syn* see TINKLE 1
rel chime
2 *syn* see JINGLE

tinker *vb syn* see FIDDLE 2
idiom play around

tinkle *vb* **1** to make a repeated light high-pitched ringing sound <wind-bells *tinkling* in the breeze>
syn plink, ting, tingle
rel clink, jangle, jingle
2 *syn* see JINGLE
3 *syn* see CHAT 1

tinsel *adj syn* see GAUDY

tint *n syn* see COLOR 1
rel tincture, touch; coloration, pigmentation; dye, stain, wash

tint *vb* to color with a slight shade or stain <white blossoms *tinted* with pale pink>
syn complexion, tincture, tinge
rel color, dye; shade, touch (up); stain, wash

tintamarre *n syn* see DIN

tiny *adj* exceptionally or remarkably small <the first *tiny* buds of spring flowers>
syn ‖bitsy, diminutive, dwarf, dwarfish, itsy-bitsy, itty-bitty, lilliputian, midget, miniature,

minikin, minute, peewee, pint-size, pocket, pocket-size, pygmy, teensy, teensy-weensy, teenty, teeny, teeny-weeny, wee, weensy, weeny; *compare* SMALL 1
rel minuscular, minuscule; infinitesimal, microscopic, minim
con colossal, enormous, gigantic, immense, mammoth, vast
ant huge

tip *n syn* see POINT 9

tip *vb syn* see SLANT 1

tip *vb syn* see TIPTOE
rel creep, mince, pussyfoot, steal

tip (over) *vb syn* see OVERTURN 1
idiom turn upside down

tip *n syn* see GRATUITY

tip *n* a piece of advice or confidential information given by one thought to have access to special or inside sources <gave him a *tip* on which horse would win>
syn point, pointer, steer, tip-off
rel advice; information; clue, cue, hint; forecast, prediction
idiom a bit of inside advice, a bug in the ear, a word to the wise

tip-off *n syn* see TIP

tipped *adj syn* see INCLINED 3

tipple *vb syn* see DRINK 3
idiom drown one's cares (*or* sorrows)

tipple *n syn* see LIQUOR 2

tippler *n syn* see DRUNKARD

tipster *n syn* see INFORMER

tipsy *adj syn* see INTOXICATED 1
rel dazed, unsteady

tiptoe *vb* to walk or proceed quietly on or as if on the ends of the toes <*tiptoed* through the dark house>
syn tip, toe
rel creep, gumshoe, pussyfoot, steal
con clomp, clump, stamp, stomp, stump

tirade *n* a violent, often protracted, and usually denunciatory speech or writing <lashed out with a vicious *tirade* of angry protest>
syn diatribe, harangue, jeremiad, philippic
rel rant, rodomontade, screed; abuse, invective, revilement, vituperation; censure, condemnation, denunciation; berating, tongue-lashing; lecture, sermon

tire *vb* **1** to deplete the strength and energy of <the plane trip *tired* him>
syn drain, fatigue, jade, wear, wear down, weary; *compare* EXHAUST 4
rel debilitate, enervate, enfeeble, sap, weaken; exhaust, wear out
con brace (up), invigorate, strengthen; animate, energize, enliven, pep (up), quicken, stimulate, vitalize
2 *syn* see BORE
rel jade, wear; irk; disgust, nauseate, sicken

---

syn synonym(s)   *rel* related word(s)
ant antonym(s)   *con* contrasted word(s)
idiom idiomatic equivalent(s)
‖ use limited; if in doubt, see a dictionary

idiom make one tired, put one to sleep

tired *adj* **1** being depleted of strength and energy <was too *tired* to go on>
syn ‖clapped-out, fatigued, jaded, wearied, weary, worn, worn-down, worn-out
rel overtaxed, overworked; drained, run-down; ‖beat, ‖bushed, dog-tired, exhausted, fagged, frazzled, overworn, ‖pooped, ‖tucked up, tuckered; collapsing, consumed, knocked out, prostrate, spent
idiom worn to a frazzle
con active, energetic, lively, strong, tireless
ant rested; fresh, untired
2 *syn* see SHABBY 1
3 *syn* see FED UP
rel annoyed, bothered, displeased, irked
idiom having a bellyful of, having about enough of
4 *syn* see TRITE

tiredness *n syn* see FATIGUE
rel collapse, prostration

tireless *adj syn* see INDEFATIGABLE
rel active, enthusiastic
con inactive, listless, tired, unenergetic, unenthusiastic, weak

tiresome *adj syn* see IRKSOME
rel dull; jading; burdensome, onerous, oppressive; difficult, hard

tiring *adj syn* see IRKSOME

Titan *adj syn* see HUGE

titanic *adj syn* see HUGE

title *n* **1** *syn* see CLAIM 1
rel argument, ground, justification, proof, reason; desert, due, merit
2 *syn* see NAME 1

title *vb syn* see NAME 1

titter *vb syn* see LAUGH
rel twitter
idiom laugh behind (*or* in) one's hand, laugh in one's beard

tittle *n syn* see PARTICLE
rel fleck, flyspeck, speck; crumb, grain, scrap, snippet

tittle-tattle *n* **1** *syn* see CHATTER
2 *syn* see REPORT 1

titubate *vb syn* see REEL 2

titular *adj syn* see NOMINAL

tizzy *n syn* see SNIT

to *prep* **1** in the direction of and as far as <was driving *to* the city>
syn into
rel toward
ant from
2 *syn* see AGAINST 2
rel on, over, upon
3 *syn* see BEFORE 1
4 *syn* see UNTIL
5 for the particular purpose of <a market study tailored *to* your needs>
syn for
idiom in contemplation (*or* consideration) of, with an eye to, with a view to
6 in complement to <played Romeo *to* her Juliet>

syn opposite

toad *n syn* see SNOT 1

toad *n syn* see SYCOPHANT

toadeater *n syn* see SYCOPHANT

toadier *n syn* see SYCOPHANT

toady *n syn* see SYCOPHANT

toady *vb syn* see FAWN
rel follow, tag, tail, trail

toadying *adj syn* see FAWNING

toadyish *adj syn* see FAWNING

to-and-fro *n* **1** *syn* see HESITATION
2 *syn* see QUARREL

toast *n syn* see DRINK 2

to-be *n syn* see FUTURE

tocsin *n syn* see ALARM 1
rel sign, signal

today *adv* at the present time <youth *today* do not know what poverty is>
syn now, nowadays, presently
idiom in this day and age, these days
con then, yesteryear

today *n syn* see PRESENT

todayish *adj syn* see PRESENT

to-do *n* **1** *syn* see COMMOTION 4
2 *syn* see COMMOTION 3

toe *vb syn* see TIPTOE

tog (out *or* up) *vb syn* see DRESS UP 1

together *adv* **1** at one and the same time <events that occurred *together*>
syn at once, coincidentally, coincidently, coinstantaneously, concurrently, simultaneously
idiom all at once, all together
ant separately
2 in succession usually without intermission <was moody for days *together*>
syn consecutively, continually, continuously, hand running, night and day, running, successively, unintermittedly, uninterruptedly
idiom on end
3 in or by combined action or effort <students and faculty protested *together*>
syn conjointly, jointly, mutually
rel collectively, concertedly, unanimously
idiom in one breath, in the same breath, with one accord, with one voice
ant separately

togetherness *n* **1** *syn* see ASSOCIATION 1
2 *syn* see SOLIDARITY

‖toggle *vb syn* see DRESS UP 1

togs *n pl syn* see CLOTHES

toil *n syn* see WORK 2
idiom sweat of one's brow, toil and trouble

toil *vb* **1** *syn* see LABOR 1
2 *syn* see DRUDGE
3 *syn* see PLOD 1

toil *n, usu* **toils** *pl syn* see WEB 2

toiler *n syn* see SLAVE 2

toilet *n* a fixture for defecation and urination
syn ‖can, convenience, ‖donicker, head, john, johnny, latrine, lavatory, ‖loo, ‖pot, ‖potty, privy, ‖throne, water closet
rel hopper

toilful *adj syn* see HARD 6

toilsome *adj syn* see HARD 6

toilsomely *adv syn* see HARD 8

token *n* **1** *syn* see INDICATION 3
rel harbinger, omen, portent; characteristic, earmark; indicator, smack
2 *syn* see REMEMBRANCE 3
3 *syn* see EXPRESSION 3
4 *syn* see PLEDGE 1

‖**tokus** *n syn* see BUTTOCKS

tolerable *adj* **1** *syn* see BEARABLE
ant intolerable
2 *syn* see RESPECTABLE 5
3 *syn* see DECENT 4
rel fair, goodish, OK, tidy
idiom better than nothing, good enough
ant intolerable

tolerably *adv syn* see ENOUGH 2

tolerance *n* **1** the capacity to bear something unpleasant, painful, or difficult <had always had a high *tolerance* to pain>
syn endurance, stamina, toleration
rel fortitude, grit, guts; strength, vigor; long-suffering, patience, sufferance; steadfastness, steadiness; opposition, resistance
ant intolerance
2 *syn* see FORBEARANCE 2
rel liberality, liberalness, open-mindedness, permissiveness
con narrow-mindedness; prejudice; dogmatism; bigotry
ant intolerance

tolerant *adj* **1** *syn* see LIBERAL 3
rel open-minded; permissive
con narrow, narrow-minded; prejudiced; dogmatic; bigoted
ant, intolerant
2 *syn* see FORBEARING
rel benevolent, humane; condoning, excusing, forgiving, sympathetic, understanding
con severe, stern; uncompromising, unforgiving, unsympathetic
ant intolerant

tolerate *vb* **1** *syn* see ACCEPT 2
rel condone, countenance; allow, consent (to), permit; have, hear (to)
2 *syn* see BEAR 10
rel sustain

toleration *n* **1** *syn* see FORBEARANCE 2
2 *syn* see TOLERANCE 1

toll *n syn* see EXPENSE 2

toll *vb syn* see LURE

toll *vb syn* see RING

‖**tomato** *n syn* see PROSTITUTE

tomb *n syn* see GRAVE
rel box, coffin, ‖trough

tomb *vb* **1** *syn* see BURY 1
ant untomb
2 *syn* see ENTOMB 1
ant disentomb, untomb

tomboy *n* a girl exhibiting boyish behavior <a *tomboy* who still rode, fished, and fought with her brothers>
syn gamine, hoyden
rel romp

tombstone *n* an inscribed memorial stone set at a place of interment <read the epitaph on the *tombstone* of her ancestor>
syn footstone, grave marker, gravestone, headstone, ledger, monument
rel memorial; cenotaph

tome *n syn* see BOOK 1

tomfool *n syn* see FOOL 1

tomfool *adj syn* see FOOLISH 2

tomfoolery *n* **1** *syn* see NONSENSE 2
2 *syn* see PRANK

tommyrot *n syn* see NONSENSE 2

Tom o' Bedlam *n syn* see LUNATIC 1

Tom Thumb *n syn* see DWARF

ton *n* **1** *syn* see FASHION 3
2 *syn* see SMART SET

tone *n* **1** *syn* see INFLECTION
2 *syn* see VEIN 1
3 *syn* see COLOR 1
rel blend
4 the state of a living body or any of its organs or parts in which the functions are healthy and performed with due vigor <diet and exercise contributed to her good muscle *tone*>
syn tonicity, tonus
rel health, healthiness; elasticity, resiliency; strength, vigor
5 *syn* see TEMPER 1
rel current, movement
idiom (the) state of things
6 *syn* see MOOD 1

toned down *adj syn* see SUBDUED 2

tongue *n syn* see LANGUAGE 1

tongue *vb syn* see SCOLD 1

tongue–lash *vb syn* see SCOLD 1
idiom give one the rough side of one's tongue

tongue–tied *adj syn* see INARTICULATE 3
con loose-lipped, loose-tongued

‖**tongue–walk** *vb syn* see SCOLD 1
idiom give one the rough side of one's tongue

tonguey *adj syn* see TALKATIVE

tonic *adj* **1** increasing or restoring physical or mental tone <the *tonic* effect of a vacation>
syn astringent, restorative, roborant
rel invigorating, refreshing, renewing, strengthening; bracing, sharp
con debilitating, enfeebling, weakening; enervating; exhausting, grueling, sapping
2 *syn* see INVIGORATING

tonicity *n syn* see TONE 4

tonish *adj syn* see STYLISH

tonus *n syn* see TONE 4

tony *adj syn* see STYLISH

too *adv* **1** *syn* see ALSO 2
2 *syn* see EVER 6
rel exorbitantly, immoderately, unconscionably, unmeasurably
3 *syn* see VERY 1

‖**toodle-oo** *interj syn* see GOOD-BYE

---

syn synonym(s)   *rel* related word(s)
ant antonym(s)   *con* contrasted word(s)
idiom idiomatic equivalent(s)
‖ use limited; if in doubt, see a dictionary

tool *n* **1** *syn* see IMPLEMENT
rel machine, mechanism
2 one used or manipulated by another to accomplish his purposes <had no intention of being used as a *tool* by either faction>
syn cat's-paw, pawn, puppet, stooge
rel agent, hireling, vehicle; chump, sucker
tool *vb* *syn* see DRIVE 5
toot *vb* *syn* see DECLARE 1
toot *n* *syn* see BINGE 1
toothful *n* *syn* see DRAM
toothsome *adj* *syn* see PALATABLE
rel agreeable, pleasant, pleasing
toothy *adj* **1** having or showing prominent teeth <a wide *toothy* grin>
syn teethy
2 *syn* see PALATABLE
too–too *adj* *syn* see GENTEEL 3
rel chichi
‖**tootsie** *n* *syn* see DOXY 1
top *n* **1** the highest point <hiked to the *top* of the mountain>
syn apex, crest, crown, fastigium, peak, roof, summit, vertex
rel acme, climax, culmination, height, pinnacle; cusp, head, point, tip
con base, foot, sole; nadir
ant bottom
2 the outer or upper part <the *top* of the table>
syn face, superficies, surface
3 *syn* see BEST
ant bottom
top *vb* **1** to remove or cut back the top of <*top* a tree>
syn crop, detruncate, pollard, truncate
rel clip, dock, prune, trim; curtail, shorten
2 *syn* see SURPASS 1
3 *syn* see SURMOUNT 3
top *adj* **1** of, relating to, or being at the top <the *top* floor of the house>
syn apical, highest, loftiest, topmost, uppermost
con bottommost, lowest
ant bottom
2 *syn* see EXCELLENT
3 *syn* see MAXIMUM
top–drawer *adj* *syn* see EXALTED 1
tope *vb* *syn* see DRINK 3
toper *n* *syn* see DRUNKARD
Tophet *n* *syn* see HELL
topic *n* *syn* see SUBJECT 2
rel proposition; issue
topless *adj* *syn* see LOFTY 6
toploftical *adj* *syn* see PROUD 1
toplofty *adj* *syn* see PROUD 1
rel inflated, puffed; egotistic
con crestfallen
topmost *adj* **1** *syn* see TOP 1
ant bottommost
2 *syn* see MAXIMUM
top–notch *adj* *syn* see EXCELLENT
top off *vb* *syn* see CLIMAX
topography *n* *syn* see TERRAIN 1
topple *vb* **1** *syn* see FALL 2
2 *syn* see TEETER

3 *syn* see OVERTURN 1
4 *syn* see OVERTHROW 2
top–ranking *adj* *syn* see EXALTED 1
topsy–turviness *n* *syn* see CONFUSION 3
topsy–turvy *adj* **1** *syn* see UPSIDE-DOWN 1
2 *syn* see UPSIDE-DOWN 2
rel cockeyed, disarranged, disjointed, disordered, unhinged
torch *n* *syn* see INCENDIARY
toreador *n* *syn* see BULLFIGHTER
torero *n* *syn* see BULLFIGHTER
torment *vb* **1** *syn* see AFFLICT
rel distress, trouble; hurt, pain, punish
2 *syn* see MOLEST
tormented *adj* *syn* see DISTRAUGHT
tormenting *adj* *syn* see EXCRUCIATING
torn *adj* *syn* see LACERATED
tornado *n* a violent destructive whirling wind accompanied by a funnel-shaped cloud extending downward from a cumulonimbus cloud <the *tornado* caused extensive destruction>
syn cyclone, twister; *compare* HURRICANE, WHIRLWIND 1
torpedo *n* *syn* see ASSASSIN
torpid *adj* *syn* see LETHARGIC
rel dull, leaden, sodden; motionless, static; numb
con lively; frisky, sprightly, vigorous; fast
ant active
torpidity *n* *syn* see LETHARGY 1
rel listlessness, passivity, stagnation
torpidness *n* *syn* see LETHARGY 1
ant activeness
torpor *n* *syn* see LETHARGY 1
rel stolidity; passivity
ant activity; animation
torrent *n* *syn* see FLOOD 2
rel flux, rush
torrid *adj* **1** *syn* see HOT 1
idiom burning hot, hot enough to roast an ox
ant arctic
2 *syn* see IMPASSIONED
rel sultry
ant frigid
tort *n* *syn* see EVIL 3
tortuous *adj* *syn* see WINDING
rel involute, vermiculate; cranky; involved
torture *vb* **1** *syn* see AFFLICT
rel oppress, persecute, wrong; hurt, wound; maim, mangle, mutilate
idiom put on the rack, put to torture
2 *syn* see DEFORM
torturing *adj* *syn* see EXCRUCIATING
torturous *adj* *syn* see EXCRUCIATING
tory *n* *syn* see DIEHARD 1
rel loyalist, traditionalist
tory *adj* *syn* see CONSERVATIVE 1
tosh *n* *syn* see NONSENSE 2
toss *vb* **1** *syn* see THROW 1
2 to rise and fall often rhythmically or with alternate motions <a small boat *tossing* in heavy seas>
syn heave, pitch, rock, roll; *compare* SEESAW
rel bob; sway

3 *syn* see DRINK 1
4 *syn* see WRITHE 1
idiom toss and turn
toss (around) *vb syn* see DISCUSS 1
rel bandy (about)
tosspot *n syn* see DRUNKARD
tot *n syn* see DRAM
tot *vb syn* see ADD 2
total *adj* **1** *syn* see WHOLE 4
rel overall; comprehensive, full, inclusive, plenary; teetotal
ant partial
2 *syn* see UTTER
3 *syn* see TOTALITARIAN 1
rel authoritative; absolute, arbitrary, despotic; omnipotent
4 *syn* see TOTALITARIAN 2
rel monopolistic
5 concentrating and employing all resources on a single objective <a *total* offensive>
syn all-out, full-blown, full-out, full-scale, totalitarian, unlimited
rel out-and-out, unreserved, unrestricted
con hampered, impeded, trammeled; restrained, restricted; stinted
ant limited
total *n* **1** *syn* see WHOLE 1
2 *syn* see BODY 5
total *vb* **1** *syn* see ADD 2
2 *syn* see AMOUNT 1
rel comprise, consist (of); stack up; equal, result (in), yield
idiom mount up to, pile up to
3 to make a total wreck of <*totaled* his car when he hit the wall>
syn demolish, wreck; *compare* DESTROY 1
rel crack up, smash
totalistic *adj syn* see TOTALITARIAN 1
con democratic; individualistic
totalitarian *adj* **1** of or relating to centralized control by one autocratic leader or party considered to be infallible <Nazi Germany was a *totalitarian* state>
syn authoritarian, total, totalistic; *compare* ABSOLUTE 4, DICTATORIAL
con democratic, popular; constitutional
2 having or exercising dictatorial powers often tending toward monopoly <antitrust legislation reversing the trend toward the *totalitarian* collectivism of big business>
syn total
3 *syn* see TOTAL 5
totalitarianism *n syn* see TYRANNY
totality *n* **1** *syn* see WHOLE 1
2 *syn* see ENTIRETY 1
3 *syn* see WHOLE 2
rel configuration, form
totalize *vb syn* see ADD 2
totally *adv syn* see ALL 1
tote *vb syn* see CARRY 1
rel cart, haul; shoulder
‖**tote** *n syn* see WHOLE 1
tote *vb syn* see ADD 2
totter *vb* **1** *syn* see TEETER

rel shimmy
2 *syn* see REEL 2
rel blunder, stumble, trip; dodder, ‖dotter; flounder
touch *vb* **1** to probe with a sensitive part of the body (as a finger) so as to get or produce a sensation often in the course of examining or exploring <*touch* an iron to test its temperature>
syn feel, finger, handle, palpate, paw
rel brush, graze; caress, fondle, rub, stroke, toy (with); palm, thumb; examine, inspect, probe, scrutinize; investigate
2 *syn* see ADJOIN
3 *syn* see EQUAL 3
4 *syn* see AFFECT
rel arouse, stir; excite, quicken, stimulate
idiom touch a chord
5 *syn* see AMOUNT 2
rel come (to), verge (on)
touch *n* **1** *syn* see CONTACT 1
rel junction; communication
2 an act of touching or feeling <woke her with a light *touch* on her hand>
syn palpation, taction
rel brush, pat, stroke; contact
3 tactile sensitivity <a blanket soft to the *touch*>
syn feel, tactility
rel feeling
4 a specified sensation conveyed through the tactile receptors <the velvety *touch* of a fabric>
syn feel, feeling
5 *syn* see HINT 2
6 distinctive manner or method <this house needs a woman's *touch*>
syn hand
rel manner, style, way
‖**7** *syn* see THEFT
touchable *adj syn* see TANGIBLE 1
ant untouchable
touch down *vb syn* see ALIGHT
touching *prep* **1** *syn* see AGAINST 2
idiom up against
2 *syn* see APROPOS
touching *adj* **1** *syn* see ADJACENT 3
rel meeting; impinging; overlapping
2 *syn* see MOVING 2
rel compassionate, responsive, sympathetic, tender; piteous, pitiable, pitiful, tear-jerking
touch-me-not-ish *adj syn* see UNSOCIABLE
touchstone *n syn* see STANDARD 3
rel check, test, trial; barometer, scale; demonstration, proof
touch up *vb* to improve or perfect by small additional strokes or alterations <*touch up* a picture>
syn brush up, retouch, tease up
rel improve, perfect, polish; do (up), fix (up)
idiom put finishing touches on
touchy *adj* **1** *syn* see IRASCIBLE

---

syn synonym(s)   *rel* related word(s)
ant antonym(s)   *con* contrasted word(s)
idiom idiomatic equivalent(s)
‖ use limited; if in doubt, see a dictionary

rel hypersensitive, oversensitive, sensitive, thin=skinned; temperamental, volatile; miffy
ant imperturbable
2 *syn* see DELICATE 7
rel dicey, risky, unpredictable; harmful, hazardous, unsafe

tough *adj* **1** *syn* see STRONG 2
rel flinty, hard, unyielding; resistant, unbreakable, withstanding
idiom tough as leather (*or* nails)
con breakable; brittle; yielding
ant fragile
2 *syn* see VISCOUS
3 advocating a persistently firm course of action <a *tough* foreign policy>
syn hard-line, inflexible, uncompromising, unyielding
rel stiff, taut; fixed, confirmed, hard-shell, narrow, rigid; arbitrary, immutable, unalterable; hard-boiled, hardened, obdurate; harsh, procrustean, rigorous, severe, strict; drastic
con liberal, relaxed; compromising, flexible, laissez-faire, yielding
ant soft
4 having or exhibiting great physical endurance (as to strain, hardship, or labor) <the rigorous climate created a *tough* people>
syn hardy, rugged
rel conditioned, hard-bitten, hardened, seasoned, steeled; fit, healthy, lusty, robust, vigorous; stalwart, strong, sturdy
con delicate, fragile, frail, tender; half-hardy, puny; weakened
ant weak
5 *syn* see OBSTINATE
rel hardfisted, hardhanded, hardheaded, tough=minded
6 *syn* see HARD 6
ant soft
7 *syn* see ONEROUS
ant soft
8 frequented by rowdy or criminal elements <lived in a *tough* neighborhood>
syn bad, rough
rel disorderly, rowdy; dangerous, unsafe; ghetto, inner-city, underprivileged
con orderly, quiet, safe

tough (out) *vb* *syn* see ACCEPT 2

tough *n* a rough or unruly person often taking part in bullying or violent behavior <attacked by a gang of *toughs*>
syn ‖b'hoy, bullyboy, mucker, mug, plug-ugly, punk, rough, roughneck, rowdy, ruffian, thug, toughie, yahoo; *compare* BULLY 1, THUG 1
rel goon, hood, hoodlum, hooligan

toughen *vb* *syn* see HARDEN 2
rel develop, strengthen
ant weaken

toughie *n* *syn* see TOUGH
rel ‖heavy

tour *n* **1** *syn* see SPELL
2 a journey in which one eventually returns to the starting point <made a quick *tour* of all the bars>

syn circuit, round, roundabout, round trip; *compare* TRIP 1
rel turn; circle tour

tour de force *n* **1** *syn* see FEAT 2
2 *syn* see MASTERPIECE 1

tourist *n* one who makes a tour for pleasure or culture <*tourists* going through the castle>
syn rubberneck, sightseer, ‖tripper
rel day-tripper, excursionist; traveler; visitor

tout *n* *syn* see LOOKOUT 3

tout *vb* to overly publicize <was *touted* as the world's most modern shopping center>
syn ballyhoo, herald, trumpet
rel proclaim, publicize; plug, promote; acclaim, laud, praise
idiom praise to the skies

tow *vb* *syn* see PULL 2
rel propel; push
idiom take in tow

toward *adj* *syn* see GOOD 1
ant untoward

toward *prep* **1** *syn* see APROPOS
2 *syn* see AGAINST 1

tower (above *or* over) *vb* *syn* see OVERLOOK 2

towering *adj* **1** *syn* see LOFTY 6
rel altitudinous, high, tall; stratospheric
2 *syn* see SUPREME
3 *syn* see MONSTROUS 1
4 reaching a high point of greatness, intensity, or violence <a *towering* rage>
syn monumental, overwhelming
rel ‖crashing; overpowering; mind-blowing
con minor, petty, piddling, puny, trivial
5 *syn* see EXCESSIVE 1

towery *adj* *syn* see LOFTY 6

to wit *adv* *syn* see NAMELY

towner *n* *syn* see TOWNSMAN

townish *adj* of, relating to, or characteristic of a town or of urban life <enjoyed a fast-paced, competitive, *townish* life-style>
syn towny
rel city, metropolitan, urban
con bucolic, rural; isolated, lonely, solitary

townman *n* *syn* see TOWNSMAN

townsman *n* a town dweller <population composed mostly of *townsmen* and a few countrymen>
syn burgher, cit, citizen, towner, townman, towny

towny *n* *syn* see TOWNSMAN

towny *adj* *syn* see TOWNISH

tow–row *n* *syn* see COMMOTION 4

toxic *adj* *syn* see POISONOUS
ant nontoxic

toxicant *adj* *syn* see POISONOUS

toy *n* **1** *syn* see KNICKKNACK
2 something for a child to play with <games, dolls, and other *toys*>
syn ‖die, ‖play-pretty, plaything, ‖pretty

toy *vb* *syn* see TRIFLE 1
rel disport, frolic, play, sport; fiddle (with), tease; caress, cosset, cuddle, dandle, pet
idiom fool (*or* mess) around with

trace *n* **1** *syn* see TRACK 1

rel evidence, proof
2 *syn* see VESTIGE 1
rel mark, token
3 *syn* see HINT 2
trace *vb syn* see TRACK 1
track *n* **1** detectable evidence that something has passed <the *track* of a sleigh in the snow>
syn trace, tread
rel impress, imprint, mark, print; sign, vestige
2 *syn* see TRAIL
rel footpath, footway, walk
idiom beaten path
3 *syn* see WAY 1
rel roadway, trackway
4 *syn* see FOOTPRINT
rel scent, slot
track *vb* **1** to follow the tracks or traces of <*track* a wounded deer>
syn trace, trail
rel follow; dog, shadow, tail; chase, pursue; find, hunt (down), smell (out)
idiom be hot on the trail of
2 *syn* see TRAVEL 2
tract *n* **1** *syn* see AREA 1
rel amplitude, spread, stretch; part, portion, section, sector
2 *syn* see LOT 3
3 *syn* see FOOTPRINT
tractable *adj syn* see OBEDIENT
rel flexible, pliable, pliant; manageable; subdued
con headstrong, unmanageable, willful; obstinate, refractory, stubborn
ant intractable, unruly
tractate *n syn* see DISCOURSE 2
trade *n* **1** a pursuit followed as an occupation or means of livelihood and requiring technical knowledge and skill <the *trade* of a carpenter>
syn art, calling, craft, handicraft, métier, profession, vocation
rel employment, occupation, pursuit, work
con avocation, hobby
2 *syn* see BUSINESS 4
rel market
3 *syn* see PATRONAGE 2
trade *vb* **1** to give one thing in return for another with an expectation of gain <*traded* furs for beads and cloth>
syn bargain, barter, exchange, swap, traffic, truck; *compare* EXCHANGE 2
rel market, merchandise, sell; deal; argue, chaffer, dicker, haggle, wrangle
idiom make (*or* strike) a bargain, make a deal
2 *syn* see EXCHANGE 2
trademark *n syn* see MARK 7
trader *n syn* see MERCHANT
tradesman *n syn* see MERCHANT
tradition *n* **1** an inherited or established way of thinking, feeling, or doing <America's puritanical *tradition* is still very much alive>
syn heritage
rel culture; convention, custom, ethic, form; birthright, inheritance, legacy
2 *syn* see LORE 2

traditional *adj* **1** of or relating to tradition <a *traditional* interpretation of the Bible>
syn conventional, tralatitious; *compare* CONVENTIONAL 1
rel ancestral, immemorial, old; customary, habitual, usual; acknowledged, established, establishmentarian, fixed; common, popular
con new; unconventional, unusual; individualistic, original, personal
2 *syn* see ORAL 2
traditionalist *n syn* see PURIST
traditionalistic *adj syn* see CONSERVATIVE 1
traduce *vb syn* see MALIGN
rel mock; disgrace; betray; violate
traducing *adj syn* see LIBELOUS
traffic *n* **1** *syn* see BUSINESS 4
2 *syn* see COMMERCE 2
rel relations, relationship; closeness, connection, familiarity, intimacy
3 *syn* see PATRONAGE 2
4 the number or volume of vehicles or pedestrians moving along a route <freeway *traffic* is heavy during the rush hour>
syn travel
traffic *vb* **1** *syn* see TRADE 1
2 to engage in illegal or disreputable business or activity <*trafficked* in drugs>
syn truck
rel deal (in), push, shove; black-market; bootleg, moonshine; fence
idiom handle (*or* deal in) under the counter
trafficable *adj syn* see MARKETABLE
trafficker *n syn* see MERCHANT
tragedy *n* **1** *syn* see DISASTER
rel blow, shock
2 *syn* see MISFORTUNE
rel unluckiness; curse, lot; woe(s)
con prosperity, success
ant triumph
trail *vb* **1** *syn* see DRAG 3
2 *syn* see DELAY 2
rel plod, trudge; falter, flag; halt
3 *syn* see TRACK 1
rel nose (out), sniff (out)
idiom follow a scent
4 *syn* see TAIL
5 *syn* see FOLLOW 2
trail *n* a rough course or way formed by or as if by repeated chance footsteps <an old Indian *trail*>
syn path, pathway, track, ‖trod
rel footpath, footwalk, footway
trailer *n* a motor-equipped or motor-drawn highway vehicle designed to serve as a place for dwelling or business <toured the country in a *trailer*>
syn camper, ‖caravan, house trailer, mobile home, motor home, recreational vehicle, RV
rel van
train *vb syn* see LURE

---

syn synonym(s)   *rel* related word(s)
ant antonym(s)   *con* contrasted word(s)
idiom idiomatic equivalent(s)
‖ use limited; if in doubt, see a dictionary

train *n* **1** *syn* see ENTOURAGE
2 *syn* see SUCCESSION 2
rel course, run; line, thread; gradation, scale, tier
train *vb* **1** *syn* see TEACH
rel cultivate, develop, shape; accustom, habituate; harden, season
2 *syn* see DIRECT 2
training *n* *syn* see EDUCATION 1
train off *vb* *syn* see SWERVE 1
traipse *vb* **1** *syn* see WANDER 1
2 *syn* see WALK 1
3 *syn* see DRAG 3
traipse *n* *syn* see SLATTERN 1
trait *n* **1** *syn* see QUALITY 1
2 *syn* see CHARACTERISTIC 1
rel denominator; attribute, quality
traitorous *adj* *syn* see FAITHLESS
rel apostate, renegade; mutinous, rebellious, seditious; alienated, disaffected, estranged; unpatriotic
con faithful; patriotic
traject *vb* *syn* see CONDUCT 4
tralatitious *adj* *syn* see TRADITIONAL 1
idiom handed down from time immemorial
tralucent *adj* *syn* see TRANSLUCENT 3
trammel *vb* **1** *syn* see ENTANGLE 3
2 *syn* see HAMPER
rel circumscribe, confine, limit; bind, enchain, handcuff, manacle
3 *syn* see STULTIFY
tramp *vb* **1** to walk, tread, or step especially heavily <heard hobnailed boots *tramping* across the square>
syn trample, tromp; *compare* PLOD 1
rel march; thud; footslog, stodge, trudge; stamp, stomp
2 *syn* see HIKE 2
3 *syn* see TRAMPLE 2
tramp *n* **1** *syn* see VAGABOND
2 *syn* see WANTON
3 a journey on foot or a walking trip <took a long *tramp* through the woods>
syn hike, walkabout
rel ramble, saunter, stroll, walk; traipse
tramper *n* *syn* see VAGABOND
trample *vb* **1** *syn* see TRAMP 1
2 to tread on forcibly and repeatedly so as to crush or injure <was *trampled* to death by his horse>
syn stamp, stomp, tramp, tromp
rel ‖stoach, ‖stramp, ‖stunt; pound; tread (on); override
trance *vb* *syn* see TRANSPORT 2
trance *n* *syn* see REVERIE
tranquil *adj* *syn* see CALM 2
rel irenic, pacific, peaceful; quiet, still; stable, steady
con stirred up, troubled
ant agitated
tranquilize *vb* *syn* see CALM
rel hush; sedate; subdue
idiom pour oil on troubled waters
ant agitate

transaction *n* *syn* see CONTRACT
transcend *vb* *syn* see SURPASS 1
idiom go beyond, rise above
transcendent *adj* **1** *syn* see SUPREME
rel accomplished, consummate, finished; entire, intact, perfect, whole
2 *syn* see ABSTRACT 1
rel absolute, ultimate; boundless, eternal, infinite
transcendental *adj* **1** *syn* see OTHERWORLDLY 1
2 *syn* see ABSTRACT 1
rel supernatural, supranatural, ultimate
transfer *vb* **1** *syn* see MOVE 4
rel carry, convey; relocate
2 *syn* see GIVE 3
rel convey, transmit
3 *syn* see TRANSFORM
4 to shift the title of (property) from one owner to another <to preserve the farm intact he *transfers* it to a single heir>
syn abalienate, alien, alienate, assign, cede, convey, deed, make over, remise, sign (over)
transfigure *vb* *syn* see TRANSFORM
transfix *vb* *syn* see IMPALE
transform *vb* to make over to a radically different form, composition, state, or disposition <the interaction of social forces *transforms* custom and produces a new tradition>
syn change, commute, convert, metamorphize, metamorphose, mutate, transfer, transfigure, translate, transmogrify, transmute, transpose, transubstantiate; *compare* CHANGE 1
rel alter; denature
transformation *n* *syn* see CONVERSION 2
transfuse *vb* *syn* see PERMEATE
transgress *vb* **1** *syn* see VIOLATE 1
2 *syn* see TRESPASS 1
transgression *n* *syn* see BREACH 1
rel erring, error, lapse, slip; overstepping; misbehavior, misstepping
transient *adj* lasting or staying only a short time <features of a *transient* culture now extinct>
syn ephemeral, evanescent, fleeting, fugacious, fugitive, impermanent, momentaneous, momentary, passing, short-lived, transitory, volatile; *compare* TEMPORARY
rel deciduous, flitting, unstable; temporal, temporary; insubstantial
idiom as transient as the clouds, here today and gone tomorrow
con lasting, perdurable, permanent, substantial; durable, stable
ant perpetual
transit *n* **1** *syn* see PASSAGE 1
2 *syn* see TRANSITION
3 *syn* see TRANSPORTATION 1
4 public conveyance of passengers or goods as a commercial enterprise <mass *transit*>
syn transport, transportation
transition *n* passage from one state or condition to another <the *transition* from boyhood to manhood>
syn alteration, passage, shift, transit

rel change, conversion, metamorphosis, transformation; development, evolution; growth, progress

transitional *adj* involving or characterized by passage from one stage, condition, or state to another <a *transitional* phase of social development>
syn transitive, transitory
rel developing, evolving; altering, changing, shifting
idiom being in a state of flux

transitive *adj syn* see TRANSITIONAL

transitory *adj* 1 *syn* see TRANSIENT
rel changeable; nonpermanent, unenduring; brief, short-term
2 *syn* see TRANSITIONAL

translate *vb* 1 to make a version of in another language <*translated* many secret documents from French to English>
syn put, render, transpose, turn
rel transliterate; transcribe; interpret; metaphrase, paraphrase
2 *syn* see TRANSFORM

translate (into) *vb syn* see PARAPHRASE

translation *n syn* see VERSION 1

translucent *adj* 1 *syn* see TRANSPARENT 1
2 *syn* see CLEAR 4
rel apparent, obvious, unmistakable
3 admitting and diffusing light so that objects beyond cannot be clearly distinguished <*translucent* amber>
syn clear, tralucent, translucid, transparent; *compare* TRANSPARENT 1
rel lucent, lucid

translucid *adj syn* see TRANSLUCENT 3

transmarine *adj syn* see OVERSEAS

transmigrate *vb syn* see MIGRATE

transmigratory *adj syn* see MIGRATORY

transmit *vb* 1 *syn* see SEND 1
rel convey, transport
2 *syn* see COMMUNICATE 1
3 *syn* see HAND DOWN
rel instill; transfuse, translate
4 *syn* see CONDUCT 4

transmogrify *vb syn* see TRANSFORM

transmundane *adj syn* see OTHERWORLDLY 1

transmute *vb syn* see TRANSFORM

transparent *adj* 1 admitting light without appreciable diffusion or distortion so that objects beyond are entirely visible <a sheet of *transparent* plastic>
syn clear, limpid, pellucid, see-through, translucent; *compare* TRANSLUCENT 3
rel crystal, crystalline, glassy; diaphanous
idiom clear as glass (*or* crystal)
con dark, smoky; cloudy, foggy hazy, misty, nubilous
ant opaque
2 *syn* see FILMY
3 *syn* see TRANSLUCENT 3
4 *syn* see CLEAR 4
rel distinguishable, recognizable; articulate, distinct, plain; unambiguous, unequivocal
con muddy, turbid

transpicuous *adj syn* see CLEAR 4

transpierce *vb syn* see IMPALE

transpire *vb* 1 *syn* see GET OUT 2
2 *syn* see HAPPEN 1
rel eventuate, result

transplace *vb syn* see REVERSE 1
rel remove; rearrange

transport *vb* 1 *syn* see CARRY 1
2 to carry away by strong and usually pleasant emotion <*transported* with ecstasy>
syn enrapture, enravish, entrance, ravish, trance
rel excite, move, provoke, quicken, stimulate; agitate, inflame, stir (up); elevate, uplift; carry away, delight, imparadise, ‖send, slay, thrill, ‖wow
3 *syn* see BANISH

transport *n* 1 *syn* see TRANSPORTATION 1
2 *syn* see ECSTASY
rel ardor, enthusiasm, fervor, passion; happiness
3 *syn* see VEHICLE 3
4 *syn* see TRANSIT 4

transportable *adj syn* see PORTABLE

transportation *n* 1 an act, process, or instance of transporting or being transported <arranged for the *transportation* of his luggage>
syn carriage, carrying, conveyance, transit, transport, transporting
rel hauling, moving
2 *syn* see VEHICLE 3
3 *syn* see TRANSIT 4

transporting *n syn* see TRANSPORTATION 1

transpose *vb* 1 *syn* see TRANSFORM
2 *syn* see TRANSLATE 1
3 *syn* see REVERSE 1

transubstantiate *vb syn* see TRANSFORM

transude *vb syn* see EXUDE

transversal *adj syn* see TRANSVERSE
rel bent; intersecting

transverse *vb syn* see TRAVERSE 4

transverse *adj* extended or lying in a direction across something else <the *transverse* arches of the cathedral ceiling>
syn crossing, crosswise, thwart, transversal, traverse
rel diagonal, oblique; across, crossed
con perpendicular
ant longitudinal

transversely *adv syn* see OVER 1

transversely *adv syn* see OVER 1

trap *n* 1 *syn* see LURE 2
rel artifice, feint, gambit, maneuver, ploy, ruse, stratagem, wile; birdlime, net; ambuscade, ambush; conspiracy, intrigue, machination, plot
‖2 *syn* see POLICEMAN
‖3 *syn* see MOUTH 1

trap *vb syn* see CATCH 3
rel mousetrap, snag

trapfall *n syn* see PITFALL

---

syn synonym(s)   *rel* related word(s)
ant antonym(s)   *con* contrasted word(s)
idiom idiomatic equivalent(s)
‖ use limited; if in doubt, see a dictionary

traps *n pl syn* see PERSONAL EFFECTS
trash *n* **1** *syn* see REFUSE
  rel leavings
  2 *syn* see NONSENSE 2
  3 *syn* see RABBLE 2
‖**trash** *vb syn* see VANDALIZE
trash *vb syn* see PLOD 1
trashy *adj syn* see CHEAP 2
  rel third-rate
trauma *n* intense mental, emotional, or physical disturbance resulting from stress <a broken home may produce persistent *trauma* in children>
  syn shock, traumatism
  rel blow, stress; traumatization; derangement, disturbance, upset; collapse
traumatism *n syn* see TRAUMA
travail *n* **1** *syn* see WORK 2
  rel task; struggle
  idiom toil and trouble
  con relaxation, rest
  2 *syn* see LABOR 2
  rel contractions, pains
  idiom birth throe
travel *vb* **1** *syn* see GO 1
  rel move (on); voyage; roam, trek; explore
  2 to journey over (as by conveyance) <certain roads can be *traveled* only on horseback>
  syn cover, do, pass (over), track, traverse
  rel cross
travel *n* **1** *syn* see PASSAGE 1
  2 often **travels** *pl syn* see JOURNEY
  3 *syn* see TRAFFIC 4
travelable *adj syn* see PASSABLE
‖**traveler** *n syn* see VAGABOND
traverse *n syn* see OBSTACLE
traverse *vb* **1** *syn* see RESIST
  2 *syn* see DENY 4
  rel oppose; dismiss; squash, squelch
  3 *syn* see TRAVEL 2
  4 to extend or lie across (something) <a highway *traversing* the entire state>
  syn cross, transverse
  rel crisscross, intersect, quarter
  idiom cut across
  5 to pass over, along, or to and fro especially on foot <deep in thought he *traversed* the terrace again and again>
  syn perambulate, walk
  rel peregrinate; track, tread; pace
traverse *adj syn* see TRANSVERSE
travesty *n* **1** *syn* see CARICATURE 2
  rel mimicry; distortion, exaggeration; ridicule
  2 *syn* see MOCKERY 2
travesty *vb syn* see MIMIC
treacherous *adj* **1** *syn* see FAITHLESS
  rel undependable, unreliable, untrustworthy; betraying, deceptive, double-crossing, false-hearted, misleading, Punic
  ant dependable; trustworthy
  2 *syn* see DANGEROUS 1
  rel deceptive, ticklish, tricky; precarious
treacherousness *n syn* see TREACHERY
  ant dependability; trustworthiness

treachery *n* betrayal of a trust or confidence <corruption in public office is little short of *treachery*>
  syn disloyalty, faithlessness, perfidiousness, perfidy, treacherousness, treason; *compare* INFIDELITY
  rel falseheartedness, falseness; double cross, double-dealing; sellout
  idiom dirty pool, dirty work at the crossroads
  con incorruptibility, reliability; probity, rectitude, uprightness; constancy, fidelity, loyalty, staunchness
  ant dependability; trustworthiness
tread *vb* **1** *syn* see DANCE 1
  2 *syn* see WALK 1
  rel march, stride; tromp
tread *n syn* see TRACK 1
treadmill *n syn* see ROUTINE
treason *n* **1** *syn* see TREACHERY
  rel deceit, deceitfulness; duplicity; Machiavellianism
  idiom breach of trust (*or* faith)
  con allegiance, loyalty
  ant staunchness
  2 *syn* see SEDITION
  rel disloyalty, treacherousness, treachery; high treason; misprision
  ant allegiance
treasure *n syn* see FIND 1
  rel catch, plum, prize; pearl
treasure *vb syn* see APPRECIATE 1
  rel conserve, guard, preserve, save; idolize, revere, reverence, venerate, worship
  idiom hold dear
treasure–house *n* **1** *syn* see TREASURY 1
  2 *syn* see BONANZA
treasure trove *n* **1** *syn* see FIND 1
  2 *syn* see BONANZA
treasury *n* **1** a place (as a room or building) where valuables are kept <priceless gold candlesticks kept in the *treasury* of the cathedral>
  syn treasure-house
  rel archive(s), gallery, museum; depository, repository, storehouse
  idiom treasure room
  2 the place of deposit, retention, and disbursement of collected funds <the union *treasury* held emergency strike funds>
  syn chest, coffer, exchequer, war chest
  rel depositary, depository
  3 *syn* see BONANZA
treat *vb* **1** *syn* see CONFER 2
  rel consider, study, weigh; deliberate, reason, think
  2 to have to do with or behave toward (a person or thing) in a specified manner <*treat* all employees fairly and impartially>
  syn deal (with), handle, play, serve, take, use
  rel conduct, do with, manage, ‖wield; regard, respect; account, consider, hold; appraise, estimate, evaluate, rate, value
  idiom act with regard to, conduct oneself toward, do by
  3 to pay for another's entertainment <*treated* her to a few drinks>

syn blow, set up, ‖shout, stand
rel stake
idiom go treat, pick up the tab for, stand treat
4 to give medical treatment to <was *treated* by an eye specialist>
syn doctor
rel attend, care (for), minister (to), nurse

treat *n syn* see DELICACY

treatise *n syn* see DISCOURSE 2
rel writing; book; argument, discussion, exposition

treaty *n* a formal, usually written, arrangement made by negotiation between two or more political authorities <the two nations finally signed an arms-limitation *treaty*>
syn agreement, concord, convention, pact; *compare* CONTRACT
rel arrangement, entente, understanding; bargain, contract; charter, compact, concordat, covenant; alliance, cartel, league; accord, reconciliation, settlement

treble *adj syn* see ACUTE 4
ant bass

tree *vb syn* see CORNER

trek *n syn* see JOURNEY

tremble *vb* **1** *syn* see SHAKE 1
rel shrink, wince
idiom tremble like a leaf
2 *syn* see SHAKE 2

trembling *adj syn* see TREMULOUS
ant steady

tremendous *adj* **1** *syn* see FEARFUL 3
2 *syn* see MONSTROUS 1
3 *syn* see HUGE
rel amazing, astounding, flabbergasting; terrific
idiom great big
ant minute

tremendousness *n syn* see ENORMITY 2
rel bigness, largeness

tremor *n syn* see EARTHQUAKE

tremor *vb* **1** *syn* see SHAKE 1
2 *syn* see SHAKE 2

tremorous *adj syn* see TREMULOUS

tremulant *adj syn* see TREMULOUS

tremulous *adj* characterized by or affected with trembling or tremors <her *tremulous* hands could scarcely hold the book>
syn aquake, aquiver, ashake, ashiver, quaking, quaky, quivering, quivery, shaking, shaky, shivering, shivery, trembling, tremorous, tremulant
rel aguish; aspen; palpitating; vibrating
idiom having the shakes
con firm, settled, stable, steady, unmoving

trench *n* a long narrow furrow in the ground <dig a *trench* for a sewer pipe>
syn cut, ditch
rel gully; drill, furrow; fosse; trough; drain, sink

trench *vb syn* see BORDER 3

trenchant *adj* **1** *syn* see INCISIVE
rel piercing, probing, razor-sharp; sarcastic, sardonic, satiric; acrid; piquant, poignant, pungent
2 *syn* see CAUSTIC 1
rel scalding, scorching

trend *n* **1** *syn* see TENDENCY 1
rel movement; flow; direction, orientation; swing, wind; progression
2 *syn* see FASHION 3

‖**trendy** *adj syn* see STYLISH
rel ultramodern
con dated, outmoded

trepidation *n syn* see FEAR 1
ant unapprehensiveness

trepidity *n syn* see FEAR 1
ant intrepidity, intrepidness

trespass *n syn* see BREACH 1
rel encroachment, entrenchment, invasion; intrusion, obtrusion

trespass *vb* **1** to commit an offense <exhibited scrupulous fairness even to those who *trespassed* against him>
syn offend, sin, transgress
rel deviate, err, lapse
idiom do wrong by
2 to make inroads on the property, territory, or rights of another <warned the hunters not to *trespass* on his land>
syn encroach, entrench, infringe, invade
rel enter, penetrate, pierce, probe; interlope, intermeddle, intrude; transgress
idiom crash the gate

trestle *n syn* see SAWHORSE

triad *n* a union or group of three often closely related individuals or things <a *triad* of deities>
syn threesome, trine, trinity, trio, triple, triumvirate, triune, troika; *compare* TRIUMVIRATE 1

trial *n* **1** the state or fact of being tested (as by suffering) <the Vietnam war period was a time of great national *trial*>
syn affliction, calvary, cross, crucible, ordeal, tribulation, visitation
rel agony, distress, misery, suffering; anguish, grief, heartbreak, sorrow, woe; adversity, misfortune; difficulty, hardship, rigor, vicissitude
idiom crown of thorns, fiery ordeal, trial and tribulation
2 a source of vexation or annoyance <living in a crowded hotel is a real *trial*>
syn care, trouble, worry
rel complication, difficulty; annoyance, distress, misfortune; ordeal
3 *syn* see EXPERIMENT
4 *syn* see ATTEMPT

trial *adj syn* see EXPERIMENTAL 2

trial and error *n syn* see EXPERIMENT

trial balloon *n syn* see FEELER
rel trial

trial run *n syn* see EXPERIMENT

tribe *n syn* see FAMILY 1

tribulation *n syn* see TRIAL 1
rel oppression, persecution, wronging

tribunal *n syn* see COURT 2

tributary *adj syn* see SUBORDINATE

---

syn synonym(s)   *rel* related word(s)
ant antonym(s)   *con* contrasted word(s)
idiom idiomatic equivalent(s)
‖ use limited; if in doubt, see a dictionary

rel conquered, subdued, subjugated, vanquished; accessory, minor; satellite

tribute *n* **1** *syn* see TESTIMONIAL 2
rel recognition; monument
2 *syn* see ENCOMIUM

trice *n syn* see INSTANT 1

trick *n* **1** an indirect, ingenious, and often cunning means to gain an end <used every *trick* in the bag to cover up the scandal>
syn artifice, chouse, device, feint, gambit, gimmick, jig, maneuver, play, ploy, ‖prat, ruse, shenanigan, sleight, stratagem, whizzer, wile; *compare* PRANK
rel contrivance, craft, expediency; blind, bluff, diversion, dodge, dodgery, red herring; curve, deception, sham, stall; fraud, ‖rort, scheme, shift, skin game
2 *syn* see PRANK
rel boutade; escapade; practical joke
3 an ingenious or dexterous act or procedure designed to puzzle or amuse <a juggler's *trick*>
syn feat, stunt
rel accomplishment
4 tricks *pl syn* see PERSONAL EFFECTS
5 *syn* see HANG
6 *syn* see HABIT 1
7 *syn* see SPELL

trick *adj* somewhat defective and inclined to function abnormally on occasion <a *trick* lock that doesn't always catch>
syn tricky, undependable
rel catchy, touchy; unreliable, untrustworthy; insecure, shaky, unstable; defective, dysfunctioning, malfunctioning

trick *vb syn* see DUPE
rel outtrick, outtrump, outwit; have
idiom take (someone) for a ride

trick (off, out, *or* up) *vb syn* see DRESS UP 1

trickery *n syn* see DECEPTION 1
rel double-cross; underhandedness
idiom underhand dealing

trickle *vb syn* see DRIP
ant gush

trickster *n* **1** *syn* see SWINDLER
idiom gyp artist
2 *syn* see MAGICIAN 2

tricksy *adj syn* see TIGHT 4

tricky *adj* **1** *syn* see SLY 2
rel deceptive, delusive; delusory, misleading; deceitful, dishonest
2 *syn* see UNSTABLE 2
rel catchy, difficult, trappy; quirky
3 *syn* see DELICATE 7
4 *syn* see TRICK

tried *adj syn* see RELIABLE 1
rel constant, faithful, staunch, steadfast; demonstrated, proved, tested; approved, certified
ant untried

tried and true *adj syn* see RELIABLE 1

trifle *n* **1** *syn* see KNICKKNACK
rel rope yarn
2 *syn* see HINT 2

trifle *vb* **1** to behave amorously without serious intent <was interested only in *trifling* with her, not marrying her>

syn coquet, dally, flirt, fool, lead on, string along, toy, wanton
rel play (with); mess around, ‖muck, mucker; philander; mash
2 *syn* see FIDDLE 1

trifle (away) *vb syn* see WASTE 2
rel misuse; burn (up), use up
con retain, save

trifling *n syn* see SMALL TALK

trifling *adj syn* see PETTY 2
rel banal, inane, insipid, jejune, vapid; empty, frivolous, hollow, idle, nugatory, otiose, vain; insignificant, unimportant

trig *adj* **1** *syn* see NEAT 2
2 *syn* see STYLISH
‖**3** *syn* see FULL 1

triggerman *n syn* see ASSASSIN

trill *vb syn* see DRIP

trillion *n syn* see SCAD

trim *vb* **1** *syn* see ADORN
2 *syn* see WHIP 2
rel ‖skin
3 *syn* see CUT 6

trim *adj* **1** *syn* see NEAT 2
rel clean, clean-cut, fit, spruce; shapely, streamlined, symmetrical
con disordered, shapeless, straggly
ant frowsy
2 *syn* see SHAPELY

trim *n syn* see ORDER 10
rel commission; whack

trine *n syn* see TRIAD

trinity *n syn* see TRIAD

trinket *n syn* see KNICKKNACK
rel plaything; frippery, showpiece, tinsel; trinketry, trinkums

trio *n syn* see TRIAD

trip *vb syn* see SKIP 1

trip *n* **1** a single passage of a vehicle between two points or to a point and return <a regular bus *trip* to and from the city>
syn run; *compare* DRIVE 1, JOURNEY, TOUR 2
rel drive; progress
2 *syn* see JOURNEY
rel run
3 *syn* see ERROR 2

tripes *n pl syn* see ENTRAILS

triple *n syn* see TRIAD

tripped out *adj syn* see DRUGGED

‖**tripper** *n syn* see TOURIST

triste *adj syn* see SAD 2

trite *adj* used or occurring so often as to have lost interest, freshness, or force <unrequited love has become a *trite* theme>
syn bathetic, chain, cliché, clichéd, commonplace, corny, hack, hackneyed, musty, old hat, shopworn, stale, stereotyped, stereotypical, threadbare, timeworn, tired, twice-told, warmed-over, well-worn, worn-out
rel common, ordinary; banal, dull, flat, jejune, mildewed, vapid; bedridden, drained, exhausted, used-up; bromidic, platitudinous, prosaic, ready-made, set, stock
con first, new, seminal; novel, unique; creative, imaginative; uncopied; memorable; distinctive

ant fresh, original

triturate *vb syn* see PULVERIZE 1

triumph *n* **1** *syn* see VICTORY 1
rel ascendancy, gain; surmounting, vanquishing, vanquishment
ant defeat
2 *syn* see EXULTATION
rel joy; festivity, merriment, reveling

triumph *vb* **1** *syn* see EXULT
rel gloat
2 *syn* see WIN 1
rel prosper, succeed; conquer, surmount
idiom get the best (*or* better) of
con lose
ant fail
3 *syn* see CONQUER 2

triumphal *adj syn* see EXULTANT

triumphant *adj syn* see EXULTANT
rel rejoicing, triumphing

triumvirate *n* **1** an administrative or ruling body of three <a monarchy replaced by a *triumvirate* of generals>
syn troika; *compare* TRIAD
rel junta
2 *syn* see TRIAD

triune *n syn* see TRIAD

trivia *n pl but sometimes sing in constr* unimportant matters <they became bored with the *trivia* of everyday life>
syn minutia(e), small beer, small change, small potato(es), triviality

trivial *adj* **1** *syn* see LITTLE 3
rel slight; negligible
idiom no great shakes
con considerable
ant momentous, weighty
2 *syn* see PETTY 2
rel captious, fribbling, frivolous; shallow, superficial

triviality *n syn* see TRIVIA
rel shallowness, superficiality, unimportance
con basic(s), essential(s), fundamental(s)

‖**trod** *n syn* see TRAIL

troika *n* **1** *syn* see TRIUMVIRATE 1
2 *syn* see TRIAD

trollop *n syn* see WANTON
idiom (a) fast number

trollop *vb syn* see SLOUCH

tromp *vb* **1** *syn* see TRAMP 1
2 *syn* see HIKE 2
rel slog, trudge
3 *syn* see TRAMPLE 2
4 *syn* see BEAT 1

troop *n* **1** *syn* see COMPANY 4
rel assemblage, assembly, collection, gathering; army, host, legion, multitude
2 troops *pl* members of a nation's military units <Marines, GI's, and Seabees were among the *troops* sent to war>
syn armed forces, forces, military, servicemen
rel combatants; soldiers, troopers
idiom fighting men

troop *vb syn* see WALK 1

trophy *n syn* see REMEMBRANCE 3

tropic *adj syn* see TROPICAL
rel baking, broiling, scorching, sweltering
con arctic

tropical *adj* of, relating to, or occurring in the tropics <*tropical* fruits>
syn tropic
rel equatorial, semitropical, subtropical; warm; hot, sultry, torrid
con temperate

tropical cyclone *n syn* see HURRICANE

tropical storm *n syn* see HURRICANE

trot *n* **1** *syn* see HAG 2
2 *syn* see PONY
‖**3 trots** *pl syn* see DIARRHEA

troth *n syn* see ENGAGEMENT 2

trot out *vb syn* see SHOW 4

troubadour *n syn* see BARD 1
rel balladist; rhymer, rhymester

trouble *vb* **1** to cause to be uneasy or upset <sorrows that *trouble* the strongest of men>
syn ail, cark, distress, upset, worry
rel agitate, concern, discompose, disquiet, disturb, perturb, rowel, ‖worrit; annoy, bother, fret, irk, vex; ‖destroy, haunt
2 *syn* see TRY 2
rel upset, worry; discompose, disconcert, disturb; harry, irritate; afflict, torment
3 *syn* see INCONVENIENCE
rel annoy, pester, plague, worry; impose (on *or* upon), intrude

trouble *n* **1** *syn* see TRIAL 2
2 *syn* see EFFORT 1
rel ado, bustle, flurry, fuss, pother; bother, inconvenience; difficulty, hardship, rigor; strain, stress
3 a condition of annoyance, disturbance, or distress <got him into *trouble* by repeating gossip>
syn Dutch, hot water
rel bind, difficulty, predicament

troubled *adj syn* see DISTRAUGHT

troublemaker *n* a person who consciously or unconsciously causes trouble <a *troublemaker* who set father against daughter>
syn bad actor, mischief-maker
rel agitator, inciter, inflamer, instigator

troublesome *adj* giving trouble or anxiety <a *troublesome* infection>
syn mean, pesky, troublous, ugly, vexatious, wicked
rel annoying, bothersome, vexing; alarming, disquieting, disturbing, upsetting; infestive; painful
con untroublesome
ant innocuous

troublesomeness *n syn* see INCONVENIENCE
rel difficulty; irritation, vexation

troublous *adj syn* see TROUBLESOME
rel troubling

trounce *vb syn* see WHIP 2

---

syn synonym(s)   *rel* related word(s)
ant antonym(s)   *con* contrasted word(s)
idiom idiomatic equivalent(s)
‖ use limited; if in doubt, see a dictionary

idiom walk all over

trouncing *n syn* see DEFEAT 1

troupe *n syn* see COMPANY 4

trouper *n syn* see ACTOR 1
rel entertainer; artiste

trove *n syn* see ACCUMULATION

truce *n* a suspension of or an agreement for suspending hostilities <the high command ordered a *truce* for the holidays>
syn armistice, cease-fire
rel break, ‖breather, letup, lull, pause, respite; de-escalation, ‖wind-down; accord, reconciliation; peace

truck *vb* **1** *syn* see TRADE 1
rel handle; peddle, retail
2 *syn* see TRAFFIC 2
idiom have truck with

truck *n syn* see COMMERCE 2

truckle *vb syn* see FAWN
rel knuckle down, knuckle under, succumb; follow, tag, tail, trail
idiom kiss (*or* lick) one's boots, lick the feet of, make a doormat of oneself

truckler *n syn* see SYCOPHANT

truckling *adj syn* see FAWNING

truculent *adj* **1** *syn* see FIERCE 1
rel browbeating, bullying, cowing, intimidating; frightening, terrifying, terrorizing
2 *syn* see ABUSIVE
rel caustic, mordacious, mordant, scathing, sharp, trenchant; harsh, rough, severe; vitriolic
3 *syn* see BELLIGERENT

trudge *vb syn* see PLOD 1

true *adj* **1** *syn* see FAITHFUL 1
rel sincere, unfeigned, whole-hearted, whole-souled
ant false, fickle
2 *syn* see UPRIGHT 2
rel creditable, estimable, worthy; high-principled, right-minded, truehearted
3 conformable to fact or to a standard, rule, or model <gave a *true* account of the accident>
syn faithful, just, right, strict, undistorted, veracious, veridical
rel careful, conscientious, meticulous, punctilious, scrupulous; finicky, fussy, overnice; accurate, precise; absolute, mathematical
idiom true to the letter
con imprecise, inaccurate, incorrect, inexact; erroneous, false
ant untrue
4 *syn* see GENUINE 3
con deceitful
5 *syn* see AUTHENTIC 2
rel genuine, kosher; sincere, unfaked, unfeigned
con artificial, fake, faked, feigned; insincere
ant false
6 *syn* see REAL 3
rel natural, normal, regular, typical
ant false
7 being such as it should be <meanings presented in their *true* relationship>
syn appropriate, desired, fitting, proper
rel acceptable; applicable, befitting, likely, suitable

con inappropriate, unfitting
8 being such by right <the *true* heir>
syn legitimate, rightful
rel lawful, legal, proper
con illegitimate, spurious, supposititious
ant false
9 that can be relied on <polls can provide a *true* projection of public sentiment>
syn authoritative, dependable, trustable, trustworthy
rel meaningful, significant; expressive, indicative, suggestive
con independable, undependable, untrustworthy; doubtful, questionable

truelove *n* **1** *syn* see GIRL FRIEND 2
2 *syn* see BOYFRIEND 2
idiom one and only

true-tongued *adj syn* see TRUTHFUL

truism *n* **1** *syn* see VERACITY 2
2 *syn* see MAXIM
3 *syn* see COMMONPLACE

trull *n syn* see WANTON

truly *adv* **1** *syn* see VERY 2
rel absolutely, positively
2 *syn* see EVEN 3
rel confidently, really
3 *syn* see WELL 7
rel probably; surely

trump *n syn* see TRUMP CARD

trump *vb syn* see SURPASS 1

trump card *n* something decisive or telling often held in reserve <kept a political *trump card* up her sleeve till election eve>
syn clincher, trump
rel ace; coup, coup de grace, coup de main
idiom ace in the hole

trumpery *n syn* see NONSENSE 2

trumpery *adj syn* see CHEAP 2

trumpet *vb syn* see TOUT

truncate *vb syn* see TOP 1
rel abbreviate, abridge; cut off, lop; shear

truncheon *n syn* see CUDGEL

trust *n* **1** complete assurance and certitude regarding the character, ability, strength, or truth of someone or something <they continue to have *trust* in his judgment>
syn confidence, dependence, faith, hope, reliance, stock
rel assurance, certainty, certitude, conviction; belief, credence, credit; positiveness, sureness; entrustment; overconfidence, oversureness
con doubt, dubiety, dubiosity, skepticism, suspicion, uncertainty
ant mistrust
2 *syn* see SYNDICATE
3 *syn* see CUSTODY

trust *vb syn* see ENTRUST 1
rel commit, consign, hand over

trust (in *or* to) *vb syn* see RELY (on *or* upon)
rel assume, imagine, presume
idiom have no reservations

trustable *adj syn* see TRUE 9
ant trustless

trustless *adj syn* see UNRELIABLE 1

rel unworthy; unfaithful; suspect, suspicious; dishonest; deceitful; treacherous
ant trustable, trustworthy

trustworthy *adj* **1 syn** see RELIABLE 1
rel truthful, veracious; honest, scrupulous, upright
con deceitful; dishonest
ant untrustworthy
2 syn see TRUE 9
rel accurate, exact; valid; realistic
con inaccurate, inexact; invalid; unrealistic; suspect
ant untrustworthy
3 syn see AUTHENTIC 1

trusty *adj* **1 syn** see RELIABLE 1
rel predictable, stable; firm, sound; responsible, ‖straight
con capricious
ant untrusty
2 syn see AUTHENTIC 1
ant untrusty

truth *n* **1 syn** see VERACITY 1
rel precision, rightness, trueness; authenticity, genuineness, veritableness; candor
idiom unvarnished truth (*or* truthfulness)
con equivocation, evasion, hedging; deception, deceptiveness, falseness
ant falsity, untruth
2 syn see VERACITY 2
rel reality
idiom (the) gospel truth, (the) truth of the matter
ant lie, untruth

truthful *adj* observant of or telling the truth <a *truthful* witness>
syn true-tongued, truth-speaking, truth-telling, veracious, veridical
rel candid, frank, honest, sincere; accurate, factual; real, realistic
con false, insincere, truthless, uncandid; inaccurate; unrealistic
ant untruthful

truthfulness *n* **syn** see VERACITY 1
ant untruthfulness

truthlessness *n* **syn** see MENDACITY

truth–speaking *adj* **syn** see TRUTHFUL

truth–telling *adj* **syn** see TRUTHFUL

try *vb* **1** to subject to testing <*try* the door to be sure it's locked>
syn check, examine, prove, test
rel inspect, scrutinize; appraise, judge, weigh
idiom make trial of, put to proof, put to the test
2 to subject to stress <the fine print *tried* her eyes>
syn distress, harass, irk, pain, strain, stress, trouble
rel annoy, bother, vex
3 syn see AFFLICT
4 syn see PROVE 1
5 to make an effort to do or accomplish something <the baby is *trying* to walk>
syn assay, attempt, endeavor, essay, offer, seek, strive, struggle, undertake
rel aim, aspire, hope, strike

idiom do one's best (*or* utmost) to, have a go at
try (out) *vb* **syn** see EXPERIMENT
rel examine, inspect, scrutinize; demonstrate, prove
idiom cut and try, put to trial, try for size

try *n* **1 syn** see ATTEMPT
2 syn see FLING 1
rel dab, jab

trying *adj* **1 syn** see TIGHT 4
rel annoying, bothersome, irksome, irritating, troublesome, vexing; strenuous; sticky, tricky
2 syn see ONEROUS

try on *vb* **syn** see EXPERIMENT

tryst *n* **syn** see ENGAGEMENT 3

‖**tub** *n* **syn** see FATTY

tub *vb* **syn** see BATHE 1

tubby *adj* **syn** see ROTUND 2
idiom plump as a dumpling (*or* partridge)

tube *n* **syn** see TELEVISION

tuberculosis *n* a communicable bacterial disease typically marked by wasting, fever, and formation of cheesy tubercles often in the lungs <Victorian heroines fading away with *tuberculosis*>
syn consumption, phthisis, TB, white plague

tuck (in) *vb* **syn** see BED
rel snug (down *or* up), snuggle

‖**tuck** *n* **syn** see FOOD 1

tuck *n* **syn** see ENERGY 2

‖**tucked up** *adj* **syn** see CRAMPED

tucker *vb* **syn** see EXHAUST 4
rel gruel; wilt; drop
idiom take the tuck out of

tug *vb* **1 syn** see CONTEND 1
2 syn see LABOR 1
3 syn see PULL 2

tug–of–war *n* **syn** see CONTEST 1

tuition *n* **syn** see EDUCATION 1

tumble *vb* **1 syn** see FALL 2
rel trip; come (down), descend
2 syn see PLUMMET
rel depreciate; sag, slump
idiom take a downward spiral, take a nosedive
3 syn see HAPPEN 2
4 syn see DISCOVER 3
5 syn see OVERTHROW 2
6 syn see FELL 1
7 syn see CONFUSE 5
8 syn see DISORDER 1

tumble (to) *vb* **syn** see APPREHEND 1

tumble *n* **syn** see CLUTTER 2

tumescent *adj* **1 syn** see INFLATED
rel bloated; bulging
2 syn see RHETORICAL

tumid *adj* **1 syn** see INFLATED
rel dilated, distended, expanded, swollen
2 syn see RHETORICAL

tummy *n* **syn** see ABDOMEN

tumulary *adj* **syn** see SEPULCHRAL 1

tumult *n* **1 syn** see COMMOTION 1

---

syn synonym(s)   **rel** related word(s)
ant antonym(s)   **con** contrasted word(s)
idiom idiomatic equivalent(s)
‖ use limited; if in doubt, see a dictionary

rel disturbance, turmoil, uproar
2 *syn* see COMMOTION 4
rel babel, din, hullabaloo, pandemonium, racket
con calm, hush, lull, quietude
3 *syn* see COMMOTION 2
rel seething; disorder, unsettlement; ferment, maelstrom, paroxysm
4 *syn* see DIN
rel noise; ‖corroboree
idiom ‖all hell broken loose
tumultuous *adj syn* see TURBULENT 1
tumultuously *adv syn* see HARD 2
tun *n syn* see CASK
rel vat
tune *n* **1** *syn* see MELODY
rel carol; composition, number, piece
2 *syn* see HARMONY 1
3 *syn* see HARMONY 2
4 *syn* see ORDER 4
tune *vb* **1** *syn* see SING 1
2 *syn* see HARMONIZE 3
rel fix, regulate
3 to adjust with respect to resonance <*tune* a TV set to a local station>
syn dial
tune (up) *vb syn* see ADJUST 2
tuned *adj syn* see MELODIOUS 2
tuneful *adj* **1** *syn* see MELODIOUS 2
2 *syn* see MELODIOUS 1
ant tuneless
tunk *vb syn* see TAP 1
turbid *adj* clouded with or as if with roiled sediment <a *turbid* stream>
syn muddy, riley, roily
rel dark, dense, obscure; mucky, thick; clouded, cloudy, murky, opaque, smoky; dull
con translucent; lucid, pellucid, transparent; crystal, crystalline; clean, pure, undefiled
ant clear, limpid
turbulence *n syn* see COMMOTION 2
rel babel, din, pandemonium, uproar; unruliness; fight, fracas
con calmness, composure, placidity, quiet
turbulent *adj* **1** given to insubordination and disorder <a *turbulent* and irresponsible group>
syn boisterous, disorderly, rambunctious, raucous, rowdy, rowdydowdy, rowdyish, rumbustious, termagant, tumultuous, unruly; *compare* UNRULY 1
rel mutinous; fast, roisterous, uncontrollable, uninhibited, wild; clamorous, loudmouthed; brawling, quarrelsome, rough, roughhouse; hell≠for-leather, rip-roaring, tempestuous
con calm, placid, quiet, tranquil; controlled, orderly, peaceful, restrained
2 *syn* see WILD 6
rel agitated, convulsed, moiling, stirred up; boiling, roily, ruffled, swirling; howling, riotous, roaring; tempest-tossed
turbulently *adv syn* see HARD 2
rel blusteringly
turf *n syn* see TERRAIN 2
rel area, region, sphere

turgid *adj* **1** *syn* see INFLATED
rel swelling, turgescent
2 *syn* see RHETORICAL
turmoil *n* **1** *syn* see COMMOTION 2
rel jitteriness, nervousness, restlessness, unease, uneasiness; disorder, disruption; moil; riot, strife, uproar
2 *syn* see UNREST
rel distress; anxiety, anxiousness
ant tranquillity
3 *syn* see COMMOTION 4
turn *vb* **1** to move or cause to move in a curved or circular path on or as if on an axis <*turned* the wheel sharply to avoid a collision>
syn circle, circumduct, gyrate, gyre, revolve, roll, rotate; *compare* SPIN 1
rel orbit; pirouette, spin, twirl, whirl; twist, weave, wind; circulate, eddy, swirl; oscillate, sway, swing, vibrate
2 *syn* see SPRAIN
3 *syn* see REVERSE 1
4 *syn* see PLOW
5 *syn* see UPSET 5
rel discompose, undo; unbalance
6 to change or cause to change course or direction <*turned* his car down a side road>
syn avert, deflect, divert, pivot, sheer, swing, veer, volte-face, wheel, whip, whirl; *compare* SHUNT 1
rel depart, detract, deviate, digress, diverge; move, shift; switch, swivel, twist, zigzag; call off, double (back), reverse; shunt, sidetrack; bend, curve, sway; detour, rechannel, turn away
7 *syn* see DIRECT 2
con call off, detract (from), distract, divert (from), draw (away)
8 *syn* see ADDRESS 3
rel employ, use; plunge (into), undertake
idiom turn one's hand (*or* energies) to
con avoid, dodge, shy (away)
9 *syn* see CURDLE
10 *syn* see DECAY
11 *syn* see CHANGE 1
12 *syn* see TRANSLATE 1
13 *syn* see DULL 3
14 *syn* see SPIN 2
15 *syn* see DEFECT
16 *syn* see RESORT 2
17 *syn* see BECOME 1
rel change (into), pass (into)
turn (on *or* upon) *vb syn* see DEPEND (on *or* upon) 1
turn *n* **1** *syn* see REVOLUTION 1
2 an often sudden change in course or trend <his health took a *turn* for the better>
syn bend, deflection, deviation, double, shift, tack, yaw
rel course, drift, trend
3 *syn* see REVERSAL 1
4 a point at which a change of course takes place <hidden by a *turn* in the road>
syn angle, bend, bow, flection, flexure, turning
rel curve, twist; corner
5 *syn* see WALK 1
6 *syn* see DRIVE 1

7 *syn* see SPELL 1
8 *syn* see CHANGE 1
9 *syn* see GIFT 2
rel bias, disposition, predisposition
10 an unusual, unexpected, or special interpretation or construction <gave a new *turn* to the old joke>
syn twist
rel construction, interpretation; device, gimmick, trick
11 *syn* see ATTACK 3
turnabout *n* **1** *syn* see REVERSAL 1
2 *syn* see RENEGADE
rel backslider, coward, quitter, turnback
turn back *vb syn* see RETURN 1
turncoat *n syn* see RENEGADE
rel deserter, straggler; betrayer, quisler, quisling, traitor; spy
turn down *vb syn* see DECLINE 4
turned on *adj syn* see DRUGGED
turn in *vb syn* see RETIRE 4
ant turn out
turning *n* **1** *syn* see TURN 4
2 *syn* see DEVIATION 1
rel detour
3 *syn* see REVERSAL 1
turning point *n syn* see JUNCTURE 2
rel climax, culmination, peak
idiom moment of truth
turnip *n syn* see DUNCE
turn off *vb* **1** *syn* see DISMISS 3
2 *syn* see HANG 2
turn out *vb* **1** *syn* see FURNISH 1
rel deck, dress (out)
2 *syn* see BEAR 9
3 *syn* see ROLL OUT
turnout *n* **1** *syn* see COSTUME
2 *syn* see OUTPUT
turn over *vb* **1** *syn* see OVERTURN 1
2 *syn* see PLOW
3 *syn* see PONDER 2
idiom turn over in one's mind
4 *syn* see GIVE 3
rel assign, confer, consign, convey, delegate, relegate; give up, relinquish, ‖turn up
idiom come across with, put into the hands of
con get back, reclaim, recover, regain, retrieve, take back
5 *syn* see COMMIT 1
turnover *n syn* see SHAKE-UP
turn up *vb* **1** *syn* see FIND 1
rel see; uncover, unearth; track (down)
idiom come across
‖**2** *syn* see RELINQUISH
3 to arrive when or where expected <*turned up* for dinner promptly at seven o'clock>
syn show, show up
rel appear, arrive, come, materialize; blow in, pop (in), punch in, roll (in), weigh in
idiom make one's appearance, put in an appearance
4 *syn* see COME 1
turtledove *n syn* see SWEETHEART 1
tussle *vb syn* see WRESTLE

rel scrap, skirmish, spar; hassle
idiom get into a tussle
tutelage *n syn* see EDUCATION 1
TV *n syn* see TELEVISION
twaddle *n syn* see NONSENSE 2
rel gabble; wish-wash
twaddle *vb* **1** *syn* see BABBLE 2
2 *syn* see CHAT 1
twang *n syn* see HINT 2
tweedle *vb syn* see CHIRP
tween *prep syn* see BETWEEN 2
tweet *vb syn* see CHIRP
twerp *n* a usually young or insignificant upstart who meddles beyond his competence or concern <ignored the protests of that insolent *twerp*>
syn pup, puppy, sprat, squirt, ‖squit
rel upstart; ‖squib; fool, jerk, ‖twit; brat
idiom small-time big shot
twice–told *adj syn* see TRITE
twiddle *vb syn* see FIDDLE 1
rel finger, manipulate, palpate; monkey (with), toy (with)
idiom twiddle around with
twiddle *vb syn* see CHAT 1
twig *vb* **1** *syn* see SEE 1
2 *syn* see APPREHEND 1
‖**twig** *n syn* see FASHION 3
twiggy *adj syn* see THIN 1
twilight *n* **1** *syn* see EVENING 1
rel afterglow, afterlight
2 *syn* see EVENING 2
rel decline; end
twin *adj* made up of two very closely matched or identical aspects, elements, individuals, or parts <the *twin* threats of inflation and recession>
syn double, dual, paired
rel bifold, binary, twofold; identical, matched, matching; like, similar
con independent, separate; dissimilar, unlike
twin *n syn* see MATE 5
twine *vb syn* see WIND 2
rel interweave; undulate; enmesh, entangle, tangle
twinge *n syn* see PAIN 1
twinkle *vb* **1** *syn* see BLINK 2
rel illuminate, light, light up; shine
2 *syn* see FLASH 1
3 *syn* see WINK
twinkle *n* **1** *syn* see INSTANT 1
2 *syn* see FLASH 1
twinkling *n syn* see INSTANT 1
idiom the twinkling of an eye
twirl *vb syn* see SPIN 2
twist *vb* **1** *syn* see SPRAIN
2 *syn* see MISREPRESENT
3 *syn* see WIND 2
ant untwist
twist *n syn* see TURN 10
twister *n syn* see TORNADO

syn synonym(s)   *rel* related word(s)
ant antonym(s)   *con* contrasted word(s)
idiom idiomatic equivalent(s)
‖ use limited; if in doubt, see a dictionary

twisting *adj syn* see CROOKED 1

twit *vb syn* see RIDICULE
  rel jive, josh, tease; chide, reproach, reprove; blame, censure, reprehend

twitch *vb syn* see JERK
  rel clutch, grasp, pluck, snatch; nip, pinch

twitter *vb* **1** *syn* see CHIRP
  2 *syn* see CHAT 1
  3 *syn* see SHAKE 1

twittery *adj syn* see NERVOUS
  rel flustered; twittering
  idiom all atwitter, all fluttery, all of a twitter

twitty *adj syn* see IRRITABLE

twixt *prep syn* see BETWEEN 2

twofold *adj* **1** having two parts, elements, or aspects <the problem is *twofold:* to find gasoline and to be able to pay for it>
  syn bifold, binary, double, double-barreled, dual, dualistic, duple, duplex
  rel dyadic; paired, twin
  con distinct, separate
  2 being twice as large, as great, or as many <a *twofold* increase in enrollment>
  syn double, double-barreled
  idiom twice over

two–handed *adj* **1** designed for or requiring the use of both hands <a *two-handed* sword>
  syn bimanual
  2 having or being efficient with two hands <*two=handed* tennis players are rare>
  syn ambidextrous, bimanual

twosome *n syn* see COUPLE

two–time *vb syn* see DECEIVE

two–wheeler *n syn* see BICYCLE

tycoon *n syn* see MAGNATE

tyke *n syn* see DOG 1

type *n* a number of individuals thought of as a group because of a common quality or qualities <political radicals of whatever *type*>
  syn breed, cast, character, class, cut, description, feather, ilk, kidney, kind, lot, mold, nature, order, persuasion, sort, species, stamp, stripe, variety, way
  rel blazon, brand, form; sample, specimen; category, group, rubric

typhoon *n syn* see HURRICANE

typic *adj syn* see GENERAL 1
  rel average, ordinary

typical *adj* **1** constituting or having the nature of a type <a *typical* instance of guilt by association>
  syn archetypal, classic, classical, exemplary, ideal, model, paradigmatic, prototypal, prototypical, quintessential, representative
  rel characteristic; emblematic, symbolic; absolute, consummate, perfect
  con uncharacteristic; unusual
  ant atypical, untypical
  2 *syn* see GENERAL 1
  rel old hat, unexceptional; collective, quintessential, representative; characteristic, specific
  idiom being the rule and not the exception
  con distinctive; exceptional, extraordinary, unusual; abnormal
  ant atypical, untypical

typification *n syn* see ALLEGORY 1

typify *vb* **1** *syn* see REPRESENT 2
  2 *syn* see EPITOMIZE 2
  rel model

tyrannical *adj syn* see ABSOLUTE 4
  rel brutal, harsh, oppressive; roughshod

tyrannize *vb* to exercise arbitrary power over often with unjust and oppressive severity <a country *tyrannized* by a dictator and his secret police>
  syn despotize
  rel dictate, dominate, domineer, overlord; crush, oppress, trample; shackle; terrorize

tyrannous *adj syn* see ABSOLUTE 4
  rel lordly; fascistic, totalitarian

tyranny *n* absolute government in which unlimited power is vested in a single usually severe and oppressive ruler <the *tyranny* of Hitler>
  syn autocracy, despotism, dictatorship, totalitarianism
  rel monocracy; absolutism, authoritarianism, fascism; domination, oppression, totality; terrorism
  idiom iron heel (*or* boot)
  con democracy; freedom; anarchy

tyrant *n* a ruler who exercises absolute power oppressively and brutally <Hitler and Stalin as twentieth-century *tyrants*>
  syn despot, dictator, duce, oppressor, strong man
  rel autocrat, totalitarian
  idiom man on horseback

tyro *n* **1** *syn* see AMATEUR 2
  2 *syn* see NOVICE

U

uberrima fides *n syn* see GOOD FAITH
ubiquitous *adj syn* see OMNIPRESENT
ugly *adj* **1** *syn* see GRAVE 3
2 unpleasing to the sight <an *ugly* decaying neighborhood>
syn hideous, ill-favored, ill-looking, unbeautiful, uncomely, unsightly
rel homely, plain; bizarre, grotesque; repelling, repugnant, repulsive; unattractive, uninviting, unpleasing, unprepossessing
idiom homely as a mud (*or* hedge) fence, not much to look at, short on looks
con comely, fair, good-looking, handsome, lovely, pretty; attractive, prepossessing
ant beautiful
3 *syn* see BASE 3
4 *syn* see TROUBLESOME
5 *syn* see SULLEN
ukase *n syn* see EDICT 1
ulterior *adj* lying behind what is manifest or avowed <an *ulterior* motive>
syn buried, concealed, covert, guarded, hidden, obscured, privy, shrouded
rel ambiguous, cryptic, dark, enigmatic, equivocal, obscure
idiom hidden under the rug, kept behind a screen, under cover, under wraps
con clear, open, overt, plain, straightforward; explicit, expressed
ultimate *adj* **1** *syn* see LAST
2 *syn* see SUPREME
3 being so fundamental as to stand at the extreme limit of the actually or conceivably knowable <*ultimate* realities>
syn absolute, categorical
rel empyreal, empyrean, sublime, transcendental; exalted, grand, lofty
ultimate *n syn* see APOTHEOSIS 1
ultimate *vb syn* see CLOSE 3
ultimately *adv syn* see YET 2
ultra *adj* **1** *syn* see EXTREME 3
2 *syn* see OUTLANDISH 3
ultraconservative *n syn* see REACTIONARY
ultrafashionable *adj syn* see STYLISH
ultraist *n syn* see RADICAL
ultraist *adj syn* see EXTREME 3
ultramarine *adj syn* see OVERSEAS
ululate *vb syn* see HOWL 1
rel bewail, lament
umbra *n* **1** *syn* see APPARITION
2 *syn* see SHADE 1
umbrage *n* **1** *syn* see SHADE 1
2 *syn* see FOLIAGE
3 *syn* see OFFENSE 2
rel annoyance, irking, vexation; exasperation, irritation, nettling, provoking; fury, ire, rage, wrath
umbrage *vb* **1** *syn* see SHADE

2 *syn* see ANGER 1
umbrageous *adj syn* see SHADY 1
umbrous *adj syn* see SHADY 1
umpire *n syn* see JUDGE 1
umpire *vb syn* see JUDGE 1
unabashed *adj syn* see SHAMELESS
ant abashed
unabbreviated *adj syn* see UNABRIDGED
ant abbreviated
unabridged *adj* not shortened by omission of parts (as words) <published an *unabridged* edition of Shakespeare's plays>
syn complete, unabbreviated, uncondensed, uncut, undocked, whole-length
rel entire, intact, whole
con condensed, cropped, curtailed, cut, incompleted, shortened, trimmed
ant abridged
unacceptable *adj syn* see OBJECTIONABLE
ant acceptable
unaccompanied *adj syn* see ALONE 1
ant accompanied, companioned
unaccomplished *adj syn* see AMATEURISH
ant accomplished, skilled
unaccountable *adj* **1** *syn* see INEXPLICABLE
ant accountable
2 *syn* see MYSTERIOUS
unaccustomed *adj syn* see UNFAMILIAR 1
ant accustomed, familiar
unacquaintance *n syn* see IGNORANCE 2
ant acquaintance
unacquainted *adj syn* see IGNORANT 2
ant acquainted
unacquaintedness *n syn* see IGNORANCE 2
ant acquaintance
unacquired *adj syn* see INNATE 1
ant acquired
unadorned *adj syn* see PLAIN 1
ant adorned
unadulterated *adj* **1** *syn* see PURE 2
2 *syn* see STRAIGHT 3
ant adulterated
unadvisable *adj syn* see INADVISABLE
ant advisable
unadvised *adj syn* see RASH 1
ant advised, thought-out
unaffable *adj syn* see UNDEMONSTRATIVE
ant affable
unaffected *adj syn* see NATURAL 5
ant affected, artificial
unafraid *adj syn* see BRAVE 1
rel composed, cool, imperturbable; assured, confident, sure

---

syn synonym(s)   *rel* related word(s)
ant antonym(s)   *con* contrasted word(s)
idiom idiomatic equivalent(s)
‖ use limited; if in doubt, see a dictionary

con apprehensive, fearful
  ant afraid
unaimed *adj syn* see RANDOM
unalert *adj syn* see INCAUTIOUS 1
  ant alert
unalike *adj syn* see DIFFERENT 1
  ant alike
unalloyed *adj syn* see PURE 2
unalluring *adj syn* see PLAIN 5
  ant alluring, attractive
unalterable *adj syn* see INFLEXIBLE 3
  ant alterable
unambiguous *adj* **1** *syn* see CLEAR 4
  ant ambiguous, obscure
  2 *syn* see EXPLICIT
  ant ambiguous
  3 *syn* see CLEAR 5
unanimated *adj syn* see DEAD 1
unanimous *adj* being of one mind <they were *unanimous* in their determination to win>
  syn consentaneous, consentient, solid
  rel agreed, agreeing, concordant, concurrent, harmonious
  idiom of one accord, of one (*or* the same) mind, with one voice
  con differing, disagreed, disagreeing, discordant, inharmonious
unanticipatedly *adv syn* see UNAWARES
unapparent *adj syn* see IMPERCEPTIBLE
  ant apparent, detectable
unappeasable *adj* **1** *syn* see INSATIABLE
  ant appeasable
  2 *syn* see GRIM 3
  ant appeasable, placable
unappetizing *adj syn* see UNPALATABLE 1
  ant appetizing
unappreciable *adj syn* see IMPERCEPTIBLE
  ant appreciable
unappreciated *adj syn* see THANKLESS 2
  ant appreciated
unappreciative *adj syn* see THANKLESS 1
  ant appreciative
unapproachable *adj* **1** *syn* see INACCESSIBLE
  ant approachable, attainable
  2 *syn* see UNSOCIABLE
  ant accessible, approachable
unapt *adj* **1** *syn* see IMPROPER 1
  2 *syn* see UNSKILLFUL 1
  ant apt
unarm *vb syn* see DISARM 2
unartful *adj syn* see NATURAL 5
  ant artful
unarticulate *adj syn* see DUMB 1
  ant articulate
unartificial *adj syn* see NATURAL 5
  ant affected, artificial
unasked *adj* **1** not asked or invited <annoyed by his *unasked* advice>
  syn unbidden, uninvited, unrequested, unsought
  rel arrogant, impudent, overbearing, presumptuous; spontaneous, voluntary; unacceptable, unwanted, unwelcome
  con desired, invited, sought, wanted; acceptable, welcome

  ant asked
  2 *syn* see SUPEREROGATORY
unassailable *adj syn* see INVINCIBLE 1
  rel stalwart, stout, strong, sturdy, tenacious, tough
  ant assailable
unassertive *adj syn* see SHY 1
  ant aggressive, assertive
unassorted *adj syn* see MISCELLANEOUS
unassuming *adj syn* see HUMBLE 1
  ant assuming, presumptuous
unassured *adj* **1** *syn* see UNSAFE
  2 *syn* see SHY 1
  ant assured
  3 *syn* see INSECURE 1
unattainable *adj* **1** *syn* see INACCESSIBLE
  ant attainable
  2 *syn* see IMPOSSIBLE 1
unattractive *adj syn* see PLAIN 5
  ant alluring, attractive
unauthentic *adj syn* see SPURIOUS 3
  ant authentic, genuine
unavailable *adj syn* see FUTILE
unavailing *adj syn* see FUTILE
unavoidable *adj syn* see INEVITABLE
  ant avoidable
unavoidably *adv syn* see WILLY-NILLY
unaware *adv syn* see UNAWARES
unaware *adj syn* see IGNORANT 2
  ant aware, conscious
unawaredly *adv syn* see UNAWARES
unawareness *n syn* see IGNORANCE 2
  ant awareness, consciousness
unawares *adv* without warning <caught *unawares* by company>
  syn aback, short, sudden, suddenly, unanticipatedly, unaware, unawaredly, unexpectedly
  rel unprepared, unready
  idiom like a bolt from the blue, off base, out of a clear sky, out of the blue
unbalance *vb syn* see MADDEN 1
unbalance *n syn* see INSANITY 1
  rel disorientation, instability
unbalanced *adj* **1** *syn* see LOPSIDED
  ant balanced
  2 *syn* see INSANE 1
unbearable *adj syn* see INSUFFERABLE
  ant bearable, supportable
unbearing *adj syn* see BARREN 2
unbeatable *adj syn* see INVINCIBLE 1
  ant beatable, defeatable
unbeauteous *adj syn* see PLAIN 5
  ant beauteous
unbeautified *adj syn* see PLAIN 1
  ant beautified, embellished
unbeautiful *adj* **1** *syn* see PLAIN 5
  ant beautiful
  2 *syn* see UGLY 2
  ant beautiful
unbecoming *adj* **1** *syn* see INDECOROUS
  rel awkward, clumsy, gauche, inept, maladroit
  ant becoming, seemly
  2 *syn* see IMPROPER 1
unbecomingness *n syn* see IMPROPRIETY 1

ant becomingness, seemliness

unbefitting *adj syn* see IMPROPER 1
ant apropos, befitting

unbegotten *adj syn* see SELF-EXISTENT

unbelief *n* the attitude or state of mind of one who does not believe <after so much deception, so many lies, she could offer nothing but *unbelief* to his words>
syn disbelief, incredulity, unbelievingness, unfaith
rel doubt, dubiety, dubiosity, skepticism, uncertainty; distrust, mistrust, suspicion; apprehension, misgiving, qualm
con assurance, certitude, security, trust; dependence, reliance, stock, store
ant belief

unbelievable *adj* 1 *syn* see INCREDIBLE 1
ant believable, credible
2 *syn* see IMPLAUSIBLE
ant believable, credible

unbelieve *vb syn* see DISBELIEVE
ant believe, credit

unbeliever *n syn* see SKEPTIC
ant believer

unbelieving *adj syn* see INCREDULOUS
ant believing

unbelievingness *n syn* see UNBELIEF

unbend *vb* 1 *syn* see RELAX 2
2 *syn* see REST 2

unbendable *adj syn* see INFLEXIBLE 2
ant bendable

unbending *adj* 1 *syn* see STIFF 1
ant bendable
2 *syn* see INFLEXIBLE 2
3 *syn* see UNSOCIABLE

unbiased *adj syn* see FAIR 4
rel aloof, uninterested
ant biased

unbidden *adj syn* see UNASKED

unbind *vb* 1 *syn* see LOOSE 3
ant bind
2 *syn* see FREE
ant bind

unblamable *adj syn* see GOOD 11
ant blamable, blameworthy

unblemished *adj* 1 *syn* see WHOLE 1
ant blemished, flawed
2 *syn* see CHASTE

unblenched *adj syn* see BRAVE 1

unblenching *adj syn* see BRAVE 1

unblock *vb syn* see OPEN 1
ant block

unblunted *adj syn* see SHARP 1
ant blunt, blunted

unblurred *adj syn* see CLEAR 4
ant blurred

unblushing *adj syn* see SHAMELESS

unbodied *adj syn* see IMMATERIAL 1
ant bodied, incarnate

unbookish *adj syn* see UNSCHOLARLY
ant bookish

unbosom *vb syn* see REVEAL 1

unbounded *adj syn* see LIMITLESS
ant bounded, limited

unbrace *vb syn* see WEAKEN 1
ant brace, reinforce

unbroken *adj syn* see WHOLE 1
ant broken

unbrookable *adj syn* see INSUFFERABLE

unbuild *vb syn* see DESTROY 1
ant build

unburden *vb syn* see RID
rel discharge, disencumber, unload
con encumber, lade, load, saddle, tax, weight
ant burden

unbury *vb syn* see EXHUME
ant bury

uncalled-for *adj* 1 *syn* see UNNECESSARY
ant required
2 *syn* see SUPEREROGATORY
3 *syn* see BASELESS
rel absurd, foolish, preposterous, silly; impertinent, intrusive, officious
ant well-founded
4 *syn* see RUDE 6

uncandid *adj syn* see DISINGENUOUS
ant candid

uncanny *adj* 1 *syn* see WEIRD 1
2 *syn* see SUPERNATURAL 2

uncared-for *adj syn* see NEGLECTED
ant cared-for

uncareful *adj syn* see IRRESPONSIBLE
ant careful

uncaring *adj syn* see CARELESS 1
ant careful

uncaused *adj syn* see SELF-EXISTENT

unceasing *adj syn* see CONTINUAL

uncelebrated *adj syn* see OBSCURE 5
ant celebrated, noted

uncelestial *adj syn* see EARTHLY 1
ant celestial

unceremonious *adj* 1 *syn* see INFORMAL 1
ant ceremonious
2 *syn* see SHORT 5

uncertain *adj* 1 not stable, consistent, or predictable <was in very *uncertain* health>
syn capricious, chancy, dicey, erratic, fluctuant, iffy, incalculable, unpredictable, whimsical; *compare* INCONSTANT 1
rel questionable, undependable, unsettled; fickle, inconstant, insecure, unstable, unsure; changeable, mutable, protean, variable; unexpectable, unforeseeable
idiom in a state of uncertainty, in suspense
2 *syn* see INCONSTANT 1
3 *syn* see MUTABLE 2
4 *syn* see DOUBTFUL 1
ant certain
5 *syn* see MOOT
ant certain
6 *syn* see OBSCURE 3
7 *syn* see VACILLATING 2
idiom at a loss

syn synonym(s)   *rel* related word(s)
ant antonym(s)   *con* contrasted word(s)
idiom idiomatic equivalent(s)
‖ use limited; if in doubt, see a dictionary

ant certain, set

uncertainty *n* a feeling of unsureness about someone or something <troubled by a growing *uncertainty* about the future>
syn concern, doubt, doubtfulness, dubiety, dubiosity, dubitancy, incertitude, mistrust, query, skepticism, suspicion, uncertitude, wonder
rel anxiety, bother, disquiet, trouble, worry; agitation, distress, perturbation, uneasiness; disfaith, distrust; hesitation, reserve, salt
con assurance, certitude, confidence, conviction; complacency, content, satisfaction
ant certainty

uncertitude *n syn* see UNCERTAINTY
ant certitude

unchain *vb syn* see FREE
ant chain

unchangeable *adj syn* see INFLEXIBLE 3
ant changeable

unchanging *adj* **1** *syn* see STEADY 2
2 *syn* see SAME 3
ant changeable, changing

uncharnel *vb syn* see EXHUME

unchaste *adj* **1** *syn* see IMPURE 1
ant chaste
2 *syn* see FAST 7
ant chaste

unchristian *adj syn* see OUTRAGEOUS 1
ant ‖Christian

uncivil *adj* **1** *syn* see BARBARIAN 1
2 *syn* see RUDE 6
rel coarse, crass, crude
con polished, smooth, urbane
ant civil

uncivilized *adj* **1** *syn* see BARBARIAN 1
ant civilized
2 *syn* see BOORISH
ant civilized
3 *syn* see OUTRAGEOUS 1

unclad *adj syn* see NUDE 2

unclean *adj* **1** *syn* see IMPURE 1
ant clean, pure
2 *syn* see DIRTY 1
ant clean, cleanly
3 *syn* see IMPURE 3
ant clean; purified

uncleanly *adj* **1** *syn* see IMPURE 1
ant cleanly
2 *syn* see DIRTY 1
ant clean, cleanly

unclear *adj* **1** *syn* see OBSCURE 3
ant clear
2 *syn* see FAINT 2
ant clear, distinct
3 *syn* see DOUBTFUL 1
ant clear

uncloak *vb syn* see EXPOSE 4
ant cloak

unclose *vb* **1** *syn* see OPEN 1
ant close
2 *syn* see REVEAL 1

unclosed *adj syn* see OPEN 1
ant closed

unclothe *vb* **1** *syn* see STRIP 1

ant clothe, dress
2 *syn* see OPEN 2

unclothed *adj syn* see NUDE 2
ant clothed, dressed

unclouded *adj syn* see FAIR 2
ant clouded, cloudy

uncluttered *adj syn* see NEAT 2
ant cluttered

uncolored *adj syn* see FAIR 4
ant colored, partial

uncombed *adj syn* see SLOVENLY 1

uncombine *vb syn* see SEPARATE 1
ant combine

un–come–at–able *adj syn* see INACCESSIBLE
ant come-at-able

uncomely *adj* **1** *syn* see IMPROPER 1
2 *syn* see PLAIN 5
ant comely
3 *syn* see UGLY 2
ant comely

uncomfortable *adj* causing or likely to cause discomfort <kept an *uncomfortable* chair for uninvited callers>
syn comfortless, discomforting, harsh, uncomforting, uncomfy
rel distressing, easeless, uneasy
con comforting, easy, soothing
ant comfortable

uncomforting *adj syn* see UNCOMFORTABLE
ant comforting

uncomfy *adj syn* see UNCOMFORTABLE
ant comfy

uncommon *adj* **1** *syn* see INFREQUENT
con commonplace, everyday, ordinary
ant common
2 *syn* see EXCEPTIONAL 1
ant common, commonplace

‖**uncommon** *adv syn* see EXTRA

uncommonly *adv* **1** *syn* see OCCASIONALLY
ant commonly
2 *syn* see EXTRA

uncommunicative *adj* **1** *syn* see SILENT 3
ant communicative
2 *syn* see UNSOCIABLE

uncompanionable *adj syn* see UNSOCIABLE
ant companionable

uncompassionate *adj syn* see UNFEELING 2
ant compassionate

uncompensated *adj syn* see UNPAID 1
ant compensated

uncomplainingness *n syn* see PATIENCE
ant complainingness, discontent

uncomplete *adj syn* see DEFICIENT 1
ant complete

uncompliant *adj syn* see INFLEXIBLE 2
ant compliant

uncomplimentary *adj syn* see DEROGATORY
ant complimentary

uncomprehensible *adj syn* see INCOMPREHENSIBLE 1
ant comprehensible, graspable

uncompromising *adj* **1** *syn* see INFLEXIBLE 2
2 *syn* see TOUGH 3

unconcealed *adj syn* see FRANK

unconceivable *adj syn* see IMPLAUSIBLE

ant conceivable

unconcern *n syn* see APATHY 2
ant concern

unconcerned *adj syn* see INDIFFERENT 2
rel collected, composed, cool, nonchalant
con anxious, careful, solicitous, worried
ant concerned

uncondensed *adj syn* see UNABRIDGED
ant condensed

unconfident *adj syn* see INSECURE 1
ant confident

unconfined *adj syn* see FREE 2
ant confined

uncongenial *adj* 1 *syn* see ANTIPATHETIC 2
rel displeasing, unattractive, unlikable, unpleasing
ant congenial
2 *syn* see INHARMONIOUS 2

unconnected *adj syn* see INCOHERENT 2
ant connected, ordered

unconquerable *adj* 1 *syn* see INVINCIBLE 1
rel insuperable, unsurmountable; proof, resistant, secure, tight
idiom more than a match for
con beatable, vincible; expugnable, pregnable, vulnerable; insecure, open, unprotected
ant conquerable
2 *syn* see INSUPERABLE
ant conquerable

unconscionable *adj* 1 *syn* see UNSCRUPULOUS
ant conscientious, conscionable
2 *syn* see EXCESSIVE 1
3 *syn* see UNREASONABLE 2
4 *syn* see OUTRAGEOUS 1

unconscious *adj syn* see INSENSIBLE 2
ant conscious

unconsequential *adj syn* see PETTY 2
ant consequential

unconsidered *adj* 1 *syn* see PETTY 2
2 *syn* see RANDOM
ant considered, planned
3 *syn* see RASH 1
ant considered

unconsolable *adj syn* see INCONSOLABLE
ant consolable

unconspicuous *adj syn* see INCONSPICUOUS
ant conspicuous

unconstrained *adj* 1 *syn* see EASYGOING 3
2 *syn* see DEMONSTRATIVE
ant constrained

unconstraint *n* freedom from constraint or pressure <had always been used to the *unconstraint* of a happy affectionate family>
syn abandon, ease, naturalness, spontaneity, unrestraint; *compare* ABANDON 2
rel impulsiveness, instinctiveness; ingenuousness, naiveté, simplicity, unsophistication
con pressure, strain, stress, tension; formality, rigidity; sophistication
ant constraint

uncontainable *adj syn* see IRREPRESSIBLE

uncontent *adj syn* see DISCONTENTED
ant content, contented

uncontented *adj syn* see DISCONTENTED

ant content, contented

uncontestable *adj syn* see POSITIVE 3
ant contestable

uncontinuous *adj syn* see INCOHERENT 2

uncontrite *adj syn* see REMORSELESS
ant contrite

uncontrollable *adj* 1 *syn* see UNRULY 1
ant controllable
2 *syn* see IRREPRESSIBLE
ant controllable

uncontrovertible *adj syn* see POSITIVE 3
ant controvertible, disputable

unconversant *adj syn* see INEXPERIENCED
ant conversant, versed

unconvincing *adj syn* see IMPLAUSIBLE
ant convincing

uncooked *adj syn* see RAW 1
ant cooked

‖**uncorporal** *adj syn* see IMMATERIAL 1

uncorrectable *adj syn* see HOPELESS 2
ant correctable

uncostly *adj syn* see CHEAP 1
ant costly

uncountable *adj* 1 *syn* see INNUMERABLE
ant countable
2 *syn* see INCALCULABLE 1

uncounted *adj syn* see INNUMERABLE

uncouple *vb syn* see DETACH
ant couple

uncourteous *adj syn* see RUDE 6
ant courteous

uncouth *adj* 1 *syn* see STRANGE 4
2 *syn* see DERELICT 1
3 *syn* see COARSE 3
ant couth
4 *syn* see RUDE 6

uncover *vb* 1 *syn* see REVEAL 1
2 *syn* see EXPOSE 1
3 *syn* see OPEN 2
ant cover

uncovered *adj syn* see OPEN 2

uncreate *vb syn* see ANNIHILATE 2

uncreated *adj syn* see SELF-EXISTENT
ant created

uncreative *adj syn* see UNORIGINAL
ant creative

uncritical *adj syn* see SUPERFICIAL 2
rel imprecise, inaccurate, inexact; careless, casual, offhand, perfunctory, slipshod
con accurate, exact, precise; careful; discerning, discriminating, penetrating
ant critical

uncrown *vb syn* see DEPOSE 1
ant coronate, crown

unction *n syn* see OINTMENT

unctious *adj syn* see FULSOME

unctuous *adj* 1 *syn* see FATTY 2
2 *syn* see FULSOME

uncultivated *adj* 1 *syn* see COARSE 3

---

syn synonym(s)   *rel* related word(s)
ant antonym(s)   *con* contrasted word(s)
idiom idiomatic equivalent(s)
‖ use limited; if in doubt, see a dictionary

ant cultivated
2 syn see BARBARIAN 1
ant cultivated
3 syn see WILD 1
ant cultivated
uncultured *adj* **1 syn** see BOORISH
ant cultured
2 syn see COARSE 3
uncurable *adj* **syn** see HOPELESS 2
ant curable
uncurbed *adj* **syn** see AUDACIOUS 4
ant curbed
uncurious *adj* **syn** see INDIFFERENT 2
ant curious
uncurtain *vb* **syn** see REVEAL 1
uncustomary *adj* **syn** see EXCEPTIONAL 1
ant customary
uncut *adj* **syn** see UNABRIDGED
ant cut
undamaged *adj* **syn** see WHOLE 1
ant damaged
undaring *adj* **syn** see TIMID 2
ant daring
undarkened *adj* **syn** see FAIR 2
undauntable *adj* **syn** see BRAVE 1
undaunted *adj* **syn** see BRAVE 1
ant daunted
undear *adj* **syn** see CHEAP 1
ant dear
undeceive *vb* **syn** see DISABUSE
ant deceive
undecided *adj* **1 syn** see PENDING
ant decided
2 syn see DOUBTFUL 1
undecipherable *adj* **syn** see ILLEGIBLE
ant decipherable
undecisive *adj* **syn** see VACILLATING 2
ant decisive
undeclared *adj* **syn** see TACIT 1
undecorated *adj* **syn** see PLAIN 1
ant decorated
undecorous *adj* **syn** see INDECOROUS
ant decorous
undefeatable *adj* **syn** see INVINCIBLE 1
ant defeatable
undefiled *adj* **syn** see CHASTE
undefined *adj* **syn** see FAINT 2
ant defined
undeflowered *adj* **syn** see VIRGIN 1
ant deflowered
undelude *vb* **syn** see DISABUSE
ant delude
undemonstrated *adj* **syn** see UNTRIED 1
ant demonstrated
undemonstrative *adj* not socially outgoing <a shy *undemonstrative* person yet capable of deep feeling>
syn aseptic, restrained, retiring, shrinking, unaffable, unexpansive, withdrawn; *compare* UNSOCIABLE
rel chill, cold, frigid, glacial, icy; emotionless, indifferent, unemotional, uninterested; aloof, distant, reserved, standoffish
con free and easy, hail-fellow-well-met, outgiving, outgoing, palsy-walsy; sociable

ant demonstrative
undeniable *adj* **1 syn** see POSITIVE 3
ant deniable
2 syn see REAL 3
undenominational *adj* **syn** see NONSECTARIAN
ant denominational
undependable *adj* **1 syn** see UNRELIABLE 1
ant dependable
2 syn see UNSAFE
ant dependable
3 syn see TRICK
ant dependable
under *adv* **syn** see BELOW 1
ant above, over
under *prep* **syn** see BELOW 1
ant over
under *adj* **1 syn** see INFERIOR 1
2 syn see SUBORDINATE
underage *n* **syn** see FAILURE 3
ant overage
underconsciousness *n* **syn** see SUBCONSCIOUS
undercover *adj* **syn** see SECRET 1
undercover man *n* **syn** see SPY
undercroft *n* **syn** see CRYPT
underdeveloped *adj* **syn** see BACKWARD 6
underdog *n* **syn** see VICTIM 2
ant overdog, top dog
underearth *adj* **syn** see SUBTERRANEAN
underfoot *adj* **1 syn** see SUBTERRANEAN
2 syn see DOWNTRODDEN
undergo *vb* **syn** see EXPERIENCE 1
rel abide, bear, endure, tolerate; bow, defer, submit, yield
underground *adj* **syn** see SUBTERRANEAN
underhand *adj* characterized by sly unobtrusive craft or deceit <ready to use the most *underhand* methods to gain his ends>
syn devious, duplicitous, guileful, indirect, shifty, sneaking, sneaky, underhanded; *compare* SECRET 1, SLY 2
rel deceitful, dishonest; crooked, oblique; crafty, cunning, insidious, sly, tricky, wily; furtive, hangdog
con candid, frank, open, plain; forthright, straightforward
ant aboveboard
underhanded *adj* **1 syn** see UNDERHAND
ant aboveboard
2 syn see SHORTHANDED
underivative *adj* **syn** see PRIMARY 5
ant derivative
underived *adj* **syn** see PRIMARY 5
ant derived
underlease *vb* **syn** see SUBLET
underlet *vb* **syn** see SUBLET
underline *vb* **syn** see EMPHASIZE
underline *n* **syn** see CAPTION
underling *n* **syn** see INFERIOR
underlying *adj* **1 syn** see FUNDAMENTAL 1
rel cardinal, essential, vital; critical, crucial; indispensable, necessary, needful
2 syn see ELEMENTAL 1
undermanned *adj* **syn** see SHORTHANDED
ant overmanned

undermine *vb* **1** *syn* see WEAKEN 1
  rel ruin, wreck; foil, frustrate, thwart
  idiom bore from within
  ant reinforce
  2 *syn* see SABOTAGE
undermining *n* *syn* see SABOTAGE
undermost *adj* *syn* see BOTTOMMOST
  ant uppermost
underneath *prep* *syn* see BELOW 1
underneath *adv* *syn* see BELOW 1
‖**underneath** *adj* *syn* see SECRET 1
underneath *n* *syn* see BOTTOM 1
underpinner *n* *syn* see SUPPORT 3
underpinning *n* **1** *syn* see BASIS 1
  2 *syn* see BASE 1
  3 *syn* see SUPPORT 3
underprivileged *adj* deficient in basic economic
  and social resources <the role of the school in
  bettering the lot of *underprivileged* children>
  syn depressed, deprived, disadvantaged
  rel handicapped; hapless, ill-fated, ill-starred,
  unfortunate, unlucky; impoverished, needy,
  poor
  idiom badly off, in adverse circumstances, out of
  luck
  con advantaged, fortunate, privileged; coddled,
  indulged, spoiled
underprize *vb* *syn* see DEPRECIATE 1
  ant overprize
underprop *vb* *syn* see SUPPORT 5
underpropping *n* *syn* see SUPPORT 3
underrate *vb* *syn* see DEPRECIATE 1
  ant overrate
underscore *vb* *syn* see EMPHASIZE
undersense *n* *syn* see SUBCONSCIOUS
undersexed *adj* *syn* see FRIGID 3
  ant oversexed
underside *n* *syn* see BOTTOM 1
understaffed *adj* *syn* see SHORTHANDED
  ant overstaffed
understand *vb* **1** *syn* see APPREHEND 1
  idiom get the drift
  ant misunderstand
  2 *syn* see KNOW 1
  idiom get the hang of
  3 to view as plausible or likely <I *understand* he
  is expected home soon>
  syn assume, believe, ‖conceit, conceive, expect,
  gather, imagine, ‖reckon, suppose, suspect, take,
  think, ‖wit; *compare* CONJECTURE
  rel conclude, deduce, infer; conjecture, guess,
  presume, surmise; fancy; consider
  con know; challenge, doubt, question
understandable *adj* of a kind to be readily understood <her style was smooth and easy, her language *understandable*>
  syn apprehensible, comprehendible, comprehensible, fathomable, graspable, intelligible,
  knowable, lucid, luminous; *compare* CLEAR 4, 5
  rel clear-cut, unambiguous, unblurred; plain,
  simple, straightforward; exoteric, lay, popular
  con mysterious, obscure, strange, vague; cryptic, esoteric, hidden
understanding *n* **1** *syn* see REASON 5

  rel discernment, discrimination, insight, penetration; awareness, intuition; apprehension,
  comprehension, grasp
  2 *syn* see AGREEMENT 2
  3 *syn* see MEANING 1
understood *adj* *syn* see TACIT 1
understrapper *n* *syn* see INFERIOR
understructure *n* *syn* see BASE 1
  ant superstructure
undersurface *n* *syn* see BOTTOM 1
undertake *vb* **1** *syn* see TRY 5
  rel begin, commence, start
  idiom put (*or* set) one's hand to
  2 *syn* see TAKE ON 3
  3 *syn* see PROMISE 1
  rel certify, warrant
  idiom stand back of (*or* behind)
undertaker *n* **1** *syn* see ENTREPRENEUR 1
  2 *syn* see MORTICIAN
undertaking *n* **1** *syn* see ATTEMPT
  2 *syn* see PROJECT 2
under–the–table *adj* *syn* see SECRET 1
  ant aboveboard
undertone *n* **1** *syn* see MURMUR 1
  2 *syn* see ASSOCIATION 4
undervalue *vb* *syn* see DEPRECIATE 1
  ant overvalue
underwater *adj* *syn* see SUBMARINE
underwit *n* *syn* see FOOL 4
underworld *n* *syn* see HELL
undescribable *adj* *syn* see UNUTTERABLE
  ant describable
undesignated *adj* *syn* see ANONYMOUS
undesigned *adj* *syn* see UNINTENTIONAL
  ant designed
undesigning *adj* *syn* see GENUINE 3
  ant designing
undesirable *adj* *syn* see OBJECTIONABLE
  ant desirable
undesired *adj* *syn* see UNWELCOME 1
  ant desired
undestroyable *adj* *syn* see INDESTRUCTIBLE
  ant destroyable, destructible
undeterminable *adj* *syn* see INDEFINITE 1
  ant determinable
undetermined *adj* **1** *syn* see PENDING
  ant determined
  2 *syn* see FAINT 2
undeveloped *adj* **1** *syn* see BACKWARD 6
  ant developed
  2 *syn* see PRIMITIVE 3
  ant advanced
undeviatingly *adv* *syn* see DIRECTLY 1
undevised *adj* *syn* see UNINTENTIONAL
  ant devised
undexterous *adj* *syn* see UNSKILLFUL 1
  ant dexterous
undifferenced *adj* *syn* see LIKE
undifferentiated *adj* *syn* see LIKE

---

syn synonym(s)   *rel* related word(s)
ant antonym(s)   *con* contrasted word(s)
idiom idiomatic equivalent(s)
‖ use limited; if in doubt, see a dictionary

ant differentiated

undiluted *adj* **1** *syn* see STRAIGHT 3
　ant diluted
　2 *syn* see PURE 2
undiplomatic *adj* *syn* see TACTLESS
　ant diplomatic
undiscernible *adj* *syn* see IMPERCEPTIBLE
　ant discernible
undisciplinable *adj* *syn* see UNRULY 1
undisciplined *adj* *syn* see UNRULY 1
　ant disciplined
undiscriminated *adj* *syn* see INDISCRIMINATE 1
　ant discriminate, discriminated
undiscriminating *adj* *syn* see INDISCRIMINATE 1
undisguised *adj* *syn* see FRANK
undisputable *adj* *syn* see POSITIVE 3
　ant controvertible, disputable
undissembled *adj* **1** *syn* see GENUINE 3
　ant dissembled, feigned
　2 *syn* see FRANK
undissembling *adj* *syn* see FRANK
　ant dissembling
undistinct *adj* *syn* see FAINT 2
　ant clear, distinct
undistinctive *adj* *syn* see FAIR 4
undistinguishing *adj* *syn* see INDISCRIMINATE 1
undistorted *adj* *syn* see TRUE 3
　ant distorted
undistracted *adj* *syn* see WHOLE 5
undivided *adj* *syn* see WHOLE 5
　ant divided
undo *vb* **1** *syn* see LOOSE 3
　2 *syn* see OPEN 1
　rel loose, untie
　3 *syn* see ABOLISH 1
　4 *syn* see DESTROY 1
　5 *syn* see OUTWIT
　idiom bring down (*or* low), bring to naught
　6 *syn* see SEDUCE 2
undocked *adj* *syn* see UNABRIDGED
　ant docked
undoing *n* *syn* see DOWNFALL 2
undomesticated *adj* *syn* see WILD 1
　ant domesticated
undoubtable *adj* *syn* see POSITIVE 3
　ant doubtable, questionable
undoubted *adj* *syn* see AUTHENTIC 2
　ant doubtful, questionable
undoubtedly *adv* *syn* see WELL 7
undoubtful *adj* *syn* see CONFIDENT 1
　ant doubtful
undress *vb* **1** *syn* see STRIP 1
　ant dress
　2 *syn* see EXPOSE 4
　ant dress up
undressed *adj* **1** *syn* see NUDE 2
　ant dressed
　2 *syn* see RUDE 1
　ant dressed, finished
undubitable *adj* *syn* see AUTHENTIC 2
　ant dubitable
undue *adj* **1** *syn* see IMPROPER 1
　2 *syn* see EXCESSIVE 1
　3 *syn* see UNREASONABLE 2

undulate *vb* *syn* see SLITHER 2
unduly *adv* *syn* see EVER 6
　ant duly
unduteous *adj* *syn* see IMPIOUS 2
　ant duteous
undutiful *adj* *syn* see IMPIOUS 2
　ant dutiful
undying *adj* *syn* see IMMORTAL 1
　rel continuing, persistent; interminable, unceasing; inextinguishable, unquenchable
　ant mortal
uneager *adj* *syn* see DISINCLINED
　ant eager
unearth *vb* *syn* see DISCOVER 3
　rel exhibit, expose, show; disclose, reveal; delve, dig
unearthing *n* *syn* see DISCOVERY
unearthly *adj* **1** *syn* see SUPERNATURAL 1
　2 *syn* see WEIRD 1
　3 *syn* see FOOLISH 2
unease *n* **1** *syn* see CARE 2
　2 *syn* see TENSION 2
　3 *syn* see EMBARRASSMENT
　ant ease, easiness
uneasiness *n* **1** *syn* see CARE 2
　2 *syn* see EMBARRASSMENT
　ant ease, easiness
uneasy *adj* **1** *syn* see TENSE 2
　rel anxious, careful, concerned, solicitous, worried; agitated, disquieted, disturbed, perturbed
　idiom on pins and needles
　ant easy
　2 *syn* see RESTLESS
　3 *syn* see DOUBTFUL 1
uneatable *adj* *syn* see INEDIBLE
　ant eatable
uneducated *adj* *syn* see IGNORANT 1
　ant educated, lettered
unelaborate *adj* *syn* see PLAIN 1
　ant elaborate
unembellished *adj* *syn* see PLAIN 1
　ant embellished
unembodied *adj* *syn* see IMMATERIAL 1
unembroidered *adj* *syn* see PLAIN 1
unemotional *adj* **1** *syn* see COLD 2
　rel dispassionate; unfeeling; impassive
　con affective, feeling; affectionate, demonstrative
　ant emotional
　2 *syn* see UNFEELING 2
unemphatic *adj* *syn* see INCONSPICUOUS
unemployed *adj* lacking a gainful occupation <the problems of *unemployed* workers>
　syn jobless, workless
　rel free, unengaged, unoccupied; underemployed; fired, laid off
　idiom at liberty, let go, on layoff, out of work
　ant employed
unending *adj* **1** *syn* see EVERLASTING 1
　2 *syn* see CONTINUAL
unendurable *adj* *syn* see INSUFFERABLE
　ant endurable
unenlarged *adj* *syn* see ILLIBERAL
unenlightened *adj* *syn* see BACKWARD 5

ant enlightened
unennobled *adj syn* see IGNOBLE 1
  ant ennobled, noble
unentangle *vb syn* see EXTRICATE 2
  ant entangle
unenthusiastic *adj syn* see TEPID 2
  ant enthusiastic
unequal *adj* **1** *syn* see DIFFERENT 1
  2 *syn* see LOPSIDED
unequalable *adj syn* see SUPREME
unequaled *adj syn* see ALONE 3
  ant equaled
unequipped *adj syn* see UNFIT 2
unequitable *adj syn* see INEQUITABLE
  ant equitable
unequivocal *adj* **1** *syn* see CLEAR 5
  ant equivocal
  2 *syn* see POSITIVE 1
  ant equivocal
  3 *syn* see POSITIVE 3
unequivocally *adv syn* see EASILY 2
uneradicable *adj syn* see INDELIBLE
  ant eradicable
unerasable *adj syn* see INDELIBLE
  ant erasable
unerring *adj syn* see INFALLIBLE 1
unescapable *adj syn* see INEVITABLE
  ant escapable
unessential *adj* **1** *syn* see UNNECESSARY
  ant essential
  2 *syn* see DISPENSABLE
  ant essential
unethical *adj syn* see CORRUPT 2
  ant ethical
unevadable *adj syn* see INEVITABLE
  ant evadable
uneven *adj* **1** *syn* see ROUGH 1
  ant even
  2 *syn* see LOPSIDED
  ant even
  3 *syn* see SPOTTY 1
  rel differing, disparate, unequal; discrepant, inconsistent
  con consistent, equal, regular
unevenness *n* **1** *syn* see DISPARITY
  2 *syn* see INEQUALITY 1
uneventful *adj syn* see COMMON 6
  ant eventful
unevolved *adj syn* see PRIMITIVE 3
  ant advanced, evolved
unexaminable *adj syn* see MYSTERIOUS
unexampled *adj syn* see ONLY 2
unexceptionable *adj syn* see DECENT 4
  ant exceptionable
unexceptional *adj* **1** *syn* see DECENT 4
  2 *syn* see COMMON 6
  ant exceptional
unexcessive *adj syn* see CONSERVATIVE 2
  ant excessive
unexpansive *adj syn* see UNDEMONSTRATIVE
  ant expansive
unexpectedly *adv syn* see UNAWARES
unexpedient *adj syn* see INADVISABLE
  ant expedient

unexperienced *adj syn* see INEXPERIENCED
  ant experienced
unexpert *adj syn* see INEFFICIENT 2
  ant expert
unexplainable *adj syn* see INEXPLICABLE
  ant explainable, explicable
unexplicit *adj syn* see OBSCURE 3
  ant explicit
unexpressed *adj* **1** *syn* see UNSPOKEN 1
  ant expressed
  2 *syn* see TACIT 1
  ant expressed
unexpressible *adj syn* see UNUTTERABLE
  ant expressible
unexpressive *adj syn* see EXPRESSIONLESS
  ant expressive
unextreme *adj syn* see CONSERVATIVE 2
unfabled *adj syn* see REAL 3
  ant fabled
unfacile *adj syn* see UNSKILLFUL 1
unfailing *adj* **1** *syn* see SAME 3
  2 *syn* see INFALLIBLE 2
  ant fallible
unfair *adj syn* see INEQUITABLE
  ant fair
unfairness *n syn* see INJUSTICE 1
  ant fairness
unfaith *n syn* see UNBELIEF
  ant faith
unfaithful *adj syn* see FAITHLESS
  ant faithful
unfaithfulness *n syn* see INFIDELITY
  ant faithfulness
unfaltering *adj syn* see SURE 2
unfamed *adj syn* see OBSCURE 5
  ant famed
unfamiliar *adj* **1** not well known <trying to find her way about the *unfamiliar* room in the dark>
  syn new, strange, unaccustomed
  rel exotic, foreign; curious, peculiar, remarkable; unknown
  con accustomed, commonplace, customary, ordinary, usual, wonted
  ant familiar
  2 *syn* see IGNORANT 2
  ant familiar
unfamiliarity *n syn* see IGNORANCE 2
unfantastic *adj syn* see REALISTIC
  ant fantastic
unfashioned *adj syn* see RUDE 1
unfasten *vb syn* see LOOSE 3
  ant fasten
unfastidious *adj syn* see SLOVENLY 1
  ant fastidious
unfathered *adj syn* see ILLEGITIMATE 1
unfathomable *adj* **1** *syn* see BOTTOMLESS 2
  ant fathomable
  2 *syn* see INCOMPREHENSIBLE 1
  ant fathomable

---

syn synonym(s)   *rel* related word(s)
ant antonym(s)   *con* contrasted word(s)
idiom idiomatic equivalent(s)
‖ use limited; if in doubt, see a dictionary

unfathomed *adj syn* see HUGE

unfavorable *adj* **1** *syn* see ADVERSE 2
  ant favorable
  2 *syn* see EVIL 5

unfavorably *adv syn* see AMISS 2

unfearful *adj syn* see BRAVE 1
  ant fearful

unfearing *adj syn* see BRAVE 1
  ant fearing

unfeasible *adj syn* see IMPOSSIBLE 1
  ant feasible, practicable

unfeeling *adj* **1** *syn* see INSENSATE 1
  ant feeling
  2 lacking in normal human sympathy <an *un-feeling* response to a plea for help>
  syn callous, cold-blooded, coldhearted, compassionless, hard-boiled, hardened, hardhearted, heartless, ironhearted, marblehearted, obdurate, stony, stonyhearted, uncompassionate, unemotional, unsympathetic; *compare* PITILESS
  rel brutal, cruel, indurated, merciless, roughhearted, ruthless, tough; exacting, severe; unamiable, uncordial, unkind; cantankerous, churlish, crotchety, curmudgeonly, surly
  idiom hard of heart
  con considerate, gentle, thoughtful; kind, merciful; compassionate, sympathetic, warmhearted
  ant feeling
  3 *syn* see NUMB 1

unfeigned *adj* **1** *syn* see SINCERE 1
  ant feigned
  2 *syn* see GENUINE 3
  ant dissembled, feigned

unfertile *adj syn* see BARREN 2
  ant fertile

unfinished *adj* **1** *syn* see RUDE 1
  ant dressed, finished
  2 *syn* see AMATEURISH
  ant finished

unfit *adj* **1** not adapted or appropriate to a particular end <land *unfit* for farming>
  syn ill-adapted, ill-suited, inappropriate, inapt, unfitted, unmeet, unsuitable, unsuited
  rel discordant, inharmonious; improper, infelicitous, unbecoming; incompatible, incongruous, uncongenial
  idiom out of drawing, out of one's element, out of place
  con adapted, appropriate, apt, suitable, suited; congruous, harmonious
  ant fit
  2 lacking essential qualifications <politicians *unfit* to govern>
  syn disqualified, incapable, incompetent, ineligible, unequipped, unfitted, unqualified
  rel awkward, blundering, bungling; butterfingered, heavy-handed, maladjusted, maladroit, unhandy; inefficient, inexpert, unproficient, unskillful
  con capable, competent, qualified; adroit, dexterous, handy; expert, skilled

unfitted *adj* **1** *syn* see UNFIT 1
  2 *syn* see UNFIT 2
  ant fitted

unfitting *adj syn* see IMPROPER 1
  ant fitting

unfix *vb* **1** *syn* see LOOSE 3
  ant fix
  2 *syn* see DETACH

unfixedness *n syn* see INSTABILITY

unflagging *adj syn* see INDEFATIGABLE
  rel constant, steady
  ant flagging

unflappable *adj syn* see COOL 2
  rel easy, relaxed

unflawed *adj syn* see PERFECT 2
  ant flawed

unfledged *adj syn* see YOUNG 1
  ant fledged

unfleshed *adj syn* see INEXPERIENCED

unfleshly *adj syn* see IMMATERIAL 1
  ant fleshly

unflexible *adj syn* see STIFF 1
  ant flexible

unflinching *adj syn* see GRIM 3

unfluctuating *adj syn* see STEADY 2
  ant fluctuant, fluctuating

unfold *vb* **1** *syn* see OPEN 4
  ant fold
  2 *syn* see SOLVE 2
  3 to disclose by degrees to the sight or understanding <shyly she *unfolded* her hopes for the future>
  syn develop, elaborate, evolve
  rel demonstrate, evidence, evince, manifest, show; disclose, display, exhibit, expose, reveal

unfolding *n syn* see DEVELOPMENT

unforbearing *adj syn* see INTOLERANT 1
  ant forbearing

unforced *adj syn* see VOLUNTARY
  ant forced

unforgivable *adj syn* see INEXCUSABLE
  ant forgivable

unformed *adj* **1** *syn* see FORMLESS
  rel unfinished
  ant formed
  2 *syn* see RUDE 1

unfortunate *adj* **1** *syn* see UNLUCKY
  rel infelicitous; deplorable, miserable, sad, wretched; malefic
  con auspicious, favorable, propitious
  ant fortunate
  2 *syn* see INFELICITOUS
  3 *syn* see DEPLORABLE

unfounded *adj syn* see BASELESS
  rel deceptive, misleading; dishonest, mendacious, untruthful
  ant well-founded

unframe *vb syn* see DESTROY 1

unfrank *adj syn* see DISINGENUOUS
  ant frank

unfrequent *adj syn* see INFREQUENT
  ant frequent

unfrequently *adv syn* see SELDOM
  ant frequently

unfriendly *adj syn* see HOSTILE 1
  ant friendly

unfruitful *adj syn* see STERILE 1

con fecund, fertile
   ant fruitful, prolific
unfunctional *adj syn* see IMPRACTICABLE 2
   ant functional
unfussy *adj syn* see EASYGOING 3
   ant fussy
ungainly *adj syn* see CLUMSY 1
   rel blundering, lubberly, maladroit
   con graceful, supple, willowy; gainly
ungarnished *adj syn* see PLAIN 1
   ant garnished
ungenerous *adj* **1** *syn* see PETTY 2
   ant generous
   2 *syn* see STINGY
   ant generous
ungenial *adj syn* see ANTIPATHETIC 2
   ant genial
ungenuine *adj syn* see SPURIOUS 3
   ant genuine
ungetatable *adj syn* see INACCESSIBLE
   ant getatable
ungifted *adj syn* see AMATEURISH
   ant gifted
ungiving *adj syn* see STINGY
ungodly *adj* **1** *syn* see IMPIOUS 1
   ant godly
   2 *syn* see INDECOROUS
   3 *syn* see OUTRAGEOUS 1
ungovernable *adj syn* see UNRULY 1
   ant governable
ungoverned *adj syn* see AUDACIOUS 4
ungracious *adj* **1** *syn* see RUDE 6
   ant gracious
   2 *syn* see SHORT 5
   ant gracious
ungraded *adj syn* see UNREFINED 3
ungraspable *adj syn* see INCOMPREHENSIBLE 1
   ant comprehensible, graspable
ungrateful *adj* **1** *syn* see THANKLESS 1
   ant grateful
   2 *syn* see THANKLESS 2
   3 *syn* see OFFENSIVE
ungratified *adj syn* see DISCONTENTED
   ant gratified
ungrounded *adj syn* see BASELESS
unguarded *adj syn* see INCAUTIOUS 1
   ant guarded
unguent *n syn* see OINTMENT
unguessed *adj syn* see MYSTERIOUS
unguilty *adj syn* see INNOCENT 2
   ant guilty
unhallowed *adj* **1** *syn* see IMPIOUS 1
   2 *syn* see FIENDISH
unhampered *adj syn* see AUDACIOUS 4
   ant hampered
unhandsome *adj* **1** *syn* see PLAIN 5
   ant handsome
   2 *syn* see RUDE 6
unhandy *adj* **1** *syn* see UNWIELDY
   2 *syn* see UNSKILLFUL 1
   ant handy
   3 *syn* see AWKWARD 2
   ant handy
unhappiness *n* **1** *syn* see MISERY 1

ant happiness
   2 *syn* see SADNESS
   ant happiness
unhappy *adj* **1** *syn* see UNLUCKY
   ant happy
   2 *syn* see INFELICITOUS
   ant happy
   3 *syn* see AWKWARD 2
   4 *syn* see SAD 1
   ant happy
   5 *syn* see BAD 8
   6 *syn* see GLOOMY 3
unharmed *adj syn* see SAFE 1
unharmonious *adj* **1** *syn* see DISSONANT 1
   ant harmonious
   2 *syn* see INHARMONIOUS 2
   ant harmonious
unhasty *adj syn* see SLOW 2
   ant hasty
unhealth *n syn* see SICKNESS 1
   ant health
unhealthful *adj syn* see UNWHOLESOME 1
   ant healthful
unhealthiness *n syn* see INFIRMITY 1
   ant healthiness
unhealthy *adj* **1** *syn* see UNWHOLESOME 1
   ant healthy
   2 *syn* see DANGEROUS 1
   3 *syn* see VICIOUS 2
unheard–of *adj syn* see OBSCURE 5
unheavy *adj syn* see LIGHT 1
   ant heavy
unheeding *adj* **1** *syn* see INATTENTIVE
   ant heedful, heeding
   2 *syn* see CARELESS 1
   ant heedful, heeding
unhewn *adj syn* see RUDE 1
unhinge *vb* **1** *syn* see UPSET 5
   2 *syn* see MADDEN 1
   3 *syn* see DISCOMPOSE 1
unholy *adj* **1** *syn* see IMPIOUS 1
   ant holy
   2 *syn* see BLAMEWORTHY
   3 *syn* see OUTRAGEOUS 1
unhonest *adj syn* see DISHONEST
   ant honest
unhorse *vb* **1** *syn* see THROW 2
   2 *syn* see OVERTHROW 2
unhurried *adj syn* see SLOW 2
   ant hurried
unhurt *adj syn* see WHOLE 1
unicity *n syn* see UNIQUENESS
unidealistic *adj syn* see REALISTIC
   ant idealistic
unification *n* a bringing together or being brought together into an integrated whole <*unification* of mass transit facilities is increasingly needed>

---

syn synonym(s)   *rel* related word(s)
ant antonym(s)   *con* contrasted word(s)
idiom idiomatic equivalent(s)
‖ use limited; if in doubt, see a dictionary

syn coadunation, coalition, combination, consolidation, melding, mergence, merger, merging, union; *compare* ALLIANCE 2
rel affiliation, connection, interlocking, joining, linkage; coupling, hookup
con dissociation, disunion, division, parting, partition, separation
ant disunification
uniform *adj* **1** *syn* see LIKE
ant various
2 *syn* see STEADY 2
rel compatible, consistent, consonant; ordered, orderly, regular
ant multiform
uniformly *adv syn* see EVENLY 3
ant variably
unify *vb* **1** to gather or combine parts or elements into a close mass or a coherent whole <minorities that are *unified* by persecution>
syn compact, concentrate, consolidate, integrate; *compare* UNITE 2
rel articulate, concatenate; order, organize, systematize; bind, tie
idiom make one
con divide, part, scatter; disorder, disorganize; disunite, divide, separate
ant break up, disunify
2 *syn* see HARMONIZE 4
ant disunify
unifying *adj syn* see INTEGRATIVE
ant disunifying
unilluminated *adj syn* see DARK 1
ant illuminated
unimaginable *adj* **1** *syn* see INCONCEIVABLE 1
ant imaginable
2 *syn* see EXCEPTIONAL 1
3 *syn* see INCREDIBLE 1
unimpaired *adj syn* see WHOLE 1
ant impaired
unimpassioned *adj* **1** *syn* see MATTER-OF-FACT 3
ant impassioned
2 *syn* see SOBER 3
rel impassive, phlegmatic, stoic, stolid; calm, placid, tranquil
con ardent, fervent, fervid, heated, keen
ant impassioned, passionate
unimpeachable *adj syn* see DECENT 4
unimportant *adj syn* see LITTLE 3
ant important
unimpressible *adj syn* see INSUSCEPTIBLE
ant impressible
unimpressionable *adj syn* see INSUSCEPTIBLE
ant impressionable
unindifferent *adj syn* see BIASED 2
ant indifferent
unindulgent *adj syn* see INTOLERANT 1
ant indulgent
uninflammable *adj syn* see NONCOMBUSTIBLE
ant flammable, inflammable
uninformed *adj syn* see IGNORANT 2
ant informed
uninhibited *adj syn* see AUDACIOUS 4
ant inhibited
uninhibitedness *n syn* see ABANDON 2

uninitiate *n syn* see AMATEUR 2
uninjured *adj syn* see WHOLE 1
ant injured
uninjurious *adj syn* see SAFE 3
uninspired *adj* **1** *syn* see UNORIGINAL
ant inspired
2 *syn* see PONDEROUS 2
ant inspired
uninstructed *adj* **1** *syn* see IGNORANT 2
2 *syn* see IGNORANT 1
unintelligent *adj syn* see SIMPLE 3
ant intelligent
unintelligible *adj* **1** *syn* see INCOMPREHENSIBLE 1
ant intelligible
2 *syn* see OBSCURE 3
ant intelligible
unintended *adj syn* see UNINTENTIONAL
ant intended
unintentional *adj* not the result of intent or design <her slight of the newcomer was quite *unintentional*>
syn inadvertent, undesigned, undevised, unintended, unplanned, unpremeditated, unpurposed, unthought; *compare* ACCIDENTAL, EXTEMPORANEOUS
rel causeless, chance, haphazard, purposeless, random; unanticipated, unexpected, unforeseen, unlooked-for; unthinking, unwitting
con deliberate, designed, devised, intended, planned, premeditated, purposed
ant intentional
uninterested *adj syn* see INDIFFERENT 2
ant interested
uninteresting *adj syn* see ARID 2
ant interesting
unintermitted *adj syn* see CONTINUAL
ant intermitted, intermittent
unintermittedly *adv syn* see TOGETHER 2
unintermittent *adj syn* see CONTINUAL
ant intermitted, intermittent
uninterrupted *adj* **1** *syn* see CONTINUAL
ant interrupted
2 *syn* see DIRECT 2
uninterruptedly *adv syn* see TOGETHER 2
ant interruptedly
uninventive *adj syn* see UNORIGINAL
ant inventive
uninvited *adj syn* see UNASKED
ant invited
union *n* **1** *syn* see UNIFICATION
ant disunion
2 *syn* see ASSOCIATION 2
3 *syn* see JOINT 1
4 *syn* see ALLIANCE 2
unique *adj* **1** *syn* see ONLY 2
2 *syn* see SINGLE 2
3 *syn* see ALONE 3
4 *syn* see EXCEPTIONAL 1
uniqueness *n* the quality or state of standing alone and without a peer <the time she rode in an old-time sleigh — never would she forget the *uniqueness* of that experience>
syn oneness, singleness, unicity, uniquity
rel curiousness, oddity, peculiarity, quaintness, singularity, strangeness; import, mark, moment,

note, significance; memorability, notability, remarkableness, unusualness
con commonness, commonplaceness, ordinariness, routineness; monotony, sameness, tediousness

uniquity *n syn* see UNIQUENESS

unite *vb* **1** *syn* see JOIN 1
rel amalgamate, blend, merge, mix
ant alienate; disunite, divide
2 to join forces especially in order to act more effectively <citizen groups *uniting* to further the fight against crime>
syn band, coadjute, combine, concur, conjoin, cooperate, league; *compare* UNIFY 1
rel affiliate, ally, associate, confederate; coalesce, commingle, fuse, mingle, weld
idiom draw together, hook up with, join forces (with), make common cause (with), throw in with
con break up, disband, separate, split (up)
ant disunite, part

unity *n* **1** the condition of being or consisting of one <*unity* — the idea conveyed by whatever we visualize as one thing>
syn individuality, oneness, singleness, singularity, singularness
rel identity, selfsameness, soleness, uniqueness, uniquity
ant multiplicity
2 *syn* see HARMONY 3
rel agreement, identity, oneness, union; solidarity; conformance, congruity
ant disunity

universal *adj* **1** *syn* see OMNIPRESENT
2 present or significant throughout the world <*universal* aspirations for a better world>
syn catholic, cosmic, cosmopolitan, ecumenical, global, planetary, worldwide
rel all-embracing, all-inclusive; broad, extensive, sweeping; all, entire, total, whole
con narrow, petty, provincial
ant parochial
3 *syn* see GENERAL 2
ant particular

universe *n* the totality of physical entities <theories of the expanding *universe*>
syn cosmos (*or* kosmos), creation, macrocosm, macrocosmos, megacosm, nature, world

univocal *adj syn* see CLEAR 5
ant ambiguous

unjust *adj syn* see INEQUITABLE
ant just

unjustifiable *adj* **1** *syn* see UNREASONABLE 2
ant justifiable
2 *syn* see INEXCUSABLE
ant justifiable

unjustness *n syn* see INJUSTICE 1
ant justice, justness

unkempt *adj syn* see SLOVENLY 1
ant kempt

unknow *vb syn* see FORGET 1

unknowable *adj* **1** *syn* see INCOMPREHENSIBLE 1
ant knowable
2 *syn* see INCONCEIVABLE 1

ant knowable
3 *syn* see MYSTERIOUS

unknowing *adj syn* see IGNORANT 2
ant knowing

unknowingness *n syn* see IGNORANCE 2
ant knowingness

unknown *adj syn* see OBSCURE 5
ant well-known

unlade *vb syn* see UNLOAD
ant lade, load

unlawful *adj* contrary to or prohibited by law <the spread of *unlawful* wiretapping>
syn criminal, illegal, illegitimate, illicit, lawless, wrongful
rel flagitious, iniquitous, nefarious; black-market, bootleg, under-the-counter; exceptionable, improper, intolerable, objectionable
idiom against the law
con condign, due, rightful; allowable, justifiable, permissible
ant lawful

unlawfulness *n syn* see ILLEGALITY
ant lawfulness

unlax *vb* **1** *syn* see RELAX 2
2 *syn* see REST 2

unlearned *adj syn* see UNSCHOLARLY
ant erudite, learned

unleash *vb syn* see TAKE OUT (on)

unless *conj syn* see EXCEPT 1

unlettered *adj syn* see IGNORANT 1
ant educated, lettered

unlevel *adj syn* see ROUGH 1
ant level

unlike *adj syn* see DIFFERENT 1
ant like

unlikely *adj syn* see IMPROBABLE 1
ant likely

unlikeness *n syn* see DISSIMILARITY
rel incompatibility, incongruousness, inconsistence
ant likeness

unlimited *adj* **1** *syn* see LIMITLESS
ant limited, measured
2 *syn* see TOTAL 5
ant limited

unload *vb* to remove cargo or the cargo of <*unload* cattle from a truck>
syn disburden, discharge, off-load, unlade, unship, unstow
rel disencumber, dump, jettison, lighten; stevedore; debark, disembark, land
idiom break bulk
ant lade, load

unloose *vb syn* see LOOSE 3

unloosen *vb syn* see LOOSE 3

unloyal *adj syn* see FAITHLESS
ant loyal

‖**unluck** *n syn* see MISFORTUNE
ant luck

---

syn synonym(s)   *rel* related word(s)
ant antonym(s)   *con* contrasted word(s)
idiom idiomatic equivalent(s)
‖ use limited; if in doubt, see a dictionary

unlucky *adj* **1** *syn* see OMINOUS
2 involving or suffering misfortune that results from chance <in spite of careful planning the expedition was *unlucky* from the start>
syn hapless, ill-fated, ill-starred, luckless, misfortunate, star-crossed, unfortunate, unhappy, untoward
rel calamitous, cataclysmic, catastrophic, dire, disastrous, tragical
idiom down on one's luck, out of luck
con fortunate, happy, providential; prosperous, successful; coming, made
ant lucky

unmake *vb* **1** *syn* see DESTROY 1
2 *syn* see DEPOSE 1
ant make

unman *vb* *syn* see UNNERVE
rel deplete, drain, exhaust, impoverish; abase, degrade; disqualify, paralyze, prostrate, unfit
idiom knock the bottom (*or* stuffing) out of
con brace, fortify
ant man

unmanageable *adj* *syn* see UNRULY 1
ant manageable

unmanly *adj* **1** *syn* see COWARDLY
ant manly
2 *syn* see EFFEMINATE
ant manly

unmannered *adj* **1** *syn* see RUDE 6
2 *syn* see FRANK

unmannerly *adj* *syn* see RUDE 6
ant mannerly

unmarred *adj* *syn* see WHOLE 1
ant marred

unmarried *adj* *syn* see SINGLE 1
ant married, wed

unmarry *vb* *syn* see DIVORCE 2

unmask *vb* *syn* see EXPOSE 4

unmatchable *adj* *syn* see SUPREME

unmatched *adj* **1** *syn* see ALONE 3
2 *syn* see ODD 1
ant matched

unmaterial *adj* *syn* see IMMATERIAL 1
ant material

unmeaning *adj* *syn* see SENSELESS 5
ant meaningful

unmeasurable *adj* **1** *syn* see INCALCULABLE 1
ant measurable
2 *syn* see EXCESSIVE 1

unmeasured *adj* **1** *syn* see INCALCULABLE 1
ant measurable
2 *syn* see LIMITLESS
ant limited, measured

unmeditated *adj* *syn* see SPONTANEOUS
ant meditated

unmeet *adj* *syn* see UNFIT 1
ant meet

unmeetness *n* *syn* see IMPROPRIETY 1

unmellowed *adj* *syn* see YOUNG 1
con developed, matured, ripened
ant mellow, mellowed

unmerciful *adj* *syn* see PITILESS
ant merciful

unmindful *adj* *syn* see FORGETFUL

con anxious, careful, concerned
ant mindful; solicitous

unmindfulness *n* *syn* see APATHY 2
ant mindfulness

unmistakable *adj* *syn* see CLEAR 5
ant mistakable

unmitigated *adj* **1** *syn* see PURE 2
2 *syn* see UTTER

unmixable *adj* *syn* see INCONSONANT 1

unmixed *adj* **1** *syn* see STRAIGHT 3
ant blended, mixed
2 *syn* see PURE 2

unmodern *adj* *syn* see OLD-FASHIONED
ant modern

unmodifiable *adj* *syn* see INFLEXIBLE 3
ant modifiable

unmovable *adj* **1** *syn* see IMMOVABLE 1
ant mobile, movable
2 *syn* see INFLEXIBLE 3

unmoving *adj* *syn* see STATIC
ant mobile

unmusical *adj* *syn* see DISSONANT 1
ant musical

unnamed *adj* *syn* see ANONYMOUS

unnatural *adj* **1** *syn* see IRREGULAR 1
2 *syn* see SUPERNATURAL 2
ant natural

unneat *adj* *syn* see SLOVENLY 1
ant neat

unnecessary *adj* not needed <*unnecessary* loss of life>
syn inessential, needless, uncalled-for, unessential, unneeded, unneedful, unrequired
rel excess, redundant, superfluous, surplus; lavish, prodigal, profuse; gratuitous, supererogatory
con essential, needed, required, vital; inevitable, unescapable
ant necessary; unavoidable

unneeded *adj* *syn* see UNNECESSARY
ant needed; unavoidable

unneedful *adj* *syn* see UNNECESSARY
ant needful; unavoidable

unnerve *vb* to deprive of strength, spirit, and vigor <a man so *unnerved* as to be bereft of sense and judgment>
syn castrate, emasculate, enervate, unman, unstring
rel enfeeble, sap, undermine, weaken; bewilder, confound, distract; agitate, perturb, upset
con brace (up), inspirit, invigorate, reinforce, strengthen; encourage, hearten, steel
ant nerve

unneutral *adj* *syn* see BIASED 2
ant neutral

unnoted *adj* *syn* see OBSCURE 5
rel unconsidered, unobserved, unremarked
ant noted

unnoteworthy *adj* *syn* see COMMON 6
ant noteworthy

unnoticeable *adj* *syn* see INCONSPICUOUS
ant noticeable

unnoticing *adj* *syn* see INATTENTIVE
ant noticing

unnumberable *adj syn* see INNUMERABLE
unnumbered *adj syn* see INNUMERABLE
  ant numbered
unobjectionable *adj syn* see DECENT 4
  ant objectionable
unobjective *adj syn* see SUBJECTIVE
  ant objective
unobservable *adj syn* see IMPERCEPTIBLE
unobservant *adj syn* see INATTENTIVE
  ant observant, observing
unobserving *adj syn* see INATTENTIVE
  ant observant, observing
unobstructed *adj syn* see OPEN 1
  con clogged, plugged
  ant obstructed
unobtainable *adj syn* see INACCESSIBLE
unobtrusive *adj syn* see QUIET 4
  ant obtrusive
unoffending *adj syn* see HARMLESS
  ant offending
unoffensive *adj syn* see HARMLESS
  ant offensive
unofficial *adj syn* see INFORMAL 1
unoften *adv syn* see SELDOM
  ant often
unordinary *adj syn* see EXCEPTIONAL 1
  ant ordinary
unorganized *adj syn* see INCOHERENT 2
  ant organized
unoriginal *adj* lacking or manifesting a lack of capacity for originality <a good man but with a
  mind stolid and *unoriginal*>
  syn noncreative, sterile, uncreative, uninspired,
  uninventive, unoriginative; *compare* ARID 2
  rel arid, barren, dry; dull, prosaic, staid, stodgy,
  stuffy, unfired
  con creative, inspired, inventive, originative;
  alert, aware, keen; constructive, productive
  ant original
unoriginated *adj syn* see SELF-EXISTENT
unoriginative *adj syn* see UNORIGINAL
  ant originative
unornamented *adj syn* see PLAIN 1
unorthodox *adj syn* see HERETICAL
  ant orthodox
unorthodoxy *n syn* see HERESY
  ant orthodoxy
unostentatious *adj syn* see PLAIN 1
  ant ostentatious
unpaid *adj* 1 serving without pay <a charity
  manned by *unpaid* assistants>
  syn uncompensated, unrecompensed, unremunerated
  rel freewill, gratuitous, voluntary, volunteer
  con compensated, recompensed, remunerated
  ant paid
  2 not cleared by payment <an *unpaid* bill>
  syn due, mature, outstanding, overdue, owing,
  payable, unsettled
  idiom in arrears
  con cleared, discharged, liquidated, settled
  ant paid
unpaired *adj syn* see ODD 1
  ant paired

unpalatable *adj* 1 lacking appeal to the sense of
  taste <threw together a greasy *unpalatable*
  meal>
  syn distasteful, flat, flavorless, ill-flavored, insipid, savorless, tasteless, unappetizing, unsavory
  rel loathsome, nauseous, sickening; thin, washy,
  watery, weak
  con appetizing, delectable, delicious, flavorsome, sapid, savory, tasty
  ant palatable
  2 *syn* see BITTER 2
unparagoned *adj syn* see ALONE 3
  ant paragoned
unparalleled *adj syn* see ALONE 3
  ant paralleled
unpardonable *adj syn* see INEXCUSABLE
  ant pardonable
unparented *adj syn* see ORPHAN
unpassioned *adj syn* see NEUTRAL
  ant impassioned, passionate
unpatient *adj syn* see IMPATIENT 1
  ant patient
unpeace *n syn* see DISCORD
  ant peace
unpeaceful *adj syn* see RESTLESS
  ant peaceful
unpedantic *adj syn* see LIVELY 1
  ant pedantic
unperceivable *adj syn* see IMPERCEPTIBLE
unperceiving *adj* 1 *syn* see IMPERCEPTIVE
  ant perceiving, perceptive, percipient
  2 *syn* see INATTENTIVE
unperceptive *adj syn* see IMPERCEPTIVE
  ant perceiving, perceptive, percipient
unperishable *adj syn* see INDESTRUCTIBLE
  ant perishable
unpermissive *adj syn* see RIGID 3
  ant permissive
unphysical *adj syn* see IMMATERIAL 1
  ant physical
unpierceable *adj syn* see IMPASSABLE 1
  ant pierceable
unpitying *adj syn* see PITILESS
  ant pitying
unplanned *adj* 1 *syn* see RANDOM
  ant planned
  2 *syn* see UNINTENTIONAL
  ant planned
unpleasant *adj syn* see BAD 8
unpliable *adj syn* see OBSTINATE
  ant pliable, pliant
unpliant *adj syn* see OBSTINATE
  ant pliable, pliant
unpolished *adj* 1 *syn* see RUDE 1
  idiom in the rough
  ant polished
  2 *syn* see RUDE 6
  3 *syn* see BOORISH

---

syn synonym(s)   *rel* related word(s)
ant antonym(s)   *con* contrasted word(s)
idiom idiomatic equivalent(s)
|| use limited; if in doubt, see a dictionary

ant polished
unpolitic *adj syn* see TACTLESS
  ant politic
unpractical *adj syn* see IMPRACTICAL 1
  ant practical
unpracticed *adj* 1 *syn* see UNTRIED 1
  2 *syn* see INEXPERIENCED
  ant practiced
unpredictable *adj syn* see UNCERTAIN 1
  ant predictable
unprejudiced *adj syn* see FAIR 4
  ant prejudiced
unpremeditated *adj* 1 *syn* see SPONTANEOUS
  2 *syn* see UNINTENTIONAL
  ant premeditated
unprepossessed *adj syn* see FAIR 4
  ant prepossessed
unprescribed *adj syn* see VOLUNTARY
  ant prescribed
unpretentious *adj syn* see PLAIN 1
  ant pretentious
unpretty *adj syn* see PLAIN 5
  ant pretty
unprevailing *adj syn* see FUTILE
unprincipled *adj* 1 *syn* see UNSCRUPULOUS
  ant principled
  2 *syn* see ABANDONED 2
  rel corrupt, crooked, unscrupulous; dishonest, unconscientious, unethical
  3 *syn* see CORRUPT 2
  ant principled
unproductive *adj* 1 *syn* see BARREN 2
  rel impotent, infecund, unprolific
  ant productive
  2 *syn* see FUTILE
  ant productive
unprofane *adj syn* see HOLY 1
  ant profane
unproficient *adj syn* see UNSKILLFUL 1
  ant proficient, skilled
unprogressive *adj* 1 *syn* see BACKWARD 6
  ant progressive
  2 *syn* see BACKWARD 5
  ant progressive
unprompted *adj syn* see SPONTANEOUS
unpropitious *adj syn* see OMINOUS
  rel adverse, antagonistic, counter
  con cheering, encouraging, reassuring
  ant propitious
unproportionate *adj syn* see LOPSIDED
  ant proportionate
unprosperous *adj syn* see POOR 1
  ant prosperous
unprosperousness *n syn* see POVERTY 1
  ant prosperousness
unprotected *adj syn* see HELPLESS 1
  rel undefended, unguarded, unsheltered, unshielded; insecure, unsafe
  ant protected
unproved *adj syn* see UNTRIED 1
  ant proved
unpunctual *adj syn* see TARDY
  ant punctual
unpurposed *adj* 1 *syn* see UNINTENTIONAL

  2 *syn* see FECKLESS 1
unqualified *adj* 1 *syn* see UNFIT 2
  rel unskilled; unsuitable
  ant qualified
  2 *syn* see SURE 2
  rel unconditional, unlimited, unreserved; clear, explicit, express; entire, perfect, utter
  ant qualified
  3 *syn* see UTTER
  4 *syn* see PURE 2
unquenchable *adj syn* see INSATIABLE
  ant quenchable
unquestionable *adj* 1 *syn* see AUTHENTIC 2
  ant doubtable, questionable
  2 *syn* see POSITIVE 3
  rel dependable, reliable; established, well=founded, well-grounded
  ant doubtable, questionable
  3 *syn* see DOWNRIGHT 2
unquestionably *adv syn* see EASILY 2
  ant questionably
unquestioning *adj syn* see SURE 2
  ant questioning
unquiet *adj syn* see RESTLESS
  ant quiet
unravel *vb syn* see SOLVE 2
  rel disentangle, extricate, untangle
unreachable *adj syn* see INACCESSIBLE
  ant reachable
unreadable *adj syn* see ILLEGIBLE
  ant legible, readable
unreal *adj syn* see FICTITIOUS 1
  ant real
unrealistic *adj syn* see IMPRACTICAL 1
  ant realistic
unrealizable *adj syn* see IMPOSSIBLE 1
  ant realizable
unreasonable *adj* 1 *syn* see ILLOGICAL
  rel incongruous, loose, self-contradictory
  ant reasonable
  2 exceeding the bounds of reason or right <the constitutional guarantees against *unreasonable* searches and seizures>
  syn unconscionable, undue, unjustifiable, unwarrantable, unwarranted
  rel arbitrary, peremptory; excessive, immoderate, inordinate, overmuch; improper, unlawful, unrightful, wrongful
  con lawful, licit; proper, right, tolerable
  ant reasonable
unreasoned *adj syn* see ILLOGICAL
  ant reasoned
unrecking *adj syn* see CARELESS 1
unreckonable *adj syn* see INCALCULABLE 1
unrecompensed *adj syn* see UNPAID 1
  ant recompensed
unrecoverable *adj syn* see HOPELESS 2
unrefined *adj* 1 *syn* see BOORISH
  ant refined
  2 *syn* see COARSE 3
  ant refined
  3 not freed from unwanted material <shipped the *unrefined* ore>
  syn crude, impure, native, raw, run-of-mine, ungraded, unsorted

rel rough, roughcast, roughhewn; coarse, natural, undressed, unprocessed
idiom in the rough
con dressed, processed
ant refined
unreflective *adj syn* see CARELESS 1
unregretful *adj syn* see REMORSELESS
ant regretful
unregular *adj syn* see IRREGULAR 1
ant regular
unrehearsed *adj syn* see EXTEMPORANEOUS
ant rehearsed
unrelenting *adj syn* see GRIM 3
ant relenting
unreliable *adj* **1** not to be counted on <it is certain that much of the testimony was *unreliable*>
syn dubious, fly-by-night, questionable, trustless, undependable, unsure, untrustworthy, untrusty
rel fickle, inconstant, unstable, vacillating; faithless, false, untrue; falsehearted, perfidious; shifty, slick, slippery, tricky; inaccurate, inexact, unfaithful
idiom not to be depended (*or* relied) on
con dependable, trustworthy, trusty; constant; faithful, true
ant reliable
2 *syn* see UNSAFE
ant reliable
unreligious *adj syn* see IRRELIGIOUS
ant religious
unremarkable *adj syn* see ORDINARY 1
unremitting *adj syn* see CONTINUAL
unremittingly *adv syn* see HARD 3
unremorseful *adj syn* see REMORSELESS
ant remorseful
unremunerated *adj syn* see UNPAID 1
ant remunerated
unrenowned *adj syn* see OBSCURE 5
ant renowned
unrepealable *adj syn* see IRREVOCABLE
ant repealable
unrepeatable *adj syn* see ONLY 2
unrepentant *adj syn* see REMORSELESS
ant repentant
unrepresentative *adj syn* see ABNORMAL 1
unrequested *adj syn* see UNASKED
unrequired *adj* **1** *syn* see UNNECESSARY
ant required
2 *syn* see DISPENSABLE
ant required
unreserved *adj* **1** *syn* see FRANK 1
ant reserved
2 *syn* see DEMONSTRATIVE
ant reserved
3 *syn* see EASYGOING 3
unresistant *adj syn* see PASSIVE 2
ant resistant, resisting
unresisting *adj syn* see PASSIVE 2
ant resistant, resisting
unresolved *adj syn* see VACILLATING 2
ant resolved
unrespectable *adj syn* see DISREPUTABLE 1
ant respectable

unresponsive *adj* **1** *syn* see INSUSCEPTIBLE
ant responsive
2 *syn* see FRIGID 3
unresponsiveness *n syn* see APATHY 1
ant responsiveness
unrest *n* a disturbed uneasy state <that popular *unrest* that, unchecked, can lead to insurrection and anarchy>
syn ailment, disquiet, disquietude, ferment, inquietude, restiveness, restlessness, storm and stress, Sturm und Drang, turmoil
rel agitation, commotion, confusion, convulsion, tumult, turbulence, upheaval; anarchy, chaos, disorder
con calm, easiness, peace, quiet
unrestful *adj* **1** *syn* see RESTLESS
ant restful
2 *syn* see NERVOUS
unrestrainable *adj syn* see IRREPRESSIBLE
ant restrainable
unrestrained *adj* **1** *syn* see EXCESSIVE 2
2 *syn* see FREE 2
ant restrained
3 *syn* see AUDACIOUS 4
rel candid, frank, open; forthright, plainspoken, straightforward; bluff, blunt, brusque
ant restrained
4 *syn* see DEMONSTRATIVE
ant restrained
unrestraint *n* **1** *syn* see UNCONSTRAINT
ant restraint
2 *syn* see ABANDON 2
unrestricted *adj syn* see OPEN 4
unriddle *vb syn* see SOLVE 2
unrighteous *adj syn* see INEQUITABLE
ant righteous
unripe *adj syn* see YOUNG 1
unrivaled *adj syn* see ALONE 3
unromantic *adj syn* see REALISTIC
ant romantic
unruffled *adj syn* see COOL 2
ant discomposed, ruffled
unruly *adj* **1** resistant to discipline or control <a stubborn *unruly* boy>
syn fractious, indocile, indomitable, intractable, recalcitrant, uncontrollable, undisciplinable, undisciplined, ungovernable, unmanageable, untoward, wild; *compare* OBSTINATE, TURBULENT 1
rel contumacious, incorrigible, insubordinate, rebellious; contrary, froward, perverse, wayward; boisterous, obstreperous, rampageous; disorderly, raffish, rambunctious, rowdy, turbulent
idiom out of hand
con controlled, easy, mild, restrained; disciplined, governable, manageable; amenable, biddable, obedient; correct, proper
ant docile, tractable
2 *syn* see TURBULENT 1

---

syn synonym(s)   *rel* related word(s)
ant antonym(s)   *con* contrasted word(s)
idiom idiomatic equivalent(s)
‖ use limited; if in doubt, see a dictionary

rel hard, ruffianly, tough
3 *syn* see DISOBEDIENT
unsacred *adj syn* see PROFANE 1
ant sacred
unsafe *adj* not to be depended on or trusted <an *unsafe* investment>
syn unassured, undependable, unreliable, untrustworthy
rel insecure, shaky, tottery, unsound, unstable; chancy, hazardous, risky; dangerous, jeopardous, perilous; erratic, uncertain
con dependable, trustworthy; secure, sound, stable, substantial
ant safe
unsaid *adj syn* see TACIT 1
unsalutary *adj syn* see UNWHOLESOME 1
ant salutary
unsandaled *adj syn* see BAREFOOT 1
ant sandaled
unsane *adj syn* see INSANE 1
ant sane
unsatiate *adj syn* see INSATIABLE
ant satiate, satiated
unsatisfactory *adj syn* see BAD 1
ant satisfactory
unsatisfiable *adj syn* see INSATIABLE
ant satisfiable
unsavory *adj syn* see UNPALATABLE 1
ant savory
unsay *vb syn* see ABJURE
unscathed *adj syn* see SAFE 1
unscholarly *adj* not devoted to scholarly pursuits <*unscholarly* concerns>
syn inerudite, unbookish, unlearned, unstudious
rel unenlightened, uninformed, uninitiated; callow, green, unripe; inexperienced, naive
con bookish, erudite, learned; enlightened, informed; experienced
ant scholarly
unschooled *adj* **1 *syn*** see IGNORANT 1
2 *syn* see NATURAL 5
unscramble *vb syn* see EXTRICATE 2
unscrupulous *adj* **1** lacking in moral scruples <*unscrupulous* conduct of political leaders>
syn conscienceless, stick-at-nothing, unconscionable, unprincipled
rel crafty, deceitful, scheming; improper, unseemly, wrongful; corrupt, crooked, dishonest; questionable, shady, sinister, underhand
con conscientious, dutiful, proper, upright; dependable, reliable, responsible
ant scrupulous
2 *syn* see CORRUPT 2
con meticulous, particular, punctilious, strict
ant scrupulous
unseasonable *adj* **1** involving or occurring at an inappropriate or unexpected time <his wife's sudden return proved most *unseasonable*>
syn ill-seasoned, ill-timed, inopportune, malapropos, mistimed, untimely
rel deplorable, inappropriate, inconvenient, unsuitable; inauspicious, infelicitous, undesirable, unfavorable, unfortunate

con apropos, opportune, timely, well-timed
ant seasonable
2 *syn* see IMPROPER 1
unseasoned *adj syn* see INEXPERIENCED
ant seasoned
unseat *vb syn* see THROW 2
unsectarian *adj syn* see NONSECTARIAN
ant sectarian
unseemliness *n syn* see IMPROPRIETY 1
ant propriety, seemliness
unseemly *adj* **1 *syn*** see INDECOROUS
rel coarse, crude, inelegant, unrefined; raffish, rowdy, ruffianly
con prim, restrained, starchy, stiff, stilted; elegant, gracious, polished, refined
ant seemly
2 *syn* see IMPROPER 1
ant seemly
unselfish *adj syn* see SELFLESS
ant selfish
unsentimental *adj syn* see REALISTIC
ant sentimental
unserviceable *adj syn* see IMPRACTICABLE 2
ant serviceable
unsettle *vb* **1 *syn*** see DISORDER 1
rel agitate, disquiet, perturb; discommode, incommode, trouble
con calm, ease, quiet, stabilize, steady
ant settle
2 *syn* see UPSET 5
ant settle
3 *syn* see DISCOMPOSE 1
unsettled *adj* **1 *syn*** see RESTLESS
2 *syn* see CHANGEABLE 1
ant settled
3 *syn* see DOUBTFUL 1
4 *syn* see PENDING
ant settled
5 *syn* see BACK 1
6 *syn* see UNPAID 2
ant settled
unsettledness *n syn* see INSTABILITY
unsex *vb syn* see STERILIZE
unshackle *vb syn* see FREE
ant shackle
unshakable *adj syn* see SURE 2
ant shakable
unshaken *adj syn* see SURE 2
ant shaken
unshaped *adj syn* see FORMLESS
ant shaped
unshared *adj syn* see SOLE 4
ant shared
unship *vb syn* see UNLOAD
unshod *adj syn* see BAREFOOT 1
ant shod
unshroud *vb syn* see EXPOSE 4
ant shroud
unshut *vb syn* see OPEN 1
ant shut
unsightly *adj syn* see UGLY 2
rel ill-shaped, unshapely; unesthetic; drab, dull, lackluster
ant sightly

unsimilar *adj syn* see DIFFERENT 1
ant similar

unskilled *adj* **1** *syn* see AMATEURISH
ant skilled
2 *syn* see INEFFICIENT 2
ant skilled

unskillful *adj* **1** lacking in skill or proficiency <an
ardent but *unskillful* home mechanic>
syn inadept, inapt, inept, inexpert, unapt, undexterous, unfacile, unhandy, unproficient
rel incapable, incompetent; unfitted, unqualified, unready
con adept, apt, dexterous, expert, handy, proficient
ant skillful
2 *syn* see INEFFICIENT 2

unsleeping *adj syn* see WATCHFUL
ant sleeping

unsmooth *adj syn* see ROUGH 1
ant smooth

unsober *adj syn* see INTOXICATED 1
ant sober

unsociable *adj* disinclined to active social intercourse <tried to hide his basically shy *unsociable*
nature under a professional heartiness of man-
ner>
syn aloof, cool, distant, insociable, offish, reserved, shut-in, solitary, standoff, standoffish,
touch-me-not-ish, unapproachable, unbending,
uncommunicative, uncompanionable, withdrawn; *compare* INDIFFERENT 2, UNDEMONSTRATIVE
rel self-contained, self-sufficient; exclusive, inaccessible, remote; prickly, sensitive; brooding,
secretive; diffident, shy, timid
con cordial, genial, hearty, outgoing; companionable, friendly, gregarious
ant sociable, social

unsoiled *adj syn* see CLEAN 1
ant soiled, sullied

unsoluble *adj syn* see INSOLUBLE
ant soluble, solvable

unsolvable *adj syn* see INSOLUBLE
ant soluble, solvable

unsophisticated *adj syn* see NATURAL 5
rel authentic, bona fide, genuine; callow, crude,
green, uncouth
con finished, polished, smooth, suave
ant sophisticated

unsorry *adj syn* see REMORSELESS
ant sorry

unsorted *adj* **1** *syn* see MISCELLANEOUS
2 *syn* see UNREFINED 3
ant sorted

unsought *adj* **1** *syn* see UNASKED
2 *syn* see UNWELCOME 1

unsound *adj* **1** *syn* see INSANE 1
ant sound
2 *syn* see WEAK 1
rel damaged, faulty, flawed, imperfect
con solid, strong, substantial
ant sound
3 *syn* see FALSE 1
ant sound
4 *syn* see DANGEROUS 1

unsparing *adj syn* see LIBERAL 1
ant close, sparing

unspeakable *adj syn* see UNUTTERABLE
rel loathsome, offensive, repulsive, revolting;
abominable, detestable, hateful, odious; distasteful, obnoxious, repellent, repugnant; atrocious,
disgusting, outrageous

unspoiled *adj syn* see VIRGIN 2

unspoken *adj* **1** not put into words <met regularly
by a sort of *unspoken* agreement>
syn silent, tacit, unexpressed, unuttered, unvoiced, wordless
rel implicit, implied, understood; hinted, intimated, suggested; mute, unsaid, unstated
con mentioned, said, stated, told, voiced
ant spoken
2 *syn* see TACIT 1
ant spoken

unstability *n syn* see INSTABILITY
ant stability

unstable *adj* **1** *syn* see MOVABLE
ant stable
2 difficult to manage because of lack of physical
steadiness <the canoe is an inherently *unstable*
craft>
syn rocky, ticklish, tricky
rel insecure, uncertain, unsteady
con secure, steady
ant stable
3 *syn* see WEAK 2
ant stable
4 *syn* see INCONSTANT 1
rel buoyant, effervescent, elastic, resilient;
freakish
ant stable
5 *syn* see CHANGEABLE 1
ant stable
6 *syn* see MUTABLE 2
ant stable
7 *syn* see DOUBTFUL 1

unstableness *n syn* see INSTABILITY
ant stability, stableness

unsteadfast *adj syn* see MOVABLE
ant steadfast

unsteadfastness *n syn* see INSTABILITY
ant steadfastness

unsteadiness *n syn* see INSTABILITY
ant steadiness

unsteady *adj* **1** *syn* see MOVABLE
2 *syn* see CHANGEABLE 1
ant steady
3 *syn* see MUTABLE 2
ant steady

unsteel *vb syn* see DISARM 2

unstop *vb syn* see OPEN 1
ant stop

unstow *vb syn* see UNLOAD

unstrengthen *vb syn* see WEAKEN 1
ant strengthen

---

syn synonym(s)   *rel* related word(s)
ant antonym(s)   *con* contrasted word(s)
idiom idiomatic equivalent(s)
|| use limited; if in doubt, see a dictionary

unstring *vb syn* see UNNERVE
unstudied *adj* **1** *syn* see NATURAL 5
  ant studied
  2 *syn* see EXTEMPORANEOUS
unstudious *adj syn* see UNSCHOLARLY
  ant studious
unstylish *adj syn* see TACKY 2
  ant stylish
unsubstantial *adj* **1** *syn* see TENUOUS 3
  ant substantial
  2 *syn* see IMPLAUSIBLE
  3 *syn* see IMMATERIAL 1
  ant substantial
  4 *syn* see WEAK 1
  rel insecure, shaky, undependable
  ant substantial
unsuccess *n syn* see FAILURE 2
  ant success, successfulness
unsuccessfulness *n syn* see FAILURE 2
  ant success, successfulness
unsufferable *adj syn* see INSUFFERABLE
  ant sufferable
unsufficient *adj syn* see SHORT 3
  ant sufficient
unsuitable *adj* **1** *syn* see UNFIT 1
  rel undesirable, unhappy
  ant suitable
  2 *syn* see IMPROPER 1
  ant suitable
unsuited *adj syn* see UNFIT 1
  rel inadmissible, objectionable, unacceptable;
  disappointing, inadequate
  ant suited
unsullied *adj* **1** *syn* see CHASTE
  ant sullied
  2 *syn* see CLEAN 1
  ant soiled, sullied
unsupportable *adj syn* see INSUFFERABLE
  ant bearable, supportable
unsure *adj* **1** *syn* see INSECURE 1
  ant sure
  2 *syn* see WEAK 2
  3 *syn* see DOUBTFUL 1
  ant sure
  4 *syn* see UNRELIABLE 1
unsurmountable *adj syn* see INSUPERABLE
  ant surmountable
unsurpassable *adj syn* see SUPREME
  ant surpassable
unsusceptible *adj syn* see INSUSCEPTIBLE
  ant susceptible
unsuspecting *adj syn* see CREDULOUS
  ant suspecting, suspicious
unsuspicious *adj syn* see CREDULOUS
  ant suspecting, suspicious
unswayable *adj syn* see INFLEXIBLE 2
  ant suasible
unswerving *adj syn* see WHOLE 5
  rel constant, steadfast, steady, unremitting;
  firm, unfaltering, unwavering
unsymmetrical *adj syn* see LOPSIDED
  ant symmetrical
unsympathetic *adj* **1** *syn* see ANTIPATHETIC 2
  rel dislikable, unlikable; displeasing, unpleasant, unpleasing

con appealing, congenial, likable; pleasant,
pleasing
  ant sympathetic
  2 *syn* see UNFEELING 2
  rel cold, cool, frigid; disinterested, halfhearted,
indifferent, lukewarm
  ant sympathetic
untactful *adj syn* see TACTLESS
  ant tactful
untangle *vb syn* see EXTRICATE 2
  ant entangle, tangle
untapped *adj syn* see VIRGIN 2
untaught *adj syn* see IGNORANT 1
untellable *adj syn* see UNUTTERABLE
  ant expressible
untempered *adj syn* see EXCESSIVE 2
  ant temperate, tempered
untenable *adj syn* see INEXCUSABLE
untended *adj syn* see NEGLECTED
untested *adj syn* see UNTRIED 1
  ant tested, tried
unthankful *adj* **1** *syn* see THANKLESS 2
  2 *syn* see THANKLESS 1
  ant thankful
unthinkable *adj* **1** *syn* see EXCEPTIONAL 1
  2 *syn* see INCREDIBLE 1
  ant thinkable
unthinking *adj syn* see CARELESS 1
unthorough *adj syn* see SLIPSHOD 3
  ant thorough
unthought *adj syn* see UNINTENTIONAL
  ant aforethought
unthrift *n* **1** *syn* see EXTRAVAGANCE 2
  ant thrift
  2 *syn* see SPENDTHRIFT
unthrift *adj syn* see IMPROVIDENT
unthrifty *adj syn* see IMPROVIDENT
  ant thrifty
untidy *adj* **1** *syn* see SLOVENLY 1
  ant tidy
  2 *syn* see SLIPSHOD 3
untie *vb syn* see EXTRICATE 2
untighten *vb syn* see LOOSE 5
  ant tighten
until *prep* up to a stipulated time <we never met
him *until* last night>
  syn before, in advance of, prior to, till, to, up
till, up to; *compare* BEFORE 1
until *conj syn* see TILL
untimely *adj* **1** *syn* see EARLY 2
  ant timely
  2 *syn* see UNSEASONABLE 1
  con opportune, pat, seasonable, well-timed
  ant timely
  3 *syn* see IMPROPER 1
  ant timely
untiring *adj syn* see INDEFATIGABLE
  con casual, disinterested, intermittent
untold *adj* **1** *syn* see HUGE
  2 *syn* see INNUMERABLE
untouchable *n syn* see OUTCAST
  rel déclassé, outcaste, outsider
untouched *adj* **1** *syn* see WHOLE 1
  2 *syn* see VIRGIN 2

untoward *adj* **1** *syn* see UNRULY 1
  2 *syn* see UNLUCKY
  3 *syn* see INDECOROUS
untowardness *n* *syn* see IMPROPRIETY 1
untrammeled *adj* *syn* see AUDACIOUS 4
untranquil *adj* *syn* see RESTLESS
untried *adj* **1** not subjected to test or proof (as by experience or use) <the fledgling's *untried* wings>
  syn undemonstrated, unpracticed, unproved, untested
  rel inexperienced, unseasoned; callow, green, immature; fresh, half-baked, unripe
  con practiced, proven, tested; accomplished, finished, skilled; initiated
  ant tested, tried
  2 *syn* see INEXPERIENCED
untroubled *adj* *syn* see CALM 1
  ant troubled
untroublesome *adj* *syn* see EASY 1
untrue *adj* **1** *syn* see FAITHLESS
  ant true
  2 *syn* see FALSE 1
  rel imprecise, inexact, unprecise; forsworn, perjured
  con exact, precise
  ant true
untruism *n* *syn* see LIE
  ant truism
untrustworthy *adj* **1** *syn* see UNRELIABLE 1
  ant trustworthy
  2 *syn* see UNSAFE
  ant trustworthy
untrusty *adj* *syn* see UNRELIABLE 1
  ant trusty
untruth *n* **1** *syn* see FALLACY 1
  ant truth
  2 *syn* see LIE
  ant truth
untruthful *adj* *syn* see DISHONEST
  rel deceptive, delusive, delusory, misleading; false, wrong; inaccurate, incorrect
  ant truthful
untruthfulness *n* *syn* see MENDACITY
  ant truthfulness
untune *vb* *syn* see DISCOMPOSE 1
untutored *adj* **1** *syn* see IGNORANT 1
  2 *syn* see NATURAL 5
untwine *vb* *syn* see EXTRICATE 2
untypical *adj* *syn* see ABNORMAL 1
  ant typical
ununderstandable *adj* *syn* see INCONCEIVABLE 1
  ant understandable
unusable *adj* *syn* see IMPRACTICABLE 2
  ant usable
unused *adj* *syn* see VACANT 4
unusual *adj* **1** *syn* see EXCEPTIONAL 1
  idiom the exception rather than the rule
  ant usual
  2 *syn* see STRANGE 4
  ant usual
unusually *adv* *syn* see EXTRA
unutterable *adj* being beyond human power to tell or describe <*unutterable* spiritual bliss>

syn incommunicable, indefinable, indescribable, ineffable, inenarrable, inexpressible, undescribable, unexpressible, unspeakable, untellable
rel inconceivable, incredible, unbelievable, unimaginable; awesome, awful, marvelous, prodigious, wonderful, wondrous
idiom beyond expression
con commonplace, humdrum, ordinary; monotonous, samely, unvarying
unuttered *adj* **1** *syn* see UNSPOKEN 1
  ant uttered
  2 *syn* see TACIT 1
  ant uttered
unvarnished *adj* *syn* see FRANK
unvarying *adj* **1** *syn* see STEADY 2
  ant varying
  2 *syn* see SAME 3
  ant variable, varying
unveil *vb* **1** *syn* see OPEN 2
  ant veil
  2 *syn* see REVEAL 1
  ant veil
unveracity *n* *syn* see MENDACITY
  ant veracity
unversed *adj* *syn* see INEXPERIENCED
  ant versed
unvigilant *adj* *syn* see INCAUTIOUS 1
  ant vigilant
unvital *adj* *syn* see PETTY 2
  ant vital
unvocal *adj* *syn* see INARTICULATE 3
  ant vocal
unvoiced *adj* *syn* see UNSPOKEN 1
  ant voiced
unwanted *adj* **1** *syn* see UNWELCOME 1
  ant wanted
  2 *syn* see OBJECTIONABLE
unwarrantable *adj* *syn* see UNREASONABLE 2
  ant warrantable
unwarranted *adj* **1** *syn* see BASELESS
  2 *syn* see UNREASONABLE 2
unwary *adj* **1** *syn* see INCAUTIOUS 1
  ant wary
  2 *syn* see CREDULOUS
  3 *syn* see RASH 1
  ant wary
unwashed *adj* *syn* see IGNOBLE 1
unwashed *n* *syn* see RABBLE 2
unwasteful *adj* *syn* see SPARING
  ant wasteful
unwatchful *adj* **1** *syn* see INATTENTIVE
  ant watchful
  2 *syn* see INCAUTIOUS 1
  ant watchful
unwatered *adj* *syn* see DRY 1
  ant watered
unwavering *adj* *syn* see SURE 2
  ant wavering
unweariable *adj* *syn* see INDEFATIGABLE

---

syn synonym(s)   *rel* related word(s)
ant antonym(s)   *con* contrasted word(s)
idiom idiomatic equivalent(s)
‖ use limited; if in doubt, see a dictionary

ant weariable

unwearying *adj syn* see INDEFATIGABLE
　rel constant, steady; interminable, unceasing

unwed *adj syn* see SINGLE 1
　ant married, wed

unwelcome *adj* **1** not of a kind to be welcome <an *unwelcome* interruption that scattered his train of thought>
　syn undesired, unsought, unwanted, unwished
　rel distasteful, obnoxious, repellent; unasked; undesirable, unpleasant, unpleasing
　con desired, sought, wanted; agreeable, desirable, pleasant, pleasing
　ant welcome
　2 *syn* see OBJECTIONABLE
　ant welcome

unwell *adj* somewhat disordered in health <had felt *unwell* from the moment she got up>
　syn ailing, ‖donsie, indisposed, low, mean, off-color, offish, poorly, sickly; *compare* SICK 1
　rel rocky, shaky, wobbly; feeble, frail, infirm, weakly; ill, sick; qualmish, queasy, squeamish
　idiom out of sorts, under the weather
　ant well

unwholesome *adj* **1** likely to be detrimental to physical, mental, or moral health <an *unwholesome* crime-ridden neighborhood>
　syn insalubrious, insalutary, noisome, noxious, sickly, unhealthful, unhealthy, unsalutary
　rel baneful, deleterious, detrimental, pernicious; harmful, hurtful, injurious, mischievous
　con healthful, hygienic, salubrious, salutary
　ant wholesome
　2 *syn* see OFFENSIVE
　ant wholesome

unwieldy *adj* clumsy and difficult to handle usually because of excessive weight and awkward form <a massive *unwieldy* sledgehammer>
　syn cumbersome, cumbrous, ponderous, unhandy; *compare* HEAVY 1
　rel awkward, inconvenient; uncontrollable, unmanageable; bulky, clumsy, lumbering, massive; burdensome, encumbering, onerous
　con compact, neat, trig, trim; adaptable, convenient, handy; easy, facile, light
　ant wieldy

unwilling *adj syn* see DISINCLINED
　ant willing

unwind *vb syn* see RELAX 2

unwise *adj* not marked by or according with good sense or sound judgment <his decision to quit school was most *unwise*>
　syn ill-advised, ill-judged, impolitic, imprudent, indiscreet, injudicious
　rel senseless, thoughtless, witless; impractical, unsound; fatuous, inane, inept; inappropriate, undesirable, unfortunate; foolish, misguided, unintelligent; childish, immature, naive
　idiom penny-wise and pound-foolish
　con discreet, judicious, prudent; sane, sensible, sound; appropriate, apt, desirable
　ant wise

unwished *adj syn* see UNWELCOME 1

unwishful *adj syn* see DISINCLINED

ant wishful

unwitting *adj* **1** *syn* see FORGETFUL
　ant witting
　2 *syn* see IGNORANT 2
　ant witting

unwitty *adj syn* see SIMPLE 3
　ant ‖witty

unwonted *adj syn* see EXCEPTIONAL 1
　ant wonted

unworkable *adj* **1** *syn* see IMPOSSIBLE 1
　2 *syn* see IMPRACTICABLE 2
　ant workable

unworked *adj syn* see RUDE 1
　ant worked, wrought

unworkmanlike *adj syn* see INEFFICIENT 2
　ant workmanlike, workmanly

unworldly *adj* **1** *syn* see DREAMY 1
　2 *syn* see NATURAL 5
　ant worldly

unworthy *adj syn* see WORTHLESS 1
　ant worthy

unwritten *adj syn* see ORAL 2
　ant written

unwrought *adj syn* see RUDE 1
　ant worked, wrought

unyielding *adj* **1** *syn* see STIFF 1
　ant yielding
　2 *syn* see OBSTINATE
　rel firm, fixed, rigid
　ant yielding
　3 *syn* see GRIM 3
　4 *syn* see TOUGH 3
　ant yielding
　5 *syn* see INFLEXIBLE 2

up *adj* **1** *syn* see BAD 1
　2 *syn* see FAMILIAR 3
　3 *syn* see UP-TO-DATE

up *vb* **1** *syn* see RISE 4
　2 *syn* see RAISE 9

up–and–coming *adj syn* see ENTERPRISING 2
　rel alert, eager, keen, ready

up and down *adv syn* see THOROUGHLY 2

up–and–down *adj syn* see DOWNRIGHT 2

upbear *vb syn* see SUPPORT 4

upbeat *adj syn* see OPTIMISTIC

upbraid *vb syn* see SCOLD 1

upchuck *vb syn* see VOMIT

upclimb *vb syn* see ASCEND 1

upcoming *adj syn* see FORTHCOMING
　rel foreseen, prospective
　idiom in prospect, on the horizon

up–country *n syn* see FRONTIER 2

update *vb syn* see RENEW 1

upend *vb syn* see WHIP 2

upgo *vb syn* see ASCEND 1

upgrade *vb syn* see ADVANCE 2
　ant downgrade

upgrade *n syn* see RISE 3

upgrading *n syn* see ADVANCEMENT 1
　ant downgrading

upgrowth *n syn* see DEVELOPMENT

upheaval *n syn* see COMMOTION 1
　rel cataclysm, catastrophe, disaster; alteration, change; churning, heaving, stirring

upheaved *adj syn* see ELEVATED 1
  ant downthrown
uphill *adj syn* see HARD 6
uphold *vb* **1** *syn* see SUPPORT 5
  rel defend, justify, maintain, vindicate; aid, assist, help
  ant contravene; subvert
  2 *syn* see SUPPORT 2
  3 *syn* see SUPPORT 4
  4 *syn* see LIFT 1
upholstered *adj* **1** *syn* see LUXURIOUS 3
  2 *syn* see FAT 2
upland *n syn* see PLATEAU
uplay *vb syn* see ACCUMULATE
uplift *vb* **1** *syn* see LIFT 1
  2 *syn* see ILLUMINATE 2
  ant degrade
uplifted *adj syn* see ELEVATED 1
upon *prep* **1** *syn* see OVER 3
  2 *syn* see OVER 4
upper class *n syn* see ARISTOCRACY
upper crust *n syn* see ARISTOCRACY
  rel (the) Four Hundred
upper hand *n syn* see BETTER 2
uppermost *adj syn* see TOP 1
  ant lowermost
‖**upper story** *n syn* see MIND 1
‖**upperworks** *n pl syn* see MIND 1
uppish *adj syn* see PRESUMPTUOUS
uppity *adj syn* see PRESUMPTUOUS
upraise *vb* **1** *syn* see LIFT 1
  2 *syn* see COMFORT
  ant depress
upraised *adj syn* see ELEVATED 1
uprear *vb* **1** *syn* see LIFT 1
  2 *syn* see BUILD 1
  3 *syn* see EXALT 1
  con bust, demote, downgrade
  ant degrade
  4 *syn* see RISE 4
upright *adj* **1** *syn* see ERECT
  2 having or manifesting a strict regard for what is morally right <an *upright* man ready to give even the devil his due>
  syn conscientious, honest, honorable, just, right, scrupulous, true
  rel ethical, moral, principled, righteous, virtuous; equitable, fair, impartial; elevated, high=minded, noble; blameless, exemplary, good, pure
  con crooked, devious, oblique; depraved; base, low, vile; ignoble, mean
  ant corrupt
uprightness *n syn* see GOODNESS
  rel nobility, reputability, worthiness; honesty, integrity
  ant corruption
uprise *vb* **1** *syn* see RISE 1
  2 *syn* see ROLL OUT
uprisen *adj syn* see ELEVATED 1
uproar *n* **1** *syn* see DIN
  rel chaos, confusion, disorder; brawl, broil, fracas, melee; commotion, confusion, turbulence, turmoil

  con calm, peace, quiet
  2 *syn* see COMMOTION 4
  3 *syn* see COMMOTION 3
uproarious *adj syn* see NOISY
uproot *vb syn* see ANNIHILATE 2
  rel demolish, destroy; overthrow, overturn, subvert; displace, replace, supersede, supplant; move, shift, transplant
  ant establish; inseminate
upset *vb* **1** *syn* see OVERTURN 1
  rel invert, reverse; bend, curve, turn
  2 *syn* see DISCOMPOSE 1
  rel bewilder, confound, distract; unman, unnerve
  idiom rock the boat
  3 *syn* see TROUBLE 1
  4 *syn* see DISORDER 1
  5 to disturb the normal functioning especially of body or mind <her stomach was badly *upset* by too many sweets>
  syn derange, disorder, sicken, turn, unhinge, unsettle
  rel afflict, indispose, lay up; ail, suffer; debilitate, incapacitate, invalid
upshot *n* **1** *syn* see EFFECT 1
  rel ending, termination; climax, culmination; completion, conclusion, finish
  2 *syn* see SUBSTANCE 2
upside–down *adj* **1** having the upper and lower parts reversed in position <*upside-down* letters>
  syn inverted, topsy-turvy
  rel reversed
  2 confused utterly even to the point of inversion of the normal or reasonable <*upside-down* logic that confused cause with effect>
  syn arsy-varsy, downside-up, topsy-turvy
  rel inverted, reversed; chaotic, confused, helter=skelter, jumbled, mixed-up; fouled-up, haywire, ‖snafu
  con orderly, well-ordered; logical, reasonable, sensible, sound; legitimate, plausible
upspring *vb* **1** *syn* see SPRING 1
  2 *syn* see RISE 1
upstanding *adj syn* see ERECT
upstart *n* a usually crude and pushing person who has recently reached a position of prominence, power, or wealth <declared the new executive an *upstart* lacking all breeding and culture>
  syn arriviste, nouveau riche, parvenu, roturier
  rel bounder, cad, outsider; guttersnipe, mucker, slob, vulgarian; boor, lout, roughneck, rowdy; comer; social climber
upsurge *vb syn* see INCREASE 2
uptight *adj syn* see TENSE 2
uptightness *n syn* see TENSION 2
up till *prep syn* see UNTIL
up to *prep syn* see UNTIL
up–to–date *adj* completely modern (as in style or outlook) <using *up-to-date* methods of study>

---

syn synonym(s)   *rel* related word(s)
ant antonym(s)   *con* contrasted word(s)
idiom idiomatic equivalent(s)
‖ use limited; if in doubt, see a dictionary

syn abreast, au courant, contemporary, down=
to-date, red-hot, up, up-to-the-minute
rel convenient, opportune, timely; expedient,
fitting, suitable; advanced, modern, stylish; a la
mode, dashing, modish
idiom abreast of the times
con dusty, rusty, stale, timeworn; antiquated,
outmoded, superannuated
ant out-of-date; archaic

up–to–the–minute *adj syn* see UP-TO-DATE

upturn *n syn* see COMMOTION 1

uranian *adj syn* see HOMOSEXUAL

uranian *n syn* see HOMOSEXUAL

uranist *n syn* see HOMOSEXUAL

urban *adj* of, relating to, or characteristic of a city
<*urban* disorders>
syn burghal, city, municipal
rel inner city; metropolitan; civic, popular, public; oppidan, town, village
ant rural

urbane *adj* **1** *syn* see COSMOPOLITAN 1
2 *syn* see SUAVE
rel balanced, poised
ant bucolic, clownish
3 *syn* see GENTEEL 1
rel affable, civil, courteous, gracious, obliging
ant rude

urchin *n* a pert or roguish youngster <*urchins* pilfering apples on their way from school>
syn gamin, imp, monkey
rel brat, bratling, cub, dickens, pup, whelp,
whippersnapper; guttersnipe, mudlark, ragamuffin, street arab; hobbledehoy

urge *vb* to press or impel to action, effort, or speed
<his conscience *urged* him to tell the truth>
syn egg (on), exhort, goad, prick, prod, prompt,
propel, sic, spur
rel hurry, hustle, push, rush, shove; blandish,
cajole, coax, encourage, incite, needle, solicit,
wheedle; constrain, drive, high-pressure, press,
pressure; provoke, set (on), tar (on)
idiom bring pressure to bear on, twist one's arm
con brake, check, constrain, curb, hold back,
inhibit, restrain

urge *n syn* see DESIRE 1
rel goad, incentive, motive, spring, spur

urgent *adj syn* see PRESSING
rel driving, impelling; demanding

usable *adj syn* see OPEN 5
ant unusable

usage *n* **1** *syn* see HABIT 1
rel choice, preference; procedure, proceeding,
process; guidance, guiding, lead
2 *syn* see FORM 3
rel ceremony, formality

usance *n syn* see USE 1

use *n* **1** the act or practice of using something or
the state of being used <all tools must be kept
ready for instant *use*>
syn appliance, application, employment, operation, play, usance; *compare* EXERCISE 1
con desuetude, disuse
ant nonuse
2 *syn* see EXERCISE 1

3 the quality of being appropriate or valuable to
some end <even the scraps had some *use*>
syn account, advantage, applicability, appropriateness, avail, fitness, relevance, service, serviceability, usefulness, utility
rel adaptability, availability, benefit, efficacy;
profit, value, worth
con inadequacy, inapplicability, inappropriateness, insufficiency, unfitness, unserviceability,
uselessness, worthlessness

4 a particular service or end <industrial *uses* of
atomic energy>
syn duty, function, goal, mark, object, objective, purpose, target
5 *syn* see HABIT 1
rel ceremony, formality
6 *syn* see NEED 3

use *vb* **1** *syn* see ACCUSTOM
2 to put into action or service <it is necessary to
use resources wisely>
syn apply, bestow, employ, exercise, exploit,
handle, utilize
rel manipulate, operate, ply, wield; control,
govern, manage, regulate
idiom avail oneself of, bring into play, fall back
(on *or* upon), make use of, press into service, put
into action, put to use
con dissipate, exhaust, use up; waste
3 *syn* see OPERATE 3
4 *syn* see SPEAK 3
5 *syn* see EXPLOIT 2
idiom make the most of, make use of
6 *syn* see TREAT 2

used up *adj syn* see EFFETE 2

useful *adj* **1** *syn* see PRACTICAL 2
2 *syn* see GOOD 1
ant useless
3 *syn* see GOOD 2
ant useless

usefulness *n syn* see USE 3
ant uselessness

useless *adj* **1** *syn* see FUTILE
ant useful
2 *syn* see IMPRACTICABLE 2
ant useful
3 *syn* see FECKLESS 1

use up *vb* **1** *syn* see CONSUME 1
2 *syn* see GO 4
3 *syn* see DEPLETE

usher *vb syn* see PRECEDE 3

usher in *vb syn* see INTRODUCE 3

usual *adj* **1** familiar through frequent or regular
repetition <the sort that would perform her
usual chores while waiting for the end of the
world>
syn accepted, accustomed, chronic, customary,
habitual, routine, wonted
rel natural, normal, regular, typical; common,
familiar, ordinary; current, prevailing, prevalent,
rife
idiom that make up one's daily round
con exceptional, rare, unaccustomed; remarkable, strange, unexpected
ant unusual

2 syn see GENERAL 1

3 syn see ORDINARY 1

usually *adv* **1** by or in accord with habit or custom <establishments of a kind *usually* restricted to back streets>

syn as usual, consistently, customarily, habitually, wontedly

2 more often than not <he is *usually* late for work>

syn as a rule, by ordinary, commonly, frequently, generally, ordinarily

rel now and again (*or* now and then), occasionally, once and again, sometimes

idiom for the most part, in the main

con infrequently, seldom, uncommonly

ant rarely

usurer *n syn* see LOAN SHARK

usurp *vb* **1 syn** see ARROGATE 1

ant abdicate

2 syn see SUPPLANT 1

utensil *n syn* see IMPLEMENT

utile *adj syn* see PRACTICAL 2

ant inutile

utilitarian *adj syn* see REALISTIC

utility *n syn* see USE 3

ant inutility

utilize *vb syn* see USE 2

rel advance, forward, further, promote

utmost *adj* **1 syn** see EXTREME 5

2 syn see MAXIMUM

3 syn see EXTREME 1

utopia *n* an often imaginary place or situation of perfection and delight <as far back as Plato, writers have attempted to portray their notion of *utopia*>

syn arcadia, Cockaigne, fairyland, heaven, lub-

berland, paradise, promised land, Shangri-la, wonderland, Zion

rel dreamland, dreamworld, never-never land

utopian *adj* **1 syn** see IDEALISTIC

rel abstract, ideal, transcendental

2 syn see AMBITIOUS 2

rel impossible, impracticable, unfeasible; arcadian, edenic, millennial, otherworldly

utopian *n syn* see DREAMER

utter *adj* being such without qualification — used especially to intensify the noun modified <acted like an *utter* idiot>

syn absolute, all-fired, arrant, black, blamed, blank, blankety-blank, blasted, bleeding, blessed, blighted, blinding, ‖blinking, blithering, ‖blooming, blue, complete, confounded, ‖consarned, consummate, crashing, dad-blamed, dad-blasted, dad-burned, damned, dang, darn (*or* durn), dashed, deuced, doggone, double-distilled, double-dyed, downright, flat-out, goldarn, gross, hell-fired, infernal, out-and-out, outright, perfect, positive, ‖proper, pure, ‖puredee (*or* pure-D), rank, regular, sheer, stark, straight-out, ‖tarnation, thoroughgoing, total, unmitigated, unqualified; *compare* PURE 2

utter *vb* **1 syn** see SPEAK 1

idiom give utterance to

2 syn see SAY 1

utterance *n* **1 syn** see WORD 1

2 syn see VOCALIZATION

3 syn see EXPRESSION 1

4 syn see SPEECH 1

uttering *n syn* see VOCALIZATION

utterly *adv* **1 syn** see WELL 3

2 syn see ALL 1

uttermost *adj* **1 syn** see EXTREME 5

2 syn see EXTREME 1

---

syn synonym(s)   **rel** related word(s)
ant antonym(s)   **con** contrasted word(s)
idiom idiomatic equivalent(s)
‖ use limited; if in doubt, see a dictionary

V

vacancy *n syn* see VACUITY 2
  rel desertedness
  ant occupancy
vacant *adj* **1** *syn* see EMPTY 1
  rel tenantless, unfilled, unoccupied, untaken
  con inhabited, tenanted
  ant occupied
2 *syn* see VACUOUS 2
3 *syn* see EXPRESSIONLESS
  rel empty-headed, inane, thoughtless, witless
4 not being put to normal or appropriate use
  <*vacant* land>
  syn idle, unused
  rel bare, empty; unfilled, unoccupied
  con filled; used
  ant occupied
vacate *vb* **1** *syn* see ANNUL 4
  rel repeal, rescind, retract, reverse, revoke
  idiom declare null and void
2 to make something (as an office, post, or dwelling) vacant or empty <*vacate* a house>
  syn clear, empty, void
  rel abandon, give up, part (with *or* from), relinquish; leave, quit
vacation *n* a period spent away from one's usual activity or work often in travel or recreation <took a two-week *vacation* to Florida>
  syn holiday, leave
  rel break, breathing space (*or* breathing spell), intermission, recess; time off; respite, rest; furlough
vacillant *adj syn* see VACILLATING 2
vacillate *vb syn* see HESITATE
  rel swag, sway, ‖swither; alternate, seesaw, teeter, teeter-totter, wag, waggle, wigwag, wobble; dally, dawdle, fiddle-faddle
  idiom blow hot and cold, hem and haw, swing from one thing to another
  con decide, resolve, settle
vacillating *adj* **1** *syn* see WEAK 2
  rel unfixed; unsettled, unsteady; changeable, fickle, inconstant; eccentric, erratic, mercurial, volatile
  con constant, steady, unchanging; strong
2 given to or manifesting hesitation or vacillation <a *vacillating* witness>
  syn double-minded, faltering, halting, hesitant, hesitating, indecisive, irresolute, pendulous, shilly-shally, shilly-shallying, tentative, timid, uncertain, undecisive, unresolved, vacillant, vacillatory, wavering, weak-kneed, whiffling, wiggle-waggle, wobbly
  rel doubtful, doubting, unsure; fluctuating, oscillating, shifting; dallying, dawdling, demurring, dillydallying, stalling
  con certain, decisive, resolute, resolved, sure; definite, positive
vacillation *n syn* see HESITATION

  rel dallying, demurral, dillydallying, stalling
vacillatory *adj syn* see VACILLATING 2
  rel alternating, seesawing, varying; indecisive, irresolute, uncertain
vacuity *n* **1** *syn* see HOLE 3
2 the condition, fact, or quality of being vacuous <the utter *vacuity* of his expression>
  syn blankness, emptiness, vacancy, vacuousness, voidness
  rel bareness, barrenness, bleakness, desolateness, hollowness; dullness, inaneness, inanity, stupidity
3 *syn* see NOTHINGNESS
vacuous *adj* **1** *syn* see EMPTY 1
2 characterized by a lack of substance, thought, or intellectual content <a *vacuous* mind>
  syn empty-headed, vacant; *compare* STUPID 1
  rel shallow, superficial; blank, empty; dull, foolish, inane, silly
vacuousness *n syn* see VACUITY 2
vade mecum *n syn* see HANDBOOK
vag *n syn* see VAGABOND
vagabond *adj syn* see ITINERANT
  rel vagabondish
vagabond *n* a person who wanders at will or as a habit <a park full of *vagabonds* sleeping on benches>
  syn arab, ‖bindle stiff, bum, canter, clochard, derelict, drifter, floater, ‖gangrel, hobo, piker, roadster, runagate, ‖shack, street arab, ‖sundowner, ‖swagger, ‖swagman, tramp, tramper, ‖traveler, vag, vagrant, Weary Willie
  rel roamer, rover, wanderer; boomer, migrant, runabout, straggler, stray, transient; bohemian, gypsy, picaro, picaroon; ‖casual; stiff; beggar, rogue
  idiom knight of the road
vagabond *vb syn* see WANDER 1
vagabondage *n syn* see VAGRANCY
vagabondia *n syn* see VAGRANCY
vagabondism *n syn* see VAGRANCY
vagabondize *vb syn* see WANDER 1
vagarious *adj syn* see ARBITRARY 1
  rel unreasonable; kinky
vagary *n syn* see CAPRICE
  rel daydream, dream, fantasy; kink, quirk
  idiom passing fancy
vagrancy *n* the act or state of wandering from place to place usually with no means of support <dropped out of society and lived a life of *vagrancy*>
  syn hoboism, vagabondage, vagabondia, vagabondism
  rel itineracy, itinerancy, nomadism; rambling, roaming, roving, wandering
vagrant *n syn* see VAGABOND
vagrant *adj syn* see ITINERANT

rel aimless, errant, erratic; straying; sauntering, strolling

vague *adj* **1** *syn* see OBSCURE 3
rel indeterminate, indistinct, unplain; cloudy, dim, hazy, nebulous; muddy
con clear, distinct
ant express
2 *syn* see FAINT 2
rel nebulous, unsubstantial; indefinite, unplain; uncertain, unrecognizable; dreamlike, dreamy
3 *syn* see HAZY
rel bleared, bleary, blurry

vain *adj* **1** devoid of worth or significance <the *vain* pursuits of a luxurious life>
syn empty, hollow, idle, nugatory, otiose
rel profitless, unprofitable, useless, valueless, void, worthless; ineffective, ineffectual, inefficacious; bootless, fruitless; abortive, futile
con useful, valuable, worthy; effective, effectual, efficacious
2 *syn* see FUTILE
rel paltry, petty, puny, trifling, trivial; delusive, delusory, misleading
3 having or exhibiting undue or excessive pride especially in one's appearance or achievements <was *vain* about his clothes>
syn conceited, ‖conceity, narcissistic, self-conceited, stuck-up, vainglorious; *compare* PROUD 1
rel arrogant, egocentric, egoistic, haughty, ‖pensy, proud, self-important, swollen-headed; boastful, self-exalting; coxcombical, dandyish, foppish
idiom stuck on oneself
con humble, meek, modest; bashful, diffident, retiring, shy

vainglorious *adj* *syn* see VAIN 3
rel boastful, bragging, vaunting; disdainful, insolent, supercilious

vainglory *n* *syn* see CONCEIT 2
rel arrogance, haughtiness; boastfulness, bombast; exhibition, flaunting, parading
con lowliness, meekness; bashfulness, diffidence, self-effacement, shyness; modesty
ant humility

vainness *n* *syn* see CONCEIT 2

vale *n* *syn* see VALLEY

valedictory *adj* *syn* see PARTING

valiance *n* *syn* see HEROISM
con feebleness, ineffectiveness; fear

valiancy *n* *syn* see HEROISM
con feebleness, ineffectiveness; fear

valiant *adj* *syn* see BRAVE 1
ant pusillanimous

valid *adj* having the power to impress others as right and well-founded <a *valid* conclusion>
syn cogent, convincing, satisfactory, satisfying, solid, sound, telling
rel persuasive, potent, strong; attested, confirmed, corroborated, demonstrated, determined, established, substantiated, validated, verified; lawful, legal, licit; effective, effectual; conclusive, decisive, definitive, determinative; acceptable

con groundless, shaky, unconvincing, unfounded, unsound; fallacious, false, misleading, sophistical; counterfeit, fictitious
ant invalid

validate *vb* *syn* see CONFIRM 2
rel approve, endorse, legalize, ratify, rubber=stamp, sanction
con abolish, abrogate, annul, cancel, repeal; void
ant invalidate

validity *n* *syn* see POINT 3
rel efficacy, gravity, soundness; persuasiveness, potency
con inconsistency; unsoundness; fallacy, falsity
ant invalidity, invalidness

validness *n* *syn* see POINT 3
ant invalidity, invalidness

valley *n* an elongate depression of the earth's surface commonly situated between ranges of hills or mountains <small farms dotted the floor of the *valley*>
syn ‖combe, dale, glen, vale
rel dell, dingle, hollow; ‖rincon; canyon

valor *n* *syn* see HEROISM
rel mettle, resolution, spirit, tenacity; indomitableness, invincibility, unconquerableness; backbone, fortitude, guts, sand
con cowardliness, fear
ant pusillanimity, pusillanimousness

valorous *adj* *syn* see BRAVE 1
ant pusillanimous

valorousness *n* *syn* see HEROISM
rel chivalrousness, chivalry; manliness
con cowardliness
ant pusillanimity, pusillanimousness

valuable *adj* *syn* see PRECIOUS 1
rel dear, expensive; appreciated, prized, treasured, valued; admired, esteemed, respected
idiom of great value
con cheap, inexpensive, trashy; unmarketable, unsalable; unworthy
ant valueless, worthless

valuate *vb* *syn* see ESTIMATE 1

valuation *n* **1** *syn* see ESTIMATE 1
rel judgment, opinion, rating
2 *syn* see WORTH 1
rel charge, cost, price

value *n* **1** *syn* see WORTH 1
rel appraisal, assessment; charge, cost, expense, price
2 *syn* see QUALITY 2

value *vb* **1** *syn* see ESTIMATE 1
rel compute, figure, gauge, reckon
idiom place a value (*or* price) on
2 *syn* see APPRECIATE 1
rel care (for); revere, reverence, venerate
idiom set much by

valueless *adj* *syn* see WORTHLESS 1
ant valuable

---

syn synonym(s)   *rel* related word(s)
ant antonym(s)   *con* contrasted word(s)
idiom idiomatic equivalent(s)
‖ use limited; if in doubt, see a dictionary

valve *n syn* see FAUCET
　rel shutoff
‖**vamoose** *vb syn* see GET OUT 1
vamp *vb syn* see MEND 2
　rel brush up, fix up, touch up; furbish, refurbish
vamp (up) *vb syn* see CONTRIVE 2
vamp *n syn* see FLIRT
　rel charmer, enchantress, enticer, femme fatale, gold digger, inveigler, seductress, siren, temptress
vandal *n* one who willfully destroys or mars something valuable <*vandals* had knocked off the head of the statue>
　syn defacer, despoiler, destroyer, ruinator, ruiner, wrecker
　rel hoodlum, hooligan, lout, ruffian; devastator, ravager, spoiler, spoliator; looter, pillager, plunderer; iconoclast
vandalize *vb* to destroy or deface (as public or private property) willfully or maliciously <youths *vandalized* the shop>
　syn ‖trash, wreck
　rel ‖rip off; destroy, tear up
vanish *vb* to pass from view or out of existence <the moon *vanished* behind a cloud>
　syn clear, disappear, evanesce, evanish, evaporate, fade
　rel dematerialize, dissolve, melt (away); die
　idiom do the vanishing act, vanish from sight, vanish into thin air, vanish like a dream
　con arise, break out (*or* through), come (forth *or* out), emerge, issue, loom (up), materialize, show (up)
　ant appear
vanished *adj syn* see EXTINCT 2
　rel expired, passed away; annihilated, no more, perished
vanity *n syn* see CONCEIT 2
　rel autotheism, self-worship
vanquish *vb syn* see CONQUER 1
　rel surmount; overturn, subvert; humble, trample
vanquisher *n syn* see VICTOR 1
　rel champ, champion
　con loser
vanquishment *n syn* see DEFEAT 1
　rel mastery, subdual, subjugation
vantage *n syn* see ADVANTAGE 3
　ant disadvantage
vapid *adj syn* see INSIPID 3
　rel flavorless, milk-toast, tasteless, weak; dull, unimaginative, uninteresting
　idiom neither hot nor cold, neither one thing nor the other
　con brisk, lively, tangy, zesty; crisp, forceful, incisive, trenchant; expressive, meaningful, pregnant, significant, telling
vaporous *adj* **1** *syn* see HAZY
　2 *syn* see AIRY 3
　rel unsubstantial, wispy; illusory, unreal
vapory *adj* **1** *syn* see HAZY
　2 *syn* see AIRY 3
　rel gaseous
variable *adj* **1** *syn* see CHANGEABLE 1

　rel fitful, spasmodic; irregular, unequable, unequal, ununiform
　con unchanging, unvarying; immobile, stable, unmoving; equable, equal, uniform
　ant constant, invariable
　2 *syn* see MUTABLE 2
　3 *syn* see INCONSTANT 1
variance *n* **1** the quality, state, or fact of being variable <a daily *variance* of 1°F.>
　syn difference, variation
　rel change, deviation, fluctuation
　ant invariance
　2 *syn* see DISCORD
　rel division, separation, severing, sundering
variation *n* **1** *syn* see CHANGE 1
　rel difference, dissimilarity; deflection, discrepancy
　con stability, unchangeableness
　2 *syn* see VARIANCE 1
　rel shift; divergence; discrepancy, disparity
　con uniformity
varicolored *adj syn* see VARIEGATED
　ant solid
varied *adj syn* see MISCELLANEOUS
variegated *adj* having a pattern involving different colors or shades of color <*variegated* leaves>
　syn dappled, discolor, motley, multicolor, multicolored, multihued, parti-color, parti-colored, polychromatic, polychrome, varicolored, versicolor, versicolored
　rel checked, checkered; piebald, pied, skewbald; freaked, streaked; flecked; stippled; marbled; mottle, mottled, spattered, speckled, spotted; calico; pinto
　ant solid
variety *n* **1** the quality or state of being composed of different parts, elements, or individuals <the *variety* of the city's cultural life>
　syn diverseness, diversity, multeity, multifariousness, multiformity, multiplicity, variousness
　rel diversification, heterogeneity, variation
　2 a collection of different things, forms, or qualities especially of a particular class <had a great *variety* of jobs in his lifetime>
　syn assortment
　rel conglomeration, medley, miscellany
　3 *syn* see TYPE
　rel classification; grade, rank
various *adj* **1** *syn* see MANY
　rel assorted, heterogeneous, miscellaneous, omnifarious, omnigenous
　2 *syn* see DIFFERENT 1
　rel changing, variant, varied, varying; distinct, separate; distinctive, individual, peculiar
　ant uniform
　3 *syn* see SEVERAL 3
　ant many, numerous
　4 *syn* see DISTINCT 1
　5 *syn* see CERTAIN 2
various *pron, pl in constr syn* see SUNDRY
variously *adv syn* see OTHERWISE 1
variousness *n syn* see VARIETY 1
varnish *vb syn* see PALLIATE
vary *vb* **1** *syn* see CHANGE 1

rel modulate, qualify
2 *syn* see DIFFER 1
3 *syn* see DIFFER 2
rel depart, deviate, digress, diverge; divide, part, separate
ant agree
4 *syn* see RANGE 3
vast *adj syn* see HUGE
rel big, large; ample, capacious, spacious; broad, expansive, far-flung, wide, widespread; astronomical, cosmic
con confined, limited, narrow, restricted
vastness *n syn* see ENORMITY 2
vatic *adj syn* see PROPHETIC
vaticinal *adj syn* see PROPHETIC
vaticinate *vb syn* see FORETELL
vault *n syn* see CRYPT
vault *vb* **1** *syn* see JUMP 1
rel upleap, upspring; overjump, overleap; clear; rise, soar; ascend, mount; surmount
2 *syn* see CLEAR 8
vaulting *adj syn* see AMBITIOUS 1
rel enthusiastic; opportunistic
vaunt *vb syn* see BOAST
rel brandish, display, exhibit, expose, flaunt, parade, show off
idiom puff oneself
vaunter *n syn* see BRAGGART
vaunting *adj syn* see BOASTFUL
vector *n* an agent capable of transmitting a pathogen from one organism to another <fleas are *vectors* of bubonic plague>
syn carrier, vehicle
veer *vb* **1** *syn* see TURN 6
2 *syn* see SWERVE 1
rel depart, deviate, digress, diverge; angle off, bear off; twist; pivot, turn, wheel
vegetate *vb* to lead a passive existence without exertion of body or mind <he never really lived his life—he merely *vegetated*>
syn stagnate
rel idle; languish; hibernate
idiom idle life away, live the life of a clam, pass the time
vehement *adj syn* see INTENSE 1
rel emphatic, pronounced; energetic, hearty, lively, zealous; forceful, potent, powerful; ardent, fervent, fervid, heated, impassioned, passionate, perfervid; delirious, frantic, furious, rabid, wild
vehicle *n* **1** *syn* see VECTOR
rel agent
2 *syn* see MEAN 2
rel implement, tool
3 a means of transporting goods or passengers <his *vehicle* was an old battered coupe>
syn conveyance, transport, transportation
veil *n syn* see MASK 2
veil *vb syn* see ENFOLD 1
rel mantle, overspread, spread (over); blanket, curtain; camouflage, cloak, cover (up), disguise, mask; conceal, hide, screen, secrete
con exhibit, lay (open), open up, reveal, uncover, unmask; bare, expose, show

ant unveil
vein *n* **1** a distinctive method of expression <wrote her speech in the proper *vein* for a very sophisticated audience>
syn fashion, manner, mode, style, tone
rel way; line; mood, tenor
2 *syn* see HINT 2
3 *syn* see MOOD 1
rel complexion, disposition, fettle, temperament; character, nature, spirit
velitation *n syn* see ENCOUNTER
velleity *n syn* see WILL 1
rel volition; wish
vellicate *vb syn* see JERK
rel nip, pinch; fidget, jig, jiggle
velocipede *n syn* see BICYCLE
velocity *n syn* see SPEED 2
rel headway, impetus, momentum; dispatch, expedition, haste, hurry
velutinous *adj syn* see VELVETY
velvetlike *adj syn* see VELVETY
idiom soft as velvet
velvety *adj* **1** having the extreme softness associated with the surface or appearance of velvet <wore a *velvety* red flower in her hair>
syn velutinous, velvetlike
rel plush, plushy, smooth, soft; glossy, sleek, slick; satiny, silken, silky
2 *syn* see SOFT 3
venal *adj* **1** open to corrupt influence and especially bribery <a *venal* legislator>
syn bribable, buyable, corruptible, purchasable; *compare* CORRUPT 2, CROOKED 2
rel corrupt, flagitious, infamous, iniquitous, nefarious, vicious; hack, hireling, mercenary, paid; ignoble, sordid; unethical, unprincipled, unscrupulous
2 *syn* see CORRUPT 2
vend *vb* **1** *syn* see SELL 2
2 *syn* see PEDDLE 2
3 *syn* see DECLARE 1
vendee *n syn* see PURCHASER
vendetta *n* a prolonged mutual enmity marked by bitter hostility and conflict <a long-standing *vendetta* between two rival gangs>
syn feud
rel dispute, quarrel; rhubarb, row, wrangle; conflict, fight, set-to; blood feud, blood vengeance
vendible *adj syn* see MARKETABLE
ant unvendible
vendible *n, usu* **vendibles** *pl syn* see MERCHANDISE
vendor *n syn* see PEDDLER
veneer *n syn* see MASK 2
veneer *vb syn* see PALLIATE
venerable *adj* **1** deserving to be venerated usually by reason of prolonged testing (as of character) <a *venerable* judge with an impressive knowledge of the law>

---

syn synonym(s)   *rel* related word(s)
ant antonym(s)   *con* contrasted word(s)
idiom idiomatic equivalent(s)
‖ use limited; if in doubt, see a dictionary

syn patriarchal, revered, reverend, reverential;
compare HONORABLE 1
rel dignified, imposing, stately; admirable, estimable; honored, reverenced; worshipful; sacred
ant unvenerable
2 *syn* see ANCIENT 1
rel elderly; patriarchal, reverenced, reverend, venerated
con contemporary, current; fresh, inexperienced, new, untried, unused

venerate *vb syn* see REVERE
rel honor; idolize
idiom put on a pedestal

venery *n syn* see HUNTING

venge *vb syn* see AVENGE
idiom even (up) the score, repay in kind, settle accounts (*or* an account)

vengeance *n syn* see RETALIATION
rel return; repayment; revengefulness, vengefulness

vengeful *adj syn* see VINDICTIVE
rel antagonistic, hostile, inimical, rancorous
con charitable, forgiving, kind; benevolent, benign, inoffensive

venial *adj* of a kind that can be remitted and that does not warrant punishment or penalty <the *venial* indiscretions of youth>
syn excusable, forgivable, pardonable, remittable
rel allowable, unobjectionable; insignificant, minor, trifling, trivial; harmless, tolerable
con criminal, damning, deadly, mortal; grievous, outrageous, serious; inexcusable, unforgivable, unpardonable, unremittable
ant heinous

venom *n syn* see POISON
rel ill will, malignity, rancor, venomousness, virulence, vitriol
con antidote, remedy

venomous *adj syn* see POISONOUS
rel malevolent, malign, malignant; baleful, malefic, maleficent; viperish, viperlike, viperous

vent *vb* **1** *syn* see EMIT 2
rel cast out, discharge, exhaust
2 *syn* see EXPRESS 2
rel utter, voice; assert, declare
idiom come out with, give vent to
con check, curb, inhibit, restrain; repress, suppress
3 *syn* see TAKE OUT (on)

vent *n* **1** *syn* see APERTURE
2 *syn* see EXPRESSION 1
rel articulation, verbalization, vocalization

venter *n syn* see ABDOMEN

ventilate *vb* **1** *syn* see BROACH
2 *syn* see EXPRESS 2
rel go into, take up; debate, deliberate, discourse (about), discuss, ‖rap (about), talk over (*or* of *or* about), thresh out; advertise, broadcast, publish
idiom chew the fat (*or* the rag)

ventilation *n syn* see CONFERENCE 1

venture *vb* **1** to expose to risk or loss <*ventured* their capital in foreign trade>

syn adventure, chance, hazard, risk, wager;
compare GAMBLE 2
rel endanger, imperil, jeopard, jeopardize, jeopardy, peril; expose, lay (open)
idiom take chances (*or* risks) on (*or* with)
2 *syn* see GAMBLE 2
rel bet, operate, play (for), speculate, stake; jeopard, jeopardize, jeopardy
idiom luck it
3 *syn* see FACE 3

venture *n syn* see ADVENTURE
rel attempt, undertaking; crack, fling; dare, gamble, risk, speculation
idiom leap in the dark

venturesome *adj syn* see ADVENTUROUS
rel stalwart, stout, sturdy; brave; overbold
con timid, timorous; afraid, apprehensive, fearful

venturous *adj syn* see ADVENTUROUS
rel aggressive, enterprising, hustling

veracious *adj* **1** *syn* see TRUTHFUL
rel direct; undeceitful, undeceptive
con equivocal; deceitful, dishonest, insincere; false, untruthful
ant unveracious
2 *syn* see TRUE 3
rel unquestionable, valid
con illusory, invalid, wrong
ant unveracious

veraciousness *n syn* see VERACITY 1
rel artlessness, openness; trustworthiness
con falseness, insincerity

veracity *n* **1** the quality or state of keeping close to fact and avoiding distortion or misrepresentation <questions the *veracity* of that witness>
syn truth, truthfulness, veraciousness, veridicality, verity
rel accuracy, correctness, exactness, factualness; frankness, honesty
con inaccuracy, incorrectness; deception, dishonesty, untruth, untruthfulness
ant unveracity
2 something that is true <can make lies sound like *veracities*>
syn gospel, truism, truth, verity
rel verisimilitude; actuality; fact
con lie, untruth
ant unveracity

verbal *adj* **1** *syn* see ORAL 2
2 *syn* see VERBATIM

verbalism *n* **1** *syn* see WORDING
rel styling
2 *syn* see VERBOSITY

verbality *n syn* see VERBIAGE 1
rel verbalism, verboseness, verbosity, wordiness

verbalization *n syn* see SPEECH 1

verbalize *vb syn* see SPEAK 1
rel air, express, give, say, state, vent, ventilate, word
idiom couch in terms, find words to express

verbatim *adv* in the same words <repeated their earlier conversation *verbatim*>
syn direct, directly, literally, literatim, word for word

rel accurately, exactly, precisely
idiom to the letter
con basically, essentially, in essence; carelessly, imprecisely, inaccurately, inexactly

verbatim *adj* using the same words <court stenographers took down the *verbatim* testimony>
syn literal, verbal, word-for-word
rel close, faithful, strict; exact, precise
idiom following the letter, true to the letter
con careless, imprecise, inaccurate, inexact

verbiage *n* **1** a stylistic fault involving excessive wordiness that obscures or unduly complicates expression <the florid *verbiage* of the dissertation>
syn circumambages, circumbendibus, circumlocution, periphrase, periphrasis, pleonasm, redundancy, roundabout, tautology, verbality; *compare* VERBOSITY
rel nimiety; repetition; expansiveness, floridity, floridness; longiloquence, long-windedness
idiom purple prose
con breviloquence, brevity, briefness, terseness
ant concision
2 syn see WORDING

verbose *adj syn* see WORDY
rel flowery, grandiloquent, magniloquent; circumlocutory, periphrastic, pleonastic, tautologous
con precise; close, compact, lean, tight
ant concise; laconic

verboseness *n syn* see VERBOSITY
ant conciseness

verbosity *n* the quality or state or an instance of being wordy <his two-hour lecture was the epitome of *verbosity*> <flowery *verbosities* weakened his speech>
syn prolixity, prolixness, verbalism, verboseness, windiness, wordiness; *compare* VERBIAGE 1
rel bombast, grandiloquence; long-windedness; redundancy
con conciseness, preciseness, succinctness, terseness; leanness, tightness

verboten *adj syn* see FORBIDDEN
rel disallowed, disapproved; unauthorized, unlicensed, unsanctioned; outlawed, taboo
con allowed, permitted; authorized, licensed; approved, endorsed, sanctioned

verdure *n syn* see FOLIAGE

verge *n* **1 syn** see BORDER 1
2 a time interval or set of circumstances marking the imminent beginning of a new state, condition, or action <on the *verge* of war>
syn brink, edge, point, threshold
rel border line

verge *vb* **1 syn** see BORDER 1
rel approach; incline, lean, tend (to *or* toward); touch (on *or* upon)
2 syn see ADJOIN
3 syn see BORDER 3

veridical *adj* **1 syn** see TRUTHFUL
2 syn see REAL 3
3 syn see TRUE 3
rel uncolored, undistorted, unvarnished; actual, real

con invalid; illusory, unreal

veridicality *n syn* see VERACITY 1
rel genuineness

verificatory *adj syn* see CORROBORATIVE

verify *vb syn* see CONFIRM 2
rel demonstrate, prove, test, try; document, establish, settle

verily *adv syn* see EVEN 3

verisimilitude *n* the quality of a representation that causes it to appear true <her characters are too stilted for *verisimilitude*>
syn color, plausibility, verisimility
rel authenticity, genuineness, veritableness; likeness, resemblance, similarity

verisimility *n syn* see VERISIMILITUDE

veritable *adj syn* see AUTHENTIC 2
rel undenied, unrefuted; actual, factual
con doubtful, questionable; imaginary, unreal, untrue; artificial, factitious; counterfeit, false, spurious

veritably *adv syn* see VERY 2

verity *n* **1 syn** see VERACITY 2
ant falsity
2 syn see VERACITY 1

vernacular *adj* of or relating to everyday speech <*vernacular* Welsh differs greatly from literary Welsh>
syn colloquial, vulgar, vulgate

vernacular *n* **1 syn** see LANGUAGE 1
rel mother tongue
idiom native tongue
2 syn see DIALECT 2
3 a commonly spoken as opposed to a prestige variety of a language <literary Chinese and the various *vernaculars*>
syn colloquial, patois, vulgate; *compare* DIALECT 2
rel dialect, lingo, slang

vernacularism *n syn* see BARBARISM

vernacularity *n syn* see BARBARISM

vernal *adj* of, relating to, or resembling the spring of the year <*vernal* sunshine>
syn spring, springlike

versant *adj syn* see FAMILIAR 3
ant unversed

versatile *adj* having a wide range of skills, aptitudes, or interests <a *versatile* artist, who is at home in any medium>
syn adaptable, all-around, ambidextrous, many-sided, mobile, myriad-minded
rel elastic, flexible, plastic, pliable; adroit, dexterous, facile; able, skilled, skillful; accomplished, conversant; gifted, talented; well≈rounded
con inadequate, limited

verse *n* **1 syn** see POETRY 1
2 syn see POEM
rel jingle; ballad, lay; sonnet; lyric; ode; epic

versed *adj* **1 syn** see EXPERIENCED

---

syn synonym(s)   **rel** related word(s)
ant antonym(s)   **con** contrasted word(s)
idiom idiomatic equivalent(s)
‖ use limited; if in doubt, see a dictionary

rel competent
con incompetent
ant unversed
2 syn see FAMILIAR 3
ant unversed

verseman *n syn* see POETASTER
versemonger *n syn* see POETASTER
verser *n syn* see POETASTER
versesmith *n syn* see POETASTER
versicolor *adj syn* see VARIEGATED
versicolored *adj syn* see VARIEGATED
versificator *n syn* see POETASTER
versifier *n syn* see POETASTER
version *n* **1** a restating often in simpler language of something previously stated or written <a simple *version* of "Tom Sawyer" for the use of children>
syn paraphrase, rendering, restatement, translation
rel rendition; clarification, interpretation; condensation, simplification; rewording; restipulation
2 syn see ACCOUNT 7
rel tale
3 syn see INTERPRETATION 2
versus *prep* **1** in conflict with <the case of John Doe *versus* Richard Roe>
syn against
rel con, contra
idiom at cross-purposes with (*or* to), at odds with, at outs with, at variance with, on the outs with
2 in contrast with <the age-old argument about free trade *versus* protection>
syn over against, vis-à-vis
idiom as opposed to
vertebrae *n syn* see SPINE
vertebral column *n syn* see SPINE
vertex *n syn* see TOP 1
rel cap; tip-top; apogee, zenith
idiom upper extremity
vertical *adj* situated at right angles to the plane of the horizon or extending from that plane at such an angle <*vertical* walls>
syn perpendicular, plumb, straight-up
rel erect, upright; steep, up-and-down
con flat, plane
ant horizontal
verticalism *n syn* see VERTICALITY
verticality *n* the quality or state of being vertical <the soaring *verticality* of the spires>
syn perpendicularity, plumbness, verticalism, verticalness
rel erectness, uprightness
con flatness, lowness
ant horizontality
verticalness *n syn* see VERTICALITY
vertiginous *adj syn* see DIZZY 2
verve *n syn* see SPIRIT 5
rel liveliness, vivacity; bounce, buoyancy, elasticity, resiliency, spring; fire, gusto, zest
very *adj* **1 syn** see AUTHENTIC 2
rel hundred-percent, perfect; correct, exact, right

con fake, fraudulent, mock, sham
2 syn see PRECISE 4
rel especial, express, special
3 syn see PERFECT 3
4 being as stated without addition or superfluity <the *very* thought of it makes me ill>
syn bare, mere
5 syn see SAME 1
idiom (the) very same
very *adv* **1** to a high or exceptional degree <a *very* successful meeting>
syn ‖awful, awfully, ‖big, ‖crazy, damned, ‖dreadful, dreadfully, eminently, exceedingly, exceptionally, extremely, greatly, highly, hugely, insatiably, ‖larruping, ‖main, mightily, mighty, ‖monstrous, ‖mortacious, mortally, most, much, notably, parlous, pesky, ‖pure, rattling, remarkably, right, ‖right smart, snapping, so, spanking, staving, strikingly, super, surpassingly, terribly, thoroughly, too, vitally, whacking, whopping
rel passing, quite, somewhat; perfectly, seriously, significantly, tellingly
idiom nothing if not
con inconsiderably, little, scarcely, slightly
2 in actual fact <told the *very* same story>
syn actually, de facto, genuinely, really, truly, veritably
rel exactly, precisely; almost, nearly, practically, well-nigh
idiom in point of fact, in truth
con apparently, ostensibly, outwardly, seemingly
vest *vb* **1 syn** see INVEST 2
2 syn see BELONG 2
vestibule *n* an entrance chamber between the outer door and the interior of a building <the *vestibule* of a theater>
syn foyer, lobby
rel entrance hall, entry, entryway; portal, portico; antechamber, anteroom; narthex
vestige *n* **1** something (as a mark or visible sign) left by a material thing formerly present but now lost or unknown <digging for the *vestiges* of past civilizations>
syn memento, relic, shadow, trace
rel remainder, remains; rag, remnant, scrap, tag
2 syn see FOOTPRINT
rel path; trail
vet *vb syn* see SCRUTINIZE 1
idiom go over with a fine-tooth comb
vet *adj syn* see EXPERIENCED
vet *n syn* see VETERAN
veteran *n* one having knowledge or ability gained through long experience <was a political campaign *veteran* of long standing>
syn longtimer, old hand, old-timer, vet
rel expert, master, past master
con amateur, freshman, youngster
ant novice
veteran *adj syn* see EXPERIENCED
rel wise; sophisticated, worldly
idiom dry behind the ears, not born yesterday, wise in the ways of the world
con inexperienced, unpracticed, unversed; unqualified, unskilled, untrained

veto *vb* to refuse to admit or approve <the President *vetoed* the bill>
 syn kill, negative, ‖nix, non-placet
 rel decline, deny, disallow, forbid, prohibit, refuse, reject; defeat
 idiom put one's veto on
 con admit, approve, assent (to); pass

vex *vb syn* see ANNOY 1
 rel ‖chaw, embarrass; plague; anger, infuriate
 con appease, mollify, pacify, propitiate, smooth (over); please, regale
 ant soothe

vexation *n syn* see ANNOYANCE 1
 rel aggravation, irritation

vexatious *adj syn* see TROUBLESOME

vexing *n syn* see ANNOYANCE 1

via *prep* **1** over a route that passes through <shipped to New York *via* the Panama Canal>
 syn by, by way of, through
 rel along; over
 2 using as a means of approach or action <reached the voters *via* mass-media advertising>
 syn by, by dint of, by means of, by virtue of, by way of, per, through, with
 idiom through the medium of

viable *adj syn* see POSSIBLE 1

viands *n pl syn* see FOOD 1
 rel fare

vibrant *adj syn* see RESONANT

vibrate *vb syn* see SHAKE 2

vice *n* **1** degrading or immoral habits and practices <an exposé of *vice* and crime in the city>
 syn corruption, depravity, immorality, wickedness
 rel decay, rot, squalor; evil, ill, sin, wrong; indecency, unchastity; debasement, debauchery, licentiousness, perversion
 con morality; respectability; uprightness
 ant virtue
 2 *syn* see FAULT 2
 rel shortcoming
 idiom weak point
 3 *syn* see BLEMISH

vice versa *adv syn* see AGAIN 5

vicinage *n syn* see LOCALITY 1

vicinity *n* **1** *syn* see LOCALITY 1
 2 *syn* see ORDER 4

vicious *adj* **1** *syn* see WRONG 1
 2 highly offensive or reprehensible in character, nature, or conduct <*vicious* parents who were a bad influence on their children>
 syn corrupt, degenerate, depraved, flagitious, infamous, miscreant, nefarious, perverse, putrid, rotten, unhealthy, villainous
 rel bad, faulty, poor, unsound; opprobrious, reprehensible; contaminated, obnoxious, septic
 con good, moral, righteous, right-minded
 ant virtuous
 3 *syn* see SAVAGE 1
 rel brutish; bloodthirsty
 4 *syn* see MALICIOUS
 5 *syn* see INTENSE 1
 rel severe

vicissitude *n* **1** *syn* see CHANGE 2
 rel alternation; reversal; transposition; progression; diversity, variety
 2 *syn* see DIFFICULTY 1
 rel chop and change, ups and downs; adversity, mischance, misfortune; affliction, trial, tribulation

victim *n* **1** a living being sacrificed (as in a religious rite) <offered up human *victims* to appease their bloodthirsty gods>
 syn offering, sacrifice
 2 one subjected to oppression, loss, or suffering <*victims* of social injustice>
 syn bottom dog, casualty, prey, underdog
 rel quarry
 3 *syn* see FOOL 3
 idiom easy mark, easy pickings

victimize *vb* **1** *syn* see SACRIFICE 1
 2 *syn* see DUPE

victor *n* **1** one that defeats an enemy <the Allies were the *victors* of World War II>
 syn conqueror, defeater, master, subduer, subjugator, vanquisher
 rel winner
 con conquered, defeated, subjugated; loser
 ant vanquished
 2 a successful contender <emerged as *victor* in the swimming meet>
 syn winner
 rel champ, champion; first, top
 idiom conquering hero
 ant loser

Victorian *adj syn* see PRIM 1
 rel old-fashioned, old-maidish; hidebound; starchy
 con easy going; trendy, with-it

victory *n* **1** the overcoming of an opponent <won a knockout *victory* in the first round>
 syn conquest, triumph, win
 rel command, control, dominion, mastery, subjugation; superiority, supremacy; walkaway, walkover
 idiom a feather in one's cap
 con loss; bust, failure, fizzle, flop, ‖floperoo, washout; comedown, cropper
 ant defeat
 2 *syn* see BETTER 2

victuals *n pl syn* see FOOD 1

videlicet *adv syn* see NAMELY

video *n syn* see TELEVISION

vie *vb* **1** *syn* see COMPETE 1
 rel challenge; match; outvie
 2 *syn* see OPPOSE 1

view *n* **1** *syn* see LOOK 1
 rel examination, inspection, scan, scrutiny
 2 *syn* see EXAMINATION
 3 *syn* see EYE 4
 4 what is revealed to the vision or can be seen <the *view* from the window>

---

syn synonym(s)   *rel* related word(s)
ant antonym(s)   *con* contrasted word(s)
idiom idiomatic equivalent(s)
‖ use limited; if in doubt, see a dictionary

syn outlook, scene, sight
rel panorama, picture, prospect, vista
5 extent or range of vision <there were still no ships in *view*>
syn sight
rel look; apprehension, scan
6 something (as an aim, end, or motive) to or by which the mind is directed <kept this *view* in mind while negotiating>
syn object
rel intent, intention, purpose; aim, ambition, goal, objective; design, plan, project; consideration, notion; expectation
7 *syn* see OPINION
rel concept, conception; deduction, inference
view *vb* **1** *syn* see SCRUTINIZE 1
2 *syn* see EYE 1
rel observe
3 *syn* see SEE 1
4 *syn* see CONSIDER 3
viewable *adj syn* see VISUAL 2
viewer *n syn* see SPECTATOR
viewpoint *n* **1** *syn* see EYE 4
2 the position or attitude that determines how something is seen, presented, or evaluated <from this *viewpoint* the picture looks askew> <consider totalitarianism from the German *viewpoint*>
syn angle, direction, outlook, side, slant, standpoint; *compare* EYE 4
rel estimation; attitude, position, posture, stand; long view, perspective
idiom frame of reference, point of view, vantage point
viewy *adj syn* see IMPRACTICAL 1
vigil *n syn* see LOOKOUT 3
vigilance *n syn* see LOOKOUT 3
vigilant *adj syn* see WATCHFUL
rel agog, anxious, avid, eager, keen; acute, sharp, sharp-eyed; attentive
idiom on one's guard, with a weather eye open
con lax, neglectful, negligent, remiss, slack; forgetful, oblivious, unmindful
vigor *n* **1** *syn* see POWER 4
2 a quality of physical or mental force or forcefulness <the *vigor* of youth>
syn bang, drive, getup, get-up-and-go, go, pep, punch, push, snap, starch, vitality; *compare* ENERGY 2, ENTERPRISE 4, SPIRIT 5
rel bounce, energy, force, might, muscularity, power, strength; healthiness, soundness; lustiness, manliness, virility
con slowness, sluggishness
ant weakness
3 *syn* see ENERGY 2
rel dash, drive, dynamism, fire, punch, starch, steam, vim, zing, zip; ability, capability, capacity
con ineffectiveness; impotence; incompetence, uselessness, worthlessness
vigorous *adj* having or manifesting great vitality and force <seemed as *vigorous* as a youth half his age>
syn dynamic, energetic, lusty, red-blooded, strenuous, ‖survigorous, vital

rel brisk, dashing, lively, slashing; exuberant, mettlesome, proud, spirited; driving, hard-driving, hard-hitting, robust, rough-and-ready, zealous; bouncing, hardy, healthy, hearty, masterful, potent, powerful, strong, tough; rude, stout, sturdy; athletic, husky, muscular, sinewy
con languorous, unenergetic; decrepit, feeble, infirm, weak; impotent
ant lethargic
vigorously *adv syn* see HARD 1
rel alertly, eagerly; boldly, firmly, purposefully, resolutely, unfalteringly, zealously; lustily, robustly
con aimlessly, languorously; falteringly, indecisively; impotently
vile *adj* **1** *syn* see BASE 3
rel corrupted, debased, debauched, depraved, perverted; coarse, gross, obscene, vulgar; disgusting, foul, nasty; abhorrent, contemptible, loathsome, offensive, repulsive, revolting
2 *syn* see OFFENSIVE
vilify *vb syn* see MALIGN
rel abuse, mistreat, misuse, outrage; assail, attack, berate; denounce
con commend, compliment; acclaim, exalt; celebrate, glorify, honor; adore, worship
ant eulogize
vilifying *adj syn* see LIBELOUS
villa *n syn* see MANSION
villain *n* **1** a low, mean, reprehensible person utterly lacking in principle <was an insufferable bully, a tyrant, and a *villain* in general>
syn blackguard, heel, knave, lowlife, miscreant, rascal, reprobate, rogue, roperipe, scoundrel, ‖slubberdegullion; *compare* SNOT 1, DEVIL 2
rel meanie; evildoer, offender, sinner; criminal, malefactor
2 *syn* see SCAMP
villainize *vb syn* see MALIGN
ant eulogize
villainous *adj syn* see VICIOUS 2
rel contrary, detestable, objectionable, offensive; debased, perverted; atrocious, heinous, outrageous; abandoned, dissolute, profligate
villenage *n syn* see BONDAGE
vim *n syn* see SPIRIT 5
rel pepper; kick, push
vinculum *n syn* see BOND 3
vindicable *adj syn* see JUSTIFIABLE
rel inoffensive, unobjectionable, venial
con indefensible, unjustifiable; inexcusable, unforgivable; heinous, mortal
vindicate *vb* **1** *syn* see AVENGE
2 *syn* see MAINTAIN 2
rel advocate, plead (for), second, support, uphold; rationalize; bear out, prove
3 *syn* see EXCULPATE
rel confute, disprove, refute; defend, guard, protect, shield
con accuse, attack, calumniate
ant convict
vindictive *adj* showing or motivated by a desire for vengeance <*vindictive* hatred for his brother>

syn revengeful, vengeful, wreakful
rel grim, implacable, merciless, relentless, unrelenting; malicious, malign, malignant, spiteful
con charitable, forgiving, merciful, relenting
ant unvindictive
vinegarish *adj syn* see CANTANKEROUS
vinegary *adj syn* see CANTANKEROUS
vintage *adj* **1** being of old, recognized, and enduring interest, importance, or quality <a *vintage* comedy from the silent movie era>
syn classic, classical
2 *syn* see OLD-FASHIONED
violate *vb* **1** to fail to keep <people who thoughtlessly *violate* the law>
syn breach, break, contravene, infract, infringe, offend, transgress
rel disregard, trample (on *or* upon); err, sin; overpass, trespass
con abide by, carry out, fulfill, submit (to); heed, keep, mind
ant observe; obey
2 *syn* see RAPE
violation *n* **1** *syn* see BREACH 1
rel break; encroachment; illegality, misdemeanor, offense, wrong
ant observance
2 *syn* see PROFANATION
rel defacement, defacing
violence *n syn* see FORCE 4
rel frenzy, fury, savagery; assault, attack, clash, foul play, onslaught, rampage, struggle, tumult, uproar
con passiveness, passivity; peace, peacefulness
ant nonviolence
violent *adj syn* see INTENSE 1
rel forceful, forcible, mighty, potent, powerful, strong; extreme, immoderate, inordinate; acute, cutting, piercing, splitting
con calm, moderate, peaceful
ant nonviolent
violently *adv syn* see HARD 2
rel combatively; destructively, ruinously
idiom like fury, with a vengeance
VIP *n syn* see NOTABLE 1
virago *n* a woman of extremely pugnacious temperament <an overbearing *virago* who screamed at her children and squabbled with her neighbors>
syn amazon, fishwife, harpy, ogress, scold, shrew, termagant, vixen, Xanthippe
rel cat; dragon; fury
virgin *adj* **1** never having had sexual relations <*virgin* girls were sacrificed>
syn intact, maiden, undeflowered, virginal
rel innocent, untouched; single, spouseless, unmarried, unwed; abstinent, celibate
2 not marred or altered from a natural or original state <a *virgin* forest>
syn unspoiled, untapped, untouched, virginal
rel primeval, pristine; fresh, new; unmarred, unsullied
virginal *adj* **1** *syn* see VIRGIN 1
2 *syn* see VIRGIN 2
virginity *n* the quality or state of being a virgin <lost her *virginity*>

syn maidenhead, maidenhood
rel chasteness, chastity, purity
virile *adj* characterized by the energy and drive considered typical of a man or of men <developed a strong *virile* prose style>
syn male, manlike, manly, masculine
rel macho, manful, mannish; decisive, driving, forceful; energetic, potent, robust; ultramasculine, ultravirile
con effeminate, womanish; emasculated, weak, weakened; impotent
virility *n* the vigor or agressiveness held to be typical of males <pundits decided that the candidate's conspicuous *virility* appealed to voters>
syn maleness, manfulness, manliness, masculinity
rel courage, dauntlessness, guts, machismo, macho, mettle, ‖moxie, pluck, resolution, spirit, spunk
con effeminacy, unmanliness; impotence, weakness; prissiness, sissiness
virtual *adj syn* see IMPLICIT 2
rel basic, essential, fundamental
ant actual
virtuality *n syn* see ESSENCE 2
virtually *adv* not absolutely or actually, yet so nearly so that the difference is negligible <that request is *virtually* an order>
syn in essence, morally, practically; *compare* ALMOST 2
rel basically, essentially, fundamentally; absolutely, actually
idiom for all practical purposes, in effect, in substance, to all intents and purposes
virtue *n* **1** *syn* see GOODNESS
rel fealty, fidelity, loyalty, piety; virtuousness
con dishonesty; disloyalty, infidelity; evil; immorality; depravity
ant vice
2 *syn* see EXCELLENCE
rel attribute, characteristic, feature, property; effectiveness, effectualness, efficacy; force, might, power, strength
3 *syn* see QUALITY 1
4 *syn* see QUALITY 2
5 *syn* see POWER 4
virtuosic *adj syn* see CONSUMMATE 1
virtuoso *n* **1** *syn* see EXPERT
2 *syn* see MUSICIAN
virtuous *adj* **1** *syn* see EFFECTIVE
ant virtueless
2 *syn* see MORAL 1
rel spotless, unsullied, untainted, untarnished; worthy
con dishonest; unjust; unworthy; impure, tainted; immodest, immoral, indecent; vicious, wicked
ant unvirtuous, virtueless
3 *syn* see GOOD 11

---

syn synonym(s)   *rel* related word(s)
ant antonym(s)   *con* contrasted word(s)
idiom idiomatic equivalent(s)
‖ use limited; if in doubt, see a dictionary

rel faultless, sinless
idiom innocent as a lamb, in the clear, without reproach
con bad, impure, unrighteous
ant unvirtuous, virtueless; vicious
virulent *adj* **1** *syn* see POISONOUS
rel malign, malignant
2 *syn* see BITTER 3
rel biting, cutting, scathing, sharp, stabbing; hateful, spiteful, unfriendly
virus *n syn* see POISON
rel corruption, taint
visage *n* **1** *syn* see FACE 1
2 *syn* see LOOK 2
vis–à–vis *n* **1** *syn* see OPPOSITE NUMBER
2 *syn* see TÊTE-À-TÊTE
vis–à–vis *prep* **1** *syn* see AGAINST 1
rel opposite
2 *syn* see VERSUS 2
viscera *n pl syn* see ENTRAILS
visceral *adj* **1** *syn* see INNER 2
2 *syn* see INSTINCTIVE 1
viscerous *adj syn* see INNER 2
viscid *adj syn* see VISCOUS
rel jellylike, slabby
viscose *adj syn* see VISCOUS
rel smeary
viscous *adj* having a glutinous adhesive consistency or quality <a *viscous* scum covered the surface of the platter>
syn tenacious, tough, viscid, viscose
rel ‖slab, slimy, thick; glutinous, gummy, ropy, sticky; semifluid; stiff
visibility *n* the quality or state of being visible <very poor *visibility* due to fog>
syn visuality
visible *adj syn* see VISUAL 2
rel seen
vision *n* **1** *syn* see REVELATION
rel apparition, phenomenon, presence
2 *syn* see FANCY 4
rel muse
idiom phantom of the mind
3 *syn* see EYE 2
vision *vb syn* see THINK 1
visional *adj syn* see VISUAL 1
visionary *adj* **1** *syn* see DREAMY 1
rel abstracted, introspective, musing; impractical
idiom out of this world, up in the clouds
2 *syn* see IDEALISTIC
rel exalted, grandiose, lofty, noble, pretentious
ant pragmatic, pragmatical
3 *syn* see AMBITIOUS 2
rel radical
visionary *n syn* see DREAMER
ant pragmatist
visionless *adj syn* see BLIND 1
visit *vb* **1** *syn* see INFLICT 2
rel afflict, bother, pain, trouble; avenge, punish
idiom bring down upon
2 to make a social call upon <*visited* friends briefly in the evening>

syn call, come by, come over, drop (in *or* by), look in, look up, pop (in), run in, see, step in, stop (in *or* by)
3 to reside with temporarily as a guest <*visited* with friends in the country for a few weeks>
syn sojourn, stay, stop (over), tarry
rel frequent; reside
4 *syn* see CONVERSE
visit *n* **1** a coming to stay with another temporarily and usually briefly <pay a *visit* to friends>
syn call, visitation
2 *syn* see SOJOURN
visitant *n syn* see VISITOR 1
visitation *n* **1** *syn* see VISIT 1
2 *syn* see TRIAL 1
rel mischance; calamity, catastrophe, disaster
visitor *n* **1** one who visits another <there are *visitors* in the living room>
syn caller, guest, visitant; *compare* COMPANY 2
rel invitee
2 visitors *pl syn* see COMPANY 2
visor *n* **1** a projecting front brim on a cap or hat for shading the eyes <the *visor* kept out the sun>
syn bill, peak
rel eyeshade
2 *syn* see MASK 1
vista *n* an extensive or distant view <a long flat tree-lined *vista*>
syn lookout, outlook, perspective, prospect, scape
rel panorama, scene, sight, view; range, scope, survey
idiom long view
visual *adj* **1** of or relating to or used in vision <the *visual* sense>
syn ocular, optic, optical, visional
2 capable of being seen <*visual* objects>
syn ocular, seeable, viewable, visible
rel discernible, perceivable, perceptible
visuality *n syn* see VISIBILITY
visualize *vb* **1** *syn* see THINK 1
rel picture, view; objectify; call up, conjure (up)
idiom bring (*or* call) to mind, conjure up a mental image (*or* picture) of, see in the mind's eye
2 *syn* see FORESEE
vital *adj* **1** *syn* see LIVING 1
rel breathing
2 *syn* see VIGOROUS
3 *syn* see ESSENTIAL 2
rel indispensable, needed, needful, required, requisite; integral, prerequisite
vital force *n syn* see SOUL 1
vitality *n syn* see VIGOR 2
rel animation, life, liveliness, pulse; endurance, energy, spirit, vim
vitalize *vb* to arouse to activity, animation, or life <atomic energy is a force that can *vitalize* or destroy human civilization>
syn actify, activate, activize, energize
rel animate, enliven, invigorate, quicken, vivify; dynamize, excite, galvanize, provoke, stimulate; pep up, strengthen
idiom put life into
con eviscerate, weaken

ant atrophy; devitalize
vitalizing *adj syn* see INVIGORATING
　ant devitalizing
vitally *adv syn* see VERY 1
vitiate *adj syn* see DEBASED
　ant purified
vitiate *vb* **1** *syn* see INJURE 1
　rel twist, warp
　2 *syn* see DEBASE 1
　rel defile, soil, sully, taint; prostitute; contaminate
　idiom drive to the dogs
　ant purify
　3 *syn* see ABOLISH 1
vitiated *adj syn* see DEBASED
　rel contaminated, defiled, polluted, tainted; impaired, injured, spoiled
　ant purified
vitriolic *adj syn* see BITTER 3
vituperate *vb syn* see SCOLD 1
　rel condemn, lambaste; asperse, calumniate,
malign, traduce; bark (at), growl (at), yell (at);
abuse, curse
　idiom rip into
　con applaud, commend, compliment; eulogize,
extol, praise
　ant acclaim
vituperation *n syn* see ABUSE
　rel blame, censure, revilement, scolding,
tongue-lashing
　con eulogy, extolment
　ant acclaim, praise
vituperative *adj syn* see ABUSIVE
　rel censorious, critical; severe; railing, scolding
vituperatory *adj syn* see ABUSIVE
　rel censorious, critical; severe; railing, scolding
vituperous *adj syn* see ABUSIVE
　rel censorious, critical; severe; railing, scolding
vivacious *adj* **1** *syn* see LIVELY 1
　rel breezy, vibrant, zesty; frolicsome, playful,
sportive
　idiom gay as a lark
　ant languid
　2 *syn* see EXUBERANT 1
viva voce *adj syn* see VOCAL 1
vivid *adj* **1** *syn* see COLORFUL
　2 *syn* see GRAPHIC 1
　rel acute, intense, keen, sharp; dramatic, dramaturgic, theatrical; eloquent, expressive, meaningful, rich; animated, lively, spirited, vigorous
vivificate *vb syn* see QUICKEN 1
　rel revive
vivify *vb syn* see QUICKEN 1
　rel refresh, renew, restore; excite, galvanize
　idiom give life to, imbue with life, put new life
into
vivres *n pl syn* see FOOD 1
vixen *n syn* see VIRAGO
vizard *n syn* see MASK 1
‖vlei *n syn* see SWAMP
vocable *n syn* see WORD 2
　rel verbalism
vocabulary *n* **1** the sum or set of words employed
by a language, group, individual, or work or in

relation to a subject <Latin contributes heavily
to the *vocabulary* of English>
　syn lexicon, word-hoard, word-stock
　idiom stock of words
　2 *syn* see TERMINOLOGY
　rel phraseology
vocal *adj* **1** uttered by the voice or having to do
with such utterance <the infant's primitive *vocal*
sounds from which language develops>
　syn articulate, oral, sonant, spoken, viva voce,
voiced
　rel intonated; expressed, uttered
　con unexpressed, unuttered, unvoiced
　ant nonvocal
　2 *syn* see VOCALIC
　ant consonantal
　3 being able to express oneself clearly or easily
<he was hardly *vocal:* he could scarcely express
the simplest concepts>
　syn articulate, eloquent, fluent, smooth-spoken
　rel expressing, voicing; expressive; outspoken,
stentorian, venting
　con faltering, halting, hesitant, stumbling
　4 *syn* see OUTSPOKEN
vocalic *adj* marked by, consisting of, or functioning as a vowel or vowels <*vocalic* and consonantal sounds>
　syn vocal, vowel, vowely
　rel vowellike
vocalism *n syn* see VOCALIZATION
vocalization *n* the exercise of the vocal organs in
song or speech <her *vocalization* of a previously
unstated thought>
　syn articulation, utterance, uttering, vocalism;
compare SPEECH 1
　rel mouth, mouthing; sounding, voice, voicing;
diction, enunciation, verbalization; speaking,
speech
vocalize *vb* **1** *syn* see SPEAK 1
　rel emit, let out; express; enunciate, pronounce;
communicate, convey, impart
　idiom execute vocally
　2 *syn* see SING 1
vocation *n* **1** *syn* see TRADE 1
　2 *syn* see MISSION
vocative *adj syn* see GLIB
　rel chatty, garrulous, loquacious, talkative,
windy; slick, smooth
vociferant *adj syn* see VOCIFEROUS
vociferate *vb syn* see CALL 1
vociferous *adj* so loud, noisy, and insistent as to
compel attention <the crowd made *vociferous*
protests against the speaker's statement>
　syn blatant, boisterous, clamorous, ‖dinsome,
loudmouthed, multivocal, obstreperous, openmouthed, strident, vociferant
　rel distracting; loud, noisy, shrill
　con close-lipped, reserved, silent, uncommunicative; noiseless, quiet, still

---

syn synonym(s)　　　*rel* related word(s)
ant antonym(s)　　　*con* contrasted word(s)
idiom idiomatic equivalent(s)
‖ use limited; if in doubt, see a dictionary

vogue *n syn* see FASHION 2
  rel bon ton, fashionableness, stylishness
voice *n* 1 *syn* see EXPRESSION 1
  rel speech
  2 the right to express a wish, choice, or opinion
  or to influence a situation <even the youngest
  had a *voice* in planning the party>
  syn say, say-so
voice *vb syn* see SPEAK 1
  rel sound; articulate, enunciate, pronounce; formulate, phrase, present, put; recount, tell
voiced *adj syn* see VOCAL 1
voiceless *adj syn* see DUMB 1
void *adj* 1 *syn* see EMPTY 1
  ant full
  2 *syn* see DEVOID
  rel scant, short, shy; bare, bereft, denuded, deprived
  3 *syn* see NULL
  rel negated
void *n syn* see HOLE 3
void *vb* 1 *syn* see VACATE 2
  rel evacuate; deplete, drain, eliminate; eject, remove, throw out
  2 *syn* see DISCHARGE 5
void *vb syn* see ANNUL 4
  idiom declare (*or* make) null and void
voidness *n syn* see VACUITY 2
  ant fullness
volage *adj syn* see GIDDY 1
volant *adj syn* see AGILE
volatile *adj* 1 *syn* see ELASTIC 2
  rel capricious, fickle, inconstant, mercurial, unstable; flighty, flippant, frivolous, light-minded;
  changeable, protean, variable
  2 *syn* see EXCITABLE
  rel explosive
  3 *syn* see INCONSTANT 1
  4 *syn* see TRANSIENT
volatility *n syn* see LIGHTNESS
  rel animation, sprightliness; inconstancy, instability, mercurialness; changeability, variability
volition *n syn* see WILL 2
  rel choice, election, option, selection; desire,
  preference
  con coercion, compulsion, duress, force
volley *n syn* see BARRAGE
volte–face *n syn* see REVERSAL 1
volte–face *vb syn* see TURN 6
  rel about-face, face (about), right-about-face
voluble *adj syn* see GLIB
volume *n* 1 *syn* see BOOK 1
  2 *syn* see BULK 1
  rel amount, content, quantity
  3 *syn* see BODY 4
voluminous *adj syn* see MANY
voluntary *adj* consisting of or proceeding from an
  exercise of free will <the law requires that a confession be *voluntary*>
  syn deliberate, intentional, unforced, unprescribed, willful, willing, witting
  rel chosen, elected, opted, volitional; autonomous, free, independent
  con coerced, compelled, forced; unintentional,
  unplanned, unwilling, unwitting

  ant involuntary
voluptuous *adj syn* see SENSUOUS
  rel indulgent, self-gratifying; abandoned, dissipated, dissolute, excessive, wanton
  con self-contained, self-denying
  ant ascetic
vomit *vb* to discharge the contents of the stomach
  through the mouth <the churning seas made
  several passengers *vomit*>
  syn barf, bring up, ‖cack, ‖cascade, ‖cast, ‖cat,
  disgorge, ‖heave, shoot, sick (up), spew, spit up,
  throw up, upchuck
  rel gag, regurgitate, retch; keck; eject, expel
  idiom ‖blow one's lunch, holler New York, lose
  one's cookies
voodoo *n* 1 *syn* see MAGICIAN 1
  2 *syn* see JINX
voodoo *vb syn* see BEWITCH 1
voodooist *n syn* see MAGICIAN 1
voracious *adj* excessively greedy (as in appetite,
  reactions, or behavior) <the wolverine is an extremely *voracious* eater>
  syn edacious, gluttonous, rapacious, ravening,
  ravenous
  rel acquisitive, covetous, grasping, greedy; de-
  vouring, gorging, satiating, sating, surfeiting;
  avid, insatiable
vortex *n syn* see EDDY
  rel spiral, spout
votary *n* 1 *syn* see ADDICT
  rel disciple; freak
  2 *syn* see AMATEUR 1
  rel hound
vote *n* 1 *syn* see BALLOT 1
  2 *syn* see SUFFRAGE
vote (in) *vb syn* see ELECT 2
  rel choose, decide
  idiom cast one's vote for
vouch *vb syn* see CERTIFY 1
  rel support, uphold; confirm, corroborate,
  prove, substantiate, verify; assure, guarantee
vouchsafe *vb syn* see GRANT 1
  rel condescend, deign, stoop; accommodate,
  favor, oblige
vow *vb* to promise solemnly <*vowed* never to leave
  each other>
  syn covenant, pledge, plight, swear; *compare*
  PROMISE 1
  rel assert, declare, ‖swan; promise
  idiom give (*or* make) a solemn promise, give
  one's word of honor
vowel *adj syn* see VOCALIC
vowely *adj syn* see VOCALIC
voyage *n* a journey by water <took the new ship
  on a long *voyage*>
  syn cruise
  rel journey, tour, trip
voyeur *n syn* see PEEPING TOM
vulgar *adj* 1 *syn* see VERNACULAR
  rel conversational, spoken; idiomatic
  2 *syn* see PUBLIC 4
  3 *syn* see COARSE 3
  4 *syn* see OBSCENE 2
  rel base, low, vile; loathsome, offensive, repulsive, revolting; indecorous, indelicate, uncouth

con decent, delicate, refined; high-minded, lofty, noble

5 *syn* see BARBARIC 1

rel inelegant, ungraceful; improper, incorrect, unseemly; uncouth, unpolished, unrefined

idiom in very poor taste

con elegant, graceful; correct, proper, seemly

vulgarism *n syn* see BARBARISM

vulgate *adj syn* see VERNACULAR

vulgate *n syn* see VERNACULAR 3

vulnerability *n syn* see EXPOSURE
  rel vincibility
vulnerableness *n syn* see EXPOSURE
  rel weakness
vulnerary *adj syn* see CURATIVE
vulpine *adj syn* see SLY 2
vulture *vb syn* see STEAL 1
vulturine *adj syn* see RAPACIOUS 1
vulturish *adj syn* see RAPACIOUS 1
vulturous *adj syn* see RAPACIOUS 1

∥wack *n* *syn* see ECCENTRIC

wacky *adj* **1** *syn* see FOOLISH 2
  2 *syn* see INSANE 1

wad *n* **1** *syn* see LUMP 1
  2 *often* **wads** *pl* *syn* see SCAD
  3 *syn* see FORTUNE 4

wade (in *or* into) *vb* *syn* see PITCH IN 1

∥waffle *vb* *syn* see BABBLE 2

wag *vb* to move to and fro <the dog *wagged* his tail briskly>
  syn beat, lash, switch, waggle, wave, woggle
  rel shake, twitch, wiggle; oscillate; wigwag

wag *n* **1** a person full of sportive humor <a gay young *wag*, always full of fun>
  syn card, comedian, humorist, joker, zany
  rel clown, cutup, madcap, prankster, show-off; jester, kidder, quipster, wisecracker, wit
  idiom life of the party
  2 *syn* see ZANY 2
  3 *syn* see HUMORIST 2

wage *n, often* **wages** *pl* the price paid a person for his labor or services <high *wages* are often seen as a factor in inflation>
  syn emolument, fee, hire, pay, pay envelope, salary, stipend
  rel compensation, recompense, remuneration, reward; earnings, income, receipts, return(s), take

wager *n* *syn* see BET

wager *vb* **1** *syn* see VENTURE 1
  2 *syn* see GAMBLE 1
  idiom lay a wager

waggery *n* **1** *syn* see MISCHIEVOUSNESS
  2 *syn* see JOKE 1

waggish *adj* *syn* see PLAYFUL 1
  rel facetious, humorous, jocose, jocular, witty; comic, comical, droll, funny, laughable, ludicrous; arch, pert, saucy
  con earnest, grave, sedate, serious, sober, staid

waggishness *n* *syn* see MISCHIEVOUSNESS

waggle *vb* *syn* see WAG
  rel sway, waddle, wobble

wail *vb* **1** *syn* see CRY 2
  idiom make an outcry
  2 *syn* see HOWL 1
  3 *syn* see BAWL 2
  4 *syn* see COMPLAIN

wailful *adj* *syn* see MELANCHOLY 2

waistband *n* *syn* see BELT 1

wait *vb* *syn* see STAY 2
  rel anticipate, foresee; await, expect
  idiom bide one's time, cool one's heels, look forward to, mark time
  con depart, go, leave

wait (on) *vb* *syn* see MINISTER (to)

waive *vb* **1** *syn* see RELINQUISH
  rel allow, concede, grant

con claim, demand, exact, require; assert, defend, maintain
  2 *syn* see DEFER

wake *vb* **1** to stop sleeping <she usually *woke* before dawn>
  syn awake, awaken, rouse, stir, waken
  rel arise, get up, roll out
  con catnap, doze, drowse, nap, nod, snooze; sleep, slumber
  2 *syn* see STIR 1
  rel freshen, renew
  con calm, ease, mollify, relax

waken *vb* **1** *syn* see STIR 1
  rel freshen, renew
  con calm, ease, mollify, relax
  2 *syn* see WAKE 1

wale *n* *syn* see WHEAL

walk *vb* **1** to advance on foot step by step <often *walked* to work on pleasant mornings>
  syn ambulate, foot (it), hoof, pace, step, traipse, tread, troop
  rel circumambulate, perambulate, promenade, ramble, stroll; hike, tramp; lumber, plod, slog, stride, stump, trudge; leg, race, run
  idiom beat one's feet, heel and toe it, ride shanks' mare
  con drive, ride
  2 *syn* see TRAVERSE 5

walk *n* **1** a usually brief journey on foot for pleasure or exercise <always took a *walk* before breakfast>
  syn constitutional, ramble, saunter, stroll, turn
  rel hike, march, tramp; deambulation, parade, promenade; airing, stretch
  2 *syn* see FIELD

walkabout *n* *syn* see TRAMP 3

walkaway *n* *syn* see RUNAWAY

walk out *vb* *syn* see STRIKE 1

walkover *n* *syn* see RUNAWAY

wall *n* *syn* see BAR 2

wall *vb* *syn* see ENCLOSE 1

wallop *n* **1** *syn* see BLOW 1
  2 *syn* see IMPACT 1
  3 *syn* see THRILL

wallop *vb* **1** *syn* see BEAT 1
  2 *syn* see WHIP 2
  3 *syn* see SLAM 1

walloping *adj* *syn* see HUGE

wallow *vb* **1** to roll or move in an indolent and ungainly yet comfortable fashion <hogs *wallowing* in a cool mudhole>
  syn welter
  rel flounder, roll, tumble; cuddle, nestle, snuggle
  2 to move or progress unsteadily and clumsily as if beset by obstacles <*wallowed* through the mire for miles trying to get help>

syn blunder, flounder, lurch, stumble; *compare* STUMBLE 3
rel reel, stagger, sway, totter, wamble, welter
idiom make heavy weather (of)
3 to become deeply or excessively involved in or with something subjectively felt as pleasant <*wallowing* in luxury>
syn bask, indulge, luxuriate, revel, roll, rollick, welter
rel baby, humor, pamper, spoil; appreciate, delight (in), enjoy, relish
con abstain, refrain; avoid, eschew, shun
waltz *vb syn* see BREEZE
‖**wambly** *adj syn* see SQUEAMISH 1
‖**wampum** *n syn* see MONEY
wan *adj* **1** *syn* see PALE 1
rel cadaverous, haggard, worn; blanched, bleached, washed-out; anemic, bloodless
2 *syn* see WEAK 4
wander *vb* **1** to move about from place to place more or less aimlessly and without obvious plan <*wandering* through the forest>
syn bat, circumambulate, drift, gad, gallivant, maunder, meander, mooch, ‖project, ramble, range, roam, roll, rove, straggle, stray, traipse, vagabond, vagabondize; *compare* SAUNTER
rel amble, saunter, stroll; divagate, diverge; trail; boom, bum, tramp
2 *syn* see DIGRESS 2
3 *syn* see ERR
wanderer *n syn* see ROVER
wandering *adj* **1** *syn* see ITINERANT
2 *syn* see ERRATIC 1
3 *syn* see DELIRIOUS 1
wane *vb* **1** *syn* see ABATE 4
ant wax
2 *syn* see FAIL 3
ant wax
wangle *vb syn* see ENGINEER
rel outflank, outgeneral, outmaneuver, overreach
waning *n syn* see FAILURE 4
ant waxing
‖**wanky** *adj syn* see WEAK 1
want *vb* **1** *syn* see LACK
idiom be found wanting, fall short, feel the want of
2 *syn* see DESIRE 1
rel choose, prefer
idiom could do with, have a mind (*or* an eye) to
3 to have as a duty or responsibility <you *want* to behave yourself>
syn must, ought, should
rel become, befit, behoove; need (to)
idiom be wise to, had better (*or* best)
want *n* **1** *syn* see ABSENCE
rel exigency, necessity, need
con sufficiency
2 *syn* see POVERTY 1
rel exiguousness, meagerness, scantiness, skimpiness; inadequacy, insufficiency
con riches
3 *syn* see REQUIREMENT 1
wanting *adj syn* see ABSENT 1

2 *syn* see SHORT 3
3 *syn* see DEFICIENT 1
wanting *prep syn* see WITHOUT 2
wanton *adj* **1** *syn* see FAST 7
rel lax, slack, wayward
idiom of easy virtue, of loose morals
con austere, puritanical, restrained, self-restrained
ant chaste
2 *syn* see SUPEREROGATORY
rel malevolent, malicious, spiteful; contrary, perverse, wayward
wanton *n* a woman who engages in lewd unseemly conduct <giddy *wantons* flaunting themselves in bars>
syn baggage, ‖bim, ‖bimbo, cyprian, hussy, jade, jezebel, ‖pig, slattern, slut, strumpet, tramp, trollop, trull, wench
idiom loose woman
wanton *vb syn* see TRIFLE 1
wantwit *n syn* see DUNCE
war *vb syn* see CONTEND 1
rel attempt, endeavor, essay, strive, struggle; challenge, engage, take on
idiom draw the sword against, lift one's hand against, take up the cudgels
warble *n syn* see MELODY
war chest *n syn* see TREASURY 2
war club *n syn* see CUDGEL
war cry *n syn* see BATTLE CRY
ward *n* **1** *syn* see GUARD 2
2 *syn* see DEFENSE 1
3 *syn* see CUSTODY
ward *vb* **1** to cause to miss an objective by or as if by turning aside <*warded* the stroke of his enemy's sword with his shield>
syn deflect, fend, parry
rel block, check, halt, stay, stymie; avert, divert, turn
idiom keep at arm's length, turn aside
2 *syn* see PREVENT 2
rel balk, foil, frustrate, thwart; check, interrupt
ant conduce (to)
ward (off) *vb syn* see FEND (off)
ant bring on
warden *n syn* see CUSTODIAN
ware *adj syn* see AWARE
warehouse *vb syn* see STOW
rel accommodate; guard, protect, shelter
wares *n pl syn* see MERCHANDISE
warfare *n syn* see CONTEST 1
warhorse *n syn* see COURSER
warlike *adj* **1** *syn* see BELLIGERENT
ant peaceable
2 *syn* see MARTIAL
rel battling, contending, fighting, warring
ant unwarlike
warlock *n syn* see MAGICIAN 1
warm *adj* **1** *syn* see ENTHUSIASTIC

---

syn synonym(s) *rel* related word(s)
ant antonym(s) *con* contrasted word(s)
idiom idiomatic equivalent(s)
‖ use limited; if in doubt, see a dictionary

2 *syn* see TENDER

rel ardent, fervent, passionate; affable, cordial, gracious; heartfelt, hearty, sincere, wholehearted

ant cool; austere

warmed–over *adj syn* see TRITE

warmhearted *adj syn* see TENDER

rel benign, benignant, kind, kindly, outgoing

con austere, cold, cool, frigid, frosty, severe, stern

ant coldhearted

warming *n syn* see DEFEAT 1

warmish *adj syn* see TEPID 1

warn *vb* **1** to let one know of approaching danger or risk <police and the weather service join to *warn* travelers of hazardous road conditions>

syn caution, forewarn

rel advise, alert, apprise, inform, notify, tip; counsel, direct, guide

idiom address a warning to, give warning, put a flea in one's ear, put one on guard

2 *syn* see INFORM 2

3 *syn* see COMMAND

warning *n* something and especially a statement that warns or is intended to warn <gave them *warning* that disobedience would lead to punishment>

syn admonition, caution, caveat, commonition, forewarning, monition

rel advice, counsel, guidance, recommendation; hint, suggestion, tip

idiom flea (*or* word) in the ear, word to the wise

warning *adj syn* see MONITORY

warp *vb* **1** *syn* see DEBASE 1

rel contort, crook, distort, twist

con disentangle, rectify, straighten, unkink

2 *syn* see DEFORM

rel bend, crook, kink, twist

3 *syn* see MISREPRESENT

war paint *n* **1** *syn* see FINERY

2 *syn* see MAKEUP 3

warped *adj syn* see BIASED 2

ant unwarped

warrant *n* **1** *syn* see PLEDGE 1

2 *syn* see BASIS 3

3 *syn* see WORD 8

warrant *vb* **1** *syn* see MAINTAIN 2

rel state; assure, ensure, insure

2 to give assurance of the worth of something especially in respect to quality, quantity, or condition <*warranted* the merchandise to be exactly as described in the catalog>

syn certify, guarantee, guaranty

rel assure, insure, secure; back, sponsor, stipulate; affirm, claim, state

idiom stand behind

3 *syn* see JUSTIFY 4

rel endorse; call (for), need, require

warrantable *adj syn* see JUSTIFIABLE

ant unwarrantable

warranty *n syn* see GUARANTEE 1

warrior *n syn* see SOLDIER

wary *adj* **1** *syn* see CAUTIOUS

rel distrustful, doubting, leery, suspicious; vigilant, watchful

idiom on one's guard

con careless, heedless, thoughtless; devil-may–care, reckless, venturesome

ant foolhardy; unwary

2 *syn* see SPARING

wash *vb* **1** *syn* see BATHE 1

2 *syn* see BATHE 2

3 *syn* see DRIFT 1

4 *syn* see SLOSH 1

washed–out *adj syn* see EFFETE 2

washed–up *adj* **1** *syn* see THROUGH 3

2 *syn* see THROUGH 4

wash out *vb* **1** *syn* see FAIL 4

2 *syn* see DISCARD

wash up *vb syn* see GO 4

washy *adj syn* see DILUTE

waspish *adj* **1** *syn* see IRRITABLE

rel contrary, impatient, perverse; malicious, sharp, spiteful; crabbed, cross-grained

2 *syn* see CANTANKEROUS

waspy *adj* **1** *syn* see IRRITABLE

rel contrary, impatient, perverse; malicious, sharp, spiteful; crabbed, cross-grained

2 *syn* see CANTANKEROUS

wassail *n* **1** *syn* see BINGE 1

2 *syn* see REVELRY 2

wassail *vb syn* see REVEL 1

waste *n* **1** an area of the earth unsuitable for cultivation or general habitation <the scattered dwellers of southern Africa's dry *wastes*>

syn badland, barren, desert, wasteland, wild, wilderness, wild land, wildness

rel brush, brushland, bush; jungle

2 *syn* see EXTRAVAGANCE 2

3 *syn* see REFUSE

rel rubble, rummage

waste *vb* **1** *syn* see RAVAGE

idiom reduce to a shambles

ant conserve

2 to spend or expend freely and usually foolishly or futilely <*wasted* his inheritance on women and gambling> <*waste* one's time on trifles>

syn blow, blunder (away), cast away, consume, dissipate, dribble (away), drivel, fool (away), fritter, frivol away, muddle (away), potter (away), prodigalize, riot (away), squander, throw away, trifle (away)

rel disburse, expend, spend; dispense, distribute; deplete, drain, exhaust, impoverish; dispel, disperse, scatter; misspend

idiom let slip through one's fingers, pour down the drain, throw good money after bad

ant save; conserve

waste (away) *vb syn* see FAIL 3

wasted *adj syn* see EMACIATED

rel meager; shriveled, withered, wizened

con healthy, robust; stalwart, stout, strong, sturdy

wastefulness *n syn* see EXTRAVAGANCE 2

ant frugality

wasteland *n syn* see WASTE 1

waster *n* **1** *syn* see SPENDTHRIFT

rel dissipater, fritterer; idler, loafer, lounger

2 *syn* see WASTREL 1

wastethrift *n syn* see SPENDTHRIFT

wastrel *n* **1** a worthless, self-indulgent, and reprehensible person <loafers and other *wastrels* lounging on the corner>
syn ‖bad lot, good-for-nothing, ne'er-do-well, no-good, profligate, rounder, scapegrace, waster
rel lecher, libertine, rake, rip, roué; blackguard, black sheep, knave, rascal, rogue, scoundrel; rapscallion, scalawag, scamp
idiom sad case
2 *syn* see SPENDTHRIFT
rel dissipater, fritterer; idler, loafer, lounger

watch *vb* **1** *syn* see SEE 2
rel examine, follow, inspect, scan, scrutinize
idiom keep an eye on, keep tabs on
2 *syn* see EYE 2
3 *syn* see TEND 2
idiom keep watch over
4 *syn* see LOOK 1

watch *n* **1** *syn* see LOOKOUT 3
2 *syn* see GUARD 2
3 *syn* see EYE 3

watch and ward *n syn* see LOOKOUT 3

watchdog *n syn* see CUSTODIAN

watcher *n syn* see SPECTATOR

watchfire *n syn* see BEACON 1

watchful *adj* paying close attention usually with a view to anticipating approaching danger or opportunity <adopted a policy of *watchful* waiting>
syn alert, open-eyed, unsleeping, vigilant, wakeful, wide-awake
rel cautious, chary, circumspect, wary; prompt, quick, ready
idiom keeping one's eyes peeled (*or* open), on the watch (*or* lookout)
con careless, heedless, thoughtless; inadvertent; absentminded, abstracted, faraway
ant unwatchful

watchman *n syn* see GUARD 2

watch out *vb syn* see BEWARE

watchword *n* **1** *syn* see PASSWORD 1
2 *syn* see PASSWORD 3
3 *syn* see CATCHWORD

water *n* **1** *syn* see TEARS
2 *syn* see SALIVA

water *vb syn* see DROOL 1

water closet *n syn* see TOILET

watercourse *n syn* see CHANNEL 1

watered–down *adj syn* see DILUTE

waterfall *n* a precipitous descent of water or the site of this <heard the roar of the *waterfall*>
syn cascade, cataract, chute, fall(s), ‖force, sault, spout
rel rapid(s), riffle, shoot; eddy, surge, vortex, whirlpool

watering hole *n* **1** *syn* see RESORT 2
2 *syn* see BAR 5
3 *syn* see NIGHTCLUB

watering place *n* **1** *syn* see SPA 1
2 *syn* see RESORT 3
3 *syn* see BAR 5
4 *syn* see NIGHTCLUB

waterish *adj* **1** *syn* see DILUTE

2 *syn* see PALE 2
3 *syn* see INSIPID 3

waterless *adj syn* see DRY 1
ant watered

waterlog *vb syn* see SOAK 1

watery *adj* **1** *syn* see DILUTE
2 *syn* see PALE 2
3 *syn* see INSIPID 3

wave *vb syn* see WAG

waver *vb syn* see HESITATE
rel palter, shift, trim; seesaw, teeter
idiom back and fill, hem and haw

wavering *n syn* see HESITATION

wavering *adj* **1** *syn* see VACILLATING 2
ant unwavering
2 *syn* see WEAK 2

wax *vb* **1** *syn* see INCREASE 2
ant wane
2 *syn* see BECOME 1

wax *n syn* see RISE 3
ant wane

waxen *adj syn* see PALE 1

waxy *adj syn* see ANGRY

way *n* **1** a public and unobstructed passage leading from one place to another <tracing the remains of an old lumberman's *way*>
syn artery, avenue, boulevard, ‖drag, highway, path, road, street, thoroughfare, track
rel course, line, passage, route; alley, byway, lane, ride, row
2 that along which one passes in going from one place to another <his *way* led through wooded hills>
syn course, line, passage, path, road, route
3 *syn* see DOOR 2
4 *syn* see METHOD 1
rel custom, habit, habitude, practice, usage, use, wont
5 *syn* see STYLE 4
6 *syn* see HABIT 1
7 *syn* see DISTANCE 2
8 *syn* see TYPE

‖**wayback** *n syn* see RUSTIC

wayfaring *adj syn* see ITINERANT

waylay *vb syn* see SURPRISE 1
rel lurk, prowl, skulk, slink
idiom lay wait for, lie in wait for

ways *n pl but sing in constr syn* see DISTANCE 2

wayward *adj* **1** *syn* see CONTRARY 3
rel capricious, fickle, inconstant, unstable, variable
con complaisant, good-natured
2 *syn* see ARBITRARY 1

weak *adj* **1** lacking physical, mental, or moral strength <a *weak* spirit in a *weak* body>
syn decrepit, feeble, flimsy, fragile, frail, infirm, insubstantial, puny, unsound, unsubstantial, ‖wanky, weakly

---

syn synonym(s)   *rel* related word(s)
ant antonym(s)   *con* contrasted word(s)
idiom idiomatic equivalent(s)
‖ use limited; if in doubt, see a dictionary

rel debilitated, enfeebled, sickly, spindly, weakened; forceless, impotent, impuissant, powerless
con stalwart, stout, sturdy, tenacious, tough; dynamic, energetic, forceful, vigorous
ant strong
2 deficient in stability <a love too *weak* to bear the trials of daily life>
syn dickey, fluctuant, insecure, rootless, shaky, unstable, unsure, vacillating, wavering, wobbly; *compare* RICKETY
rel hesitant, irresolute, trimming, uncertain; insubstantial, undependable, unreliable
con certain, secure, solid, stable, sure; dependable, reliable, substantial
ant strong
3 *syn* see IMPLAUSIBLE
4 not equal to the requirements and demands of a situation <a *weak* executive>
syn boneless, emasculate, forceless, impotent, inadequate, ineffective, ineffectual, invertebrate, slack-spined, spineless, wan
rel unfit, unqualified, unsuitable; bungling, incompetent, inept
con able, competent, effective, efficient; adequate, fit, qualified, satisfactory, sufficient, suitable; manly, masculine, virile
ant strong
5 *syn* see DILUTE
ant strong
weaken *vb* **1** to lose or cause to lose strength, vigor, or energy <his hesitation *weakened* the force of his argument>
syn attenuate, blunt, cripple, debilitate, disable, enfeeble, sap, unbrace, undermine, unstrengthen; *compare* PARALYZE 1
rel emasculate, enervate, incapacitate, unman, unnerve; damage, impair, injure; lessen, minimize, reduce; dilute, thin
con better, improve; activate, energize, invigorate, vitalize
ant strengthen
2 *syn* see FAIL 1
3 *syn* see FAIL 3
4 *syn* see DILUTE
weak–headed *adj syn* see SIMPLE 3
weak–kneed *adj syn* see VACILLATING 2
weakling *n* a person lacking in stamina and character <her speech deplored the characterless *weaklings* in critical positions>
syn baby, doormat, invertebrate, jellyfish, milksop, Milquetoast, ‖molly, mollycoddle, namby≠pamby, nebbish, pantywaist, sissy, sissy-pants (*or* sissy-britches), sop, wimp
rel butt, mark, pushover, sucker; drip, mama's boy, misfit, mother's boy, nerd, sad sack, weak sister
idiom shrinking violet
weakly *adv syn* see SOTTO VOCE
ant strongly
weakly *adj syn* see WEAK 1
weak–minded *adj syn* see SIMPLE 3
weakness *n syn* see APPETITE 3
weal *n syn* see WHEAL
weald *n syn* see FOREST

wealth *n* **1** *syn* see MEAN 3
2 one's worldly possessions <at that point his *wealth* consisted of the clothes he stood in and a solitary quarter>
syn fortune, property, resources, riches, substance, worth
rel assets, estate, goods, holdings, possessions
wealthy *adj syn* see RICH 1
con impoverished, penniless, poor
ant indigent
wean *vb syn* see ESTRANGE
ant addict
wear *vb* **1** *syn* see ABRADE 1
2 *syn* see TIRE 1
wear (away) *vb syn* see EAT 3
wear down *vb syn* see TIRE 1
wearied *adj syn* see TIRED 1
ant refreshed; unwearied, unweary
weariful *adj syn* see ARID 2
weariless *adj syn* see INDEFATIGABLE
weariness *n syn* see FATIGUE
wearisome *adj syn* see ARID 2
wear out *vb* **1** *syn* see EXHAUST 4
‖**2** *syn* see WHIP 1
weary *vb* **1** *syn* see TIRE 1
rel debilitate, enfeeble, weaken; depress, oppress, weigh
con animate, energize, vitalize; enliven, quicken, vivify
ant refresh
2 *syn* see BORE
weary *adj* **1** *syn* see TIRED 1
ant refreshed, unwearied, unweary
2 *syn* see FED UP
Weary Willie *n syn* see VAGABOND
weasel *n syn* see SNEAK
weasel *vb syn* see EQUIVOCATE 2
weathery *adj syn* see CHANGEABLE 1
weave *vb syn* see LURCH 2
web *n* **1** *syn* see TEXTURE 2
2 something by which one is ensnared, held fast, or inextricably involved <diplomacy caught in its own *web* of double-dealing>
syn cobweb, entanglement, mesh(es), toil(s); *compare* ENTANGLEMENT 1
rel complexity, complication; labyrinth, maze, morass, skein, snarl, tangle; embroilment, enmeshment, ensnarement, entrapment, involvement
idiom a tangled web
3 *syn* see MAZE 1
wed *vb* **1** *syn* see MARRY 1
2 *syn* see MARRY 2
3 *syn* see JOIN 1
wedded *adj syn* see MATRIMONIAL
con unwed, unwedded
wedding *n* the marriage ceremony usually with its accompanying festivities <one of the most elaborate *weddings* of the social season>
syn bridal, espousal(s), marriage, nuptial(s), spousal
wedlock *n syn* see MARRIAGE 1
wee *adj syn* see TINY
weed *n syn* see MARIJUANA

weensy *adj syn* see TINY

weeny *adj syn* see TINY

weep *vb* **1** *syn* see DEPLORE 1

  2 *syn* see EXUDE

  3 *syn* see CRY 2

  4 *syn* see DRIP

weeping *adj syn* see TEARFUL

weepy *adj syn* see TEARFUL

weigh *vb* **1** *syn* see CONSIDER 1

  rel appraise, evaluate, rate

  2 *syn* see BURDEN

  3 to carry intellectual weight ·<this evidence *weighed* heavily against him>

  syn count, militate, tell

  rel import, matter, register, signify

  idiom amount to some shucks, be something, carry weight, cut (some) ice

  4 *syn* see MATTER

weigh down *vb syn* see DEPRESS 2

  ant raise (*one's spirits*)

weight *n* **1** *syn* see LOAD 2

  2 *syn* see IMPORTANCE

  3 *syn* see INFLUENCE 1

  rel effectiveness, efficacy; forcefulness, forcibleness, potency, powerfulness

  4 *syn* see LOAD 3

weight *vb* **1** *syn* see ADULTERATE

  rel burden, cumber, encumber; contaminate, corrupt, foul up, spoil

  2 *syn* see BURDEN

weightiness *n syn* see IMPORTANCE

weightless *adj syn* see LIGHT 1

  ant weighty

weighty *adj* **1** *syn* see IMPORTANT 1

  2 *syn* see SERIOUS 1

  3 *syn* see SERIOUS 2

  4 *syn* see HEAVY 1

  ant weightless

  5 *syn* see FAT 2

  6 *syn* see ONEROUS

weird *n* **1** *syn* see FATE

  2 *syn* see PREDICTION

weird *adj* **1** fearfully and mysteriously strange or fantastic <shuddered at the *weird* unearthly glow that swept across the sky>

  syn eerie, spooky, uncanny, unearthly

  rel creepy, haunting, unnatural; preternatural, supernatural; supernal; curious, odd, peculiar, queer, strange; inscrutable, mysterious; awe-inspiring, awful, dreadful, fearful, horrific

  con common, commonplace, everyday, quotidian; natural, normal, ordinary

  2 *syn* see STRANGE 4

welcome *adj syn* see PLEASANT 1

  rel congenial, cordial, genial, sympathetic; contenting, satisfying

  ant unwelcome

welfare *n* a state of thriving and progress <parents who seek their children's *welfare*>

  syn advantage, benefit, good, interest, prosperity, well-being

  rel fortune, luck, success; contentment, felicity, happiness, satisfaction

  ant illfare

welkin *n syn* see SKY

well *n* **1** wells *pl syn* see SPA 1

  2 *syn* see SOURCE

well *adv* **1** in a good, proper, or acceptable manner <the children behaved very *well* at the party>

  syn aright, befittingly, correctly, decently, decorously, fitly, fittingly, justly, nicely, properly, rightly

  rel bearably, passably, tolerably, unobjectionably; considerately, pleasantly, thoughtfully, white; appropriately

  con badly, improperly, objectionably, obnoxiously, outrageously

  ant ill

  2 in a pleasant, cooperative, or thoughtful manner <he speaks *well* of your new proposal>

  syn considerately, generously, heedfully, kindly, thoughtfully

  rel concernedly, interestedly; approvingly

  con contemptuously, disdainfully, scornfully

  3 to a full extent or degree <you are *well* aware of the problems we face>

  syn à fond, altogether, clear, ‖cleverly, completely, entirely, fully, perfectly, ‖plumb, quite, right, roundly, ‖slam, ‖slap, thoroughly, utterly, wholly

  rel certainly, obviously, surely, undoubtedly, unquestionably; sublimely

  idiom all the way

  con barely, hardly, scarcely

  4 in an adequate or appropriate manner <any large box will answer our need very *well*>

  syn acceptably, adequately, amply, appropriately, becomingly, fittingly, properly, right, satisfactorily, suitably

  5 in a desirable or pleasing manner <everything went *well* on the trip>

  syn favorably, fortunately, happily, prosperously, satisfyingly, successfully, swimmingly

  rel comfortably, easily, smoothly

  con amiss, wrong

  ant badly

  6 *syn* see EASILY 1

  7 in all likelihood <the fighting may *well* continue for years>

  syn doubtlessly, easily, indeed, really, truly, undoubtedly

  rel conceivably, perhaps, possibly; likely, probably

  8 to a considerable extent or degree <they landed *well* beyond the wharf>

  syn considerably, far, quite, rather, significantly, somewhat

  idiom by a long way, by a wide margin

well *adj* **1** *syn* see PROSPEROUS 3

  2 *syn* see HEALTHY 1

  ant ill, unwell

  3 *syn* see LUCKY

well–behaved *adj syn* see GOOD 13

---

syn synonym(s)   *rel* related word(s)
ant antonym(s)   *con* contrasted word(s)
idiom idiomatic equivalent(s)
‖ use limited; if in doubt, see a dictionary

well–being *n* **1** *syn* see PROSPERITY 2
  ant ill-being
  2 *syn* see WELFARE
  ant ill-being
well–bred *adj syn* see GENTEEL 1
  ant ill-bred
well–conditioned *adj syn* see HEALTHY 1
well–developed *adj syn* see CURVACEOUS
well–disposed *adj syn* see SYMPATHETIC 2
  ant ill-disposed
well–favored *adj syn* see BEAUTIFUL
  ant ill-favored
well–fixed *adj syn* see PROSPEROUS 3
  ant badly off
well–founded *adj* having a firm foundation in fact
  or logic <offered *well-founded* arguments to
  support his position>
  syn cogent, good, just, justified, well-grounded
  rel sound, substantial, telling, valid; rational,
  reasonable, reasoned; fundamental, meaty, pithy
  con unjustified; insubstantial, invalid, unsound;
  irrational, unreasonable
well–groomed *adj* **1** *syn* see NEAT 2
  2 *syn* see DAPPER
well–grounded *adj syn* see WELL-FOUNDED
wellhead *n syn* see SOURCE
well–heeled *adj syn* see PROSPEROUS 3
  ant badly off
well–hung *adj syn* see GLIB
well–known *adj* much talked about <a *well-known*
  hospital>
  syn famous, leading, noted, notorious, popular,
  prominent; *compare* FAMOUS 2
  rel conspicuous, important, outstanding
  idiom on everyone's tongue
  con inconspicuous, obscure, unheard-of, unimportant, unnoted, unpopular
  ant unknown
well–liked *adj syn* see FAVORITE 2
well–liking *adj syn* see HEALTHY 1
well–mannered *adj syn* see CIVIL 2
  ant ill-mannered
well–nigh *adv* **1** *syn* see NEARLY
  2 *syn* see ALMOST 2
well–off *adj syn* see PROSPEROUS 3
  ant badly off
well over *vb syn* see OVERFLOW 2
well–paying *adj syn* see ADVANTAGEOUS 1
well–proportioned *adj syn* see SHAPELY
wellspring *n syn* see SOURCE
well–thought–of *adj syn* see RESPECTABLE 1
well–timed *adj syn* see TIMELY 1
  con premature, untimely; behindhand, late,
  tardy
  ant ill-timed
well–to–do *adj syn* see PROSPEROUS 3
  ant badly off
well–turned *adj syn* see SHAPELY
well–worn *adj syn* see TRITE
welsh *vb syn* see BACK DOWN
welt *n* **1** *syn* see WHEAL
  ‖**2** *syn* see BLOW 1
weltanschauung *n syn* see IDEOLOGY
welter *vb* **1** *syn* see WALLOW 1

  rel strive, struggle; toss, tumble, writhe; grovel
  2 *syn* see WALLOW 3
welter *vb syn* see WITHER
wench *n* **1** *syn* see GIRL 1
  2 *syn* see WANTON
wend *vb syn* see GO 1
western *n* a motion picture or radio or television
  play with its scene laid in the western U.S. and
  having cowboys as its main characters <young
  boys delighting in Saturday morning *westerns*>
  syn horse opera, oater
  rel shoot-'em-up
wet *vb* to make wet by or as if by saturating with
  water <they were *wet* thoroughly by the pouring
  rain>
  syn deluge, douse, drench, drown, soak, sop,
  souse; *compare* SOAK 1
  rel damp, dampen, moisten; humidify, humify;
  fill, impregnate, saturate; irrigate; lave, rinse,
  wash
  ant desiccate, dry
wet *adj* **1** containing or impregnated with liquid
  <change *wet* clothing for dry>
  syn drenched, dripping, madid, saturate, saturated, soaked, soaking, sodden, sopping, soppy,
  soused, wringing-wet
  rel soggy, water-logged; damp, dank, moist,
  wettish
  idiom dripping (*or* soaking *or* sopping) wet
  con bone-dry, dehydrated, desiccated, parched,
  sere, waterless
  ant dry
  2 *syn* see INTOXICATED 1
‖**wet** *n syn* see DRAM
wettish *adj syn* see DAMP
whack *vb syn* see STRIKE 2
whack *n* **1** *syn* see BLOW 1
  2 *syn* see FLING 1
whacking *adj syn* see HUGE
whacking *adv syn* see VERY 1
whale *n syn* see GIANT
whale *vb syn* see WHIP 1
whaling *adj syn* see HUGE
wham *n syn* see BANG 2
whammy *n syn* see JINX
whangdoodle *n syn* see NONSENSE 2
wharf *n* a structure used by boats and ships for
  taking on or landing cargo and passengers
  <brought the boat alongside the *wharf* and
  moored her>
  syn berth, dock, jetty, levee, pier, quay, slip
what–do–you–call–it *n* a thing or person that the
  speaker cannot (as from not knowing or from
  forgetting) name <hand me one of those little
  what-do-you-call-its> <went to *what-do-you-
  call-her's* house last week>
  syn what-is-it, whatsis, what's its name, what-
  you-call-it, what-you-may-call-it, whatyoumayjigger; *compare* DOODAD, GADGET 1
what–is–it *n syn* see WHAT-DO-YOU-CALL-IT
whatnot *n syn* see KNICKKNACK
whatsis *n syn* see WHAT-DO-YOU-CALL-IT
what's its name *n syn* see WHAT-DO-YOU-CALL-IT
what–you–call–it *n syn* see WHAT-DO-YOU-CALL-IT

what–you–may–call–it *n* *syn* see WHAT-DO-YOU= CALL-IT

whatyoumayjigger *n* *syn* see WHAT-DO-YOU-CALL-IT

wheal *n* a ridge raised on the skin by or as if by a stroke of a lash <the convict's back was covered with *wheals* and old scars>
syn wale, weal, welt, whelk, ‖whelp
rel strake, streak, stripe

wheedle *vb* *syn* see COAX

wheel *n* **1** *syn* see CYCLE 1
2 *syn* see REVOLUTION 1
3 *syn* see LEAGUE 4

wheel *vb* **1** *syn* see REEL 2
2 *syn* see DRIVE 5
3 *syn* see TURN 6

wheeze *vb* *syn* see HISS

wheeze *n* *syn* see PRANK

whelk *n* *syn* see WHEAL

whelm *vb* **1** *syn* see DELUGE 1
2 *syn* see DELUGE 3
3 *syn* see OVERWHELM 4

‖**whelp** *n* *syn* see WHEAL

when *adv* *syn* see THEN 1

when *conj* *syn* see THOUGH

whence *n* *syn* see SOURCE

where *adv* **1** *syn* see WHEREVER
2 *syn* see WHITHER 1

where *n* *syn* see PLACE 1

whereabouts *adv* *syn* see WHITHER 1
con hereabouts, thereabouts

whereas *conj* **1** *syn* see BECAUSE
2 *syn* see THOUGH

‖**whereaway** *adv* *syn* see WHITHER 1

wherefore *n* *syn* see REASON 3

whereto *adv* *syn* see WHITHER 2

whereunto *adv* *syn* see WHITHER 2

wherever *adv* at, in, or to any or every place in or to which <he goes *wherever* he is needed>
syn everywhere, where
con here, there

‖**wherret** *vb* *syn* see SLAP 1

‖**wherret** *vb* *syn* see WORRY 1

whet *vb* **1** *syn* see SHARPEN
2 *syn* see STIR 1

whet *n* ‖**1** *syn* see WHILE 1
2 *syn* see APPETIZER

whether or no *adv* *syn* see WILLY-NILLY

whetted *adj* *syn* see SHARP 1

whicker *vb* *syn* see NEIGH

whiff *n* *syn* see HINT 2

whiffet *n* *syn* see NONENTITY

whiffle *vb* *syn* see HESITATE

whiffling *adj* *syn* see VACILLATING 2

whiffy *adj* *syn* see MALODOROUS 1

whigmaleerie *n* **1** *syn* see CAPRICE
2 *syn* see KNICKKNACK

while *n* **1** a somewhat indefinite period of time <sat down to rest for a *while*>
syn bit, space, spell, stretch, time, ‖whet
2 *syn* see OCCASION 5
3 *syn* see EFFORT 1

while *conj* *syn* see THOUGH

while *vb* to pass time and especially leisure time without boredom or in pleasant ways <*whiled* odd hours away in dreaming>

syn beguile, fleet, wile
rel amuse, divert, entertain; brighten, enliven, lighten

while (away) *vb* *syn* see SPEND 3

whilom *adj* *syn* see FORMER 2

whim *n* *syn* see CAPRICE
rel idea; disposition, inclination, thought; dream, fantasy, vision

whimper *vb* to cry feebly and often plaintively or peevishly <a baby *whimpering* in his sleep>
syn pule, whine; *compare* CRY 2

whimsical *adj* **1** *syn* see ARBITRARY 1
2 *syn* see UNCERTAIN 1

whimsied *adj* *syn* see ARBITRARY 1

whimsy *n* *syn* see CAPRICE
rel idea; disposition, inclination, thought; dream, fantasy, vision

whim–whams *n pl* *syn* see JITTERS

whine *vb* **1** *syn* see WHIMPER
2 *syn* see COMPLAIN

‖**whinner** *vb* *syn* see NEIGH

whinny *vb* *syn* see NEIGH

whiny *adj* *syn* see IRRITABLE

whip *vb* **1** to strike repeatedly with or as if with a lash or rod <*whip* a dog for stealing from the table>
syn flagellate, flog, hide, ‖larrup, lash, lather, scourge, stripe, thrash, ‖wear out, whale, ‖yerk
rel beat, belabor, drub, wallop; bastinado, birch, bludgeon, cane, cudgel, quirt, switch
2 to defeat utterly <*whipped* their traditional rival by a score of 40 to 7>
syn beat, blast, ‖bowl (down *or* out), ‖clean up (on), ‖clobber, ‖cream, curry, drub, dust, lambaste, ‖larrup, lick, mop (up), overrun, overwhelm, rout, shellac, skunk, smear, smother, steamroller, thrash, trim, trounce, upend, wallop, whomp; *compare* CONQUER 1, DEFEAT 2
rel conquer, defeat, overcome, subdue, vanquish
idiom cook one's goose, deal a crushing defeat, settle one's hash, snow one under
3 to agitate with an instrument so as to stiffen and increase the bulk of by incorporation of air <*whip* cream for a shortcake>
syn beat, whisk
4 *syn* see TURN 6

whip (up) *vb* *syn* see INCITE
ant calm (down)

whip hand *n* *syn* see BETTER 2

whippersnapper *n* *syn* see NONENTITY

whipping boy *n* *syn* see SCAPEGOAT

whippy *adj* *syn* see ELASTIC 1

whipster *n* *syn* see NONENTITY

whirl *vb* **1** *syn* see SPIN 1
2 *syn* see SWIRL
3 *syn* see TURN 6
4 *syn* see HURRY 2
5 *syn* see SPIN 2

---

syn synonym(s)   *rel* related word(s)
ant antonym(s)   *con* contrasted word(s)
idiom idiomatic equivalent(s)
‖ use limited; if in doubt, see a dictionary

whirl *n* **1** *syn* see REVOLUTION 1
  2 *syn* see EDDY
  3 *syn* see COMMOTION 4
  4 *syn* see STIR 1
  5 *syn* see FLING 1
whirlblast *n* *syn* see WHIRLWIND 1
whirligig *vb* *syn* see SPIN 1
whirlpool *n* **1** *syn* see EDDY
  2 *syn* see STIR 1
whirlpool *vb* *syn* see SWIRL
‖**whirlpuff** *n* *syn* see WHIRLWIND 1
whirlwind *n* **1** a rotating windstorm of limited extent that is often accompanied by a column of dust or vapor <*whirlwinds* moved across the plowed land>
  syn whirlblast, ‖whirlpuff, whirly; *compare* HURRICANE, TORNADO
  rel dust devil, rainspout, sand column, sand spout, waterspout
  2 *syn* see STIR 1
whirly *n* *syn* see WHIRLWIND 1
whish *vb* **1** *syn* see HISS
  2 *syn* see HURRY 2
whisk *vb* **1** *syn* see HURRY 2
  2 *syn* see WHIP 3
whisker *n* *syn* see HAIR
whiskered *adj* **1** *syn* see BEARDED
  2 *syn* see HAIRY 1
whiskers *n pl* *syn* see BEARD
whisper *vb* **1** *syn* see HISS
  2 *syn* see CONFIDE 1
whisper *n* **1** *syn* see MURMUR 1
  2 *syn* see HINT 2
whispering *n* *syn* see REPORT 1
whist *adj* *syn* see STILL 3
whistle–stop *n* *syn* see BURG
whit *n* *syn* see PARTICLE
white *adj* *syn* see FAVORABLE 5
  ant black
white *n* *syn* see REACTIONARY
  ant red
white *vb* **1** *syn* see WHITEN 1
  2 *syn* see PALLIATE
whited sepulcher *n* *syn* see HYPOCRITE
white–haired *adj* *syn* see FAVORITE 1
white–headed *adj* *syn* see FAVORITE 1
white–hot *adj* **1** *syn* see HOT 1
  2 *syn* see IMPASSIONED
white lightning *n* *syn* see MOONSHINE 2
white–livered *adj* *syn* see COWARDLY
whiten *vb* **1** to free from color and make white or whiter <*whiten* linen in the sun>
  syn blanch, bleach, blench, decolor, decolorize, white
  rel dim, dull, fade, lighten, pale; etiolate; frost, grizzle, silver
  con color, darken
  ant blacken
  2 *syn* see PALLIATE
white plague *n* *syn* see TUBERCULOSIS
whitewash *vb* *syn* see PALLIATE
whither *adv* **1** to what place <*whither* did they go?>
  syn where, whereabouts, ‖whereaway

  2 to what point, conclusion, or end <*whither* is our nation drifting?>
  syn whereto, whereunto
whiz *vb* **1** *syn* see HISS
  2 *syn* see HURRY 2
whiz *n* *syn* see EXPERT
  ant dub, dud, duffer
whiz–bang *adj* *syn* see EXCELLENT
whizzer *n* *syn* see TRICK 1
whole *adj* **1** free from damage, defect, or flaw <feared the eggs were broken but found them *whole*>
  syn entire, flawless, good, intact, perfect, sound, unblemished, unbroken, undamaged, unhurt, unimpaired, uninjured, unmarred, untouched
  rel complete, plenary; healthy, well
  con broken, damaged, defective, impaired, injured, marred
  2 *syn* see HEALTHY 1
  3 lacking nothing that properly belongs to it <the effect of the *whole* mural>
  syn choate, complete, entire, full, integral, perfect
  rel orbicular, rounded, well-rounded
  ant partial
  4 including every constituent element or individual <the *whole* community rose to his defense>
  syn all, complete, entire, gross, outright, total
  ant partial
  5 not scattered or dispersed <gave the matter her *whole* attention>
  syn concentrated, exclusive, fixed, undistracted, undivided, unswerving
whole *n* **1** the total supply or amount <the *whole* of our creative literature>
  syn aggregate, all, be-all and end-all, entirety, gross, sum, sum total, tale, total, totality, ‖tote
  rel amount, supply; result, resultant, summation; bulk, mass, quantity, quantum
  con detail, division, fraction, fragment, portion, section, segment, share
  ant part
  2 an organized array of parts or elements forming or functioning as a unit <stars, planets, galaxies — all but parts of one stupendous *whole*, the universe>
  syn entity, integral, integrate, sum, system, totality; *compare* SYSTEM 1
  rel being, organism, organization; coherence, cohesion, linkage; unity
  con accumulation, aggregation, heap, pile, mass; section, segment; selection
  ant part; agglomeration
wholehearted *adj* **1** *syn* see SURE 2
  2 *syn* see SINCERE 1
  rel ardent, fervent, impassioned, passionate; earnest, serious; authentic, bona fide, genuine
whole–hog *adj* *syn* see EXHAUSTIVE
whole–length *adj* *syn* see UNABRIDGED
wholeness *n* **1** *syn* see HEALTH
  rel integrity; heartiness, robustness, vigor
  2 *syn* see ENTIRETY 1
  3 *syn* see INTEGRITY 2
whole number *n* *syn* see NUMBER

wholesale *adj syn* see INDISCRIMINATE 1
wholesome *adj* **1** *syn* see HEALTHFUL
  ant noxious; unwholesome
  2 *syn* see CURATIVE
  3 *syn* see HEALTHY 1
  4 *syn* see SAFE 3
  ant noxious
whole–souled *adj syn* see SINCERE 1
  rel ardent, fervent, impassioned; earnest, intense, serious
wholly *adv* **1** *syn* see WELL 3
  2 *syn* see ALL 1
whomp *vb syn* see WHIP 2
whoop *vb syn* see SHOUT 1
whoop *n syn* see PARTICLE
whoop–de–do *n syn* see REVELRY 2
whoopee *n* **1** *syn* see REVELRY 2
  2 *syn* see MERRYMAKING
whoopla *n* **1** *syn* see COMMOTION 4
  2 *syn* see REVELRY 2
whoop–up *n syn* see REVELRY 2
whoosh *vb syn* see HISS
whop *vb syn* see BEAT 1
whop *n syn* see BLOW 1
whopping *adj syn* see HUGE
whopping *adv syn* see VERY 1
whore *n* **1** *syn* see HARLOT 1
  2 *syn* see PROSTITUTE
whoredom *n syn* see PROSTITUTION
whorehouse *n syn* see BROTHEL
whoreson *n syn* see BASTARD 1
whorish *adj syn* see FAST 7
whorl *vb syn* see SWIRL
who's who *n syn* see ARISTOCRACY
why *n* **1** *syn* see REASON 3
  2 *syn* see MYSTERY
whyfor *n syn* see REASON 3
wicked *adj* **1** *syn* see WRONG 1
  ant upright
  2 *syn* see PLAYFUL 1
  3 *syn* see RISQUÉ
  4 *syn* see MALICIOUS
  5 *syn* see DANGEROUS 1
  6 *syn* see TROUBLESOME
  7 *syn* see OUTRAGEOUS 1
  8 *syn* see SKILLFUL 2
  9 *syn* see ABLE
wickedness *n* **1** *syn* see EVIL 2
  2 *syn* see VICE 1
wide *adj* **1** *syn* see SPACIOUS
  2 *syn* see EXTENSIVE 1
  3 *syn* see LIBERAL 3
wide–awake *adj syn* see WATCHFUL
  rel alive, awake, aware, conscious, sensible
widen *vb syn* see BROADEN
wideness *n syn* see BREADTH 2
widespread *adj syn* see PREVAILING
widget *n syn* see GADGET 1
width *n syn* see RANGE 2
wield *vb* **1** *syn* see HANDLE 2
  rel conduct, control
  2 *syn* see EXERT
wieldy *adj syn* see STRONG 1
wiener *n syn* see FRANKFURTER

wienerwurst *n syn* see FRANKFURTER
‖**wienie** *n syn* see FRANKFURTER
wife *n* the female partner in a marriage <a sense of humor is a requirement for his potential *wife*>
  syn ‖ball and chain, lady, ‖little woman, ‖missus, Mrs., ‖old lady, ‖old woman, ‖rib, ‖squaw, ‖woman
  rel consort, helpmate, helpmeet, mate, other half, spouse; bride, dowager, matron; concubine
  idiom better half
  con maid, maiden; widow
wig *n syn* see REBUKE
wig *vb syn* see SCOLD 1
wigging *n syn* see REBUKE
wiggle *vb syn* see WRIGGLE
wiggle–waggle *adj syn* see VACILLATING 2
wiggle–waggle *vb syn* see HESITATE
wiggy *adj syn* see POMPOUS 1
wight *n syn* see HUMAN
wild *adj* **1** living and growing in a state of nature and without human intervention <lived on *wild* plants and game animals>
  syn agrarian, agrestal, native, natural, uncultivated, undomesticated; *compare* SAVAGE 1
  rel escaped, feral; unsubdued, untamed
  ant cultivated, domesticated
  2 *syn* see SAVAGE 1
  ant tame, tamed
  3 *syn* see IRRESPONSIBLE
  rel adventurous, audacious, daring, dashing; brash, cocksure, rash
  4 *syn* see FURIOUS 2
  rel bewildered, distracted, perplexed; agitated, perturbed, upset; addled, confused, muddled; crazy, demented, deranged, mad
  con easy, relaxed
  5 *syn* see UNRULY 1
  6 marked by turmoil and fury especially of natural elements <a *wild* night of howling winds and driving snow>
  syn blustering, blustery, ‖coarse, dirty, furious, raging, rough, stormful, stormy, tempestuous, turbulent
  rel blatant, boisterous, clamorous, ungovernable, unruly; brutal, harsh, severe
  con calm, peaceful, placid, quiet, stormless; halcyon, irenic, serene
  7 given to unrestrained self-indulgence and pursuit of pleasure <her son got in with a *wild* bunch and took to drink>
  syn devil-may-care, fast, gay, raffish, rakehell, rakish, sporty
  rel boisterous, roisterous, rollicking, swaggering; careless, heedless, irresponsible, thoughtless; lewd, loose, unchaste, wanton
  con moderate, restrained, sober, sparing, temperate; bridled, controlled, curbed; self-controlled
  8 *syn* see EXTRAVAGANT 1

---

syn synonym(s)   *rel* related word(s)
ant antonym(s)   *con* contrasted word(s)
idiom idiomatic equivalent(s)
‖ use limited; if in doubt, see a dictionary

9 *syn* see BARBARIAN 1
ant cultivated, cultured
10 *syn* see BARBARIC 1
wild *n syn* see WASTE 1
wilderness *n syn* see WASTE 1
rel backcountry, backland(s), hinterland
idiom back of beyond
wild land *n syn* see WASTE 1
wildly *adv syn* see HARD 2
wildness *n syn* see WASTE 1
wile *n syn* see TRICK 1
rel chicane, chicanery, trickery; cunning, deceit, dissimulation, guile
con candor, frankness, openness, plain dealing, straightforwardness, unconstraint; artlessness, naturalness, sincerity
wile *vb* **1** *syn* see ATTRACT 1
2 *syn* see WHILE
wiliness *n syn* see CUNNING 2
will *vb* to be inclined <you may decide whichever way you *will*>
syn choose, elect, like, please, wish
rel crave, desire, want
idiom have a mind to, see (*or* think) fit
will *n* **1** a desire to act in a particular way or have a particular thing <I've no *will* to be sociable tonight>
syn fancy, inclination, liking, mind, pleasure, velleity
rel appetite, desire, passion, urge; hankering, longing, pining, yearning
idiom heart's desire
con aversion, dislike, distaste, repugnance, repulsion, revulsion
2 the aspect of mind involved in choosing or deciding <problems arise when one's *will* and judgment come in conflict>
syn volition
rel design, intent, purpose, wishes; character, disposition, temper
3 power of controlling one's actions, impulses, or emotions <a self-indulgent man of feeble character and little *will*>
syn discipline, self-command, self-control, self=discipline, self-government, self-mastery, self=restraint, willpower
rel aplomb, assurance, confidence, poise, self=possession; control, discretion, restraint
con gratification, indulgence, self-indulgence
will *vb* to give to another by will <*will* family treasures to a relative>
syn bequeath, devise, leave, legate
willful *adj* **1** *syn* see OBSTINATE
rel contumacious, factious
idiom having the bit in one's teeth, not yielding an inch
con amenable, docile, obedient, tractable
ant biddable
2 *syn* see VOLUNTARY
rel intentional, purposive; decided, determined, resolved; dogged, obstinate, pertinacious, stubborn
con accidental, chance, involuntary, unintentional, unplanned

willies *n pl syn* see JITTERS
willing *adj* **1** prepared in mind or by disposition <*willing* to help>
syn disposed, fain, inclined, minded, predisposed, prone, ready
rel agreeable, compliant, favorable; forward, game, prompt
idiom in the mood
con averse, disinclined, indisposed, loath, reluctant, unminded
ant unwilling
2 *syn* see VOLUNTARY
rel disposed, inclined, predisposed; open, prone
will–less *adj syn* see SPONTANEOUS
willpower *n syn* see WILL 3
willy–nilly *adv* surely and without regard to plans or inclination <it seems that we must drift *willy=nilly* toward disaster>
syn helplessly, inescapably, inevitably, perforce, unavoidably, whether or no
idiom as a matter of course, come what may, of necessity, without let or choice
‖**willy–willy** *n syn* see HURRICANE
wilt *vb* **1** *syn* see WITHER
2 *syn* see COLLAPSE 2
3 *syn* see DROOP 3
wily *adj syn* see SLY 2
rel sagacious, shrewd; clever, knowing
con aboveboard, forthright, straightforward; guileless, open, trusting
wimp *n syn* see WEAKLING
win *vb* **1** to gain the victory <the home team *won* by a wide margin>
syn beat, overcome, prevail, triumph; *compare* CONQUER 1
idiom bear off the palm (*or* prize), bring home the bacon, carry the day, come out first (*or* ahead), finish in front
ant lose
2 *syn* see GAIN 1
3 *syn* see EARN 1
rel produce, yield
4 *syn* see GET 1
ant lose
win (over) *vb* **1** *syn* see DISARM 2
2 *syn* see INDUCE 1
win *n syn* see VICTORY 1
wince *vb syn* see RECOIL
rel dodge, duck, jib, sheer, swerve, turn; cower, cringe
wind *n* **1** *syn* see NOTHING 1
2 *syn* see HINT 1
wind *vb syn* see BLOW 1
wind *vb* **1** *syn* see DEFORM
2 to follow a circular, spiral, or writhing course <the vine *wound* its way up the pillar>
syn coil, corkscrew, curl, entwine, spiral, twine, twist, wreathe; *compare* CURVE
rel bend, curve, meander, weave; circle, encircle, enlace, gird, girdle, surround; enclose, envelop
windbaggery *n syn* see NONSENSE 2
windiness *n syn* see VERBOSITY
winding *adj* curving repeatedly first one way then another <a *winding* country road>

syn anfractuous, convoluted, flexuous, meandering, meandrous, serpentine, sinuous, snaky, tortuous; *compare* CROOKED 1
rel bending, curving, twisting; crooked, devious; circuitous, indirect, roundabout
con direct, straight
window dressing *n syn* see MASK 2
windrow *n syn* see PILE 1
wind up *vb* 1 *syn* see CLOSE 3
2 *syn* see SETTLE 7
windup *n syn* see FINALE
windy *adj* 1 marked by more wind than usual <a *windy* March day>
syn airy, blowy, breezy, gusty
rel brisk, fresh; drafty
con breathless, motionless, still
ant windless
2 *syn* see INFLATED
3 *syn* see WORDY
wing *n syn* see ANNEX
rel expansion, prolongation; bulge, projection, protrusion, protuberance
wing *vb syn* see FLY 4
wink *vb* to close and open the eyelids quickly <*winking* involuntarily as the light struck his eyes>
syn bat, blink, nictate, nictitate, twinkle
rel squinch, squinny, squint; flutter
wink (at) *vb syn* see CONNIVE 1
wink *n* 1 *syn* see INSTANT 1
2 *syn* see HINT 2
winker *n syn* see EYE 1
winner *n syn* see VICTOR 2
ant loser
winning *adj syn* see SWEET 1
winnow *vb* 1 *syn* see BLOW 1
2 *syn* see SORT 2
winsome *adj syn* see SWEET 1
rel adorable, lovable, lovesome
wipe (out) *vb* 1 *syn* see ERASE
2 *syn* see ANNIHILATE 2
3 *syn* see SLAUGHTER 3
wipe *n* 1 *syn* see HIT 1
‖2 *syn* see HANDKERCHIEF
‖**wiped out** *adj syn* see DRUGGED
‖**wiper** *n syn* see HANDKERCHIEF
‖**wire** *n syn* see PICKPOCKET
wiredraw *vb syn* see THIN 1
wiry *adj syn* see MUSCULAR 1
wisdom *n* 1 *syn* see KNOWLEDGE 2
2 *syn* see SAGACITY
3 *syn* see SENSE 6
rel judiciousness, sageness, saneness, sapience; perspicacity, sagacity, shrewdness
ant folly
wise *n syn* see METHOD 1
wise *adj* 1 having or exhibiting a capacity for discernment and the intelligent application of knowledge <to be *wise* is to use knowledge well>
syn discerning, gnostic, insighted, insightful, knowing, knowledgeable, perceptive, sagacious, sage, sophic, wisehearted
rel aware, grasping, intuitive, sensing; acute, keen, perspicacious; cogitative, contemplative, reflective, thoughtful; astute, sharp, shrewd

con dull, obtuse, slow, slow-witted; insensitive, unaware, unknowing
ant unwise
2 exercising or involving sound judgment <*wise* management of scarce resources>
syn judgmatic, judicious, prudent, sage, sane, sapient, sensible; *compare* SHREWD
rel canny, discreet, foresighted, provident; astute, perspicacious, sagacious, shrewd; alert, bright, intelligent, keen, smart
con careless, heedless, injudicious; improvident, imprudent, indiscreet, short-sighted
ant foolish, unwise
3 *syn* see EXPEDIENT
4 shrewdly aware and subtly resourceful <a *wise* operator with his eye always on the main chance>
syn canny, hep, knowing, nimble-witted, quick, quick-witted, sharp, sharp-witted, slick, smart; *compare* INTELLIGENT 2, SHREWD
rel cagey, foresighted, shrewd; artful, crafty, cunning, slippery, smooth, tricky, wily; steel=trap
idiom in the groove, not born yesterday, on the beam
con narrow, prim, puritanical, straitlaced; conservative, plodding, ‖square
5 presumptuously confident and self-assured <a bunch of *wise* kids tearing up the neighborhood>
syn ‖biggety, bold, bold-faced, cheeky, forward, fresh, impudent, nervy, pert, procacious, sassy, smart, smart-alecky
rel arrogant, brash, cocky, insolent; flip, flippant, impertinent, lippy, saucy
con demure, mannerly, modest, proper; dull, priggish, stuffy
wise (up) *vb syn* see INFORM 2
wiseacre *n syn* see SMART ALECK
wisecrack *n syn* see JOKE 1
wisecracker *n syn* see SMART ALECK
wise guy *n syn* see SMART ALECK
wisehead *n syn* see SMART ALECK
wisehearted *adj syn* see WISE 1
wise man *n syn* see SAGE
wisenheimer *n syn* see SMART ALECK
wish *vb* 1 *syn* see DESIRE 1
rel expect, hope; fancy
2 *syn* see WILL
3 *syn* see IMPOSE 4
wishy–washy *adj* 1 *syn* see INSIPID 3
rel enervated, languid, listless, spiritless; flavorless, savorless
idiom neither flesh, fowl, nor good red herring, neither one thing nor the other
2 *syn* see CHARACTERLESS
wistful *adj syn* see PENSIVE 2
‖**wit** *vb syn* see UNDERSTAND 3
wit *n* 1 *syn* see MIND 1

---

syn synonym(s)   *rel* related word(s)
ant antonym(s)   *con* contrasted word(s)
idiom idiomatic equivalent(s)
‖ use limited; if in doubt, see a dictionary

rel perspicacity, sagacity; apprehension, awareness, comprehension

2 *often* **wits** *pl* mental soundness and health <frightened nearly out of her *wits*>
syn lucidity, ‖marbles, mind, reason, saneness, sanity, sense(s), soundnesss
rel balance, rationality
con aberration; craziness, derangement, insanity, lunacy, madness, mania
ant witlessness

3 acuteness of perception or judgment <had the *wit* to know that he was out of his depth in such a discussion>
syn acumen, astucity, astuteness, clear-sightedness, discernment, discrimination, keenness, penetration, percipience, perspicacity, shrewdness; *compare* PRUDENCE 1
rel awareness, comprehension, grasp, insight, perception, understanding; prudence, sagaciousness, sagacity, sageness, sapience, wisdom; clairvoyance, divination, ESP, sensing
con aridity, dullness, prosaicness, unimaginativeness; fatuity, foolishness, inanity, silliness, stupidity

4 *syn* see INTELLIGENCE 1

5 a talent for banter or persiflage <a jolly man, noted for his kindly *wit*>
syn esprit, humor
rel alertness, keenness, quick-wittedness; brilliance, cleverness, intelligence, smartness

6 *syn* see HUMOR 5

7 *syn* see HUMORIST 2

witch *n* **1** a woman who practices the black arts <ancient laws against *witches*>
syn bruja, enchantress, hag, hex, lamia, sorceress, witchwoman; *compare* MAGICIAN 1

2 *syn* see HAG 2

witch *vb* *syn* see BEWITCH 1

witchcraft *n* **1** *syn* see MAGIC 1
2 *syn* see CHARM 3

witchery *n* **1** *syn* see MAGIC 1
2 *syn* see CHARM 3

witching *n* *syn* see MAGIC 1

witchwoman *n* *syn* see WITCH 1

witchy *adj* *syn* see MAGIC

with *prep* **1** *syn* see OVER 3
2 *syn* see FOR 2
3 *syn* see VIA 2

withal *adv* **1** *syn* see ALSO 2
2 *syn* see HOWEVER

withdraw *vb* **1** *syn* see REMOVE 2
ant deposit
2 *syn* see ABJURE
3 *syn* see GO 2
rel quail, recoil, retreat, shrink; recede
idiom give ground, give way
con advance, progress; arrive, come
4 *syn* see RETREAT 2
ant advance

withdrawal *n* *syn* see DEPARTURE 1
ant approach

withdrawn *adj* **1** *syn* see UNDEMONSTRATIVE
ant outgiving
2 *syn* see INDIFFERENT 2

3 *syn* see UNSOCIABLE
ant outgoing

wither *vb* to lose substance and freshness by or as if by loss of natural moisture <projects that *wither* and die from lack of popular interest>
syn dry up, mummify, mummy, shrivel, welter, wilt, wizen
rel cave in, collapse, deflate, fold; constrict, contract, shrink; decline, wane
con freshen, revive, revivify; develop, grow, increase, wax
ant flourish

withhold *vb* **1** *syn* see RESTRAIN 1
2 *syn* see KEEP 5
con award, concede, grant, vouchsafe
ant accord
3 *syn* see DENY 2
4 *syn* see REFRAIN 1

within *adv* *syn* see INDOORS
ant without

within *n* *syn* see INTERIOR
ant without

withindoors *adv* *syn* see INDOORS
ant withoutdoors

withinside *adv* *syn* see INDOORS
ant withoutside

with–it *adj* *syn* see STYLISH

without *prep* **1** *syn* see BEYOND 1
2 not having <living *without* decent housing or adequate food>
syn awanting, lacking, minus, sans, wanting

without *adv* *syn* see OUTDOORS
ant within

without *n* *syn* see OUTDOORS

‖**without** *conj* *syn* see EXCEPT 1

withoutdoors *adv* *syn* see OUTDOORS
ant indoors, withindoors

with respect to *prep* *syn* see APROPOS

withstand *vb* *syn* see RESIST
rel bear, endure, stand, suffer, tolerate
con capitulate, submit, yield

witless *adj* **1** *syn* see SIMPLE 3
2 *syn* see INSANE 1

witlessness *n* *syn* see FOOLISHNESS

witness *n* **1** *syn* see TESTIMONY
2 *syn* see SPECTATOR

witness *vb* **1** *syn* see CERTIFY 1
rel affirm; endorse, subscribe
2 *syn* see INDICATE 2

witticism *n* *syn* see JOKE 1

wittiness *n* *syn* see HUMOR 4

witting *adj* **1** *syn* see AWARE
ant unwitting
2 *syn* see VOLUNTARY
ant unwitting

witty *adj* provoking or intended to provoke mirth <a whimsical *witty* discussion on the foreignness of honesty to politics>
syn facetious, humorous, jocose, jocular
rel amusing, diverting, entertaining; scintillating, sparkling; penetrating, piercing, probing; funny, ridiculous, risible
con foolish, senseless, silly; brash, cheeky, fresh; earnest, serious, sober, solemn

ant unwitty

wiz *n syn* see EXPERT

ant dub, dud, duffer

wizard *n* **1** *syn* see MAGICIAN 1

2 *syn* see EXPERT

ant dub, dud, duffer

wizardly *adj syn* see MAGIC

wizardry *n syn* see MAGIC 1

wizen *vb syn* see WITHER

rel decrease, diminish, dwindle, reduce

wobble *vb* **1** *syn* see LURCH 2

2 *syn* see TEETER

3 *syn* see SHAKE

wobbly *adj* **1** *syn* see RICKETY

2 *syn* see WEAK 2

3 *syn* see VACILLATING 2

woe *n* **1** *syn* see SORROW

rel bemoaning, bewailing, deploring, lamentation

con bliss, felicity, happiness

2 *syn* see MISERY 1

3 *usu* **woes** *pl syn* see DISASTER

woebegone *adj* **1** *syn* see DOWNCAST

rel lugubrious, melancholy

con alert, concerned, interested, spirited; lively, vigorous; avid, eager, keen

2 *syn* see GLOOMY 3

rel dilapidated, outworn, shabby, worn

con bright, crisp, fresh, gay

woeful *adj* **1** full of or expressive of woe <a *woeful* countenance>

syn afflicted, doleful, dolent, dolorous, miserable, rueful, ruthful, sorrowful, wretched

rel harrowed, racked, tortured, wrung; crushed, overcome, stricken; disconsolate, heartsick, inconsolable; dejected, depressed, dispirited, downcast, downhearted, low-spirited

idiom cut to the heart, cut up, in the dumps (*or* depths *or* doldrums), on the rack

con content, satisfied; easy, peaceful, quiet; cheerful, gay, lighthearted

ant joyful

2 *syn* see MELANCHOLY 2

3 *syn* see DEPLORABLE

rel dismal, grave, sad; unprecedented

woggle *vb syn* see WAG

wolf *n* a man forward, direct, and zealous in amorous pursuit of women <known far and wide as a lecherous old *wolf*>

syn Casanova, chaser, Don Juan, ladies' man, lady-killer, masher, philander, philanderer, womanizer

rel amorist; lecher, libertine, Lothario, profligate, rip, roué, rounder

idiom man on the make, skirt chaser

wolf *vb* **1** *syn* see GULP

2 *syn* see PHILANDER

wolfish *adj syn* see FIERCE 1

woman *n* **1** a female human being <a health club that caters to *women*>

syn ‖dame, ‖doll, female, gal, gentlewoman, ‖girl, lady, she, ‖skirt, ‖squaw

rel ‖bird, ‖chick; milady

‖**2** *syn* see WIFE

3 *syn* see MISTRESS

womanish *adj syn* see FEMININE

womanize *vb syn* see PHILANDER

womanizer *n syn* see WOLF

womanlike *adj syn* see FEMININE

womanly *adj syn* see FEMININE

wonder *n* **1** something that causes fascinated astonishment or admiration <the seven *wonders* of the ancient world>

syn marvel, miracle, phenomenon, portent, prodigy, sensation, stunner

rel curiosity, cynosure, gazingstock, spectacle

idiom one for the book(s), something to shout (*or* write home) about

2 the complex emotion aroused by the strange and incomprehensible and especially the awe-inspiring <stood gazing in wide-eyed *wonder* at the scene unveiled before her>

syn admiration, amaze, amazement, marveling, wonderment

rel awe, fear, reverence; bewilderment, perplexity, puzzlement; astonishment, marvel, shock

con disinterest, incuriosity, indifference, unconcern; dispassion, impassivity; casualness, offhandedness; boredom, ennui

3 *syn* see UNCERTAINTY

rel assailability, vulnerability

con unconcern

wonderful *adj* **1** *syn* see MARVELOUS 1

2 *syn* see MARVELOUS 2

ant lousy

wonderland *n syn* see UTOPIA

wonderment *n syn* see WONDER 2

wondrous *adj syn* see MARVELOUS 1

wont *n syn* see HABIT 1

wont *vb syn* see ACCUSTOM

wonted *adj syn* see USUAL 1

ant unwonted

wontedly *adv syn* see USUALLY 1

ant unwontedly

woo *vb syn* see ADDRESS 8

idiom bill and coo, pitch woo

wood *n, often* **woods** *pl but sing or pl in constr syn* see FOREST

wooden *adj* **1** *syn* see STIFF 4

rel awkward, clumsy; heavy, ponderous, weighty

con limber, supple; plastic, pliable, pliant

2 *syn* see AWKWARD 2

woodenhead *n syn* see DUNCE

woodland *n syn* see FOREST

woods colt *n syn* see BASTARD 1

woodsy *n syn* see RUSTIC

wooer *n syn* see SUITOR 2

woolly *adj syn* see HAIRY 1

word *vb* to convey (as an impression, a thought, or a need) in words <seemed scarcely to know how to *word* her appeal>

---

syn synonym(s)   *rel* related word(s)
ant antonym(s)   *con* contrasted word(s)
idiom idiomatic equivalent(s)
‖ use limited; if in doubt, see a dictionary

syn couch, express, formulate, phrase, put; *compare* EXPRESS 2

rel convey, offer, submit; say, state, tell

word *n* **1** something that is said <didn't tell a *word* about his plans>

syn statement, utterance

rel announcement, declaration, pronouncement

2 a pronounceable sound or combination of sounds that expresses and symbolizes an idea <be sure you learn the meaning of each *word*>

syn term, vocable

rel expression, idiom, locution, phrase

3 *syn* see COMMAND 1

4 *syn* see NEWS

5 *syn* see REPORT 1

6 *syn* see MESSAGE 1

7 *syn* see SAYING

8 a statement whose weight or worth depends on the truthfulness or authority of its maker <had the doctor's *word* that no operation would be needed>

syn assurance, guarantee, pledge, warrant; *compare* PROMISE

rel commitment, engagement, undertaking; oath, vow; promise

9 *syn* see PROMISE

10 *usu* **words** *pl syn* see QUARREL

11 *syn* see PASSWORD 3

12 *syn* see PASSWORD 1

wordage *n syn* see WORDING

word for word *adv syn* see VERBATIM

word–for–word *adj syn* see VERBATIM

word–hoard *n syn* see VOCABULARY 1

wordiness *n syn* see VERBOSITY

con crispness, pithiness, trenchancy

ant laconicism, laconism

wording *n* manner or style of verbal expression <take care with the *wording* of a formal invitation>

syn diction, parlance, phrase, phraseology, phrasing, verbalism, verbiage, wordage

rel language, mode, style

wordless *adj* **1** *syn* see TACIT 1

2 *syn* see SILENT 2

3 *syn* see SILENT 3

4 *syn* see UNSPOKEN 1

ant wordy

word–of–mouth *adj syn* see ORAL 2

word–stock *n syn* see VOCABULARY 1

wordy *adj* using or marked by the use of more words than are needed to express an idea <tired of dull *wordy* editorials>

syn diffuse, long-winded, palaverous, prolix, redundant, verbose, windy

rel flatulent, inflated, tumid, turgid; garrulous, glib, loquacious, talkative, voluble; bombastic, highfalutin, rhetorical

con compendious, concise, pithy, succinct, summary, terse; lean, taut

ant laconic

work *n* **1** the activity that affords one his livelihood <laborers hurrying to *work* at dawn>

syn business, calling, employment, job, line, occupation, pursuit, ‖racket; *compare* JOB 2

rel art, craft, handicraft, métier, profession, trade, vocation, walk

2 strenuous activity that involves difficulty and effort and usually affords no pleasure <had done much hard *work* during her life>

syn bullwork, donkeywork, drudge, drudgery, grind, labor, moil, plugging, slavery, slogging, sweat, toil, travail

rel effort, exertion, pains, trouble; chore, duty, job; elucubration; striving; spadework

ant play

3 **works** *pl syn* see FACTORY

work *vb* **1** *syn* see OPERATE 3

2 *syn* see TILL

3 *syn* see SOLVE 1

4 *syn* see LABOR 1

5 *syn* see FUNCTION 3

6 *syn* see ACT 5

work (for) *vb syn* see BENEFIT

workable *adj syn* see POSSIBLE 1

rel applicable, exploitable, usable

ant unworkable

workaday *adj* **1** *syn* see PROSAIC 3

2 *syn* see ORDINARY 1

workday *adj syn* see PROSAIC 3

worker *n* one who earns a living by labor and especially by manual labor <weary *workers* straggling home each night>

syn hand, laborer, ‖mozo, operative, roustabout, workhand, workingman, workman

rel artisan, craftsman, handicraftsman, mechanic; employee

ant idler

workhand *n syn* see WORKER

workhorse *n* **1** *syn* see SLAVE 2

2 *syn* see SAWHORSE

work in *vb syn* see INSINUATE 3

working *adj* **1** *syn* see ACTIVE 1

2 *syn* see BUSY 1

workingman *n syn* see WORKER

workless *adj syn* see UNEMPLOYED

workman *n syn* see WORKER

workmanlike *adj syn* see SKILLFUL 2

ant unworkmanlike

workmanly *adj syn* see SKILLFUL 2

work off *vb syn* see FOIST 3

work out *vb syn* see SOLVE 1

work over *vb syn* see REVISE

work–shy *adj syn* see LAZY

work up *vb syn* see GENERATE 3

world *n* **1** *syn* see EARTH 1

2 *syn* see UNIVERSE

worldly *adj* **1** *syn* see EARTHLY 1

ant otherworldly

2 *syn* see MATERIALISTIC

ant otherworldly, unworldly

3 *syn* see SOPHISTICATED 2

ant unworldly

worldly–wise *adj syn* see SOPHISTICATED 2

rel callous, hard-boiled, hardened

con naive, unsophisticated, unworldly

worldwide *adj syn* see UNIVERSAL 2

con parochial

world–wise *adj syn* see SOPHISTICATED 2

world–without–end *adj syn* see EVERLASTING 1
world–without–end *n syn* see ETERNITY 2
worm *n syn* see WRETCH 1
worm *vb* **1** *syn* see INSINUATE 3
　2 *syn* see WRIGGLE
wormling *n syn* see WRETCH 1
worn *adj* **1** *syn* see TIRED 1
　2 *syn* see HAGGARD
worn–down *adj syn* see TIRED 1
worn–out *adj* **1** *syn* see EFFETE 2
　2 *syn* see TIRED 1
　3 *syn* see TRITE
worried *adj syn* see DISTRAUGHT
　ant unworried
worry *vb* **1** to disturb one or destroy one's peace of
mind by repeated or persistent tormenting at-
tacks <vain regrets that *worry* his spirit>
　syn annoy, bedevil, beleaguer, dun, gnaw, hagride, harass, harry, hassle, needle, pester, plague,
tantalize, tease, ‖wherret
　rel beset, bother, fret, pelt, trouble, vex; goad,
test, try; afflict, torment, torture; aggrieve, oppress, persecute, wrong
　idiom give one gyp
　con comfort, console, solace; alleviate, assuage,
ease, relieve
　2 *syn* see TROUBLE 1
　3 to experience concern, disquietude, or anxiety
<*worrying* over her children's health>
　syn cark, fret, fuss, pother, stew, ‖tew
　rel carry on, take on; despair, give up; bother,
concern (oneself); agitate, disquiet, disturb,
trouble
　idiom be upset, bite one's nails
　con accept, submit; abide, bear, endure, stand,
support; disregard, ignore, overlook, pass over
worry *n* **1** *syn* see CARE 2
　rel presentiment; doubt, mistrust, uncertainty;
anguish, heartache, woe
　con composure, equanimity, sangfroid; assurance, certainty, certitude, confidence, security
　2 *syn* see TRIAL 2
worrywart *n syn* see PESSIMIST
worsen *vb syn* see DETERIORATE 1
　rel blast, blight, debase, degrade, humble,
lower; corrupt, foul, taint
　idiom get worse, grow worse
　ant better
worship *n syn* see ADORATION
worship *vb* **1** *syn* see REVERE
　con contemn, despise, disdain, flout, scorn;
curse, execrate, vilify
　2 *syn* see ADORE 3
　ant abominate; scorn
　3 *syn* see LOVE 2
worst *vb syn* see DEFEAT 2
worth *n* **1** equivalence in good qualities (as utility,
importance, or desirability) express or implied
<impossible to estimate the *worth* of such a man
to the community>
　syn account, valuation, value
　rel class, excellence, merit, perfection, quality,
virtue; rate; use, usefulness, utility; consequence,
importance, mark, moment, note, significance,
weight

　con baseness, meanness, paltriness, poorness
　ant worthlessness
　2 *syn* see QUALITY 2
　3 *syn* see WEALTH 2
worthless *adj* **1** lacking all excellence or value
<gave me a *worthless* check>
　syn draffy, drossy, good-for-nothing, inutile,
‖no-account, no-good, nothing, unworthy, valueless
　rel inferior, mediocre, poor, second-rate; defective, flawed, imperfect; bootless, ineffectual, unavailing, useless; contemptible, dusty, mean,
sad, sorry
　idiom dear at any price, of no earthly value (*or*
worth)
　con esteemed, precious; useful, valuable, worthwhile; invaluable, priceless
　ant worthful
　2 *syn* see FECKLESS 1
　rel incapable, incompetent, unqualified
worthwhile *adj syn* see ADVANTAGEOUS 1
worthy *adj* **1** having worth or merit <a *worthy* custom handed down from our ancestors>
　syn admirable, commendable, deserving, estimable, laudable, meritable, meritorious, praisable, praiseworthy, thankworthy
　rel invaluable, precious, priceless; desirable,
pleasing, satisfying; divine
　con good-for-nothing, ‖no-account, no-good,
valueless; contemptible, sad, sorry
　ant worthless
　2 *syn* see HONORABLE 1
　ant unworthy
wound *vb syn* see INJURE 3
wow *n syn* see SMASH 6
‖**wowser** *n syn* see PRUDE
wrack *vb syn* see DESTROY 1
wrackful *adj syn* see DESTRUCTIVE
wraith *n syn* see APPARITION
wrangle *vb* **1** *syn* see QUARREL
　2 *syn* see ARGUE 2
wrangle *n syn* see QUARREL
wrap *vb syn* see ENFOLD 1
　rel camouflage, cloak, mask
　ant unwrap
wrap (up) *vb* **1** *syn* see BUNDLE UP
　2 *syn* see SWATHE
wrapped *adj syn* see INTENT
wrapped up *adj syn* see INTENT
wrap up *vb syn* see CLOSE 3
wrath *n syn* see ANGER
　rel acerbity, acrimony, asperity; offense, resentment
wrathful *adj syn* see ANGRY
wrathy *adj syn* see ANGRY
‖**wraxle** *vb syn* see WRESTLE
wreak *vb syn* see INFLICT 2
wreakful *adj syn* see VINDICTIVE

---

syn synonym(s)　　　*rel* related word(s)
ant antonym(s)　　　*con* contrasted word(s)
idiom idiomatic equivalent(s)
‖ use limited; if in doubt, see a dictionary

wreath *n* a circlet of intertwined leaves or flowers worn upon the head as an ornament or as a mark of honor or esteem <received the laurel *wreath* of victory from the emperor's own hand>
syn chaplet, coronal, coronet, crown, garland
rel bay(s), laurel

wreathe *vb syn* see WIND 2

wreck *n* **1** *syn* see CRASH 3
2 *syn* see COLLAPSE 2
3 *syn* see JALOPY

wreck *vb* **1** *syn* see VANDALIZE
2 *syn* see DESTROY 1
rel despoil, loot, plunder, ravage; cripple, disable
3 *syn* see TOTAL 3
4 *syn* see SABOTAGE
5 *syn* see SHIPWRECK 1
6 *syn* see RUIN 2
7 *syn* see INFLICT 2

wreckage *n* **1** *syn* see SABOTAGE
2 *syn* see DRIFTWOOD

wrecker *n syn* see VANDAL

wreckful *adj syn* see DESTRUCTIVE

wrecking *n syn* see SABOTAGE

wrench *vb* **1** to shift the position of or move by or as if by vigorous twisting <suddenly *wrenched* her around to face him>
syn wrest, wring, wry
rel bend, twist; coerce, compel, constrain, force; drag, rend, tear; contort, distort
2 *syn* see SPRAIN
3 *syn* see MISREPRESENT
4 *syn* see EXTORT 1

wrest *vb* **1** *syn* see WRENCH 1
rel arrogate, confiscate, usurp; elicit, extort, extract
2 *syn* see EXTORT 1
3 *syn* see MISREPRESENT

wrestle *vb* to struggle with an opponent at close quarters <determined to solve the problem if he had to *wrestle* with it all night>
syn grapple, scuffle, tussle, ‖wraxle
rel contend, fight, struggle; endeavor, essay; labor, moil, toil, travail, work; exert, strain, stretch, strive

wretch *n* **1** a worthless and often vicious or contemptible person <a treacherous drink-sodden *wretch*>
syn ‖blighter, lowlife, mucker, no-good, worm, wormling
rel good-for-naught, good-for-nothing, ne'er≠do-well; blackguard, caitiff, devil, knave, rapscallion, rascal, rogue, rotter, scalawag, scoundrel, villain
idiom sad case
2 *syn* see SNOT 1

wretched *adj* **1** *syn* see WOEFUL 1
rel melancholy; abject, mean, sordid; piteous, pitiable, pitiful; despairing, despondent, forlorn, hopeless
con animated, gay, lively; content, contented, satisfied; gratified, pleased
2 *syn* see BASE

wretchedness *n syn* see MISERY 1

wriggle *vb* to move or advance with wormlike motions <the attackers *wriggled* stealthily through the underbrush>
syn squiggle, squirm, wiggle, worm, writhe
rel flow, glide, ooze, slide, slip

wring *vb* **1** *syn* see EXTORT 1
2 *syn* see WRENCH 1
rel press, squeeze
3 *syn* see AFFLICT

wringing–wet *adj syn* see WET 1

wrinkle *n* a small linear prominence or depression on a surface <a benign old face netted with *wrinkles*>
syn corrugation, crease, crinkle, fold, furrow, plica, ridge, rimple, rivel, ruck
rel crow's foot; pleat, pucker

wrinkle *vb syn* see CRUMPLE 1

write *vb* to form characters or words on a surface (as of paper) usually with pen or pencil <learned to *write* at an early age>
syn engross, indite, inscribe, scribe
rel dot (down), jot, note; chalk, pen, pencil; scratch, scrawl, scribble; draft, draw, make out; write down, write up
idiom push one's pen, put in writing, take down

write down *vb syn* see DEPRECIATE 1
ant write up

write off *vb* **1** *syn* see DEPRECIATE 1
2 *syn* see DECRY 2

write–up *n syn* see PUFF 3

writhe *vb* **1** to twist and turn in physical or mental distress <*writhing* in anguish with a throbbing toothache>
syn agonize, squirm, toss
rel blench, flinch, recoil, shrink, wince; contort, distort; bend, twist; thrash, tumble
2 *syn* see WRIGGLE

writing *n syn* see PRINT 2

writing desk *n syn* see DESK

wrong *n* **1** *syn* see INJUSTICE 2
2 *syn* see EVIL 2
3 *syn* see EVIL 3
4 *syn* see INJUSTICE 1

wrong *adj* **1** rejecting or deviating from the dictates of moral or divine law <had a *wrong* outlook on life> <*wrong* principles of conduct>
syn bad, evil, immoral, iniquitous, reprobate, sinful, vicious, wicked
rel blamable, blameworthy, censurable, reprehensible; corrupt, debauched, depraved; abandoned, dissolute, infamous, villainous; blasphemous, unholy, unrighteous; accursed, unblessed
con ethical, high-principled, moral, righteous, upright; chaste, innocent, pure, virtuous
ant right
2 *syn* see FALSE 1
idiom at fault, barking up the wrong tree, in error, on the wrong track
con exact, precise
ant right
3 *syn* see BAD 1
rel improper, inappropriate, inapt, infelicitous, unfit, unfitting, unhappy, unsuitable
con appropriate, fit, fitting, proper, suitable

4 *syn* see MISTAKEN
  ant right
  5 *syn* see INSANE 1
wrong *adv syn* see AMISS 2
  ant right
wrong *vb* to inflict injury on another without justification <these men who have *wronged* the public trust deserve no consideration>
  syn aggrieve, oppress, outrage, persecute
  rel abuse, ill-treat, maltreat, mistreat; harm,
hurt, injure; offend
  idiom do wrong to (*or* by)
  con guard, protect, safeguard; care (for), cherish; honor, love, respect

wrongdoing *n* **1** *syn* see EVIL 3
  2 *syn* see MISCONDUCT
wrongful *adj syn* see UNLAWFUL
  ant rightful
wrongheaded *adj* **1** *syn* see OBSTINATE
  2 *syn* see CONTRARY 3
wrongly *adv syn* see AMISS 1
  ant rightly
wroth *adj syn* see ANGRY
wrothful *adj syn* see ANGRY
wrothy *adj syn* see ANGRY
wry *vb syn* see WRENCH 1
wry *adj syn* see SARDONIC

---

syn synonym(s)   *rel* related word(s)
ant antonym(s)   *con* contrasted word(s)
idiom idiomatic equivalent(s)
‖ use limited; if in doubt, see a dictionary

XYZ

x *n syn* see ERROR 1

x (out) *vb syn* see ERASE

Xanthippe *n syn* see VIRAGO

Xmas *n syn* see CHRISTMAS

yahoo *n syn* see TOUGH

yak *n syn* see CHATTER

yak *vb syn* see CHAT 1

‖**yak** *n syn* see JOKE 1

yakety–yak *n syn* see CHATTER

yakety–yak *vb syn* see CHAT 1

yak–yak *n syn* see CHATTER

yak–yak *vb syn* see CHAT

yammer *vb* **1** *syn* see GRIPE
  2 *syn* see CHAT 1

yank *vb* **1** *syn* see JERK
  rel tug; clutch, grab, snatch
  2 *syn* see EXTRACT 1

yap *n* **1** *syn* see RUSTIC
  ‖**2** *syn* see MOUTH 1

yard *n syn* see COURT 1

yardstick *n syn* see STANDARD 3

yare *adj syn* see AGILE

yarn *n* **1** *syn* see STORY 2
  2 *syn* see CHAT 2

yarn *vb syn* see CONVERSE

yatter *n syn* see CHATTER

yatter *vb syn* see CHAT 1

yaw *n syn* see TURN 2

yaw *vb syn* see SEESAW

yaw *vb syn* see YAWN

yawn *vb* to breathe deeply with jaws widespread usually in reaction to fatigue or boredom <*yawned* again and again in the stuffy room>
  syn gape, yaw
  rel doze, drowse, nap, snooze

yawn *n syn* see TEDIUM

yawning *adj syn* see CAVERNOUS 1

yawp (or yaup) *vb* **1** *syn* see SQUALL 1
  2 *syn* see GRIPE

yea *adv* **1** *syn* see ALSO 2
  2 *syn* see YES 1
  3 *syn* see EVEN 3

yearbook *n* a book issued yearly to chronicle a particular part of the preceding year's activities <sports editor of his school *yearbook*>
  syn annual, annuary

yearn *vb syn* see LONG
  rel covet, desire, wish; pant
  ant dread

years *n pl syn* see OLD AGE

yeast *n syn* see FOAM

yeasty *adj syn* see GIDDY 1

yegg *n syn* see ROBBER

yell *vb* **1** *syn* see SHOUT 1
  2 to complain vigorously or vociferously <let the opposition *yell;* we got the vote>
  syn howl, scream, squeal, yip, yowl

rel cry, lament, squall, wail, weep; bemoan, bewail, deplore
  idiom beat one's breast, make an outcry, tear one's hair, yell to high heaven
  con acclaim, applaud, cheer, hail
  3 *syn* see CALL 1

yellow *adj syn* see COWARDLY

yellowback *n syn* see DIME NOVEL

yellowbelly *n syn* see COWARD
  rel fink, rat, stinker

yellow dog *n syn* see CAD

yen *vb syn* see LONG

‖**yep** *adv syn* see YES 1
  ant ‖nope

‖**yerk** *vb syn* see WHIP 1

yes *adv* **1** —used as a function word to express assent, agreement, understanding, or acceptance <*yes*, I can do that>
  syn agreed, all right, aye, OK (*or* okay), ‖okey-doke, yea, ‖yep
  rel assuredly, certainly, gladly, willingly; undoubtedly, unquestionably
  idiom beyond a doubt, beyond any shade (*or* shadow) of doubt, with all my heart, without the least doubt
  2 *syn* see EXACTLY 3

yes *vb syn* see ASSENT

yes–man *n* **1** *syn* see STOOGE 1
  2 *syn* see SYCOPHANT

yesterday *n syn* see PAST
  ant tomorrow

yesteryear *n syn* see PAST

yet *adv* **1** beyond this — used as an intensive to stress the comparative degree <in spite of her protest he went *yet* faster>
  syn even, still
  2 at some future time <just wait, we'll get there *yet*>
  syn eventually, finally, someday, sometime, somewhen, sooner or later, ultimately
  idiom after a while, in due course, in the course of time
  3 *syn* see ALSO 2
  4 *syn* see HITHERTO 1
  5 *syn* see HOWEVER

yet *conj syn* see ONLY

yield *vb* **1** *syn* see RELINQUISH
  con appropriate, arrogate, confiscate
  2 to give way before a force that one can no longer resist <*yielded* to temptation>
  syn bow, buckle (under), capitulate, cave, defer, knuckle, knuckle under, submit, succumb
  rel accord, award, concede, grant; cede, surrender, waive; break, fail
  idiom give ground, give place, give way
  con bear up, hold out, resist
  ant withstand
  3 *syn* see BEAR 9

4 *syn* see GIVE 7
  rel discharge, eject, emit, vent
5 to produce as return or revenue <an investment that *yields* 10 percent>
  syn bring in, pay, return
  rel afford, furnish, provide, supply; hold out, offer, proffer, tender
  idiom afford (*or* give *or* provide) a return of, put at one's disposal
6 *syn* see GIVE 12
yield *n syn* see OUTPUT
yielding *adj* **1** *syn* see SOFT 6
  ant unyielding
2 *syn* see PASSIVE 2
yip *vb syn* see YELL 2
‖**yob** *n syn* see RUSTIC
yoke *n* **1** *syn* see BONDAGE
2 *syn* see BOND 3
yoke *vb* **1** *syn* see HITCH 2
2 *syn* see JOIN 1
yokel *n syn* see RUSTIC
yon *adv* **1** *syn* see BEYOND 1
2 *syn* see THERE
yonder *adv syn* see BEYOND 1
yore *n syn* see PAST
young *adj* **1** being in an early stage of life, growth, or development <interested in molding *young* minds>
  syn callow, green, immature, infant, juvenile, unfledged, unripe, youthful
  rel fresh, new; crude, raw, unfinished, unformed
  con full-grown, grown-up, mature, ripe; aged, elderly, superannuated
  ant old; adult
2 *syn* see INEXPERIENCED
youngling *n syn* see CHILD 1
young man *n syn* see BOYFRIEND 1
young one *n syn* see CHILD 1
youngster *n syn* see CHILD 1
youth *n* **1** the period of life in which one passes from childhood to maturity <the thought of regaining one's *youth*>
  syn adolescence, greenness, juvenility, prime, puberty, pubescence, salad days, spring, springtide, springtime, youthfulness, youthhood
  rel callowness, immaturity, inexperience, unripeness; dewiness
  idiom awkward age, flower (*or* springtime *or* May) of life
  ant age
2 *syn* see CHILD 1
youthful *adj syn* see YOUNG 1
  rel beardless, boyish, puerile; maiden, virgin, virginal
  con adult, matured
  ant aged, elderly
youthfulness *n syn* see YOUTH 1
youthhood *n syn* see YOUTH
yowl *vb* **1** *syn* see YELL 2
2 *syn* see BAWL 2
yule *n syn* see CHRISTMAS
yuletide *n syn* see CHRISTMAS
yummy *adj syn* see DELIGHTFUL
zakuska *n syn* see APPETIZER

zany *n* **1** *syn* see CLOWN 3
  rel comic, farceur, funnyman
2 one who makes an exhibition of himself for the amusement of others <tired of having her parties spoiled by drunken *zanies*>
  syn clown, cutup, farceur, joker, jokester, wag
  rel practical joker, pranker, prankster, trickster; exhibitionist, show-off
3 *syn* see WAG 1
4 *syn* see FOOL 4
zany *adj syn* see FOOLISH 2
zeal *n syn* see PASSION 6
  rel energy, gusto, spirit, zest; fierceness, intensity, vehemence; avidity, keenness, readiness, urgency; earnestness, seriousness, sincerity
  con coolness, halfheartedness, indifference, lukewarmness; carelessness, heedlessness, insouciance, negligence, unmindfulness; disinterest, lackadaisy, unconcern
  ant apathy
zealot *n syn* see ENTHUSIAST
  rel adherent, disciple, follower, partisan, sectary
zealous *adj syn* see ENTHUSIASTIC
  rel afire, ardent, fervent, fervid, fired; avid, eager; dedicated, fanatic, frenetic, rabid, wild=eyed; infatuated, obsessed, possessed
  con cool, halfhearted, indifferent, lukewarm; careless, heedless, insouciant, negligent, unmindful; disinterested, lackadaisical, uninterested
  ant apathetic
zemi *n syn* see CHARM 2
zenith *n syn* see APEX 2
  ant nadir
zero *n* **1** a numerical symbol 0 denoting the absence of all magnitude or quantity <wrote a row of *zeros* after the decimal point>
  syn aught (*or* ought), cipher, goose egg, naught (*or* nought), nothing, zilch
  rel blank, nil, void
2 *syn* see NONENTITY
zero (in) *vb syn* see DIRECT 2
zero hour *n syn* see JUNCTURE 2
zest *n syn* see TASTE 4
  rel ardor, eagerness, enthusiasm, fervor, passion, zeal; delectation, delight, enjoyment, pleasure, satisfaction; bliss, ecstasy, elation
zesty *adj syn* see PUNGENT
zetetic *n syn* see SKEPTIC
zilch *n* **1** *syn* see ZERO 1
2 *syn* see NONENTITY
zing *n* **1** *syn* see EAGERNESS
2 *syn* see SPIRIT 5
Zion *n* **1** *syn* see HEAVEN 2
2 *syn* see UTOPIA
zip *vb* **1** *syn* see BREEZE
2 *syn* see HURRY 2
zippy *adj syn* see AGILE
  rel alert, keen, ready; dynamic, forceful, intense

---

syn synonym(s)   *rel* related word(s)
ant antonym(s)   *con* contrasted word(s)
idiom idiomatic equivalent(s)
‖ use limited; if in doubt, see a dictionary

zoetic *adj syn* see LIVING 1

Zoilus *n syn* see CRITIC

zombie *n* **1** *syn* see DUNCE

  2 *syn* see ECCENTRIC

zone *n syn* see AREA 1

  rel section, sector, segment

zonked *adj* **1** *syn* see INTOXICATED 1

  2 *syn* see DRUGGED